# A Chronology

| 1928 | "Black Production" begins. |
|------|---------------------------|
| 1929 | Firing tests held for the navy. |
| 1930 | Hitler pays a visit. |
| 1931 | Alfried joins the SS. |
| 1931–32 | New weapons demonstrated to the army. |
| 1933 | Krupp finances Hitler. |
| | Gustav appointed Führer of industry. |
| 1935 | Hitler proclaims "military sovereignty." |
| 1936 | Krupp subs threaten France during Rhineland crisis. |
| 1938 | Krupp rewarded after Austrian putsch. |
| | Alfried, back from Spain, rises swiftly. |
| 1939 | Gustav's first stroke. |
| | Alfried writes his first annual report. |
| 1940 | Claus killed in action. |
| | Alfried shells England across the Channel. |
| 1942 | Alfried appointed chief director. |
| 1943 | January: first real RAF raid on Essen. |
| | Battle of the Kursk salient: a Krupp disaster. |
| | Lex Krupp: Hitler honors Alfried. |
| 1944 | Krupp gases a Rothschild at Auschwitz. |
| | Arrest of Barbara Krupp. |
| | Capture of Harald by Russians. |
| | Alfried rules 100,000 slave laborers. |
| 1945 | Eckbert killed in action. |
| | Americans capture Ruhr and seize Alfried. |
| | Internment of Bertha and Gustav. |
| | Eviction of Barbara and the baron. |
| 1946 | Second dismantling of the factories. |
| 1948 | War Crimes Tribunal convicts Alfried at Nuremberg. |
| 1950 | Death of Gustav. |
| 1951 | John J. McCloy releases Alfried. |
| 1953 | Alfried again rules the Ruhr. |
| 1955 | Release of Harald. |
| 1957 | Death of Bertha. |
| 1963 | Alfried becomes the most powerful industrialist in the Common Market. |
| 1967 | Krupp completes Germany's first nuclear plant. |
| | Collapse of the firm's finances. |
| | Arndt II opts for a carefree life. |
| | Death of Alfried, last of the Krupps. |
| 1968 | Dissolution of *die Firma*. |

# The Arms of Krupp

## 1587-1968

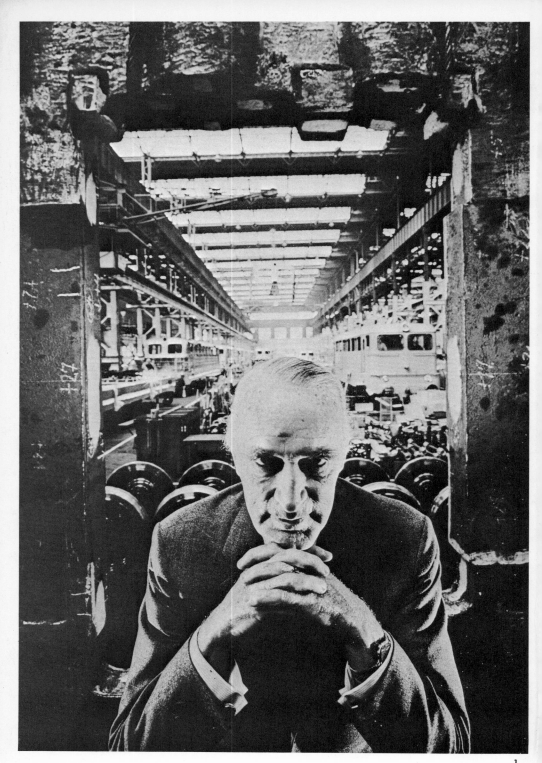

Alfried Krupp

Portrait by Arnold Newman

# The Arms of Krupp

## 1587-1968

✠ ✠ ✠

by William Manchester

LITTLE, BROWN AND COMPANY · BOSTON · TORONTO

Lines from the song "Lilli Marlene" are reprinted by permission of the
Music Publishing House: Apollo-Verlag Paul Lincke, Berlin. Sole Licensing
Agent for the United States of America, Edward B. Marks Music Corporation.

* * *

*Published simultaneously in Canada*
*by Little, Brown & Company (Canada) Limited*

PRINTED IN THE UNITED STATES OF AMERICA

*For*
*The children of Buschmannshof*
*Who lie at Voerde-bei-Dinslaken*
*And have no other monument*

*Oh Deutschland, bleiche Mutter!*
*Wie haben deine Söhne dich zugerichtet*
*Dass du unter den Völkern sitzest*
*Ein Gespött oder eine Furcht!*

—Bertolt Brecht
*Deutschland*

Oh Germany, pale mother!
How have your sons ill-served you
That you are scorned by all people —
A thing of obloquy and terror!

*Noch weiz ich an im mêre / daz mir ist bekant.*
*einen lintrachen / sluoc des heldes hant.*
*er badet sich in dem bluote: / sîn hût wart hurnîn.*
*des snîdet in kein wâfen: / daz ist dicke worden schîn.*

*Das Nibelungenlied*

And I know even more, more I can tell.
Once, by his violent hand, a dragon fell.
He bathed in blood, grew hard, and can't be slain.
And many have seen this again — and yet again.

# Order of Battle

✠ ✠ ✠

# Illustrations

✠ ✠ ✠

# Glossary

✠ ✠ ✠

*A.G.* (*Aktiengesellschaft*)  corporation
*alleinige Inhaber*  sole proprietor (of the Krupp firm)
*Allerhöchsteselber*  All-Highest (Kaiser)
*Attentat*  attempted assassination of Hitler July 1944
*Ausländer*  foreigner(s)
*feldgrau*  field gray (uniform)
*die Firma*  the Krupp firm
*Fremdarbeiter*  foreign workers (slave laborers)
*Generalbevollmächtigter*  General Plenipotentiary (Berthold Beitz)
*Generalregulativ*  General Regulations of 1872
*Generalstab*  German General Staff
*G.m.b.H.* (*Gesellschaft mit beschränkter Haftung*)  company of limited liability — similar to "Inc." or "Ltd."
*der Grosse Krupp*  the Great Krupp (Alfred Krupp)
*Gusstahlfabrik*  cast steel factory
*Hauptverwaltungsgebäude*  Krupp's central administration building, Essen
*Jubiläum*  jubilee
*Justizpalast*  Palace of Justice (Nuremberg)
*Kanonenkönig*  Cannon King
*kleine Haus*  wing of Villa Hügel, Krupp castle
*Konzernherr*  owner of the Krupp concern
*Kruppianer*  Krupp worker(s)
*kruppsche*  Krupp (adj.)
*Kruppstahl*  Krupp steel
*Kumpel*  Krupp miners
*Lagerführer*  Concentration camp commander
*Lex Krupp*  Hitler's Krupp decree
*Menschenjagd*(*en*)  man (slave) hunts
*Muttergesellschaft*  holding company
*Oberlagerführung*  Krupp's foreign workers administration
*Offizierskorps*  officer corps
*Pickelhauben*  spiked helmets
*Prinzgemahl*  prince consort
*Prokura*  management committee

*Ruhrgebiet*   Ruhr industrial region
*Schlotbarone*   steel (Ruhr) barons
*Sieg*   victory
*Sklavenarbeit*   slave labor
*Sklavenhalter*   slaveholder (Alfried Krupp)
*S.M.*   His Majesty (Seine Majestät)
*Stammhaus*   "ancestral home" of Alfred Krupp
*Stücke*   livestock (slave laborers)
*Übermenschen*   master race
*Untermenschen*   subhumans (slave laborers)
*Urgrossvater*   great-grandfather
*Villa Hügel*   300-room Krupp castle overlooking the Ruhr
*Waffenschmiede des Reichs*   arsenal of the empire (*die Firma*)
*Werkschutz*   Krupp's company police

# The Arms of Krupp

## 1587-1968

# 𝔓rologue

## ✠

# Anvil of the Reich

IN 1914 Archduke Franz Ferdinand of Austria was assassinated at Sarajevo, and little of the Europe he had known survived him. His wife, his titles — even his country — vanished in the red madness of the time. The assassins had unhinged the world, which is the only reason we remember their victim. The blunt truth is that he had been brutal and mulish — a *Klotz*. Yet every funeral has its pathetic personal details, and among the petty but vexing problems raised by the archduke's unexpected demise was the issue of what his executors were to do with his hunting lodge near Werfen, Austria. For four hundred years the lodge (really an immense villa), had been one of the homes of the archbishops of Salzburg, who had commuted between there, their Renaissance cathedral, their theological seminary east of Munich, and their two archepiscopal palaces on the Salzach River. In the new, enlightened Europe, however, the ecclesiastical hierarchy had yielded to royalty. The dull click of rosary beads had been replaced by the clean, sharp crack of sportsmen's rifles. Franz Ferdinand, whatever his other weaknesses, had been a superb shot. In the teeming forests surrounding his lodge he had broken all slaughtering records. His trophies filled the halls.

Thus the sentimental Viennese felt that the new owner of Blühnbach should know something about guns. But the eighty-room château was expensive. Eventually their dilemma was solved brilliantly by Gustav Krupp von Bohlen und Halbach of Essen, Germany. Gustav Krupp was well acquainted with guns. He was, in fact, the continent's leading cannon manufacturer. The Krupps had been looking for a new country home far from their weapons forges in the sooty, smelly Ruhr valley, so Gustav and his family acquired the estate, with its superb view of the Austrian Alps, beneath one of whose peaks the legendary twelfth-century Emperor Frederick Barbarossa is said to lie asleep in a cave, ready to spring to Germany's aid whenever the black ravens circling overhead warn him that the sacred soil of his First Reich is in danger.[1]

In the long sweep of history the sale of Blühnbach seems scarcely worth a footnote. Yet in a way it is a parable of the era. Since the dawn of modern Europe the mysterious, powerful Krupp dynasty had flourished on war and rumors of war. Its steel forges had disgorged armor, bayonets, field guns, shells, battleship armor and flotillas of submarines, always at immense profit to the House of Krupp. After Franz Ferdinand's death the Central Powers sprang to arms, thereby confronting the House with a stupendous market. Thus there is a fine analogue in members of the family entering archducal forests, trigger fingers tense, stalking prey. They were, in fact, symbols of the Fatherland's national mood.

Everything about the Krupps was remarkable: their way of life (secretive), their appearance (vulpine), their empire (international), and their customers (chiefs of state), but nothing was quite so phenomenal as this habit of matching the Teuton mood of the moment. In the Middle Ages, when Germany was weak, the Krupps appeared and plied their trade modestly in the walled city of Essen. During the Napoleonic era, when the country felt servile, the head of the house donned a French cockade and became a Francophile. Then, in the next half-century, Germany rose. The drums of conquest rolled in 1870, 1914, and 1939, and each time it was a Krupp who honed the Junker blade on the family's anvils. Nowhere in American industry — or that of any other country — can you find a match for the ties that have bound German governments to the Krupp family. For a century the two were inseparable partners, often acting as instruments of one another. And never has the parallel been more striking than in the appalling spring of 1945, when it appeared to have become deadly.

When Gustav bought Blühnbach he never dreamed that he might be buying a tomb. Nevertheless, thirty-one years later the lodge became that to him, for as the Third Reich crumbled it seemed that the country and the Krupp dynasty were about to expire together. Throughout that extraordinary season the head of the house lay as prostrate as the nation — helpless, paralyzed, in an upstairs bedroom surrounded by thousands of stuffed deer heads, mounted skins, and bric-a-brac fashioned from animal bones. He was not surrounded by his family. Twelve years earlier Gustav had reached the *kolossal* conclusion that Barbarossa's new name was Adolf Hitler, and four of his sons had departed to become, in the words of the Führer's *Mein Kampf* exhortation to all German youth, "hard as Krupp steel" (*hart wie Kruppstahl*).[2] Of the paralytic's children, five sons and two daughters, only one was here: thirty-two-year-old Berthold, a delicate, Oxford-educated scientist who had been released by the Wehrmacht for penicillin research in Munich.

The third person in the room was the most famous woman in the Reich.

Her name was Bertha Krupp, and she was Gustav's wife. For nearly a half-century she had been Germany's richest individual. Born in cheerless, forbidding Villa Hügel, the three-hundred-room Krupp castle in Essen, Bertha had been bred to be a Teutonic version of Queen Mary — faithful, regal, erect as a candle. In her youth Kaiser Wilhelm II had been almost a member of the family. He had had a suite at Hügel, he had presided at her wedding, and he had been godfather to her eldest son. Later she had become an international figure. The world knew her as Big Bertha, because in the Kaiser's war Krupp's giant mortar had been christened for her (*die dicke Bertha*, literally "fat Bertha") and in World War II her name had been given to the Berthawerk, a Krupp howitzer plant in Silesia built and manned by Jewish slave labor from Auschwitz, which had a Krupp automatic weapons plant within the camp, where, according to the Nuremberg testimony of one of Gustav's own employees:

> *Vom Fabrikgelände aus konnte man die drei grossen Schornsteine des Krematoriums sehen . . . die Häftlinge erzählten von den Vergasungen und Verbrennungen, die im Lager stattfanden.*

> From the factory one could see the three big chimneys of the crematorium . . . the inmates told of the gassing and burning that took place in the camp.[3]

Today virtually all Germans and a majority abroad believe that German industrialists had no choice, that the Nazis forced them to use slaves of all ages and sexes, that the industrialists themselves would have been exterminated had they behaved otherwise. This is untrue. The forgotten mountains of Nuremberg documents are quite clear about this. They reveal that the Reich's manufacturers not only had a choice; most of them took advantage of it:

> The Flick concern did not accept women, because the work was too heavy for them. [*Der Flick-Konzern hat die Frauen nicht angenommen, weil die Arbeit für sie zu schwer war*]. The Röchling group displayed no interest in foreign labor. . . . Hitler himself did not then consider it practical for so important a concern as Krupp to employ foreign labor. . . . Himmler was opposed to allowing this valuable labor pool, which he wished to manage himself, to work for the armaments industry.[4]

Krupp felt otherwise. According to the firm's wartime reports, the family-owned concern believed that "automatic weapons are the weapons of the future" (*automatische Waffen sind die Waffen der Zukunft*) and used the great prestige of Krupp's name to conscript Auschwitz prisoners — men, women, and children — for heavy labor in its shops. Setting an example of vigor and enterprise, the Essen *Konzern* refused to be turned back when the army, uneasy about the camp's proximity to the fluid eastern front, vetoed automatic weapons manufacture there. The firm's own records show that

> . . . *schlug Krupp vor, in der bereits in Auschwitz zur Verfügung stehenden Fabrikhalle die Fertigung von Flugzeugbestandteilen und Zündern aufzunehmen, da inzwischen die Zünderfabrik in Essen ausgebombt worden war.* . . .

> . . . Krupp proposed that the factory building, which already stood complete in Auschwitz, be used for the manufacture of aircraft parts and shell fuses, since, in the meantime, the Essen fuse factory had been bombed out. The essential point that influences the decision is, once again, the availability of labor in the concentration camp. For this very reason, Krupp opposed a proposal to employ German workmen. When the army wanted to give the fuse contract to another firm, arguing that Krupp was not in a position to fulfill the production quotas, Krupp objected violently, laying particular stress on the firm's close connection with the Auschwitz concentration camp.[5]

To an outsider the implications of all this are clear, and are reflected in Krupp's dreadful reputation abroad. Inside Germany the image is quite different. There the memory of Bertha is still beloved (she died in 1957), and she herself was always puzzled by bitterness toward the family in *das Ausland*, that revealing German word which welds all nations outside the Reich into a single collective noun. Actually the firm's military activity didn't interest her. That was for men; as a woman she was preoccupied with the social welfare of the two hundred thousand Germans who toiled for the Krupp Konzern. For as long as she or anybody else could remember, these *Kruppianer* had been wards of the family. The challenge had always been met with imagination; in the nineteenth century Bismarck's great social legislation had been inspired by Krupp programs.[6]

Now in 1945 it appeared that the hegemony was to end. In its four centuries the dynasty had known madness, shocking sex scandal, the humiliation of military occupation, and even insolvency, but there had been nothing comparable to this blood-colored smog. A Wagnerian night was descending over Germany. Not since the Thirty Years War had there been anything like it, and Krupp had at least profited then. Heinrich Heine's bleak prediction appeared to be coming true: civilization faced destruction in an orgy of fighting for fighting's sake. In Bertha's youth such a catastrophe would have been inconceivable, though her mother, Margarethe von Ende Krupp, may have had an intimation of it. To Baron Tilo von Wilmowsky, who married Bertha's sister Barbara, Margarethe once said, "You know, I am frequently depressed that I have lived to see such a glut of good fortune, and so many honors from the Kaiser . . . it is almost too much. . . . Often I am afraid, as in a nightmare, that all this may one day collapse" (*Oft bedrückt mich wie ein Alpdruck die Furcht, dass all dieses einmal zusammenbrechen könnte*).[7]

Yet it is unlikely that even Margarethe could have glimpsed how total that collapse was to be. From the capital Goebbels repeatedly broadcast the assurance that "Berlin stays German! Vienna will be German again!" (*Berlin bleibt deutsch, Wien wird wieder deutsch!*), but each hour it became clearer that Austria had seen its last coal-scuttle helmet, its last Wehrmacht jackboot. Six months had passed since General Jodl scrawled in his diary on September 28, "Black day" (*Schwarzer Tag*). Now in April, the cruelest month, all days were black, and this family was among the hardest hit. Essen was a broken, cratered wasteland. Bertha's sister, who shared her contempt for Hitler as a parvenu, had been seized after the July 20, 1944, attempt on the Führer's life. Bertha's titled brother-in-law had been sent to Sachsenhausen concentration camp for the same reason; a son-in-law lay dead in the Russian snows; a nephew was at the bottom of the Atlantic — drowned, ironically, when the British ship upon which he was being transported to Canada as a prisoner of war was torpedoed by a Krupp U-boat. Worse, three of Bertha's own sons had left as officers of the Reich and vanished into the haze of battle. Adventurous, athletic Claus had died in the Luftwaffe in 1940. His brother Harald, lanky and intro-spective, had been captured in Bucharest four years later by Soviet troops. And though none of the Krupps knew it yet, Eckbert, the baby of the family, had just been killed in action in Italy. Now, at Blühnbach with Gustav, Bertha was reduced to the role of practical nurse, a handler of bedpans. Götterdämmerung was not only turning out to be worse than advertised; it was also vastly more vulgar.[8]

"*Ach, mein Gott!*" the wintry figure on the bed would croak. "Bertha! Berthold!" Swiftly they attended him. A distant door would slam, and he would rage, "*Donnerwetter! Himmel! Verfault, verdammt, geistesschwach!*" — for in the deepening twilight of senility this old man, who had given his own name to Fat Gustav, the mighty siege gun of Sevastopol, was infuriated by the faintest noise.

This too was ironic, and perhaps it was also just. Indeed, it may be argued that the paralysis itself was a fitting climax to Gustav's career. All his life he had been a parody of Prussian rigidity. To make sure that he would be peppy in wintertime, he had kept his office temperature at 55 degrees and his Hügel study at 64 — Bertha labored over her social problems on the other side of the desk swathed in furs, and the rooms are chilly to this day. Hügel dinners were notorious. Gustav believed in brisk meals. Several visitors can remember that when they tried to make amiable conversation, their plates were snatched away; "You had to eat so fast," according to one of them, "that your teeth hurt." Gustav, who ate with remarkable skill and speed himself, felt that table talk was inefficient.[9]

Efficiency was his religion. One of his oddest hobbies was reading train timetables, looking for typographical errors. When he found one he would seize his telephone and denounce the railroad. Leaving for the office each morning, he expected his chauffeur to have the engine running; he didn't want to hang around all those seconds while the key was turned in the ignition. And Hügel guests learned that their host retired at 10 P.M. precisely; at 9:45 a servant would whisper to them that it was time to go. Once Gustav broke this rule. He agreed to attend a civil celebration until midnight. Ernst von Raussendorf, a Krupp executive, was standing at the bar that evening with Gustav's older daughter Irmgard when she said quietly, "Look at your watch." He did — as the watch of a Kruppianer it was naturally on time — and told her that twelve o'clock was just a moment away. "Father will be leaving now," Irmgard said. When the sweep-second hand noted the hour, Raussendorf glanced up, and sure enough, there was his employer, rising from the chair.[10]

More significant to the world outside Essen was Gustav's absolute loyalty to the leader of his country. It didn't much matter who the leader was. After the Kaiser's exile in 1918 he had remained *kaisertreu*, writing Doorn each year on Wilhelm's birthday to reaffirm his loyalty. Yet at the same time he would leave a room rather than hear a slur against the President of the Weimar Republic. With the rise of Hitler he became what a fellow industrialist called a "super-Nazi" (*Obernazi*). He was quite prepared to accept the ultimate consequences of his new faith. When Claus's plane crashed in the Eifel Hills a friend offered condolences. The father replied icily, *"Mein Sohn hatte die Ehre, für den Führer zu sterben"* (My son had the honor to die for the Führer).[11]

This was the Gustav Allied intelligence knew — the robot, the fanatic party leader, the proud wearer of the Golden Party Badge. Even as he moaned beneath his Blühnbach eiderdown, agents were fanning across Europe searching for him, for with Göring and Ribbentrop he stood high on the list of men wanted as war criminals. Gustav was familiar with this sort of thing. Like Wilhelm, he had been named a war criminal after World War I, and when the French occupied the Ruhr in 1923 they had sent him to prison. This time, however, the Allies were determined that he should end his life at the end of a Nuremberg rope. His name had become so odious that Harald, in a Russian prisoner of war camp, found it wise to adopt an alias. Every Allied power had a dossier on Gustav, and virtually everything they had was unimpeachable.[12]

And yet there were some striking omissions. No man is really a robot. Gustav's very excesses are suspect. Like the Kaiser, whose strutting had masked bitter shame over his withered arm, Gustav was trying to be something he was not. Outside Hügel he deceived nearly everyone; his sons' friends called him "the Bull," which he doubtless found gratifying. But no man looked less like a bull. In the family he was known by the absurd nursery nickname Taffy. Taffy was slight, dainty, and a head shorter than his wife; he had been schooled as a diplomat, and retained the diplomat's elegant mannerisms. (Sometimes this training even shone through at the Hügel dining table. Once a visiting Russian technician, who had never seen a finger bowl, picked his up and drank from it. Gustav watched thoughtfully, then lifted his own and drained it.[13])

If this suggests that there was something bogus about him, it is accurate. For forty years he had been playing a part. He had been posing as the owner of a firm in which he didn't have a share of stock, and he had been masquerading as a Krupp although he had never met anyone by that name until he was thirty-six years old.

The real Krupp was Bertha. She had inherited her father's vast industrial empire when she was sixteen. In the Fatherland it was unthinkable for a woman to hold such power, so she had married Gustav von Bohlen und Halbach. There is some reason to believe that the Kaiser himself was the matchmaker; young Bertha's arms forges were a priceless asset to Germany, and every German military man of any consequence showed up at the Hügel wedding to give away the bride. After the vows Wilhelm announced in his nasal voice that henceforth Gustav's last name would be "*Krupp* von Bohlen und Halbach." In popular usage this was quickly shortened to Gustav Krupp. But the emperor himself addressed the groom as "my dear Bohlen," and no imperial edict could inject an ounce of Krupp blood into Gustav's veins. His surviving sons refer to him today as the "prince consort" (*Prinzgemahl*).[14]

This is confusing. Indeed, the deeper one dives into the family's lore, the murkier the waters become. But in 1945 the victorious powers were in no mood for complexities. Already a corps of eminent lawyers, led by United States Supreme Court Justice Robert H. Jackson, were culling the Krupp dossiers. Presently American troops reached Blühnbach. Gustav, under guard, was moved to an inn on a nearby road, where Bertha continued to nurse him. Buses stopped there, and sometimes the drivers would help her with soiled bedding, but otherwise she carried on alone, for Berthold had left on urgent family business.[15]

The jurists continued to cull. It took them some time to discover that the Krupp in the inn was the wrong Krupp.

They had been obsessed with Gustav. He was the demon, they thought, because he had led the firm so long. It was true that the prince consort had still been very much in charge when Hitler attacked Poland. Since then, however, night and fog had blanketed the Reich, and the Allies didn't know that there had been a change of command in Essen. Gustav's senility had already become advanced when Claus died in 1940. Throughout most of the intervening years — when a monstrous Krupp gun on curved railway tracks in a cave bombed Chatham from Cap Gris-Nez on the other side of the English Channel, firing at a range of 134 miles and throwing shells so enormous that to this day the British survivors believe that they were being pounded by high altitude Luftwaffe bombers; through the years of Auschwitz and slave labor, when the inmates of 138 concentration camps toiled for Krupp, and Robert Rothschild was gassed because he wouldn't sign his French firm over to Krupp — the leader of the family (who would remain so until his strange death in the late 1960's) had been the eldest son of Bertha and Gustav.[16]

His name was Alfried Felix Alwyn Krupp von Bohlen und Halbach. Here one must dip into those cloudy waters for a quick briefing on Krupp surnames. The Kaiser's wedding decree of 1906 meant that in future generations only the senior male would be named Krupp von Bohlen und Halbach. Claus, Berthold, Harald, Eckbert and their sisters bore the name of their father. Their older brother had been similarly christened. He had even remained Alfried von Bohlen after March 31, 1942, when he became the firm's *Vorsitzender des Vorstandes*, Director of Directors. As such, according to his own files, he

> . . . assigned Jewish prisoners from concentration camps to many different places [*hat . . . jüdische Gefangene aus Konzentrationslagern an den verschiedensten Arbeitsplätzen beschäftigt*], including the Friedrich Krupp Bertha Works (AG) in Markstädt near Breslau, in the concentration camp at Auschwitz, in the concentration camps at Wüstegiersdorf, Riespot near Bremen, Geisenheim, Elmag (Elsässische Maschinenbau A.G., Mulhouse, Alsace), and in the Essen (Humboldtstrasse) camp.[17]

At this last camp, according to one of Alfried's workmen, who was put on the Nuremberg stand in the vain hope that his testimony would help the defense, fantastic conditions prevailed even after it was obvious that the Reich had lost the war:

> . . . *Krupp hielt es für [eine] Pflicht 520 jüdische Mädchen, zum Teil noch fast Kinder, unter brutalsten Bedingungen im Herzen des Konzerns, in Essen, arbeiten zu lassen.*

> . . . Krupp considered it a duty to make 520 Jewish girls, some of them little more than children, work under the most brutal conditions in the heart of the concern, in Essen.[18]

Alfried's own wartime words reveal that he was exploiting his special relationship with Berlin, first to get Jews and then, having them, to get contracts which could be handled only by a firm with a limitless reservoir of labor. In a letter dated September 7, 1943, he wrote a Lieutenant Colonel (*Oberstleutnant*) Wedel:

> *Was die Mitarbeit unseres technischen Büros . . . in Breslau angeht,*

*kann ich nur sagen, dass zwischen diesem Büro und Auschwitz die engste
Zusammenarbeit besteht und für die Zukunft gesichert ist.*

As regards the cooperation of our technical office in Breslau, I can only
say that between that office and Auschwitz the closest understanding exists
and is guaranteed for the future.[19]

Really there was no job he could not undertake. His manpower pool was
almost bottomless. Auschwitz prisoners were only a fraction of it. His
papers show that apart from German workmen he had assembled 69,898
foreign civilian workmen, 23,076 prisoners of war, and 4,978 concentration
camp prisoners (almost exclusively Jews). With 97,952 slaves, he was the
sovereign of the Ruhr. Yet he still lacked the crown. He wanted it, and in
the eyes of National Socialist ideologues he was entitled to it. Gustav's
condition was plainly hopeless. It was time he surrendered the prized
"Krupp." One-man rule was a family tradition, and as early as 1941
Gustav and Bertha had agreed that the industrial monarchy should go
to Alfried — provided he divorce his objectionable young wife, which
he speedily did.[20]

Passing everything along to one child was illegal, however; it would
disinherit the others. Extraordinary measures were required, and on August
10, 1942, Alfried, a tall, aquiline, middle-aged man who bore a strong
physical resemblance to his mother, presented himself at the Führer's
underground headquarters in East Prussia to thrash the matter out. As
one of the party bigwigs (*Bonzen*), true to the Führer since youth, he
was assured of a warm welcome. After a lengthy correspondence with
Martin Bormann, Hitler's deputy, and Hans Lammers, the Nazi constitutional oracle, everything was settled. The Führer proclaimed:

> *Die Firma Fried. Krupp, ein Familienunternehmen seit 132 Jahren,
> verdient höchste Anerkennung für ihre unvergleichlichen Leistungen bei
> der Verstärkung der militärischen Macht Deutschlands. Es ist daher mein
> Wunsch, dass das Unternehmen als Familieneigentum erhalten wird.*

> The firm of Fried. Krupp, a family enterprise for 132 years, deserves the
> highest recognition for its incomparable performances in boosting the
> military power of Germany. Therefore, it is my wish that the enterprise be
> preserved as a family property.[21]

With his signature, this decree became a unique law, the "Lex Krupp."
Alfried was now his mother's sole heir. At the same time Hitler re-
christened him Krupp, and when the U.S. Ninth Army captured Essen on
April 11, 1945, they found Alfried more or less lashed to the mast, carrying
on — as he had since 1931, when he became a sponsoring member of the
SS — for Führer and Reich.[22]

Thus it was Alfried who mounted the dock at Nuremberg, Alfried who stood trial before three U.S. state supreme court justices on charges of planning aggressive war, spoliation of property in occupied countries, and, above all, crimes against humanity — the slave labor count, the heart of the case. He was acquitted of aggression. That, the tribunal ruled, lay in Gustav's era. On the other charges he was found guilty, however, and sentenced to twelve years in prison and the confiscation of all his property.[23]

So shocking had the evidence against him been that all the Allies, East and West, were determined to purge Europe of the Krupp name. The nightmare had grown darker and darker, until now it was blacker than the bottom of the deepest Krupp mine. The dynasty's holdings were being systematically carved up; dismantlers with long sticks of chalk were drawing lines across factory floors, dividing plant and machinery among the nations which had suffered most from the Nazi occupation,[24] and in Landsberg Fortress, where Hitler had written *Mein Kampf* two decades before, Alfried wore convict garb. To the family his imprisonment was the most grievous blow of all. Raised to be a prince of industrialists, he now lay rusting in jail, condemned and humiliated. The Krupps had always been fiercely proud. This burden was almost insupportable. And yet, apparently, it had to be borne.

☩    ☩    ☩

No one then would have thought it possible that within five years he would once more control his fortune, or that twenty years after he had become Adolf Hitler's most famous industrial protégé he would be the richest man in Europe, the most powerful industrialist in the Common Market. Even he himself became impressed with the speed of his recovery — at one time he had estimated that it would take him fifty years to clear the rubble in Essen alone. Yet he had never doubted that redemption would come, or that he would be ultimately vindicated. After the Nuremberg verdict Friedrich von Bülow, the fellow prisoner who had directed Krupp's slave labor program, had wanted to plan an escape. According to Bülow, Alfried had put a stop to that. He had said calmly, "Time will settle all."[25]

On the surface this seemed to be absurd optimism. The U.S. Supreme Court had rejected an appeal from his attorneys. On August 21, 1948, three weeks after the verdict, Alfried had written to General Lucius Clay, military governor of West Germany's American zone, asking him to intervene. There had been no reply. Then the general had endorsed the findings of a review board and confirmed the Nuremberg sentence, an act which apparently exhausted the prisoner's legal remedies. Yet Alfried's faith was justified by the striking parallels between the Krupp saga and German history. "After the Kaiser left," a Villa Hügel servant once told me, "this became the first family of Germany."[26] In some ways the Krupps had a greater claim to primacy than the Hohenzollerns, and as the 1940's ended the nation began to take an upward turn. The economic miracle of the country's recovery had begun. So had the Cold War, and NATO diplomats wanted Germany committed to their side.

The devotion of the conquered people to the Krupps could hardly be lost on the occupation authorities. In the early 1960's a Hamburg news-paper editor told this writer, "If I retranslated the Nuremberg testimony and documents that condemned Herr Krupp into German, and published them in this country, I'd be out of a job. There's always been a feeling here that other companies make profits, but that *Krupp* is doing something for *Germany*." That sentiment was even stronger during Alfried's imprison-ment. When Bertha came to see her son during visiting hours, the Germans there treated her as royalty, and once a young girl rushed up and kissed her hand. Above all, the grand alliance which was forming against the Soviet Union needed the power of the Ruhr. That meant Alfried. "The Ruhr is Essen," Germans say, and "Essen is Krupp," and "*Wenn Deutschland blüht, blüht Krupp*" (When Germany prospers, Krupp prospers). In theory there were two ways to detour around him. The first was nationalization. But even the British Labour government was against that. The second was forced emigration. Although a U.S. Cabinet mem-ber had proposed that "no Germans should be left in the Ruhr at all," the plan was neither workable nor desirable, and there is no indication that any other solution was seriously considered until seven months after the out-break of the Korean War, when U.S. High Commissioner John J. McCloy, in a historic act of clemency, removed the problem by restoring Alfried's holdings and pardoning him.[27]

With that act, a penniless convict was restored to his former exalted status. Once more a Krupp held the key to Europe's greatest treasure.

It was, and remains, an extraordinary treasure.

✠      ✠      ✠

Across central Europe the great coalfields lie like a glittering black belt, waiting to flame into power. This priceless lode, without which the indus-trial revolution would have been impossible, starts in Wales and ends in Poland. There is nothing uniform about it, however. The seams in France and Belgium vary enormously in yield and quality, and between Saxony and Polish Silesia, where the vein ends, stands a vast tract of sterile ground. By any standard, the most valuable jewel in the tiara is that corner of Germany where the Rhine emerges from the hulking hills and turns westward toward the plains of Holland. Here the great river is fed by a sluggish, polluted tributary — chemists estimate that its waters pass through the human body eight times — which rises in the Sauerland, over a hundred miles to the east. That stream is the Ruhr. As a waterway it has slight value now. It is so insignificant that long ago it lost exclusive right to

its own name. By "the Ruhr" we really mean the Ruhrgebiet, the surrounding region, and there the story is very different. In that basin
Germans mine as much coal as the rest of the continent combined, and
produce more fine steel. The relationship is not casual. This is Europe's
prime source of coke — pure carbon, acquired by cooking coal to draw off
its gases — and it is spongy, brittle coke which is indispensable for the
conversion of iron into steel.

Dominating the Ruhr are fewer than a dozen *Schlotbarone*, "smokestack
barons." The figure is apt. In the nineteenth century their families
replaced the declining feudal aristocracy. Led by the Krupps, the industrialists played on German habits of obedience to crush struggling unions,
and their workmen became docile and immobile. Even today the typical
Ruhr worker is determined to live out his life within view of the church
where he was baptized. One underground manager of a Krupp mine was
among the Luftwaffe's first jet pilots in World War II. Afterward he was
offered a future in commercial aviation. The pay would have been better,
the life cleaner. He declined. Over schnapps I asked him why. He replied,
"My father was underground manager of this mine." The abiding loyalty
of such men evokes images of feudal society; so do the customs of their
employers. The smokestack barons *act* like barons. The men build castles
and keep to themselves, and the women behave like ladies of the manor,
visiting sick dependents and contributing to charities. Bertha Krupp was
famous for her good works. When fatally stricken by a heart attack,
she was putting on her hat, preparing to visit the widow of a
Kruppianer.[28]

Despite its prominence, the Ruhr is a tiny fief, a mere scar on the map
of the continent. It taps hydroelectric sources as far away as Aachen, the
Black Forest, and Switzerland, yet it occupies less than one percent of
truncated West Germany. Counting every forge and shaft, it is no larger
than metropolitan New York. You can drive over most of it in three hours
on the Dortmund-Düsseldorf Autobahn or commute from one end to the
other on its famous streetcars. The inner Ruhr — fifteen cities which run
into one another — covers only two hundred square miles. As the RAF
demonstrated in the early 1940's, this leaves it vulnerable to a determined
assault. But concentration has another side. Because the geologic freak
beneath the soil has been brilliantly exploited, the Ruhr has become, as
Gustav Stolper wrote, "an industrial organization which in its compactness
and intensity is unparalleled in the world." German ingenuity has made it
the continent's most awesome economic force, with political consequences
which have been felt by five generations of Europeans and three of
Americans. Aware of their strength, the Schlotbarone wrung vital concessions from Berlin under the Second Reich (the Kaisers) and the Third
Reich (Hitler), and it was here that the German sword was forged
three times in the past century. "The German Empire," John Maynard

Keynes observed, "has been built more truly on coal and iron than on blood and iron."[29]

Blood and iron has proved to be a more memorable phrase because it is more stirring. Rolling drums and glittering medals have a greater romantic appeal than slide rules and smog, and on the whole they have been more favored by historians. Schoolchildren are taught that Sparta won battles because she put superior warriors in the field. The lesson disregards recent research, which has revealed that while the Spartans' enemies were limited to bronze and soft wrought iron, they themselves were armed with swords of superb steel — a decisive advantage. Professional soldiers are more sensitive to such distinctions. In the days when the Ruhr was disgorging staggering quantities of tanks, cannon, shells, aircraft, and submarines, the German General Staff fully appreciated their arsenal. In both world wars it lay at the core of their strategy. Indeed, their anxiety to shield it in 1914 may have weakened the right wing of the Schlieffen Plan to invade France. After World War II, General Franz Halder declared at Nuremberg that the Ruhrgebiet was "the most decisive factor in the German conduct of the war." This was no news to Halder's former antagonists. Once the Normandy landings had been completed, Allied generals agreed that the Wehrmacht's armory was their chief target. They disagreed only on which route to it was quickest.[30]

Today the Ruhr produces few weapons. It has become the powerhouse of the European Economic Community and, because of Krupp's immensity and technical skills, of underdeveloped countries around the globe. The barons, stronger and wealthier than ever, look eagerly to the future. Inquiries into their past, on the other hand, are discouraged, and even resented. Yet it is impossible to understand the German present without jacking open lids and prying into crypts and memories which have been sealed. To grasp Krupp's Ruhr, we must know both what it is and what it has been. Luckily geography doesn't change, and one way to start is by looking at the Ruhr — actually eying it — from three points: a tunnel, the surface above, and a small plane cruising overhead.

✠     ✠     ✠

The tunnel lies a half-mile underground. It is at the bottom of Essen's one-hundred-year-old Amalie shaft, named for Alfried's great-great-great-great-grandmother, and reaching it is something of an expedition. *"Glück-auf!"* (Good luck!), the burly men around you call to one another as the party vanishes into the cavernous entrance. Helmeted and booted, equipped with a flashlight and a carbon monoxide mask, you descend for two hours via cart elevators, clanking miniature trains, and — most of the time — by hiking down ancient, arched passageways hewn from rock.

It is not a pleasant journey, nor is it entirely safe. Certainly mining conditions have improved since Amalie's first years, when men toiled in the bowels of the Ruhr aided only by crude lamps, mules, and their own picks. Mechanization has changed all that. However, it has also permitted Kruppianer to go deeper, and danger increases with depth;* each year four or five men die in this shaft. One dodges live wires and coal carts. The air is thick with black powder, and the ignition of a single match here could bring catastrophe.

Approaching the face, the tunnel shrinks. You go to your knees, and then to your belly. At the same time, the temperature rises spectacularly. In places where the rock is damp (in a mine, water is hotter than stone) the thermometer reaches 122 degrees Fahrenheit. Dead ahead one dimly perceives naked, soot-covered men groveling in the rich dust. These *Kumpel*, miners, earn nine dollars a day. Although the men at the face are carefully picked, they can't take more than five hours of such work at a stretch. Each day they tear four thousand tons from Amalie's hoard: an extraordinary yield, for the seam is only a yard high. Sprawling among them, you watch the face gleam fitfully in the swinging beam of your light. It is craggy and blue-black, and as you watch, it recedes slightly. An automatic knife slices across it. Great chunks fall to a conveyor belt, which, moving jerkily, carries them off to the carts and elevators.

There are over one hundred and fifty miles of such caves under Essen alone, and they are moving all the time; as the knives slash at one side, roof jacks are shifted to fill in the opposite side with slag. The city is literally founded on coal. And Krupp's vertical concentration is literally vertical, for when the coal goes up it is fed directly into furnaces.

✠   ✠   ✠

This relationship is seen clearly when you surface and mount the corrugated iron roof of a Krupp mill in nearby Bochum. Looking across the mill yard, you watch processions of trains arriving, freighted with iron ore. Their cargo comes from all over the world. Less than 20 percent of it is German; less than half is European. Most of the ore has been shipped from Africa, Asia, and the Western Hemisphere.[31] Meanwhile, as the trains dump their cascades of glinting rock into bins, chains of buckets brimming with coal appear from holes in the earth and are shuttled upward, on moving ropes, toward the factory. Good coke is more precious than ore; the plant is here because the coal is just below.

Like the mine, the mill is uncomfortably hot — in an old Ruhr story a steel baron arrives in hell and cries, "*Verdammt!* I forgot my winter coat!" Unlike the tunnel, however, the plant provides spectacles of blinding beauty. A major steel tap, with hundreds of tons of liquid metal streaming from several open-hearth furnaces simultaneously, throwing off great

---

* There is a limit, even with mechanization; since the above was written commercial mining has been suspended in the Amalie shaft.

clouds of sparks as they race through the earthen forms provided for them, is breathtaking. Crusts of iron oxide flaking off hot ingots, the cherry-red glow of metal moving through blooming mills, the way monster forgings repeatedly burst into gouts of flame as automatic presses five stories high shape and trim them — the whole pageant is exciting, even glorious.

It is exciting because it makes sense. In the mine every movement seemed to be pointless drudgery, but upstairs the meaning of the Ruhr begins to emerge. And leaving Bochum and striking out across the centers of heavy industry, one acquires a feeling for the setting. The peculiar, introverted society that has grown up in the shadow of the towering chimneys is a milieu all its own. It becomes evident in little ways. You are struck by the angular, topheavy silhouettes of the terra-cotta houses; by the dark, smoke-colored patina that gives even the newest buildings an aura of age; by the endless crocodiles of domed, grimy boxcars which, though they are now stenciled EUROP, haven't changed since the early 1940's, when they were used for infamous purposes.

You hear the workers speaking that harsh north German which, as the Bavarians say, "makes the ears bleed." Most of the voices are deep. The Ruhr is largely a man's society, even after hours. Among executives dinner parties without women are still very common. (To an Ausländer this seems rather Wilhelmine, and here, as in Wilhelmine Germany and Victorian England, illicit sex flourishes. Although there are only three hundred registered prostitutes in Essen, the police estimate that there are two thousand unregulated "wild girls" — *wilde Dirnen* — part-time free-lance women, many of them young matrons, who have sprung up to answer a felt need.)

Not all the voices are guttural. The proud, monocled class distinguished by its slashed cheeks, homburgs, and chauffeured black Mercedes is as insular as ever, but when you leave the industrial hierarchy and move on the denimed level you are in a more cosmopolitan world. There is nothing new in this. During the nineteenth century Polish and east German labor built the factories. Today seventy thousand migrants form the base of the Ruhr's economic pyramid, evoking memories of the years when foreigners were not recruited but impressed. Since the immigration of wives and children is discouraged, the newcomers add to the Ruhr's masculinity. On Saturday nights there isn't much else for them to do, so they get drunk. You see them staggering around shopping centers in lonely little clusters, staring enviously at the glittering display windows.

During the week, when German women invade the stores shoulder to shoulder in mass formation, the outsiders have no time for window shopping. Ruhr workers really work. Indeed, one's most enduring impression of the region is of activity. Each of its industrial complexes seethes, and every artery in and out of the arena is crowded with trucks, trains, barges, and planes, bringing fodder for the plants and departing with finished products. It is noisy, it is incredibly busy, and it is best seen from the sky.

✠　　✠　　✠

Flying over the Ruhr is like dodging traffic in a dense fog. On the sunniest day the visibility is less than a mile. The pall of smoke starts north of Cologne and rises ten thousand feet; you can see it boiling up from the forest of chimneys below: black smoke, red smoke, yellow, white, and orange smoke, blending into an immense greasy overcast as the toiling chefs below season and spice their entrées of liquid metal.

Though hazy, the landscape is anything but colorless. You are constantly aware of the spectrum of hues, and watching a steam locomotive puff beneath you (inasmuch as coal is all around, the engines have not been switched to diesel) you realize why. You have seen this before. Twenty-five years ago, when the Ruhr was known as Flak Alley, every Allied fighter carried cameras synchronized with its wing guns. Those reels have been reproduced in a thousand films and documentaries — the strafing of a German plane has become a movie cliché — but they are all black-and-white, and witnessing the real thing one is vividly aware of the rust-brown of Krupp's bottle-shaped furnaces at Rheinhausen on the left bank of the Rhine; of the red switches in the great railroad marshaling yard at Hamm, whose fringes are still pitted by bomb craters; of the chalk-and-lemon-colored concrete plants; of the bright blue of coiling canals bearing beetlelike barges around Duisburg; of the bilious mists spiraling up from the octagonal cooling towers which squat beside each mill like bizarre gasworks. Nothing is entirely gray. At Kettwig the castle of August Thyssen has a cerulescent tint, and at Essen, on the north bank of the Ruhr River, the sprawling mass of Krupp's Villa Hügel is a mottled tan.

The most surprising color, however, is green. It is startling because there is so much of it. Confined on the surface to the ganglia of Ruhr power, you had expected to see a gigantic complex of workshops and sheds, criss-crossed by mean streets and surrounded by dreary slums. There is plenty of squalor. The cities of Wanne-Eickel, Castrop-Rauxel, and Gelsenkirchen are grimed, stained, weathered, almost Dickensian; *Gelsenkirchener Barock* is a German synonym for hideous taste. But there is countryside, too. In fact, only a tenth of the Ruhr is really congested, and half of it is under the plow. While it is rarely lovely — Mirabeau dismissed one of its reaches as *"froide, stérile, d'un aspect hideux"*[32] — much of it is genuinely rural. Thick stands of forest separate the outlying towns. Meadows appear, inhabited by cattle. Between Herne and Lünen, above Dortmund, are flourishing estates owned by Westphalia's landed aristocracy. This soil is rich in more than minerals. Before the Ruhr became an industrial gem it was an agricultural gem, and the banks of the river itself are lined with iridescent shoulders of swaying foliage.

Indeed, so blessed is the Ruhr that its violent history cannot possibly be attributed to the land. In few strips of the world has nature been so generous. Not only is it wealthy and fertile; its position athwart the natural trade routes of Europe made it an anchor of commerce for the whole continent six centuries ago, and cruising over the larger cities at a thousand feet you can still discern the crooked pattern of medieval alleys below.

It is to these cities that one repeatedly returns in fascination, for there — jagged, jumbled, yet awesome all the same — is the true majesty of the Ruhr. There is nothing pastoral about it. The factories loom through the refracted light like cathedrals, and if you bank and drift down a few hundred feet your attention is riveted on the intricate maze beneath the wings, and you quickly forget the idyllic landscape behind the tail. The overwhelming impression is of stark Teutonic power. Although the cornucopia of the Ruhr disgorges peaceful products now, anyone with memories of another generation feels vaguely disquieted. The very pattern of the key centers is menacing. On a map they suggest the shadow of the gigantic Fenris-wolf, offspring of Loki and the giantess Angurboda and brother of the Mitgard serpent. The evil wolf was bound by a magic cord until he burst free to swallow Odin, and it is unfettered that his silhouette appears on the map, lunging eastward. Hamm is the eye, Recklinghausen the ear, Dortmund the mouth, Bochum the throat. Wuppertal and Solingen form the front leg, Mülheim and Düsseldorf the rear. Rheinhausen is the tail. Gelsenkirchen, Bottrop, and Duisburg trace the hunched back. And the heart is Essen.

✠     ✠     ✠

The Ruhrgebiet as we know it is scarcely a century old. Armenians were producing wrought iron nearly three thousand years ago, and the blast furnace appeared in Europe toward the end of the Middle Ages. Industrialization came late to Germany, however, and when it arrived the impact was shattering, for reasons deeply embedded in the nation's history.[33]

The greenery of the Ruhr is the clue to those reasons. Even today deep woods typify much of Germany, and at the dawn of written European history the entire country was one enormous jungle. To the Romans that Hercynian forest was a marvel. East of the Rhine it stretched on and on, dark, solid, and terrifying. Caesar talked to Germans who had journeyed through it for two months without a glimpse of sunlight. Tacitus was appalled by its vastness, its impenetrable marshes, its brutal winters and its cloaking, soaking fog.

The Rhine was Caesar's outpost. The land beyond never became part of his empire. In Gaul there were roads down which his legions could march, conquering what would later become France and giving it political cohesion. In the trackless wildwood to the east this was impossible, and so we see the beginning of an unhappy chain of events. It is notable that the earliest known altar in what is now Bonn, on the Rhine's left bank, was dedicated by Caesar's embittered legionnaires to Nemesis, the goddess of retribution. Germany, remaining formless, failed to develop into a national state during the Middle Ages; it was, as Will Durant wrote, "not a nation but a name." The Thirty Years War robbed it of its Renaissance. *Obrigkeit*, authority, remained in the hands of some three hundred independent princes (nowhere was this fragmentation more extreme than in the Ruhr) who suppressed half-formed nationalism during the French Revolution and throttled liberalism in 1848. Then Prussia, "the germ cell of the Reich," as Hitler called it, imposed its martial strength on the crazy quilt of states, bringing unity without democracy.[34] The rest of the bleak story is familiar: lack of a parliamentary tradition made the Wilhelmine Reichstag a farce, destroyed the Weimar Republic, and is a nagging fear in Bonn today.

But politics is only a symptom. The primeval forest had a profound effect on the people themselves, and it may be the most important single key to the mystery of why the Germans have behaved as they have. As early as the second century A.D., a hundred years before Frenchmen were known as Franks, Tacitus warned them that "It is for your sake, not ours, that we guard the barrier of the Rhine against the ferocious Germans, who have so often attempted, and who will always desire, to exchange the solitude of their woods and swamps for . . . Gaul." The Roman historian was so depressed by the habitat of the Teutonic tribes that he decided they must have always lived there: "No one, apart from the perils of an awful and unknown sea, would have left Asia or Africa or Italy to look for Germany. With its wild scenery and harsh climate it is pleasant neither to live in nor to look upon unless it be one's home."[35]

That was snobbish of Tacitus. Being illiterate, the natives were unable to reply. Doubtless they would have been insulted, for love of the bush sounds as a constant note throughout the German centuries; give a German an afternoon off and he will pack a lunch, assemble his family, and vanish into the trees. Certainly the first primitive Teutons were capable of emigrating had they so wished. Even Tacitus was impressed by them. To him they were noble savages, hardy warriors. All accounts of that time agree that they were supple and powerfully built, with fair complexions and reddish-brown hair.* They wore the skins of wild beasts, carried hatchets or what they called *frameae* — javelins — and they were loyal only to their chieftains. Looking back from the perspective of eighteenth-century England, Edward Gibbon observed that "the forests and morasses of Germany were filled with a hardy race of barbarians" who "delighted in

---

* In the *Nibelungenlied*, Siegfried's hair is described as "golden-red of hue, fair of fashion, and falling down in great locks." Tacitus says all Germans had "fierce blue eyes, red hair, tall frames." They had, he comments, kept their race "untainted." In short, they were Aryans.

war," who "spread terror and destruction from the Rhine to the Pyrenees," and who, "through their poverty, bravery, obsession with honor, and primitive virtues and vices, were a constant source of anxiety." He concluded: "The Germans despised an enemy who appeared destitute either of power or of inclination to offend them."

Virile, sentimental, insecure and melancholic, distrustful of outsiders and haunted even then by fear of enemy encirclement (*Einkreisungspolitik*), the ancient German evolved into a tribal creature, happy only with his own *Volk*. To the German, Germany became a kind of communal secret society. The worst thing that could happen to him was exile — "to be given forth," in his pagan phrase, "to be a wolf in holy places." In time his outlook was complicated by a new religion, and particularly by the Protestant work ethic. But he continued to carry with him ancestral memories of tribal rituals: of the Germans of Moravia lighting bonfires atop hills on Midsummer Eve, say, or of a dying Teuton chieftain who would deliver a farewell sermon to his people and then ceremoniously burn himself to death in front of the sacred oak tree.[36]

Always there was the interplay of light and darkness. Around the flickering fire, all was familiar. There lovers dallied, and boys learned to fight pitilessly, and the strongest man ruled by right of club law (*das Faustrecht*). But out in the tangled forest, out among the wild lupines beneath the brooding moon, lay the mysterious unknown. Grim forces lurked there, the *Volk* confided to one another as the flames whispered low and the tortured shadows grew; werewolves crouched beneath the writhing treetops, trolls and warlocks feasted on serpents' hearts, women transformed themselves into slimy beasts and coupled with their own brothers; and in a cave Brünnhilde dreamed of the dank smell of bloodstained axes.

Thus were born the morbid themes that have tormented the Gothic soul ever since: the dream orgy, the death wish, the fascination with the grotesque, the emotional convulsion, the exultation in what an unknown Middle High German poet called "overweening pride . . . and awful vengeance."[37] The dark images are gripping; in the twentieth century they have become as familiar to the rest of the world as phantoms in a recurring nightmare. Each tribe had its own version of the superstition, and since it was hardy, with roots older than recorded history, it was unthreatened by the rise of Christianity. The grossest forms of barbarism proved astoundingly durable. The murder of unwanted baby girls at birth persisted into the eleventh century. During the seventeenth century some hundred thousand Germans were executed for witchcraft. And there was nothing chivalrous about Teutonic tournaments. The object was mayhem. A knight entered the lists determined to hack to death as many fellow knights as he could; in one medieval tourney near Cologne, over sixty men were slain. Conversion to Rome had been deceptive. The old and the new were simply fused together. In time the Germans adorned the feast of the Nativity with colorful pagan symbols (notably the Christmas tree), and in some communities they transformed the local pagan legend into a Christian tale.

That happened in the Ruhr. At the end of the eighth century, when Charlemagne captured the Saxons' hilltop citadel south of Dortmund, a group of monks appeared across the Ruhr River from Essen and founded Werden Abbey, whose Romanesque walls still stand. Fifty years later Christians entered the village of Essen itself and built a convent which also survives, together with several processional crosses and an ancient seven-branched candelabrum. The first bishop arrived there A.D. 852, but the thousand-year-old legend of his coming resembles nothing Biblical. In the infidelic *Vorstellung* elves and sprites are usually dancing in a haunted glen when the blond hero suddenly strides out of the woods. So it is in this fantasy. The "wild and savage people" are in "a wilderness, full of foul marshes, and covered with impenetrable thickets and noisome weeds." Then a godlike figure makes his supernatural appearance and lo, the demons are foiled and the land flourishes. He tells the *Volk* to stop worshiping false idols, and they do. Instead they worship him, to the great profit of the entire Ruhr valley. Their extraordinary deity is the prelate, but that is only a gesture toward the cross. He could just as easily be a pre-Christian chief. Even his name seems more significant than his faith. In the Essen myth he is actually called Alfried.[38]

# 1

✠

# The Walled City

THE first Krupp came out of the woods. He was named Arndt, and nothing is really known about his antecedents. Family researchers suggest that he was descended from Dutchmen called Kroppen, or Krop, who had lived on the lower Rhine during the previous century. At Gendringen references to such a family appear in 1485, 1522, and 1566, but any link between them and Arndt is sheer speculation. He could just as easily have sprung, order pad in hand, from the hot loins of a dragon. All we can be sure of is that in January 1587 he wrote his name in Essen's Register of Merchants, and even this must be qualified, for his handwriting was dreadful. The signature may be variously read as Krupp, Krupe, Kripp, or Kripe. Indeed, his fellow townsmen deciphered it in each of those ways until well into the seventeenth century, when his descendants settled on the present form.[1]

All this is unsatisfactory. Yet we needn't leave Arndt's background a complete void. While no documents can be cited, it is possible to make a few educated guesses. Barring the marvelous, he was a man of means. Only in folklore did ragged boys enter medieval towns and rise to become burghers clothed in gold. In practice the poor had almost no way of improving their station. Not only did society discourage such mobility; the typical peasant hadn't the necessary skills anyhow — he was an unlettered clod with a vocabulary of perhaps six hundred German words.[2] Messy as Arndt's calligraphy is, it marks him as a person of some consequence. Besides, he couldn't have joined the Merchants' Guild unless he had arrived with some of the gauds of affluence. It wasn't allowed.

Again, while the record indicates nothing beyond a faceless blob, it is safe to hazard something about the first Krupp's physiognomy. Almost certainly he lacked the gauntness of later Krupps. Arndt was a sixteenth-century German merchant, and we know quite a lot about the customs of that class. They were above all dedicated gluttons. Girth was proof of prosperity; the man who could outeat his neighbors was admired everywhere. One performer devoured thirty eggs, a pound of cheese, and a large quantity of bread at a single sitting. He then fell dead, and became a national hero. Seven-hour meals were not uncommon; it has been estimated that the well-to-do spent half their waking hours either masticating or defecating. In these circumstances only an abnormal metabolic rate could prevent a rich man from becoming obese.

Thus, in our imagination, Arndt makes his debut with elephantine tread. It is the late 1500's. The Essen of Charlemagne's day has changed mightily. In the tenth century it became a city. Since then, as a member of the Hanseatic League, it has acquired a population of five thousand, which sounds tiny but really makes it one of Europe's largest, tightest urban concentrations. The Hansa has been declining for some time now. Its key city of Lübeck is exhausted from a long war with Sweden (1563–1570), Dutch ports are expanding, and the Atlantic has been opened to trade, which can thus bypass the German rivers. Still, Essen remains prosperous. Seen from afar, its profile is an exuberant Brueghel dream. Above its castellated walls — thirty feet high and nearly as thick — towers and spires hang needlelike against the sky, and beneath them lie the gabled roofs of the great merchants' homes, five stories high and built of heavy beams filled in with lath, mortar, and terra-cotta.

Scrutinized more closely, however, Essen was less attractive. Every foot of space inside was valuable. Apart from the market square there was little breathing room. Today, four hundred years later, the square still stands in the center of Essen, and near it are the hoary walls of the town hall, the eleven-hundred-year-old cathedral, and the ancient Marktkirche. It is difficult to recapture the spirit of the age in which they were erected — there are so many department stores, so much plate glass — yet the sixty blocks within the oval-shaped old city remain cramped and bewildering. In Arndt's time it was much worse. Houses leaned drunkenly against one another; upper stories jutted out, each above the other, darkening the Hogarthian alleys below. Livestock roamed the unpaved lanes, appalling fires swept the community from time to time. Despite the wall, wolves managed to penetrate the town; there was a bounty on them. Night was a time of fear. Curfew horns blew at dusk. Thereafter no one left his hearth if he could help it, for footpads lurked outside — chains, hung across intersections to discourage them, were ineffective — and timid burghers listened anxiously for the clank of the watchman's iron-shod staff and his mournful call, "Pray for the dead!"

They might have done more than pray. Wolves and thieves were certainly nuisances, but no one saw the greater evil, the utter absence of sanitation. None perceived the civic menace in the practice of dumping

sewage from the nearest window, or thought it dangerous that the city's
Jewish moneylenders should be mobbed every Good Friday and left to
fester the rest of the year in a squalid angle of the wall. Rich families
alleviated the stench of human waste with rose leaves and lavender and
turned to other matters. The inevitable happened. Disease broke out again
and again. Epidemics were attributed to sin, cures to a return of piety, and
the cycle recurred without benefit to anyone. Arndt Krupp became an
exception. It was his genius that he saw a way to exploit an epidemic.
Twelve years after he had settled in a building facing on Essen's Salt
Market the bubonic plague struck. Midsummer plague was the most horrid
of medieval nightmares, and Essen's visitation was particularly ghastly.
Stricken houses were quarantined, the healthy people inside left to rot with
the ill. Delirious men, finding the mark of the disease upon them, waylaid
and raped women in their final convulsions. At night dead-carts creaked
down lanes piled high with corpses; outside the wall half-witted drunks
rolled the naked bodies into mass graves. Then municipal employees quit.
The city reeked with mingled odors of vomit, urine, and feces. In many
quarters there was no one left to complain; according to a chronicle of the
time, entire streets were like cemeteries "in their sad desertion" (*in ihrer
betrübenden Einsamkeit*). As the pestilence grew, panic swept Essen.
Men sold their property for what it would bring and went off on a final
binge. Arndt, betting he would survive and winning, bought extensive
"gardens and pastures" (*Gärten und Trifte*) outside the city gates, acquiring parcels of land which would still be part of the family empire nearly
four centuries later.[3]

To credit him with foresight would be absurd. Invoked from the mists
of centuries, the first Krupp merely emerges as a shrewd chandler with a
keen eye for the main chance. Although he joined the Guild of Smiths
later in life, there is no sign that he had any thought of establishing an
industrial dynasty. If he had, he would have moved in other directions. For
years strip miners had been shipping boatloads of fuel coal down the Rhine
to the Low Countries. Arndt ignored the omen. Similarly, he failed to join
those who were diverting waterpower in the hills south of the Ruhr River
to drive hammers and bellows, converting the iron ore there into wrought
iron. Bellows were now large enough to melt the ore for casting, as bronze
had always been cast, and in the shops of Solingen fourteen miles below
Düsseldorf swordsmiths were tempering and polishing the blades of
German knights.

Arndt had nothing to do with this. He wasn't an armorer. He was a
trader. In retrospect we see him before his Salzmarkt house, waddling out
in his loose robe and broad-brimmed, hard felt hat to greet the morning
Rathaus bells and nod to cronies on the square: the watchman, the town
clerk, the hangman. He is dressed in linen and felt, and as a leader of the

community he sometimes changes his clothes. His neighbors know him as an active Lutheran, which may be why he immigrated here; although Essen is nominally ruled by the abbess of the convent, which has become a Benedictine nunnery, she suffers the presence of Protestants. Equally important (and equally rare) she smiles on trade. As a merchant Arndt is a member of a growing but controversial class. Most ecclesiastics are wary of creeping materialism. One of them complains that men seem interested only in carnal love and gain; another frets that "nowadays, alas, men honor a rich boor before poor lords without right; a man is wretched without possessions, whatever his knowledge or his deeds."[4]

Arndt has possessions. He may even be a boor. Yet in thinking of him as a businessman we must remember that he is not *our* type of businessman. The payroll he meets is tiny. In fact, he may need no outside help at all; almost immediately after his arrival here he married one Gertrud von der Gathen, who swiftly produced four bright children. They have grown up learning to mind the store, for although his trade (primarily in cattle, wine and schnapps), has made Arndt one of the city's wealthiest men, he has no separate shop; all dealing is done, and all books are kept, either on the ground floor of his home or on the street just outside. He is, in short, a typical medieval entrepreneur. In communities of small stores and fledgling industries, the mercantile masters form a tight oligarchy. They own the streets, they run the fairs, they see to it that the wall is mended and that Jewry knows its place. Even the public officials are appointed by them — and usually they choose their own relatives. The ruling clique is virtually a closed corporation, and we can only attribute Arndt's speedy acceptance into its highest councils to his extraordinary piece of luck with the plague.

This is not merely a picture of Essen in 1600; it is Essen for the better part of the next two hundred years, until the eruption of political and economic revolutions in the late eighteenth century. Today the twentieth century has become so plastic that we find it difficult to realize how immobile civilization in central Europe once was. It was almost untouched by the cultural tides of its time. Elsewhere the Age of Reason dawned and illumined man's horizons. Here there were only vague rumors in the dark. The long centuries stretched on and on, silent, inert, cold-drawn, rigid. Princes died, bands of mercenaries marched and countermarched; but society, and especially mercantile society, remained stagnant. Disciplined, imperturbable, hostile to change, jealous of its privileges, the trading class bred generation after generation, each precisely like its predecessor. Individual fortunes rose and fell, but the range of success or failure was sharply limited. Not even a national calamity could shake the established order much.

The Thirty Years War was a national calamity. Between 1618 and 1648 Germany served as a bloody doormat for five foreign armies — Danes, Swedes, Spaniards, Frenchmen, Bohemians. Villages were obliterated by the hundreds, and anywhere from one-third to two-thirds of the population perished. In many devastated tracts people survived only through cannibalism; mothers devoured their babies, starving mobs cut warm corpses from gallows and tore them apart with their teeth. Essen, as the natural crossroads of the Hellweg, the Westphalian plain, lay in the midst of this horror. Moreover, the war was a religious war, and the reigning abbess, Maria Klara von Spaur, abandoning tolerance for counterreformation, denounced the city to the Spaniards as heretical. That the Krupps should have endured those years is remarkable enough. What is singular is that they seem to have been almost untouched by the tragedy. Arndt did expire in 1624 — after prudently investing in a headstone from the public "stone quarry" (*Steinkuhle*) — but his time had come anyhow. The year before, his son Georg had died with his young wife; the city archives attribute their deaths to an epidemic. Georg's sisters Katharina and Margarethe lived through the butchery and raised children of their own. It is of passing interest that Katharina, in marrying Alexander Huyssen, allied the Krupps with another future family of Schlotbarone. She lived to be eighty-eight, surviving her husband by a half-century, and accumulated an independent fortune in real estate.[5]

Most interesting of all, however, was the career of Arndt's other son. Anton Krupp is one member of his generation who is not a cipher. Though fragmentary, the chronicles suggest a man of ingenuity and even of pugnacity — on one occasion he was fined heavily* "for beating Dr. Hasselmann in the street" (*weil er Dr. Hasselmann auf der Strasse geschlagen hat*). In 1612 he married Gertrud Krösen. The elder Krösen was one of Essen's twenty-four gunsmiths. Anton adopted his father-in-law's trade, and during the war he sold a thousand barrels a year. We know nothing of their caliber or quality; we can't even be sure who his clients were. In 1641 he was described in a town council minute as "our highly honored patriot lord, the nobly born Herr Anthon [sic] Krupp" (*unsern hochgeehrten Herrn Patriot, den Markischen Ritterbürtigen Herrn Anthon Krupp*), which indicates that he had prospered. Conceivably those profits could have come from the family store, but the source and size of Anton's income is unimportant; he is significant because he was the first member of the dynasty to deal in arms and because he entered the field so early. After him came a long hiatus. The next military transaction would not be entered in the family books until the Napoleonic era. Nevertheless, there it is: a Krupp was selling cannon in the Ruhr nearly three centuries before Verdun, three and a quarter centuries before Stalingrad. Like a flash of gunfire on a distant horizon, the event is ominous. A flash may only register a gun. But it leaves the gunner with a range.[6]

At mid-century the Peace of Westphalia ended the Teuton agony.

---

* The fine was ten thalers. In terms of modern purchasing power, a seventeenth-century thaler was worth ten dollars. Later it became half that.

France, faithfully following Richelieu's design, became the dominant power in Europe — one of a string of Gallic triumphs which the Germans would never forget. For the present, however, the tribal grudge was left to fester. The great need was to rebuild, to regain strength. In Essen the family which would later play such a spectacular role in the national revenge reopened the Salzmarkt shop and broadened its markets. Presently the city was booming again. The last alien troops departed, paid out of pocket by the mercantile oligarchy. A new abbess presided over the nunnery. And in the Rathaus a youthful clerk named Matthias Krupp took office.

Matthias was Georg's son. Orphaned at the age of two, he was characterized by that implacable conservatism frequently found in men who have been reared in times of widespread disorder, and with him the Krupps enter their dull period. Now in the third Essen generation, they have become local patricians. Stolid and solvent, they are entrenched members of the establishment, the very proper Esseners. There is no more untidy confusion about the family name. It is writ large and clear, in bold black cursive script. Plague no longer afflicts Krupps, and nobody loses his temper and beats up Dr. Hasselmann in the street.

As true Brahmins, they become men of property. The compulsion to collect deeds is not a new trait with them. Arndt and Katharina have been conspicuous examples of it. But now it becomes a mania. Beginning with Matthias — who buys the precious fields east of the wall which will later be the heart of the dynasty's great gun factory — each Krupp succumbs in turn to the yearning for more *Lebensraum*. In the end they owned just about everything worth having; by the sixth generation a flattering chronicler was describing them as "Essen's uncrowned kings" (*Essens ungekrönte Könige*).[7]

Very likely the writer of this was himself a Krupp, for among other things the family controlled city hall. That was another trend established by Matthias. At the time of his death in 1673 he left three sons. The eldest, Georg Dietrich, was only sixteen, but the family was so powerful that the office of town clerk was kept vacant until he had reached his majority. Georg Dietrich wielded the *secretarius* seals for sixty-four years, and when *he* died the job went to a nephew. Meanwhile another of Matthias's sons had served as Bürgermeister. A third concentrated on the business, opening a sideline in textiles, and ran the Essen orphanage.

In 1749 Krupps had held the orb and mace of municipal authority for exactly a century, so they threw a party to celebrate. It was ill-advised. Prospects weren't as bright as they seemed. The dynasty seemed to be running out of steam. Of the three brothers only the Bürgermeister, Arnold Krupp, had left sons. There were two of them, and both were disappointing. The new clerk, Heinrich Wilhelm Krupp, dabbled in strip mining, lost everything, and had to sell some property to meet his bills.

Heinrich's marriage was fruitless. That left the extension of the male line up to his brother, Friedrich Jodocus Krupp. Jodocus never became a power in the government, and under his uninspired leadership the business dwindled to little more than a grocery. But he did manage to avoid bankruptcy and hold on to the sheaf of deeds, and — in 1737 — to move the big store to an imposing house at the corner of Limbeckerstrasse and the Flax Market. Most important, he sired a son.

He almost failed there. His first wife had died barren. At forty-five he was a childless widower and seemed fated to be the last of the Krupps. Then, in 1751, the dynasty was granted a reprieve. Jodocus married nineteen-year-old Helene Amalie Ascherfeld.

Because Germans are male chauvinists, there is a tendency to ignore the role Krupp women played in establishing and guarding Krupp primacy. Throughout these quiet years handsome dowries were adding to the family fortune, and although the unsung daughters left to raise broods of their own, their descendants stuck to the Ruhr and would, in the next century, contribute wealth and talent to the family. Helene Amalie has a further distinction. Beyond doubt she was the strong Krupp of her generation. It would be incorrect to say that she brought the clan new blood (Arndt Krupp had been her great-great-grandfather) but she did introduce a style which her masculine cousins sadly lacked. She was acute, energetic, and industrious. She was also fertile. Although Jodocus had only six years to live at the time of the wedding, Helene Amalie needed less than one; she became pregnant almost immediately.

The child, Peter Friedrich Wilhelm Krupp, is transitional. All his life he was overshadowed by his mother, whom he served as accountant. As the Widow Krupp (Witwe Krupp) Helene Amalie expanded the Flachsmarkt store, adding a butcher shop, a paint department, and dress goods while her son fooled around in the local rifle association and honored ancestral memories by serving on the municipal council. At twenty-six he married a Düsseldorf girl; at forty-two he was dead, and his mother began tutoring his eight-year-old son in the mysteries of trade.

They were becoming more mysterious. The Ruhr hadn't even reached the threshold of greatness, but it was making certain curious discoveries about itself. Men were starting to understand the blast furnace. Its use had been slowly spreading, and gangs now trooped regularly into the woods to mine the iron ore there. Tainted though it was by sulfur and phosphorus, the ore was abundant, and the smelters worked it right there in the forest, using the trees for charcoal, which, they had learned, united with the ore's oxygen at high temperatures, ridding the iron of its oxides. The necessary heat was generated in various ways. In the beginning smelters simply built a fire atop the nearest hill and hoped the wind would whip up the flames. Concluding that water-driven bellows would be more efficient, they then

moved their hearths to the banks of the dashing little streams that fed the
Ruhr River. It was all very crude. The valley remained agricultural, and the
iron was chiefly used for local farm tools. It really wasn't good enough to
export, and even if it had been worth shipping, exporters would have been
thwarted by the incredible tangle of river tolls. This was still feudal
country — as late as 1823 Essen hadn't grown to the limit of its medieval
walls — and every landowner on the shores of the Ruhr and the Rhine
exacted his toll from passing barges.[8]

Only a canny merchant could have recognized the seeds of profitable
heavy industry in this sporadic, hobbled activity. But the Widow Krupp
was one of the shrewdest Germans of her time. She acquired a mill north
of Essen, and she bought shares in four coal mines. She had the means to
plunge still deeper; according to her son's accounts, she was worth 150,000
thaler. Scanning possible investments, she selected the Gutehoffnungshütte, an iron forge on nearby Sterkrade brook. It was a superb choice.
Established in 1782, the forge was owned by an ironmaster who was short
of charcoal and had already begun to experiment with coal. Unluckily for
him, he was an incompetent businessman, and in 1800 he had to disappear
from the Ruhr to avoid his creditors. Chief among these was Helene
Amalie Krupp, who held first mortgage on the works. The widow moved
swiftly. "As he fled privily," she noted in her records, "his estate went into
bankruptcy, due to my heavy claims on it, and I was able to buy it at the
public auction, paying 12,000 thalers, that is, 15,000 thalers Berlin currency, for all the buildings, plant, rights, and good will" (*mit allen Gebäu-
den, Rechten und Gerechtigkeiten*).[9]

Seven years later she appointed her nineteen-year-old grandson, Friedrich Krupp, to manage the works.

✠   ✠   ✠

One of the greatest family ironies lies in the present name of the firm,
emblazoned on twentieth-century factories all over the world as FRIED.
KRUPP OF ESSEN, for the widow's heir is unique among the Krupps. In
eleven generations of merchants and executives, he is without doubt the
most incompetent.

Born exactly two hundred years after Arndt Krupp's arrival at the city
gate, Friedrich was the great-grandson of Arndt's great-grandson, and hence
entitled to the assured manner of the patrician. His problem was that he
had altogether too much of it. He was determined to become the Ruhr's
first real industrialist, and in his anxiety he stumbled blindly from disaster
to disaster. Indeed, he failed with such appalling regularity that one suspects that the manner may have been bogus — that he may have been
feigning a confidence that he should have had but somehow lacked.
Certainly he seems to have been a young man of wild contradictions. On
the surface he was dynamic, flamboyant, full of ginger; privately he was

confiding to his journal, "Ach, I am doomed to be in want. . . . From our foolishness we harvest distress, misfortune" (*Jammer, Elend, sind die Garben, die die Torheit ernten kann*).[10]

The Gutehoffnungshütte was to be his first misfortune. Under Helene Amalie the forge had become a highly profitable enterprise, producing kitchenware, stoves, weights, and, under a subsidy from Berlin, cannonballs for Prussia. Like Anton Krupp's gun barrels, the cannonballs are a flash in the distance; events since have given them greater significance than they had then. They were, however, a clear sign of the times. The specter of Bonaparte had darkened the entire continent. The Ruhr, a march from the border, could not escape involvement. Beyond the Elbe, Prussia had begun to stir. In 1802 Prussia — "not a state with an army," in Mirabeau's mot, "but an army with a state" — seized Essen and Werden, ending the millennium of abbesses' reign. To Berlin a forge capable of turning out solid shot was of obvious value. The Widow Krupp was interested; a thaler was a thaler. Still, her intuitive caution held her back from wholesale conversion, and the next six years vindicated her. In 1805 Prussia dumped its Austrian and Russian allies and came to terms with Napoleon. Parcels of land were exchanged, among them a piece of the Ruhr, which became the French Grand Duchy of Berg. The duchy's ruler was Joachim Murat, marshal of France and husband of Caroline Bonaparte, who set up headquarters in Düsseldorf. As it happened, Essen hadn't been part of the bargain, but the marshal decided to take it anyhow. He moved troops in. The Prussians, accepting the challenge, swarmed over the crenelated old wall one night and evicted the French. It was awkward for Napoleon. He denounced Murat publicly, privately told him to wait awhile, and settled accounts three years later at the Peace of Tilsit, when Essen, then a city of fifteen thousand, was incorporated into the duchy anyhow.[11]

Meanwhile the widow had gone back to making pots and pans. With so many lunatics running around in epaulettes, it was the only sensible course. However, her grandson had other ideas. Since childhood he had been shackled to the counter at Flachsmarkt No. 12, haggling over petty sales, and when Helene Amalie turned him loose in the foundry he sacked the veteran foreman, then canceled the tedious manufacture of traditional hardware, and retooled for highly technical production: pistons, cylinders, steam pipes, engine parts. It was absurd. His workers lacked the necessary skills, and his own experience had been limited to the Essen store. In a single stroke he had transformed a modest sinecure into insolvency, and he celebrated this triumph by getting married — in the Gutehoffnungshütte.[12]

His wife was ill prepared for the bizarre life that lay ahead of her. Still in her teens, Therese Wilhelmi had celebrated her engagement by dancing through the streets of Essen, clutching a doll and shouting lustily in low German, "*Ick sin Brut!*" (I'm a bride!). Apparently she never suspected that the bridegroom was a fool. In that society reverence for the breadwinner approached the absolute, even when he was a consistent loser. The new *Brut* had been raised to breed strong children. She bred four, and no more could have been expected of her. From her portrait she appears to have been a thin-lipped, birdlike woman. She looks determined, even stubborn, but she does not look intelligent, and the painting was done late in life, when she had at least learned to read. Although the daughter of a merchant, she was virtually inarticulate; as late as nine years after the wedding Friedrich's brother-in-law wrote of their wives, "They cannot even speak German, their mother tongue, correctly, much less write it."[13]

Therese's husband's *Grossmutter* did not share this disability. She was especially good at reading figures, and after one glance at his accounts she decided to act. Shortly after the marriage Friedrich fell ill. When he recovered he discovered that Helene Amalie had sold the Gutehoffnungs-hütte to three colliery operators named Gottlob Jacoby, Gerhard Haniel, and Heinrich Huyssen. Another grandson might have pondered the lesson. Not Friedrich. He saw only that his grandmother, striking her usual hard bargain, had increased her estate by 47,250 thalers, and immediately he began thinking of ways to spend it. On August 3, 1809, we find him traveling to Bremen with a passport signed by Napoleon. Had Bonaparte known what young Krupp was up to, he wouldn't have allowed him to travel farther than the nearest prison. The emperor had thrown a cordon of customs posts around Europe. Between his taxes and the English block-ade, Ruhr merchants were at their wits' end; the husband of Friedrich's sister Helene, Friedrich von Müller, had been driven to brewing ersatz coffee, and others were studying the powders of medieval alchemists, frantically hoping to plug the gaps on their shelves somehow. Krupp, how-ever, was taking a different tack. He was determined to break the law, smuggling products into the continent from Dutch colonies. That Novem-ber he and his agents planned to ship goods from Amsterdam to Essen. The Rothschilds could bring this sort of thing off. He couldn't. Somehow he managed to wheedle 12,500 thalers from his usually prudent grand-mother. Then the agents, who may have been swindling him from the outset, wrote him that all was lost; the French couldn't be outwitted.[14]

That was the way it went. That was how it had always gone with him, and now he was going to raise the stakes. On March 9, 1810, Helene Amalie died in her seventy-ninth year. She might have named other heirs. Her granddaughter Frau von Müller was living in Essen, and so was Georg Dietrich's great-grandson Georg Christian Sölling. Certainly the widow could have had no illusions about the rabbity young would-be smuggler under her roof. Nevertheless, he was the eldest son of her eldest son. The rights of the direct male line were strongly supported by custom. She couldn't find it in her heart to disinherit him, so virtually everything fell into his hands — the Flachsmarkt store, two hundred and twenty-three years' accumulation of deeds and mortgages, and a fortune in cash: two hundred thousand thalers, roughly equivalent to a million dollars today. Friedrich's dreams soared. His first move was to change the Flachsmarkt store. Its long life as a retail outlet was about to end. In the future it would be devoted to commodity wholesaling. Perhaps wholesale trade just sounded refined, though it is likelier that he still had his eye on Amsterdam; the commodities he specified, coffee and sugar, were subject to French duties. But that was only a beginning. Opulent and independent, he was after something more spectacular. He wanted a grand coup, and it was then, while his grandmother's will was still being probated, that he decided he would find the almost legendary *Geheimnis des Stahlgiessens,* the secret of cast steel.

In the Napoleonic era cast steel had a special cachet. It was the nuclear fission of its day: mysterious, glamorous, seemingly limitless in its possibilities. Steel — low-carbon iron, tough and malleable — is not a natural phenomenon, and in a time when chemistry was poorly understood it was regarded as a marvel. In the past, smelters had produced small quantities of it by manipulating ore and carbon with rods, meantime regulating the flow of air through bellows. To produce the metal they worked on its "feel," on its appearance, on hunches, and on sleights and arcana handed down from fathers to sons. Until the nineteenth century these hit-or-miss methods were good enough, but now, in the spring of the machine age, Europe was crying for big chunks of high-quality steel. The old smiths couldn't help. Nor could the operators of blast furnaces; furnaces produced only cast iron, which, with its high carbon content, was too brittle to be satisfactory. Attempts were made to fuse several small ingots of steel and cast them as a single block; the smiths were frustrated because the oxygen in the air combined with the carbon in the steel, ruining a whole batch.

Yet some men could bring the thing off. The secret existed and had been discovered. To the great annoyance of Napoleon, the discoverers were Englishmen. Not only had the British cornered cast steel; they had held their monopoly of it for seventy years. In 1740 a Sheffield clockmaker named Benjamin Huntsman had excluded air by heating metal in small, enclosed, earthenware cupolas.* He called the cupolas crucibles, and eventually the result became known as crucible steel, or, in Prussia, cast steel (*Gusstahl*). In Friedrich Krupp's youth it was still called English steel. Huntsman and his successors had guarded their process carefully. Europeans who wanted fine cutlery, or durable watch springs, or, most important, machined parts, were obliged to import from Sheffield.

Nelson's victory at Trafalgar and the Royal Navy's subsequent blockade had stopped all that. Continental industry was in trouble, and Napoleon had offered a reward of four thousand francs to the first steelmaker who

---

* Actually, Huntsman had rediscovered an ancient process. It had been produced in India, used in the celebrated swords of Damascus, and described by Aristotle in 384 B.C. Then the formula was lost. See Fisher, *The Epic of Steel,* pp. 21–22.

could match the British process. This was the prize which had drawn young Krupp's attention. Others had been similarly attracted. The year of Helene Amalie's death, a mining superintendent "in the services of the Napoleonic King of Westfalia" was reported to have found "the Englishman's secret." The following year the men who acquired the Gutehoffnungshütte from Friedrich announced that they were "in possession of the secret process,"[15] and other claims were filed in Liège, Schaffhausen, Kirchspielwald, and Radevormwald. Later, Friedrich's descendants would vehemently assert that the honor was his, and charge that all other claimants were frauds. Really it is impossible to choose among them.

Unriddling the cast steel process was meaningless in itself. The trick lay in first designing a battery of strong, airtight cupolas and then in so organizing them that their liquid fillings would pour simultaneously into a central mold. It was, in short, a matter of organization and detail — the very sort of challenge Friedrich Krupp was least equipped to meet.

This aspect of the problem was imperfectly understood when, on September 20, 1811, he founded his Gusstahlfabrik — Cast Steel Works — "for the manufacture of English cast steel and all articles made thereof." The works' first home was an annex of the Flachsmarkt house, a shed no larger than a photographer's darkroom, beside and to the rear of the main building. After a chimney had been installed there was scarcely room to turn around. So inadequate was the hutch that one wonders about the founder's early intentions. It seems incredible that he — even he — really thought that he could solve the greatest industrial puzzle of his time in a back bedroom. Possibly he regarded the Gusstahlfabrik as a hobby. His daily schedule seems to support this; wholesaler by day, he would slip into the shed evenings, literally playing with fire. With a more patient man this approach might have made sense. In Friedrich's case there were certain obvious difficulties. If his pursuit of the prize money was serious, every hour away from his experiments was an hour wasted. Furthermore, timid wading didn't fit his character. As a born sport he longed to plunge into deep waters, and more and more he found excuses to leave his desk, shed his cutaway, and hurry back to the shed. Finally, his speculative fever had developed a familiar symptom: premonition. He felt sure he was on the track of something.[16]

He may have had some justification. Two months after his announcement that he was in the steel business he signed a contract with two brothers from Wiesbaden, Wilhelm Georg Ludwig von Kechel and Georg Karl Gottfried von Kechel. The Kechels were Prussian army officers. Retired now, and hoping to supplement their pensions, they had stumbled across the information that cupolas were used in Sheffield. In Essen they offered Krupp a proposition. If he would admit them as partners and put up capital, they would provide the cast steel recipe. The papers were drawn up, signed, and witnessed — and then the curious episode of the elderly brothers vanishes in the mists of controversy. According to one account, the Kechels were raffish adventurers who bilked an innocent youth. According to another, they built practical crucibles, designed proper feed-ins, and were ruined by Friedrich's ignorance and impetuosity. Either version is possible, yet neither is entirely satisfactory, for each omits the wild background of that year. Napoleonic Europe was approaching its final agony. Essen was about to be embattled once more, and it is highly doubtful that any new enterprise could have flourished in the alarums and excursions of 1812.[17]

For Krupp it was a twelvemonth's nightmare. The first tremors of upheaval caught him while he was busy moving the factory. His new partners had sensibly pointed out that the shed wouldn't do. Even if he made big steel, he couldn't have done anything with it — shaping large ingots required more than human muscle, so he built a mill on a family plot beside a small Essen stream and joined its waterwheel to a tailhammer with a 450-pound thrust. Meanwhile the wholesale business languished. His ignorant wife couldn't help him there, and besides, she was pregnant for the second time; on April 26 she gave birth to their first son, who, with the Kechels standing by as godfathers, was christened Alfried in memory of Essen's legendary hero.* Tinkering with the new hammer, watching the aged Kechels sweat over the cupolas, and returning behind the city wall each evening to a glum bout of bookkeeping, the young father blundered through the autumn. To be charitable, Friedrich's troubles here were not entirely of his own making. Someone had to take the first step toward fine steel, and he was paying the penalty of the pioneer. Still, it is fair to point out that his motives were not unselfish. He coveted Napoleon's gold napoleons. And he had a remarkable talent for making a bad situation worse. Although he has been portrayed to subsequent generations of Germans as a man of vision, he consistently misread the signs of history, and as the year waned he made a stunning miscalculation. Since his grandmother's death he had been wavering over whether to collaborate with the French. Now he took the plunge, swearing allegiance to Bonaparte on December 17 — just as the emperor's Grande Armée was disappearing into the snows of Russia.[18]

In collaboration, as in other forms of rapid descent, it is impossible to stop; momentum takes over. Friedrich's oath was only a beginning. He joined the government as city councilman, hoisted the French tricolor, supervised the quartering of French troops in Essen homes, and loaned money to two French rifle makers. By April he had reached the dead end of collusion: he was under arms himself as adjutant of the First Essen

---

* He remained Alfried until his first trip to England in 1839, when, in a burst of Anglophilia, he changed it to Alfred. However, to avoid confusion we shall call him Alfred in all future references.

Defense Battalion. If this has a romantic ring, it is deceptive; the adjutant's last task was fated to be grimy. When Gebhard von Blücher's Prussians raced after the Grand Army's survivors that fall, Napoleon's ragged remnant tried to make a last stand on the Rhine, and Krupp was put to work with a spade, digging trenches for them. In our own less forgiving century, such behavior would have meant the end of Friedrich's career, and probably the scaffold. But nationalism was more casual then. While there had been some uprisings against French rule in the Ruhr, it is hard to say where his loyalty should have been. The only local sovereign he had known had been the last abbess, and he was a Protestant. Germany didn't exist; Prussian soldiers were almost as alien as the Parisians. Krupp's neighbors appear to have been willing to let bygones be bygones, and Blücher's officers were tolerant. Krupp was even permitted to remain in the city government.[19]

Nevertheless a corner had been turned. The disorders had been expensive. Ditch digging had kept Krupp away from the store. And Napoleon was no longer in a position to reward a successful young steelmaker. Indeed, Sheffield was again exporting to the continent. In commerce there are times when a man should hibernate, and this was one of them. The only sensible course for Friedrich would have been to postpone work at the foundry, put the ex-officers on half-pay, and burn late candles over his Flachsmarkt desk, at least until the House of Krupp was in order. He did just the opposite. The idea of casting steel had begun as a diversion; now it was an obsession, the glittering pot of gold at the end of his rainbow, and he was determined to pursue it even if the chase cost him both his life and his fortune, which, in the end, it did.

His relatives became alarmed. Already the foundry had cost forty thousand thalers. Both his wife's father and his sister's husband were familiar with sound business practice, and they were appalled at this squandering. Not only was the foundry's waterwheel still turning; Krupp was taking on new men. Worse, he was coddling them. As early as 1813 two workers named Stuber and Schurfeld were given sick pay, and on January 9, 1814, Krupp paid an Essen surgeon two thalers for giving an injured worker a bloodletting, an alcohol rub, an enema, and a blowing of "air into the lungs through the mouth." Such concern for employees' welfare was then regarded as a grand gesture of *noblesse oblige;* the young industrialist, following the example of the feudal aristocracy, was ministering to his own. In fact the precedent became Friedrich's one solid contribution to the Konzern he had established and to the nation which Bismarck would one day forge with the help of Krupp steel. To the Müllers and Wilhelmis it seemed to be the act of an irresponsible spendthrift. Six months after Napoleon's abdication at Fontainebleau a family council was called. Friedrich capitulated. More impetuous than resolute, he bowed to the advice of his elders: he vowed not to touch another drop of steel.

The waterwheel creaked to a halt, the martial brothers clicked their heels and marched off into oblivion. The Gusstahlfabrik was closed.[20]

But only for a few months. The following March, as the emperor came roaring ashore from Elba, the former Gallic adjutant revived his own dreams of glory. Sketching plans for a new shop with sixty cupolas, he cashed in assets worth ten thousand thalers and negotiated a loan — the first of many — from "the Jew Moses" (*Jude Moses*). His venture capital is diminishing; the quicksands of disaster have begun to tug at his feet. The pattern of the first venture is repeated. There is even a Prussian officer, a Captain Friedrich Nicolai, who appears with credentials testifying that he is expert in "every kind of machine" (*Maschinen jeder Art*). Like his predecessors he formed a partnership with Krupp, and like them he would be blamed as a low intriguer; twenty years later Friedrich's son demanded restitution from the government on the ground that Nicolai, though ignorant, had carried a state "patent for crucible steel manufacture" (*das Patent der Gusstahlfabrikation*). Of course, there was no such patent; there could be none. The captain may have known something about casting, or he may have been a glib soldier of industrial fortune looking for an easy mark, which Krupp certainly was. In either case the result would have been the same. It was a time of trial and error in continental steelmaking; no one was going to make much headway against the British in this generation. Friedrich's hopes were dashed once more. Again the elders gathered, again the works were closed; and again the founder, shorn of his last partner, crept back to kindle the fires.[21]

Late in 1816 he produced his first steel. But it wasn't cast steel. After five heartbreaking years the best he could do was match the yields of the hill smelters; when finished, these tiny bars were marketed as files for tanners in neighboring Ruhr towns. Inching ahead, he sold bayonets to Berlin — the third warning gun on the rim of history — and filled a few orders for tools and dies. The dies were good; on November 19, 1817, the Düsseldorf mint, in response to his plea for a testimonial, agreed that of all the work done for it, that "by Herr Friedrich Krupp of Essen is the best." His difficulty was that he couldn't produce enough to balance his books. The Gusstahlfabrik, despite its drain on his fortune, was still in the village smith class. Friedrich's solution was characteristic. Although he hadn't yet solved the basic casting process, his mind was ranging ahead to complex copper alloys. The present shop couldn't handle that kind of smelting, so he would build a new *Schmelzhaus* with an 800-pound hammer. The site he chose was on the shore of Essen's little Berne River, a ten-minute walk from the city wall, on what is now Altendorferstrasse. Today the Berne goes underground a block north of Altendorferstrasse, but then it flowed straight down to the Ruhr, and in 1818 it became, as it has been ever since, the heart of Fried. Krupp of Essen. When the works were finished in August 1819, the owner was delighted. He was certain that it would save him. He would — indeed had — bet his bottom thaler on it. A long, narrow, one-story building, the factory had ten doors, forty-eight windows, eleven chimneys and ventilators, and — on paper — a daily capacity of one hundred pounds of forged steel. It faced the city and was, as the new owner exulted, "lovely and expensive" (*schön und kostspielig*).[22]

This was his final undoing. His elaborate plans had overlooked one staggering fact: the Berne was an intermittent, unreliable, highly temperamental stream, and when its level fell the waterwheel naturally stopped. That first year was one long drought. Friedrich lacked *Glückauf*. He was going down for the third time, and there were no lifelines left. Desperately he cast around for some. The last of his grandmother's fortune was ebbing from him in a frightful hemorrhage of capital, and in a frantic effort to stanch the flow he turned to the government. It didn't much matter which government; he just wanted a patron. Twice he proposed to Saint Petersburg that he establish a state-aided foundry in Russia, and three applications for subsidies were sent to Berlin. The last one was dispatched in 1823.[23] Like the others it was denied, and Friedrich was left to his final agony. The Gusstahlfabrik was falling apart — actually disintegrating, with cupolas cracking and hot metal gushing across the floor. Drought returned. He was perched by a dry creek, which meant that his waterwheel was wasted; he might as well have been back in the old shed, except that it wasn't his any more. In April 1824 the great Flachsmarkt house, a reminder to all Essen that one mercantile family had withstood the whims of fate for two hundred and thirty-six years, passed from his hands. The new owner was his father-in-law. Kinship was all very well, but business was business, and Friedrich had borrowed 18,125 thalers from Herr Wilhelmi. The old man went to court, acquired a judgment, and was awarded the homestead in settlement.

Krupp had lost a cherished status symbol. In addition he lacked a roof, so he moved Therese and their four children into a cottage beside the Gusstahlfabrik. To friends he explained, "I can keep a better eye on affairs at the works. Besides, I need the country air" (*die frische Landluft*).

The friends were undeceived. His new house was a hut. Originally intended for his factory foreman, it hardly had room for an active bachelor. Square, half-timbered, with green blinds decorated by heart-shaped carvings, the cottage did possess a certain homely appeal, and later, when the greatest of the Krupps spurned his patrician past and christened it his "ancestral home" (*Stammhaus*), it became famous throughout Germany.* When the family moved in its charm was less evident. The entry hall was closet-sized, and the three downstairs rooms, which Friedrich and his wife shared, weren't much larger. Everyone ate in the kitchen, around the cast-iron stove that was the cottage's sole source of heat. On one side of the

---

* Destroyed by bombing in 1944, the cottage has been rebuilt and has much of the original furniture. It stands just outside the office Alfried Krupp occupied.

stove stood a pair of huge black hand-hewn clogs, which Friedrich slipped over his shoes whenever he went into the works. On the other side a narrow flight of stairs curved up to the attic, where four pallets lay under the low eaves for the next Krupp generation: Ida, fifteen; Alfred, twelve; Hermann, ten; and Fritz, four.

After losing the Flachsmarkt home their father appears to have thrown in his hand. He was obliged to resign his city office, and his name was stricken from Essen's tax list, which, for a merchant, was the ultimate disgrace. Needing twenty-five thousand thalers for proper equipment, owing ten thousand to creditors, he left his affairs to one Herr Grevel, an accountant who kept up pretenses, meeting the foundry's payroll by liquidating Krupp real estate. According to one account, Grevel had to call Friedrich from a tavern to sign the transfer papers, but this may have been malicious gossip. By the autumn of 1824 he was confined to his bed. We do know that for two years he lay in the room beside the kitchen, staring at the ceiling, a ruined man brooding over his humiliation. His clogs gathered dust. Birds nested in the inactive waterwheel, while crucibles crumbled and the workless men loafed. An air of unreality hung over the works. Since Waterloo, Essen had become passionately Prussian, and elsewhere in the valley men toiled relentlessly, harried by the prickly north German conscience. Here there was only silent despair. For two years Friedrich's anguish dragged on until, on Sunday, October 8, 1826, he quietly turned his face into his straw tick and died. He was just thirty-nine. The doctor told Therese that her husband was a victim of "the pectoral dropsy" (*der Brustwassersucht*).[24]

Three days later the widow's embarrassed relatives filed into the front room and carried the plain coffin to the family graveyard near the Flachsmarkt.[25] Trudging there, the pallbearers could not have doubted that they were witnessing the end of a dynasty — that they were burying Friedrich's dream with him. Still, there were faint portents. Since the French had eliminated all Ruhr tolls, river traffic had grown more profitable each year. A few weeks before the funeral the Ruhr's first locomotive had made its maiden run, hauling squat cars crammed with coal. More auspicious than either of these, however, was the behavior of the dead man's eldest son. The expression of the new *paterfamilias* was anything but funereal. Awkward and nervous, wild, driven, with an air of almost unbearable tension, he could scarcely wait for the graveside service to end. He wanted only to be back at the factory.

# 2

ZWEI

✠

# The Anvil Was His Desk

I N the florid lore of nineteenth-century capitalism there are few episodes more dramatic than Alfred Krupp's arrival on the floor of the works that afternoon. All the ingredients of high theater are there: the grieving widow, the helpless younger children, the fresh-faced stripling springing to the defense of the family honor. It would be a century and a quarter before another lean and hungry Krupp faced the world at bay, and even Ausländer are drawn by the spell of that scene in 1826. To Germans it is irresistible. So is the temptation to wallow in *Schmalz*, and after the hero had become a national figure his tale was gilded and embossed until he appeared as a compost of Horatio at the bridge *cum* Siegfried dispatching the dragon. It is impossible to exaggerate the impact of this legend on the German people; for the better part of a century the Reich's schoolchildren were taught to look back in admiration on young Alfred's feat, marveling at the gallant youth who had coaxed strange fires from the cold jaws of the flyblown Gusstahlfabrik.*

One hesitates to deface monuments. Nevertheless, it didn't happen quite that way. Outwardly, nothing much occurred the first day. In the factory Alfred was confronted by its seven sullen workers — five smelters and two forgers — and there was little he could do to help them feed their families. As her husband's heir, Therese could claim a pitifully small legacy: this shop; the Stammhaus, worth 750 thalers; a few pawned properties in town; one cow and some pigs. Any sudden shift in the family's fortunes would have required a miracle, and Alfred wouldn't be in a position to deliver miracles for quite some time. He was just fourteen years old.[1]

---

* The teaching continues today, using Bernhard Woischnik's *Alfred Krupp, Meister des Stahls* (1957).

Nevertheless, he was an unusual boy. Tall and rail-thin, with a long bony skull and spidery legs, he had that peculiar strength of will often found in extreme ectomorphs. Sensitive, proud, possessed of violent hidden drives, he had watched his father's tragic decline with a sense of mounting frustration. The memory of that broken figure lying supine in the Stammhaus while everything went smash would be with him always, to recur vividly in times of peril. In physique Alfred resembled his mother, but his behavior was closer to his father's. Like Friedrich, he was to display a flamboyant streak, and it was to be his good fortune that, unlike him, he lived in an era in which fustian schemes were possible. Friedrich believed the government of Prussia was obligated to back the works; so did Alfred. The father had served his business apprenticeship as his grandmother's manager; the son served his as his mother's. And both men responded to crises by going into hiding. Significantly, whenever things went wrong at the shop — and on the roller coaster of Adam Smith laissez-faire the most astute entrepreneur had airsick moments — Alfred would flee home, lock his door, and lie down, sometimes for weeks at a time. He had learned at his father's inert knee that the bedroom door was an excellent escape hatch.

But although Alfred was his parents' son, he was not a carbon of them. Really he was *sui generis,* a true maverick — restless, brilliant, imaginative, tormented, farsighted, and, despite some rather extraordinary eccentricities, supremely practical. He comes very close to that stock character in Victorian three-deckers, the mad genius. If he wasn't demented, he was certainly a crank. Even as an adolescent he had begun to display the odd traits and phobias which would later fascinate the capitals of Europe. Although he worked among gouts of flame, he was terrified of fire. Smells intrigued him; he believed some to be auspicious and some evil. Horse manure, in Alfred's view, was a particularly enriching odor. He thought its scent was inspiring, and in the presence of fresh dung he became creative. Unhappily he was convinced that his own exhalations were toxic, so he tried to keep on the move. That was fine during the day. After he had retired it wasn't so easy, and as a consequence he slept badly. Yet his chronic insomnia, which would have crippled another executive, actually may have made Alfred more efficient. He was such a bundle of neurotic quirks that they seem to have supported one another. At night, for example, he wrote business memoranda. A compulsive writer — over thirty thousand of his letters and notes are extant — he trained himself to scribble in the dark, crouched sweating under his eiderdown. After dawn flushed his workers from their beds they would find Krupp's scrawled praise or scorn propped on their benches. To them his energy was a marvel. To us the greater marvel is that he kept this up for over fifty years without once being institutionalized.[2]

Alfred's great talents were slower to emerge; His progress was hampered by the sluggish pace of Germany's industrial revolution. Nevertheless, he was clearly a bright youth. On November 26, 1825, when he was thirteen, his Essen teacher had sent Friedrich a report card with the red-ink comment: "I have to compliment him in every respect, especially his endeavors in math. He should continue in the same manner and I am sure we shall be satisfied (*Befriedigung finden*) with him." He wasn't able to continue. Before the next marking period he had become a dropout. The troubles at home had ended his formal education; thereafter, as he noted, he had "no time for reading, politics, and that sort of thing (*keine Zeit für Lektüre, Politik und dergleichen*). . . . The anvil was my desk." It was, and he approached it intently; with a painstaking thoroughness which his father had so conspicuously lacked he taught himself to be a master smith. Before he was twenty he would be producing fine steel. He was learning the "feel" of the virtuoso, how "in working up this steel, as also in hardening it, only a dark glowing heat is needed, and that with a dark glow it becomes just as hard as the English steel (*englischer Stahl*) with a much greater degree of heat." But that skill was only a beginning. The ultimate secret was perfectionism. Alfred's version of the Sheffield process was to cook his metal in little sixty-pound graphite pots and then pour them together. One false move and *pfui*; the steel had turned to iron. The first Krupp to have been born in Prussia, he imposed a goose-step discipline on his chefs, and while his habit of flying into screaming rages over trifles was doubtless unpleasant for them, it was also the making of him.[3]

Thus Kruppstahl became a product of Alfred's character. His ordeal began on the evening of the funeral, when he left the silent factory and rejoined his grieving family in the cottage where, as he recalled later, "my father had, without success, sacrificed to the manufacture of cast steel a considerable fortune, and besides that his whole stock of vitality and health." Alfred would remember his childhood as a time of "misery and sorrow." Now, at the onset of puberty, he had "the care of a family father during the day, added to hard work at the factory, and at night I had to study how to overcome the difficulties in the way." He lived "on bread and potatoes, bread and coffee, and scant portions of meat." His chief recollection of that period was to be of "the growing danger of total ruin, and my endurance, suffering, and hard labor to avert the calamity"; of lying sprawled, gray with fatigue, "in the attic, in fear and trembling anxiety, with little hope for the future," during "hundreds of sleepless nights." He had to do almost everything himself:

> Forty years ago the cracking of a crucible meant insolvency [*dann war das ein Bankrott*]. . . . In those days we lived from hand to mouth [*Damals lebten wir von der Hand in den mund*]. Things simply had to turn out right. . . . I myself acted as clerk, letter writer, cashier, smith,

smelter, coke pounder, night watchman at the converting furnace, and took on many other jobs as well.[4]

In these passages one perceives a shade of primitive terror. "*Es musste alles gelingen*": Things simply had to turn out right. Why? Under the circumstances there would have been no disgrace in failure. His father had botched things properly. If there was nothing to be salvaged, that was hardly the boy's fault. But that wasn't how it had been presented to Alfred. No woman cheerfully admits that she has been married to a block-head. In the blindness of devotion, his mother refused to face the awkward truth about her husband. Therese Krupp had an emotional investment in Friedrich's reputation; she meant to protect it. Stubborn and still ignorant, she had nevertheless mastered her letters, and no sooner was the grave-stone in place than she advertised that

> *Das Geschäft wird hierdurch keines Weges leiden, da mein Mann aus Vorsorge das Geheimnis der Zubereitung des Gusstahls meinen ältesten Sohn gelehrt hat.*

> The business will not be hampered in any way, for my husband took the precaution of instructing my oldest son in the secret formula for the preparation of cast steel.[5]

*Und so*: that left things squarely up to Alfred. Of course, it was absurd. A young boy couldn't see that, though. He viewed his father through the prism of his mother's faith. Once, she told him, he had been in the works with Friedrich. Apparently the exotic process had been revealed to him there. Frantically he searched his memory, sorting out chaotic impressions of ore dust, noise, and workbench smells, trying to remember what the familiar gruff voice had told him. It was no good. *Dummkopf* that he was, he hadn't paid attention. And now he was in a dreadful fix; now he must either rediscover the secret and redeem his mother's promise or face damnation.

Innocent of the cruel deception, he compounded his mother's lie with others. That same week he wrote the Berlin mint that he had been running the factory for some time, and that "the satisfaction of merchants, mints, etc. with the crucible steel which I have turned out during the past year has gone on increasing, so that we often cannot produce as much as we receive orders for." He was soliciting customers. Luckily for him, few took the bait, for he was in no position to satisfy them. The Düsseldorf mint did. It ordered three hundred pounds and then had to reject shipment after shipment. "That the crucible steel last sent to you has again turned out badly is as unpleasant to me as it is surprising," he wrote the mintmaster in anguish, adding the plea, "I beg you therefore to make another test with it." Meantime he was doggedly groping toward flawless metal, hoarding his mother's few assets. Friedrich, with his careless generosity, had turned an Essen house over to a local official. Alfred promptly turned out the squatter, and the enraged ex-tenant wrote Therese, "Hardly are his father's remains laid to rest when the fourteen-year-old son sets himself to domineer over one of his oldest friends!" Alfred's mother backed him up — all things considered, it was the least she could do — and he returned to the works, hoping he could coax enough marketable steel from the foundry to support a household of five and still meet his payroll.[6]

For three years the exhausted, half-starved youth drove his smelters mercilessly until sundown and then pored over foolscap, chasing Friedrich's will-o'-the-wisp, the arcana of metallurgy. His force dropped to six men, then to five. Perhaps this was an economy measure, perhaps two pessimists quit; we cannot tell. Eking out driblets of tool steel at the melting furnace, forging them into fleshing knives and dies, luring mintmasters and toolsmiths to Essen for fruitless sales talks, he kept waiting in vain for the big break. Two hurdles seemed insurmountable. English drummers were overrunning the continent, displaying their superior line. And each time Alfred landed an order and mobilized the half-dozen Kruppianer to fill it, his power failed.

The Berne continued to be an exasperating stream. At best it was a whimsical rivulet washing weakly against the paddles of the shop wheel; at worst it brought the works to a quivering halt. Alfred first thought there must be some obstruction upstream. He wrote the Bürgermeister of Borbeck, then a hamlet just above Essen, asking him to consult a forester "on the method of clearing my hammer brook." It wasn't that simple. After a spell of wet weather the flighty branch was quite capable of changing character completely, turning into a brawling torrent that threatened the shop's very foundations. One month we find him apologizing to a buyer because "the water here rose to such an extent, following an extraordinarily heavy rain, that all works situated by the water have been put entirely out of action, and I am thus unfortunately prevented from effecting dispatch of your requirements within the promised time." Later the stream bed is dry again, and the engraver of the Royal Sardinian Mint is mournfully informed that the forge has been immobilized by "lack of water." By the following autumn Vulcan had been impotent so long that young Krupp appealed to the Royal Prussian Arms Factory at Saarn-on-Ruhr, begging to use its forge for rush orders. It was *die alte Tour*, the same old song and dance: "My hammer shop has been in great difficulties this summer owing to lack of water . . . I have been unable to produce anything approaching my requirements."[7]

German gunsmiths had no time for an insolent whelp named Krupp, and he was subjected to a singular indignity: renting the Gutehoffnungshütte hammer, which his great-grandmother had once owned. Alfred was furious at his government. Aged sixteen, he complained of "the still prevailing prejudice which ascribes such superiority to the English article," and suggested to authorities that "since the Prussian state is concerned to further the growth of home manufacture, I venture to request that the state may cooperate in establishing the success of this solitary Prussian crucible steel factory, which is so useful to the state." But the Prussian state wasn't thinking along those lines at all. When Therese, at her son's insistence, asked King Friedrich Wilhelm for an interest-free loan of 15,000 thalers for twelve years, the treasury tactfully pleaded poverty. Berlin was still opposed to handouts.[8]

Yet the government wasn't so blind to trade as Krupp thought. It had a long-range policy, cannier than he knew. Since 1819 Prussia had been quietly expanding the Zollverein, the German Customs Union. In effect this was a common market, the first surge toward a reunited Reich, and on January 1, 1834, its architects reached an agreement with thirty-six Teutonic states. All intra-union tariffs were abolished. Economically the pact created a single nation of thirty million Germans, and Alfred was in an excellent position to exploit it. His declaration that he was ready to meet all cast steel needs of the Zollverein (a million pounds a year) was a preposterous example of Krupp bombast; nevertheless, his career was beginning its upward path. On January 27, 1830, he had excitedly reported to a friend that

> I have just succeeded in the important invention of a completely weldable crucible steel, which like any other steel can be welded with iron in the ordinary way at welding heat, and the experiments with it for facing the heaviest sledgehammers as well as for small cutting tools have been a thorough success, the joiners' chisels from it having extraordinary cutting power and the hammers such a high degree of hardness [so vorzügliche Härte].[9]

There was only one crucible of it, to be sure, but it was the real thing. That year he broke even for the first time, and despite Berlin's indifference the firm had new capital; Fritz von Müller, his Aunt Helene's son, had advanced him 10,000 thalers. Alfred's brother Hermann, now twenty, had joined him on the Gusstahlfabrik floor, freeing him to train five more Ruhr farmers as Kruppianer. Most important, Krupp finally had something worth selling. Shelving more grandiose plans, he had concentrated on small rolls of exact specifications. His work was flawless,* and in March 1834 he packed a case of sample rolls and set out on a tour of the new market's nerve centers — Frankfurt, Stuttgart, Munich, Leipzig, Berlin. Three months later he galloped home, his pockets stuffed with orders. Fried. Krupp of Essen, nearly a quarter-century old, was solvent at last. Imme-

---

* In the 1960's this writer tested a retired flattening roll for gold which Alfred made for Messieurs America Alves de Sousa e Silva of Portugal in the 1830's, and found it to be in excellent condition after a century and a quarter of use.

diately he hired two salesmen and redoubled his training program. The number of Kruppianer jumped from eleven to thirty and then, in a sudden spurt, to sixty-seven. Alfred had quintupled his pre-Zollverein production of steel. In a confidential letter that December he trumpeted that "the past year has been so favorable" it had "inspired courage to work on, despite all sacrifices."[10]

The letter was confidential because he was again asking the government for money. The firm had not broken out to the broad plain of prosperity, nor would it until Alfred had grown gnarled, splenetic, ravaged, and misanthropic. Reading his correspondence and watching him move through young manhood and middle age — the 1830's, '40's, and '50's — is like watching an animal in a maze. He progresses. But there are so many dead ends, so many false hopes raised and then dashed, that the aggravation of his youthful idiosyncrasies is hardly surprising. Summers, for example, he would repeatedly face a familiar crisis. The weather would be exceptionally dry. Each morning he would rise anxiously, creep down from the attic to glare back at the glaring sun, and then inspect the parched trough beneath his becalmed wheel. Obviously it was pointless to bring in business unless he could deliver the goods. Equally obvious, he couldn't depend on the Berne. The stream was much too fickle. There was only one solution. He needed a steam engine.[11]

And who made the Ruhr's new steam hammers? The Gutehoffnungshütte. He had to drink from that bitter cup again. He also had to pay for the privilege, which is why he was resuming his attempts to wangle money from the tight-fisted Treasury. He failed — he was to fail again in 1835 and 1836 — and since his father had destroyed both the firm's reputation and its credit, he too was becalmed. That Christmas Cousin von Müller agreed to guarantee his signature. The following spring a 20-horsepower hammer was installed in the forge. It wasn't much of a machine. According to Alfred's notes, the valves leaked, the damper didn't fit, the piston required constant repacking, and since he couldn't afford pipes he and Hermann were obliged to organize the men in bucket brigades to fill the tanks. Nevertheless the hammer worked. The first faint spiral of steam had appeared over Essen. Krupp salesmen were corralling occasional clients in Athens, Saint Petersburg, Flanders, and Switzerland; and Alfred himself, trotting over to the Düsseldorf mint, was assured that the old scars there had been healed. Things were looking up. He might, with some justice, have advertised himself as one of the more promising men in Essen, or even in the Ruhr. Alfred never understated his prospects, however. Writing to the Prussian consul in Christiana (who had never heard of him) he boasted, "It is well known that my works, established twenty years ago and now doing well are the only ones of their kind on the continent" (*auf dem Continent ist . . . keine andere aufgekommen*).[12]

✠    ✠    ✠

This was more than conceit. It was an extremely shrewd tactic. Repeated endlessly, it came to be accepted fact long before it was true. It was, in truth, a big lie, told a century before Berlin discovered the technique. Indeed, those Kruppianer who argue that Alfred was the first modern German leader have a strong case, though their reasoning may be somewhat skewed. They see him as a strong man. His strength was evident, but his maturity was doubtful. Raised in insecurity and instability, he had become arrogant, aloof, Janus-faced, self-pitying in adversity, vindictive in triumph, fascinated by the grotesque, an enigma to others and to himself. His suspicions bordered on paranoia — in these years he began requiring loyalty oaths of his workers, and the doors of his hardening room and polishing shop were kept locked to enforce them. Efficiency, that German totem, was a fetish with him. His methods were curious, but when he did a job, it was done right.

The old German had been a paradigm of *Gemütlichkeit*: coarse and genial, a connoisseur of heavy foods who lay back belching after a long meal, unbuttoned and chuckling, his large, blank, sagging face creased by jovial wrinkles and his twinkling glasses perched at the end of his nose. Alfred viewed all this with cold scorn; he was in open revolt against Prussia's past. He had that compulsive devotion to work which would one day be celebrated as a national trait and its ancilla, that almost sensual pleasure in the gears and cams of technology. Writing of fine steel, he could grow lyrical: it "must be fine-fibered — not crystalline — moreover, with a metallic sheen — not like most of it, breaking off blackish and dull — but quite soft and tough, both cold and in a glowing state." It was his devotion to quality which was partly responsible for his letter to the consul in Scandinavia. He had learned a few things about chemistry, and one of them was that Swedish iron, unlike Prussia's, was virtually untainted by phosphorus. For the moment the information was worthless, because the Swedes couldn't be bothered with his tiny orders. Nevertheless he persisted, goaded by a new incentive. In the past only goldsmiths and silversmiths and watchmakers had been interested in his hard, tough rollers. Now the rollers had to be harder and tougher than ever, for the factory had discovered a virgin market for them.[13]

The discoverer had been Hermann, but under the new leader that was inconsequential. Despite his allegiance to industrialization, the emerging German was in many ways a throwback to the original Teutonic tribes. A figure of absolute authority, he demanded soldierly obedience from members of his own family — even if this meant ignoring Prussian common law. By rights Alfred's brother should have received some recognition for the firm's first genuine invention. For generations spoons and forks had been produced by stamping patterns from metal and finishing them by hand. One afternoon Hermann was examining a defective roll. Feeding scraps into it, he noticed the obvious — that the roll created identical creases in each scrap — and then drew the brilliant conclusion: what were forks and spoons except strips of metal with calculated imperfections? Experimenting in a corner of the shop, he engraved patterns on rollers. The resulting hand mill was then used to crank out superior tableware. Alfred came, he saw, he confiscated; he adopted the innovation as his own and set about exploiting it with his inexhaustible energy, and Hermann dutifully acceded.[14]

In the summer of 1838 Alfred packed his *Handkoffer*. For a year he had been planning a trip abroad, and now he was ready. His motives were various. Peddling rollers was one. Another was curiosity. Krupp's traveling man in the Lowlands and France had been bringing back strange accounts not only of opulent markets but also of sprawling factories almost obscured by their own boiling smoke. To one isolated by the poverty and frugality of early nineteenth-century Prussia such marvels were astounding; Alfred had to see them for himself. It was a good time to go. There was enough work to keep the seventy Kruppianer busy. Annexes were going up, dwarfing the original building. The steam hammer piston was packed and thumping. Hermann was a seasoned foreman; Fritz, wan and bespectacled, was nearly twenty, old enough to do the bookkeeping and take the road now and then with samples; Ida could help her mother with the housekeeping. More important than any of these, however, was Alfred's fierce desire to see England. The curious ambivalence which would mark the twentieth-century German attitude toward Britain had begun to stir. It would be eighty years before the exiled Kaiser Wilhelm II, arriving in Holland, requested "a cup of really hot, strong, English tea,"[15] and ninety years before Krupp sons began attending Oxford, but the Anglophilia which later infected his country's aristocracy was already evident in Alfred. There is one difference. His successors admired England's upper class. Alfred was attracted by the technical competence in the Midlands. Sheffield, a magic name since his boyhood, had become Mecca for him. The British had not only launched the industrial revolution; they were still leading it — leading it even in the Ruhr, where their engineers, wise to the new uses of coke, had just taught German miners how to sink shafts deeper than three hundred yards. It was the English who monopolized Swedish ore, the English who were still swamping the continent with superior tool steel and case-hardened rolls. Apparently Sheffield still had a few secrets squirreled away, and if the only way to unearth them was to go there, then: *nach* Sheffield.

But first: *nach* Paris. Alien though the British might be, they were nevertheless racial cousins of the Germans, and therefore likely to be wily. It was better to train a bit before crossing the channel. The French were less spartan. They were self-indulgent, oversexed — one still heard whispered stories about the Grande Armée's occupation — and notoriously fond of decking out their bawdy women with expensive trinkets. The Paris barnyard, in short, was certain to be eager for *schöne* rollers. On departing from Essen this was a normal attitude for Alfred. The singular thing is that he left Paris with the very same impressions. The boulevards, the arches, the cathedrals, the enchantment of Europe's most magnificent city didn't touch him at all. He didn't dislike it; it simply wasn't there for him. Travel couldn't broaden him because he was incapable of being broadened. The businesslike reports of his salesmen were confirmed, and that was all that interested him.

Thus his letters tell almost nothing of France. As usual, however, they reveal a great deal about himself. Now in fine copperplate, now in a hasty scrawl, he informs the family that he is out there hustling. "God willing," he writes on July 8, "I shall get to work and see what can be done here. There will be a huge mass of manufacturers to be visited here, if the directory can be trusted." (The directory is accurate. He is picking up clients everywhere.) "Now I shall add the addresses of the customers, together with the prices, and then close, for it is half-past 2, and I have not stood up from my chair since 7 in the morning." Later in the month he scribbles that "Herewith I send you more orders," that "I expect confirmation of 3,000 francs' worth any day, others of several thousands of francs are under negotiation," and that "if I were not absolutely obliged to go to England for much greater advantages . . . I could easily get orders for 4 times as much as up to now." A Krupp travelogue follows ("Paris is the sort of place where a skilled salesman can find something to do, year in, year out, in all the kinds of things we make"); then back to business: "In the remaining 3 days of July I shall make a sketch of a machine that will perhaps cost 2-to-3,000 francs; I am also thinking about hardened rollers of 12 and 10 and 8 inches; this is not definite, but something will come of it" (*dies ist aber noch nicht fest, doch wird noch was buttern*).[16]

Outside the seductive Parisian summer lies, warm with bonhomie. Alfred is anxious to quit his room, but not for revelry: "Just see — I must cut it short now, as I have been writing since 4 o'clock, and it will soon be midday; so I have lost some orders for today, as I generally go out at 8 o'clock — just see, I was going to say, whether rollers of old steel, which is known to be hard, show the same insufficiency of hardness, and whether, when they are being ground fine, they can still be handled. To get steel strong and hard, you must keep to the correct melting time and not too high a degree of heat. . . ." And so it goes, decrescendo, deadpan, businesslike shoptalk, through endless sheaves of foolscap. Again and again he reminds the Stammhaus that he is making twenty to thirty calls a day, and that he is not wasting his time, even when walking between appointments: "I make notes all day, stop in the street 10 times an hour and note down what occurs to me." Even his postscripts pant. "This makes some 30 pages of writing. I only wish I may not have to repeat anything, as I have lost a lot of time over this." Or: "This morning I made a sketch of a rolling mill at 10 thousand francs to lay before a certain man; I am not sure that it will be accepted, but I am just going to put on my boots, and shall have more to say in my next."[17]

The man approved the sketch. If he hadn't, one feels, Alfred would have shot himself — he seems that close to panic. But this is hyperbole. He wouldn't have done anything of the sort. Instead he would merely have collapsed, groaning, until the alarmed *hôtelier* summoned a physician. One sketch *was* rejected, and the dreadful consequences were described for Hermann and Fritz in a subsequent dispatch. His hand shaking, Alfred wrote:

> . . . for five days I have not been out of bed [*5 Tage lang bin ich nicht aus dem Bett gewesen*]; I had the most dreadful pains in all my limbs, so that I could not get up for the bed to be made; I had plasters all over my back, bleeding at the nose, headache, could not eat — in short, all the inconveniences which the devil has invented.[18]

Such digressions aside, the only emotional chords he strikes are homesickness ("Do get someone — Ida in any case, because there is no one else to do it, to write me something from Essen about relations and friends. I feel the need") and a lurking suspicion that some hanky-panky may be going on in his absence. "If a bride expected me (*Wenn mich zu Hause eine Braut erwartete*) I couldn't be in a greater hurry," he writes of the grimy Gusstahlfabrik. But will it be in proper shape to receive him? The dark thought haunts him. Is Hermann selecting too brittle a steel for slender rollers? Details, *bitte*. Does he have a double stock of valves for the engine and those pesky pumps? And what about housings? And covers and plugs for cupolas? And crucible clay? Brooding further, he remembers the night watchman. Can the man be trusted? "I suppose we might have a second night watchman to check the first, and a third to keep his eye on the second." He reflects, and concludes gloomily, "In the end all three would be asleep together." The worry continues to nag him. "It is annoying that the night is not in the day, because one never knows whether the strictest injunctions will be even remotely obeyed." Alfred isn't concerned about the watchman's honesty. No one can sneak away with a factory, or even a steam hammer. The issue cuts deeper, it touches one of his most terrible fears: "How easily a fire can break out, you know, and a fire would destroy everything, everything!"[19]

Assured by Hermann that the factory is still there, Alfred marches on England. By October he is in the Midlands, and there his performance goes beyond the bizarre; it becomes quite incredible. There is something almost Chaplinesque about his British adventures. Reading the correspondence, one half expects him to write, "And then my pants split," or "Today a man hit me in the face with a custard pie." His dark goal is industrial espionage. Before leaving Prussia he acquired a passport made out to "A. Crup," which he imagines sounds English, and in his baggage is a pair of little swan-neck spurs, the mark of a gentleman. He has a confederate: Friedrich Heinrich Sölling, a kindly, frog-faced Essen merchant and the great-great-grandson of Georg Dietrich Krupp. Cryptic letters have been mailed to Sölling from Paris; the plotters will rendezvous in Liverpool and then advance stealthily on Sheffield, Hull and Stourbridge. In fact this happens. The two bogus toffs check their covers, don disguises, and set out. But let Alfred tell it:

> Only yesterday, at a place 5 miles away, where I had gone for a walk with Fritz Sölling [*Noch gestern habe ich hier, 5 Meilen entfernt, wohin ich mit Fritz Sölling spazierte*], I saw, without any introduction, a new rolling mill for copper plates, which has only been working for a short time and where no one is admitted. I was properly booted and spurred, and the proprietor was flattered that a couple of such good fellows should deign to inspect his works [*dass so ein Paar fideler Freunde sein Werk zu besichtigen würdigten*].[20]

*Hurra! Glück!* But had the expedition really been successful? In reality it had been a farce. All Alfred had learned is that good steel comes from fine workmanship and good iron, or, as he put it, underscoring the line, "*We shall never get from Bruninghaus the iron to make the kind of steel that is satisfactory for edged tools.*" Very true, but he didn't have to go to Sheffield to find that out, as Hermann knew; that is why they had been trying to get Swedish ore. And the stratagem was pointless anyhow. In planning it, Alfred had been setting his sights on the Midlands of a generation ago, the bogey that had killed Friedrich Krupp. By the late 1830's the Huntsman principle was known everywhere. The English were aware of that, and if their visitor had come to them decently they would doubtless have told him a great deal more than he heard in masquerade. J. A. Henckel, who founded a Ruhr factory at Solingen, was stopping in Sheffield at the same time. Henckel introduced himself as himself, and no one clammed up; he wrote home that he was free to tour all mills "from ten o'clock in the morning until ten at night."[21]

Moreover, if the British *had* wanted to keep Krupp out, Alfred's mummery wouldn't have saved him, because it couldn't possibly have deceived anyone. In presenting themselves as gentry he and Sölling toiled under an obvious handicap. Neither spoke English. Discovering this to be awkward, Alfred took a crash course in the language, meanwhile embellishing his counterfeit story with an account of a continental childhood and feigning a dark, Slavic look. He still wouldn't admit the truth to Englishmen, though. That winter in Liverpool he became acquainted with a Prussian diplomat, Hermann von Mumm, who later described him in his memoirs as "quite young, very tall and slim, looked delicate, but . . . good-looking and attractive." One day Alfred drew Mumm aside and confided that he was traveling under an assumed name. This was scarcely news to the confidant, whose friends, amused by the lanky stranger's quirk of wearing his little spurs on all occasions, had gaily christened him "the Baron." The Baron was no mystery to the diplomat. Mumm had already identified him as an Essen man who had come over "to try to pick up information in British steelworks. His name," he added, "was Krupp."[22]

Krupp remained in England five months, picking up no information he couldn't have acquired at home. Since he was living in what was then the industrial capital of Europe, he couldn't expect to write orders. Besides, that would have broken his cover. Lonely — Sölling had returned to the Ruhr via Rotterdam — he had been taken in by a Liverpool family named Lightbody. Forty years later he wrote his host's grandson that the Lightbody home "was and will remain in my memory for all times a sacred spot," but at the time he made it sound like a dreadful hole, and himself like a nervous wreck. There was some comfort in Liverpool hospitality, which was allowing him to eat "at less than one-third of the cost." Yet the thought that "This trip costs money and eats into the year's profits" continued to harrass him. His worries about the factory returned. There was a storm in Liverpool, some chimney pots were toppled, and tossing on the alien bed he remembered the squat, ugly silhouette of his own beloved smokestacks. "I hope nothing of the sort has happened over there," he wrote Hermann as the wind rattled his window. "I should be anxious about our roofs." That was all he could do, fret. He was rusting away, reduced to dreaming up schemes for Hermann to save postal money:

> If you write to me in London on a sheet like this and put "single" on the outside, it will cost only single postage; there must of course be no envelope. Little sketches, &c., can always be made to fit, as you can still so arrange them that they will not be seen by anyone peeping into the letter.[23]

This was shabby of Alfred, unworthy of a man who had advertised his works as the only one of its kind on the continent. At the end of the winter he gave up the Midlands as a bad job. He had been defeated, and he knew it. Far from being resentful, he was — and would for the rest of his life remain — awed by the British, a reaction which casts some light on one of the dark recesses in his convoluted mind. He had "hated Englishmen till I went to England and there found such good, genuine men and women." Back in Paris he instructed Hermann that "iron from England must only be used for the finest things," and it was then, on March 13, 1839, that he decided to Anglicize his first name. At the same time there was another, more familiar backlash to the Midlands disaster. The symptoms began in the middle of March. He had queer sensations in his throat. These were rapidly followed by complaints of headache, catarrh, asthma, lumbago, and strange discharges. He twitched. He was gassy. He was constipated. The syndrome continued, enlivened by odd rashes and fits of dizziness — by everything, indeed, except writer's cramp — and reached a climax the following month, when he became twenty-seven years old. Unable to remember when he had had his last bowel movement, he retired to his lodgings with a douche. "I celebrate my birthday in my own way," he wrote glumly that night; "last year with cough medicine, this year with enemas" (*das Jahr vorher mit Zuckerwasser und dieses Jahr mit Klistierspritzen*).[24]

⊠     ⊠     ⊠

On one of Alfred's last mornings in Paris his scampering pencil was interrupted by harsh, banging sounds in the street outside. Crossing impatiently to the window, he looked out and — *Himmel! du grosser Gott!* Now what? Barricades were going up, wagons were being overturned, scowling men with muskets were darting back and forth. He raced downstairs to investigate and next day sent the Stammhaus an exclusive dispatch concluding:

> *Es ist noch nicht ganz gedämpft, aber es wird heute wohl enden. Wenn es die Geschäfte verbessert . . . so mögen sie sich in Teufels Namen klopfen.*
>
> It is not quite suppressed yet, but will probably end today. If it improves business . . . then in the devil's name let them bash in each other's heads.[25]

The revolt, precipitated by the resignation of Foreign Minister Louis Molé, was one of those fulminations which eventually culminated in the overthrow of the July Monarchy. But the bad guess didn't trouble Alfred. It just wasn't his field. He still had "no time for reading, politics, and that sort of thing." And it is impossible to fault him. The factional maneuvers of Molé, Thiers, Guizot, and de Soult were incomprehensible to most Germans, including politicians. Elsewhere the roll of French gunfire encouraged liberal insurgents; the Belgians won independence from Holland, the Poles rose, and even the plucky little Papal States tried — if vainly — to break away from His Holiness. In central Europe, however, the *Volk* slumbered on. Metternich was still dictator of Austria, and Prussia remained the citadel of absolutism. Prussians felt themselves above claptrap about constitutions, suffrage, freedom of the press. Alfred's attitude was typical. Leaders, he declared, "must only be forced to do their duty or be sent to the devil. Then all will go right."[26]

But it wasn't going right. Hoary walls were tumbling down, and since they weren't all political walls, Krupp couldn't remain immobile without being crushed by the debris. Nor did he always try: "I go with the times, and I do not stand in the way of progress," he said, meaning technical progress, bigger and better steam hammers, tougher Kruppstahl. Unfortunately it wasn't that simple. The Metternichs who thought they could sponge away memories of Napoleon were as doomed as the Luddites who smashed machinery. The new ideas and the new skills were linked. For example, in every land conquered by the Grand Army the antiquated guild system had been abolished. This created a free labor market — the same sort of market which had existed in England for over a century, and which had triggered Britain's industrial advances. On the continent the pattern was repeated; English machines were first adopted and then improved. Meanwhile the liberated guild workers became factory hands, the middle class grew, industrial titans emerged, the ferment continued — it was all of a piece. Like every wind of change, this one blew off some roofs. Economically it brought alarming cycles of boom and bust. Wealth acquired overnight would encourage capital investment, and then panic, howling down out of nowhere, would dump investors into a depression. The cycle could move with alarming speed. When Alfred left Paris, everything was fine. Returning to Essen after a whirlwind two-week door-to-door sales campaign in Brussels, Ghent, Antwerp, Liège, and Cologne, he found Hermann and the entire Ruhr in an acute case of economic anxiety.[27]

England had passed through this stage. Dread of an uncertain future was one of an industrial society's growing pains. Without stockholders, credit was tight. And when machines displaced *Handwerker*, purchasing power dropped; the flower of prosperity rapidly withered. For Fried. Krupp of Essen, the general depression was exacerbated by special irritants. The British were waging a price war on continental manufacturers of steel rolls, and now Krupp had a competitor in his own backyard; Jacob Mayer, in nearby Bochum, had succeeded in casting steel.* One would have supposed that Alfred's brilliant salesmanship in France would have given him a substantial lead, but no; hardly had he unpacked when a letter arrived reporting one of his customers was dead. In a few years nearly all of them were in Gallic cemeteries. It seemed queer, and still does. He himself wondered whether "a great pestilence"[28] had struck Paris — a curious plague which singled out smiths. God's hand appeared to be against him again. *Die alte Tour*: once more he was cast as Job. And indeed, his rash, predictably, worsened.

---

* Old rivalries die hard. In 1962 an official history of Britain's chief munitions firm described Mayer, not Krupp, as Germany's cast steel pioneer, and gave him full credit for inventing Krupp's steel railroad tires. (J. D. Scott, *Vickers*, p. 14.)

It passed. Beneath Alfred's other qualities lay an implacable will. It was his bedrock; as long as he was anchored in it, he couldn't collapse. Therese treated his rash with ointment, and sprawled on his attic paillasse he studied the sky for a sign of hope. Presently he found a promising patch. Although the market for rolling mills had shrunk, the *size* of the rolls in demand had vastly increased. Therefore, while clients were harder to find, a few of them would go a long way. Still scratching himself angrily, he left the Ruhr again to stalk contacts. It was to be a long trek. On Christmas Eve, 1839, he wrote the Ober-Präsident of his state requesting introductions to officials in Austria, Italy, Russia, "and the remaining European states," and that was only the beginning. He appeared in Warsaw and Prague, reappeared in Paris and Brussels, sought a meeting with James von Rothschild (he was trying to get his foot in the door of the French mint) and even pondered "doing business soon in North America." For the next several years he was absent from the factory almost constantly, riding trains, carriages, horses; staying in cheap, unheated rooms; presenting credentials and testimonials wangled from Prussian bureaucrats; showing sample spoons and forks; earnestly pointing out that "It is sufficient to have patterns of the forks and spoons, in order to arrange the rollers to turn out similar shapes with any ornamentation or engraving desired"; and posting signed contracts to Essen.[29]

His life, always lonely, grew lonelier. Each time he unpacked, a fresh crisis sent him packing again. "Now that my travels are over, I can prepare with an easy mind to remain at home in the future," he wrote on February 27, 1841, and the very next letter to the same correspondent is from Vienna: "You will be surprised to hear that I have already been here a week. . . ." His relatives rarely saw him. "You have become like the Wandering Jew," Sölling wrote him, "always traveling from one place to another." In the musty air of spooky rural inns his phobias increased. He thought of Kruppianer smoking pipes, lighting all those matches, and he shuddered. Tobacco must be *verboten*, and apprehensive that some spy in the shop might intercept his instructions — fears of persecution are creeping into his letters — he put them in French: "*Marquez dans la liste des ouvriers ceux qui fument.*" Occasionally he tried to break out of his narrow routine, to make and keep a friend. After a luncheon with a Berlin client there was a polite argument over whether he should have picked up the tab. Alfred's lead skipped merrily: "You demand a bill for rye bread! As a punishment for this impropriety, the largest rye loaf Westphalia has ever produced is going to you by the next opportunity, and I nearly wrote . . . for a cheese to be sent to you in the rind of which you could take your afternoon nap." But the jovial note was false, off-key, screeching; and in the very next paragraph he shifted to his normal gear: "The machine will go to you at your expense," he noted flatly, "and if not suitable will be returned at your expense." He could afford a loaf of bread, but shipping costs to Berlin — that was business, and Herr Jürst must be left with no legal loopholes.[30]

Gauche? Well, yes; Alfred was always that. But there was just no other way he could be. Remembering his family, remembering the ninety-nine Kruppianer now dependent on the works, remembering his father and vowing that he would not follow Friedrich's sad example, he had to weigh every pfennig. The wolf was always there, gnawing at the Stammhaus door. Hermann, too, was on the move, and between them they were picking up just enough customers to survive. In Saint Petersburg the firm of C. Tehelstein bought fork and spoon rollers; in Berlin a Herr Vollgold was buying others; and Austria looked promising, though "Strangely enough the Viennese stick tight to the old shape of their forks and spoons, and refuse to take imitations of Paris fashions," with which he hoped to score a success. Rather spitefully Alfred added, "The Austrian likes to take a respectable mouthful, and on this account some people consider the spoons too small."[31]

If Alfred disliked Austria — and he did, intensely — he had good reason. In Vienna he was subjected to a harrowing ordeal which turned him gray before he was thirty. It wasn't his fault. He was cheated blind. Perhaps he should have been warier; by now he had been through several scorchings from foreign fire. Yet in many ways he remained naïve. Although bribery of public officials was then established business practice, he continued to be outraged by it, describing his Russian bribees as "*Schwindler.*" And greasing palms, as he should have learned, guaranteed nothing: the rule in chancelleries was *Caveat venditor.* Vienna, however, was not Saint Petersburg or Paris. It was Germanic, Nordic, a brother country. As a good Prussian, Alfred respected *die Obrigkeit,* authority, and that was his downfall. Under Metternich, Austria was a full-fledged police state. Police state *Obrigkeit,* Krupp was to discover, was far more ruthless and treacherous than the clienteles with whom he had haggled elsewhere. "The Austrians," Napoleon had observed, "are always late, with their payments, with their armies, in their policies." Sometimes they didn't deliver at all. Moreover, since Austrian contracts were big, an official reverse there could be overwhelming. This one came closer to crushing Fried. Krupp of Essen than anything since the death of the founder.

The autumn of 1840 found Alfred negotiating with Vienna's Imperial Mint. The gentlemen there wanted a new rolling mill. They also wanted a guarantee. He obliged, and noted the terms in his travel diary: "Should the rollers, or any part of the mechanism supplied, break within two years or lose its serviceability, I bind myself to make replacement free of charge" (*den Ersatz unentgeltlich zu besorgen*).[32]

Fair enough. Sketches were submitted to the Austrians, who blandly approved them and later accepted delivery of the finished product. Then the trouble started. He couldn't get his money. Everyone was polite, but each time he mentioned payment he received evasive answers. Pressing the issue, he was told that his product wasn't quite satisfactory. No, no, nothing to worry about, but — another time. He came back, and came back again, and yet again, with mounting anxiety. For a year and a half he was in and out of the capital. Nothing changed. The mint kept his mills and paid him nothing. Desperate, he appealed to Baron Kübeck von Kübau, the Austrian Minister for Mining and Coinage. His case, he protested, had been limned "in the most unfavorable light" by "favored persons — whose names and disgraceful measures to injure me I am prepared to communicate verbally to Your Excellency, together with proofs." He was distraught:

> Being forced to stay here until the matter is settled [*Genötigt bis zur abgemachten Sache hier zu bleiben*], I have lost over 20,000 florins through neglect of my works, and have in addition incurred here unnecessary expenses amounting to over 7,000 florins. . . . Because of these losses, and because of being deprived of the (for me) considerable sum due for the rolling mills supplied, I have been brought to the brink of ruin.[33]

No reply. Three weeks passed, and he tried the minister again. His plight had become acute. In Metternich's Vienna, he had discovered, he could "make no claim in law on Your Excellency." Without recourse, with his spindly back to the wall, Alfred flung himself on His Excellency's mercy, trusting in the baron's "gracious considerateness." He begged for "at least part of the purchase price." Forming each letter in his best hand, he explained to the minister that "A flourishing factory, which was making a fine yearly profit, will be hopelessly lost unless my petition is granted," and prayed "that at any rate the amount of the one contract of 23 December 1840, which has been fulfilled in all respects, may be at once paid to me." Overstatement was habitual with him, but this time he was close to the bone. That same morning a fresh report from Essen had advised him that the first estimate of losses had been based on a miscalculation; actually the Austrian misadventure had cost 75,000 thalers, thrice what he thought. He was at the end of his tether: "At this moment I stand on the brink of the abyss (*am Rande des Abgrundes*); only immediate assistance can still save me."[34]

It was a moving plea. It moved the baron a few inches. He received Alfred and granted him token redress. Crawling back to the Ruhr, Krupp stared down bleakly at the long columns of red ink. Fifteen years of managing the Gusstahlfabrik had been the death of his father. The son's fifteen years seemed to have brought little improvement. Once more the same dirges were sung in Essen — Berlin was asked to help, the petition was denied, emigration to Russia was considered ("The Prussian government has done nothing for me, so I cannot be considered ungrateful if I decide to leave my country for another, whose authorities possess the wisdom to foster industry in every possible way"), and once more cousins rallied round the embattled family. His credit with Fritz von Müller had been exhausted, so Sölling was persuaded to step into the breach. Under the circumstances it took some persuading; he was promised 4½ percent on his capital, 25 percent of any profits, and no liability for losses. That understood, he put up an initial sum of 50,000 thalers and became a sleeping partner. Meanwhile a third relative had joined the brothers. In 1843 Adalbert Ascherfeld, a burly goldsmith who was descended from Helene Amalie's family, arrived from Paris to take over as floor boss.[35]

The Stammhaus diet had again been reduced to bread, potatoes, and coffee. The spoon and fork patent kept them going. On February 26, 1847, it was recognized in England (instantly it was sold outright to a British firm), and a brisk trade grew up with Hungarian silversmiths. Alfred's biggest spoon contract, ironically, was in Austria. While awaiting Baron Kübeck's pleasure he had met a wealthy merchant named Alexander Schöller. Examining his samples, Schöller suggested a partnership. At the moment Alfred preferred to see all Viennese in hell, but he was in no position to indulge his temper. Fritz Krupp was in his twenties and blossoming; Ascherfeld, bullheaded and built like a safe, was an effective foreman. Hermann could be spared, so after a family council he departed to establish the new factory at Berndorf, outside Vienna. As with all Alfred's transactions south of the border, this looked better than it was. The Berndorferwerk wasn't of much use to him. The works there quickly grew into an independent enterprise and didn't return to the Essen fold until 1938, a half-century after his death. Even then the reunion required an *Anschluss* by Adolf Hitler and some rather crude bargaining with Hermann Göring.[36]

Nevertheless the rise of the Berndorf works did have one enormous, immediate advantage for Alfred. It got Hermann out of town. *Bruderliebe*, brotherly love, was all very well; but if it meant sharing your birthright, then *nichts zu machen*: nothing doing. Alfred had become convinced that the factory was his birthright. It had been several years since he had diffidently described it as "the crucible steel works which I manage for my mother"; it was now "*my* works," "*my* shop," "*my* hammer"; or, in tenderer moments, "my child," "my bride." In part this was an understandable consequence of his long struggle. His toil and tears for the foundry had been greater than those of Hermann, Fritz, and Ida combined. In larger part, however, his attitude was the projection of a totalitarian spirit. Like his father, he believed that industrialists were the natural successors of feudal barons. The rights of a lord were incontestable, and bore no relationship to those of vassals. His first work rules, in 1838, stipulated that Kruppianer who ran up debts should be sacked. Three years later the whip cracked again. If any man were five minutes late he was to be docked an hour's wages. His Kruppianer were bound by absolute obligations; on October 12, 1844, he wrote Sölling that he expected every worker to "remain loyal to the factory that supports him." He intended to rule his fief with an iron hand, and he regarded it as his because the first of noble rights was primogeniture.[37]

Of course, it really wasn't his, and as Therese approached her sixties in declining health the question of inheritance dominated all other family issues. Mortgaged though it was, the factory was nevertheless her sole estate. And although hard times had grown harder — the depression of 1846–1847 lay over the land — each of her children wanted a piece of the works. Her verdict came in 1848. Hermann, absent and unable to argue his case, was given what he already had, the Berndorf partnership. Apparently he was content; his correspondence from Vienna was confined to detailed (and very sound) advice to Alfred about the need to watch "differences of carbon content in crucible steel."[38] As a woman, Ida needn't be taken seriously; she was to receive a cash settlement. That left Fritz, who was present, male, and, in the showdown, unexpectedly mulish. Alfred, however, had a powerful ally. Fritz Sölling, the hitherto silent partner, spoke up for him. That convinced Therese. The precedent was important. In the future the Krupp fortune would be reserved for the eldest child, and as Krupp power grew in Germany, echoes of the decision were to be heard in government policy (for example, the Nazi hereditary law of September 29, 1933). Thus children yet unborn were affected when Fritz lost his case. Like his sister he was given money — to add to the humiliation he was required to swear that he would never reveal the firm's trade secrets — and he stalked away to become a Bonn merchant. He glared as he left, and the heir glared after him. Alfred, given to unbounded rages himself, had no patience with bad temper in others. To him his brother was being inexcusably "sullen" (mürrisch).

On February 24, 1848, Alfred rather churlishly noted that his mother had turned over to him "das Wrack der Fabrik" (the wreck of a factory). Therese had allowed him to select the date of transfer, and unwittingly he had innocently picked the very morning when Parisian mobs were assaulting the Tuileries and overthrowing Louis Philippe. The continental chain reaction followed, and this time central Europe was not spared. The fall of Metternich evoked no sobs in the Stammhaus, but when the inhabitants of Berlin rose there were gasps; this sort of thing wasn't supposed to happen in Prussia. It actually didn't; after yielding to the March revolt Friedrich Wilhelm IV played for time until the Frankfurt Parliament offered him the imperial crown. It was an insufferable affront to a monarch who regarded himself as God's viceroy and looked upon any constitution as "a plotted parchment, to rule us with paragraphs, and to replace the ancient,

sacred bond of loyalty." Ultimately he rejected it in scorn, thus ending
the democratic insolence. But that triumph of the true Germany was far
away when the new proprietor took title to the works. He was worried.
"Alfred assembled the workpeople yesterday," Ida wrote a friend, "and
spoke of the general unrest. He said he hoped it would not spread to
Essen, but that if it should, he expected his men by their influence to do
all they could to stem it."[39]

Privately he was even less sanguine. "We must face the possibility of the
working classes proceeding to smash up machinery," he warned one of his
French clients on March 3. Hardly had he mailed this when rumbles of
discontent were heard in Essen. The workmen had their blood up and
their heads down. Ominous disorders were reported in shabby neighborhoods, and the frightened Bürgermeister proclaimed a state of siege.
Alfred acted swiftly. The instant one of his workers became *mürrisch* (it
turned out to be one of the original seven) he was summarily dismissed.
During the siege city gates were locked, so Ascherfeld assumed responsibility for the remaining one hundred and twenty-three men, thereby
becoming the first Krupp guard. In the morning the Rathaus bell would
toll — "*Lauft, es läutet*" (Run, run, the bell is ringing!) Kruppianer wives
would cry in low German as their men dashed down the narrow, twisting
streets. His truculent muzzle thrust forward, Ascherfeld would bark commands, escort them to the works, and march them back in the evening,
counting cadence.[40]

This was one side of Alfred's first response to social unrest. Doubtless it
was as harsh as it sounds, yet workers of that era were accustomed to
regimentation. Furthermore — and here we see the beginnings of Kruppianer devotion to Krupp — Alfred recognized that the rank of industrial
baron carried heavy responsibilities. As a patriarchal employer he had to
keep the men working, the families fed; to find some nostrum, whatever
the cost. In 1848 the initial cost was his family plate. It had survived
previous vicissitudes. Now, like Frederick the Great, he melted it down
to meet his wage bill, and when it was gone he tossed in his pitchers,
cutlery, and his English spurs, rolled them through a Krupp roller, and
marketed the result. Sölling meanwhile had arranged a loan from Salomon
Oppenheim, a Cologne banker. It was no small feat in that year of banking
failures, and though Alfred, loathing interest charges, began his long feud
with "speculators, stock exchange Jews, share swindlers, and similar parasites," the payroll was met again. Then, after the Russians had crushed
Kossuth's Hungarian revolt at Temesvar in 1849, they turned to domestic
affairs and offered Krupp 21,000 rubles if he would build a huge spoon factory in Saint Petersburg. He began to see a gleam of hope ahead, though
only a gleam; on June 10 he wrote, "Who is there who is not suffering from
the present conditions? We must just keep our heads above water (*Man
muss nur den Kopf oben behalten*).[41]

☒    ☒    ☒

In Alfred's first photograph, taken at this time, he *looks* like a man who is just keeping his head above water. He was thirty-seven, and although he hadn't gained a pound since adolescence he could have passed for fifty. His thin, smarmed-down hair was receding rapidly (he couldn't afford a wig yet) and three permanent wrinkles puckered his pasty forehead. The eyes were narrowed and wary; they had a haunted, harrowed, hunted cast. Alfred had learned to distrust luck, foreigners, even his own men. Most of all he was apprehensive about the future, which shows how deceptive fate can be, for the future was about to encircle Fried. Krupp of Essen with a dazzling, money-colored rainbow. No extraordinary invention was required to bring this to pass. The seeds of coming affluence lay all around him. The quelling of the Frankfurt upstarts assured an autocratic regime which would be indispensable to Krupp. Dead ahead lay the great age of railways. Abroad, the United States was about to gird a continent with rails; America still lacked a steel industry of its own, and Alfred's experimental railroad castings were being fashioned even now in the Gusstahlfabrik.

The most auspicious innovation, however, was the one which seemed to show the least promise. It had been lying around for years, had attracted no interest whatever, and wouldn't even become a topic of Stammhaus dinner conversation for several years more. It was Alfred's pet project. Each of his brothers had displayed a bright technical flair. Hermann had contributed the cutlery rolls. In 1844, at Berlin's Deutsche Gewerbe-Aus-stellung — industrial exhibition — the Krupp display had featured the latest model of his machine, "which, by means of roller pressure, converts sheets of raw silver, German silver, or any other ductile metal, into spoons and forks of any shape and with any usual ornamentation, cutting them out flat, and stamping them sharply and cleanly." Fritz, a putterer and tinkerer, had attempted prototypes of the vacuum cleaner and horseless carriage. These had failed, but he didn't always fail; at the Deutsche Gewerbe-Ausstellung his tubular bells had brought Krupp the gold medal which was to be sacrificed in fire four years later. Alfred's own contributions were ignored in the 1844 exhibit. He himself didn't think much of them. His papers mention them casually, almost in passing.

They were two hollow-forged, cold-drawn musket barrels.[42]

# 3

✠

# Der Kanonenkönig

No one can be certain what prompted Alfred to turn out his first musket. The family hadn't dabbled in arms since his father honed bayonets, and inasmuch as the last shipment of them had left Essen when Alfred was seven years old, any memories he may have had of it were, at most, exceedingly dim. Weaponry, to be sure, was an old Ruhrgebiet tradition. Yet it had no meaning for a fledgling industrialist of the new era. The traditional weapons turned out by the Ruhr were swords, the swordsmiths' ancient seat was Solingen, and they had been converting to knives and scissors anyhow. Lacking evidence, conjecture flourishes. Modern Krupp admirers suggest that Alfred was inspired by national pride. One of them notes that in those proud days "the poetic genius of the youth of Germany was saturated with militaristic ideals, and death in battle was prized as a sacred duty on behalf of Fatherland, home, and family." This says more about German legend than Krupp history. If Alfred was an idealistic youth, he was extremely close-mouthed about it. According to another story, Alfred simply looked at one of his eight-inch rolls and whimsically reflected that if reamed out it would have a martial look. Somehow that account isn't convincing either, and there isn't a jot of evidence to support it. Indeed, there is no record of early Krupp rolls that thick.[1]

According to a third account, Hermann visited Munich on a sales trip at the age of twenty-two, was asked by a gun dealer whether it would be possible to cast steel weapons, and sent the suggestion home.[2] This is the likeliest of the three. Hermann was in southern Germany then. And he was twenty-two in 1836, the year Alfred started trying to forge a gun with his own hands. It was slow work. Like Hermann's first roller and Fritz's gadgets, it was a hobby to be indulged after hours, and he had less leisure time than his brothers. Away most of the time, he would return, sink into

Friedrich's old brown leather Stammhaus chair, and instantly be confronted with a thousand petty administrative details. Under this hectic schedule the forging took seven years. In the end, however, it was a brilliant technical success: by the spring of 1843 he had produced his first tapered, silver-bright barrel. Elated, he did what came naturally — he tried to sell it. And then the familiar, sour feelings of frustration began aborting his hope. They were to last longer than the forging had. For over a decade they seeped through his system, poisoning his faith until he came to regret the whole undertaking.

Prussia was approached first. On the hottest Sunday of that summer he brushed and mounted his finest horse and rode over to the Saarn arsenal. This opening move was unpropitious. Saarn's sweating guard was rude; Alfred was turned away. Calling again, he learned that the officer on duty, a Lieutenant von Donat, thought the idea of steel weapons rather funny. However, von Donat intimated that a brother officer, a Captain von Linger, might feel otherwise. The lieutenant, one gathers, regarded the captain as something of an eccentric. Unfortunately, the armory's nonconformist was absent. Doubtless this explanation had been offered to let Alfred down easily, but he galloped back and dispatched his best gun to Saarn. In an accompanying letter he proudly announced,

> *Ew. Hochwohlgeboren habe ich die Ehre — Ihre gütige Bewilligung benutzend — hierbei einen vom mildesten Gusstahl massiv geschmiedeten Gewehrlauf zu übersenden. . . .*

> Taking advantage of your kind permission, I have the honor to send you a musket barrel forged from the best crucible steel. . . . At the top of the barrel I have left standing a wedge-shaped piece, which can be cut off cold, and on which any desired test of the tenacity of the material can be made.[3]

He didn't expect the army to change its small arms policy. Muskets weren't really what he had in mind. He was seeking a judgment on "the fitness of this material for *cannon*" (*die Tüchtigkeit dieses Materials für Kanonen*) and declared that his next step would be to make "an attempt to forge such crucible steel barrels directly as tubes" (*einen Versuch . . . dergleichen Gusstahlläufe gleich als Rohre zu schmieden*). Anticipating an enthusiastic response to his first specimen, he was packing two others; they would be on their way shortly.[4]

They went. And they were returned. Linger had his little ways, but he wasn't *that* odd. Exasperated, Alfred turned to his favorite foreigners, the British. In his awkward English he informed a Birmingham firm that he was sending "in 1 packet in linnin" two barrels "which it will please you to submit to severe essays and comparisons to gun barrels of iron, especially with regard to the solidity of the material and to the consequence of the greater purity and polish of the soul."* Should the firm order more than ten thousand pieces — clearly he had reconsidered the value of a musket order; it would be better than nothing — he was prepared to quote a price of ten to twelve shillings per piece. If the order were larger, he would go still lower. But the British, like the Prussians, weren't interested in steel arms at any price. They were frightfully sorry. They hoped he understood. But there it was.[5]

*Also:* he would give the home country another chance. Saarn didn't have the final say in military questions, and after the industrial exhibition he decided to approach Berlin's General War Department. For the time being his artillery project was shelved; he was definitely concentrating on small arms. Incessant lobbying, and perhaps a few palmed coins, had persuaded Saarn to test one of his barrels. It had performed superbly, even after the metal had been filed to half the regulation thickness and the test charge raised to three ounces of powder. All this Alfred submitted to General Hermann von Boyen, a septuagenarian who had served as Bülow's chief of staff in the struggle against Napoleon, and who had come out of retirement to become Minister of War. Three weeks after the submission, on March 23, 1844, Krupp had his answer:

> In reply to the offer transmitted to me in your communication under date of 1st inst. [*Auf das in Ihrem unter dem 1. d. Mts. an mich gerichteten Schreiben enthaltene Anerbieten wird Ihnen eröffnet*], you are hereby informed that no use whatever can be made thereof as regards the production of musket barrels, since the present manner of manufacturing these, and the quality of the barrels so produced, at a cost not inconsiderably less, meets all reasonable requirements and leaves hardly anything to be desired.[6]

Even in those days men of war were inarticulate. And after the turgidity had been stripped away, what was left was discouraging. Nevertheless the general did leave the door open to "further deliberation" on "the production of cannon from crucible steel." Eagerly, Alfred dusted off his artillery plans and proposed that he build an experimental gun. A six-pounder, he believed, would be beyond his present capacity. Eventually he hoped to invest over 10,000 thalers in a complete gun shop (flywheels, new furnaces, a 45-horsepower steam hammer) but there was no point in plunging until Berlin approved the weapon and, he added tactfully, Krupp had orders. He suggested a three-pounder. He could supply one "within a couple of weeks." The general warmed a bit — he became tepid — and on April 22, 1844, Alfred was given the green light. Unhappily, he had grossly underestimated the time he required; three years later he was still assuring a new minister that the weapon was on its way. It was delivered to the Spandau arsenal outside Berlin in September 1847.[7]

---

* He meant "bore." *Die Seele* means both "soul" and "gun bore" in German.

Prussia had received Krupp's first cannon. And it couldn't have cared less. Later the political upheavals were blamed for official preoccupation, but they were six months away, and when they did come the critical period was brief. Actually no one was interested in finding out whether or not the gun would fire. There it sat, 237 pounds of Krupp's best Kruppstahl, lacking even a protective canopy. For almost two years spiders spun webs across the 6.5-centimeter (2.5-inch) muzzle until Alfred, beside himself, finally goaded the sluggish Artillery Test Commission (*Artillerie-Prüfungs-kommission*) into action. In June 1849 the gun was fired on the Tegel range. Three months later the report reached Essen. Alfred, reading it, was stunned. His weapon shot well, he was told patronizingly; only excessive overloading could destroy it. But "the need for an improvement of our light guns and our field guns, specifically, hardly exists. All that might be desired is longer life for heavy bronze barrels and greater capacity for those of iron." Having made an unequivocal point, the commission hedged:

*Wir können Sie daher nicht aufmuntern, die Versuche fortzusetzen, wenn Sie nicht im Voraus ersehen, dass es Ihnen gelingen wird, das aus den grossen Kosten entspringende Hindernis für die Einführung derartiger Rohre zu beseitigen.*

We are therefore unable to recommend that you continue the experiments unless you can see your way in advance to eliminating the obstacle to the introduction of barrels of this type which arises from their high cost.[8]

Boyen, at least, had been straightforward. To Alfred, shredded with rage, it seemed that the testers were talking out of both sides of their mouths. Actually no one wanted his invention. It represented change, and the ossified brass regarded all progress with slit eyes. In retrospect the commission's verdict seems amazingly shortsighted. Yet it wasn't confined to Prussia, or, for that matter, to soldiers. Like all upheavals, the industrial revolution was roiled by counterrevolution; the same year Alfred began forging his original musket, Samuel Morse perfected his telegraph, and he was to spend eight years hammering on Washington doors before the first strand of wire went up. The military mind has always been especially immune to new ideas. Nineteenth-century officer corps fought furiously against the notions of America's Richard Gatling, England's Henry Shrapnel, and Germany's Count Ferdinand von Zeppelin.

Alfred's gun was not only rejected; it was deeply resented. Until he blundered on the scene the profession of arms had been stable and predictable. A field marshal could draw up his battle plans with confidence that the tactics employed would be those he had learned as a cadet. In some branches there had been nothing new for centuries. Gunpowder was essentially the same explosive Chinese rocketeers had used against the Tartars in 1232, and there had been no significant development in heavy weapon design since the appearance of cast bronze artillery in the late

1400's. In the stubby, thick-walled, kettle-shaped cannon of the 1840's one could still perceive the profile of the improved catapults which had appeared in the fourteenth century, when the artisans who had been casting iron church bells altered their molds to make pots capable of hurling rocks.

Refinements had been minor: better casting, better boring, broader tubes. In 1515 the Germans had introduced the wheel lock at Nuremberg; a few years later the French invented cannonballs. Napoleon's chief contribution had been to mass his batteries and blaze away at short range (*"Le feu est tout"*); for all his reputation as a master of artillery, he couldn't alter medieval gunsmith technology. War's fascination had tempted many of Europe's most brilliant minds to devise new ways of killing human beings, and three centuries before Alfred Krupp's birth Leonardo da Vinci had dreamed of breech-loading fieldpieces. The perennial obstacle had been metallurgy. At the time of Krupp's debut armorers were still woefully ignorant of chemical principles. The few advances they did make were largely through trial and error, and since they were experimenting with death they often returned to their drawing boards with bloody hands. No metal was really reliable. Any big weapon could explode at any time. Cast-iron cannon had been used effectively by Gustavus Adolphus in the Thirty Years War, yet it remained dangerously brittle because of its high carbon content; at the siege of Sevastopol, seven years after the commission snubbed Krupp, cast iron took an appalling toll of British gunners. Wrought iron, with even less carbon than steel, was coming into use. But here the difficulty was the exact opposite. It was too soft. In 1844 a twelve-inch wrought-iron smoothbore blew up on a gala voyage of the U.S.S. *Princeton,* killing the secretaries of State and Navy and subjecting relations between the Cabinet and admirals to a severe strain. Each such incident strengthened the innate conservatism of the gold-braided mossbacks. Bronze was the safest bet, and most of them stuck to that. It was heavy and dreadfully expensive, but for early Victorians it had one extraordinary commendation. Wellington had defeated Napoleon with it. That was the most telling argument against Krupp's three-pounder. Berlin's Inspector General of Ordnance, Alfred later wrote a friend, had bluntly told him that he *"wollte von Gusstahlkanonen nichts wissen, denn die alten Bronzekanonen hatten bei Waterloo ihre Überlegenheit bewiesen"* (would have nothing to do with cast steel cannon, because the old bronze guns had proved their superiority at Waterloo).[9]

Waterloo: in 1849 it was an unanswerable argument. Faced with it, even Alfred wavered, and as he made plans for his world première he again shelved his cannon blueprints. The première was to be in England's Crystal Palace. The British were about to hold the first world's fair in 1851. There wasn't much room for Prussia, then obscure; still, Krupp could hire space if he wanted it. He wanted it very much, and with his instinctive flair for publicity he foresaw that any triumph in London, however small, would be noted by the entire world. Actually he counted on an immense triumph. European industrialists were then vying to see who could produce the biggest block of cast steel. Everyone was boasting of "monster ingots," and London would show who could come up with the largest monstrosity. It was a great chance for status. In Alfred's view, the winner would be the man with the most disciplined workers — the boss who cracked the sharpest lash. Assembling his Kruppianer, barking commands as they moved in lockstep, he achieved an extraordinary feat. Ninety-eight crucibles were poured simultaneously without a hitch. He had produced a technical miracle: a 4,300-pound ingot cast in one piece.[10]

Early April found him in London in the mad Victorian ironwork of the Crystal Palace, sending back a play-by-play account of preparations for the unveiling. Now that Hermann was gone, Alfred addressed the factory collectively — "Gentlemen of the Establishment," or "Gentlemen of the Collegium" when he felt grand, or, in jauntier moments, "Dear Works" (*Geehrte Gusstahlfabrik*). He had brought along a helper to unpack crates, and the man was too busy to do anything else. ("Hagewiesche says, tell his wife he is well, and would like to have her news. He has little time now for writing.") Shirt-sleeved and steaming with sweat, he himself was feverishly prying off boards and examining the more delicate exhibits. ("Breil offered to bet his head on the firm packing of the tinsel rolls. . . . His head now belongs to me.") Awaiting the curtain's rise, he busied himself with minutiae. On April 13 he reminded the works that "When I return, there is the tire to be made" (*Wenn ich zurückkomme, bleibt der Tyre zu machen*), his first reference to Krupp's weldless steel railroad tire, and in the anterooms of the Crystal Palace he met a Mr. Thomas Prosser, an American who would set the tires spinning across a continent.* [11]

His chief concern, of course, was the monster. Inevitably there were dramatic snags. It wouldn't have been a Krupp show without them. Anticipating his prodigy's arrival, he crowed, "We shall make the English open their eyes!" He warned his assistant to keep his mouth shut, but forgot his own: "An English paper says that Turton of Sheffield will send a 27-cwt.† piece of crucible steel to the exhibition. It is probably my own doing that he is making a big ingot, for I spoke of it. . . ." Creeping around, he scouted the opposition. A Krupp myth has it that he whipped out a pocketknife of Kruppstahl, scraped off a piece of the British ingot, and snorted, "Well, it's big, but it's no good." Certainly he was disdainful.

---

* Their subsequent contract, dated August 16, 1851, is still in the business files of Prosser's great-grandson. Prosser's family represented Krupp in the United States until World War I. After 1918 the two firms reached a new agreement. Since World War II there has been no association (Roger D. Prosser to the author, September 23, 1963).

† Actually, it was only 24 hundredweight (2,400 pounds).

He wrote home scornfully:

> *Die Engländer haben einen Guss von 2400 Pfd. hier liegen, worauf
> geschrieben steht . . .*

The English have a 2,400-pound casting lying here, with an inscription "Monster casting," and a lengthy description of the magnificence of the article and the difficulty of producing it. None of it is forged, and there is nothing so far to prove that it is not cast iron. I have been saying that we make little bits like that every day, and that I shall introduce them to its grandfather.[12]

Yes. But Sheffield's ingot was there, and Krupp's had not arrived. No eyes could be opened by what wasn't there, and Alfred, priming his pump of small inventions, assembled the displays he had: rolling mills for mints, carriage and buffer springs, railroad axles. Hopefully he included in the fair catalogue: *Forged cast-steel containing a small quantity of carbon; exhibited for purity and toughness.* The exhibition committee was unimpressed. In the catalogue he was listed as No. 649 and identified as a "Manufacturer and part Inventor" from "Essen, near Düsseldorf" — Essen itself wasn't on British maps. Pacing the *Kristallpalast* in a frenzy, he dispatched an SOS to the Gentlemen of the Collegium — "Let us send whatever else can be got ready." It was one of those historic moments, like Newton's watching the apple fall, or Grant's taking the road to Fort Donelson. Krupp's afterthoughts were to be the sensation of London. Hastily inserted at the end of entry 649 after *et cetera*, they were described as: *gun and carriage, cast-steel cuirass breastplates.*[13]

The monster showed up at the last minute and created its own sensation. Steelmakers were agog; Krupp was awarded his second gold medal and acclaimed as a genius. The more the experts examined its texture, the more excited they became. These finer points were lost on the public, however. For them the main attraction in the palace was Alfred's sideshow. Awaiting the tardy ingot, he had devoted hours to the staging of the cannon. It was the gun he had planned years before, a six-pounder polished to mirror finish and mounted on hand-rubbed ash, the wood favored by ancient Teutons for javelins. Around it lay six glittering armor breastplates; overhead a military tent served as a canopy, crowned by the royal Prussian flag and a shield. The shield's inscription was no help. "German Customs Union" (*Deutscher Zollverein*) sounded dull in any tongue. But cannon and cuirasses recalled the universal, thrilling language of the Corsican: *la gloire, en avant, à la baionette, offensive à outrance.* The pure steel, invested with chivalric glamour, reminded sighing ladies in poke bonnets of the romantic panoply of Prince Hal, and Saint George and Saint Crispin's Day, and all that. After Queen Victoria had paused by the tent to murmur appreciatively, every London newspaper felt obliged to take a close look at Krupp. Piqued by Sheffield's humiliation, some journalists let chauvinism blind their judgment. The *Observer's* man observed that "the brittleness of steel is so great that we doubt whether it would resist any successive charges of powder." Still, both the *Observer* and the *Daily News* conceded that the cannon was beautiful to behold, and the *Illustrated London News* extolled "the magnificent steel cannon of Herr Krupp" as "the very coxcomb of great guns."[14]

Alfred didn't sell his great gun in London. The report of the juries was extravagant in its praise of his ingot ("The Exhibition does not show from any other country a bar of cast and forged steel of such large dimensions and of equal beauty. The members of the Jury do not remember to have seen anywhere a similar example"), but it ignored his cannon. Yet the public acclaim, his first, and from a British audience at that, stirred him. He began to see genuine possibilities in munitions, and the Crystal Palace had taught him how to realize them. Fairs were superb advertisements. Henceforth he would attend every one in Europe, accompanied by batteries of murderous coxcombs. That was the lesson he had drawn from England's cheers, and he cannot be blamed. One British reporter did regret that Krupp hadn't shown devices "for grinding corn, or surgical instruments, or something more appropriate to this peaceful age, and to the Exhibition, than a model fieldpiece." But it was the reporter, not Krupp, who had misjudged the temper of the time. Peaceful steel hadn't been absent from the exhibit. The United States section of the fair had displayed an elaborate plow, fitted with costly woods, adorned with American paintings, and burnished as brightly as Alfred's six-pounder. Everyone, including Krupp's journalistic critic, had ignored it.[15]

✠     ✠     ✠

Alfred was now in his fortieth year. Already he seemed venerable; in Essen he was known as *der alte Herr*, a wizened, emaciated, perennially jackbooted figure with the stiff, jerky movements of an old codger. Kruppianer marveled at the codger's horsemanship. On the friskiest stallion he would sit rigidly erect, determined that any concessions should be made by his mount. He had never learned to unbend, and now he was past learning; henceforth each business triumph would merely whet his appetite. The triumphs were coming now. Even before London the railway boom had begun to brighten his factory fires. In 1849 he had perfected his cast steel axles and springs, signed a big contract with the Cologne-Minden Eisenbahn, and built a spring shop whose future was assured. That should have mellowed him a bit. It didn't; obsessed with the need to achieve, he couldn't break away from his ledgers and blueprints for more than a few moments at a time. In the summer of 1850 Therese's long decline ended in death. Hermann was profoundly affected, and Berndorf was going through a financial convulsion unmatched in Essen. Alfred was terse, stark. "Two things . . . alone can move me, honor and prosperity," he wrote, and neither was involved here. He mentioned his loss briefly in one letter and quickly switched the subject to his new line of teaspoons and the pair he was having engraved.[16]

Still, there was a gap in his life. Ida had drifted away, and he felt widowed. Therese had known how to prepare his favorite dishes, sweep the floor, make his bed, and keep the Stammhaus shipshape. He hadn't time for housekeeping. Besides, it was woman's work. And so, like many another middle-aged celibate suddenly deprived of a doting mother, he began looking around for a wife. Returning from the Crystal Palace, he pondered the life of one of his unmarried Polish customers:

> *Ein alter Junggeselle in Warschau muss was Schreckliches sein und bitter überall. — Was mich anbetrifft sagen Sie ich wäre ein L—— wenn ich nicht binnen . . . bin . . .*

To be an old bachelor in Warsaw must be terrible; it is unpleasant anywhere. As for myself, call me a l—— if I am not . . . within . . .[17]

"Within . . ." was, of course, an escape clause. Still, Alfred was no liar. To be sure, he wasn't married either that year or the next. Shopping for the right bargain took time. As a suitor he had certain obvious shortcomings. Yet he had never been fainthearted; if he kept the file open, he felt, eventually the deal would be closed, and closed it was, on April 24, 1853. Next day he wrote from Cologne:

> Years after I gave my word that I meant to marry, I have at last found the one with whom — from our first meeting — I have hoped to find happiness, with a confidence that I had never thought possible. The lady, to whom I became engaged yesterday, is Bertha Eichhoff, and lives here in Cologne.
>
> This news is for your friendly interest, and please forward this letter to Warsaw for my friends and well-wishers, Hoecke and Luckfield.
>
> Yours sincerely and happily,
>
> ALFRED KRUPP

You will realize that I cannot write much in my fiancée's home, and will excuse my brevity. What will your father say? [*Dass ich im Hause meiner Braut nicht viel schreiben kann denken Sie wohl selbst u. entschuldigen die Kürze. Wass wird Ihr Papa sagen?*][18]

Bertha's sensations are unrecorded. Perhaps she felt too numb for any. Her courtship had been highly unorthodox. That first moment of meeting had been in a Cologne theater. Bertha, in the audience, had been unnerved to discover that she was being eyed by a tense, rawboned horseman, wearing mud-spattered jackboots and standing, arms akimbo, in the aisle. He meant no harm; quite the opposite. Having just ridden in to execute another contract, Alfred had attended the play on impulse. Spotting her, he made, so to speak, a horseback decision. He pursued her for a month, repeatedly informed her (so he later said) that "*Wo ich glaubte, ein Stück Gusstahl sitzen zu haben, hatte ich ein Herz*" (where I supposed I had nothing but a piece of cast steel, I had a heart) and wooed her until she said *Ja*. The sequel was equally bewildering. In Essen the betrothal was announced at a great Gusstahlfabrik feast, and all that night mortars were fired into the Ruhr sky while chanting, torch-bearing Kruppianer paraded through the narrow streets of the old city.[19]

Given Alfred's temperament, domestic happiness was impossible. No one could live with such a man. He could barely stand himself. The match was doomed, and all that remained was to define the exact nature of the distress. Here the character of the first Bertha Krupp becomes decisive. It is elusive — everything about her is elusive. Little is known of her antecedents. Clearly she was no patrician; her grandfather had been an archbishop's pastrycook, her father an Inspector of Rhine Customs. In 1853 she was twenty-one, fair, and blue-eyed. Her pictures show a bunched-up, sharp-featured girl; the expression is hard and steady, the chin juts. It is an image of robust strength. Yet as *die Frau vom* Alfred Krupp she created an impression of extreme frailty — created it with such success that no one, including her husband, ever suspected fraud. Had she been really weak, he would have quickly drained her. In a few years she would have wasted away. Instead, she survived by cultivating poor health with neurotic intensity, and it was too good an act to be just an act. Bertha, physically powerful, actually seems to have believed that she was delicate. The hypochondriac, in short, had married a hypochondriac.[20]

Her feelings toward him are an enigma. He, on the other hand, showed every sign of being in love, and in his frenzied way tried to make her happy. The Stammhaus, he agreed, was unsuitable for them. It was to remain where it was, a monument to his father and a reminder to Kruppianer that their leader's origins had been as humble as theirs. (To ram home the point, he later affixed a plaque to the cottage, saying precisely that.) The wedded couple, having exchanged rings on May 19, moved into a new home. The groom called it their *Gartenhaus*. Photographs of it are extant, and they are appalling. One would call it the most insane structure in a period of artistic lunacy, except that late in life Alfred was to demonstrate how wild an architect he could be when he really put his mind to it. Nevertheless, the Garden House had its own peculiarities. Built right in the middle of the works, it was surrounded by hothouses sheltering peacocks, grapevines, and pineapples. Atop the roof, a glassed-in crow's nest permitted the head of the household to peer out at the factory gate and spy tardy workers. Before the front door stretched an intricate maze of formal gardens, fountains, islands gay with flowers, and grottos fashioned of slag. The Gartenhaus faced away from the Gusstahlfabrik, and Alfred was confident that his wife — provided she stayed out of his crow's nest — need never be reminded of its presence.[21]

He was mistaken. The Ruhr had changed mightily since the 1840's. Five years earlier, an English traveler had described Essen as "poetically agricultural," but now that idyll was gone. The city was awakening from its long slumber; soon its picturesque little cottages, fashioned of timber with wattle and daub filling, would vanish entirely. Germany was on the verge of the great industrial surge which would, within a half-century, sweep English supremacy aside. The coal and iron industries had made their fateful union. Each year the sky overhead grew grayer; each year the smelters used more coke. By puddling they were transforming iron to wrought iron and then adding coke to increase the carbon content. It was sound chemistry, if somewhat intricate, but Alfred, of all people, should have realized that it was bound to smother his domestic paradise.[22]

The factory air was filthy, and there was no way to keep it out of the house. Billowing clouds of oily grit withered his flowers, blacked his fountains, coated his hothouses with soot. At times he couldn't even see through the panes of his roof nest. The tainting smoke penetrated every room, ruining his bride's trousseau and besmirching her freshly washed antimacassars and linens before the laundress was out the door. Nor was this all. Alfred was installing heavier and heavier machinery, and the grunt of his steam hammers rocked the foundations of his home. Bertha couldn't keep glasses on her sideboard. If she put them out after breakfast, all would be cracked by lunch. Alfred didn't seem to mind. He was proud of the house, and to his wife's annoyance he became a homebody. When she complained about the dishes; an admiring friend jotted down her husband's reply: "It's only a few porcelain plates; I'll make the customers pay for them" (*das muss alles die Kundschaft bezahlen*). And when she countered with a plea that he take her away for just one evening, to a concert, he answered sharply, "Sorry, it's impossible! I must see that my smokestacks continue to smoke, and when I hear my forge tomorrow, that will be music more exquisite than the playing of all the world's fiddles" (*habe ich mehr Musik, als wenn alle Geigen der Welt spielen*).[23]

Bertha had conceived in the first week of marriage. On February 17, 1854, she gave birth to a son — flabby and sickly, though Alfred didn't notice that, either, then. Exultant, he christened the child Friedrich Alfred Krupp in honor of his father and himself, and to further herald the arrival of little Fritz he named his noisiest steam hammer *Schmiedhammer Fritz*, which, thanks to a new night shift, thundered around the clock. With it, he announced, he expected to "*selbst die Antipoden aus dem Schlaf zu schrecken*" (startle the Antipodes themselves out of their slumbers). That decided Bertha. She began to moan and twist her hands, and for the rest of her life she was never to be out of the hands of physicians. Alfred was all solicitude. He sent her away to spas, hired the best Berlin doctors, and took the boy off her hands for long periods. He also displayed intense interest in her symptoms. Fascinated by illness, he fired off advice: "Exercise is good for the digestion and improves the humors and the blood." In his view, activity, any activity, was better than this everlasting, swooning languor, and he attempted to prod her to her feet: "Please go to the furniture store and see whether they have some cane chairs and leather-upholstered furniture that will go together for the Gartenhaus. . . ." Confidence was needed ("You need not be in doubt about the progress of the treatment"), and spirit: "If a little recuperation is still necessary from time to time at present, why, that is nothing very terrible!" Sometimes he took a firm line: "When you leave Berlin you must be stronger and livelier, otherwise, instead of staying here in the summer, we shall have to spend it at watering places." Even at a distance he couldn't refrain from trying to run her life for her:

*Liebe beste Bertha!*

I quite agree with Frau Bell that plain silk does not suit you, but traveling clothes are not meant to be ornamental; on a trip one wears the plainest dustlike materials, as journeys are always accompanied by dust, which would be very unsightly with taffeta, and to be seen beating the dust off would be quite vulgar. Cuffs, blouse fronts, and all the flummery that is worn in formal dress should be left off when traveling. Also gold and jewels. One should be downright simple. Knowing that you have clean underwear beneath your dress should be enough [*Man ist ganz einfach gekleidet. Das Bewusstsein saubere Unterwäsche zu tragen genügt*].[24]

Anxious that she shouldn't exhaust herself in correspondence with spa acquaintances, he devised a form for her:

I have received your note of . . . ., and note therefrom with ${pleasure \atop sorrow}$ that things are ${going \atop not\ going}$ well; as for myself, ${\text{I am very well, thank goodness, and} \atop \text{certainly not yet plump and fat, but}}$ hope this will ${remain\ so. \atop soon\ come.}$ Since my last letter, I have been for a drive regularly every day through the delightful Tiergarten, and go twice every day for one hour walking there in the most charming company, which a king would give millions to see. In the end, however, the thing is becoming monotonous, and I am longing to be back with my dear husband, and hope above all that he will be pleased with me. Only do not write to me too often; that embarrasses me, because I cannot reply.

Yours as ever,

BERTHA

As an afterthought he added: "This form for other people. But for me, I want a few lines in writing, please" (*Dieses Schema ist für die andern. Ich bitte dagegen um einige Zeilen Geschriebenes*).[25]

He got precious few. Really there was little to discuss. Her Essen trauma behind her, Bertha wrinkled her nose at what she called "factory people" (*Fabriker*), so she was reduced to gossip and petty complaints. Fleeing from one fashionable resort to another, she formed her little friendships, made her little enemies. Alfred tried to remain part of her life. On flying visits to spas he strove earnestly to like "Clara" and "Emmy," "Otto" and "dear, sweet Anna," and he displayed manly indignation when his wife complained that a "loathsome Jew" had eyed her lewdly, though he pointed out that there was no law against looking: "If he should ever lift his hat, ignore it as though he had lifted it to someone else."[26]

In the Alfred-Bertha dialogues — manic starlinglike chatter on one side, yawning inattention on the other — one's sympathies lie with him. Granted that he was exasperating — whenever they met he insisted that she console and comfort him — still, he *was* working under great strain, he *did* cancel important meetings to see her, he *had* taken two of her cousins, Ernst and Richard Eichhoff, into the works management, and she could have displayed, or simulated, kindness. His affection, however grotesque, was genuine. In his stream of poignant notes he greeted her as "Dear Sweetheart," "Dear Berth," "Dear Best of Berthas," "Dear Old Woman." Toward their son he was, in these early years, unfailingly tender. "Kiss Fritz wet for me!" he implored when the child was with her, and whenever the boy arrived in the Ruhr the father was enraptured, chronicling every detail: "I found Fritz as cheerful as ever, and yesterday he ate like a navvy. . . . I received *such* an outburst of joy." Dejected reaction always followed separation from his wife and son. In the solitude of the soot-streaked Gartenhaus, pacing the floor, his boots crunching on fragments of shattered tumblers, he would sink into temporary despondency: "*Ich bin wirklich allein nichts wert u. mir ist schlecht zumute ohne dich*" (I am really no good alone, and I am in poor spirits without you).[27]

✠     ✠     ✠

Actually he was at his best alone — desolate, no doubt, but creative nevertheless — and with the factory belching smoke outside he would revive swiftly. The foundries, the forges, the ugly piles of slag and staining coke: these were his true family, and in lucid moments he knew it: "I always look upon the works here as my child, and a well-brought-up one at that, whose behavior is a joy; who, indeed, would not want to have as much as possible to do with such a child?"[28] Bertha didn't; that was the bone between them. Another man could have reconciled his family and his career. Not Alfred. He had to have as much as possible to do with his works, had to go all out, trying this scheme and that, putting one aside while he pushed another; otherwise he would be dishonoring his father and betraying his mother's trust. He couldn't budge, Bertha couldn't. Thus they drifted, unaware that long after their deaths, the child they both cherished would become a spectacular victim of their conflict.

At the time of Alfred's marriage the prospects of Krupp guns were again waning. By early 1852 it was clear that his London cannon had been a flashy curiosity, nothing more. Since no customers had come forward, he decided to give it away. On January 19 he directed that it be disassembled, cleaned, reassembled, "polished as nicely as possible," and sent with his compliments to the King of Prussia. Ostensibly this was a gracious gesture. In fact he was playing a deep game. He anticipated a windfall in free publicity — "The gun must be completed quickly, in time for the Emperor of Russia to see it," he scribbled to Ascherfeld — and he got it. Friedrich Wilhelm IV, not knowing what else to do with such an unusual gift, replied that he would be pleased to display it in his palace. "Yesterday," Alfred noted gleefully, "I received the decision that the gun was to be set up in the marble hall in the Potsdam Stadtschloss. Today we did it with six artillerymen. The King said the Emperor of Russia should see it there."[29]

Czar Nicholas I was a potential client. At the time, his state visit seemed to be the main chance. It was certainly a golden opportunity, and eventually Alfred's maneuver was to reap a harvest in Saint Petersburg. Meantime, however, the Potsdam cannon had won him a powerful ally who would later help him financially, see that his key patents were extended, and let it be known that the Krupp works were *"ein vaterländisches Institut"* (a national institution).[30] The name of this very useful angel was Wilhelm Friedrich Ludwig von Hohenzollern. Today he is remembered as Wilhelm I, "the old Kaiser," predecessor of the Wilhelm II who led Germany to defeat in World War I, but in 1852 he was a grizzled, ramrod-backed sleeping giant, chiefly known for his intransigence in the Berlin rioting of March 18, 1848. The German blood spilled that day had been on his hands; bitter liberals had denounced him as a reactionary, and to appease them his royal brother had been obliged to send Wilhelm into a brief exile. Lately palace insiders had been studying him with fresh interest. Since the sovereign was childless, Wilhelm was Prussia's heir presumptive. His reign might begin at any time, because Friedrich Wilhelm's mind had become increasingly clouded. He was given to medieval dreamings. Year by year he was sinking into madness, and already Wilhelm had been awarded the title Prince of Prussia — in effect, Crown Prince, or, as the unreconciled liberals would have it, the Cartridge Prince.

That was more than an epithet. Sharing his mooning brother's faith in divine right, the prince fortified it with a fierce reverence for the God of battles. His military background was impressive. In his teens he had led bayonet charges against the French, winning an Iron Cross in the lines before Bar-sur-Aube at the age of eighteen. At twenty-one he was a major general. If, as seemed likely, he was to become Prussia's first soldier king since Frederick the Great, he was a key figure for an aspiring munitions manufacturer. Luckily for Alfred, Wilhelm's conservatism was only political. Unencumbered by the officer corps' hostility toward new weapons, he was an ideal critic of the Potsdam gun, and when he strolled into the Stadtschloss marble hall and beheld it, he found that where he had supposed he had a heart he had a piece of cast steel. He wouldn't rest until he had met "this Herr Krupp," and the following year he expressed a wish to come to Essen.[31]

This news, relayed through channels, electrified Alfred. "Of course" (*selbstverständlich*), he replied; a Hohenzollern could drop in on him any time; the Gusstahlfabrik latchstring was always up. Bertha, then in the first months of her pregnancy, swept away the broken crockery and hid her gray doilies and counterpanes as the Cartridge Prince dismounted outside. Chin in and chest out, Wilhelm marched through the factory, *links, rechts*; left, right. On emerging he congratulated Alfred. The shop, he observed, was as tidy as a parade ground (it really was), and *die Kruppianer* were true soldiers of industry. Because Friedrich Wilhelm's mental fugues hadn't yet reduced him to an idiot king — and weren't to do so for another five years — the prince couldn't throw any business Krupp's way yet. Nevertheless, he wanted to show his appreciation, so he pinned Alfred's narrow breast with the *Roter-Adler-Orden*, Order of the Red Eagle, fourth *Klasse*, a distinction normally reserved for gallant generals. It wasn't better than a commercial order — in Alfred's view, nothing was — but he saw it, correctly, as a royal promise, an invisible pivot.[32]

If the factory had been honored, so had His Highness. A tour of the shop was not only unusual; it was almost unprecedented. Since the Berlin industrial exhibition of 1844, when an Elberfeld spoonmaker had tried to pass off Kruppstahl as his own, Alfred's passion for secrecy had become an obsession. "Please do not leave the works when I am away," he wrote Ascherfeld from Berlin's Hotel de Russie in the summer of 1852, "and take the greatest care that an eye is kept on the people who come to the works outside working hours." One never knew when a sly knave might show up with a false passport and little swan-neck spurs. Even a cousin of Ascherfeld's was excluded:

> Now there is another matter which I must mention. I remember that a relative of yours — Herr Pastor, Jr., who is in Austria, has frequently visited you and stayed with you. This gentleman now wants to set up a cast steel factory in Hungary, and is coming to Essen with that in mind. I need say no more to you to put you on your guard concerning conversations and questions, visits to the works, and everything of that sort. He is

trying also to get suitable workmen [*Er hat die Absicht, zugleich taug-liche Arbeiter zu erwerben*].³³

His embarrassed foreman noted sadly that "no assurance" would "shake his conviction" that the cousin was a spy. Subsequently these suspicions became ludicrous; Alfred shipped one display to an industrial exhibition and then, gnawed by doubt, instructed the Krupp man in charge to hide it from the public — "let it rust away . . . in a damp corner, rather than give information to the French, English, and Americans, who will only pick up ideas from us."³⁴

Still, he had some justification. Over in Bochum, Jacob Mayer, like Alfred, was requiring his workers to take oaths that they would never reveal his cast steel technique. There *were* industrial spies in the Ruhr, and in the months after the Cartridge Prince's call Krupp had precious treasures to guard. Exhilarated by his conquest of London, he was plotting a new European coup. German fairs were walkovers now; in 1854 he won ribbons in Munich and Düsseldorf. What he really wanted was a triumph at next year's Paris World Exhibition, France's answer to the Crystal Palace challenge. He now had a French agent, who was bombarded with advice. The great thing would be to get prominent space in the main hall. "Do not spare nice talk and money to make yourself friends who will help you," Alfred advised Heinrich Haass, and forwarding instructions on the new monster ingot he was shipping, he ordered Haass to demonstrate the interior consistency of the steel block by making "a fracture" which "must strike every expert."³⁵

Experts were struck by the ingot. Several of them, in fact, were nearly crushed by it. A line of jurors was about to wind past when the ingot, weighing a hundred thousand pounds, crashed through the exhibition's wooden floor, plunged into the basement, and reduced everything below to pulp. Alfred, hearing of the disaster, had a nervous breakdown. For once he wasn't just Bertha's visitor; he fled to Pyrmont to become a fellow patient. Industrialists who knew him strongly suspected a Krupp publicity stunt. If so, it was a successful one, for the judges, surveying the wreckage, were enthusiastic. *La sacrée tête carrée d'Allemand*, they reported, was indeed *formidable, bravo, bravissimo*; the new age demanded big slabs of steel, and here, obviously, was the biggest yet. Several viewers hinted to Haass that they would like to see the maker set up shop in their own countries. The three-year-old Crédit Mobilier openly proposed a Krupp factory in France, and there were invitations from as far away as America. Haass relayed these reactions to Pyrmont, and suddenly Alfred was well — well enough to air the snappish charge that the cast steel bells Jacob Mayer had sent to the fair were "*Roheisen*," pig iron.³⁶

Mayer, infuriated, called him a liar and proved it by breaking off a clapper, heating it, and forging it on the spot. Briefly he held the spotlight.

Unfortunately he couldn't keep it, because Alfred was prepared to show more than an ingot. Church bells, like America's plow four years earlier, couldn't compete with ordnance, and this time Krupp unveiled a cast steel twelve-pounder. Napoleon III, an artillery enthusiast, was enchanted. He ordered the weapon weighed — it was two hundred pounds lighter than bronze fieldpieces of the same caliber — and then tested at Vincennes. After three thousand shots had been fired without even scarring the bore, the emperor created Alfred a Chevalier de la Légion d'Honneur. Like being a Red Eagle, that was at first gratifying. It soon soured, however; Haass informed the new chevalier that French officers, eager to learn more about the cannon, were planning to overload it and burst the barrel. Alfred was alarmed. This was worse than Ascherfeld's cousin. He shot back:

> It cannot be my wish that the gun should now be torn to pieces [*Es kann nicht mein Wunsch sein dass die Kanone jetzt zerrissen wird*] and the material given to the French factories to imitate, for I have no intention of having my invention exploited by others, but claim above all to assure the interest in it exclusively to myself. Does the French government want to trick me, and am I in the end even to thank them for the powder which they have used in the interest of their research into this important question? [*Will die franz. Regierung mich umgehen und soll ich am Ende noch für das Pulver danken was sie im Interesse der Prüfung einer so wichtigen Frage aufgewendet hat?*][37]

He needn't have worried. Vincennes was merely indulging an imperial whim. There was no real enthusiasm for the test there. He could have buried all the constables of France in a salvo of Krupp shells and their allegiance to bronze would have been unshaken. Wilhelm excepted — and he was then powerless — no European field marshal felt otherwise. Blind to the practical implications of Kruppstahl performance, they treated it as an amusing oddity. Alfred, convinced that he had a good thing going and resolved to catch *someone*'s eye, presented gift guns to Switzerland, Austria, and Russia. His Russian experience was typical. The most distinguished generals of the new Czar Aleksandr II arranged an elaborate test of the gun. Day after day their men bombarded distant targets with it, and after four thousand rounds they examined every inch of the barrel. Not a scratch. Bronze, they agreed, could never have survived such punishment. Indeed, the performance had been so remarkable that they decided to do something about it. By unanimous consent, they ordered the cannon preserved as a freak in the Artillery Museum of the Fortress of Peter and Paul.[38]

✠　　✠　　✠

Thirty years later, in the last weeks of his life, Alfred confided to one of his directors, "It was only through the manufacture of tires, under the protection of our patents, that the works were able to make enough profit to lay down the gunmaking plant."[39] That was the nub of it. In these middle years Alfred was like a gambler who lays a wager, wins, and leaves his winnings on the table. Each success formed the nexus for the next thrust. His spoon rollers had underwritten the tire experiments. Now the tires were to finance munitions.

Railroads were the heart, soul, and symbol of nineteenth-century expansionism, and no industry depended so heavily on the gropings of the new steelmakers. Iron simply wasn't good enough for iron horses. Actually it never had been satisfactory for travelers, but broken stagecoach springs had merely brought discomfort; a cracked axle, delay. On a train lives were at stake. Springs, axles, rails, and tires (wheels) had to be made of sterner stuff. Alfred had quickly solved the first three. Wheels were a special problem. They had to be seamless, they couldn't be welded. At the same time, they were a potential source of fantastic profits, for if they could be mass-produced the market was almost unlimited. Here was an immense challenge to his technical genius, and he solved it brilliantly. Scribbly sketches, yellowed now but still clear, show how. His answer was centrifugal motion, with finishing on a lathe. In mid-January 1852 the first tire was ready, and he directed "the second one to be forged complete as quickly as possible and as nicely as possible, dirty places or places of unequal thickness, which have been worked down with a cold chisel or a file before the last shaping, being forged over so that no one can guess that a chisel or file has been used." Krupp went into production in 1853, exhibited the results at the Munich fair the next year, and was soon selling fifteen thousand wheels a year. The boom continued through his lifetime, and in 1875 he recognized the tremendous contribution of this single invention by designating three interlocked circles as his trademark. It is still the Krupp trademark, and is so recognized everywhere in Europe, though Americans frequently confuse it with the symbol of Ballantine beer.[40]

The tire was a masterstroke. There was almost no competition; undoubtedly he was the inventor. There remained the matter of patents, which turned into a typical Krupp battle, with stormy rages, threats, high confusion, and touches of low comedy. The issue was: how unlimited were his rights? The longer his exclusivity lasted, the more valuable it was; once his technique entered the public domain his margin would be cut sharply. Berlin recognized the patent on February 3, 1853. Alfred wanted it to last ten years, the government suggested six; they compromised at eight, although he protested that that would mean expiration *"before I have gained anything by it."*[41] He wasn't serious. He was going to gain a lot at once, and knew it. Objections were for the record, to lay the groundwork for a future campaign. It was to be a bruising struggle, and what made it especially humiliating was that it would be fought in his own country. Every other European country was treating his wheels handsomely. Not a single licensing dispute had arisen abroad. Only Prussia was being niggardly.

Alfred's troubles in Berlin were of his own making. Lacking any talent with people, he had managed to alienate Prussia's powerful Minister of Commerce, a sausage-fingered banker named August von der Heydt. The Crystal Palace medal had inspired the minister to come and inspect Krupp's works. He had thought he was paying tribute to a successful manufacturer, but he wasn't royalty. Alfred, ever alert to espionage, had snubbed him. That had been very stupid. Von der Heydt had been mortally offended. He vowed vengeance for this *Schweinerei*, and he was in a position to hurt Krupp grievously, for Prussia had replaced Austria as Europe's model police state. The autumn after the first patent skirmish Alfred, realizing how badly he had blundered, turned contrite. Of course, he overdid it. He always overdid everything; that was his signature. Acquiring a portrait of von der Heydt, he hung it over his desk and let the subject know that it was "intended to encourage and inspire me . . . to make a success of things, just as Christ must strive in His way of life after nothing meaner than the Godhead."[42]

The Godhead was unmoved. Let Christ strive away; the Ministry of Commerce was Krupp's implacable foe. To spite him, von der Heydt vowed that orders for Krupp wheels to be used on Prussian rails would be reduced to a bare minimum. His office had jurisdiction over the national railroads, and instructions were handed down: stick to puddled steel tires. Alfred was horrified. The honor of Prussia was threatened! Also Krupp's profits! "Who would believe that in one month of this year we have delivered to France — as well as to one single Austrian company — goods to a greater value than we have to the Prussian State Railways during the whole of their existence?" he cried on Easter Sunday, 1857. Early the following year he pointed out to Baron Alexander von Humboldt that despite recognition in other countries, "the Prussian State Railways persist unchangingly in being an exception, and their total orders in the past year did not reach the necessary minimum of a single day." When the author of the boycott still wouldn't budge, Alfred protested directly to von der Heydt that ministry buyers "have *to an inexplicable degree disregarded my establishment and all applications for work*," and that "up to now *the Royal State Prussian Railways have not taken one-half of one percent of all the tires manufactured*."[43]

More than money was involved here. The capitalist of a hundred years ago wasn't a board chairman worrying about quarterly dividends and price-earnings ratios. The issue for him was nothing less than survival. In the headlong race to exploit the opportunities of the time — the fantastic prizes available to a handful in that giddy moment of history — a conservative stance was impossible. To maintain momentum one needed great tanks of capital. By British standards, German industry was still a poor cousin; nevertheless, a juggernaut was assuming shape in central Europe, and a few figures suggest the speed of its growth. Between 1850 and 1860, the annual production from Ruhr blast furnaces increased fifteen times. In 1857 the number of Kruppianer passed one thousand men. The Gusstahlfabrik shops had octupled and now comprised a rolling mill, a power press, a fitting shop, and a score of steam hammers, furnaces, and foundries.

Alfred had agents in London, Paris and Vienna — Matthias von Ficzek, his man in Vienna, also represented the Rothschilds. Since the Paris exhibition Kruppstahl had acquired a special cachet, and he had begun to turn out screws and crankshafts for foreign ships. Yet with the ruthless need for expansion, his fiscal position remained precarious. All gains could be wiped out in a fortnight. As yet, Krupp had no special position in Germany.* He had to establish himself with his own muscle, and his greatest asset was that tire patent. With it, he could build a commanding lead; without it, the future of Prussia would belong not to Krupp's virile cannon but to Jacob Mayer's effeminate church bells.

Alfred needn't have pushed quite so hard. In his lust to corner sources of raw materials he was already overreaching himself, and his insistence on one-man ownership repeatedly jeopardized the Konzern. His descendants were later grateful to him on both counts. Without the strength they provided, the firm would have gone the way of I. G. Farben in the trust-busting which followed World War II. In the depression-ridden 1850's, however, they seemed unreasonably foolish — a fact not lost on his sleeping partner. As Krupp's borrowings increased, Fritz Sölling became troubled. It was foolish to dance on such a tightrope, he argued; why not form a corporation? To Alfred this was like asking him to share Bertha. He could imagine no more ghastly fate than falling "into the hands of a joint-stock company." To his friend Gustav Jürst he wrote, "I do not want to submit the balance sheet to anyone"; his cousin must realize that he was "not a partner, that is, not on a percentage basis." Sölling persisted. He believed that he was entitled to an audit, and he was right. It made no difference. Like Alfred's brothers before him, Sölling found himself frozen out. "I must be what I have given myself out to be, 'Alfred Krupp, Sole Proprietor' " (der alleinige Inhaber), Alfred wrote Ascherfeld. "The fact that Herr Sölling is entitled to a certain share . . . for a term of years is of no concern to the public." His partner had committed an unpardonable sin, and there was to be no forgiveness, not even at the grave. Sölling's

---

* Or, for that matter, in Essen. He was known to fellow craftsmen and government ministers, not to the public. On April 10, 1854, Essen's Police Commissioner, in notarizing a testimonial to Krupp crankshafts by the Rheinish Steamship Company of Cologne, identified Alfred as "Herr Friedrich Krupp." (Krupp Werksarchiv IV, 88.)

worries about mounting credit grew; when the long Panic of 1857 broke, he became an insomniac. Lacking the constitution of *der alleinige Inhaber*, he succumbed. Alfred's eulogy was curt and cruel: *"Binnen acht Tagen war er gesund und tot"* (One week he was well, the next he was dead).[44]

August von der Heydt was a tougher opponent. Here two Prussian tyrants were at loggerheads: both vulpine, resourceful, and possessed of a jugular instinct. For a while it appeared that von der Heydt had won. On June 3, 1859, Alfred made what seemed to be his final appeal for extension of the railroad tire patent. Icily it was rejected. Bitterly Alfred wrote that "v.d. Heydt never wanted my works to prosper," that his antagonist had "neglected nothing to make me seriously regret that I did not exploit my inventions abroad years ago, and if I still have to adopt this course, no one but the Minister v.d. Heydt will be to blame." That sounds like a threat, and it was; his correspondent was General Constantin von Voigts-Rhetz, director of the General War Department in Berlin and an enthusiastic advocate of steel cannon. The general made an ideal emissary to Wilhelm. And Wilhelm, who had been appointed regent for his crazy brother the previous autumn, was now in a position to help the sole proprietor.[45]

Alfred was preparing to outflank the Minister of Commerce. In the spring of 1860 he moved in for the kill, wrapping himself in the Prussian flag. Voigts-Rhetz having smoothed the way for him, he wrote His Highness himself, asserting that "in spite of the higher gains which could indubitably be realized, I have refused to supply any cast steel guns to foreign countries when I believed I could serve my native land thereby." He thereupon renewed his plea for an extension. On March 19 Wilhelm urged the ministry to approve. On April 14 v.d. Heydt, fighting desperately, recommended refusal. Finally, on April 25, the regent assured the future of the Krupp dynasty by overruling him, citing "the patriotic sentiments which Commercial Counselor Alfred Krupp, of Essen, has frequently displayed, particularly in declining foreign orders offered to him for guns."[46]

⚒   ⚒   ⚒

Note the crafty wording of Alfred's message to the prince. He had refused to sell cannon "when I believed I could serve my native land thereby." The more you read it, the less it says. In assuming it meant sacrifice, Wilhelm had been led into an arrant lie. Alfred had declined nothing. He had, in fact, been soliciting cannon customers all over Europe. It was true that the market remained listless, but not because Krupp had been aloof. After the Paris exhibition he had nearly sold Napoleon III three hundred twelve-pounders. The deal fell through because of the patriotic sentiments, not of Alfred, but of the emperor, who felt obliged to support the Schneider family's new gun works at Le Creusot — thus giving the first fillip to the international arms race which was to play such a spectacular role during the next hundred years. While Krupp had failed there, the fair had led to his first sale. The Khedive of Egypt, admiring the gun in the booth, had ordered twenty-six of them. These were being polished when the Czar, having decided that perhaps there was a place for military freaks, asked for one sixty-pounder for coastal defense. If it went well, he was prepared to spend rubles like water.

Krupp complied, though he was becoming somewhat weary of sovereigns. A gunsmith couldn't live without them, but their imperious ways could be maddening. The Duke of Brunswick, for example, had accepted delivery of a Krupp gift gun and had then failed even to send an acknowledgment; the King of Hanover had ordered a 1,500-thaler cannon, had offered 1,000 thalers for it — and then had paid nothing. How could you dun a king? Alfred's solution was to hint that he would like gifts in return: thoroughbred horses, "something tangible, from which one gets pleasure daily, and more solid than little crosses and stars and titles and similar shabby baubles." Bavaria had presented him with the Order of Merit of St. Michael, Knight's Cross; Hanover with the Guelphic Order, fourth class. He regarded these as so much wampum, yet they were all he had got from either monarch. The steeds remained in their royal stables, and on January 19, 1859, with his cannon virtually spiked, he seriously considered scrapping all his arms designs. He informed Haass that while he had been toying with the notion of "a monster gun with a bore 13 inches in diameter and 15 feet in length" (*ein Monster-Geschütz von 13 Zoll Seelendurchmesser und 15 Fuss Seelenlänge*), it scarcely seemed worth the bother: "Although, as in the case in question, I still pay some attention to guns, I have a desire to give up gun production." It made no money; it was troublesome; there was no prospect of "finding compensation in bulk deliveries." Egypt excepted, he lacked any large orders. All in all, it seemed a bad job. Nothing came up "to the expectations which I have been led to form from certain quarters, and especially from France." Haass himself was being fobbed off "with empty verbal promises, not even written ones"; the emperor's army had just acquired rifled bronze guns for eighty batteries; Schneider, encouraged, had invested in a gigantic steam hammer. Alfred was inclined to see his own future in directing his attention "exclusively to a more profitable activity, the production of cast steel tires and cast steel shafts and axles for seagoing and river vessels, railway locomotives and wagons." He would devote his tools "for use in the arts of peace."[47]

Darkness: then flaming dawn. Even as he pondered throwing in the towel, the new regent was preparing to order one hundred six-pounders. Voigts-Rhetz persuaded the prince to raise this to 312 — worth 200,000 thalers — and by May 20 (when Kruppianer were exempted from military conscription), Alfred had received a 100,000-thaler advance from the Prussian War Office. Already Krupp's first gun shop was rising. A ripple of fresh interest stirred the pavilions of royal Europe. Thoroughbreds now began arriving in Essen, and also carriage horses. In October, Prince William of Baden came as a Gartenhaus guest, and after he had left, gasping and wheezing and ordering new shirts, Berlin issued a proclamation. Friedrich Wilhelm IV had finally been carted off to Valhalla; Wilhelm was King of Prussia. As one of his first regal acts he would return for a second Gusstahlfabrik tour, this time accompanied by his son and his royal entourage. He had sent ahead another Order of the Red Eagle — *third* class this time, with clasp (*der Schleife*) — and was going to add the Knight's Cross of the House of Hohenzollern. More wampum, but Alfred didn't scorn it. This was Prussian, this was the real thing. Trembling with patriotic ardor, he expressed his "joy and excitement" to the government,[48] and then, his script charging across the sheets of foolscap, he issued a communiqué to the entire works, setting the stage for His Majesty.

If Wilhelm had seen it, he might have changed his mind, for it was a staggering example of Teutonic thoroughness masquerading as efficiency. Alfred prescribed (a) a hundred-foot-square hall to house an exhibition of steelmaking, beginning with coke and crude ore and ending with products; (b) a tableau revealing the difference between pig iron (i.e., Jacob Mayer's bells) and cast steel (Kruppstahl); (c) specimens of axles, tires, and guns, showing "every stage of the process"; (d) completed guns "with improvements in design and mounting"; and (e) wooden models of two future Krupp cannon. As a grand finale, His Majesty was to witness the actual, hour-by-hour casting and forging of a red-hot gun.[49]

It was an exhausting schedule. It was more: it amounted to impertinence. Only a megalomaniac could assume that he was entitled to that much royal time. Yet Wilhelm went through with it. Gorgeous in his gilt braid, his crimson sash, his shimmering medals and burnished helmet, the monarch admired miles of slag, murmured over clay molds, and bestowed royal approval on endless sample springs and dull displays of shop paraphernalia while behind him, aghast but silent, his gaudy retinue shuffled nervously, flicking batons in vain attempts to rid plumes and tunics of the ubiquitous grime. None of them enjoyed it, and Prussia's *Kriegsminister*, General Graf Albrecht Theodor Emil von Roon, who had already quarreled with Alfred by mail, was so insulted that he became a second von der Heydt. Nevertheless the show went on and on until night fell and only the flickering forge fires illumined the eerie scene. The king stayed to the end because he was bent on pleasing Krupp. He had become convinced that he needed him.

Why?

Prussia was why. The soldier king was looking beyond his boundaries, to Germany and — *der Kriegsgott gebe es!* — to a reborn Reich.

Today it is difficult to recapture Wilhelm's mood, to remember how small a man he seemed to be in the eyes of the world, to realize that only a century ago the Germans were the laughingstock of Europe. No one now alive can recall a time when the Teutonic shadow did not threaten, dominate, darken, or even blot out the rest of the continent. Yet when Wilhelm I ascended his throne Prussia was still a comic opera country led by braggarts and introspective, professorial bureaucrats. It had long been insignificant, and there was little reason to believe that the future would change things much. Certainly no one suspected that Berlin would become the capital of the greatest aggressive power in modern history, that its troops would repeatedly lunge across their frontiers, provoking three decisive wars and soaking European soil with the blood of three generations.

Military might was inconceivable without political stability, and politically Germany was a swamp. The old Holy Roman Empire, the First Reich — which, generations of teachers explained, had been neither holy, nor Roman, nor an empire — had degenerated into a bewildering jigsaw puzzle. Its resurgence appeared as improbable as a united Africa would now. Napoleon had reduced Germany's three hundred states, bishoprics, and free cities to a hundred, and the coalition against him had brought further consolidation, yet even the *Bund* of 1815 had thirty-eight petty states, each independent and jealous of the others. Of these, Prussia and Austria were strong enough to dispute hegemony, and in a showdown Prussia had come out second best. The Frankfurt Parliament of May 1848 having failed to revive national integrity, Friedrich Wilhelm IV had proposed that the princes form a new union, Austria to be excluded. Vienna had thereupon issued a counterplan — a return to the weak *Bund*. The motive behind this was to keep the King of Prussia another insignificant Teuton prince, and it worked; in the autumn of 1850 the small princes, cherishing their sovereignty, sprang aboard the Austrian bandwagon. Friedrich Wilhelm could have resorted to the final argument of kings, but thanks to the Spandau officers who had left Alfred's first gun to the spiders, he lacked persuasive cannon. Besides, for all his daydreams of tournaments, he was, in his saner moments, a coward. Craven and impotent, he submitted to a treaty of capitulation, forever after known to fervent German nationalists as *die Scham von Olmütz* (the shame of Olmütz).

This is what his brother was up against. Heroic and resolute, Wilhelm meant to avenge the honor of the crown, and from the moment he donned it he began taking steps up — or down — the road to glory. His call at Essen was one. Another was military reform; overriding all opposition, he expanded conscription and gave Prussia a huge standing army. Most important, he found an incomparable political deputy in Otto Eduard Bismarck-Schönhausen, an aristocratic Brandenburg Junker and passionate defender of royal prerogative who was just three years younger than Alfred. The year after his fiery ordeal at Krupp's forges, the king appointed Bismarck his chief of cabinet, and the liberals began to get an inkling of what they were in for. "Germany looks not to Prussia's liberalism, but to her force," he told them, and — most memorably — "The great questions of the day will not be settled by resolutions and majority votes . . . but by iron and blood" (*Eisen und Blut*). Weighing this, Wilhelm sent Bismarck to the place where the iron was. Unable to stand the stench of the Gartenhaus any longer, Alfred was building a new home, and Bismarck was his last guest before he moved. The two neurotics got along famously. They sat around talking and admiring the inane peacocks and pineapples, and found that they agreed on everything from divine right to the beauty of old trees. Alfred was particularly pleased to learn that his guest loved horses. (The host hadn't lost his unusual sense of smell: "Young horses jumping around in a meadow, that is a delightful thing to see!") At dinner Bismarck slyly suggested that the Empress Eugénie was a bit randy, and when Napoleon III's name came up he murmured in a droll undertone, "What a stupid man he is!" (*Eigentlich ist er dumm!*). Just how stupid the fellow was wouldn't be clear until several years later, when the two diners joined forces, but Alfred, perhaps remembering his Paris frustrations, found his guest's interjection sidesplitting.[50]

The state visit had become an Essen convention; in a matter of months Alfred's prospects had changed dramatically. When von der Heydt humbly asked him to serve as a Prussian judge at the London Industrial Exhibition of 1862, Krupp crisply suggested that he find "some other person more suitable for the position,"[51] and Alfred's relationship with Wilhelm was to improve until he was virtually a member of the court. He would continue to have his giddy ups and sickening downs. That was in the nature of both the man and the industrial revolution, and possibly it was also characteristic of Germany. But henceforth he was to be a privileged figure in the quadrangular Potsdam Palace; he and his salesmen were invited to offer their line in private audiences with the king. The link uniting Krupp and Hohenzollern was unbreakable. Alfred wanted to make guns, Wilhelm wanted to buy them. It was a marriage of convenience, perhaps of necessity, and not even death could end it; each of Wilhelm's successors was bound to be allied with the senior Krupp of his generation. To fathom that interdependence is to grasp the new, historic meaning which the dynasty now assumed. Henceforth Krupp would be identified with the nationalistic aspirations of the *Volk*. And because of the favors granted him and his heirs, they would become the country's leading industrial family. The fact that he continued to manufacture tools of peace is quite beside the point. Krupp's success with peaceful production was a direct consequence of his military production. If he hadn't made cannon, he wouldn't have become a national institution, and it was the institutionalizing of the Krupps which gave them their supremacy. Wilhelm would never have intervened to save the tire patent if Alfred hadn't been ready and able to forge the new Prussian sword. Krupp himself understood the source of his power very well. In a crisis he would come to attention and salute the flag. If that failed, he would growl threats — he was going to move away, he was going to find a sovereign who appreciated him.

It nearly always worked. Sometimes it failed, for the monarch and his armorer weren't alone. Violent tides and crosscurrents were swirling around Potsdam and Essen, yanking them this way and that and straining their bond. Alfred's failures were few, but the reasons behind them were significant. The first was technical: as a pioneer he sometimes strayed. The second lay in the Prussian army: Krupp wasn't the only man indispensable to the king's grand design, and the military brass still clung to their beloved bronze artillery. These two — his fallibility and standpat officers — had led to his row with Baron von Roon. In the last weeks of Wilhelm's regency Alfred decided to build breech-loading cannon. It was a revolutionary idea. His notion of rifling barrels was shocking enough* and had, in fact, been rejected; after a test firing at an old fort near Jülich, the army had stipulated that should any of his 312 guns be rifled, they would be promptly returned. Now he was proposing to load his barrels from the *rear*. The officer corps considered the idea funny as a crutch.

Doggedly he asked Prussia to buy it. The breech, he explained, would be closed with a wedge, and he wanted a fifteen-year patent on the notion. The application reached the desk of Roon, who, since he was to play a key role in the future history of the Krupp dynasty, must be observed in passing. A stubborn, mustachioed martinet, he was regarded as a stuffed shirt; a colonel confided to his diary, "God protect us from our friends! . . . He [Roon] appears to stand as a strategist on about the same level as Count Bismarck; but as a comedian anyhow he ranks immeasurably higher." Walter Görlitz, in his *Der deutsche Generalstab*, pictures him as "a great mountain of a man, whose dark blue eyes and aggressively up-turned mustache suggested the stereotype of the Prussian sergeant. Indeed, 'the king's sergeant' was what he liked to call himself. Others, however, had different names for him, and in a thoughtful desire to distinguish him from other members of his family they spoke of him as 'Ruffian Roon.'" Certainly he was rough on the Konzernherr from Essen. He used Alfred's petition as toilet paper and then advertised the fact among colleagues in the Offizierskorps.[52]

One of them told Alfred, who demanded that the king intervene. Unfortunately Wilhelm couldn't. He needed his vulgar Kriegsminister quite as much as he needed his armorer, for Roon, in his own way, was a genius; designing railroad systems, he was perfecting a plan for speedy mobilization which would discount the numerical superiority of Prussia's potential enemies. Moreover, Wilhelm owed the king's sergeant an irreparable debt. While he was still Regent Prinz the Diet had refused to pass his army

---

* A year later, when Union and Confederate gunners first dueled at Bull Run, their standard fieldpieces were bronze smoothbores.

estimates. Without that budget, the sovereign could never raise Prussia to a first-class European power. For five years the issue kept Berlin in an uproar; duels were fought, *coups d'état* against the Diet were plotted, and at one point the Offizierskorps planned to occupy the capital with 35,000 men, alerting reinforcements in Stettin, Breslau, and Königsberg. Had the War Minister ever broken faith with his sovereign, had he flinched for a moment, the Second Reich would have died stillborn. He never budged. Indeed, according to Görlitz,

> The struggle against the Diet was led by War Minister General von Roon [*Den Kampf gegen das Parlament führten der Kriegsminister General v. Roon*], who took the view that people must guard the army against the Diet, openly identifying themselves with the speeches of Moltke and the leader of the Military Cabinet, General von Manteuffel.[53]

All this was an outgrowth of the abortive "revolution" of 1848, and the loyalty of the Junkers to their class may be judged by the fact that they were locked in a bitter internecine *Kampf* of their own. The *Chef* of the military Cabinet and the War Minister each looked upon himself as the monarch's chief of staff. All officers agreed with Roon that their army was "the aristocrat's professional school; its natural head, the king." Ruffian Roon's goal was "to preserve the constitutional theory of Frederick the Great against an imitation of the 'Mock Monarchy of England,' and to maintain the integrity of the sovereign's position as supreme war lord (*allerhöchsten Kriegsherrn*) in the midst of . . . 'confusions of constitutional thought.'" Manteuffel went farther. For him, Prussia "was simply the army, and anything in Prussia that was *not* martial incurred on his part not merely a lack of understanding but something like a positive hatred." One would have thought that Roon and Manteuffel would have been blood brothers. Instead they and their disciples were sworn enemies, and only the menace of the Diet — ultimately solved by the Byzantine intrigues of Bismarck — averted an insurrection.[54]

Grateful to Roon, needing him to complete the organization of swift conscription at vital railheads, Wilhelm could only forward Alfred's repeated pleas for a favorable decision to the Kriegsministerium. But the Konzernherr was uninterested in Berlin's vicissitudes. He wanted his breechloader approved, and he brought every conceivable pressure to bear upon Roon. The invention, Krupp argued, had been "worked out primarily for my own country." If the ministry let him down, "I should be compelled to depart from my own intention and past practice, and to cease from continuing to deny to certain other states the benefit of my invention in accordance therewith."[55] The attempt at intimidation was clear. It left Roon unshaken, however; the application was denied. No breechloaders for

Prussia were forthcoming, and no patent. Alfred, bitter, petitioned Wilhelm, who remained mute. Only after England and then France had approved the patent did Roon grudgingly accept it. But the last gory laugh was his. Although he had brushed the design from Essen aside, a careful scrutiny would have revealed that the wedge mechanism really was defective. Unhappily for Alfred, the fatal flaw was passed over — only to be discovered six years later on the field of battle.

Defects could be corrected, diehard generals could be retired. A third strain on Krupp's role as Prussia's gunmaker was far more grave — graver for him and, eventually, for all Europe. It was to haunt the world long after his death, and it arose from a monstrous contradiction. Cannon were patriotic, business was international. In the laissez-faire spirit of the times, an industrialist was entitled to peddle his line to clients in any country. This put a private arms manufacturer in a very odd position, and it was further complicated by the fact that only in wartime could he thrive on local trade. Since no one knew when war might break out, he had to support his shops by selling abroad. Thus, beginning in the early 1860's, Krupp delivered guns to Russia, Belgium, Holland, Spain, Switzerland, Austria and England. Berlin knew this. The government not only encouraged him to maintain a large establishment; it was prepared to act as his accomplice. On October 12, 1862, Alfred wrote Crown Prince Friedrich Wilhelm that the British had just finished trials of his guns at Woolwich. They had reported "extraordinary satisfaction, owing to the complete tightness and safety of the breech mechanism" — the name of the Colonel Blimp responsible for this blunder has been mercifully lost — and Krupp had been invited to London to discuss prices. "A star of hope has risen for me," he exulted. Unfortunately he had no friends at court. Would the crown prince be gracious enough to write letters of introduction for him? His Highness was delighted — and sent them by return post.[56]

Alfred saw this as sound business practice. On the following February 27 he inquired of Friedrich Wilhelm, "Why should not England, in urgent circumstances, obtain the material from her friends abroad, until her own industries can make it" (bis es dasselbe innerhalb seiner Industrie selbst schafft)?[57]

To him the argument was unanswerable. Yet since no one could guarantee that friends abroad would be friends forever, his repeated assurance that he would not arm an enemy of Prussia was reduced to an absurdity. He had promised Roon that he would never peddle a gun "which might some day be turned against Prussia." How could he make such a promise? Who knew who those enemies were going to be? As it turned out, the various combinations of power which formed to stem German militarism were going to include nearly every country in Europe, which meant that cannon made in Essen were going to be turned on millions of German soldiers. Curiously, no one anticipated this awkward possibility, and to add to the lunacy, officers in other countries frequently saw no need to support home industry. Alfred was well received in London. (On his return he gratefully acknowledged an endorsement from the Duke of Cambridge, adding, "I am firmly resolved to be deserving of it, by delivering to England something worth having.") The deal fell through because the emerging English firm of W. G. Armstrong and Company turned the screws on Parliament, but the Admiralty secretly purchased Krupp barrels anyhow. Then, to Alfred's horror, he discovered that *Prussian* admirals were eager to buy *British* guns. They had fallen in love with Armstrong muzzle-loaders and saw no reason why they shouldn't have them. Discovering that his own ox was about to be gored, Krupp went straight to Bismarck and told him the navy's treachery made him "utterly sick." Bismarck agreed — it simply wouldn't do. "He was glad to see me," Alfred noted with relief; the talk "was grist for my mill."[58]

The arrival of Armstrong completed Europe's deadly triumvirate. Krupp, Schneider, Armstrong: over the next eighty years they were to be celebrated first as shields of national honor and later, after their slaughtering machines were hopelessly out of control, as merchants of death.* However, there was never any question of who was Number One. Alfred had been first, Alfred was biggest, Alfred had the most satisfied customers. His dominance of London's 1862 exhibition was absolute. Past fairs had taught him that the mob doted on weapons, and he played to the gallery. An artist from the *Illustrated London News* sketched "a group of objects exhibited by Mr. Krupp of Essen, Prussia," and the sketch bristles with objects of murder. One journalist did find a pair of railroad wheels "which have been run nearly 74,000 miles, without having been again put into the lathe," but he was a digger, an exception. His colleagues' eyes were riveted on Alfred's artillery, and their cheers were strident. The *Morning Post*, the *Daily News*, the *News of the World* were enthralled; the *Spectator* rapturously told of "ladies standing in mute delight," of men dreaming of "the battle music of the future." Even *The Times* saluted the "almost military discipline which prevails" in "Krupp's steel works at Eissen [*sic*]," and concluded, "We congratulate Krupp on the pre-eminent position which he occupies."[59]

This, as *The Times* was unkind enough to point out, was Sheffield's backyard. Armstrong's men, just entering the gun business, stiffened their upper lips and did what they could. They picked up odd orders in Italy, Spain, the Low Countries, South America, the Middle East. Armstrong

---

* In 1888 Armstrong was joined by another British arms firm, Vickers Sons & Company, Ltd. However, the two were on the same team and finally merged as Armstrong-Vickers, Ltd. on October 31, 1927. Interestingly, Tom Vickers's production of cast steel railway tires — beginning in 1863 — supported his early experiments with guns. His technical education had been in Germany. (Scott, *Vickers*, pp. 14–15.)

himself was hopeful. Ignoring Schneider, he wrote of Alfred that "He, at any rate, can be the only person besides ourselves who deals with any European power." He regarded every Krupp step backward as a step forward for Armstrong; when a report reached England that a Krupp gun had blown up, he gleefully informed his works manager that it had burst "with a vengeance, flying into a thousand pieces. All the fragments were sound so that the failure was purely due to the intrinsic unsoundness of the material. I have had this nice piece of news conveyed to [Under-Secretary for War] Lord Grey." Yet the best he could do was small beer. Armstrong thought his stock must be soaring when the Russians offered to abandon their munitions works at Aleksandropol (Leninakan) if he would set up shop there. He was unaware that for years they had been pressing the same proposal on Alfred, and that he had declined because he could "supply Russia more cheaply from Essen."[60]

Certainly he was supplying Russia with a lot. Aleksandr II had become his chief client. Not even Wilhelm could match him. The sixty-pounder Krupp had sent to Saint Petersburg had been a spectacular weapon, and in the autumn of 1863 Aleksandr's generals dumbfounded Alfred by placing a million-thaler order, five times larger than Potsdam's. It permitted — indeed required — the construction of a second gun shop, and Krupp foremen traveled as far as Poland to recruit new Kruppianer. Alfred was overwhelmed. His Prussian chauvinism diminished perceptibly; he became something of a Cossack. In the spring of 1864 he entertained a Russian artillery mission at the Gartenhaus, which he had decided to retain as a guesthouse; he entered into a lengthy correspondence with Lieutenant General Count Frants Eduard Ivanovich Todleben, and even tried to decipher a Russian book on the defense of Sevastopol. For the moment he thrust aside all thoughts of serving *Vaterland* or Britain. His energies were consumed in serving that million thalers. The Gusstahlfabrik, he wrote Todleben, "now employs nearly 7,000 men, of which the greater part is working for Russia."[61]

Inevitably the surge in Krupp activity attracted outside attention. Alfred was staying in an Unter den Linden hotel when a Berlin newspaper published details of his Muscovite contract. Returning to the Linden after a spat with Roon, he read the article and found himself described as *"der Kanonenkönig."* Delighted, he sent the clipping to Bertha. Foreign papers had picked it up; in a few weeks he was *"le Roi des Canons"* in Paris and "the Cannon King" in London. It was one of those casual phrases which strike a popular chord, and it stuck — stuck so thoroughly that thereafter the head of the Krupp family in each generation was to be known as the Cannon King.[62]

# 4

✠

# More Efficient Than Brand X

$\mathbf{A}$LFRED's domain was growing swiftly. As the 1860's passed midpoint an accelerating sense of momentum became perceptible; his wheels were grinding large and quick and smooth. He demolished the old Gusstahl-fabrik and rebuilt it from scratch, adding three machine shops, three rolling mills, a wheelwright's shop, an axle turnery, a gun hammer house, and a boiler shop. Each month the glum, gravy-colored air overhead grew more morose. The entire Ruhr was changing as men explored coke's marvelous uses; the last of the picturesque old hillside blast furnaces were extinguished, the last streamside waterwheels creaked to a halt. Industry was moving to the coalfield in force, and with it came the new German proletariat: ex-farmers who had never seen a machine, who were crammed in housing meant for half their number — Essen's population rose 150 percent during the decade — and who insisted, even there, in keeping a cow or pig, or in tilling a tiny plot of land, as a reminder of pastoral life. The migration was a dreadful wrench for them, with dreadful conse-quences. England's working class had had a half-century to become accustomed to the new life. The Prussians had only a few years, and they simply couldn't make the adjustment. Uprooted too swiftly, they remained an insular folk, yearning for the simple ignorance they had known before the railroads gridded their feudal land.[1]

Their arrival solved Krupp's manpower problem. The capital shortage remained. Alfred should have handled it better than he did. He had excel-lent advice. The works now benefited from bright new proconsuls — Sophus Goose, a clever young lawyer; Carl Meyer, an owlish former book-seller with a rattail mustache who became Essen's ambassador to Potsdam; and Alfred Longsdon, a turnip-faced, languid British aristocrat who served as London agent, who refused to learn German — and whom Krupp trusted more than any of his own countrymen. All were destined to spend much of their careers trying to convince their employer that he must put some sort of checkrein on his craving for vertical integration. All warnings against extravagance were airily dismissed: *"Hätte ich erst dann arbeiten wollen, wenn alle Einrichtungen vollkommen waren, so würde ich heute Tagelöhner sein"* (If I had waited to set to work until all arrangements were complete, I should be a journeyman today).[2]

Despite generous credits from Berlin, his acquisition of raw materials continued to grow past all reason. He felt he must have his own coal mines, his own coking ovens, his own iron ore beds — fifty of them in the Ruhr — and even that wasn't enough; tussling nights with his eiderdown, his fists and his mind clenched, he concluded that his stocks of raw materials were still inadequate: he would have to buy the Sayn foundry from Prussia's Royal Treasury. The subsequent negotiations provide an example of the terrible price he paid in such transactions. The financial drain was bad enough — apprehensive that the Sayn talks might collapse, he impulsively settled for 500,000 thalers, 100,000 more than the sum for which the government would have settled. But the toll on his ragged nervous system was far greater. After the foundry deed had changed hands he wrote that "never in all my business life, even in times of want, have I ever spent such days of anxiety as during the two months when objections were being raised to the completion of the contract." As usual, he believed sinister forces had been allied against him: "The intrigues which went on, the breaches of undertakings, and contemptible conduct of people in the highest places shall have a separate account from me. . . ." The worry had made him "ill and old" (*krank und alt*).[3]

Then came the Bessemer process. Sir Henry Bessemer's converter had been patented in England several years earlier. Now Longsdon, a close friend of Sir Henry's brother, told Krupp that he could have the Prussian license if he liked. Alfred seized the chance. His German subordinates thought he needed the process as much as another hole in the ground, and they were right. Bessemer had enjoyed a stunning success at home, melting pig iron in an egg-shaped crucible, passing a blast of hot air through it, uniting the air's oxygen with the iron's carbon and leaving steel. It was magnificent — in England. English ores, though not so pure as Sweden's, had relatively little phosphorus. German ores were so laced with it that they almost glowed in the dark, and Sir Henry's invention couldn't do a thing about it. Krupp spent years trying to justify his investment. Fifteen years later he was hoping "we can still use the Bessemer process at a profit,"[4] and when that proved impossible he — typically — plunged heavily in phosphorus-free Spanish mines. At the outset, however, he didn't even know that the problem existed. Working in secret, as always, he built converters, gave his new product the code name C & T Steel, and used it for King Wilhelm's new cannon.

Der Kanonenkönig's hour of trial was fast approaching. Wilhelm's new army was on the march. Early in January 1864, Prussia and Austria allied to invade Schleswig-Holstein; and, in a lightning campaign, tore the two duchies from Denmark. Alfred sounded the charge for the Gusstahlfabrik: "We must put all our energy into serving Prussia quickly (*Wir müssen Preussen mit aller Energie rasch bedienen*), and obtain as rapidly as possible what is lacking, rifling machines and the like."[5]

The machines were important. His lobbying had defeated Roon; the new weapons were rifled breechloaders. Prussian caissons trundled them north, but they saw little action, partly because of the speed of the blitz and partly, perhaps, because the Offizierskorps continued to feel skittish about untried ordnance. After the peace Roon balked at the question of more steel artillery until the king intervened again, placing an order for three hundred more Essen cannon. Still, Alfred ground his teeth. He had hoped for great things in Schleswig-Holstein: thundering salvos, fields of maimed Danes. He needn't have fretted. Presently the drums of battle were rolling again; the two allies were quarreling over their spoils, and he looked forward to the new fray with confidence — with overconfidence, as it turned out, for every war has its unpleasant surprises, and the *Brüderkrieg* with Austria was to stun Krupp. In the tumultuous months ahead, each of his weaknesses was to be cruelly exposed: his trading with potential enemies, his capital drought, his inferior Bessemer steel, his erratic breeches, and above all, the equally erratic behavior of the gunsmith himself.

Essen greeted 1866 with an earsplitting din of steam hammers. Business had never been better, and as spring greened the stands of tall, spreading ash along the Berne and Ruhr rivers, every shop was working at capacity. The U.S.A. couldn't get enough railroad wheels — some American orders now were worth $100,000 each. The political crisis in the South was especially exciting. Baden, Württemberg, and Bavaria asked for batteries of cast steel; Austria had requested 24 guns, and Wilhelm had come through with a really superb new order — 162 four-pounders, 250 six-pounders, and 115 twenty-four-pounders. The fact that requests from Berlin and Vienna might prove conflicting and embarrassing hadn't occurred to Alfred. It occurred to Roon. On April 9, 1866, the day after the two nations began to mobilize — Bismarck had signed an alliance with Italy twenty-four hours earlier — the War Minister sent an urgent dispatch to Essen:

I venture to ask whether you are willing, out of patriotic regard to present political conditions, to undertake not to supply any guns to Austria without the consent of the king's government [*ohne Zustimmung der Königlichen Regierung keine Geschütze an Österreich zu liefern*].[6]

In Essen five anguished days passed without a reply. Then Alfred answered with hauteur (and obvious humbug) that "Of political conditions I know very little; I go on working quietly." He explained that Vienna's first sample of the new cannon wasn't due until June, that the entire contract wasn't to be fulfilled until six weeks later, and, shrewdly, that Berlin could confiscate his shipments if the king wished. Then, unwittingly, he came to the crux of the argument and withdrew in confusion:

> With reference to this subject, I trust your Excellency will attain your object without any conflict between my patriotism and my reputation abroad [ohne einen Konflikt zwischen meinem Patriotismus und meinem Ruf nach Aussen]. . . . We are, praise God! not yet at war, after all, and may God grant that we stay at peace.[7]

There was much more, but in sum the answer to Roon was an evasive no. The reaction was inevitable. Had Krupp had stock, the price would have plummeted. Yet on this matter he was singularly obtuse. Blind to the conflict of his interests and Prussia's, he visited the capital and called on Roon, on a Hohenzollern prince, and on Bismarck. Their altered manner left him unaffected. "War with Austria," he noted blithely, "is imminent." Bismarck brought up the question of arming the enemy ("He urged me not to supply the Austrians with their guns too quickly"), but Alfred didn't see the warning: "I said that we must . . . fulfill obligations which we have undertaken." Alfred even frightened his host by observing that Prussia's defenses were inadequate. "That evidently startled him, which was what I wanted," he jauntily reported to his lieutenants in Essen, adding that Bismarck had "consoled himself for the present with the fact that the Austrian guns might well be intended for Austrian forts . . . against Italy." More than consolation was available to the king's deputy. Alfred's awakening quickly followed. He was, he confided to Bismarck for the nth time, in need of funds. Could the Prussian State Bank advance him two million thalers? In the past the government had always been accommodating. Now he was rudely told that he would have to take out a private mortgage on his raw materials with the Seehandlung Bankinstitut. Enraged, he appealed to the king. Wilhelm's rebuke was crushing. He advised Krupp to apply for the mortgage, to stop behaving "so obstinately," to "drop this stubborn attitude" and to "Come to your senses while there is still time!" (Besinnen Sie sich noch zur rechten Zeit!). Dazed, Alfred agreed, then collapsed, scribbling to Nice, where Bertha and twelve-year-old Fritz were tanning themselves, that he was prostrate from "Rheuma und Nervotismus."[8]

Berlin had no time to commiserate with a nervous rheumatic. The capital itself was suffering from a bad attack of nerves. Bismarck had bitten off a lot. Napoleon III thought it was too much. Viewing the alliance against Wilhelm — Bavaria, Württemberg, Baden, Saxony, and Hanover had joined Austria — the French emperor placed his diplomatic bets on a long war which would exhaust both belligerents. He was spectacularly wrong. The war lasted just seven weeks. By midsummer victorious Prussia had absorbed Austrian Silesia and all north Germany. Piece by jigsaw piece, a great nation was assuming shape. The triumph had been a triumph of technology. General Helmuth von Moltke had carefully studied the American Union's skillful use of railroads in the South; moving his troops in boxcars, coordinating their movements with corps of trained telegraphers, he had massed decisive forces before the Bohemian fortress Königgrätz (Sadowa). On July 3, exactly three years after the decision at Gettysburg, the defenders had been overwhelmed. Tactically, Prussian small weapons had performed especially well. Early dispatches raved about Johann Nikolaus von Dreyse's breech-loading "needle" guns, which had permitted attacking waves of infantry to fire prone at standing Austrians armed with muzzle-loaders.[9]

But what about the artillery? Limping uneasily back to Essen, Alfred awaited reports. The first one was encouraging. On July 9 General Voigts-Rhetz wrote him from Bohemia that

> *Ich konnte Ihnen nur das Wort "Sieg!" zurufen, als die Schlacht vorbei war, und das war in jener Zeit auch genug. . . . Eins Ihrer Kinder wurde übrigens auch verwundet.*

> When the battle was over I could only shout the word "Victory!" to you, and that was enough, too, at that time. You knew that we had overthrown proud Austria, and you were particularly concerned, apart from your patriotism — for you have helped us in the most effective way, with your guns. These children of yours conversed for long hot hours with their Austrian cousins. It was an artillery duel with rifled guns, highly memorable and interesting, but also very destructive. One of your children, indeed, was wounded.[10]

That was one way of putting it. It was the kindest possible way, for Voigts-Rhetz was a strong partisan of steel cannon. The facts were worse. Improper angles in his breechblock slots had badly marred Alfred's combat debut. Leakages of gas and flame from the seams of the breeches had repeatedly burst his four-pounders and six-pounders, butchering the men who had loaded them. Nor could the dead gunners be blamed. The disaster wasn't confined to the Prussian army. A curt complaint from Saint Petersburg disclosed that a nine-inch Krupp cannon had exploded there during maneuvers. Suddenly everything was going to pieces — men, Kruppstahl, profits, prospects. Even the railroad tire market was threatened; a British firm was returning Essen's first batch of Bessemer wheels as unsatisfactory. Kruppianer wages were cut, men were idle.[11]

Faced with this string of calamities, Alfred simply absconded. Leaping aboard the first train, he ran aimlessly to Coblenz, to Heidelberg, to the dense Black Forest. He paused to catch his breath in Karlsruhe, that quaint city with a peculiarly Teutonic inspiration, built to conform with the dream of a grand duke who fell asleep during a hunt. But Germany wasn't big enough for Krupp. Hadn't he massacred his own country's brave cannoneers? He would be locked up as a homicidal maniac! What was the king saying? And Bismarck? And Roon — well, that was predictable. The disparaging old bashaw would be derisively reminding Potsdam that he had foretold this; that bronze, at least, didn't burst. Sweating bullets, Alfred bought a ticket to Switzerland. En route he penned Roon a pitiful, hangdog note:

*Berlin oder im Hauptquartier S.M. des Königs. Privat. Eigenhändig.*

*Ew. Exzellenz*
   *Fühle ich mich gedrungen — mitten in der Freude über die wunderbaren Erfolge der unvergleichlichen Armee — . . .*

Berlin, or at the Headquarters of H.M. the King. Private. Personal.

Your Excellency
   In the midst of my joy at the wonderful success of our incomparable army, I feel obliged to confess my overwhelming grief at the news, which has just reached me, that in the case of two four-pounders the breech flew off in action, and that the same thing happened . . . to a four-pounder and a six-pounder. . . .[12]

Alibis followed. Sir Henry Bessemer was a *Schwein*. The fault lay with gun parts made of "unsuitable material, which material was not supplied by me." Still, he wanted to be fair. There was no getting around it, a cannon "ought not to endanger those serving it." The miscreant offered to replace all of Prussia's steel guns free of charge, and the letter was posted by a trainman while its contrite author, in the unaccustomed garb of sackcloth and ashes, went into exile.

It was to be a protracted exile. He stayed away a year, for in Berne he read that demobilized soldiers had brought cholera to the Ruhr — his own head groom had died of it — and he had pain enough without *that*. What he needed was peace and solace. In a word, he needed his wife. To her consternation, he showed up in Nice, haggard with grief and grotesque in a new wig. Bertha's physician has left us a sharp vignette of his arrival at the Château Peillon. It is depressing; château veterans stared at the skinny, hard-faced fugitive and hesitated to approach him. He was fifty-four and already looked senile. Dr. Künster, who had met him before, wrote that

He was a misfit, who attracted attention everywhere because of his unusual height and striking leanness. His features had once been very regular, even attractive, but he had aged rapidly. His face was lifeless, pale, and wrinkled. A thin remnant of gray hair, topped by a toupee, crowned his head. He rarely· smiled. Most of the time his face was stony and immobile [*Selten belebte ein Lächeln diese Züge, gewöhnlich waren sie steinern, ohne jede Regung*].[13]

Coming here had turned out to be a mistake. He was lonelier than ever. There was no one for him to talk to. Rumors that invisible horns had crowned the wig are highly speculative; certainly Frau Krupp had had opportunities for affairs exceptional in that era, and photographs hint at an astonishing change in her, suggesting a buxom, vigorous woman in her early thirties who appeared to be sensual, tousled, dissolute. (However one considers her expression, it *is* disturbing; she was either wanton or — another distinct possibility — deeply disturbed.) But that may have been the photographer. It doesn't matter. Chaste or indiscreet or mad, she had withdrawn from Alfred. His ill son was a stranger, and the rest of the inhabitants were dull or odious. He fell to wrangling with one of Bertha's idle relatives. According to Künster:

> *Krupp ist ohne Zweifel ein technisches Genie . . . Er war gewöhnt, wie ein Fürst aufzutreten, konnte aber daneben kleinliche Züge verraten.*

> Krupp is undoubtedly a technician of genius . . . but apart from that he was extremely narrow-minded. He took no interest in anything unconnected with his professional work. As a consequence, he concluded that a relative of his wife, Max Bruch, later a famous conductor, was completely wasting his time in devoting it to music. If Bruch had been a technician, Krupp remarked in all seriousness, he would have been of some use to himself and to mankind, but as a musician he was leading an utterly pointless existence. . . . There was nothing he thought beyond his reach once he had set his sights on it. His own career had raised his self-confidence to such a pitch that his conduct at times bordered on megalomania. He could behave in princely fashion. Yet he was capable, at the same time, of mean actions.[14]

In his own hand Krupp summed up his judgment of Germany's cultural genius.

> *Ich frage weder Goethe noch irgendein Wesen in der Welt, was Recht ist; — das weiss ich selbst und niemanden stelle ich so hoch, dass er besser wisse.*

> I don't have to ask Goethe or anybody else in the world what is right; — I know the answer myself, and I don't consider anyone entitled to know better.

His work had always been his salvation. Yet it wasn't much help now. That November he pondered rebuilding his reputation, suggesting that his salesmen get "in touch with the appropriate editors of respectable newspapers." But his heart wasn't in it. The Cannon King appeared to be dethroned, kaput. Even when it developed that the situation wasn't as bad as he had thought, his convalescence lagged; a year later he noted that he was "still frequently troubled by headaches." Then, bit by bit, he came back. He began gift-shopping again, buying fine horses for foreign clients and, if they were sovereigns, sending them silver-chased guns. All this was managed from Nice, however, and back at the Gusstahlfabrik workmen began to wonder what had happened to their field marshal. Except for flying visits, Kruppianer seldom saw him. After forty years at the helm, standing watches around the clock, he had abandoned ship. It was an odd performance, quite out of proportion to the Königgrätz disaster. Perhaps he had developed an aversion to his shops, perhaps he was hoping to win Bertha back. In any event, long after the cholera epidemic was over and prosperity had returned to the factory, he continued his bizarre spa-hopping, a bloodless, unkempt turkey-cock chasing his shadow around Europe and leaving his factory power in the hands of Essen's *Prokura,* a four-man board of managers. "The state of my health does not permit me to trouble myself with the business of the works," he wrote them from the Dutch seaside resort of Scheveningen. Henceforth he proposed to meditate on how he might best move "from a life of activity to the eternal world to come."[15]

How long he would have wallowed in the doldrums if external events hadn't intruded is an open question; it is also highly academic. Events were constantly shouldering their way into his life, for he was a steelmaker, this was the Age of Steel, and nearly every day some ingenious young engineer was shaking the kaleidoscope of progress and forming a brilliant new pattern. In the long run Alfred was bound to prosper, just as his father had been bound to fail. History was riding with him. If an inventor improved upon the Bessemer process the invention was certain to be drawn to the source of coke — the Ruhr, which is to say Krupp. While he was languishing unhappily with Bertha's swanky friends on the Riviera, Karl Wilhelm Siemens perfected the open-hearth furnace in Britain, achieving chemical changes in melted pig iron and steel scrap by burning gases in the chamber. Though slower than Bessemer's converter, the new minestrone produced more steel, of higher quality. It was ideal for impure ore. Siemens promptly offered it to Alfred as *"dem an der Spitze der Industrie stehenden"* (our leading industrialist), and abruptly the exile again found a life of activity attractive. Resurrected, he alerted the Prokura: "We must keep a watchful eye on the matter and let nothing slip through our fingers — if it is good, we must be first in the field."[16]

Meanwhile his allies in the Prussian army had been busy healing scars.

Every maneuver in the seven-week war had been subjected to detailed scrutiny. The mutilated breeches hadn't been acquitted. However, other breeches had held. Here military judgment had to be suspended — owing to faulty deployment, it was impossible to assess the fusillades — but two generals, Voigts-Rhetz and Gustav Eduard von Hindersin, who had been chief of artillery in Bohemia during the Austro-Prussian War, were zealots: they wanted the entire army re-equipped with heavy steel mortars and rifled, breech-loading, cast steel guns from Essen. Alfred, they pointed out, had volunteered to swap 400 new four-pounders for his pre-1866 cannon, and was following through. Masterminding the negotiations in letters to Essen, Krupp arranged meetings between his managers and Bismarck, bypassed Roon (through Roon's deputy), and acquired the king's blessing. His reason for "making the sacrifice," as he put it, wasn't patriotic. He wanted rehabilitation, an end to scandal; "inquisitions of that sort are bound to annoy everyone, and the . . . authorities poke their noses into everything." His Majesty agreed to make peace. Alfred had been in simultaneous correspondence with his engineers, and the angular breechblock slot defect had been eliminated. On Tegel range the improvement was demonstrated to the satisfaction of the king, Bismarck, and Moltke; even Roon was temporarily silenced, and, as Krupp noted, "the breech-loading system" was "adopted as a principle in Prussia." The sacrifice had been no sacrifice at all. It had been good business. All the ground lost in Austria had been regained, and by early 1867 Alfred was actually trying to influence royal appointments in the War Department. To Albert Pieper, the energetic young chairman of his Prokura, he wrote:

> I intend to speak my mind on this subject to the king himself at the very first opportunity [*Ich habe mir vorgenommen, bei erster Gelegenheit dem Könige selbst meine Meinung darüber zu sagen*], to remind him that Prussia was backward because the department was badly administered, and that there will be another fiasco if the department is torn limb from limb. I can say anything to him [*Ich kann ihm alles sagen*].[17]

✠   ✠   ✠

Thus was the fallen mighty again. He ought to have learned several lessons. Burned in Vienna, he should at least have become shy of foreign gun trade. But no: in less than a year, at the peak of 1868's Franco-Prussian crisis over Luxembourg, we find him trying to arm the French during the second Paris exhibition. The crisis worsens — Napoleon III, frightened by Wilhelm's waxing power, is trying to annex the duchy — and Alfred hesitates. He wants Berlin to understand that "In the event of war I am prepared to do all in my power that can be of service." Then he

lunges ahead. At the exhibition he displays an 88,000-pound ingot (the
wary jury insists that the floor be reinforced) and a gigantic fourteen-inch
gun. His advertisements acclaim the cannon as *"ein Ungeheuer, wie es die
Welt noch nicht sah"* (a monster such as the world has never seen), and
they are no exaggeration. The barrel alone weighs fifty tons, the carriage
forty; the powder charge for each projectile is a hundred pounds. *En-
chanté*, the emperor awards Krupp a Grand Prix and an officer's rank in
the Legion of Honor. Prospects grow hotter. In September the Luxembourg quarrel ends in Napoleonic humiliation. Maybe the emperor is in
the mood to make something of it. If so, Krupp has some nice persuaders
for sale. On January 31, 1868, Alfred had sent the Tuileries a catalogue of
his weapons. "Encouraged by the interest which Your Gracious Majesty
has shown in a simple industrialist," he begged the emperor to inspect "the
enclosed report of a series of firing tests which have just taken place," and
suggested that "the steel cannon which I manufacture for various high
powers of Europe will be worthy of Your Majesty's attention for a
moment, and will be an excuse for my boldness." Boldness was an understatement. The two nations were armed camps. It nearly led to something,
too. Then General Edmond Leboeuf, Minister of War and a Schneider
intimate, intervened. Despite a brilliant piece of intelligence by a French
artillery mission which had observed the superior range and accuracy of the
new Krupp breechloaders during Belgian maneuvers, the French declined
Alfred's proposition. On March 11, 1868, the War Ministry in Paris closed
its Krupp file with the terse note: *Rien à faire.*[18]

Nothing doing. And a lucky thing for Alfred too. Yet he didn't see it
that way. Disappointed, he gave the Paris gun to Potsdam, writing 150,000
thalers off to "credit and good will" — and then shipped the Czar of All
the Russias a second big gun to make sure his chief customer didn't feel
slighted. The patriot in him and the internationalist continued to coexist,
partly because the lines of nationalism hadn't quite hardened in central
Europe, partly because he had become something unique. Jérôme Bonaparte, stopping in Essen as a visiting diplomat, described the firm as *"ein
Staat im Staate"* (a state within a state). That was close. In a period of
wildfire militarism the munitions manufacturer was a figure of world
admiration, and Krupp had, as he put it in Saint Petersburg, "the greatest
of existing gun factories." Because of his remarkable works, he was
honored by sovereigns whom Wilhelm didn't dare offend. Japan and
Sweden sent members of their royal families to Essen; Russia, Turkey,
Brazil, and Belgium decorated Alfred; Portugal admitted him to the sacred
Order of Christ (Commander's Cross).[19]

The armorer's sword didn't cut both ways, though. Essen might ignore
Berlin, might even jeopardize Prussian security — there can be no other
interpretation of the flirtation with Louis Napoleon — but Berlin must

buy arms from Essen alone. Krupp's logic here was specious. He argued that

> *Wenn wir für Preussen arbeiten, auch wenn es die Lieferungen bezahlt, so verlieren wir doch dem gegenüber . . .*

> When we work for Prussia we lose relatively, although she pays for our goods, since we turn our time and craftsmanship to more profitable ways when we devote them to other governments.[20]

Thus he felt entitled to take the position that should Berlin order "so much as one cannon" from a competitor, he would "give the whole world what it wants."[21] The fact that he was already making deliveries to anyone with ducats, guilders, guldens, livres, marks, maravedis, or rubles was conveniently ignored. Letters tactfully pointing this out were read by him in the depths of his insomniac's night and impatiently thrust aside. Double standard or no, the game was going to be played his way, by his rules. He frequently threatened to desert the banks of the Berne, and one wonders just what he had in mind. Nice? Scheveningen? Not Essen, at any rate: the Ruhr was a place to celebrate good fortune; during a setback it was intolerable, and when Alfred's sky darkened in 1868 he entrained for Saint Petersburg.

Hard on the heels of his French disappointment word had come that the navy of the new North German Federation (Prussia and all other states north of the river Main) was weighing a new approach from Armstrong. That was definitely not playing the game, and leaving Bertha, Krupp bought his ticket to the Finland Station. He chose Russia because he was one of Czar Aleksandr II's favorites and, as he put it, could count on "enormous orders" to fortify his self-esteem. Setting up his portable files in a hotel room there, he began an anxious exchange of telegrams with his man in Berlin, Carl Meyer. Meyer's facts were alarming. Nine-inch British muzzle-loaders had been fired at Tegel and had pleased an eminent jury: Wilhelm, Bismarck, and the admirals. (*"Die filzige Suite,"* Alfred scrawled mutinously; "a vile gang"). Berlin was considering open bidding. This was shocking. It was nothing less than raw, unabashed free enterprise. How could he combat it? There was only one way — make the two-headed Prussian eagle scream. "That equal justice has not been meted out to me, the native manufacturer, is the thing of which I have to complain," he complained. "That the Royal Prussian Navy should not draw its guns from abroad so long as it has an opportunity of obtaining better guns at home, is for me much more a matter of honor than of financial interest." And sitting in the Russian capital, begging additional business from officials on the left bank of the Great Neva, adjourning each evening to the Aleksandrinki theater with epauletted officers of the Russian navy he had armed, he asserted vigorously that "a foreigner" (Armstrong) should not be permitted to compete for the North German navy's funds with a native (himself). "Such a proceeding on the part of Prussia," he protested, "would be, more than anything else, an exposure of the Essen establishment to humiliation in the eyes of the whole world."[22]

The humiliation was avoided through an extraordinary stratagem. Alfred actually collected testimonials from the Czar's admirals. All swore that Krupp eight- and nine-inch cannon were more efficient than those bearing any other trademark. They urged Wilhelm not to switch to Brand X, and Alfred forwarded these remarkable documents to Meyer, who laid them before His Majesty. The king backed down. Bewildered, the Englishmen departed. Perhaps the episode seemed so fantastic to them that they never told their home office the details; no reference to it appears in Armstrong's official history. We do know that they gave up on the Germans, just as Krupp had given up in France, and never came back. After such a farce they can't be blamed. The British had won every battle but the last one, and had lost that because Krupp accused them of being unsporting. Each year Germany became more unfathomable.

The king's capitulations to Alfred baffled many in his own entourage. Roon, that intransigent spoilsport of the Krupp game, was especially perplexed. Time was about to treat the Prussian Minister of War unkindly. Stupendous events were to discredit his technical judgment and make it seem that he had been deliberately fouling the armorer of the Reich. Yet he wasn't the complete fool. His preference for bronze — or, that failing, for Armstrong's wrought-iron barrels strengthened by exterior coils — had strong support among intelligent ordnance experts. They continued to distrust steel, pointing out that it cooled unevenly during casting, and that consequent flaws could shatter guns. It had happened. It had happened to Krupp cannon. Long after rifling and breech-loading had been accepted, this basic objection was to be raised repeatedly. It appeared six months after the end of the naval battle. Alfred had thought the issue resolved. Ordering a two-million-thaler expansion of Essen's gun shops in anticipation of navy contracts, he had returned to his wooing of Bertha, and he was nursing a blistering sunburn when Roon administered an agonizing slap on the back. Seven days before Christmas, 1868, the minister advised him that the whole matter had been tabled. The British were out, but no one was in. What was to be done about ship armament wasn't apparent. Perhaps he was thinking of catapults or marlinespikes; he didn't say. He did state flatly that there would be no contracts for Essen, and Alfred was obliged to cancel the expansion. To Roon he wrote, "I . . . bow to the inevitable."[23]

He bowed — like a jackknife. Clearly there was more here than met the eye, and he meant to get to the bottom of it. He went straight to his supporters in the department. They shared his concern. They knew even better than Krupp how bitter the gun quarrel in Berlin had become, and they were also aware that the decision was of enormous import. The stakes were nothing less than the life of Prussia and the future of Europe. Alfred's assessment of Louis Napoleon's mood had been correct. After his Luxembourg mortification he *had* wanted to turn to the last resort of kings. He still did; he was looking for a final reckoning with Prussia. The Junkers were delighted to oblige. Since October 29, 1857, when Moltke had been appointed chief of the general staff six days after Wilhelm became prince regent, the staff had been planning an *Aufmarsch* against France.[24] It was only a matter of time before the two powers sprang at each other. Before the cannon question was settled it was to be a matter of months.

That settlement came in the late autumn of 1869, and the royal nod once more went to Krupp. Voigts-Rhetz sent him the glad tidings. The two men had been in constant contact, and the general had become an authority on Alfred's headaches. Now he believed they would end, and he was right. In June, Roon's clique had moved for a showdown. They wanted the steel decision reversed, and they were quietly planning a complete return to bronze artillery before war broke out.* It is a sign of the bitterness in the army that Voigts-Rhetz flatly called this "treason." His own clique had been in a dilemma. Offizierskorps honor being what it was, none of Roon's antagonists could broach the question with Wilhelm. The solution was to call in a civilian. Missives had flown back and forth between Nice and Essen, and finally Alfred sent Meyer to the king. Now it was in the open. Perturbed, His Majesty called in Voigts-Rhetz (which indicates where the sovereign's sympathies lay) and asked his opinion. The general was concise. Krupp, he reported, had brought muzzle velocity up to 1,700 feet per second and could raise it to 2,000 feet. "The king," the general reported to Alfred, "saw at once that bronze couldn't stand that strain, that the soft metal would melt, and that the weight of the gun would have to be increased so much that the four-pounder would be too heavy for field use." That was the end of that. Jubilantly describing the rout of the opposition, Voigts-Rhetz sent Alfred a carol about the King:

*Als ihm H. Meyer die Mitteilungen über jene feindselige Perfidie gebracht hat, habe er es gar nicht glauben können, dass es möglich sei. . . . Wenn er von jenen Leuten nur nicht stets gehindert und aufgehetzt würde.*

When Herr Meyer brought him news of this malicious piece of treachery, he simply could not believe it possible. . . . It appears that he did not handle those stupidly hostile gentlemen very tenderly. . . . It is a real joy to discuss such matters with the king, as he shows so much good

---

* Not impossible. The construction of heavy guns then took one year. If ordnance men had started the big switch then, they would have just finished it at the outbreak of hostilities — thus virtually ensuring the defeat of Prussia.

will, such sympathy and grateful interest, combined with such understanding. If only he were not continually hampered and stirred up by those people.[25]

Sometimes the general sounds like a Krupp salesman. "Those people" might have been, not brother officers, but Armstrong men.

☩ ☩ ☩

April 1870. Paris and Berlin are squaring off. In the Palais Bourbon there is talk of cutting Prussia down to her pre-Königgrätz size. Bismarck's finger is on the trigger. Wilhelm orders him not to squeeze, but intrigue is leading to hostilities all the same. The Spaniards have expelled their nymphomaniac queen, Isabella II. Her successor has yet to be chosen, and Bismarck is quietly backing Prince Leopold, a Hohenzollern.

Quite by coincidence, one of Prince von Hohenzollern's clerks lost his job that month and applied to Alfred. The reply from Essen was:

I am sorry to hear that you are ill. If it is any consolation to you, I may say that this has been the case with me for years. I am very nervous, ought not to write, and shall not get through this letter without a headache afterward. [*Ich bin sehr nervös, darf nicht schreiben, schreibe diesen Brief nicht ohne Kopfweh nachher zu bekommen*]. So excuse the brevity.[26]

What had happened? Voigts-Rhetz didn't understand; Krupp had so many Prussian orders that Wilhelm was replacing Aleksandr II as his leading client. Bertha was confused; her Old Man had left Nice in sunny spirits. Essen was similarly bewildered; the Cannon King lay behind drawn blinds in Friedrich Krupp's old posture day after day, staring at the ceiling. A physician was summoned. Sigmund Freud was still a Viennese youth, and when a thorough physical examination disclosed nothing, the doctor departed as perplexed as the others. But we know what was wrong. We know that Alfred scampered frenetically from one critical situation to another. Emergencies were a way of life for him, and all that remains is to discover the nature of his plight then.

It was housing. Anticlimactic? Not with him; he could invest the most humdrum predicament with an air of suspense, and his housing problem was no ordinary one. The Gartenhaus, as we have seen, had been a disaster. In 1864 he reluctantly conceded as much. He didn't mind the noise and the filth (by now his larynx was about destroyed anyhow) but he had concluded that the atmosphere was toxic. Deciding that country air would be "a means of prolonging life for myself," that "if I live a single year longer because of it, I can surely employ a year's profits there," he had directed Pieper to select a suitable site. This wasn't easy. Fresh air had just about disappeared from Essen. The best land was on the slopes of the river

Ruhr, yet even there shallow strip mines pocked the banks, and Alfred's instructions to Pieper complicated the task. He not only wanted to be free of "the dust and smoke of black coal"; he insisted on a large enough tract to support "the house, stabling, riding track, courtyards, park and garden grounds, wells, fountains, cascades, fishponds on the hill and in the valley, game cover, viaducts over hollows, bridges, pasture on the Ruhr for horses and other animals" — and he wanted all this done without anyone becoming aware of what was afoot. He was afraid of "inconvenient neighbors, miserable hovels with inhabitants of doubtful character, thievish neighbors" (since all Essen newcomers were Kruppianer, he could only have meant his own employees); and he suspected that once "it is known that I intend to build and lay out the grounds, I shall ever after have to pay gold for what can still be got at present for silver."[27]

Pieper found an artful front man to buy up lots. Inevitably word leaked out; some gold was required, but by the end of the year he had a temporary house. Firedamp had been replaced by inspiring aromas from a "flat ground suitable for pasture, to keep a bit of stud." Then Alfred tackled the permanent building, and then the circus began. It was to continue for a decade, because he was designing more than a home. He intended to (a) lure Bertha back, or at least Fritz — pathetically he noted that his "only boy" lived "with my wife and far away from me"; (b) inhabit a palace worthy of entertaining crowned heads; and (c) leave a monument to himself. (a) was impossible. (b) could have been achieved by buying a mortgaged castle elsewhere — a possibility which had been rejected when Krupp learned that landed barons regarded smokestack barons as *nicht Salonfähig*, socially unacceptable. There remained (c). In this the owner succeeded brilliantly. He built the German equivalent of the Albert Memorial.[28]

Alfred Krupp had reviewed the talents of all leading architects on the continent and decided the most highly qualified was Alfred Krupp. For five years he had toiled intermittently over the plans. They may still be seen in the family archives, a frightful jumble of penciled pothookery, with innumerable directions and admonitions in the margins. All reflect his potpourri of phobias. Wooden beams were out. They were inflammable, so Krupp's castle would be constructed entirely of steel and stone. Gas mains, of course, were unthinkable. By now he wrote as fluently in dark as in light, and visiting crowns could glitter just as well by the light of candelabra. The privacy of the householder was to be sacred — his bedchamber would be guarded by three barriers of triple-locked doors. Since he hated drafts (they led to pneumonia), all windows would be permanently sealed. Ventilation would be provided by unique ducts invented by the architect. That raised the problem of manure. He gave a lot of thought to this; then it came to him in a flash. *Gott sei Dank*, what an idea! He could build his study directly over the stable, with shafts to waft the scent upward! And that is precisely what he decided to do, crowing, so to speak, on his private dunghill.[29]

Villa Hügel, the Hillside Villa: so it would be known. After three centuries in Essen the House of Krupp was to have a permanent house — two of them, actually, for the mansion proper (which would include a second-floor private apartment for Wilhelm) was to be linked by a low two-story gallery to *das kleine Haus*, the small house, an independent wing. *Der Hügel* would be more than a family seat; it would become a monument which would astonish all Europe.

In conception Alfred's villa was an edificial nightmare. In execution it was to become worse. Even today one boggles at a description of it. There is something quite incredible about the castle. Presumably the façade was meant to be Renaissance, but here and there the limestone mass is broken by bleak square entrances curiously like those of German railroad stations, and indeed, the grotesque superstructure on the roof bears an uncanny resemblance to the train terminal in Cologne. Strolling the perimeter, one unexpectedly encounters accusing eyes carved in the stone, and statues of lionesses sprouting bomb-shaped human breasts. Inside, the feeling of lunacy is heightened. If these walls could talk, one feels, they would say something preposterous. It is characteristic of the place that no one really knows how many chambers there really are. Krupp's present family archivist believes that there are 156 rooms in the big house, 60 in *das kleine Haus* — total 216 — but a recent count reached 300. It depends on what you call a room. The interior is a mad labyrinth of great halls, hidden doors, and secret passages, and it is unwise to drink too much schnapps in Villa Hügel.

In the 1860's all this was on paper. Krupp still wasn't sure where he wanted to put it. He did know this: the decision must be entirely his. No surveyors; *he* would make the survey. He ordered construction of a wooden tower, taller than the tallest Ruhrgebiet tree. Wheels were affixed to the bottom, Alfred clambered to the top, and grunting, sweating Kruppianer in round brimless caps pushed the cumbersome frame through arcadian underbrush while the Kanonenkönig stood aloft in a top hat, scanning the landscape through a spyglass. There was more here than met the eye. Underground, a small firm was driving horizontal mines, and he had to consider the possibility that his contractor, sinking foundations, might squash molelike Kumpel toiling below. Soils were sampled, experimental shafts dug. Finally, in 1869, he made up his mind. *Der Hügel* would sit on the brow of a hill overlooking the river.[30]

As it happened, the hill he chose was naked, and though Alfred disliked wooden interiors, he wanted trees outside. He was approaching sixty. There wasn't time to plant seedlings and await their growth; therefore he would assemble majestic groves elsewhere and move them here. Whole avenues of trees were bought up and brought in from neighboring Kettwig and Gelsenkirchen. In bitter winter, roots frozen and stark branches decked with gay streamers, the mobile forest was transported to the wind-swept slope on special vehicles. To the gaping workmen who gathered along the route the transplanting seemed marvelous. The first operation was an unqualified triumph. That spring every branch obediently budded. The nude hill was a haze of green. And in April 1870, Alfred laid the cornerstone of the castle.[31]

Instantly it was threatened by a series of disasters. A hurricane blew the first scaffolding away. Driving rains turned the excavations into mudholes. Walls went up slowly, and the southwest corner had hardly been finished when Alfred galloped up one morning and found, to his horror and indignation, that it was scored by deep fissures. Like the Germany of which it was to be an architectural allegory, Villa Hügel was in danger of be-coming a public joke. Yet like the Reich it *was* rising, beam by beam and block by ugly block. Indeed, they were about to rise together. On June 19 Prince Leopold of Hohenzollern, with Wilhelm's approval, decided to accept the Spanish crown. There was a leak, Paris found out, and the hotheaded Duc de Gramont, who had only recently taken over the French Ministry of Foreign Affairs, threatened Berlin. Wilhelm hesitated, then advised Leopold to withdraw. But Gramont and the Empress Eu-génie weren't satisfied. They demanded a royal apology. At Ems spa the king declined.[32]

Bismarck saw his chance. On July 13, with Roon and Moltke at his elbow, he edited Wilhelm's telegram of refusal, sharpening a sentence here, honing a phrase there, until the telegram had become an instrument of provocation. "His Majesty the King," Bismarck's version concluded, had "decided not to receive the French ambassador again, and sent to tell him through the aide-de-camp on duty that His Majesty had nothing further to communicate to the ambassador." This, Bismarck assured Moltke (who was egging him on, pointing out that it would be better to fight now than in a few years' time, when French military reforms would be taking hold) would have the effect of a red rag on the Gallic bull. It did. Indeed, under the intricate rules of nineteenth-century diplomatic etiquette it could have no other effect. It was so insulting that Louis Napoleon was deprived of choice. His honor was now the issue. He had to declare war, and two days later he did, thereby bringing on one of Alfred Krupp's most agonizing headaches. At first this is puzzling. For him this war was, after all, the opportunity of a lifetime. Eventually he came to see that, but at the moment he was engrossed in the building of his castle, and he had just discovered a ghastly error. His plans for it were all based on the use of a specific building material — French limestone from the quarries at Chan-tilly, outside of Paris.[33]

# 5

✠

# Now See What Has
# Done Our Army!

The Ems dispatch, by Wilhelm out of Bismarck, had reached Paris on Bastille Day, 1870. At 4:40 P.M. Louis Napoleon's ministers drew up the orders for mobilization. On second thought they hesitated, but six hours later they felt the full force of the Teutonic goad: Bismarck had officially communicated the text of the telegram to all the governments of Europe. It was like spitting in a man's face and then crowing to his friends about it. By the following day the capital seethed with war fever. Even Émile Ollivier, leader of the peace party, agreed that he accepted war *"d'un coeur léger,"* with a light heart, and on the floor of the Senate the powerful Guyot-Montpayroux trumpeted, "Prussia has forgotten the France of Jena and we must remind her!"[1]

French sabers were not only rattling; they were being unsheathed. Count Alfred von Waldsee, the Prussian military attaché in Paris, wired his king of Napoleon's clandestine preparations for war. Troops were being hurried home from Algiers and Rome, officers were being recalled from leave, military commissions were on their way to railroad depots, the cavalry had placed huge orders for oats in the United States, and artillery parks were teeming. Alarmed, Wilhelm secretly called reservists to the colors. Then, on July 12, he set *die Mobilmachung* in motion. The south German states followed, Bavaria and Baden on the 16th and Württemberg on the 18th. That was it: next day France declared war. In less than three weeks 1,183,000 Germans had donned *Pickelhauben*, spiked helmets. Over 400,-000 of them were massed on the Franco-Prussian frontier, backed by 1,440 cannon.[2]

Looking back over a century it is hard to recapture the shock of what was to follow. Conditioned by 1870, 1914, and 1939, one feels that the world ought to have anticipated Teutonic might. It didn't. On the contrary, all eyes were on the French emperor. The day after Wilhelm's order the *London Standard,* pondering the military situation, devoted itself to an analysis of invasion routes into Prussia. It was "impossible," the paper explained, for Moltke and his generals "to take the initiative." The *Pall Mall Gazette* of July 29 agreed that events could take only one course, and *The Times* felt an Englishman would be justified in laying his "last shilling on Casquette against Pumpernickel." Generals Burnside and Sheridan had arrived from the United States to see precisely how the upstarts from central Europe were to be crushed; Kate Amberly (who two years later was to give birth to Bertrand Russell) wrote on July 17, "It makes one miserable to think of that lovely Rhine a seat of war." Those were the views in neutral capitals. Wilhelm's subjects were equally certain that the enemy would be at their doors. German peasants were cutting their corn green so that Gallic hobnails could not trample it, and in the newly acquired states to the south Bürgermeisters were preparing to collaborate. Under the treaty which had ended the *Brüderkrieg* four years earlier there was no way for them to evade their military obligations, but in Mainz and Hanover tricolors were ready for display when the victors marched in. Even the Prussian leaders assumed that hostilities would open with a French *offensive à outrance.* Wilhelm himself was so sure of it that he decided there was no reason to issue maps of France at the outset. The French commanders made the same decision — a ghastly error. General Carl Constantin Albrecht von Blumenthal, Crown Prince Friedrich Wilhelm's chief of staff, expected the first French drive to reach Mainz. Moltke thought Napoleon would throw 150,000 men into a spoiling attack up the Saar valley to the Rhine, and while he was ready for it, he never dreamed he would make the first moves. As the days passed with no sign of enemy activity the crown prince wrote in his war diary: "It may well happen that, for . . . all our age-long preparations against a sudden onslaught, we shall be the aggressors. Whoever could have thought it?"[3]

The foe did not think it. The French *Military Almanac* had evaluated Moltke's troops as "a magnificent organization on paper, but a doubtful instrument for the defense . . . which would be highly imperfect during the first phase of an offensive war." During the opening two weeks of hostilities a resourceful publisher enriched himself by issuing a French-German dictionary for the use of the French in Berlin, and on assuming command of his armies on July 28 the French emperor told them, "Whatever may be the road we take beyond our frontiers, we shall come across the glorious tracks of our fathers. We shall prove worthy of them. All France follows you with its fervent prayers, and the eyes of the world are upon you. On our success hangs the fate of liberty and civilization." To be sure, equipment was piling up faster than men — on the fourteenth day of mobilization his Army of the Rhine had assembled less than 53 percent of its troops — but that seemed a trifle. The French were so sure. For three generations the long shadow of the first Bonaparte had dominated military thought. Now his nephew was in the saddle, and behind him stood what were, by universal agreement, the finest legions in Europe. Seasoned by thirty years of continuous fighting in Africa and Mexico, blooded on the continent by victories over Austria at Magenta and Solferino, bearing battle flags emblazoned by combat streamers from the Crimea and Asia, gaudily uniformed in dashing kepis, tunics striped with light blue and yellow, and *pantalons rouges*, they were the envy of every foreign chancellery. Turkey, in 1856, and Japan, in 1868, had chosen French officers to guide them in building their armies. The élan of Louis Napoleon's soldiery could scarcely have been higher; they eagerly looked forward to heroic attacks carried out by gallant men crying *"En avant! À la baïonette!"* to the strains of *La Marseillaise*. Their faith in their leadership was absolute. The emperor himself was a student of artillery and had published two treatises on it, the first of which, his *Manuel d'Artillerie*, had commanded professional admiration for thirty-five years. Edmond Leboeuf, marshal of France, had distinguished himself with the new rifled artillery in the Italian campaign. Now he assured Napoleon that the army was ready "even down to the buttons on their gaiters," and no one doubted him.[4]

To imperial France, Prussia's martial stance seemed nothing less than an impertinence. Had Parisians been told that King Wilhelm, despite his seventy-three years, was a far more effective commander than their Napoleon and that Leboeuf was not worth a single braided strand from the great Moltke's epaulettes, they would have been incredulous. If anyone had suggested to them that the enemy's morale was as high as their own, they would have been amused — though it was certainly true; the Junkers were spurred by a desire to avenge a thousand years of inferiority, and the German privates in their uniforms of Prussian blue, singing the Protestant hymn *In allen meinen Taten* and chanting *"Nach Paris!"* around their campfires, believed they had embarked upon a mighty crusade to humble the city Prussian newspapers called "the new Babylon."

The emperor's officer corps regarded them with contempt. Moltke's stunning triumph of 1866 was discounted. Anybody could defeat the Austrians, and nearly everyone had. Anyhow, that had been largely a stroke of efficiency, which, in French eyes, was a pedestrian virtue. The fact that Prussia had built its railroad grid with war in mind, had studied General Sherman's brilliant use of railways in Tennessee, and had mastered the coordination of telegraph and troop trains was considered of small consequence in Napoleon's headquarters. Should anyone have insisted otherwise he would have been dismissed as a dreamer.

Really they were the dreamers. This was the year that Jacques Offenbach, that fugitive from a Cologne synagogue choir, reached the peak of his popularity in the French capital, and the French concept of war was far closer to one of his operettas at the Comédie Française than to reality. The industrial revolution had transformed the profession of arms, but in their martial illusions they refought the battles of Napoleon I. They saw *la grande guerre* as it had been depicted in florid paintings of *la Grande Armée*, with picture-book charges, hedge-leaping hussars, romantic dragoons in knightly cuirasses, and moonlight glinting on the lances of the emperor's cavalry. In their imagination they envisaged intrepid formations of grenadiers wheeling in on exposed flanks, of horses bedecked with tassels rearing against the sky, their sinews delineated with precision and their hot carmine-red nostrils dilated. "*C'était*," as Théophile Gautier said later, "*trop beau*." Since there was no place in such fantasies for the dull clatter of Morse keys and the duller click of locomotive wheels, they convinced themselves that these didn't matter. Instead they heard the trumpets of heralds as brave men marched under bright banners to the field of glory, to the field of honor, to the sound of the guns.

*To the sound of the guns:* that was the rub. With his immense manpower, his hardened veterans, and his strategic frontiers, Louis Napoleon could have overcome his other handicaps. France's fatal weakness was ordnance. His marshals were not so preoccupied with *la gloire militaire* that they had overlooked the significance of firepower. Their infantrymen's new .43-caliber, cartridge-firing chassepot rifle had twice the range of the Dreyse needle gun with which Prussia had crushed the Hapsburgs four years earlier, and with some justification they expected much of their mitrailleuse, which, like the six-barreled American Gatling gun, was a primitive ancestor of the coming machine gun. The mitrailleuse had twenty-six barrels; they could be fired in rapid succession by turning a crank. But the Frenchmen's artillery was hopelessly obsolete. They possessed 30 percent fewer fieldpieces than Moltke's *Geschützbedienung*, and French barrels, though rifled, were all bronze. Schneider hadn't even adopted Sir Joseph Whitworth's invention of wrought-iron barrels strengthened by exterior coils, which had become the backbone of Britain's artillery. Leboeuf, in short, was in roughly the same plight as Königgrätz's Austrian defenders of 1866. It was his own fault. When *Les Papiers Secrets du Second Empire* was published in Belgium after the war it was discovered that the marshal himself had scribbled the "*Rien à faire*" across Krupp's offer to supply France with cast steel breechloaders. His colleagues had been anxious to protect Schneider's fledgling works — which, in 1870, were to be paralyzed by the first successful Communist strike. And Leboeuf himself didn't think the barrels from Essen were any good. Gunnery specialists, sharing the convictions of Roon's technicians, had persuaded him that the difficulties of cooling steel evenly during the casting process were insuperable.* Moreover, he himself remained stubbornly loyal to muzzle-loaders. Even if breeches could be made safe for gunners, he argued, there remained the problem of gas leakage and the consequent loss of range. He was, of course, wrong on all counts. Wilhelm, Bismarck, and Moltke had learned the vital lesson on Tegel range, and now the world would be shown — in France.[5]

Thus the guns of August 1870 became the smoking muzzles of Alfred Krupp. They had twice the range of the enemy's bronze pieces, and in accuracy, in concentration, and in rapid fire (which the French ordnance experts had deprecated on the ground that it would encourage gunners to use too much ammunition), the cannon from the Ruhr surpassed anything the enemy could field. Although the mitrailleuses were so secret that they weren't issued to the army until the last days of mobilization, Prussian intelligence had warned Berlin of them. The Germans, unlike the French, took their spies seriously. Batteries were ordered to spot the chattering machine guns and knock them out in the first stages of each engagement, reducing the enemy to small arms. Since soldiers in those days literally did march to the sound of the guns — in the fog of war that was the only way they could find out where the action was — Frenchmen would be tramping to their death. The opening skirmish came at Wissembourg in Alsace on August 4; the French general was killed by a Krupp shell. Then came the first great ordeal, at Wörth, in northeast France, on August 6. Marshal Patrice MacMahon considered a Prussian attack so unlikely that he neglected to have his men dig trenches. His chief concern was that the enemy might slip away. "Never," wrote one of his subordinates, "were troops so sure of themselves and more confident of success." Then Alfred's maul struck. The opposing infantry divisions were evenly matched, and the battle might have been a draw. It wasn't. It was a rout, because after eight hours of hammering by Krupp cannon the French lines broke and retreated in wild disorder.[6]

Wörth — called the battle of Fröschwiller by the French — was an omen; villagers required a full week to recover the splendidly pantalooned corpses from vineyards and forests. The crown prince's losses had also been heavy, but gradually his commanders realized that henceforth they didn't have to charge the chassepots; they could leave the decision to their magnificent artillery. In the words of the official French account of a subsequent encounter, Krupp's breechloaders "smashed all the attempts of French gunners to retaliate and rained shells on the massed lines of infantry which waited with no trace of cover to repel an attack that never

---

* Louis Napoleon would have been better served had he consulted his most imaginative novelist. In March 1868, when Leboeuf was scrawling "Nothing doing" on Essen's proposal, Jules Verne was writing Chapter 12 of *Twenty Thousand Leagues Under the Sea*. Verne's Captain Nemo, taking Professor Aronnax on a tour of the *Nautilus*, explains that the submarine's engine is constructed of the finest steel in the world, cast "by Krupp in Prussia."

came." The war diaries of the participants are more vivid; a Prussian saw the distant blue blouses reacting "like a startled swarm of bees," a French observer wrote that tunics littered the ground so thickly that it looked "like a field of flax," and a historian noted that the records of Louis Napoleon's regiments revealed "a gradual disintegration under the weight of German shells." While the exultant Prussians, Saxons, Hessians, and Silesians sang the newly popular *Die Wacht am Rhein* and *Deutschland über alles,* their embittered enemies slogged into position chanting, "*Un, deux, trois, merde.*"[7]

Machiavelli said of Charles VIII that in the winter of 1494–1495 he "seized Italy with chalk in hand," meaning that he had but to encircle a strongpoint on a map and his iron cannonballs would level it. Charles had conducted sixty successful sieges in sixteen months. In the summer of 1870 Wilhelm's gunners settled the outcome in less than one month. On the eve of August 6 the French had been drawn up in two main bodies, MacMahon's in Alsace and Emperor Louis Napoleon's in Lorraine. Louis had divided them by the spine of the Vosges mountains, and in the light of established military practice it is hard to criticize him. But he hadn't reckoned on the terrible guns. Even as the right wing was falling back from Wörth, the left was losing the towering Spicheren heights forty miles to the northwest, in the Saar. Within twenty-four hours the French dream had become a nightmare. MacMahon abandoned Alsace and Louis Napoleon retreated to the mighty fortress of Metz. After three ferocious battles Moltke flung Uhlans across the only road to Verdun and surrounded Metz. Louis Napoleon escaped at the last moment and galloped south to MacMahon, frantically urging him to cut through the Germans and relieve the fort. The consequence was disaster. On Thursday, September 1, the emperor's exhausted right wing met King Wilhelm's flushed corps seven miles from the Belgian border at Sedan, a small, obsolete fortress on the Meuse with seventeenth-century works. To MacMahon the irregular high ground north of the town was a "*position magnifique,*" but General Auguste Ducrot, a veteran of Wörth, knew what was coming. Hunched under a cloak by the bivouac fire of a red- and blue-turbaned Zouave regiment, he saw the grim truth: "*Nous sommes dans un pot de chambre, et nous y serons emmerdés.*" "Chamber pot" described their position perfectly, and *la merde* which was about to descend upon them was Kruppstahl.[8]

The fighting began before dawn. Although Moltke wanted to wait until his two wings had tightened around the enemy, the First Bavarian Corps was too eager to wait, and at 4 A.M. they pushed across the Meuse in a thick, cold mist. Panicking, the French barricaded themselves in the town's solid stone houses, which were swiftly demolished by shellfire. As dawn lightened the valley sixteen Krupp batteries, brilliantly deployed on the slopes above, far beyond the range of the French guns, annihilated an entire Zouave division, including the commanding officer and his chief of staff. No one was safe from the murderous bursts. With daylight less than an hour old a shell fragment wounded MacMahon himself; carried back into the tiny fort on a litter, he passed his baton to Ducrot. At 8 A.M. the man who had seen the inevitable coming ordered a breakout to the west. General Emmanuel Wimpffen contested the command, refused to obey, and spoke of "pitching the Bavarians into the Rhine." To Ducrot's anguished arguments he replied stolidly, "We need a victory." Ducrot replied, "You will be very lucky, *mon général,* if this evening you have a retreat!" He wasn't exaggerating; every minute the uncannily accurate gunfire grew more intense, and at midmorning Moltke threw columns across the Sedan-Mézières road, blocking the last possible escape hatch. The sun had now burned off the early haze. It was a magnificent day. Moltke's staff, in the words of Professor Michael Howard,

> . . . had found for the king a vantage point from which a view of the battle could be obtained such as no commander of an army in western Europe was ever to see again. In a clearing on the wooded hills above Frénois, south of the Meuse, there gathered a glittering concourse of uniformed notabilities more suitable to an opera house or a racecourse than to a climactic battle which was to decide the destinies of Europe and perhaps of the world. There was the king himself; there was Moltke, Roon and their staff officers watching . . . while Bismarck, Hatzfeld and the Foreign Office officials [also] watched. . . . There was . . . a whole crowd of German princelings . . . watching the remains of their independence dwindling hour by hour as the Prussian, Saxon and Bavarian guns decimated the French army round Sedan.[9]

Altogether the Prussians and their fellow Germans had five hundred Krupp cannon. Wilhelm, raising a telescope to see the fruits of Essen's labor, beheld an extraordinary spectacle — mile after mile of thrashing red trousers beneath the long gun line of the Second Bavarian Corps and, beyond their flashing muzzles, the deep green ridges of the Ardennes. By noon even Wimpffen knew the day was lost. He then tried the breakout, couldn't even assemble enough troops for an attempt, and at one o'clock sent to Sedan for Louis Napoleon. The emperor wouldn't come. He wasn't afraid. On the contrary, he mounted his horse and galloped recklessly through the blizzard of shrapnel, preferring death on the battlefield to the dishonor of surrender. But clearly someone was going to have to offer his sword. By two o'clock the Germans were mopping up. By three o'clock the leaderless French infantry was hiding in the woods. In a last, desperate measure Ducrot tried to use the emperor's cavalry to hew a hole in the tide of Prussian blue to the west. The horsemen's commander raised his saber — and instantly fell back, his face a mass of gore. Two aides dragged him back through the squadrons. Seeing him, the cavalrymen growled,

"*Vengez-le!*" Gallantly they charged again, and again, and then again, until the last of them lay writhing in their own blood beside the carcasses of their slaughtered mounts. The King of Prussia lowered his spyglass. He murmured, "*Ah! Les braves gens!*"[10]

"Never before," wrote Howard, "had gunfire been used in war with such precision." The astonished king watched the flickering bracelets of fire created by the exploding shells as they girded each strongpoint, scything the defenders. Yet death spurned Louis Napoleon. Shells engulfed his cavalry, his massed infantry, his staff, and his lieutenants, but not a splinter fell near him, and he returned to Sedan unharmed. At dusk he sent a sergeant with a white pennant to ask terms and ordered the white flag hoisted over the fort itself. Moltke, sighting it, dispatched a Prussian nobleman to inquire what it meant. The officer returned with a letter which might be called the baptismal certificate of the Second German Reich:

*Monsieur mon frère,*

*N'ayant pas pu mourir au milieu de mes troupes, il ne me reste qu' à remettre mon épée entre les mains de Votre Majesté. Je suis de Votre Majesté le bon frère.* [Since I could not die in the midst of my troops, I can only put my sword in Your Majesty's hands. I am Your Majesty's good brother.]

NAPOLEON[11]

But neither the emperor nor his sword were in the hands of Wilhelm. The king, after studying it, wordlessly handed it to Bismarck, who dictated a reply in his behalf, suggesting "*la capitulation*" and concluding: "*J'ai désigné le Général de Moltke à cet effet.*"[12]

That night the German troops thankfully chanted the great Lutheran chorale *Nun danket alle Gott* (Old Hundred) around their campfires. They were as stunned as the French. In Howard's words, no one on either side had foreseen that "the effectiveness of the Prussian artillery was to be the greatest tactical surprise of the Franco-Prussian war." Its impact on the participants varied according to their situations. The Prussians and their allies were exultant. The French were embittered; nearly a half-century later at Versailles, Georges Clemenceau, who was now mayor of Montmartre and whom this disaster brought into national politics, would recall the taste for *revanche* he had acquired in his twenties and use it to demolish Woodrow Wilson's policy of mercy toward the then prostrate Germany. Louis Napoleon was in a state of collapse. One of his officers, Jean Baptiste Montaudun, described him as "much aged, much weakened, and possessing none of the bearing of the leader of an army." Moltke and Bismarck were ruthless, and when Wimpffen met them — he didn't want to go, but Ducrot said savagely, "You assumed the command when you thought there was some honor and profit in exercising it . . . Now you cannot refuse" — they rejected his plea that "a peace based on conditions which would flatter the *amour-propre* of the army and diminish the bitterness of defeat would be durable, whereas rigorous measures would awaken bad passions and perhaps bring on endless war between France and Prussia."[13]

Bismarck, in declining to be generous, fixed the French general with his pale blue eyes and replied that "One should not, in general, rely on gratitude, and especially not that of a people." Instead the Junker demanded the surrender of the entire French force at Sedan, including Louis Napoleon himself, as prisoners of war. Wimpffen was aghast. Bismarck, extracting the last ounce of pleasure from the triumph, observed that as a nation Frenchmen were "irritable, envious, jealous, and proud to excess. It seems to you that victory is a property reserved for you alone, that the glory of arms is your monopoly." The Germans, on the other hand, he went on, were a peaceful people who had been invaded by France on thirty occasions during the past two centuries — fourteen times between 1785 and 1813. Now all that was over: "We must have land, fortresses, and frontiers which will shelter us for good from enemy attack." Still Wimpffen recoiled. Moltke stepped in. In one day the emperor had been reduced from 104,000 to 80,000 troops, he observed, while Wilhelm had a quarter-million. Then the German commander unrolled a map, showing him the ring of batteries which invested the French army with *"fünfhundert Kanonen — cinq cents canons."*[14]

That argument was unanswerable, and the truce was extended while Wimpffen rode back to consult his emperor. In desperation, Napoleon resolved to lay an appeal before Wilhelm, one sovereign to another. The next morning he remounted his steed and galloped off once more, but Prussian sentries intercepted him and brought him straight to Bismarck and Moltke. Fearing that their generous king might soften their terms, they took Napoleon to a cottage. He could, they said, see Wilhelm *after* the instrument of surrender had been signed. That was soon. Even as the bourgeois emperor fumed, Wimpffen was scrawling his name on it in the Château de Bellevue on the river. Moltke had yielded one infinitesimal point: officers who agreed not to take up arms again would be paroled. It is a symptom of the hardening feeling that only five hundred and fifty took advantage of the loophole. The document completed, the imperial POW was granted his audience. The meeting was short and awkward (both monarchs blushed) and Napoleon, as Wilhelm's advisers had predicted, did ask a favor. He begged the king to let him be taken to prison through Belgium. If he were marched through France, he pointed out, he would be subjected to intolerable humiliation. Wilhelm glanced at Bismarck, who shrugged. With one French army bottled up at Metz and this one in captivity, the king's minister-president observed sardonically, "It would not even do any harm if he took another direction . . . if he failed to keep his word it would not injure us." The emperor turned to the king. To Moritz Busch, who later became Bismarck's biographer, the captive looked "too soft, I might say too shabby." He said to his conqueror, "I congratulate you on your army, above all on your artillery. My own was so" — he groped — "inferior." The embarrassed Wilhelm looked away.[15]

The following day Napoleon III, Emperor of the French, was carted off to a *Stalag* at Wilhelmshöhe with his elegant baggage, his periwigged footmen, and his huge entourage. The splendid weather had been replaced by a driving rain. Napoleon's surviving troops were huddled in a hastily improvised internment camp on the banks of the river. From *le camp de la misère*, as they called it, they shouted epithets at him. Moltke and Bismarck stood together, watching the emperor's carriage roll away.

"There is a dynasty on its way out," Bismarck murmured.[16]

He might have added that two others were remorselessly rising: those of Hohenzollern and Krupp.

✠　　✠　　✠

Alfred, meanwhile, had had no inkling of the spectacular change in his fortunes. The war had seemed to him to have come at a dreadful time. He hadn't completed the converting of his factory to the Siemens-Martin process, and Albert Pieper had chosen this extremely inconvenient time to die. When another correspondent sent word that he too was on his deathbed, Alfred replied irritably that he was unwell himself: "I am not equal to my business, rarely receive visitors, and lack sufficient strength and vitality to perform what the works and the building of my house demand of me (*die Fabrik und der Neubau eines Wohnhauses mir auferlegen*).[17]

His house was demanding more and more. On the hill the complicated business of transplanting another grove of trees was in process; roots dangled from burlap bags. And now there was this trouble with the French. It seemed to be a blow aimed at him personally. He demanded that his French stonemasons continue to work on Villa Hügel (they did) and that Chantilly continue to send him more stone (incredibly, this too was done, through Belgium, while he continued to ship rollers and railroad wheels to France through England until the bitter climax of early September destroyed the two-way traffic). So great an obsession had the mansion become that his first response to the king's general mobilization of July 12 had been to ignore it. Hügel must continue to go up, he told the four directors of his Prokura: "*Um jeden Preis, selbst mit der Beseitigung von Arbeitern der Fabrik!*" (At all costs, even if we have to take men from the works!).[18]

With France's declaration of war he completely reversed himself. During an earlier Franco-Prussian row he had offered to donate a million thalers' worth (about $420,000) of cast steel guns to Berlin "in case of a war with France" (*im Falle eines Krieges mit Frankreich*); news of Paris's proclamation reached Essen July 20, 1870, and instantly he wrote Roon offering "to redeem that promise" and stipulating only that his generosity be kept "entirely secret." He knew Roon. He didn't want his offer to be interpreted as an exploitation of the crisis for the sake of free publicity. The gift was turned down anyhow, for the typically Roonian reason that extra cannon would upset the army's sacred Table of Organization. But Krupp's zeal was undampened. He had signed the letter to Roon "God protect Prussia!" (*Gott schütze Preussen!*) and for the next several months he adopted the habit of ending missives with that or similar spread-eagle phrases, saluting *patriotische Begeisterung*, patriotic enthusiasm; *dem Drang, dem Vaterland zu dienen*, yearning to serve the Fatherland; and, with a thrill of pride, *den unübertrefflichen Leistungen unseres tapferen Kriegsheeres*, the "incomparable deeds of our valiant army."[19]

Eight days after the outbreak of hostilities he had posted his own fighting orders to the men in his shops and sheds. Breaking one of his most hallowed rules, he authorized subcontracting whenever it would speed the war effort. He called for shifts "working day and night in every shop with all the men and machines at our command, shrinking from no expense or sacrifice." Substitute mountings and parts were to be turned out against the possibility of Prussian reverses in the field. "Similarly," he wrote:

> *Ebenso wolle man von Geschossen das maximal Quantum anfertigen, welches für unsere Geschütze im Falle der grössten Aktion nützlich sein könne. . . . Daher rechne ich auf äusserste Tätigkeit und weises Über-legen.*

> Let us prepare the maximum number of projectiles which can be used by our guns in the event of a battle on the largest conceivable scale. Apart from the 9-inch guns, we should anticipate the commitment of even the partly finished 11-inch ones. Regardless of whether this approach finds favor with the authorities, of whether it is approved, whether the fruit of our labor is accepted, and regardless of whether we ever receive payment for them, I expect, from the patriotism of all whose services are devoted to cannon, that he will think of nothing except the possible crisis of arms ahead of us, in which our toil may be justified and be of incalculable value to the Fatherland. I therefore look for the utmost activity and prudent reflection.[20]

At the same time, he was reflecting prudently upon what the war meant to him and to his future. He was not, as one of his German admirers was to insist, "the very image of a patriot, marching in extraordinary obscurity with the rank and file." Alfred couldn't be obscure under any circum-stances, and while his patriotism was real enough, his attitude toward the war was bound to be influenced by his special role. He couldn't restrain himself from requesting permission to use the Tegel range during certain hours, although he knew the request was hopeless. When Roon asked him to deliver certain parts which had been earmarked for Russia, he replied that as a businessman he must first secure the permission of his clients. Like everyone else he had supposed that the conflict would open with a French thrust across the Rhine. Essen was within lunging distance, but Meyer's suggestion that Kruppianer be armed with rifles was tartly rejected. That, Krupp remarked, would be *eine grosse Torheit*, a monumental blunder; should Louis Napoleon's troops reach the Ruhr, "we will offer them roast veal and red wine, otherwise they will destroy the factory." His greatest concern, however, was the performance of his product on the battlefield. Memories of 1866 were painfully fresh, and another Teutonic conquest would turn sour for him if accompanied by reports of faulty cannon.[21]

The news was long in coming. He heard of the victories in Alsace and Lorraine, but didn't know how they had been achieved. His first word of Sedan arrived in a letter from Wilhelm Ludwig Deichmann, a banker who had loaned money to the government and taken the precaution of sending agents to the front. The note was exasperating:

> *Welche glückliche Wendung haben die Kriegsereignisse genommen!*
> . . . *Hoffentlich wird Paris rasch von uns besetzt und dem Schwindel ein*
> *Ende gemacht werden.*

> What a fortunate turn the war has taken! That wicked scoundrel Napoleon has been properly punished for challenging, without the slightest provocation, our peace-loving Fatherland and bringing anguish and misery upon thousands and thousands of families. I should consider that the war was over had not the Paris catastrophe faced us with new trouble. Let us pray that we shall seize the French capital without delay and thus end this disgraceful business.[22]

Krupp was in a mood to put an end to the disgraceful Deichmann. All his suspicions of bankers seemed confirmed. The letter was a gush of bombast without one word about artillery. *Gott schütze Krupp!* Then the great tidings began to filter through from his faithful Voigts-Rhetz. The general's C Corps was seventy miles from Sedan, in the ring of troops encircling Metz. He had been either in combat or on the move since August 6, but now that he had time to catch his breath he began firing off dispatches to Essen. He could describe the action he had seen, and as Sedan veterans joined C Corps he interviewed them and relayed their observations. Forget about Königgrätz, Voigts-Rhetz advised Alfred. To be sure, "the shells from the French rifled thirty-six-pounders are flying about our ears at five to six hundred paces"; nevertheless the general stated that the first weeks of combat "have already proved the superiority of our artillery to that of the French, and have repeatedly shown this arm to be our best defense against the chassepot rifle"; *"der Bronze Humbug"* was as good as dead. At Sedan, Krupp had met "the acid test" (*die grosse Probe*). The superiority of his steel breechloaders over Napoleon's bronze muzzle-loaders had been clearly demonstrated (*Überlegenheit . . . ganz eindeutig*). Indeed, there was no need to manufacture spare parts. Essen's field-pieces had proved to be *"unverwüstlich"* — indestructible.[23]

Krupp felt transported. For three winters he had languished at Nice. Now, though the builders hadn't succeeded in getting a roof over his castle, he was going to spend this year with *kruppsche* workmen. It was like old times; young journeymen to whom the great proprietor was only a legend would arrive at their benches mornings and find furious notes from him beside their toolboxes. For the first time in years he felt that there was some point behind all this clatter of machinery and puffing of smoke. In his youth he had been vindicating his father's memory. Now he was proving himself, passing *die grosse Probe* in the service of his country. Writing Roon, he declared that since his offer of free guns was unacceptable, he was finding other ways to pledge allegiance to the flag. He had set aside 120,000 thalers for a Victoria National Foundation for Disabled Soldiers (Victoria-Nationale-Invalidenstiftung) — and was contributing to funds for war widows, sending his own elaborately equipped hospital to France for wounded heroes, and shipping supplementary provisions to selected officers. Since Krupp himself made up the list, it was naturally headed by Voigts-Rhetz, who expressed his gratitude in the terms his benefactor cherished most.

> *. . . ich weiss, dass das Schreiben ein grosses Opfer für Sie ist, da es Ihre Gesundheit angreift. . . . Heute ist es ruhig vor unseren Fronten und ich hoffe, dass die Franzosen nicht irgendein boshaftes Attentat hinter den dichten Nebelschichten ausbrüten, die das weite Moseltal bedecken.*

> . . . I know that writing is a great trial for you, since it injures your health. So the pleasure of hearing from you is always bound up with regret that you must suffer for the sacrifice made to friendship. No day, no hour passes but I think of you with truest devotion, and rejoice with all my heart in your friendship and affection. If these thoughts were all set down, they would fill an entire library. It is quiet today on our fronts, and I hope that the French are not hatching some evil plot behind the thick layers of fog which blanket the broad valley of the Moselle.[24]

"The chest of valuable cigars," he added, getting down to the graft, "which you, my dearest friend, were so kind as to send me, arrived safely. My warmest thanks and those of my large staff for them. You have kept us plentifully supplied with the choicest brands — so much so that we can revel in them through a very long campaign! . . . The fame of your private hospital, which has already done so much good, has reached us even here. You think of everything for everyone." That was as humbug as the bronze. Alfred wasn't thinking of everyone at all. Cigars and brandy went to officers who had supported cast steel breechloaders; those who opposed them could live on black Westphalian pumpernickel. Excluding them from the hospital and Victoria-Nationale-Invalidenstiftung was clearly impractical, but deciphering Krupp's correspondence of 1870–1871 leaves the distinct impression that his compassion for them was slight. Nor can he be much blamed. They were an extraordinarily mulish lot; it is a matter of record that the diehards continued to stonewall *after* Sedan. As late as December 11 the crown prince wrote in his diary at Versailles that "In yesterday's cannonade before Beaugency twenty-four of our cast steel four-pounders were completely shot out, so that the barrels had to be sent back as unusable and new ones substituted in their place. Krupp's artillery critics are rejoicing over this failure, at the head of them being General von Podbielski."[25]

Quartermaster General Eugen A. Theophil von Podbielski was a powerful opponent. In Moltke's army he should also have been a soldier of great sagacity, but his interpretation of the duel outside Paris on Saturday, December 10, was wholly unjustified. Far from quenching the faith of Krupp partisans, it merely proved that four-pounders were too small, and hence obsolete; the great lesson of Sedan was that cast steel guns need never be brought within range of bronze counterbattery fire. As one of his backers wrote Alfred, Prussia "would be still more successful if we already had the 1,700-foot muzzle velocity, the possibility of which we owe to you." Voigts-Rhetz, in other words, had been right. If the cannon were large enough they really *were* indestructible. Krupp was toiling away at the possibility of gigantic barrels. Writing Roon, he reported that he had been experimenting with a new field gun before the outbreak of war. He proposed that Prussia order twenty-four of these pieces "very soon." The Minister of War, with his customary lack of graciousness, asked Krupp to please stop bothering him. Krupp wouldn't stop. Carried away, he telegraphed Roon that he had designed a fantastic monster:

MÖGLICHE VERWENDBARKEIT VOR PARIS ANNEHMEND . . . WEITERES SCHRIFTLICH. SOLLTEN ABER SOLCHE MÖRSER NICHT VERWENDBAR SEIN, SO BITTE UM UMGEHENDE TELEGRAPHISCHE NACHRICHT.

ASSUMING POSSIBLE USE BEFORE PARIS AM PUTTING IN HAND AT MY OWN RISK SO AS NOT TO LOSE TIME SIX SMOOTHBORE CAST STEEL MORTARS OF 21½-INCH CALIBER, 60 DEGREES ELEVATION, 300 CWT. WEIGHT, FOR 60-POUND CHARGES AND THOUSAND-POUND BOMBS WITH 60-POUND EXPLODING CHARGE, EFFECTIVE AT FIVE THOUSAND PACES, TOGETHER WITH MOUNTINGS, TRANSPORT WAGONS, AND SIX HUNDRED SHELLS. HOPE TO COMPLETE TWO MORTARS ABOUT MIDDLE FEBRU-

ARY. FURTHER DETAILS IN WRITING. SHOULD SUCH MORTARS NOT BE
USEFUL PLEASE TELEGRAPH REPLY NOW.

In an accompanying letter he again promised *"schnelle Lieferung,"* early
delivery, with two of the 56-cm. mortars (22-inch) ready by the middle of
February. His concern, he explained, arose from reports "bruited abroad"
that "certain forts, especially Mont Valérien," dominated Paris and could
not be reduced without "serious sacrifice of time and men." Roon could
prevent that merely by saying *Ja.* "I am convinced," Alfred concluded,
"that no structures above or below the ground can withstand the mortars
now put in hand, and in particular that they will destroy foundations and
inner spaces by the weight of the impact and the force of the explosion."[26]

Roon said *Nein.* For once the mossbacks were right; the army didn't
need thousand-pound bombs or gaping muzzles. It was doing very nicely
with the Krupp guns it had. Last spring 15-cm. siege cannon and 21-cm.
mortars had been ordered from Essen, and these were being tested in
action for the first time. Meanwhile the complexion of the war had continued to change dramatically. *La Débâcle,* as Émile Zola was calling it,
grew more stupendous each week. Two days after Louis Napoleon's surrender of Sedan, Paris had risen. Eugénie, whom her husband had appointed regent during his absence on the battlefield, fled the city. The
Parisians proclaimed a republic and dug in. They were determined. They
were also doomed. In July, Austria, Italy, and Denmark had intimated that
they would be honored to serve as allies of the Second Empire. They had
assumed they would be backing a winner. After the staggering defeats of
August, culminating in that bloody day on the Meuse, their foreign
ministers murmured excuses and sidled away.[27]

France's last professional army, Marshal François Achille Bazaine's
173,000 veterans, was bottled up in Metz. Bazaine was weak and indecisive,
yet there wasn't much he could do; even Moltke, in his place, would have
been paralyzed. The faith of France in the impregnability of Metz was
groundless. For ten centuries the scarred old fort on the Moselle had
barred the way to invaders from across the Rhine. Now its hour had struck.
Ringed by *Pickelhauben,* pinned down inside the fortifications beneath
Metz's steep bluff by *"les canons terribles,"* Bazaine abandoned all thought
of counterattack. "I absolutely forbid anyone to advance a yard," he
ordered. While German bands jubilantly played the stirring *Heil dir im
Siegeskranz,* Krupp guns slowly pulverized the thick old works. With no
prospect of relief, his supplies dwindling and his walls crumbling, Bazaine
surrendered on October 24, bitterly refusing the honors of war.[28]

Paris was left alone. The embattled citizen leaders were far more game
than either the emperor at Sedan or the marshal in Metz, and for nearly
fourteen more weeks they defiantly rejected the verdict of the guns. *La
ville lumière,* the heart of the cosmopolitan world, simply could not accept

what had happened. In July people had flocked to the streets shouting "À Berlin! À Berlin! Vive la guerre!" and on August 6 stock exchange speculators, trying to rig the market, had spread the word on the Rue Vivienne that the entire army of the Prussian crown prince had been captured. When the exact opposite came to pass, they were incredulous. Léon Gambetta, Minister of the Interior in the new republic, vowed that "a nation in arms" could not be overcome. He called for a levée en masse. "Tied down and contained by the capital," he predicted, "the Prussians, far from home, anxious, harassed, hunted down by our reawakened people, will be gradually decimated by our arms, by hunger, by natural causes." Paris, he insisted, was far stronger than any fortress in the provinces. This was actually true. The rumors Krupp had heard "bruited abroad" about the city's defenses were not entirely baseless. In 1840 Thiers had exploited a Near East crisis to give it a 30-foot-high enceinte (wall), a 10-foot-wide moat, and 94 bastions, 15 forts and 3,000 cannon covering approaches to Paris. What Gambetta overlooked — in the light of professional near-sightedness he can scarcely be blamed — was that in three decades the new firepower had rendered this massive system obsolete.[29]

Using French railroads, Moltke moved swiftly toward the Marne. On September 15 he was in Château-Thierry, planning the siege. Two days later a great pincers movement began, with the Kronprinz of Prussia sweeping around from the south and the Kronprinz of Saxony meeting him from the north. The envelopment was completed in twenty-four hours. The last mail train left the city on September 18. Next day telegraph lines were cut; Paris was isolated, exposed to the merciless guns. Even as the lines went down — the Journal Officiel obliquely broke the news to Paris that it was surrounded by suggesting that the population "not . . . feel surprised at the absence of telegraphic intelligence from the country" — the first French defenders to sortie from the enceinte were fleeing back in panic from Krupp muzzles on the Châtillon plateau, a commanding eminence just outside the gates. A Parisian who met a squad of retreating Zouaves recorded in his journal that "One of them, laughing nervously, told me that there had been no battle, that it had been a general rout straightaway, that he had not fired a single shot. I was struck by the gaze of these men . . . vague, shifty, glassy, settling nowhere." It was a look which was to become increasingly familiar to Frenchmen over the next seventy-five years.[30]

The literary capital of civilization was crowded with diarists, and their entries during the siege are full of similar allusions. After the smoke had rolled away from the Châtillon heights another, who described himself in his postwar memoirs as a "besieged resident," made "a few calls" and noted that everyone "seemed to be engaged in measuring the distance from the Prussian batteries to his particular house. One friend I found seated in a cellar with a quantity of mattresses over it, to make it bomb-proof." To the more perceptive citizens it quickly became evident that the reduction of their defenses was merely a matter of time. "If in our sorties," one wrote, "we have been invariably driven back by the Prussian field artillery, what hope is there of breaking through the enemy's lines now that the terrible Krupp cannon are at length in position all round Paris, in works which we have all along been assured were being destroyed by our naval gunners as fast as they were constructed?" The heaviest concentration of batteries was on the Châtillon prominence. Quartermaster General Podbielski gloated over each requisition for new barrels from Essen, yet the fact was that the artillerymen were deliberately wearing them out. Krupp's superheavy guns threw a projectile 5,600 meters — 6,130 yards — which only reached the suburbs of Paris. By deliberately overloading charges and raising barrels to thirty-degree angles, however, the gunners discovered that they could consistently hurl shells 7,500 yards, a hitherto unheard-of distance. Between three and four hundred fell in the city each day, exploding in the Île St. Louis, the Salpêtrière, the Panthéon, the Sorbonne, and the Convent of the Sacred Heart. The Left Bank bore the brunt of the bombardment, but it was the talk of the entire capital. At the end of December the Ministry of Agriculture, hoping to increase morale, announced the distribution of supplementary rations. It was greeted with cynicism. As one observer wrote sardonically, "Enjoy your New Year's Day, Parisians, and fatten yourselves up for Krupp of Châtillon."[31]

In a three-week period 12,000 shells struck 1,400 buildings; 20,000 Parisians were left homeless. To bombard one stronghold east of the city Moltke assembled seventy-six of Krupp's most powerful cannon. An astonished defender measured one of the resulting craters; it was a yard deep and four and a half feet wide. The shallow French trenches were swiftly obliterated, burying some troops alive. Their commander had no choice; he had to evacuate the fort. Archibald Forbes, a veteran war correspondent for the London *Daily News,* marched in with the victors on October 30, 1870, and described the mutilated corpses of *les braves gens* to his shocked readers.

> The terrible ghastliness of those dead transcended anything I had ever seen, or even dreamt of, in the shuddering nightmare after my first battlefield. Remember how they had been slain. Not with the nimble bullet of the needle gun, that drills a minute hole through a man and leaves him undisfigured, unless it has chanced to strike his face; not with the sharp stab of the bayonet, but slaughtered with missiles of terrible weight, shattered into fragments by explosions of many pounds of powder, mangled and torn by massive fragments of iron.[32]

As 1871 dawned Alfred was the employer of 10,000 men, over 3,000 of them newcomers since July. The French would remember the new year as *l'année terrible*, but Krupp saw it differently. For the first time Prussia was far and away his leading customer. Refusing to be discouraged by Roon, he kept thinking of new weapons. One of them had caught hold. Carrier pigeons excepted, the enemy capital's sole means of communication was by balloon. Therefore he and Wilhelm Gross, his finest technician, had designed a *preussisches Ballongeschütz* — the world's first antiaircraft gun. In some respects it looked much like its celebrated great-grandson, Alfried Krupp's .88 of World War II. The barrel was six feet long; the mounting fifteen feet high, including a steel stock, trigger, and trigger guard, like a rifle. The muzzle could be swung around rapidly. The gunner would thrust a shell into the breech, turn a crank to cock it, brace the stock against his shoulder, aim through a rear sight, and fire. On December 3 Crown Prince Friedrich Wilhelm noted in his war diary, "Krupp from Essen has sent us a model of a balloon gun, as it is called, and believes that with this, an invention resembling a rocket battery, the balloons ascending from Paris can be hit and destroyed." The model was instantly approved. Hawks from Saxony had intercepted and killed a number of the carrier pigeons (evoking, in that naïve day, a storm of Parisian protests against this "barbarity and cruelty"), but riflemen had been singularly unsuccessful against balloons, and though cavalry had galloped after some for miles they always returned disappointed. Presently the first balloon cannon arrived from the Ruhr. A British war correspondent cabled his editor that the range was said "to exceed 500 yards" — actually it flung a three-pound grenade up 666 yards — and that the arrangement was "indeed not unsimilar to that of some large stationary telescopes." Testimony to its effectiveness varied sharply. The number of balloons sent up during daylight hours dropped abruptly, and Krupp partisans cheered lustily. His critics, on the other hand, insisted that Paris was running short of skilled aeronauts.[33]

On January 28, the 113th day of investment, all argument ended. Paris capitulated. Ahead lay the Commune, civil war, a second siege, and the horrors of starvation. For the victors the spoils were glittering. In signing the treaty Bismarck exacted a billion-dollar indemnity and the ceding of Alsace and eastern Lorraine. Though nowhere near the severity of those France had imposed upon Prussia in 1807, the terms were sufficient to assure burning irredentism in the conquered country, and by redrawing the frontiers along linguistic and strategic lines, disregarding industrial considerations, Bismarck had left the Ruhr dangerously close to the border. But tomorrow was far away; in 1871 the conquerors could only feast on glory. There was enough for everyone. Nothing like this had happened to the balance of continental power since Gustavus Adolphus's crushing of the mighty Catholic alliance in a few weeks of 1631. Prussia and her German allies, Professor Howard wrote, had "totally destroyed the military power of imperial France. For nearly eighty years the defeated nation had given the law in military matters to Europe, whereas the victor, ten years earlier, had been the least of the continent's major military powers. . . . Prussia established a military pre-eminence and a political hegemony which made the unification of Germany under her leadership a matter of course, and which only an alliance embracing nearly every major power in the world was to wrest from her half a century later."[34]

Unification was achieved while the muzzles on Châtillon were still blazing. On December 2 King Ludwig of Bavaria had addressed a letter to the King of Prussia (Bismarck had drafted it) inviting him to assume the imperial title, and ten days before the fall of Paris, Bismarck crowned Wilhelm emperor (*Kaiser*) of the new empire (*Reich*) in the Hall of Mirrors at Versailles. According to the diary of William Howard Russell of *The Times* of London, who was present for the investiture, at exactly noon on January 18 the boom of a Krupp cannon

> far away rolls above the voices in the Court hailing the Emperor King. Then there is a hush of expectation, and then rich and sonorous rise the massive strains of the chorale chanted by the men of regimental bands assembled in a choir, as the King, bearing his helmet in his hand, and dressed in full uniform as a German General, stalked slowly up the long gallery, and bowing to the clergy in front of the temporary altar opposite him, halted and dressed himself right and front, and then twirling his heavy mustache with his disengaged hand, surveyed the scene at each side of him.

It was the ultimate humiliation: Wilhelm was standing beneath a painting of Frenchmen chasing Germans dedicated "À *toutes les Gloires de la France.*" In the words of Alistair Horne, "Not only had something of the old order of Europe died; to the injury of the bombardment of Paris an appalling insult had been added, and the combination of the two would jointly inject a special bitterness into Franco-Prussian relations for the next three-quarters of a century." The players continued to play out their roles, but the issue had been decided on the anvils of Essen before the first shot was fired. In Horne's words, "As the French were to discover again in 1914, their fortifications were simply not adequate to face the latest products of Herr Krupp." Europe began to have second thoughts about the nature of the Prussian character. *The Times* protested the brutal behavior of German troops, Prussian guns sank five British colliers in the lower Seine, and Archibald Forbes recorded in his diary the arrogant remark of a young Junker who informed him that his regiment "would, before two years were over, be besieging Windsor Castle."[35]

At Versailles the new Kaiser made Bismarck a prince and his chancellor. This time there was no grumbling from the south. The divided Fatherland also belonged to the past. Welded together by the magnificence of the feat of arms, both German federations gladly abandoned their sovereignty and submitted to the spirit of the time: the Saxon chaplains at Versailles preached — a knell — "Already one race, one people, we are now one nation." Thus the beginnings of *Ein Volk, ein Kaiser, ein Reich*, which — with later the substitution of *Führer* for *Kaiser* — was to hold central Europe spellbound for almost a hundred years. The only real loser in Germany was parliamentary government; its champions had been the liberals, who had opposed the new chancellor's policy of *Eisen und Blut* and were now discredited. For *das Zweite Reich* the prospects ahead were dazzling. The new empire, with the Ruhr to give it industrial muscle for military adventures, dominated *Weltpolitik*. Soldiers abroad were quick to pay tribute. In America, West Point cadets had worn the kepi of the great Napoleon's armies. Suddenly both the Point and the U.S. Marine Corps adopted spiked helmets. The war of 1870 was the most splendid moment in Germany's military history, and the subjects of the new Kaiser, not knowing that it was also Germany's last triumphant conflict, were variously awed, reverent, and increasingly haughty. Alfred Krupp exulted. To Longsdon in London he wrote in his broken English, "Now see what has done our Army!"[36]

✠   ✠   ✠

In 1963 this writer found Alfred's *Ballongeschütz* standing in an obscure corner of the Zeughaus, East Berlin's old military museum. Its Communist caretakers were ignorant of its significance; they didn't even know who had made it, though the legend *Friedr. Krupp Essen* was still legible on a brass plate. Generals, not manufacturers, are the celebrities of war. The end of the Franco-Prussian War, like that of the American Civil War six years earlier, was followed by the raising of triumphant statues in town squares. Typically, a hatless, dying hero was depicted sprawled on the battlefield, one hand holding the Prussian flag aloft, the other hand braced on a Krupp cannon. The inventor of the gun was not depicted. On a column in what is now West Berlin the government erected the golden *Siegessäule*, the 1870 angel of victory. Berliners called (and still call) her "the heaviest woman in Germany, the most expensive, and the cheapest, because for sixty pfennigs you can mount her and have a beautiful view of the city." Included in the view are Tiergarten statues of Bismarck, Moltke, and Roon, who had tried so hard to ban steel cannon. Essen excepted (Alfred commissioned three statues of himself), the Fatherland raised no monuments to Krupp.[37]

But none was necessary. He was receiving his tribute in every world currency. Everywhere he was identified with the triumph. A successful war, he discovered, was an even better advertisement than a world's fair. His product had been proved effective in the laboratory of battle. Being Alfred, he looked for a dark thread in the silver cloud, and presently he found one:

I am very tired, nervous, played out, and can't go on like this [*Ich bin sehr müde, nervös, kaputt und kann so nicht mehr weitermachen*]. Who would protect Krupp's works, which are so close to the frontier, against the French if the ratio of firepower were reversed in a new *revanche* war?[38]

Yet by the first anniversary of Sedan even he felt sanguine. The years before the Berlin Congress of 1875 were the first golden age of arms manufacturers. The firm was being swamped with orders; Krupp cannon had become the new status symbol of nations. Turkey used them to guard the Bosporus, Rumania to protect the forty bastions of Bucharest. According to legend, tiny Andorra bought a long-range gun and then discovered that it couldn't be fired without hitting French soil. In 1873 the Kruppwerke payroll was half again as large as in 1870; the firm had surpassed the peak of its wartime production. Then came the Sino-Japanese war scare of 1874–1875, the first in a long series of plums which fell into Alfred's lap. Tokyo had purchased cannon from Schneider and the Chinese warlords had been buying from Armstrong, but by now memoirs of men who had fought at Sedan, Metz, and Paris were being read all over the globe; when Krupp wrote flattering letters to Li Hung-chang ("the Bismarck of Asia") and sent him a model railroad, Li responded by ordering 275 field guns, another 150 cannon to arm the Taku fort guarding the approach to Tientsin, and complete armament for eight warships. In gratitude Alfred hung over the head of his bed a portrait of Li, despite his fear of combustible objects in the castle. Word of his Chinese coup reached Potsdam, and the Kaiser chortled, "*Krupp schreibt den Regierungen vor, was sie kaufen müssen*" (Krupp tells governments what they must buy). If governments were poor enough, he really did. Backward countries were given shipments of obsolete weapons. Despite the huge bill paid by Asia's Bismarck, Li Hung-chang didn't receive Essen's latest model, which was being delivered to Saint Petersburg that winter. The Taku forts got outdated cannon, and a handsome order from Bangkok was filled from the same prescription. Alfred wrote tartly,

> *Was könnten Chinesen und Siamesen nicht für Löcher damit in ihre Feinde schiessen!*"

Chinese and Siamese can blow their enemies to bits well enough with these![39]

# 6

✠

# Der Grosse Krupp

THE awesome Second Reich of 1871 — an amalgam of four kingdoms, five grand duchies, six duchies, seven principalities, three free cities, and the imperial domain of Alsace-Lorraine, all united under a single *deutscher Kaiser* or, as his court came to know him, *"der Allerhöchsteselber"* (the All-Highest), ought to have adopted a sophisticated, cosmopolitan outlook. But the conversion had been too swift. Its Junker leaders retained their Prussian *Störrigkeit* (pigheadedness), which had blinded them to the value of Essen's cannon before and which, incredibly, thwarted Krupp in what should have been his hour of vindication. Every engagement from Wörth to Paris had demonstrated that in time of war Kruppstahl was more priceless than gold. The world recognized it: not only China and Siam, but even far-off Chile came to the Gusstahlfabrik door, inviting a Krupp mission to Santiago and thereby initiating the arms race which has plagued Latin America ever since. Essen's competitors saw it: Armstrong and Schneider-Creusot salesmen were sent coded messages ordering them to shadow Alfred's agents around the clock. Perceptive Germans realized it: like Görlitz, studying the lessons of the war, they concluded that

> *Neben Clausewitz als Philosoph des Krieges wurden Alfred Krupp als Rüstungsindustrieller oder Werner von Siemens als Telegraphenbauer die Väter einer modernen Kriegsführung.*

> Along with Clausewitz, as military philosopher, the fathers of modern warfare were Alfred Krupp, the arms industrialist, and Werner von Siemens, the telegraph builder.[1]

Yet *der Allerhöchsteselber's* professional staff remained divided over the value of what was now popularly known as *die Firma*. Podbielski tried to convince the All-Highest that increased muzzle velocity was "a matter of small importance" (*es macht nicht viel aus*), an extraordinary argument from a professional soldier who had just witnessed Prussia's greatest military achievement, not excepting Blücher's forced march over the moist twilight plain of Waterloo, and Roon, carrying his feud with Krupp into the postwar era, suggested that the Kaiser scrap his cast steel barrels and reintroduce bronze guns.[2]

Alfred fought back. He felt certain that "the French, conscious of their inferiority in the artillery duels," would devote their energy to rapid rearmament; if the victory was to be retained, Germany must stay "ahead of them." On April 13, six weeks after the terms of the peace treaty had been accepted by France's new National Assembly at Bordeaux, he was in Berlin, writing Moltke,

> . . . *erlaube ich mir ganz gehorsamst zu melden, dass ich eine Versuchsstation für Geschütze aller Gattungen zu errichten beabsichtige . . . möglichst eben, an einer Eisenbahn liegend und nahe meinem Etablissement oder wenigstens dem Regierungsbezirk Düsseldorf.*

> . . . I beg most obediently to inform you that I contemplate starting a trial ground for guns of all kinds, seeing that, with the degree of efficiency that has been attained and the further development which still has to be aimed at, there is no available place in the country which is adequate as regards safety and observation. The site should be approximately two German miles long, one wide, uninhabited, uncultivated, not intersected in the middle by roads running down the length, as flat as possible, situated on a railway, and near my establishment or at least near the governmental district of Düsseldorf.[3]

Moltke's reply suggested he should apply to "*seine Exzellenz den Kriegsminister von Roon*." That was unkind. The field marshal knew of their feud. Nevertheless Krupp flung down the gauntlet to Roon on April 17, arguing that "prompt rearmament" (*Beschleunigung der deutschen Bewaffnung*) was absolutely vital and offering "to put down a contribution of 25,000 thalers for defraying the cost of the most comprehensive comparative trials, which, it may be assumed, will be held between the cast steel and bronze field guns."[4]

The Kriegsminister's answer of April 22 was infuriating. For the present, he said, he would "refrain from any definite comment on your proposals" except to marvel at "the lightness with which you treat your own financial interest." Next day Alfred appealed directly to the Kaiser. Noting "the preference, now making itself felt in influential circles, for the introduction of . . . a bronze four-pounder" and attributing it to officers who, "with their well-known opposition to every progress which proceeds from my establishment, and their clinging to bronze, dominate the opinion and decision of the majority," he stated flatly (and accurately) that "Using bronze for guns is a squandering of men, horses, and material (*Verschwendung an Menschen, Bespannung und Material*), a waste of priceless powers which are sacrificed in vain, but which play a decisive role if harnessed to the finest and most effective cast steel guns (*besten, wirksamsten Gusstahlrohren*)." Despite "all the resistance of hidebound prejudice," he argued, "cast steel has won its present position as the most indispensable material in war as in peace." Europeans of 1871 must realize that they were living in the Steel Age. "Railways, the greatness of Germany, the fall of France, belong to the Steel Age; the Bronze Age is past." He renewed his appeal for "comparative trials." Already, he said, the Krupp cannon which crushed Louis Napoleon were obsolescent: "The present type of gun stands to the new one in much the same relation as the needle gun to the chassepot." A muzzle velocity of 1,700 feet was now essential. Alfred was ready to test such a weapon, and he wanted to provide Wilhelm's army with two thousand of them.[5]

Privately Wilhelm was inclined to agree; the Kaiser told Podbielski that he was talking "*Blödsinn*" (nonsense). And Bismarck agreed with Krupp that a large part of the victors' indemnity must be spent fortifying the new frontier against the vengeful French. But this was no time to ride roughshod over Roon. In his own way he, too, had contributed mightily to the new empire. His organization of the army had made possible the lightning mobilizations of 1866 and 1870, and the Offizierskorps was well aware of it. Later he could be outflanked. Meanwhile the Cannon King was told that he must be patient. Alfred couldn't be that, of course; for five weeks he had been camped in the capital on the War Ministry's Berlin doorstep, and on the last day he wrote Voigts-Rhetz, vowing, "I will do all in my power to get Prussia better armed than hitherto to combat the growing inclination of the most influential people to reintroduce bronze guns." Nevertheless he returned to the Ruhr defeated. Apparently Sedan had changed nothing; the prophet was still honored in every land save his own. Saint Petersburg was again courting him (he shrewdly backed away on the ground that if "there were war between Germany and Russia, which is by no means impossible, obviously I could not make munitions to be used against the Fatherland"). His own wooing of Louis Napoleon had been a near thing, and he now knew it. Similarly, the civic leadership in Birmingham, Alabama, wanted him to move his shops there. He stayed where he was, confident that the Prussian tide would turn; "All the military authorities and the Test Commission have always been against me. I shall come out on top in spite of them all, as in the past."[6]

Yet he was getting a little old to play the waiting game. He felt, not unreasonably, that arms makers, like armies, were entitled to intervals of peace. His private life continued to be chaotic. That April he lacked even primitive creature comforts. Owing to his unfortunate choice of French building materials — not to mention his designation of himself as architect — Villa Hügel remained unroofed. He had expected the peace treaty to bring a resumption of limestone shipments from Chantilly, but the Paris Commune and its aftermath kept the quarries closed until autumn. Nice was inaccessible for the same reason, so in mid-September Alfred took his wife and seventeen-year-old son to England. They settled down for the winter at Torquay, which Bertha liked because its Mediterranean palms reminded her of the Riviera, and whose docks, her husband noted with relish, had played a key role in repulsing the Spanish Armada.

Frau Krupp lolled about. Young Fritz, a zealous botanist, collected specimens. Alfred bombarded the Fatherland with letters. The thickness of his Torquay correspondence and his interpolated comments in it — "I must close today, for I am ever so tired"; "I can't help it if the pencil wants to run"; "Now time to go to bed. God assist you to understand my writing" — suggested he did little else. He continued to lob oleaginous missives into Berlin, assuring the crown prince that "I keep your portrait in front of me early and late." To the Prokura he sent detailed instructions on how to clean boilers, warnings against "the use of inferior qualities of iron ore [which] might be the ruin of the works," moralistic sermons, and certain building orders. He wanted work begun on three housing developments for Kruppianer. Then, "as soon as the season permits," the Stammhaus must "be raised as much as necessary, provided with new sills and doorposts in place of any which may have rotted, and restored to the exact state in which it was originally. Room A must have only one window as formerly, and all the window shutters a ventilation hole like this ♡ . . . . The little house is to have no business purpose at all. I wish it to be maintained as long as the works exist, that my successors, like myself, may look with thankfulness and joy at this monument, this source of the great works. May the house and its history give courage to the fainthearted and imbue him with perseverance. May it be a warning not to despise the humblest thing, and to beware of arrogance."[7]

The humblest thing in Essen continued to be the great castle which was to replace the Stammhaus and the Garden House. Although the limestone was now coming through and a housetop of sorts had been erected, the builders informed Alfred that the interior fittings would not be in place until next summer and that occupancy was out of the question until 1873 — three years late. "It looks more and more as though I am to be disappointed," he wrote. "I always get a belated explanation of the latest lack of activity from Herren Funke and Schürenberg [the builders]. . . . Words and promises will not satisfy me. I expect deeds, and I shall take care that anyone who shows himself too weak to fulfill his promises, or who once imposes on me, shall have no chance to do so again." To Voigts-Rhetz he wrote on March 2, 1872, "Since I have been here I have occupied myself with nothing except arranging about my house in Essen." That was untrue. In the same letter he requested a report from the general on "what success you and Prince Bismarck have had with the Kaiser." Allegations from the Royal Test Commission could be quickly disproved, he said, "since my Essen Testing Committee has been through them all and can answer any question on the spot." Then, the following day, a telegram reached Torquay from Ernst Eichhoff. Bertha's aging cousin reported dissension in the works. Alfred fired back demands for more information:

> *Warum soll ich nicht wissen wer gährt und was gährt? . . . so kann jetzt nur mündlich das letzte Wort geäussert werden, worauf ich durchaus gefasst bin.*

> Why should I not know what is brewing and who is brewing it? Who is in opposition and who is in revolt, and why? — The truth is nothing like so bad as the apprehensions one can entertain. I shall not write any more, and if all that I have written already has not sufficed, I can only settle matters by coming in person, and to that I have quite made up my mind.[8]

Before leaving he snatched off his wig and thrust his fringe of real hair under Bertha's eyes, insisting she agree that it had grown whiter since he left the Ruhr. She did, and then confided to her own notepaper, "*Was man alles erleben kann, ist wirklich fabelhaft*" (It's really remarkable what a lot one can put up with).[9]

✠    ✠    ✠

The row in Essen was between the Prokura and the technical department. It was insignificant, but this was a good time for the Cannon King to come back; Voigts-Rhetz had succeeded in staging a bronze vs. steel test at Tegel. His fervent account of it awaited Krupp: ". . . A trial of the gun has recently been made on a considerable scale with the *most brilliant* results . . . and this has led to the intelligent majority of the Test Commission all declaring themselves in favor of your gun as the *only* gun for the artillery." In consequence, the general reported, Bismarck had "now harnessed himself to your triumphant chariot with all his energy." Jubilantly Alfred scrawled across the paper, "Now we have the great arbiter (*Gebieter*) of Germany's destiny pulling with us!" and circulated it among members of the Prokura. He promised Berlin a thousand cannon this year and a second thousand by the end of 1873. In January the Czar had ordered five hundred, specifying caliber and design which would make them "as destructive in effect," but Alfred directed that Saint Petersburg's guns be built "much heavier, and therefore less maneuverable." If this seems less than fair to a client who, after all, had been far more generous than Berlin, Krupp's delicate position must be borne in mind. In pushing for this contract he had repeatedly insisted that his sole motive was patriotism.

The commitment to the Romanovs was awkward. He had to do something to explain it away.[10]

He had to do something else: deliver the guns to the Reich and the Russians. Producing four flawless giant barrels each day and meeting his other obligations was clearly beyond the present capacities of the Gusstahlfabrik. *Also:* he would have to expand. Actually he had begun to multiply his capital outlay while still in England. From Torquay he had authorized the purchase of a controlling interest in the Orconsera Iron Company, which was about to begin mining a million-dollar field near Bilbao, Spain. Pondering the problem of transporting ore from the Bay of Biscay, he decided that he needed a fleet. "English ship prices are absolutely enormous and the plates are bad," he wrote Eichhoff in June. "I simply cannot get rid of the idea that . . . we ourselves must build." He commissioned the construction of four vessels by Dutch shipwrights in Vlissingen and Rotterdam, and that was only the beginning of his new expansion fever. In Germany he made down payments on three hundred mines and bought out two of his competitors, the Hermannshütte at Neuwied and the Johanesshütte in Duisburg. Johanesshütte alone owned four blast furnaces, and he paid inflated prices for both. The Konzern was dangerously exposed. As Meyer wrote Eichhoff, "The possibility is by no means a remote one that Krupps may find itself involved in serious embarrassment within a very short time. And even if in the end they manage to recover, you will nevertheless be left with heavy obligations to meet. Herr Krupp suffers from a mania for buying things (*die Manie alles kaufen zu wollen*). The Cologne bankers are beginning to have grave doubts and are against any further commitments to him."[11]

The mania was widespread in the new empire. Between 1871 and 1874 German heavy industry doubled, and while no other industrialist went to Alfred's lengths — he had increased his liabilities by 32 million marks — virtually everyone with a stake plunged. Fueled by French reparations, the flame swelled ever larger. Even the prudent Bismarck was quietly dabbling in stocks with his broker Bleichröder. *Eisen und Blut* had been replaced by *Bereichert Euch*, feather your nest. Then came the crash. In September 1873 the French made their last payment. The slide began with a series of Viennese bank failures, spread across the continent, vaulted the Atlantic, and hit Wall Street September 20, when the New York Stock Exchange was forced to close for ten days. Alfred's obvious course was to retrench. Meyer pleaded with him to cut back. But here he was his father's son. Instead he extended his short-term credits — paying 900,000 marks for one mine and 4,000,000 for another — and thereby reduced his financial advisers, as *die Firma*'s chronicle notes, "to a state of sheer incomprehension." He was obsessed with the thought that this, of all times, was the moment to corner the market in raw materials. He wanted enough for his son, grandson, and great-grandson. "In order to assure a future worthy of them," he wrote, "it is essential that the works shall have their own independent sources of ore and minerals, and should extract them and work them as they now draw their water: pure, from their own estates, free of agents and middlemen, and under their own uninfluenced control."[12]

On paper he was the proprietor of the largest industrial enterprise in Europe. As the short-term notes came due, however, the flimsiness of the structure became appallingly evident. Every day huge floating debts drifted in, and only one solution seemed possible — to convert Krupp into a stock company. Alfred rejected it; he bluntly wrote, "We have and will have no shareholders waiting for their dividends." Yet he couldn't wish away the debtors waiting for their cash. It was an impasse, the beginning of what became known among his twentieth-century descendants as *die Gründer-krise*, the Founder's Crisis. To *der Gründer* the way out was clear. He would appeal to the Kaiser. Writing Wilhelm at Ems, he begged "the favor of an audience" to discuss "a private matter, a desire." His Majesty was polite but unresponsive. Early in February, brooding over his desk on his twenty-fifth anniversary as owner of *das Wrack der Fabrik*, Krupp had composed a homily and posted it on the Stammhaus for all Kruppianer to weigh: "The Goal of Work Shall be the General Welfare; Work then is Blessing, Work then is Prayer." Prayerfully he now went to work on the emperor anew. He regarded his establishment, he wrote Wilhelm, "as a national workshop." The factories were "in a certain degree inseparable from the conception of the growth and importance of the state, and consequently indispensable." Therefore to class him with those industrialists who were "just smart businessmen" would be a manifest injustice.[13]

Unfortunately that was precisely how he had to be classed. At the outbreak of the war with France, Prussia had had just eighteen limited liability companies. Now there were over five hundred, and half of them, undercapitalized, were being swept away. To grant one exception would be to open a dam. The most the government could do was to advance sums against future gun orders. But Alfred refused to accept the imperial veto. To him it was inexplicable. His Majesty just didn't understand. Somehow he must be made to see the light, and as late as March of the following year Alfred was still trying to reach him through his chancellor. By now Berlin had begun to wonder whether he could even be called smart. From the capital Meyer wrote Eichhoff: "The boss will probably hear from Prince Bismarck within the next twenty-four hours that there is no possibility whatsoever of his requests being met from public funds. I trust that I can prevent him from making this sort of demand, which can only bring him more harm than good" (*Hoffentlich gelingt es mir, ihn überhaupt von solchen Versuchen abzuhalten, es könnte mehr schaden wie nützen*).[14]

No one could slam a door harder than the Iron Chancellor, and when his thundering *Nein* reached Essen *der Herr Chef* headed for bed. "I don't feel particularly unwell," he wrote his son, "but I don't have the strength for anything, and I suffer every time I try to get up." A succession of doctors named Schweninger, Künster, and Schmidt attended him. The first had the best luck. Ernst Schweninger was personal physician to the chancellor, who, though he couldn't put Krupp on the dole, did want the gunsmith to stay in business. Bismarck's own seizures were much like Alfred's — when things didn't go his way he would retire to his estate at Friedrichsruh and brood beneath its trees for weeks at a time. The doctor had enjoyed a remarkable success in rousing him from such trances. Schweninger's prescription was simple. It consisted of standing over his eminent patient and bellowing, "GET UP!" Arriving in Essen, he went straight to the Gartenhaus, where Krupp was holed up, strode into the master bedroom, and screamed, "AUFSTEHEN!" The scarecrow on the mattress bounded off the mattress and *stand auf*. Then the physician screwed his monocle in place. Staring at the bewildered industrialist, he lectured him: he must give up cigars, limit himself to one glass of red wine a day, and get plenty of fresh air. Alfred obeyed the first, bilked on the second, and defied the third. His method of cheating was ingenious. He could truthfully report that he was, in fact, drinking only one tumblerful each twenty-four hours. But Schweninger hadn't specified how *large* the glass should be, and from Düsseldorf Krupp had acquired one which would hold two liters, nearly a half-gallon. As for oxygen, Alfred didn't believe in it. He was convinced that the scent of dung was more salubrious. Bertha's Dr. Künster, appearing at her insistence, lasted less than a quarter-hour. He gazed down at the inert figure and confessed himself baffled. The figure on the bed stirred angrily. He growled, *"Das müssen Sie selbst ja am besten wissen, was mir fehlt, wozu sind Sie Arzt"* (You ought to know what's the matter with me, you're a doctor). Just then the doctor, accustomed to the more agreeable fragrances of the Riviera, inhaled a powerful whiff of fresh manure. He flashed, *"Entschuldigung, Durchlaucht, ich bin nie Tierarzt gewesen!"* (Excuse me, Sir, I've never practiced as a veterinarian!). The physician then diagnosed his patient's ailment as *"Hypochondrie, die an Geisteskrankheit grenzt,"* hypochondria bordering on insanity. That was the end of Künster. Krupp dismissed him on the spot. Clearly the man didn't know his business. The sole proprietor retained Schmidt, whose chief qualifications seem to have been meekness and a bottomless reservoir of sympathy.[15]

Confined, propped up on pillows, Alfred tried to deal with the financial crisis by drowning it in prose. All his letters and orders were in pencil now ("Ink has a worse effect on my nerves"), and the lead point raced wildly over the paper in a jagged script so large that frequently a full page would hold fewer than a dozen words. To his son he proclaimed, "We must overcome a serious misfortune, parry a heavy blow, avert a disaster." With the Prokura he was less assured. He wondered where to turn — "so many highly placed people cannot *bear* me" (*so viele hochgestellte Leute können mich nicht leiden*) — and finding no haven he became desperate: "There must on no account be any question of slowing down work, closing foundries, working at half-strength or half-time, or only partial employment of the men, for that amounts to mortification, and that would be the *beginning of the end.*" Behind this bombast lay Alfredian cunning; training new Kruppianer would be expensive. Yet something had to give. From Berlin, Meyer wrote Goose, "We are no longer making a profit, and are on the road to ruin! Herr Krupp refuses to believe it; he thinks that an *increase* of talent among the men will quickly secure everything that he understands by 'order'! I warn him every day against illusions of this sort, but quite in vain!" Reluctantly Alfred recognized that a wage cut was inevitable. "With the exception of the machine shops for guns," he decreed, workmen "must get accustomed here, as in England," to their toil being rewarded "handsomely when a large profit is made, and on a low level when it is low." He consoled himself with the thought that he would pick up skilled hands from other depressed factories: "Gradually discharged men from elsewhere will present themselves (also scamps). The best, however, will of their own accord content themselves with lower wages."[16]

It was too late. His creditors were howling for an inventory, and reluctantly he permitted Meyer to bring in a team of auditors. Their verdict was unnerving. His assets — plant, raw materials, unfinished products — had been grossly overvalued. "After the fresh disclosure of yesterday," he wrote Goose next morning, "I am crushed." He pondered "what I must now do, both as a man of honor and as one who does not seek anyone's unhappiness." In a frenzy he scrawled, "*I need ten millions.*" That, too, was a bad estimate. Actually he needed thirty millions — $17,500,000. Dead set against public ownership, he had but one recourse: the bankers. Credit had never been tighter, but in Berlin Meyer dutifully trudged from money changer to money changer. "Bleichröder lacks the resources to grant loans of this magnitude," he reported. "Deichmanns, too, believe that only the Rothschild *Gruppe* . . . would be in a position to do so. Anyway, I would ten times rather do business with Hansemann than with Bleichröder." As it turned out, no one financier was prepared to shoulder the burden. A group of them raised the cash under the supervision of the Prussian State Bank's Seehandlung (Overseas Trading Company). Before Alfred could touch a pfennig of it he was required, on April 4, 1874, to sign what he regarded as "a shameful document." Really it was generous. The Seehandlung merely reserved the right to appoint a comptroller, and the man designated was his own Carl Meyer. That made no difference to Alfred. He regarded April 4 as a black day, marking the firm's capitulation to the "*Judenschwindler*" — despite the absence of Jews among the negotiators.[17]

Krupp's lack of judgment in this business confirmed his worst suspicions about other people; he blamed everyone except himself, and the full weight of wrath fell upon his faithful Prokura. In 1871 he had written from Torquay that the Gusstahlfabrik had "the health and vigor of a fifty-year-old oak tree"; of his directors, he had asked only, "See that you protect the root!" (*Beschützt nur ihre Wurzel!*). Now they had betrayed him. On August 22, nearly five months after his surrender, he wrote Longsdon in London, "I have not slept since. All those who have enjoyed in full measure my confidence and friendship have so much neglected their duty of acting according to principles known to them. . . . I tell you in these few words what miserable feelings occupy my head. . . . I want some rest." He got little, and gave the Prokura less. A stream of abusive notes descended upon its five members. Ernst Eichhoff, embarrassed, died. So did Heinrich Haass, who had never recovered from the stigma of having been Krupp's representative in Paris in 1870. Sophus Goose began to lose interest, and Richard Eichhoff became so maddened by *der Herr Chef* that although he stayed on as his foundry manager, he refused to speak to him. When reproached by Meyer, Alfred would either insist that he could not recall what he had written or reply bitingly, "*Ich habe die Bilanzen nicht gemacht*" (It was not I who drew up the balance sheet) — which was, of course, beside the point. Uncivil with his lieutenants, he formed a strange friendship with "Schwarze Helene," an eccentric woman who lived alone on a cliff overlooking the Ruhr a mile downstream. Afternoons he would gallop over and pour out his troubles to her. Among his colleagues, he was openly called *der grollende Alte*, the old grouch.[18]

He was now permanently entrenched in *der Hügel*. A great iron fence surrounded the estate, and on Sundays workers and their families would press their faces against the bars, peering in at the scape of thick woods and clear rippling water. The cracks had been repaired, the foundations were secure; the Kaiser's apartment was ready for occupancy. Over it a staff stood ready to receive his purple pennant. On the front lawn were ten other flagpoles. Four of them would bear Krupp's personal ensign, now being designed; from the other six would fly the colors of whichever nation he chose to honor. To spare visiting monarchs the indignity of alighting in Essen's train station Alfred designed a special spur for Hügel Park.*

Inevitably the stone-and-steel interior was stark. Remembering the Hügel of her childhood, Alfred's octogenarian granddaughter Barbara, once summed it up to the author in a single grim word: "*Cold.*" Certainly the dimensions were imperial. The entrance hall, with its five great chandeliers, was nearly half as long as a football field, and the length of the dining room table was sixty feet. The castle was large enough to house any crowned head in Europe and his retinue. Eventually virtually all of them

---

* Like everything else on the hill the construction of this private line (*Zechenbahn*) took longer than he expected; it was not operational until 1887, the year of his death. However, it survived the last of the Krupps in 1967.

came, though as a lure for *der Alte*'s wife and son it remained unappealing. Probably Bertha would have stayed away in any event, but Alfred had a chance with Fritz, and the boy did spend a holiday there with a classmate, Alfred Körte. Unfortunately the householder's temper was at its most vile. Körte never saw his host. Instead he encountered notes pinned to doorways, reprimanding him on his conduct. Since the details were specific and accurate, he realized that unseen eyes were watching him all the time. It gave him, he recalled later, a creepy feeling.[19]

Krupp's behavior had nothing to do with his guests. One afternoon nearly a century later his great-grandson Alfried said to this writer, "You know, he was really infuriated by this house." That was the nub of it: a genuine hatred had sprung up between a man and the atrocity he had built. If this suggests that the castle reciprocated his animosity, one can merely note that Alfred thought of it that way; he invested it with a personality, and certainly its conduct toward him was far more malicious than the Prokura's. His elaborate heating system was a failure. That first winter Krupp almost froze. Summer was, if anything, worse. The iron roof turned the interior into a caldron. The ventilators didn't work, and since he had ordered the windows permanently sealed he was constantly gasping for air. Incensed, he had the whole system torn out. The new one was as ineffective as the old — ten years later it, too, was removed.[20]

Two aspects were pleasing: the size of Hügel and its foliage. His conviction that his own body odors were toxic had grown as he aged and was reinforced by the belief that his lungs could exhaust a room's supply of oxygen within an hour, leaving their sole proprietor to be quietly asphyxiated. Now, with three hundred rooms, his guards and servants could bed down for the night and leave vast corridors down which he could roam, napping awhile in one chamber and then, after sniffing the air suspiciously for a trace of carbon dioxide, moving on. He was a living ghost, haunting his own castle; in the darkness he would prowl restlessly from hall to hall on his pipestem legs, a spidery, tortured specter.

Sometimes he paused and looked out upon his trees with satisfaction. The thick stands of sequoia were particularly lovely, but most striking was the single *Blutbuche* (blood beech) by the cavernous main entrance. It was immense then, and in the three generations since its transplanting it has become enormous. There are those in the Ruhrgebiet who say its blood-red leaves became redder each decade, though this, of course, is sheer imagination.[21]

✠     ✠     ✠

On September 1, 1877, the anniversary of Sedan, Kaiser Wilhelm I arrived for his fourth tour of the Gusstahlfabrik and his first stay at *der Hügel*. Accompanying him was a phalanx of generals and princes in glittering *Pickelhauben* and the rumor, widely credited in the press, that *der Allerhöchsteselber* was checking up on a small investment he had made in the works. Understandably it irked Alfred, who wished it were true, and the monarch was obliged to issue repeated denials through his Finance Minister. The Kaiser's sole motive was his consuming passion for military details. His impression of the sprawling new castle is not extant, but he was delighted with Krupp's gift of two highly polished guns designed to fit his yacht *Hohenzollern.* In turn he presented Alfred with a life-size portrait of himself in *"ewiger Dankbarkeit"* (eternal gratitude) for the Cannon King's contribution to Prussia's victory seven years earlier.[22]

Despite Alfred's dislike of paintings, Hügel was becoming rather cluttered with them.* Foreign sovereigns were indifferent to his accounting problems; figures defining range and muzzle velocity were far more interesting to them, and since the fall of France virtually every chief of state with martial aspirations had either exchanged gifts with Krupp or struck a medal in his honor. The only notable absentees were Victoria of England and MacMahon of France, who were nursing arms industries of their own, and the Presidents of the United States. Alfred ought to have found some way of paying tribute to the U.S.A., for thanks to American orders he was speedily paying off his great debt. He had not seen Thomas Prosser since 1851, but under the contract they had signed in London the correspondence between New York and Essen had grown thicker each month. From Prosser's first advertisement in his behalf — "Gents much prefer KRUPP's STEEL for all kinds of Road Tools, such as cold chisels, claw bars, punches, etc." — a mighty transatlantic business had boomed. Now it was Prosser's clients who advertised; the Canadian Pacific Railway told its passengers that "Krupp Crucible Steel Tires are used exclusively throughout the whole C.P.R. SYSTEM for your safety." The New Haven, Central Railroad of Georgia, Chicago, Burlington and Quincy, Erie, Louisville and Nashville, Michigan Central, Chicago and Northwestern, Boston and Maine, and Philadelphia and Reading were also equipping their cars with Alfred's seamless steel tires. Nearly all railroads were using Krupp rails: the New York Central, Illinois Central, Delaware and Hudson, Maine Central, Lake Shore and Michigan Southern, Bangor and Aroostock, Great Northern, Boston and Albany, Florida and East Coast, Texas and Pacific, Southern Pacific, and Mexican National. A few years after the Kaiser's visit a young American railroad magnate named E. H. Harriman placed a single order for 25,000 tons of 80-pound rails in behalf of the Southern Pacific — a year's supply. In 1874, when Alfred was going through his ordeal with the Prussian bankers, Essen had shipped 175,000 tons of rails from Hamburg

---

* It still is. Among others Wilhelm I, Friedrich III, and Wilhelm II, each in full uniform, hang on the walls of the main hall with their bejeweled Kaiserinnen beside them. Only Hitler — who occupied the place of honor from 1933 to 1945 — has been removed.

to east coast ports. Prosser's books in New Jersey show that cables ordering rails and tires were being dispatched to the Ruhr almost daily. The volume was running into several millions of dollars annually; Kruppstahl was crisscrossing a nation.[23]

Schneider and Armstrong were helping, though far behind, the British grossing a half-million dollars a year from American railways. At the time, this traffic in peaceful steel appeared to be an unmixed blessing. Actually its implications were sinister. The U.S. steel industry was still a fledgling giant. As it approached its full height in the 1880's — the rate of growth was already fantastic — it would dwarf Europe's forges. The American market would then be closed to the continent's steelmakers. To stay in the black they would be obliged to plunge ever deeper into munitions. Since they were competitive and backed by their governments, the consequence was to be a deadly arms race. To be sure, that race was fueled by other fires: chauvinism, a wobbly balance of power, the adventurism of the first Kaiser's grandson, Balkan nationalism, and France's yearning for revenge. Yet all these stimuli might have been damped down had not the Ruhr, the Midlands, and Le Creusot given them the tools to finish the job.[24]

The merchants of death could not read the future. They had no idea that they were digging graves for the flower of European youth. In a message to his Kruppianer, Alfred wrote,

> *Wir gehen mit Frieden einer günstigen Zeit entgegen und ich war von grosser Hoffnung für die Zukunft erfüllt. Was nützen aber alle Aufträge, wenn Arbeit und Transport durch Krieg gehemmt werden! . . . Den Gram möchte ich nicht erleben.*

> With peace we have been progressing toward a time of prosperity, and I have been filled with immense hope for the future. But what would be the use of all our contracts if work and transport were throttled by war! Our factory might even be destroyed; in all events it would be necessary to be prepared for discharges, even for the complete halt of all work. And then, in the place of earning, there would come distress, the pawnshop, and the moneylender, for my own assets and the welfare funds would rapidly be exhausted. I pray I may never live to see that tragedy.[25]

Here Alfred may have originated that bleak justification for all arms races — that there can be no peace without sharpened swords — though historians have recognized instead a Bismarck paraphrase of it. In a famous speech on February 6, 1888, seven months after Krupp's death, the Eisenkanzler was to tell the Reichstag that increased armaments were the best guarantee for peace: "That sounds paradoxical, but it is true. With the powerful machine which we are making of the German army, no aggression will be attempted." By then it was to sound so persuasive that the delegates supported him unanimously.[26]

Thus, while praying against war, Alfred stoked the furnaces for it. The very occasion for this proclamation was a general election in which he was urging his men to vote for "patriotic members of the Reichstag, so that the military estimates, which alone can assure peace, may become law. Only then will the Reich be protected."[27] He meant it; he really believed that the one way to avoid a general European war was to build an invincible Teuton juggernaut. And though he appears to have been unaware of the extent to which American dollars were rescuing him from his follies in the Panic of '73, he certainly appreciated the value of his peaceful products. At his direction the Konzern's trademark had become the three interlocking circles. In the twentieth century thousands of Europeans came to assume that it represented the muzzles of three cannon, but on June 7, 1875, when Longsdon first registered it in England's *Trade Marks Magazine,* no one was confused. Although Krupp cannon had increasingly dominated his displays at the big international exhibitions of those years in Sydney, Melbourne, Amsterdam, Berlin, and Düsseldorf, the firm continued to be celebrated for its railroad products.

In the Ruhr the decade after Kaiser Wilhelm I's coronation was largely devoted to experimentation in technology, management, politics, and, to Alfred's anguish, the financing of the new heavy industry. The great technical breakthrough came in 1875 with Gilchrist Thomas's invention of what is now known as the basic process of steelmaking. Patented two years later, it eliminated Henry Bessemer's "fatal enemy" phosphorus by lining Bessemer converters with limestone and dolomite. These absorbed the phosphorus from pig iron and passed it off as slag. At first Krupp was alarmed by the process. He had just invested a fortune in Spain to acquire phosphorus-free ores. As it happened, his ores there did decline in value, but the basic process gave him something far more precious. Alsace and Lorraine were rich in phosphorescent ore fields. And now, thanks to the Iron Chancellor, they belonged to Germany. In the words of one of Thomas's biographers, "Alsace-Lorraine became worth fighting for."[28]

Krupp's managerial difficulties were solved in 1879 with the appointment of a beefy, walrus-mustachioed strong man named Hanns Jencke to the chairmanship of the Prokura. Alfred liked him because he sat a horse well. He had another, more significant recommendation: he came to Essen from the Kaiser's official family, where he had been a key official in the Reich Treasury. For the next twenty-three years Jencke directed the firm's international activities, serving as the Konzernherr's executive officer and consulting him only on vital issues of policy. His arrival at the works marked the beginning of regular exchanges of personnel between the government and *die Firma;* henceforth Krupp proposals were far likelier to receive a sympathetic hearing in Berlin. At the same time Alfred — the empire's most powerful industrialist — backed Bismarck to the hilt. He would have done so anyhow out of conviction, but a *kaisertreu* board meant enthusiastic support from his staff.[29]

Like it or not, the Cannon King was deep in domestic politics. Every move he made was watched and judged for its impact on the electorate. So simple a project as the construction of workers' settlements took on political overtones. As the Gusstahlfabrik had expanded, so had the need for manpower. The first immigrants had been farmers from the ridges on either side of the Rhine; they had been followed by Saxons, Silesians, East Prussians, Poles, and Austrians. The Ruhr had become an ethnic crucible. Essen, Dortmund, and Düsseldorf had been rural hamlets in Alfred's youth. Now they were urban giants, spreading across the countryside and absorbing surrounding villages. When Krupp recruited 7,000 migrants in the early 1870's the city's population grew by 25,000. With the sprawl had come congestion — the number of people in Essen's old city had increased from 7,200 in 1850 to 50,000; most Kruppianer were living in huts — and, inevitably, disease. Alfred, hypersensitive to germs, ordered the Prokura to clear the area "where the cholera pesthouses are." He authorized "the erection of family residences on our own sites," and as the finishing touches were put on Villa Hügel he opened workers' barracks for 6,000 people. Essential services were provided for residents: stores, churches, playgrounds, and schools.[30]

On the surface nothing could be less controversial than the building of classrooms. The Reich of the 1870's, however, was riven by Bismarck's *Kulturkampf*. To the chancellor the Catholic Church represented separatism. He had declared war on it by breaking off diplomatic relations with the Vatican, making civil marriage compulsory, and suppressing parochial education. In Torquay, Krupp had planned to build separate schools for the children of Catholic workers. In less than two years he executed a complete about-face. "If we take a hand in separating people," he wrote on June 22, 1873, "the consequence would be Catholic and Protestant districts in our settlements, enemy quarters opposite one another, quarrels and fights between the schoolchildren, despotism of the priest in the Catholic quarters, the ultimate necessity of entirely removing one creed and allowing only one to exist. They must all live mixed together." He became a convert to secular education. "The priests," he decided, merely wanted "to increase their power." To thwart this "scheme of clerical ambition and its tools" he insisted upon classrooms "in which children of all creeds get used to one another at an early age, get to know one another, play (and quarrel) together." Bismarck himself could not have presented his own case more deftly.[31]

The Second Reich was not a dictatorship. To retain the loyalty of the Kaiser's new subjects the chancellor had vested legislative power in two houses, the Bundesrat, representing the member states, and the Reichstag, elected by all German men over twenty-five. From the years before the war the empire had inherited three parties: the Conservatives, Progressives, and National Liberals. Now the embittered Catholic Party made four and the even more bitter Social Democrats five. It was this fifth which was to haunt the last years of *der Grosse Krupp*, as Alfred was now known. The founder of the Sozialdemokratische Partei Deutschlands (SPD) had been Ferdinand Lassalle, a gifted, eccentric disciple of Marx who began to organize German workingmen in Leipzig in 1863. The following year he was killed in a duel. The Great Krupp regarded him with contempt. The fact that Schneider's gun shops had been crippled in 1870 by a strike whose leader had been Adolphe-Alphonse Assi, an equally erratic member of the Marxist International given to delicate embroidery (he had met disaster in 1871 as chairman of the Paris Commune) amused Alfred no end. Then the SPD called a strike of all miners in the new Reich. Krupp's Graf Beust field was included. Suddenly the Social Democrats weren't funny any more. He scribbled orders that "neither now nor at any future time" should a former striker "be taken on at our works, however shorthanded we may be." Alfred wanted it clearly understood that he meant "Strikes in all spheres (*Streike in allen Sphären*) . . . Whenever a strike appears to be imminent in any clique, I shall come there at once, and then we shall see about settling the lot. I intend to act quite ruthlessly, for there is, as I see it, no other possible course. . . . What does not bend can break (*Was nicht biegt mag brechen*).[32]

On reflection he now concluded that "Lassalle with his philosophy has sown devilish seed." To stamp it out he drew up one of the most significant documents in the four centuries of the Krupp dynasty. Alfred called it the *Generalregulativ* of September 9, 1872. Issued twelve weeks after the miners' walkout, the General Regulations comprised seventy-two articles, signed by Alfred as sole proprietor and distributed to every worker. For nearly a century the *Generalregulativ* was to remain the Konzern's basic constitution. It is not too much to call it a blueprint for all German industry. Everything which was to emerge in the decades ahead — the rigid chain-of-command system, vertical and horizontal integration, the establishment of cartels — was tersely set forth in its fine Gothic script. At the time, however, the sole proprietor was preoccupied with labor unions. The rights and responsibilities of each Kruppianer were spelled out, with the overwhelming emphasis on the worker's obligations to the firm:

> *Untreue und Verrat muss mit aller gesetzlichen Strenge verfolgt werden . . . denn wie aus dem Samen die Frucht hervorgeht und je nach seiner Art Nahrung oder Gift, so entspringt dem Geist die Tat — Gutes oder Böses.*

The full force of authority must be used to suppress disloyalty and conspiracy. Those who commit unworthy acts must never be permitted to feel safe, must never escape public disgrace. Good, like wickedness, should be examined through a microscope, for there truth is to be found. Even as a seed bears fruit in direct ratio to the nourishment or poison it is given, so is it from the spirit that an act, benign or evil, arises.

The shop was entitled to a man's "full and undivided energy," and workmen were expected to display punctuality, "loyalty," a love of "good order," and freedom from "all prejudicial influences." Lest anyone misinterpret this last, there was a further provision that "refusing to work" or "inciting others thereto" meant an employee "may never again become a member of the concern." Indeed, "no person known to have taken part in troublemaking of a similar kind elsewhere may be given employment in the firm." The blacklist, in sum, was now official.[33]

What may strike the Ausländer as odd is that Alfred's General Regulations were regarded — and in Essen are still regarded — as liberal. For the first time a German firm was spelling out its duties to its men. Kruppianer could lay claim to "a health service, a relief fund . . . a pension scheme, hospitals and homes for the aged" and, though this would not come into effect until 1877, Krupp's "Life Insurance Institution." Nothing remotely resembling this may be found in the archives of the other titans who were emerging from the industrial revolution. What Alfred was achieving was the transformation of Essen into the largest, most stable company town in history. His low-cost housing colonies, each of them named for a Krupp ancestor, were already functioning. He had established a bread factory, a wine store, a butcher plant, a hotel, and a charity fund for families left destitute by the periodic flooding of the Ruhr. Soup kitchens and public works projects startlingly like those which would appear sixty years later during the Great Depression were available to the unemployed. Before the SPD could establish workable cooperatives, Krupp's Konsum-Anstalt — a chain of nonprofit retail outlets open to all employees and their families — was in business. Of course, a man dismissed from his job lost everything, including his pension. Elsewhere, however, pensions didn't even exist. Alfred may have been a mad genius, but that he was a genius cannot be doubted.[34]

Such paternalism, Norman J. G. Pounds pointed out in his study of the Ruhr, "was contrary to the social and political development of the time." Krupp meant it to be. Despite his repeated insistence that as a businessman he was "unpolitisch," the Generalregulativ was a political document. Alfred sent the Kaiser a copy, which survives in the Krupp family archives; on the title page, in his bold, jagged hand, is the inscription, *Originally determined for the protection and flowering of the works. Besides that, it is useful for the prevention of socialistic errors.* Among those who saw the moral was Wilhelm's chancellor. The parallels between Alfred's text and Bismarck's social welfare legislation of 1883, 1884, and 1889 are unmistakable. In 1911 the Reich's Workmen's Insurance Code was to extend to all laborers the rights *der Grosse Krupp* had given his men nearly four decades before, and the following year Kaiser Wilhelm II declared in Essen that the Iron Chancellor had been prodded by Krupp. Echoes of the General Regulations were to be heard in the Third Reich. Hitler wrote in *Mein Kampf* that his own program had begun with a study of Bismarck's social reforms, and the slogan of the Führer's Labor Front leader Robert Ley — *"Die Volksgemeinschaft muss exerziert werden"* (Community spirit must be drilled) — was taken almost verbatim from Alfred's fourth article.[35]

It is the judgment of history that between the Franco-Prussian War and World War I, German workmen traded freedom for security, with ghastly consequences for themselves, the Fatherland, and the entire world. By American standards the Reich's labor movement never passed the forelock-tugging stage; it was Michael Bakunin, the exiled Russian anarchist, who observed that the Germans' passion for authority made them shrink from freedom: "They want to be at once both masters and slaves." Yet the swap of liberty for creature comforts was not made meekly. The SPD continued to be a vital, abrasive force. The Ruhr, with its tremendous influx of people from the far corners of the empire and beyond, was especially vulnerable to agitators who told them that industrial feudalism was not the only answer to their plight. Alfred, uneasy despite his preventive measures, told the Prokura he favored *"Gesinnungsschnüffelei"* (snooping). He ordered "a constant quiet observation of the spirit of our workers, so that we cannot miss the beginning of any ferment anywhere; and I must demand that if the cleverest and best workman or foreman even looks as though he wants to raise objections, or belongs to one of those unions, he shall be discharged as quickly as practicable, without consideration of whether he can be spared." The first report from *die Firma*'s snoopers stunned him. Lassalle's followers were not only present in Essen; the Gusstahlfabrik had become *"ein Brutstätte der Sozialdemokratie,"* a hotbed of Social Democrats. Henceforth the specter of the Red movement hulked ever larger in Alfred's web of private fears, and his first, impulsive reaction was also destined to be remembered and quoted by the Nazis:

> *Ich wollte, dass jemand mit grosser Begabung eine Gegenrevolte zum Besten des Volkes anregte, mit fliegenden Arbeiterbatallionen von jungen Leuten!*

I wish somebody with great gifts would start a counterrevolution for the best of the people — with flying columns, labor battalions of young men![36]

✠     ✠     ✠

In the last quarter of the nineteenth century the Ruhr barons, discovering that they were indispensable to the Second Reich's martial might, drew up their own terms for coexistence with Berlin. In Alfred's case those terms were high, and were met in full. The exact extent of his contribution to the ensuing campaign against the SPD is a matter of conjecture. He himself had no way of measuring it. He pressed certain views upon Berlin; action followed. Since the All-Highest and his chancellor shared his beliefs, something would have been done in any event. Nevertheless there is little doubt that the vehemence of the repression owed much to *der Grosse Krupp*. The men in denim caps, unlike those in spiked helmets, had no claim upon the emperor's affections. Alfred knew more about them than Wilhelm. He was the most influential industrialist in the empire, the one closest to the All-Highest, the one most hostile to the Social Democrats. Under these circumstances he could not hold his tongue.

To the Kaiser he wrote that unless the strongest possible measures were taken, "one enterprise after another will close down. The iron industry will die out. Ironworks will be indistinguishable from ruined castles. My own establishment, I do not hesitate to declare, will meet with the same fate. It may well be that my successor will be left with nothing but the determination to emigrate to America" (*nach Amerika auszuwandern*). Steps must be taken to "undermine" the "social danger on the horizon." He had provided Kruppianer with benefits out of his own pocket, knowing there was no prospect of any return, but he intended "to be and to remain master in my own house" (*in meinem Hause*). The Second Reich should not "nurse a serpent at the breast"; those "who want to disturb the peace" should be treated with "the utmost rigor." Bismarck was "Germany's greatest creditor. We owe him more than any benefactor of German blood since Luther." Alfred prayed that "the great prince will overcome his malicious opponents."[37]

From Essen the task of Prussian leadership appeared to be clear. As a misanthropist, Krupp had no faith in the electorate, and he wanted universal manhood suffrage abolished — "the franchise (*Stimmrecht* should be withdrawn from people without property." That price was too high; much as the hardheaded chancellor would have enjoyed turning back the clock, he knew it was impossible, and elections to the Reichstag were scheduled nineteen months later, for June 30, 1877. On February 11 Alfred began coaching his men; he posted a proclamation in all shops warning that a vote for the SPD was a vote for "*die Faulen, Liederlichen, und Unfähigen*" (the idle, dissolute, and incompetent). He went on to admonish them to "Enjoy what you have. When work is over, stay in the circle of your family with your wife, children, and the old people, and think about household problems and education. Let that be your politics. Then you will be happy. But spare yourself the excitement of big questions of national policy. Issues of high policy require more time and knowledge than the workman has at his command (*Höhere Politik treiben erfordert mehr freie Zeit und Einblick in die Verhältnisse, als dem Arbeiter verliehen ist*).[38]

Nearly a half-million voting Germans dissented; in the general election the SPD elected a dozen men to the 397-member Reichstag. To the twentieth-century political eye their victory seems slight. They held but 3 percent of the seats in one of the empire's two parliamentary bodies. As presiding officer of the Bundesrat, Bismarck initiated legislation and appointed administrative officers. His rule could hardly have been regarded as threatened. Moreover, judged by the brands of Socialism which were arising in other European countries, the demands of the Reich's Social Democrats were ludicrously mild. They suggested that more power be vested in the Reichstag, and they urged free public education, civil liberties, free trade, income and inheritance taxes, the elimination of military influences from the emperor's court, and greater cooperation with other nations in the interests of peace.

In Germany, however, all this was heresy. The morning after the returns had been totted up Krupp — who had found their campaign for peace particularly odious (he paraphrased it as "defenselessness is no disgrace") — summarily dismissed thirty men on suspicion of "spreading Socialist doctrines," and in Berlin Bismarck, weighing the "black" evil of Catholicism against the "red" evil of Socialism, opted for *schwarz*. He called on Pope Leo XIII and agreed to a truce. Back home he rammed through the most reactionary measures since the heyday of Metternich, his celebrated "law dealing with Socialism" (*Sozialistengesetz*). Abetted by threats against the All-Highest's life, he persuaded the Reichstag to outlaw SPD societies, meetings, and newspapers. Although the majority refused to gag debate or interfere with the new SPD deputies, it did ban the collection of funds which, "by means of Social Democratic, Socialistic, or Communistic designs, aim at the overthrow of the existing order of state or society." Anyone circulating SPD literature or even speaking favorably of it was to be fined and jailed. Labor unions were to be supervised by the state police, who were authorized to expel from the Reich "any person accused of being a Socialist," and industrial unrest was to be met by martial law. It was the harshest body of German legislation since the Carlsbad Decrees of 1819 crushed liberalism in the German Confederation. It also gave every appearance of being effective. The SPD leaders fled to Switzerland. In Essen, Krupp's archives note, Alfred was "overjoyed."[39]

The plain fact is that his convictions had become those of an out-and-out tyrant. Even in his twenties he had treated Kruppianer as though they were his property. In growing older, he had grown worse; severe as the chancellor's *Sozialistengesetz* was, it was a parody of the despotism at Villa Hügel and in the Gusstahlfabrik. Alfred had now reached his late sixties, and with the onset of senescence the streak of irrationalism in his personality broadened and deepened. For long periods he withdrew from society, communicating only by pencil. One day word reached him that a certain foreman had declined to deliver crucibles in the rain, arguing that the quality of the steel would suffer. In the morning the man found a note on his toolbox: "The most delicate thing in the world, a newborn infant, is taken to church in all weathers. No need to look for a more striking example." The note was unsigned. A signature was unnecessary. Everyone knew that handwriting. His behavior toward his guests on the hill was often wild. The castle attracted some of the most powerful and sophisticated men in Europe, with their wives. They were there as potential customers. Prudence, let alone civility, should have prompted their host to receive them hospitably. Yet when the mood was on him he treated them as he had his son's friend Körte. If he saw or heard of the most innocent flirtation between an unmarried couple, he didn't wait until the sinner had retired; among his surviving documents are several slips of paper slashed with that unmistakable calligraphy and reading: "A carriage is waiting at the door to take you to the station. Alfr. Krupp."[40]

But it was his employees who felt the full force of his whip hand. In one of his stranger "Dear Works" letters he actually proposed that all Kruppianer wear uniforms, with hash marks (*Insignien*) for years of service, chevrons for foremen, and epaulettes for managers. Sketches were enclosed. The five members of the Prokura, studying them, realized that they would look like the doormen at the Essener Hof, Alfred's new hotel for visiting salesmen. Jencke tactfully pointed out to him that the grimy factory air made gilt impractical, and Alfred (who presumably would have dressed himself as a *Feldmarschall*) withdrew the plan. Nevertheless he never stopped trying to dictate attire. The notices on the doors of his guest bedrooms specified required dress. His preferences were always out of style. Discovering that Hügel maids were wearing black stockings — obviously the sensible thing to do, for the factory smog reached the hill — he sharply reprimanded them; white stockings had been customary among domestic help when he was young, and they must wear white here. Writing to his son he remarked petulantly that "luxury has increased in all classes and remarkably in the lower class"; the result of this "German fat living" was that "women in the journeyman's class (*Gesellenklasse*) wear lace-up boots nowadays and every silly youngster puts on Wellingtons. The masses are no longer content unless they have nothing left to save. The women spend everything on outward show; a dairy maid wants to look like a great lady. . . . Compared with all this, how simply people lived forty to fifty years ago! They were happy and on the whole they fared better. In those days wooden clogs were worn, and they did not let in the water. I wore them myself at work. A pair cost only five silver groschen. I wore them at the damp dripping hammer, on the cold earth, and we warmed them every now and then by shaking inside them glowing ashes from the fire." He informed the Prokura that since "the children of wise parents wear clogs," no flooring was necessary in Krupp schools. Indeed, he thought it mightn't be a bad idea for the directors themselves to slip them on in the Gusstahl-fabrik. Jencke's reply is not extant.[41]

In the plant he became obsessed with punctuality and efficiency. There were fines for everything: tardiness, insolence, running up debts in the Konsum-Anstalt, and misdemeanors which, in another community, would have been handled by city authorities. There were more Krupp policemen than Essen policemen. Workers who wanted to leave their posts for a few minutes, even to answer a call of nature, were required to obtain written permission from foremen. Still Krupp was dissatisfied. All his life he had yearned for "order," and in his own opinion he never got it. In the 1850's he had decreed that "The running around in the turning shop is to cease entirely. Anyone who wants a drink is to tell the foreman, who will have enough fetched for everyone to have some. Anyone who is not content with the regulations can go." Ten years later he had complained, "I want once more to call attention to . . . idleness and waste of time, such as can be seen daily," and on the eve of the war with France he had torn right through a sheet of foolscap, scrabbling furiously, "If one walks around one finds shop dawdlers and loafers everywhere." At the height of the financial crisis he took time to inspect the shops again. "I intend to see order introduced at last," he wrote, "and there is no question of patience, more patience. For years I have been patient in vain; now I cannot be patient for as much as another fortnight." Yet he had to be. Two years later he was raging, "The workman takes a positive pleasure in consuming plenty of gas and oil, if it does not come out of his pocket; he has no feeling for loss of this kind."[42]

Loyalty oaths were now required of every employee, though Alfred had little faith in them. He continued to maintain certain "locked departments" — the men were literally locked in during their shifts — but here, too, he realized that any stocker or welder who quit could take the firm's most cherished technical secrets with him. Once a foreman at one of the new, sensitive Gilchrist Thomas converters walked out and took a job in Dortmund. Krupp pursued him there, and tried to talk the Dortmund police into arresting the man. In a letter back to the firm he fumed:

*Alle anderen Rücksichten sind Nebensache, ob der L——— jemals ein tüchtiger Arbeiter wieder bei uns werden wird und welche Kosten und Mühe wir von der Verfolgung haben werden. . . .*

All other considerations — whether L——— will ever do good work with us again and what expense and trouble will come to us by suing him — these matters are of secondary importance. We must make certain that our contracts and our discipline are respected. A dodger must not have a moment's peace. His position is insupportable. We must attack him with damage suits and public stigma as long and as much as the law allows.[43]

The thought that not even a German court would be offended by the spectacle of a man changing employers, and that no public stigma could be attached to it, never occurred to Alfred. He found the injustice unbearable; the freedom of men to come and go meant that any disgruntled *Dümmling* could sell him down the Ruhr. To him "day pay," as he contemptuously called it, was equally unfair, and he would have reintroduced piecework had he not been warned that his best men would leave. He liked piecework because it seemed so much more efficient. In his passion for efficiency he devoted hours to speculating how he might utilize the Konzern's refuse. It seemed criminal to let all that ash, slag, and dross be carted away; suspecting that some enterprising entrepreneur might be taking advantage of him, he dispatched a team to shadow the wagons. (To his dismay they reported that the rubbish was dumped in the river upstream from *der Hügel*.) Since he was providing his employees with homes, schools, hospitals, and food, he reasoned that their hours away from work belonged to him, too. It is an astonishing fact that most of them agreed, or at any rate displayed no signs of mutiny.* There is no evidence that he provoked either indignation or amusement with what was, by any yardstick, his most extraordinary order to "the Men of My Works." He had been thinking it over, he said, and had come to the conclusion that a faithful workman's places of work included the marriage bed. Just as the sole proprietor was acquiring enough raw materials to last the house of Krupp and *die Firma* for the next ninety-nine years, so must every conscientious Kruppianer strive "*dem Staate recht viele treue Untertanen liefern und der Fabrik Arbeiter eigener Race*"† (to provide the state with plenty of loyal subjects and to develop a special breed of men for the works).[44]

☒   ☒   ☒

Breeding in the night, toiling in the day — let that be their politics. But not all of them were content to confine their electioneering to the forge and the mattress. The "*rote Gefahr*" (Red menace), as he called it, continued to haunt him. From Zurich the SPD exiles were mounting a skillful propaganda campaign, and Essen continued to be vulnerable. In vain Alfred leveled a barrage of manifestos at the shops. Overcoming his fear of ex-Kruppianer betraying him he cried: "I expect and demand complete trust, refuse to entertain any unjustifiable claims, and will continue to

---

* An ancient (Catholic) Kruppianer, whose family had worked for the Krupps since the year of the battle of Waterloo, once told this writer that pictures of the Krupp family always hung in his grandparents' parlor. He was asked, "Where?" He replied, "Just above the saints."

† The English word had not yet been Teutonized to *Rasse*.

remedy all legitimate grievances, but hereby invite all persons who are not satisfied with these conditions to hand in their notices, rather than wait for me to dismiss them, and thereby to leave my works in a lawful manner to make way for others" (*und so in gesetzlicher Weise das Etablissement zu verlassen, um anderen Platz zu machen*).[45]

Even the local newspaper stirred his wrath: "The *Essener Blätter*, among others, is trying by every kind of invention to bring into suspicion the character of the management of my works. . . . To this and similar barefaced lies from malicious enemies I now reply with the following solemn admonition. Nothing, and no consequences to follow, will induce me to allow anything to be bullied out of me."[46]

*Störrisch* workers failed to see the connection between staunch service at the forge and lathe and an abiding desire for the abolition of tariffs, the introduction of an income tax, and free speech. In vain the Master in his House painted gory pictures of Paris in the spring of '71. Social Democrats, he warned: "want to see the French Commune set up here (*wollen die französische Commune aufgeführt haben*). However, once they succeeded in overthrowing all existing situations and conditions, these disciples would only begin quarreling among themselves for dominance. Indeed, that is the hidden aim of all of them. At present they are fighting in a common cause, but that is in the back of their minds. The greater their zeal to bring the victory of their new legislation, the less intention any one of them has in obeying it himself. What they seek is to exploit the misguided masses as the soldiers in their struggles and then to sacrifice them to their own self-seeking."[47]

It left no discernible impression. The mulish masses *wanted* to be misguided. Yet Alfred thought he had found their range, and when a demented anarchist named Emil Hödel tried to assassinate the Kaiser on May 11, 1878, and Bismarck dissolved the Reichstag in hopes of securing an absolute majority for the Conservative (National) Party, Krupp agreed to stand for office as the local Nationalist candidate. It was an appalling miscalculation. With the influx of Poles and South Germans, Essen had become heavily Catholic. The incumbent, Gerhard Stötzel, represented the Catholic (*Zentrum* — Center) Party. *Gemütlich*, extroverted, a former fitter and turner at the works who had become editor of the *Blätter*, he was highly popular. In light of the fact that Alfred was opposed by both the Socialists and the Centrists, he make a remarkably good showing; when the votes were counted on the evening of July 28, Stötzel had a plurality of less than a thousand out of some 27,000 votes cast. But Krupp had never even considered the possibility of defeat. His managers soothed him by reporting that they had canvassed the factory and discovered that Kruppianer, accustomed to seeing the name Alfred Krupp printed on everything, hadn't realized that its presence on the ballot meant he was an applicant for office; they had thought it an imprimatur. The explanation sounds absurd, but may have been true. He hadn't campaigned, and he believed them. He refused to risk mortification twice, however, and when the Conservatives asked him to try again in the next election he swiftly declined. To Herr Baedeker, an editor and the party's Essen chairman, he wrote that the proposition was *"ausgeschlossen"* (out of the question). While "very grateful for the honor," he had "neither the equipment nor the strength and time to occupy myself with any sort of public affair."[48]

That was untrue. The old totalitarian was absorbed by public affairs. His strength and time were occupied by the Bismarckian program closest to his heart: rearmament. The chancellor had urged the Reichstag to approve a peacetime army of 400,000 men. It did. Then he had asked that financial grants to the military be made, not annually, but in perpetuity. The deputies had balked. He had proposed seven-year grants as a compromise, and this had become the Reich's key political issue. Increasingly the government discovered that obituaries of the SPD had been premature. Despite the *Sozialistengesetz* its intended victims had rapidly rebuilt an underground strength of 550,000 voters, and were now surging toward a million. They wanted a Reichstag which would turn Bismarck down, and the Centrists, who had neither forgotten nor forgiven the Kulturkampf, joined them. To Krupp's horror, jolly, beery, fun-loving Stötzel followed the Catholic party line. In the past he hadn't even taken a clear stand on Pius IX's *Syllabus of Errors*. Now he was stumping Essen, denouncing munitions. It was like attacking shipbuilding in Hamburg or chinaware in Dresden. The man had to go, and to dispatch him Alfred personally selected the Nationalist candidate. Stötzel's opponent, *der Grosse Krupp* informed Baedeker, would be his own son Fritz.

This time there would be no confusion about an imprimatur. The name Friedrich Alfred Krupp hadn't been printed on anything except his birth certificate and company records. Furthermore, *der Kanonenkönig* decided to mount an all-out campaign in his behalf. It was to be the firm's most stupendous triumph since Sedan, and much noisier. First the sole proprietor of the Gusstahlfabrik passed the word to the Prokura that Fritz was clearly the man most qualified to serve V*ater* and V*aterland*. Then, in one of his enormous broadsides to employees, he dealt with the issue of rearmament: "In the certainty that I have honorably earned the trust of all, I am now obeying the urge once again to address a few words of advice to our present-day personnel, as I have so often done in the past, and with such good results. Then the questions dealt with security and peace — the purely domestic interests of the factory and of your family life. Today I wish to address myself to the interests of the entire German Reich, interests which are, of course, also our own" (*meine heutige Ansprache betrifft dagegen das grosse Interesse des ganzen deutschen Reiches, welches ja auch das Unsere ist*). After "passing over events which are familiar," he declared that he wanted to "make some remarks in connection with" the general election of members of the Reichstag which the All-Highest had ordered.

*Von dem Geiste der Majorität des nächsten Reichstages wird die Frage abhängen, ob Krieg oder Frieden. . . . und wäre es dann nicht unmöglich, dass bei ungenügender Militärmacht die deutsche Armee, trotz ihrer geschichtlich unvergleichlichen Grosstaten, der Übermacht würde weichen müssen, dass dann das Innere des Reiches mit Krieg überzogen, entkräftet, verheert und das Ganze vielleicht wieder zerrissen werden könnte.*

The question of war or peace will depend upon the spirit of the new Reichstag. If we assemble there united and powerful, France will not dare attack us. But if we appear to be weak and quarreling among ourselves, war is inevitable, and in that event it would not be beyond the realm of possibility that, despite the incomparable valor of its past history, the German army might be obliged to give ground before superior force, and the territory of the Reich might be trampled by war, devastated, and perhaps even its unity torn to shreds.[49]

His real purpose was to see Gerhard Stötzel yield to superior force, the alliance between the SPD and the Centrists torn to shreds at the polls, and perhaps Stötzel himself back in the shops in a lowly capacity. Elaborate plans were laid for the incumbent's destruction, including the crudest forms of intimidation within the works. Not all of them were practical. Alfred demanded that every foreman send him a list of his men, with the political affiliation of each noted beside his name. Since most Kruppianer craftily replied that they were undecided, the scheme failed. But Krupp found out anyhow. Since he controlled the Rathaus, he dictated polling procedures. His most loyal subordinates were appointed *Wahlhelfer* — assistants to the supervisor of elections. Explaining that they wished to "simplify" procedures, they introduced what were, in effect, marked ballots; of varying sizes and colors, these could be traced back to the voter. But something went wrong. Perhaps the men resented Alfred's threats; perhaps they were unmoved by Fritz, who lacked his father's commanding presence. In any event, while Bismarck was winning nationally, his man in Essen was defeated by the embattled Stötzel.[50]

The Kanonenkönig went up in smoke. The whole thing had been a fraud, he declared, a diabolical plot (*Ausgeburt der Hölle*) to discredit his family name. Very well. Now, he told the Prokura, the enemy would see his true mettle. Warily Jencke asked what he meant to do. "Blow up the works!" Alfred cried. His chairman murmured that that would look bad in the annual report. As the representative of the bankers Meyer was bound to object, and besides — how would you blow up a mine? Alfred was momentarily silent. Then: "I'll sell out! I'll settle up with all loyal employees to their satisfaction; no one will lose a penny if I retire." Selling out was possible, Jencke conceded, but why do it now, of all times? The Nationalists were now assured of a fine working majority in Berlin. Bismarck would get his seven-year appropriation, and the firm would receive splendid orders. Alfred stalked out without a word, leaving him the field.[51]

But he wasn't finished with the SPD. In a Berlin hotel room he drafted a fresh order for his sorely tried Prokura. He demanded that all Social Democrats be discharged without notice and that a placard be posted in the shops, announcing the fact: "The next time I go through the works I want to feel at home, and I would rather see the place empty than find some fellow with venom in his heart, such as every Social Democrat is" (*einen Kerl, der nur Feindschaft im Herzen trägt wie jeder Sozialdemokrat es tut*). Detailed instructions followed. Inspectors were to examine every trash bin in the shops and housing developments; anyone who had read literature critical of management or the government was to be sacked. No explanations were to be accepted — and none were. An elderly watchman who had been on the payroll for thirty-three years was dismissed, and so was a worker whose landlady had wrapped his lunch in a *verboten* newspaper. Encouraged by these successes, Alfred ordered the hiring of another inspector to check wastepaper and "used toilet paper" for seditious notes.[52]

"*In diesem Jahrzehnt der grossen Wandlungen altert Krupp zusehends*," the family chronicle reveals; "In this decade of great changes Krupp aged visibly." The fate of the unknown *Klosettpapier Inspektor* is not disclosed.[53]

# 7

✠

## The Rest Is Gas

ALFRED KRUPP's twilight years were the heyday of the small war, and it was this hemic turmoil which established him as Europe's most powerful industrialist. As Winston Churchill observed, war, which later became "cruel and sordid," was then still "cruel and glorious" and the simplest way of resolving international disputes. In the sixteen years between the fall of Paris and Alfred's death the world was in an almost constant state of declared hostility. Not counting insurrections, annexations, *coups d'état*, and crises, there were no fewer than fifteen conflicts involving France, Austria, England, Russia, Afghanistan, Tunis, Italy, Eritrea, Sudan, Serbia, Bulgaria, Montenegro, Peru, Bolivia, Chile, Uruguay, Brazil, Argentina, Paraguay, Turkey, Burma, and China. Spain was preoccupied with what was left of her New World colonies. Even the United States was fighting Indians. Germany was the only great power which was not on the march, and in the peaceful Ruhr Krupp could study battlefield communiqués and apply the lessons in his shops. Each bloodletting served as a testing ground. In addition, most provided a source of favorable publicity. After two of his clients had locked horns in the Russo-Turkish War of 1877–1878 Krupp secured testimonials from *both* sides, and the following year copies of these were dispatched to every member of the House of Commons via Longsdon. In effect Parliament was asked why it should stick with Armstrong when the killing power of Krupp merchandise was superior and, owing to mass production, cheaper.[1]

The variety of *kruppsche* wares now included built-up heavy guns, mountain batteries, coastal defense cannon, and huge howitzers, all of which could be fed from a new turnery with a daily capacity of 1,000 shells. By the middle of the '80's he was the employer of 20,000 Kruppianer, many of whom he had never seen. His proclamations took on an imperial tone; they were addressed to:

DIE ANGEHÖRIGEN MEINER GUSSTAHLFABRIK UND DER MEINER FIRMA
FRIED. KRUPP GEHÖRENDEN BERG— UND HÜTTENWERKE

THE PERSONNEL OF MY CAST STEEL WORKS AND THE MINES AND
SMELTING WORKS BELONGING TO MY FIRM OF FRIED. KRUPP

With a fleet of ships in the Netherlands, ore fields in Spain, and agents in every major capital, he had become an international institution. Nevertheless his own gauge of size continued to be what he could touch and weigh, his measure of success the massiveness of the equipment on his factory floor. When the steam hammer Fritz broke down he introduced 5,000-ton hydraulic presses, and in photographs of Essen at this time one is struck by the disparity between the men and their machines. The Kruppianer in their brimless blue skullcaps appear to be tiny, antlike. All around them are chains with links as large as a man's head; gears twice their height, with teeth thicker than their arms; looming gantries whose rivets are wider than their fists; and fiery forges which could inhale a half-dozen men on their Bessemer-hot breaths. If only as an advertisement, Alfred was determined to remain the producer of the world's biggest pieces of cast steel. At the Philadelphia Centennial Exhibit of 1876 he displayed a gigantic shaft for a German warship and seven cannon, led by a 60-ton leviathan which fired half-ton shells through a 35.5 cm. (13.85-inch) muzzle. It was exactly a quarter-century since he had exhibited his little six-pounder with its 6.5 cm. bore in London, which shows how swiftly the industrial revolution had swept the Ruhr.

The Philadelphia leviathan — "Krupp's killing machine," American newspapers called it — found no market in the United States. (It would have been useless at Little Bighorn, fought in June of that year.) Alfred gave it to the Sultan of Turkey, following the custom which had proved so effective in the past. Even as the presentation of his London gun to Potsdam Palace had eventually extracted the first thalers from the talons of the Prussian eagle, so now did the shipping of Gala fieldpieces and gewgaws reap pleasant harvests; the little model railway he had sent to Li Hung-chang brought steel orders for China's first railroad networks, keeping the Gusstahlfabrik at its daily production capacity of 500 seamless tires and axles, 450 springs, and 1,800 rails just as American demands were beginning to level off. But Krupp had much more than his own ingenuity working for him now. Increasingly the resources of the German government were at his disposal. A Krupp triumph was considered a plume in the Reich's Pickelhaube; a Krupp reverse, a blow to Teuton Blut. Furthermore, the day had passed when slights to Prussian pride were passed off with self-deprecating shrugs. Until 1870 the country's image had been that of the *gemütlich* professor, typified by Professor Bhaer, Jo's kindly suitor in *Little Women* (1868). No more. The crushing of imperial France had given the victors a new, ominous arrogance; these were the years when the Kaiser's soldiers met civilian "insolence" in Alsace-Lorraine with corporal punishment, and when even German ladies were expected to step off a sidewalk to let Offiziere pass. As part of the military establishment Krupp prestige was identified with the army's now sacred honor, and hence inviolable.[2]

Thus a small incident in Serbia was inflated out of all proportion. Already the Serbs were the most difficult of the Balkan states. Internally they had lost one king to assassins, and they were still fuming. Abroad they had signed no fewer than four secret military treaties — with Montenegro, Rumania, Greece, and Austria — and during the '70's they declared war on Turkey twice. Defeated in every battle, Belgrade was anxious to improve its artillery. Competitive tests were staged outside the capital between Krupp, Armstrong, and a French designer affiliated with Schneider. The British were quickly eliminated, but Alfred's luck was bad. After repeated firings his breeches warped. The crew from Essen required thirty minutes to shoot thirty shells at ranges from 1,100 to 4,000 yards; Frenchmen under a Colonel de Bange finished in twenty-three minutes. Realizing that his reputation was at stake, Alfred swiftly cabled instructions to cut his bidding price in half. It was too late. The order had gone to Paris.*[3]

The repercussions were immediate. The *Norddeutsche Allgemeine Zeitung*, Bismarck's newspaper, began printing a series of lurid stories describing hidden defects in the French guns. Horrible accounts told how Serb gunners, making trial runs with the first batch of barrels to be delivered, were butchered by bursting breechblocks, their slimy intestines draped around the bores and mounts. Meanwhile Krupp had discovered a way to recoup. King Carol I of Rumania was coming to Berlin. The Rumanians, like the Serbs, were dissatisfied with their cannon; entering the Russo-Turkish War on the side of Russia, they had been hard pressed at the siege of Plevna. Fritz Krupp was in the Reich capital, and his father instructed him to make an appointment with Carol. "I shall be glad if the audience is favorable to you," he wrote. ". . . It might be well to prepare the ground — not on account of guns, which we can sell at all times and which will, in any event, *be recommended by the All-Highest in Berlin,* but if you can get a chance, tell him about our successes with armor plates." (Author's italics.) Not only Wilhelm but Bismarck and Krupp's admirers on the general staff enthusiastically praised the workmanship of Germany's gun-

---

* To no avail. On November 13, 1885, the hapless Serbs confidently loaded their new 3.1-inchers and made war on Bulgaria. Four days later they were routed at Slivnitza. Only the intervention of the Austrians saved them from complete extinction. With satisfaction Alfred noted, "Bad customers."

smith, and the consequence was a huge new order for the fortress of Bucharest.[4]

Occasionally, to Alfred's intense irritation, rumors of such machinations appeared in the press. On January 17, 1883, he wrote Jencke: "I think the Kaiser knows me well enough to scorn the suggestion, should anyone make it to him, that we stoop to intrigue, to the detriment of the prestige of the nation's power, in order to acquire orders for guns. Our first concern is to serve Kaiser and Reich, and to offer the first fruits of progress in their entirety to the Fatherland (*Allerdings wollen wir vor allem dem Kaiser und Reich dienen, alle ersten Früchte des Fortschritts dem Vaterlande anbieten*).[5]

This was a characteristic Krupp evasion. Presumably the strengthening of Rumanian ordnance resulted in no "detriment of the prestige" of the Reich. It did not preclude conniving and manipulation, though; they were real enough. That same year Germany sent a military mission to Constantinople. The chief of the mission, Baron Kolmar von der Goltz, then a brilliant forty-year-old general — in 1916 he was to die at the front, fighting for Turkey — was specifically instructed to "get the Turks to buy their guns from the firm of Krupp." Alfred himself regarded German diplomats in Turkey as his salesmen. Posting an album of photographs of his cannon to the sultan, he wrote the Prokura, "Undoubtedly the ambassador, who can easily discover my relationship with the All-Highest if he does not already know of it, will give any necessary advice, indicate ways and means, or act as intermediary himself." There is no record that the embassy roused itself in his behalf. Goltz did, however, and with dazzling results. In July 1885 the Turks made a down payment for 926 howitzers, fieldpieces, and coastal defense guns. Until the debt had been paid off, all revenues from the Constantinople customshouse were to be sent directly to Essen. Once again Krupp guns barred the Dardanelles to Krupp's loyal old customer, the czar.[6]

It is impossible to ascertain how great a role bribery played in the arms tariff of these years. Unquestionably money changed hands. The presentation of gifts did not stop at oil portraits, model trains, and *Gala* guns.* In some countries subornation was probably the decisive factor. This seems to have been true in Japan, where Krupp and Schneider vied for the Mikado's favor. The Germans came to Tokyo under a heavy handicap; their hosts, lacking the sophistication of Turks and Russians, regarded Alfred's close

---

* Georges Clemenceau once described the plight of an engineer in a banana republic who had gone out "to execute a contract for a cruiser which a branch establishment of his firm had procured from the government of a European power. On his arrival he began to pay 'commissions' to various people, great and small, who were interested in the contract. At last, to an officer who came with an exorbitant demand, he cried: 'How can I build the cruiser?' The reply was: 'What does that matter, so long as you get paid and we get paid?' " (Engelbrecht and Hanighen, *Merchants of Death* [New York, 1934], 150.)

relationship with Li Hung-chang as an unfriendly act. That misunderstanding might have been cleared up. Like Constantinople, however, Tokyo had felt the need of European military advice. Here the mission was French, and its chief, Louis Émile Bertin, was charged with designing new Japanese warships. Gunnery tests were performed in the Mikado's presence, and the Krupp men carried the day, but the order for new battleship guns went to Schneider. On the other hand, there was a distinct fragrance about the manner in which Krupp acquired a contract to modernize all Belgian forts on the Meuse. Here he was competing with both Schneider and local industrialists in Liège. Brussels newspapers suggested that Ruhr weapons were old-fashioned, and Liège appeared to be the winner until a Captain E. Monthaye of the Belgian general staff published an extraordinary monograph, *Krupp et de Bange*. Monthaye argued — sensibly — that Belgium was too small a country to support native munitions manufacturers. He then charged that French steel was inferior and ended with an encomium to Alfred which could only have been inspired in Essen.

Serbia, Japan, and Belgium were atypical; in most countries Krupp neither lost to rivals nor needed local allies. The authority of German officers was so great that a word from one of them was usually sufficient. Krupp sent Armstrong packing in Italy without scheming simply because Sedan was more recent than Waterloo and more impressive; similarly, the British retreated in disorder from Buenos Aires when a Lieutenant Colonel Sellström, noting that Argentina planned to rebuild its navy, wrote in a local periodical of the technical accomplishments of Kruppstahl before Metz and Paris. When Alfred sent his son to Saint Petersburg on December 9, 1880, with instructions to see "His Majesty the Czar and the Czarevitch, and also Grand Duke Constantine," in "the hope that we may be on the way to a good time, thanks to big contracts, success, and increased profits," he did not find it necessary to repeat the lessons of 1870–1871; all the chancelleries in the world had heard the echo of those cannonades, and his clientele included Switzerland, Holland, Portugal, Sweden, Denmark, Italy, Russia, Belgium, Argentina, Turkey, Brazil, China, Egypt, Austria, and every Balkan capital except Belgrade. Altogether 24,576 Krupp cannon were pointing at each other, provided one includes those in the Reich, which Alfred of course did not do.[7]

✠    ✠    ✠

Alfred didn't, but the Kaiser had wondered. During the maddening lull of '71, when Krupp was pleading for *Beschleunigung der deutschen Bewaffnung* and Roon was toying with the thought of returning to bronze, the powerful new field gun had been kept waiting in the wings. It couldn't remain there forever. Too much had been invested in its design, and the

Prokura was setting aside the firm's best ores for production.[8] Besides, the thing worked. It was certain to make a spectacular impression on any range, and Alfred, knowing that, had refused to wait until some sense had been knocked into the pigheaded panjandrums of Berlin. By the time of the Tegel trials which brought Wilhelm and Bismarck round, two big customers had bought. It was easy enough to fob off the *Allerhöchste-selber* with explanations that Russia didn't threaten the Reich at the moment, and that peace in the east was the keystone in the chancellor's arch of policy anyhow. But peace in the south was less certain. The new empire had been built at Austria's expense. Bismarck was determined to reconcile the Hapsburgs and Hohenzollerns. In 1873 he did it, persuading Franz Josef to expand southeastward through the Balkans and establishing an alliance of Germany, Russia, and Austria — the League of the Three Emperors. Meanwhile Carl Meyer and Wilhelm Gross had sold Vienna a large shipment of the new weapon. Wilhelm I had scarcely signed his new Essen contract when he learned that a potential enemy on his border was going to get the same cannon. The upshot was a crisis of confidence between the House of Krupp and the House of Hohenzollern. Meyer telegraphed Alfred to *komm schnell*, Alfred took the next train, and the following morning the two old men met in Potsdam. It began as the worst audience in Alfred's life. Until now their meetings had always been affable; Wilhelm was courteous by nature, and Krupp had behaved the way he wanted model Kruppianer to behave toward *him*.

Today the climate was frigid. The All-Highest did not smile, did not invite his subject to sit, did not begin with his usual small talk. Instead he began by drawing from his pocket a pamphlet which Gross had written at Alfred's direction, and which Meyer had published — *Geschichte der Gusstahlkanone* (*History of the Cast Steel Gun*). It was, the emperor observed dryly, "a technical work of limited appeal." Unfortunately, its most enchanted readers would be military men abroad. The details were so specific that the *Geschichte* would be invaluable to any general confronting a foe armed with the new fieldpiece. Krupp was speechless. For once he had violated his own code of secrecy. His motive had been to win supporters among the Prussian military caste. It had never occurred to him that the booklet might be read by the attachés of foreign powers stationed in Berlin. Luckily for him his antagonists on Moltke's staff, who had made certain that a copy reached the Kaiser, had overplayed their hand. They had told Wilhelm that Franz Josef's divisions would be equipped with a *better* gun. Alfred saw the opening and plunged into it. Far from being better, he said swiftly, it was inferior. The Austrian cannon, like the czar's, would be cumbersome. The All-Highest came down a little. He expressed surprise, asked a few questions, and warmed visibly. Encouraged, Alfred pushed his luck — and won. He seized the opportunity to teach the emperor the facts of life about the arms industry. He had to ship munitions to *"befreundete Staaten"* (friendly states); otherwise *"dann würde der Gusstahlfabrik, so wie sie heute arbeitet, die Grundlage entzogen"* (the foundations of the factory in its present form would be threatened). Experiments with weapons, he went on, were extremely costly. The armorer of the Reich had to maintain a large establishment. Without global markets he would go under unless — well, there was an alternative, of course: the Kaiser could subsidize the works.[9]

Hastily Wilhelm withdrew. He had no intention of matching the military budgets of some twenty foreign capitals, whose money, under the present arrangement, poured into Essen. Momentarily he had seen a flicker of things to come. Had he known how expensive the international arms industry would become in the long run, how much German blood and treasure would be spent in its behalf, and how truncated it would leave his empire three-quarters of a century later, he might have seized the chance to nationalize the Ruhr. But Alfred's case seemed irrefutable, and the mollified emperor nodded as his richest blacksmith bowed out. Krupp, for his part, damned himself for permitting publication of the *dumm* booklet and became more furtive than ever. He had planned to display the gun at the International Exhibition in Vienna. Now he telegraphed the Prokura: "This thought strikes me — unfortunately not until so late" — that it could be "said of us in Berlin that our efforts to keep it secret from other states are all humbug. . . . If we feel inclined to offer such guns to one state or another, they should be invited to Essen; I think, however, that for the moment we must on no account offer field guns for sale at all, because we must remain free for Prussia." The cannon was to be recrated at once and returned to the Ruhr.[10]

In less than two years Wilhelm's moment of pique was forgotten in a war scare, one of those near eruptions which kept European diplomacy in ferment during the four decades before Sarajevo. The French Chamber of Deputies passed a strong army bill. A Berlin newspaper published a provocative account of it headed "Is War in Sight?" In Paris, where the article was considered to have been inspired by Bismarck, the government panicked; the Foreign Minister appealed to England and Russia for support, Czar Aleksandr himself came to Berlin, and grave discussions were held. The ominous clouds rolled away. Aleksandr's chancellor cabled anxious capitals, "Peace is now assured." Meanwhile, during the interim the Kaiser had sent another wire from Ems, ordering two thousand 8.8-cm. (3.5-inch) Krupp guns. Alfred, responding with celerity, jubilantly replied that thanks to "the exalted and breathtaking interest shown by the king . . . Prussia is now the best-armed state."[11]

His relations with Wilhelm had improved, and it was well for Krupp that they had, for he faced two more showdowns with the Prussian military caste. First he was confronted once more by army diehards. His most influential ally in uniform, Constantin von Voigts-Rhetz, had retired.

While Gross was writing *Geschichte der Gusstahlkanone* Alfred had wistfully advised him, "I should be very glad to see everything possible said in honor of the general, particularly now, in the evening of his life, when he is no longer playing any active part, so that at least he might see that we are loyal and fair and grateful to him. Who knows how much longer he may have to live?" Constantin lived long enough to be mortified by Gross's candied flattery in the pamphlet which violated security and to see his younger brother lead the army's last charge against his old friend in Essen. Julius von Voigts-Rhetz had succeeded his brother as chief of the General War Department. Like his brother officers he had accepted the Kaiser's dictum that the Reich's gunsmith must be allowed to sell to *befreundete Staaten*. But the more he and they thought about it, the more convinced they were that there was a hole in Krupp's case. To graduates of the Kriegsakademie at Lichterfelde, Prussia's West Point and the nursery of the Offizierskorps, it seemed logical that the sword should be permitted to cut both ways. If Krupp could sell abroad, they argued, why couldn't they buy abroad?[12]

Thus the old hobgoblin was resurrected. Alfred learned of this dangerous line of reasoning eight months after the war scare. He instantly concluded that it would cut him to pieces. His faith in his merchandise was unlimited, but he had learned in the past that superior quality meant little to Lichterfelde alumni. On January 11, 1876, he wrote Julius a long letter, reviewing the history of his feuds with officers, starting with the rejection of his first hollow-forged barrels in the 1840's, and begging the young man to follow the example of his brother. It was absurd to suggest that Krupp had been favored by his countrymen: "Other great states experimented at their own cost and (as England, for example) not only indemnified the investor but showed him great favor; I have experimented at my own cost and have offered the results for the service of the state. In so doing I have saved the state expense, risk, and time." Yet his loyalty had met with ingratitude: "Here in Prussia every effort was made as recently as 1868 to abandon cast steel and go over to the English make." He described the "shameful document" he had been forced to sign two years earlier, omitting the fact that his prodigal behavior had led to it ("I have expended a great fortune and fallen into debt. I have to meet my liabilities and repay a large capital sum in a few years, and the future has thus no attractive appearance") and added that "Apart from this, it would be doubly unjust to employ other works, which have done nothing toward the creation of the cast steel gun, and which merely imitate what they have found out by fair means or foul, and on whose soil seed would be sown that is mine." Judged from "a commercial point of view," he insisted, "the gunmaker must be a spendthrift; he must make only the best, regardless of cost." Krupp concluded with an appeal in behalf of his own future and that of the German Reich: "I must make certain that the present product of the factory continues to be a credit to me twenty and fifty years from now, so that my remotest descendants savor the benefit of it (*dass die fernen Nachkommen davon den Segen geniessen*); whereas the shares of a company frequently change the management within a few years, and all the shareholders ever think of is the next dividend."[13]

Unpersuaded, Julius invited Krupp to submit nine unfinished 15-cm. guns — and extended the same invitation to Armstrong and Schneider. "A tender," Alfred wrote bitterly, "has been issued to other works. . . ." He felt isolated, and he was; his own directors felt he was taking too strong a line. "Only I have the right to supply guns to the state," he retorted sharply. He repeated his threats either to sell out or to take the czar at his word and move the factory to Russia. Then he decided to go straight to Wilhelm. On March 16 he sent the Kaiser a copy of the *Denkschrift* (memorial) he had vainly submitted to Julius. With it went a blunt letter. "Of all the institutions in the world with which I have had dealings," he wrote, "our country's ordnance department alone has lately been once more showing hostility to my establishment, and more than ever; it will not rest until the works have passed into the slavishly subservient hands of a joint-stock company. . . . I have hesitated whether I should trouble Your Majesty with this none too pleasant communication; but I have been considering the consequences of a breach and the ultimate disposal of my establishment, and as this would certainly be a still more unpleasant surprise, I was bound to prefer the present step." He concluded: "I hope that this justifies me before Your Majesty. My conscience assures me the protection of my Judge, even against the All-Highest's displeasure, on which certain members of those authorities have often speculated in the past (*auf welche einzelne Glieder jener Behörden bereits oft spekuliert haben*).[14]

In other words, the Highest was with him even if the All-Highest wasn't. This was perilously close to lèse-majesté. Alfred sounded very sure of himself, and he was, with reason. Julius hotly denied that he even knew what a stock company *was*. To no avail: on March 29 the Kaiser received Alfred from 12:30 to 1 P.M. A Dr. Pieper of the imperial staff took notes on the conversation. They survive, and since they mark the German government's final capitulation, with consequences which were still felt ninety years later in Bonn, they deserve to be reprinted in their entirety. Pieper began with a description of the imperial mood: "General impression. H.M. was most kind and sympathetic, so dispersing at once any anxiety that had been felt. On the whole H.M. seemed to share the views expressed by Herr Krupp in his memorial" (*Im Ganzen schien S.M. die von Herrn Krupp dargelegten Besorgnisse, resp. in der Denkschrift enthaltenen Anschauungen zu teilen*). Then:

*The audience.*[15]

SEINE MAJESTÄT: I have read your *Denkschrift*; as you authorized me to
    make official use of it I have made a few remarks on it and sent it to
    Albedyll.*

HERR KRUPP: In so doing Your Majesty has met an urgent desire of mine;
    in the hope that something of the sort might have happened I
    brought a second copy of the *Denkschrift* for Your Majesty. I do not
    want anything but justice and fair dealing, but I must fight the matter
    through, however much it may cost me, even if it cost me my head.

S.M. *went into some of the points in the* Denkschrift, *remarking from
    time to time,* "I have said so myself."

HERR KRUPP: Not long ago Major Trautmann† asked General von Voigts-
    Rhetz straight out: "What is it exactly that they have against the
    works?" Instead of giving a plain answer v. V.-R. threatened that the
    time might come when the works might be forbidden to export. Your
    Majesty, it is surely in the best interest of the state that there should
    be friendly relations between the works and the state. I have made
    provisions for insuring that the works shall continue to remain in the
    future in the hands of my family; I have bought mines for ninety-nine
    years in the hope that this will be so for at least that period. But when
    views of this sort are held, and that by the man who is supposed to be
    our next War Minister (*at this S.M. was greatly taken aback*) how
    can that be hoped for?

I am not conscious of having given offense to General von Voigts-
    Rhetz; of all men I should have expected that he would have inherited
    a friendly feeling from his brother. At the present the works are too
    weak to absorb oppressive measure; what they want is help.

(*Extracts from the accounts were then placed before S.M., who
    retained them.*)

I do not want to get away without speaking about the Minister of
    War. The more I hear of him the more I am convinced that he is a
    man of sterling uprightness. If injustice is done, therefore, it cannot be
    his fault. It is impossible for him to be acquainted with every detail.
    The fault lies with the small men, the place hunters who make inaccu-
    rate representations to him.

S.M. *agreed altogether with this view.*

HERR KRUPP: The matter must be decided now, one way or the other. I
    shall be staying here in Berlin indefinitely. If desired I should be ready
    to give Your Majesty further information at any time.

---

* General Emil von Albedyll, who had replaced von Roon as Kriegsminister and
chief of the Prussian Military Cabinet in 1872, and who held that office until the year
after Alfred Krupp's death.

† A retired officer on Carl Meyer's payroll.

*(Herr Krupp asked whether he might wait on the Kaiserin. S.M.
said that she was probably just going for a drive. Anyhow, he would
soon have an opportunity of seeing her at dinner.)*

S.M.: Do you realize that you are going to bring a hornet's nest around
your ears *(in ein Wespennest stechen)*?

HERR KRUPP: Yes, I know, but it has got to be cleared up. This position of
uncertainty must be ended, be the consequences what they may.

I was glad of this journey because it was a pleasure to me to convey
at last to Your Majesty the guns that have been ready for so long. I am
all the more sorry that at the same time I have had to trouble Your
Majesty with these unpleasant matters.

S.M. Please, please — it is very kind of you to let me know about these
things, *(Bitte, bitte, es ist mir sehr lieb, dass Sie mir diese Sachen
mitteilen).*

Pieper was struck by the fact that "All the time Herr Krupp pressed for
'light, clarity, and truth.' " What is far more striking is that the subject did
virtually all the talking, made all the demands, pressed himself forward as
the empress's companion, insisted upon an immediate solution — and was
answered by *"Bitte, bitte."* Had a Social Democrat used such language he
would have found himself in a dungeon; many were imprisoned for far less.
The Kaiser was being told to toe the mark. And he did. Far from stirring
up a hornet's nest, Alfred was rewarded with news that the invitations to
Armstrong and Schneider had been withdrawn. On October 5 Alfred sent
his own plans for German weapons to Count von Flemming of the cabinet
at Karlsruhe, asking him "to be good enough to oblige me by handing the
enclosed communication to His Majesty the Kaiser. I have chosen this way
to avoid attracting notice and giving rise to idle talk by a direct address to
His Majesty." In the return mail the count replied, "His Majesty graciously accepted your communication. I think I may infer from some
things he said about you and your good work that you will not lack, with
respect to your latest invention in the field of gunnery, the support which
you have enjoyed from the Kaiser in the past."[16]

It was all over but the shooting, when unforeseen difficulties arose in an
unexpected quarter. Krupp had defeated the German army. The navy, he
believed, was already in his pocket. In sending the *Denkschrift* to Wilhelm
he had told the All-Highest that "On the other hand I recognize with
gratitude that so far as the Royal Prussian Navy is concerned, though at
first it was prejudiced against my product and was notoriously an admirer
of British ordnance, I have since enjoyed its unvarying recognition and
confidence. . . ." He spoke prematurely. He had scarcely received the
soldiers' sword of surrender when the sailors mutinied against him. He had
thought every eventuality covered; the Konzern could trade freely with
foreign war ministries, while generals and admirals of the Reich could buy

only from him. But one possibility had been overlooked. Suppose the goods he sold proved to be worthless? Under the exacting Gross that was supposed to be impossible. Nevertheless it happened. The Kaiser's warships were on maneuvers in the North Sea when *Bums! Paff!* — clouds of smoke erupted around gun turrets and the decks were littered with dead and dying seamen. A frantic telegram arrived from Kiel: Kruppstahl tubes had exploded. The infuriated Reichsmarineamt refused to accept another barrel from Essen unless the shipment was accompanied by a guarantee.[17]

It was one thing for Alfred to say airily that Chinese and Siamese could "blow their enemies to bits well enough with these," something else again when the victims were Bavarians and Saxons. A team of picked technicians, dispatched to Kiel from Essen, returned with long faces. There could be no doubt; the guns had been defective. The Cannon King sat uneasily on his throne. He scrawled stern manifestos for posting in the shops, ordering stricter inspection of ores, raw steel, and finished bores. The humbled Prokura urged him to agree to guarantees. It was hard enough to know that the firm had German blood on its hands. Refusing pledges of good workmanship now would seem an act of extraordinary arrogance. It was. But Alfred was an extraordinarily arrogant man. Submitting to the Admiralty's demands, he said, was *ausgeschlossen*. It would be "the ruin of the works." Should he give in here, every little South American dictator and Asian warlord would insist upon similar assurances. "If," he wrote his son, "we . . . give the guarantee, that is only a palliative, and a costly one, for within a year's time the news may arrive that similarly defective guns have burst in other states and disasters have resulted." He would be at their mercy. It was intolerable. He said no.[18]

And he made it stick. Berlin ordered the navy to sweep down its bloody decks, recruit new gunners, and forget the whole episode. Krupp's powerful will had achieved the ultimate triumph; after a half-century of battling Prussian officialdom he had risen from the weedy boy to whom all doors were closed to the mighty Kanonenkönig whose every ultimatum, however outrageous, was accepted. He himself did not look at his victory over the Reichsmarineamt in that light, however. To him the mere fact that he had been obliged to listen to so insolent a proposal was monstrous, and he wrote his son, then in Saint Petersburg, that they must reach a position in which a repetition of the insult would be impossible: "To make every effort to reach that goal and to hew to the standard is everybody's sacred duty. Once we have reached it, we can call the tune, laying down conditions and standards ourselves and wiping out forever the humiliation imposed upon us from another quarter (*verwischen für immer das Schmachvolle, was uns von einer anderen Seite widerfahren ist*).[19]

The other "quarter" was the navy, but he couldn't bring himself to set down the odious word.

✠   ✠   ✠

Like most nineteenth-century captains of industry Alfred was gifted with an instinctive flair for showmanship. Now he began looking for a proper theater, which, for a manufacturer of long-range cannon, wasn't easily acquired. He couldn't display his wares to foreign customers at Tegel — the War Office drew the line at that — and besides, Tegel was too small for his new artillery. In his letter to Moltke six weeks after the French surrender he had specified a private proving ground two miles long. In 1874 he had acquired an even longer range at Dülmen, forty-three miles from Essen, but its 6,561 yards were obsolete before Kruppianer finished leveling its trees. What he really needed was a cleared tract ten and a half miles long, with four and a half miles of uninhabited woods beyond to compensate for overshoots. There was no such place in the heavily populated Rhineland. Indeed, since the land had to be relatively flat, there were precious few in Germany, and they would become far more precious if it were known that Alfred Krupp was a potential buyer. Roaming the country on horseback, he found just the place he wanted at Meppen, in Hanover province near Osnabrück. There was just one problem. It was owned by one hundred and twenty different farmers, each with his own plot. The negotiations could take forever, he reflected gloomily. Then he hit upon the solution. Of all his lieutenants, only Wilhelm Gross shared his sense of urgency. Gross's incentive was Krupp's new 35.5-cm. bombardment cannon. Armstrong had developed a similar weapon, and the Dutch, Swiss, and Norwegians had expressed interest in it. Like Krupp, however, the British lacked a stretch of real estate long enough to accommodate thousand-pound, high-explosive missiles fired through a bore nearly fourteen inches wide, and buyers wouldn't buy until they had seen the gun in action.[20]

Get Meppen, Alfred told Gross, and I'll get the orders. Gross got it by posing as an eccentric who wanted solitude and was willing to pay for it; in the end he signed one hundred and twenty separate long-term leases. Then Alfred arrived with teams of Kruppianer. The area, three miles wide, was surrounded by a heavy wire fence. Signs warned strangers ACHTUNG! GEFAHRENPUNKT! The *Gefahrenpunkt* (danger point) was traversed by three main roads. Observation towers much like those which would overlook *kruppsche* concentration camps seventy years later were built where each highway entered the proving ground. During trials the thoroughfares were closed, quite illegally, by uniformed Krupp guards. Within, technicians and distinguished visitors could be housed in elaborately furnished shellproof bunkers buttressed, roofed, and equipped with facilities to serve champagne to potential clients as they peered through slits. Meppen not only met all Krupp's needs; it was superior to the proving grounds of any nation in the world, including, most conspicuously, the German Reich. To his vast delight the Offizierskorps of the Prussian Artillery Test Commission came to him, spiked helmets in hand, and begged to use it. He replied that they might rent it during the off-season, if any.[21]

He didn't want there to be any. Now that he had his own incomparable trial ground he was eager to try it out. His first thought was to challenge Armstrong to a duel. Let the British and German goliaths stand hubcap to hubcap and blaze away, he gleefully told Gross; customers would be invited to watch and then to write their checks — in millions of marks. Gross was horrified. Had he swindled all those peasants for nothing? The point of the thing was to get something Armstrong lacked. If the British were to use Krupp's range, they would be competing on equal terms. Besides, there was always the possibility that the enemy might win; because of their naval contracts heavy guns were an Armstrong specialty. As it turned out, they weren't interested anyhow. Alfred had sent the invitation through Longsdon. It was declined with cool thanks. The British plainly suspected a trap. Krupp's *Gefahrenpunkt* could be a lethal danger point for a cannon maker with new, secret improvements. Alfred, disappointed, had a few rounds hurled for his own benefit — the 14-incher registered at 10,000 yards — and then brooded over ways to exploit his new toy.[22]

The upshot was his "Bombardment of the Nations" (*Völkerschiessen*), the military sensation of the late '70's. Actually there were two bombardments. The first Völkerschiessen was held in 1878 with twenty-seven artillery officers from twelve foreign countries attending it. On the eve of the big shoot Alfred wrote Sophus Goose, "You can imagine how I am on thorns as to the result and what the visitors will say, for I have long felt that success in this will be the first and surest means of getting all our hammers and the whole works fully occupied." His plans were elaborate. All the foreign officers were to be taken first to the works, where "there will be a big show"; after lunch in the Gartenhaus they would refresh themselves at the Essener Hof. Then: *Nach* Meppen! The great day dawned crisp and clear, but Alfred could not show his guests the way. He was laid up, suffering from mysterious discharges; his son stepped into the role of host. Alfred's anxieties proved groundless. The Völkerschiessen was a tremendous success. Between thundering barrages the rustle of order pad pages being turned could be heard in the bomb shelters, and the visitors left in so fervid a state of enthusiasm that the following year, when Krupp sent out another batch of invitations, eighty-one ordnance experts from eighteen nations accepted. There might have been more, but he had snubbed the Turks — otherwise the czar's officers would have stayed away, and Saint Petersburg was a bigger customer than Constantinople — and had cut the French out of deference to Berlin.[23]

That was his only concession to Kriegsakademie alumni. Albedyll's delegation was disagreeably surprised to find itself outnumbered by English officers (Alfred never abandoned hope of becoming Britain's armorer) and dismayed to discover that at Meppen German was the one language which was *not* spoken. Teams of Krupp executives jabbered away in Italian, English, and French; the Prussians had to stand about mutely and await translations. Nevertheless they stayed. For anyone with a professional interest in artillery the firings of August 5–8, 1879, were irresistible. Krupp had a new showpiece: a 44-cm. (17-inch) built-up gun which hurled 2,200-pound shells. Strengthened by shrinking a tempered steel envelope over the barrel and then looping the envelope with coiled bars, it resembled a huge black bottle. Peering out from their luxurious bunkers, the cosmopolitan guests watched popeyed as the projectiles, each weighing over a ton, soared aloft and burst in the distance. The earth rocked, and since programs had been distributed, informing them in advance just which target was to be demolished in a given test, they could judge the accuracy of the weapon. Krupp's gunners behaved flawlessly. The Italians, who had been buying their heavy ordnance from Armstrong, peppered their escort with questions. He answered them fluently, making graceful allusions to the virility of Rome's modern legions. *Adulati*, they ordered four 17-inchers for the defense of La Spezia — and then learned, after their return home, that not a bridge in Switzerland was strong enough to support them. Alfred obligingly shipped them by sea.[24]

The Völkerschiessen was a brilliant publicity coup, and as Krupp had promised Gross, it more than paid its way. Nevertheless he was disappointed. His pet project had been rejected. For over two years he had been obsessed with what he called his *Panzerkanone* — literally, an "armored gun." Artillerymen would be protected by a heavy steel shield. The barrel would not protrude through it; instead it would be fitted into the shield with a ball-and-socket joint. He had unveiled the first specimen on the Kaiser's visit to Essen in 1877; certain of success, he had been prepared to quote prices for S.M. and his staff "when I have finished showing its value on account of its safety and the saving of men and guns, and when they are satisfied that such a gun will destroy a whole battery, with every soul, without itself being damaged." But the invention was altogether too gimmicky. Wilhelm looked doubtful. Even Gross and Fritz Krupp, who had been skeptical all along, were discreetly silent. And the officers of the emperor's entourage were derisive. As Alfred wrote bitterly, "Moltke shook his head because sighting would be impossible. [Julius] Voigts-Rhetz argued that no human being would be able to stay inside the armored compartment because of the tremendous noise of the discharge," and their staffs had dismissed it "as a mad folly."[25]

The stationary tank — for that is what his *Panzerkanone* really was — became Alfred's last big crusade. It never had a chance. Quite apart from its novelty, which was enough to doom it in the military mind, it relied to a large extent upon the strength of the shield, and armor plate was the one metallurgical problem he never solved. In December 1873 he had visualized "bar armor" — thick, bar-shaped, forged iron ingots — and had offhandedly concluded, "I leave the design and the troublesome work to the experts." It was too troublesome for them. They tried and threw up their hands. Their mistake, he retorted, was that their plate was too thin; "The mass must be made of such a thickness that it does not bend, and so soft that it does not break." His own technicians shared the general feeling that Hermann Gruson, inventor of the case-hardening process, was turning out far better plate in his shipyards. Though Krupp shells had bounced off Gruson armor at Tegel in 1868, Alfred jeered at Gruson's case-hardened turrets, which had been adopted by the navy, as "iron pots," and complained to the Kronprinz that he was being "pigeonholed." The *Panzerkanone*, he told the future Kaiser Friedrich III, was the *Kanone* of the future; eventually it would be used to "protect coasts, estuaries, fortresses, and passes from attack." With characteristic ambiguity he combined greed and idealism in his closing sentence: "I want to find a great deal of work — bread — for my people, and could find room for another 3,000 men; it is for that reason that I am working to obtain acceptance for my idea, and not from ambition or desire of gain." How he could gainfully engage 3,000 more Kruppianer without profiting he did not say.[26]

Actually his shields were far stronger than his critics thought. They weren't in the same class as Gruson's, but they were quite good enough to give gunners the necessary protection. Julius Voigts-Rhetz's objection was absurd. Alfred knew it was, and counted on the Meppen shows to vindicate him. There was one way of settling the issue once and for all. A human being would have to crouch behind the shield while it was shelled. His son, his managers, even the Prussian generals were appalled. He noted dryly, "All those who are now coming have learned from their school days that there is no stopping the recoil. It has even been suggested that sheep or goats should be put inside during the shooting. If they could also serve the guns, I should have no objection" (*Wenn die auch die Geschütze bedienen könnten, dann hätte ich nichts dagegen*).[27]

He asked for volunteers. Unexpectedly a young major from the Viennese Military Science Association presented himself. Afterward the major appeared unharmed, but that proved nothing; the gun crews, to Alfred's fury, had deliberately shot wide of the shield. Moreover, while cooped up the Austrian officer had thought of a new objection to the *Panzerkanone*. Krupp had met Moltke's argument by equipping the shield with a slit which could be closed under fire and unlatched afterward for sighting. Major Count von Geldern submitted that "In his opinion the enemy would wait his opportunity to fire when the shutter was opened."[28]

Maddened, Alfred struck back with a plan to silence all his enemies. At first they were indeed speechless. Had he gone through with it, he too would have been silenced — forever. He proposed that he himself sit behind his armor while cannon of increasing calibers pounded away at him. He would take minute-by-minute notes, which would survive him,

THE REST IS GAS 173

and periodically he would peep out through the shutter, defying them to hit him. *Wunderbar!* The Bombardment of Krupp! As the cannon reached a crescendo of violent orchestration he would die a hero's death! With eighty-one officers looking on! Including all those Englishmen!

> . . . *ich werde selbst in meinen Turm gehen. . . . Es ist nicht mehr als billig, dass man mit seinem Leben Sicherheit verbürgt, bevor man andere Leute in den Turm gehen lässt.*

> . . . I shall go into the turret myself. . . . It is no more than just that one should risk one's own life before asking others to go into the turret.[29]

His Prokura gently dissuaded him from public suicide. He was bombarded, all the same. His beard flapping in the wind, he stalked down the range and disappeared inside the *Panzerkanone.* For several minutes shells crumpled around him; then the cease-fire was sounded and he emerged with a peculiar, hammered look. Jubilantly he wrote Goose:

> *Die mir gewordene Drohung, dass die Polizei es nicht erlauben würde und dass keiner auf den Panzer schiessen würde, wenn ich darin wäre, hat sich nicht bestätigt. . . . so darf noch keinem der Insassen deshalb ein Finger weh tun.*

> The threat that the police would forbid it, and that no one would fire against the armor as I was behind it, did not materialize. Thus I had no occasion to dismiss any of the gunners for insubordination, nor did I see any lack of courage among our people. Actually one is safest there behind the armor, and on Wednesday, when we fire a storm of shells against it, no one should have so much as a finger hurt.[30]

He was right. On Wednesday, the last day of the Bombardment of the Nations, a clutch of terrified Kruppianer were locked in the turret and subjected to a ferocious cannonade. Afterward they stumbled out, temporarily deaf but otherwise sound. Alfred reached for his pencil. The foreign officers merely stared at him. In disgust he scrawled, *"No orders!"*

&#9672; &#9672; &#9672;

"I am presently nearly only a skin with some bones," he wrote Longsdon in the middle of the night; "the rest is gas. It may happen that one fine day the gas will overwhelm by its lightness and quantity the weight of the poor bones and suddenly, if they don't hold me, I shall go up directly into heaven with my earthly dress, probably the first host* of such an appearance in yonder quarter since creation. What a saving of a dirty roundabout way through the damp tomb and the hot purgatory — and what a comfort to one who believes in the latter."[31]

---

* He meant guest. The two words are much alike in German.

His wife was one who believed in the latter, and during their infrequent visits his sacrilege grated on her more and more. It was becoming increasingly difficult to keep up appearances, though they managed when distinguished visitors called. One of them left a circumstantial account of the successful front the Krupps presented. The Baroness Hilda Elizabeth Bunsen Deichmann was one of the few women Alfred admired; she was the daughter of a minor Ruhr baron, she had been born in the Prussian legation in London, and she was more English than German. In her privately printed memoirs she told how

> Herr Krupp lived in princely style at an enormous country house with a very large guesthouse [the "small house"] attached. It could be compared with a large embassy, for people from all parts of the world came to persuade him to make business arrangements with their governments. Thus there were a great many large dinner parties, and once we arrived to be told that many hundreds of people were expected at a ball that evening. This was a very brilliant affair, but all the preparations were made without any commotion, and next morning all was cleared away and the enormous rooms presented their usual appearance.

Alfred was still active then. Hilda Deichmann was struck by his determination to continue his education to the last — and, inevitably, by his dedication to horseflesh:

> During one of our visits [to Hügel], an Italian professor had been engaged to teach Herr Krupp Italian, as he was anxious to control all business arrangements with Italy. Being so busy, he hit upon the idea of the professor accompanying him on his daily rides; but, as this gentleman had never mounted a horse before, the Italian conversation did not make much progress!

Hilda found both the sole proprietor and his wife charming —

> Close to the works was a very tiny and poor-looking house which Herr Krupp showed us as his birthplace [sic], and which he religiously preserved intact. Frau Krupp, his wife, was an old lady when I first knew her, who was always dressed in light blue. She seemed pleased and proud to receive visitors.[32]

Doubtless Bertha was, in fact, delighted to see the baroness; her presence meant that Alfred would behave. He would even preen himself, for Hilda, or another young woman like her, would be an ideal matrimonial prospect for his son. Unfortunately Fritz and Bertha had other ideas — which led to their final row.

Since Alfred and his wife had been strangers for thirty years, it is perhaps inaccurate to say that she "left him" in the spring of 1882; nevertheless that is when she departed for good. That she had maintained a token residence under his roof for so long is a tribute to the power of nineteenth-century social conventions. Each meeting had been capped by a quarrel. Once he became jealous of a handsome young coachman, banished the unfortunate youth, and was startled when she departed in a huff. They disagreed about everything. She could endure his abuse, his ravings, his nocturnal wanderings, his fetishistic admiration for manure, even his militant atheism. What she could not bear was his proprietary attitude toward their son. Alfred was taking Fritz away from her. Worse, the young man himself seemed desperately unhappy about it. Now twenty-seven, he had a chance for happiness, and she was determined to see that he got it. He couldn't speak for himself. He was developing peculiarities of his own and was spending that April beneath the almond trees of Málaga, recuperating from one of his periodic bouts of illness. Therefore his mother came up from the Riviera, reached Villa Hügel in the evening, and went straight to her husband. Fritz, she told him, wanted to get married.[33]

She could scarcely have chosen a worse time. Alfred had just lost a game of dominoes to a member of the Prokura. He was always a terrible loser, and often accused the winner of cheating. Turning his back on her, he refused to discuss the subject. She persisted. Since she wanted a final answer, he thundered, he would give her one; it was *"Nein!"* This time it was she who turned away, and the next he knew a servant was whispering to him that Frau Krupp was packing not only her clothes but everything she owned in the castle. Alfred hurried upstairs. Sure enough, she was bossing maids around, ordering boxes filled. He scolded, he wheedled, he raged, he threatened. She said nothing. She wouldn't even look at him. When the last carton had been filled and carried away, she strode after it. In anguish he shouted down the deep bleak stone stairwell, *"Mach' kein Unsinn! Bertha, bedenke, was du tust!"* (Don't be foolish! Think, Bertha, what you are doing!). They were the last words he would ever speak to her. Fritz, returning from Spain, heard every detail of the scene from the help. He learned nothing from his father. Krupp was silent, set, withdrawn. In his own horrid way he tried to make amends; sulkily he consented to the marriage, making it quite clear that his son had, in his opinion, made the worst possible choice. It didn't bring his wife back. Spitefully he ordered her suite converted to storerooms and never mentioned her again. In his correspondence we find but one oblique reference to the separation. The following April 10 he wrote Fritz Funke, a fellow Ruhr Schlotbaron, "You always say straight out whatever occurs to you, and I made a remark to you yesterday in a friendly way with regard to giving information to any who might be curious about my household arrangements. I can only repeat what I said then. If I receive confidential information from anyone or see into his family affairs or household arrangements, I am not free to pass on what I have learned. If a stranger asks me questions about such matters, I tell him straight out that they are no business of his and that I have no right to satisfy his curiosity."[34]

The next line is instructive: *"Ich liege im Bette mit Rheuma und habe daher Zeit zu schreiben"* (I am in bed with rheumatism and so have time for letter writing). That was the story of his life now. He had four years to live, and he spent much of them on his back in Villa Hügel, a stub of a pencil held fast in his fist. Occasionally he had himself driven down to Düsseldorf, where he made pathetic attempts to strike up friendships with members of the artistic community, including Franz Liszt, whose life span (1811–1886) matched his own almost to the year. The old Kanonenkönig was a very lonely man. Of his three siblings Hermann and Ida were dead, and his other brother, who had never forgotten their inheritance quarrel, communicated with him only through the firm. Longsdon was the sole contemporary he trusted, and he was across the channel. In the castle's candle-lit darkness ("You know I am a night bird") Alfred wrote him long screeds suggesting he "come here to the hill" and "then we will go every day on horseback together and you shall choose your horse and we will ride to Düsseldorf as I did yesterday and study paintings, and go again as often as we like. And thus we will amuse ourselves and talk only from time to time of business and fabric [the factory], just as much as is far from harming health. Now, my dear friend, don't loose a day. . ." Longsdon didn't come. He couldn't speak a word of German and thought the Prussians a race of cads. But Alfred's lifelong, unrequited love affair with Britannia burned bright to the end. The grandson of his British landlord of nearly a half-century earlier read about him and wrote him, and Alfred's reply was pathetic in its ardor; he recalled that "when I was young and your father and aunt and also the grand-eldren so friendly and alltogether so kind toward me — a mere foreigner — that Birchfield was and will remain in my memory for all times a sacred spot." Krupp's yearning for England almost leaped from the pages — as, in a very different way, did his hatred for his home, "my prison." With the arrival of his daughter-in-law Villa Hügel had become, if anything, even more unpleasant than before, and the fact that he was responsible for the unpleasantness did not make it more endurable.[35]

Down in Essen his 20,000 Kruppianer continued to feed his forges and fertilize their wives. From the hill the city resembled one enormous shed — nearly a million square yards were roofed — blanketed by a scudding gray haze. The Social Democrats were present, but not troublesome. Business was good; reports from visiting members of his management told him that. The bankers were being paid off. Now and then he would fire off one of his intemperate salvos; employees must not be permitted to start farms in the housing developments ("The men would work at home and rest in the works") or keep goats ("Goats have gnawed Greece bare") or improve upon their homes ("I have several times seen small lattice bowers . . . and find most of them very ugly"). The government was becoming lax — "Never were the national roads so bad as they are now." Artisans no longer took pride in their work — "The repairs to Friedrichstrasse and Schederhof could not conceivably be more crudely done." He accused the management of treating the sole proprietor lightly. Its reports to him were "all too short." Although his holdings were now reckoned at eight million marks, small entries should not be omitted from the balance sheet. Krupp's success, Krupp reminded them, had sprung from a passion for detail. *Also:* why had they failed to include the value of the old Stammhaus, 750 marks ($561.40)?[36]

Yet these were asides. The dominant theme of his senility was a dark, endless brooding over new ways to kill people. His career as a peaceful industrialist had been distinguished, and had he echoed the spirit of his trademark he and his descendants would be remembered by history in a very different light. Secluded in his castle, however, he forgot axles, springs, rails, and seamless tires and contemplated the prospect of a general European war. "It would," he wrote Longsdon on April 13, 1885, "be a sad thing"; but it would be even sadder if Britain and Germany (whom he assumed would be allies) lacked ingenious weapons. Therefore he concentrated on new devices. After the disappointing failure of a Krupp mountain gun in Italian trials at Vinadio he turned toward the sea. What Germany needed, he concluded, was a first-class navy, and he was just the man to design it. Some of his suggestions were clairvoyant. He advocated the introduction of smoke screens "produced on a movable carriage, which can be shifted about to confuse the enemy," and his "pivot gunboat" anticipated PT boats by nearly sixty years. "Assume," he wrote, "that two or three small ships tackle one or more big ones. They must proceed to their rear, since they are not armored, but at the proper moment they steam ahead, circle round the enemy ships at full speed, and fire on them as rapidly as they can load." The outcome seemed to him inevitable, although, like Douglas MacArthur in 1941, he minimized the range and power of warships' long guns in battling light craft. Of the PTs he declared enthusiastically that "With their great speed and their maneuvering around a central target their aiming problems are simplified. The enemy ship is large and lies dead in the center, while the small one is almost invisible and difficult to sight because of its speed. The big ship is in ten times the danger, and if the small one is actually hit and sunk, the loss in equipment and human lives is only one-tenth as much. . . ." His difficulty was that he was long on vision, short on technical expertise. Arthur Whitehead's invention of the "automobile fish torpedo" was several years away; Krupp proposed to arm each gunboat with one of his largest cannon. According to the specifications, his engineers informed him, the vessel would be capsized by the recoil. Very well, Alfred flared; he would build a gun which would fire in two directions *simultaneously*, the second shot absorbing the recoil of the first. "You probably think I'm crazy" (*Nun können Sie mir höchstens noch sagen, ich wäre verrückt*), he wrote. Unable to think of a reply, they made none, so he sent them another snappish note: "If you think ignoring me is going to make any impression on me you're wrong."[37]

He wouldn't quit hatching schemes, even though his doctors begged him to surrender his pencil; after a lifetime of imaginary ailments he was now plainly failing. In the autumn of 1884 Düsseldorf prepared to receive Bismarck. The chancellor wanted to stop in Essen, but Krupp confessed he would be "unable to meet the Prince at the railway station or to accompany him to the works, or even receive him there with his escort; for I am simply not well enough . . . to do anything except vegetate and avoid all excitement." The following April he took a short trip and noted next day, "I returned with a lumbago. Now they plaster me, and if that doesn't do, then Dr. Dicken will electrify me." To his indignation, Dicken died two weeks later. It was, Krupp raged, typical of the medical profession; the idiots couldn't even cure themselves. "I am now the very old man," he sadly wrote Longsdon. "I tread [dread] to go by carriage, but after two hours driving I could scarcely get up the staircase. . . . I have a doctor here from Berlin." The newcomer was none other than Professor Schweninger, the Iron Chancellor's iron-willed physician. Fearfully Alfred referred to him as "my torturer." This time, however, the doctor did not order Krupp to stand at attention. Instead he left several bottles of fluid which, from its effects, sounds suspiciously as though it may have been fortified by alcohol. Distrustful of German physicians, Alfred asked Longsdon to get an opinion from "a Doctor of London," but he conceded that "the stomach is much pleased by that liquid."[38]

He pondered the hereafter. Did it exist? Krupp was dubious. Yet he could be wrong. If so, he was ready for an audit of his books "in the presence of the Lord" (*vor seinem Herrgott*). He certainly wasn't going to compromise his principles by "haggling with God for a second-class seat in Paradise" (*keinen Kompromiss, versucht nicht, Gott ein Plätzchen im Paradiese abzuhandeln*). That would not be "manly" (*männlich*). He preferred to hammer away at his anvil to the end, and so, though he recorded on March 1, 1887, that "I am forbidden to work," he justified disobedience on the ground that "success can do me nothing but good." Unfortunately the new successes were being harvested by others. Four weeks later he learned that an American electrical engineer named Hiram Maxim had invented a crankless machine gun which used its own recoil to fire, eject empty cartridges, and reload itself. "What I know," Alfred wrote on March 31, "is astonishing, and I envy the inventor."[39]

His own final effort to revolutionize warfare — and, at the same time, to provide a suitable platform for his ill-starred armored gun — was what he variously described as a "cell ship," "floating battery," and "hollow island." "Soon," he observed, "we shall supply the proof that every armored ship is destroyed above and below water by our shells. These ruined, expensive vessels will then be useless. The next thing will be to find a substitute for them" (*Nun ist es die Aufgabe Ersatz dafür zu finden*).[40]

His substitute was preposterous. Shaped like a dish, supported by chambers of air, the battery would pound away at coast fortifications, and depart on the outgoing tide. In his shaky old man's hand Alfred sketched the plans in a single night on forty-two quarto pages filled with cramped, barely legible notes:

> . . . no external armor [*ohne jeden Panzer von aussen*]. . . . The ship must be of such a size that she has a sufficient number of cells to keep her above water, even though she might sink to deck level. . . . An armored ship with her hull penetrated by a few shells must inevitably sink; with this ship, the shells may go right through, and where the armored ship fills with inrushing water each shot will perhaps bring just a few hundred cubic feet of water into the vessel, and where with heavy armor all are quickly lost, here the only men who would perish would be those who received direct hits [*Wasser in dieses Schiff und wie beim schweren Panzer rasch alles verloren ist, werden bei uns nur die Leute getötet, die getroffen werden*].

Of course, he conceded, there would be doubting Thomases, the sons of those who had rejected his cast steel cannon. They would heckle, cavil, jeer. But he was ready for their frivolous objections.

> *Je grösser die Aufgabe, je schwieriger die Lösung erscheint, desto grösser der Verdienst. . . . so denke ich mir doch, dass man durch Anker und Ketten solche Verbindungen herstellen kann mit dem Geschütz, dass man später, wenn Ruhe wieder ist, es heraufholen kann.*

> The bigger the task and the more difficult its solution appears to be, the greater the achievement. Suppose we examine a weak aspect of the gun on the hollow island. Immobile, it may be rammed and sunk by an enemy warship. However, before that happens the ramming ship has shots in her hull which are fatal to her. Therefore, though we lose a gun, the foe loses his vessel. If we have towed our island into the ocean so far that we prevent the enemy from bombarding the coasts, and if we are actually unable to save the battery from superior force, to bring it back to safe harbor, it seems to me that we can still leave a buoy on the spot so that later, when peace has been signed, the gun can be raised again.[41]

His son and his doctor studied the plans together. The physician muttered the single oath "*Je!*" (*Jesus!*). Fritz instructed the factory to ignore the sole proprietor, and Schweninger extracted from Alfred a vow never to communicate with his beloved works again.[42]

On July 13, 1887, the physician examined his gaunt patient in one of the cavernous stone bedrooms upstairs and found his condition unchanged. Fritz left on a trip. The next day the seventy-five-year-old Cannon King, alone in the castle with his servants, succumbed to a heart attack and toppled into the arms of his mute valet, Hans Ludger. There was a sudden spasm; he stiffened and then went slack, and as his lifeless hand opened a two-inch pencil fell to the marble floor. In Paris, where it was Bastille Day, the French nation was overjoyed. Savage articles in the capital's press reported that Krupp had stolen his cast steel process from Bessemer, that in Alfred's last years all his guns had "fouled and burst," and that he had prospered only because the firm's real owners were Bismarck and the Prussian royal family. "French artillery is superior to the German on all points," Le Matin said in an account which was read with indignation by one member of Germany's royal family, twenty-eight-year-old Friedrich Wilhelm Viktor Albert, the Hohenzollern who was destined to be remembered in history as the Kaiser Wilhelm. But Parisian newspapers were an exception. Most editorials abroad linked Krupp's name with those of the chancellor and the emperor as one of the chief architects of victory in 1871 and, therefore, a founding father of the Reich.[43]

To be sure, few nations were in a position to take a critical look at Alfred's career; he had armed forty-six of them. In Hügel were a diamond ring from Russia's Grand Duke Mikhail Mikhailovich, a solid gold snuffbox from Franz Josef of Austria, and a two-thousand-year-old vase from Li Hung-chang. As much as any other single individual Krupp had set the stage for the great holocausts which would begin in 1914, and in recognition of his achievements the grateful governments of his day had awarded him forty-four military medals, stars, and crosses, including multiple honors from Spain, Belgium, Italy, Rumania, Austria, Russia, Turkey, and Brazil. Sweden had decorated him with the Order of Vasa, Japan with the Order of the Rising Sun, and Greece had presented him with the Commander's Cross of the Order of the Redeemer.[44]

He had planned his own funeral in detail, and Essen followed each instruction to the letter. For three days he lay in state in the main hall of the castle.* On the third night the scraggy corpse was carried down the long road to the works, past walks lined with solid black flags and twelve thousand Kruppianer holding smoking flambeaux aloft. Before it was entombed it was displayed again briefly in the cottage from which his bankrupt father had been buried. Because of the restoration the Stammhaus looked much as it had on the morning of his father's funeral sixty years before, when he had left it as a skinny, scared child. At his direction

---

* The "White Room," as it was then called; it is now the Music Room.

everything had been preserved, down to the hand-hewn black wooden clogs in which he had walked to the Gusstahlfabrik. Here the mourners viewed him for the last time. Then a gun carriage bore the coffin to the family plot in Kettwig Gate cemetery, by the remnants of the city's medieval wall, where Jencke eulogized:

*Er war das Beispiel eines glühenden Patrioten, dem kein Opfer zu gross war für sein Vaterland.*

The noble gentleman who was an example of that patriotism which considers no sacrifice for the Fatherland too great.[45]

☒    ☒    ☒

In death, as in life, Alfred's body proved restless. Kettwig Gate had to be demolished to make room for a new train station. Like his father — whose cadaver was shifted about so many times that eventually it was lost — the Kanonenkönig's tranquility was disturbed by the constant expansion of the city he had put on the map and the consequent need to move graveyards. In 1956, however, he was sealed in a permanent vault by his great-grandson Alfried, who, while restoring the honor and prosperity of the dynasty, decided to reunite all the family dead. Alfried brought the ashes of his father Gustav to the Ruhr from a remote family estate. Alfried's youngest brother Eckbert was found under a Wehrmacht cross in Italy, and the bones of other Krupps were collected and reinterred in Essen's exclusive suburb of Bredeney.[46]

The cemetery is private, guarded, and awesome. A walk of pink granite winds through an immaculate park, past tulips and evergreens. Then, abruptly, one comes upon the burial ground, a startling array of huge black marble tombs. Gustav and his wife, the second Bertha, lie together under a single stone; their fallen sons are at their feet. The Krupp trademark is carved on the crypt of Alfred's son Fritz. And looming over all is the monument of Alfred himself. Once more the old Cannon King dominates the Krupps; his sepulcher, ascending in tiers, is twenty feet high. Here and there bronze figures perch on marble ledges, keeping watch over the graves. Some are of angels, and one is an enormous crouching eagle. Since the eagle holds a wreath in his talons, he is presumably in mourning, though his expression is anything but sad. It is unsettling. He looks enraged.[47]

# 8

✠

# Prince of the Blood

Aₙₙ so we come to Friedrich Alfred, alias Fritz Alfred, alias Fritz — the most successful, baffling, charming, repulsive and (with the sole exception of his grandson Alfried) most enigmatic of all the Krupps. Absent from Fritz's modern black vault in Bredeney is the small brass plaque which was affixed to his headstone after he, like his father and grandfather before him, had been borne from the Stammhaus to Kettwig Gate. "*Ich verzeihe allen meinen Feinden,*" it read; "I forgive all my enemies." That he actually said it is doubtful; nevertheless it is in the spirit of the man. He was unfailingly charitable, generous, and kind. Separating him from the storm clouds which rolled about him isn't easy, and the clumsy attempts of his public relations men to burnish his image are no help. These were the years when the firm became conscious of its reputation abroad. A planted article in the *Outlook*, an American weekly, gives some insight into the coarse texture of Prussian gray flannel at the turn of the century. Describing the Konzern's concern for its workers' welfare, a contributor named Edward A. Steiner wrote on January 25, 1902:

> I have stood in the presence of many great, the titled and the throned, but I have seldom made my bow with greater reverence than before this busy businessman, who has not been too busy to think of those who have helped to create his wealth.
>
> "You have come from America to see us; that's very nice. What do you want to see — our peace products or our war products?"
>
> "Your heart products, Mr. Krupp," I replied; and a smile passed over the rather stern face.[1]

It is unlikely that Steiner ever laid eyes on the sole proprietor's sole heir, whose aspect was anything but stern. (He resembled no one so much as the late actor Jean Hersholt.) Still, he *was* devoted to his W*ohlfahrtsein-richtungen*, his institutions to improve the lot of Kruppianer. He *did* break the niggardly Schlotbarone tradition by becoming the Ruhr's first (and last) munificent philanthropist. Enlightened industrial policies *were* dear to him, and he detested the violence of which, ironically, he was an international symbol; as he once told Wilhelm II, "My fortune is my curse. Without it I would have dedicated my life to art, literature, and science."[2]

Nevertheless the fact remains that the number of enemies whom the headstone plaque was meant to absolve, who beset him in life and gloated over his death, was extraordinary. So deep was the hatred he inspired that after the burial Krupp police had to guard his grave around the clock, fending off men who were determined to desecrate the coffin.[3] In part this enmity sprang from his spectacular end. In part it was a sign of the times; no Kanonenkönig — unlike his father he loathed the sobriquet, but it stuck all the same — could have eluded *fin-de-siècle* notoriety. Most of all, the implacable hostility which focused upon this shrewd, sensitive introvert was a piece of his legacy. Krupp *père* had sown the wind; Krupp *fils* was fated to reap the whirlwind. He would have been able to avoid it only if he had been a nonentity, and he was anything but that; in his own complex way he was abler than Alfred.

In his youth this ability had been well camouflaged. A keen eye, appreciative of subtleties, might have perceived the latent *Geist* behind that intricate facade. His father lacked that vision; to the day of his death he had grave doubts about his successor. Alfred had wanted another Alfred, and the two Cannon Kings could not have been less alike. The father had been "Herr Krupp" at the age of fourteen. Friedrich Alfred was "Fritz" all his life.[4] Despite Alfred's imaginary illnesses he had the constitution of Kruppstahl. Despite the son's robust appearance he was genuinely frail, a chronic sufferer from high blood pressure and asthma which may have been attributable, as his resentful mother believed, to his birth in the soot-laden air of the factory yard. The older Krupp was rawboned and cranky. The boy was fat, myopic, and placid, and his only real childhood interest was natural science. As a youth he appeared to spend most of his time weighing himself and then rolling his eyes at the result, or in labeling samples of flora and fauna.

The Great Krupp was appalled. Exultant over the arrival of a male heir, he had christened his mightiest steam hammer of that decade after him. Now his hopes, like the unwieldy hammer, were broken. The dynasty seemed doomed; he had sired a slug. For a time he seriously considered disinheriting the youth and setting him up as a gentleman farmer.[5] Then, as Fritz reached adolescence, his health improved. Alfred changed his mind. Instead of disowning him he would train him. Specimens were *verboten*. So was formal education; the boy had just said good-bye to private tutors and was beginning to enjoy Essen's *Gymnasium* when, to his dismay, his father ordered him to quit school.

Alfred's motives were mixed. One was selfish. He was fond of his bland son; as he wrote a member of the management, Fritz was his "only boy" and had spent most of his childhood "with my wife and far away from me." The thought that he should be deprived of precious hours of companionship while Fritz was in a classroom vexed him. Being the sort of man he was, he therefore declared schooling forbidden, too. Being Alfred, he also rationalized the order. To him it was obvious: the sole proprietor could provide invaluable information, facts and insight which could not be found in any curriculum. He would be his son's *Gymnasialdirektor*. He wrote, "The best I can hope and do for Fritz — and I believe it will be more valuable to him than his inheritance — is to advise him to collect and file all my writings, so that he will always know the spirit and ambitions of my career and save himself much anxiety, provided that he accepts with confidence what I myself, with equal confidence, have written down and wanted him to understand" (*So wird er mehr und mehr sich hineinfinden in den Geist und das Streben meines Lebens und viel eigenes Denken und eigene Sorgen wird er sich ersparen, wenn er mit Überzeugung das aufnehmen wird, was ich mit Überzeugung geschrieben und gewollt habe*).[6]

The instruction began in Torquay the autumn after the Franco-Prussian War. He gave the boy a thick notebook and a fistful of well-sharpened pencils; whenever an inspiring idea crossed Alfred's mind he would speak up, and it was Fritz's job to record it. On October 11 Krupp wrote the Prokura that he wanted his entire correspondence preserved "so that my son may study it later." Back in the Gusstahlfabrik he sent a communiqué to Torquay ("Alfred Krupp to Friedrich Alfred Krupp") observing that priceless lessons were to be learned by copying a wise man's words. "I therefore recommend," he concluded, "that you assemble and record all original letters from me." Now then, he asked, didn't that sound better than collecting biological specimens?[7]

Fritz can hardly have thought so. The seventeen-year-old boy realized that the task would be staggering; his father was a human letter-writing machine. But good-naturedly he agreed. Life with father had taught him to be devious, and the education of the industrial crown prince — or, as Alfred would have it, *"wahrscheinlicher Erbe des Etablissements"* (the heir apparent of the establishment) — proceeded. "This advice will be more valuable to you than your inheritance," the father wrote, and the son dutifully copied, "This advice will be more valuable to you than your inheritance." A spate of Krupp prejudices followed. Fritz must cultivate distrust of people so that "Nobody will be able to fool you," and he should learn to think out "every possibility in advance, generally ten years in advance"; while "many clever people may regard that as superfluous, and all mentally lazy people always will . . . I have always found it pays, just as a chief of staff always has his farthest movements prearranged for every conceivable case in the event of victory or defeat." Victory, for a sole proprietor, meant absolute rule of his domain. Defeat would be falling into the hands of "stock-company-promoting beasts of prey." If Fried. Krupp of Essen became a corporation, Alfred would rise from hell to haunt his son. There was one exception. Much as he despised stockholders, he detested matriarchies even more; should Fritz fail to produce male issue, he would prefer public ownership to having the firm fall into the hands of women.[8]

And that reminded him of something else. He wasn't wasting all this time on one generation. He expected these teachings to be handed down to his child's children's children — *"für ewig Zeiten,"* as he subsequently wrote his son; "for all time." Accordingly, when he drew up the *General-regulativ* the boy served as his amanuensis. Alfred's epistle to Bertha's cousin Ernst from Torquay, alerting the Prokura to the imminent arrival of its new constitution, gives some idea of what the youth was going through. "About regulations," he wrote,

> *Ich schicke Dir später mein Originalschreiben (in Bleistift), welches Fritz abgeschrieben hat. . . . Das ist mir eine Freude und eine Beruhigung.*

> I will send you later my original draft (in pencil) which Fritz copied. Fritz has now bought himself a book, in which I shall write diverse things for him; he will also copy this long letter into it, and please send him what I wrote about the control of the shop managers and foremen, or a copy of it, so that he may include it in his collection. I am glad that he is doing this task at his own volition and is fascinated and delighted by it, constantly volunteering; he already takes his future career seriously. That pleases and comforts me.[9]

That was rubbish. Fritz hadn't volunteered for this drudgery, and certainly it could have neither fascinated nor delighted him. Occasionally he found a gem in the slag. His father's suggestion that *"Du musst beim künftigen Kaiser das sein, was ich beim jetzigen war\** was the most important piece of advice he ever received; though vulnerable to hindsight now, in the light of what was then known it was canny. It was also an exception. Most of the time the son floundered in a torrent of empty words. As he later conceded with his instinctive tact, "Because of my father's high ideals, the years of my apprenticeship (*Lehrjahre*) were not easy." In fact they became unbearable. He developed writer's cramp. He was desperate. He joined the army.[10]

---

\* Literally, "You must have the same relationship with the future Kaiser that I used to have with the present one." This was written in 1872, during the misunderstanding between Alfred and Wilhelm I over the shipment of Krupp's new field gun to the Austrians.

Fritz didn't enlist — that would have brought an open breach with his father — but the effect was the same. Being the Cannon King's heir apparent had given him entree to select Offizierskorps circles, and he contrived to be called up for compulsory military service. It was a brilliant stroke, providing him with the one escape hatch he could enter without dishonor; Alfred, who was making a fortune out of German militarism, couldn't possibly object. Posted to the Baden Dragoons in Karlsruhe, Fritz was deliriously happy. After his father's drill, Prussian discipline was a lark. Back in Villa Hügel, Krupp fumed impotently — and, as it turned out, needlessly, for within a few weeks his scribe was back at his elbow; the dragoons had discharged their recruit for "shortsightedness, asthmatic attacks, and corpulence." Fritz, shattered, sobbed bitterly. Alfred presented him with a ream of paper and a box of brand-new pencils. With them was a note of greeting. It began cheerily,

*Lieber Fritz!*
*Ich kam in den Zug, aus dem einen ins andere, so werde ich fortfahren für Dich meine Überzeugungen niederzulegen.*

Dear Fritz,
My train of thought leads me from one thing to another, so I shall just continue to put down my views for you.

After a rambling denunciation of *"Kanalschwärmer"* (canal fanatics) — sinister figures who were improving the Ruhr's waterways with his tax money — it ended, *"Ich wünsche Dir viel Vergnügen. Dein treuer Alter"* (I wish you a good time. Your affectionate Old Man).[11]

The Old Man really thought he was giving the boy a rare treat. Doctors disagreed. The army physician in Karlruhe hadn't had any choice; he had to reject a fat, bespectacled young man whose breath, after he had goose-stepped the length of the parade ground, rasped like a file. Fritz wasn't fit to be a soldier, wasn't even well enough to spend all his time in the Ruhr. Plainly he was wobbly, and his father became alarmed. The ubiquitous Ernst Schweninger arrived from Berlin, listened to Fritz's gasps, and screamed, "LIE DOWN!" He kneaded the fleshy chest with his bony fingers. *"Gelenkrheumatismus,"* he spat, arising — rheumatoid arthritis. Was it catching? the worried parent asked. No, the doctor said testily, but it couldn't be cured in this house, which smelled like a horse's latrine, or this valley, with its filthy air. What was needed was a long trip in a restorative climate, accompanied by a physician. Schweninger recommended the valley of the Nile. He himself couldn't go, but his colleague Schmidt was available.[12]

That was in September 1874. Three months later Fritz and Dr. Schmidt were in Cairo, presumably beyond Alfred's reach. Not so: wherever there was a mailman, there was Krupp. His first letters were solicitous. On December 22 he wrote, *"Freue ich mich über Dein gutes Befinden"* (I'm glad that you are doing well), though in the very next sentence he launched into a string of waspish complaints designed to make Fritz feel guilty for vacationing while his poor *treuer Alter* battled single-handedly against staggering odds:

> *Ich vegetiere mit fortwährendem Wechsel von Nerven und Erkältungs-leiden, welche von denen, die sie nicht haben, sehr gering geachtet werden. . . . Das Widerstreben ist grösser als die Treue, und meine frühere Vorstellung von der Allgemeinheit der Treue stellt sich immer mehr als Illusion heraus.*

> I am vegetating still with alternating nerve trouble and colds, things that people who don't have them think are nothing. My time is as full of cares as ever, and I just have to go on and on writing. I wouldn't have all these burdens and anxieties and all this work if those responsible had done their duty. In time order will emerge. Maybe it won't be too late. But it is very hard to instill a sense of order and duty where the climate has encouraged the weeds of laziness and irresponsibility. There is more hostility to me than loyalty, and each day I realize more and more that my old notion, that loyalty is to be found everywhere, is just an illusion.[13]

*Ordnung:* order. It remained his passion, and as he had grown older he had become convinced that everyone around him was engaged in a conspiracy to deprive him of it. A quarter-century before John Fiske popularized the word paranoia in the *Atlantic Monthly* Alfred was a full-fledged paranoid — Germany's greatest, perhaps, until the champion of the New Order appeared and infected a nation. Actually Fritz had more justification, for he really was being persecuted. He sent his father pictures of himself taken by the Nile, and he must have eyed the first sentence of Alfred's reply warily:

> *Mein lieber Fritz!*
> *Mit grosser Freude habe ich aus den übersandten Photographien ersehen, dass Du bereits kräftiger aussiehst als je.*

> My dear Fritz,
> I noticed with great pleasure that in the photographs you sent me you already look stronger than you ever did before.[14]

In the snapshots the boy looked anything but well, nor was he; he suffered constant pain and was in no condition to work. All the same, that was what his Old Man had in mind. Alfred had never forgotten that his first cannon sale had been to Khedive Said of Egypt. Now Said's nephew Ismail sat on the throne. Surely there must be *some* business there to be picked up. On New Year's Eve his eye lit upon a newspaper paragraph.

Earlier in the year Ismail had annexed the Sudanese province of Darfur; now there was speculation that the Egyptians might build a railroad there. It was nonsense. The Khedive was so bankrupt that in less than a year he would be obliged to sell his Suez Canal shares to the British, but Alfred seized upon the item, dispatched his Constantinople agent to Cairo, and telegraphed Fritz instructions to open sales talks. That evening he wrote him, "I am prepared to undertake the whole railway to Darfur (*die ganze Bahn nach Darfur*), including all the earthworks. Therefore you may go directly to talk to such people as may be interested in the scheme and have notions of their own about it." (*welche sich dafür interessieren mögen und eine Stellung zu solchem Unternehmen einnehman*). This has a strong flavor of busywork. Alfred admitted as much: "It is possible, of course, that the report is baseless and that there is no question at present of any such work, that the report is only correct in part or not at all. Even in that case none of the brainwork or writing will have been wasted (*ist kein Nachdenken und keine Zeile deshalb vergeudet*); a similar case will turn up later, and we shall have thought it through in advance and can exploit our present conclusions."[15]

It was improbable. *This* case, as Alfred conceived it, did not exist. The astonishing fact is that he had no idea where the Sudan was. He thought it must be somewhere in the Middle East; next morning he mailed Fritz another letter, explaining that the contract appealed to him because "For a long time I have been turning the idea of connecting Europe and eastern Asia by a railroad, and I find that there has been a surprising amount of preliminary work done along these lines, much more than I had expected, much of it cutting across my original plan and modifying it" (*welches meine ursprüngliche Idee durchkreuzt und läutert*).[16]

He had anticipated putting the Reich's *Drang nach Osten* on the tracks by thirteen years, but his ignorance of geography meant that he was merely inflicting meaningless punishment upon his son. Obediently the heir dragged himself to the palace and then reported that Ismail wasn't interested. Still dissatisfied, Alfred cabled him to seek an audience with "Zeki Pasha." Zeki was rumored to be powerful. He might know the right strings to pull. Fritz limped off again and found the pasha unsympathetic and vocal about it; he nursed a passionate hatred of all trains.

At this point Dr. Schmidt intervened. His patient was deteriorating, and he saw no hope of recovery unless he severed all lines of communication between father and son. Therefore he took a drastic step. He bought two three-month passages aboard a lazy Nile steamer — and whisked Fritz aboard without telling Essen. The correspondence which follows is one of the most entertaining in the Krupp family archives. Alfred writes, suggesting a new approach to the Khedive. No answer. Well, maybe it wasn't a good idea, the Old Man concedes; however, that doesn't mean that Fritz should waste his time "*herumreisen und herumtreiben*" (dawdling and fooling around): "without interfering with your recovery, you will have time to study. Who knows how long I may have to live!" Still no reply.[17] On January 26 Alfred sounds an ominous note. Maybe Fritz doesn't know it, but there have been a few changes in the shops. Everyone, and he means *everyone*, must toe *der Alte's* line: "Laziness and indifference (*Trägheit und Gleichgültigkeit*) are out. All, without exception, who cannot cooperate or work harmoniously in the same spirit as the others will have to go."[18]

Assuming that this lecture will be taken to heart, he resumes his course of instruction next day, writing, "There is still an enormous amount of advice that I want to pass along to you as you start your career. Today I have time only for what is essential. I shall enlighten you regarding several contacts that we have and the characters of certain individuals, their value or lack of it" (*ihren Wert oder ihre Unbrauchbarkeit*).[19]

Three weeks pass, and each day the Hügel postman spreads his hands helplessly. The voice in Egypt continues to be mute. Can Fritz be paralyzed? Has he fallen victim to a tropical disease? No; Schmidt would have relayed such news. Annoyed, Alfred fires off a primer on bookkeeping. He begins, "Today I will only touch upon what I intend to explain in more detail at an early date. The first point is the nature of accountancy, finance, and calculation. You must study these until you feel completely at home with them" (*In diesen Dingen musst Du immer vollständig zu Hause sein*).[20]

This memorial languishes in Cairo, unread. Next comes a bale of paper, with instructions to sift every word of it. Hearing nothing, the Old Man dispatches a sharp note:

*Mein lieber Fritz!*

*Ich bedauere, dass Du nicht dazu gelangt bist, die Kopien meiner Schreiben an die Prokura nachzulesen. . . . Sie enthalten die Erfahrung meines Lebens und meiner Grundsätze, denen ich allein mein Wohlergehen verdanke und deren Nichtachtung allein die Ursache des Rüttelns an solchem Wohlergehen war.*

I regret that you have not gotten round to reading the copies of my letters to the Prokura, making extracts from them, and registering the contents, as well as reading other letters that I sent to the Prokura. They contain the experience of my life, and my principles, to which alone I owe my prosperity, and the ignoring of which was the sole cause of the jeopardizing of this prosperity.[21]

Silence. Apparently nobody in Egypt gives a hang about Krupp's life experience, principles, or prosperity. *Hei! Buh!* What's going on down there? February 17 is the heir's twenty-first birthday. In the castle on the hill Alfred and Bertha, reunited for the occasion, blow out candles on a cake and telegraph greetings, which are unacknowledged. Now Alfred's blood is up. The letters and cables from Essen reach a crescendo of rage, the threat of disinheritance is renewed — it is always possible, he writes on February 18, "to make other dispositions in order to preserve, without misgiving of any kind, the edifice I have brought into being" (*anders zu disponieren, um mit grösstmöglicher Zuversicht das Geschaffene zu erhalten*) — and the grizzled gunsmith reaches an agony of frustration. Then comes the simple explanation. The slow boat to nowhere redocks and Dr. Schmidt wires that his patient is completely restored. While Krupp's splenetic notes have been piling up in an Egyptian postal bin, his son has been admiring herons. Schmidt is ordered home to give a full account of the unauthorized expedition; Fritz, exculpated, remains to inspect a batch of Krupp cannon whose gun carriages have been warped by the arid climate.[22]

Somehow Fritz always had an answer; he always avoided the fatal clash. To survive he had cultivated an extraordinary gift for intrigue which, in his father's last years, was an incalculable asset to the firm. In the '70's and '80's international arms manufacturers were tacitly recognized as independent powers. As such, they dealt directly with sovereigns. Alfred made a dreadful envoy. In Potsdam his bombast was understood, for he was dealing with fellow Prussians. Even there his temperament had left lifelong scars, however, and abroad its eruptions would have been catastrophic. Thus it was Fritz who called upon Balkan monarchs and the Czar of All the Russias, Fritz who represented the firm at international exhibitions. His silky gifts were equally useful in Essen. Since his father had given him no specific assignment, he set up a desk in the Stammhaus and pored over memoranda between Alfred and Alfred's staff. There is no sign that his resulting contributions were appreciated at the time (indeed, the behavior of the Prokura after he took over indicates that the managers had seriously underrated him) but he repeatedly served as a buffer between them and the Old Man. Twice he persuaded valuable men (Sophus Goose and Wilhelm Gross) to withdraw resignations after rows with the Cannon King. Once the Old Man drew up an elaborate report "On the Prevention of Gas at the Base of Projectiles, the Guiding and Centering of the Projectile, and the Lining of Its Casing or Powder Magazine with Plate, as well as on Progressive Spiraling." He forwarded it to Gross, who, never dreaming it would be returned to Hügel, scribbled an obscenity across it. Alfred saw the slur. As retribution, he tried to play Major von Trautmann off against Gross. Fritz heard of the scheme and wrote the major:

> *Diese ganz privaten Zeilen schreibe ich in der Hoffnung, das Gute zu fördern, aber auch böse Folgen zu vermeiden. . . .*
> *Herzlichen Gruss und nehmen Sie diese Zeilen nicht übel.*
> > *Ihrem ganz ergebenen . . .*

I am writing you this entirely private letter in the hope of advancing what is desirable, but also of preventing what would be most unfortunate. . . . Before you enter into any discussion you should send for all pertinent documents. You will find there that Gross has answered a number of questions. You will, I am confident, find yourself in agreement with him on most matters. If so, it would be desirable, in every instance, for the answers to be mutually consistent. I want to be very certain that my father will not think that your views and Gross's are opposed when they are basically in agreement. My father is very much inclined to make this error, which would cause enormous confusion and must be avoided if possible. . . .

All my best wishes. Don't be angry with me for having written this.

Most sincerely yours,

F. A. KRUPP[23]

Forewarned, Trautmann supported the ordnance designer. Of course, had Alfred found out that his son was sabotaging him, his thunder would have shaken the entire Ruhr. He never had an inkling. He had trained Fritz well, though not as he had intended. He had thought to impose his will, his passions, his behavior patterns upon the boy; and instead he had created a mirror image of himself. Old Krupp was direct, young Krupp was oblique. The testator was virile, his heir feminine. Alfred was crude, Fritz crafty. The father was obvious, the son deceptive. It could not be otherwise; the youth had had to cultivate these traits because he lacked the emotional equipment to do battle with a man who never hesitated to gouge and bite in a scrap, and who, unlike Fritz, had not been crippled by a ravaging split between his parents. The child may have loved his father. One cannot tell. But there can be no doubt that he was mortally afraid of him. He would go to any lengths to avoid a showdown, and because he was clever and resourceful one never came.

✠　✠　✠

His marriage was a near thing. Alone even he could not have bypassed his *treuer Alter* and reached the altar. As it was he needed two powerful allies, his mother and his wife, each of whom was more masculine than he. Indeed, it is entirely possible that Bertha, not Fritz, chose Margarethe von Ende as her future daughter-in-law. It was she who took an instant liking to Marga, introduced her to her son, arranged trysts, and planned the union — thus achieving the prize which eluded her husband: an extension of her personality into the next generation.

Outwardly the two women appeared to have little in common. Bertha was a plebeian malingerer, Marga a patrician activist. Nevertheless their values were the same. Each was asserting a woman's right to be herself, and in a country so dominated by men that coeducation was actually a prison offense, both were strong-minded, wily competitors. Alfred's wife had got her way at a terrible cost to him, herself, and their child. She had with-drawn into a strange world peopled by fellow parasites and, perhaps, by her own disordered fancies, from which she returned only on her own condi-tions. In the twentieth century it is difficult to appreciate the tactics and triumphs of the rich female neurotic a hundred years ago. Her base of operation has been swept away. Today she would be diagnosed and treated, freeing her men from the anxieties which were such powerful allies in her war against them.

Marga is more understandable. She was the presuffragette, the emanci-pated spirit determined to flee the oppressive cocoon society had fashioned for her. She could not run far. It would be quite wrong to suggest that she was sophisticated, worldly, or even as knowledgeable as, say, a fourteen-year-old of the 1960's. In her Düsseldorf home neither Baron August von Ende nor his wife would acknowledge to their children that babies were born naked, and the baroness attempted to conceal her later pregnancies from Marga. The girl knew her mother was with child, but her information stopped right there. Moreover, she was wholly ignorant of the more exotic aspects of sex, and later this innocence would magnify the great tragedy in her own life and her husband's.[24]

Nor did she know much more about politics. When she was seventeen she had been taken to Berlin to stand wide-eyed under a sky of forget-me-not blue as the victorious Prussian army, *Pickelhauben* flashing in the sun, marched through the Brandenburg Gate to the thrilling silver flourishes of trumpets, ophicleides, and kettledrums; and once she had heard the Iron Chancellor speak. Yet most of the history she knew was family history. The von Endes were of that lackluster breed which had been reduced to genteel poverty by the great Bonaparte. Indeed, they had been on the decline for two centuries, and to find an ancestor of genuine eminence they had to reach back still another two hundred years, to Franz von Sickingen (1481–1523), a Rhineland knight and Reformation leader who had served Charles V as imperial chamberlain. By the 1870's the women of the family had been reduced to washing servants' clothing and making their own dresses.

Yet a title retained a certain magic; August von Ende represented Düs-seldorf in the first Reichstag, and in the capital his impressionable daugh-ter heard of girls who supported themselves by teaching. She mentioned this to her mother, who swiftly replied that if she did anything of the sort her family would disown her. Marga went ahead anyhow. Lacking suffi-cient education to teach, she exploited her facility with languages to become a governess, first to the children of a British admiral on the bleak island of Holyhead, off the Welsh coast, and then, more agreeably, to a princess in the little German state of Dessau. From time to time she visited her home. The door wasn't barred. The baroness hadn't disowned

her after all (though Marga was obliged to sleep in a maid's bedroom so
that her siblings would realize that their eldest sister had chosen the
primrose path), and to avoid scandal she was included on family trips,
which is how she happened to meet the Krupps at Villa Hügel. August
had official business with Alfred. He brought his wife and children along to
see the fantastic castle. Bertha took Marga aside, discovered that she was
exactly Fritz's age, and began pushing the alliance.

The details of the subsequent tug of war are obscure; one of the few
reliable accounts comes from the memoirs of Baroness Deichmann.

> The Krupps had only one son, Fritz. I was very sorry for him. He was
> very delicate and suffered from asthma, but his father would not realize
> this and expected him to do all the work that he himself had done at his
> age. A special train was always in readiness to take the unfortunate Fritz to
> any part of Germany on business, and he returned quite exhausted from
> these tours.
>
> Fritz often came to see us in Chester Street and at the Garth, to get
> away from Essen. He became engaged to a charming lady, Fräulein von
> Ende. The father objected to this arrangement, being anxious that his son
> should marry into some great industrial factory. It was a long time before
> permission was granted. . . . Herr Krupp must have been very peculiar in
> his old age, as he repudiated his wife and refused to allow her to return to
> his home. Krupp was a wonderful man in many ways, and cared for his
> thousands of workpeople in a fatherly manner; but he was very severe with
> them. He would issue commands like an emperor, which had to be obeyed
> to the letter.[25]

In point of fact, it is doubtful that any prospective daughter-in-law
would have suited Bertha's husband; his own experiences with women had
been too bruising, and he was too jealous of Fritz. Though compelled to
deal with August, he looked upon him as a petty bureaucrat. As a self-made
man he detested the Prussian nobility, and he put forth specific objections
to this daughter of it. She was willful, she was pious, and in his opinion she
was also homely. Whether Fritz sprang to the defense of his love is unknown. Silence would have been consistent with his character. Since his
mother was embattled there was no need for him to stir himself, and after
she had withdrawn from Villa Hügel, never to darken its hideous door
again, Alfred told Fritz that if he was bent on taking the *Hündin* to the
altar he could go ahead. He did; next day he wrote August,

*Hochverehrter Herr von Ende!*
   *Gestatten Sie mir bitte eine Zusammenkunft . . . oder wo Sie sonst
befehlen, damit ich um Ihre Genehmigung in einer Angelegenheit ein-
komme, von der mein Lebensglück abhängt. . . . In erregter Spannung
Ihr seit lange Ihnen treu ergebener*

                                                  F. A. KRUPP

Esteemed Mr. von Ende:
    I beg you to grant me an audience . . . to permit me to ask your sanction in a matter on which my happiness in life depends. . . . In great anxiety and suspense I remain, as I have always been, yours most devotedly,

F. A. KRUPP[26]

Approval came speedily. Very likely the baron could scarcely believe his good fortune. Last year Marga had been regarded by their relatives as little better than a streetwalker. Now she was marrying the Fatherland's most affluent scion, and in that summer of 1882 they all came to celebrate the engagement at Wörlitz and the wedding in Blasewitz.

Bertha was present, Alfred not. After the ceremony he received them on the castle steps with a formal, written speech of welcome. (More homework for Fritz.) Replacing it in his pocket he indulged himself in one of his pet polemics, a denunciation of the absurd pretensions of that overrated Saxe-Weimar shyster, Johann Wolfgang von Goethe. As his son waggled a pencil, trying furiously to keep pace with the soaring vowels and crashing consonants, Krupp solemnly proclaimed: "I don't care how great a philosopher Goethe is supposed to have been or how many other people dispense with vast quantities of worldly wisdom and respect for society and the overbearing masses. I don't give a fig for any of them. Those who stare at their navels and emit the judgment of idiots, no matter how highly they may be regarded elsewhere, make guttersnipes of themselves, and that is my opinion of them. So far as I am concerned, in conducting my business I pay no attention to their hogwash. I go my own way and never ask anybody what's right" (*Ich für mich nehme auf keinen Menschen Rücksicht, gehe immer meinen eigenen Weg, frage niemanden, was Recht ist*).[27]

Alfred smacked his lips. He liked his remarks so much he decided to put them in a letter to a Düsseldorf acquaintance, and he confiscated Fritz's notes on the spot. Then, frowning heavily, he informed the dismayed bride and groom that he had no place to put them.

It was true. Der Hügel was going through one of its periodic tearing-out of systems; of its three hundred rooms, only one suite, his own, was inhabitable. The young Krupps went off to Madrid and stayed with the royal family — presenting a long-range cannon as an expression of their gratitude — and returned to find that "*der alte Herr*" (the old gentleman) as Marga always called him, had decided to house them in Hügel's rambling "small house." Once she was settled there, he proceeded to stalk her from the castle proper. Spiteful notes lectured her on the behavior of her guests. If she and Fritz were going out he would watch from behind drawn curtains until they were ready to enter their carriage, whereupon he would send a servant with word that he wanted to see her at once on what would turn out to be a trivial matter. Marga refused to be drawn. She invited him to lunch daily, sat attentively through his long monologues, and solicited his advice on household problems. He replied by insulting her. She was wasting his money, he told her; she was living like a queen. She asked how he thought she might cut expenses. He suggested that she reduce the grocery bill by raising vegetables on the lawn. She ignored that one, and she insisted on entertaining von Endes despite the old gentleman's conviction that his son's new in-laws were all germ carriers. In a typical screed he wrote Longsdon, "Fritz returned today ill from Meppen, his wife is still suffering and besides his father and mother-in-law, visitors here, are both also ill. It is here a perfect hospital on the hill." With Marga he went further. He accused her of turning his castle into a "pesthouse" (*Spital für Pestkranke*). She came over to apologize for her constitution and he hid, fearing contamination.[28]

This went on for five years. Meanwhile Fritz was trying to create a role for himself down at the works. During his betrothal his father had appointed him to the Prokura. He was to receive 20 percent of the firm's annual profits or 100,000 marks, whichever was the greater, so he should have been carefree.[29] In truth he was under a tremendous strain. In his early thirties, he looked fifteen years older; his hair was gray, his eyes peered out weakly from behind gold-rimmed spectacles, and he had developed a tremendous middle-aged spread. Lacking an assignment from above he chose his own tasks and tackled them zealously. First he set out to master all technical aspects of steelmaking. Next he appointed himself Krupp's foreign minister. Gradually his Florentine presence became felt in Peking, Buenos Aires, Rio, Santiago, and all the Balkan capitals. He became expert in the methods of Armstrong, Schneider, and the Mitsuis. In his files were the name and background of every foreign arms salesman, gunnery statistics, analyses of military spending in every government, and a growing correspondence with Gustav Nachtigal, the German explorer, whom he had met in Cairo and whose African annexations were inspiring the first demands for a powerful German navy. Unnoticed by the rest of the management, Fritz became the best-informed man in Essen. Behind his dull façade lurked a first-class mind, and its qualities should have been evident when he made his debut as Villa Hügel's host. A mission of Japanese economists, engineers, and officers came to the Ruhr after a disappointing reception in Paris. Alfred designated Fritz his deputy. Before the mission left, its allegiance and its yen had been switched from Schneider to Krupp — a brilliant coup and a direct consequence of young Krupp's dogged study, though his older colleagues could not see it.

On a Hügel wall today there hangs a curious portrait of Fritz, showing him rising hastily from his desk. In the background Alfred looks down sternly. One feels that the son has just become aware of his father's presence and is springing to his feet, and doubtless that is how he appeared then to the senior men in management — an intimidated, ineffectual youth whose successes sprang from the old man's genius. The old man would have agreed. During his last months he wrote each of his associates, telling them he counted upon them to help the heir through the difficult period which, he was certain, would follow his own death. He looked upon Fritz as genial but soft, well-meaning but lacking in good judgment; e.g., his picking of Marga. Alfred remained his daughter-in-law's implacable enemy to the end. Nothing she did pleased him, and in his eye her worst blunder was giving birth to a daughter in March 1886. Christening the infant Bertha Antoinette didn't help. It was, he thought, a gratuitous reminder of his own domestic unhappiness. He visited the nursery once and then slunk back to the castle's main hall, loudly advertising his view that all children were "Gewürm" (vermin). During the following summer, his last on earth, Marga conceived again. He died convinced that the new infant would also be a girl. He was right, and naming her Barbara after the patron saint of artillery didn't alter the fact that there was no male Krupp in line.[30]

But though the far horizon was obscure, the immediate future was assured, and in eleven months the House of Krupp plunged into an era so different from anything Essen had known that the effect was intoxicating. One by one the dominant figures of the old order were passing. Alfred was in Kettwig Gate cemetery, and the following winter his wife joined him. Nursed to the end by Marga — and refusing to set foot in Villa Hügel, or even to sanction funeral services there — Bertha slipped away unnoticed. Doubtless her death would have been overlooked in any event, for all eyes were on Berlin. Twice that year the leadership of the Reich changed hands. On March 9, 1888, the first Kaiser died, and the humane Kronprinz became Kaiser Friedrich III. His reign lasted exactly ninety-eight days. Riddled with cancer, he succumbed on June 15, and the flame of German liberalism, which had flickered hopefully, was extinguished when Friedrich's handsome, mustachioed, twenty-nine-year-old son replaced him at the helm. His own father had concluded that he was pompous and vain; now all Europe was to learn it. Kaiser Wilhelm II's first message was addressed, not to his people, but to the military. In bristling language he reaffirmed his faith in divine right — "The king's will," he declared, "is the supreme law of the land." The man who, next to Adolf Hitler, was to become the Krupps' most influential patron, had mounted the imperial throne. The era of what was to be known as Wilhelmine Germany had begun.[31]

✠    ✠    ✠

Wilhelm I had still ruled the Fatherland, and Barbara had been in her mother's womb, when Fritz paid his first visit to the capital as sole proprietor of the world's largest industrial establishment. The new head of the family didn't look like a king, but he certainly traveled like one. His private train set out from Hügel's *Zechenbahn* bearing trunks packed with ceremonial costumes and handsomely mounted gifts in various calibers, and his huge entourage was headed by Hanns Jencke; Carl Menshausen, another director; Felix von Ende, Fritz's brother-in-law; and *Doktor der Medizin Ernst Schweninger, the Second Reich's Merlin.* Their leader had been planning this trip for a long time. He called it *"die Fürstenrundreise,"* his "royal tour." Actually he was just calling upon the firm's chief customers, but since they were all sovereigns, attaching a purple ribbon to the expedition seemed appropriate. After an amiable chat with Seine Majestät the tour wound back and forth across Europe, stopping while the lord of Essen exchanged pleasantries with King Leopold of Belgium, King Albert of Saxony, King Carol of Rumania, and Sultan Abdul Hamid of Turkey.[32]

Each of the host monarchs was, in the family's benign phrase, "an old friend of our House," though admittedly the sultan was a controversial one. While the nineteenth century took a permissive attitude toward regal whims, the most indulgent had to concede that the ruler of Constantinople was an unholy terror. "Abdul the Damned," a red-bearded small-arms enthusiast who carried three pistols in his sash and could write his name with them on a wall at twenty paces, liked to while away the hours by butchering his subjects. He had exterminated Kurds, Lycians, and Circassians in Asia Minor, Greeks in Crete, Arabs in Yemen, Albanians on the Adriatic Coast, and Druses in Lebanon, and now he had fixed his blood-colored eye on the Armenians.

Fritz, of course, was too tactful to refer to the sultan's genocidal little ways. Instead he addressed him as the *"Wohltäter des Türkenvolkes"* (benefactor of the Turkish people). Abdul showed off with his revolvers, and then — a sign of the quasi-official role which Krupps would play in successive German governments — entrusted him with a message to Bismarck which he regarded as too delicate for Wilhelm's ambassador. As Fritz explained it that evening in a letter to the Iron Chancellor: "His Majesty the Sultan finds himself in an exceedingly critical position at the moment. The key to it is the Bulgarian question. The Turkish people and the Sultan himself want peace and most ardently wish to preserve it. Therefore the Sultan, both in his own behalf and that of his people, pleads for the benign support of Your Highness at this difficult time" (*in dieser schweren Zeit*). Details followed, and action came in the wake of Bismarck's receipt of young Krupp's aide-mémoire; Prince Ferdinand of Saxe-Coburg, the new ruler of the Bulgars, was not recognized by Berlin.[33]

Back in Essen, Fritz decreed that *"alle unnötige Schreiberei vermieden und das Notwendige mündlich besprochen werde"* (all unnecessary writing will be avoided and even crucial arrangements settled orally). His purpose was to end the blizzard of intrafirm billets which had descended on the works from Hügel. It was misunderstood. According to the unpublished memoirs of Ernst Haux, Krupp's treasurer, who is our most valuable source for this period, the members of the management "looked like Guards officers" and treated the heir like a raw recruit. They thought he preferred to remain in the background, which was precisely where they wanted him. When they discovered that he meant to cut down on memoranda by presiding in person, they were amazed. Jencke led the mutineers. The old man had wanted the Prokura to run the firm, he said. Surely the son did not want to profane his father's memory. Fritz, he suggested, should avoid excessive burdens; he should remember that he was not a well man. Like Alfred they had been deceived by Fritz's ineffectual expression and sphinxlike self-possession; they assumed they were dealing with a lump.[34]

They were dealing with a Krupp, and in his own serpentine fashion he let them know it. In one of his rare written instructions he gently put the fiery Jencke in his place: "I do, of course, intend to pay stricter attention to the contracts under way and to the proceedings of management than my father could, owing to his old age and deteriorating health. My motives, surely, are comprehensible" (*Die Motive hierfür sind ja leicht begreiflich*).[35]

First he abolished *die Prokura*, the committee of management, and replaced it with *ein Direktorium*, a board. Next he enlarged the board and packed it with younger, more sympathetic members. Finally he amended the *Generalregulativ* to transfer the power of executive decision from the directors to the owner. The regency was over; an *alleinige Inhaber* was in charge once more. Next he launched an expansion program. The Gusstahlfabrik's smelting department was rebuilt. A technical school rose to train apprentice Kruppianer. Since the shallow Ruhr could not accommodate the gigantic ore barges from Sweden, he ordered a second steel mill built on a two-mile meadow at Rheinhausen, along the west bank of the Rhine. It would take proper advantage of the basic process and would be known, he announced, as the Friedrich-Alfred-Hütte. His modesty had been sham. Behind his mask he was just as flamboyant as his father. A foreign visitor noted that

> Everywhere the name of Krupp appears: now on the picturesque marketplace, on the door of a mammoth department store, then on a bronze monument, now on the portals of a church . . . over a library, numerous schoolhouses, butcher shops, a sausage factory, shoemakers' shops and tailoring establishments, over playgrounds and cemeteries. . . . There is a German beer garden close to each park, and over them is written plainly, "Owned by Friedrich Krupp."[36]

The first generation of Ruhr barons, whom Alfred had led, had been maestros of the factory floor. Fritz, the new trailblazer, never touched an anvil and rarely even saw one. Indeed, he was seldom in Essen. He was off meeting fresh challenges with his sly skills, and in the fifth year of his reign he offered a dazzling example of how he could crush an antagonist who had successfully defied his father. Hermann Gruson had first crossed Alfred in 1848, when, as master mechanic for the Berlin-Hamburg railroad, he had sent sample axles from Krupp to a rival firm for testing. For nearly forty years the two men had been bitter enemies. Alfred's armor could never match Hermann's, and to prove it Gruson had set up his own proving grounds at Tangerhütte, where foreign officers watched shells bounce off his plate and demolish Krupp's. His factory in the Saxon city of Magdeburg held so commanding a lead that Jencke advised Fritz to forget about turrets; they were hopelessly outclassed. But Gruson had made the one fatal slip that Krupp had avoided. During the panic of '73–'74 he had incorporated his company. In the spring of 1892 the shareholders of Gruson A.G. (*Aktiengesellschaft* — joint-stock company) assembled and were astonished to find Friedrich Alfred Krupp among them. While Hermann stared across the table, his old foe's son counted out certificates. At the end he produced a pencil and did a simple sum. He owned 51 percent of the stock. Gruson now belonged to Krupp. Crushed, Hermann went home to die, and by the following May, when Magdeburg was formally absorbed by the Essen empire, Krupp-Panzer had become a synonym for quality steel plate throughout Europe.[37]

By now Krupp's reputation for excellence was self-perpetuating; if an inventor had a really good thing he headed for Villa Hügel. On April 10, 1893, a thirty-six-year-old German mechanical engineer appeared with patent number 67207, for a new kind of internal combustion engine employing autoignition of the fuel. Clipped to it was his explanatory text, *Theorie und Konstruktion eines rationellen Wärmemotors*. His name was Rudolf Diesel, and he impressed upon Fritz that "The whole of my engine must be made of steel." Krupp nodded, riffling through the blueprints with one hand and reaching for a contract with the other. Four years later he gave the world the first, 32-horsepower diesel engine. Hiram Maxim came to the hill with a license permitting Krupp manufacture of his machine guns, and so did Alfred Bernhard Nobel, bringing his revolutionary formula for smokeless gunpowder, ballistite. Ballistite meant that soldiers need neither reveal their positions to the enemy nor be enveloped in black fog. Smokeless powder was essential to the rapid-firing Maxim gun, and because it burned slowly, providing maximum thrust, ballistite altered artillery design. The big steel bottles were gone forever. Cannon became long and graceful — and far more deadly.[38]

Beneath its gray skies the Ruhr, in Norman Pounds's words, "lay bright with promise."[39] The heavy throb of industrialization was changing the valley almost daily. Kumpels burrowing ever deeper beneath the works had found that the rich black veins of coking coal between Essen and Bochum were inexhaustible, and the great highway of the Rhine accommodated Krupp's growing fleet of steamships and barges, which docked from abroad and then fed moving chains of bins that rose like ski lifts, bearing chunks of ore toward the insatiable furnaces. The new generation did not, of course, create this phenomenon. The coal had always been there. Alfred Krupp's passion for vertical integration had established the essential base for growth. Bismarck's harsh peace of 1871 had virtually awarded the glittering lodes of Alsace and Lorraine to him, and the chancellor's fusion of *ein Volk* into *ein Reich* provided the political cohesion without which the Ruhrgebiet would have been merely an outsized heart in a stunted body. To these assets must be added the great unfathomable, the German national character. Elsewhere in Europe workmen and tycoons coexisted in a climate of sullen distrust. Not the *Volk*; in Churchill's mot, "the German is always at your throat or at your feet," and in the Ruhr he groveled. Whatever his political allegiance, he never struck. His wife remained preoccupied with her four K's — *Küche, Kemenate, Kinder, Kirche* (kitchen, bedroom, children, church) — and the children were trained to follow parental patterns. In Essen they hadn't much choice. The company town Alfred had built put each generation on the treadmill of the last. Kruppianer were born in Krupp maternity wards, taught in Krupp schools, and housed in Krupp developments. When they married they wedded the daughters of other Kruppianer, thus starting the process all over again.

Fritz was responsible for none of this. The forces of expansion had been ready to bound ahead when he came into his birthright. Yet the new Krupp channeled them with remarkable skill. Alfred could not have done it half so well. His genius is unquestioned, but it was the genius of the pioneer. The old man's creative life had really ended at Sedan. During his last sixteen years his craving for innovations had throttled the firm. What was needed was an exploiter, and nobody could exploit like Fritz. At the end of his sixth year in power he had modernized every toolbench in his realm. Steam hammers had been discarded for forging presses, belt-geared cranes for electrical equipment, obsolescent furnaces for Martin converters — five Martin factories in Essen alone, each larger than the old Gusstahlfabrik, which had also been refitted for the basic process. In addition, Krupp's realm was spreading in all directions. Outside Essen he owned three steel plants, any one of which would have made him a major industrialist: the Grusonwerk, Rheinhausen, and a new factory at Annen, six miles southwest of Dortmund, on the eastern fringe of the Ruhrgebiet. Elsewhere in the Reich he held title to four ironworks, three mammoth coal mines (Hannover I, Hannover II, and Sälzer und Neuack), 547 ore fields, and the Meppen range; and overseas he had added Scandinavian tracts to his Spanish possessions.[40]

The heart of his dominion remained in Essen. Within the city he had over five million square feet — 127 acres — under roofs. There were an electrical plant, a steam plant, a coking plant with 281 ovens. There were forge hammer shops and annealing, hardening, puddling, spring, and machine and boiler shops; rail, plate, rolling, and cogging mills; gasworks and waterworks; and kilns, foundries, and chemical laboratories. Each year Essen's sheds devoured 1,250,000 tons of ore and regurgitated 320,000 tons of finished Kruppstahl. And that was only production. Besides serving the Fatherland as industrialist, gunsmith and diplomat, Krupp wore another hat in the Ruhr. He was a feudal suzerain, holding deeds to the homes and barracks occupied by his 43,000 subjects. Among the supervisors of the hundred departments over which he and his staff presided were division heads administering his educational system, police force, fire brigade, and a communications grid with 196 telephone exchanges and 20 telegraph stations linked to the Kaiser's imperial network. Fritz was Essen's butcher, Essen's baker, Essen's candlestick maker. He operated 92 groceries, a slaughterhouse, a flour mill, two hotels, two clothing mills, factories manufacturing shoes, clocks, furniture and ice — even a housekeeper's school where young brides could learn how to keep Kruppianer happy. The very Bibles, vestments, and crucifixes used in the city's churches were stamped BEWEGLICHE HABE FRIED. KRUPP (personal property of Krupp).[41]

In seven years his fortune rose by 68,000,000 marks and his personal income tripled. Yet all the time the silent engine of history was pulsing beneath the surface of events, and for those who could read them there were signs of what lay ahead. There was, for example, the disappointing correspondence in the once prosperous file of Thos. Prosser & Sons. As early as January 25, 1888, Prosser reported from Manhattan's 15 Gold Street that there were "difficulties with the NY Central RR" because W. H. Vanderbilt had been persuaded that some of the railroad's business should go to home industry "for political services rendered." Complaints that deliveries from Bremen were too slow came from the Northern Pacific on July 9 and the Union Pacific on November 4. Two months later there was trouble with J. J. Hill. Prosser wrote, "Enclosed please find letter received from Mr. Hill, President of the St. Paul M&MRR, enclosing a statement of mileage of tires, by which you will see that the record made by the American Martin steel tires (Standard & Midvale) in many cases are almost equal to the mileage made by your Crucible, and in the case of the Moguls the American tire is ahead of yours. Mr. Hill has always been a strong believer in your tires but at the last interview we had with him he stated that he could not see any economy in paying an extra price for your Crucible Tires as they were now getting nearly as good results from American Martin tires. . . . He said he believed that if he came into the market with a good order he could get Martin steel tires for half the price of

Krupp Crucible Steel tires." That is exactly what happened, and there was worse to come. By the summer of 1890 Prosser was informing Essen that Krupp railway steel was "being disposed of as scrap."* But in the booming Ruhr the loss of U.S. accounts was a trifle. The *Werksarchiv* indicate that the question was never even raised at a board meeting. Fritz wrote off America and more than made up the deficit by erecting four new cannon factories.[42]

From Hügel the possibility that the new Kaiser might turn out to be a leftist politician — absurd as it now sounds — appeared far more grave. On March 18, 1890, Wilhelm II dismissed Bismarck and set about running his own Reich. The bone between them was the prince's anti-Socialist legislation. Naïvely hoping to woo workmen away from the SPD, the emperor proposed to restrict child labor, make the Sabbath a day of rest, and encourage participation in management by workers' committees. The press christened him "the Labor Emperor," and he was pleased. Fritz wasn't. He was disturbed, and after drafting a long letter of protest he took it to Bismarck. The chancellor was squatting beneath one of his trees. He agreed, he groaned, but he felt "like an old circus horse"; he had been through all this too many times. He was in no mood to intervene, and under the circumstances he could accomplish little. On the other hand, he mused, eying his guest shrewdly, Fritz himself might achieve something. He carried a great name, and the monarch knew it. There was, Bismarck observed, a significant difference between *der Allerhöchsteselber* and the Deity (*der Allerhöchste* — the Most High).† Although *Gott sieht die Person nicht an*, the young ruler *was* a respecter of persons. Fritz took the chancellor's advice and forwarded his letter to Hohenzollern Palace.[43]

There was no reply. Given time Krupp would doubtless have approached the Kaiser slowly through his advisers, but speed was important. He applied for an audience. Thus their first formal confrontation bore undertones of heavy irony. Wilhelm, who had no genuine concern for the lot of working people, appeared as their champion. Fritz, who recoiled from outbursts, had to rage at his emperor. The *Sozialprogramm* was unacceptable, he said. He quoted the Kaiser's own words: "Only one man is master over the land and that is I" (*Nur ein Mann ist Herr des Landes, und das bin ich*) and looked inquiring. "*Ja?*" he asked. "*Jawohl,*" Wilhelm replied distantly. Very well, said Fritz; then an employer must be "*Herr in eigenen Haus.*" He was quoting his own father, and Alfred would have been proud of him; those years of writer's cramp were bearing fruit. The

---

* The firm continued to manufacture Alfred's seamless wheels until September 1, 1939, when his granddaughter's tanks lunged into Poland. (WM/Alfried.)

† God was the one superior officer to Whom the Kaiser deferred. Even so, he sometimes seemed to be insubordinate. One Monday *Der Reichsanzeiger* noted that the day before at church "the All-Highest paid his respects to the Most High." On November 11, 1918, there were those in Germany who felt that the Almighty was getting back a little of His Own. Perhaps so. R.H.I.P.

All-Highest stroked his preposterous mustache, and Fritz hurried on. If he couldn't run his factories his own way, he declared, he might have to move elsewhere — another quote, straight from the family archives. Besides, he argued, leniency with lazy workmen merely encouraged the Social Democrats. If you gave them a centimeter they took a meter. Krupp punished disloyal Kruppianer ruthlessly, and the policy worked very well.[44]

The Kaiser wouldn't budge. Fritz left feeling he had failed. Wilhelm forced repeal of Bismarck's *Sozialistengesetz*. But the subsequent election vindicated Krupp. To the astonishment of all Europe, the rehabilitated SPD polled nearly a million and a half votes, one out of every five, and won thirty-five seats in the Reichstag. The emperor was beside himself. In subsequent statements he branded the Socialists a "gang of traitors" who did not "deserve the name of Germans"; the members of any party which criticized "the All-Highest Ruler must be rooted out to the last stump" as "vagabonds without a country" (*vaterlandslose Gesellen*). The stung emperor forgot about children, Sunday, and denimed representatives on *Direktoriums*. Instead he began reading industrial statistics. They dumbfounded him. The Reich's steel production was increasing seven times faster than Great Britain's — German steelmakers were second only to that remote prodigy, the United States, and the man paying the highest income tax in the empire was F. A. Krupp of Essen; it was greater even than that of the Kaiser himself.[45]

Meanwhile Wilhelm had been obliged to come to the defense of Krupp artillery in his own official household. The issue is difficult to credit, yet there it is, spelled out in the private papers of Friedrich von Holstein, Bismarck's ex-subordinate and the evil genius of Germany's foreign policy. Nearly twenty years had passed since the Franco-Prussian War, and the army was still pining for bronze cannon. On September 21, 1890, a Prussian diplomat wrote Holstein of a meeting between the Kaiser, Chancellor von Caprivi, and General Julius von Verdy de Vernois, Wilhelm's new Minister of War. "The chancellor," Holstein reported, "told me that there had been a new development in the bronze versus cast steel dispute, in which S.M. had sided with Krupp and advocated cast steel while Verdy had advocated bronze. The devotees of bronze were constantly making great play of the fact that bronze does not crack. Now, three bronze cannon have recently cracked. The chancellor said to me: 'That's a great triumph for S.M.' "[46]

It was also a triumph for Fritz, though one wonders what three bronze guns were doing in the army at so late a date. S.M. lacked his grandfather's patience; on October 1 Verdy was sacked. Shortly thereafter Fritz became the favored recipient of imperial correspondence. The Kaiser wanted to make amends. Though he never knew it, he chose the worst possible approach. Understandably Fritz had developed a lifelong aversion to turgid prose. To his horror, he found that Wilhelm was an indefatigable correspondent. Having buried one hack writer, young Krupp was saddled with another, who bombarded him with such profound advice as

> *Für tausend bittere Stunden sich mit einer einzigen trösten, welche schön ist, und aus Herz und Können immer sein Bestes geben, auch wenn es keinen Dank erfährt.*

> Take comfort for a thousand bitter hours in one that is sweet, give the best that heart and brain can provide, even if no thanks is forthcoming.

and

> *Die Welt ist gross und wir Menschen sind so klein, da kann sich doch nicht alles um einen allein drehen.*

> The world is so great and we men are so little that the universe can scarcely be expected to be concerned with one individual.[47]

It was not only banal, it was plagiarized. Wilhelm should have been Alfred's son. He was laboriously copying dreadful passages from the work of Ludwig Ganghofer, a fifth-rate novelist of the '90's. Furthermore, the Kaiser didn't believe any of it. He was convinced that the universe was concerned with one individual, himself, and when in a subsequent epistle he meticulously wrote (*i.e.*, lifted from Ganghofer), "*Wer misstrauisch ist, begeht ein Unrecht gegen andere und schädigt sich selbst*" (The suspicious are guilty of injustice to others and only injure themselves), the groggy Krupp suspected that the drudge in Berlin must be leading up to something.[48]

He was leading up to an invitation, not to spout bromides but to talk about ordnance. Fritz accepted with alacrity. He had been trying to resolve the half-century feud between the House of Krupp and the Offizierskorps, but the rancor was still there. Everything had been tried — invitations to Meppen, offers to hold special showings of experimental weapons for them, cut-rate prices. None of the stratagems had worked, and when the Kaiser asked whether he had any complaints, Krupp replied he had plenty. Why did the German army snub his shooting trials? Why did the Reich always place its orders for cannon at the last minute — and then insist upon immediate delivery? Why did the War Office refuse even to see Krupp's engineers? Wilhelm stared. Was this actually true? Fritz said he was glad the All-Highest had asked that question, because he just happened to have a set of blueprints in his pocket, plans for a rapid-fire fieldpiece using Nobel's smokeless powder. German soldiers wouldn't look at them, but perhaps their commander-in-chief could spare time for a glance. The Kaiser did. He was instantly impressed, and thrusting them aside he began pounding the table with his fist, shouting that he wanted to see his general staff. The *Generalstab* had enjoyed a thousand sweet hours at Krupp's expense; now they were in for a bitter one. The next day, Black Friday as they later called it, they were summoned into the Kaiser's presence. While Fritz sat silent, looking in repose as though he were dreaming of Egyptian herons, Wilhelm visited his private furies upon them. High in oath, he demanded that they adopt the new quick-firer, send regular missions to Essen, and attend every Meppen test. To make sure they obeyed him, he himself would ride out to the proving ground from time to time. It would be a holiday for him, he said, just to get away from stuffy, pigheaded Junker bureaucrats and *"sich . . . etwas vorschiessen lassen"* — be shown a bit of shooting.[49]

# 9

NEUN

✠

# Oscar Wilde of the Second Reich

T<small>HE</small> Kaiser came and hurrahed. This was *it*: actual shells bursting, targets disintegrating, the ground beneath his jackboots trembling with a deep, manly rumble. With a little imagination — and he had a lot — one could envisage the real thing. To Wilhelm that was a prospect of indescribable grandeur. The mere thought of battle moved him to tears, not of grief but of pride, and Fritz saw to it that the effect was heightened by Krupp's band blaring out *Heil Kaiser Dir* and *Was blasen die Trompeten?*, and by the firm's all-male glee club booming:

> *Gloria Viktoria!*
> *Ja, mit Herz und Hand*
> *Für Vaterland. . . .*[1]

S.M.'s visits to Meppen so enchanted him that Ernst Haux's profits curve soared right off the chart, and the army, having survived the humiliation of Black Friday, faced an even darker moment when Krupp introduced the All-Highest to a new metal on his range. During his years as *wahrscheinlicher Erbe des Etablissements* Fritz had observed the world's navies expanding their battleship armor from four-and-a-half inches at the waterline to a thickness of two solid feet. He had a hunch that a strong alloy might solve this absurdity, and one of his first acts as owner had been to order experiments with nickel steel. It worked brilliantly. Moreover, by holding the alloy at 2,000 degrees Fahrenheit for two weeks while coal gas was passed over its surface, and then treating it to a water- and heat-hardening process, Krupp produced a metal hard outside and resilient inside. At a stroke every other plate patent had been rendered obsolete. Not only would the new armor be useful to fleets; its adoption by field artillery was absolutely necessary, for while the unfortunate General Verdy had been misguided, there had been a thread of reason in his argument: Nobel's new gunpowder, with its picric acid base, was so powerful that it shattered both bronze *and* cast steel. Krupp thought nickel steel cannon could handle it, and by the early '90's his first barrels were ready for testing. He asked the War Office to send a committee. The son met the same treatment his father had received when he first proposed steel guns: the generals answered that they liked what they had. Fritz appealed to Seine Majestät, and S.M. appeared at Meppen practically dragging the Korps by its chin straps — "The officers of the committee attended," a chronicler noted, "cursing heartily." They were foiled again. The new fieldpieces could contain the mightiest charge, and the All-Highest decreed that unalloyed steel was now as obsolete as bronze.[2]

Nickel steel cemented the marriage between young Hohenzollern and young Krupp. The Kaiser appointed Fritz a *Geheime Kommerzienrat* (privy councillor), conferring upon him the title *Exzellenz,* and he made it a point to visit at least once a year the Hügel apartment which had been built for his grandfather. The emperor was a trying guest. Time has blurred the sharp edges of Wilhelmine Germany, but it hasn't done much for the image of Wilhelm himself. He was an irresponsible, pompous, impulsive popinjay, and he never stopped playing war. Thinking to break the Social Democrats with bombast, he would debouch from the castle and issue outrageous statements; "As in 1861, so now — division and distrust prevail among our people," a typical one ran. "Our German Reich rests upon a single steadfast cornerstone — the army. . . . If it should ever again come to pass that the city of Berlin revolts against its monarch, the Guards will avenge with their bayonets the disobedience of a people to its king!" He had to militarize everything. His office was "General Headquarters," and even the meekest of his civil servants were issued uniforms and ranks. The Minister of Education was made a major, the Minister of Finance a lieutenant. If a man ran his bureau well, he was promoted; if not, informal courts-martial would be held, sometimes at the Hügel dining table. (One morning after the budget had failed to balance Finanzminister von Scholz picked up *Der Reichsanzeiger* and found he had been broken to sergeant.) *S.M.* was forever saber rattling — literally clanging a real sword blade in a real scabbard, because he always came to the castle dressed as a *Feldmarschall,* complete with spurs. Storing his wardrobe was a major logistical problem; it contained two hundred uniforms and required the full-time services of twelve valets, or, as he insisted upon calling them, "Officers of the Imperial Bodyguard."[3]

Thanks to his patronage, Exzellenz Krupp had acquired the absolute monopoly of which *der Grosse Krupp* had dreamed. As Fritz's annual income jumped from 7,000,000 marks to 21,000,000 marks, the firm's business with Berlin rose from 33 percent of its gross product to 67 percent. Since taxable fortunes had become a matter of public record, anyone could read the details in the *Jahrbuch der Millionäre in Preussen,* and with the All-Highest's purple pennant being hoisted over Villa Hügel so often, there was a revival of the old rumors that the emperor was getting a share of the profits.* The Krupp archives do not disclose that a single pfennig changed hands during those visits, but even some of Wilhelm's counselors assumed that he was lining his pocket. While Holstein doubted that the Kaiser was drawing dividends from Albert Ballin, the Hamburg shipowner, he took it for granted that Essen provided part of the imperial income; "Incidentally," he wrote the new chancellor, "the rumor is gaining ground in political circles, probably unjustly, that S.M. has big investments with Ballin, as he does with Krupp." Bismarck's cynical protégé wasn't outraged; he added that the emperor "simply behaves incautiously, in this as in other matters." The chancellor was painfully aware of it. So was everyone in the government. A few members of the government thought Wilhelm's reckless pronouncements too fantastic to be taken seriously. Count August zu Eulenburg, chief marshal to his court, wrote that "It's really a blessing, after all, that in this witches' kettle, not to say madhouse, there should be something to laugh at." Ausländer were less amused, and a chill ran through Europe when the Kaiser, dispatching German troops to the mixed force gathering to smash the Boxer Rebellion, told them:

> *Kommt ihr vor den Feind, so wird derselbe geschlagen. Wer euch in die Hände fällt, sei euch verfallen. Wie vor tausend Jahren die Hunnen mit ihrem König Etzel sich einen Namen gemacht . . . so möge der Name Deutscher in China auf tausend Jahre durch euch in einer Weise betätigt werden, dass niemals wieder ein Chinese wagt, einen Deutschen auch nur scheel anzusehen!*

> If you meet the enemy you will beat him. If you take prisoners their lives will be forfeit to you. Even as a thousand years ago the Huns under their King Attila made their name . . . so may the name of Germany stand in China by your deeds for a thousand years, to such a degree that never again will a Chinese dare look twice at a German![4]

The All-Highest himself had said it: the Germans were Huns. The tag was to stick through the two greatest wars in history, and is still heard today. The affinity between the emperor and his armorer was an attraction of opposites. Fritz never uttered a colorful phrase and never even swore under his breath — though his directors were shouting *Verdammt, Donnerwetter,* and *Hol' dich der Teufel* at the height of the Boxer crisis. They were mad at the Kaiser, not the Chinese. The struggle in Peking provoked

---

* The illusion that the Kaiser was "a large shareholder" in Krupp's persists among modern historians, e.g., A. J. P. Taylor's *The Struggle for Mastery of Europe 1848–1918* (Oxford: 1954), p. 508.

the one serious misunderstanding between Krupp and S.M. It was the sequel to Alfred's icy audience with the first Kaiser twenty-eight years earlier. The germ of the problem was the same — Essen's sale of arms to foreign countries. Wilhelm was especially excited by the uprising in Peking because it had been touched off by the assassination of his ambassador there, and he was beside himself with joy when a German gunboat achieved a spectacular victory. The international expeditionary force, pressing to relieve the beleaguered Europeans and Americans in Peking, was pinned down on the left bank of the Hai River by fire from the old Taku forts. S.M.'s tiny *Iltis*, Commander Lans at the helm, sailed up the Hai and took on the forts single-handed. Shellfire quickly reduced the ship to a blazing hulk. Lans was gravely wounded; nevertheless he put a party of marines ashore. They took the Boxer artillerymen from the flank, spiked the guns, and then noticed that the metal plates affixed to the breeches read *Fried. Krupp, Essen*. From General Headquarters in Berlin the ecstatic All-Highest sent word that Lans was to receive the *Pour le Mérite*, Prussia's highest military decoration. In return the *Allerhöchsteselber* received a message from his valiant captain reporting, "We were hit seventeen times, most of the shells bursting in the ship and killing and wounding my brave men. And the irony of it! (*Und welcher Hohn!*) All the enemy's cannon and shells come from our own country — they are all modern Krupp quick-firers."[5]

Maddened, the Kaiser dispatched a telegram to Fritz:

ES PASST SICH NICHT, IM MOMENT, WO ICH MEINE SOLDATEN AUSRÜCKEN LASSE ZUM KAMPF GEGEN DIE GELBEN BESTIEN, AUS DER ERNSTEN SITUATION NOCH GELD HERAUSSCHLAGEN ZU WOLLEN.

THIS IS NO TIME, WHEN I AM SENDING MY SOLDIERS INTO BATTLE AGAINST THE YELLOW BEASTS, TO TRY TO MAKE MONEY OUT OF SO SERIOUS A SITUATION.[6]

For Essen the situation was serious; Lans had become a national hero. Patiently Fritz explained that while the *Kapitän*'s gallantry was beyond question, there were grave doubts about his accuracy. It was regrettably true that the forts had been equipped with Krupp guns, but they weren't quick-firers. They were obsolete. His father had sold them to Li Hung-chang a generation ago, when Fritz was a little boy. How could the Kaiser blame a little boy? For that matter, how could he blame the little boy's father? At the time of the sale Li had been a good friend of Germany. Indeed, he still was. Li bore no responsibility for the uprising in Peking. He was now seventy-seven years old, and as governor of Chihli Province he had, at considerable risk to himself, opposed the *gelben Bestien*. But the emperor already knew that — he knew Li, and had been among the sovereigns who had appointed him commissioner to restore peace after the Boxers had been wiped out.[7]

The silence from Berlin was deafening. It was hard to acknowledge that an officer with the *Pour le Mérite* at his throat could have erred, harder still to concede that the Kaiser himself had blundered. For a month the telegraph wires between Berlin and Essen were cold. Then Wilhelm, missing the godlike thunder of Meppen, invited Exzellenz Krupp to Berlin for a talk. They talked of other things. The emperor pretended nothing had happened. Fritz had already forgiven him anyhow. He was incapable of bearing a grudge, and when the emperor's impetuousness was criticized by a mutual friend, Baron Armand von Ardenne, Krupp was taken aback. Major (later General) Ardenne recalled that Bismarck had once said Wilhelm wanted a birthday every day. Ardenne agreed; he thought their monarch a shallow fellow. Not so, said Fritz. Recently he had dined at General Headquarters, and over brandy with the men the Kaiser had spoken authoritatively about Röntgen rays, the Conservative Party, England, Frederick the Great, and scientific and technical questions. "There was genius in that imperial flow of speech," Krupp said warmly. "One might call it a spiritual eminence." And what, asked Ardenne, did the other guests say? "Oh, naturally no one talked but the All-Highest," Fritz replied. *"Natürlicherweise,"* said the baron. And to Fritz's confusion his friend burst into laughter.[8]

✠     ✠     ✠

As the battle of the *Iltis* became a national legend — with no explanation of how the mysterious Boxers had managed to wreak such havoc upon a German warship — everyone in Essen and Berlin forgot the moment of imperial wrath. The Kaiser had been piqued, then contrite. Yet his penitence was unnecessary. Krupp's elucidation had answered all questions, but that was because Wilhelm II, like Wilhelm I, had chosen a poor example. The basic problem of the international arms industry remained. Each new invention made it more complex, and now there were five colossi battling for their share of the world's treasuries. Krupp, Schneider, Armstrong, and Vickers had been joined by Mitsui and then, when an Austrian named Emil von Skoda converted a forty-year-old machinery factory in Pilsen to a munitions plant, by Czechoslovakia's sprawling Skoda works.

So immense were the rewards in their game that a player could absorb tremendous losses without flinching. In the '90's King Alfonso XII, harassed by Cuban rebels, let it be known that Madrid was in the market for new hardware. Fritz swiftly dispatched his ace salesman, Friedrich Wilhelm von Bülow, who had virtually appropriated the arms treasuries of Turkey, Portugal, and Italy. Unluckily for Bülow, he was up against the greatest drummer of them all, Sir Basil Zaharoff, a former Balkan refugee who had spent his childhood in the bazaars of Constantinople, had cele-brated his puberty by becoming a thief, and had so mastered the art of bribing war ministries for the greater glory of Vickers that his adopted motherland had gratefully created him a Knight of the Grand Cross of the Bath and a Doctor of Civil Laws (Oxford). For five years Bülow and Zaharoff were locked in a ferocious duel. Eventually almost every Spanish officer above the rank of major was an employee of either Krupp or Vickers. But nobody could be as sneaky as Sir Basil when he was really trying; he bought Krupp weapons and contributed them to the insurgents in Cuba, betrayed the insurgents to Spaniards on his payroll, and went to Alfonso with the evidence. That broke the stalemate. Royal pesos were converted not into marks but into pounds and — because Zaharoff owned Schneider shares — francs. The delighted French later invested him with the Grand Cross of the Legion of Honor. Bülow came home discouraged. Fritz cheered him up. Finanzrat Haux's charts, he assured him, wouldn't even show a dent. Next time Bülow would do better.*⁹

Similarly, Krupp expended a fortune on the Chicago World's Fair of 1893. To house his displays he constructed a separate pavilion, a replica of Villa Hügel with his name emblazoned across the façade. It cost $1,500,-000. The *Scientific American* devoted an issue to it. "Of all the foreign nations that are taking part in the World's Columbian Exposition at Chicago," the front page article began, "Germany takes the lead, in extent, variety, cost, and superiority in almost every characteristic. Of the private exhibitions, Krupp, the great metal manufacturer of Germany, stands at the head. His exhibit is wonderful, and by its greatness almost dwarfs all other exhibits in the same line." Drawings showed "a cast steel bow frame for a new German ironclad," "one of the Krupp traveling cranes, used for slinging and moving the great Krupp guns," and three 16.24-inch cannon mounted on hydraulic carriages. "A special interest attaches itself to this particular gun," one caption read, "because it was tested in the presence of the German Emperor at Meppen on April 28, 1892. On that occasion it was fired nearly thirteen miles." The salesmanship couldn't have been more flagrant had the articles been written in Essen (which was, of course, entirely possible), but no one strained for the bait. America was satisfied with its hardware, and rightly so; five years later United States guns demolished Zaharoff's merchandise at Manila Bay, El Caney, San Juan Hill, and Santiago. One wonders how the Spanish-American War would have gone if Bülow hadn't failed in Madrid. The following year the Boers, who had acquired their guns (and gun crews) from Krupp, staggered the

---

* He didn't, though. In 1914, as Krupp's London agent, he was accused of spying and imprisoned for four years. Appointed to the firm's postwar office in Berlin, he was an efficient instrument of secret rearmament, but the Bülows seemed to be plagued by bad luck. Together his son and Fritz's grandson were to be convicted for operating one of the most ghastly slave labor empires in the Third Reich (see chapters 19–22).

British Empire by defeating three English armies in a single week and surrounding Kimberley and Ladysmith. (The Kaiser, with his unfailing tact, promptly wrote the Prince of Wales, advising him that Britain should quit: "Even the crackest football team, when it is beaten after a plucky game, puts a good face on it and accepts defeat.")[10]

Fritz had not only maintained his father's superiority in the field; he was steadily increasing it. The only conflict of the '90's in which Krupp arms were defeated was the Sino-Japanese War of 1894, when the Chinese, Alfred's clients, were driven from the field by the Japs — who had become customers of Fritz. By the turn of the century, a dozen years after he had assumed control of the firm, the son was official armorer in Moscow, Vienna, and Rome and had sold 40,000 cannon to the capitals of Europe — "enough," the *Nation* subsequently predicted, "to make them believers in the necessity of armed peace." Like his father he had been showered with decorations (sixteen of them for extraordinary heroism) bearing such imposing titles as Commander's Cross of the Order of the Crown of Rumania. Grand Cross of the Vigilant White Falcon, Commander's Cross of Henry the Lion, and Order of the Crown First Class with Gems — this last from the All-Highest, who had been impressed by Fritz's cool performance under fire at Meppen.[11]

There appeared to be no end to Krupp's stratagems. Probably the most profitable of them was what the amused Kaiser called his *Schutz- und Trutzwaffen schaukeln,* his defensive and offensive weapons seesaw. It worked this way. Having perfected his nickel steel armor, Fritz advertised it in every chancellery. Armies and navies invested in it. Then he unveiled chrome steel shells that would pierce the nickel steel. Armies and navies invested again. Next — this was at the Chicago fair, and was enough in itself to justify the pavilion — he appeared with a high-carbon armor plate that would resist the new shells. Orders poured in. But just when every general and admiral thought he had equipped his forces with invincible shields Fritz popped up again. Good news for the valiant advocates of attack: it turned out that the improved plate could be pierced by "capped shot" with explosive noses, which cost like the devil. The governments of the world dug deep into their exchequers, and they went right on digging. Altogether thirty of them had been caught in the lash and counterlash.[12]

Fritz showed the figures to the emperor, who chuckled. He would have gagged if he had known the truth: he himself was being trapped in a variation of the seesaw. Berlin had just invested 140 million marks in Krupp's newest ("Pattern 96") field gun. Like all cannon in the history of warfare until then, it was rigid; that is, the barrel lacked a recoil mechanism. It bucked when fired and had to be reaimed for the next round. Schneider was watching from Creusot. The day Essen delivered the last shipment of the consignment to Tegel, Paris began arming with Schneider's 75-mm. fieldpiece, which absorbed its own shock. The Generalstab was in a funk. Then Fritz telegraphed them to *Stillstand;* he was on his way. In Berlin he proudly revealed that his laboratories had just perfected *das kruppsche Rohrrücklaufgeschütz,* Krupp's recoil cylinder gun. It was just as buckproof as the French 75. In the general relief no one questioned his exquisite timing or asked how much the new weapon would cost. It was expensive: the switch swelled *kruppsche* profits by 200 million marks.[13]

Now and then eyebrows were raised, but events were moving too swiftly; before a perceptive critic could clear his throat Fritz was exploring a new approach whose very existence was unsuspected. In the last four years of the nineteenth century he actually contrived to siphon cash from competing steelmakers. His instrument was a primitive munitions trust. By 1897 there were two basic processes for case-hardening armor plate. One was Krupp's; the other had been invented by an American, H. A. Harvey. Under the Harvey United Steel Company, which existed only on paper and whose chairman was Albert Vickers, the patents were exchanged. All member organizations — Krupp, Vickers, Armstrong, Schneider, Carnegie, and Bethlehem Steel — agreed to pool information about refinements of hardening techniques, and Krupp received a royalty of $45 on each ton of hull armor produced.[14]

Armor is defensive, but shells are not, and in 1902 Krupp and Vickers concluded a second agreement whose implications no one seems to have thought through. Fritz's engineers had perfected the finest time fuses in the world, and Albert Vickers liked them so much he wanted his customers to have them. Fritz sent the blueprints to Sheffield and promised to forward details about any future improvements. In return, Vickers would stamp each shell *KPz* (Krupp patent fuse), and pay Essen one shilling threepence for each one fired. Should hostilities break out between Asian or South American clients of the two firms the arrangement would be relatively harmless. But in the event of war between England and Germany the situation would become extremely ugly; Krupp would be profiting from Reich casualty lists.[15]

☒     ☒     ☒

That possibility was beginning to loom large. German and British students, meeting on the continent, spoke frankly about the conflict — each with disquieting optimism, though they did not see it that way. Wilhelm's naval officers adopted the custom of drinking toasts to *"Der Tag."* As early as 1891 the newly formed Alldeutsche Verband (Pan-German League) had distributed display signs to merchants reading *Dem Deutschen gehört die Welt* (The world belongs to Germans), and in his General Headquarters the Kaiser, the force behind all these incendiary words, continued to play with matches. The dismissal of Bismarck had eliminated the only effective checkrein on his policy of expansion. As the emperor saw it, the Franco-Prussian War had unleashed a magnificent surge of Teutonic conquest, and he was anxious that it not be stopped.[16]

In Villa Hügel, Fritz thought of ways to help his friend. One was to add to the torrent of inflammatory prose. Accordingly, in 1893 he founded a daily newspaper in the capital, the *Berliner Neueste Nachrichten,* and started a wire service.* The editorial policies of both were clear. They supported the firm of Krupp, the All-Highest, the army, the navy, German industry, and the Alldeutsche Verband. Wilhelm was appreciative. Yet words weren't enough, the Kaiser sighed unhappily. How about a deed? Why not stand for office? Fritz winced. He had tried that once. Then try it again, Wilhelm urged. There were altogether too many treacherous delegates. He had asked them to vote him a hundred million marks so he could add sixty thousand men to the army. The *Schweine* had had the effrontery to reply that they had already given him twelve billions, that the size of the army had trebled since Sedan, and that enough was enough. To meet this impudence, he had been obliged to dissolve the old Reichstag, and he would be most grateful if Krupp would run for the new one.

As a loyal German, Fritz reluctantly obliged, and as loyal Kruppianer, his foremen escorted their men to the polls and watched them vote. The first result was inconclusive: 19,484 for Krupp, 19,447 for the Catholic candidate, and some five thousand for the SPD. In the runoff Fritz won a hairbreadth victory, however; the Social Democrats now had as little use for the Catholics as for Krupp. The loser complained that the Konzern's electioneering techniques had been irregular, but the election officials reported they had noticed nothing odd.† The jubilant victors provided free beer for everyone in Essen, organized a torchlight procession, and tramped up the hill. Embarrassed, his Exzellenz appeared briefly and mumbled a few words, which no one heard. It was a fitting debut; though he sat as deputy from Essen between 1893 and 1898, he never rose to speak and seemed bewildered by the need for strict party discipline in a house barely controlled by the emperor's admirers. The army bill passed with Fritz's support, but that was the extent of his contribution. Once he voted against his own leadership, and twice his feeble grasp of political decorum became a source of national concern. In 1894 he declared at a large dinner party that failure to sign a commercial treaty with Russia would mean war. He knew, he went on, because Bismarck had said as much to his doctor, and the doctor had reported his words to Fritz. Next day the sensational statement was spread across the front page of every Berlin paper except his own. The retired chancellor was obliged to issue a formal denial. To Fritz

---

* The news service was short-lived, but the paper continued publication until 1919, when it perished in the German revolution.

† Certainly they had seen nothing unique. In this same election a Saar industrialist-politician, Baron Karl von Stumm-Halberg, marched *his* Neunkirchen constituents to the polls in columns.

he wrote testily: "I can't imagine Schweninger expressing himself as reported. This notion has never crossed my mind and is directly opposed to my views. Clearly I wouldn't have palmed off a judgment contradicting my own on Schweninger. It would have been senseless" (*Ich kann Schweninger doch nicht das Gegenteil meiner Ansicht ganz zwecklos aufgebunden haben*).[17]

Here Bismarck is suspect. The idea *must* have occurred to him — some sort of arrangement was needed to draw the teeth of the new Franco-Russian military entente. But that was beside the point; Krupp should never have blurted out a confidence. His tongue was almost as loose as his sovereign's. Four years later, at the height of the Anglo-French crisis over Fashoda, he was dining at Hohenzollern Schloss when the Secretary of State for Foreign Affairs casually remarked that if he were Prime Minister of England he would declare war on France immediately, using Fashoda as an excuse, because it was a rare opportunity; the balance of power temporarily favored Britain (". . . *denn so günstige Verhältnisse kämen für England so bald nicht wieder*"). Fritz returned to his hotel and wrote a letter to a friend in London, asking that the German minister's views be brought to the prime minister's attention. The result was predictable: mortified explanations in Berlin and a strengthening of the British conviction that all Germans suffered from foot-and-mouth disease.[18]

Fritz was at his worst in public life, at his best behind the scenes. He had always known it, and now the Kaiser agreed. For once S.M. was tactful. He was in no position to censure another man for reckless speech. Besides, while Krupp's term in the Reichstag gave every outward appearance of failure, the monarch knew better. In his own circuitous fashion the deputy from Essen had been shaping the empire's future in ways far beyond the capacity of any other man in the chamber. Wilhelm dreamed of a powerful German navy, and in 1895, at the ceremonies formally opening the canal between the North and Baltic seas, he had asked Krupp to help him get one. The situation was intolerable, the Kaiser observed; the Fatherland had become the second greatest trading nation in the world, yet its fleet was fifth. Even Italy had more warships. In the history of civilization no commercial nation had held its own without the support of sea power. Besides, there was the scramble for colonies. Men-of-war were absolutely essential if the Reich expected to pick up the few plums left. Would Krupp join him in this crusade?[19]

Krupp would. He increased his support of the Alldeutsche Verband, which was already agitating for a strong fleet, and he contributed heavily to the Flottenverein (Navy League), whose hundred thousand members, corps of paid lecturers, and magazine *Die Flotte* were flooding the empire with chauvinistic literature. But Fritz could do more than back a navy. He could build one. After conferring with Friedrich Hollmann, *Vizeadmiral* and head of the Imperial Admiralty (Reichsmarineamt), he prepared to retool the Gruson works for mass production of nickel steel battleship armor and to construct nine new armor-plated ships in Essen. The following year, 1896, Wilhelm's campaign took two giant steps forward. Hollmann, who had stepped aside to become state secretary of the Imperial Naval Office, was succeeded by the most brilliant naval man of his time, Alfred von Tirpitz, and Krupp bought a shipyard in Kiel. Lying at the end of a stunning Baltic fjord and looking down on one of the finest natural harbors in Europe, Kiel had been chiefly known as the home of Wilhelm's private yacht, the magnificent new gold and white *Hohenzollern,* which swung regally from its gleaming anchor chain on the deep blue water. No one had paid much attention to the sailors there — in Germany the army had a corner on military glory — and even natives of the city were indifferent to the Germaniawerft, a navy yard which had been built by Danes and had languished under a series of owners. Now Kiel swarmed with Kruppianer. Fritz's facilities here, and his factories in Essen, Annen, Rheinhausen, and Magdeburg meant he could construct an entire fleet, from rivets to shells. He celebrated by adding an anchor to his coat of arms.[20]

Before he could provide the tools to finish whatever job his imperial patron had in mind, however, funds had to be extracted from the Reichstag. This became a drama in two acts: the navy bills of 1898 and 1900. Tirpitz's first program coasted through the chamber. It was relatively modest; the superiority of England and France would remain unchallenged, and the sea force provided would be just large enough to keep supply routes open in case of war. The second act was very different. Krupp had scarcely finished laying the keels for this first fleet when Tirpitz changed his tack. He wanted a force so immense, he said, that the strongest naval power in the world would think twice before challenging it. This was a direct challenge to the British, who to some extent had brought it on themselves; frustrated by the reverses in South Africa, one of Victoria's warships had seized the German merchant ship *Bundesrath,* bound for the Boers. The Pan-German and Navy leagues cried foul. Wilhelm told the nation that it must demand its *"Platz an der Sonne"* (place in the sun) and that *"Deutschlands Zukunft liegt auf dem Wasser"* (Germany's future lies on the water). In a xenophobic frenzy a majority of the Reichstag swept aside delaying tactics of an SPD-Centrist-Progressive coalition and authorized the building "regardless of cost" of thirty-eight battleships, enough to meet Britain's home fleet on equal terms.[21]

Cost-plus was an immense incentive. Fritz had gone to sea in a big way; while drawing royalties through the Harvey trust for all steel armor used in the fleets of England, France, Japan, Italy, and the United States — *i.e.,* the sea power which would confront embattled Germany within fifteen years — Fritz built nine battleships, five light cruisers, and thirty-three destroyers for Tirpitz. The admiral should have been satisfied. He wasn't. Priggishly he insisted that the Reichsmarineamt should get a mark's value for a mark spent. It wasn't; it was getting half that. Krupp was charging 279 million marks for the battleships' armor, and Tirpitz discovered that Fritz's profit was exactly 100 percent. Nor was Krupp satisfied with that. His Berlin newspaper mounted a vigorous campaign charging that the Reichsmarineamt was haggling over prices while the Fatherland's security was in peril. Prince Otto zu Salm-Horstmar, the new president of the Flottenverein, wrote Tirpitz and begged him to sacrifice money in the interests of speed. Questioned sharply, the prince conceded that he had been asked to write the letter; the askers were "gentlemen connected with German industrial interests" — specifically, Krupp. Enraged, Tirpitz tried to cross Fritz's T. Permitting reporters to identify him as a "well-informed military source," he charged profiteering and demanded an end to Krupp's "monopolistic price policy." Counterbattery fire bracketed him at once. From Essen a well-informed industrialist branded the admiral with the forked beard a "father of lies" (*Vater der Lügen*). Tirpitz demanded to see Fritz's books, and Fritz fled to the Kaiser.[22]

The All-Highest ordered the admiral to quit. The feuding could only give aid and comfort to the Reich's enemies, and when Tirpitz suggested that the empire's taxpayers might be aided and comforted too, Wilhelm pretended to have not heard him. In his relationship with Krupp the Kaiser had crossed a kind of Rubicon, invisible to the old sea dog but vivid in perspective. As events were about to demonstrate, Wilhelm felt obliged to defend Krupp against all charges, however shocking. He needed his armorer. His reign was now committed to militarism. In battle the Kruppstahl muscle provided by Fritz's *Staat im Staate* would be indispensable; without the House of Krupp the House of Hohenzollern would be a house of cards. These were the years when pressure from peace advocates forced heads of state to send elegantly dressed delegates to disarmament conferences at The Hague. The emperor loathed the meetings on principle, of course, but his obligations to Essen made them especially unwelcome. As the King of Italy pointed out, the Kaiser would never agree to "clipping the wings of Krupp." He wouldn't — he couldn't; in the margin of one peace proposal he scrawled, "What will Krupp pay his workers with?"[23]

Meanwhile Kiel, like Essen, was experimenting with fascinating new forms of warfare. Despite the vocal opposition of Tirpitz, the Germaniawerft engineers had concluded that diving submarines were practical. The perfection of the gyroscopic compass made submerged navigation possible, and Rudolf Diesel's engine meant they could dispense with dangerous, smoky gasoline. Production was several years away, but already they had complete blueprints for Germany's first undersea boat. Rather unimaginatively they christened it *das Unterseeboot-eins*: the U-1.[24]

✠   ✠   ✠

On January 1, 1900, Essen greeted the new century — appropriately — with a thunderous display of fireworks. From the Gusstahlfabrik, Limbeckerstrasse, and from the ancient square between the old Flachsmarkt and the Rathaus rockets spluttered and soared, painting the night sky with a fiery mural — an omen, though no one there realized it, of the retribution which lay ahead. On the hill two Krupps who would live to see the grim sequels watched furtively from the Kaiser's apartment. They weren't supposed to be up. Aged thirteen and twelve, Bertha and Barbara lived spartan, isolated lives. Occasionally, however, they were permitted to join their father for a cruise aboard one of his two yachts *Maja* and *Puritan*, and the snapshots Barbara has preserved from those voyages provide a clue to what the girls were like. They look small, dark, fragile, and painfully vulnerable. In their heart-shaped faces, the wide eyes peering out beneath bonnets, one perceives the cameo innocence of very privileged children in a very sheltered time. Doubtless they were merely bemused by the gyrations of the funny photographer (*Mädchen! Ach, passen Sie auf!*), but they seem to be gazing across two-thirds of a century of brutality and murder and worse, and it is hard to gaze back.[25]

The worst, for them, came in these tender years. They were about to become the victims of their father's misconduct, or, if one believes that all forms of sexual behavior are equally acceptable, of a society which took a different view. Gert von Klass has given us a memorable picture of Wilhelmine Germany's stolid middle class: "This *fin de siècle* was very unlike that of the eighteenth century, when the phrase had first come into vogue. . . . Now came the humdrum heyday of plush, trinkets, and knickknacks in the front parlor. This tastelessness was accompanied by the "stuffiness" of the common masses, an outgrowth of a "hypocrisy" which had been blessed with a pious aura, including a spurious notion of "sexual morality." These notions were typical of the era" (*Begriffe der Zeit*).[26]

In such an atmosphere the secret activities of the Reich's richest industrialist were to identify him as a monster — and indeed, even today the most permissive are likely to feel that buying boys for carnal purposes is bestial. Yet he did not look like a beast. Fritz appears in the old yacht photographs, too, and unlike his father he never seems forbidding, or like his mother a trifle mad. He is simply a stooped, overweight, somewhat comic businessman dressed in tight white ducks and a yachting cap, fussing over bowls and vases. Reading his expression is impossible, for he never glances up at the camera. But there is nothing evasive about this. He has the best possible excuse. He is lost in his hobby, examining specimens.

None of those close to Krupp begrudged him his diversions. It was generally felt that for all his wealth he had led a difficult life — an unnatural childhood, a demeaning apprenticeship, and then crushing responsibility. The Social Democrats, of course, were unsympathetic. Their newspaper *Vorwärts* conducted a vigorous campaign against him; in a typical cartoon he was depicted in a silk hat, white tie and tails, looking down contemptuously on a bearded foreman. The foreman was saying, "The people are very bitter about the wage reduction and are threatening to kill me," while Fritz replied, "But my dear Müller, why should I be concerned?"[27] That was crude propaganda. There had been no pay cuts at Krupp since the '70's, and though the SPD's favorite anti-Krupp epithet was *kaltblütig* (coldblooded), Essen knew better. Fritz had not only continued his father's paternalistic programs; he had taken a personal interest in the firm's new colony for retired workmen, donated a million marks to the care of injured workers, and organized boating, fencing, and glee clubs for white-collar Kruppianer. Unlike her mother-in-law, Marga collaborated enthusiastically. Later, *kruppsche* public relations to the contrary, she was not known throughout the Ruhr as an "angel of charity"; nevertheless she was responsible for a women's hospital and a staff of visiting nurses, and she did teach her daughters to visit the homes of ailing workmen. The Krupp family was highly regarded in Essen. That was why the *Vorwärts* attacks on Fritz were so bitter. His popularity with his men contradicted Social Democratic dogma. It was killing the SPD with kindness.

To the Marxist eye Krupp was the quintessence of the evil capitalist. He manufactured engines of death, advised the emperor on *Weltpolitik*, reaped a fortune from the sweat of the proletariat, and squandered it on bacchanalian feasts. His private kingdom included three private estates: Hügel; a lavish shooting box on the Rhine at Sayneck; and Meineck, a lodge in Baden-Baden which Marga had inherited from a distant relative. At Sayneck and Meineck he entertained the Reich's social elite; in his Essen castle he was host to crowned heads — the Kaiser, King Carlos of Portugal, King Leopold of Belgium, Emperor Franz Josef of Austria, and the Prince of Wales on the eve of his ascension as Edward VII of England. Fritz's receptions at Berlin's Hotel Bristol, a few steps from the intersection of Unter den Linden and Wilhelmstrasse, were major social events. In February 1898 *Volkszeitung* described one of Fritz's more casual entertainments:

> *Der Abgeordnete Krupp gab im Hotel Bristol am Sonntag Nachmittag 1 Uhr etwa 250 Personen ein Frühstück. . . . Herr Krupp ist in der glücklichen Lage, ein Jahreseinkommen von 7 Millionen Mark zu versteuern.*

Deputy Krupp gave a luncheon at the Hotel Bristol at 1 P.M. Sunday for about 250 guests. Nearly all Cabinet ministers and many members of the Berlin aristocracy, including a large number of politicians, were present. Separate tables were laid; ten to twelve people sat at each. Every setting was flanked by a miniature ship tastefully decorated with violets or by a tiny gun loaded — not with lethal shot and shell — but with violets or other flowers. After the meal guests were treated to a special performance presented by entertainers from the Central Theater and the Winter Garden, by Tyrolean yodelers, Negro minstrels [Negerminstrels], and an Italian concert group. Herr Krupp is in the enviable position of paying taxes on an annual income of seven million marks.[28]

This was the SPD view of Fritz — a bloated magnate belching contentedly with his fellow exploiters while Mr. Bones made jokes about the old plantation. Had they been told that he hated every minute of it, they would have hooted. Who could hate great platters loaded with rich food? Fritz could. He averted his eyes because he wasn't allowed to touch the culinary triumphs of the Bristol's chef. Often he had to limit himself to a glass of mineral water. Even cigars were forbidden, and still he suffered; Schweninger had ordered him to lie prone for an hour after each meal. Krupp's banquets were torture for Krupp. Apart from the food, he shrank from the self-assured chatter of his poised guests, bumbled when he tried to join it, and retreated wretchedly back to the Ruhr, where the climate played havoc with his asthma, vertigo, and high blood pressure. In Essen he stubbornly battled the weaknesses of his flesh. A gym was installed in Villa Hügel. Each morning he rose early and put himself through a punishing workout, and each afternoon he made a pilgrimage to the weighing machine in the Stammhaus. A typical entry read: "15 May, 1894. F. A. Krupp. 88.4 kilos. Without vest and jacket, 85.7 kilos." It wasn't good enough, and reflecting that the only robust years of his life had been those spent with his mother in the elegant spas of Italy and southern France, he began eying the Mediterranean longingly.[29]

A great passion, as George Moore observed, is the fruit of many passionless years. After his barren youth Fritz doubtless felt that he was entitled to ardor, and the hot Latins seemed to be the people to provide it. Naples attracted him first, because it was the home of Anthon Dohrn, the German zoologist. In the beginning Dohrn ignored the overtures from Essen. His zoologische Station was for professionals, and he was chary of amateur marine biologists. But Fritz was no ordinary enthusiast. For one thing, he could afford equipment far beyond Dohrn's means. In Kiel he had the Maja rebuilt and outfitted for expeditions in search of oceanic fauna. Moreover, the scientific bent his father had tried to unbend was still there. After the Maja's early cruises both Dohrn and Dr. Otto Zacharias of the biologische Station in Plön conceded that Krupp was making a genuine, if limited, contribution to research. In hauls off Naples, Salerno, and Capri he had collected and correctly identified thirty-three new species of "free-swimming animal forms," five kinds of marine worms never before found outside the Atlantic, four fish, twenty-three types of plankton and twenty-four crustaceans. Enchanted, Fritz ordered Germaniawerft to design improved apparatus for deep-sea dives and resolved to spend each winter and spring near Italy. His base would be Capri. And there, beginning in 1898, he took up an annual residence of several months. For once he was doing something he wanted to do — for once the long sterile years were yielding rich fruit. When Vizeadmiral Hollmann wrote him in 1898 that he was missed, Krupp replied offhandedly: "I hear from Essen occasionally. Yet nothing good on the whole. They babble on about the War Office, the Navy, or the Foreign Office. And what good can come from places like that" (*und was könnte auch Gutes von diesen Stellen kommen*). It seemed far wiser to remain here and mount his specimens of *Scopelus crocodilus, Cyclothone microdon,* and *Nyctiphanes norwegica sars,* whose presence in the Mediterranean hadn't even been suspected.[30]

It wasn't wiser. It was criminal folly, for Fritz wasn't confining his studies to primitive forms of life. He was also collecting *Homo sapiens,* and a handful of Germans knew it. The first Berliner to suspect that Krupp had become an ardent pederast was Conrad Uhl, proprietor of the Hotel Bristol. Learning that Fritz had adopted the practice of sending his wife to a different hotel when he and Marga were visiting the capital together, Herr Uhl was puzzled. The mystery was quickly cleared up; Krupp called upon the *Hotelier* and informed him that from time to time he would be sending young Italian men to the Bristol with letters of introduction. They were his *Schützlinge* — protégés — and he would be grateful if the Bristol would employ them as waiters. He would pay their wages, of course. All he asked in return was that they be released from their duties whenever he was in town, to provide him with companionship. Uhl was taken aback, but he supposed a great industrialist must be indulged. At the outset he had no idea how much indulgence Fritz expected. The boys who came were very young, spoke no German, were insubordinate, and lacked the dexterity to serve as porters, pages, or cook's helpers, let alone wait on table. That was when Krupp was away. When he checked in it was worse. The entire stable of handsome youths would crowd into his suite, and the hosteler, listening to the giggles and squeals echoing within, drew the obvious conclusions. He spoke no Italian, he told Kriminalkommissar Hans von Tresckow of the Berlin police, but he didn't need an interpreter to understand *that.*[31]

Thus began the first *Fall Krupp* (Krupp case), which before it had run its course would shake the throne of the *Allerhöchsteselber* himself. To grasp the full implications of Fritz's diversions one must appreciate the peculiar status of male homosexuality in the Second Reich. It was the vilest of offenses — and, paradoxically, the most prestigious. Under the notorious *Paragraph* 175 of the German penal code anyone remotely associated with inversion was an unspeakable criminal, subject to a long sentence at hard labor. That was what had driven Uhl to Tresckow. Friedrich

Alfred Krupp of Essen was his star guest, but he had placed the Bristol in a hideous position. As nominal employer of Krupp's passive lovers Herr Uhl was, in the eyes of the law, a pimp for deviates. Perhaps a Kanonenkönig could survive the scandal, but a humble *Hotelier* faced ruin.

On the other hand, it is significant that Tresckow wasn't startled. As he explained many years later in his memoirs, V*on Fürsten und andern Sterblichen*, the Kriminalkommissar was at that time engaged in several hundred major investigations, each involving an eminent citizen of the Reich. Wilhelmine *Kultur*'s emphasis on masculinity had produced a generation of perverts. Abroad sodomy was delicately known as "the German vice"; the most virile men in the empire wrote gushing letters to one another. Among the skilled practitioners of anal and oral sex were three counts, all aides-de-camp of the Kaiser; the Kaiserin's private secretary; the court chamberlain; and the All-Highest's closest personal friend, Prince Phillipp zu Eulenburg und Hertefeld, who was sleeping with General Count Kuno von Moltke, the military commandant of Berlin. The King of Württemberg was in love with a mechanic, the King of Bavaria with a coachman, and Archduke Ludwig Viktor — brother of Austro-Hungary's Emperor Franz Josef — with a Viennese masseur who knew him by the endearing nickname Luzi-Wuzi. In Tresckow's files were intimate descriptions of mass fellatio orgies among officers of the elite Garde du Corps regiment. During one party on the estate of Prince Maximilian Egon zu Fürstenberg, General Count Dietrich von Hülsen-Haeseler, the chief of the Reich's military cabinet, appeared in front of the Kaiser dressed in a pink ballet skirt and rose wreath. The general's ramrod back dipped low in a swanlike bow; then he whirled away in a graceful dance as the assembled officer corps sighed passionately in admiration. Hülsen-Haeseler circled the floor, returned to the imperial presence for his farewell bow, and then, to Wilhelm's horror, dropped dead of a heart attack. Rigor mortis had set in before his brother officers realized that it would be improper to bury him in the skirt. They had a terrible time stuffing the stiff corpse into a dress uniform. Still, everyone had to agree that he had "danced beautifully."[32]

Naturally the Berlin police weren't going to arrest such men. The Kriminalkommissar and his superior, a Polizeikommissar named Meerscheidt-Hüllessem, who stood watch over the Berlin *Verbrecheralbum* (criminal records file), were determined to protect the empire from pimps and moronic male homosexuals who might — and often did — attempt to blackmail its leaders. Meerscheidt-Hüllessem's carefully alphabetized indexes described the behavior of the most famous deviates and the characteristics of their partners. Generals and counts who were having affairs with one another were safe (safe, that is, until the sinister Holstein decided to discredit his enemies at court by forcing four public trials in the wake of the Krupp case), but Fritz was in jeopardy, because his protégés were anonymities. They had nothing to lose by talking, and the authorities couldn't intimidate them without implicating their patron. In the midst of this dilemma Meerscheidt-Hüllessem died. His will specified that the incriminating documents be dispatched under seal to Hermann von Lucanus, head of Wilhelm's civil cabinet. The testament directed Lucanus to submit them to the Kaiser, together with a letter from the late Polizeikommissar explaining their contents. Meerscheidt-Hüllessem's foresight had been in vain, however; the All-Highest refused to stoop to such matters. He declined to break the seal. These belonged to the police, he said curtly, and back they went to Tresckow. Meanwhile *Fall Krupp* appeared to have been solved. Uhl had screwed up his courage and told Fritz that hostelers, like industrialists, must be masters in their own houses. He could not tolerate interference with his management; therefore he had sacked the gigglers and squealers, leaving Krupp, so to speak, empty-handed.[33]

But not for long. The situation was far graver than the police knew. Fritz's wildest partying had been confined to the little lotus-eating nodule of Capri, where he was beyond their protection and where its intensity mounted each season. He thought he had taken adequate steps to avoid exposure. He always stayed at the exclusive Quisisana, whose owner, unlike Uhl, was both broad-minded and a power in the local government. Fritz had contributed to local charities, built a road across the island, and sent presents to all the natives he met. Then, in the words of a fellow expatriate, he "let himself go"; according to one of his German friends, Capri Krupp enjoyed cheerful conversation, jesting, and "even more boisterous amusement." That was one way of putting it. A grotto was transformed into a terraced, scented Sodom. Favored youths were enlisted in a kind of Krupp fun club. Members received keys to the place and, as a token of their benefactor's affection, either solid gold pins shaped like artillery shells or gold medals with two crossed forks, both designed by him. In return they submitted to sophisticated caresses from him while three violinists played. An orgasm was celebrated by skyrockets, and now and then, when the boys were intoxicated by wine and Krupp by his passion, the love play was photographed. That was careless of Fritz. Prints were hawked by a local vendor of pornography. The Konzernherr was guilty of other lapses. From the pictures it was clear that some of his companions were mere children. Even worse, his grotto — "the Hermitage of Fra Felice" — was regarded as semisacred, and he had dressed its caretaker in the robes of a Franciscan monk, thus deeply offending the local clergy. This seems to have been his undoing, though an English writer living on the island believes that Italian authorities decided to intervene after jealousy erupted between two youths and one, feeling Krupp wasn't paying enough attention to him, went to the police on the mainland. The surfacing of the scandal is rather hazy. What is clear is that in the spring of 1902, after an extensive investigation by high-level *carabinieri*, the government of Victor Emmanuel II asked Fritz to leave Italian territory and never return.[34]

Had the incident ended there, the Cannon King would have been home free. He had planned to cut this year's stay short anyhow; his daughters were to be confirmed at Easter, the Kaiser was coming to Meppen for gunnery trials the following week, and then Krupp was to open the Rhineland and Westphalia Industries Fair at Düsseldorf, where he would exhibit a gigantic fifty-yard steel propeller shaft. He proceeded with his schedule, his aplomb intact. Wilhelm visited Essen to celebrate the city's one hundredth anniversary as part of Prussia, and he and Fritz heaped honors on one another. That summer Krupp attended the Kiel regatta as the emperor's guest of honor. Afterward he held a full-dress review of the Konzern's finances with Ernst Haux, and by September, when he visited London to approve indefinite extension of the Vickers royalty arrangement for shell fuses, it looked as though he would be spared. The grotto was lost, of course. His young lovers would have to console one another. Even an explanatory note to them would be madness. Still, there were other islands. With discretion he could pursue his peculiar pleasures elsewhere. There seemed to be no reason why he should ever hear the name Capri again.

✠　　✠　　✠

He forgot the press. He was a police character now. He hadn't been charged and tried, but sworn statements had been taken from witnesses, the awful photographs lay in Italian files — and *carabinieri* inspectors did not share Berlin's anxiety over his good name. For six months official circles in Italy had been buzzing with particulars of Krupp's *dolce vita*; eventually, enterprising reporters were bound to verify the facts and publish them. The story broke while Fritz was in London. Almost simultaneously Naples's *Propaganda* and Rome's *Avanti* printed lengthy accounts. Accompanying editorials deplored the corruption of children. Only yesterday Fritz had reigned over his private Babylon, enjoying imaginative exhibitions of sodomy. Now his asylum was gone; even his security in Germany was jeopardized. Under this strain his appearance rapidly deteriorated. The Baroness Deichmann, traveling with her eldest daughter, met him by chance on a steamer. So disheveled was he that she was under the impression that he "was living in two small rooms at a small hotel . . . imagining that no one knew him there, and that all thought he was poor." As an old friend of the family she frankly told him she was "shocked to see his pitiable condition. . . . In vain I entreated him to send for his wife to nurse him, and to have proper care taken of his health. He wished, he said, to . . . live with the fishermen. It was a sad instance, indeed, of the inefficiency of great wealth and influence to make one happy."[35]

The baroness's aside is a sad instance of the naïveté of Victorian and

Wilhelmine ladies; Frau Krupp was the last woman on earth Herr Krupp wanted to see. In the words of a more perceptive commentator,

> His apparently harmless diversions ended abruptly with the eruption of that sad and ugly episode which became christened "the Krupp scandal." It rocked the very foundations of the House of Krupp. The world was told, in details which were shocking and which should have been suppressed, that the beneficiary of one of the greatest international fortunes was a criminal according to the statutes of his own country. Equally disturbing was the sudden revelation that the powerful little man — not at all the chaste, humdrum, driven company man his father had thought him to be — lived a secret double life [ein Doppelleben führte].[36]

Now that the news was out anything could follow. What actually happened was tragic; in October anonymous letters, with clippings enclosed, were sent to Marga at Villa Hügel. Distraught, she took the next train to Berlin and went straight to the Kaiser. Wilhelm expressed his extreme displeasure (with her); then he summoned a council of his advisers and suggested that it might be necessary to delegate management of the Krupp factories to a board of trustees. Admiral Hollmann vigorously dissented. A moral principle was at stake, he protested. The Krupps stood for absolute authority vested in the family's senior male. Violate that and you would be setting a precedent; the next thing you knew someone would be proposing that the Reich be run by trustees. That gave the emperor pause. He left the issue unresolved, and the instant the meeting broke up Hollmann cabled the details to Krupp. He added a piece of advice. He and Fritz's other friends in the capital had resolved upon a course of strategy. They would tell S.M. that Marga was not responsible, that she suffered from hallucinations and was "in urgent need of prolonged treatment in an institution for nervous disorders" (. . . deren Unterbringung und unter Umständen dauernde Sistierung in einer Nervenheilanstalt nötig sei).[37]

Fritz, at his wits' end, agreed. The ensuing scene in Villa Hügel can only be imagined — Frau Krupp wild-eyed and hysterical as Herr Krupp returns and orders her bundled off to Professor Binswanger's asylum in Jena. Some members of the firm were told she had gone to Baden-Baden for a rest, but most knew the truth; too many servants had seen her carried by force to the train waiting within the castle grounds. That was on November 2. Events were moving rapidly now. Six days later the Catholic Augsburger Postzeitung ran a long article under a Rome dateline. Although Fritz was not named, one ominous sentence suggested that identification was imminent: "Unfortunately the case closely concerns a great industrialist of the highest reputation (der Name eines Grossindustriellen von bestem Klang) who is intimately connected with the imperial court."[38]

Frantically Fritz considered a lawsuit against the two Italian publishers.

He sent for Haux. Later the Finanzrat remembered that on a bleak autumn evening

> I called at the castle in reply to Herr Krupp's summons. It was almost as though he knew that he had but a short time to live; he was preoccupied with a thorough revision of his will. The great mansion was still as death. Frau Krupp was away. . . . Herr Krupp gave me a message to carry to his private attorney in Berlin, Crown Counsel von Simson. It was imperative that I leave for the capital that very night. As we two sat in the gloomy library talking of this and that . . . [I thought that] Herr Krupp was a sensitive, vulnerable person. . . . He ought to have had a thicker skin [*eine dickere, empfindlichere Haut*].[39]

Simson advised against suit. Since the Italian government hadn't prosecuted *Avanti* and *Propaganda*, legal action by Germans would be hazardous. The best course was to lie low and hope the storm would ebb. The *Augsburger Postzeitung* hadn't dared use Krupp's name; perhaps no one else would. That was wishful thinking. One journal in particular was bound to pick up the gauntlet, and its editors reached the largest audience in the empire. The blow fell November 15. On that day, *Vorwärts* issue number 268 published a long article under the headline KRUPP AUF CAPRI. "For weeks the foreign press has been full of the shocking details about the 'Krupp case,' " it began. After describing Fritz's establishment on Capri and reviewing the provisions of Paragraph 175, the paper declared that Exzellenz Krupp, "the richest man in Germany, whose yearly income since the navy bills (*Flottenvorlagen*) had risen to 25 million and more, who employs over 50,000 persons in his works . . . indulged in homosexual practices with the young men of the island. The corruption took on such proportions that certain candid (*nach der Natur aufgenommene*) photographs could be seen at the establishment of a Capri photographer. The island, after Krupp money had paved the way, became a center of homosexuality." *Vorwärts* reported the investigation of an Italian police inspector, the deportation of Fritz, and the possibility of further developments: "As long as Krupp lives in Germany, he is subject to the penal provisions of Paragraph 175. After perverse practices have resulted in an open scandal, it is the duty of the public prosecutor's office to take legal action."[40]

Now Fritz *had* to sue. Within hours of the paper's appearance he telegraphed the capital appealing to the government to join him. That same afternoon the chancellor agreed to charge *Vorwärts* with criminal libel. By evening issue number 268 had become a collector's item. Imperial police confiscated every copy they could find; subscribers' homes were raided, and even the desks of Reichstag deputies were searched. The All-Highest's arm couldn't reach everywhere, however. The whole empire knew of *Fall Krupp*. On November 18 Fritz ordered the following notice posted in every Essen, Annen, Rheinhausen, and Kiel workshop and at the entrance of every coal mine and ore field he owned:

*Ein Berliner sozialdemokratisches Blatt hat vor einigen Tagen unge-
heuere Beschimpfungen und Verdächtigungen gegen Herrn F. A. Krupp
gerichtet. . . . Ausserdem ist die sofortige Beschlagnahme des Berliner
Blattes und anderer Blätter, welche den Artikel verbreitet haben, gericht-
lich angeordnet worden.*

A Berlin Social Democratic newspaper has recently published insults and insinuations of a disgraceful character against Herr F. A. Krupp. It is hereby announced that at the request of Herr F. A. Krupp criminal proceedings are being taken in open court against the responsible editor by the Royal Public Prosecutions Office in Berlin. Judicial orders have also been given for the immediate confiscation of the Berlin newspaper and other papers which reproduced the article.[41]

It was an impressive gesture, and doubtless the SPD wondered whether it could survive the showdown. Knowing that unimpeachable evidence lay in Roman police files was one thing; producing it in a German courtroom was very different. Should the Kaiser's government decide to exercise pressure on the Italians, those precious documents and photographs — even the witnesses — might vanish. Krupp's friends were thinking along the same lines. Messages from Berlin assured him that the machinery of suppression was ready. It awaited only the imperial word of command, and the Kaiser would issue that command if Krupp requested it. Fritz would not only be vindicating himself; he would be rendering an immense service to the Reich. The SPD could be dealt a *coup de grâce.*

He nearly went along with them. On November 21 he addressed a note to the imperial chamberlain. "*Hochverehrter Gönner!*" it began — "Most esteemed patron!" —

*Ew. Exzellenz werden, von England heimgekehrt, erfahren, wie mir
seitens der Sozialdemokratie mitgespielt wird. . . . die ja angeblich meine
Ausweisung verfügt haben soll.*

Your Excellency will have been made aware, on your return from England, of the trick played upon me by the Social Democrats. The blow was all the harder for me to bear because of the grief caused me a few weeks before by the illness of my wife. My friends in Berlin are unanimously of the opinion that I have no alternative in these circumstances but to beg His Majesty to grant me an audience and for me to show myself in Berlin. Should the opportunity arise I would venture, if the audience were granted, to beg most humbly that the Italian government might be moved to make some explanation or give some satisfaction regarding its orders for my banishment.[42]

In conclusion he wrote that "I must take the advice of my friends" as "an extremely painful and disagreeable necessity." That was not the language of a fighter. And only a fighter — an Alfred Krupp — could have beaten this charge. Ruthlessness and a savage disregard of Fritz's own children were required. Their mother was already in a mental hospital. Tomorrow, November 22, four doctors were coming to the castle to confer with Krupp over her fate. She could be committed for life, unjustly consigned to a cell while her daughters grew up believing her to be a lunatic. Fritz couldn't go through with it. He would rather die. And so he did.

On his last evening alive he dined with Bertha and Barbara and then played Salta, a new parlor game, with them. Retiring early, he explained that he felt unwell. Outside, a dark bank of clouds hung low over the castle. By morning the sky had cleared, and all day the hill was washed by sunshine so bright that it burned right through the factory smoke, but Fritz did not see it. Precisely how and when he committed suicide will never be known; all that can be said with certainty is that the official accounts were so riddled with discrepancies that they were obviously a fabric of hastily constructed lies. Haux, the most reliable observer, was attending a mass meeting of Krupp officials that morning, debating how they could help the embattled man on the hill. All of them knew that the doctors were pondering Marga's future, and Haux with two colleagues decided on a trip to Villa Hügel. They were determined to find out what, if anything, had been decided. The three men drove up the hill in a hansom, and

> . . . Als wir am grossen Haus angelangt waren, stürzte Assessor Korn, der Privatsekretär, aus dem Hause heraus mit der Schreckensnachricht, dass Herr Krupp soeben gestorben sei. . . . Wir betraten das einfache Schlafzimmer, in dem der stille Mann, der nun alles Erdenleid und alle Unruhe dieses Lebens überwunden hatte, in seinem Bette lag.

> . . . Just as we arrived at the mansion Attorney Korn, Krupp's private secretary, raced out with the staggering news that Herr Krupp had died a few minutes earlier. He had succumbed to a stroke. The big house was still as death. We saw no member of the family. The grieving butler led us upstairs, and we entered the simply furnished bedroom. There lay the corpse of the man who was now beyond all earthly suffering.[43]

The presence of the physicians was sheer luck, but someone capitalized on it. They agreed to sign a statement, which read in part:

> Herr Krupp hatte sich seit dem, Abend des einundzwanzigsten November unwohl gefühlt, jedoch hatten die Diener keinen Arzt hinzugezogen, da Dr. Vogt sowieso am andern Morgen um 6 Uhr erwartet wurde. . . .

ABOVE: The Stammhaus before its destruction by bombs in 1944. A replica now stands on the site. BELOW: Friedrich Alfried Krupp's study in the Stammhaus.

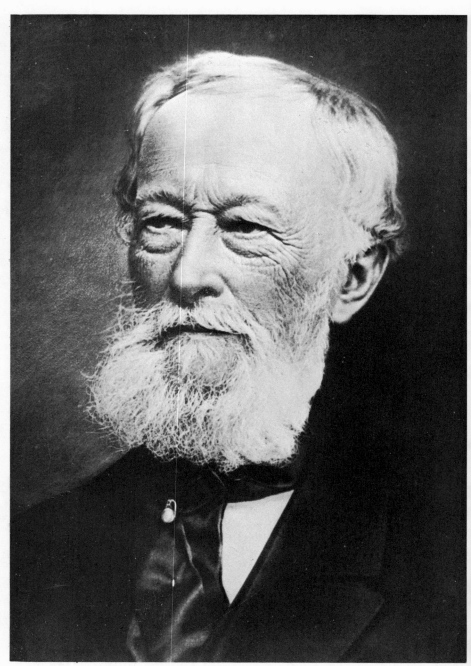

Alfred Krupp (1812-1887)

The Cannon King's handwriting — a letter to his London
agent Alfred Longsdon.

ABOVE: The great steam hammer Fritz, named by Alfred Krupp for his son. BELOW: Krupp Bessemer converters in 1900. Installed in 1862, they were the Ruhr's first.

One wing of Villa Hügel

Bertha Eichhoff Krupp
(1831-1888)

10

11

Margarethe von Ende Krupp
(1854-1931)

Friedrich Alfred Krupp (1854-1902) — the family's favorite portrait.
In photographs he was far less Prussian.

*Es bestanden die Symptome eines Gehirnschlages. . . . Nachmittags um
3 Uhr trat der Tod ein.*

Herr Krupp had not been feeling himself since the evening of November
21, but the servants, on his orders, had not yet sent for a physician. In any
event, Dr. Vogt was due at the castle the following day at 6 A.M. When he
appeared on the morning of November 22 he found Herr Krupp unconscious. . . . Soon after the administering of two injections the patient
awoke and was reasonably aware of his surroundings. He requested Dr.
Vogt to remember him to his two daughters and to attend to funeral
arrangements. At about 8:15 A.M. shortness of breath, a slackening heart,
and a cold skin became more and more obvious. . . . The symptoms of
cerebral hemorrhage were conspicuous. . . . Death came at 3 P.M.[44]

Late that afternoon Amtliche Deutsche Telegraphenbüro, the official
German news agency, sent this flash across the incredulous Reich:

VILLA HÜGEL, 22. NOVEMBER. EXZELLENZ KRUPP IST HEUTE NACH-
MITTAG DREI UHR GESTORBEN. DER TOD IST INFOLGE EINES HEUTE
FRÜH SECHS UHR EINGETRETENEN GEHIRNSCHLAGS ERFOLGT.

VILLA HÜGEL, NOVEMBER 22. EXZELLENZ KRUPP DIED AT THREE
O'CLOCK THIS AFTERNOON. DEATH WAS DUE TO A STROKE WHICH HE
SUFFERED AT SIX IN THE MORNING.[45]

According to Haux's account, he saw Fritz dead at noon. The exact time
at which the second Cannon King succumbed became the first inconsistency — the recollections of servants place it anywhere from the hour
before dawn to the middle of the afternoon — and it was rapidly followed
by others. Under the circumstances the question of Krupp's last words was
disquieting. He might have said anything. The Direktorium decided he
had kept his mouth shut; reporters were told he had died "without regain-
ing consciousness" (*ohne dass er das Bewusstsein zuvor wiedererlangt hätte*). However, in the general confusion they had failed to check with the
doctors' statement, and when they realized it reported that Fritz had been
awake and "reasonably aware," they huddled and recalled their release.
Apparently they had concluded that if there had to be last words, they had
better be the right ones. In any event, the press was now told that the last
sentence on the industrialist's lips had been, *"Ich gehe ohne Hass und
Groll aus diesem Leben und verzeihe allen denen, die mir weh getan
haben"* (I depart this life without hatred and forgive all those who have
injured me).

Oddest of all was the behavior of the physicians. At the turn of the
century medicine was an inexact science; nevertheless it is astonishing to
read their statement that a "cold skin" (*Abkühlung der Haut*) was notice-
able before "a progressive loss of consciousness set in." Even unsophisti-

cated laymen knew that skin cannot grow cold while there is still life in the body. Indeed, the medical imprecision of this document (shortness of breath and a slow heartbeat are described as "the symptoms" which led the doctors to believe Krupp had been the victim of a stroke), together with its general vagueness, suggests that it may have been drawn up by someone else. Whatever the doctors had seen in Fritz's bedroom, they were the last to see it. In the most shocking development of all, the corpse was placed in a sealed casket. It was to be opened for no one, including relatives, friends, and members of the Direktorium. There wasn't even an official autopsy. The reason given for this extraordinary (and illegal) omission was that the manner of death constituted "important evidence in the prosecution of Vorwärts, in view of the connection between the libelous attacks and the stroke which followed them." Assuming such a connection, the findings of a coroner would, of course, be essential. By sealing the coffin the physicians were putting both themselves and the dead man under a dense cloud of suspicion. The Kölnische Zeitung published the whisper which was being hissed throughout the empire: "Hat er sich selbst im Bewusstsein einer Schuld gerichtet" (Has the knowledge of his own guilt compelled him to take his life)?[46]

The Right denied it. Der Tag, the archconservative right-wing daily, published an inflammatory obituary headed "Barbarism," declaring that the SPD had made Fritz "a hunted animal." Abroad this was the accepted interpretation — "But for savage attacks upon him by the Socialist press his life would have been prolonged," was a typical American newspaper comment, and nowhere was it voiced more eloquently than in the hour after Fritz had been lowered into his grave. Marga had been released from her asylum as soon as the German news agency's bulletin reached Jena (in keeping with the general atmosphere of unreality, no one thought it peculiar that her sanity had been restored by word of her husband's unexpected death), and a private railway coach brought her to Hügel's branch Zechenbahn in good time for the funeral on November 27. But she wasn't chief mourner. The Kaiser reserved that privilege for himself. Incredibly, he appeared in full battle dress, accompanied by the Generalstab and Tirpitz's Reichsmarineamt officers. The Krupp family has preserved a movie showing the caisson's progress from the Stammhaus to the cemetery. The widow cannot be seen; instead, there is Wilhelm, marching alone behind the gun carriage. With his right hand he holds the sword beneath his ankle-length hussar's greatcoat. Behind him the generals and admirals advance in massed formation. Like all films of that era the movement is quick and jerky, and one has the impression that they are in a hurry to get the coffin underground.[47]

They hopped along past forty-three hundred Kruppianer standing at attention, and after the graveside service at Kettwig Gate the emperor, twirling his upturned mustaches, declared that he wanted to address the leading men of Essen at the railroad station. There he told them that he had come to the Ruhr "to raise the shield of the German emperor over the house and memory of Krupp" (*unter dem Schild des deutschen Kaisers das Haus und das Andenken von Krupp zu erhalten*). The Social Democratic Party was guilty of "intellectual murder" (*intellektueller Mord*), and since it was obvious to every loyal German that they had *ermordet* a gallant leader of the Reich, "He who does not cut the tablecloth between himself and those scoundrels shares the moral guilt for the deed" (*Wer nicht das Tischtuch zwischen sich und diesen bösen Leuten zerschneidet, legt moralisch gewissermassen die Mitschuld auf sein Haupt*). He could not understand, he continued, his voice rising, how men could be so base. But he wanted faithful Kruppianer to hear from their emperor that "I repudiate these attacks upon him . . . a German of the Germans . . . his honor so assailed. Who made this infamous attack upon our friend? Men who till now have been looked upon as Germans, but who henceforth are unworthy of that name. And these men come from the Reich's working classes, who owe so infinite a debt of gratitude to Krupp!"[48]

Exit the All-Highest, stamping furiously. Among the strapping, helmeted Teutonic aides whose glittering jackboots swung after him were at least six incurable homosexuals, some of whom must have marveled that the demise of one of their number should be the occasion for national mourning. By now Wilhelm must have known the truth. Dr. Isenbiel, his public prosecutor, was a man of exceptional ability. Over the next several years he was to display remarkable zeal in pursuing German violators of Paragraph 175, and on the day of Krupp's burial he must have known that there was sufficient evidence in Berlin and Rome to have put Fritz, not the editor of *Vorwärts*, in the dock. Nevertheless the Kaiser held fast to his position. His motives may have been various: friendship for the man who lay by Kettwig Gate, animosity toward the SPD, and concern over Kruppianer morale. Whatever his convictions, they were strongly felt; at his insistence every Krupp workman was asked to sign a declaration thanking their emperor for his campaign against *intellektuellen Mord*. (Two veterans at the Grusonwerk, with thirty-eight years of service between them, refused and were dismissed.) On December 5 he received a delegation of the signers, whose spokesman told him of their "deep, respectful" gratitude toward their dead employer. In reply, he assured them the crusade against the SPD would go on.

It did, but not under the banner of the *Fall Krupp*; that cause was doomed. Marga had demonstrated her mental health by quietly insisting that the charges against *Vorwärts* be dropped. Ten days after Wilhelm's audience with the respectful Kruppianer, Isenbiel announced that the widow was "extremely desirous of ending the publicity involved by the proceeding relating to the deceased"; that the plaintiff, being dead, was "unable to put in a sworn statement in answer to the attack made on him"; and that "it would not be in the public interest to proceed with the charge of criminal libel, which is accordingly withdrawn." Confiscated copies of the newspaper's issue number 268 would be returned to their rightful owners. The Kaiser didn't quit easily, and when Georg von Vollmar, a Social Democratic deputy, rose in the Reichstag on January 20 to deplore the exploitation of Fritz's funeral for political purposes, he was not even permitted to speak. Outside the government the case was as dead as Krupp. Even the conservative press quit and engaged in what briefly became a necrophilic obsession throughout the empire — guessing the whereabouts of Friedrich Alfred Krupp. Encouraged by the sealed coffin and the absence of an autopsy, rumor spread that Fritz hadn't died at all, that he had just slipped away quietly. Over the next four years newspapers periodically published interviews with travelers who reported having seen him in America, South America, Jerusalem, and the Far East.[49]

The *Allerhöchsteselber* only wished it were true. The Krupp factories, as important to his mailed fist as any branch of his armed services, were now controlled by a woman whose one appeal to him for help had led her to an insane asylum, who frankly told visitors that she had a low opinion *"vom Kaiser und seiner Art,"* and who had been so scarred by the nightmarish autumn that she had aged prematurely and was already called Granny (*das Mütterchen*) by her own family. Furthermore, from Berlin the future looked almost as bleak. The Konzern had no heir, only an heiress: a leggy child named Bertha. *Was nun?* What now? This, Wilhelm observed with some asperity, was supposed to be the *Fatherland.* You couldn't expect proud German officers to click their heels to a girl. In the end he decided that there was only one solution to the Krupp problem: he would have to find Bertha a stud.[50]

# 10

✠

# Cannon Queen

Sᴇʟᴇᴄᴛɪɴɢ the right mate would take time, and an adolescent Bertha really wasn't ready for breeding, so she and her sister were shipped off to a *Mädchenschule* in Baden-Baden. The newspapers of the time described it as "a fashionable finishing school." The phrase suggests bridle paths, sedate classes in decorum, lyceum lectures, and curtsying exercises. Barbara doesn't remember it as being at all like that. There were occasional music lessons (she scratched at a violin while Bertha hammered out Chopin on a battered, out-of-tune piano), but the rest of the curriculum resembled a school for cooks and maids: "It was cooking, sewing, housekeeping, ironing" — grimacing, Barbara makes ironing motions — "and very dull." About all that the future Cannon Queen learned which would be useful when she became mistress of Villa Hügel was how to stop servants from stealing in the daytime and from intramural sex at night.[1]

Though the sisters didn't feel especially rich in Baden-Baden they nevertheless were, and a large staff of lawyers was struggling with the consequences of their father's sudden death. Barbara was easy. Fritz's will left one fortune in stocks and bonds to her and another to his widow. Bertha was the hard one. Faithful as always to Alfred's wishes, Fritz had stipulated that since his wife had failed to produce a son (under the circumstances that was an unfair way of putting it, but here again the second Cannon King was merely copying his father's language), the firm should become a corporation. Actually that step would have been necessary anyhow, will or no will; otherwise Marga couldn't serve as trustee until Bertha reached her majority. Yet Fritz had also remembered Alfred's loathing of outside stockholders. Therefore he had directed that Krupp shares were never to be quoted on any exchange.

Satisfying that specification while observing the letter of the law presented a dilemma, and in most countries it would have been unsolvable. The fact that it was overcome sheds a dazzling light both on German corporate practices and on Berlin's determination to maintain the Armory of the Empire (*Waffenschmiede des Reichs*), as the firm had come to be known. On July 1, 1903, the original enterprise of Fried. Krupp was transformed into Fried. Krupp A.G. (Inc.), which served as both an operating company in Essen and a holding company (*Muttergesellschaft*) for assets in Kiel, Rheinhausen, Annen, Magdeburg, and elsewhere. "Fräulein Bertha Krupp" was designated "owner and leader of the family business"; the title was to be passed along to "the oldest heir" in successive generations. All the formalities of incorporation were observed, and all were rendered meaningless. The Direktorium was rechristened Vorstand, the term for board of directors in publicly owned industries. It was only a ritual. They were the same men. German law provided that an *Aktiengesellschaft* must issue stock and have at least five stockholders. Accordingly, Krupp A.G. printed 160,000 shares. One went to Marga's brother Felix, three to members of the board, and the other 159,996 to the teenager who was taking piano lessons. Bertha owned 99.9975 percent of the Konzern. (Forty years later, when she passed it along to her oldest son, the Third Reich took an even more benign view of Essen's *Waffenschmiede*. Bertha had been permitted to increase her holdings to 99.999375 percent. She owned all the shares but one. The outstanding certificate belonged to Barbara and was ridiculously undervalued at 500 Reichsmarks, less than a hundred dollars.)[2]

All this would fall into the lap of one young girl when she reached her majority, and her first act upon learning of it was to write the Kaiser that "In my thoughts I kiss Your Majesty's hand most submissively" (*In Gedanken küsse ich E. M. alleruntertänigst die Hand*). Her twenty-first birthday was still four years away, however. Until then, Fritz's will declared, all profits were to go to his widow. That didn't sit well with the All-Highest, who had never forgiven her for what he called "that Capri affair," but providing the regent with incentive was only sensible. The House of Krupp was in desperate need of another widow with the determination of Katharina in the seventeenth century, Helene Amalie in the eighteenth, and Therese Wilhelmi in the nineteenth. Marga became one. Like them she was now known in Essen as Witwe Krupp, and like them she presided over account books whose figures grew more and more impressive. In her first fiscal year she made the equivalent in marks of thirty million dollars, and during the following three years the earnings on the capital she held in trust escalated from 6 percent to 7.5 percent to 10 percent.[3]

Marga was no wizard. As she confessed to Haux, she was "*eine Gans*" (a goose) about figures, and if he were to put her own death sentence in front of her she would sign it "*glatt*" (blind). The point is that Haux wouldn't have deceived her, and she knew it. Having made one mistake in judging male character, she never made another. She was a shrewd appraiser of executives, and she realized that the destiny of Fried. Krupp A.G., like that of Fried. Krupp, was bound to the throne. She even swallowed her pride and invited Wilhelm to Hügel ("Such a sign of grace would give me and my daughters the consoling reassurance that Your Majesty's benevolence toward, and interest in, the Firm of Krupp continues without a change"), and though he declined to bestow such a sign of grace at this time, she doggedly recruited men he favored as her advisers. Fritz's suicide had broken Hanns Jencke; he resigned after the funeral. To replace him as board chairman she chose Alfred Hugenberg, a peppery walrus-mustached high Treasury official who was to play a vital role in German politics for the next three decades, culminating in the fateful year 1933. The rest of the Vorstand consisted of a retired cabinet minister, a retired naval officer, a banker from the imperial household, seven ranking civil servants from Berlin, and nine engineers, administrators, and attorneys, all of them known to Seine Majestät.[4]

Marga left the business of business to them. She herself concentrated on the restoration of *Kruppgeist* — plant morale — which had been badly shaken by the catastrophe of 1902. Each morning she rose in Hügel's "small house" (after her return from the asylum she never again slept in the castle proper) and was driven by carriage to her husband's former office. Mornings were devoted to the Konzern, afternoons to Kruppianer. She became the model of the considerate Schlotbaronin. Widows of workers, sick men, and factory families in trouble could always count on a visit from Frau Krupp. Word was passed in the shops that if any workman wanted to see her, he had but to post a letter *auf dem Hügel*; she never failed to respond in person. On her desk at the small house were plans for housing developments: Alt-Westend, Neu-Westend, Nordhof, Baumhof, Schederhof, Cronenberg, and Alfredshof and Friedrichshof, named for the two men who had crossed her life with tragedy.

All her work was marked by extraordinary thoroughness. If at times she seemed to be the lady bountiful, there were other times when she was more like a Prussian drill sergeant. The houses in colonies for retired Kruppianer looked like half-timbered huts designed by Hans Christian Andersen, and their occupants were encouraged to dress like senescent elves. In new settlements Marga calculated the exact number of steps from a man's front door to his shop; he was informed of the result, to encourage promptness. One of her charities outside the Ruhr was a home in Baden-Lichtenthal for "ladies of the educated classes who are without means." It was free, but there must have been times when its occupants wondered whether streetwalking wasn't a better solution to their problems. Everything was rationed, including water. Regulations posted in each room demanded "cleanliness, punctuality, thrift, adaptability to others, and discipline"; lights were to be "turned out at 10:15 in the evening and not switched on again till 7:30 in the morning." Karl Dohrmann, a manservant whose employment at Villa Hügel dates from the years of Marga's regency, recalls that she was "very energetic, very exacting," and Bertha's tribute to her late in life strongly suggests domination: "Our mother seemed infallible to us in every respect, and we clung to her in deepest devotion, not without certain feelings of inferiority, since we children . . . were always scared that we might not completely satisfy her demands."[5]

One semester at Baden-Baden was all the girls could take. They preferred Hügel; if the taskmaster in the castle was demanding, she was also lovable. Back there, Marga brought them in tow when she called at employees' homes. Her effectiveness among Kruppianer families was so impressive that Bertha adopted the custom, continuing it literally until her last hour on earth, and Barbara became a lifelong social worker. Attempts to educate the sisters in the mysteries of steelmaking were less successful. At appointed hours each week picked technicians guided the girls past forges and mills. They listened dutifully — and agreed after each session that they hadn't the faintest idea what the men had been talking about. At intervals they would also make carefully rehearsed appearances in the capital. These, too, were unsuccessful, though the girls weren't to blame. Ignorant of the reason for their father's death, they were unselfconscious about it. Berlin was still buzzing with gossip, however, and adults felt awkward with them. Gräfin Therese Brockdorff, Mistress of the Robes to Kaiserin Augusta Victoria, noted condescendingly in her diary that "It was quite moving to see the lengths to which Frau Krupp had gone to dress and raise her two daughters, charming young girls, in as simple and modest a fashion as she could. The challenge, of course, was no small one in this environment" (gewiss keine kleine Aufgabe in dieser Umgebung).[6]

In the history of the Krupp dynasty the years between November 1902 and August 1906 stand apart. The firm's sprawling industrial empire had never been busier, yet social life on the hill had come to a Stillstand. The Kaiser had never stayed away so long. Since S.M. wasn't coming, Marga decided to have no imperial guests at all. All the exotic foreign flags were furled because she didn't want to risk offending Wilhelm; the Vorstand was left to deal with the monarchs of Europe. Yet war ministers abroad were still very much aware of the family. So were its critics, as George Bernard Shaw demonstrated brilliantly in December 1905 when his Major Barbara, a thinly veiled satire largely based on the Krupps, opened in London. In the play Barbara is substituted for Bertha, the head of the munitions family is named Sir Andrew Undershaft, and Bertha-Barbara is given a pacifist brother called Stephen. Stephen complains, "I have hardly ever opened a newspaper in my life without seeing our name in it. The Undershaft torpedo! The Undershaft quick-firers! The Undershaft ten-inch! The Undershaft disappearing rampart gun! The Undershaft submarine! And now the Undershaft aerial battleship!"[7]

Shaw is uncanny. Although he could not possibly have had access to Alfred's correspondence, the "disappearing rampart gun" is straight out of the Kanonenkönig's last mad scribbles about the *Panzerkanone*, and while he couldn't have penetrated Germaniawerft's secret pens in Kiel, his submarine reference came less than a year before the launching of the U–1 there. Moreover, the discussion in Act III about the family's nursing home, libraries, schools, insurance fund, pension fund, and building society bears an extraordinary resemblance to Marga's memoranda to the Vorstand, now filed in the Krupp archives.

The curtain fell on Shaw's first performance exactly five months before the announcement of Bertha's engagement, and the Konzern's publicity men fought back. One feels a certain compassion for them. They were hopelessly outclassed.* Lacking wit, skill, sensitivity, or even a solid grounding in facts — repeatedly articles inspired in Essen identified the Krupps as members of Prussia's titled aristocracy — the firm's journalistic Hessians bludgeoned their way into print with articles so unsubtle, so transparently bogus, that the only wounds they inflicted were upon their young client. A typical piece in the American *Review of Reviews* was entitled "The Head of the House of Krupp a Peace Advocate." Its anonymous author breathlessly described his encounter with a delegate to the International Peace Conference of 1907, who told of meeting Bertha Krupp and

> alleged that he had the Baroness's own words as authority for the statement that she had personally objected to the manufacture of a particular gun known as a "bomb cannon." The possibilities of this weapon were so great that the woman who is virtual owner of this enterprise became alarmed and frankly admitted that she was an advocate of peace. . . . It is interesting to note the fact that when, in commenting on the report, the Baroness [Bertha] had expressed herself as unwilling that this weapon should be manufactured in Essen, one of the German dailies observed editorially, with humorous naïveté: "The experts explained to Her Grace that the gun was so dangerous that few would get in its way, and that it would therefore tend toward peace."[8]

There is so much of the era in that account. The works never produced any "bomb cannon." The very term was the ludicrous inspiration of some layman at a time when new weapons were exciting but poorly understood. Had Essen's gun shops come up with one, Bertha wouldn't have dreamed

---

* But not without allies. "When *Major Barbara* was produced," the playwright sardonically noted a quarter-century later, it was "deplored by a London daily as a tasteless blasphemy." (*Collected Works of George Bernard Shaw* [New York: 1930], XI, 221.)

of objecting; according to her brother-in-law, when Big Bertha was named for her "She took it with resignation" (*Sie nahm es resigniert hin*) because it was "something the firm did" (*eine Anordnung der Firma*). The awed references to "the Baroness" and "Her Grace" are superb examples of Edwardian toadying to the opulent. The "humorous naïveté" speaks volumes about an age in which the ignorant were gleefully playing with the fire which was about to engulf them. And the assumption that the artless girl was an intellectual waif in a world dominated by masculine wisdom characterized the decade, the German Empire, and the situation of that empire's wealthiest heiress. The possibility that she might manage her own affairs was never considered, because everyone in Fried. Krupp A.G. knew the Kaiser wouldn't sanction it. Bertha simply had to get married. In France *la femme* was esteemed for what she was, a woman, but in Germany she acquired status only when she became *die Frau*, keeper of the four K's and the family hearth.[9]

One is tempted to speculate about what sort of marriage prospect Fritz Krupp's elder daughter would have been had she been penniless, yet the question is really an idle one. Her fortune had made her what she was. When she lay in her cradle her dying grandfather, glowering down at it, had predicted that before she was twenty she would be surrounded by "dozens of suitors." Alfred was wrong only because the Kaiser was personally screening all eligible young men. In her late teens she was one of the most desirable maidens in the world, and if her physical attractions had matched her financial allurement, she would have stood alone. She wasn't *un*attractive — she was simply rather plain. More than anyone else she resembled her father's father. His genes seemed to have skipped a generation. Fritz hadn't looked at all like him, but Bertha, tall, and with a firm jaw, high brow, and penetrating eyes, might have been her grandfather's daughter.[10]

At the birth of each girl Marga had purchased a thick scrapbook, elegantly bound in blue leather; she made entries until they were of age and then turned the books over to them. Bertha's vanished during the 1923 troubles in Essen, when a French general briefly served as head of Villa Hügel's household. Barbara's survives. Riffling through it a reader senses the difference between the girls. Barbara was dainty and refined; Bertha stately, hearty, regal. The older sister's instincts were competitive. She liked horseback riding, and when she came into her legacy she built a yacht, *Germania*, which became *Hohenzollern*'s chief rival at Kiel regattas. Unlike her sister she scorned Paris fashions. During most of her life she wore expensive, dowdy tweeds. In her youth — until the great disillusionment of 1918 — Bertha's politics were summed up in a single word then popular throughout the Reich: *Majestätsgläubigkeit* (faith in the All-Highest). Heinrich Class, founder of the Alldeutsche Verband and a close friend of Hugenberg, was invited to the castle as a dinner guest; after spending the evening expounding his imperialist, anti-Semitic ideas he left with the conviction that Bertha was *"ein leidenschaftlich deutsche Frau"* (a passionately German woman).[11]

Yet her true loyalty was to Krupp's empire, not Hohenzollern's. She seems to have regarded herself as a quasi-official figure, a sovereign who must always consider the needs of her own realm first. The fact that she was a German woman complicated matters no end. She could not rule in her own right. She must delegate her authority. Still, she never forgot her obligations to the sixty-three thousand Kruppianer who came with her estate, which is one reason that her memory is cherished in the Ruhr today. Each year she received at Hügel twenty-five-year and fifty-year veterans of the shops and pinned silver and gold replicas of the firm's three-ring trademark in their lapels. The annual ritual always produced a crop of charming stories. One old oaf wandered through the castle, swiping cigars and stuffing them in his breast pocket. As he made his farewell bow to his hostess they spilled all over the floor. Bertha beamed. "Why, Herr Schmidt," she reproached him, "you must never bring your own cigars when you come to visit us!"[12]

Her duties on the hill, her regular trips through the plants, and her matriarchal duties as uncrowned queen of the Ruhr left her with very little time to herself, even for her immediate family. But *Pflicht* (duty) was *Pflicht*. The daughter of an imperial house had no choice. Late in life she sat for a bust. As he fashioned the clay the sculptor commented that it must be very hard on the Queen of England to have so few private moments with her children. Bertha replied, "Well, she does have three weeks with them sometimes in the country, and that's quite enough for people like us."[13]

⚔     ⚔     ⚔

In the early spring of 1906, when Fräulein Bertha was twenty, the Kaiser decided it was time she sacrificed her maidenhead to the Reich. At the time, the sisters were on their way to visit their father's zoological friends in Naples and inquire about his activities in the Mediterranean. It seems unlikely that their arrival could have been anticipated with any great relish, but the scientists needn't have worried; the girls never reached them. In Rome they were adroitly sidetracked, and Bertha met her future husband at, of all places, the Royal Prussian Embassy to the Holy See. He was an attaché there, a thin-lipped, tightly corseted career diplomat who was sixteen years older, and a head shorter, than his prospective bride. The suitor's name was Gustav von Bohlen und Halbach. Exactly how he became Bertha's *Blitzfreund* is uncertain; Barbara is the only remaining witness, and she was bewildered by the pace of events. She herself had just become betrothed to a scion of Prussian aristocracy, Freiherr (Baron) Tilo von Wilmowsky, grandson of Wilhelm I's last civilian adviser, son of one of Wilhelm II's cabinet ministers, and a Villa Hügel guest of the family several years before. There had been no flicker of romance in her sister's life until this trip into the south. And now Bertha had accepted a proposal from an undistinguished, stiff little coxcomb. Since neither Bertha nor Gustav was the type to fall in love at first sight — and since he had never spared anyone five seconds unless it meant a firmer purchase on the next rung of his career — there was little doubt in Essen that the alliance had been contrived and managed by the imperial Cupid in Berlin.[14]

The few skeptics were converted by S.M.'s reaction. Marga announced the engagement in May. In August the Kaiser appeared at Villa Hügel, jovially claiming his apartment and brandishing medals. Two members of the board were decorated with the Red Eagle, and Marga herself stood at attention while the Order of Wilhelm was pinned to her frock. When, the Kaiser inquired, would the wedding be held? They had settled on October 15, and he promised to be on hand with Tirpitz, the Generalstab, and the chancellor. He was as good as his word; there had never been a civil ceremony like it. The emperor, his brother Prince Heinrich, his cabinet, and the army and the navy gave the bride away. Afterward, at the banquet, the groom was ignored. Wilhelm rose to address the new wife. "My dear Bertha" (*meine liebe Bertha*), he began, and after recalling that her father had been his "valued and beloved friend" (*teurer und geliebter Freund*), he expressed the hope: "When you stride through the factory may the worker take off his cap before you in grateful love" (*Wenn Sie durch die Fabrikräume schreiten, möge der Arbeiter in dankbarer Liebe die Mütze vor Ihnen lüften*). Then he got down to business. This wasn't an ordinary marriage, he reminded her. More was expected of it than the usual issue. Naturally it was that. One must think of future generations. The Reich would always need its anvil. But right now the safeguarding of the immediate future was essential. Therefore he proposed a toast: "May you be successful, my dear daughter, in maintaining the works at the high standard of efficiency which they have attained and in continuing to supply our German Fatherland with offensive and defensive weapons of a quality and performance unapproached by those of any other nation!" (*welche in Fabrikation sowohl wie auch in Leistungen nach wie vor von keiner Nation erreicht werden!*)[15]

Having brightened the day, S.M. decided to indulge himself. The party moved down to the first floor ballroom, and he spotted a woman he had known in his oat-sowing youth. As the monarch and his old *Liebling* stood chatting in the center of the hall, the rest of the guests filed in and stood against the walls, whispering to one another. They couldn't sit down until he did. Whether through thoughtlessness or design — the infuriated Haux, who suffered from varicose veins, was convinced that the scene was calculated — the emperor kept them standing for two hours. During the whole of that time, the Finanzrat noted bitterly, they were obliged to listen to the All-Highest's "forced, nasal laugh" echoing through the chamber.[16]

Before leaving he sprung his surprise on the newlyweds. After most weddings, he announced sonorously, the wife takes her husband's name. This time, "to ensure at least an appearance of continuity of the Essen dynasty" (*damit wenigstens eine äusserliche Fortführung der Essener Dynastie ermöglicht ist*), it was going to be the other way around. Henceforth Gustav's last name would be *Krupp* von Bohlen und Halbach. Furthermore, the emperor granted the couple the right to pass along the "Krupp" and the fortune which went with it to their eldest son. All this was proclaimed in thick Gothic script, with many flourishes and illuminated letters, on what must be one of the largest formal documents in history. It survives today in the Hügel. The red wax seal alone is seven inches in diameter, framed in metal. The silver cord dangling from it has the thickness — and, with the passage of over a half-century, the coloration — of a grown man's small intestine. At the bottom of the parchment is the imperial signature, huge and jagged, and the countersignature of Theobald von Bethmann-Hollweg, Prussian Minister of the Interior and the Reich's next chancellor. The instrument reaffirmed "the special position of the House of Krupp" (*die besondere Stellung des Hauses Krupp*), although, as the beaming Kaiser remarked, it was up to the bridegroom to prove himself "a real Krupp" (*ein wahrer Krupp*).[17]

Compound surnames were nothing new to Gustav. He was the descendant of two zealous German-American families, one of which, the Halbachs, had settled at Remscheid on the southern fringe of the Ruhr three centuries earlier and had, in the 1660's, produced cannonballs from a nearby mine. In the second decade of the nineteenth century they had emigrated to Pennsylvania and acquired substantial holdings in the coalfields of Scranton. After the Civil War one Gustav Halbach had married the daughter of Colonel Henry Bohlen, who had led a German-American regiment — the 75th Pennsylvania Volunteers — against the South. Because the colonial had died heroically in the second battle of Manassas, the groom honored his memory by hyphenating his own name, making it Bohlen-Halbach. Then came the glorious rise of the new Reich. To Bohlen-Halbach its appeal was irresistible; he left the United States for the home of his ancestors, taking with him his share of the family's profits from Scranton coal. The Grand Duke of Baden eagerly welcomed both the returned son of the Fatherland and his bankroll; he ennobled him, changing his name once more, to von Bohlen und Halbach, which was passed along to Gustav, Jr., the middle-aged little man whose monarch had now ordered him to become *ein wahrer Krupp*.[18]

Doubtless all this had been known to the emperor before he chose Gustav, and possibly S.M. had relished some of the peregrine offshoots on the prince consort's family tree. Colonel Bohlen, for example, had been a warrior after Wilhelm's heart. Before fighting Robert E. Lee he had served valiantly in the Mexican War and, as a soldier of fortune, under the French in the Crimea. The closing lines of the regimental anthem he wrote for the 75th Pennsylvania might have been composed by one of Moltke's commanders: *"Und opferst du dich auch, wohlan/Vergebens stirbt kein Ehrenmann"* (And if in battle you should fall/Be proud: you've answered duty's call). When he himself fell, Philadelphia proclaimed a full month of public mourning, which proved that the buck the All-Highest had picked was descended from heroic stock.

It cannot be said that these bold bloodlines were visible beneath the pale skin of the new Krupp von Bohlen und Halbach — or, as everyone soon called him, plain Krupp. Gustav Krupp was one of the least flamboyant men ever to emerge in public life. He never lost his temper. Indeed, he rarely displayed emotion of any sort. With his domed forehead, spartan nose, set mouth and quick mechanical gestures he was the paradigm graduate of that Prussian diplomatic training which Bismarck had contemptuously dismissed as *die Ochsentour*, the school for dullards. There was nothing in Berlin's police files on Gustav; he had never mounted Italian youths in a grotto or, if it came to that, even spoken a kind word to anyone beneath his station. Until 1906 he had been known as *der Legationsrat*, legation councillor, and that sums him up. He was the man who never does anything wrong, never misses an appointment, and never shows the faintest flicker of imagination. It is in fact doubtful that he entertained a single original thought in his entire life.

But he knew how to get on. At eighteen he had volunteered for the 2nd Baden Dragoons and served one year at Bruchsal as an *Oberleutnant*. After carefully hanging up his uniform he studied law at the correct schools — Lausanne, Strasbourg, and Heidelberg. Eventually he earned an LLD and passed into the civil service. Before assignment to the Vatican he had served in Berlin's Washington and Peking embassies. His diary indicates that he had learned nothing about Americans, Italians, or Chinese; his account of the Boxer crisis has the fire and charm of a Bureau of Sanitation report. One feels that he would have regarded any inclination to broaden his horizons as disloyal — a symptom of independence, and therefore a yearning to be crushed. Testifying at Nuremberg forty years later, Baron von Wilmowsky told the war crimes court that his brother-in-law "had a very definite way of subordinating himself to the authority of the state," that this "main characteristic" was "exaggerated," and that "I remember in various conversations he charged me with subversion when I dared criticize measures taken by the government."[19]

He was, in sum, a forerunner of what would become known a half-century later in West Germany as *der Organisationsmann*. With his fanatical love of order he had no use for the Reichstag — *"die verwüstete Arena der parlamentarischen Kämpfe,"* he contemptuously called it; "the sordid area of parliamentary conflict." That was the kind of thinking the All-Highest appreciated. *"Regis voluntas suprema lex,"* Wilhelm had written; "the king's will is the highest law." There are a number of words and phrases which describe this attitude, and most of them, significantly, are German. Often it is called *Befehlsnotstand* ("an order must be obeyed"), a concept which is considered mitigating by the Fatherland's courts to this day. Others know it as *Rechtpositivismus,* the Teuton belief that any law, however outrageous, must be executed — carried out, to use one of Adolf Eichmann's pet words, with *Kadavergehorsam,* "the obedience of corpses." Gustav would have understood Eichmann perfectly. When the SS colonel quoted Heinrich Himmler's SS motto, "My honor is my loyalty," his Israeli judge branded it "empty talk." Eichmann retorted that they were "winged words" (*geflügelte Worte*), and Krupp von Bohlen would have cried *"Jawohl!"*[20]

*"Jawohl,* Bertha!" he would snap out when, out of earshot of everyone except the servants, she reminded him who the real owner of the Konzern was. Similarly, if others debated the morality of submarine warfare, he maintained what one of his admirers called his *strenge Reserve,* another clutch of those winged words which means, literally, "unyielding impassivity." He worshiped means and ignored ends; whenever anyone brought up the human consequences of *kruppsche* policies he would bark, "Politics is forbidden here" (*Hier wird nicht politisiert*). To outsiders this seems senseless. But it must be remembered that the new Krupp was a little man. His targets were low. He had toiled for eighteen years. In return he had received minor decorations from England, Japan, China, and Austria. Another man might have looked upon them as meaningless gewgaws. To Gustav, however, they were tokens of respectability, and that, really, was all he had been aiming at. Now he had been thrust into a position of immense responsibility. He was too old to bow before new icons. He could only follow the lights which had carried him this far: efficiency, self-discipline, single-minded concentration on the job at hand, and, above all, punctuality.[21]

In a nation which prided itself upon its punctiliousness, Gustav's prompt habits became legend. Overnight guests at the castle were informed that breakfast was served at 7:15. If they arrived downstairs at 7:16, they found the dining room doors closed. He breakfasted for exactly fifteen minutes, then strode outside, where the carriage — or, beginning in 1908, the car — began to move the instant his feet left the ground. In his pocket he carried a small book with each day's schedule clearly outlined: so many minutes for this, so many for that. There was even a set period for preparing tomorrow's schedule, and, in the back, a schedule of schedules. Alfred Krupp would have gloated. The great days of paperwork had returned to Essen, and the new Krupp's syllabi were as inflexible as the Schlieffen Plan, or, for that matter, the *Generalregulativ* of 1872, which he embraced like a lost child. Precisely fifty minutes were allocated to the evening meal, unless there were visitors, in which case the dinner party ended at 9:45. It had to be over then, because at 10:15 Gustav and Bertha slid between the sheets. After all, bed, too, was one of Krupp's obligations to both the All-Highest and the dynasty; Alfred the Great had been as clear on that point as the Kaiser. Here Gustav's production record was superb. Nine months and twenty-eight days after the wedding Bertha gave birth to a son. Informed in the castle library, where he had been briskly pacing back and forth like a sentry on his post, the new father instantly dictated a memorandum to the senior officials of the firm:

Hügel, August 13, 1907, 2:15 P.M.

To the Directors of Fried. Krupp, Essen:
  I feel compelled to inform the board personally and in my wife's name at this earliest possible moment of the birth to us of a healthy son. It is our intention to name him Alfried in memory of his great ancestors. May he grow up in the midst of the Krupp establishment and prepare himself by practical work for assuming those solemn duties, the great significance of which I grasp more and more every day [*möge er in den Krupp'schen Werken aufwachsen, in praktischer Arbeit sich die Grundlagen schaffen zu der wichtigen Übernahme der verantwortungsvollen Pflicht, deren Grösse ich mit jedem Tag mehr erkenne*].[22]

It sounds like the announcement of a successful business deal, and in a way it was; a male heir had just entered the Konzern's inventory. Inspired, Gustav returned to the 10:15 rite, and his efficient performance of his solemn duties continued to bear fruit. It was all there in his file copies. Second son: 1908. Third son: 1910. First daughter: 1912. Fourth son: 1913. Fifth son: 1916. Second daughter: 1920. Sixth son: 1922. The Schlieffen Plan failed, the Reich foundered, but Krupp's conjugal advances continued unchecked on all fronts.[23]

*Eisenbahn* officials who knew that their timetables constituted his vacation reading were amused. What they didn't know was that the miniature train in Villa Hügel's third-floor picture gallery would have put them to shame. Technically it belonged to Krupp's children. Actually they only worked on the railroad. His master schedule called for sixty minutes a week with them, and he spent it letting them watch him play with the transformer. The toy was an elaborate grid, with quadruple underpasses, triple switches, roundhouses, and tiny repair shops. It was also equipped with timetables. Preparing these was the job of the younger generation; checking them was Gustav's. Stopwatch in hand, he would observe the progress of the locomotives, the coaling operations, the taking on and discharging of passengers, the loading and unloading of freight cars. It was, he explained to his sons and daughters, good training for them. Because parental approval was at stake, and because no one could be icier than Gustav Krupp when he withheld it, they toiled until they had achieved perfection. The trains in Villa Hügel always ran on time.

So did everything else. Luncheons in the castle were invariably business luncheons. Bertha handled the logistics, Gustav placed the guests according to protocol, and the staff watched the clock. Visitors weren't allowed to come in their own cars; their chauffeurs might be lax. Under the regulation drill, Krupp drivers dropped them off at the main entrance at 1:29 P.M. At 1:30 they entered the reception room to chat with Gustav and Bertha until 1:40, when they were led into the dining room. The moment Krupp finished a course, servants removed all plates from the table; poky or garrulous eaters were left hungry. The meal ended at 2:15, coffee at 2:29. At 2:30 on the dot the guests stepped into the waiting limousines and were driven away. Nothing was left to chance, including the temperature of the coffee, which might have thrown everything out of whack and which, therefore, was never too hot. That was the story of Gustav's life: any craving for warmth, in his opinion, was a sign of weakness. He further believed that surrender to one temptation inevitably led to others. He kept his office frigid not merely because he enjoyed the discomfort; gelidity also encouraged subordinates to speak their pieces in the shortest possible time. At night Hügel's windows were thrown open (here he broke with Alfred, his idol in all other ways) so that everyone would stay where he belonged, under his blanket. The only prowler allowed in the halls was his wife, who wanted to make certain that there was only one body to a bed. According to an observer, "One of her pet self-assigned tasks was to conceal herself at night near the servants' bedrooms. The long rows of tiny cells were in two wings, separated by sex and joined only by an iron bridge. If she saw a footman or maid in the corridor connecting one wing to the other, she fired him then and there" (*Sah sie einen Diener in dem Korridor, der von dem einen zum andern Flügel führte, entliess sie ihn auf der Stelle*).[24]

In winter this was a hardship post; because her husband was a fresh-air fiend she had to bundle up like a picket on the eastern front in 1944. Yet it cannot be argued that Gustav was worried about the cost of the coal. His diplomatic career had taught him that nothing impresses people more than lavish spending, and he made Villa Hügel the most impressive private household in the world. Outbuildings, moats, and turrets were added until the castle resembled a Disney dream of the Middle Ages. In the basement kitchen two chefs reigned over twenty subordinates. Hügel had its own poultry farm, greenhouses, workshops, a painting shop, and a domestic staff of 120, not counting gardeners and the stablehands who watched over Krupp's eight riding horses and four pairs of carriage horses. Riding was Gustav's one passion. He didn't smoke, didn't drink, had no small talk, and discouraged fraternization with members of his own household by arranging his Hügel desk so that his back would always be turned toward the doorway, but even after the stables had been enlarged to make room for four limousines he continued with his daily canter. He expected his sons to join him, too. Sunday morning his daughters were allowed to sleep in, but the boys had to swing into their saddles after breakfast. When they grew old enough to pose for portraits, he chose Germany's finest painter of horses. "And that's what he got," one of his sons once remarked to me wryly. "Horseflesh."[25]

☩   ☩   ☩

Gustav was an unreal bridegroom, and as he grew older he became incredible. Alfred had been psychotic but believable, Fritz perverted but pathetic. The Prinzgemahl who had become consort to their princess was a machine. One pores over his papers for some sign of humanity. One turns away defeated. Even his horsemanship is suspect; that, after all, had been Alfred's enthusiasm, and it would have been just like Gustav to take it up for that very reason. There was one moment when he might have let himself go. It came late in life, when Germany had overrun Europe and Krupp tanks were poised on the beaches of the English Channel. He owed no one anything then, and the Third Reich's leader, unlike the Second's, owed him quite a lot. Yet his words then might have been cranked out by Goebbels. In *Krupp*, the firm's magazine, he wrote such trivia as "I have often been permitted to accompany the Führer through the old and new workshops and to experience how the workers of Krupp cheered him in gratitude," "We are all proud of having contributed to the magnificent success of our army," and "I have always considered it an honor as well as an obligation to be the head of an armament factory, and I know the employees of Krupp share these feelings."[26]

Did he believe it? Loyalty to his superiors was probably the one thing he *did* believe in. Everything in his life was directed toward that end. Early in his marriage he and his brother-in-law were inspecting a plat of property near the Dutch border. Freiherr von Wilmowsky observed with admiration that the farmers on Holland's side were harvesting magnificent crops, while the Germans weren't doing much. Gustav took this to be a slur on the Reich, and he promptly bought five hundred hectares of the German land and set about trying to turn it into a model farm. The project was hopeless. Gustav lacked a green thumb. Still, he wouldn't quit, and for the next thirty years he strove to outdo the Dutch, who weren't even aware of the contest. All he could show for his massive efforts were a few withered leaves. Nevertheless the attempt had been a matter of national honor, and von Wilmowsky, who rather liked him — the baron's feelings were a blend of pity and fascination — wished a thousand times that he had kept his mouth shut.[27]

Until the Kaiser toasted Bertha as his cannon queen that October day in 1906 the lives of the two sisters had been indistinguishable. Indeed, since both became engaged the same spring the German press had assumed there would be a double wedding. Wilhelm vetoed that. He had no objection to Barbara, but royalty stood in splendid isolation; Bertha and Bertha alone must be the cynosure of the empire's eyes on her wedding day. Thus, while Gustav was flinging open Hügel's windows and synchronizing all watches, Tilo took *his* bride to the Wilmowsky estate in old Prussia that winter and introduced the genuflecting staff to their new *Freifrau* in front of Schloss Marienthal, his family home. Architecturally Marienthal was far more pleasing than Villa Hügel, and it was nearly as large; its two huge quadrangles were approximately the size of Harvard College's yard. The manor hall of the castle bore the date 1730, which made it an upstart in Wilmowsky history. Tilo's ancestors had been members of the Brandenburg hierarchy since the Thirty Years War; for three hundred years before that they had lived baronial lives in the Silesian dukedom of Teschen, and before *that* they had been feudal knights in western Germany.[28]

One wonders what the fate of the Krupp dynasty would have been had Tilo married Bertha. Aged twenty-eight, he was closer to her age, and in nearly every way he was Gustav's opposite. To be sure, he dressed elegantly, wore a monocle, and clicked his heels. But that was liturgical — it went with Marienthal. Under his Teutonic surface the baron was humane, modest, and idealistic, and in his forties he was to become one of Germany's first Rotarians. Youthful years in England had changed him, as Gustav's travels had not; he was an admirer of British democracy and British understatement — though his estates made him one of the largest landowners in Europe, he persisted in identifying himself to strangers as "a farmer." Nor was this sham. Tilo was a keen student of agricultural science. He used intricate fertilization formulas, carefully rotated crops, and became an authority on hybrids. He could have made a hundred flowers bloom on those frontier hectares where his brother-in-law grew weeds.[29]

The one thing Gustav could do which Tilo couldn't was abandon his conscience for blind obedience. The Freiherr never forgot why the Wilmowskys had shown Silesia their heels after the Thirty Years War. They had been Protestants and the rest of the duchy was Catholic. When Tilo's forebears went to church they meant it. So did he; he was a practicing Christian. As two World Wars were to demonstrate, he was capable of disregarding brutal orders from Berlin, and if he had been the ruler of Essen history might read rather differently. It is worth noting that his first visit to Hügel, in 1896, had been in response to an invitation from Fritz, who was then quite normal. Tilo von Wilmowsky was the sort of son-in-law Fritz would have chosen. Only a Kaiser Wilhelm II could have approved of a Gustav.

Thus the Wilmowskys and the Krupp von Bohlen und Halbachs went their own ways. There was no estrangement. The sisters were too close for that. They could not bear to be apart for long, and Gustav repeatedly sought Tilo out. Unsure of himself, deprived of the lineage which permitted the baron to carry his title comfortably, the new Krupp begged his brother-in-law to join the firm's board. Tilo consented. He even agreed to serve as Gustav's deputy, because, as he explained at Nuremberg, Gustav told him that the Vorstand was only legal "camouflage"; the real decisions were made in Villa Hügel by Bertha and himself. That being understood, neither the baron nor his wife played any significant role in the factories.* They were interested in seedlings, harvests, the life in Marienthal — which had scarcely altered its pattern in the past three hundred years — and occasional travel.[30]

The sun of Pax Britannica was now very low in the sky. The epoch which had begun at Waterloo had reached its twilight hours, and in retrospect the shadows cast by Essen's ugly chimneys seem sharply delineated. They were not so clear then. To the young couples it seemed that the golden years would stretch on endlessly, and examining the snapshots they took, the diaries they kept, and the letters they wrote each other one senses a curiously static quality. Doom lay dead ahead, yet they did not know it; they behaved as though this Indian summer would last forever. For the vast majority of the world's population it was not a serene era, but for the very rich it was glorious, and they enjoyed it enormously. Even Gustav was persuaded to break his pattern of self-regimentation. He slipped off with Bertha to a quiet London hotel, where they sat for Sir Hubert von Herkomer, the Bavarian-born professor of fine arts at Oxford who had painted Wagner, Ruskin, Lord Kelvin, and the Marquess of Salisbury. (Krupp conducted less tranquil business there on the sly, but of that, more presently.) Meanwhile Barbara and Tilo were touring the United States.[31]

The Wilmowskys' four-month tour during the winter of 1909–1910 was a high-water mark in Krupp's reputation abroad. In future years members of the family crossing the seas would be obliged to dodge delegations bearing placards reading BUTCHERS! BLOODSTAINED HUNS, or KRUPP KILLERS OF JEW BABIES!, but that season the aura was still untarnished. On trains they were always accompanied by the president of the railway, who would often tell them that the wheels on which they were riding had been manufactured in Essen. All the headlines were benign: KRUPP BARONESS

---

* Until the Austrian Anschluss, thirty years later. For the baron's curious role in the acquisition of the Berndorferwerk, founded by Bertha's great-uncle Hermann in the 1840's, see below, chapter 15.

LIKES HOME, HAS NO INCLINATION FOR WOMAN SUFFRAGE OR CLUB LIFE, SAYS SHE "KEEPS HOUSE"; LAUGHTER ONE OF JOYS OF TITLED COUPLE VISITING CHICAGO; NOBLE DAUGHTER OF KRUPP, GUN MAN, VISITS NEW YORK; "RICHEST WOMAN" SEES IN BOSTON MODEL FOR WHAT WORLD MUST BE; and AMERICA WINS KRUPP HEIRESS, BARONESS BARBARA VON WILMOWSKI ENTHUSIASTIC IN PRAISE OF U.S., SEES GARY STEEL MILLS.[32]

The trip to Gary was their only industrial call, and was made to please the Imperial German Commissioner of Agriculture, who accompanied them throughout and urged them not to offend the eager American Schlotbarone. What Barbara wanted to see most was Chicago's Hull-House. Jane Addams was the Wilmowskys' hostess there, and she and the faculty of Bryn Mawr in Pennsylvania left a lasting impression on Barbara and Tilo. Apart from the issue of votes for women — the *Freifrau* flushed delicately and whispered that she thought the mere asking of such a question was "unbelievable" — everything in America delighted them. The zealous reporters in turn noted admiringly that a framed photograph of Bertha and little Alfried was always on the baroness's writing desk, that Barbara was "a tall, slender woman of the pure German type, with the rosy Teutonic complexion, blue eyes, an oval face of attractive expression, and a great deal of hair that is dressed in so simple a way as to emphasize her youthfulness," and that "the baron, slight, tall, of military bearing, with an air distingué, caressed a very small, light-colored mustache as the baroness talked of her observations in America." Those observations are a clue to how bright destiny looked to Europe's privileged classes. America, the baroness told a Chicago newspaperwoman, "represents in advance what the world must be like in some future time when, with the annihilation of time and distance through the genius of Zeppelins, Wrights, and Marconis, the world will be fused into one great whole, speaking one language and pursuing but one ideal, the good of humanity."[33]

Before leaving for New York, where Mr. and Mrs. Thomas Prosser were to see them aboard the Hamburg-bound North German Lloyd steamer *Kaiser Wilhelm II*, the Wilmowskys dined in Washington with S.M.'s ambassador, forty-seven-year-old Count Johann Heinrich von Bernstorff. After gossiping about mutual friends — the ambassador's family had been in diplomatic service since 1733, and Wilmowskys and Bernstorffs had been friends for three generations — the count entertained them with stories of his years as first secretary in London and consul general in Cairo. Then, coughing delicately, he inquired about Krupp's new *Unterseeboote*. It was his information that Germaniawerft was laying the keel for the U–18, that monstrous torpedoes had been perfected with a range of 6,000 yards and a speed of 40 knots, and that the Reichsmarineamt was seriously considering the possibilities of a war in which merchant ships would be targets. Did they know anything about that? They shook their heads dumbly. They really didn't, but it sounded absurd. Agreed, said their host; his years in

London had convinced him that England would not tolerate such an atrocity. He shrugged his shoulders. One heard so much. Probably there was nothing to it. At any rate, it wasn't his problem. He had been here less than two years, and expected to be in Washington at least until 1917.[34]

# 11

ELF

✠

# A Real Krupp

Gustav's perusal of Alfred's papers had been even more intense than Fritz's — only his son's would be so thorough — and one of the old man's secrets, he had concluded, had been his flair for drama. While Gustav himself lacked theatrical talent, he could at least erect a stage. Essen was approaching the Great Krupp's hundredth birthday, and the new Krupp planned to make a big thing of it. The impending festivities were advertised as the firm's centennial, but it wasn't so; Bertha's luckless great-grandfather had founded Fried. Krupp in 1811. Gustav, however, preferred 1912 to 1911 for a commemoration, partly out of admiration for Alfred but also because the postponement gave him one more year to consolidate his position.[1]

On paper that position was impregnable. With Bertha's shares in his pocket he was a two-legged stockholders' meeting. Thanks to the Kaiser, he even bore the family name. But somehow his nursery nickname had leaked out; behind his back he was known as Taffy, and his finicky mannerisms were contrasted with the earthiness of his fellow Schlotbarone — Thyssen, Stinnes, Klöckner, Reusch, Kirkdorf. His greatest handicap was the fact that he could never be his own man. In one popular Ruhr joke he was described as one of Bertha's offspring: "only the doctor threw the baby away and kept the placenta." As his wife's creature, he couldn't hope to surmount that obstacle. He would have to bypass it.[2]

Here his extraordinary dedication was an asset. No one who watched him at work could come away with the feeling that he was treating his job as a sinecure. He appointed himself chief company spy, sneaking around to make certain everyone was giving Krupp his money's worth. One of his unnerving habits, which accounted for rapid turnover among telephone employees, was timing his own long-distance calls and darting out the moment he hung up to see whether the figure in the company operator's log agreed with his. At the end of each day he demanded a full accounting from his chauffeur, his valet, and his secretary, Fräulein Kröne. He insisted upon being told how each had spent the day. He also wanted to know exactly how much money they had disbursed — his or theirs, it made no difference — and what they had bought. That was the extent of the conversation; he never exchanged a pleasant word with them, never commented on the weather, never even wished them a Merry Christmas. (The secretary found these sessions especially grueling. Now a very old woman living in retirement, she finds it impossible to discuss them. The mere memory, she explains, makes her "too nervous.")[3]

Unlike Alfred Krupp, Gustav Krupp could not impose his forceful personality directly upon the firm's employees. There were far too many of them now. To most he would remain remote, and therefore he borrowed the carrots and sticks implicit in the *Generalregulativ*. Employee benefits soared; so did the demands upon those who got them. The thirty thousand Kruppianer in colonies were occupants of the finest workmen's dwellings in the Ruhr. In return for their housing they agreed to renounce labor unions and the SPD and to suffer supervision by uniformed inspectors, who were entitled to enter their houses at any hour of day or night "to see that the regulations laid down for conduct and mode of life are strictly observed." An American reporter toured the city and cabled his editor a sympathetic account of the "stalwart sons of Vulcan." He compared the "luxury" of Krupp cottages with the "filthy homes in the Chicago Stockyards' Packingtown." There was, he observed at the end, just one "fly in the amber. . . . Those who work for Krupp must sacrifice political liberty. . . . For all practical purposes the people of Essen are body and soul the property of the Krupps."[4]

If the new Krupp read the dispatch he probably approved of it, though naturally he was less explicit in his addresses to his men. He told them, he later explained, that he regarded himself as "the trustee of an obligatory heritage." Upon arriving among them he had realized that they were "accustomed to seeing in the Krupp family, which I now embodied next to my wife, not only the employer but also the leading co-worker. This made me proud and modest at the same time." Lyrically he added, "The sapling which was once planted by Alfred Krupp and was nursed carefully by Friedrich Alfred Krupp, not to forget his wife, my mother-in-law Margarethe Krupp — that sapling of loyalty and mutual trust had meantime grown to be a formidable tree whose branches and twigs were spreading afar. I stepped in under their protective shade and learned that a century of Krupp tradition had already borne prolific fruit."[5]

Some of the branches and twigs were so far away that no one in the Ruhr had ever seen them. Between 1906, when he became the firm's chairman-designate, and 1909, when he assumed the full powers of the chairmanship,

Krupp learned to his astonishment that, among other things, the firm owned much of Australia's base metal industry, held concession rights to the rich monazite sands of Travancore in India, and had become sole proprietor of New Caledonia's vast nickel mines through a French dummy company, the Société des Mines Nickélifères. By cartels and gentlemen's agreements, Fried. Krupp's reserves had been strengthened in every industrial country. Though Bertha didn't know it, her Finanzrat had invested a million marks of her money in the stocks of British munitions firms — that was what kept Gustav busy in London when he wasn't sitting for his portrait — and Bertha and the Schneiders owned as much of Austria-Hungary's Skoda Werke as any Austrian.[6]

In Essen alone Krupp was responsible for a constellation of eighty smoke-shrouded factories. Gustav's first sight of them had left him speechless. They used more gas than the city surrounding them, more electricity than all Berlin, and constituted a huge city within a city, with its own police force, fire department, and traffic laws. But the miles of grimy sheds spreading in every direction from the old Gusstahlfabrik obscured Fried. Krupp A.G.'s greater role as a holding company. Essen was only the apex of an iceberg. In western and northern Germany the Muttergesellschaft was responsible for eight other gigantic steel plants (Rheinhausen alone housed six towering blast furnaces and fifteen blowing engines); for the Germaniawerft shipyard at Kiel; for foundries, coal mines, ore fields, clay pits, and limestone quarries as far away as Silesia; and for three proving grounds at Meppen, Dülmen, and Tangerhutte — each of which was superior to any governmental firing range in the world. Every year Bertha's holdings outside Essen produced 2,000,000 tons of coal, 800,000 tons of coke, 100,000 tons of iron ore, and 800,000 tons of pig iron, and Gustav's first annual report revealed that 48,880 shells and 25,131 rifle bullets had been fired at the ranges, enough for a major Balkan war. His fellow board members spoke only in superlatives. *Die Firma*, they boasted, had "*das grösste Vermögen, die höchsten Dividende, den bedeutendsten Konzern, die gefährlichste Kanone*" (the greatest fortune, the highest dividends, the largest business concern, the most formidable gun) — and they were right.[7]

Could he improve upon this record? Could he give the grizzled specter of *der Grosse Krupp* a present worthy of the old blackguard? He could and did. Krupp was big; *also*, Krupp must become bigger. First, however, it needed a symbol. Villa Hügel was a nice place to live, or would be, once Gustav redecorated it in dark paneling and stuffed it with heavy Wilhelmine furniture. But hadn't Alfred said that his work was his prayer? Gustav resolved that the firm's headquarters must be as striking as the castle. During his three years as chairman-designate he designed and supervised the erection of a citadel of toil. The Hauptverwaltungsgebäude, or chief administration building, as it is still known, is the second most famous structure in Kruppdom. It may also be the ugliest office building in Europe. Ponderous, decorated in vulgar crenelated style, it was constructed of a porous stone which rapidly absorbed soot, giving it the appearance of an immense slag heap. One little bay window, decorated with the three rings, overlooked the street from the second floor. This was Krupp's office. Had he looked out, which of course he never did, he would have seen the stricken expressions on the faces of arriving visitors.[8]

Ensconced in this nightmare, with its smell of dungeons, Krupp issued his expansion orders. Three shooting grounds weren't enough; he wanted a fourth. Rheinhausen needed more blast furnaces. Studying reports of the Russo-Japanese War, the world's most recent conflict between great powers, he noted that shellfire had led to protective entrenchments shielded by barbed wire. With frightful but flawless logic he foresaw that in any future hostilities barbwire would be in great demand; therefore in 1911 he bought the Hamm Wireworks, Germany's largest, in the northeast corner of the Ruhr. (Within a year the First Balkan War had confirmed his judgment.) Industrialists elsewhere had licensed Rudolf Diesel's patent. If Kiel was to produce the mightiest U-boat armada in the world, Krupp must become the world's greatest producer of diesel engines, and it was done. "Rustless" (stainless) steel was the coming thing; he insisted that he have a patent for that, too, and in 1912 he got it. All these projects required tremendous injections of capital. Unhesitatingly he invited subscriptions to a 50-million-mark loan; unhesitatingly the public responded. *Die höchsten Dividende* grew higher each year. In 1911 the return on Bertha's investment was 10 percent; in 1912 12 percent, and in 1913 it was to be 14 percent, a German record. The *Jahrbuch der Millionäre* reported that the third richest individual in the Reich was Baron von Goldschmidt-Rothschild, son-in-law of the last male descendant in Germany of the Frankfurt banking house. Goldschmidt-Rothschild had 163 million marks. Prince Henckel von Donnersmark was second, with 254 million, and Bertha Krupp, with 283 million, was first. Her annual income exceeded six million American dollars. And investors were bound to feel bullish; the arms market was getting better all the time.[9]

✠     ✠     ✠

The Krupp Centenary opened in the early summer of 1912 with the distribution of 14 million marks among the firm's workmen, and then it started to become lavish. It was the Reich's equivalent of Victoria's Diamond Jubilee of 1897 — an orgy of spending, chauvinism, self-congratulation, and misty nostalgia. The anniversary, wrote the *Nation*, was being celebrated in Germany "much as if [Krupp] were a branch of the government, as in a sense it is." Newspapers devoted thousands of columns to the parallels between the family and the *Volk*. Magazines explained how the rise of Krupp's industrial empire was inextricably bound up with that of the Reich. Editorial writers reminded their readers that a hundred years earlier, when Alfred Krupp wriggled free of his mother's womb, Germany was just beginning to throw off the Napoleonic yoke and feel the stirrings which were to flower at Versailles in 1871, and in every little town square the local Bürgermeister took his stance beneath the Franco-Prussian victory statue to salute the enterprise which, in the words of one of them, "is today, as it has been for decades past, the greatest maker of war materials the world over."[10]

In Essen the celebrations were scheduled to cover three days. Wilhelm arrived from Berlin wearing the uniform of the All-Highest Warlord — *des allerhöchsten Kriegsherrn*, as he liked to style himself these days. Accompanying him were all the princes of Prussia, Chancellor von Bethmann-Hollweg, the Kaiser's cabinet leaders, and every general and admiral in the empire. A remarkable oil painting in the family archives shows all these dignitaries gathered in the new marble reception hall of the Hauptverwaltungsgebäude. Gustav is addressing them; his waxen manikin figure rises from a sea of foliage. To his right is the Generalstab; to his left, Tirpitz's blue-and-gold disciples. The All-Highest watches the speaker from a chair in the middle of a garish rug, facing Gustav; around him are three ladies in the fantastic flowered hats of the period — the Kaiserin, Marga, and Bertha — and behind him sit the leaders of the civil government. They appear to be daydreaming. Wilhelm seems impatient, either because he cannot bear Gustav's lethal prose or is impatient to open his own fiery address.[11]

The All-Highest seldom bored an audience. Echoing the jingoist editorials, he began by recalling that the birth of the Gusstahlfabrik coincided with the beginning of the German nationalist movement, "which the following year at Leipzig's Battle of the Nations (*Völkerschlacht*) was to shake the nation free from the oppressor." Since then, he continued, "Krupp cannon have thundered over the battlefields where German unity was fought for and won, and Krupp cannon are the energy of the German army and navy today. The ships constructed in the Krupp yards carry the German flag into every sea. Krupp steel protects our vessels and our forts." Almost as an aside he interpolated, "But the Krupp works has not only been an exploiter in this sense. It has also been the first in Germany to recognize the new social problems and to seek to solve them, thus leading to social legislation." Raising his adenoidal voice, he urged his listeners to remain *"treu den Traditionen des Hauses, zur Ehre des Namens Krupp, zum Ruhme unserer Industrie und zum Wohle des deutschen Vaterlandes."* Then, caressing his curly locks with two strokes of his good right hand, he shouted, *"Das Haus und die Firma Krupp: hurra, hurra, hurra!"* His audience sprang to its feet and responded, *"Heil Kaiser und Reich!"*[12]

That over, everyone there was presented a copy of *Krupp 1812–1912*, a huge book glorifying the achievements of house and firm. Although the second day was devoted to exhibits, demonstrations, tableaux, and marathon banquets in a temporary hall constructed for the occasion on Hügel's south grounds overlooking the sluggish waters of the Ruhr, whenever possible Gustav and Bertha slipped away from the Kaiser and sneaked off into the woods. They were rehearsing a pageant. Gustav had decided to climax the third day's festivities with a feudal tournament — not a mock ceremony, but the real thing. The spectacle was entitled *"Hie, Sankt Barbara! Hie, Sankt Georg!"* after the patron saints of gunnery and chivalry. Jousters were to carry real lances capable of inflicting real wounds. For the past month a Düsseldorf costume house had been working in shifts to outfit the participants. Krupp himself had a tailor-made suit of burnished armor (high-carbon *Kruppstahl*; none of his antagonists would be carrying offensive weapons capable of penetrating it). Bertha was to be dressed as a medieval lady, Krupp executives as vassals — and picked Kruppianer as serfs.[13]

It was not an aesthetic era, yet there is something almost heroic about the tastelessness of this production. Ernst Haux read the scenario and rushed to Krupp, appalled. Tournaments were anachronistic to the Krupp tradition, he pointed out, wagging his stubby beard and close-cropped head. Germany's last recorded joust had been held in the reign of Maximilian I, who had died in 1519, nearly seven decades before Arndt Krupp's appearance in Essen. Moreover, even the early generations of the family were irrelevant to the glory Germany was toasting now. Foundries, rolling mills, and smokestacks would be far more appropriate symbols. Warriors didn't fight in the saddle with pikes, halberds, and épées any more. If they did, Fried. Krupp wouldn't be a going Konzern. Gustav wavered, but it was too late; word of the show had reached the All-Highest, and he had read with delight Hugenberg's fustian prologue: "Your Kaiser's eye gazes once more upon us and proudly follows the victorious course of our industrial enterprise. . . . To the virtues of our people, which must be preserved if it is to remain young and energetic, belong also the old Germanic valor and love of arms" (*die alte germanische Tapferkeit und Waffenliebe*).[14]

This suited S.M.'s *Teutschtümelei* — love of medieval mannerisms — perfectly. He repaired to his apartment and selected his gaudiest uniform, shiniest helmet, sharpest sword, and most evil-looking dagger. Even Haux conceded that the tourney couldn't be scratched now, so ambulances at the Krupp hospital were alerted to remove casualties.

Next day the All-Highest entered his imperial box armed to the teeth. Bertha sat between him and the chancellor; the Kaiserin was with Marga. In the second rank were Tirpitz, Minister of War Josias von Heeringen, Rudolf von Valentini, head of the civil cabinet; Rheinhold Sydow, State Secretary of the Reich Finance Office; and Klemens Delbrück, a leader of the Reichstag. The Offizierskorps occupied the rest of the grandstand. Choice seats were reserved for foreigners representing client nations, but it was catch-as-catch-can for the others, with the Americans and Australians seated behind posts beyond the left field foul line. Gustav's pageant script was distributed among the spectators, and a copy of it reposes in the family archives, a tribute to one man's faith in his own talent. His opening lines were:

> *Ihre Kaiserliche Hoheit, lang lebe Ihr Reich!*
> *Dies ist der Turnierplatz, liebe Bertha,*
> *auf dem ich vor Dir und dem Kaiser reiten werde:*
> *Ich bitte nun um deinen Segen, Liebste.*
> (Sie gibt ihm ihr Tuch; er küsst ihre Hand.)
> *Danke!*
>
> Your Highness, long live your empire!
> This is the jousting place, dear Bertha,
> On which I shall ride before you and before the Kaiser:
> I ask now for your blessing, dearest.
> (*She gives him her scarf; he kisses her hand.*)
> Thank you![15]

He then rode "up and down with the small boy." The boy was Alfried, not quite five years old, astride a tiny gray pony. A photograph taken during the dress rehearsal shows him thus, dressed as a page, with a chaplet of leaves on his forehead and a preoccupied expression on his face. Bertha regards him fondly from a nearby sidesaddle; her broad-brimmed hat trails plumes. She looks like something out of an amateur production of *The Student Prince*. Gustav is ignoring both of them. In full armor and bearing a broadsword, he is straddling an enormous stallion. He gives the impression that he may fall off at any moment, knows it, and is petrified.

He didn't fall, because he didn't ride. Just as a team of workmen was about to hoist him up, a breathless messenger arrived with a dispatch for Herr von Valentini. For twenty years engineers had been warning the managers of Ruhr coal mines that they must combat dust by periodic watering. The incidence of silicosis, a lung disease to which miners are prone, was alarmingly high, and the dangers of firedamp were mounting. Now the inevitable had happened. The Lothringen shaft had blown up near Bochum; one hundred and ten Kumpels were dead. There was a quick huddle in the grandstand. Under the circumstances, Wilhelm's advisers suggested, a frolic here might be misunderstood by S.M.'s subjects. The *Allerhöchsteselber* agreed. Reluctantly he strode up to the imperial apartment to shed his warlord's gear. Bertha slid down, master mechanics unscrewed Gustav's mail, and the little boy was led off to Marga Brandt, his governess.[16]

If the miners' mishap hadn't spoiled the joust, Alfried would doubtless have given a good account of himself. He had been trained to ride as royalty is trained, with forty-five minutes of instruction each day from a master who, as a commoner, trotted a half-length behind his pupil, calling out respectfully, "Master Alfried, head up! Master Alfried, toes down!" Bertha's second child had died a few months after birth, so at this age the boy benefited from the teacher's exclusive attention. He could have managed his pony more adroitly than Gustav his stallion. Nor would the imposing uniforms in the gallery have given the young heir stage fright. As long as he could remember (and well before) he had been the subject of special attention. In the Ruhr he was more fawned upon than the Kronprinz. The Vorstand had responded to Gustav's memo announcing his birth with a prayerful bulletin expressing the hope in behalf of fifty thousand Kruppianer that "God's blessing" (*Segen Gottes*) would be conferred upon the future Krupp. Alfried's christening had been a national event. Programs had been printed, seats reserved in the first-floor salon, and standing room provided on temporary platforms for Krupp's castle servants (*Hügelangehörige*). All the dignitaries who had come to Bertha's wedding — and who would later attend Gustav's abortive tournament — had been present, with the Kaiser himself selected as the infant's god-father. Program notes explained the meaning of each name: Alfried for his illustrious great-grandfather, Felix for Margarethe's brother, and Alwyn for Gustav's brother. The baby's father personally drew up a timetable for the ceremony, which assured that Alfried Felix Alwyn von Bohlen und Halbach — some day to be *Krupp* von Bohlen und Halbach — would be baptized as promptly as he had been born. Thenceforth every scrap of news about him became an item of significance to the entire Reich. The decision to follow Fritz's example and incorporate an anchor in his coat of arms was interpreted as a good omen; Germany's navy would grow ever more powerful until Britannia was swept from the waves. Whenever Bertha paraded through downtown Essen, all eyes were on the child in her wake; the watching *Hausfrauen* were well aware that the future of their own children would one day depend upon him.[17]

Thanks to Gustav's passion for records, there exists a mass of data about the early years of the boy who would one day be the most powerful Krupp in history — the idol of German youth in another, more sinister Reich. The father's scrupulous hand noted that Alfried was twenty-two and a half inches long at birth; his growth was to be measured on each subsequent birthday until, upon reaching his majority, he exceeded six feet. At the age of twelve months he could stand. His first books were *Gulliver's Travels* and the works of Karl May, the German James Fenimore Cooper: *Der Mahdi, Im Sudan,* and *Old Surehand II.* But one observation of Bertha's is more revealing than the whole of Gustav's facts. Of all her children, she noticed, Alfried was "the most earnest." Public adulation and private statistics had nothing to do with that. His seriousness, his introspection, and the awful loneliness which was to be his greatest strength and greatest weakness may be traced to his upbringing. Later his brothers and sisters received some of the same discipline, but they had one another to lean upon, and since none of them was destined to inherit the name Krupp, parental attention was easily diverted. Alfried was never free of it. As soon as he was old enough to understand the geography of the great barn his family inhabited he learned that the basement was for servants; formal rooms were on the first floor; his mother, father, and emperor had apartments on the second; the third was reserved for drawing rooms; children, nurses, and governesses lived on the fourth; and guests on the fifth. However, that did not mean that the fourth floor was a refuge for him. He had no asylum anywhere. During his toddling years maids and footmen were instructed to submit to Gustav daily reports on the child's activities. Taught by private tutors, under a regimen drawn up by his father, he spoke fluent French before he learned German. That set him apart; so did every other influence in his life. A dozen times a day he was told that he must expect to be different, that he must never hope for a normal life. The reason was always the same: *Verantwortlichkeit*, responsibility. He must become one of the most *verantwortlich* men in the world; it was his duty.[18]

Duty, Marga Brandt explained as the pageant broke up, required him to doff his page's costume and forget the canter before the All-Highest. He would not be allowed to ride up and down the jousting place with his father. He must remove his trappings and return to his lessons. That was the *verantwortlich* thing to do. After all, it had only been a game, she consoled him. Perhaps one day he would have a chance to serve the Reich in a real war.

✠ ✠ ✠

The cold war — in those days they called it the "dry war" — had become a rigid groove confining Gustav's single-track mind. Except for stainless steel and experiments with tough Widia (tungsten carbide) steel, he evinced little interest in the tools of peace. The international arms trade was racing toward an unseen precipice, and he was swiftly approaching it along with Schneider, Skoda, Mitsui, Vickers and Armstrong, Putiloff (Russia), Terni and Ansaldo (Italy), and Bethlehem and Du Pont (America). There was this difference: Krupp led the pack. And Berlin expected him to stay in front. Repeatedly Conservative deputies to the Reichstag raised the question "Is Germany the armaments race leader" (*Ist Deutschland der Rüstungstreiber*)? and it was up to Essen to make certain the answer was always *Ja*. It always was. In May 1914 Karl Liebknecht, leader of the Social Democratic deputies, summed it up: "Krupp's is the matador of the international armament industry, pre-eminent in every department." To be sure, scattered voices deplored the contest.

Liebknecht scorned the "bloody international of the merchants of death" (*blutige internationale Händler des Todes*). Andrew Carnegie, pondering the munitions budgets of the great powers, confessed that he was "gravely worried," and at the other end of the political spectrum Nikolai Lenin wrote that Europe had become "a barrel of gunpowder."[19]

Twenty years later, when the great reaction against martial virtues had set in, oversimplifying the competition between the great arms merchants became an intellectual fashion. Any aggressive move by France was attributed to Schneider; any unfurling of the Rising Sun to Mitsui. In practice the rivalries were more sophisticated than that. Apart from Krupp, virtually all the large weapons emporia were listed on the world's stock exchanges, and through the cross-pollination of investments, patent interchanges, and out-and-out cartels their interests often coincided. The Kaiser's growls during the Moroccan crisis of 1911 have often been attributed to Gustav, on the erroneous assumptions that France and Germany were jockeying for commercial privileges there and that Wilhelm dispatched the gunboat *Panther* to scare Frenchmen. Six years earlier, when the emperor landed at Tangier and demanded an open-door policy, he *had* been egged on by Marga Krupp's directors, who had been using Morocco as a dumping ground for obsolete cannon and were alarmed at the prospect of tariff walls which would favor Schneider. At the time of the *Panther*'s here-comes-the-cavalry ride to Agadir, however, the situation had altered. The country's attraction for steelmakers was no longer as a market but as a source of minerals. And though the Wilhelmstrasse and the Quai d'Orsay were still at odds over who should pull its political strings, Krupp and Schneider had joined their claims, together with those of Thyssen, in a dummy Union des Mines. The firms had agreed to split the sultan's iron ore three ways. The last thing they wanted was a Franco-German diplomatic showdown. One arose because Reinhard Mannesmann, a Remscheid ironmaker, had been excluded from the agreement. Mannesmann had paid the Moroccans a heavy subsidy for mining concessions. If the country became a French protectorate he would lose everything. He convinced several Reichstag deputies that he was being victimized, and the flag-waving Alldeutsche Verband did the rest. The gunboat sailed, Britain rallied to France's side, Wilhelm's gesture failed. Morocco became French, and Schneider, no longer in need of allies, quit the cartel. All three Germans — Krupp, Thyssen, and Mannesmann — were left to sulk.[20]

Such intricate maneuvers were rare, however. In most backward countries salesmen who had mastered the old eye-gouging, knee-to-the-groin tactics continued to chalk up striking successes. One of the greatest victories in the history of foul play was Krupp's seizure of a Brazilian contract from Schneider's hands. At the outset the Germans seemed to be hopeless underdogs. Their rivals had a far better gun, the French 75, and Krupp's men knew it. When Rio scheduled the first tests Essen's quick-firers hadn't even reached the country. The 75's, on the other hand, were housed in a heavily guarded warehouse up-country. On the morning of the demonstration Schneider's agent received a hysterical message from his watchman. The barrels were useless and the warehouse had burned down. A mob had surrounded it and flung torches on the roof. The sample battery was ruined. Frantic cables to Le Creusot brought a second shipment, but when the vessel reached the Brazilian port where the guns were to be transferred to river steamers it appeared that money had changed hands; the native captains refused the cargo on the ground that 75-mm. shells were explosive and therefore dangerous. Next day a Rio paper reported in end-of-the-world type that Peruvian troops had invaded the Brazilian state of Amazonas. The newspaper's special correspondent — he bore the curiously un-Latin name of Hauptmann von Restsoff — disclosed that Peru was equipped with Schneider cannon. Rio, he warned, must acquire modern arms immediately. That night hostile demonstrations outside the French legation eliminated rational discussion, and next day word arrived from the Ruhr that a Krupp artillery park had already sailed. It was bought sight unseen. As the guns came ashore a band played *Deutschland über Alles*, von Restsoff came to attention, and the Schneider man strode away raging.[21]

Like every other member of the European establishment, Gustav was worried about the Balkans, though for a singular reason. Others were disturbed by the incessant warfare there. Krupp didn't mind that. He liked a good scrap. But he was troubled by the way things were going. Although each of the armies carried miscellaneous equipment from Sheffield, Le Creusot, and Essen, spheres of influence had been carved out for heavy ordnance. Greek and Bulgarian cannon, for example, came from Schneider. The Ottoman Empire's artillery had been forged by Krupp, and the *dumm* Turks kept losing. In the autumn of 1912 they practically destroyed the splendid image which had been created at Sedan. Retreating before the Greeks, Bulgars, and Serbs, the sultan's troops were thrashed at Kirk Kilissé, Kumanovo, Lulé Burgas, and Monastir. It was embarrassing for Gustav, and he was immensely relieved when the outbreak of the Second Balkan War found Rumania on Turkey's side. Rumanians were both hard fighters and Krupp customers, and when they routed the Bulgars there was jubilation in the Hauptverwaltungsgebäude. Every time a Krupp shell struck its target Essen made sure the world knew it, just as each German who broke a world's record, won a prize, or excited admiration in other countries was feted in Berlin.[22]

Gradually other Europeans came to weigh the potency of the Teutonic tribal spirit and conclude that the easy victories of 1870 had gone to Berlin's head. The more the new German generation thought about those battles, the more convinced they were that German blood *was* superior, that German soldiers *were* invincible, and that if any antagonist proved intractable they would repeat the triumphs of their fathers. This bellicosity, embodied in their sovereign, had come to exercise profound influence in neighboring capitals. None was immune to it; Britain was the least volatile of them, yet in the first decade of the twentieth century Englishmen had become persuaded that eventually they were going to have to fight Germans. In 1908 a British aristocrat declared, "The danger now is that in Europe we have a competitor the most formidable in numbers, intellect and education with which we have ever been confronted." In London men wearing *Pickelhauben* walked the streets to promote a novel about German invasion, and a play with the same theme ran a year and a half.[23]

To outsiders the Reich looked monolithic, the Kaiser arrogant, his officers aggressive; and Essen's sole function seemed to be that of Germany's arsenal. Since Krupp's special position at home was important to the firm, nothing was done to correct the impression. Nevertheless it was invalid. In 1911 the old Gusstahlfabrik sold its fifty-thousandth cannon. Of these, over half had gone to nations beyond the Fatherland's borders — fifty-two client governments in Europe, South America, Asia, and Africa. When identity with the Fatherland was useful, the firm encouraged it, of course; Krupp salesmen were reporting items of military intelligence to the nearest German embassy as early as 1903. In return they naturally expected certain favors. Ambassador Maximilian von Brandt had been recalled from Peking for criticizing defects in the Krupp cannon delivered there, and Gustav's agent in Constantinople was housed in a mansion next door to Wilhelm's embassy. But the firm was really an international institution. The salesmen — or, as Gustav liked to call them, the "Plenipotentiaries of the firm of Krupp" (*Bevollmächtigte der Firma Krupp*) — were usually citizens of the governments with which they dealt and, in nearly every case, men with unusual connections. Vienna's plenipotentiary was a friend of the Rothschilds; New York's, a relative of J. P. Morgan; Copenhagen's, the future Danish Minister of War; Brussels's, the brother-in-law of Belgium's War Minister; Peking's, a nephew of Yüan Shih-k'ai, the acting chief of state; and Rome's, Mario Cresta, president of the chamber of commerce, who found himself in an extremely awkward situation during the Tripolitan War which grew out of the second Moroccan crisis. Italy, determined to grab its share of North Africa before the French seized everything, landed a force to annex Tripoli. Turks under Enver Bey struck back. Signor Cresta was delivering an impassioned address at a patriotic rally, exhorting Rome's new legions to fight like Caesar's, when word arrived that one of them had just been annihilated by fifty Krupp cannon.[24]

But those were the risks Bevollmächtigte took — risks taken, for that matter, by the head of the firm himself. Just as his workmen voted the SPD ticket and remained fiercely loyal to Krupp, so Gustav managed to unite allegiance to his country and to his wife's profits. In a letter to von Valentini he wrote, "*Weder die Firma Krupp noch ihr Inhaber müssen sich in den Vordergrund der politischen Kämpfe schieben lassen*" (Neither the firm of Krupp nor its owner must be pushed into political struggles). This was nonsense. If you do business with fifty-two foreign governments and sell 24,000 field guns to your own country you are obviously as deep in politics as a layman can get. Yet Gustav, like Alfred, wanted it both ways, and having persuaded himself that conflict between his merchandise and his patriotism was impossible, he went on to consummate a number of transactions which clearly affected Germany's security. Disclosing shell fuse secrets to Vickers wasn't his responsibility. The last renewal of that agreement had been signed in 1904, two years before he joined the board. Nor could he be held accountable for leasing Krupp's split trail for field artillery pieces to the U.S. Army, even though the use of that patent would ultimately augment American mobility at Saint-Mihiel and in the Argonne, with the Kaiser's troops the losers; like Count von Bernstorff in Washington, Krupp never dreamed that Washington and Berlin would be at war before young Alfried's tenth birthday. Gustav did have every reason to be wary of Saint Petersburg. Since 1907 Russia, France, and England had been joined in the Triple Entente. The Entente's antagonists were the three powers of the Triple Alliance: Austria, Italy, and Germany. Nevertheless Krupp left no palm ungreased in an all-out effort to outbox competitors and become the chief stiffener of morale for the czar's military establishment, vitiated by the Japanese victories. Every barrel he shipped east increased the dreaded encirclement of the Reich, yet he sent all the Russians would take. And he gave them their rubles' worth; when Hindenburg's troops overran the fortresses of the great Polish triangle in 1914 they found them equipped with the latest Krupp howitzers.[25]

Long before then Gustav had demonstrated that he intended to keep his twin obligations sealed in logic-tight compartments, that he wouldn't permit the empire's international relations to hamstring his business. Sometimes he seemed to court military displeasure. In 1906 Count Ferdinand von Zeppelin began manufacturing dirigibles for the Reich at Friedrichshafen. Three years later Krupp electrified Frankfurt's International Aircraft Fair by an exhibit of "anti-Zeppelin" guns, which were then bought furiously by the three powers most in need of them: France, England, and Russia. That same year Reginald McKenna, First Lord of the Admiralty, created an even greater sensation in the House of Commons; the dreadnought race between Germany and Great Britain was then in its fourth year, and McKenna informed Parliament that Krupp's Kiel shipyards were prepared to provide England with eight warships a year. That deal fell through. It was too much — for once Tirpitz, Armstrong, and Vickers were bedfellows — but Krupp did succeed in maintaining two prices for naval armor, charging Berlin nearly twice as much as Washington. Karl Liebknecht read out the figures in the Reichstag, Tirpitz admitted that they were correct, the Kaiser's eyebrows shot up, and he asked Herr Rötger, a senior director of Krupp's board, why this should be.

The only answer he got was that Gustav and his directors were acting as executors of Fritz's will (*Testamentsvollstrecker*). The reply was given stonily, and there was no appeal from it.[26]

In 1912 Krupp crossed a line which would have spelled utter ruin for any other company in any other country. Irrefutable evidence appeared proving that Essen agents had stolen over a thousand documents from War Office files. Several Junkers were caught with Krupp jam on their mustaches, and at the same time it was revealed that Krupp money had fomented anti-German attacks in the French press to stir up Berlin and create new business at home. Ernst Haux was the first director in the Hauptver-waltungsgebäude to know that something was wrong. "One morning — it was in the middle of September — Mühlon, one of the accountants, entered my office in a state of great excitement," his account begins. "He informed me that Eccius, head of our commercial branch dealing with war material, was at that moment in conference with detectives and an examining magistrate from the Criminal Investigation Department in Berlin. They had come to confiscate secret reports from our Berlin representative. They were mainly concerned with the so-called 'granulating rollers' (*Korn-walzer*), our code name for confidential documents, received from Brandt, the secretary. Captain Dreger, our Berlin representative, and Brandt himself had been arrested. Dreger, however, was soon released."[27]

But Brandt and Kruppdirektor Eccius weren't, and their trial became the high point in what to Haux was "*Der Krupp-Prozess 1912/1913*," to the SPD "the *Kornwalzer* affair," and to the general public simply the *Skandal*. Under any name it was fragrant. The first scent of it had reached Liebknecht, probably because his hostility to the Berlin-Hügel axis was so well known, in a plain envelope with no return address. Inside were seventeen slips of paper, each headed "*Kornwalzer*" and bearing highly classified information. The sender was never found, and Liebknecht turned the slips over to Minister of War von Heeringen. At the minister's request police began reading mail to and from No. 19 Voss-strasse, Krupp's office in the capital. They found that Brandt systematically paid out large sums to men in uniform; eight naval officers had received 50,000 marks and one army artillery officer 13,000 marks. The intelligence received was priceless; it included specifications of every German weapon, contemplated designs, war plans, and correspondence with and about other arms firms. With it, Krupp could manipulate key military figures. Every move by generals and admirals was anticipated. A profitable war scare could be created by leaking a few selected facts in Paris, which was what had happened. At Heeringen's request the police had rounded up the bribers and bribees simultaneously and raided No. 19 Voss-strasse, where they learned that seven hundred stolen documents were kept in the Essen safe of a retired Krupp executive.[28]

The authorities had everything — the documents, confessions, receipts for the bribes — and for seven months they did nothing. It is impossible to say who was pulling which string, but clearly someone was active behind the scenes. Not a word appeared in the press, and all the prisoners were freed, including Brandt. That was too much for Liebknecht. On April 18, 1913, the Social Democrat rose in the Reichstag. He dryly conceded that "Obviously it is impossible, without alluding to Krupp, to sing all those patriotic hymns lauding Germany which are customary in veterans' associations, Young German clubs, and other such military societies. The collapse of the good name of Krupp would unquestionably deal a staggering blow to the brand of patriotism we Germans have patented" (*hat unser deutscher Patentpatriotismus einen schweren Schlag erlitten*). Nevertheless it was equally indisputable that "This celebrated firm systematically uses its fortune to tempt senior and junior Prussian officials to betray military secrets." Liebknecht thought the Reichstag should know that *die Firma* stood accused of "Obtaining information regarding the contents of secret documents concerning designs, results of tests, and particularly prices quoted by or accepted from other companies for the purpose of private gain" (*Kenntnis von geheimen Schriftstücken zu erhalten, deren Inhalt die Firma interessierte, insbesondere über Konstruktionen, Ergebnisse von Versuchen, namentlich aber über Preise, die andere Werke fordern oder ihnen bewilligt sind*).

He sat down amid consternation. Heeringen added to the general dismay by acknowledging that Liebknecht's description of Krupp's method was correct and that he wanted to express his own "unqualified disapproval of such a procedure." He added that "there is, however, no evidence (*noch in keiner Weise festgestellt*) that the Essen directors were a party to it." Certainly there is no evidence that Gustav knew the sordid details — though he must have had some inkling, because every appropriation over 10,000 marks had to be approved by him — but the suggestion that the entire board had been hoodwinked was too much. The public didn't accept it, nor did the directors; one of them challenged their SPD accuser to a duel, and Alfred Hugenberg sounded the keynote for the defense by announcing at a press conference that "*Es gibt keinen Fall Krupp, sondern nur einen Fall Liebknecht!*" (There is no Krupp case, but only a Liebknecht case!) Then the Kaiser leaped into it. Ten years earlier he had staked his name on the heterosexuality of Fritz Krupp, and now he let it be known that he intended to shield Gustav. With accusations and denials arching back and forth over Berlin like dumdums he summoned Krupp to the Schloss and pinned on his breast Prussia's Order of the Red Eagle, Second Class, with Oak Leaf Cluster.[29]

But of course there was no way of suppressing the scandal now. Heeringen had resigned, and the conservative Berlin press — *Germania, Tageblatt, Vossische Zeitung,* and Bismarck's old mouthpiece, *Norddeutsche Allgemeine Zeitung* — had joined *Vorwärts* in demanding scapegoats. The All-Highest strode about muttering "those owls, those muttonheads" to himself; less than two years ago he had proclaimed that his royal crown had been "granted by God's grace alone and not by parliaments, popular assemblies and popular decision. . . . Considering myself an instrument of the Lord, I go my own way." It was absurd for the Kaiser to go one way and the rest of the Reich the other, and to him the patriotic piety of the Social Democrats was insufferable. (Here one sympathizes with Wilhelm. The SPD had no real concern for the sanctity of military secrets. They had found a good stick and were brandishing it.) He turned his back and let the courts deal with the rearrested suspects as best they could.

There the furor continued unabated. Hugenberg took the stand and declared that he was unable to produce minutes of Krupp board meetings because nobody ever took any. The men in the courtroom who knew Gustav laughed aloud. Finally the judge elicited the fact that over a period of six and a half years Brandt had purloined 1,500 papers, half of which were then submitted as exhibits for the prosecution. In late October 1913, over a year after the accountant had burst into Haux's office, sentences were passed. Each military officer who had accepted bribes was cashiered and imprisoned for six months. Brandt went to jail for four months; Eccius, the director, was fined 1,200 marks. Although no one had paid much attention, the saddest and most ironical words in the entire affair had been spoken by Heeringen in his valedictory as a cabinet member. The Reichstag record reads,

> . . . It is not the case that I favor private industry. But we are dependent upon it. In critical times we must have great masses of materials immediately ready. This cannot be secured in a state factory. On the other hand, we cannot give the private firms enough orders to keep them solvent in peacetime. Hence they are dependent upon foreign orders. Who gets the advantage of that? Unquestionably the class they support! [*Loud laughter.*]

✠　　✠　　✠

Astonishingly, the thirteen-month uproar hadn't touched Krupp. If the generals had wanted to crucify Bertha's prince consort the *Kornwalzer* case would have been a sturdy cross. But that was the last thing they had in mind. The trial hadn't hurt him because OHL (*Oberste Heeresleitung*, the Army High Command) needed him for its western operations, a swift thrust across the gentle hills and plains in the northeast corner of the European peninsula — that serene tract which, as Telford Taylor observed, has "witnessed the ebb and flow of military power in Europe." There Marlborough had defeated the forces of Louis XIV at Ramillies and Oudenaarde, there the first Napoleon had come to Waterloo and the second to Sedan, and there the General Staff proposed to strike when their day of reckoning came with the grandsons of the men who had been defeated in 1870.[30]

Count Schlieffen, the author of the Reich's *grosse Plan*, as the Offizierskorps christened it over a decade before its execution, never executed it. He was not, in fact, a man of action. To the privileged few who wore the Generalstab's tight blue tunics and glittering buttons, and who goose-stepped* into the red-brick Georgian building on Berlin's Königsplatz which housed *Stabs* leaders, their *Chef* was singularly lacking in what they proudly called *stramme Zucht* — the Prussian military stiffness, with its squared shoulders, scornful mouth, and mackerel-cold eye; he, for example was quite unlike his bullet-headed, neckless aide, Major Erich Ludendorff, who allegedly wore his monocle during the act of love.

Schlieffen was Prussia's great *Philosoph des Krieges*. The children of Ludendorff whispered to one another, "Father looks like a glacier!" Not Schlieffen. He was effete, eccentric. "Crazy Schlieffen," he had been nick-named in 1854 when he had joined the 2nd Garde-Ulanen. He rescued his career by marrying his lovely cousin and by distinguishing himself as staff officer, first at Königgrätz under Prinz Albrecht of Prussia's Uhlans, and then, in 1870, on the Loire under the Grand Duke of Mecklenburg-Schwerin. In 1884 he became *Chef* of the "Great General Staff" (*Grosse Generalstab*), as it was known to the army. By now *ein grosser Plan* existed, and in 1905, on the eve of his retirement, it was perfected by Schlieffen.

Under his tutelage, the *preussische-deutsche Generalstabsoffiziere* were taught that they must create a swinging door (*Klapptür*) by which a northern group and a southern group would pivot around a key hinge and smash the French. There were certain basic premises in the *Operationsplan*, notably the invasion of neutral Belgium and the deployment of a powerful right wing; on his deathbed in 1913 the Feldmarschall's last words were *"Macht mir den rechten Flügel stark"* (See that you make the right wing strong). Meantime the burgeoning importance of Essen's *Waffenschmiede* had altered the semisacred plan in two respects. The first weakened it. Too strong a punch on the right would leave a vulnerable left. The swinging door might open the wrong way. As Ludendorff subsequently explained in *Kriegsführung und Politik*, "a technical change" was necessary; Hermann von Kuhl frankly pointed out that "In no case must the enemy be allowed to get to the Rhine; for then our . . . industrial region would be extremely endangered. . . ."[31]

The second modification removed a basic flaw in the plan. The

---

* Nearly everyone, including Germans, assumes that they originated the goose step. Not so; they merely perpetuated an eighteenth-century British innovation. Two centuries ago all English regiments paraded stiff-legged. On February 11, 1806, Sir Robert Wilson, then a brigade commander under Wellington in the Peninsular Campaign, scrawled in his diary, "The balance-, or goose-step, excited a fever of pain." In 1825 D. L. Richardson submitted a formal complaint against it to the Royal Military Academy in Sandhurst; as late as 1887, the year of Alfred Krupp's death, T. A. Trollope, the novelist's brother, was urging its abolition. By then it was restricted to recruits who had just taken the king's shilling. Shortly thereafter it disappeared from England. But in the Reich it remained, a singular, significant national anachronism.

Ruhr was worth protecting, for without Krupp's second contribution the invasion might falter. "When you march into France," Schlieffen had said, "let the last man on the right brush the channel with his sleeve." That assumed the Germans would reach the channel. It took a lot for granted, for barring the path into Belgium stood the mightiest fortress in Europe, the fortified city of Liège. Situated on a commanding eminence over the broad Meuse, Liège had been reinforced in the 1880's by a thirty-mile circle of forts protected by moats, linked by chains of underground passages, and equipped with 8.4-inch (210-mm.) guns which disappeared into impregnable turrets when not being fired. In the words of Barbara Tuchman, "Ten years ago Port Arthur had withstood a siege of nine months without surrender. World opinion expected Liège certainly to equal the record of Port Arthur if not to hold out indefinitely." The Germans had assigned a separate Army of the Meuse to the bastion, six crack brigades equipped with a secret weapon which would create as much excitement and awe then as the primitive nuclear weapons of three decades later. It was a squat, stubby Krupp howitzer which was more powerful than any cannon in the world, including the 12-inch rifles on Britain's new, "all-big-gun" dreadnoughts. This was the 16.8-inch (420-mm., or 42-cm.) Big Bertha. Each of the Berthas required two hundred specially trained artillerymen and threw its armor-piercing, delayed-action shells (Busy Berthas) nine miles. Its muzzle velocity was equal to that of five express trains weighing 250 tons each, traveling at a speed of 62 mph.[32]

Essen had been experimenting with *die dicke Bertha* since Gustav's elevation to the Vorstand chairmanship. Producing a howitzer capable of pulverizing Liège's defenses had been relatively easy; the trick was to make one which could be moved. The first model had to be shipped in two sections, each drawn by a locomotive, and because of its fantastic recoil it couldn't be fired unless it was first embedded in cement, which meant it could only be moved by blasting. The army designated a smaller (though still prodigious) 305-mm. Skoda mortar for supplementary firepower. Meanwhile Fritz Rausenberger, Krupp's chief ordnance technician, worked year after year at breaking his monstrous Bertha down into two sections which could be mounted on wheeled carriages. Early in 1914 Wilhelm watched the testing of this new, more mobile model and departed beaming.[33]

Even greater improvements were expected by autumn, and a second round of Meppen firings was scheduled for October 1. They were never held, because that summer the world went mad. Touched off by the assassination which gave Krupp his new country home in Austria and, ultimately, a new global reputation, the thunder of gunfire rolled across the continent. After issuing his historic "blank check" to Austria-Hungary, S.M. confided to Gustav that he would "declare war at once if Russia mobilized." To the Kaiser's confidant in Essen it seemed that his sovereign's "repeated protestations" that no one would ever again be in a position to reproach him for indecision were "almost comical to hear." There was nothing funny about cannon, however, and here Krupp encouraged the All-Highest, assuring him that the foe's artillery was neither good nor complete, while Germany's had "never been better."[34] At two o'clock on the afternoon of August 1 an official telegram arrived in the Hauptverwaltungs-gebäude from Berlin. It comprised two letters: "D.K." — *drohende Kriegsgefahr* (imminent threat of war). At 4 P.M. mobilization was an-nounced, at 7 P.M. Germany declared war on Russia, and within twenty-four hours Germany and Austria began marching against their neighbors. The neighbors swiftly countermarched. Before the polarization of nations into "the Central Powers" and "the Allies" was complete, fifty-seven countries had issued declarations of war against one another. In every lan-guage they agreed that it was the World War, *der Weltkrieg, la Grande Guerre*. Even today the strange passions which were unleashed, the glee with which millions raced off to be slaughtered, are murky. One thing was clear: there had never been anything remotely like it before.

But Gustav thought there had. To him the parallels with the Franco-Prussian War were irresistible, and he saw himself following in the foot-steps of Alfred the Great. Like Bertha's grandfather, he had the finest can-non in the world — a new shipment of 180 field guns ordered by Brazil was hastily rerouted to the Belgian frontier — and Wilhelm II, like Wilhelm I, commanded the most magnificent troops on the continent. Even Villa Hügel was a shambles once more. Krupp had chosen this season to have the interior of the castle completely redecorated, and Uncle Felix von Ende, the family Bohemian, was adorning the dining room walls with romantic murals, though that didn't stop the business lunches and eminent guests, which proceeded with the usual clockwork precision. In those first feverish days of August, Gustav was host to Emil Fischer, the great German chemist who had been awarded a Nobel prize in 1902. One evening Fischer confided that he was worried; the Reich's nitrate stocks, he said, were especially low.[35]

Krupp waved away the guncotton problem. Within a year, he assured the scientist, I. G. Farben would be producing synthetic nitrates (he was right), and in almost every other respect preparedness was letter-perfect. Two million reservists were arriving at their prearranged posts, receiving Mauser magazine rifles, *Pickelhauben* with gray linen covers, and the new *feldgrau* uniforms which had replaced Prussian blue in 1910. Mobilization trains, the timetables for which Gustav had proofread and found flawless, carried the men to frontier concentration points with minimal delay; thanks to the foresight of the Generalstab, four double railroad lines ran straight across the Reich, with feeder lines which had been laid with swift assembly in mind. As the Fatherland bunched its awesome fist, morale was extraordinary. Krupp's Berlin office, under new management since the

*Skandal,* reported that cars filled with handkerchief-waving officers were racing up and down the Linden while sidewalk crowds bayed *Deutschland über Alles* and

> *Lieb Vaterland, kannst ruhig sein,*
> *Fest steht und treu die Wacht,*
> *Die Wacht am Rhein. . . .*[36]

To the delight of the entire Fatherland, the hundred SPD deputies, now the strongest single bloc in the Reichstag, had voted unanimously to support the war credits. Answering their *Hoch* "For Kaiser, people, and country," S.M. — whom Krupp had escorted aboard the *Hohenzollern* during Kiel Week on the very day Franz Ferdinand was shot — had delightedly replied that "I see no parties any more, only Germans."

Gustav's sky, unlike Wilhelm's, was not entirely cloudless. To be sure, he could hardly complain about his Kruppianer. They were cheerfully working shifts round the clock, lustily singing *Heil dir im Siegeskranz* and *Siegreich woll'n wir Frankreich schlagen* as they assembled guns and mounts and toiled desperately to start the gross howitzers rolling toward Liège. Krupp's difficulty was that even at this early date, before a single shot had been fired, he was being branded abroad as a war criminal. An alert *Daily Mail* correspondent had spotted him in Kiel; learning now that Gustav and Bertha had just come from London, he jumped to the conclusion that they had been inspecting British munitions plants and had reported to the All-Highest "what the Master of Essen had gleaned in guileless Albion." It was annoying and untrue — they had crossed for their last portrait sittings — but it was believed in Great Britain, where H. G. Wells was writing, on the eve of his country's war declaration, "At the very core of all this evil that has burst at last in world disaster lies Kruppism, this sordid, enormous trade in the instruments of death." England was entering the conflict because Germany was invading Belgium, whose premier, Comte Charles de Broqueville, suddenly recalled that last year the Belgian Parliament had ordered heavy artillery from Fried. Krupp A.G. The guns had never been delivered. And now, the premier said, the world knew why. The implications of premeditated conspiracy against peace were obvious.[37]

To cap it all, a Krupp director named Wilhelm Mühlon had lost his mind. A brilliant young attorney, Mühlon had served the firm first as Gustav's private secretary and then, since 1911, as a member of the elite board. The moment S.M. ordered mobilization he disappeared from Essen. To the utter astonishment of his employer he had just surfaced in Switzerland, where he had announced his resignation from the firm, denounced the Reich for its war preparations, and declared that "Six months before August, Krupp received secret advice about the coming war from Berlin and thereupon proceeded to extend the factories to cope with the additional work" (*daraufhin seien die Werke sofort entsprechend umgestellt worden*).[38]

The charge rankled. It retained its sting for nearly twenty years; in 1933, another year during which obtuse Ausländer were misunderstanding him and his country, Krupp testified for the prosecution in the trial of one of his former director's friends and scouted "the lying statement of Mühlon." Far from having plotted conflict nineteen years earlier, he declared, Berlin had been taken by surprise: "*Der Mangel an Sprengstoffen im Jahre 1914 hat uns an der Front viele Leben gekostet*" — The shortage of explosives in 1914 resulted in great loss of life for us at the front). That was after Gustav had had nearly two decades in which to become accustomed to his protégé's treachery. At the time, with Dr. Fischer, he came very close to dropping his mask of detachment. Mühlon's ingratitude was too much, his falsehood too outrageous. Why, he asked his guest, should one director insist that the firm could be conspiring with a government which had just fined another director for peering through its keyholes? How could anyone even suggest that there were any *Konnexionen* between his peaceful, industrious shops and docks and international political intrigue — between builders like himself and the arrogant, upstart, would-be destroyers who had encircled the Fatherland? Wagging his head solemnly, the great chemist agreed that obviously there could be no connection, none whatever.[39]

# 12

✠

# The Last Love Battle

K RUPP neatly entered the winged words of the works' wartime slogan in his black notebook: *Dass viele Feinde viel Ehre seien* (The greater the foe the greater the honor).[1] In reality the opening honor of 1914 should have been bestowed upon him; though Belgium wasn't a very impressive foe, the lion's share of credit for its swift conquest belonged to the Reich's gunsmith. But military custom requires that first recognition go to the soldier in the field. Thus the blue, white, and gold cross of the *Pour le Mérite* was suspended from the oxlike neck of Erich Friedrich Wilhelm Ludendorff, that blubbery, friendless, obscure professional soldier who, at the outbreak of the war, had commanded a brigade of quiet garrison troops in Strasbourg. Because he wore the prized crimson stripes of the Generalstab, he was posted to the elite Army of the Meuse as liaison officer, and because his commandeered Belgian automobile happened to be outside the great gates of Liège on August 7, 1914, he pounded on them with the hilt of his sword, was admitted by defeatists, and drove straight in to accept the formal surrender of the city.

When the news reached General Headquarters the Kaiser was so delighted that he embraced Helmuth von Moltke, nephew of the great marshal, and, according to Moltke, "rapturously kissed" him. The pulse of the entire Fatherland quickened. Even Mühlon, the apostate Krupp director, entered in his diary, "August 8th. Yesterday evening the news came that Liège had been taken by storm. . . . No one of us would have thought it possible that the first quickly mobilized troops could take such a fortress offhand (*aus dem Stegreif*). I was almost tempted to an involuntary pride over this exploit." It was to be a long war, but its patterns were fixed and frozen in those opening days. The unknown victor of Liège was a made man. Though he lacked the customary "von," in two years he was to become military dictator of the empire, with absolute powers unheard of in Europe since the death of Frederick the Great.[2]

What makes Ludendorff's meteoric rise especially ironical is that the first reports of Liège's capitulation were greatly exaggerated. The ceremony of August 7 had been almost meaningless. S.M. had bussed young Moltke for nothing. The city had quit, but the all-important forts were fighting on. If the thirty-mile circle of strongpoints held out, nobody in field gray was going to brush the channel with his sleeve. Already the stubborn defenders had forced a three-day postponement in the First Army's advance. Since the tyranny of the Schlieffen Plan compelled all the Germans in Belgium to march in concert — all or none — two million men were being held up. Thus Ludendorff's first act, upon emerging from the redoubt which he had presumably taken, was to call for siege cannon. There the story became less one of heroics than of engineering prowess, brute strength, and perspiration. Moving the black, *kolossal*, 98-ton *dicke Berthas* was an even greater challenge than had been supposed. Two days after Ludendorff's desperate order the enormous howitzers were still squatting in Essen, surrounded by yelping Offiziere and grunting Kruppianer. On the night of August 9–10 they were hoisted, levered, winched, craned, jacked, windlassed, pried, and clawed aboard freight cars, and the rails to Belgium were cleared. The following night they raced across the frontier, but twenty miles beyond that the locomotives came to a grinding halt; the Belgians had blown a tunnel. *The Times* of London reported that the Kaiser's assault on Liège "has been very handsomely beaten," and indeed, S.M. had gone over to the defensive; everything depended upon the flatulent, tumescent, unlovely but unquestionably deadly fat Berthas.[3]

The demolished tunnel was at Herbesthal, twenty miles from the fortress. The saboteurs had achieved a stunning success. Repairs were impossible, and at midnight offloading began, starting with the yard-long shells. This was worse than Essen, because the engineers lacked heavy moving equipment. Trucks broke down. Uhlan steeds were pressed into service; their harnesses snapped. Since the guns had a range of nine miles, they needed to be advanced only eleven, and the roads were good. Nevertheless the backbreaking struggle continued all night and through the next day with a combination of motor vehicles, horses, and detachments of soldiers inching the gun carriages of the Kruppstahl giantesses forward. Late in the afternoon of August 12 one of them was assembled and in position, the brutal black mouth gaping skyward. Its two hundred attendants swarmed over it and then, wearing special padded equipment which protected their vital organs, they huddled on the ground three hundred yards away. At 6:30 P.M. came the command: "*Feuer!*" An electric switch was turned. The Belgian defenders felt a jarring in the earth so alarming that some wondered whether hell had risen. A Busy Bertha emerged from the bore's dark mouth, sailed up a mile and, after remaining airborne a full minute, struck its target, Fort Pontisse, dead center. Moments later a spiraling cloud of concrete, steel, and human flesh and bone was boiling a thousand feet overhead.[4]

Ludendorff had watched this appalling horror, and he entered the choking debris of another strongpoint, Fort Loncin, minutes after it, too, had been hit. Miraculously there were a few survivors. In his memoirs he recalled that

It had been hit by a shell from one of our 42-cm. [420-mm.] howitzers. The magazine had been blown up and the whole work collapsed. A number of dazed and blackened Belgian soldiers crawled out of the ruins, accompanied by some Germans who had been taken prisoner on the night of August 5–6. All bleeding, they came toward us with their hands up, stammering, "Don't kill, don't kill" [*Blutend, mit hocherhobenen Händen, kamen sie uns entgegen. "Ne pas tuer, ne pas tuer" brachten sie stammelnd hervor*].[5]

"*Wir waren keine Hunnen*," the general added wryly; "We were no Huns." He was right, of course; Attila had never dreamed of anything so ghastly. In those days men had still been awed by Plutarch's description of Archimedes' huge catapult, which drove the Romans away from Syracuse by throwing 1,800-pound stones at them; the Roman commander, confounded, had said, "Archimedes really outdoes the hundred-handed giants of mythology." But that had been a slingshot. Krupp's new siege gun was a weapon of mass murder. The Belgians waiting in their reinforced concrete bunkers, which they had been told would resist any direct hit from any projectile, would hear the shriek of a Busy Bertha homing on them. Then the shell would penetrate the steel-buttressed cement and the delayed-action fuse would set off the ton of explosive. Hour after hour this nightmare went on, until the maze of subterranean corridors linking the thirty miles of redoubts became choked with gas, fire, and men who, one witness later recalled, had become "hysterical, even mad, in the awful apprehension of the next shot."[6]

After forty-eight hours all the great keeps shielding the northern and eastern moats of Liège had been reduced to blood-soaked debris; one redoubt had absorbed forty-five shells before quitting, but now a brief silence fell over the battlefield. The cobweb of defensive belts there had disintegrated. Then came a hush. It was followed by the thump of hobnailed boots. The First Army was on the move, the sleeve reaching for the channel. Next, to reduce the underground blockhouses on the far side of the city, the Germans laboriously moved one of the Big Berthas downtown. Célestin Demblon, a Liège *député* and professor at L'Université Nouvelle de Bruxelles, was in the Place Saint-Pierre with some friends when he saw, coming round a corner,

*. . . au milieu de soldats allemands, une pièce d'artillerie si colossale que nous n'en pouvions croire nos yeux. . . . Les soldats l'accompagnaient roidement, avec une solennité presque religieuse. Le Bélial des canons!*

*. . . Effroyable fut la détonation! Les curieux avaient été refoulés; le sol fut secoué comme par un tremblement de terre — et toutes les vitres du voisinage volèrent en éclat!*

. . . in the middle of German soldiers a piece of artillery so colossal that we could not believe our eyes. It was one of the eight giant cannon that the Germans call the "surprise of the war," the "420"! Their invention, known only to the emperor and certain intimates, has been, one hears, totally secret. The metal monster advanced in two parts, pulled by 36 horses, if memory serves. The pavement trembled. The crowd remained mute with consternation. Slowly it crossed the Place Saint-Lambert . . . attracting crowds of curious onlookers along its slow and heavy passage. Hannibal's elephants could not have astonished the Romans more! . . . The soldiers who accompanied it marched stiffly, with an almost religious solemnity. It was the Belial of cannons!

At the end of the Boulevard d'Avroy . . . the monster was carefully mounted and scrupulously aimed. . . . Then came the frightful explosion! The crowd was flung back; the earth shook as if there had been an earthquake and all the windowpanes in the neighborhood were shattered![7]

On August 16 the last fort fell — the unconscious body of the general commanding Liège's defense was found pinned beneath a mass of shattered masonry — and Krupp's Belials lumbered off to end the week-long, but less critical, sieges of Namur, Antwerp, and Mauberge. As the meticulous after-action reports filtered back to Wilhelm's GHQ, he and his allies gradually came to appreciate the extraordinary role Essen's strutting little civilian had played in the subjugation of Belgium. Though Gustav's collection of military decorations had started late, he was now following the tradition of Alfred and Fritz. Each month brought new finery to his left breast. In addition to the medal bestowed upon him at the height of the *Skandal* he already held Saxony's Commander's Cross Second Class of the Order of Albert, Prussia's Order of the Crown Second Class, Bavaria's Military Order of Merit of Saint Michael Second Class, Mecklenburg's Grand Commander Cross (*Grosskomturkreuz*) of the Order of the Griffen, Bavaria's Star for the Order of Merit of Saint Michael Second Class, and the Bavarian Military Order of Merit Second Class with Star. Now the All-Highest summoned him to the imperial presence and pinned upon his frock coat the Iron Cross First Class, an award ordinarily reserved for men who had distinguished themselves on the battlefield and which did not come to Corporal Adolf Hitler of the 16th Bavarian Reserve Infantry until he had fought for four years, suffered two grave wounds, and captured fifteen enemy single-handed. Nor was that the end of Gustav's honors. Prussia added the Cross of Merit for War Aid (*Verdienstkreuz für Kriegshilfe*) — Bertha got that one, too — and Turkey the Order of Mejidieh First Class and the Iron Crescent. To cap everything, Bonn University decided that Krupp was more than a military hero. Its faculty concluded that the performance of the fat Berthas had advanced the cause of human civilization. Therefore they conferred upon him the degree of *Ehrendoktor der Philosophie.*[8]

In the showering of encomia no one was so tactless as to mention the fact that the great howitzers had been tardy at Liège. It had been such a small delay; just two days. Undiscovered by a hundred thousand galloping French cavalry, the Teutonic forces had continued their sweep through Belgium, lapped at the breakwater of Verdun, and reached the Marne. But that was the extent of the invader's penetration. Those forty-eight hours had been all the Allies needed. The British Expeditionary Force crossed the channel and took up position on the French left, six hundred racing Paris taxicabs delivered six thousand *poilus* to the hard-pressed front, and after a seven-day battle involving over two million men the Germans recoiled to the river Aisne and dug in. Then the sidestepping began, the lines of the opposing armies extending westward and northward as each tried to out-flank the other. Eventually they ran out of land; a snakelike chain of trenches began on the Swiss border and ended 466 miles away on the channel at Nieuport. Mobility, and the opportunity for maneuver, were gone.*

No one grasped that then. The sacrifices in the opening battles had been so great on both sides that the thought of stalemate was intolerable. With the expensive and ingenious arsenals available to strategists an early break-through somewhere seemed inevitable. When Tirpitz inspected the Ger-maniawerft in February 1915, five months after the Marne, he peered quizzically at the submarines under construction and remarked to Krupp, "*Na, die kommen für diesen Krieg ja doch zu spät*" (Well, you know, these are going to be much too late for this war). He may have meant that the issue would be resolved in France; he may have thought that the subs already christened were sufficient. In either case he was wrong, and if he had the second in mind his error was monumental. For the *Unterseeboot* was to be the decisive weapon of the war, and in a way no one had envisaged. At the time of the admiral's visit to Kiel, Berlin planned to counter British sea power with unrestricted *Unterseeboot* warfare, and on the morning of the following May 1 a Lieutenant Commander Schweiger, prowling off the Irish coast in his *kruppsche* U–20, torpedoed the Cunard liner *Lusitania*. Over 1,100 drowned, 138 of them American

---

* Schlieffen had predicted that the army's breakout from Belgium would be Ger-many's Cannae. It was. He forgot that while Hannibal routed the Romans at Cannae, he failed to take Rome. (Alfred Schlieffen, *Cannae* [1922], 4.)

civilians. In that gentler age, when war was still thought of as chivalrous, the sinking seemed almost unbelievable. President Woodrow Wilson, outraged, drafted a protest so strongly worded that Secretary of State William Jennings Bryan refused to sign it. The note went to the Wilhelmstrasse anyhow, a virtual ultimatum. In his headquarters at Luxembourg the All-Highest brooded over it and then called off his subs, but the meaning of the incident was clear. Wilson had drawn a line. If the Schweigers were unleashed again, America would fight.[9]

✠    ✠    ✠

In those first months the Ruhr's beribboned hero of Belgium was pre-occupied with annexation schemes and raw material statistics. He enthusiastically endorsed the Alldeutsche Verband doctrines of Heinrich Class, who wrote that "Russia's face must be turned back to the east and her frontiers must be reduced, approximately, to those of Peter the Great," and in November 1914 Gustav drew up his own agenda of war aims for Foreign Minister Gottlieb von Jagow and "some other friends of mine in the government." Convinced that "the peace can and must be dictated to the enemy," Krupp rejected any suggestion of negotiations. The Reich, he was convinced, was Europe's hub. Around it he wanted to consolidate a Teutonic *Mitteleuropa* including Austria-Hungary and the neutral states of Holland, Switzerland, and Scandinavia. First France had to be humbled. French territory was to be annexed along the line of the Moselle and the Meuse, and this breathtaking plan was justified on grounds that made excellent sense in the Hauptverwaltungsgebäude: "A France lacking any considerable reserves of iron and coal can no longer present an economic danger on the world market or a political danger in the council of great powers."[10]

Krupp's vision ranged far. He foresaw the re-emergence of Poland as a "buffer state," with a Germanized strip between it and the Reich to provide "a firm bolt" against Polish yearning for Prussian land once governed from Warsaw. He anticipated an expanded Teuton colonial empire in Africa (*Mittelafrika*) ringed by naval bases and coaling stations, and he argued that "If these aims are achieved, German culture and civilization will direct the progress of humanity; to fight and conquer for such a goal is worth the price of noble blood." But more than the spilling of blood would be necessary. Belgium must be held in permanent subjugation (Gustav rather thought that the north coast of France should be a province of the Reich, too) and, most important, ships from the Germaniawerft must rule the waves of the Channel:

Here we should be lying at the very marrow of England's world power, a position — perhaps the only one — which could bring us England's lasting friendship. For only if we are able to hurt England badly at any moment will she really leave us unmolested, perhaps even become our "friend," insofar as England is capable of friendship at all.[11]

The raw material invoices, though tiresome, were more urgent. I. G. Farben's wizards of ersatz were accomplishing marvels; nevertheless there was no substitute for the basic minerals Krupp's kettles required. Gustav had anticipated the problem. Once more his coach had been Alfred. The prince consort had studied the Franco-Prussian War with admiration, and that was one reason he had invested so heavily in overseas firms. Moltke, who agreed with him, had canceled Schlieffen's proposal that the Netherlands be invaded, explaining that Holland "must be the windpipe that permits us to breathe." That first embattled autumn this foresighted policy drew a handsome dividend. In September the Norwegian freighter *Benesloet* picked up 2,500 tons of priceless nickel in New Caledonia. After it had sailed French colonial authorities discovered that the consignee was Fried. Krupp A.G., who had paid in advance. Stopped at sea by the French cruiser *Dupetit-Thouars*, the vessel was brought into Brest. A prize court declared the cargo to be contraband of war, but Paris, anxious not to offend Oslo, ordered the ship freed. On October 10 the *Benesloet* left Brest for Norway, and by the end of the month the shipment had reached the Ruhr. That winter British exporters also sent Gustav nickel and copper through Holland. At first there seemed to be no reason why these arrangements should not continue indefinitely. Allied feeling was hardening, however, and on the last day of spring Krupp read the following paragraph in his evening paper:

> London, June 20 (TU). The metal merchants [*die Eisenhändler*] Hetherington and Wilson of Edinburgh, who made deliveries of ore via Rotterdam to the firm of Krupp after the outbreak of the war, were each sentenced to six months' imprisonment and a fine of two thousand pounds.[12]

Gustav produced his black book and drew a sharp line through the two names. The verdict wasn't catastrophic (except for Hetherington and Wilson), but it did call for new wariness and fresh ideas. Henceforth Holland was to be avoided. It was too obvious. Thanks to Scandinavian faith in free enterprise, Norway and Sweden were still available, and from them came a steady flow of the rare condiments and thymes which guaranteed the splendid temper of the silver-gray molten alloys in Essen, Rheinhausen, Annen, Kiel, Hamm, and Magdeburg. As insurance the Germaniawerft constructed a unique vessel which could defy the Allied naval blockade without offending Woodrow Wilson. It was a submarine freighter with a cargo capacity of 800 tons and a cruising radius which could take it across the Atlantic. Christened *Deutschland* on June 23, 1916, the vessel immediately began fetching minerals and raw rubber from the Reich's isolated colonies.[13]

By then Krupp's empire had been so transformed that uniformed Kruppianer, coming home on leave, had trouble finding their homes. At the outbreak of the war the firm had employed 82,500 men, roughly half of them in Essen. The payroll jumped to 118,000 and then to 150,000, including 20,000 women, most of whom were assigned to the sensitive task of fitting fuses. A neutral war correspondent touring the Gusstahlfabrik was astounded to come upon a dining room with 7,200 seats, in which 35,000 workers were fed daily by rotation. Toiling in two twelve-hour shifts to assemble guns, mounts, ammunition, and ship armor, the workmen saw new construction rising around them almost overnight. In the first year of the war thirty-five huge shops were built and equipped in Essen alone. Blueprints were drawn up for a 23,000-square-yard shell factory in January 1915; by July it was in operation.[14]

The production figures were incredible. In the first year of the war Essen replaced over 900 field guns and 300 light howitzers. In the second year the new munitions factory delivered nearly 8,000,000 shells. And in the third year Krupp reached a breathtaking plateau; each *month* the assembly lines shipped out 9,000,000 shells and 3,000 cannon. Had quality deteriorated under these conditions the army could scarcely have objected. But there was no reason for complaint. When the Germans sprang at Verdun on February 21, 1916, the assault was preceded by a twelve-and-a-half-hour "curtain of fire" from 1,200 artillery pieces pouring 100,000 shells an hour on an eight-mile front, and the thirteen Big Berthas — now called "Gamma guns," or simply "the 420's" — were just as accurate there as their older sisters at Liège. OHL's code name for the operation was *Gericht* (place of judgment). Railways were no longer a problem; each howitzer was dissassembled into 172 pieces and carried forward on twelve freight cars. Twenty hours were still required to get one into action, however, and as artillerymen struggled with its ponderous steel anatomy infantrymen would stand about gawking at the shells. Once the firing started they scattered or suffered ruptured eardrums. The receiving end was, of course, much worse. In *The Price of Glory*, his brilliant account of the war's greatest battle, Alistair Horne described "a roaring descent as noisy, prolonged and demoralizing as a Stuka." He added,

From February onwards the 420's had kept the Verdun forts under steady bombardment from their one-ton projectiles. . . . One (fortunately unexploded) 420 shell was discovered to have penetrated six feet of earth, ten feet of concrete, and finally a wall thirty inches thick. In several places the shells burst inside the fort, with terrible effects. Casualties were high, with many simply asphyxiated by the deadly TNT gases trapped inside the fort. . . . The terrifying noise of the descending shell . . .

drove many of the occupants out of their wits. After one bad shelling, the commandant, finding himself confronted with a minor mutiny by shell-shocked "lunatics," was forced to round them up at pistol point and lock them up in a casemate. Then the fort M. O. himself went mad and ran out of the fort into the neighboring woods, where he was later discovered sitting on a tree stump, in a state of complete amnesia.[15]

The emperor, more and more impressed, fired off congratulatory messages to Gustav. After the battle of Jutland he telegraphed him:

> WILHELMSHAVEN JUNE 5, 1916 — HERR KRUPP VON BOHLEN UND HALBACH, ESSEN — AS AN IMMEDIATE RESULT OF THE IMPRESSION MADE UPON ME BY THE EYEWITNESS ACCOUNTS OF THE BATTLE IN THE NORTH SEA, I WISH TO PLACE ON RECORD THAT OUR SUCCESS WAS DUE TO OUR EXCELLENT GUNS AND ARMOR AND MORE ESPECIALLY TO THE DESTRUCTIVE EFFECT OF OUR SHELLS. THE BATTLE IS, THEREFORE, ALSO A DAY OF TRIUMPH FOR THE KRUPP WORKS [SO IST DER SCHLACHTTAG AUCH EIN EHRENTAG DER KRUPP-WERKE].[16]

The results were less conclusive than the Kaiser thought. The Reich's navy had sunk fourteen warships to the British eleven and inflicted twice as many casualties, but the English were still in control of the sea. Jutland had been a draw, and one reason was that both fleets had been shielded by the same plate. Prewar deals couldn't be undealt. In France, British duds falling behind German lines bore the tiny stamp *KPz 96/04,* 1896 being the year Vickers first licensed Krupp's fuse patent and 1904 the year the agreement was renewed. S.M.'s soldiers weren't suspicious, but the House of Commons was. In late April 1915 Lord Charles William de la Poer Beresford, an outspoken critic of British naval policy, had asked Prime Minister Asquith whether it was true that the Krupp family was being paid "a royalty of a shilling a shell." This was horribly embarrassing for everyone, and the question was not answered until the first week in May. Then the reply was equivocal. The House was told that although provision had once been made for a royalty of one shilling threepence, the agreement had expired on July 16, 1914, and that "since that date no royalty on any of the fuses has been paid." Of course there had been no payment. The countries were at war. But the assertion that the agreement had lapsed was wholly untrue. Legally it was still binding, and both firms were keeping book on it, Vickers in an account marked "K" and Gustav under a rough formula which reckoned that Albert Vickers owed him 60 marks for every dead German soldier.[17]

It was, of course, quite impossible to explain this sort of thing to Wilhelm, let alone the men at the front. The arcana of the munitions industry had been intricate enough in peacetime. Now they had become so complex that in Germany Krupp and a half-dozen other Ruhr barons inhabited a world of their own, speaking a separate language and facing and mastering challenges incomprehensible to nearly everyone else. The season the *Deutschland* was launched, for example, they were obliged to bring every conceivable pressure to bear upon Chancellor Bethmann-Hollweg before he would authorize the seizure of Belgium's industrial resources. The chancellor, protesting that it was piracy, yielded reluctantly. His order set a frightful precedent for the next generation, when most of Europe would become one vast Belgium occupied by the sons of the Germans now under arms, and that autumn another command with even more ominous implications for the future reached the military governor in Brussels. Despite a labor conscription act which impressed every able German male between the ages of fifteen and sixty and drafted healthy females for work in arms factories, there was a shortage of hands in the shops. Therefore the new decree conscripted Belgian civilians for manual labor in Ruhr plants. Tilo von Wilmowsky, then a cavalry officer serving as the governor's aide-de-camp, was shocked. He wrote his brother-in-law, urging him to lay the matter before the emperor. Krupp regretfully declined. One must, he explained, obey.[18]

Although Tilo didn't know it, Krupp himself was largely responsible for the conscription. On August 27, 1916, Rumania had entered the war on the Allied side. Next day Hindenburg had been appointed supreme commander of the army, with Ludendorff as chief of his general staff. There was virtually no limit to their authority; when Bethmann-Hollweg's conscience continued to trouble him, the chancellor was curtly dismissed. In the second week of their reign the two generals toured the western front together, and riding back through Belgium on September 8 Ludendorff was joined by Krupp and Carl Duisberg of I. G. Farben, the two most influential industrialists in the empire. In his words, "On my way next afternoon I discussed this matter [war production] with Herr Duisberg and Herr Krupp von Bohlen und Halbach, whom I had asked to join the train. They considered it quite possible, in view of our stocks of raw material, to increase our output of war material if only the labor problem could be solved" (*Sie hielten eine Erhöhung des Kriegsgeräts auf Grund unserer Rohstofflage durchaus für möglich, wenn die Arbeiterfrage gelöst würde*). Ludendorff solved it. He issued the edict which appalled Baron von Wilmowsky, and as a result the smokestack barons were able to assure the government that "The resources available to the industry of Germany are such as to enable it to supply all the munitions and war material that may be required by our valiant troops and our faithful allies for many years to come" (. . . *auf viele Jahr hinaus mit der notwendigen Munition und dem sonstigen Kriegsmaterial zu versorgen*).[19]

The little exchange sounds like a toneless exercise in Teutonic bureaucracy, and that is what is so dreadful about it. These men weren't dealing with spare parts. They were disposing of people. The essence of their message was that the war was going very well. The machines were holding up splendidly. The present situation could continue indefinitely, if only they didn't run out of human beings. That was their attitude toward the Belgian conscripts; that was how they talked about their own soldiers. The Generalstab spoke dispassionately of the need for *Menschen*, human material. Yet inferring that this callousness was confined to the Reich would be quite wrong. It was found in every embattled capital, nowhere more strikingly than in that citadel of decency, London. Lord Edward Henry Carson, a civilized graduate of Trinity College, Dublin, told his peers that "The necessary supply of heroes must be maintained at all costs," and British officers responsible for logistics, calculating the average toll of shellfire casualties in inactive sectors, called it "normal wastage."[20]

They sound like monsters. Actually they were creatures of a historic metamorphosis. In that remote day of derbies, ostrich plume bonnets, and hansom cabs, civilization was in the midst of a profound transition. Culturally it remained gyved to the horsy past, while signs increased that the machine age had arrived. Europe lay half in one period, half in another, and the agony was multiplied by the fact that of all societal institutions the military profession was the one most rooted in the folklore of the past. Its traditional leaders — the emperors, princes, potentates, and field marshals — were the most conservative men in society, the least capable of understanding the new mechanized war they had to lead. Junkers cherished their monocles, spotless white gloves, black-and-silver saber knots, and concrete *Kommandantur* with Prussian eagles molded above the entrances, while the yearning of the French for *la gloire* continued to be almost as great as their talent for self-hypnosis. Even as their soldiers were baaing like sheep to show that they regarded themselves as lambs marked for slaughter, *maréchaux* spoke glowingly of the natural *élan* of the poilu. Of course, this was for the younger men, *les jeunes turcs*. At their age they had to take care of themselves. When Falkenhayn attacked Verdun the courier who brought the news was informed that "Papa" Joffre, the Constable of France, was asleep behind a double-locked door and couldn't be disturbed.[21]

England's military Boeotians were equally convinced that a chap could smash through that barbed wire if he had enough sand, and they were even more devoted to peacetime military routine and Quetta manners. They strode around in gleaming field boots and jingling spurs and toured the lines in Rolls-Royces, cursing bad march discipline. It was a pretty thin time for the regular service, they agreed; so many of the officer replacements weren't really gentlemen. Something must be done about it. The new fellows were sharply reminded that they should keep servants in their dugouts, strike slack privates on sight, and make certain that the senior company was on the right before going over the top. In rest camp subalterns were actually required to attend riding school and learn polo, and during the worst fighting on the Somme divisional horse shows were held just behind the front.

As the slaughter grew through 1915 and 1916 some of the more fantastic anachronisms disappeared from field uniforms. The Germans shed the impractical spikes on their *Pickelhauben;* the British and French, who hadn't had any helmets at all during the battle of the Marne, were now protected. French infantrymen no longer wore scarlet trousers and blue coats, nor French artillerymen black and gold, and the British army had abandoned the practice of having newly commissioned junior officers visit an armorer to have their swords sharpened, like Henry V, before sailing for France. The decision wasn't made lightly; sword sharpening had been a sentimental ceremony. The idea of attacking a machine gun with a saber is inconceivable today, but the generals hadn't been thinking about the machine gun much. They had considered it and decided that it was, in the words of England's Sir Douglas Haig, "a much overrated weapon." Each year Krupp, Schneider, Vickers, and Armstrong clanked out new engines of death, while the alumni of the Kriegsschule, Sandhurst, and Saint-Cyr accepted them grudgingly or not at all. They belonged to that older generation which still called electric light "the electric" and distrusted it as newfangled. Foch thought the airplane silly. Kitchener dismissed the tank as a "toy" and von Hindenburg, warned of Allied tanks, scoffed, "The German infantry can get along quite well without those peculiar motor cars." The invaluable Stokes mortar was rejected twice at the British War Office and finally introduced by Lloyd George, who begged the money for it from an Indian maharajah. In the gleaming châteaux where generals in dress uniforms moved colored pins on beautiful maps this was regarded as both bad form and foolishness. The epauletted marshals placed their main reliance in great masses of cavalry — as late as 1918 General John J. Pershing, U.S.A., would be cluttering up his supply lines with mountains of fodder for useless horses — and their staffs rarely visited the front, where a very different kind of war was being fought.[22]

✠    ✠    ✠

There, by the junk heap of no-man's-land, the great armies squatted across France year after year, living troglodytic lives in candlelit dugouts and trenches hewn from Fricourt chalk or La Bassée clay, or scooped from the porridge of swampy Flanders. The efficient Prussians dug deep emplacements for their heavy Krupp guns — they had ten times as many long-range cannon as the Allies — and tacked up propaganda signs (*Gott strafe England; Frankreich, du bist betrogen*). Then they settled down to teach the children German while the Allies furiously counterattacked. The struggles which followed were called battles, but although they were fought on a stupendous scale, with 60,000 young Englishmen lost in a single day on the Somme, strategically they were only siege assaults. Every attack found the German defenses stronger. In letters to the Fatherland soldiers referred to their enemies as *Kanonenfutter*, cannon fodder, and the enemies would have agreed. The poilus and Tommies who crawled over their parapets before daybreak, lay down in front of jump-off tapes, and waited for their officers' zero hour whistles would face as many as ten aprons of wire with barbs thick as a man's thumb, backed by pullulating *Soldaten*. A few trenches would be taken at shocking cost — one gain of seven hundred mutilated yards cost 26,000 men — and then the siege would start again. At home newspapers spoke of "hammer blows" and "the big push," but the men knew better; a soldiers' mot had it that the war would last a hundred years, five years of fighting and ninety-five of winding up the barbwire.[23]

The western front had become an endless inferno, a weird, grimy life unlike anything in the upbringing of the fighters, except, perhaps, the stories of Jules Verne. There were a few poignant reminders of prewar days — the birds that caroled over the lunar landscape each gray, watery dawn; the big yellow poplar forests behind the front — but most sound and color was unearthly. Overhead, shells warbled endlessly; below, bullets cracked and ricochets sang with an iron ring. There were spectacular red Very flares, saffron shrapnel puffs, snaky yellowish mists of mustard gas souring the ground. Little foliage survived here. Trees splintered to matchwood stood in silhouette against the sky like teeth in a broken comb. Arriving draftees were shipped up in cattle cars and marched over duckboard to their new homes in the earth, where everything revolved around the trench — you had a trench knife, a trench cane, a rod-shaped trench periscope and, if you were unlucky, trench foot, trench mouth, or trench fever.

The survivors were those who developed quick reactions to danger. An alert youth learned to sort out the whines that threatened him, though after a few close ones, when his ears buzzed and everything turned scarlet, he also realized that the time might come when ducking wouldn't do any good. If he was a German Krupp-Maxim machine gunner he knew that his life expectancy in combat had been calculated at about thirty minutes, and in time he became detached toward death and casual with its appliances. His potato masher grenades were used to stir up fish in French ponds. Cartridges were removed from the right places in gun belts to rap out familiar rhythms. Gunners sprayed the enemy lines with belt after belt from water-cooled barrels to boil the water for *Suppe*, and if the British or French were known to be low on canister and improvising, the trenches would be eagerly searched after a shelling to see whether they had thrown over anything useful. Sometimes you could find handy screws, bolts, the cogwheels of a clock, or even a set of false teeth that just might fit.[24]

To the most idealistic youth the world has ever known this hideous life came as a crisis of the spirit. They had marched off to the lilt of *Die*

*Wacht am Rhein* or *Tipperary* or the *Marseillaise*, dreaming of braid and heroism. When they found that their generation was bleeding to death, with each month's casualty lists redder than the last, the thoughtful among them recoiled, stunned, and fled into cynicism and despair. Erich Maria Remarque, who had been a sixteen-year-old Westphalian *Gymnasium* student at the outbreak of the war, wondered why communiqués should insist that all was quiet on the western front; thrice wounded young Harold Macmillan of Britain retreated into a study of Horace; the composer of *Keep the Home Fires Burning* acquired an exemption and lolled around a London apartment in a silk dressing gown, burning incense; Siegfried Sassoon flung his Military Cross into the sea and wrote bitterly,

> . . . *Pray you'll never know*
> *The hell where youth and laughter go.*[25]

They were the sensitive. Most men fought stolidly. They had been bred to valor, taught fealty to the tribal deities of *Gott* or God or *Dieu*, and with numb certitude they sacrificed themselves to a civilization that was vanishing with them. Perceived down the corridor of time they seem to have been marked by a quiet sense of dedication that could only have been instinctive. In that war, said Dick Diver, touring old trenches in F. Scott Fitzgerald's *Tender Is the Night*, "You had to have a whole-souled sentimental equipment going back further than you could remember. You had to remember Christmas, and postcards of the Crown Prince and his fiancée, and little cafés in Valence and beer gardens in Unter den Linden and weddings at the *mairie*, and going to the Derby, and your grandfather's whiskers." This, he said, "was the last love battle."[26]

In the Entente offensives the lines moved a few feet a day, "leaving the dead," said Dick Diver, "like a million bloody rugs." For the Central Powers the passage of events was quite different. After their failure to take Verdun the western front really had become comparatively quiet for their assault troops. Elsewhere was plenty of news, however, nearly all of it good for them. They didn't deserve it. Like Allied commanders they were bewitched by Clausewitzian faith in the "decisive battle," the Napoleonic doctrine of "big battalions." Ludendorff, indeed, scouted all action in other theaters as "sideshows" (*Jahrmarktsbuden*). But sideshows were winning the war for the Germans. Blessed with interior lines, they needed no risky amphibious operations, England's undoing at Gallipoli. They could strike anywhere by rescheduling trains, and as the deadlock continued in the west they crushed a weak eastern ally each autumn — thus releasing more of their troops for France every year.

In 1914 they mauled the Russians at Tannenberg. In 1915 Bulgaria joined them to knock Serbia out of the war. In 1916 it was Rumania's turn. The Rumanians had doubled the size of their army in the past two years, but strategically they were isolated, and a blooded German force, withdrawn from Verdun, swarmed up the Carpathian mountains. Just before the winter snows sealed the passes they broke through and Rumania quit. It was of a piece with the whole dismal pattern in the East. The Middle East was much the same — only the camel-raiding parties of a young English archaeologist named T. E. Lawrence offered a ghost of hope — and in 1917, with a succession of revolutionary governments slipping ever farther to the left in Russia, Ludendorff sent a phalanx of picked divisions to reinforce Austria's Caporetto sector in Italy. On October 24 they attacked out of the Julian Alps in a thick fog. It was a brilliant stroke. The Italians collapsed. In twelve hours they were on the run; by the end of November terrified Venetians were hiding the bronze horses of Saint Mark's and preparing to flee. When the defenders finally rallied they had lost 600,000 men and were back on the Piave. The most ardent disciple of *la gloire* agreed that it looked like a bad war.

Nor was that the worst. In France 1917 had become a freak of horror. Both the French and British had felt bullish in the spring. Each had planned independently to make this the decisive battle in the West, and each had massed its biggest battalions for a breakthrough. The French were to open the ball with an "unlimited offensive" under their swashbuckling new Constable, Robert Georges Nivelle, who had replaced the bovine Joffre. Unfortunately Nivelle's plan of attack reached Ludendorff. The offensive had been advertised in the newspapers and orders circulated as low as company level, which meant the Germans picked up prisoners carrying them. Nivelle knew this. He also knew that Ludendorff was riposting with a strategic withdrawal called *Alberich* after the evil dwarf in the Nibelungen legend, fouling wells and sowing booby traps as he went. The French commander insisted that this didn't change a thing. In fact it ruined everything. The new German line was a defender's dream, a mincing machine for poilus. The drive against it turned into slaughter, and the moment it halted revolt spread among French troops fed on the promise of victory. France had, in effect, been knocked out of the war.

Now the Allies turned desperately to Haig. He responded by giving them the horror of Passchendaele. Attacking out of the old Ypres salient — a strategic incubus, but sacred since the last stand of British regulars there in 1914 — Haig took dead aim on Krupp's submarine ports in Belgium. He never had a chance. There wasn't a flicker of surprise. A long preliminary bombardment merely destroyed the Flemish drainage system. The water, having nowhere else to go, flooded the trenches, and to make things soggier the rains were the heaviest in thirty years. After three months in this dismal sinkhole the English had barely taken the village of Passchendaele. Their army was exhausted. In London ambulance trains unloaded at night, smuggling casualties home out of consideration for civilian morale, and in Flanders fields the poppies blew between the crosses, row on uncompromising row, that marked 150,000 fresh British graves.

Yet the penultimate year of the war is not remembered for the Italian rout, the French mutiny, or the senseless murder of England's youth, because two developments outside Europe eclipsed them. The first was America's entry into the war. Von Bernstorff had sent reams of dispatches from Washington begging Wilhelm not to resume unrestricted submarine warfare, but as the efficiency of the Allied blockade grew the All-Highest was under pressure to take the plunge. Krupp had built up a fleet of 148 subs, and Hindenburg and Ludendorff wanted them used. Early in 1917 S.M. had what he regarded as a bright idea. He had his Foreign Secretary wire the Mexican government, suggesting that it invade the United States and recover Texas, New Mexico, and Arizona. If the Americans were fighting at home, he told his dazzled court, they couldn't take on the Central Powers. Unluckily for him the British decoded the telegram; it was published throughout the United States and stirred up considerable resentment, especially in Texas. By now the Generalstab was crying for action, so the Kaiser sent for Gustav. U–boat construction must have overriding priority, he said. Krupp raced to Kiel and began a complete reorganization of the Germaniawerft, and the emperor pushed the button. For the next two months the Atlantic fairly churned with torpedo wakes. President Wilson tried to dodge the inevitable by arming merchant ships, but when enthusiastic sub commanders started sinking homeward-bound American ships he gave up, and on April 6 Congress declared war.[27]

At first the German gamble seemed worth the risk. Though the Allies sank 50 submarines, Krupp maintained the Reich's underwater fleet at 134 in October, and the destruction of Allied shipping actually exceeded German expectations. In April alone 875,000 tons went down, over half of it British. England's Admiral Jellicoe told America's Admiral Sims that the U–boat campaign had his country on its knees. Rations were tight and growing tighter. The government was doing everything it could — draft notices were being sent to the maimed, the blind, the mad, and in some cases even the dead — but it wasn't enough. One ship in four was going down. There was only six weeks supply of corn in the country. Jellicoe predicted an Allied surrender by November 1. Finally the Admiralty accepted Lloyd George's suggested solution: the convoying of merchant vessels. From the first it was a brilliant success. At the same time an increase in destroyer construction and the development of the depth bomb controlled the peril of Gustav's black hulls. Enough British bottoms were available to bridge the Atlantic, bringing over the desperately needed American Expeditionary Force.[28]

It was a race against time, for the second development of 1917, the capstone of the German victories in the East, eliminated that front and gave them, for the first time, overwhelming numerical superiority in the

West. In November the Bolsheviks seized power in Russia and sued for peace. Overnight it became a new war. Ludendorff moved map pins by the fistful. Wilhelm's imperial locomotive steamed up to the Hindenburg-Ludendorff headquarters in the little French town of Avesnes, southeast of Valenciennes, to watch the triumph of Germany's arms. No one suspected that S.M. would be denied his victory. The armistice with the new Russian government had freed 3,000 Krupp cannon and a million men in gray-green uniforms and coal-scuttle helmets, enough to give Ludendorff the whip hand, provided he struck before America's waxing strength erased his edge. Designing a brilliant new technique stressing shock troops, stealth, surprise bombardment, gas, and infiltration, he prepared a concert of thrusts and encoded the operation *Kaiserschlacht* (Kaiser's battle). Hindenburg promised the emperor they would be in Paris by April 1.

Ludendorff knew his enemies. *Kaiserschlacht's* first blow, delivered on March 21, fell on the weak seam joining the French and British armies in the Somme valley, and its objective was Amiens, through which ran the only line of communication between the two Allies. After a tremendous cannonade from Essen's muzzles the Germans lunged out of a heavy fog with five times their Verdun strength. By night the line had been broken in several places. During the second day the British, weakened by Passchendaele, fell back ten miles. The bulge grew deeper each hour; on the sixth day one of the railways between Amiens and the capital was cut, but that was the end. The starved assault troops had turned aside to pillage, the Tommies held on grimly, and Ludendorff readied his next stroke for April, in Flanders. He had fog again, and again he broke through, this time on a thirty-mile front. Everything Haig had won six months before was lost. The enemy was within five miles of Hazebrouck, a vital railway junction and his goal, when Ludendorff wavered. He couldn't decide whether or not to exploit the capture of the tallest hill in Flanders, and by the time he made up his mind the stubborn British were dug in. All he had was a second salient, which wasn't Paris.

Yet no one doubted that his masterpiece was still to come. Having pounced twice he was certain to lunge again. The Allies were distraught. "We are fighting with our backs to the wall!" Haig told his troops. Marshal Foch, who in this dark hour had been made generalissimo of all the armies, called for a "foot-by-foot" defense of the ground, and Pershing put every doughboy he had at Foch's disposal. Curiously it was the Americans, the freshmen, who picked the spot where the Germans' greatest storm would break. The Chemin des Dames ridge, north of the Aisne, was such a natural stronghold that the French had treated it casually — had, in fact, manned it with five exhausted British divisions sent to them for rest. It happened that this was the sector closest to Paris. Ludendorff's plan was to crash through and head for the capital. He expected every Allied reserve to be committed to the defense of the city then, and when that happened he was going to wheel and drive on Haig's channel ports.

His preparations were superb. No one took the American guess seriously because there wasn't a trace of activity in the German lines. Observation posts reported nothing, aerial photographs were a blank. Apparently there weren't even any batteries there. Actually there were nearly 4,000 Krupp guns. You just couldn't see them. Moving at night and hiding in the woods by day, with horses' hooves wrapped in rags and the sounds of creaking Konzern gun carriages muted by creaking frogs, Ludendorff had massed fourteen crack divisions in a wild weald of giant trees opposite the ridge. On the morning of May 27 the attackers sprang out of nowhere behind a gale of gas and shrapnel. The British disintegrated. By dusk the German assault columns had moved twelve miles. They crossed the Vesle River and surged on, boots thumping and *feldgrau* tunics swishing in the sunshine, and by the fifth day, when Soissons fell, they had overrun five French defense lines. There weren't any after that. They were on the Marne, the tip of their salient just thirty-seven miles from the Eiffel Tower at a place called Château-Thierry. The Allied Supreme War Council convened hurriedly. The European marshals had agreed that the Americans wouldn't be ready until 1919, but there wasn't anyone else available, so they sent in the United States Marines.

Arriving after an all-night march, the 5th and 6th Regiments of Marines were thrown across the road to Paris. Opposite them was a rolling field of summer wheat, thick with scarlet poppies, and four hundred yards beyond the field lay a forbidding Dante thicket of dark, tortured foliage. That was Belleau Wood. The Germans had two divisions coming through there; they were expected to break out shoulder to shoulder at any time. There wasn't any Allied line, an excited French officer told the Americans, and there wouldn't be any unless they formed one. It was hard to hear him, because refugees were fleeing past with birdcages and clothing packed in rattling baby carriages. One of them shouted, "*La guerre est fini!*" and an American shouted back, "*Pas fini!*" — thereby giving the sector its name. For five days the marines held five miles of Pas Fini against the solid gray columns that came hurtling across the field. The Germans reported encountering enemy "shock units" (*feudale Regimente*). Clemenceau announced that the Americans had saved Paris, and when they went over to the offensive, stormed Belleau Wood, and cleared it, they became national heroes at home — OUR GALLANT MARINES DRIVE ON 2½ MILES, NOTHING STOPS THEIR RUSH, cried a *New York Times* streamer. Of the eight thousand men who had straddled the road in the crisis, only two thousand were left. Over a hundred were awarded the Distinguished Service Cross.[29]

Pershing had a million men in France now. He was taking over more and more of the Allied line, and when the Germans tried to take advantage of Bastille Day by attacking again, precipitating the second battle of the Marne, five divisions of doughboys counterattacked. Ludendorff's hopes were fading with the summer poppies. He had given his July 14 drive a tremendous buildup. It had been christened the *Siegessturm* (stroke of victory), and he had ordered a tall wooden tower built behind the lines so the Kaiser could watch. Wilhelm perched there for six days, squinting through telescopes at distant blurs, trying to figure out which army was his. When he climbed down stiffly all the news was bad. The final cast had failed. This time the Germans didn't even have a bulge. Their morale was sinking fast; pitiful letters told the troops of hunger at home, and quartermasters with bare shelves were issuing soldiers commandeered women's clothing. Then came what Ludendorff called *"der schwarze Tag"* of the war. On August 8 the British massed nearly five hundred tanks in front of Amiens, cracked the German line and gained eight miles. It was an omen. That week Ludendorff offered to resign. He was put off, but a corner had been turned. Henceforth the Generalstab would be occupied with thoughts, not of victory, but of striking a bargain with the Allies and saving the army.[30]

☩   ☩   ☩

The All-Highest was unconvinced. At the height of the *Siegessturm* he had bestowed upon Hindenburg the Iron Cross with the crown in gold, the second such award in history. (The first had gone to Blücher after the defeat of Napoleon.) To be sure, he did mutter to Ludendorff after the sickening reverse of August 8, "I quite see now that we must strike a balance. . . . The war must be brought to an end . . . I will expect you, gentlemen, at Spa within the next few days." Yet in the Spa conference six days later he was indecisive. He was toying with the hope that the introduction of genuine parliamentary democracy might save the Hohenzollern dynasty. And he still hadn't abandoned the hope of a satisfactory solution in the field.[31]

Wilhelm was dreaming, but he was a hardheaded realist compared to Krupp. In the words of a German writer, Gustav suffered from an inability "ever to admit that the war was lost. . . . He therefore put up shutters on his mind which blinded him to what was really going on." According to his calculations, Ludendorff was about to triumph at any moment. The army had defeated the Fatherland's foes on every front except one, and there German troops remained deep in French territory. Like Alfred Krupp, Gustav Krupp was sending cannon to bombard Paris. The historical parallel was too strong to be denied. Kaiser, Reich, Volk, and Kanonenkönig would prevail together.[32]

The shelling of the French capital coincided with Ludendorff's 1918 offensives almost to the day. It began on March 23, just forty-eight hours after the first attack had gone in, when artillery specialists took over the freshly won Laon salient near Crépy, and it ended the morning after the black day of August 8. During those 139 days a shell was launched every twenty minutes. The bombardment was pointless and wanton, and more than any other German *Schrecklichkeit*, including the U–boats, it was identified with the name of Krupp. It was also a remarkable technical achievement. Though the world knew the gun as Big Bertha (a misnomer that persists today, even in Essen) there was no resemblance between the sawed-off siege howitzer which won Germany's first battle of the war and the long, tapered *Pariskanone* that played such a spectacular role in its last drive. The Berthas flung a projectile weighing a ton nine miles. The Paris cannon's shells were less than a quarter of that weight — they varied between 200 and 230 pounds — and the bore was only 8.3 inches (21 cm.), half the size of the howitzer's. What made the *Pariskanone* extraordinary was its range. Originally it had been designed as a naval gun. In the autumn of 1914 Rausenberger, working at Meppen with a primitive model, had perfected a barrel which would fire thirty-one miles. In forty-one months of experimentation he had increased this to eighty-one miles. At the same time he had improved its accuracy, so that although the Laon salient was seventy-seven miles northeast of the capital, the first shell burst in the very center of the Place de la République.[33]

The German navy still regarded the weapon as its own, and it was serviced by a crew of sixty seamen commanded by a full admiral. All had been carefully trained for this one task, for their 150-ton prodigy required exceptional care. The thirty-pound disparity in shells was deliberate. The sailors had been taught that each projectile must be *"vorgewärmt"* (pre-heated) in an underground chamber before firing, and that after every round the barrel must be slung from blocks and *"gerade gebogen"* (straightened). But even the most painstaking attention to detail could not repeal metallurgical laws. Firing expanded the bore slightly. Therefore the tapered projectiles were numbered, each slightly longer and thicker than the last. The caliber was never constant. Although officially listed at 8.3 inches, in practice it varied between 8.2 and 8.4 inches. After 65 firings a barrel was useless and had to be replaced.

Appointing a flag officer to one gun may seem absurd, but he presided over an instrument panel as large as a warship's. Extensive exercises in higher mathematics preceded the launching of every shell. The commanding officer and his staff pored over last-minute data on atmospheric pressure, humidity, temperature, and the curvature of the earth's surface. Because no artillery observer could see eighty miles, reports from spies within Paris told them whether or not they were enjoying good shooting, and, if not, where they were off. When countdown time came, a special telephone alerted thirty surrounding batteries, who opened fire to confuse Allied teams trying to pinpoint the *Pariskanone*'s location, and forty Fokker pursuit planes were held in readiness on a nearby airfield against the possibility that the teams might succeed anyhow and send bombers over. On the command *"Feuer!"* a projectile arched into the sky, reaching a maximum height of twenty-six miles in the ionosphere before the trajectory began its descent. Approaching the city it sounded like an enormous dachshund vomiting. Results varied; in twenty weeks the weapon killed over a thousand Parisians, but there were days when the agents reported nothing more than a few damaged cornices. A particularly impressive score came on Good Friday, March 29, when a shell crashed through the roof of Saint-Gervais-l'Église and exploded in the transept during Mass, killing ninety-one worshipers and wounding over a hundred. But the overall record hardly justified the expenditure of 35,000 marks a shot. *"Sie sorgt nur für neuen Hass gegen Deutschland,"* wrote Gert von Klass — it only made Germany more hated than ever.[34]

By late summer everybody hated Germany, including a lot of Germans. Famished and ill-housed, the Kaiser's subjects had invested all their hopes in the all-or-nothing drives of the spring. Now they had nothing and were rebellious. The news from the west grew progressively worse; the British and French retook Roye, Bapaume, Noyon, and Péronne, and the Americans were converging on both sides of the Saint-Mihiel salient. Abruptly, in the midst of this gloom, Wilhelm decided to inspect the works at Essen. He was preceded by his Kaiserin. The ubiquitous Ernst Haux was present when Augusta Victoria walked down a line of Gusstahlfabrik executives, pinning decorations on the lapels of their frock coats, and he wrote, "She did not look very robust then, as she had on former visits, when her appearance so truly typified the mother of seven splendid children. Now she seemed quite frail. . . . It was said that she took strong medicine to stay slim. . . . Outside, a storm raged while the empress passed along the long file, addressing a few friendly words to each person." Even the weather, Haux reflected gloomily, was against Germany.[35]

Krupp was informed that S.M. himself would be pleased to arrive on Monday, September 9, rest in his Hügel apartment, see how the war effort was coming along, and stay overnight. Gustav instinctively reached for a pencil and prepared a timetable:

Monday, September 9
3:00 P.M.   Departure from Villa Hügel
3:15 P.M.   Arrival at Hauptverwaltungsgebäude
            Introductory remarks, with maps and charts
3:50 P.M.   Machine Shop I
4:10 P.M.   Gun Cradle Shop IV
4:30 P.M.   Recoil Cylinder Shop I
            Gun Shop III . . .[36]

And so it went. Or rather, that was how it was supposed to go. The Kaiser was restless. He hurried through the long schedule, which continued into Tuesday with calls at hot pressing shops, fuse shops, shell turning shops and the Essen firing range. Then, after lunch in the Friedrichshalle Restaurant — Gustav had allowed him just twenty minutes to eat — he cleared his throat. What he really wanted, he said, was a chance to talk to the men. In the past selected audiences of white-collar executives and trusted foremen had been picked for him, but this time he was determined to address grimy Kruppianer. As he entered gate no. 28 by the Hauptverwaltungsgebäude, Haux noted that the emperor had been to a hairdresser: "He came with curled locks, the way he was pictured on coins then, and had a leather strap over his uniform shoulder, a custom among English officers, but one that had not been introduced in the German army. He carried a walking stick, with a small hatchet for a grip, which the Hungarians had given him."[37]

Pointing the cane at the top of a coal dump, Wilhelm suggested that he speak from there. Krupp was dismayed: the Kaiser was dressed in his *Feldmarschall's* uniform, with the golden Prussian eagle spread across the front of his glittering helmet; one trip up the coal pile and he would be indistinguishable from a Kumpel. Even Alfred had never done *that*. In his most diplomatic manner Gustav suggested that the stage was inauspicious; only those in front would be able to hear their sovereign. Krupp pointed to a huge shed nearby, and Wilhelm stalked into it, ducking cranes. On such short notice choosing politically reliable workers was impossible; the foremen had to round up those in the vicinity. Some 1,500 foundrymen were assembled, and they stood, impassive and curious in their paper shirts and wooden clogs, while the emperor mounted a low platform for what was to be his last speech in the Ruhr. *"Meine Freunde!"* he began, and launched into a rousing talk:

It is just a question of making a supreme effort — the whole issue hangs on that. . . . There is disaffection in the interior of the country, but it does not come from the hearts of the people; it is artificially inspired. Anybody who listens to such disloyal talk and spreads rumors in trains, factories, or elsewhere, is committing a crime against his Fatherland and is a traitor deserving harsh punishment, no matter whether he be a count or a worker. I know quite well that each of you agrees with me [*Ich weiss sehr wohl, dass ein jeder von euch mir darin recht gibt*].[38]

It was becoming increasingly obvious that they didn't at all agree with him. Whatever their feelings about the forces in the field, the Kaiser himself was being treated with an unprecedented lack of respect. It was his own fault. He had never been more off-key. In a singularly unfortunate choice of metaphor he asked them to hold up their end as he was holding up his — *"Ich auf meinem Thron und du an deinem Amboss"* (I on my throne and you on your anvil). The shops that day were unusually warm; the contrast between sweltering foundries and imperial comfort was too much. The men leered openly and muttered among themselves. As Wilhelm's adjutant observed later in his memoirs, "Looks became grim, and the more excited the emperor grew, the more clearly his audience expressed its negative reaction." It worked both ways; their evident discontent aroused him still further. As Haux noted sadly, Germany's imperial ruler evoked all the clichés of the *patriotische Blätter*, even to evoking the support of the Most High — he "begged the workers to stand by him, assuring them that God, Who had always fought at Germany's side, would never let the side down now."

The Kaiser spoke rapidly, and more shrilly; forgetting himself, he gestured frantically with his withered left arm.

> *Werdet stark wie Stahl, und der deutsche Volksblock, zu Stahl zusammengeschweisst, soll dem Feinde seine Kraft zeigen. . . . Dazu helfe uns Gott! Und wer das will, der antworte mit Ja!*

> Be strong as steel, and the solidity of the German people, welded into a single steel block, shall show the foe its strength. Those among you who have been moved by this appeal, those whose hearts are in the right place and who will keep the faith, let them stand up and promise me in the name of all the workmen of Germany: We shall fight and hold out to the last man, so help us God! Let those who will do this answer me by saying Yes!

There was silence in the shed. According to the official account, one of the last papers in the archives of the Second Reich, the hush was followed by "loud and prolonged cries of 'Yes.'" If there were such shouts, Finanzrat Haux, the emperor's adjutant, and the reporter for the *Essener Volkszeitung*, who had taken down S.M.'s remarks in shorthand, were all deaf to them. According to the newspaper's surprisingly frank account of September 11, 1918, supported by the memories of surviving Kruppianer who were there, not a single affirmative response was heard. One man called, "*Wann ist endlich Frieden?*" (When will we have peace?) — and another cried "*Hunger!*" Wilhelm paled. Conspicuously agitated, he plunged into his coda.

> *Ich danke euch. Mit diesem Ja gehe ich jetzt zum Feldmarschall. Jeder Zweifel muss aus Herz und Sinn verbannt werden. Dazu helfe uns Gott. Amen. Und nun, Leute, lebt wohl!*

> I thank you. With this Yes I will go to the field marshal [Hindenburg]. Every doubt must be removed from my heart and mind. God help us. Amen. And now, men, farewell![39]

He was driven straight to the Hauptbahnhof in his long gray limousine; his special train charged out through the smoke-veiled shops, past the Hügel spur, and westward along the banks of the placid Ruhr. He was bound, not for the front, as he had intimated, but for the soothing mineral springs of Spa. The All-Highest was feeling very low. He needed a tonic. So did Krupp executives; behind him Wilhelm had left managerial consternation. Haux thought the episode "quite disagreeable." Even Frau Haux, who until now had been an ardent believer in *Majestätsgläubigkeit*, had been shaken; in his journal the Finanzrat noted that "My wife, who attended the meeting, was much distressed about this speech." So disastrous had the exhibition been that by the time work shifts changed later in the afternoon a rumor far worse than any the speaker had deplored was sweeping Essen. The emperor had shown himself, the story went, and the workers had tried to kill him. Official denials were necessary, which was humiliating. In fact there was a poetic truth to the tale. To the 1,500 men who had been in that shed, the Kaiser they knew *had* died. As long as he had remained remote, mystical and powerful, his aura had been intact. By appearing in the flesh and revealing himself as a crippled, distraught victim of events, he had broken the spell. A god, which he had seemed to be, could not be defeated. An old man, which he clearly was, could be and undoubtedly had been. He had lied when he said he had heard them say yes. Therefore he had been lying about the rest.

Krupp's workers had disclosed their feelings, Krupp himself had not. What he had thought of the spectacle by gate 28 is unknown. Had Alfred been in charge we would have streams of memoranda, minute-by-minute bulletins on his splenetic reflections or, at the very least, on the state of his health. But Gustav, for all his attempts to ape the first Cannon King, was a different creature. In time of crisis he retreated into a trance of obedience and saw only what he chose to see. He ought to have been anticipating the coming capitulation. Unlike the foundrymen he had received an appraisal of the military situation from the best possible authority. Late in August, Ludendorff had summoned Krupp, Duisberg, Stinnes, and Ballin, led them to his map, and showed them how impossible things were. He suggested that the industrialists go straight to the Kaiser and open his eyes. Outside the map room the others looked to Gustav, their natural leader. But Krupp couldn't open Wilhelm's eyes; his own were too firmly shut. Instead he listened to imperial hangers-on who approached the four tycoons and told them that the general was unnecessarily pessimistic, that the fortunes of war were about to change, and that if they went to the emperor as Cassandras he would never forgive them. Gustav nodded gravely, the other three shrugged, and the delegation dissolved itself on the spot.

If the Reich's plight were as serious as the general thought, the Cannon King seems to have told himself (we can only judge him by his actions, for he committed nothing to paper), Wilhelm would know it without being told by a quartet of busybodies from Hamburg and the Ruhr. Certainly the view from Essen's Hauptverwaltungsgebäude was nowhere near as gloomy as Ludendorff's. Orders for war material continued to pour in; finished products poured out. The Germaniawerft had moved into mass production of U–boats; despite the British navy there had never been so many German subs at sea. After the black-day breakthrough Berlin had placed an urgent order for 85 tanks; an assembly line was tooling up for the "peculiar motor cars" Hindenburg had so airily dismissed. The army wanted armored cars and antiaircraft guns; designers had the blueprints ready. The Gusstahlfabrik was turning out 4,000 shells an hour and a sparkling new cannon every 45 minutes, and glowing reports from Meppen indicated that three new weapons — a heavy but highly mobile howitzer and 4- and 6-inch field guns — were so superior to anything in Allied artillery parks that they might very well split the western front wide open.[40]

It was pleasanter to think about that, so Gustav thought about that and spent a great deal of time going over Haux's books. They made superb reading. Since August 1914 the Konzern had paid for all new construction and accumulated a staggering gross profit of 432 million marks. Of course, all of it (except for the treasure sequestered in Holland, which was so secret the members of the board didn't even discuss it among themselves) was on paper. An Allied victory could reduce it to scrap paper. Indeed, if Ludendorff had been right Krupp might face more than insolvency; diplomats from neutral countries brought fresh reports of an official Allied war criminal list, and to Gustav's indignation he was high on it. There was also an outrageous editorial which had appeared in the May 4, 1918, issue of the influential *Littell's Living Age*. It reached the Ruhr that autumn via Scandinavia, and a bilingual executive leafing through it had come upon the preposterous leader, which suggested that Essen's Kanonenkönig was as responsible for the war as the emperor. Of course, it was all the doing of Mühlon, that lying *Schweinehund*. He had just published his diary under the astonishing title *The Vandal of Europe: An Exposé of the Inner Workings of Germany's Policy of World Domination, and its Brutalizing Consequences*, "by Wilhelm Mühlon, Former Director in Krupps." It was unspeakable. But Gustav knew the English. They were too sensible to be trapped by such sludge. You could do business with them. Doubtless they were as offended and embarrassed by this as he was. Nevertheless it was disquieting to read in *Living Age* that "The destiny of the country and the firm are interwoven, and if Germany falls, Krupps and Kruppism fall with it."[41]

✠    ✠    ✠

Meanwhile reality crept closer each day. In a series of local battles Ludendorff's spring gains disappeared from war maps. Germans were being pinched off all along the front, and Foch was charting an "arpeggio" of drives against the Hindenburg Line. "Everyone is to attack as soon as they can, as strong as they can, and as long as they can," he said, and "*L'édifice commence à craquer. Tout le monde à la bataille!*"[42] Actually it was better organized than that. There was a plan, and the American army was its fulcrum. Pershing's troops held ninety-four miles on the extreme right of the Allied line. In the center were the French, with the British to their left and King Albert of Belgium on the sea, leading a combined group, including two American divisions.

Much was expected on Albert's end, not so much on the other. Pershing was to be the Allied anchor. He faced the toughest link in the Hindenburg Line, the one part of the field the Germans could not yield and still retire with honor. It was the fantastic Forêt d'Argonne, within which the Germans had prepared four positions stretching back fourteen miles, manned by double garrisons and cunningly woven with interlocking belts of machine gun fire. They had taken every possible precaution there because the Sedan-Mézières railroad, their only line of escape to Liège and the Fatherland, lay behind the Argonne fastness. Once it was broken their army couldn't be withdrawn; it would lie at the mercy of the Allies. Foch knew how strong the enemy was here, and that was why the Americans' chief mission was to hold. They would join in the attacks, but their big job was to crack the whip, with the Belgians swinging free on the other end.

But the Yanks, with the only really young army left in Europe, were eager. And Foch had been right the first time: the edifice was cracking wide apart. When Pershing threw nine green divisions against the Germans on the misty morning of September 26, Ludendorff's forward positions were overrun, and the doughboys joined in the growing orchestration of battle beneath which all France trembled. At first the forest was wrapped in a blinding, clammy fog. Runners, officers, command posts — and a famous battalion — got lost. One patrol literally vanished Indian file into the haze; the men didn't return, their bodies were never found, they weren't in POW camps after the war, and are listed as missing to this day. Then, abruptly, the weather cleared. The trees were revealed in their autumnal splendor, coppery, golden, purplish, deep scarlet. All along the front the war was rapidly approaching a solution in the field. Albert was re-entering his channel towns in triumph, the French were ringing their own church bells in the little long-lost villages around Lille, and the British were approaching Mons. Everything was slipping away from the Kaiser, including the other Central Powers. An Allied army which had been mired in Salonica since 1915 sent a spearhead of Serb mountain fighters against Bulgaria, and on September 20 the Bulgarians quit. That same day the British took Damascus; Turkey then bowed out. Even the Italians were attacking, which meant Austria's end was near.

When Pershing renewed his advance the Germans' last scribbly ditches caved in, and they were left without any front at all. Apart from the stolid Krupp machine gunners, who kept their murderous barrels hot to the end, German soldiers had become a disorderly mob of refugees. They had lost heart. During this final agony, their rearguard in France, Sergeant Alexander Woollcott wrote in *Stars and Stripes*, resembled an escaping man who "twitches a chair down behind him for his pursuer to stumble over."[43] Each chill dawn poilus, Tommies, and doughboys went roaring over the top in fighting kit, driving the fleeing wraiths in *feldgrau* against the hills of Belgium and Luxembourg. It was a chase, not a battle. The horses, caissons and camions could scarcely keep up with the racing troops. With the vital railroad in his hands Pershing told his commanders to forget about flanks, light up the trucks, and see how far they could go — an order which touched off a frantic race for Sedan.

Within the disintegrating Reich everyone who could get the Kaiser's ear was telling him to quit while he still could, under any terms. On the third day of the great Allied drive Hindenburg demanded that a peace proposal be made "at once." On the seventh day, at a council of war in Berlin chaired by the All-Highest, Hindenburg insisted that "The army cannot wait forty-eight hours." That evening the *Feldmarschall* wrote that it was absolutely essential to "stop the fighting," and two days after that he reported in despair that there was no hope of restraining the enemy. The Wilhelmstrasse was frantically trying to reach Woodrow Wilson through Switzerland, suggesting a peace based on Wilsonian proposals made nine months before. At the time they had been scornfully branded "the Fourteen Points" by the *Norddeutsche Allgemeine Zeitung*. Now they were all the Germans could get — more, in fact, for Wilson coldly referred their note to Foch. The President could read maps, too.[44]

The Kaiser couldn't, or wouldn't. Wilhelm, who had urged the English to be good sports and admit the other chaps had won the Boer War, clung to his crown and his pitiful hopes while the scope of the disaster mounted. On October 27 Ludendorff quit and was succeeded by General Wilhelm von Gröner. On November 3 the fleet at Kiel, ordered off on a death-or-glory ride against the British, mutinied. Four days later revolution broke out in Munich, and Prince Max of Baden, the new chancellor, advised Wilhelm that the only hope of preserving the monarchy lay in his immediate renunciation of the throne. The Kaiser pouted at Spa. In a final display of bombast he reminded Gröner, who also insisted that he step down, of the army's oath of loyalty to the All-Highest. Sorrowfully the general replied, *"Der Fahneneid ist jetzt nur eine Idee"* (The oath of loyalty is now only a fiction).[45] Despairing, Prince Max announced the abdication anyhow. Philipp Scheidemann, an ex-printer who had become leader of the Social Democrats — SPD zeal for the war had soured — proclaimed a republic in Berlin. Already a German armistice commission headed by the leader of the Catholic Centrists was receiving directions beamed from the Eiffel Tower, telling them which trenches to approach and where to pick up their guides to Foch's railway coach near Compiègne. On November 10 Hindenburg and Gröner advised the emperor that they were unable to guarantee the loyalty of the army. That, and only that, stirred Wilhelm. Too listless to hide his withered arm under his cape, the emperor crept into his limousine and fled to Holland.

At 5 A.M. the following morning the German envoys signed Foch's dictated terms. A cease-fire was to begin six hours later, and the moment the hills were tinged with the first faint promise of morning motorcycles spluttered up and down the front, passing the word. After ten o'clock the trenches grew noisy — everybody wanted to get in the last shot — but eyes glued to a million watches finally saw minute hands creep upright, and then there was utter quiet. It lasted a moment and was followed by a deafening cheer on both sides. Generals might haggle over words, but soldiers knew this was more than an armistice. It was the end of the war, of all wars, and it had come, as editorial writers everywhere noted profoundly, at the eleventh hour of the eleventh day of the eleventh month.

Yet for once the generals were right. It was to be a long truce, but it wouldn't be peace, because more than the German command was finished. There were omens, for those who could read them. The belfries Edith Wharton heard calling joyously to one another across Paris that morning might also have been tolling for a French army broken in spirit and left to politicians like André Maginot. Something had died in France, just as something had been born in Russia; that very morning, as rockets of victory streaked innocently over the conquered Argonne, Bolshevik troops mounted an offensive against 5,000 American soldiers who had been unwisely diverted to Archangel in the hope of rescuing a fallen ally. American voters had just discredited Woodrow Wilson, torpedoing his League of Nations and confirming the fears of Winston Churchill, who wondered, as he stood in a London window and heard Big Ben strike eleven, whether the world would return to international anarchy. [46]

It would. But it would not be the same anarchy. An age had reached Journey's End. The door of history had shut on the princes and potentates and plumed marshals and glittering little regular armies — on all the elegance and fanfaronade that marked that disciplined, secure world. The grinning doughboys stacking their Springfield rifles and swapping cigarettes for souvenirs might not know it; their new Congress back home certainly didn't, and the hysterical crowds in Times Square, the Champs-Élysées, and the Buckingham Palace grounds knew it least of all, though the English had a sign. As they romped over the mall with firecrackers and confetti the sky suddenly darkened. It began to rain, hard. Some of the celebrators climbed into the arms of Queen Victoria's statue, but after huddling there a few minutes they climbed down. They had found little shelter, and less comfort. The arms had been stone-cold.[47]

Inside Germany feelings were mixed. The famished, the lonely, the working classes, those who had been convinced by Social Democratic propaganda and who admired the fearlessness of Karl Liebknecht were immeasurably relieved. But those whom deprivation had not touched were bewildered. The ardently nationalistic middle class had waited four years for triumph. Now it was confronted by defeat. The taste was bitter and, for millions, unbearable. Already the search for scapegoats had begun, and it was to be quickly resolved when the civilians who had signed the peace terms were christened the "November criminals." Within a few months the two German generals who had presided over the collapse in France were to cosponsor a myth which would slake the parched imagination of the nation. Dining with the head of the British military mission in Berlin one evening, Ludendorff complained that the Generalstab had never been supported properly by civilians at home. "Do you mean, General," the British officer asked helpfully, "that you were stabbed in the back?" Ludendorff started visibly. "Stabbed in the back? Yes, that's it exactly," he said excitedly. "We were stabbed in the back." Informed of the exchange, Hindenburg, forgetting his own panicky pleas for terms, blandly told the country, "as an English general has very truly said, the German army was stabbed in the back."[48]

In a Pomeranian military hospital a twice decorated German noncom who had been temporarily blinded during a heavy gas attack on the night of October 13 learned of the capitulation from a sobbing pastor. The minister wasn't ready to quit, and neither was Adolf Hitler. The invalided corporal was still ready to charge, but now there would be no more charges. Six years later the future Führer set down a description of his reaction. He could not sleep. He was ablaze with hatred for those he called responsible for the betrayal:

> *Elende und verkommene Verbrecher!* . . . *Mit dem Juden gibt es kein Parieren, sondern nur das harte Entweder–Oder. Ich aber beschloss, Politiker zu werden.*

> Wretched and miserable criminals! . . . What was all the pain in my eyes now, compared with this misery? What now followed were terrible days and even worse nights . . . In the days that followed I became aware of my own destiny. . . . With the Jews there is no bargaining, but only the hard either–or. My own fate became known to me. I resolved to go into politics.[49]

After Hitler had reached his crest Krupp liked to declare grandly of World War I that:

*Es blieb oberster Grundsatz vom ersten Tage des Krieges an, dass die Inhaber des Unternehmens am Kriege kein Geld verdienen wollten.*

It was a basic principle, dating from the day the war broke out, that the owners of the business had no desire to make money out of it.[50]

The Führer liked to hear it, but it was nonsense; the firm's records read otherwise. The nature of a man's commitment to the conflict may be judged by his response to the calamity of early November, and here Gustav's behavior is revealing. Wilhelm fled when he found he couldn't be Kaiser any more, Hitler was seized with a lust for revenge, and Krupp was stunned when Berlin canceled all contracts and suspended payments to the Konzern. That break came on November 8, as the German armistice commission headed for the French lines. It was a violent shock, and not only because profits were at stake. Krupp was the sole source of support for inhabitants of the Krupp empire. In Essen alone the Gusstahlfabrik provided sustenance for 105,000 families. Gustav telegraphed Berlin, asking what he was to do with them. The reply was exasperating. No Kruppianer was to be dismissed, the new government said; Gustav must keep them busy "somehow or other" (*irgendwie*).[51]

As Haux noted dryly, the Social Democrats now ascendant in the capital had an imperfect grasp of economics. Keeping the workmen occupied was possible only if they were paid, and the wage bill couldn't be met unless Krupp's sole customer resumed the disbursement of funds. Again the telegraph wires crackled. The exchange was fruitless, so Gustav decided to close the shops; shifts reporting for work on the morning of November 9 discovered that they were locked out. Presses, wheels, belts, hammers were motionless. For the first time within living memory the Gusstahlfabrik was silent. Early that afternoon a brief, brisk storm washed away the pall of smoke overhead. The sky quickly cleared, leaving Essen bathed in unaccustomed sunshine. Its brilliance had an unsettling effect on the population; men averted their eyes and winced.[52]

Next day a large crowd gathered outside the Hauptbahnhof. Rumors spread that foremen were organizing a demonstration, and the workers, having nothing else to do, converged on the station. There were no foremen, only SPD orators and some speakers from the far Left jubilantly waving red flags. The Kruppianer listened, became interested when popular men among them were nominated as their spokesmen, and entered the discussions in earnest. In Villa Hügel, Krupp waited impassively. He had agents on the spot; they would bring messages if anything serious happened. Presently the first arrived. His news was grave. The specter which had haunted Alfred *der Grosse* was again present in Essen and was assuming an ominous form. Anticipating the imminent return of their brothers and sons now in France, the workmen were forming *Arbeiter- und Soldatenräte,* proletarian councils modeled after those which had been so successful in Russia the year before. Indeed, there was actually talk of a German revolution.[53]

# 13

✠

# The Groaning Land

THE behavior of the Krupps between the collapse of Ludendorff's *Siegessturm* and the success of the Blitzkrieg makes no sense unless one massive fact is grasped: the Germans' war did not end on Armistice Day. In Allied countries statues of lean bronze soldiers began appearing on Lest-We-Forget plinths in city and town squares, bearing the inscription 1914–1918. In Germany the second date would have been incorrect. The fallen Reich, like France after the Franco-Prussian War, was racked by civil strife. A frightening new phenomenon — Hans Kohn called it "the sudden brutalization of politics" — had emerged. During one two-year period beginning in 1919 political assassins (*Femen*) committed at least 354 murders. The shadow of primitive terror appeared variously in every corner of the fledgling Teuton republic, and for a quarter-century its dark menace would always be just a scream away. German infants born in that first winter of peace would grow up in a nation ruled, during their teens, by terrorists waiting for them to reach military age so that they could storm across their frontiers in anger. But the swastika of 1933 did not bring the hobgoblins of fear. They were present in strength from the moment firing stopped on the western front. On January 15, 1919, Karl Liebknecht, Krupp's most effective prewar critic, was murdered on a Berlin sidewalk — shot in the back by police agents who were never brought to trial. Five months later, when the Versailles Treaty was signed, an army *Freikorps* was executing leftists in the Baltic provinces. Every city had neighborhoods hoarding surplus rifles and Krupp machine guns; the adult male inhabitants, at that time the most seasoned killers in history, awaited only a motive. Since each man nursed private grudges, in the poisonous postwar atmosphere any day could bring a witches' Sabbath. Only in Amerongen, Holland, one of

Wilhelm's German biographers wrote bitterly, could the Kaiser block his ears against "the groaning of his land."[1]

During the first turbulent year of peace the Krupp complex seethed but did not erupt. The parallel between the Fatherland and its most powerful family still held, but Essen's two bloody climaxes — the Easter weeks of 1920 and 1923 — lay ahead. Averting an immediate explosion was largely Gustav's personal triumph. Potentially Essen was among the most flammable communities in the humbled empire, because with no prospect of armament orders massive dismissals were inevitable. Reports of discontent around the Hauptbahnhof were so alarming that all Villa Hügel servants were armed and a seamstress was instructed to fashion a red flag which could be hoisted as a friendly sign should mobs storm the hill. When none came, Gustav, in a remarkable display of personal courage, went down into the city. His bowler set square on his head, he deliberately strode through the idle crowds. They didn't cheer him, but then, he had never been cheered; he wasn't that sort of man — "When he mingled with the crowds of factory workers, none of them came too close to him. He walked with his usual upright carriage and stiff gait" (aufrecht, mit eckigen Bewegungen).[2]

Some doffed their caps, the traditional sign of respect when Krupp passed through his shops. Entering the Hauptverwaltungsgebäude he called an emergency meeting of the Vorstand and announced his decision. All men who had been employed on August 1, 1914, were to be kept on the payroll, whatever the cost. The rest — over 70,000 in the Essen factories alone, nearly half of them Poles — would have to go. There was a stirring among the board members, and Gustav quickly said he knew; they were a threat. Accordingly they must be given some incentive to leave the Ruhr. A general announcement would be made: all who departed before November 18 would be given fourteen days' pay and a free one-way railroad ticket.[3]

It worked. Gustav's published reminders that "the traditional welfare policy of my firm," including sick leave and pensions, was available only to loyal workmen, sobered those Kruppianer who had been assured that they still had their jobs and gave them a vested interest in tranquillity. The temporary wartime employees were appeased by cash and train fare. Most of them were homesick, and photographs of their departures suggest that they were also scared; the depot platforms were jammed with tense men in crude peasant caps rolling their eyes whitely at the camera. By the morning after the deadline, according to the arithmetic of Krupp police, 52,000 passengers had departed by rail and another 18,000 on foot.[4]

There remained the fate of the Konzern. Gustav had shelved his war cry — obviously "The greater the foe the greater the honor" had been wide of the mark — and twice within the three weeks following the great exodus he substituted other mottoes. The first was inspired by a challenge within his own board. The Vorstand suggested that the firm be liquidated. Gustav and Bertha riffled through her grandfather's papers. Alfred's mandate had been clear. His descendants should preside over the Gusstahlfabrik forever. Therefore the first shibboleth became "There will always be a Krupp empire!" (*Krupps Reich wird ewig bestehen!*). It sounded good, but then, so had its predecessor. It was followed by "*Nie wieder Krieg*" (No more war). What was needed was something practical, however, and on December 6, 1918, Gustav supplied it. On shop posters, in catalogues, and in newspaper advertisements Krupp told Germans, "*Wir machen alles!*"[5]

*Wir machen alles:* We make everything. It was nearly true. That same afternoon the prince consort unveiled a showroom on the first floor of the Hauptverwaltungsgebäude, displaying designs and prices for Krupp's peacetime production line. For the first time since Alfred's prime the firm would turn out spoon and fork rollers. There were a few big items — agricultural and textile machines, dredgers, crankshafts. The bulk of the products, however, were small. Kruppianer who had given Europe the hundred-ton monsters which had pulverized Liège and butchered Parisians eighty miles from the Laon salient would now make motor scooters, cash registers, adding machines, movie cameras, typewriters, tableware, water sprinklers, and optical and surgical instruments. They considered it debasing, and their employer, agreeing, blamed their inglorious plight upon the November criminals. Gustav erred; Schneider, Armstrong and Vickers were making identical conversions. That winter the Vickers Peace Products Committee addressed itself to "the relative selling merits of 'boy rabbits (squeaking)' and 'girl rabbits (nonsqueaking).' "[6]

There had always been a certain flair about Krupp, a gift for carrying the absurd to the fantastic, and it manifested itself now. Gustav ordered the list submitted to the shops and offered awards to men who suggested practical additions. One returning veteran sent in a slip with a single word upon it: *Jaws*. Puzzled, Krupp summoned him. What sort of *Kinnbacken* did he have in mind? Human jaws, the man explained. There was a long silence. Then Gustav said distantly, "We don't really make *everything*." Of course not, the veteran said hastily; what he had in mind was a new use for the firm's stainless V₂A steel. It would make superb false teeth, rustless and guaranteed tasteless, and shellfire had damaged the jaws of a great many young soldiers. The Kruppianer won a prize. In Essen, Gustav set up a special hospital where Krupp dentists and surgeons installed dentures in the mouths of over three thousand Germans who had been wounded by projectiles armed with Krupp patent fuses.[7]

Because of political repercussions Gustav postponed raising the issue of patent fees with Vickers until July 1921, though he must have been sorely tempted to approach Sheffield earlier. Legally, he believed, the English owed him over a quarter-million pounds, and Haux was hard pressed for liquid assets. Converting the holdings in Holland was inconvenient. Therefore the Finanzrat was restricted to the balance sheets in Essen, which made ghastly reading. At the outbreak of the war Krupp had been 130 million marks in the black; the day the chimneys stopped he was 148 million in the red, and the first year of peace was no help — at the end of 1919 the firm had lost another 36 million. The production of gadgets was a blunder. Krupp was the very symbol of heavy industry; the adjustment to motor scooters and typewriters was too great a leap. The manufacture of steel bridges turned out to be more profitable, and in June 1919 Gustav took a giant step forward by achieving something which had always eluded Alfred, an agreement with the Prussian State Railways. Four years of shifting troops ceaselessly from one front to another had left Germany's rolling stock depleted. The following December, Krupp put the first of two thousand locomotives on the tracks. All Essen turned out for the ceremony and delivered an ovation when twelve-year-old Alfried stepped into the cabin, yanked the whistle cord, and gave the throttle a tug. It was a good start. The assembly of freight cars had already begun. Yet it would be years before the line paid off. Meanwhile key executives were quitting the Hauptverwaltungsgebäude — Rausenburger retired because he couldn't make cannon any more; Alfred Hugenberg left to found the new German National People's Party (the Green Shirts) — and the first wave of violence approached Essen.[8]

On January 10, 1920, the Versailles *Diktat*, as the treaty was beginning to be called, was ratified by Germany, and at 5 A.M. on March 13 a specter of the future appeared: Rightists attempted to overthrow the seven-month-old Weimar Republic. General Walther Freiherr von Lüttwitz, commanding officer of military units stationed in Berlin, seized the capital and proclaimed Friedrich Wolfgang Kapp, an ultraconservative politician, "Imperial Chancellor." Friedrich Ebert, the Social Democratic president, fled to Dresden and then to Stuttgart, trying frantically to find out where the army stood. Although reduced to 100,000 men the army was crucial, because officers had been secretly distributing arms to *Freikorps* which had sprung up all over Germany. These bands were dedicated to the suppression of liberal parties on the local level, which made Ebert's quest seem bleak. It was: General Hans von Seeckt, the commander of Weimar's army, the truncated Reichswehr, stood aside and prepared to watch the republic fall. But the SPD had a formidable weapon of its own, the general strike. In desperation Ebert used it. He ordered every worker in the country to leave his job. When Germans obey, they really obey; next day not a single water tap, gas range, electric light, train or streetcar would function. Within a week the putsch collapsed and Kapp fled to Sweden.

While communications shut down, however, rumors had spread that the coup was succeeding, and as a result the workers of the Ruhr had risen. Under Versailles the Ruhr was out-of-bounds to both Allied and Reichswehr troops. The leftist but anti-Communist Rote Soldatenbund (Red

Soldiers League) seemed invincible. Seizing a cache of arms in Bochum, 70,000 men led by ex-noncoms marched toward Essen. On March 19 the Soldatenbund fought a pitched battle with local police and a *Freikorps*; three hundred men were killed, the red soldiers won, and Krupp factories were occupied.* During the next week Mülheim, Düsseldorf, Oberhausen, Elberfeld, and Kettwig fell to the workers. In each a local republic was proclaimed. Public officials were elected, sentries were posted to prevent looting. But it was all in vain. Ebert, back in Berlin, was dismayed by the success of the insurgents. All street fighters were a threat to the republic, whatever their sympathies. He petitioned the Entente Commission to allow the Reichswehr to suppress the revolt. The reply was ambiguous (largely because France wanted an independent Rhineland state as a buffer), but on April 3 General von Watter, commander of the regular troops in Rhenish Westphalia, invaded the Ruhr anyhow. The issue was decided within twenty-four hours. One by one the local councils were cut off from each other and annihilated. It was a savage, bloody business, and Essen's last stand in a fortified red brick water tower on Easter Sunday was fought out against the incongruous background of churchgoers in new finery and children hugging toy bunnies. Two sisters in their teens left their parents to serve as nurses. They watched the ruthless massacre of workers taken prisoner, and when Walter Duranty of the *New York Times* interviewed them their frocks were still bloodstained. The younger girl sobbed, "I think all soldiers ought to be put in front of their own machine guns and shot till there are none of them left."[9]

With military courts of *Freikorpskämpfer* trying Soldatenbund members and sentencing them to be shot, the Ruhr, it seemed, could sink no lower. But the French, who in these years were always ready to make a bad situation worse, seized upon the presence of regular troops in the neutral zone as an excuse. They were still dreaming of a separate Rhineland republic — one of the few German advocates of this scheme, curiously, was Konrad Adenauer of Cologne — so poilus also marched in, broke out the tricolor, and shot seven youths who protested. The operation was pointless. It helped neither party to the intramural strife. If France's intervention had any immediate purpose it was to remind people who had won the war and instill respect for the conqueror. The only lasting conseqeunce was fresh bitterness throughout the Ruhr and in Berlin. It was little things like that which made the French remembered.[10]

☒    ☒    ☒

On the evening of March 20 a workers' armored car, appropriately painted bright red, turned off Alfredstrasse, wound through a maze of quiet little streets named for other members of the Kanonenkönig's family,

---

* That same day the United States Senate defeated the Versailles Treaty for the second time.

and approached the silent, forbidding mass of Villa Hügel. The domestic staff within nervously fingered their weapons. They had been expecting this; if Russian Reds murdered the Romanovs, what would German Reds do to the Krupps? But they misjudged their visitors. Karl Dohrmann went to the door. Of all the footmen, he had seen the most military service; he thought he could deal with fellow ex-soldiers, and he did. When the armed callers explained that they had no intention of molesting anyone, that they were merely hungry, Dohrmann was unsurprised. He led them down to the kitchens, gave them all they could carry, and sent them packing. They hadn't even asked about the family.[11]

If they had, they would have been disappointed. Apart from the servants nobody was at home. Bertha was four months pregnant with her seventh child, and Gustav didn't want her disturbed by gunfire. At the first flash of trouble — a demonstration outside the Rheinhausen plant — he had put his wife and children in cars and headed for Sayneck, Fritz Krupp's old hunting lodge on the Rhine. Marga had remained behind. She hadn't been near Sayneck since her husband had entertained Italian youths there. For several days she stayed in Arnoldhaus, the Krupp maternity ward named for Bertha's lost child. Then the street fighters began blazing away at each other under her windows. She changed her mind about Sayneck, and setting off alone with characteristic self-possession, passed through the heaviest fighting to join her daughter. When Waldtraut was born in August, Marga was by Bertha's side.[12]

Gustav wasn't around Sayneck much. As a diplomat he believed in keeping up appearances, and the more disorganized Germany became the harder he worked at pretending everything was normal. It took a lot of effort that season. In the first place, he had been officially branded a war criminal at Versailles. According to Article 231 of the treaty the All-Highest, Crown Prince Rupprecht, Admirals Tirpitz and Scheer, Gustav Krupp von Bohlen und Halbach, and generals Hindenburg, Ludendorff, Mackensen, and Kluck were among those whose lawless activities had shattered Europe. Krupp was confident that German refusal to cooperate would kill that article, and he was right, but other unpleasantnesses were harder to ignore. The uprising in the Ruhr was no small thing; it created a major international incident, and until the back of the rebellion was broken an enlisted man sat in Krupp's private office. (When Gustav returned the thermometer there was over 70 degrees. He ordered all the windows flung open and refused to re-enter until the temperature had dropped.) Lastly, and most disagreeable of all, was the dismantling of his factories.

On May 29, 1920, eight weeks after Easter, an Allied Control Commission registered at the Essener Hof and encamped in the Hauptverwaltungsgebäude. Colonel Leverett, the British officer in command, described his task as purely supervisory. The destruction of Krupp shops was to be achieved by German laborers, paid by Krupp. Leverett hoped they would be quick about it, because there was a lot to do. Before he left he had to see the Gusstahlfabrik cut down to half its size; his Essen schedule called for the scrapping of nearly a million tools and 9,300 machines weighing 60,000 tons, and the clearing of 100,000 cubic yards of ground. Then he had to move on to Kiel, where, he "believed," Krupp owned a shipyard. There were "some warships there." They had to be "sunk, and all keels laid demolished."[13]

The colonel was delayed, for a reason Lewis Carroll would have relished. Before dismembering the plant, he said, he must first satisfy the requirements of the treaty's Article 168. All war material on hand had to be turned over to him. He knew precisely how much there was, because General Charles Marie Édouard Nollet, chief of the Military Inter-Allied Control Commission in Berlin, had given him a detailed list of nearly a million items drawn up by French intelligence, starting with 159 experimental fieldpieces. Krupp's Vorstand studied it and explained to Leverett that the French had exaggerated the size of Germany's artillery parks and munitions stockpiles; there weren't that many cannon and shells in the country. The colonel brooded and improvised what seemed to him to be a brilliant solution. Orders were orders, he said. Surely they understood that. Therefore, before the shops were torn down they would resume full-scale production of arms. Thus it happened that Essen's *Waffenschmiede des Reichs* once more roared ahead, turning out ton after ton of weapons which Leverett then shipped to Nollet, who then destroyed them.[14]

That done, the forges were shut down and dismantling proceeded. It was a grim business. Toiling in the summer heat, the workers lacked Geist. Nobody sang *Siegreich woll'n wir Frankreich schlagen*; they scarcely spoke to one another. "Everybody can gather the significance of the outcome of the war for the Krupp works as well as for my wife and myself," Gustav wrote afterward. "It is general knowledge that hardly any works were as hard hit by the Treaty of Versailles as Krupp." He was right, but as events were to prove, the firm's industrial potential was unaffected by the ritualistic crushing of bricks and steel. Versailles's attempt to remove the Krupp threat failed, not because the provisions were too harsh but because the approach was ineffectual. Like the Iron Chancellor a half-century earlier, the drafters of the treaty were obsessed by military strategy. They wanted to give the French a defensible frontier, preferably on the Rhine. All they achieved was to reinforce Germany's fear of encirclement. The Ruhr's productive capacity was left intact, and within five years the output of coal and steel was to bounce back to the levels of July 1914. Indeed, in the long run Krupp benefited from the razing and gutting of obsolete equipment. Unlike the gunsmiths of the triumphant powers, Gustav would enter the crucial 1930's with modern facilities and techniques.[15]

Still, Colonel Leverett's scuttling operation *was* degrading. Krupp refused to watch it. Instead he drove down to the Black Forest during the last month of Bertha's pregnancy for the postwar reopening of Baden-Baden's fashionable horse racing. Sigrid Schultz, then a young assistant correspondent for the Chicago *Tribune*, recalls that Gustav gallantly squired her about, sent her roses, and proudly told her of his American ancestry. On the last evening of the season he held a formal dinner for the most eminent of his fellow visitors. Nothing was spared to create the illusion that there had been no war, no defeat, no humiliation. Miss Schultz wondered why the tableware wasn't silver. Thinking it might have been fashioned from some interesting new alloy, she examined it carefully and saw it was solid gold. Gustav had ordered it shipped from Villa Hügel for the occasion.[16]

At summer's end the family continued to avoid Essen; the dismantling was still going on. They scarcely knew their way around the late archduke's estate in Austria and were curious about it, so once Bertha could travel Gustav took them to Blühnbach. They were now a large family: Alfried, thirteen; Claus, ten; Irmgard, eight; Berthold, six; Harald, four, and little Waldtraut. With the birth of Eckbert two years later the new generation would be complete. Inevitably their childhood was abnormal; from birth they were reminded of their special position in Germany. At Berthold's christening six years earlier Ernst Haux had proudly written that "the Kaiser, Privy Councilor (*Geheimrat*) von Simson, and your humble servant (*meine Wenigkeit*) were asked to be godfathers." Being designated godfather to a Krupp son or daughter was an honor, and the children knew it, because Bertha never let them forget. In other ways they reflected their father's eccentricities. The *Prinzgemahl*'s household was obsessed with protocol. There was a pecking order, and everyone knew his place in it.[17]

Alfried might as well have been an only son. He was coached by special tutors, permitted to dine with his parents, taken on special tours of mines and, when in the Ruhr, driven to the Hauptverwaltungsgebäude for weekly indoctrination sessions. Though he might watch his brother Claus build model Fokkers and go ice skating with young Fritz von Bülow, other children were never permitted to forget that they were in the presence of the next Krupp. From time to time he tried to emerge from his splendid isolation. When Gustav released him from his tutors and permitted him to attend Bredeney's *Realgymnasium*, the boy went out for crew. Gustav presented the school with a new scull, and to no one's surprise the coach gave his son the honored position of stroke. Alfried's classmates, envious and resentful, would heckle him when masters were absent, shouting, *Na, Krupp, alter Junge, was tut man wohl augenblicklich auf deinem Schutthaufen"* (Well, Krupp, old boy, what are they doing up at your scrap heap these days)? He was a friendless adolescent. Once he followed a group of boys into a tavern. Inside, he sat tongue-tied. The owner said gently, "*Sie müssen nicht immer so ernst sein*" (You shouldn't be so serious *all* the time). Alfried reddened and squirmed. The proprietor was wrong. Being serious all the time was the boy's lifelong obligation. When his father enrolled him as a Krupp apprentice, Alfried rode a motorcycle between Hügel and the shops. It accomplished nothing. Gustav, unimpressed, waited until the machine broke down one day and ordered his son's name posted on a list of tardy workers.[18]

To Berthold and Harald their two older brothers were, in Harald's word, "gods." Alfried's godliness had been bestowed upon him; Claus created his own. Husky and extroverted, he dominated the younger boys. Unlike them, he had been old enough to understand the war. His idol was Baron Manfred von Richthofen, and while airplanes were only a hobby now, he dreamed of flying for Germany some day. Irmgard, shy and plain, was ignored by the boys. Waldtraut grew to be a pretty, spirited girl, but Eckbert was so much younger than his brothers that he was as unnoticed as Irmgard. Thus the children were aware of both an adult hierarchy and of caste distinctions among themselves. On certain issues they were united, however. They all hated Villa Hügel. There their parents were busy with formal receptions and banquets, and they were expected to behave like dolls. Escaping the servants' spy system was almost impossible. Their one lark was to hide behind the carved oak staircase when a distinguished guest arrived and watch him cross the hundred-foot main hall. At the far end, beyond five stupendous chandeliers, Gustav and Bertha would be waiting. Their sons and daughters always hoped that one of the important visitors would slip and fall on the highly polished parquet flooring. But it never happened, their conduct was always reported to Gustav, and they were always punished. Among themselves they called Hügel "the tomb."[19]

Blühnbach, on the other hand, was "paradise." The four-storied ivy-covered castle was beautiful and luxurious — "*wollüstig*," as the Austrians say. There were tiger skins on the floors, mounted chamois horns on the walls, and, on the roof, tiny cannon pointing in all directions. These Wilhelmine touches appealed immensely to youthful imaginations. Most important, at Blühnbach the children had their mother and father to themselves. There was no state banquet protocol, no need to don starched clothes and be paraded around like marionettes. The Austrian Alps were too inaccessible. Even after a visitor had reached the main gate he faced a long journey to the castle. Once, years later, Berthold was showing the hunting trophies there to an American writer. Looking out from a stone balcony across the thick forests of conifer and the craggy, snow-clad mountains, the American inquired curiously, "How far do you own?" "Do you see that ridge?" said Berthold, pointing to a vague blue line on the horizon. "*That* far?" asked his astonished guest. "No," Berthold said; "to the ridge beyond."[20]

The Krupps were continuing to live on their prewar scale, and every outward sign suggested a miraculous recovery from the war. The number of Kruppianer increased each month until, on July 1, 1921, the Gusstahlfabrik's payroll exceeded that of early 1914. In the winter of 1920–1921 Gustav had bought five hundred acres for a new plant in Merseburg, near the finest lignite mines in Germany, and acquired a string of collieries which gave the firm a coal reserve of ten million tons. This expansion is rather mysterious. Where was the credit coming from? Not from sales; the new gadget line was barely breaking even, and although Krupp's locomotives were popular, his insistence upon excellence limited production to three hundred a year, entailing rejection of orders from Brazil, Rumania, South Africa, and India. Some cash was acquired by closing Annen and liquidating Bayrische Geschützwerke, a small Munich subsidiary, but hardly enough to keep the hammers throbbing in Essen, let alone Rheinhausen, Magdeburg, Hamm, and Kiel.

The fact is that Krupp's prosperity was largely show. For three years after the armistice Gustav was spending more than he earned. For almost any other company in any other nation this would have brought ruin. One clue to Krupp's splurging lies in what was, on the surface, his most hopeless project of the decade. In 1922 he told his board a German army officer had told him that Lenin had said, "The steppe must be turned into a bread factory, and Krupp must help us." Accordingly, Krupp machines were sent to plow up 62,500 acres between Rostov and Astrakhan, on the Manytch River. Gustav, who was still struggling with his little farm on the Dutch border, was the last man to turn anything into a bread factory, and Tilo von Wilmowsky, a genuine agricultural expert, realized that the attempt was "hopeless from the start." Nevertheless Tilo agreed that they must try. According to his recollection,

> Immediately after the Treaty of Rapallo, Rathenau, who was Foreign Minister at the time, and one of the shrewdest and most highly educated men in world affairs I have ever met, strongly urged my brother-in-law to take over a big concession in Russia, so as to prove that German commercial interests were prepared to collaborate in a practical way in furthering the aims of the treaty. It was quite typical of Bohlen that he at once consented, though it was obvious that there could be no question of the firm — then fighting desperately for its very existence — profiting from the transaction [dass dabei von Rentabilität für die im schwersten Existenzkampf stehende Firma keine Rede sein konte].[21]

Significantly, the only other director to understand Gustav's motives was Otto Wiedfeldt, who later became Weimar's ambassador to Washington. Walther Rathenau's signing of the Rapallo Treaty was one of the most controversial political acts of the decade. In addition to extensive trade agreements, the pact gave the Soviet Union its first important de jure recognition and canceled all war claims between the two countries. Russia's thirty-four other creditor nations were alarmed — they regarded bonds between Moscow and Berlin as ominous — and Germany's powerful rightists were enraged. On June 24 Rathenau was shot dead in the street, the third Weimar moderate to be assassinated that year.

The Russo-Krupp concordat went ahead without him; among other things, the USSR became the only foreign country to receive locomotives from Essen. Historically the firm had always turned eastward when the West became inhospitable, and the present agreement had two distinct advantages. It pleased the republic in Berlin and was approved by General von Seeckt, who was making his own private arrangements with the Russians. Since the Soviets had not signed the Versailles Treaty, they were under no obligation to respect its provisions — specifically, nothing prevented them from abetting secret German rearmament. Therefore the Krupp money thrown away on the Manytch project was money well lost. The destiny of the house of Krupp rode with the destiny of Germany. The firm could prosper only if the nation, and particularly the nation's army, was rising. Given a powerful, aggressive government, all else would follow. The present government was neither. But elements within it were ambitious. As long as Krupp cooperated with them, they would not permit the great House to fall. And when their hands found the helm, the dynasty in Essen would ride to glory with them.

✠ ✠ ✠

In the West the Rapallo pact was regarded as the illegitimate child of what had begun as a respectable conference in Genoa, where an international congress had gathered to ponder Russia's general problems and Germany's debt. Finding the other delegates hostile and unrealistic, the Weimar and Soviet diplomats had departed and struck their own bargain. The French were furious, and when the Germans begged for a reparations moratorium at the end of the year, the vindictive Premier Poincaré decided to occupy the Ruhr. On January 10, 1923, the troops marched. Belgians joined them, and military government was established by a Mission Interaliée de Contrôle des Usines et des Mines (Micum). Micum's proclamation of martial law was followed by censorship of the press, confiscation of private property, and the expulsion of 147,000 people. The Italians declined to participate. The British went further. In a stiff note they protested that the "Franco-Belgian action . . . was not a sanction authorized by the treaty." It was, in fact, extraordinary. That sort of thing wasn't supposed to happen in peacetime Europe. Despite the tragic sweep of events since then, to Kruppianer who remember the 1920's "the invasion" still means the occupation of 1923. The invaders felt they were dealing from strength; the area they had sealed off was only sixty miles long and twenty-eight miles wide, but because of the intense concentration of German industry there, poilus had seized 85 percent of the country's coal, 80 percent of its steel and iron production, and the source of 70 percent of its marketable goods. Weimar, though aware of this, knew that all this wealth would be useless to Paris and Brussels unless the natives cooperated. Therefore the German government called for passive resistance. The French and Belgians countered by declaring the Ruhr to be in a state of siege.[22]

On January 9, two days before the first troops in horizon blue entered Essen, Gustav sent word to his men to be calm. For over two months they obeyed. The resistance, though sullen, remained submissive. But daily the pressures within men mounted. The invaders' stranglehold on Germany's economy began to tell in thousands of little ways and in one big one which every workman understood. Inflation was driving the mark down at bewildering speed; a year of this and all savings and pensions would be forfeited. Kruppianer called the occupation "die Bajonette," the bayonet. They were in a mood to strike back, and as Easter approached, with its reminders of the violence two years ago, workers and management reached a tacit agreement. Siren cords hung in every shop; in the event of trouble — an accident, say, or a burst furnace — anyone could pull them. It was now understood that should französische soldiers attempt to enter the factories the tocsin would be sounded. No one planned beyond that. They seem to have believed that a show of muscle by a mass of German men would intimidate die Bajonette.[23]

At 7 A.M. on the morning of Easter Saturday, March 31, a Lieutenant Durieux of the 160th French Infantry appeared on Altendorferstrasse with eleven men and a machine gun. They were there to take an inventory of the vehicles in Krupp's zentrale Garage, directly across the street from the Hauptverwaltungsgebäude. The lieutenant hadn't even been authorized to borrow a truck, and Krupp knew it; yesterday French headquarters in Düsseldorf had telephoned him, explaining the purpose of the patrol. But he hadn't passed the word along. Perhaps his domestic situation was accountable for his silence. Villa Hügel's guest rooms were now occupied by a French general and his staff. Forty years later Alfried would remember this as the most bitter experience of his youth, and undoubtedly it heightened family tempers. Naturally no one spoke to the uninvited guests, but that didn't prevent the general's giving orders to the servants, including instructions to shut windows and turn up the heat. Gustav left the castle perspiring each morning and arrived in his office bloody-minded. He was disposed to disregard French messages from Düsseldorf, though whether he deliberately ignored this one or actually forgot it is irrelevant. From the first day of die Bajonette bloodshed had been inevitable. If Gustav Krupp was to blame for what followed, so was Raymond Poincaré, un imbécile, that year, malgré lui.[24]

Lieutenant Durieux, a very small man who was about to appear briefly in the very center of the European stage, had trouble getting into the zentrale Garage. The superintendent was two hours late for work — difficult to credit at Krupp's, but there it is. At nine o'clock the man appeared, gave the kepis a lowering glance, unlocked the door, and admitted them. Instantly the Krupp fire department siren next door began to shriek. Durieux, seeing the red trucks, naturally assumed there was a blaze somewhere. Methodically he started to count bumpers. But now the Hauptverwaltungsgebäude whistle was screaming too. Within the next several minutes they were joined by over five thousand other *Sirenen*. Astonished, the young French officer sought out the superintendent and asked him what the hideous concert meant. "Down tools," the man replied. Durieux rushed to the door, and sure enough, as far as he could see Altendorferstrasse was one dense mass of workers' caps. At the subsequent trial he estimated the crowd at thirty thousand, and no German accused him of exaggerating.[25]

Meanwhile, what of Gustav? He was in a position to intervene — the bay window of his office overlooked the entire scene — and he did nothing. Arguing that he was out of touch is absurd. His elaborate switchboard reached every foreman in the plant. Moreover, we know that he used it to telephone the main garage. He inquired anxiously whether his limousine had been scratched in the melee, then told the superintendent to keep an eye on it. That, incredibly, was his only order while the sirens continued to sound. They blew for an hour and a half. During that period the lieutenant concluded that his position here was precarious. He had, after all, less than a dozen men. At any instant this vast herd of grimy men might sweep in and take the entire patrol from the rear; therefore he retreated to another, smaller garage on the side opposite the fire station. The machine gun was set up in the entrance and trained on the mob, which edged back a bit. Durieux's new position had one fatal defect, however. The structure was equipped with steam jets for cleaning machines, and the controls were on the roof. (Five days later a Krupp executive convinced a group of foreign correspondents that there were no such jets, but as surviving Kruppianer recall, he was showing them the other, *zentrale Garage*.)

As long as the *Sirenen* kept keening the crowd was quiet. It stood, transfixed. Here a cap bobbed, there a soot-smudged face peered over a shoulder; otherwise no one moved. Then, at 10:30, the shrieking whistles died away. It was like a signal. The front rank began to edge forward. Exactly what happened during the next thirty minutes is unclear. Some of Durieux's men said they were pelted by stones and lumps of coal, and two poilus insisted they saw workmen holding revolvers. If pistols were there, the lieutenant himself missed them. He was struck by no flying objects, saw none around him, and had made up his mind to stare down the mob when the steam began to hiss. Two Kruppianer on the roof had turned the cocks wide open; a thick, scathing mist was filling the building. Durieux, half blinded by his own sweat, ordered the riflemen and the machine gunner to fire a volley over the heads of the throng. Either the workmen were too excited to be intimidated or — more likely — those in front were pushed from behind. In any event, they pressed closer, and this time, at 11 A.M., the lieutenant told the patrol to aim at the men. He waited a moment, decided that there was no other solution, and gave the command, "*Commencez le feu!*"

The stuttering gunfire was heard everywhere. Next morning's edition of the *New York Times* carried the page one headline FRENCH KILL 6 MEN, WOUND 30 OTHERS IN FIGHT AT KRUPP'S.[26]

It was worse than that. When Kruppianer belonging to the German Red Cross had moved into the no-man's-land between the machine gun and their retreating comrades (a rescue operation requiring conspicuous bravery, for they wore no brassards) Altendorferstrasse was a chaos of smoke, steam, and blood. Clearly the marksmen had aimed at vital organs, and at that range they couldn't miss. As the first Krupp doctor to reach the casualties observed, the proximity of the victims had produced "terrible gaping wounds." Altogether there were thirteen dead, including five apprentices in their teens, and fifty-two wounded.[27]

All Germany was outraged. "Many a heart breaks viewing this misery," said former chancellor Karl Josef Wirth, and the SPD issued a statement denouncing the "bloody Easter in the Ruhr." The French general at Villa Hügel ordered tanks and a battalion of machine gunners from Düsseldorf in hope of preventing reprisals. It was impossible. That same afternoon a Belgian motorcyclist, a French police agent, and two French engineers were attacked, beaten, and robbed. Saboteurs blew up an Essen bridge. In neighboring Mülheim veterans of the Rote Soldatenbund stormed the city hall and held it for twenty-four hours. Hand grenades were thrown at French soldiers in Düsseldorf, and a poilu sentry was murdered in Essen's Hauptbahnhof by a gunman lurking in a ventilator shaft. The sentinel received no sympathy abroad. The massacre on Altendorferstrasse had preempted the world's attention. French editorial writers were mute, and the British and American press was almost as indignant as Germany's. The *Nation* called it "savagery" and declared that "a handful of French soldiers lost their heads in Essen and slaughtered eleven [*sic*] workmen at the Krupp works without a hair of their own heads being touched or threatened." "This," warned the *Spectator*, "is the way to increase German resistance, not to stop it."[28]

By now even Poincaré should have understood that. The general in Hügel did; he announced that his troops would be withdrawn from Essen for the funeral. But Paris remained implacable. Essen was stiffly informed that since the sentry's killer had escaped, the city would be fined 100,000 marks. For Germans the penalty was merely one more nail in the cross; a Berlin newspaper cartoonist depicted Poincaré at a table, knife and fork in hand, carving up a mutilated child labeled *Krupp*. Delegations from everywhere were approaching Essen for the burial, which had to be delayed ten days while Nationalists, Communists, Socialists, Catholics, Protestants, and even freethinkers and Christian Scientists disputed as to who should dominate the services. In the end Gustav swept them all aside. The men had died for *die Firma*, he declared. Therefore *he* would be the chief mourner. The visiting deputations would, however, be allowed to march in the cortege. Given the national fever, a memorable spectacle was inevitable, but Krupp had spent his youth studying ceremonial pomp; he had resolved to give the thirteen victims a state funeral, and the consequent ritual eclipsed every other funeral in the history of the Ruhr, including the obsequies for Alfred and Fritz.[29]

Actually it was a national rite. An hour after dawn on April 10 flags were lowered to half-staff all over Germany, and church bells began tolling in every town and city. The Reichstag met as a congregation, praying for the slain workers. In Essen, Kruppianer wearing white armbands directed traffic as three hundred thousand mourners lined the four-mile route from gate number 28 to Ehrenfried Cemetery — reserved for Esseners who died performing acts of heroism — where thirteen graves had been dug. Inside the great marble entrance hall of the Hauptverwaltungsgebäude the thirteen coffins lay in a single rank, draped in red, white, and black national colors and flanked by a Catholic bishop and a Protestant pastor. In the gallery overhead the Konzern's five-hundred-man choir had been divided into two groups; half sang a recessional while the other half chanted a Mass. The haunting scene was illumined only by candelabra, and as the entire chorus joined voices in the amen, Krupp stepped into this dim light to deliver his eulogy. He was incapable of a moving oration, but the magic of his name and the drama he had created were enough; when he crossed the hall to embrace the martyrs' widows and children they sobbed convulsively.[30]

Outside the procession formed: four hundred massed German flags; the caissons, Gustav marching alone behind them with bowed head; the surviving relatives; and forty delegations of men bearing black wreaths on their chests, led by Kumpels in their traditional costumes, their mine lights focused on Krupp like spotlights. The miners were there because one of the victims had been a Kumpel — no one ever asked why he hadn't been underground the morning of the massacre — but most of the other mourners weren't even from the Ruhr. They were Bavarians, Silesians, Saxons, Pomeranians, Württembergers, East Prussians; they represented every social and economic class and Germany's entire political spectrum; and when, at the graves, the bishop flung wide his arms and cried the single word *"Totschlagen!"* (Murder!), the deep passions of the fallen Reich were rekindled in a long, heavy silence. The hush was broken by the sound of an approaching aircraft. Though French infantrymen were absent, a single flyer had been observing the cortege from a Nieuport overhead. He chose this moment to buzz the cemetery. The biplane roared overhead at treetop height. The *Bajonette* was still doing its utmost to see that the wound remained unhealed.[31]

✠     ✠     ✠

And now it was about to be salted. The triumph of Krupp's pageantry seems to have unhinged Micum. Those who felt contrite went all the way; a young French lieutenant named Étienne Bach emerged from an Essen church after Holy Communion, apologized to his German fellow worshipers in a broken voice, and then publicly divested himself of his uniform. Bach's superiors went the other way. They were determined to humiliate Krupp. Twice during the next three weeks he was interrogated by French officers, and when he left for Berlin at the end of the month with two of his directors to attend a meeting of the Prussian Privy Council, warrants were issued for the arrest of all three of them, charging them with "inciting a riot" on Easter Saturday. The French timing strongly suggests that this was meant to be no more than a gesture, that Krupp was expected to stay out of the Ruhr. Expatriated, he could have been traduced as a fugitive and a coward. Indeed, certain questions asked of him after his return May 1 suggest that he had been marked as a scapegoat. On the third day of his trial an officer angrily demanded why he had come back. His colleagues had remained in the capital. Hadn't he known he faced prison? Gustav nodded shortly and answered, "My absence might be construed as incriminating my directors or as evidence of a guilty conscience on my own part." Why then, he was asked, hadn't he insisted that the other two join him? According to the transcript he replied, "I am ready enough to go to jail myself, even though I know I am innocent. But I do not choose to ask others to do it!" (*Von anderen Herren verlange ich das nicht!*)[32]

It is entirely possible that he had asked them *not* to do it. Krupp alone in the dock was far simpler for people to grasp. The funeral on April 10 had taught him the pull of martyrdom, and from the opening session of the hearings in Werden, just across the Ruhr River from Villa Hügel, he deliberately courted that fate. It was a skillful performance. The corseted little martinet had more blind spots than most men, and he was confounded by the great strategies of his time, but he was a crafty tactician. It should be added that his antagonists were extremely stupid. They frankly described the proceedings as military, and German headlines shouted, KRUPP VOR DEM FRANZÖSISCHEN KRIEGSGERICHT! (Krupp in front of a French court martial!). Naturally every German was on his side. The prosecution compounded this blunder. They had the facts of the massacre all wrong. Indeed, the officer who made the final plea to the court, a Captain Duvert, didn't even know how many poilus had been in the garage. Though German newspapermen were excluded from the courtroom, *Figaro* reported Duvert's summation: "Picture to yourself the directors, the great leaders of the immense Krupp works, remaining impassive in their offices when the mob, at their instigation, threatened to massacre ten poor French soldiers! Imagine their smile as they watched the spectacle from behind the windows of their offices — that smile that they had during the war — their generals wore that smile when German troops burned French villages and massacred their inhabitants!"[33]

The court fined the unsmiling Krupp 100 million marks and sentenced him to fifteen years in prison. "For a verdict like this," the *Berliner Tageblatt* thundered, "we have a parallel only in the Dreyfus case. . . . Those who witnessed the pleadings on Tuesday must have come away with the feeling that the object of the trial was not to attain justice, but frankly to destroy an enemy, to crush an obstacle in the path of French ambition." On May 9 Krupp was transferred to Düsseldorf prison under heavy guard, and German saboteurs observed the day by blowing up the French barracks in Dortmund. (The French retaliated by arresting the German chief of police.) Yet Gustav's life in jail was not the hardship that the public thought it to be. The prison was run by Germans, and his cell was twice the size of any other in its block. Bernhard Menne, a Düsseldorf journalist who had been picked up for making francophobic speeches, noted that the warden gave the eminent inmate from Essen the freedom of the prison yard. Krupp's door was never locked, and each day a committee from the German Red Cross called upon him bearing gifts — to the irritation of the other inmates, who got none. He even had visitors, though the French had expressly forbidden it. Tilo von Wilmowsky called on a British friend in Cologne and acquired forged English passports for himself and Bertha. As his wife entered the cell Gustav rose, beaming. He said, *"Nicht wahr, jetzt darf ich mich doch wirklich mit Recht einen Kruppianer nennen"* (Well, now I really have a perfect right to call myself a Kruppianer, haven't I)?[34]

He did indeed. Alfred *der Grosse* couldn't have handled himself better. Nor could Gustav have chosen a better time to be behind bars. Outside, galloping inflation was running away with the country. In June the mark declined to 100,000 for the dollar, in July to 200,000, in August to 5,000,000. On October 23, the day of the final collapse, a dollar bill brought 40 billion marks in banks and 60 billion in the black market. Tilo, running the firm while his brother-in-law lay back chewing Red Cross candy, was paying the men every other day, and a worker still needed a wheelbarrow full of bills to buy a loaf of bread. On June 10 the baron had, with the permission of the government, begun issuing *Kruppmarks* — notes varying in value between 100 marks and 200 million marks. They looked more impressive than the government's, and in Krupp stores they were worth more. Subsequent issues were dated July 10, August 14, September 5, and December 31. By then they were the only currency in the Ruhr worth anything at all, which was good news for Kruppianer who lived from day to day but shattering to those whose future security was tied to the firm's pension plans, now bankrupt. The heaviest blow fell upon a handful of loyal workers who had become stockholders in the firm. The previous year Gustav, casting about for ready cash and finding none, had offered 100,000 of Bertha's shares to his employees. Some thirty men had exchanged their savings for certificates. When the mark began to tumble he had bought the shares back with money which was now worthless. Their disillusion might have spread quickly if he had remained in his office, but as a national hero he was immune.[35]

Had he remained free, doubtless his prestige would have shrunk in other ways, for he was a member of established authority, which was having a dreadful year. During Krupp's third week of imprisonment heavy guerrilla fighting broke out all over the Ruhr. At the end of May, and again on August 20, three-quarters of a million steel and coal workers, including Kruppianer, went on strike. They struck blindly; the walkouts solved nothing. In Essen and Düsseldorf terrorists stalked Frenchmen. Incidents became so frequent that they were no longer reported in the foreign press — that summer was one continuous eruption of sniper shots and grenade explosions. Events were hopelessly out of control, though the government in Paris was reluctant to admit it. On October 22 its puppets proclaimed a Ruhr-Rhineland Republic in Aachen and Düren. Too weak to survive a plebiscite, it dissolved, and the dreary task of withdrawing the bayonet began. France had lost face, but so had Weimar's leaders. Chancellor Wilhelm Cuno's government fell; Gustav Stresemann, his successor, abandoned passive resistance, and the Germans agreed to discuss a resumption of reparations payments. It was not a popular decision. In November, Ludendorff, who had been brooding in Munich, joined the new Nationalsozialistische Deutsche Arbeiterpartei in an attempted putsch. Though the attempted uprising was a failure, the name of Adolf Hitler was heard outside Bavaria for the first time, and the name of his party appeared in headlines so often that it was abbreviated to Nazi. As an outsider ragging the country's entrenched plutocracy he had a large following, while everyone trying to maintain order was on the defensive. In Essen a newspaper cameraman photographed Bertha and Hindenburg during a street corner conversation. The *Feldmarschall* was in uniform; Bertha (who had become progressively more dowdy) wore a long baggy overcoat and spats. Abroad the picture appeared under the caption *German Hearts That Beat As One in the Ruhr*, which was probably correct, though they certainly do not appear to have been beating happily. Both faces were strained and anxious. Studying them, one feels that they would have been delighted to share Gustav's dungeon.[36]

His days there were numbered. The Ruhr had become too important to be immobilized for long; the impact of the occupation could not be confined to Germany. When the franc declined 25 percent Paris was under pressure to get out fast, and after seven months of Krupp's sentence had been served he was granted a "Christmas amnesty." Micum required him to sign a paper declaring that he had been justly convicted, but that fooled no one. Upon his return to Essen the entire city turned out to welcome him, and when he entered the *preussische Staatsrat* meeting room in Berlin his fellow councillors rose to their feet in silent tribute. Henceforth anyone who crossed Gustav would be courting trouble. Konrad Adenauer was a vigorous, popular Bürgermeister of Cologne, yet when he rejected Krupp's design for an arched bridge over the Rhine — Adenauer thought a suspension bridge more practical — his mail suddenly turned ugly. Anonymous correspondents felt he had betrayed Germany. Krupp's debt to the blundering French was that great.[37]

The firm's postwar recovery began that winter, though no one would have guessed it at the time. Conditions in Essen were appalling. The retreating French army took 21 new locomotives and 123 trucks with them, and in their wake they left disorder. On his first visit to the Hauptverwaltungsgebäude after his release Gustav saw looters staggering from Krupp stores, their arms loaded with plunder. The streets were unsafe, even in daylight. Armed men roamed the center of the city; there had been holdups in the administration building itself. The boardroom was guarded, and inside it the Vorstand slumped gloomily in their chairs. Once more they recommended that Bertha sell out, and once more Gustav wouldn't hear of it. Krupp reserves included huge blocks of shares in foreign corporations, he reminded them. The cushion was there if they needed it. Meantime he intended to clear away the confusion left by inflation. As things stood now they had no idea how solvent they were, therefore he instructed Haux to transfer all bookkeeping to the gold standard. He had also been giving some thought to that farm project on the Russian steppe. If the project really was impossible, they had better write it off, and he wanted his brother-in-law to go there and see. Tilo went. He found acres of sunflowers, flax, and wild tulips, but not a grain of wheat. The young German manager was devoting himself to the works of Goethe and Kant. Sowing grain was pointless, Herr Klette explained — the lusty spring gales blew it away, and if the topsoil were plowed, the wind took that, too. "Doomed to failure," Tilo wired Gustav, and turned the vast tract over to a thirty-year-old Soviet functionary named Anastas Ivanovich Mikoyan.[38]

From the Hauptverwaltungsgebäude Krupp launched a dozen new projects. To compensate the USSR for his failure on the steppe he trained young Russians in his school for apprentices. His salesmen entrained for Moscow and Peking with brochures advertising his agricultural equipment; their missions were profitable from the start. His laboratories produced a new steel tougher than anything in metallurgical history. They crushed cobalt and tungsten carbide to powder, pressed it in 1,600-degree heat, and honed it with diamonds. Christened Widia (from *wie Diamant*, like diamond), the steel was first exhibited at the Leipzig trade fair of 1926. By 1928 the firm had enrolled 30,000 new Kruppianer, and the following May Gustav opened a blast furnace factory in Borbeck, an Essen suburb. Next year American engineers employed by Chrysler concluded that his Enduro KA-2 (Krupp Austinitic Steel) was the finest stainless steel anywhere; accordingly, it was used to cap the tower of the Chrysler Building in Manhattan, where it has sparkled ever since. Other Krupp technicians had developed a new method of converting low-grade iron ore into high-grade steel. They called it the Renn bloomery process and installed it in the Grusonwerk. With it, the firm overcame its wartime loss of ore fields in Lorraine, Spain, and Latvia. Mining rights were bought up all over Scandinavia and Newfoundland. They came cheap, for no other steel-maker could afford them, and with their yield Krupp re-established his prewar pre-eminence.[39]

The drafters of Versailles hadn't anticipated this. Schneider assumed that the return of Lorraine would guarantee French supremacy. But after the occupation of 1923 Paris lost its militancy and shrugged off warnings that the anvil of the Reich was beginning to look alarmingly like the weapons forge which had devastated France twice in a half-century. The Weimar Republic, on the other hand, was supporting Gustav and his fellow Schlotbarone in an intricate strategy based on subsidies, superior *kruppsche* technology, and one conspicuously unfair trade practice. Concentrating on the new ores, the Germans built a high-cost steel industry which monopolized the Ruhr's coal production. Deprived of that coal, the French mills fell behind. Hoping to redress the balance, they proposed the formation of a cartel. The Internationale Rohstahlgemeinschaft, established at Luxembourg in 1926, looked foolproof on paper. In practice it institutionalized French inferiority. Each of the member nations — France, England, Belgium, Luxembourg, Austria, Czechoslovakia, and Germany — agreed to eliminate "ruinous competition" by sticking to an annual quota. The Germans signed, watched the others hew to the line — and then broke the rules themselves. That was the sharp practice. The cartel provided that any member who did that would have to pay a penalty. At first the smokestack barons quietly paid. Then they threatened to quit the agreement unless their fines were cut and their quota increased. By then the cosignees had become afflicted with that peculiar paralysis which was to typify all victims of Teutonic bluster in the 1930's. They stood by impotently while the throbbing Ruhr exceeded its quota by four million tons a year. Those who wondered aloud where all that steel was going were reprimanded for warmongering.[40]

✠    ✠    ✠

Most Kruppianer had never heard of a *Kartell* and were probably incapable of grasping the concept. They had fathomed the meaning of the Easter Saturday massacre, however—with that maddening lack of logic which had become the despair of Germany's neighbors, they held annual services for the slain thirteen and forgot the much bloodier Easter three years earlier—and they had grasped the motives behind the sentencing of Gustav. They knew that pension payments had been resumed. Krupp's name retained its magic; if something was wrong, someone else must be to blame. Something, in that dismal decade, was always wrong. Gustav stayed on his feet, but he stumbled often. For all its brilliant local successes the firm lacked its old momentum. In 1928, and again in 1929, payrolls had to be cut back. Workmen blamed Berlin, never the Hauptverwaltungsge-bäude. They doted on Bertha and her children and hung pictures of the family on their parlor walls, and when Margarethe Krupp died on March 24, 1931, all Essen went into mourning; every house wore broad stripes of crepe like huge black bandages. The only outsider to witness the rites in Villa Hügel was Karl Sabel, an enterprising young Ruhr newspaperman. Sabel had rented a silk hat, frock coat, and the biggest limousine in Düsseldorf. Alighting from it, he eyed the Krupp footman at the square castle portico coldly. The man bowed low and Sabel walked in on what at first seemed to be a re-enactment of a Teuton myth. In the garden room, surrounded by her brother Felix's romantic murals and two hundred invited guests, the body of Fritz Krupp's widow lay on an elevated slab like a dead queen. The services had just opened with a long eulogy from the Bürgermeister. He finished and Hügel's maids, dressed in spotless blue uniforms, approached the coffin one by one, each laying a single flower on Marga's breast. (Gustav, the efficiency expert, had allowed them four minutes and 35 seconds for this. Upon departing, Sabel noticed, they immediately took up their chores.) Outside, three hundred thousand people lined the route to Kettwig Gate cemetery. Most of them were too young to remember the golden years of Fritz, and only a handful recalled the night the great Alfred had been carried down the hill. Nevertheless Marga had been a link with the enchanted past, when guns were made and sold profitably but never fired in anger; and so they were bereft.[41]

She had represented something else that was cherished: Krupp's benevolent paternalism. That wasn't mourned because it was still very much alive. The average *kruppsche* workman blessed the family for whatever prosperity he enjoyed, was grateful for its many small generosities, and was never curious about what was going on in the front office. It is too bad no one peeked, for quite a lot was happening—enough, in fact, to have startled every chief of state in the world. Gustav made a great fuss over Widia, Enduro KA-2, and his excellent locomotives. Most of his time was occupied with other matters, however, and in them lies the answer to the nagging riddle of how he kept going under the crippling restrictions of Versailles. Deprived of his chief source of revenue, he became a financial manipulator. At one time he was operating entirely with Dutch guilders; putting up some of the stock squirreled away in Holland as collateral, he received the equivalent of 100 million marks from the Netherlands. Then, in 1925, he had acquired a massive transfusion from the United States. The loan was for ten million dollars, though he was rather surly about it. Under German law, Krupp shops had to be posted with notices announcing that they had been mortgaged until the loan was paid off. Gustav called a meeting of all white-collar workers and told them, "*Tun sie alles, damit die verdammten Schilder so schnell wie möglich wieder verschwinden!*" (I hope everybody will do his best to make certain that these damned things are torn down as soon as possible!).[42]

They came down within two years, though white-collar perseverance had nothing to do with their removal. In the winter of 1926–1927 Gustav achieved two coups. The first was the settlement of his dispute with Vickers. In July 1921 he had filed his claim in Sheffield, asking £260,000 for the use of his *Krupp-Patentzünder* during the war. Under the circumstances this seemed to him to be quite reasonable. Translated into battlefield terms, it estimated that the British had fired 4,160,000 shells and killed a German with every other one. Vickers demurred. The matter was referred by Krupp to the Anglo-German Mixed Arbitration Tribunal, and hearings were held in 1924. Understandably there are few references to this delicate issue in the Krupp archives, but Vickers's records disclose that "After several adjournments the final hearing was postponed *sine die*. Eventually, in August 1926, a compromise was reached under which Vickers paid Krupps £40,000 and in October of that year the proceedings before the Tribunal were closed." It was some compromise. Sheffield was insisting the English had used only 640,000 shells. Again translated, so slight an expenditure would have meant four casualties for each shot. That was preposterous, but losers can't be choosers, and in the 1920's forty thousand British pounds was most welcome in the Hauptverwaltungsgebäude.[43]

Even better was a loan of 60 million gold marks from German banks which permitted Haux to pay off the *verdammte* Yankees, and best of all was an outright grant of 75 millions from Berlin to compensate Krupp for his losses under the French, though here we are getting into something else. Determining exactly how much money the government gave Essen in the fifteen years between the fall of the Second Reich and the rise of the Third is impossible, because both the giver and the receiver were keeping several sets of books. According to Haux's balance sheet for the fiscal year 1924–1925, for example, the firm lost 59 million marks. Deficits during those twelve months ranged from less than a million at Rheinhausen to nearly 17 million in Kiel. But these figures are meaningless, because they omit income from certain illicit activities abroad and the steady siphoning of funds from the Weimar Republic's tax coffers. These subsidies to Krupp have been calculated at anywhere from 300 millions up. To maintain his

Bertha Krupp (1886-1957) in 1909 with two-year-old Alfried (1907-1967)

Gustav Krupp (1870-1950) addressing Krupp centenary guests in the reception hall of the Hauptverwaltungsgebäude, August 8, 1912. To th the German General Staff. To the left, Admiral Tirpitz with his staff.

, the Kaiser with his Kaiserin and Bertha and Margarethe Krupp. The
y and civil cabinets sit behind them.

Bertha, five-year-old Alfried, and Gustav rehearsing for the Krupp
centennial tournament in 1912.

Kaiser Wilhelm II marches through Essen with Gustav
on the eve of World War I.

The Gusstahlfabrik in 1912

A "Big Bertha" captured near Ypres in World War I.

Artist's conception of Krupp's *Pariskanone* of 1918.

Blühnbach, the Krupp castle in the Austrian Alps.

Krupp gunworks early in the century.

Walzwerk I (Rolling Mill) in 1920.

idle arms forges that long they must have been tremendous. Yet surviving documents provide only fragments of evidence; *e.g.*, two comments from ex-chancellors: an entry in Stresemann's diary for June 6, 1925 *"Dann mussten wir für Krupp 50 Millionen Mark verschaffen"* — (Then we had to raise 50 million marks for Krupp) and a letter from Karl Josef Wirth written to Gustav on August 9, 1940, immediately after Krupp became the first German to receive the War Merit Cross First Class.[44]

Wirth's congratulatory message is jarring to those who believe that Weimar was a noble experiment which was sabotaged by the Nazis. In addition, it contradicts the view that democracy and rampant militarism cannot coexist. They were working together smoothly less than two years after the armistice, when a Sternberg dentist was designing the first swastika and Adolf Hitler was still an obscure demagogue furtively organizing brown-shirted squads (*Ordnertruppen*) for street fighting. Not only was Wirth the leader of the German government in this period; on May 11, 1921, he signed Weimar's official acceptance of the Versailles Treaty, promising to respect his country's obligations under it:

> On the strength of the decision by the Reichstag, I have been charged to declare, as requested, the following, in the name of the new government and in connection with the resolution of the Allied Powers dated 5 May 1921:
> The German Government is determined. . . . To carry out without reservation or delay the measures relative to the disarmament of military, naval, and aerial forces as specified in the memorandum by the Allied Powers dated 21 January 1921.[45]

His word was no more reliable than Hitler's. Although this committed him, both as chancellor and as a man of his word, to seeing that "The manufacture of arms, munitions, or any war material, shall only be carried out in factories or works the location of which shall be communicated to and approved by the Governments of the Principal Allied and Associated Powers, and the number of which they retain the right to restrict," and bound him to prohibit "importation into Germany of arms, munitions, and war material of every kind" and the dispatch "to any foreign country" of "any military, naval, or air mission," he was flagrantly violating both the letter and spirit of his pledge at the moment he signed it. As he later wrote Gustav, he recalled "with satisfaction the years of 1920 till 1923, when together with [Krupp] Director Dr. [Otto] Wiedfeldt both of us were able to lay new foundations for the development of the German armament technique (*um neue Grundlagen für den technischen Fortschritt der deutschen Rüstung zu legen*) through your great and most significant firm. Herr Reich President von Hindenburg . . . had been informed of it. His reaction also was very creditable, though nothing of this has as yet been disclosed to the public. I also write down these lines to add them to my files, which already contain the . . . letter of Dr. Wiedfeldt of 1921, stating that your most respected firm was assured of ten years service for the government on account of my initiative as the Reich Chancellor and Reich Minister of Finance, by releasing considerable sums of the Reich for the preservation of German armament technique" (*wurden beträchtliche Summen vom Reich an die Firma gezahlt, um die deutsche Rüstungstechnologie zu erhalten*).[46]

Wirth cautioned that he was setting all this down "in a purely personal and confidential way," since the government of the Third Reich had spread the word that "any publication about previous preparations for the recovery of national freedom would be discouraged. All the same, he added, "our hearts are very much in the events of those days." Gustav's heart certainly was. Nor could he see any reason to keep quiet about it. The summer he received Wirth's letter he had become convinced that the betrayal of the November criminals had been avenged and that he would end his life in a Europe ruled by Germany's New Order. Therefore he triumphantly set down the facts of Krupp's secret rearming after the armistice of 1918. Captured by American troops in April 1945, his papers show a remarkable talent for international intrigue. Though he omitted the size of Weimar's subsidies (that was in Haux's department, and by then Haux was dead) he included virtually everything else, including details which would have rung alarm bells in the chancelleries of the '20's. Together with certain military documents which also fell into American hands, they reveal the degree to which Krupp anticipated Hitler. At Versailles Ausländer thought they had deprived Germany of the tools of aggression. They were dreaming. And as they dreamed, Gustav carefully "*schmiedete das neue deutsche Schwert*" (forged the new German sword).

# 14

✠

# We've Hired Hitler!

Chancellor Wirth had been converted to the crusade for "military freedom" (*Wehrfreiheit*)[1] by Generaloberst von Seeckt, who was both *Chef* of the Reichswehr and, behind the scenes, rearmament's gray eminence. Gustav needed no persuasion. As he wrote twenty years afterward, "Everything within me revolted against the idea . . . that the German people would be enslaved forever." He felt that "If Germany should ever be reborn, if it should shake off the chains of Versailles, the Krupp concern had to be prepared." Out of "the conviction that Germany must fight again to rise," understanding "the feelings of my workers, who to date had worked proudly for German arms," he had looked out across the still shops and unnaturally clear sunlight on Armistice Day 1918. "At that time," he recalled, "the situation appeared hopeless." Yet he believed he "knew the German man; therefore I never doubted that, although for the time being all indications were against it — one day a change would come." During the postwar troubles, while escorting his expectant wife to Sayneck and feasting on gold plate, he was pondering choices:

> *Die Maschinen waren zerstört, die Werkzeuge waren vernichtet — geblieben aber waren die Menschen: die Männer in den Konstruktionsbüros und in den Werkstätten, die den Geschützbau in glückhafter Zusammenarbeit zur letzten Vollendung gebracht hatten. . . . Gerade jetzt fühlte ich mich in den magischen Kreis einer festgefügten Werksgemeinschaft aufs stärkste einbezogen . . .*

The machines were destroyed, the tools were smashed, but the men remained, the men in the construction offices and workshops who, working in joyous harmony, had brought the technique of manufacturing German cannon to its ultimate perfection. Their skill had to be maintained at all costs . . . Despite all opposition I both wanted and had to maintain Krupp as an armament plant . . . I never felt the inner obligation for all my deeds more compellingly than in those fateful weeks and months of 1919 and 1920. Then I felt myself drawn into the magic circle of an established working community . . .[2]

Looking down from the pinnacle of 1941 into the trough of 1919–1920, Krupp thought that "The decisions I had to make at that time were perhaps the most difficult ones in my life." Yet he felt he could not shirk his duty, which was "through years of secret work, scientific and basic groundwork," to be ready "again to work for the German armed forces at the appointed hour without loss of time or experience." Later he came to believe it the greatest achievement of his career that "After the assumption of power by Adolf Hitler I had the honor to report to the Führer that Krupp stood ready after a short warm-up to begin the rearmament of the German people without any gaps of experience. The blood of the comrades of Easter Saturday had not been shed in vain."[3]

He might have added that his months in jail, by investing him with martyrdom, had not been wasted. But how did he achieve his miracle? The agreement which Wirth had signed, published in the July 15, 1921, evening *Deutscher Reichsanzeiger und Preussischer Staatsanzeiger* (German Reich Gazette and Prussian State Gazette), specified that "Friedrich Krupp A.G., Essen-Ruhr" was restricted to the manufacture of a single type of gun and could make only four of them a year. For the navy the firm was confined to just enough cannon, gun mountings, ammunition hoists, mechanical firing devices, and armor as might be needed to replace rusting equipment in Weimar's small fleet. Even this pittance was subject to supervision and inspection by the Allied Control Commission, which had been sent to Essen to breathe down Krupp's neck. Gustav loathed the commissioners and the SPD members in the factories who served as their unpaid staff.* He regarded them all as "snoopers" (*Schnüffler*), and even after the enemy officers had left the Ruhr he was incensed by the memory of the "uncouth, irreconcilable attitude, especially on the part of the French members of the Control Commission, as well as a widespread network of spies and denunciators. . . ."[4]

In those first years still another *ausländisch* force was poking around the Gusstahlfabrik. These were foreign correspondents who had come because there was so much curiosity abroad about the sinister name of Krupp. To a man they were, as Gustav gleefully put it, "hoodwinked." A representative of the *Christian Science Monitor* marveled at the ease with which designers of cannon were adjusting to railroad production. "Peace is taking its

---

* At great risk to themselves. As the decade advanced, more and more Social Democrats became victims of the right-wing *Femen* (political assassins), toward whom the Weimar courts were astonishingly lenient.

revenge at Krupp's," wrote the *Manchester Guardian*; "one can have no hesitation in affirming, after a visit at Krupp's, that everything connected with war industry has been scrapped away." The *Review of Reviews* was delighted to find that "a ridiculously small enclosure in one corner of a great shop is all that can now be devoted to the manufacture of ordnance"; *Living Age* observed that "The 1919–1920 balance sheet of Fried. Krupp contains the following memorable words: 'During the reported year, and for the first time in two generations, the Krupp works, according to the dispositions of the Treaty of Versailles, have produced no war materials' "; and the *Scientific American*, at Gustav's insistence, publicly apologized for giving its readers the impression that gun mounts were being illicitly shipped from Essen to Brazil. (The unfortunate magazine had seized upon the one transaction which was legal. Krupp was fulfilling a prewar order.) Several writers grew lyrical. One dispatched a lavish description of the Stammhaus — "Fried. Krupp's respected shrine, and the only tangible evidence to evoke the tradition of a mighty name" — while another, a correspondent for the *Literary Digest*, charmed his readers with an account of his reception by a *gemütlicher* old watchman "smoking a Rhineland pipe and smiling a wistful smile." The *Digest* man told how he toured the Gusstahlfabrik with Georg Karl Friedrich "Bruno" Baur, a Krupp director. "Germany's past is buried here," he quoted Herr Baur in conclusion, "and Germany's future lurks here likewise, in these old furnaces."[5]

Lurks was the word for it. If the newspapermen had put their heads together they would have noted an odd coincidence: all who had brought cameras were subsequently dismayed to find that their film couldn't be developed. Somehow every roll had been overexposed. Had they checked they would have further recalled that before leaving the plant they had been invited into a Hauptverwaltungsgebäude canteen for a light snack, courtesy of Krupp. While they ate, an infrared ray homed on their lenses. The reason for this was not — as an Essen legend has it — that one of the *Pariskanone* barrels had been set upright and surrounded by bricks, camouflaging it as a chimney. Nor — another myth — was it because Krupp was manufacturing baby carriages which would be disassembled and reassembled as machine guns. Kruppianer were subtler than that. Forbidden work was in progress, but at that stage nothing was being turned out. It was all on the drawing boards, and there was some apprehension that a newspaper photograph, innocently taken, might produce a print which would later be scanned by the skilled eye of an ordnance engineer.[6]

The futility of the Control Commission during its six years in Essen is something of a mystery. Its hourly movements were telegraphed ahead to the Hauptverwaltungsgebäude, of course, and hiding papers was easy; when the French occupied the Ruhr, Gustav summoned his artillery designers to his office, turned them and their plans over to an alert young executive, and sent them to the Berlin suburb of Spandau, where work continued in temporary quarters. Still, Krupp wasn't always so furtive. In late November 1925 Seeckt arrived at Villa Hügel to occupy the Kaiser's old apartment and make a five-day tour of the shops. The commission's mandate had four months to run, yet there is no record that the Generaloberst's visit stirred the curiosity of its members, or that their suspicions were aroused by the frequent departures of key ordnance technicians for countries which had been neutral during the war. Perhaps the sheer size of the works defeated them; perhaps their protracted exile in a bleak and hostile city had sapped their vitality; perhaps they had become embroiled in intramural squabbles. Gustav believed that the source of the "ridicule" directed at him, the advertisement of so long a list of peaceful products, diverted them: "Thus to the surprise of many people Krupp began to manufacture products which really appeared to be far distant from the previous work of an armament plant. Even the Allied snooping commissions were duped. Padlocks, milk cans, cash registers, track repair machines, trash carts, and similar small junk appeared really unsuspicious, and even locomotives and automobiles made an entirely civilian impression" (wirkten durchaus zivil). There is no doubt that the unwelcome guests were in fact "duped" by the "small junk" and by the big lie, periodically reiterated in Berlin by the legal division of the Weimar Reichswehrministerium, that "the Peace Treaty of Versailles is also a law of Germany, and by reason of this it is binding on all German citizens. This commitment even outranks the provisions of the German constitution." At the "behest of the Reichstag," members of the government who participated in "preparations for the mobilization of a Wehrmacht" could be "indicted before the state judicial court for criminal violation of their official duties under Article 59 of the constitution."[7]

These soporific words were last declaimed in January 1927. In the light of what is now known, it is scarcely possible that any general or flag officer wearing Weimar's uniform could have listened to them with anything except cynicism. The Diktat was discredited everywhere. To invoke its phrases, to agree that Germany should be limited to a 100,000-man army and a tiny navy, would have been regarded as a despicable act of collaboration. But the Offizierskorps knew the Defense Ministry wasn't serious. Far from trading with the enemy, the Reichswehr's civilian watchdogs were turning a blind eye toward feverish preparations for a rematch with the triumphant powers of 1918.

In imperial Germany it had been possible to keep the chancellor ignorant of military planning. Not so now. The Reichswehrminister, a politician, dominated his absurdly small staff — a lowly adjutant's office (Adjutantur). The lordly title of Commander-in-Chief (Oberbefehlshaber) had been abolished and replaced by the pedestrian Chief (Chef). There were two Chefs for the two services; they presided over the Army

Command (Heeresleitung), Seeckt's domain, and the Navy Command (Marineleitung). One army subdivision, the Troops Department (Truppenamt) was in fact functioning as a Generalstab, but no one admitted it, because Versailles had proscribed a German General Staff. Weimar's laymen were as tight-lipped as the uniformed men who, theoretically, were subordinate to them. "In 1938," General Telford Taylor would write after World War II, "a stupefied world was to gape in frightened amazement at the nation which had suddenly achieved such terrifying strength. How? Much of the story was in the Krupp files at Essen. . . . Truly, there was a deep continuity from the Weimar Republic to the Third Reich, as the Krupps and the generals knew."[8]

Obviously it was impossible to conduct rearmament in whispers. Once Gustav had pulled out all the stops "a visitor to the Ruhr," noted William L. Shirer, was "struck by the intense activity of the armament works, especially those of Krupp, chief German gunmakers for three quarters of a century," and even before the arms forges were rekindled there were portentous signs for those who could, or would, read them. As early as May 20, 1921, less than fourteen months after Gustav had taken his historic plunge and started the clandestine forging of *das neue deutsche Schwert*, the United States Army concluded an inquiry into new Krupp patents. "The investigation," it reported, disclosed "a rather striking circumstance in view of the conditions which Germany is supposed to observe as to disarmament and manufacture of war materials under her treaty obligations." American intelligence officers had found that of recent Essen patents 26 were for artillery control devices, 18 for electrical fire control apparatus, 9 for fuses and shells, 17 for field guns, and 14 for heavy cannon which could be moved only by rail. Secretary of War John W. Weeks made details available to the press, which ignored them. The reaction against Versailles was also strong among the victors. Feeling that they had gone too far in saddling Germany with war guilt, the former Allies entered that fateful period of overcompensation which eventually led to Munich. Circumstantial accounts of German air aces training a future Luftwaffe in Russia should have been verified. In fact they were dismissed or even applauded. England's *New Statesman*, then as now an eccentric publication, advanced the remarkable argument that France was a more fit subject for inspection of military activities than the defeated enemy, and that there was "no conceivable reason from the British point of view why Germany should not possess as many airplanes as France."[9]

The precise nature of Krupp's postwar activities in eastern Europe is elusive. Governments there are understandably closemouthed about it, and sources are confined to diplomats' autobiographies and Seeckt's incomplete, posthumous papers, which appeared during the early 1950's. Visiting Budapest on an official mission, Nicholas Snowden called upon a member of the Horthy-Bethlen cabinet in 1921. His host casually mentioned that German technicians were busily employed in a new Hungarian mill. Snowden became curious and, according to his memoirs, "learned that the Krupps, although ostensibly devoting the plant to the making of agricultural implements, were actually and secretly manufacturing arms."[10] This is doubtful. It is hearsay, it is unsupported by the Krupp archives, and it would have been pointless; Krupp had already acquired a weapons factory in Scandinavia. He needed only one, because he and Seeckt, agreeing that cannon rapidly became obsolescent, had decided to restrict production during the early '20's and concentrate on design. It is, however, entirely possible that Snowden's informant had correctly identified men from the Ruhr as Krupp gunsmiths. Their role would have been advisory, with Essen billing Budapest for their services. That was the pattern within the Soviet Union. Immediately after the signing of the Rapallo pact, Karl Bernardovich Radek, Trotsky's chief lieutenant, came to Berlin to solicit technical guidance for the USSRs' munitions industry. An agreement with him was negotiated in the apartment of Kurt von Schleicher, a future Weimar defense minister and chancellor who had served on Ludendorff's staff during the war. Seeckt's papers do not reveal the names of the negotiators, but evidently he and Schleicher represented the army; Gustav's emissary would logically have been Friedrich Wilhelm von Bülow, then manager of the Berlin office. Whoever they were, and whatever the fine print in their contract, the results benefited both parties. Krupp artisans presided over the manufacture of projectiles on assembly lines in the Urals and near Leningrad, including the Putilov works, which — like Schneider's shops in 1870 — had been strikebound when the government needed them most, and which were still disorganized. In return for Krupp know-how, Moscow set aside tracts of land for the Germans, who used it to test heavy artillery and instruct young fighter pilots. The terms of the bargain were scrupulously observed until 1935, when the Führer's repudiation of Versailles and affirmation of "military sovereignty" ended the need for dissembling. By then Seeckt's Russophilism had reaped a stunning harvest in technical advances and trained manpower.[11]

Throughout these furtive years Gustav's finest designers stayed in Berlin. Even after the *Bajonette* had been withdrawn from the Ruhr they continued to draft sketches in the capital's suburbs, where they could forget about control commissioners and consult ranking officers daily, and after two years they moved from Spandau into an office building in the heart of the capital. The decision, made by Krupp on the advice of the Heeresleitung, was one of the best-kept secrets of the decade. Berliners working on other floors had no idea of what was going on; neither did the men's wives. Indeed, there is much about the operation which evokes memories of Eric Ambler's early spy novels. On the hot, lazy morning of July 1, 1925, a van parked in Potsdam Square and perspiring workmen moved desks, file cabinets, and draftsmen's boards up nine flights of stairs to a suite on the top story. That afternoon nineteen nondescript men in business suits occupied the rooms and installed a new lock. Downstairs a small brass plate identified their firm as:

KOCH UND KIENZLE (E)
Primus Palast
4 Potsdamer Platz[12]

Koch and Kienzle sounds like a comedy team, but the operative letter (E) stood for *Entwicklung* (development). Here, a short walk from Seeckt's Inspection Office for Arms and Equipment (IWG), the ablest team of ordnance designers in the world quietly drew up specifications for the weapons which were to change the map of Europe. One of them was Fritz Tubbesing, then a chunky youth who was to become chief of the artillery construction office three years later and who, at this writing, is still active in the Hauptverwaltungsgebäude. As Tubbesing recalls, "Nobody noticed us, nobody bothered us, nobody even knocked on our door. There we were, practically on top of the Reichstag, and they didn't know it." Though the Reichstag didn't, the Reichswehr did. IWG locked files contained a Krupp code book; with it, officers could translate the cover names being used at Koch and Kienzle. The first tank, for example, was called an "agricultural tractor" (*landwirtschaftlicher Ackerbau Schlepper*). Later there were light, medium, and heavy tractors (*leichter Schlepper, mittelschwerer Schlepper, schwerer Schlepper*). Sometimes the engineers at 4 Potsdamer Platz forgot themselves. Once they submitted sketches for a heavy tractor equipped with a 7.5-cm. cannon. Another lapse — for which they were to pay dearly at Nuremberg, where Krupp's lawyers argued that the weapons the craftsmen worked on had been purely defensive — was a marginal reminder that "specifications for power tractors" (*i.e.*, self-propelled guns) "must meet the requirements for transportation on open railroad cars in Belgium and France." At the time, however, these slips passed unnoticed. IWG had nothing but praise for their paper work, and in a file memorandum Krupp himself described it as "an important step on the road to freedom." Toiling late, the men on the tenth floor developed eight types of heavy artillery, howitzers, and light field guns; a new, mobile 21-cm. mortar; and the tank family.[13]

In 1926 Seeckt retired. He was content. "There is only one way in which we shall be able to provide for the arming of great masses of troops," he had written after the armistice — to make "suitable arrangements with the industrialists of the nation." He had reached an understanding with just one, but Krupp counted more than all the others combined. Gustav's commitment to rearmament was total. As an intrafirm budget memo noted, he was pledging to the armed forces every coin he could lay his hands on, including "large hidden reserves entered on the first gold mark balance sheet from the profits of the pre–World War years."[14] In an annual report he wrote:

> In spite of numerous doubts, since 1919 the firm has decided, as the trustee of a historical heritage, to safeguard its irreplaceable experiences for the military potential of our nation, and to keep the employees and shops in readiness for later armament orders, if or when the occasion should arise. With this in mind, we set up our new production program in a pattern in which our employees could achieve and improve their experiences with arms, although the manufacture and sale of some of the products entailed big losses [. . . *schwere Verluste in sich schlossen*].[15]

✠ ✠ ✠

Two years before Seeckt bowed out, Admiral Paul Behncke, a Jutland veteran who had served as chief of Weimar's naval command, was piped ashore for the last time in Kiel. Unlike the flamboyant Tirpitz he was quickly forgotten by his countrymen, and in 1937 he died in obscurity, unhonored by his Führer. Yet Behncke, together with Krupp and Seeckt, had made the early Nazi triumphs possible. Unable to see over the horizon — with only their faith in the German character to assure them that a strong leader would emerge at the appointed hour — the admiral, the general, and the armorer had staked everything on the eventual resurrection of the mighty Reich they had known and loved. They had joined hands early, less than nine months after Chancellor Wirth had accepted the Allied terms on behalf of the country. After they had conferred, a Krupp memorandum noted that while "an official contract" between them was impossible "for political reasons," they had nevertheless reached "a gentleman's agreement" (*die Vereinbarung*). It added: "These most significant agreements of 25 January 1922 are the first step jointly taken by the *Reichswehrministerium* and Krupp to circumvent, and thereby to break down, the regulations of the Treaty of Versailles which strangle Germany's military freedom."*[16]

But Gustav's yearning for *Wehrfreiheit* exceeded even that of the officer corps. The year before, with no encouragement from Berlin, he had struck

---

* The extent of rearmament under the Weimar Republic may raise eyebrows. Skeptics are referred to two startling documents which were largely overlooked in the mountain of documents collected at Nuremberg. The first is a closely typed, 72-page Krupp memorandum bearing the title *Die Abteilung Artilleriekonstruktion der Fried. Krupp AG. und die Entwicklung der Heeresartillerie von November 1918 bis 1933* (The Artillery Construction Department of Fried. Krupp A.G. and the Development of Army Artillery from November 1918 to 1933). The second is a 76-page secret naval report written by a Captain Schüssler for the German Admiralty in 1937: *Veröffentlichung Nr. 15, Der Kampf der Marine gegen Versailles 1919–1935* (Service Publication No. 15, The Struggle of the Navy Against Versailles, 1919–1935). Since both were written under the Third Reich, when the government in power was claiming credit for *all* rearmament, they are doubly impressive.

the first blow at Versailles. Exchanging his patents and licenses for shares in the Swedish steel firm of Aktielbolaget Bofors, he had picked up enough voting rights to give him control over the firm's production. On April 1, 1921 one Chief Engineer Daur had checked out of gate 28 for a ten-year stay in Sweden. Daur wasn't a drafter of blueprints. He was a production man, and by the end of the year Bofors was turning out a weapon developed in Essen during the war, the 7.5-cm. mountain gun L/20. The L/20 had been shelved because it would have been useless on the western front. It was a matchless performer in hill country, however, and the Dutch immediately bought a consignment for troops stationed in the Netherlands East Indies. The sale was exciting and provocative. Though Germans sometimes had the impression that they had been fighting the whole world for four years, it wasn't true; some nations had backed away from the bloodbath, and one major power, Russia, had quit. By operating on the neutral soil of Sweden and selling to others who had been neutral, Krupp could keep his forgers' hands nimble and make money at the same time. For the next fourteen years Bofors served as a substitute Gusstahlfabrik, disgorging, to the pride of its foster parent in the frigid Hauptverwaltungsgebäude office, "the latest types of heavy guns, tanks armed with a machine gun capable of firing a thousand rounds a minute, antiaircraft guns, gas bombs, and many other things" (*und vieles Andere mehr*).[17]

By the time the second of the new customers (Denmark) had signed up, the gentleman's agreement had been reached. In Krupp's words he then "introduced German officers into the Bofors plant to inspect guns and munitions and to be spectators during firing tests. Bofors also made experimental ammunition for armored vehicles which was fired in the presence of German officers. Thus the Krupp-Bofors relationship proved beneficial for the further development of the German army's artillery." It proved so beneficial that Karl Pfirsch, a Kruppianer for twenty years and a member of the board, was sent to Scandinavia to supervise it. In 1927, six years before the National Socialists came to power, Pfirsch's official title was director of Krupp's War Material Department. Although his profit margins were insignificant, the coming and going of so many monocled members of the *Junkerherrschaft* aroused the interest of Swedish Socialists. Unlike Germany's SPD, the Swedes were not exposed to the intimidation of *Femen* bullets, and in 1929 Stockholm's Riksdag — Parliament — passed a law forbidding foreign participation in the ownership of Swedish munitions factories. But Krupp lawyers had been bypassing such legislation for a half-century. They merely created a holding company of Bofors stockowners. Gustav's name appeared nowhere in the firm's records, and its managers could assert with a straight face that he held no investments in the plant itself, although in fact *die Firma* fueled Bofors until the masquerade ended in 1935.[18]

Krupp's most extensive holdings abroad, however, were in Holland. His maneuvers there predated the armistice. In 1916 British intelligence had been astonished to find that a Hague firm with the very English name of Blessing and Company was importing ore for Essen. They blacklisted it; then, hearing that it was moribund, they forgot about it. Actually it was only dormant. Krupp owned 100 percent of Blessing, and in the weeks before the abdication of the All-Highest, Blessing "bought" Gustav's stockpiles in Essen, Magdeburg, and Düsseldorf, thus accounting for the discrepancy between the figures Colonel Leverett brought to Essen on May 29, 1920, and the actual arms on hand. Next Krupp began a series of stunning moves, each more bewildering than the last. Blessing was sold, with all its assets, to the Hollandsche Industrie en Handel Maatschappij, whose name was changed to Siderius A.G. Siderius in turn became a holding company for three Dutch shipyards: Piet Smit in Rotterdam, Maschinen en Apparaten Fabrik in Utrecht, and Ingenieur-Kantoor voor Scheepsbouw in The Hague. Two Krupp directors, Siegfried Fronknecht and Henri George, held all the shares in Siderius. In 1922, after Krupp, Seeckt, and Behncke had reached their agreement, Fronknecht and George moved to the Netherlands with forty German engineers — the vanguard, as it turned out, of a much larger force.[19]

It took Allied intelligence years to unravel this ingenious snarl. French agents began with the figures General Charles Nollet had given Leverett. Something was very wrong here; reliable informants had reported a 1,500-gun artillery park in Essen. Professional spies didn't make mistakes of that magnitude, and nobody could hide that many cannon. Studying railroad records (the Germans often insisted upon recording everything in the years between 1918 and 1945, even when their ledgers spelled their own doom), the French traced the shipments across the Netherlands border to the city of Groningen and the banks of the river Ijssel, the Rhine's northern mouth. They asked the natives whether there were any cannon depots about. Vraag-en antwoordspel, the Dutch replied: yes and no. Big guns had been stored here. They had been taken away on flat freight cars. Fingers pointed southward. More checking of manifests, more interrogation, and the exhausted agents finally made the Blessing–Hollandsche Industrie–Siderius connection and traced the German background of its managers. But now it was 1926. Krupp had sold blocks of Siderius stock to influential Dutchmen. Handsome dividends had been paid, and when Paris protested through diplomatic channels, Amsterdam curtly replied that Queen Wilhelmina's government had no intention of intervening in what was, under the laws of Holland, a koninklijk geodgekeurde vennootschap, a private corporation.

The heart of Krupp's Dutch complex lay in The Hague. His Ingenieur-Kantoor voor Scheepsbouw (Engineering Office for Shipbuilding), known in Essen's files as I.v.S., had been established with the approval and co-operation of Admiral Behncke's Marineleitung in Berlin. According to German naval documents, two lieutenant commanders named Bartenbach and Blum joined thirty Germaniawerft engineers in setting up "a German U-boat construction office" on Netherlands territory. In the beginning they were desperately in need of capital, and Berlin sanctioned the sale of submarine blueprints to certain countries, beginning with Japan. All this was a flagrant violation of Versailles, and Gustav knew it. One of his memoranda from these years — its only date is "12 April," but it was almost certainly written in 1922 — noted that the entire operation in The Hague would be a violation of treaty articles 168, 170, and 179. Krupp added, "This risk must be run, however, if U-boat construction is to be further pursued at all. . . . Hence, the presentations below are based on the further prerequisite that the company to be formed in Holland must have no traceable connection with the Germaniawerft." At this point further doubts apparently assailed him, for he crossed out "Germania-werft" and substituted "shipyards."[20]

He needn't have worried. Paris dropped the matter, and the Dutch businessmen seemed more than satisfied with their investment. The Japanese were happy with their plans, and I.v.S. sold duplicate sets to Spain, Finland, Turkey, and Holland itself. Krupp nautical engineers and German naval officers left The Hague to supervise the construction; their fees went into the I.v.S. war chest. The Finns, appreciative of the excellent craftsmanship in their boats, then allowed men from the Ruhr to build the prototype of the Marineleitung's 250-ton subs (U–1 to U–24), which would be used in World War II. At the same time, I.v.S. reached a secret understanding with the Spanish dictator Miguel Primo de Rivera y Or-baneja under which Krupp constructed a 740-ton U-boat in Cadiz; this in turn became the archetype for the Reich's "flag subs" U–25 and U–26. These blueprints were shown in Ankara and Helsinki, Turkish and Finnish admirals juggled their budgets to permit further expansion, and Krup-pianer arrived from Kiel to make certain the big black sausages would be seaworthy when launched. They brought along apprentices to watch. Moreover, shipbuilders weren't the only Germans to gain experience through the dummy company in the Netherlands. One of Behncke's officers became chief adviser to the Finns, and Madrid, Ankara, and Helsinki permitted German commanders and crews to break in the boats. As *Der Kampf der Marine gegen Versailles* put it, the operational plan permitted "the training of camouflaged German navy personnel without diplomatic unpleasantness for the Reich."[21]

On March 16, 1926, the Allied Control Commission left Essen, and "although this did not mean the end of spying," as Gustav put it, the sole agents left were SPD amateurs who could be dispatched by the *Feme*. That same year Rausenberger died and Krupp recruited a gifted thirty-year-old Luxembourger, Dr. Eduard Houdremont, professor of the science of iron production (*Eisenhüttenkunde*) at Aachen. The mills were beginning to grind faster. It was time some of the exiles came home. The men at Bofors and I.v.S. had to remain where they were; Krupp couldn't show his fist just yet. Nevertheless he was determined to be prepared for "mass production upon command" (*Massenproduktion auf Befehl*). Accordingly, he ordered the men at 4 Potsdamer Platz to wind up those projects which no longer required daily supervision by IWG officers and, after a discreet interval, to entrain for the Ruhr. In his words,

> Als diese Aufgaben Ende 1927 erfüllt waren, wurde KuK E aufgelöst, die Herren wurden nach Essen zurückberufen, wo inzwischen mit der Artillerie-Konstruktionsabteilung begonnen worden war.

When at the end of 1927 these tasks had been finished, KuK (E) [Koch and Kienzle] was dissolved and the men returned to Essen, where, meantime, the reconstruction of the artillery design department had started.[22]

The firm now entered the period of what was known as *schwarze Produktion*, black production. Work was stepped up on self-propelled guns, tanks, torpedo compressed-air containers, ship propellers, periscopes, airplane crankshafts, armor plate, devices for remote control of naval fire, and primitive rocket design. In 1918 Rausenberger had been working on a high-velocity 88-mm. gun for the navy; this was converted to an antiaircraft weapon, and designers speculated that its versatility might make it useful on a tank. According to a subsequent Krupp memo, written during the war, "Of the guns which were being used in 1939–1941, the most important were already fully developed in 1933." Some jobs were completed much earlier: "With the exception of the hydraulic safety switch, the basic principles of armament and turret design for tanks had already been worked out in 1926," and the Grusonwerk began manufacturing tanks on a limited scale in 1928.[23]

In the spring of 1931 Tilo von Wilmowsky, an incorrigible joiner, was in Paris for a meeting of one of those vague organizations that flourished during the 1920's, advocating international harmony and recoiling from any practical steps toward it. During the farewell banquet a Frenchman declared that he was vehemently opposed to Weimar's proposal for a customs union (*Kreditanstalt*) with Austria. The baron asked, "Why?" The man cried, "Forty more divisions for Germany!" Swiftly Tilo said, "But better than that — one general staff!" The Frenchman stared across the table. "I think," Tilo later remarked with a chuckle, "that he thought I was drunk."[24]

The baron was sober, his remark relevant; Germans had begun to think along those lines once more. As a member of the Konzern's board Tilo was aware that Meppen, reconverted to farmland in 1919, was again a proving ground, and that secret firing tests had been held there for naval officers in

1929. A second range was built in Essen, east of the Helene Amalie mine; in June 1931 both were used to demonstrate the new weapons for the army. Mass firings on iron targets were held in January 1932 and again the following spring. Each month now saw tighter security in the shops, the purchase of new equipment, the introduction of new weapons. Berlin's contempt for the *Diktat* was becoming more and more open. Arguing that a liberal interpretation of Versailles would permit the building of a German "pocket battleship" (*Taschenpanzerkreuzer*), Hermann Müller-Franken, head of the coalition cabinet of 1928–1930, overrode the SPD slogan of *"Kinderspeisung oder Panzerkreuzer?"* (Food for the children or armored cruisers?) and persuaded the Reichstag to appropriate 80 millions for one. Krupp hastily recalled a group of engineers and resettled them in Kiel, where neighbors marveled that their children spoke Dutch.[25]

Gustav acquired a monstrous 15,000-ton press, useful only in the manufacture of giant cannon, rejoiced that Borbeck was now prepared to turn out whole panzer divisions, and brightened the days of his board with crisp little memos about the military value of Widia tool steel: "The use of these tools reduces the processing time to an extent never thought possible. For instance, during the 1914–1918 war the turning of a certain grenade with high-speed tool steel required approximately 220 minutes; the introduction of Widia enables the construction of automatic machines which do this work in about 12 minutes. Modern production of grenades without Widia is, therefore, unthinkable." As Talleyrand said of the Bourbons, Krupp had learned nothing and forgotten nothing. In "Objectives of German Policy," an extraordinary article written in English for the November 1932 *Review of Reviews*, he protested that Germans were being treated as second-class world citizens:

. . . the vital rights of national defense enjoyed by all other peoples are withheld from them. Not *increase* in armament, but *equality* of armament must therefore be the aim of every German government. In Germany we have no interest in any increase in armament throughout the world. . . . There is a fairy tale spread all over the world that the munitions industry desires and works for a general increase in armaments . . . as a businessman I am of the opinion that international disarmament must be the general aim.[26]

This is depressing reading. It may be that the real evil done at Versailles was not the treaty itself — as these things go, it was no *Diktat*; the Germans' own settlement with the Russians at Brest-Litovsk had been far harsher — but rather the conversion of a nation's leadership into habitual liars. While Krupp set down these pious words, one of his executives was proudly gathering data for a list of his chief's contributions to a new, heavily muscled Reich ("3.7-cm. gun for armored cars; 5-cm. gun for armored cars; 7.5-cm. heavy antitank gun, tank turrets ZW38, heavy field howitzer 18; heavy 10-cm. gun 18; gun carriage and limbers, heavy field howitzer 18 and 10-cm. gun 18; 21-cm. mortar 18 . . ."), and adding that all this was possible because "the firm, acting on its own initiative and believing in a revival, has, since 1918, retained at its own expense its employees, practical knowledge, and workshops for the manufacture of war material." Indeed, the month after Gustav's eloquent plea for Germany's right to protect herself, he received a New Year's message from a Colonel Zwengauer, a department chief in the army's ordnance inspection office, which provides some indication of the strength of the bond between Krupp and the military establishment under the Weimar Republic. On December 28 the colonel wrote, "The department is convinced that, thanks to your active cooperation and valuable advice, our armament development in 1932 has made considerable progress which is of great significance to our intent of rearming as a whole."[27]

There wasn't much peace and good will toward men in that greeting, but then, it had been a bad year. The whole world was wallowing in the trough of economic depression. "After long years of losses," Haux wrote, "the [fiscal] year 1931–1932 showed a loss of 30 millions, of which only 16 millions appeared in the annual report." Idle men were hired to widen the Ruhr River, improving the view from the rear of Villa Hügel, but the outlook from the city side of the castle was bleak. Of Essen's 40,000 Kruppianer, only 18,000 were working, and they were on a three-day week. At the onset of winter the prospect had become so grim that to save fuel Gustav and Bertha moved into the sixty rooms of the kleine Haus, leaving the rest of the great pile unheated.[28]

Alfried once told this writer, "My father took no active interest in politics, except in economic policy." If one concedes that every great political issue has an economic root, this is true. Decidedly Gustav wanted no truck with footling deals and jobbery. Nevertheless he, like Alfred and Fritz before him, was deeply involved in affairs of state. In "Objectives of German Policy" he declared that "It has been shown, in the September dissolution of the Reichstag, that the political parties have eliminated themselves from all active work for the welfare of the nation and the people . . .[they] have shown themselves incapable of forming and supporting a government which with vigor and determination replaces, by practical deeds, theoretical consideration of possible betterment." He added that inasmuch as "the internal political situation can no longer be mastered by political parties," President von Hindenburg should name "a government enjoying his confidence . . . to step into the breach." Krupp was looking for a man on horseback. But which one? The country had a score of them, straining in their stirrups and glaring at one another. Until recently he had been contributing heavily to the National People's Party

(DNV) of Alfred Hugenberg, last seen by the Essen public as a costumed vassal in the firm's centennial pageant. Hugenberg believed in a return to the Kaiser's Reich, and until recently it had seemed possible that he would become the new national leader. During the current crisis, however, his popularity had declined sharply. Now he was frisking up to the bigger Nazi Party, which had attracted so many idealistic young men, Alfried among them.[29]

As the nation's chief manufacturer, Krupp would have to decide soon. His wife regarded — and would continue to regard — the leader of the National Socialist movement as an ill-bred guttersnipe. Bertha declined to utter his name, referring to him patronizingly as "that certain gentleman" (*jener gewisse Herr*). Still, Gustav had to admit that that certain gentleman had come a long way since his bumptious visit to the Hauptverwaltungsgebäude just before the depression. At the main gate a huge sign had accosted him:

WIR ERSUCHEN, UM ÜBERFLÜSSIGE UNZUTRÄGLICHKEITEN ZU VERMEIDEN, VON DER BITTE UM BESICHTIGUNG DER WERKE ABSEHEN ZU WOLLEN, DA DIESE IN KEINEM FALL GEWÄHRTWERDEN.

IT IS REQUESTED THAT, TO PREVENT MISUNDERSTANDINGS, NO APPLICATIONS BE MADE TO VISIT THE WORKS, SINCE SUCH APPLICATIONS CANNOT BE GRANTED UNDER ANY CIRCUMSTANCES WHATSOEVER.

Unintimidated, the visitor had demanded a tour of the Gusstahlfabrik, and it is diverting to note that he was barred from the shops because he was too unknown to be trusted; Krupp was afraid that he might see rearmament work and squeal. Instead he had been fobbed off with a visit to the firm's historical exhibit. Even there he had displayed a sense of theater. Recognizing the political value of any association with Krupp, he had signed the exhibit register with a flourish and underscored his signature, as though he knew that soon the Krupp destiny would be inextricably entangled with his own. The name was still there, slashed across the guest book like a jagged prophecy: *Adolf Hitler*.[30]

✠   ✠   ✠

To place events in context: Hitler's unsuccessful attempt to penetrate the high walls and guarded gates of Germany's *Waffenschmiede* had come a year before Tilo's Paris banquet, when the Grusonwerk was entering its fourth year of tank production, when Krupp was regularly showing off new weapons at Meppen — and when National Socialism, with only twelve seats in the Reichstag, was regarded as a wild-eyed splinter party. In the Reichstag elections of September 14, 1930, that changed. The Nazis emerged with 107 seats, second only to the Social Democrats. Now they had to be taken seriously. They had popular support, including the allegiance of every non-Communist hoodlum in the country. In the spring campaigns of 1932, when Hitler unsuccessfully challenged Hindenburg's presidency, his storm troopers smashed the windows of shops owned by Jews and beat up Social Democrats and Communists indiscriminately in the streets. And this was while they were forbidden to demonstrate. When the old Feldmarschall lifted the brown shirt ban that June, Berlin and Brandenburg became so chaotic that they had to be put under martial law. In the following months new elections gave the Nazis 230 deputies — not enough for a majority but more than any other party. All that stood between Hitler and the chancellorship was his own will. He refused to accept the office with restricted powers, enter a coalition, or become vice chancellor. Thus the weak and discredited government stumbled along blindly while the people surged to the polls again and again, unable to resolve the issue.

Krupp found this very confusing. With his reverence for chiefs of state he had continued to mail submissive letters to S.M. in Doorn, and although he agreed with his fellow industrialists that Weimar was a *Zwischenreich*, a temporary regime, he had stalked indignantly from a meeting when one of them referred to former President Ebert as "that saddlemaker." Gustav wanted to obey. He asked only that he be given firm leadership. Lacking that, yearning for a return to order, he concluded that there would have to be a "big change" (*grosser Umschwung*). His position, and the eminent name he bore, meant that any new leader would encounter rough sledding without his active support. Aware of this responsibility, he hesitated while others leaped. As early as 1925 Carl Duisberg of I. G. Farben had called for "the strong man" who "is always necessary for us Germans"; now Duisberg had found his man and was delighted with him. Similarly, Fritz Thyssen had joined the Nazi Party in December 1931 and contributed a hundred million marks to it, and even Seeckt, raised in the tradition of total separation between state and army, advised his sister to vote for Hitler, explaining, "Youth is right. I am too old."[31]

Some of Krupp's reservations were snobbish. Like Bertha, he saw Hitler as an upstart; both of them, one feels, would have felt warmer toward the ex-corporal if he had been an ex-*officer* named Adolf *von* Hitler. But Gustav also distrusted intemperance. A chief of state should be majestic, poised, judicious. The Nazis' hero was none of them. At times he seemed to go out of his way to offend businessmen, denouncing them as "stupid fools who cannot see beyond the wares they peddle," permitting Goebbels to scorn the Reichsverband der Deutschen Industrie, Germany's national manufacturers' association, as "liberalistic, Jew-infested, capitalistic, and reactionary," and even writing as point twelve of the National Socialist program, "We demand the total confiscation of all war profits." To be sure, he had quietly dropped that last plank from his platform, and

Hugenberg assured Krupp that if they once got Hitler into the government "Papen and I will handle him." Nevertheless Gustav continued to hang back, spreading his campaign contributions among all right-wing parties, including the National Socialists but not favoring them.[32]

Krupp's conversion came late, and because certain records were later destroyed, pinpointing the date is impossible. We know that he was holding out as late as January 27, 1932, when Thyssen arranged a Hitler speech to the Schlotbarone in Düsseldorf's Industrieklub. Gustav didn't go, didn't hear the appeal to his fellow barons, and didn't contribute to the flow of contributions which the address attracted. But he was being drawn by the magnet. He had sent a member of his board to the Industrieklub with instructions to bring back a complete report. The emissary returned with more; he himself had caught the bug, and to the disgust of Tilo — who thought Hitler a raving demagogue — he spouted intoxicating passages of National Socialist propaganda. Krupp wavered. Hugenberg had joined Hitler in a united front. The man must have *something*.[33]

On March 22 J. K. Jenney, an agent for the foreign relations department of Du Pont, reported to Wilmington that "It is a matter of common gossip in Germany that I.G. is financing Hitler. Other German firms who are supposed to be doing so are Krupp and Thyssen." Jenney was wrong about Gustav, who was backing Franz von Papen and Kurt von Schleicher that season, but the swastika had begun to look more attractive to him. At Thyssen's urging, the Nazis had abandoned their plans for the nationalization of industry and were promising active support for German business. And to Gustav the former corporal's advocacy of the *Führerprinzip* began to sound like Alfred's insistence that an employer must be master in his own house. In Essen this was sacred writ. As its apostle Gustav had become one of the most anti-union industrialists in Europe. In 1928 he had led the Ruhr's steelmakers in a lockout of 250,000 men, and when that was over he persuaded the government to impose an "emergency" wage reduction of 15 percent (a cut which Kruppianer then laid at the door of Weimar, not Villa Hügel). Now Hitler was sending word (through Thyssen and Hugenberg) that he agreed about organized labor. Krupp moved a step closer to him. He felt he had to. He was not only the Fatherland's leading capitalist; the previous autumn he had succeeded Carl Duisberg as president of the Reichsverband, and though his obligation to take a stand weighed heavily upon him, he could not escape it. If the Führer would make each manufacturer Führer of his own domain he might deserve the support of all big business. In the words of a Konzern writer, *"Er hat nichts gegen Hitler, warum sollte er etwas gegen ihn haben"* (The firm had nothing against Hitler. Why should it object to the man)?[34]

The turning point for Gustav seems to have been the elections of November 6, 1932. The Reichstag had been dissolved because Hitler had refused to form a government with Papen. He had demanded *"entweder im vollen Ausmasse od. überhaupt nicht einzutreten"* (all or nothing), and when the returns were in it seemed that he had gambled and lost. The endless campaigning had exhausted the patience of the party's big contributors. "Money is extraordinarily hard to obtain," Paul Joseph Goebbels had written in his diary on October 15. "All the gentlemen of 'property and education' are standing by the government." As a consequence, the Nazis had lost two million votes and thirty-five Reichstag seats while the Communists gained three-quarters of a million votes and eleven deputies. Thyssen declared that he could make no further contributions to National Socialism, and Goebbels faced the prospect of an empty treasury and the need to pay Nazi functionaries, printers, and the SA (Sturmabteilung) thugs, who alone cost over two million marks a week. The little *Doktor* despaired. "Deep depression is prevalent in the organization, money worries prevent any constructive work," he wrote on December 8. ". . . We are all very discouraged, particularly in the face of the present danger that the entire party may collapse and all our work be in vain. We are now facing the decisive test." Three days later he noted, "The financial situation of the Berlin organization is hopeless. Nothing but debts and obligations." And in the last week of the year, while Colonel Zwengauer was expressing his gratitude to Gustav for "our armament development in 1932," Goebbels touched bottom: "1932 has brought us eternal bad luck. . . . The past was difficult and the future looks dark and gloomy; all prospects and hopes have quite disappeared."[35]

His dawn was a few days away. All autumn German industrialists had been groping toward an understanding with Hitler. Eight days after the dissolution of the Reichstag, August Heinrichsbauer, the coal baron who was acting as their liaison man, wrote Gregor Strasser, then the second most powerful man in the party, that certain unnamed tycoons were preparing to suggest to the "decisive offices in Berlin" that "Hitler be appointed Chancellor of the Reich." Heinrichsbauer's discretion is maddening, for had he identified his clients it is entirely possible that Krupp would have been among them. He didn't, and we cannot know. The Communist gains in the new Reichstag had shaken Gustav, however, and now we come to a document which is generally accepted as authentic. After the election a Nazi leader named Wilhelm Karl Keppler prepared a draft of the letter Heinrichsbauer had proposed, *"zur Bekämpfung des Bolschewismus"* (to combat Bolshevism). Keppler then passed it along to a rabid Nazi, Baron Kurt von Schröder of the powerful I. H. Stein banking house in Cologne, who collected the necessary signatures and sent it to the president's secretary on November 28.[36]

The original was destroyed with the bombing of the Reich Chancellery a decade later. The Stein building was also reduced to ruins, but after the war an American officer searched its rubble and came up with Schröder's copy. Clearly the industrialists had been scared. The elections had convinced them that they had to choose between the extreme Right and the extreme Left, that the present government simply would not do. The letter opened with a solemn requiem for Papen: the returns "demonstrated that the former cabinet, whose sincere intentions no one among the German people doubted, did not find adequate support within the German people." It was imperative, the argument continued, to "exclude the Communist Party, whose attitude is negative to the state." The letter urged that "Entrusting the leader of the largest national group with the responsible leadership of a presidential cabinet which harbors the best technical and personal forces will eliminate the blemishes and mistakes with which any mass movement is perforce affected; it will incite millions of people, who today are still standing apart, to a positive attitude." Eliminating prolixity, the message was clear — pick Hitler; the office will make him responsible; the alternative is chaos. If the Schröder copy is accurate, the thirty-eight signers were led by Schacht and Krupp.[37]

Hindenburg had already offered Hitler the chancellorship — four days before the letter was delivered. The president wanted to tie strings to it, however, and Hitler still refused. Kurt von Schleicher formed a presidential cabinet December 2, and according to Thyssen, "It was mainly Herr Krupp von Bohlen who then advocated a rapprochement between Strasser and General Schleicher." This suggestion almost destroyed the Nazis, for Strasser wanted to follow it. Hitler denounced Strasser for stabbing him in the back, sent him off on a vacation, and during his absence stripped him of all power within the party. Nevertheless the National Socialist position remained precarious until Schleicher, in an act of incredible stupidity, alienated all men of "property and education" in a nationwide radio broadcast. He pleaded with his listeners to forget that he was a general and promised them a planned economy with price controls, an end to wage cuts, and the confiscation of Junker estates for peasants. In a stroke he had lost all his friends, including Hindenburg, himself a landowner. Since Schleicher was also trying to woo the unions, money from the disgusted Ruhr barons began flowing into the Nazis' empty coffers. On January 16 Goebbels wrote that the fiscal situation had "fundamentally improved overnight." How much of the money came from the Hauptverwaltungs-gebäude is unknown. Undoubtedly some of it was Krupp's (if only through Hugenberg), though Gustav's greatest contribution to the Nazi revolution was yet to come.[38]

The president dismissed Schleicher January 28. Two days later Hindenburg named as chancellor the man he had scorned as "that Austrian corporal" (den österreichischen Gefreiten). Hugenberg became minister of economy and agriculture, and Papen vice chancellor. On January 4 Papen, conferring with Hitler in Schröder's Cologne home, had thought he had reached an understanding with him. Now he gleefully told Hugenberg, "*Wir haben Hitler engagiert!*" (We've hired Hitler!)[39] Certainly if they had been dealing with an ordinary politician his chances of survival would have been slight. The National Socialists were a decided minority in the Reichstag, but although anti-Nazis appeared to hold all the important posts in the new chancellor's government, they had been guilty of a grave oversight. Hermann Göring had become minister without portfolio. It was understood that he would preside over the Luftwaffe when Germany got one. Meanwhile, unnoticed, he had been made responsible for the Prussian police. That was all Hitler's evil genius needed. Before the new elections, scheduled for March 5, he planned to turn his SA bullies loose and introduce two *dei ex machina*: the Reichstag would be burned and the Communists blamed for it, and he would collect enough money from German capitalists to underwrite the most expensive political campaign in the country's history.

Apart from his cabinet role, Göring was president of the Reichstag. His position entitled him to a house. An underground passage led from the basement to the Reichstag, and it is the consensus of historians that this tunnel was about to play a key role in the consolidation of Nazi power — that SA arsonists were planning to dart through it on the evening of February 27. Exactly one week earlier the Präsidentspalast was used for the more sedate but equally essential harvesting of contributions, and the host sent telegrams to the twenty-five wealthiest men in the nation. Gustav's read:

KRUPPBOHLEN INVITED RESPECTFULLY TO A CONFERENCE IN THE HOUSE OF THE PRESIDENT OF THE REICHSTAG, FRIEDRICHEBERSTR, ON MONDAY FEBRUARY 20TH 6 O'CLOCK AFTERNOON, DURING WHICH THE REICH CHANCELLOR WILL EXPLAIN HIS POLICIES. (SIGNED) PRESIDENT OF THE REICHSTAG GÖRING, MINISTER OF THE REICH.[40]

Naturally Krupp accepted. To him this wasn't a baffling maneuver by an ambitious politician; it was an order delivered in behalf of the head of the state. In appointing Hitler, Hindenburg had given him the sanctity of office and, with it, the unflinching loyalty of the head of Germany's industrial first family.

The guests sat in carefully arranged armchairs. Krupp, because of his wealth and his presidency of the Reichsverband, was closest to the low rostrum; behind him were four I. G. Farben directors and Albert Vögler, head of the powerful Vereinigte Deutsche Stahlwerke. Göring spoke first, introducing his leader to those who, like Krupp, were seeing him in the flesh for the first time. Then the chancellor rose. "We are about to hold the last election," he began, and paused to let the full implications of that sink in. Naturally the transition to *Nationalsozialismus* would be smoother if the party was swept in by a landslide. Therefore he solicited their support. In backing the dictatorship they would be backing themselves: "Private enterprise cannot be maintained in a democracy" (*privates Unternehmertum könne in der Demokratie nicht bestehen.*) To clear up any lingering doubts about his meaning he added that among the evil forms democracy assumed was trade unionism; the Reich, if left to such institutions, "will inevitably fall." It was the noblest task of leadership to find ideals which would bind the German people together, and he had found those ideals in nationalism and the strength of "authority and personality" (*Autorität und Persönlichkeit*). He assured them that he would not only eliminate the Communist threat; he would restore the Wehrmacht to its former glory. Like all Hitler speeches this one rambled, but the point of it could scarcely have been plainer. He intended to liquidate the Weimar Republic, and he needed their treasure. "Regardless of the outcome" at the polls, there would be "no retreat." If he lost he would stay in office "by other means . . . with other weapons."[41]

He sat down, Krupp sprang up. In a brief memo dated two days later and filed in his *Personal Correspondence 1933–34* folder, Gustav merely noted that "On the 20th of this month I expressed to Reich Chancellor Hitler the gratitude of approximately twenty-five industrialists present for having given us such a clear picture of the conception of his ideas." His commitment had been deeper than that. At Nuremberg, Hjalmar Schacht deposed that "After Hitler had made his speech, the old Krupp answered Hitler and expressed the unanimous feeling of the industrialists in support of Hitler." Göring reminded them of the point of the meeting. Repeating Hitler, he said, "The sacrifice asked for will be so much easier to bear if industry realizes that the election of March 5 will surely be the last one for the next ten years, possibly for the next hundred years." Schacht put it more bluntly. He cried, "*Und nun, mein Herren, an die Kasse!*" (And now, gentlemen, pony up!). There was a whispering among armchairs. Once again Krupp rose as senior man. He led his colleagues with a pledge of a million marks, and Schacht collected two million more from the others.[42]

"In financing the terror election of 1933," Professor Arthur Schweitzer wrote twenty years later, "the leaders of big business made a substantial investment in the new government and became thereby a full partner in the Third Reich." Luckily for the chancellor, the fund was big enough to support his party after the election, for the results were surprisingly inconclusive. Hitler had everything going for him — money, the machinery of the state, Goebbels's ingenious propaganda devices, the prestige and backing of the Krupp name, and a decree, signed by President Hindenburg the day after the rigged fire, which among other things curtailed freedom of the press, the right of assembly, and even the sanctity of private correspondence. The storm troopers left no enemy nose unbloodied; from the raid on the SPD's Karl Liebknecht Haus by Göring's police to back street whippings of Jewish shopkeepers, the campaign was an orgy of violence. Yet with all this the National Socialists won only 44 percent of the vote. Combining their 288 seats and Hugenberg's 52 they had a majority of 16, enough to govern but not nearly enough for the two-thirds mandate Hitler needed to legalize his dictatorship. Thanks to his new wealth, however, his deputies were in a position to grease palms for the first time. The National Socialists' *Gesetz zur Behebung der Not von Volk und Reich* of March 23, literally a "law for removing the distress of people and Reich" but actually an enabling act establishing a totalitarian regime, was passed 441–84, with the support of every party except the Social Democrats. The Third Reich, in Nazi jargon the "Thousand-Year Reich," was a reality. Jubilant, the uniformed National Socialist deputies sprang to their feet and burst into that haunting anthem which had been composed four years before by a raffish young demimondain Nazi named Horst Wessel —

> *Die Fahne hoch! Die Reihen dicht geschlossen.*
> *S.A. marschiert mit ruhig festem Schritt. . . .*
>
> Raise the banners! Stand rank on rank together.
> S.A. march on, with steady, quiet tread. . . .[43]

Hitler's authority now surpassed the Kaiser's at his zenith, and in the words of the prosecutor's opening statement at Nuremberg thirteen and a half years later, "The ouster from the Reichstag of his political opponents and the aid of the [Hugenberg] Deutschnationalen Volkspartei, which was heavily financed and supported by Krupp, gave him the votes needed for its enactment." This was the basis for the SPD charge *"dass Krupp Hitlers Weg an die Macht finanziell gepflastert habe,"* that "Krupp financially paved Hitler's road to power."[44] Like most political accusations it was overstated and oversimplified — Krupp had been paving the way for whatever leader might rise. He had considered several, and had in fact come late to the Hitler rally. Nevertheless he had arrived in the nick of time, and he was about to make amends for his tardiness with enthusiasm.

# 15

FÜNFZEHN

✠
## The Führer Is Always Right

O N the threshold of totalitarianism Krupp briefly hesitated. Visiting the capital the week before the passage of the enabling act, he called at his Berlin office, where Fritz von Bülow had succeeded his father. Overhead the swastika snapped viciously from a new flagpole. What, Gustav demanded, had happened to the German colors? The younger Bülow nervously pointed out that they, too, were flying; there were *two* poles. That was the new custom here, he said, and pointed out the double standards over the Dresdner Bank branch next door. Krupp nodded moodily, but he still hadn't gone all the way. On the streets Nazis and their growing legion of converts were greeting one another with the stiffened upraised arms of the *Hitlergruss*, the Hitler salute. To Karl Stahl, his Berlin chauffeur, Gustav issued careful instructions: whenever he emerged from a meeting, the chauffeur should watch his gloves. If Krupp carried them in his right hand, Stahl must click his heels and touch the bill of his cap in the old Prussian salutation. Should the gloves be in Gustav's left hand, however, Stahl would throw out his arm and they would exchange the *Hitlergruss* together.[1]

Then the Reichstag capitulated, and Krupp plunged. Overnight he was heiling everyone in sight. Within twenty-four hours of the enabling act he sent word to the chancellor that he and his fellow manufacturers agreed that Germany now had "the *basis for a stable government*. Difficulties which arose in the past from constant political fluctuations, and which obstructed economic initiative to a high degree, have been eliminated." The endorsement from his colleagues was faked — the Reichsverband board hadn't met — but the Nazis didn't care. This was the kind of language they understood. Hitler, pleased, received him at the Reich

Chancellery on Saturday, April 1. Three days later Krupp wrote him on the official stationery of the Reichsverband's Berlin office:

*Sehr geehrter Herr Reichskanzler!*
I wish to express my gratitude to you for the audience you granted me on Saturday, despite the fact that you are very busy these days. I welcomed this opportunity all the more because I am aware now of new and important problems which, as you will understand, I shall be able to handle in my capacity as chairman of the Reich Federation of German Industry only if I am sure of the confidence of the Reich government and, in particular, of your confidence in me [*und insbesondere Ihres Vertrauens mir gegenüber*]. . . .[2]

These veiled allusions to momentous developments became clearer on April 25, when Gustav wrote Hitler of his "wish to coordinate production in the interest of the whole nation . . . adopting the leadership conception (*Führerprinzip*) of the new German state." A reorganization of the manufacturers' association would be carried out "in line with the wishes and plans I have fostered and expressed since assuming the chairmanship of German industry." His goal was "to coordinate the economic facts of our existence with political necessities and, further, to bring the new organization into complete alignment with the political aims of the government of the Reich" (*die neue Organisation in volle Übereinstimmung mit den politischen Zielen der Reichsregierung zu bringen*).[3]

In short, the factories, like the nation, needed a dictator. Obviously his name should be Krupp.

There is no way of knowing whether this idea was born in the chancellery or Villa Hügel, but probably it was Hitler's. Gustav was too much of a traditionalist to suggest dramatic breaks with the past, and his ambitions were confined to the family dynasty anyhow — he had never displayed any interest in dominating his fellow capitalists. It was the chancellor who would gain, by using the name of Krupp to institutionalize the alliance between big business and National Socialism. This having been said, it should be added that he could scarcely have found a more willing pawn than Gustav. In a second conference on April 28 the two men hammered out the details of the agreement, and the newspapers of May 4 carried an official communiqué announcing that Krupp was now the Führer of German industry. His first act was to expel all Jews from the Reichsverband, which was then converted to the quasi-official Reichsgruppe Industrie. On May 22 he ordered the members of the board to resign and forbade further meetings, formal or informal, among them. In underwriting an end to political elections, they now discovered, they had unwittingly liquidated their own independence.[4]

Yet there were no complaints. The Jews withdrew into silence — that long, tragic silence which seemed to be their wisest choice at the time, and later turned out to be the worst — while the others waited for the chancellor to fulfill his pledge of February 20. This was one promise Hitler kept. On May 2 storm troopers raided every trade union office in the country, seized their treasuries, and herded the leaders off to concentration camps.

Hitler outlawed collective bargaining, then banned the SPD (together with every other party except his own). Robert Ley, head of the National Socialist Labor Front, declared that the new government intended "to restore absolute leadership to the natural leader of the factory — that is, the employer . . . only the employer can decide. Many employers have for years had to call for the 'master in the house.' Now they are once again to be the 'master in the house.' "[5] *Der Herr im eigenen Haus:* once more Essen heard that familiar, thrilling ring. Forty-six years after Alfred the Great's death his prayer for a counterrevolutionary leader, backed by "flying columns" of young men, had been answered.

Gustav had anticipated that it would be. The month before, he had become National Socialism's chief fund raiser, soliciting contributions to the party from his fellow Ruhr barons and telling them urgently, "Whoever helps quickly, helps doubly!" Eight days after the brown-shirted flying columns had shattered German trade unionism he hatched "a scheme" as a Du Pont agent described it in a report dated July 17, "whereby industry could contribute to the party organization funds."[*] This was the *Hitler Spende,* the Hitler Fund. Its purpose, Krupp wrote Schacht, was "to represent a token of gratitude to the leader of the nation." Its practice — as revealed by a Rudolf Hess directive found twelve years later in the file of Gustav's private secretary — was twofold. The first was to support "the SA, SS, staffs, Hitler Youth, the political organizations. . . ." The second was to free businessmen from harassment by party thugs. Should storm troops force their way into contributors' offices, Hess wrote, "The donors will identify themselves with a certificate bearing my signature and the party stamp." *Spende* money, in short, was protection money.[6]

Year after year, until he was succeeded by his eldest son, Gustav voluntarily served as chairman of this instrument of systematic blackmail. The fund became the Nazis' greatest private source of wealth. Krupp alone put over six million reichsmarks in it, plus another six million for other National Socialist causes, and the more he gave, the better he felt. After a particularly lavish shower of gold (RM 100,000) he wrote:

---

* Du Pont files became public records during the congressional (Nye) munitions hearings of 1934. The American firm was not, of course, connected in any way with the political activities of German capitalists; its European representatives were merely gathering information about competitors.

*Auf dem Hügel,*
*Essen-Hügel, 2. Januar 1936*

*An den Führer und Reichskanzler*
*Herrn Adolf Hitler*
*Berlin W 8*
*Wilhelmstr. 78*

*Mein Führer,*

With reference to my letter of last November 1, I declare my willingness to continue to head the Board of the Adolf Hitler Spende of German Industry again in its fourth year, to conform with the wish expressed in your letter of last October 31.

May I be permitted to take this opportunity, my Führer, to express my most sincere wishes to you for the year 1936, for the continued preparation of your far-reaching plans and the confidence that this fourth year of its development will bring this first part of your program much nearer to fulfillment than could have been hoped or expected three years ago. It remains a deep satisfaction to me to have been able to serve you in a modest way during this time [*dass ich Ihnen während dieser Zeit auf eine bescheidene Weise dienen durfte*].

With German greeting,

Your obedient servant,

Signed:   Dr. Krupp von Bohlen
und Halbach[7]

There is a horrid fascination in the Krupp-Hitler correspondence, for it limns a deliberate surrender of identity. At the beginning of 1933 Gustav had been a responsible member of the traditional German establishment. Within five years he was to become a thrall. His loss of freedom was unaccompanied by pain. On the contrary, he yielded with an awful exaltation. The pattern is evident in his signatures. The first letters to the chancellery were courteous exchanges between equals. Krupp signed them, "*mit vorzüglichster Hochachtung*" (very respectfully yours). Then he turned to the warmer, more submissive "*mit deutschen Gruss*" (German greeting). Finally he abdicated entirely, ending each note with "Heil Hitler!" There was a word for this sort of transformation in those years. It was *Gleichschaltung*, conformity, or coordination. No man was more *gleichgeschaltet* than Gustav. In April 1933 he directed the members of his Vorstand to join the party. In August the Nazi salute became compulsory in his factories, and Kruppianer who kept their arms at their sides were dismissed. That winter he was among the signers of a petition to President Hindenburg asking that the old field marshal step aside and let Hitler be both chancellor *and* president. Already the petitioners were calling their leader by his new title: "The Führer again has asked us to stand by him faithfully. . . . None of us will be missing when it is up to us to testify to this." Hindenburg declined, but it made no difference; when he died the following August the corporal he had once despised and had distrusted to the end took over anyhow. This was clearly illegal. The enabling act had put the presidency beyond his grasp. Yet law had already become a mockery in Germany, and Krupp waved aside Hitler's flagrant abuse of the order he had once cherished with a pet Nazi mot: *"Wo gehobelt wird, da fallen Späne"* (Where there is planing, shavings fall).[8]

Order had been replaced by the New Order, *Neuordnung.* Gustav's endorsement of *die Neuordnung* was total; he refused to listen to a word against it. For years he had met with an informal group called the Ruhrlade, the cream of the smokestack barons. One evening Karl Bosch of I. G. Farben spoke of the corruption in the new government. Krupp arose, accused Bosch of insulting the Führer, declared that he would never attend another Ruhrlade session, and walked out, thereby scuttling the association, which became meaningless without him.[9] In Essen huge portraits of the Führer were hung in Villa Hügel, the Essener Hof, and every office of the main administration building. Even in Alfred Krupp's prime the city had known more freedom of speech. The Hauptverwaltungsgebäude was linked to Gestapo headquarters on Kortestrasse, eleven blocks away, by telephone, and all known Social Democrats and all employees overheard sniping at the regime were sent there for questioning.

Fortunately for domestic tranquillity Gustav excluded members of his own family. Tilo von Wilmowsky had joined the party, for reasons which are obscure. He later said that he hoped to reform it from within — *"um Schlimmeres zu verhüten"* (to stop something worse from happening). His subsequent behavior suggests that he became for a time a more ardent Nazi than he would concede afterward, but he wasn't in the same class with his brother-in-law. According to the baron, "Within the family you were a little safe in speaking your mind, though not when Gustav was around. Once in Villa Hügel I made a mildly critical remark about the men around Hitler. Gustav asked me never to talk like that again while I was in his home." The head of the household couldn't threaten to banish Bertha, since both the castle and the business belonged to her. If she behaved disloyally, however, he could deprive her of the pleasure of his company, and he did. When he ordered the flags of imperial Germany hauled down from Hügel's poles and Nazi ensigns raised in their place, she watched stolidly. Then she wheeled and strode inside. To her maid, Fräulein Achenbach, she said bitterly, *"Gehen Sie in den Park, und sehen Sie, wie tief wir gesunken sind"* (Go in the park and see how low we have fallen). Her husband, who had been following on her heels, spun away. As he strutted off he snapped over his shoulder, *"Der Führer hat immer recht!"* (The Führer is always right!)[10]

His family and his friends speculated about this uncompromising attitude. Some concluded that Gustav was merely being consistent; he had always been rigid, and fifteen years of uncertainty and flux had tried him sorely. Others thought he was overcompensating. Unlike Bertha and Tilo he had not been born to his position. Nothing, not even Wilhelm's decree, could make him a real Krupp, and so he lacked assurance. To Hermann Bücher of the Allgemeine Elektrizitätsgesellschaft his fellow industrialist's betrayal of the Reichsverband was revealing: "In normal times he was an outstanding president. He was, however, not equal to meeting the conditions that developed in 1932–33. . . . He found himself unable to shake off his upbringing in an *Obrigkeitsstaat* [a nation in which the authority of the state is all-powerful] and in his former diplomatic career. Instead he considered himself — as he himself frequently expressed it — the trustee of his wife's fortune and the guardian of the Krupp tradition."[11]

But this is hindsight. Gustav believed he *was* safeguarding that fortune and that tradition. He was trying to do what his wife's grandfather would have wished, and judged by that standard he cannot be blamed. Alfred had been a prophet of the Third Reich while the Second Reich was in its infancy. He would have been the first to support a national leader who was both a strikebreaker and a sworn enemy of the SPD, and he wouldn't have hesitated to invoke its powers in his behalf. German business had never pledged allegiance to the creed of free enterprise. Like the first Kanonen-könig, who had sought official favors from his youth onward, the titans of the Reich's industry regarded Berlin as an ally and were eager to identify themselves with an authoritarian regime. The history of the house of Krupp eloquently supported the argument that the closer the ties between Essen and the country's rulers, the greater the chances for national glory and Krupp prosperity. From Wilhelm I's first visit to the Gusstahlfabrik in the autumn of 1859 to Wilhelm II's farewell in the autumn of 1918, the alliance had seen Germany and German industry rise from insignificance to continental pre-eminence. If they had fallen, the November criminals were to blame. If they were to rise once more, the bond must be reforged. By that interpretation it was Bertha, not Gustav, who wanted to betray the dynasty. *Der Grosse Krupp* would have been ashamed of his bloodline.

He would have been proud of his grandson-in-law when a *Führerbefehl* (Hitler decree) in the spring of 1934 named Gustav the Reich's *Führer der Wirtschaft* (leader of the economy) *"alter kruppscher Tradition entsprechend"* (according to the old Krupp tradition).[12] And the ghost of the half-mad genius would have exulted when Hitler decided to visit the works two months later.

The motivation behind the Führer's presence in Essen on June 28–29 has never been adequately explained. Certainly the timing was singular. The reason given then — that he was coming to attend the wedding of Josef Terboven, the North Rhineland–Westphalia Nazi *Gauleiter* (district leader) — was patent nonsense. Krupp was more important than a hundred Terbovens. At that moment in the history of the Third Reich he was more controversial, however, and the *Gauleiter*'s wedding may have been a convenient excuse for the dictator's first tour of his *Waffenschmiede*. There is another, more sinister possibility. Krupp had become a center of controversy because he was a tycoon. The Nazi Party had begun as the German Workers Party (*Deutsche Arbeiterpartei*). But Hitler's grasp of economics was feeble. The thrust of his yearnings had been revealed when he grafted *Nationalsozialistische* on the tiny party's name.[13]

After the dismissal of Hugenberg, who as a former Krupp director had been looked upon as Gustav's representative in the cabinet of the new government, a sharp critic of the Schlotbarone had been appointed to the Ministry of Economics. Throughout its first year in power, therefore, the National Socialist Party had been an uneasy marriage between nationalists and anticapitalistic middle-class socialists. Now in the second spring a divorce was imminent. The Nazis were on the brink of civil war, cutthroat against cutthroat. Hitler's racist, imperialistic, oligarchic ideology was threatened by revolt among the socialists in his ranks. The crisis was grave; the cry for a "second revolution" was being raised by Ernst Röhm, chief of staff of the SA, whose two and a half million storm troopers had propelled the chancellor into office.

On June 4 four SA men, at Röhm's express orders, had appeared on Altendorferstrasse and forced their way past gate 28. Their leader, Chef des politischen Amts der obersten SA-Führung von Detten — Chief of the Political Bureau of the Supreme Headquarters of the Storm Detachments — had insisted upon interrupting a Gusstahlfabrik assembly line and delivering a speech predicting the *"zweite Revolution."* Krupp had complained to Hitler, the Führer brooded. Should Röhm unleash all his thugs the consequences would be catastrophic. Therefore the Führer resolved to move first, within twelve hours of his conference with Krupp. If during that meeting he withheld news of the imminent bloodbath from Gustav (who in the new power structure would be an even more vital figure, representing both heavy industry and military ties) his silence was extraordinary. There is not a shred of evidence either way, but logic suggests that the Nazi Chancellor, like the Iron Chancellor before him, probably confided in the armorer of the Reich.[14]

Hitler was not received at Villa Hügel. Bertha wouldn't have it. For one thing, she was mortified. The family was still confined to the sixty rooms of the small wing. She refused to have a plebeian politician see the proud dynasty humbled. Before his next visit to the Ruhr that source of discomfiture had been removed, but although he rode up the hill as often as Wilhelm thereafter, he never spent a night in the Kaiser's suite; after tea or dinner in the castle's great banquet hall he would be driven to the home of an old friend in nearby Mülheim. Bertha's disapproval was not political. Indeed, once the Führer had disassociated himself from the socialist rabble she thawed visibly. She simply could not see a man from the gutter occupying the exalted place of her beloved S.M., and on this first visit, with his conservative credentials still suspect, he wasn't even invited to tea.

He and his retinue stayed at the Kaiserhof, an old Goebbels haunt and the only hotel in Essen which was not owned by Krupp. After Terboven and his bride had left on their honeymoon, the Führer was welcomed in the marble reception hall of the Hauptverwaltungsgebäude, where Krupp and the All-Highest had opened the centennial celebration of 1912. With his wife pleading a headache, Gustav chose as hostess his oldest daughter, Irmgard. Irmgard had turned twenty-one four weeks before. At that age she should have been pretty. She wasn't, and this was the worst moment of her youth. Dark, shy, and painfully aware of her lack of charm, she was obliged to act as official greeter. She fidgeted in the ornate doorway, intensely embarrassed. Then Hitler stamped up in his glittering boots, took the bouquet she offered, beamed as she curtsied, and swept on to embrace her father. To the cheering, heiling Krupp executives, watching the leader of economy and the leader of the Fatherland withdraw to Gustav's private office that sunny Friday, it seemed that sixteen years of shame had been rolled away. It was, they agreed, a splendid climax.[15]

But it wasn't the climax. That came early Saturday. Leaving the Ruhr, the Führer motored south and stopped at a Godesberg hotel managed by a wartime comrade. In the small hours of the morning he made his move. The SS men who were to purge the SA were tensely awaiting his command. Landing at Munich, he gave the green signal. In that ghastly night of long knives German Rightists tortured and murdered over four hundred fellow German Rightists, including Röhm. It was a *Schreckensherrschaft*, a reign of terror. An untold number of bystanders were killed out of sheer malice. A priest whom Hitler was known to loathe was shot three times in the heart and thrown in a forest; another man who had crossed the Führer eleven years earlier was hacked to death with pickaxes and left in a swamp near the then obscure Bavarian town of Dachau; and at least one martyr, an eminent Munich music critic, was butchered by mistake because he and a local SA leader had the same name.

Elsewhere the reaction would have been shock and outrage — one may imagine how America would have responded had Franklin Roosevelt ordered the FBI to slaughter his critics — but the German attitude was very different. A throb of admiration ran through the Reich. Here was a man who *acted*. Wernher von Blomberg, the ranking general of the Offizierskorps, publicly congratulated Hitler. So did the cabinet, which passed a decree "legalizing" the executions ex post facto. Even Hindenburg thanked his chancellor for his "gallant personal intervention." Gustav — who had been rescued from middle-class socialism by the purge — said nothing. Today in Essen any mention of the Röhmputsch is met with the evasive answer that since nothing like this had ever occurred in Germany before, Krupp "refused to admit that it was happening now." This is claptrap. He knew what had happened, may very well have known of it in advance, and was in any event among the chief beneficiaries of the new alignment, "which," in Professor Schweitzer's memorable phrase, "had now been cemented through the blood of the murdered victims."[16]

✠   ✠   ✠

A second major beneficiary was the army. Röhm's SA had been so large and so well organized that it threatened to replace the armed forces at the very moment when they were about to cast aside the shackles of the *Diktat* and become the mightiest military machine in European history. To resurrect the Wehrmacht the officer corps needed the Führer's unqualified support. Of course, Krupp's was needed, too, but that could be assumed. The long years of clandestine cooperation had given the *Offizierskorps* and its gunsmith a common goal; it had been Blomberg's endorsement of the new government which had been the occasion for the hoisting of the swastika over Hügel, and Hitler's inauguration of a secret rearmament program on April 4, 1934, had assured him the fidelity of the General Staff and the Master who reigned over his House by the Ruhr.

Since it also meant the quiet scuttling of all hopes for a higher standard of living, the dreams of the middle-class socialists had been doomed from the outset. They had wanted butter; *Mein Kampf* Nazis, guns. The purge had settled the issue, though the country at large was unaware of it because an armament program meant full employment. Three years after the Zentralbüro für deutsche Aufrüstung (Central Bureau for German Rearmament) opened its offices at Berlin's No. 9 Margarethenstrasse in Berlin the number of idle German men dropped from six million to less than one million. On orders telegraphed from Margarethenstrasse to Essen the old Gusstahlfabrik alone increased its payroll from 35,000 to 112,000. The Haupverwaltungsgebäude became known as *der Ameisenhaufen*, the busy anthill. *Die Firma* expanded its two firing ranges and put 40 million reichsmarks in new facilities. Gustav now admitted to his shop supervisors that the line of peace products had been camouflage. Its sole purpose, he said, had been "to keep our personnel and our plants occupied." Henceforth they would have more than enough to do for the army and navy. They did, too, "*Das Tempo War hinreissend*," a survivor of those days later recalled — the pace was terrific.[17]

Though these first strides toward *Aufrüstung* were giant steps they passed unnoticed. In the spring of 1933 the chancellor had announced an elaborate public works program, and Goebbels exploited it brilliantly. To the superficial eye Hitler appeared to be preoccupied with welfare goals. He even appointed Carl Goerdeler, mayor of Königsberg and Leipzig, as price commissioner.[18] Goerdeler was known abroad as an advocate of free enterprise and an archenemy of militarism; his rise was noted and applauded. His subsequent resignation in protest against the drift of Nazi policy was shrugged off. While Goerdeler would later play a strange role in the lives of Gustav Krupp, Alfried Krupp and — on July 20, 1944 — Adolf Hitler, his disappearance seemed of small consequence when weighed against the government's initial public works budget of 5.4 billion marks.

That sounds like a lot. But the arms budget was 21 *billion*. How could so vast an investment be concealed? The answer is a name: Schacht. His bag of tricks was bottomless. Krupp and his fellow industrialists were not paid in marks. They received "mefo bills," IOU's which were accepted in Berlin by the Metallurgische Forschungsgesellschaft G.m.b.H., a dummy company representing four private concerns and two ministries, who in turn were backed by the national treasury. Since the Central Bank eventually rediscounted all these notes, everyone was paid without a single digit appearing on the record. At the same time, the Führer abolished the eight-hour day, making overtime cheap for employers. Schacht thought of everything; when the Olympic Games came to Berlin he made certain that all foreign currency spent by visitors went to Essen, and whenever possible accounts were blocked and assets frozen. As he wrote Blomberg in a confidential letter on June 6, 1936, "The Central Bank has the German mark funds of foreigners under its control almost exclusively reinvested in rearmament bills. Our armaments are thus partly financed from the deposits of our political enemies."[19]

In a series of cabinet meetings following the Röhm purge, rearmament was given absolute priority over every other Nazi program. This was the will of the three power blocs to emerge from the massacre triumphant: the party, the army, and big business. But the initiative came from Krupp, the only industrialist who had defied Versailles and was ready to produce. As early as March 1933, Gustav, presuming to speak for the Reichsverband, had rejected "any international control of weapons." The following October he and his lieutenants in the Reichsgruppe Industrie had publicly welcomed the Führer's withdrawal from the European disarmament conference and the League of Nations. In the spring the Reich Chancellor quietly handed the armed forces a blank check. The Generalstab and Marineleitung were told to draw up their own budgets. It would be up to the government to find the money for them. Throughout that summer Berlin's obsession with arms increased. On September 4 the government gave munitions makers first call on raw materials from overseas. Iron ore imports shot up 170 percent, and Krupp's steel production at the Gusstahl-fabrik and Rheinhausen increased from a million and a half tons a year to four million.[20]

The cabinet was moving fast, but not fast enough for Gustav. He hadn't waited for the decrees of 1934. His private *Aufrüstung* having picked up momentum under the Weimar Republic, he had accelerated during the transition. Krupp had no contracts, merely verbal understandings with individual officers. As Colonel Wilhelm Keitel told an officer in the Margarethenstrasse Zentralbüro on May 22, 1933, "Matters communicated orally cannot be proven. They can be denied." Thirteen months later the government was still wary; Admiral Erich Raeder wrote in his notebook, "Führer's instructions: No mention must be made of a displacement of 25–26,000 tons . . . the Führer demands complete secrecy on the construction of U-boats."[21]

Gustav understood the need to remain tight-lipped; he knew he was acting with Hitler's approval. The chancellor had expressed himself clearly at that first evening meeting in Göring's official residence, and Krupp had issued appropriate orders next morning: they were to clear the shops for mass production. The Vorstand moved with unprecedented celerity. By the end of April, Krupp's imports for the first four months of 1933 had exceeded the total tonnage for 1932. Stockpiles skyrocketed; scrap iron went from 10,000 tons to 83,000; iron ore from 35,000 to 208,000; copper from 8,000 to 15,000; and for the first time since early 1914 the firm was receiving Brazilian shipments of high-grade zircon ore, used only in gun steel. Meanwhile, Gustav noted, only 6 percent of Germany's iron was being exported to "enemy countries" like England, France, Belgium, Russia, and Czechoslovakia.[22]

Krupp profits did not mark time while formal agreements were drawn up. Today in Essen, Gustav's heirs insist that he only obeyed orders and "put a good face on a bad business" (eine gute Miene zum bösen Spiel machte). In fact it was superb business, the finest in the history of the dynasty. Rearmament proved to be a boon to all German industrialists; nationally their profit average rose from 2 percent in the prosperous year 1926 to 6.5 percent. That was a figure to warm baronial hearts. But look at Krupp. From the moment the enabling act made Adolf Hitler dictator the Konzern's financial worries were over. Ernst Haux, now over seventy, was preparing to retire after a half-century of devoted service. Under Weimar, coming into his Finanz office each morning hadn't been much fun. Suddenly that changed. In the last chapter of his unpublished memoirs he tells how a sudden flood of credits from Berlin allowed him to screw the top on his bottle of red ink: ". . . in [the fiscal year] 1932–33 for the first time we ended this year with a small profit, and one could start to build some small reserve." Furthermore, "the general business trend kept improving from month to month, so that we could employ new workers." He sums up the reason in his chapter title: "Wieder Kriegsmaterial bei Krupp" (Once More War Material by Krupp). Gustav, he relates, confided in him that "no business in war material was being carried on abroad as yet; first everything possible must be done to equip the new German army." In a trembling hand Haux added his own comment: "The firm of Krupp had moved back into its old position as first armorer of the German Reich. A new page of its glory-filled history has been turned over." Ecstatic, he ended his autobiography with a chauvinistic quatrain —

*Gott segne das Haus und die Firma Krupp*
*wie bisher, so auch in alle Zukunft.*
*Zum Heil der Werksangehörigen und*
*des ganzen deutschen Volkes.*

God bless the House and Firm of Krupp
As hitherto, so in all the future.
For the blessing of the employees and
Of the whole German people.[23]

He died believing this was true. In practice, of course, the blessings were largely confined to the family in Villa Hügel. Technically they had been conferred upon "Fräulein Bertha Krupp," though naturally she gave Gustav all the spending money he wanted. Even after she had reoccupied the main wing of the castle she had more assets than she could count. *Die Firma's* receipts were up 433 percent; her personal income had increased tenfold. As the 1930's advanced it continued to grow. One-sixth, and then one-fifth of Germany's national income was being spent on arms. By 1939 Hitler, pointing with pride to the Gusstahlfabrik, would be able to declare that "For more than six years I have worked for the strengthening of the German Wehrmacht. During this time more than 90 billions have been spent for the building up of our army. It is today the best equipped in the world and in every respect surpasses that of the year 1914." The figures of Haux's successor reveal what this meant in Essen. The year following the blood purge Bertha's profit after taxes, gifts, and reserves was 57 million reichsmarks; three years after that it was 97 million, and two years after that 111 million.[24]

Meanwhile, down in the Hauptverwaltungsgebäude, her husband was increasing her capital investment every day. Each great war had seen an ingenious ordnance designer standing at the elbow of the reigning Krupp. In 1870 it had been Wilhelm Gross, in 1914 Fritz Rausenberger, and now Gustav hired as head of the Artillery Designing Department a strapping blond forty-three-year-old Berliner and former storm trooper named Erich Müller. His first name was quickly forgotten. Krupps, Kruppianer, and his admiring Führer knew him as "Kanonen-Müller," the first technician in the Reich.[25] Together with Gustav and Professor Houdremont, he planned the exploitation of Bertha's new wealth. To relieve Wehrmacht anxieties over petroleum reserves they built the *kruppsche* Treibstoffwerk, a synthetic fuel plant, in Wanne-Eickel, northeast of Essen's city line. Seven Renn kiln factories were erected, and the Renn patents were leased to Japan for installations in Korea and Manchuria.

Smaller Schlotbarone were bought out in Bochum, Hagen, and Düsseldorf. New buildings were erected at Hamm and Rheinhausen. In Essen the Cronenberg workers' colony was razed and the Gusstahlfabrik, after spreading in that direction, tripled its output. The Führer sent word that he wanted a hundred new tanks by March 1934 and six hundred and fifty a year later. Employees of the late firm of Koch und Kienzle (E) whipped out the blueprints. Bofors foremen came home from Sweden, and Krupp's Krawa truck assembly lines closed down to retool. Another Führer message ordered the building of six submarines and preparation for a sub-a-month program. Coded instructions were flashed from I.v.S. in Holland to Kiel, and, in the words of Der Kampf der Marine gegen Versailles 1919–1935, the Germaniawerft was able to lay two keels immediately, commission the first of them within three and a half months, "and then, at intervals of about eight days, to put new submarines continuously into service."[26] At Meppen, Kanonen-Müller tested new quick-firing howitzers with motorized traction; in the shadow of Gustav's office Kruppianer began producing shell cases on lathes, transforming precast steel blocks into gun barrels, and erecting new rolling mills capable of handling heavy armor plate. Krupp and his men were transported, deafened to the sound of their own hammers by what the jargon of the time called the Third Reich's "ringing fanfare of trumpets" (schmetternde Fanfare).

On Saturday, March 16, 1935, trumpets and drums throughout the Reich joined in exuberant, ear-splitting concert when a Führerbefehl decreed universal military conscription and an army of twelve corps and thirty-six divisions. It was the end of Versailles. Hitler had buried it and was reading its obituary. This blast at the coalition which had defeated imperial Germany seventeen years before was accompanied by significant revisions in military terminology. The Reichswehr became the new Wehrmacht. The Luftwaffe was unveiled, to the dread of Europe. The Truppenamt was publicly known as the Generalstab once again, and Weimar's Marineleitung, Kiel's chief customer, the Kriegsmarine. The new names sounded virile and were popular — Hitler, with his instinctive grasp of the Teutonic personality, had struck precisely the right chord. That Sunday was Heldengedenktag, Germany's Memorial Day. An official observance of the occasion had been scheduled, and William L. Shirer attended to see how yesterday's dramatic announcement had been received.

I went to the ceremony at noon at the State Opera House and there witnessed a scene which Germany had not seen since 1914. The entire lower floor was a sea of military uniforms, the faded gray uniforms and spiked helmets of the old imperial army mingling with the attire of the new army. . . . At Hitler's side was Field Marshal von Mackensen, the last surviving field marshal of the Kaiser's army, colorfully attired in the uniform of the Death's-Head Hussars. Strong lights played on the stage, where young officers stood like marble statues holding upright the nation's war flags. Behind them on an enormous curtain hung an immense silver-and-black Iron Cross. Ostensibly this was a ceremony to honor Germany's war dead. It turned out to be a jubilant celebration of the death of Versailles and the rebirth of the conscript German army.

The generals, one could see by their faces, were immensely pleased. Like everyone else they had been taken by surprise. . . .[27]

Gustav wasn't; he had had nearly four months' warning. Thus, the Vorstand's annual report noted, "When . . . we were again called upon to manufacture war materials in large quantities, we were immediately ready to do so." By now the Germaniawerft and the Grusonwerk were turning out armor plate and naval guns for *Deutschland, Tirpitz, Admiral Graf Spee, Admiral Scheer,* and *Bismarck,* the world's largest battleship (45,000 tons). Kiel was also building an aircraft carrier and flotillas of battle cruisers, destroyers, and minesweepers, and Essen, Borbeck, and Rheinhausen were disgorging tanks, tank turrets, gun carriages, howitzers, mortars, siege guns, and field guns. The Swedish and Dutch operations were closed down. Every available man was needed in the Ruhrgebiet or the shipyards. Once they were back Gustav found that his potential was greater than he had thought. He could not only arm the Wehrmacht; he could re-enter the international munitions market. Hitler's shattering announcement had provoked a weak protest from Paris, a tremulous expression of hope in London that Anglo-German relations would not be impaired — and a flood of arms orders for Krupp. Turkey, Greece, Brazil, Bulgaria, and the USSR wanted Essen cannon; Fritz von Bülow was relieved of his duties in Berlin and sent to Rio de Janeiro, an arms salesman like his father before him, resurrecting the cloak-and-dagger Krupp tradition which had flourished for nearly a half-century before Sarajevo.[28]

It was a sentimental journey for Bülow, and it was followed by an ironic sequel. Berlin took the position that Krupp should not be dependent upon foreign sources in wartime. In the Führer's words, "The duration of our existence is dependent on possession of the Ruhr," and the forges there were useless unless they could be fed. "Shortage of ore," Göring told Krupp, as though he needed reminding, "must not endanger the program of munitions production or armaments in case of war." In 1914 the younger Moltke had decided against invading Holland to keep an open channel with neutral nations for the Ruhr. The Netherlands had served Gustav well then, but the German navy now felt that Dutch neutrality had, on the whole, been a mistake; toward the end the Allies had been thoroughly searching cargoes bound for there. Besides, the U-boat commanders who had trained with Krupp's I.v.S. wanted bases in the Netherlands. Thus Holland was to be absorbed by the Reich. Occupied, it could not be used as a back door for raw materials. Therefore Krupp was ordered to so design all weapons earmarked for Berlin that they could be produced in an encircled Reich. This meant ersatz alloys, second-class steel. Since the edict did not apply to foreign shipments, Rio and the Balkans acquired guns superior to the Wehrmacht's.[29]

But parallels between Krupp's Wilhelmine trade and arms manufacture in the New Order really lack validity. In the prewar era the firm had traded as a free competitor in a wide-open market. Now all its movements, including export licenses, were scrutinized in the capital. This does not mean, as Alfried Krupp later argued in the dock at Nuremberg, that the firm was the creature of "a system which we did not create, which we only incompletely knew, and of which in many cases we disapproved." Alfried conceded that his father "was the only industrialist, the only private person in a circle of the highest political and military leaders."[30] It would be more accurate to say that Gustav, having done much to create a system in which individualism counted for little, was hewing to the party line.

He did this gladly — and so did his son, the future Konzernherr. As the tempo of the 1930's quickened they eagerly endorsed each of the Führer's steps toward the charnel house. In speeches on April 7 and 8, 1938, they approved the Austrian *Anschluss*; on October 13, 1938, they applauded the Nazi occupation of the Czech Sudetenland; on September 4, 1939, they acclaimed the invasion of Poland; on May 6, 1941, they spoke in ardent terms of the subjugation of the Lowlands and France the year before.[31] They didn't need to scramble around for orders in tiny Balkan capitals and South American banana republics. The magnitude of Hitler's rearmament boom and their special position in the Reich guaranteed their affluence in the present and, so far as they could see, the future. When the Third Reich reached flood tide they would become the most privileged firm in the history of commerce, but long before then they had acquired advantages which left Schneider and Armstrong-Vickers openmouthed.

Only after the capitulation of France in 1871, for example, had Alfred Krupp been in a position to build a private firing range, and even then Gross had been obliged to sign 120 leases before acquiring Meppen's fifty square miles. Hitler gave Gustav an entire country, Spain. On the night of July 22, 1936, the Führer received an urgent plea for assistance from Francisco Franco. Apart from the Condor Legion, a Luftwaffe unit, Hitler merely sent a few troops to the *Caudillo*, but matériel was another matter; altogether the Germans spent a half-billion marks on equipment for him. Civilian technicians from Essen and Kiel went down to study the experiments in mass bombing, the seaworthiness of *Deutschland* in its maneuvers off Ceuta, and the prowess of tanks and ordnance in the field. Krupp's most pleasant surprise was the astonishing versatility of the six batteries of 88's he had contributed to Franco. The reports were so glowing that Generalmajor Hugo Sperrle forwarded them to Hitler, who, according to Sigrid Schultz, later cited them in moving up the date for general war. To the family they were an even deeper source of pride. At the height of the Loyalists' great Teruel offensive against the insurgents, *wahrscheinlicher Erbe des Etablissements* Alfried had been appointed Vorstand member in charge of the War Material and Artillery Construction departments. The improvement of the 88, which he delightedly described as "above all the guns which stood the test of actual performance," had been the first important task of Bertha's first son.[32]

☒   ☒   ☒

On December 17, 1936, Gustav once more led the Schlotbarone to Berlin in response to another telegraphed invitation from the *Reichstagspräsident*. Addressing the industrialists in the Preussenhaus, Göring briefed them on the goals of the Nazis' Four-Year Plan, which required their cooperation, and discussed the inevitable outbreak of hostilities. It was nearly eleven months before the Führer's war decision of November 5, 1937; nevertheless those around him were already convinced that he would fulfill his destiny as Germany's greatest warlord. "Our whole nation is at stake," the Reichsgruppe Industrie was told by their host, who had been appointed *Kommissar* of the plan. ". . . the battle we are approaching demands a colossal measure of productive ability. No limit on rearmament can be visualized. The only alternative in this case is victory or destruction." Then he added, "If we win, business will be sufficiently compensated."[33]

*Unser Hermann* meant to whet their appetites, and he did. Yet it would be wrong to attribute Gustav's enthusiasm for National Socialism to greed. Although his wife's wealth and the vastness of his industrial empire assured him a continuing role in the councils of government, he had, at the time of the Preussenhaus speech, resigned as Reichsgruppenführer. Kurt Schmitt, the Nazi Minister of Economy, had been jealous of Krupp's title. Schmitt had persuaded Hitler to divide business into seven units and to demote Gustav to the leadership of just one of them. Krupp, contemptuous of such squabbling, quit. His name was mightier than any favor Berlin could bestow and he knew it. Repeatedly he declared that he declined to be regarded as just another entrepreneur. Though profits were naturally gratifying, he saw himself as a selfless patriot. With pride he noted in an annual report that despite the cost of the plans drafted by I.v.S., Bofors, and Koch und Kienzle (E) in time, talent, and capital — not to mention risk — "we let other firms profit from our experience," charging them no fee. Similarly, when the Nazis balked at a general rise in steel prices in 1937 and launched the state-owned Hermann Göring steelworks, Krupp, unlike his fellow tycoons, put veteran Kruppianer and successful pilot plants at its disposal.[34]

The zealots of any generation are puzzling to their successors. After Götterdämmerung Gustav's behavior seemed comprehensible only if attributed to a lust for private gain. But National Socialism at its height was one of the most potent political medicines the world had ever known. For xenophobic Germans the tug was irresistible; whatever their reservations about *die Neuordnung*, they joined ranks behind Hitler whenever the Reich seemed threatened. He knew they would, and he made certain that the threat was never far off. That was part of the Führer's genius. His foreign policy made war inevitable, yet each link in the chain of aggression toughened the loyalty of the *Herrenvolk*, and especially that of the *Herr im eigenen Haus*.

Hitler first ruptured the borders of Versailles Germany at daybreak on March 7, 1936, when three battalions of German soldiers goose-stepped across the Rhine bridges, headed for Aachen, Trier, and Saarbrücken, and reoccupied the Rhineland buffer. Gustav's reaction is revealing. The tension of the next two days was almost too much to be borne. The normally rigid faces of the Generalstab twitched with anxiety. Blomberg had only four brigades in combat dress; if the French had blown a single bugle or rolled a single drum he was prepared to execute an about-face and goose-step back over the bridges. That would have been the end of the Thousand-Year Reich, and its leader knew it. If the French had retaliated, the Führer said afterward, "we would have had to withdraw with our tails between our legs, for the military resources at our disposal would have been wholly inadequate for even a moderate resistance." The Reich's most formidable weapons at that time were Krupp's new U-boats. As *Der Kampf der Marine* put it, "On March 7, 1936, during the critical period of the occupation of the demilitarized zone on the western border, eighteen submarines were at our disposal, seventeen of which had already passed their test period, and in case of emergency could have been deployed without difficulty on the French coast as far as the Gironde."[35]

Twenty days after the crisis, when it had become clear that Paris was even more terrified than Berlin, the Führer came to Essen to thank Gustav for the fertile pens of Kiel. Krupp had drawn up the reception timetable with the exquisite attention to detail once reserved for S.M. Over ten thousand Kruppianer had been herded into the Gusstahlfabrik's locomotive shed on Helenenstrasse. Today the huge barn is called the Maschinenfabriken; then it was known as Hindenburg Bay. It was the largest arena in Essen, as long as a football field and almost as wide. At one end a small stage had been erected. While the company band played *Heil Hitler Dir* (formerly *Heil Kaiser Dir*), the Führer, Rudolf Hess, and Karl Otto Saur sat on straight chairs; then Krupp introduced the Führer. A photograph of this scene survives, and at first glance one suspects an optical illusion. Gustav is wearing *two* swastika armbands. Even Hitler has only one. There is no trick. Both brassards were there, and Krupp's behavior after Hitler had snarled his way through one of his more vicious speeches confirmed his mood. Peering at his watch Gustav announced that in ten seconds it would 4 P.M. He had ordered all sirens to sound, as they had that fateful morning thirteen years ago, and while they shrieked he wanted everyone present to stand in silence and hold "inner communion" with their Führer. The tocsins screamed. Twenty thousand workmen's boots clamped down as they rose. Hitler sat mopping his lips while a *Krupp Nachrichten* reporter noted that "tears started from the eyes" of Gustav. The prayerful hush was followed by an ovation; then Krupp declared that "the blood of the comrades of Easter Saturday 1923 was not shed in vain." He wanted the entire world to record that "he publicly honors our great leader Adolf Hitler, to whose service he pledges himself" (*in aufrichtiger Verehrung und im Gelöbnis treuer Gefolgschaft feiert er unsern grossen Führer Adolf Hitler*).[36]

Gustav had pledged his wife's fortune and his own sacred honor, and for a busy executive he devoted a remarkable amount of time to strengthening his Nazi ties still further. Some of these activities were essential to the party. Like other industrialists he had to see that each Kruppianer was enrolled in the Labor Front and weekly "dues" deducted from pay envelopes. In his role as chairman of the Hitler Spende he was obliged to keep up a regular correspondence with Martin Ludwig Bormann, the dour convicted murderer who served his Führer as private secretary, and when manufacturers protested that they couldn't convert to war production without cutting their donations, Krupp had to pass along Bormann's warning that four million reichsmarks must be contributed immediately, "under compulsion if it should not be forthcoming voluntarily."[37] Other gestures were in the tradition of the firm. Like the Great Krupp, Gustav enjoyed sending the chief of state highly polished *Gala* guns. There were also ceremonial Gusstahlfabrik tours for eminent German statesmen — *e.g.*, Bormann, Goebbels, Göring, Ribbentrop, Himmler, Hess, Neurath, Blomberg, Fritsch, Keitel, Raeder, Mackensen, Todt, Speer, Funk, Ley, and Sauckel — and for the leaders of friendly nations, notably Japanese conservatives and Benito Mussolini, who was first shown around by Hitler himself the last week of September 1937.[38]

All these were echoes of the past. But on a personal level Gustav went much farther than either of the two Cannon Kings before him to endear himself to the Berlin establishment. In his anxiety to be accepted as a fellow member of the Nazi club he extended himself in countless little ways, and some which weren't so little. He contributed 20,000 reichsmarks to Alfred Rosenberg's Nazi propaganda in other countries, for example, and designated members of his foreign sales force members of the government's espionage network. Their liaison man with Berlin was Max Ihn, a party member and Krupp departmental director (*Abteilungsdirektor*). Beginning in October 1935 all foreign firms licensing Essen patents were required to submit detailed production figures to Ihn. With these, engineers working under his supervision estimated the industrial potential of possible enemies, including the United States, and forwarded their appreciations to Berlin.[39]

The Nazis responded warmly. In 1935, the year Gustav's salesmen became spies, he turned sixty-five. On August 7 Admiral Raeder wrote Villa Hügel of "my heartfelt desire to express to you my sincere congratulations. . . . I remember gratefully in this connection your great work for the imperial navy and thank you in a similar manner for having again placed at our disposal for the reconstruction of the navy your whole personality and your works." (Gustav, never forgetting that he was only Bertha's *Prinzgemahl*, replied that "My wife wishes to thank you very much for your kind greetings and remembrances, which she fully returns. I add my expression of the most sincere respect to hers and remain with Heil Hitler! Yours very sincerely, Krupp von Bohlen und Halbach.") Five months later Göring threw the Third Reich's biggest party in Berlin; the enormous Opera House was completely redecorated in white satin, over a million marks was spent on entertainment, and Krupp, wearing all his bejeweled decorations, was among the cynosures of the elaborate reception.[40]

By now Schmitt's jurisdictional dispute with Krupp had been forgotten. The Führer, who liked to think of new titles for people, named Baron von Wilmowsky Managing Director (*Vorstandsmitglied*) of the National Motor Road Company (Reichsautobahn Gesellschaft), set up to handle transportation problems which would arise upon mobilization, and both Gustav and Alfried became "War Economy Leaders" (*Wehrwirtschaftsführer*), charged with rallying industry at the outbreak of war. Hitler also enjoyed drawing up loyalty oaths to himself, and on February 6, 1937, he demanded that the Krupps, in their new capacity, sign what he called a "declaration of political attitude": "I herewith declare that I stand by the National Socialist conception of the State without any reserve and that I have not been active in any way against the interests of the people. . . . I am aware that in case of any expressions or actions of mine in the future which might be understood as an offense against the National Socialist conception of the State I must expect, in addition to a legal prosecution, my dismissal from the post of *Wehrwirtschaftsführer*."[41]

When Alfried's copy of this document was read at Nuremberg the presiding judge interrupted to say abruptly, "I don't understand that." It was indeed hard for an *Ausländer* to grasp. Elsewhere businessmen weren't required to swear that they wouldn't do what they obviously had no intention of doing, and asking them formally to deny that they would do it would have been regarded as insulting. But the Krupps made the pledge without a murmur, and afterward Gustav cast about for new opportunities to tug his forelock. One presented itself that September. The year before, he had attended the annual Nazi Party congress, sitting in a dreamy trance as the storm troopers paraded into the stadium to the rousing strains of *Die Fahne hoch* and stood immobile in flawless formations beneath immensely long swastika banners. Gustav yearned to return every year, but somebody in the family had to watch the works, so this time he sent Alfried and Claus. After they returned to Villa Hügel their father wrote Martin Bormann; the letter was discovered eight years later in the scattered rubble of the Reich Chancellery at what had once been Wilhelmstrasse 78. After apologizing for his own absence at the rally Gustav proudly reported that

. . . our two sons both returned from Nuremberg deeply moved. I am very pleased that they have gained these tremendous and lasting impressions [*diese gewaltigen und unvergesslichen Eindrücke*]. My own experience in Nuremberg was that only there could one fully understand the purpose and the power of the movement [*den Zweck und die Kraft der Bewegung*], and I am therefore doubly pleased with the foundation that has thus been assured for our sons.[42]

Birthdays were always festive occasions among the movement's elite; on one of Gustav's Hitler awarded him the Golden Party Badge, making him the most decorated civilian in the Third Reich. To return like for like the Krupps worked furiously each evening, designing a present for the Führer's own fiftieth anniversary. The fruit of their labor was a remarkable piece of furniture, a table which Gustav and Alfried ceremoniously delivered to their leader in his Bavarian mountain villa at Berchtesgaden on April 20, 1939. Unlike the Krupp-Bormann correspondence — which was to grow in historical value as the Thousand-Year Reich aged — the gift did not survive the wartime bombings. Photographs of the presentation are extant, however, and the May 15, 1939, issue of *Krupp Nachrichten* described it in loving detail. Of dark oak, spangled with swastikas and iron crosses fashioned from Krupp Enduro KA–2 steel, its top was engraved with a quotation from *Mein Kampf*. There was a trick lid; it could be removed by pressing two stainless steel lions. Inside, in metal polished to blinding brilliance, was a bas-relief portrait of the Gasthof Zum Pommer, the shabby hostel in the Austrian town of Braunau am Inn where the infant son of Alois Hitler, *né* Schicklgruber, had first blinked at the world the year before Fritz Krupp's formal introduction to Wilhelm II. Though the Führer ordinarily disliked any reminder of his early life, this clearly delighted him. He danced a little jig and then, in that effeminate way he had, cocked his left wrist against his canted hip and extended a limp hand. Gustav didn't allow himself to smile often, but this time he giggled; in the blurred photographs he looks like a rejuvenated old dwarf. The impression of Alfried is very different. Tall and somber, clothed in a tight sheath of what his SS extolled as *Sachlichkeit* (objectivity), he bowed gravely and thumped his heels.[43]

✠   ✠   ✠

To define now the precise relationship between Altendorferstrasse and Wilhelmstrasse in the '30's is difficult. Since the war an entire generation of Germans has been taught that Gustav had become a helpless victim of events who "now merely acted as the executive organ of a will that knew no bounds," whose only alternative was to flee the Reich, and who couldn't do that because there was "no going ashore from this ship" (*aus diesem Schiff steigt niemand aus*). It was more complicated than that. There was the waxing influence of Alfried. There was Bertha, who, after all, owned the business, and who, despite her conviction that she was superior to the Führer, retained her intense patriotism. Finally, Gustav himself was constantly aware of the example of Alfred Krupp.[44]

The sunken eyes of the first Cannon King would have glowed at the March 30, 1938, issue of the *Essener Allgemeine Zeitung*, which observed the fifteenth anniversary of the Easter Saturday episode by presenting the unfortunate Lieutenant Durieux as a sadistic monster who had recruited his men from French institutions for the criminally insane and joined them in gloating over the corpses of blond Aryan children. Still, Alfred had resisted bureaucratic intrusions from Berlin, and while that can scarcely be said of Gustav, the House of Krupp did not always bend to Hitler's will in the '30's. The point is important, for it demonstrates that the nation's greatest industrial family could and did defy the Nazis with impunity. That being established, it follows that the Krupps, father and son, followed the path they did because they preferred it. There is no question that they enjoyed freedom of choice. Although armament offered the greatest profit margin, the Konzern had to look beyond the coming war. Therefore nonmilitary heavy production was never abandoned. Despite vehement objections from Berlin, the firm continued to manufacture locomotives, bridges, and dredging equipment. Göring came to the Hauptverwaltungsgebäude determined to change Gustav's mind and left defeated. To a member of the Vorstand he said bitterly, "*Euer oller Geheimrat würde lieber Nachtpötte statt Kanonen machen*" (Your silly old privy councillor would rather make chamber pots than guns). In 1938 the Berlin cabinet, backed by the Führer, delivered two ultimata to Krupp: the Krawa shop must quit making trucks and convert all assembly lines to tanks, and Kiel must abandon everything except warships. Gustav said no to both. There was an ominous silence in the capital. Then the government, attempting to save face, demanded that a Kruppianer housing development be demolished for munitions shops. Again Krupp's reply was negative. For two years beginning in 1936 he even insisted upon keeping a Jew on the payroll, an electrical engineer named Robert Waller who had worked for him for twenty years. After the *Kristallnacht* of November 9–10, 1938, the "night of broken glass" when synagogues were desecrated and Jews were stalked like animals in a nationwide pogrom, the engineer's fellow employees insisted that he be dismissed. Gustav reluctantly agreed, but made a point of awarding Waller eight months' separation pay.[45]

Every Nazi, Hannah Arendt acidly observed, had his favorite Jew. Krupp's mulishness in this case demonstrates his independence; it does not mean that he opposed the government's anti-Semitic policy. Gustav then — and later, to a far greater extent, Alfried — benefited from the elimination of Jewish competition and the availability of valuable Jewish properties at bargain prices. Indeed, the house of Krupp continued to enjoy one small but symbolic *Kristallnacht* windfall twenty years after the Führer's death. In the wake of the pogrom Hitler ordered Göring to call a meeting of Nazi leaders and settle the "Jewish question" (*Judenfrage*) "once and for all." A stenographic report of the conference survives:

GÖRING: How many synagogues were actually burned?

HEYDRICH: Altogether there are 101 synagogues destroyed by fire, 76 synagogues demolished, and 7,500 stores ruined in the Reich.

GÖRING: What do you mean, "destroyed by fire" (*durch Brand zerstört*)?

HEYDRICH: Partly they are burned down (*abgebrannt*) and partly gutted (*ausgebrannt*).[46]

Goebbels spoke up, noting that "new, various possibilities exist to utilize the space where the synagogues stood." Some cities wanted to erect new buildings, some wanted parks, some parking lots. The Jews must pay for it (*Die Juden müssen das bezahlen*). However, several shrines had such thick walls that they could be leveled only by prolonged blasting, which would be a nuisance to Aryan neighbors. Perhaps these could be rebuilt as museums. One such synagogue stood in downtown Essen. For a quarter-century its massive dome had been the center of the city's Jewish community. After Alfried's postwar release from prison, old Hebrew inscriptions were left on the stone exterior, but a modern architect redesigned the interior. A sign outside the portal read *Industrieform;* the rooms inside were used to exhibit Krupp products, exactly as the little *Doktor* wished.[47]

Krupp's greatest steal during the bloodless conquests of the '30's was a byproduct of German aggression in Austria, and the man who managed it was, of all people, Gustav's mild-mannered brother-in-law. Gustav was *hors de combat* with excruciating dental pains. He had fled to Badgastein spa to convalesce. Tilo von Wilmowsky, as senior member of the Vorstand's five-man executive committee (*Aufsichtsrat*), was obliged to step in. He had already been drawn into the maneuver by his deep interest in the history of his wife's family. Leafing through old documents and deciphering Alfred Krupp's erratic Gothic calligraphy, he had become fascinated by the fact that the Berndorfer Metallwarenfabrik, now Austria's principal metalworks, had been founded by Alfred's brother Hermann in 1843. To the baron it seemed a shame that there was no tie between the Berndorferwerk and Essen.

Briefly a merger had seemed imminent. Hermann's son Artur was childless; in the 1920's he had written a will naming Bertha's second son as his heir. Unfortunately for Claus his first cousin twice removed was in no position to leave anyone anything. In 1927 the Berndorferwerk had foundered, control had passed to new management, and the firm was now the legal property of anonymous Austrian stockholders. Although Claus had gone on to study civil engineering in Krupp's Grusonwerk, preparing himself for what had appeared to be a bright future, the training seemed a waste of time. Barring a miracle, that future was doomed.

Tilo contrived the miracle with the assistance of the Wehrmacht. On February 3, 1937, a full year before the Anschluss, he was in Berlin laying Claus's case before the Nazi leadership. "Dear Taffy!" he wrote Gustav from his estate. "I talked to State Secretary (Hans) Lammers today. He is going to try to have the Führer receive you, if at all possible, week after next. I told him that you wanted to speak to him about the possibility of acquiring Austrian shares and . . . asked him to see to it that the audience take place as soon as possible, as you were very anxious to have the matter definitely settled; and, besides, the Führer himself had promised to receive you. You told me that you would be here on Monday the 8th. I can then tell you the details personally."[48]

One longs for a transcript of that Monday meeting between Tilo and Gustav, for this brief note provides the first evidence that the Krupps, alone among the Third Reich's 69,642,000 private citizens, had access to the most sensitive documents of the Secret Cabinet Council (Geheimer Kabinettsrat). Except under one condition Hitler's intervention in behalf of Krupp's son would be pointless and — even for him — a remarkable breach of diplomatic etiquette. The exception would be a redrawing of the map of Europe, placing the Berndorf factory within his frontiers. So far as the world knew there was no prospect of that. Berlin had recognized Vienna's sovereignty in the Austro-German treaty signed seven months earlier, and the Führer had promised to leave his southern neighbor alone. In secret clauses, however, Dr. Kurt von Schuschnigg had betrayed the Ostmärkische Sturmscharen, the patriotic organization dedicated to Austrian independence which he himself had founded. Attempting to appease Hitler, he had agreed to free Nazi political prisoners and give them posts of "political responsibility." Under Artur von Seyss-Inquart, the leader of the Austrian Nazis, Viennese storm troopers planned to rock the country with daily demonstrations and bombings throughout 1937. During the spring of 1938 they would hoist the swastika and declare open rebellion. All this was foretold in orders to Seyss-Inquart from Rudolf Hess, who promised that before a shot could be fired the Wehrmacht would intervene to stop "German blood from being shed by Germans." Austria would be incorporated into the Reich. Then Krupp could redeem the Führer's promissory note; Claus would receive what the family regarded as his birthright.[49]

That is precisely what happened. After the "Four Weeks' Agony" (February 12–March 11, 1938), the Führer's soldiers marched. Schuschnigg collapsed; the two countries were united in the Union of the Greater Germany; jackbooted Viennese Nazis collared Jews and led them off to clean SS latrines; Baron Louis de Rothschild's Plösslgasse palace was looted — later he bought his way out of Austria by signing his steel mills over to the Hermann Göring Works — and Tilo politely reminded Berlin that as one of the victors Krupp was entitled to one of the spoils. On April 2 Tilo received an answer from Wilhelm Keppler, known to him as the organizer of the Freundeskreis der Wirtschaft, a group of businessmen who venerated Heinrich Himmler and contributed millions to his "Aryan" research. Keppler had just been appointed Reich Commissioner for Austria. He disclosed that he had "spoken to Feldmarschall Göring and he raised no objection to your firm taking over the majority of shares of the above-mentioned firm. I shall presumably discuss the matter also with the Commerce Ministry here today. . . . The transfer of blocks of shares has been stopped by the decree of the Reich Minister for Economics; thus you will not be confronted with *faits accomplis* which might be undesirable to you." The negotiations dragged on until late June. Three other German firms were interested in the factory and had to be rebuffed. In Essen the Berndorfer file (KA–14) grew thick with carbons of waspish exchanges between Nazi functionaries ("I already *told* you in Vienna that State Secretary Keppler had informed me that Feldmarschall Göring had promised Herr Krupp . . . that the shares of the Berndorfer Metallwarenfabrik Artur Krupp A.G. were to be sold only to him"); with Gustav's complaints about his inflamed gums and his spa (". . . the baths are always somewhat trying"); and with explanations to him that the Kreditanstalt Bank, representing Berndorf's Viennese stockholders, was raising impertinent objections to the liquidation. That summer the forced sale was finally consummated, and Krupp paid eight and a half million marks for assets which, according to Essen's own balance sheet, were worth twenty-seven million.[50]

Compared with Alfried's later thefts this was petty larceny. Nevertheless it was an omen, and provides some indication of what had happened to the moral fabric of Germany's privileged classes since 1914. For two centuries the Prussian code had proscribed looting; after Napoleon routed Höhenlohe-Kirchberg and Rüchel at Jena the defeated Teuton troops shivered throughout the bitter winter of 1806–1807 rather than cut wood in privately owned forests. Tilo had been raised in that tradition. Yet he saw nothing wrong in this confiscation of Austrians' savings. That year the National Socialists continued to encourage the revival of German folk songs, and in the Ruhr *Im Wald da sind die Räuber* (In the Woods There Are the Robbers) enjoyed a special vogue. Kruppianer sang it lustily. No one thought the lyrics sardonic. The acquisition was, indeed, a source of pride. After the new factory had been converted to the manufacture of munitions and integrated into Göring's Four-Year Plan, Wilhelm Berdrow, the family's official historian of that era, wrote that "the Anschluss of Austria to the German Reich in March 1938 had the gratifying result, as far as the Krupp firm was concerned, that an old plant established by the Krupp brothers [*sic*] . . . could be incorporated in the Muttergesellschaft in Essen." That is what happened: Claus was on active duty as a Luftwaffe Oberleutnant, so Bertha held the deed. Until he crashed over the Hürtgen Forest on January 10, 1940, while testing a new type of oxygen mask for high-altitude flying, he served as her viceroy, spending his leaves in the Berndorfer head office — a junior officer presiding over a multimillion-mark concern.[51]

There was no chance that Alfried would be expected or even permitted to prove his own fealty at the front. The death of Claus increased the burden which was being speedily transferred to him. Since the denunciation of Versailles it had grown at a staggering rate. Three years before the Kruppstahl juggernaut lurched toward Warsaw, while the Konzern was arming the Reich and building shutters, turrets, and machine gun mounts for the *Westwall* (Siegfried Line), Gustav had been picking up deeds all over the Führer's expanding empire. Economic writers of that period describe the gigantic vertical enterprise as an "octopus," and the old muckraking term, though dated even then, was apt. The rebuilt Gusstahlfabrik — an amalgam of eighty-one separate factories — continued to be the monster's heart. With the contiguous shops in Borbeck, these plants formed a tear-shaped blob on the Ruhr map. From it invisible tentacles reached in every direction. Apart from the wholly owned subsidiaries in Rheinhausen, Magdeburg, Hamm, Annen, and Kiel, Krupp held a controlling interest in 110 firms, including the Skoda Works, and substantial investments, often enough to dictate company policy, in 142 other German corporations. Nothing could touch this dominance, including competition, for an *ad hoc* Reichsverband committee, appointed by the regime and led by Gustav, had urged compulsory membership in existing cartels for all industrialists, arguing that free enterprise could wreck the German economy. Even the Nazis had boggled at this. The barons applied pressure and the government gave way. Two such cartel laws were issued. They were described as emergency measures, but in the Third Reich emergencies tended to become permanent; the decrees became part of the state's legal code.[52]

Abroad, Bertha's smokestacks stained the sky over almost every continental country, from Belgium to Bulgaria, from Norway to Italy. Her reinvested armaments profits had bought over half the stock in 41 foreign plants and large blocks of shares in another 25. There were thousands of Krupp ore pits and coal mines, some with shafts penetrating more than 3,250 feet of the earth's crust. If a heavy industrial enterprise was profitable and German, the probability was that the deed belonged to "Fräulein Krupp." In addition she owned a chain of hotels, a group of banks, a cement works, and — should the industrial revolution end and the clock be turned back two centuries — a score of estates producing enough grain and livestock to support the family for three generations. Thus Gustav could assure his wife that whatever happened to Hitler's Reich, her bloodline would survive it.[53]

Despite Gustav's passion for detail he could not keep up with all this. Like the President of the United States he had a constitution (the Generalregulativ of 1872), a staff of special assistants (the Aufsichtsrat), a cabinet (the Vorstand), a subcabinet (the Prokura), and a congress (Bertha). He rarely went to Berlin except to visit the Führer. Similarly, Villa Hügel guests were limited now to Hitler, Mussolini, a few Japanese, high-ranking Nazis, and certain selected generals and admirals. So close was Krupp to the makers and breakers of reputations that an officer receiving his first invitation to visit Essen could be certain that promotion and a vital mission lay just ahead. Krupp attendance at any National Socialist function automatically gave it status, and like any chief executive he had to think of ways to dodge inferior honors. Here his early training in the Prussian civil service was invaluable. He sent emissaries, and the importance of a group could be judged by the power of the Krupp executive who occupied Gustav's place at the head table.

In the autumn of 1938 the *Kommissar* of the Four-Year Plan was expected to address a conference of iron and steel magnates in Düsseldorf. Whatever his schedule, the prince consort would have to attend. Göring's star, already high, had begun to soar; in the last few months he had been anointed as *Feldmarschall* and appointed economic dictator of the Reich. Then, at the last moment, he sent his regrets to the meeting, and Krupp naturally sent his too. Still, it was going to be an important occasion. *Unser* Hermann's staff was going to review the Fatherland's recent economic achievements. On November 4 the industrialists assembled in an atmosphere of heartiness and elation. Even before the speakers told them they were doing a good job they knew it. They were the chief beneficiaries of the armament boom. Their bookkeepers were breaking all records. During the current year the tycoons had cleared and banked five billion marks (there were just two billions in Germany's savings banks) and since their last annual meeting Krupp alone had doubled the armaments orders on his books. The horizon continued to brighten: in the future plants would not only be strike-free; the Four-Year Plan's administrators had completed the vassalage of wage earners by decreeing labor conscription. Workmen would have to toil wherever they were assigned. Absenteeism was to be swiftly punished by fines and stiff prison sentences.[54]

Under this cheery glow in Düsseldorf there was but one discordant note. Gustav's emissaries were his two most trusted lieutenants, but sharp-eyed barons noticed that they had arrived in separate black limousines and ignored one another during the proceedings. One of them was Alfried, who, having completed his long apprenticeship, was now a full member of Krupp's Vorstand. The other was a bluff fifty-year-old industrial genius named Ewald Oskar Ludwig Löser, who bore an astonishing physical resemblance to Göring. Löser had been a member of the firm less than fourteen months, yet he was already known throughout the Ruhrgebiet as the most gifted executive to join it since Hanns Jencke quit after Fritz Krupp's suicide. He was the director of nine of the Konzern's companies and the powerhouse behind ten affiliates.

Outsiders assumed that the tension between the two men arose from a baronial feud, a struggle for the power that had already begun to slip from the aging Gustav's hands. In part this was true. Alfried remained Bertha's legatee, but he was in trouble. His mother had objected vehemently to his marriage to a divorcée. There was actually a strong possibility of disinheritance, in which case the dynamic Löser would probably become Gustav's successor. But the two Krupp delegates to the Düsseldorf conference would have been at swords' points in any case. There was something between them. Alfried couldn't put his finger on it. Later, in an affidavit written for an American interrogation team, he explained: "I myself could exert no influence on Löser, on account of my younger age, and I probably did not recognize his business policies then — until about 1941 — to their full extent. . . . I realized that in Löser's departments the old Krupp traditions had already vanished to a large extent. . . . Löser's position with Krupp became extraordinarily strong. . . . He was considered within and without the firm as the true representative of Krupp" (*der wahre Vertreter des Krupp Konzerns*).[55]

It was more personal than that. Alfried and Löser were executives with conflicting creeds and personalities, and those differences had led the older man down a dangerous path. Alfried didn't know it. He would have given a great deal for the information, for it would have solved his problem; with it, he could have eliminated his rival. Paradoxically, Löser's secret handicap lay behind his recruitment by Gustav. The senescent Krupp, aware that his wife had cast a dark cloud over their son's prospects, had been looking for a businessman of conspicuous talent. In 1937 he had been introduced to

Carl Goerdeler on Tilo's Saxony estate. Greatly impressed, he had asked him to join the firm. The sequel had been awkward: the Führer had vetoed the choice. He had given no reason, but he had had an excellent one; Goerdeler had just resigned the mayoralty of Leipzig in protest against the Nazi pulverization of Mendelssohn's statue.[56]

When Krupp had stammered that he had to withdraw his proposal, Goerdeler had suavely told him to forget about it. He had other plans anyhow. Had he gone into detail Gustav, as a loyal Nazi, would have been compelled to denounce him. The former mayor intended to tour England, France, and America, urging their leaders to fight Hitlerism. After a coup, he himself would become Germany's prime minister. This was the inception of that strange intrigue which was to reach its climax six years later in the attempt on the Führer's life. Already the plot had become elaborate and included a shadow cabinet. But Krupp, ignorant of it and feeling a sense of obligation to the man whom the inscrutable Führer had chosen to humiliate, had continued to apologize. He had even solicited his advice over promising managerial material. Goerdeler had given him one name — Ewald Löser, who had been his *Bürgermeister* when he was *Oberbürgermeister*. Krupp had met Löser and been captivated by him, and Hitler had let this one get past him. The lapse was understandable. No one except the man who had recommended him to Gustav knew that Löser was a key figure in the shadow cabinet which would be formed when the Führer was purged. He hadn't changed his views since coming to Essen. The brightest star in the Krupp constellation of executives, the threat to Alfried's future, had become as disloyal as a German could be in the 1930's and was, in fact, prepared to collaborate in the assassination of Hitler himself.[57]

# 16

✠

# It Is an Honor to Be an SS Man

THE last of the Krupps had reached his majority on August 13, 1928, two years after Koch und Kienzle had perfected the design of the Reich's new panzers and nineteen months before his contemporary, Horst Wessel, was murdered on a Berlin street. The perspective is important. After his Nuremberg trial a *die Firma* spokesman told the foreign press that Alfried had been a misguided youth during World War II, and the explanation was widely accepted; John J. McCloy, in releasing him from prison, declared that there was "reasonable doubt that he was responsible for the policies of the Krupp Co., in which he occupied a rather junior position."[1] Actually he was a year older than General Telford Taylor, who prosecuted him. He belonged to the generation of Martin Bormann, Heinrich Himmler, and Reinhard (*"der Henker"*) Heydrich. Baldur von Schirach, Gauleiter of Vienna, was born the same year as Alfried; Adolf Eichmann, the year before.

"It was the times. All of them were idealists in their twenties," an elderly acquaintance of the Krupp family later mused. Alfried had made his commitment early. While Gustav was just beginning to weigh the advantages of putting the family's resources behind Hitler, his son was already contributing to the Nazi Party from his allowance. He had also identified himself with its darkest fringe. "In the summer of 1931," Otto Dietrich later wrote, "the Führer suddenly decided to concentrate systematically on cultivating the influential industrial magnates," and that season, the year before Eichmann donned the black shirt of the Schutzstaffel (SS), Alfried joined the SS Fördernde Mitgliedschaft (sponsoring members) — the organization's elite subdivision. He was then a civil engineering student at Aachen Technical College. In exchange for his monthly dues and oath of allegiance to the SS he received a subscription to the

Schutzstaffel magazine, a numbered swastika armband with the circular inscription on its perimeter *Dank der SS für treue Hilfe in der Kampfzeit* (Thanks to the SS for faithful assistance in time of battle); and a membership book bearing a rousing poem by Reichsführer Himmler, leader of the blackshirts:

> *Es ist eine Ehre, SS-Mann zu sein,*
> *Es ist eine Ehre, Förderndes Mitglied zu sein;*
> *Tue jeder weiter seine Pflicht,*
> *Wir SS-Männer und ihr Fördernden Mitglieder,*
> *    jeder an seiner Stelle:*
> *Und Deutschland wird wieder gross werden.*

> It is an honor to be an SS man,
> It is an honor to be an FM;
> Let each of us continue to do his duty,
> We SS–FM men at our posts:
> And Germany will become great again.[2]

Alfried's Nazi Party number — 6,989,627 — was high. He remained aloof from the parent body until 1938, when the Führer had consolidated his power. The son may have been waiting for his father, or for the suppression of the middle-class socialists. It is of small consequence; his faithful assistance to the embattled SS in 1931 clearly puts him in the vanguard of the movement. Equally clear, he was proud of his status as an old fighter. He continued his contributions to Himmler until the outbreak of the war, when his branch of the SS was disbanded. Meanwhile he had joined several other National Socialist organizations, including the Nazi Flying Corps. Claus's enthusiasm for aviation had become infectious. But Alfried spurned the Luftwaffe and chose a party squadron. He was good, too; in six years he rose from second lieutenant (NSFK-Sturmführer) to colonel (NSFK-Standartenführer).[3]

Yet he didn't look the part. To be sure, there was a strong physical resemblance between himself and the Great Krupp. Like Alfred, Alfried was distinguished by a narrow head, high brow, hawklike nose, sunken cheeks, a sardonic mouth, and a long, lean face. The two were alike in other ways, too: shy, lonely, uneasy; each with the same locked mind. But in some respects we know Alfred better, because he was such a compulsive writer. Alfried rarely committed an unnecessary word to paper. And though his support of Nazi causes leads one to expect a certain stance — something like the icy stare and outthrust chin of Otto Skorzeny, another of Alfried's contemporaries in the party — it wasn't there. He had no dueling scars, no monocle. He seldom clicked his heels and never shaved his head; indeed, much of the time he needed a haircut. His handshake was spongy, and his manner with strangers wistful, anxious, wary. He smiled tightly, just crimping the corners of his mouth and scarcely moving his rather pendulous lower lip. Most surprising of all were his eyes. They were flat and faded, and they roved all the time, as though he were wearing contact lenses that didn't quite fit.

Sir William Elliot, the English flyer, met him in the home of a mutual friend and commented afterward that Alfried was the very opposite of his concept of a Prussian tycoon.[4] In reality Alfried's understated, impersonal manner was more British than Prussian. That was not entirely illogical. The German aristocracy's streak of Anglophilia had survived 1918. Gustav had sent Claus and Berthold to Oxford. Tilo von Wilmowsky's son Kurt was preparing to follow them there, and on her afternoon walks Barbara Krupp Wilmowsky wore an English lady's tailored tweeds, mouse-colored scarf, floppy felt hat, and blunt-toed shoes; she carried a stout stick, and when she returned she poured high tea. Barbara's most famous nephew could have passed as British. With his bony, equine features Alfried might have been an unemployed English actor, say, or an eccentric Midlands bookkeeper. He didn't look like gentry, though. Something was lacking: a certain buoyancy, a sense of assurance; and he was fated never to acquire it. This is puzzling, for his subsequent achievements, outstripping in some respects those of Alfred, were to argue the presence of these very traits. And indeed, the closer one examines Alfried the more one is aware of the wild contradictions in him. There is no pattern there. He comes close to being one of those Men of Mystery whom prewar journalists cherished, the Men Nobody Knew.

Perhaps no one ever knew Alfried. One of his brothers once remarked to this writer, "He has enormous control. It's not always easy even for me to establish contact with him." To an acquaintance he himself said after the war, "You know, I'm not close to any of my brothers and sisters except Waldtraut, and she lives in the Argentine now." One of his oldest acquaintances was bewildered by their reunion the year after Landsberg War Crimes Prison No. 1 freed Alfried. The two men had last met in Berlin in January 1942. Ten momentous years had passed. There couldn't have been more to talk about. Alfried entered the room and nodded briefly. He said, "Oh, hello."[5]

By then he had become *the* Krupp, entitled to spend his time and his fortune as he pleased. His preferences are instructive. Over most of the Hügel estate barbered grass rises and falls in even swells, but one corner is laced with thickly wooded ravines, and there, as far as possible from the castle, Alfried built a fifteen-room home. Privacy was assured by the erection of barbwire and a manned sentry box. Inside he lived quietly with five servants, often spending his evenings in solitude, drinking White Horse Scotch and chain-smoking Camels from a fluted gold cigarette case, a habit which dated from the early 1930's.

He attended no church. He never went to a concert. He seldom picked up a book. Philanthropy bored him. Yet he did spend a great deal of money. His afternoons and holidays were devoted to expensive hobbies — sailing his sixty-six-foot yacht *Germania* V from his hideaway on the North Sea island of Sylt, flying around in his private Jetstar, taping classical music records, and photographing his travels. He really worked at photography, adding his own sound track to his movies in an elaborate home laboratory; his meticulous darkroom log shows that he spent 522 hours on a single film. When he returned from a trip abroad, his color snapshots were collected in book form and published in editions of four hundred. The volumes cost him forty dollars each and were sent free to chiefs of state and cabinet ministers — that is, to potential customers — in the countries depicted. Like his christening in 1907, they were good for business.[6]

They were not good photography. Equipped with the finest German cameras, schooled by experts in the use of them, Alfried stalked his subjects. He would line up the Taj Mahal, check his light meter, and *click!* — he had taken a banal postcard shot. One can pick up a similar view in Delhi for a few annas. In Egypt he approached the Sphinx, adjusted his knobs and dials, and left with a stolid picture you have seen a thousand times. His movies had the same defects. A safari reel, taken from an automobile, showed a lion. On the sound track Alfried's bleak voice identified the beast as a lion. And that was all. Of his feelings, the element of excitement, even the speed of the car, there was nothing. *Sachlichkeit* — objectivity: the Reichsführer would have approved.

Nearly all his pictures had this in common: the absence of people. In art as in life he remained aloof from the crowd. One pored over his prints of Japanese landscapes, Siamese temples, the bathing ghats of Benares, the sunsets of Ceylon — and then, unexpectedly, a human being appeared. It was Alfried himself, and it was no ordinary self-portrait. By posing between facing mirrors he had created a stunning spectacle of countless Alfrieds receding into the distance, half of them facing the lens, half turned away. The result was a graphic allegory of his global presence, and because it was imaginative it baffled all previous judgments of him.[7]

The metaphor goes deeper. For every image we have of Alfried facing us there is an opposite. He was inarticulate. He was also brilliant. He looked vague. Yet when British troops assembled senior Ruhr industrialists at Recklinghausen in 1945, the other prisoners instantly elected Alfried camp leader. He appeared to be hesitant. But he made every major decision in the Konzern for a quarter-century, and differences arising among his middle-aged siblings were resolved by big brother, who was always watching them. Although he was introverted, he had an adventurous life. Early in the Nazi regime he was a daring flyer; thirty years later in his custom-built sports cars he covered Essen streets at lightning speed. He would sail the North Sea in the teeth of a force-eight gale until his shaggy eyebrows were encrusted with salt, and when an airline captain was discharged for alleged recklessness and negligence, Alfried promptly hired him to fly the Jetstar.[8]

Significantly, friends assumed that his motive was to acquire a good pilot. No one credited him with compassion. He was so detached that in some ways he was almost an emotional cripple. Nevertheless, he had his commitments, some of them very strong. Before his postwar trial he frankly told Dr. Max Mandellaub, an American interrogator, that he had supported Nazism from the outset as "the only chance to put Germany on its feet again," and he went to his grave declining to disown Hitler.[9] His loyalty to the House of Krupp was undivided. No matter how late he had been up the night before, however low the whisky in the bottle, whatever the number of cigarette stubs in the ashtray, when in the Ruhr he rose early and started for the Hauptverwaltungsgebäude in his low-slung pearl-gray Porsche, skillfully executing the racing changes at each corner.

Really it would have been very difficult for him to forget himself in Essen. Ten city license numbers were reserved for his personal auto-grandfather, his great-great-grandmother and great-great-grandfather, and his mother's great-grandfather's great-grandfather's great-grandfather Arndt, who started it all by exploiting the bubonic plague. Altogether, more than a hundred city streets were named for Krupps and faithful employees, not to mention parks, hospitals, and housing projects. Other German Wilhelmstrasses honored S.M.; Essen's was a tribute to Therese Wilhelmi Krupp (1790–1850). Elsewhere Graf-Spee Strasses glorified the name of the German admiral; here it evoked memories of a Krupp mobiles, and they all began with the letters ERZ, because Erz means "ore" in German. Reminders of his dynastic heritage were posted all around him. On his morning drive he passed streets named for one of his sisters, four of his brothers, his father, his grandmother, his great-grandmother and great-product, the armament of the pocket battleship which fought valiantly for Führer and Reich in the first major engagement of World War II.[10]

Arriving at the office — always at 9:30 A.M. precisely — the Porsche was greeted by a blue-uniformed Krupp policeman, who sprang to attention and brought a rigid hand to the bill of his cap in a martial salute. Alfried flapped his arm in a casual response and left the car parked on the sidewalk. He never got a ticket, perhaps because the city had more Krupp policemen than traffic policemen. By any yardstick it was a municipal anachronism, the biggest company town in the world. The three circles of Krupp's trademark stared at you everywhere, from walls, matchbooks, flower vases, coat lapels, and, if you tried to escape them by fleeing into a *Bierstube*, from the bottoms of shot glasses fashioned of Kruppstahl. The *Bürgermeister* of Essen was a retired Kruppianer. The city auditorium was reserved for important company functions. It was illegal to erect any new buildings on the south bank of the Ruhr, which would spoil Alfried's view from Hügel, and if you were looking for an important city record you found it in the family archives on the hill. Even the Roman Catholic Bishop of Essen wore a ring set with a piece of Krupp coal. When Essen designed a ring of its own in the early 1960's, to be awarded to international celebrities of uncommon distinction, municipal authorities agreed that only one person was worthy of the honor — Alfried Krupp von Bohlen und Halbach.[11]

This atmosphere of the '60's was pretty much what it had been in Alfried's youth, when the title Krupp belonged to Gustav and Alfried was still Herr von Bohlen und Halbach. The difference was that in the '30's he had not yet mounted the throne; he was the future king, being trained by the most zealous of prince consorts. Young Herr von Bohlen spent five full years studying at Aachen, and that was his third college. Beginning in 1925 he had devoted four years to chemistry, physics, and metallurgy, first in Munich and then in Berlin-Charlottenburg. In 1934, after nearly a full decade in classrooms and laboratories, Aachen graduated him with honors as a certified engineer (*Diplomingenieur*). One might assume that he had had education enough. Gustav didn't think so. He wanted to be sure that the next Konzernherr was familiar with all aspects of the business. Alfried's 12-pfennig-an-hour apprenticeship had been a start in that direction. As sole proprietor he wouldn't be spending much time at forges and slag heaps, however; he needed experience on loftier levels, so for six months after graduating with honors from Aachen he served as an unpaid employee (*Volontär*) in Berlin's Dresdner Bank, learning about high finance. In November 1935 he left Berlin and began an eleven-month orientation course in the Hauptverwaltungsgebäude. On October 1, 1936, ten months before his thirtieth birthday, he was appointed deputy director in an elaborate ceremony at the Kapenhöhe, a Krupp auditorium. Carl Görens introduced him to the assembled executives; then Alfried strode up and down the aisles, shaking hands with his future subordinates and receiving congratulations.[12]

✠   ✠   ✠

He had already seen Hitler once, during that emotion-packed appearance in Hindenburg Bay, and when the Führer next visited Essen, Alfried was introduced to him as a full-fledged member of the board in charge of rearmament. Meanwhile he appeared to be living the best of lives in the Third Reich. On the third floor of Villa Hügel his parents had built him a private suite, walled in rich dark leather. His name and his position automatically gave him a voice in the management of twenty-four other German corporations and banks. The mounting responsibilities on Altendorferstrasse were his chief preoccupation, of course; in the words of one writer, *"Er empfand dieselbe Liebe für seine Firma, die andere für ihr Vaterland und ihren Glauben empfinden"* (He pledged the same devotion to the company which others give to their Fatherland and their faith). Still, a healthy man had to relax occasionally. Weekends Alfried could choose from a variety of diversions. He belonged to the Reich's Yacht Klub, Automobilklub, Aero-Klub, Hochseesport-Verband Hansa (Sea Sports Association), Turn- und Fechtklub (Gymnastics and Fencing Club), and Luftsportverein (Air Sports Club); to the Deutsch-Öster-reichischer Alpenverein (German-Austrian Alpine Club), and, for rainy days, the Deutsche Adelsgenossenschaft, the Association of German Nobility, under whose auspices everyone with a privileged *von* in his name was entitled to consort with his peers and enjoy their aristocratic company.[13]

Yet his skies weren't as blue as they seemed. As long as his father was in command they would be menaced by a cloud no bigger than a stopwatch and equally exasperating. Satisfying such a parent was extremely difficult. In the summer of 1934 the family was vacationing in Schleswig-Holstein, and Gustav discovered that the yachting school at Glücksburg had just been taken over by the Marine SA. Most SA activities were suspect after the Röhm purge, but its navy was an exception. Besides, Gustav believed all his sons should have military training. Being only eleven, Eckbert was exempted; Harald declined for the convincing reason that, as a member of the luckless class of 1916, he was obliged to spend six months in the Nazis' compulsory labor service plus two years as a military conscript. Alfried, Claus, and Berthold had no excuse. They were enrolled and drilled day after day. Furthermore, their names were now in the SA files. For years afterward Berthold was approached by brownshirts demanding that he attend this or that meeting, and he hated it.[14]

Claus enjoyed it. Gustav's second son came very close to the Aryan ideal. He was handsome, fair, and a physical brute; he dreamed of martial glory. No one in the family remembers any serious conflict between Claus and his father. The youth's prospective future in Austria's Berndorferwerk pleased him immensely, and on September 22, 1938, six months after the *Anschluss*, he married a Viennese girl in Baden. Gustav and Bertha were overjoyed; the alliance strengthened the dynasty, and it was the family's second that year. To the surprise and delight of her parents, Irmgard, the least comely of their children, had won the heart of a nobleman. On April 6 she had become the Baroness von Frenz in a civil ceremony at Bredeney Rathaus. The wedding had been followed by an extravagant reception at Hügel, the last big occasion there before Claus's funeral. If Irmgard could marry well anyone could, and the aging *Prinzgemahl*, now approaching seventy, should have contemplated the end of his life serenely.[15]

Unfortunately Alfried had become a problem. Conflict between Gustav and the strongest of his sons was inevitable; the question was where it would arise. In politics and at the office they saw eye to eye, and Hitler's designation of the coming Krupp as Wehrwirtschaftsführer on August 11, 1937, with Four-Year Plan responsibilities equal to his father's, had gratified the old Krupp. The difficulty lay in Alfried's personal life. As early as 1926, when he was eighteen, he had become the subject of parental frowns. According to his own account, Gustav had accused him of frivolity, of spending insufficient time preparing for examinations, and of wasting his time "playing around Munich." Alfried won their first quarrel. He wanted a fast racing car, and after a long wrangle his father gave him the money. In Munich he careened through the old city in a red Simson; later in Aachen he traded up for a souped-up Austro-Daimler, which he took with him to Berlin. During the summer and fall of 1935 he left exhaust trails over much of western Europe. Perhaps he was weary of his endless training; perhaps the life of a Dresdner Bank *Volontär* was dull. In any event, he was seen in the resorts of southern Europe, in Paris, and in the smart night clubs of Estoril, on the Portugese coast. It was no way for an *SS-Mann* to behave, let alone a Krupp. Gustav's frown deepened.[16]

The spree was brief, and perhaps it was also pitiful. Before winter settled in Alfried was back in the Ruhr, congratulating Max Ihn on his new appointment as the firm's "counterintelligence" (*Spionageabwehr*) chief and poring over U-boat blueprints at his new desk. For the rest of his life he would be shackled to responsibility. Unhappily for familial harmony, however, he had sowed one oat which was hard to uproot. In Berlin he had fallen in love with Anneliese Bahr, the quiet blond daughter of a Hamburg merchant, and he was determined to marry her. This time he was up against his mother. Bertha was so vehement about divorce that she had forced the resignation of a Krupp director who had left his wife, saying it upset her to see him (*da es sie jedesmal aufregte, ihn zu sehen*). When she learned that Anneliese had been married before she was implacable. At the same time, Gustav's discreet inquiries brought the astonishing news that the girl's sister had married a Jew and gone off to Latin America with him. Did Alfried want to be related to people like that? he asked indignantly. Alfried did. Legally there was no way of stopping him — to prevent "racial pollution" other SS men were forbidden to wed without Himmler's permission, but those with numbered swastikas were exempt — and on November 11, 1937, according to the family archives, he contracted what his parents regarded as a morganatic marriage in the Berlin suburb of Wiesenburg. On January 24, 1938, according to a biographical stipulation signed by his lawyer at Nuremberg, the bride gave birth to a son in Berlin-Charlottenburg. The new grandmother's comment is not recorded.[17]

The child was christened Arndt Friedrich Alfried von Bohlen und Halbach, thus naming him after (1) his father, (2) the first Krupp, and

(3) Anneliese's mother-in-law's father. Bertha was unappeased. Like Fritz and Marga a half-century earlier, the couple and their baby were consigned to the castle's *kleine Haus*. Left to themselves they were, by all accounts, quite happy; as an old Hügel servant puts it, "Those were the only years when I saw Alfried smile, and when he was with Frau Anneliese he smiled all the time." But love could not conquer all. They were in an impossible situation. The pressure from the big house grew and in the encapsulated society of the Ruhr's managerial class there was nowhere to turn for relief. Crude jokes were circulated about the new Frau von Bohlen's background. It was really quite respectable. Her father was a former cavalry captain; her union with her first husband had been brief, and she had borne him no children. Had she been accepted on the hill, she would have been accepted everywhere. Lacking that sanction she was everywhere rejected. Her reputation was cruelly mauled. In a crude pun on her maiden name she was called the *"Bardame."* The future looked hopeless, and Alfried's inheritance was threatened. Clearly it meant a great deal to him; he once said, "I believe I have to follow my great-grandfather's will even though it is a hundred years old" (*selbst wenn er jetzt schon hundert Jahre alt ist*). There could be no doubt that Alfred would have wanted his granddaughter's son to preside over his Gusstahlfabrik, and so, at the end of four years, Alfried and Anneliese capitulated. After the divorce she moved to the Bavarian lake of Tegernsee and raised young Arndt there. Arndt's father, alone and lonely once more in his leather-walled suite, withdrew more deeply into himself. His eyes grew colder, his manner more carefully impersonal. To Tilo it seemed that his attitude was one of "ironical sarcasm," even toward National Socialism. He himself said, "My life has never depended on me, but on the course of history."[18]

His career and history were now about to merge. Aware of it, he gave himself entirely to his work. Although Gustav had tried to emulate old Alfred, he had been handicapped by his role as an outsider. In his early thirties Alfried not only looked like the family's idol; he sounded like him, too. He spoke contemptuously of the weakness of stock companies, stressed the responsibility of Kruppianer to their employer, and, in contemplating the coming struggle for Europe, sounded a note of Alfredian vigor: "The only way to stop us is to kill us all." In mastery of shop details and technical competence he quickly outstripped his father, who had never overcome his diplomatic training. Alfried had steeped himself in the tradition of the House. Soon the bold initials AK would once more appear on orders to the firm, and he intended to be worthy of them. One day a visitor, looking down on the swarming traffic of Altendorferstrasse, asked, "Why do you have your office here on the main street?" Without looking up Alfried replied, "Because my great-grandfather's office was here."[19]

In directing *die Firma*'s armory during the stupendous conflict which was about to begin, he held one trump which the original AK had lacked.

When Roon had asked Krupp in the spring of 1866 not to supply any guns to Austria without the consent of the king's government, the best Alfred had been able to do was to assure him that Berlin would be kept informed of any consignments for Austria. He would gleefully have exchanged all his Viennese orders for the Kriegsministerium's long-range plans, but Roon, Moltke, Podbielski, and even Bismarck and Wilhelm I would have been outraged at the suggestion that they share military secrets with a layman. Hitler wasn't outraged. He realized that his struggle had become the Krupps' too, and that the more they knew the likelier were the prospects of victory. Thus the minutes of his Geheimer Kabinettsrat were promptly forwarded to the Hauptverwaltungsgebäude. Krupp responded with alacrity. On October 12, 1937, Max Ihn had assigned an executive named Sonnenberg to meet regularly with a naval captain representing the Intelligence Bureau (*Abwehr*) of OKW (*Oberkommando der Wehrmacht*, the high command of the armed forces), forwarding reports from Krupp agents abroad and receiving strategic information in return. On December 29, 1938, OKW forwarded a suggestion through Sonnenberg that they form a joint committee to create an agency for "disrupting enemy industry and commerce" — in a word, sabotage. Krupp not only agreed; the firm had an overseas force-in-being ready to go. In the United States, for example, Kruppianer had been operating out of Wilmington since the 1920's. Through Otto Wiedfeldt, Weimar's ambassador to Washington and a former Krupp director, American loans meant to put Germany back on its feet had been channeled to the Krupp-Nirosta Company, licensed under the laws of Delaware.*[20]

There is no evidence that the Krupps saw Blomberg's fateful appreciation of June 24, 1937, in which he alerted the armed forces to "the military exploitation of politically favorable opportunities," but that is unsurprising; there were only four copies of it. In view of the close ties to OKW the Vorstand probably heard of it. Certainly the firm's leaders must have known of the Führer's four-hour speech to his generals and admirals in the Wilhelmstrasse that autumn. Hitler had assembled them to discuss war eventualities (*Kriegsfälle*). According to the transcribed shorthand of his young adjutant, Oberst Friedrich Hossbach, he declared that Germany's problem could be solved only by force, and that was never without peril: "If one accepts as the basis of the following exposition the resort to force, with its risks, the only remaining questions are 'when' and 'where'" (*dann bleibt noch die Beantwortung der Fragen "wann" und "wie"*).[21]

A lunge by the new Wehrmacht was now assured, and in the subsequent exposition Hossbach noted that if the Führer was "still living," it was his

---

* In January 1940 its name was shortened to Nirosta and Swiss ownership was attempted as camouflage. Nirosta was an invaluable cog in the Nazis' Argentine apparatus until Pearl Harbor, when the FBI, which had been watching it all along, moved in and padlocked its offices.

"unalterable resolve to solve Germany's problem of space (*die deutsche Raumfrage*) at least by 1943–1945." During the next year Hitler advanced the date, and Essen was aware of it. On March 18, 1939, "Kanonen-Müller" began holding regular meetings with him, briefing him on Alfried's progress, and on May 17, a full week before the Führer called a meeting of the Nazi leadership in the Reich Chancellery and disclosed his intention to attack the Poles, he advised the Konzern to cut off all arms shipments to Warsaw. Alfried obliged; among his postwar files was this record of a telephone conversation: "Subject: Exports to Poland. Instructions for the immediate future. All exports to Poland are to be stopped immediately. Contracts should not be canceled. Polish customers pressing for delivery can be given evasive answers (such as — consignment not complete, or freight cars lacking, etc.)."[22]

✠ ✠ ✠

That was a deft way to allay suspicion, and Alfried had no doubt that suspicions would be justified. As he later put it in a Nuremberg affidavit, it had become "quite clear to me that German policy was not guiltless as far as the outbreak of war was concerned"; he discounted Goebbels's "propaganda declaration" that Germany was the helpless victim of aggressive neighbors. He could hardly claim otherwise. Not only had he honed the tip of the lance which ripped open the Reich's eastern frontier; in two August meetings the Führer had told him that the Westwall must be ready to repel a French offensive by August 25. At OKW the safety of the *Waffenschmiede* in Essen was a matter of grave concern. Afterward Franz Halder, describing the Ruhr as the "most decisive factor in the German conduct of the war," declared that if the French had screwed up the courage to end their sitzkrieg and climb out of the reinforced concrete vaults André Maginot had designed for them, seizing the heart of Krupp's complex while the Reich's troops were tied down on the Vistula, Hitler would have had to sue for peace.* The Führer knew the danger. When he did turn to the west his war directive declared that the offensive was necessary to win "a protective area (*Vorfeld*) for the Ruhr."[23]

In Essen the tension was unimaginable. No one at Villa Hügel spoke of it; a wartime invasion of Essen would eclipse the troubles of 1923, and the closest the family came to discussions of the great lurking fear was in Alfried's proud recital of the statistics of his gun production and his four brothers' display of their immaculate uniforms. Claus was ruddy and gay in Luftwaffe blue, the others struck poses on the lawn in *feldgrau*. All three, appropriately, were in the artillery: Berthold, twenty-five, and Harald, twenty-three, as *Oberleutnants*, and Eckbert, who had just turned seven-

---

* Halder's anxiety over the Ruhr is strikingly like the younger Moltke's in 1914, which resulted in disastrous weakening of the German right wing (see Kuhl 174).

teen, as a *Leutnant*. Watching their horseplay by the portico, Gustav choked up. He often became moist these days, and in an office at 9 Kirchmannstrasse his personal physician, Dr. Gerhard Wiele, pondered the old Krupp's growing emotionalism with apprehension. Wiele's star patient obviously showed his age. Allied intelligence officers, monitoring the broadcasts of DNB (Deutsches Nachrichtenbüro), Goebbels's official news agency, had no way of knowing that he was coming unstuck. As late as 1944 DNB announcers would report a Gustav speech to the students of Berlin University exalting martial virtues and the miracles wrought by the Führer, neglecting to add that it had been read for him because he was incapable of delivering it himself. By then any layman could arrive at Wiele's diagnosis. Goebbels himself had done so a year earlier. In his diary for April 10, 1943, he had written, "Old man Bohlen, now seventy-two and a half years old, is already somewhat gaga" (*verrückt*).[24]

There is no way of tracing Krupp's medical history in these years. His doctor is dead; an RAF bomb destroyed the medical records at 9 Kirchmannstrasse. But senility cannot be pinpointed anyhow. It manifests itself in odd little acts, blurred vision, and spells of childlike irrationalism which come and go. The first such incident of consequence was precipitated by the imminence of war. As long as saber rattling was confined to Nuremberg rallies, audiences with the Führer, and intrafirm memoranda, Gustav enjoyed it. He knew the timetable as well as Alfried; he had approved it. Still, it was one thing to contemplate the hostilities in the vague future and something else to stare at the calendar and realize that the last days of peace were slipping by. Suppose the Reich should lose? It had happened once, and the thought of another 1918 was insupportable. He had been elated by Chamberlain's surrender at Munich. This was *Kaiserwetter*, and he wrote the woodchopping All-Highest in Doorn to tell him so. He was adding a sentimental postscript (S.M. would turn eighty on January 27) when Fritz von Bülow, now his confidential secretary, tiptoed in with disturbing news from Hjalmar Schacht. To the astonishment of everyone around him, Hitler hadn't been at all appeased. He was furious with Chamberlain. "That *Kerl*," Schacht had heard him say to his SS bodyguards, "has spoiled my entry into Prague!" The Führer had really wanted war. He was convinced his troops could overwhelm Czechoslovakia in a week. Gustav knew better; the old Koch und Kienzle team had expressed great professional respect for the Skoda equipment carried by the thirty-five Czech divisions. In dismay he stammered to Bülow, "I — I don't understand the Führer at all! He has just signed a wonderful agreement. Why is he being bitchy?"[25]

The secretary left, shaken. Hitler had never been mentioned in this office in anything except the most reverent terms. Accusing him of being *nörglerisch* — for Gustav had used the vulgar form — was *lèse-majesté*. It was an unaccountable lapse, and next spring Alfried noticed another. The order to cut off Poland's arms thrilled the younger generation. Not Gustav; he developed a tic, and his familiar strut lost its bounce. At first he convinced himself that the threat was a myth. Hitler must be bluffing. In early August, with Kruppianer toiling feverishly on the Siegfried Line, he came to his senses. According to Karl Fuss, then director of the firm's educational department, Krupp summoned him and asked his help in drafting a letter in English. Significantly, he did not call Alfried. His son's English was flawless, but so was his allegiance to the Führer, and the father's intentions bordered on subversion. One message, he remarked cryptically, was going to "a leading British politician" (einem führenden englischen Politiker) whom he had met once and whom he now begged to help him stave off war. To Fuss he muttered, "I don't know whether the gentlemen in Berlin have any idea what it means to become involved with the British Empire." Then he requested Fuss to translate another appeal — this one, he said, would be dispatched to a man "high in the industrial world of the United States" (führend auf dem Gebiet der Industrie der Vereinigten Staaten).[26]

Meanwhile, during the period in which he had convinced himself that the danger didn't exist, he had given his brother-in-law tragic advice. Earlier in the summer the baron and his wife had been packing for Oxford. They planned to visit their son. Like his father before him, Kurt had completed his studies at Balliol, reading politics. The Wilmowskys were eager to celebrate; afterward Kurt intended to sail for South Africa for a holiday. But his father was worried. Since Hitler's March 15 entry into Prague, or, as the Führer preferred to put it, the "liquidation of the rump Czech state," British attitudes had hardened. When Sir John Simon rose in the House of Commons and delivered a cynical speech in what it was fashionable to call the "Munich spirit," it met with what newspapermen described as "a pitch of anger rarely seen." Next day Chamberlain stowed his umbrella. In a speech broadcast from Birmingham the prime minister apologized for Munich and promised to mend his ways. Of the rape of Czechoslovakia he asked rhetorically, "Is this the end of an old adventure or the beginning of a new? Is this the last attack upon a small state or is it to be followed by others? Is this, in effect, a step in the direction of an attempt to dominate the world by force?" If so, and if "Herr Hitler" assumed that "this nation has so lost its fiber that it will not take part to the utmost of its power in resisting such a challenge," he was making a fatal miscalculation. Berlin was amused. The Wilhelmstrasse couldn't believe that Arthur Neville Chamberlain had found his spine. Yet he had. He had been cheated; he was enraged; and on the eve of All Fool's Day (as Goebbels sarcastically observed) the discredited hero of the previous September stunned the Commons by a unilateral guarantee of Poland's frontiers. "I may add," he concluded in his reedy voice, "that the French government have authorized me to make it plain that they stand in the same position in this matter."[27]

Six months earlier, while a crowd outside 10 Downing Street sang, "For he's a Jolly Good Fellow," Chamberlain had appeared in a second-floor window and reminded them of Disraeli's triumph at the Congress of Berlin in 1878. "My good friends," the jolly good fellow had cried, "this is the second time in our history that there has come back from Germany to Downing Street peace with honor. I believe it is peace in our time." Now, with the troops scarcely demobilized, there was once more talk of a general European war, and Barbara and Tilo, about to cross the channel for a reunion with a son who expected to spend the rest of 1939 in a dominion of the British Empire, were uneasy. They didn't know what to do because they had no idea what the Führer had in mind. Gustav knew. He and his son had access to state secrets which were withheld from other members of the Aufsichtsrat. They were among the privileged handful authorized to hold friendly (*kollegiale*) discussions with the Wilhelmstrasse on policy, so the baron went to his relative and friend of thirty-three years for advice. At the mention of war Gustav became highly agitated. As Tilo later recalled, "He answered, and in a rather excited manner, and I remember it very well, that there could be no question of war because such madness could not happen."[28]

It happened less than three months later. At dawn on September 1, as the first olive light appeared in a lowering, overcast heaven, Hitler's gray steel juggernaut roared across the border and took dead aim on Warsaw, led, as Günter Grass later wrote sardonically in *The Tin Drum*, by "the German tanks, stallions from the studs of the Krupps von Bohlen und Halbach, no nobler steeds in all the world." In Essen over two thousand of the Reich's top ballistics experts had reported to Alfried for duty; they were poring over Krupp's 1,800,000 cannon designs and listening to DNB accounts of the offensive, hoping to hear that the poilus were staying in their hideouts and that Kruppstahl was doing its job on the eastern front. They were, and it was. No weapons director in the history of the House, including Wilhelm Gross in 1870, could match the Alfried–Kanonen-Müller performance of 1939. Even when their opportunities to experiment in Spain are discounted, the record remains dazzling. Naturally Goebbels couldn't reveal details over the radio, but the technical appreciations crossing Alfried's desk were ecstatic. The Panzers were singled out for special praise. One report glowed that "the latest tank developed by Krupp, *viz.*, type PzKw IV, has gained particular distinction during the campaign in Poland. There have been surprisingly few breakdowns"; and an intrafirm memorandum pointed out that "The fact that we manufactured both tanks and antitank guns stood us in good stead . . . and gave us a knowledge of both tanks and how to combat them."[29]

But no one weapon accounted for the stunning success of the blitzkrieg. Krupp had fashioned an incredibly sophisticated arsenal, and one official summary indicates how pitifully outclassed the gallant Polish cavalrymen were: "The great fighting strength of the German artillery, the superiority of the German tanks, especially the tank IV, over those of the enemy, the performance of the 8.8-cm. antiaircraft gun in support of other formations in attack as well as in defense against enemy tank attacks, the masterful power of the German Luftwaffe, of the submarines and the battleship *Bismarck*, speak clearly for the quality of these weapons." A later account described how "Krupp's assembly lines in his hundred factories turned out guns in all calibers — antiaircraft guns, antitank guns, and heavy naval guns — in addition to tank, submarine, and other warship and aircraft parts, and, last but not least, the steel which was used by other munitions producers" (*den anderen Waffenfabriken*).[30]

Writing his first annual report for the entire Konzern on October 1, 1939, three days after the Kremlin banquet at which Ribbentrop and Stalin divided up Poland, Alfried was at his bloodless best:

We take great pride in the fact [*Wir sind sehr stolz auf die Tatsache*] that our products have come up to expectations during the war, and we have been strengthened in our desire to do everything in our power to maintain the technical quality of German ordnance equipment, thus playing our part in reducing the Wehrmacht casualties [*dadurch unseren Beitrag zur Verminderung der Wehrmachtsverluste zu leisten*].

Profits for the last fiscal year, he announced, were 12,059,000 marks. Their products just having received the best possible commercial, another boom year loomed, and in anticipation of it Alfried declared a Christmas bonus for all Kruppianer.[31]

It didn't help his cousin Kurt. After toasting Balliol's seven centuries at a final high tea with his parents, young Wilmowsky had sailed for Capetown, and he was camped on a veldt when he learned that a state of war existed between his hosts and his Fatherland. He was on the sidelines; he could have remained there. But Teutons of his generation would have regarded that as dishonorable, and Kurt, like Claus and like Hans Adenauer, nephew of the future chancellor, was to join that roll of Balliol Germans who made the supreme sacrifice for the Reich. In Capetown he tried to return to the Reich by signing aboard a freighter as a common seaman. Spotted, he was interned and sent to a prison camp in England, where he charmed his guards by playing Bach on the piano each evening. They were sorry to see him go, but embattled Britain had decided to transfer enemy aliens to Canada. So he sailed once more, and for the last time. At Schloss Marienthal, Tilo and Barbara received word through Switzerland that their son had drowned. The bitter details came later. In mid-Atlantic his ship had been sunk — by a Krupp U-boat firing a Krupp torpedo.[32]

☩   ☩   ☩

In the first two years of the war the number of Krupp victims multiplied by geometric progression. To lay the full horror of those months at the ornate door of the Hauptverwaltungsgebäude would, of course, be fatuous; nevertheless the firm had become much more than a weapons forge. To an extent unprecedented in the history of industry, a corporation had become an integral part of a warlord's apparatus. In foreign policy the mesh was perfect. Less than a month after Claus had had the honor to lay down his life for his Führer, and two months before the invasion of Denmark, Krupp's Copenhagen agent was sending OKW coded information on Danish armaments establishments.[33]

He was working under intense pressure; Hitler's formal directive for the conquest of Scandinavia (Weserübung) was not issued until three weeks later, and when the fleet sailed north at 5:15 A.M. on April 9, 1940, Krupp's representative in Norway was caught off guard. Fifteen miles south of Oslo, where the fifty-mile Oslo Fjord narrows perceptibly, stood the eighty-five-year-old fortress of Oscarborg. Essen's man in the Norwegian capital had been ordered to send OKW detailed information on the defenders' strongpoints, but in his haste he had overlooked the fact that Oscarborg was armed with ancient 28-cm. Krupp cannon. Despite their age they were in superb condition. In a blaze of deadly fire they crippled one heavy cruiser, Lützow, and sank another, Blücher, with a loss of 1,600 seamen and several Gestapo officials who were on their way to proclaim Vidkun Quisling dictator of Norway. Oskar Kummetz, the admiral commanding the squadron, was obliged to swim ashore. The rest of his ships had to turn back for twenty-four hours. The Wilhelmstrasse was outraged by this insult to the German flag, and Altendorferstrasse, feeling partly responsible for it, was humiliated. Forty years earlier the Boxers had done the same thing at China's Taku forts. The All-Highest had visited his wrath upon Fritz Krupp then, and the new leader's temper was even shorter. There was no telling what he would do. In fact he did nothing. He was far more understanding of the pitfalls of the arms trade than any of his predecessors. Even when he learned that the firm's last big foreign sale before the beginning of hostilities in Poland had been a warship delivered to the Soviet Union, he kept his patience. After all, he observed tolerantly, it wasn't always possible to tell who tomorrow's enemies would be, and at present Russia was an ally anyhow.[34]

Krupp's record in the Low Countries was better. There tomorrow's enemies were identified early. At 11 A.M. on October 10, 1939, Hitler had issued his War Directive No. 6, ordering preparations "for an attacking

operation . . . through the areas of Luxembourg, Belgium and Holland."
Six days later Alfried received an inquiry from Holland about a shipment
of howitzers and antiaircraft guns; it was set aside with the marginal
notation "Not to be answered." That proved awkward. Because the conquest of Denmark and Norway delayed the thrust westward, Amsterdam
began to react sharply to Essen's tergiversation, and on March 16, 1940,
one of Alfried's aides sent him a frank appraisal of the problem: "They
greatly mistrust us, and even more so since the Dutch officers who were to
come to Essen to inspect the materials for the 10.5-cm. field howitzer, and
who had applied for visas to enter Germany, have not been issued these
visas to the present day, although private Dutch individuals have had their
visas issued without any trouble." Despite the necessity for evasion, he
added, "the Dutch should on no account become aware of this." The
shifting and dodging continued for eight weeks more; then the visa applications became pointless, since Holland had been incorporated into the
Reich.[35]

The pattern was repeated in the Balkans. Early the following year the
Hauptverwaltungsgebäude, alerted to the Wehrmacht's imminent blitz of
Greece and Yugoslavia and determined not to repeat the blunder of
Oscarborg, sent OKW a list of all Krupp guns delivered to Belgrade and
Athens, some of them dating back to Alfred's time. Yugoslavia was of
special interest to the rising young Kanonenkönig because of its priceless
deposits of chrome ore. Chrome was essential to the production of fine gun
steel; imports from outside Europe had been cut off in the autumn of
1939, and as early as the following spring Alfried had cast a covetous eye
upon the Balkan fields. That May a Krupp mining expert named George
Ufer was told that henceforth he would serve three masters: the Konzern,
the Hermann Göring Works, and the Führer. As director of a dummy
firm, Ufer crossed the border and began a geological survey of Yugoslavia,
reporting his findings directly to the Reich's nearest consul general.[36]

That summer the invasion of Russia marked the end of the war's first
phase. On September 3 the casualty list reported that Corporal Hanno
Raitz von Frenz had been *"in der Schlacht gefallen"* (killed in action).[37]
Irmgard went into mourning and Hügel's footmen redecorated the castle
with their bolts of crepe for her husband of three years. The death of
Claus could no longer be regarded as an isolated tragedy. Victory, it
seemed, was going to take a little longer than everyone had assumed.
Already some members of the Vorstand were looking back longingly to the
war's first year, when everything had gone perfectly — when Gustav's fears
had seemed unfounded and he himself had forgotten that he had ever
nursed them.

In its hour of shining triumph the regime had not forgotten its armorer.
Three of the Reich's most eminent Nazis, Rudolf Hess, Fritz Todt, and
Hitler himself had paid tribute to the Gusstahlfabrik's wartime efforts, to

its secret rearmament before 1933, and to Gustav himself. Hess had come first. At 11 A.M. on May 1, 1940, he had appeared in Hindenburg Bay with an immense flag — the Nazi "golden banner," designating the firm a "National Socialist model plant." Robert Ley had stood beside Hess; Alfried beside his father. The Krupp magazine of May 15 proudly re-created the scene.

> After the Essen Trumpet Call, our proven Krupp band of wind instruments under the baton of Leader Schnitzler plays Paul Hoffner's *Musik zum Frankenburger Würfelspiel,* a unique composition which is especially suited to the occasion because of its solemn character. Next, Amtsleiter Schröder . . . reads the names of the plants which have already received awards. The name of Krupp leads them all. Every fellow worker who had the privilege of sharing it must have felt his heart beat faster with pride and joy at this moment.
>
> The stirring address by Rudolf Hess, the Führer's deputy, is known to our colleagues from the daily press. It was characterized by a most timely political note — settling final accounts with the Jewish-plutocratic-democratic world.[38]

After the *Sieg Heils* had died away it occurred to Gustav that *he* had taken timely steps toward settling with the Jewish-plutocratic-democratic world while Rudolf Hess was still an economics student at Munich whiling away his free time distributing anti-Semitic pamphlets. Old Krupp still had lucid moments, and in this one he decided it was high time the Reich started paying him back for his investments of those years. He asked Todt to come to the Gusstahlfabrik. According to Alfried's file note of July 25, 1940, his father "gave an impressive account of Krupp's development after 1918," relating "how, at the time, he had discussed at length with the Reich Chancellor [Wirth] the question of whether or not he should, in the conversion of the plants, keep in mind any future restoration of Germany's military power, in spite of the fact that the regulations of the Treaty of Versailles prohibited Krupp from producing any war materials except in a negligible amount." He felt that repayment was due. Todt agreed warmly and "assured the firm of Krupp that the present government would not fail them."[39]

Two weeks later Gustav celebrated his seventieth birthday. This time he was not so lucid. He was dazed, partly from gratitude; the previous evening he had learned that Hitler intended to descend upon Essen like the Kaiser of old, bearing bright ribbons and glittering medals. As always, Krupp's limousine drew up at the Hauptverwaltungsgebäude within ten seconds of 9 A.M., but today Bertha sat beside him, and Alfried, Irmgard, and Waldtraut rode in a smaller car just behind. They all waited in the marble hall, surrounded by directors and executives, until the Führer strode in. After embracing Alfried he announced that "In the name of the German people I confer upon Dr. Exzellenz Gustav Krupp von Bohlen und Halbach the Shield of the Eagle of the German Reich with the inscription 'German Führer of Economics.'" This *Adlerschild des deutschen Reichs*, he decreed, must be displayed in the center of the north wing of the administration building throughout the remainder of the Thousand-Year Reich. In addition he conferred upon Krupp the title Pioneer of Labor (*Pionier der Arbeit*) and the War Cross of Merit (*Kriegsverdienstkreuz*). The cross came in two orders — regular and commander's. Hitler was awarding Gustav both. Standing beneath his golden banner, wearing his Golden Party Badge, and glorified by his Wehrwirtschaftsführer title, the septuagenarian prince consort would cut as spectacular a figure as Göring.[40]

The Führer stepped aside and his anile gunsmith walked robotlike to the lectern and spoke briefly. A colleague who had not seen him since Hess's visit was appalled at his evident deterioration. He saw "a man with snow-white hair, holding himself even more stiffly than he had in the past, his features set like a mask, his gestures strictly disciplined, his whole body rigid" (*maskenhaft starren Gesichts, unfrei in jeder Bewegung, verkrampft*). Afterward, in his office, Gustav told his secretary that he didn't understand it. He couldn't think what he had done to deserve such glory. After all, he had merely followed the path of duty [*seine Pflicht getan*].[41]

# 17

✠

# Crier Havot!

AT daybreak on May 10, 1940, the Wehrmacht crossed the frontiers of Belgium, Holland, and Luxembourg — three little nations whose neutrality Hitler had promised to respect — and wheeled westward and southward in a great arc of *feldgrau* tunics and coal-scuttle helmets stretching 175 miles, from the North Sea's Frisian Islands to the vaults of Maginot. In the chaos of war it is always difficult for the press to find out what is going on, but here commentators were faced with a revolution in military technology, an army of Krupp tanks which, as William L. Shirer discovered, was "unprecedented in warfare for size, concentration, mobility and striking power" and which, when it began lurching into the Ardennes Forest, "stretched in three columns back for a hundred miles far beyond the Rhine." On the fifth day the French dam broke. Two German tank divisions crossed the Meuse near Sedan on a pontoon bridge; by dusk their bridgehead was thirty miles wide and fifteen miles deep. Winston Churchill, Britain's new prime minister, flew to Paris May 16 and asked the commander-in-chief, General Maurice Gamelin, "*Où est la masse de manoeuvre?*" Gamelin had no strategic reserve. He shrugged. "*Aucune,*" he replied: "There is none." Within seventy-two hours an unstoppable phalanx of seven panzer divisions, hurtling westward past the caved-in, quarter-century-old trenches of the Hindenburg Line, was fifty miles from the English Channel. The British Expeditionary Force, every Belgian soldier under arms, and three French armies were ensnared in a taut net of Kruppstahl. On Saturday, May 18, Churchill ordered troops home from the Near East. "I cannot feel that we have enough trustworthy troops in England," he informed the chief of the Imperial General Staff, "in view of the very large numbers that may be landed from air carriers preceded by parachutists."[1]

At noon that same day a Bavarian art dealer named Artur Rümann sat down for lunch in an exclusive Düsseldorf club with three Ruhr industrialists. No one then knew that the fluid front had jelled. When the dimensions of the success became clear, General Alfred Jodl scrawled in his diary, "Führer beside himself with joy." Rümann kept a diary too, and in its own way it is as valuable a contribution to history as the general's. Like Jodl he felt hopeful that noon, though for an entirely different reason; he had been openly critical of the regime and had, in consequence, found it increasingly difficult to make a living. Lately he had been working as a cultural agent; today he hoped to make a sale. His host, a Henkel plant manager (*Betriebsführer*) named Lübs, had married an old friend of the Rümann family. Lübs was an astute collector, and Rümann represented the owner of a valuable picture. The agent needed the commission and expected to get it. He failed. Like the BEF, the Belgians, and the French, he was trapped by the Sedan breakthrough.[2]

During the meal the telephone in the private dining room rang. Lübs excused himself. "The young Krupp will come here," he said upon returning, and just as they were putting their napkins aside Alfried entered. The art historian was introduced to him, but there wasn't much time to talk, because everyone wanted to hear the two o'clock DNB news broadcast. In an adjoining room they gathered around a radio on a small smoking table. One of the businessmen had brought a map. He spread it out and their eyes darted across it, searching for place names as the announcer identified the depth of the Wehrmacht penetration. As yet the communiqués hadn't mentioned France, but "in Holland," Rümann noted, "the situation had so consolidated that there was a possibility that outstanding members of the economy would be able to travel there now. The tension of these gentlemen grew perceptibly; the radio was shut off or was lowered and now the four gentlemen pointed with their fingers to certain places in Holland." He heard them babbling excitedly: "Here is village ———. There is Müller; he is yours," and "There is Herr Schmidt, or Huber . . . he has two plants, we will have him arrested." At one point Alfried said to one of the others, "This factory is yours."[3]

They were, in short, responding to the medieval European call, "*Crier havot!*" — the fourteenth-century Teutonic command to pillage. Rümann, standing behind them, recoiled:

> They resembled vultures gathered around their carrion [*um ihre Beute versammelten Aasgeiern*], and you may believe that a man like me, an art historian, who has dedicated his life to the preservation of culture, was bound to be very much shaken by this.

Disgusted, he put his hand on his host's shoulder and said, "Herr Lübs, may I take my leave? I don't seem to be in the right place here." He knew that he had "lost this deal which was vital to me, but at that moment I didn't care at all." Lübs was busy telephoning his office to acquire special passports for himself and the others, who were engrossed by the map. Rümann quietly slipped out to reappear in Alfried's life as a Nuremberg witness.[*4]

Even before the thrust into Poland the Führer had invited German tycoons to submit lists of properties lost in 1918, and Gustav had asked for restitution of his Lorraine holdings. The Weimar Republic had already compensated him for them, but the request was reasonable compared with what actually happened. With the crushing of all Allied resistance conditions were completely altered. One needn't have a legal claim to enemy property. It was necessary only to get there first and persuade the army's military government officers to intercede. This was, of course, outright brigandage. Technically the plundering masqueraded as "leasing," but like most Nazi subterfuges it was exceedingly transparent. As the exhausted French troops fell back on Vichy, Göring sent Krupp secret instructions via the Armed Forces Operations Office (*Wehrmachtsführungsamt*) noting that "One of the goals of the German economic office is the increase of German influence in foreign enterprises. It cannot be seen yet if and in which way the peace treaty will deal with the transfer of holdings and so on, but it is necessary even now that every opportunity be used to make it possible for the German economy to gain a foothold even during the war." The Hauptverwaltungsgebäude, responding, alerted all representatives of the firm traveling in occupied countries: since "Krupp's interests must be pursued as opportunities arise" and "information must be received on time," news of available factories should be promptly dispatched to Essen.[5]

The firm's special status with the armed forces enhanced its role as exploiter. Doubtless that prestige alone would have been sufficient to guarantee an excessive share of the spoils, but the Reich's debt to Krupp continued to grow. In the Netherlands, agents left behind when the undercover manufacture of U-boats ceased at I.v.S. were able to inform occupation authorities where valuable caches were. Frequently they led them to the spot. The Dutch naturally thought this uncivil — without their indulgent hospitality the sub fleet of OKM (*Oberkommando der Kriegsmarine*, high command of the navy) could never have achieved its present might — but the military governors were grateful. Of even greater importance was Alfried's membership in two official organizations estab-

---

* Dr. Rümann has since been derisively described in Essen as an *"ältlicher Kunsthändler"* (elderly art dealer), but he is not so easy to dismiss. The author of four books, he held degrees from the universities of Berlin, Munich, and Heidelberg. In the spring of 1940, when he recorded the above episode in his diary, he was fifty-two years old, and during the author's last visit to Munich his mind was lucid.

ished to organize looting, the Reichsvereinigung Eisen (Reich Iron Association, or RVE) and the Reichsvereinigung Kohle (Reich Coal Association — RVK).[6]

As a member of the RVK's praesidium and chairman of its organization committee, he was strategically placed, but his role in the RVE was still more significant. Formed in the third year of the war, the iron association was one of those semiautonomous cliques which wielded absolute power in the name of the Führer. Alfried, jubilant over his appointment, wrote his father:

> Essen, 29. Mai 1942
> *Gusstahlfabrik*

*Lieber Papa,*

Many thanks for your letter dated the 26th of this month.

Dr. Müller and I went yesterday to Reich Minister Speer, who promptly named me to the Rüstungsrat. Furthermore, he informed me that he, together with the Reich Minister for Economy, had suggested me as deputy chairman for the Reich Iron Association which is to be formed. . . . I accepted this post mainly because I am convinced that Fried. Krupp must play a leading part in the new Reich Iron Association [*Ich habe diese Ernennung hauptsächlich aus dem Grunde angenommen, weil ich davon überzeugt bin, dass Fried. Krupp eine führende Rolle bei der neuen Reichsvereinigung Eisen spielen muss*].

Herr Speer promised once more to come to Essen, but was not yet able to fix a day.

With many greetings to you and Mama,

> ALFRIED[7]

Albert Speer later said that he came to regard the deputy chairman as one of RVE's "three wise men" (*drei weise Männer*).* According to RVE records, on July 22, 1942,

> . . . *Alfried Krupp, der die RVE vertrat, wohnte mit Speer einer Sitzung des Zentralen Planungsausschusses bei . . . sowie anderen, im Laufe derer beschlossen wurde, 45.000 russische Zivilarbeiter in die Gusstahlfabrik, 120.000 Kriegsgefangene und 6.000 russische Zivilisten in die Kohlengruben einzusetzen, sowie auch gesundheitliche Forderungen für den Einsatz von Kriegsgefangenen zu stellen, welche niedriger waren, als die Forderungen für in den Kohlengruben beschäftigten deutschen Arbeiter.*

> . . . Alfried Krupp, representing the RVE, attended a session of the Central Planning Board with Speer . . . and others, in the course of which it was decided to impress 45,000 Russian civilians into the steel

---

* The other two were Hermann Röchling, the Saar's steel king, and Walter "Panzer" Rohland of the Deutsche Edelstahlwerke.

plant, 120,000 prisoners of war and 6,000 Russian civilians into the coal mines, and to place the medical standards for recruiting prisoners of war lower than those required of Germans employed in the coal mines.[8]

Among Alfried's more devious creations was Holland's Rijksbureau voor Ijzer en Staal, a German office which systematically ordered Dutch firms to deposit, at confiscation depots, specific consignments of iron, steel, and alloys. Here his years of engineering training proved invaluable. He knew what the Dutch had, what Krupp needed, and how to spot inferior ores.[9]

The victors' cool, methodical approach, combined with the ruthless use of force, reaped historic harvests. Berlin was able to exact occupational assessments of over seven billion dollars a year from France alone, four times the reparations which the Weimar Republic had paid annually under the Dawes and Young plans — and which Hitler had denounced as criminally unjust. Yet Alfried was always thinking of new ways to improve the yield. Casting a covetous eye upon the European assets of United States citizens, he wrote a fellow member of the Vorstand, inquiring what steps had been "undertaken to secure trusteeships of enterprises of interest to us in case American property were confiscated as a retaliation against the Americans." A second letter suggested seizure of a specific United States firm: "Singer Sewing Machines is, to my knowledge, American property. The appointment of trustees as a retaliation against the Americans is to be expected shortly. Perhaps a Krupp man could then become trustee."[10]

The Hague Peace Conference of 1899, which Count Georg Münster had signed in behalf of Germany, was explicit about the sanctity of private property in wartime. It declared that "if, as a result of war action, a belligerent occupies a territory of the adversary, he does *not*, thereby, acquire the right to dispose of property in that territory. . . . The economy of the belligerently occupied territory is to be kept intact. . . . Just as the inhabitants of the occupied country must not be forced to help the enemy in the waging of war against their own country or their own country's allies, so must the economic assets of the occupied territory not be used in such a manner." Hitler had torpedoed the Versailles Treaty, but he had not denounced the Hague Articles, and Alfried knew it. As a member of the Verbindungsstelle Eisen für Schrifttum und Presse, an organization which provided the most powerful Nazi industrialists with confidential information, he received a cutting from the British *Financial Times*, together with a translation into German. After the war both were found in his personal file. The article was terse and to the point:

Sooner or later, the Allies will have to draw up their lists of war criminals . . . it is expected that those who have ordered or executed looting of all sorts will not be overlooked. It is an undisputed principle that spoliation of occupied territories is considered to be a war crime.[11]

✠    ✠    ✠

In occupied Paris the victorious Germans tended to cluster around the Arc de Triomphe: in the wired-off Avenue Kléber, down the Avenue Foch (where Gestapo headquarters were located), and in the elegant homes of French millionaires. Alfried's office was at 141 Boulevard Haussmann, nine blocks from the arch. The building — it still stands — is a tan four-story brick mansion with an elaborately sculptured façade and much highly polished brasswork, and there is a story behind Krupp's acquisition of it. Before the fall of France it had belonged to the Société Bacri Frères, a Jewish firm. Krupp's Paris agent, Walter Stein, had had his eye on it during the Munich crisis. When the Nazi commissar for Jewish questions arrived, Stein persuaded him to confiscate No. 141 and turn it over to the newly organized Krupp Société Anonyme Française. His office manager was a Kruppianer named Leon Schmitt, who was on excellent terms with Richard Sandre, provisional administrator of Rothschild holdings.[12]

Alfried himself wasn't in Paris much. He was traveling almost continually through occupied territories in his new role as one of *die Firma's* ruling triumvirate. As early as 1937, when Löser moved to Essen, Gustav had confided to him that he wanted to be a *konstitutioneller Monarch*. After the Führer had ingested France the old man published an announcement in Essen declaring that in the future "The decisions of the Directorate in technical matters are to be made by Görens, in commercial and administrative affairs by Löser, and in matters of mining and armament by Alfried von Bohlen und Halbach" (*auf dem Gebiete der Bergwerk- und Rüstungsindustrie von Alfried von Bohlen und Halbach*).[13] Foreign acquisitions, it was decided, lay in Alfried's domain. Furthermore, since he would be touring the Low Countries, France, and later Yugoslavia, looking for plants, equipment, and raw materials, he might as well handle other problems there as they arose.

Robert Rothschild[14] was a problem. He needn't have been. Had he listened to reason, capitulated to Krupp, and signed papers assigning title of his Société Anonyme Austin in Liancourt on the Oise, he would have survived the war and might be alive today. But he was a stubborn man. In the last spring of peace he had bought 91 percent of the twenty-year-old factory's shares for four million francs, and he was proud of his acquisition. During the first week in June 1940 he had to evacuate it. On the advice of French authorities he left his home at 42 Rue Victor Hugo six days before the entry of German troops and moved — temporarily, he thought — to Lyon. When Vichy struck its bargain with the Führer at Montoire in October, the industrialist prepared to return north. His business was the manufacture of tractors; now that hostilities had ended he saw no reason why he shouldn't resume it. To his surprise the Lyon Chamber of

Commerce detained him. His journey, he was advised, would be most unwise. Rothschild couldn't understand why. After all, he wasn't even a Frenchman; technically he was a citizen of Yugoslavia, which at that date was still neutral. It made no difference, the French businessmen replied. In the eyes of the conquerors his Yugoslav papers were bogus. To them he was just another Jew. The Reich had rules about Jews. Monsieur Rothschild would find the climate more agreeable here on the Rhone.

There was a way out, or so it at first appeared. His wife Vera was a Gentile, and her brother Milos Celap, an energetic thirty-one-year-old Yugoslav, knew the business. That autumn Milos, to whom we are indebted for the full account of what happened,* rode to Liancourt and found the factory occupied by German troops. Their commanding officer, Lieutenant Bröckler, explained that there could be no question of a Rothschild repossessing the works, and that it would be extremely dangerous for him to recross into occupied France. However, if he transferred his stock to an Aryan — in Bröckler's opinion Celap himself was Aryan — the wheels could begin turning once more. In Lyon the dispossessed proprietor was first dismayed, then resigned. He agreed "in the interest of my family, to save my heritage, and also in the interest of the factory workers and my agricultural clients in France." All assets were put in his brother-in-law's name, and at Liancourt Bröckler accepted Celap as owner. The troops marched away, the workmen returned to their benches and lathes. Tractor production began once more, and that seemed to be it.

It wasn't. In Essen the Konzern was vexed by the Wehrmacht's rising demand for trucks. The buildup for the invasion of Russia had begun; Berlin expected Krupp to deliver thousands of DB–10's heavy Daimler-Benz *Blockwagen*. Ten weeks after Celap's resumption of production a Vichy Frenchman presented himself at the factory door and said he was taking it over as "provisional administrator" (*commissaire gérant*). Rothschild's transfer of shares to his wife's brother had been illegal, he explained; all transactions involving Jews after May 23, 1940, lacked validity. That left things exactly as they had been: Rothschild still owned the plant. Upon learning this, he dug in his heels. He had hesitated to step down for a trusted member of his family; he had no intention of giving his shops to a stranger, and a predatory, anti-Semitic stranger at that. At first glance his intransigence seemed irrelevant. Ten German firms were competing with one another for the seized property, and OKW and the Nazi Party's Office for Foreign Commerce (Aussenhandelsamt) awarded it to Krupp. In an announcement dated August 27, 1942, Alfried formally renamed the plant Krupp S.A. Industrielle et Commerce, Paris.[15] Subsequently he supervised the transfer of his Krawa production to Liancourt. A subordinate reported that Alfried "gained throughout a favorable impression, which he also

---

* See note 14.

communicated to me. He takes the view that we should continue to support the efforts to produce in the west."[16]

Still, Germans like things *blitzsauber*, neat as a pin, and the exasperating fact remained that Liancourt's deed was held, not by the Aryan Krupp, but by the Jew Rothschild. At 141 Boulevard Haussmann, Walter Stein was applying every conceivable pressure upon the military authorities and Vichy. A succession of provisional administrators was appointed; each was dismissed for failing to resolve the issue. In the beginning they tried to deal with Celap, but his own position became precarious when Germany invaded Yugoslavia; on April 6, 1941, he fled into the unoccupied zone. Nearly twenty months later, on November 25, 1943, Stein believed he had found a solution. The *commissaire gérant* was Richard Sandre, described in contemporary documents as "persona grata with Krupps."[17] Moreover, in a memorandum to Essen, Stein reported the establishment of "a closer contact with the French government"; he had made "the acquaintance of Count de Janchais, who is the liaison officer of Marshal Pétain. . . . The man is talented and has been specially entrusted with the task of collaboration by the marshal." By now it had become obvious to everyone concerned that remarkable talents would be required. Rothschild hadn't budged, though he knew Krupp was in dead earnest. Discovering that the marshal was as indifferent to his Yugoslav citizenship as the Führer, he had tried to escape to Portugal through Spain in September 1942 and had actually crossed the Spanish border when French police raced after him, apprehended him, and sent him to a concentration camp at Saint Privat on the Ardèche River. Celap persuaded (or bribed; the record is unclear) the prefect to release his brother-in-law. Rothschild then moved to a villa at Cleon d'Andran. It was a precaution. The little hamlet was in the Italian zone and thereafter appeared safe to him.

He erred. In Cleon d'Andran he was accessible to Stein, Stein's man Schmitt, Schmitt's collaborator Sandre, and Sandre's Lyon contact, a Vichyite attorney named Damour, whom Pétain had appointed to the Commissariat for Jewish Affairs. Together they represented Liancourt's bureaucratic regency, the House of Krupp, and the vassal French regime. Rothschild's appraisal of the Italian position was correct. As the German Foreign Office noted petulantly, "the lack of zeal" shown by Italian officials made solution of the Jewish problem in French territory occupied by Italy exceedingly difficult.[18] But the Nazis were in a position to change all that. They had the muscle and the will, and to a degree which has been vastly underrated they were actively supported by French Fascists. Confronted by this power Mussolini's benevolent despots were impotent, a fact which Sandre tried to impress upon Rothschild in a personal call on February 6, 1944. According to Celap, who was present, Sandre pointed out that transfer of title to Krupp was virtually a *fait accompli*. Resisting it was pointless; Krupp already had the machines and had signed a lease with the authorities responsible for Jewish property. As ex-proprietor, however, Rothschild could clarify the title by approving certain papers. (The places where he should sign were neatly checked in pencil.) In addition he could surrender the firm's books, which he had taken with him during the collapse of the French army and without which Alfried could not properly "assess the valuation of the company's shares of stock." Rothschild set his jaw. He declined to accept the status of former owner. Indeed, he refused to cooperate in any way, despite his blackmailer's repeated threats, couched each time in the same language: "If you don't want to give me that information — well, you can just imagine what will happen to you."

It happened two weeks later. On the night of February 21 a gang of Vichy's anti-Semitic Parti Populaire Français swooped down upon the villa, kidnapped Rothschild from the Italians, and delivered him to Montluc prison in Lyon. From there he smuggled a letter to his brother-in-law via Maître Levigne, a notary public and mutual friend:

> . . . I am sorry to cause you so much trouble and annoyance. Thanks and sincere friendship.
>
> ROBERT

*This blow is due to Damour and Sandre. Precise information.*[19]

Damour and Sandre now proceeded to consummate their crime. They filled out the necessary forms in triplicate, converting the last vestiges of the Société Anonyme Austin to Krupp S.A. Industrielle et Commerce; Schmitt accepted in behalf of Alfried Krupp. They were all behaving as though Rothschild were legally dead, and by the time the last signature had been witnessed he was. The two French turncoats were, as they explained to Boulevard Haussmann, weary of petty Jew-baiting (they called it *Judenverfolgung;* local collaborators spoke the Aryan language), so they were going to turn this *Dummkopf* over to the Eichmann apparatus. At the end of February Rothschild was sent to the huge Nazi concentration camp in Drancy, northeast of Paris. It was at Drancy that Prussian diligence reached one of its ghastliest *culs-de-sac;* anxious to allay suspicions that the cattle cars rolling eastward were headed for *Vernichtungslager* (extermination camps), Eichmann's local deputy ordered the mixing of adults and children in exact proportion to the percentage of each in the general population — "The Jews arriving from the unoccupied zone will be mingled at Drancy with Jewish children now at Pithiviers and Beaune-la-Rolande."[20] Rothschild was assigned to the first such train; his last seventy-two hours were spent trying to comfort orphans who were too small or too terrified to understand the orders barked at them by members of Death's-Head detachments (*Totenkopfverbände*) — storm troopers in this SS branch wore skull-and-bones shoulder insignia on their black tunics.

The first such train was assembled quickly. On the eve of its departure Drancy's commandant recorded that as of 1900 hours he had "deported" a gratifying number of inmates. The figure, give or take a Jew, was 49,000. Next morning his graph soared. While dawn lightened the eastern sky over the German Reich an enormous *Gruppe* was crammed into boxcars and headed for the horizon. Robert Rothschild was among them. Krupp's *Judenfrage* was about to be solved by the most shocking version of the Final Solution; the locomotive's destination was Auschwitz. There, beneath the great and now famous gate inscribed ARBEIT MACHT FREI (work makes you free), the haggard passengers stood dumbly while the selector, frequently advised by a Krupp executive, cried *"Links!"* or *"Rechts!"* directing which way they should go. It was *Links* for Rothschild, though Celap's Nuremberg affidavit merely states that his wealthy brother-in-law was "sent on 7 March 1944 to Auschwitz, from which camp he never returned nor ever gave a sign of life." He put it that way because he couldn't bear to set down the details. Krupp's thirty-seven lawyers, assuming he had none, pounced on this. Two of them hammered at him in cross-examination, with an unexpected result:

Q: . . . he never returned. From that, you conclude that he died there. Do you have any exact information concerning your statement?

A: I wasn't there, of course, when he died, if that is what you mean, but I have met a person who was deported at the same time as he was, and he was together with him on the three days and three nights of the transport to Auschwitz. They arrived at Auschwitz on or about the night of 10 or 11 March, and out of 1,500 people, 100 men and 30 women were placed to the right; the others were put to the left, and those who remained in the camp were never heard of again. I think that is sufficient explanation.

Q (A *pause*): You know nothing conclusive, witness?

A: If you want to put it that way. . . . I think it is a reasonable assumption to say that he will never come back.

The German attorney swiftly changed the subject, but as the tribunal later observed in its verdict, the brutal point had been made: Rothschild had been gassed to enrich Krupp.

✠     ✠     ✠

Liancourt was more complicated than most Krupp responses to the "Cry havoc"; two famous European names were involved, and observing the proprieties was important if possible. Awkwardness was an inevitable by-product of the failure to intimidate the old Jew. "Witness, you leveled a grave charge against Krupp," Alfried's associate counsel sternly told Celap four years after the murder. "We are not dealing with a company now, but with human beings of flesh and blood." *Fleisch und Blut*: it appeared to bother counsel no end. Yet the full transcript suggests otherwise. Most of the charges against his client dealt with human beings, most were ghastlier, but few victims received as much legal attention as this one. The difficulty here was that the quarry had been entitled to as impressive a coat of arms as those who dispatched him. That was why Krupp had wanted everything *blitzsauber*. In no other case of plunder was a victim given over three years to haggle. More often he was simply evicted, or, if his property would be more useful in the Ruhr, thrust aside while *it* was evicted.

On an April afternoon in 1941, for example, Robert Koch, technical director of the Alsthom Société[21] in Belfort and a twenty-year veteran of the shop floor, was supervising boiler production when he glanced through a window and saw the firm's most valuable piece of machinery, a massive sheet metal bending machine worth nearly 700,000 francs, under scrutiny by a German naval officer and several strange civilians. As he hurried toward them they attached a huge one-word sign to it: BESCHLAGNAHMT (seized property).[22] Later he remarked dryly, "None of these people — neither the naval officer nor the people who accompanied him — gave me the honor of introducing themselves. You see, they were the masters and they felt they could do whatever they wanted." After Koch had protested that the equipment was essential to his rolling of boiler drums and high-pressure tubes for hydraulic machines, one civilian stepped forward and identified himself as Herr Eisfeld, a Krupp engineer. The bender was required, he explained, to roll thick plate for the German Reich. Koch became indignant. It was designed for *thin* plate; misuse could destroy it. He put his objections in writing that same evening and received in return an offer of payment. Since the bid was less than one-sixth the bender's value (quite apart from the fact that replacement was impossible in wartime), he wrote again. A *Generalstabsintendant*, a military government civilian with the rank of major general, replied stiffly that failure to accept the offer meant "the payment of compensation must be refused on the part of the German Reich for all time." Application elsewhere was pointless; Vichy's Ambassador Extraordinary to occupied France had decreed that in all such cases the owner must negotiate directly with the Germans. Three days later dismantlers arrived and loaded the bending machine aboard freight cars for Rheinhausen. Later Koch learned that Krupp was using it for OKM's Jäger program — the mass production of submarines.[23]

Alsthom was a subsidiary of a much larger and more prestigious concern, SACM (Alsatian Corporation for Mechanical Construction), or, as the Germans had renamed it, Elsässische Maschinenbau, A.G. (Elmag).[24] SACM–Elmag had been producing textile machinery in Mulhouse since 1816; its reputation was international. For nearly thirty-six months after the French collapse in 1940 the great factory was unneeded and undisturbed. Then Essen began to feel the full weight of the RAF's new punch. On August 9, 1939, Göring, boasting of the Luftwaffe's invincibility, had promised the Schlotbarone that "The Ruhr will not be subjected to a single bomb. If an enemy bomber reaches the Ruhr my name is not Hermann Göring: you can call me Meier!" Krupp hadn't believed him. The Alfried-Löser-Görens triumvirate had expected *some* raids. They hadn't counted on whole acres of shops being obliterated, however, and when the Krawa sheds were wiped out in two nights they began looking at maps again. Blaming the discredited *Reichsmarschall* was a waste of time. Hermann Meier had withdrawn from reality to Karinhall, his country palace. As he deteriorated, so did the Reich's air arm, and on the morning of March 16, 1943, Alfried resolved to move what was left of Krawa out of the Ruhr. There were two possibilities: Czechoslovakia's Tatra Works and Elmag. After inspecting both he opted for the second.[25]

The owners, as usual, were not consulted; on March 31 he negotiated a contract for seizure (*Betriebsüberlassungsvertrag*) with the military government of Alsace. The seller informed the buyer that "as an Alsatian enterprise with predominant participation by enemy interests, Elmag is subject to the regulations covering enemy property." Until now the firm had been supervised by a "provisional management" (*kommissarische Verwaltung*). This would now be replaced by Krupp leases. SACM's stockholders strenuously opposed the change, but by the time they learned of it Kruppianer were swarming through the gate. Alfried had no intention of ever relinquishing his hold on the plant. A note found in his files dated March 27 bears the notation "As regards Ministerialrat [Karl Otto] Saur's suggestion that Krupp purchase Elmag, this can be handled in negotiations. It must not, however, hold up the relocation." Nor did it; by now Krupp had acquired remarkable skill in taking over other people's property and converting it to arms production. SACM–Elmag's assembly lines were rapidly retooled for armor plate, military tractors, and 88's. Special searching missions roamed France, confiscating additional equipment.[26]

After D Day in Normandy native Alsatian labor began vanishing into the hills at an alarming rate, but Essen was ready for that; on July 5 a teletype message informed the Krupp executives in Mulhouse that Oranienburg KZ (*Konzentrationslager* — concentration camp), northwest of Berlin, was sending *"ein Maximum von 1,250 KZ-Arbeiter"* (a maximum of 1,250 concentration camp workpeople). The manner of their treatment may be deduced from the fact that after the war a Denazification Panel sentenced the head of the camp, Ernst Wirtz, to eight years at hard labor, and from Nuremberg testimony that

An advance party of 30 to 60 concentration camp inmates came to the Elmag Works in order to build a concentration camp there which would accommodate 1,000 people. . . . The local Alsace workmen were so indignant at the conditions that they openly protested and threatened to strike as long as the concentration camp prisoners continued to be so ill-treated [*so lange die KZ Arbeiter so misshandelt würden*].[27]

It made no difference. Krupp had prepared for every contingency, including the Allied seizure of Alsace. As American troops approached in August 1944, another memo found in Alfried's files reveals, "for security reasons the first contingent of KZ inmates allotted to us was . . . removed from the factory. The KZ operation has been stopped." Then Krupp simply picked up Elmag's plants — there were three of them — and lumbered off to Bavaria with them.[28]

As the pillage reached its height, Alfried toured Europe in a souped-up Luftwaffe fighter with special markings. He never piloted himself because, as he once explained to this writer, "It was impossible to distinguish between private and military planes."[29] His experience and rank as a Nazi Flying Corps Standartenführer qualified him to take over the fighter's controls, but with so much paper work he couldn't permit himself that luxury; instead he sat in the copilot's seat, a clipboard in his lap, doing sums. As the intricate web of spoliation was spun, his directors back on Altendorferstrasse entered new acquisitions on the ledgers of the *Muttergesellschaft,* cautiously giving each a book value of one mark. Estimating their real value is impossible, but certainly Hitler's conquests had made Krupp the greatest mogul in the chronicles of world trade. Before the Nazi tide ebbed Alfried ruled an economic colossus sprawling across twelve nations, from the Ukraine to the Atlantic, from the North Sea to the Mediterranean. He owned factories everywhere, a complex of shipyards in the Netherlands, and ore mines in Greece, Russia, France, the Sudetenland, Norway, and Yugoslavia. Before D Day and the initiation of *Ruhrhilfe-Aktion* (literally, Ruhr assistance action), under which the victims' plants were stripped of tools and equipment, leaving businessmen in occupied nations destitute, the *kruppsche* Holland manager alone was responsible for enterprises in Rotterdam, Hilversum, Dordrecht, and Gorinchem. Had anyone in the Hauptverwaltungsgebäude suggested that the family would soon lose it all, the man would have been dismissed as a fool. No one was so rash. Even during the *Ruhrhilfe-Aktion* confidence radiated from Alfried and all around him. They had faith in *Sieg.*

In subjugated territories the artless — and they were many — had expected generosity from the victors. Nothing of the sort happened. The least attractive characteristics of both *die Firma* and the Reich surfaced during these years. There was a brutish strain in their behavior, the memory of which is still vivid in the countries which the Wehrmacht overwhelmed. Like the Scythian warriors who, centuries before Christ, drank the blood of their fallen enemies and used their skulls for wineglasses, the Germans of 1939–1945 were unmellowed by triumph. They boasted that they came "as conquerors, not liberators" (*als Eroberer, nicht als Befreier*). Later they would talk about "Hitler's mad policy" (*Hitlers wahnsinnige Politik*); at the time they had no such misgivings, and if his conduct at times raised questions about his sanity, so did theirs. Those whose mood was piratical, as Alfried's was, looted until their passion for booty was slaked.

In his case that was never. Indeed, as the war progressed his exercise of power grew more naked. At first he was devious. In September 1940 he reached a secret agreement with Herr Neuhausen, Germany's consul general in Belgrade. Seven months later the Wehrmacht overran Yugoslavia and the understanding bore fruit; all stock in the country's Chromasseo Mining Company was seized from its owner, Moses Asseo, and split equally between Krupp and Göring, and a young executive from Essen was appointed War Administrator, *Kriegsverwaltungsrat*. (Göring insisted on a token payment of 400,000 dinars; his partner couldn't understand why he was "insisting so emphatically on payment . . . for the benefit of Jewish property.") In an intrafirm memo Krupp proudly observed that "there was no other [firm] which made efforts for a more intense exploitation of Yugoslav chromium ore." But in Belgrade, at least, the forms of legality had been observed. During the next two years Alfried peeled off his velvet glove. After Pearl Harbor he founded Krupp-Brussels S.A. to dismantle factories in Belgium and cart their machinery off to the Ruhr. On June 11, 1942, noting that a shipbuilder in Holland was resisting eviction, Krupp concluded, "Herr Wortelboor is a Dutchman. He plainly has no interest in furthering the interest of the German navy. . . . Dr. Knobloch will inform the navy of our way of looking at things, and will suggest that the navy exert a certain amount of pressure on Wortelboor."[30]

Under the guise of RVE and RVK missions Alfried seized the Montbelleux tungsten mines in northern France "without notice," as a Nuremberg judge later declared, "and without the issuance of a requisition." That was in August 1942. By then the masquerade of "buying" or "leasing" plants in occupied countries was over. In its verdict the Nuremberg tribunal wrote: "We conclude that it has been clearly established by credible evidence that from 1942 onward illegal acts of spoliation and plunder were committed by, and in behalf of, the Krupp firm in the Netherlands on a large scale, and that particularly from about September 1944 to the spring of 1945 certain industries of the Netherlands were exploited for the German war effort in the most ruthless way, without consideration of the local economy and in consequence of a deliberate design and policy." Occasionally Kruppianer went too far even for their fellow Germans. In December 1944 they arrived in the Dutch city of Dordrecht, twelve miles from Rotterdam, to confiscate equipment belonging to the Lips firm. Two German occupation officials arrived at the height of the activity and called the Krupp men "robbers."[31]

☩   ☩   ☩

Holland had been neutral. Hitler's sole quarrel with the Dutch had been that their dikes and windmills stood between the Wehrmacht and France. In Russia the situation was very different; to the Nazi mind *Fall Barbarossa*, as the Führer called the war in the east, was a crusade against evil.[32] "When Barbarossa begins," he told his ranking generals on the afternoon of February 3, 1941, "the world will hold its breath and make no comment!" (*Wenn Barbarossa steigt, wird die Welt den Atem anhalten und sich still verhalten!*). Even now comment seems inadequate. The scope of the crime, the unscrupulousness of the men behind it, and their premeditation were and are unique. As early as January 1941 the United States commercial attaché in Berlin learned of Barbarossa and the plans which were being made for economic exploitation of the defeated USSR. They were elaborate and frightful, for the Führer decreed in early March that "The war against Russia will be such that it cannot be conducted in a knightly fashion. The struggle is one of ideologies and racial differences and will have to be conducted with unprecedented, unmerciful, and unrelenting harshness. . . . Russia has not participated in the Hague Convention and therefore has no rights under it." Later Hitler decided that the convention didn't cover *any* of the Reich's enemies, but the war in the west never reached the ferocity of the eastern front, because nowhere else was the savagery organized so thoroughly. Looting was part of the master plan. All Soviet assets were declared to be "property marshaled for the national economy" (*Wirtschafts-Sondervermögen*), and the haphazard dividing of spoils conducted by Alfried and his three friends that May afternoon in Düsseldorf was replaced by an official assignment of priorities.[33]

The highest industrial priority was Krupp's. Of all the targets on Russia's map the most coveted was the vast, enormously rich Ukraine, that "plum of the golden pheasants," as it was called by Fritz Sauckel, Hitler's drafter of civilian manpower in the occupied territories. The Ukraine was Stalin's food belt, and with its iron fields, coal mines, and steel factories it was also his Ruhr. After the peace, Alfred Rosenberg explained to the Reich's industrialists in May 1941, its 40 million inhabitants would become subjects of "an independent state allied to Germany" — in short, a colony. Meanwhile it must be picked clean by quasi-official agencies. Assets would be held in trust by an organization called the Berg- und Hüttenwerksgesellschaft Ost G.m.b.H. (BHO) — literally, the Mining and Foundry Works Company East, Inc. Alfried dominated the BHO's administrative board (*Verwaltungsrat*). Thanks to that key position and to a piece of great good luck, he was probably the one man in Europe to make money out of Barbarossa.[34]

The luck lay in the Reds' Ukrainian leadership. When Feldmarschall Walther von Brauchitsch's legions burst across a 2,000-mile front on June 22, 1941, the anniversary of Napoleon's crossing of the Niemen in his drive on Moscow, Stalin's marshals, as the Generalstab's chief of staff observed in his diary, "were tactically surprised along the entire front." On July 8 one Hitler subordinate completed a study of the more recent intelligence reports and declared that the war was "practically" won. No one disagreed. The Reds in the south seemed to have given up. That same day Soviet General I. I. Fedyuinsky withdrew his troops to the Korosten fortified line in the Ukrainian steppes, well inside the old borders of Russia. Five weeks later he was summoned to Moscow and the line disintegrated.

The defenders had to retreat. Brauchitsch commanded three million Germans, Italians, Rumanians, Hungarians, and Finns. Facing them were two million ill-prepared, badly shocked Russians. In the north, Kliment Voroshilov, recklessly stripping the Finnish battlefield of all reserves, fled from Wilhelm Ritter von Leeb's Army Group, fought a brilliant rearguard action in the suburbs of Leningrad, and dug in with sixty divisions for a two-year siege. Semën Timoshenko desperately rallied the buckling, concave front in the center, and Moscow was saved. The dispatches from the southwest, however, continued to foretell Russian disasters.

Hitler was partly responsible for this. On August 4 he tentatively gave the Ukraine priority over the Soviet capital. Two weeks later the blitz swept into Dnepropetrovsk, at the far end of the Dnieper bend, and on August 23 the Führer flatly rejected General Heinz Guderian's plea for a march on Moscow, explaining that the Ukraine's industry and raw materials were essential to the war. "My generals," he told that day's conference, "know nothing about the economic aspects of the war." Thus the Wehrmacht's crack units were flung across the steppes. In the first week of September, Stalin, begging for a second front, cabled Churchill: "The position of the Soviet troops has considerably deteriorated in such vital areas as the Ukraine. . . . The relative stability of the front, achieved some three weeks ago, has been upset by the arrival of thirty to thirty-four German divisions and enormous numbers of tanks and aircraft . . ."

Perhaps the coming collapse was inevitable, but certainly the character of the commanding officers on both sides hastened it. The invaders were led by the Reich's ablest tactician, Gert von Rundstedt, and laboring opposite him was the USSR's most inept, Semën Mikhailovich Budënny. Budënny, who had been a cavalry officer in 1918, represented the worst traditions of World War I; he had simply no concept of a war of maneuver. A Bolshevik hero of the Russian civil war, a Kremlin favorite, and a senior marshal of the Soviet Union, he was ordered to stop the invasion and given a million men to do it. Ten million wouldn't have been enough for him. He stubbornly insisted on fighting by the book — the trench warfare book which had been discredited a generation earlier.

To be sure, he couldn't possibly have matched Rundstedt's mobility. In that first summer of the eastern conflict the Germans had Krupp tanks; the Russians, horses. Yet even Hannibal seems to have moved faster than Budënny. On July 20 he took his one pathetic stand. It was a set piece: a three-minute artillery barrage followed by twelve waves of unsupported foot soldiers. He had turned the calendar back to Tannenberg, and the results were identical. After the slaughter he sat motionless for five days, staring across the plain with a dazed expression while the racing tank columns of Guderian and Hasso von Manteuffel butchered his supply lines, rolled up his rear, and, when Guderian executed a 90-degree spin, cut him off from Timoshenko. The trap was closing fast. Odessa was invested. The Black Sea flank was open. Rundstedt tightened the noose while his elated men photographed Red trucks which had been shredded by Alfried's 88's, and on August 19, less than nine weeks after hostilities had begun, most of the Ukrainian strongpoints had fallen. OKH (*Oberkommando des Heeres* — army high command) concluded that the Reds were "no longer capable of creating a firm defensive front or offering serious resistance in the area of Army Group South." The Germans had ripped open a 200-mile hole in the defensive line. Nothing could stop them from occupying the entire Ukraine and most of the Crimea. Indeed, they were not destined to pause until they had captured Rostov on the Don, the legendary "gate to the Caucasus," on November 19. By then their rear was quiet. In the second week of September, Budënny had telegraphed Moscow that he was abandoning the Ukraine. Stalin sent Timoshenko to relieve him, but seventy-two hours after the new marshal's arrival Rundstedt had completed his encirclement of four Russian armies. One-third of the Red Army had been annihilated; a half-million Slavs were prisoners. It was, the Führer proclaimed, "the greatest battle in the history of the world," and both Soviet marshals flew out of the trap with Budënny's political commissar, a lieutenant general named Nikita Khrushchev.

In the Hauptverwaltungsgebäude Alfried had been brooding over his own map board. To him the rout meant millions of marks, for his red pins identified scores of industrial complexes which had been earmarked for "sponsorship" (*Förderung*) by the Konzern. The Communists, aware of the House of Krupp, knew exactly what was behind the Ukrainian drive. They were determined to thwart it if they could, transplanting heavy industry to the Urals, the Volga country, central Asia and western Siberia — anywhere beyond the range of the Luftwaffe and Krupp. As early as July 2 the government decided to move an armor plate mill from Mariupol, although the fighting was still hundreds of miles to the west, and on August 2 factory managers were told to dismantle the sprawling tube-rolling mill at Dnepropetrovsk, load it on ten groups of trains, reassemble it at Pervouralsk in the Urals, and resume full production there by December 24. The evacuations were directed by L. P. Korniets of the Ukrainian government. They were an extraordinary effort. Shifts toiled nonstop around the clock. Alexander Werth, who watched them for the BBC and the London *Sunday Times,* concluded that this transplantation of industry to the east "must rank among the most stupendous organizational and human achievements of the Soviet Union during the war." Though there were failures, it had been possible to rescue a great deal; "283 major industrial enterprises" had been evacuated from the Ukraine between June and October, "besides 136 smaller factories."[35]

Werth added that "a very important quantity of . . . equipment was left behind." Fortunately for Alfried, that included most of the plants which had been set aside for him. The complicated armor plate mill, for example, defied frantic dismantlers, and at Dnepropetrovsk the Wehrmacht was too fast for L. P. Korniets, whose timetable called for a final shipment of equipment on September 6. By then Germans had held the city three weeks. As a rule, steel factories — Krupp's specialty — stayed where they were. To rebuild its shattered armor Moscow had to ration all metals. On September 11, 1941, with the loss of the Ukraine confirmed, a government instruction decreed that steel and reinforced concrete were to be used "only in cases where the use of other local materials, such as timber, is technically wholly out of the question." The Ural shops where the new Soviet tanks would be born were built of wood.

Krupp, on the other hand, could now turn out enough armor to shield a dozen armies. The capitulation of Dnepropetrovsk made him sole proprietor, in effect, of the gigantic Molotov works, 120 miles southwest of Kharkov. The fall of Kramatorsk in the eastern Ukraine brought a temporary, unexpected snag; occupation authorities balked at turning over factory keys to Kruppianer. Alfried himself was obliged to write them testily: "As long as these questions are not clarified, it will be impossible for the Krupp firm to start work at Kramatorsk. Notwithstanding, five Krupp gentlemen have arrived at Kramatorsk in the meantime. Direktor Dr. Korschan will be at your disposal at any time in order to discuss this proposal with you. I would be grateful to you for giving him an appointment as soon as possible. I myself shall be in Berlin only next week." His trip to the capital was successful; the keys were yielded, and he took possession of two of the finest and most modern machine factories in Europe, the Ilyitch and the Azov A.[36]

The capture of Debaltsevo was less exhilarating. Its equipment, he knew, was obsolescent. Nevertheless he dispatched a team of scavengers there, and after surveying the shops they reported that they were prepared to salvage enough spare parts to fill eighty boxcars. Unfortunately they lacked a train. Could Herr von Bohlen . . . ? He could; he telephoned the right number in Berlin, and the rolling stock arrived at the abandoned factory before nightfall. The climax of Budënny's humiliation brought Krupp a triple prize; when Army Group South's southernmost pincer gripped the Sea of Azov on October 7 and anchored Rundstedt's right flank, Alfried acquired an agricultural machinery factory at Berdyansk and two mills in Mariupol. Through prearrangement with the BHO he also picked up countless mining and smelting properties, notably those around Stalino. Since the bulk of Europe's chrome ore is in the USSR, and since chromite is an invaluable alloy in the manufacture of armor plate, Krupp could replace and reinforce the bruised *Panzergruppen*. His success as an exploiter was astonishing. Taken as a group, the smokestack barons in the Ukraine extracted from there only one-seventh of the spoils which were being taken from France, but in the first thirteen months of occupation BHO sent home 6,906 tons of chromium ore, 52,156 tons of scrap iron, 325,751 tons of iron ore, and 438,031 tons of manganese ore. Krupp's salesmen were actually exporting finished Ukrainian machine products to Bulgaria, Turkey, and Rumania.[37]

✠     ✠     ✠

No one is more fascinated by Germans than Germans, and they dwell endlessly on how they have used their passion for trivia to defeat themselves. Obsessed with details, they mismanage larger issues. Their occupation of the Ukraine is a superb example. It made France's clumsy seizure of the Ruhr two decades earlier look like a masterstroke. The *poilus* then had faced a hostile population. Here the natives received their conquerors hospitably. Their memories of the Austro-German occupation of 1918 were rather pleasant. Life under the Communist dictatorship had been dreary and arduous for the Ukrainians, who considered themselves a separate nation.

Elsewhere in the Soviet Union, and particularly in Moscow, the standard of living had risen with the end of the second Five-Year Plan. Comrades in the capital accepted Stalin's official slogan — *"Zhit' stalo legche, zhit' stalo veselei"* (freely translated, "You never had it so good"), but in Kiev, Kharkov, and Odessa the Little Russians (which is what "Ukrainians" means in Slavonic) spat it out like an oath. Weary of the dictator's tyrannical whims, cherishing their fourteen-year vision of independence, they had greeted the Teutonic legions as liberators. Orthodox clergymen declared themselves subservient to the invaders; nationalists began publishing a newspaper, *Nova Ukraina*.[38]

The Nazi answer was to jail the priests, ban the paper, and ravage the land. They declared that they intended to treat their hosts as chattels. Able-bodied Little Russians were to be shipped westward in boxcars, to toil as drudges. The Germans had their own ideas about the future of "Ukraina." The newcomers meant to realize their dream of *Lebensraum* by repopulating the region with *Herrenvolk*. Slavs — all Slavs — were alike, the astonished people were told. Like Jews they were *Untermenschen*, and this smiling countryside was too good for subhumans. In private the victors were even more outspoken. Göring proposed that they "kill all the men in the Ukraine . . . and then send in the SS stallions." Erich Koch, a Göring protégé, a sour little martinet who habitually carried a stockwhip, was appointed Reich Kommissar of the Ukraine. Attending his first conference as the Führer's proconsul, he announced that he had asked Himmler for his *Einsatzkommandos* (extermination squads). Alfried dryly asked who would run his new factories, and Fritz Sauckel protested that "the unparalleled strain of this war compels us, in the name of the Führer, to mobilize many millions of foreigners for labor in the German total war economy, and to *make them work at maximum capacity*. . . ." Thus in March 1942, the Nazis created the Generalbevollmächtigter für den Arbeitseinsatz (Special Office of Labor Allocation).[39]

Obviously, the sane policy would have been to keep the labor conscripts in the Ukraine. There was plenty to do there. Instead they were exported to the Reich; in a single month green-uniformed German police reduced the population of Kharkov from 700,000 to 350,000, and altogether nearly four million Ukrainians were shipped westward as "eastern workers" (*Ostarbeiter*). As draft evasion became a major problem, the occupation authorities met it with coercion. An OKW report of July 13, 1943, mentions "an intensification of countermeasures: among others, confiscation of grain and property; burning down of houses . . . tying down and mishandling of those assembled; forcible abortion of pregnant women."[40] The anonymous chronicler mechanically noted that these measures were ineffective — "The population reacts particularly strongly against the forcible separation of mothers from their babies, and schoolchildren from their families." Inevitably these episodes increased the labor problems of Krupp managers on the scene. One executive was found hanged from a light fixture in his office. A second was killed by cyanide poisoning; and the Ukrainian mistress of a third presented him with a large hot-water bottle which turned out to be a camouflaged land mine; he took it to bed and was blown up. Alfried's native miners became more and more inefficient. To his annoyance he was actually obliged to import coal for his Ukrainian works from the Ruhr and Silesia.

Yet he himself was contributing to the Führer's difficulties. He cannot be accused of incompetence. His problem was that his responsibilities had become enormous, and he couldn't be everywhere at once. Görens was an able technician. His morale had disintegrated, however; he had lost his only son in combat, didn't consider it an honor, and contemplated suicide with increasing earnestness. Löser balanced the books and was a superb administrator. Indeed, in his anxiety to shield his clandestine contacts with Allen Dulles in Switzerland he countersigned document after damning document, masquerading as an ardent Nazi so convincingly that, to his subsequent astonishment, he wound up in the Nuremberg dock beside Alfried. Still, his zeal was counterfeit. He wasn't *führertreu.* There was a limit to how low he could force himself to bend. Whenever he saw a chance to toss a wrench into the Hauptverwaltungsgebäude machinery he did it.

Thus, although responsibility was theoretically divided between three men, Alfried bore the full burden. And he couldn't carry it. He couldn't even devote adequate time to armaments design. That was his specialty; he was trained for it, he had a gift for it. No one else in the firm could match his grasp there, and had he watched the erratic Erich Kanonen-Müller as his great-grandfather had watched Wilhelm Gross, the titanic struggle in the east might have had another outcome, for virtually all the key engagements there were to be decided by artillery and tanks. Krupp superiority might have won the war. In practice, Krupp inferiority contributed a great deal to its loss. Of all the paradoxes in the history of the dynasty, one of the sharpest is that at the height of his historic duel with Stalin, Hitler honored Kanonen-Müller's low party number (263734) and subsequent devotion with the grandiloquent title *Herr Professor honoris causa.* In addition he awarded him the *Kriegsverdienstkreuz* for extraordinary proficiency in the design of new arms.[41] Yet the blunt truth was that even Löser couldn't have sabotaged *die Firma's* war effort as effectively as Müller did unintentionally.

Gustav, Alfried, and Hitler himself were among his collaborators. The origin of one of their fiascos may be traced back to 1936. Among the conspicuous flaws of National Socialism was its irrational yearning for the past. Eager to match the triumphs of Sedan and Liège, the Führer had proposed the design of a new monster gun while visiting the works after his remilitarization of the demilitarized zone. The French, he pointed out, were in a position to devastate much of the Rhineland with their Maginot Line batteries. Would it be possible to develop a counter weapon whose projectiles could penetrate eleven yards of earthworks, ten feet of concrete, or five feet of steel armor? Müller agreed to try, and Krupp earmarked ten million marks for the new gun. It wasn't ready in 1939, but it wasn't needed then; the French held their fire. In the summer of 1940 the prodigy was unveiled. Its gaping muzzle was nearly a yard wide. Its range was 25 miles. It weighed 1,465 tons and could be moved only on double railroad tracks — the base was that wide. Alfried conducted tests at Hillersleben, with shells fired against armor and concrete; the following spring he led Hitler and Speer to Hügenwald, serving as host during formal firings, even as his grandfather and great-grandfather had once entertained the Kaisers. Afterward craters were measured at over ten yards wide and ten yards deep. By the following spring this dinosaur was inching toward the front on groaning freight cars. Kruppianer had christened it Big Gustav; artillerymen, who for some obscure reason preferred to think of their weapons as feminine, called it Dora. On July 2, 1942, Sevastopol fell after 250 days of siege, and Gustav wrote Hitler:

*Auf dem Hügel,*
*24. Juli 1942*

*Mein Führer!*

*Die grosse Waffe, die dank Ihrem persönlichen Befehl hergestellt wurde, hat nun ihre Wirksamkeit bewiesen . . . Es ist für meine Gattin und mich eine angenehme Pflicht, Ihnen, mein Führer, für das unseren Betrieben sowie uns persönlich geschenkte Vertrauen, indem uns ein solcher Auftrag erteilt wurde, unseren Dank auszusprechen.*

*Sieg Heil!*

*G. v. Bohlen und Halbach*

*Zur persönlichen Übergabe durch Alfried*

The Hill
July 24, 1942

My Führer!

The big weapon which was manufactured thanks to your personal command has now proved its effectiveness. It remains a page of glory for the Krupp works community and was made possible through close cooperation between the designers and the builders. Krupp gratefully recognizes that the confidence displayed in the family by all agencies, and especially by you, my Führer, has facilitated an undertaking which, for the most part, was achieved in wartime.

Faithful to an example set by Alfred Krupp in 1870, my wife and I ask as a favor that the Krupp works may refrain from charging for this first finished product. It is for my wife and me a pleasant duty to express our thanks to you, my Führer, for the confidence bestowed on our works as well as on us personally in your giving such an assignment to us.

*Hail victory!*

G. v. BOHLEN UND HALBACH

*To be presented by Alfried in person.*[42]

The gesture was meaningless; Krupp charged seven million marks for each successive Big Gustav, further enriching the family treasury. More important to the Reich, Gustav's letter erred; the cannon were as worthless as Fritz Rausenberger's great Paris guns of 1918. Alfried and Kanonen-Müller had personally supervised their use during the siege, and the young Krupp's staff reported that the first barrel had been "fired 53 times in all, sometimes with the most successful results against fortified targets. After the fort was captured, opportunity was given to study the good aiming and also the exceptional efforts of the semi-armor-piercing shells on fortifications."[43] But this was evasive. The fine print revealed that only one projectile in five had reached the Russians. The heavy damage had been wreaked by the Luftwaffe; in six days bomber pilots dropped 50,000 high-explosive and incendiary bombs on the city. And the real captors of Sevastopol had been heroic German infantrymen, who fought in the streets wearing gas masks to offset the reek of bodies rotting in the summer sun, and whose losses had been staggering. Big Gustav, or Dora, was entitled to no share in the triumph. The last of the great Krupp fieldpieces hadn't "proved its effectiveness." Instead it had been unmasked as a grotesque fraud.

Gustav's jaunty air to the Führer notwithstanding, the war was witnessing a nightmare of reverses in the east, and much of the blame lay in Essen. Müller's eccentric virtuosity, unchecked by Alfried, undermined the Wehrmacht's Russian campaigns. The semiliterate "Kanonen Professor" and dominant member of the Reich's Weapons Development Committee (Waffenentwicklungskommission) was too faithful a National Socialist for the good of National Socialism. He believed — and Alfried, also hewing to the party line, believed with him — that genuine competition between Slavs and Aryans was inherently impossible. The master race was bound to master the subhumans; there could be no other outcome. As ordnance experts they had taken a professional interest in A. A. Shcherbakov's Red Army report during the Lenin commemorative ceremony at the Bolshoi Theater on January 21, 1939. Unfortunately for their cause, they had been merely amused when the Politburo member announced that the government had built up "a mighty armaments industry" and had "lined with steel and concrete the frontiers of this land of triumphant socialism." Casually, almost indifferently, they had dismissed Scherbakov's declaration that "the Soviet Union, which was weak and unprepared for defense, is now ready for all emergencies; it is capable, as Comrade Stalin said, of producing modern weapons of defense on a mass scale, and of supplying our army with them in the event of a foreign attack.[44]

✠     ✠     ✠

Russia's military weaknesses were strategic, not tactical. The Soviet Stavka was no match for the Generalstab. In the February 6, 1939, issue of

*Pravda* a Red Army spokesman asserted that "The dashing 'theories' about a lightning war — the so-called *Blitzkrieg* . . . arise from the bourgeoisie's deathly fear of the proletarian revolution."[45] He asserted that the raw courage of the private soldier, not the intelligence of his officers, was what won wars. Communists could be hamstrung by ideology, too. But Soviet technicians weren't. Shcherbakov may have been guilty of indiscretion; his audience had included German intelligence officers, and it is astonishing that Stalin didn't purge him. But he wasn't exaggerating. Russia's arms forges had superb blueprints. And because of a heroic national effort, beginning in the summer of 1941 and led by Colonel General of the Artillery Voronov, the Red Army actually had, by 1943, achieved ordnance predominance in the field.

In addition, Red armor was to prove more effective than Krupp's during the coming crisis. It wasn't as effective on paper; its edge lay in practical application. Erich Kanonen-Müller was altogether too inventive, too clever, too enthusiastic, too enchanted by gimcracks; and he attracted men like himself. The engineers behind Stalin's troops stuck to two basic tanks, thus simplifying their spare parts problem. (Americans cherish the myth that the USSR rode to victory on United States treads. It isn't true. The only western tank employed by the Reds to any extent was the Sherman. The Sherman was very good. However, by the time it reached Vladivostok in the autumn of 1942, Russia's T–34, superior to it in every respect, had been in full production for a year and a half.) Kanonen-Müller and his creative colleagues went to the opposite extreme. They wanted the panzer generals to field an elaborate, Disneylike family of tanks. And that was what happened.

Müller was ardently supported by a two-man brain trust, Dr. Ferdinand Porsche and his thirty-four-year-old son Ferry. Both were recent additions to the Krupp payroll and star attractions. Twenty years earlier the father had achieved an international reputation as the inventor of Mercedes S and SS sports cars, and when the Führer had ordered him to make an unbeatable Grand Prix car he had responded with the six-liter Auto-Union, which is still the fastest car ever built; three drivers were necessary and even so there were fatalities. Hitler, delighted, sent Ferdinand and Ferry to the Gusstahlfabrik. It was madness. They belonged in a toy shop, not a weapons forge. Nevertheless they enjoyed an immense, if brief, vogue in Essen, thanks largely to Erich Müller. In the West German *Who's Who* today Ferry notes that he "developed the Volkswagen and other products." He is too modest. The two Porsches spawned variegated subcultures of forty-five-ton Panthers; of useless, unlandworthy Leopards, for light reconnaissance, which consumed hundreds of thousands of factory man-hours in 1942; and Tigers, which did work, as by the law of averages they should have. Porsche "other products" included a preposterous supertank weighing

180 tons (three times the Tigerpanzer) and a "land monitor," which mercifully never saw combat, of a *thousand* tons. The Führer approved. Krupp
was elated. But Müller should have been called Meier.[46]

Mechanical inferiority was something new in the German experience,
and they never really accepted it. If an engineering problem couldn't be
mastered, most of them thought, it must be insurmountable. In their first
Russian spring, watching Krupp treads wallow and halt in the gluey
Ukrainian muck, they gave up and christened the season *Schlammperiode*,
the deep mud period. Yet the Soviets' all-purpose, wide-tread T–34's were
moving. This wasn't the Wehrmacht's first intimation of the enemy's
technical skills; as early as November 1941 a team of German experts had
toured the front and proposed that the Fatherland produce a copy of the
T–34 from captured blueprints. Alfried was absent as usual, overseeing the
*havot* in Belgrade, and Müller, deeply offended, rejected the suggestion as
an insult to *kruppsche Geist*. Thus Germany's *Waffenschmiede*, in the
absence of its captain, yawed and broached throughout 1942 like a vessel
with no one at the helm, and the following year the Wehrmacht's basic
panzers were still the PzKw III and IV. They had been superb against
Polish cavalry and the defeatist French, but the Russians were more resourceful, and they outclassed Krupp's best. Improvising, General Guderian
ordered self-propelled tank destroyers (*Jagdpanzer*) and infantry support
cannon (*Sturmgeschütze*). Both were created to overcome the conspicuous impotence of towed 37-mm. and 50-mm. guns against the T–34.
Experimenting with the 75's mounted on Skoda 28-T chassis, German
tank performance improved. Turning out *Jagdpanzer* was quick, easy and
cheap.[47]

More important, the Führer was enthusiastic, and when Hitler glowed
the Konzern burst into flame. This was Müller's big chance. He
missed it. Again, Krupp's historic passion for size was the firm's undoing.
The aging bright young men of Koch und Kienzle and Dr. Porsche created
a mammoth *Jagdpanzer*. Troops at the front called it *der Elefant*. It was,
in fact, a monstrosity. Armed with a 100-mm. cannon on a fixed mounting,
it suffered from a narrow field of fire, cramped crew space, and the lack of
secondary armament. At the same time, its thick underbelly armor made it
as expensive as an orthodox tank. In the perspective of history, the Nazi
conduct of the war evokes little compassion, yet there is something
pathetic about the common soldier's faith in the legendary Krupp armorer
he had been taught to revere in school and whose blunders were now
destroying him. He never realized it, despite heartbreaking reverses. At
Ploesti gunners christened their two most successful antiaircraft 88's
Bertha and Friedrich after the Cannon Queen and her father; four white
rings were painted around Bertha's muzzle, and artillerymen were still
proudly explaining to visitors that each represented a destroyed American

bomber when, on August 31, 1944, the failure of Krupp armor admitted Soviet troops to the city. Earlier, on July 2, 1943, Sergeant Imboden, a *Tigerpanzer* crewman, wrote in his journal: "Ivan, with his usual cunning, had held his fire . . . But now the whole front was a girdle of flashes. It seemed as though we were driving into a ring of flame. Four times our valiant Rosinante shuddered under a direct hit, and we thanked our fates for the strength of our good Krupp steel."[48]

The Kruppstahl was matchless, the use of it appalling. Three days after the sergeant's entry German and Russian armor at Kursk were locked in what may be the least understood engagement of the war. Undeniably it was the most fateful — afterward Walter Görlitz, the German historian, wrote that though Stalingrad was the "psychological turning point," the "military crisis" came at Kursk[49] — and it was here that Alfried posted his greatest failure. Preoccupied with the Berthawerk, Elmag, the fuse factory in Auschwitz, manhunts in the Low Countries, and his imminent succession to the leadership of the family dynasty, he had permitted the struggle for superior weapons to drift beyond hope of recovery. The Germans were now going into battle with equipment of poorer quality than the Slavs', and the Third Reich was about to pay the price.

In the high summer of 1943 Hitler needed a victory. His North African front was crumbling; an invasion of Italy was expected before autumn. Since autumn the Führer had lost nearly 700,000 men in Russia. Striking out from the rubble of Stalingrad, the Soviets had crossed the Donets southwestward at Izyum and spread westward to capture Lozovaya junction, undercutting the German position at Kharkov, which fell into their hands on February 16, and nearly intercepting the armies of Manstein and Kleist. For a time the German situation seemed hopeless. Then the second half of February brought a dramatic change. An early thaw prevented the overextended Russians from bringing up reinforcements and supplies. They lost their momentum. The retreating Nazis fell back on the Dnieper, regrouped, and counterattacked under Manstein, snapping off enemy forces southwest of Kharkov and recovering the line of the Donets. The Red tide, it seemed, had been turned back.

Declaring that he intended to make up what had been "lost in winter," Hitler put his finger on the map. The Kursk salient, which had been recaptured by the Russians on February 8, six days after the surrender of Stalingrad, and which they regarded as a springboard for the reconquest of the Ukraine, was a conspicuous target. OKW encoded the operation *Zitadelle*. The ground between Orel in the north and Belgorod in the south was to be reduced by a massive concentration under Manstein, the new commander of Army Group South — 37 panzer divisions, two motorized, and 18 infantry. Moscow's Stavka was deeply concerned; when news reached the capital that the Nazi offensive had begun, *Red Star*, abandoning ideology, struck the deeper chords of patriotism: "Our fathers and our forebears made every sacrifice to save their Russia, their homeland. Our people will never forget Minin and Pozharsky, Suvorov and Kutuzov and the Russian partisans of 1812. We are proud to think that the blood of our glorious ancestors is flowing in our veins, and we shall be worthy of them. . . ." Hitler, for his part, had complete faith in Krupp's Panther, Elefanten, Jagdpanzer and Tigerpanzer. To those around him he predicted that the coming German triumph would "fire the imagination of the world."[50]

It was the greatest armored battle in history — 3,000 tanks on each side pitching and tumbling toward one another to the orchestration of artillery barrages and the Soviets' Katyusha mortars. On the evening of July 5, the first day, Stavka's communiqué disclosed that "Preliminary reports show that our troops . . . have crippled or destroyed 586 enemy tanks." The Jagdpanzer had disintegrated in the first wave. The Elefanten had also been doomed. Krupp had turned out 90 of them. All had gone into action that first morning at Kursk. All had failed, and the Russians celebrated the next dawn by committing to combat a stunning new Brobdingnagian machine with 122-mm. cannon and infrared sights. Hitler's mighty drive was already faltering. On successive days the Russian score was 433 Essen tanks, then 520, then 304. "The Tigers are burning!" one Soviet dispatch from the front began. Prisoners were quoted as describing "the carnage among the German troops, the like of which they had never seen." By July 22, when action was broken off, the Führer had lost 70,000 soldiers killed and 2,900 tanks destroyed. The myth that Nazi summer offensives were invincible was dead. A Stalin order of July 24 announced "the final liquidation" of the German gains; Red counterthrusts had gained between fifteen and thirty miles. Alexander Werth inspected the desolate salient. He saw a hideous desert, in which every tree and bush had been smashed by shellfire. Hundreds of burned-out tanks and wrecked planes were still littering the battlefield, and even several miles away from it the air was filled with the stench of thousands of half-buried . . . corpses." *Zitadelle* had been a catastrophe — from Orel to Belgorod the scarred land was strewn with jagged fragments of Alfried's finest steel.[51]

✠   ✠   ✠

Now the Stavka switched to the offensive, and the Red Army became a hammer smashing Krupp against the anvil of the steppes. The Hauptuerwaltungsgebäude map had looked ominous since Stalingrad. After Feldmarschall Friedrich Paulus's surrender there Ukrainian factories had changed hands several times, among them *die Firma*'s two at Kramatorsk. Workmen never knew whether the swastika or the red flag would fly over their shops next day. During the German counterattack in late February, Werth noted that he left Kharkov "with a feeling of foreboding." He added: "The Germans returned, not at once but over a fortnight later, on March 15. One of the first things the SS did was to butcher 200 wounded in a hospital, and set fire to the building. [This] was their 'revenge for Stalingrad.' "[52]

The Ilyitch and Azov A plants had been returned to Alfried in that campaign. Encouraged, his works managers had informed Essen that "we plan to add a wire drawing plant, a nail factory, and an electrode factory to the existing screw factory. Some of the machines for these purposes have already been bought." At Alfried's request, Müller had drawn up a detailed plan for the proposed expansion, adding, "I should also like you to apply . . . for the transfer of the Boltov works in Brushkovka." Before committing further capital, however, Krupp had wanted to know more about the military situation. His Ukrainian executives had assured him that if the Wehrmacht still held Kramatorsk in the spring "our ownership of the works would undoubtedly be assured for the future."[53]

The investment was made on the assumption that Manstein would conquer Kursk. The rout there changed everything. In August General Konev retook Kharkov and Rokossovsky drove deep into the northern Ukraine. On September 10 Marshals Malinovsky and Tolbukhin, supported by a naval landing west of the city, recaptured Mariupol. Kramatorsk was lost to Russian infantrymen the same month, and on October 25 Malinovsky seized Dnepropetrovsk in a lightning attack. Retreating German foot soldiers became increasingly cynical; they called the Russian campaign *"Kaukasus — hin und zurück"* (Caucasus round trip). Such crack SS Panzer divisions as Leibstandarte, Das Reich, and Totenkopf were decimated. The Führer's Dnieper line had been breached. Alfried had lost all his Russian factories — or rather, to be precise, he had lost the buildings. L. P. Korniets had taught him something about speedy dismantling. Evacuation plans had been drawn up and awaited only a warning siren. Before Malinovsky and Tolbukhin had completed their amphibious operation on the Sea of Azov, Kruppianer had shipped Mariupol's complete electrosteel mill to the Berthawerk in Silesia, together with a giant turbine, countless Ivan (ammunition) machines, 10,000 tons of steel alloy, and 8,000 tons of chrome steel. Krupp executives appealed for 280 boxcars to evacuate Kramatorsk equipment. The army could provide only a hundred, but they were enough to cart away the heart of the plant.[54]

⌘　　⌘　　⌘

By then the German war was irrevocably lost. Yet at the time the outlook was murky even to the Allies, and for those whose sole sources of information were Goebbels newspapers, Goebbels films, and Goebbels broadcasts, the Führer's eventual triumph still seemed inevitable. Nazi Germany controlled more territory than the Holy Roman Empire at its peak. American power was despised, and the alliance between Communist Russia and the capitalistic democracies seemed doomed to disintegration anyhow. After the collapse this writer asked Alfried why he had assumed the Krupp title. He replied, "I feel I did the only thing possible. My father was seventy-three; he was pretty tired. I believe he was happy to be out of the responsibility and out of the front line. . . . It was easier for me, because I didn't have my father's diplomatic background, which of course didn't fit into the circumstances of Germany at the time" (*die Verhältnisse des damaligen Deutschlands*).[55]

Undeniably Gustav's age, infirmity, and training in diplomacy were of little use in the embattled Reich, and certainly the son's youth and engineering skills were invaluable. Furthermore, with his unflagging support of the principles of Alfred Krupp and the practices of Adolf Hitler he had won the right to claim his birthright. After an interregnum of nearly four decades it was time the prince consort stepped aside: a real Krupp was at last ready to assume control in name as well as in fact.

# 18

✠

# Alfried
# Commands the Kruppbunker

SHORTLY before her death in 1957 the wrinkled, majestic Bertha Krupp posed for several artists. After a French painter had finished two portraits of her, Otto Kranzbühler, the lawyer who had unsuccessfully defended her son Alfried at Nuremberg, inspected them with Waldtraut and Berthold. "I thought one was good and one not," he recalled afterward. "The one I liked showed a benevolent, radiant expression. They disagreed. The one they preferred showed a severe queen. Unknowingly, the painter had portrayed the two sides of her character — and since I had only known her after she had been softened by suffering, I had never seen the queen."[1]

Bertha's ordeal began in 1941, when Gustav suffered his first stroke. Only she, Waldtraut, and Dr. Gerhardt Wiele, the family physician, knew of it; Alfried was away in the conquered countries, his brothers were in uniform, and Gustav himself refused to admit that anything had happened. Nevertheless he had obviously suffered brain damage. From time to time he was afflicted by spells of dizziness. She begged him to give up riding, but he refused; each morning before breakfast two grooms would help him into the saddle and off he would gallop, Learlike, into the wind. Worried, she ordered a second horse readied for her and followed him at a discreet distance, expecting to see him topple off at any moment.[2]

He didn't fall. Early in 1942 he himself decided to give up riding, for by now he was suffering from double vision. Evenings he would sit in a corner of the massive second floor with Bertha, his golden swastika glittering in his lapel, affecting to read reports from the Hauptverwaltungsgebäude while she pretended not to notice that he was holding them upside down. Hour after hour they would sit silently, staring down while the radio played the Horst Wessel song over and over, exhorting the *Herrenvolk* for the millionth time to "clear the streets" for the "brown battalions" — for the "storm trooper":

> *Die Strassen frei den braunen Bataillonen!*
> *Die Strasse frei dem Sturmabteilungsmann!* . . .

Then he would rise stiffly and totter off to bed. According to a family chronicler:

> The Hill had become a quiet place [*Auf dem Hügel ist es still gewor-den*]. The stream of visitors had been reduced to a trickle. . . . The desolate state of the castle was evocative of the atmosphere which had been dominant there during the last years in the life of Alfred Krupp. The world beyond seemed very far away. Even the war was somewhat unreal. Gustav persisted in a regimen which was governed exactly by the clock. But in fact his activities were only a way of passing the time, the days and weeks that slipped slowly yet steadily past. . . . He would quietly retire each evening at the same hour [*Unbekümmert geht er zur gewohnten Stunde schlafen*].[3]

Until his second stroke, his wife, doctor, and servants tacitly shared his conspiracy of silence. After that, dissembling became more difficult. His secretary was now painfully aware of his handicaps. Fräulein Kröne would ride up the hill to take his dictation, but after barking out a few sentences he would lose focus and digress into incoherent descriptions of long-ago meetings with S.M., of his Peking days, of his youthful service with the Second Baden Dragoons at Bruchsal. For a time his speech was so garbled that only Bertha could understand him. Gradually it improved, and his secretary, accustomed to his style, could pick up the thread of his meaning from an isolated phrase and complete the letter herself. Once his brother-in-law arrived from Marienthal; abandoning all pretense, Gustav tapped his forehead and told the baron, "Please give me a word when you notice I can't find it." Tilo professed to look astonished, though by now everyone close to the household was aware of the old Krupp's disability. As Fritz von Bülow later put it, "Obviously he wasn't himself. At one period he couldn't speak a word. It was clear to all that the time had come for Herr Alfried to take over." Fritz Wilhelm Hardach, who joined the firm in 1941, afterward remembered that "When I came Gustav was already failing. He took little interest in the firm that year, and none the next." And one Hügel visitor saw the once mighty lord of Essen "walking up and down the grounds picking up pieces of enemy shrapnel and carefully placing the iron splinters in a basket — to help along with the old metals collection of the government."[4]

His final message to his Kruppianer, written out in his large slanting handwriting and published in 1942, was a hymn of praise "to mutual trust between management and labor":

In the areas menaced by air attack the armament worker of 1941 is exposed to the same material danger as the soldier. Again I must affirm that under these unusual conditions he does his duty gallantly and calmly [*Ich muss nochmals bezeugen, dass er unter diesen aussergewöhnlichen Verhältnissen seine Pflicht tapfer und ruhig tut*].[5]

The premise was untrue then. Apart from a token RAF strike the day Germany invaded the Low Countries in 1940, Essen was virtually untouched in the war's early years. Both Krupp records and the United States Strategic Bombing Survey agree that the first Allied raid of any consequence against Essen was carried out on the night of January 7, 1943. Even then the damage was confined to two foundries and quickly repaired. One vagrant bomb had exploded harmlessly on Hügel's grounds; otherwise the estate was untouched. At the outbreak of hostilities Gustav had ordered the castle's 1913 indoor swimming pool drained, but that was merely a gesture to the national spartanism. A soldier's life, as his own soldier sons could have told him, was rather more difficult than that.[6]

Still, the first three years of the war were wholly unlike the last three. The Third Reich stood at high tide, the Fatherland's mood was jubilant, and Alfried's brothers gloried in it. After two exhausting months as a junior officer with the horse-drawn artillery in Belgium, Holland and France, Berthold had been assigned to a comfortable staff job. Harald, too, was a staff Oberleutnant, instructing the Rumanians in the finer points of Krupp 88's; Hermann Hobrecker, encountering him in Bucharest, was struck by his immaculate grooming and his casual air. To be sure, the continuing hostilities meant deferred careers for Harald, who had passed his bar examination shortly before the invasion of Poland, and for Berthold, a fledgling chemist; yet that was true of almost everyone their age. Eckbert had been spared even that disappointment. He was too young. The evening before the invasion of Poland he had celebrated his seventeenth birthday; he had just been graduated from Bredeney Realgymnasium and hadn't thought much about what he would do as a civilian. At the moment being a Wehrmacht Leutnant stationed in tranquil Italy seemed rather grand.[7]

They rarely saw their ailing father. By sheer force of will Gustav held himself together on family occasions; when Waldtraut married a Berlin textile tycoon in the castle on March 12, 1942, he was elegant and lucid. Berthold, arriving home on leave, found his father almost normal, though he sensed an air of strain. Gustav, Bertha, and Alfried seemed unnaturally tense, and Berthold privately decided to spend his future furloughs elsewhere. Fortunately the old Krupp had provided for just this contingency.

Aware that his children preferred Blühnbach to Hügel, he had announced, at a family dinner late in the 1930's, that each member of the family might have the use of the Austrian castle thirty days a year. (Typically, he decreed that they must pay for their own drinks and those of their guests; the Blühnbach *maître d'* would make a full accounting to him.) Thus the leaves of the Bohlen lieutenants became vacations from both their parents and the army. In 1942, by coincidence, Eckbert and Harald reached the family's Alpine retreat the same day and skied together for a full month. They enjoyed it immensely. Yet on the whole none of the brothers seem to have missed one another much. They had an odd relationship. Berthold and Harald were — and were to remain — close, but Alfried and Claus had been aloof, and Eckbert had been small and unnoticed. Of their skiing holiday Harald once remarked to me, "He was just twenty. I was surprised to find that he was a person, someone to talk to man to man. Of course, I never saw him again."[8]

✠     ✠     ✠

At Nuremberg, Otto Kranzbühler became convinced that the martial sacrifices of Claus, Berthold, Harald, and Eckbert had been a decisive influence on Alfried's conduct during the early 1940's. "He was the eldest of five brothers — four, after the death of Claus," Kranzbühler explained. "The others were serving in the field as officers of the German Reich. He felt that this was the least he could do, that it was his duty." Unquestionably his wartime responsibilities obsessed him. Like his great-grandfather in 1870–1871, his grandfather in the fight for the first German Navy Law of 1898, and his father in 1914–1918, he was engrossed in his role as the empire's gunsmith. He gave up his hobbies. He had no home life. His closest friends had been those he made as a university student, but beginning in 1941 he stopped attending the annual meetings of their alumni association. Chain-smoking his Camels (he had built up a towering stockpile before Pearl Harbor), he worked endlessly for the firm, the RVE, the RVK, the National Armaments Council (Rüstungsrat), the Rhine-Westphalian Coal Syndicate, and the Northwest Iron-Producing Industry Group, of which he was deputy chairman.[9]

As his power grew, so did his party responsibilities; he succeeded his father in key party posts. While Gustav mechanically leafed through statements and dispatches he could no longer understand, his heir toiled beneath a portrait of Hitler and the red-on-black slogan, MIT UNSEREM FÜHRER ZUM SIEG! (WITH OUR FÜHRER TO VICTORY!), deciphering complex statistics and issuing orders to the Ukraine, Yugoslavia, Denmark, the Low Countries, and France. Berlin was watching him anxiously. Goebbels noted in his diary, "I paid a short visit to Krupp's. . . . I was received by young Bohlen, who has taken over the management of the plant in place of his father. . . . Only time will tell whether he is equal to managing this gigantic undertaking, employing nearly two hundred thousand workers, including branch offices and plants."[10] On reflection Goebbels concluded that his impression had been favorable, and that same spring Alfried was ceremoniously decorated with the *Kriegsverdienstkreuz.*

The path of duty was less clear to a *Führer der Betriebe* than to an *Oberleutnant.* Unlike his brothers Alfried faced intricate choices, and if he appears to have been overzealous, it is only fair to point out that his reactions were affected by extraordinary circumstances. There were the traditions of his dynasty, in which he had been indoctrinated since childhood. There were the perils which he knew were being faced daily on battlefields by other Germans of his generation. Moreover, the Krupp empire was far too vast to be managed by one man. Much that was done was done without his knowledge. That was why Erich Müller and Fritz von Bülow, among others, were also to be held answerable at Nuremberg later. Finally, only those blinded by prejudice would reject out of hand Alfried's Nuremberg defenses that "Economics go beyond national borders in peace as well as in war," and "We worried and toiled under conditions which are very difficult to understand and judge in retrospect."[11]

This having been said, one must add that it is hard to assess the deeds of millions of Europeans who were trapped in the crucible of World War II, including countless inmates of concentration camps who sought favoritism at the expense of their fellow prisoners. Excepting those who, like Gustav, were no longer accountable for their actions, virtually every adult on the continent had something to justify — something done or left undone. Nevertheless the world was not completely mad. Decency was not extinct. Industrialists other than the young Krupp worried and toiled under identical conditions and emerged with clear consciences, undamaged reputations, and what Germans call a *weisse Weste* (a white vest, i.e., a clean bill of health). It is possible to draw a line; and having done so it is then possible to pore over Alfried's files for those years and determine when he crossed it and entered foul territory. Auschwitz has been mentioned. Krupp's role there is indefensible by any civilized standards; it was, among other things, in flagrant violation of German labor laws. Alfried could not afterward argue, as uniformed guards did, that he had been given the option of either obeying the commands of superior officers or perishing himself. The Führer had not asked him to take advantage of the victims of Auschwitz. He exploited them voluntarily.

That episode does not stand alone. According to the testimony of Karl Otto Saur, chief of the Speer ministry's technical office, Krupp built the Berthawerk in Silesia with Auschwitz Jews over the objections of government engineers. The project had first been suggested by Alfried on February 5, 1942. In June, Saur tried to table it. To bypass this opposition, von Bohlen, as he was still known then, went directly to Hitler. On August 8 Saur, Speer, and Alfried met in Hitler's office with the other two leaders of the RVE — Rohland and Röchling. "At the conclusion of this meeting," Saur told the Nuremberg tribunal, "Mr. von Bohlen went to see Hitler and together with Speer came from Hitler's headquarters to the park area of Rastenburg, where I was walking around with various other gentlemen. Speer approached me in the presence of Mr. von Bohlen, and informed me of the order that Hitler had now definitely issued that the construction had to be carried out and that we had to give him all the help he needed. . . . I had to conclude that this was an explicit order from Hitler which we had to follow." Asked by the tribunal why the Führer had intervened, Saur explained that "Hitler himself had a great admiration and weakness for the name Krupp, and the family Krupp as such, because, to repeat his own words, that was 'the weapons forge for all Germany.'" The witness added that "The relationship between Krupp and ourselves was different from our relationship with other firms because of the unique position which Krupp held. I would like to quote another example. For instance, the Hermann Göring Works were in a similar position."[12]

After Alfried's conviction as a war criminal, Baron Tilo von Wilmowsky published a bitter attack on Saur, charging that he had been "designated in Hitler's will as Speer's successor (*Nachfolger*), and that "Saur had created an insupportable atmosphere in the German economy with his boorish manners." The baron accused Saur of being a racist and charged that his bigotry had won approval among Americans:

> The fact that he once used the disparaging term "Polacks" in an official letter did him no damage [*Dass er die Polen in einem amtlichen Schreiben mit dem Schimpfwort 'Polacken' bezeichnet hatte, hat ihm nichts geschadet*]. The fact that during a tour of a factory he once gave a Russian worker standing nearby a slap in the face for no reason — the Krupp court took no cognizance of this. This man, who truly embodied the "slave labor program" of the men in power in Germany, and who should have exchanged roles with the accused — this man again did his best against his victims, just as he had done under Hitler [*tat genau wie unter Hitler, wieder sein Bestes gegen seine Opfer*].[13]

Tilo's loyalty to his embattled nephew is admirable; his scrupulosity isn't. Although Saur and Speer were mentioned in Hitler's last testament, which was largely a fulmination against world Jewry, Saur at Nuremberg had nothing to gain by appearing as a prosecution witness. But that is beside the point. What is basic is that the implications of the August 8 *Führerbefehl* were obvious to everyone, and Alfried has never denied that he grasped them then or that he later saw the consequence with his own eyes. In an affidavit signed for Allied intelligence officers on June 26, 1947, he conceded that "With particular reference to the Berthawerk in Markstädt near Breslau, it is a fact that for the construction work preceding the opening of this plant . . . the labor of a great many prisoners of *Konzentrationslager* was being utilized, which was known to me personally," and he acknowledged that "I, myself, have been to Markstädt four or five times. At least once, during one of my other visits to Markstädt, I have seen the *Konzentrationslager* Fünfteichen" — the camp where Berthawerk prisoners were penned up at night. There and elsewhere he took the lead in ordering efficient use of slave labor. On November 16, 1943, he expressed the opinion to Johannes Schröder, then chief of the firm's accounting department, that one plant was "far from being adequately utilized" and that "something should be done to employ 300–400 workers there."[14]

Those who protested that labor conscription was immoral and, under international law, illegal, were overruled or ignored. As early as 1941 the herding of vast masses of prisoners of war into Krupp shops disturbed the conservative *Junkerherrschaft*. In Berlin, Admiral Wilhelm Canaris protested that it violated the Hague agreements, the Geneva Convention, and military principles which had been evolving for a century and a half. "Since the eighteenth century," he declared, "these have gradually been established along the lines that war captivity is neither revenge nor punishment, but solely protective custody, the only purpose of which is to prevent the prisoners of war from further participation in the war. This principle was developed in accordance with the view held by all armies that it is contrary to military tradition to kill or injure helpless people." Among those who pondered the admiral's logic was a Kruppianer named Albert Schrödter. For fifteen years Schrödter had managed Krupp's great Germaniawerft. In 1941 he began receiving hordes of Dutch, Belgian, and French soldiers dressed in striped prison garb. Realizing that "the employment of prisoners of war on immediate armament work was not legal," he took his dilemma straight to Essen. Alfried explained to him that POWs were already toiling in the Gusstahlfabrik. He took him on a tour to prove it. Then, according to Schrödter, the future Konzernherr said, "You come to see us on all these problems. We will show you how we do it." Kiel's manager was told he could "arrange matters" to suit local conditions, but that did not mean that he was free to leave his wards idle. "The legitimacy of employing foreign workers on war work," Alfried warned him, "is not to be discussed."[15]

The counterargument to the Canaris position was tersely set forth by Feldmarschall Wilhelm Keitel, who, referring to the eastern front, wrote on the back of the admiral's memorandum that "The objections arise from the military concept of chivalrous warfare. This [war] is [for] the destruction of an ideology. Therefore I approve and back the measures." So stated, the disagreement takes on aspects of a polite debate. It was in practice that the measures became appalling. Keitel, who was hanged for endorsing them, never profited from the POW policy or saw it in action.

Alfried, who was to survive his own conviction, benefited from the Nazi labor program, observed its effects in his factories, and was repeatedly reminded of the growing horror in Krupp camps by his medical staff. On December 15, 1942, Dr. Wiele, his own family physician, sent a lengthy report describing, among other cases, the autopsy of a prisoner who had literally died of starvation: "No organic ailment . . . was found, although a condition of malnutrition to an extreme degree was determined. The fat tissue had disappeared from the entire organism and only a so-called gelatinous atrophy was left. The liver was small, lacking fat and glucose; the musculature was weak." Dr. Wilhelm Jäger, a senior Krupp doctor, inspected the fenced-in compounds and reached the conclusion that

> Die Lebensbedingungen in allen Fremdarbeiterlagern waren ausserordentlich schlecht. Sie waren stark überbelegt . . . Tuberkulose war besonders weit verbreitet. Die TB-Rate war viermal so hoch wie die normale Rate. Dies wurde hervorgerufen durch schlechte Unterbringung, elende Qualität und unzureichende Quantität der Ernährung und durch Überanstrengung.

Conditions in all camps for foreign workers were extremely bad. They were greatly overcrowded . . . The diet was entirely inadequate . . . Only bad meat, such as horsemeat or meat which had been rejected by veterinarians as infected with tuberculosis germs, was passed out in these camps. Clothing, too, was altogether inadequate. Foreigners from the east worked and slept in the same clothing in which they had arrived. Nearly all of them had to use their blankets as coats in cold and wet weather. Many had to walk to work barefoot, even in winter. Tuberculosis was particularly prevalent. The TB rate was four times the normal rate. This was the result of inferior housing, poor food and an insufficient amount of it, and overwork.[16]

In his postwar grillings Alfried rarely pleaded, as did so many other defendants, that details eluded him or that his memory had become vague. On the contrary, he recalled names, dates, and figures. To Maximilian Koessler, an Allied interrogator, he revealed a particularly astonishing anecdote which disclosed how widespread and indiscriminate Fritz Sauckel's Menschenjagden (roundups) had been. One day Alfried had glimpsed a familiar face in a passing blur of KZ uniforms. The man was Voss van Steenwyk, husband of a second cousin. He had been seized at his estate in Noordwijk, a watering place twelve miles north of The Hague, and had been jeered by German soldiers when he insisted that he was a Krupp relative. Alfried acknowledged him — and, later, acknowledged that he had no idea of van Steenwyk's subsequent fate. Die Firma had so many dependents. He admitted, "I know that the Krupp coal mines employed about fifty percent foreign workers and that about four-fifths of these foreign workers came from the east." He even volunteered that he had received "a letter, addressed to me personally and signed by eighteen Dutch Krupp workers employed at Essen-Bergeborbeck and dated 16 December 1952." The Dutchmen were complaining about their working conditions. He said he passed their petition along to a subordinate.[17]

It was this issue of humanity, Ewald Löser insisted after the war, which led to his break with the Konzern. He declared that he had been opposed to involuntary labor, that "I had arguments about these questions with Gustav Krupp, Alfried Krupp, and [Paul] Görens," and that these clashes "finally led to my leaving the firm." Löser's attempt to disassociate himself from the conscription of aliens touched off Alfried's one flash of temper at Nuremberg. He denied that his old rival had ever raised objections to the program and added vehemently, "It is incorrect that this was one of the reasons for his resignation."[18]

The tribunal believed him, and understandably so. To be sure, Löser had loathed the camps. In Berlin, in the autumn of 1942, he had told Sauckel, "You must be careful that history some day does not consider you a slave dealer." The pig-eyed little "Plenipotentiary for the Allocation of Labor" had replied, "That is not my intention, but I must procure the workers; that is my task." Löser had begged Sauckel to visit Essen and see how dreadful conditions there were, and he hounded Gustav about them so mercilessly that when Berthold came home on leave Bertha confided in him that she hated to see Löser coming up the hill: "He always upsets us so. Whenever he leaves your father comes down with a dreadful headache, and we have to give him something to put him to sleep." But Löser, too, had been dealing in slaves. His judges could not overlook it; he had affixed his signature to too many incriminating papers and ordered too many plant leaders — including Schrödter at Kiel's Germaniawerft — to employ prisoners of war, impressed civilians, and concentration camp inmates.[19]

In the 1960's he abandoned that line of defense. "Krupp had been a share company," he says. "For all practical purposes, Alfried became sole owner on April 1, 1943. The position I had held — with direct responsibility to the Vorstand — was abolished. In the future there would only be one leader. I didn't want to serve under him, and Alfried Krupp didn't want me there, either." That is closer to the truth. Löser's motives, like those of most of his fellow conspirators, were mixed; had the *Attentat* of July 20, 1944, succeeded they would have become the dominant figures in the Reich, and wherever Löser worked, in government, in industry, or in the underground, he would have been a hard-driving, fiercely ambitious executive.[20]

Yet his friction with Alfried was more than a naked struggle for power. The ideological gulf was still there. Had he merely yearned for prestige and authority Löser need never have come to the Ruhr; with his conspicuous gifts he could have flourished in his native Saxony and, ultimately, in Berlin. He was the sort of man who has always risen to the top in Germany — in the Second Reich, in the Third, and in Bonn today. The fact is that he *did* provoke a crisis with Alfried over the requisition of 80,000 new foreign workers. His stand took courage, for more than his future in the Hauptverwaltungsgebäude was at stake. Behind the scenes he was courting an even greater danger.

In 1937, immediately after joining the firm, Löser had become a member of the subversive Kleine Kreis (Small Circle), a group of seven Ruhr executives who met monthly, pondering ways to get rid of Hitler. Meanwhile the conspiracy of anti-Nazi German conservatives was growing. That same year Carl Goerdeler, Löser's former chief in Leipzig, had toured the western democracies. In the United States he talked to Cordell Hull, Sumner Welles, Henry Wallace, Henry Morgenthau Jr., and Senator Robert A. Taft, trying to persuade them that the Führer wasn't bluffing — that he really meant to wipe them out. Goerdeler had traveled to London in the summer of 1939 to warn Chamberlain, Churchill, and Lord Halifax that the Wehrmacht would invade Poland at the end of August. His source was Baron Ernst von Weizsaecker, the new Holstein of the Wilhelmstrasse and a key plotter. The following October, with England and France already at war with Germany, Goerdeler again crossed the border with a Weizsaecker tip, this time to alert the Belgians to a German invasion. Since Goerdeler's convictions had been widely advertised, and since he was a bluff, extroverted man who spoke his mind with almost suicidal candor, he was taking immense risks. Löser shared them; while a member of the Essen triumvirate he had secretly strengthened his ties with Goerdeler. In March 1942 the conspirators established a formal organization, and in November they established radio contact with Allen Dulles in Switzerland. Beginning January 22, 1943, regular meetings of the shadow cabinet were held. Two months later, after the quiet resignation of Krupp's dynamic *Finanzdirektor*, Dulles learned, as he later recalled, that after the successful revolt "the ministry of finance was to go to a conservative named Löser."[21]

Heartbreaking mishaps were to dog the conspirators to the end. On March 21 a coup was attempted at the Zeughaus Unter den Linden. Hitler came to celebrate *Heldengedenktag* and nearly became a fallen hero himself; he was rescued by a last-minute schedule change. "Operation Flash," as the plotters had called it, was shelved, and they scattered.

Ten days later in Essen Dr. Friedrich Janssen, speaking for *die Firma*, told the press that Herr Löser, exhausted and ill from overwork, had left the Konzern and was convalescing in Switzerland. He had gone — but he came back. His inspiration was Goerdeler, who visited the Ruhr that July, waded through the debris of bombed-out homes, and wrote that "The work of a thousand years is but rubble" that something must be done to end the Nazi "madness." Re-entering the Hauptverwaltungsgebäude would have been humiliating for Löser, and perhaps impossible, but it wasn't necessary. Dr. Hans Beusch, director of the firm's social welfare program, had worked with him in Goerdeler's Leipzig administration and was committed to the apparatus; Beusch could keep posted on the young Krupp's movements and, through his Berlin contacts, with government plans for the Ruhr. Therefore Löser accepted a sinecure. He became trustee of a confiscated radio factory in Eindhoven, Holland (ironically the appointment put his name on the Allied war criminal list) while he prepared to run the financial affairs of a Führerless Reich.[22]

In photographs of these years the sleek, overfed, supremely confident Löser of the 1930's (and the 1960's) is missing. Instead one sees a grim, passionate man. He is slender; his clothes hang loosely; his teeth seem to be continually clenched. His manner is that of a dedicated political leader about to address a doubtful audience. He is always leaning forward, his spectacles gripped in his white-knuckled fist. No wonder; during the six months after his departure from Krupp he was an accessory to at least six attempts on Hitler's life. Each disappointment seemed more unbelievable, each tomorrow promised success, and by now he had staked his life on the outcome. At times the future seemed to promise nothing but despair. There was dissension within the movement. Yet one goal united them all. Once Hitler had been destroyed, they agreed, Germany would be free again, and that fall hope focused on a relatively obscure conspirator and a plan (code name Valkyrie) which seemed flawless. The key figure was an *Oberstleutnant* (lieutenant colonel) who was exactly Alfried's age. Henceforth the fate of Löser and Dr. Hans Beusch would ride with this idealistic descendant of Gneisenau, thirty-six-year-old Count Klaus Philip Schenk von Stauffenberg.

&#10010;   &#10010;   &#10010;

If the Führer had been blown to bits in 1943, thirty-six-year-old Alfried Felix Alwyn von Bohlen would have been indignant, and not only because he was devoted to Hitler. While Löser was going underground that year, Alfried was rising to the very top. Already *de facto* leader of the Konzern, now he was reaching for *de jure* possession. His great-grandfather's will of 1882 had set up what, at that time, had seemed to be a foolproof plan. As the firm's lawyers explained to the author, Alfred Krupp had provided for a *fideikommiss*, literally inheritance by entail, "establishing for three heirs the line of succession in such a way that the industrial part of the estate would not be divided, but would, instead, fall to one successor each time it changed hands. These three were Friedrich Alfred Krupp, Bertha Krupp, and Bertha Krupp's oldest son." This had worked smoothly enough at the turn of the century, when Fritz's estate passed into Bertha's hands. Since then capitalists had been introduced to the inheritance tax, however, and the German statutes regulating the transfer of property were particularly intricate. An act of 1920, tied to the Prussian common law code of 1794, barred the naming of a single heir unless he was an only child, which Alfried patently wasn't. Furthermore, the firm was at the crest of its greatest prosperity in the family's three-hundred-and-fifty-six-year history. Taxes based on its present value would demolish the estate.

Obviously something had to be done, but whatever it was wouldn't be easy. At first glance the answer seemed simple enough. Hitler was not only a friend; his destiny was tied to the family's. And he could do anything he pleased in Germany — on April 26, 1942, his rubber stamp Reichstag had actually given him the right to pass the death sentence on every human being in the Reich. Even a totalitarian regime must weigh the danger of establishing precedents, however, and other Ruhr barons were watching closely. A month after Alfried's divorce in 1941 Gustav had begun work on a solution. During his coherent spells he drafted legislation for the introduction of "industrial bequests" (*industrielle Erbhöfe*), which would be limited to "estates left by firms of world-wide reputation which have acquired a special position as a consequence of their services and traditions"[23] — in short, to Krupp. The owners of such firms would be permitted to name their successors, who, in turn, would pay a minimal annuity to the Reich. It was a clever scheme, and doubtless Alfried helped his father hatch it, for it was the future Krupp who delivered the outline nine months later to Hitler's Wolfsschanze (Wolf's Lair) at Rastenburg in East Prussia, where Stauffenberg's briefcase was to be left two summers later. The heir apparent's visit had been preceded by detailed correspondence between the failing lord of Essen and Martin Bormann. Nevertheless Alfried's call elicited no immediate response. Bureaucracies are alike the world over, and the Wolf had other things on its mind, *e.g.*, its invasion of the Soviet Union, the British and Russian thrust into Iran, and Rommel's duel in the sun with Montgomery.

Gustav jogged the Wolfsschanze repeatedly, with no success. The impairment of his faculties had begun to alarm him; he wanted this thing settled. On the twenty-fourth anniversary of the November criminals' crime he tried once more:

11 *November 1942*

*Mein lieber Herr Bormann!*

Today I once again refer to my letter of July 27, acknowledging at the same time the receipt of your letter of the 21st of the same month, and referring to the conversation which you had with my son Alfried at the Führer's headquarters on August 10 with regard to safeguarding the Krupp firm for the future. . . . Should there still be any questions concerning the fundamental ideas of the draft of the law, I shall always be at your disposal, during your stay in Berlin. My son Alfried, for his part, would be glad to call upon you as my representative at any other place which might be convenient to you [*mein Sohn Alfried seinerseits würde sich freuen, Sie als mein Vertreter an irgendeinem anderen Ihnen passenden Ort besuchen zu dürfen*]

*Mit alter Hochachtung und Dankbarkeit und*

*mit Heil Hitler*

*Ihr*

*KBH*

Their subsequent correspondence reveals that Bormann carefully studied this letter, the full text of which included a hodgepodge of Gustavian thoughts. Although he was aware that his Kruppianers' social welfare "will be taken care of by the party and the state more and more in the future," he believed that the people who worked for him were entitled to added inducements for "promotion of intellectual and technical talents" and "a further social claim to which especially the workers of Krupp are entitled." He was thinking of establishing "a kind of company-owned training place" for craftsmen; modestly he proposed that "the name 'Gustav-Haus' shall serve this idea in the widest sense of the word." There was more of this sort of thing, but Bormann saw through it to the kernel, which was very hard. Something had to be done for Alfried, and fast: "On considering this question we have ascertained that under the present laws the principal solution of the question cannot be carried out. We have to find an entirely new way . . . creating new legislation."[24]

What the old Krupp wanted was an absolute industrial monarchy. He insisted that the Reich recognize the existence of the family's autonomous *Staat im Staate*, ruled by an independent Konzernherr. This was something more than the protection of the firm's efficiency, the preservation of a legacy, and tax exemption. It was an entirely new concept, repealing a long roll of statutes which had begun with the inception of the industrial revolution. Nevertheless Hitler approved. In his harsh, inimitable voice he told Bormann, "*Jawohl*."

However, there must be no nonsense about fresh legislation for all businessmen. That would open a Pandora's box; everyone in the government would be busy turning down claims, and there would be no time left to fight the war. They might as well call a spade a spade; this was to be one law for one family, exempting it from the Reich Ministers for Justice, Economics, and Finance. If their advice was sought they would naturally protest. Therefore they would be told nothing. This unique privilege was being granted because of the Krupp dynasty's long history of loyalty to the aspirations of German militarism, and, in particular, its unswerving loyalty to the National Socialist German Worker's Party. The reigning Krupp and the Krupp-to-be had been faithful to their Führer. In consequence they were rewarded — but by the party, not the Reich. The panjandrums of the Reichstag were to be ignored. Bormann, the Nazis' deputy leader and chief of the party chancellery, and Hans Lammers, the Nazis' state secretary, who had served as legal counsel for the Führer's decree of June 29, 1941, designating Göring as his own successor in the event of death, would hammer out the details between them.

Four days before Christmas they sent the dynasty a present. A gleaming black Mercedes skidded to a halt beside the Krupp castle's blood beech, and one of the Reich's "asphalt soldiers" — impeccably groomed SS troops — bounded out, a leather dispatch case strapped to his wrist. As head butler Karl Dohrmann held the door; the messenger marched into the library and handed Gustav a large envelope. The letter inside read:

*Der Führer der Partei-Kanzlei*
*An:  Dr. Krupp von Bohlen und Halbach*
PERSÖNLICH

*Essen, auf dem Hügel*

*Lieber Herr von Bohlen!*

It is already a fortnight since I verbally informed Reich Minister Dr. Lammers that the Führer wishes a "Lex Krupp" entirely designed for the preservation of the Krupp family enterprise. Reich Minister Dr. Lammers has promised me that he would discuss the whole matter with you verbally [*Herr Reichsminister Dr. Lammers hat mir versprochen, die ganze Angelegenheit mit Ihnen mündlich zu erörtern*]. He would be pleased to come to Essen, since, in any case, he has never seen the works.

I heartily wish you, your family, and the works all the best for the New Year, with a request to be remembered. I am always

*Ihr* [Yours]

gez. BORMANN[25]

The small print took time, but by the New Year letters from Bormann and Gustav were crisscrossing, and Alfried was conferring regularly with Lammers. In drafting the Lex Krupp, Lammers acted as a constitutional seer. On January 9, 1943, Gustav wrote:

*Lieber Bormann,*

My son Alfried and I had a conversation with Dr. Lammers today which showed perfect mutual agreement. [*Mein Sohn Alfried und ich hatten heute eine Unterredung mit Dr. Lammers, aus der sich vollständige gegenseitige Übereinstimmung ergab.*] I did not want to fail to inform you of this and at the same time gratefully acknowledge receipt of your friendly letter of the 31st of last month. Alfried will, in a short time, together with our notary public, submit further documents and present them to Herr Reichsminister Lammers. My wife and I send you and your family the best wishes for 1943. May it be a year of well-being and benefit for our people and particularly for our Führer, as their symbol.

Heil Hitler!

*Ihr*

G.v.B.u.H.[26]

G.v.B.u.H.'s good wishes notwithstanding, Russia's second winter offensive opened twenty-four hours later. At 8 A.M. on January 10, 1943 — the very hour at which Gustav's eldest son was breakfasting with five Berlin functionaries, arguing that the Krupp dynasty was entitled to special recognition because the family had always provided the Reich with Europe's finest arms — the Russian lines encircling Stalingrad erupted in one continual, ear-shattering roar from seven thousand Soviet cannon. The twenty-two Nazi divisions in the pocket were hopelessly outgunned.

Inside the city which the Russian dictator had named after himself in 1925, the effects were devastating. The Germans were caught in a bloody arena. In November the Soviet trap had closed on 330,000 of them. "Now," *Red Star* noted grimly, "there is no sun for them, they are rationed to twenty-five or thirty rounds a day, and they are to fire only when attacked. . . . Here, in the dark cold ruins of the city they have destroyed they will meet with vengeance; they will meet it under the cruel stars of the Russian winter night."[27] Even Junker 52's were unable to get through with supplies. When Paulus surrendered to a Russian lieutenant on the twenty-fourth day of the Voroshilov salvos there were barely 80,000 survivors left in the blackened lunar wasteland, trembling pitifully in the 44-degree-below-freezing cold. The Führer proclaimed three days of national mourning. Over and over the radio in Hügel's second-floor hall played the *Siegfried* funeral march and *Ich hatt' einen Kameraden* —

> *Wird mir die Hand noch reichen,*
> *Wieweil ich eben lad':*
> *Kann dir die Hand nicht geben,*
> *Bleib' du im ew' gen Leben*
> *Mein guter Kamerad!*
>
> His hand he tries to reach me,
> As I my charge renew;
> My hand was never given,
> But he will be in heaven
> My comrade tried and true!

Alfried was in the capital, renewing his charge against the ramparts of corporate law with three *Kameraden*, subordinates of Lammers. On February 24 — when, for the first time, DNB used the ominous word *Götterdämmerung* — Gustav wrote Lammers from Bad Gastein, near Blühnbach, that "My son informs me that he, together with Dr. Jöden, had a discussion with State Secretary Kritzinger last Saturday, at which Herr Winnuhn was also present. The conference had the splendid result that agreement was reached on the principal question. . . . We have to call on the assistance of the state in this context because, to preserve the unity of the management in the hands of one man, a settlement regarding the inheritance legislation must be made which differs from the regulations of the inheritance law valid today. . . ."[28]

✠ ✠ ✠

Gustav's condition was deteriorating rapidly. His nervousness had become more pronounced, and for the first time in his life he was becoming careless of his personal appearance; occasionally he would urinate in his trousers and neglect to change them. Alone, Alfried mounted fresh assaults on Lammers, Bormann, and the Führer himself. They had no time for him. Originally Gustav had scheduled his formal abdication for March 31. He postponed the ceremony three months, and still nothing had happened. The Wolf in East Prussia was preoccupied with the battles of Kharkov, Tanganrog, Bryansk, Smolensk, and Kiev, all of which were lost by the Wehrmacht; by the loss of North Africa and Sicily; by the invasion of Italy; and by the overthrow of Mussolini, which depressed morale in the Lair. Finally, on November 12, convinced that the Russians had been stopped and that the Allies were pinned down at Salerno, Hitler paused to scan domestic affairs and affixed his signature to the document Lammers had prepared. After citing the dynasty's unique contributions to German aggression in three wars, the Führer provided, among other things that

> Der Eigentümer des Vermögens der Krupp-Familie ist dazu berechtigt, dieses Vermögen zur Errichtung eines Familienunternehmens mit genau festgelegter Nachfolge zu verwenden.

> The owner of the Krupp family's wealth is entitled to use this fortune for the establishment of a family enterprise with a specially regulated succession.

and that

> Der jeweilige Eigentümer des Unternehmens soll den Namen "Krupp" vor seinem Familiennamen tragen.

> Whoever be the owner of the enterprise shall carry the name Krupp before his family name.[29]

The following day an asphalt soldier delivered the historic decree to Villa Hügel, and forty-eight hours later, on the somber afternoon of November 15, a motorcade of Mercedes limousines wound up the hill. Nazi Gauleiters, Gestapo men, SS functionaries, generals, admirals, and, most important, the firm's lawyers, joined Gustav, Bertha, and Alfried in the big hall. The old Krupp's chair was a few steps from the toilet; footmen stood on either side of it, alert for a distress signal. But there was no need for the prince consort to rise. Indeed, his attendance wasn't necessary; he held no financial interest in the firm.

The presence of only two individuals was essential: the Cannon Queen and the future Cannon King. Bertha stood first. At fifty-seven she was still a vigorous woman, and reading from a paper her attorneys had prepared she declared firmly, "I renounce the ownership of the family undertaking in favor of my son Alfried, who thus, in accordance with the statute drawn up on the basis of the Führer's decree, becomes the owner of the family undertaking." Having disinherited Berthold, Harald, Eckbert, Irmgard, Waldtraut, and Claus's widow and son in one sentence, she continued, "In accordance with the Führer's decree my son will be known by the name of Alfried Krupp von Bohlen und Halbach from the time that he becomes the owner." She beamed at her firstborn and sat. He rose. "I am in agreement with the above declaration by my mother," he said quietly, "and I take over the ownership of the family undertaking." There was a long, impressive silence while he eyed each witness. Then his father spoiled it. When Alfried Krupp's stare reached Gustav the old man's hands fluttered nervously. Swiftly the two servants hoisted him between them and half carried him into the *Klosett*. In the embarrassed hush the sound of flushing could be heard.[30]

The Lex Krupp was published in the *Reichsgesetzblatt* (*Reich Law Gazette*) of November 20. Three weeks later the directors of the firm went through the motions of ratifying it. The Führer then formally "passed" *die Firma*'s enabling act, and during the Christmas holidays Gustav, with Bertha's help, struggled through his last coherent letter. It was addressed, appropriately, to Adolf Hitler.

*Dezember 29, 1943*

*Mein Führer!*

*Gemäss Verordnung vom 12. November 1943 haben Sie Ihre Einwilligung gegeben, der Nachfolge bei den Krupp Familienunternehmen eine besondere Grundlage zu gewähren . . .*

*Auf diese Weise haben Sie einen Wunsch verwirklicht, den ich und meine Frau seit Jahren hegten, und unsere Herzen ihrer grossen Sorge um die Zukunft der Krupp Werke entlastet . . . Dieser Grundauffassung von Alfred Krupp zufolge wünschen meine Frau und ich ebenfalls, die Nachfolge so zu bestimmen, dass nur ein Nachfolger unserer Familie das Betriebseigentum erben würde. . . .*

By virtue of the decree of November 12, 1943, you have given your consent to the foundation of the Krupp family enterprise on special principles of succession, and on December 21, 1943, you passed the statute of the family enterprise established here on December 15, 1943.

By this you have made a wish come true which my wife and I had cherished for years, and thereby you have relieved our hearts of great anxiety over the future of the Krupp works. The preservation of the Krupp works in the hands of one person, and thereby the assumption of full responsibility by one member of the family, had already been the wish of my wife's grandfather, Alfred Krupp. This aim has found clear expression in his will, where, to prevent any division of the ownership of the works, he stipulated the succession of inheritance for three generations in such a manner that only one of the future heirs, the oldest, was to inherit the family property. Following this basic conception of Alfred Krupp, my wife and I also desire to stipulate the succession in that manner whereby only one successor of our family would inherit the family property. . . .[31]

In his own tedious fashion, Gustav then reviewed the history of German corporate law, German common law, and the contributions of the dynasty to the glorious feats of arms achieved at Sedan, the first bombardment of Paris, Liège, Jutland, Verdun, Tannenberg, the blitzkrieg of 1940, the siege of Sevastopol, and the submarine offensives of two wars. It was, he said, his greatest wish that the Berlin-Essen axis might be strengthened, assuring future generations of German men that they, like their forefathers, might enjoy ecstatic moments of Teutonic conquest.

By your decree, my Führer, this aim has now been achieved [*Durch Ihre Verordnung, mein Führer, ist dieses Ziel nun erreicht worden*]. My wife and I, as well as the whole family, will be deeply grateful to you for this proof of your confidence, and we shall do everything that is within our power to equip our son Alfried, the present owner of the family enterprise, for the task of maintaining, and, if possible, increasing the production of the Krupp works, in both peace and war, in your spirit and for the benefit of our people.

Our special thanks go to you, my Führer, also for the great honor and recognition which you have awarded, in your introduction to your decree, to 132 years of Krupp work, done by many generations of faithful followers, and steered and directed by four generations of the family Krupp [*von vier Generationen der Familie Krupp gesteuert und geleitet*].

Your grateful

BERTHA KRUPP VON BOHLEN UND HALBACH
GUSTAV KRUPP VON BOHLEN UND HALBACH[32]

The second signature was now, of course, a forgery. From this moment forward Alfried would hold the title and the power. He had come into a remarkable inheritance, and the 300,000 shares didn't begin to represent its real value, for their book evaluation of 500 marks each was obsolete. Since Hitler seized power in 1933 the Konzern's assets had jumped from 72,962,000 marks to 237,316,093 marks. Moreover, that evaluation didn't include the confiscated companies in conquered nations. Despite the war, business had never been better. In 1943 Krupp sales had reached an all-time peak, surpassing the record year of 1939. Furthermore, the family had received generous allotments from Hitler's occupation assessments in France. Alfried had become monarch of the continent's greatest industrial complex. Apart from the Führer, who had made it all possible, no one in Europe could challenge him; he held seven high offices in the government and the National Socialist Party, each of which would have entitled him to immediate access to Hitler even if his name hadn't been Krupp.[33]

On the morning of the same day that his parents dispatched their gratitude to the Wolfsschanze, the new *alleinige Inhaber* authorized the first order of his reign:

*An die Betriebe, Büros und Zweigwerke — Betrifft: Umwandlung der Aktiengesellschaft in die Einzelfirma Friedrich Krupp. . . .*

*Gemäss Entscheid durch die Generalversammlung vom 15. Dezember 1943, wurde die Friedrich Krupp Aktiengesellschaft in die Einzelfirma Friedrich Krupp, mit Sitz in Essen, umgewandelt . . .*

*Der Inhaber des Familienunternehmens trägt die volle Verantwortung und leitet das ganze Unternehmen. Um ihn in seiner Aufgabe zu unterstützen, hat er eine als "das Direktorium" bezeichnete Geschäftsführung ernannt.*

To plants, offices and branch enterprises

Subject: Conversion of the Aktiengesellschaft to the individual firm of Fried. Krupp.

On the decision of the general meeting of December 15, 1943, the Fried. Krupp Aktiengesellschaft was converted into the individually owned firm of Fried. Krupp, with headquarters in Essen. On the same date and upon simultaneous establishment of articles of incorporation of Fried. Krupp, the firm was vested in the sole ownership of Herr Alfried von Bohlen und Halbach. Upon resignation of the appropriate officers, the family enterprise thus established will have the future trade name of

Fried. Krupp . . .

Herr Alfried von Bohlen und Halbach will henceforth bear the name of Herr Alfried Krupp von Bohlen und Halbach.

The owner of the family enterprise is answerable for the direction of the entire enterprise. To assist him in the management of the business he has appointed a directorate.[34]

Actually, he added in a wry aside, the Direktorium would be identical to the old Vorstand "with the exception of Herr Löser, resigned." Like most of his countrymen, he found nomenclature engrossing; he ordered new rubber stamps, new letterheads "and other standard forms," and he exulted in the fact that also on December 15, by command of Adolf Hitler, he had taken over his father's duties as Nazi "Leader of the Plants."

But his concern with designations and salutations was only the means to an end. He possessed absolute authority now, and he wanted a quarter-million Kruppianer to know it. That first order had been issued by Görens and Janssen in his behalf, possibly because he wanted to dispel the notion that he had dismissed Löser. Now it was time he acted in his own name. On January 11, in honor of the Nazi regime's eleventh anniversary, he promulgated a decree setting forth the duties of the Direktorium and clarifying his own role in two unequivocal sentences which were to haunt him at Nuremberg:

> *Der Inhaber des Familienunternehmens trägt die alleinige Verant-*
> *wortung für die ganze Firma und ist deren Haupt. . . . Alle wichtigen*
> *Angelegenheiten müssen mir sowie auch den Mitgliedern des Direktoriums*
> *zur Entscheidung vorgelegt werden.*

> The owner of the family enterprise alone carries the responsibility for, and is the head of, the entire firm. . . . All matters of importance must be submitted to me as well as to members of the directorate for a decision.[35]

In retrospect the haggling with Bormann, the dickering with Lammers, and the ultimate rejoicing over the Führer's decision may seem like an exercise in futility. The Third Reich, after all, had less then three years to run. But the most singular fact about Krupp today is meaningless unless seen in the context of those days. It centers around that single date, December 15, 1943. Krupp publications and West German school books note that Alfried became sole owner of the firm on that day. The significance of the date lies in the fact that on that bitterly cold Wednesday a quarter-century ago the Vorstand, in obedience to Hitler's decree, dissolved itself and bowed to the new ruler. It was the day the Lex Krupp really took effect.[36]

The implications of this are unappreciated in Germany; even the Social Democratic opposition, which has been battling the dynasty for a hundred years and knows that many Nazi laws are still in effect, is unaware of this one. But in a meeting with this author twenty years after Alfried's first order to the Konzern as sole proprietor, his lawyers confirmed that the "special 1943 agreement between the government and Krupp" was the legal basis for his postwar rule over the family's seigniory, and they were convinced that the Lex Krupp, with its extraordinary tax advantages, would apply should his son claim the dynastic legacy.[37] Stripped of technicalities and learned footnotes, this had just one meaning — Alfried Krupp, the wealthiest and most prestigious individual in Europe's Common Market during the early 1960's, held his position until his death under a special authorization from Adolf Hitler, Führer of the Reich. The Wolf had been slain, its Lair was destroyed; but one member of the old pack retained his claws.

✠ ✠ ✠

Retreating from the Wolfsschanze, Hitler returned to the Reich Chancellery in Berlin, that enormous palace of marble, feldspar, red stone, massive doors, and baroque candelabra which he himself had designed and which, second only to Villa Hügel, was the most hideous building in Germany. Each day it became less habitable. Allied raids were reducing it to a gutted skeleton. Fifty feet beneath the garden of the old chancellery, however, a shelter had been built. Approached from within the chancellery by stairs leading down through the butler's pantry, the suite comprised twelve rooms, none larger than a closet, and a curved stair descending to an even deeper (though equally cramped) second chamber. This was the Führerbunker, "the stage," in the words of H. R. Trevor-Roper, "on which the last act of the Nazi melodrama was played out."[38]

As Hitler dug in, so did the new Krupp. One of his first acts as ruler of the family empire had been to issue a proclamation boasting of "the glorious history of the Krupp weapons forges," pointing "with pride" to the workers as "active adherents of Nazi ideology," and promising "revenge against the Allies"; but like his Führer he didn't want to fall victim to vagrant shrapnel. Summoning a team of picked miners and engineers, he set them to work scooping out a Kruppbunker beneath Villa Hügel. Between August 10, 1942, when he had visited East Prussia with the first draft of the decree which would establish his sovereignty, and its publication in the Reichsgesetzblatt over a year later, RAF Lancasters had dropped 6,926 tons of bombs on Essen. Bertha and the prince consort spent more and more time in Blühnbach, but Alfried's post was here, and naturally he preferred not to die at it.[39]

His hideout was bizarre. Even today a visit to the entrance of his private bunker is eerie. Opening a concealed door in the family library, you descend a steep flight of stairs and pass through the Chinese Room, lacquered in red and black as a sentimental reminder of Gustav's Peking career. Here you encounter labyrinthine white-tiled catacombs; a cavernous cellar; the bright green swimming pool adorned with marble Wilhelmine figures; more white tile; and then the formidable portal marked in stark Gothic letters: LUFTSCHUTZBUNKER: 50 PERSONEN. Today the shelter is filled in — after the war it threatened the castle's foundations — but twenty-five years ago the door led to a steep 120-step staircase, which the new Krupp would illumine with the aid of a candle or flashlight. At the bottom, no matter who was with him, he would remain silent, his presence marked only by the glow of a cigarette.

Incessant chain-smoking was one sign of the tension in him. Another was his growing devotion to skat, a kind of Teutonic bridge game in which a player matches his wits against two opponents, fighting, so to speak, on two fronts. (Other admirers of skat have included Adolf Eichmann and

Wilhelm I. During most of the battle of Verdun S.M. played in the lonely grandeur of Schloss Pless. He lost consistently. Alfried always won.) In every other respect, however, Krupp's self-control was magnificent. Each morning after a raid he would slide behind the wheel of his dark Bayerische Motoren Werke (BMW) sports car and carefully pick his way through the night's debris. While secretaries swept broken glass from the floor of his office — and, on four occasions, repaired the framed pictures of Hitler and Alfred Krupp which hung side by side behind his desk — he received reports from the Direktorium of damaged rolling mills, of water rising in his coal mines, of broken power lines. Swiftly he issued orders for repairs, sending squads of crack Kruppianer to vital shops and power stations, dispatching task forces of Kumpel with heavy duty pumps to the mines, allocating details of foreign workers and POW's to reconstruction, and requisitioning new equipment from seized plants in the occupied territories.

By 7:30 P.M. the rakish BMW was parked outside Villa Hügel once more and Alfried was attacking the castle's hoard of British Scotch. During dinner he brooded. His guests could never guess what was on his mind or even appraise his mood, and since they were all Krupp subordinates they tended to speak carefully and keep a wary eye on the head of the table. The likeliest reason for their host's preoccupation was that he was listening for enemy bombers. If they were coming they usually arrived during brandy. A few minutes after 9 P.M. sirens would wail, Krupp would glance stoically at his watch — this, after all, was business — and then the Kruppstahl ring of 88's around the Ruhr, manned by 100,000 troops of the Reich's Flieger-Abwehr-Kanone (Flak) command would open up. You couldn't mistake that sound. You could actually see it; the snifters on the table would start to tremble. There was so much steel in the sky that Allied pilots christened the Ruhrgebiet "Flak Alley."

As the engineer behind the first 88's used in Spain, Alfried could gauge exactly when the raid was approaching its crescendo. Once the drone of motors became audible he could estimate from experience the number of attacking planes, their type, and their altitude. Still, he liked to see for himself. Crushing his cigarette stub and pinching the stem of his goblet between his thumb and forefinger, carefully placing it where, if upset, it wouldn't stain the linen, he would lead his executives to the elegant grounds outside and glance up calmly, almost nonchalantly. Even children would know that this was the time to race for cover; overhead the black Pathfinders (swift, all-wood, twin-engine RAF Mosquitoes) would be flitting about, sowing Essen with red and green signal flares, outlining the target for approaching Lancaster bombardiers.

"The flares would fall in cones, and if you didn't pause to think what they meant, they were really a lovely sight," recalls Dr. Friedrich Wilhelm Hardach, who lived on the hill during the last two years of the war. "We called them 'Christmas trees.' Herr Alfried would remain erect and motionless, just watching them. The rest of us would be very nervous. We knew that in precisely ten minutes the bombers would be up there, and what they would drop wouldn't be so pretty. But *we* couldn't move until *he* did. Sometimes he would remain there under the *Blutbuche* during the entire raid." More often he headed for the shelter; it was thirty-six yards deeper than the basement and had a separate exit in one of the far gardens, in case the vast mass of the castle collapsed and blocked its main door. Yet no one has ever suggested that Alfried was not a man of exceptional personal courage. Once a stray incendiary started a small fire in the servants' quarters over the main ballroom. A trapped footman appeared on the castle dome in his nightshirt, peered around wildly, and scrambled down a ladder which had been erected by Bredeney's *Luftschutzwart* (air raid warden). The Direktorium was hopping up and down with excitement, but Krupp's equine face merely crinkled in one of his rare, sardonic smiles. He displayed no anxiety, nor did the peril appear to disturb him. Once the Lancasters had left, his *maître* of those days remembers, he casually returned to his unfinished brandy and lit a fresh Camel. He certainly never lay awake fretting, as his great-grandfather would have done. In the *maître's* words, *"Herr Alfried schlief immer ganz ruhig, wie ein Kind"* (Herr Alfried always slept as peacefully as a child).[40]

Although divorced and separated from the rest of his family, he was probably surrounded by more friends then than at any other period, with the possible exception of his prison term. He had the RAF to thank for that. With the overwhelming triumphs of the early years Krupp officials seem to have persuaded themselves that Göring had been right, that the Luftwaffe could turn back most enemy bombers. In any event, they built few shelters. Alfried could construct a last-minute bunker because his name was Krupp; no one else had access to the necessary men and materials. When the heavy raids began early in 1943, Essen's Kruppianer were for a time virtually helpless. Directors who had relatives in the country sent their wives and children there, defying a Führer decree which forbade anyone to desert the Ruhr. Hardach packed his family off to a hamlet in northern Westphalia. After Dr. Paul Hansen's home had sustained a direct hit in 1943 he found a refuge for his wife 155 miles from the Ruhr. Twice another executive saved his own house, a block away from Altendorferstrasse, from incendiaries; then he lost it and took everyone in his household to the train station. Dr. Hermann Hobrecker drove his wife and children to his father-in-law's house in Wiesbaden — where, oddly, they were bombed out while the Hobrecker home in Essen survived the war.[41]

Evacuation was largely a privilege of rank; workmen found it almost impossible to get travel permits. The craftsmen in the colonies of Schederhofstrasse, Swanenkamp and Segerothstrasse emerged from the ruins and carried on in their littered cellars, and those neighborhoods remain barren to this day. Krupp figures show that of the 32,013 workers' houses owned by the firm at the outbreak of the war, 13,388 were totally destroyed and 16,117 severely damaged. Essen was stippled with naked chimneys. A few men of influence managed to wheedle authorization for repairs; since Albert Speer and Robert Ley often stayed at the Essener Hof, the manager reconstructed the top floor with reinforced concrete in 1943, to prevent further damage. Even so, his shipment of cement was withheld until the hotel had been hit three times.[42]

Learning that so many of the Konzern's key men were being forced to live as homeless bachelors, Bertha had begun inviting them to move into Hügel's guest rooms, and later into the children's rooms. Alfried expanded her policy. It wasn't a sacrifice; parts of the castle were never used, and since shedding Anneliese and returning to his quarters in the big house, Alfried's *kleine Haus* had been entirely vacant. This way he had skat partners, dinner guests who couldn't beg off with familial excuses, and companions whenever the roll of 88's telegraphed news of coming fireworks. In addition he could discuss business with the Direktorium after dinner. If a member of the board was troubled by a particularly intricate problem, he and the Konzernherr could unravel it at breakfast or while riding downtown together afterward. And should the main administration building be razed, Krupp's empire could be run from his castle.

The Hauptverwaltungsgebäude never toppled. Its durability was marvelous. On all four sides outbuildings had been reduced to junk, and the bridge connecting Alfried's artillery wing with the main building lay in the street, but despite great fissures, some large enough for a man to walk through, the ugly walls stood. As an architect Gustav had been hopeless, but he had laid a solid foundation. The building had been erected on a single slab of concrete; it would be safe as long as that slab remained intact, and no bomb short of an atomic device could dent it. To be sure, the RAF had made life in the Hauptverwaltungsgebäude extremely trying. Fritz Tubbesing, a veteran of Koch und Kienzle, had been charged with keeping it livable. Fritz was a resourceful Kruppianer. The challenges of secret rearmament hadn't vexed him. But this edifice, as he later conceded, virtually defeated him.

Whenever the Lancasters arrived, Tubbesing would conscientiously leave his wife and children and sprint to the Hauptverwaltungsgebäude three miles away, hoping to save it. "And all the time," he said afterward, "I would be wondering whether they would be there when I got back." His tale is typical of those who stayed in the embattled city. Again and again his house was rocked by high explosives. Throughout 1943 and the first half of 1944 he repaired it with tin sheets. Finding a Krupp carpenter who had been bombed out, Tubbesing gave him a free room in exchange for help. The roof was demolished; the two men repaired it. It vanished once more; once more they rebuilt it. Then, in the great RAF attack of October 23–24, when 4,522 tons of bombs were dropped on Essen, the roof, walls, and floor were annihilated. The Tubbesings and the carpenter hastily put together a crude lean-to. Reporting at the administration building next day, Fritz learned that during the night eight armor plate mills, seven machine shops, six foundries, and miscellaneous shell shops, plate shops, and gun mount shops were out of action. Discouraged, *die Firma's* accountants closed their books and kept no further record of damage from raids.[43]

In that month, according to Marshal of the RAF Sir Arthur Travers "Bomber" Harris, the tonnage of explosives dropped by British airmen was twice that in any previous month. Bomber Command's chief targets were the Ruhr and the Rhineland, and Germany's leaders were understandably anxious. In 1914 the Fatherland had forfeited the first battle of the Marne to shield its great anvil; now, with a powerful air arm, the enemy had found a new way to threaten it. Goebbels's diaries reflect the official anxiety. On March 13, 1943, he dictated: "Later in the evening the news reached us of another exceedingly heavy air raid on Essen. This time the Krupp plant has been hard hit. I telephoned to the Deputy Gauleiter, Schlessmann, who gave me a rather depressing report. Twenty-five major fires were raging on the ground of the Krupp plant alone. Air warfare is at present our greatest worry . . . Things simply cannot go on like this. The Führer told Göring what he thought, without mincing words. It is expected that Göring will now do something decisive." The Reichsmarschall didn't; he couldn't. A week later Goebbels noted: "Even if the claim that Krupp has been 80 percent destroyed is terribly exaggerated, we must nevertheless expect serious stoppages of production." In May he commented glumly: "The 800-acre Krupp plant bombarded from the air for the fifty-fifth time . . ." and, on July 28: "The last raid brought about 100 percent stoppage of production in the Krupp works. Speer himself is much concerned and worried about it."[44]

Had the RAF limited itself to Krupp's weapons factories — and Essen was exclusively a British show; the American Air Force never approached the city — its conduct would have been above reproach. But with the best intentions bombing remains an inexact science. At Nuremberg a Belgian chaplain who had been imprisoned in Essen described the impact of the attacks on women and children as "completely chaotic," and when a Krupp lawyer referred bitterly to "the final phase of the war, during which Essen was transformed into a battlefield, and finally into a heap of trash," the prosecution sat silent and troubled. Goebbels's firsthand impressions are revealing. On April 10, 1943, he appeared for a personal inspection, and his first reaction was that of the efficient, objective Nazi: "We arrived in Essen before 7 A.M. Deputy Gauleiter Schlessmann and a large staff awaited us at the Hauptbahnhof. We go to the hotel on foot because driving is quite impossible in many parts of Essen. This walk enables us to make an estimate of the damage inflicted by the last three air raids . . . The building experts of the Stadtbehörden calculate that it will take about twelve years to repair the damage."[45]

He debated asking Alfried to move the Gusstahlfabrik elsewhere and concluded, "There would be no purpose in it, for the moment Essen is no longer an industrial center the English will pounce on the next city, say Bochum or Dortmund or Düsseldorf. A position must be held as long as possible." All this was set down with chilling detachment. Yet behind Goebbels's demonic façade lay memories of his boyhood as the son of a foreman in the nearby industrial town of Rheydt. Having paid his respects to both the old Krupp and the new Krupp, he struck out toward familiar landmarks. "Only by going on such a trip can one really estimate the damage," he wrote. "It was terrible. One's heart shudders upon revisiting and seeing, in their present condition, the streets and squares that were once so beautiful. I suffer almost physically at the sight, for I have known the city of Essen well ever since my childhood. I can draw comparisons between what was and what now is." He did, and then he wept.[46]

✠    ✠    ✠

Goebbels didn't cry over the damaged shops; even he realized that they were legitimate quarry. He was moved by the smashed homes, the ravaged parks, and the mutilated civilians, and in mentioning them one must touch upon one of the more controversial issues of the war. The basic facts are indisputable. In the beginning they were trivial; toward the end of a memorandum to Alfried a subordinate noted, almost as an afterthought, that "Through enemy action on January 13, 1943, the Altenessen Store was partly destroyed. However, the clothing still available was saved for the greater part."[47] Raids were still insignificant then. The heavy attacks started the following spring. Their object was to terrorize the German population; in the press briefing after the first thousand-plane-raid — on Cologne — Bomber Command claimed that 250 factories had been destroyed, but photographs clearly showed that downtown Cologne had been the bull's-eye. Between 14,000 and 15,000 people had been slaughtered. The English were stalking inhabitants, not industry.

The next thousand-bomber target was Essen. When the mission had been accomplished, Winston Churchill promised the Commons that Germany "will be subjected to an ordeal the like of which has never been experienced by a country in continuity, severity, and magnitude." In a note to Stalin the prime minister was equally candid and more specific: "We sent 348 heavy bombers to Essen on Saturday, casting 900 tons of bombs in order to increase the damage to Krupp's, which was again effectively hit, and to carry ruin into the southwestern part of the city which had previously suffered little." No one has ever accused Churchill of being ignorant of continental geography. He should have known that the suburbs of southwestern Essen — Fulerum, Haarzopf, Frohnhausen, and Holsterhausen — were entirely residential. Sensing that the Russian dictator would be appreciative, Churchill added that a second assault had leveled the housing of the Germaniawerft's Kruppianer: "Last night 507 aircraft, all but 166 being heavies, carried 1,400 tons to Kiel."[48]

Kiel was a sideshow. After the war Sir Arthur Harris conceded that Bomber Command had decided to saturate the Ruhr, concentrating on "the complete destruction of four Ruhr cities," and statistics gathered for *United States Strategic Bombing Survey* leave no doubt that these were all vital centers in that belt of walled cities which had bound the Ruhr since the Dark Ages, with Essen as the buckle. Essen and Dortmund suffered the most; the destruction in Bochum, Duisburg, Düsseldorf, and Hamm was less appalling. In the great raids heavy industry was battered least. The real targets were homes and stores. The pattern was too consistent to be anything but intentional. According to the *Survey*, "24 percent — nearly one-fourth the total tonnage dropped, and almost twice the weight of bombs launched against all manufacturing targets together — was dropped in attacks against large cities . . . In sheer destructiveness these raids far outstripped all other forms of attack."[49]

To be sure, the British had been provoked. During the fall of France the RAF's impotence, the fruit of appeasement, had been almost insupportable. Except for lone sorties on May 10 and June 16, 1940 (a total of 51 bombs), Krupp had been unaware that enemy aircraft existed. William L. Shirer had been in the Ruhr that spring, and the clear night skies had baffled him. On May 19 he had written in his diary that "the night bombings of the British have done very little damage." Later that same day he observed that the RAF had "not only failed to put the Ruhr out of commission, but even to damage the German flying fields." On June 16 an entry noted that "in the Ruhr there was little evidence of British night bombings." This frustration had been followed by the London blitz. "Whoever sets fire to his neighbor's house cannot complain if the sparks land on his own roof." The proverb is German, but Bomber Command adopted it grimly. The Nazis had started this atrocious form of warfare. Now they were to taste it with a vengeance.[50]

Military men are professionals, however, and though retribution is understandable to a layman, it lacks sufficient dignity for them. Thus they evolved what they called "the higher strategy." The advocates of strategic bombing have been with us for a half-century now, from the Argonne to Vietnam. World War II was the golden age of their faith. To them their solution was the only route to victory. It sounds so simple: destroy a nation's capacity to make war and it must sue for peace. This dogma has, moreover, a subtle advantage over direct confrontation. Your own men are relatively safe. If they do die, death is clean. Most important, you never see the real results of their work until the enemy has surrendered. A reconnaissance photograph is impersonal, dehumanized; the scale is too small to show, say, a dismembered child. Warfare almost becomes an intellectual exercise. So regarded, the annihilation of the Möhne and Eder dams twenty-two miles east of Essen on the night of May 16, 1943, takes on the aspect of a remarkable feat. Sixteen Lancasters under Wing Commander Guy Gibson deftly skip-bombed the faces of the structures, opening breaches a hundred yards wide and a hundred feet deep. Immediately 334 million tons of water came hurtling down the Ruhr valley. The effect of this tidal wave was felt fifty miles away; all summer the railroad spur below Villa Hügel was flooded. No one has attempted to guess how many thousands of sleeping people perished that evening. The question hasn't even been raised. Vickers's official historian merely describes the operation as "one of the most illustrious episodes in the history of the Air Force."[51]

Conceivably Wing Commander Gibson's achievement affected the Reich's military potential, since a few bridges were washed out and some factory floors were drenched, but that wasn't the purpose of Sir Arthur's air offensive. The urban Ruhr was being demolished, according to the marshal himself, "with a view of breaking German morale." The analysts of the comprehensive *Survey* wrote, "It was believed that city attacks offered a means of destroying German civilian morale. It was believed that if the morale of industrial workers could be affected, or if laborers could be diverted from the factories to other purposes, such as caring for their families, repairing damage to their homes . . . war production would suffer."[52]

The failure of these theorists was total. Harris subsequently offered the explanation that Bomber Command rapidly reached a point of diminishing returns: "Effective additional damage could only be done to the already devastated cities . . . by an enormous expenditure of bombs, as much as four or five thousand tons in a single attack and sometimes up to 10,000 tons in two attacks in close succession." But in Essen he achieved that staggering total twice, and as he ultimately conceded, "morale bombing was completely ineffective against so well organized a police state as Germany." The authors of the *Survey* — they included George W. Ball, John Kenneth Galbraith, and Paul H. Nitze — concluded that "The mental reaction of the German people to air attack is significant . . . they showed surprising resistance to the terror and hardship of repeated air attack, to the destruction of their homes and belongings, and to the conditions under which they were forced to live." They not only resisted; they were defiant. Each morning as Alfried drove from the castle to the

Hauptverwaltungsgebäude he saw, on those walls which were still standing, freshly chalked swastikas and the interlocking circles of Krupp.[53]

The RAF staff was hypnotized by the Gusstahlfabrik legend; it was almost impossible for London to avert its eyes and examine Alfried's chimneys elsewhere. To be sure, the *Waffenschmiede* continued to be the heart of the Konzern, producing each year over 20 million metric tons of shells, 128-mm. antiaircraft weapons, howitzers, tank hulls and turrets, and special (380-mm.) and heavy (240- to 280-mm.) guns. Yet this was only the capital of Krupp's empire. He offered other inviting targets. His Gruson-werk in Magdeburg, for example, was an endless source of tanks, guns, submarine parts, and 105- and 88-mm. guns; each month it delivered 18,800 75-mm. shells to the Wehrmacht. Lancasters also passed directly over Alfried's Borbeck foundry, Germany's most modern munitions plant, during each Ruhr raid. Under Borbeck's roofs were 75,000 tons of new machinery, a thousand square miles of priceless blueprints, and 60,000 Kruppianer converting Scandinavia's richest ores into Tiger tanks. Finally, the glowing forges of the mighty Friedrich-Alfred Hütte in Rheinhausen, just across the Rhine, were more vital to the Führer's war economy than the Gusstahlfabrik, the Grusonwerk, or Borbeck. The *Survey* concluded that Rheinhausen was "the most highly integrated steel plant in the Krupp combine . . . it is more important than any single Krupp plant in the Essen area."[54]

Had the commanding officers in London's war rooms been dispassionate, all this would have been reflected in the number and strength of British raids. It wasn't. Lancasters dropped 1,465 badly aimed tons of explosive on Magdeburg; "The damage," the *Survey* concluded, ". . . was negligible." Of RAF attacks on Borbeck it found that "only one" appeared to have "affected" the Borbeck plant. Most astonishing, fewer than 100 tons of bombs were earmarked for Rheinhausen's 1,500 acres of coke ovens, blast furnaces, Thomas converters, open hearths, and rolling mills. Indeed, there was "no evidence that any bomb of the aforementioned 76 tons aimed at or near Rheinhausen hit the plant." Meanwhile the old cast steel factory was absorbing a murderous 16,152 tons — and that doesn't include Harris's last raid, which was so massive that no one bothered to keep score. After the war excuses were offered. Rheinhausen had been "overbombed" (a forerunner to "overkill"). The Germans had outfoxed the RAF: "Preraid intelligence seemed to overlook its importance as a producer of steel ingots" while overestimating "the importance of Krupp-Essen as a producer of steel and heavy ordnance." Then Allied spies protested that they were being libeled. Since the victors' spoils include the right to write military history, the chroniclers agreed upon an ingenious solution: "The Krupp management considered Krupp-Essen as a decoy in the heavy bombing attacks of 1943 and 1944, inasmuch as they had finished their primary function of developing equipment for this war long before the heavy bombing started." The Gusstahlfabrik doubtless did serve as a decoy, but the illusion was born in Britain, not the Ruhr. Harris and his staff had been in pursuit of revenge, and they had got it.[55]

Presumably saturation bombing should, at the very least, have dealt a severe blow to *die Firma.* Inevitably its impact was felt — a single attack took out 25 acres of Krupp sheds; the next raid, 37 sheds. This was no triumph of marksmanship. It was almost impossible for bombardiers to miss. Krupp had six million square yards of factory space in Essen — an area seven times larger than the center of the city — and by the end of the war 30 percent of it had been demolished. The October 23–24, 1944 raid knocked out electric power; the final assault on March 11, 1945, paralyzed the Gusstahlfabrik. According to management records, production was curtailed after each heavy attack, and not all Kruppianer shook their fists at the sky. During 1944 absenteeism rose 33 percent. Meanwhile the 3,189,000 people in the inner Ruhr, of whom 2,300,000 lived in the six largest cities, were caught up in the turmoil. If they couldn't leave, they could at least create pandemonium, and occasionally some did. According to British figures (which have been challenged), between the first and fourth quarter of 1944 the Ruhr's hard coal production dropped from 32.1 millions of tons to 17.8; the crude steel yield from 3.4 millions of tons to 1.5.[56]

If true, this appears to be a partial vindication of Bomber Command. But figures are plastic; you can do with them what you like. The statistics of damaged shops do not reveal Alfried's immense recuperative powers. He was rebuilding all the time. The Gusstahlfabrik was hurt, the *Survey* conceded, "but as an ordnance target it undoubtedly received more attention than was justified by its importance." Dropping a bomb on a mill didn't necessarily wipe it out, even if the bombardier achieved a direct hit: "Many of the older, brick wall structures were completely demolished, but the modern steel frame buildings sustained little more than roof damage."[57]

The greatest blow to Bomber Command's pride was delivered by those Allied intelligence officers who later retrieved the Ruhr's wartime performance figures. The one consequence strategic bombing votaries hadn't expected, and which they have been trying to explain ever since, was an *increase* in output during heavy raids. Nevertheless that is what happened. The "serious stoppages" Goebbels anticipated never occurred. Afterward Willi Schlieker — number three man in the Ministerium for Armament and War Production, after Speer himself and Karl Otto Saur — revealed after the war that "as the bombings grew, so did German production, until on the very eve of defeat, when Germany had collapsed within, the Ruhr was producing more than ever before." Schlieker recalled that Hitler had told Speer, "Give me six hundred tanks a month, and we will abolish every enemy in the world." The Generalstab, said Willi, echoed the Führer — "600 tanks a month, 600 was the magic figure. By the end of 1943 Germany was producing 1,000 tanks a month . . . By November 1944, when the Allies had already made their first breach of German soil, Germany was producing 1,800 tanks a month. . . . Production rose and soared. . . . By mid-1944 airplane production had reached a peak of 3,750 aircraft a month."[58]

Despite the drop in war materials (which, if correct, would of course have become crucial had the war been prolonged), the Ruhr was breaking records even as the Pathfinders flitted against the stars and the cumbersome bomb bay doors swung open. In 1944 the Schlotbarone delivered three times as much armor as in 1943, tripled the Luftwaffe's reserve of new fighter bombers, and manufactured *eight times* as many night fighters. Not only was 1944 a more impressive production year than 1942; in many ways the last quarter of 1944 was an improvement over the first quarter. Feldmarschall Walther Model might still be holding the Ruhr today if transportation hadn't broken down. His supply lines disintegrated because the railroad grid had become a hopeless snarl. Schleiker told American bombing experts that the Ruhrgebiet "ultimately collapsed, not because of the bombing of plants, mills and mines but because the railway exits were so clogged with blowouts, breaks, and burned-out locomotives that they could not carry away the 30,000 tons of finished goods the Ruhr produced every day. The Ruhr strangled finally, in January and February 1945, on its own production; it did not cave in under blast."[59]

Judging the efficacy of what Sir Arthur hailed as the "third front" does not, however, eliminate the moral issue of bombing women and children (and Allied POW's and concentration camps), which for some critics — including Englishmen with special qualifications — is hardest to bear. Major General J. F. C. Fuller, the most vehement of them, called the air offensive a "massacre of civilian populations." Chester Wilmot wrote that "in cities like Cologne and Essen there was nothing left to burn, and the blast bombs, which had caused such havoc when the buildings were intact . . . did little more than convulse the rubble," and B. H. Liddell Hart compared "the higher strategy" with the methods of thirteenth-century Mongols. The RAF marshal, stung, replied that "in all normal warfare of the past, and of the not too distant past, it was the common practice to besiege cities and, if they refused to surrender when called upon with due formality to do so, every living thing in them was in the end put to the sword." General Fuller replied acidly that Sir Arthur's grasp of history was as inadequate as his bombing. Although thirty thousand people had been butchered in Magdeburg during the Thirty Years War for ignoring Tilly's demand that they capitulate, Fuller pointed out, all Christendom had protested, and though British troops were guilty of "fearful excesses" after the storming of Badajoz, Wellington had reprimanded, not condoned, them. During the eighteenth and nineteenth centuries many cities had been stormed, yet purposeful atrocities were the exception to the rule.

England, Fuller insisted, now stood condemned by her own conscience.[60]

These were questions for honorable men to ponder; the Nazis had forfeited their right to pass judgment upon anyone. As Hannah Arendt observed two decades later, "The saturation bombing of German cities" was "still the stock excuse for killing civilians," despite the fact that the Nazi exterminations had begun long before.[61] Alfried offered no excuses. In defeat, as in triumph, he was *Sachlichkeit*. It was impossible to shake him. At Villa Hügel, still largely unscarred, the mad routine continued from season to season, sustained by a desperate conviction that, appearances notwithstanding, the Führer must know what he was doing. Executives in the guest rooms and the "small house" could envisage no other outcome; therefore they persuaded themselves that Germany's fortunes would turn any day now.

It was like a Brecht play. One December a flight of Lancasters took advantage of the early twilight and arrived during cocktails. Alfried declined to go and watch. Doubtless he was bored with Christmas trees in the sky, and besides, it was cold out. The soup was late. He looked annoyed. Then the *maître* did the unforgivable; he served a Moselle with meat. Alfried eyed his pale glass and inquired what had become of the red wines. The *maître* explained; there had been a brief fire in the servants' quarters. Krupp's eyebrows shot up: what did the fire have to do with *der Wein*? Fidgeting, the *maître* stammered out that a bomb had hit a pipe. The castle had no water. The castle owner's forehead remained crinkled. How, he asked, had the blaze been brought under control? "*Mit dem Châteauneuf-du-Pape*," the wretched man mumbled. Alfried stared at him incredulously, and, like a member of the Reform Club, murmured, "*Nicht möglich! Extraordinär. Das ist aber wirklich zu viel*" (Indeed! Extraordinary. Really, this is too much). He toyed with a solid gold fork, toyed with a solid gold spoon — and then solemnly tasted the white wine. "*Ach so, er ist gut*," he said quietly. Dinner proceeded without further incident, followed by a game of skat which he won handily.[62]

# 19

✠

# Who Are All These People?

S TRIPPED of his Nazi duties, Gustav von Bohlen had crept off to Austria; in the spring of 1944 he and Bertha retired to the snowy peace of Blühnbach. Before leaving the Ruhr he dined with her and his successor on his last night in the Essen castle. The old man was attended by his usual flock of menservants. By now meals were a trial for everyone; he had become wholly unpredictable. Among other things he was subject to hallucinations, and on this final evening, according to the recollection of one of the menservants, he startled Bertha and Alfried with a disquieting spectacle. Clutching his napkin, he struggled to his feet. He pointed a palsied finger toward the shadowy end of the long room and whispered:

"*Wer sind denn eigentlich all diese Leute?*" "Who are all these people?"[1]

Bertha assured him that there was no one there, and he sank back. Yet he may have been more perceptive than she thought. To be sure, the alcoves beneath Uncle Felix's murals were uninhabited, but as Krupp executives were shipping their families to the comparative safety of the countryside, tens of thousands of newcomers had arrived, and the city's population had altered dramatically. Since Tilo had observed the strangers gnawing bark from trees, it is entirely possible that Gustav, on one of his expeditions outside, had glimpsed the change.[2]

Those in possession of their faculties couldn't miss Essen's transformation. The immigrants didn't look like, dress like, or speak like Kruppianer or even *Stammarbeiter*, the cadre of skilled veterans in other Ruhr firms. The aliens were led by armed guards wearing the black shirts of the SS Totenkopfverbände, or the smart blue uniforms of Alfried's company police, with swastika armbands and KRUPP on their jaunty visored caps. *Ausländer* were marched from their barbwire compounds through the city streets to the shops where they toiled, and their emaciated appearance and tragic bearing evoked memories of Alfred the Great's wildest schemes for SPD punishment.

*Wer waren denn eigentlich all diese Leute?* The answer is a monosyllable. These people were slaves. In postwar accounts and in certain contemporary documents Krupp resorted to elaborate euphemisms to avoid that word. Men who had once borne arms under other flags were *Kriegsgefangene* (POWs), even though they were now chained to milling machines. Workers from abroad became simply *Fremdarbeiter*, foreign workers — a bland, impersonal denomination unsuggestive of coercion. This detachment is even reflected in concentration camp documents. Paragraph 14 of the Krupp-Auschwitz agreement, for example, noted impersonally that the SS had contracted *"aus den Insassen des KZ die benötigten Arbeitskräfte zu stellen"* (to supply the necessary labor from among the concentration camp inmates).[3]

*"Hier wohnt Stille des Herzens,"* newly arrived foreign workers were told by recruiters describing Essen — "Here dwells the heart's repose." It was a cruel hoax, yet at the outset it wasn't deliberate. During the early months of the conflict there were no instances of Krupp sadism; the firm's paternalistic policy was still inviolate. A witness described Fritz von Bülow in this period as "a very obliging, charming man; a man of moderation; a conciliatory person."[4] *Fremdarbeiter* were still a curiosity. There was no reason to abuse them, and since there was enough of everything to go around, the first arrivals were treated with an apologetic hospitality — the war had made this dislocation necessary, they were told, but Krupp would see that it was as painless as possible.

One of them was a forty-eight-year-old Czech, a civil engineer who had been a fighter pilot in World War I and who later appeared before the Nuremberg tribunal. On June 3, 1939, eleven weeks after the Nazis had seized Prague, Constantin Sossin-Arbatoff was among 150 men who were ordered to appear at the central train station by 4 P.M. the following afternoon. They went expecting the worst. Instead two Krupp functionaries greeted them warmly, led them to five new sleeping cars, and "gave every one of us a large parcel of sandwiches with white bread, sausages, and various other food articles." Next morning at nine o'clock the train reached the Ruhr, where "several representatives of Krupp at Essen welcomed us and helped us with our luggage." Checks were issued for the baggage, which was transported separately while the newcomers were invited to board buses.[5]

According to Sossin-Arbatoff, "Those buses, too, were entirely new and nice, and we were very much surprised at this treatment." After a two-hour tour of the city they disembarked at the Koppenhöhe, a Krupp club, where waiters served them a three-course meal, cigarettes, all the beer they could drink, and postcards for writing home. At the end of the afternoon they were billeted in a large building on Bottreperstrasse. There were bathrooms, there was fresh linen — there were even German maids. Two days later the Czechs went to work in Apparatenbau I (Appliance Construction Shop I). Sossin-Arbatoff was designated a locksmith and paid 94 pfennigs an hour. It wasn't like life in Prague, but it wasn't like slavery, either.[6]

Foreign workers continued to be a rarity for nearly two and a half years, and as late as January 1942 the Gusstahlfabrik rolls showed relatively few Russians and Poles among the foreign conscripts. By that summer, however, nearly 7,000 more Slavs had been logged in, and Krupp had requisitioned almost 9,000 more. Their race was portentous. For a decade the Führer had preached that the peoples living to the east were subhuman. Now signs posted outside Krupp shops proclaimed SLAWEN SIND SKLAVEN (Slavs are slaves). The ugly word was out in the open, and with it came a new jargon. Increasingly, intrafirm memoranda alluded to *Sklavenarbeiter* (slave labor), *Sklavengeschäft* (the slave trade), *Sklaverei* (slavery), *Sklavenmarkt* (the slave market) and *Sklavenhalter* (the slaveholder — Alfried). Once Adolf Eichmann's trains began rolling the patois expanded. Assembly lines, Alfried's subordinates were informed, would be augmented by *Judenmaterial* (Jewish livestock). In German the verb to eat is *essen*. The feeding of farm creatures is *fressen*, and that was the word used for slaves; often as they jumped from their boxcars in the terminal the first words they heard were *"Keine Arbeit, kein Fressen"* (No work, no feeding).

The first recorded instance of physical brutality occurred there at the Hauptbahnhof. The victims, significantly, were from the east. According to Adam Schmidt, a railroad worker, "In the middle of 1941 the first workers arrived from Poland, Galicia, and the Polish Ukraine. They came crammed in freight cars. The Krupp foremen rushed the workers out of the train, and beat them and kicked them. . . . I watched with my own eyes while people who could barely walk were dragged to work" (*Mit eigenen Augen konnte ich sehen, dass auch Kranke, die kaum gehen konnten, zur Arbeit herangezogen wurden*).[7]

No three-course meals now, no immaculate linen, no fresh-faced Aryan maids. In the beginning the change was directly attributable to the ideological distinctions. Every ethnic, racial, and national group had its place in the Nazi scheme of things. After new arrivals had been issued wooden clogs, Krupp blankets stamped with the three interlocking wheels, and the firm's prison uniforms — blue with a broad yellow stripe — the Oberlagerführung (Foreign Workers' Camp Administration) turned them over to the Werkschutz (plant security police), the factory guard (Werkschar), or the auxiliary plant security police (Erweiterter Werkschutz). There segregation began. Jews, at the bottom of the totem, wore yellow cloth tags, and whenever practical heads of Jewish girls were shaved to form grotesque designs. That wasn't always possible, because it conflicted with another *Rassenhass* (race hatred) principle: the touching of Hebrew heads by Krupp barbers was regarded as an imposition upon German racial comrades (*Volksgenossen*) and therefore prohibited. Thus the ruling: no foreign barbers, no eccentric haircuts.

Russian slaves wore white initials SR for Sowjetrussland (Soviet Russia) on their backs. Poles were painted with a big P. Other eastern workers wore a blue rectangle reading OST sewn on the right side of their breasts, and prisoners from elsewhere received white, blue, red, or green-on-white brassards.* Names were forbidden; individuals were known by their numbers, which were stitched in white on their garb. Dehumanization was complete. Here the dynasty's century-old insistence that each worker in the shops was a member of the family had collided head-on with National Socialist dogma. Dogma had won, partly because it, too, was rooted in the legacy of Alfred the Great. In the words of one observer, there was in Essen

> *Etwas, was sich mit den Nazi Ideen zusammenschloss und das Dritte Reich mit dessen Lebenskraft erzeugte . . . Die Tradition des Krupp-Konzerns und die "sozialpolitische Anschauung," die er vertrat, passten genau zum moralischen Klima des Dritten Reiches.*

Something which fused with Nazi ideas to produce the Third Reich and its vitality . . . The tradition of the Krupp firm, and its "sociopolitical attitude," exactly suited the moral climate of the Third Reich.

The breakdown of the labor draftees into ethnic subgroups pleased the party ideologues, but it was too tortuous for outsiders; they couldn't grasp its subtleties, and in practice eventually some of the Krupp and SS guards at Alfried's 138 camps didn't even know whether they were standing watch over Jews, Ukrainians, and Poles swept up by labor conscription, or French, Dutch, and Belgian workmen who had come to the Ruhr as *Freiwillige* (volunteers) and were now trapped behind barbwire under compulsory extension of their contracts. To the artisans of Essen all armbands looked pretty much alike. Once the initial curiosity had faded, Kruppianer, like the foremen charged with the supervision of the slaves, simply lost interest. The important thing was to get on with the job. Any diversion was dismissed with a shrug, or — if it became a serious impediment — was kicked aside.

By 1943 the solicitous greeters who had welcomed Constantin Sossin-

---

* There were variations on this. Prisoners directly under the SS, for example, wore on their sleeves an O (for *Ostarbeiter*, eastern worker) until the summer of 1944, when Himmler, for some strange reason, decreed that it should be replaced by a patch resembling a sunflower.

Arbatoff four years earlier had abandoned all thoughts of separate but equal treatment. Sheer numbers had defeated them. As the endless trains of steaming, rust-red boxcars puffed into the Hauptbahnhof, the Oberlagerführung was overwhelmed by a vast human frieze. There were so many strangers. Their command of German was so atrocious. And all of them seemed to emit a foul, indescribably offensive odor. In captivity their skins had acquired a peculiar pearly gray color, their livid faces were strained, they stood around dumbly with lowered heads, like beasts of burden waiting to be driven. *Und so:* they would be driven. The exasperation of their hosts was replaced by fury, and the order came down from the Hauptverwaltungsgebäude: "*Fahrt mal dazwischen!*" (Get them moving!). Fists were used, then boots, and finally blackjacks and whips of Kruppstahl. The uniformed escorts suffered a perennial shortage of cudgels, as one memorable exchange attests:

*Martinwerke,* 7
21 IX 1944

Fried. Krupp, Essen

To: Herr von Bülow

We still urgently need ten leather truncheons or similar weapons for clubbing for our shock guards [*Lederknüppel, oder ähnliche Waffen, die unsere Stossmannschaften zum Verprügeln gebrauchen könnten*]. As we have learned that you still have such items in stock, we beg you to give this messenger the requested ten pieces.

LINDER

For discussion with H. Wilshaus:

Do we still have any weapons of the blackjack type [*Waffen ähnlich wie Knüppel*]?

VON BÜLOW

25 September

To: Herr von Bülow

I can supply the ten leather truncheons, or steel birches [*Lederknüppel oder Stahlstäbe*].

WILSHAUS[8]

At some point — it varied from individual to individual — most Germans stopped thinking of the alien slaves as human beings. Krupp's postwar historian writes that "The sullen features (*trostlosen Züge*) of the foreign workers from east and west continued to be conspicuous," but to the average Essen native the imported workers appear to have been not merely inconspicuous but quite faceless. Kruppianer slang reflected the change in the front office. The popular wartime term for the new-comers was *Stücke* — stock, cattle. Marching down Helenenstrasse on a bitter autumn morning while a truncheon-swinging guard counted out his cadence of *"Links! Rechts!"* — "Left! Right!" — one highly educated Czech woman saw a group of German housewives standing near the steel mill where she worked as a drudge. The guard was preoccupied with his other wards, so the Czech slave briefly greeted the bystanders in their own language. "They were amazed," she later recalled. "It was as though a dog had spoken aloud. They had thought of me as an animal, something out of the woods."[9]

&#x2720;   &#x2720;   &#x2720;

The Reich's manpower problem grew as the Reich grew. With the widening war it became critical, and troubled reports from the Ruhr began to accumulate on Albert Speer's desk. Hands were needed, *any* hands. They needn't be skilled, they needn't even be willing; it was necessary only that they be present and pliable. There was one obvious solution: drafting German women. Ludendorff had conscripted them in 1916, and Speer urged Hitler to follow his example. The Führer's veto was flat — "The sacrifice of our most cherished ideals is too great a price." Thus the origins of the Third Reich's slave labor program lay in what might be called the soft underbelly of National Socialism, the maudlin "idealism" which doted on middle-class sentimentality. When military drafts left a vacuum in Allied shops, femininity filled it. But German women belonged in the home; the New Order was fighting to keep them there. Over three million U.S. mothers and daughters, a third of them in their teens, were working in war industries, and English munitions factories had hired 2,250,000 girls. German shops, meanwhile had employed only 182,000 — roughly the number of female cooks and maids in the country. Even those who came willingly were resented; a Krupp file note of April 22, 1943, discloses that the SS viewed "with great distrust" women from the Ruhr who were training Jewish prisoners in mass fuse production at Auschwitz.*[10]

So the Fatherland turned to the only alternative, foreigners. Until Speer turned over his labor responsibilities to Fritz Sauckel, manhunts had been sporadic and uncoordinated. The new manpower czar cooperated zealously with willing manufacturers. Dealing with Essen required infinite patience, he found, for *die Firma* was his most persistent customer. Afterward most family friends stopped trying to offer rational explanations of why this

---

* In the end Speer won a paper victory. On July 25, 1944, the Führer decreed that all German women from the ages of seventeen to fifty must register for work. By then it was too late. The millions of slaves were already in the Reich, and Allied bombing disrupted the canvassing of eligible German females. In Berlin, Goebbels noted sardonically, only 200 of 5,000 called up actually reported for work. (ED 83/1 Institut für Zeitgeschichte [Munich]).

should have been so, although former Brigadeführer (Brigadier General) Walther Schieber, who worked closely with Alfried (and who conceded at Nuremberg that Krupp "did negotiate directly with the SS for concentration camp inmates"), offered an apologia for sending the prisoners into arms plants. It was "humane," he argued; even though a slave who worked "never really escaped the barbwire, nevertheless, according to my personal feeling, spiritually at least this man had a better opinion of himself, and more self-respect." The Konzern had saved prisoners' morale, the ex-Brigadeführer explained. It had taken their minds off their troubles by providing jobs.[11]

Unlike the witness, Krupp never tried to justify his conduct to the western democracies. Erich Müller declared that Alfried "did not have any particular misgivings about the employment of concentration camp inmates in the plants,"[12] and addressing the tribunal himself, Alfried spoke as though the prosecution had actually accused him of mistreating Kruppianer:

> *Wir bemühten und plagten uns unter Umständen, die im Rückblick schwer zu verstehen und zu beurteilen sind. Den Vorwurf der Gleichgültigkeit unseren Arbeitern gegenüber verdienen wir nicht.*

> We worried and toiled under conditions which are very difficult to understand and judge in retrospect. Indifferences toward the fate of our workers is a charge which we do not deserve.[13]

His attorneys, more wary of the bench, offered the curious argument that Krupp had faced the prospect of accepting slaves or losing his own head — that if Alfried had failed to produce enough weapons, the Führer would have sent him to the gas chamber. In rebuttal Karl Otto Saur, whose Essen reputation had tumbled since that glorious sun-drenched day when he had joined Hitler in awarding Krupp the golden banner, testified that "In the last three years I have not been able to find a single case, nor have I heard of a single one, in which someone was sent to a concentration camp because he failed to fulfill his production quota" (*seine Produktionsquote nicht erfüllte*).[14]

Krupp's lawyers insisted that he had played no role in the impressment of foreign civilians. All the great roundups, they vowed, had been official acts of the German government. In theory this was true. In practice, however, initiative usually lay in the hands of the Ruhr barons, and after Wehrmacht kidnappings of foreign women and children, industrialists were invited to take their share. Many refused. There is no record that Krupp ever did, and the slave labor drafts, through which countless thousands disappeared from their homes into the wartime Ruhr, were customarily masterminded by Krupp executives.

Alfried's files are full of this. Early in the third year of the war reports reached the Hauptverwaltungsgebäude that *Fremdarbeiter* were reaching the shops as late as two and sometimes even three months after they had been requisitioned. Immediately three executives were dispatched to lodge formal protests with the Wehrmacht, the Gestapo, and the SS. These conferences concluded, Alfried appointed Heinrich Lehmann liaison man with the DAF (German Labor Front) and director of the firm's new Arbeitseinsatz A (labor procurement and recruiting). In subsequent campaigns Lehmann swept through five occupied countries. If he didn't find able-bodied *Stücke* in one capital, he set off for another — always with the cooperation of the occupying authorities. From France he drafted entire factories of workmen, from Holland he dispatched 30,000 ironworkers and shipwrights to the Germaniawerft, and when *Freiwillige* showed signs of reluctance they were sent into Germany wearing manacles. As a consequence the Konzern became known everywhere in the Netherlands as *Pest Firma* (a plague firm).

A generation inured to excesses may not appreciate the extent to which this represented a break with precedent. It was nothing less than a counterrevolution. Slavery had begun to disappear from Europe in the tenth century and had vanished altogether with the last vestiges of feudalism. France hadn't seen a serf since the French Revolution; Germany, since 1781. Even the czars had abolished serfdom in 1861. Since then civilized nations had methodically persuaded backward lands to rid themselves of slaves. Brazil's capitulation in 1888 had freed the last country in the Western Hemisphere; the Berlin Conference of 1885 and the Brussels Act of 1890 had brought most of Africa and Asia in line. Yet so odious was the concept of servitude that educated men could not rest until it was gone entirely, and in the aftermath of World War I five international meetings had toiled toward this end. Two of them, the Slavery Convention of 1926 and the Forced Labor Convention of 1930, had been judged historic achievements. Both had been sponsored by the League of Nations, and the second, defining forced labor as "work or service (other than penal labor) exacted under menace of a penalty," had declared that "any form of compulsory labor for private enterprise is prohibited."[15]

Nevertheless, here was Alfried — the alumnus of three German universities — ordering chattels in thousand-head lots one hundred and sixty-one years after Joseph II had emancipated the last Hapsburg bondsman. To be sure, Krupp's Frenchmen, Dutchmen, and Belgians were still being signed up as "volunteers," but that was only a gesture toward their racial status. The very word *Freiwillige* had its origins in the conquerors' curious glossary of euphemisms, or *Sprachregelungen* (language rules), other memorable examples of which included *Aussiedlung* (evacuation), *Arbeitseinsatz im Osten* (labor in the east), *Sonderbehandlung* (special treatment), *Umsiedlung* (resettlement), and, most memorably, *Endlösung* (final solution).[16]

Krupp preferred his records to read as though workmen from the western democracies had come to the Ruhrgebiet of their own free will. In the east, of course, there was no need for such evasions. *Slawen waren Sklaven,* and the name of any nonconforming Kruppianer who suggested otherwise went on the hot line between Altendorferstrasse and local Gestapo headquarters on Kortestrasse. Krupp treated deliveries of human meat from the Soviet Union as inanimate raw material, sometimes approving of its quality, sometimes objecting. A file note written in the summer of 1942 observed waspishly, "I am under the impression that the better Russian workers are at this time being chosen for works in central and eastern Germany. We really get the rejects only. Just now 600 Russians, consisting of 450 women and 150 juveniles . . . arrived."[17]

In Berlin any cavil from the Hauptverwaltungsgebäude drew instant attention. On July 8 an anxious subordinate submitted a lengthy report to Albert Speer denying that Alfried was getting a poor grade of Slavs. During May and June *Slawen* had been delivered to Essen. The functionary insisted that "The requirements of the firm Fried. Krupp A.G. for replacement for German workers drafted into the armed forces have been met currently and in time," and continued heatedly, "The complaints of the firm Krupp about allegedly insufficient labor allocations are unfounded. . . . I have once again asked Sauckel to send Krupp 3,000 to 4,000 more workers in entire convoys from the Russian civilian workers presently arriving in Service Command VI."[18] Here, surely, was a historic commitment. The diplomats from forty nations who signed the convention of 1930 had thought they were stamping out isolated examples of exploitation in remote jungles. They never dreamed that within twelve years Europe's mightiest tycoon would be bargaining for "entire convoys" of bondsmen.

✠　　✠　　✠

There was trouble over the Jews. They had always been troublesome, of course, but this difficulty was unprecedented. As early as October 18, 1940, General Franz Halder had mused in his diary that Polish Jews could be "cheap slaves." However, powerful SS figures were vehemently opposed to the enslavement of *Judenmaterial.* In their view the issue was clearly one of principle: National Socialism was committed to the elimination of every living *Jude* and *Jüdin,* and on July 31, 1941, Göring had written Reinhard Heydrich, "I hereby charge you with making all necessary preparations . . . for bringing about a complete solution (*Gesamtlösung*) of the Jewish question in the German sphere of influence in Europe . . . I request . . . the desired final solution (*Endlösung*) of the Jewish question."[19]

In obedience to the Reichsmarschall's command, beltlines of extermination were set in motion. To the dismay of German industrialists in those first months, however, the blackshirts took all orders literally. To them *Endlösung* meant what it said. The solution had to be irrevocable. But there was nothing final about slave labor. It was an expediency; it solved nothing. If Jewish livestock were being fed, quartered, and led to machines, they had not, obviously, been murdered, and despite the most rigid precautions there was always the possibility that crafty couples might contrive to breed, defeating the Führer's goal and leaving the problem to another generation of Germans.

Until the labor crisis of 1942 these SS purists had their way. Then the SS began to have second thoughts. *Endlösung* was working, but the cost in ammunition was shocking. In the spring of 1942 Himmler ordered a German physician named Beckar to experiment with gas vans. These mobile units were in turn abandoned (because of limited capacity and high fuel consumption) for *Vernichtungslager* (extermination camps), of which the most celebrated soon became Oświęcim, a former Austrian cavalry barracks in the marshes of southern Poland which would later be immortalized in its German rendition, Auschwitz. Meanwhile the realists and the idealists continued their tug-of-war. Essen's position was clear. A Hauptverwaltungsgebäude memorandum of April 25, 1942, noted that to "turn out 80 s.i.g." (*Schwere Infanterie Geschütze* — heavy infantry guns) "new expansion" was necessary; accordingly Alfried recommended manufacture by *die Firma* "in the concentration camp in the Sudetengau (Sudetenland)."[20]

No one knows who coined the ingenious phrase "extermination through work," but four weeks later Krupp put it to the Führer. Ignoring the language rules, he said that every party member favored liquidation (*Beseitigung*) of "Jews, foreign saboteurs, anti-Nazi Germans, gypsies, criminals, and antisocial elements" (*Verbrecher und Asoziale*), but that he could see no reason why they shouldn't contribute something to the Fatherland before they went. Properly driven, each could contribute a lifetime of work in the months before he was dispatched. Hitler hesitated. Himmler continued to be mulish, though not out of loyalty to *Endlösung*. Himself an empire builder, he had begun employing prisoners in business ventures of his own. The trick was to persuade him that cooperation with the Schlotbarone would be wiser. The answer, it turned out, was a simple matter of economics, or, if you like, of bribery; Krupp proposed to pay the SS four marks per diem per inmate, from which seven-tenths of a mark would be deducted for feeding. In addition, "The SS would receive a commission on the sale of arms, to compensate for not having the use of its own prisoners" (*um sie für den Verzicht auf die Verwendung ihrer eigenen Gefangenen zu entschädigen*).[21]

Opposition vanished overnight. In September, Hitler authorized the new policy and ordered a KZ canvass to determine how many prisoners were fit. The answer was 25 percent, of which 40 percent were suitable for munitions plants. Alfried had anticipated the directive; on September 18 a teletype to Sauckel's Berlin office at Mohrenstrasse 65 began, "Subject: Employment of Jews. Instead of making a report to the individual labor committees, we request you to note that the Krupp firm is prepared to employ 1,050–1,100 Jewish workers." The application went on to list turners, mechanics, milling machine operators, drill press operators, lathe operators, grinders, and planers, and ended with the caveat, "It is desirable that the people be examined with regard to their abilities before they are assigned."[22]

Krupp had an immediate objective: *Zünderanfertigung,* fuse manufacture. The Sudetenland camp was too small for mass production, so he had taken dead aim on Auschwitz, and as the range of skills available there became evident, he added gun parts to his plans. Six weeks later his directors assembled in the Hauptverwaltungsgebäude board room. The agenda was confined to a single item — *"Einrichtung einer Fertigungsstelle für Teile von automatische Waffen in Auschwitz"* (construction of a manufacturing plant for automatic weapons parts in Auschwitz). Assured that "The Auschwitz concentration camp will supply the necessary labor," the executives authorized two million marks for the project, whose plans were then inscribed "Approved [*genehmigt*] by the Direktorium on October 31, 1942."[23]

That was in the Krupp tradition — brisk, specific, and to the point. Unhappily, the Third Reich was infested with intriguers whose motives weren't as lofty as those of the *Endlösung* crusaders, and other concerns were plotting to get the same craftsmen. Despite repeated assurances of SS cooperation, the winter passed uneventfully. In late March, Alfried sent an emissary into southern Poland with instructions to find out what was wrong. To the Kruppianer's amazement, an officer at the camp expressed the opinion that "German employees ought to be used for this production if at all possible." On April 5 Alfried recorded his own view:

> The main purpose of the move to Auschwitz was to make use of the people available there [*der Hauptzweck der Verlagerung nach Auschwitz sei, die dort vorhandenen Leute einzusetzen*]. . . . The whole reason why it was decided to make the best of the unusual difficulties presented by Auschwitz — i.e., the free availability of labor — would no longer apply, since, at the very least, the best labor [*die besten Arbeitskräfte*] would no longer be there.[24]

The pick of the crop *was* still there, and Alfried knew it. After a full century of dealing with spiked helmets and coal-scuttle helmets there was little *die Firma* didn't know about intramural scheming; the stratagem was to find the right man and use him. His name, which had already been acquired through a diligent search of party records, turned out to be Obersturmführer Sommer, a junior SS officer stationed in Berlin and assigned to Special Committee M3 of the Speer ministry. Contacted by a Krupp agent several months before, Sommer had agreed to keep a record of all the skilled Jews picked up in the capital and shipped to the east. On March 16 he had turned the list over to his contact. With it, Krupp could forward a list of 500 prized prisoners and demand immediate action. He got it; Rudolf Franz Höss, the forty-three-year-old convicted murderer who now reigned over Auschwitz as *Kommandant des KZL* (*Konzentrationslager*, concentration camp) capitulated. Later, at Nuremberg, Höss declared that he had supervised the destruction of three million people. "*Der Rest wurde ausgesucht und für Sklavenarbeit in den Industrien der KZL verwendet*," he added — "The rest were selected and used for slave labor in the concentration camp industrial plants."[25]

That selection began on April 22, 1943. Studying his camp map, Höss assigned Krupp area number 6. Squads of Kruppianer immediately moved in; working around the clock, by May 28 they had constructed a rail junction, a huge double shed, and a washroom annex. A second shed was rising alongside, and barracks had been leased from the SS. These and subsequent structures were found after the war on the Kommandant's meticulous map. Krupp's accounting of the fiscal arrangements began in June, when the first Jewish captives were shepherded inside the finished shed to begin work. The entry for one month reads,

> *Laut Forderungsnachweis 1/43. 2/43 vom 3. Juli 1943 hat die Firma Krupp für die Zeit vom 3. Juli–3. August 1943 der SS RM 28.973, — für die Arbeit der Gefangenen überwiesen. Der Tagessatz für den Arbeiter war RM 4, —, für Hilfsarbeiter RM 3, —.*

> According to confirmation of orders 1/43 and 2/43 of July 3, 1943, the firm of Krupp paid the SS the sum of RM 28, 973 — for work done by the prisoners during the period July 3–August 3, 1943. The daily rate for a workman was 4 marks, and for an auxiliary workman 3 marks.[26]

Neither Höss nor Krupp recorded the conditions under which the *Stücke* toiled. However, two Kruppianer did. Erich Lutat, a specialized craftsman with an inquiring mind, was one of twenty-five Germans who traveled from Essen to Auschwitz in June and remained, training prisoners, for five months. Since most of his wards had learned to speak some German, he began asking questions, and to the edification of the Nuremberg tribunal five years later, Lutat rapidly acquired a thorough understanding of life within the camp. He watched the smoke rolling from the crematorium chimneys; he learned to recognize the smell of burning human flesh; he saw that the people he was instructing lacked adequate food, clothing, or shelter. Despite ironclad orders to the contrary, both Lutat and Paul Ortmann, a

Bertha and Gustav with their children.

ABOVE: In 1931, the Krupps' silver wedding anniversary. From left, Berthold, Irmgard, Alfried, Harald, Waldtraut, Eckbert, and Claus. BELOW: In 1940. From left, standing, Berthold, Claus, Harald; seated, Waldtraut, Eckbert, Alfried, and Irmgard.

LEFT: Alfried congratulates Hitler on his fiftieth birthday, April 20, 1939. RIGHT: With Gustav they admire the family's birthday present to the Führer.

25

A gathering of friends at Hügelschloss in 1942. Left, Hitler and Mussolini.
Right, Gustav and Alfried. Center, Goebbels and the Nazi hierarchy.

28

Three views of the Hauptverwaltungsgebäude (administration bu[ild]ing) of the Krupp works. ABOVE: Modern views; at right, from the [?] At left, note the bay window in Gustav's office. BELOW: Surroun[ded] by rubble after the RAF's fifty-fifth and last raid on Essen.

29

30

ABOVE: Essen's prewar synagogue, now a showplace for Krupp products. BELOW: The symbolic coffin outside the synagogue commemorating the twenty-five hundred Essen Jews who perished in the 1933-1945 catastrophe.

**33**

Tunnel in Essen where Krupp slaves hid during air raids. Note the bomb scars.

Father Come on his return
elgium from *die Firma* slavery.

**34**

Elizabeth Roth outside Villa
Hügel after the war.

**35**

Alfried Krupp's wartime headquarters at
141 Boulevard Haussmann, Paris.

Memorial to the sixty-one Krupp slaves who died in the
company's Dechenschule concentration camp in the
massive bombing of October 23-24, 1944.

fellow technician, shared their bread, potatoes, and cigarettes with trainees. Ortmann was appalled by the frequency with which guards whipped inmates, and Lutat once intervened when an SS man, with no apparent provocation, forced a Jewish craftsman to hop around the factory on his knees. Lutat testified: "The prisoners were escorted to the factory by the SS at 6 A.M., later on at 7 A.M. Here, they remained under the supervision of the factory guards . . . The workmen were Poles, Dutchmen, Czechs, Frenchmen, and a great many Jews. . . . Many of the prisoners were in pitiful physical condition" (*Viele Gefangene waren in bemitleidenswerter physischer Verfassung*).[27]

Ortmann and Lutat never suspected then that they were witnessing an early (and comparatively mild) rehearsal of a spectacle which would reach its climax in the streets and fields of the Ruhrgebiet itself, but they were present when the Krupp curtain fell at Auschwitz. Alfried had hard luck there. He had hoped to reach peak production in the camp by October; that would be a pleasant surprise for the Führer and the dignitaries who would gather in Hügel's great hall to see him take the orb and mace of authority from his father the following month. His hopes were dashed. As the Russian offensive gained momentum in the Ukraine, factory after factory was abandoned. Bitterly disappointed, he and his Essen specialists transferred the equipment to two Silesian camps — Wüstegiersdorf and the great Berthawerk sheds rising at Markstädt.[28]

Auschwitz is a familiar name, but it was only one of many camps. Until the collapse in 1945, Krupp employed forced labor in nearly a hundred factories sprawled across Germany, Poland, Austria, France, and Czechoslovakia. The figure is inexact, because all Konzern papers mentioning foreign workers, prisoners of war, or concentration camp inmates were stamped *Geheim* (secret) by Alfried's Oberlagerführung, and bales of them were later burned.[29] Similarly, there is no way of determining exactly how many concentration camps were built by Krupp and the SS, or the number of *Stücke* penned in them. An educated guess exists, however. Hans Schade, a research analyst retained by the Americans at Nuremberg, studied all surviving documents carefully, and his estimates are by far the best available.

With the extension of the war and the growth of Alfried's power, Schade's graphs reveal, there was a remarkable acceleration in Krupp's slave population. As late as August 1943 the drafts were relatively small. The flow from France was only a trickle, and virtually all the Dutch were then going to Kiel; the eighty-one factories of the Gusstahlfabrik complex in Essen had enrolled just 11,557 foreign civilians, 2,412 POWs — and no KZ inmates. Prior to his coronation the new Krupp was already a power in the Reich, of course. As vice chairman of RVE he had attended a meeting of the Führer's Central Planning Board on July 22, 1942, when he joined Speer, Sauckel, General Erhard Milch, and Paul Körner, chairman of the

Hermann Göring Werke, in deciding to impress 45,000 unskilled Russians for work in German steel mills and another 126,000, including several thousand POWs, for mine labor. But Alfried was unable to bring the full force of his personality to bear upon his fellow Nazi *Bonzen* until the end of that year, when he became sole proprietor. Then he was in a position to negotiate directly with the government, leasing slaves at four marks a head and even insisting upon the firm's right to return damaged goods:

> *Es gilt jedenfalls als vereinbart, dass für die Fabrikation gänzlich un- geeignete Leute ausgetauscht werden können.*

> However, it has been agreed that people who are totally unsuitable can be exchanged.[30]

Since KZ labor often reached Essen badly shopworn, that stipulation represented a defeat for Heinrich Himmler, Reichsführer of the SS, chief of the home front, and commander of all Wehrmacht troops stationed within the Reich's prewar frontiers. But Alfried Krupp could deal from strength, too. As an honored friend and early supporter of Adolf Hitler, as sole proprietor of Fried. Krupp, as one of the RVE's "three wise men," as a member of the Wirtschaftsgruppe Eisenschaffende Industrie, and as Reich Wehrwirtschaftsführer, the Konzernherr was permitted to draw almost endlessly upon the rapidly accumulating pool of alien conscripts. Schade's figures prove that he did; an undated document picked up by an American soldier in Essen after the collapse revealed that on the day it was filed, the Gusstahlfabrik alone was using approximately 75,000 slaves. During the first months of Alfried's ascension to supreme power within the firm the rolls fluctuated wildly — Schlotbarone were like women in a bargain basement, grabbing stock from one another — but by the end of that summer they had stabilized, and on September 30, 1944, when he was the employer of 277,966 workmen and office staff (*Arbeiter und Ange- stellte*), he also ruled a slave empire whose population was roughly that of Knoxville today. In the grave words he was to hear when he stood indicted at Nuremberg, he was personally responsible for "about 100,000 persons exploited as slaves by Krupp in Germany, in countries alien to them, and in concentration camps."[31]

By then, as Eugene Davidson has perceptively noted, many Germans "talked as though they had been awakened from a fantastic dream in which they had somehow played a part." After the collapse of their armed forces "they found themselves in a prosaic non-Nazi world where murders of innocent people had to be accounted for, and they stared at the pictures of atrocities in disbelief and horror. They confessed and squirmed and alternately blamed themselves and even more readily the men and creeds they had served." It must be remembered, however, that that mood emerged only when the Reich had been defeated in the field. As long as Hitler remained in power, there was no contrition. The problems of the *Sklavengeschäft* were handled with determination and efficiency, and, occasionally, with gamy wit. In the fifth summer of the war the barrels of *Einsatzgruppen* machine pistols were still hot. Livestock was often retrieved in last-minute rescues, and Alfried's report for July 1944 observed laconically that the conscription of five hundred Jews "was negotiated at the shooting range" (*auf den Schiesständen*).[32]

His chief viceroy in this bizarre domain was Fritz von Bülow, then in his mid-fifties. Short, pink, and slightly popeyed, Bülow would have preferred reclining in his handsome Bredeney library beneath his family's twelfth-century coat of arms, wearing his favorite houndstooth sports jacket and reading sophisticated French fiction. He was cultivated and sensitive — and that was precisely his problem. On paper he was qualified to play the iron man. Berlin had appointed him both military and political *Hauptabwehrbeauftragter* (chief counterintelligence agent in private industry); he had been awarded the *Kriegsverdienstkreuz* second class; he was director of the plant police. But all these honors had been showered upon him because he had been confidential aide to Gustav Krupp, who in turn had chosen him because of his father's services to the dynasty. Actually Krupp's chief slavedriver was feckless; he was incapable of coping with the terrifying rage now mounting in the embattled nation. In crises he would either turn his head while less squeamish subordinates wrought horror, or overcompensate and try to outdo them himself.

Bülow was the one weak link in Alfried's chain of command. Elsewhere the system functioned smoothly. Krupp's manpower administration was in many ways a duplicate of the Führer's. Under Hitler, Sauckel brought forced labor into the Reich and Speer doled it out. Under Alfried, Lehmann's Arbeitseinsatz A traveled abroad recruiting foreigners while the men of Arbeitseinsatz I distributed incoming *Stücke* through the Oberlagerführung to the owner's factories. The camps varied enormously in appearance, population, and size — from Fünfteichen's five thousand Jews to Saal Saes and Saal Fiedler in the Essen suburbs of Dellwig and Borbeck, each with sixty Poles and Frenchmen, neither larger than a vacant lot. Seen from Alfried's office in the Hauptverwaltungsgebäude, the complex jigsaw seemed sensible and effective. It appeared to meet the great test; it worked. In the words of one observer, "The efforts of Krupp in the slave market bore rapid and abundant fruit" (*schnelle und reiche Früchte*).[33]

✠　　✠　　✠

In the gathering Wagnerian murk of Hitler's aging New Order the name Krupp looked mightier than ever. The dynasty couldn't bear close inspection, however. After dominating European industry for four generations, it had begun to fester; to adopt a nineteenth-century Austrian mot, the Konzern had become less an autocracy than a state of emergency. The slaves proved it; they had become the most conspicuous symptom of the disease which had infected all Germany. No country, no business, no individual could descend to such a level and still flourish. Effective as forced labor may have appeared — and opinions about that vary — it was doomed in the end, for the keepers became the kept, caged by their growing uneasiness, suspicion, and, in some cases, feelings of guilt. Their anxieties sapped their vitality. Meanwhile the slaves became less and less useful as the conditions of their enslavement vitiated *them*.

Some had been worthless from the outset. The *Menschenjagden* had been unbelievably indiscriminate; Sauckel and Lehmann dragnets had swept up the halt, the lame, and, in some cases, the blind. By the autumn of 1943, when Alfried suspended his Auschwitz operations, Essen was jammed with bewildered mobs of ragged, emaciated Ausländer from four continents — Poles, French, Belgians, Danes, Dutch, Luxembourgers, Czechs, Hungarians, Slovaks, Russians, Ukrainians, Yugoslavians, Greeks, Italians trapped after the surrender of their government, Algerians, and even some Chinese. Young priests, farmers, and prisoners of war were suitable, of course, but mingled with them were senile men, pregnant women, and infants. Though babies were obviously inadequate, the minimum working age in shops and mines did drop appallingly from year to year. In the beginning it was seventeen. Then, according to a postwar affidavit from Max Ihn, "Youths were employed . . . from fourteen years on." The Nuremberg tribunal found that in 1943 twelve-year-old boys were being put to work not as apprentices but as laborers, and that "In 1944, children as young as six years of age were being assigned to work." The gaunt faces of these small slaves stare up at us from yellowing photographs on old work cards.[34]

That summer a spectator seated in a helicopter high above Alfried's Altendorferstrasse office and granted immunity from the clumps of 88-mm. *Flakgeschütze* that ringed the city would have looked down upon a remarkable panorama. Beneath him, beginning a few blocks from the Hauptverwaltungsgebäude and extending outward in a radius from two to five miles, he would see 55 Krupp–SS *Konzentrationslager*. Unlike those Germans who lived near extermination camps and later disclaimed any knowledge of them, Essen's natives were never far from their strange guests. The camps went where they would go: in bombed-out sheds, on school playgrounds, sandwiched into suburban neighborhoods.[35]

There was no uniformity of housing. Inmates lived in sturdy buildings, in heatless huts, under tents, or in ruins; and some slept on the ground, unprotected from the rain. Even so, it was impossible to mistake the camps' purpose. In one revealing fragment of Nuremberg testimony Fritz Führer, a former Krupp gatekeeper who had put on the blue Werkschutz uniform and risen to become commandant of a camp, argued that he had successfully avoided any appearance of restraint. The foreign workers lived in two stone schoolhouses, and that was all. Or almost all — "I can say," he confidently told the astonished tribunal, "that the Dechenschule camp did not give the impression that it was a prison, except that it was surrounded by barbed-wire fences, and that guards were at the gate, and there were armed guards patrolling the grounds."[36]

Boxing the compass from his perch high above the Hauptverwaltungsgebäude, the hypothetical observer would first behold the stockade of Seumannstrasse three miles to the north, where 3,000 Russians, western workers, and German criminals were penned behind concertinas of wire and towers equipped with searchlights and automatic weapons. The eye of the airborne watcher would move nearly 180 degrees across densely populated eastern Essen before lighting upon Schlageterschule (160 prisoners), directly across the Ruhr from Villa Hügel. Here, as in most of the other camps, machine guns were absent; the Werkschutz was equipped with obsolete Mannlicher rifles, relics of the Franco-Prussian War. Moving up the western arc of vision, the witness would see Kraemerplatz (2,000 Slavs and French), twenty blocks to the southwest of his roost overhead; Raumerstrasse (1,500 Russian prisoners of war); and, due west, Fritz Führer's Dechenschule, from which 300 eastern slaves had been moved the previous spring to make room for "westerners." In the last week of August a new arrival was beginning a secret diary which he would later fling before Alfried in Nuremberg's Palace of Justice:

> Le camp de Dechenschule, situé à la limite ouest de la ville d'Essen, vit des arrivages de prisonniers originaires de Belgique, dès le printemps 1944. . . . En fait le camp . . . était administré par la Werkschutz ou police privée de la firme Krupp.

> During the spring of 1944, prisoners from Belgium began arriving at the Dechenschule camp, located near the far western border of the city of Essen. . . . The official name of this camp was Sonderlager der Geheimstaatspolizei Dechenschule," i.e., a Gestapo camp. But that organization exercised its control only at the top administrative level. According to what the prisoners could find out, the camp was . . . administered by the Werkschutz, or private police force of the Krupp firm.[37]

West-northwest of the mythical helicopter lay three camps: Hafenstrasse III (1,000 Czechs), Nöggerathstrasse (1,100 French POWs), and Spenlestrasse (2,500 Russians). All three were repeatedly condemned by responsible Kruppianer in memoranda forwarded to the front office. Nöggerathstrasse was particularly loathsome to Dr. Wilhelm Jäger, Krupp's chief camp physician, whose repeated pleas for humane behavior toward the firm's conscripts verge upon the heroic. In a confidential memo dated

September 2, 1944, he wrote that the French there had been "for nearly half a year in dog kennels, public urinals, and old baking houses." The kennels were "three feet high, nine feet long, six feet wide." Five men slept in each of them, and the prisoners had to "crawl into these kennels on all fours." There was "no water in the camp."[38]

The thickest cluster of camps — over twenty — was northwest of the Hauptverwaltungsgebäude. There, among others, were Frintoperstrasse (1,000 Slavs), Rabenhorst (1,000 "easterners"), Bottroperstrasse (2,200 Italians and French). Again and again the pattern was repeated. Krupp doctors, fearing contamination, finally refused to enter the human stockyards. Jäger reported to Alfried that the situation in the camps was extremely grave, and there was apprehension that epidemics among slaves might spread to Germans. Contemporary documents do not reveal any reflection of this concern on Altendorferstrasse. A typical file note, dated July 6, 1944, covered a vast range of details (including 500 slaves personally "requested" by Alfried "from the office of District Attorney Joel, Hamm"), but mentioned no improvement in conditions within the stockades. One passage read, "Herr Pfister found the former camp for Italian military internees . . . to be suitable. Accommodation can be provided for 2,000 prisoners altogether by using triple-deck bunks instead of the double-deck bunks used heretofore. A guard tower of the simplest form should be erected at each of the four corners of the camp for security reasons. . . . To this end the barbed wire must be rearranged accordingly. Other changes are not necessary in the camp." The reason changes were unnecessary was that the firm had to look ahead, and housing German Kruppianer in such structures, as a financial report submitted the previous March 24 had noted, was unthinkable:

> The accommodation huts, since they are at present being used to house the Jews and concentration camp employees [Juden und KZ-Häftlinge], ought to be considered worthless for peacetime purposes [in Friedenszeiten wertlos], since it should be out of the question to put personnel in such huts in the long run.[39]

As a staunch National Socialist, Alfried never forsook his doctrinaire distinction between the treatment of "easterners" and "westerners." On paper, at least, men from France and the Low Countries had come to the Ruhr of their own free will, and Freiwillige, in the words of an order circulated to Krupp plants during Alfried's third month as sole proprietor, were to be "released from service, as before, on the expiration of their contract." "Eastern workers and Poles," by contrast, were "subject to indefinite service." An undated Werkschutz instruction stipulated that Russians "must be strictly segregated from the German population, the other foreign civilian workers, and all prisoners of war. They will be accommodated in closed camps, which they must leave only to go to work, *under escort* of the guard." (Italics in original.) It was in practice that the disparity vanished; once the volunteers decided to exercise their rights, they lost them. "The one-year contracts of a great number of our French, Belgian, and Dutch workers of the Gusstahlfabrik will expire within the next two months," a Krupp letter to the Essen employment office noted. "Since these people are not prepared to renew their contracts we intend to have them conscripted."[40]

The theory of dual treatment collapsed within a few weeks; eastern and western detention quickly became indistinguishable. All inmates were required to doff their caps when SS or Werkschutz officers appeared within their compounds. Those who defiantly destroyed headgear were subjected to the ultimate humiliation: their heads were shaved in crosses. When Hermann Brombach, a Krupp agent in the Netherlands, sent back word that "a steady increase" of Dutch workers were overstaying their leave "without justification," and Brussels and Paris reported the same problem, Bülow made plans in October 1943 for "the operation of a penal camp (*Strafanstalt*) of its own by the Krupp firm at the Gusstahlfabrik." Thenceforth all the excesses to which Slavs and Jews had been subjected became familiar to the European conscripts.[41]

Dechenschule was the first *Strafanstalt*. In a postwar affidavit Bülow explained that frequently he was obliged "to denounce foreign workers to the Gestapo . . . because of absenteeism," and that when Kriminalrat Peter Nohles, the local Gestapo leader, told him the prisons were overcrowded, Bülow conceived the notion of a separate camp from which workers would be "escorted to and from work by members of the Krupp plant police." At the time he put it differently. According to the shorthand notes of a Hauptverwaltungsgebäude conference in January 1944, Bülow took the floor to tell Alfried that "Foreigners must be treated with greater severity and strictness. For them, punishment away from work is especially desirable. Dechenschule will become a penal camp . . . under the supervision of the Gestapo . . . officers are invited to enumerate especially difficult and dirty tasks for which these foreigners may be used in groups of fifty to sixty."[42]

Nohles, the Gestapo chief, committed suicide in Nuremberg prison during Krupp's trial, but before taking his life he left an affidavit and seventy-one pages of testimony. The gist of his account is that his role at Dechenschule was largely that of a figurehead. Though few Germans willingly implicated themselves in war crimes, this contention is supported by the recollections of surviving prisoners, of Krupp guards, and of the firm's documents. To be sure, the Werkschutz described Dechenschule as "a labor discipline camp, supervised by the Gestapo and guarded by the plant police," but there was no evidence of such supervision. On the other hand, inmates were very much aware that the guards who beat them with four-edged leather truncheons wore the name KRUPP on their badges, caps, and armbands. Fritz Führer, the *Lagerführer*, was on Alfried's payroll, and Führer later testified that Bülow's specification of "difficult and dirty work" was carefully carried out at furnaces and slag piles. Gestapo files seized on Kortestrasse in 1945 noted the camp's address (Dechenstrasse 22) and telephone number (Essen 20597), but Nohles had been far too busy to dial it, let alone inspect the grounds.[43]

Doubtless he would have approved the security precautions. They could scarcely have been improved upon. Windows were equipped with thick iron bars, a double apron of barbwire encircled the compound, and guards were informed that "At the slightest sign of unruliness and disobedience, ruthless action has to be taken. Also, firearms must be used relentlessly to break resistance. Escaping internees are to be fired at immediately with firm intent to hit them." Prisoners worked twelve hours a day seven days a week, were allowed no holidays, and were, of course, paid nothing. Bülow was so proud of the stockade that on March 15, anticipating the arrest of "many more of these Belgians and Frenchmen," he urged that the firm "open another special camp in the Kapitän-Lehmann Strasse." It was never built. Indeed, Dechenschule itself was destroyed in enemy bombing; its prisoners had to be moved overnight to a hastily erected compound in Oberhausen.[44]

Bülow was distressed, but his pride really hadn't been justified. On paper the camp seemed to be an excellent solution to absenteeism. It wasn't. Fritz Führer, examining the records of his wards, was amazed to find that most of them couldn't possibly have been guilty of breach of contract, because they had never been inside Germany before. The Reich had committed a colossal error. A very high percentage of these men were civic leaders, professors, and clergymen who had been arrested as temporary hostages, shipped to the Ruhr, through some incomprehensible error, and sent to Dechenschule because bunks were available there. By any standard of intelligence or achievement they were the most distinguished foreigners in Essen. Yet here they were, singled out for punishment. Their present jail, carefully conceived, skillfully built, and patrolled rigorously, was admirable in every respect save one. It was being used to cage the wrong men.[45]

# 20

✳

# The Gods Themselves
# Struggle in Vain

**K**RUPP's attitude toward the firm's temporary employees was an inaccurate reflection of the official position in Berlin. General Adolf Westhoff of OKW stated that Alfried's treatment of Russian prisoners of war did not meet with the approval of the Wehrmacht, and among the prosecution exhibits at Nuremberg was the transcript of a telephone call from an OKW colonel in Berlin who protested on October 14, 1942, that "*Oberkommando der Wehrmacht* has lately received from their own offices and recently also in anonymous letters from the German population a considerable number of complaints about the treatment of POWs at the firm Krupp (especially that they are being beaten, and furthermore that they do not receive the food and time off that is due them. Among other things the POWs are said not to have received any potatoes for six weeks). All these things no longer occur anywhere else in Germany."[1]

The Nazi leadership took a more tolerant view of such abuses, yet Krupp was at odds even with the party. In his Führer Record of March 21–22, 1942, Albert Speer noted, "Point 20 — The Führer declared unequivocally and at great length that he did not agree that the Russians should be fed so poorly" and "Point 21 — The Führer is surprised that the civilian Russians are kept behind barbed wire fences like prisoners of war." Speer and Sauckel promised that these practices would be discontinued — both felt barbwire hurt worker morale — and the following month, on April 22, the order was reinforced by an SS decree which forbade such fencing in of civilian camps, adding "barbed wire already in use for this purpose must be removed unless no other wire can be procured." Krupp ignored both Führer and Reichsführer SS. An inspection in March 1943 revealed that the stakes around the Essen camps had been restrung and that the new wire was both thicker and more heavily barbed.[2]

Drexel A. Sprecher, an eminent Washington attorney who observed all the Nuremberg trials and then edited the bales of testimony and exhibits left behind, confessed that he found the Krupp case the most baffling of all. Sprecher concluded that "Alfried's exploitation of slave labor was worse than that of any other industrialist, including I. G. Farben. Nowhere else was there such sadism, such senseless barbarity, such shocking treatment of people as dehumanized material." The reason, he suggested, lay in Krupp's one-man rule. "His power was absolute, and therefore absolutely corrupting. At the same time, the men beneath the sovereign could be checked only by him. When he failed to restrain them, they let themselves go, and when the Germans go they really go."[3]

Perhaps. Yet there is another possibility. There was more to Krupp tradition than sole ownership. Since the founding of the dynasty, *die Firma* had stressed familial virtues. Whatever may be said against paternalism — and there is little criticism which is not implicit in the history of this family — the fact remains that in no other industrial empire were lifelong workers more loyal to their employer, or workmen's families more stable. Their content was rooted in the Krupps' long history of genuine interest in their welfare, and that very concern was quickened by the abnormal conditions in the wartime Ruhr. For six years the ratio between German men and German women was in dramatic imbalance. At one point in the agony of 1939–1945 every able male between sixteen and sixty was called up. There were at that time 48,970 foreign men in greater Essen. It was easy for Hitler, Himmler, and Speer to speak of removing the barriers between the slaves and German civilians. But not all the women in the Ruhr regarded the *Fremdarbeiter* as subhuman, or, if they did, cared enough to ignore them. Tattered and haggard though they might be, the strangers were nevertheless masculine. Those were the days when Essen girls — and middle-aged *Hausfrauen*, too — prowled the evening streets in pairs. To Krupp executives, brooding about the suffering men at the front, the danger of promiscuity was very real, and reports from the city supported their apprehension. *Rassenschande* (shaming the race; i.e., copulating with *Untermenschen*) was the ultimate crime for Germans. Nevertheless, according to a report issued in the second year of the war, Ruhr girls as young as thirteen years old found it "daring and exciting" to have sexual intercourse with camp inmates.[4]

Thus the Hauptverwaltungsgebäude posters put up all over the city on March 13, 1942, were directed not to the prisoners but to the *Volk*. They declared that "In spite of repeated instructions and admonitions, numerous employees continue to infringe upon the regulations regarding relations with prisoners of war. Thus, lately . . . transactions have been discovered between German male and female workers or foreign civilians on one side and prisoners of war on the other." The only major Nazi who had demonstrated any real sympathy for Krupp's plight was the ill-starred Reinhard Heydrich; three weeks earlier, on February 20, he had forbidden the shipping of Asiatics to Germany and prohibited social contacts between the German population and Russian POWs. But Krupp went further. The people of Essen, the warning of March 13 continued, "must be made to realize that all prisoners of war — including the French — belong to hostile nations. *The Russian civilian workers are to be treated in the same way as prisoners of war.* Any sympathy is false pity, which the courts will not accept as an excuse." (Italics in the original.)[5]

The fear of community *Rassenschande* meant that Wehrschutz "supervisors" (*Beaufsichtige*) of Krupp wards became exceptionally callous. Bülow prohibited church visits, mail home, slackness in the display of ethnic insignia, and, above all, fraternization with the local population. Against the possibility that German men might be seduced by Russian women, the ominous note was added that "Female eastern workers who become pregnant should no longer be reported to the SS" — instead, Krupp would take its own steps. Impregnation within and without the stockades was a growing problem, and its extent is a tribute to the reproductive instinct, since only the most resourceful couples could conceive, or even embrace, in the wartime Ruhr. On paper, at least, prisoners were never free of supervision. "Particularly deserving" foreign workers were only "allowed to take walks under the supervision of a German guard" on "alternate Sundays." Their days were bracketed by the Werkschutz predawn shriek, "*Aufstehen und beeilen Sie sich!*" (Get up and hurry up!) and the evening yell, "*Halt's Maul!*" (Shut up!).[6]

Fear that German girls might convert themselves into amateur *Prostituierte* expressed itself only in tighter restrictions. Removing the source of masculine temptation never occurred to Krupp. Instead every slave was closely watched as a potential escapee. Today this is vehemently — and, on the whole, successfully — denied in Essen. It collides head-on with Krupp's insistence that "All these men and women were victims of a compulsory labor system forced upon businessmen by the State" (*die der Staat seiner Industrie oktroyiert hatte*). At Nuremberg, Speer, testifying that firms had no control over camps, argued that "The head of a firm could not bother about conditions in such a camp." There is some truth in this. Alfried could not inspect each compound. He was, however, responsible for overall policy. Essen directives unquestionably came from the top, and obviously the firm guarded its wards with extraordinary zeal. A memo of Alfried's dated January 12, 1944, stated that "An application for special leave from Italian civilians is prima facie (*auf den ersten Blick*) untrustworthy," complained that "Frenchmen are refusing to extend their contracts," and declared that "Berlin . . . must be made aware once more that stricter measures must be taken for [French] personnel returning from leave. In spite of Sauckel's intervention, the returns are difficult to enforce, especially in France, where there is no police registration."[7]

The absentees were not lazy. As Alfried's file note observed, "Reports from France indicate that Frenchmen who have broken their contracts have no difficulty finding work in France." Nor were they merely bored with Teutonic regimentation, or jaded by foul billets in rusting baking houses, kennels, and public urinals. They were simply terrified. The clusters of *Flakgeschütze* and searchlight batteries surrounding the great semicircle of camps were ineffective. Lying naked under the bombsights of Sir Arthur Harris's Lancasters, Essen had become a place of death. Krupp was discovering that

The time was approaching an end when the Gusstahlfabrik had been permitted to produce unmolested [*Die Zeit geht zu Ende, da die Gusstahlfabrik ungestört arbeiten durfte*]. On March 5, 1943, Essen and the Krupp works received its first big bombing. Two years later, on March 11, 1945, the last and greatest blow was to fall on both. In between, the bombers came regularly. The monotony of this form of warfare made a habit of terror [*Die Monotonie dieser Kriegsform lässt Schrecken zur Gewöhnung werden*]. The missiles did not distinguish between the just and the unjust, nor did they spare the innocent, and they seldom landed on the guilty.[8]

In point of fact, the bombs almost *never* found the guilty; the Krupp-bunker was not hit, and the directors' homes in Bredeney came off relatively lightly, while the prisoners of war, foreign workers, and concentration camp inmates crouched helplessly in the eye of the target. Eugen Lauffer, technical manager in Alfried's housing administration, conceded in a Nuremberg affidavit that "the camps were without exception in the areas which were most affected." During one raid medical attention was withheld from the survivors for over twenty-four hours, and critically injured Catholics who then asked for last rites were denied them. In March 1943 the British wiped out a hundred Poles at Hafenstrasse, a complex of camps on the northwestern outskirts, in the suburb of Borbeck. Altogether, according to an undated report sent to Alfried late in the war, three camps were "partially destroyed," thirty-two "destroyed," and twenty-two "twice destroyed." None escaped intact. On a single night, October 23–24, 1944, City Engineer Gross of Essen listed 820 people killed and 643 wounded.*[9]

In part the tragedies were a consequence of indiscriminate bombing, but in this as in everything else Krupp had a policy; the just were to suffer more than the unjust, and some innocents more than others. On one street two camps stood side by side. When the tocsin of alarm sounded, Jewish girls took refuge in the remnants of a pulverized cellar behind the barbwire

---

* This may have included some Germans. The record is unclear.

of their camp; Poles, in a ditch within theirs. During a minor raid a stray bomb fell in the ditch. Over a hundred Polish corpses were counted, and then the order came down — in the future the Jewesses would lie in the exposed ditch, the Poles in the safer cellar. Here Polish men were lucky. They were not so lucky as the "westerners," however; that was why the casualties had been so heavy at Hafenstrasse. In death the pecking order held: a *Jude* had less chance than an *Ostarbeiter*, whose odds were smaller than a *Freiwilliger*, who in turn ran greater risks than the *Herrenvolk*. One Jewish girl who survived recalled that "When there was an air raid, we were the only ones expressly forbidden to go into the air raid shelter; we just had to stay where we were, exposed to the air raid and without any sort of protection (*waren dem Luftangriff ohne irgendwelchen Schutz ausgesetzt*). . . ."10

No one was really safe, of course (except the elite huddled in the bunker beneath the castle on the hill), but makeshift shelters had been provided for Kruppianer. Slaves lacked these *Luftschutzeinrichtungen*. At best they had *Splittergraben* (slit trenches) dug by themselves. In a Nuremberg affidavit, Alfried insisted that "As far as . . . the heavy air raids are concerned, the cause of this difficulty must be attributed to the fact that the erection and construction" of shelters was not "immediately possible," thereby "making demands on an intensified scale on camps and other suitable accommodation not damaged by bombs." This is crude obfuscation, and we have the notes of a fellow smokestack baron to prove it. In October 1944, when the war was in its sixth year and the initial turmoil which had made safeguards "not immediately possible" had subsided, Bernard Weiss of the Flick group inspected a Krupp factory. His visit was interrupted by enemy bombers, and after the all-clear he wrote:

> "Since there were no adequate air raid shelters, we were advised to leave the works [*Da keine ausreichenden Schutzräume vorhanden waren, wurde uns empfohlen, das Werk zu verlassen*]. All the employees, too, *with the exception of the concentration camp inmates* [*mit Ausnahme der KZ Insassen*], jumped into buses or on bicycles, while others made off at a run into the surrounding countryside up to 2 kilometers from the works." (Author's italics.)11

In brief, everybody was free to hide except the prisoners, who had to stay and take it. At first not all suffered in silence. At 10:30 P.M. on January 9, 1943, after the debris of England's first real raid on Essen had settled, the Werkschutz put through an emergency telephone call to Lehmann, who minuted the conversation for Alfried: ". . . Captain Dahlmann rang me up and told me that the guards in our prisoner of war camps in Raumerstrasse were barely able to suppress a revolt among the Russian prisoners of war. . . . In the opinion of Captain Dahlmann the reason the prisoners of war became so restive is that in the Raumerstrasse camp there are no slit trenches."[12]

Two months later, when the Lancasters dropped 908 tons of bombs in the great raid of March 5–6 and created a temporary power failure, there was no hint of panic. The slaves passively buried their dead and then rapidly rebuilt the shops, whose productivity had been halved. By then they had accepted their lot, knowing that they had no choice. If they stayed they might be blown up by RAF bombs; if they ran, they knew they would be gunned down by Mannlichers and Mausers. Their plight was pitiable and evident, yet almost nothing was done to resolve it. In that first memorandum Lehmann told Alfried that Dahlmann "urgently requests such trenches be dug in order, among other things, not to disturb the surrounding civilian population in case of serious trouble." Disregarding the captain's peculiar order of priorities, his reasoning was sound. Yet the ground remained unbroken. On October 16 a routine report noted that at Raumerstrasse "there are no air raid installations for the guards or the prisoners of war." Indeed, the inmates were not even provided with sand to extinguish phosphorus bombs.[13]

Similarly, the Lagerführer of Hafenstrasse warned the front office that his 1,400 Poles, Czechs, and Russians were dangerously vulnerable. Again Lehmann dutifully minuted that "yesterday Captain Fiene of the local Werkschutz called me and said that slit trenches for protection against splinters would have to be provided as soon as possible. . . ." Two months later, when the Hafenstrasse complex of camps was annihilated in March 1943, it still lacked slit trenches. The camps were then completely rebuilt, fresh *Stücke* was imported to inhabit them — but again protection was ignored, and again they were obliterated. The pattern kept repeating itself. Lehmann's reports were slighted or shelved, yet he himself pigeonholed some protests made to him. On October 13, 1942, one of his subordinates forwarded a report on a tour of Herdenstrasse stating, among other things, that "Air raid precautions are missing altogether. Air raid slit trenches for both guards and prisoners are also missing." Lehmann thrust it aside. The following year Herderstrasse was leveled, with a loss of 600 Soviet prisoners of war.[14]

Trenches offered only the most primitive asylum. Nevertheless they were better than open ground, and as Bomber Command's offensive gained momentum the slaves desperately excavated craters with their bare hands. The Werkschutz and SS neither tried to stop them nor did they offer help. Dechenschule's guards erected a strong bunker for themselves. There was room for their dependents, too, but pleas for sanctuary were ignored; the slaves were limited to a shallow fissure they had scooped within their compound. An almost identical situation developed at Walzwerk II (Rolling Mill II). According to Gerhardt Marquardt, a veteran machinist who had been a Kruppianer since 1920, his German co-workers converted a

recreation room into a shelter by rebuilding the ceiling and walls of reinforced concrete. When sirens sounded the French war prisoners who
worked alongside them were pointedly excluded; the POWs had to burrow
into a slag heap outside the mill.[15]

When RAF Pathfinders darted overhead, watched by the impassive
Konzernherr at Villa Hügel, the luckiest slaves were those who lived near
railroad tunnels. Two miles west of the Hauptverwaltungsgebäude three
such underpasses passed beneath the Essen-Mülheim line at Nöggerathstrasse, Grunertstrasse, and Böhmerstrasse. The last was far the best — 75
yards long and 20 feet wide, with an arched ceiling 35 feet high. A structure that could support a locomotive was safe against the terrors of
bombers in that war. Even today its advantages are obvious to a veteran of
those years. Although the discolored cement façades are pocked by the
bursts that scarred them a generation ago, the interior is solid and reassuring.

This haven lay five blocks, or four-tenths of a mile, from the camp at
Raumerstrasse. An agile man could easily reach it in three minutes at the
most, and since the near mutiny of January 1943 the guards had permitted
their prisoners to join them in the sprint. That is, the most nimble of them
were allowed to come; the tunnel couldn't hold everyone. In the words of a
contemporary account, "At this camp there were from 1,200 to 1,500
prisoners and . . . the passageway could not accommodate that number,
so that during an air raid the remainder had to stay in camp." The first
dash there separated the swift from the slow. Thereafter those who knew
they couldn't make it stayed behind. To the Werkschutz this was an ideal
solution, the survival of the fittest. Actually it was a survival of youth. The
men who lagged and dropped out were the middle-aged and the elderly.
Thus life expectancy was sharply altered by age; the prisoners Bomber
Command slew at Raumerstrasse were all old.[16]

Unfortunately for the inmates of Nöggerathstrasse, the underpass nearest them was an artery in the civil defense network. At the height of a raid,
fire engines from Altendorf and Frohnhausen roared back and forth
through it, and pedestrians were *verboten*. That left the underpass at
Grunertstrasse, which wasn't much; really it was little more than a bridge.
Moreover, the tunnel was too far from the camp. The Lagerführer
announced that inmates who wanted to go there would have to stay there;
a separate detachment of guards would be assigned to them. Though life in
the underpass meant sleeping on jagged old cobblestones, every French
POW volunteered. The issue was solved by a lottery, and the 170 winners
Dr. Jäger on "prisoner of war camp number 1420 in Nöggerathstrasse."
moved. On June 12, 1944, a Dr. Stinnesbeck reported to the indefatigable
Stinnesbeck was distressed. Medical treatments at the camp were being
given outdoors; sick call was held in the charred toilet of a burned house;

medical orderlies were sleeping in the men's lavatory; there were no drugs or wound dressings. What disturbed the physician most about the prisoners, however, was that "170 of them . . . are no longer housed in huts." Instead, they were living in the Grunertstrasse underpass, and "This tunnel is damp and not suitable for human beings."[17]

For once Jäger was unmoved. He had been at this longer than his colleague, and he had learned to cope with realities. The situation at Nöggerathstrasse was a matter of simple arithmetic. A year earlier, the camp had housed 1,100 Frenchmen. Since then, 286 of those who had remained in the huts had been killed in raids. The tunnel might be wet, uncomfortable, and, under any other circumstances, unfit for habitation, but 170 had gone in and 170 were still there. The winners of the lottery had won their lives.

✠ ✠ ✠

In the last tortuous days of the Thousand-Year Reich two of Goebbels's secretaries fled Berlin on bicycles, and the crippled *Doktor*, though already preoccupied with plans for his own suicide, cried out, "How can there be any guarantee now of keeping regular office hours?" The Hauptverwaltungsgebäude was alternately amused and infuriated by the unrealism of National Socialist bureaucrats, and christened the Wilhelmstrasse *das Idiotenhaus*. Thus the pot on the kettle. Nothing in the capital was more idiotic than Essen's senseless dissipation of its *Sklavenarbeit*. The most brutal Arabian *Sklavenhalter* knows the value of his human livestock. He may humiliate it, abuse it, and even mistreat it up to a point, but he is always careful to preserve the spark of life. Otherwise his investment becomes a total loss. Krupp's squandering of lives that were useful to him is therefore an insoluble riddle, and his failure to shield them from the murderous bombings is but one example of it. "*Mit der Dummheit kämpfen Götter selbst vergebens*," wrote Schiller in *Die Jungfrau von Orleans* — "The gods themselves struggle in vain against stupidity."[18]

Though the Nazi *Weltanschauung* demanded ruthlessness toward racial subhumans, Germany's requirements for mass labor were so urgent that even the most fanatical members of the hierarchy recognized the need for some restraint. A contented slave, they realized, was a competent slave. Excesses were thus condemned, not because they were unconscionable but because they were inefficient. After a particularly vicious *Menschenjagd* in the autumn of 1942, the office of Alfred Rosenberg protested against "'Recruiting' methods . . . which probably have their precedent in the blackest days of the slave trade." Göring grumbled that as inferiors *Ostarbeiter* should be shod with wooden clogs and fed "special food" ("cats, horses, etc."); nevertheless he agreed with Goebbels that only a man who received sufficient food could do a proper day's work. To Speer there was "nothing to be said against the SS taking drastic steps and putting those known as slackers in concentration camps"; still, he insisted on adequate food and housing on the grounds that the alternative was hopeless inefficiency.[19]

Surprisingly, the most earnest advocate of decency was Fritz Sauckel, the Reich's chief slaver. In captured documents his position is repeatedly disclosed, and it is always explicit and unequivocal. Although Sauckel died on the scaffold, the guilt for the most odious crimes of which he was convicted is shared by men who survived him and flourished in West Germany's postwar Bundesrepublik. His speeches and reports reveal that he begged his superiors, his subordinates, and above all the Schlotbarone to consider what they were doing. A former merchant sailor, he lacked the intellect of a Schacht or Alfried Krupp; on March 9, 1943, Goebbels wrote pessimistically in his diary, "Sauckel is one of the dullest of the dull." Yet the master slaver saw the core of the issue. Sauckel implored the industrialists who received deliveries from him to provide their dependents with medicine, food, and proper quarters, arguing that "Slaves who are underfed, diseased, resentful, despairing, and filled with hate will never yield that maximum of output which they might achieve under normal conditions."[20]

Krupp, unpersuaded, continued to run the sickest slave program in the Reich. Foreign workers in his 81 major factories were habitually underfed and diseased. In consequence they really *were* resentful, despairing, or filled with hate. Understandably, with that attitude, they never achieved maximum production. But then, Alfried hadn't expected that they would. "Naturally," he declared in an affidavit signed July 3, 1947, "we could not obtain from them the work output of a normal German worker." Naturally: how could subhumans compete with humans? Of course, he *did* load the dice. As early as March 20, 1942, when German silos were bursting with the largest food surplus in the country's history — owing to the confiscation of harvests in occupied territories — a revealing interoffice memo disclosed that during a diet conference at Raumerstrasse "Mr. Hassel from the Werkschutz, who was present at the time, butted in and said . . . that one was dealing with Bolsheviks and they ought to have beatings substituted for food." The spokesman for this enlightened approach was one of Alfried's most influential lieutenants; he represented Altendorferstrasse's attitude; and it was in 1942 that a team of Wehrmacht officers inspecting POW camps reported, "Edema cases existed only in Krupp camps." Alfried later conceded that he knew at the time that slaves were starving: "The fact that complaints were frequently made on account of insufficient food for the foreign workers . . . [is] well remembered by me."[21]

He blamed "technical difficulties" and "the official regulations, which determined the rations in detail." They did indeed. And they were sensible. As of February 9, 1942, Russians and Poles who had been drafted for forced labor were supposed to be receiving a miminum of 2,156 calories a day. The figure for those engaged in heavy work was 2,615; in very heavy work, 2,909. Yet what was happening at Krupp during those months? On March 14 the supervisor of a tool shop complained that "the food of the Russians working here is so pitifully bad that they are getting weaker and weaker every day. Investigations have shown, for example, that some Russians are not strong enough to tighten a turning part sufficiently, for the lack of physical strength. Conditions are exactly the same at all other places where Russians are employed. If care is not taken to change the feeding arrangements sufficiently so that a normal output may be expected from these men, then their employment, and all the expense connected with it, will have been in vain."[22]

Elsewhere in the Konzern conditions *were* the same. Four days later one Krupp foreman wrote another foreman, describing a daily visit by Ober-lagerführrung chefs: "What these men call a day's ration is a complete puzzle to me. The food was a puzzle, too, because they ladled out the thinnest of already watery soup. It was literally water with a handful of turnips, and it looked like dish water. . . . The people have to work for us. Good, but care must be taken to see that they get at least the bare necessities. I have seen a few figures in the camp, and a cold shudder actually ran up and down my spine. I met one there, and he looked as though he'd got barber's rash. . . . If this continues, we shall all be contaminated. It is a pity, when just at this moment the motto is 'increased production.' Something must be done to keep the people capable of production."[23]

Nothing was done. Eight days later the manager of a boiler construction shop reported on the performance of his Russian soldiers and civilians. Six weeks had passed since their arrival and the beginning of *fressen,* he noted, and they were "in a generally weak physical condition. . . . 10 to 12 of the 32 Russians here are absent daily on account of illness. . . . The reason why the Russians are not capable of production is, in my opinion, that the food which they are given will never give them the strength for working which you hope for. The food one day, for instance, consisted of a watery soup with cabbage leaves and a few pieces of turnip." This was Krupp's famous "bunker soup" (*Bunkersuppe*), which contained perhaps 350 calories. Sometimes it was supplemented by a second meal, a wafer-thin piece of bread smeared with jam, but the survivors' most vivid memories of twilight would be of returning from the shops to confinement and standing in line, racked by hunger cramps, holding out tin cups to receive this vile garbage. *Die Firma* was one of the few firms whose SS contract permitted it to make its own arrangements for feeding slaves, thus cutting its four marks per diem payments to Himmler. I. G. Farben was another, but Farben slaves were given the full ration, with supplementary meals provided for men assigned to heavy duty. Not so Krupp. At Nuremberg, Kruppianer testimony revealed the desperate straits to which prisoners were reduced:

> The warm meal consisted of soup, the cold one of bread with jam or margarine. The so-called "bunker soup" that was served at Krupp was not touched by many German workmen [*Die sogenannte Bunkersuppe, die bei Krupp serviert wurde, wurde von manchen deutschen Arbeitern nicht angerührt*]. After the air raids in October of 1944, however, even this was no longer available. The night shift never received any extra food* . . . Krupp received .70 RM for feeding the prisoners per head per diem [*Krupp erhielt für die Ernährung der Gefangenen .70 RM pro Tag und Person*]. [24]

At mealtimes, as at other times, Krupp tried to maintain the double standard: conscripts from the west were *Untermenschen*, but prisoners thickened the distinctions blurred. When a Krupp lawyer, cross-examining a Dutchman three years after the war, inquired about his rations, the reply was, "Well, so far as I can remember we only got one slice a day." (The slice, he added, weighed about an ounce and a half.) On that diet prisoners deteriorated rapidly, and some of the most poignant stories this writer heard from survivors were of men who returned from Essen to their homes in France and the Low Countries and were ejected — the doors literally slammed in their faces — because their wives and mothers didn't recognize them. In general, however, captives from the east received less of everything except brutality. "Of all the military prisoners they fared the worst," the Nuremberg tribunal concluded, and the judgment is supported by over five hundred pounds of testimony, documents, and exhibits. The decision to abuse them had been made on the very highest level. In one memorandum the office manager of the firm's locomotive factory recorded that Lehmann, who received his own orders directly from Alfried, had told him that each Russian would receive "300 grams of bread between 0400 and 0500 hours." The manager added, "I pointed out that it was impossible to exist on this bread ration until 1800 hours, whereupon Dr. Lehmann told me that the Russian prisoners of war must not be allowed to get used to western European ways of feeding."[25]

Among the defendants who were to stand beside Alfried in Nuremberg's Palace of Justice was Max Ihn, who had been appointed to the board in March 1941. In an affidavit written two years after the Nazi collapse Ihn conceded, "The food rations for Russian workers were so low that . . . it was almost impossible to put these people to work." He blamed the government and insisted that rations "were at last gradually increased." In fact, the reverse was true. Rations became so insignificant that chefs

---

* Sauckel had specified that workers on night duty be given 2,244 calories a day.

sometimes forgot them altogether; on his first anniversary as a board member Ihn received this handwritten chit from the armored car shop: "Herr Balz informs me that the food for 9 Russian civilians on the night shift on March 19–20 was forgotten. Foreman Grollius therefore refused to bring these people to work. Only then did they receive their food." Plainly Grollius was insolent, if not insubordinate. Still, he was not alone. Later in 1942 a band of Kruppianer protested against the Russian diet. In a police state public expressions of sympathy required rare courage, but the tiny minority persisted in them, and deserves to be remembered. In the last winter of the war, when others had abandoned compassion, one worker noted the concern of fellow Kruppianer toward Jewish girls: "The German workmen saw how inadequately the girls were fed and not infrequently would sneak them something edible, out of pity" (*steckten ihnen manchmal aus Mitleid etwas Essbares zu*).[26]

Unfortunately these mites were insignificant. There was too much suffering for private charity. As early as the winter of 1942–1943, when Alfried had established his *de facto* control of the firm, the most casual riffling through Hauptverwaltungsgebäude reports would have revealed that only a massive rescue operation could avert catastrophe. Here are three of them, plucked from their folders:

October 20, 1942, from a junior executive who had just toured Raumerstrasse, to Lehmann: "Guards who have been on duty for some time declared that they had on various occasions noticed new transports of prisoners who, on arrival, were in the best of health and appeared sturdy and strong but who, after only a few weeks, were in an extraordinarily weakened condition. Wehrmacht medical inspectors have also made remarks in the camps along these lines and stated that they had never met with such a bad general state of affairs in the case of Russians as in the Krupp camps."[27]

November 19, 1942, from Instrument Workshop No. 11 to the Oberlagerführung: ". . . We have again and again discovered that the food for the Russian prisoners of war who, in our plant, are exclusively employed on heavy work, is totally inadequate. We have already expressed this in our letter to Herr Ihn dated October 30, 1942. We discover again and again that people who live on this diet always break down at work after a short time and sometimes die. . . . For this heavy work" — aircraft armor plate, *very* heavy work — "we must insist that the food be sufficient actually to keep these workers with us."[28]

May 7, 1943, from Dr. Gerhard Wiele, Alfried's personal physician and chief of Krupp hospitals: "Subject: Deaths of eastern workers. Fifty-four eastern workers died at the Lazarettstrasse, four of them due to external causes (*äussere Einwirkung*) and fifty of disease. The causes of death for these fifty who died from disease were tuberculosis, thirty-eight (including two women); malnutrition, two; hemorrhage of the stomach, one; intestinal diseases, two; typhus, one (female); pneumonia, three; appendicitis, one (female); liver disease, one; abscess, one. The compilation therefore shows that four-fifths died of tuberculosis and malnutrition, i.e., 80 percent."[29]

The doctor coupled tuberculosis and malnutrition because in 1943 they belonged together. Every member of the medical profession was aware that the incidence of pulmonary tuberculosis had risen sharply throughout Europe since the outbreak of the war — it would not drop again until 1947 — and that while everyone was inhaling tubercle bacilli, symptoms rarely appeared unless the victim's resistance had been weakened, usually by poor diet. In a normal community a doctor's first orders after confirmation of diagnosis would have been improved diet and rest. In Essen everything had been inverted, and so physicians, like foremen and Werkschutz guards, could merely tot up columns of figures and submit their necrotic audits while prisoners lay in the barren compounds exhibiting the advanced tubercular symptoms which were so meticulously described in Dr. Wiele's textbooks: coughing (*Husten*), difficulty in breathing (*Kurzatmigkeit*), and expectoration of blood (*Blutspeien*).

In Nuremberg's Palace of Justice Dr. Theodor Rohlfs, who had served as camp physician of Stalag VI-I, an 80,000-prisoner assembly camp in Düsseldorf, provided a stunning example of how Prussian logic can turn black into white.[30] Dr. Rohlfs appeared as a defense witness. Unlike Dr. Jäger, he didn't think Krupp camps had been so bad. He testified that the *Fremdarbeiter* had arrived there "in a really deplorable physical condition," which, he said firmly, had been "certainly caused by the strains of the transport and perhaps also during their stay in the collection camps." Then came a rapid-fire recitation of statistics. It seemed impressive; the rate of illness among Italian workers had been 4 percent, among Germans 3 to 4 percent, among the French 2.5 percent. Frenchmen, apparently, had been healthier than Kruppianer. Admittedly the initial Soviet figure had been "extremely high." However, Dr. Rohlfs asserted, that statistic had been dramatically altered by Krupp care. Krupp's lawyers stepped down and Max Mandellaub, a bilingual American attorney, cross-examined the witness. The sparring was brief; the *coup de maître* breathtaking. Mandellaub asked whether Rohlfs "can here state, under oath, that the situation of the prisoners of war in Essen, and particularly that of the Russian prisoners of war, was satisfactory."

A: Yes, it was satisfactory, as far as possible under then prevailing conditions.
Q: You said . . . the Russians had a rate of sickness of 35 percent. If I remember correctly, that must have been 35 percent.
A: Yes.

Q: This percentage then was reduced to 6 percent. Is that correct?
A: Yes. I remember this figure very decidedly.
Q: Of what date?

At this point Rohlfs's self-assurance wavered, and he replied, "I am afraid I can't say that. We were successful in reducing the rate of illness in the case of the Russians to such an extent that the percentage of illness fluctuated around 6 percent." The American closed in:

Q: How many cases of death did you have?
A. I'm afraid I can't give you any figures for that . . . because of extreme weakness and exhaustion many of them died. . . .
Q: Is it therefore correct to assume that part of this reduction of illness in the case of Russian prisoners of war might also be caused by death?
A: Yes, of course. . . .

Of course. Since they had died a natural death, the doctor saw nothing odd in his reduction of 35 percent to 6 percent by neglecting to distinguish between those who had been cured and those who had succumbed. Thus the number of actual fatalities in *die Firma*'s camps is unknown, even when the patients were in Dr. Jäger's wards, where the reason for discharge *was* noted. Probably bombs destroyed some records; certainly Krupp destroyed others. Survivors seldom remembered the last hours of the starving. Often the victims would quietly drift into coma and then slip away while other slaves were in their shops; Werkschutz or SS men removed the cadavers, and most camp registries were lost or burned before Allied troops arrived. Yet now and then an exceptional inmate, brooding over the doom ahead, displayed spirit. These were remembered, and sometimes recorded. In one of those singular vignettes which illumine the full scope of a far greater tragedy, a slim dossier of reports, now yellow and brittle, but with the official stamps and signatures of all the proper officials still legible, describes what was called "Subject: Death of Soviet Russian Prisoner of War 326/39004 Schosow, Sergei, caused by shooting."[31]

On the morning of April 29, 1944 — it was a Saturday, warm and dank — Schosow was assigned to a work party (*Arbeitsabteilung*) clearing away the rubble of a bombed-out Krupp bakery. Toward noon a Werkschutz guard named Wilhelm Jacke saw him reach for the blackened heel of a bread loaf. In the next moment, a Wuppertal military court found, "the prisoner of war was killed by a shot through the breast." On the recommendation of a *Heeresjustizinspektor* (judge advocate official with the equivalent rank of first lieutenant), a *Kriegsgerichtsrat* (judge advocate with the equivalent rank of major) decided that "According to the investigations made, Wilhelm Jacke acted according to regulations, and there is no cause for taking action against him."

This being the Ruhr, the verdict was forwarded to Essen for approval. Bülow wanted "to praise Jacke in public." On June 14 a subordinate persuaded him to send the guard a letter of commendation, on the ground that such a gesture "should put an end to the matter." It did: an endorsement was filed in the personnel record of the murderer, and the corpse vanished. We know almost nothing of Sergei Schosow — his age, his rank, his appearance, or his family, if any — and shall never learn more about him. The Krupp figure 326/39004 means as much to us as his name. But he was a man. He was famished. He knew that it was worth his life to reach for that crust, yet he had to try, and picturing him crouching among the smashed timbers and crumbled oven of that company bakery, extending his cramped hand until the sudden Mannlicher bullet slew him, we glimpse in tableau the anguish that was *Sklavenarbeiter*.

✠    ✠    ✠

His executioner is also an anonymity. Wilhelm Jacke's local celebrity lasted a year and a day; when Hitler committed suicide in the Führerbunker, Jacke suffered an abrupt change in status, and like so many others whose names cropped up in the Palace of Justice, he disappeared. Nevertheless he, too, is more than a cipher. Jacke was not a brutish anthropophagite; he had grasped the essentials of a sophisticated *kruppsche* policy. So had the guards at the terminal: in shouting "No work, no feeding" at newly arrived foreign workers they were stating the terms of the workers' contracts. As a more detached observer put it, "In many cases, food was denied the prisoners as a punishment."[32]

Because the diminishing efficiency of *Stücke* was reflected in production figures, the firm cast about for a solution. On October 27, 1942, Bülow called a meeting of all camp leaders. The first item in the memorandum which followed dealt with falling in for work and reads in part: "All the camp leaders complained that they had the greatest difficulty in bringing the male and female . . . workers to work in the morning. In the darkness (the roll call for the first shift takes place at 0430 hours) some of the workers sneak away, hide themselves in the latrines, or under the beds, or lie down in beds in other barracks, etc. The camp leaders are of the unanimous opinion that the only possible way to combat this is to treat the shirkers harshly and bring them to work by force."[33]

The uniformed Kommandants in black and blue then set to in earnest. In the future, they announced, slaves who let them down would be found "seriously disloyal" (*grob pflichtwidrig*). At predawn musters inmates were told that jail awaited "foreign shirkers" or others guilty of "loitering, breach of work contract, or absenteeism, etc." The threat was real; there is extant a handwritten file note reading: "The Italian civilian worker Antonio Molinari, Factory No. 680–187" (electrosteel works in Borbeck), "born April 21, 1918, in Venice, was arrested for refusing to work. Concentration camp requested." Beneath the illegible signature is the endorsement, "For antisocial behavior — concentration camp." No allowance was made for arduous tasks. In the words of Kruppianer Adolf Trockel, as the bombings mounted, "Mostly they had to lug bricks and corrugated iron sheets (*Ziegelsteine und Wellblech*). This hard physical work had to be done in cold weather, in inadequate clothing, without gloves or protective clothing of any kind (*ohne Handschuhe oder Schutzkleidung*).[34]

Kicks, blows, and confinement in Essen cells having proved inefficacious, Bülow's Lagerführers recommended "Instantaneous measures of corporal treatment . . . especially in cases where the steadily increasing thefts from kitchens and breaches of discipline toward the guards are to be dealt with. . . . Furthermore, the Werkschutz will, in the future, be at liberty to punish slackers and insubordinate workers by depriving them of their meals." This gave the guards the power of life or death, and it was to continue during the two and a half years left before the German surrender. A German workman later told how "Anyone who did not work fast enough (*Wer nicht im nötigen Tempo arbeitete*) was forced to work harder by kicks and blows. Alleged shirking was punished by deprivation of meals or cutting the offender's hair in the shape of a cross." Henceforth the withholding of food became increasingly common. To be sure, rations in the best compounds continued to be unspeakable — one western survivor described "pitchforking dirty, decaying spinach from a wagon directly into the cooking pots," with the consequence that "disease and dysentery were rife." It was eaten, all the same; *some* sort of sustenance was essential. It is hardly surprising that there were "thefts from kitchens."[35]

Excessive demands upon workers were another frequent form of oppression, and it was this that inspired a thirty-two-year-old French employee named Robert Ledux, who like Sergei Schosow made a desperate gesture. Ledux was employed in Factory No. 494261, a tank construction plant of the highest priority. Shortly before noon on February 13, 1944, he and two other workers were ordered to move a 330-pound machine by hand. The Frenchman refused. This, he said, was a job for the shop crane, and turning Krupp's slogan upon the firm, he shouted, "No food, no work." To the indignation of the German foreman, he mounted a box and began a speech urging other Frenchmen to strike. The foreman pushed Ledux aside, Ledux punched the foreman in the nose, and the Werkschutz carted the rebel off. Four days later Bülow notified the Gestapo, but before they could act the prisoner somehow contrived to escape Essen, Ruhr, and Reich; he was never again seen in Germany.[36]

After Stalingrad, German morale sank perceptibly. For the first time, new conscripts arrived manacled to one another, and while individual Kruppianer displayed compassion, the company line hardened. Any foreman with a reputation as "a tough guy" (*ein scharfer Hund*) was encouraged from above. The toughest of all — and one of the most conspicuous absentees at Nuremberg — was Deputy Chief of the Werkschutz Hassel, who wore his SS uniform while drawing Krupp pay. He was universally regarded as a sadist, and was granted a wage increase in 1943 upon Bülow's recommendation that "in these recent months Herr Hassel has been especially efficient." One of Hassel's post-Stalingrad efficiencies was the organization of "Enlarged Werkschutz II." Eight German workmen on each shift were appointed to it and furnished with clubs and whips. Their ostensible purpose was to suppress riots. In practice they were encouraged to use their scourges freely.[37]

Under Hassel, careers were built on brutality. Camp guards who murdered prisoners were freed on the ground that they had acted in self-defense or in "line of duty." Duty, as interpreted by Hassel's subordinates, was typified by the record of one who supervised all foreign workers at the Krawa shop in Essen and who, after the war, was sentenced to eight years' imprisonment by a German court. Over a period of four years, it was found, he had been guilty of "beating eastern workers, male and female, with a wooden board, a rubber hose, and his fists; waking eastern workers with a water hose; throwing a French civilian down a stairway; and ruthlessly beating a Russian prisoner of war to death with a four-edged piece of wood." He was not a Nuremberg absentee. He testified that he had acted on instructions from his superiors, who told him that if slaves were tardy or lazy he should "interfere energetically," and who then showed him how to go about it. Inasmuch as he had already been convicted, his word may be suspect. But his personnel record was found in *die Firma*'s files. If Krupp had disapproved of his conduct, Krupp had had four years in which to discipline him or demote him, and nothing had been done.[38]

Bülow witnessed beatings, examined victims after beatings, and permitted brutal treatment to continue as long as there was any hope that corporal punishment would improve production. Savagery having failed, the fate of an unproductive slave was scribbled on his record jacket — "Buchenwald Concentration Camp," or simply "KZ." Later, other executives and supervisors could feign ignorance of what such a disposition meant, arguing that they had never seen Buchenwald and had no idea what was going on there. Alfried's viceroy of the camps wasn't among them. He had signed one document too many. Drawn up on October 7, 1943, it discussed what was to be done with prisoners of war whose insubordination had been so great that neither detention nor bread and water seemed adequate punishment. Recalcitrants, Bülow ordered, were to be "brought before the Gestapo." He continued, "In such cases, the Gestapo always passes death sentences, for the execution of which a detail of other Russian prisoners of war may be used," and added in a postscript, "I request that the contents of this note be treated as confidential, particularly in view of the death penalty."[39]

Thus the vicious circle grew still more vicious: the spindly chattels, driven through the streets of Essen with steel whips, were unequal to the physical tasks asked of them; failing to perform, they were abused and starved further; collapsing, they were exterminated. In retrospect it seems obvious that Krupp's 100,000 involuntary employees were scarcely worth their *Bunkersuppe*. Their emaciation was conspicuous; so was their despondency. But the Reich was in no mood to ponder the weaknesses of its wards. The most extravagant gestures of despair passed unrecognized for what they were. One Russian, unable to bear his lot another day, actually amputated both his hands by laying his wrists on a train track moments before a locomotive roared up. He was charged with "work sabotage."[40]

# 21

✠

# NN

Dₑcₑₘbₑᵣ 7, 1941, lives in infamy in Europe for a crime vaster in scope and, in its affront to humanity, far more shocking than the Japanese attack on Pearl Harbor, for it was on that Sunday that the Führer promulgated *den Nacht und Nebel Erlass*, the Night and Fog Decree. The decree's original goal was to winnow out people "endangering German security" (*die deutsche Sicherheit gefährden*), but two months later Feldmarschall Keitel expanded it to include all persons in occupied countries who had been taken into custody and were still alive eight days later. In such cases

> . . . *sollen künftig die Beschuldigten heimlich nach Deutschland gebracht . . . werden. . . .*

> . . . the prisoners are to be transported to Germany secretly . . . these measures will have a deterrent effect because
> a) the prisoners will vanish without leaving a trace,
> b) no information may be given out as to their whereabouts or their fate.[1]

At Nuremberg, Keitel confessed to the International Military Tribunal that of all the atrocities in which he had collaborated, this was "the worst."[2] It was indeed. Behind the order was the reasoning, explicitly stated, that "effective intimidation" of captive nations could best be achieved by a measure under which "the relatives of the criminal and the population do not know his fate." Since the "criminals" were to include children, the illiterate, and the retarded, the *Erlass* also assured that in the chaos of postwar Europe the fate of many would *never* be known. Today there are countless men and women who lost a member of the family a quarter-century ago and are tormented by the thought that he may still be alive somewhere. In 1945 the seized *Sicherheitsdienst* (SD) records were found to contain merely names and the scrawled initials NN (*Nacht und Nebel*). How many died will never be known. For once the German passion for records was overcome. Even the sites of graves went unchronicled. The victims had vanished forever in the night and fog of the Third German Reich.

Krupp's camps included massive shipments of slaves who had been consigned to NN. Yet in a sense the dreadful double initial applies to every one of them, for after all the documents have been studied, all the testimony reread, all the affidavits examined and all the statistics tabulated, one is left with the haunting question: Who were the slaves? We see a face here and there in isolated vignettes — the Russian who reached for bread, the brave Frenchman who tried to call a strike. We know that they represented every country in Europe, every age group of both sexes, every level of intellect, culture, and aspiration. We have some idea of what they endured, and of why those who died succumbed. Yet that still doesn't tell us who they were. Like the Germans who passed their dense formations every day and stared right through them, we are apt to think of the *Stücke* as an immense, anonymous blur receding into the darkness and drifting mists of the past. And this is unjust. Since they are an integral part of the Krupp story — since the Krupps themselves always held that those who worked for them were members of the family — they must be seen and heard. The mind cannot encompass a hundred thousand people, but it is possible to focus on a half-dozen here.

✠   ✠   ✠

Tadeusz (Tad) Goldsztajn, a dark, slight, wiry adolescent, celebrated his sixteenth birthday on July 25, 1943, in Sosnowiec, an industrial city of 130,000 in southwestern Poland.[3] The war had scarcely touched the boy's family. Germany prized Sosnowiec's mines and mills; its railroad marshaling yards were crucial to the Russian campaign, and the inhabitants had been largely ignored. Hernyk Goldsztajn, Tad's father, was a newspaperman. He continued to report to his office every day, and at home his wife Regina kept house for him, the boy, and Hernyk's husky unmarried brother. But the Goldsztajns were Jews. They were living in a deepening shadow, although, of course, they had no concept of the nightmare ahead. Then, three weeks after the birthday party, as the Russian counteroffensive roared out of the Kursk salient, terror struck Sosnowiec's Jews. All four Goldsztajns were herded into a boxcar and sent to Auschwitz. Disembarking under the ARBEIT MACHT FREI sign, they heard the customary command to segregate themselves by sex. Tad obediently left his mother, thinking the separation temporary. It wasn't until later, behind the wire, that he learned that she had been taken straight to the crematorium.

By then the two men and the youth had been billeted in Auschwitz's
Birkenau Lager, a subcamp. They vowed they would stick together, and for
five weeks they held out. Then an SS officer entered their barracks carrying
an *Offiziersstock*, a swagger stick. Beside him stood a heavyset Berthawerk
executive. The prisoners were stripped naked and slowly paraded past the
Krupp selector, who, after examining their muscle quality and skin texture,
signaled his choices to the officer. Tad and his powerfully built uncle were
picked; Hernyk Goldsztajn was motioned aside for extermination. Frantically the newspaperman and his son appealed to the SS man. Keep the
family united, they appealed; all three would work much better that way.
The Germans looked astonished; *Judenmaterial* never spoke during these
rites. Abruptly the Krupp man flicked a finger toward the older Goldsztajn's spectacles — all he was wearing — and with a blow of his short
cane the SS officer struck the glasses, pulverizing them. That was the
last Tad saw of his father. Moments later Hernyk was being led toward
the gas chambers, plucking bits of crushed lenses from his bleeding lids.

On September 30, 1943, the boy, his uncle, and some six hundred other
Jewish men and boys were packed, standing, in a chain of cattle cars and
sent, via Breslau, to Fünfteichen KZ in Markstädt, Silesia, where each
received his tattooed *Häftlingsnummer* (literally, "prisoner's number") on
the left forearm and was told that he would be employed in the Berthawerk. Starvation began immediately. Their only ration was a single bowl of
broth which Tad later described as a "tasteless, watery substance . . .
prepared out of some sort of grass"; in his subsequent affidavit he declared
that "In the fifteen months which I spent working for Krupp I was always
hungry, sleepy, filthy, tired beyond any human comparison, and most of
the time, by any normal standards, seriously ill." On January 6 his uncle,
reduced from a strapping workman to a wraith, died in Fünfteichen's
hospital. Of the six hundred who had made the trip, twenty were alive a
year later.

Here again, Krupp's motives are inexplicable. The Berthawerk was never
envisaged as a fast-profit, in-and-out wartime operation. Christening it had
been one of Gustav's last official acts before stepping aside for his son, and
it was meant to honor his wife; when complete, its steel capacity was
expected to equal that of Essen and Rheinhausen combined. Set up in
January 1943, with a capital of 100 million reichsmarks, it was wholly
owned by Alfried Krupp, who bore the title of *Vorsitzender des Aufsichts-
rats*, chairman of the board, and who eventually invested another 120
million reichsmarks in it. Ground had been broken with high hopes for
rapid erection of sheds and an impressive yield from this capital. Using
"building Jews" (*Baujuden*) from Auschwitz, engineers from Essen had
broken ground even before Alfried had approved their blueprints. In one of
the first reports they told him how "The construction work is being carried

out under especially favorable conditions. The workmen consist mostly of workers and Jews under sentence (*Die Bauarbeiter setzen sich zum grössten Teil aus Strafarbeitern und Strafjuden zusammen*). There are already 1,200 men in one camp." That had been when Tad was a fifteen-year-old schoolboy, his father was covering general news assignments in Sosnowiec, and no one in the Goldsztajn family had heard of either the Berthawerk or Fünfteichen. On July 21, 1943, four days before Tad's birthday party, a Krupp intrafirm memorandum further reported that "a concentration camp is being built for 4,000 prisoners (*es wird ein KZ aufgebaut, für 4.000 Gefangene*). The completion of the camp and the bringing to it of the prisoners must be accelerated."[4]

By the third week in September, when Tad and his uncle were chosen to be *Baujuden* and his father was gassed and cremated, Alfried's chief lieutenants were meeting at the site with high SS officers. Target dates were set: on October 1 the camp would be ready to receive 800 inmates — this was to be Tad's group; as we have seen, it was 200 men short, another reason for hoarding manpower — and the entire KZ, inhabited by the full complement of prisoners, was supposed to be ready and on the mark by December 1. On the first day of October, which was also the day Tad was led from his boxcar to his Fünfteichen bunk with his uncle, Alfried signed a general order to his directors headed "Subject: Berthawerk" and noting with pride that "Notwithstanding many difficulties we have pushed through the Berthawerk construction." The RAF raids in the Ruhr, he pointed out, made the Silesian project more vital than ever: "As a result of the damage to our Essen plants, this plant is of particularly outstanding significance. The start of production on schedule and without hindrance, and the further development and the stepping up of production, is, consequently, of the greatest importance."[5]

Alfried made on-the-spot inspections. At Nuremberg he recalled his tours, and one of his German subordinates there, Klaus Stein, testified that "Krupp was thoroughly informed upon working conditions at Markstädt" (*Krupp war über die Arbeitsbedingungen in Markstädt voll informiert*). The new Konzernherr's optimism, based almost entirely upon faith in his Auschwitz livestock, continued to grow. Indeed, on February 2, 1944, he asked his colleagues in RVE to approve two new *kruppsche* projects, a steel plant and an armor plate factory, both of which would rise and flourish with the help of *Judenmaterial* drafts. The request cited Krupp experience at the Berthawerk, where, "Above all, there is a concentration camp available that can house 4–5,000 concentration camp prisoners, but which at present is occupied only by 1,200. In addition the 3,300 Jews doing construction work right there will soon be available for assignment to this work" (*Ferner werden in Kürze 3.300 Juden, welche an Ort und Stelle Bauarbeiter sind, für diese Arbeit freigemacht werden können*).[6]

Unfortunately he had already passed his own Berthawerk deadline two months earlier. Indeed, the lag between Alfried's promises and the actual performance at Markstädt widened to six months. The issue was solved only after the Speer ministry formed a Working Committee of the German Armaments Industry (*Arbeitsgemeinschaft der deutschen Waffenindustrie*), whose howitzer technicians and efficiency experts — at what cost we shall presently see — organized gun production and then returned the management to the humiliated Alfried. He seems to have never understood what had gone wrong or why the Berthawerk remained a disappointment, though the reason lay buried in his file for December 13, 1943. A monthly report had warned him that *"Es liegen bisher unerfüllte Rotzettel über nahezu 1.000 Mann vor. Ursache ist die äussert angespannte Arbeitslage im ganzen Reich"* (Requisitions for almost 1,000 men are still unhonored, and the reason for this is the acute labor situation throughout the Reich).[7]

*Stücke*, in other words, must not be wasted. In the light of this and other warnings Tad Goldsztajn's ordeal, which mounted as Alfried's problems mounted, becomes as confounding as the plight of Essen's serfs. Tad said later, "We were not slaves; our status was much lower. True, we were deprived of freedom and became a piece of property which our masters put to work. But here the similarity with any known form of slavery ends, for we were a completely expendable piece of property. We did not even compare favorably with Herr Krupp's machinery, which we tended. The equipment in the shop was well maintained. It was operated with care, oiled, greased and allowed to rest; its longevity was protected. We, on the other hand, were like a piece of sandpaper which, rubbed once or twice, becomes useless and is thrown away to be burned with the waste."

Fünfteichen issued each new arrival a shirt, undershorts, jacket and overcoat (all of burlap), and a pair of wooden clogs. That was the beginning and end of the clothing allowance — no replacements were ever distributed, although within days the cheap fabric had begun to tear. Tad's body became, and remained, black with oil; he was infested with lice; and the clogs were wholly inadequate for the three-mile, fifty-minute march to the Berthawerk, which began each morning after a 4:30 reveille gong and roll call on Fünfteichen's *Appellplatz* (parade ground). Flanked by SS guards and trained dogs, the inmates moved through the predawn darkness in ranks of five to a guard's quickstep cadence count of *"Links! Rechts! Links! Rechts!"* Prisoners who dropped were carried back and often never seen again, for Fünfteichen had its own gas chamber. Nights, after returning from the factory, young Goldsztajn actually saw ritualistic murder done in the floodlit *Appellplatz*, where "the public executions took place and the daily punishment was meted out with rubber hoses."

Berthawerk slaves averaged from four to four and a half hours' sleep each night, although they spent only twelve hours a day in the factory,* broken by three roll calls to discourage flight. The long marches, the parade ground ceremonies, and the witnessing of medieval retribution took time. More time was wasted by Fünfteichen's insufficiencies — feeding took two hours each evening because there were just fifty soup bowls to go around — and though the inmates were theoretically through at 11 P.M., the guards kept them up until past midnight doing camp chores. Thus many shop accidents were attributable to simple exhaustion.

The Berthawerk could not have been an easy place to work under the best of circumstances. At its height, six gigantic sheds employed nearly a thousand slaves each. Tad was assigned to *Kolbenstangen* (piston rods) department number 10 in the main machine shop. Nineteen other departments shared the same roof, each making one part of a light howitzer. After the Saur reforms one complete artillery piece left the floor every sixty minutes. Speed was bought at a price — there were now industrial hazards which had been considered intolerable since the early days of Alfred the Great. As Tad moved between his lathe, boring machine, and grinder, white-hot fragments of sharp metal fell into his open clogs. The wounds grew infected; he bears the scars today.

The percentage of suffering men would have been high in any event, if only because of their inadequate clothing. In the plant named for the most celebrated woman in the Reich, emerging cannon were hot, men were not. Throughout the winter of 1943–1944 there was no warmth for the working slaves. Large coke stoves had been set up for German workmen from Essen, but these were off limits to Jews. Any prisoner who sneaked over to hold out his stiff hands was chased away. As often as not, he was also beaten. Here discipline was handled by working Kruppianer, and except for beheadings, every brutality seen in Fünfteichen, including canings and other torture, was repeated in the factory. According to Tad,

> At work we were Krupp's charges. SS guards were placed along the wall to prevent escape, but seldom interfered with the prisoners at work. This was the job of the various "Meisters" and their assistants. The slightest mistake, a broken tool, a piece of scrap — things which occur every day in factories around the world — would provoke them. They would hit us, kick us, beat us with rubber hoses and iron bars. If they themselves did not want to bother with punishment, they would summon the Kapo [KZ trusty] and order him to give us twenty-five lashes. To this day I sleep on my stomach, a habit I acquired at Krupp because of the sores on my back from beating.

---

* There were exceptions to this. At Nuremberg a witness testified that during a three-week period he was required to work thirty-six-hour shifts with twelve hours off between each shift. (Jaroslav Brandejs testimony at Nuremberg January 29, 1948, Krupp case transcript 2643–2677.)

In *Kolbenstangen* number 10 all work was supervised by "Meister" Malik, assisted by a Czech named Klechka. Once the German foreman lashed Tad's face so badly that the boy was nearly disfigured; he was saved by the intervention of an SS man. At other times, Tad remembered, Malik "spat in my face and tore my clothes. He even prevented me from going to the toilet." This was a grave penalty, for the youth, like nearly all his co-workers, suffered from dysentery. It was an inevitable consequence of their diet, and those who failed to recover from it disappeared up the camp chimney. Malik had no patience with their disability. When a man spent too long in the toilet, the German ordered the Kapo to follow him and spray him with cold water until he returned. In sub-zero temperatures this could be more dangerous than mutilation, yet the SS did not interfere. Malik was administering what had become an established chastisement. "My case was in no way special," the boy later deposed. "Many of the Krupp personnel acted the same way, and all the prisoners suffered the same fate."

His own crisis came less than two months after the death of his uncle. Inflamed by Tad's frequent trips to the *Wasser-Klosett*, Malik decided to make an example of him; on the German's command, the Kapo drenched him. Tad's resistance was low. That night his fever rose. He dreaded the *Revier* (sick bay), for most prisoners who reported there were never seen again. Tad kept working; then one day he fell out of the morning march and was returned to Fünfteichen. In sick bay he quickly learned why so few patients were cured. There was no medical care. For every bunk, there were two and sometimes three prisoners. Patients were forced to sleep in turns. The nearest latrine was in another building a hundred yards away, and since everyone admitted to the *Revier* was forced to surrender his clothes, inmates were obliged to sprint naked through the bitter cold. Those too weak to go were told to move their bowels in their bunks. Tad never did that (though he had to share a pallet fouled by others), but undoubtedly his condition was grim; "After the first few days I began spitting blood," he subsequently declared, though, "To this day I do not know what I was suffering from, for no doctor bothered to examine me, either upon arrival or during my stay in the hospital." Had a physician seen him, the diagnosis under these circumstances would most likely have been dysentery *and* pulmonary tuberculosis.

His youth and his constitution brought him back from the brink, through three more seasons on the factory floor, and past the anniversary of his uncle's cremation. By now the mood of the Germans had altered dramatically; their confidence in the future had been supplanted by blind panic. The foremen heard Berlin broadcasts announce that the Wehrmacht had abandoned Tannenberg, blowing up the huge war memorial. DNB warned of *Terrorbomber* all over the Reich, and here in Silesia, Marshal Ivan S. Koniev's First Ukrainian Army was pushing back Army

Group Center and preparing to breach the Oder. Breslau was doomed, and with it, Markstädt.

Here the recollections of another eyewitness are pertinent. Dr. Paul Hansen, a brilliant Krupp engineer who had joined the firm in 1929 and who later retired in Essen, spangled with honors, on January 1, 1963, was the master builder of the Berthawerk. He was never told to evacuate it — "As usual," he dryly remarked to this writer, "the order was to stay there to the last man." Amazingly, there *was* a last man. Hansen had left, but one of his draftsmen was still in a Berthawerk office, toiling diligently. The telephone on his desk rang; he picked it up and found himself talking to a Russian down the hall. Somehow he got out with a half-hour to spare. It is worth noting that after the war his superior directed first the rebuilding of the Essen plants, and then Krupp's *Industriebau* department, which profitably erects steel plants in underdeveloped countries, "the same sort of thing," Hansen explains, "that we did in Markstädt. In 1945 the Berthawerk seemed to be a complete loss. Actually it was excellent experience."[8]

The captivity of Tad Goldsztajn ended at Gross Rosen, another concentration camp southeast of Liegnitz. The SS, less optimistic than the procrastinatory draftsman, had marched its prisoners, now a hodgepodge of Jews, Poles, and Russians, into safer territory. Very shortly, however, the lightning thrusts of Koniev's advance made all Silesia unsafe. In the general disorder Tad fled. He stumbled through the terrified towns of Thuringia, found asylum with an American army motorized patrol, and eventually made a new life for himself in another country, under another name. Unlike Hansen, he finds no saving grace in the Markstädt experiment; like most other survivors of Krupp enslavement he remains embittered. Although he was graduated from a university and has become a successful financier, he cannot forget those he left behind in Fünfteichen's gas chamber. He is, he says, "one speaking for thousands." As late as 1951, when he was living in a dormitory, two fellow students entered his room and, finding him dozing, waggishly shouted *"Aufstehen!"* Afterward Tad recalled that "I rolled out of my bed, hit the floor, and sprang to attention. We all realized it was no joke." Even now he drifts off at night hearing the cadence *Links . . . Links . . . Links.* Sleeping on his stomach, he sometimes dreams of broken spectacles.

✠   ✠   ✠

In fleeing alone and never retracing his wartime steps, Tad is a typical *Sklavenarbeit* survivor. Today he remembers but one German from those days: the Krupp selector at Auschwitz, who later appeared from time to time in the Berthawerk. Time has reduced the others to shadows. It is unlikely that he would even recognize Meister Malik today, and since he knows no other survivor of Fünfteichen or the Berthawerk, there is no one to jog his memory. But there are survivors with common memories —

among them a Dutch student, a radio technician, and a priest whose experiences crisscrossed in wartime Essen. Unlike Tad, they testified at Nurenberg, and since their stories were mutually supportive they made a strong impression upon the tribunal.

In January 1943 Hendrik Scholtens, a nineteen-year-old youth who had been born in the Netherlands East Indies of Dutch parents, was studying aeronautical engineering in southwestern Holland.[9] Scholtens was in Delft, at Julianalaan 99, when he received a notice from The Hague's Gewestlijk Arbeidsbureau (Provincial Labor Office) ordering him, in the name of Dr. Arthur Seyss-Inquart, to report for work in Germany. The student knew Seyss-Inquart only by his nickname — "the Butcher Governor of Holland" — but he was fully aware of the implications of the summons. Accordingly, he instantly applied for a six-months student deferment and, once it had been granted, cast about for help. Unfortunately he was alone in the world. His parents couldn't help; they had been trapped on Borneo and were prisoners of the Japanese. Lacking money, unable to contact the underground, he nevertheless postponed the inevitable for six months after the expiration of his deferment. Then, early in the new year, his last excuse was rejected. Reporting to The Hague, he was sent to Willi Messerschmitt's Flugzeugwerke in Mannheim to make fighter planes. Scholtens remained there just ten days. Then, unwisely, he escaped. On January 31, 1944, while trying to recross the Netherlands border, he was picked up and shipped straight to the Hauptverwaltungsgebäude, where the SS turned him over to the Werkschutz. His coat, tie, belt, and watch were confiscated with the explanation that they were "luxury articles"; his sleeves were cut off above the elbow; and for the next four hours he and a group of other newcomers were marched through the winter afternoon to Neerfeldschule, or, as it was known to insiders, Neerfeld X.

Neerfeldschule, like Dechenschule, was a punishment camp. The slaves were housed in a two-story school building surrounded by two rows of barbwire with a brick wall between the rows. This wasn't Fünfteichen: the guards wore *die Firma*'s blue, not SS black. In the rather awkward phrasing of Scholtens's English affidavit, "Neerfeld X was a Krupp camp. With the exception of the camp leader, who wore civilian clothes — he however wore a badge which had the word Krupp on — all the guards had the word Krupp on their caps, and some of them had a band round the sleeve which also had the word Krupp on it." Otherwise, however, the stockade could easily have been taken for one of Himmler's Schutzstaffel camps. The new prisoners were assigned numbers and stripped nude. A guard saw Scholtens trying to keep a snapshot of his mother and father, seized it and tore it up, and beat him about the face and head until he bled. The youth struggled into his yellow-striped convict clothes, but when ordered into a barber's chair for a prison haircut he was too dazed to respond promptly. Inferring that he was holding back, two Krupp men fell upon him, ripped off his jacket, and thrashed his back with rubber truncheons until he collapsed. After that, he and others were, in his words, "kicked to a room opposite the administration, where my hair was shaved off. This shaving was done with a knife without any previous soaping. The result was that after this treatment we walked about with bleeding heads."

The old schoolhouse had been damaged by bombs. There really wasn't enough room for the slaves already there, so the fresh *Gruppe* was sent to the cellar. Most of the floor was covered with several inches of water, but because it was uneven there were a few dry spots. The newcomers had been chattels less than a day; nevertheless, they had already been reduced to animals. A ghastly fight broke out for these precious patches — it was to recur each night — and Scholtens heard one guard remark to another, *"Das ist recht schön, sie erziehen sich selber"* (That's fine, they educate themselves). Next morning they were routed out before daybreak. After standing at attention in the snow for two hours in their thin clothing, they were marched back into Essen to repair bomb damage. It hardly seemed worth the trip. They didn't arrive until noon, and the hike back required another four hours. Under such a regimen, Saur's 2,909 calories scarcely seem excessive, yet when food appeared that evening (for the first time in two days), it was the familiar bowl of "warm water with cabbage leaves," accompanied by a single slice of black bread. Once a week, older slaves told Scholtens, they would also receive a smear of margarine, a smear of jam, and a small sausage.

He knew that wouldn't be enough. One veteran suggested to him that he search Neerfeldschule's straw pallets for mice — "However horrible, this will be the only fresh food you will be able to get hold of." The student thought he must be joking. Yet as the nocturnal chaos was repeated again and again, with filthy prisoners brawling in the dark over a few feet of dry floor and sick prisoners doubled up in the water fighting cramps (use of the toilet was forbidden until dawn) the revolting advice seemed less disgusting. Obviously Scholtens wasn't going to last long this way. He could see what was happening to weaker men: "When there were enough sick people they were put on a truck till the floor of the truck was covered. They vanished from the camp, and I never saw them again." The youth was determined to avoid that sort of exit at all costs, so he and another Dutchman began stalking mice in earnest. Finally they found one.

At Nuremberg these little episodes appeared to disturb the defense far more than the larger implication — the disappearance of the ill men. Under cross-examination an incredulous Krupp lawyer challenged Scholtens's account of what the attorney called this "particularly unsavory incidents":

Q: Can you describe in detail how you caught the mouse?

A: Yes. We were terribly hungry in those days . . . we became a little bit crazy, so to speak, and were looking for anything that could be eaten. And we saw other prisoners eating, and just seeing one chewing made us more hungry for something. And they said, "Well, you can eat it, too." Well, there were lots of those mice in the straw beds, and my friend and I, we got one, and although we didn't eat it with appetite, we did try to.

Q: You caught the mouse with your own hands?

A: Yes, of course I did.

Q: And on the following day, as you say, you cooked it in the factory?

A: Yes.

Q: Did you have the possibility of so doing?

A: Yes. Near the works we found some wood and we made a fire. Sometimes we were allowed to make a fire when it was terribly cold, and in the iron saucepan which we always carried with us when there was something to put in it we, so to say, fried it in order not to eat it raw.

Q: I'd like to ask one more question on this subject. A mouse has a skin. Did you skin the mouse before you cooked it?

A: Of course, we ate only the meat.

Q: Did you have tools to do that?

A: Well, not tools, but pieces of glass and little iron pieces we could always find around the grounds.[10]

The lawyer moved on, which is too bad, for the issue wasn't really resolved. Mouse meat is largely protein; Scholtens's share of the catch could hardly have kept him going long. Nor did it. Six weeks after his arrival in Essen he became feverish, fainted, and awoke with double pneumonia. The truck looked unavoidable now, but he was saved by a bureaucratic freak. Scholtens was an escapee. Legally he was a Messerschmitt slave. Krupp couldn't dispose of another industrialist's property. Therefore the fever-racked student, whose weight had dropped to ninety-seven pounds, was transferred, via a transit camp and Heidelberg, to Mannheim town prison, where he slowly recovered.

✠ ✠ ✠

On April 4, 1944, when Scholtens was returned to his rightful owner, the radio technician and the priest were still at large in the Low Countries. Indeed, they didn't even meet him until after the liberation of Europe. What tied his life to theirs was Neerfeldschule, where they were transferred that autumn after two months at Dechenschule, and a common ability to identify the men who had mistreated them there. It is precisely this sort of corroboration, the fitting together of thousands of tiny pieces in the immense jigsaw puzzle of Krupp slavery, which makes the 4,200 exhibits and the 13,454-page transcript of Alfried's Nuremberg trial so compelling. Because fragments of recollection are mutually supportive, the accounts of individual witnesses gain in credibility. Without that binding skein they would be dismissed as improbable or, in some instances, quite unbelievable.

Paul Ledoux did not astonish the court — like Scholtens, he is chiefly remembered for what in his case was called a "disagreeable topic" — and the attitude of Krupp's counsel suggests that they felt he belonged in captivity. Before the war Ledoux, a short, frail, bespectacled craftsman then in his mid-thirties, had owned his own radio shop in Brussels.[11] The Wehrmacht closed it down; men who could build transmitters were dangerous. Actually Ledoux, despite his meek appearance, was even more menacing to the Reich without his tubes and wires. By day an inconspicuous employee of the Brussels air raid defense network, he became a formidable resistance leader after dark. Ledoux was the man Scholtens should have reached when he wanted to evade conscription in 1943. For three years the resourceful technician provided the quarries of Sauckel and Speer with false papers, meanwhile publishing underground newspapers and organizing sabotage.

On the night of August 12, 1944, he was responsible for the destruction of all telephone lines in Luxembourg, cutting off German reinforcements hurrying to Paris. That was his greatest single coup. It was also his last. The Gestapo had been on his track for four months. In April he had fled his home a jump ahead of them, and he was roving Belgium under the assumed name of Delamarre when, just five days after his *pièce de résistance*, Belgian fascists picked him up in Lecambon railway station. The arrest seems to have been routine, however; the SD grilled him at length, but had they known who he really was he would have been executed. Instead, they appear to have concluded that he was another *Sklavenarbeit* draft dodger. No motive was given for his arrest, and on August 22 his interrogators, after scribbling NN beside his alias, dispatched him into the night and fog of the Ruhr.

Next day he arrived at Essen's Hauptbahnhof. His fighting days were over. A sensible man, he coolly examined Dechenschule's elaborate wire, heard the Werkschutz guards say they were ready to shoot to kill, and believed them. Even if he could concoct a plan, his fellow prisoners were too feeble to help him, and very soon he would be in the same condition. Therefore he took advantage of his deceptive appearance. Once he had been in a Belgian Red Cross first aid class, and during air raids he adopted the role of camp samaritan, tending wounds and telling the injured what they must do to avoid infection. He was so effective in the great raid of October 23–24, when Dechenschule was totally destroyed and its prisoners moved to Neerfeldschule, that the Lagenführer named him camp *Sanitäter* (medic), and it was in that capacity that he testified at Nuremberg.

His appointment had been necessary, Ledoux explained: except for the voluntary ministrations of German nuns the slaves had been without medical attention. He cited cases of men who had died for lack of care and tersely described the only occasion when his pleas for professional advice had been answered. "The physician was drunk," he said. "He listened in on the heartbeat of the body." In fact, he explained to the tribunal, the doctor had been so intoxicated that he hadn't realized that there was no heartbeat there; before his arrival Ledoux himself had pronounced the patient dead of diphtheria. After that, Neerfeldschule was not visited by any Krupp physician, drunk or sober. The Belgian *Sanitäter*, equipped with only the most elementary knowledge of tourniquets and artificial respiration, coped alone with casualties which would have strained the facilities of a general hospital's emergency room.

Krupp's lawyers protested that the bombings were to blame for this sort of thing; RAF *Terrorbomber* had been destroying camps, homes, German civilians, and *Fremdarbeiter* alike — Alfried hadn't created this chaos and couldn't be held responsible for it. Ledoux's really damning evidence, however, was an account of Dechenschule's dispensary *before* the 4,500-ton October bomb raid and his subsequent appointment as medic. *Die Firma*, he dryly told the court, had decided how many slaves would be permitted to be sick at any given time. The figure was 10 percent. Unfortunately, Dechenschule at that time was inhabited by four hundred prisoners, and the dispensary had not forty beds but six, one of which was occupied by the German medic who preceded Ledoux as *Sanitäter*. Ledoux was assigned to room 2A, directly above the dispensary and divided from it by a floor of planks with large gaps between them. Room 2A was almost a war crime in itself. Within it were forty slaves "who were," he said, "locked in that room during the whole of the night; to accomplish their human needs," he went on, "they had only two jelly pots, and these jelly pots served as night pots for all of these forty men — big jelly cans, but as the food contained lots of liquid (it mainly consisted of soup), and as also most of the inmates from the very beginning suffered from dysentery, or at least a disease very similar to it, these two pots were absolutely inadequate for the forty men who had to perform their needs and, therefore, the results were what one can imagine." Even the dullest of the guards came to grasp the implications; "*Wie viele sind heute nacht krepiert?*" they would shout in the morning — "How many of you died during the night?" Ledoux's cross-examiner asked whether anyone had protested. Someone had; the Krupp medic had. At roll calls, Ledoux related, "the *Sanitäter* would complain to the guard that, for instance, urine had again come down from the room above, into the dispensary." Dissatisfied, the German lawyer persisted with such questions as "Could it come through the ceiling?" and "Did the ceiling have holes or cracks in it?" Although all this had been explained in rather more detail than the even least squeamish members of the prosecution staff thought necessary, the defense insisted upon pursuing this "disagreeable topic."

It was a familiar pattern during the war crime trials. Whether from disbelief or because the defense counsel, following continental judicial procedure, were anxious to make certain that the tribunal had all the facts, the cross-examination drove home the point until the revolting scene was graven upon the minds of all present — the twoscore men in 2A staggering to the two brimming slop jars, the semiliquid feces spreading across the crude boards and dripping on the feverish patients below, the sound and stench of seeping sewage in the night. Because of their unusual attainments, a great many of Dechenschule's prisoners would have been welcome guests in Villa Hügel five years earlier. Now, a block away from the Altendorferstrasse route Alfried followed in his drives between the castle and the office, they were forced to defecate upon their own sick. Had any groom deprived the family thoroughbreds of their balanced oats, he would have been instantly dismissed and sent to look for a job elsewhere. Of course, he wouldn't have had much trouble. There were always openings in the Werkschutz.

✠   ✠   ✠

Nineteen years after Bomber Command's annihilation of Dechenschule the author was having tea in the palace of Dr. Franz Hengsbach, the vigorous young Roman Catholic Archbishop of Essen, surrounded by sacred local relics — some dating back nine hundred years — which had miraculously survived all the raids. Overhead hung portraits of the last two lady-abbesses to rule the city before Napoleon's arrival in 1802 and of Pope Pius XII. The archbishop himself, wearing his scarlet cap, his purple robe trimmed with scarlet piping, and the bright crucifix at his waist, seemed to belong to another age.[12]

But not for long. Outside, a six-foot neon sign atop the Hotel Handelshof acclaimed West Germany's economic comeback — ESSEN DIE EINKAUFSSTADT (ESSEN THE SHOPPING CENTER) — and through a tinted window one could glimpse, directly across the street, the hulk of the city's former synagogue and present exhibition hall for samples of the latest Ruhr products. Even the Church offered no sanctuary from the throbbing spirit of the Ruhrgebeit, nor did its dynamic local prelate wish it to. On his finger twinkled a ring set with a piece of coal from Alfried's Hannover-Hannibal mine, and on his table lay a copy of *Kreuz über Kohle und Eisen*, an account of the fruitful union between Cross, Coal and Iron. At the mention of Alfried himself, His Excellency sighed affectionately, "*Ach, Krupp! Die drei Ringe!*"

He explained. Although the dynasty has never been joined with Rome, over half the population of greater Essen is Catholic, and informal ties between Villa Hügel and the Vatican began with the charitable work of Margarethe Krupp and Bertha Krupp. They were quickly strengthened; when Gustav was imprisoned in 1923, a thirty-seven-year-old monsignor visited his cell and begged the French to release him. In September 1962 the same dignitary, now Gustavo Cardinal Testa and a papal delegate, traveled to Hügel to confer upon Alfried a gold *Gedenkmedaille*, or commemorative medallion, in the name of the pontiff.[13] The dynasty's ecclesiastical admirers could easily have remained silent during its hour of trial. They preferred to speak out strongly. Essen did not become a diocese until ten years after Alfried's conviction, but on March 14, 1948, when the prosecution's presentation of its case was approaching a climax in Nuremberg, Josef Cardinal Frings, the sexagenarian Archbishop of Cologne, delivered a forthright address in ruined Essen, declaring, "When I refer to Krupp and to the family of Krupp, I mean those things which have made Essen as big as it is now. I believe I may say that this firm and this family has always showed great social understanding and cared very much for the welfare of their workers and employees. I know that all the people in Essen have been proud of being Krupp workers, employees, and officials. If there is anyone entitled to be an honorable citizen of the city of Essen, then surely it is the head of this house." The prelate contended that he did not want to influence the tribunal. However, he expressed confidence that "nobody will think ill of me if I say I feel very deeply for the fate of this family who was once so well thought of."[14]

If anyone thought ill of the speech he kept quiet, and Dr. Hengsbach, arriving in the Ruhr a decade after the defendant's conviction, became increasingly impressed by the family's contributions to Catholicity since Krupp's release from prison. Alfried donated the largest stained-glass window in Essen's cathedral; played a major role in the reconstruction of Münster-in-Westfalen's nearby church, which had been largely destroyed during the Lancaster raids; contributed heavily to a Catholic hospital and to the Catholic University in Tokyo; and sponsored an exhibition of early Christian art in Villa Hügel, to which the Pope had sent an emissary. Reviewing the Konzernherr's gifts, His Excellency told this writer, "A Bishop of Essen can only be grateful to Alfried Krupp." Indeed, in discussing Rolf Hochhuth's controversial *Der Stellvertreter* (*The Deputy*) over tea, Dr. Hengsbach displayed almost as much indignation over Hochhuth's treatment of Krupp as over his depiction of Pius XII. Reminded that the play had been dedicated to the memory of Father Maximilian Kolbe, inmate number 16670 at Auschwitz, he replied that that was irrelevant; told that Alfried had maintained his own concentration camps in this very city, *Seine Exzellenz* shook his head and answered sharply, "Slave labor was a Nazi crime. It had nothing to do with Krupp."

✠    ✠    ✠

The Archbishop's assertion would have surprised Father Alphonse
Charles Gyseline Come,[15] who had been immured at Dechenschule KZ as
inmate number 137, who shared his fate with two other Roman Catholic
priests from the Low Countries, and who often returns to the site of the
camp, now marked by a small gray stone to which a brass plate has been
affixed. The inscription reads:

> Am 23, 10 1944
> Starben Hier
> Für die Freiheit
> 61 Europäer
>
> On October 23, 1944
> Here perished
> For freedom
> 61 Europeans

A group of German laymen drafted the inscription, which never seems
to arouse the curiosity of the children skipping past, perhaps because it is
so bland. Even the nationality of the slain Europeans is missing. Father
Come is a source of greater detail. He was the author of *Témoignage sur
les Camps de Dechenschule et Neerfeld*, the clandestine diary crammed
with charts and statistics which he wrote in the dark during his captivity
and concealed between planks, and which was being scrutinized in Nuremberg as a major prosecution affidavit even as Cardinal Frings supported
Alfried — a difference of opinion which some may impute to the tugs of
chauvinism, but which may also be traceable to the gulf between members
of the Roman Catholic Church.

Father Come, not being a monsignor, never met Krupp. Today he is
shepherd of a small flock in Leignon, Belgium, one of those tiny Meuse
towns of crooked lanes and weathered stone which have never capitulated
to the twentieth century, and in the summer of 1944 his parish was Smuid,
thirty-five miles east of Bastogne and even smaller than Leignon. His war,
he thought then, had ended with the surrender of King Leopold III four
years earlier. At that time Alphonse Come had been a chaplain in His
Majesty's army, a tall, slender man with an intense, ascetic expression
whose features, in contemporary photographs, always seem drawn to a
point. Krupp's lawyers tried strenuously to identify him with the Belgian
resistance — they never abandoned the position that preslavery underground activity was a mitigating factor — but in his case they hadn't much
luck. When Paul Ledoux spoke in the witness box of "my three other
comrades, one of whom was Father Come,"[16] he was merely describing a
relationship forged in the KZ crucible. He had never met them before, and

under normal circumstances would never have been in a position to refer to the priest as a comrade. The father in Smuid never forged papers, bombed bridges, or destroyed Wehrmacht communications. Under Nuremberg cross-examination the most he would concede was that "As a Catholic priest it was my duty to oppose the tendency turning the world into pagans . . . the haven of the German army." On a continent ruled by swastika, Generalstab and Schlotbarone, that may have been considered subversive, yet it hardly ranks with Ledoux's exploits.

Another of Father Come's duties as vicar was to rise early on the humid morning of August 15, 1944, and prepare for the Feast of the Assumption, the annual commemoration of the Virgin Mary's miraculous ascent into heaven. Of all days upon which a Catholic priest might anticipate arrest — assuming that there are such occasions — this was among the least likely. Even the Wehrmacht honored the holy day; a hundred and sixty-five miles away in Antwerp Cathedral, Rubens's painting depicting the Assumption had been carefully sequestered against the possibility of damage, and similar frescoes by Correggio and Gaudenzio Ferrari had been provided with elaborate cushions to absorb bomb shock. Unluckily for European clerics, however, there was a curious ditheism in the conqueror's mood. During the ten weeks since the Normandy landings guerrilla activity had waxed from the Waddenzee to Vichy France, and in each guilty community German reprisals had been directed at those most highly esteemed by their neighbors. The violated corpse of Kaj Munk, one of the continent's most revered clergymen, had been left on a road with a placard reading *Schwein, du hast dennoch für Deutschland gearbeitet* (Swine, you worked for Germany just the same) pinned to its frock, and small Belgian towns had become accustomed to black-bordered red posters:

Cowardly criminals in the pay of England and Moscow killed the Feldkommandant of Mol on the morning of July 2, 1944. Until now the assassins have not been arrested. As retribution for this murder I have ordered that fifty hostages be shot, beginning with . . . Fifty more hostages will be shot should the guilty still be at large at midnight July 25, 1944 [*Falls die Täter nicht bis zum Ablauf des 25 Juli 1944 ergriffen sind, werden . . . weitere fünfzig Geiseln erschossen werden*].

Early in August a subtle policy shift had been adopted by the occupation authorities responsible for the Low Countries. As Alfried's tribunal noted, "brutal recruitment drives were conducted in Belgium"; beloved citizens were engulfed by NN, and these "were employed by the Krupp firm."[17] One such operation was directed at the Ardennes. On the eve of the Assumption an adjutant to General Alexander von Falkenhausen, military governor of the country, juggling a red crayon, had pondered a map of the forest. His deliberations finished, he had drawn a large red circle around all

Luxembourg province, and troop movements into the Ardennes were complete when, at 5:10 the next morning, Father Come escorted his mother into their front hall, on their way to church. The cleric's sister Eugénie went first. Before opening the door she glanced through a window and clapped her hand over her mouth. *"Les allemands!"* she shrieked. Her brother stared out. Sure enough; the vicarage was surrounded by the Führer's soldiers, armed and in battle dress. Every exit from the village had been blocked, and the mayor, the town clerk, two magistrates, and two councillors, most of them still in their nightshirts, were being led toward a truck. Father Come stepped outside and was seized by a Wehrmacht corporal. The noncom yelled, *"Sie sind verhaftet!"* (You are under arrest!), and when the bewildered vicar asked why, he was merely told that it was an order.

Another order directed that the prisoners, accompanied only by overnight bags, be transported to Germany. First, however, they were driven sixty miles south and delivered to Arlon Prison, near the border. Arlon had become famous as the Bastille of the resistance — Ledoux had been held there by the SD for two days — but its cells had never before been graced by so much eminence. At noonday the prison yard looked like a convention of the province's leaders. "In the neighboring village, ten more were taken, ten more in another village nearby and twelve in another village," Father Come would later testify. And so it went: the mayors, the clergy, the medical profession, the attorneys and the scholars had been singled out for banishment. The guards treated them like their predecessors. Paris rose on August 25 (a black day for Alfried — Staff Sergeant Norbert Barr, a middle-aged Austrian-American who had been Paris correspondent of the *Berliner Tageblatt* before the war, led a team of four U.S. VII Corps intelligence men to 141 Boulevard Haussmann and seized Krupp's files), but no word of the revolt penetrated Arlon's ancient stone walls. At four that morning the inmates were roused and told to change their clothes. A guard ordered Father Come and the other two priests to discard their soutanes. As they entrained an officer told them that whatever the outcome of the war their epitaph would be *Schwein, du hast dennoch für Deutschland gearbeitet.*

*Was sonst noch?* one of the swine asked timidly. The blazing answer was, never mind what next; he would find out soon enough. They all found out at 5:30 P.M., when they tumbled out of boxcars in Essen's Hauptbahnhof and formed ranks beside the tracks. A Wehrmacht *Feldwebel* ran his eye over them, then burst into laughter. "Now you are going to work for Krupp, and for you that is going to be boom! boom! boom!" he cried. Since they looked mystified, the sergeant explained, "I mean *bombing!*" The Belgians remained baffled. He left chortling at his little joke, and a fresh detachment of armed men marched them off toward Hindenburgstrasse.

An hour later the Belgians began to understand: they were issued blankets into which the firm's *drei Ringe* had been woven. Dressed in yellow-striped gray-blue burlap adorned with the same three rings, they were assigned to Dechenschule's room 2A, with its two gigantic chamber pots and its profusion of filth.

At 8:30 that evening the door was chained and padlocked and the nightly torment of the sick men below them began. Eight hours later the chain rattled, the door burst open, and a squad of blue-uniformed men skidded in on the accumulation of waste, yelling, "*Wie viele sind heute nacht krepiert?*" and "*Aufstehen!*" and lashing out in the dark with rubber hoses. The daily routine had begun. The prisoners were due at a Siemens-Martin furnace before six o'clock, and before then they had to clean up the mess on the floor. That very evening, after twelve hours of dragging hundred-pound bags of cement up and down forty steps, Father Come began drafting his statement; within a week he had made a fair start. His tone was objective:

> This camp, surrounded by walls lined with barbwire, was guarded in military style day and night by armed men of the Werkschutz. The inmates were marched in different groups to and from their work in various Krupp shops by armed Werkschutz men, who kept them under surveillance during work [*Les hommes étaient menés et remenés de travail, en différents kommandos, à plusieurs ateliers de Krupp, par des Werkschutz armés qui surveillaient durant le travail*]. . . . There were two daily roll calls, one in the morning and one in the evening. Their food was the same as that served to the lowest classification of prisoners from the east (bowls of watery soup and some bread, without extras).[18]

It had taken him a while to realize that he had been singled out for special attention. Only priests, so far as he could see, were expected to stagger up and down staircases lugging concrete. The heaviest work was assigned to them. By turn he moved 110-pound ingots at Martin Works I, swung a pick for Krupp's *Stollenbau* (tunnel construction), installed barbed wire at camps and put iron bars in the windows, pushed crates in detachment ABA (*Apparatenbau Abteilung*, apparatus manufacture), carted away debris, dug trenches, and cleaned Werkschutz quarters. Wherever he worked he carried the heaviest loads, was given the dirtiest tasks, and received the shortest breaks. Wondering whether he had violated any regulations, he searched his memory. He couldn't recall any infractions. Then he realized that whenever one of his fellow slaves called him *mon père, monsieur le curé,* or *l'abbé,* foremen would deliberately address him by number. "*Los, Hundertsiebenunddreissig! Rasch!*" they would call and No. 137 would obediently hurry over. He didn't mind the slight, though the use of *Stücke* to describe all the Belgians offended him deeply.

As distress grew in the camp his position became more and more awkward. Evasion of his priestly responsibilities was impossible. He had to give dying Catholics extreme unction, whatever the Werkschutz thought, and he wanted to say Mass. Repeatedly other prisoners begged the Lagerführer to grant this permission. The answer was always negative, and ultimately, as the *curé* later recalled, the commander "had me called to his office and repeated to me specifically the prohibition against fulfilling my religious duties under threat of the severest punishment that could exist, that is, capital punishment."[19] Because of Essen's huge Catholic population, some guards were members of the Church. Threatening a priest with death for praying dismayed them. They resented it, and secretly told Father Come so. One slipped him four marks, told him his name, asked that he pray for him; another gave him a tiny crucifix. But the official attitude toward No. 137 never changed.

The night of October 23–24, memorialized today on the playground plaque, was the busiest in the vicar's career. No one interfered with his final rites, either then or during the following forty-eight hours, when the critically injured succumbed one by one. The Werkschutz was giving the smoldering ruins a wide berth; as the priest noted, "The survivors remained for two days, always under the surveillance of their guards (*sous la surveillance de leure gardiens*), at a safe shelter some ten meters away from the ruins of the camp." That afternoon the walking wounded were marched to Neerfeldschule. Any new stockade, they uneasily assured one another, would be an improvement. They erred.

> Again, this camp was enclosed by barbwire fences, and there was wire mesh netting over the windows. . . . The camp was patrolled day and night by one or two armed sentries. . . . In fact, the situation at Neerfeld was far worse than that at Dechenschule. The abusive forced labor, the scraps of food doled out to the inmates, the complete lack of the most basic and fundamental hygienic and sanitary measures, as well as proper medical care, caused the death of dozens of prisoners for whom these circumstances made it impossible to procure from outside the camp the things they lacked [*causèrent la mort d'une douzaine de détenus qui avait été mis par ce régime, dans l'impossibilité de trouver hors du camp tout ce qui y manquait*].[20]

At Neerfeldschule the Belgians were introduced to certain *Sklavenarbeit* refinements. There was the official camp beater. There were also punitive visits to the camp, hitherto unheard of, by dissatisfied foremen who had been displeased with the performance of this or that slave during the day and who would drop by, after brooding in a corner *Bierstube*, to borrow a Werkschutz whip and thrash the miscreant; among such victims was

Ferdinand Thieltgen, who had been administrative assistant to the governor of Luxembourg province.

By now Father Come was rather out of things. He had become Fritz von Bülow's batman. (In one of Nuremberg's dramatic moments the gaunt cleric, once more wearing his soutane, faced his dwarfish ex-master across the courtroom and said evenly, "In my convict uniform with yellow stripes I even entered Herr von Bülow's Werkschutz office and . . . started the fire, though I hardly think he remembers that today."[21]) It was humiliating to serve as the personal slave of a man Hitler had designated *kruppscher Hauptabwehrbeauftragter;* nevertheless the priest now had greater opportunities to fill page after page of the graph paper he had filched with his tiny crabbed handwriting.* Though the cleric never glimpsed Krupp himself, Bülow was as close to the sole proprietor as any man in the Konzern. If he could understand Alfried's stand-in, the enslaved priest felt, he would come close to comprehending the heart of the darkness which was enveloping them all.

He failed. The rosy little Prussian patrician with restless hands and protruding eyeballs, whose name had been proudly borne for three centuries by ten Feldmarschalls, statesmen, writers and composers, remained an enigma. After one bombing Bülow "came to deliver a speech to us — incidentally, in excellent French — and from the way he talked to us it became apparent that if he wasn't the man who had our destiny in his hands, he was still the man who could shape our very existence down there. He promised us that we would have better housing facilities, better food. He said they had been mistaken concerning us. He congratulated us. He said that it wasn't Germany's fault that we had all these victims on account of the air raids, that the reason was the war, and that the war had been forced upon Germany by the Allies." Then, in his strange, hushed voice, Bülow asked any man with a complaint to speak up. After so many sticks this carrot was bewildering; the men were tongue-tied. Paul Ledoux wasn't, but he remained silent because, as he said afterward, he knew that "we were just beings who were being ordered around. We had nothing to ask." However, there was an articulate innocent among them. Taking the *Hauptabwehrbeauftragte* at his word, a Belgian named Decoune stepped toward the dais and reported that Werkschutz guards, themselves hungry, had been stealing the little food the prisoners had. Bülow departed hastily, looking hurt. After he had passed through the gate Decoune was turned over to the camp beater.†[22]

---

* Today the diary is almost illegible; Father Come had to decipher some blurred passages for the writer.

† Yet he had been justified. Die Firma's records reveal, "The SS complained that senior members of the Oberlagerführung were stealing the prisoners' sugar" (*Beschwerte sich die SS, dass die Oberlagerführung zu Unrecht Zucker einbehalten habe, der für die Ernährung die Gefangenen bestimmt war*). (NIK–7014.)

Alfried excepted, Bülow was to receive the stiffest sentence at the Krupp trial. If he accepts their verdict — and he does — so must we. Still, his guilt was not simple. More than anyone else in the history of the dynasty he evokes memories of Friedrich Alfred Krupp, and it is conceivable that his father, who had spent four years learning sophistry and intrigue from Fritz Krupp at the turn of the century, may have passed their subtleties along to his son. In his own way the plant police *Chef* of 1939–1945 was as wicked as Hassel, the SS Obersturmbannführer who was on Krupp's payroll as the Werkschutz's deputy chief, and upon whom Bülow blamed everything during his pretrial interrogations. Absentee scapegoats are always suspect. Bülow was in command. He was resourceful and imaginative. If, for example, he didn't hatch the scheme, he certainly knew about the plant police's disposal of the Belgians' Red Cross postcards on Christmas Day 1944, an exquisite psychological torture which Father Come still recalls as the cruelest moment in his imprisonment. When the cards were distributed the slaves had been jubilant. Though cynical of their wardens, they trusted the Red Cross and didn't see how anything could go wrong. Each man was allowed to address his own card to his family and set down exactly twenty-five words. After the guards' collection the prisoners never expected to see them again until the peace.

But they did see them, or what was left of them, whether by design or accident. It was their lean priest who made the discovery. In the charred embers of a stove fire over which the Werkschutz leaders had warmed their hands, Bülow's minion found bits and pieces, each with its laboriously written fragment of tender message. The Belgians had thought they were giving those closest to them a merry Christmas just by letting them know they were still alive. Each had hoarded his twenty-five-word ration and spent it in love. And then the Krupp guards had kindled them. Worse: they had permitted the slaves to know of it so that each would face 1945 seared by the knowledge that his fate remained cloaked in night, fog, and worse.[23]

# 22

✠

## Noth kennt kein Gebot

IN the late spring of 1884 a destitute Scandinavian woman had rapped on the great door of Villa Hügel and been turned away by servants of the great Kanonenkönig. That evening she had written Alfred directly. The prospect of a foreign woman in trouble had touched him, and he had forwarded her appeal to Pieper with instructions that she was to be paid 1,000 marks from petty cash:

> Von einer hier bereits abgewiesenen Norwegerin erhalte ich solben dies Schreiben. Es kann ja alles Lüge und sie kann schlecht sein, aber es ist ja auch möglich, dass sie nur einmal leichtsinnig war und verstossen wurde von der Familie. . . . Noth kennt kein Gebot.

> I have just received this letter from a Norwegian lady who has already been ejected from here. It may be all lies, and she may be wicked, but it is also possible that she has been indiscreet once and has been turned out by her family. She speaks here of jumping into the Rhine. — Even assuming that she is worthless, it might be that she could be saved, and that would still be worthwhile. First, she must be rescued from the menace of going under through indigence, dying of hunger, losing her mind, or yielding to vice. Necessity knows no law.[1]

Krupp solicitude had been the family's pride ever since; the assertion that they cared deeply about the welfare of others was stressed by commissioned historians and splashed across company brochures. It still is. Yet there was a time when Alfred's great-grandson not only abandoned helpless women from abroad, but exploited them, abused them, and then left them to a doom far more unspeakable than the turbid gray waters of the Rhine. The bonfire of the Third Reich was rapidly being reduced to embers. No sources of manpower were left and so, necessity knowing no law, Krupp turned to girls, to mothers, and, in the end, to the construction of a private concentration camp for children.

✠ ✠ ✠

In February 1944 Hendrik Scholtens had found himself working beside Jewish girls from Hungary. Although conversation was forbidden, the youth managed a whispered exchange with one of them. Later she passed him a note. "She wrote me," he later recalled, "that she had been arrested in Budapest during a *Razzia* (police raid), and that she was a Jewess."[2]

This is baffling. *Judenmaterial* came to Essen relatively late in the war. Hungary was near the bottom of Adolf Eichmann's timetable; the first official *Razzia* was carried out that spring. According to a deposition from SS Hauptsturmführer Dieter Wisliceny, who was present, Eichmann's Budapest meeting with Auschwitz's Höss to work out the details came "in June or July 1944" — at least two months after Scholtens had left the Ruhr. The origin of the working party he encountered remains a mystery; there is no reference to it in extant documents, and one can only conclude that its victims had been swept up in a premature foray. One of Father Come's recollections is far more illuminating. Marching to Walzwerk I one September morning, his group was halted beside several hundred women waiting at the corner of Helenenstrasse and Bottroperstrasse. Despite guards and the linguistic barrier, the priest heard soft voices calling out in broken French. He caught the words *juif* and *Hongrie* and concluded that they were Hungarian Jewesses. He wondered where they worked and where their camp was.[3]

Today we know that and much more. The date, the intersection, and the clandestine calls identify them as surely as the vicar's soutane had identified him. That dawn 520 young women and girls were standing opposite the men from Dechenschule, ready to enter Krupp's Walzwerk II. Earlier in the year they had belonged to a community of some 300,000 Jews living in Hungary or in adjacent territory seized by Hungary after Munich. The fate which had originally been assigned to all of them is set forth in a sheaf of brisk letters which define the peculiar relationships that existed between Höss and German industry. The Auschwitz Lagerführer, having chosen Zyklon-B crystals as the most efficient means of dispatching human life, turned to the problem of crematoria and solicited bids from the makers of heating equipment. Several replied, for the competition in such commerce was intense. One firm claimed that its Dachau furnaces had provided "full satisfaction in practice" (*sich in der Praxis ausgezeichnet bewährt haben*). Another went into particulars, explaining:

> We propose the use of a simple metal fork, moving on cylinders, to put the cadavers into the furnace . . . We suggest light carts on wheels to

move the dead bodies from the storage points to the furnaces. Please note enclosed diagrams, drawn to scale [*Für den Transport der Leichen vom Aufbewahrungsraum bis vor die Öfen empfehlen wir, auf Rädern laufende leichte Transportgestelle zu verwenden und geben wir Ihnen auch für diese eine Masskizze*].[4]

The winner in the Auschwitz rivalry was Saxony's Firma I. A. Topf und Söhne, who, in a letter dated February 12, 1943, acknowledged Höss's approval with a businesslike reply addressed "*An die Zentralverwaltung der SS und Polizei, Auschwitz*," announcing under the letterhead that it would treat of "*Betr.: Krematorien für das zweite und dritte Gefangenenlager*" (Subject: Crematoria for camps two and three), and then going straight to the point:

> This is to acknowledge receipt of your order for five triple furnaces, together with two electric lifts for raising the corpses and one emergency elevator. Also ordered by you were two practical installations, one for stoking and the other for moving ashes [*für die Entfernung der Asche*].[5]

The Höss-Eichmann conference modified plans somewhat. Although the Lagerführer estimated that "only 20 or at the most 25 percent of these Hungarian Jews could be used for labor," including "women and some children aged twelve or thirteen," the SS was now committed to extermination through work, and Krupp selectors were already stationed at the KZ gate. In the early summer of 1944 the SS notified munitions firms that from fifty to sixty "Hungarian Jewesses" (*ungarische Jüdinnen*) would be available. Inquiring, Krupp was advised "to get in touch with the Buchenwald concentration camp on the subject of an allocation" (*sich direkt mit dem KZ Buchenwald in Verbindung zu setzen*) but told that the firm "must expect to take a certain number of women" (*mit einer Anzahl Frauen rechnen müsse*). Actually Krupp seems to have preferred feminine labor for certain tasks — "Our last request was for 700 women" read a July 28 note in Alfried's file summarizing a conference with a Buchenwald SS captain. The experience with Russian women had been encouraging, and that same month Standartenführer Pister, Buchenwald's Lagerführer, came to the Hauptverwaltungsgebäude for a detailed discussion of the proposed employment of Jewesses at the rolling mill.[6]

Those details, forwarded to Alfried by Bülow, provided that Krupp would sign the customary lease with the SS. The firm agreed to issue each girl one blanket in summer and two in winter. The girls would be housed in Humboldt, a camp twenty blocks from Dechenschule which had been evacuated recently by Italian military internees. Alfried's subordinates thought this compound admirable. "The main things" to be done, he was informed, "are the erection of a barbed wire fence in front of the hall which allows a small exit and the erection of a small barracks for the commander of the guard and his duty officer and for the German female guard personnel." Precisely why barbwire and guards had been unnecessary for Italian men but would be needed to pen in Jewish girls was unexplained, though the SS officer raised no objection. Inspecting Humboldtstrasse, however, he became dubious on other counts. For one thing, the quarters seemed cramped. This, he was assured, could be remedied by placing "three beds over each other, instead of two" (3 *Betten übereinander statt bisher* 2). Then there was the problem of distance. *Judenmaterial* coming from Auschwitz wore inadequate footgear, the Buchenwald commandant pointed out; the girls couldn't possibly march back and forth between Humboldtstrasse and Walzwerk II. Therefore he made the shipment conditional upon the firm's agreement to transport them by streetcar. Krupp agreed. Now all that remained was the actual selection of individual slaves — which brings us to the fantastic ordeal of the Roth sisters.[7]

☧    ☧    ☧

Today, in a dresser drawer directly over a Main Street grocery in a very small American town, a snapshot of a family group lies wrapped in tissue paper.[8] The picture was obviously posed, and in some ways it resembles a formal portrait of the Krupp family, painted in 1931 to mark the silver wedding anniversary of Gustav and Bertha, which hangs today in Villa Hügel's main hall. The chief difference is that the snapshot is more modest. The head of the household was well-to-do, but as a wholesale wine merchant he could scarcely afford the artistic talents of George Harcourt, and though the background is neat and attractive, it lacks the murals, vases, and hand-painted screens which distinguish the Krupp tableau.

The centerpiece in the photograph, a small sofa, is occupied by the family's parents — Ignatz Roth, bald and mustachioed, and his buxom, dark-haired wife, Maria. Children hover around them: six-year-old Irving, clinging to his mother's lap, and, behind the couch, Olga, seventeen, Elizabeth, fifteen, and Ernestine, thirteen. The sisters look eager and dutiful. Maria is sedate, and little Irving is restlessly biting his lip, but their father appears unaccountably stern. And here, perhaps, is another variation between Hügel's portrait and the picture in the bedroom dresser, a sign of the times. Although 1931 was a critical year for the Krupps, their expressions were blank; one cannot even tell whether Alfried wore an SS insignia, for his left shoulder is turned away from the artist. But Papa Roth may have been eying the lens severely because the photographer, his elder son Josef, was about to emigrate to Israel. Since the creation of Czechoslovakia in 1918, Ignatz and Maria had been proud of their Czechoslovak citizenship. Their home was in the center of Uzhorod, a prosperous city of thirty thousand; Uzhorod was the capital of Podkarpatská Rus province (Carpathian Russia — Ruthenia), at the eastern tip of the country; to Roth senior it seemed improbable that the echo of distant Teuton trumpets could reach Jews here.

Young Josef thought it probable. The time was early November 1938. Chamberlain had just struck his Czech bargain with Hitler, and on the last evening of September, General Alfred Jodl, then commanding an artillery division in Vienna, had jubilantly confided to his diary:

> The Pact of Munich has been signed. Czechoslovakia is through as a power factor [*Die Tschechoslowakei hat als Machtfaktor ausgespielt*]. . . . The Führer's genius and his resolve not to be cowed even by a world war have once more achieved a triumph without force. It is now to be hoped that this naïve, dubious and weak people have been converted and will remain converted.[9]

Because Josef was neither naïve, nor dubious, nor weak, he and the photograph he took exist today. In occupying the Sudetenland Hitler had, of course, guaranteed the integrity of the rest of Czechoslovakia, with, of course, no intention of keeping his word. Once the nation's "little Maginot Line" was in his hands, he swiftly moved to liquidate the rest of its provinces, absorbing most of them into the German Reich and throwing a few bones to greedy (and shortsighted) neighbors. Ruthenia was such a bone. Uzhorod lay two hundred miles from Germany, but the Hungarian army, now massed on the border, was a few hours' march to the south. Ties tightened between Berlin and Budapest until, on March 14, 1939, alarmed Ruthenians proclaimed their independence and begged the Führer for protection. They were too late. After the war Allied intelligence officers sifting the Reich's diplomatic files found a communication from Miklós Horthy to Hitler, dated March 13, thanking him for the award of Ruthenia:

> Excellency! Heartfelt gratitude! [*Eure Exzellenz! Herzlichen Dank!*] I cannot tell you how overjoyed I am, for this headwater region is, for Hungary — I dislike verbosity — a critical issue. . . . We are tackling it zealously. Orders have been cut. Thursday, the 16th, there will be a border incident [*Grenzzwischenfall*] and then an all-out offensive.[10]

Why wait? Hitler replied, and the delighted Hungarian regent agreed. At 6 A.M. Wednesday his troops broached the frontier. The Republic of Carpatho-Ukraine had lasted less than twenty-four hours. There hadn't even been time to design a flag; from the sidewalk outside their home the stunned Roth family watched Hungary's colors rise over the buildings of the provincial government. Now their people were officially designated as inferior, and the city's new rulers made certain that they never forgot it. Elizabeth and Ernestine were expelled from school; the family was watched. One Friday afternoon Papa Roth, walking home with Elizabeth, saw a strange official slapping the child of a friend. He protested, and when the man said the boy had been fishing without a license, Ignatz told him the offense hardly justified a public beating. Next day policemen appeared at the Roths' door and took the wine merchant away. He was accused of making derogatory remarks about Hungarians, found guilty, and sentenced to three months' imprisonment.

On the day he was freed the family began to plan an escape. Olga was needed to help her father at the office, but Elizabeth pored over German and English grammar books at home, and Ernestine and Irving attended a Hebrew school each day, studying geography. The Roths hoped to join Josef; the more they knew about foreign countries, and the greater their knowledge of foreign languages, the better their chances would be. It was a pathetic scheme, because it was doomed. The same dream was alive in tens of thousands of other Jewish homes, and the SS knew it. To identify potential fugitives, *Judenmaterial* were required to wear the yellow Star of David. The desperate Uzhorod plots went on, but all were foiled. The penultimate step was taken in April 1944. Eviction notices were served; Jews were gathered in a ghetto, taking with them only what they could carry. For some inexplicable reason, as the warehouses of Auschwitz were later to reveal, wearers of the yellow star throughout eastern Europe tended to choose two items of apparel which have since passed from fashion. The men and boys wore cloth caps, the women and girls rubber galoshes, and in retrospect those caps and galoshes (together with the stuffed toys clutched by children) have become symbols of their martyrdom. Films taken by the officers who were herding them together show the multitudes passing in confused array, cap visors tugged low over foreheads, unbuttoned galoshes flapping in the bright sunlight of what was, for virtually all of Ruthenia's Jewry, their last spring.

The six Roths were among them. Ignatz and Maria had changed little since 1938, and though Irving was now twelve, he was small for his age; with his narrow, pinched face he could have passed for nine. But the daughters had blossomed. Olga, Elizabeth and nineteen-year-old Ernestine — the two younger sisters had been born just fourteen months apart — were pretty, graceful, and alert, if somewhat frail. Marching toward the railroad station, none of them had the remotest idea of what lay ahead. Elsewhere word of what "resettlement" meant had spread from city to city, but this farthest tip of what had been Czechoslovakia was too remote. Even the pretty picture postcards which were distributed among them for mailing to relatives aroused no suspicion; the fact that they were instructed to write identical messages on the back was dismissed as a typical German quirk. In that province some villages spoke Hungarian, some Slovakian, some Czech (a Slovakian offshoot). The officers knew that the language of Uzhorod was Czech, and these Jews were therefore told to write: "*Máme se velmi dobré zde. Pracujeme a kazdy je dobry a milý knam. Ocekavame vaš přijezd*" (We are doing very well here. We have work and are well treated. We await your arrival).[11]

"In May 1944," Hannah Arendt later wrote of Auschwitz, "the trains began arriving from Hungary right on schedule. Very few 'able-bodied men' among the passengers were selected for labor, and these few were put to work in Krupp's."[12] That sounds orderly. Actually it was chaotic. Höss's *Vernichtungslager*, where the excellent facilities of I. A. Topf und Söhne awaited them, was five hundred miles to the northwest, but the route they followed nearly doubled the trip. There were, moreover, interminable delays in the rail junctions of Michalovce, Zakopane, Nowy Targ, and, finally, at Cracow, thirty-three miles from their destination. Afterward Elizabeth recalled, "We were moved in cattle cars. There was no room to sit, there were no facilities, and the odor was terrible. No windows were open: there were none to open. The journey took almost a week. Then, suddenly, in the middle of the night, we were there. Everything happened at once. Doors flew open, floodlights blinded us. Some man was shrieking, 'Men here, women over there.' "

In the confusion Irving became separated from his father. The crying boy fled to his sisters — Maria was already in the floodlit line, being examined by SS women — who held a ten-second consultation. "I'm older, I'll take him with me," Olga volunteered, drawing her weeping brother to her waist. "I'll tell them I'm his mother." This seemed a sensible solution. In fact Olga was unwittingly forfeiting her own life. As Höss explained in his Nuremberg affidavit, "Children of tender years (*Kinder im zarten Alter*), being unable to work, were exterminated without exception" (*unterschiedslos vernichet*).[13] The SS *Frauen*, making what the commandant described as a "spot decision" (*Entscheidung*), judged small-boned Irving to be of tender years, and Olga, as his "mother," had to go with him, following her already condemned parents to Topf's furnaces. Like Tad Goldsztajn, Elizabeth and Ernestine were saved by their age. The selectors would have preferred huskier young women, but experience had taught them that vitality accompanied nubility.

All this the two sisters learned afterward. "We were in a daze, we didn't know what was happening," Elizabeth remembered years later, and Ernestine added, "The fact that our sister was gone and we weren't was fate." The breakup of the family occurred early on the morning of May 19, 1944. Sent off to the right, the Jewish women chosen for labor were deprived of the few personal belongings they had. In the unfurnished barracks to which they were assigned, they found themselves among other eastern

Europeans. As Krupp was subsequently briefed, these were "girls between fifteen and twenty-five who had been transported with their relatives from homes in Czechoslovakia, Rumania, and Hungary to the Auschwitz camp." The Konzernherr then learned that:

> In Auschwitz wurden die Familien getrennt, die Arbeitsunfähigen vergast, die Überlebenden als Häftlinge zur Zwangsarbeit ausgesucht. Die Mädchen wurden kahl geschoren und mit Häftlingsnummern tätowiert. Ihr ganzes Besitztum einschliesslich Kleider und Schuhe wurde ihnen abgenommen und durch Häftlingskleidung und Gefangenenschuhe ersetzt. Das Kleid war ein einteiliges Kleid aus grauem Stoff mit einem roten Kreuz im Rücken und dem gelben Judenfleck am Ärmel.

At Auschwitz the families were separated, those unable to work gassed, and the remainder singled out for conscription. The girls were shaved bald and tattooed with camp numbers. Their possessions, including clothing and shoes, were taken away and replaced by prison uniforms and shoes. The dress was in one piece, made of gray material, with a red cross on the back and the yellow Jew-patch on the sleeve.[14]

For six weeks they did nothing. Pregnancy tests were being administered, and any woman with child was sent to the crematoria. In addition, the slightest illness, even a common cold, meant death; regulations, specifying that "the sick" should join the infirm and the infirm must join the impregnated, were followed to the letter. Then "the girls were brought, in a group of about 2,000 fellow prisoners, to the Gelsenberg camp, which was supervised by the commandant of Buchenwald" (das unter der Aufsicht des Kommandanten von Buchenwald stand).[15]

The exact location of this slave replacement depot (which is what it really was) is uncertain. Elsewhere Krupp records identify it as Gelsenberg-Benzin. Almost certainly it was in the outskirts of Gelsenkirchen — other file notes refer to a nearby canal, and Ernestine is certain that they were already in the Ruhr. At Nuremberg she testified that "this shipment of 'ungarischer Jüdinnen' " (eventually the young women came to think of themselves as freight, and to accept their designation as Hungarian) arrived at the camp on July 4, 1944. The Lagerführer was an elderly SS officer; discipline was relatively lax. His 2,000 wards were housed in four enormous canvas pavilions. "There were five hundred in each tent," she testified, "but it was August, and we didn't mind." She paused. She added, "Then Krupp came."[16]

Alfried didn't arrive in person, of course; he was represented by a five-man team who had been told to examine "the suitability of the women there for work in the factory" (die Eignung der dort beschäftigten Frauen für die Arbeit in der Gusstahlfabrik). Awaiting the fresh draft, Essen's labor allocation office had plunged ahead with preparations. The planners expected robust, well-nourished stock. Until now Walzwerk II had employed scarcely a hundred female Kruppianer, all limited to light duties. Sturdy feminine arms were needed in the actual rolling departments — the heating furnaces and annealing beds — where only men had worked. In addition, Alfried was informed on August 9 that "the plant railroad has obtained very good results with female switch operators, and intends to use female stokers for steam locomotives." Standartenführer Pister may have been partly responsible for the impression that the Konzern would receive a band of Amazons, for as part of the Krupp contract Buchenwald's commandant insisted that Alfried provide forty-five strong Aryan girls who would take the SS oath, submit to three weeks' training at Ravensbrück KZ, Himmler's largest concentration camp for female prisoners, and then guard the new inhabitants of the Humboldtstrasse stockade. *Die Firma* attracted volunteers from its German women employees by a 70-pfennig-an-hour bonus; then, at Krupp's request, the Ravensbrück course was accelerated. Karolin Geulen, a German girl who had been working in Walzwerk II, who was exactly Elizabeth's age and whose industrial career was to become intertwined with the careers of both Roth sisters, later deposed that she spent "not quite two weeks" at Ravensbrück. Nevertheless, mustering a large party of athletic women, giving them whips, and teaching them sophisticated methods of inflicting pain suggested anticipation of a caliber of workers quite different from what Krupp in fact got.[17]

The discrepancy was discovered by the first member of the inspection team to reach Gelsenberg. Johann Adolf Trockel, a department director, appeared in the temporary camp a few days after the Jewesses had detrained. After watching them clear away air raid debris he reported that although his examination "could only be very superficial," he was struck by their "extremely primitive dress and equally primitive footwear" — they "wore only a shirt, underpants, and a light-gray gown." What really startled him, however, was their frailty. "Compared to the Polish and eastern women," who were "usually quite rugged" on debarkation in Essen, these were "fragile-looking creatures unsuited for heavy work" (*zartgliedrige Geschöpfe, für schwere Arbeit untauglich*).[18]

Momentarily Krupp was discouraged; all the hurry to equip and outfit the Karolin Geulens in black uniforms — and now this. For over a month the fragile creatures were left in their tents. Then, in mid-August, the rest of the inspection team called on them. Its leader was Theodor Braun, a short man in his fifties with a game leg who had joined the firm at the height of the furious production drive in 1917, was now a Walzwerk II plant leader, and, luckily for his present mission, knew how to take orders. His mandate was to cull 520 girls from the 2,000 inmates. At first he didn't see how he could meet it. Confirming Trockel's observations, he noted in addition that the youngest of the fit prisoners were "fourteen years old," and that "footwear consisted of galoshes, double-buckled shoes, or worn-out shoes, and must be described as poor."[19]

Braun called for volunteers. There was no response, for since May 19 the young women had been wary — as Elizabeth later told the tribunal, "We didn't know whether he really meant work or the gas chamber." Lacking a response, Braun proceeded with the selection arbitrarily. He insisted afterward that he was as humane as possible: "While making our choices we soon noticed that some of the women or girls among those remaining cried, and that others in pairs or larger groups held one another's hands. . . . The camp director agreed with our suggestion to allow relatives or friends to be together." The Roths had another impression. Ernestine testified that he "picked the youngest and strongest girls." Elizabeth described Braun as "what we called 'a real Nazi.' He was very unfriendly; you could tell we were nothing to him. The other man, Hammerschmidt, was much kinder, and we felt that if it weren't for the Nazis he would not be in this sort of thing." The ritual would have been unpleasant in any event, and the anonymity of the prisoners heightened it. At Nuremberg an American attorney asked Elizabeth, "Did they call you by name, how did they — ?" She interrupted him: "Well, we didn't have any names. We had only a gown, on the left arm we had our numbers, but they didn't ask our numbers. With their fingers they just showed at each person whom they wanted."*[20]

Braun limped off, followed by his three fellow slavers. On Altendorferstrasse their achievement was summarized:"*In Gelsenberg wurden aus diesem Trupp 520 Mädchen von den Angestellten der Firma Krupp für die Arbeit in Essen ausgewählt*" (At Gelsenberg 520 girls were selected by officials of the Krupp firm for work in Essen).[21]

The two sisters had no idea what had happened. For all they knew, the truck convoy now drawing up might be taking them to crematoria. They kissed the friends they were leaving — nothing is known of the 1,500 women who had *not* been chosen — and were marched off. Later Elizabeth said, "We were going, but we did not know where we were going. We did not even know who these German men had been, we were seeing them for the first time. It was when we reached Essen that we found out we were working for Krupp."

❖    ❖    ❖

Q: Will you tell the tribunal where you stayed in Essen?
A: In Essen, at the camp Humboldt.
Q: That was in Humboldtstrasse?
A: Yes. . . .
Q: Were you in a position to know or were you told that this camp was on the property of and belonged to the Krupp firm?

---

* Elizabeth testified in English, Ernestine in Czech.

A: That is right.

Q: Was the camp open? Were you free to come and go to any extent?

A: No, there were SS guards on the gate and the camp was around with barbed wire.

PRESIDING JUDGE: I didn't get that last.

ATTORNEY (H. RUSSELL THAYER): The camp was surrounded by barbwire.

Q: When you got up in the morning and then went to work, did you walk to work or did you ride to work?

A: . . . We went [at first] by streetcar. The rest of the time we walked back and forth.

Q: You walked in a large group?

A: Yes.

Q: Under guard?

A: SS men and SS women.

Q: You walked through the open streets of Essen?

A: Yes.

Q: Under guard?

A: Yes. . . .

Q: Can you estimate in your recollection how often it happened that you went without any food at all for a period of at least 24 hours?

A: I can't remember the number, how often it was, but it was very often that I didn't receive any food. . . . The answer from the SS men and women was, "You work for Krupp, ask from Krupp."

Q: Will you tell the tribunal whether or not, if you were ill, some care was taken of you? Will you tell the tribunal what care?

A: We had a dispensary where very, very sick people could go with a very high temperature, I could say, half dead. We could be very, very sick, but we could not go, since we were afraid that we would be taken to the gas chamber.

Q: I would like to ask the witness if she recognizes this instrument as one similar to that with which she herself has at one time or another, in Essen, while working for Krupp, been struck?

A: Every SS man had that. I got it once in my face. . . .

PRESIDING JUDGE: Pass that thing up. Let me see it. (*The instrument was handed to the judge.*) Go ahead.

MR. THAYER: You have been — or have you been, pardon me, have you ever been struck with an instrument such as that which you were shown?

WITNESS ROTH: Yes, once.

Q: While you were working in Essen?

A: Yes.

Q: For Krupp?

A: It was one evening, I came home, I was tired. . . . I don't know why and how it happened, one of the SS soldiers walked up to me and hit me over the face.

Q: And you say that you were struck, and the other workers were struck, with this. Did you ever see other workers struck with an instrument such as this?

A: In the factory they used to kick us with SS boots.

Q: I think you didn't understand my question. Did you ever see other members of this group of concentration camp workers also struck with an instrument such as this?

A: You mean that they struck somebody else?

Q: Yes, did you ever see them strike somebody else?

A: I could see that — ten, twenty every minute. . . . I was lucky I got it only once, but I have seen people kicked red and blue on the whole body; they couldn't get up and still they kicked them.

Q: This mistreatment also occurred —

PRESIDING JUDGE: Excuse me, this has been referred to and is not marked. Do you want it marked for identification?

MR. THAYER: Yes, I do want it marked.

PRESIDING JUDGE: 556 for identification.

Q: Were you ever kicked by a civilian worker of Krupp, not an SS man?

A: Yes, I was.

Q: A civilian?

A: Yes, I was.

Q: You are sure that that person was working at the time as a Krupp employee, are you?

A: Yes. He was in charge, to watch how fast we worked, and if we worked hard enough. . . .

Q: And do you — did it ever occur to you that you were punished at any time after a Krupp official asked an SS man to punish you?

A: It very often happened, and when Braun was making inspections in the factory . . . he just walked up to the SS man and he asked him to punish us; and then it happened we didn't get food and were punished. . . .

Q: And will you tell the tribunal whether or not any threats had been made prior to the time . . . Allied troops did enter the city?

A: The SS say we have always five minutes; the last five minutes we shall kill you.

Q: You say the SS men said that during the last five minutes they would kill you?

A: Yes. . . . We heard that every day from the SS men and the SS women. . . .

PRESIDING JUDGE: Well, now, the conditions that you have described that you worked under, did those conditions exist during all the time you worked at Krupp, so that anybody coming into the part of the Krupp factory where you worked could see the conditions you worked under?

WITNESS ROTH: Yes, everybody could see.

Q: That was day after day?

A: Day after day.

Q: And night after night?

A: Night after night.[22]

☩　　☩　·　☩

The area occupied by Humboldtstrasse KZ was — and, at this writing, still is — a large field approximately a thousand yards long and half again as wide. It was a peculiarity of nearly all German cities, including Berlin, that urban areas were broken up by such green patches. Before the war they had been a source of great charm; now they became convenient to slavers. Humboldt plain was bordered by Südwest cemetery, a trolley terminal, and, farther away, streets of small, squat, half-timbered homes whose occupants were later able to assert, truthfully, that they couldn't possibly have heard shrieks in the stockade. Grounds keepers at the cemetery were within earshot, but they had to be careful. A large part of Südwest had been reserved for Nazi party members who had fallen in battle. The ground was sacred; periodic visits assured that the martyrs' graves were receiving meticulous attention. Any man charged with its care who protested odd noises in the Juden KZ was likely to wind up screaming himself and knew it.

The Jewesses had first marched past Humboldtstrasse's new watchtowers on August 25, 1944. After each had been issued a Krupp blanket and a pair of clogs, they were addressed by Lagerführer Oskar Rieck. By all accounts Rieck seems to have stepped straight from a wartime B-movie. Short, scarfaced, and jackbooted, he always carried a rubber hose in one hand and a long leather whip in the other. If this description were based solely on the recollection of his victims, one might wonder, but it is supported in every detail by the commandant's staff. Karolin Geulen thought Rieck "particularly brutal" and "inhumane." He was an expert with the dogwhip. Sometimes, on a whim, he would enter the wooden barracks and thrash the girls while they were undressing. Although most of his *Jüdinnen* were between fourteen and twenty-five, one was in her thirties, and when he was informed that she couldn't keep up with the others he methodically whipped her to death that night. His real gift, however, was accuracy. At eight feet he could make a lash snap within the diameter of a pfennig piece. After the prisoners had returned from the rolling mill he would seek out the tiredest and try to strike the pupils of her eyes before she could avert her face: "That was the Lagerführer's specialty, that he whipped everybody in the eyes. It happened once that a woman was slow and she was blinded."[23]

Assessing responsibility for what happened within the camp is difficult. Oskar Rieck was a member of the SS. His name does not appear on any Krupp payroll, and Alfried cannot be held answerable for the camp leader's repeated statement to the girls, "Krupp can't keep you here if you don't work hard; if you don't, he will have to send you back to Auschwitz." His guards were also in the SS (though the SS women had been enlisted in Essen and *were* on the payroll). The failure to provide a second blanket and warmer clothing is unclear. At Nuremberg, Theodor Braun vaguely suggested that Buchenwald was to blame: "To my knowledge of these things, Herr Pister said at the time that we shouldn't give them any clothing because of the danger of escape. What was done in negotiations with the firm and the SS about the clothing, I don't know."[24]

Still, the Konzern owned the field and had built the stockade. Here, as in all Essen KZ, Krupp kitchens controlled the diet, which, after the first few weeks, was reduced to the usual slice of bread and bowl of *Bunkersuppe*. Above all, firm memoranda determined the working conditions ("in a locked room in armor plate shop number 4 under . . . supervisory conditions") and the hours of work, 6 A.M. to 5:45 P.M. Though conspicuously unsuited to heavy labor, Humboldtstrasse's prisoners were never assigned to anything else. Elizabeth toiled at a steel-hardening oven inside Walzwerk II. Ernestine mixed concrete and carried bricks and corrugated iron sheets in the yard outside. As the days grew colder her hands, unprotected by gloves, froze to the sheets. Her palms began to shred. By winter they were bloody pulp. Two other Jewesses who were to escape with the Roths submitted signed statements to the Nuremberg tribunal describing factory punishments. One, Rosa Katz, declared, "We were supervised by the SS, both men and women, who watched all the time in case one of us wanted to rest for a few moments. Then the offender would be hit with an iron bar until her body was covered with bruises." And Agnes Königsberg — a distant cousin of the Roths — stated that "We received kicks and blows, both in camp and at the place of work, from the SS men and from the Germans. This mistreatment happened very often, frequently without any visible reason, and sometimes on the slightest pertext. . . ." Agnes went on to name three Krupp foremen who, she said, ordered corporal punishment in her presence.[25]

Multiple deaths would have followed quickly without the intervention of those Kruppianer who shared rations with the Jewesses, whispered encouragement, and relayed word, from their own clandestine radio sets, of reports from London describing Allied successes. Some seemed to share the girls' suffering vicariously. Peter Gutersohn, an elderly builder of tank turrets, believed that sympathy was strongest among veterans who, like himself, had been employees of the firm since before World War I. Gutersohn first saw the *Jüdinnen* on a streetcar in Kraemerplatz. "Their entire clothing," he later certified, "consisted of one ragged dress made of burlap. They wore wooden slippers on their naked feet." He was "deeply shocked" and felt "really ashamed to be a German when I saw what had been done to these women." At the same time, he was painfully aware that younger German workmen disagreed with him. Over and over he heard "these rather aggressive National Socialists" ask rhetorically, "What are we going to do with this rabble? Why don't you kill them?" Killing them, Gutersohn concluded, seemed to be the objective of Werkmeister Wunsch, because "the work for which these women were used had never been done by any of the German women employed in our plant." The girls

. . . had to load rubble and ride on trucks and lug iron girders, and they were also engaged in other cleaning-up work. These Jewesses had neither clothing nor protective gloves suitable for such work [*Diese Jüdinnen besassen für diese Arbeit weder Arbeitskleidung noch Schutzhandschuhe*]. . . . If, on such occasions, the women wanted to dry themselves in front of a coal fire, or tried to wash some of their rags, they were immediately driven away by Wunsch.[26]

Peter Hubert, another Kruppianer, supervised eight of the girls for a three-week period. On his first day he discovered, to his astonishment, that bare-handed fourteen-year-olds weighing less than ninety pounds were pushing loads of stone on all-metal wheelbarrows — work he himself could not have done — "*Ich habe, ohne dass ich die kalten Griffe anfasste, doppelte Handschuhe tragen müssen, um mich vor der Kälte zu schützen*" (Even without touching the cold handles I had to wear double-thickness gloves to protect my hands from the cold). Hubert loaned his to one of the smaller girls, whereupon a superior intervened, tore them from her hands, and threw them in a coke fire. Turning on Hubert he shouted, "*Wenn Sie so nicht arbeiten wollen, dann treten Sie sie in den Arsch!*" (If they don't want to work like that, just give them a kick in the ass!).[27]

In some ways the most persuasive testimony is that of the Jew beaters. Karolin Geulen was a reluctant witness. In her first statement she insisted that the girls had been given light work, adequate food, straw mattresses, "two or three blankets," warm clothing, and leather shoes. Recalled four months later, Karolin completely reversed herself; indeed, she admitted whipping a girl and volunteered that "if I were treated in such a way, I should certainly have the feeling that I was being treated inhumanely" (*ich würde, wenn ich selbst so behandelt werden würde, das bestimmte Empfinden haben, dass ich unmenschlich behandelt wurde*). Similarly, Selma Nolten, an SS supervisor who worked with Braun, and whom the Roth sisters and Agnes Königsberg were to remember by name ("The SS women were worse than the men, they liked to use their whips," said Elizabeth), vehemently denied that she herself had struck anyone, but recalled that her own superior, SS Oberaufseherin Emmi Theissen, had beaten a prisoner in her early teens for seeking shelter during an air raid. Selma conceded that the prisoners' clogs broke quickly, that they had to rip strips from their one blanket and bind up their feet, and that the daily marches to and from Walzwerk II were an appalling ordeal:

> Some women suffered frostbite because they had to trudge their way to the factory over snowy and icy roads [über die vereisten und verschneiten Strassen den Fussweg zur Fabrik machen mussten] wearing such miserable footwear, i.e., stockingless and with shoes that consisted only of a wooden sole and were usually damaged.[28]

Determining the guilt of Karolin and Selma is impossible, nor can one define that of Walter Thöne, under whom imprisoned girls swung ten-pound picks and carried thirty-pound steel sheets. Thöne was a Nazi. He confessed to kicking and beating the women. Yet he refused to accept responsibility; the real culprit, he insisted, was another party member, who, unfortunately, couldn't be produced. Once again, les absents ont toujours tort. According to Thöne this absentee, named Reif,

> . . . supervised this work and saw to it that I kept an eye on the speed. . . . Nearly every day this man, who had no conscience, stopped me and, in an unmistakable way, told me to drive the Jewesses harder so as to get even more work out of them. He also continually stressed that I should not worry too much about what methods I used, and if need be, hit them hard, like a piece of iron. . . . Yet the poor women were poorly protected against the cold, since they were wearing only thin rags; most of these unfortunate people wore no stockings with the severe frost. In the wintertime their legs were always blue with cold and bore rough marks of frostbite — as big as a five-mark piece [Die Beine waren im Winter immer blau gefroren und zeigten schorfige Froststellen, so gross wie ein 5-Markstück].[29]

Thöne or Reif — it makes no difference. Perhaps Reif never existed; possibly he was Thöne's other self. What matters is that his story supports those of Peter Gutersohn, Peter Hubert, Karolin Geulen, Selma Nolten, and the surviving girls. The working conditions are established beyond question, and the responsibility for them lay not in Berlin, but at the great door of the three-hundred room castle auf dem Hügel.

✠   ✠   ✠

As stipulated in the Krupp-Buchenwald agreement, the Jewish women and girls had been transported from the trolley depot to Walzwerk II in open summer streetcars during the first month of their captivity, and though Humboldtstrasse's barracks and huts were uncomfortably crowded, they *had* provided shelter from the weather. Besides, it had still been fall; the weather had been mild. The girls' crisis began on the night of October 23–24. In the great raid which destroyed Dechenschule and knocked out thirty-one shops, Humboldtstrasse, twenty blocks away from Father Come and his comrades, was also demolished. The trolley depot lay in ruins, its tracks twisted in weird patterns. Every wooden structure in the camp had been leveled — the occupants of one locked hut had been burned alive — and only the tin kitchen still stood.[30]

Dechenschule's men were moved to Neerfeldschule, but the women of Humboldtstrasse stayed where they were. Though the guards kept telling them that the outcome of the war was of no concern here, that "We'll always have the last five minutes," this was one camp that really did worry Krupp. It was unproductive. The girls were simply too small and too weak to do the work. They had become laborers in a kind of horrid make-work project. Rather than invest further capital in them, Krupp's Oberlager-führung let it deteriorate; the camp's 500 inhabitants were moved into the kitchen.[31]

None of the bombs had struck Walzwerk II, though the factory lay near the center of the industrial complex and Humboldtstrasse was on the outskirts of Essen. Lacking transport, the Jewesses began their nine-mile daily round trip on foot at 4:30 A.M. October 25, following a crooked route down Kruppstrasse, Mülheimerstrasse, Frohnhauserstrasse, and Böckler-strasse (crossing Altendorferstrasse beneath Alfried's office) and then out Bottroperstrasse to Helenenstrasse and the plant. The trip took two hours each way. *Bunkersuppe* had produced edema, swelling their bodies grotesquely, and as the autumn waned their condition worsened in other ways. By now the last of their disintegrating clogs had been discarded. Feet were wrapped in rags or left naked. In chill rain, then in sleet, they hobbled along frantically, trying to keep up with the *Links-Rechts* cadence and avoid the whips' sting, their burlap gowns in tatters and their drenched blankets, which doubled as overcoats, draped over their shoulders. Before the first snow their soles were raked with open wounds. Behind them they left a track of blood and pus.

As compassion for abused slaves grew among the older generation of Kruppianer at Walzwerk II, the tolerance of the young men and the supervisors diminished. One day in the shop a French *Fremdarbeiter* slipped a letter to a friendly German and asked him to mail it. That evening the Samaritan was caught at the post office, and next day Ernestine Roth saw him being marched round the factory, a placard on his back stating his crime and announcing that he had been sentenced to death for it. Since the girls' families had been gassed, they were not tempted by mail.

It seemed that they had been spared nothing, that no shocks were left. Nevertheless there were a few, which were now introduced. Since leaving Auschwitz their hair had thickened. Now, upon orders of dissatisfied Werkmeisters, strips were shorn from the heads of unproductive slaves. It was done cunningly. Intricate designs were fashioned, each more absurd than the last; the less efficient the worker the uglier her coif became, and with their bloated torsos and mutilated hands and feet some really did look inhuman. Finally, to impress upon the young women that they were all *Unterfrauen*, factory toilets were barred to them. To relieve themselves they had to squat in the yard outside, voiding like animals in full view of passersby.[32]

"I was so miserable," Elizabeth later testified, "I used to lie awake at night hoping that the bombs would fall near me so I wouldn't have to work the next day." Her sister actually sought death. December 15 was to be Ernestine's twentieth birthday. She didn't want to live to see it, and during an RAF attack three days before, "I left the [kitchen] cellar and ran out into the open. I was glad there was an air raid and I might get killed, because I didn't mind about life, I wanted death before a birthday." The Lancasters spared Humboldtstrasse that night. On January 12, however, concussion flattened the kitchen, and the cellar became the girls' permanent home. There was no light, no heat, no water. Asked at Nuremberg where they slept, Elizabeth replied, "On the floor. We were lucky when we could find a piece of wood, take it down to the cellar and sleep on the wood. . . . We were five hundred, but if there were thirty straw mattresses it was much." The stronger young women battled for dry patches, thus repeating — except that this winter was far more severe — the scenes Hendrik Scholtens had witnessed a year earlier. A literal translation of one fragment from Ernestine's Czech testimony, with its moving rhythms and Slavic repetition, offers some idea as to what nights were like in the girls' camps: "The winter was very cold for us. There was great snow, and it was very cold, and the cellar where we lived had no insulation, was always wet, the roof of the cellar was very wet, and also the walls, and we had only one blanket, so it was very cold."

Another view was furnished when Dr. Jäger, who had somehow kept his title of *kruppscher Oberlagerarzt*, called at the camp. Jäger reported to Alfried's physician:

> Upon my visit I found these females suffering from open festering wounds and other diseases [*Bei meinem ersten Besuch in diesem Lager fand ich Personen, die an eiternden offenen Wunden und anderen Krankheiten litten*]. . . . They had no shoes and went about in their bare feet. The only clothing of each consisted of a sack with holes for the head and arms. Their hair was shorn [*Ihr Haar war abgeschoren*]. The camp was encircled by barbwire. . . . A person could not enter the prisoners' quarters

without being attacked by fleas. . . . I myself left with huge boils from them, on my arms and the rest of my body [*Ich hatte grosse Beulen an meinen Armen und an meinem ganzen Körper*].[33]

By now the dreadful winter was at its height, yet though blizzards and bitter cold, gale-driven rain whipped the Ruhr, nothing was done to improve the girls' lot. Instead a very different solution was proposed — the final solution. In February, Johannes Maria Dollhaine, who had participated in the Gelsenberg selection with Trockel and who worked under Lehmann in Arbeitsatz A, discussed the issue with Oskar Rieck and then made a verbal recommendation. Dollhaine, Lehmann, and Friedrich Janssen were in an air raid shelter at the time. The proposal to Lehmann was ". . . *auf keinen Fall die Insassen des KZL lebend in die Hände der herannahenden amerikanischen Truppen fallen zu lassen*" (that under no circumstances should the inmates of the concentration camp be allowed to fall into the hands of the approaching American troops).[34]

Lehmann asked Janssen to canvass the management. There, too, the recommendation was that the young women must go. During his postwar imprisonment Alfried conceded in an affidavit that he had been "very disagreeably affected" by their presence and therefore decided "to get rid of them as soon as possible." In the Palace of Justice defense witnesses protested that Krupp merely wanted the bondswomen moved "in the interests of the girls' safety" — a peculiar argument, in the light of all they had endured and, more significantly, their new destination. As Alfried added in his affidavit, negotiations were proceeding with "a gentleman from Buchenwald." Even if one accepts the doubtful contention that Krupp was more concerned about the protection of these girls than that of the German women who must remain, plainly the prisoners had become a hideous embarrassment to him. Karl Sommerer, a subordinate who participated in the arrangement of transport, told the tribunal that during their camp-to-factory marches, they traveled right through the central part of the city. At no time were they secluded: "Every day anyone could see them at work and in their spare time." Anyone with foresight who observed their condition, and anticipated the probable reaction of U.S. soldiers, was bound to have grave second thoughts. Janssen's thoughts are a matter of record. In an affidavit Max Ihn recalled the "suggestion that the 520 Jewesses who were employed at Krupp's should be taken away before the occupation took place, namely back to Buchenwald." Subsequently Lehmann, in his role as Alfried's DAF liaison man, was ordered in behalf of *die Firma:*

. . . *den Abtransport der Frauen nach Buchenwald zu arrangieren. Die SS stimmte der Evakuierung der Frauen zu, war aber nicht mehr in der Lage, Transportmittel zur Verfügung zu stellen. Es gelang der Abteilung Lehmann, einen Zug zusammenzustellen.*

. . . to arrange for the transportation of the women to Buchenwald. The SS agreed to the evacuation of the women, but was no longer in a position to supply transport. Lehmann's department accordingly succeeded in assembling a train.[35]

"At last I have managed it!" Lehmann told Sommerer one day early that March. In Sommerer's words, "the time had come when the necessity for the removal of these girls had become acute." Despite the prestige of the firm, such an evacuation at this stage of the war was going to require great skill. Essen's Hauptbahnhof was rubble; no locomotive could negotiate its wreckage. Ten miles away, however, the Bochum terminal was intact, and the train Lehmann had acquired — fifty coaches headed for the Buchenwald killing center, with 1,800 victims already aboard and room for another 500 — would pause there on March 17. Since there had been so much "bomb damage to the traffic routes," as Sommerer put it, the girls and their SS guards were going to need a guide for their march there. He himself would lead them and explain the situation to railway officials. Sommerer expected that some bureaucrat would say, "I can't do it" (he was to be justified), and he surmised (again correctly) that the magic of the name of Alfried Krupp, who was determined that the tracks should be cleared for this shipment "as soon as possible," would surmount petty difficulties.[36]

Unfortunately for the Konzernherr, complete suppression was now impossible. Too many people knew of the plot, and the details were too lurid. The SS men and women kept quiet, but rumors drifted down from the Hauptverwaltungsgebäude to departmental heads and supervisors, and from them to foremen. In a few days the men knew of it. A sympathetic Kruppianer outlined Elizabeth Roth's future for her in a few muttered phrases; during the march back to Humboldtstrasse that night she passed the word to the others. Cremation was now very close, and their chances of avoiding it appeared hopeless. They weren't quite. Rosa Katz had struck up a friendship with Gerhardt Marquardt, a simple man who lived in a hutch on the Stadtwiese with his common law wife. One afternoon when his companion was absent, Marquardt had actually smuggled Rosa out of Walzwerk II and shown her his tiny home. The Roths had no such contact, but trooping back on Böcklerstrasse, Elizabeth recognized a worker from their shop, Kurt Schneider, entering his house with a key. At work he had seemed understanding. And now she knew where he lived. Between Marquardt and Schneider some sort of outside arrangements might be made.

First, of course, they had to break through Humboldtstrasse's barbwire. Examining the stakes and aprons surreptitiously, the Roth sisters found a stretch weakened by previous bombings. Lately RAF bombardiers had avoided Essen; perhaps they had written it off. If not, if another raid struck near here and drove the Lagerführer and his guards to their bunker, Elizabeth intended to lead a herd of *Stücke* through the wire — which is precisely what she did.

✠     ✠     ✠

Awkward as an Allied encounter with maimed young women would be, the discovery that Krupp had maintained a *Konzentrationslager* for infants would have incited ghastly retribution, and because the very prospect was appalling, the decision to liquidate Buschmannshof — for there was such a concentration camp, and that was its name — had preceded the requisition of the Buchenwald train.

The suppression of Buschmannshof's story was an almost unqualified success; when Rolf Hochhuth suggested in his appendix to *Der Stellvertreter* that "if the largest employer in Greater Germany and the members of his family" had not invoked a double standard in the treatment of Germans and foreigners, "then possibly ninety-eight out of one hundred and thirty-two children would not have died in the camp of Voerde near Essen," an indignant Krupp executive told this writer that the playwright had "turned an act of generosity into a monstrosity" — that "Bertha Krupp built the quarters with the guidance of the Red Cross for homeless orphans."[37] Bertha and the Red Cross had nothing to do with it, the inmates were not orphans, and Hochhuth had only grazed the truth. Yet fewer than a dozen people knew it, and they were keeping very quiet. Their silence went unchallenged, partly because the facts are so incredible, partly because the infants, far from being "near Essen," had been twenty-six miles away — and chiefly because there are no known survivors.

Indeed, Krupp was so confident that Buschmannshof would be forgotten that its buildings weren't even torn down. Today they still stand, seven long low dingy barracks with small windows, indistinguishable at first glance from the sheds of Auschwitz. There are a few differences. Discipline was never a problem at Buschmannshof, or Voerde-West as it was also called. The oldest prisoners were two years old, and all were extremely weak. Therefore there are no barbwire stakes. And a visitor familiar with the history of the compound is startled to see television antennae sprouting from the barrack roofs; the sheds have been converted to a housing project for the indigent. There is no mistaking the architecture of the buildings, of course. Anyone familiar with concentration camps is instantly aware that one stood here once. But strangers are not likely to stumble upon it. A thick birch grove screens it from the nearest street, Bahnhofstrasse, and the nearest town, Voerde-bei-Dinslaken (not Voerde, as Hochhuth thought, a different place altogether) is such a small hamlet that it appears on no map.

Anna Döring, Buschmannshof's last matron, no longer lives at Hindenburgstrasse 186A. She is still chunky and buxom, with abundant curly brown hair, a pudgy face, stubby arms, and expressive hands, however, and on hard questions she is as intractable as she was on May 31, 1948, when she took the stand at Nuremberg. Years later, thinking her caller must be an acquaintance from the old Germany, she greeted this writer with that winning smile which has given *Hausfrauen* the deserved reputation of being the most hospitable housekeepers in Europe. Then she remembered; she was reminded. The victims were mentioned, and she turned sulky. No, she had forgotten all that. No, she never visited the graves. Yes, they were still there. Of course. *So wahr mir Gott helfe!* Do graves ever move?

Some do; some of these did. In Henn op den Damm tavern on Hindenburgstrasse an old man recalled disinterring and reinterring tiny corpses, and with his help the author found a strange enclave in a distant corner of nearby Waldfriedhof, the Friedershof town cemetery. On a barren patch of land were seven lines of graves — over a hundred altogether, the old man observed, laboriously counting them and then explaining that the rest were in Friedrichfeld, another, larger cemetery down the road. Each grave was marked by a three-by-six-inch stone slab bearing only the number which the camp had once assigned to the infant lying beneath; row on row the diminutive markers were set in the hard Ruhr soil, each rank presenting its digits as neatly as a logarithm table.

Carefully one noted the figures: 149, 250, 211, 18, 231. Here they were meaningless. Among the Nuremberg documents, however, there is extant a register of deaths which was kept during the war by Ernst Vowinkel, a clerk in Voerde-bei-Dinslaken's registry office (*Standesamt*), who submitted it with a sworn statement certifying that it contained "the names of eastern workers' children who died in the children's camp Voerde-West of the Gusstahlfabrik of the firm in Fried. Krupp of Essen between August 1944 and March 1945."[38] From Vowinkel's pages we learn that 149 was Valentina Rabzewa, who lived less than a month and died of "general weakness"; that 250, Eduard Moltschiusnaja, perished of "malnutrition" after four months and twenty days; that 211, Wladimir Chodolowa, expired for "unknown" reasons at the age of six and a half months; that 18, Lidija Solotawa, succumbed to pneumonia on the fifty-ninth day of life; and that 231, Nikolaj Kotenko, died, aged two months and fifteen days, of tuberculosis. If the skeptical doubt Herr Vowinkel, finding it inconceivable that a twentieth-century industrialist could be implicated in a modern massacre of innocents, there are the confiscated files of the firm itself. One report dated January 2, 1945, reads:

Subject: Death of child of eastern worker [*Tod des Kindes einer Ostarbeiterin*]

| Last name: | Bodanowa | Born: | May 26, 1944 |
| First name: | Lydia | In: | Essen |

*Family status:* Child [*Familien-*
   *stand: Kind*]
*Camp:*       Voerde-West
*Died on:*     December 30, 1944
*Time of death:*  6 A.M.
*Cause of death:*  Scarlet fever
*Address of relatives:* ——

*Mother:* Bodanowa, Wara
*Employment number* [*Arbeits nu-*
   *mmer*]: 519837
*Burial will take place* [*Beerdigung findet*
   . . . *statt*] *on:* January 4, 1945
*By:*      Main Camp Administration
*Cemetery:* Friedrichfeld
*Legacy:*   None

Signed: SCHULTEN[39]

How did this happen? Krupp blamed it on incompetent subordinates and sloppy Sauckel recruitment. At Nuremberg one defense witness supported the contention that *Menschenjagd* procedures had been inept; Dr. Walter Schrieber of the Speer ministry, who proudly informed the court that he had been awarded the SS Sword, the Himmler Ring, the Knight's Cross, and the Golden Party Badge ("for setting up cellulose factories and manufacturing celluloid from potatoes"), lectured the Allied judges in the manner of an impatient pedant: "Herr Vorsitzender, I don't know whether you know that if an industrialist in 1943 and 1944 received a few hundred of them [foreign workers], many were children, whom, of course, he couldn't use at all. . . . I am myself an industrialist, and so have some basis on which to speak."[40] By "children," Schrieber meant conscripts five years old or younger; six-year-old foreigners were entitled to wear the white jackets with vertical stripes of the slave youth. Buschmannshof's inhabitants were an entirely different category, however. They had been born on Reich soil, in Krupp captivity. Their existence was a consequence of the firm's decision "to allow relatives . . . to be together." Doubtless the policy was meant to be merciful, but no one had thought it through. In practice its implications were dreadful. When husbands and wives were permitted to live together the wives conceived; and when the firm decided that the women must return to their machines, the offspring became Krupp's frailest wards.

Their births began in 1942, nine months after the first families from the east arrived in Essen. As Lagerführer complaints about pregnancies grew, the problem reached the desk of one of Alfried's chief lieutenants, Hans Kupke, a former artillery designer and supervisor of firing ranges who had just been appointed Oberlagerführer. First Alfried's obstetricians were summoned. "When female eastern workers employed at Krupp's were expecting a child the confinement took place in one of the hospitals of Krupp," Oberlagerführer Kupke later wrote. "One part of the hospital was fenced off. There the women were delivered. After a certain time, it might have been three or perhaps six weeks, the women resumed work, while the children remained in the hospital."[41]

But this could only be a temporary solution. Pediatricians had to replace obstetricians. At first a Dr. Seynsche treated the infants. By late summer the birthrate was skyrocketing; Seynsche's wards were overrun, and Kupke agreed "after much persuasion" — he did not identify his persuader, but his superior was Alfried Krupp — "to a camp being set aside to accommodate these children." Eventually, he continued, they "fixed up" Buschmannshof, which had been acquired from the Todt organization: "At that time — January 1943 — about 120 children were concerned. I do not remember the exact number. The children were taken care of by a woman who was cook and all-round help at the same time, and who did her best for the children. She had at her disposal quite a number of female eastern workers."[42]

In the beginning she had twenty, each a Ukrainian who had given birth to a Buschmannshof baby. They were lucky, for of all Krupp's slaves, including the girls in Humboldtstrasse, the most wretched must have been those mothers who had been separated from their newborn infants. In theory each was entitled to a weekly visit, but this rarely worked. Asked how many came, Anna Döring replied, "Sometimes fifteen, and as many as sixteen occasionally, on Sundays."[43] They weren't indifferent; they just couldn't get there. Many had been transferred to Krupp factories outside the Ruhr; others were restricted to quarters, and even those who were free faced formidable difficulties. By streetcar Voerde-bei-Dinslaken was thirty-seven miles from Essen, with many transfers. Even today a round trip is trying to one who speaks German; for a Russian woman, in wartime, the linguistic barrier and the complicated detours around bombed-out lines doubtless seemed defeating. Indeed, it is a marvel that any made it at all.

The crime of Buschmannshof cannot be pinned to any one man. Alfried was answerable for it, of course, but so far as is known he never inspected the camp. Apparently most of the Kruppianer employed there did what they could with what they had, but the terrible system created by an embattled Volk gave them little. Johann Wienen, appointed Lagerführer of Buschmannshof in 1944, wanted "nice, large, bright" rooms, beds with sheets and covers, and hot water. At night he tenderly addressed each of his charges as Kindchen (my little child), and in his pathetic and revealing affidavit he later wrote, "We even provided some underwear." The infants needed more than that. They were ill even before the trucks bearing them braked beside his barracks. He said, "I remember when two transports, I believe of twenty or twenty-five children each, arrived from Essen. We noticed then that these children were in a bad physical state. They seemed to be sick, and we did not believe that they would live."[44]

He inspected them every day. Summoning all his resources, he pleaded with the Hauptverwaltungsgebäude, and, "when the first cases of diphtheria occured in the fall of 1944," appealed directly to Dr. Jäger. Jäger, being Jäger, saw to it that the necessary serum was dispatched at once. Yet so inept was the camp staff that it hardly knew what to do with the vials. The camp's only physician, Dr. Kolesnik, was an elderly Ukrainian. "His German," said Wienen, "was but halting," and meanwhile the quality of Wienen's aides was rapidly declining. His first *Verwalterin*, one Fräulein Howa, had broken her leg. She was succeeded by the cook, Frau Makowski, who caught diphtheria from one of the infants and died in December. That left Anna Döring, the cook's assistant. At Nuremberg, Anna was an exasperating and hostile witness, but that may have been partly because she had been so incompetent. Lacking nursing training, she acknowledged that she hadn't the faintest idea of what scurvy is, what rickets are, or what hydrocephalic (*wasserköpfig*) meant. In short, she was ignorant of the gravest diseases threatening the camp. Anna was equally vague about statistics; she didn't know how many infants had passed through the barracks, had no idea how many had been alive or dead, and couldn't even guess. Asked, "Would you say that a death rate of 85 children would be a high one?" she replied warily, "As far as I remember there could never have been that many deaths"; asked, "Do you know there are death certificates in evidence for at least that many?" she answered, "I do not know." Anna didn't know much. Excerpts from the transcript give a fair sample of her testimony under cross-examination:

Q: How many children were alive at any one date? Can you remember?
A: *Nein.*
Q: Do you know how many died from September 1944 to January 1945?
A: No, I don't know [*Nein, ich weiss es nicht*].
Q: Do you know what the cause of death of most of these children was supposed to be?
A: No, I cannot find an explanation for that and never could [*Nein, ich kann keine Klärung dafür finden, und habe es nie gekonnt.*][45]

Ernst Wirtz, an unskilled Kruppianer, was no more qualified to answer medical questions than Anna Döring, and as a Werkschutz guard who had been sentenced to eight years in prison for the abuse of Krupp slaves in Essen, Mulhouse, and Kulmbach he had even less reason to cooperate with the court. He does seem to have been more curious than Anna, however, and since he hadn't been assigned to Buschmannshof he had no reason to feel defensive about it. When Wirtz called at the camp in January 1945 on an errand, Wienen had been replaced by Lorenz Scheider. In testifying about a meeting of Krupp Lagerführers, Scheider recalled that during his regime prisoners "might receive an occasional kick or something," and that any slave who crossed him "might be gripped harshly." (Q: So, in other words, he was beaten? A: Well, yes.) Under Scheider the outlook for

Voerde-bei-Dinslaken's infants dwindled alarmingly, though here again assignment of individual responsibility is risky. The firm was preoccupied with other things. *Unterkinder* under two years old could make no contribution to *totaler Krieg*, and so Buschmannshof's *Kindermord* began. There were no machine pistols, no Zyklon-B crystals, no I. A. Topf triple furnaces. But the outcome was the same.[46]

Wirtz saw the camp's babies lying "in sort of prison bunks — on paillasses (*Strohsäcke*) with rubber sheets. The children were quite naked." They were being fed a slimy gruel from bottles; many had "swollen heads," and "there was no child at all whose arms or hands were thicker than my thumb." By now deliveries of pregnant *Ostarbeiterinnen* had been transferred from Essen, where Krupp hospitals were filled with air raid casualties, to Voerde-bei-Dinslaken, yet Anna's Ukrainian helpers had been cut from twenty to four. With the help of the interpreter, Wirtz struck up a conversation with these matrons. He inquired about the futures of new mothers and learned that "As soon as an eastern worker had given birth to a child she was allowed six weeks, and after these six weeks she went back to work, and the child was kept in the camp so that the female worker could go to work again." Next, as he testified, "I asked them how it came about that these children were so undernourished, and I was told they had very little to eat." (At dinner that evening Wirtz raised this question with Scheider, who "told me that he didn't get enough food from the Oberlagerführung." Meals for Kruppianer, the Lagerführer's guest noticed, were "plentiful and better than at Mulhouse. . . . I was surprised that we got such good food.")[47]

Back with the Ukrainian matrons, the ex-guard wondered how all this would end. They told him: it was ending, they said bitterly, all the time. At first he didn't understand. Then, speaking through the interpreter, they explained. According to his account three years later, the women said that "Fifty or sixty children died every day, and as many were born every day, because there was a constant influx of eastern female workers with children." Really inquisitive now, their visitor pressed them for details. "I asked the interpreter," he recalled on the witness stand, "how it came about that so many of the children died, and if the children were buried, and the interpreter told me the children were cremated inside the camp."[48]

"No child was cremated!" Anna Döring cried when confronted with this. "They were always put in nice coffins and got a proper funeral!" It made little difference. Probably both witnesses were right. In or out of caskets, some bodies went into the ground. In the Third Reich numbered headstones weren't erected over *Fremdarbeiter* ashes. On the other hand, the numbered graves in the two cemeteries off Hindenbergstrasse do not coincide with the mortality rate of Buschmannshof's helpless inmates who perished, General Telford Taylor found, "by the scores, of disease and neglect." Although figures are necessarily incomplete, 74 percent of the original infant population died, 90 percent of these fatalities coming in the last seven months of the camp's existence. Shown Krupp records and Ernst Vowinkel's death certificates — which attributed about half the mortality to "general weakness" — Oberlagerführer Kupke declared, "I admit this is due to a measure of maladministration," and Alfried too complained that he had been ill served by his "subordinate gentlemen." The judges, more judgmental, noted that "Vivid descriptions have been given by *defense* witnesses of the pitiable condition of these most innocent victims of the cruel slave labor program. A large number of these babies died of malnutrition."[49]

Yet they didn't all die, and the presence of survivors as Allied tanks raced to encircle the Ruhr led to Buschmannshof's final atrocity. Whoever perpetrated it was guilty of a very great war crime. Regrettably, his identity eluded American intelligence. Oberlagerführer Kupke could only recall that someone — obviously he had to be someone of immense power — ordered him to see that "the children were moved to Thuringia." Thuringia is two hundred miles east of the Ruhr; it was, at that stage in the hostilities, as far as offensive objects could be shipped and still be shielded by the retreating Wehrmacht. Feverish infants, like mutilated young girls, were a potential source of discomfiture; they had to go, and so they went, though how, and precisely when, we shall never know. Anna Döring could only tell the court that the evacuation came "at the end of February." She had been conveniently at home then; the bombings had become an intolerable nuisance for her. Thus, "I wasn't present that day, unfortunately, and therefore I cannot make any statements about it." Anna was asked whether her wards left "well and healthy." She didn't respond.[50]

The implications of Buschmannshof's resettlement eclipse anything else in the four centuries of the Essen dynasty, for this camp was unique. Relatives of other Krupp prisoners had no idea where they were, and when peace came they would have to await the return of living slaves of NN, but for each naked infant who had lain trembling on a straw pallet behind that birch thicket in Voerde-bei-Dinslaken there was at least one parent who knew her child had been there, awaiting her. Those mothers who returned that summer "W Projedennoj Germaniji," as they said then, "in conquered Germany," found the unpainted barracks deserted. Before U.S. troops could free them and care for them, "the children," in the words of General Taylor, had been "turned over to the Reich authorities and moved without the knowledge of the parents." In fact, we have only the assurance of Hans Kupke, who wasn't even there, that the four Ukrainian matrons accompanied the babies — had the move been responsible, the camp leader and Anna Döring should have led them — and Kupke acknowledged that it had been "impossible to inform the other mothers, many of whom had been transferred from Essen with their plant."[51]

"That," the Oberlagerführer concluded, "is all I can state here on the subject of these children of eastern workers."[52] Given the chaos of 1945 and the age of the nurslings, it is too much to hope that any *Ostarbeiterin* could add more than a wail of anguish. Hendrik Scholtens could find his parents even though they were in the Dutch East Indies; Father Come could make his way back to Mère Come in Smuid. But what could 234, 243, 249, and 256 do, had they still been alive? They didn't know their last names were Petrowa, Amelina, Sasaschkowa, and Taranin. If they did, they could have told no one; they couldn't walk, let alone talk. Even if their mothers had come upon a truckload of babies, the consequences would have been unpredictable. The vast majority had seen their children for but a few moments at birth. Identification now would have been almost impossible, and the maternal yearning for reunion would, at best, have produced indescribable mental agony.*

Before Hans Frank was led to the rope in Nuremberg he said: *"Tausend Jahre werden vergehen und sie werden diese Schuld von Deutschland nicht wegnehmen"* (A thousand years will pass and Germany's guilt will not be expunged).

Those words have been adopted as the epitaph of the *Tausendjährige Reich*, but its most helpless victims haven't any. No monument stands near Buschmannshof's incongruous TV antennae, nor even by the tiny numbered slabs in Waldfriedhof and Friedrichfeld. Were one inscribed, it might bear Goethe's last words: *"Licht, mehr Licht!"* (Light, more light!), for the children's graveyards, situated in the darkest recesses of their cemeteries, have scarcely any light at all. Indeed, the very markers can't last much longer. Once their files and columns stood as erect as asphalt soldiers on the Führer's birthday, each presenting its figures sharply etched. Time, however, has been unkind to them. Elsewhere in the graveyards German plots are admirably tended. No one has cared for these. After nearly a quarter-century the numerals on some stones are indecipherable, and others have been toppled by frost. Many are disintegrating already. Within another decade there will be no trace of them at all.

---

* But the issue is probably academic. Toward the end of the war it was Reich policy in the East to exterminate babies of Polish and Russian women who had been working for German industry by injecting poison in their veins. (Earl M. Kintner, ed. *Hadamar Trial of Aleons Klein, Adolf Wallmann, et al.* London: 1948.) One matron testified in her defense that she bought toys for such children who, according to the euphemistic jargon of Germany's *Sprachregelung*, had been condemned for being "useless feeders." (Ibid., testimony of Irmgard Huber.)

# 23

✠

## Götterdämmerung

IF Krupp's slaves were far from home, so were his relatives. It was a time of unprecedented turmoil — not even the upheavals of 1618–1648 had uprooted so many millions of Germans — and the climax was reached in the last summer of the war, when death stalked the Führer in his own remote Wolfsschanze. Thereafter the *Volk* would be hungrier and more terrified, but never again so widely dispersed. So it was with the dynasty. During that final season under the swastika the family, once so tightly knit, had been strewn across five countries.

Alfried alone remained in Essen. Berthold had been appointed a staff officer in Russia, Harald was adjutant to a German artillery colonel in Bucharest, and Eckbert lay entrenched in northern Italy on the Reich's Gustav Line. By now Gustav himself had permanently withdrawn to the Austrian Alps with Bertha, and messages between Blühnbach and Villa Hügel were rare. With the retirement of the old patriarch there had been a general loosening of familial ties. Alfried was far too busy masterminding the thousandfold schemes of his firm to remember birthdays and anniversaries or write encouraging letters from home. Inasmuch as he had become leader of the dynasty, his silence invited silence. Communications dwindled among all those who, only five years earlier, had risen from the great banquet table beneath Uncle Felix's murals depicting *The Chase for Food* and toasted Eckbert's seventeenth year.[1]

Even within the borders of prewar Germany those bound to Alfried by blood had been separated by the war. Waldtraut was in Bremen with her shipbuilding husband, Irmgard mourned Corporal von Frenz. Alfried's divorced wife Anneliese was rearing their six-year-old son Arndt beside the quiet waters of the Tegernsee, outside Munich; Barbara Krupp Wilmowsky lived on the majestic, isolated grounds of Marienthal Castle, over two hundred miles from Hügel and nearly three hundred from her sister. As far as the rest of the family knew, she and the baron were raising tons of wheat with the help of eastern *Fremdarbeiter*. Certainly no one was worried about her. For a half-century Barbara had been the gentlest, most selfless, and least controversial of the Krupps. Thus it was with incredulity that Alfried learned that his elderly aunt had been arrested by the Gestapo for high treason, thrown into a small cell in Halle-an-der-Saale's common jail with a dozen teen-aged prostitutes, and set to work slicing sausage skins while awaiting trial.

Barbara and Tilo were as surprised as their nephew. Their imprisonment (the baron had been picked up, too) was a direct consequence of the July 20 *Attentat*. Neither had even known of the plot against Hitler's life, but that made little difference; the failure of Count Klaus von Stauffenberg's bomb to exterminate the beast in the lair unleashed a massacre of members of the Offizierskorps, the aristocracy, and the conservatives of the old regime — against all, in short, who at the outset of his regime had regarded "that Austrian corporal" as an upstart and who, now that things were going badly, wanted *der österreichische Gefreiter* dead. It was enough for Himmler that Carl Goerdeler, Johannes Popitz, and Ulrich von Hassel, the three chief conspirators, had been frequent guests at Marienthal. The guilt of their hosts was assumed. Into the bag they went, together with some seven thousand other Germans whose culpability, according to an official source, was "based on names and places"; i.e., guilt by association. Of these, 4,980 were shot, hanged, or tortured to death.[2]

Ironically, some directors of the attempted coup survived for weeks and even months while the innocent were butchered. This was due partly to Goerdeler's eluding his pursuers for twenty-three days, partly to Himmler's hope that he could use the intriguers' Swiss contacts to bargain with the Western powers, and partly to his own inefficiency.[3] Although justly dreaded, the Gestapo lacked counterespionage skills. The files in Himmler's ornate red brick and marble headquarters on Berlin's Prinz-Albrecht-Strasse carried the names of over two million German "suspects," but little of the data had been sifted. Indeed, the schemers had had the Reichsführer's own file clerks in their pay. One of them had warned Goerdeler of his imminent arrest three days before the bomb in the lair went off. Instantly he went into hiding. Hitler put a million marks on his head, and his face was on every front page in the Reich, yet he remained at large until August 12. Then a woman recognized him outside a country inn in Konradswalde, seventy miles from Danzig. By noon he was behind bars.

Next morning Alfried, rising from his Villa Hügel breakfast table, received a telephone call advising him to follow a circuitous route in driving to the office. The home of one of his Bredeney neighbors had been cordoned off; an archcriminal of the Reich was about to be taken into custody. His name — as great a shock as the Marienthal arrests — was Ewald Löser. Alfried didn't even know his old rival was back in the Ruhr. Though Löser had kept his membership on the *Aufsichtsräte* of several Krupp firms, he was presumed to be in Holland, running Philips Radio as the Führer's trustee. Unlike Goerdeler, he hadn't been on the run, because the only written records of his complicity were in his Essen home and in Allen Dulles's ciphers. Learning that Stauffenberg had failed, the Finanzdirektor-designate of the doomed shadow government headed for home, where he and his wife had burned all incriminating documents. Since yesterday they and Dr. Hans Beusch, the physician who was director of Alfried's welfare program in public and, in private, Löser's aide, had been awaiting the heavy knock on the door.[4]

It came at 9 A.M. Five plainclothesmen flashed their leather identity disks and then raced through the house, sweeping books from shelves and ripping apart the huge overstuffed chairs favored then, as now, by Krupp executives. To this day Frau Löser can show precisely where the implicating papers had lain on July 20. While the absence of hard evidence doubtless saved her husband's life, nothing could have prevented his imprisonment. He and Dr. Beusch were handcuffed and led to a waiting black Mercedes, and it was a week before she found out that they were in a damp Berlin dungeon under the palatial Prinz-Albrecht-Strasse headquarters. Even though she brought great baskets of food, Beusch's constitution couldn't withstand Gestapo confinement; that winter the doctor sickened and died. Löser also fell ill, but his immense vitality kept him alive until spring brought peace. He wouldn't have been spared had his accusers uncovered any sort of verification of their distrust; on February 2 Himmler, deciding that Goerdeler and Popitz were useless to him, sent them to hang from meat hooks in Plötzensee prison.* Löser, however, was never even brought to trial. When the Russians entered the capital he was still arguing his ignorance of his friends' disloyalty. His only sin, he contended, had been singularly bad luck. It was a lie, yet it worked.[5]

In Barbara's case it was true, and Gestapo agents couldn't prove otherwise without perjured testimony. The fact that they actually resorted to that suggests they were convinced Marienthal really had been a nest of intrigue. Arraigned before a Nazi *Volksgerichtshof* (People's Court), she was first asked why she had refused membership in a National Socialist organization for charitable activities. Her reply was that she preferred to work through the church. Then one of the castle's forty maids took the stand. On July 17, the girl declared under oath, her mistress had said, "If

---

* *"Sie sollen gehängt werden wie Schlachtvieh,"* the Führer ordered — "String them up like cattle." Filming the executions, Goebbels cameramen accumulated eighty miles of celluloid. Germans, including Nazis, couldn't watch the edited result; they fled from theaters. But Hitler never tired of the movie. Watching it became his favorite diversion.

Hitler died tomorrow all Germany would be happy" (*Wenn Hitler morgen stirbt, freut sich ganz Deutschland*). In the late summer of 1944 that was enough to hang anybody, and the prosecution produced two supporting witnesses. It looked very much as though a granddaughter of the great Krupp was about to be executed for treachery.[6]

Then, abruptly, the judges recalled Barbara's accuser to the stand and inquired why, if she had heard such an incendiary statement three days before the planting of the bomb, hadn't she reported it to the authorities at once? Stauffenberg might have been seized before he could smuggle his legal briefcase into the Wolfsschanze. As it was, the maid was casting grave suspicion on herself. The frightened girl immediately withdrew her charge. Back in her cell, Barbara read Biblical passages to the soiled young doves around her until she was released. Krupp's own explanation for her acquittal was that "Eventually an intelligent prosecuting attorney and a reasonable court (*ein einsichtsvoller Staatsanwalt und ein verständiger Gericht*) restored her freedom." Very likely Alfried had done more than that for his aunt. People's Courts were notoriously unreasonable; their prosecutors acted sensibly only when powerful forces intervened. Barbara's vindication was too good to be true. It becomes comprehensible only if one assumes that the path of Nazi justice had been crossed by the gaunt shadow in Villa Hügel.[7]

Tilo wasn't a real Krupp, the case against him was more substantial,* and his *Volksgerichtshof* behaved differently. To be sure, no one could prove that he had participated in the attempt on the Führer's life. His abhorrence of violence was well known, and he remained a loyal member of the party. Still, his roots lay too deep in Wilhelmine Germany for him to be successfully *gleichgeschaltet* by National Socialism. He had written letters criticizing the SS, he had tried to help a Jew. After lengthy interrogations he was accused of knowing the July 20 plotters, of appearing in Protestant churches as a lay reader, and of demanding better treatment for foreign workers. He "affirmed" all three. For his mischief the court formally expelled him from the party and packed him off to a concentration camp.[8]

The camp was Sachsenhausen on the Havel River; before three seasons had passed its stockade would become the grave for 100,000 people. Bertha, learning of Tilo's plight from Barbara, tried to send her chauffeur there with food — one wonders what her picture of KZ life must have been — and the baron's daughter Ursula brought parcels to the gate. None reached him. As winter deepened his situation became desperate. He was nearly sixty years old, until his arrest he hadn't known a day of deprivation, and his endurance of the cold took on miraculous aspects; afterward he attributed it to a life spent in the open. Yet the worst lay ahead of him. As

---

* For example, his July 26, 1937, guarantee to Gustav that Löser was loyal to the party (NIK-12522).

Zhukov's spearheads approached the camp, a doctor representing the Swedish Red Cross begged the Lagerführer, SS Standartenführer Keindel, to turn Sachsenhausen over to him. Keindel refused. Instead he formed the 40,000 surviving prisoners into two columns and marched them off in a driving rain. Those who couldn't keep up with the others were murdered as they fell out; the Red Cross physician, trailing the rearguard, counted twenty corpses in the first four miles, all of them shot in the head. And that was only the beginning. Before the twin columns were intercepted by American troops, their trek had continued for eleven days. Nursed back to life, the baron vowed he would never forget "this crime," this "shame and dishonor to the German nation." In his memoirs he afterward wrote, "It became completely obvious that Germany had collapsed!" (*Deutschlands völliger Zusammenbruch wurde hier physisch greifbar!*).[9]

✠   ✠   ✠

To informed insiders it had been obvious since the Normandy landings six weeks before the *Attentat*. That was why so many eminent men had committed themselves to the attempt on the Führer's life. Assassination having failed, bereft now of even a shadow government, the Reich drifted toward the abyss. Henceforth each reverse in the field promised personal grief for countless families, and the Krupps were no exception. Barbara's humiliation had been the first blow, Tilo's imprisonment was the second, and the third came on the night of August 26–27, 1944. Aware that the Russian summer offensive would be irresistible, King Michael of Rumania had been secretly negotiating with the USSR since March. A Wehrmacht defeat in the Bessarabian sector, it was agreed, would trigger the king's defection from the Axis; Rumania would join the United Nations and declare war on Germany. He did it August 25. The Führer's troops were trapped, and among the junior officers forced to surrender in the next forty-eight hours was Harald von Bohlen und Halbach.[10]

He gave his right name to his Soviet captors, who, not grasping its significance, herded him into a POW encampment with thousands of others. Very quickly he realized his error. Enemy propaganda agents, turning Goebbels's techniques against him, were courting the prisoners with Marxist ideology; they were especially attentive to German war profiteers, and they had fixed upon Krupp as a symbol. It was only a question of time before a sophisticated commissar linked Harald with Alfried. Transferred to a new POW cage, he destroyed all identification and gave his name as Harald Bohlen. Bit by bit he drifted into a bland anonymity, grew a beard, and awaited repatriation. He nearly made it. By spring most of the prisoners had been sent to Russia. Rumania retained custody of five hundred sick Wehrmacht veterans, among them one Oberleutnant Boller, as Harald now called himself. In May he was put on a train for home and reached the Oder before a German Communist recognized him and betrayed his alias. The Russians sent him straight to a political prison in Moscow. In a remarkably short time they accumulated a three-foot-high dossier on him; then he and a team of interrogators settled down to eleven straight months of questioning.[11]

One Soviet contention was that Krupp's allegiance was to profits, not patriotism. Their unfortunate prisoner knew little of such matters, of course, and as usual the Communists were overstating their case against the family. Nevertheless there was a case to be made. Devoted as Alfried was to the war effort, his chief concern was the firm's solvency. Some proof — it is slight — suggests that the major Schlotbarone formed an alliance for postwar progress on August 10, 1944, three weeks after the *Attentat* and two weeks before Harald's capture. The source is a French double agent, considered reliable, who reported to American military intelligence that representatives of Krupp, Röchling, Messerschmitt, Rheinmetall-Borsig, and the Volkswagenwerk gathered that Thursday in Strasbourg's Hotel Rotes Haus to weigh their future. The Frenchman, who said he was present, declared that the men planned a commercial campaign for the period following capitulation. The keystone of the plan was to be "building foreign credits for Germany."[12]

Whether or not Krupp considered joining forces with fellow industrialists (there is a distinct possibility that the agent in the Red House was himself a Communist), the Konzern had already considered its own position and drawn up an independent blueprint. It was more daring than foreign credits, and far more illegal. Had the Führer heard of it he would have struck hard. But the alternative was bankruptcy. In 1942 Gustav had accumulated more than 200 million marks in Reich treasury bonds. This bale of engraved paper was the nucleus of Alfried's legacy, and he had to get rid of it. The ease with which Allied aircraft dominated the skies over Essen strongly suggested that liens against the present Berlin government were of dubious value. At the same time, the damage wrought by the bombings demanded new capital; as Dr. Friedrich Janssen pointed out at the time, "We must make our financial position so strong that after the end of the war we can reconstruct those shops from our own funds." Therefore liquidation of the Führer's currency began in the first days of the new Krupp's reign.[13]

His lieutenants agreed that the policy was sound. At Nuremberg Johannes Schröder, who had been Janssen's assistant, testified:

> Under the impact of these air attacks and the war situation, we felt that Germany had lost the war and in strictest confidence we said so among ourselves. . . . In view of the coming defeat, Krupp managers were more interested in at least saving something for the postwar era [*Im*

*Anblick der kommenden Niederlage waren die Krupp-Direktoren indessen mehr daran interessiert, wenigstens etwas für die Nachkriegszeit zu ersparen].* We wanted to lead the business into the future in a state of financial health that would permit its survival. . . . . Rather than invest assets in war production and lose them, the firm followed a new policy of secretly keeping all assets as liquid as possible [*Anstatt die verfügbaren Mittel in der Kriegsproduktion anzulegen und zu verlieren, befolgte die Firma insgeheim einen neuen Kurs, nämlich die Guthaben so flüssig wie möglich zu halten*]. It rid itself of war bonds, cashed in claims for war damages, and collected outstanding debts from the Reich.[14]

In practice complete liquidation proved unwise; Stauffenberg saw to that. As Schröder explained, "We had to be particularly careful, especially after July 20, 1944 . . . because the Reich then demanded that industry make all liquid assets available to finance the war. Since we could not use the mails, Dr. Janssen personally went to each subsidiary firm and explained this policy of ours." It was a hazardous venture. Schröder conceded that Alfried and his staff "realized the risk we were running" (*Wir wussten, was wir riskierten*). Their one advantage was that Himmler was baffled by the legerdemain of high finance. He had no idea of what Krupp was up to. Neither, at first, did one member of the Nuremberg tribunal. What, he inquired four years later, had all this accomplished? Schröder's answer was crisp. By "piling up large bank reserves," he explained, *die Firma* remained viable. Altogether some 162 million marks of worthless paper was sold off, "so that when the war was over we had only 68 million marks left in bonds." They too could have been peddled, he added, but that "would have smacked too much of defeatism." There was a long, thoughtful silence in the Justizpalast. Then the witness, reflecting, perhaps, upon how this would sound to his countrymen, cried out, "*Wir waren keine Verräter!*" (We were no traitors!).[15]

The countless dead* who had fallen defending the Fatherland in those last two years might have disagreed, but Alfred Krupp wouldn't have given the question a second thought. His House hadn't been betrayed, and that was what would have mattered to the first Kanonenkönig. It was a matter of priorities, which are different for soldiers and tycoons. Beyond it, however, there is another issue. In Schröder's words, Alfried and those around him persisted in recovering the treasure which Gustav had pledged to Berlin, "although this would have been regarded as a grave act of sabotage and could have sent those involved to a concentration camp" (*obwohl dies als schwerer Sabotageakt die Beteiligten ins KZ-Lager hätte bringen können*).[16] Perhaps he thought that heroic, but to others who had heard all the witnesses it had another ring. The defense of "superior orders," of

---

* Some three and a half million Germans were killed in action; civilian casualties, it is estimated, doubled the Reich's loss.

"blind obedience," of *Befehlsnotstand* and *Rechtspositivismus* — the doctrine that *any* law must be carried out under *all* circumstances — was forever dead. Having risked prison for a fortune, Krupp could never lay the blame for his slaves' fate at the scorched threshold of the Führerbunker.

&#9880; &#9880; &#9880;

The big sell-off reached its peak in midsummer of 1944. In those long weeks of heat and smog the Hauptverwaltungsgebäude functioned in a state of controlled panic. Not all of it was attributable to the mad gleam in the wounded Führer's eye. Once the first Normandy beachhead was consolidated, the Gusstahlfabrik itself was in jeopardy. Alfried had every reason to believe the Anglo-American armies in France had their eye on this arsenal, and he was right. The only disagreement among the enemy commanders was how to approach it best. Montgomery favored "one powerful and full-blooded thrust." The Germans were momentarily demoralized, he argued that August; once in the Ruhr the Allies had but to "maintain forces there for a maximum of three months — and that would be the end." Although Eisenhower preferred an advance on a broad front, he gave the British field marshal his chance at Arnhem. Three airborne divisions were to seize a bridgehead there, outflank the Westwall, and race into the Ruhr. The parachutist gamble ended in a bitter withdrawal; miserable weather, lack of adequate support, and the unexpected presence of two SS panzer divisions on the ground gave the anvil of the Reich a reprieve, and in November the Allies turned to a series of staggered attacks, one of which, Eisenhower hoped, would leap over the Rhine and bring him the great prize.[17]

While the prizeholder in Essen worked against time, his father's condition deteriorated. Until late autumn Gustav remained active. He had to be watched, but he could walk and, frequently, talk. Still, he wasn't the brisk executive he had once been. At the end of the summer Berthold was discharged from the army and assigned to penicillin research in Munich. On visits to Blühnbach he noticed how his father's mind would "fade, come into focus, and fade again." When Ursula von Wilmowsky visited the family's eighty-room Austrian castle in September to describe her own parents' trials Gustav didn't even recognize her. That was an exception, though. He could identify other callers, he was spasmodically coherent (sometimes he would wonder aloud how the Führer's scrap metal drive was going) and though he became vague whenever Berthold tried to describe the grand strategy of the war, there was no reason to believe he would become vaguer. His condition seemed arrested.[18]

On November 25 it plunged. Walking alone in Blühnbach's gardens, the former Krupp whirled toward the castle and began running hard. Before Bertha and the servants could reach him he tripped, fell headlong, and lay sprawled on his back, moaning. One arm was bent oddly; clearly he was hurt. Bertha helped him into a car and told the chauffeur to rush him to the nearest hospital, at Schwarzach–Sankt Veit. But the Austrian Alps are not built for fast driving. The roads are narrow, they double back on themselves in fantastic turns, and at that time of year they are likely to be slippery. Afterward the chauffeur said another car had nearly forced him off the blacktop. Whatever the reason, he did swerve and stand on the brake. Gustav, half conscious, was thrown forward; his head smashed against a metal bar behind the driver. For eight weeks he lay in the hospital, and while there he suffered a paralytic stroke — his second, the doctors told Bertha. After his return to Blühnbach she nursed him almost constantly. Never again, she had been told, could he be left alone. In March, Berthold arrived from Munich and found the old man seated on a balcony, watched by a footman, staring sightlessly across the exquisite valleys. "Papa, we have lost the war," the son said. His father turned and cried, "Berthold!" Yet no one knew, then or ever, whether he had understood. For six years his pathetic silence was to be broken only by occasional oaths and outbursts of inexplicable weeping. To Berthold laboratory research seemed pointless now. He decided to return to Munich and pack up. When the enemy arrived, he assured his mother, he would be here beside her.[19]

Claus in a Luftwaffe grave, the baron in Sachsenhausen, Kurt von Wilmowsky torpedoed on the Atlantic, Irmgard's young husband buried under the Russian snows, Harald missing in action, Gustav stricken and speechless — one by one they were slipping away. The next blow was the loss of Eckbert, and there is something mysterious about it. In April 1945 Bertha received a letter from him. He was well, he expected to remain well. There was no way of telling when the envelope had been posted, however, and when peace came and her youngest child didn't return she grew uneasy. One month of silence followed another until, in August, an officer in his brother's regiment wrote that Eckbert had been killed in March. After corresponding with other men who had been his brother's comrades, Berthold went to Italy and found him buried in San Marino. That is the riddle: San Marino had been occupied by British troops since September 23, 1944. The likeliest explanation is that Eckbert had joined in the retreat from the Gustav Line, had been isolated from his company during the frenzied regrouping on the Gothic Line, and had wandered into unfriendly territory, where he had been shot by a sentry or by partisans.[20]

By the time his death had been confirmed, however, no one was much interested in details. They had too many details as it was; the visitation of night and fog upon the Krupp family itself had lost impact because the crisis seemed to have passed. It had reached its height in the third month of that year, when the Third Reich still existed, *die Firma* was intact, and the thoughts of everyone in the Blühnbach castle except Gustav — and possibly even he, during his crying spells — were upon the castle overlooking the river Ruhr. In the second week of March came word that Allied troops had crossed another, far greater river. For the first time since the Napoleonic invasions, enemy infantry was on the right bank of the Rhine. The Americans had seized a railroad bridge at Remagen.[21]

✠ ✠ ✠

The bridge was taken March 8. Years later, reflecting on that season of violence and disorder, when every day's dispatches brought news of historic alterations in Europe's ancient frontiers, Alfried understated the tension that month in Essen itself. The troubles elsewhere had been far greater, he said; the Ruhr wasn't the worst place to be: "Here we were lucky on the whole (*Hier haben wir im allgemeinen Glück gehabt*), except, of course, that work was constantly being interrupted when people had to go to the air raid shelters" (*als die Leute in die Luftschutzkeller hinunter mussten*).[22]

The last such interruption came on the night of March 11, three days after Remagen's Ludendorff bridge had fallen to a patrol of the 14th U.S. Tank Battalion. At dusk Lancasters appeared over Essen in force. It was two days before the debris settled, and Alfried, carefully stepping through the twisted girders and deformed masonry — 700 unexploded bombs lay among millions of cubic yards of junk — realized that the back of Krupp's one-hundred-and-thirty-four-year-old cast steel factory had at last been broken. One blockbuster had blown a statue of *der Grosse Krupp* from its marble plinth to a shallow crater, though even there the first Cannon King stood on his feet, like a soldier in a foxhole, his beard against the parapet and his furious eyes glaring across the wasteland of smoking sockets.[23]

Alfried's inventory of finished and semifinished steel, stored in warehouses outside the city, exceeded 100,000 — two months' production — and with the raw materials on hand Borbeck and Rheinhausen could produce 100,000 more. Once that was gone, however, there would be no more. Although two-thirds of Krupp's industrial plant in Germany remained intact, communication was hopeless. The following week Hitler, concluding that the German people were unworthy of him, issued a *Führerbefehl* commanding the destruction of all power plants and coal mines. Speer was appalled, Krupp sardonic. In Essen the job had already been accomplished by the obliging *Engländer*. Bombs hadn't reached the priceless tunnels underground, of course, but they had demolished the surface pumps, permitting underground wells to fill the shafts hewn by four generations of miners. Any *Kumpel* who tried to report for work now would be drowned. Thus the new Gauleiter's order to evacuate all shops was gratuitous, though Alfried dutifully endorsed it and even decided to hole up in Villa Hügel on the ground that his appearance in his office might encourage faithful Kruppianer to re-enter their smashed factories. ("*Befehl ist Befehl*," he said — "An order is an order.") Fritz Tubbesing was appointed full-time caretaker of the Hauptverwaltungsgebäude. From his office directly above Alfried's he looked out wonderingly on the forest of idle, stunted chimneys. Later he said, "During my thirty years of work for the firm I had never known such stillness" (*In den dreissig Jahren meiner Tätigkeit für die Firma habe ich niemals eine solche Stille erlebt*).[24]

The approach of peace should have brought a respite for the slaves. They had been brought here to work; now that Germany's defeat was only a matter of time — now that their jobs had lost all meaning — they should have been left alone to await their deliverers. But the *Sklavengeschäft* had never been sensible, and with the failure of Rundstedt's Ardennes offensive the prospects of Krupp's conscripts had taken an ominous turn. A kind of madness swept some of the guards; realizing that the end was near, they cast about for scapegoats and flung themselves upon their emaciated chattels. Toward the end of that winter, when two feet of snow had blanketed the Reich and Germans without face masks had suffered constant headaches, Ukrainian women in unheated barracks were awakened at 4 A.M. (for no reason whatever) by icy jets of water. Once the prisoners were up, guards attacked them with solid rubber hoses, lashing at their breasts. Male slaves were struck in the groin, and few were left unbruised, for beatings had now been incorporated into the daily routine.[25]

The sources for this last act of Krupp's slave labor tragedy are almost all German Kruppianer who voluntarily came to the Palace of Justice, telling their stories in the presence of the one man who might give them jobs or pensions once Allied troops had been withdrawn from the Ruhr. If Teutonic sadism is a prodigy, so is Teutonic idealism, as the selflessness of the July 20 martyrs had demonstrated. There were workmen in Essen who had been deeply offended by Werkschutz brutality, had protested at the time, and wanted justice done, whatever the cost to themselves. The defense never attempted to answer them, and they were, in fact, unanswerable. No single incident was damning in itself, but the cumulative effect was overwhelming. And when unimpeachable witnesses declared that some of the most revolting episodes had occurred within earshot of Alfried's office, there was an uneasy stirring in the dock — though the chief defendant sat impassive, tuning testimony out now as he may have tuned out screams then.[26]

The witnesses agreed that mistreatment had accelerated as broadcasts from Hans Fritzsche, Goebbels's official radio commentator, conceded that the Wehrmacht was falling back. For his tens of millions of listeners, the newscaster's introductory "*Hier spricht Hans Fritzsche*" (This is Hans Fritzsche) had become as familiar as Edward R. Murrow's "This is London" was elsewhere. Fritzsche was trusted, and when he prophesied

Götterdämmerung, his listeners knew they were for it. Their response appears to have been almost reflexive. One Krupp torturer who appeared before a Nuremberg commission was Heinrich Hümmerich, a veteran member of the Werkschutz's elite Werkschar. "At the beginning, this kind of punishment was rare," he said, "but as the end of the war approached it happened more and more often that people were seized and turned over to us."[27]

Fastidious guards and foremen sent slaves to the Werkschar. Those with thicker skins administered their own punishments. A worker named Vogelmann swore that a fellow employee "ruthlessly beat a Russian prisoner of war" with a homemade truncheon "until the prisoner collapsed, covered with blood, and died shortly afterwards from head injuries." A German called Käfer told how another Kruppianer struck a foreigner "with a wooden board in which there were nails, in such a brutal manner that the prisoner lost consciousness and had to be taken away." A man named Guseinow described how inflamed a certain guard became whenever one of his Ostarbeiterinnen complained that she had been separated from her baby in Buschmannshof; once "an eastern female worker, who was too unhappy about the death of her child to work, was driven to work by him with blows."[28]

Intervention in behalf of victims was imprudent. Franz Beduhn, an employee of the firm since 1927, objected to the methods of Heinrich Buschhauer, the supervisor of Russian POW's in the boiler construction department. One day, according to Beduhn's affidavit — which was supported by signed statements from four fellow craftsmen — "Buschhauer picked out an especially weak man and ordered him to move, by himself, heavy iron blocks weighing nearly 1,000 pounds." The prisoner couldn't do it; it was physically impossible. When he failed the supervisor "fell upon him and hit him in the face with his fist. The Russian immediately collapsed. However, Buschhauer did not leave him alone, but kicked the poor man without mercy. He kicked him in the stomach, in the neck, and in the back." Beduhn flung himself between them, Buschhauer shouted that he would report him to the Gestapo, and the mediator was saved only by swift action by the shop manager. The subsequent fate of the Russian is, as usual, unknown. There was really only one sure way to flee a determined persecutor: enlistment in the Wehrmacht. Several Poles suffering from chilblains volunteered just to get shoes. This escape hatch, of course, was restricted to males.[29]

Actual torture was carried out in the Hauptverwaltungsgebäude basement, a vast, gloomy, concrete cavern. Werkschutz and Werkschar headquarters were there, and in one of their offices off-duty guards constructed an ingenious device to humble exasperating slaves. It looked like a metal cupboard, but Fritz Fell, a night shift switchboard operator who worked thirty feet away and saw it in use, christened it with the name by which it became known and feared: "the cage" (*der Käfig*). He later explained, "I saw eastern female workers locked into the cupboard and said to myself, 'This is a cage.' I don't know the reason exactly. Well, because an animal — a bird — you lock into a cage."[30]

The *Käfig* was designed for people, and was therefore much larger than a birdcage. American officers thought it so unusual that they photographed it, and three of their prints were submitted at Nuremberg as exhibits. The pictures show a windowless, heavy steel apparatus five feet high — four to six inches too low for the average adult to stand erect. The interior was divided by a vertical partition, creating two cells, each 22 inches wide and 22 inches deep. Two perforations in the lid provided the only ventilation, and two heavy bolts in front securely held prisoners inside. As General Taylor told the tribunal, "slave workers were crammed in a crouching position and left for periods of hours up to several days. A refinement of torture was to pour water during winter weather onto the victims through [the] air holes in the top of the cupboard."[31]

Unterführer Gerlach, to give him his Werkschar title, was the keeper of the cage. When Hitler invaded Poland, Gerlach had been an obscure Krupp locksmith; he was one of those gifted sadists whose talents emerged in the *Sklaverei* pens. By turn he had become a Werkschutz guard, a Lagerführer, and finally deputy leader of the company police. It was Gerlach who first saw the possibilities in the ventilation slots. One bitter winter night Josef Dahm, a German civilian whose duties sometimes brought him to the guardroom, saw the Unterführer lock slaves in the cage. Then, in Dahm's words, "Gerlach took a pail of water and emptied it on the top of the cupboard and the water dripped into the cupboard." From inside Dahm heard "a moaning."[32]

Gerlach was among those who were irritated by women with infants in Buschmannshof. One mother insisted on making a weekly round trip there. His annoyance increased when he heard that she had conceived a second time, and he put her in the cage. The details of this incident subsequently came from Fritz Fell, who was subjected to one of the sharper cross-examinations in Nuremberg's Justizpalast. Fell testified that at the time of her *Käfig* torment the Slavic wife was in the seventh month of pregnancy. Heinz Wolf, a Krupp counsel, was derisive. How, he asked, could the witness have known that? Fell's answer seems straightforward enough: "Because her fellow worker, a certain Herti Scartipa, told me that. And it could be noticed pretty easily." Once Gerlach noticed it, he began stalking her. She was due back from Voerde-bei-Dinslaken at 10 P.M. each Sunday. Missing a trolley transfer once, she checked back at 10:15. The Unterführer had her brought directly to his office. "I've waited for that for a long time — for you to overstay your leave," the switchboard operator heard him shout, and into the cage she went. For an expectant mother in her condition the agony must have been indescribable. Fell went off duty at 6 A.M. When he returned she had vanished.[33]

"Bad as beatings were," the Justizpalast tribunal observed in its summation, "women confined in the 'cage' begged for beatings rather than undergo the torture of being in the 'cage.'" Some Krupp prisoners got both. At the end of December, as Rathaus bells greeted the last New Year of the Third Reich, eastern workers assigned to Tank Construction Shop IV began what Dahm called a "kind of festivity." Summoned, Gerlach found three *Fremdarbeiter* in female barracks. He took them to headquarters and gave each a standard beating with a rubber truncheon. Then he locked all three in the *Käfig*, one on the left side and two on the right. They groaned and he dumped water on them. After an hour the muffled cries of the stooping prisoners on the right became unbearable to Dahm. He suggested to Gerlach that one be released, and one was, but the others remained caged until the next day.[34]

The courtroom performance of men like Dahm and Fell, Aryans who had enjoyed the privileges of *Übermenschen* and who spoke out against Alfried now that he had been defeated, incensed Krupp's thirty-seven lawyers. If in fact these alleged abuses had taken place in the Hauptverwaltungsgebäude, they asked bitingly, why hadn't the witnesses complained at the time? The stratagem wasn't clever. It ignored evidence that some outraged Kruppianer *had* spoken up, and it assumed that Krupp would have sided with the complainants — that the Gerlachs were not instruments of an official policy. Everything pointed the other way. Dahm said, "I was afraid that if I said anything Gerlach would have done something to me," that although the Unterführer had no authority over him, "he could have reported me, and I would have been taken away." Similarly, Fell replied that a protest from him "would have meant my arrest at the very least." In this they were supported by a Werkschutz guard who had seen other company policemen murder slaves. Explaining why he had held his own tongue, he said, "Those occurrences were generally known. I knew the authorities already knew what had happened."[35]

The authorities must have known. Torture is noisy, and the beatings and cagings were staged, not on the outskirts of Essen, but in Alfried's Hauptverwaltungsgebäude. Fräulein Ilse Wagner, one of the Konzernherr's secretaries, told the court that sitting at her desk she could hear the victims' cries. In pondering the guilt of her employer and his board, the Nuremberg tribunal found such evidence probative. "The beatings . . . were known to the members of the Werkschutz," the judges observed in their verdict. "They were known to secretaries who were employed in the building. Could they have been unknown to these defendants whose offices were in the building?"[36]

✠    ✠    ✠

No more cries were heard from Humboldtstrasse after Saint Patrick's Day. That morning Karl Sommerer led the approximately five hundred Jewish girls to Bochum on schedule and put them aboard the Buchenwald train. Sommerer didn't bother to count heads. There wouldn't have been much point in it. In three raids camp records had vanished in flames, and no one knew how many inmates had perished then, at the mill, or under Lagerführer Rieck's cunning whip. A check seemed unnecessary anyhow. The prisoners were too feeble to stray and too conspicuous to avoid notice. With their swollen bellies, running sores, and eccentric haircuts, dressed in torn burlap gowns and ripped blankets, lacking rations or reliable contacts or even a primitive knowledge of Essen's street plan — without, in sum, a strand of hope, they apparently hadn't a chance. It was inconceivable that one of them could walk a block without being challenged by a loyal Kruppianer.[37]

Incredibly, five of them hobbled sixty blocks and found a precarious sanctuary. At the height of the March 11 bombing, with Rieck and his guards in their shelter, Elizabeth Roth had crept to the slack span of barbwire with her sister Ernestine and with Agnes and René Königsberg, Rosa Katz, and a sixth girl, a virtual stranger who had joined them at the last moment. The wire parted easily; one by one they crawled through, examined the rusty barbs by the light of the overhead flares to make sure they had left no telltale shreds of burlap, and started across the field beyond. At this point the strange girl's nerve broke. It is a common phenomenon among escapees; the known, however ghastly, seems preferable to the unknown. The reluctant runaway turned back, tremblingly re-entered the gap, and was never seen again by the others.[38]

They, too, were confused. Elizabeth wanted to find Kurt Schneider, Rosa preferred Gerhardt Marquardt's hutch. Both lay to the northeast, and so, after a whispered consultation, they struck out in that direction. Soon they were lost. Next day they had no idea where they had been, but years later this writer, with the help of the girls, retraced their route through suburban Frohnhausen, past the ruins of Dechenschule and Raumerstrasse, across the Essen-Mülheim railroad tracks, into the blazing heart of the Gusstahlfabrik itself, and out again.

Their survival of the great raid was a marvel. Yet without it they would have had no chance. All around them frantic Kruppianer were running about. A second glance from a single German would have identified the fugitives as *Stücke*, but as the marker flares sparkled overhead, followed by wave after wave of heavy aircraft, no one had the patience or the presence of mind for that. Four miles to the south Alfried could stand on the steps of his castle watching the havoc with relative poise. Here equanimity would have seemed suicidal, and consequently the five escapees emerged on Zangenstrasse without being hailed or even noticed.

They didn't know they were on Zangenstrasse, and had a street sign remained standing it wouldn't have helped much. Briefly the swirling pall lifted; on either side of the street, they saw, were cemeteries. For a sickening moment they thought they had followed a great circle and returned to Humboldtstrasse. Neither graveyard was Südwestfriedhof, however. Had the blanket of smoke lifted entirely, they would have glimpsed the hulking sheds of what was left of Walzwerk II, four blocks to the west. Despite their intricate detours they had instinctively paralleled the *Links-Rechts* of the SS guards and were a short walk from their shop. Indeed, it was nearly worktime. To the east, through the gray shroud blanketing the city, they perceived a faint ribbon of light. Dawn was imminent. Already the first sickly glow illuminated the cemetery on the eastern side of the street. It appealed to Elizabeth; of the two burial grounds, Segerothfriedhof, though they did not know its name then, looked safer. The plots appeared to be ill kept; the grass was long; they could burrow in it and sleep securely through the day. In fact, she had chosen the best place of concealment in all Essen, and once they were inside and the light had grown stronger they realized it. Though chipped and desecrated with crudely painted yellow swastikas, the headstones around them were familiar. Some were tablets inscribed in Hebrew, others bore the Star of David. Unwittingly they had blundered into the city's old Jewish graveyard — the one place where no one would look for living *Jüdinnen*.

The solution was only temporary. They were desperately in need of food and water. Here again they were in luck — not much, but some — for on the far side of Segerothfriedhof, across a narrow meadow, Rosa Katz saw a long low line of tiny tarpaper and brick huts, each with a vegetable garden and outhouse behind and an untrimmed hedge to shield it from its neighbors. This, she told them excitedly, was the Stadtwiese, Marquardt's home. While Elizabeth and the Königsbergs established a crude bunker in a bombed-out cellar between the cemetery and the meadow, Rosa and Ernestine fetched Marquardt. Elizabeth, testifying in her imperfect English, later told the tribunal of his reaction. Apparently Marquardt had expected to help Rosa, not her friends:

> He was shocked when he saw my sister. When they explained to him that we escaped he said, "I can't help you. Better go back." But I knew that we couldn't go back. . . . I asked him to give me a pistol. I would kill myself better. He said he couldn't do that, he will see what he can do. I said I will do everything I can, but he must help. So he helped us. We couldn't stay in that cellar, it was open, no place to sit down. We find another cellar. We move there. At night, at one o'clock, he used to bring

us each a potato, a slice of bread. The first three days he didn't bring anything. He was afraid to say to his wife he is going to help us. The fourth day he brought us a bottle of water. We didn't know what to do with that water, drink from the water — to drink or to wash ourselves. It was then for one and a half weeks that he used to come and see us at night.[39]

Marquardt's recollection is quite different. In the courtroom he cast himself in an admirable role, insisting that he had found them the cemetery, defied SS men who told him, "If we ever find the man who is giving shelter to the girls we will certainly hang him," and provided the girls with potatoes, rabbit meat, and cooking utensils. After they had left Germany, he continued, they sent him parcels. Marquardt went further: he maintained that they told him they were "glad to have left the Auschwitz camp" and "quite liked it at Krupp." All this is unlikely. Their discovery of the graveyard had been fortuitous. There is no reason to believe that either Krupp or the SS was aware of their absence. The Roths have no memory of sending him parcels, and while they were doubtless glad to have seen the last of Auschwitz, it is inconceivable that they would have voluntarily endorsed Krupp.[40]

Rosa was absent more and more often, and one day she disappeared altogether. Since Marquardt vanished at the same time, the Roths and the Königsbergs assumed they had drifted off together. In any event the four left were now quite destitute. How long they remained so is difficult to determine, but since they remember artillery shells falling in the Stadtwiese they must have stayed until late March. Obsessed by the craving for food, they entirely forgot the possibility of recapture. One afternoon Elizabeth was resting her back against the cellar wall, sipping rainwater, when she saw a man staring down at her. "*Was für eine Blume ist das?*" he asked ironically — "What is this flower?" Terrified, frantically coping with the strange idiom, she blurted out the first thing that came to mind; she said they were German women who had escaped from the Americans and were returning to the Fatherland. Turning solemn, he studied their gowns, wounds, arm numbers, and hair and asked the obvious. Weren't they *Häftlinge*, prisoners of state? Certainly not, Elizabeth replied indignantly; they were *Damen*. Thoughtfully he said, "You had better watch out, because the Gestapo found twelve *Häftlinge* who escaped from a camp, and they were just killed." She decided to confide in him. He seemed compassionate and, as she said afterward, "there was no choice, we had to tell him."

He realized it. He said he had a wooden hut, and he said, "If you like to stay there, you take it." So we chose that. We stayed there for a few days, but after a few days he couldn't feed us. He was a very, very poor man who didn't have enough for himself to eat. A few days later he said he couldn't feed us, and he couldn't come back, because he was afraid of his neighbors. They would find out that we were there.[41]

Kurt Schneider was their last hope. Ernestine and Agnes were sure they could find his house. Late one night they did, skulking through wreckage and darkened backyards. They told him their plight — and he threw up his hands. Schneider himself was near the end of his tether. Besides, he argued reasonably, his home would offer no asylum. The very prominence of his street — which had attracted him to Elizabeth's attention in the first place — militated against it. No one could go unnoticed there for long. Nevertheless he thought he knew someone who *could* help them. Fritz Niermann, a pious grocer, had been deeply offended by Berlin's imprisonment of Martin Niemöller. The grocer occupied a large, undamaged flat on the second story of Markscheide 15, a stone apartment house halfway down a narrow dead-end street just off Altendorferstrasse. He was offering refuge to enemies of the regime, and Schneider would tell him to expect four girls.[42]

Markscheide 15 could have existed only in the last days of Hitler. Understandably, the young women were skittish. They hadn't really known Schneider well, didn't know Niermann at all, and discovered next evening that to reach the flat they had to pick their way back through the eerie remnants of the Gusstahlfabrik. Passing the Hauptverwaltungsgebäude was the worst of it. There was no way to bypass the sprawling administrative complex. Indeed, they actually had to walk by Werkschutz headquarters — crossing the street to skirt Gerlach and his legendary *Käfig*. Even after they had reached the side street they were only a brisk fifteen-minute walk from Alfried's office, and the first people they saw in the apartment foyer were three tall, slender SS officers in full uniform. That seemed to be the end of the girls. In reality it was the end of their suffering. Niermann and his wife came forward slowly, but there was nothing inauspicious in that; the grocer, in his sixties, suffered from heart trouble. Both were generous, *gemütliche* Germans, both greeted them warmly. The girls were given their own room, with an exit to the street. There was only one rule of the house: never speak to fellow guests or, if possible, glance in their direction. The host didn't even explain the SS men. It wasn't necessary. Within a week the big central hall was swarming with black, brown, and gray tunics — defecting soldiers and party *Blockwart* whose treason had placed their lives in peril as great as that of any Jewess. Agnes even learned to recognize the tiny identifying badges which distinguished members of the SS, the criminal police, the security police, and the SD. At any other time the girls would have been perplexed by the swarm of turncoats, but their immense feeling of relief eclipsed curiosity. It was enough to lie on clean linen, let their hair grow, follow the Niermanns' diet, and watch the symptoms of their dropsy diminish.

✠    ✠    ✠

On their third afternoon all four were roused by a commotion outside. Sidling up to the curtains they saw a harsh glow against the flawless spring sky. Something was burning outside, and since there were no Lancasters overhead they wondered fleetingly what it could be. Scarcely anyone knew then, including Kriminalrat Peter Nohles and his Gestapo superiors in Düsseldorf. Today, however, Fritz Tubbesing speaks freely of it. Krupp safes were stuffed with sensitive documents, intrafirm memoranda and correspondence, and transcripts of conferences. Some were classified, some were embarrassing, and some were downright incomprehensible to men who had not lived and worked in the Führer's shadow. Assembling his directors in the subcellar below the Werkschutz — the offices upstairs were littered with window glass, and no one could be sure that the March 11 raid had been the last — Alfried ordered a massive deportation of paper. Reports of minor significance could be stored down here in safes; only Schröder and Tubbesing would retain keys to them. His shaggy eyebrows arched: *Verstehst du?* They nodded, they understood — *Das versteht sich von selbst*; it went without saying. The Konzernherr went on to explain that other sensitive papers would be shipped from the Ruhr and stored in 150 caches. A list had been prepared. The chief hiding places would be ore mines in the Harz mountains in central Germany; Baron von Wilmowsky's two Saxony estates, Friedrich Alfred Krupp's old shooting box, an unused Bohlen castle, and a Blühnbach alp.*[43]

The most delicate files were saved for last. That was bad planning, for they were still in their vaults, awaiting transport, when word of catastrophe reached Villa Hügel. In the third week of March, Eisenhower had authorized Bradley to broaden the Remagen bridgehead. The Ninth American Army's offensive roared out of its riverside bridgeheads in the first light of March 23. Feldmarschall Walther Model was being encircled. Generals George Patton and Courtney Hodges, joining forces near Giessen, cut loose from their supply bases and raced up the Frankfurt-Kassel corridor in a great sweep east of the Ruhr. Meanwhile Lieutenant General J. Lawton Collins spun his VII Corps north and sliced across the unprotected rear of German troops still clinging to the Rhine between Cologne and Duisburg.[44]

In one day American tank columns covered fifty-five miles. Patton, Hodges, and Collins now had a common target: the Prussian city of Paderborn, fifty miles east of Münster. To the Führer it was sacred

---

* Krupp's scheme failed. Allied infantrymen unearthed the strongboxes in all 150 crypts. (WM/Tubbesing.)

ground. Here his panzer divisions had been born, and here his finest tank specialists were training picked cadets in the newest Krupp models. Teachers, pupils, and machines fought gallantly against the converging spearheads, but their valor had been star-crossed before they sighted the first enemy turret. On April 1 they were overwhelmed. The trap had closed: Hamm became its padlock. Inside were 350,000 Reich soldiers. It was a greater disaster than Stalingrad, the most stupendous in German military history, and Model, after ordering his disintegrating garrisons to fight on for eighteen days, contemplated suicide.[45]

Doubtless the Konzernherr was in a mood to shoot the Feldmarschall himself. Now there was no way to smuggle out his files. Among them were blueprints for secret weapons, invaluable assets for a munitions firm and potential contributions to a new Germany which might rise from the ashes of a second Versailles. Now they themselves must be reduced to cinders. Furthermore, there wasn't much time. In Berlin the Führer had nearly a month to live, but already U.S. Long Toms were throwing 155-mm. shells into what was left of Essen from Hamborn, a town outside Duisburg, seventeen miles away. One of them had struck the span between the Hauptverwaltungsgebäude's two wings, dumping what was left of the structure into Altendorferstrasse like a revolutionary barricade. Tubbesing, examining the wreckage, momentarily wondered which American family made Yank *Kanonen*. But this was no hour for reflection. Telephoning the caretaker from the Hill, a director demanded of him, "Is the parking lot burning yet?"[46]

During the 1930's the garage from which Lieutenant Durieux had cried "*Commencez le feu!*" — creating thirteen Krupp martyrs and endearing Gustav to the defeated nation — had been leveled. The square had then been paved to receive the 990-mark ($396) Volkswagens which the Führer had promised German workmen and never delivered. Now history was about to transpire in this vacant *Parkplatz* once more. The subsequent event has been variously described, and its meaning is imprecise. Noting the frequent absence of links between Alfried and specific crimes (for example, executions, instructions to Krupp selectors at Auschwitz, the Buchenwald deportation, and the outrages of Buschmannshof), Cecelia H. Goetz, a member of the Nuremberg prosecution team, said flatly, "Of course, the most damning documents went up in the fire before the Americans arrived." No one contradicted her, and the tribunal, sharing her view, observed pointedly in its ruling that "It appears from the evidence that a great volume of documents from the files of the Krupp firm were burned . . . shortly before the entry of the Allied troops into Essen. The significance of the burning of these documents is not to be overlooked."[47]

There was really no way to justify this eleventh-hour incineration. Later Tubbesing conceded, "Some papers were destroyed by the firm. They were secret papers." To the idle Kruppianer who ringed the pavement, watched the caretaker and his staff lug out carton after carton until a towering pyramid had been erected, stood back while it was doused with *Benzin*, and headed for cover as Tubbesing held a match to the fuse, it became known as "the bonfire." *Das Freudenfeuer* is as good a name as any, for every condemned sheet of paper was incinerated in the leaping flames.[48]

Each morning now the shellfire grew in intensity. Daytime strafers had replaced the lumbering night bombers; the streets were dangerous. Krupp's slaves knew liberation was close. They could tell, for one thing, from the attitude of German civilians. The SS forfeited its last five minutes and melted away, and the worst of the Werkschutz sadists followed them. On January 9 Willi Toppat,* the swart camp beater (*Untier*) at Neerfeld-schule, had flogged Father Come for the last time. As the Toppats and Hassels and Gerlachs faded into the countryside, distinctions between *Übermenschen* and *Untermenschen* became blurred. Paul Ledoux and the Belgian priest had been beavering away at a Neerfeldschule tunnel. Now they were befriended by Frintop families who wanted to share food with the prisoners.[49]

On April 8 a member of the Direktorium decided to call Wolfgang Schleicher, technical director of Jacob Mayer's old factory in Bochum. An American voice answered — though the Bochumer Verein was seventeen miles *east* of Essen, it was already in U.S. hands. By that evening Alfried, on the hill, and Tubbesing, in the empty Hauptverwaltungsgebäude, had acquired a nervous habit of glancing at clocks from time to time. The war had seen it once before, in Britain fifty-five months earlier. On September 4, 1940, Hitler had kept the Sportspalast roaring with laughter when he said craftily, "In England they are consumed with curiosity and keep asking, 'Why doesn't he come?' Be calm, he's coming! Be calm, he's coming!" (*Beruhigt euch, er kommt!*)[50]

Now it was the Herrenvolk's turn to be calm, for the enemy was coming *here*. On the night of April 9 patrols were reported crossing the Rhein-Herne Canal, the northern boundary of Greater Essen. Advance platoons were in Vogelheim and Dellwig next day, littering Katenberg and Kaiser Wilhelm Park with discarded Ten-in-One rations and setting up Browning automatic rifles and 60-mm. mortars in Schonnebeck, Stoppenberg, and Altenessen. In these northern suburbs Kruppianer and Hausfrauen eyed the lanky, unkempt, bearded Yanks warily. They came from a country "whose conceptions of life," Hitler had told Essen, "are determined by a greedy shopkeeper's outlook (*habgierigsten Krämergeist*) and who love none of the loftiest expressions of the human spirit (*die höchsten Äus-serungen des menschlichen Geistes*), such as music."[51]

---

*On May 18, 1948, Willi — who had been a prewar grinder (*Schleifer*) in the Gus-stahlfabrik's Rolling Mill No. 1 — frankly described the professional tricks of Krupp's camp beaters to the Nuremberg tribunal. In the dock Alfried whispered, "Before this trial I never knew what faults and idiocies my people were capable of."

Whatever their shortcomings — and his scathing analysis was to be echoed and rephrased during the next twenty years by intellectuals in every European country — there was something to be said for the unshaven infantrymen. For example, they had come prepared. Over three centuries they too had developed a national character, and one quality which they shared with their checkmated foe was a passion for efficiency and productivity. On the other hand, they cherished a sentimental affection for underdogs, never a Teutonic weakness. Even before arriving in the Ruhr they had heard rumors of slave labor. Now the sights and smells of the system itself incensed them. Krupp had been right; though their own country had been the last civilized nation to abolish slavery, they would never understand his KZ *Lager*. On every level they recoiled angrily. GIs waving M1's forced *Hausfrauen* to empty their pantries for freed prisoners, officers paraded Kruppianer through the foulest camps, knocking down the arms of those who tried to hold their noses; and corps headquarters, more practical, dispatched flying squads of displaced person experts.

In the hiatus between freedom and benevolent regimentation (there was no other solution) *Sklaven* roamed about in bands of hundreds, even thousands. Afterward Germans would spin lurid tales of murder, rape, and plunder. Retribution would have been understandable. Certainly the sadists had been wise to flee, and General Taylor cannot be taxed for his subsequent observation in the *Columbia Law Review* that "quite apart from considerations bearing on the security of the occupation, it would have hardly been a kindness to Krupp and other prominent suspected war criminals to leave them at large." Essen, he pointed out, had been thronged with Krupp's forced labor. "Had prominent Nazis been left at large," he wrote, "they would have been the target for acts of private vengeance and a stimulus to political violence on a large scale."[52]

Only the last phrase is doubtful. The U.S. army would have suppressed any uprising, and the emancipated slaves were incapable of organization. A handful wandered up the hills and held out there until July, waylaying Germans rash enough to travel alone. But the highwaymen were exceptional. A poll of Ruhr households exposed the stories of violence as hearsay. Repeatedly Kruppianer wives recalled watching as a ragged horde approached their kitchens, reaching for their carving knives (suicide, they had been taught, was preferable to *Rassenschande*, coitus with Sklaven) — and then learning that the menacing Ausländer merely wanted water, a few tins of food, and compass bearings. They were eager to go home; they just wanted to know the way. In all Kruppdom there was but one recorded instance of Slavic pillage. On their first day of liberty a band of Ukrainians broke into the firm's Konsum-Anstalt between Altendorferstrasse and the Essener Hof and emptied the wine cellar. Next day they were desperately ill. Germans describe the scene sympathetically; they are far more bitter toward the GIs who seized their watches and cameras. (Today Ninth

Army veterans confess that this was outright theft. They expected to meet the Russians soon, and wanted gadgets to barter for souvenirs.)[53]

Most released prisoners were too weak for thoughts of the *Sklavenhalter* in his castle, for the Krupp policemen who had tormented them, or for reprisal in any form. Father Come had been a slave only seven months, yet he weighed less than a hundred pounds. Despite professional care from the Belgian Red Cross he couldn't walk into Smuid until May 4, five weeks after his liberation, and even then he was unrecognized in his own parish. As a westerner, the priest was provided with guides. Russians were fed from military canteens and left to themselves until the two fronts merged. Some Allied officers expressed apprehension that with nourishment they might become unruly, but the conquerors had no concept of what prolonged subjugation does to the spirit. In his remarkable *roman à clef, The Birthday King,* Gabriel Fielding describes the life of a German industrial family led by a protagonist named Alfried and his blind mother (and opposed by a close relative, a baron who perishes in the *Attentat*) between 1939 and 1945. Though the fictive slaves are always milling about in the novel's background, there is an eerie air of unreality about them. Emancipated by American troops in the spring, "the prisoners in their striped camp wear, tiring too soon, had sat down . . . in groups looking like hundreds of clowns escaped from a giant circus. A number of them had died where they sat or lay; of joy or sadness or of simple dysentery which had been rife in the camp for months."[54]

Fielding's inmates were Russians, Ukrainians, and Poles, whose repatriation had yet to be worked out. Like Alfried Waitzmann in *The Birthday King,* Alfried Krupp had populated most of his stockades with *Ostarbeiter* and *Ostarbeiterinnen;* they had been more plentiful and cheaper. Other nationalities were contacted by the DP squads with celerity, however. Ninth Army had brought officers who spoke French, Flemish, Dutch, Italian, all the Scandinavian languages and — to the astonishment of the Roths and Königsbergs — many languages of eastern Europe, too. After the deserters in Niermann's flat had changed to mufti and hurried away, Elizabeth, Ernestine, Agnes, and René ventured to the corner of Markscheide and Altendorferstrasse with their hosts. The thoroughfare was impassable, crowded with slogging infantrymen and their equipment. It was like a victory parade, she thought, and she wanted to wave a flag. Suddenly she saw a real flag. Stepping back, she gripped her sister's arm. In a jeep cruising slowly past them sat a captain whose shoulder patch bore twin stripes of red and white intersected at one end by a blue triangle — the ensign of prewar Czechoslovakia.[55]

Elizabeth cried out, the other three girls waved, and the captain ordered his driver to stop. Easily shouldering pedestrians aside — the Germans seemed hypnotized by the Americans' nonchalant gait; they had never seen such a slovenly parade — he loomed over the young women. "Where are you from?" he asked, in Slovakian, Hungarian, and Czech. In Czech they replied together, "Uzhorod!" Then they all began babbling at once. The DP officer held up his hand and said he would lead them to a central collecting point. They froze, but he had been schooled to deal with fears. Rapidly he added that they must come voluntarily; there would be no roll calls or barbwire, and no one would be expected or even allowed to work. From his musette bag he drew four salmon-colored identity cards. These, he explained, were for Czech DPs. Once they had been completed and returned, the bearers would be entitled to extra rations — more, he explained casually, than the Germans were going to get.

To the Niermanns, Elizabeth whispered lightly — but prophetically — "Maybe we'll be sending you food."

She had spoken in German. The captain started and asked her to speak louder. When she began her reply in Czech, he interrupted: "*Wie sagt man das auf deutsch, bitte?*"

Obligingly she shifted to German, and he looked thoughtful. "*Gut! Sehr gut!*" he said at last. "*Das ist richtig* (That is right). *So Sie sprechen deutsch.*"

"*Jawohl,*" she said, curtsying. "English, too, pretty good."

He smiled. "Good — maybe they can use you as a receptionist."

"Receptionist?" The word was new. Her English wasn't that good.

"*Sprechstundenhilfe.*" The German was equally strange to her, so he said in Czech, "*Úředník v čekárně — v předpokji.*" He added, "To meet people, maybe up at Villa Hügel."

Elizabeth looked blank. "What's Villa Hügel?" she asked.

# 24

✠

# I Am the Owner of This Property

O N page one of April 10's *New York Times* a four-column map depicted the Ruhr surrounded by a broken white loop labeled by a tiny U.S. flag: "9TH ARMY." Beneath the flag three black arrows pointed at Essen, but though an Associated Press correspondent reported that he had been inside the city — and his description of damage confirms him — the battle wasn't over. LIMITED GAINS MADE IN RUHR, a gloomy copy editor wrote. They were very limited. "What is there left to a commander in defeat?" the anguished Model asked his staff. "In ancient times they took poison." He then shot himself, leaving behind a plea to fight on which needlessly prolonged the agony of embattled Kruppianer and their conscripts. To be sure, thousands of exhausted soldiers did down their arms. However, in Werden, directly across the Ruhr from Essen, a motley phalanx of twelve-year-old Werewolves, seventy-year-old members of the home guard (*Volkssturm*), *Volks* Grenadiers, *Flaktruppen* without 88's, panzer crews without tanks, Luftwaffe pilots without planes, and diehard paratroopers dug in to defend the south bank of the Ruhr. Alfried didn't need the *Times* or the AP to know what was happening here. He could hear it; shells were crisscrossing the sky over Hügel, sounding like titanic locomotives, and one of his directors silently prayed that the Ami munitions *Meister* were as sharp-eyed as Krupp's, that none of the Long Tom fuses had been cut short.[1]

All day the weather had been magnificent, and with time on his hands for the first time since his youth, the idle Konzernherr had strolled through Hügel Park. The grounds had never been lovelier. Beyond the portico the *Blutbuche* was a fiery ovoid. The air was heavy with the scent of roses.

Vivid beds of tulips dotted the elegant meadow — scarlet, orange, yellow, pink, white, and purple blossoms — and between the castle steps and the first towering row of sequoias were countless shrubs and hedges, charming in their various shades of green. One bush west of the entrance was fifteen feet high and forty yards wide — a bantam forest in itself. As Alfried crossed to study it, his custom-made shoes sank into the springy turf, he noticed a proliferation of wild flowers in a shallow dimple. Tiny buttercups and daisies had sprouted on the lawn, scattered between them lay multitudes of minute pink blossoms, and over all a squadron of dazzling butterflies were balanced in swaying echelons, like Stukas hovering over a crowded road. The sole proprietor waited and waited in the dreaming heat, but the butterflies didn't dive, the little flowers didn't panic, the serenity remained unbroken. Over drinks that evening he tried to describe the scene to his directors. Description wasn't enough; he wanted them to see it, and glasses in hand they emerged from the main hall. It was too late: the magic had gone. The butterflies had returned to whatever base sheltered them, and a dense fog, rolling in from the river, obscured the foliage. While they strolled, the duel between Werden's Krupp howitzers and the Amis' 155's resumed with rude ferocity. The disappointed Konzernherr led his men inside, signaled a footman to stiffen his drink and, to drown out the artillery din, ordered the radio turned on *"Laut."*[2]

This was DNB's hour. The rich baritone of Goebbels's most accomplished pitchman was loud enough as it was, and when Alfried's servant obediently spun the *Lautstärkenkontrolle* to the right the resonant introduction could be heard throughout the castle: *"Hier spricht Hans Fritzsche!"* The head of the household gestured impatiently and the volume knob was adjusted. Fritzsche was a disappointment, all the same. He had been incomparable in the days of Hitler's great victories — mocking, exultant, taunting, sarcastic, boastful, witty. Now his pickings were slim. In a hoarse imitation of his old gloat he announced that Pastor Niemöller, freed by the Allies, had told his liberators that "Germans are not suited for democracy and prefer to be governed." This was followed by a drumfire of jargon. The plutocratic-democratic-degenerate Jew barbarians were being held at bay in the Ruhrgebiet. During the first week of President Rosenfeld's criminal attack on Okinawa the Führer's intrepid samurai allies in Tokyo had gutted 102 tanks and killed 3,600 aggressor-rapists — cold comfort to Germans or, for that matter, to Japanese who could read a map and see how close to Tokyo Okinawa was. Then Fritzsche's voice rose excitedly. The treacherous Austrians who had betrayed Vienna to the Russians had been arrested! All had been executed! This was an oblique way of conceding that Vienna had fallen, and with similar periphrasis the newscaster revealed that 80,000 Wehrmacht troops had been surrounded in Holland by Canadians, that ten of the Führer's jet bases had been blown up, that U.S. and British forces were racing toward the Elbe, and that the Americans were 114 miles from Berlin. Fritzsche concluded on a note of heavy sarcasm. U.S. engineers, throwing new bridges across the Rhine, were forced to use structural steel from captured Krupp plants![3]

He signed off, and a husky feminine voice began to croon the sad song which, by then, had become the anthem of the Reich:

> *Vor der Kaserne,*
> *vor dem grossen Tor,*
> *Steht 'ne Laterne*
> *und steht sie noch davor.*
> *Dort wollen wir uns mal wiederseh'n,*
> *Bei der Laterne wollen wir steh'n*
> *Wie einst, Lilli Marlene*
> *Wie einst . . .*

Halfway through Alfried rose and stalked into the dining room. It was too humiliating: Rheinhausen's Friedrich-Alfred-Hütte, christened by his mother to honor his grandfather's memory, now served as the enemy's *Waffenschmiede.*

Krupp's companions that last evening were Karl Eberhardt, Eduard Houdremont, and Friedrich Wilhelm Hardach. Fritz Hardach was uncomfortably outranked. With his bullet head, rigid back and glinting rimless spectacles he looked like a member of the inner circle, but he had been with *die Firma* less than four years and didn't even belong to the party. He was here only because Bertha, hearing that his home had been gutted in 1943, had pitied him. Eberhardt and Houdremont belonged to another world; they were directors, holders of Führer decorations for Krupp contributions to the Third Reich. When the Konzernherr invited his guests to join him in a high-stake game of skat after brandy, therefore, Hardach tactfully declined.[4]

He missed a tour de force. Alfried had never been more adroit. Sitting by the black marble fireplace in his third-floor study beneath the oil painting of Hitler, he outscored his lieutenants in game after game. By bedtime, when they dejectedly mounted the stairs to their rooms above, he had won what for another man would have been a small fortune. Characteristically, neither his triumph at the table, the thundering artillery overhead, nor the imminent fall of his city troubled his rest. In two years of air raids he hadn't known a night of insomnia, and tonight he dropped off quickly.[5]

⌗ ⌗ ⌗

As Krupp slept, a squad of steel-helmeted American infantrymen moved uncertainly through a draw by the great shrub, their combat boots crushing daisies and buttercups. They were scouts, and their sergeant had been told to find out whether or not he could dig in on the Ruhr's north bank and send for reinforcements. Since everything turned on the efficiency of the German firepower across the river, he and his men had to draw fire before he could reach any decision. They exposed themselves, found the enemy's marksmanship intimidating, and hastily retired. As they withdrew through Hügel Park, however, one of them held a fragmentary, high school German conversation with an elderly retainer who lived in one of the estate's outbuildings and who had been aroused by the latest eruption from Werden. Approaching the river, the GI's curiosity had been aroused by the blacked-out hulk on his left. Squinting through the thickening mist, he had swiftly calculated its dimensions and realized that he had never seen any building, private or public, quite so large. He asked what it was, the old man told him, he passed the word, and the sergeant sent it back through the chain of command. His company commander decided this was too big for him. The squad should report directly to battalion headquarters.[6]

Six miles to the north, Lieutenant Colonel Clarence M. Sagmoen and Louis Azrael, war correspondent for the Baltimore *News-Post*, were sitting wearily in the battalion command post while the CO frowned at a map. This was the 313th Regiment of the 79th U.S. Division. According to Colonel Ed van Bibber, the West Pointer who led the 313th, G–2 had sworn that "There isn't a Kraut in Essen." Thus the only problem was to plot an approach march. Lacking resistance, subterfuge was unnecessary. They would use the main streets: Dortmunder Strasse, Gladbeckerstrasse, Altendorferstrasse, and Alfredstrasse. G–2 reported two hotels in the city, the Essener Hof and the Kaiserhof. Both would be reserved for staff billets.

Tomorrow's plans were altered slightly when the sergeant and two of his men arrived to report that they had actually seen Krupp's legendary castle. Sagmoen rose quickly. Blond, and nearly six and a half feet tall, he led the men to the map and asked them whether they could trace the way on the plastic overlay. Considering the unfamiliar terrain and poor visibility, their directions were remarkably precise. The sergeant ran his finger down Alfredstrasse to Frankenstrasse, east to Kruppallee, and through the maze of crooked little streets which would later be named Eckbertstrasse, Arnoldstrasse, Waldtrautstrasse, and Haraldstrasse to "a front yard bigger than New York's Central Park." (It really was bigger, 4.6 square miles to Central Park's 2.6.) The castle wasn't larger than Versailles, as the GIs suggested; nevertheless, their description of its silhouette impressed Colonel Sagmoen. He doubted it was fortified — all enemy shells were coming from across the river — but conceivably there were lookouts directing counterbattery fire from Hügel.

In any event it was best to show force, flex muscle, break out the flag. Six weeks in the Reich had persuaded him that graciousness was lost on its inhabitants. Niemöller was right — G-2 monitored DNB broadcasts; *Hier spricht Hans Fritzsche* — in insisting that his countrymen enjoyed being mastered, and the best way to greet Herr Krupp was with the muzzle of an air-cooled .50-caliber machine gun. The battalion commander agreed. He even loaned Sagmoen his German-speaking adjutant, Captain Benjamin G. Westerveld, and ordered him to set everything up. Westerveld drew a jeep from the motor pool, told the pool sergeant to clean, load, and bolt the weapon to the rear mounting, and picked the most ferocious-looking bruiser in headquarters company to man it. None of this was standard operating procedure. Colonels didn't arrest civilians, adjutants weren't chauffeurs, and the ETO's customary antipersonnel machine gun was the .30-caliber Browning; the .50-caliber was for tanks and planes. SOP had become irrelevant, however; there were no precedents for a Krupp capture. Louis Azrael knew that. He had walked in on a spectacular story, and he begged to come. Certainly, Colonel Sagmoen replied — just report here in the morning. Of course, Azrael would have to sit in the back, but then, so would Krupp.

✠    ✠    ✠

The Konzernherr was tranquil, troops in the 313th's battalion cleaned their weapons, and Fritz Tubbesing sat alone and wretched.[7] Tubbesing was no coward. Powerfully built, with thick coarse hair, jagged teeth, and a deep, commanding voice, he was as fearless as the men who had made the armies of S.M. and the Führer the terror of Europe. Still, he was uneasy tonight. Somewhere beneath his perch high in Krupp's headquarters building GIs were moving stealthily through Essen's back streets. The caretaker had never seen an American, but DNB descriptions of them were unsettling. Though he could take care of himself, his wife and children were another matter; for two years now they had been living in a roofless house beside the cemetery where the victims of the Easter Saturday massacre lay buried, for Tubbesing lacked sufficient status to arrange a haven for them in the countryside. As he brooded over what might be happening to them, his anxiety waxed.

The Hauptverwaltungsgebäude, moreover, had become a scary place. Bomb damage had created weird noises. Tubbesing was not an imaginative man, yet among the sounds of dripping, creaking, and banging of unfastened doors he thought he could hear chains rattling, spectral groans, and, now and then, a quavering, high-pitched shriek. It was almost as though the dead of three wars had returned to haunt the House of Krupp. Had phantoms invaded his office, he could have dealt with them, but they seemed to be far off — in an abandoned wing, at the end of a forsaken corridor, or in that depressing basement. Odd reverberations were inevitable, he reassured himself; there were gaping fissures in the walls.

Capricious gusts of wind could play strange tricks in such crevices, with every room transformed into an echo chamber. That was it, he decided, settling back; a spring breeze had rattled his nerves. *Pfui, schäme dich!* Then a heavy chain clattered. Something moaned. A screech like chalk on a blackboard came from the deserted Werkschutz headquarters, and in an instant the caretaker was bolt upright again.

Fancy aside, the Hauptverwaltungsgebäude had become virtually uninhabitable. Like its paralyzed architect it continued to exist, but like Gustav it was also quite useless. Not a pane of glass remained whole. Nothing worked, not even doorknobs. Worst of all, the entire edifice emitted an indescribable, nauseating stench. Tubbesing felt guilty about that. Since the previous autumn, when the sole proprietor had handed him this thankless task, he had worked tirelessly to repair damage after each bombing. Every conceivable solution had been tried, yet he had toiled with increasing frustration; every sheet of pressed wood fitted into a shattered window would be blown to splinters in the next raid. The disruption of plumbing had been worst of all. For months now every toilet had been filled to the brim. The halls reeked of sewage; other Kruppianer would glance at him reproachfully, as though *he* were responsible for the *Terrorbomber*.

In January he had been seized with what seemed to be an inspiration. The Berne, he remembered, had been Alfred Krupp's original source of power. In raising this building Gustav had diverted the stream underground, but old charts showed it was still down there. Mobilizing his men, Tubbesing built immense vats on the roof and ran firehoses from there to the submerged river. Watches were synchronized, pumps manned, a pistol was fired, and all the Berne water which had been sucked up into the garret tanks shot down through the Hauptverwaltungsgebäude's pipes. In less than a minute every toilet in both wings flushed simultaneously — from a block away, it sounded like the Gasteiner Ache waterfalls. That should have been the caretaker's finest hour. Instead it was a disaster. He had assumed that the Berne was pure. In fact it was hopelessly polluted. At a stroke he had ruined the administration building's drinking water, and his parched colleagues looked more reproving than ever. Herr Krupp pretended not to notice, but Tubbesing noticed that the Konzernherr's chauffeur brought him a large flask each morning.

Now they were all gone, and he worried about his unprotected family. Who would know if he visited the ruin he called home? No one, unless the Americans came in the night, and what could one man do against an army? Maliciously he hoped they *would* come and try to use the befouled washrooms. The thought diverted him and strengthened his resolve; he pushed back his chair and set out for home. The streets were very quiet. He was sure he was being watched. But at least there were no spooks here, and in his basement he found all the Tubbesings asleep and unharmed.

✠    ✠    ✠

At 7 A.M. Tubbesing was back at his desk.[8] Looking out, he saw two of his assistants in another office, diagonally across a little ell. Twenty minutes later he again glanced out his glassless windows and beheld, under the rising fog, two lines of helmeted soldiers loping up Altendorferstrasse, one on each side of the street, with jeeps, trucks, command cars, and tanks bearing large white stars advancing between them. Unconsciously, he realized, he had been expecting a repetition of 1923. But then the French had sent merely a token force. These columns, stretching back for miles, seemed endless. As the first troops came closer he was struck by their youth, their physiques, and the excellence of their equipment. To a German they appeared to lack discipline, but there was a certain jauntiness about them. He couldn't remember when he had seen such élan in Wehrmacht men.

On an absurd impulse, he decided that Fritz Tubbesing should meet Essen's conquerors, and slipping into his coat (and silently damning the plumbing, which made ablutions impossible) he hurried down to the entrance, where he discovered that the 79th Division wasn't looking for hosts. Before he could welcome them a jeep drew over, an officer leaped out, and, ordering the caretaker to about-face, jammed a tommy gun in his back. The threat was impersonal; troops entering vacant buildings elsewhere had encountered booby traps or sniper fire, and Fritz was to be used as a shield during a hasty inspection. Satisfied, the officer ended his tour back at the front door and drove off. Minutes later a second jeep, dominated by a mounted .50-caliber machine gun and a fierce, powerfully built gunner, pulled up. Without alighting, a tall lieutenant colonel in front asked casually, "*Wo ist Herr Krupp?*" Without thinking Tubbesing replied, "*Auf dem kruppschen Hügel Schloss,*" at which the driver burned rubber in a racing start.

Under other circumstances the caretaker might have had second thoughts about this exchange, but he hadn't time to assess its implications; by now jeeps were arriving regularly. One bore a pair of immaculately uniformed men who explained, in flawless German, that they were intelligence officers. Would he be good enough to lead them to Krupp's office? He did, and there, after a brief interlude of unprofessional horseplay — they were wrestling over possession of a large howitzer model — they tried to open Alfried's desk drawers. All were locked. "*Schlüssel?*" one inquired of Tubbesing. He shook his head; he had no key. The other man shrugged, drew a .45-caliber pistol from a holster, and began shooting out locks. The caretaker was horrified. One simply didn't open fire on the sole proprietor's furniture. Simultaneously he was struck by the thought that his assistants across the ell would think the Americans were shooting *him*. To hearten them he showed himself in the window. They looked relieved, though the gesture almost cost him his life; thinking it a signal, the first officer had unsheathed his own pistol and was pointing it at his head.

The caretaker stuttered an explanation, the muzzle was lowered, and suddenly Tubbesing found himself the protagonist of a strange one-act play. The office had been invaded by a score of newcomers. Some were shooting open locked files, others were confiscating typewriters, a third group was removing signed photographs of eminent Nazis from their frames — anything that moved, it appeared, was a souvenir[9] — and a fourth team was interrogating Tubbesing. Talking compulsively, he described the most intricate details of cannon manufacture, the history of the House, the Führer's visits here, and Krupp's personal relationships with Göring, Goebbels, and Bormann. (Later in the day he realized that one of the questioners must have been holding a microphone. Every word that he said had been recorded. Hour after hour his answers were broadcast, over loudspeakers, to the population of Essen.) After that a GI shoved a second submachine gun at him. Once more he was required to lead a circuit of the building, though the soldiers, to his relief, shied away from the forbidding cellars. The fear of hidden gunmen and camouflaged bombs was still daunting; for the present, at least, there would be no awkward questions about the safes down there.

At the height of this uproar Tubbesing felt a plucking at his sleeve. Turning, he discovered that he was face to face with Finanzdirektor Johannes Schröder. Schröder flicked his forefinger to his lips, and the caretaker repressed a start. His superior was really quite safe; with so many strangers running around, Alfried himself might have walked through the Hauptverwaltungsgebäude unmolested. Tubbesing assumed that *die Firma's* Finanzdirektor was here to take inventory, and felt contrite, for typewriters were disappearing at an alarming rate. Instead the treasurer hurriedly whispered an order: at one o'clock the caretaker was to slip away, make his way to the Bredeney home of Dr. Janssen, on Tirpitzstrasse, and submit a full report on the day's activities to the Direktorium. Tubbesing felt a surge of pride in the ancient *Haus*. It was incredible — on this, of all days, the board was holding a formal meeting.

Though there was such a session, it couldn't accomplish much. The chair at the head of the table was unoccupied, and Alfried's telephoned instructions had not been helpful. In Berlin, he had reminded them, "The authorities are still at the helm, and we must listen to them" (*Die Behörden sind noch am Ruder, und wir müssen ihnen noch gehorchen*).[10] Here, Tubbesing pointed out, the Americans were in complete control. Having been threatened twice by tommy guns and once by a .45, he reported his impression that disobedience of Ami authority would be extremely unwise. The caretaker could continue to play on their fears of the gloomy basement, but any show of resistance would merely mean the death of another German. Since the name on the gravestone would be Tubbesing, he was doubtless biased. Still, he couldn't see what would be achieved. The Direktorium didn't argue. Indeed, they instructed him to avoid danger, surrendering his keys if necessary, and he trudged back to cope.

During his brief absence the keys had become obsolete. Mastering their apprehension, infantrymen had explored the cellars, engineers had removed the safes with cranes, and demolition teams had blown them open. Meanwhile a new problem had arisen. The Ninth Army had held the center of Essen less than eight hours, yet already, Tubbesing discovered, his own countrymen had set up some fifty junkyards on the fringes of the ravaged Gusstahlfabrik and were assembling scrap for sale elsewhere. Indignant, he found military government headquarters in the Essener Hof, encountered a colonel, and begged that something be done to stop this plunder. The cast steel factory was private property. Its owner's assets were being pilfered in broad daylight. Meanwhile, in the central administration building, victorious soldiers were carting off machines, trophies, and pictures of statesmen. Surely the Americans did not believe in looting? No, the colonel coolly replied, they did not; he would post military policemen at all Hauptverwaltungsgebäude entrances, and no one, including Tubbesing himself, would be allowed to enter. Guarding the remains of the city's eighty factories would take a little longer, but there was one obvious solution. Didn't the firm have a plant police? The ex-caretaker nodded, adding that it was very efficient. "Then use it," said the colonel, dismissing him. Thus the first irony of the occupation: while every other Krupp force was being disbanded, the one institution to remain at full strength — indeed, it was soon enlisting fresh recruits — was the Werkschutz.[11]

✠     ✠     ✠

It was Lieutenant Colonel Clarence Sagmoen, of course, to whom Tubbesing had disclosed that the Konzernherr was in his castle. Captain Westerveld had been driving the armed jeep, with war correspondent Azrael perched beside the sinister gunner, and behind them, in a second jeep, five more men of the 313th carrying automatic weapons. The arrest of men on Allied war criminal lists was not taken lightly; in the minds of the Reich's enemies they were responsible for the war, and some were known to have SS escorts. At this stage, it must be remembered, the name Krupp was largely symbolic. None of the men riding up the half-mile conifer-lined drive toward Villa Hügel could distinguish between Gustav and Alfried, all thought the family belonged to Germany's titled nobility, and some were convinced that the tenacity of Werden's resistance was no coincidence — that Nazi fanatics had rallied on the Ruhr to defend "Baron Krupp." Given these misunderstandings, the designation of a small task force was inevitable.

There were misconceptions in the castle, too. Alfried had been on the telephone; he knew the situation in the city; he had been expecting un-invited guests since daybreak. Nevertheless he wasn't ready. This seems to have been a matter of face. It would be unseemly for a German of his eminence to appear anxious, so he decided to keep the Americans waiting. Karl Dohrmann had thought he would honor the invaders by dressing in his most expensive livery, but to the GIs he merely looked like a rich man's flunky, and his aloof manner was interpreted as arrogant condescension (which, in part, it was). Lastly, Hügel's one hundred and twenty-five servants had assembled by the portico. In the great homes of Europe this is a familiar form of greeting; the householder himself is so welcomed when he returns from a long journey. The soldiers in the two jeeps, on the other hand, were bound to regard a mass of Germans as ominous, and they were edgy even before their wheels stopped rolling. Thus the account of Alfried's arrest must be pieced together from the recollections of many individuals who were under severe strain, who misconstrued the motives of one another, and who, in most instances, were further confused by the language barrier.

Colonel Sagmoen dissolved the human barrier by charging it. As Captain Westerveld set his brake, the colonel sprang out, pistol in hand, and darted toward the servants. They scattered. Striding into the foyer with Wester-veld and Azrael at his heels, he was confronted by the splendid figure of Dohrmann. A butler who had dealt with the Kaiser, the Führer, and the Duce declined to be cowed by an Ausländer who, in his eyes, showed every sign of being an ill-bred movie gangster with a gun. To his amazement, the officer spoke German — Sagmoen was bilingual — and they were off on a rapid-fire, bark-and-bark-back exchange:

"*Wer is hier zu Hause?*" (Who lives here?)

"*Mein Herr, Diplomingenieur Alfried Krupp von Bohlen und Halbach.*"

"*Wo ist Krupp?*"

"*Oben*" (Upstairs).

"*Holen Sie ihn sofort 'runter*" (Bring him down at once).

"*Meine Herren, Herr Krupp erwartet Sie; darf ich Sie bitten, näher zu treten*" (Gentlemen, Herr Krupp is expecting you; may I ask you to enter)?[12]

In English, Dohrmann's tone sounds excessively polite. That is precisely what it was — the fruity tone a butler uses with tradesmen, not colonels. Sagmoen understood the snub, but he refused to be baited. Instead he paced the hall with the captain and the foreign correspondent, examining paintings, a collection of cannon models, the chandeliers, and the leather spines in the library beyond (several thousand volumes, most of them about politics). Ten minutes passed. The colonel returned and peered up the carved oak staircase. Dohrmann was standing there like a sentry. Again the officer inquired "*Wo ist er?*" and was told Krupp would be down directly. He didn't come, though; the ten minutes became fifteen, then twenty, and

Sagmoen was fuming. To his adjutant he muttered, "I'm going to see what's keeping him." Brushing the butler aside, he bounded up two steps at a time. According to Azrael, "In a moment or so, I followed. Sagmoen apparently had looked into several rooms among those on the second floor to the left (as I recall) of the staircase. Just as I got there he was entering the front room and I, seeing him and following, saw tall, slender, immaculately dressed Krupp adjusting his necktie in front of a bureau mirror."[13]

Alfried was wearing a pinstripe business suit; on the table beside him lay a black felt hat. As he slowly donned it, facing the glass, he and the colonel exchanged another volley, this time led by the Konzernherr:

*"Ich bin der Inhaber dieses Gutes; was wünchen Sie"* (I am the owner of this property; what do you want)?

*"Sind Sie Krupp"* (Are you Krupp)?

*"Ja, ich bin Krupp von Bohlen."*

*"Sie sind verhaftet!"* (You are under arrest!)[14]

What happened next is a matter of dispute. According to Azrael, "The lieutenant colonel ordered him to come along. The two walked down the steps and, with the servant standing there with a bewildered expression, Krupp got into the back seat of the jeep. I sat near him. The officer sat in front." Smiling faintly, Alfried merely commented later, "It was an astonishing time." Dohrmann's version was more dramatic. Before the appearance of his *Herr*, he remembers, many soldiers were running through the castle halls, wrenching open doors, and he has a vivid picture of Alfried's captor leading him out *"mit einem brutalen Polizeigriff"* (with a brutal police hold). No enlisted men entered Hügel that morning, and it is improbable that a staff officer would have humiliated a prisoner who, by all accounts, was behaving with dignity. The butler's account may well have been colored by the atmosphere on the Hill that morning. The hundred-odd vassals gathered in Hügel Park were stunned. To them, watching the head of the House led off was as great a shock as the arrest of the chief of state would have been for inhabitants of the Führerbunker. One footman ran out with a weekend bag and lunch from the castle kitchens. He was too late: the lead jeep was already rolling. As it passed the ranks of servants Azrael heard them gasp, "Krupp! Krupp! Krupp!" It was a prayer, a chant, like a muted *Sieg Heil.*[15]

The gunner stood erect, as immobile as one of the great Krupp's statues, and Alfried, learning that the war correspondent was a civilian, broke into English. During the long drive to regimental headquarters — now situated between Essen and Düsseldorf — they had what the reporter later described as "quite a chat." The prisoner "insisted he really had nothing to do with the war. He was merely a manufacturer who took orders and filled them. He didn't even make vast profits on his work for the government, since prices were fixed, he said."[16]

Sagmoen, proud of his quarry, took him straight to the 313th's command post. As they drew up, the lieutenant colonel and the correspondent raced inside, Sagmoen shouting, "Colonel, I've got Krupp. Do you want to talk to him?" Van Bibber, unshaven, spat, "I don't want to see the son of a bitch. Take him to the prison cage."[17] Despite his executive officer's crestfallen look, the regimental commander's instincts were probably correct. At Villa Hügel Alfried had felt obliged to keep his arresting party waiting; here the senior officer believed that dealing directly with him would be improper. The POW cage, on the other hand, was not the place for an accused war criminal. Civilians didn't belong with Wehrmacht captives, and intelligence specialists had a prior claim on this civilian anyhow.

Their first interrogation of him was conducted that afternoon in the kitchen of a damaged Ruhr apartment. Krupp agreed to a dialogue in English, and an officer asked, "Why didn't you leave the Ruhr?"[18]

Alfried shrugged. "I wanted to stay with my factory, where I belong, with my fellow workers."

"Are you a Nazi?"

"I am a German."

"Are you a member of the Nazi Party?"

"Well, yes, but most Germans are."*

"What is your present salary?"

Obviously annoyed, Alfried snapped, "Must I answer that?"

"Yes," the officer snapped back.

Producing a silver case, Krupp extracted a Camel, tapped it thoughtfully, lit it — no one had offered him a match — and replied, "Four hundred thousand marks a year."†

"Do you still think Germany will win the war?"

Having just liquidated nearly 200 million RM in Reich bonds, Alfried peered incredulously through a haze of cigarette smoke and replied flatly, "I do not know. Politics is not my business. My business is making steel."

"What are your plans after the war?"

"I hope to rebuild the factories and produce again."

They glared, assuming he meant the production of weapons, and dismissed him, concentrating instead on Signal Corps photographs of unfinished weapons found in the Gusstahlfabrik: two *Schwerer Gustav* barrels, duplicates of those which had been used at Sevastopol, and the hulls of new 177-ton (*Maus*) tanks. The session had not been illuminating;

---

* Most Germans weren't. Of 79,529,957 German citizens, 5,000,000 (6 percent) were National Socialist Party members and 1,040,520 (1.3 percent) belonged to the party leadership. (Nuremberg record *Nazi Conspiracy and Aggression*, chart 14, 693261 O–47 VIII.)

† At the official prewar exchange rate, $160,000. But any figure would have been unrealistic. The question revealed the questioner's ignorance. Alfried had hesitated because he didn't work for a "salary." As sole proprietor he owned everything. On April 11, 1945, he had no idea what that was worth.

there would be more. Alfried, however, thought that he was through. When he was returned to Villa Hügel and told that he must remain in the sixty-room *kleine Haus* under "house arrest" he assumed his detention would last no more than a few days. That seemed reasonable to him. The Allies, after all, had routed the Wehrmacht. To a visiting friend he recalled philosophically that when Hindenburg had been asked whether he or Ludendorff had won the battle of Tannenberg, the field marshal had replied, "I don't know, but if we had lost it, I would be remembered as the loser." As sole proprietor of the Führer's anvil, he must expect to share, as his father had shared, the degradation of defeat.[19]

His awakening came slowly. As the days passed the security measures in the little house tightened. No more correspondents were allowed to interview him, and in the absence of information rumors appeared in the world press. 800-ROOM HOUSE OVERRUN BY U.S. TROOPS read a headline in the April 16 *New York Times; Time* wrote of "the high-walled Villa Hügel, secluded estate of powerful, mysterious Alfred [sic] von Bohlen und Halbach"; the Associated Press reported that he had been locked up in a Hügel gardener's cottage, and the *London Sunday Express* informed its readers that American troops referred to Krupp as Little Alfie. Actually GIs didn't refer to him at all, because they were unaware of him. On May 21 he was removed from the castle under heavy escort. A month later the *Times* disclosed that he was in English hands, and on the evening of August 13 the British Broadcasting Corporation announced that he had been taken to an "undisclosed destination." The destination was Recklinghausen, where the lesser Schlotbarone elected him camp leader. In a subsequent communiqué he was officially described as "an internee of the British Army of the Rhine." In fact he had been under formal arrest as a suspected war criminal since the day of the BBC broadcast. That date is significant; Gustav wasn't indicted by the Allies until August 30, and the prosecution at that time was wholly unaware of his senility, yet two weeks earlier the English had been convinced that whatever the outcome of the father's case, there was sufficient evidence to convict the son.[20]

Alfried didn't believe it. Already he had decided upon his defense — that he was being persecuted because of the dynasty's reputation. Three summers later, in his Nuremberg summation, he would have it honed to perfection: "When in 1943 I became the responsible bearer of the Krupp name and tradition, little did I anticipate that this legacy would one day bring me into the defendant's dock. . . . And yet the name of Krupp was on the list of war criminals long before the end of the war, not because of the charges which the prosecution is compiling against us now, but because of a notion which is as old as it is fallacious: Krupp wanted war and Krupp made war." By disregarding the firm's pillage of the continent and the massive documentation of slave labor crimes, he was to convince the

German audience outside the courtroom — and, ultimately, businessmen in Allied nations — that he had been condemned by an accident of birth.[21]

Once a German-American guard asked him how he preferred to be addressed: as Herr Alfried, Herr von Bohlen, or Herr Krupp von Bohlen und Halbach? The Konzernherr answered curtly, "*Nennen Sie mich Krupp. Wegen dieses Namens bin ich hier. Diese Zelle ist mein Anteil an dem grossen Krupp-Erbe*" (Call me Krupp. I'm here because of that name. This cell is my share of the great Krupp inheritance).[22]

✠ ✠ ✠

Krupp's arrest had been especially shattering for Villa Hügel's butler, and may have converted him into one of Europe's first postwar anti-Americans. Everything he saw in the days immediately following Alfried's arrest seemed to confirm that prejudice. He could understand the billeting of infantrymen in the main body of the castle. He could even look on indulgently while GIs consumed half the family's cellar — he himself, after all, had been on the western front in World War I. It was their manners which he found inexcusable. Later, when the combat troops had left and a footman pointed out that the behavior of U.S. occupation forces had become unexceptionable, Dohrmann replied tersely, "Of course. They are Germans. They crossed the sea when they were young. But blood tells."[23]

They weren't Germans, they were in Europe for the first time, and blood is mute. What the butler failed to grasp was that while peacetime soldiers can afford courtesy and are even ordered to show it, men in action are professionally discourteous. The departure of Colonel Sagmoen's two-jeep task force was followed by an invasion of mud-spattered, foul-mouthed men who burst through the foyer, scarred the priceless oaken balustrade with their swaying metal gear, and streaked up the spiral stairway leading to the Cyclops eye of Hügel's huge skylight. If Nazi guerrillas didn't want it as an observation post, the 79th Division did. Artillery observers are a nervous lot. Perching on landmarks they become conspicuous targets, and if this crew was brusque with the help it was because they expected to be dislodged from their roost at any moment. As the days passed without sniper fire from across the river, their immunity mystified them; either Werden regarded Villa Hügel as a shrine, they concluded, or the enemy was short of ammunition.

Despite the intensity of the firepower which was being directed from Villa Hügel's roof, the American offensive bogged down. For six days patrols trying to cross the river were turned back, and on April 17 the castle received its first visit from an American general. Major General Matthew Bunker Ridgway, commander of the XVIII Airborne Corps, took this stalemate personally. He had just celebrated his fiftieth birthday, and the mélange of bitter-enders on the opposite side of the Ruhr had done their best to spoil it. Hand grenades dangling from his combat jacket, he climbed to the skylight, eyed the wooded shore on the far bank, and then climbed down and asked whether any of the Germans present spoke English. Fritz Hardach stepped forward. Hügel had changed hands and the sound of gunfire had grown worse, but Hardach had clung to his guest room on the fourth floor. GI behavior didn't offend him. If the Amis didn't bother him, he wouldn't bother them. He was under the impression that Eisenhower's nonfraternization order thwarted communication anyhow, and was surprised at Ridgway's request.[24]

The general not only wanted to talk; he was friendly. What, he asked Krupp's lieutenant, was the point of continuing this bloodshed? Two days ago he had sent an aide to Model's headquarters under a white flag to point out that the Nazi situation was hopeless. Citing Robert E. Lee's decision at Appomattox eighty years ago that month, Ridgway had written, "The same choice is now yours. In the light of a soldier's honor, for the reputation of the German Officer Corps, for the sake of your nation's future, lay down your arms at once. The German lives you will save are sorely needed to restore your people to their proper place in society." A member of Model's staff replied verbally that the Offizierskorps, bound by oath to the Führer, could never entertain such a treasonable thought. "Why," the corps commander inquired of Hardach, "don't the civilians over there rise up against those nuts?" Choosing his words carefully, Fritz delicately pointed out that for nearly a week the United States Army had been trying to establish a bridgehead on the south bank of the river. If the USA couldn't dislodge the nuts, what could the people of Werden do? Ridgway was momentarily silent. Then he said, "I get it."[25]

Turning restlessly, he asked for a tour of the castle. Hardach showed him all of it: the Kaiser's private apartment, the desk where Bertha and Gustav had worked, Alfried's leather-walled study, the dining room table which would seat sixty-five, Uncle Felix's murals, the three *Liebschaft der Venus mit Adonis* tapestries woven by Van Den Hecke in 1709, the Grotto, the Chinese Room, the green tile swimming pool, the life-size portraits of Krupps and Kaisers — Hitler's had been discreetly removed — and the secret passage leading to the Kruppbunker. At the end, standing in the main hall, the general noticed an American private practicing golf shots with a putter. "Where did you get that?" he asked. The soldier pointed to a closet. Hardach volunteered that it belonged to Gustav, and Ridgway — who was then unaware that a 137-car freight train had brought 4,174 cases of French works of art into the Reich to adorn the homes of wearers of the Golden Party Badge — said firmly, "Put it back." Summoning a first lieutenant he said, "This place is a kind of museum. I want everything here kept here. Future generations should see what I've just seen."[26]

That future chiefs of state would be entertained here by the reigning

Krupp, with a new German leader at his side and assembled Kruppianer outside singing Deutschland über Alles, was inconceivable that spring. In any event, before Villa Hügel could become anything, the nuts across the river had to be brought to their senses. For the present, Ridgway ordered, the castle must remain an observation post, "which meant," as Fritz later put it, "that the shells kept zooming overhead." On May 1 there was a surge of hope. Radios in Essen and Werden picked up a strong signal from Hamburg. First came Anton Bruckner's Seventh Symphony, played as a dirge; then a long roll of drums and then the deep, breaking voice of an announcer: "In his operational headquarters our Führer, fighting to his last breath against Bolshevism (bis zum letzten Atemzug gegen den Bolschewismus kämpfend), died for Germany this afternoon in the Reich Chancellery. On April 30 the Führer appointed Grand Admiral Dönitz as his heir. The Grand Admiral, heir to the Führer, now speaks to the German people."[27]

Thus the Lex Dönitz. Clearly its beneficiary had but one course: immediate capitulation. But harsh truths had been obscured in this strange land for twelve years, and the admiral, with his country split into fragments, astounded the world by declaring that he intended to go right on fighting Russians: "So long as we must continue to defend against you and fight you, the Americans are not fighting for themselves but only for the spread of Bolshevism in Europe" (sondern allein für die Ausbreitung des Bolschewismus in Europa).[28]

This delighted the filibustering army of extremists across the Ruhr, and despite Anglo-American explanations to them that a separate peace now would betray every member of the new United Nations, the holdouts continued to cherish (and fulfill) their death wish until the night of May 6–7. At midnight there was a sudden lull along the south bank; somehow word of the Reich's imminent surrender had reached the Werewolves, Volksstürmers, and paratroopers there. Less than three hours later General Alfred Jodl and Admiral Hans von Friedeburg signed the instrument in a little red schoolhouse in Rheims. Laying down his pen, Jodl said, "I can at this time only express the hope that the victor will treat us generously" (dass der Sieger uns mit Grossmut behandeln wird).[29] In the east his hope was dashed. Though V–E Day was proclaimed May 8, the Red Army continued to slaughter Volk until the official headline of 12:01 A.M. May 9, and in the final hours of fighting, after their allies had stacked arms, they captured the ruined Saxon capital of Dresden.

By then the sounds of battle had rolled away from the devastated Ruhrgebiet. No more firing was heard in Werden. Little boats crisscrossed Baldeney See below Villa Hügel bearing food and medicine, and Major General Ernest N. Harmon's XXII U.S. Corps chose the Konzernherr's estate as its temporary billet. The air raid protection ladders (Luftschutz-leitern) which Alfried had ordered propped against Hügel's façade were carried away, the ballroom became a map room, the CO slept in the Kaiser's bed, and the dining room was reserved for staff officers. Krupp's home proved an admirable setting for all the little conveniences with which American soldiers are surrounded by a grateful government. Banquets were prepared in Hügel's enormous kitchens while noncoms sunned themselves in the Grotto or fished in the outer garden lake.[30]

The rambling castle was ideal for junior officers. For the first time since 1913 its underground pool was filled and dressing rooms outfitted. Billiard tables appeared in Gustav's Chinese Room, and Margarethe Brandt, who as a young woman had become governess to Bertha and Barbara over a half-century ago, gave GIs German lessons.[31] At least once a week Karl Dohrmann and his footmen moved charts from the ballroom and the corps band moved in. Since Fräuleins were still excluded, there were always more men than women, but WACs and female civilians from other European countries kept the floor lively. One of the dancers was Ernestine Roth. She and her sister, released after hospitalization, had finally discovered what and where Villa Hügel was. It continually astonished them. Sometimes, passing through the dining room, Ernestine would pause and touch the gold tableware, realizing that Krupp had feasted with it here while children starved in the city below.

Elizabeth rarely danced. Her legs still bothered her. In warm, dry weather she felt fit, but the slightest touch of dampness in the air triggered waves of pain. Thus, at the height of one ball, she was seated at the receptionist's desk in the foyer when a smartly dressed woman in her early thirties entered and asked in German whether she might go to her room. Elizabeth was startled; as far as she knew, only men lived in the castle. Shyly the visitor explained: she was Irmgard von Bohlen Raitz von Frenz — a member of the Krupp family. This was, or had been, her home, and in a closet upstairs hung one of her fur coats. With times as hard as they were, she thought she might need it during the months ahead. Winters in this part of the country, she explained, could be very cold. After a pause Elizabeth quietly replied that she knew. Beckoning to a servant, she ordered him to fetch the lady's coat.[32]

✠    ✠    ✠

At dawn on April 11, the day Alfried fell into American hands, Colonel Otto Skorzeny had zigzagged wildly across Vienna's Floridsdorfer Bridge under heavy sniper fire to radio Hitler from the nearest Gestapo headquarters that the city was lost. Austria had unexpectedly become a major theater of war. The NKVD was setting up a puppet regime in its capital, and although the Americans (unlike Winston Churchill) were undismayed by Stalin's territorial ambitions, they were obsessed with the myth of the *Alpenfestung,* the National Redoubt in the south to which the

Führer would withdraw for a last stand. No one knew precisely where this fortress was supposed to be, but Shaef had tentatively circled Berghof, Hitler's celebrated retreat at Berchtesgaden. Berchtesgaden was within a few miles of Salzburg. So was Blühnbach.[33]

The origins of the *Alpenfestung* legend are obscure. In 1944 rumors of a formidable defense system in the Austrian Alps reached Allen Dulles, who sent Washington a warning from Switzerland. Somebody on Massachusetts Avenue talked out of turn at a cocktail party in a neutral embassy, a coded dispatch was relayed to Berlin, and Goebbels elatedly exploited the fable. By Christmas every American commander, including General George Marshall, believed it. "After the Ruhr was taken," Eisenhower's chief of staff General Walter Bedell Smith wrote the year after the war, "we were convinced that there would be no surrender at all so long as Hitler lived. Our feeling then was that we should be forced to destroy the remnants of the German army piece by piece, with the final possibility of a prolonged campaign in the rugged Alpine area of western Austria and southern Bavaria known as the National Redoubt."[34]

Once Model had been sealed off, therefore, the supreme commander had concentrated the bulk of his forces under Omar Bradley in the Kassel area. Lunging eastward into central Germany, Bradley had turned his right wing southward into the Danube Valley, west of Vienna, and radioed the Russians that he would seize the Redoubt before linking up with them. Senior German officers were so aware that the *Alpenfestung* was merely a Führer dream that one Feldmarschall who later claimed he had flown there to organize last-ditch resistance became a symbol of cowardice to his comrades.[35] Its existence in Eisenhower's mind was enough for Bradley, however, and thus it happened that Blühnbach, lying between Vienna and Munich, became trapped between the Russians and Americans. His ear to the radio, Berthold heard Fritzsche cry over and over, *"Männer, tut Eure Pflicht! Ihre haftet mit Eurem Leben und Eurer Ehre!"* (Men, do your duty! Your life and honor depend on it!) Alfried's brother found the appeal singularly uninspiring. Obligations to duty and honor were becoming cloudier by the hour, but clearly both the lives of his parents and his own future depended less on valor than on good judgment. Unlike the millions whom Fritzsche was rallying to the swastika for the last time, Berthold understood English. He had been monitoring American shortwave broadcasts, and, though the ciphers baffled him, signals between "Able," "Easy" and "Fox" were becoming more distinct. Obviously an Ami juggernaut was on its way. That was good news to Blühnbach's intent listener; if Alfried wasn't worried about enemy interest in the dynasty, Berthold was. Unhappily nothing was simple that month. Other language broadcasts warned that a second juggernaut was advancing up the broad basin of the Danube. Moscow had discounted a Shaef intelligence summary which claimed that "some of the most important ministries and personalities of the Nazi regime are already established in the Redoubt area,"[36] but the Russians were grabbing all the land they could. Therefore, as a third of the Anglo-American armies drove toward Austria under Lieutenant General Jacob L. Devers, a fourth of the Soviet forces — two Army Groups led by Marshals Rodion Y. Malinovsky and Fyodor Talbukhin — were sweeping up from Vienna. Berthold didn't know the extent of the commitment, but the idyllic landscape around him was the goal of several million troops. Understandably he was anxious to keep his father out of the Red Army's hands. To the world Gustav was still the symbol of Krupp, and the Communists, more interested in images than in justice, were quite capable of trying him before their own judges as a representative capitalist. His paralysis wouldn't prevent a mock trial. They were experienced stage managers.

The race was close. At 10 A.M. on April 25 two waves of U.S. heavy bombers appeared over the crest of Hohe Göll and shattered the Führer's beloved Berghof; infantrymen of Devers's Sixth Army Group, bypassing the mountain fastness, had overrun Berchtesgaden by a scant twelve miles when Jodl and Friedeburg finally laid down the Nazi sword. Gustav was safe, and historians can be at least as grateful for that as Krupps, since the distinction could now be drawn between his responsibility and his son's. Yet the rescuers had no inkling of what they had rescued. They had never heard of Blühnbach. It wasn't on their maps, and even if it had been, officers without guides would have been confounded by the passes. One sentence in that Shaef intelligence summary had been correct: "This area is, by the very nature of the terrain, practically impenetrable." Berthold knew it; therefore he approached the Americans as soon as he heard they were in the neighborhood. In late April, with his brother under house arrest in Hügel's *kleine Hause*, he made his way to a village six miles away and spoke to a group of young American officers there. Later he recalled, "I told them who we were and where we were. They were very correct. They came and inspected the house and interrogated my mother, though they didn't approach my father. He was sitting on a balcony, staring out at the view. I showed them that he was there. They verified it by staring through a window, but they didn't disturb him."[37]

Some of Berthold's guests may have wondered why they had been summoned. To them the wintry invalid must have appeared, as he did to a sympathetic German, an old man "still forgotten by death" (*noch immer vom Tode vergessen*). Certainly the Americans had no way of knowing that they were looking at the Nazi who would stand thirteenth among the first twenty-two major war criminals scheduled to be tried six months later before an international military tribunal; the IMT was not created until August 8. Nevertheless American generals were aware that there would be trials. The United Nations War Crimes Commission had been established on October 7, 1942, every government had its list, and "Gustav Krupp," in the words of the IMT's historian, "was regarded by all the Allied powers as one of the most important of the war criminals." This being so, one would assume that the first inspection of Krupp's Austrian castle would be quickly followed by others. Berthold expected them, but none came. The senile Schlotbaron was ignored; May passed, June passed, and the former hunting lodge of the archduke whose death had set off this thirty-year spiral of European warfare dozed on in the summer sun.[38]

It is altogether fitting, and quite in keeping with the high drama and absurd coincidence which marked four centuries of Krupp history, that the first high officer to reach Blühnbach should be a distant relative who stumbled into the valley for the wrong reason. Colonel Charles W. Thayer, West Point '33, was then a member of General Mark Clark's staff. Thayer knew of the superb chamois shooting in the Austrian Alps, and in July he and a classmate from the Point decided to liberate a lodge and take a vacation. Two decades later his fellow officer would be a distinguished general, but in 1945 neither of them held sufficient rank to commandeer an estate on his own. Therefore Thayer proposed to identify himself as a representative of the general, who, he would explain, was keen on hunting. Few soldiers would have dared take Mark Clark's name in vain, but nothing about Charles W. Thayer was ordinary. He was a Saint Paul's graduate, a member of what Society calls a well-connected family, and a man of great charm. His sister Avis had married another Saint Paul's alumnus, Charles E. "Chip" Bohlen, the brilliant forty-year-old American diplomat who had served as first secretary in the United States Moscow embassy, advised President Roosevelt at Teheran and Yalta, and had played a vital role in San Francisco's U.N. founding conference the month before. Although Chip Bohlen never advertised the fact, his grandfather and Gustav's father had been brothers.[39]

Colonel Thayer knew of the relationship, had told his aides about it, and had grasped the significance of Blühnbach as soon as he learned he was near it. Like Colonel Sagmoen in Essen, he drove up the castle's pink granite driveway with a crowded jeep in his wake, and like Sagmoen he was greeted by a frock-coated manservant. "American colonels don't do business with butlers," he said sharply. Deliberately turning his back, he waited until he heard another, tentative footstep. It was Berthold, white-faced, trembling, and trying very hard to smile. "He was scared to death — as he had every right to be," Thayer said later. This, the colonel decided, was a man with whom he could do business, and after weighing effective approaches he decided to be "appallingly rude." He was certainly that; in his words, "If I'd had spurs, I'd have dragged them across the dining room table."

But which table? And which dining room? Only after Berthold had invited him in did Thayer appreciate the magnitude of the castle. There were suites and subsuites, forked stairways leading to multiple corridors, courtyards and gardens and tiers of outbuildings. It was a miniature city. He and his friend couldn't stay here. Neither would ever know where the other was. Clearing his throat, he asked sternly whether Herr von Bohlen had heard of Mark W. Clark, the four-star general who commanded all U.S. occupation forces in Austria. Berthold nodded. General Clark wanted a hunting lodge, Thayer said, not a castle. Berthold quickly replied that he was certain he could provide something suitable; the family owned many in the surrounding ranges. But perhaps the colonel had come to see his parents? His father was infirm, and his mother was nursing him in the room just beyond that door. However —

Lighting a pipe, the American officer shook his head. He had what he wanted, and as they retraced their way through the warren of paneled trophy rooms Berthold assured him that the accommodations would be adequately furnished with weapons, ammunition, linen, silver, and, of course, servants. By now there had been a subtle change in relationships between the two men. Berthold was no longer frightened, and he had guessed his caller's true purpose. Therefore he gently suggested a trade. It was a peculiarity of his father's condition, he explained, that the old man was offended by the slightest noise, and lately there had been a great deal of gunfire in the forests. Thayer nodded. "I heard it. Sounds like a regular battle. It's the 101st Airborne, butchering chamois." Possibly, Alfried's brother suggested, the four-star American general would find his stay more pleasant if Blühnbach were declared out-of-bounds to enlisted men. Thayer grunted and made a mental note to speak to Max Taylor. (Next day he did, and the divisional commander obliged.) "Berthold was terribly pleasant," Thayer afterward said, "and not too dumb. He knew how to get around me. He knew what I wanted. He satisfied me and got what *he* wanted — peace and quiet."

As they were standing in the driveway, surrounded by the colonel's staff, Berthold inquired politely, "Would you by any chance know my dear cousin in the American foreign service, Chip Bohlen?"

The colonel pulled on his pipe. He replied stonily, "No foreign service officer could possibly be your cousin."

Instantly he realized that he had slipped. Everyone around them knew Chip was his brother-in-law, and a ripple of laughter ran through the ranks. Leaping into his seat, he ordered his driver to take off. The two jeeps vanished down the carefully raked drive, leaving Berthold to wonder when, if ever, the Allies would begin to think earnestly about the dynasty.

✠    ✠    ✠

They were in dead earnest, and on the very highest levels. Later it became popular in certain circles to attribute all plans for the "deindustrialization" of the Ruhr to Henry Morgenthau, Jr., the American Secretary of the Treasury. This was wholly untrue. The victors were united in their determination to destroy the economic basis of German militarism. Referring to Krupp arms, Franklin Roosevelt had said before his death, "Defeat of the Nazi armies will have to be followed by the eradication of these weapons of economic warfare," and Attorney General Francis Biddle proposed to a congressional committee that "we break the power of the German monopolistic firms." As late as October 1945 the State Department was seriously considering the establishment of a Ruhr-Rhineland state, with the forcible eviction of the German population. London objected, but Paris thought the idea had merit.[40]

Some wondered whether the Ruhr was worth the effort. It seemed finished. Its own Schlotbarone were crushed by the devastation. In surrendering to Montgomery, Dönitz said, "My generation will never again see a flourishing Germany." Alan Moorehead, one of the most astute war correspondents, considered all the talk of neutralizing the Fatherland's war potential nonsense; in his opinion, the job had already been done. The Reich "is ruined and exhausted beyond the recall of this and perhaps the next generation," he wrote; "we have only to stick to our program of occupation and Germany will lapse into a small agricultural state, owning no great industries." Yet that was not a unanimous view. "Even in desolation, the Ruhr spoke of Teutonic power," another reporter wrote. "Nor was there a better vantage point to view the spectacle than from that pinnacle of the Vulcan's temple known as the Krupp Hauptverwaltungsgebäude."[41]

The more extravagant proposals were quashed before they could reach the conference table. Germany's reborn SPD proposed the nationalization of Krupp but couldn't even enlist the support of England's new Labour government; Britain, herself exhausted, needed Washington's help, and American businessmen wouldn't tolerate so dangerous a precedent. Nevertheless the Allied blueprint for Germany, as drawn in Potsdam that August by Truman, Stalin, and Attlee, staggered the defeated tycoons. All factories of any conceivable military use were to be dismantled; undamaged machinery was to be exported as reparations; the rest would be destroyed. The country's steel production was to be arbitrarily limited. (Seven months later this first Level of Industry Plan set a ceiling of seven million ingot tons a year, 9 percent of America's production. Surplus steel capacity was to be removed, thus, in effect, penalizing those ravaged continental Allies which needed the powerhouse of the Ruhr to rebuild their own economies.) Finally, Potsdam's signatories pledged themselves to eliminate "the excessive concentration of economic power as exemplified by cartels, syndicates, trusts, and other monopolistic arrangements."[42]

The administrator of American-occupied Germany was Lieutenant General Lucius Clay. The landscape he governed was scenic but unproductive; as he observed in his memoirs, "The highly industrialized British Zone contained the majority of the large enterprises." That included the Ruhr. In June 1945 Harmon's XXII U.S. Corps withdrew southward and British regiments marched into Essen with bands playing, bagpipes skirling, and battle flags snapping triumphantly in the wind. Troop commanders moved into the Essener Hof — they were to remain five years — and Villa Hügel became the headquarters of the U.S./U.K. Coal Control Group. Ineluctably the castle became a showplace for visiting VIPs. Montgomery sipped tea in the study where Alfried had played his last game of skat; Margaret Bourke-White photographed generals on the carved staircase; the Düsseldorf Ballet Troupe performed in the ballroom for junketing congressmen and members of Parliament.[43]

Kruppianer warily eyed the battle dress and guards mustaches of the *Landser*, as British soldiers were known. The Englishmen were better marchers than Americans, which won respect, and their military music was more stirring. But the Amis had been kind. *Landser* were not so gentle. Everyone expected them to be strict, and they were — though, to the vast amusement of Krupp artisans drifting back from POW camps, they lacked the technical skills of GIs; Hügel's master safe resisted the blasting and boring of a British engineering company for a full week, after which the infuriated Tommies found that it was empty.[44] English specialties were ceremonial flourishes, flexing the steel hand in the velvet glove, and lampooning *Herrenvolk* postures. In their first week they fired nearly six hundred Krupp executives who had been Nazis. Since Hermann Hobrecker had never joined the party, he was named chief of personnel.

Then red-tabbed officers pondered what sort of production should be resumed. To their astonishment, they discovered that it had never really stopped. Like some low but indestructible form of life, the Gusstahlfabrik had endured the saturation bombing, and here and there wisps of smoke still curled up from broken slabs of masonry. Even on April 11, while dealing with souvenir hunters, interrogation teams, and his board in hiding, Fritz Tubbesing had repaired enough power lines to operate the bakery and several consumer cooperatives. Now Kruppianer were turning out a small line of steel roofing. Operating under strict supervision, with military permits, other shops were allowed to train apprentices and begin construction of an assembly line for locomotives. Everywhere Ruhr craftsmen were doing what they could. In Bochum, Theodore H. White found, the Bochumer Verein "added two musicians to their staff and learned to cast enormous silvery bells of alloy steel — Protestant bells with one particular distinctive pitch of tone, Catholic bells with another distinctive tone. On the collar of the bells they molded the words: 'God is Love.'"

It was rather dull after Tigers, Panthers, 88's, and *Schwere Gustavs*, but it was work, and men were desperate for jobs. According to the occupation authorities' own statisticians, the average German was receiving 1,040 calories a day — a *Sklaven* feast, perhaps, but still only 67 percent of the subsistence level for adults. And beyond the borders of the humbled Reich, nations which had endured years of humiliation under German conquerors were also in straits. Graciously, the U.S. State Department agreed that the Ruhr should deliver 25 million tons of coal to France and Belgium — a cruel, irresponsible promise, for although there had been a time when the fabulous Kumpel could comply, flooded shafts had reduced total production to three million tons a month. Essen's Rathaus did what it could for the local economy. After convalescing from his Gestapo imprisonment, Eward Löser, appointed *Finanzdirektor*, introduced an imaginative public works project. The city's last dole had merely broadened Baldeney See, improving the view from the family's castle windows, but this one would clear the way for a larger, more efficient Hauptbahnhof. One casualty of progress would be the ancient Kettwig Gate Cemetery — there was no other direction in which the train terminal could expand — and so the coffins of Friedrich Krupp, Alfred Krupp, Fritz Krupp and Claus von Bohlen began their wanderings on November 10.[45]

The occupying authorities wanted Alfried's staff out of the way; it was time to enforce the decisions ratified at Potsdam. On November 16 the British Military Government announced the seizure of the firm of Fried. Krupp, together with all subsidiaries and assets, and appointed Colonel E. L. Douglas Fowles as comptroller. Taking over on a foggy, drizzly fall afternoon, Fowles received a group of subordinate executives who had been cleared by denazification courts. Led by Hobrecker and Paul Hansen, they hesitantly entered the colonel's refurbished Hauptverwaltungsgebäude office — the Union Jack had replaced Hitler's portrait — and wondered whether they would be asked to sit. Immediately the British colonel waved them to a row of chairs. His manner was friendly but detached. He was, he reminded them, a professional soldier. He didn't make policy; he carried out orders. Therefore argument with him was pointless. Even if they convinced him that his superiors' instructions were unwise, he would be helpless. He did what he was told; they must do what they were told. With that, he gave them their orders, speaking in German, he said, so that there would be no misunderstanding. Pointing out at the drenched landscape of bombed-out shops he declared: "Out there, gentlemen, no chimney will ever smoke again. Where the cast steel factory once stood there will be shrubs and meadows and parks. The British military government has decided to finish Krupp forever. That is all, gentlemen" (*mit Krupp für alle Zeit Schluss zu machen. Das ist alles, meine Herren*).[46]

It wasn't all. When Kruppianer learned that they were expected to ship intact machinery to foreign countries and tear down what was left, there was a flicker of mutiny. Despite threats that rations would be withheld, some workmen downed tools. Again the sub-Direktorium was summoned, this time to Düsseldorf. In Fowles's office the Germans had been stunned, but now their relationships with the *Landser* were vastly more complex. Apart from the abortive strike (it was only a gesture; the strikers had no bargaining power), other forces had intervened. Archbishop Frings had driven up from Cologne to beg the British to be sensible, and although the German executives Fowles had appointed held ostensible power, as loyal servants of the dynasty they were receiving secret instructions from Berthold, the one member of the family still at large. Indeed, the colonel's whole chain of command was meaningless. He had appointed Hansen "custodian," but of the four executives called to Düsseldorf — Hansen, Hobrecker, Fritz Hardach and Johannes Schröder — Schröder was the true leader. To the victors he was suspect, a man who had served the Reich too well. His colleagues accepted his seniority, however, and to cap that he had Bertha Krupp's blessing, via Berthold.

They were ushered into the office of a Brigadier Noel. "No one said *Guten Tag*," one of the four later said wryly. The atmosphere was arctic; "*Das Schwert des Siegers lag auf dem Tisch*," another German said afterward — "The conqueror's sword lay on the table." It lay, invisible, on one of two tables, around which red-tabbed officers sat silently. The second table had not been provided with chairs. A sergeant motioned them to it, and they stood awkwardly while the brigadier told them there would be no more strikes, no more interference from the church, no disobedience, no sabotage. If their men wouldn't dismantle the factories, they themselves would do it, brick by brick, under armed guard. There was a pause, then a brief, bitter exchange between Noel and Schröder. The German asked,

"*Wie sollen wir unsere Schulden bezahlen und die Forderungen eintreiben, Sir*" (How can we pay and collect our debts, sir)?

The brigadier snapped, "*Mit welchem Recht stellen Sie mir Fragen*" (By what right do you ask me questions)?

"*Mit dem Recht eines zum Tode Verurteilten, der Anspruch auf ein letztes Wort hat*" (By the right of a man who has been sentenced to death, and who is entitled to a last word).

Noel said cuttingly, "*Kriegsverbrecher treiben weder ihre Schulden ein, noch bezahlen sie sie an andere Kriegsverbrecher*" (War criminals do not collect debts, nor do they pay debts to other war criminals).[47]

He rose. The meeting was over. The men from Essen were led out. Although no one yet knew precisely what a war criminal was, a general officer of the occupying power seemed certain of their guilt. Or was it the company's guilt? Could an industrial enterprise be a *Kriegsverbrecher*? The issue was never fully resolved, for the success of Tubbesing's April bonfire meant that certain felonies could be only attributed to the Konzern and the Konzernherr, its supreme commander. This much seemed evident to the Germans: *die Firma* as a firm had already been tried, condemned, and sentenced to death in the Allies' private chambers, and those who had remained faithful to it were expected to participate in the execution.

The task was huge. Had the concern been confined to Krupp's deeded holdings of September 1, 1939, the amount of paper work would still have been enormous, but the books in the uncovered caches included all those seized factories in territory which had been held by the Wehrmacht. Machinery, some of it very expensive, had been moved from plant to plant — a Belgian forge might now be in Prague, and the Red Army might object to its restoration. To sort everything out, bilingual delegations arrived in Essen from Moscow, Warsaw, Rome, Athens, Oslo, Copenhagen, Belgrade, Paris, London and Washington. Each was given quarters in the Hauptverwaltungsgebäude, and Paul Hansen hurried from floor to floor with the necessary documents, provided, of course, they had not been confiscated by the Nuremberg prosecution.[48]

Some large problems were quickly solved. The Berndorferwerk was returned to its Austrian stockholders and their heirs, who merged it with the Ransdorfer Metallwerke, thereby ending the hundred-year-old offshoot of Hermann Krupp. Trustees took over Meppen, the dynasty's fabled proving grounds; twelve years later, in July 1957, they were to formally present it to artillery officers of West Germany's new army. Since the Grusonwerk was in Magdeberg, in the Russian zone, there was little anyone in Essen could do about it; the USSR simply claimed it as a prize of war. It was quite a prize. In its vaults were Krupp's secret tungsten steel formulas, which 12,000 East German Kruppianer, now comrade-employees of the Sowjestiche Maschinenbau AG, incorporated in the USSR's first MIGs. *Die Firma* had been reconciled to the loss of the Grusonwerk. Russians, after all, could only behave like Russians. British behavior in Kiel was another matter. Led by teams of technicians from the Clyde, Kiel's shipwrights were forced to destroy every submarine pen and then level the entire Germaniawerft — a spiteful act, the Germans remonstrated, designed only to cripple postwar maritime competition.[49]

All such protests were either written off as Prussian arrogance or ignored entirely. The Reich's enemies had Krupp by the throat, and in their impersonal, bureaucratic way they were almost as ruthless as Alfried had been when Hitler had seemed unstoppable. Essen workmen watched dourly while Midlands engineers smartly paced shop floors, marking with colored chalk the lathes, machine tools, drop forges, and milling machines to be shipped abroad. Once cranes had hoisted them away, the dynamiting began. Each morning at 6 A.M. the day's first demolitions rocked Essen. Over seven thousand Krupp workmen were feeding their families by destroying their place of livelihood, and the destruction was to continue for nearly five years. On one day early in 1948 a *Business Week* photographer shot pictures of a gigantic boiler headed for the Ukraine, of massive steel ingots en route to England, of captured French naval guns on their way home, and of monstrous machines, useful only to cannon makers, being blown apart. Blast furnaces went to Greece; the Gusstahlfabrik's mighty 15,000-ton press was shipped to the Yugoslavs, who didn't know what to do with it and who left it on the shores of the Adriatic, where it was later found coated with rust. Even bricks were dumped in boxes marked "Reparations for Holland" by gaunt, bitter Kruppianer.[50]

Bricks for the Dutch, a useless press to Tito, obsolete weapons to Brest — these were of small consequence. Giving the USSR heavy industry was another matter, and farsighted men were worried about it. Luckily the Soviets, as usual in Stalin's last decade, proved to be their own worst enemies. A share in the Ruhr lode should have been worth almost any price to Moscow. Instead, by reneging on their agreement to operate the Russian zone as part of a united Germany, the Reds left themselves open to reprisal, and on May 3, 1946, General Clay seized the chance. Except for "advance plant," he announced, the delivery of all reparations which had been destined for the Soviet Union was suspended. Unhappily for Krupp, Clay had no authority over the British, who had already agreed to present the Soviet Union with the most priceless asset still standing in the Ruhrgebiet: the Borbeck open hearth smelting installations and steel rolling mills. Begun in May 1929, Borbeck was the most modern steel plant in the Reich, the largest producer of steel ingots in the Essen area, and it was virtually unscathed. The factory had cost Krupp 28 million dollars; it could be stripped down and shipped east for six million. Moscow was eager to have it, and London went along. In February 1946, over a year before the Allies published their first formal dismantlement plan, the walls began to come down. Two years later the job was done, the reassembled plant stood deep in the USSR, and with it were towering stocks of priceless Krupp blueprints.[51]

No published list of dismantled German factories exists today, but a few figures suggest the extent of the Konzern's loss. Between the arrival of English regiments on Altendorferstrasse and the outbreak of the Korean War just five years later, Allied policy cost the firm more physical assets than all World War II air raids against Krupp plants. Over 130,000 tons of finished machinery went to Russia alone, over 150,000 tons of scrap to the United Kingdom. Nine out of every ten buildings Alfried had inherited in 1943 were gone. Nothing was left of the original cast steel factory but twisted junk; everything else had been sliced away with blowtorches and loaded on freight cars.[52]

In late March 1945 Hitler had ordered Albert Speer to eliminate all industrial plants, all significant electrical facilities, waterworks, gasworks, food stores and clothing stores [*die Zerstörung aller Industrieanlagen, aller wichtigen Elektrizitäts-, Wasser- und Gaswerke und so weiter, aber auch der Lebensmittel- und Bekleidungslager*] . . . all bridges . . . all railway and communication installations . . . all waterways, all ships, all freight cars and all locomotives.[53]

"*Verbrannte Erde,*" the Führer had called it in Russia — "scorched earth." In disobeying him now in Germany, Speer believed he had made national recovery possible. Yet it was hard for Alfried's executives to see much difference between Hitler's scorched earth and the victors' dismantlement policy. One would have been industrial suicide, the other industrial murder. To be sure, the skills of 100,000 Kruppianer were intact; the British, lacking an SS, did not resort to final solutions. *Die Firma's* rich coal remained in the earth, and Rheinhausen still loomed over the west bank of the Rhine, but under the Allied High Commission's Law 27 Alfried would never again be permitted to control any of them. Law 27 was aimed at the eleven most powerful smokestack barons, chiefly Krupp, who had owned 55 percent of the Ruhr's coal and 90 percent of German steel production. To "decentralize the German economy," eliminate "excessive concentration of economic power," and prevent "the development of a war potential," the law provided, the commission would not permit "the return to positions of ownership and control of those persons who have been found, or may be found, to have furthered the aggressive designs of the National Socialist Party."[54]

As General Clay put it afterward, "We early prepared a law to break up cartels and excessive concentrations of power, and submitted it to the Allied Control Council." Though a Republican and a conservative, Clay represented his country's traditional zeal for trust-busting, an enthusiasm which German businessmen have never understood. Even in the depths of defeat they thought it impractical and unrealistic; the Schlotbarone actually doubted that it was possible to break up a concern as tightly woven as Fried. Krupp. Though no outsider has ever shared their emotional commitment to monopolies, it was a Wall Street financier who had stated their case most crisply. "You can't unscramble eggs," J. P. Morgan had said. The Americans in Germany didn't believe mines and mills were eggs. They didn't see how, with a conviction at Nuremberg, they could fail to unscramble Krupp's omelet. What they neglected to take into account was that the vanquished Reich had become one vast Bedlam — and that Essen's historic dynasty was an accurate reflection of the national chaos.

# 25

✠

# Krupp...
# You Have Been Convicted

I N the waning autumn of 1945, as the first frost found German children huddling in the cut-down Wehrmacht uniforms of their fathers, German girls selling themselves to soldiers for boxes of cereal, and German mothers exchanging priceless Dresden for cartons of cigarettes, everyone in the Krupp family except Alfried, Bertha, and Gustav was on the move. None of them at any given moment was likely to have the faintest notion of where the others were. Berthold, as he later put it, was "wandering like a tramp through Germany." Harald was hiding behind his alias in a Rumanian POW cage; the whereabouts of Waldtraut and Irmgard were unknown. Ursula von Wilmowsky von Waldhausen and her husband Rolf were living like squatters in a vacant Essen house. Ursula's last word from her parents was that they had recovered from their ordeal and were once more at Marienthal, welcoming home battle-scarred farmers and planning a fruitful harvest. Barbara's daughter had no reason to think otherwise. Wilmowskys had been caring for their Saxon peasants seventy-five years before Saxony became a kingdom. Where else would they be?[1]

The answer — the girl couldn't believe it when she heard it — was that they were trudging the open road with all they owned on their backs, as helpless and as hungry as the hordes of other fugitives around them. "Your brother-in-law is Krupp?" a Red Army officer asked Tilo in September. The baron admitted it, and the officer told him his estate was confiscated. The four-story castle would become a children's home; the land would be converted to a collective farm. Next day a messenger brought a slip of paper. On it were orders to leave within twenty-four hours. Knapsacks would be permitted, but no baggage. Barbara took her blue lifetime scrapbook. Then, from an ancient trunk she exhumed a peculiarly shaped, leather-encased clock which Fritz Krupp had bought in Paris the month before the Franco-Prussian War broke out. The timepiece was her only other tie to her childhood, and she asked a maid to hide it in the church belfry. (Years later it arrived safely at Villa Hügel in an unmarked parcel.) Leaving Marienthal, as she explained afterward with a cheerful shrug, "we put sacks on our backs and left." They couldn't possibly reach the Ruhr on foot, but that wasn't necessary. Unlike the DPs around them, the elderly couple belonged to the old patriciate, whose estates were scattered all over Germany. One of Barbara's lay just across the West German border, near Kassel. She hadn't seen it for years, and it was small, but it was enough to see them through the winter. They survived by barter. Neighbors were given prized bottles from the wine cellar and firewood cut from the hunting forest by old Krupp retainers. In return they brought the Wilmowskys black bread, milk, eggs, and now and then a chicken.[2]

Barbara's sister was in even worse straits. At Blühnbach Bertha would have been comfortable, but she too had been evicted from her castle. Both Alfried's parents were internees of the United States Army; the Krupps' private *Alpenfestung* was too remote for security-minded Americans, so the fifty-nine-year-old grandmother had been ordered to bring her seventy-five-year-old husband to a hostel on the nearest road. Gert von Klass has left us a poignant picture of how, as his relatives frantically searched for one another, Gustav

lay at a coaching inn by Blühnbach [*im Posthaus zu Blühnbach*], where country buses sometimes stopped. It stood not far from his property, which was now all he had left. Still incapable of any motion whatsoever, he was attended by Bertha Krupp and a professional nurse. The bus driver occasionally pitched in with the daily making of his bed. . . . He had been examined by American physicians. They had only shrugged their shoulders. The sentinel continued to sit near the sickroom door, where the inert patient, in his mental haze, sank silently toward the end [*Der Wachtposten sitzt nach wie vor neben der Türe des Kranken-zimmers, in dem der Gelähmte seinem Ende entgegendämmert*]. The women had grown used to the soldier's presence; they hardly noticed him.[3]

Berthold hadn't forgotten the sentry, however, and it was this probing by American doctors, together with the indictment of his father, which was responsible for his frantic *Wanderlust*. If the conquerors really were bent upon hanging a Krupp, he, the only man in the family free to come and go, had to do something about it. Even Berthold's freedom was limited. While raising a defense fund in Essen, he heard a rumor that Carl Görens was dead. It was true: Görens's depression over his only son's battlefield death had become unendurable, and he had jumped from a tower of Schloss Vehlen, the Westphalian castle where Alfried and his staff were now imprisoned. Berthold had to verify it, for he had counted on the dead man as a vital witness. After all, Alfried, Görens, and Löser had once ruled the firm as a triumvirate, and Löser, it was now known, had been politically unreliable. Because of this *nationale Zuverlässigkeit*, he would doubtless give unfriendly evidence.

Operating out of a small Hauptverwaltungsgebäude office, Alfried's brother sought Görens's prewar residence on Hohenzollernstrasse that first postwar fall. His information was limited; he didn't even know that two days earlier the Direktorium had been clapped in jail. On his first expedition he learned what the bombings had earlier done to Essen. Hohenzollernstrasse, to his consternation, had disappeared. The RAF had obliterated the entire street — homes, gardens, sidewalks, curbstones, drains, lampposts, hydrants, paving, even sewers. A stranger told him the Direktor was dead. At the Essener Hof he tried to verify the report. A tight-lipped redtab said, "I won't tell you. All I can say is that he's better off than you are." (Berthold later sought out Frau Görens, who went to the hostel herself, learned she was a widow, and was allowed to bury her husband.) The reason for his plight, Berthold was informed, was that he was a Krupp. "My name is von Bohlen und Halbach," he said. "You're a Krupp, Krupp, Krupp," the officer repeated, jabbing his forefinger at the once elegant, now fraying lapel, "and if you're found within Essen's city limits after sundown, you'll be shot."[4]

Baron von Wilmowsky was told the same thing when, hearing of Berthold's mission, he left Barbara on the Kassel estate and came to help. Though he wasn't a Krupp, his wife was, and that, to the English, was enough. Neither man obeyed the ultimatum. Moving about only at night, they hid for days in Ursula von Waldhausen's attic. Later Berthold encountered Jean Sprenger, an old friend, on a darkened Bredeney street corner. Himself the son of a smokestack baron, Sprenger had attended the University of Munich with Berthold, and his brother had been a classmate of Harald's in Essen's Realgymnasium. Now the brother, like Harald, was gone. But not Jean; tall, blond, and athletic, he was a poster of Goebbels's ideal Aryan, and he seemed indestructible. As an infantry officer he had endured four winters on the eastern front and was hardier, if leaner, than ever. In a way Sprenger was deceptive. He looked tough, yet he was to prove himself one of the most gifted and sensitive sculptors in postwar Germany. Already he had taken over the unoccupied home of one of the Krupp directors imprisoned in Vehlen Castle and rebuilt a gutted wing as a studio. He offered to share it with Berthold — they were fated to live together there for the next ten years — and to do what he could for the Krupp defense.[5]

Sprenger couldn't accomplish much; neither could the baron. Essentially Berthold's was a one-man task, hampered by difficulties which would have defeated almost anyone except a gallant and devoted son. He knew nothing of what had happened in Essen during the past decade. To this day he can only spread his hands when asked about the evidence revealed at Nuremberg; he had been at Oxford during the prelude to war and in the Wehrmacht or working on penicillin research thereafter. His father had done little to inspire filial loyalty, and Alfried had always been cool and aloof with him, but he knew how his mother felt about her husband and her eldest son, and he worshiped Bertha. Thus he put himself to the test. The frailest of four brothers, he traveled endlessly on trains, sitting up at night in dirty, leaking Hauptbahnhöfen and standing throughout journeys between the Ruhr, the coaching inn, lawyers' offices, and Nuremberg.

There were few seats on German coaches that fall and winter. Berthold was roving a 143,200-square-mile madhouse. He was hiring legal counsel in a European country whose national currency was American cigarettes and gathering evidence in a Reich reduced to half the size of France — 48,000,-000 people were jammed into a strip narrower than the distance between Washington and New York — a humbled empire where bridges lay awash in her riverbeds, ten-year-old Autobahnen had been chewed to pieces by heavy tank treads, whose churches were charred hulks, cities reeked of corpses and sewage, children collapsed at school for lack of nourishment, former leaders lived in disguise, aristocrats bribed cooks for jobs as dishwashers in the overflowing kitchens of the triumphant armies, countesses wore unsightly prewar woolen stockings perforated with ragged holes, and workmen toiled outdoors in soleless boots and cracked *Lederhosen.* The elite in this strange land were black market gangsters, and the country's struggle for life was frustrated, first by the arrival of eight million panicky fugitives from the east and then by an occupation government administered by three victorious powers and an invited guest, France.[6]

In this turmoil, paradoxically, lay the dynasty's salvation. Sharing it as Krupps in the past had shared the *Volk's* other moods, Berthold, trading in Lucky Strikes and sleeping on the wooden benches of train stations, seemed no match for United States Supreme Court Justice Robert H. Jackson. Yet he beat him and saved his brother's life. To be sure, Mr. Justice Jackson contributed to his own defeat. If he hadn't insisted so fiercely that the guilty Krupp was Gustav, or if he had restrained himself from an astonishing legal blunder, Alfried might have been doomed anyhow. But in large part the failure of Allied prosecutors to put the right Krupp in Nuremberg's first dock was a failure of communication. Germany was in such a state of anarchy that even the conquerors had difficulties reaching one another. The U.S. doctors had submitted their report on Gustav's incapacity, but it didn't reach Jackson, who since May had been chief war crimes prosecutor for the United States. Thomas Harris, a brilliant young New York attorney, had become the first investigator to discover that the Konzern's extant documents demanded the indictment of the fourth Kanonenkönig, not his father, but Harris's finding stopped short of Jackson's desk.

Both items of information were vital. Had they reached the American justice — or Sir Hartley Shawcross of Britain, General R. A. Rudenko of the Soviet Union, or François de Menthon and Auguste Champetier de Ribes of France, Jackson's fellow prosecutors — it is highly improbable that Krupp would have left Nuremberg alive. That first tribunal was a quartet of hanging judges. Twenty-two defendants faced it, and twelve were condemned to the noose. One, Hermann Göring, took his life by biting a cyanide capsule on the eve of his execution. Göring would have been condemned by any Allied court. It is generally conceded by scholars of the trial, however, that several of the eleven who were hanged in the Palace of Justice on the morning of October 16, 1946, were victims of the time. Alfred Jodl, for example, would have certainly been spared by a later tribunal. Generals far more culpable than he — such as Manstein, Kesselring, and Erich von dem Bach-Zelewski, who had led the bloody SS suppression of the Warsaw revolt — were freed within a few years. Indeed, one of the judges who had sentenced Jodl later declared that the verdict was a mistake, and restitution was made to his widow.[7] He died for a fraction of the crimes of which Alfried was later found guilty, and for which he could have been convicted before that first court. Chance favored Krupp, the dedication of his brother helped, Jackson's slip contributed heavily; but most of all he benefited from the national tumult he had done so much to create. In it, he managed to dodge the sweep of the enemy's searchlights just long enough.

⚔    ⚔    ⚔

To Germans of the war generation, the name Nuremberg is synonymous with disgrace — disgrace because the city cradled National Socialism, the dream which betrayed them, and because there the enemy imposed foreign justice upon them. Anglo-Saxon legal procedure was adopted for the trials, a decision which, defense counsel rightly protested, put them at a disadvantage. Frankfurt's *Die Neue Zeitung* skillfully summed up the handicaps which the accused men faced. They were accustomed to a continental courtroom whose judge held the defendant's record in his hands, was acquainted with every detail of the police investigation, was under legal obligation to trust an official's word more than that of a private citizen, and had the power to prevent cross-examination. Now all that was turned round. The judges listened while prosecutors and defense lawyers led the proceedings. Defendants were considered innocent until proven guilty. Only what was said in court under oath counted. Every witness was subject to cross-examination, and a defendant was entitled to remain silent without prejudice to his case — a right which was to be exercised in but one of the Nuremberg war crimes trials, the Krupp case.[8]

Manifestly the Germans could not try their own. At Versailles they had been asked to pass judgment upon a hundred men; only six had been arrested, and all were acquitted. Yet even some Allied leaders had reservations about the new approach. Secretary of State Cordell Hull had wanted the German leaders given a drumhead court-marshal. Winston Churchill, agreeing, thought the top Nazis should be led out some morning and shot. But Hull had resigned in 1944, and the British electorate had overthrown Churchill. A majority agreed with Walter Lippmann, who compared the Nuremberg concept to the Magna Carta, *habeas corpus*, and the Bill of Rights. President Truman thought a new trail to international justice was being blazed. The *New York Times* concurred, and no one felt this crusading spirit more strongly than Robert Justice Jackson. He went to Bavaria with what Justice Holmes once called "fire in the belly," convinced that he was an emissary of morality and historic justice.[9]

"The entire prosecution," wrote Eugene Davidson in his study of the International Military Tribunal, "was united on the desirability of trying a member of the Krupp family." Jackson was their leader. When the indictment was signed on October 6 in Berlin the American singled out the dynasty in his bill of particulars as the most vicious instrument of Teutonic aggression. Already the case against Gustav was formidable. Based on prewar documents, it had been amassed during the war and implicated him a dozen times over in the secret rearmament of the Reich and the plotting of Nazi aggression. Already a seat had been reserved for him in the second row of the Palace of Justice dock; he and Karl Dönitz were to sit directly behind Göring and Hess, with Sauckel, Seyss-Inquart, Speer, SD chief Ernst Kaltenbrunner, and Hitler's crony Julius Streicher, among others, to their left.[10]

On October 20 the first rumor of Gustav's illness appeared in the press. No one bothered to investigate it until, on November 4, his court-appointed lawyer submitted two medical affidavits, fruits of Berthold's toil. One had been signed by Dr. Karl Gersdorf of Werfen, Salzburg, on September 9, the other by Dr. Otto Gerke of Bad Gastein on September 13; both urged that proceedings against the patient be deferred until his health permitted him to appear. To the prosecutors the motion looked bogus, a dodge as familiar to Anglo-Saxon lawyers as to the continent. Nevertheless the tribunal appointed a medical commission to examine the defendant. Lord Justice Geoffrey Lawrence of Britain, the president of the court, assembled an impressive panel: Brigadier R. E. Turnbridge, medical officer of the British Army of the Rhine; Dr. Bertram Schoffner, an American neuropsychiatrist; Dr. René Piedelièvre, professor of medicine in Paris; and three Soviet specialists. The six physicians appeared at the coaching inn on the morning of November 6, two days after Krupp's stopgap lawyer had filed his plea. Bertha and the nurse led them to the sickbed. The patient greeted them with two hoarse words, "*Guten Tag*," and immediately lapsed into a coma. Next day Justice Lawrence read their conclusions to a stunned battery of Allied attorneys:

> We unanimously agree that the invalid is suffering from senile softening of the brain . . . and that the state of his health is such that he is unable to follow the proceedings before the court or to understand or cooperate in any interrogation. The physical condition of the invalid is such that he cannot be transported without danger to his life. We believe, after due consideration, that his condition is not likely to improve but rather to deteriorate. Consequently we are unanimously of the opinion that he will never be in a physical or mental state to appear before the International Military Tribunal.[11]

The IMT voted to weigh the matter carefully, but in the light of the doctors' clear-cut language there could be no doubt what its decision would be, and in a preliminary hearing on November 14 the prosecutors, petitioning for a trial *in absentia*, were sharply questioned by the Lord Chief Justice. "Do you believe," Lawrence asked Jackson, "that it would be in the interests of justice to sentence a man who, on account of illness, is not in a position to conduct his defense properly?" The embarrassed American replied that he did not. Lawrence then turned to Sir Hartley Shawcross.

LAWRENCE: Do you agree with me that according to the law of Great Britain — as well as the law of the United States — a man in Gustav Krupp's mental and physical condition would be pronounced incapable of pleading?
SIR HARTLEY: Yes, indeed.[12]

The court therefore ruled against an *in absentia* trial for Gustav — though Martin Bormann was to be so tried, and condemned to death should he be found. Three days after their first Krupp ruling the judges announced an indefinite postponement in proceedings against Gustav, adding that he would be haled before the bench the moment he was fit. That evening the chief prosecutors conferred. Jackson and Charles Dubost, the French attorney, proposed the indictment of Alfried. Sir Hartley agreed. General Rudenko, the Russian, was ready to convict both Alfried and Gustav on the spot.

Debating strategy *in camera* was one thing. Rising in open court was something else, and it was when Dubost and Jackson addressed the tribunal that Friday that they irreparably botched the true case against Alfried. Granted that Jackson couldn't possibly have examined all the evidence at his disposal — the SS documents alone filled six freight cars — he was still a Supreme Court justice. He knew courtroom procedure, and his flaunting of it is incomprehensible. Since the father could not sit in the dock, he argued, the son should take his place on the ground that "no greater disservice to the future peace of the world could be done than to excuse the entire Krupp family from this trial." This became the source for the legend that Alfried later paid for Gustav's crimes. Justice Lawrence wanted no part of it — "This is not a football game where another player can be substituted for one who is injured," he said sharply, and he inquired whether such a motion would be acceptable in an American courtroom. After Jackson had conceded that it would not, Dubost offered an identical motion. The French judge bluntly asked his compatriot, "Do you really believe that you can request the court to substitute one name for another on the bill of indictment?" Dubost's reply was negative, Lawrence curtly thanked him, and the tribunal agreed that Krupp's seat in the dock would remain unoccupied.[13]

Yet already the tentative probing of Alfried's wartime conduct had persuaded junior members of the prosecution staffs that he was a felon in his own right. Meeting in extraordinary session Saturday, the court heard Sir Hartley, de Menthon, and Champetier de Ribes present that argument. The IMT wavered. Time was short; opening statements were scheduled to begin Monday. Before the first of them, the judges handed down their ruling: though Alfried Krupp had been excluded from the present hearings, he would enter the dock "immediately after the close of the present trial." It was perhaps with that in mind that Jackson delivered his moving summation before the tribunal: "They stand before the record of this trial as bloodstained Gloucester stood by the body of his slain king. He begged of the widow, as they beg of you: 'Say I slew them not.' If you were to say of these men that they are not guilty, it would be as true to say that there has been no war, there are no slain, there has been no crime."[14]

✠ ✠ ✠

Thus the industrial symbol of *furor teutonicus* had been granted a reprieve. It lasted far longer than anyone then would have thought possible; two years were to pass before Alfried would enter the paneled courtroom and, as chief defendant, take Hermann Göring's old seat at the end of the dock. Trying him "immediately after" Göring's suicide and the executions of Ribbentrop, Jodl, Keitel, Kaltenbrunner, Rosenberg, Frank, Frick, Streicher, Sauckel, and Seyss-Inquart had proved impossible; during the nine-month trial Germany, Europe, and the world had changed beyond belief.

In the ravaged Reich, confusion and pandemonium had increased. Each day's testimony before the IMT had set off a fresh chain of indictments. Exhausted clerks were asked to translate and screen 100,000 new documents; the U.N. War Crimes Commission now had a list of 36,800 suspects, and the Russians — who in those days were indignant with everyone — were boycotting the commission. Some witnesses crucial to the Krupp trial went underground. Thousands of Nazis emigrated to Egypt or followed Otto Skorzeny's improvised escape route through Spain to Argentina, which offered "political asylum" to such SS fugitives as Dr. Fritz Mengele, who was charged not with holding unpopular political opinions but with the slaughter of thousands of concentration camp inmates. Meantime Krupp's ex-slaves were finding their way home or vanishing into displaced person camps. Allied prosecutors placed advertisements in DP newspapers, urging survivors of the company's camps to come forward, but most had had enough; they wanted to leave Germany forever, and since there was no legal way to hold them, much evidence evaporated.

The greatest reason for the delay, however, was the breakup of the International Military Tribunal. Repeatedly during the trial the position of the three western democracies had been compromised by their embarrassing eastern ally. *Tu quoque* (You, too) is an ancient legal stratagem — a retort charging the prosecutor with having committed the defendant's offense, and Nazis in the witness box had used it to score heavily against General Rudenko. Charged with the rape of Poland, a German could reply that the Soviet Union had joined in the rape. Accused of massacres, he had but to mention the Red Army's mass murder of 11,000 Polish soldiers in the Katyn forest — a crime documented by British and American intelligence and by investigations of the Poles themselves.[15]

The knowledge that a bloodstained Gloucester was among those passing judgment disquieted Britons, Frenchmen, and Americans. The Russians were equally unhappy. They didn't enjoy being indicted in a free court; their lawyers were accustomed to trials in which the accused recited prepared confessions. Soviet police even wanted to use *Sippenhaftung,* the arrest of a defendant's relatives to intimidate defendants. With chilling Slavic candor, their lawyers blandly explained that a man in their custody was already guilty — that, after all, was why he had been picked up — and they had expected every Nazi in the dock to hang. When other members of the IMT overrode the protests of Major General I. Nikitchenko, the USSR judge, Moscow was confounded. And when the tribunal merely sentenced Hess, Funk, Dönitz, Raeder, Speer, and von Neurath to jail and released Schacht, von Papen, and Fritzsche outright, the Reds stormed out of the Justizpalast. In the future, they announced, they would hold their own trials.[16]

They did; so did every European power which had been at war with Germany. The Pentagon suggested that the United States withdraw too, but strong men in the American Military Government, notably General Clay and General Taylor, were vehemently opposed. An SS man who had murdered a Parisian could be tried in Paris as a war criminal, but major war criminals were a different breed; they had committed crimes throughout the continent. America, the transatlantic power, had a special responsibility here. On American Military Government books were the cases of 1,762 Germans, including 420 who were later sentenced to death for Dachau atrocities. Of these, 199 were accused of major war crimes. Clay and Taylor grouped all prisoners into twelve cases, covering extermination squads, Nazi officials, medical "experiments," the SD, and so on. Of these Krupp, largely because of the mass of data, was to be case number ten. As the trial date approached, rumblings of discontent increased in the international financial community, but, General Taylor later recalled, "General Clay supported me unfailingly. He's from Marietta, Georgia, a really small town, and he had the rural Southerner's distrust of 'wicked bankers.' "[17]

Throughout the winter and spring of 1946–1947 the accumulation of evidence went on, despite the withdrawal of allies, the indifference of bored foreign correspondents, and a growing feeling in the Truman administration that Germans should be enlisted in the Cold War. The prosecution's greatest single obstacle was Chief Justice Fred Vinson's decree that federal judges would no longer be granted leaves of absence to serve on the Nuremberg bench. Undismayed, Clay combed state supreme courts and recruited their ablest judges. The Krupp tribunal would be Justice H. C. Anderson of the Tennessee Court of Appeals, Justice Edward J. Daly of the Connecticut Superior Court, and Justice William J. Wilkins of the Superior Court of Washington.

All this took time. But time worked for both sides. Over two years General Taylor assembled a working staff (shaking out one eminent bureaucrat who actually wanted to try Bertha Krupp). Rawlings Ragland, the crisp young Kentuckian who was to lead the Krupp prosecution, divided the four main charges among his ten associates. Documents were classified, affidavits submitted, depositions taken. At the same time, Alfried's brother, at work now in a healing Germany, had retained Krupp's chief counsel. Otto Kranzbühler's defense of Dönitz before the IMT had clearly demonstrated that he was the most dignified and learned attorney in Nuremberg, and his subsequent appearances for Hermann Röchling and for Odilo Burkhart in the Flick case strengthened his mastery of American courtroom sparring. "Kranzbühler was the one German who really understood the art of cross-examination," Drexel Sprecher, leader of the I. G. Farben prosecution, was to say later, while to Cecelia H. Goetz, who would subsequently argue cases before the U.S. Supreme Court, he was "the greatest lawyer I've ever seen — a dream lawyer, a Hollywood lawyer, always pulling rabbits out of his hat." The former naval captain had one further advantage. His distinguished wartime service for the Reich wouldn't impress the tribunal, but it might daunt some Kruppianer on the stand.[18]

Kranzbühler's new staff was enormous. Berthold was no longer reduced to doling out cigarette money. Exactly how many of Krupp's foreign assets were liquidated during these months is unknown, but the holdings were there, and fragments of information here and there suggest their extent. Once, when Alfried's chief counsel wanted to expand his staff, he asked Anderson to "release some of Herr Krupp's investments in Sweden, Spain, France, Belgium, and the United States." Asked how much he needed, Kranzbühler replied, "About a hundred thousand pounds." Since the pound was then worth four dollars, this was $400,000, and it was only a fraction of the money available to Alfried abroad. Later he sold off $1,700,000 to finance Kruppianer pensions and put up collateral valued by commercial banks at $20,000,000. The sell-off and reinvestment of Nazi bonds in 1943 and 1944 — the best guess is that this had been done through Switzerland and Sweden — was, among other things, underwriting a titanic defense; for every U.S. lawyer marshaling documents there were three Germans counterattacking, and it is a measure of Krupp's untarnished prestige among his countrymen that Kranzbühler was being assisted by no fewer than twenty-four advocates who held the prestigious degree of *Doktor der Rechte*. There was even an expensive American attorney — former U.S. Colonel Joseph S. Robinson — in his retinue. Among them they assembled 1,309 affidavits (to the Americans' 380) and two defense witnesses for every prosecution witness.[19]

The contention that Alfried was defenseless in the Palace of Justice is therefore absurd, despite the subsequent report in an American magazine that he had been tried "without benefit of counsel."[20] After his conviction Germans angrily pointed out that the judges, the rules of procedure, the bailiffs — even the flag behind the bench — were American. Those were reasonable complaints. The Nazi banner could scarcely have been displayed, of course, and the U.N. standard would have been inappropriate, but there was really no need for any ensign at all. Yet a scrupulous examination of the transcript suggests that Kranzbühler, too, entered the courtroom with certain tactical advantages. The documents were in German. Most of the key witnesses had to be Alfried's countrymen, and Germans tended to regard prosecution testimony as collaboration with the enemy. Moreover, no prosecution attorney in Nuremberg could put a man on the stand without first waiving the right to try him later for crimes of his own, and many individuals with damning evidence were themselves awaiting trial.

Finally, the nationality of the jurists was less decisive than it seemed. Hu Anderson, the presiding judge, was a political conservative. He appeared impressed by Dr. Walter Siemens's charge that the prosecution was prone "to see a criminal in every German industrialist," and he leaned forward attentively when Alfred Schilf, another Krupp *Doktor der Rechte*, intimated that the proceedings against Krupp and I. G. Farben were "definitely anticapitalistic." An exchange between Justice Anderson and SS

Brigadeführer Walther Schrieber on May 27 was to be particularly illuminating. The judge seemed to feel that the Speer ministry's intervention in the Berthawerk had constituted bureaucratic meddling. "Well, now," he said, "there is nothing unusual for a private enterprise that had been successful many, many years objecting to the government putting a man down there telling them how to run their business. Nothing strange about that, is there?" As the holder of the Knight's Cross, the Golden Party emblem, the SS Sword, and the Himmler Ring, Schrieber was well aware that the Third Reich hadn't been at all like the New Deal, and he replied, "In Germany it was to say the least dangerous, if not actually dangerous to one's very life." Nettled and confused, Anderson commented testily, "Well, you obviously didn't understand my question." Perhaps the SS general hadn't, but clearly the justice hadn't understood the answer. Though he was to agree with his two colleagues that Alfried was a war criminal and should be imprisoned, he would submit a dissenting opinion objecting to the confiscation of Krupp's property; to him that was the violation of a sacred right.[21]

Alfried first conferred with *die Firma* attorneys in August 1946, but Kranzbühler didn't meet him until the following summer. From the outset the hatchet-faced German lawyer realized that Berthold's eldest brother was a man of exceptional acumen. Another year would pass before the judicial machinery began to grind out indictments; both counsel and client knew judgment day was inevitable, however, "and," Kranzbühler predicted, "it will be like the first trial. It won't be a lawsuit; it will be political." Since General Taylor was a Roosevelt Democrat, the German attorney felt that the intrusion of New Deal ideology would be unavoidable — that "although the parallels between fascism and German industry are ridiculous, they will be drawn." There was, he warned, no way to avoid the stigmata of war crimes: "to the winner, the loser will always be an aggressor." Alfried nodded thoughtfully, asked technical questions, proposed specific tactics, and shared strategic planning to a degree rare in any client. Already he was a silent but powerful influence upon his own Generalstab.[22]

He relished their conferences, which is unsurprising, for over the past sixteen months he had been shunted from stockade to stockade — Recklinghausen, Schloss Vehlen, Bielefeld, and finally the collecting depot for Nuremberg defendants known to the British as Dustbin and to Americans as Ashcan. The long wait, Fritz von Bülow later said, "was the worst time of all, even worse than after the sentencing." Between his legal meetings Krupp would often grow morose, neglect his appearance, and go unshaven for as long as a week. His ten Direktorium lieutenants worried about him. Then, shortly before the trial, his day — and theirs — was unexpectedly brightened by a new arrival. The chief and his staff were to be joined by a twelfth defendant; Ashcan's latest guest was Ewald Löser, only yesterday Essen's *Finanzdirektor*. His former colleagues, who had remained *führertreu*, were in no mood to reward his treachery by verifying it, and so, lacking any other living witness to his July 20 role except his wife, the man who had nearly died in a Prinz-Albrecht-Strasse dungeon under Himmler was now behind American bars. To him it seemed madness. It seems so now; the only sensible explanation is the incoherence of the era.[23]

Berthold visited Ashcan four times, twice bringing Fritz Hardach and Jean Sprenger. The excursions were a greater sacrifice than Alfried appreciated at the time, for his brother's wanderings were far from over. Despite Kranzbühler's corps of aides, certain jobs must be done by a member of the family. Veteran Kruppianer would confide in no one else, former Hauptverwaltungsgebäude clerks would show salvaged correspondence only to a son of Bertha's, and relatives of men in hiding were mute unless they heard the magic name of Krupp. Even then they looked blank when the runagate's life was at stake. "I kept trying to find people who had known Alfried when he was making major decisions," Berthold said long afterward, "and none of them seemed to be in Germany any more." His most trying duty, now that Kranzbühler and Alfried commanded the defense, was reassuring his mother. Whenever he could spare time he made the long trek to the roadside hostel. Bertha, herself an Austrian internee, was forbidden to visit her imprisoned son. Kranzbühler sent teams of lawyers to question her, but she could tell them nothing, she knew nothing, and in the end she submitted no affidavit. To Berthold she expressed bewilderment: "Why do they attack *Papa*? What is this talk of blood? Why do foreigners feel so violently about Krupp?"[24]

He thought he knew one reason. In his opinion, "The top Americans in Germany were OK, but the fire in the prosecution staff came from German Jews who had become naturalized Americans and then lawyers. In the courtroom they were acting from hate. They made the trial political."[25] Berthold is a man of exceptional intelligence, but here his reasoning defies understanding. Krupp had been indicted by Robert H. Jackson. The chief prosecutor was Telford Taylor. Rawlings Ragland was to be Taylor's field marshal in the courtroom, and the leader of the Krupp trial team was H. Russell Thayer. If there was any ethnic imbalance in that staff, it favored white Anglo-Saxon Protestants, and the presence of Anderson, Daly, and Wilkins on the bench strengthened it. All the same, to this day Essen remains convinced that Alfried was the victim of vindictive, embittered *Juden*.

✠ ✠ ✠

As the second year of his captivity waned, Alfried was convoyed down Nuremberg's Königstrasse in an armored car. There were so many military policemen around him that he caught only a glimpse of the city, but it was enough; nothing remained of the intoxicating backdrop he had seen during the great September rally when marching bands had blared *Heil Hitler Dir*, jackboots had thumped in unison on the cobblestones, and millions had shrieked ecstatically. In a single half-hour two years earlier, Allied bombers had wiped out ancient Nuremberg: the steep-pitched roofs, dormer windows, and dark narrow medieval streets. All Krupp could see were heaps of rusting rubble, the *Frauenkirche* bell tower, nearly six centuries old — which tolled now for the condemned — and the quaint red shell of Albrecht-Dürer-Haus, miraculously held upright by its great central beam, in which Germany's greatest artist had created his woodcuts and engravings for two of the last rulers of the First Reich. The bombardiers had spared but one major public building, the rambling gray sandstone Justizpalast, whose walls contained a score of courtrooms, a penitentiary, a prison yard, and a scaffold. A man could be dragged in off the street, charged, convicted, and hanged, all under one roof and all legally. The structure was a monument to German efficiency, and had been used often.

It was here, on September, 15, 1935, that the Führer's famous Nuremberg Laws had been promulgated, officially designating Jews as *Untermenschen*. Here the most savage parodies of National Socialist justice had been staged, with crowds drenching defendants with spittle while judges wearing swastikas on their robes juggled gavels. And now, nearly twenty months after his arrest, Krupp was led to a Palace of Justice cell and told the new rules. MPs would be stationed outside his door day and night. He would be permitted one twenty-minute exercise period and one shower a day, but conversations with fellow prisoners would be forbidden until after the trial had begun, and then only in the dock during recess. If he thought his clothes unpresentable, the prison tailor would make him a suit, but it must be removed each time he returned to his cell.[26]

Alfried scorned the tailor; Berthold had brought a wardrobe. He also disdained the English language — "It was," he later explained, "a matter of principle." Arraigned on August 15 before seventy-five-year-old, holloweyed Judge Anderson (who reminded a Reuters correspondent of "a desiccated eagle"), he prematurely snapped "*Hier. Unschuldig*" — not guilty — when his name was called. The judge asked whether he was represented by counsel. "*Ja.*" Had the indictment been served upon him in the German language more than thirty days ago? "*Ja.*" Was he familiar with the charges and specifications, and had he read them? "*Ja.*" Was he now ready to plead? "*Ja.*" How did he plead to this indictment, guilty or not guilty? "*Unschuldig.*"[27]

Three weeks later he was led from his cell to an elevator. Debouching on the second floor, he passed a series of checkpoints, each of which relayed word of his arrival to the next. Six hundred spectators filled the gallery behind the railing in the great paneled courtroom, but he ignored them. Sitting in the dock, his eyes fixed on the distant wall, he waited impassively while his fellow defendants filed in and took their places beside him: Houdremont (Nazi Party No. 8301922), Eberhardt (No. 4038202), Lehmann (8303913), Janssen (3421734), "Kanonen-Müller" (2637734), Max Ihn (3421752), Hans Kupke (1988328), Karl Pfirsch (5608734), Heinrich Korschan (3419293), and, of course, Löser and Fritz von Bülow, one of whom had refused to join the party out of principle, while the other had been too preoccupied with its demands. Altogether the defendants held fifty-three Nazi decorations, awards, and official titles, and until the collapse their collective wealth, quite apart from that of Krupp himself, had been immense.

Two helmeted GIs wearing campaign ribbons stood at parade rest behind Krupp and Bülow — the Nazis, sensitive to racial distinctions, noted indignantly that both were American Negroes — and as the ornate clock above the dock reached 9 A.M. the three robed justices moved toward the bench. Meanwhile instructors finished coaching the defendants in the use of translation earphones and the lights on the witness stand. There were two bulbs there, yellow and red. If the first flashed, it meant "Please speak slowly, the interpreter is behind you." The red bulb was literally a stop light; the witness must stop altogether until the interpreter had caught up. Pauses between questions and answers were essential — otherwise translations might become hopelessly garbled. This briefing, important to witnesses, was of little interest to these prisoners; on instructions from Alfried, none of them would testify in his own defense. When the time came to make a statement, he would speak for all, and only Löser, the outcast, had decided to defy him.[28]

Now the instructors withdrew. The tribunal was in place. Anderson was pale; his health was poor. Justice Daly, fifty-five, grave, bespectacled, and intent, stood at his right; Justice Wilkins, handsome and leonine, at his left. A uniformed marshal clicked his polished heels and called, "The Honorable, the Judges of Military Tribunal III A! Military Tribunal III A is now in session. God save the United States of America and this Honorable Tribunal!"

Alfried donned his earphones and deliberately switched the dial to "Deutsch."* They crackled, "Die ehrenwerten Richter des Militärtribunals

---

* Kranzbühler, whose English was as flawless as Alfried's, followed his client's lead. Word of this spread among prosecution witnesses, with dismaying consequences. Elizabeth Roth's German was much better than her English, but while Kranzbühler would speak nothing except German, she would not respond in it. Similarly, when Milos Celap was asked at the outset of his cross-examination on January 27, "I understand, witness, that you also speak German. Would it not be easier for the proceedings here if you would answer in German?" Celap snapped, "No, I prefer to speak French." The defense attorney quickly said, "Of course; I only suggested it to make matters easier here." It would have made matters easier. But confusion may have been Alfried's motive. (WM/Ernestine Roth; Celap testimony 1/26–27/48 Ntr 2398–2438.)

*III A! Das Militärtribunal III A hat mit der Sitzung begonnen. Gott schütze die Vereinigten Staaten von Amerika und dieses ehrenwerte Tribunal!"*

As frequently happens in a lawsuit whose chief counsel are virtuosos, the trial had already begun with a brief joust in chambers. Otto Kranzbühler complained that "the entire material of the Krupp files has been confiscated . . . probably something like several thousand documents." How could the court expect him to prepare a case without them? General Taylor quietly agreed that the request was reasonable. Counsel's allegations notwithstanding, however, he added sharply, a great many of the files had been opened to the defense staff since late summer, and the rest would be forthcoming shortly — as, indeed, they were. On the surface Taylor was the winner. Nevertheless, Kranzbühler had scored, suggesting that the conqueror was abusing his police powers. The colloquy had cast his client in the role of victim. He was never to relinquish that pose.[29]

The general, on the other hand, was an avenger. "Of all the names which have become associated with the Nuremberg trials," he declared from the lectern, launching the opening statement for the prosecution, "I suppose that none has been a household word for so many decades — indeed for nearly a century — as that of Krupp." The tribunal, he went on, must understand that the prosecution was not attacking the business of manufacturing armaments, which, inherently, was no more unlawful than diplomacy or the military profession. Despite the "sinister sheen" which the name had acquired over the years, the men in the dock were not on trial as symbols. None was named because of his association with the firm. Each was answerable for specific acts committed in an individual capacity. Yet, it must be remembered that although these men were National Socialists, they, unlike most Nuremberg defendants, had not risen to power on the crest of the Nazi wave. Nazism was, after all, only a temporary manifestation of something much older "which fused with Nazi ideas to produce the Third Reich and its pernicious vitality," or, as Alfried heard it, *"was sich mit den Nazi Ideen zusammenschloss und das Dritte Reich mit dessen Lebenskraft erzeugte."* Therefore, Taylor continued, while the defendants were accused of crimes committed in the recent past, judgment of their guilt or innocence was impossible without some familiarity with the history and traditions of a dynasty which had long ago made the name of Krupp "the focus, the symbol, and the beneficiary, of the most sinister forces engaged in menacing the peace of Europe." In Krupp's earphones the interpreter's flat voice droned, ". . . *der Mittelpunkt, das Symbol, und den Nutzniesser, der unheimlichsten Kräfte, die den Frieden Europas bedrohen."*[30]

As the tribunal sat back in high-backed leather chairs, Taylor presented his charges. There were four of them, and they were identical with those

Buschmannshof, Krupp's concentration camp for children. ABOVE: The
barracks. BELOW: Two of the numbered gravestones.

Alfried Krupp's arrest at
Villa Hügel, April 11, 1945.

40

Alfried in the dock at Nuremberg with his Nazi aides (to his left)
and his legal staff (foreground).

Krupp's famous 15,000-ton press being dismantled as reparations after World War II.

Alfried and Vera Krupp
at their wedding, May 19, 1952.

One of Alfried's weekend shooting parties. From left, Alfried, United States Ambassador David Bruce, Berthold Beitz, British Ambassador Sir Christopher Eden Steel, and the firm's London representative, Count Klaus Ahlefeldt-Lauruiz.

45

ABOVE: Alfried at unveiling ceremonies for the Kiel Yacht Club's memorial to his grandfather Friedrich Alfred Krupp. BELOW: Alfried's brother Harald returns from a Russian prison, October 1955. From left, Waldtraut, Harald, Bertha, Alfried. The sign says, "Heartfelt welcome."

46

Bertha Krupp with her son Berthold and Chancellor Konrad Adenauer
at Villa Hügel, 1953.

Alfried is host to Ludwig Erhar
Essen. Alfried's son Arndt and
Berthold Beitz are in the rear.

Emperor Haile Selassie of Ethiopia greeted by Bertha and Alfried at Villa Hügel, November 11, 1954. Beitz stands behind the emperor.

49

Bertha and Alfried Krupp welcome King Paul and Queen Frederika of Greece to Rheinhausen, September 1956.

50

Sir Alhaji Ahmadu Bello, Premier of Northern Algeria, at the castle with Alfried in 1962.

Modibo Keita, President of Mali, and his wife arriving at Hügelschloss in 1962, escorted by Alfried Krupp (right) and Berthold Beitz (left).

52

Jackson had laid before the IMT: crimes against peace, plunder, crimes against humanity (slave labor), and "conspiracy" — an umbrella covering the first three. At length, in the final paragraph of his 36,000-word declaration, the general returned to his opening theme. The dynasty was a continuum, he said; one must see it in that light. Because of the family's legacy, its men had been ready to follow Hitler before he appeared to lead them. Indeed, he had been the perfect instrument for ideas carefully nursed in Essen three generations ago, and his National Socialism had been the ultimate realization of Kruppdom:

> The tradition of the Krupp firm, and the "social-political" attitude for which it stood, was exactly suited to the moral climate of the Third Reich. There was no crime such a state could commit — whether it was war, plunder, or slavery — in which these men would not participate.[31]

The German had a different ring. It was somehow familiar:

> Die Tradition des Krupp-Konzerns und die "sozialpolitische" Anschauung, die er vertrat, passten genau zum moralischen Klima des Dritten Reiches. Es gab kein Verbrechen, das ein solcher Staat begehen konnte — sei es Krieg, Plündern oder Sklaverei — woran diese Männer nicht bereit wären teilzunehmen.

Alfried, son of Gustav, grandson of Fritz, and great-grandson of Alfred, sat motionless, staring at the erect general. His eyes were hooded. He might have been fascinated. He might have been bored.

✠     ✠     ✠

After it was all over — after sympathetic Americans had expressed regrets for humiliating the Ruhr's most illustrious baron (and furious Germans had rejected the apology) — a writer depicted Alfried in the dock, chilled by a "feeling of isolation (Gefühl der Isoliertheit), increased by the character of press reports wholly under the influence of the changes in the prosecution's indictment."[32]

Alfried's chill had a more pedestrian explanation. He was cold. Everyone in the courtroom was. Justice Anderson attributed his own stifled shudders to age and illness until Wednesday, January 21. By then the court had been sitting in refrigeration for seven straight weeks. Cecelia Goetz, questioning witnesses, clomped back and forth in ski boots. Otto Kranzbühler wore insulation under his robes, and Paul Hansen, coming down from Essen to testify in the eighth week — by which time members of the tribunal were angrily banging stone-cold radiators with their gavels — wondered whether this was Bavaria or Siberia. Hansen suffered in the box for two days. Toward the end of his ordeal he tried to stammer a brief description of how the Berthawerk had been conceived, "a project for an evacuation plant for Krupp in Essen." The first phrase came out *"Pro-pro-projekt für ei-einen Aus-ausweich-weichbetrieb-b-b . . ."* Both the yellow and the red light flashed on, and as men hunched forward, straining to hear, there was a sudden, eerie rustling of crumpled newspaper throughout the courtroom. In that instant Hansen realized that half of them had stuffed sheets of newspapers under their shirts.[33]

If newspaper stories were influenced by General Taylor's charges, the innuendos were well concealed. Germans read that the prosecution was "making no attempt to hide its lust for hatred and vengeance," that it "attached a collective guilt to the German people," and that the chief argument against Alfried was that "Germans differ basically from all other European nations because of their greed, their love of fighting, and their wickedness" (*ihre Raubgier, Kriegslust, und Schlechtigkeit*).[34]

Here the press was distorting the position, not of Krupp, but of his accusers, and it is depressing to find that other misrepresentations appeared in the United States. Accounts in the financial newspapers read like handouts from the Hauptverwaltungsgebäude; those of the *New York Herald Tribune* like sermons on the need for a united Europe built around a Ruhr guided by Essen's Konzernherr. One correspondent languished in a villa outside the city and telephoned Kranzbühler's staff daily for details of recent developments. Another, waging a private war against the American occupation in general and Clay in particular, used the Krupp case as a flagrant example of AMG's irresponsibility.

One expected more from the *New York Times,* and one got more. Kathleen McLaughlin's reports were objective, concise, and accurate. But somehow the *Times* rarely found room for them. Alfried's trial, like Adolf Eichmann's thirteen years later, lasted nearly nine months, longer than any ever held in the United States. The court proceedings ran over four million words. Yet between the late winter of 1947 and the summer of 1948, when the last evidence was heard, America's newspaper of record published exactly four of Miss McLaughlin's accounts of trial testimony — a total of forty-seven paragraphs, less than two columns, all of it buried on inside pages.[35]

The absentees missed a lot, for every great trial has a special *ambiance,* and Krupp's was in many ways surprising. There was, for example, the setting. Inasmuch as judgment was rendered upon him at Nuremberg, a generation of scholars has assumed that the entire case was heard in the enormous mahogany and marble hall on the second floor of the Palace of Justice. It wasn't. The cast assembled there for the first and last day (when the press *did* come), but with so many other proceedings demanding space General Taylor, knowing how long this one would last, moved it to a fourth-floor chamber, leaving the ornate furnishings, to the I. G. Farben tribunal. Upstairs there were no pageantry, no ornate furnishings, and, as noted, no heat. The room looked much like an American police court. In an attempt to relieve its bleakness, MPs had spread a silken canopy across the ceiling. The gesture was well meant, but the effect was ghastly; more and more the cloth resembled a shroud. Glancing around you could see (and hate) the steam pipes, and each time a member of the tribunal spoke his listeners were distracted by the valve cock behind Justice Anderson's left ear. During recesses one attorney would dart up and desperately wrench the wheel, always in vain; like so many gadgets in Germany that winter, this one was rusted solid.

Despite its barren props the room had become a stage for high theater. The tribunal was sober and majestic, and certain performers provided color. Ragland was the Southern gentleman, Taylor the New England aristocrat, Kranzbühler the haughty genius of the bar. Some were deceptive. Benjamin B. Ferencz, Taylor's executive counsel, slumping carelessly like a preoccupied college instructor, was really an idealist with a first-rate mind and extraordinary dedication. Cecelia Goetz — casually mussed, dressed in a checked wool blouse — smiled easily and thought grim thoughts. Other participants weren't themselves. Löser, sick and a pariah to both sides, propped his hands on a cane. His eyes were like bruises, his chin sank upon his chest. Often he was absent in the prison infirmary.

Krupp, however, dominated them all. This was his trial, he was the most famous man in Nuremberg, and everyone in the courtroom felt his silent power. Miss Goetz found him endlessly fascinating. He was, she kept reminding herself, "the German equivalent of Henry Ford II." She wrote, "It is hard to equate that elegant patrician face with such ruthlessness and cruelty as he, in fact, displayed during this Hitlerian period."[36] Unlike most Nuremberg defendants, including the mass murderers, he never expressed contrition. The most shocking testimony made no discernible impression upon him, though he never missed a word of it; in his conferences with Kranzbühler, the counsel was astounded by Alfried's memory. To Taylor, Krupp was a challenge. Both men were of the same generation, and the general felt they should be capable of understanding one another. He never reached Alfried, though. The barrier between them was impenetrable. After nine months the ruler of Hügelschloss was still a sphinx.

By joining the SS Alfried had, in the words of his membership certificate, made himself "responsible with this signature," but that issue was never raised during the trial; as Taylor said later, "We had enough on him as it was." His case wasn't faultless. The prosecution staff was aware of two notable weaknesses. Kranzbühler was certain to exploit the absentees: it happened in all Justizpalast proceedings. As a defense witness was to note when Eichmann stood in his Jerusalem dock, "It was customary at the time of the war crime trials to put as much blame as possible on those who were absent or believed to be dead." Furthermore, the aggression charge dangled from the slenderest of threads. Alfried's role in the last years of his father's reign was obscure. According to four Paris-to-Washington cables dispatched by Ambassador Bullitt in March 1937 and marked "Eyes Only President," however, Gustav's son had been one of twenty industrialists whom Hitler had addressed that month. After reviewing the Nazi plan of conquest ("Austria, Czechoslovakia, the rest of Europe") the Führer had unrolled a map, traced his finger across the Atlantic, and said, "The amount of Jewish blood in the streets of Europe will be as nothing compared to the gutters of New York then." Unfortunately, Bullitt's cables had implicated certain figures in Argentina. The State Department was reluctant to release the originals. "If State will give us those telegrams, we can prove aggressive warfare," said Norbert Barr, then an adviser to the general. "Otherwise that count will fall."[37]

State didn't, and the count fell, yet even if the prosecution staff had known that at the outset their confidence would have retained its edge. No case as massive as this could be flawless. The rupture of peace had been the act of one man — even Göring had tried to roll back the Wehrmacht in the middle of December 1939. Doubtless Alfried had gone along with his Führer, but nobody had influenced Hitler. Besides, evidence of aggression, like SS zeal, was unnecessary. Krupp's plunder of the continent was an incontestable violation of international law. On July 29, 1899, Count Georg Münster, at the express direction of Wilhelm II, had joined twenty-five other nations in signing the Convention on the Laws and Customs of War of the International Peace Conference at The Hague. The agreement had not been entered into lightly; at one point S.M. had written, "In practice, however, I shall rely on God and my sharp sword! And I shit on all their decisions." Nevertheless in the end the Fatherland had agreed that "if, as a result of war action, a belligerent occupies a territory of the adversary, he does *not*, thereby, acquire the right to dispose of property in that territory, except according to the strict rules laid down in the regulations." Alfried had violated every one of those rules. Until the Third Reich's sword was blunted, he had covered The Hague's decisions with *kruppscher Scheisse*, and the prosecution could prove it.[38]

Americans at home who read the indictment reacted variously. Men of property were inclined to feel that plunder was the gravest charge. Crimes against humanity seemed more outrageous to a majority, and Taylor and his staff, agreeing, thought slave labor the key to their case. Salvaged documents bearing Alfried's name and stamp tied him to the use of slaves at Auschwitz and the Berthawerk, though proof of his personal participation wasn't really necessary. The fact that Krupp himself had never murdered a prisoner of war, tortured a pregnant woman, or buried babies by the numbers was irrelevant. In sentencing Eichmann an Israeli court was to observe that "the legal and moral responsibility of him who delivers the victim to his death is, in our opinion, no smaller, and may even be greater, than the liability of him who does the victim to death." The principle's relevance to the Konzern was set forth with even greater clarity by a spokesman for it, who, reviewing the awesome responsibilities which successive heads of the Krupp family had borne throughout the history of the dynasty, declared that, "No anonymity was possible in this business. It was always one man who remained answerable for all its operations (*Immer stand ein Mann für das Werk, trat eine Gestalt hervor, die alles verantwortete, was geschah*). Decisions were never made by the managers, but solely by the owners, whether the owner in question happened to be great or a mediocrity."[39]

Judge Anderson continued to worry some of the team of prosecutors. Of Krupp's decision to rearm secretly immediately after Versailles he said from the bench, "Considered objectively and in the proper context, it is at least plausible that Gustav's decision made in 1919 was a calculated business risk. Here was a man faced with the loss of a large part of what doubtless was a profitable business that had been built up over a long period of years." But the aged Tennessean's very insistence upon viewing the family's unusual way of making profit "from a strictly private business standpoint" suggested that Alfried's seizure of other men's private businesses would inflame him all the more.[40]

General Taylor and his aides were invested with a crusading spirit, but all trials recess, and when the defendants were led off at the end of each day, everyone else fled the Palace of Justice. Most headed for the bright pink, newly hewn sandstone of the Grand Hotel, beside the Hauptbahnhof. The food was good, the service excellent, and the rooms were warm. Since even Otto Kranzbühler came, the prosecution, the defense, and the judges met almost every evening in Nuremberg's first shrine to Ludwig Erhard's growing boom. There, fortified by drink and food, they fraternized to a degree which would have been unthinkable in any other trial. Kranzbühler didn't unbend much. Still, he did speak English. One American asked why he clung to German in the courtroom. "It is dangerous," he replied. "One may become entangled in the subtleties and idioms of another language." And yet, his antagonists noticed, he never missed an idiom in the Grand Hotel; in nine months of chats never split an infinitive, never ended a sentence with a preposition, and never misused "whom." They respected him without understanding him. In an uncharacteristic outburst he snapped, "I would like you to show me the American industrialist who would say no to his government in time of war." There was an uneasy silence. His understanding of them, they realized, was equally deficient. Despite his intellect he didn't grasp that rules were different outside

Germany, that there were some things no U.S. government would dare ask and that no major U.S. tycoon, with or without official sanction, could possibly do.[41]

One evening an American boarded a streetcar and rode out to the stadium where, each September before the war, Hitler had addressed his annual party rallies. Under a ghostly moon the blocks of shadows lay as motionless as the squares of storm troopers who had once stood here at attention, and who were now among Germany's seven million war dead. Once the sound of music had been earsplitting. Tonight there was nothing but the whisper of a bitter December wind. The visitor had never seen a Nuremberg rally, but American networks had carried the Führer's speeches, and looking up at the vacant, moon-washed podium he could hear, in memory, the hoarse, guttural intonations of the twentieth century's greatest spellbinder —

*Das nervöse Zeitalter des 19. Jahrhunderts hat bei uns endgültig seinen Abschluss gefunden! In den nächsten tausend Jahren findet in Deutschland keine Revolution mehr statt!*

With us the nineteenth century's age of nerves is ended! There will be no other revolution in Germany for the next thousand years![42]

Riding back to the hotel he wondered how many of the men he faced each day had heard that *Führerproklamation* here, had raised their stiffened right hands with thirty thousand others in the *Hitlergruss*, had believed that Germany would remain unchanged for a millennium — and remembered now.

⌗　⌗　⌗

Another wind was blowing through the postwar Reich, warming the defeated nation. Otto Kranzbühler was sensitive to it, set his sails to catch it, and — with Krupp's advice and consent — conducted a defense wholly unlike any other at Nuremberg. The prosecution lived in the immediate past, the world of *Die Fahne hoch*. Alfried's chief counsel saw that regardless of the outcome here, politics would be far more important to his client's future than justice, for the new wind, now approaching gale force, was political.

Its first stirring had been felt the autumn before Alfried's indictment, when, on a Thursday evening in September, U.S. Secretary of State James Byrnes boarded the dead Führer's palatial private train and rode southward across the still, beaten countryside, the Secretary sleeping in Hitler's bed and his adviser, Benjamin V. Cohen, in Göring's. Alighting by Stuttgart's bomb-gutted Hauptbahnhof, they rode to the Staats-Theater, where Secretary Byrnes invited German leaders to stand with the western allies in the Cold War. In return, he offered them an opportunity to reform their Reich. They would be permitted to run their own affairs under proper safeguards. Moreover — and this was of intense interest to Krupp and his chief counsel — the United States would see to it that the Ruhr remained Teutonic, that German industry was restored, and that all plans for an agrarian West Germany were abandoned. Byrnes's audience had roared its approval.[43]

When Fritz Thyssen had broken with Hitler he had written him, "Your policy will terminate in a *finis Germaniae*," but Thyssen hadn't counted on the unbelievable stupidity of Russia's German policy. One wonders whether anyone in the Kremlin had bothered to study the geography of the Reich. Every miscalculation the Soviets made, beginning at Potsdam, was based on the assumption that they were dealing from strength. They weren't. The Red Army held Berlin. That was an ace. But nearly every other card was held by the West. Essentially East Germany was one big farm, while West Germany was larger, more heavily populated, and richly endowed with natural resources. Powered by the Ruhr, it was the Reich's reservoir of vigor, skills, drive, and industry.

The consequence was that Washington — which deserved little, because the State Department also lacked a coherent Germany policy — won triumph after triumph. Stalin tried to bar France from the postwar settlement and failed, thus driving the affronted Quai d'Orsay into a military alliance with the United States. Then the Soviet dictator decided that there was really no difference between British Conservatives and the British Labour Party, disillusioning the new men in Whitehall and adding a third power to what would soon become NATO. The Kremlin's balance sheet has to be read to be believed. At the time of the Jodl-Friedeburg capitulation, Russia presented her claims — control of the Dardanelles, a slice of Turkish territory, a fixed share of Near Eastern oil, Caspian territory to shield her Baku fields, a Titoist Trieste, an Austrian Carinthia, a role in the occupation of Japan, and a physical presence in the Ruhr. Not one of these demands was met. What Stalin got, Theodore H. White wrote, was "one-third of the captured German Navy, one hundred million dollars' worth of reparations from Italy, three votes and the right of veto in the United Nations."[44]

All this must be seen as a global backdrop to the trial on the fourth floor of Nuremberg's Justizpalast. Whatever the tribunal's verdict, Krupp was convinced that his future would be determined by statesmen, not jurists. The solution wouldn't come quickly, but events were moving in an encouraging direction. On the very day that General Taylor mounted the podium to present his case against Alfried, the conquerors' Four Power alliance was disintegrating at a meeting between Molotov and George Marshall in London. Then, as the Krupp proceedings approached midpoint — Baron Tilo von Wilmowsky was on the stand at the time, passionately defending his relatives* — a military policeman passed a message to the bench, which called a brief recess. Moscow had just committed its greatest folly yet; the Red Army had blockaded Berlin.

Friedrich Flick testified next day on behalf of his fellow industrialist. His appearance was a fiasco; cross-examined by Ragland, Flick couldn't cite a single German businessman who had been sent to a concentration camp for failing to meet production quotas, thereby contributing to the demolition of Krupp's defense against the slave labor charge. The prosecution was elated. Kranzbühler, watching developments through his larger prism, was undismayed. Ragland had scored a legal point, but Krupp's long-range position was improving hourly. On that first day of the blockade some one hundred C–47 transport planes carrying a total of 250 tons of supplies had landed at Templehof Airdrome. The first great East-West crisis, triggered by General Clay's withholding of Soviet reparations shipments, by currency reform, and by the first moves toward an independent German state led from Bonn, was on. Nine days later Clay called on the Russian commander-in-chief. "How long do you plan to keep it up?" he inquired. General Sokolovsky answered, "Until you drop your plans for a West German government." The Americans didn't drop their plans, and when the daily capacity of the C–47's touched the 13,000-ton mark Stalin called off the blockade. Meantime international justice had, almost unnoticed, become a casualty of the confrontation. A writer observed dryly, "When the Nuremberg tribunal decided to invite the Soviets to Essen and asked them to participate in the Krupp concern management (*beschloss, die Sowjets nach Essen einzuladen und sie am Krupp-Konzern zu beteiligen*), the Soviets had started their blockade of West Berlin, which the United States defended by its great airlift."[45]

By coincidence, the prosecution had completed its three-month parade of witnesses the week before the crisis began. As Krupp's day in court opened, a British plane was shot down over Berlin by a Soviet fighter, Clay dissolved the Allied Council, and the United States closed its zonal border to all Russians. Partial mobilization had begun. In Nuremberg Taylor and everyone on his staff felt the tension. American Military Government now wanted all Justizpalast proceedings to end soon. Messengers brought word that fresh troops were arriving from America, that elite airborne divisions were being deployed, and that a new field was being built for the 36th Jet Fighter Wing, which had taken off from the Atlantic coast. While the arguments droned on in the courtroom, the Soviet Union formally withdrew from the Berlin Kommandantura, completing the split of the city's administration; the Pentagon pondered provoking a showdown by sending an armored column through Russian Berlin; Georges Bidault publicly expressed the fear that any incident might bring war; and the Soviet Air

---

* April 1, 1948.

Command, as though looking for an incident, announced night flights over western Berlin.

This was the atmosphere in which the Nuremberg tribunal wrote their verdicts. The Krupp and Farben cases ended within twenty-four hours of one another; the nervous judges fled Europe before General Taylor could speak to them. The judgments seemed sound, but appellate review lay ahead, and there were those among the prosecutors who remembered the winter cold with nostalgia.[46]

✠ ✠ ✠

Only if the darkening shadow of Berlin is borne in mind does the Krupp transcript make sense. It was a peculiar trial anyhow. Repeatedly the hearings were interrupted by queer little incidents: Archbishop Frings's attempted intervention, the suicide of Essen's Gestapo chief Peter Nohles, the neat bundles of organized petitions for clemency which methodically arrived in the judges' chambers, and defense efforts to induce Kruppianer to alter their affidavits. There was even attempted intimidation in the courtroom itself — Ragland discovered that whenever a Krupp workman testified for the prosecution one of Alfried's lawyers, a ferocious Prussian with cheeks crisscrossed by dueling scars, would glare at him until he stepped down. (The Americans countered by having their huskiest lawyer stare at *him*. He then quit.)

Gradually the cordial exchanges in the Grand Hotel became infrequent. The trial was assuming an ugly, explosive character. Attorneys abused witnesses, opposing counsel, and the court itself. One Thursday late in April, for example, an American attorney was asking one of Alfried's executives about the firm's use of secret couriers to withhold information from Reich officials in occupied France. He made his point; the witness agreed that "the transfer of the plant from Mulhouse to the German side of the Rhine . . . was not caused by an order but was done in the interest of Krupp." A member of the defense staff bounded up and demanded to know the purpose of such questions. He shouted, "They sound to me more like an interrogation before a German People's Court, asking why one had concealed something from the Nazi authorities!" Comparing the tribunal to a *Volksgerichtshof* — a kangaroo court dominated by party thugs, with sham lawyers and the presentation of witnesses friendly to the defendant forbidden — was an insult to the three justices on the bench, and Judge Daly, presiding, replied coldly, "We have never had that experience, Doctor, so we don't know what kind of interrogation that is."[47]

No prosecution grilling matched the ferocity of the German attack on General Taylor's last witness. He was Karl Otto Saur, and his appearance out of the past that June 8 stunned the thirty-three German lawyers sitting before Alfried like a protective black shield. They were helpless against Saur. He had been too close to the Führer, he knew too much, and he swore under oath that Alfried's personal intervention with Hitler was directly responsible for Krupp's use of Auschwitz Jews in the Berthawerk. Though less dramatic than the concentration camps for girls and children, this was the most damning evidence yet heard against the head of the House himself; in a stroke it swept away every argument which had been advanced to explain Alfried's *Fremdarbeiter* program. There was only one possible counterattack: inpugning the integrity of the witness. To Otto Kranzbühler Saur was "like a Chinese mandarin, a man who takes all the opportunities available under a dictatorship" and then finds it convenient "to pretend he was only an errand boy." A second German scorned the beefy, red-faced Saur as "a filthy pig," and a third said, "To try to refute the existence of compulsory production . . . by calling, of all people, this witness . . . was virtually the same as calling Goebbels as a witness for National Socialist 'democracy.' "[48]

It wasn't at all the same, but that was irrelevant. What was important was to insist that the Ruhr barons had merely been "howling with the wolves," in Flick's memorable phrase — in other words, they had been obliged to feign allegiance to a dictatorship which they had actually despised. A secondary goal was delay of the trial. The grimmer the news from Berlin, the more intransigent defense counsel became. Repeatedly German lawyers were warned against making speeches while examining witnesses; defiantly they would outshout the gavel and finish anyway. There were other ways of killing time. Once the court was diverted by a long home movie which showed, among other things, young Alfried at the tiller of a 1919 Krupp locomotive. ("Very moving," Ragland drawled, "but what does it prove?") And then there was the defense's endless recital of the Konzern's production statistics.[49]

Here Kranzbühler's ostensible purpose was to convince the tribunal that all depictions of Alfried as a *Kanonenkönig* were myth. The notion was absurd, he insisted; Skoda had made Wehrmacht guns. Fried. Krupp of Essen was not now, nor had it ever been, the Reich *Waffenschmiede*. That was a fiction of the Kaiser's, and everyone knew what a loudmouth *he* had been. The defense even produced Kruppianer who had worked in the Gusstahlfabrik for fifty years without once laying eyes on a weapon. To be sure, *some* arms had been produced, and this touched off what the exasperated prosecution christened "the numbers game."

The defense version of the facts started on July 1, 1914, when, the tribunal was told, the firm had provided the world with 2,750,000 seamless steel railway tires and was turning out between a fifth and a third of the German *Eisenbahn*'s "rails, tires, wheels, axles, locomotive frames, boilers, fireboxes, and forged pieces." At that time 5 percent of Krupp steel had been set aside for ordnance. (Another estimate, equally reliable, put the figure at 39 percent; the weary prosecution let it pass.) Between 1911 and

1943, Baron von Wilmowsky testified, 8 percent of the firm's products had been for war purposes; between 1919 and 1935, "when the Führer ordered rearmament," guns had accounted for but 7 percent of production; overall, between the two wars 14 percent of the turnover had been military. In 1939 a mere 26 percent of the workers had been assigned to munitions. The following year this actually dropped to 25 percent, and the year after that to 24 percent. A rise to 25 percent came the next year, and then, when the Führer proclaimed total war, to 42 percent. But even then, over half of Essen's Kruppianer had nothing to do with munitions.[50]

Evaluation of the numbers was impossible, witnesses contradicted one another, and their evidence had nothing to do with the indictment against Alfried. Nevertheless the minutiae went on hour after hour, and whenever an American protested, a German would reply in a wounded tone that he heard "the harsh bark of the oppressor"; that the Palace of Justice was in danger of becoming the setting for a *Volksgerichtshof*.

The prosecution should have refused to be drawn, but the provocation was too great, the passions of the war too recent, the German taunts too skillful. For example, when the tribunal unanimously threw out counts one and four (aggression and conspiracy) on April 5 — Ragland, still presenting witnesses, wasn't even permitted to submit a brief, which hardly suggests a Germanophobic bench — the delighted Germans acclaimed the ruling as "the equivalent of a collapse of the political aspect of the indictment, the theoretical basis of the whole proceeding" (*Grundthese des Verfahrens*).[51]

Thwarted because Krupp refused to enter the witness box, American lawyers looked down in dismay at the material they had prepared for his cross-examination. He was to have been examined in relays, each interrogator exploring in turn the train carrying five hundred Jewesses to Buchenwald, the Auschwitz factory, the training of Krupp women in SS methods at Ravensbrück, and the construction of the Berthawerk. Now those questions would forever remain unanswered. In chagrin they denounced his "silence strike," although they were well aware that he was entitled to remain mute without prejudice to his cause.

That was one American lapse. Three months before, there had been another, and the two are linked, for the first provided Krupp with an excuse not to testify. (Afterward Kranzbühler conceded that they had been looking for an alibi; under no circumstances would Alfried have subjected himself to cross-examination; his answers, on the record, would have been used against him to the end of his life.) That earlier slip had arisen from the vexing confusions over the two legal systems. It began, innocently enough, with a routine motion from Dr. Alfred Schilf, Janssen's lawyer, on January 17. To speed up the proceedings, the tribunal had ordered that depositions be taken from minor witnesses elsewhere in the Justizpalast. Schilf wanted the defendants present at these sessions. He was overruled, his colleagues vehemently protested, the tribunal reaffirmed Anderson's decision, and Krupp's defense staff, enraged, walked out of the courtroom. In continental trials this was an acceptable form of protest. In America and England it was illegal. The two chief counsel were absent; General Taylor was attending the Flick proceedings and Otto Kranzbühler was defending Hermann Röchling, "the Krupp of the Saar," before a French tribunal. Ragland telephoned Taylor, who urged immediate adjournment.[52]

It was the only sensible course, but the three judges, unfamiliar with continental law, believed that they had been deliberately slighted. After seething for several hours, Justice Anderson ordered the marshal to round up all the Krupp attorneys they could find. Six were haled before him, told that they were guilty of contempt, and sent to cells. Their protests were gaveled down, which was unwise. Unknown to the tribunal, summary power to punish for contempt does not exist in the continental code. To the Germans the Tennessean's action seemed despotic, and their resentment is understandable. After a weekend behind bars five of them apologized to the bench, but the sixth, Dr. Günter Geisseler, refused to express regrets and was disqualified from further participation in the defense. For Kranzbühler the arbitrary decision was a windfall. Krupp counsel could loftily reveal that "The accused accordingly decided to abstain from any personal statement in the future, in the conviction that anything they said could only make matters worse" (*dass jedes Wort die Lage nur verschlechtern würde*).[53]

It was strange logic, made stranger by the fact that five men in the dock — Bülow, Ihn, Janssen, Korschan, and Kupke — subsequently *did* testify in behalf of Alfried and one another. But it gave Krupp his pretext, and it persuaded millions of Germans that Nuremberg's most celebrated defendant of 1948, like his father before him, was a martyr to the Fatherland.

✠  ✠  ✠

During the trial Kranzbühler presented another piece of intricate staging which, though equally effective in the court of public opinion, was pure sleight of hand. He convinced the press that his client was being deprived of counsel of his own choice, and by repeating this absurdity in subsequent lectures he even managed to implant it in the minds of some historians. Since the barred attorney was to reappear during Krupp's clemency hearings two years later, both the argument advanced in his behalf at Nuremberg and his credentials should be eyed carefully.

Alfried Krupp, Kranzbühler declared, needed an American lawyer. Able though his German staff was, a defendant facing United States justice was entitled to an attorney familiar with Anglo-Saxon procedure. Accordingly, he asked the tribunal to accept as his colleague Earl J. Carroll, a former captain in the United States Army and a member of the law firm of Thomas Foley and Earl J. Carroll, of Haywood, California. Kranzbühler added that if the judges' ruling were negative, he himself would withdraw as Krupp's counsel. The ruling was negative. He begged the court to reconsider. When it refused again, he attempted to resign; he remained only because Judge Anderson ordered him to stay as Alfried's court-appointed lawyer. This is the basis for the charge, made in the *Columbia Law Review* in January 1953 by Professor Heinrich Kronstein of Georgetown Law School, that "Krupp selected an American attorney of good standing" — Carroll — but the tribunal "refused to admit the American and appointed *ex officio* a German substitute."* The *ex officio* substitute, of course, was Otto Kranzbühler, who had been defending his client for three months before Carroll appeared. Moreover, the implication of Nuremberg critics that foreign lawyers were barred from the Justizpalast is quickly disproved. Colonel Robinson was already on Krupp's staff, Dr. Walter Vinessa of Switzerland was representing Dr. Walter Häflinger, an I. G. Farben director, and Warren E. Magee of Washington, D.C., was defending Baron Ernst von Weizsaecker, Ribbentrop's deputy, in the so-called Ministries Case.

That leaves the issue of Mr. Carroll's "good standing." It is an odd tale. Brash, likable, and genially Irish, Carroll had an instinctive gift for publicity, plunging eagerly from one controversy to another. In the spring of 1946 *Newsweek* had described him as "flamboyant." Others thought him insubordinate. While still in uniform he had won an impressive string of court-martial acquittals for enlisted men challenging various military regulations. Suddenly, and rather mysteriously, he himself faced the prospect of a court-martial. In September 1946 he sailed home after telling a press conference that he was being "shanghaied" because of his "crusade" against "grave abuses" in the army and the American Military Government.[54]

AMG thought it had seen the end of Earl Carroll, but after changing into mufti he sailed back and opened an office in Frankfurt. His official position was sharply defined. His papers limited him to the defense of U.S. soldiers and four American civilians awaiting trial — not enough, on the face of it, to build a satisfactory practice. But Carroll was enterprising. In fact, he was so resourceful that on May 5, 1947, he brought down on his head the wrath of General Lucius Clay himself. In a public statement the U.S. military governor accused him of "abusing his German entry permit by acting as a commercial representative of a foreign liquor concern." He

---

* Professor Kronstein's article was a favorable review of *Warum wurde Krupp verurteilt?* (*Why Was Krupp Condemned?*) by Tilo von Wilmowsky. (See below, pp. 662–663.) Nowhere did the professor identify the author as a relative of the convicted war criminal. Instead the baron was presented as a dispassionate German scholar. General Taylor replied in the February 1953 issue of the *Columbia Law Review*.

could continue to appear before AMG courts, representing soldiers and the four indicted civilians. That had been the understanding, and Clay would abide by it. He expected Carroll to leave after those cases were closed, however. No "further violations" would be permitted.[55]

Obviously this excluded the Californian from any role in the Krupp case. Under AMG Ordinance No. 7 the Nuremberg tribunals were governed by the London Charter of the International Military Tribunal and subject to "the powers of the Military Governor for the United States Zone of Occupation within Germany" — i.e., the very general who had insisted that the attorney Kranzbühler wanted to recruit must either stick to his bargain or be deported. Clay's position may seem harsh, but the Reich was still in a state of anarchy. All foreign civilians were suspect. Thousands were deep in the black market, and though the motives of non-German lawyers varied, and may in some instances have been noble, AMG regarded them all with suspicion. Indeed, in the light of what later happened, it is worth noting that it was John J. McCloy, then a former Assistant Secretary of War, who regarded Carroll as a "carpetbagger."

The tribunal rejected the applicant in biting language. Anderson, speaking for the court, observed that Alfried's request for the services of another American attorney had not been filed before the trial, that this alone disqualified him, and that Dr. Kranzbühler, whose defense of Dönitz before the IMT had saved the Grossadmiral's life, was providing "able and competent" advice. Then the judges went after Carroll. To the court "this alleged attorney" from an "alleged law firm" was "not qualified and not available." Since the military governor's ban still held, he had better confine himself to the cases then in hand.[56]

The target of this polemic strode from the courtroom and held a press conference in the hall. Ignoring the fact that he was under orders to leave the American Zone of Occupation as soon as his desk was clear, he attacked the legality of all the tribunals sitting at Nuremberg. Because the judges were Americans, he said, their courts were not international. Then he dropped out of sight. Presumably he had returned to the West Coast. He hadn't. Ignoring Clay, he had joined Flick's legal staff, and when Flick's judges sentenced the manufacturer to seven months in prison Carroll announced at another press conference that he would file a writ of habeas corpus in Washington and ask that all the Nuremberg rulings be thrown out.[57]

On April 6, 1948, a district court dismissed his petition for a writ; on May 11, 1949, an appellate court upheld the ruling, and the following November 14 the Supreme Court denied his plea for a writ of certiorari. The appellate judgment was perhaps the most lucid defense of the Nuremberg trials ever written. The U.S. Court of Appeals for the District of Columbia Circuit declared that the tribunals were not courts of the United States. Upon Germany's surrender the victorious powers had agreed that supreme authority over the conquered Reich would be exercised by their four commanders in chief, acting as a Control Council — the governing body of Germany. The council's Law No. 10 of December 20, 1945, defined war crimes, prescribed punishments, and provided for tribunals which were to be "determined or designated by each Zone Commander for his respective Zone." The authority of the courts, therefore, was rooted in the sovereignty of the United States, the United Kingdom, France, and the Soviet Union. Legally it was just as international as that of the International Military Tribunal — and would be fully justified in adopting that designation.[58]

Even a dauntless Irishman, one might think, would have become discouraged by now. Newspapermen had forgotten him, AMG had forgotten him, the official historian of the IMT didn't mention him. But the Germans remembered. The scrappy Carroll had built a European reputation. Like Kranzbühler, he would be vindicated when the fate of defendants was determined not by judges and soldiers but by statesmen and diplomats. Quietly reopening his Frankfurt office, he bided his time.

✠　　✠　　✠

The Berlin airlift notwithstanding, political pressures had not yet intruded upon the war crimes proceedings when Krupp's defense rested, blaming everything that had gone wrong in Essen on Alfried's elderly advisers — Kranzbühler's picture was of an innocent youth who had been run over by massed wheelchairs. On June 30 Krupp made his personal statement to the court. He was preceded by Löser, who described his underground role and concluded, "It culminated before the People's Court. That the latter's death sentence was not executed and that I am now here is more than a miracle." Löser's voice broke with emotion. Alfried, rising slowly, was tightly sheathed in his enigmatical *Sachlichkeit*. As a Krupp, he wasn't going to beg or show weakness. He was, he told the tribunal, speaking for his codefendants, who had joined his firm with the conviction that its good reputation was unshakable. Now they found themselves victims of a legend. Though the Konzern was only a business, it was being used as a symbol of Teutonic aggression. Never in Villa Hügel, as a child or as a man, had he ever heard anyone speak approvingly of war, and the judges should remember that "the symbol of our House does not depict a cannon, but three interlocked wheels, an emblem of peaceful trade."[59]

Had Gustav Krupp von Bohlen stood trial, Alfried was convinced, the International Military Tribunal would have acquitted him. Now, as the son, he had to take his place. But his own position was much more difficult. His father, at least, had known from the first days of the Third Reich what was going on in Berlin. Therefore, he would have brought an encyclopedic knowledge of his own role to the courtroom. As an understudy, Alfried was at a cruel disadvantage. He was being asked to answer for a system which he did not create, which he imperfectly understood, and of which he often disapproved. In essence, he charged, the prosecution's case came down to three words: *"Sie haben zusammengearbeitet"* (You cooperated). And now, raising his strong baritone for all Germany to hear, he replied that it was true, that he had, and that he was proud he had: "No one will be able to hold it against us that in the emergency of war we followed the path of duty, a path which millions of Germans had to take at the front and at home, and which led them to death (*einen Weg, dem Millionen von Deutschen, sowohl an der Front wie auch zu Hause, folgen mussten und der zum Tode führte*)."

He dismissed "plunder of the occupied territories" with the observation that big business is international. Slave labor was pricklier, and Alfried's solution tells as much about him as anything he ever said or wrote. He simply ignored it — not deliberately, one can be sure, for he knew what the tribunal could do to him — but because for him the problem didn't exist. It wasn't there, just as the slaves hadn't been there. To the court he explained that throughout the history of his firm "man was always more important than money. My whole education taught me to make our firm serve the men who worked in it, many of them in the second and third generation. This spirit filled the entire plant. Can you believe that something which took a century to grow can suddenly disappear?" He was serious. What is difficult to grasp is that he was talking about *German* men. *Sklaven* weren't *Kruppianer*. Not being human, they could not be mistreated. It was this fantastic mental block which permitted him to declare solemnly that he was "conscious of no violation of the laws of humanity."

The three justices pondered their verdict for a full month. None questioned Alfried's guilt. From the first draft their opinion on the slave labor count was unanimous and very strong. Only three issues divided Anderson, Daly, and Wilkins. Anderson believed Löser and thought he should be acquitted. Daly, however, was strong for conviction, and Wilkins, after weighing the evidence, agreed with misgivings. Wilkins wanted a more vehement spoliation judgment, citing Krupp's pillage of certain French, Yugoslavian, and Russian properties. His colleagues felt the evidence in these cases was ambiguous and that there was enough on the record without it to condemn Alfried on that count ten times over. Lastly they debated the sentence. They agreed on imprisonment, but Daly and Wilkins wanted to seize his property, too. As Wilkins wrote in a penciled note to himself, "Now we decided to do away with the Krupp firm and ordered its properties confiscated, feeling that the plants would pass into the hands of peaceful-minded Germans. . . ."[60] Under Council Control Law No. 10 they were entitled to do this. Article II, section 2 provided that anyone convicted of crimes against humanity was subject to any one or all of six punishments, among them "forfeiture of property." Anderson demurred. After writing the long majority opinion, he and Wilkins decided to add brief dissents on marginal questions.[61]

The verdict, read in the big paneled courtroom on July 31, 1948, was 60,000 words long. Both the defense and the prosecution were stunned by the harshness of the language from the bench. Under Alfried, they heard,

> This huge octopus, the Krupp firm, with its body at Essen, swiftly un-folded one of its tentacles behind each new aggressive push of the Wehrmacht and sucked back into Germany much that could be of value to Germany's war effort and to the Krupp firm in particular. . . . That this growth and expansion on the part of the Krupp firm was due in large measure to the favored position it held with Hitler there can be little doubt. The close relationship between Krupp on the one hand and the Reich Government, particularly the Army and Navy Command, on the other hand, amounted to a veritable alliance. The wartime activities of the Krupp concern were based in part upon spoliation of other countries and on exploitation and maltreatment of large masses of forced foreign labor.[62]

Judge Anderson announced that the tribunal was ready to pronounce sentence, and Judge Daly commanded, "The defendant Alfried Felix Alwyn Krupp von Bohlen und Halbach will arise." Alfried stood. There was a pause. Then Daly read gravely, "On the counts of the indictment on which you have been convicted, the tribunal sentences you to imprisonment for twelve years and orders forfeiture of all your property, both real and personal." He added that the time already spent in confinement should be credited to the term, beginning April 11, 1945. He concluded "You may be seated."[63]

Krupp had difficulty finding the seat. Of those who had been watching him, two would later recall his reaction. He had expected jail. A German in the translation booth observed that Alfried responded "as if the whole show didn't concern him" (*als ob das ganze Theater ihn nichts anginge*), and Rawlings Ragland agreed that he was indifferent to the first part of the verdict: "He had been sphinxlike throughout the trial, and the twelve-year sentence came as no surprise; he didn't bat an eyelash." But the loss of the dynasty's holdings was something else. Ragland noted that "when confiscation was announced he went white as a sheet. I thought he was going to faint. He seemed to be on the point of collapse."[64]

Even the prosecution lawyers were astonished. They hadn't asked for it, though Taylor and Ragland agreed in whispers that it was just; after all, thousands of small-fry party members were paying heavy fines each day to German denazification courts, and the principle was the same. The application, of course, would be something else again. To an ex-Nazi *Blockwart* the imposition of a $500 fine might be the equivalent of taking "all your property, both real and personal," but sequestering the fortune of an international multimillionaire was certain to be complicated. In commenting on the decision, the New York Times asked "What is Krupp property? That is the key question. The tribunal . . . did not say what it considered to be his alone. And that is the rub, because even the Krupp family does not completely agree on that." A banner headline in Stars and Stripes read, KRUPP SEIZURE IS FIRST ORDERED IN WAR TRIALS. It wasn't the first. On June 30 Hermann Röchling's tribunal had ordered an identical confiscation. Yet some printed errors never die, especially if they are convenient; to this day the Stars and Stripes banner is quoted in the Ruhr.[65]

If the Americans were amazed, the Germans were dumbfounded. They scarcely heard the imposition of lesser sentences on Krupp's aides. In the corridor Joseph Robinson promised to fight the verdict through American courts — to the Supreme Court, if necessary. Otto Kranzbühler told reporters that the Americans had "given the Russians an entry ticket into the Ruhr." His countrymen were equally bitter. Perhaps because Taylor was a general and German respect for generals abided, he was exempt from personal attack. Of his staff, however, a German wrote that "The exaggerated character of their charges and their insistent disregard of every mitigating circumstance gave them the aspect of instruments of vengeance, not of the law."[66]

Justice Daly was depicted as a man whose "features concealed, rather than expressed, a mind not without an inclination to hedge," while Wilkins was described as a kind of predatory beast whose eyes "sparkled ferociously" (blitzen von Angriffslust) and whose "muzzle was razor-edged" (Mund ist messerscharf). Krupp, the Fatherland was sadly told, would emerge from prison a fifty-one-year-old pauper.[67]

That wasn't quite true; Krupp still had access to untapped resources. Before exchanging his suit for a convict uniform he arranged, through Berthold, to pay his legal staff from foreign assets. And he recovered quickly from the verdict. A photograph taken in the prison yard after Anderson, Wilkins, and Daly had left to board their plane for New York shows Alfried with two of his directors. In the picture they are hunched over, playing skat. Alfried's face is turned from the camera. They are playing for matches, and the size of his stack shows that, as usual, he is winning heavily.

# 26

✠

# Hoher Kommissar John J. McCloy

The first week in August Krupp and his convicted Direktorium were transported to Landsberg, one of the loveliest cities in southern Bavaria, and locked up in War Crimes Prison Number One, a medieval stronghold overlooking the river below. It was here that Adolf Hitler had been confined during Alfried's youth after the unsuccessful Nazi putsch in Munich, here that the Führer had written *Mein Kampf*. For those who cherish legends, and millions of *Volk* do, it was an incomparable stage for the martyred Krupp.

Thus a whole mythology arose during his thirty months in Landsberg. Some stories are true. He did rise at 6:30 each morning, don red-and-white-striped dungarees, empty his urine bucket, and take his turn as a dishwasher like any ordinary prisoner. But the yarns of Alfried's volunteering to work in Landsberg's blacksmith shop, matching his great-grandfather's feats at the anvil, and turning out magnificent wrought-iron candlesticks for the altar where fellow prisoners prayed for National Socialists executed here by the Americans — those tales are sheer nonsense, and with his typical candor he once admitted it to me.[1]

Striped garb, cells, chamber pots and KP were disagreeable, but he and those who shared his imprisonment agree now that it was unexpectedly pleasant. The warden and Krupp hit it off at once; ten years after Krupp's release they were still exchanging Christmas cards. No one in the fortress ate *Bunkersuppe*. Quite the contrary — the food was far better than the rations in the town. Apart from an occasional shift in the laundry or kitchen, Alfried's time was his own. For the first time since his arrest in Villa Hügel he could chain-smoke Camels all day long. The prison library was stocked with books and newspapers in several languages, paper and ink were available, and usually he read novels or wrote. "Landsberg," Fritz von Bülow was to recall, "was one long sunlit holiday."[2]

Krupp wrote his first letter in the medieval penitentiary on August 21. Addressed An den amerikanischen Militärgouverneur General Clay, APO 742, Berlin, it can only be described as a nine-page mistake. He repeated everything he had said at the trial. The House of Krupp had been tried as a symbol ("I suddenly came to take my father's place in the criminal proceedings"); convicting him of looting was unfair because the Hague rules were vague. It was arrogant: Clay was told that he needed but to reflect that Alfried's firm consisted of well over seventy companies, of which one alone — the Gusstahlfabrik — comprised nearly a hundred factories, and he would realize that these other matters "were trifles to the Krupp Konzern." The prosecution witnesses had lied. The Nazis in Berlin had been to blame for the mistreatment of foreign workers. However, if excesses had been committed by Kruppianer, "I simply cannot grasp the fact that my staff and I are to bear criminal responsibility for excesses committed by individual subordinate members of this large organization." The only explanation was a "biased and prejudiced" tribunal. Therefore Krupp demanded that Clay disavow the verdict, release him at once, and quash the "unlawful" confiscation of his property.[3]

It was not a plea likely to win the sympathy of a gray-eyed Georgian who had reservations even about American tycoons. Alfried's greatest error, however, was in writing it at all. Nuremberg apocrypha to the contrary, convicted defendants had recourse to an appellate body, and Krupp's letter, which no lawyer would have sanctioned, constituted an appeal by a prisoner acting as his own attorney. The general, taking it as such, turned it over to his review panel: Judge J. Warren Madden, Alvin Rockwell, and Colonel John Raymond, who subsequently became deputy legal adviser to the State Department. For seven months they pored over the transcript and documents, appraising the evidence against Alfried and Fritz von Bülow, who had sent a similar letter to APO 742. Acting on their recommendations, the military governor "in all respects confirmed" their jail sentences on April 1, 1949, and went out of his way to issue a statement declaring that in his opinion the full evidence of the trial would provide history with "an unparalleled record of how greed and avarice, in unscrupulous hands, bring destruction and misery to the world." The general modified the judgment in but one respect. Disposal of Krupp's various holdings was to be handled by the various American, British, French, and Russian zone commanders. General Clay later explained to this writer, "There was no other solution, as our courts had jurisdiction only in our zone of occupation."[4]

This exhausted Krupp's legal remedies. He had been tried and been convicted, had appealed and been rejected. The one recourse left was pardon, which seemed preposterous. Other Nazis had been hanged for smaller crimes; even now twenty-eight of his fellow prisoners, including the SS officers who had permitted the shooting of seventy-one unarmed American POW's near Malmédy during the Battle of the Bulge, wore red jackets which marked them for the rope. In Washington Senator Joseph McCarthy was waging a one-man crusade for the Malmédy convicts, charging that they had been "treated brutally to extort confessions," but not even McCarthy spoke up for Krupp. Indeed, support for forfeiture of his property was strong in Congress; on February 28, 1949, a delegation of senators headed by James E. Murray of Montana presented Clay with a "Memorandum in Support of Affirmance of Property Confiscation Decree." Any U.S. proconsul who ignored his own appeals court *and* the Hill would have provoked a violent storm at home, and it is hard to see how he could have survived it.[5]

Yet nothing really happened. The Austrians had reclaimed the Berndorferwerk, the Russians had seized the Grusonwerk; but those shops would have changed hands had Alfried never been tried. Virtually all of Alfried's factories, mines, and ore fields lay in the British zone. General Clay had notified his British counterpart of the confiscation decree. There was no reply. French industry had irrefutable claims against Krupp. The French general also was silent. There was no way to touch Krupp assets in neutral countries, but certainly his shares in American corporations were available, and his legal staff today confirms that no one reached for them. This is not to suggest an international conspiracy of financiers in behalf of a humbled capitalist. A more sensible explanation is that the Konzern's affairs were so tangled, and so many vital records were missing, that the only feasible course seemed to be to leave everything under military trusteeship until the skein could be unraveled.

Once each month Berthold called at Landsberg with a fat briefcase. In theory the one Ruhr firm entitled to a German management was the Gutehoffnungshütte that Friedrich Krupp had gambled away a century and a half earlier. In practice the English devoted their energies to dismantling, and let Germans act as custodians. Essen's custodianship rapidly took on the character of a shadow management. With his elder brother's approval, Berthold headed a *Familienrat*. Each director in Landsberg had appointed a deputy before leaving Nuremberg; guided by the long arm in Landsberg, the deputies planned reconstruction and a renewal of production. Now and then there was a flare-up between them and the redtabs in the Essener Hof. Once Major General William A. Bishop discharged Paul Hansen for "fomenting anti-British feeling." Next day Hansen was back. As dismantlement mastermind he was indispensable to Bishop.[6]

Without Krupp, Kruppdom (*Krupp-Reich*) languished. Apprentice training and locomotive repair continued; the rest was busywork. Even with dismantling at its peak, a profitable line of peacetime production could have been started. Though lacking machines, the firm retained its social capital — the skills of its workingmen, the craftsmanship of its engineers, the organizational ability of its supervisors. But the Konzernherr was missing. At the time this seemed an ill wind. In the long run there was good in it for him. His martyrdom contributed to his stature as a full-fledged "real Krupp," the equal of Alfred, Fritz, and Gustav. Tilo von Wilmowsky's pamphlet, *Warum wurde Krupp verurteilt?*, dashed off after his nephew's conviction, argued that Alfried's slaves actually owed their lives to him; if it hadn't been for Krupp, they would have perished in gas ovens. Karl Otto Saur was dismissed as an upstart with "boorish manners" (*Fuhrknechtsmanieren*). The baron scathingly dismissed the prosecution's last witness as "This man, who truly embodied the 'slave labor program' of the men in power in Germany (*Dieser Mann, der das 'Sklavenarbeits-programm' der deutschen Machthaber wirklich verkörperte*), and who should have exchanged roles with the accused — this man again did his worst against his victims, just as he had done under Hitler."[7]

How Saur, a technician with no responsibility for manpower, could have been held responsible for the Sauckel-Krupp *Menschenjagden*, was ignored. Yet he may have come to regret his June 8, 1948, testimony in the Justiz-palast. After a brief stab at setting up an office in Munich as consulting engineer, he dropped out of sight. Essen workmen whose evidence had damaged their *Chef* similarly vanished; even Gerhardt Marquardt, Kurt Schneider, and Fritz Niermann, the three men who had helped the escaping Roth sisters and their companions, disappeared. The baron was believed by every *krupptreue* German when he justified the shocking history of the Berthawerk by writing, "Gustav Krupp and his associates did not favor the plan, since they wished to maintain the Essen works as the principal center of production." It had been Alfried, of course, not his father, who had been responsible for carrying out plans for the Silesian factory. And the whole point of the construction had been to provide an *Ausweichbetrieb*, an evacuation plant, should RAF bombing completely destroy the Gusstahlfabrik. Tilo ignored that. He even insisted that "during the whole time needed for the building and commissioning of the works, the Krupp firm was made to feel the weight of Hitler's order and the constant pressure of the Munitions Ministry."

Isolated at Marienthal, the baron could not have known that the Munitions Ministry had felt the full weight of Alfried Krupp, backed by the Führer — that he was writing black and calling it white. Blinded by grief over the humbling of his nephew, he insisted that "Refusal to employ foreign workers would have been a public demonstration of protest; it would have amounted to suicide" (*sie wäre einem Selbstmord gleichge-kommen*) — this in the teeth of Nuremberg testimony about manufac-turers who had declined drafts from Sauckel's pool and had gone unpunished. To Tilo any rumor, however baseless, or any charge, however unsubstantiated, was welcome provided it helped him clear his wife's family name. Thus he didn't even attempt to cope with documents revealing Gustav's, and then Alfried's, participation in party leadership. To him they were merely two more victims of Nazism, and he adopted Alfried's explanation for the tribunal's miscarriage of justice: "The judges were obviously so influenced by the 'Krupp Legend' that it was inconceivable to them that this industrial concern, blessed as it was with the myth of omnipotence, could have been under the thumb of the National Socialist leaders (*der Gewalt der nationalsozialistischen machthaber*), just as every other concern was."

At APO 742 Tilo's distortions were ignored. He had ended his pamphlet with a quotation from Lincoln: "Nothing is settled until it is justly settled." American occupation authorities agreed, and were now preparing a 1,539-page volume of trial excerpts, in German, to be deposited in the libraries of all three western zones. This would set the record straight, correct the baron's flagrant errors, and tell the *Volk* what had really happened and what Alfried's crimes had been. Unfortunately they miscalculated. The book might have contributed much to that, but it was never given a chance. Clay's successor, feeling that it would damage German-American friendship, suppressed it.[8] Thus the only book-length version of Krupp's trial available in Germany has been, and at this writing still is, his uncle's expanded account.

☒    ☒    ☒

"*Herr Krupp brütet Tag und Nacht über seine Geschäfte,*" a fellow prisoner wrote home: "Herr Krupp broods day and night over his business." It was a minority opinion. "*Die Zeit schwindet ihm unter den Händen,*" one closer to him recalled afterward: "Time passed swiftly." That seems closer to the truth. To be sure, Krupp was lonely. The visits of his mother, brother and uncle were infrequent, and prolonged confinement produces a spiritual malaise all its own. Still, the core of strength and pride was untouched. His letters to Anneliese Bahr, inquiring about their son, were polite but impersonal; when Anneliese came to Landsberg he received her courteously without attempting to renew closer ties. His correspondence with one of her friends was warmer. Unknown to Anneliese, a sophisticated, aggressive, kittenish blonde whom he had met as Vera Hossenfeldt during his youth had begun writing Alfried on her own. Something in her letters touched a chord in him, and he responded, but a convict under a twelve-year sentence, with highly uncertain prospects, has little to offer any woman. Though isolation was a hardship, he had resolved to endure it without dreaming idle dreams or deteriorating. Any sign of weakness would be capitulation. He must remain strong. He had refused to beg in his letter to General Clay, and when offered a look at the world outside seventeen months later he spurned it.

The occasion was his father's death. On January 16, 1950, Gustav moved his head on the pillow for the last time; Bertha, holding his hand, felt it grow cold. The funeral presented extraordinary problems, for at first no one could think where to put the old man. The family plot at Kettwig Gate was now part of Essen's new Hauptbahnhof. Blühnbach was still in American hands; and Viennese officials who might have been helpful did not share Germany's awe of the dynasty. Clearly advice from the head of the House was needed. The family was still in disarray. Harald, now in a VIP prison outside Moscow, had been told four years earlier by a Red Army officer that Gustav was dead, and now, to his utter confusion, another officer gave him the same message. The baron heard the news from an anonymous telephoner. Berthold received a wire from his mother and immediately dispatched another wire to Alfried, who went to the warden.[9]

It was true, the warden said. He expressed his condolences while the tall convict stood rigid; then Alfried asked whether he might be released to help his mother. The warden checked with superior authority. It was possible, he replied, provided Krupp was accompanied at all times by a tight security guard. Krupp spun about and departed the office. That left the distressing problem of burial with Berthold, who reached the coaching inn later in the day. Bertha, exhausted by over five years of bedside nursing, was in no condition to make decisions. Somehow the innkeeper's yard seemed inappropriate; Gustav, the nineteenth-century social climber who had reached the top rung, would have been indignant. Under pressure to do *something*, Berthold ordered cremation in Salzburg. "Really," he sighed afterward, "it was the only way." It was; yet in those years the family was spared nothing. As the crematorium's squat trolley was wheeled toward the flames, a *Life* magazine photographer darted up, snapping a frame which was to be reproduced around the world within a week.[10]

The widow and her son left with the filled urn. What to do with it? Berthold's temporary quarters in Essen? They didn't belong to him. A safe-deposit box? No; rumors would spread, unfortunate conclusions might be drawn. Besides, Bertha insisted that there be a service. Suddenly Berthold smacked his forehead with the heel of his hand. *Verdammter Idiot!* Why hadn't he thought of it before? There was Obergrombach, a small Bohlen estate in Baden. No one lived on it; the ashes could go there. Again Alfried was informed, again he asked permission to leave, and again, upon being told that he must submit to a plainclothes escort, he stalked away. The interment ceremony, therefore, was almost unattended. SS crematoria excepted, it would be hard to conceive of a burial less like the state funeral the old man would have wanted. But then, he had died at a bad time.

Telford Taylor had predicted that Gustav's death would signal an attack on the confiscation verdict. Kranzbühler couldn't miss such an obvious opportunity, and sure enough, within a week Bertha claimed the dynastic fortune, estimated by her and her attorneys at well over 500 million dollars. The German public, which had never heard of the Lex Krupp, now learned through a brief news broadcast that Hitler had apparently issued an unusual decree at Frau Krupp's request and that she was now asking the conquerors to set it aside. Perplexed, they heard that according to her the law

> . . . which established her son Alfried as the sole heir and proprietor is unlawful since it was issued by the Führer in violation of the law of the land [. . . *ihren Sohn Alfried als einzigen Erben und Eigentümer einsetzte, sei ungültig, da der Führer sie in Verletzung des Gesetzes erlassen habe*]. She petitioned the occupation authorities to disinherit her imprisoned son and to permit her and her other children to share the legacy. Alfried's brothers and sisters support the plea.[11]

There was no reply. Krupp couldn't even be disowned by his own mother. Disgusted, he returned to his newspapers and his exquisite view of the river Lech. Both had become unexpectedly engrossing. By now he had been locked up for almost five years. The last time he had looked upon the Reich he had seen total ruin. Nine out of every ten German plants had been still. There had been no telephone wires, no mail, no drugs for the maimed soldiers and civilians jamming the hospitals. The mighty Rhine had been barred by 754 sunken barges in the American zone alone, the railway system crippled by 885 bombed railroad bridges, the roads made impassable by demolished highway bridges beyond number. Since then less than half a decade had passed, yet the fabulous Fatherland was roaring again. Peering down, Krupp could see brightly painted barges, sparkling with brass fittings, plying the Lech. If they were here, they must be on the Rhine and the Ruhr, too. The road along the shore was thick with shiny new cars whose pictures he had seen, and not quite believed, in the prison library — Volkswagens, Opels, Kapitans, and Mercedes-Benzes darting past enormous triple-trailer-trucks bearing goods to market. Landsberg's men were smoking long Havana cigars, Landsberg's women were chic and nyloned, Landsberg's boys were sturdy and tough, roughhousing in gleaming *Lederhosen*.[12]

The Germany Krupp had left was gone forever, altered past recall by momentous events. Outside, his countrymen were talking of West Germany's "economic miracle" (*Wirtschaftswunder*) and of the country itself as an "economic wonderland" (*Wirtschaftswunderland*). Marvelous changes had been wrought everywhere. A few figures are revealing. In five years the nation's gross national product was up 70 percent, exports had multiplied sevenfold, and credits were higher than in any other European state. For every new house built in France, the Germans had built eight;

they were now putting up nearly a half-billion homes a year. In heavy industry the French were rapidly falling behind. German coal production had doubled, steel production had increased from 2,500,000 tons a year to 11,000,000 — and would have soared even higher if the Allies hadn't insisted upon that as a ceiling. Powered by the germ cell of the Ruhr, the truncated Reich had surpassed the economic peak of 1936, Hitler's best year, and the manufacture of radios, automobiles, and hardware was roughly twice as great as in that year. Unemployment was down to 3.5 percent and shrinking. In defeat the *Volk* were realizing all the promises the Führer had failed to redeem. Already Germany was neck and neck with the United Kingdom in the renewed race for economic supremacy. And all this, it must be remembered, was being accomplished with 30 percent of the old Deutsches Reich in Soviet hands.[13]

What was the explanation? *U.S. News and World Report* wrote that "In West Germany, under a system of free enterprise, fortunes are being made by many." Fortunes *were* being made — "The Mercedes," ran a popular slogan, "is the Volkswagen of the Ruhr" — but the Schlotbarone who drove them would have been annoyed by the suggestion that their new prosperity owed anything to what they scorned as *"freie Wirtschaft."* Undoubtedly, Ludwig Erhardt had something to do with it. The Minister of Economics was no more a champion of laissez-faire than Schacht had been, however; his great contributions were government-backed credits and liberal tax concessions for manufacturers. And useful as his intervention was, Secretary of State Byrnes's successor dwarfed it when, on June 5, 1947, he mounted the commencement podium in Harvard Yard and invited western Europe to join the United States in a massive bootstrap operation. Through the Marshall Plan, the European Recovery Program, and other money-colored funnels, four billion dollars were to be infused into the parched economy of the Reich. Once the *Wirtschaftswunder* had been accomplished, most of its beneficiaries adopted the same attitude as Gustav Krupp's toward the Dawes Plan of the 1920's. That was understandable; they were proud, and they had been hurt. A young Speer protégé who briefly flourished in the Wonderland told Charles Thayer, "We in the Ruhr didn't see much of it. Perhaps you should have hired better public relations men to tell us about all your help." A steelmaker remarked to this writer, "Marshall had nothing to do with it. This was a German miracle." A chemical manufacturer said, "We got back on our feet because we worked hard. ERP had little to do with it."[14]

Although $4,000,000,000 must have had *something* to do with it, the *Wirtschaftswunderland* wasn't created by the dollar alone. It sprang from many sources. One, beyond question, was the powerful Teutonic urge to dominate the continent. Germans had always been born toilers, and now they drove themselves harder than ever. Another source, though the Ruhr barons hotly deny it, was the American breakup of cartels, which cleared the way for bright upstarts. At the same time, the Germans, disqualified from the Cold War, were freed from the dead weight of military budgets. The French contribution to NATO was several billions a year, British defense absorbed over 10 percent of the U.K. national product, but there wasn't a single German in uniform.

Paradoxically, the defeated industrialists had emerged from the smog of 1945 with one unnoticed but vital asset. Though their factories had been reduced to twisted steel and powdered masonry, their stocks of machine tools were intact. These heavy duty instruments, essential to peacetime production, had been augmented by the Führer's great aggressive thrusts. At the time of Munich, Germany had had 1,281,000 of them. When the Reich collapsed, the machine tool inventory in the U.S., British, and French zones had actually risen to 2,216,000. During six years of victories and defeats the potential productive strength of the Ruhr had, in other words, doubled. In Essen, Alfried's deputies hid his model of the *Prinz Eugen* from their British keepers on the roof of the Hauptverwaltungsge-bäude. To them it was a reminder of the glorious cruise of February 11–12, 1942, when Krupp's mighty warship sailed unmolested up the English Channel in broad daylight — "Nothing more mortifying to the pride of sea power has happened in home waters since the seventeenth century," *The Times* of London had written — and for some unreformed Kruppianer it suggested the possibility of even greater glory to come. But that was sheer bravado. Tools weren't exposed on the roof. They were housed in insulated vaults, greased lovingly twice a week, and hoarded against the day when *die Firma*, like other Ruhr concerns, would be allowed to use them.[15]

Though full tribute must be paid to Teuton vitality and Teuton crafts-manship, the economic wonder of the late 1950's was largely spawned by external forces. Some were economic. The Ruhrgebiet was indispensable to an exhausted continent struggling toward salvation. Britain feared German competition. But Englishmen were hungry, too, and London couldn't justify the export of food to Bremen and Hamburg because Germans were prohibited from earning their own keep. The Dutch were caught in a different bind. With the Reich prostrate, the port of Rotterdam was functioning at less than half of capacity. The same was true of Antwerp and Norwegian merchant ships, and Swedish mines and the Belgian pits which had provided casting sand for Kruppstahl were deserted. Even the Swiss were caught; without their largest German customer, vast electric power stations stood idle. Desperately trying to fend off protests from the Low Countries, Scandinavia, and the Alps, Allied experts attempted to develop light industries in the inner Ruhr. It was no use. Textile and consumer goods factories were unsuitable for the anvil. It was a forge, not a spindle.[16]

The barons knew this. They were fully aware of Europe's need for them. It entitled them to a place at the bargaining table, and the strength of their position grew as the Cold War temperature plunged. Byrnes's Stuttgart speech had been the first straw on the rising wind. The second appeared the following March, when Herbert Hoover's economic mission to Germany and Austria, reporting to President Truman, criticized dismantling and the restriction of Ruhr production. In April the Moscow Conference ended in a dismaying uproar, revealing to the entire world the unbridgeable gulf between Stalin and his former allies. Then came the Berlin blockade, the airlift, the fascinating change in GI and Tommy attitudes toward the beaten Reich ("they" became "we") and the shift in international alliances which provided an outlet for pent-up energy and skills.[17]

The western powers did not end their state of war until 1951, the year Washington also reversed its attitude toward Krupp. But diplomatic rituals always lag far behind events. If one were to choose a single day which marked the beginning of the new Germany, it would be May 12, 1949. That morning the Russians, defeated by the airlift, ended their long blockade, and even as the first trucks and trains from the west entered the capital General Clay flew from there to a historic Frankfurt conference. Since September seventy Germans without Nazi pasts had been meeting in a commandeered girls' normal school in Bonn, drafting the constitution for a new nation. Clay worked out the final details, approved it, and then left for home and retirement. Three months later Bonn held elections; Konrad Adenauer became the first German chancellor since Adolf Hitler's suicide over four years before. As a gesture of faith in the new country, the United States, France, and the United Kingdom ended military government. In the future each victor would be represented by a high commissioner.[18]

"The tide," Fritz von Bülow later said, "had turned." Though Krupp would remain in Landsberg Fortress for another year and a half, the momentum of events was building rapidly. Essen myth to the contrary, he had made no contribution to the *Wirtschaftswunder*, but the change in the continent's political and economic climate had altered his own prospects immensely. Later, talking to a writer about it, he observed,

In what is unfortunately called the miracle, there is really nothing miraculous. First, the Germans learned after the First World War that they could come back from defeat. This lesson inspired us constantly, until we too recovered again. Hard work was the chief factor [*Der Hauptfaktor war harte Arbeit*]. This time we had to start from the bottom, and we had to drive ourselves even more relentlessly. The Marshall Plan and other American aid gave us a shot in the arm. Another lift was political. We could rise again while the wartime anti-German coalition broke up and the united effort to persecute Germany was abandoned. But there was another guide to lead us over the mountain. We had good luck — don't underestimate our good luck [*wir hatten viel Glück — unterschätzen Sie das Glück nicht*]. Add all these things together and you have recovery — but not a miracle.[19]

✠   ✠   ✠

Luck revealed itself to him with *kolossal* impudence. In the hundred years since Alfred Krupp had nervously unveiled his glittering steel field gun in Hyde Park's Crystal Palace, only one weapon had crossed steel with *Waffenschmiede* products and hopelessly routed them — Russia's T–34. Guderian had credited it with stopping his drive on Tula and Moscow; in the ghastly crucible of the Kursk salient it had shattered Alfried's last great shield. Memories of it still haunted his dreams, though in the womb of American imprisonment he was gradually learning to forget it. Yet it still existed in large numbers, nursing itself from fuel nozzles in vast Siberian armor parks, and its low, menacing silhouette was about to reenter his life.[20]

At eight o'clock German time Saturday evening, June 24, 1950 (he was playing skat at the time), the T–34 was the same tank — 32 tons, broad-treaded, protected by exceptionally thick steel plate and mounting an 85-mm. cannon and two 7.62-mm. machine guns. Eight P.M. in Landsberg was four o'clock the following morning in Korea. There the calendar read Sunday, June 25, though no one on the northern side of the thirty-eighth parallel could read it; a North Korean general named Chai Ung Jun had ordered total blackout. In darkness and scattered rain General Chai, having received a green light from Premier Kim Il Sung and his Soviet advisers, had just deployed 150 T–34's and 90,000 men across the parallel in a forty-mile arc. On the clocks of world capitals it was wartime again.[21]

Chai's tanks were headed for Seoul, and for the House of Krupp they had abruptly become the most auspicious weapons since Alfred's breech-loaders blew Louis Napoleon's Second Empire into oblivion at Sedan. Four generations of Kruppianer, describing that golden day on the Meuse, had told their apprentice sons, "*Wenn Deutschland blüht, blüht Krupp*" (whenever Germany flourishes, Krupp flourishes). Now Alfried's private economic miracle was about to appear, and all because of an ugly spread of squat-hulled Bolshevik monsters manned by Asian *Untermenschen* on the opposite side of the globe. That was insolent of luck, a crude joke. But of course the convict whose cell door swings wide doesn't inquire into the politics of the locksmith.

The one principal in the Krupp story who denies that the locksmith's name was Chai is John J. McCloy, who, by taking over as America's high commissioner exactly eleven months earlier, had inherited General Clay's powers. Short, brisk, and blunt, the New York banker insists that *he* turned the key. "There's not a goddamn word of truth in the charge that

Krupp's release was inspired by the outbreak of the Korean War," he snaps. "No lawyer told me what to do, and it wasn't political. It was a matter of my conscience." No sensible man differs lightly with John McCloy. He is, deservedly, among the most respected men in public life, and no one who knows him would challenge his integrity. It was slanderous to traduce him because he had favored a moderate denazification policy while in the War Department, or to hint that German businessmen were turning the new *Hoher Kommissar's* head with flattery.[22]

McCloy was his own man. He was, moreover, a superb choice for the new post in Frankfurt. As a captain in World War I he had served with the AEF occupation forces at Coblenz. Though he had little courtroom experience, he held a law degree and was responsible for the Hague conviction, twenty years later, of Germany's Black Tom saboteurs of 1916. A world traveler, he knew Europe almost as well as any European; a skilled negotiator, he engineered the collaboration between Generals Giraud and de Gaulle in the spring of 1943, and he was certainly better qualified to administer the American zone than anyone in the State Department. His character was above reproach, his abilities matchless. He was not, however, infallible. As we shall presently see, the record suggests that he really hadn't much to do with the Krupp decision, and no man, not even a John J. McCloy, could remain untouched by the cyclone that blew out of Korea in the second half of 1950.[23]

It was far graver than the Berlin confrontation. Less than five years after the capitulation of the Japanese Empire, the western powers, led by the United States, were once more fighting a major war. Washington was peering out across both oceans, for the bulk of western military strength was tied down in the occupation of Germany. That was the fulcrum, and everyone knew it. "There *had* to be a change in the U.S. attitude toward Nuremberg," Otto Kranzbühler said afterward, while Benjamin Ferencz, who had sat across the chilly Justizpalast room from Kranzbühler, said, "At that time there was a sense of panic about the Russians, a feeling that there was an urgent need for an understanding with the Germans. McCloy couldn't detach himself from that atmosphere." The *New York Times* pointed out that "reviving Ruhr industry and holding down the industrialists" were conflicting goals. Overnight a major gear of the Marshall Plan shifted into reverse. Its original drafters had specified that not a dollar from it could be spent on defense. Now Washington told European capitals that the larger their military budgets, the greater their share in ERP would be. Above all loomed the urgent question of the partitioned Reich. The British high commissioner, General Sir Brian Robertson, declared privately, "We *must* get Germany committed."[24]

"For the Germans," T. H. White later wrote, the Asian conflict "brought quick, complete and unconditional profit. . . . The post-Korea boom drew German industry back into the world markets at such prices that it was able to re-equip huge sectors of its run-down plant." The Schlotbarone also brought new strength to the bargaining table, which may puzzle Americans since grown accustomed to seventy-billion-dollar defense budgets and a gigantic military establishment. It wasn't baffling then. It was a grim symptom of a grimmer reality. In June 1950 the three western allies held West Germany with seven undermanned divisions. Across the zonal frontier stood twenty-two Red Army divisions backed by Walter Ulbricht's new East German army. All Soviet satellites were under arms and equipped with artillery and T–34s. The Free World, as it was now known, was defended by a thin line of riflemen. The supplies which should have backed them had been sold as war surplus or steel scrap. It is a caustic fact that when NATO asked Paris for its order of battle, the embarrassed French replied that they could contribute but two weak divisions, one of whose regiments was armed with obsolete Krupp tanks — the same model which had been chewed into junk by Russian armor. But France couldn't even field her Tigers. They lacked spare parts.[25]

Spare parts had once been available at the Hauptverwaltungsgebäude. And the Germans, her former enemies in the West suddenly remembered, had almost defeated the Soviet Union single-handed. As 1950 waned and the seething Korean front disintegrated under the weight of Chinese manpower, Pentagon strategists grappled with the question of what to do with two rediscovered factors: Germany's martial prowess and the Prussian militaristic tradition. In war a symbol can be more effective than an army corps. To the Ruhr, Professor Pounds wrote, "Krupp became a legend. Essen owed its existence as an industrial city to him, and even in 1950 the legend had political significance." Thus the complex interweaving of Ruhr politics, NATO requirements, and shifting military fortunes eight time zones away combined in a plural theme which, though unnoticed at the time, seems startlingly clear in retrospect.[26]

That summer the terror spread by North Korean armor was so great that, according to the U.S. Army's official historian, "prepared demolitions were not blown, roadblocks were erected but not manned, and obstacles were not covered by fire." In September, however, the United Nations command was holding the dreaded T–34's at bay on the Pusan perimeter by a desperate combination of arms — electrically operated 3.5-inch aluminum bazookas, Corsair strafers carrying napalm and 500-pound bombs, and a tank collection comprising M–26 Shermans, M–46 Pattons, and M4A3 Shermans which provided a five-to-one superiority. Heartened, the U.N. commander made his end run at Inchon and then, disregarding warnings from India, advanced toward the Yalu. Late in October, Peking entered the war, attacking Australian and Scottish battalions on the western side of the Taeryong River. Britain, France, and the U.S. promptly tore up West Germany's 11,000,000-ton steel limit and urged the barons to go all out in the fight against Communism. (At that time Allied engineers doubted that the Ruhr's old-fashioned methods could yield more than 13,500,000 tons a year at most. They didn't know Alfried Krupp and the new generation of smokestack barons. It is a tribute to their genius that within eleven months of Alfried's release the Germans would be pouring the full 13,500,000, that within two years they would add another million, and that the year after that they would hit 18,000,000 tons.)[27]

On November 21, 1950, Douglas MacArthur sighted the Yalu. Ten days later Alfried held his first Direktorium meeting since the fall of the Third Reich. To be sure, he was still a convict. But four Chinese armies had just begun a full-scale offensive; suddenly MacArthur was in full retreat, and the Landsberg warden set aside a large room for Konzern business. Executives came down from Essen accompanied by representatives of the firm's legal staff. Conferences were held regularly in the prison from then on:

Herr Krupp would sit at the head of the table flanked by his directors [Herr Krupp sass am Ende des Tisches, mit seinen Direktoren auf beiden Seiten]. Some of them would smoke American cigars or peel oranges or bananas sent in from outside while they soberly discussed production figures and financial statements.[28]

The evacuation of 205,000 U.N. personnel by sea from Hungnam was begun in December. Simultaneously, representatives of the western powers, meeting in Brussels, chose Dwight D. Eisenhower as supreme commander of the Western European Defense Force; the three high commissioners were instructed to raise a German army. Returning from Belgium, they summoned Chancellor Adenauer to the Petersberger Hof — the snow-white villa directly across the Rhine from Bonn where Chamberlain had betrayed Czechoslovakia to Hitler before the formalities in Munich — and pleaded with him to help them recruit a new German striking force. It was the first time they greeted the chancellor hat in hand, and the last time he was to be beckoned to the Petersberger Hof. Each three weeks for the past year and a half he had promptly reported and received his instructions. All that had been washed away by the blood in the Yalu. West Germany was essentially sovereign. The West's decision to rearm her had not been unanimous; both France and England had at first recoiled from it. But the United States had insisted, and since Americans were doing 58 percent of the dying in Korea, Whitehall and the Quai d'Orsay had submitted to Washington's steamroller, expertly driven by Hoher Kommissar der Vereinigten Staaten John J. McCloy.[29]

On January 4, 1951, the week the Reds retook Seoul, the United States commissioner resolved upon another step. "It is better to abandon a whole province than to divide an army," Schlieffen had written, and with abandonment of the Ruhr now unthinkable a united barony had become a matter of some urgency. The smaller manufacturers sorely missed the great Schlotbaron. While it would be politically inexpedient for him to preside openly over the production of Pusan-bound steel — indeed, the Control Council's deconcentration decree forbade it — his expertise could be equally effective offstage, and the *Volk*, grasping the significance of the act, would cheer it and turn more firmly westward.

Krupp himself saw the design. It may even be said that he shared in it. Calling him a consultant would be going too far, but he certainly held one of the highest security clearances of any convict in penal history. The red-striped denim he donned each dawn had become a droll costume. The homburg, though invisible, was back on his head. He had known the outcome of the Brussels conference before it met; in November he had been quietly informed of Washington's determination to see a new German sword forged. His discharge, he was told in confidence, was "only a question of a short time." His brother Berthold and Otto Kranzbühler had also heard from privileged sources that a proclamation of clemency was being prepared. They hoped to have him out by Christmas, and though that proved impossible, he and his staff celebrated the imminent decree with a discreet Christmas feast. The diners dallied long at the table, rising at approximately the same hour that the last elements of the First Marine Division's rearguard were debarking from Hungnam.[30]

McCloy's Frankfurt aides had decided to keep the clemency timetable from Alfried until forty hours before the fortress gates swung open. However, shortly after the New Year rumors, verification, and even details began to reach all the inmates. There was to be a general amnesty; twenty-one of the twenty-eight men in War Crimes Prison Number One who had been condemned to death, including all who had been convicted of the Malmédy murders, were to shed their red jackets. Krupp would not only regain his freedom; he would be rich again. To be sure, the British needed time to evacuate Villa Hügel, and occupation authorities counted on the reinstated Konzernherr to sell his coal and steel holdings to another German industrialist as part of the decartelization program. Meanwhile the hearths, mines, ore fields, and seventy-odd enterprises worth a half-billion dollars would once more be his.

In Washington Senator Joseph McCarthy nodded and smiled. "Extremely wise," he commented.[31]

✠ ✠ ✠

So sensitive to history are twentieth-century soldiers and statesmen that research can usually pinpoint the place, and frequently the exact time, when great decisions were reached. A culling of a translator's notes, for example, reveals that the Munich Pact was signed at a few minutes past

1 A.M., September 30, 1938, in the Führerhaus on the Bavarian capital's baroque Königsplatz. NATO was conceived on the evening of December 16, 1947, in the home of the United Kingdom's foreign minister at 22 Carleton Terrace, London, after Vyacheslav Mikhailovich Molotov had spat Nyet a hundred times and flown off angrily. U.S. soldiers first collided with North Korean troops at precisely 8:16 A.M., July 5, 1950, just north of Osan. But there are exceptions to the rule of access. The public has never been told where or when the Truman administration resolved to unsheathe German bayonets once again, or who recommended it, and no scholar has yet fixed responsibility — the who, when, where, why, and how — for John J. McCloy's momentous repudiation of a distinguished Nuremberg tribunal and General Lucius Clay. We have the version which was circulated by occupation authorities. It is worthless. Under scrutiny it proves to be fatally flawed, a fragile cover story that shatters the instant anyone leans upon it.[32]

One of the first leaners was Mrs. Franklin D. Roosevelt. Disturbed by the reports from Landsberg, she wrote the high commissioner, "Why are we freeing so many Nazis?" In his reply McCloy explained that he had "inherited these cases from General Clay, who, for one reason or another, had been unable to dispose of them." He informed her he had received "many letters and petitions" asking him to set aside the Nuremberg rulings — in the light of the tribunal's blizzard of organized mail, this was probably an understatement — and that he considered it "a fundamental principle of American justice that accused persons shall have a final right to be heard. . . ." So it is. That was why the general had appointed his appellate board, which, after sifting the entire record, had advised him that there was no reason to show mercy. Later the commissioner told this writer that Clay, in transferring authority to him, referred to Landsberg and said, "This is a hell of a job." It was a reasonable remark; he was passing along responsibility for the lives of nearly thirty men whose death sentences could be changed to life imprisonment by a squiggle of the pen. State governors frequently spare the condemned. But they rarely pardon prisoners, and they never appoint an appellate court to review the decision of another appellate court. They can't: it is illegal. Yet that is what McCloy did. In police idiom he was "acting on information received." But it was information solicited by a Clemency Board he appointed because, he told Eleanor Roosevelt, "unlike criminal cases in the United States and England there was no provision for further court review of these cases for possible errors of law or of fact after the court of first instance passed upon them." The commissioner's correspondence strongly suggests that he was unaware that precisely such a review had been conducted by Judge Madden, Mr. Rockwell, and Colonel Raymond.[33]

General Clay's appellate board had convened in Germany. Commissioner McCloy's first met in Washington three months before the outbreak of Korean hostilities. The appointment of its members on March 20, 1950, is, as McCloy rightly points out, irrefutable evidence that his decision to pore over the verdicts was wholly unrelated to the new war. It does not attest that the war and its catastrophes had no effect on the judgment of the members, however; it does not even prove that some cases were not glossed over and new ones introduced. To be sure, that would have been unusual. Yet everything about this second review was unusual. The commissioner appointed three men with impeccable records: the Honorable David W. Peck, presiding justice of the New York Supreme Court's appellate division; Frederick A. Moran, chairman of the New York Board of Parole; and Brigadier General Conrad E. Snow, assistant legal adviser to the Department of State. He then gave them an impossible task. Clay's attorneys had had seven months to ponder one case. McCloy provided five months for a complete review of all twelve Nuremberg trials which had followed the IMT — that is, a thorough study of the cases against 104 defendants whose collective proceedings had required the equivalent of five judicial years and whose transcripts, exclusive of documents and briefs, were ten times the length of Webster's unabridged dictionary and covered 330,000 pages, a stack of paper 110 feet high.

In Munich the judge, the parole officer, and the brigadier sat for forty days. After reading the twelve verdicts (over 3,000 pages in themselves) they were introduced to members of the German bar as the Advisory Board on Clemency for War Criminals. This was quickly shortened to the Peck Panel, and under that name the triumvirate opened hearings. When the reviewers reported their findings to the high commissioner on August 28, 1950, they noted that they had examined the judgments, that Moran had interviewed each prisoner in Landsberg, and that fifty lawyers representing ninety defendants had stated their cases before the board. That sounded impressive, sensible, and reasonable. It wasn't. No court of appeals would dream of reversing any judge — and it must be borne in mind that Krupp had been found guilty by three eminent justices from appellate benches — without inviting briefs from both defense *and* prosecution. In the proceedings before the Peck Panel, counsel for convicted criminals were heard and permitted to file extensive comments. There was no rebuttal. As Telford Taylor pointed out in his own letter to Mrs. Roosevelt, "Even in a clemency proceeding before the governor of any of our states, the views of the district attorney and of the judge who tried the case are invariably obtained and considered. None of these elementary and established practices were observed by Mr. McCloy."[*34]

---

* With Eleanor Roosevelt's permission, the high commissioner published his letter to her in *Information Bulletin,* the official publication of the American occupation. On June 29, 1951, Taylor, having received the same courtesy from her, asked *Information Bulletin* to follow up by printing his answer to McCloy. The editor, H. Warner Waid, did not even acknowledge receipt of his request. After waiting eleven weeks, Taylor again wrote Waid (September 14), appealing for publication "to correct certain

By the summer of 1950 the prosecution team which had convicted Krupp in 1948 was scattered around the world. General Taylor was preparing to join the new war effort; most of those who had helped him had retired to private practice. The Peck Panel could have written them. It didn't. It could have solicited the views of the tribunal. The justices did not even know their verdict was being questioned. The slighting of fellow countrymen who had sacrificed two years to what they had hoped would become a new code of international law went beyond that, however. By coincidence, one of Nuremberg's senior prosecutors was on the spot during the Peck deliberations. As an army officer in 1945 Benjamin B. Ferencz had entered captured concentration camps while the crematorium ovens were still hot. He had become one of the first members of the War Crimes Commission, and now, five years later, he was still in Germany. His mission, ironically, was restitution of the property of murdered Jews to their heirs — an issue which, had the sanctity of private property been a burning issue in Frankfurt, should have evoked as much official zeal as respect for Krupp's holdings. Learning of the Peck review, Ferencz wrote each member of the triumvirate, explaining that he had been executive counsel to Telford Taylor during the trials and offering his services. He received a curt acknowledgment from the panel's secretary, informing him that the board would let him know if they wanted him. They didn't. Out of curiosity he dropped into the high commissioner's office from time to time during the Peck deliberations. On his first visit, at the very beginning of the new inquiry, he found the records of the Krupp trial. They were packed in crates six feet long and shaped curiously like coffins. Knowing the evidence that lay inside, he kept wondering when the lids would be removed. They never were. After McCloy had freed Alfried, Ferencz called for the last time and saw that not a screw had been turned.[35]

This is not to suggest that the commissioner regarded his mandate lightly. Scanning the entire record was literally impossible; a top-notch speed reader, absorbing 1,200 words a minute, couldn't get through the Nuremberg transcripts in less than seventeen months. John McCloy was, among other things, responsible for the administration of a third of West Germany. He would have been justified in delegating the entire Landsberg issue to Peck, but he worried about the convicts. Ferencz thought him "generous and kindly, anxious to make a gesture toward the Germans." Whatever pressure he may have felt from Washington, however much he may have been influenced by the slaughter of American youth in Korea, McCloy was genuinely disturbed by the Krupp verdict. "We'd tried him reluctantly," he later told me, "and the confiscation troubled me. I con-

damaging inaccuracies in Mr. McCloy's letter to Mrs. Roosevelt, which you published in your May issue." Once more he was ignored. This gratuitous insult to a general officer of the United States, who had served both the Attorney General and the U.S. Senate as a legal expert, indicates how far the pendulum had swung in the U.S. zone since the rendering of justice at Nuremberg.

sulted my French and British colleagues, and they agreed with me. My feeling — it was a feeling — was that Alfried was a playboy, that he hadn't had much responsibility. I felt that he had expiated whatever he'd done by the time he'd already served in jail. Oh, I don't doubt that he'd supported the Nazis early; he was a weakling."[36]

Brooding over the 104 convicted men, determined to touch every possible base in the little time he had, the *Hoher Kommissar* personally traveled to Landsberg and talked to many whose future, if any, lay in his hands. ("Some, particularly the generals, were arrogant; they deliberately turned their backs. But others were quite decent. They walked right up and shook hands with me.") For some reason he didn't see Krupp. ("Later we met socially, of course, at cocktail parties.") The confrontation would have been interesting. One cannot imagine a greater contrast in the world of commerce. While both were men with first-class minds, the American was humane, outgoing; the German almost unapproachable. Alfried probably wouldn't have turned his back. It would have been more like him to have stared right through McCloy. Though disappointing to historians, the lack of an encounter did strengthen the commissioner's objectivity. "I went both ways with the Peck Panel," he said years afterward. "Sometimes I was harder than they suggested, sometimes softer. But in Krupp's case their recommendation was unanimous."[37]

Writing the author long after the event, Judge Peck was, in one letter, extremely hazy about the panel's advice on how to dispose of the Krupp question; "I cannot give you the information requested," he confessed, "because I have no recollection on the subject." This is hardly surprising. Over a hundred convicted war criminals, 3,000 pages of verdicts, pleas and briefs from fifty lawyers speaking a strange tongue, deliberations and the submission of a report in a whirlwind of sessions — it is a wonder that anything came of it, and had the Advisory Board on Clemency been obligated to weigh arguments from the Nuremberg prosecutors, confusing it and shading its convictions with doubt, quite possibly nothing would, in fact, have been achieved. Therefore it is rather marvelous that from that swarming, jabbering, forty-day night court Peck should, in another letter long after the event, have remembered that the name of Alfried Krupp's counsel was Earl J. Carroll.[38]

✠　　✠　　✠

The pariah of Nuremberg, the "alleged attorney" from an "alleged law firm," had made a dazzling comeback. Krupp's legal staff had concluded that he had to have American counsel because the Americans had behaved so queerly since the verdict. Although the U.S. Supreme Court had declared itself incompetent to pass upon it, the threat of confiscation remained as vague as ever; the Konzern seemed destined to spend eternity in suspended animation. Carroll exuded confidence, he spoke the Peck Panel's language, and he had been retained once more to prepare a writ of appeal and take it to Munich.

Here the waters become exceedingly muddy. According to Carroll's subsequent account, he had told Clay that the confiscation order would "further the Communist design"; now he "took up the matter" with McCloy. McCloy recalls no conference with Carroll, and it is improbable that any such meeting would have advanced his client's cause. To the commissioner the Californian remained unrehabilitated, an expatriate "in bad odor." Carroll dealt not with him, but with the Peck Panel. In the absence of refutation, his arguments doubtless sounded impressive. Passed up to the front office by the panel, they were to form the core of McCloy's public position. Three are typical: (1) Alfried had actually held "a rather junior position"* in the firm; (2) under American law, assets may be forfeited only if they have been acquired through illegal acts, which wasn't true of Krupp's prewar capital; and (3) obviously Carroll's client was the victim of discrimination, since he was the only war criminal whose property had been confiscated; Flick and Farben, for example, had retained all their holdings.[39]

An answering brief would have pointed out that (1) a 1943 intrafirm circular declared that Alfried Krupp had "the full responsibility and direction of the entire enterprise"; (2) the Nuremberg trials had been governed not by American statutes but by a law promulgated by the four-power coalition which had defeated the Third Reich, specifying "forfeiture of property" for men found guilty of war crimes; and (3) Krupp wasn't the only convicted industrialist upon whom this blow had fallen. In the Flick and Farben cases, moreover, the pattern had been different. Slave labor evidence had been far less shocking, and both firms were stock companies. Confiscation there would have been like declaring all General Motors stock void because of management crimes. In Krupp management and owner-ship had been vested in one man, which made forfeiture just. Here the prosecution might have introduced another question, unmentioned at the time. If the Peck Panel really believed that the Konzernherr hadn't had much to do with the running of his firm, why was it planning to free all his directors with him?[40]

For five months the panel's recommendations lay on McCloy's desk. World news grew worse and worse. "American troops," a wire service reported, "are taking a terrible beating in Korea from the Chinese Com-munists, and the U.N. forces, mostly our men, are retreating south of Seoul." General MacArthur asked the Pentagon whether Washington had considered the possibility of being driven out of Korea altogether. On

---

* Much later Rawlings Ragland commented mordantly, "I daresay that never before has the sole owner of a half-billion-dollar enterprise been described as occupying 'a rather junior position.'" (Ragland to WM 3/19/63.)

Capitol Hill the "great debate" over Europe's vulnerability had opened; Senator Robert A. Taft said the President had already "usurped authority" in defending South Korea and had no right to increase American troop strength and arms on the continent. In the public discussion Herbert Hoover added that such an increase would be pointless anyhow; should the Russians plunge into West Germany, we could only harass them from aircraft carriers. On January 17 Peking rejected a new peace appeal from the United Nations and the high commissioner prepared his amnesty statement, to be announced two weeks later.

Krupp didn't know it, but his brother did. Reflecting how far the dynasty had come since the collapse, he felt "at the end of a long winter." Earl J. Carroll was jubilant. In the fall of 1946 he had fled home under the threat of a court-martial. Now he was rich. The size of his Krupp commission is a matter of some dispute, but it was certainly historic. In 1954 a magazine interviewed him and reported that "The terms of Carroll's employment were simple. He was to get Krupp out of prison and get his property restored. The fee was to be 5 percent of everything he could recover. Carroll got Krupp out and his fortune returned, receiving for his five-year job a fee of, roughly, $25 million." Kurt Schürmann, Friedrich von Batocki, and Gertrud Stahmer-Knoll, three members of the firm's permanent legal staff, concede that while the fee was "very high," it wasn't *that* high. They hint at a figure somewhere between two and three million. Foreign correspondents for the Chicago *Daily News* and the New York *Daily News* estimated that Carroll was paid two million and Colonel Robinson, who had joined him in preparing the brief, another two million. On one point there is general agreement: the lawyer wanted his commission in cash. After Alfried's negotiations over the details of restitution two years later, Carroll showed the Ruhr his heels. Some said he retired in Massachusetts; others reported him still in Germany, practicing German law and earning $100,000 a year. In any event, his relationship with the House of Krupp had ended, though he had served it ably.[41]

On Wednesday, January 31, 1951, Radio Frankfurt was describing the plight of a U.S.-French regimental combat team trapped twelve miles north of Yoju when a newscaster broke in with the U.S. High Commissioner's official announcement of war criminal amnesties. McCloy had liquidated Alfried's case by signing two documents, one to release him and the other to restore his property. He said, "I can find no personal guilt in Defendant Krupp to distinguish him above all others sentenced by the Nuremberg courts." Alfried would, of course, remain subject to Allied High Commission Law 27 ("Reorganization of the German Coal, Iron, and Steel Industries"). But all his holdings would be restored to him because, the *Hoher Kommissar* declared, the confiscation of property was "repugnant to our American concepts of justice." Once General Thomas T. Handy, commander in chief of the U.S. European Command, had countersigned the necessary papers, 101 prisoners would be freed from Landsberg Fortress.[42]

In Essen, at Wallotstrasse 16, Frau Ewald Löser listened intently as the names were read. Then she wept. Her husband hadn't been among them. Pardon had been withheld from the one anti-Nazi in the firm's management. For reasons no one can explain — McCloy calls it "a dreadful mistake" — the survivor of the Gestapo dungeon was to remain in his Landsberg cell for five more months. Ailing, he was released on June 1 to his wife's care and convalescence in a Recklinghausen hospital.*[43]

✠   ✠   ✠

John McCloy had supposed that had he failed to act in the Krupp case, he would have been subjected to severe criticism — that, in his words, there would have been "a hell of a howl if I let the confiscation go through." Why he thought so is puzzling. The howlers had already been heard from. Now they were placated. "McCloy did the only fair and possible thing," Otto Kranzbühler said. Louis Lochner, a strong backer of German industrialists, believed the commissioner's reasoning "clear and cogent"; restitution, in his opinion, was "the moral and American thing to do." And one of the most respected leaders of the SPD thought that "If the Amis really believe in the sanctity of private property, there was no choice."[44]

He kept his reflections to himself, because leaders of his own party — the largest in Germany — were issuing a statement charging that western capitalists and the Bonn government were plotting to restore "the old managers to politics and economy." They added, "We have now arrived once more at the point where the German catastrophe began." Many of the Reich's recent enemies were in a towering rage. No single act of the occupation created a greater emotional shock than McCloy's rejection of the Krupp verdict. The clumsy way in which the matter had been handled salted the wound. Justice Wilkins, riffling through a Seattle newspaper in his superior court chambers, learned of it from a small wire service item. He wrote McCloy, "As you know, trial judges are very often reversed, but at least they have the opportunity to know the reasons by reading the advance sheets and the reports." In Washington Joseph W. Kaufman, who had served on the prosecution staff, called Alfried's release "appeasement of the Germans" which "flies in the face of General Clay's action last year in confirming the sentences after giving the matter unusually protracted study and deliberation." Max Mandellaub thought clemency under these circumstances was actually illegal, and in New York Cecelia Goetz bitterly reproached herself for persuading Kruppianer to take the stand against Krupp, believing that now they would be marked for reprisals.

---

* In August, seventy-eight-year-old Hermann Röchling's verdict of confiscation was reversed; the "Krupp of the Saar" went home to die (NYT 8/21/51).

Elizabeth Roth, whose legacy consisted of a cheap snapshot and the memory of her murdered family, wondered why the right to property should be more sacred than the right to life.[45]

Representative Jacob J. Javits protested to Secretary of State Dean Acheson, requesting that the family be fined its entire fortune for "misdeeds against humanity." The Jewish War Veterans denounced "a disservice to justice." Drew Middleton wrote savagely in the *New York Times*, "Some day the Krupp family will be back in Villa Hügel and the Krupp works will be making all sorts of new weapons with which a new generation of Europeans can be killed. As they are fond of saying in the Ruhr, 'You have to look at these things realistically.' "[46]

That was an American reaction. It was comparatively mild. As an editorial writer noted in the same day's issue of the *Times*, there was "a sharp difference between European and American attitudes toward people like Krupp." The British attitude was summed up in a Vicky cartoon in the London *News Chronicle*; Hitler and Göring were depicted staring at a newspaper headed KRUPP FREED while the Führer asked, "Should we have hung on a little longer?" An anonymous Briton left a wreath "To the Dead from Krupp" on the Royal Artillery Memorial at Hyde Park Corner. Winston Churchill rose in Commons to remonstrate in behalf of the loyal opposition, and Prime Minister Attlee made a statement — a preposterous statement — that "There is no question of Krupp being allowed to assume either ownership or control of the former Krupp industrial empire." Undeceived, Fleet Street raged on. The *Observer* declared, "The American decision means that dangerous lunatics will again be at large." The *Sunday Pictorial* described Bertha Krupp as an old woman rubbing her hands "with glee" because her eldest son would soon be producing cannon again, and caricatures in the *Daily Express* and the *Sunday Express* represented Bertha and Alfried as loathsome creatures. Across the channel the Foreign Affairs Commission of the French National Assembly passed a resolution of displeasure and forwarded it to Frankfurt. *Paris l'Aube* advised Alfried, "Disappear! We have seen enough of you!" and the *Paris-Presse* saw "all that the French detest in Germany — the Prussian spirit, pan-Germanism, militarism, industrial dumping — walking abroad again."[47]

McCloy was baffled and angry. Outrage in Paris and London was incomprehensible to him. Unlike the British and French high commissioners, who never consulted him, he always solicited their views before making a major move. Both had been invited to submit appraisals of the Krupp situation; both had agreed with his decision. Moreover, while an American was now releasing Alfried, England and France had conveniently forgotten that he would never have been tried and sentenced if McCloy's predecessors hadn't insisted upon it. He was particularly indignant with the British. It was pure hypocrisy for Churchill and Attlee to shake their heads and roll their eyes. Alfried had been their responsibility. He had been arrested and first imprisoned in the British zone, where most of his property was. They had turned him over to the United States because they weren't interested in evidence against him. And though two and a half years had passed since the Nuremberg tribunal had told Alfried that he must submit to "forfeiture of all your property," the English hadn't seized a single Krupp company.

In a letter to a friend at the Stanford Research Institute, McCloy expressed his anguish:

I am very much puzzled by the English reaction to the release of Krupp. In the first place, the English refused to try any industrialists, and rather criticized us for our vindictiveness in doing so. They could have tried Krupp if they had been willing to but they early indicated that they had no interest. . . . Now, when we let this man out after he has spent five years or more in prison, the English newspapers are making a great howl about it, implying that I took this action as a matter of expediency. Certainly if it had been expedient I would not have dealt in any way with anyone by the name of Krupp. But . . . I could see no reason to keep this man in jail merely because his name was Krupp. Of all the places from which I would least have expected criticism in this case England was first.[48]

He ended by observing that "in a decision such as this, one can only follow one's conscience and not the likelihood of approbation or criticism." There can be no doubt that the American high commissioner was conscientious, dedicated, and determined to do the just thing. Sincerity illumines every line he writes. He was as detached as any man in that difficult position could have been: he had acted as no one's tool; he had done the right as he saw the right.

And yet . . .

✠    ✠    ✠

His vision was exceedingly limited. To Eleanor Roosevelt he wrote, "After detailed study of this case, I could not convince myself that Alfred [sic] Krupp deserved the sentence imposed upon him." It is singular that anyone completing a thorough study of Nuremberg proceedings could confuse Alfred Krupp with Alfried Krupp, and this lapse appears more than once in McCloy's 1951 correspondence. The truth seems to be that no one involved in the clemency decision had taken a really close look at the record. While the commissioner's reply to Justice Wilkins hinted tantalizingly at fresh disclosures ("The evidence, some of which was new, indicated a rather lesser responsibility on his part, if anything"), those revelations were not cited, as, to a member of the overruled tribunal at the very least, they should have been.[49]

There are other anomalies in the commissioner's files for that year. He assured Mrs. Roosevelt that "My finding has no effect on the status of the Krupp plants. The bulk of them have been dismantled . . . what remains is subject to deconcentration law." Yet that same month he suggested to Wilkins a justifiable doubt over the enforceability of that law in dealing with an exonerated defendant: "Krupp, I am told, does not intend to re-engage in the steel business, but whether or not this is merely a present worthy intention which may be altered upon the passage of time I cannot say." Over and over he repeated that he had "inherited these cases" from General Clay, that Krupp had had a right to appeal, that the review was needed for "possible errors of law or fact" — though he enumerated no errors which could have withstood a prosecutor's rebuttal. At times the explanations which went out over his signature verged on sophistry; the confiscation decree had "already been partly rescinded by General Clay" (Clay had merely pointed out that he couldn't enforce it outside the American zone), and in his references to foreign workers he merely mentioned Krupp's "use" of them, never Krupp's *treatment* of them, the hard rock upon which Telford Taylor had built his case.[50]

Obviously the high commissioner was unfamiliar with Taylor's indictment. The story he heard was the tale Alfried had told the tribunal and retold in his appeal to Clay. His lawyers had offered a version of it to the Peck Panel. The panel accepted it — having heard no conflicting account — and passed it up to McCloy. Thus we find the commissioner using, in defense of clemency, the rejected arguments of a convicted defendant. A few examples:

| KRUPP | McCLOY |
|---|---|
| *On prejudice against the family*<br>". . . the name of Krupp was on the list of war criminals . . . because of a notion which is as old as it is fallacious: Krupp wanted war and Krupp made war." (To the Nuremberg tribunal, June 30, 1948.) | "As for the particular case of Alfried Krupp, I find it difficult to understand the reaction on any other basis than the effect of a notorious name." (To Javits, May 10, 1951.) |
| *On bias against arms manufacturers*<br>"Although we were not conscious of any war guilt, we were familiar with the old myth of the war guilt of the armament industry." (To General Clay, August 21, 1948.) | "It is true that the name of Krupp stands as a symbol of the German armaments industry. I was not concerned with a symbol." (To Javits.)<br><br>"It is true that the name of Krupp has become a symbol of evil: the |

KRUPP

McCLOY

German armaments industry; I was concerned, not with a symbol, but with the guilt of an individual, Alfred [*sic*] Krupp." (To Mrs. Roosevelt.)

### On Alfried as a scapegoat

"I consider myself my father's successor in this defendant dock . . . I am here in place of my father." (To the tribunal.)

". . . his father was on his deathbed when these trials took place and this [Alfried] Krupp was next in line." (To Mrs. Roosevelt.)

"Due to the state of his health he [Gustav] was not indicted. Therefore my staff and I were put on trial." (To Clay.)

"I am inclined to think that the son took his father's place in the dock largely because his father was on his deathbed at the time." (To Javits.)

"I never understood how I suddenly came to take my father's place in the proceedings." (To Clay.)

"This man, as you know, was not the real Krupp . . . but was a son who only came into the board late in the war and exerted very little if any influence in the management of the company." (To Karl Brandt at Stamford.)

### On confiscation

"I request you to quash the confiscation of my property . . . as unlawful." (To Clay.)

"No other person has had his private property confiscated." (To Mrs. Roosevelt.)

". . . in no other case was any individual's personal property confiscated." (To Brandt.)

### On crimes against humanity

"It appears that the tribunal [believes] I approved of the government's 'slave labor program' and exploited it in favor of the firm. To me, the government recruitment and allocation of manpower to the armament industry was a measure of

"I also found it very doubtful that he had any responsibility for the use of slave labor in the Krupp plant." (To Javits.)

"Moreover, he was convicted on the slave labor charge. Every plant in the Ruhr of any size had forced

| Krupp | McCloy |
|---|---|
| war economy which we could no more evade than the numerous other government regulations during the war." (To Clay.) | labor, and it was assigned by the government and supervised by the SS and SD groups, the companies having very little if anything to do with the conditions under which they were employed." (To Brandt.) |

So close are these parallels that had the high commissioner known that Alfried had used such language his repetition of it would be inconceivable. Judge Peck and his two colleagues, also men of probity, must have shared his innocence. Inevitably some aspects of the clemency decision remain murky. Everyone was keeping at least one eye on the Korean peninsula. MacArthur's troops had just sustained a grave defeat. Under such circumstances embattled governments withdraw into themselves and make policy in private. The Americans in Germany were, after all, subordinates. We have no way of knowing whether key figures on lower levels received urgent advice from Washington and, believing that the security of the West was in peril, quietly stage-managed the summary reversal of Krupp's conviction. The commissioner and his Clemency Board never have seen the painted scenery, the stage props, the actors, the claque. Anyone sophisticated in the ways of great powers knows how easily these things are done once the right man is given the order. Thereafter the task is completed by cipher clerks, translators, special assistants, public relations men and, of course, lawyers. All this, to repeat, is speculation. If anything of the sort happened it is concealed by bureaucratic haze.

We only know the results. In throwing out the Nuremberg verdict the U.S. proconsul in Frankfurt had in effect reaffirmed Adolf Hitler's special grant, bestowed upon Alfried by a grateful Führer eight winters earlier, affirming that, Reich inheritance laws to the contrary, *die Firma* should be solely owned by Bertha's eldest son. While turning back the Ruhr clock to 1943 McCloy had also made a number of inaccurate statements which damaged General Taylor, General Clay, and the tribunal. In forty days his Clemency Board had made a travesty of years of interrogation and painstaking documentation, and now he cast doubt upon their capacities and even their integrity. One of them bitterly recalled Hitler's "Political Testament," written in his Berlin bunker less than twenty-four hours before he took his life. Predicting that the western democracies would one day beg Germany to join them against Russia, the Führer had dictated to one of his secretaries, Frau Gertrud Junge, ". . . the seed has been sown that will one day lead to the glorious rebirth of the National Socialist movement (*zur strahlenden Wiedergeburt der nationalsozialistischen Bewegung*) of a truly united nation."[51]

Though National Socialism remained discredited, the dream of a truly united nation one day seemed closer to many on that last January afternoon in 1951. But the powers of a superpower are limited. Its Frankfurt viceroy could pardon Alfried Krupp. Its spokesmen could join German newspapers in scouting those who had condemned him. Yet it could not cancel half a line nor wash out a word of history. It could not even rewrite the report of the Peck Panel, which on page 17 of its introduction had declared that while clemency was its goal, "no law can be called upon to defend the murder of Jews and gypsies, the enslavement and accompanying cruel treatment of masses of people, and the wide program . . . which determined who would be resettled and who would be enslaved or destroyed." The report continued, "Murder, pillage and enslavement are against law everywhere and have been for at least the twentieth century."[52]

Murder, pillage, enslavement, and the cruel treatment of masses of people had been practiced on a vast scale within the Konzernherr's *Staat im Staate* in the last mad effusion of National Socialism. The judgment reached at Nuremberg was sound. A large staff of Hauptverwaltungsgebäude publicity men — trained, now, on Madison Avenue — continues to cry out against it, but it cannot be shaken. To paraphrase Mr. Justice Jackson, "Krupp stood before the record of his trial as bloodstained Gloucester stood by the body of his slain king. Gloucester begged of the widow, as Krupp begged: 'Say I slew them not.' And the Queen replied, 'Then say they were not slain. But dead they are.' If you were to say that Krupp was not guilty, it would be as true to say that there had been no Auschwitz fuse factory, no company concentration camps, no Rothschild gassed, no basement torture cage, no infant corpses, no slain, no crime, no war."[53]

The author handed John J. McCloy an audit of discrepancies between his 1951 statements about Alfried and the Nuremburg transcript. The retired commissioner read it carefully. Then, he handed it back, commenting, "That's ancient history." By then it was indeed history, though hardly ancient. The murder of thirteen-year-old King Edward V and his younger brother in the Tower of London is quite different, however. It goes back to the first weeks of August 1483, and like so many of history's legendary figures the victims' thirty-one-year-old uncle, who became King Richard III, has been distorted by the lens of time. Britain flourished during his brief reign, for he was the innovator of wise legislative measures and an energetic administrator. His fatal flaw, in the eyes of a contemporary, was his "innate ferocity." Another chronicler wrote, "He was not a monster; but a typical man in an age of strange contradictions of character, of culture combined with cruelty, and of an emotional temper that was capable of high ends, though unscrupulous of means."

His means were his undoing. Despite his personal heroism he died at

Bosworth Field because Englishmen were convinced that he had been responsible for the deaths of the two princes in the Tower, "for which cause," the *Chronicles of London* tell us, "King Richard lost the hearts of the people."

In this Gloucester differed from Krupp, who emerged from Landsberg's heavy doors at the stroke of 9 A.M. on the bitter morning of Saturday, February 3, 1951, and led the twenty-eight other freed prisoners, including four former generals, out through a thick smoke-colored fog. He heard a great shout, accompanied by the running of many feet, and discovered that he had become a national idol.[54]

# 27

✠

# The Germans
# Are Being Treated Like Niggers

B EYOND the mist stood Berthold, holding a floppy bouquet of jonquils and tulips and shivering in a fur-collared coat. On one side of him Otto Kranzbühler, the Direktorium, and their staffs were lined up shoulder to shoulder; they had been up all night driving the three hundred miles from Essen to be here. Bertha was absent. She felt no charity for the Amis and refused to give them the satisfaction of knowing that she had come to see her son released by grace of America's *Hoher Kommissar*. Bertha Krupp was really the person to whom Eleanor Roosevelt should have written. The exchange would be invaluable.[1]

On the other side of Berthold there was, of all things, a laundry truck. It was a ruse. The week before, he had bought a big new Porsche, one of the first of the *Wirtschaftswunderland*'s expensive sports cars to be sold in the Fatherland. Picking up his brother in a gleaming status symbol wouldn't help the family's reputation, so he had parked the Porsche in a borrowed garage several blocks away and, rather in the style of Metternich's improvised flight from Vienna on a laundry wagon, hired this Volkswagen microbus. *Schneeweisse Wäsche*, read the lettering on the side — Snow-White Laundry. In the fog it emitted a ghostly glow, but renting it had been a sensible precaution. Behind the solid rank of directors stood virtually every reporter, foreign correspondent, and motion picture cameraman in Germany.

As Alfried strode into view Berthold realized that his brother was in no condition for a press conference. A Krupp, their father had taught them, should always be *ein Mann mit hochmütigem Auftreten*, a man of haughty appearance. Alfried seemed healthy and in good spirits, but his skin was colorless, and the Americans had dressed him in outsized ski pants and a blue-gray jacket of coarse weave. He looked less like a tycoon than a Wehrmacht POW returning from Russia. Nothing could be done about the prison pallor; the journalists would (and did) describe him as "drawn." The clothes could be remedied, however. Luckily, the foresighted younger brother had rented a suite in Landsberg's finest hotel and brought a change of attire. While the directors warded off the press, promising a press conference once Krupp had breakfasted, Berthold whisked Alfried into the hotel. After a hot shower the pardoned industrialist slipped into a silk shirt, white tie, and the tailor-made suit Karl Dohrmann had carefully pressed last evening. Downstairs the breakfast arrangements appeared to be proceeding admirably. The proprietor, Herr Schmidt, had set one table for the delegation from Essen and another, on a lower level, for the press. No one could question Krupp until he had collected himself and been briefed on the latest developments in the world beyond bars.

Then, in a stroke, Schmidt destroyed all the meticulous arrangements for a good image. To Berthold's horror, he saw a waiter approaching with champagne. It hadn't been ordered; it was a gesture from the hosteler, who wanted to show Alfried how every good German felt that morning. Nearly fifteen years later Berthold still winced at the memory: "The reporters were watching, and naturally they all wrote that we were having a 'champagne breakfast' (*Champagnerfrühstück*). It was in headlines all around the world." Alfried himself once murmured, "Two bottles for forty people — it didn't seem like too much. But Mr. McCloy was very annoyed." That was a typical Alfriedian understatement. In Frankfurt the commissioner was beside himself. He too had to think about his image, and he thought a businessman should have a better sense of what was fitting.

By 10:45 the dishes had been cleared away. Outside, the street by the laundry van was clear; the twenty-eight other pardoned Nazis had slipped away unnoticed. Berthold decided to meet the press out there, hoping the weather would discourage correspondents. It didn't. And in performance the Germans among them were the worst offenders. They thought Herr Schmidt's taste flawless, and wrote — inaccurately, since the Austrian border was closed to Krupp — that he had enjoyed an admirable cuisine "prior to his departure for Blühnbach Castle, where his mother was waiting for him."

"At his press conference," Jack Raymond of the *New York Times* cabled his office, "he was greeted like a returning hero. Photographers and newsreel men milled about, taking his picture from all angles for nearly a half-hour."[2] Those films and negatives survive. In them Berthold is radiant, Kranzbühler thoughtful, and the directors anxious for some sign from Alfried, some signal of what he wants them to do. There was none. After nearly six years of imprisonment he was the same Krupp: impassive and a trifle bored. He might have been pondering whether it had been a good wine or a bad wine.

Except that he wasn't. His replies to questions from the more persistent foreign correspondents reveal that on a loftier level he was as image-conscious as his brother. He didn't fawn. He wouldn't have known how. For the most part he shrewdly refrained from comment. Asked whether the Pope and Bethlehem Steel had intervened in his behalf, he looked blank. Asked whether he had any views on codetermination, under which workers would share in management decisions, he had none. Inquiries about his immediate plans were turned aside with the reminder that his plants remained in the hands of Allied trustees. He sidestepped the issues of deconcentration and decartelization and deftly pointed out that since the confiscation decree had never been carried out, he expected no red tape, legal tangles, or bookkeeping problems.

Some journalists had come with honed blades. It wasn't always possible to dodge them, though he deflected the worst. One dealt with his Justizpalast conviction. He replied quietly, *"In Nürnberg wurde ich von der Hauptanklage freigesprochen, jedoch zweier leichterer Anklagen schuldig gefunden"* (I was acquitted of the main charge at Nuremberg and found guilty on two lesser charges). He might have been asked why he considered crimes against humanity and plunder "lesser charges," but the anomaly flew by unnoticed. Another reporter invited him to renounce the Führer. This was the twentieth anniversary of his association with the SS, an excellent opportunity to shed the past. He shrugged his shoulders and declined: *"Wir müssten noch einmal den ganzen Verhandlungsbericht durchkauen. Ersparen Sie mir das, bitte"* (We would have to rehash the whole trial record. Please spare me all that). There was little they could say. They hadn't hashed it in the first place. The most awkward question dealt with rearmament: Would he produce guns and tanks again? He couldn't nod without arousing the fifty-one nations which had warred with the Reich; on the other hand, a negative answer might require subsequent retraction: he was keenly aware of the critical situation south of Seoul.[3]

He walked a tightrope: "Personally, I have neither the inclination nor the intention of doing so. Actually, I think, the problem will be resolved by the German government, not by my own desires. I hope that events will never again compel Krupp to enter the munitions business, but what a plant makes depends, after all, not only on the decisions of its owner but also on official policies. My life has always been determined by the course of history, not by me" (*Mein Leben ist immer vom Lauf der Geschichte, nicht von mir selbst, bestimmt worden*).[4]

With that, his brother had him in the microbus. The press, scribbling, was taken unawares; before the first of them could pull away Berthold had turned two corners. The switch to the Porsche went off without incident. Skirting Munich on the back roads south of Dachau, they reached the tiny village of Walsertal by early afternoon, and there, in a hotel overlooking a deep, snow-filled valley, their sixty-four-year-old mother awaited them. From Walsertal they drove to Berchtesgaden. Blühnbach lay just across the border, and the Austrians were unlikely to remain difficult. Once the right Viennese were approached in the right way Alfried would be able to reoccupy the castle. After all, it belonged to him. He wanted an active vacation; it would be good to race down the Alps on skis once again. Nevertheless his first concern was the Konzern. He was eager to see it and see what could be done with it. Gently Berthold reminded him that a return wasn't that simple. Although the American high commissioner had overruled an American verdict, he had no authority in the British zone. To be sure, the redtabs had evacuated the Essen Hof last fall, but Villa Hügel remained the headquarters of the Combined Control Group, supervising the production of all Ruhr coal. There was also the matter of decentralization. The Allies had strange feelings about cartels and economic power. Lawyers would have to handle that.[5]

After a long reunion with Bertha and a longer holiday, Alfried bought a souped-up Porsche of his own and drove home to Essen. At the foot of Hügel hill, on Frankenstrasse, just three doors from an inn occupied by English officers working for the Control Group, Berthold and Uncle Tilo had taken over a "Drei-Zimmer," a three-room house. Berthold and the baron had furnished two offices there; the third became Krupp's. Alfried moved in with his brother and Jean Sprenger and began an intensive study of Allied High Commission Law 27, the barrier that stood between him and reoccupation of his throne. Its authors had believed that it would break the great German monopolies which had dominated European industry, fueling three wars in three generations, and provide the country with viable, competitive firms. Krupp, like his fellow barons, saw it as a bludgeon whose real purpose was to reduce German economic strength. If enforced, they believed, it would permanently transform old Reich markets into British and French spheres of influence.[6]

The enforcement of Law 27 was vigorous. Flick, for example, was being forced to sell his basic industries and buy into Mercedes-Benz. The Vereinigte Stahlwerke had been broken up into thirteen independent companies. I. G. Farben was becoming a name from the past. Very soon 90 percent of the Third Reich's industry would be wholly decartelized, and Krupp's directors, crowding into the drei-Zimmer for their first meeting out of stir, were pessimistic. In a hopeless monotone Fritz von Bülow said, "We might as well pull down Villa Hügel." Another director suggested he sell out. "Never!" Krupp snapped. "I won't sell my people like cattle." Again that word: Stücke. But after six years it had a quaint ring.[7]

That evening he strolled up the winding streets toward Hügel Park. He came up over the brow of the hill and glimpsed, in the fading twilight, the huge limestone castle where he had been born and where he had at various times seen the Kaiser, a vindictive French general, the Führer, and the Duce; the ceremony celebrating his own succession under the Lex Krupp; the massive RAF bombings; and his arrest on that drowsy April morning in 1945. Impulsively he stepped toward it. After fifteen steps he stopped dead. Around a corner he had encountered a sign ten feet tall reading:

KEINE BESUCHER AUSSER FÜR AMTLICHE ZWECKE!
(NO VISITORS EXCEPT ON OFFICIAL BUSINESS!)

He turned his back and strode swiftly back to Frankenstrasse. Looking out on the layers of rust coating the moonscape of the Gusstahlfabrik in the city below Bredeney he felt like an "outcast in his ruins" (*ein Paria zwischen Ruinen*), the victim of "injustice rampant" (*die Übersteigerung des Unrechts*).[8]

❧       ❧       ❧

Yet he had known it would be a long, deep game, and despite outward appearances his position was excellent. To be sure, Kruppstahl was no longer needed in Korea; two days after Alfried's release the Chinese had launched a major offensive, but MacArthur blunted its spearhead in four days, and less than a month later the United Nations reoccupied Seoul. The war was a stalemate. The Cold War temperature seemed perfectly fixed below zero, however, and the dynasty's three traditional specialties — research, quality, and the most highly skilled work force anywhere in the world — were vital to a militant Europe. The Ruhr, in Norman Pounds's phrase, had become "a political weapon, a symbol and source of military strength and potentially an instrument of a sort of political blackmail." Moreover, the instrument had grown larger. Excluding isolated Berlin, Essen was the third largest city in Chancellor Adenauer's new Bundesrepublik Deutschland — the Federal Republic of [West] Germany. "*Dieu*," Voltaire observed, "*est toujours pour les gros bataillons.*"[9]

Voltaire also wrote, "*L'histoire n'est que le tableau des crimes et des malheurs*," but the Germans Adenauer led refused to believe that their history was a scroll of crimes and misfortunes. They had left a shocking record of one and had been cruelly penalized by the other. Even so, their faith in idealism, stability, and dependability remained intact. The story of early Germany had not been titled *Vaterländische Historie* by chance.[10] The Fatherland was the land where fathers had ruled, ruled in 1951, and rule today. In Essen, where Kruppianer doffed their caps when they recognized the pardoned Konzernherr, that national characteristic was Alfried's political trump. Some four million German widows, mourning their martyred husbands in lonely rooms, and a million and a half crippled Wehrmacht veterans, many of them begging in the streets, rejected Nuremberg's indictments of the warlords and their armorer. Deceived by two virile father figures in two catastrophic wars, they nevertheless yearned for new symbols of severity, masculinity, and paternalism. Adenauer suited them for that reason; so did Krupp.

The suzerain of an anachronistic feudal kingdom whose roots lay nearly four centuries in the past and which had endured into the second half of the twentieth century, Alfried was as Teutonic as the Black Forest. His countrymen applauded the firm's discrimination between blue-collar workers and white-collar employees. They thrilled to his repetition of the dynastic demand that "*der Fabrikeigentümer Herr in seinem Hause sein und bleiben müsse*" (The factory owner must remain master in his own house). And from the Franco-German frontier to the Russian watchtowers on the Thuringian ridges the people approved his vow, "*Krupps Reich wird ewig bestehen*" (There'll always be a Kruppdom). Even in the Deutsche Demokratische Republik of East Germany designers of the Leipzig Industrial Fair, erecting an exhibit for the Ernst Thällmann Werk added "(formerly Krupp)" to attract spectators. The entire Reich had become aroused by Alfried's demand for a return to "*das monarchische Prinzip*" and to the old Krupp spirit. There was even a phrase for that: *der alte Krupp-Geist*.[11]

In his study of Vickers, J. D. Scott wrote that the British arms firm, like Krupp, was "a national institution." He added candidly, "And Vickers has, of course, a kind of innate understanding of the working of Whitehall, of the relations of civil servants to ministers, and the operations of government" — a concession that no one in the Hauptverwaltungsgebäude has ever made. Vickers is so service-minded that decorated combat veterans are given preference and the dining hall is called a mess. *Krupp-Geist* is rather more complicated. Undeniably there was a muted sound of rolling drums in the Ruhr when Alfried was released. Yet Ruhrgebiet workmen were more dedicated than Midlands workmen — the departing British officially noted that they had found the typical Kruppianer to be "industrious, efficient and an exceedingly knowledgeable worker, knowing fully what he wanted to accomplish" — because they saw their employer in a different light. They were stirred by the memories of great battles won by Krupp weapons, but their fidelity was more filial than chauvinistic. Krupp fulfilled their longing for a strong, benevolent *geistiger Vater*.[12]

This was the Krupp the Palace of Justice had never seen, who sponsored sewing and home economics schools for women, apprentice shops for all boys beginning at the age of fourteen, an 85,000-volume public library, free hospital care for every citizen of Essen (including employees of other companies), three-room apartments at ten dollars a month for families awaiting reopening of the shops, and exhibitions on "Creative Leisure Time." Harald von Bohlen has suggested that "The name of Krupp projects what in physics is called radiation." His political opponents agree. Although 52 percent of Essen's postwar voters belong to the SPD, Fritz

Heine, a former member of the party's executive committee, said thoughtfully, "The whole town is still fascinated by Krupp. It's unique, amazing; even our own people are caught up in it. The workers marry these two — Krupp and the SPD. I don't know how they do it, but they do it."[13]

Once the author was sharing a dinner pail with Heinrich Heyer, Albert Gregorius, and Hermann Frisch, the three leaders of the Gusstahlfabrik union. All were Social Democrats. If anyone knew the temper in the shops, they did; among them they represented one hundred and forty-one years of service to the firm. One said solemnly, "You know, I would die for Alfried Krupp." To appreciate the significance of this an American must try to imagine Walter Reuther saying that he would die for Henry Ford. A hard core of Communists, about 3 percent of the whole, remained card carriers. But even Krupp Communists are different. Debating the issue of guns against Russia, they voted: "If the company begins making arms again the workmen should protest, but not strike" (*protestieren, aber nicht streiken*). Alfried knew why: "They know I am responsible for their lasting employment, as Krupps have been since my great-grandfather" (*wie es die Krupps seit meinem Urgrossvater immer waren*).

Had they — and the rest of the Federal Republic — believed in his guilt, his bargaining power vis-à-vis the western allies would have dissolved. Few did. Much later a younger generation of German intellectuals would grope toward an understanding of the essence of the National Socialist government in which Alfried had been so deeply involved, though the revisionists never had much luck penetrating the inner Ruhr. As late as 1964, when *Der Stellvertreter* was produced in Essen, the scenes depicting Krupp at Auschwitz were eliminated.[14] (Again, a hypothetical parallel: one cannot conceive of a major play about the sitdown strikes of the 1930's appearing in Detroit with all references to Ford cut. If it did happen every newspaper editor in the country would put the story on page one. In West Germany the scissoring of Hochhuth's drama passed unnoticed.) A quarter-century after Stalingrad and the *Endlösung*, Essen engineers explain Hitler as a phenomenon created by seven million jobless men, a national leader who, despite his flawed foreign policy, should also be remembered for his magnificent skein of superhighways and "the Volkswagen, which he personally created in 1938 almost in its present design, right down to the organization of cylinders." In the last two years of the war, of course, "Hitler lost his mind." Note the tense. The Führer's sanity was unchallenged until he began to lose.

The accepted version of Alfried's own record is highly colored, and its hold on the Ruhr in 1951 was a political reality of incalculable value. Some canards were diverting. It was widely believed, for instance, that the first GIs to enter Essen had been "Polish mercenaries" ordered to avenge the Poles in Krupp camps, and that they had sacked much of Villa Hügel. Misapprehensions about Nuremberg were less trivial. Indeed, some members of General Taylor's staff came to believe that McCloy's release of Alfried was far less damaging than his failure to approve German publication of the Justizpalast proceedings. Lacking facts, Kruppianer absorbed specious distortions. They were persuaded that the firm's rearmament after Versailles had been entirely legal, that Hitler had threatened Krupp with confiscation if he refused to build the Berthawerk, that Alfried had been sentenced by the tribunal solely because he had manufactured arms. The most sensitive topic was slave labor. Understandably, those who had testified against the Konzernherr kept quiet or vanished altogether. Others who had seen chattels at work or in the camps refused to discuss them. Thus the fable arose that all workers who had taken the stand had denied slave abuse, and that Krupp had actually been reprimanded by the SS and SD for overfeeding foreign workers.

In Germany, as in India after the Raj, a prison record was a badge of pride. It was in this climate that an industrialist said, "If I attacked Herr Krupp publicly I'd be out of a job. In fact, if I even dictated a letter criticizing him, I'd have trouble with my secretary." A Düsseldorf economist explained why decentralization wouldn't work in Essen: "Most Germans feel that Krupp is entitled to keep his property. They feel this way because of Krupp's previous role. Public opinion would be against any person who tried to buy properties he was forced to sell. If an American firm did so this would be especially true; the newcomer would have trouble in the Ruhr." On this issue, the magazine *Capital* noted, "the Ruhr stands together; no buyer could be found."

The Allied high commissioners approached Alfried gingerly. All three of them were involved now; Krupp's humpty-dumpty couldn't be put back together again, even in part, without their consent. Beginning in September 1951 the sessions, which were to stretch over eighteen months, were held around a long, highly polished table in Mehlem, the commissioners' headquarters. Alfried, flanked by lawyers and aides, faced teams of Americans, British, and French. It was an unprecedented tableau: after the greatest war in history a private citizen was negotiating a peace treaty with three nations. And Alfried had come determined to drive a hard bargain. At the first meeting a U.S. lawyer handed him a pen and a prepared statement:

> I have no intention of returning to the basic coal and steel industries in Germany [*Ich beabsichtige nicht, wieder in Deutschland in die Grundstoffindustrien Kohle und Stahl zurückzukehren*], and I promise not to

use any of the moneys which I may receive from the sale of properties or investments under this plan to buy into the basic coal or steel industries in Germany.[15]

It wasn't even a good try. Krupp handed back pen and paper. His lawyers, he said, had advised him that such a pact would violate the

Bundesrepublik constitution. (The Allies neglected to mention the Lex Krupp, which had also been unconstitutional.) At the next summit conference — these were held at irregular intervals, with attorneys quibbling in between — Alfried submitted a counterproposal limiting whatever pledge he might make to ten years. Here, as at Nuremberg, he insisted that the proceedings were entirely political. He added that political issues, as everyone present had observed during the past year, were subject to rapid change. Justice wasn't involved. To be realistic, the agreement was a form of appeasement: "After all, this is nothing more than a political declaration designed to throw a sop (*Beruhigungsbrocken*) to certain elements of public opinion among the populations of the nations which formed the coalition against the Reich."[16]

McCloy accepted the ten-year provision. Sir Brian Robertson rejected it and so, more passionately, did André François-Poncet, France's high commissioner. His countrymen were painfully aware that the Germans always treated Frenchmen shabbily, but lately the Teutons had been surpassing themselves. While receiving four billion dollars in aid, they had repaid less than one percent of the havoc their Wehrmacht had created in France; countless thousands of French citizens had been murdered between 1940 and 1945, yet the Allies had hanged or jailed scarcely a thousand culprits, most of whom, like Krupp, were now free again; of the 80,000 machine tools pilfered from French plants, fewer than one in ten had been returned.[17]

Krupp was unmoved. He held the strong hand. François-Poncet's own government had, at the moment, every reason to oppose decentralization. The Ruhr's coking coal was still Europe's best; Krupp foundries were the natural market for the continent's richest iron beds — in French Lorraine. Now Robert Schuman had advanced a revolutionary proposal. Hitler had hoarded his coal. Under the Schuman Plan, Germany would sell coal to all buyers. In return, her heavy industry would be unshackled. The Plan would be administered by a High Authority and an assembly responsible to no government. Like it or not, any economist who had studied the history of European customs unions knew that the forces generated by Schuman would be centripetal. It was a time for making omelets, not unscrambling them.

Alfried dropped his proposal that he confine his pledge to ten years; Sir Brian and François-Poncet made certain concessions. Krupp then implied that he might accept the principle of segregating his heavy industry from his other holdings, and the wrangling went on, month after month, over definitions. "*Stahl-oder eisenerzeugende Industrie*" was too vague, he insisted; in German it meant *all* steel- or iron-producing industries, which, technically, would include the Widia tungsten carbide works. Widia wasn't a mass producer of steel; he meant to keep it. For a long period everything bogged down while linguistic experts reworked phrases in three languages. Eventually they hammered out a "letter of definition," to be attached to the final accord as an appendix.[18] Actually it was unnecessary. Krupp had no intention of abiding by it. He privately called it a form of blackmail (*Art von Erpressung*), an extorted signature which would be used to placate American newspapers. His sole purpose in haggling was to drill as many holes as possible in the final document. In the end he was to reduce it to a sieve.

☒    ☒    ☒

During the first two years of his new freedom Krupp's whereabouts were unknown for weeks at a time. Later some of these absences were to be explained, to the dismay and fury of the Mehlem negotiators, but no one thought them odd then; he was notoriously antisocial. His headquarters continued to be in Bredeney, yet he postponed his first post-Landsberg public appearance in Essen for a full year. Even then, it was perfunctory. The occasion was the seventieth birthday of Theo Goldschmidt, owner of a large chemical company and a Ruhr baron. The party was held in Essen's Kaiserhof. Karl Sabel, the ubiquitous star reporter of the *Westdeutsche Allgemeine Zeitung*, sidled up to Alfried. What, he wanted to know, did the Konzernherr think of the Allied bombing of German civilians? The orthodox response would have been that it had been an atrocity; Alfried, however, shook his head. He said, "All that's happened, we want to forget about that. We want to go forward."[19]

In point of fact he had no intention of forgetting. His humiliation in British prison camps and at Nuremberg, the stigma of conviction as a major Nazi war criminal, burned within him and would one day blaze high. At the same time, there can be no doubt that he was sincere in wanting to look ahead. He couldn't hate intensely just now because, among other things, he was in love. Shortly after his release he had begun dating the girl he had known as Fräulein Vera Hossenfeldt. Here Alfried was getting into something wholly beyond his experience. He was accustomed to his regal mother, his meek first wife, stodgy *Hausfrauen*, and overdressed Schlotbaroninnen who treated their husbands like lords. Vera belonged to a new breed. Beautiful, petite, with a heart-shaped face, a stunning figure, a yearning for adventure and no conspicuous inhibitions, she was one of the charter members of the jet set. Krupp was defenseless against such a woman. She could devour him. She did.

Her origins — a tradition in such alliances — are obscure. Apparently her father sold insurance. Somehow she was introduced to highly eligible bachelors, including a baron named Langer, who proposed, was accepted, and, once the new baroness had shed her bridal veil, rejected for a certain Frank Wisbar. Frank hadn't a title. He was in motion pictures, however, and that sounded exciting, especially when he proposed that they try their luck in Hollywood. Unhappily, neither Frank nor Vera read newspapers much. German stock was very low in California, and Herr and Frau Wisbar found every studio gate closed to them. Vera was reduced to a job as salesgirl in a department store. But clever girls with her charm are meant to buy, not sell. She quickly switched employers, becoming receptionist for a refugee doctor. Dr. Knauer was busy, rich, and a naturalized American. Frank was still haunting the studios in vain. In a brilliant triple play Vera divorced Frank in Las Vegas, married the doctor, divorced *him*, and returned to the Fatherland with a thick roll of alimony, a new coiffure, a trunk packed with the latest fashions, and a sheaf of letters from a Landsberg convict.[20]

Alfried was enchanted. Any man who has seen his property snatched from him, his family decimated, and himself fined a half-billion dollars and locked in a cell with a tin bucket can be fairly said to be on the rebound. The same, of course, is true of any girl who has survived a German baron, a discredited Reich, show business, clerking in a Los Angeles department store, and handling medical patients. They quickly caught one another and were married in Berchtesgaden on May 19, 1952. In some ways the episode was like Krupp's flight from Herr Schmidt's champagne breakfast. Berthold, who had become the Otto Skorzeny of the family, laid on a baker's truck for transportation, bribed the mayor to keep his mouth shut after officiating, asked the proprietor of Berchtesgaden's swankest inn — Freddi Stöll, the former skiing star — to serve with Frau Stöll as witnesses, and parked his brother's high-powered sports car outside for a quick getaway.[21]

Borrowing Freddi's battered auto, Alfried drove Vera to the office of the local registrar. Before the Rathaus could spread the word, the wedding was over. At the wedding dinner in the inn's dining room (quaintly decorated with empty Chianti bottles) the groom gave the bride fifteen tulips, a dozen roses, and title to the most expensive Porsche on the market. She, wearing a light suit, a striped scarf, and a hat which looked rather like a warped land mine, responded that whatever the record showed, Alfried was the only man she had ever loved. At that he beamed. Freddi took a picture of it; though scarcely credible, there is Krupp, looking positively jolly. After rapid-fire good-byes they made a run for it. The Porsche engine roared and Alfried raced down the mountain beside a woman with a colorful past who had just acquired the astonishing name of Frau Vera Hossenfeldt von Langer Wisbar Knauer Krupp von Bohlen und Halbach.

It was a long honeymoon. It had to be; Krupp still had no fixed base, and at times Vera must have had the impression that they were on the lam. During that first year they were almost constantly moving between Mehlem and five separate residences. As a fixed base the Bredeney house which Berthold and Jean Sprenger had confiscated would have been ideal, but it had become overcrowded. Jean had enlarged his workshop, and

Jean's brother had acquired a new wife and moved in. Therefore the Berchtesgaden newlyweds shunted between there, Blühnbach, Walsertal, Fritz Krupp's old shooting box near Coblenz, and a villa Alfried leased at Hösel, a village between Kettwig and Ratingen about twenty minutes from Essen. The British continued to wear out their welcome in Hügel, though that didn't much matter; Vera took one look at the castle's north façade and almost threw up. Alfried didn't intend to live there anyhow. For symbolic reasons it must remain his official residence. Their day-to-day life, however, would be spent in a smaller, ultramodern mansion which was rising inside the park.[22]

Like his great-grandfather he had personally chosen the site and picked the workmen. With fifteen rooms and five personal servants, not counting bodyguards, Alfried thought he, Vera, and their stable of racing cars could live comfortably. She agreed, though she was less enthusiastic than he was about Bertha's decision to leave Austria and occupy the Villa Spingorrum, an old red brick house just fifty yards down the street at number 10 Berenberger Mark. The old woman needed only one servant, but no sentry in Germany could have kept her away from her son. Already Vera was muttering to a friend, "Seine Mutter Bertha hat ein zu strenges Hausregiment geführt" (His mother Bertha ran house discipline like a tyrant).[23]

No one noticed interfamilial friction, for the new couple was moving too fast. Vera enjoyed being a nomad, and at this period in Alfried's life she was the perfect company wife, drawing him out and skillfully manipulating his re-emergence into public life. When Irmgard was remarried in Dortmund to a Bavarian landowner on June 19, she guided Krupp to his pew and gracefully helped her timid sister-in-law become Frau von Bohlen und Halbach Raitz von Frenz Eilenstein. (Irmgard wasn't as frail as she looked; during the next decade she gave birth to six children and, in the long run, proved an astute manager of her husband's estate.) Vera's next stroke was brilliant. On July 4 the big American consulate in Düsseldorf traditionally opened its door to all Americans in the Ruhr, and as Dr. Knauer's ex-wife she claimed eligibility, towing her lanky, brooding husband behind her. The call turned into a diplomatic coup. The German public was delighted, which pleased the surprised consulate, which made the bargaining in Mehlem a trifle smoother. Although Alfried Krupp was as uneasy at public functions as Alfred Krupp had been, they were important to him; as Vera dragged him to exhibitions, concerts, one-man shows, and gala openings the legend took on flesh and blood. Admittedly the flesh was gaunt and the blood thin. In Hügel's family archives there is a photograph of the Konzernherr striding past a gigantic granite bust of his grandfather, unveiled at Kiel in these years to honor "Friedrich Alfred Krupp's longtime membership in the Kiel Imperial Yachting Club, as a member of which he participated in many pre–World War I regattas." Alfried looks stonier than

Fritz, but the dense throng of camera-toting Germans in the background is obviously pleased.[24]

Left to his own devices — and there were times when Vera did leave him, prowling the fashionable shops of Düsseldorf's Königsallee and stuffing her Porsche with loot — he toyed with his own new cameras, listened to Wagner, or haunted the Essener Hof as Gustav, Fritz, and Alfred had before him. The hotel hadn't been returned to him yet, but a celebrated hotelier had completely redecorated it, hurling the swagger sticks left behind by redtabs into trash cans and modernizing the guest rooms. The lounges and public rooms had been restored to their nineteenth-century style. All the Wilhelmine horrors were back, and here, surrounded by ornate balconies, crooked stairways, drab carpets and ponderous furniture, Krupp felt like a Krupp.[25]

One evening in the summer of 1952 this overdressed tomb was invaded by the unlikeliest guest in its long history, a thirty-eight-year-old Pomeranian named Berthold Beitz. Beitz was a product of the *Wirtschaftswunderland;* in the old Germany he could never have achieved eminence. The son of a Greifswald bank teller, he had served his own teller's apprenticeship when war broke out. Joining the German Shell Company in Hamburg, he had avoided military service by managing the Boryslav oil fields in occupied Poland. After the war his lack of a Nazi Party number earned him a job in the British zonal insurance administration. Though he had never even seen an actuarial table, he prospered on bluff, hiring ex-Nazis with insurance experience to work for him. By the end of the airlift he had become general manager of the Germania-Iduna Insurance Company, and in four years his salesmanship had raised the firm from sixth to third place in the Bundesrepublik's insurance industry.[26]

Handsome, extroverted, and fast-talking, Beitz made no secret of his admiration for *die neueste Madison-Avenue-Mode.* When rivals contemptuously christened him *"der Amerikaner,"* he elatedly advertised the fact. He wore charcoal-gray flannel suits, became a jazz addict (*jazzsüchtig*), and used American slang. Every proposal to reach his desk was tagged either "OK" or, if he intended to torpedo it, "KO"; and he affectionately described his mother as *"ein tough baby."* In a nation devoted to titles and protocol Beitz insisted upon aggressive informality. He had a set speech for new employees: *"Nennen Sie mich einfach Beitz, wenn mir Ihre Arbeit gefällt, werde ich Sie beim Vornamen anreden"* (Call me Beitz. If I like your work, I'll call you by your first name).[27]

Given a choice that summer evening in Alfried's second year of freedom, *der Amerikaner* would have preferred to be at home in Hamburg, listening to Louis Armstrong or Muggsy Spanier and tapping his well-shined shoe. To him the renovated Essener Hof was as square as a toy block. But Jean Sprenger's studio was here, and Beitz, to shake up old Hamburgers, had commissioned Sprenger to carve a nine-foot slick nude for Germania-Iduna's new glass-walled administration building. Unable to survive Essen's depressing night life without a martini and spirited company, he invited Sprenger and Berthold von Bohlen to join him for dinner. At Alfried's customary corner table, to the left of the fireplace, Berthold asked Beitz whether he would like to meet his famous brother. "OK," said Beitz, beaming. As he later recalled, "After all, I was young and the name of Krupp had a magic sound (*einen magischen Klang*) for me."[28]

Berthold said he would arrange it within the next few days. He was, of course, wholly unaware that he had just ignited a slow fuse that would eventually help demolish the ancient edifice which had survived the All-Highest, the French occupation, the Führer, the Royal Air Force, and Nuremberg.

✠　✠　✠

In Mehlem the three "blackmailers" from Washington, London, and Paris were less affected by the *Klang* of Alfried's name. They insisted he renounce privileges which he considered his birthright. The negotiators tried to keep their tempers, but once a hoarse voice on Krupp's side of the table muttered "*Die Deutschen werden wie Nigger behandelt!*" (The Germans are being treated like niggers!), and Alfried, in a swift diversion, demanded that Sir Brian restore three hundred and seventy art treasures which, servants had told him, had been stolen from Villa Hügel. It was an indication of the ebbing Allied tide that Whitehall immediately put a top agent on the job and tracked most of them down. By September 1952 the basic terms of the treaty had been hammered out. Each of Alfried's four brothers and sisters and his nephew, Arnold von Bohlen, were to receive ten million marks (2.5 million dollars) in cash or equivalent stock in two of his companies, Capito und Klein (rolled steel) in Düsseldorf and Westfälische Drahtindustrie (wire) in Hamm. All Bertha's children except Alfried would share ownership of Klausheide, a small seed factory near the Belgian border on the site of Gustav's agricultural fiasco, with young Arnold; it had been named in memory of his father's Luftwaffe heroism. Harald's funds would be held in escrow until whenever, if ever, the Russians released him. Under Allied High Commission Law 27, all German coal and steel companies were to be removed from Krupp control. He would retain his truck, locomotive, and shipbuilding interests. In compensation for his losses he would receive 25 million pounds sterling — 70 million dollars.[29]

When the announcement of this tentative decision was made in October, its echoes made Parliament tremble. "The uproar caused by the McCloy decision was remarkably violent, especially in the British press," Alistair Horne wrote in the London Daily *Telegraph*, "but it was nothing compared to the furor which arose when the Allied High Commission were forced to reveal . . . the terms of their plan to 'liquidate' the Krupp empire." A cartoonist for the *Sunday Pictorial* depicted Alfried looking out over a forest of smoking chimneys while the figure of Death egged him on with bony fingers. In the House of Commons, Foreign Secretary Anthony Eden survived a torrent of questions only by blaming the Labour government, which, he said, had provided for compensation. Allied law, he declared, made no provision for confiscation — an outright fiction which slipped past the opposition.* Indeed, he said, the law actually required payment.[30]

Even that wasn't good enough, so he went farther. "It is the government's purpose," he added, "to ensure that Herr Krupp shall not be allowed to use the proceeds of sale of his holdings to buy his way back into the coal and steel industries or otherwise to acquire a controlling interest. The means of achieving that end are under discussion in Germany between the High Commission and the Federal government." Krupp did not reply directly. However, he did order Hardach, acting as his spokesman, to issue a statement describing all attempts to bar him from his mines and foundries as "a barrier which is against the German constitution, a denial of ordinary human rights and a suppression of freedom of trade." That set off another tumult in England. On Armistice Day, James Cameron published a polemic in the *Daily Mirror* under the headline, THE LAPDOG OF WAR IS STILL HOWLING FOR JUSTICE, and in the House, Clement Davies again raised the issue of compensation. "The restoration of such a vast sum of money to the family whose activities were of such assistance to Hitler has deeply shocked people everywhere," he said. "Inasmuch as Krupp has been found guilty of using slave labor and taking other people's property, is it not possible to devote some of this wealth to the people who have suffered?"[31]

It was an awkward question, and since some of the people who had suffered had lawyers, too, it was to bedevil Alfried to the end of his life. Unfortunately for them, they weren't much use in the Cold War. German public opinion and Krupp expertise were more useful, and so, after a lull of nearly four months, the Krupp Treaty was drawn up in its final form. The *Definitionsbrief* stipulated that Alfried was banned from

> . . . *legierten Stahl auf irgendeine andere Weise herzustellen als in kleinen Quantitäten, wie es Eigenart der Unternehmen sei, die im Besitz von Alfried Krupp bleiben.*

> . . . manufacturing alloy steel by any formula except in small amounts incidental to the firms which are to remain the property of Alfried Krupp.

---

* Reprise: Allied Control Council Law No. 10, dated Berlin, December 20, 1945, and signed on behalf of the U.K. by Field Marshal B. L. Montgomery, specified "forfeiture of property," without qualification. (*Official Gazette of the Control Council for Germany*, Berlin, 1946.)

This was also to be true of "the hot rolling of steel" (*das Warmwalzen von Stahl*). However, the letter of definition declared:

> . . . *die Produktion von Widia ist nicht als Teil der stahlerzeugenden Industrie anzusehen.*

> . . . the manufacture of Widia is not to be considered as part of steel production.[32]

Then the fine print started. Krupp's Hannover-Hannibal and Constantin der Grosse coal mines in Bochum were to be transferred to trustees who might, under certain circumstances, sell them to foreign buyers. The rest of Alfried's heavy industry was put under an umbrella to be known as the Hütten- und Bergwerke Rheinhausen Dachgesellschaft. This holding company would own all the Konzern's steel mills, coal mines, and ore fields — the Rheinhausen plant, Essen's Bergwerke shafts, the iron subsidiary of Sieg-Lahn Bergbau, the coal veins of Rossenray, Rheinberg, and Alfred, and the mines of Gewerkschaft Emscher-Lippe. The holding company would be capitalized at $12,792,000 in common stock and $7,466,000 in convertible bonds, all to be held by three respectable *deutsche Treuhänder*: ex-Chancellor Hans Luther, and Herbert Lubowski and Carl Goetz, bankers without Nazi pasts. For a commission of 0.5 percent, these trustees undertook to sell the holding company's holdings to "independent persons" within five years of the following January 31; if no buyers had stepped forward by then, the firms were to be offered to the first bidder. The only prospective buyers excluded would be Krupp himself, members of his "immediate family, or . . . persons acting on their behalf." Kruppianer working for the "segregated properties," as they came to be known, might buy up to 10 percent of the holding company's stocks and bonds.[33]

Alfried remained a multimillionaire. Among his financial resources would be a 24 percent royalty on coal from the Rossenray and Rheinberg shafts, which, under British administration, were yielding an annual output worth £830,000, or $2,324,000. And though he had been cut off from his raw material base, he was still sole proprietor of all of *die Firma's* fabricating mills, plants, factories, shipyards, and outlets. *Fortune*, analyzing the clauses and subclauses, concluded that "the Kingdom of Krupp was sliced up not only vertically but horizontally."[34] Even so, Alfried was left with a fortune assessed at 140 million dollars. He wasn't the fabulous tycoon he had been under the Third Reich, but then, the thousand years were over. Measured in any currency, or any exchange, he was one of the world's richest men. In any event, after the signing in Mehlem on March 4, there seemed to be no way for him to reconcentrate the dynasty's economic power.

Yet there were doubts even then. In the Bundesrepublik accounts of Essen's new *Neuordnung* were studied with intense interest, and from their own reporters Germans learned what correspondents from other countries had missed: "The accord he was compelled to sign made no allusion in this connection to any obligation to abstain from the production of arms (*der Rüstungsproduktion*) in the future." It was a strange omission, and raises grave doubts about the motives of the Allied negotiators. After Nuremberg, one might think, such a postulate would have taken precedence over all others. The Widia appendix provided a second loophole. Taken literally, and in its entirety, it permitted him to produce as much steel as he liked; he merely had to buy raw ingots from other Schlotbarone and let clever lawyers write the contracts. That would have been an evasion, to be sure, but any man who has been called a "lapdog of war" and whose staff feels that they have been "treated like niggers" is not likely to balk at trickery. Alfried had always been a tergiversator, and he was reconciled to the fact that any attempt to bleach the family's reputation abroad would be doomed to failure and humiliation. To the world, Krupp meant tools of war. When he recited the long list of his peaceful products to Vera, she was thunderstruck. "Why don't more people know that?" she asked. "Why can't you tell them?" He sighed. "No one would believe me," he replied. "Everyone believes we make weapons, only weapons, even Germans."[35]

His countrymen had always been proud of their *Waffenschmiede*, but the rest of Europe was wary. One problem was the family's name. To Ausländer, Norbert Mühlen noted:

> Krupp is not a melodious name. No matter how you say it, it sounds like the crump of a field gun [*der Schuss einer Kanone*], the detonation of a shell [*die Explosion eines Geschosses*], a Tiger tank [*das Donnern eines Tigerpanzers*] — in brief, like all the lethal goods mass-produced on Krupp belt lines for a century of war.[36]

Reconciled to Allied abuse from abroad, confident of German approval, Alfried felt free to treat the Mehlem agreement as he liked. His independence was strengthened by other flaws in the treaty. Its five-year deadline was meaningless. Unless the prospective buyer was a German, Krupp need only sell at prices acceptable to him — "*zu Preisen, die für ihn annehmbar waren.*" If he found the terms unacceptable he could appeal for an extension of time — meanwhile controlling his coal and steel assets through the holding company and the loyalty of its subordinate Kruppianer. Legally there would be no way to force an auction. Under the amended occupation statute Bonn was becoming more autonomous each month. Already German newspapers were asking of Mehlem, "Can the subject of a sovereign state sign away his birthright to three foreign powers?" Two Hauptverwaltungsgebäude lawyers who had been at Mehlem said he couldn't; one called the agreement "a scrap of paper," and the other said, "A promise given under compulsion is not a promise."

*Pacta sunt servanda* — treaties must be observed — is one of the oldest cornerstones of international stability. But the fledgling Bundesrepublik didn't see how *it* could enforce expiring Allied statutes ordering German industrialists to "deconcentrate" (*entflechten*); already the occupation's International Ruhr Authority had been supplanted by the supersovereign European Coal and Steel Authority. Therefore Adenauer had avoided full responsibility for Mehlem. The high commissioners, accordingly, had demanded ironclad personal guarantees from Krupp. Keeping his word, they told the chancellor, was Alfried's "personal and moral obligation" (*seine persönliche und moralische Verpflichtung*). He had led them to believe this was true. Within a week of the signing and stamping of the pact, Krupp granted one of his rare exclusive interviews to Ian Colvin of the London *Sunday Express*. Among other things he said, "I have signed an undertaking not to produce coal and steel and I stick to it" (*ich werde mich daran halten*).[37]

A year later he repeated his vow to Henry Luce in Vera's presence during a luncheon at the London airport. Luce believed him then and, later, never forgave him. There were a few skeptics. Colvin noticed that Krupp added absently, "There is a clause in the disposal law which provides for revision of it if the Allies consent" (*falls die Alliierten einverstanden sind*).[38] We know now that he meant he might apply for an extension again, and then again, and yet again — to the end of his life. At the time the hint passed unnoticed. Gordon Young of Reuters later thought the commissioners had "rather ingenuously" accepted Alfried's word. That was an extravagant understatement; they had, in fact, accepted a *verbal* commitment. Incredibly, Alfried hadn't even been in Mehlem on March 4. The date was suitable for three High Commissioners, but Krupp thought it would be rather interesting to race his lovely wife down the ski slopes of a remote Swiss resort; someone else could sign for the Konzern. There was an air of unreality about all this. Nevertheless *The Times* of London, endorsing the pact in which his signature was conveniently absent, argued, "Herr Krupp's great wealth is in itself no proof of special guilt."

Krupp now wanted his empire back intact, and he believed he had found the man who could help him get it. After Berthold had mentioned Beitz to him, Sprenger had remarked, "He really is an extraordinary self-made man, aged thirty-seven and the *Generaldirektor* of an insurance firm. You could do something with him." Alfried asked whether Beitz would be coming back to see the completed statue, the sculptor nodded, and Alfried suggested that the three of them have a drink then in Sprenger's studio. Rounds of drinks were followed by another Essener Hof dinner and a quickly forged friendship between Krupp and Beitz. The two men skied at Saint Moritz almost weekly. Business was never mentioned, but one afternoon while they were sipping whisky Bertha Krupp, the last woman in Europe one would expect to see in ski boots, clomped out of nowhere, joined Beitz while her son occupied himself elsewhere, and began a long, skillful interrogation about his career. Later this was followed by a regal Bertha visit to Erna Stuth, Beitz's mother. "That wasn't Bertha's idea," Tilo von Wilmowsky recalled later. "It was Alfried's. He consulted no one; I didn't even know what was in his mind until it was a *fait accompli*. But he valued his mother's intuition about bloodlines."[39]

All this preceded the signing of the Krupp Treaty. On September 25, 1952, while the Mehlem bargaining was still in progress, the peripatetic Alfried and Vera were dining with the Beitzes and Jean Sprenger in Hamburg's rebuilt Hotel Vier Jahreszeiten, overlooking the dark waters of the Binnet Alster. Vera and Else Beitz were chatting merrily at the Four Seasons bar with the blond artist when Alfried took *der Amerikaner's* arm and invited him to stroll along the shore. On another evening it would have been a sensible suggestion, but tonight it seemed distinctly odd: a heavy rain was falling. Vera and Jean exchanged a wink; after the two men had left they laughed aloud, for they had an inkling of what was coming. Beitz hadn't any. Afterward he remembered, *"Offen gesagt, ich nahm an, er wollte wegen einer Anleihe nachfragen"* (To be honest, I really thought he was going to ask me for a loan). They walked until midnight, getting wetter and wetter. Beitz's gray flannel creases had vanished and his knees were soggy bags when the Konzernherr finally said, "I believe you and I could work together. Will you move to Essen and help me rebuild my firm" (*meine Firma wiederaufzubauen*)?[40]

Explaining his motives a decade later, Alfried said, "We had shops all over West Germany; we had to think of some way to get the best production from them. We needed a new way of thinking, especially in light of the decartelization threat. We were like horses with blinders — and the blinders had grown long. We simply had to have someone with no blinders at all." He continued, "I knew I needed a man who was completely free of the 'steel mentality' — the less he knew about steel, the better. And I had found him more or less by chance" (*mehr oder weniger per Zufall*).

Although startled, Beitz was shrewd enough to ask terms. The Konzern, Krupp explained, was unlike any other industrial combine. There was a board of directors, but its function was limited to carrying out the instructions of the sole proprietor and, should Beitz join him as deputy, of Beitz. Their range of decision would be unlimited, with three exceptions: "First, no weapons can be manufactured. Second, there must be no question of following the Allies' discriminatory demand (*die diskriminierende Auflage der Alliierten*) that the coal and steel holdings be sold. Third, the company must remain a family firm (*Familienunternehmen*) for the time being."[41]

The nominee replied he would have to sleep on it for several nights — thus convincing Alfried that he had made the right choice. Actually Beitz wanted not sleep but information. For him, as for most Germans, Krupp was a misty legend. He knew no more about it than the average Frenchman knows of the taxicabs of Paris, the Briton of the City, the American of the FBI. Beitz wanted facts, figures, data. Early in the morning after Alfried's offer he telephoned his friend Axel Springer, Germany's press lord, and asked him to send over every clipping he had on the firm. He studied all carefully, then furiously read every book he could find about the Ruhr, its prospects, and the stability of the Konzern. Finally he called Essen and gave Krupp his answer: "*Ja, ich bin einverstanden, wenn mein Aufsichtsrat mich gehen lässt*" (Yes, I'll do it if my board of directors will release me).[42]

Germania-Iduna was reluctant to let *der Amerikaner* go. He had a contract with them, they severely reminded him; treaties must be observed. Contracts expire, however, and this one would lapse in a year. Beitz telephoned Krupp that he would be ready to report to the Hauptverwaltungsgebäude in November 1953.

☩      ☩      ☩

The exiled sovereign formally re-entered his capital on Thursday, March 12, 1953, eight days after the promulgation of the Mehlem treaty, eight years after his arrest in Villa Hügel, and exactly a century after King Friedrich Wilhelm IV of Prussia had granted a patent for seamless steel tires to Alfred Krupp. Alfred had been forty-one then, Alfried was forty-five now, and his great-grandfather was very much on the Konzernherr's mind as his snub-nosed sports car crawled through the narrow streets of the ancient city, passed the Essener Hof, and headed up the rough cobblestones of Altendorferstrasse. Some aged Kruppianer in the applauding crowd remembered the mad old beanpole, too; one, pointing to a restored statue of him, cried, "*Nehmen Sie ihm den Bart ab, und Sie glauben, es ist Herr Alfried!*" (Shave off the whiskers and you have Herr Alfried!)[43]

The *Westdeutsche Allgemeine Zeitung* called the throng pressing against Werkschutz lines on either curb "festive," and so it was. Children waved flags bearing the three black interlocked rings. *Hausfrauen* tossed bouquets under the car wheels and curtsied as Vera, ruddy from the Saint Moritz sun, watched wonderingly. Beside her Alfried nodded but slightly as well-scrubbed workmen shouted "*Lang lebe das Krupp-Reich!*" Inwardly, however, he was moved. Outside the Hauptverwaltungsgebäude he heard Essen's Oberbürgermeister — a retired Krupp smith who administered this metropolis of 695,000 — respectfully express the city's gratitude and happiness in welcoming back its most distinguished citizen. Then, turning to the assembled Direktorium, Alfried said quietly, "I thought it might take a half-century, or even more, before we could stand erect, but I never doubted that the day of our new rise (*der Tag eines neuen Aufstieges*) would come."[44]

Here he sounded like Gustav, who, in undertaking secret rearmament in the wake of the Versailles Treaty, had resolved "not to lose hope, but . . . think of a brighter future." Alfried's staff was less sanguine. After kissing the hand of the new Frau Krupp, they withdrew to the scarred boardroom with the sole proprietor and observed that the firm could hardly be described as standing on its own feet. Doubtless the cheers outside had been heartening, but half of them were avaricious; Friedrich Janssen's figures showed 16,000 workers on the rolls and 16,000 pensioners. Obviously one man at a lathe couldn't support one on a park bench. Agreed, Krupp replied, but "Human beings have come first with us for a hundred years." The directors exchanged exasperated glances, and Janssen opened a book-length survey which concluded that only an investment of nearly two billion marks — $457,000,000 — would bring Fried. Krupp of Essen back to its 1943 crest. It was out of the question.[45]

Alfried's face froze. *Nothing* was out of the question: "In my life I have never learned the notion of impossibleness (*Ich habe den Begriff Unmöglichkeit in meinem Leben nie kennengelernt*). I am convinced that I must follow the last will of my great-grandfather, even though it is a hundred years old. Defeatism is forbidden. *Meine Herren*, I have been in this business for seventeen years. Recovery of trade is certain."[46]

Janssen had been in the business thirty-five years, and he pulled a long face. But Krupp had an advantage over his Direktorium. While they had been riffling through balance sheets and statistical reports, he had been eying the world's economic profile. A Korean truce was imminent; within a year every continent would be a wide-open market for heavy hardware. While he needed more capital, a Krupp could always find credit, and Bonn would be as cooperative as Berlin had been. Politics demanded it. The new chancellor would welcome a thriving Ruhr, and he certainly wouldn't want to incur the dynasty's enmity. Therefore Alfried remained sanguine. When one executive suggested a moratorium on pension payments, he snapped, "*Nein!*" They would begin by paying retired workmen 50 percent of their support and increase it to 100 percent within a year. Pensions were the firm's best investment. To prove it, he led them outside and sent for Hermann Waldeck, a hard-bitten SPD veteran with fifty years on the factory floor. Pointing out across the black and rust-red ruins of the Gusstahlfabrik, Krupp asked the old man whether he thought they could rebuild again. Waldeck grunted, "*Gewiss, wir sind ja alle immer noch Kruppianer*" (Sure we can; after all, we're still Kruppianer).[47]

Starting next day, Alfried appealed to the old *Krupp-Geist*, sounding the tocsin for craftsmen who had learned their trades at Konzern benches to return. He had little to offer in wages now; nevertheless, the working force doubled, redoubled, and continued to grow at the rate of a thousand a month. To them his stand for pensions was fresh proof that he was *ein echter Krupp*. Some of his subordinates had thought the tug of tradition would be stronger among older Germans. Curiously, it was just the other way round. The personnel department reported that men with family responsibilities asked about hourly rates and fringe benefits. The young merely wanted to work for Krupp.

They seldom saw him. During that first year of the restoration Alfried and his wife were again absent on mysterious journeys. But these weren't vacations. Flying his own plane once more, he visited London for the first time in seventeen years, entertained Vera in the Savoy Grill, and took off next morning for the Bahamas. No one knew exactly where the couple had gone. In fact they were guests on the Nassau estate of Axel Wenner-Gren, an influential Swedish financier, Germanophile, and family friend. In the clandestine '20's Wenner-Gren had been useful to Gustav. Now Alfried was suggesting they collaborate in a secret power play which would create an earthquake in Fleet Street. With Wenner-Gren committed, Krupp lifted his wings again, first "to open a German exhibit" in Mexico City — actually he was conferring with Argentine millionaires — and then back across the Atlantic to Dublin. No one could understand what he could possibly see in Ireland. He said it was the scenery; really it was a fresh field of mineral deposits. Returning to London, the Krupps toured Farnborough Air Display, just to check on what was available to the RAF these days. The three-hour lunch with Henry Luce followed, which was eventually followed by a *Time* cover story, "The House That Krupp Built."[48]

The three-hundred-room house that Alfred Krupp had built in the 1870's was once more the property of his great-grandson. Two weeks after Alfried's grand re-entry into Essen it had been the scene of the family's first postwar meeting. The occasion was the confirmation of fifteen-year-old Arndt von Bohlen in Bredeney's Evangelische Kirche. The ritual was without religious significance. The last Krupp to praise God vigorously had been Margarethe, who had given the land for this church. Alfried now presented it with an organ, but that was merely a gesture to the First Estate from the Second. The ceremonies of March 29, 1953, are chiefly interesting because, while reuniting father and son, they provided an opportunity for Bertha Krupp to appear with her new daughter-in-law in public. Bertha nodded — once. Having forced Alfried to turn out Anneliese Bahr because there had been a divorce in her past, the queen mother could hardly be jovial to a triple divorcée. Vera, nettled, displayed her soignée enchantment to Arndt, which was doubtless exciting for him. It may have been more, an omen. Anneliese, who had stayed home in her

Tegernsee villa, had become far more worldly in the past few years; one of her closest friends was now Mady Rahl, a shopworn blonde actress who enjoyed an immense celebrity in Hitler's court, and through Mady the boy was learning that men of great wealth can enjoy unusual pleasures. Nevertheless Mady wasn't a Vera. In meeting his father's Corinthian second wife Arndt was being introduced to his own spectacular future.[49]

Meanwhile the most recent Frau Krupp, in coming within closer range of her imperatorial mother-in-law, had been given an unsettling glimpse of *her* destiny. The conquest of an impressionable youth was a hollow coup for her. Winning Bertha really counted, and the confrontation had been a disaster. Vera had been routed, snubbed, scorned. A second checkmate followed several months later, on the same chessboard. Beitz had just appeared on the familial scene, snapping his fingers and humming Dixieland, and to impress *die Media* with the firm's nonexistent affluence he proposed a Christian Dior fashion show in Villa Hügel. Alfried consulted his mother, and the Hauptverwaltungsgebäude held its breath. Beitz won. The very qualities Bertha found objectionable in Vera were endearing in him. He was a German *man*; that made the difference. Then — to the astonishment of everyone, including herself — the Dior exhibition became a Bertha Krupp triumph.

"That was the day," Beitz told me, "that I realized she was *die grosse Bertha*, not *die dicke Bertha*. Her greatness was illumined by her sense of humor. She was so amused because the reporters came to look at her, not at the good-looking girls in the show." She may have been even more diverted because among the girls she had so successfully upstaged was her own daughter-in-law. Vera had spent a full day in the salon of Düsseldorf's most expensive *Kosmetiker*, submitting to masseurs and baking under hair dryers. Nothing in the show could match her own Pucci frock, designed exclusively for her. Yet there she stood, glowering alone in a corner beside the carved staircase. *She* was supposed to be mistress of the household here, and the press was as oblivious to her as though she had been an upstairs maid.[50]

That could have been solved by her husband. Unhappily for her, he wasn't there. Since Mehlem she had seen less and less of him, and his long absences were another source of discontent for her. As a sympathetic friend later explained it, he "worked too hard for her taste" (*für ihren Geschmack hatte Alfried Krupp zuviel gearbeitet*). London, Nassau, Mexico, and Dublin had been exciting for her. Here Alfried was either bowed over his desk with Beitz, or in Bonn, or across the river in the grimy smog of Rheinhausen. Even when he drove to Düsseldorf, the only Ruhr city which in Vera's opinion had genuine flair, he avoided Königsallee and Flingerstrasse and haunted the countinghouses. Reproached, he would evoke the ghost of Alfred, whose charisma baffled her. As Konzernherr, he said, he had to think of his Kruppianer.

Given the *monarchische Prinzip*, he had no choice. This wasn't General Motors or Du Pont, he patiently told her. The firm had no shareholders; everything depended upon him. But why not sell out? she protested. He stared back, appalled, as though she had uttered some vile blasphemy. They were just discovering that they spoke in different tongues. To Vera there was no conceivable reason for a man to drive himself day after day when he could write a check for a hundred million dollars. Krupp regarded the money as wholly irrelevant. And, to widen their growing rift, there was little time to discuss it. "For Alfried the firm was everything," said Jean Sprenger, who served as a mutual confidant. "Being a Krupp is a big thing. It requires dedication." Alfried himself put it to his wife in much that way. She, in return, asked why he never attended a concert, read a book, or threw a lavish party for *real* people, *fun* people. He answered simply, "A man like me, living a life like mine, has very little free time" (*hat sehr wenig freie Zeit*).[51]

In the United States they might have worked it out. She was childless; she could have accompanied him on his excursions within the Bundesrepublik. But in the Fatherland women stayed home. She did attend one official function and suffered the humiliation of being introduced as "Frau Cook" by a confused host who never dreamed that she could be related to Alfried. Even recreation was largely masculine. Studying Fritz Krupp's faithful record of Alfred's methods, Alfried noticed how heavily Alfred had relied on Longsdon. The firm's British representative now was Klaus Ahlefeldt-Lauruiz, a Danish count with a home in London's Eaton Square. The *alleinige Inhaber* solicited the count's advice, and Ahlefeldt suggested weekend shooting parties; hunting game was private, off the record, and brought influential men together under informal conditions. Unfortunately for Vera, such gatherings were stag. When Krupp stalked fowl with the American and British ambassadors to Bonn on Grandfather Fritz's old hunting grounds, Beitz and Ahlefeldt could join them, but Frau Krupp was excluded. At about the same time Alfried launched the *Germania* V in the North Sea. Thereafter he never missed a Kiel Regatta. She missed them all.

According to Ruhr custom her role should have been confined to admiring his trophies and finding nooks in his den where they might be displayed to advantage. She preferred to investigate his business. A lively interest in a man's career is expected of American wives. In the Ruhr it is shocking, but Vera was unintimidated. She was forever asking straightforward questions of him and of his associates. One of the few casual affairs which brought mixed company together was *das Einzugsfest des Herrn und der Frau*, the housewarming for their 200,000-mark villa on Berenberger Mark. All the barons came to Hügel Park that day, together with the most eminent financiers and survivors of the old nobility. Their wives had been brought up faithfully to observe the axiom which had been laid down by an adviser of the Kaiserin over half a century earlier:

*Die Töchter aus gutem Haus sollten ein gutes Französisch lernen, Manieren bekommen und tüchtige Hausfrauen werden.*

Daughters of society are to learn proper French, be taught manners, and turned into efficient housewives.

The Hossenfeldts weren't a noble family, the French Vera knew would have amazed the Marseilles waterfront, and she never boiled an egg. Therefore, while the other women were murmuring over the decor and the floral arrangements, Frau Krupp dogged Herr Krupp. She had picked an awkward time. The head of one of the wealthiest and most prestigious banking houses in Europe had come down from Hamburg for the occasion. As the banker explained it ten years later, "I was trying to talk business with Alfried. It was an extremely delicate matter, but we couldn't shake her. She just wouldn't go away — she wanted to be in on everything of his. Finally I shrugged and left it for another time. It was no small matter, and it was more important to him than to our house. When they split up later I think he would have given anything to get rid of her." There he was wrong. Members of the family unanimously agree that the Konzernherr was deeply in love with her. "It was Frau Anneliese all over again," said an elderly Hügel servant. "The only time I saw him smile after the war was when he was with Frau Vera."[52]

*"Sie verbrachte den grössten Teil ihres Lebens damit, auf Krupp zu warten,"* a mutual friend remembers; "She spent most of her time waiting for Krupp." Yet when he came to her and took her away, she saw no cheering neon-lit bars, heard no merry rolls of dice, was warmed by no Mediterranean sunshine. Alfried's idea of an outing was his annual reunion with the Gesellschaft der Freunde der Technischen Hochschule Aachen, the circle of comrades he had formed during his university days. Counting women and children, there were now twenty-two members. Until the late '30's they had met each year on *Pfingsten* (Whitsunday), and since they hadn't seen one another in fifteen years, Alfried proposed that *die Freunde* resume the annual tradition as his guests at Blühnbach. Horst Hosmann, who had ridden the economic miracle to a front office job with Siemens Elektrogeräte Aktiengesellschaft, remembers that when their host greeted them on the steps of his Austrian castle, "He was older and had more gray hairs, but the changes were purely physical. He was not made more timid by adversity, or any more arrogant. He was simply our Alfried."[53]

Vera, however, wasn't their Vera. Everywhere she turned there were noisy, squalling children underfoot. The men ignored her, and she had nothing in common with their wives. Moreover, the program read like a bad joke: "We will climb mountains, hike, and show lantern slides of our families and our friends." Whitsun fell early that year; the trails were unsuitable for outdoor activity, even if Alfried's *Frau* had been the out-doorsy type. She hadn't any lantern slides of her three other husbands or her travels to Hollywood casting studios and the L.A. bargain counter. Therefore she suffered through hour after hour of Walther learning to walk, Hans on a swing, Anna's first recital. Leaving in their sleek black BMW she blurted out, "*Ist das lästig!*" (What a nuisance!). Krupp looked startled. He had, she realized, enjoyed every moment of it.

So the symptoms of discontent multiplied. Worst of all, she thought, was the Ruhr itself: its smog, its hideous skyline, its greasy air. "I have artist's blood," she told Sprenger desperately. He had never seen any sign of talent in her, but he knew what she meant; it was a matter of tempera-ment. Flinging her arms wide she cried, "Oh, how I miss Las Vegas, Los Angeles, my golden California sunshine! How can I stay under this gray heaven?" Here the parallel between Alfred and Alfried is relevant. In February 1854, the family archives recorded, Bertha Eichhoff Krupp had despaired of Essen:

> Shortly thereafter she began journeys in search of health, leaving the family home, crammed between the steel factory with its coke ovens and the forge with the shattering thunder of its hammers, even those being drowned out by the noise from the railroad wheel works. It was music to Krupp's ears, but not to those of a delicate woman [*nicht aber für eine zarte Frau*].[54]

Now, a hundred years later, incompatibility was repeating itself. There was one difference. Women's status had changed vastly. Until she reached the Riviera, at the very least, the earlier Frau Krupp had slept in only one man's bed. Vera had been bedded by a nobleman, a showman, and a doctor, and she had developed a lusty connubial appetite. A freedom the first Bertha had never dreamed of was available to her great-grandson's wife. In addition, she could enlarge that independence and diminish the capital base upon which the hated Konzern depended by the scraps of information she had picked up. She had found out quite a lot. Among other things she knew that, quite apart from his holdings in the Bundes-republik, her husband had deposited over a quarter-billion dollars in Swiss, Bahaman, Indian, Argentinian, German, and American bank accounts.[55] This figure in itself, if known, was enough to influence any fiscal negotia-tions pending at any time, and the time of disclosure was swiftly approach-ing. When it arrived, a member of the Direktorium cleared his desk of all paper with one sweep of his arm and cried, "What power a woman can bring to bear (*Welchen Einfluss kann eine Frau . . . ausüben*), although she doesn't realize it, upon the prospects of a firm!"

But of course Frau Vera Hossenfeldt von Langer Wisbar Knauer Krupp von Bohlen und Halbach *did* realize it.

&#10013;   &#10013;   &#10013;

The editor of *Die Welt am Sonntag,* one of West Germany's largest newspapers, once recalled how, as a boy in the Ruhr, "I was convinced that Krupp must have secret lists, secret agents, hired murderers, an international espionage network." Then he grew up "and found what the company's deep secret *really* was. All of them, from Krupp down, don't think of it as a place for making profit. They're convinced that they are a kind of state." He fingered his file and drew out an announcement from the Hauptverwaltungsgebäude. At a glance it seemed routine: Alfried Krupp and his son were about to leave on a commercial mission to Tokyo. The key lay in the last sentence. Alfried and Arndt would fly on separate planes. This, an Essen spokesman explained, was a precaution adopted *"auch von den Mitgliedern der königlichen Familie von Grossbritannien"* (also by the members of the royal family of Great Britain).[56]

By the autumn of 1954 the royal family of the Ruhr concluded that it was time Krupp resumed entertainment of fellow monarchs. Bonn thought so; from Bonn, Ludwig Erhard reported that visiting chiefs of state were eager to include a Hügel stop on their Bundesrepublik tours, and since the government was as proud of its chief industrialist as its constituents were, Chancellor Adenauer agreed. Apart from providing a swift view of the nation's famous powerhouse, such calls would offer the studied formalities to which regal guests were accustomed, and which, at present, were beyond the talents of provincial Bonn. Gustav had worked out all the finer touches before World War I. The Hungarian government had adopted Krupp protocol in toto. Why should the Fatherland be deprived of it?[57]

Charles W. Thayer thought there was an excellent reason. The omnipresent Colonel Thayer's contacts were endless. In 1945 they had won him a Blühnbach shooting box, and on the day Villa Hügel was reopened to crowned heads he appeared in the entourage of Greece's King Paul and Queen Frederika. Thayer wasn't actually related to them, nor had either been a West Point classmate, but he did know the *Herald Tribune* foreign correspondent who had covered Alfried's Nuremberg trial and whose stories about Justizpalast injustice had caught Krupp's eye and won him a place on *die Firma*'s public relations payroll. Thus the colonel received an invitation, met Alfried, reminisced with Berthold — and gagged at the spectacle staged for the sovereigns. "That reception was really in dreadful, appalling taste," he said after it was over. "The queen, who has good taste, boggled at it." Alfried would have been puzzled by Thayer's censure. He never doubted the value of dynastic ceremony. "Of course, I don't need all those rooms," he said to me one morning. "My great-grandfather did.

Now, however, when a prime minister or chief of state wants to see me he flies in or motors up after a chat with the chancellor and leaves a few hours later. Still, Hügel serves its purpose. It is impressive. When I need it, it is there."[58]

For a while there had been doubts that it would remain there. To Germans the castle was, as one writer put it, "as symbolic of Kruppdom as growing factories (wachsende Werkanlagen) and booming prosperity." To Janssen, however, it was a white elephant. The British returned the architectural monstrosity to Alfried after the Mehlem ceremonies, and reluctantly he offered it to the state of Rhineland-Westphalia as a histori-cal treasure. To his astonishment the provincial government politely de-clined. So did Bonn, and for the same reason; it was associated with all the aspects of Teutonic character the new Germany wanted to forget: arro-gance, the Offizierskorps, the Generalstab, S.M., the Führer, and profits reaped from murder and thievery. Yet there was a curious ambivalence in the Bundesrepublik's attitude toward Hügel. The leaders of four succes-sive Berlin regimes had never declined an engraved invitation from the hill, and when Alfried and Bertha sent one to Konrad Adenauer, der Alte came. On November 13, 1953, the week Beitz left Hamburg for Essen, the chancellor beamed at Bertha, clasped her hand, and bowed low by the life-size oil portraits of his imperial predecessors.[59]

Alfried's first Hügel reception for an African chief of state, Emperor Haile Selassie of Ethiopia, came almost exactly a year later, on Armistice Day. Five hundred guests were invited, including a hundred and twenty diplomats, who were driven from Bonn in seven-passenger black Mercedes limousines. Presumably they were coming to dine, though in each car a blue-uniformed hostess served sandwiches and champagne all the way. (Labels and matchboxes were also solid blue; Krupp had abandoned the family's heraldic color of red — "a change," he tactfully explained to me, "which seemed appropriate.") He was standing just outside the castle, awaiting the Lion of Judah. With him were twenty miners in silk costume, their Kumpel lamps hanging from their necks; eighteen trumpeters dressed in hunters' uniforms; Krupp's company band; a choir of one hundred Kruppianer wearing Lederhosen; two hundred apprentices holding paper Ethiopian flags; and a scowling, scar-faced majordomo in tailored black enlivened by gold frogs, gold epaulettes, and a glittering gold shako. The colors of Krupp hung from the four inner flagpoles, the Lion of Judah's from the outer eight.[60]

That was outside. Inside, at the far end of the great hall, Bertha Krupp could be dimly perceived. She was wearing a black suit, a triple strand of pearls, and a dowdy little black hat, but there was an undeniable majesty in her carriage. Two diminutive flower girls flanked her. In the hall between the castle proper and the "small house," Beitz, brisk as Broadway, straightened his regimental-striped tie and formed the Direktorium and lesser Schlotbarone who had been honored with engraved invitations into a hollow Kipling square. From time to time a chef in a billowy white tam darted across the great hall holding a long skewer at port arms. Tables in the state banquet room supported gold platters crowded with stuffed lobster, *foie gras*, and two-pound tins of black caviar. Behind them stood bottles of chilled Moselle, row on row.

Suddenly all the musicians started tuning up at once. Bugles rasped. The choir hummed. Three orchestras took a tone. The band blared in several octaves, then cooperated. Someone on Hügel's roof blew a whistle, and the cacophony died away; the choir and the orchestras were whisked inside to take up positions behind screens. Haile Selassie was approaching the hill. In the distance a squad of motorcycles cleared their rough throats for the climb from Frankenstrasse. Their muttering grew to a deep jabber, and abruptly they appeared at the far end of the lane of trees which had been transplanted under Alfred's fierce eye in the winter of 1871. Their riders, uniformed in white from helmets to boots, led the Mercedes to the entrance while the buglers sounded *Hail to the Prince*. The emperor dismounted in a simple business suit — had he been better briefed, he might have worn purple — and stood erect beside Alfried as the company band, in black and gold livery, struggled through Ethiopia's Coptic hymn, an intricate air never meant for brass. This orchestra had been trained to play more virile strains. Now, with gusto, they trumpeted the hundred-and-thirteen-year-old

> *Deutschland, Deutschland, über alles, über alles in der Welt!*
> *Wenn es stets zu Schutz und Trutze brüderlich zusammen hält,*
> *Von der Maas bis an die Memel, von der Etsch bis an den Belt.*
> *Deutschland, Deutschland über alles, über alles in der Welt!*

Inside, the muted choir picked up the even more moving melody which was celebrating its centennial this autumn:

> *. . . zum Rhein, zum Rhein, zum deutschen Rhein!*
> *Wer will des Stromes Hüter sein!*
> *Lieb Vaterland, magst ruhig sein,*
> *Lieb Vaterland magst ruhig sein:*
> *Fest steht und treu die Wacht, die Wacht am Rhein!*
> *Fest steht und treu die Wacht, die Wacht am Rhein!*

Haile Selassie moved precariously toward Bertha; Alfried, towering over both of them in a double-breasted suit, murmured introductions; Bertha smiled benignly; and *der Kaiser von Äthiopien* extended his hand and bowed deeply. Beitz led his square forward, flannel seams swinging in unison, and everyone advanced on the lobster. But this was more than a feast. It was a symbolic rite. The tapestries, the oil paintings of former Krupps and mustachioed Prussians in spiked helmets, the choir singing *Lieder* (and humming a chorus whose words, when last heard here, were *"Heil dir im Siegeskranz, Herrscher des Vaterlands, Heil Hitler dir!"*), the oak-paneled banquet room, and the pagan ball of fire which eerily blazed up from the baroque hearth — all were evocative of a past which only the ignorant or the unimaginative could banish from thought.

It is entirely conceivable that the Emperor of Abyssinia remembered a fragment reported in the '30's; when his tribesmen were being exterminated by Italy's legions DNB had trumpeted that the *"kruppsche Konzern"* was *entzückt* (delighted). But of course he was too much the king to mention it. His *ausländische* predecessors in this hall — Edward VII of England, Franz Josef of Austria, Leopold II of Belgium, Mussolini himself — had never trespassed upon Krupp hospitality, and it would have done no good anyhow. The fourth Cannon King would have pretended he hadn't heard. In a way the Lion of Judah was honored. He was the first black monarch for whom the red (now blue) carpet had been unrolled. Therefore he ate the lobster, caviar, and *foie gras*, drank the Moselle, and talked of his need for heavy industry. Alfried, Bertha, and Beitz listened gravely, the men making occasional notes. The four of them sat at a roped-off table near the hearth; no other guest, not even a Krupp director, was permitted within earshot. The scar-faced majordomo stood facing the crowd, his arms crossed, scanning faces.

Abruptly it was time to go. The five hundred guests, some of them staggering, rose to their feet and were awarded presents, bottles of brandy and silver-plated cigarette lighters. Then they were escorted to their limousines. The choir, the band, the trumpeters joined in a final flourish. The white-liveried motorcyclists gunned their accelerators and the caravan began its descent of the hill. As Haile Selassie passed the blood beech he passed the two hundred boys in immaculate denim, each smiling mechanically and waving Abyssinia's ensign. One wondered whether they knew who the little black man could be, or that he was from Africa, or where that might be.

✠    ✠    ✠

No one had asked about Vera during the reception; that would have been more indiscreet than mentioning the Duce. Breeding aside, any inquiry about the lovely Frau Krupp would have been turned aside, for her precise whereabouts were something of an enigma. Gossip columnists reported her surfacing in New York café society, emerging from Las Vegas gambling casinos, bathing in the California sun. Alfried's wife had become a swinger before the word was known. She preferred to dine with actors, mobsters and rich European expatriates. She had no desire to feast the Lion of Judah — and she was determined never again to be seen in the old castle overlooking the river Ruhr.

# 28

ACHTUNDZWANZIG

✠

# Heute die ganze Welt

O N the night of January 16–17, 1942, Adolf Hitler, relaxing in his
Wolf's Lair while the faithful Bormann transcribed his "table talk"
(*Tischgespräche*), had indulged in one of his rare allusions to sex. Speak-
ing of his years at Berchtesgaden he said,

> I knew a lot of women then. A number of them were in love with me.
> So why didn't I get married? To leave a wife behind me [*Sollte ich eine
> Frau zurücklassen*]? . . . There could be no question of a wedding for
> me. Thus I had to turn my back on certain opportunities that presented
> themselves.[1]

Eventually there was a Frau Hitler, but Eva Braun's married life hardly
attenuates his argument that dedicated men should remain bachelors;
within twenty-seven hours of the ceremony husband and wife had committed suicide. The Goebbelses were an even worse example. Magda
Goebbels poisoned their six children, and then an SS orderly shot both
parents at her husband's command. Of course, the inhabitants of the
Führerbunker that night were exceptional people; it is highly implausible
that we shall look upon their like again soon. But Alfried Krupp was also
unusual, and while his growing estrangement from his wife is relatively
unspectacular — Vera was no martyr — the dead Führer had put his
finger on the reason for their incompatibility. *Why get married?* he might
have asked Krupp. *To leave a wife behind you?* To be sure, there was a
remote possibility that an attentive spouse might have reconciled Vera to
the Ruhr's "gray heaven," but an absent spouse could do nothing, and
during her rare calls in Essen there was little time for solitude. Finally she
stamped off for the last time, hurting Kruppianer feelings by denouncing

their "*hässliche, provinzielle und freudlose Stadt*" (hideous, provincial, joyless city).

An ominous lull followed, a dusk before fireworks. The rockets were touched off, perhaps, by Frau Krupp's appearance as the pivotal figure in a marital scandal. Somewhere along the way she had acquired a construction firm from one of the various men whose name she had borne. Its president was an executive named Louis Manchon, and in the autumn of 1956 Manchon's wife Annabel charged that he had "openly and notoriously carried on a romance." She named the correspondent as that Hossenfeldt von Langer Wisbar Knauer Krupp von Bohlen und Halbach woman. It didn't fit easily into a headline; most newspapers ignored the story. But in October Vera decided it was time she filed a suit of her own, and the legal documents a trembling secretary quietly left on the corner of Alfried's desk made front-page news throughout the Bundesrepublik, *das Ausland*, and even in Las Vegas, whose postmark they bore. Marriages made in heaven are dissolved in Nevada every day, but this one, made in Berchtesgaden, was breaking up with a *kolossal* barrage of accusations, demands, financial figures, and allegations.[2]

Vera listed her husband's far-flung holdings, bank accounts, and safe-deposit caches (or all she knew about; she missed quite a few). For the first time the general public was given a glimpse of how far Krupp's tentacles reached across continents through complex license deals, patent exchanges, investments, holding companies, and even marriage ties. After describing the size of the pie, Plaintiff Hossenfeldt, etc., specified the dimensions of the piece she wanted: an immediate settlement of over five million dollars and yearly alimony of a quarter-million dollars. It was the least he could do for her, she argued. According to her complaint, Alfried had refused to support her, had denied her a home life, had forced her to submit to *Mutter* Bertha's intolerable *Hausregiment*, and had demanded that she give up her American citizenship. Dramatically she told a German reporter, "*Ich schätze meine Freiheit in Amerika mehr als all sein Geld*" (I prize my freedom in the United States more than all his gold).

The fortune was characterized in the Bundesrepublik press as "her price for freedom and silence" (*der Preis, den sie für Freiheit und Still-schweigen verlangte*), a strong hint that she was holding back a lot. If so, it wasn't personal. The plaintiff felt strongly that her sexual needs had been neglected, and the paragraph in her bill that really shocked Essen declared that

> *Der Angeklagte hat sich willkürlich und ohne Grund dem Ehebett entzogen und hat sich ständig geweigert, ehelichen Verkehr mit der Klägerin zu haben.*

The defendant did, willfully and without cause, withdraw from the marriage bed and has persistently refused to have matrimonial intercourse with the plaintiff.[3]

That was unfair of Vera. Krupp could hardly be blamed for withdrawing from a bed which at that time was over five thousand miles away and in a country from which he, as a convicted war criminal, was barred. As his partisans saw it, she had refused to behave like a sensible wife. The rest of the family hardly knew her. During the high moments of the past two years — Berthold's marriage to the daughter of a former Weimar ambassador, Arndt's school graduation in Bavaria, and Harald's miraculous reappearance after ten years in Russian prisons — she had been in Monte Carlo, the Lido, or the Strip. Her husband, typically, did not comment on her reproaches. He turned the divorce bill over to his legal staff and never mentioned his second wife's name again. *Krupp vs. Krupp* was quietly settled three months later — settled illegally under Bonn's divorce law, which outlawed *in camera* proceedings, though everyone was far too concerned to mention that. The incident had embarrassed an entire nation. The Bundesrepublik was glad enough to be rid of it.

Shucking reminders of Krupp's ex-*Frau* wasn't that easy, however; she retained her glamour, and columnists found her good copy. Eventually she was persuaded to dim her neon and lie low. The persuader was Alfried; she needed a hobby, he advised her advisers through his advisers, and he had found just the thing: a 518-acre ranch about twenty-five miles west of Las Vegas. Lately Chet Lauck, the Lum of the Lum and Abner radio program, had been using it as a hideaway. If Lum could hide there, so could Vera. She agreed, and the estate cost Krupp slightly more than a million dollars.

It seemed a good idea, and for a while it worked. But some women are fated to make headlines. The retreat was *too* secluded. In 1959 three men forced their way into the house, tied up Vera and her foreman, and departed with a 33.3-carat, $250,000 diamond Alfried had once given her. What it was doing there, or how the thieves knew of it, was never explained, but the crime didn't pay; the jewel was recovered in Elizabeth, New Jersey, by federal agents. Seven men went to jail, and no more was heard from the ranch until the spring of 1967, when its owner grew weary of it. She offered it to the government as a park for $1,110,000. That price seemed to exclude private bids. Krupp, however, was not the world's only billionaire. On June 20, Howard Hughes, just as rich and just as mysterious, took over the deed. Newspapers identified the seller as "a former film actress and the ex-wife of German munitions magnate Alfried Krupp."[4] Like it or not — and plainly Essen's first family didn't — the public would continue to regard Vera as Frau Krupp until her death that autumn.

✠      ✠      ✠

In the Ruhr, Vera is darkly limned: "She trapped him, and she hurt him, and she made a fortune — ach!" Those closest to Alfried were convinced that he was still in love with the sophisticated Cinderella who had stalked him in Landsberg. Clearly she left a void in his life. Beitz never stopped trying to interest him in syncopation ("New Orleans, *sehr* cool"), yet Krupp refused to be lured from the consolations of Wagner. The Konzernherr lived alone with his chauffeur, cook, butler, housekeeper, valet, cameras, darkroom, Porsches, BMWs, cases of White Horse whisky and crates of Camels — and despised them all. "Our Herr Alfried is a lonely man," sighed one of his servants. "A most unhappy gentleman," said a member of the *Germania* V crew, and a hard-core German Communist murmured, "I feel so sorry for Krupp, and it hasn't anything to do with politics; he's just so miserable" (*Er ist eben ein armer Kerl*).[5]

Blaming his second wife for that, however, would be as absurd as saddling Bertha Eichhoff with her wretched husband's hypochondria. Both women were shallow, indolent, and addicted to resorts. But each had married a Krupp in his forties whose character had been formed long before and whose first allegiance was to the struggling Konzern. Fritz Krupp and Gustav had taken over flourishing empires. Alfred had to build, and Alfried had to rebuild. To appease Vera her husband would have been obliged to abandon the dynastic dream while his mother, the symbol of the family's past, looked on. He couldn't do it. Restoring the power and prestige of the three-ring trademark had been an obsession with him since the foggy morning he had shed his convict uniform in Landsberg. Rather than forsake it he would have deserted her, and to a degree that is what he had done. He had not withdrawn "willfully and without cause," as she had charged, though doubtless his conduct had been incomprehensible to her. In the crucial months after Mehlem he was keeping hundreds of statesmen guessing. If they couldn't see his motives, and few did, her confusion is unsurprising.

To her (and to them) he was behaving like a recrowned monarch, preferring the company of fellow sovereigns to his hearth. For two months at a time he would be on the wing, paying state visits to Turkey's Menderes, Ceylon's Bandaranaike, and Indonesia's Sukarno between calls on the capitals of Venezuela, Brazil, Argentina, Thailand, and the Philippines. Sometimes he would circle for hours over wasteland blank as a plate. Everyone knew there was nothing in the Sahara desert but sand and smelly camels, yet Krupp explored it. Even more amazing, he and Cyrus Eaton, Jr., sat for hours in a helicopter on the rim of the Arctic Circle, peering down at some snowdrifts Eaton owned. The Cleveland industrialist was a notorious eccentric, of course, but what was the Reich's gunsmith doing there? Were the Eskimos preparing to march on Canada? It was, the press concluded, preposterous.[6]

It wasn't. It was brilliant. Alfried had changed roles. He now saw himself as contractor to the world (*Weltlieferant*), and he was looking for markets. The identity of his Hügel guests should have provided a clue to the spheres of influence he was carving out for the Konzern. Except for King Paul of Greece and the Archbishop of Canterbury, they came from the emerging nations: Keita of Mali, Badr of Yemen, Radakrishnan of India, Ahmadu of Nigeria, Kubitschek of Brazil, the Shah of Iran and, after Cameroon became a republic, President Ahmadao Ahidjo. Krupp was wooing them all. Eventually *die Firma*'s flag rooms contained standards of one hundred and forty countries. A dinner guest found his nation's ensign before him, affixed to a tiny flagpole. To those whose colors were new the gesture meant a great deal. They were most appreciative, and they were the customers Alfried was courting. To them he sent his magnificent albums, bound in leather and gold leaf, of the dull photographs he had taken during his travels through their swamps and jungles.

After the fanfare, the toasts, the national anthems, the gift albums, and the return home, the salesmen moved in. None were Germans. Alfried was aware that the white man's burden had become a stigma. Therefore he signed a pact with the East Asiatic Company, a Danish union of forty trading firms whose chairman was the King of Denmark's cousin. In each of what Krupp called "*die unterentwickelten Länder*" (the underdeveloped countries) the company maintained an office staffed entirely by natives. The cabinet member pondering a choice among various machines never felt that he was being asked to return Hügel's superb hospitality. He was, after all, dealing with a fellow countryman, and while he may have guessed at the reason for the apparatus he was still grateful for the display of tact.[7]

Krupp offered more. On Altendorferstrasse a battery of sophisticated devices printed instructions in every language. Some directions were visual, like a child's think-and-do book, for before submitting a big bid teams of Essen experts would ponder a dossier describing a country's literacy level. Krupp sized up new markets the way the Generalstab had prepared for invasions. Advance scouts sent ore samples back to the Ruhr for analysis. Pilots took aerial photographs. Uncharted terrain was mapped, and customs, local superstitions, and climate were examined, with highly practical results. Within six months of the Mehlem treaty Krupp's engineers had perfected an engine-compressor brake ideal for trucks working in back country. Locomotives were built to withstand tropical heat and humidity; and gearshifts were simplified by engineers familiar with the limited mechanical training of the men who would have to use them.

Behind these details was a powerful surge of emotion. One had to live in Essen during that period and talk to the exotic men in colorful robes to grasp why they felt a common bond with Krupp. "We sympathize with the Germans," one of them told me, "because we have had a common foe.

For two centuries my homeland was exploited by the English. In World War II Krupp was fighting the imperialists." Visiting Britons and Americans found that interpretation of the struggle against Hitler unsettling, even outrageous — until Versailles the Reich had been an eager competitor for colonies abroad. Yet somehow that argument had no effect upon Afro-Asian attitudes.

Precisely when Alfried first became aware of this rapport and saw the opportunities for exploitation is a Konzern secret. I once asked him. "The idea," he replied with one of his enigmatic half-smiles, "grew in a garden." The garden may have been Landsberg; he was a prisoner there when President Truman announced America's Point Four program, and six years later Krupp called his own program Point Four and a Half. Their motives, of course, were very different. The President's was geopolitical, the Konzernherr's commercial. To Alfried the *unterentwickelten Länder* of the early 1950's were what he called "the trading partners of tomorrow," and sure enough, before long half his trade was with them. Conceivably he would have boxed the compass anyhow, but a Bundesrepublik survey agreed in 1955 that

> Because of the Allied shackles the Krupp firm was obliged to assume a growing role in the world market [*Die von den Alliierten der Firma Fried. Krupp auferlegten Beschränkungen zwangen sie, ihre Aktivität in wachsendem Umfang auf den Weltmarkt zu verlegen*]. . . . This is a paradox, for, as a direct consequence of Allied economic policies, the Krupp firm has had no choice but to compete successfully against British manufacturers in their established markets, *e.g.*, India and Pakistan. Here is a consequence of the decartelization decrees which could never have been anticipated by their authors [*Dieses Ergebnis der Entflechtungspolitik hatten ihre Urheber nicht vorhergesehen*].[8]

It should have been anticipated. The trustbuster had barred the head of the family from his foundries. Within the next fifteen years sixty new countries would enter the United Nations, all of them clamoring for industrialization. Krupp could be locked out of his steel mills, but there was no way to lock the minds of his Kruppianer; if he couldn't sell ingots, he could sell his expertise, teaching the freed states how to build the plants they yearned to own. Here, as so often in Krupp history, the garden's first seed had been planted long ago. Two months before Alfried's third birthday, the Ruhr magazine *Stahl und Eisen* had carried an advertisement offering to "erect complete factories." Nothing had come of it then, but now the Konzernherr put his full weight behind just such a program.[9]

He began by creating a department of "consulting engineering." Then came the Industriebau, staffed by Berthawerk veterans. Its technical director was Dr. Paul Hansen, and he had one product, factories. If you wanted to build a Gusstahlfabrik of your own, Hansen was your man. His advice was expensive — fees ranged from $25,000 to $450,000 — but he provided ironclad guarantees and attractive pay-as-you-forge plans. Usually, in fact, the dark-skinned customers who came to Essen (via Bonn, which steered them toward the Hauptverwaltungsgebäude) paid more, for the Industriebau invited them to shop around in two other new Krupp companies. Die Firma offered good buys in excavating machinery, cement plants, suspension bridges, irrigation systems, hydraulic steel structures, and dams. A special treat awaited guests from the tropics. Multilingual Kruppianer displayed ingenious devices for extracting oil and processing coconuts, rubber, and sugar cane at bargain prices.[10]

Hansen's first sale had been two Renn kilns to Spain.[11] Within two years a wanderer could find die drei Ringe on Mexican rolling mills, Alexandria paper mills, Iranian foundries, Greek refineries, a vegetable oil processing plant in the Sudan, and harbor installations in Chile, Thailand, Iraq, and Holland. Krupp prospectors were sifting the sands of Sinai and the snows of Antarctica. Krupp metallurgists were eying veins of rock in France and Turkey, and if they liked what they found it was shipped home to the Fatherland on Krupp merchant ships built in Bremen by Weser A.G., yet another of the firm's new companies, manned by Kiel Kruppianer who had built Graf Spee, armed Bismarck and Deutschland, and welded together the litters of U-boats now rusting on the floor of the Atlantic. Krupp bridges spanned rivers in Portugal. Krupp smelteries smelt in Spain. The family flag had been planted in Java, South Africa, and Bolivia; and a Philippine steel factory, a Bosporus bridge, and a Turko-Persian railroad had reached the blueprint stage.

Overnight Alfried had created the biggest hardware store in history. He was capable of altering geography; one of his machines, all steel and longer than a city block, could scoop up a mountain and dump it elsewhere. But why stop with earth? Why not move populations, too? The gleaming cranes and open-hearth furnaces would sink into the swamps unless Mexicans, Arabs, Moslems and Hindus were on the spot to man them. Someone suggested the designing of replicas of Essen, the finest industrial community in the world. It was agreed, and Krupp advertised

Complete planning and erection of self-sufficient installations for the manufacture of iron, steel, and metal, together with total construction of adjacent housing projects, transportation systems, and power plants.[12]

The funny little gadgets translated it into every language from Arabic to Zyrian, and in New Delhi Jawaharlal Nehru envisaged a metropolis of 100,000 families, a beehive which would make Peking lose lots of face. There was competition, however. In December 1953, nine months after he had reoccupied his old office in the Hauptverwaltungsgebäude munitions wing, Alfried received a troubling letter from Nehru; the Soviet Union was offering to do the same job dirt cheap. Krupp was exceptionally busy at the time. He was negotiating with King Paul to construct a huge nickel works outside Athens, selling a hundred locomotives each to Sukarno and to Pretoria's Daniel Malan, and starting a Bombay cement factory. He couldn't fly to Asia, so he rerouted his man in Bombay, sending him specific instructions. Nehru was told that he could sign up with the Russians if he liked; he wouldn't pay much, but on the other hand he wouldn't get much. *Kruppstahl* would be high-quality steel, produced by the new oxygen-blowing process. Quality was expensive. The prime minister could take his choice.

Nehru replied that he liked to talk to leaders, not ambassadors. Since he was wavering, Alfried went down for what was to be the first of four protracted Indian visits, yielding the best steel and some of the worst photography ever to come out of Asia. The German price was over 150 million dollars, plus $4,410,000 in consultation fees. That was a lot of advice, Nehru said reflectively. Krupp conceded as much, but argued it was worth every anna; indeed, he said, in a regal gesture, if the job wasn't finished within the prime minister's four-year deadline, the firm would forfeit the fees. He had already become known as his own best salesman, and this dazzling stroke proved it. Nehru signed.[13]

Because of his British education, he anticipated a new Sheffield. He was to be disappointed. Krupp's architects designed Rourkela, as the city was to be known, along lines familiar to everyone who has ever lived between Mülheim and Bochum. Konrad Steiler, Alfried's Rourkela deputy, led his men to the Orissa site in eastern India, two hundred miles from the nearest city, and told them they had come to build a *"neues Essen."* Steiler wanted a community as Teutonic as prewar Saigon had been French. He got it. Rourkela today has a hotel evocative of the Essener Hof, a square like Bismarckplatz, a park like the Stadtwald, an encircling Autobahn; housing colonies in which each unit has two tidy rooms, a kitchen, and a bathroom; and a central shopping area in which automobiles are *verboten.* Economic colonialism in some ways is identical to imperial colonialism.[14]

But the Indians were delighted. Steiler, who slept beneath a calendar for four years, beat the timetable. The city's sewage system, electricity, and plumbing were superb, and the architects had thoughtfully surrounded each compound with a wall tall enough to discourage stray beasts. The rice paddies had vanished; Steiler had condemned them with a sweep of his arm. Later he explained, "It had been understood that there would be no sentimental nonsense about the primitive structures already there." Krupp had also insisted upon hospitals, schools, recreational areas, and theaters. These had satisfied the needs of five generations in Essen, and they showed every sign of working as well here. Best of all, from the government's point of view, was the Gusstahlfabrik itself. The chief of state personally tapped the first blast furnace; Alfried made his last appearance, to collect some 155 million dollars and take a hideous snapshot of the setting sun, and Steiler's team left the immaculate shops to the natives they had trained and christened "*Neokruppianer.*"[15]

This was good business, and Essen never saw it as anything else. But the Konzern had been so subtle for so long that men couldn't quite believe its motives were confined to profit. Local newspapers read extravagant meanings into Alfried's visits to Tokyo, Rio, Bangkok, Cairo, Colombo, Ottawa, and Ankara. Usually he was haggling over contracts or seeking replacements for his exhausted Swedish mineral fields. Nevertheless Afro-Asian statesmen depicted him as a savior and converged on Villa Hügel. The most dramatic visit there was that of President Mobido Keita of Mali, who delivered a long oration thanking Alfried for the survival of his country. Senegal's secession from the Mali Federation had left Keita landlocked, cut off from food supplies; a massive shipment of Krupp trucks had saved him. Alfried acknowledged Keita's tribute graciously, and everyone in the castle was deeply moved.

France's truck manufacturers were moved to comment acidly that had it not been for the maddening intrigues of African politics, they would have reached the Bamako depot first. Mali didn't believe them. The *Manchester Guardian,* the first Allied newspaper to see Alfried's grand design, warned in October 1953 that "Krupp is emerging as Britain's most dangerous competitor as an exporter of constructional machinery to the underdeveloped areas of the world." Those areas received Krupp, not as a competing exporter, but as a Samaritan. The *New York Times* noted the firm's "spectacular recovery." The Germans saw it that way, too. By 1956, when Vera filed her divorce bill, Alfried had a two-year backlog of orders on his books. As Norbert Mühlen observed

> *Wo Hitler als Eroberer versagt hatte, dort waren Krupp-Verkäufer erfolgreich.*

> Where Hitler's soldiers had failed, Krupp's salesmen succeeded.[16]

✠　　✠　　✠

Essen was naturally jubilant. Yet the magnitude of Alfried's achievements, his lightning thrusts into remote continents, and his stunning reversal of the dynasty's prospects had an awkward side. In the Justizpalast Otto Kranzbühler had insisted that his client had been callow and feckless, incapable of the dynamic action attributed to him by the prosecution. That had been the keystone of Earl J. Carroll's brief to the Peck Panel, and McCloy, in reversing the tribunal, had accepted it. Yet every step taken by the Konzernherr since his return to power argued that he was anything except ineffective — that he was, as General Taylor had insisted at Nuremberg, an exceptionally gifted industrialist.

In the Hauptverwaltungsgebäude's boardroom directors put their heads together and arose with a solution. Newspapermen were told that the real architect of industrial victory was Berthold Beitz. That pleased Krupp's extroverted deputy, and it also suited the introverted genius who had chosen him. Another tycoon might have been too vain to step into shadows. But Alfried loathed limelight, scorned applause, and was wholly unconcerned with where the credit went. All that really counted with him was results; he was content to hold himself aloof while journalists wrote him off as the worn-out victim of paternal sins, military defeat, imprisonment, and two divorces.

Though agreeable to many, the solution doesn't hold together. Beitz first reported to Altendorferstrasse in November 1953, the month after the *Manchester Guardian* editorial. Eight months had passed since Mehlem, and the most casual glance at Janssen's figures for that period reveals breathtaking achievements. With Krupp making major decisions every day, Essen had begun to lose the appearance of an enormous junkyard by the end of spring. New shops were rising over the cleared concrete slabs of the old Gusstahlfabrik foundations, barges were gliding up the river with raw materials, freight trains snaked between new plants and already gray with a patina of fresh soot, diesel tractor-trucks roared toward the Autobahn bearing products ready for the market. Breaking with the past, Alfried had written off his Kiel docks, his low-grade ore installation at Salzgitter, his line of agricultural machinery, and — the greatest wrench — the firm's production of seamless steel railroad tires.[17]

New machinery, he believed, would give him a head start on competitors. Here he was following in Gustav's steps. His exploration of untapped markets was far more imaginative than his father's, however. In May 1953, while Beitz was still presiding over Germania-Iduna, Krupp rocked the world of big business by moving into East Pakistan. Alfried offered Dacca new methods, new processes, and blueprints for new plants. With them, he predicted, Neokruppianer could turn out 300,000 tons of Pakistanistahl a year. Modestly, he asked only that he be given a 10 percent royalty on all gross profits. The system worked, Dacca was delighted, and he, of course, had augmented his guaranteed annual income.

During that first summer he sold trucks in the Middle East, railroads in South America, and mills to Salonika. Those who had written him off as a Krupp in name only should have studied his ingenious maneuvering with Nehru or the complex treaty he signed in Rio. Brazil wanted ponderous machines suitable for its *campos*. Alfried was confident that his laboratories could develop them. There was just one difficulty. The Brazilians hadn't much cash. Krupp suggested that they draw on Brazil's debit trade balance with the Bundesrepublik in the form of blocked cruzieros. Rio agreed, converting its debt by assigning Alfried shares in mineral fields, and his technicians extracted the ores — for a fee, naturally.[18]

The Dacca and Rio contracts are one clue to a question which puzzled all outsiders that year: where was Krupp getting his capital? Later Vera provided other answers, but he wasn't nearly as affluent as he seemed. In some respects Alfried's most impressive performance in 1953 was the grand manner with which he toured the world, dealing as an equal with presidents, kings, and premiers, when back in his counting rooms Janssen was squeezing every pfennig. Later the Finanzdirektor confessed that "If we had been forced to open our books, we would have been finished. Our situation was far more desperate than anyone could have guessed" (*Unsere Situation war weit schlechter, als irgend jemand ahnte*).[19]

It was not so desperate as many thought, however. The sources of Krupp's fiscal strength were various and broadly based. One was the 70 million dollars the Allies had set aside in return for a promise he never meant to keep. Another was the era. Like his father in 1923, he had been sent to jail during a period of economic chaos and funny money; since then things had been set right, and German banks, with their faith in the indestructibility of the firm, loaned him 20 million dollars. Still another asset, whose true dimensions will never be known, was West Germany's indemnification program. As Max Mandellaub observed, "Krupp was one of the first German industrial firms which prepared its claims against the Bonn federal government because of the dismantling policy of the occupying powers after 1945." Once the Bundestag had authorized compensation for these losses, Mandellaub pointed out, Krupp was "in the advantageous position to estimate the loss without any real control, since nobody can estimate how many of the machines and installations left over in Essen on the day of armistice were still in working order or smashed during the last months of the war."[20]

This much was certain: the Bundesrepublik wasn't going to challenge Alfried's figures. Krupp's position as the nation's most favored firm had rarely been more secure, and this was its real fount of stability. Bonn awarded the sole proprietor contracts to rebuild sixteen major Rhine bridges, allowed him substantial tax write-offs, and advanced him remarkable sums of credit — 63 million dollars from the Frankfurt Export Credit Bank alone. In the light of these sums, the 20 million dollars Krupp spent in rebuilding his Essen shops seems unimpressive. It hardly need be added that the government would never have acted so benignly, nor the banker have been so munificent, towards an unknown Pomeranian insurance salesman named Berthold Beitz.[21]

At the end of the restoration's first fiscal year, Alfried broke precedent by inviting all Kruppianer with twenty-five, forty, or fifty years' service to the castle on the hill. This was the first of what would be annual "Jubilee" ceremonies. As a spectacle the *Jubiläum* was dismal. Reporters were excluded; Dr. Carl Hundhausen, a member of the Direktorium, briefed them outside. The workmen were ill at ease in the forbidding hall, and Krupp, as master of ceremonies, lacked suavity. Nevertheless the content in his terse speech transformed it into a personal triumph. He disclosed that new projects were under way in Spain, Greece, Pakistan, Iraq, Thailand, Chile, Sudan, and Iran. In the production of trucks alone, Krupp was second only to Daimler-Benz. Still, one had to look ahead. He was establishing a new subsidiary to investigate industrial planning and construction abroad, and soon, with patents licensed from New York, he would be building textile machinery and selling it through a Swiss corporation. The balance sheet, of course, was not available for inspection; unlike managers of stock companies, he plowed his profits back into expansion. However, he could tell them that the year's turnover had been nearly a billion marks — 238 million dollars.[22]

At that there was a gasp. Krupp held up a hand. "Let us not be too proud of this work we have done," he said, "and above all, let us not be too haughty. For it is no secret that we are not yet safely across the mountain." No industrialist is invulnerable, but certainly Alfried had left the valley far behind. Subsequent *Jubiläen* had to be moved to the Saalbau — theoretically Essen's civic auditorium, though really Krupp's whenever he wanted it — because Hügel could no longer hold the audience. There were already 91,000 names on the firm's payroll, and they rapidly rose to 125,000. Each spring Alfried noted the tremendous range of products listed in his catalogue and the new fields he was entering: communications, artificial textiles, water purification, plastics, and devices to remove dust from the atmosphere (which, unfortunately, were never attached to his own vomiting chimneys). Krupp's Weser A.G. was building 15 percent of Germany's new shipping. Two hundred scientists had developed a bright new metal, titanium: rustproof, strong as steel and 80 percent lighter, ideal for jet planes. Within three years of that first Jubilee the Konzern's turnover had quadrupled. Kruppianer were now doing a billion *dollars'* worth of business a year, a fifth of it overseas.[23]

Even that was an understatement. Alfried discreetly omitted a billion and a quarter dollars from the segregated *Holdingfirma* Hütten- und Bergwerke Rheinhausen Dachgesellschaft. As a gentleman, he explained, he would not even enter his coal and steel properties, and his employees there could neither call themselves Kruppianer nor receive the three golden rings after fifty years on the job. The German code of honor has peculiar blind spots. Under his written pact with Paris, London, and Washington, he had agreed to begin liquidating those holdings. He had done nothing of the sort. It was, it seemed, ungentlemanly for him to visit the forges and mines, but quite all right to keep them and pocket the profits. Since West German steel production had now passed 28 million tons, putting the Bundesrepublik third in the world behind the United States and Russia, those profits were considerable. After an extensive investigation the French periodical *Réalités* reported that the Konzern was already Europe's fourth largest company, hard on the heels of Royal Dutch Petroleum, Unilever, and Mannesmann. Alfried's personal fortune was estimated at 800 million dollars. Already his steel capacity was 5,500,000 tons a year, comparable with Jones and Laughlin, number four in the U.S. steel race. Reuters pointed out that Alfried's comeback in the 1950's had outstripped Gustav's in the 1920's, and a German writer concluded, "From the economic standpoint, it is healthy progress" (. . . *ist diese Entwicklung gesund*).[24]

&#x2629; &#x2629; &#x2629;

From the public relations standpoint, it was a splitting headache. In one of the more diverting understatements of the period Dr. Hans Günther Sohl disclosed to a *New York Times* reporter that "the Ruhr complex" (the fear of economic concentration in the Reich's historic armory) had "not been overcome in some quarters." Those quarters included some of the nations Alfried was visiting. Less than ten years had passed since the holocaust of the century, and soldiers maimed by 88's and Tiger treads were incensed by accounts of Krupp's growing wealth. In Melbourne he descended from his aircraft to the accompaniment of hisses and shouts of "Jew killer! Butcher!" — looking steadily over their heads he remarked evenly that he was "a little sorry that some people are sorry I am in Australia" — and in Ottawa his hotel was picketed by Black Watch veterans carrying placards reading, BACK TO NUREMBERG, WAR CRIMINAL![25]

Even in emerging nations there would sometimes be a moment of anxiety after Krupp's Jetstar wheels touched the airport tarmac; as *The Times* of London explained after one of Alfried's Rourkela visits, "When Herr Krupp arrived in India recently he was immediately received by Mr. Nehru; yet there is always the fear that some immigration official will refuse him entry." European criticism continued unabated. In the House of Commons a Conservative MP periodically deplored "the way this large-scale employer of slave labor has been treated," in the House of Lords a peer rose from time to time to demand that "this infamous war criminal be punished," and even in the Bundestag hard-line Social Democrats continued to mutter about "*die blutige Internationale der Händler in Tod.*"[26]

Krupp turned this disagreeable problem over to Dr. Hundhausen and a staff of forty trained manipulators of public opinion. At first glance the challenge seemed insuperable; nevertheless they met it, in large part because they were buttressed by the long tradition behind them. Superlatives are hazardous, but it would be hard to find a munitions firm with longer experience at planting stories in the press. Friedrich Krupp had recorded in 1819,

Since accountant Grevel has succeeded in getting an enthusiastic article published in a Frankfurt newspaper, sales have slightly increased. The royal gun factories on the Rhine have placed orders for steel for bayonets and gun barrels [*Aus den königlichen Hütten am Rhein kommt eine Bestellung auf Stahlblöcke für Bajonette und Kanonenrohre*].[27]

Alfred Krupp was more sensitive to the value of favorable publicity than American tycoons a half-century later. In his prime, when Madison Avenue was still an unpaved road, he was circulating releases among members of the Berlin press and distributing handbills in Parliament, and on November 27, 1866, nearly seventy years before I. G. Farben hired Ivy Lee to improve its image, he wrote a remarkable letter to Albert Pieper:

> I think therefore that now is the time for accurate accounts of our works, from the pen of authorities, to be sent at regular intervals to periodicals which enlighten the whole world [*durch Zeitungen, welche die ganze Welt erleuchten*]. We can furnish the material, and, to the extent to which we cannot find proper authorities ready to offer assistance, we might get in touch with the appropriate editors of respectable newspapers.[28]

Both the first and second Kanonenkönig turned industrial expositions into *kruppsche* carnivals. Alfred became a world figure by unveiling his steel cannon in London, Fritz stunned Philadelphia's exhibition of the '90's with gigantic howitzers, and Alfried, following their example, attracted fresh attention by displaying a seventy-five-ton nuclear reactor vessel cover at the Hanover Fair of 1963. Each generation of Krupps was unhappy with its *ausländische* reputation, and each burnished it.

At the turn of the century foreign magazines published a rash of articles under suspect pseudonyms describing Fritz Krupp's Essen as a quaint fairyland where artisans puffed on long-stemmed pipes, the fragrance of their tobacco blending with the scent of roses and rosemary as they peered merrily over octagonal spectacles. Then, between 1914 and 1918, Allied writers were extremely rude to the family. Afterward the curve of flattery rose again, only to plunge sharply in the 1940's. *Life* concluded then that "At least as much as Adolf Hitler, the Krupp family is responsible for the casualties of Allied soldiers in World War II." *Time* described Alfried as "Herr Krupp, merchant of death." After his return from prison and penury, however, the graph of praise resumed its climb. Two American writers especially successful in attacking the Nuremberg verdict were Freda Utley and Louis Lochner. Lochner wrote that he had spoken to Kruppianer in Essen and that they had assured him that foreign workers had been as well treated during the war as German workers; the court, however, "chose to ignore such testimony." Miss Utley, who had served in the Moscow Institute of World Economy and Politics between 1930 and 1936 and had then leaped over the wall, argued that Control Council Law No. 10 was a conspicuous example of "the influence of Communists" which indicted "most of the capitalist class." She said she had heard reports that the Krupp tribunal was the most "prejudiced and unAmerican" in Nuremberg — in this passage, she confused Justice Anderson with Justice Daly — and that there were grounds for suspecting that General Telford Taylor "was sympathetic to the Soviet Union."29

Even in the McCarthy era, which this was, Louis Lochner and Freda Utley reached only a small audience. But editors with large circulations picked up their refrain. The Brooklyn *Tablet* opened a full-fledged assault on General Taylor, criticizing his conduct during the Bergen-Belsen case. (He had played no part in it.) Of the Krupp case the *Reader's Digest* said that "It was tried in an atmosphere of supercharged emotions. . . . But the Allied prosecutor was determined to make an example of the House of Krupp." *Time*, reversing itself, quoted anonymous observers as hoping that "the ban on [Krupp] arms production would soon be withdrawn" on the ground that "The sooner Krupp pitches in to do its share in the rearming, the better." *Newsweek* wrote that Alfried "had had little to do with Hitler." Krupp's fate, *The Times* of London stated, had been to be sentenced "in place of his ailing father."30

These comments were appreciated in the Hauptverwaltungsgebäude, where a staff of *PR-Männer* under Hundhausen prepared a daily world press summary for Krupp's scrutiny. The image, everyone agreed, positively glowed, and as the years passed subtle refinements were introduced for each of the Konzern's markets. Awed visitors from abroad were shown the full scope of Krupp's empire; in Villa Hügel an electric globe resembling a Pentagon situation map pinpointed Konzern bases and projects in the Middle East, Australia, North and South America, Africa, Europe, India, Pakistan, and Southeast Asia. Special attention was drawn to three refineries Krupp had built in the Soviet Union, to a 250-ton steel foundry in the Philippines, Manchurian Renn plants, and, slyly, to a coal-loading installation on the American shore of Lake Erie. The Yankees might tell Alfried to go home, but they had no objection to becoming Krupp customers.

For economics ministers with limited educational backgrounds Hundhausen built a library of audiovisual aids, including twenty-five feature-length color movies — two in English, two in French — but most diplomats and businessmen were fluent in several languages, and for them the firm prepared beautifully bound books. Some of the indoctrination in them was superb: "While the Englishman is having his first whisky and soda and changing for dinner, the Krupp agent is still out in the desert demonstrating equipment," and "When a dealer in an underdeveloped area writes for aid, the American sends him a letter in reply — but Krupp sends a salesman."

Krupp did not, of course, send such choice jabs to the U.K. or the U.S.;

there Krupp was depicted as a selfless contributor to the world's technological future. Americans were reminded of the *Kruppstahl* which protected the bathyscaphe *Trieste* in its search for the lost U.S. submarine *Thresher*. The dive wasn't much for the *Trieste*. Three years earlier the bathyscaphe, shielded by vacuum-degassed Cr-Ni-Mn steel, had made the deepest ocean descent in history, seven miles down, to the bottom of the Marianas Trench in the Pacific.[31]

Particular attention was devoted to elaborate press releases telling the entire world how Krupp engineers had volunteered to raise the red granite obelisk of Pharaoh Sesotris I from thirty-eight centuries of muck for a token fee of 3,500 Egyptian pounds. Gamal Abdul Nasser wanted to erect the Pharaoh's curious tribute to himself in a Cairo square, so Alfried sent down a crack team of engineers. Using hydraulic presses, technicians hoisted the massive obelisk from the depths of the Upper Nile; then they scrubbed it, transported it to the square, and set it down on a concrete base with cranes. Blonde hostesses wearing the three rings on blue uniforms distributed brochures telling how Krupp had done it. A genial public relations man from Essen introduced the girls as "Krupp's blue angels," and Hundhausen's chief assistant, a young baron who had served his apprenticeship with McCann-Erickson in New York, wrote the story of Krupp in a book called *Tu Gutes und rede darüber* (*Do Good and Talk About It*).[32]

✠     ✠     ✠

Amused Nazi exiles in Egypt dismissed the project as "Operation Eau de Cologne," and in Essen cynics who remembered the immediate past applied the sobriquet to the firm's entire PR program. They had a point. Alfried's resurrection of the obelisk of Heliopolis hadn't been at all altruistic. He had been stalking Nasser's good will, and the president surrendered it; in return for *die Firma*'s investment Krupp was awarded contracts for a paper factory, a shipyard, and two Nile bridges, one connecting downtown Cairo with Cairo University. That should have been enough, but the Konzernherr had his eye on something much bigger. An interoffice memo read: "The true goal of Krupp in Egypt is the multimillion-dollar Aswan Dam" (*Das nächste Ziel Krupps ist das Milliardenprojekt des Assuan-Damms*). When he didn't get it — on October 24, 1958, Nasser resolved Aswan's future by striking a hundred-million-dollar bargain with Khrushchev — he sulked. American prestige was bruised, but so was Essen's; Alfried warned sympathetic *Jubiläum* guests, "There is a real danger in economic penetration drives by the Soviets that are concentrated on strategic points and carried out without regard to cost. Thus they might conquer a country from within, as they are about to do in Egypt."[33]

*Hund* in the manger, jeered his chiders; the Russian penetration of Egypt was no greater than Krupp's in Brazil. But what really gave Altendorferstrasse's PR program a distinct fragrance was its extraordinary selectivity. No one could blame Hundhausen's men for trying to suppress the fact that a Swiss editor of *Neue Zürcher Zeitung*, scanning photographs taken during a meeting between Alfried and his Argentinian salesmen, had spotted the six-foot-four hulk of Otto Skorzeny. For seven years the former SS Obersturmbannführer had been quietly serving as liaison officer between Perón and Krupp. Now his cover was broken; his usefulness had ended; at fifty-two he was through. The publicity men who dodged questions about Skorzeny were doing their job, sparing their employer embarrassment. But the rule book does not permit image-makers to have things both ways. Hundhausen's staff did, and that was why they became known as *Parfümeriehändler*. They insisted, for example, upon advertising the glorious past of *Haus* and *Familie*. In 1961 *Krupp*, a magnificently illustrated book, listed "Milestones in the Firm" during the previous century and a half for the concern's foreign clientele. Yet there were no pictures of the Kaisers, Feldmarschalls, Grossadmirals, or the Führer, and not a single weapon manufactured by the family was mentioned.

Alfried was so anxious to forget his career as armorer of the Reich that his huge department store in Essen wasn't even permitted to sell toy soldiers or water pistols. If you pointed a Leica at the guard beside S.M.'s Hügel portrait he would flee. One director vowed, "We will never make another gun." When a group of German university students raised the issue with Fritz Hardach he replied solemnly, "Better to make milk cans than cannon." Beitz mused that fieldpieces were becoming obsolete in today's world. "If the continent were threatened by an arms race," he said, "we should get hold of Schneider-Creusot, Vickers-Armstrong, and Skoda, and say, 'Hello, let's have a drink and sit down and see if we can't do something better than make guns.'" Here, interestingly, Alfried himself was less adamant. Though he shook his head when asked about the possibility of a reawakened Reich, his line of reasoning was less assuring: "Producing munitions isn't good business. Civilian production is more stable in peacetime, and besides, there is always the chance that you might lose the war" (*Rüstungsproduktion ist kein Geschäft. Die zivile Produktion ist kontinuierlicher im Frieden, und einen Krieg riskiert man immer zu verlieren*). No moral issue there: if guns were profitable and victory certain, all obstacles would be removed. There were other qualifications. Should a chancellor ask him to retool for a new Wehrmacht, Krupp conceded, his position would be "difficult." Under those conditions, he supposed, "We would. We must not forget reality."[34]

In one of the more intriguing aspects of *Eau de Cologne*, admiring writers attempted to expunge any link between Gustav Krupp and the rise of Adolf Hitler. The year after Mehlem, Gert von Klass wrote that

Beginning in 1934 Hitler tried to persuade the Krupp firm to build weapons whose manufacture was interdicted under the Versailles Treaty. His demands were followed by lengthy negotiations in Berlin, which grew increasingly abrasive as time passed [*Diese Wünsche lösten zahlreiche Verhandlungen in Berlin aus, die im Laufe der Monate immer unangenehmer wurden*]. . . . Gustav . . . was extremely hesitant to violate the Treaty of Versailles, for he considered treaties sacred by their very nature.[35]

Two years after Klass, Ferdinand Fried, a respected German historian, flatly declared that not until 1936 was "arms manufacture once more resumed at Krupps (*dass . . . mit der Waffenproduktion wieder begonnen wurde*) as it was at many other steelworks." This is wholly untrue. The firm's leadership in Germany's secret rearmament is borne out in Krupp's annual reports and Gustav's extant files. Also, if it *were* true, the Konzern cheated the Führer out of a fortune. Arguing the Gusstahlfabrik had been ready to rearm "without a moment's delay" (*ohne einen Augenblick zu zögern*) when Hitler seized power, Essen had demanded compensation. In a memorandum to the government on July 18, 1940, Johannes Schröder submitted that "Without a state contract, Krupp kept up its personnel, workshops, and experiments from 1918 to 1933 and consumed for this purpose not only the total profits from its coal mines and steelworks, but also large hidden reserves entered on the first gold mark balance sheet from the profits of the pre–World War years. [Thus] Krupp was in a position, when rearmament began, to produce the most modern apparatus immediately in serial manufacture, and to instruct many other firms." Berlin, knowing this to be so, paid *die Firma* the 300 million.[36]

If so incontrovertible a fact as Krupp's fifteen-year conspiracy against Versailles could be ignored, those who took the postwar breast-beating of *PR-Männer* without a dash of salt were, to put it gently, artless. It was true that you couldn't buy a tin gun in Essen's Konsum-Warenhaus. It was also conceivable that the Konzern might be manufacturing the real thing, and if you probed a bit you would find that in fact this was true. In 1953 Krupp's Flugzeugbau G.m.b.H. began assembling jet fighters in Bremen. Americans might have protested to their congressmen, but it wouldn't have done much good, because Alfried had protected himself against that sort of flank attack by selling a 43 percent interest in the subsidiary to United Aircraft. Krupp, one was told in Washington, was making weapons for the Free World.

Alfried acknowledged his submissiveness to *die Obrigkeiten*, the established German government, and added that should Bonn ask for more than jets, he would give more. However, when Krupp's Ruhr *Mirakel* was at its height — with the family's prewar holdings more than doubled — any change in the status quo seemed folly. In the Kaiser's heyday the Alldeutsche Verband had chanted "*Dem Deutschen gehört die Welt*"

53

Two views of Alfried Krupp's atomic pile at Jülich.

54

Alfried's brother
Harald (1916-    )

Alfried's brother
Berthold (1913-    )

Berthold Beitz (1913-

Alfried Krupp with his aunt, Barbara Krupp von Wilmowsky, and her
husband, Baron Tilo von Wilmowsky.

Krupp's Mechanische Werkstatt (Heavy Mechanical Workshop) at
the time of Alfried's death.

Ore wharf and blast furnaces of the Krupp iron and steel works at Rheinhausen.

A Krupp block-long excavator and loading unit.

Alfried's son Arndt. ABOVE: With Alfried at Hanover in 1960, and with his mother Anneliese. BELOW: At carnival balls; left, with Gina Lollobrigida.

64

Günter Vogelsang, who became general director of Fried. Krupp A.G. in 1968.

Hermann Abs, president of the Deutsche Bank and chairman of the new Krupp corporation.

68

The author; above, outside Villa Hügel just before a Krupp dinner party in 1963; below, at work in Krupp's Friedrich-Alfred Hütte, Rheinhausen.

(The world belongs to Germans) and *"Heute Deutschland, morgen die ganze Welt"* (Today Germany, tomorrow the whole world). But now it was *übermorgen*, the day after tomorrow, and Krupp had achieved a global empire without firing a single shot. He had jumped off from his line of departure at 0900 on the morning of 10 February 1951, moved resolutely through Landsberg's murk, and captured all his objectives. Now he was master of nearly everything he saw, which, from the cockpit of his Jetstar, was quite a lot. There was no conceivable reason to re-create the *Waffenschmiede*. In a jocular mood *der Amerikaner* said, "When the next war's over, it will be the electronics firms and the missile manufacturers *die Fabrikanten elektronischer Geräte und die Raketenmacher*) who will be put in the dock before a war crimes tribunal, not us."[37]

Today a Krupp world. But what about *morgen?* There was nothing to prevent Alfried from entering the electronic, missile, and atomic fields. Indeed, he was already in two of them; somewhere in north Germany, not far from Meppen, his scientists were perfecting his first three-stage rocket, and his first atomic pile had been completed. For a glimpse at this hour of Krupp's tomorrow you needed a pass, a map, and enough gasoline to carry you sixty-two miles southwestward on Bundesstrasse No. 1, past the fantastic radio towers of the Deutsche Welle, whose square acre of coiled steel spider webs beam the Bundesrepublik's broadcasts in German to expatriates in South America twenty-four hours a day. In the sleepy Westphalian town of Jülich, twelve miles from the Dutch border, you turned down a narrow country road and passed an old red brick mansion, now used as a railroad repair shop. The scene was evocative of Gloucestershire, of the ghostly gray stone villages between Cheltenham and Tewkesbury, and here, as there, one wondered how men supported themselves.

Abruptly the question was answered. Round an unexpected curve the road improved dramatically and broadened to four lanes. A traffic light turned red as a vehicle approached — the controls were in a sentry box labeled SICHERHEITSZENTRALE (ALARM CENTER). Dead ahead lay a black and white striped gate. Presenting your pass, you proceeded through a maze of streets (without a thorough advance briefing, no one could hope to negotiate it) to a second gate marked ATOMKRAFTWERK and produced your credentials for a second armed sentinel. Beyond that, in a heavy forest, stood Alfried's pride, a tall, queerly shaped structure bearing the familiar three rings and the sign ATOMREAKTOR.

The Kruppianer there called the fifteen-megawatt test reactor KFA, short for Kernforschungsanlage (Nuclear Research Plant). Partly subsidized by a Bonn ministry, it was founded by a Konzern subsidiary, the BBC-Krupp Institut für R-Entwicklung (Institute for Reactor Development). If your papers were in order, the youthful director, Dr. Claus von der Decken, would explain how Krupp ingenuity achieved a critical mass in 1967. Over 100,000 graphite balls made from coke — there is almost no end to the uses of Krupp coke — shielded the uranium. That was an experiment, and it worked. Now Dr. von der Decken was building a gigantic pile. At the outset he expected to have it ready sometime between 1972 and 1975. In fact he unveiled a fifteen-megawatt reactor well before the end of the 1960's, using 100,000 of his odd balls.[38] Von der Decken had been under some pressure. Herr Krupp, with his extensive engineering background, seemed mesmerized by the project; he was forever driving out to examine it and ask sophisticated questions.

The new pile, Dr. von der Decken explained, would be a breeder-reactor. To a layman this was portentous: "After the pilot works, you can get plutonium from the breeder, and with that you can hatch a plutonium bomb." He added, "This one will only produce juice for the power stations, of course." Of course. Krupp's U-235 was provided by the U.S. Atomic Energy Commission. That showed how long ago yesterday was, though naturally it offered no hint of when tomorrow would arrive, or what it would be like.

☒   ☒   ☒

On March 29, 1956, Bertha Krupp had celebrated her seventieth birthday in Villa Hügel, and the family paused in its headlong plunge into the future for a moment of homage. Bertha was still the queen of the Ruhr and, for many, of Germany. Exactly seven decades earlier her gaunt, septuagenarian grandfather had glared down at the female infant in the small wing of the castle. Seventeen months later his emaciated corpse had been slowly carried down the hill by the light of flickering torches, and now that she herself was approaching the age he had been then, her subjects realized how remarkable a link to the past she was.

She observed the last March Thursday in 1956 by setting a flat fur hat squarely on her head, draping a fleece shawl over her weeds, and walking over to Villa Hügel for a review of the Direktorium. Followed by Alfried, a head taller, and Arndt, a head shorter, she trooped the line. It was a scene from the Wilhelmstrasse 73 she had known as a girl; candlelight illumined the tapestried walls, and the directors, in striped trousers, stood at attention with their hands folded over their loins and bowed deeply as she passed. Following the protocol of such occasions, she ignored them, staring straight ahead and gliding across the parquet with that slow, graceful, heel-and-toe gait which must be learned in childhood or never. Afterward she donated a new door to a Salzburg church; dedicated Bertha-Schwestern-Wohnheim, the modern Essen nursing home which had been named for her; and received gifts.[39]

Though heartwarming, it was all rather anticlimactic, for she had received the greatest present in her life five months earlier. Stukas, 88's, and the mammoth howitzers had been christened in her honor, and none had impressed her, but her patrician poise had been shattered on the morning of October 11, 1955, by a telephone call to her red brick villa at Berenberger Mark No. 10 informing her that among the last eight hundred Wehrmacht soldiers to be returned from Siberia was a lanky, ragged officer who, despite his beard, bore the unmistakable high brow of the dynasty. It was Harald, long ago given up as killed in action or executed.[40]

At that moment he had been milling around in Friedland Stalag, near Göttingen. An alert Essen reporter had identified him. Harald had volunteered nothing; like his comrades, he was in a state of bewilderment. Bertha was too overwhelmed to make the trip. Alfried was busy capturing Krupp markets, and Berthold was on holiday in Greece with his wife, celebrating the birth of their first son, so Waldtraut raced down from Bremen, picked up a new Mercedes from the family garage, and found her brother huddled in a corner of the compound, wary and frightened. She wanted to take him directly to a hotel and call a tailor, but he begged off. Too much was happening too fast — he felt dizzy. He asked her to leave him there and come back next day. "Then, having sent her away," he recalled afterward, "I discovered that I had to spend seven or eight hours talking to newspaper people. But it worked out very well. I had no real idea of the situation in the Bundesrepublik, or, for that matter, in Villa Hügel. They filled me in, and I gave each of them his little anecdote."

In the morning Waldtraut returned with the tailor and drove her confused brother to a secluded hotel suite in Kassel, twenty-five miles away. For two days he slept, was measured, adjusted to a richer diet, and sorted out ten Orwellian years for her. It was an extraordinary story; his sister listened with horror and fascination.

Betrayed at Frankfurt-an-der-Oder just as he was about to be repatriated, he had been confined in a Moscow political prison from May 1946 to March 1947; then, for the next three years, in solitary confinement on the outskirts of the city — just where, he never knew. His fellow inmates were Wehrmacht generals, KZ Lagerführers, German scientists, party *Bonzen*, and Reich diplomats, though the Russians designated all of them prisoners of war. The first year of interrogations seemed interminable. Eight summers later he wryly told an American writer, "We called these sessions 'studies,' because they were studying us and we were studying them."

Really there wasn't much to learn from Harald. Like Berthold, he had only the haziest idea of what Gustav and Alfried had been up to. His questioners tried every conceivable psychological technique. Once, told to prepare a speech on "The Childhood of the Son of a Capitalist," he offered two reminiscences: playing with flowers and falling down in a boys' game. His captors were infuriated. That sort of thing, they spluttered, might have come from a speech on the childhood of the son of an exploited worker.

In disgust they flung him in a cell for three years. Alone, he pieced together a spotty, distorted, but not altogether inaccurate picture of the world outside. He knew of Alfried's trial at Nuremberg, for example, and though the newspapers slipped under his steel door were crowded with gloomy reports of chronic unemployment in West Germany and accounts of the postwar Volkswagen's abysmal failure, none of it deceived him: "You learn to sift the truth from totalitarian papers, and I'd had great training under Goebbels."

By December 1949, when his eldest brother was beginning his seventeenth month of imprisonment at Landsberg and Gustav was rapidly approaching the end in the inn below Blühnbach, Harald thought he saw a chance of freedom. All the Germans against whom any sort of evidence had been gathered had been tried and dispatched. His hopes were quickly dashed, however; the remaining two thousand convicts were summarily indicted as "criminals of war." In January (it was the week of Gustav's cremation, although, of course, Harald was ignorant of that) his dog-eared dossier was brought into his cell, accompanied by three judges and an interpreter who addressed him as *"Kriegsverbrecher"* — he had, he realized, already been condemned. The court accused him of teaching Rumanians how to use Krupp guns, of espionage in Bessarabia, of having been in contact with C–1 (Wehrmacht intelligence), and of being a top Nazi.

He replied that there was nothing illegal in artillery instruction during wartime, that he had only been in Bessarabia two days showing untrained troops how to sight howitzers, and that he had known only one C–1 officer, whom he had met in a Soviet POW cage. ("That doesn't matter," a member of the court snapped.) The last charge was the most serious. Harald pointed out that he had been a National Socialist just two years. He couldn't deny having met Hitler, Göring, Goebbels, and Himmler, but the circumstances had been somewhat unusual; he had been a youth and they had been guests in his father's house. The drumhead court-martial was unimpressed. He was sent out of the cell for five minutes; when he returned he was informed that he had been sentenced to twenty-five years in a labor camp.

Thus, while the Americans were preparing to free Alfried, who had been deeply involved in the Nazi regime, his innocent brother, whom the Führer had disinherited in the Lex Krupp, was being transported to the eastern slopes of the Urals. Clad in grimy coveralls and ill-fitting boots, Harald toiled for five years in the iron mines near Sverdlovsk, nearly two thousand miles from home and closer to Mongolia or New Delhi than to Essen. Those who suffered in Krupp concentration camps may find a historic justice in this, but the blow could have fallen on a guiltier member of the family. In the spring of 1955 he had just completed a fifth of his term; lacking a pardon, he wouldn't be returned to Germany until the eve of his fifty-ninth birthday in 1975. Then, that spring, the Russians released all Austrian "criminals of war" slaving in the Urals. The two thousand Germans jubilantly told one another that their turn would come soon, and 40 percent, Harald among them, were right. The fate of the other twelve hundred, some of whom had become his closest friends remained — and would remain — obscure.

He finished his account as the Mercedes roller-coastered over the Rothaar range, Waldtraut skillfully twisting the big wheel as she negotiated the tricky fifteen-hundred-foot passes north of Kahler Asten's jagged peak. Her brother was in no condition to drive. He wouldn't have known where to look for the ignition switch. He had never seen a car like this, roads like these, or, for that matter, a suit like the one he was wearing. Until this morning, he hadn't put on civilian clothes in more than sixteen years. Adenauer was a meaningless name to him; he had never heard of John J. McCloy or Berthold Beitz, though he was intrigued by the transformations wrought by Ludwig Erhard. Another Schacht, he supposed — Alfried would know him. He would have to ask Alfried a lot, for the Reich he had left at the age of twenty-three wasn't at all like the Bundesrepublik he was seeing through the window of an onrushing car seven months before his fortieth birthday. The month before Eckbert had turned seventeen — he had been killed in Italy over nine years ago, Waldtraut had just said, but Harald thrust that out of his mind; one could absorb just so much — he himself had qualified as a junior lawyer (*Rechtsbeistand*). Now all he knew of law was that a man could be transported to a quarter-century of penal servitude because he had played *Fussball* on the lawn while his father was entertaining the Führer inside. It was useless to try to go back to courtrooms. He would have to find a new career. Perhaps Alfried could find him something.

The Konzernherr had darted back to be on hand when Harald reached Essen and to order the erection of a sign, festooned with Hügel evergreen branches, over the door of Berenberger Mark 10. HERZLICH WILLKOMMEN, it read — heartfelt welcome. The greeting was extended on the steps by Bertha and Alfried, and a Pressebild Krupp photographer has carefully preserved the scene. Waldtraut had a hand under Harald's arm — in fact she appeared to be holding him up. She had not begun to put on weight then. Her divorce and second husband lay ahead, and she was still the vivacious girl they had always known. Alfried, on the far right, wore the broadest grin of his life. Bertha stood between the two men in a light gray suit. Mother, brother, and sister were looking off toward their right; Harald alone stared straight at the lens. He too was beaming, but the beard had been trimmed into too tight an imperial, the hair was too slick, the novelty of the expensive suit, shirt, and tie was too obvious. His flesh was gray. His eyes alone were alive; the rest was wax. He felt restored only after the cameraman retreated and Alfried and Waldtraut tactfully remained by the entrance while mother and son wordlessly stepped inside. To him their talk was "deeply moving." Presently they emerged arm in arm, walking slowly through the grounds of Hügel and talking little. "A mother waits," Harald later said simply. "She knew why they had been keeping me in Russia. She knew it wouldn't have happened if my name had been Schultz or Schmidt."

✠   ✠   ✠

Had he been a Schultz or a Schmidt, that would have been the extent of his return: embraces, tender exchanges, and, afterward, intimate gossip. But no Krupp reunion is complete without the family lawyers, who in this case had astounding news for the dynasty's Lazarus. In the Urals he had thought of himself as penniless. Alfried, after all, had been the sole heir. Now Harald learned that he was a capitalist. While breaking rocks into stones with a sledgehammer outside Sverdlovsk he had become a millionaire. Under the Krupp Treaty signed at Mehlem, the Konzernherr owed him 2.5 million dollars — not much to Alfried, but enough to make his fellow ex-con financially secure. With this windfall Harald, like Waldtraut, Irmgard, Arnold, and Berthold, had become independent of the head of the house. Berthold had put most of his money into two firms — Wasag A.G., an Essen chemical company, and Gurid G.m.b.H., a Hamburg brake lining factory. Back from Greece, he took the resurrected Harald in as his partner, and Jean Sprenger decorated modern offices for them at Rolandstrasse 9, a block from the Saalbau.

In time Harald found a bride in Wuppertal-Barmen, twenty miles away, and built a home in Hügel Park; the television antennae of the three brothers crowned an eminence east of the castle, with Alfried's, naturally, the highest. Eventually twelve grandchildren were born to Bertha. The Konzernherr excepted, Gustav's sons and daughters had followed his advice and married into Germany's patriciate; Harald's wife, Doerte Hillringhaus, was the daughter of a Ruhr manufacturer; Berthold's father-in-law had been Ago von Maltzan, Weimar's ambassador to Washington between 1925 and 1927; and when Waldtraut's divorce came through she married a shipbuilder, a member of the new Teutonic aristocracy forming in Argentina. The daughters naturally followed their husbands. The sons remained in the looming shadow of *Urgrossvater's* vision of what a palace should look like; "This way," Berthold explained, "we all live together there at *der Hügel* behind the fence, and it is nice because our children play together and come to know one another."[41]

Thus Bertha's last years were blessed by a quiescence she had never known before. Damned in her cradle because she had been born a girl, left fatherless in her teens by Wilhelmine Germany's most sensational scandal, married to a xenophobic automaton sixteen years her senior, she had, while still a young matron, seen her childhood home threatened by bands of German Communists. To bear Waldtraut she had had to go into hiding. Two of her sons had been killed wearing the uniform of a Führer she despised. When her husband died she hadn't known where to put his ashes; his eldest son and heir had spent the day of the secret funeral confined in a Bavarian jail.

Women from freer cultures may carp. After all, they may argue, *she* was the Konzerndame from 1902 to 1943, the most critical years in the history of firm and Fatherland, and she had stepped down only after petitioning Hitler to transfer her power to Alfried. She was a woman of character and convictions. Why hadn't she asserted herself? To ask the question is to display a complete ignorance of Bertha and her Reich. It would never have occurred to her to rebel against Germany's patriarchy. In Gabriel Fielding's *roman à clef* about the Krupps, "*die Frau Kommerzienrat,*" as she is known, worries about her son's Nazism. To the baron in the novel she confides, "Alfried is a little different. Ever since he was a child —" But she goes no farther, and it never crosses her mind to intrude in his management of the firm she owns, even though slave labor camps crowd the landscape around the family castle. When Bertha visited Gustav in Düsseldorf prison with Baron von Wilmowsky, her only thought, as a German woman, was to comfort him; Tilo noticed, "Tearfully his wife assured him that he had proved himself worthy of her forefathers" (*dass er der Vorfahren würdig sei*).[42]

As she began her seventy-second year, peace at last came to her. If anything Alfried had become more withdrawn since his divorce, but his mother didn't miss Vera, and the details of the divorce suit and settlement were carefully kept from Berenberger Mark 10. Elsewhere all was tranquil. Her son's genius had restored *die Firma* to its former opulence and power. Berthold and Harald returned from business trips with stories of the Bundesrepublik's affection for the family. Her sons, her sister, her brother-in-law, two daughters-in-law, and the rising generation surrounded her red brick house, and on pleasant mornings she would stroll across the superbly contoured grounds of Hügel Park to have tea with Barbara beneath the copper-red leaves of the *Blutbuche,* around which they had played as little girls and behind which they had hidden when Marga Brandt had frantically searched for them. If the Ruhr became dull, Bertha's children could retire to their estates: Alfried's Blühnbach; Irmgard's Gildehaus, near Hanover; Berthold's Obergrombach, outside Karlsruhe; and young Arnold von Bohlen's villa, vacant now that the boy was preparing to enter Balliol College in Oxford, following his great-uncle Baron von Wilmowsky, his cousin Kurt von Wilmowsky, and his own father, who had walked the High Street with Hans Adenauer while General Hans von Seeckt and

Gustav Krupp were quietly perfecting the machine which would overrun France on Arnold's first birthday.[43]

Waldtraut was negotiating for an estate, and although Harald had returned too late to acquire one of the family's country homes, he had found refuge in hobbies. Alfried, his childhood hero, was still his idol; he consciously imitated him, acquiring a custom-built Porsche, a battery of expensive cameras, a private pilot's license and a plane. Berthold, meanwhile, had sold his Porsche. The favorite of Essen's younger generation, he drove his own Volkswagen and mocked familial tradition by hiring Johannes Schröder after Alfried had angrily fired him.

Bertha was closest to Kruppdom's older generation, to the widowed, and to the ill. Kruppianer in trouble who wrote her always received a personal answer, or, if they were ill, a bedside call. Beitz was away on business when his wife was rushed to Krupp's six-hundred-bed Krankenanstalt; Bertha, who had been visiting her nurses next door, was at Else's side before physicians had readied the surgical amphitheater, and she was still there when the distraught husband raced in to see his convalescent wife. But emergencies and tragedies were rare. Bertha was at her best in remembering their victims after others had forgotten. Each morning she would stand before the ornate, old-fashioned window in her front hall, anchoring one of her little hats in place with a long hatpin. Then, after a severe inspection, she would depart to call on other women in the Krupp community who, like her, wore lonely weeds.[44]

At 8:30 A.M. on the gray day of September 21, 1957, she rose from the table in especially good spirits. Five weeks earlier Alfried had turned fifty. A special issue of *Krupp Mitteilungen* had been devoted to his birthday. Gert von Klass had written a biographical sketch beginning with the memorandum Gustav had written to his executives at 2:15 P.M. August 13, 1907, announcing the birth of the next Konzernherr, and citing Alfried's triumphs in overcoming the injustices of the Justizpalast. Photographs had shown Krupp addressing the directors of the firm's subsidiary companies on the progressive theme of 1957, which had been named a *Jubeljahr* (jubilee year) in his honor. On the back of the issue Alfried, Bertha, and Arndt were pictured over the caption "*Drei Generationen Krupp,*" and she had been delighted to find this portrait framed on the parlor walls of the Kruppianer widows she visited. Reaching for her hat, she wondered aloud to her maid how many she would see that day.[45]

She saw none. The flat black pillbox was in place atop her white marcelled hair and the pin was poised to run it through when she crumpled to the carpet. Frantically the maid telephoned the hospital and then tried to reach members of the family. Alfried and Harald were away; Berthold himself was on the sick list with a heart attack. He was improving, but his mother's coronary was fatal. She lay unconscious with the doctor and the maid for two hours before succumbing. Two minutes later there was a skirr of rubber outside; Beitz dashed in. The physician had just crossed her hands and covered her with her favorite black shawl.[46]

Four days later, as her coffin lay in state in the castle's great hall, banked with flowers from virtually every capital in the world, Alfried reentered his old leather-walled study, closed the door, and wrote:

*Nach einem gesegneten und vielen Prüfungen unterworfenen Leben entschlief am 21. September 1957 im 72. Lebensjahr . . .*

After a life of blessedness and one subjected to many vicissitudes, there took place on September 21, 1957, in her 72nd year, the death of

Frau
Bertha Krupp von Bohlen und Halbach
née Krupp

For us she was always the kindhearted, understanding mother [*die gütige, immer verständnisvolle Mutter*], the loving family counselor and the guiding light of our house.

With her great human dignity and unchanging inner peace, she remained, even in the most trying of difficult times [*auch in den schwersten Notzeiten*], untouched by the passage of time and an example and incentive to us all.

In deep mourning

(for the family)
Alfried Krupp von Bohlen und Halbach

The funeral services will take place Wednesday, September 25, at eleven o'clock at Villa Hügel. The burial will then take place with immediate family only.

At the same time the urn of Dr. Gustav Krupp von Bohlen und Halbach, which has been brought to Essen, will also be buried.[47]

Hügel servants had lowered to half-mast the ten Krupp flags on poles outside and the eleventh on a roof staff. Dressed in black, Bertha lay in an open coffin for eight hours, and it seemed that the whole population of Essen had come to say farewell to her. Four abreast, they slowly circled the bier. It was that afternoon, for the first time, that an unknown pensioner discovered that death had literally divided the Krupps of pre-Nazi Germany. On the west wall of the hall hung a portrait which had commemorated the silver wedding anniversary of Bertha and Gustav. Within an hour the painting had become the most popular work of art in the Ruhr. The pensioner had found that if you drew an imaginary line down the canvas, you would separate the living from the dead. All those on one side were gone: Claus, Eckbert, Gustav, and now Bertha. On the other side were the survivors: Alfried, Berthold, Harald, Irmgard and Waldtraut.

Until Alfried's death spoiled the symmetry, the uncanny division continued to exercise a morbid spell over Kruppianer, and every Sunday during visiting hours fascinated visitors traced their fingers over the glass, evoking memories of those Auschwitz selections in which the condemned were sent to the left and those saved for Krupp labor went to the right.

Next morning at the precise stroke of eleven — as Gustav would have wished — the funeral services began. Earlier in the year Alfried had staked out the new family graveyard just outside the park, and slowly the hearse wound down the hill past streets renamed by the Konzernherr — Waldtrautstrasse, Arnoldstrasse, and Haraldstrasse, west on Eckbertstrasse, and north on Kruppallee to the peaceful, heavily fenced sanctuary off Westerwaldstrasse. Arndt stood behind his father; Anneliese had come up from her Tegernsee retreat to be with him. In a halting, barely audible voice Barbara whispered her last good-bye, from notes written in longhand under the flaming *Blutbuche* at dawn:

*Unvergesslich ist sie von uns gegangen.*
*Möge aber Frau Berthas Geist fortleben in Werk und Familie.*
*Das wollte Gott.*

Unforgettable, she has left our midst.
May Frau Bertha's spirit live on in her work and family.
So be it.[48]

The mourners withdrew; the sentinel resumed his post at the gate. Workmen raked smooth the pink granite walk, gardeners pruned the shrubs, and men with shovels covered the coffin. Beside it stood the urn bearing Gustav's ashes, and when the spades had banked the earth, a flat black marble slab was lowered over both. On a black marble scroll atop the stone craftsmen had chiseled

<table>
<tr><td align="center">*Gustav Krupp*<br>*von Bohlen und Halbach*</td><td align="center">*Bertha Krupp*<br>*von Bohlen und Halbach*<br>*Geb. Krupp*</td></tr>
<tr><td align="center">*7 August 1870 — 16 Januar 1950*</td><td align="center">*29 Marz 1886 — 21 September 1957*</td></tr>
</table>

The towering black monument to A. *Krupp   26 April 1812 — 14 Juli 1887* dominates the plot, and all the other inscriptions face away from it. Had Gustav been born a Krupp, doubtless some way would have been found around that, for the Germans, with their love of symbolism, would have cherished the coincidence of his birth on the very day that Napoleon III, battered by Krupp's cast steel cannon, ordered the entire French army to fall back on Châlons, where, in the words of his biographer, he "returned to his headquarters in a state of moral and physical collapse." He realized that "the Empire is lost"; in the words of Professor Michael Howard, "By the decision he took in the railway carriage in Metz station on the morning of the 7th of August, Napoleon acknowledged defeat."[49]

But that date was hidden from A. Krupp's tombstone. From its incredibly high ledges one could see, to one side, only the white plaque in memory of the lost bones of Alfred's father and, on the other side, the crypt of the great Kanonenkönig's son, adorned with a wreath and *die drei Ringe*. With a weak predecessor and a corrupt successor it is perhaps understandable that the master's grave and its attached bronze figures should look forbidding. Yet the displeasure seems to be directed toward neither plaque nor crypt. Partly this is a trick of landscaping; the walk curves westward, the seats face that way, and the tulips, pansies, and evergreens planted around the monument above the lean skeleton of A. Krupp are so arranged that its ghostly inhabitant appears to be glowering at the double slab. It is as though Grossvater were unable, even in death, to forgive Bertha her femininity.

# 29

✠

## Not a Stone Shall Be Sold

Alfried's every step now seemed to be guided by a conscious effort to match the achievements of the great ancestor he most resembled. On September 6, 1850, Alfred had dismissed his own mother's death in four terse sentences: "The first news I must tell you is anything but pleasant. Four weeks ago I lost my mother (*Ich habe Ihnen leider keine angenehmen Nachrichten zu geben. Vor 4 Wochen habe ich meine Mutter verloren*). Her pain was indescribable. Her end, when it came, was a release for which she had long yearned." Thereupon he had immediately plunged into an intricate discussion of business ("I have to tell you of the outstanding accessories for teaspoons of the filleted type"). His great-grandson, forged from the same block of Kruppstahl, shook aside familial suggestions that the firm observe a period of mourning after Bertha's death.[1]

Instead he insisted that Barbara drive to Bremen and christen the flagship of his seafaring subsidiary — MS *Tilo von Wilmowsky*, a 17,000-ton, 546-foot vessel powered by four Krupp diesel engines. Kruppianer *Geist* demanded it, he said firmly. A more probable incentive was Alfried's impatience to see the three-ringed prow of his new ship plowing water, hurrying his swelling cargoes of Konzern exports abroad and returning — in flagrant violation of his agreement with three governments — carrying its share of the 5,000,000 tons of ore now hauled to Krupp steel mills each year on Krupp bottoms.[2]

Thus, with the earth still fresh on her sister's grave, Barbara mounted the Bremen platform in a black coat and black beret and gently pushed the monstrous bow with her right hand. As she shoved she murmured, "*Ich taufe Dich auf den Namen* Tilo von Wilmowsky *und wünsche Dir allzeit glückliche Fahrt*" (I christen you *Tilo von Wilmowsky* and wish you auspicious sailing for all time). Alfried called hoarsely, "*Gott mit uns, und wir mit Gott — so setzen wir die Schiffahrt fort*" (God with us, and we with God — so we send our fleet onward), and Tilo, a trifle stooped now, watched a hull nearly twice as large as the largest warship *die Firma* had been allowed to build under Article 190 of the Versailles Treaty roar down its cradle and into the waters of Wesermünde.[3]

Yet although Krupp continued to reign as unchallenged head of the House, his mother's passing had released certain latent tensions. Their focus became Berthold Beitz. From the moment he arrived in Essen, Alfried's chief of staff had antagonized the Schlotbarone establishment. Behind his back he was called *Ruhrfremd* (alien to the Ruhr) and *Krupps Stössel* (Krupp's pounder). His manners, his scorn for convention, and his disregard for titles offended the firm's old guard, not all of whom were timeservers. Johannes Schröder had the keenest financial mind in Essen after Löser. He had joined the company as Löser's assistant in 1938, and as director of Krupp's Berlin office he had worked out the intricate scheme to circumvent Hitler's Wirtschaftsgruppe and liquidate the Reich bonds. Yet Beitz treated him like a fogy. He seemed to go out of his way to alienate traditionalists. Generations of *Kopfarbeiterinnen* had proudly typed the firm's correspondence under the letterhead *Fried. Krupp, Essen, Altendorferstrasse 103*. Beitz barred it from his office. He worked for Alfried, not the firm, he declared, and in a lapse of taste which shocked every executive he publicly announced his own salary: a million marks ($250,000) a year. His sycophants encouraged the slogan "In Essen there is but one prophet, and his name is Berthold Beitz." Alfried's Mohammed was capable of saying anything. At one of his first meetings in the paneled boardroom he told a Prussian count, "I know one woman who has held both you and me in her arms at different times." A glacial silence gripped the big cigar box. Beitz smiled. "Yes," he continued blandly, "you probably didn't know that Erna Stuth, who was your nurse in your childhood home in Demmin, is my mother."[4]

He prohibited heel clicking in his presence, frowned on monocles, and addressed foremen by their nicknames. "*Die Paternoster*," the queer man-size boxes which move in a perpetual vertical ellipse, serving the Hauptverwaltungsgebäude as crack-the-whip elevators, were speeded up on his instructions — a hazard for the infirm, since anyone who missed his timing could be crushed upon stepping on or off a paternoster. At times he didn't seem to trust any functionary over thirty. In an interview he lightly elucidated his concept of his relationship with his directors: "I think of myself as a sort of lion tamer (*Löwenbändiger*). I keep the lions — that is, the staff — performing properly; I don't allow them to devour one another (*dass sie einander nicht auffressen*); and I amuse myself and enrich Alfried by inventing new tricks for them."[5]

*Um Gottes Willen!* Imagine Herr Direktor Keller trying to eat Herr Doktor von Knieriem! Referring to them as beasts was bad enough on Altendorferstrasse; on the hill Beitz's novel behavior created the greatest sensation since Fritz Krupp's indiscretions in Capri. Not only had he built a home behind the fence; his futuristic house on Weg zur Platte was actually closer to Bertha's grave than were the homes of her children or her sister, and he jubilantly advertised himself as "a real Krupp." Real Krupps were disdainful. They thought him vulgar. Had he been a Friedrich von Bülow, a Graf Zedwitz-Arnim, or especially a Count Klaus Ahlefeldt-Lauruiz with his Savile Row suits, his flat on Eaton Square, and his charming Britishisms ("ruddy," "damme," "jolly fine") he might have received a marginal acceptance. But Beitz was not only hopelessly lower *Klasse*; he gloried in it. That a man in his position should be the son of a nursemaid was awkward enough; for him to make an off-color joke of it in the boardroom was intolerable. To all who would listen he told with relish how, when the Wehrmacht had finally drafted him from the management of Poland's Boryslav oil fields late in the war, he had rejected a commission and become a *Feldwebel* like his father before him. "The smartest thing I ever did," he would chortle, an unmistakable allusion to the higher casualties among officers. No *Heldentod* for Beitz, and no forelock tugging; of the German aristocracy he said contemptuously, "I can't stand them" (*Ich kann sie nicht leiden*). He openly preferred the company of brash, toadying upstarts, crying, "They're my boys!"[6]

"*Das sind meine Boys*" grated; clearly the epithet "*der Amerikaner*" was no exaggeration — the man was the greatest Amiphile in the Bundesrepublik. He was forever flying over for conferences in Fairfield County, Evanston, or Grosse Pointe, and no one was surprised when he announced the engagement of his daughter Barbara to an American businessman. He himself sounded like a member of the NAM, denouncing Bonn's civil servants as a *Bürokratie*. His taste in music was appalling; a visit to Weg zur Platte meant a torturous hour of shouting above cacophonous trombones, trumpets, saxophones, and tribal drums. He boasted that he was "introducing Krupp to the twentieth century." His employer's sisters-in-law struck back by remarking tartly that "Herr Beitz has steel elbows — with tungsten carbide tips." Among them, the Beitz garage became a legend. It was said to be modeled after Jayne Mansfield's bathroom, and there were rumors that he presided over arcane "bar-b-q's" wearing an apron decorated with coy slogans, cooking the steaks himself on an outdoor grill, and executing a peculiar little soft-shoe dance. Obviously the son of Erna Beitz, née Stuth, belonged with *seine Boys*.

So the family froze him out. Berthold and Harald told Alfried that they doubted he was *ernst*. Certainly he lacked seriousness on holiday. Camping out with Alfried in the Konzernherr's hideaway on the North Sea island of Sylt he dressed like a tramp. Aboard the *Germania* V he cakewalked the sixty-six feet from stem to stern, and at Sayneck, the elaborate shooting box Fritz Krupp had built on the Rhine to entertain attractive youths from his grotto and gay Offizierskorps friends, he ran about in the forest firing his gun like a berserk *Flakgeschütz* triggerman, terrifying the staff and hitting nothing. For years Alfried and Berthold had shared the lodge under a tacit understanding; even Tilo and Harald, who enjoyed stalking game with cameras, had stayed away. Beitz, identifying himself with Alfried, simply drove up in his sporty Mercedes and took over. The consequence was that Berthold avoided the place and his wife, Beitz's most implacable foe, now cut him dead. Whenever a confrontation seemed imminent, Frau Edith Carola von Maltzan von Bohlen und Halbach would scoop up her young son and descend upon 43 Rue Foch, Paris, where her brother, Baron Dr. Vollrath von Maltzan, having followed his father and his wife's distant cousin Chip into the diplomatic corps, was the Bundesrepublik's ambassador to France. Naturally Harald's wife didn't want to cope alone, so the father of Frau Doerte Hillringhaus von Bohlen und Halbach would be favored by a visit from his daughter. That left Beitz alone with the Bar-b-q pit, Muggsy Spanier, the all-tile garage, and his family. It was a pity Vera hadn't waited nine months before divorcing Alfried. With Bertha gone, she might have made the marriage work; she and Else Beitz had been such good friends.

The Konzernherr's brothers never let him forget their disapproval of his right-hand man. Socially the man was a *Klotz*, they insisted, and in business he was a dangerous visionary. It would be exaggeration to call this a family quarrel. They didn't argue. Their father's indoctrination had been too thorough. One didn't cross the head of the House. Whatever the women might do, the men could never feud with Krupp. Nevertheless, one was allowed to show independence. Berthold and Harald politely declined sinecures in the Konzern. They decided that only one member of the family should have offices in the Hauptverwaltungsgebäude, and unlike their mother, they declined to share the responsibilities for their own affairs with Beitz. Instead they asked Otto Kranzbühler to join them as chairman of their board.

The closest sign of an outright rift among Bertha's children was the Schröder affair. In the spring of 1962 he was among the half-dozen most respected economists in the Ruhr. Abruptly Alfried, on Beitz's advice, dismissed him. The ex-Finanzdirektor then published *"Der finanzielle Herzinfarkt"* (The Financial Coronary) in the Düsseldorf *Handelsblatt*, the *Wall Street Journal* of the Ruhrgebiet. It was a perceptive, thinly veiled attack on Krupp's fiscal policy, and Alfried's brothers thought it made so much sense that they put him on *their* payroll. He replied distantly that he had sacked the old man for another reason entirely. Schröder had shown up in Japan while Alfried was there with Arndt. He hadn't told Krupp he was coming; he had just appeared. This had been outright insubordination, a direct violation of the Konzern's *Organisationshandbuch*, and it had been intolerable. Alfried therefore had no intention of reading "*Der finanzielle Herzinfarkt.*" It had nothing to do with him.

He couldn't have been farther wrong. Indeed, it is doubtful that any Krupp made a graver error in the four centuries of the bloodline. As subsequent events were to prove, in suggesting that he read Schröders' nineteen cogent paragraphs his brothers had given him the best advice of his career, and in spurning it he betrayed the great-grandfather whose memory he cherished.

⍟   ⍟   ⍟

*Das Organisationshandbuch*, promulgated by Alfried three months after Bertha's death, had been designed as a tribute to Alfred's memory, as a new edition of the *Generalregulativ* of 1872. First drafted by Beitz after frequent consultations with American corporation lawyers, it pointed up once more the parallels between the two most gifted leaders of the family.

His relatives to the contrary, Alfried's appointment of Beitz had also been inspired by the past. In the *Familien-Archiv*, now housed in Hügel's *kleine Haus* and guarded by Schröder's waspish brother Ernst, Alfried had read that after the end of Alfred's war and the mighty forward thrust of the Gusstahlfabrik in its aftermath, the sole proprietor of the 1870's "was searching for an alter ego, to take his place at the head of the enterprise (*an der Spitze des Unternehmens*) and manage it precisely as he would himself."[7]

*Der Grosse Krupp*, his third successor had been excited to find, had ruled out steel executives. He himself could provide the best technical advice in the Ruhr. More important to him were managerial skills, and he had discovered them in Hanns Jencke. Alfred had approached Jencke eight years after the last Krupp shell had been fired from Châtillon plateau — Alfried had made his offer to Beitz eight years after *his* last shell had been fired in World War II — and the subsequent transformation in the character of the enterprise had been startling:

> With Jencke a new epoch opened [*Mit Jencke beginnt insofern eine neue Ära*]; the supervisors, and later the Krupp board of directors, were assigned their proper functions, consulting the proprietor of the company only on issues of vital importance. . . . A worldly man in the best sense of the term, a superb organizer with a good business mind, a self-reliant individual ever prepared for fresh responsibilities, Jencke saw to it that stability was restored under his leadership. His forcefulness and innate executive ability made bluffs and cover-ups impossible [*Seine grosse Sicherheit und natürliche Autorität schliessen es aus, dass man ihm Szenen machen kann*]. . . . In practice, if not in name, he became chief

of the enterprise's worldwide ventures until the death of Friedrich Alfried Krupp in 1902.[8]

Beitz looked like a second Jencke to Alfried. He wasn't. The bespectacled, walrus-mustachioed Prussian who had paraded through the shops in jackboots was as different from *der Amerikaner* as two bright entrepreneurs could be. To his post as *Vorsitzender der Prokura* (chairman of the board) Jencke had brought not only the record of his dazzling performance as a railway executive but also a wealth of contacts in the establishment of the Second Reich and, most important, years of solid experience at the high old-fashioned desks of the first Kaiser's treasury department. To the grander title of *Generalbevollmächtigter* (General Plenipotentiary) Beitz brought a shoeshine and a smile. He was a superb salesman with a first-class mind, but he lacked Jencke's grounding in economics and resented Johannes Schröder's attempts to instruct him.

Both men were products of their eras. Vorsitzender Jencke represented the serenity and self-confidence that followed Prussia's industrial revolution, crowned by her feat of arms at Sedan. Beitz, on the other hand, was typical of post-Hitler Germany. Outwardly he was cocky, but his inner insecurity was revealed by his aping of the customs popular, so he thought, in the nation which had overwhelmed the Führer. While Jencke had methodically climbed the ladder of achievement one rung at a time, Beitz had bounded up it, fleeing from the memory of that first ghastly winter of peace, when he, Else, Barbara and little Bettina had nearly starved in a bombed-out, one-room summer house outside Hamburg. On the way up his quick mind and extraordinary memory had picked up the jargon, slick mannerisms, and superficial skills of a *Generalbevollmächtigter*. Yet he gave himself away at every turn. "I fly to Poznan, Poland, this weekend in my own Jetstar," he once said to me with studied carelessness. On another occasion he jabbed his finger at the air and remarked, apropos of nothing, "I told Khrushchev, 'Yes, we are capitalists, but we are three hundred and fifty years old, and I am a self-made man.' " Only the last was true. Beitz was too big a spender to accumulate capital, and he had risen from obscurity. The son of the Pomeranian Lancer sergeant and bank teller was an incomparable actor, but the fact remains that he was playing a part.[9]

He was enchanted by the role in which Krupp had cast him. "I'm Alfried's alter ego," he would say, adopting the archivist's phrase. A new constitution for the firm pleased him, too, and his appearance in Essen marked the resurrection of a title which, though authorized for Alfried by the Lex Krupp, had lain among yellowing papers since the first Kanonenkönig's funeral in the summer of 1887. In the future his *Chef* would be the firm's *alleinige Inhaber*, its sole proprietor.[10]

On September 9, 1872, the eccentric scarecrow had signed the last page of his *Generalregulativ*, "Alfred Krupp, *alleinige Inhaber*." Searching for ways to translate Alfried's reorganizational needs into prose, Beitz drove to the *kleine Haus* and asked Ernst Schröder for the original. The first paragraph fired his imagination:

> *Die wachsende Ausdehnung der Werke und Geschäfte der Firma Fried. Krupp lässt es wünschenswert . . . für gegenwärtige und kommende Zeiten eine gesicherte Ordnung und ein harmonisches Zusammenwirken zu verbürgen, und damit das Gedeihen des Ganzen, wie die Wohlfahrt jedes einzelnen zu sichern.*

> The increasing growth of the works and business of the firm of Fried. Krupp makes it desirable, indeed mandatory, to solidify and perfect those precepts and laws which are responsible for the present prosperity of the enterprise, and simultaneously to set forth clearly the rights and duties of each department and position in the shops and in the management, determining their exact limits in order to assure, insofar as this is possible, well-grounded business procedures and harmonious action by all, both in the present and in the foreseeable future, and the stability of the enterprise and well-being of its employees.[11]

Afterward Beitz told a reporter, "I went back to an old document, the General Regulations set out in the year 1872 by Alfried Krupp's great-grandfather. I gave it out again in modern form, just adding a few sentences." That wasn't exactly what happened. It was Alfried, not Beitz, who issued the *Organisationshandbuch* of January 1, 1958, and both men did much more than retouch the original.

They had no choice; the *Generalregulativ* was outdated. The chief difficulty, as Beitz conceded afterward, was *"die Betriebe,"* the associated companies. The nineteenth-century Krupp had owned a cast steel factory. The only purpose of his other holdings had been to feed it. Alfred's twentieth-century descendant was the proprietor of an array of companies offering 3,500 products and services, including mineral water, locomotives, orchids, soft drinks, supermarket goods, hotels, pastries, greenhouses, slaughterhouses, furniture factories, books, bridges, phonograph records, false teeth, false hair, false limbs, and falsies. Alfried shared ownership with others in a few of them, and in the front offices of these "companies of limited liability" responsibility was divided. Beitz was not alone in viewing elderly, starched-collar Kruppianer skeptically; Krupp had reservations about them, too. The enterprise had become so vast that many senior officials had never seen the Konzernherr. They were proud to hang his photograph on their office walls, but in practice they tended to regard themselves as civil servants, each Führer of his own domain. "The great problem," Alfried explained in an interview, "was that in the years immediately after the war, partly through Allied but also even through German influence, all our factories had been working a little apart from one another. Each was indepentent of the rest, and there was no feeling of belonging together (*Zusammengehörigkeit*). So the first thing to be done was obviously to get all the different factories and companies working together again — and to build up a new central administration."[12]

In practice his solution was the precise opposite: decentralization. He believed in bigness. Therefore, he concluded, the only way to eliminate the dangers of bureaucracy was to introduce federation, converting his empire into a commonwealth within which "individual initiative will be combined with unquestioning obedience" (*individuelle Initiative ist mit unbedingter Diszin zu verbinden*). Essen would continue to be Krupp's center of gravity. Supreme leadership would come from the tall, dark, and unhandsome Hauptverwaltungsgebäude, and eighty junior vice presidents would have permanent offices there. But the old Firma Fried. Krupp would now be, in essence, a *Muttergesellschaft*. "The Proprietor, or his General Plenipotentiary, shall lead the whole firm," read the opening clause of the new manual. That was at the very top of the structure; Krupp reigned and Beitz ruled, assisted by a streamlined executive board of five members: Hermann Hobrecker, Hans Kallen, Paul Keller, Paul Hansen, and, at the outset, Johannes Schröder. Under them were twenty-eight chief companies (*Konzernhauptbetriebe*) and fifty-two companies (*Konzernbetriebe*). Each was led by a technical director and a commercial manager — in the Industriebau, for instance, Hansen supervised production and Hans Seboth led the salesmen. All were invited to go their own way. Their workers weren't encouraged to think of themselves as Kruppianer any more. Indeed, executives weren't even required to buy their raw materials from other Krupp subsidiaries; they could shop around the Ruhr for low bids. Any given subsidiary was to have "the maximum freedom possible, limited by the fewest possible instructions while it meets its obligations, unhampered by red tape (*um seine selbstständige Aufgabe verantwortungsbewusst zu übernehmen*). . . . The skills and initiative of individuals are to be given free rein, restricted solely by the general well-being of the enterprise."[13]

As Alfried commented in signing the *Handbuch*, "The structure of the concern has changed considerably as a result of the war and its aftermath. While previously the concern was built around a central core, the Gusstahlfabrik, it now consists of a number of divisions, all ranking equally within the organization."* That was clear enough, and the reorganization made sense. It was efficient, it introduced healthy intrafirm rivalries, yet the chain of command remained. Krupp's revised lines of authority held up admirably under the vicissitudes of a decade. Still, the second *alleinige Inhaber*, like the first, insisted upon adding his own imprint. The name was too simple; he had to change it to *Der Plan und die Bestimmungen über die Neuorganisation der Firma Fried. Krupp* (The New Plan and

---

* For Krupp's organization chart, see Appendix II.

Precepts of Organization of the Firm of Fried. Krupp). Carl Hundhausen, brooding over *Image*, proposed that all references to the first Kanonen-könig and his General Regulations be deleted. Reminders of the past, he pointed out, might arouse pride within the Bundesrepublik, but they would stir up bitterness abroad. Alfried bridled; he even insisted on adopting certain phrases of his great-grandfather verbatim. The constitution, he inserted in his own hand,

> . . . *führt die Tradition des Generalregulativs für die Firma Fried. Krupp, das im Jahre 1872 von meinem Urgrossvater erlassen wurde* . . .
>
> . . . carries forward the tradition of the General Regulations of the firm of Fried. Krupp, as laid down *by my great-grandfather* in the year 1872. Their purpose was to set forth the rights and duties of each department and position in the shops and in the management, determining their exact limits in order to assure, insofar as this is possible, well-grounded business procedures and harmonious action by all, both in the present and in the foreseeable future, and the stability of the enterprise and well-being of its employees.[14]

The final touch was the stringing together of aphorisms which might have been lifted from the works of Ganghofer. Krupp was a child of Wilhelmine Germany — a very late child, to be sure, but *kaisertreu* all the same, with an unslakable thirst for the pablum his godfather had ladled out. S.M. would have been as entranced as the original sole proprietor to read such musty dust catchers as:

> Individuals must combine all their energies into absolute cooperation [*Die Einzelanstrengungen aller Mitarbeiter müssen in echter Zusammenarbeit zu einer Gesamtanstrengung werden*]. It is not enough for a man to do his own job. He must also bear in mind the needs of other subsidiaries.

Or:

> He who perseveres, following the light of his conscience, need never be wary of his superiors; rather should he consider them essential to the completion of his tasks [*für seine eigene Tätigkeit*].

Or:

> Every man has the right to state his case until the directors have made their ruling [*Jeder hat das Recht, seine eigenen Ideen darzulegen, bis das Direktorium seine Entschlüsse gefasst hat*]. Then he must toe the line, whether he believes it right or wrong.[15]

Beitz couldn't have written such lines. He was capable of absurdity and shallow economics, but he knew the idiom of his own time. Only a throwback could have coined these barren maxims, stressing the duties of loyal employees and skirting his own obligations to them. Alfried and his father had always been at odds, and he rarely mentioned his grandfather. So, with Bertha's death, he had grown even closer to the Krupp whose baptismal name he bore, whose very bone structure he had inherited, whose domestic life had been very like his own, and who had given voice to his own authoritarian ideology three wars, 200 million casualties, and a thousand billion dollars in war budgets ago.[16] When a Parisian columnist read of Alfried's intention to *décentraliser* he taunted him, "*Alfrieda, ma vieille, tu faiblis!*" But the Konzernherr wasn't weakening. Really he was restating autocratic propositions which other European industrialists had struck out a generation earlier. Indeed, scanning Alfred's *Generalregulativ* of 1872 and Alfried's *Neuorganisation* of 1958, one is almost tempted to cross-examine those who scoff at reincarnation.

✠    ✠    ✠

The new *Organisationsplan des Krupp-Konzerns* diagram was checkered with blue-bordered boxes bearing the name of each subsidiary and straight lines showing channels of responsibility. Yet something was missing. In the lower right-hand corner of the chart the largest box of all stood alone, unlinked to the skein. In thick black letters it was headed *Grundstoffbereich* (basic sphere). These were the segregated properties which Alfried had promised to sell by January 31, 1959, a month after the promulgation of his new charter. He remained unreconciled to the bargain he had struck at Mehlem almost six years earlier; even as West Germany mourned the Reich's lost territories to the east, so did Krupp lament the isolation of his coal mines and steel mills.

In retrospect one wonders why. Once I asked him outright whether it wouldn't have been wiser to abide by the word he had given the Allied High Commissioners and sell out. The question merely set off fresh recollections of the gospel according to Alfred. He reviewed his great-grandfather's wishes and added coolly, "This firm has felt for a hundred and fifty years that if you want to produce good steel, you must stick to vertical integration." It wasn't really an answer. Integration wasn't the issue; he had sworn to the world that he would never produce any steel, good or otherwise. Nevertheless, others who raised the same question received essentially the same reply. To intrafirm suggestions that he confine himself to manufacturing and distribution — the profits from his Essen groceries alone would have made him a millionaire — he answered firmly, as he did with this writer, that he was a steelmaker born and bred. "A cobbler," he said in his favorite phrase, "must stick to his last" (*Schuster bleib bei deinem Leisten*).[17]

Much later, on the tenth anniversary of the Mehlem signing, Fritz Hardach sat gloomily in his Ruhr study and mused, "Suppose Herr Krupp gave in now. Who would buy the stock? The prices are too low. It's coal versus oil these days, especially oil from the Middle East, and also British and even American coal." In an office on the Elbe a man who had known the Krupps since his youth said that same spring, "He should have sold. But to understand the Krupps you must first understand that *they don't give in*. The old man wrote Fritz in 1874 that he wanted his order preserved for all time. Alfried can never forget that. Moreover, he still believes that the Third Reich was right, that he was battling for a moral cause, and that capitulation would be a betrayal of the Führer."[18]

In the months after the signing of the treaty Alfried could easily have divested himself of his sequestered holdings. To be sure, there were no German offers — it was "a point of honor among the Schlotbarone not to bid," a *Handelsblatt* editor explained — and interest abroad was slight. There was a token bid from Holland, there was a ten-million-dollar offer from America's Colorado Fuel and Iron Corporation. Alfried rejected both as inadequate, and the three trustees agreed. They were right: his compensation had been set at 70 million. Very few capitalists invest that much in a foreign country, especially if they face a surly labor force and a hostile population. Nevertheless there was an alternative. Though the German people are wary of common stocks, Volkswagen had proved that a breakthrough was possible. If others could coax marks from savings accounts, certainly the tremendous prestige of Krupp would send Düsseldorf's *Aktienindex*, the German equivalent of the Dow-Jones industrial average, soaring. But Altendorferstrasse remained mute, and issue after issue of *Capital*, the financier's bible, reported, *"Keine Krupp Kapital-Gesellschaft, keine Käufer"* (No Krupp stock corporation, no offer).[19]

On Wall Street, John J. McCloy exploded, "The Germans have tried to get me to intervene and have this covenant discarded. I've said, and I still say, that he volunteered to sign it and he should stick to it. He says it was extorted from him under duress. That's absolutely untrue." In the large American consulate at Düsseldorf, in effect an embassy to the Ruhrgebiet, a large framed photograph of the Rheinhausen works was hung at the head of the stairway where no visiting Schlotbarone could miss it. The barons turned away. "The Ruhr," they said, "sticks together." That intransigence raised their morale, but it didn't do much for their government's. Konrad Adenauer had made a pledge of his own in 1954. In exchange for full sovereignty, NATO membership, and partnership in the Western European Union, the Bundesrepublik had reluctantly assured its Allies in Paris that Bonn would undertake responsibility for carrying out Law 27. That made the chancellor Mehlem's policeman. Seeing the trap, he had foxily added that since the law was about to expire, "I must therefore reserve the right to raise this question again at some suitable time" (*Ich muss mir deshalb das Recht vorbehalten, dieses Thema bei einer passender Gelegenheit wieder anzuschneiden*).[20]

Three years later Krupp reminded *der Alte* of his reservations and, in a rare public address, argued that big business had the right and even the obligation to become as large as possible: "If we stand by and watch our great, integrated industries shrink and be forced to break up, we can be very certain that other countries will not follow our example. To drive Germans out of the markets of the world (*werden uns von den Weltmärkten vertreiben*) they will exploit the very methods of cheap, efficient mass production (*Grossproduktion*) that Germans invented. Strong as he was, Adenauer knew that no German chancellor had successfully defied Krupp, and already he was wavering. All the same, he was no rubber lion. He said, "We face a grave future menace (*Darin liegt eine grosse Gefahr für die Zukunft*). It is that a small band of economic giants will seize the German economy with so tenacious a stranglehold that the government will be obliged to move against them."[21]

The chancellor had no intention of moving. He was a realist, and henceforth he and his obese economics minister would be reduced to Krupp panjandrums while the hierarchy of the Ruhr, freed from Silesian competition, grew tighter and more inbred than ever. An octopus, someone once said, is hard to kill. Now that Krupp owned more than a hundred factories in the Bundesrepublik alone, he seemed immortal. Bonn's anticartel laws remained on the books, but they were dead. With each passing week smaller barons grasped the fact that Alfried had successfully "reconcentrated" his holdings, and within a year of Adenauer's paean to free enterprise over a hundred German firms had applied for mergers. There was one brief flare-up, when

. . . Beitz came with Alfried Krupp to the Schaumburg Palace in Bonn to get federal aid for the Krupp firm. The Essen concern wanted to divest itself of the Allied order to sell its iron and steel holdings by 1959 [*der Essener Konzern wollte die alliierte Auflage loswerden, seinen Stahlbesitz, das Hüttenwerk Rheinhausen, bis zum Jahre 1959 zu veräussern*]. When the owner of the firm explained in well-chosen words how greatly the sales order shackled him by making him keep separate books, thus preventing him from pooling his profits and losses, Manager Beitz aggressively asked the old chancellor if the Krupps were "second-class people" [*"Menschen zweiter Klasse"*], who were not entitled to that free choice of vocation which was guaranteed in German law. When the chancellor asked that he be given time, Beitz threatened to fight for their rights all the way to the federal court.[22]

To me Beitz said, "The segregated properties would never stand up in a German court. That treaty violates our law. But Alfried — well, you know, he insists on being correct. I say to him, 'Go to Africa for two or three months. I'm your General Plenipotentiary, I'll take care of it; I'll sell to somebody, maybe to Arndt.' Alfried is such a gentleman. He just looks at me sadly and shakes his head." He was right to shake his head. Had Beitz studied the pact he would have realized that no sale could be consummated without trustee approval, and that as a member of the family Krupp's son was an ineligible buyer. Moreover, if the Generalbevollmächtigter had read the Paris Pacts of 1954 he would have known that West Germany was committed to support of the Krupp Treaty. The pacts had become part of the Bundesrepublik constitution. A courtroom was the last place to plead the sole proprietor's case.[23]

Instead Alfried chose to opt for the court of public opinion and the quieter council rooms of the Atlantic alliance. Conservative German newspapers waged a vigorous campaign arguing that a forced sale by a free citizen of the Bundesrepublik would be outrageous, that the terms were impractical, and that the treaty was "a leftover from the Morgenthau Plan and the era of Allied economic oppression in Germany." As early as 1954 Beitz demanded that "our" coal and steel holdings be returned. "Whatever Alfried can't say because he stands by his promise I'll say for him instead," he declared, adding that as long as he himself remained in the firm "Not a stone shall be sold" (Kein Stein soll verkauft werden). The following year Schröder told a meeting of industrialists that Krupp without steel was "like a woman without the lower part of her body" (Krupp ohne Stahl war wie eine Frau ohne Unterleib) — an earthy simile which Beitz promptly adopted.[24]

By 1957 Adenauer was openly backing the treaty scrappers; subsequently Erhard described Mehlem as "out of date." Meanwhile Alfried had been moving toward open defiance of Luther, Lubowski, and Goetz, the three trustees of his sequestered properties. He had begun by sending his extroverted Generalbevollmächtigter as an uninvited guest to board meetings of sequestered firms from which he himself was excluded. ("Er war aus Neugier gekommen," Krupp blandly explained; "He came out of curiosity.") Next, two hundred managers of segregated firms were abruptly summoned to Essen for an inspection of their books and a full accounting of what had been going on in their shops. The penultimate move was made in September 1957. Seven months earlier Konrad Adenauer, in a letter addressed to the State Department, Whitehall, and the Quai d'Orsay, had formally requested that the Krupp Treaty be allowed to die on the books. The French reserved judgment. Washington, which by now had become Essen's tacit collaborator, agreed. However, the British, in whose country anti-Krupp sentiment ran strongly,* asked the chancellor for a detailed report on progress in "breaking up concentrations of German industry." Beitz, a man of words, protested, "We must all row our hardest

---

* Hard to understand, because England was the one of the European Allies which had never heard the harsh bark of the oppressor on its own soil. One possible explanation is the close ethnic relationship between Englishmen and their oppressors. The British may expect much more from their cousins.

for the West; there is no point in tying the arms of one of your best oarsmen." Krupp, a man of action, crossed his Rubicon or, to be more apt, his Rhine. Carefully waiting until three days before the new Bundesrepublik elections, when public attention would be pre-empted by campaign charges, he quietly announced that he had just appointed Herr Berthold Beitz chairman of the Hütten- und Bergwerke Rheinhausen holding company for sequestered properties, that all members of the board would be Krupp directors, and that the holding company's head offices were being moved from Duisburg on the Rhine to the Hauptverwaltungsgebäude.[25]

After the chancellor's landslide third-term victory on September 15 the implications of the Konzernherr's deft unilateral move began to be appreciated by the sophisticated readers of *Handelsblatt* and *Capital:*

> It was generally understood that this step meant Krupp's defiant reoccupation of those parts of his empire from which he was still banished by the treaty [*Jedermann begriff, dass diese Geste die Wiederkehr Krupps in diesem Teil seines Reiches symbolisierte, aus dem er noch immer durch den Vertrag verbannt war*]. . . . Alfried Krupp's protests that he was merely waiting for buyers was merely a thin screen to save the face of the Allies while he tore up his promise. Krupp statisticians once more listed the plants with their overall profits and output as though they still belonged to the Konzern, or, to be precise, as if they again belonged to it.[26]

Three more years were to pass, and many more moves were to be made on the great chessboard, before Alfried would tell a *Jubiläum* that "all my holdings have now been amalgamated into a single company." But that was merely a formality. The deed had been done with his seizure of the holding company, and no one was more aware of it than Luther, Lubowski, and Goetz. The two bankers and ex-chancellor — the "three new wise men," as the German press sarcastically called the trustees — hadn't even been notified of the coup. Appointed by London, Paris, Washington, and Krupp himself, they had now been publicly snubbed. They appealed to Bonn, citing their mandate and Alfried's flagrant violation of the treaty. The Bundesrepublik answered that it could find no infringement of any existing agreement — a curious reply, since the three trustees held 100 percent of the holding company's shares. At the Deutsche Industrial Institute in Cologne the lesser barons rallied behind the big baron. The new watchword on the Rhine was "rationalize or die," which, in the jargon of the Schlotbarone, meant an even tighter concentration of productive capacity than they had achieved in their prewar heyday when, led by Krupp, fewer than a dozen men had controlled 90 percent of the Ruhr's steel flow. Under the Allied decartelization decree, the seven mightiest titans had been ordered to withdraw from the coal and steel industry. By the end of the 1950's all had complied — all but one, Number One.[27]

In his addresses to annual rallies of aging Kruppianer in Villa Hügel and at the Saalbau, Number One's belligerency grew with the decade. By 1958 he was openly defiant. The treaty, he said, was an "intolerable" invasion of the Bundesrepublik's sovereign rights. The Bonn-Essen alliance was now firmly forged; Erhard introduced a five-dollar-a-ton tariff on imported coal, designed to cut off nine million tons which had been scheduled for shipment from the United States during the coming year. Only if the agreement were torn up, Alfried insisted, could he and the western powers coexist. "I think we have been very patient," he told a Jubilee gathering, "but I believe that the time has now come when we must have the situation clarified." Before flying off on a tour of his Asian holdings he cited three reasons why he should be allowed to keep his steel mills and coal mines: German history proved that big cartels brought prosperity, the European trend was toward concentration anyhow, and German combines weren't so large as American corporations. "Faced with these problems," he concluded, "we fail to have any sympathy with talk about 'excessive concentration.' "28

He had left out quite a lot. American corporations listed on the New York Stock Exchange were owned by some twenty million shareholders; his firm, by one. And his "personal and moral obligation," as it had been described at Mehlem, remained unmet. As the head of one of Europe's oldest and proudest houses he resented accusations of fraud. Nevertheless he was clearly engaged in an elaborate campaign of deception. After his release from Landsberg he had publicly declared that he had "signed an undertaking not to produce coal and steel" and would "stick to it" (*ich werde mich daran halten*). Asked about this three years later by a *Time* correspondent he had repeated, "We have a moral obligation, and I will not look for escapes." In fact he was looking for little else. His colleagues, embarrassed by the record, explained that "Alfried is torn; he wants to keep his word, but he wants to make steel, too." But that is not what he said when the British evacuated Essen and returned the bulk of his Konzern to him. Nor was it true, as Beitz claimed, that "Alfried Krupp never promised to *break up* the coal and steel concerns. The agreement was only that he would not use his money to buy new interests in coal and steel." And even if that *had* been the agreement, Alfried would stand guilty of violating it, for during the five years when he was presumably divesting himself of heavy industry he was secretly acquiring vast new forges, furnaces, and shafts.29

Krupp's duplicity was unsuspected at the time, and none of his speeches, handouts or exchanges with foreign ministries hinted at the reasons behind it. Some were rooted in continental practice; the Common Market had retained certain built-in benefits which European cartels had always enjoyed and which were unknown in the United States. For example, transactions between Alfried's subsidiaries, including his sequestered properties, were exempt from turnover taxes. This peculiar practice, which was under investigation by Senator Estes Kefauver at the time of his death, encouraged the expansion of industrial giants at the expense of small business, and continues to handicap American concerns competing with Market firms.

But the Krupps have always transcended balance sheets. Beyond the tide of orders and contracts moving from in-baskets to out-baskets there were grander goals, chiefly the indestructible dream of a Teutonic Europe, to be achieved now, at last, in the global marketplace. *Réalités* wrote, "Krupp believes that Europe's past, her resources, and her techniques make her unbeatable when it comes to building the foundations of industrialization." Understandably Alfried did not tell a Parisian journal that he thought he could sweep aside the industrialists of France, with their depleted plants and low machine tool inventories. He was certain of it, though. One of his directors told this writer, "Charles de Gaulle reminds me of the typical German staff officer. The Generalstab was convinced that it could handle the Nazis — and de Gaulle is just as positive he can handle the Ruhr. The only reason Paris accepted the Schuman Plan was that the French had no doubt whatever that France would lead the economy of a united Europe. They actually thought they would swing more weight than Herr Krupp!"[30]

✠   ✠   ✠

When McCloy was told that Krupp was once more the richest man in Europe, he said, "I'm not surprised. Given the base from which he had to move and the resurgence of Germany, it was almost inevitable." McCloy's decision to unleash the Konzernherr had given Alfried his springboard. The Ruhr's key position in the realigned continent had assured him his goal; as *Réalités* conceded grudgingly, "from the standpoint of a united Europe — if you agree that the six Common Market countries will either prosper united or fall divided — Krupp is probably indispensable to the smooth running of Europe's economy tomorrow."[31]

The article was titled *"Roi Krupp."* Economically the dynasty's last König and the geologic freak over which his family had perched for nearly four centuries were far more important than the fluctuating politics of provincial Bonn. To a rational economic statesman like Jean Monnet, Krupp and the Bundesrepublik were one. Germany's other neighbors felt the same way, but unlike Monnet they wanted no part of the discredited Reich. However, U.S. policy, born in the airlift, sustained in central Europe by the introduction of Adenauer's democracy, and succored there by a hard German currency, pivoted on Bonn. Since Washington was injecting twelve billion dollars into the anemic continent, Americans felt they had a right to call, or at least to suggest, the tune. America's goal was to re-create the productivity of Western Europe. It could be done. The United States had done it, demolishing interstate barriers to create the greatest gross national product in the history of the world. George C. Marshall, extrapolating, had proposed to force a similar amalgamation across the Atlantic. The economists in Europe's ancient nation-states agreed. Only one, the United Kingdom, stood aloof — to the dismay of later British statesmen who were to hammer at the door of the Common Market, pleading for admittance.

Thus, at the outset, the Market comprised what were called the Five — Italy, France, and the three Benelux countries: Belgium, the Netherlands, and Luxembourg. Savage memories of steel-helmeted *Ubermenschen* haunted them all; Bonn was pointedly ignored. The omission crippled the proposed union, and during a small dinner at the Quai d'Orsay the winter before the Korean War the five foreign secretaries quietly tabled it. A year later Krupp emerged from Landsberg, and the countries which had suffered at his hands were obliged to restudy John Maynard Keynes's Cambridge lectures, delivered in the wake of Versailles thirty years earlier. "The statistics of the economic interdependence of Germany and her neighbors," he had said, "are overwhelming."[32]

Professor Pounds, a contemporary observer of the debate over whether Bonn should be admitted to the coalition, was a geologist, not an economist, and he was appalled by Krupp's past. Like Keynes, however, he recognized the inevitable. "An overall plan for European industry is impossible without the willing cooperation of the Ruhr industrialists," he wrote the year Alfried was freed. "The possession of the coalfield of the Ruhr puts western Germany into an immensely strong bargaining position, an advantage which she appears at the present time to be using to the full." Certainly America could export coal — could, indeed, sell it on the continent more cheaply than the Schlotbarone could. But the United States couldn't match the barons' quality: "The Ruhr has a near monopoly at least of the export of coking coal and coke. The commodity is urgently needed — especially in view of the concentration of British exports — in most other countries. No amount of political maneuvering can overcome this geographical fact, or rob the Germans of the power it gives them."[33]

Therefore the Five, in January 1959, became the Six. At number 24 Avenue de la Joyeuse Entrée in Brussels, the headquarters of the European Economic Community, Dr. Karl-Heinz Narjes, *chef de cabinet*, formally presented Bonn's representative to Dr. Walter Hallstein, the former Wehrmacht Oberleutnant who had become president of the Common Market. As a German, Hallstein preferred to call it the Europäische Wirtschaftsgemeinschaft. That pleased his countrymen. The Ruhr had another greater reason to be elated. The barons were destined to dominate the union. None of them took French industrial pretensions seriously, and Great Britain and the United States, the two economic powers whose efficient techniques might threaten them, were to be outsiders. To be sure, they themselves were committed now. A writer pointed out that "Europe's new Iron and Steel Community binds Krupp, and all West Germany, closer to the West, of which it is now an integral part" (*dessen integriertes Mitglied es jetzt ist*).[34]

The shrunken Reich was, at that low moment in its history, without choice. In the past trade had tugged its firms eastward. Later that pull might be felt again. Meanwhile, barring a thaw in Moscow and its buffer states, Germany's power base lay either in the Atlantic community or nowhere. If this attitude suggests something less than a rapturous embrace of the Free World, it is accurate. Totalitarians do not become antitotalitarian overnight. Krupp led his colleagues into the union with alacrity; he displayed no affection. For him, for them, and for their country this was a marriage of convenience, and no one knew better than Germany's former partners how quickly it could be dissolved if its ties became inexpedient. The skeptics reserved judgment. Though the *Wall Street Journal* approvingly reported that "a continuous series of group and individual conferences" were "constantly cementing the union of the Six," the *Nation* observed that "Krupp could wield monopoly powers, and could form part of a newly aggressive Germany," and Theodore H. White wrote that "If the Germans are swept again by one of those sea-tides of emotion which so violently seize them, then the new Union of Europe is useless; better it were that it had never been born." At times the vexing crises of the Cold War obscured the fact that for all the friction between them, none of the confrontations between Russia and the United States had flared into open conflict, while Germany had been the world's one great threat to twentieth-century peace. Should Bonn quit NATO, Americans would be hurt. But they couldn't claim martyrdom. One should always read the small print in the contract.[35]

# 30

DREIZIG

�֍

# Most Powerful Man
# in the Common Market

Alfried Krupp entered the Common Market as its richest individual and most powerful single industrialist. His Konzern was one of seven member firms in the great customs union with a four-billion-mark turnover, and the only one which was privately owned. He and his satellite Schlotbarone produced half the coal used by the Six, and in theory he could, with a crisp order to Beitz, halt three out of every four ships entering and leaving Rotterdam. Of course, he did no such thing. He wanted those cargoes even more than the Dutch wanted to unload them. Profit lay in cooperation; therefore he plunged enthusiastically into the new adventure. His exhibits at industrial fairs outdid all others in those gaudy displays of color which appealed so to the postwar continent. Boxcars shuttling between his factories bore the Market's ensign EUROP. To prove that he was a European first and a German second, he invested in equipment from the other Five (all lathes in Essen's *Maschinenfabriken* carried tiny metal plates identifying them as products of Les Innovations Mécaniques, the first French machines to be used by Kruppianer since the last plundering expedition in Mulhouse on November 20, 1944), and because of his eminence he was naturally invited to Brussels for those price-fixing sessions which were already giving Whitehall pause.[1]

But all this was peripheral. Most of his energy was absorbed by a tremendous double deal — not quite the same thing as a double cross, though it was that, too — which, if he could bring it off, should entitle him to a monument as tall and ornate as that of his *Urgrossvater* Alfred. D day was to be January 31, 1959; H hour at dawn. At Mehlem he had vowed that when the sun rose over the Ruhr that morning he would have completed his withdrawal from mines and mills. For five years he had been planning the exact opposite, yet so complex were his strategics and so baffling his tactics that the Allies, fellow Germans, and even friends and relatives were bewildered. Alfried Felix Alwyn Krupp von Bohlen und Halbach, they argued among themselves, was no Austrian corporal. He was a member of fourteen patrician clubs. Again and again he had assured Washington, London, Paris, and his own countrymen that he had made a moral commitment and meant to keep it. That a man of his breeding and background could be guilty of perfidy was inconceivable.

Nevertheless he was, and the omens, for those who could read them, were there. His attitude toward the Avenue de la Joyeuse Entrée was quite odd. Referring to himself in the monarchic plural he said, "The speeding up of economic integration offers us rather fewer opportunities [and] more risks. However, we maintain our favorable attitude toward the European community in the interests of international collaboration." It made no sense. Leveling tariff hedgehogs within the Six provided him with magnificent openings, not risks, and if Krupp was prepared to sacrifice profit for world harmony, this was the first anyone had heard of it — unless, of course, he was sidling up to Walter Hallstein and Karl-Heinz Narjes. But what could Brussels's street of joyous admission do for the Konzernherr? Speaking to three hundred *Jubiläum* veterans — like Nuremberg's September rallies, these spring ceremonies had become occasions for policy statements — he softly dropped the other shoe. Once more he solemnly declared that he could not break his Mehlem word; once more he asked that he be released from it. To the astonishment of those who had studied the treaty he suggested that it really wasn't a binding agreement. Then he added portentously: "We want to enter the Common Market on a level footing with other big undertakings, in order to compete with them."[2]

That was the first intimation of treachery — the first sign that he might proclaim what was to be known as *"die Annullierung der kruppschen Unterschrift"* (the withdrawal of the Krupp signature) unless the Mehlem *Diktat* was torn up and the Konzern given its proper place in the sun. Those who missed the clue needn't blush. It was blurred and faint; otherwise Alfried wouldn't have left it. The most revealing aspect of his conduct was not what he did, but what he did not do. Two months before the expiration of his five-year limitation he had consummated exactly two sales: the Emscher-Lippe and Constantin der Grosse mines. On the Seine and the Potomac there were uneasy stirrings; in the House of Lords there was a question. Viscount Elibank, DSO, requested assurance that the government would hold Alfried to his word. Lord Gosford, speaking for the Foreign Office, answered that other capitals must be consulted. The *Evening Standard* found Gosford's reply unsatisfactory: "What possible reason can there be for Britain to be soft toward Herr Krupp?" it demanded editorially. "Apart from growing prosperous, he has done nothing in the past years to justify a change of mind."[3]

☒    ☒    ☒

He was about to do even less. Lord Elibank should have asked one more question of his fellow peer: to whom had Alfried sold those mines? Emscher-Lippe had gone to the Hiberner Combine, in which the Bundesrepublik, under Erhard's strange financial structure, held a controlling share. In view of the *Stahlpakt* between Essen and Bonn there was no guarantee that the architect of the Economic Miracle might not sell it right back.

It was the second sale, however, which should have widened eyes throughout the industrial world, for it clearly suggested that something was afoot in the Ruhrgebiet. If there was one deed more priceless to the dynasty than any other it was Constantin's. The bottomless vein of pure anthracite had taken ten years off Alfred's life. It led directly to the Founder's Crisis, which made him a ward of a banking coalition, saddled him with a 30-million-mark mortgage he paid off only a few weeks before his death, and led Carl Meyer to write Ernst Eichhoff in desperation, "Herr Krupp has a mania for buying things." But Herr Krupp had never regretted it. Without vertical concentration, he had believed, dynastic supremacy "for all time" would be a pitiful, ill-starred dream.

Yet Alfried, who worshiped at his great-grandfather's shrine, had bargained away this trove capable of yielding ten thousand tons a day — enough coke for 75 percent of the steel mills to which he still held title, Mehlem notwithstanding. Furthermore, he had transferred the deed early in 1954, less than a year after the signing of the treaty. That was mysterious enough. The capstone, however, was the new owner. Any industrialist in Europe would have ransomed his safe for a piece of Constantin. Alfried had sold all of it to the one firm the Great Krupp had loathed more than Armstrong, Vickers, or Schneider-Creusot — Jacob Mayer's Bochumer Verein in Bochum.[4]

To appreciate the dimensions of this incongruity one must cast back a century or more, to the tumultuous years when the Ruhr became a major force in Europe. Some time in the 1830's Mayer, until then a Württemberg watchmaker, had perfected a successful method of producing high-quality cast steel. On December 6, 1842, four months after Krupp had returned penniless from Metternich's corrupt Vienna *"Mit beschnittenen Schwingen, durch Kummer und Sorge mit 30 Jahren ergraut"* (With clipped wings and hair turned gray at thirty by strain) to submit his first forged steel musket barrel to Oberleutnant von Donat at Saarn, his great rival had moved from Lendensdorf to Bochum and built his own Gusstahlfabrik eighteen miles east of Altendorferstrasse. At the Paris Exposition of 1855, Mayer became the only serious rival in Ruhr history to the Kanonenkönig's boast that Kruppstahl was Prussia's first cast steel. To Alfred that challenge was a gauntlet flung on the factory floor, and the war for raw materials followed. The fading Gutehoffnungshütte had become the first Ruhr factory to explore the possibilities of vertical integration, buying a small mine in 1854, but the real struggle didn't open until 1868, when both Krupp's Werke and Mayer's began picking up shafts by the dozens: the competition heightened until a fifth of all German coal was coming from their "tied" mines (*Hüttenzechen*).[5]

Mayer's weakness, unhappily, was fatal to his dream. A benign, deeply pious man, he actually believed in public ownership and had deliberately created the Bochumer Verein für Bergbau und Gusstahlfabrikation, holding his first stockholders' meeting on September 1, 1854. As a humanitarian he was shocked by Krupp's cannon; he himself preferred to specialize in church bells, three of which, blackened by a hundred years of Ruhr soot, hang to this day on Jacob-Mayer-Strasse just outside the mill he founded, with the barely legible inscription *Gusstahlglocken gegossen von Mayer u. Kühne im Jahre 1854.* After King Wilhelm I was crowned Kaiser in Versailles, Mayer lost heart, and on July 31, 1875, Bochum's newspaper carried the heavy black headline *Jacob Mayer Gestorben.* He had died young, without issue, leaving his fortune to the Lutheran Church.[6]

As part of the Führer's Vereinigte Stahlwerke between 1933 and 1945, the Bochumer Verein had lost all identity to the *Ruhrfremden.* Kruppianer have very long memories, however, and Ernst Schröder, for one, believed the sale of 1954 was a desecration. Even Ernst's astute brother Johannes hadn't an inkling of what lay ahead. Beitz, then a total stranger to the intricacies of the Ruhrgebiet, later confessed, "*I thought the Bochumer Verein was a football team.*" Airborne from Düsseldorf, en route to the Bahamas, Alfried enlightened him. In the entire Reich, he explained, there had been just three firms capable of producing quality steel: the Gusstahlfabrik, now a wasteland; the Ruhrstahl A.G., which had been dismantled, and the Bochum works, scarcely touched by the RAF. Bochum's shops had suffered but one heavy raid, on November 4, 1944. The British had ordered dismantling two years later, then rescinded the order after Wolfgang Schleicher, the senior member of the management, had eloquently pleaded that the memory of Mayer's nineteenth-century calliope chimes deserved better.[7]

Deconcentrated from the Vereinigte Stahlwerke, the intact firm had become a stock company once more, expanded rapidly, and was now flourishing. It would, Alfried felt, serve as an admirable replacement for the annihilated shops of Essen. Beitz nodded vigorously. But how, he asked, could the Konzernherr get his hands on it? Quietly Krupp explained how his grandfather had seized control of the Grusonwerk in

1892. Like Hermann Gruson, Mayer had sacrificed his role as sole owner to public ownership. Krupps, too, were members of the public. The difference was that, having more money, they could buy out a competitor. Instead of selling in 1959, Alfried proposed to buy — and in buying the Bochumer Verein, of course, he would automatically regain ownership of his biggest mine.

The scheme was breathtaking, unscrupulous, and risky. Yet Alfried was now at the height of his powers. As his jet approached Nassau, he told Beitz of Axel Wenner-Gren's past services to the Reich. In his thirties the Swedish financier had cloaked Krupp's foreign holdings between 1914 and 1918. In his forties he had collaborated with Gustav's illicit rearmament at Aktienbolaget Bofors. In his fifties he had applauded while Krupp forged the new German sword, had proudly identified himself as an Aryan, and had greeted the Führer with the *Hitlergruss*. In his sixties he had toiled as hard as Alfried or Speer to keep Sweden's best ore moving southward into the Ruhr. He had just celebrated his seventieth birthday when Alfried and Vera visited him, and he had sworn that he was ready for one more mighty lunge toward the grail which had fascinated him since youth — a German Europe.[8]

Vera hadn't overheard that conversation; though Krupp trusted his bride, he had known that the old millionaire would never speak freely in a woman's presence. She wouldn't have learned much anyhow. Nothing had been decided. In his dealings with Krupps, Wenner-Gren had always been a follower, not a leader. In 1954 he had merely promised to join any grand design Alfried created. Now, Krupp told Beitz, the operational planning was complete. In outmaneuvering Hermann Gruson, Fritz Krupp had worked behind stage props, knowing that an unmasking would have touched off a skyrocketing of shares. Alfried's pledge to the Allies intensified the need for absolute secrecy. Unknown to its trustees, the Hütten- und Bergwerke Rheinhausen Dachgesellschaft would, through its financial directors, pick up small lots of Bochumer Verein shares — 27 percent of the total over a four-year period. Wenner-Gren, meanwhile, would buy 42 percent and later another 6 percent. All the stock would be deposited in the vaults of the Vermögensverwaltung (Vigau), a cover holding company which administered the Swede's German holdings, until 1958. Then Wenner-Gren would sell to Krupp. Alfried, in announcing his acquisition, would formally demand that the Allies scrap their treaty with him.[9]

The details were worked out in the Bahamas; thereafter Krupp and his collaborator conferred frequently. No one even guessed at the existence of a plot. Both men were enthusiastic yachtsmen, and together they were building the Alweg Monorail, a transportation novelty, for the forthcoming Seattle fair. It seemed altogether natural that they should encounter one another in Kiel, Hamburg, and Stockholm. The first solid hint that their talks had been less than innocent came in February 1958, when Carl

Hundhausen was appointed director-general of the Bochumer Verein. *Handelsblatt* quickly pointed out that Hundhausen remained a member of Krupp's Direktorium. Within a few days the financial press learned that Wenner-Gren, whose Bochumer Verein holdings had been estimated at less than 25 percent, controlled over half the stock, and that together he and Krupp held 75 percent of it.[10]

Two months later Krupp delivered the most defiant of his *Jubiläum* speeches. Foreign demands that he sell were "unconscionable," he said; the Bundesrepublik was an independent country and should not permit a German to be treated like a subhuman. Now the Allies, and especially the economic wizards in the American consulate at Düsseldorf, knew what was coming. It was a question of timing. Alfried held his fire. Although Wenner-Gren transferred his Bochumer Verein shares to Krupp that spring, the Konzernherr didn't move until the end of the year. He did, however, alter his strategy. Adenauer, he decided, was in a better position to deal with the Allies. He himself would apply directly to the High Authority of the new European Coal and Steel Community. Its supranational status meant its decisions could not be questioned by any government, and the pattern of its recent rulings — notably in banking — suggested a strong bias in favor of reconcentration. In a policy statement it had declared opposition, "not to 'bigness,' but to 'abuses of bigness.' " Alfried asked approval of his purchase of the Bochumer Verein. The Authority granted it on Christmas Eve, and Krupp formally merged the Bochum works with Rheinhausen under Beitz's chairmanship. The last papers were signed in January, three weeks before the expiration of the Mehlem deadline. In the Konzernherr's words, "The reorganization of the Krupp Konzern is now virtually complete. The Bochumer Verein . . . has now taken the place of the former Fried. Krupp Gusstahlfabrik."[11]

In diplomacy ownership is ten-tenths of the law. The cables and dispatches now crossing between London, Washington, Paris, Bonn, Luxembourg, and Brussels were very correct, precisely worded, and quite meaningless. Prodded by an aroused Viscount Elibank, Whitehall asked the Bundesrepublik to intervene. After a long silence Bonn elegantly replied that the request had been sent to the wrong address; this was a matter for the High Authority. The Authority, in turn, observed that it had not been party to the Mehlem agreement and could not, therefore, be expected to assume responsibility for it. In February 1959 Chancellor Adenauer suggested to President Eisenhower, Prime Minister Macmillan, and the newly inaugurated President de Gaulle that they grant Krupp a twelve-month extension of his deadline. They should, he observed, be "well aware that Krupp's rebuilding job has helped spark West Germany's postwar boom."[12]

That was rubbish. The *Wirtschaftswunderland* had been created while

Alfried was in Landsberg, and it was equally odd that *der Alte*'s appeal should follow the expiration of Alfried's five years — after he had reneged on his pledge, that is, and taken a new giant step toward economic mastery of Europe. But the statesmen were merely going through the motions now. Under the terms of Bonn's agreement with the Allies, a "mixed committee" was appointed to ponder Krupp's case: Judge Spencer Phenix of the United States, Sir Edward Jackson of Britain, François Leduc of France, three Germans, and Dr. E. Reinhardt, Switzerland's most eminent banker and director of the Crédit Suisse, who was elected chairman. It was June 3 before the committee held its first meeting. After another six months of inactivity the seven members solemnly announced that Krupp had been granted a twelve-month reprieve. The press ignored the decision, and rightly so. It had been a ponderous ritual which, like some ancient Aztec ceremony, was to be repeated each year until the aftermath of Alfried's death, when, on February 26, 1968, the Konzern issued a formal statement declaring that Mehlem was invalid, indefensible, and an "anachronistic relic of Allied occupation rights." Washington and Paris privately agreed. London quietly explained that acquiescence would create a political storm at home, but acknowledged "a new situation" deserving serious study. By then, of course, the original order had become a legal fiction. In practice the sole effect of the annual January respite had been to let time pass, blurring memories and diminishing the wrath aroused by the name of Krupp.[13]

Much of that wrath had already been dissipated when Alfried made his bold moves in the winter of 1958–59. *The Times* of London felt the High Authority had acted wisely. Almost as an aside, the *New York Times* observed that Alfried's acquisition of the Bochumer Verein indicated a "scrapping of curbs" on Common Market trusts. One American news-magazine saw the dimensions of the coup. The merger, *Newsweek* pointed out, "will not only make Krupp Europe's largest steel producer . . . it will also bring the huge Constantine the Great coal mine back into the fold and enable Krupp to supply 75 percent of its own coal mines. The new $1 billion combine will employ 120,000 workers, and its annual sales should top Krupp's prewar $1.2 billion." Actually Krupp had more than doubled his prewar steel capacity. Rheinhausen was the largest steel mill on the continent. The Bochumer Verein covered over five million square yards, consumed forty million cubic feet of coke-oven gas every day, and was capable of casting a single ingot of 380 tons — seventy-six times as large as the Krupp ingot which had crashed through the floor of the Paris Exhibition hall in 1855 and excited the continent.[14]

That winter Wolf Frank, one of the Nuremberg trial interpreters, was skiing near Salzburg. In a lodge he encountered Alfried, who recognized him and asked, "How is that General Taylor?" Frank answered, "He's doing fine, Herr Krupp, but not as fine as you." Herr Krupp laughed. He liked a good joke, and this came near being the biggest economic joke of the century. Apparently pfennigless a decade ago, he was now the richest man in Europe. Moreover, his fortune was growing, for, being sole proprietor, he retained little more than a million dollars a year for his personal use and plowed the rest of his profits back into the Konzern. The yearly rites of the international committee merely amused the *alleinige Inhaber*. They did not handicap him. Deconcentration was dead; he had shot it down. He wasn't even inconvenienced by the Bundesrepublik's corporation tax structure, for, as the chief of his legal staff explained to this author, "All his taxes, including those for Rheinhausen and the Bochumer Verein, are handled here in the Hauptverwaltungsgebäude, because Herr Krupp, as far as taxes are concerned, is one man." Herr Krupp made certain there was no confusion about this. At his April 14, 1960, Jubilee he announced that all his holdings had been "amalgamated into a single company."[15]

Kruppianer have a sense of humor, too. On the day they formally took over the Bochumer Verein they cast a gray steel bell, a wry tribute to the unlucky Jacob Mayer. Its inscription was a droll, if sacrilegious, commemoration of Alfried's great victory over England, France, and the United States. It may be seen today in the yard outside the Bochumer Verein's largest blooming mill. From twenty yards away you can clearly read: *Christ ist erstanden* — "Christ is risen."

✠   ✠   ✠

In the early 1960's, when the Krupp dynasty stood at flood tide, a book published in Germany calculated that "At present his personal fortune, at the very least, is over 4 billion marks" (*Nach den vorsichtigsten Schätzungen überschreitet sein Vermögen zur Zeit 4 Milliarden Mark*). Four billion marks was one billion dollars. And the guess was modest. At that time Alfried was really worth $1,120,000,000 — nearly a billion and a quarter dollars, more than John D. Rockefeller had accumulated in a taxless America. Rockefeller's wealth could have been greater. It wasn't because, as a devout Baptist, he spoke of it as "God's gold," and long before he had reached the peak of his earning power he had begun to establish universities, scientific laboratories, and public parks. So thoroughly did he instill the concept of philanthropy in his son that John D. Rockefeller, Jr., devoted his entire life to it. In the Reich traditions were just the other way around. Employees excepted, Alfred Krupp had confined his charitable activities to an occasional handout. Fritz Krupp had put Capri on the dole, but that wasn't selflessness; he was merely bribing an island. Gustav had never given a pfennig to anyone except the Führer, and even there his son's stealthy Reich bond liquidation had made the Krupps renegers. Alfried, no man to break with tradition, kept his hoard. Thus his fortune continued to reproduce itself. As one financial analyst observed, Krupp's assets were so international that he had a stake in every foreign economy; he was as interested in the Dow-Jones average and the Macmillan budget as any American or British capitalist. His numbered accounts, his investments in Asia and South America, and the yard-high stacks of stock certificates in his fireproof, air-conditioned Hauptverwaltungsgebäude crypts dwarfed the opulence of Fords, Mellons, Morgans, and Du Ponts. The financial analysis concluded that although he had owned but 120 million dollars in cash at the time of his release from Landsberg (Flick, with 200 million, was then the richest German) Alfried was now one of five men in the world who could reckon their wealth in ten figures:

> Together with King Abdul-Aziz ibn-Saud of Saudi Arabia, Sheikh Sir Abdulla as-Salim as-Sabah, the Sheikh of Quatar, the Nizam-ul-Mulk of Hyderabad, and a taciturn American oilman named J. Paul Getty, Herr Krupp is a member of that select club each of whose members can, in theory, write a check for a billion dollars [. . . gehört Alfried Krupp zu jenem ziemlich exclusiven Klub, dessen Mitglieder über mehr als eine Milliarden Dollar verfügen].[16]

Alfried never discussed his capital with outsiders. To all inquiries his set explanation, delivered with that lopsided smile, was "People are likely to put in too many zeros." Beitz insisted that the press consistently exaggerated his employer's treasure — "Wir sind nur kleine Fische" (We're just little fish). This was not diffidence. Had the full scope of Krupp's fortune been disclosed, his embarrassment with others, including members of his own family, would have been acute. Because of Hitler's affection for him he had become heir to Bertha's full legacy. His only gifts to his brothers and sisters had been those extracted by the Allies, Mehlem's one enduring achievement. The source of his largesse was something he would rather that the public, so ready to misunderstand his Führer, forget about.[17]

Introverted and secretive by nature, Alfried would have preferred to be ignored by everyone outside Hügel Park. But that was impossible. As owner of the largest privately owned industrial empire in history he ruled a hundred and twenty factory towns. He was producing more steel than Potsdam had allocated for the entire Reich, and American businessmen regarded him as their greatest competitor. His annual sales had passed a billion dollars and were growing at a rate of nearly a hundred million dollars each year; as he reminded jubilant Jubiläum guests, "Today there is hardly a country in the world to which we have not made deliveries. One in every five of us works for foreign customers." Some of those customers lived in communities so remote that the female inhabitants, never having seen a white man before, offered their favors to arriving Kruppianer in gratitude for the comic relief; others were in provinces whose men would have arrested an American on sight — Manchuria, where Alfried was building Renn plants for Mao Tse-tung, and Russia's Nowo-Kuibyschewsk, Stalinogorsk, and Kursk, where he had erected chemical factories.[18]

Beitz himself may have been a little fish, but Krupp had become monstrous. Ten years after his reoccupation of the Hauptverwaltungsgebäude on March 4, 1953, he had octupled his payroll. In the Bundersrepublik alone he commanded more men than the Duke of Wellington had led at Waterloo, Lee at Gettysburg, Moltke at Königgrätz, or Napoleon III at Sedan, and in Brazil alone 1,750 South Americans producing Kruppstahl on the converted coffee plantation of Campo Limbo identified themselves to a visiting American as *Neokruppianer*, that new breed, successor to the Fuzzy-Wuzzies and Gunga Dins. In Asia, Arabia, and Africa there were natives who had never heard of Eisenhower, Adenauer, Macmillan, or de Gaulle, yet who nodded vigorously at the mention of Alfried's name. Therefore there was no way, short of the melting down of all movable type in the world, that Krupp's yearning for privacy could be satisfied. It was unrealistic to hope that journalists would ignore a man whose achievements regularly brought him foreign decorations, honorary degrees, and the toast "Krupp!" from chiefs of state visiting his castle. There was a magic about the man; it touched everyone around him. When his Generalbevollmächtigter arrived at the 1962 Gridiron dinner in Bonn he was invited to join the leader of the SPD (no one visited the family graveyard to see whether Alfred's tomb heaved and trembled that night), and in New York Beitz, attending the centenary dinner of the American Steel Institute at the Waldorf Astoria in May 1957, was seated in the place of honor beside Vice President Richard M. Nixon. The hosts may have had private reservations about Krupp, but as men who admired success they could scarcely withhold approval from a man who, against all odds, had more than tripled his $300,000,000 annual turnover under Hitler.[19]

In these remarkable years, with the Konzernherr enjoying vigorous health while his heir, now in his early twenties, received the finest education in Europe, doubts about the future would have been inconceivable. In retrospect we see it as a strange hiatus between debacle and debacle, yet the coming events cast no shadows. For eleven generations the family had ruled Essen, and there seemed to be no doubt that the Ruhr would remember Alfried as the greatest of the Krupps, the dynastic leader who had actually achieved his great-grandfather's impossible ambitions. His mastery of the Common Market was unchallenged. Old age lay ahead, with its unfathomable prospects, but his restless expansionism seemed to guarantee an even more stupendous Krupp-Reich then.

While in the Ruhr he conferred twice each day with Beitz, at 10 A.M. in his office and in the evening, over drinks, in his home. The aide brought problems, the sole proprietor provided solutions. Krupp's manner was always the same: soft-spoken, deceptively hesitant, almost deferential. His replies betrayed the true Alfried, however, for they revealed an uncanny knowledge of his vast domain and a remarkable instinct for correct answers to the riddles vexing Beitz. One typical session began with coal. Beitz told him that *kruppsche* mines were then producing 21,041 tons a day. Though this was a tremendous volume, more than enough to feed his thousands of maws, mining expense increases notoriously with depth; some Kumpel were toiling in sixty-year-old shafts. Alfried nodded, thought a moment, and, producing a map, pointed to untapped sources in the northern Ruhr, the lower Rhine, and the Netherlands. Then, dismissing routine, he unfolded a new map, this one of Spain. The Americans were extracting U-235 here, here, and here. Jülich couldn't depend upon the generosity of the Atomic Energy Commission forever. *Die Firma* should have its own sources. Krupp surveyors had been sending back analyses of Spanish minerals for nearly a century; Alfried had been reviewing their latest reports, and he suggested that Beitz send crack Geiger-Müller teams there, there, and there.[20]

A third map appeared, of Canada. Algoma Steel shares were available. Buy them. Algoma had excellent ore fields; a takeover was possible. A fourth map: Labrador. Prospectors from the British-controlled Rio Tinto combine had been seen on Ashuanipi Lake, and Krupp needed the iron ore deposits on an adjacent plateau. Fifth — Beitz blinked — a huge chart of the French Riviera. As carelessly as though he were discussing a new racing car to which he had taken a fancy, Alfried murmured that he was thinking of buying the Riviera. *"Alles?"* gasped his lieutenant. Alfried chain-lit another Camel. He had been chatting with Fritz von Opel and Count von Zeppelin. They had agreed that European vacations were growing longer and more frequent, so the Riviera would be a superb investment. Begin with a bid for the Côte d'Azur. Certain real estate prices had been artificially depressed (Krupp never revealed the sources of such information, even to Beitz), and a strong move behind the right French front man might sweep up everything — beaches, parasols, hotels, amusement parks; the lot.[21]

*"Er ist, wer er ist, der Mann"* (He's the whole show). And so he was. The Konzernherr would say, "I think our whole future lies in high-quality work. The time is past when you could build an industry like Krupp on mass production of steel for armaments and railroads. The future lies in special steels for high-grade machinery." Later that same day his parrotlike lieutenant would issue a press release proclaiming that, in his opinion, "We must keep a step ahead, we need to produce new sorts of machinery, made of high-quality steel, which will always have something that the others haven't got. Then people will be *forced* to buy from us." The press naturally gave the credit to Beitz. Less than a score of people knew that Alfried reigned as an absolute monarch. No one could even see him

without passing through his aide's office. He worked in isolation beneath an oil painting of his great-grandfather, his long feet firmly planted on a pale green rug. In the words of his son he was "a man very much turned in upon himself, who loves solitude and does not like people around him." Beitz commissioned Jean Sprenger to produce a bust of Alfried for his office. Completed, the bronze effigy looked nearly as lifelike as the real thing across the hall.[22]

With a firm handclasp, manly greeting ("*Hi! Ich bin Beitz!*"), efficient manner, and the marvelous grace with which he dominated Villa Hügel state occasions, pirouetting from dignitary to dignitary as deftly as a ballet virtuoso, the General Plenipotentiary even persuaded some insiders that he was the real mastermind, that Krupp was merely a figurehead — which was precisely what Krupp wanted the world to think. The handful who knew both men were undeceived. When, shortly after the historic walk in the rain on the shore at Hamburg, Beitz had ecstatically blurted out to Count Klaus Ahlefeldt-Lauruiz, "I'm going to act as the owner of Krupp!" the count had been incredulous. "I thought," he recalled afterward, "that he must be drunk." Over a year later the subtlety of the appointment hit him: Beitz was to *act* as owner. The *alleinige Inhaber* and his chief of staff were as ideally matched as Hindenburg (whose strategic skills have been largely overlooked by historians) and the more flamboyant Ludendorff. Choosing Beitz, Ahlefeldt thought admiringly, had been one of Krupp's greatest achievements, "a task suited to his genius" (*Entsprechende Aufgabe Genie seiner Anlage*).[23]

*Verkaufsgewandtheit*: salesmanship. That was how the patricians behind Hügel's iron fence described *der Amerikaner's* true gift. But to display the full range of his virtuosity Beitz really needed another setting. The Hauptverwaltungsgebäude was all wrong. He had come to loathe it, and with Krupp's permission he designed a modernistic, two-story, two-block-long office building adorned "with a few arty figures . . . naked women, or dolphins and buffalo, or slightly profane angels and images of the Virgin Mary."[24] His new Hauptverwaltungsgebäude would have been a travesty of Rockefeller Center, just as he was a parody of George Washington Hill, but his sketches suited the mood of West Germany's crazy quilt *Wirtschaftswunderland*. In the manic Bundesrepublik nothing was too wild. Doubtless fellow countrymen would have greeted his architectural atrocity with murmurs of admiration. They didn't, because the builders never broke ground. Bonn vetoed the plans — not for aesthetic reasons, but because there was a national shortage of building materials. Unless a firm's administration building was condemned as unsafe, it had to stand. Thus Gustav's memorial, like Alfred's on the hill, may still be eyed by those tourists who are loath to believe that taste in yesterday's Fatherland was just as grotesque as today's.

The best place to see the exquisite meshing of the talents of Krupp and Beitz was Hanover's annual ten-day industrial fair. Before the partition, German industrialists had shown their new stock in Leipzig each spring for two centuries. Now Leipzig was in the Russian zone, however, and while some titans crossed the line, the general boycott was so effective that Leipzig hadn't held a full exhibition since 1960. Consequently, the great baronial show was held yearly in the sprawling *Industrieausstellung* area southeast of Hanover's baroque Herrenhausen Gardens. Fried. Krupp naturally had its own pavilion, in the very bull's-eye of the fairgrounds. The showmanship was the work of Alfried's jazzy Generalbevollmächtig-ter; the wares of the Konzernherr himself.

As a spectacle, the pavilion dominated the entire *Jahrmarkt*. Its superb central position wasn't the fruit of intrigue. German capitalists didn't compete for status. Each knew his place, and *die Firma's* role as a national institution was unchallenged; the halls of Stinnes, Thyssenstahl, and the heirs of I. G. Farben had been erected at a respectful distance. Surrounded by one hundred and forty flags of kings, sheikhs, sultans, and presidents who were its chief customers, the concern's central *Halle* was roofed by an enormous concrete disk which seemed to hang in the air unsupported. At the entrance stood a black steel shaft bearing the three rings. Beside the shaft a peculiar work of stainless steel statuary formed in varying thicknesses, bizarre curves and coils. To stare at it too long was unwise; the effigy invited vertigo.

Within, the prospect was more pleasing. Rejecting *Urgrossvater's* gorgeous exhibition colors of red, white, and gold, Beitz had chosen a blue and white motif. Since the *Muttergesellschaft* of Fried. Krupp had become a constellation of firms, each had been provided with its own booth under the intimidating central dome. Blond, heavy-breasted blue angels wearing three-ring badges pointed out blown-up wall photographs in full color. There was Rheinhausen, seen from the air; Rourkela, a confusing blend of the exotic and the Teutonic; a blue and white wall chart of the Konzern's organizational structure; and twelve-foot pictures of Ruhr engineers peering at Burmese ore through magnifying glasses, drilling holes in Egypt's eastern desert, and tinkering with geophysical magnetometers in the Punjab. From outside, one heard a muted humming and, peering up, saw a Bundesrepublik helicopter decorated, as Fokkers were a half-century earlier, by black-and-white iron crosses. Then the hum was briefly lost in a deep-chested laugh near the shaft. Three *Offiziere* in the new Bundesrepublik army were strolling past, their blue uniforms and swooping caps startlingly like those of the Werkschutz guards who greeted Alfried with a *Kruppgruss* on his arrival at the Hauptverwaltungsgebäude each morning.

In its way, the pavilion was a visual masterpiece. Aestheticism aside — the ostentatious flagpoles, the giddy stainless steel roller coaster, the gross photography, and the alarming cement dome — it achieved remarkable

MOST POWERFUL MAN IN THE COMMON MARKET 751

effects. Everything had been done by suggestion. Certainly the swivel-hipped guides attracted attention. The complex of booths conveyed the impression that every industry in the Bundesrepublik was represented here. The fluttering national colors and the big pictures implied that Krupp was more international than the United Nations (which did not, after all, have a delegation in Peking), and the German officers and the iron cross over the Nuremberg-sized Krupp banner atop the dome provided a subtle nostalgic touch. In the universities, at least, the rising generation of Germans had little affection for their national past. But Hanover's visitors were middle-aged or older. Some remembered the Kaiser, and all retained vivid memories of the Führer's exhilarating twelve-year *Totentanz*. The combined symbols of Krupp, the Offizierskorps, and the *eisernes Kreuz* on the helicopter drew them like a clear flourish from the ringing swastika-bedecked trumpets of yesterday.

Yet all this, in the end, was merely the feat of an accomplished pitchman. Had nothing been offered but sex and chauvinism the crowds would have quickly dispersed. What held them was the Konzernherr's contribution — less colorful, perhaps even less dramatic, but infinitely more solid. One's first impression of Alfried's exhibits is summed up in a single word: power. The sheer weight of the precisely forged displays was astounding — a 55-ton generator rotor, a 35-ton hot roll cast from a single ingot, a 15-ton, 1,650-horsepower cylinder liner for a marine diesel engine, a 25-ton forged steel rollweight, and two 50-ton chilled iron rolls side by side. The second impression was quality. He offered a precision-forged blade of Krupp titanium LT–31 steel for a giant steam turbine, another turbine blade three times as large (already sold to a Cincinnati company), and an intricate refrigerated shipping container for meat and fruit (sold to the Guinea State Railways).[25]

Finally, power and quality merged with ingenuity. Krupp unveiled steel monsters which had never been seen or even conceived of before. There was a truck-mounted crane 200 feet high for very heavy duty. On the other side of the pavilion stood a crawler-mounted limestone crushing plant, higher than a four-story building, that weighed 200 tons — heavier than 250 automobiles. Alfried's masterpiece, which seemed to have been tugged from the pages of Jules Verne, was an automatic concrete factory with remote electronic control. Its function was to reduce rocks the size of mansions into siltlike gravel, which could then be mixed with heavy concrete and used to blacktop highways. Inside its mechanical bowels were crushers, screens, bins, belt conveyors, processing machines, and a ninety-foot mixing and batching tower. This goliath — its shape is indescribable — could be operated by one man sitting in a cockpit a hundred feet away. The tower was linked to a ticket printer; the customer was served exclusively by machines, from the moment he placed his order until he received the computerized bill.

Even a crowd of German industrialists yields few customers for automatic concrete factories. But mingling among the gaping visitors were economic ministers and chiefs of state — including, one week, the President of the Cameroons — from nations with thousands of miles of unpaved roads, and some foreigners bought. Just one purchaser for so big a machine justified the entire exhibition, and the layman, leaving the pavilion and averting his eyes from the drunken statuary at the entrance, grasped the elementary fact that the Konzernherr wasn't in Hanover to overawe anyone. He had come here to make money, and in various currencies he was accumulating it by the millions of marks.

✠ ✠ ✠

*Time's* cover story on Alfried was followed by several dispatches reporting that Fried. Krupp of Essen had become one of the twelve largest firms in the world and the only one owned by a single individual.[26] Among the fascinated readers was Benjamin B. Ferencz, the Nuremberg prosecutor who had never stopped haunting Nazis. Despite his benign mien, he had parachuted behind enemy lines during the war, had gone to great lengths to hale fugitive war criminals before tribunals, and, since his marriage to a Hungarian Jewish girl (not one of Humboldtstrasse's slaves), had kept a thickening file on Krupp. It occurred to him, as it had to Napoleon III's emissary to the Ruhrgebiet in the 1860's, that the Konzern was really an independent kingdom. The symbols of authority were handed down to the heir from generation to generation. The ruler received visiting potentates in one of Europe's largest castles. At one time or another whichever Krupp was occupying the throne had displayed all the trappings of sovereignty: the family had decorated loyal subjects, built private prisons, ordered executions, maintained a private army, and, in 1923, issued *kruppsche* currency. In the Hauptverwaltungsgebäude members of the Direktorium spoke proudly of *"das kruppsche aussenpolitische Programm"* (Krupp's foreign policy). So far, the banner of *die drei Ringe* hadn't been hoisted over the U.N. Plaza on the East River, but then, Krupp-Reich wasn't the only country excluded from the General Assembly. Bonn itself was barred, yet in 1953, in a display of sovereignty, it had acknowledged German crimes against the Jewish people to the International Court of Justice in The Hague and agreed to pay Israel six billion marks over a period of twelve years.

If Bonn could, why couldn't — why shouldn't — Essen? That was the last link in Ferencz's chain of reasoning. The Bundesrepublik was paying reparations despite vehement objections from the Arab bloc. The Konzern, which had been conducting its affairs as an independent state a hundred years before the creation of West Germany, ought to recognize a similar obligation. Krupp could afford it. And Krupp owed it; unlike Adenauer and Erhard, he had enriched himself with slave labor, paying no wages, substituting filth for rations, and treating his conscripts as *Stücke*.

All this the American lawyer knew from Nuremberg, and since leaving the Justizpalast he had learned a great deal more. A specialist in international law, he advised the little community of Auschwitz survivors who now lived in Brooklyn. As counsel for the Conference on Jewish War Material Claims Against Germany he had represented Israel before the World Court in the early 1950's and won the $1,500,000,000 judgment against Bonn. Moreover, he knew that no Ruhr baron could claim that he had been covered by that verdict; within the past year he had quietly settled with the splinter companies which had once formed I. G. Farben. They had agreed to pay five thousand marks ($1,200) to each Jewish *Sklavenarbeiter*. There was no possibility of fraud; claimants were being screened by the survivors themselves. Ferencz felt certain that his case in Essen would be far stronger. He was eager to press it, and after amassing all his documents he flew to Germany, where by prearrangement he was met by a German attorney who would serve as his assistant. Only General Taylor and Mrs. Ferencz knew that here, as at The Hague, with Farben, and in all his dealings in behalf of the Third Reich's Jewish victims, the American would be serving without fee.

He was awarded a mechanical smile from the blue angel behind the Hauptverwaltungsgebäude reception desk. No one in the plush waiting room on the first floor of the old armory wing felt threatened. The New Yorker seemed so tame. But reliving the past, Santayana wrote, is the fate of those who forget it, and the recent past should have taught Germans that not all tigers wear stripes. Hitler had chewed carpets, Göring had worn real horns, Goebbels had ranted, yet in some ways the most terrifying murderer in the lot had been Heinrich Himmler, who had impressed men meeting the Führer's clique for the first time after the 1933 takeover as mild-mannered and gentle. *"Ein sanft aussehender Mann,"* was how one old acquaintance had described the Reichsführer — "a man of kindly manner" — and Ferencz's bland manner was equally deceptive.[27]

*"Hi! Ich bin Beitz!"* the General Plenipotentiary began, and was quietly handed a 15,000-word legal brief headed *Die Zwangsarbeit jüdischer KZ-Lager Insassen im Krupp Konzern* (The Forced Labor of Jewish Concentration Camp Inmates Within the Krupp Combine). Subclauses crowded with document citations dealt with the Auschwitz factory, the Berthawerk, Wüstegiersdorf, Mulhouse, Fünfteichen, Humboldtstrasse, the attitudes of the SS and the Speer ministry, and Alfried's requisitions of Jewish prisoners and his defiance of Berlin's insistence that they be treated properly. The Generalbevollmächtigter's eyes widened. This was even worse than the day the Swiss newspaperman had found Otto Skorzeny on the payroll. He riffled through the long pages until he came to the last of seven conclusions:

The firm of Krupp exploited the prisoners' labor without ever paying them for it, nor did it ever attempt to compensate its forced laborers for the injuries to life, health, freedom, and honor which were sustained. It is a demand of basic justice [*ein Gebot der elementarsten Gerechtigkeit*] that Krupp should fulfill, even belatedly, its responsibility before the law, making good the damage done [*Schadenersatz für seelische und körperliche Leiden*], through its own fault, in its factories.²⁸

Beitz, a secretary later recalled, first went "white as a sheet" (*leichenblass*); then he cried, "*Erpressung!*" (Blackmail!) and fled across the hall to the Konzernherr. It wasn't blackmail. Under German law, anyone found guilty in a criminal court is liable to civil suits from those who have been damaged by his crimes. Bonn had formally recognized the validity of the Nuremberg verdicts. Despite McCloy's pardon, Krupp had been judged guilty, and tens of thousands of plaintiffs had the legal right to claim substantial redress. But civil claimants rarely carry their litigation into the courtroom. Pretrial settlements are customary, and Ferencz had every reason to believe that Krupp would act swiftly and generously. Court awards might be much higher than the Jews' demands — Ferencz was asking for the Farben sum, $1,250, which seems absurdly small in the light of the victims' ordeals. The overriding cause for optimism, however, was a matter of elementary mathematics. Five percent of the *Waffenschmiede*'s slave laborers had been Jewish, according to the firm's own records, and most of them couldn't be traced or had perished, leaving no relatives. An out-of-court settlement with this one lawyer should cost *die Firma* no more than ten million marks — two-and-a-half-million dollars. On the other hand, it was conceivable that any ruling against Krupp might encourage suits from the Gentiles. At the very least this would cost fifty million dollars, not to mention the hideous public relations scar.²⁹

Had Ferencz been dealing with any other war criminal he could have counted on what the Ruhr calls *Kaiserwetter* — blue skies. After a proper interval Beitz should have recrossed the hall, called in the firm's legal staff, and begun negotiating. But Krupp was still Krupp. Beitz didn't reappear. Indeed, Ferencz never saw him again. The Konzern's lawyers did turn up, and there were negotiations, yet nothing went right. Each session was marred by recriminations, accusations of bad faith, anti-Semitic remarks. At times the Germans seemed to be inviting Ferencz to call their bluff. They had far more to lose than he did, but an attorney must consider his clients. Bringing witnesses back to Germany would be expensive, and many would not return under any circumstances; they wanted no more of the Reich, whatever the ruling chancellor's name, as long as Krupp still reigned over the Ruhr. Their fears were irrational. But their lives had been ruined by the greatest eruption of irrationalism in history, and Ferencz, understanding their apprehension, had to bargain.

The dickering, as he later put it, was "long and difficult." His antagonists found him far more formidable than they had suspected, and their *Chef* was under pressure from the one man to whom he owed an irreparable debt. John J. McCloy, apprised of the facts, sent word that he would issue a sharp public statement unless the firm yielded. Nevertheless the interminable sessions went on. The enmity was almost tangible; skirmishes unexpectedly grew into roaring battles. Farben had agreed to set aside a fund for non-Jewish slaves. Ferencz suggested Krupp do the same. "Are you authorized to represent Gentiles?" asked a German across the table. Curtly he conceded that he wasn't. "Then forget about it!" he was told. Krupp counsel insisted that as part of the pact the Jews must abstain from any future criticism of Krupp, and they added that any compensation whatsoever for dead Jews, or the dependents of those who had died, was not to be even discussed. *Der Endlösung der Judenfrage*, apparently, had literally meant the final solution of the Jewish question; Krupp had no intention of being blackmailed by chimney smoke.[30]

That left the lawyers with a perplexing *Judenfrage* of their own: how many Krupp Jews had survived? After the collapse in 1945 they had scattered or disappeared into DP camps; Jewish groups had no idea of whether the multitude had perished or found sanctuary. Though the most vital records of *die Firma* had been reduced to cinders in the great Altendorferstrasse bonfire of 1945, those remaining indicated a maximum of 1,200 men, women, and children had outlived Krupp's Third Reich and were alive today. At $1,250 each, the Farben figure, this would cost Krupp a million and a half dollars. Ferencz suggested that the records might be in error, and after further haggling Alfried's advisers agreed to set aside another million dollars. The agreement was announced two days before Christmas 1959. To the infinite disgust of the American lawyer, the Germans "immediately started gushing a lot of moral hokum about sacrifice." Beitz announced that Krupp was making this voluntary gesture "to heal the wounds suffered during World War II" (*zur Heilung der Wunden des zweiten Weltkrieges beizutragen*). It worked; what could have been a disastrous rout was converted into a public relations triumph. Krupp's reformation was hailed by editorial writers everywhere, and the editor of *Overseas Weekly* even reported, erroneously, that "The claims of heirs will also be honored."[31]

Ironically, many recipients later came under the impression that lawyers were deducting excessive commissions. Accounts from Essen had told them they would receive $1,250 each, but their checks were for $750. Some never learned that there had been no fee at all. The reason for the discrepancy was that the Conference on Jewish War Material Claims, uneasy over the fact that no one could make even an educated guess at the number of living *Judenmaterial* once ruled by Krupp, was making a down payment.

Later, when all returns were in, the remaining funds would be distributed evenly.

Then the blow fell. There would be no surplus. In fact, even after the four-million-mark reserve fund had been exhausted there wasn't enough money to buy a bowl of *Bunkersuppe* for those who were tardy in filing their forms. Krupp's confident estimate, it developed, was off. In 1945 his Werkschutz and Werkschar squads had efficiently dispatched boxcars of *Stücke* to the Reich's death camps, but the performance of the exterminators in the last months of the war, it now appeared, had been a disgrace to the Führer. KRUPP SIGNS TO PAY JEWS — the headline Elizabeth Roth saw in a Christmas Eve edition of the New York *Journal American*[32] — was simultaneously translated into every language that same day, and presently two thousand survivors appeared from the Berthawerk alone. To the astonishment of Krupp, actual, breathing Jews with unimpeachable qualifications were popping up everywhere.

One reason for the miscalculation was quickly uncovered. Everyone had assumed that, apart from the Roth group, all Humboldtstrasse inmates had been gassed and cremated at Buchenwald. The truth was that the SS commandant there had rejected them, explaining to their distraught guards that the war was going to end at any moment and he had his hands full trying to murder the Jews he already had. The mad train had gone shrieking off into the night looking for an accommodating executioner. In Lower Saxony the Lagerführer of Bergen-Belsen, had been more cooperative, but Belsen had been overrun just twenty-four hours after Buchenwald; time ran out while the girls were patiently waiting in line to be slaughtered. The British army broke through the barbwire and freed them. Of the Jewesses who, Krupp assumed, had vanished forever from *die Firma* records, 384 were alive, and under the terms of his promise "to heal the wounds of World War II" all were entitled to cash.*

So no individual received $1,250. The pie was cut into smaller and smaller pieces. Administrators reduced the $750 to $500 and then ran out of funds. Ferencz appealed to Altendorferstrasse for a supplementary appropriation and received the brusque answer *gar nichts*, nothing doing. Meanwhile the Gentiles who had been penned in Krupp warrens had been reading the newspapers with increasing interest. In Belgium Father Come told me

---

* General Taylor, Benjamin Ferencz — even the Roth escapees — were amazed. No one in the Ruhr could believe it. The news that the Buchenwald death train had failed triggered the only outburst of temper the author saw in Otto Kranzbühler. He was sitting in his Düsseldorf study at Arnoldstrasse 15 when this writer told him that 311 of the 394 Humboldtstrasse claims had been approved. He slammed a fist into a palm. "We were deceived in the Justizpalast!" he said. "How could several hundred people have disappeared? An impossibility! The prosecution said only six had survived. They had every opportunity to check, and I cannot believe they did not know. The Americans lied to us!" He was unconvinced by the observation that thousands of people had vanished in the chaos of postwar Germany.

bitterly, "Krupp has never acknowledged what he did to me and has never given anything to me." Individuals wrote to Altendorferstrasse. The answers were not only evasive; they actually intimated that Krupp was unable to accommodate non-Jews because the settlement with the Conference on Jewish War Material Claims had been so expensive. Ferencz dryly referred to them as the "greedy Jews" letters, pointing out that they never mentioned an elementary fraction — Krupp's "healing" of wounds suffered by those *Judenmaterial* lucky enough to escape and be paid had cost him less than one-fifth of one percent of the family fortune.

Like his great-grandfather, Alfried was skillful at defending contradictory positions. His settlement with the Jews had constituted a clear confession of guilt. Nobody pays damages unless he is responsible for them. Furthermore, if there was any establishment in which Alfried was more implicated than in others, it was the Berthawerk and its Fünfteichen barracks. On his orders his foremen had entered Auschwitz to select fit workers — and to consign the unfit to the chimneys. *Stücke* had built the factory at Alfried's insistence, despite the protests of lesser Nazis that it was impractical. He had toured the immense complex of plants named for his mother, and in a subsequent affidavit he had admitted to inspecting the slaves. Nevertheless, when a request for compensation reached Essen from a Herr Wandner, a Gentile who had been caught up in the Fünfteichen dragnet and had lost his right leg to a Berthawerk crane, the former slave was informed:

> May we point out in this connection that the employment of prisoners was the consequence of instructions from the authorities [*durch behördliche Anordnungen*], and that those firms which had contracts with the government of the Reich were, in order to meet their contractual obligations, forced to use concentration camp inmates because of the catastrophic labor shortage [*des katastrophalen Arbeitskraftsmangels*].[33]

Krupp hastened to add that the absence of Wandner's leg was, in its own way, something of a catastrophe. He was sorry about that. The applicant was merely asked to bear in mind that:

> The fate of the Jews formerly imprisoned in concentration camps [*Das schwere Schicksal der jüdischen ehemaligen KZ-Häftlinge*] prompted us as early as 1959 to conclude the agreement with the Conference on Jewish War Material Claims Against Germany, Inc., with which you are familiar. . . . Thus, to our regret, we are obliged to inform you that we are not in a position to fulfill your request [*Wir bedauern daher, Ihnen mitteilen zu müssen, dass wir uns nicht in der Lage sehen, Ihrer Bitte zu entsprechen*].[34]

Members of the Jewish community, handicapped in almost every other way, had emerged from the war with one tremendous advantage: superior organization. But other ethnic groups had also been forced together in the vise of Nazi exploitation, and one, comprised of Anglo-Saxon Krupp victims, had an office at 18 Queens Gate Terrace, London. Two weeks after Beitz's Christmas "wound-healing" release the members of its governing council wrote the Hauptverwaltungsgebäude, stating their case. Their reply came seven weeks later, brief and brusque:

> Wir nehmen Bezug auf das Schreiben von 7. Januar 1960 und dürfen Ihnen mitteilen, dass wir uns über die erheblichen finanziellen Aufwendungen zugunsten jüdischer KZ-Häftlinge hinaus zu weiteren freiwilligen Zahlungen leider nicht in der Lage sehen. Wir bitten Sie hierfür Verständnis zu haben.

We have received your letter of January 7 and wish to explain that because so much money has been used to the advantage of the Jews, we are not in a position to make voluntary contributions. We trust you will understand.[35]

They understood. Recognizing the insinuation, they forwarded the letter to Benjamin Ferencz and General Taylor. Somehow it was evocative. On the night before his death Hitler had written: "Centuries will pass, but from the rubble of our monuments and cities the loathing for those responsible will always turn to the ones we have to thank for all this: international Jewry and its helpers!" (dem internationalen Judentum und seinen Helfern!).[36]

# 31

✠

## You Can See the Ones in the Light

LIKE a Haydn melody, certain haunting themes recurred throughout the House's history, and as the 1960's advanced two of them grew progressively more menacing. For the second time in less than a century a strong sole proprietor was baffled by the intricacies of banking and by a son whose exotic weaknesses neither he nor their empire could tolerate. Both problems were to develop in concert and would, in the end, overwhelm the last giant of Essen.

Meanwhile there was a hiatus. The theme most cherished by loyal subjects of the Deutsche Reich and the Krupp-Reich was their common past, present, and future. At Fritz's funeral the Kaiser had told white-collar Kruppianer, "Through your craftsmanship I have seen the name of our German Fatherland glorified in foreign countries everywhere" (*Mit Stolz habe ich im Ausland überall durch Eurer Hände Werk den Namen unseres deutschen Vaterlandes verherrlicht gesehen*). So now, in Bonn's Haus des Bundespräsidenten, President Heinrich Lübke of West Germany wrote out the opening lines of a major speech to be delivered in Essen: "In the history of your firm are mirrored in a fateful way the highs and lows, the triumphs and disasters, of our German people" (*In der Geschichte Ihrer Firma spiegeln sich in schicksalhafter Weise Höhen und Tiefen der Geschichte unseres ganzen Volkes wieder*).[1]

The address was being prepared for a very special occasion. There had been nothing like it since the deaths of one hundred and ten coal miners had canceled Gustav's tournament, sending S.M. home in a sulk and forcing five-year-old Alfried to dismount from his pony. That centennial had been observed in 1912, on what had been Alfred's hundredth birthday. After some wheedling his great-grandson was persuaded to change the date. Now that Krupps had abdicated as Kanonenkönige it seemed more fitting to celebrate the sesquicentennial on November 20, 1961, two months after the hundred and fiftieth anniversary of the day Friedrich Krupp had founded *"eine Fabrik zur Verfertigung des Gusstahls und aller daraus resultierenden Fabrikate"* — a "factory for the manufacture of cast steel and all the products issuing therefrom." Certainly that had been luckless Friedrich's target, but everyone except the public relations department knew he had missed it by a mile. Nevertheless, once Alfried had endorsed the plan with a scrawled AK — he had adopted the custom of using not only the initials but even the calligraphy of the man they would really be honoring — the Bundesrepublik mobilized with the lightning speed of a resurrected Albrecht Theodor Emil von Roon cramming Pickelhauben aboard trains bound for the Franco-Prussian frontier. It was to be the most stirring German function since the Führer's award of thirteen Feldmarschall's batons after the fall of France, and the most magnificent since Gustav, wearing all his party decorations, had been led into the satinwalled Berlin Opernhaus by Hermann Göring. Teams of protocol experts from Bonn's Reichskanzlei and Essen's Hauptverwaltungsgebäude carefully went over the guest list. Chancellor Adenauer, President Lübke, ex-President Theodor Heuss, and Ludwig Erhard would lead the national delegation. Accompanying them would be thirty ambassadors, mostly from Africa and Asia, and their wives. Greeting the guests would be the Konzernherr, his twenty-three-year-old heir, Beitz, and two hundred and sixty Krupp representatives from fifty-nine countries. Alfried excepted, the cynosure was certain to be Arndt, who, as one of the firm's official histories pointed out, "is destined one day to continue the tradition of the House of Krupp."[2]

That was not likely to be soon. His father was still very much in command, and every detail of the ceremony was conceived and supervised by him. He went over the rebuilt Stammhaus inch by inch, seeing to it that Fritz's scales and even the black clogs Alfred had worn to the Gusstahlfabrik were properly placed. He reviewed a motion picture, *Die Drei Ringe: Krupp Heute;* he staked out the lot where the Alweg Monorail was to be reassembled, reviewed the script for the awarding of papal decorations to himself and Baron von Wilmowsky, and stipulated the dimensions for the great signs over the stage, which would be adorned by the three rings and the house-high lettering 150 JAHRE KRUPP 1811–1961. At his insistence, all Kruppianer who had been on the firm's payroll at the time of the abortive tournament were to be honored guests, and he was elated to learn that there were over five hundred of them.[3]

The protocol teams were appalled. That meant two thousand guests. Villa Hügel couldn't accommodate them. Even the Saalbau was too small. Suppose it should rain? The Konzernherr, undismayed, drafted plans for an edifice at least as remarkable as the turret inside which *Urgrossvater* had valiantly proposed to crouch while his own cannon bombarded him into extinction. Alfried's structure was perhaps the largest single tent ever built — a fantastic, inflated, blue-and-white perlon sphere which would house the leaders of the Bundesrepublik, fellow Schlotbarone, all diplomatic missions, the five hundred elderly Kruppianer, all Alfried's servants (including his car washer), the stage, and the Stammhaus. It had one handicap. Unlike Alfred's turret, Alfried's tent could be brought to earth by a needle thrust. Accordingly, the *Ballonhaus* was surrounded day and night by armed guards. The PR men deplored the need for them. Actually their presence gave the festival a certain air. And though no one was prescient enough to say so at the time, Krupp's vulnerability to a pinprick was singularly appropriate, though only a Cassandra would have said so then. Schröder, then still in office, reported five billion marks in sales for the current fiscal year. The Krupp men from abroad, many of whom had not seen the Ruhr since it had been a wasteland ten years earlier, were amazed at the transformation of Essen; one had to search the suburbs for a bomb crater, and downtown 140 consumer outlets glowed at night with towering blue, yellow, and green neon Krupp K's. For six days and nights the guests staggered from punch bowls to movies, from monorail rides to candlelit dinners in the castle, from chamber music recitals to dances given by the *"Herr im Haus."*[4]

The speeches came on the last day. At the stroke of noon Alfried delivered his Jubiläumsrede. *"Herr Altbundespräsident, Exzellenzen, Herr Bundestagspräsident, meine Herren Minister, meine Herren Präsidenten, Herr Oberbürgermeister, Magnifizenzen, meine sehr verehrten Damen und Herren!"* he began, all in one breath. Characteristically he gave them no inkling of his future plans. He dwelt, rather, on the past glories of Konzern and Reich, the solidity of the firm, and the magnificent empire his son would lead. Oberbürgermeister Wilhelm Nieswandt was brief, humble, and almost inaudible, as befitting a former Krupp smith; the governor of Nordrhein-Westfalen was unctuous; the men from Bonn trumpeted confidence, almost arrogance. Lübke, enervated by the week's revelry, was unable to mount the platform. His speech, read for him, denounced those swinish Ausländer who spread *"falsche Klischees"* abroad about the former armorer of the Reich.[5]

Theodor Heuss went a step farther. Those false clichés, he said, could be traced to "hatred spurred by war." They had created an outrageous image of *die Firma* as an "annex to hell," while, he commented sarcastically, Schneider-Creusot, Skoda, Vickers-Armstrong, and the Bethlehem Steel Corporation were depicted as heavenly angels (*Himmlische Engel*). Perhaps foreigners disapproved of the Fatherland's industrial hierarchy, perhaps they thought it autocratic. That was too bad, because it wasn't going to change. Each Kruppianer was and would remain in one of three castes: the workers, the white-collar employees, and the executives — all of them patriotic company men (*Betriebspatriotismus*).[6]

Erhard, speaking last, declared that Krupp's tomorrow and Germany's were locked together like nut and bolt. And he demanded, as Alfried had, that France, England and America join Germany in tearing the Mehlem *Diktat* to shreds. The agreement was absurd, he cried; it was hopelessly out-of-date. He had a point. The treaty wasn't a dead letter yet, but in the Ruhr it was rapidly becoming a public joke.

✠  ✠  ✠

In that golden autumn of 1961 the family had attained a kind of incredible idyll in which every ambition was realized, every want satisfied, and every source of mischief stifled by the all-powerful *alleinige Inhaber*. Krupp himself was not happy, *natürlich*, but what great man had known serenity? Not Alexander, not Friedrich the Great, not Napoleon, not Bismarck, nor S.M., nor the Führer, nor any of the Krupps who had led the dynasty to its present eminence. Happiness was something they gave others; like Siegfried, they held a mighty shield over the tribe and found inner solace in the knowledge that their wisdom and valor provided contentment for those they loved.

Waldtraut, busy as ever, had made a new home with her second husband in Argentina, among friends of the '30's who, for political or other reasons, found residence in Europe awkward. Each year she flew home — always a little plumper but as vivacious as ever — called on all her relatives, and left the most exclusive dressmakers on the continent counting stacks of Krupp gold. Irmgard, on the other hand, was rarely seen; Alfried's plain sister raised her brood and helped her husband supervise their estate in placid Bavarian obscurity. The others seldom heard from her except when she announced the birth of another child. Behind Hügel's fence there were good-natured jokes about Irmgard's *Kraft durch Freude*, but she had in fact found both strength *and* joy in her quiescent haven, and they really rejoiced for her. She had never been the cleverest of them, yet she had become the only one to avoid the glare of publicity. Harald, mortified by the sesquicentennial, secretly envied her.[7]

Harald's recovery from his Koestler ordeal was slow. For over two years after his return from the Urals he was troubled by insomnia, remembering the comrades he had left behind. Nights in the castle's shadow he would toss fitfully, recalling Brecht's *Threepenny* lines:

> *Denn die einen sind im Dunkeln*
> *Und die andern sind im Licht.*
> *Und man siehet die im Lichte*
> *Die im Dunkeln sieht man nicht.*

> And these are in the dark
> And those are in the light
> And you can see the ones in the light;
> Those in the dark you can't see.

Marriage helped, and the birth of a child. So did time, his warm bond with Berthold, and his diversions. As the fastest gun in the Ruhrgebiet, Berthold put most of the family's hunting lodges out-of-bounds — the forests were unsafe when he was armed and at large — but Berthold had taught his introverted brother the more civilized pleasures of art, music, and literature. (Berthold, the most humane and sensitive of Gustav's sons, resembled his father most in physique, least in temperament; he was an astute businessman, and their two firms prospered.) As the well-bred daughter of a Schlotbaron, Doerte von Bohlen encouraged her husband's enthusiasms, took out her own flying license, and became Harald's copilot. His convalescence lasted nearly eight years. Eventually he overcame his inner tension. He would never again be the single-minded junior officer who had marched eastward to conquer Russia, but he had become a finer, more mature man: a symbol, like Berthold, of the Bundesrepublik's hope.

Led by Axel Springer, West Germany's Hearst, most journalists in the shrunken Reich shared the national yearning to forget yesterday's phantoms. Fritz Sauckel had ended his life at the end of a Justizpalast rope fifteen years before the Konzernherr's sesquicentennial, and Albert Speer, serving twenty years, still languished in Spandau; yet no one even whispered that Alfried had worked side by side with them and had been found guilty of the same crimes in the same courtroom. Now and then there were muffled protests. In Frankfurt a Konzentrationslager guard sentenced to life for murder cried out, "It's us, the little ones, who pay, but what about the *Bonzen* who gave the orders? They sit in their castles on the Ruhr and get richer and fatter!" The story was buried. The man was a thug, unacceptable in polite society. Besides, he was guilty. He had been condemned and sentenced by a tribunal.

Copies of the German documents which had convicted Krupp — or, as even American correspondents put it, which had convicted him of his father's crimes — became harder and harder to find. Justice Wilkins had retained his records, and Justice Daly deposited his in a Hartford law library, but they were in English. Washington thoughtfully returned the original documents to Bonn on the ground that they were Bundesrepublik property. Cecelia Goetz of the prosecution staff had lost her notes in a basement fire "of unexplained origin."[8] Rawlings Ragland, General Taylor's deputy chief counsel, had sent a complete copy of the trial transcript to his sister in Lexington, Kentucky, thinking it might eventually be of historical interest; it was still there, stacked in a barn loft, when this writer began his inquiry ten years ago. Because of the high commissioner's suppression of a German version, the transcript's contents have remained unknown to citizens of the Bundesrepublik. Indeed, the average Essen citizen's ignorance of his country's past is staggering. The author asked a *Taxichauffeur* whether he knew that Burgplatz used to be known as Adolf Hitler Platz, and that a nearby street had been Adolf-Hitler-Strasse. He burst into laughter; he chortled that I must be joking — though when I began humming *Die Fahne hoch* I caught him watching me in the rearview mirror, and there was no mirth in his eyes. He was of that generation.

Tilo and Barbara lived on in the tan brick house beside Villa Hügel, once a gatekeeper's home and now rather grand. *"Freiherr!"* my driver always snapped at the Hügel guard when I arrived for afternoon tea, and the lean, smartly uniformed young man obediently clicked his boots and gave me that inimitable salute foreigners ordinarily see only in old Erich von Stroheim films. The autumn before Krupp's sesquicentennial the baron had written his memoirs.* Although dedicated to Barbara and the memory of Bertha, they were, in large part, a history of three centuries of Wilmowsky suzerainty over Marienthal, his lost home. He gave the first volume to his wife, who in exchange surprised him with an exquisitely bound one-copy edition of *Humor bei Krupp*, a collection of witty sketches her grandfather had doodled in the margins of his letters. The baron and his baroness always found them sidesplitting. Their guest could only feign a weak smile. If the Frenchman's sense of humor is in the bedroom, someone wrote, the German's is in the bathroom, and *der Grosse Krupp*, obsessed with horses, often found merriment in something funny happening on the way to the stable. Sometimes there were variations upon this: a man falling off a horse — taking a really dreadful spill — or a *Dummkopf* sawing himself off the end of a branch from a great height. They were third-rate, nineteenth-century vaudeville, and a courteous visitor's comments could only be vague.

Yet the Wilmowskys were unfailingly kind. To cross their threshold was to leave behind the crass new Germany, the twelve-year nightmare before it, the Weimar experiment, and those four years in the trenches which had been a kind of cultural hinge between the age of stability and the age of anxiety — to turn, if only in fantasy, to that serenity in which the very few worshiped *der Allerhöchste* in Lutheran pulpits on Sundays, cheered *der Allerhöchsteselber* and his bulging wardrobe of uniforms the rest of the week, believed him implicitly when he told them the Fatherland was threatened with encirclement, and never challenged the assumption that the only people worth knowing were those you read about in Berlin's *Der Reichsanzeiger*. Like nuclear warfare the Reich's martial stance had been all right — for them — as long as no one did anything about it.

Seventy years near the seats of power had not cured the baron's artlessness. "Let us hope Herr de Gaulle will not follow the ambition of Napoleon," he once murmured; the baroness nodded dutifully, and one envisioned *Le Grand* Charles leading a Grand Armée through the Berlin Wall, over Ulbricht's dead body, and into the snows of the Soviet Union.[9] Again: "Do you remember I once told a Frenchman Germany and Austria

---

* *Rückblickend möchte ich sagen* . . . (Oldenburg and Hamburg: 1961.)

should have one Generalstab, and he thought me drunk! But *now* we *have* it, with a German general sitting in Washington!" (He referred to Hans Speidel, who had been Rommel's chief of staff and held a NATO post in the late 1950's.)

Tilo wasn't chauvinistic; merely chimerical. He was as unpredictable as the sudden Ruhr windstorms which blow up out of nowhere on the finest spring day. The baron was proud of Patrick Duncan, a friend of his son's, who was then campaigning against apartheid in South Africa. He was amused by Christine Keeler. (His wife was not; she pursed her lips.) Although he had been a Nazi, he readily agreed that the Hitler era was a *Schweinerei*, and he was skeptical of the Teutonic national character. "You know, we have a special god for envy. His name is Loki. No other people have that." (Here Barbara could not keep silent; she protested, "That's not very fair to the Germans!" and he cried, "It's true, it's true!") Yet any implied criticism of the family name — his or hers — angered him. After a moment of dignified silence, he would stiffly move the party into his study, displaying the treasured trophies of a very old man: the fading snapshots of his lost son, and photographs of his grandson, of Bertha Krupp, Gustav Krupp, Margarethe Krupp, Hermann Krupp's son Artur, and, incongruously, the mounted horns of an African eland over a plaque inscribed *1911, Torrenjau, W.* He explained — referring to the Wilmowskys' eviction from Marienthal — "That was all the Russians would let me take then. Hunting was the great passion of my youth."

The baron and his baroness were Alfried Krupp's one link with the past. In 1911, one realized with astonishment, Tilo had been thirty-three years old. Perhaps because he had grown up in an age free of bitterness, he and his wife were incapable of malice. On November 20, 1961, the president of the Bundesrepublik had reminded his audience of the sole proprietor's postwar crucifixion — "the surrender and dismantling of the factories, the announcement that all was at an end, the catastrophes" — but he failed to add that while the Konzernherr had recovered and redoubled his holdings, his ancient aunt and uncle, once masters of a castle nearly as large as Villa Hügel, were now his tenants, waited upon by his servants as they watched over their shabby souvenirs: a scrapbook, warped pictures, whitened game horns, and the quaint leather clock Papa Fritz had picked up in Paris early in 1870.[10]

The odd thing was that Alfried was vindictive and they were not. He had been raised to believe that the invincible Reich had been betrayed by Weimar's November criminals, that hatred was a catharsis, and that to be virile was to be, in effect, paranoid. Throughout his formative years Hitler had been the national idol, and as the Führer's only boyhood friend wrote in retrospect, "Everywhere he saw only obstacles and maliciousness. . . . He was forever taking up cudgels against something and out of sorts with the world (*mit aller Welt überworfen*). . . . I never saw him take anything lightly."[11]

Krupp was not Hitler. He was a more subtle and, in the early '60's, a more successful antagonist. Yet he, too, took a grim view of the world; he, too, saw himself surrounded by antagonists. For both the *Einkreisen* had become real enough, but each had created his own encirclers. One answer to the riddle of Alfried's character may be found in the chilling philosophy Hitler fashioned in Landsberg from what he erroneously believed to be the secret of the SPD's successes at the polls. To historians the reasons for Socialist pluralities in the Weimar years are obvious: dedication to lower taxes, more employment, and the full dinner pail. To the future Führer that was too simple. In his Landsberg cell he had dictated to Hess:

> I grasped the infamous mental terror [*infamen geistigen Terror*] this party wields, especially on the middle classes, which are not equipped to meet such attacks, either morally or intellectually. On signal the Social Democrats set loose a storm of lies and slander against whoever threatens them most until their opponent cracks under the strain. . . . This is a scientific stratagem based on an intuitive understanding of all human vulnerability, and its victory is to be guaranteed with an almost mathematical precision [*Es ist eine unter genauer Berechnung aller menschlichen Schwächen gefundene Taktik, deren Ergebnis fast mathematisch zum Erfolge führen muss*] . . . Simultaneously, I understood the power of physical terror toward the individual and the masses. . . . For while among the rank and file their triumph appears to be the triumph of justice, the loser usually abandons hope.[12]

It would be hard to find a more brilliant exposition of fascist psychology. Yet only a Hitler or a Bazarov can peer into the stark core of his negativism without flinching. Most Nazis couldn't endure the still dark night of reflection. Göring escaped into Karinhall, Himmler fled to an asylum, Goebbels invented an ideological pablum. With his immense inner resources, Krupp came closer to stoicism, but he felt the need to lean upon the tranquillity and mercy he had learned from his mother, just as Fritz had sought solace from Bertha Eichhoff, and as young Arndt now found comfort in Anneliese Bahr.

That, it seems, was the meaning Tilo and Barbara held for Krupp. Within his lifetime the propertied classes had turned upon themselves. The brutality of National Socialism had represented a 180-degree pivot from the genteel code of the Wilhelmine patriciate. Contemporaneous letters suggest the completeness of the *volte-face*. A friend of the baron's, congratulating him on his departure for Oxford as an undergraduate, had advised him, "Off you go. Defend the altar, the throne, and the hearth (*Kampfe für den Altar, für den Thron und für die Hütte*). But remember

that the altar should be the Almighty's footstool, not the refuge of hypocrisy; that the throne should never be dependent upon the lusts of any self-
seeking party but upon the well-being of the entire country; and that the
meekest hearth is a free man's castle. Always remember — take sides with
the poor and helpless." Similarly, whereas fourteen-year-old members of
Hitler's Bund deutscher Mädel were encouraged to seek impregnation by
Aryan youths during their *Landjahr* summers, Barbara, as she recalled in
old age, had been taught that "Children must learn to fit in, and not make
a fuss about themselves. Any eccentricity was forbidden. This was more
than prudery: parents hesitated to concede that babies were born nude.
They covered up the unbeautiful, the dangerous, and the doubtful" (*man
deckte das Unschöne, das Gefährliche und Zweifelhafte zu*).[13]

Krupp saw the gulf and sought to bridge it. His reach was never quite
long enough, but the effort strengthened his sense of the past, and that was
terribly important to him. It was a soil in which he could put down roots,
an emotional legacy he could leave to his son. Thus, while indifferent to
the honors a grateful Reich had showered upon himself — he had been
amused by Gustav's ostentatious display of his golden party badge —
Alfried was curiously moved when, on the tenth anniversary of Mehlem,
the president of West Germany awarded Tilo the Star of the Great Order
of Merit of the Federal Republic. The baron trembled with emotion when
the president pinned him with *der Stern zum Grossen Verdienstkreuz der
Bundesrepublik*. Afterward he told me quaveringly, "You can think what
you will of decorations, but if the chief of state of one part of the divided
Reich drives you from your three-hundred-and-sixty-three-year-old manor
with a scrap of paper — gives you only twenty-four hours to leave — if you
can only take the clothes on your back and what you can carry and must
leave the rest — and then after fifteen years the chief of state of the rest of
this Siamese twin country gives you a star, well . . ." His voice faded, then
rose. "Well, I esteem it."[14]

�333    �333    �333

To the delight of Baron and Baroness von Wilmowsky, the autumn of
1962 saw the emergence of two clean-cut adventurers named Winston
Churchill II and Arnold von Bohlen, both of them in the finest Karl May
tradition. To Barbara's relief Tilo even tossed *Der Spiegel's* provocative
account of Britain's Profumo scandal into the *Papierkorb* (she swiftly
disposed of it) and lost himself in the serialized accounts of Churchill,
who had just turned twenty-two, and the accompanying photographs of
Gustav's eldest grandson, twenty-three.[15]

They had been introduced at Oxford, where Arnold was president of the
university's ski club and Winston was its secretary. As the former prime
minister's grandson explained to a writer on the eve of the trip which

captured the imagination of Hügel and Chartwell from its inception, he and Arnold had first become friends "three years ago when we both skied for the university in Austria. He was at Balliol; I was at Christ Church. In 1961 he went on safari in Tanganyika, and in the same year I had made a five-thousand-mile expedition by Land Rover across the Sahara from Libya to the Tibesti Mountains and back." Cleaning a .38-caliber revolver while checking a survival kit which contained a week's supply of food and water, waterproof matches, and morphine tablets, he added, "The Tibesti's really quite impressive. Highest peak's Emi Koussi — over eleven thousand feet; didn't try *that*. But this trip will be a lark. We'll be flying twenty thousand miles and visiting over forty countries. No idea how long we'll be gone."

They were to be away nine months, and while the pistol and survival kit may sound a trifle melodramatic, the two youths were taking a genuine risk. Churchill had bought a new Piper Comanche for the occasion, but its range was only 850 miles, its maximum speed scarcely greater than a Jaguar's, and its map bag crammed with charts which perplexed more than they edified. Neither of them knew much about navigation. Young Winston had a classical education; his companion was preparing for graduate work at Fontainebleau — a substitute for the Harvard Business School, which his father had attended but which the family now rejected because of America's treatment of Krupp. When Churchill stepped from his cockpit in Geneva in an open-neck shirt and a duffel coat, he conceded to a Swiss newspaperman that their first lap had been disquieting. No wonder; between them, he confessed as he offered Arnold a helping hand out, they had less than two hundred and fifty hours flying experience. Veteran fliers were alarmed. That first hop should have been safe as houses, but the rest of the route would be bewildering. The youths gaily explained that *Queen* magazine was underwriting their expenses; with Sir Winston's classic *My African Journey* in mind, its editors were advertising the grandson's forthcoming series as *In the Steps of My Grandfather*. There were those who wondered whether it would ever see print. Grandfather, unhampered by the complexities wrought at Kitty Hawk, had traveled at a more leisurely pace through Omdurman, Ghana, Togo, Pretoria, and the Transvaal. To be sure, he had faced the Mahdi and the Boers, but at least he had known where he was, and the ground had always been beneath his, or his horse's, feet.

In seeing the pair off from Gatwich Airport, Surrey, on November 11, 1962, Flight Lieutenant Busby, Winston II's instructor, had begged them to be careful. One wonders whether they had heard him. "On the takeoff from Annam," as Churchill described it afterward, "we flew over the Dead Sea with our altimeter registering 1,275 *below* sea level." He seemed elated by his ability to read an altimeter and added, "You see, the surface of the lake is approximately 1,285 feet below sea level." What he omitted was that simple arithmetic put them ten feet over the waves, and an Arabian *khamsin* — the most sudden and ferocious windstorm imaginable — could have torn their single-engine aircraft to shreds and sent them to salty depths untraced by the steps of anyone's grandfather. Apparently that sort of jeopardy never intimidates pilots in their twenties, which may explain why Arnold's father and his finely tuned Messerschmitt had vanished into the Hürtgen Forest that cloudless January morning in 1940 without a hostile flyer on the horizon. Told gently of the hazard later, Winston looked blank. He replied, flatly, "We were going to Cairo." In his mind there had never been a possibility of a ten-foot detour. It is a point of view which makes men prime ministers, cannon kings, and cadavers.

Peril aside, the expedition was generating almost as much good will among the powerful as a royal tour. Even before the two Oxonians had left, the nations on their itinerary, hearing the names Churchill and Krupp coupled, had extended invitations to state banquets over the signatures of Emperor Haile Selassie, King Hussein I of Jordan, President Nazem el-Kodsi of Syria and Premier Ibrahim Abboud of Sudan, who escorted them to Khartoum and expressed his profound regrets over the demise of the late Chinese Gordon; and a Yemenese chieftain with the disconcerting habit of gesticulating wildly with both hands clutching daggers. Rank didn't impress them — they took it for granted. After their return Winston remarked indifferently, "In Beirut we were invited to lunch by some wealthy Lebanese bankers. There were twenty-two guests, with excellent food served on the finest silver. Outside the house were parked an assortment of E-type Jags, Mercedes, Aston-Martins — you know." In almost any other undergraduate such insouciance would have been suspect, but as a Churchill he was above (or beyond) foppery. Similarly, Arnold was merely making conversation when he reported, as though it were news, that in Egypt President Nasser hadn't been at the airport to greet them personally. Instead Nasser sent Hassan Sabray, his chief adviser; Sabray led them up the Nile to accommodations at Luxor, and through an inspection of the High Dam being built at Aswan by Sovietianner.

Ahead lay Kenya, Tanganyika, and Zanzibar — lands that Churchill, out of a habit picked up in public school, kept referring to as "British East Africa." Neither knew that on this leg they were following the steps of Arnold's *great*-grandfather until, pausing at a Togoland village in that spring of 1963, Winston mentioned to a group of chieftains that his companion was a member of Germany's Krupp family. There was an astonished pause among the three most elderly natives; then one stepped forward, bowed deeply to Arnold, and addressed him in stilted German: "*Dass es mein innigster Wunsch ist, Ew. Exzellenz meinen ehrfurcht-vollsten Dank und meine unbegrenzte Verehrung zu Füssen legen zu dürfen*" (It is my deep desire to lay before Your Excellency my most respectful gratitude and unbounded veneration).[16] That summer Winston wrote a book about their trip,[17] and Arnold published his photographs, which, family seniority notwithstanding, made his Uncle Alfried's look like Brownie snapshots. In the shade of the coppery *Blutbuche* Tilo and Barbara agreed that their flight was finer in every way than Claus's had been. The little four-seater, the baron reminded the baroness, had left Surrey on what was known as Armistice Day in the United States, Remembrance Sunday in the United Kingdom, and Jahrestag des Waffen-stillstandes in Germany — the anniversary which had so embittered Arnold's grandfather Gustav that he had secretly rearmed the Fatherland, enrolled his sons in paramilitary Nazi *Gruppen*, and brought the dynasty to the brink of extinction. A Churchill and a Krupp in the same cockpit, Tilo contended, proved that Europe had said good-bye to all that.

Barbara, busy with her embroidery, didn't point out that though Arnold was a member of the family, he wasn't really a Krupp. He had Alfried's *Geist*, he was a natural leader, and he was the most virile youth in the dynasty. Had Claus been Bertha's eldest child, Arnold would have become a future Konzernherr at birth. As it was, however, the legatee was Alfried's son. And Arndt Friedrich Alfried von Bohlen und Halbach, it had developed, was everything his cousin wasn't.

⊠    ⊠    ⊠

The latest (and, as events were to prove, the last) heir of the establishments looked upon all cities as nasty smellpots, but until he pressed Rio to his bosom he regarded Paris as the least odious of them, and the sad story of his peculiar life is summed up in a Parisian proverb — *L'adversité fait l'homme, et le bonheur les monstres:* adversity makes men; good fortune makes monsters. Still, one must be fair. The character of Alfried's *wahrscheinlicher Erbe des Etablissements* — then no more than a name to the 125,000 Kruppianer who confidently expected that he would one day reign over them — must be judged in the context of mid-twentieth-century history. Like all male infants destined one day to rule *der Hügel* and Essen's Krupp-Reich, Arndt had grown to manhood in a Europe which had been altered past understanding, roiled by changes which made even his own father's early years seem comparatively serene. The chasm between January 24, 1938, when Alfried's son had arrived in the world, and November 20, 1961, when monocled strangers in striped trousers first bowed low to their future sovereign, is almost unbridgeable.

Consider the turbulent life he had led, the world from which, in revulsion, he was slowly withdrawing. He was born the year of the *Anschluss* in Charlottenburg, an exclusive western suburb of Berlin, then the capital of the world's greatest military power. Five months before his second birthday the anarchy began, and his earliest memories were of dazzling uniforms, brass bands, *Sieg Heils*. He was too little to distinguish much, but he could sense moods, and the battlefield deaths of two uncles were ominous.

When he was four, his father divorced his mother to please his paternal grandparents, and she brought him up in the elegant villa overlooking Tegernsee. At the age of seven, the designated Krupp-to-be learned that every close male relative was either a captive, a fugitive, or a certified madman. At ten, he was poring over the daily issues of Munich's *Abendzeitung*. One evening he read that three eminent justices had convicted his father of unspeakable charges, sentenced him to prison as a major war criminal, and confiscated all his property — expropriating, that is, the legacy which Arndt had been told would one day be his. His mother consoled him with the fiction that the real criminal had been his grandfather. Somehow it didn't help.

Yet that pattern was at least consistent. Three years later it became wild. Alfried was released and his fortune was restored. Now the Fatherland acclaimed him as a great man, though the precise nature of his achievements was obscure. Apparently they had something to do with an exceedingly odd man who had tried to conquer the world, had failed, had ordered the entire country destroyed, had committed suicide with his bride of a few hours, and then, at his last wish, had been drenched with gasoline and set afire. Whoever he had been, he was exalted as the paradigm of German manhood.

After Arndt's father had been pardoned, perplexity followed confusion. The following year the boy, now in his teens, was confirmed in the *evangelische* (Protestant) church near the family castle, which was separated by a belt of forest from a metropolis owned, it seemed, by his father. Under the terms of their divorce, Alfried and Anneliese had agreed to share custody of the boy. This turned out to be impractical; during Arndt's early years his father was frequently absent in countries which had been conquered by the then invincible Wehrmacht and were inhabited by subhuman people; later he was in jail or, again, abroad. Even when the two could share a few days in Villa Hügel, the child found out that in Essen his mother, whom he adored, was still called the *Bardame*. He asked what a barmaid was, was told, and acquired a dislike for the Ruhr. Father, he gradually decided, was altogether too preoccupied with his work; Mother was much more fun. Tegernsee was always jolly. The guest list there usually included Mady Rahl, the voluptuous blonde who had been a favorite of Hitler's court and was an intimate friend of Anneliese, though in the decade after the war mother and son spent less and less time on German soil. They leased permanent apartments at Copacabana Beach, to assure their presence during the wildest days of the Rio festival; at Bayreuth, for the spring frolic; on the Côte d'Azur; and in the interior of Brazil, where Arndt eventually bought his own estate, with a private airfield for visiting guests. His appearances in Essen were chiefly confined to Alfried's annual *Jubiläum*.[18]

At the sesquicentennial, where he glassily eyed his servile Direktorium-to-be, he lightly referred to Alfried and Beitz as V-1 and V-2 — a play on "Vater-1" and "Vater-2." The witticism was ill-received in Britain and Belgium, thousands of whose civilians had been killed by the pilotless missiles — Antwerp alone had counted 3,470 corpses — and who knew that the V had really stood for Vergeltungswaffen (weapons of revenge). But Arndt hadn't spoken in malice. There was some feeling within the family that if Arnold could play the man, so could his cousin; they were, it was pointed out, members of the same generation who had suffered the same handicaps. The parallel didn't hold, though. Arnold was never confirmed in a ceremony from which his own mother was excluded and Vera, a sexy stranger, substituted; nor was he expected to understand Vera's disagreeable divorce action, nor the grotesque double funeral of Bertha and Gustav.[19]

In a sesquicentennial aside, seventy-seven-year-old Theodor Heuss, who had known Fritz Krupp when he himself was seventeen, remarked upon the modern paintings now hanging in Villa Hügel and wondered aloud what Fritz would say if he could see them. Alfried's grandfather, he concluded, would shrug and murmur, "Immerhin: Krupp!" (Well, anyway: it's Krupp!)[20] That was the general attitude toward Fritz's great-grandson. Arndt was a Krupp, or would be one day, and after Alfred, it was agreed, no sole owner could be faulted for excessive eccentricity. Yet Alfried's heir was beginning to reveal one peculiarity which had never appeared in the bloodline: a total indifference toward the future of the Konzern, a blindness to the splendor of the family name. It was inconceivable that a man who had been prepared for the day when the king must die could be an unconcerned, lackadaisical lightweight. If he seemed so, those who met him reasoned, it was because he was still rummaging through his tangled past, trying to sort it all out. Immerhin: Krupp — that was the unvarying explanation, the widening umbrella which shielded the conduct of Arndt Friedrich Alfried von Bohlen und Halbach, der wahrscheinliche Erbe des Etablissements.

In naming his only child for his grandfather, himself, and for the mysterious stranger who had stalked into the Ruhr in the sixteenth century and founded the dynasty upon the infectious schwarze Tod, Alfried Krupp had disclosed his hand. His ambitions for his son were boundless. He himself would outstrip Alfred's achievements, but then the namesake and eleventh direct descendant of the original Arndt would dwarf his own. Remembering Gustav's straitjacket discipline, the Konzernherr charted a permissive course. He even presented Arndt with an expensive racing car when the youth graduated from the Liceum Alpinum, a Swiss boarding school near Zuoz which Harald had attended during his periodic illnesses in the early 1930's. On March 13, 1959, six weeks after Krupp had abrogated the Mehlem treaty, he proudly announced to the press, "Tonight, together with my son, I am leaving on a trip to Japan." Traveling in their separate jets they returned from Tokyo via Iran, Morocco, Spain, and an ore field on the banks of the river Kwai, investigating, according to daily bulletins issued from the Hauptverwaltungsgebäude, industrial prospects. Their journey was identified as the Krupp-to-be's "first business trip"; Konzern brochures noted respectfully that after landing in the Bundesrepublik the son drove to the Black Forest to enroll in the University of Freiburg im Breisgau, where, as "the only son of Alfried Krupp," he would major in economics.[21]

His academic career was rather more complicated than the brochures suggested. Obviously he was brilliant; entering Freiburg, he already spoke six languages fluently. Equally clearly, he was a spectacular underachiever. At his Zuoz commencement he had been twenty, the oldest member of his graduating class. Part of his difficulties arose from the war. As a young schoolboy he had been shunted from school to school, eventually finishing his grammar school education at Bavaria's Landschulheim Stein an der Traun. Of course, the schooling of all Europeans his age was handicapped by mobility (or worse), but Arndt's steepest slide began after the continent had settled down. His university career lasted just two semesters; he never even took an examination. Evasive relatives talked vaguely of difficult curricula; he was obliged to travel frequently for *die Firma*, they explained, and had to switch schools because certain sophisticated courses in business administration were not offered at Freiburg. In plain fact he was drifting. Over a period of four years he was enrolled at universities in Munich, Bonn, and Cologne. His father turned a blind eye to all this, insisting that the idle scholar was admirably equipped to assume his future responsibilities because he had no memory of S.M. or the Führer, that he knew only the reformed Reich, and that Kruppianer understood this: *"Die Leute sprechen vom jungen Krupp, und nicht vom jungen Bohlen und Halbach"* (The people speak of young Krupp, not of young Bohlen und Halbach).[22]

But Kruppianer didn't understand. They spoke of Arndt less and less, for his knowledge of them and their country was feebler than that of foreign correspondents covering Bonn, who at least were in Germany, while he and his souped-up *Sportwagen* were seen only at Alfried's annual Jubilees, at the hundred and fiftieth anniversary celebration, and in the jagged countryside surrounding the country house near Rottach-Egern in upper Bavaria to which he and Anneliese now returned each year for a two-month holiday in the Fatherland. Mother and son spent much more time in Brazil. Since it was impossible to suppress rumors of their movements, visitors to Krupp's Hanover pavilion learned from the suave narrator of the documentary film *Campo Limbo* that the heir was "serving a long apprenticeship" there "as is the Krupp custom." Delivered casually while the screen showed furious activity in Alfried's Brazilian steelworks, this suggested that Arndt was somewhere offstage, supervising the casting of a monstrous ingot. He wasn't. He was languishing on his estate south of Rio.

Had Campo Limbo test-fired a new Big Bertha, he couldn't have risen to honor his grandmother. He wouldn't have heard it; he was too far away. Counting his private airstrip, the park modeled after Versailles, the stables — Brazil's largest — and the dwellings for a hundred and eighty servants, including over a score of gardeners, Arndt's manor covered forty-three square miles, eight times the area of Capri.[23]

Beitz, his V–2, contended that Arndt "thinks of himself as a trustee, like his father." That was merely *Beitzisch* huckstering; the V–2, it was recalled, had made a much louder noise than the V–1. Alfried had come to dislike his son's droll identification of him with the least loyal of the Führer's *Wunderwaffen* (on June 17, 1944, an erratic V–1, turning round in mid-course and scoring a direct hit on the Führerbunker, had sent Hitler in full flight to Berchtesgaden), and after their Japanese trip Krupp retreated into his *Sachlichkeit*, withholding all comment about his son's strange conduct. Other members of the family dutifully followed his example, even with acquaintances. "He makes a friendly impression," one told this writer, staring out a Hauptverwaltungsgebäude window, and then swiftly changed the subject. Another said hesitantly, "He's a nice young man; it's too early to tell what he'll become." As it happened, Beitz had just adopted the habit of accosting passing workmen and asking bluntly, "How old are you? Thirty? Well, when are you going to begin to do something with your life?" Reminded of this, the relative suddenly became fascinated by the budding leaves of a nearby tree. Harald warily described his nephew as "sympathetic, empathetic, with a good understanding of others." He was asked what interests Arndt had. After a long pause he said, "Heraldry."[24]

"Agronomy," Arndt himself replied to the same question, when interviewed in the Rottach-Egern villa on May 31, 1967. He explained that he planned to "establish an agricultural model enterprise in South America." But that Wednesday he was very much on the defensive, reacting to journalistic charges that he was leading a playboy's life. "As we Krupps know from bitter experience, money certainly doesn't always make one happy," he said. "Suddenly I have been exposed in the way that Jacqueline Kennedy or Princess Soraya is exposed before the public eye. Yet I do want to point out that I never consider myself in the focus of public interest, being neither an unhappy widow nor a deposed empress. I'm not an unhappy person, either." Nor was he. To adopt a Bavarian verdict, "Arndt is as conceited as a peacock," which is the most reasonable explanation for his ready granting of an interview at a time when he was, or said he was, avoiding fame.[25]

In the light of the heir's exhibitionism, his long years of obscurity are remarkable, and may be set down in part to German newspapermen's fierce protection of the family reputation. His very existence was as unknown to most Germans as Eva Braun's during her twelve years as Hitler's mistress. Yet Arndt, despite his disclaimer, worked hard at his celebrity role, and he was an individual of striking appearance — a limp, dainty, almost beautiful man who enjoyed escorting starlets or full-fledged stars (*e.g.*, Gina Lollobrigida) to nightclubs, though it was noted that none of these friendships flowered into romance; virtually all the European acquaintances who flew back to Brazil with him were men.

Once a hundred German girls were interviewed by an agency commissioned to select Arndt's feminine companion for a Parisian holiday. It was like picking Fräulein Deutschland, and the winner, a Munich model named Eva Gassner, afterward reported that her only souvenir of the expedition was a set of earrings which had been designed by her escort. The gift was more revealing than she knew, for the bleak fact is that the heir's real hobby was neither heraldry nor agronomy, nor, as he put it rather desperately during his Rottach-Egern interview, raising "rice, pigs, dairy products, maize, honey, and poultry."[26] It was fashioning designs for costume jewelry which were then executed by French craftsmen. Most of the finished pieces were presented to his mother, whose collection became her own chief source of diversion.

Arndt's first, brief appearance in the Bundesrepublik press had been at Anneliese's side, when he accompanied her to the Bayreuth spring festival in 1956. The following year a paragraph noted that he had given her a cocker spaniel named Regina, as a birthday present. The year after that he was mentioned as the "steady companion" of Mady Rahl — the fading ex-actress, his mother's choice, was twice Arndt's age — and following his Zuoz graduation he was listed as a party guest of Prince Joachim Fürstenberg at a Bayrische Hof reception. The reporter of this trivia was Hannes Obermaier, the Winchell of Munich's *Abendzeitung* and one of the few German journalists unintimidated by the colossus of Essen. Like most successful gossip columnists, Obermaier was on cordial terms with the men and women whose names he sprinkled through his prose. He knew Anneliese well enough to visit her and Arndt in their Copacabana Beach suite, and he likened his days on the Brazilian estate to "life in the Old South, *Gone with the Wind* with Arndt playing Clark Gable's role."[27]

Flattered, the owner of the Rio plantation grew sideburns. Yet the version of Baroness Renate von Holzschuher, a fashion model who flew to Rio as a jet guest of the young lord, sounded less like Margaret Mitchell than Harold Robbins. There was no mention of magnolias or banjos, no rice, pigs, dairy products, etc. To savor her account: "I had the most marvelous dinner party given for me by our dear Arndt. Arndt is a complete dear. Together with dear Johannes (Prince Thurn und Taxis), Hattie (Princess Auersperg), and Ruppie (Prince Hohenlohe) he is forming the funniest and most wonderful group. But the nicest of all are our meetings at the poolside. . . . I must admit that such a trip is not only worth the effort, but is worth the collapse afterwards."[28] This is more than *Gemütlichkeit*. The correct word is *Überschwenglichkeit*, gushiness, and no one would have been quicker to spit it out and reach for the mouthwash than Alfred Krupp, whose message to his Kruppianer, published early in February 1873 on the twenty-fifth anniversary of his sole ownership, is still the most widely quoted maxim in the Ruhr:

> Der Zweck der Arbeit soll das Gemeinwohl sein, dann bringt Arbeit Segen, dann ist Arbeit Gebet.

> The goal of work shall be the general welfare; work then is blessing, work then is prayer.*[29]

✠   ✠   ✠

Young Baroness von Holzschuher mentioned no work, no welfare, and certainly no prayers. Had she done so, they might have resembled the incantations muttered sixty years earlier in the grotto of Fra Felice by Capriotes dressed in Franciscan robes while the naked young lovers of Fritz Krupp, adorned by the golden medals he had designed for them, fondled the then Konzernherr. Those were private rituals, of course. So were Arndt's parties. No Neapolitan newspaper accused Fritz's great-grandson of indiscretions. Yet externally, at least, fin-de-siècle decadence had been a pale forerunner of its *milieu-de-siècle* sequel. The cultivated fatigue was more studied, the bored aestheticism more obscure, the escapism, world-weariness, and fashionable despair carried to a higher pitch. The very rich moved to faster rhythms; everything was revved up; Baroness von Holzschuher's gushing was almost a regurgitation.

Before the Capri blowup Wilhelmine patricians arched their eyebrows at the tale that "For several years Dr. Schweninger has commanded Herr [Fritz] Krupp to strip and lie on his stomach for a full hour after each meal (. . . *nach dem Essen eine Stunde auf dem Bauch liegen sollte*) while Herr Krupp's companions, to prevent him from becoming bored, join him in this activity." But that was another civilization. By mid-century the jet set was accustomed to well-bred ladies who used four-letter words in mixed company, to impulsive performances between intoxicated guests who didn't even know each other's names, to extended trips abroad by people who had spouses elsewhere, and to extraordinary exhibitions between men and women. One chose one's country, of course. Lawyers briefed their clients

---

* This was part of a five-paragraph *Erlass zur 25 jährigen Wiederkehr des Tages der Besitzübernahme durch Alfred Krupp* (Decree on the Twenty-fifth Anniversary of Alfred Krupp's Proprietorship). Attached to it was a drawing of the Stammhaus, suitable for framing. Some of these pictures may be found in Essen parlors today, nearly a century later.

on local statutes, though certain individuals, too preoccupied to solicit advice, did commit grave offenses. It was possible to be worth a fortune, to winter in Acapulco and summer in Saint Moritz, to see one's photograph in *Stern, Paris-Match, Epoca,* and *Look* — and to be wanted by the police of several countries. Warrants often remained outstanding for frequently there was no statute of limitations on the crimes committed. Popular mythology to the contrary, *au milieu de siècle* class barriers remained, and at the top the gap had widened.[30]

Arndt F. A. v. Bohlen und Halbach was at the top. Chaperoned by an understanding mother, backed by a billion dollars, the possessor of a private aircraft which could easily accommodate his custom-built Rolls-Royce in its luggage bay, and the holder of deeds to homes in Brazil, Germany, France, and Lebanon, he seemed far safer from the press than Fritz Krupp had been. But the peacock in him refused to be tamed. For years the Hauptverwaltungsgebäude had successfully pleaded with editors to remember the boy's youth. By January 24, 1967, that had become difficult. Arndt was in his thirtieth year. *Die Zeit, Abendzeitung,* and *Der Spiegel* would be watching his every move. It was a good time to lie low, to take a long cruise on the new yacht he had generously given himself.

Instead he anticipated his approaching middle age by throwing postwar Germany's biggest birthday party as a lavish gesture of self-esteem. *Abendzeitung* devoted a full half-page to the guest list, and in his column "Hunter notiert," Hannes Obermaier reported next day that:

> One imperial highness, dozens of princes, and countless aristocrats [*Eine kaiserliche Hoheit, mehrere königliche Hoheiten, Prinzen zu Dutzenden*] mingled with uncrowned millionaires at Arndt Krupp von Bohlen's gigantic birthday bash [*Geburtstagparty*]. The scene was Humplmayr's, and it was beyond doubt the most extravagant ball in the history of the establishment. All stops were pulled out for the exclusive guests. There were fancy floral arrangements, there was formal dress, and rare caviar was served from two-pound tins [*Kaviar in Kilobüchsen*], like a Hollywood movie when Russian grand dukes are at table.[31]

The Reich had seen nothing like it since the Führer's fiftieth birthday on April 20, 1939, when Hitler had proclaimed a national holiday, opened a new *Autobahn,* issued a stamp with his picture on it, received a congratulatory telegram from King George VI — Franklin Roosevelt sent none* — and admired his favorite gift, brought by *lieben* Gustav and *treuen* Alfried. There were few other guests at Berchtesgaden that day, however, for he had been preoccupied with the liquidation of Slovakia and making certain that the Jews reimbursed Aryan insurance companies for enthusiastic SS excesses during *Kristallnacht,* the night of broken glass. *Abendzeitung's*

---

\* *Dieser Lumpenstaat . . . Räuberstaaten!*" Göring had raged — "That nation of villains . . . That gangster state!" (Shirer *Aufstieg und Fall* 460.)

columnist to the contrary, Alfried's son hadn't succeeded to the title; thus, having no business, he needn't mix it with pleasure. He could play both host and guest of honor.

Considering the company he kept, one would have expected the festivities to be very far out. On the contrary; they were a curious anachronism, a throwback to the turn of the century mood upon which its celebrants doted. With its pageantry, billboard-sized menus, and swarms of titled guests (one marveled that so many still existed), the affair seemed more evocative of the Hotel Bristol in the 1890's than Humplmayr's in the 1960's:

> The dance itself opened according to formal protocol, with Arndt leading the cotillion, escorting former Empress Soraya to the floor [*Arndt bat Ex-kaiserin Soraya um den ersten Tanz*]. They were followed by Prince Johannes von Thurn und Taxis guiding Charlotte Franzen, wife of the restaurateur.[32]

Herr Conrad Uhl, the forgotten restaurateur of the old Bristol, could have strained eyes and ears without detecting a false note. The formal dress of the men arriving at Maximiliansplatz 16 was immaculate; the women's gowns were designed by France's most exclusive couturiers. *Die Firma*'s billionaire-designate pranced across the center of the Cuvilliés ballroom, and facing him during the German waltz was one of the most extraordinary *Weltdamen* in the history of the *haut monde*. Princess Soraya, it may be said, symbolized everything in the life of Alfried's son. Born of a Persian chieftain and a Bavarian mother the year Hitler tore up the Versailles Treaty, she was a beautiful, green-eyed, barren, thirty-one-year-old veteran of Cannes, Sun Valley, Central Park West, the West End, le Boulevard Saint-Germain, the *dolce vita* of Via Venti Settembre, and, of course, the agrarian mutations of Rio. At seventeen she had been married to the Shah of Iran. For seven years she had shared Teheran's peacock throne with him, her exotic tastes lubricated by Iranian oil. Then, in March 1958, her husband threw her out "for the good of the country"; his army was ordered to destroy every portrait and photograph of her, inside the palace and out. The disgraced wife shrugged. With what Moslem women call *"Insh' Allah"* — Islam's equivalent of the SS *Sachlichkeit* — she sighed huskily, "I have cried enough," and settled in Cologne, depositing, with an indifference which only the Nizam of Hyderabad could match, seven million dollars' worth of jewels in a local bank. She was an exquisite, voluptuous, provocative corsair costumed by Pucci and attended daily by Lilly Daché. Millions of women disapproved of her. Tossing restlessly in the night brooding over the life she led, they bit their bed sheets in envy.[33]

Herr Uhl would have especially enjoyed the finesse with which Arndt's

other guests whirled in concentric circles, displaying that almost geometric respect for distinctions of peerage which had become embedded in
highborn tradition before the *Allerhöchsteselber* had mounted his throne.
There had been a few changes since the war, but the oldest rule of all still
held: length of bloodline took precedence over resonance of title. Leading
the roll of priority that evening were Prince Rupprecht zu Hohenlohe-
Langenburg, Prince Johann Georg von Hohenzollern and Princess Birgitta,
Count and Countess Hans-Veit Toerring-Jettenbach, and Baron Camillo
von Thalhammer; surrounding them was a crush of other counts and
barons, a British peer, and several consuls. Baroness von Holzschuher could
be glimpsed now and then, and on the outskirts, like a ghost from the
white satin walls of Berlin's Kroll-Opernhaus opening thirty years earlier,
stood the bottle-blonde coif of Mady Rahl, still cherishing her fashionable
Munich address at Wiedermayerstrasse 23, her membership in the Tanz-
und Theaterausbildung, and her five-line entry in *Wer ist Wer?* Mady's
wasn't the last name on the list. To be at the bottom here was a form of
inverted snobbery, and the privilege had been reserved for Maria Estele
Kubitschek, the elder daughter of the Brazilian President who had made
her host's South American *Staat im Staate* possible.

A clock struck *zwölf*. Abruptly the dancing stopped completely. There
was an embarrassed pause.

> It was midnight — time for congratulations to begin. But what does one
> give Croesus on his birthday [*Was schenkt man einem Milliardenerben zu
> seinem Geburstag*]? Prince von Bayern presented him with a single carna-
> tion. Nightclub owner and man-about-town James Graser rendered his
> off-color "Dudlhofer" dairy. Most of the guests had arranged clever bou-
> quets beforehand. After the clock's tolling Arndt spent the bulk of his time
> dancing with Hildegarde Neff. . . . Ysabel (Diamond Lil) Style had
> brought along her own butler, to be served exclusively by him. Prince Tas-
> silo Fürstenberg announced to an attentive crowd that his daughter Ira
> had been chosen for a movie role in Rome [*dass seine Tochter Ira im April
> ihren ersten Film in Rom drehen wird*].[34]

Obermaier noticed an assortment of "*homosexuelle Modezeichner* [fash-
ion designers] *aus ganz Deutschland*" and some who weren't German.
One group was from London. In a whimsical interval between intraprofes-
sional flirtations and indulgence in the dining specialties of the house —
"breast [chicken] à la Sophia Loren" and "back [lamb] à la Mustapha"
— they sang. One chorus had been especially popular the autumn after
Arndt's birth, and back in the United Kingdom some of the singers'
parents still identified it with Munich:

> *For he's a jolly good fellow,*
> *For he's a jolly good fellow . . .*

And so said all of them. But their host, master of six tongues, was momentarily nonplussed. Hesitating in midstep he asked Fräulein Neff, "*Was ist das für ein Liedlein?*" She was speechless. She couldn't tell him what that little song was. Hildegarde was as sophisticated as Arndt; the star of West Germany's first postwar film, *Mörder sind unter uns* (Murderers Are Among Us), she had played opposite Erich von Stroheim in Hollywood and won awards in Locarno, Milan and Vichy. Yet although she was much older than Arndt and had entered her fortieth year last month, Hildegarde had been but a child of ten when the Right Honorable Arthur Neville Chamberlain (whose social position would have warranted an invitation to Maximiliansplatz 16 that night) had briefly gratified his countrymen by letting down the Czechoslovak side with the BBC cry, "How horrible, fantastic, incredible it is that we should be digging trenches . . . here because of a quarrel in a faraway country between people of whom we know nothing!"* To Arndt and Hildegarde, Munich was a city, no more, a wide-open Bundesrepublik town celebrated for the shaded benches on Leopoldstrasse, where *lesbische Fräulein* publicly caress one another, thereby attracting more tourists than Munich's huge zoo. Had one of the Englishmen who created miniskirts in the warren of shops behind Berkeley Square House presented the birthday king with an umbrella, Arndt probably would have laughed, but that would have been because all life had become a joke to him; the real point would have completely escaped him.[35]

To his lovely partner he whispered again, "*Was ist das für ein Liedchen?*" (He had now concluded that it was a ditty.) She shook her head, they exchanged a blank glance, and the Britons, who had been watching carefully, held a mirthful conference. They raised their tenors in a reprise *lentissimo*. Their puzzled host stared at them, people from a faraway country of which he knew nothing. At that they lost control. Harmony was transmogrified into cacophony, and the nightingales from Berkeley Square, abandoning song, commenced to giggle.

✠   ✠   ✠

There was no giggling *auf dem Hügel*, no celebration of the heir's anniversary, and certainly no rejoicing over the photograph which appeared on the front pages of German newspapers next morning exhibiting "Krupp-Sohn Arndt" wearing not only white tie, but a scarlet diagonal ribbon across his pearl studs and, dangling from his neck, a military cross bestowed by some unknown (and doubtless underdeveloped) government. Four of Arndt's uncles had worn the Wehrmacht's *Feldgrau*, and one Göring's

---

* The following day Goebbels' Reichspropagandaministerium rebroadcast this quotation throughout Germany, together with the news that a "*Konferenz zwischen Deutschland, Italien, Frankreich und Grossbritannien*" was imminent. Arndt's nurse heard it over the radio while feeding Alfried's seven-month old son.

Luftwaffe blue; three had been killed in action and a fourth imprisoned for a decade. To be sure, his own father had never strapped on a *Stahlhelm*. Nevertheless Alfried's survival of the RAF's 1943–1944 bombings had been something of a feat, and he fully merited the two *Kriegsverdienstkreuze* Hitler had pinned on his chest; in the words of an international biographical dictionary, Alfried had "almost single-handedly kept Adolf Hitler's huge war machine rolling." Yet neither he nor his brothers ever wore their medals. Now his only child — and no longer a child at that — was parading before the press displaying a preposterous gewgaw which might have been purchased in the toy department of Krupp's Essen department store. It was disgraceful. It was humiliating. It was worse; it was ominous.[36]

On certain topics Krupp servants are discreet, and properly so. How many Camels and how much White Horse whisky the Konzernherr consumed that long lonely weekend on Sylt is privileged information, though we do know that he sat alone hour after hour listening to taped Wagner: *Tannhäuser, Lohengrin, Die Meistersinger von Nürnberg, Tristan und Isolde,* and, appropriately, *Die Gotterdämmerung.* Financially his empire was shakier than all but a handful suspected. And now this blow had fallen. People would start talking, men who were in a position to know and who would be heard attentively. You could trust valets, and if you were Alfried Krupp you could trust yourself, but that was just about the lot. One close friend, a member of the Direktorium, volunteered to this writer, "You know, I saw young Krupp at the sesquicentennial. That was the first and last time. And Herr Alfried is an old man. It could come at any time." Another said: "Arndt *is* a problem. It's not so much that he plays around, though ye gods and little fishes (*heiliger Strohsack*), the records he sets — if the Führer were alive he'd be climbing all over us! The real difficulty is that the next in line doesn't *want* to assume command. Leading an enterprise of such enormity requires great dedication, and I'm afraid that when that particular gene was passed out Arndt was next door (*im nächsten Haus*). Naturally this is a great trial to his father. The Konzern is his whole life."[37]

The immediate threat to Alfried, however, lay in the Bundesrepublik press. *Abendzeitung* had beaten every other newspaper and newsmagazine in the country. The Munich columnist had, with the complete cooperation of Arndt and his guests, set down the basic facts about the *Geburtstag* and the *Geburtstagsgeschenke.* He hadn't libeled anyone; nevertheless he had crossed a line. The author of "Hunter notiert" had depicted Arndt as an indolent fool. Others would be quick to make certain that Arndt's ensign remained nailed to the Krupp mast so that all might see it, which, for the nation's most eminent dynasty could only be catastrophic. And presently that happened. As expected, the catastrophe began in *Der Spiegel.* Until now Rudolf Augstein, the editor-in-chief of Germany's newsmagazine, had largely confined his sniping to Beitz. No more; he would be un-locking his arsenal. The periodical which had hacked the Flick dynasty to pieces three years earlier over a minor family quarrel wouldn't ignore Alfried's unfortunate son, and sure enough, after a lull — the editor had been imprisoned for attacking a member of the Bonn government — *Spiegel* breathlessly disclosed to its readers that mighty as Alfried was, Krupp dominance of the Ruhr, as old as modern European history, would end with his death: "His only son Arndt, who reached maturity long ago, demonstrated that he lacks both the inclination and the ability (*dass er nicht geneigt und kaum fähig ist*) to lead the firm, now or ever." Nothing like that had ever been published about a Krupp crown prince. Augstein added that despite Arndt's exceptional university opportunities at Frei-burg, Munich, and Cologne, he had opted "*für die Laufbahn des Play-boys*" (the career of a playboy), and that "His most serious occupation is cruising around in his Rolls-Royce (*Seit einiger Zeit tummelt er sich mit seinem Rolls-Royce*), exploring the playground of international Snobiety. At a nightclub brawl in Nice during 1965 he lost a platinum ring with a fourteen-carat solitaire worth $40,000."[38]

Even Arndt was stung by that, though for a startling reason. Augstein had mentioned the limousine and the diamond but had slighted his yacht, *Antinoüs*. Therefore, in an interview two months later, he rephrased *Der Spiegel* to include it: " 'Arndt has shown that he has neither the inclina-tion nor the capacity to run his father's enterprise. He has a Rolls-Royce and a motor yacht.' What a puzzling connection!" It baffled him, he said, because he knew a self-made man who owned several Rolls and yachts. (He overlooked a conspicuous distinction; unlike himself the tycoon worked for a living.) Arndt asserted that he regarded such "allusions to my private life" as "extremely tasteless . . . whatever form this life may have assumed." He insisted that "the impression given by the press that I am incapable of running Krupp . . . is not true. I'm also not a playboy member of the international jet set, as the boulevard press has been de-scribing me. Admittedly, I enjoy my life during my leisure time, yet I'm a very hardworking, serious man when I'm in Brazil." He didn't want people in the Fatherland to think that he had become a Latin American, though. "How can I deny that this is the country of my birth, the country of my family?" he asked passionately. "I shall always keep a *pied-à-terre* in this country. I don't deny being a European, a German. I intend to return again and again to recharge my spiritual batteries."[39]

Nobody bought his story. Somehow grimy Kruppianer couldn't envisage a Versailles replica on another continent as the appropriate place for their eventual *alleinige Inhaber* to recharge or even discharge his spiritual batter-ies. They didn't expect him to wriggle through a mine shaft among a band of Kumpel, but at the very least he could have paid token calls at Villa Hügel and the Hauptverwaltungsgebäude. Arndt's continuing absence from the Ruhr created something of a problem, for any public encounter between him and his father would now attract swarms of reporters. Thus, while it was essential that they discuss the Konzern's future, their meetings had to be furtive and carefully arranged. During the winter of 1962–1963 they began a series of clandestine conferences, first on Waldtraut's Argentinian estate and then in the North Sea fogbanks off Sylt, where Alfried's *Germania V* would anchor within hailing distance of Arndt's *Antinoüs*. Somehow newspapermen found out anyhow, with the upshot that Arndt, debarking from *Antinoüs's* gangplank and reading magazines and newspapers, would conclude that the press wasn't taking him seriously. It wasn't. Its skepticism was virtually unanimous. *Fortune* flatly declared that Arndt "showed not the slightest talent or inclination for becoming the sixth head of the firm." By then, he himself had quit pretending. To one journalist he said wearily, "The Krupp tradition has brought my forebears a lot of unhappiness"; to a second, "I am not like my father, who sacrificed his whole life for something, not knowing whether it is really worth it in his own time"; to a third, "My father has worked more than he has lived. I'm not like him, and I'm not about to be." Asked about his own destiny, he called a deuce a deuce. Henceforth, he said, he would *"ein sorgenfreies Leben führen"* (lead a carefree life).[40]

The stupidest Kruppianer knew that a man couldn't be both hedonist and Konzernherr. The brightest, brooding with his American cigarettes, Scotch whisky, and Wagnerian tapes, contemplated a fresh draft of his will. A century before, on April 1, the eve of the Paris Exhibition of 1868, his great-grandfather had personally flicked the lint from his glittering fourteen-inch showpiece cannon, a thousand-pounder with a fifty-ton barrel and a forty-ton, swivel-frame steel carriage. This was the weapon he had grandly described to the King of Prussia as "a monster such as had never been seen by the world" (*ein Ungeheuer, wie es die Welt noch nicht sah*), and which he had then presented to His Majesty as a gift. After polishing the muzzle and then reinforcing the floor beneath his 88,000-pound cast steel ingot, Alfred had returned to his Paris hotel room and pondered the future of the dynasty. Like Alfried a hundred years later he had been chilled by the approaching shadow of his sixtieth birthday, and he had dispassionately weighed the disquieting fact that his only son was, in the words of the family chronicles,

. . . a weakling [*ein kränkelnder Knabe*]. How could his frail physique support such an enormous burden of responsibilities, and where could one recruit assistants sufficiently able, faithful [*so fähig, so treu*] and dedicated to be privy to the young man's confidences? Alfred despaired. His feeling of debilitation, of being utterly worn out, engulfed him once more. Every time he tried to run away from his burdens they bound him all the tighter. The richest man in Germany was truly one of the most miserable [*Der reichste Mann Deutschlands ist wahrlich einer der elendsten*]. He tore at his fetters. But the sound of their rattling only told him he would never be rid of them.[41]

One can almost sympathize with the brooder of 1967. The sole heir of Alfred *der Grosse* had been sickly and reluctant, but at least he had been there, he had been dutiful, and he had been prepared to take over. Moreover, the underpinning of the family legacy — money — had become exceedingly shaky. Alfred would have understood that, though it was doubtful that Arndt would; few members of the Direktorium did, and the financial community is still trying to decipher it. "*Der reichste Mann Deutschlands*" had been an accurate description of the great-grandfather, and in 1967 *Newsweek* was also correct in identifying the great-grandson as "the richest man in Europe — the sole owner of 150 factories and mines turning out 3,573 products." But capitalists can accumulate fantastic debts. In 1875, with all his shops flourishing, Alfred had been forced to shoulder 30,000,000 marks in obligations, the funds to be provided by a syndicate of financiers under the management of the Prussian State Bank. To his humiliation he had been obliged to submit to a comptroller, and though he regarded the contract he signed that April 4 as a capitulation, even those terms would have been impossible without the active intervention of S.M. Now, in another spring ninety-two years later, Alfried Krupp found himself in a plight which dwarfed that long-ago Founder's Crisis. No one on the continent could match his personal fortune. At the same time he was, paradoxically, the Bundesrepublik's largest creditor. For all his inventory of absorption towers, refineries, steel mills, chemical plants, shipbuilding and locomotive construction yards, truck, bridge, and turbine shops — not to mention wine cellars, merchandise marts, and bins containing nuts and bolts of every size used anywhere in the world — in spite of all this, Krupp owed nearly 700 million dollars. He was indebted to 263 German banks and insurance companies. There had never been anything like it in industrial history. No benign Kaiser sat in Potsdam now, and even if he had it wouldn't have mattered. There was no exit. Beaufort's scale stood at force twelve for Alfried Krupp. His eleven-generation dynasty faced total ruin.[42]

# 32

✠

# The Flag Follows Trade

ALFRIED KRUPP's life — it has "never depended on me,"[1] as he once said — had been an extraordinary culmination of dynastic drives since his birth; like all the men who had borne his name, he had mirrored the fluctuating fortunes of Germany, and during a sharp Bundesrepublik recession in his sixtieth year he was to step right through the looking glass, shattering the dreams of his ancestors. Like Adolf Hitler, the focus of his early life, he felt (perhaps justifiably) that his tragic momentum was being accelerated by those closest to him. Alfried's own son had turned his back on nearly everything a Krupp should cherish. Now Berthold Beitz, the hand-picked deputy to whom he had entrusted the tactical fate of *die Firma*, blundered incredibly, bringing *Haus*, *Familie*, and *Dynastie* down in a debacle which shook the capitals of the world. It broke the Konzernherr's heart, and when it was all over the frail son and the strong friend were to stand over the silent grave of the last, and perhaps the greatest, of the Krupps.

In his obituary of the family's four-hundred-year-reign, James Bell of *Fortune* was to observe of *der Amerikaner* that "Because he was a salesman rather than a financial man with an eye out for profitability, a considerable portion of his enemies came to be concentrated in the powerful banking community." By a freak of European economics — a playback of the 1873 crisis — it was in that very community that Krupp's lieutenant needed friends most. The man who really should have been standing at Krupp's elbow was Johannes Schröder. Schröder was a graduate of the universities of Freiburg, Vienna, and Berlin; in 1929 the Weimar Republic had honored him with a *Diplom-Volkswirt* (state diploma in national economy); and for fifteen years before joining the firm in 1938 he had been accepted as a member of the Ruhrgebiet's tight-knit financial establishment. Moreover, he knew what was wrong with the Krupp-Beitz policies. Writing in *Handelsblatt* after he had been dismissed on the absurd charge that his surprise appearance in Japan had embarrassed Arndt, Schröder noted that in family firms

> . . . there is usually only one sole proprietor, one man at the head of the concern [*über die Personalgesellschaften und Einzelfirmen heerscht meistens ein Kopf*].He may be a gifted technician; he may be a fantastic salesman. He creates marvelous situations and gains marvelous sales [*Er schafft wunderbare Betriebe und erzielt herrliche Umsätze*]. He tolerates the presence of no one near him, and looks upon finance as something which is — unfortunately — necessary, but which will never trouble him because of his remarkable achievements, even if cash has to be scratched out of all corners. He mixes up money and capital and is dumbfounded when, one day, despite his dazzling successes, he finds himself tottering on the very brink of ruin.[2]

Schröder's camouflage was clever. Going after Krupp himself was unthinkable. Therefore he had substituted the name of Willi Schlieker. As a former Speer protégé, Schlieker had tried to parlay his wartime miracles into a fortune. The Ruhr establishment, quietly enjoying *Schadenfreude* (malicious gloating), had watched impassively as Willi miscalculated, overextended himself, and was crushed under a millstone of debt. The victim had been in his thirties, a graduate of what the Schlotbarone had disdainfully called "Speer's kindergarten." Schröder was free to pillory him in public, although, of course, *Handelsblatt*'s knowledgeable readers knew that he was after far bigger game:

> I always compare this kind of modern economic leader with a man who has a brilliant mind and powerful muscles, but who disregards his circulatory system. He looks healthy, glowing, in the pink. Suddenly he suffers a heart attack; he falls ill or dies [*Während er noch gesund und strahlend aussieht, wir der plötzlich, von einem Herzinfarkt betroffen und fällt krank oder tot um*]. The danger of such financial coronaries is especially dire in firms which do not publish their balance sheets. They are not subject to medical (or, in this case, public) control. Thus they cannot be warned in time.

In the aftermath of the war, he realized, such warnings had been impossible. "If one wishes to rebuild, one has to overlook the difference between capital and money. *Any* credit which could be obtained was invested. Whether it was short-term or long-term was of no consequence. Necessity knows no laws!" Once more: *Noth kennt kein Gebot*. But with the return of stability a strong concern had to maintain liquid assets:

> *Man muss sich über eines klar sein: Liquidität ist teuer, aber Illiquidität ist viel teurer; denn sie kostet die Existenz!*

One thing must be clear: Liquidity is expensive, but illiquidity much more so, because it destroys the very existence of a firm![3]

Schröder was addressing himself, as passionately as an economist can, to the Konzernherr. He might as well have left his pen corked. Alfried had been trained as an engineer. Arndt was to have received a thorough economic education, but his detour to the founts of pleasure had permitted *der Amerikaner*, who thought of assets in terms of Goldfinger, to strike out on his own. One German banker, so close to Alfried that he prefers that his name not be used, believes that the sole proprietor's fortunes began to turn in "the middle of 1966. The consolidated balance sheet figures for 1965, which were ready then, showed an alarming profit situation. The reasons? The deterioration of steel prices, the crisis in coal mining, the decline in sales, rising costs." He slid a clipping across his mahogany desk —

KRUPP HÜTTENWERKE
BLIEBEN OHNE GEWINN

KRUPP STEELWORKS
WITHOUT A PROFIT

But the banker was diagnosing the financial coronary after the vessels had ruptured. Schröder had predicted the attack nearly five years in advance, and if his prognosis was sound in other ways, the real turning point may have come when Berthold Beitz, deplaning from Bulgaria after a whirlwind tour in which he had outsold salesmen from England, Japan, Italy and France, said airily. "Why go to Indonesia or Bolivia when eastern Europe is on our doorstep?"[4] Schröder could have answered him swiftly. In underdeveloped countries Bonn handled the financing for ten years and guaranteed 80 percent of it. Once the Konzern crossed the curtain the Bundesrepublik was absolved of fiscal responsibility — was, indeed, officially opposed to all exchanges with the *kommunistischen Block*.

The doctrine sparked a first-class row between Adenauer and Beitz in May 1958, when Alfried's chief of staff tentatively sought to exploit his wartime contacts in Poland. He was greeted so warmly there that he flew on to Moscow — and returned to face Adenauer's wrath. *Der Alte*, censuring his visit, issued a public statement from the Palais Schaumburg declaring: *"Mann müsse an der nationalen Zuverlässigkeit des Herrn Beitz zweifeln"* (One must doubt the national reliability of Herr Beitz).[5]

To dab a businessman with red paint seems absurd, but the severe old chancellor was the rock of West German anti-Communism, and the very ardor of Beitz's reception on the other side of Europe's threshold made him suspect. After Adenauer's denunciation Russia, in an attempt to help, made a characteristic mistake; despite Beitz's high role in Hans Frank's

Generalgouvernement Polen, the Kremlin proclaimed, the USSR had given him a clean bill of health. In Warsaw, Premier Josef Cyrankiewicz, equally well-meaning, released a statement in German describing Beitz as "an outstanding emissary of Germany, for twenty years a tried and proven friend of my country."[6]

That helped the Generalbevollmächtigter's reputation among the Reds, but in the Ruhr it merely confirmed the distrust of unrepentant ex-Nazis who had been wary of the Hamburg salesman from the outset. The Führer hadn't sent Frank, Seyss-Inquart, or their staffs into the General Government as emissaries. No one had told them to win Jewish friends or influence the Polish people, and any German sergeant who had saved *Stücke* had been guilty of treason. Even Adenauer, no Nazi, was raising questions of patriotism. Beitz was in trouble and knew it, and in April, for the first time in his career, he

> . . . stirred up his superior, Alfried Krupp, to send a protest letter immediately [*bewog seinen Arbeitgeber Alfried Krupp alsbald zu einem Protestbrief*]. The Chancellor backed away [*retirierte*] and capitulated. He denied outright that he had used the phrase "national reliability."[7]

Behind that skirmish lay an issue as old as Prussian politics. Lacking national frontiers yet dominating central Europe, the Reich had never been able to decide who its friends should be. This indecisiveness had led to two two-front wars in thirty years, and Krupp's inability to resolve it was about to set the stage for his decline, fall, and death.

Before moving to Brussels, the president of the Common Market had been Adenauer's foreign secretary. His most memorable achievement had been the so-called Hallstein Doctrine, under which the Bundesrepublik withheld diplomatic recognition from any country which recognized East Germany, the sole exception being Russia, on the ground that it was an occupation power. However, as generations of Allied diplomats have learned to their despair, Germany's ruling classes have always taken it as an article of faith that they can handle Russians better than London, Paris, or Washington. In 1939 Joachim Ribbentrop had signed a nonaggression pact with the Soviet Union, privately confiding: "That we will advance militarily up to Moscow and beyond is, I believe, unquestionable."[8] Now *die Firma*'s General Plenipotentiary was covertly violating the Hallstein Doctrine, and here as elsewhere the family was prepared to represent the Fatherland. Bonn was committed to NATO, yet strong figures in the government wanted the firm "to negotiate quasi-diplomatic relations between West Germany and the Soviet satellite states of eastern Europe." Krupp's "trade missions" in the satellite countries would serve "not only to drum up exchange but also as thinly veiled diplomatic posts" manned by German diplomats trained during the Third Reich. They would render the Hallstein Doctrine obsolescent.[9]

One May weekend this writer was informed that Herr Beitz would be unable to keep an appointment of long standing; he was in Moscow, talking to Nikita Khrushchev. They were discussing politics, not business, and after flying back Beitz reported to Bonn before returning to Essen. That same Sunday Baron von Wilmowsky was the guest of Klaus von Bismarck, great-grandson of the Iron Chancellor, at Haus Villigst, the Ruhr estate of young Bismarck who, with a group of contemporaries, was vehemently opposed to Beitz's Russian visit. Their debate pointed up the size of the Fatherland's eternal geopolitical riddle. In his memoirs the great *Eisenkanzler* of the Nineteenth Century had concluded that the freedom of Reich policy in the east was a distinct advantage — that Berlin could always outwait and outwit the bear. On May 21, 1864, with Prussian troops fighting in Schleswig-Holstein, Alfred Krupp had proudly notified Saint Petersburg that his firm "now employs 7,000 men, of which the greater part is working for Russia." The Kaiser, General Hans von Seeckt, and Adolf Hitler, the most effective Russophobe in German history, had echoed the Kanonenkönig's ambivalence. Dictating to Hess from his Landsberg cell, the Führer observed with rare dispassion that "*Wäre ich selbst Franzose . . . so könnte und wollte auch ich nicht anders handeln, als es am Ende ein Clemenceau tut*" (Were I a Frenchman . . . I would conduct my foreign affairs just as Clemenceau has). Later in the same prison he wrote that National Socialism must strike hands with Russians:

> We are taking up where the First Reich broke off six hundred years ago. We shall stop the ceaseless *Volksdeutschen* emigration to the south and west and turn our eyes toward the opportunities in the east . . . When we speak today in Europe of new land and territory, we can only first think of Russia and the dependent states which border her [*Wenn wir aber heute in Europa von neuem Grund und Boden reden, können wir in erster Linie nur an Russland und die ihm untertanen Randstaaten denken*].[10]

While six million Germans dutifully bought six million copies of *Mein Kampf*, few were loyal enough to trudge through its 782 prolix pages. There were exceptions; Alfried Krupp kept a copy of his party bible on his bedside table to the day of his death, and Joachim Ribbentrop rarely made a move without checking the dog-eared pages of his copy. In the last week of May 1939, while briefing his ambassador to Russia, he prepared a carefully worded eyes-only minute for Hitler, suggesting that "no real conflict of interests (*kein realer aussenpolitischer Interessengegensatz*) afflicts the Reich and the USSR. . . . It is even possible to go so far as to say that when resolving the German-Polish question — whatever the solution — we would take Russian wishes under advisement insofar as that is possible.[11]

The Führer's marginal notes in Ribbentrop's captured files show that he himself couldn't make up his mind. A *détente* with Stalin attracted him. The ambassador in Moscow was instructed to tell Molotov that the Reich desired "a resumption of normal political relations, stressing that Germany had "no aggressive intentions" toward the USSR, which, in that last spring before the war, was quite true. The leader of the Germans was backing, filling, backing, filling. If Otto von Bismarck, Alfried Krupp, the All-Highest, Hans von Seeckt, and Adolf Hitler had been unable to resolve the Fatherland's schizophrenic attitude toward the east, it is too much to expect that the trick could have been brought off by a former champagne salesman in 1939 — or, twenty years later, by a former insurance salesman.[12]

❊ ❊ ❊

Beitz thought he saw a *Stern im Osten.* Alfried Krupp had actually managed Ukrainian factories; he had more experience with Russian industry than any industrialist in the Ruhr, and he might have warned his aide. But Krupp was preoccupied with the problem of Arndt, and his chief of staff was the only man at the controls. In 1949 the Ruhr had turned eastward during a mild recession. Now, eight years later, business was slack again, and again the remedy seemed attractive. Most Schlotbarone refused to deal with Communists, but Krupp himself told them that any industrialist who raised a political objection (*politischen Einwand*) might as well start drawing up bankruptcy papers, that the only sensible cairn in the world of commerce was "economic reason" (*wirtschaftliche Vernunft*), which, at the moment, appeared to lead to Beitz's star. The man who was following it tried to dismiss his critics with a quip. Describing the masters of the Kremlin at a Bonn reception, Beitz arched his brows and whispered in mock surprise, "Those people actually have fingernails as clean as ours!" Adenauer, unamused, shot back, "Why not wear a red carnation in your lapel, Herr Beitz?" Beitz spluttered of "building bridges between East and West," and, turning to those around him, said plaintively, "I cannot understand these critics (*Ich kann diese Kritiker nicht verstehen*). Is there anything wrong with shaking hands with a customer who has just bought fifty million marks' worth of equipment from you? . . . I am a simple businessman. I want to know nothing about politics and would like to stay far away from political questions. . . . Let Adenauer handle his diplomacy and let us handle our trade. Free enterprise doesn't pay much attention to political viewpoints while the governments change" (*Privatindustrie kümmert sich nicht um politische Gesichtspunkte, während die Regierungen wechseln*).[13]

In the Hauptverwaltungsgebäude that would have received an ovation. In the Palais Schaumburg it was followed by a gelid silence. The reminder that German governments change was not tactful, and to this audience the proposition that Krupp's double operations beyond the curtain could be divorced from Bonn's foreign policy was inane. Luckily for Beitz, the Konzernherr himself was present. Speaking quietly he said, "Our commercial goals in the eastern bloc are being judged from a political viewpoint (*Unsere Geschäftsinteressen im Ostblock werden nach politischen Gesichtspunkten beurteilt*). This attitude couldn't be wider of the mark; our interests are wholly economic. We sell goods in the eastern nations, not for political reasons, but to create new jobs for German workmen" (*zur Erhaltung der Arbeitsplätze, nicht aber aus politischen Beweggründen*).[14]

He was echoing his father, who had cried "*Hier wird nicht politisiert!*" while financing Hitler's terror election of 1933, and he made no more sense than Gustav. But tradition carried the argument. Nobody in the government was going to argue with a Krupp. After a polite pause the conversation was changed to trivia. Beitz had not been exculpated, of course. He was a handy scapegoat then, and the sacrifice of his reputation became even more convenient less than a decade later, when the sky darkened over the Ruhr again, for the firm's miscalculations in its last years were not confined to the Ostblock. Despite Bonn's 5 percent coal tariff, Pennsylvania smokestack barons were underselling Germans in their own country, fueling the furnaces of the Bundesrepublik with inferior anthracite. Meanwhile, all over the world, steelmakers were suffering one of their periodic, prolonged, inexplicable crises. Logic should have suggested a cutback. But the records show that

> In the fiscal year 1965 alone, the General Director invested $82,500,000 in the firm's coal and steel holdings. At the same time, he was setting aside but $36,750,000 for the manufacture of goods and trade. The General Director did not close down the highly unprofitable Essen coal mines Amalie and Helene until 1965–66. [*Erst 1965/66 liess Beitz die unrentablen Essener Zechen Amalie und Helene stillegen*].

Again:

> In 1965 the truck factory lost a total of $5,000,000 [*1965 machte die Lkw Fabrik 20 Millionen Mark Verlust*].

And finally:

> Actually, a careful breakdown of statistics discloses that the manufacturing companies of Krupp are still in the black [*Tatsächlich arbeiten die meisten der Verarbeitungs betriebe bis heute mit Gewinn*]. Among those subsidiaries operating at a loss, in addition to the truck factory, are coal and steel holdings, the Bremen shipyards, and the Fried. Krupp Universalbau.[15]

Neil McInnes of *Barron's* comparing these figures with Krupp's disastrous trade through the not-so-iron curtain, wrote that it looked to him as though "Berthold Beitz's supersalesmanship in East Europe" was putting "the Krupp family out of business for keeps"[16] It *did* look that way. And by and large, that is the way it was. Yet those who blamed Beitz were reading German periodicals; few in the Fatherland were prepared to hold *der alleinige Inhaber* answerable. Nevertheless Alfried *was* the sole proprietor. Essen was rooted in *das monarchische Prinzip,* and an absolute monarch cannot escape responsibility by sacrificing an inept vassal. To be sure, there were special circumstances. De Gaulle cut Alfried out of western European markets, vetoing his plan to share in the production of "Concord," the Anglo-French supersonic jet airliner. Similarly, most American business simply ignored a nationwide advertisement directed at them in U.S. magazines, headed KRUPP — SYMBOL OF LEADERSHIP IN INDUSTRIAL PROGRESS, guaranteeing that "More than 110,000 employees, more than 20,000 sub-suppliers, and over 150 years of experience enable Krupp to attack any problem, any task, irrespective of magnitude." The slamming of these doors encouraged Beitz to make his fatal turn eastward. So did the Bundesrepublik chancellor, who became reconciled to the use of Essen trade missions as cover legations in satellite countries; so did the chancellor's pfennig-wise country, which, according to a Strauss report in 1967, had spent only $2,800,000,000 in the vital area of research and development the previous year, a mere 2.3 percent of the GNP, compared with 4 percent for the U.S.A. and 3.2 percent in England.[17]

Still, all Schlotbarone shared that handicap. What set the Konzern apart was its size and the fact that its ruler was often an absentee landlord. Alfried's flair for adventure hadn't entirely vanished. In the spring of 1963, when he was desperately needed in the Hauptverwaltungsgebäude, he chose to end a visit to South America with a long sea voyage, sailing the *Germania* V to Bremen and taking films along the way. Racing cars had never lost their fascination for him. He had an advanced case of what someone once called "West Germany's auto-eroticism," and for three days each year he would stand over his Porsche 911, wearing overalls, watching mechanics tune the engine in Stuttgart. He never allowed anyone else to lay a finger on the wheel; "It would," he said, "be like loaning your toothbrush." His bent for fun and games never matched Arndt's. The Konzernherr was a hard-driving executive, wily and imaginative. Yet his flaws were portentous. He had mistaken Beitz for a Jencke, and his dedication to his dynastic past crippled Schröder and Schröder's successors.[18]

In the great recession of 1966–1967 Hermann Josef Abs, Germany's most eminent banker, pleaded with the Fatherland's industrialists to pare their payrolls, eliminating wasteful practices. Abs was a close friend of Krupp. They belonged to the same generation, the same clubs, the same cliques. As chairman of the board of both Hamburg's Deutsch-Asiatische and Frankfurt's Kreditanstalt für Wiederaufbau, Abs stood at the center of the Bundesrepublik's financial establishment and commanded more baronial respect than anyone in the government, including Erhard. Nevertheless, Alfried had to refuse him. Similarly, the sole proprietor was singularly obtuse when a Krupp executive pointed out to him that the firm's heavy commitment to coal and steel was becoming dangerous. Over the past four years the firm had invested 300 million dollars of capital in this sector, including $88,750,000 for a new hot strip mill which was flooding the West German market with new ingots at a time when foreign steel salesmen were waging a price war on them. Alfried's loyalty to his grimy Kumpel had converted much of the Ruhr into a replica of the industrialized Welsh countryside — its meadows were dotted with 23 million dollars' worth of unwanted Krupp coal. The executive discreetly refrained from pointing out that the Konzernherr could have avoided this dilemma had he stuck to his Mehlem bargain, but apparently that possibility never crossed Alfried's mind.[19]

Beitz suggested they shut down the Lokomotiven aller Art. Krupp shook his head. "My great-grandfather made locomotive parts; we shall go on making locomotives," he said flatly. "Profit is important, but it cannot be isolated from our social responsibility." Riffling through the pages of that day's *Westdeutsche Allgemeine Zeitung*, he turned to the columns headed *Ehemänner gesucht* (Husbands Wanted). On the working class level, courting in Germany is very direct. A man may enumerate the qualifications of the female he has in mind, and women, who advertise just as frequently, are likely to name the prospective groom's trade. Alfried's long finger ran down the fine type, pausing again and again to point out the frequency with which unmarried women or war widows had indicated that Kruppianer were preferred. They preferred Kruppianer, the Konzernherr reminded his chief of staff, because men employed by him were guaranteed steady jobs, fringe benefits far beyond the program of any welfare state, and a secure retirement. He knew the Lokomotiven assembly line. The great-great-grandsons of Kruppianer were working on it. Rising, he stepped into his darkroom, and presently der Amerikaner heard the deep brasses of Wagner coming over the villa's loudspeakers. The interview was over. Next morning Beitz told an acquaintance, "Krupp feels a deep obligation to his men. Some workmen represent the fifth generation of Kruppianer — certainly many of their grandfathers toiled at the works — and they endured the hardships and destruction of the wars, remaining true to him even during his long imprisonment, staying until the firm was healed. Therefore his attitude is: Kruppianer cannot simply be sold" (*Kruppianer können nicht einfach verkauft werden*).[20]

*Er war, wer er war, der Mann:* Alfried was still the whole show. However, warnings were being repeated by others in much stronger terms. Abs and his fellow bankers presented Krupp with a table comparing Bundesrepublik industrial production for the winter of 1966–1967 with identical months in the previous winter — October down 6 percent, November 9 percent, December 1.8 percent, January 4.1 percent, February 4.6 percent, March 7.4 percent. Already, Bonn's Gridiron authors were preparing skits turning *Wirtschaftswunder* into *Wirtschaftsgleiten* and *Wirtschaftsabgleiten* (sliding economy); *Wirtschaftsniedergang* and *Wirtschaftsabschlag* (depression); and *Wirtschaftswunderkater* (financial hangover), *-fall* (collapse), *-stille* (stagnancy), *-herbst* (autumn), *-rückgang* (recession) and, cruelest of all, *Wirtschaftswunderpause* (the snoozing economic miracle). Alfried thrust them aside as figments of journalistic imagination.[21]

But now the Cassandras were not confined to the press. Schröder's successors in *die Firma*'s counting rooms found themselves in an impossible position. Other great firms were raising capital by issuing fresh stock. The sole owner continued to rely upon his personal fortune and bank credit. In West Germany's sliding economy, however, credit was becoming drum-tight. No *Allerhöchsteselber* reigned in the capital now, fingering the tip of his *Pickelhaube*. Instead, Bonn's new Minister of Economics, bespectacled Karl Schiller (who preferred to rechristen the *Wirtschaftswunder* the *Talfahrt*, down the hill) was a Social Democrat and a firm believer in government intervention. Even Count Klaus Ahlefeldt-Lauruiz was worried about Campo Limbo. The Brazilian government was altogether too unstable for his liking; it was dangerous, he insisted "to have all one's eggs in one basket" (*alles auf eine Karte setzen*). Krupp replied crisply that at the last rendezvous of *Germania V* and *Antinoüs* his son reported *kolossal* progress in Brazil. He didn't say when Arndt had last visited *die Firma*'s South American steelworks.[22]

With that, Alfried took off for an African safari, giving Beitz full powers. By now foreign correspondents were asking awkward questions. Wasn't Fried. Krupp a dinosaur, they inquired of the Hauptverwaltungsgebäude? Here was one of the world's twelve largest firms, doing over one and a third billion dollars' worth of business each year — and its sole proprietor was off shooting elephants while his stand-in kept store. The *New York Times* Bonn bureau warned its international desk to expect bad news from Essen, and *Fortune*'s representative, echoing German sentiment, cabled home that "Some Ruhr experts feel that Krupp lost the chance of a lifetime when he didn't unload his coal and steel holdings as he had agreed to do in his compact with the American, British, and French high commissioners fourteen years ago. . . . Krupp held on to his properties, and the coal-steel part of his business accounted for fully half of the $12,500,000 loss in 1966."[23]

✠   ✠   ✠

Krupp had been charged with war crimes, bloody-mindedness, and unrepentant Nazism, but he had never been accused of disloyalty to the dynasty. Approaching his sixtieth birthday, he retained one of the most able minds in international finance, and the Great Krupp's grotesque tomb remained his shrine. Five years earlier he had divested himself of all illusions about Arndt. As the then heir later conceded in his Bavarian villa, he had agreed to renounce his right to the name Krupp "after my father approached me with the request to consider this step." Arndt added, "I have long been familiar with what the Fords did with their enterprise, and I have always admired their decision." Whether or not he had admired it, he was certainly aware of it. His father had briefed him thoroughly. In the winter of 1962–1963 Krupp sent Beitz to McCloy's elegant mini-office overlooking Manhattan's East River at 1 Chase Manhattan Plaza. The former *Hoher Kommissar* and the convict he had pardoned moved in the same circles, and Alfried's token payments to surviving *Stücke* had arisen in part from his benefactor's prodding. Now Krupp wanted *wie du mir so ich dir*, tit for tat. Foundations were almost unknown in Germany — the law discouraged them — and he needed advice on the best way to set one up. McCloy sent Beitz over to Shepard Stone, his special counsel under the occupation, now on the Ford Foundation staff. Later Beitz briefly consulted Robert F. Kennedy in Washington.[24]

*Der Amerikaner* is an easy man to follow. A correspondent for the London *Sunday Telegraph* spotted his jaunty figure and sent back a dispatch under the headline FINANCE CLOUDS OVER KRUPP EMPIRE. Reporters perched outside every Direktorium meeting, ballpoints at the ready. In November 1965 a Reuters correspondent broke the first story at Krupp's Hütten- und Bergwerke Rheinhausen in Düsseldorf. On Alfried's orders the holding company met in extraordinary session, authorizing a formal merger with the Bochumer Verein. The new company would be called Fried. Krupp Hüttenwerke A.G.; it was to constitute the first step toward a Krupp Foundation. On December 10 the directors of Bochumer Verein, on orders from Hügel, agreed that Krupp's two coal and steel enterprises should mesh; the largest company owned anywhere by one man had taken a giant step into the twentieth century. But more than a few meetings were required. The empire was so enormous, the legal knots so complex, that Krupp's advisers told him they would need another twenty months to pull it off. With luck it could be done by the summer of 1967, and he agreed to that target date.[25]

He might have goaded them. But the maneuver wasn't simple for him, either. Alfried was determined to remain faithful to Alfred; he had reexamined *Urgrossvater*'s letters, and reconciling their advice was often difficult. Sometimes it was reassuring. At the height of the 1848 political crisis, with the debates in the Prussian Constituent Assembly becoming increasingly more radical, the indomitable scarecrow had written two French businessmen, "Who isn't suffering from the present situation? We must just keep our heads above water" (*Wer leidet wohl nicht unter den jetzigen Verhältnissen? Man muss nur den Kopf oben behalten*). Other times Alfred's counsel was disquieting. Although European foundations had been established by Benedictines as early as the sixth century, they were unknown to nineteenth-century capitalists, and *der Grosse Krupp* had never given them a thought. His opposition would have been violent. His antagonism to stock companies largely arose from his fanatical yearning for secrecy, and there could be no *alleinige Inhaber* in a foundation. As early as Easter Sunday 1857 he had written Carl Meyer:

> Secrets are our capital [*Die Geheimnisse sind unser Kapital*]. And capital is squandered as soon as they are known on the outside. Business these days swarms with . . . parasites who are happy to profit from anything they can pilfer and to milk talented and intelligent men so that they may stuff their pockets and lie back in stuffed chairs.

It was the Konzern's great strength, he had declared, that "We have no shareholders waiting for their dividends," and obviously his great-grandson couldn't disinherit Arndt without sacrificing that. Nevertheless the thing had to be done.[26]

Despite the Krupp-Beitz disclaimers, their balance sheet was tippy, and the weight dragging it down lay in eastern Europe, Russia, and beyond. But here, too, Alfried felt he had no option. Of all *Urgrossvater's* maxims, one, dashed off on the eve of Sedan, overrode all others:

> I count on the national spirit of every man whose duty calls him to the lathe that he will think only of the country's crisis [*dass er nichts Anderes bedenke, als den möglichen Nothfall*] and the possible value of our firm, which, conceivably, may now become invaluable to the state.[27]

Krupp had always been a national institution, never a mere siphoner of profits. Whenever the Reich had needed the family, it had been ready, and as the last of the line Alfried had decided that it was his duty to do one thing more — something really big — for Germany.

✠   ✠   ✠

Among the motifs which reappear in the history of all three Reichs is *die Wiedervereinigung*, reunification. There was nothing odd about the Bundesrepublik's covert Ostblock policy, initiated in the Hauptverwaltungsgebäude and adopted by Bonn. Once the shock of defeat had diminished Germany was left with but one national issue: a passionate yearning for fusion with the lost lands to the east. The western allies could offer no help. But in different ways Bismarck and Alfred Krupp had shown the way, and Berthold Beitz, as indifferent to Johannes Schröder's economics as the Iron Chancellor had been to the whining voices of miserly

Prussia, was determined to follow his gleam of light just over the eastern horizon.

In 1958 he pushed the firm's Ostblock business to ten million dollars. Moscow was his most eager customer. Anastas Mikoyan, re-entering Krupp records for the first time since his farewell to Baron Wilmowsky thirty years earlier on the Ukrainian steppes, flew to the Bundesrepublik and approached Beitz directly. Chairman Khrushchev, he reminded Alfried's Generalbevollmächtigter, had told the world that the Soviet Union would overtake American production. It was possible, he continued in German, "provided we have the benefit of technological advice from the west. Krupp wares have a great name in Russia. And a canny businessman always keeps two irons in the fire" (*Krupp-Waren haben einen grossen Ruf bei unserem Volk. Und ein geschickter Geschäftsmann hat immer zwei Eisen im Feuer*).[28]

The *rapprochement* began with a down payment of 2,702,702 gold rubles and an announcement by the chairman himself that "the Soviet Union has entertained good trade relations with the Krupp firm in Essen in the past." Whether this astonishing assertion referred to the baron's unhappy wheat fiasco or to the battle of the Kursk salient, it passed unnoticed; the great thing was that rubles and kopecks were flowing westward, and that Khrushchev, like Aleksandr II, was sharing his vodka with Germans. Beitz's first call at the Kremlin was an immense success. He jovially referred to his assistants as "*meine Sputnike, Moll und Wrede*," was presented with an enormous hunting piece (in Hügel there were groans from members of the family who cherished hopes of returning to the shooting box at Sayneck), and received an affectionate, "*Da swidanija, Gospodin Beitz*" farewell from his host.[29]

The chairman promptly struck Krupp's name from Moscow's war criminal list and ordered an immediate end to all denunciations of him. Unfortunately for the dynasty's east European image, Khrushchev was a maverick; the typical Communist lacked geniality, and nothing in the Slavic experience had encouraged him to be optimistic about Krupp. Furthermore, Russian bureaucracy hadn't changed essentially since the Romanovs. It appears doubtful that Khrushchev's instructions were heard beyond the grim corridor outside his office. Leipzig posters continued to identify the world's warmongers as WALLSTREET, ROCKEFELLER UND KRUPP. To be sure, these signs were hastily removed in March 1959, when the chairman himself arrived from Moscow to reopen the fair's Krupp exhibit and accept a stainless steel tumbler adorned with *die drei Ringe*. Khrushchev "regretted that he could not meet Herr Alfried Krupp himself," drank cognac to "the continued health and affluence of the company," and conveyed his "warmest personal wishes to Herr Krupp."[30]

The chairman could convince the block wardens who decided which posters would be displayed at Deutsche Demokratische Republik's trade fair, but he couldn't reach everybody, and one golden June day after his edict this writer, strolling past the Maxim Gorki Theater and the replanted Unter den Linden in East Berlin, encountered an elaborate display of Krupp photographs in the lobby of the German History Museum. One caption read *Alfried Krupp auf der Anklagebank*. The picture did indeed depict Krupp sitting in the Nuremberg dock; however, a skilled artist had transformed the guards' helmets from American to Russian and Negro GI complexions had been airbrushed white. The accompanying text explained that Alfried, convicted as a war criminal by the USSR, had been pardoned by the Wallstreet capitalist John J. Mc-Cloy. It concluded: "Between the years 1946 and 1948 the criminals were sentenced. Afterward they were freed by the western powers and instantly assumed powerful positions in the west zone regime" (*Die meisten von ihnen nahmen bald wieder beherrschende Positionen im Westzonen-Regime ein*). Another showed *Geschützproduktion*, cannon production, and the finishing of a 10.5 grenade launcher. Here the peruser learned that "In spite of the most widespread acquisition lust of German capital, the firm of Krupp remains the most reactionary segment of German industry" (*Die Firma Krupp verkörperte stets die weitgehendsten Eroberungsgelüste des deutschen Kapitals, die reaktionärsten Teile der deutschen Industrie*).[31]

Most ludicrous was a photograph of Tilo von Wilmowsky examining a cluster of blossoms. The explanation:

> *Während der Hitler Ära war der Krupp Konzern durch Krupp von Bohlen und Halbach und dessen Schwager Tilo Freiherr von Wilmowsky im Verwaltungsrat der Reichbahn, dem grossen staatlichen Betriebe, vertreten.*

> During the Hitler era the Krupp concern was run by the elder Krupp von Bohlen und Halbach and his brother-in-law Baron Tilo von Wilmowsky, a high official in the state railways.

Tilo was there, all right, but to imply that his appointment had been useful to the Führer was absurd. One evening Gustav permitted him to run the transmitter of the family's electric train. In three minutes the baron overturned two locomotives, ran through four signals, smashed a switch, demolished a station, and, just as Gustav was frantically lurching across the table to stop him, short-circuited the transformer. Had he been appointed to the lowliest railroad position, Hitler would have lost the war at the Polish frontier.

Yet what visitors thought of the Linden's museum exhibits was of no significance to Chairman Khrushchev — nor, for that matter, to Chancellor Adenauer. In Germany a strong Reichskanzler makes his own foreign policy. This had been true under the Kings of Prussia, the Kaisers,

Weimar, and the Führer, and *der Alte* had merely to decide whether the most auspicious trade winds were blowing from the east or the west. As an admirer of Bismarck he thought he could read the signs. Vodka toasts were being raised once more. The forbidding door of the Kremlin had swung open. With his encouragement, the Bundesrepublik would follow Beitz's star and the currents of trade would shift. Late in 1960 he made the most disastrous decision in Krupp history; gazing across Russia's vast spaces, feeling the Bismarckian spell, he reached out to return the embrace of the great polar bear. The Hauptverwaltungsgebäude rejoiced, and Krupp, having already sanctioned *die Firma*'s role in the fatal move, shared the Direktorium's enthusiasm. Under Wilhelmine imperialism, he reminded them, trade had followed the flag. Now the Konzern would reverse it. In the new Reich schoolboys would learn, *"Die Fahne folgt dem Handel."*

# 33

✠

# Krupp ist tot!

$A$RCANA IMPERII, state secrets, proscribe research into the eighty-four-year-old chancellor's motives, but those who watched him brood beneath the sprinkling *Glockenspiel* of his shelf clock — always fifteen minutes off, a reminder of how little time he had left — are entitled to an educated guess. He had held that flag aloft for fourteen years. He felt, with a conviction which would be swiftly vindicated, that the Rubber Lion was an inept heir, even in economics. There was time for one more bold stroke. His personal friendship with Dwight Eisenhower was about to end; in a few weeks the President would leave the White House. De Gaulle was trying to use him, and twice in the past year the West had flagrantly insulted him. On May 24 the British and Russians had signed a five-year trade agreement in Moscow — Sir David Eccles, president of the British Board of Trade, had been quoted as estimating that during the first year alone Anglo-Soviet trade would increase by 50 million dollars. That was Krupp's total business with the *Ostblock*. Then, in August, the Allies agreed to a five-year freeze of the partition of the Reich at a conference to which the Germans had not even been invited.[1]

The press later described the eve of Beitz's departure to Germans:

> Am 19. December 1960 konferierten Konrad Adenauer und Berthold Beitz 45 Minuten lang unter vier Augen über die Reise. Das vertrauliche Palaver im Kanzleramt befriedigte nicht nur den Diplomaten Beitz: Bis dahin war auch das persönliche Verhältnis zwischen dem Rhöndorfer und dem forschen Krupp-Star sehr kühl gewesen.

> On December 19, 1960, Konrad Adenauer and Berthold Beitz conferred privately for 45 minutes about the trip. The opportunity to exchange views with the chancellor was undoubtedly a deep source of satisfaction for

Beitz the diplomat. Until that time personal relations between the leader of the government and the Krupp spokesman had been very cool.[2]

Subsequent accounts in Western newspapers were more circumstantial. An editorial in the *Baltimore Sun*, noting the exchange of trade missions, observed that "on this minimal diplomatic level Germany is following businessmen into Yugoslavia, Czechoslovakia, and Hungary. . . . Beitz is conceivably carrying no government portfolio on his trip, but since Krupp in so many ways *is* Germany, the appearance of Beitz in foreign places always has more than ordinary significance." The *Times* of London assumed that Krupp's emissary must be carrying an official portfolio; after all, it pointed out, "Herr Beitz . . . keeps in close touch with Dr. Adenauer." The *New York Times* had quoted *der Amerikaner* himself as saying that economic ties with eastern Europe could and should lead to political ties, and *Newsweek* reported that "Bonn's 'new men' are quietly building up contacts with the Poles, Rumanians, and Russians. Dr. [*sic*] Berthold Beitz, foreign trade manager of the huge Krupp combine, recently announced that the Russians will soon accept a permanent Krupp mission in Moscow."[3]

While his chief of staff was touching base with every puppet regime except East Berlin — and hiring Ulbricht consultants even there — Alfried Krupp was putting his prestige behind the new program. That fall he announced the Konzern had completed contracts for "substantial sales of railroad and construction equipment," and that negotiations for a new treaty with the Soviet Union had begun. Five months later he told Jubilee guests satellite countries were receiving 6 percent of Krupp's business and "We are of the opinion that this should be increased." It was; at the next *Jubiläum* he reported *Ostblock* sales had been doubled and asked for "all-out efforts to reach a substantial improvement." Beitz was using every trick he knew, some of which aroused concern in Washington. By the mid-1960's he was signing new contracts in Manchuria, and since Peking was shipping tanks and artillery into North Vietnam, Secretary of State Rusk suggested, in a March 25, 1966, press conference, that the Germans "go slow" in building a 150-million-dollar steel plant for Mao. His appeal was unheard. By now the Bundesrepublik, led by Krupp, was carrying half the Common Market's trade with the East. In Poland, in Rumania, in Bulgaria, in Hungary, in Albania, in Czechoslovakia, and in Russia itself the same Kruppianer who had moved behind the Wehrmacht in the early 1940's were putting up oil refineries, foundries, and textile mills. To West German industrialists, Krupp's aide became a new miracle worker. Of him they read, "*Dank seiner Aktivität stieg der Ost-Anteil am Krupp-Export von fünf auf 23 Prozent*" (Thanks to his efforts, Krupp export business with countries in the eastern bloc rose from 5 to 23 percent).[4]

You can do anything with figures. In March 1967 *Der Spiegel* subscribers learned:

> The code name was "K" and for six weeks ministers and bankers treated it as a state secret [*Der Kode hiess "K," and sechs Wochen lang behandelten Minister und Bankiers die Sache wie ein Staatsgeheimnis*] . . . but on the ninety-sixth day of Chancellor Kiesinger's new Bonn government the secret was out: the largest single firm in Germany was in financial trouble [*Die grösste Einzelfirma des Bundesrepublik, Fried. Krupp. in Essen, hatte Finanzierungssorgen*]. For one entire day the nation was shocked. Not a single newspaper had printed a word about it.[5]

*Capital* immediately followed with "Das war Krupp" — an obituary, in effect, of the 380-year-old dynasty:

> . . . on December 31, 1968, Krupp will cease to exist [*am 31. Dezember 1968, wird es die Einzelfirma Fried. Krupp nicht mehr geben*]. By then it will have been transformed from a private company, solely owned by one man, to a foundation. The last word will belong, not to a board of directors, but to an administrative council.[6]

Business news rarely reaches front pages. This made headlines all over the world; even *Izvestia* described it as "probably the greatest sensation in German industrial history since the war."[7]

What had happened? Alfried and Arndt retained their private Jetstars, yachts, and castles; Essen remained the largest company town on earth; and von Bohlen and von Wilmowsky estates in West Germany were intact. The Konzern's turnover of nearly a billion and a half dollars had set a record during the past fiscal year; it made Haux's figures during the All-Highest's booms and Schröder's for the years when Krupp's prosperity under the Führer reached its peaks, seem puny. To the layman Krupp should have been mightier than ever. The answer lay in Schröder's *Handelsblatt* article. "Liquidity is expensive," he had warned, "but illiquidity is much more so, because it destroys the very existence of a firm."

Now the firm had lost its liquid assets, and, with them, the capacity to survive. After the crash Beitz said glumly, "We were rolled over by events." In a sense this was true. Without the economic hangover of 1966–1967 "*kruppsche schillernde Seifenblase*" (Krupp's glittering soap bubble), as it is now wryly known in the Ruhr, could have floated splendidly from fiscal year to fiscal year, just as Alfred's empire would have remained impregnable if the Vienna stock exchange hadn't collapsed in the summer of 1873. Each crisis found the Konzern vulnerable, and in each the fragility arose from overexpansion. Every spring other European industrialists returned from Hanover and Leipzig complaining that Beitz was shoving them aside with his tungsten-carbide-tipped elbows, snatching up the lion's share of *Ostblock* trade by offering bargain basement terms. It was true; he was giving the Communists up to fifteen years to pay and interest as low as 4.5 percent. Since the Konzern dominated West Germany's economy, the Reds were receiving a quarter of the Bundesrepublik's long-term investment credit while buying only 4.1 percent of its exports. So miraculous an economic wonder couldn't last forever, and when it ended Alfried would be caught in the trap which Beitz, unwittingly, and Khrushchev, perhaps wittingly, had set for him.[8]

The details of any *Wirtschaftswunderpause* are dull to the layman, but these can be quickly explained. Ludwig Erhard had given the *Volk* a high ride by borrowing heavily against the future, and all the bills came due at once. Chancellor Kurt Kiesinger and Karl Schiller, the new Erhard, inherited a vat of red ink. During that first winter of their regime, as the GNP dropped steeply month after month, the Bundesrepublik's economy was dramatically weakened, reducing its growth rate to the lowest level in postwar history. Everything was down: production, consumption, investment plans, and morale; both Bonn and the Bundesbank (the equivalent of the Federal Reserve) were drafting anticyclical policies at the Economics Ministry, on Bonn's outskirts. A few selective statistics provide a sharp profile of the slump. By comparison with 1965, the output of raw steel had plunged 50,000 tons a month, foundries had orders for barely a million tons of rolled steel on their books, and over-all industrial orders had sunk 13.5 percent. Industrialists, reacting accordingly, were spending 13 percent less on capital improvements. Düsseldorf's *Aktienindex* was down to 109.3 — to find a Dow-Jones parallel one must reach way back — and in a single month the sales of shares dropped 6.1 percent. Dr. Heinrich Irmler, the Präsident of Hanover's Landeszentralbank, Vizepräsident of Düsseldorf's Landeszentralbank and Direktor of Frankfurt's Deutsche Bundesbank, attributed the slide entirely to the export crisis: "In foreign trade, Germany needs an annual surplus of eight or nine billion DM [from two to two-and-a-quarter billion dollars]. But our exports are really under the 1966 and 1965 levels."[9]

Only two indicators had risen, both of them ominous. The cost of living was up and unemployment had increased from 150,600 to 501,300 — a staggering figure, equivalent to 11,000,000 in the United States. No one seemed to know what to do about it. Chancellor Kiesinger proposed an excess profits tax on industries, an across-the-board surtax, and public works. This chilled those who remembered Heinrich Brüning's remedy for the Great Depression: additional taxation, restrictions on business, and altered social services. All Brüning had achieved was the stigma *"Hungerkanzler"* and a rapid growth in extremist political parties, who, in fact, were appearing with impressive results for the first time in the 1966 Bundesrepublik election. The prospect of a major financial catastrophe was, in that last year before outsiders were permitted to examine the Hauptverwaltungsgebäude's books, very real. It was also too shattering to contemplate, for the force which had swept Hitler to power had been set in motion by the failure of the Kreditanstalt, the great Austrian banking house, in the summer of 1931. The closing of the Kreditanstalt's doors had ruined banks all over the Weimar Republic, forced Brüning to Draconian measures, and led to his dismissal.[10]

The first whispers that Alfried was in straits circulated in 1963; a wholly unforeseen rumor swept the Düsseldorf exchange one spring day that Krupp, caught in a credit squeeze, was going public. I recall racing southward on Autobahn No. 1 with a high Krupp executive bent upon stamping out the hearsay. He succeeded, and when the London *Sunday Telegraph* sent up its balloon that November 3 predicting Krupp collapse, the distinguished Hermann Josef Abs shot it down by announcing that the Konzern had "adequate and unused credit lines." In Essen a spokesman ridiculed the notion that Alfried was staggering under short-term loans which could not be converted into long-term notes as another example of the British "Krupp trauma"; the notion, Beitz added, was "completely without foundation." Some of those present noticed that his voice trembled, though. Krupp was not yet overburdened, but neither was the short-term dilemma absurd, and the last thing the Direktorium wanted was a run on the bank.[11]

For one thing, there were so many banks. Afterward Americans were amazed by the ease with which Essen's mastodon had extracted credit from respectable institutions, but no one who knew the Fatherland was surprised. To Germans, serving the *Waffenschmiede* was an honor. Moreover, none could imagine the possibility that Bonn would permit the Konzern to go bankrupt. Neither could Bonn, if it came to that; it was the one solution no one considered. Even members of the international financial establishment hesitated to discuss the problems of *die Firma* openly. On November 26, 1966 — over four months after Bundesrepublik President Karl Blessing had reluctantly loaned Krupp 20 million dollars from the European Recovery Program — London's *Economist* cautiously reported that "various stories have been given increasing credence outside Germany that any day now one or the other of the big internationally known companies might fail to meet its obligations." No names were mentioned. The *Economist* was playing the game.[12]

Because of his own Nazi past, Blessing had acted with grave misgivings; one was reluctant to be identified with old comrades these days. But for the moment he was safe. The public couldn't read between the lines. Enormous as the firm remained, it no longer stood alone on the continent. Beginning with Beitz's eastern adventures a kind of attrition had set in.

Alfried wasn't even Europe's biggest steelmaker any more; Phoenix-Rheinrohr and August Thyssen-Hütte had merged and bypassed him. Bad luck dogged Krupp subsidiaries. The worldwide shipping depression had hit his Bremen yards hard, despite the launching of nearly a million tons; every truck and locomotive to roll off its assembly line represented a loss; Rheinhausen was hemorrhaging four million marks a year; and the Flugzeugbau and Flugtechnik were deadweight.[13]

These blows could have been absorbed without the intensification of the credit crisis. But to pick up new Communist customers, Beitz was slashing his prices 20 and 40 percent, and the company's sole base was Alfried's narrowing wealth. He was now doing over 200 million dollars' business in the east annually, and all of it was ruinous — every Russian kopeck, Polish zloty, Czech koruna, Rumanian leu, Bulgarian lev, Chinese yuan, Yugoslav dinar, Hungarian forint, and Albanian lek. The German bankers had a glimpse of the approaching thunderhead, but no more than a glimpse. They knew about the ships, trucks, trains, and the Rheinhausen holding company, because those balance sheets were public record — one of Mehlem's few enduring achievements. In its hundred and fifty-five years of transactions Fried. Krupp itself, however, had never opened its books to any outsider. Alfried certainly had no intention of breaking precedent now. Abs, his powerful ally in the financial community, had hand-picked Arno Seegar as Schröder's successor, yet even Abs was barred from the Hauptverwaltungsgebäude's counting rooms.[14]

Had he been admitted, he would have been appalled. There was so little to count. At each spring's *Jubiläum* Krupp spoke confidently of billion-dollar-plus turnovers. He never added that his income varied from 15 to 70 million and that in 1967 his obligations would exceed 50 million. Since two of his customers had privately informed him that they intended to default, he cast about desperately for alternatives. Bankers were assigned shares in 24.9 percent of the Fried. Krupp Hüttenwerk — some 35 million dollars. Knowing they suspected his ratio of equity capital to debt was alarming, he drew up plans for a new subsidiary, to be called Fried. Krupp Export A.G., which they would manage in exchange for 100 million dollars in export credits. In New York, his American agent negotiated a 15-million-dollar ship-charter mortgage with Roger M. Blough of the United States Steel Corporation. Despite incursions, his personal fortune remained largely intact, but when matched against his interest payments it shrank. The sky continued to darken; as the recession deepened, money grew tighter. Bayerische Motorenwerke, Borgward, Hugo Stinnes, and the big Haenschel Locomotive Works at Kassel followed Willi Schlieker into oblivion. Finally one of Krupp's exasperated lieutenants took the unprecedented step of issuing a statement on his own. "We are making a mistake in trying to sell our products abroad by offering ever easier credit terms," he declared. "The only competitive standards should be the quality of our products." In London the *Illustrated News* commented late in 1966: "The plain fact is that by mid-November this year, Krupps of Essen, whose turnover exceeds 460 million pounds, had got itself into a serious financial mess. . . . the specter of bankruptcy has risen again."[15]

Too late, Krupp retrenched. The year before, an iron-cold winter had frozen central Europe hard, and every ton of coal the Kumpel could slash from the old mines had been needed, but now the weather turned unseasonably mild: 40 percent of the yield went begging. In one swift signature Alfried dismissed 8,800 miners, bitterly turning his back on the paternalism Friedrich Krupp had introduced in 1813. To save face the decision was attributed to Beitz. Actually the firm's Generalbevollmächtigter had been given his head but once, in the lands beyond the Oder-Neisse, and now the man who had trusted him had to suffer the consequences. Beitz voluntarily reduced his quarter-million-dollar annual salary by 5 percent and asked 55,000 other Kruppianer to follow his example. With six more strokes of his pen Krupp closed four Essen coal mines, the Bremerhaven docks, and the Dortmund shaft of the Krupp-Dolberg factory. These cutbacks were expected to save about 20 million dollars a year. With his interest payments exceeding his profits, the Konzernherr was caught in a squeeze as tight as the tolerances on the machined breech of his first 88.[16]

✠   ✠   ✠

To Philip Shabecoff of the *New York Times* it was a marvel that in the final third of the twentieth century the Krupp family could continue to "run the vast industrial holdings as a private fief." Alfried's advisers, most of whom were ignorant of the trap which held him fast, nevertheless concurred with *The Times*'s comment in London that "there is no longer any room for private concerns of this size and kind." Alfried disagreed until the last week of autumn in 1966. His heir had been a heartbreaking disappointment to him, yet nothing had been done to establish a foundation, and the plans he did discuss with his Direktorium were for a sham foundation, solely owned by him, operating through camouflages. Arndt, if Arndt changed, could take it over at his death as easily as he could *die Firma*.[17]

The financial crisis was hideous. All the same, there had been others before it. The German government had saved Alfred in the 1870's, Gustav in the 1920's, and Alfried himself fifteen years ago. But dispassionate analysis is too much to expect of anyone in a vise. While Krupp was being squashed in this one, a close friend mused that the predicament was "not without a tragic note. Alfried Krupp is a hurt and embittered man. . . . He has always considered his imprisonment after the war by the Allies unjust. . . . Krupp has had little luck with his family; he had two divorces, and his only son is absolutely uninterested in running the business. The owner of a dynastic company like this will always strive to preserve it as a family firm. So Krupp has become a sensitive, lonesome man burdened by a great tradition."[18]

Repeatedly Beitz submitted plans to transform the Konzern into a *Kapitalgesellschaft*; repeatedly the Konzernherr brushed them aside. Then, abruptly, events took over. Whatever hope remained for a stable transition to a reformed Arndt was based on the Lex Krupp, with its unique tax benefits covering both the present and, in Hitler's words, "any taxation arising from the death of the owner (*Erbschaftsteuer*) or from change of ownership (*Schenkungsteuer*)." As Krupp's legal staff had interpreted future obligations to this writer, the firm's "special" relationship with the German government remained untouched. But there was, it turned out, a huge, unnoticed pitfall. The Bundesrepublik constitution approved by Lucius Clay on May 12, 1949, had established a Supreme Tax Court which met in Munich. Since it had rarely attracted the attention of the Schlotbarone, they seldom gave it much thought. Nevertheless the court's power was absolute — no counsel could appeal its rulings — and on November 17, 1966, it unexpectedly opened fire on Krupp. In the sour words of Hermann Schenck, a sixty-six-year-old former director of Bochumer Verein, "The decision of the court came as a surprise, even in Bonn; judges always act according to their own pleasure."[19]

That decision, which became effective on New Year's Day, decreed that while subsidiaries of corporations would continue to be exempt from West Germany's *Umsatzsteuer* (the sales tax imposed on transactions between firms), the exemption no longer applied to solely owned corporations. To Alfried the judgment meant an annual levy of 15 million dollars. Then the justices delivered their *coup de grâce*. Since he had been paying a token inheritance tax for Arndt from current income, certain details were left unresolved; nevertheless the dynasty's historic shield — its protection by the Prussian common law of 1794, under which a proprietor might establish a "line of succession in such a way that the industrial part of the estate would not be divided, but would rather fall to one successor each time it changed hands" — had been formally removed. In deference to the Kaiser's exemption decree, and then Hitler's, Krupp had been untouched by the tax code of 1919. Now the judges reversed their predecessors; now that immunity was gone.[20]

And now catastrophe escalated. Six weeks after the ruling in Munich, the clouds which had been gathering over Herr Seegar's books began to close in. Early in January, Alfried's chief creditors — Krupp's five "House banks," including the Dresdner and Deutsche banks — requested a consolidated, confidential balance sheet. Seegar glumly drew it up, and its five readers, including Abs, lay awake that night with the Finanzdirektor's summary spinning in their minds:

The firm of Fried. Krupp is indebted to 263 creditor banks for 2.5 billion marks [625 million dollars] [*Auf den Konten von 263 Gläubiger-Banken steht die Firma Krupp mit 2.5 Milliarden Mark in Debet*]. With delivery debts and open-market credit added to this, Krupp's total debt outstanding rises to 5.2 billion marks [two billion one hundred and twenty million dollars]. Last year the Konzern had to pay out almost 300 million marks [75 million dollars] in interest and recorded a net loss of 50 million marks [12.5 million dollars] [*Im vergangenen Jahr musste der Konzern fast 300 Millionen Mark Zinsen zahlen, er buchte mehr als 50 Millionen Mark Verlust*], though in 1965 the firm had earned 60 million marks [15 million dollars].[21]

The House banks wavered. It is possible for a debtor's obligations to reach such heights that his creditors cannot afford to let him go out of business, for that way they would lose everything. Furthermore, Seegar had drawn an exasperating profile. Measured in marks and pfennigs, Alfried was the greatest failure in the history of European finance. Yet privately he remained a billionaire, and it was quite possible that he might pull *die Firma* together within two or three years. In 1966 customers had bought five billion marks' worth of his products — a billion and a quarter dollars — which meant a sudden turnabout in the economy could avert disaster. If the long-term loans he desperately needed were extended now and followed by a sudden shift in the nation's economic prospects, West Germany would once more be blessed by easy money. That turnabout could solve what seemed, in Seegar's ledgers, insoluble. Its possibility couldn't be dismissed, for Krupp retained the greatest reputation in the nation's industry. Counting dependents, nearly a half-million people — the rough equivalent of jobless men in the Bundesrepublik — depended on his prosperity. As the *New York Times* Bonn correspondent put it, "Government and industry, already concerned by new doubts abroad of the essential soundness of the West German industrial economy, could not afford to permit the financial health of the greatest name in German industry to remain in question."[22]

So the House capitalists stood around the sickbed, praying. Obviously a crisis was approaching; obviously the patient's condition couldn't be kept secret long. Over 250 other banks were involved, 54 of them members of the Bundesrepublik's Ausfuhrkredit, the consortium which backed foreign loans by German firms. Alfried already owed the Ausfuhrkredit 90 million dollars. Its credit committee had been watching the Ruhr vigilantly since the outset of the country's business slump, and news of Krupp salary cuts, layoffs, and shutdowns had created an inevitable climate of apprehension.

Only one more straw was needed, and in early January Beitz provided that with a request for 25 million dollars more. Suddenly the sickbed became the vortex of a traffic jam. Anxious credit committee members respectfully suggested on January 27 that they, too, were entitled to a look at the books. Krupp replied, "Nothing doing" (*Durchaus nicht*). He knew these men. Unlike the House banks they had never been his allies. They wanted his sprawling empire transformed into a corporation, they wanted shares in it, and one of them openly urged him to fire Beitz. That suggestion ended the meeting. Alfried summoned his secretary and dictated a new twelve-year contract for his chief of staff — which, though no one thought of it at the time, would carry the Generalbevollmächtigter to his sixty-fifth birthday, five years after he had hoped to retire to the joys of taped Dixieland.[23]

Dismissed by the *alleinige Inhaber*, the Ausfuhrkredit's credit committee informed the House banks they would have to carry any new risks themselves. When they refused, Karl Blessing went to Bonn, proposing 75 million dollars of government-backed export credit in exchange for major changes in the Hauptverwaltungsgebäude.[24] It was now February 1967, ninety-four years after Bismarck and Wilhelm I had forced Alfred Krupp to mortgage his Gusstahlfabrik to *die Seehandlung*, the Overseas Trading Company of *die preussische Staatsbank*, and the parallels between the Founder's Crisis and the Last Heir's Crisis are uncanny in other ways; throughout that spring identical agreements were reached on identical dates. There was one significant difference: Alfred's trustee had been Carl Meyer. Berlin, in short, had appointed Krupp's own man to supervise Krupp. Alfried, on the other hand, had to deal with Professor Doktor Karl Schiller.

The *Bundeswirtschaftsminister*, not *der Amerikaner*, was the man the dynasty's last Kanonenkönig should have chosen as his Hanns Jencke,[25] but the lean, scholarly Schiller's politics had ruled him out. He was not only a Social Democrat; he had turned his back on the Reich in the Führer's hour of need, withdrawing from the total war effort to teach economics in university cloisters. Schiller would have made a wretched salesman, yet in his field — which, presumably, was also Beitz's field — he had one of the finest minds in Germany, Erhard not excepted. While still a youth he had been honored by the universities of Kiel, Frankfurt, Berlin, and Heidelberg. In the years when Alfried was planning his *Mirakel an der Ruhr* Schiller had published two books, *Aufgaben und Versuche zur neuen Ordnung von Gesellschaft und Wirtschaft* (1953) and *Sozialismus und Wettbewerb* (1955), revealing a remarkable understanding of the new Europe and the future of German industry. It is inconceivable that Schiller would have financed long-term, low-interest loans with short-term paper whose interest rates would skyrocket, the moment capital grew scarce, to 8 and even 10 percent.

In any other nation a magnate facing ruin might have sought an appointment with the Minister of Economics. Not Krupp. He waited impassively until the cabinet member came to Altendorferstrasse. Despite Schiller's political convictions he recognized the peculiar status of *Firma*, *Familie*, and *Dynastie*, and he knew that any minister who summoned a Krupp to Bonn would never be forgiven by his constituency. Thus it was he who telephoned Essen, he who drove to the Hauptverwaltungsgebäude on February 21 and sat where Erhard, Schacht, and Funk had sat (and, before his birth and when Alfried was seventeen months old, where Bernhard von Bülow had called on Gustav in behalf of the All-Highest to discuss the Reich's inheritance tax bill, then pending before the Reichstag). Throughout their session Alfried was stiff and wary, his thoughts clothed, as always, in a caliginous veil. Eyes hooded, he listened while the *Bundeswirtschaftsminister* bluntly stated that if Krupp wanted Bundesrepublik help, Krupp would have to go public — convert the Konzern to a corporation and issue stock. Schiller later said that he left with the impression that Krupp "wasn't happy, but he was convinced." In fact, the Konzernherr had what he wanted: a commitment from Bundeskanzler Kiesinger's new coalition government. What Bonn would receive in return seemed vague, for the sole proprietor, having suffered the indignity of watching a Social Democrat sit at the oval conference table in his private office beneath *Urgrossvater's* portrait, left Europe immediately afterward. Inquiring colleagues were told that the *Chef der Dynastie* had departed for the dark continent once more to shoot beasts. No one outside Hügel knew precisely where he was. Karl Schiller, Karl Blessing, Hermann Josef Abs, and Werner Krueger of the Dresdner Bank received identical answers: *"Konzernherr Krupp war auf eine Reise nach Afrika ausgewichen."*[28]

The disappearance — which resembled Alfred's headlong flight to the Riviera after the Königgrätz fiasco of 1866 — couldn't have come at a worse time. This was the period which the press later called *"der Alarmbrief des Bundesbankchefs"* and *"die Krupp-Bombe."* The only man left to defend the Hauptverwaltungsgebäude bridge was that unlikely Horatio in the regimental-striped tie and button-down shirt, Berthold Beitz, whose awkward position was heightened by his abrasive relationships with Germany's financial community. Throughout the remainder of February and the first week in March the country's most eminent bankers were in marathon session, seeking a resolution acceptable to both Essen and Bonn. Had Alfried's chief aide not been considered déclassé by members of the German establishment, he would have been at ease and the discussions fruitful. But to them he was still the *Ausländer* from Pomerania, and now his debts, like Alfried's, had come due. He had no bargaining power whatever; Abs, Krupp's closest friend in the banking world, was taking a hard line with Schiller's full backing. At one conference which Schiller attended, *der Amerikaner* secured a place at the table only by resorting to muscle; hitching a chair behind him, he shouldered his way between two financiers. They regarded him icily. His charm hadn't deserted him; he responded with a light comment: "We can be humble." He had to be. Humility was the only course left to him. It was at this meeting that a broker remarked *sotto voce*, "For fourteen years this outsider, the son of a Pomeranian civil servant, has collected enemies the way some people collect postage stamps" (. . . *Feinde gesammelt wie andere Leute Briefmarken*).[27]

The climactic meeting began at four o'clock on the afternoon of March 6, 1967, in Düsseldorf's Dresdner Bank. Beitz, Schiller, Blessing, and the twenty-eight greatest figures in German finance were present. Theoretically 235 presidents of insurance companies and savings banks were also entitled to debate and vote, but there simply wasn't room for all Krupp's creditors. Moreover, their presence would have complicated public relations. Already the press had picked up a strong scent. News of Operation K had been withheld from them for six weeks. This was no time to jeopardize secrecy, and the convergence of nearly three hundred banking leaders on Krupp's chief House bank would have alerted every newscaster in the continent. Even Karl Blessing had slipped in the bank's back door. Heinz Kühn, Minister-Präsident of North Rhine–Westphalia — governor, that is, of West Germany's richest state — was as deeply involved as Blessing. His appearance would have created a sensation among the reporters, however, so he stayed in touch by telephone.[28]

He was on the line a long time. Substantial agreement was reached by 5:30 P.M. That left specifics, not all of which were clarified then. Nevertheless, when the gathering broke up at 1:35 A.M. the great knot had been unraveled and Schiller scheduled a press conference the following day. Conditions on both sides were remarkably stiff, perhaps unique. When the Prussian State Bank had loaned Alfried's great-grandfather 30 million marks in March 1874, he had described it as *"ein schmachvolles Dokument"* (a humiliating document) and *"eine Riesenlast"* (a colossal burden), despite the selection of Meyer as his *Treuhänder* and the lack of any suggestions for reform in the Gusstahlfabrik's management. Gert von Klass observed that

> The ill-tempered old crank on the hill [*der grollende Alte auf dem Hügel*], as he was now known, became senile shortly after the signing ceremony. No aspect of the company failed to excite his suspicion. His oldest and most loyal lieutenants were subjected to shocking accusations. He was convinced that they were culpable and he blameless, that he had been betrayed, swindled, cheated.[29]

Like a budget sheet the Düsseldorf settlement had two facing pages, chronicling the exchange in commitments. Some insight into the difference between the *Krupp-Bombe* of 1874 and this one may be found in a single figure. The burden Alfred had shouldered had seemed humiliating to him, but it was merely 5 percent of his great-grandson's new obligations. First, Schiller agreed that Tuesday morning to guarantee the Konzern 75 million dollars in new *Exportkredit*. Second, the bankers voted to extend all outstanding Krupp obligations until the end of 1968 and — backed by a Schiller guarantee — to offer Krupp 100 million dollars of new credit. If Alfried's books balanced on December 13, 1968, normal export financing would be resumed. Kühn, the weary telephoner, promised that North Rhine–Westphalia would back long-term loans to wipe out $37,500,000 in short-term "Eurodollar" notes (*Verbindlichkeiten*) held by the firm. Thus *die* anemic *Firma* was to be infused with 150 million dollars — 600 million marks of new blood — at the height of a debilitating national recession which was forcing old, established Schlotbarone into bankruptcy every day.[30]

Obviously some concessions would be expected in return. There is reason to believe that Alfried had made private pledges before flying into the jungle. On March 4, the day before Beitz squeezed up to the conference table, Krupp had personally written out a Declaration of Intent, taking his first half-step toward "preparations in order to transform the firm into a stock company." He had found his own scapegoats: the tax judges. Their ruling, he asserted, had been "decisive." Later Arndt stated that "our decision was in no way influenced by financial difficulties. The firm of Krupp is sound." Its plight, he insisted, had arisen from the new death duties imposed by the Munich court: "Since inheritance would have left me with about 50 percent of the enterprise, this partition naturally meant the end of Krupp."[31]

There was something of the martyr in Arndt's expression that May afternoon; he seemed momentarily transfixed by the magnitude of his own gift to the Fatherland. "I am of the strong conviction that all members of the Krupp family through the generations have been possessed by a profound sense of duty and obligation to the works. Each generation has done something vitally important to preserve the firm. And now, when Krupp's further survival is only assured by being turned into a foundation, I personally thought that I, as the last link in a chain . . . would be under the same obligation to do my constructive bit. I believe I have done this by my renunciation, having fulfilled my duty toward the enterprise, toward my family, and thus also toward my country." He sounded like Nathan Hale. What he neglected to add was that in exchange for his sacrifice he would receive a million marks a year until his father's death and then two million a year until his own.[32]

Krupp's promise "to transform the firm into a stock company" sounds revolutionary until one remembers that when he took over in 1943 it had already *been* a stock company — with Bertha owning 159,999 shares and

Barbara one. That hadn't been good enough for Karl Schiller, and when he faced a hundred and fifty reporters after the settlement he explained the intricate safeguards which had been established. By April 15 Krupp would have to name a six-man supervisory council. Its members would reorganize the Konzern. Then, by January 31, 1968, family control would end; Fried. Krupp of Essen would become a corporation. In the beginning there would be one shareholder, Alfried, but over a period of two or three years partners would be admitted. Lastly, when the books would bear reading, the doors would be opened for other investors.[33]

Schiller stressed that this was an exceptional action, that it was without precedent in the Bundesrepublik, and that any tycoon who expected the precedent to be broken again would be grievously wrong. Moreover, he pointed out, everything was being handled by "only a few banks"; the government would not be represented on the supervisory council. That was an evasion, however; Krupp couldn't have been saved without the hostaging of tax funds, a lifeline which had been withheld from all other drowning tycoons. A German reporter drew Finanzminister Franz-Josef Strauss aside, and they dueled.

Q. Up till now, the government has avoided such Samaritan actions (*Samariteraufgaben*). What is so special about the Krupp case (*am Fall Krupp*)?

A. Krupp suffered far more than most from the war's aftereffects (*Krupp hatte unter den Kriegsfolgen besonders stark gelitten.*) On his release from prison, Krupp also behaved generously toward workers who were released after the war, and he paid them additional social aid.

Q. Is the government paying a sort of national gratitude debt by its action?

A. Krupp is our most important single-ownership firm (*Krupp ist die bedeutendste Einzelfirma.*)

Q. Have you already asked Krupp to publish his balance sheets?

A. We do not have the legal power to do this. Krupp is owned by a single man and is under no obligation to open books (*Krupp ist eine Einzelfirma, die keiner Offenlegungspflicht unterliegt*) . . .

Q. What will happen if the Krupp firm does not fulfill the conditions?

A. We are assuming that the firm will fulfill its contractual obligations (*vertragliche Verpflichtungen*).[34]

Bonn's foreign correspondents assumed instead that the Bundesrepublik's treasury lid was being lifted because *die Firma* had once more extended itself in behalf of the Reich, had been mauled, and was receiving nourishment from a government which could not ignore its own debts to generations of men bearing the greatest name in German industry. Staging a skit the newspapermen sang:

*In klein Bonna an dem Rhein*
*Wir sind zur Zeit ein bisschen knapp bei Kasse —*
*In klein Bonna an dem Rhein*
*Das Wirtschaftswunder wird ja immer blasser*

*Der Haushalt, sagte Franz-Josef Strauss, hängt an 'nem dünnen Faden,*
*Die Bauern und Beamten steigen auf die Barrikaden,*
*Doch Krupp bekommt Entwicklungsgeld, sonst geht die Firma baden.*

In little old Bonn by the Rhine
We're a trifle hard up at the time —
In little old Bonn by the Rhine
The Wirtschaftswunder's passed its prime.

The budget, Strauss says, hangs by a thread,
Clerk-and-farmer barricades lie ahead,
Krupp might get hurt too — but gets cash instead.

✠　　✠　　✠

He got cash, and *die Firma* was saved, but at a price Alfred the Great couldn't have imagined in his wildest castle-stalking nightmares. Now there could be *no* sole proprietor. The title was meaningless. Great-grand-father's great-grandson, who shared his strengths and weaknesses but lived in another century, had to abdicate.

The formal ceremony was held in Villa Hügel's main hall, where the great Krupp's body had lain in state eighty years earlier. It was April 1, 1967, a date which, in the Ruhr as elsewhere, is usually celebrated by tricks. This year there was no *Aprilscherz*, no April fooling; the one overwhelming prank of fate was enough. Besides, the weather didn't seem to fit the calendar. It was an afternoon out of season, overcast and cold. Roaring fires had been built in each fireplace, yet the rooms remained as chilly as they had been in the wake of the Franco-Prussian War, when their amateur architect had denounced them and stormed off to Torquay.[35]

Today a horde of uniformed Werkschutz huskies lined the walls, watching attentively as though ready to bludgeon rowdies into silence and haul them off to the now forgotten Kruppstahl cage in the Hauptver-waltungsgebäude basement. They were unnecessary. The bleak castle had rarely been quieter, which was just as well, for although the lectern at the library end of the hall had been equipped with a microphone and loud-speakers, the Konzernherr's monotone was barely audible. Bony, gray, and haggard, he stepped to the rostrum and stood immobile for a long moment, coldly scrutinizing his sympathetic audience. In four months he would be sixty years old. Surrounded as he was by life-size oil portraits of Krupps and Hohenzollerns, he should have been prepared to justify his heritage with a startling disclosure of splendid new developments. Instead the only unexpected news he could offer those attending his last *Jubiläum* was that on March 2, anticipating the Dresdner Bank conference by four days, he had established a Krupp G.m.b.H. which would keep book on the fortune he had felt certain that the government and the banks would place at his disposal after his return from safari. The new subsidiary would be responsible for long-term exports. Germany needed exports, just as the firm had been in desperate need of "an ample amount of ownership capital." He had hoped to acquire that capital in 1966. Instead he had encountered "a difficult year." Kruppstahl went begging for lack of customers, 2,900 Kruppianer had to be dismissed by the foundries, shorter shifts "could not be avoided," and the yield from Krupp mines had dropped by 32 percent.

He was still aware of "the great role that the concept of social responsibility has played in the history of my family and our concern." For once a thread of emotion stitched his baritone and burred his words: "I say openly — I am proud of it." But to underwrite paternalism he had to have broader capitalization. Then, almost listlessly, came the historic announcement, "I have thus decided to transform the firm into a stock corporation over a foundation." He intended to see to it that profits from the foundation were dedicated to the furthering of scientific research in the Reich. The establishment of a public Krupp corporation was deplorable and offensive, but "such a transformation is in accord with the economic necessities of our time." In conclusion — and now his tone was utterly dead — he expressed gratitude to the banks, the government, Beitz, and "my son Arndt," without whose "renunciation of inheritance" the end of the dynasty would have been impossible: "For his responsible understanding I would publicly like to thank him." One familiar with Arndt's way of life tried to picture him as Arndt Krupp, Konzernherr and dynastic patriarch. One wondered how much coaxing had been required.

Abruptly the Jubilee was over. For the last time a Krupp had presided over an official function in the capital of his kingdom; not until Alfried himself lay in state beneath Waldtraut's portrait (on the east wall, where the Führer's used to hang) would a member of the family be the focus of world attention in the grimy limestone palace. His guests, erect in faultlessly creased pinstripe trousers, lined up to say farewell. Each of them shook his hand, bowed jerkily from the hips and filed on, receiving a small gift, a final token of esteem from the Konzernherr. There was, if possible, less conversation than usual. Shortly the last of them had walked out into the harsh wind, leaving a tall gray-faced man surrounded by burly Krupp troopers, tongues of hearth fire, endless corridors and history. Gaunt and unmoved, he watched them go, his roving eyes faintly suggestive of the hallucinative, even the suicidal.

"*Wohin Krupp?*" asked the title of a leading article in one of the Bundesrepublik's monthlies; "Whither Krupp?" "Despite the Bonn government's dramatic intervention," it concluded, ". . . well-informed German experts predict that the biggest problems still lie ahead." Ill-informed

Ausländer could tell that there would be problems. The castle ceremony was held on a Saturday. Before two more Saturdays had passed Alfried was pledged to name a streamlining *Verwaltungsrat*, administrative council. Predictably he chose Abs and Werner Krueger of the Dresdner Bank. They had to be there, if only for sentimental reasons; the bank had been welded to Krupp ever since its agent at Sedan sent back word of Prussia's feat of arms. "What a fortunate turn the war has taken!" Deichmann had written Alfred from Düsseldorf, and now that there were no Prussian armies for Krupp to arm and misfortune had overtaken the family — now that Essen was bereft of what used to be called *Aprilglück* — Deichmann's third-generation successors had to try to soften the impact of the falling star. They were joined by Professor Doktor Ludwig Raiser of Tübingen University; Professor Doktor Bernhard Timm, chief executive of the Common Market's most tightly managed chemical corporation; Professor Doktor Hans Leussink, Bonn's adviser on research and development; and Otto Brenner, president of West Germany's metalworkers' union.[36]

There was one other name on the list — Berthold Beitz. With Alfried's abdication *der Amerikaner* had been shorn of his title as Generalbevollmächtigter. He was on the administrative council as his patron's personal representative, and outside the Ruhrgebiet both the well-informed and the ill-informed, including veteran industrial spies reporting to what Londoners call "the City," assumed that he would become managing director of the new corporation. But to the "considerable surprise" of London's *Economist* the council voted to shelve Krupp's own choice. Instead they chose a forty-seven-year-old CPA and ex-Kruppianer, the son of a Krefeld Schlotbaron. Günter Vogelsang was a man with whom other rulers of the Ruhr would be at ease. In the war's wake he had briefly worked for Willi Schlieker. After Schlieker's own enterprise had tumbled because its capital base was too thin, Beitz had hired Vogelsang to study auditing procedures in the Hauptverwaltungsgebäude and then, that done, to reorganize the management of the Bochumer Verein. In 1960 Mannesmann had lured him away from Krupp. Now he was designated "chief adviser" to the Verwaltungsrat, restructuring the corporation he would lead. An unemotional man, he described his task as "diagnosing the patient so I can prescribe a therapy." Early in his analysis the Konzern was further shaken by a cycle of secondary tremors — the sort which follow every major earthquake. Essen announced that Finanzdirektor Arno Seegar had "resigned without notice." In keeping with his commitment of April 1, Alfried assured Bonn that Krupp profits, which members of the family had rarely even discussed with outsiders in the past, would be set aside *"zur Förderung der Wissenschaften"* (for the advancement of science). On April 13, however, he signed another document whose implications were unappreciated at the time. Entitled a *"Förder-Rentenvertrag,"* the instrument provided that Arndt's present income of a quarter-million dollars a year in marks should come from the firm's basic industries and that after Alfried's death the matching sum would be paid to his son by the Augsburg office of Krupp's Nationale Registrier-Kassen G.m.b.H.[37]

Meantime the council of trustees plunged ahead, making no attempt to camouflage their immediate goals. They wanted to get rid of the firm's Generalbevollmächtiger, its coal, and its steel — in that order. One of them remarked privately, and with *Schadenfreude*, "Beitz will move out of the active management to function on the supervisory council. In other words, Beitz is no longer the boss." He had never been boss, of course — a real Krupp, which Alfried was, made his own decisions — but the extroverted Pomeranian *had* exercised vast powers in the name of Essen's sovereign and even of the government's. He took his defrocking like a man. During an interview late one evening in his incongruous, wired-for-sound, modern ranch home on Weg zur Platte he brooded over an empty wineglass and said, "In three or four years we" — as always, his *"wir"* meant Krupp and Beitz — "will be happy we made these decisions, even if under outside pressure. Sometimes you are bitter when you have to take medicine. But you have to do what the doctor says, and then you thank God you did, because he finds the cause of the poison and the reason you were sick. I will admit I was shocked by what happened. I had been working on a conversion to a foundation for eight [sic] years with the full support of Herr Krupp. It was all going wonderfully and would have been a first-class affair. Then came this outside force and all our plans lost their brilliance, for they were taken out of our hands." Recapitulating, he said bravely, "As a capital company we'll pay dividends, high or low, depending on the times. We'll come out of this stronger than before."[38]

Once more he was wrong. The future of Berthold Beitz would remain cloudy. Alfried Krupp was another matter, though. That summer his personal fate was revealed in teletype flashes, diplomatic codes, and hastily convened meetings in virtually every world capital. Alfried wouldn't be able to come out of the crisis stronger, because he wasn't going to come out of it at all.

✠　　✠　　✠

Some time before midsummer the Konzernherr tidily drew up his will. It would have dismayed his parents. Gustav's faithful execution of his conjugal duty and Bertha's gravid years had been in vain. Alfried might as well have been an only son. None of his siblings were mentioned — in part, perhaps, because of their hostility toward Beitz. While no member of the family was to be apprised of it until the Saturday after his funeral, when the seals were to be broken, the testament's three executors would be Beitz, Arndt, and Dedo von Schenck, a member of the Konzern's legal staff who had insisted during an interview earlier in the spring that the Lex Krupp was dead on the books.[39]

Then, at 10 o'clock on the smog-shrouded evening of Sunday, July 30, Alfried died. It was the most trying night the dynasty's public relations men had known since Fritz Krupp's demise in 1902; now, as then, they took twelve hours to inform the press, and even so their releases were confusing. On only one point were they exasperatingly consistent; his guarded, exquisitely appointed modern villa in Hügel Park was uniformly described as a *Häuschen*, a cottage. The greatest riddle was the cause of his death. One spokesman issued a release describing it as "sudden and un-expected." A second handout disclosed that he had been suffering from an "incurable disease," a third that he hadn't been ill at all, and a fourth that his silver-gray Porsche hadn't been parked on the sidewalk outside his office for a month because his medical staff, examining him in July, had dis-covered that he was dying from bronchial cancer caused by smoking too many American cigarettes. Eventually everyone settled on this last. It grew more circumstantial. *Der Tumor* had eluded the physicians until it was so far advanced that treatment was pointless; Krupp had been confined to his little hut since mid-July; when he expired the only other person present had been a Krupp nurse. All this was astonishing. Certainly the secret had been well kept. The entire family had been caught off guard. Arndt, indeed, had just finished issuing a statement criticizing his father's com-pulsive work habits and everything he represented, including "Krupp tradition."[40]

Arndt was a young man of the world, Teutonic in name only. Every *treue* German over the age of thirty-five had cherished that tradition, however, and on that Monday, as July melted into August, Bundesrepublik flags and black-on-white Krupp flags dipped to half-mast all over the Ruhr. Messages of commiseration poured in addressed to the new *Hausherr* (perplexing the Hauptverwaltungsgebäude communications center, since no one seemed to know who the real head of the family was now). The condolences crossed both political and ideological lines. President Heinrich Lübke wrote from Bonn, "The life and work of Alfried Krupp are in-extricably linked with the fate of our nation"; a labor leader praised Herr Krupp's "farsightedness"; and all the members of one union local joined in signing a telegram describing the deceased as "a progressive employer con-scious of his social responsibility." Among themselves Kruppianer were as confused as the firm's press releases. "*Herr Krupp ist tot!*" they cried across the shops; "Krupp is dead!" Some thought his end meant the end of the business, and here one detected that sharp difference between the reactions of different generations, so typical of Germany in the late '60's. To very young workmen who had never heard the roll of distant drums or the summons of martial trumpets, a job was a job. "If there's no more work here, I'll just move on," they shrugged. But their seniors were inconsolable. To each Alfried had been a member of the immediate family, and they asked in tears, "What will happen now?"[41]

What happened was pagan. Following the dynastic custom, Krupp's corpse was laid in an open oak coffin in the castle's great hall, an immense candle burning behind its cushioned head and its flanks guarded by six uniformed Kumpel wearing gaudy uniforms and feathered shakos. Members of the family came singly and in pairs. Beitz called alone, unconsciously crossed his own hands as Alfried's were crossed, then wept. On Wednesday the door was opened to thousands of waiting Kruppianer. They shuffled across the parquet floor, took a last look at their employer (for most, it was also their first look), and departed blinking and inhaling the thick scent of banked blossoms.[42]

The funeral was on Thursday. There were five hundred official mourners — a delegation from Bonn and a clutch of labor leaders — who were admitted to the castle while the masses stood outside in a downpour, crowding around loudspeakers to hear the eulogies. For the most part they listened to repetitions of the telegrams, letters, and formal statements which had been arriving from all over West Germany (but rarely from elsewhere) since the first of the week; doubtless President Eugen Gerstenmaier of the Bundestag was justified in declaring that he spoke, not for the Kiesinger regime, but for the entire country when he said of Alfried, "We thank him and the house of Krupp for everything it has meant in more than one hundred and fifty years to many Germans; nay to the whole nation,"[43] The final tribute paid, the services over, the Krupp band struck up "Glückauf." Moving in step to its strains, ten more costumed coal miners bore the coffin out into the rain while — on a signal flashed across the Ruhrgebiet and beyond — 125,000 Kruppianer downed tools and stood erect by their lathes, gantries, open hearths and launching docks. They were silently honoring the last of his breed. Eleven weeks later, on October 16, Alfried's second wife, the last woman to receive the name of Krupp, died in Los Angeles at Mount Sinai Hospital; her collection of Russian art was auctioned off in New York in May 1968.)[44]

Following the route of Alfred's, Fritz's, Margarethe's, Claus's and Bertha's pallbearers, Alfried's cortege wound down the hill. At the bottom it veered left toward the family's private-cemetery-within-a-private-cemetery, and there the body was lowered into the stony Ruhr soil beneath Urgrossvater's tiered monument. The band hurriedly shoved its drenched instruments into cases and departed. The miners marched off, soggy plumes dripping. Beitz backed away. Arndt fled, Baron von Wilmowsky escorted Barbara to their waiting Mercedes, and all the von Bohlen und Halbachs departed, leaving the plot which Alfried had staked out eleven years earlier, and which Alfred still dominated, enveloped in sheets of rain.

The graveyard is no place to visit in a squall or after dark, for while the Krupps will never again evoke terror beyond the Reich's frontiers, their long saga is so saturated in melodrama that any new stage business seems an imposition. Even in Bredeney's broadest sunlight one fancies them raging at one another — Anton Krupp, say, son of the first Arndt, boasting how he had sold a thousand gun barrels a year during the Thirty Years War and demanding an accounting of his legacy, or Friedrich Krupp, asking plaintively what had become of the single-mindedness with which he had honed bayonets for Prussia, or, more likely, the greatest Kanonenkönig roaring that he had sounded the alarm against "*Speculanten, Börsenjuden, Aktienschwindler und dergleichen*" (speculators, stock-exchange Jews, swindlers, and similar parasites), and that in a letter to Fritz, then in Egypt, he had specifically cautioned his descendants to be on the alert for "a stock-company-promoting beast of prey" (*ein Gründer Raubthier*), admonishing the family,

> The first point is the nature of accounting, finance, and calculation. You must study these until you feel completely at home with them [*In diesen Dingen musst Du immer vollständig zu Hause sein*]. Then you cannot be led astray by anyone. And then and then only will you be absolutely safe from the one great menace against which I must warn you — from ever permitting persons motivated by selfishness and intrigue to coax you into deserting your post and falling into the hands of a joint-stock company [*in die Gewalt einer Gründer-Gesellschaft zu fallen*].[45]

Alfried might retort that Alfred hadn't practiced what he preached, that his own troubles had begun with his allegiance to the Führer — whom his great-grandfather had anticipated and blessed — and that he was far from having been the worst of his strain: a common scold like Anton Krupp, a weakling like Friedrich, or a public scandal like Fritz. He had merely shared the strengths and the infirmities of most real Krupps, particularly a lack of genetic vigor (it was astonishing that a surname could have survived for eleven generations on so little virility) and the absence of any real understanding of accounting, finance, and calculation. As his Generalbevollmächtigter had wryly observed a few weeks earlier:

"Now that the floods have receded we can finally see what's on the bottom: very little gold but lots of old bottles" (*wenig Gold und alte Flaschen*).[46]

Were there a Krupp Valhalla, this would doubtless be greeted by bitter laughter. The sequence was more interesting than that, though the revelation of its true nature was slow in coming. On November 29, 1967, the Hauptverwaltungsgebäude dutifully announced the establishment of an Alfried Krupp von Bohlen und Halbach Foundation (*Stiftung*). The joint-stock company was formed on January 2, 1968, with all the former

Konzernherr's assets pooled in it. In the last week of that month, as the dynasty formally expired, Vogelsang was confirmed as Generaldirektor, Abs became chairman of a fifteen-man Aufsichtsrat, and *die Firma's* mysterious, semisacred books were opened at last. Wading through them took Abs's new board awhile. At first they were awed by the sheer size of the family's industrial accumulations. The list of one hundred major companies left by Alfried filled nine closely typed pages; his shareholdings in other corporations took up another ten pages; and the factories he had owned outright occupied eighty-eight square miles of Reich soil.[47]

Then the full scope of Krupp's disastrous adventure in the east emerged. Abs and his fourteen colleagues had expected that their venture would join the ranks of Thyssen-Stiftung and Volkswagenwerk-Stiftung, two foundations which, between them, contribute over forty million dollars a year to the German people. Those hopes were dashed. Fried. Krupp G.m.b.H. was so shaky that it wouldn't even be able to pay its taxes for at least four years. To be sure, there would be profits, but — and this was the blow — under the Förder-Rentenvertrag drawn up by Alfried fifteen weeks before his death, his son was entitled to siphon off his $500,000 a year before the Aufsichtsrat could meet any other obligations, including those to the government. The document was airtight. Legally Bonn couldn't do a thing. In the words of one Hamburg editor, masses of Kruppianer would continue to sweat so that *"der prominenteste Playboy von der Ruhr"* (the most prominent Ruhr playboy) could spend two million marks a year for *"Brot und Spiele"* (bread and circuses).[48]

Thus the bottom which was finally glimpsed after the floods had passed was occupied, not by old bottles, but by the second Arndt, who celebrated his triumph over the West German establishment by declaring that he preferred the exotic pleasures of jet set expatriation to the harsh obligations which had been imposed over the centuries by his familial stock. *Glückauf:* good fortune. So the oddly dressed Kumpel had blared as the spirit of the last Herr Krupp departed the chill halls of Villa Hügel. Yet the fortune stayed behind, *Kapital* fueling an allowance for a perennial child who, having disowned his forefathers, was being showered with more spending money than any of them — the builders of the empire he was cheerfully deserting — would have known how to spend.

And should this news be spread among other bloodlines in that strange land beyond the great gas oven in the sky, the sardonic laughter would grow. For the Krupp story, laced with ironies throughout its four centuries, had been crowned in the end by the most massive irony of all. Arndt could have succeeded his father as the most powerful individual in the Common Market. In exchange for signing his "inheritance waiver" (*Erbverzicht*), he was being rewarded with a staggering bonus. But what was the source of the rights he had renounced? It was the Lex Krupp. Stated otherwise,

Arndt, playmate of the Western World, could gleefully look forward to a lifetime of squandering among Beautiful People, thanks to a special decree issued on a raw November day nearly a quarter-century before and still regarded as valid.[49] The author of the decree, Arndt's true patron and the real source of his affluence, was Adolf Hitler, Führer of the Third Reich.

## Epilogue

### ✠
# Silver in an Old Mirror

In a shop the Ruhr tourist may pick up Dr. Hans Tümmler's *Essen: Ein Bildband* and read,

> *Die Kirchen, denen sich nun die neue Synagoge zugesellt hat, und die wachsende Zahl schöner, lichter Schulneubauten für alle nur denkbaren Bildungswege können hier nur in ganz wenigen Beispielen erscheinen . . .*
>
> The churches, including a new synagogue, and the increasing number of attractive, sunny schools dedicated to all the branches of education, are represented here by a few examples. . . .[1]

The synagogue exists — Bonn paid the builder under its indemnification program — but there is something peculiar about it. Inasmuch as the city's prewar ghetto housed 5,500 people, one looks for a building at least half the size of its predecessor and finds, instead, a Lilliputian place of worship. At that it is too large for the 250 Essen Jews who survive into the 1960's, and part of the building has been converted to a seed shop and offices for a dentist and a tax consultant. Inside, the Star of David looks down from a lovely skylight on just twelve narrow rows of seats. After the dedication in 1960 Siegfried Neugarten, an elder, began watching over them like a sentinel when the annual epidemic of anti-Semitic incidents in the Bundesrepublik passed a thousand. Not long ago, after 685 swastika smearings and other profane acts in a single month, Herr Neugarten said that in time there would be no need for any Essen synagogue. "We are decreasing," he explained. "Most of us are of the older generation, and we are not too happy when a Jewish youth comes here, because he has no future. The number of Jews is too small. And there is no contact with the Aryans because we cannot forget what happened. For those reasons we tell him to go to another country, *any* other country." He shrugged. "So. Within twenty or thirty years Hitler's plan for a Jew-clean (*judenrein*) Germany will be realized after all."[2]

To an authentic *Amerikaner* living in the shadow of Villa Hügel during the last years of Krupp sovereignty and retracing the past, the period 1933–1945 was, not surprisingly, more fascinating, baffling, and provoking than any other. Sometimes every street corner seemed to offer mock clues to that chapter in the Krupp history. On the outskirts of the shopping area a white-on-blue neon sign announced the presence within of "RVE," and for a fleeting instant one remembered Alfried's strong role in the Nazi organization for parceling out shipments of human livestock. It was no more than fleeting; a second glance revealed that the initials now stood for a Westphalian business firm. World War II steam engines continued to snuffle and grunt in and out of the Hauptbahnhof's marshaling yards. Behind them they trailed the same ominous rust-red boxcars. Now in the era of the Common Market, however, the contents were inanimate, though until the *Wirtschaftswunderpause* there were disquieting moments when, outside store windows in the evening, herds of ragged *Fremdarbeiter* could be seen peering yearningly at displays and jabbering at one another in Polish, Italian, Flemish, French, and Greek. In Essen these workers lived, wrote Professor Pounds, "under conditions that are scarcely better than those in which the wartime conscripted laborers existed."[3] But that was an exaggeration. The new foreign workers were paid wages and were free to come and go; slavery in Germany died with the Führer.

More accurately, Pounds noted that the bomb-blasted wasteland of the Ruhr was being rebuilt along its former lines, following prewar street plans and re-creating appalling congestion.[4] Inevitably, many of yesterday's footprints vanished in the reconstruction. To cite one example, landmarks which would have been familiar to Elizabeth and Ernestine Roth have disappeared. They could have found their camp site — because it was so far from Krupp shops, the vast, littered, thinly grassed field was unchanged — and a streetcar called "Nr. 227," its sides advertising women's footwear, hauled passengers from there to the Essener Hof. But Walzwerk II, where the girls toiled and suffered in the daytime, had been torn down in 1962; the Stadtwiese, where Gerhardt Marquardt gave them food, was slowly shrinking as the neighborhood was built up; and Fritz Niermann, the grocer in whose home they found asylum, was no longer at Markscheide 15. The two Czech sisters might have made their way to the Jewish cemetery a second time, though they would have been puzzled by the Krupp padlocks on the gate. The locks, meant to discourage desecration, were only partly successful. The graveyard had become a favorite trysting place for young bucks from the shops and dates with blonde haystack hairdos and courage enough to leap over the wall, and before the introduction of *die*

*Pille* the ground between monuments and crypts was littered with mementos of robust lust.

Elizabeth and Ernestine never went back. Father Come and Paul Ledoux did. Thirty miles from the Belgian priest's new parish a monument at Saint-Hubert was dedicated to "*Les Victimes du Camp Spécial de la Gestapo des Usines Krupp, Dechenschule — Neerfeld, 1940–45*," and after an annual reunion on the Sunday nearest the anniversary of the great October 23–24 bombing in 1944 a delegation of survivors proceeded to Essen and left flowers at the site where Dechenschule once stood. They were glad it was now a playground, glad that children — with that innocence which knows no nationality — laughed where the former slaves knew only fear. The neighborhood had become one of the Ruhr's most thickly populated, but none of the Germans whose windows looked down on the school recalled the crimes committed there a quarter-century before. And soon no delegates would arrive yearly to remind them. The life span of former *Sklavenarbeiter* was turning out to be tragically short. They lived until fifty and were then prey to diseases which afflict other men twenty years later. Of the 270 original members of Father Come's Amicales des Camps de Dechenschule et Neerfeld fewer than a hundred were alive; he himself was suffering from heart disease. Regardless of sex or race, all those still alive reported chronic insomnia. Nearly all, moreover, had developed other problems. In New York Benjamin Ferencz was obliged to set up a separate office to interview Alfried's former slaves. "They burst into tears, they weep. . . ." He paused and spread his hands.[5]

"Most American businessmen think Krupp did as Du Pont or any other U.S. businessman would do," General Taylor said with a trace of bitterness. "Even lawyers say the victors were trying the vanquished." Of all the figures in Alfried's trial Taylor had become one of the hardest to find; he spent less and less time at his law firm and more and more at Columbia Law School. On the other hand — and on the opposite side of the country — Mr. Justice Wilkins, the sole survivor of Krupp's Nuremberg tribunal, could be found by any lawyer in the state of Washington. He was back reviewing appeals in Seattle. Rawlings Ragland, Taylor's chief of staff in the case, practiced law in Washington, D.C., where he often lunched with Drexel A. Sprecher, chief of staff in the I. G. Farben case. Cecelia Goetz was a member of a Manhattan law firm. John J. McCloy won new fame (and, unexpectedly, entered another controversy) after President Kennedy's assassination; as a member of the Warren Commission he was still turning up on front pages. He could be frequently seen in paneled boardrooms, and he was as vehement as ever in his opposition to a German translation of the trial on the ground that it was pointless to "rake up the coals."[6]

Nevertheless the coals were being raked up in the Bundesrepublik by

Otto Kranzbühler. When not serving in his various capacities as chairman of Alfried's brothers' Wasag A.G., executor of Bertha's and Gustav's estates, chief legal adviser to the Flick family, and attorney-at-law, the former naval captain toured West Germany lecturing on Nuremberg. The Justizpalast rulings were an American farce, he told attentive Germans, citing McCloy's pardon of Alfried as proof. With the passage of time there were fewer and fewer witnesses to support or rebut Kranzbühler. Arthur Rümann, the art dealer who watched Alfried and his fellow Schlotbarone anticipate the plunder of France and the Low Countries during the Blitzkrieg of 1940, was in and out of Munich hospitals. For a while (unknown to either of them) Rümann's Ausfahrtsallee neighbor had been Karl Otto Saur, consulting engineer and, in the eyes of Krupp partisans, the archvillain of Nuremberg. With his disappearance, there was no one to swear that Alfried had gone over Speer's head to get the Führer's approval for the Berthawerk except Speer himself, and he, after his release from Spandau within a few months of Alfried's death, went into seclusion.

Many key figures were dead, among them Eduard Houdremont, Alfried's fellow defendant in 1947–1948; Vera Krupp; and Axel Wenner-Gren, who had gone to a Swedish grave in 1962 at the age of eighty without betraying nearly a half-century of Krupp trust. Other participants in the Krupp drama had never known much. Anna Döring lived two miles from the sinister sheds of Buschmannshof, Krupp's concentration camp for infants. She bunched up trying to understand a visitor's German, flushed when she did, and spluttered just enough to reveal that she was no more than a wartime cog in a machine whose designers had been in Essen. Still others had emigrated to South America, and at least one was enjoying the affluence of postwar America. As a major, Horst Krüger had commanded the great railroad gun which shelled England from the outskirts of Calais until, reversing too fast on its way back into its sheltering cave when British Blenheims approached, it blew itself up. Later, as a brigadier general in the West German army, Krüger attracted the interest of visiting ordnance technicians and joined the faculty of the Massachusetts Institute of Technology.[7]

Many Kruppianer remained in the Ruhr on the Konzern's payroll — Hermann Hobrecker, executive in charge of "exports to the east" from 1941 to 1945, was director of personnel. Finanzdirektor Janssen was drawing a pension. So was Paul Hansen, who regarded the erection of the Berthawerk as "excellent experience," and Karl Dohrmann, who as Villa Hügel's butler remembered the castle when Margarethe Krupp was "Queen Mother" and Bertha was a bride. The pensioners even included Ewald Löser, who continued to be dubious in the eyes of middle-aged Kruppianer; die Firma honored its obligations to retired executives under all circumstances. Löser shrugged off the criticism of neighbors. His rare managerial talents had brought him a new career as an industrial consultant; he was often absent from Essen, and when at home he and his wife cherished that close bond which is often found in aging, childless couples who have endured much together.[8]

If the city had a pariah he was, curiously, the man who — with the exception of the Konzernherr himself — had received the heaviest sentence in the Krupp case. Not even Kranzbühler would put in a good word for Fritz von Bülow. Whatever other Germans who shivered in the Palace of Justice's coldest courtroom may have thought of the tribunal, they had been shocked by the testimony and documents which backed every word of General Taylor's slave labor indictment. The prosecution blamed Herr Krupp. For those who pledged allegiance to the Ruhr's ancient House, that was unthinkable; therefore it turned on the man who had been Krupp's chief slaver, leaving him with pride in his ancient lineage, the knowledge that he had served Alfried as faithfully as his father served Gustav, his childhood memories of ice skating with the future ruler of the dynasty — and with very little else. "My wife can't stand the climate," he explained hollowly. "This is a lonely house." Retired now, von Bülow dressed carefully once each week and sought the company of Baron Tilo von Wilmowsky and Berthold von Bohlen at the one place where he could not be refused: the Tuesday meetings of Essen's Rotary Club at 1 P.M. in the Kaiserhof.[9]

&#9960;   &#9960;   &#9960;

Should a stranger have the time, the money, and an interest in a chronological tour of the Krupp past, he would begin in one of the gaping squares between downtown Essen's medieval Marktkirche and the Staatarchiv, with its invaluable files of the *Essener Allgemeine Zeitung* and the *Essener Tageblatt* backed by the city's two gentle, perceptive archivists, Frau Clara Müller and Fräulein Anneliese Sprenger. The foreigner would first pay a token call at the Rathaus, part of which survived the wartime bombings. Touching the old stone is a reminder that Alfred wasn't the first Krupp, that before he clanged on the scene emitting sparks and strange noises family bureaucrats and merchants had dominated Essen in the sixteenth, seventeenth, and eighteenth centuries. And the preposterous three-color neon sign affixed to the building — "Ratskeller–Stern-Pils," a beer ad on city hall — sets a proper tone of blatancy. Krupp appeals to patriotism can be confusing. It should be fixed in the mind that from Arndt to Arndt the dynasty attained and achieved hegemony by keeping a firm eye on the thaler, pfennig, and mark.

A short walk away, at the corner of Limbeckerstrasse and Vienhoferstrasse, is the site of the old Flachsmarkt. There, in the window of a store selling Miele washing machines, a stainless steel plaque informs passersby that

*An dieser Stelle*
*stand das Geburtshaus*
*von Alfred Krupp*
*Geb. 26.4.1812*
*Gest.14.7.1887*

In this place
stood the birthplace
of Alfred Krupp
born April 26, 1812
died July 14, 1887

And between the Rathaus and the plaque, a hand grenade's throw away from an eleventh-century church, stands the old man himself. During the Thousand Year Reich this statue of him crowned a taller plinth and was venerated by various winged females who reached up (in vain) to feel his skinny legs. Alfried brought him closer to our level. We can see, as the Führer could not, that he is bracing himself with his left arm on an anvil. That is appropriate. What is less seemly is that his bronze eyes should stare out at a store displaying feminine fashions: microskirts, plunging necklines, and the huge brassieres that so many German women seem to require. Involuntarily one steps back, half expecting the bearded figure to hurl his anvil through the panes. He doesn't. He can't, and presently the visitor sees one reason why. In putting him back on his pedestal workmen gave him a slight backward tilt; should the figure acquire life and move a finger of that left hand, the entire statue would crash at the foot of the church toward which its back is firmly turned.

Alfried did a better job in restoring the Stammhaus. With its black clogs, its old-fashioned illumination, and the original furniture, it re-creates the atmosphere of the Ruhr between Waterloo and Sedan. But for a glimpse of the power and poetry of steel, which enticed the first Kanonen-könig, one should stop by Altendorferstrasse 30 at the Press- und Hammer-werk, which was among the few shops to come through the RAF holocaust unscathed. Under the direction of its veteran *Meister* forty-ton, flaming ingots cross the shop floor in cradles made of chains. Bursting into fire from time to time, they are hammered, squashed, squeezed and squeezed until they take on the appearance of a roll — a convenient shape from which almost anything can be made and almost everything has, here; photographs of the Gusstahlfabrik in the 1860's differ from those taken in the 1960's only in detail, none of it significant to the layman.

Essen is approaching the centennial of the Franco-Prussian War and can scarcely contain itself. "In 1945 there was hope that the [democratic, middle-class] temper of 1848–49 would be revived," Hans Kohn wrote in the summer of 1967. "Now the centenary of 1870 is fast approaching and with it the glorification of Bismarck, the civilian chancellor who almost always appeared in a cuirassier uniform."[10] He appears so in bas-relief at Bismarckplatz; the artist sculptured him listening while *der Grosse Krupp* lectured. Alfred may be talking horse manure, but both men seem enchanted with it. In Burgplatz and across the river in suburban Werden are other statues which might be found anywhere in Germany: Kaiser Wilhelm I on horseback, observing a dying soldier holding the Prussian flag aloft with one hand while he props himself on a Krupp cannon with the other. Overhead an angel holding the wreath of victory is about to drop it on his head. It is unaccountably heavy; the soldier, one feels, knows it; his expression conveys more terror than gratitude.

There are no angels hovering over the statue of "Friedrich Alfred Krupp/1854–1902" on the grounds of the hospital his elder daughter built. Indeed, the frock-coated, stocky figure appears to have been deliberately presented as a dull man. He looks more like a defeated alderman than the deviate who disgraced himself on Capri before coming home to commit suicide in the gloomy castle. And there is no monument whatever to the All-Highest, despite the vital role he played in Krupp destinies, perhaps because *he* disgraced *him*self on his last Essen visit. Considering how completely Fritz and Wilhelm reigned over the Ruhr at the turn of the century, the almost total absence of reminders of either is singular. Nothing fails like failure. Imagination is needed to summon their ghosts. Fritz's may lurk behind the immense black iron gates beside the Essen-to-Düsseldorf train's special Hügel stop: the snarled forest, deep ravines, and steep hills beyond haven't changed in the two-thirds of a century since Margarethe, hurriedly released from her insane asylum, alighted from the *Zechenbahn* here to supervise her husband's funeral. And S.M. seems to hover over the unaltered underpass at Hagen and Trentelgasse, where he used to parade during each visit to the Ruhr, and the Hauptverwaltungsgebäude's former entrance hall. But the visitor to the underpass must be agile. The traffic is shocking. And finding the hall is something of a trick; you have to know the building well. Since the war its bomb-blackened marble floor — over which damaged false balconies frown down with broken stone rungs looking like discolored, distorted teeth — has been virtually sealed off. Once there the stranger will be reminded of Wilhelmine pomp, but unhappily he will be reminded of something else, for Hitler used to come in this way. The Kaiser's specter must coexist with the Führer's, and sharing is something neither was much good at.

On the other hand Bertha, who made generosity her career, is everywhere — in little Villa Hügel touches, in the hospital and nursing home, in her sister's scrapbook, and in the red brick house at 12 Berenberger Mark where she died. Reminders of her crop up all over Germany. She even appears far beyond the iron curtain in Silesia's Berthawerk, now run by Polish Communists. An expedition there is hardly worth the trouble, but the curious foreigner should make a few other side trips, notably to

Blühnbach, to Barbara and Tilo's beloved Marienthal, and, of course, to Berlin. Inasmuch as the last four generations of Krupps (like the last four German governments) swung the dynasty's weight back and forth between east and west, it is fitting that virtually all Krupp memorabilia in the former capital should be within a few blocks of the wall. There is Alfred's 1870 *preussisches Ballongeschütz* in its forsaken gallery across from the Maxim Gorki theater, a few hundred yards from the Zoo Station entrance. The celebrated statues of Moltke and Roon are in the Tiergarten, adjoining Checkpoint Charlie. The site of the conservative Hotel Bristol, where Fritz Krupp made unconventional love to imported Capriote youths, is on the Linden, a few blocks from the wall, and to see the ruins of the brick and marble Gestapo prison on Prinz-Albrecht-Strasse, the scene of Löser's suffering, and the Potsdamer Platz building which housed Koch und Kienzle — Gustav Krupp's name for the planners of secret rearmament in the 1920's — one must go to the wall itself, prop a stepladder against the cinder blocks, and peer over into the no-man's-land between what veteran agents call the Friendlies and the Unfriendlies.

Activities at Koch und Kienzle, as Fritz Tubbesing recalled recently, were directed from the Hauptverwaltungsgebäude office whose window is distinguished from all others by its bay window and the three interlocked rings carved in stone.[11] It was here that Gustav Krupp lovingly sketched the sluglike 420-mm. mortar named for his bride in 1909, here that he toiled throughout World War I, here that he dreamed of a second chance afterward and decided to put the prestige and wealth of his wife's name behind Adolf Hitler. Today the third Kanonenkönig's office is used by a typing pool. The girls there haven't the vaguest idea of what went on between these walls for thirty years, and the visitor steeped in Krupp lore resents the lack of a plaque, if only because it was from this window on Easter Saturday, 1923, that a leader of the world's greatest munitions-making family actually heard shots fired in anger and, as the staccato burst died away, the cries of the wounded and the dying.

There are no reminders below, either. The firm's fire department of 1923 has been replaced by a zipper factory; the garage used by Lieutenant Durieux's poilus was torn down and the space converted to that parking lot best remembered for its bonfire of documents. During the sixteen years between the French invasion of the Ruhr and the Wehrmacht's invasion of Poland it was inconceivable that Essen could ever forget the victims of the massacre. Yet Essen has. Even their graves are ignored. The thirteen stone crosses, separated from the rest of the cemetery by hedges, provide only names, dates of birth, and the 1923 date of death — another sign that Gustav was confident the slain were immortal. Today none of the care-takers know who the thirteen were, for after the war this Ehrenfriedhof (Cemetery of Honor) was incorporated into the huge Südwest Cemetery. Memories of their deaths have been overwhelmed by the deaths of millions, and the error of some anonymous clerk has been repeated on the graveyard map, which identifies the Easter Saturday martyrs as casualties in a "bombing" (*Bombenabwurf*). When the author explained the lapse, the chief custodian — a man too young to recall the drama of the incident — looked surprised. Then he shrugged. What did it matter?

What did it matter? "*Ohne mich*" (Without me) had become the slogan of the postwar generation. It meant that for the present Germany was turning its back on the Cold War. It did not mean a complete withdrawal, as Arndt interpreted it, but in either event traditional landmarks and keepsakes lost their value. The family's Hügel model of Gustav's *die dicke Bertha* was lost to some unknown British souvenir hunter. No one missed it. During Krupp's Landsberg imprisonment Karl Dohrmann saved models of the Konzernherr's 88 gun and *Prinz Eugen*. Later the butler discovered that his efforts were unappreciated, his souvenirs untreasured. On the green-tinted second floor of the Hauptverwaltungsgebäude's munitions wing, which replaced Gustav's office as the Ruhr's most sacred ground, emphasis was on recovery and new trade records. Alfried presided over his sleek elmwood conference table as the greatest entrepreneur of his time; reminders of his years as armorer of the Reich were suppressed.

In the Essener Hof American businessmen from Indiana raised their glasses to toast "Krupp!" and Englishmen, masters of Essen in the late 1940's and early 1950's, haggled over contract clauses. Commercial relations with the Low Countries was a recurring theme; a downtown sign urged, "Visit lovely Rotterdam!" Adolf-Hitler-Strasse was Kettwigstrasse again; Krupp's Hindenburg Bay, used within living memory to inspire the *Waffenschmiede*'s gunmakers with stirring ovations, was devoted to the assembly of locomotives destined for Greece. One by one Krupp bulldozers leveled most of Alfried's wartime concentration camps for new housing developments, and no one talked about the Jews any more, partly because there were so few to attract attention. Even before Alfried's decline and death *die Firma* was acquiring the faceless aspect of a corporation. The Konzernherr was an anachronism, and everyone knew it. Suddenly Beitz's *Drang nach Osten* boomeranged, followed by Arndt's stunning decision that the Konzern would have to carry on *ohne ihn* because he had other affairs which were more urgent. Then the break with the past became complete. As Günter Vogelsang said in the late spring of 1968, a half-year after his appointment as general director, today the firm "has a professional, paid, elected management and both decision-making and responsibility are collective. The leadership style at Krupp is no longer patriarchal."[12] Fried. Krupp of Essen is becoming as impersonal and as bland as General Motors or Ford, which the younger executives frankly hope to imitate. Older Kruppianer are brokenhearted. They can't believe it. For them the thrill is gone. Nevertheless the emphasis on the corporate image grows stronger every weekday, and each Sunday, when Villa Hügel is open to the public, the crowd arriving to stare up at portraits of Germany's first family dwindles perceptibly. Plainly Essen, the Ruhr, and the Bundesrepublik have said *Lebe wohl* to all that.

✠   ✠   ✠

Yet behind the transformation, behind the neon booster sign advertising Essen as "the City of Trade," behind the glittering plate-glass windows of the present lies the mystic, stained-glass past. Like the silver in an old mirror, it gleams fitfully when the light strikes it right. Crossing Essen's Gildenplatz you hear strident music. A music box big as a freight car is playing marches; a crowd has gathered and everyone, unconsciously, is standing at attention. At a late party a brooding man slams down his stein and cries, "If *only* Paulus had broken through at Stalingrad!" Those around him nod sympathetically, leaving the inexpressible to deep thought. A Krupp salesman, back from abroad, complains bitterly of home office arrogance: "They think Essen is the capital of the world!" Passing Bismarck's statue a taxi driver identifies him as "one of our famous generals." Another monument at Burgplatz, *"Wachsames Hähnchen"* (Vigilant Rooster) is topped by a golden rooster; it is meant to hallow the memory of natives who fell in the two World Wars, and the heroic figure on the column is carrying a bow and arrow. Essen should be the last city on earth to think that the Wehrmacht was armed with bows and arrows, but there it is. There will always be a German, and he will always see reality through a romantic, hazy, highly colored nimbus. A real stained-glass window in Villa Hügel's "small house" depicts the coat of arms of each Krupp, including Alfried's. One looks in vain for symbols of the true Krupp might. They glitter with medieval helmets, plumes, and coronets; above them stands a golden Aryan knight in spotless armor; beneath them, in Latin, is the family motto, *Cave Gryppen* (Beware of the Griffin).[13]

The griffin is a mythical beast, half lion and half eagle. If one existed, it would be found in the Reich's dark, haunting forests, symbols of the tortured Teuton soul since Tacitus first wrote of their vast swamps, their dense vapors, and their interminability. Of course, there is no griffin. It is only a dream of evil, a Grimm brothers nightmare. The forests are real enough, though. More than a third of the country is still wooded. Even the Ruhr can be unexpectedly green, especially along the banks of the river. Heavy shoulders of ash and gnarled oak crowd the shores below Hügel, and if you hike a mile downstream to the crest of Schwarze Helene, the view is spectacular.

Here, on a fine spring evening, you may look out over brows and slopes shaggy with foliage and sailboats dancing on the Ruhr. It is difficult to believe that Krupp's massive concentration of industry can be so close, or that the water can be polluted. Yet even here one cannot forget the family. The castle is below, squat and square. Inland rises the green tower of

Bredeney's *Realgymnasium*, where Alfried first went to school. Indeed, the very hill on which you stand is named for the eccentric old woman who enjoyed a local celebrity a century ago because Alfred Krupp, whenever he was in trouble, would gallop over here to pour out his troubles to her, and since the hill is very near the homes of his other great-grandsons, they sometimes come here to dine in Zur Platte, a chic little restaurant on the summit, and exchange the latest tidings.

And perhaps, with that strong sense of continuity which distinguishes this extraordinary old family, their thoughts sometimes regress, like a movie reel rewound, the film whirring backward, spinning into the past over episodes remembered, over stories told them in their childhood, and deeper ancestral memories. To scenes of Alfried, gaunt and tight-lipped, in the dock at Nuremberg . . . of themselves frisking on the Hügel lawn in their new *feldgrau* uniforms with Claus and Eckbert . . . of greeting the Führer with a stiff-armed *Hitlergruss* as he strode briskly across the great hall of the castle . . . of Alfried pledging himself to the newly formed SS. Back farther, to tales of Gustav's wedding to Bertha Krupp, and S.M.'s mustaches that morning, and how the elegant young baron danced and danced . . . of Fritz's ghastly death, of Margarethe's meekness with her irascible father-in-law, of Fritz in his youth, sobbing bitterly because the Prinz Karl Regiment of the Baden Dragoons had rejected him as a physical weakling . . . of how the manners of Essen's visitors changed in the wake of the Franco-Prussian War, the old thoughtfulness yielding to the haughty, strutting Prussian artillery *Offizier* . . . of spidery Alfred lying alone in the dark, scribbling of apprehensions lest some future catastrophe prevent him from avenging his father's failures:

> *Wie leicht ein Brand entstehen kann, weiss man, und ein Brand würde alles, alles zerstören!*

> How easily a fire can break out, you know, and a fire would destroy everything, everything![14]

Back and back, past the Friedrich Krupps and the Anton and Georg and Wilhelm and Heinrich Krupps — and the Katharinas and Helenes and Gertruds and Theodoras, the Krupp Valkyrie — back beyond the first glinting razor-sharp bayonets, the first sluglike cannonballs, the agony of the Thirty Years War and the Black Death — back past the early black-and-white Westphalian cottages into other times, older than the written record of Essen's original Krupp or even the Dark Ages; back to the jumbled terror of the Hercynian forest, when the Rhineland was a Roman outpost, and men believed in monstrous things, and the barbaric Ruhr lay dark under the moon, its oak and bloodbeech tops writhing in the evening wind like a gaggle of ghosts, and the first grim Aryan savage crouched in his garment of coarse skins, his crude javelin poised, tense and alert, cloaked by night and fog, ready; waiting; and waiting.

# Acknowledgments

✠ ✠ ✠

I n gathering the information here presented, the author has received assistance from Count Klaus Ahlefeldt-Lauruiz, Louis Azrael, George Norbert Barr, Friedrich von Batocki, Berthold Beitz, James Bell, M. P. Belmore, Oskar Belplate, Berthold von Bohlen und Halbach, Harald von Bohlen und Halbach, D. Bosse, Kay Boyle, Hans Buchheim, Friedrich von Bülow, Hans Erich Campen, Franz Cesarz, Father Alphonse Come, Henrik Georg van Dam, Heinrich Deichmann, Karl Dohrmann, Benjamin B. Ferencz, Richard D. Forster, Hermann Frisch, Heitz Gegenhorst, Cecelia H. Goetz, Werner Gohmert, Tadeusz Goldstajn, Albert Gregorius, Paul Hansen, Friedrich Wilhelm Hardach, Fritz Heine, Wilhelm L. Heinrichs, Archbishop Franz Hengsbach, Heinrich Heyder, Richard Hildebrandt, Dieter Hirschfeld, Hermann Hobrecker, Horst Hosmann, Carl Hundhausen, Ted Kaghan, Karl Kesselring, Otto Kranzbühler, Alfried Krupp von Bohlen und Halbach, Ewald Löser, Frau Ewald Löser, John J. McCloy, Eugene McCreary, Max Mandellaub, Siegfried Maruhn, Fritz Meininghaus, Bernhard Menne, Friedhelm Mittler, Clara Müller, Siegfried Neugarten, John W. Paton, Otto Proksch, Rawlings Ragland, Roger D. Prosser, Heiner Radzio, Ernst von Raussendorf, Elizabeth Roth, Ernestine Roth, Erhard Reusch, Wilhelm Rüttherodt, Karl Sabel, Wolfgang Schleicher, Franz Schmidt-Wulffsen, Ernst Schröder, Sigrid Schultz, Kurt Schürmann, Hans Seyboth, Drexel A. Sprecher, Anneliese Sprenger, Jean Sprenger, Gertrud Stahmer-Knoll, Telford Taylor, Charles W. Thayer, Fritz Tubbesing, Eric Warburg, Alfonse Baron Werwilghen, Hans-Günter Weymann, George Williams, Tilo Frhr. von Wilmowsky, Barbara Krupp von Wilmowsky, Georg-Volkmar Graf Zedtwitz-Arnim, and Walter Zimmerman.

In his research role the writer owes them much, and the debt is gratefully acknowledged. In interpreting the material, however, he owes them nothing; indeed, many of them will wish to disassociate themselves from some of the views in this text. Let it be done here. All responsibility is mine alone.

W.M.

# Appendices

✠ ✠ ✠

### APPENDIX I
# Krupp Genealogy

### APPENDIX II
# Die Firma

### APPENDIX III
# Chronology

# Krupp Family Tree

Arndt Krupp
arrived in Essen
d 1624

Anton Krupp   **m**   Gertrud Krösen     Katharina Krupp   **m**   Alexander Huyssen     Georg Krup
1588-1661   1612      d 1676    1619       1590-1623

Matthias Kru
1621-1673

Georg Dietrich Krupp   **m**   Anna Elisabeth Huyssen      Arnold Krup
1657-1742   1690    1661-1735      1662-1734

Theodora Maria Krupp   **m**   Johann Müller     Juliane Krupp **m** Johann Zopf     Friedrich Jodocus
1703-1786   1731   1703-1780     1702-1749   1722   1691-1774     1706-1757

Marie Müller   **m**   Arnold Theodor Sölling      Peter Friedrich Wilhe
1740-1813   1760    1727-1795      1753-1795

Georg Christian Sölling   **m**   Caroline Schemmann      Friedrich Kru
1775-1857   1810    1790-1850      1787-1826
     Founder of Firma Fri

Friedrich Heinrich Sölling     Marie Baum   **m**   Hermann Krupp    Ida Krupp    Alfred Krup
1815-1859     1821-1879   1847   1814-1879    1809-1882    1812-1887
      Co-owner Berndorfer Metallwarenfabrik       Owner of Fried.
      (Two sons and five daughters)

Margret Rudolf   **m**   Artur Krupp      Friedrich Alfred
1858-1920   1881   1856-1938      1854-1902
Owner Berndorfer Metallwarenfabrik      Owner of Fried.

Bertha Krupp
1886-1957
Owner of Fried. I

Harald      Berthold      Waldtraut      Alfried Krupp
1916-      1913-      1920-      Bohlen und Hal
**m** Doerte     **m** Edith von    **m** 1942; divorced    1907-1967
Hillringhaus    Maltzan     **m** 1961-     Owner of Fried. I
(one child)     (one son)    (two children)

Arndt von Bo
und Halbac
1938-

von Bohlen und Halbach

Gertrud von der Gathen
d 1633

Brigitta Klocke
d 1623

Margarethe Krupp   **m**   Arnold Erlsberg
d 1652

Anna Katharina Voss
d 1698

Anna Gertrud Burckhardt
1681–1725

Matthias Arnold Krupp   **m**   Anna Elisabeth Sölling
1660–1729     1694     1669–1757

1. Janna Elbers 1727
1696–1739
2. Helene Amalie Ascherfeld 1751
1732–1810

Heinrich Wilhelm Krupp   **m**   Katharina Wuppermann
1711–1760     1742     1711–1760

Petronella Forsthoff
1757–1839

Therese Wilhelmi
1790–1850

Helene Krupp   **m**   Friedrich von Müller
1782–1833   1803   1771–1839

Bertha Eichhoff      Friedrich Krupp
1831–1888      1820–1901

Carl Friedrich von Müller
1804–1874

Margarethe Freiin von Ende
1854–1931

Gustav Krupp von
Bohlen und Halbach
1870–1950

Barbara Krupp   **m**   Tilo von Wilmowsky
1887–   1907   1878–
(Two sons and four daughters)

1. Anneliese Bahr 1937    Arnold      Claus      Irmgard      Eckbert
(divorced 1941)      1908–09      1910–40      1912–      1922–45
2. Vera Hossenfeldt 1952           m 1938      m 1938
(divorced 1957)          (Son: Arnold)    Hanno Raitz v. Frenz
d 1967                          d 1941
Remarried (six children)

von Bohlen und Halbach

# *Die Firma* at the Time of Alfried Krupp's Death

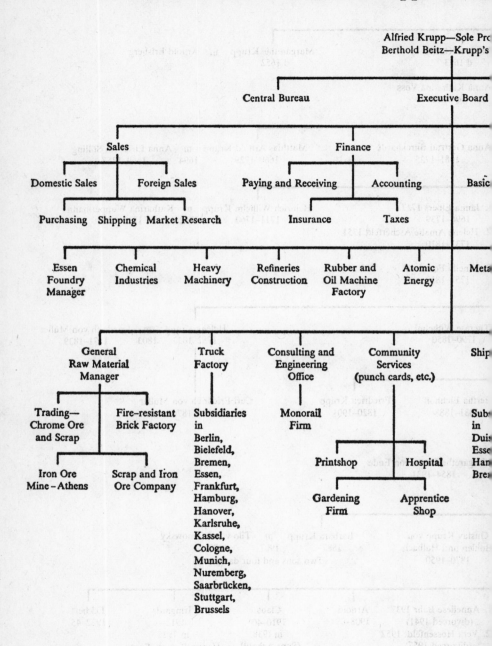

Alfried Krupp—Sole Pro
Berthold Beitz—Krupp's

Central Bureau

Executive Board

Sales

Finance

Domestic Sales

Foreign Sales

Paying and Receiving

Accounting

Basic

Purchasing  Shipping  Market Research

Insurance

Taxes

Essen Foundry Manager

Chemical Industries

Heavy Machinery

Refineries Construction

Rubber and Oil Machine Factory

Atomic Energy

Meta

General Raw Material Manager

Truck Factory

Consulting and Engineering Office

Community Services (punch cards, etc.)

Ship

Trading— Chrome Ore and Scrap

Fire-resistant Brick Factory

Subsidiaries in Berlin, Bielefeld, Bremen, Essen, Frankfurt, Hamburg, Hanover, Karlsruhe, Kassel, Cologne, Munich, Nuremberg, Saarbrücken, Stuttgart, Brussels

Monorail Firm

Sub in Dui Esse Han Bre

Iron Ore Mine–Athens

Scrap and Iron Ore Company

Printshop

Hospital

Gardening Firm

Apprentice Shop

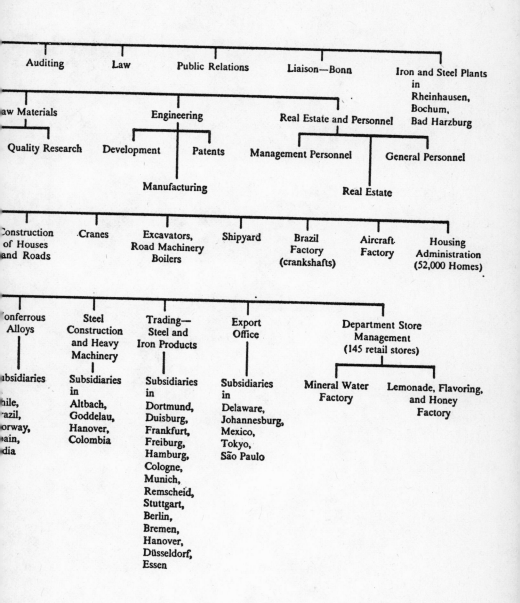

Auditing    Law    Public Relations    Liaison—Bonn    Iron and Steel Plants in Rheinhausen, Bochum, Bad Harzburg

Raw Materials    Engineering    Real Estate and Personnel

Quality Research    Development    Patents    Management Personnel    General Personnel

Manufacturing    Real Estate

Construction of Houses and Roads    Cranes    Excavators, Road Machinery Boilers    Shipyard    Brazil Factory (crankshafts)    Aircraft Factory    Housing Administration (52,000 Homes)

Nonferrous Alloys    Steel Construction and Heavy Machinery    Trading— Steel and Iron Products    Export Office    Department Store Management (145 retail stores)

Subsidiaries in Chile, Brazil, Norway, Spain, India    Subsidiaries in Altbach, Goddelau, Hanover, Colombia    Subsidiaries in Dortmund, Duisburg, Frankfurt, Freiburg, Hamburg, Cologne, Munich, Remscheid, Stuttgart, Berlin, Bremen, Hanover, Düsseldorf, Essen    Subsidiaries in Delaware, Johannesburg, Mexico, Tokyo, São Paulo    Mineral Water Factory    Lemonade, Flavoring, and Honey Factory

APPENDIX III

# Chronology

✠   ✠   ✠

1587    Arrival of Arndt Krupp in Essen.
1599    The Black Death: a windfall for Arndt.
1618–48   Thirty Years War: Anton Krupp produces 1,000 gun barrels a year.
1811    Friedrich Krupp founds the family cast steel factory.
1812    Friedrich digs trenches for Napoleon.
       Birth of Alfred Krupp.
1816    Krupp bayonets to Berlin.
1826    Death of Friedrich.
1838    Alfred spies in England.
1836–42   Alfred produces hollow-forged muskets.
1847    Prussia receives Alfred's first steel cannon.
1851    Alfred's debut at London's Crystal Palace Exhibition.
1855    Krupp steel smashes floor of Paris Exhibition.
1866    Prussia invades Austria with Krupp cannon.
1870    Sedan: Krupp guns defeat Napoleon III.
1871    First Krupp bombardment of Paris.
1878    "Bombardment of the Nations."
1886    Birth of Bertha Krupp.
1887    Death of Alfred Krupp.
       Fritz Krupp's Royal Tour.
1900    Fritz builds the Kaiser a navy.
1901    Plans for U–1 drawn.
1902    Fritz's suicide.
1906    Marriage of Bertha and Gustav Krupp.
1907    Birth of Alfried Krupp; joy in the Reich.
1909    Construction of Big Bertha.
1914    Big Berthas crush Belgium.
1916    Verdun: a Krupp masterpiece.
       Jutland: Krupp vs. Krupp.
       Gustav and Ludendorff confer.

| | |
|---|---|
| 1918 | Gustav shells Paris. |
| | Kaiser says farewell in Essen. |
| 1919 | Gustav named a war criminal. |
| | Allies dismantle the factory. |
| 1920 | Workers rise, seize Essen. |
| | Gustav begins secret rearmament. |
| 1923 | French occupy the castle. |
| | Bloody Saturday at the office. |
| 1925 | Von Seeckt inspects the shops. |
| 1926 | Allied commission leaves Essen. |
| | Design of 1940 tanks completed. |
| 1928 | "Black Production" begins. |
| 1929 | Firing tests held for the navy. |
| 1930 | Hitler pays a visit. |
| 1931 | Alfried joins the SS. |
| 1931–32 | New weapons demonstrated to the army. |
| 1933 | Krupp finances Hitler. |
| | Gustav appointed Führer of industry. |
| 1935 | Hitler proclaims "military sovereignty." |
| 1936 | Krupp subs threaten France during Rhineland crisis. |
| 1938 | Krupp rewarded after Austrian putsch. |
| | Alfried, back from Spain, rises swiftly. |
| 1939 | Gustav's first stroke. |
| | Alfried writes his first annual report. |
| 1940 | Claus killed in action. |
| | Alfried shells England across the Channel. |
| 1942 | Alfried appointed chief director. |
| 1943 | January: first real RAF raid on Essen. |
| | Battle of the Kursk salient: a Krupp disaster. |
| | Lex Krupp: Hitler honors Alfried. |
| 1944 | Krupp gases a Rothschild at Auschwitz. |
| | Arrest of Barbara Krupp. |
| | Capture of Harald by Russians. |
| | Alfried rules 100,000 slave laborers. |
| 1945 | Eckbert killed in action. |
| | Americans capture Ruhr and seize Alfried. |
| | Internment of Bertha and Gustav. |
| | Eviction of Barbara and the baron. |
| 1946 | Second dismantling of the factories. |
| 1948 | War Crimes Tribunal convicts Alfried at Nuremberg. |
| 1950 | Death of Gustav. |
| 1951 | John J. McCloy releases Alfried. |
| 1953 | Alfried again rules the Ruhr. |

1955    Release of Harald.
1957    Death of Bertha.
1963    Alfried becomes the most powerful industrialist in the Common
        Market.
1967    Krupp completes Germany's first nuclear plant.
        Collapse of the firm's finances.
        Arndt II opts for a carefree life.
        Death of Alfried, last of the Krupps.
1968    Dissolution of *die Firma*.

# Notes

✠　✠　✠

# ✠
# Chapter Notes

Abbreviations used in these notes in the interest of brevity are:

AK    Alfred Krupp
DGFP  Documents on German Foreign Policy 1918–1945 Series D
        (1937–1945)
DNB   Deutsches Nachrichtenbüro (German news service under
        Hitler)
FAK   Friedrich Alfred Krupp
IMT   International Military Tribunal
KFA   Documents from the Krupp Familien Archiv, Krupp His-
        torische Archiv, and Krupp Werksarchiv
NCA   *Nazi Conspiracy and Aggression* (see bibliography, p. 927)
Ntr   Nuremberg transcript of Military Tribunals Case No. 10,
        United States of America vs. Alfried Felix Alwyn Krupp
        von Bohlen und Halbach *et al.* (the Krupp Case), Novem-
        ber 17, 1947–July 31, 1948.
NYT   *New York Times*
SB    *United States Strategic Bombing Survey* (Washington:
        1947)
Test  Testimony in the Alfried Krupp case
TMWC  Nuremberg trials of the International Military Tribunal
TWC   *Trials of War Criminals* . . . (see bibliography, p. 930)
WM    Author's interviews

Nuremberg documents filed in the National Archives Virginia annex and
at the International Court of Justice, The Hague, are identified only by
number. The most frequent prefixes are:

DE }
D  }  Defense exhibits

NIK   Nazi industrialist Krupp

Others — for example, C, EC, KI, L, NI, OKW, PS — were arbitrarily
assigned at Nuremberg.

ED and NG indicate material from The Institut für Zeitgeschichte (Munich).

Short forms of names as used in the notes are: Alfried (Alfried Krupp); Barbara Krupp (Barbara Krupp von Wilmowsky); Bertha I (Bertha Eichhoff Krupp); Berthold (Berthold von Bohlen und Halbach); Gustav (Gustav Krupp); Harald (Harald von Bohlen und Halbach); Hermann (Hermann Krupp); Lauruiz (Count Ahlefeldt-Lauruiz); Wilmowsky (Baron Tilo von Wilmowsky).

Works cited by short title or by simply the last name of the author are listed in full in the bibliography (p. 915).

### PROLOGUE: ANVIL OF THE REICH

1  Blühnbach sources: WM/Schröder, Barbara Krupp v. Wilmowsky (hereinafter Barbara Krupp), Berthold v. Bohlen u. Halbach (hereinafter Berthold), Tilo Frhr. v. Wilmowsky (hereinafter Wilmowsky); Charles W. Thayer and his *Unquiet Germans* 95–97; Kohn *Mind of Germany* 1.
2  Mühlen 157.
3  NIK-11504, -7445, -11674.
4  NIK-11200, -11804, -11504, -382.
5  NIK-2868,  -9232,  -805,  -3757, -11975, -2965, -4721.
6  WM/Wilmowsky; KFA IV 320 S. 42, 44 (1872); also *Hundertjähriges Bestehen* 179–185.
7  Wilmowsky *Rückblickend* 47 (hereinafter Wilmowsky).
8  Görlitz *Kleine Geschichte* 659; Wilmowsky 223–4.
9  WM/Hansen, Hobrecker.
10  WM/Bülow, Raussendorf.
11  WM/Bülow (who drafted them); Lochner 32; NCA I 1080; NIK-3725; Mühlen 167.
12  NCA I 85 (Gustav listed 13th of 24 defendants in indictment signed in Berlin 10/6/45); WM/Harald v. Bohlen u. Halbach (hereinafter Harald).
13  WM/Sprenger; Klass *Ringe* (hereinafter Klass) 17; *Der Spiegel* 6/5/63.
14  WM/Berthold, Harald.
15  Klass 495.
16  Horne *Power* (hereinafter Horne) 110; NIK-10214, -10590 (Celap affidavit).
17  Ferencz 3–4.
18  *Test* Pleyer Ntr 5702–3.
19  NIK-2965.
20  NIK-13173,  -14207;  *Der Spiegel* 6/5/63.

21  Gustav Krupp (hereinafter Gustav) to Bormann, D-99; Bormann to Gustav, D-103; *Reichsgesetzblatt* 11/20/43 (Führer's decree 11/12/43).
22  NIK-12074.
23  Order 4/5/48 Nuremberg, signed by Presiding Judge H. C. Anderson, also Opinion of same date; Opinion and Judgment, Military Tribunal III, Nuremberg 7/31/48.
24  *Business Week* 5/8/48.
25  Mühlen 219; WM/Bülow.
26  WM/Dohrmann.
27  WM/Menne, Kranzbühler, Heine (who, then an SPD executive committee member, was rebuffed in London on socialization of Krupp works); Morgenthau 23.
28  *Atlantic* 10/1960.
29  Stolper *German Realities* quoted in Pounds 269; Keynes quoted in Pounds 17.
30  *NYT* 1/30/61; Görlitz *General Staff* 36; TWC XII 1084.
31  *Bochumer Verein* 24.
32  Mirabeau 200.
33  Brodie 19; Pounds 37.
34  Hitler 124.
35  Tacitus 267.
36  Frazer 229, 625.
37  Ryder, strophe 1003.
38  Tümmler lx; Conway in *Harper's*.

### 1. THE WALLED CITY

1  Essen Stadtarchiv (signature in register for 1/1587, righthand page, 4th line); Menne 3.
2  Coulton 393.
3  Menne 11.
4  *Villa Hügel* 1; *Freidank's Bescheidenheit* (1877) 41–2.
5  Berdrow *Familie Krupp* (hereinafter Berdrow) 20.

6 Ibid. 62; Menne 17.
7 Mühlen 13.
8 Pounds 37; Kraft li.
9 Pounds 34; Menne 36.
10 Ca. 1807; the journal is in KFA.
11 Menne 46; Essen history: Ribbeck passim.
12 Menne 38.
13 Klass 27.
14 Pounds 54; passport KFA; Menne 39–40.
15 *Westfälischer Anzeiger* no. 84, 1810, 1811.
16 *Fried. Krupp Essen 1811–1946.* (Date disputed by Krupp firm as unknown and possibly as early as 1810. Kechel contract date seems to confirm 1811.) Krupp documentary film *Pioniere deutscher Technik* shows reconstruction of original building and annex.
17 Klass *Asche* 87–98.
18 WM/Hundhausen (who identified the stream as the Walkmühle); *Beiträge zur Geschichte* 12–13.
19 *Beiträge zur Geschichte* 15; Wiedfeldt *Friedrich Krupp* 2.
20 *Krupp Past and Present* 41.
21 Klass *Asche* 94–5; AK to Essen Bürgermeister Pfeiffer 12/23/1834.
22 WM/Hundhausen; Mühlen 20; *Krupp in the Service of Engineering Progress* 5; Klass 25.
23 Menne 51.
24 Therese Wilhelmi Krupp; quoted in Klass 22.
25 AK to Gödeking of Berlin Mint 10/15/1826.

2. THE ANVIL WAS HIS DESK

1 Klass 126; Berdrow 296; Menne 54.
2 Mühlen 37–8; AK to Ascherfeld (n.d.; early 1850's); Klass 85; AK to Hermann Krupp (hereinafter Hermann) 9/9/1838.
3 Villa Hügel exhibit 1963; Klass 34; *Krupp in the Service of Engineering Progress* 14; AK to J. Ravené's Sons 1/23/1835.
4 AK to Pfeiffer 12/23/1834; Steiner in *Outlook*; AK to Prokura 1/14/1872; Klass 35.
5 Therese Krupp to business associates 10/19/1826.
6 AK to Gödeking 10/15/1826; AK to Noelle of Düsseldorf Mint 1/9/1828; Griesenbeck to Therese Wilhemi Krupp 11/24/1826.

7 AK to Borbeck Bürgermeister Stock 11/14/28; AK to Bruckmann and Company 12/22/1833; AK to Lendy of Sardinian Mint 10/1/1834; AK to Trenelle at Saarn 11/16/1834.
8 AK to Essen Bürgermeister Kopstadt 2/6/1829.
9 Pounds 56; AK to Moldenhauer 1/27/1830.
10 Berdrow *Alfred Krupp* 52, 73, 77, 94; AK to Pfeiffer 12/23/1834.
11 AK to Jacobi, Haniel, and Huyssen 12/21/1834; 7/6/1836.
12 AK to Consul Grüning 9/1837.
13 White 173; AK to Brüninghaus 3/2/1837.
14 Berdrow *Alfred Krupp*, 52, 73, 77, 94.
15 Edmond Taylor 334.
16 AK to *die Firma* 7/8/1838; AK to Hermann 7/27/1838.
17 AK to Hermann 7/27/1838 and 5/13/1839.
18 AK to Hermann 8/12/1838.
19 Ibid.; Mühlen 36; AK to Hermann 9/9/1838.
20 Menne 61–2; Berdrow *Alfred Krupp* 122; AK to Hermann 1/28/1839.
21 AK to Hermann 1/28/1839; Menne 63.
22 Mumm *Meine Erlebnisse zu Pferde,* quoted in Menne 62.
23 AK to Lightbody 1/12/1881; AK to Hermann 1/24–28/1839.
24 AK to Prokura 10/16/1879; AK to Hermann 3/13/1839; WM/Hundhausen; Mühlen 34.
25 AK to Hermann 5/13/1839.
26 Klass 34; AK to Longsdon 11/28/1875.
27 Berdrow *Briefe* 54.
28 Ibid.
29 AK to Ober-Präsident Bodelschwingh-Velmede 12/24/1839; AK to v. Rother, Chef des Seehandlungs-Instituts, 4/5/1845; AK to Richter and Hagdorn 6/10/1848; AK to Tegelstein 9/14/1839.
30 AK to Henniger 2/27/1841 and 4/14/1841; Sölling to AK 2/5/1850; AK to Ascherfeld (n.d.; early 1850's); AK to Jürst 3/27/1851.
31 AK to Sölling 2/18/1846.
32 Berdrow *Briefe* 58.
33 AK to Kübeck 7/16/1842.
34 AK to Kübeck 8/2/1842.
35 AK to Sölling 3/31/1846; Berdrow *Alfred Krupp* 201, 209–11.

36   Fried. Krupp *Krupp* 1812–1912 98, 69–70; TWC IX 469–482.
37   AK to Jürst 9/6/1851 and to Ascherfeld and Gantesweiler 2/9–10/1852; *Times* (London) 2/25/1862; AK to Sölling 10/12/1844.
38   Hermann to AK 1/1/1848.
39   Berdrow *Briefe* 85; Menne 70; Berdrow *Alfred Krupp* 201, 209–11; Menne 71.
40   AK to Hagdorn 3/3/1848; Menne 68.
41   AK to Meyer 4/13/1857; AK to Richter and Hagdorn 6/10/1848.
42   AK to Central-Commission für die Gewerbe-Ausstellung 8/24/1844.

### 3.  DER KANONENKÖNIG

1    Pounds 83; Klass 18–19; WM/ Hundhausen.
2    Fried. Krupp *Krupp* 1812–1912 140; Hermann to AK 1/1/1848.
3    AK to Donat 7/16/1843.
4    Ibid.
5    AK to Sargant Brothers 9/21/1843.
6    AK to Boyen 3/1/44; Boyen to AK 3/23/1844.
7    AK to Rohr 10/23/1847.
8    Klass 40; AK to Artillery Test Commission 9/4/1849.
9    Brodie 109; Millis 81; AK note 12/17 on letter from Meyer 12/15/1878.
10   *Times* (London) 2/28/1862; *Illustrated History* 148.
11   AK to *die Firma* ca. 4/18/1851; AK to Gusstahlfabrik ca. 5/11/1851; AK to Collegium (Board) of *die Firma* 4/13/1851.
12   AK to Collegium 4/13/1851; to *die Firma* 4/18/1851; to Gusstahlfabrik ca. 5/11/1851.
13   *Catalogue of Exhibition* entry 649; *Economist* 8/16/1851; AK to *die Firma* ca. 4/18/1851.
14   *Report of the Juries* (London: 1851) 13; *Observer* 6/15/1851; *Daily News* 6/10/1851; *Illustrated London News* 8/2/1851.
15   *Report of the Juries* 13; *Illustrated London News* 7/26/1851.
16   AK to Pieper 2/23/1869; AK to Jürst 9/6/1850.
17   AK to Jürst 9/6/1851.
18   AK to Jürst 4/25/1853.
19   Young 18; Menne 83–4; Berdrow *Briefe* 136n.
20   Mühlen 54; Klass 50; Mühlen 54ff.

21   Wilmowsky *Der Hügel* 6.
22   Banfield 47–50; Fisher 50–51; Pounds 72–3; AK to Meyer 10/30/1859.
23   Mühlen 55.
24   *Krupp* 1811–1961 38; AK to Haass 1/19/1859; Klass 64; AK to Bertha Krupp (hereinafter Bertha I) dated "Thursday," probably 1861; 6/12/1860; dated "Thursday midday 1 o'clock," probably 1857; dated "Early Monday," probably autumn 1857; dated "Thursday," probably 1861; apparently in Cologne, dated "Tuesday, noon."
25   AK to Bertha I dated "Thursday," probably 1861.
26   AK to Bertha I 6/12/1860.
27   Ibid.; AK to Bertha I dated "Thursday," probably 1861; dated "Wednesday, 5:00," probably autumn 1855.
28   AK to Henniger 2/27/1841.
29   AK to Gusstahlfabrik 1/19/1852; to Ascherfeld 7/1852.
30   Menne 95.
31   Emery in *Living Age*.
32   Mühlen 45; Menne 92.
33   AK to Ascherfeld 7/1852 and undated letter probably 1857.
34   Berdrow *Briefe* 151n; AK to Prokura 4/15/1873.
35   AK to Haass 4/23/1855 and undated letter probably 6/1855.
36   Menne 80; AK to Haass (n.d.) probably 6/1855).
37   Baedeker 33, 70; AK to Haass 2/23/1856.
38   Klass 57.
39   AK to Budde 3/1/1887.
40   AK to Gusstahlfabrik 1/19/1852; *Trade Marks Magazine* no. 6, 6/7/1876.
41   AK to *das Ministerium für Handel, Gewerbe, und öffentliche Arbeiten* 3/3/1853.
42   AK to Heydt 11/12/1853.
43   AK to Meyer 4/13/1857; to Humboldt 1/4/1858; to Heydt 4/7/1858.
44   AK to F. A. Krupp (hereinafter FAK) 2/18/1875; to Jürst 9/6/1851; to Ascherfeld and Gantesweiler 9/10/1852; Klass 59.
45   AK to Voigts-Rhetz 10/13/1859.
46   AK to the Prince Regent 3/8/1860.
47   AK to Meyer 4/13/1857; Schröder "Verzeichnis Alfred Krupp"; AK to Haass 1/19/1859.

48 AK to Geh. Staats- und Kabinettsrat Illaire 10/2/1861.
49 Ibid.
50 Werner Richter 88; AK to Pieper 1/26/1864; Klass 70; Berdrow Briefe 199.
51 AK to Heydt 2/21/1862.
52 Görlitz Generalstab 79, 102–3.
53 Görlitz, Kleine Geschichte 78.
54 Ibid.; Görlitz Generalstab 79, 69
55 AK to Roon 6/1/1860.
56 AK to Crown Prince 10/12/1862.
57 Scott 32.
58 AK to Roon 6/1/1860; to Duke of Cambridge 3/26/1863; to Prokura 5/18–20/1862.
59 Illustrated London News 11/18/1862; Reynold's Newspaper 6/22/1862; Spectator 5/24/1862; Times (London) 2/28/1862.
60 Scott 33, 32; AK to Pieper 2/23/1869.
61 AK to Todleben 5/21/1864.
62 Menne 92–3.

## 4. MORE EFFICIENT THAN BRAND X

1 Klass 66; Mühlen 50; Pounds 78–83.
2 AK to die Firma 3/12/1865.
3 Berdrow Alfred Krupp 73; Baedeker 61; AK to Pieper 1/26/1868.
4 AK to FAK 3/18/1877.
5 AK to die Firma (n.d.; probably 3/1864).
6 Roon to AK 4/9/1866.
7 AK to Roon 4/13/1866.
8 AK to Prokura 5/18 and 20/1866; Roon to AK 5/27/66; Klass 76; AK to Bertha I 5/23/1866.
9 Barail III 64.
10 Voigts-Rhetz to AK 7/9/1866.
11 AK to die Firma 2/3/1867.
12 AK to Roon 7/30/1866.
13 Menne 101; AK to Ernst Eichhoff 12/6/1871; Künster quoted in Klass 80–81.
14 Künster quoted in Klass 80–81.
15 AK to Pieper 11/27/1866 and 1/26/1868; to Prokura 9/13/1867.
16 Klass 112; Krupp in the Service of Engineering Progress 19.
17 AK to Pieper 1/26/1868; to Meyer 6/7/1868; to Pieper 2/4/1868.
18 AK to Pieper 4/8/1867; Berdrow Briefe 181; Les Papiers Secrets 7–14; Baedeker 72.
19 Jérôme Bonaparte quoted in Menne

144; AK to Meyer 6/8/1868; Schröder "Verzeichnis Alfred Krupp."
20 AK to Pieper 2/4/1868.
21 Mühlen 48.
22 Ibid.; AK to Meyer 6/18/1868.
23 Bessemer 130ff.: Howard 5–6; Reybaud in Houille, "L'Usine d'Essen et les Canons Krupp" passim; AK to Roon 12/21/1868.
24 Moltke Militärische Korrespondenz 11.
25 Voigts-Rhetz to AK 11/8/1869.
26 AK to Krausnick 7/4/1870.
27 Berdrow Briefe 187; AK to Pieper 2/29 and 1/26/1864.
28 AK to Pieper 2/29/1864.
29 KFA (see also Klass facing 80); Menne 123; Klass 68, 93.
30 Klass 90.
31 Ibid. 97; NYT 2/18/1951.
32 Klass 94; Werner Richter 157–166 passim.
33 Bismarck-Schönhausen II 96; Howard 54; Klass 93–4; Woischnik 123; Menne 114.

## 5. NOW SEE WHAT HAS DONE OUR ARMY!

1 Howard 55; Gramont 212–23; Allivier XIV 422; Lehautcourt Les Origines 581.
2 Lehmann 25.
3 Howard 77; Horne Paris 38; Schneider II 139; Howard 77; Frederick III (English tr.) 7, 19.
4 Howard 78; Lebrun II 63; Lehautcourt Guerre de 1870–1 II 129; Allivier XIV 100, 451; Horne Paris 42; Millis 213.
5 Brodie 130, 137, 138, 145; Baedecker 75; Lebrun 33–43; Menne 101; Fried. Krupp Krupp 1812–1912 151.
6 Horne Paris 42; Brodie 145; Howard 102; Bonnal 205.
7 Army of France, État Major, Section Historique, La Guerre de 1870–71, publiée par la Revue d'Histoire, rédigé à la Section historique de l'État Major de l'Armée; L'Armée de Châlons III, Docs. annexes 104, 215; Generalstab II 247; Sarazin 53; Howard 214.
8 Machiavelli quoted in Brodie 51; Howard 205; Horne Paris 51.
9 Howard 209; Horne Paris 51; Lebrun 111–12; Sarazin 123; Howard 212.

10  Howard 220; Horne *Paris* 51; Howard 216.
11  Howard 217; Generalstab I ii 402.
12  Ibid. 403.
13  Frederick III 93; Howard 6; Ducrot 51–3.
14  Howard 220, 221.
15  Busch *Bismarck in the Franco-Prussian War* 159; Schneider II 219.
16  Bronsart v. Schellendorff 65.
17  AK to Krausnick 7/4/1870.
18  Menne 113, 114.
19  AK to Roon 7/20/1870.
20  AK to *die Firma* 7/27/1870.
21  Klass 103; Menne 113.
22  Klass 103–4.
23  Voigts-Rhetz to AK 10/5/1870.
24  AK to Roon 11/15/1870; Voigts-Rhetz to AK 10/5/1870.
25  Frederick III 221.
26  Voigts-Rhetz to AK 10/5/1870; AK to Roon 11/15/1870 and 1/2/1871.
27  Howard 120–21.
28  Ibid. 282.
29  Hermann v. Müller passim; Horne *Paris* 62–3.
30  Moltke *Militärische Korrespondenz* 297–8; Baldick 28–9, 30; Horne *Paris* 78.
31  Howard 324–5; Baldick 62–3; Horne *Paris* 86; Baldick 182–3; Horne *Paris* 76, 204; Berdrow *Alfred Krupp* 152; Baldick 186.
32  Horne *Paris* 210, 217.
33  Menne 113–14; Horne *Paris* 129; Baldick 120–21; Mühlen 51; author's own observation of surviving *Ballongeschütz* in East Berlin's historical exhibit in the Zeughaus on Unter den Linden (1963); Frederick III 228; correspondent quoted in Baldick 121; Horne *Paris* 129.
34  Howard 1
35  Russell of *Times* quoted in Horne *Paris* 218; ibid. 165.
36  AK to Longsdon 11/28/1875.
37  Zeughaus, author's observation.
38  Mühlen 67.
39  Menne 114–15; 155; Hallgarten 128; AK to Prokura 7/26/1873; Menne 153; *Vorwärts* 12/4/1915; Menne 156; Berdrow *Alfred Krupp* 292; Mühlen 68; Menne 134.

## 6. DER GROSSE KRUPP

1  Görlitz *Kleine Geschichte* 66.
2  AK note on letter from Meyer 12/17/1878; *American Historical Review* 10/1930, 145.
3  AK note to Meyer letter 12/15/1878; AK to Moltke 4/13/1871.
4  Moltke to AK 4/4/1871; AK to Roon 4/17/1871.
5  Roon to AK 4/22/1871; AK to Wilhelm I 4/23/1871.
6  AK to Voigts-Rhetz 5/1/71; Berdrow *Briefe* 359n.
7  Berdrow *Briefe* 276ff; AK to *die deutschen Kronprinzen* (filed) 1/16/1880; to Prokura 1/14/1872.
8  AK to Loerbroks (Prokura member 1867–77) 9/26/1870; to Voigts-Rhetz 3/2/1872; to Ernst Eichhoff 3/7/1872.
9  Klass 66, 86.
10  Voigts-Rhetz to AK (n.d.) ca. 2/15/1872; AK to Prokura 2/22/1872; AK to Voigts-Rhetz 1/6/1872.
11  AK to Prokura (n.d.) 6/1872; Meyer to Eichhoff 3/1874 quoted in Klass 119–20.
12  Menne 124; Berdrow *Briefe* 291; AK to *die Firma* 10/11/1871.
13  Berdrow *Briefe* 278; AK to Wilhelm I, proposed agenda for audience 7/17/1872; AK *Erlass zur 25 jährigen Wiederkehr des Tages der Besitzübernahme durch Alfred Krupp* (early February 1873) Berdrow *Briefe* 285; AK to Prokura 7/26/1873.
14  Meyer to Eichhoff quoted in Klass 120.
15  AK to FAK 1/27/1875; Klass 205–6.
16  AK to Eichhoff 12/6/1871; to Prokura 10/9/1873; Meyer to Goose 4/6/1877; AK to Prokura 3/30/1874 and 7/16/1874.
17  Berdrow *Briefe* 293; Klass 119, 121.
18  Berdrow *Alfred Krupp* 157–160.
19  WM/ Barbara Krupp; author's observations and *Villa Hügel* passim; Klass 204–5.
20  WM/ Alfried Krupp von Bohlen und Halbach (hereinafter Alfried); *Villa Hügel* passim.
21  WM/ Barbara Krupp.
22  Menne 141–2.
23  Roger Prosser to WM 9/23/63.
24  Scott 13–14.
25  AK *Ansprache an die Angehörigen meiner Gusstahlfabrik und der meiner Firma Fried. Krupp gehörenden Berg-und Hüttenwerke* 2/1887.
26  Kohn in *Saturday Review*.

27  AK *Ansprache* (see note 25).

28  Pounds 108; AK to FAK 3/18/1877; Thompson 277.

29  Klass 169–70; Menne 137.

30  Pounds 130; AK to Meyer 11/7/1873; Ribbeck passim; AK to *die Firma* 6/15/1871; Klass 114; Berdrow *Alfred Krupp* 145–71; *Krupp Past and Present* 41; Hunter in *Review of Reviews*.

31  AK to Prokura 6/22/1873 and 10/16/1879.

32  AK to FAK 1/16/1885; Klass 135; AK to *die Firma* 2/24/1870; to Eichhoff 1/31/1872.

33  AK to FAK 1/16/1885; Alfred Krupp *Generalregulativ für die Firma Fried. Krupp* (Essen: 9/9/1872) *mit einer Vorbemerkung von Ernst Schröder* (Essen: 1961), pars. 11–12, 69–71 inter alia.

34  Alfred Krupp *Generalregulativ* . . .

35  Pounds 81; KFA IV 320 S. 42, 44 (1872); *Hundertjähriges Bestehen* 179–85; Lochner 178.

36  Shirer 96; Noman 169 n. 5; Klass 158; AK to *die Firma* 2/24/1870; Klass 158; AK to FAK 1/16/1885 (also see Menne 150 and Kürenberg 331).

37  Klass 160; AK *An die Arbeiter der Gusstahlfabrik* 6/24/1872.

38  AK *Ein Wort an meine Angehörigen* 2/11/1877.

39  Menne 145; KFA.

40  KFA.

41  Menne 144; Mühlen 62; Klass 205; AK to FAK 1/16/1885.

42  AK to Ascherfeld (n.d.; early 1850's); AK to Prokura 1/28/1874.

43  AK to *die Firma* 10/6/1871; Berdrow *Alfred Krupp* 236.

44  Menne 144; (see also Mühlen 63).

45  AK *An die Arbeiter der Gusstahlfabrik* 6/24/1872.

46  Ibid.

47  AK *Ein Wort an meine Angehörigen* 2/11/1877.

48  Menne 147; AK to Prokura (headed *Zur Aufnahme an Hr. Baedeker. Erklärung*) 9/27/1881.

49  AK *Ansprache* (see note 25).

50  *Berliner Volksblatt* 5/8/1887.

51  Menne 119; see also letters making these threats, e.g., AK to *die Firma* 2/24/1870 and to Eichhoff 1/31/1872.

52  AK to Goose and Erhardt 4/6/1877 (aging rapidly, he merely redrafted an earlier polemic); Menne 148.

53  KFA.


## 7.  THE REST IS GAS

1  Baedeker 308–11

2  Menne 134; Mühlen 70; Berdrow *Alfred Krupp* 114; Tuchman *Tower* 243.

3  Menne 151–2; Baedeker 208–9.

4  Baedeker 208–9; Menne 152; AK to FAK 3/22/1887.

5  AK to Jencke 1/17/1883.

6  Hallgarten 128.

7  Menne 153; AK to FAK and Jencke 12/9/1880; Menne 115, 150; Mühlen 71; Fried. Krupp *Krupp 1812–1912* 248; Menne 170.

8  AK to Prokura 7/26/1873.

9  Klass 151; AK to Voigts-Rhetz 1/6/1872.

10  AK to Prokura 4/15/1873.

11  AK to Prokura 10/1874, 2/23–25/1881.

12  AK note on Meyer letter 12/17/1878; AK to Wilhelm Gross (filed) 1/31/1875.

13  AK to Julius v. Voigts-Rhetz 1/11/1876.

14  AK to Wilhelm I 3/16/76.

15  Transcript of audience: "*Bericht über den Verlauf der Audienz, die S.M. Herrn Krupp am 29. März 1876 von 12½ bis 1 Uhr ertheilt hat* (*Niederschrift des Dr. Pieper*)" KFA passim.

16  Ibid.; AK to Flemming 10/5/1876; Flemming to AK 10/7/1876.

17  AK to Wilhelm I 3/16/1876; Berdrow *Briefe* 376–7.

18  AK to Jencke 9/21/1880; to FAK 9/1/1880.

19  AK to FAK and Jencke 12/9/1880.

20  AK to Moltke 4/13/1871; Klass 155; Menne 138; *Statistische Angaben über die Krupp'sche Gusstahlfabrik*.

21  Klass 155–6; Menne 138–9; Berdrow *Alfred Krupp* 234–6.

22  Klass 156.

23  AK to Goose 11/5/1878; *Fried. Krupp Essen 1811–1946*; Menne 139, 140; Berdrow *Briefe* 362.

24  Berdrow *Alfred Krupp* 300; *Fried. Krupp Essen 1811–1946*.

25  AK to Erhardt 8/25/1877; to Goose 5/11/1877.

26 AK to Prokura 12/7/1873; to Comptoir. — *Canonisches* (gun office) 12/25/1873; to Longsdon 6/12/1880; to *die deutschen Kronprinzen* 1/16/1880.
27 AK to Goose 11/5/1877.
28 AK *Reisebericht über Rücksprache mit österreichischen Marine- und Artillerie-Fachleuten. Einige Bemerkungen.* 5/22/1879.
29 AK to Budde (filed) 6/11/1885.
30 AK to Goose 11/5/1877.
31 AK to Longsdon 1/7/1886.
32 Deichmann 237, 238.
33 Mühlen 72.
34 Klass 192; Mühlen 72; Klass 192; AK to Funke 4/10/1883.
35 AK to Graf v. Schell-Schellenberg 2/7/1886; to Longsdon 4/3/1882; to Lightbody 1/12/1881.
36 AK to Gussmann 5/17/1887; to Prokura 5/10/1887.
37 AK to Longsdon 4/13/1885; to Budde 5/8–9/1881; Berdrow *Briefe* 371; AK to *die Firma* (n.d., probably 8/1881); to Budde 11/24/1882; to Haedenkamp 8/5/1878; Klass 208; Mühlen 73.
38 AK to Jencke 9/17/1884; to Longsdon 4/13 and 5/4/1885, 6/7 and 7/30/86.
39 Klass 209–10; AK to Budde 3/1/1887.
40 AK to Budde 11/24/1882.
41 Ibid.
42 Klass 209; AK to Budde and FAK 2/17/1887.
43 Menne 165–72; Klass 210; *Time* 8/19/1957; obituaries in Paris *Matin, Rheinisch-Westfälische Zeitung, Kölnische Zeitung,* and *Essener General-anzeiger.*
44 Menne 169–70; Baedeker 264; Schröder "Verzeichnis Alfred Krupp."
45 Steiner in *Outlook;* Klass 212; Menne 169.
46 WM/ Schröder.
47 WM observation.

## 8. PRINCE OF THE BLOOD

1 *Essener Volkszig* 11/27/02; Steiner in *Outlook.*
2 "Personal Characteristics of the Late Herr Krupp," *Review of Reviews* 1/1903.
3 *Essener Volkszig* 11/27/02.
4 Berdrow *Alfred Krupp* 115.
5 Klass 138.

6 AK to Pieper 2/29/1864; Klass 142; Bell in *Fortune* 2/1956.
7 AK to *die Firma* 10/11/1871; AK to FAK (filed) 5/29/1874.
8 Klass 148; AK to FAK 12/31/1874 and 2/18/1875.
9 AK to FAK 2/18/1875; to Eichhoff 12/6/1871.
10 Klass 167.
11 Berdrow *Alfred Krupp* 115; Klass 170–1; AK to FAK (filed) 1/16/1885.
12 Klass 143–5; Mühlen 79.
13 AK to FAK 12/22/1874.
14 AK to FAK (filed) 1/26/1875.
15 AK to FAK 12/31/1874.
16 AK to FAK 1/1/1875.
17 AK to FAK (filed) 1/27/1875.
18 AK to FAK 1/26/1875.
19 AK to FAK 1/27/1875.
20 AK to FAK 2/18/1875.
21 KFA.
22 AK to FAK 2/18/1875; Klass 148.
23 Klass 166–7; Berdrow *Briefe* 133n.
24 Margarethe's early years pp. 199–201: Klass 180–94; Menne 174–5; Mühlen 79–80.
25 Deichmann 238.
26 Quoted in Klass 193.
27 Klass 204.
28 AK to Longsdon 4/13/1885.
29 Klass 195.
30 Klass 207; Mühlen 81.
31 Menne 175; *Ludwig Wilhelm Hohenzollern* 69.
32 Mühlen 83.
33 Menne 174; FAK to Bismarck quoted in Klass 229.
34 Klass 223; Haux 38.
35 FAK to Jencke quoted in Klass 222–3.
36 Steiner in *Outlook.*
37 Pounds 125–6; Menne 175–7; *Die Zukunft* (1893) II 91.
38 *Krupp in the Service of Engineering Progress* 33; Mühlen 72; Tuchman *Tower* 235.
39 Pounds 96.
40 *Statistische Angaben über die Krupp'-sche Gusstahlfabrik;* Kellen 4–14, 22.
41 Ibid.
42 Prosser & Sons to Fried. Krupp 1/25/1888.
43 Klass 235.
44 Krupp's imperial audience was entitled "Arbeiterausschüsse und Massnahmen beim Ausbruch des nächsten Streiks" (Workers Committees and Steps to Be Taken at

the Outbreak of the Next Strike): in KFA.

45 Rudolf Martin II 5, 15.
46 Alfred v. Kiderlen-Wächter to Holstein 9/21/1890; quoted in Rich and Fisher *Holstein Papers* III 358.
47 Klass 269.
48 Ibid.
49 Klass 240.

## 9. OSCAR WILDE OF THE SECOND REICH

1 Klass 239–41.
2 Menne 177–8; Brodie 127.
3 Ludwig *Wilhelm Hohenzollern* 294; Edmond Taylor 14.
4 Holstein to Bernhard v. Bülow 5/21/08 quoted in Rich and Fisher *Holstein Papers* IV 529; Klass 275; Bülow 418.
5 *Vorwärts* 8/17/1899.
6 Klass 275–6.
7 Maximilian v. Brandt to Holstein 9/21/00 quoted in Rich and Fisher *Holstein Papers* 203–4.
8 Klass 237.
9 Baedeker 200–202; WM/ Bülow.
10 *Scientific American* 7/15/1893; *Die Grosse Politik der Europäischen Kabinette* XV 4721; *Vorwärts* 1/13/00 and 1/10/01; Tuchman *Tower* 57.
11 Schröder "Verzeichnis Alfred Krupp."
12 Fried. Krupp *Krupp 1812–1912* 366–70; Menne 176–7; Brodie 160; Mühlen 86.
13 Haussner 14, 30–35, 46–47, 51–52, 57, 59, 94–97.
14 Engelbrecht and Hanighen 111; Scott 86–7.
15 Scott 86–7, 150–51.
16 Usher *Pan-Germanism* 1; Tuchman *Tower* 343.
17 *Essener Volkszig* 5/16/ and 6/1/1893; Klass 256.
18 Ibid.
19 Kehr *Schlachtflottenbau* 101, 168–75.
20 Ibid.; Rich and Fisher *Holstein Papers* III 358; IV 51; Kellen 38–42; Menne 179; Fried. Krupp 1811–1946; Edmond Taylor 323; KFA.
21 "Krupps and Kruppdom"; Fischer 7; Menne 184.
22 Klass 267; Berdrow *Alfred Krupp* 281.

23 *Die grosse Politik der Europäischen Kabinette*, IV no. 423; quoted in Tuchman *Tower* 241.
24 *Rheinisch-Westfälische Zeitung* 8/7/06.
25 Recollections of retired Kruppianer; Barbara Krupp's scrapbook (unpublished).
26 Klass 261–2.
27 *Vorwärts* 100 *Jahre SPD* (1963) 59.
28 *Review of Reviews* 1/1893; Klass 263.
29 "Personal Characteristics," *Review of Reviews* 1/1903; (journal) Stammhaus exhibit, Essen.
30 WM/Barbara Krupp; "Personal Characteristics," *Review of Reviews* 1/1903; Klass 275–6.
31 Menne 217–18.
32 Tresckow 114–16; Edmond Taylor 151; Rich and Fisher *Holstein Papers* III 608–15; Baumont *L'affaire*, Tuchman *Tower* 330, 331.
33 Tresckow 126–7.
34 Aldington 112–13, 117, 118, 205; Menen in *Holiday*; Douglas 257; *Die Zukunft* (1902) 41, 333; *Vorwärts* 1/15 and 12/30/02; Tresckow 127–30.
35 Deichmann 289.
36 Mühlen 92.
37 Ibid. 92–3; Menne 225.
38 *Augsburger Postzeitung* 11/8/02.
39 Haux 60–61.
40 *Vorwärts* 11/15/02.
41 *Die Verhandlungen des Deutschen Reichstags* 1/20/03; Klass 282.
42 Klass 282–3.
43 Haux 60–61.
44 *Essener Volkszig* 11/22/02.
45 Ibid.
46 *Der Fall Krupp* 41–52.
47 "Personal Characteristics," *Review of Reviews* 1/1903; Pounds 212; *Pioniere deutscher Technik*.
48 *Essener Volkszig* 11/27/02; Ludwig 294–5.
49 *Vorwärts* 12/16/02; *Die Verhandlungen des Deutschen Reichstags* 11/20/03.
50 Klass 307; personal information.

## 10. CANNON QUEEN

1 WM/ Barbara Krupp.
2 Fried. Krupp *Krupp 1812–1912* 398; Hasse 8; Wilmowsky *Test* 4/1/48 Ntr 5240.
3 Mühlen 97; Baedeker 300–302.

4 Marga's trusteeship pp. 242–245: Baedeker 300–2.
5 Klass 307; WM/ Dohrmann.
6 WM/ Barbara Krupp; Brockdorff quoted in Klass 301.
7 *Major Barbara*, Shaw's complete works (New York: 1962).
8 "Head of the House of Krupp," *Review of Reviews* 10/1910.
9 WM/ Wilmowsky; Pritchett in *Holiday*.
10 Klass 208.
11 WM/Barbara Krupp; Mühlen 116.
12 WM/ Dohrmann.
13 WM/ Sprenger.
14 WM/ Barbara Krupp.
15 Menne 257; *Berliner Tageblatt* 11/16/06; Mühlen 104.
16 Haux 76–7.
17 Hügel exhibit 1963; *Berliner Tageblatt* 11/16/06.
18 Gustav's background pp. 249–251: Baedeker 300–302; Seiss passim; WM/Schultz; Mühlen 103–108; Menne 257–8; Klass 312–14; Young 25–6; WM/Wilmowsky.
19 Wilmowsky *Test* 3/31/48 Ntr 5225, 5164.
20 Klass 321; Edmond Taylor 149; Arendt in *New Yorker* 3/2 and 2/23/63.
21 Mühlen 110; Schröder "Verzeichnis Gustav Krupp."
22 WM/Dohrmann; Klass 325.
23 TWC IX 233–4.
24 Mühlen 110.
25 WM/Berthold.
26 *Krupp* 3/1/42; D-94; TWC IX 264.
27 Wilmowsky *Test* 3/31/48 *Ntr* 5162–5242.
28 Wilmowsky 9–17.
29 Wilmowsky *Test* 3/31/48 *Ntr.* 5177–8, 5224.
30 Ibid.
31 "Herr Krupp in England," *Literary Digest* 9/5/1914.
32 WM/Barbara Krupp, Wilmowsky; 1909 *Chicago Journal* clipping (n.d.); *Chicago Evening American* 12/8/09; *New York Herald* 1/5/10.
33 WM/Barbara Krupp, Wilmowsky; *Chicago Evening American* 12/8/09.
34 *New York Herald* 1/5/10; *Chicago Evening American* 12/8/09; WM/ Barbara Krupp, Wilmowsky.

## 11. A REAL KRUPP

1 Haux persistently pointed out that *die Firma* had been founded in 1811; see Haux 88–90.
2 TWC IX 403–404; Klass 17.
3 Mühlen 109; Klass 323–4; Mühlen 109; WM/Cesarz.
4 Kellen *Die Firma Krupp* 155–68; Düwell 11–18; Hunter in *Review of Reviews*.
5 NCA VI 1044.
6 "Krupps and Kruppdom"; Seldes 17, 19.
7 Fried. Krupp *Krupp 1812–1912* 363, 409; Hasse 9, 12, 30; Edmond Taylor 154; Menne 309; *Vorwärts* 8/2/08.
8 WM/Wilmowsky, Schröder, Hundhausen, Dohrmann, Raussendorf.
9 *Vorwärts* 2/14 and 4/14/11, 2/18/15; Hasse 9; Klass 332; Menne 308–309.
10 "The Krupp Centenary" in *Nation* and *Outlook*.
11 *Outlook* 9/14/12.
12 *Hundertjähriges Bestehen* passim.
13 *Krupp 1812–1912* (Jubiläumswerk); "The Krupps" in *Life*.
14 Haux 88–90; *Hundertjähriges Bestehen* 179–85.
15 Klass 336; Young 32.
16 Mühlen 112; Young 33; Klass 336.
17 Bell in *Fortune* 2/1956; Menne 258; Klass 325; WM/Dohrmann.
18 Young 29; WM/Alfried; Mühlen 173; WM/Harald, Berthold.
19 Edmond Taylor 159; *Krupp Past and Present* 37; Seldes 59; D-191; Seldes 20; Carnegie 6; Ruth Fischer 23.
20 *Berliner Tageblatt* 5/20/13; Hallgarten 187; Taylor *Sword and Swastika* (hereinafter Taylor) 465; Wile 152.
21 Maitrot 20–22.
22 *Vorwärts* 3/26/13; Hallgarten 267.
23 I. F. Clark "The Shape of Wars to Come" in *History Today* 2/1965.
24 Fried. *Krupp Essen 1811–1946*; Mühlen 107; Menne 211–12; Fried. Krupp *Krupp 1812–1912* 196–7; Menne 238.
25 Mühlen 108; Lochner 36; Borkin and Welsh 73; *Vorwärts* 10/13/05; Seldes 37.
26 *Die Zukunft* (1908) 241; Fried. Krupp *Krupp 1812–1912* 357–8; "Krupps and Kruppdom"; *Die Verhandlungen des Deutschen Reichstags* 3/1-21/01; WM/Menne.
27 Haux 102–105.
28 *Skandal* pp. 278–280: *Die Verhandlungen des Deutschen Reichstags* 4/18-26/13; *Vorwärts* files 1913 passim, Menne 277–9; Haux 102–

105; Klass 337–41; Seldes 340–41; Usher in *Nation;* "Verdict in Krupp Scandal," *Literary Digest* 12/6/13.
29 Schröder "Verzeichnis Gustav Krupp."
30 Taylor *March of Conquest* 206.
31 Görlitz *Kleine Geschichte* 145; Kuhl 174.
32 Tuchman *August* 163–4; Menne 303; Fried. *Krupp 1811–1946;* Klass 345–6; Henschen in *Forum.*
33 "Austria's Famous 'Skoda' Mortars," *Scientific American* 7/3/15.
34 Fischer 55, 59.
35 Klass 345; *Villa Hügel* 18; Klass 346; Taylor 95.
36 Klass 346; Taylor 95.
37 "Herr Krupp in England"; Seldes 65; Tuchman *August* 102.
38 Menne 309.
39 *Rheinisch–Westfälische Zeitung* 12/11/33.


12. THE LAST LOVE BATTLE

1 Menne 314.
2 Moltke *Erinnerungen-Briefe-Dokumente* 24; Mühlon 70.
3 Schindler passim; Tuchman *August* 501.
4 Schindler passim.
5 Ludendorff *Meine Kriegserinnerungen* 31.
6 Ibid. quoted in Brodie 9; quoted in Tuchman *August* 92.
7 Demblon 110–111.
8 Schröder "Verzeichnis Gustav Krupp"; Menne 315.
9 Klass 347; *American Heritage* 6/1955.
10 Boelcke 147ff.
11 Ibid.
12 *Kammerdebatte Journal officiel* 1/24/19; *Vörwarts* 6/21/15. General descriptions of the conflict pp. 292–314 are from WM "The First World War," *Holiday* 11/62.
13 Klass 349; Fried. *Krupp Essen 1811–1946.*
14 Klass 344.
15 *Fortune* 2/1956; *Literary Digest* 4/12/19; Menne 314; Klass 347; Mühlen 120; Horne *Glory* 42, 247.
16 *Berliner Tageblatt* 6/6/16; Lehmann–Russbüldt 27; *Vorwärts* 100 *Jahre SPD* (1963) 59.
17 Menne 316; *Vorwärts* 4/27/15; *Times* (London) 5/5/15.
18 Goodspeed 196; WM/Wilmowsky.
19 Ludendorff 216.
20 Graves 318; Wolff 10.

21 Liddell Hart 42.
22 Graves 125; Liddell Hart 74; Wolff 35; Liddell Hart 73, 246.
23 Slossen 72.
24 Wolff 261; Graves 236.
25 Graves 298–9; 311; Siegfried Sassoon, "Suicide in the Trenches," *Counter-Attack and Other Poems.* New York: 1918.
26 Fitzgerald *Tender Is the Night* ch. 13.
27 Klass 355.
28 Crutwell 384–5.
29 Metcalf 489; NYT 6/8/59, 6/8/18.
30 Ludendorff 547.
31 Ibid.
32 Klass 417–18.
33 The Paris gun pp. 305–306: Paxton 381–2; Fried. *Krupp Essen 1811–1946;* Menne 328–9; Eisgruber passim.
34 Mühlen 120; Menne 329; Klass 356.
35 Haux 116–17.
36 Ernst Schröder "Verlauf des letzten Kaiserbesuchs."
37 Haux 116–17.
38 Kaiser's speech pp. 308–309: *Essener Volkszeitung* 9/11/18.
39 WM/Menne.
40 Mühlen 119; TWC IX 64, 267; Taylor 20, 43; *Literary Digest* 4/12/19.
41 Klass 363, "Krupps and Kruppdom."
42 Liddell Hart 259.
43 *Stars and Stripes* 11/8/18.
44 Liddell Hart 266; Churchill *World Crisis* (hereinafter Churchill) III 538.
45 Goodspeed 273.
46 Churchill III 541.
47 Wolff 272; "As the Guns Fell Silent," NYT *Magazine* 11/9/58.
48 Goodspeed 280; Görlitz *Kleine Geschichte* 220–21.
49 Hitler 224–5.
50 Menne 333.
51 Klass 358.
52 Haux 118–20.
53 TWC IX 258.


13. THE GROANING LAND

1 NYT 1/18/19, 1/20/19; Ruth Fischer 87; Ludwig 509.
2 Mühlen 122; Klass 368.
3 Klass 322; Mühlen 123.
4 Ibid.
5 Menne 339.
6 Scott 137.
7 Klass 382.

8   Ibid. 366; Fuchs 85–6; *Steel* 4/1958; *Fried. Krupp Essen 1811–1946;* "From Swords to Plowshares," *Scientific American* 9/3/21; *Pioniere deutscher Technik.*
9   *NYT* 1920: 3/20–22, 24–26, 31; 4/5, 8, 14.
10   *NYT* 4/7, 8/20.
11   *NYT* 3/21/20; WM/Dohrmann; Haux 126–9.
12   NIK-12074.
13   TWC IX 66.
14   *Fortune* 2/1956; NCA VI 1031; *NYT* 3/26/20; Mühlen 125.
15   NCA VI 1031.
16   *NYT* 6/22/20; WM/Schultz.
17   Haux 107.
18   Young 36; Mühlen 173, 174.
19   WM/Harald, Berthold.
20   WM/Berthold; Thayer 96.
21   *Test Wilmowsky Ntr* 5162–5242; *Living Age* 12/12/25; WM/Wilmowsky; *Der Spiegel* 6/5/63; Wilmowsky 178–81.
22   Pounds 250–51.
23   Easter Saturday massacre pp. 330–334: *NYT* 4/1, 2, 5/23; *Süddeutsche Monatshefte* (Munich) 6/23; Raphael *Krupp* 121–2; Ruth Fischer 257; *Essener Allgemeine Zeitung* 3/30/38.
24   WM/Alfried.
26   *NYT* 4/1/23.
25   Ruth Fischer 258.
27   WM/Deichmann, Frisch, Gregorius, Heyder, Menne, Tubbesing; *NYT* 4/3/23.
28   *NYT* 4/2/23; *Living Age* 6/19/23.
29   *NYT* 4/10/23; Ruth Fischer 258.
30   *NYT* 4/10, 11/23.
31   *NYT* 4/11/23.
32   Heinrich Grüber "Zwischen Thron und Altar" in *Freitag* 8/7/64 *NYT* 4/3/23; Klass 373.
33   *Living Age* 6/19/23.
34   Ibid.; Ruth Fischer 258; *NYT* 5/10/23; WM/Menne; Wilmowsky 166.
35   KFA; Raphael *Krupp* 117–18, 123; Raphael *Stinnes* 110–111; Alfred Baedeker 210.
36   *Current Opinion* 4/1923.
37   Wilmowsky 166; Weymar 69–71.
38   *Living Age* 12/12/25; Wilmowsky 180; *Der Spiegel* 6/5/63.
39   *Fried. Krupp Essen 1811–1946; Krupp heute-Menschen und Werk* TWC IX 309; *Metlfax Magazine* 5/1961.
40   Martin in *Nation.*

41   Haux 136; WM/Sabel; Wilmowsky 165.
42   *Die deutsche Schwereisenindustrie* 32; Klass 391.
43   Scott 151; Lehmann-Russbüldt 50.
44   Raphael *Stinnes* 110–111; Menne 348.
45   NIK-12114.
46   NIK-8575; *NYT* 2/18/51.
47   Klass 20.

14.   WE'VE HIRED HITLER!

1   TWC IX 76.
2   TWC IX 263–4, NCA 1031; *Krupp Nachrichten* 4/5/51; *Erinnerungen an Herrn Gustav Krupp v. Bohlen und Halbach* (n.d.); NI-764.
3   Ibid.
4   NIK-12114, -7352; D-94; NIK-9041.
5   D-94; *Christian Science Monitor (Current Opinion)* 6/21; *Manchester Guardian (Literary Digest)* 2/28/20; *Review of Reviews* 9/1928; *Living Age* 1/1/27; *Scientific American* 5/1922; *Living Age* 1/1/27; *Literary Digest* 4/12/19.
6   Young 43; Taylor 43.
7   WM/Tubbesing; Taylor 45; TWC IX 74; D-94; NIK-12057.
8   Taylor 84.
9   Shirer 282; Borkin and Welsh 255–6; Taylor 50.
10   Quoted in Borkin and Welsh 256.
11   Taylor 37–8; Raphael *Krupp* 115; *Vorwärts* 10/23 and 11/5/20; Edmond Taylor 258.
12   WM/Tubbesing.
13   TWC IX 76–7; NIK-9041; WM/Tubbesing; TWC IX 86n., 77; Taylor 44–5.
14   Taylor 93; NIK-12315.
15   NIK-1284.
16   NIK-9041.
17   TWC IX 272–3, 279; Menne 353.
18   NIK-9041; TWC IX 44; Rikstag report 4/3/35, *Neue Zürcher Zeitung* 4/6/35; *Berner Tagwacht* 4/5/35.
19   Menne 351ff.; *Het Volk* 11/6, 13/30.
20   C-156; NIK-12294; TWC IX 292n.
21   TWC IX 289; C-156.
22   NIK-9041.
23   TWC IX 283; NIK-10499 (TWC IX 128).
24   WM/Wilmowsky.
25   TWC IX 12, 281–2.
26   D-168; Gustav Krupp von Bohlen in *Review of Reviews.*

27 NIK-9041, -11775.
28 Haux 138; WM/Hansen; *Villa Hügel* 11; WM/Dohrmann.
29 WM/Alfried; Gustav Krupp von Bohlen in *Review of Reviews.*
30 WM/Dohrmann, Tubbesing, Bülow.
31 Lochner 32; Taylor 98, 60.
32 Taylor 120; Bernstein 62.
33 TWC IX 210; Wilmowsky *Test Ntr* 5179.
34 *Hearings, Special Committee Investigating the Munitions Industry, U.S. Senate, 73d Congress, Report No. 944,* Part 3 (Washington:1934) 270; Lochner 41; Klass 414.
35 Shirer 172, 178; Taylor 66; NI-6522.
36 Berndorff 220–22.
37 Lochner 25–6; 3901-PS translated NCA VI 796–7.
38 Thyssen 107; Shirer 179.
39 Lochner 137.
40 D-201 (NCA VI 1080).
41 TWC VI 12–13; D-203 (NCA VI 1080–85).
42 D-204 (NCA VI 1085); NI-406 (Farben case); NI-910; D-203 (NCA VI 1080–85); 3725-PS (NCA VI 465).
43 Schweitzer *Big Business* 106; 2001-PS (NCA IV 638–9); Hans Buchheim to WM 4/18/63.
44 TWC IX 82.

15. THE FÜHRER IS ALWAYS RIGHT

1 WM/Bülow, Berthold.
2 Krupp to Hitler NI-910, -904.
3 Krupp to Hitler D-157.
4 Mühlen 153–4; Lochner 166.
5 Shirer 283.
6 Krupp to Springorum 4/26/33 D-208 (NCA VI 1088); Borkin and Welsh 258; Krupp to Schacht 5/29/33, 5/30/33 (NCA VI 1060), TWC IX 344–5; D-151 (Prosecution Exhibit 211D); Schweitzer 521–3; NCA IV 465.
7 Krupp to Hitler 1/2/36 NI-312.
8 Krupp to Grossadmiral Erich Raeder 8/10/35 D-88; Young 46; Schweitzer 592; Bernstein 47.
9 Thyssen 108.
10 WM/Wilmowsky; Wilmowsky *Test Ntr* 5185, 5200; Wilmowsky 169.
11 Lochner 169.
12 Krupp D-62.
13 2950-PS (NCA V 654–5); *Rheinisch-Westfälische Zeitung* 1/27/34,

1/26/35; TWC VI 22; WM/Winkelmann (Kaiserhof manager); WM/Deichmann.
14 Menne 368–9.
15 WM/Dohrmann, Winkelmann; Mühlen 159–60; WM/Berthold.
16 Klass 417; Schweitzer 246.
17 Menne 365; Mühlen 159; Menne 366; TWC IX 265–6; Menne 365.
18 *Berliner Börsen-Zeitung* 12/21/34.
19 Schweitzer 51, 308–309; *Börsen- und Wirtschaftskalender* ( Frankfurt: 1934); *Wehrwirtschaft- und Rüstungsstab* (German War Ministry microfilm) 5.203, roll 35, T-77.
20 NI-910; *Effects of Stategic Bombing* 247.
21 EC 177 (NCA VII 333); C-189 (NCA I 431).
22 Menne 366; *Neue Weltbühne* (1933), 948, 986; *Effects of Strategic Bombing* 247; TWC IX 89.
23 Haux 138.
24 *Rheinisch-Westfälische Zeitung* 1/27/34, 1/26/36; *Deutsche Allgemeine Zeitung* 1/25/36; NCA I 89; TWC IX 85; Schweitzer 398; Edmond Taylor 393; Schweitzer 333; TWC IX 128; NCA I 89.
25 TWC IX 42.
26 C-156.
27 Shirer 284; Shirer *Berlin Diary* 31–3.
28 NIK-9041; Klass 425; WM/Bülow.
29 Klass 426–7.
30 *Test* 6/30/48 *Ntr* 13215–20.
31 NCA I 88–9.
32 TWC IX 16, 96, 99; Young 48.
33 *Military Tribunals Case No. 10* (hereinafter Case No. 10) 7–8.
34 NIK-11625; TWC IX 22.
35 Schmidt 320; TWC IX 128.
36 Young 47; D-94, Menne 373.
37 Lochner 123–4.
38 TWC IX 22.
39 NCA I 88–9; *Case No. 10* 11; TWC IX 44–5.
40 Raeder to Krupp 8/7/35 NCA VI 1042–3; Krupp to Raeder 8/10/35 NCA VI 1043; Goebbels *Diaries* 19.
41 NIK-12074; D-63.
42 Krupp to Bormann (n.d.) quoted in Young 48.
43 *Krupp Nachrichten* 5/15/39.
44 Klass 428.
45 Lochner 208; TWC IX 1447; DE-2767.
46 TMWC XVIII 508.
47 Ibid.; *Weihe der neuen Synagogue Essen* 14–19.

48 Wilmowsky to Krupp 2/5/37 (handwritten) NIK-8700.
49 *Akten zur Deutschen Auswärtigen Politik* (Baden-Baden: starting 1953), Series D I, No. 152.
50 Keppler to Wilmowsky 4/1–2/38 NI-766; Olscher to Heller 5/4/38 NIK-11183; Krupp to Löser 6/19/38 Löser Doc. 26; Löser to Krupp 6/24/38 NIK-8438.
51 Berdrow, *Alfred Krupp und die Familie* 310; NIK-12076, -12074.
52 *Fried. Krupp Essen 1811–1946.*
53 TWC IX 11; Pounds 197; *Case No. 10* 5; Berlin Document Center Reichswirtschaftministerium, box 391, folder 564.
54 NCA VI 89; "Aufwand und Ertrag" in *Wirtschaft und Statistik* 576–7.
55 Young 53.
56 WM/Wilmowsky; Wilmowsky 225–7.
57 Wilmowsky *Test Ntr* 5202, 5237–8; Dulles 181; WM/Löser.

16. IT IS AN HONOR
TO BE AN SS MAN

NOTE: Much of the material on Alfried Krupp is based on the author's observations while Alfried was alive.
1 McCloy to Javits *Congressional Record* 5/10/51, A2812.
2 Personal information; Arendt *Eichmann in Jerusalem* 31; Buchheim to WM 4/18/63; Buchheim 350–51.
3 NIK-12074.
4 WM/Ahlefeldt-Lauruiz (hereinafter Lauruiz).
5 WM/Berthold, Lauruiz, Hosmann.
6 *Buenos Aires Freie Presse* 5/25/63; WM/Lauruiz.
7 *Life* 5/10/54.
8 WM/Sprenger.
9 Mandellaub to WM 8/28/63.
10 Wittkamp in *Krupp Mitteilungen* 186.
11 WM/Hengsbach; Hügel Exhibit 11/17/61.
12 NIK-12074 II; *Financial Times* 3/31/62; WM/Sabel.
13 Mühlen 207; NIK-12074 IV.
14 WM/Berthold.
15 WM/Schröder; NIK-12074 I.
16 NIK-12074 IX; Mandellaub to WM 8/28/63; Young 38.
17 *Fortune* 2/56; Mühlen 174; WM/Schröder; NIK-12074 I.
18 NIK-12074 I; Mühlen 179; *Der Spiegel* 6/5/63; Mühlen 260; WM/

Hosmann; Wilmowsky *Test* 3/1/48 *Ntr* 5177; *National Observer* 3/4/63.
19 *Fortune* 2/56; WM/Lauruiz.
20 Bernstein 63–4; NCA I 88–9; *Case No. 10* 10–11; TWC IX 18; Morgenthau 39.
21 TMWC 402–13.
22 NIK-11625, -11619, -11626 (memo of 8/22/39).
23 NIK-10336; Taylor *Conquest* 158.
24 Goebbels *Diaries* 323.
25 Schacht *Test* TMWC XII 531; WM/Bülow.
26 Young 49–50.
27 Shirer 610.
28 Wilmowsky *Test Ntr* 5169–70.
29 Young 54; *Fried. Krupp Essen 1811–1946*; NI-764 (Krupp memo 7/16/40); NIK-1049 (Krupp memo 2/9/42).
30 Young 54–5.
31 WM/Schürmann; Young 55.
32 *Ntr* 5169–70; WM/Wilmowsky; Wilmowsky 223–4.
33 TWC VI 99.
34 Taylor *Conquest* 116; Shirer 702–703.
35 TWC VI 18; D-168.
36 NIK-13330, -13383, -13243, -13156, -13159, -13158.
37 NIK-12074 I.
38 NIK-12630.
39 NIK-6472.
40 WM/Berthold; D-66 (NCA VI 1034); Mühlen 160.
41 Klass 432; personal information.

17. CRIER HAVOT!

1 Shirer 723; Churchill to General Ismay 5/18/40, Churchill *Finest Hour* 55.
2 Shirer 746; Rümann *Test* 1/23/48 *Ntr* 2058–4.
3 Rümann *Test* 1/23/48 *Ntr* 2058–84.
4 Ibid.
5 NI-048; TMWC IX 633; TWC IX 105; EC-137 (NCA VII 309); NIK-3990.
6 TWC IX 106–108, 1370; *Case No. 10* 20.
7 NIK-12074 VI; TWC IX 107, 115, 1362; Young 56.
8 TWC VI 826; TWC IX 114–15.
9 TWC IX 107.
10 Shirer 943; TWC IX 1372.
11 James Brown Scott passim; *U.S. Technical Manual* 27–251, *Treaties* 31–5; TWC IX 1341; *Financial Times* 7/15/43; NIK-13025.

12 Moorehead *Eclipse* 161; J. Schröder *Test Ntr* 6106–6249; TWC IX 569, 574, 1351; WM's observation; NIK-7012, -7206; Alfried's affidavit 5/3/47 (NIK-10332); NIK-13018.

13 NIK-10497.

14 Rothschild narrative pp. 421–426: Celap affidavit (NIK-10590); Celap *Test* 1/26–27/48 *Ntr* 2398–2438; NIK-10587, -8011, D-526, NIK-13002, -13018, -12999, DE-425, NIK-10485, DE-426, NIK-7025, -7012, -7017, -7023, DE-427.

15 NIK-13018.

16 Johannes Schröder to Habermaas 11/16/43 (NIK-7025).

17 NIK-7012.

18 Arendt in *New Yorker* 3/9/63.

19 Photostat of Rothschild's letter, certified by Celap 7/24/47; Rothschild's widow has original (TWC IX 510).

20 Reitlinger 75, 310, 312, 319, 325–6.

21 Alsthom Société pp. 427–428: Koch *Test* 1/22/48 *Ntr* 2110–48; Erich Thiess *Test* 4/30/48, 5/1/48 *Ntr* 6407–65; NIK-13448, DE-1, NIK-6547, -6549, -13447, -6552, -13450, -6556, DS-126, NIK-6557, -6560, -13451.

22 TWC IX 651.

23 NIK-6476.

24 Ehmag pp. 427–429: Kurt Biegi *Test* 4/29/48 *Ntr* 6251–92; DE-448, NIK-6268, DE-2456, NIK-6254, DE-449, NI-2884, NIK-6258, -8908, DE-479, -481, -480, -483, -482, NIK-6273, -10804, DE-438.

25 IMT *Test* Birger Dahlerus 3/18/46 quoted in Shirer 517n; Schröder *Test* 4/27–29/48 *Ntr* 6106–6249 TWC IX 1391.

26 3/1/43 secret contract (NIK-6254); NIK-6268.

27 NIK-15403; NIK-12380, -8911, -11914.

28 TWC IX 1355.

29 WM/Alfried.

30 NIK-13222, -13156, -13159, -13158, -13383, -12908, -5997.

31 NIK-12908, -8068, -8066, -12908; TWC IX 1461–4; NIK-7441.

32 Descriptions of Russo-German war pp. 431–444 based on Clark *Barbarossa*, Werth *Russia at War*, Dallin *German Rule in Russia 1941–1945*, Erikson *The Soviet High Command*, and Allen and Muratoff *The Russian Campaigns of 1941–1943 and 1944–1945*.

33 Halder affidavit 11/22/45 NCA VIII 645–56; TMWC 240–41.

34 Clark 349; TWC IX 1472.

35 Werth 215; *Sunday Times* quoted in Werth 213.

36 NIK-3895, -13228, -13994; *Case No. 10 21*; TWC IX 1473.

37 TWC IX 1480; NIK-13971; Dallin 385; Young 57; Dallin 407; NI-4332; NIK-12848; WM/Holbrecker; *Fortune* 2/1956.

38 Werth 7, 613.

39 Dallin 123; Sauckel *Ausführung des Generalbevollmächtigten für den Arbeitereinsatz* 2/5–6/43, 1739-PS TMWC XXVII 586–7; OKW/Gen Ou *Arbeit Erfassung im Osten* 7/13/43 E4–1 YOVO.

40 Clark 350.

41 TWC IX 42.

42 TWC IX 90–91; *Fortune* 2/1956; Mühlen 161; Young 59–60; TWC IX 11–12; Gustav to Hitler 7/24/42.

43 TWC IX 91.

44 Werth 8–9.

45 *Pravda* 2/6/39.

46 Ogorkiewicz chapter "Organization of German Armored Forces."

47 Guderian 299ff.

48 Ibid.; Dugan and Stewart 32.

49 Görlitz *Paulus* 288.

50 Werth 682, 681.

51 Ibid. 682–3, 684.

52 Ibid. 618.

53 NI-2959; TWC IX 1480; NI-2959.

54 TWC IX 1483; *Case No. 10 21*.

55 WM/Alfried.

## 18. ALFRIED COMMANDS THE KRUPPBUNKER

1 WM/Kranzbühler.

2 WM/Bülow; Young 71–2.

3 WM/Dohrmann; Klass 435.

4 WM/Bülow; Young 72; WM/Wilmowsky, Bülow, Hardach; Lochner 209–10.

5 D-94.

6 SB *Gusstahlfabrik Friedrich Krupp, Essen*, Appendix II, i; WM/Hundhausen; *Villa Hügel* 24.

7 WM/Berthold, Hobrecker.

8 WM/Berthold, Harald.

9 WM/Kranzbühler, Hosmann; NIK-12074 VI.

10 Goebbels *Diaries* 323 (entry for 4/10/43).

11 *Ntr* 13215–20 (6/30/48).

12 Saur *Test* 6/8/48 *Ntr* 11798–11869.

13 Wilmowsky *Warum wurde Krupp* 175–6.

14 NIK-11231, -7025.
15 TMWC I 232; Albert Schrödter Test 1/29-30/48 Ntr 2678-2709, 2723-67.
16 TMWC I 232; NIK-9301; D-288 (NCA VII 2-7).
17 Krupp affidavit 6/26/47 NIK-11231; WM/Alfried, Berthold; NIK-11231; TWC IX 806.
18 Löser affidavit 4/28/47 NIK-8283; Krupp affidavit 6/28/48 NIK-11231.
19 NIK-8283; WM/Berthold.
20 WM/Löser.
21 Lochner 175; Rothfels 96; Dulles 124-46.
22 WM/Sabel; Dulles 145; TWC IX 41.
23 Klass 434.
24 Gustav to Bormann 11/11/42 D-99 (TWC IX 348-50).
25 Bormann to Gustav 12/21/42 D-103.
26 Gustav to Bormann 1/9/43; Young 62-3.
27 Werth 535-6.
28 Gustav to Bormann 2/24/43; D-106.
29 Reichsgesetzblatt 11/20/43; 1387-PS; TWC IX 351-2.
30 Young 63.
31 Gustav and Bertha Krupp to Hitler 12/29/43 D-135.
32 Ibid.
33 WM/Schröder, NCA I 89.
34 NIK-9294.
35 Alfried Krupp to die Firma 1/11/44; Young 66.
36 Krupp Mitteilungen 8/1957, issues of Unser Profil, etc.
37 WM/Krupp's legal staff.
38 Trevor-Roper 94.
39 TWC IX 21; SB Gusstahlfabrik Friedrich Krupp, Essen 8.
40 WM/Dohrmann; Villa Hügel 21; WM/Dohrmann.
41 WM/Hardach, Hansen, Meininghaus, Hobrecker.
42 Fried. Krupp Essen 1811-1946; Krupp in the Service of Engineering Progress; "Catchwords about the Essener Hof" (unpublished memorandum, 1963).
43 WM/Tubbesing; SB Gusstahlfabrik Friedrich Krupp, Essen 8, 9.
44 Goebbels Diaries 297, 312, 351, 417 (each entry is headed Die Lage—the situation).
45 WM/Come; Alfred Schilf 3/22/48 Ntr 4761-74 (TWC IX 171-2); Goebbels Diaries 321-2.
46 Goebbels Diaries 321-2; Fortune 2/1956.

47 D-202.
48 Fuller 228; Hansard House of Commons Debates vol. 380 p. 55 col. 553; Churchill to Stalin 4/6/43 Hinge of Fate 756.
49 Harris 77, 88; Pounds 223; SB European War quoted in Fuller 229.
50 Shirer Berlin Diary 347, 406.
51 Die Welt 5/15 and 6/8/63; Scott 280.
52 Harris 77-8; Fuller 229; see also The Times (London) 6/25/43.
53 Harris 78-9; Fuller 229.
54 SB Rheinhausen 1.
55 SB Grusonwerke 5; SB Borbeck 1; SB Rheinhausen 3; SB Gusstahlfabrik Friedrich Krupp, Essen 8, 2, 3.
56 Fortune 2/1956; Fried. Krupp Essen 1811-1946 13; Life 5/23/60; Klass 436; Pounds 223-34; SB Gusstahlfabrik (Exhibit E); Wilmot 554.
57 SB Gusstahlfabrik 20, 19.
58 White 177-8.
59 Ibid. 178.
60 Fuller 405; Wilmot 553; Liddell Hart quoted in Fuller 406; Harris 177; Fuller 405.
61 Arendt in New Yorker 3/2/63.
62 Personal information.

## 19. WHO ARE ALL THESE PEOPLE?

1 Young 73; WM/Dohrmann.
2 WM/Wilmowsky.
3 NIK-11972.
4 Test Josef Borchmeyer 5/11/48 Ntr 7251-7331.
5 Test Sossin-Arbatoff 5/5/48 Ntr 6711-78.
6 Ibid.
7 Test 1/2-3/48 Ntr 2968-3012; Mühlen 164.
8 NIK-13090.
9 Klass 435; WM/Elizabeth Roth.
10 Führer conference 3/13/43; NIK-4723; WM/Elizabeth Roth.
11 Test 5/27/48 Ntr 9983-10022.
12 Müller affidavit 7/1/47 NIK-11803.
13 Krupp to tribunal 6/30/48 Ntr 13215-20 (TWC IX 1326).
14 Saur Test 6/8/48 Ntr 11798-11869.
15 See also Annex to Hague Convention No. IV 10/18/07 (36 Stat. 2277; Treaty Series No. 539; Malloy Treaties II 2269) as cited in U.S. Technical Manual 27-251, Article 52, 33.
16 Arendt Eichmann in Jerusalem 85.
17 DE-971; file note of 8/14/42 D-348.

18  NIK-15513.
19  720-PS TMWC XXVI 266–72, NCA III 524–6.
20  NIK-8485.
21  NIK-1504; K1 48, Ferencz 9.
22  NIK-5860.
23  NIK-2868.
24  NIK-3754, -4728.
25  NIK-6565; NI-034, PS-3868.
26  NIK-4728; NIK-11977, -2877.
27  Lutat Test 2/16–17/48 Ntr 4122–37; NIK-11674; Ortmann Test 2/25/48 Ntr 4654–83.
28  NIK-11975, Artman Test 4671.
29  NIK-12431.
30  NIK-7269.
31  NIK-13173, -14204; Ntr 18–113 (12/8/45); TWC IX 115.
32  Davidson 7; NIK-12334.
33  NIK-8981; Ferencz 28.
34  TWC IX 116, 1409; D-274; TWC IX 1409.
35  NIK-10214.
36  Führer Test 5/17–18/48 Ntr 8277–8328 (TWC IX 1107).
37  Come 1.
38  D-399.
39  NIK-7440, -89890.
40  NIK-6405; DE-1572; NIK-15402.
41  DE-1272; TWC IX 1399.
42  NIK-11233; TWC IX 119.
43  DE-1362; Test 5/22–24/48 Ntr 9156–9210, 9301–16; DE-1363; Gestapo report DE-2999.
44  Bülow 1/11/44 letter NIK-15376; DE-2999; NIK-15383.
45  Führer Test 5/17–18/48 Ntr 8277–8328 (TWC IX 1107).

## 20.  THE GODS THEMSELVES STRUGGLE IN VAIN

1  Test 5/11/48 Ntr 7334–75; NIK-12356.
2  Speer report on conferences with Hitler 3/21–22/42 DE-1580; 1519-PS TWMC XXVII 273–83; Himmler decree of 4/25/42 TWC IX 1407; Opinion and Judgment of Military Tribunal III 7/31/48 Ntr 13231–13402 TWC IX 1407.
3  WM/Sprecher.
4  Reichsjugendführer passim.
5  NG 848 Institut für Zeitgeschichte (Munich); NIK-6115.
6  NIK-9301; NIK-9206; Tribunal Judgment TWC IX 1405.
7  Klass 435; TMWC XVI 546; NIK-9803.
8  Klass 436.

9  Lauffer affidavit 3/5/48 DE-1828; Tribunal Judgment TWC IX 1402; DE-2992 (TWC IX 1235).
10  WM/Elizabeth Roth; NIK-11728.
11  NIK-13364; NIK-11231; NIK-7454, -9034.
12  NIK-12361.
13  Ibid.; N-1394.
14  DE-1158 (TWC IX 1231–32); TWC IX 1394; DE-1146; NIK-10214.
15  Marquardt Test 5/12–13/48 Ntr 7511–31, 7638–7700.
16  Tribunal Judgment TWC IX 1394.
17  D-335.
18  Toland 419; Schiller Die Jungfrau von Orleans vi, 28.
19  TMWC III 432, 549; Buchheim et al. II, 92–3; see also Davidson 495.
20  Goebbels Diaries 325; TWC VII 58; TMWC XXXVI 32.
21  Krupp affidavit 7/3/47 NIK-11231; D-318; Tribunal Judgment TWC IX 1386; NIK-11231.
22  TMWC XV Sauckel 47, 268; NIK-3991.
23  D-310.
24  D-297; TMWC XV Sauckel 47, 268; Test Hermann Lux 5/27–28/48 Ntr 10277; NIK-7014.
25  Test Scholtens 2/10/48 Ntr 3616–27; WM/Come; D-164.
26  NIK-10753; D-319; Tribunal Judgment TWC IX 1408; Marquardt Test Ntr 7531; Geulen Test 5/25/48 Ntr 9548–62.
27  NIK-12359.
28  NIK-12358.
29  D-283.
30  Rohlfs narrative DE-1023; Rohlfs Test 5/19/48 Ntr 8551–73.
31  Schosow narrative NIK-4378.
32  NIK-11423, -8765, -10214.
33  D-144.
34  DE-1363; Adolf Trockel Test 5/13/48, 5/21/48 Ntr 7715; Maria Hermanns Test 5/12/48 Ntr 7561, 7571; NIK-8766, -3731.
35  DE-1363; D-144; Marquardt Test Ntr 7675, 7649, 7670.
36  NIK-13867; Josef Lorenz Test 5/19–20/48, 6/12/48 Ntr 8480–96, 8576–8632, 12384–12407.
37  Borschmeyer Test 5/10–11/48 Ntr 7221–47, 7251–7331; Tribunal Judgment TWC IX 1410–11.
38  Lorenz Test 5/19–20/48 Ntr 8480–96, 8574–8632; 6/12/48 Ntr 12384–12407; Ernst Wirtz Test 2/18/48

*Ntr* 4307–47; NIK-12380; Tribunal Judgment TWC IX 1410.
39  NIK-13899, -13887, -12362.
40  Berlin Documents Center, Gestapo Reports 9/1942.

## 21. NN

1  L-90 NCA VII 871–2.
2  NCA VII 873–4.
3  Goldsztajn narrative pp. 519–525: sworn statement of Theodore Lehmann (formerly Goldsztajn) attested by notary public.
4  Ferencz 6; NIK-7445, -7456.
5  NIK-7269, -15512.
6  Klaus Stein *Test* 2/25/48 *Ntr* 4632–53; NIK-5941; NIK-12342.
7  Saur *Test* 6/8/48 *Ntr* 11798–11869; NIK-7426.
8  WM/Hansen.
9  Scholtens narrative pp. 526–528: his *Test* 2/10/48 *Ntr* 3616–27; his affidavit NIK-12802.
10  TWC IX 1062–63.
11  Ledoux narrative pp. 529–531: his *Test* 2/4/48 *Ntr* 3137–72.
12  Hengsbach interview pp. 531–532: WM/Hengsbach.
13  Schröder "Verzeichnis Alfried Krupp."
14  Quoted by Dr. Fritz Wecker, associate counsel for Alfried, 3/22/48 *Ntr* 4714–31.
15  Come narrative pp. 534–540: his *Test* 2/2–3/48 *Ntr* 2968–3012; WM/Come; Come "Dechenschule et Neerfeld."
16  TWC IX 1069.
17  Tribunal Judgment TWC IX 1399.
18  Come "Journal."
19  TWC IX 1052.
20  Come "Témoignage."
21  TWC IX 1054.
22  Ledoux *Test* 2/4/48; TWC IX 1074.
23  WM/Come.

## 22. NOTH KENNT KEIN GEBOT

1  AK to Pieper 6/6 and 7/29/1884.
2  Scholtens NIK-12802.
3  WM/Come; Come *Test* 2/2–3/48 *Ntr* 2968–3012.
4  TMWC VII 585.
5  Ibid. 584.
6  Zeigler 103, 106; NIK-2891, -7679; D-238.
7  D-238; NIK-7440, -11167.
8  Roth narrative pp. 544–562: WM/

Elizabeth Roth, Ernestine Roth; Elizabeth *Test* 1/8–9/48 *Ntr* 1251–1326; Ernestine *Test* 1/9/48 *Ntr* 1327–75.
9  1780-PS (NCA IV 238).
10  DGFP IV 241.
11  Elizabeth Roth to WM 4/7/67.
12  Arendt in *New Yorker* 3/9/63.
13  Höss affidavit NCA VI 789–90, ND 3868-PS.
14  NIK-11728, -8763.
15  Ibid.
16  Adolf Trockel affidavit 12/30/47 DE-1014; Ernestine Roth *Test* 1/9/48 *Ntr* 1327–75.
17  DE-1014; NIK-9802; Trockel cross-examination 5/21/48 *Ntr* 8973–9004; Geulen affidavit 4/14/48 DE-1112; Geulen *Test* 5/25/48 *Ntr* 9548–9562.
18  NIK-11676.
19  Braun affidavit 2/18/48 DE-1054, Braun *Test* 5/26/48 *Ntr* 9861–9904.
20  Ibid.; WM/Elizabeth, Ernestine.
21  NIK-11728, -8763.
22  Extracts from Elizabeth Roth's *Test* 1/8–9/48 *Ntr* 1251–1326.
23  Geulen cross-examination; WM/Elizabeth Roth.
24  Braun cross-examination 5/26/48 *Ntr* 9861–9904.
25  NIK-3581; D-277; NIK-11728.
26  NIK-8766; Gutersohn *Test* 2/17/48 *Ntr* 4142–75; NIK-8766.
27  NIK-7855.
28  Ferencz 43; NIK-11731, -11732; Ferencz 42.
29  D-355.
30  Recollections of survivors; SB *Gusstahlfabrik Friedrich Krupp, Essen.*
31  WM/Cecelia Goetz.
32  Geulen cross-examination.
33  NCA VII 2–7; D-288.
34  *Test* Dollhaine *Ntr* 8942.
35  NIK-11231, -10346; *Test* Karl Sommerer 6/3/48 *Ntr* 11074–11101; Ihn affidavit D-274.
36  Sommerer *Test Ntr* 11074–11101.
37  Hochhuth 336; WM/Zedtwitz-Arnim.
38  NIK-12922.
39  NI-2916.
40  Schrieber cross-examination 5/27/48 *Ntr* 9983–10022.
41  NIK-10766.
42  Ibid.; N-1113; *Test* Ernst Wirtz 2/18/48 *Ntr* 4307–47.
43  Döring cross-examination 5/31/48 *Ntr* 10677–10700.
44  Wienen affidavit 4/27/48 DE-2103.

45 Ibid.; Döring cross-examination 5/31/48 Ntr 10677–10700.
46 Wirtz Test 2/18/48 Ntr 4307–47; Lorenz Scheider Test 6/10/48 Ntr 12113–87.
47 Döring Test 5/31/48 Ntr 10677–10700; Wirtz Test 2/18/48 Ntr 4307–47.
48 Wirtz Test 2/18/48 Ntr 4307–47.
49 Döring Test 5/31/48 Ntr 10677–10700; TWC IX 122, 1408; NIK-10766; NIK-11231; TWC IX 1408.
50 NIK-10766; Döring Test 5/31/48 Ntr 10677–10700.
51 TWC IX 122.
52 NIK-10766.

## 23. GÖTTERDÄMMERUNG

1 WM/Alfried, Barbara Krupp, Wilmowsky, Berthold, Harald.
2 Wilmowsky 225; Wilmowsky Test Ntr 5176; Zeller 283; Rothfels 9, 14.
3 Ritter 419–29.
4 WM/Löser and Frau Löser.
5 Ibid.; WM/Zedtwitz-Arnim.
6 Wilmowsky 226; Wilmowsky Test Ntr 5177–8.
7 WM/Wilmowsky; Klass 437.
8 Wilmowsky/Gustav correspondence of late July 1937 guaranteeing Löser's party loyalty (NIK-12522); Wilmowsky Test Ntr 5176; Wilmowsky 228–9.
9 Mühlen 172; WM/Wilmowsky; Wilmowsky 229.
10 Wilmot 437–8.
11 WM/Harald.
12 Morgenthau 10–11.
13 TWC IX 872.
14 Schröder Test 4/27, 29/48 Ntr 6106–6249; Mühlen 176–7.
15 TWC IX 872.
16 Schröder Test Ntr 6106–6249.
17 Moorehead, Montgomery 1206–7; Eisenhower 305; Shirer 1089; Wilmot 521–22.
18 WM/Berthold, Wilmowsky; Mühlen 173.
19 Young 72–3; Klass 438; Mühlen 180; WM/Berthold.
20 WM/Berthold.
21 Hechler 116–28; Fuller 357.
22 Young 69.
23 SB Gusstahlfabrik Friedrich Krupp Essen 8; Life 8/27/45; Weekly Post 11/26/60; Mühlen 182; Life 8/27/45; Mühlen 183.
24 SB Rheinhausen 5–6; Lochner

252–53; Führer Conferences on Naval Affairs 1945 90; WM/Meininghaus, Tubbesing; Mühlen 182.
25 Fritz Fell Test 2/4/48 Ntr 3108–36.
26 Tribunal Judgment TWC IX 1411; Ntr 3687–3703.
27 Heinrich Hümmerich Test 5/21–22/48 Ntr 9068–86, 9126–45, TWC IX 952.
28 German Denazification Board Substantiation 10/30/47, NIK-12380.
29 NIK-7155; Fell Test TWC IX 939.
30 TWC IX 938.
31 Nuremberg exhibits D-382A, D-382B, and D-382C; Case No. 10, 24.
32 Josef Dahm Test 2/3–4/48 Ntr 3080–3108, TWC IX 329–31; Dahm affidavit D-382.
33 TWC IX 936.
34 TWC IX 1410 (Tribunal Judgment), 930.
35 TWC IX 931–2, 937, 1022.
36 Ilse Wagner Test 2/10/48 Ntr 3687–3703; Tribunal Judgment TWC IX 1411.
37 Sommerer Test 6/3/48 Ntr 11074–11101.
38 Escape narrative pp. 585–589: Elizabeth Roth Test 1/8–9/48 Ntr 1251–1326; Ernestine Roth 1/9/48 Ntr 1327–75; Marquardt 5/12–13/48 Ntr 7511–31, 7638–7700; WM/Elizabeth Roth, Ernestine Roth; correspondence with Elizabeth and Ernestine Roth; WM personal investigation.
39 TWC IX 1150.
40 TWC IX 1171.
41 TWC IX 1151.
42 Elizabeth Roth to WM 3/27/63; TWC IX 1151.
43 WM/Alfried, Tubbesing, Goetz.
44 Fuller 359–60.
45 Ibid.; Wilmot 683–4; Moorehead Eclipse 238–46.
46 WM/Hardach, Tubbesing.
47 Shirer 266–67; WM/Goetz; Tribunal Judgment TWC IX 1332.
48 WM/Tubbesing.
49 WM/Come.
50 WM/Schleicher; Deutsches Nachrichtenbüro files 9/4/40.
51 Ciano 449–52.
52 Taylor in Columbia Law Review 2/1953.
53 WM/John W. Paton.
54 WM/Come; Fielding 292.
55 The rescue pp. 593–594: WM/Elizabeth Roth.

## 24. I AM THE OWNER OF THIS PROPERTY

1 NYT 4/10/45; Toland 391.
2 WM/recollections of various Hügel servants.
3 NYT 4/11/45, 4/10/45, 3/27/45.
4 WM/Hardach, Alfried.
5 Ibid.
6 Closing in on Hügel pp. 597–599: *Time* 4/23/45; Young 74–5; Louis Azrael to WM 9/17/64.
7 Vigil in the Hauptverwaltungsgebäude pp. 599–600: WM/Tubbesing.
8 Seizure of the Hauptverwaltungsgebäude pp. 601–603: WM/Tubbesing.
9 DE-2275; Mühlen 183.
10 Mühlen 182.
11 Ibid. 185.
12 Young 75.
13 Azrael to WM 9/17/64.
14 Young 75.
15 Azrael to WM 9/17/64; WM/Alfried; Sagmoen to WM 2/24/65; Mühlen 182; *Time* 4/23/45.
16 Azrael to WM 9/17/64.
17 Ibid.
18 Krupp interrogation *Time* 4/23/45; *Fortune* 2/56.
19 *Fried. Krupp Essen* 1811–1946; NYT 5/22/45.
20 NYT 4/16/45; *Time* 4/23/45; NYT 1945: 4/16, 5/22, 6/22; BBC file 8/14/45.
21 *Nation* 3/21/59; Krupp's statement to Tribunal 6/30/48 *Ntr* 13215–20.
22 Mühlen 211.
23 WM/Dohrmann.
24 NYT 2/18/51; WM/Hardach.
25 Toland 384–5.
26 1015-B-PS TMWC III 666–70; WM/Hardach.
27 DNB files 5/10/45.
28 Ibid.
29 Dönitz 472–3.
30 *Villa Hügel.*
31 *Life* 8/27/45.
32 WM/Elizabeth Roth.
33 Toland 354.
34 Toland 262–3; Smith in *Saturday Evening Post* 7/6/46.
35 Toland 582.
36 Wilmot 690.
37 Ibid.; WM/Berthold.
38 Klass 465; NCA I 85; Davidson 5, 26.
39 Thayer-Bohlen confrontation pp. 614–16: WM/Berthold and Thayer; Thayer 95–7.
40 *Nation* 3/1/59; Pounds 253.
41 Dönitz 472; Moorehead *Eclipse* viii; NYT 12/6/59.
42 WM/Heine; Pounds 254; Potsdam Agreement iii, B Clause 12.
43 Clay 356; *Life* 8/27/45.
44 NYT 9/24/45.
45 White 135, 136, 141.
46 NYT 11/17/45; Klass 439; WM/Hobrecker; Mühlen 186.
47 Mühlen 186.
48 WM/Tubbesing; NYT 4/18/50.
49 Schröder *Fabrik in Berndorf;* Horne 115; *Newsweek* 1/4/54; *Fortune* 2/1956.
50 NYT 10/21/48, 2/10/49; *Business Week* 5/8/48; *Fortune* 2/1956; NYT 3/29/59.
51 White 143; *Fortune* 2/1956.
52 Pounds 256; Stolper 149–52; *Fortune* 2/1956.
53 TMWC XVI 497–8.
54 Text of Allied Control Council Law No. 10 *Official Gazette of the Control Council for Germany* No. 3 1/1946 50–55; Clay 325–6.

## 25. KRUPP . . . YOU HAVE BEEN CONVICTED

1 WM/Berthold, Sprenger.
2 WM/Wilmowsky; *Ntr* 5230; WM/Barbara Krupp.
3 TWC IX 1; Klass 465.
4 WM/Berthold.
5 WM/Wilmowsky, Sprenger.
6 White 134–7.
7 Davidson 363n.
8 *Frankfurter Neue Zeitung* 10/18/49.
9 Davidson *Life and Death of Germany* 105–6.
10 Davidson 26.
11 NYT 10/20 and 11/4/45; NCA I 85, 91–2.
12 NCA I 84; NYT 11/9/45; Heydecker 87–8.
13 TMWC I 138; NYT 11/13/45; Thayer 97; NCA I 85; NYT 11/17/45; Heydecker 88; NYT 11/18/45.
14 NYT 11/20/45; Taylor in *Columbia Law Review* 4/1955.
15 Clay 251.
16 Ibid.
17 The distinction between war criminals and major war criminals is

spelled out in Arendt *Eichmann in Jerusalem* 258; WM/Taylor.

18 WM/Taylor, Sprecher, Goetz.
19 Young 120–21; TWC IX 2.
20 *True* 8/1954.
21 Siemens 3/22/48 *Ntr* 4815; Schilf 3/22/48 *Ntr* 4761–74; Anderson/Schrieber exchange 5/27/48 *Ntr* 9983–10022.
22 WM/Kranzbühler, Alfried, Berthold.
23 WM/Alfried, Bülow; *NYT* picture 8/16/47.
24 WM/Berthold.
25 Ibid.
26 Davidson 21.
27 WM/Kranzbühler, Young 83; TWC IX 2; *NYT* 11/18/47. Indictment published in *NYT* 8/16/47.
28 Tribunal Judgment 7/31/48 *Ntr* 13233.
29 Prosecution's opening statement 12/8/47 *Ntr* 18–113.
30 Ibid.
31 Ibid.
32 Klass 454.
33 *Ntr* 2307–47, 2465–74 (1/24, 27/48).
34 Klass 454, 444, 446.
35 *NYT* 1947: 11/12, 12/12, 12/13, 12/16. Other stories dealt with matters apart from testimony and documents.
36 Goetz to WM 5/6/63.
37 Buchheim 45–55; *History of U.N. War Crimes Commission* 303; WM/Taylor, Barr.
38 Bross 211; *Die grosse Politik der Europäischen Kabinette* XV 4320.
39 NIK-7248, -1178, -2965, etc.; Arendt in *New Yorker* 3/9/63; Klass 15.
40 Concurring opinion on Dismissal of Aggressive War Charges 7/7/48 TWC IX 417.
41 WM/Kranzbühler.
42 Shirer *Aufstieg und Fall* I 265.
43 *NYT* 9/7/46; *Time* 9/16/46.
44 White 335–40.
45 Flick testimony 4/2/48 *Ntr* 5409–24, 4/19/48 *Ntr* 5444–88, *NYT* 4/20/48; White 145; Mühlen 209.
46 WM/Taylor.
47 Kurt Biegl *Test* 4/29/48 *Ntr* 6251–92; TWC IX 625 (Dr. Gerhart Weiz and Judge Daly).
48 WM/Kranzbühler; Wilmowsky *Warum wurde Krupp* 175.
49 Taylor in *International Conciliation* 4/1949; WM/Ragland.

50 Wilmowsky *Test Ntr* 5201, *Krupp Engineering* 11, *Review of Reviews* 9/1927, *Scientific American* 9/1932; *Krupp Past and Present* 39, Lochner 201–2, *Fortune* 2/1956, Klass 429, *Weekly Post* 11/26/60, and *Newsweek* 1/4/54.
51 Klass 456.
52 *NYT* 1/18/48.
53 Ibid.; Klass 455.
54 *Newsweek* 4/15/46; *NYT* 9/5/46.
55 *NYT* 5/6/47.
56 *NYT* 12/20/47.
57 *NYT* 12/23/47.
58 *Official Gazette of the Control Council for Germany* No. 3 1/1946 50–55; *Federal Reporter* 983.
59 Löser and Krupp statements pp. 655–656 6/30/48 *Ntr* 13215–20; TWC IX 1012.
60 Wilkins note on letter Clay to Wilkins 6/24/51.
61 *Landsberg Documentary* 26–7.
62 Klass 459–60.
63 Tribunal Judgment 7/31/48 *Ntr* 13231–13402.
64 WM/Ragland.
65 *NYT* 8/2/48; *Stars and Stripes* 8/2/48.
66 Klass 463.
67 Ibid. 451.

## 26. HOHER KOMMISSAR JOHN J. McCLOY

1 WM/Alfried.
2 WM/Bülow.
3 Krupp to Clay 8/21/48: stamped "Filed 21 August 1948 with Secretary General for Military Tribunals, Defense Center."
4 Taylor in *Columbia Law Review* 2/1953; TWC IX 1487–8; Mühlen 209; Clay to WM 3/22/63.
5 TWC IX 1485n (1).
6 *NYT* 4/18/50.
7 Quotations pp. 662–663 are from Wilmowsky *Warum wurde Krupp* 176–80.
8 WM/Barr.
9 WM/Wilmowsky, Berthold.
10 WM/Alfried, Berthold; *Life* 2/6/50.
11 Mühlen 210.
12 White 140.
13 White 157.
14 *U.S. News and World Report* 2/27/59; Thayer 104.
15 White 157; Shirer 914n.

16   Pounds 256.
17   Hoover *Report* introduction.
18   White 146–8.
19   WM/Bülow; Mühlen 254.
20   Guderian 162, 233–8.
21   Appleman 11–12, 19.
22   NYT 7/25/49; WM/McCloy.
23   *Current Biography* 4/49.
24   WM/Kranzbühler, Ferencz; Young 104.
25   White 250, 152, 275.
26   Pounds 115.
27   Appleman 31, 157, 381, 508; White 156.
28   Young 103.
29   White 151–2; Appleman 605.
30   Young 105; WM/Berthold, Kranzbühler.
31   NYT 2/18/51.
32   Shirer 415–17; White 287; Appleman 68–9.
33   Eleanor Roosevelt to McCloy 2/15/51; McCloy to Eleanor Roosevelt 3/12/51; WM/McCloy.
34   *Landsberg Documentary* 13; Telford Taylor to Eleanor Roosevelt 6/19/51.
35   WM/Ferencz.
36   WM/McCloy.
37   Ibid.
38   Peck to WM 8/14/63, 3/22/63.
39   *True* 8/1954; *Department of State Bulletin* XXIV no. 623 6/11/51.
40   NIK-9299; TWC VI, XIX.
41   *True* 8/1954; WM/Schürmann, Batocki, Stahmer-Knoll.
42   NYT 2/1/51; TWC XV 1173–4; *Landsberg Documentary* 10; *Atlantic* 10/1960.
43   WM/Frau Löser; NYT 6/2, 5/51.
44   WM/Kranzbühler; Lochner 250; WM/Heine.
45   NYT 8/20/52; Wilkins to McCloy 2/21/51; NYT 2/1/51.
46   NYT 9/30/52; 2/18/51.
47   *Newsweek* 2/12/51; *Horne* 109; Young 108; *Sunday Pictorial* 2/8/51; NYT 3/10/51; *Time* 2/12/51.
48   Quoted in Klass 477–8.
49   McCloy to Mrs. Roosevelt 4/12/51; McCloy to Wilkins 4/19/51.
50   McCloy to Mrs. Roosevelt 4/12/51; McCloy to Javits quoted in *Department of State Bulletin* XXIV 623 6/11/51.
51   1387-PS; *Reichsgesetzblatt* 11/20/43; 3569-PS.
52   *Landsberg Documentary* 17.
53   Taylor in *Columbia Law Review* 4/1955.
54   NYT 2/4/51.

## 27. THE GERMANS ARE BEING TREATED LIKE NIGGERS

1   Alfried's release pp. 688–690: WM/Alfried, Berthold, Bülow.
2   NYT 2/11/51.
3   Mühlen 217.
4   Mühlen 217–18.
5   WM/Berthold.
6   WM/Berthold, Wilmowsky.
7   WM/Bülow; *Fortune* 2/1956.
8   WM/Alfried.
9   Pounds 126.
10   Benjamin Disraeli *Current History* 1858.
11   TWC IX 669n; WM/Hundhausen.
12   Scott 368, 260; quoted in Pounds 190.
13   WM/Harald, Heine.
14   Williams, "An American at Krupp."
15   Mühlen 226.
16   Ibid. 227.
17   White 250.
18   Mühlen 228.
19   WM/Sabel.
20   Young 109; personal information.
21   Alfried's marriage pp. 698–699: WM/Berthold.
22   WM/Sprenger.
23   Mühlen 259.
24   KFA; Young 128
25   "Catchwords about the Essener Hof" (unpublished ms 1963).
26   WM/Beitz; Young 123–5.
27   WM/Beitz; Mühlen 223–4.
28   WM/Beitz, Berthold, Springer
29   WM/Schürmann, Batocki, Stahmer-Knoll.
30   Young 111.
31   Ibid.; *Daily Mirror* 11/11/52.
32   Mühlen 227.
33   Young 113–14.
34   *Fortune* 2/1956.
35   Klass 479.
36   Mühlen 272.
37   Quoted in Davidson 13; Young 117.
38   Young 117.
39   WM/Sprenger; *Fortune* 2/1956; WM/Wilmowsky.
40   Events of 9/25/52 pp. 708–709: WM/Alfried, Beitz, Sprenger.
41   *Der Spiegel* 3/13/67.
42   Mühlen 223.

43 Krupp's return to Essen pp. 709–710: *Westdeutsche Allgemeine Zeitung* 3/13/53.
44 Young 108: Mühlen 219.
45 TWC IX 264; *Reader's Digest* 9/1955.
46 Personal information.
47 KFA; WM/Alfried; *Fortune* 2/1956; Mühlen 266.
48 Young 129; Luce to WM 4/15/63.
49 KFA; *Abendzeitung* (Munich) files 1958.
50 WM/Beitz.
51 WM/Sprenger; Mühlen 259.
52 Personal information; WM/Dohrmann.
53 WM/Hosmann.
54 WM/Sprenger; Klass 50.
55 *NYT* 10/25/56.
56 WM/Menne; Mühlen 270.
57 WM/Zedtwitz-Arnim.
58 Thayer 97–9; WM/Thayer, Alfried.
59 Mühlen 256; *Westdeutsche Allgemeine Zeitung* 11/14/53.
60 Haile Selassie's visit pp. 719–722: *Westdeutsche Allgemeine Zeitung* 11/12/54; WM/Alfried.

## 28. HEUTE DIE GANZE WELT

1 Picker, entry for 1/16–17/42.
2 Young 137–8; *NYT* 10/25/56.
3 Mühlen 258; Young 137.
4 *Los Angeles Times* 6/22/67.
5 Mühlen 260.
6 *Time* 8/19/57.
7 WM/Lauruiz.
8 Mühlen 236.
9 *Stahl und Eisen* 6/15/10.
10 WM/Hansen.
11 *Krupp Engineering* 41.
12 KFA.
13 *NYT* 3/28/55.
14 Rourkela pp. 730–732: *Rourkela* passim.
15 Young 127.
16 *NYT* 1/9/60; Mühlen 236.
17 *NYT* 4/4/54; *Business Week* 5/5/51.
18 Young 125–6.
19 Mühlen 232.
20 Mandellaub to WM 8/28/64.
21 *Time* 8/19/57.
22 *NYT* 3/28/55.
23 Ibid.; *Krupp Products*.
24 *Réalités* 8/1959.
25 *NYT* 4/16/60; Young 142.
26 *Times* (London) 1/14/60.
27 Menne 50.

28 AK to Pieper 11/27/1866.
29 *Outlook* 1/25/02; *Time* 4/23/45; Lochner 245; Utley 169, 172, 177, 182, 169.
30 *Reader's Digest* 9/1955; *Time* 9/15/52; *Newsweek* 4/18/63.
31 Villa Hügel exhibit 1963.
32 Zedtwitz-Arnim 3.
33 Mühlen 240; *Fortune* 2/1956; *U.S. News and World Report* 3/14/60.
34 *Fortune* 2/1956; Mühlen 252; *Time* 9/18/57.
35 Klass 419–20.
36 The firm's leadership in arms is borne out: NIK-11625, -9091, -12294, -6577, -755, -6576, D-94, C-156, 1387-PS; Schröder memo 7/18/40: NIK-12315.
37 Tuchman *Tower* 243; Mühlen 225.
38 *Newsweek* 1/15/68.
39 *Krupp Mitteilungen* 11/1957; *Krupp Past and Present* 45.
40 Captivity and return of Harald pp. 745–748: WM/Harald, Sabel, Dohrmann, Barbara Krupp; *Krupp Mitteilungen* 8/1957.
41 WM/Berthold.
42 Fielding 29, 37; Wilmowsky 166.
43 Wilmowsky 224.
44 WM/Beitz.
45 *Krupp Mitteilungen* 8/1957.
46 *NYT* 9/22/57.
47 *Krupp Mitteilungen* 11/1957.
48 Ibid.
49 *Revue de Paris* 154 (9-10/1929), 505–7; Napoleon III *Oeuvres Posthumes* ed. Chapelle 43; Frossard 79.

## 29. NOT A STONE SHALL BE SOLD

1 AK to Gustav Jürst 9/6/1850.
2 *Krupp Mitteilungen* 12/1957; *NYT* 9/18/57.
3 *Krupp Mitteilungen* 12/1957; TWC IX 242.
4 *Weekly Post* (England) 11/26/60; *Test* 4/27–29/48 Ntr 6106–6249; *London Observer* 2/12/61.
5 WM/Beitz; *Fortune* 2/1956.
6 *London Observer* 2/12/61.
7 Klass 168.
8 Ibid. 161, 169–70.
9 Ibid. 161; Young 123–4; WM/Beitz.
10 WM/Beitz.
11 AK *Generalregulativ* 41.
12 Young 119–20.
13 AK *Generalregulativ* passim.
14 *Krupp Past and Present* 23; Klass 260.

15 Mühlen 262–3.
16 Benns 474; *Information Please Almanac 1952* 231–2.
17 WM/Alfried.
18 WM/Hardach, Menne; AK to FAK 12/22/1874.
19 "Das war Krupp."
20 WM/McCloy.
21 Mühlen 251.
22 *Life* 8/27/45; *Newsweek* 1/19/59; *Der Spiegel* 6/5/63.
23 WM/Beitz.
24 *Atlantic* 10/1960; Young 147–8; WM/Schröder.
25 NYT 11/21/61; *Fortune* 2/1956; *Atlantic* 10/1960; Young 153; *Atlantic* 10/1960.
26 Mühlen 249.
27 *Handelsblatt* 4/16/60; NYT 1/25/59, 1/26/60.
28 *Nation* 3/21/59; NYT 3/14/59; *Atlantic* 10/1960.
29 Young 117; *Time* 8/19/57.
30 *Réalités* 8/1959.
31 WM/McCloy; *Réalités* 8/1959.
32 Keynes 14.
33 Pounds 21–2.
34 Mühlen 254.
35 *Wall Street Journal* 8/17/62; *Nation* 3/21/59; White 16.

## 30. MOST POWERFUL MAN IN THE COMMON MARKET

1 WM/Alfried; *Test* 4/29/48 *Ntr* 6251–92.
2 *Financial Times* 3/31/62, 3/14/59.
3 Young 153–4.
4 WM/Meininghaus; *Unser Werk* 4.
5 Berdrow *Briefe* 66; Däbritz 4–7; Pounds 82, 102–3.
6 *Unser Werk* 59; Pounds 185; *Unser Werk* 23.
7 Young 131; Pounds 185; WM/Schleicher.
8 *Nation* 3/21/59.
9 WM/Wilmowsky; *Atlantic* 10/1960.
10 *Krupp 1811–1961* 196; WM/Wilmowsky; Young 154; *Time* 1/19/59.
11 Young 154; NYT 1/11, 25/59; *Newsweek* 1/19/59; *Krupp Past and Present* 7.
12 *Newsweek* 1/19/59.
13 Young 156; NYT 1/26/60, 2/27/68.
14 NYT 1/7/59; *Newsweek* 1/19/59; *Unser Werk* 4.
15 WM/Taylor, Schürmann; NYT 4/15/60.

16 Mühlen 253; Young 122; Mühlen 260.
17 *Newsweek* 1/4/54.
18 *Fortune* 8/1961; Alfried Krupp "Address Delivered at a Jubilee Gathering of Long-Service Employees, Held in the Saalbau, Essen, March 5, 1950" (privately printed); *Krupp Past and Present* 9.
19 Schröder "Verzeichnis Alfried Krupp"; Young 150.
20 WM/Alfried, Beitz, Meininghaus.
21 *Parade* 9/9/62.
22 Young 136; NYT 8/1/67.
23 WM/Lauruiz.
24 Mühlen 220.
25 *Krupp Mitteilungen* 6/1963; *Fried. Krupp Hannover-Messe 1963 Verzeichnis der Ausstellungsstücke* passim.
26 Henry Luce to WM 4/15/63; *Time* 8/19/57.
27 Shirer *Aufstieg und Fall* 143.
28 Ferencz 49.
29 NIK-13173, -14207.
30 Ferencz to WM 3/22/63.
31 NYT 12/24/59; *Nation* 1/4/60; Bornberg 168.
32 New York *Journal American* 12/23/59.
33 NIK-9209, -11312, -12005A, -8672, -12328, -9304, -12342, -7246, -7247, -7454, -11231, -5939; Saur *Test* 6/8/48 *Ntr* 11807, 11809, 11860; Knoll to Wandner 11/27/64.
34 Knoll to Wandner 11/27/64.
35 Mosche and Knoll to the Central Committee of Nazi Victims, Refugees of the Free World 2/25/60.
36 3596-PS.

## 31. YOU CAN SEE THE ONES IN THE LIGHT

1 *Der Spiegel* 11/12/57.
2 *Krupp: Informationen über den Konzern* 51; WM/Beitz; *Krupp Past and Present* 31; *Life* 5/5/61.
3 *Krupp 1811–1961*; WM/Schröder.
4 WM/Williams; *Times* (London) 7/7/61.
5 *Krupp 1811–1961*; "Jubiläumsrede von Herrn Dr. Alfried Krupp von Bohlen und Halbach am 20. November 1961" (unpublished).
6 NYT 11/21/61; Heuss 125.
7 WM/Barbara Krupp, Harald.
8 WM/Goetz.
9 WM/Wilmowsky.

10 Heuss 8.
11 Kubizek 110.
12 Hitler 454–6.
13 Klass 179; Shirer *Aufstieg und Fall* 143; WM/Barbara Krupp; Klass 141.
14 Heuss 8; WM/Wilmowsky.
15 Winston Churchill II and Arnold von Bohlen pp. 804–807: *Queen* 5/8/63; London Daily Express 11/13/62; *Weekly Tribune* (Geneva) 11/15/63; WM/Barbara Krupp, Wilmowsky, Harald.
16 WM/Wilmowsky.
17 *NYT* 8/25/63.
18 Arndt von Bohlen pp. 808–813: *Abendzeitung* (Munich) 1956–67 passim.
19 WM/Beitz; Wilmot 661n.
20 Heuss 22.
21 WM/Harald; *NYT* 3/14/59; *Krupp Past and Present* 31.
22 WM/Schröder; *NYT* 8/1/67; *Réalités* 8/1959; Mühlen 285.
23 Campo Limbo film (Krupp documentary 4/1962); 5/12/67 interview with Hannes Obermaier.
24 WM/Beitz; Shirer 1040–41; Young 139; WM/Harald.
25 Interview with Arndt von Bohlen 5/31/67.
26 Ibid.
27 Obermaier interview.
28 *Abendzeitung* (Munich).
29 "Erlass zur 25 jährigen Wiederkehr des Tages der Besitzübernahme durch Alfred Krupp" (Decree on the 25th Anniversary of Alfred Krupp's proprietorship). Berdrow *Briefe* 285.
30 *Vorwärts* 11/15/02; Mühlen 90–91.
31 *Abendzeitung* (Munich) 1/25/66.
32 *NYT* 4/26/39; *Abendzeitung* (Munich) 1/25/66.
33 *NYT* 1958: 3/6, 11, 14, 15, 17, 21; 4/6, 9, 15, 23, 28; 5/17, 22; 6/22.
34 *Abendzeitung* (Munich) 1/25/66.
35 BBC Log 9/27/38 (2030).
36 *Der Spiegel* 3/13/67; NIK-12074 IX; Cleveland Amory *Celebrity Register* 415.
37 Personal information.
38 *NYT* 1965: 2/7, 5/15–18, 6/4, 7/16; *Der Spiegel* 3/13/67.
39 Arndt von Bohlen interview 5/31/67.
40 WM/Beitz, McCloy; *Fortune* 8/1967; *Time* 8/11/67; *NYT* 8/1/67; *Newsweek* 8/14/67; *NYT* 8/1/67.
41 Klass 85–6.

42 *Newsweek* 8/11/67; "Das War Krupp."

## 32. THE FLAG FOLLOWS TRADE

1 *National Observer* 3/4/63.
2 *Fortune* 8/1967; *Handelsblatt* 7/27/62.
3 *Handelsblatt* 7/27/62.
4 *Fortune* 8/1967.
5 *Der Spiegel* 6/5/63.
6 *London Observer* 2/12/61; *Der Spiegel* 6/5/62.
7 *Der Spiegel* 6/5/62.
8 Davidson 148, 155.
9 *National Observer* 3/4/63.
10 Bismarck-Schönhausen II 292; AK to Todleben 5/21/1864; Hitler 102, 103–4.
11 *Akten zur Deutschen Auswärtigen Politik* VI 490–93.
12 Ibid.
13 *Der Spiegel* 3/13/67.
14 Ibid.
15 Ibid.
16 *Barron's* 5/22/67.
17 *London Sunday Telegraph* 6/21/64; *Newsweek* 11/22/65; *Die Welt* 5/18/67.
18 *Buenos Aires Freie Presse* 6/5/63; WM/Alfried.
19 *Die Welt* 5/18/67; *Fortune* 8/1967; Rodenstock interview 5/19/67.
20 *Time* 8/11/67; *Newsweek* 3/20/67; *Der Spiegel* 3/13/67.
21 *Die Welt* 5/18/67.
22 WM/Lauruiz.
23 *NYT* 8/1/67 and 4/4/67; *Fortune* 8/1967.
24 Arndt von Bohlen interview 5/31/67; WM/McCloy; *NYT* 4/8/63; WM/McCloy, Ted Kaghan.
25 *London Sunday Telegraph* 11/3/63; *NYT* 11/17/65 and 12/11/65; WM/Beitz.
26 AK to Richter and Hagdorn 6/10/1848; to Meyer 4/13/1857.
27 AK to *die Firma* 7/27/1870.
28 Mühlen 242–3.
29 *Der Spiegel* 6/5/63.
30 Mühlen 245.
31 Captions for exhibits: Museum der deutschen Geschichte, Berlin. Exhibit 1963.

## 33. KRUPP IST TOT!

1 *NYT* 5/25/60; Krupp's *Jubiläum* speech 4/4/64; *NYT* 8/61/60.

2   Der Spiegel 6/5/63.
3   Baltimore Sun 5/25/63; Times (London) 1/14/62; NYT 12/7/60; Newsweek 8/19/63.
4   Wall Street Journal 11/7/63; Krupp's Jubiläum speech 4/4/64; Associated Press files 3/24/66; Die Zeit 5/26/67.
5   Der Spiegel 3/16/67.
6   "Das War Krupp."
7   Quoted in Capital 4/1967.
8   Beitz press conference 3/7/67; Barron's 5/22/67.
9   Die Zeit 3/26/67 and 5/19/67; Heinrich Irmler interview 5/9/67.
10   Die Zeit 5/19/67; Collier 19.
11   Fortune 8/1967; NYT 11/17/63.
12   Barron's 5/22/67; Economist 11/26/66.
13   Newsweek 9/21/64; NYT 11/17/63.
14   Der Spiegel 3/13/67.
15   Die Welt 6/6/67; Wall Street Journal 3/8/67; NYT 11/17/63 and 4/5/67.
16   Krupp's Jubiläum speech 4/4/64; Newsweek 3/20/67; "Das war Krupp"; Der Spiegel 6/13/67.
17   NYT 4/1/67; Times (London) 3/8/67.
18   Interview with Dresdner Bank executive.
19   Der Spiegel 3/13/67; Reichsgesetzblatt 11/20/43; Schürmann memo re inheritance tax 6/20/63; Hermann Schenck interview 5/24/67.
20   Schürmann memo 6/20/63.
21   Frankfurter Allgemeine 3/7/67; Der Spiegel 3/13/67.
22   Krupp's Jubiläum speech 4/1/67; NYT 11/17/63.
23   Barron's 5/22/67; Heinrich Irmler interview, Deutsche Bundesbank, Frankfurt 5/9/67; Financial Times 7/6/60.
24   Fortune 8/1967.
25   Klass Asche 161.
26   Der Spiegel 3/13/67; Rich and Fisher Holstein Papers IV 616n. 1; Schiller press conference 3/7/67; Der Spiegel 3/13/67.
27   Die Zeit 3/26/67; Fortune 8/1967; Der Spiegel 3/13/67.
28   "Das war Krupp."
29   Ibid.; Klass 122–3.
30   Der Spiegel 3/13/67; National Observer 3/13/67.
31   Alfried Krupp, Vorhaben-Erklärung; Arndt von Bohlen interview 5/31/67.
32   Arndt von Bohlen interview 5/31/67; NYT 4/2/67.
33   Schiller press conference.
34   Der Spiegel 3/13/67.
35   Ceremony in Hügel's main hall: Krupp's Jubiläum speech 4/1/67; Spiegel 4/10/67; NYT 4/2/67; Fortune 8/1967; Westdeutsche Allgemeine Zeitung 4/2/67.
36   German International XI (4/1967), "Whither Krupp" 9; Fortune 8/1967; Klass 103.
37   Economist 4/22/67; Der Spiegel 1/22/68.
38   Fortune 8/1967.
39   NYT 8/5/67.
40   NYT 8/1/67; Frankfurter Allgemeine 8/1/67; Associated Press files 7/31/67; NYT 8/1/67; Time 8/11/67.
41   NYT 8/1/67; Newsweek 8/11/67.
42   Alfried's funeral: Die Welt, Frankfurter Allgemeine, Handelsblatt, Westdeutsche Allgemeine Zeitung, NYT 8/4/67; Time 8/11/67; Newsweek 8/14/67.
43   NYT 8/4/67.
44   NYT 10/17/67.
45   AK to Meyer 4/13/1857; to FAK 2/18/1875.
46   Der Spiegel 3/13/67.
47   Der Spiegel 1/22/68.
48   Ibid.
49   1387-PS; WM/Schürmann and colleagues; Schürmann memo 6/20/63.

## EPILOGUE: SILVER IN AN OLD MIRROR

1   Tümmler IV.
2   Weihe der neuen Synagogue 20–22; WM/Neugarten.
3   Pounds 233.
4   Ibid. 224.
5   WM/Come, Ferencz.
6   WM/Taylor, McCloy.
7   WM/Döring; Horne 110; WM/Horne.
8   WM/Hansen.
9   WM/Bülow.
10   Kohn in Saturday Review 8/19/67.
11   WM/Tubbesing.
12   NYT 6/22/68.
13   WM/Lauruiz; Essen mit Einführung 17.
14   Mühlen 37.

# ✠
# Bibliography

A LARGE part of this book is based on material which does not fit comfortably in a formal bibliography. Much of it comes from the author's explorations and interviews in several countries. Other sources are fragmentary: letters, affidavits, scrapbooks, photographs, scenes from documentary films. The transcript of the Krupp trial at Nuremberg, for example, contains, quite apart from testimony, over 4,200 written exhibits, and many of these interoffice memoranda and reports are vital to an understanding of Krupp between 1918 and 1945.

Obviously the author's debt to archivists and librarians is immense. Sometimes the curators are dispassionate. The Berlin Documents Center and the Institut für Zeitgeschichte in Munich are, deservedly, Meccas for scholars investigating the Third Reich. Other times the custodians view the family with obvious distaste. Those responsible for the Sozialdemokratische Partei Deutschlands Parteivorstand Archiv and Düsseldorf's Zentralrat der Juden Deutschlands can hardly be expected to applaud Krupp, nor do they. Nevertheless they are content to let the record speak for itself — and so, it must be added, are the caretakers of the central treasures of documents in Essen. Those treasures are great. It is astounding that so much should have survived two world wars. Many firms in the United States, lacking Krupp's sense of history, have far less to show for the past, and I am deeply grateful to the men and women of Essen's Stadtbücherei and Stadtarchiv and Krupp's Familien-Archiv, Historische Archiv, and Werksarchiv for their cooperation. They have only part of the story (the Nuremberg material, for example, is a mystery to them), but without their part the rest would be meaningless.

Among published works, I am particularly indebted to Konrad Ribbeck's history of the city of Essen, Professor Norman J. G. Pounds's study of the Ruhr, and books and articles by previous chroniclers of Krupp; viz., Diedrich Baedeker, Wilhelm Berdrow, Hermann Frobenius, Helmuth de Haas, Herman Hasse, Otto Hué, L. Katzenstein, T. Kellen, Gert von Klass, I. Meisbach, Bernhard Menne, Norbert Mühlen, Friedrich C. G. Müller,

Victor Niemeyer, Gaston Raphael, Franz Richter, and Gordon Young. The books to which I turned most frequently are those by Berdrow, Klass, Menne, Mühlen, and Young, and I wish to express my gratitude to them here.

## BIBLIOGRAPHY

Abeken, Heinrich. *Ein schlichtes Leben in bewegter Zeit, aus Briefen zussammengestellt.* Berlin: 1898.

Adam, J. *Mes illusions et nos souffrances pendant le siège de Paris.* Paris: 1906.

*Akten zur Deutschen Auswärtigen Politik 1918–1945; Series D, 1937–1945.* Baden-Baden: 1950–56.

Albers, Johann Heinrich. *Die Belagerung von Metz . . . von 19 August bis 28 Oktober 1870, nach französischen Quellen und mündlichen Mitteilungen.* Metz: 1896.

Aldington, Richard. *Pinorman, Personal Recollections of Norman Douglas, Pino Orioli, and Charles Prentice.* London: 1954.

*Alldeutscher Verband, 20 Jahre alldeutscher Arbeit und Kämpfe.* Leipzig: 1910.

Allen, W. E. D., and Paul Muratoff. *The Russian Campaigns of 1941–1943.* 2 vols. London: 1944 and 1945.

Allivier, Emile. *L'Empire libéral. Études, récits, souvenirs.* Vol. XIV. Paris: 1895–1912.

"Amazing Comeback: Krupp Rises from War's Ruins." *Newsweek,* January 4, 1954.

"Amnesty Storm." *Newsweek,* February 12, 1951.

Anderson, Omer. "The Cannon King Assumes a Cold War Role." *National Observer,* March 4, 1963.

"Ansprachen bei der Trauerfeier in Villa Hügel am 25 September 1957." *Krupp Mitteilungen,* November 1957.

Appleman, Roy E. *United States Army in the Korean War: South to the Nakong, North to the Yalu (June–November 1950).* Washington: 1961.

"Approach to Clemency Decisions." *Information Bulletin* (monthly magazine of the Office of U. S. High Commissioner for Germany), May 1951.

Arendt, Hannah. *Eichmann in Jerusalem: A Report on the Banality of Evil.* Rev. ed. New York: 1964.

———. "Eichmann in Jerusalem." *The New Yorker,* February 23, 1963; March 2 and 9, 1963.

Assmann, Kurt. *Deutsche Schicksalsjahre.* Wiesbaden: 1950.

"Aufwand und Ertrag bei den industriellen Aktiengesellschaften." *Wirtschaft und Statistik.* Berlin: 1938.

Baedeker, Alfred. *Jahrbuch für den Oberbergamtsbezirk Dortmund.* Essen: 1926.

Baedeker, Diedrich. *Alfred Krupp und die Entwicklung der Gusstahlfabrik zu Essen.* Essen: 1889 and 1912. (Chapter note references to "Baedeker" are to this work.)

Baedeker, Karl. *Ruhrgebiet.* Freiburg: 1959.

Baldick, Robert. *The Siege of Paris.* London: 1964.

Banfield, T. C. *Industry of the Rhine* (series 1, *Agriculture*). London: 1848.

Barail, François Charles du. *Mes Souvenirs, 1820–1879.* Paris: 1894–96.

Bartz, Karl. *Als der Himmel brannte.* Hanover: 1955.

Bauer, Colonel M. *Der Grosse Krieg in Feld und Heimat.* Tübingen: 1921.

Baumont, Maurice. *L'Affaire Eulenberg et les Origines de la Guerre mondiale.* Paris: 1933.

*Beiträge zur Geschichte von Stadt und Stift Essen.* Essen: 1903.

"Beitz — Star im Osten." *Der Spiegel,* June 5, 1963.

Bell, James. "The Comeback of Krupp." *Fortune,* February 1956.

———. "End of a Long Road for House of Krupp." *Washington Star,* August 6, 1967.

———. "The Fall of the House of Krupp." *Fortune,* August 1967.

Benns, F. Lee. *European History Since 1870.* New York: 1941.

Bénoist-Méchin, Jacques. *Histoire de l'Armée allemande depuis l'Armistice.* Paris: 1936–38.

Berdrow, Wilhelm. *Alfred Krupp und die Familie*. Berlin: 1943.
———. *Die Familie Krupp in Essen von 1587 bis 1787*. Essen: 1931. (Chapter note references to "Berdrow" are to this work.)
———. *Friedrich Krupp, der Gründer der Gusstahlfabrik in Briefen und Urkunden*. Essen: 1914.
———. *Alfred Krupp*. 2 vols. Berlin: 1927.
———. "125 Jahre Krupp." *Krupp*. November 20, 1936.
———, ed. *Alfred Krupps Briefe 1826–1887 im Aufrage der Familie und der Firma Krupp*. Berlin: 1928.
Berndorff, H. R. *General zwischen Ost und West*. Hamburg: n.d.
Bernhardt, F. von. *Deutschland und der nächste Krieg*. Stuttgart-Berlin: 1913.
Bernstein, Victor H. *Final Judgment: The Story of Nuremberg*. Introduction by Max Lerner. New York: 1947.
"Berthold Beitz: The Man Behind Krupps." *The London Observer*, February 12, 1961.
Bessemer, Sir Henry. *An Autobiography*. London: 1905.
*Bewegung, Staat und Volk in ihren Organisationen*. Berlin: 1934.
Binder, David. "Alfred Krupp, Last Sole Owner of German Steel Empire, Dies." *New York Times*, August 1, 1967.
———. "Bonn: The 'Village' Goes Urban." *New York Times*, January 8, 1967.
Bismarck-Schönhausen, Otto Fürst von. *Gedanken und Erinnerungen*. Stuttgart and Berlin: 1922.
Bismarck-Schönhausen, Otto Eduard von. *Bismarck the Man and Statesman*. Vol. II. London: 1898.
*Bochumer Verein für Gusstahlfabrikation AG, Bochum: Ein Bericht über das Werk, seine Geschichte, Erzeugnisse und Leistungen*. Bochum: n.d.
Boelcke, Siegfried. *Krupp und die Hohenzollern*. Berlin: 1956.
"Die Bomben auf fielen aus achtzehn Meter Höhe." *Die Welt*, May 15, 1963.
"Bomben die Möhnetalsperre." *Die Welt*, June 8, 1963.
"Bonn Banks Force Krupp to Open Up Its Books." *New York World Journal Tribune*, March 8, 1967.
"Bonn Comes to Aid of Krupp Empire, but the Price Is a Corporate Image." *National Observer*, March 13, 1967.
Bonnal, Guillaume Auguste. *Froeschwiller: récit commenté des événements . . . du 15 Juillet au 12 Août 1870*. Paris: 1899.
Bordier, Henri. *L'Allemagne aux Tuileries de 1850 à 1870*. Paris: 1872.
Borkin, Charles, and Charles A. Welsh. *Germany's Master Plan: The Story of Industrial Offensive*. Introduction by Thurmond Arnold. New York: 1943.
Bornberg, John. *Schizophrenic Germany*. New York: 1961.
Brady, Robert A. *The Spirit and Structure of German Fascism*. Foreword by Harold J. Laski. New York: 1937.
Brodie, Bernard, and Fawn Brodie. *From Crossbow to H-Bomb*. New York: 1962.
Bronsart von Schellendorff, Paul. *Geheimes Kriegstagebuch 1870–71*. Ed. by Peter Rassow. Bonn: 1954.
Bross, Werner. *Gespräche mit Hermann Göring*. Flemburg and Hamburg: 1950.
Brunel, Georges. *Les Ballons au siège de Paris, 1870–71*. Paris: 1933.
Buchheim, Hans. *Fördernde Mitgliedschaft bei der SS*. Munich: Gutachten des Instituts für Zeitgeschichte im Selbstverlag des Instituts für Zeitgeschichte (pp. 350–351), 1958.
———. "Die SS in der Verfassung des Dritten Reichs." *Vierteljahreshefte für Zeitgeschichte*, April 1955.
———. Letter to the author. April 18, 1963.
Buchheim, Hans, and others. *Anatomie des SS-Staates*. Alten and Freiburg: 1965.
Bülow, Prince Bernhard von. *Memoirs*. Boston: 1931–32.
"Die Bürgschaft ist ein Sonderfall." *Der Spiegel*, March 13, 1967.
"Burial for Krupp at Shrine in Essen." *New York Times*, August 4, 1967.
Busch, Moritz. *Bismarck: Some Secret Pages of His History*. London: 1898.
———. *Bismarck in the Franco-Prussian War, 1870–71*. Translated. London: 1879.

Cadoux, Gaston. "Les Magnats de la Ruhr." *Revue Politique et Parlementaire*, CXV, 1923: CXVI, 1923.
Callender, Harold. "A New View on Krupp." *New York Times*, February 1, 1959.
Cameron, James. 1914. New York: 1959.
"The Cannon King Assumes a Cold War Role." *National Observer*, March 4, 1963.
Carnegie, Andrew. *Armaments and Their Results*. New York: 1909.
*Case No. 10* (see *Military Tribunals Case No. 10*).
*Catalogue of the Great Exhibition*. London: 1851.
"Changing Krupp from a War to a Peace Factory." *Current Opinion*, June 1921.
Churchill, Winston S. *Their Finest Hour*. Boston: 1949.
———. *The Hinge of Fate*. New York: 1951.
———. *The World Crisis*. London: 1927. (Chapter with references to "Churchill" are to this work.)
Churchill, Winston II. "In the Steps of my Grandfather." With photographs by Arnold von Bohlen. *Queen*, May 8, 1963.
Ciano, Count Galeazzo. *Ciano's Diplomatic Papers*. Ed. by Malcolm Muggeridge. London: 1948.
Clark, Alan. *Barbarossa: The Russian-German Conflict, 1941–45*. New York: 1965.
———. *The Fall of Crete*. New York: 1962.
Clay, Lucius D. *Decision in Germany*. Garden City, N.Y.: 1950.
———. Letter to the author. March 27, 1963.
Coblenz, Gaston. "Big 3 Giving Krupp Time to Sell Out." *New York Herald Tribune*, January 31, 1959.
Collier, Basil. *The Second World War: A Military History, from Munich to Hiroshima*. New York: 1967.
"Combines: Baron of the Ruhr." *Newsweek*, January 19, 1959.
Come, Father Alphonse. "Témoignage sur les Camps de Dechenschule et Neerfeld." 3 pp. Unpublished.
———. "Journal, August 15, 1944 — May 4, 1945." 100 pp. with charts. Unpublished.
"Comeback for 'Men of Essen.'" *Life* (international Ed.), May 23, 1960.
Conrad von Hötzendorff, Franz. *Aus meiner Dienstzeit, 1906–18*. 5 vols. Vienna, 1921–25.
Conrady, Alexander. *Die Rheinlände in der Französenzeit*. Stuttgart: 1922.
Conway, Moncure D. "An Iron City Beside the Ruhr." *Harper's New Monthly Magazine*, March 1886.
Coulton, G. G. *The Medieval Village*. Cambridge: 1926.
"Crisis at Krupp." *Newsweek*, March 20, 1967.
Crutwell, C. R. M. F. *A History of the Great War 1914–1918*. Oxford: 1934.
Däbritz, W. *Bochumer Verein für Bergbau und Gusstahlfabrikation in Bochum*. Düsseldorf: 1934.
Dallin, Alexander. *German Rule in Russia, 1941–1945*. New York: 1957.
Daluces, Jean. *Le Troisième Reich*. Paris: 1950.
Darmstädter, F. *Bismarck and the Creation of the Second Reich*. London: 1948.
"Das war Krupp." *Capital*, April 1967.
Davidson, Eugene. *The Life and Death of Germany*. New York: 1959.
———. *The Trial of the Germans*. New York: 1966. (Chapter note references to "Davidson" are to this work.)
"The Death of Friedrich Krupp." *Scientific American*, December 6, 1902.
Deichmann, Baroness Hilda. *Impressions and Memories*. London: 1926.
Demblon, Celest. *La Guerre à Liège*. Paris: 1915.
*Der Deutsch-Französische Krieg 1870–1871*, Redigiert von der kriegsgeschichtlichen Abteilung des Grossen Generalstabes. Vol. II. Berlin: 1872–81.
*Die deutsche Eisen- und Stahlindustrie 1933*. "Das Spezialarchiv der deutschen Wirtschaft." Berlin: 1933.
*Die deutsche Schwereisenindustrie und ihr Arbeiter*. Stuttgart: 1925.
Deutscher Metallarbeiterverband. *Konzerne der Metallindustrie*. Stuttgart: 1924.
Diels, Rudolf. *Lucifer ante Portas*. Stuttgart: 1950.
Dietrich, Otto. *Mit Hitler in die Macht*. Munich: 1934.
*Documents authentiques annotés: Les papiers secrets du second empire*. Brussels: 1871.

*Documents on German Foreign Policy 1918–1945.* Series D, 1937–1945. Washington: n.d.

*Dokumente der deutschen Politik, 1933–40.* Berlin: 1935–43.

Dönitz, Karl. *Zehn Jahre und zwanzig Tage.* Bonn: 1958.

Dornberg, John. "Anti-Semitism Blights Germany." New York *Herald-Tribune,* June 27, 1965.

Douglas, Norman. *Looking Back.* New York: 1933.

Dredge, James. *The Works of Messrs. Schneider & Co.* London: 1900.

Ducrot, Auguste Alexandre. *La Journée de Sédan.* Paris: 1871.

"Düsseldorf, Essen and Other Parts of the Ruhr Quiet and in Perfect Order." *New York Times,* March 25, 1920.

Dugan, Charles, and Carroll Stewart. *Ploesti.* New York: 1962.

Duffield, Isabel McKenna. *Washington in the 90's.* San Francisco: 1929.

Dulles, Allen Welsh. *Germany's Underground.* New York: 1947.

Du Pont, Bessie G. *E. I. Du Pont de Nemours and Company: A History, 1802–1902.* New York: 1920.

Duranty, Walter. "Last Stand at Essen Told by Girl Nurse." *New York Times,* April 14, 1920.

Düwell, Wilhelm. *Wohlfahrts-Plage.* Dortmund: 1903.

"Economics Catches Up with the House of Krupp." *New York Times,* April 9, 1967.

*The Effects of Strategic Bombing on the War Economy,* Washington: 1945.

Eisenhower, Dwight D. *Crusade in Europe.* New York: 1948.

Eisgruber, Heinz. *So schossen wir nach Paris.* Berlin: 1934.

Emery, Luigi. "The House of Krupp." *Littell's Living Age,* January 1, 1927.

"End of the Dynasty." *Time,* August 11, 1967.

"End of the Krupps." *Business Week,* May 8, 1948.

Engelbrecht, N. C., and F. C. Hanighen. *Merchants of Death: A Study of the International Armament Industry.* New York: 1934.

Erikson, John. *The Soviet High Command.* London: 1962.

"Es war ein festlicher Abend." *Unser Profil* (Rheinhausen), January-February 1963.

*Essen mit einer Einführung.* Essen: n.d.

"Essen Soviet Claims Many Guns and Prisoners." *New York Times,* March 24, 1920.

Eulenberg-Hertefeld, Fürst Philipp zu. *Aus 50 Jahren.* Berlin: 1923.

"Ewald Löser, Last of Jailed Krupp Executives, Freed." *New York Times,* June 2, 1951.

*Der Fall Krupp.* Munich: 1903.

Faure, Paul. *Les Marchants des Canons contre la Paix.* Paris: 1932.

*Federal Reporter,* vol. 174, 2d series, p. 983 (1949). "Decision of the United States Court of Appeals for the District of Columbia Circuit, May 11, 1949, Affirming Order of District Court of the United States for the District of Columbia, No. 9883. Friedrich Flick, appellant, v. Louis Johnson, Secretary of Defense, et al., appellees."

Ferencz, Benjamin B. "Die Zwangsarbeit jüdischer KZ-Lager Insassen im Krupp Konzern." Unpublished legal brief in the author's files.

——. Letter to the author. March 22, 1963.

Fest, T. C. *Das Gesicht des Dritten Reichs.* Munich: 1963.

Feuchter, Georg W. *Geschichte des Luftkrieges.* Bonn: 1954.

Fielding, Gabriel. *The Birthday King.* London: 1962.

Fife, Robert Herndon, Jr. *The German Empire Between Two Wars: A Study of the Political and Social Development of the Nation Between 1871 and 1914.* New York: 1916.

Fischer, Fritz. *Griff nach der Weltmacht.* Düsseldorf: 1961.

Fischer, Georg. *König Wilhelm und die Beschiessung von Paris.* Leipzig: 1902.

Fischer, Ruth. *Stalin and German Communism.* Cambridge: 1948.

Fisher, Douglas Alan. *The Epic of Steel.* New York: 1963.

Fitzgerald, F. Scott. *Tender is the Night.* New York: 1934.

"Flick-Erbe — Von Friederichs Gnaden." *Der Spiegel,* June 5, 1963.

"Flying off to Asia . . . A Churchill and a Krupp." *Daily Express* (London), November 13, 1962.

Fodor, Eugene. *Germany 1967*. New York: 1967.

Foerster, Wolfgang. *Ein General kämpft gegen den Krieg*. Munich: 1949.

Forbes, Archibald. *My Experiences of the War Between France and Germany*. London: 1871.

*Foreign relations of the United States. The Conference of Berlin (the Potsdam Conference) 1945*. Vol. II. Washington: 1960.

Fortsche, Colonel H. *Kriegskunst heute und morgen*. Berlin: 1939.

Fraiken, J. "L'Industrie des Armes à Feu de Liège." *Revue Economique Internationale*, September 1929.

François, General Hermann von. *Marneschlacht und Tannenberg*. Berlin: 1923.

Frank, Hans. *Die Technik des Staats*. Munich: 1942.

Frazer, Sir James. *The New Golden Bough*. Ed. by Theodore H. Gaster. New York: 1959.

Frederick III. *The War Diary of the Emperor Frederick III 1870–1871*. Trans. and ed. by A. R. Allinson. London: 1927.

*Freidank's Bescheidenheit*. Berlin: 1877.

"French Kill 6 Men, Wound 30 Others, in Fight at Krupp's." *New York Times*, April 1, 1923.

Freytag-Loringhoven, Freiherr von. *Menschen und Dinge wie ich sie in meinem Leben sah*. Berlin: 1923.

Fried, Ferdinand. *Krupp-Tradition und Aufgabe*. Godesberg: 1956.

Fried. Krupp A.G. *Erwiderung auf das Rundschreiben der Rheinischen Metallwaren- und Maschinenfabrik*. Essen: 1905.

———. *Krupp 1812–1912*. Jena: 1912.

———. *Die Krupps*. Essen: 1912.

"Fried. Krupp Essen, 1811–1946." Compiled by Krupp Control, Essen, B.A.O.R. Mimeographed. December 1946.

Friedjung, Heinrich. *Das Zeitalter des Imperialismus*. Berlin: 1919.

Friedman, Filip. *This was Oswiecim* [Auschwitz]. London: 1946.

*Friedrich-Alfred Hütte, Rheinhausen, Germany*. The United States Strategic Bombing Survey, Munitions Division. Washington: January 1947.

"Friedrich Alfred Krupp — the Essen Philanthropist." *Review of Reviews*, January 1903.

*Friedrich Krupp A.G. Borbeck Plant, Essen, Germany*. The United States Strategic Bombing Survey, Munitions Division. Washington: January 1947.

*Friedrich Krupp, Grusonwerke A.G. Madgeburg, Germany*. The United States Strategic Bombing Survey, Ordnance Branch. Washington: January 1947.

Frischauer, Willi. "How Germany Will Help Others." *Weekly Post* (London), December 3, 1960.

———. "The Ruhr Goes Atomic." *Weekly Post* (London), November 26, 1960.

Frobenius, Hermann. *Alfred Krupp, ein Lebensbild*. Dresden: 1889.

Frobenius, Lieut. Col. H. *Kriegsziele und Friedensziele*. Berlin: 1915.

"From Swords to Plowshares — A Survey of the Post-War Activities of the Huge Krupp Works." *Scientific American*, September 3, 1921.

Frossard, Charles Auguste. *Rapport sur les Opérations du deuxièmes corps de l'armée du Rhin dans la campagne de 1870*. Paris: 1871.

Fuchs, Rudolf. *Die Kriegsgewinne*. Zurich: 1918.

Fuller, J. C. S. *The Second World War, 1939–45: A Strategic and Tactical History*. London: 1948.

"Fünfzehn Jahre." Essener Allgemeine Zeitung, March 30, 1938.

"A Gallery of German Business Leaders." *Fortune*, August 1961.

Generalstab. *Der Deutsch-Französische Krieg 1870–1871. Redigiert von der kriegesgeschichtlichen Abteilung des Grossen Generalstabes*. Vol. II.

*The German Campaign in Russia — Planning and Operations 1940–42*. Washington: 1955.

"Germany's Krupp: Can He Keep His Empire?" *U.S. News and World Report*, January 30, 1959.

Giese, Friedrich. *Die Kriegsmarine im grossdeutschen Freiheitskampf*. Berlin: 1940.

Gilbert, G. M. *Nuremberg Diary*, New York: 1947.

*Glaubenskrise im Dritten Reich.* Stuttgart: 1953.

Globke, Hans. *Kommentare zur deutschen Rassegesetzbung.* Munich, Berlin: 1936.

Goebbels, Joseph. *Diaries, 1942–1943.* Trans. by Louis P. Lochner. New York: 1948.

———. *Vom Kaiserhof zur Reichskanzlei.* Munich: 1936.

Goecke, Rudolf. *Das Grossherzogtum Berg unter Joachim Murat, Napoleon I und Louis Napoleon.* Cologne: 1877.

Goepel, Otto. *Essen, Montanindustrielle Entwicklung und Aufbau der Ruhr-Emscherstadt.* Essen: 1925.

Goetz, Cecelia H. Letter to the author. May 1, 1963.

Goldstajn, Tadeusz. Sworn statement regarding Berthawerk conditions; in the author's files.

Goncourt, Edmond et Jules de. *Journal: Memoires de la vie littéraire.* Paris: 1956–1959.

Goodspeed, D. J. *Ludendorff, Genius of World War I.* Boston: 1966.

Göring, Hermann. *Reden und Aufsätze.* Munich: 1938.

———. *Aufbau einer Nation.* Berlin: 1934.

Görlitz, Walter. *Der deutsche Generalstab, Geschichte und Gestalt 1657–1945.* Frankfurt: n.d.

———. *History of the German General Staff, 1657–1945.* Trans. by Brian Battershaw. London: n.d.

———. *Kleine Geschichte des deutschen Generalstabes.* Berlin: 1967.

———. *Paulus and Stalingrad.* London: 1963.

———. *Der zweite Weltkrieg, 1939–45.* Stuttgart: 1951.

Goure, Léon. *The Siege of Leningrad.* Stanford: 1962.

Gramont, Duc de. *La France et la Prusse avant la Guerre.* Paris: 1872.

Grävenitz, Georg von. *Die militärische Vorbereitung der Jugend in Gegenwart und Zukunft.* Ed. "Der Deutsche Krieg," No. 67, 1915.

Graves, Robert. *Good-bye to All That.* New York: 1930.

*Great Exhibition, 1851, Official Descriptive and Illustrated Catalogue, Part II, Classes V. to X., Machinery.* London: 1851.

"The Great Krupp Works." *Scientific American,* August 22, 1896.

Greiner, Helmuth. *Die Oberste Wehrmachtsführung, 1939–45.* Wiesbaden: 1951.

Greiner, Josef. *Das Ende des Hitler-Mythos.* Vienna: 1947.

Groos, Otto. *Was jeder vom Seekrieg wissen muss.* Berlin: 1940.

*Die Grosse Politik der Europäischen Kabinette 1871–1914.* 40 vols. Berlin: 1922–1927.

Gruson, Sidney. "German Concerns Ask New Mergers." *New York Times,* January 11, 1959.

———. "Krupp Denies Aim Is Bigger Empire." *New York Times,* January 18, 1959.

———. "Krupp Paces West Germany's Comeback." *New York Times,* February 5, 1961.

———. "Krupp Permitted to Buy Steel Unit." *New York Times,* January 7, 1959.

Guderian, Heinz. *Erinnerungen eines Soldaten.* Heidenberg: 1951.

———. *Panzer Leader.* New York: 1952.

Guillemin. *L'héroïque défense de Paris, 1870–71.* Paris: 1959.

*Gusstahlfabrik Friedrich Krupp, Essen, Germany.* The United States Strategic Bombing Survey, Munitions Division. Washington: January 1947.

Haas, Helmuth de. *The Lure of Steel: 150 Years Krupp 1811/1961.* Essen: 1961.

———. *Wir im Ruhrgebiet.* Photographs by Fritz Fenzl. Stuttgart: 1960.

Habatsch, Walther. *Die deutsche Besetzung von Dänemark und Norwegen, 1940.* 2nd ed. Göttingen: 1952.

Haeften, Oberst von. "Bismarck und Moltke." *Preussiche Jahrbücher* CLXXVII (1919).

Halder, Franz. *Hitler als Feldherr.* Munich: 1959.

Hallgarten, George W. F. *Hitler, Reichswehr und Industrie.* Frankfurt: 1955.

Hallgarten, Wolfgang. *Vorkriegsimperialismus.* Paris: 1935. (Chapter note references to "Hallgarten" are to this work.)

———. "La Signification politique et économique de la mission Liman von Sanders." *Revue d'Histoire de la Guerre Mondiale,* January 1935.

"Hannover 1963: Weltweiter Wettbewerb." *Krupp Mitteilungen,* June, 1963.

Harris, Sir Arthur T. *Bomber Offensive.* London: 1947.

Hasse, Hermann. *Krupp in Essen. Die Bedeutung der deutschen Waffenschmiede.* Berlin: n.d.

Haufhofer, K., and J. Märtz. *Zur Geopolitik der Selbstbestimmung.* Munich: 1923.

Haussner, Karl. *Das Feldgeschütz mit langem Rohrrücklauf.* Munich: 1928.

Haux, Ernst. "Bei Krupp 1890–1935. Bilder der Erinnerung aus 45 Jahren von Finanzrat Dr. Ernst Haux." Typescript. 138 pp. The only copy is deposited in the Werksarchiv Fried. Krupp. (Chapter note references to "Haux" are to this work.)

—————. *Was lehrt uns der Krieg?* Essen: 1918.

"The Head of the House of Krupp a Peace Advocate." *Review of Reviews,* October 1910.

Hechler, Kenneth William. *The Bridge at Remagen.* New York: 1957.

Helms, Karl Heinrich. *Krupp und Krause, Roman einer Epoche.* Recklinghausen: 1965.

Henk, Emil. *Die Tragödie des 20 Juli 1955.* 1946.

Henschen, Sigmund. "Busy Bertha." *Forum,* May 1917.

Hérisson, Maurice d'Irisson d'. *Journal d'un officier d'ordonnance, Juillet 1870–Février 1871.* Paris: 1885.

"Herr Krupp in England." *The Literary Digest,* September 5, 1914.

Heusinger, Adolf. *Befehl im Widerstreit — Schicksalsstunden der deutschen Armee, 1923–25.* Stuttgart: 1950.

Heuss, Theodor. *150 Jahre Krupp, Gedenkrede zu Essen am 20. November 1961.* Tübingen: 1962.

Heydecker, Joe J., and Johannes Leeb. *Der Nürnberger Prozess.* Berlin, Köln: 1958.

Heyking, E. von. *Tagebücher aus vier Weltteilen.* Leipzig: 1926.

Hilberg, Raul. *The Destruction of the European Jews.* Chicago: 1961.

Hindenburg, Paul von Beneckendorf und von. *Aus meinem Leben.* Leipzig: 1934.

*Historische Sammlung Krupp.* Essen: November 18, 1961.

*History of the United Nations War Crimes Commission.* London: 1948.

Hitler, Adolf. *Mein Kampf.* Munich: 1932.

Hochhuth, Rolf. *Der Stellvertreter.* (*The Deputy*) Berlin: 1963. Trans. by Richard and Clara Winston. New York: 1964.

Hoffbauer, E. *Die deutsche Artillerie in den Schlachten und Treffen des Deutsch-Französischen Krieges 1870–71. Heft I: Das Treffen von Weissenburg.* Berlin: 1896.

Holborn, Hajo. *A History of Modern Germany, 1648–1840.* New York: 1964.

Hönig, Fritz. *Gefechtbilder aus dem Kriege, 1870–71.* 3 vols. Berlin: 1891–94.

Höppner, General von. *Deutschlands Krieg in der Luft. Ein Rückblick auf die Entwicklung und die Leistungen unserer Heeres-Luftstreikräfte im Weltkrieg.* Leipzig: 1921.

Horne, Alistair. *Back to Power: A Report on the New Germany.* London: 1955. (Chapter note references to "Horne" are to this work.)

—————. *The Fall of Paris, the Siege and the Commune, 1870–71.* New York: 1965.

—————. *The Price of Glory: Verdun 1916.* New York: 1962.

Hossbach, Friedrich. *Zwischen Wehrmacht und Hitler.* Hannover: 1949.

"The House of Krupp." *La Stampa* (Turin), October 7, 1926. Trans. and repub. in *Littell's Living Age,* January 1, 1927.

"House of Krupp Observes Its 150th Anniversary." *New York Times,* November 21, 1961.

"The House That Krupp Built." *Time,* August 19, 1957.

Howard, Michael. *The Franco-Prussian War, the German Invasion of France 1870–1871.* London: 1962.

Hué, Otto. *Krupp und die Arbeiterklasse.* Essen: 1912.

*Hundertjähriges Bestehen der Firma Fried. Krupp und der Gusstahlfabrik zu Essen a. d. Ruhr.* Essen: Jahresbericht der Handelskammer für die Kreise Essen, Mülheim-Ruhr und Oberhausen zu Essen (pp. 179–185). 1912.

Hunter, Robert. "The Krupps' Model Town: A Type of German Feudalism." *Review of Reviews,* June 1915.

Huret, Jules. *In Deutschland.* 1907.

*Das Hüttenwerk Rheinhausen.* Essen: January 1961.

*Illustrated History of the International Exhibition.* London: 1862.

*India: A Reference Manual.* Delhi: 1953.
"An Injustice to the Krupp Works." *Scientific American,* May 1922.
"Iron and Steel," *The Morning Post* (London), July 3, 1862.
Jacobsen, Hans-Adolf. *Dokumente zur Vorgeschichte des Westfeldzuges, 1939–40.* Göttingen: 1956.
Jaspers, Karl. "Beispiel für das Verhängnis des Vorrangs nationalpolitischen Denkens." *Lebenfragen der deutschen Politik.* 1963.
"Jubiläumsrede von Herrn Dr. Alfried Krupp von Bohlen und Halbach am 20. November 1961." Unpublished.
Justrow, Karl. *Der Technische Krieg im Spiegel der Kriegserfahrungen und der Weltpresse.* Berlin: 1938.
"Der Kaiser bei Krupp in Essen." *Vorwärts,* 100 Jahre SPD, May 1963.
"The Kaiser's Death Factories Are Silent Now." *The Literary Digest,* April 12, 1919.
Kaltenbusch, F. *Das sittliche Recht des Krieges.* Giessen: 1906.
Kantorowicz, Hermann. *Der Geist der englischen Politik.* Berlin: 1929.
Katzenstein, L. "Les deux Krupp et leur Oeuvre." *Revue Économique Internationale,* May 1906.
Kehr, Eckart. *Schlachtflottenbau und Parteipolitik, 1894–1901.* Berlin: 1930.
——. "Soziale und finanzielle Grundlagen der Tirpitzschen Flottenpropaganda." *Gesellschaft.* September 1908.
Keim, General A. "Wachet, liebe Volkserzieher!" *Volkserzieher,* No. 29, 1910.
Kellen, T. *Friedrich Alfred Krupp und sein Werk.* Braunschweig: 1904.
——. *Die Firma Krupp und ihre soziale Tätigkeit.* Hamm: 1903.
Kelly, Daniel F. "Sees Decline of Germany's Jews Nearing." United Press International, November 23, 1963.
Keynes, John Maynard. *The Economic Consequences of the Peace.* London: 1919.
"King Krupp." *Réalités,* August 1959.
Kintner, Earl W., ed. *Haldamar Trial of Alfons Klein, Adolf Wallmann, et al.* London: 1948.
Kirchoff, Vice-Admiral. *Englands Willkür. 1914–1915.*
——. "England und Amerika." *Süddeutsche Monatsschriften,* January–May 1915.
Klass, Gert von. *Die Drei Ringe, Lebensgeschichte eines Industrieunternehmens.* Tübingen: 1953. (Chapter note references to "Klass" are to this work.)
——. *Aus Schutt und Asche, Krupp nach fünf Menschenaltern.* Tübingen: 1961.
——. *Stahl vom Rhein, die Geschichte des Hüttenwerkes Rheinhausen.* Essen: 1957.
——. "Am 13. August 1957 vollendet Alfried Krupp von Bohlen und Halbach, der alleinige Inhaber der Firma Fried. Krupp, Essen, sein fünfzigstes Lebensjahr." *Krupp Mitteilungen,* August 1957.
——. "Bertha Krupp von Bohlen und Halbach." *Krupp Mitteilungen,* March 20, 1956.
Klee, Karl. *Das Unternehmen Seelöwe.* Göttingen: 1949.
Kleist, Peter. *Zwischen Hitler und Stalin.* Bonn: 1950.
Klindender, General A. D. "Der deutsche Offizier." *Hamburger Volksheim,* n. 14. Hamburg: 1915.
Klose, Werner. *Generation im Gleichschritt.* Oldenberg and Hamburg: 1964.
Klotz, Helmut. *Der neue deutsche Krieg.* Berlin: 1937.
Knieriem, August von. *The Nuremberg Trials.* Chicago: 1959.
Knorr, R. H. "The Krupps and Their Steel Works at Essen." *Review of Reviews,* January 1903.
Koepper, Gustav. *Das Gusstahlwerk Friedrich Krupp und seine Entstehung.* Essen: 1897.
Kohn, Hans. *The Mind of Germany: The Education of a Nation.* New York: 1960.
——. "Three Goals for Prussia." *Saturday Review,* August 19, 1967.
Koller, General Karl. *Der letzte Monat.* Mannerheim: 1949.
Kordt, Erich. *Nicht aus den Akten (Die Wilhelmstrasse in Frieden und Krieg, 1928–1945).* Stuttgart: 1950.
Krafft von Dellmensigen, General. *Die Führung des Kronprinzen Rupprecht von*

*Bayern auf dem linken deutschen Heeresflügel bis zur Schlacht in Lothringen im August, 1914,* Wissen und Wehr, Sonderheft. Berlin: 1925.

Kraft, F. G. "Bürger, Häuser, und Strassen in Essen," *Beiträge zur Geschichte der Stadt u. Stift Essen.* Essen: 1933.

Kranzbühler, Otto. "Nuremberg Eighteen Years Afterwards." *De Paul Law Review,* XIV, No. 2, Spring-Summer 1965.

————. *Rückblick auf Nürnberg.* Hamburg: 1949.

————. *Kreuz über Kohle und Eisen. Herausgegeben im Auftrage des Bischofs von Essen,* Dr. *Franz Hengsbach.* Essen: 1958.

Kronstein, Heinrich. Review of *Warum wurde Krupp verurteilt? Legende und Justizirrtum. Columbia Law Review,* January 1953. Reply by Telford Taylor. "The Krupp Trial: Fact v. Fiction." *Columbia Law Review,* February 1953.

Krosigk, Graf Lutz Schwerin von. *Es geschah in Deutschland.* Tübingen: 1951.

*Krupp 1811–1961, Auslandsvertretertagung 1961.* Essen: 1961.

"Krupp Again a World Leader in Heavy Industry." *The Times* (London), July 7, 1961.

Krupp, Alfred. *Generalregulativ für die Firma Fried. Krupp.* (Essen: September 9, 1872) *mit einer Vorbemerkung von Ernst Schröder* (Essen: 1961).

————. "Humor bei Alfred Krupp." Alfred Krupp's sketches and cartoons, bound as a volume. The only copy is in the possession of Baron Tilo von Wilmoswky.

"Krupp auf Capri." *Vorwärts,* Nr. 268, November 15, 1902.

"Krupp auf Leibrente." *Der Stern,* March 21–27, 1967.

"Krupp-Bürgschaft; Höhen und Tiefen." *Der Spiegel,* March 13, 1967.

"The Krupp Centenary." *The Nation,* August 22, 1912.

"The Krupp Centenary." *Outlook,* September 14, 1912.

"Krupp Dead Buried with Pomp in Essen." *New York Times,* April 11, 1923.

"Krupp Directors to Face Army Trial." *New York Times,* April 3, 1923.

"Krupp Empire's Big Blowout." *Life,* May 5, 1961.

"The Krupp Exhibit at the Great Fair." *Scientific American,* July 15, 1893.

"Krupp: Father or Child of History?" *Newsweek,* September 23, 1963.

*Krupp Heute.* Essen: 1963.

*Krupp: Information über den Konzern; seine Geschichte, seine Erzeugnisse, seine Leistungen.* Essen: 1963.

*Krupp in the Service of Engineering Progress.* Essen: n.d.

"Krupp Is Back in Business." *Business Week,* May 5, 1951.

"Krupp-Krise: Schulden und Sühne." *Der Spiegel,* March 13, 1967.

"Krupp Marches On." *The Times Review of Industry* (London), February 1962.

"Krupp on the March." *Time,* January 9, 1959.

*Krupp Past and Present: A Short Outline.* Essen: 1961.

"The Krupp Phoenix Rises Again." *The Times* (London), April 18, 1963.

*Krupp Products and Services from A to Z.* Essen: 1961.

"Krupp Receives the 'Golden Banner.' " Trans. at Nuremberg. *Krupp,* May 15, 1940.

"Krupp Reports Company Held Its Own During 1962." *New York Times,* April 8, 1963.

"The Krupp Scandals in Germany: Foreign Comment." *The Literary Digest,* May 10, 1913.

"The Krupp Steel Works." *The Literary Digest,* June 1915.

"The Krupp Verdict." *Littell's Living Age,* June 16, 1923.

"Krupp-Verkauf sauflage: Dem deutschen Volke." *Der Spiegel,* February 26, 1968.

Krupp von Bohlen und Halbach, Alfried. *Vereinigte Staaten von Amerika gegen Alfried Krupp und andere. Inhalt: Berufung der Verteidigung* (Application for revision of sentence) *an General Clay vom 21. August 1948; Antrag der Verteidigung auf Einberufung einer Plenarsitzung der Militärtribunale vom 10. August 1948.* Mimeographed; in author's collection.

————. Three speeches to retiring Krupp workers, reprinted in the *Financial Times* (London), April 29, 1959; March 6, 1960; and May 4, 1962.

————. *Vorhaben Erklärung.* March 4, 1964.

Krupp von Bohlen und Halbach, Gustav. "Objectives of German Policy." *Review of Reviews*, November 1932.
——. "Plant Leaders and Armament Leaders." Trans. at Nuremberg. *Krupp*, March 1, 1942.
——. "Works Leader and Armaments Works." Trans. at Nuremberg. Essen: April 5, 1941.
"Krupp vor dem französischen Kriegsgericht." *Süddeutsche Monatshefte* (Munich), June 1923.
"Krupps and Kruppdom." *Littell's Living Age*, May 4, 1918.
"Krupp's Great Plant Converted to the Arts of Peace." *The Literary Digest*, February 28, 1920.
"Krupp's Steel." *Illustrated London News*, November 15, 1862.
"Krupps in the Steppe." *Frankfurter Zeitung Wochenblatt*, September 24, 1925. Trans. and repub. in *Littell's Living Age*, December 12, 1925.
"The Krupps: The Cannon Makers of Essen Face the End of Their Dynasty." *Life*, August 27, 1945.
"Krupp's Will Leaves All to a New Foundation." *New York Times*, August 5, 1967.
"Krupp-Stiftung: Unterm Strich." *Der Spiegel*, January 22, 1968.
Kubizek, August. *Adolf Hitler, mein Jugendfreund*. Graz: 1953.
Kuhl, Hermann Joseph von. *Der deutsche Generalstab in Vorbereitung und Durchführung des Weltkrieges*. Berlin: 1920.
Kurenberg, Joachim von *Krupp, Kampf um Stahl*. Berlin: 1935.
Labouchère, Henry. *Diary of a Besieged Resident in Paris*. London: 1871.
Lachmann, Kurt. "Alfried Krupp Takes a Look at the Future of Europe." *U.S. News and World Report*, March 14, 1960.
*Landsberg: A Documentary Report*. Reprinted from the February 1951 issue of *Information Bulletin*, official magazine of the U. S. High Commissioner for Germany. Frankfurt: 1951.
"Last of the Krupps." *Newsweek*, August 14, 1967.
"The Late Herr Krupp as a Patron of Zoology." *Review of Reviews*, February 1903.
Launay, L., and J. Sennac. *Les Relations Internationales des Industries de la Guerre*. Paris: 1932.
Leber, Annedore, ed. *Conscience in Revolt: Sixty-four Stories of Resistance in Germany 1933–45*. London: 1957.
Lebrun, Barthélemi Louis Joseph. *Souvenirs Militaires 1866–1870*. Vol. II of *Preliminaires de la Guerre, Missions en Belgique et à Vienne*. Paris: 1895.
Lehautcourt, Pierre. *Les Origines de la Guerre de 1870: 1a Candidature Hohenzollern 1868–1870*. Paris: 1912.
——. *Guerre de 1870–71*. Vol. II of *Aperçu et commentaires*. Paris: 1910.
Lehmann, Gustav. *Die Mobilmachung von 1870–71*. Berlin: 1905.
Lehmann-Russbüldt, Otto. *Die blutige Internationale der Rüstungen*. Berlin: 1933.
Lenard, Philipp. *Deutsche Physik*. Munich-Berlin: 1938.
Lévai, Eugene. *Black Book on the Martyrdom of the Hungarian Jews*. Zurich: 1948.
Levinson, Leonard Louis. *Wall Street: A Pictorial History*. New York: 1961.
Lewinsohn, Richard. *Die Umschichtung der europäischen Vermögen*. Berlin: 1925.
Lewis, Flora. "Rebirth — and Challenge — of the Ruhr." *New York Times Magazine*, March 29, 1959.
Lichtenberger, Henri. *L'Allemagne Nouvelle*. Paris: 1936.
Liddell Hart, B. H. *The War in Outline 1914–1918*. New York: 1936.
Liebert, General E. von. *Ziele der deutschen Kolonial — und Auswanderungspolitik*, 1907. 2nd ed., 1910.
*Le Livre Jaune Français Documents diplomatiques, 1938–39. Paris* (Ministère des Affaires Étrangères): 1939.
Lloyd-Jones, Patricia. "Krupps Go Public Next Year." London *Times*, March 8, 1967.
Lochner, Louis P. *Tycoons and Tyrant: German Industry from Hitler to Adenauer*. Chicago: 1954.
Long, Wellington. "Banks Get Krupp to Open Up Its Books." United Press International, March 8, 1967.
Lossberg, Bernhard von. *Im Wehrmacht-Führungsstab*. Hamburg: 1950.

Luce, Henry. Letter to the author. April 15, 1963.

Ludendorff, Eric. *Auf dem Weg zur Feldherrnhalle*. Munich: 1937.

———. *Meine Kriegserinnerungen 1914–1916*. Berlin: 1919. (Chapter note references to "Ludendorff" are to this work.)

———. *Kriegsführung und Politik*. Berlin: 1922.

———. *Der Totalkrieg*. Berlin: 1933.

Ludwig, Emil. *Bismarck, Geschichte eines Kämpfers*. Berlin: 1927.

———. *Wilhelm Hohenzollern*. New York: 1926. (Chapter note references to "Ludwig" are to this work.)

Luedde-Neurath, Walther. *Die letzten Tage des Dritten Reiches*. Göttingen: 1951.

Luetkens, W. L. "First Full Krupp Accounts." *Financial Times*, February 25, 1968.

Maitrot, General. *La France et les Républiques Sud-Américaines*. Nancy: 1920.

"Making War Pay." *Nation*, January 9, 1960.

Malik, Rex. "Krupp Marches On." *Times Review of Industry*, February 1962.

Manchester, William. "The First World War." *Holiday*, November 1962.

———. "The House of Krupp." *Holiday*, October, November, December, 1964; January, February, 1965.

Manstein, Eric von. *Verlorene Siege*. Bonn: 1955.

Martin, James Stewart. *All Honorable Men*. Boston: 1950.

———. "The Rebirth of Krupp." *Nation*, March 21, 1959.

Martin, Rudolf. *Jahrbuch des Vermögens und Einkommens der Millionäre*. Berlin: 1912.

Maschke, Hermann M. *Das Krupp-Urteil und das Problem der "Plünderung."* Göttingen: 1951.

Matschoss, Conrad. *Ein Jahrhundert deutscher Maschinenbau*. Berlin: 1922.

McCloy, John J. "The Present Order of German Government." A letter to Representative J. K. Javits. *Department of State Bulletin*, June 11, 1951.

Meinhold, Eberhard. *Deutsche Rassenpolitik und die Erziehung im nationalen Ehrgefühl*. Munich: 1907.

Meisbach, I. *Friedrich Alfred Krupp*. Cologne: 1902.

Meissner, Otto. *Staatssekretär unter Ebert-Hindenburg-Hitler*. Hamburg: 1950.

Melzer, Walther. *Albert Kanal und Eben-Emael*. Heidelberg: 1957.

Menen, Aubrey. "The Be-Witching Isle of Capri." *Holiday*, January 1959.

Menne, Bernhard. *Krupp — Deutschlands Kanonenkönige*. Zurich: 1936.

"Merger Favored by Krupp Group." *New York Times*, November 17, 1965.

Metcalf, Clyde H. *A History of the United States Marine Corps*. New York: 1939.

Metsch, Horst von. *Wehrpolitik*. Berlin: 1939.

Mews, Karl. *Geschichte der Essener Gewehrindustrie*. Essen: 1909.

Middleton, Drew. "The Fabulous Krupps: a New Chapter." *New York Times Magazine*, February 18, 1951.

Military Tribunals Case No. 10: United States vs. Krupp, Löser, Houdremont, Müller, Jansen, Pfirsch, Ihn, Eberhardt, Korschan, Bülow, Lehmann, and Kupke. Nuremberg (U.S. Military Government): 1947.

Miller, F. C. G. *L'Usine Krupp*. Lausanne: 1898.

Millis, Walter. *Arms and Men*. New York: 1956.

Mirabeau, Honoré Gabriel Riquetti, Compte de. *De la Monarchie prussienne, sous Frédéric le Grand, avec un appendice contenant des recherches sur la situation actuelle des principales contrées de l'Allemagne*. London: 1788.

"Missglückte Mohrenwäsche der Industrie." *Der Gewerkschafter*, May 1963.

Moland, Louis. *Par Ballon monté: septembre 1870–10 février 1871*. Paris: 1872.

Moltke, Helmuth Johannes Ludwig von. *Erinnerungen-Briefe-Dokumente, 1877–1916*. Stuttgart: 1922.

———. *Militärische Korrespondenz aus den Dienstschriften des Krieges 1870–71*. Berlin: 1896.

Monneray, Henri. *La Persécution des Juifs en France*. Paris: 1937.

Montaudon, Jean Baptiste. *Souvenirs militaires*. Paris: 1898–1900.

Montegelas, Max von. *Die Folgen der Friedensverträge für Europa*. (*Handbuch der Politik*, 3d ed. Band 5.) Berlin: 1922.

Mooney, Richard E. "Krupp Takes First Steps to Public Ownership." *New York Times*, December 11, 1965.
Moorehead, Alan. *Eclipse*. New York: 1945.
―――. *Montgomery: A Biography*. New York: 1946.
Morgenthau, Henry, Jr. *Germany Is Our Problem*. New York: 1945.
Mourin, Maxine. *Les Complots contre Hitler*. Paris: 1948.
Mühlen, Norbert. *Die Krupps*. Frankfurt am Main: 1960.
Mühlon, Wilhelm. *The Vandal of Europe, an Exposé of the Inner Workings of Germany's Policy of World Domination, and its Brutalizing Consequences*. Trans. with an introduction by William L. McPherson. London: 1918.
Müller, Friedrich C. G. *L'Usine Krupp*. Lausanne: 1898.
Müller, Hermann von. *Die Entwicklung der Feldartillerie von 1815 bis 1870*. Berlin: 1893.
―――. *Die Tätigkeit der deutschen Festungsartillerie bei den Belagerungen, Beschiessungen und Einschliessungen im Deutsch-Französischen Kriege 1870–71*. Berlin: 1899–1904.
Museum der deutschen Geschichte, Berlin. Exhibit 1963. East Berlin.
Napoleon III. *Oeuvres posthumes et autographes inédits de Napoléon III en exil*. Recueillis et co-ordonnés par le comte de la Chapelle. Paris: 1873.
*Nazi Conspiracy and Aggression*. Vols. I. and VI. Office of United States Chief of Counsel for Prosecution of Axis Criminality. Washington: 1946.
"Neubeginn unserer Seeschiffahrt — MS Tilo von Wilmowsky vom Stapel gelaufen." *Krupp Mitteilungen*, December 1957.
"Die neue Versuchsanstalt der Fried. Krupp WIDIA-Fabrik." *Technische Mitteilungen Krupp*, December 1957.
Neuss, Erich. *Geschichte des Geschlechts von Wilmowsky, die Biographie von Herrn Baron*. Privately printed: 1963.
Nichols, A. *Neutralität und amerikanische Waffenausfuhr*. Berlin: 1931.
Nicholson, H. *Die Verschwörung der Diplomaten*. Frankfurt: 1930.
Niemeyer, Victor. *Alfred Krupp: A Sketch of his Life and Work*. New York: 1888.
Noman, Max. *Apostles of Revolution*. Boston: 1939.
Obermaier, Hannes. "Hunter" columns in Munich *Abendzeitung* 1956–1966.
*Official Gazette of the Control Council for Germany*. Berlin: 1946.
Ogorkiewicz, Richard Marian. *Armor: The Development of Mechanized Forces*. London: 1960.
Olsen, Arthur J. "Krupp Problems Focus Attention on German Industry and Financing." *New York Times*, November 17, 1967.
―――. ."Ruhr Industry Back to Pre-War Structure." *New York Times*, January 25, 1959.
Oven, Wilfred von. *Mit Goebbels bis zum Ende*. Buenos Aires: 1949.
*Papiers Secrets de Second Empire, Les*. No. 12. Brussels: 1871.
*Para a Inauguração da Krupp Metalurgia Camp Limpo S.A. em Junio 17, de 1961*. Campo Limpo, Brazil: 1961.
Paxton, Frederic L. *America at War 1917–1918*. Boston: 1939.
Pechel, Rudolf. *Deutscher Widerstand*. Zurich: 1947.
Peck, David W. Letter to the author. March 22, 1963.
Perbandt, H. von. *Ist die Monopolstellung Krupps berechtigt?* Berlin: 1909.
―――. *Das Persönliche im modernen Unternehmertum*. Leipzig: 1920.
"Personal Characteristics of the Late Herr Krupp." *Review of Reviews*, January 1903.
Pertz, G. H. *Das Leben des Feldmarschalls Grafen N. von Gneisenau*. Berlin: 1864, 1880.
Peyrefitte, Roger. *Exil in Capri, mit einem Vorwort von Jean Cocteau*. Karlsruhe: 1960.
Pflug-Hartung, Julius von. *Krieg und Sieg 1870–71: Ein Gedenkbuch*. Berlin: n.d.
Picker, Henry. *Hitlers Tischgespräche*. Bonn: 1951.
*Pioniere deutscher Technik*, Krupp documentary film.
Plumb, Robert K. "Sparta's Might Laid to Secret Weapon — Steel." *New York Times*, January 30, 1961.
Poliakov, Léon. *Auschwitz*. Paris: 1964.

Poliakov, Leon, and Josef Wulf. *Das Dritte Reich und die Juden.* Berlin: 1955.
Pounds, Norman J. G. *The Ruhr.* Bloomington: 1952.
Pritchett, V. S. "Germany." *Holiday,* May 1959.
Prittie, Terence. "The Krupp Empire." *The Atlantic,* October 1960.
Rabenau, Friedrich von. *Seeckt, aus seinem Leben.* Leipzig: 1940.
Ragland, Rawlings. Letter to the author. March 19, 1963.
Raphael, Gaston. *Hugo Stinnes.* Berlin: 1925.
———. *Krupp et Thyssen.* Paris: 1925.
Raymond, Jack. "Krupp on Release Is Hailed as Hero." *New York Times,* February 4, 1951.
"Rebirth at Essen." *Time,* September 15, 1952.
"Red Army Captures Essen." *New York Times,* March 20, 1929.
Reichsjugendführer, ed. *Kriminalität und Gefährdung der Jugend.* Berlin: 1941.
Reitlinger, Gerald. *The Final Solution.* New York: 1953.
"The Renaissance of Krupp." *The Financial Times* (London), July 6, 1960.
"Reprieve." *Time,* February 12, 1951.
Reybaud, Louis. *La Fer et la Houille.* Paris: 1874.
Ribbeck, Konrad. *Geschichte der Stadt Essen.* Essen: 1915.
Ribbentrop, Joachim von. *Zwischen London und Moskau. Erinnerungen und letzte Aufzeichnungen.* Leone am Starnberger See: 1953.
Rich, Norman, and M. H. Fisher. *Friedrich von Holstein: Politics and Diplomacy in the Era of Bismarck and Wilhelm II.* Cambridge: 1965.
———. eds. *The Holstein Papers.* Vol. III. Cambridge: 1961.
Richter, Franz. "Alfried [sic] Krupp und das Ausland." *Nord und Süd.* 1917.
Richter, Werner. *Bismarck.* Trans. by F. H. Hinsley. New York: 1965.
Ritter, Gerhard. *Carl Goerdeler und die deutsche Widerstandsbewegung.* Stuttgart: 1955.
Robertson, H. Murray. *Krupp's and the International Armaments Ring.* London: 1915.
Roth, Elizabeth. Letters to the author. June 3, March 27, April 2, March 23, 1963; April 7, 1967.
Rothfels, Hans. *The German Opposition to Hitler.* Hinsdale, Ill.: 1948.
*Rourkela.* Calcutta: Lalchand Roy & Company, n.d.
Rupprecht, Kronprinz. *Mein Kriegstagebuch.* Vol. I. Munich: 1929.
Russell, William Howard. *My Diary During the Last Great War.* London: 1874.
Rüstow, Friedrich Wilhelm. *Die Feldherrnkunst des neunzehnten Jahrhunderts.* Zürich: 1857.
Ryder, Frank G. *The Song of the Nibelungs.* Trans. from the Middle High German Nibelungenlied. Detroit: 1962.
Sarazin, C. *Récits sur la dernière guerre franco-allemande.* Paris: 1887.
Sasuly, Richard. *I. G. Farben.* New York: 1947.
Saternus, A. *Die Schwerindustrie in und nach dem Kriege.* Berlin: 1920.
Scharnhorst, Gerhard T. D. *Briefe.* Ed. K. Linnebach. Munich: 1914.
Schaumburg-Lippe, Prinz Friedrich Christian zu. *Zwischen Krone und Kerker.* Wiesbaden: 1952.
Schiller, Johann. *Die Jungfrau von Orleans.* Frankfurt/M: 1963.
Schindler, Oberleutnant D. *Eine 42 cm Mörser-Batterie im Weltkrieg.* Breslau: 1934.
Schlieffen, Alfred. *Cannae.* (English trans.). Fort Leavenworth: 1936.
Schmid, Heinz. *Kriegsgewinne und Wirtschaft.* Berlin: 1935.
Schmidt, Paul. *Statist auf diplomatischer Bühne 1923–1945.* Bonn: 1949.
Schmitthenner, Paul. *Volkstümliche Wehrkunde.* Berlin: 1935.
Schneider, Louis. *Aus dem Leben Kaiser Wilhelms 1849–1873.* Berlin: 1888.
Scholl, Inge. *Die weisse Rose.* Frankfurt: 1952.
Schramm, Wilhelm von. *Der 20. Juli in Paris.* Bad Woerishorn: 1953.
Schröder, Ernst. "Angaben darüber, wem die Fabrik in Berndorf jetzt gehört und darüber, ob zur Familie Krupp familiäre Bindungen bestehen." Unpublished. 1963.
———. *Krupp-Geschichte einer Unternehmenfamilie.* Göttingen: 1957.
———. "Verlauf des letzten Kaiserbesuchs bei Krupp am 9. und 10. September, 1918." (Schedule of the Kaiser's last visit to Essen.) Unpublished; 1963; in author's collection.

——. Letter to the author. July 20, 1963.

——. "Verzeichnis der Orden Alfred Krupp 1853–1887." Unpublished. 1963.

——."Verzeichnis der Orden Alfried Krupp von Bohlen und Halbach." Unpublished. 1963.

——. "Verzeichnis der Herrn Dr. Gustav Krupp vBuH verliehenen Orden. Unpublished. 1963.

Schröder, Johannes. "Der finanzielle Herzinfarkt." *Handelsblatt*, July 27, 1962.

Schubart, Captain H. *England und die Interessen des Kontinents*. Berlin: 1914–15.

Schultz, Joachim. *Die letzten 30 Tage — aus dem Kriegstagebuch des O.K.W.* Stuttgart: 1951.

Schürmann, Kurt. Memo to author "Concerning Inheritance Tax." Dated June 20, 1963. Unpublished.

Schüssler, Captain. *The Fight of the Navy Against Versailles 1919–1935.* Trans. at Nuremberg. Berlin: 1937.

Schweitzer, Arthur. *Big Business in the Third Reich*. Bloomington: 1964.

——. "Business Policy in a Dictatorship." *The Business Review*, XXXVIII, No. 4, 1964.

Scott, J. D. *Vickers: A History*. London: 1962. (Chapter note references to "Scott" are to this work.)

Scott, James Brown. *The Hague Peace Conference of 1899 and 1907*. Baltimore: 1909.

"Sechs feiern ihr Goldenes." *Unser Profil* (Rheinhausen), March–April 1963.

Seeckt, Johann von. *Deutschland zwischen West und Ost*. Hamburg: 1933.

——. *Wege deutscher Aussenpolitik*. Leipzig: 1931.

"Segelregatta Buenos Aires–Rio de Janeiro im Film." *Buenos Aires Freie Presse*, May 25, 1963.

Seiss, D. D. *Remarks Made at the Funeral of Henry Bohlen, Brigadier-General U. S. Army*. Philadelphia: 1862.

Seldes, George. *Iron, Blood, and Profits*. New York: 1934.

Shabecoff, Philip. "Economics Catches Up with the House of Krupp." *New York Times*, April 9, 1967.

——. "Krupp: An Empire That Wobbled. *New York Times*, April 5, 1967.

——. "Krupp Announces End of Family Rule." *New York Times*, April 2, 1967.

——. "Krupp Challenges Allies on Order." *New York Times*, February 27, 1968.

Shaw, Stanley. *William of Germany*. New York: 1913.

Shirer, William. *Aufstieg und Fall des Dritten Reichs.* 2 Vols. Munich and Zurich: 1963.

——. *Berlin Diary*. New York: 1941.

——. *The Rise and Fall of the Third Reich: A History of Nazi Germany*. New York: 1960. (Chapter note references for "Shirer" are to this work.)

Sievers, Eduard. *Der Nibelungen Not*. Leipzig: 1921.

Slossen, Preston Williams. *The Great Crusade and After*. New York: 1930.

Smith, Walter Bedell. "Eisenhower's Six Great Decisions, No. 6." *Saturday Evening Post*, July 6, 1946.

Soldau, Georg. *Der Mann und der künftige Krieg*. Oldenburg: 1925.

Sondern, Frederic, Jr. "The Remarkable Rebirth of the House of Krupp." *Reader's Digest*, September 1955.

"Soviet Proclaimed at Essen." *New York Times*, March 21, 1920.

Spengler, Oswald. *Jahre der Entscheidung*. Munich: 1935.

*Statistische Angaben über die Krupp'sche Gusstahlfabrik nebst den zugehörigen Berg- und Hüttenwerken*. Essen: 1892.

Steinboemer, Gustav. *Soldatentum und Kultur. Die Wiederherstellung des Soldaten*. Hamburg: 1935.

Steiner, Edward A. "A Visit to Herr Krupp." *Outlook*, January 25, 1902.

Steinmuth, Hans. *England und der U-Boot-Krieg*. Stuttgart: 1916.

Stern, Michael. "My Fee Will be $25 Million." *True*, August 1954.

Stolper, Gustav. *German Realities*. New York: 1948.

Stonner, Anton. *Nationale Erziehung und Religionsunterricht*. Regensburg: 1934.

Strache, Wolf. *Essen*. Stuttgart: 1959.

Sturgkh, Josef. *Im Deutschen Grossen Hauptquartier*. Leipzig: 1921.

Suarez, Georges, and Guy Laborde. *Agonie de la Paix*. Paris: 1942.

Tacitus. *De Germania*. Ed. by T. E. Page and W. H. Rouse. London: 1914.

Taylor, Edmond. *The Fall of the Dynasties: The Collapse of the Old Order, 1905–1922*. New York: 1963.

Taylor, Telford. "The Krupp Trial: Fact vs. Fiction." *Columbia Law Review*, February 1953.

———. *The March of Conquest: The German Victories in Western Europe, 1940*. New York: 1958.

———. "The Nuremberg Trials." *Columbia Law Review*, April 1955.

———. "Nuremberg Trials: War Crimes and International Law." *International Conciliation*, April 1949.

———. *Sword and Swastika: Generals and Nazis in the Third Reich*. New York: 1952. (Chapter note references to "Taylor" are to this work.)

Tetens, T. H. *The New Germany and the Old Nazis*. New York: 1961.

Thayer, Charles W. *The Unquiet Germans*. New York: 1957.

Thompson, L. G. *Sidney Gilchrist Thomas*. London: 1940.

Thorwald, Juergen. *Das Ende an der Elbe*. Stuttgart: 1950.

Thun, H. *Die Industrie am Niederrhein und ihre Arbeiter*. Leipzig: 1879.

Thyssen, Fritz. *I Paid Hitler*. Trans. by Cesar Saerschinger. New York: 1941.

Tirpitz, Alfred von. *Erinnerungen*. Leipzig: 1919.

Tirpitz, W. von. *Wie hat such der Staatsbetrieb beim Aufbau der Flotte bewährt?* Leipzig: 1909.

Tissandier, Gaston. *En Ballon! Pendant le siège de Paris*. Paris: 1871.

Toland, John. *Last 100 Days*. New York: 1966.

Tresckow, Hans von. *Von Fürsten und andern Sterblichen*. Berlin: 1922.

Trevor-Roper, H. R. *The Last Days of Hitler*. New York: 1947.

*Trials of War Criminals Before the Nuremberg Military Tribunals Under Control Council Law No. 10, Nuremberg October 1946–April 1949*. Vols. VI ,VII, IX, XII, XIII, XIV, and XV. Washington: 1950, 1952.

Tuchman, Barbara W. *The Guns of August*. New York: 1962.

———. *Proud Tower*. New York: 1966.

Tümmler, Hans. *Essen, ein Bildband*. Essen: 1961.

Ullrich, Johannes. *Das Kriegswesen im Wandel der Zeiten*. Leipzig: 1940.

U. S. *Army Technical Manual 27–251: Treaties Governing Land Warfare*. Washington: 1944.

*United States Strategic Bombing Survey* (Washington: 1947).

*Unser Werk: Bochumer Verein für Gusstahlfabrikation A.G., Bochum*. Bochum: December 1956.

Usher, Roland G. "The Liebknecht Disclosures." *Nation*, May 15, 1913.

———. *Pan-Germanism*. Boston: 1913.

Utley, Freda. *The High Cost of Judgment*. Chicago: 1949.

Vabres, Donnedieu de. Le Procès de Nüremberg. Paris: 1947.

Valois, Admiral. *Nieder mit England!* Berlin: 1915.

"Vera Krupp, Ex-Wife of Industrialist, 57" (obituary). *New York Times*, October 17, 1957.

"The Verdict in the Krupp Scandal." *The Literary Digest*, December 6, 1913.

Vermeil, Edmond. *L'Allemagne Contemporaine, Sociale, Politique, et Culturale, 1890–1950*. 2 vols. Paris: 1952–53.

*Villa Hügel*. Essen: Headquarters, UK/US Coal Control Group, n.d.

"Villa Hügel im Zeichen der Trauer-Abschied von Frau Bertha Krupp." *Krupp Mitteilungen*, November 1957.

Voigts-Rhetz, Constantin von. *Briefe des Generals der Infantrie von Voigts-Rhetz aus den Kriegsjahren 1866 und 1870–71*. Berlin: 1906.

Vossler, Karl. *Gedenkrede für die Opfer an der Universität München*. Munich: 1947.

Vowinckel, Kurt. *Die Wehrmacht im Kampf*. Vols. 1–11. Heidelberg: 1954.

Wassen, H. M. *Was geschah in Stalingrad? Wo sind die Schuldigen?* Salzburg: 1950.

Waldersee, Alfred von. *Denkwürdigkeiten*. Stuttgart: 1922–23.

*Weihe der neuen Synagoge Essen*. Düsseldorf: Kalima-Druck, October 21, 1959.

Weisenborn, Guenther. *Der lautlose Aufstand.* Hamburg: 1953.

Werth, Alexander. *Russia at War, 1941–1945.* New York: 1964.

Werner, Rear Admiral Barthomaeus von. *Deutsches Kriegsschiffleben und Seefahrt Kunst:* 1895.

———. *Die Kampfmittel zur See:* 1896.

———. *Die deutsche Kolonialfrage:* 1897.

"West Germany's Millionaires — from Rubble to Riches." *U.S. News and World Report,* February 27, 1959.

Weyer, Bruno. *Deutschlands Seegefahren. Der Verfall der deutschen Flotte und ihr geplanter Wiederaufbau.* Munich: 1898.

Weyersberg, Albert. *Johann Abraham Henckels.* Münster: 1931.

Weymar, Paul. *Adenauer: His Authorized Biography.* New York: 1957.

White, Theodore H. *Fire in the Ashes: Europe in Mid-Century.* New York: 1953.

Wichert, Erwin. *Dramatische Tage in Hitlers Reich.* Stuttgart: 1952.

Wiedenfeld, Kurt. *Ein jahrhundert rheinischer Montanindustrie.* Bonn: 1916.

Wiedfeldt, Otto. *Friedrich Krupp als Stadtrat in Essen.* Essen: 1902.

Wile, Fred W. *Rings um den Kaiser.* Berlin: 1913.

Wilkins, William J. Letter to the author. March 19, 1967.

Wille, R. *Ehrhardt-Geschütze.* Berlin: 1908.

Williams, George. "An American at Krupp." Unpublished manuscript. 1965.

Wilmot, Chester. *The Struggle for Europe.* New York: 1952.

Wilmowsky, Tilo Frhr von. *Der Hügel.* Essen: n.d.

———. *Warum wurde Krupp verurteilt? Legende und Justizirrtum.* Stuttgart: 1950.

———. *Rückblickend möchte ich sagen . . . An der Schwelle des 150 jährigen Krupp-Jubiläums.* Oldenburg and Hamburg: 1961. (Chapter note references to "Wilmowsky" are to this work.)

Winschuh, Josef. *Der Verein mit dem langen Namen.* Berlin: 1932.

*Wirtschaftswissenschaftliches Institut der Gewerkschaften GmbH*· Cologne: 1962.

Woischnik, Bernhard. *Alfred Krupp: Meister des Stahls. Das Lebenbild eines grossen Deutschen.* Bad Godesberg: 1957.

Wolff, Leonard. *In Flanders Fields.* New York: 1958.

Wylie, I.A.R. *The Germans.* Indianapolis: 1911.

Yorck von. Wartenburg, Graf. *Weltgeschichte in Umrissen. Federzeichnung Deutschen. Bis zur Gegenwart fortgeführt von Prof. Dr. Hans F. Helmolt.* 25th ed. Berlin: 1922.

Young, Gordon. *The Fall and Rise of Alfried Krupp.* London: 1960.

Zeller, Eberhard. *Geist der Freiheit.* Munich: 1954.

Zola, Emile. *La Débâcle.* Paris: 1892.

Zoller, A., ed. *Hitler Privat.* Düsseldorf: 1949.

*Zur Hundertjahrfeier der Firma Krupp 1812–1912.* Essen: 1912.

# Picture Credits

# Index

✠ ✠ ✠

# The Krupp Dynasty

| | |
|---|---|
| 1587 | Arrival of Arndt Krupp in Essen. |
| 1599 | The Black Death: a windfall for Arndt. |
| 1618–48 | Thirty Years War: Anton Krupp produces 1,000 gun barrels a year. |
| 1811 | Friedrich Krupp founds the family cast steel factory. |
| 1812 | Friedrich digs trenches for Napoleon. |
| | Birth of Alfred Krupp. |
| 1816 | Krupp bayonets to Berlin. |
| 1826 | Death of Friedrich. |
| 1838 | Alfred spies in England. |
| 1836–42 | Alfred produces hollow-forged muskets. |
| 1847 | Prussia receives Alfred's first steel cannon. |
| 1851 | Alfred's debut at London's Crystal Palace Exhibition. |
| 1855 | Krupp steel smashes floor of Paris Exhibition. |
| 1866 | Prussia invades Austria with Krupp cannon. |
| 1870 | Sedan: Krupp guns defeat Napoleon III. |
| 1871 | First Krupp bombardment of Paris. |
| 1878 | "Bombardment of the Nations." |
| 1886 | Birth of Bertha Krupp. |
| 1887 | Death of Alfred Krupp. |
| | Fritz Krupp's Royal Tour. |
| 1900 | Fritz builds the Kaiser a navy. |
| 1901 | Plans for U–1 drawn. |
| 1902 | Fritz's suicide. |
| 1906 | Marriage of Bertha and Gustav Krupp. |
| 1907 | Birth of Alfried Krupp; joy in the Reich. |
| 1909 | Construction of Big Bertha. |
| 1914 | Big Berthas crush Belgium. |
| 1916 | Verdun: a Krupp masterpiece. |
| | Jutland: Krupp vs. Krupp. |
| | Gustav and Ludendorff confer. |
| 1918 | Gustav shells Paris. |
| | Kaiser says farewell in Essen. |
| 1919 | Gustav named a war criminal. |
| | Allies dismantle the factory. |
| 1920 | Workers rise, seize Essen. |
| | Gustav begins secret rearmament. |
| 1923 | French occupy the castle. |
| | Bloody Saturday at the office. |
| 1925 | Von Seeckt inspects the shops. |
| 1926 | Allied commission leaves Essen. |
| | Design of 1940 tanks completed. |

# MORE
# EXPOSITORY
# SERMON OUTLINES

### CHARLES SIMEON
and Others

**BAKER**
A DIVISION OF
Baker Book House Co

Reprinted 1996 by Baker Books
a division of Baker Book House Company
P.O. Box 6287, Grand Rapids, MI 49516-6287

Printed in the United States of America

ISBN 0-8010-9016-4

# CONTENTS

# PUBLISHER'S PREFACE

The book here reprinted as *More Expository Sermon Outlines* has been assisting preachers in the preparation of sound, biblical sermons for much of the last 150 years. This work was originally published in three volumes under the title *Theological Sketch-Book: Skeletons of Sermons.* A two-volume edition was released, four years later, in 1848. This edition of *Theological Sketch-Book* carried an expanded subtitle:

> *Skeletons of Sermons, Carefully Arranged in Systematic Order So As to Constitute a Complete Body of Divinity; Partly Original but Chiefly Selected from Simeon's "Horae Homileticae" and "Skeletons."*

The anonymous editor of this compilation favored sermon "skeletons" (or outlines) written by Charles Simeon, an eminent Anglican preacher of the early nineteenth century. *Theological Sketch-Book* drew largely on the following two works by Simeon:

> *Horae Homileticae: Discourses (in the Form of Skeletons) upon the Whole Scriptures.* 17 vols. London, 1819–28.
> *Helps to Composition: 600 Skeletons of Sermons* . . . 5 vols. 2d ed. London, 1808.

Of the 226 outlines in volume 2 (reprinted here) of *Theological Sketch-Book,* 97 are drawn from Simeon's two multivolume sets.

The remaining outlines are drawn from the following sources: (1) *Joseph Benson's Sermons, and Plans of Sermons, on Many of the Most Important Texts of Holy Scripture;* (2) *The Pulpit Assistant: Containing 300 Outlines or Skeletons of Sermons, Chiefly Extracted from Various Authors;* (3) *The Pulpit: A Magazine of Sermons;* (4) *The Preacher: Containing Sermons by Eminent Living Divines;* and (5) *Sketches of Sermons, Preached to Congregations in Various Parts of the United Kingdom and on the European Continent.* (See Abbreviations of Sources.)

Who was Charles Simeon, the preacher whose work is featured in the *Theological Sketch-Book?* Simeon (1759–1836) was, with William Wilberforce, one of the two leading evangelicals in the Church of England during the early 1800s.

During his first year as a student at King's College, Cambridge, Simeon came under conviction of his sinfulness and his need of a Savior. By Easter morning, culminating months of seeking, he experienced the assurance of salvation. During Holy Communion that day he had "the sweetest access to God through my blessed Saviour."

Simeon became a Fellow of King's in 1782, and later that same year he was appointed to serve the Church of the Holy Trinity in Cambridge (the same pulpit that had been occupied by Puritans Richard Sibbes and Thomas Goodwin). Simeon remained in this parish for the rest of his life, despite many opportunities to accept more prestigious ecclesiastical posts.

Simeon's evangelical convictions were nurtured by his friendship with John Venn and his father, Henry. He did not mute these convictions when preaching, though evangelical preachers were a distinct minority in the Church of England and were granted no respect by the students and professors of Cambridge University.

Simeon suffered for his evangelical beliefs for many years, even at the hands of his parishioners. But he held firm and, after many years, finally earned the admiration of his parish, the university community, and the Church of England generally. Eventually he came to exercise greater influence in that church than any archbishop.

Simeon played a major role in the establishment of such evangelical organizations as the British and Foreign Bible society, Religious Tract Society, Church Missionary Society, and London Jews Society. He personally founded what came to be known as the Simeon Trust. He was also a pioneer in ministering to university students and in providing (however unofficially) theological and homiletical training to those planning to seek ordination.

According to Marcus Loane, "Simeon was a preacher of no mean fame in an age when preaching was too often defaced by artificial style and monotonous voice."His style, by contrast, was simple and direct. He aimed, above all, to be understood, to reach his hearer's heart and conscience. ". . . the gravity of that purpose and the dignity of his message kept his diction always free from tameness and raised it at times to noble heights of grandeur."

"His style of delivery as a young man," Loane continues, "was earnest and impassioned to a degree; it was still in old age lively and impressive in no common measure. Voice and gesture were marked by the natural and unstudied power of purest sincerity and strongest reality; he could not fail to hold his audience with the unlaboured utterance and the tremendous reverence with which he spoke."

The real secret of Simeon's effectiveness as a preacher, however, was his lifelong habit of arising early each morning and devoting four hours to prayer and the rigorous study of Scripture. At least twelve hours of work went into the preparation of each sermon.

According to Canon Smyth in *The Art of Preaching,* Simeon was "almost the first man in the history of the English pulpit since the Middle Ages to appreciate that it is perfectly possible to teach men how to preach." In 1792 Simeon began his sermon classes, which he held regularly for forty years. In each class fifteen to twenty undergraduates received instruction in the technique of constructing and delivering sermons.

To assist both his students and other preachers (most of whom had received no instruction in homiletics), Simeon began to publish shortened versions of his sermons. By the end of his life he had published more than 2,500 of these extended outlines in a final edition of *Horae Homileticae*, which, according to Kenneth Hylson-Smith, "were much appreciated by preachers and others in his day."

In the preface to *Horae Homileticae*, Simeon expressed the following concern: "Does it uniformly tend to humble the sinner, to exalt the Saviour, to promote holiness? If in one single instance it loses sight of any of these points, let it be condemned without mercy."

Was Simeon concerned about the outlines in *Horae Homileticae* becoming a crutch for preachers? "If it leads the ignorant to preach the truth, and the indolent to exert themselves, and the weak to attain a facility for writing their own, and the busy and laborious to do more and with better effect than they otherwise could have done," wrote Simeon, "I shall be richly repaid for my labour."

Baker Book House is pleased to make *Expository Sermon Outlines* and *More Expository Sermon Outlines*, volumes 1 and 2 of *Theological Sketch-Book*, available once again. We trust that this reprint edition will be of real assistance to many preachers and that they will be inspired to preach in the enduring tradition of Charles Simeon.

## FOR FURTHER READING

Bishop, John. "Charles Simeon: Preaching to Exalt the Savior, Promote Holiness." *Preaching* (November 1994), 56–7.

Hopkins, Hugh Evan. *Charles Simeon of Cambridge.* Grand Rapids: Eerdmans, 1977.

Hylson-Smith, Kenneth. *The Evangelicals in the Church of England: 1734–1984.* Edinburgh: T. & T. Clark, 1989. Pages 70–76

Loane, Marcus L. *Cambridge and the Evangelical Succession.* London: Lutterworth, 1952. Pages 171–220.

McGraw, James. *Great Evangelical Preachers of Yesterday.* Nashville: Abingdon, 1961. Pages 80–85.

Pollard, Arthur, and Michael Hennell, eds. *Charles Simeon (1759–1836): Essays Written in Commemoration of His Bi-Centenary by Members of the Evangelical Fellowship for Theological Literature.* London: SPCK, 1959.

Toon, Peter. "Charles Simeon." In *Who's Who in Christian History.* Edited by J. D. Douglas and Philip W. Comfort. Wheaton: Tyndale, 1992. Page 625.

# ABBREVIATIONS
## FOR SOURCES

B.      Benson, Joseph. *Sermons, and Plans of Sermons, on Many of the Most Important Texts of Holy Scripture.* 3 vols., 6 parts. London: Cadell, 1824–27.

H.      *The Pulpit Assistant: Containing 300 Outlines or Skeletons of Sermons, Chiefly Extracted from Various Authors, with an Essay on the Composition of a Sermon by Thomas Hannam.* 5 vols. London, 1819.

H.H.      Simeon, Charles. *Horae Homileticae: Discourses (in the Form of Skeletons) upon the Whole Scriptures.* 17 vols. London, 1819–28.

P.      *The Pulpit: A Magazine of Sermons.* 8 vols. London, 1824ff.

Pr.      *The Preacher: Containing Sermons by Eminent Living Divines.* London, 1831–35.

Sk.      Simeon, Charles. *Helps to Composition: 600 Skeletons of Sermons . . .* 5 vols. 2d ed. London, 1808.

S.S.      *Sketches of Sermons, Preached to Congregations in Various Parts of the United Kingdom and on the European Continent, Furnished by Their Respective Authors.* 8 vols. London, 1822–25.

*Note:* One of the sermons is credited to Man., a source the publisher has been unable to identify.

*its one thing all believers can do No matter what their gifts, Longevity, beginner. Strong, weak,*

# CHAPTER 1.

## THE MEANS OF GRACE.

### CONTINUED FROM VOLUME FIRST.

### NEED OF DIVINE ASSISTANCE IN PRAYER.

Romans viii. 29.—Likewise the Spirit also helpeth our infirmities: for we know not what we should pray for as we ought: but the Spirit itself maketh intercession for us with groanings which cannot be uttered. (Pr.)

PRAYER has been the distinguishing practice of the godly in all ages, and no real believer can live without it. Yet for this, as well as for all other spiritual duties, we are insufficient, and need the Holy Spirit to teach and help us. Yea, more than in any other duty, as it is of all others the most spiritual, and therefore the most difficult to be performed aright. There is no nearness to God in this exercise, without a considerable degree of spirituality, and abstraction from the present world.

*need Help*

I. CONSIDER OUR INSUFFICIENCY FOR THIS GREAT DUTY: "WE KNOW NOT WHAT WE SHOULD PRAY FOR AS WE OUGHT.

*I.*

It is intimated that we are insufficient in two respects, both as to the matter and manner of prayer.

1. As to the *matter of prayer:* "we know not *what* to pray for."——— We know some things that we want, and should ask for; but on the whole we are exceedingly ignorant and uninformed.

*we are Lacking*

Particularly, *we are apt to pray for many things which if granted would be for our hurt:* and "who knoweth what is good for man in this life?" We may think uninterrupted health and prosperity would be desirable: yet afflictions are often amongst our greatest blessings, and continued prosperity might have been our ruin.——— We may think it good that the life of our children and friends should be spared; yet we know not what they would be to us, if our desire were granted. Paul had a thorn in the flesh which he wished to have removed, but the Lord saw it needful to be there.——— We may desire a station in the church, which we are not qualified to occupy; like the two disciples who wanted to sit, one on the right hand and the other on the left, in the kingdom of their Lord; but were told "they knew not what they asked."——— In all such cases our feelings and wishes must be subordinated to the will of God, saying with our blessed Lord, Not my will, but thine be done. We may ask as he did, to have the bitter cup removed; but we must also submit as he did.

*Hurt or good*

*only God.*

*Power Prestige Pride Greed*

Again: *We omit praying for many things which are essential to our good.* It is well that God's giving is not measured by our asking, and that he gives exceeding abundantly above all that we ask or think, Ephes. iii. 20.——— We know not the difficulties that lie before us, and therefore cannot ask specifically for what is necessary. David saw none of these when he was anointed king, nor what troubles would attend his reign. If Peter had been duly aware of the temptation that would befall him, he might have prayed against that fatal hour: but it was well that Christ foresaw it, and

*Wrong Things*

*First*

3

*[handwritten margin notes: Lord's prayer — Our father which art in heaven Halowed be thy name]*

prayed for him that his faith might not fail. —— Every day of our lives we know not what to ask in particular, and can only commit our way unto the Lord, that our goings may be established.

2. As to *the manner of praying:* "we know not what we should pray for *as we ought.*" —— Even in those things which we know we ought to pray for, we know not how to ask aright, or in a proper manner. There are some things which we know we need, as our daily bread, the forgiveness of our sins, and to be kept from temptation: yet we know not how to pray for them in such a manner as is required. —— It is intimated in the text that there is something belonging to the manner of true prayer, which is necessary to render it acceptable in the sight of God; and that those who draw near to him are required to pray "as they ought." This may include the following particulars—

1. That *our hearts be fixed,* and engaged with God in this sacred duty. It must be the prayer of faith, pleading the promises, and relying on their fulfilment. —— But how difficult it is to have our hearts thus engaged, thus intently fixed on the great object of prayer: how prone to turn aside like a deceitful bow!

2. That we approach God *with humility and deep abasement.* The gospel has placed us on low ground, and there we must stand whenever we appear before God; as sinners ready to perish, as utterly unworthy, crying out with the publican, God be merciful to me a sinner. The Pharisee prayed, but knew not how to pray as he ought, and it availed nothing. —— See the case of the poor woman, who did pray as she ought. Matt. xv. 22—28. It is such importunate prayer that takes the kingdom of heaven by violence.

3. That *our expectations' from God should be enlarged.* To pray "as we ought," we must desire much and hope for much. We must believe in God's truth and goodness, in Christ's alsufficiency and willingness to save. "Open thy mouth wide, and I will fill it." We must pray always, and not faint; and then like Jacob we shall prevail. —— This however is the manner of prayer for which we feel our insufficiency, and need the influence of the Holy Spirit. We find it difficult, as Job did, to order our speech aright before him, by reason of darkness; but if we possess the spirit of faith, we shall prevail notwithstanding.

4. That we urge *those pleas which God delights to honor.* What these are we may see in some examples of successful prayer, and shall find that they were all derived from the honor and glory of God, his covenant faithfulness and truth, and the prevailing name of the Lord Jesus. —— When Moses pleaded for Israel, he pleaded the name and the faithfulness of God. Exod. xxxii. 10—14. —— When Solomon asked great things for Israel, and that God would forgive his people, his plea is the covenant promise which he had given. 1 Kings viii. 25, 30, 39. —— Hezekiah did the same, and also the apostles of our Lord, Isa. xxxvii. 14; Acts iv. 30.

*[handwritten margin note: come from God given to us. for his honor & Glory.]*

II. Observe how much we are indebted to the assistance of the Holy Spirit, in the performance of this important duty.

He is said to "help our infirmities," and to "make intercession for us." Without his influence there is no true prayer: we must pray with the Spirit and with the understanding also. —— Saul had been in the habit of prayer while a pharisee; yet when he was converted it was said, "Behold he prayeth," for he had never truly prayed before. —— The inhabitants of Jerusalem were no doubt accustomed to attend the worship of the sanctuary; yet it was not till the Holy Spirit was poured out upon them that they began

4

*we can't Be Victorious if* ~~we succeed~~

to pray in real earnest. Zech. xii. 10. —— Nor do believers ever prevail in prayer and supplication, but by his assistance. Such are their "infirmities," their ignorance, weakness, and wanderings of heart.

The " intercession" of the Holy Spirit, is not like that of Christ's :. the latter is for us, but this is in us. It is the Holy Spirit that inspires us with a spirit of prayer, and it is he that teaches us both how and what to pray for as we ought. —— He never excites desires, but such as are according to the will of God. The Lord also is said to know the mind of the Spirit, or what is of his inditing; and knowing this, he will assuredly answer. —— It is the Holy Spirit that endues the mind with sacred fervor and earnestness, and furnishes it with sweetness of expression in prayer. When the mind is overwhelmed with grief and anguish, and unable to give utterance to the heart, he interprets " the groans that cannot be uttered, and maketh intercession for us."

### IMPROVEMENT.

1. We are taught to acknowledge our utter insufficiency for what is good, and that the whole of our salvation is of grace. We can do nothing as we ought, and therefore nothing to deserve mercy at the hands of God.

2. While we feel and own our insufficiency, let us not presume to deny our obligations; for we are not only at the same time to pray, but required to pray as we ought.

3. We are from hence furnished with a criterion by which to judge of our own religion; for it is here taken for granted that the Lord's people are a praying people, and that they account it good to draw near unto God.

4. We are here taught to cherish the influence of the Holy Spirit, to depend upon *him* it in the performance of every spiritual exercise, and to admire the infinite compassion of God the Holy Spirit *to us.* to our manifold infirmities.

———————

### PRAYER PROVED TO BE A PROFITABLE EXERCISE.

Job xxi, 15.—" What profit should we have, if we pray unto him." (Sk.)

" I am the man that hath seen affliction," said Jeremiah; and with equal propriety might Job have adopted similar language. What affliction did he see in his family; in his substance; and in his person! and how afflictive were the ill-natured and sarcastic reflections attached to his character by his mistaken friends! they were puzzled to understand, why God had thus dealt with Job. As his afflictions were so sudden, so complicated, and so overwhelming they thought that some secret thing, some hidden wickedness, had drawn down the heavy judgments of God upon him. But Job confutes their unfounded assertions, and vindicates his own character, by showing, that this world, though the theatre of crime, is not the scene of punishment. "Wherefore doth the wicked live ?" &c. verse 7. Why does not God punish them ? They are not afflicted—neither in their persons, " The rod of God," &c. verse 9. Nor in their families, "Their seed is established," &c. verse 8. Nor in their property, "Their bull gendereth," &c. verse 10. Nor have they any inward depression of spirits, " for they take the timbrel and harp," &c. verse 12. But this prosperity could not be the result of innocence on their part, or of approbation on the part of God  For "they say unto God, Depart from us," &c.  "What is the Almighty that we should serve him, and what profit?" &c.  That is, there is nothing in God to excite our homage, nor is there any thing in prayer to promote our welfare.  Thus the sentiment in the text is as false as it is impious.  But let us try to profit by this passage, while we consider,

I. THE EXERCISE ASSUMED—"If we pray unto him."

II. THE INQUIRY INSTITUTED—"What profit should we have?"

I. THE EXERCISE ASSUMED—"If we pray," &c.  Prayer implies four things :

1. *A consciousness of want.*  Man is a needy creature.  He wants every thing! nothing is absolutely his own.  Destitution is his inheritance; if God abandon him, he has nothing, and is nothing.  He wants earthly blessings to support his body, and heavenly blessings to sustain and satisfy his mind.  But many never pray, because they know not their necessities ; they are ignorant of themselves, of their poverty, guilt and wretchedness.  They are best qualified to pray who know most of themselves.

2. *Prayer supposes an object capable of supplying our wants.*  This Being must know our necessities, and possess sufficient benevolence and power to supply them.  Such is the Almighty, who is considered in this verse as the object of prayer.  He knows us altogether, and his benevolence is equal to his knowledge, and his name is sufficiently indicative of his power to do us good.  Prayers to saints or angels are impious, as they transfer the homage from the creator to the creature ; and absurd, as angels are as dependant as men.

3. *Prayer implies an approach towards the Almighty.*  Man is an alien from God ; far gone from original righteousness.  God is not in all his thoughts.  The lusts of the flesh, the lusts of the eye, and the pride of life, absorb his whole attention.  But when he begins to pray, his mind turns towards God.  Hence prayer is called feeling after God, looking to him, seeking his face, and pouring out the heart before him.

4. *Prayer includes an expression of our wants.*  They who pray speak to God : "Behold now I have taken upon me to speak unto the Lord," &c. Gen. xviii. 27.  "While I was speaking in prayer," &c.  Hannah spake in her heart, when she prayed, but her voice was not heard, 1 Sam. i. 13. "When ye pray, *say*, Our Father," &c.  "Take with you words, and turn unto the LORD," Hosea xiv. 2.  Let us express our wants *fully ;* let us not dissemble nor cloak our sins before the face of Almighty God ; but confess them in all their variety, their malignity, and demerit.  Let us do it *humbly.* God is an awful being ; we are not worthy of the least of his mercies. Pride is hateful to God ; but "he shall save the humble person."  Let us do it *importunately:* God suffers us to plead with him, Luke xi. 5—10. xvii, 1—7.  Do it by *faith ;* and especially do it in *the name of Jesus,* John xiv. 13, 14.

II. THE INQUIRY INSTITUTED.  "What profit should we have?" &c. Selfishness is universally prevalent in the world.  Wicked men are invariably selfish men ; "All seek their own, not the things which are Jesus Christ's."  Hence the inquiry concerning profit in the text ; and because prayer is deemed unprofitable, therefore it is neglected.  But there is no exercise under heaven attended with so much profit as prayer.

1. *Prayer contributes to the removal of evil.  Of moral evil.*  Jabez prayed that God would keep him from evil; and God granted him that which he requested.  David said, "I will confess my transgressions unto the LORD,

6

and thou forgavest the iniquity of my sin. *Of natural evil.--Affliction.*
"Is any among you afflicted? let him pray." "Then they cried unto the
LORD in their trouble, and he delivered them," &c. Psa. cvii. 6. Hezekiah
prayed, and wept in his affliction, and God said, " Behold 1 will heal thee."
1 Kings xx. 5.— *Sorrow.* "I found," said David, "trouble and sorrow:
then called I upon the name of the LORD," &c. Psa. cxvi. 1—4. Christ
" offered up prayers and supplications, with strong crying and tears, unto
him that was able to save him from death, and was heard in that he feared."
—*Oppression.* Look at Israel in Egypt, "I have heard their cry," saith
God, "by reason of their task masters, and am come down to deliver them,"
Exod. iii. 7, 8. See Peter shut up in prison; but prayer was made for him,
and God delivered him, Acts xii, 5—16, 25.

2. *Prayer is instrumental in procuring good.* All good, for body and
soul, for time and eternity, is promised to prayer. *Is it profitable to possess wisdom?* Yes, "if thou be wise, thou shalt be wise for thyself."
Wisdom procures happiness, Prov. iii. 13. Length of days, iii. 16. Pleas
ure, verse 17. Promotion, Prov. iv. 8. And glory, iii. 35, iv, 9. But he
who never prays is devoid of wisdom. See 1 Kings iii. 9; Dan. ii. 18, 23;
James i. 5; Acts x. 31. *Is it profitable to possess power?* Power to resist the devil, to conquer our corruptions, and to vanquish and put to flight
the armies of the aliens? Prayer supplies this strength. "In the day when
I cried, thou answeredst me, and strengthenedst me with strength in my
soul," Psa. cxxxviii. 3. The spirit helpeth our infirmities, but they who
pray most acceptably to God have the largest effusions of that spirit, Luke
xi. 13. Prayer is a most important part of the christians armour. *Is it
profitable to possess protection?* See Psa. xviii. 3, lvi. 9. To possess *peace?*
Phil. iv. 6, 7. To have *an assurance of heaven?* See the penitent thief,
Luke xxiii. 42, 43. And the profit of prayer infinitely outweighs all other
profit.—It is *divine.* Worldly profit consists in flocks, herds, money, &c.
This, in faith, grace, love, happiness, &c.—It is *mental.* Worldly profit is
sensual, all for the outward man; but he who prays is enriched inwardly;
all his intellectual powers are profited.—It is *comprehensive.* Worldly profit is circumscribed, and bounded by time; the profit of prayer illimitable.
—It is *universal.* Worldly profit affects us partially; this, in body, and
soul, and substance. And the profit arising from prayer is secured without
*risk,* and retained without any fears of *deprivation.* In conclusion observe,

1. *The conduct of the wicked is impious.* They not only live without
prayer, but live as if God had no right to exact this duty of them. "What
profit should we have, if we pray?"—But is it optional with you whether
to pray or not? Are duties matters of opinion? No, God has made prayer
imperative upon you; it is his commandment, and it cannot be violated with
impunity.

2. *The conduct of the wicked is erroneous.* They consider prayer a
profitless exercise, and therefore neglect it. But this calculation is totally
unfounded. Prayer avails much. How strange that men who reason so
conclusively in matters of science, should suffer themselves to be so grievously deceived as to the duties of religion!

3. *The conduct of the wicked is ruinous.* Without prayer salvation is
unattainable, Prov. i. 24—31.

7

## THE APOSTLE'S PRAYER FOR AN INCREASE OF FAITH.

Luke xvii. 5.—And the apostles said unto the Lord, Increase our faith. (Sk.)

In the verses preceding the text, our divine Redeemer instructs his disciples in the nature and importance of a most difficult duty, that of forgiving injuries; a duty totally unknown or utterly disregarded, till taught by his doctrines, and enforced by his example; as the wisest moralists of the most enlightened nations represented the desire of revenge as the mark of a noble mind, and thought it more magnanimous to revenge an injury, than forgive it. "If thy brother tresspass against thee," &c. ver. 3. "Offences will come:" our views are dissimilar, our passions discordant, and our interests diversified; some offend by their dispositions—others by their manners—others by their conduct; some by their ignorance, and others by their wickedness; but whatever motive may actuate the offending person, or however frequently he may repeat the offence, yet, if he repent, "thou shalt forgive him." The apostles seemed aware of the difficulty attendant on the practice of this duty, and therefore said unto the Lord, "Increase our faith." In the text there are four general ideas implied.

I. That the disciples of Christ possess faith. There can be no *increase* where there is no possession. We may infer the truth of the above assertion,

1. *From the nature of faith.* Definitions of faith are abundant; genuine faith implies the entertaining Scriptural views of the person and offices of Christ, accompanied by an implicit dependence on him for salvation, and a cordial reception of him in the heart. And if this view of faith be correct, it can exist only among the disciples of Christ. Infidels deny his existence —Arians and Socinians reject his atonement—Pharisees trust in themselves that they are righteous, and are ignorant of Christ's righteousness—and practical sinners of all kinds refuse to admit him into their hearts.

2. *From the character of Christ's disciples.* As disciples they are all instructed by him. In what?—the doctrines of faith. What do they learn? —to believe in his name, to submit to his authority, and to depend upon his truth. As disciples they follow him; does not this suppose the exercise of faith? Acts xiii. 38, They rejoice in him, Luke xix. 37. But their joy is the joy of faith, 1 Pet. i. 8.

3. *From the testimonies of revelation.* Jesus said to one, "O woman, great is thy faith!" To another, "Thy faith hath saved thee." He prayed for Peter, that his "faith fail not." Stephen was "a man full of faith," &c.

II. That an increase of faith is possible. This will appear,

1. *From the power and goodness of its Author.* Faith is not an earthborn virtue, begotten by the mere exercise of the human faculties, but a grace that owes its existence to the agency of Jesus Christ. He is "the author and finisher of our faith," &c. Heb. xii. 2; Eph. ii 8; Phil. i. 29. And cannot he who bestows the gift, increase that gift? He who opens the eye of the mind to behold the glories of eternity, can shine with clearer light, and beam with greater lustre. His power is infinite, and his goodness unlimited.

2. *From the progressive nature of religion.* Religion is all progression, and every christian grace admits of an increase; its first implantation in the heart resembles a seed, which when cast into the earth germinates, and, by progressive and gradual growth, becomes a great tree. Christians are regarded as walking, running, pressing forward, all of which expressions de-

8

**note** increase and advancement. Religion must not be considered in detached parts, but as a complete system of holy principles, and heavenly fruits, which have a necessary dependence upon each other ; and our increase in one, necessarily ensures an increase in the whole.

3. *From the admonitions of the Bible.* Christians are exhorted to "grow in grace," &c. 2 Pet. iii. 18. Earnestly to contend for the faith, &c. Jude 3. To build yourselves up, &c. ver. 20. These with many other texts in the New Testament, prove that an increase of faith is possible.

4. *From the experience of the saints.* Faith increases by exercise : every act of faith tends to give permanency and stability to the principle which gives it birth. Christians depend upon God for providential, spiritual, and eternal benefits ; and that dependence increases in proportion as they know more of God, Psa. ix. 10.

III. THAT AN INCREASE OF FAITH IS GREATLY TO BE DESIRED. We infer this,

1. *From its nature.* It is a divine gift, and its existence is attributed to the operation of God, Col. ii. 12. That which God works in us must be desirable : as he is an infinitely good being, his works must necessarily bear a resemblance to himself.

2. *From its effects.* These refer—*To our own personal salvation.* We are justified by faith—saved by faith—Christ dwells in our hearts by faith—we stand by faith—live by faith—walk by faith—and have boldness of access to God by faith. *To the victories we gain over our enemies.* By the shield of faith we quench the fiery darts, &c. Eph. vi. 16. We conquer the world by faith, 1 John v. 4. The ancient worthies by faith "subdued kingdoms," &c. Heb. xi. 33, 34.—*To the moral influence of our example.* True faith produceth good works ; for "faith without works is dead ;" and good works are profitable unto men, Matt. v. 16 ; Titus iii. 8. That on which such high encomiums are bestowed in the bible, by which such amazing effects have been produced, and the absence of which involves men in condemnation here and eternal damnation hereafter, must be desirable. And as the most certain way of retaining faith, is by increasing in it, we may infer the truth of the above position.

IV. THAT MEANS SHOULD BE USED TO SECURE AN INCREASE OF FAITH. To accomplish this object,

1. *Study the character of its author.* Meditate on the power, wisdom, and goodness of our Lord Jesus Christ. Reflect on what he has done for mankind ; contemplate what he has promised to do. Think meanly of the Saviour, and you will have little confidence in him ; but think greatly and highly of him, and you will trust in him heartily, and believe in him fully.

2. *Get a more extensive acquaintance with the promises of God.* Read them frequently ; treasure them up in your memories ; hide them in your hearts ; meditate on their greatness, variety and immutability ; and labor to realize them in your own personal experience.

3. *Be on your guard against every thing that will deaden or damp the ardour of your faith.* Carnal company, worldly cares, spiritual supineness, filthy and foolish conversation,—all tend to sap the foundation of your faith, and destroy your dependence upon God. Chiefly,

4. *Pray for an increase of faith.* "The apostles said unto the Lord, increase our faith ;"—"Go thou, and do likewise." Say it *humbly*, from a deep conviction of thy unworthiness, and the infinite dignity and goodness of thy Saviour :—say it *fervently ;* pour out strong cries and fervent supplications in behalf of this blessing :—say it *importunately ;* recollect the im-

9

portunate widow, and the poor blind beggar;—say it in thy closet;—say it in the assemblies of the saints;—say it as thou walkest by the way;—say it for thy own sake, and for the sake of others.

In conclusion, we address a word,

1. *To those who have no faith.* Your case is awful, you are condemned already, and the wrath of God abideth on you. You need say unto the Lord, Give us faith, impart the heavenly gift to us, and let us believe to the saving of our souls.

2. *To those whose faith has declined.* "Remember from whence you are fallen, and repent, and do your first works."

3. *To those whose faith remains in full vigour.* "Hold fast whereto ye have already attained, and walk by the same rule," &c. Keep faith in lively exercise, and soon you will receive the end of your faith, even the salvation of your souls.

---

## THE DEBTOR'S PRAYER.

Matthew vi. 10.—*Forgive us our debts.* (Sk.)

THIS petition is taken from that comprehensive and well known compendium of devotion, which we call, for the sake of distinction, the Lord's prayer. A prayer which Christ condescended to teach his disciples; and a prayer which is designed to be a model for all our prayers. Forms of prayer were common among the Jews, and every public teacher presented one to his disciples; these forms were sometimes drawn out to a considerable length, and from them abridgments were not unfrequently made. We have the satisfaction to learn from God himself what prayer is, and what language we should use in our addresses to the throne of grace; and when a sovereign dictates a petition which he allows condemned culprits to present to him, who can question his willingness to grant their request?—The text is of universal consequence, and suggests to us;—that we have debts,—that these debts may be forgiven,—and that it is highly important and desirable for us to obtain forgiveness.

I. WHAT ARE OUR DEBTS? This term *debts*, is by St. Luke xi. 4, rendered *sins.* St. John defines sin as a transgression of the law; of that particular law which every man is under to God. Jesus Christ has seen fit to reduce the whole of the moral law, which in the Old Testament is amplified into various precepts, into two positive injunctions, "Thou shalt love the Lord thy God," &c., Matt. xxii. 37—39. God's law is *universally binding;* wherever there are rational creatures in any part of the creation, there they are obligated to love God according to the extent of their capacities.— It can never be abrogated. Human laws change, worldly maxims vary, and many of the Jewish precepts were designed only for a single people and to be in use for a certain period, but this law is unchangeable. *It allows of no deviation.* It requires perfect, uniform, and undeviating obedience; and every man, through all the periods of his being, with an unchangeable intensity of desire, is required to love God, &c. This law we have all violated in instances innumerable.—We have done it, by omitting to do what the law positively enjoins; and by doing what the law plainly prohibits.—These deviations, sins, or trespasses, are in the text termed *debts.*

1. *Debts suppose two parties, the one of which has received goods, valuables, or commodities from the other.* This is our case. From God we have received all we possess; we owe our being to him, Acts xvii. 25—28. Our bodies are his workmanship, Psa. cxxxix. 13—16. He is the father of our spirits, Heb. xii. 9. For our property we are indebted to his blessing, Deut. viii. 18. He fixeth the bounds of our habitation, Acts xvii. 27. Indeed to each of us it may be said, " What hast thou that thou didst not receive ?"

2. *Debts imply, that the returns made have not been proportioned to the property received.* Here also we all stand impeached. How deeply are we in arrears! Unnumbered benefits we have received from God, but what returns have we made? It is said of Hezekiah, " that he rendered not again according to the benefit done unto him:" and his conduct we have all too successfully imitated. Our time has been wasted,—our talents prostituted,—our hearts set on idols.—The members of our bodies have been instruments of unrighteous unto sin; and the powers of our souls have been darkened and degraded: and God and his benefits forgotten.

3. *Debts place their subjects in circumstances of embarrassment and danger.* How wretched is the man who is deeply in debt! Wherever he turns, he is sure to meet a creditor. who harasses and torments him for sums which he is totally unable to discharge. He lives every day under the expectation of an arrest, and calculates upon nothing but confinement in a jail. How descriptive is this of the state of sinners who are deeply in debt to God! who have made no returns of gratitude, love, nor obedience to their Maker! who are tormented with fearful apprehensions! liable to an arrest from Divine Justice, and in danger of being cast into the prison of hell.

II. OUR DEBTS MAY BE FORGIVEN.

1. *When we ask forgiveness for our debts, it supposes that we have no hope of discharging them.* We cannot pay them off: the immense and incalculable value of the benefits received, leaves no possibility of our making adequate returns for them : if God had never done any thing for us, but that of giving his Son to die for our sins, this would have laid us under such a mighty debt of obligation, that an eternity of gratitude would have failed to discharge the amazing sum; but he has given us his Spirit, his gospel, his ordinances, and his ministers. " Oh to grace what mighty debtors !" We cannot pay off our debts; they have been so long standing, accumulating, and increasing. Most of all, we have nothing to pay, we are insolvent debtors.

2. *When we ask forgiveness, it implies that our future obedience can never atone for our past defects.* If we had contracted a debt, our payment for goods in future would not discharge the old debt: we can never go beyond the requirements of the law; " Therefore by the deeds of the law," &c., Rom. iii. 20. But our debts may be forgiven. We infer this,—*First, from the character of God as revealed by himself.* He proclaimed his name to Moses; " The LORD God, merciful and gracious, long-suffering, and abundant in goodness and truth; keeping mercy for thousands; forgiving iniquity," &c., Exod. xxxiv. 6, 7. " He is ready to pardon," Neh. ix. 7. " Ready to forgive," Psa. lxxxvi. 5. " To him belong mercies and forgivenesses," &c., Dan. ix. 9. " I, even I, am he that blotteth out," &c., Isa xliii. 25.—*Secondly, from the atoning sacrifice of Jesus Christ.* That the sufferings of the Redeemer were sufferings for our sins, is a fact which the inspired writers most clearly demonstrate. " He was wounded for our transgressions," &c., Isa. liii. 5. " He hath made him to be sin for us," &c., 2

Cor. v. 21. "Christ was once offered," &c., Heb. ix. 28. "Who his own self bare our sins," &c., 1 Peter ii. 24. And the atonement of Christ for sin is the foundation of our hope of pardon. Hence remission of sins is preached in his name, Luke xxiv. 47; Acts xiii. 38, 39. And "God forgives men for Christ's sake," Ephes. iv. 32.—*Thirdly, from the promises of the Bible* "Come now and let us reason together," &c., Isa. i. 18. "Let the wicked forsake his way," &c., lv. 7. "All manner of sin and blasphemy," &c., Matt. xii. 31.—*Fourthly, from the testimonies of the saints.* Moses said to God, "Thou hast forgiven this people from Egypt even until now," Num. xiv. 19. "He being full of compassion, forgave their iniquity," Psa. lxxviii. 38. David said, "Thou forgavest the iniquity of my sin," Psa. xxxii. 5. Hezekiah declared, "Thou hast cast all my sins behind thy back," Isa. xxxviii. 17. "We have redemption through his blood, even the forgiveness of sins," Colos. i. 14. And if any other evidence be deemed necessary, to prove that our debts may be forgiven, the prayer in the text is sufficient. Christ has taught us to ask forgiveness; and what we are directed to ask, we may confidently hope to receive. But to whom is this forgiveness administered? To penitent believers; "He," (God) "pardoneth and absolveth all them that truly repent and unfeignedly believe his holy gospel." Repentance prepares the mind for the reception of pardon; and induces the sinner humbly and importunately to plead for it, Acts viii. 22. Faith enables him to claim the promises of forgiveness as his own, Acts xiii. 39.

III. THAT IT IS HIGHLY IMPORTANT AND DESIRABLE FOR US TO OBTAIN FORGIVENESS. Two things will serve to confirm the truth of this observation.

1. *A state of forgiveness is a state of positive enjoyment: Enjoyment*, arising from a consciousness of having escaped punishment; an unpardoned sinner is in danger of perdition; he is a child of wrath; God is angry with him, and punishment is threatened him; but when God forgives him, that wrath which was revealed from heaven against him is removed; and he has the knowledge of salvation, &c., Luke i. 77. *Enjoyment*, flowing from the peace of God which passeth all understanding. "For being justified by faith," &c., Rom. v. 1. *Enjoyment*, springing from the testimony of a good conscience, 2 Cor. i. 12. And how highly desirable is that state, which gives birth to enjoyments so divine, so rational, so pure, and so permanent!

2. *A state of forgiveness is a state of absolute security.* What has that man to fear, against whom Heaven has no accusation? "If God be for us, who can be against us? Who shall lay any thing to the charge of God's elect? It is God that justifieth. Who is he that condemneth?" A man who has obtained forgiveness from his God, may look every enemy in the face.—With his conscience he is at peace;—God will bruise Satan under his feet;—death will be to him a vanquished foe;—and heaven is his by title and by promise, Rom. viii. 17; 1 John ii. 25. Contemplating such privileges,—who can help exclaiming, "Blessed are they whose iniquities are forgiven, and whose sins are covered."

### INFERENCES.

1. *If sins are debts, we cannot fail to recollect how awfully we are in arrears.* Let us make up our accounts, and as far as we can, form an estimate, ascertain how much we owe to God. Some of us are old and gray neaded! Oh what a debt is ours! How much have we received, but how little paid?

**2.** *Oh how promptly and earnestly should we sue for pardon.* Forgiveness is now offered, but if we delay to accept the generous offer, our great Creditor will issue an arrest against us, and we shall be cast into prison, and be confined in chains of darkness to the judgment of the great day.

3. *Has God forgiven your debts?* Cease not to reflect on the returns which duty binds you to make.—*Be grateful,* "Bless the LORD, O my soul," &c., Psa. ciii. 2, 3. *Cultivate a spirit of forgiveness towards others,* Matt. xviii. 23—35. *Let your love to God bear some proportion to the greatness of the obligations you are under to him.* "There was a certain creditor which had two debtors," &c., "and when they had nothing to pay, he frankly forgave them both; which of them will love him most?" Luke vii. 42.

---

## PROPER METHOD OF PRAYING TO GOD.

Ps. xxv. 11.—For thy name's sake, O Lord, pardon mine iniquity! for it is great. (H. H.)

GOD is a mighty Sovereign, "who doth according to his own will," "neither giveth account to us of any of his matters." We may indeed mark the traces of wisdom and goodness in every thing which he does; but "his ways and his thoughts are very different from ours, and far above them." In the dispensations of his providence he pays no regard to the moral characters of men, but "makes the sun to shine equally upon the evil and the good." In the dispensations of his grace too he is far from preferring those whom we should think he would select. He often inclines the hearts of "publicans and harlots to enter into his kingdom," while he leaves less abandoned Pharisees and Formalists to perish in their sins. This if it be an humiliating truth, is also replete with comfort. If it take away all grounds of boasting, it cuts off at the same time all occasion for despondency. If he "have a right to do what he will with his own," the vilest person in the universe may approach him with a comfortable hope of acceptance, and may address him in the language of the text.

In these words of the Psalmist we may notice,

I. HIS CONFESSION—

David was not ashamed to confess that his sins were exceeding great—

There is no reason to think that David in this psalm adverts to his transgression with Bathsheba. It is probable that the psalm was penned many years before that event. The Royal Penitent speaks rather of his in-dwelling corruptions. He had long been accustomed to observe the workings of his own heart, and had often besought God to search and try him to the uttermost. Ps. cxxxix. 23, 24. In this way he had marked both the defects of his duties, and the evil propensities of his nature; and, from a review of all his actions, words, and thoughts, was led to acknowledge that his sin was exceeding great. Nor was this confession peculiar to him. Holy Job, as soon as he beheld his true character, exclaimed, "Behold, I am vile!" Job xl. 4. And Paul no sooner became acquainted with the purity and extent of God's law, than he saw himself a condemned sinner, and confessed, that "in him dwelt no good thing." Rom. vii. 9, 18.

And does not a similar confession become *us* also?

Let us only review our past lives, and we shall find too much occasion for the deepest humiliation. Have not many of us been addicted to open, known iniquities? and do not the consciences of such persons testify against

13

them that their sin is great? Have not many also devoted all their time and
attention to *secular* concerns? and will they account it a light thing thus to
despise God, and idolize the world? Have not others satisfied themselves
with a formal round of duties, in which their souls were never earnestly engaged? and can they suppose that God is pleased with a mere lip-service,
when their hearts are far from him? Have not others professed Godliness indeed, but walked utterly unworthy of their profession, being as proud, and
passionate, as worldly too, and covetous, as those who have made no such
profession? and can *they* suppose their sin is not great, when sinners are
hardened, and God is blasphemed through their means?— — —But why
do we speak of the *profane* and *worldly*, or the *formal* and *hypocritical?*
Must not even the *saints* themselves blush and be confounded, when they
consider how miserably they have fallen short in every thing? Must they
not exclaim with St. Paul, "O wretched man that I am!"? Surely we must
know little indeed of ourselves, if we do not all see how much the confession in the text is suited to our state.

When, like David, we are duly humbled under a sense of our guilt, we
shall readily adopt,

II. HIS PETITION—

David could not rest without imploring forgiveness at God's hands—

He found a sense of guilt to be an intolerable burthen to his soul; Ps.
xxxviii. 4; and well knew that it would "eat as a canker," till he had obtained the pardon of his sin. Hence he humbled himself before his God,
and cried for mercy.

Nor shall *we* restrain prayer before God, if we will but consider the state
of an unpardoned soul—

No words can fully express the misery of one who has all the guilt of
his sins upon him. He has *no peace with God*, seeing that "God is angry
with him every day," and "the wrath of God abideth on him." He has
*no peace in his own conscience;* for though he may drown reflection for a
while in business or pleasure, he is like the troubled sea which cannot rest,
but casts up mire and dirt. Isa. lvii. 20. He is also *destitute of* any well-
founded *hope:* he may buoy up himself with blind presumption; but he
will feel many misgiving fears, and forebodings of evil. He has *no comfort
in his afflictions;* for, not having God for his friend, he cannot go to him
with confidence, or obtain those refreshing consolations which strengthen
and uphold the godly. *In a dying hour* he is yet more *wretched:* if he be
not insensible as a beast, how does he regret his mis-spent hours, and wish
that God would prolong his state of probation! But *in the eternal world
his misery is completed:* he comes to the tribunal of Justice without any
Mediator to reconcile him to God, or any Advocate to plead his cause: yea,
the very voice which just before importuned him to accept of mercy, now
bids him "depart accursed:" and from that moment his doom is fixed in everlasting burnings. Now can any man reflect on this, and not see the need
of crying earnestly for mercy? Can our petitions be too earnest, or too
constant, when they are appointed, and the only means of escaping all this
misery?

But in our application for mercy, we must be careful to use,

III. HIS PLEA—

The Psalmist derived all his hope of mercy from God himself—

He pleaded not the smallness of his offences or the multitude of his services,
the depth of his penitence, or the fervor of his petitions. He knew that
name, which had long before been proclaimed to Moses, to which, as to " a

strong tower, the righteous runneth and is safe ;" and to *that* he fled for refuge ; from *that* he derived his only hope, his only plea.

Nor can we present any other plea than the name, the sacred name of Jesus—

Under the Gospel we are taught more clearly to ask in the name of Jesus, and are assured that petitions so offered shall never fail of acceptance. John xiv. 13, 14. But it is no easy matter to offer that plea in sincerity. Perhaps there is not any thing in the world more difficult. *We naturally prefer any other plea that can be devised :* and, even when we find that we have not in ourselves any worthiness on which we can rely, we are still averse to rest on the name of Jesus. We either *deem it insufficient* to procure acceptance for our prayers, or *make our unworthiness a reason for declining to urge it as our plea* with any confidence before God. But, unless we renounce every other hope, and rest entirely on the mediation and intercession of Christ, our prayer will never enter into the ears of our heavenly Father—

OBSERVATIONS :

1. The vilest of sinners has no reason to despair—

The confession, petition, and plea, which David presented at the throne of Grace, are suited to the very chief of sinners : nor, as the subsequent experience of David proves, can there be any state in which they shall not prevail. Let none then despond. Be it so, Our iniquities are great : but are they greater than Christ's merits, or beyond the reach of God's mercy ? If not, let us exalt our adorable Saviour, and determine, if we perish, to perish crying for mercy in the name of Jesus.

2. The most eminent saints have no ground to boast—

There never was a creature that had any righteousness of his own to plead. And if God has had mercy upon any, it was purely and entirely for his own name sake. Ezek. xxxvi. 22, 32. Could we ascend to heaven, and ask the glorified saints what had been the ground of their acceptance, they would all " cast down their crowns at the feet of Jesus," and shout, with one consent, ' 'Salvation to God and to the Lamb !" Rev. iv. 10, and vii. 10.—Let the saints on earth then lie low before God, and say continually, " Not unto us, O Lord, not unto us, but unto thy *name* be the praise."

3. Persons of every description must guard diligently against pride and unbelief—

Sin, of whatever kind, is both evil in itself and dangerous to us. But the consequences of pride and unbelief are peculiarly fatal. There is not any other sin which may not be forgiven, provided we seek mercy with real penitence and faith. But if we be too proud to confess our sins, and to plead the name and merits of Jesus for the forgiveness of them, we insure and seal our own condemnation. Let us then guard against *all* sin ; but especially against these, which rivet all our other sins upon us. So shall we obtain favor with God, and " be to him for a name and for a praise for evermore. Jer. xiii. 11.

## THE BENEFIT OF PRAYER.

John xvi. 24.—Ask, and ye shall receive, that your joy may be full. (H. H.)

THIS world is justly characterized as a vale of tears. Even they who experience the most happiness, find many interruptions of it: nor is there any way of securing permanent tranquility, but by waiting upon God in prayer.

The disciples were sorrowful on account of the approaching departure of their Lord, with whom they had hitherto enjoyed the most familiar fellowship. Our Lord tells them, that though they would no longer be able to *inquire*, ver. 23, ἐρωτήσετε, of him, yet, if they would *ask*, ib. αἰτήσητε, of the Father in his name, he would grant them whatsoever they should need; and that the answers which they should receive to their prayers would abundantly overbalance the loss of their present privileges, and fill them with unutterable joy.

In the direction given them, we may notice,

I. OUR DUTY—

It is comprised in one word, "Ask." Now this is,

1. An easy duty—

We do not mean that it is always easy to pray, (for there is nothing more difficult when the heart is indisposed for that exercise;) but that is the easiest condition that could possibly be imposed— — —and that, when the heart is in a proper frame, prayer is as easy to the soul, as breathing is to the body: it is the first, and most natural, effort of a living soul: "Behold, he prayeth!" Acts ix. 11.

2. A reasonable duty—

Man is a dependent creature; and it is but reasonable that he should acknowledge that dependence at a throne of grace, and ask for those mercies which he stands in need of. The very heathens have felt the propriety of supplicating their deities, and have established ordinances whereby they might conciliate the favor of their gods. It is true, that God knows our necessities before we ask: yet is it highly proper that we should spread them before him, in order that we ourselves may be humbled under a sense of them, and that God's mercy in relieving them may be more clearly seen.

3. A necessary duty—

Though God cannot be prevailed upon by dint of importunity,* yet he has appointed prayer as the means of obtaining his blessings. He has said, "I will be inquired of to do it for them." Ezek. xxxvi. 37. There is no room therefore left for us to speculate upon the use of prayer: it is quite sufficient that God has required it as means to an end: and if we will not comply with his injunctions respecting it, it is utterly in vain for us to expect his blessings.

4. An acceptable duty—

Prayer offered to the Deity without any respect to the mediation of Christ, is not acceptable; but when presented in an humble dependence on his atonement, and intercession, it comes up before God as incense, and prevails beyond the utmost extent of our conceptions. It is to prayer *offered in this manner*, that the promise in the text is given. Ver. 23, 24. And this has been the qualification of all acceptable prayer from the beginning. Abel was heard on account of his sacrifice. Heb. xi. 4. The penitents under the law obtained mercy in no other way. Heb. ix. 22. The Jews, when unable

* The expressions, Luke xviii. 7, 8, must not lead us to think of God as though he were wrought upon as we are.

by reason of their captivity, to offer their accustomed sacrifices, were to look towards the temple, which was a type of our incarnate God. 1 Kings viii 47, 48; Dan. vi. 10. And to that same Jesus must we look, trusting in him as "our Advocate with the Father, and as the propitiation for our sins." 1 John ii. 1, 2. Nor did any one ever ask *in this manner* without obtaining a supply of all his wants.

To counteract the backwardness of our hearts to this duty, let us consider,

II. OUR ENCOURAGEMENT TO PERFORM IT—

The promise of acceptance is without any limit or exception—

There is no exception with respect to the persons who may apply to God. The vilest person in the universe, provided he ask *in the manner prescribed in the text*, shall be heard as readily as the very chief of the apostles. His past iniquities, of whatever kind they have been, shall not operate as any bar to his acceptance with God— — —

Nor is there any limit respecting the blessings we implore : provided they will really conduce to our good, and to God's glory, they shall be given. However "wide we open our mouths, God will fill them"— — —Ps. lxxxi. 10; John xiv. 13, 14. The frequent and solemn repetition of this truth by our Lord himself, must of necessity remove all doubt upon the subject. Matt. vii. 7, 8.

And instances of its accomplishment occur in almost every page of the sacred writings—

Whether Abel's prayer was answered by fire from heaven which consumed his sacrifice, or by some other token of the divine favor, the acceptance of it was equally manifest, and the fact is equally encouraging to us. To recount the various instances that occurred from that period to the times of Christ and his apostles, would be a pleasing task, but would occupy many hours. Suffice it to say, that whether men's prayer has been offered for themselves Jonah ii. 1, 7, or for others, Exod. xxxii. 11—14; Acts xii. 5—9, and whether it has been of a more stated and solemn kind, Ps. xviii. 6, or only in a sudden ejaculation, Neh. ii. 4—6, it has equally prevailed; it has prevailed speedily, 2 Kings xx. 2, 4, 5; Dan. ix. 20, 21, 23, and to a most incredible extent; Jam. v. 17, 18; and shall yet prevail, by whomsoever it may be offered, ib. ver. 16.

This encouragement to prayer is greatly heightened by what is added respecting,

III. THE CONSEQUENCE OF A DUE AND ACCEPTABLE PERFORMANCE OF IT—

God delights in the prosperity of his people ; and desires that they should be happy here, as well as in the world to come. It is with this view that he has enjoined prayer as a duty ; because, when performed aright, it is the means of filling the soul with the sublimest joy.

1. It tranquilizes the most perturbed mind—

Let a person under any sudden irritation, or calamity betake himself to prayer, and he will speedily find the tempest calmed, and his agitations quieted. No other thing will operate like this. It will enable him to educe good out of every evil : it will not only blunt the edge of all his trials, but will turn his sorrows into joy. Ps. xxx. 8—11, and xl. 1—3.

2. It brings God nigh unto the soul—

God in answer to prayer will take away the veil which intercepts our views of him, and "manifest himself to us, as he does not unto the world." What an exhibition of his glory was that which he vouchsafed to Moses! What a bright display of Christ's excellency was that which the three favored disciples were admitted to behold on Mount Tabor ! We say not indeed that any similar vision of the Father or the Son shall ever be presented to our bodily eyes: but God will certainly "shine into the hearts of those who call upon him, to give them the light of the knowledge of his glory in the face of Jesus Christ;" 2 Cor. iv. 6; and will enable them to say, "Truly our fellowship is with the Father, and with his Son Jesus Christ." 1 John i. 3. What ineffable delight must such manifestations bring with them!——

3. It gives us an earnest and foretaste of heaven itself—

The happiness of heaven consists in the vision and fruition of God: and this, as far as it can be enjoyed by faith, is enjoyed in prayer. There is not any one who has abounded in the performance of this duty, but has had frequent occasion, when in his closet, to exclaim with Jacob, "This is none other but the house of God, this is the gate of heaven!" Gen. xxviii. 17. In such seasons as these a man has no occasion to search out evidences of his acceptance with God, or of his title to heaven; for the very intercourse which he has with the deity is, if we may so speak, heaven brought down to earth; it is an actual anticipation of heaven, and a pledge of his complete possession of it in due season.

ADDRESS,

1. To those who ask without receiving—

Think not that God has violated his promise. The reason of your not receiving is, that "you ask amiss." Jam. iv. 3. Your petitions are cold, formal, hypocritical; and you have not a due respect to the name of Jesus in presenting them to God. Perform your duty as you ought, and you shall never complain of a want of acceptance in it.

2. To those who have received answers to prayer—

Let not your communion with God puff you up with pride, but rather abase you in the dust. If once you grow vain and secure, you will provoke God to hide his face from you, and to withhold the communications of his grace. Rejoice in the glorious privileges you possess; but "rejoice with trembling."

---

## THE BREAD OF LIFE.

John vi 34.—Lord, evermore give us this bread. (Sk.)

THERE is displayed in the gospel a most admirable and delightful combination of doctrines, precepts, and promises; and the performance of each christian duty entitles us to the enjoyment of some gracious promise. This sentiment is exemplified in no employment more than that of prayer: an engagement in which all good men have delighted, and the pleasure of which increases in proportion to the frequency of its repetition and the fervor of its exercise. Thank God hone need be at a loss for words in his addresses to the Divine Being: for, in addition to that comprehensive form of prayer, significantly designated "the Lord's Prayer," sentiments of petition, supplication, and intercession are interspersed through the inspired volume, many of which were used by holy men, who were disciples of our Lord, who heard the gracious words that dropped from his lips, and who were favored by his immediate instruction; one of these is recorded in the text. Our Lord had been pointing out the amazing superiority which he and his dispensation possessed over the dispensation of food which miraculously sustained the Israelites in the wilderness. The disciples heard with attention, and when he had ended his instructive observations, they unanimously cried out, "Lord, evermore give us this bread." Observe in this prayer,

I. A BLESSING REQUESTED ;—"This bread;" that is, the true bread from heaven," for the bread of God is He that cometh down from heaven, and giveth life unto the world," ver. 33. Bread is here, by Jesus Christ, represented as a type of himself; and to show its propriety, remark,

1. *Bread is of a vivifying quality.* Metaphors, which are drawn from earthly objects to represent heavenly ones, must necessarily be defective in expressing their full meaning. Bread, though of a reviving nature, cannot restore animation, when life is extinct; but the bread of heaven finds us in a state of death, and its efficacy is manifested in communicating life to our souls, Eph. ii. 1, as well as in supporting that life in all circumstances, Psa. xxiii. 2, 5.

2. *Bread is congenial to all appetites.* All have *naturally* a disposition for bread; and in the same manner, Christ, the bread from heaven, is exactly suited to satisfy the spiritual appetites of mankind; and as some tastes are vitiated to such a degree, that they do not relish bread, so many sinners prefer feeding on ashes and husks rather than on Christ, Luke xv. 16; Isa. lv. 2, xliv. 20.

3. *Bread is the common gift of God to the world.* Only a few possess the luxuries of life; but bread is for all, it is the greatest blessing that God ever bestowed for the support of animal life; and "God so loved the world, that he gave his only begotten Son, that whosoever believeth in him might not perish, but have everlasting life," &c., John iii. 16, 17; and this is the greatest blessing the Almighty ever bestowed for the benefit of our souls. John xv. 5.

4. *Bread can only be useful as we partake of it.* It may be in our hands, but unless we feed upon it, it will be of no benefit to us. We hear Christ preached, we attend on his ordinances; but in vain is all this, unless we stretch forth the hand, eat, and live for ever, John vi. 27; 1 Cor. xi. 24.

II. A PERSON ADDRESSED ;—"Lord;" who is the proper object of prayer, because,

1. *Prayer is the language of need;* and of this humanity is full. No sun rises that does not cast his beams on our wants; and whither should we go, but to Him, in whom dwelleth all the fulness necessary to supply the wants of mankind, John vi. 68; Col. ii. 9.

2. *Prayer is the expression of a dependent to a superior.* And who gave us life? who has supported it to the present moment? That God on whom we and all other created beings depend, Gen. i. 26, 27; Acts xvii. 26, 28.

3. *Prayer is the result of hope;* and surely, if ever there was a foundation for hope, it is in God, Psa. xlii. 11. He has condescended to assume the most endearing and encouraging characters, in his relations to mankind, Psa. xlviii. 14; 2 Cor. vi. 18. He has deigned to promise the full supply of our wants, and abundance of both temporal and spiritual blessings, 1 Pet. i. 4; Psa. cxxx. 8, xxxvii. 25. He has been the God of our fathers, 2 Cor. i. 10. Hope in the Lord is therefore founded upon a sure and rational basis.

III. A MODE OF COMMUNICATION STATED ;—"Give us this bread."

1. *Because we can no more maintain spiritual life without it, than our bodies can live without food.*

**2.** *Because we cannot borrow it with any possibility of returning it,* on account of our necessitous circumstances. Nor do we ever receive more of this bread than we can use, Rev. iii. 17.

**3.** *Because we cannot purchase it;* having been plundered by sin of every valuable we possessed, Acts viii. 20, 21.

**4.** *Because we cannot earn it;* we have been disabled, nor can we move till we receive this invaluable restorative; and if we receive it, it must be as a gift, Luke x. 30; Tit. iii. 5.

IV. A PERIOD FOR ITS CONTINUANCE SPECIFIED?—"evermore."

**1.** *Because in this world we shall always need it.* To whatever state of grace a man may attain, he is still liable to fall, as appears from a variety of petitions and cautions which the scriptures contain, Psa. li. 12; Prov. i. 24—32; Matt. xxiv. 13; Luke ix. 62; 1 Tim. i. 19, 20; Heb. x. 38. 39. Let the Almighty withdraw his support for one moment, and we must die, and die eternally, Psa. lx. 11; Lam. iv. 16, 17.

**2.** *Because the stores of divine goodness cannot be exhausted.* Gratitude to an earthly benefactor will often prevent us from being importunate in our requests, lest by giving to us, he should impoverish himself; but this cannot be the case with the bread that cometh down from heaven, for that is undiminishable, Eph. iii. 18, 19.

**3.** *Because it always will retain its efficacy and virtue.* Unalterable in quantity, it is also unchangeable in quality, Heb. xiii. 8.

**4.** *Because it does not induce satiety.* Earthly food is too gross to allow its unintermitting use; but on the contrary, as we receive this divine bread, our capacities to make use of it are enlarged, and our appetite increased for its continued communication.

**5.** *Because in the world to come it will constitute our joy and felicity.* Christ will still be the only delight of his saints, and will be their exceeding great reward for ever and ever, Rev. vii. 9—17.

NOTICE,

1. This bread must be sought with penitence, Matt. v. 4.
2. This bread will be found by faith, John iii. 36.
3. This bread must be received with gratitude, Psa. xcii. 1.

Have my hearers ever received the blessing of which we have spoken? if not, let the language of your hearts be, "Lord, evermore give us this bread;" for "Blessed is he that shall eat this bread in the kingdom of God."

---

## FEEDING ON CHRIST THE ONLY MEANS OF SPIRITUAL LIFE.

John vi. 53—58.—Verily, verily, I say unto you, Except ye eat the flesh of the Son of Man, and drink his blood, ye have no life in you. Whoso eateth my flesh, and drinketh my blood, hath eternal life; and I will raise him up at the last day. For my flesh is meat indeed, and my blood is drink indeed. He that eateth my flesh, and drinketh my blood, dwelleth in me, and I in him, As the living Father hath sent me, and I live by the Father; so he that eateth me, even he shall live by me. This is that bread which came down from heaven: not as your fathers did eat manna, and are dead: he that eateth of this bread shall live for ever. (B.)

THE circumstances under which these words were spoken, are the following.

Consider,

I. What we are to understand by "eating the flesh of the Son of Man, and drinking his blood."

Eating his flesh, and drinking his blood, literally and carnally, as the Jews supposed, ver. 52, is not here meant; and this notion Jesus refuted and repelled. Ver. 63.—

Nor is the eating his flesh under the form of bread, and drinking his blood under that of wine, intended here, as the Papists suppose; nor the partaking the signs of his flesh and blood, as the Protestants speak, in the holy Eucharist.—For the Lord's Supper was not then instituted, and however Jesus might have the design of that sacrament in his mind, and make use of terms applicable to it, it is certain his hearers could not understand him as speaking respecting it.—In the case of the converted thief, and all that died in the faith, before the institution of that ordinance, it was not necessary to salvation, but the eating and drinking Christ's flesh and blood, is here declared to be necessary. Ver. 53.—It may be observed, also, that a participation of the Lord's Supper does not necessarily and universally produce the effects which are ascribed to the feeding on Christ, which is treated of in this discourse. Ver. 54—58.

The eating of Christ's flesh and drinking his blood, spoken of in the text, is of a spiritual kind, and means a participation in his merits, or an interest in his sufferings and death, in his blood and righteousness, his atonement and mediation, for our justification, sanctification, and spiritual consolation.—This is done by the agency of the Holy Spirit.—And hence it implies that we partake of his Spirit; ver. 63; 1 Cor. xii. 13; John iv. 10; vii. 37, 38; as the fruit of his death and resurrection, viz. to quicken, renew, Tit. iii. 5—7, strengthen, and comfort us.— — His Word also is implied; ver. 63; confirmed by his death, being the means of feeding us with knowledge, of refreshing, supporting, and nourishing our minds. The doctrines of the Word are often represented under this metaphor. Prov. ix. 5; Isa. lv. 2; Eccles. xxiv. 21. Now we are thus to partake of Christ by faith; by which we are persuaded of the sufficiency of his merits, and rely thereon for justification; persuaded of the efficacy of his Spirit, and apply for it, in order to regeneration, and renewal in righteousness; convinced and assured of the truth and importance of his Word, and yield a due attention to it, maturely considering and inwardly digesting it.

II. The necessity of this, and the advantages that result from it.

Without feeding thus on Christ, we "have no life in us;" ver. 53; we may have natural and animal life, vital heat, and motion: we may breathe, and speak, and use our bodily senses; we may have rational life, may apprehend, reason, judge, choose, and so forth. But we have not spiritual life; the favor of God, Psa. xxx. 5, union with him, Eph. iv. 18, a spiritual mind, Rom. viii. 6, spiritual warmth, or zeal breathing in prayer and praise, spiritual senses, a discerning and understanding mind, a vigorous choice, just judgment, and lively affections towards God. We have not eternal life, no title to it, no meetness for it, nor earnest of it. 1 John v. 11, 12.

If we do eat Christ's flesh and drink his blood, we have eternal life; ver. 54; a title to it in our justification; a fitness for it in our progressive sanctification; an earnest, or the beginning of it, in communion with God.

This is proved by the following verses. His, "flesh is meat indeed;" or is truly meat, and the most excellent meat; and his "blood is drink indeed." Ver. 55. Hereby we are refreshed, as with meat and drink; strengthened for our spiritual warfare, duty, and suffering, and nourished up to eternal life.—Hereby we have union with Christ, and a continuance thereof; ver.

56, we have the present life of grace; ver. 57; and shall have the future life of glory. Ver. 58.

III. How WE MAY THUS EAT THE FLESH AND DRINK THE BLOOD OF CHRIST, AND THE STEPS TO BE TAKEN IN ORDER TO IT.

We must prefer this spiritual meat before the bodily " meat which perisheth," ver. 27, and all earthly things.—We must expect it from Christ, as a *free gift*, ver. 27, 31—34, and must have no reliance on our own merit.— We must " come to him" for it, ver. 34—37, by prayer, in faith, being persuaded he will give it, and depending entirely on his power, love, and faithfulness.—We must, therefore, be " taught of God," by his Word, Spirit, and Providence ; ver. 45 ; receiving thereby illumination, conviction, discipline.—We must be " drawn" by the Father. Ver. 43, 44. An attention to the great principles of natural religion, and obedience to its dictates, is a preparation for christianity. " If any man will do his will, he shall know of the doctrine, whether it be of God." John vii. 17.— — The miracles of God, the promises of God, the dispensations of Providence, especially afflictive ones, the influences of the Spirit, are given, and free for all. Thus he draws, " first by the iron chains of legal convictions, and secondly by the silken cords of redeeming love."* Instances of the former method we have in the Jailor, Acts xvi. 30, in David, Psa. xxxii. 4, in the Jews, Acts ii. 37, in Saul, Acts ix. 5, in the Woman of Canaan, Matt. xv. 22—28 ; and of the latter in the Woman of Samaria, John iv. 7—26, in Zaccheus, Luke xix. 2—10, in the Disciples,—in Lydia. Acts xvi. 14. Without this drawing, no man can or will come to Christ, whether he be moral or immoral, Jew or nominal christian, learned or unlearned, young or old. For, naturally, he neither feels nor sees his need of coming to Jesus ; he has neither power nor will to come, being chained down by ignorance, pride, and self-conceit, by sloth, by unbelief, and hardness of heart.—This is a true, but humbling doctrine : and that the Father is " not willing any should perish,", but is ready to draw all to Christ, is most encouraging.

### APPLICATION.

Have you eaten the flesh and drunk the blood of Jesus Christ? Examine yourselves particularly.— —If you have not, your state is wretched and dangerous ; and you have need to come without delay ; and, therefore, to be drawn by the Father.—Be willing, be desirous to be drawn, or to hear him say, " Depart, ye cursed ;" pray that he would draw you ; yield to his attraction, " hear and learn of the Father ;" hear the voice of his works, his Providence, his Word, his promises, his threatenings ; hear the still small voice of his Spirit, and follow his direction.—Are you mourning for him ; hungering for the bread of life, that " you may eat thereof, and not die ?" Ver. 50. Then, he is drawing you ; be encouraged and thankful.—Have you come to him, and partaken of his flesh and blood ? Then, again, be thankful, and continue to feed on him, and use the strength you have received to his glory

* Fletcher.

## BAPTISM

**Acts** ii. 38—41.—Repent, and be baptized every one of you in the name of Jesus Christ, for the remission of sins, and ye shall receive the gift of the Holy Ghost : for the promise is unto you, and to your children, and to all that are afar off, even as many as the Lord our God shall call. And with many other words did he testify and exhort, saying, Save yourselves from this untoward generation. Then they that gladly received his word were baptized : and the same day there were added unto them about three thousand souls. (Pr.)

WE here see the apostles in a very interesting situation, making their first general attack on the kingdom of darkness ; opening their commission which Jesus gave them at his ascension, and " beginning at Jerusalem."

There were several important circumstances which attended the commencement of the apostolic mission. —— 1. It was preceded by prayer : ch. i. 12—14. —— 2. By intimate union among themselves : ii. 1. —— 3. By an extraordinary outpouring of the Holy Spirit : ii. 2, 3. —— The people beholding these things, some doubted, and others were filled with reproach ; and this gives occasion for Peter's address in the words of our text. —— The effect is, the murderers of Christ are pricked to the heart, and are exhorted to be baptized.

I. OFFER SOME EXPLANATORY REMARKS UPON THE TEXT.

1. They are exhorted to *repent*, and this previous to their being baptized. —— Repentance is not a mere *reformation* of conduct, for that would not have been connected with " the remission of sins." —— Nor does it consist merely in being *alarmed* at the consequences, for they were already in a state of alarm. —— But it denotes *a change of heart*, sorrow for having sinned, not in that instance only, but in every other, though conviction might begin with that. It was a spiritual and evangelical repentance which the apostle required, such as is connected with faith in Christ and the remission of sins, and such as John preached. Acts xix. 4.

This exhortation does not merely point out what was their immediate duty : it also contains an intimation of mercy. —— The fallen angels were not so admonished when they had sinned, but were pronounced accursed : and if we also had been left under the curse, there would have been no place for repentance.

2. They are next exhorted to be *baptized*. —— Baptism is a solemn institution of Christ, by which we profess his name, and acknowledge ourselves to be his. It was therefore exhorting them to become his disciples, and to make an open profession of their love to him, even as they had formerly avowed their enmity against him. —— They were required to believe in him, to own him as their Lord, and to take his yoke upon them. —— It was also an act of obedience, to prove their faith in Jesus, and their love to him. Our submission to this ordinance must also be performed in obedience to the same authority.

3. Be baptized *every one of you*, is the divine command. Every one that heard the gospel was exhorted to repent, and every one that repented was commanded to be baptized. —— We here see that it is not left as a matter of discretion, much less of indifference ; but baptism is binding on all those who are the subjects of repentance and of faith. —— Some indeed admit it to be a duty to those who *see* it to be so : but they think that is all. —— True indeed it is, that a blind obedience is not required ; but that those who profess the gospel should read and understand and obey from the heart the precepts which it inculcates.

**4.** This obedience is to be performed *in the name of the Lord Jesus.* ——— This denotes not so much the form of administration, as the authority on which it rests, and at the same time points out the medium of salvation. ——— Christ is Lord of the church, and of the souls of men; and what is done in religion is to be to his glory, and from regard to his authority.

**5.** Baptism is to be attended to, for *the remission of sins.* ——— When Paul was converted, it was said to him, "Arise and be baptized, and wash away thy sins;" not literally, as if it possessed such a virtue in itself; but in the same sense, as we are said to "eat the flesh and drink the blood of Christ," in the sacred supper. ——— Baptism was a sign of forgiveness, and an emblem of the fountain opened for sin and uncleanness. ——— The real and only ground of forgiveness is the atonement of Christ: and this is intimated in their being baptized in his name, as in chap. x. 43.

**6.** They shall receive *the gift of the Holy Spirit:* this was extraordinary. ——— They should receive that very blessing of which they doubted and wondered—the spirit of prophecy: ver. 16, 17.

**7.** The promise is *to you and your children.* This was the encouragement addressed to the primitive converts, and the same is addressed to us—

**1.** Observe, the *promise* refers not to that which was made to Abraham, which included all his spiritual seed; but to that mentioned by Joel, and which is referred to in ver. 16, 17; compared with Joel ii. 28.

**2.** The term *children* here does not mean infants, but adults, the "sons and daughters that should see visions, and prophesy;" that is, the Jewish posterity; as when we speak of the "children of Israel," we do not mean the infant offspring of Jacob, but all his descendants in the times of Moses.

**3.** That which rendered the promise so peculiarly seasonable now was, that it stood against *the curse* which they had so awfully imprecated: "his blood be on us and on our children." Being pricked to their hearts, they might now think that the curse was coming upon them.

**4.** While it encouraged the penitent Jews, it also excluded their national prejudices and vanity; for the promise was to them that were *afar off*, among the Gentiles, as well as to them that are nigh.

**5.** The whole, whether to Jews or Gentiles, is restricted to *as many as the Lord should call.* This promise therefore cannot apply to any who are not called.

**8.** With many other words did Peter exhort his hearers *to save themselves* from that generation. ——— Repentance for sin, faith in Christ, and being baptized in his name, is the way in which they were to "save themselves:" not as authors of their own salvation, yet as being active in fleeing for refuge, as Lot did out of Sodom, or as the manslayer from the avenger of blood.

**9.** It is added, "Then they that gladly received his word *were baptized*," though probably not all who were pricked in their hearts: for there might be many left. and we still see various characters in whom convictions have not this issue. True faith is receiving the word with gladness; not merely having the truth forced upon the conscience, but the heart open to receive it, and that with cordial approbation and inward joy.

II. DRAW SOME CONCLUSIONS FROM THE SUBJECT.

**1.** Observe, that God's truth sometimes finds its way to *men's consciences*, and that only: but this is not conversion. ——— It is not enough to be pricked to the heart: we must repent and believe the gospel. ——— Many rest in their convictions, and too many preachers give encouragement to such, as if these were evidences of grace. But not so with Peter, nor Paul and Silas, when they addressed the convicted and trembling jailor. Acts xvi. 31.

**2.** If we truly repent and believe the gospel, we must prove *the sincerity* of our faith by taking the yoke of Christ upon us, and keeping his commands. ———— It is a sad way of reasoning, that because we believe, we need not therefore obey; and that because baptism is not essential, we may therefore be saved without it.

**3.** The argument from the text, in favor of *infant baptism*, is utterly groundless; for "as many" as received the word were baptized, and such only.

**4.** We learn the satisfaction there is in following the example of *primitive christians*, in keeping the commands of our Saviour. This has the promise of his abiding presence. Matt. xxviii. 20.

---

## THE DESIGN AND IMPORTANCE OF THE LORD'S SUPPER.

**1 Cor. xi. 24, 26.**—This do in remembrance of me . . . . for as often as ye eat this bread, and drink this cup, ye do shew the Lord's death till he come. (S. S.)

THE Corinthians had shamefully profaned the Lord's Supper—
St. Paul reproves them, and rectifies their views of that ordinance—
I. THE DESIGN OF THE LORD'S SUPPER.
Our ungrateful hearts are prone to forget the richest mercies—
To keep up "the remembrance" of his death, Christ instituted his last supper—
When we celebrate that ordinance, we "shew forth" his death.
The passover was a memorial of the deliverance vouchsafed to the Jews from the sword of the destroying angel—
At every returning celebration of it the reason of that ordinance was declared—*
Christ in his death has effected a greater deliverance for us—
In partaking of the bread and wine we "shew forth" his death—
We shew forth *the manner of it* as excruciating and bloody—†
We shew forth *the end of it* as a sacrifice for our sins—‡
We shew forth *the sufficiency of it* for our full salvation—‖
We shew forth his death "till he come"
Christ will, in due season, come again to judge the world—
Then his people will no longer need such memorials as these—
They will incessantly enjoy the brightest vision of his person, and the richest fruits of his death—

* In reference to Exod. xii. 26, 27, a custom obtained among the Jews that a child should ask the meaning of the passover, and that the person who presided should then give an account of its intent and origin, that so the remembrance of God's mercy might be transmitted to their latest posterity: and this was called "the declaration" or "shewing forth." Dr. Gill on the text.

† The breaking of the bread and the pouring out of the wine seem well calculated to impress this idea.

‡ In this light it is represented by St. Paul, 1 Cor. v. 7, and by our Lord himself, Matt. xxvi. 28.

‖ We express our affiance in his blood as the Jews did in the blood of the Paschal Lamb, when they sprinkled their door-posts with it, and eat of the flesh that had been roast with fire.

But till then the remembrance of his dying love, and the expectation of his future advent, must be thus preserved—

Such was Christ's end in instituting, and such should be our end in observing it—

To enforce the observance of this ordinance, we will proceed to shew,

II. THE NECESSITY OF ATTENDING IT.

The duty of commemorating our Lord's death is much neglected.

But a neglect of it involves us in the deepest guilt—

It implies,

1. Rebellion against the highest authority

Christ, the supreme governor of heaven and earth, has said, "Do this"—

Yet the language of too many is, "I will not"—

But they who disregarded *the passover* did not go unpunished—*

Much less shall they who slight the invitations to *Christ's supper*—Luke xiv. 24.

Surely it is no less than madness to persist in this rebellion—

2. Ingratitude towards our greatest benefactor

Christ has even "given his own life a ransom for us"—

And shall we disregard his dying command?—

*On the same night that he was betrayed,* did he institute these memorials of his death—

Had he *at that season* such a concern for us, and can we refuse to do so small a thing in remembrance of him?—

The Jews went thrice every year up to Jerusalem, from the extreme parts of Judea, to commemorate their deliverance—

And shall we turn our backs on the table when it is spread before us?—

Shall not God visit for such ingratitude as this?—†

3. Contempt of the richest mercies

To communicate, without discerning the Lord's body, can profit us nothing—

But to approach the table in humility and faith is a sure mean of obtaining all spiritual blessings—

Christ sometimes reveals himself in the breaking of bread, to those who had not so fully discovered him in the ministration of the word—Luke xxiv. 30, 31.

And do they not manifest a contempt of these mercies, who will not use the means of procuring them?—

How may the Saviour take up that lamentation over them!—Matt. xxiii 37.

4. A renunciation of our baptismal covenant

In baptism we covenanted to renounce the world, &c., and to serve God—

This covenant we ought to renew and confirm at the Lord's table—

But our refusing to confirm it is a tacit renunciation of it—

And can we hope that God will fulfil his part while we violate ours?—

---

* If a man had contracted any ceremonial defilement, or were on a journey, he might omit eating the passover at the appointed time; only he must eat it a month afterwards. But if he forbore to eat of it without any such impediment, God said concerning him, "that soul shall be cut off, *that man shall bear his sin.*" Numb. ix. 7—11.

† Let such conduct be expressed in words: "Thou didst indeed give thy body to be broken, &c., for me; and only requirest me to eat bread, &c., in remembrance of thee; but I account even that too much to do for thee:" Who could dare to utter such language? Or who would endure it if spoken by his servant or his child? Yet such is the language of our actions.

**Will** he be our God when we refuse to be his people?—
We shall CONCLUDE with answering some excuses.
"*I am not prepared*"—How then can you be prepared to die?—*
"*I am afraid of eating and drinking my own damnation*"—
Are you not afraid of damnation for neglecting your duty?—†
"*I am afraid of sinning afterwards, and thereby increasing my guilt*"—
If sins after receiving the Lord's Supper were unpardonable, none should receive it till the last moment of their lives—‡
"*The time of administering it interferes with other engagements*"—
To those who cannot deny themselves in any thing, we say with Paul—Rom. iii. 8, ad fin.
But where the difficulties are insurmountable, God will accept the will for the deed—Matt. xii. 7.
They however, who are at liberty, should attend "as often" as they can—
Only they must be careful to communicate with reverence, humility, faith, and gratitude.

---

## ON THE PREPARATION REQUISITE BEFORE THE LORD'S SUPPER.

1 Cor. xi. 28.—Let a man examine himself, and so let him eat of that bread and drink of that cup.  (S. S.)

GOD is an holy and jealous God, and greatly to be feared—
In all our approaches to him we should be filled with awe—
But a want of reverence prevails among the generality of mankind—
Even real christians manifest it sometimes, and that too even in the most sacred ordinances—
St. Paul, reproving the Corinthians for their conduct at the Lord's Supper, lays down an universal rule for communicants—"Let a man," &c.
I. THE DUTY OF SELF-EXAMINATION IN GENERAL—
This is an important but much neglected duty—
It is strongly recommended in the scriptures—
The apostle expressly enjoins it on all—2 Cor. xiii. 5.
This injunction is remarkably strong and energetic— — —
There is great reason for it—
We cannot ascertain the state of our souls without it
It is evident that the generality of men deceive themselves—
We also are liable to the same deception through pride and self-love—
Nor can we form a right conclusion without a strict investigation—
A mistake respecting our state would be fatal
There is no repentance in the grave—
As we die, so shall we continue for ever—
The benefits to be derived from it are exceeding great.

* Is not this acknowledgment the strongest reason for immediate repentance?

† In neglecting duty you insure condemnation; in practising it as well as you can (to say the least) you *may* avert it.

‡ If you really desire strength, where would you so soon obtain it? But if you determine to live in sin, your condemnation will be equally sure whether you come or not.

If our state be found good, we shall rejoice in the testimony of a good conscience—

If it be bad, we shall be stirred up to flee from the wrath to come—

We should therefore live in the habitual practice of this duty—Ps. lxxvii. 5.

But self-examination is more especially needful on certain occasions—

II. THE NEED OF IT BEFORE THE LORD'S SUPPER IN PARTICULAR.

This is intimated in the text; "Let a man examine himself, and *so* let him come"—

And indeed there is peculiar reason for it at that time—

That ordinance is a season of remarkable solemnity

There we see Christ crucified, as it were, before our eyes—

There we contemplate the most stupendous mysteries—

There we commemorate the greatest of all mercies—

There we are admitted to most familiar fellowship with God—

And does it become us to engage lightly in such an ordinance?—

It is a season that calls for the exercise of all our powers

The understanding should be occupied in devoutest meditations—

The affections should be engaged to the uttermost—

And can we thus command our faculties without any preparation?—

The neglect of self-examination may rob us of all the benefit of the ordinance.

Who can estimate the benefits we might receive if we came prepared?—

But who has not often communicated in vain?—

And has not our neglect been the true cause of this?—

We should therefore be peculiarly attentive to it at such a season

To assist in the discharge of this duty we shall shew,

III. THE SUBJECTS WHICH WE SHOULD THEN MORE ESPECIALLY ENQUIRE INTO.

We should examine ourselves respecting

Our knowledge of the ordinance itself.

To come without a proper discernment is dangerous—Ver. 27.

We should enquire what we know of the nature and ends of the ordinance—

On a distinct view of these our profiting much depends—

The state of our souls before God

At the Lord's table we receive " the children's bread"—

We should enquire therefore whether we be God's children!—

The immediate frame of our souls

We ought to have all our graces in lively exercise—Cant. iv. 16.

APPLICATION.

Begin this necessary work without delay— — —

Yet set not about it in a legal manner or for self-righteous ends—

Do not trust in your preparation, or expect acceptance on account of it—

But look to Christ as the only ground of your hope towards God—

Neither stay away from the table because you have not spent so much time in preparation as you could wish—

Whether you have used more or less diligence you must go as the publican—Luke xviii. 13.

Be assured however that your profiting will for the most part be proportioned to your preparation.

## THE CELEBRATION OF THE LORD'S SUPPER A CHRISTIAN DUTY.

1 Cor. v. 7, 8.—Purge out therefore the old leaven, that ye may be a new lump, as ye are unleavened.—For even Christ our passover is sacrificed for us: therefore let us keep the feast, not with old leaven, neither with the leaven of malice and wickedness; but with the unleavened bread of sincerity and truth. (Fk.)

The age of the apostles has sometimes been styled the golden age of Christianity. On many accounts it stands entitled to this high character. Then men became Christians, not because Christianity was the religion of the state, or because their predecessors were Christians, but from a conviction of its divine origin, truth, and excellence. Then they placed religion not in mere morality, or in the external observance of the institutions of Christianity, but in the renewing of the Holy Ghost.—Then the preachers of the gospel were alike eminent for piety, zeal, and gifts, workmen needing not to be ashamed. But even that age was not all gold;—there was some dross. False teachers crept in privily, and brought with them damnable doctrines. One of these, during the absence of St. Paul, had found his way into the Corinthian church. He preached another gospel. The demoralizing influence of such preaching was soon visible in the licentiousness of one of the members. The apostle ordered his excommunication, reminding them that vice is contaminating; "a little leaven leaveneth the whole lump."—Here he alludes to the Jewish passover; *then* all leaven was to be removed from their houses; *here* all sin from our hearts. "Purge out therefore," &c.

Our text teaches us three things.

I. That Christ crucified is the true passover, of which the Jewish was a type. For an account of the Jewish passover read Exodus chap. xii. Several things here demand attention.

1. *The passover was of divine appointment.* It did not originate with Moses or Aaron, or any of the elders or people of Israel. It was not the offspring of human policy, but of God, ver. 1. So its antitype originated neither with angels nor men, but with God. It was neither in the *power* nor *wisdom* of man to devise and execute a plan, by which the divine attributes could be harmonized, and the sinner saved. But that which man could not do, God *has* done.

2. *The passover was appointed for the deliverance of the Israelites from bondage and death.* They were slaves, oppressed with labor, tormented with cruelty, Exodus i. 11—16. The Lord heard their cry, and stretched out his hand to save: so Christ's death was intended to deliver mankind from the slavery, guilt, love, pollution, and punishment of sin;—to lead from spiritual Egypt to the heavenly Jerusalem.

3. *The passover would benefit none unless the blood were applied*, ver. 7, and 13. So also the death of Christ will profit us nothing, unless through faith we become the personal subjects of its mystical application—*to our consciences*, "in purging them from dead works," Heb. ix. 14,—*to our hearts*, in cleansing them from all sin, 1 John i. 7.

4. *The passover was not only to be slain, and its blood sprinkled, but it was also to be eaten;* see the eighth and following verses. So we must eat the flesh of the Son of God, John vi. 53.—Spiritual life is sustained by Christ—by furnishing the understanding with *instruction*, and *motives*—and by pouring grace into the heart to act upon the *will*—to raise the *affections*—to purify the *heart*—and to produce *power* to please God.—Christ is indeed our passover.

29

**II.** THAT AS THE FEAST OF THE PASSOVER WAS TO BE CELEBRATED BY THE JEWS, SO THE EUCHARIST OR LORD'S SUPPER IS TO BE CELEBRATED BY CHRISTIANS. The Jews were to celebrate it—all the Jews and proselytes, Exod. xii. 47, 48,—but none else, verse 43,—it was to be celebrated as long as their dispensation should continue, verse 24,—as a memorial of their deliverance from Egypt, verse 27.—So the Lord's Supper is to be celebrated by all Christians—all who receive Christ as their Lord and Master—who make his word the rule of their faith and practice—who propose his glory as the object of their desire—and who, deeply conscious of the deceitfulness and weakness of the human heart, rely continually and implicitly upon Christ for the promised aid of the Holy Spirit to enable them to *will* and to *do* of his good pleasure. Those who are not Christians have no right to it ;—Christ appointed it for his disciples only, Luke xxii. 14, &c.,—its being celebrated as a political test to qualify for civil offices is an awful profanation of the ordinance, and ranks among our national sins. But *all* Christians ought to celebrate it.

1. *Because Christ has commanded it*, Luke xxii. 19. Whatever he has commanded must be implicitly obeyed. To refuse obedience in any case because we do not perceive the necessity of the things enjoined, is totally to reject the authority of him who commands, and to make our obedience depend upon our perception of the fitness of the thing commanded.

2. *Because it keeps alive the important doctrine of salvation through the death of Christ.* The death of Christ is not to be viewed as an *ordinary* event—nor as the death of a martyr ; but as a *propitiation* for sin, Rom. iii. 25. Our Lord's words perfectly agree with this view, and explicitly teach this doctrine. So long as this rite is performed, so long will the doctrine of Christ's sacrificial death be received in the church.

3. *Because it eminently tends to excite holy affections.*—*Godly sorrow*, arising from a conviction that our sins, in common with those of others, occasioned the sufferings and death of Christ, *Ardent love to Christ.*—Love begets love ; remember its greatness as manifested in his incarnation—preaching—labor—suffering—death—resurrection—intercession—gift of the Holy Ghost—and all the blessings of the Christian dispensation. *Grateful obedience.*—Love is a constraining principle, it delights in doing the *will*—and copying the *example* of him whom we love. As the passover was to be an ordinance to the Jews forever, so the Lord's Supper is to be perpetuated in the Christian church to the end of time, 1 Cor. xi. 26

**III.** THAT IN ORDER TO ITS ACCEPTABLE CELEBRATION SEVERAL THINGS DEMAND ATTENTION.

1. *We should have correct views of its nature.* A fondness for mystery has led the Romish and Greek churches to interpret literally, what can only be metaphorically understood. Hence the absurd doctrine of *transubstantiation.* Neither the body nor blood of Christ is any more in the Lord's Supper, than the body and blood of the paschal lamb slain in Egypt in the time of Moses, was in the passover celebrated by our Lord and his apostles in Jerusalem.—In both cases the ordinances are merely *commemorative rites.*

2. *We should not ascribe an efficacy to it which it does not possess.* Many substitute it in the place of regeneration.—Hence the vilest debauchee, when he thinks himself dying, sends for a minister to come and give him the sacrament—having received it, he concludes his peace is made with God, and in this horrible delusion expires. Ministers should never administer it

30

to any person without explaining its nature, and showing that it is *not a Saviour*, but, like prayer, and hearing the gospel, *a means of salvation.*

3. *We should celebrate it with suitable dispositions. Not with malice.* For here we commemorate not malice but love—love to the worthless—love to enemies—love, where wrath and indignation had been merited. *Not with wickedness.*—For here we read God's aversion to wickedness of every kind—his method of removing it,—and our obligation to universal holiness. *But with sincerity and truth*—with purity of intention—and with an agreement between our principles and outward profession.

Conclude by answering a few objections.

*I dare not keep the feast, for it is a solemn ordinance.*—For the same reason you should neither pray—read the Scriptures—sing God's praises—nor hear his gospel preached; for they are all solemn.

2. *I am not prepared to receive it.* If you have not made up your mind to forsake sin, dare not to approach the table; but if you are resolved to be the servant of Christ, draw near.

3. *I have kept the feast formerly, but since then I have relapsed into sin.* Let this humble you, but let it no more hinder you from coming to the table, than from approaching the throne of grace.

---

## THE APOSTLES' COMMISSION.

Matt. xxxviii. 18—20.—And Jesus came, and spake unto them, saying, All power is given unto me in heaven and in earth, go ye therefore, and teach all nations, baptizing them in the name of the Father, and of the Son, and of the Holy Ghost; teaching them to observe all things whatsoever I have commanded you: and lo, I am with you alway, even unto the end of the world. Amen. (S. S.)

THE apostles spoke and wrote in a most authoritative manner—
They issued commands, promises and threats, in the name of God.
We therefore naturally enquire, by what authority they acted—
The passage before us gives a most satisfactory account—
In these words of our Lord we observe,
I. THE AUTHORITY HE CLAIMED.
Jesus, as God, possessed all power equally with the Father—
But, as Mediator, he received his power from the Father—
He received it, partly, that by means of it he might execute his mediatorial office. John xvii. 2.—
And, partly, as a reward for executing it. Phil. ii. 8—11.—
This power extended over heaven and earth.
Less than this would not have sufficed for the ends for which it was given—
But by this he is enabled to overrule every thing for the accomplishment of his own purpose—
Nor is it at all diminished by the lapse of ages.
It shall indeed cease to act at the last day. 1 Cor. xv. 28.—
There will not then be any occasion for the exercise of it.—
But till all the members of the church be glorified, Jesus will exert this power for their good—
And his authority will be the hope and consolation of them all—

It was upon this that he founded,

II. THE COMMISSION HE GAVE TO HIS APOSTLES.

He had formerly sent them to instruct the Jews—

He now extends their commission to the gentiles—

They were to *teach* all nations.

As they were to baptize men in the name of the sacred THREE, no doubt they were first to make known the persons and offices of the holy Trinity—

They were to declare " the Father," as our offended, but reconciled God and Father—

They were to make known " the Son," as the sinner's advocate and propitiation—

They were to set forth " the Holy Ghost," as the enlightener, comforter, and sanctifier of God's elect—

They were to *baptize* their converts in the name of the sacred Three.

Having proselyted men to the Christian faith, they were to initiate them into covenant with God by baptism—

But though they first taught adults, and then baptized them, they reversed this order with respect to infants—

They took care, however, that in all cases the doctrine they preached should be recorded in the baptismal rite—

And that every christian should either expressly or virtually acknowledge it—

They were also to *instruct* their hearers in *practical religion.*

It is evident they were not to be *merely* moral preachers—

They must of necessity insist much on the offices of the Father, Son, and Holy Ghost—

But they were also to inculcate every moral duty—

And to enforce every obligation whether toward God or man—

This commission was arduous—We proceed to notice,

III. THE PROMISE HE ADDED FOR THEIR ENCOURAGEMENT.

The Apostles might well have been discouraged from attempting to execute so difficult a service.

They were, in themselves, poor, mean, and illiterate—

They had to propagate principles new, strange, detested—

——————— to oppose the lusts and prejudices of mankind—

——————— to bring men from sin to a life of holiness and self-denial—

And this, not only without human aid, but in opposition to all the power and policy of the world—

They could not therefore but feel themselves unfit for such a task—

But our Lord gave them a most encouraging promise.

When Moses declined the service to which he was called, God promised to be with him, Exod. iv. 15—

Thus Christ engaged to succor his disciples in their work—

He assured them of his presence to direct, assist, and uphold them

And to give effect to their labours—

To this promise he called their particular attention ; " lo"—

Nor will he fail to accomplish it to the end of the world—

Nor was the affirmation added to it without peculiar energy,

"Amen" may be considered as an affirmation or a petition—

In either view it should not be overlooked—

The promise it confirms was the solace of all the Apostles—

And has been the support of all succeeding pastors—

**Let every** one then add "Amen," as importing both his wish and affiance—

INFER

1. How clearly is the doctrine of the Trinity revealed !

The Father, Son, and Holy Ghost, are here distinctly mentioned—

They are all mentioned *in the same manner*, and *for the same end*—

Whatsoever is meant by " the name" of the Father, must be understood also in reference to the Son and Holy Ghost—

And the baptizing of persons in their name must be considered as the most solemn act of worship to them—

Let none then doubt the truth or importance of this doctrine—

Let every one rather be daily worshipping the sacred Three—

And looking to them to perform their respective offices—

2. How highly should we value the ordinances of religion !

Many excuse themselves from attending on public ordinances, by saying, that they are equally profited at home—

But the converting and edifying of souls is the appointed labor of Christ's ministers—

And Christ has promised his special presence with them—

It must therefore be the duty of all to attend on their ministrations—

Let us then reverence his institutes, and seek his blessing—

Thousands yet daily experience the truth of his promise—

The poor, the weak, the desponding, are enriched, strengthened, comforted—

Nor shall any that truly hunger be ever sent away empty.

〰〰〰〰〰〰

## CHAPTER II.

## EXHORTATIONS.

### AN INVITATION TO PARTAKE OF GOSPEL BLESSINGS.

Isaiah lv. 1, 2.—Ho, every one that thirsteth, come ye to the waters, and he that hath no money : come ye, buy and, eat ; yea, come, buy wine and milk without money, and without price. Wherefore do ye spend money for that which is not bread ? and your labor for that which satisfieth not? hearken diligently unto me, and eat ye that which is good, and let your soul delight itself in fatness. (B.)

IN the text, we have a most encouraging invitation to us Gentiles. Consider we,

I. TO WHOM THE INVITATION IS MADE.

" Ho every one that thirsteth,"—" and he that hath no money."—

Those who *thirst* are invited. Thirst implies want, and, therefore, the needy are invited ; all who need happiness. We naturally seek it in present things, in carnal pleasure, or worldly honor and wealth; but these things neither do nor can afford it.

Thirsty persons are sensible, keenly sensible, of their wants. Hence, those are especially invited, who are sensible of their need of these things.—

Those who are thirsty feel a desire for refreshing draughts ; a strong, constant and increasing desire. Such, therefore, are particularly welcome.—

33

The thirsty are uneasy, distressed, and restless till they drink, and can be satisfied with nothing else. So those who are uneasy, unhappy, and restless to obtain pardon, the divine favor, a birth from above, and the sanctifying influences of the Spirit, and will be satisfied with nothing else, that is, the " weary and heavy laden," are still more particularly called.

The thirsty are active, and will take pains to gain refreshment. These are most of all invited.

But suppose they be very guilty, and have lived in the neglect of all their duties to God and man, and the commission of all kinds of sins ?—still, they are welcome. Those, who have *no money*, no good works, no righteousness, if they only thirst, shall be welcome.

II.  WHAT IT IMPLIES, OR THE NATURE OF THE INVITATION.

"Come to the waters." This may be interpreted, " Come to the keys, wharfs, and ports, on navigable rivers, where foreign commodities are imported.— "

Buy what you absolutely want. Buy what is of infinite value,—pardon, of your sins, acceptance with God, adoption, regeneration, &c. Buy what will do you infinite good, will remove all your miseries, and make you happy, truly, continually, and lastingly happy ; what will enrich you, elevate your nature in the highest degree, and make you most glorious. Buy an estate, an inheritance, a kingdom, a crown.

Come and buy for nothing, " without money and without price." The blessings offered to you are invaluable; no price can be set upon them .

" Their value vast ungrasp'd by minds create."

We are indeed, poor, and have nothing, but the blessings are already bought and paid for.—We may have them gratis, as free undeserved gifts.— And yet they shall be as much our own, as if bought and paid for by us.

Buy very cheap. You must part with clay, thick clay, that defiles, burdens, and destroys—the world, and sin. You must part with poison, and buy food ; you must part with rags, and buy costly and splendid clothing; you must part with chains, and buy crowns ; you must part with disorders and death, and buy health and immortality. Again,

Come to the waters and wash. Come, ye filthy ; ye that are defiled with guilt, come to the " fountain opened for sin and uncleanness;" ye that are defiled with the power and pollution, the ulcers and leprosy of sin, come and receive the Spirit of God, the washing of regeneration.

Come to the waters and drink. Ye thirsty ; come, and be refreshed with peace with God ; peace of mind, and the consolations of God's Spirit; in " the times of refreshing from his presence." Come, ye weary, and " I will give you rest."

Come and be healed. These are medicinal waters. The blood of Christ, the Spirit of God, the word of God, the waters of the sanctuary, are intended for the cure of spiritual diseases.

Come and be quickened, and made immortal. These are *waters of life*. Drink of them, and live ; yea, live for ever.

Fear not lest you should drink the waters dry. They shall increase continually, and impart their salutary effects to all who use them. (See Ezek. xlvii. 1—12.

The waters when you shall drink of them, shall become " milk;" sweet, balmy, and nourishing. Such are the truths and promises of the Gospel ; such the grace and love of Go in Jesus Christ.

The " milk" shall become "wine," cheering, invigorating, strengthening. Gospel truths and promises, God's grace and love shall be productive of hope, joy, and strong consolation.

It is not enough that we come and look at the blessings which are offered , we must partake of them. We must *buy* them; they must be ours. We must *eat* them: applying them, in their several particulars, for our own use and benefit. But how ? By faith. We must hear: hearken diligently." Come, not only to the ordinances, but " unto me," by faith in prayer.

III. THE ARGUMENTS WHEREBY THE INVITATION IS ENFORCED.

" Wherefore do ye spend money for that which is not bread, and your *l*abor for that which satisfieth not ?"

The rich live by their money , and the poor by labor. Both are gone out of the way of truth and happiness. The things which men pursue, the riches, honors, and pleasures of this world are not *bread*, they are not the proper food of the soul, are not suited to its nature, are not calculated to fill its capacity, and supply its wants ; to refresh it, to restore its wasted strength, to preserve its health, to nourish and make it grow. They do not invigorate, strengthen, or improve it.—

Neither do these things *satisfy* us. They do not even at present ; but if they did, we have no hold upon them ; they are perfectly uncertain, and will certainly leave us, when we shall be in greatest need of consolation.

Wherefore, then, do ye follow after these things ? Is it reasonable ? Is it wise ? Is it for your honor ? Is it for your interest? Is it your duty ? Quite the reverse. — — Is it necessary ? Cannot you do otherwise ? Yes ; the grace of God is sufficient for you, and free for you.

But, do you object, we have nothing better to pursue, and must be active. Not so. Come unto me, and your soul shall live ; shall be quickened, in the possession of the favor of God, a union with him, his image, his nature, fellowship with him, holiness inward and outward, happiness present and eternal, according to an everlasting covenant.

Wherefore, " Ho, every one that thirsteth," all of you in general, and every one in particular, " come ye to the waters," &c. — —

---

## GOD IS DESIROUS OF SAVING MEN.

Jer. xiii. 27.—Woe unto thee, O Jerusalem! Wilt thou not be made clean? When shall it once be? (H. H.)

THROUGHOUT all the sacred writings we behold the goodness and severity of God : sometimes the one attracts our notice, and sometimes the other ; and in many places, as in that before us, we are both struck with the union and combination of them both. Jerusalem was the city of the living God, the residence of his peculiar people ; yet he denounces woe against them : but at the same time he declares, in very pathetic language, the ardent desires of his soul to exercise mercy towards them.

From these most affecting words we shall take occasion to shew,

I. THE WOES WHICH IMPENITENT SINNERS HAVE REASON TO EXPECT— This is a painful, but necessary, subject of our inquiries— The punishment that awaits sinners in most tremendous—

The loss of heaven is one part of it: and who shall declare how great a loss this is?— — —The miseries of hell (which is the other part) are equally beyond the powers of language to describe, or of imagination to conceive— — —

This, however, the impenitent have but too much reason to expect—

" Woe unto thee !" says my text: and this is the voice of reason*— — — of scripture†— — —of experience‡— — —of the compassionate Saviour himself ||— — —What stronger evidence can any man wish for? and how blind must he be that is not convinced by it!

But however merited and awful these woes, are, we see from the text,

II. How unwilling God is to inflict them—

He complains of men's obstinacy in rejecting the overtures of his mercy—

It is their sin only that exposes them to his displeasure: were that once removed, he would " rejoice over them to do them good." And whence is it that they are not cleansed from it? Has not God provided such means for their cleansing, as should certainly be effectual, if only they were applied? Has he not opened a fountain to cleanse them from guilt? Zech. xiii. 1; 1 John i. 7,— — —Has he not promised to sprinkle them with water that should purify and renew their very inmost souls? Ezek. xxxvi. 25—27, — — —Yes: but they are averse to that purification: they hate the very means by which it is to be attained, and the regimen whereby it is to be preserved— — —God would gladly effect the work for them, if only they would submit to it; but they will not. Ezek. xxxiii. 11. Hence those com plaints so often uttered by the prophets, Ps. lxxxi. 11–13; Jer. vii. 23–26, and by Christ himself— — —John v. 40; Matt. xxiii. 37.

He expresses also an impatient longing for an opportunity to bless their souls—

Long has he waited to no purpose: yet still " he waiteth to be gracious unto us :" " he stands at the door of our hearts, and knocks." His address to us is, " Turn ye, turn ye from your evil ways; for why will ye die, O house of Israel ?" Every day appears to him an age: Hos. viii. 5; Jer. xv. 6. " I am weary with repenting ;" he is at a loss, as it were, what to do, whether to give us up, or to use any further means. Hos. vi. 4, and xi. 8; Jer. iii. 4, 19. The complaint in the text is scarcely less the language of despondency, than of compassion; " When shall it once be?" It is as though he said, " My patience is almost exhausted : your return to me is the most earnest desire of my soul : but I fear I shall be forced, in spite of all my efforts to save you, to abandon you at last, and to execute the judgments which you so obstinately provoke."

Address,

1. Those who imagine that they have no need of cleansing—

What child of man has not need to be cleansed from that taint which we inherit from our first parents? Job xiv. 4, and xv. 14, and xxv. 4. And who has not contracted much moral defilement by means of actual transgression ?— — —Let none entertain such proud conceits. The best amongst

---

* There must be a difference between the righteous and the wicked.

† Against ten thousand passages to this effect, there is not one syllable that has an opposite aspect.

‡ The union of sin and misery is felt by all. Where is there a sinner that is truly happy? See Isaiah lvii. 20, 21.

|| See how often woe is denounced, Matt. xxiii. 13, 14, 15, 16, 23, 25, 27, 29, 33.

us, no less than the worst, need to be washed in the blood of Christ and be renewed by his Spirit; and without this cleansing, must inevitably perish.

2. Those who are unwilling to be cleansed—

Many are unwilling to part with even the grossest lusts. What then must we say to them? Must we speak peace to them, instead of denouncing woes? If we were to do so, God would not confirm our word: so that we should only delude them to their ruin. But indeed they themselves would not be deluded by any such assertions: for, with whatever confidence they utter them themselves, they would not endure to hear them if uttered from the pulpit.

But it is not gross sin only that must be put away: we must be "cleansed also from secret faults:" whatever stops short of this, is ineffectual. The right hand, the right eye, must be sacrificed; and the whole heart be turned unto God— — —

3. Those who desire the cleansing of their souls—

It is of infinite importance that you seek this blessing aright. It is not in floods of tears that you are to be cleansed; though floods of tears are proper and desirable: it is the blood of Christ alone that can cleanse from the guilt of sin; and the Spirit of Christ alone that can cleanse from the power and pollution of sin. To apply these effectually, we must embrace the promises, and rest upon them, trusting in God to accomplish them to our souls. We must not first cleanse ourselves, and then embrace God's promises of mercy; but first lay hold on the promises, and then, by virtue derived from them, proceed to "cleanse ourselves from all filthiness both of flesh and spirit." 2 Cor. vii. 1, with Acts xv. 9.

~~~~~~~~~~

## INVITATION TO COME TO CHRIST.

Rev. xxii. 17.—And the Spirit and the Bride say, Come: and let him that heareth say, Come: and let him that is athirst, come: and whosoever will, let him take of the water of life freely. (H. H.)

RICH beyond expression are the blessings held forth to us in the Word of Life: and as free as light are the invitations given us to partake of them. Not only in the epistles to the Seven Churches, and in the other parts of this prophetic book, but throughout the whole scriptures, is every possible encouragement afforded to the sinners of mankind, to repent of sin, and to "lay hold upon the hope that is set before them" in the gospel. And here, in the close of the inspired volume, are invitations to us reiterated from every quarter, that we may be prevailed upon to accept of mercy, ere the door of mercy be for ever closed.

Let us consider,

I. THE BLESSINGS TO WHICH WE ARE INVITED—

They are here designated by "the water of life." We will notice them,

1. Generally—

The source from whence this water flows, is no other than the Lord Jesus Christ, the Saviour of the world. In the very chapter before us, "the pure river of the water of life" is said to "proceed out of the throne of God and of the Lamb." Ver. 1. As in the wilderness, the water gushing from the rock that had been smitten supplied the necessities of all Israel; so the Lord

**Jesus Christ,** when smitten with the rod of the law, poured forth the waters of salvation for the benefit of the whole world. 1 Cor. x. 4. He is "the fountain of living waters;" Jer. ii. 13; and whosoever cometh to him, may drink and live for ever. In the chapter before our text, the Lord Jesus Christ declared this to the apostle John: "I am Alpha and Omega, the beginning and the end. I will give to him that is athirst of the fountain of the water of life freely." Ch. xxi. 6. In the days of his flesh, he spoke repeatedly to this effect. To the Samaritan woman, of whom he had asked a draught of water, he said, "If thou knewest the gift of God, and who it is that saith unto thee, Give me to drink, thou wouldest have asked of him, and he would have given thee living water." John iv. 10. On another occasion, when the people had, according to custom, drawn water from the pool of Siloam, he stood in the place of public concourse, and cried, "If any man thirst, let him come unto me and drink: and out of his belly shall flow rivers of living water." This latter expression is then explained by the Evangelist, who adds, "This spake He of the Spirit, which they that believe on him should receive." John vii. 37–39. Now here we have, *in a general view*, the import of the expression in my text. The Holy Spirit is that water of life which Christ is empowered to bestow: and wherever that blessed Spirit is imparted, there is within the person's own bosom a principle of life, seeking for vent in all suitable expressions of duty to God; or, as our Lord elsewhere expresses it, "there is within him a well of water springing up unto everlasting life;" John iv. 14; to which the Holy Spirit, in all his tendencies and operations, leads us to aspire.

2. More particularly—

Three blessings in particular I will specify, as granted by our Lord Jesus Christ unto all who come unto him; namely, *pardon*, and *holiness*, and *glory*.

The Lord Jesus will in the first place bestow the *pardon* of our sins. He is said by the prophet to be "the Fountain opened for sin and for uncleanness:" Zech. xiii. 1; and all who come to wash in that fountain are cleansed from all their sins. In it even "sins of a crimson dye" are made "white as snow:" Isa. i. 18; as it is said, "The blood of Jesus Christ cleanseth from all sin." 1 John i. 7.

For the purposes of *sanctification* also shall this gift be bestowed: for, by the prophet Ezekiel, he says, "I will sprinkle clean water upon you, and ye shall be clean: from all your filthiness and from all your idols will I cleanse you. And I will put my Spirit within you, and cause you to walk in my statutes, and to keep my judgments to do them." Ezek. xxxvi. 25–27.

Eternal *glory* also will he confer upon them: for, when they have "washed their robes, and made them white in the blood of the Lamb, he will lead them unto living fountains of waters," Rev. vii. 14, 16, and will cause them to "drink of the rivers of pleasure which are at God's right hand for evermore." Ps. xxxvi. 8, and xvi. 11.

Let us now turn our attention to,

II. THE INVITATION ITSELF—

Here we cannot but notice the very peculiar urgency and freeness of it—

1. The urgency, to overcome reluctance—

"The Spirit says, Come." The Holy Spirit of God has undertaken the office of revealing Christ to men, and of bringing sinners to Christ for the remission of their sins. John xvi. 8, 14. He descended visibly on the day of Pentecost for these ends: and by the ministry of the apostles, as also by his operation on the souls of men, wrought powerfully upon multitudes.

whom he " made willing in the day of his power," and effectually subdued to the obedience of faith. Thus at this time also is he carrying on the work that has been assigned him in the economy of Redemption. In the written word, he speaks to us : by the ministry of his servants, he pleads with us : by the convictions which he fastens on our mind and conscience, he strives with us individually ; if by any means he may constrain us to accept the blessings offered to us in the gospel. His voice to us every day and hour is, " Come," come to Christ as the Saviour of your soul.

" The Bride also says, Come." The Bride is the church, " the Lamb's wife," who has experienced in her own person all the blessedness of that salvation which she is so desirous of imparting to all around her. The church of old addressed her Lord, saying, " Draw me, and we will run after thee :" Cant. i. 4 ; that is, " Draw me, and I will not come alone : I will surely labor to the utmost of my power to make known to others the wonders of thy love, that they also may be partakers of my felicity, and unite with me in honoring and adoring thee." Thus the church does in every age. She is " the pillar and ground of the truth," 1 Tim. iii. 15, supporting it firmly in the world, and exhibiting, as by public inscriptions that are visible to all, the glory and excellency of the gospel salvation. She then unites with the Spirit of God in saying to all around her, " Come :" Come to Jesus and see what a Saviour he is. See in me what he both can and will do for you also ; however far off you may now be, you may draw nigh to him with a full assurance of acceptance with him ; and though now " aliens from the commonwealth of Israel, and strangers from the covenants of promise, you may become fellow-citizens with the saints and of the household of God." Eph. ii. 19.

" Let him also that heareth, say, Come." Those to whom the foregoing invitations are announced, should unite their efforts to make them known, and to induce every creature under heaven to accept them. Think not, brethren, that you have performed your duty when you have heard these invitations from the lips of your minister ; no, nor when you have yourselves complied with his advice. You are all to be preachers in your own circles ; all to repeat to your friends and relatives, your families and dependents, the glad tidings which you hear of a free and full salvation ; and, with one heart and one voice, should join in saying to all around you, " Come, come, come." This was the conduct of Andrew and of Philip, when they had found the Saviour ; John i. 40, 41, 43, 45 ; and this must be the conduct of us all, in our res pective spheres.

2. The freeness, to counteract despondency—

" We are all invited to " take of the water of life freely." If we are " athirst," we are the very persons whose names, if I may so speak, are especially written on the cards of invitation. Indeed, if our names had been expressly recorded in this passage, we should not have had a thousandth part of the assurance of God's willingness to accept us that we now have ; for there might be other persons of our name : but no mourning penitent in the universe can err in tracing his name in the designation that is here given.

It may be, however, that some may say, " I am not sufficiently athirst to be able to appropriate to myself this character. I should be glad indeed to obtain mercy of the Lord ; but I do not pant after it as the hart after the water-brooks, and therefore I have not in myself the qualification that is here required." To counteract such desponding fears, the Saviour says, " Whosoever will, let him take of the water of life freely." If you have not all the thirst that you can wish, have you the inclination? have you the desire?

39

Then you are the person invited: and you must not dream of staying till you can bring certain qualifications along with you, but come and take these blessings "*freely*, without money and without price." Isa. lv. 1.

To impress this subject the more deeply on your minds, let me ADDRESS a few words,

1. To the reluctant—

Many are the excuses which you urge for your declining the invitation sent you in the gospel: and to you they appear perhaps sufficient to justify your refusal. But your Lord and Saviour will not be deceived: he sees the radical indisposition of your mind to the blessings which he offers you; and will say of you, as he did in reference to those of old, "They shall never taste of my supper." Luke xiv. 16–24. You may be offering a variety of pleas: but he will put the true construction on them all, "Ye *will* not come unto me that ye may have life." John v. 40. O think, how bitterly you will regret your present conduct, when you shall see unnumbered myriads, who were once as far off from him as you now are, sitting down at the marriage supper of the Lamb, and you yourselves be cast out into outer darkness! What weeping, and wailing, and gnashing of teeth will you then experience to all eternity! Matt. viii. 11, 12. How will those words sound in your ears at the last day, "Often would I have gathered thee, as a hen gathereth her chickens under her wings; but ye would not!" Matt. xxiii. 37. Do but reflect on this one moment,—"*I would; and ye would not.*" Verily, that reflection will constitute the very summit of your misery in hell. I pray you, hold not out any longer against the urgent invitations which are now sent you; but come unto the Saviour, and accept the rest which he has promised to all that are weary and heavy-laden.

2. To the desponding—

What can the Saviour add to convince you of his willingness to accept and bless you? Perhaps you will say, "I have tried to come to him, and I cannot: and I have tried so long, that I think it in vain to entertain a hope of final success." Is this the case? Then hear what the Saviour says to you by the prophet Isaiah: When the poor and needy seek water, and there is none, and their tongue faileth for thirst, I the Lord will hear them, I the God of Israel will not forsake them: I will open rivers in high places, and fountains in the midst of the valleys: I will make the wilderness a pool of water, and the dry land springs of water. Isa. xli. 17, 18. Now I cannot conceive a case more desperate than that which is here depicted: The person is in himself "poor and needy." (There you will easily recognize your own character.) He has "sought for water," even for the waters of salvation. (That represents what you also profess to have done.) He has "found none." (There is your unhappy lot painted with the utmost precision.) "His tongue faileth for thirst;" so that he is ready to sink in utter despair. (What can you add to that, to bring it home more fully to your own case?) Yet this is *the very person for whom God has reserved his blessings, and to whom he engages to impart them.* "But I am in such a state, that it is almost impossible to deliver me: you might as well expect a river to be running over the highest mountains, as for the waters of salvation to reach me." Is that the case? says the Saviour: then "*I will open rivers in high places;* I will make the wilderness a pool of water, and the dry land springs of water." See here, my brethren, what wonderful condescension there is in your Lord and Saviour, that he will so describe your case, that it should not be possible for you to fail in recognizing your own character, or to doubt any longer his ability and willingness to save you. Take then this

40

passage; and rely upon it; and plead it with him; and expect the accomplishment of it to your own soul. Then shall "your light rise in obscurity, and your darkness be as the noon-day." Isa. lviii. 10. You shall find that the Saviour is not "a fountain sealed," Cant. iv. 12, but "a fountain opened;" Psa. xxxvi. 9; Joel iii. 18; and "out of that well of salvation you shall drink water with joy" for evermore. Isa. xii. 3.

---

## EXHORTATION TO A HOLY WALK.

Isaiah ii. 5.—O house of Jacob, come ye, and let us walk in the light of the Lord. (H. H.)

MANY prophecies there are which are not yet accomplished, especially among those which are to be fulfilled "in the last days," The last days were understood even by the Jews themselves as relating to the days of the Messiah; and they comprehend all the time from his first advent in the flesh, to the period when his kingdom shall be fully established upon earth. Hence the prophecies relating to that period must have different degrees of accomplishment; being partly fulfilled in the first triumphs of the gospel, but having a further and more entire accomplishment when all the kingdoms of the world shall become the kingdom of our Lord and Saviour Jesus Christ. Thus it is that we are to understand the prophecy contained in the preceding context. "The mountain of the Lord's house," that is, the gospel church, was established on the top of the mountains in the apostolic age, when it triumphed over heathen idolatry and Jewish superstition; and myriads of converts encouraged one another to serve and glorify their God: but we have not yet seen the time when "swords have been beaten into ploughshares, and spears into pruning-hooks, and nations have ceased to learn and practice the art of war." That time however will come; and we should long, and labor to the utmost of our power, to hasten it forward. We should even now anticipate it; yea, we *will* anticipate it: "O house of Jacob, come ye, and let us walk in the light of the Lord!"

Let us walk in the light
I. OF HIS TRUTH—
His truth now shines in its meridian splendor—
"The darkness is indeed past; and the true light now shineth." 1 John ii. 8. "The day-star has arisen," 2 Pet. i. 19; "the day-spring from on high hath visited us," Luke i. 78, 79; "the Sun of righteousness," Mal. iv. 2; shineth forth in his brightness: and the way of salvation through a crucified Redeemer is now so plain, "that no wayfaring man though a fool can err therein." Isa. xxxv. 8. —— —— "On the face of Moses there was a veil, that they who received the law should not see its full import: but if the gospel be hid, it is from those only whom the god of this world hath blinded;" since "we may all with open (that is, *unveiled)* face behold as in a mirror the glory of the Lord." 2 Cor. iii. 13—18. —— ——
Let us then walk in it—
Having the light, we should "believe in the light, that we may be the children of light." John xii. 35. 36. We should embrace with all thankfulness the way of salvation revealed in the gospel. We should "*come to Christ*" as the appointed Saviour of a ruined world: Matt. xi. 28; we

should "*look to him*," as dying upon the cross for us: Isa. xlv. 22; we should "*build upon him*, as our only foundation;" 1 Cor. iii. 11; and "*cleave unto him* with full purpose of heart;" Acts xi. 23; and "determine to know non but him;" 1 Cor. ii. 2; and to "glory in nothing but the cross of Christ;" Gal. vi. 14; ——— "Arise then, and *be enlightened*, for the light is come; and the glory of the Lord is risen upon you." Isa, lx. 1. *The marginal reading.*

Whilst confiding in God as reconciled to us by the blood of the cross, we should endeavor to walk in the light,

II. OF HIS COUNTENANCE—

This is the privilege of a true believer—

So it is declared to be, by one who experienced it richly in his own soul. Ps. lxxxix. 15. God presents himself to us in the gospel under the endearing relations of a father and a friend, to whom we may carry every want, every trial, every difficulty; and from whom we may expect a supply according to our need. He will be not only "*our God.*" but "*a God unto us,*" 1 Chron. xvii. 24. Putting forth all his wisdom, all his love, and all his power, to make us truly blessed. He will engage in this work "with his whole heart and with his whole soul;" Jer. xxxii. 41; so that it must be utterly our own fault if we be not as holy, and as happy, as our hearts can wish. ——— ———

Let us then enjoy our privilege—

Let us "walk with God," as Enoch did; and "glory in him as the God of our salvation." See what holy joy David found in communion with him, Ps. lxiii. 1—5, and cxlv. 1—12, and cl. ——— ——— and shall we who live under a so much nobler dispensation experience less? Shall not *we*, who have so much clearer views of Christ, "rejoice in him with joy unspeakable and glorified?" O let us "*delight ourselves in God*," and have even now, "in the secret of his presence" and the consolations of his Spirit, an earnest and a foretaste of our heavenly inheritance. Ps. xxxi. 20. Eph. i. 13, 14. ——— ———

But we shall in vain hope to enjoy his presence, if we walk not also in the light,

III. OF HIS COMMANDMENTS—

These are given by him "as a light to our feet and a lantern to our paths."—

Without them we should not "know how to walk and to please God;" but by them we are fully informed in all things that are needful for us to do. Prov. vi. 23. They do not indeed descend to every particular circumstance in which we can be placed; but they afford principles which are universally applicable, and which are quite sufficient for our direction when duly applied. The duty " of doing to others as we would be done unto," is so comprehensive as to embrace every part of our social duty, whilst it is so simple that it may be comprehended and applied by every one who desires to please God.

Let us then make these the one rule of our conduct—

Let us not attempt to reduce them to the standard of the world, but endeavor rather to raise our conduct to the standard of God's revealed will. Let us treasure up in our minds the most exalted precepts, and "hide God's word in our hearts, that we may not sin against him:" for " then shall we not be ashamed, when we have respect unto all God's commandments ———

In ADDRESSING " the house of Jacob," we must speak to,

1. Those who are nominally so—

**It is** but too true, that " all are not Israel, who are of Israel :' and those who are only of the house of Jacob by name and profession, may know it by their walk and conversation. Consider, I pray you, in what light you have walked : Is it not manifest, that the generality who call themselves christians are influenced only by the things of time and sense ; and that their principles and pursuits are altogether earthly? Know then, ye lovers of this present evil world, that, if God's word may be depended on, you are deluding yourselves to eternal ruin. Isa. l. 11. You " sow the wind and you shall reap the whirlwind. Hos. viii. 7. When will you begin to see, that " one thing," and one thing only, " is needful?" When will you learn to say, " Whom have I in heaven but thee? and there is none upon earth that I desire in comparison of thee?" That you should seek present as well as eternal happiness, we grant: but you should seek it where David did ; " Who will shew us any good? Lord, lift thou up the light of thy countenance upon us ; and that will put more gladness in my heart than any increase of corn, wine, and oil can ever do." Ps. iv. 6, 7.

2. Those who are really so—

You have found that God in Christ is " a fountain of life; and in his light you have seen light." Ps. xxxvi. 9. You therefore are " children of the light and of the day." But if you are so highly distinguished in your character, think how distinguished you should also be in your conduct. Eph. v. 8. 1 Thess. v. 5. 6. The eyes of all are upon you : they will look particularly to see whether religion is such a source of happiness, as you profess. O shew them that " you need neither the sun to lighten you by day, nor the moon by night, since the Lord has been a light unto you, and your God your glory." Isa. lx. 19. Shew them that even in the greatest troubles you have a fountain of consolation to go unto : and that " when you walk in darkness, the Lord is a light unto you." Job xxix. 3. Mic. vii. 8. And, as it is eminently characteristic of Gospel times to encourage one another in the ways of God, see that you do so, " speaking one with another in psalms and hymns and spiritual songs, singing and making melody in your hearts unto the Lord." Then, from enjoying God in his courts below, you shall be taken to serve him in his temple above, where your largest desires shall be satisfied, and your utmost capacities be filled Rev. xxi. 22, 23. Ps. xvi. 11.

---

### DAVID'S ADVICE TO SOLOMON.

1 Chron. xxviii. 9. And thou, Solomon my son, know thou the God of thy father, and serve him with a perfect heart, and with a willing mind : for the Lord searcheth all hearts, and understandeth all the imaginations of the thoughts : if thou seek him, he will be found of thee ; but if thou forsake him, he will cast thee off forever. (H. H.)

**Whatever** may have been their own conduct through life, it is the wish of most men in a dying hour, that their children should walk in the ways of probity and honor. But men of piety have higher views : they wish their children not merely to pass through this world with credit, but to obtain happiness beyond the grave.—The advice of David in the words before us, is precisely such as every religious parent would wish to give to his surviving family. Let us observe,

43

**I.** The advice here given—

The occasion was most solemn. David had desired to build a temple for the Lord, but was forbidden; and was directed to devolve that office on his son Solomon. All the princes and great men of the nation were convened to assist at the solemnity: and in the presence of them all did David direct his son,

1. Whom to seek—

The terms here used have doubtless a peculiar force. David does not say to his son, "Know thou the God *of Israel;* but "Know thou the God of *thy father;*" by which expression he evidently called the attention of Solomon to the character of Jehovah as exemplified in all his dealings towards *him:* it is as though he had said, "Know thou that *sovereign* God, who chose me above all to rule his people Israel ——— Know that *almighty* God who, in all my dangers from Saul or other enemies, has preserved me to the present hour ——— Know that *merciful* God who forgave me all my great transgressions in the matter of Uriah ——— and that *faithful* God who has fulfilled to me all his great and precious promises, in raising up thee to sit on my throne, and to build a temple to the Lord" ———

"*Know*" this God: study his character as displayed in all his conduct towards me: acquaint thyself with him in the most intimate and endearing manner: and seek him as thy friend, thy portion, thine eternal great reward! But remember that it is in Christ only that this character of God can be fully seen ——— Seek then to know God as reconciled to you in the Son of his love; and let "this God be your God for ever and ever."

2. How to serve him—

Integrity of heart is indispensable in all who would serve their God aright. *Absolute* perfection is not to be expected by fallen man: but that measure of perfection which consists in a total freedom from all guile, not only may, but must, be attained. To be "Israelites indeed," we must be "without guile." There must be no lust, which we desire to retain; no duty, from which we draw back; no sacrifice which we are averse to make: the will of God, even his whole will, without any limitation or exception, must be that to which we aim to be conformed ——— And in our labors to fulfil our duty, we must not be constrained by slavish fear, but by filial love. We must feel the service of our God to be perfect freedom; and find all our delight in it, like the angels, who "do his will, hearkening to the voice of his word" ——— As we are to love our God, so also are we to serve him, "with all our heart, and mind, and soul, and strength."

The importance of this charge is strongly marked in,

**II.** The considerations with which it is enforced—

Two arguments are here used to impress the more deeply on Solomon's mind the foregoing exhortation. They are briefly these;

1. That God is privy to our inmost thoughts—

If God could judge only by the outward appearance, we might with less danger be inattentive to our hearts: but the heart of man is as visible to him as the sacrifices when flayed and divided asunder were to the priests of old. Heb. iv. 13, τετραχηλισμένα. Not the thoughts only, but "the imaginations of the thoughts," the very first risings of them before they are formed into a distinct apprehension of the mind, are all seen and marked by him, so as to ascertain with precision their nature and quality; and to make them infallible grounds of condemnation or acquittal in the day of judgment. Not actions only, but "the spirits of men are weighed by him," so as to discern how much there is of good or evil in every inclination, affection, appetite, and motion of the soul.

What a reason is this for attending to the frame of our minds in the service of our God! That, and that only which is according to his word, will be accepted by him: whatever there is of formality, or hypocrisy, or of any evil principle, will all be separated as chaff from the wheat, to be consumed in the fire, when the wheat is treasured up in his garner. Alas! how little that is truly good, will be found even in the best of men! Consider this, all ye who would find acceptance with God; and endeavor to approve yourselves to Him, "who searcheth the heart, and trieth the reins."

2. That he will deal with us according as we conduct ourselves towards him—

It is grievous that men should explain away the plainest declarations of God, in order to accommodate them to human systems. There is nothing clearer in all the inspired volume, than that "God will be found of them that seek him, and cast off those who forsake him." We appeal to the experience of all who are in the slightest degree acquainted with vital godliness. "Did God ever say to any man, Seek my face in vain?" ———— On the other hand, Who ever turned back from him, without suffering loss in his soul? Who has not found that the Spirit of God may be grieved and provoked to withdraw his gracious communications? Most assuredly he will not always strive with man, but will give us up to our hearts' lusts, if we wilfully harbor those dispositions or affections which are hateful in his sight. Moreover, in the eternal world, he will recompense every man exactly according to his works; adjudging to his diligent servants a reward propor tioned to their diligence in improving their talents, and to the disobedient servants a punishment proportioned to their guilt.

Who can reflect on this, and not feel the force of the advice given in our text? Our happiness both in time and in eternity depends on our present diligence and fidelity. Let us therefore implore help from God, that we may so devote ourselves to him now, as to be approved by him in the day of judgment.

ADDRESS—

1. To parents—

You see in David, what should be your chief desire in behalf of your children. We say not that you should be indifferent about their worldly ad vancement; for that also is important in its place: but your great concern should be to have them truly pious and devoted to God. Labor then, by every possible means, to attain this point. Call them to you. and address them each by name with all tenderness and fidelity; remembering that you yourselves must answer unto God for the influence with which he has invested you for their good; and that, if they perish through your neglect, their blood will be required at your hands.

2. To those who are coming forth into life—

Such advice as that which is given in our text, you are ready to judge premature, or at least to think you have good reason for delaying your attention to it. But are you young, and moving in an elevated sphere, and engaging in concerns of vast importance? So was Solomon: yet were these no reasons for David to withhold the advice, or with Solomon to reject it. Remember, it is for eternity, and not for time only, that you should live; and, if you disregard the admonitions of your parents, they who now so long for your welfare, will be swift witnesses against you at the day of judgment.

**3.** To all who are here present—

It is not unbecoming a minister of Christ to regard his flock with **parental solicitude**, or to address them in the language of our text. Let me then address each of you, as it were, in the presence of the whole collective body, and urge you to seek after God with your whole hearts. Rest not in a formal routine of duties, or in a partial conformity to his revealed will : but see that your "hearts are right with him ;" and never rest till you have " the witness of his Spirit," and "the testimony of your own conscience, that in simplicity and godly sincerity you have your conversation in the world." Such a state of mind is most desirable for every one of us ; and it is the best preparative, no less for the duties of this life, than for the enjoyments of the life to come.

---

## RELIGION IS NOT A SOURCE OF EVIL TO THOSE WHO EMBRACE IT.

Jer. xxv. 5, 6.—Turn ye now every one from his evil way, and from the evil of your doings, . . . . . and I will do you no hurt.

Sin is the greatest of all evils ; because it is the source from which all evils flow. Nor can the miseries which it has introduced be ever remedied, but by a thorough turning unto God. This, Jeremiah tells us, was the remedy prescribed by *all the prophets:* ver. 4, with the text : and certainly it is the only one that can ever prove effectual.

The passage from whence the text is taken, contains, in addition to the words which we have cited, a dehortation or dissuasion from idolatry ; together with an intimation, that a continuance in that sin would accelerate their ruin, and insure their exclusion from the promised land : they would persist in it " *to their hurt.*" Ver. 7. On the contrary, if they would return to God, he would forbear to inflict upon them his threatened judgments, and " *do them no hurt,*"

But we omit that which related to the temporal state of the Jews, in order that we may fix your attention more immediately upon that part of the subject which is applicable to all persons in all ages of the world.

The text consists of,

I. An exhortation—

As idolatry was at that time the national sin of the Jews, so every one has some evil way to which he is more particularly addicted. We cannot pretend to trace all the shades of difference that are found in different men : we will rather arrange the whole under three great and comprehensive classes: to one or other of which, all, except true. christians belong. We therefore say, Turn.

1. From profaneness—

That this is a common sin amongst us, needs no proof ; we cannot open our eyes or our ears but we must be speedily convinced of it. —— ——

Let then as many of you as have entertained licentious principles, or indulged in vicious practices, " turn from the evil of your doings," yea turn from it speedily, and with utter abhorrence.

2. From wordliness—

While the young and gay are rushing into vice, and pouring contempt upon every thing that is serious, a great part of mankind are immersed in

**wordly** cares, and as regardless of religion as their more dissipated **bre-**
**thren** —— ——

True it is, that these persons have more specious grounds on which to
vindicate their conduct, inasmuch as it seems nearly allied to prudence and
diligence. Still, however, while we highly approve of those virtues, we
cannot but condemn a worldly spirit as evil : since it is declared to be incompatible with the love of God : 1 John ii. 15—17 : and therefore we say to
all, " Turn from it," lest you deceive yourselves to your utter ruin.

3. From formality.

There is a very considerable number of persons, whose strictness of prin-
ple, and correctness of manners, screen them effectually against any charge
of profaneness; while their indifference to riches and aggrandizement shews
that they are not open, in any great degree, to the imputation of worldliness.
But their religion consists in a mere round of duties, in which they have no
real enjoyment of God, but only a self-righteous, self-complacent approbation
of their own minds —— ——

That this also is evil, we cannot doubt, if only we bear in mind that God
requires our *hearts* : Prov. xxiii. 26; and that every service, in which the
heart is not engaged, is declared to be vain and worthless in his sight. Matt.
xv. 8, 9. Compare 2 Tim. iii. 5.

In exhorting such persons to turn from the evil of their doings, we would
by no means be understood to discourage diligence in attending on divine
ordinances, whether public or private ; but only to guard against a resting
in the performance of duties, and a substituting of that in the place of Christ.
In appreciating our religious observances, let us judge of them by their spirituality, and by our enjoyment of God in them : and, if they be ever so devout, still let us remember that they make no atonement for sin, nor do they
confer any obligation whatever upon God ; yea, rather, the more devout they
are, the more we are indebted to God for that grace whereby we are enabled
so to worship him.

To confirm the exhortation, God has been pleased to add,

II. A promise—

At first sight the promise appears to be unworthy of God, and incapable
of affording any great encouragement to those to whom it is made. But,
if taken altogether abstractedly, it surely is no light matter for those who deserve all the judgments that God can inflict, to be assured, that he will never
do them any hurt : and if considered in connexion with our fears and apprehensions, it will be found to contain the richest consolation. *In this view,*
we observe, God will do us no hurt in respect of,

1 Our intellect—

When we begin in earnest to be religious, our friends are ready to suppose
that we are, or shall soon be, beside ourselves : see Mark iii. 21. Acts xxvi.
24. 2 Cor. v. 13: nor can we altogether wonder at their judgment, when
we consider how great the change is, (like a river turning back to its source,)
and how unable they are to account for it. But they may spare themselves
their fears; for God gives his people, not a spirit of delusion, but " of a
*sound mind.*" 2 Tim. i. 7. The prodigal's return to his father's house was
the first proof of sanity, not of insanity : nor has any person a spark of true
wisdom in him, till he begin to fear the Lord. Ps. cxi. 10. In conversion
a man is made to form a correct judgment respecting his most important concerns ; and not only to view things in the same light that God views them,
but to act agreeably to those views. As well therefore might the man whose
eyes Jesus had opened be said to have suffered injury in his organs of vi-

sion, as a person thus enlightened in his judgment be said to have suffered in his intellect.*

2. Our friends—

We are taught to expect, that, on our becoming decided followers of Christ, " our greatest foes will be those of our own household :" Matt. x. 35, 36; and experience accords with the declarations of scripture on this head. But are we therefore injured in this respect? Our Lord has told us, and experience accords with that also, that if we lose any friends for his sake, he will repay us in kind, as it were, an hundred-fold. Mark x. 29, 30. A merchant who should part with his goods to such advantage as this, would surely not be thought to have sustained any loss. But besides this recompense in the present world, God himself will be our friend, both now and for ever. And would not *this* amply repay the loss of all earthly friends?

3. Our reputation—

Though the whole of our conduct be visibly improved, yet shall we, on turning to God, be loaded with opprobrium and contempt; and though something may be gained by prudence, or conceded to us on account of our celebrity in learning, there is no religious person that occupies the same place in the estimation of the world that he would do if he were not religious. If our Lord himself was " despised and rejected of men," Isa. liii. 3, and the apostles were deemed " the off-scouring of all things," 1 Cor. iv. 13, it is in vain for us to expect honor from man. Matt. x. 24, 25, with John v. 44. But are we therefore without honor? No: our very disgrace, when so procured, is a very high honor, inasmuch as it assimilates us to Christ, 1 Peter iv. 13, and is a testimony to us of our fidelity. Luke xxi. 13. But suppose that ignominy had nothing to counterbalance it here, should we have any reason to regret it when Christ " confessed us before his Father, and his holy angels ;" and when they who despised us, shall " awake to shame and everlasting contempt?" Dan. xii. 2.

4. Our interests—

The laws of the land certainly afford us very great protection. Nevertheless it is no uncommon thing at this day for children and servants to be called to make very great sacrifices for the gospel sake. But be it so: they are forced, like St. Paul, to serve the Lord " in cold and nakedness," and in a privation of all earthly comforts. But are they eventually " hurt?" What if their spiritual consolations be proportioned to their temporal afflictions : have they not made a good exchange? Is not peace in the bosom incomparably better than money in the purse? The riches of this world are easily appreciated : but those which Christ imparts, are " unsearchable." Their despisers would, at a future day, give all the world for a drop of water only to cool their tongue. How rich then must they be who are drinking living waters eternally at the fountain head!

5. Our happiness—

Doubtless the godly have grounds of mourning peculiar to themselves: but are they therefore losers in respect of happiness? No: their sorrows, if I may so speak, are sources of joy : they would on no account be without them : they rather regret that they cannot sorrow more : they mourn because they cannot mourn, and weep because they cannot weep : and if at any time they have been enabled to abase themselves before God in dust and ashes,

---

* That people who are insane, may fix their thoughts upon religion, or that a person may become distracted by *misapprehensions* of religion, is confessed : but if religion would drive a man mad, the more religious he was, the more likely to be mad. Who does not shudder at the consequences that would result from that opinion?

48

tney look back upon such seasons as the most precious in their whole lives. But if they have sorrows unknown to others, have they not "joys also, with which the stranger intermeddleth not?" Let a promise be applied with power to their souls, or "the love of God be shed abroad in their hearts," have they not a very foretaste of heaven upon earth? Compare their state with that of others, on a dying bed: follow them in the instant of their departure from the body: see them welcomed to the bosom of their Lord: contemplate their eternal state, in contrast with that of their despisers; and then say whether they have any reason to complain, that their fidelity to God occasioned on the whole a diminution of their happiness?

ADDRESS,

1. Those who are yet following their evil ways—

We inquire not, What are the ways you follow: if you do not turn from *every* evil way to God, and devote yourself unreservedly to your Lord and Saviour, the issue will be the same, whatever course you take. Your guilt may be more or less aggravated, and your misery be apportioned accordingly: but, without entering into the different degrees of punishment, let me ask, Will not *sin* "do you *hurt?*"— — —And would not God do you *good*, if you would return unto him?— — —"Turn then from all your transgressions; so iniquity shall not be your ruin." Ezek. xviii. 30.

2. Those who are turning from their evil ways—

Halt not between two opinions: strive not to reconcile the inconsistent services of God and Mammon. Matt. vi. 24. "If Baal be God, follow him: but if the Lord be God, then follow him." There is a certain kind of turning unto God, by which you will suffer hurt on every side, and receive no benefit whatever. If your "heart be not whole with God," no good can accrue to you, nor can any evil be averted from you. The world will not approve of you, because you are too precise for them: and God will not approve of you, because you are not upright before him. Be not then temporizing and hypocritical, but open, decided, and consistent characters. "Follow your Lord fully:" "follow him without the camp, bearing his reproach." Heb. xiii. 13. Thus, though "your life may be accounted madness, and your end to be without honor, yet shall you be numbered among the children of God, and have your lot among his saints." Wisd. v. 4, 5.

---

## THE SOURCE AND REMEDY OF DESPONDING FEARS.

Job xxxv. 14.—Although thou sayest thou shalt not see him, yet judgment is before him. therefore trust thou in him. (H. H.)

IN controversy there is need of the utmost candor; nor without it can we ever hope for a favorable issue. The friends of Job were grievously defective in it; and therefore utterly failed, either to convince him, or to be convinced themselves. But Elihu, who was an attentive auditor of the dispute, and who, on account of his youth, judged it indecorous to offer his sentiments till he saw that his elders were silenced, took up the matter with incomparably better temper and judgment, and, instead of bringing railing and unfounded accusations as the others had done, called Job's attention to many expressions he had used, and endeavored to convince him out of his own mouth. This was wise, and well adapted to the end proposed: and it is observable, that when God reproved the manner in which the other three had conducted the controversy, he said nothing to the disparagement of Elihu, nor required any sacrifice on his account.

It is certain that Job, though far from being a hypocrite, as his friends had represented him, had not always spoken quite advisedly with his lips. His self-justification had been occasionally too strong, and his complaints of God's conduct towards him somewhat irreverent: he had yielded also too much to despondency. He had complained that he could not understand God's dealings with him, and that he had no hope or prospect of deliverance from his troubles. Ch. xxiii. 8, 9. This is noticed by Elihu in the words before us; and the proper remedy for such desponding fears is pointed out to him: " although thou sayest thou shalt not see God, yet judgment is before him; therefore trust thou in him;" that is, place in God that confidence he deserves; and all will yet be well.

From the words thus explained we shall be led to consider,

I. The source of desponding fears—

There is far more of despondency in men than is generally supposed: perhaps it is, as much as any other thing whatever, a ground of their continuing impenitent in their sins.

The *ostensible* ground of men's fears is usually a sense of the extreme difficulty of their case—

Thus it was with Israel at the Red Sea, at the waters of Marah, at the borders of Canaan also, when the spies represented the cities as impregnable, and the inhabitants as irresistible. Thus it was even with the pious Hezekiah, when his sickness appeared to be unto death: Isa. xxxviii. 10–13, and thus it is with multitudes amongst ourselves, who imagine that their circumstances are so calamitous, as to be beyond the reach of any remedy. More particularly is this the case with persons under spiritual trouble; they are apt to imagine, that their sins are unpardonable, and that their corruptions are too inveterate ever to be subdued— — —

The *real* ground is a low apprehension of the perfections of their God—

This is the interpretation which God himself puts on the unbelieving fears of his people. When Sarah laughed at the promise made to her, the answer was, " Is there any thing too hard for the Lord ?" and the complaint of God against the unbelieving Israelites was, that " they limited the Holy One of Israel." In fact, a just view of God's perfections would silence all fears: for if his wisdom, his power, his love, his faithfulness be really infinite, we have nothing to do, but to repose our confidence in him, and we are safe— — —

But it is a small thing to know the source of desponding fears, unless we apply,

II. The remedy—

This is prescribed in the words of our text:

1. Contemplate God—

What we are to understand by that expression, " Judgment is before him,' may be ascertained by consulting a similar passage in the prophet Isaiah. Isa. xxx. 18. He will do nothing but what is right and good; nor will he omit any thing which it becomes him to do.

*Consider what he has done* in a way of power and grace— — —and is he not the same God as ever?

*Consider what he has engaged to do:* is there any thing that we can need, which is not made over to us by an express promise? Has he not said, that 'his grace shall be sufficient for us;" that "we shall have no temptation without a way to escape;" that "as our day is, so shall our strength be;" that "he will give grace and glory, and withhold no good thing" from his believing people? "Hath he then said these things, and will he not do them? hath he spoken, and will he not make them good?"

Consider, above all, the gift of his only dear Son! What else will he, or can he, withhold from us? Rom. viii. 32. Surely he will be " a strength to the poor, a strength to the needy in his distress, a refuge from the storm, a shadow from the heat, when the blast of the terrible ones is as a storm against the wall." Isa. xxv. 4.

Did we but duly consider his glorious perfections as already exercised for his people, and as specially pledged to be exercised for us, we should never entertain a doubt of his constant and effectual care. "His name would be to us as a strong tower, to which we should run, and be safe."

2. Trust in him—

"They that know his name will trust in him:" and to trust in him is the certain way to dissipate all fear. See how a confidence in God operated in the case of David: Psa. xlvi. 1—3, and Psa. xi. 1—4; and the same effect will it produce in us: "if we commit our ways to him, our very thoughts," (which are by nature fluctuating as the wind,) "shall be established." This then is what we must do: we must "cast all our care on Him who careth for us." It is the very direction which God himself gives to "those who walk in darkness and have no light:" Isa. l. 10; and if we follow this direction, "God will keep us in perfect peace;" Isa. xxvi. 3; and we shall be as Mount Zion, which cannot be removed, but standeth fast for ever." Psa. cxxv. 1.

ADDRESS,

1. To those who overlook difficulties—

This is the habit of men in general: and hence it is that they are so much at their ease. But it is no easy matter to turn to God aright. To repent and to believe in Christ are works far beyond the ability of man; nor can any man do either the one or the other, but by the influence of the Holy Ghost. Acts v. 31; Phil. i. 29. O let this be duly weighed! Let us remember, that "we cannot even say that Jesus is the Lord," (we cannot feelingly and believingly say it,) "but by the Holy Ghost:" 1 Cor. xii. 3; and let us not delay one hour to seek his effectual aid.

2. To those who unduly magnify them—

We certainly magnify our difficulties too much, when we deem them insuperable: for "the things that are impossible with man are possible with God." See the state of Jonah in the whale's belly: could any be conceived more hopeless? Yet from thence did he cry, and his prayer entered into the ears of the Lord of Hosts. Jonah ii. 1—7. Thus let us "never stagger at the promises of God through unbelief, but be strong in faith, giving glory to God." Rom. iv. 20. The greater our difficulties, let our application to him be the most earnest, and our expectations of his gracious interposition be the more enlarged: "Be of good courage, and he shall strengthen your heart all ye that hope in the Lord." Ps. xxxi. 24.

## SEEKING THE LORD EXPLAINED AND ENFORCED.

Isa. lv. 6, 7. Seek ye the Lord while he may be found, call ye upon him while he is near: Let the wicked forsake his way, and the unrighteous man his thoughts: and let him return unto the Lord, and he will have mercy upon him; and to our God, for he will abundantly pardon. (B.)

In the verses now before us, the Prophet earnestly exhorts the wicked of all nations to seek the knowledge and favor of God by repentance and prayer, adding the most gracious assurance of his readiness to show "mercy and abundantly pardon."

But to enter into the meaning and force of the exhortation, let us consider,

I. What is implied in seeking the Lord.

It is to seek the KNOWLEDGE of the Lord, lost by the fall.—We do not mean the knowledge of his being, that he is; or, of his nature, what he is, a *Spirit*. This, however, the heathen did not know, or they would not have "changed the glory of the incorruptible God into an image made like to corruptible man, and to birds, and four-footed beasts, and creeping things." Rom. i. 23. Nor could hypocrites, if they were sensible of his spiritual nature, hope to please him by ceremonies, or any mere external services.— Nor do we mean the knowledge of his attributes, such as his eternity, omnipotence, omniscience, his infinite wisdom, equity and goodness; nor of the relations in which he stands to his creatures in general, or to mankind in particular, as our Creator, Governor and Benefactor. The works of creation, and the dispensations of Providence, manifest God in these respects. Rom. i. 20.—But we mean that knowledge of him which is by supernatural revelation, and communicated through his word, especially "the Word made flesh," and his Spirit. John i. 18; Eph, i. 17; 2 Cor. iv. 6; 1 John v. 20; Matt. xi. 27.

This is that acquaintance with him,—in his glory and majesty, producing the fear of him, which we have not by nature; Rom. iii. 18; a fear of reverence, a fear of awfulness, a filial fear of offending him.—In his holiness and justice, which produces humility. Job. xlii. 6; xl. 4.—In his mercy and grace, Jer. xxxi. 34, which produces confidence. Ps. ix. 10.—In his love and goodness, which produces returns of love, not only esteem, and desire, but grateful, complacential love, attended with zeal for his glory, and obedience to his will.

It is to seek HIS FAVOR, lost also by the fall, for "by nature we are the children of wrath;" Eph. ii. 3; and to be "accepted," or taken into favor. Eph. i. 6.

It is to seek HIS IMAGE, in which man was created, Gen. i. 27, but which he has lost, being earthly, sensual, devilish. James iii. 15. We are to "put off concerning the former conversation, the old man," &c. Eph. iv. 22—24.

It is to seek COMMUNION WITH HIM. This we have not by nature, "being alienated from the life of God, through the ignorance that is in us:" Eph. iv. 18; Col. i. 21; but we may attain it. 2 Cor. vi. 16; John xiv. 23; Eph. ii. 21, 22; 1 John i. 3.

It is to seek the EVERLASTING VISION AND ENJOYMENT OF HIM. Matt. v. 8; 1 John iii. 2; Rev. xxi. 3—7; xxii. 3 4.

II. How, or in what way, the Lord must be sought.

As a preparation for seeking him, we must be sensible of our entire, or great want of him in all these respects; of the knowledge of him; of his favor; of his image; of communion with him, and the enjoyment of him.

We must be sensible of the excellency of these blessings; of their attainableness; of the absolute necessity of attaining them, in order to our salvation present and eternal.

We must feel desires; earnest, increasing, restless desires after him. Thus David, Ps. xlii. 1; lxiii. 1; Isa. xxvi. 8, 9.

Conscious these blessings before mentioned are God's gifts, we must seek them in prayer: Matt. vii. 7; and not only in *mental* prayer, though this be important, but in *vocal*. We must "call upon him."—In private. Matt. vi. 6. We mean not the *saying* our prayers, but really presenting our requests to God, for blessings which we know we want, and must obtain, or perish. We must pray sincerely, earnestly, importunately, perseveringly, and in faith, nothing doubting.—In our families, also, we must join in prayer to God.—In social meetings.—And in the public congregation; and, therefore, we should take care to be present in time.

But in the use of these means we must be consistent. The "wicked" must "forsake his way;" his ungodly, unrighteous, intemperate way. Tit. ii. 11, 12. "The unrighteous man," *the man of iniquity:* of injustice, fraud, violence, oppression; "his thoughts," his deceitful imaginations, that these things are reconcileable with religion, or that he can finally prosper in such a way, or escape the Divine vengeance.—*The man of vanity;* who pursues things unattainable, unsatisfactory, uncertain, transitory; "his thoughts," his delusive schemes, and contrivances to obtain happiness in this way. Or, let him who vainly thinks to enlighten his own mind, expiate his own sins, change his own nature, or do the will of God of himself, in other words, who vainly "goes about to establish his own righteousness, not submitting himself to the righteousness of God," desist from such thoughts.— And let him turn to the Lord, and expect these things only from him, and seek his happiness only in him. We must turn to him in judgment,—in choice,—in intention,—resolution,—affection,—in faith, believing his truths, declarations, promises in Christ, and coming to God only through him.

III. WHEN WE MUST SEEK THE LORD.

" While he may be found."

—In life, with which, when it closes, will terminate all opportunities of seeking the Lord.—In health, not " in the floods of great waters." Ps. xxxii. 6.—In youth, the period of life more favorable than any other for obtaining true religion, and wherein a special promise is given, for the encouragement of those that begin early to seek the Lord. Eccles. ix. 10.—At least, while our day of grace lasts, and " he is near," by his Word, and the ordinances he has instituted among his people, and by his Spirit, convincing, alarming, drawing, assisting us in our endeavors.

We should remember, we cannot tell how long our day of grace may continue. With many it has ended on this side the grave. It was so with the Israelites in the wilderness, Ps. xcv. 8, 9, 11, and those who rejected our Lord's ministry, to whom he said, " Ye shall die in your sins." John viii. 21. Thus we may be given over to hardness and impenitence of heart, if we neglect to improve our present means, and the grace given to us. Prov. i. 28, 29.

We shall notice,

IV. THE GRACIOUS PROMISE MADE TO SUCH AS SEEK HIM IN THAT WAY, AND AT THAT TIME.

"He will have mercy upon him." Hebrew, "He will have the bowels of a mother to a child." Although past sins may have been many, great, aggravated, long continued; although present corruption, temptation, and habits of sin be very strong; although hinderances and oppositions be many; and apparently insurmountable; he will "pardon" us freely and fully.—He will subdue our iniquities, and "renew" us in the spirit of our minds."—He will "strengthen us with might in our inner man," and, "strong in the grace that is in Christ Jesus," we shall more than overcome all that oppose. 2 Tim. ii. 1; Rom. viii. 37.

"He will *abundantly* pardon." Hebrew, "will multiply to pardon." When such as have been guilty of very great wickedness, come to have a serious sense of their sins, and of the holiness and justice of God, they are almost inconsolable, and are wont to think their guilt too aggravated to be forgiven; hence the Prophet makes use of strong terms, and to encourage them, and lead them to repentance, he assures them God will multiply pardons as their sins have been multiplied. Rom. v. 20.—He will also again forgive, if we fall off and return to him in repentance. "He will heal our backslidings."

---

## THE TENDER EXPOSTULATION OF HEAVEN.

### Ezek. xviii. 31.—Why will ye die? (H.)

How can we, without a melting heart, see and hear those compassionate words of the good God, saying to us, "Why will ye die, O house of Israel?" The house of Israel was the church of God, the company of those who had the book of God, the covenant and ordinances of God among them, and yet God asks them, "Why will ye die," and be lost for ever? Supposing him asking us the same question, you professed christians, you that now belong to the Israel of God, "Why will ye die?" Why will ye sin on, and refuse mercy and peace, and run yourselves wilfully unto eternal death and damnation?

Consider, and meditate the extent and importance of this question. How many more are contained in the bowels of it, or may be drawn suitable thereto? Many serious and weighty questions we may ask ourselves upon every word of the question in the text. As,

I. "WHY WILL YE DIE?"

1. Why will you continue spiritually dead—Dead in your guilt, ignorance, unbelief, hardness of heart; dead to God, to religion, the ways of God, to heaven? Is there no such thing as communion with God? A having the conversation in heaven? A better country? Why continue dead to all this?

2. Why will you refuse the Author of life? Why put him to complain? John v. 40.

3. Why do ye reject and refuse the way of life, the good way that will bring you to eternal life? John xiv. 6, and the path he hath made known?

4. Why will you imbitter your own death? What a terrible death will you die, if you die in your sins?

5. Why will you venture on eternal death? Rom. vi. 23.

II. "WHY WILL YOU DIE?"

1. You, who are such noble, rational creatures; you who are the first-born of the creation, Job xxxv. 11; you who have immortality written on your minds and consciences.

**2.** You, who are put in the Redeemer's hand.

**3.** You, who have a Bible, the book of God, put into your hand.

**4.** You, who have life so freely and frankly offered. Isa. lv. 1, 2.

**5.** You, who have a Saviour standing and knocking at your doors. Rev. iii. 20.

**6.** You, who have the Spirit striving with you. 1 Thess. v. 19.

**7.** You, who have the ministers of God's word.

**8.** You, who have the Lord urging the case with you. "Why will you die?"

**9.** You, who live within the compass of the christian church. Heb. xi. 40.

III. "WHY WILL YOU DIE?"

**1.** Are you resolved that the blessed God shall have no more glory in your salvation? Luke xv. 32.

**2.** Are you resolved that the Redeemer shall have no honor or satisfaction in you, or praise for you? Rev. i. 5, 6; Isa. liii. 11.

**3.** That the holy angels shall have no joy or comfort in you? Luke xv. 10.

**4.** Do you design that the devil and damned spirits shall have your company for ever?

**5.** Is it not enough in your eyes, that angels have sinned and died, but you must die also? 2 Peter ii. 4.

**6.** Is it not enough that your first parents died, but you must die too?

**7.** Is it not enough that the old world died, but you must die too? Gen. vi. 11—13. That Sodom and Gomorrah died, &c., but you must die also? Gen. xix. 24; 2 Peter ii. 5, 6.

**8.** Is it not enough that the old house of Israel generally died, but you must also die? The prophets complained. Isa. liii. 1.

**9.** Are the numbers to be saved so great, that you will not be one of that number?

**10.** Is heaven and life so dreadful a state, that you are resolved you will not come thither? Is death and hell so happy a state, that none but that will serve you?

**11.** Is the misery of the heathen world so small, that you are resolved your's shall be greater? Matt. xi. 20—24.

**12.** Are you such enemies to yourselves, that you are resolved to die, whatever is the consequence? Is it not enough to die once, but you will die twice? Rev. xxi. 8.

**13.** Have you a mind to try by experience what this death is? and to defeat the Redeemer's design in going to prepare places above for such as you? John xiv. 3.

And, lastly, Are you resolved to glorify no other attribute of God but his wrath and vengeance? Is this life hastening to an end? Is death approaching apace? Is the Judge at the door? Must you, in a few days, be either in heaven or hell? among the blessed or the damned? And yet, will ye not think of these things? "Why will ye die?"

## THE SALVATION OF SINNERS DESIRED BY GOD.

Ezekiel xxxiii. 11.—" As I live, saith the Lord God, I have no pleasure in the death of the wicked," &c. (Sk.)

It is evident from the uniform conduct of Ezekiel, that he well understood, and faithfully discharged his duty, as a watchman unto the house of Israel. To this office God had appointed him, verses 7—9; and, in the execution of it, he plainly set before his people both their sin and their danger. But the house of Israel, being hardened in transgression, hated reproof, and endeavored to evade the force of it, by casting the blame of their sin and misery upon God himself. This they did in effect, by the plea of necessity, verse 10. " If our transgressions and our sins be upon us, and we pine away in them, how then shall we live?" As if they had said, "Our case is hopeless, for it appears that God has decreed our destruction; and if we sin and suffer by the decree of God, how then can we be blamed? can we alter his purpose, and live when God has doomed us to die?" This impious reflection on God he strongly resents, and fully proves the injustice of it, in the language now before us: " As I live saith the Lord God, I have no pleasure in the death of the wicked; but that the wicked turn from his way and live: turn ye, turn ye from your evil ways; for why will ye die, oh house of Israel?" These words lead us to observe,

I. The state of mankind as sinners. Here we learn that it is,

1. A state of moral evil. They walk in evil ways. By the term "way" is meant a course of moral conduct, including the habitual actions, words, and thoughts, of mankind, Isa. liii. 6. The plural term "ways" is here employed, to intimate that the courses pursued by sinners are various in their kinds. They are ways of rebellion, or opposition to God's authority: they are open and avowed, such as St. Paul describes, 1 Cor. vi. 9, 10; Gal. v. 19—21; or they are secret and concealed, such as our Lord describes, Mark vii. 21—23. There are ways of impenitence, or contempt of God's mercy: in which God is forgotten, Jer. ii. 32; and not sought, Psa. x. 4, cvii. 10, 11. There are ways of self-deception, or vain delusive hope, Prov. xiv. 12; such is the way of self-righteousness, Jer. xvii. 5, 6; Isa. i. 11: and such also is the way of Antinomianism, Prov. xxx. 12; Matt. vii. 21; Heb. xii. 14. But all their ways are evil however diversified. They are evil—because they are iniquitous: contrary to the rule of rectitude, 1 John iii. 4.—Because they are painful: occasioning present misery, Prov. xv. 19; Jer. ii. 19.—Because they are destructive: leading to certain ruin, Ezek. xviii. 30; Rom. vi. 21. Hence our text assures us that the state of mankind as sinners, is

2. A state of imminent danger:—a state in which they are certainly exposed to death, even to eternal death, Rom. vi. 23. By eternal death is meant the punishment inflicted on sinners in a future state, Rev. xxi. 8. This punishment is called death—not because it implies annihilation ; for the wicked still live, when they leave this world. Their continued existence is evident from their state before judgment, Luke xvi. 23, 24; from their sentence at judgment, Matt. xxv. 41—46; and their torment after judgment, Rev. xiv. 10, 11.—But this punishment is called death, because in it there is some resemblance to natural death. To omit other circumstances, the subjects of natural death are separated from the society of the living, and become the prey either of worms or of fire. Are the subjects of natural death removed from the society of the living? so the subjects of eternal death are banished from the presence of God, and of those who live to him, 2 Thess. i. 7—9; Matt. xiii.

**40—42.** Are the subjects of natural death the common prey either of **worms or of fire?** This they are, according to the different customs of different countries; some being committed to the silent grave, and some being consumed on the funeral pile. Thus also the subjects of eternal death are represented as being preyed on both by the *worm* and the *fire*, Mark ix. 43, 44. Their worm is an *accusing conscience*, which condemns them as being the authors of their own misery, Jer. iv. 18. The worms of the grave indeed, though dreaded, are not *felt*, and soon *die;* but this worm *never dies*, and the torture it inflicts must be endless. The fire that consumes the bodies on the funeral pile is only a *material fire*, kindled by feeble *mortals*, and must soon become *extinct;* but the fire of hell, if not material, must be something much more dreadful: it is kindled by the wrath of *God*, Isa. xxx. 33: and will *never* be quenched, Matt. iii. 12. However, the state of sinners in this world, though alarming, is not yet hopeless. Let us therefore observe,

II. THEIR DUTY AND PRIVILEGE AS SINCERE PENITENTS.

1. *Their duty.* This is, to turn from their evil ways;—"Turn ye," &c Turn from your ways of *rebellion*, by entire *reformation*, Isa. lv. 7; Ezek. xviii. 27.—Turn from your ways of *impenitence*, by earnest *prayer*, Hos. xiv. 1, 2; Luke xviii. 13. Turn from your ways of *self-deception*, by coming to God, trusting in Christ's mediation. John xiv. 6; and by seeking a new creation, Gal. vi. 16; Psa. li. 10.—Turn *seasonably:* without delay, Isa. lv. 6; Job xxii. 21.—Turn *perpetually:* without defection, Jer. 1. 5.— Turn *believingly:* in confident expectation of salvation, Heb. x. 19—22. That as gospel penitents your confidence may be strengthened, observe,

2. *Their privilege.* This is, to be *saved from death*, and *enjoy life.*— To *be saved from death*, Ezek. xviii. 28. All genuine believers in our Lord Jesus Christ are saved from death by being delivered from the dominion of spiritual, and the sentence of eternal death, John xi. 25, 26. By means of this salvation from death, they are brought also—*To enjoy life.* The life enjoyed by them is comprehensive; including an interest in God's manifested favor, Psa. xxx. 5, lxiii. 3;—actual devotedness to God's service, Rom. vi. 13:—and the eternal possession of heaven, Rom. ii. 6, 7. Observe,

3. *The attainment of this privilege is as certain as it is desirable.* It is certain, from God's earnest *command;* "Turn ye, turn ye from your evil ways." This interests you in God's sincerity, Isa. xlv. 19.—It is certain, from God's solemn *oath;* "As I live, saith the Lord," &c. This interests you in God's *veracity*, Heb. vi. 18.—It is certain from God's gracious *expostulation;* "Why will ye die, O house of Israel?" This interests you in God's most affectionate regard. Almost every word in this kind expostulation emphatically expresses the great concern of God for the salvation of mankind. These words, therefore, "Why will ye die?" most forcibly suggest the most direct and distinct APPLICATION of our text.

1. *Why will ye* DIE? By continuing in sin, you choose death, the worst of all evils; and eternal death, which is the worst of all deaths. Carelessly to squander away your earthly goods and possessions is bad; to impair and destroy your health is worse; to waste and murder your time is worse still: for 'Time destroyed, is suicide: where more than blood is spilt.'—But to plunge your immortal souls into death eternal, is the very worst of crimes; for this is murder, self-murder, and even self-murder of the blackest description: it is an exploit of *wickedness* which can never be forgiven, and for which no atonement has ever been made.

2. *Why will ye die?* By what arguments can you justify your conduct at the bar of your own conscience? Is not God a better master than the de-

vil ? Is not holiness better employment than sin! Are not the treasures of grace and heaven better enjoyments than hell and damnation ? Is not the pursuit of life more rational and more conducive to happiness than the pursuit of death?—If it be, then in choosing death instead of life, your *folly* is as great as your wickedness. Every sinner therefore may justly exclaim with Saul;—" I have played the fool, and have erred exceedingly," 1 Sam. xxvi. 21.

3. *Why will* YE *die?*—Ye *men!* concerning whom there is still hope of salvation. You are not devils, for whom a Redeemer was never provided ; you are not lost souls in hell, who are out of the reach of divine mercy ; Christ still seeks you, that he may save you, Rev. iii. 20.—Ye Americans ' the peculiar favorites of heaven ; who enjoy the clearest gospel light, the greatest religious liberty, and the highest advantages for piety, in the richest abundance, Psa. cxlvii. 20.—Ye professing *Christians!* who are called by the name of Christ, and are encouraged in his word to seek him, 2 Chron. vii. 14 ; who are baptized in the name of Christ, and bound by the most solemn vows to serve him alone, Eccl. v. 4.—Ye *Protestants!* who are delivered from, and protest against the pernicious errors which have crept into the visible church of Christ; if you continue in sin, your *inconsistency* will be as great as your wickedness and your folly : and when judged at the bar of God, you must be found without excuse, Matt. xxii. 12, 13.

4. *Why* WILL *ye die?* Remember, if thou die eternally, it must be because you *will* die ; your death must be the result of your own deliberate choice ; for *God wills your salvation.* This is evident, not only from his word and oath here recorded, but also from his *long-suffering*, 2 Pet. iii. 9 ; —from the *tears* of Christ over perishing sinners, Matt. xxiii. 37 ; Luke xix. 41, 42 ; —and from his being *given* to die in our stead, Rom. viii. 32. And *Divine grace renders you capable of seeking salvation*, with the utmost certainty of success, Phil. ii. 12, 13. Then *resolve* with the prodigal ;—" I will arise," &c., Luke xv. 18, 19. Imitate David in resolute *promptitude,* Psa. cxix. 59, 60. And confidently *hope* with Micah, Mic. vii. 18, 19.

---

## REST FOR THE WEARY AND HEAVY LADEN.

Matthew xi. 28.—Come unto me all ye that labor and are heavy laden, and I will give you rest. (Sk.)

THE numerous miracles which our blessed Lord performed, proved that his mission was divine ; and the various sermons and parables which he delivered, constrained those who heard him to exclaim, " Never man spake like this man !" Grace was poured into his lips ; and in him were accomplished the words of the prophet,—" The Lord God hath given me the tongue of the learned, that I should know how to speak a word in season to him that is weary." He warned the unruly, instructed the ignorant, comforted the distressed, and poured the balm of consolation into the wounded spirit. Many were the gracious words which proceeded out of his mouth ; and a few of his discourses have been recorded for the instruction, encouragement, and edification of those upon whom the ends of the world are come. Our text, found in one of these discourses, has ever been salutary to those who have felt distressed on account of their sin ; and if there were no

58

**other** passage of the same complexion in the Bible, this would be sufficient to inspire hope, and to banish despair. The subject connected with these words, comprehends,

I. THE PERSONS ADDRESSED are described as "laboring, and heavy laden."

1. *They labor.* This expression signifies, the act of doing something which requires strong exertion. Many of the Jews labored hard to recommend themselves to God, by observing various rites and ceremonies, Rom. x. 3. They were required by divine authority to offer a great number of costly sacrifices;—to travel to Jerusalem three times a year to worship God, and to observe various ritual precepts. In the days of our Lord, their teachers bound heavy burdens, and grievous to be borne, and laid them on their shoulders; and thus the Jewish yoke became intolerably oppressive;—" A yoke," said St. Peter, " which neither our fathers nor we were able to bear."

The Jews are not the only persons who have labored to merit heaven, by the performance of what are called religious duties: many who name the name of Christ, and profess to believe the articles of the christian faith, are not less sanguine in their expectations of being saved by their own endeavors;—they toil and labor to cancel the debt which they have contracted, to atone for the sins which they have committed; and thus to obtain that heaven, which they are conscious they have forfeited. But Jesus Christ is the only way to the Father,—the only Mediator between God and man,—the only Physician of souls,—the only Saviour of sinners, John xiv. 6; Acts iv. 12; 1 Cor. iii. 11.

2. *They are heavy laden.* They feel the burden of sin, Psa. xxxviii. 4; Isa. xxxviii. 14,—the reproaches of a guilty conscience, Prov. xviii. 14; Acts ii. 37,—the wrath of God abiding on them, Psa. xxxii. 4. Such persons are prepared to receive the blessing of the gospel, Matt. v. 4,—they are the individuals to whom the promises of pardon and salvation are addressed, Isa. lv. 1,—the very characters which Christ came to save, 1 Tim. i. 15; Luke xix. 10. Hence,

II. THE INVITATION GIVEN TO THEM;—" Come unto me ;" which signifies, that,

1. *We must address Christ in prayer.* Prayer is the desire of the soul expressed to God; it is God's appointed means, in the use of which he hath engaged to give us whatever we need, Matt. vii. 7. Prayer may be as effectually expressed by the sighs and groans of a broken and contrite spirit, as by the most suitable words. This duty is not only easy to perform, but it is indispensably necessary; without prayer we cannot be saved, Ezek. xxxvi. 37; Rom. x. 13. Let us not, however, suppose, that there is any thing meritorious in prayer; our prayers cannot purchase the favor of God, or the remission of sin.

2. *We must come in the exercise of faith.* Unbelief pours contempt on the Saviour, and excludes us from any share in the blessings of salvation; but faith honors God, and secures an interest in all that Jesus has done and suffered for sinners; see 1 Tim. v. 10; Rom. iv. 5; Acts x. 43, and xiii 38, 39; Heb. xi. 16. *We must believe that Christ is a suitable Saviour* Are we ignorant of God, of our duty, and of our privileges? Christ is our wisdom. Are we under guilt and condemnation? Christ is our righteousness. Are we in a state of moral defilement; polluted with sin, and altogether filthy and abominable? Christ is our sanctification, 1 John i. 7; 1 Cor. i. 30, 31. Our stubborn wills he can subdue—our defiled consciences he can purge—our wicked hearts he can cleanse. In coming to Christ, we

should keep this in mind; " He is able to save" me ; though my sins are ever so numerous, or aggravated, he can pardon them; though my nature is ever so much depraved, he can renew me : see Heb. vii. 25. *We must believe that he is a willing Saviour.* Why should we question his willingness ? Did he not voluntarily take our nature—endure the contradiction of sinners—and submit to be condemned, and scourged, and crucified ? Every groan he heaved, every tear he shed, every drop of blood he poured out, tells us that his heart is made of tenderness, and that he is full of mercy and of grace. *The text embraces all kinds and degrees of sinners :*—" Come unto me *all* ye that labor and are heavy laden." Whatever you have been, or whatever you have done, if you only come to the Saviour with an humble, lowly, penitent, and believing heart, he will receive you graciously. *And to whom would you go ?* The law condemns you, your own consciences condemn you; you are wretched, Rev. iii. 17. Your repentance, your tears, your prayers, cannot save you ; you must come to Christ, or perish. Let me entreat you to make an *early* application to Christ, Heb. iii. 15 ; 2 Cor. vi. 2, and you shall realize,

III. THE BLESSING PROMISED TO THOSE WHO ACCEPT THE INVITATION. A guilty conscience is compared to a troubled sea, which cannot rest : there is no peace to the wicked ; no peace with God—no peace in the mind. As long as we continue under the guilt of sin, and the curse of the law, and the wrath of God, how can we expect to be at rest ?· That soul must be dreadfully oppressed, and grievously tormented, which has such a load to sustain ; but if we accept the Saviour's invitation, he will deliver us from all our perplexing doubts, and from all our tormenting fears.

1. *The cause of misery and distress will be removed.* All the anguish of mind which we ever felt, was the effect of sin ; nor is it possible for us to be happy while under the guilt and power of moral evil. Our iniquities must be forgiven—our persons must be justified—before we can have peace with God. When the laboring and heavy-laden sinner comes to Christ, believes in him, and receives him in all his saving offices, he obtains the remission of sins, receives the Spirit of adoption, and is accepted in the Beloved Rom. v. 1, 11 ; Heb. iv. 3. His conscience no longer accuses him, 2 Cor i. 12 ; the law no longer condemns him, Gal. iii. 13 ; Rom. viii. 1,—the wrath of God no longer oppresses him, Isa. xxxviii. 17, and xii. 1,—he is no longer the slave of sin, Rom. vi. 14, 22, or the captive of Satan, 2 Tim. ii. 26 ; Col. i. 13,—he is saved from the fear of death and the dread of eternity. *Another cause of misery is removed*, by the renewal of the mind—· the regeneration of fallen nature ; in consequence of which, the evil tempers and dispositions no longer predominate, and distress the soul, see Gal. v. 17—24.

2. *The comforts of religion are communicated.* These are genuine, various, and extensive, Prov. iii. 13—18. Oh what a change is produced in the views and feelings of a person who is justified freely by divine grace ! He thinks on the horrible dungeon out of which he has been brought ; he calls to mind the wormwood and the gall—the guilt and anguish under which he labored ; and contrasting these with the privileges of his present state, and the glory of his future prospects, he says, or sings, with the .Psalmist, Psa. cxvi. 7—12. " Return unto thy rest," &c.

3. But we shall never realize the full import of the Saviour's gracious promise, until we enter upon that rest which remaineth for the people of God Isa. lvii. 2 ; Rev. xiv. 13. and xxi. 3, 4.

Let the subject teach

*i. The self-righteous Pharisee*, who is laboring to meet heaven by his imaginary good works, that such an attempt is foolish, and dangerous, and destructive, Rom. iii. 19, 20 ; Matt. v. 20, and xxi. 31 ; Isa. l. 11.

*z. The mourning penitent*,—that Christ kindly invites, and is waiting to receive him, 2 Pet. i. 4 ; Isa. lv. 7—9 ; Micah vii. 18, 19.

3. *The soul happily pardoned*,—to be thankful, Psa. cxvi. 12, 13,—to be humble, Ezek. xvi. 63,—to be watchful, 1 Cor. x. 12,—and steadfast, Rev. ii. 10.

---

## AN INVITATION TO PARTICIPATE IN THE GOODNESS OF THE LORD.

Ps. xxxiv. 8.   O taste and see that the Lord is good.   (Sk.)

IF there be any exercise upon earth that bears a resemblance to the employment of heaven, or any sensation that men feel in common with angels, it is that of gratitude to God ; and among all the inspired writers, no man engaged more heartily in this delightful occupation than David, who was the author of this psalm.   It is in a peculiar sense a psalm of praise.   David begins it by declaring, "I will bless the Lord at all times," &c.   There are certain exercises in the Christian life suited to peculiar seasons, but praise is never unsuitable ; gratitude is never ill-timed ; "My soul shall make her boast in the Lord."   Some boast in their wealth, others in their personal accomplishments : David gloried in the Lord ; and not satisfied with doing this alone, he invited others to engage in the same exercise—"O magnify the Lord," &c., ver. 3.   He then assigns the reason why he magnified the Lord, ver. 4—6 ; and in the text, under the influence of the same spirit, he adds, "O taste and see that the Lord is good."   We have in this passage,

I. SOMETHING ASSUMED :—That "the Lord is good."   There are few expressions that occur more frequently in the Psalms than this, and there is no sentiment that should be more deeply or constantly impressed upon our minds.

1. *God is infinitely good.*   His goodness knows no bounds, limits, nor dimensions ; so that we may well exclaim, "How great is thy goodness!"

2. *God is independently good.*   His goodness is all his own ; there are good men and good angels, but these are dependently good : their goodness is not essential to their natures.

3. *God is absolutely good.*   His goodness can never be extended, nor diminished ; our goodness is capable of increase ; it may be augmented, perhaps to all eternity ; but God's goodness is always the same.

4. *God is unchangeably good.*   There is no variableness in his goodness : our goodness is mutable ; we are liable to change every day, but God changeth not.

5. *God is universally good.*   He is good to all, and good every where : his goodness is the same in every part of the globe, and in heaven and earth the same.

6. *God is eternally good.*   His goodness endureth for ever ; he cannot cease to be good.

II. SOMETHING IMPLIED :—That the goodness of the Lord may be *seen* and *tasted.*   There are various mediums through which the goodness of the Lord may be seen.

1. *The creation is a kind of glass or mirror, which reflects the goodness of the Lord.* There was a period in eternity, in which God alone existed; he was not necessitated to form any creatures; but he was pleased to do it, not so much to exhibit his eternal power, as to communicate his infinite goodness; hence when God finished his works of creation, he "saw every thing that he had made, and behold it was very good."

2. *The goodness of the Lord may be seen in the provision made for all creatures.* "These all wait upon thee," &c., Psa. civ. 27. "The eyes of all wait upon thee," &c., Psa. cxlv. 15. "Consider the ravens, for they neither sow nor reap," &c., Luke xii. 24.

3. *The goodness of the Lord may be seen in the redemption of the world by Jesus Christ.* Man, by his personal transgression, forfeited all title to the divine favor, and exposed himself to eternal punishment; but oh! the riches of God's goodness induced him to deliver up his own Son to death for our ransom. What but goodness, unmerited and unparalleled goodness, would provide for us such a Saviour? so *suitable* to our necessities, so *powerful* to help us, and so *willing* to do us good.

4. *The goodness of the Lord may be seen in the means of grace with which we are favored.* Here is the gospel, containing glad tidings and good news, spread before us. Here are the ambassadors of peace crying, "Ho! every one that thirsteth," &c. Here is the Spirit of God ready to work in us all goodness, and righteousness, and truth. Here are friends saying, "Come thou with us, and we will do thee good" And here are many personal, social, and religious advantages, all of which serve to display the divine goodness.

5. *The goodness of the Lord may be seen in the rewards of heaven;* rewards beyond the power of human conception, gratuitously bestowed, and lasting as eternity. But the goodness of the Lord may not only be seen but tasted. The soul has its appetites as well as the body. *Tasting,* literally, is proving the quality of any thing by the mouth, or palate. David said, "How sweet are thy words unto my taste!" St. Paul mentions some who had "tasted of the heavenly gift." To taste that the Lord is good, is to enjoy his goodness: we do this, 1. *When we receive a knowledge of salvation by the remission of our sins.* A soul laboring under a sense of guilt tastes the bitter bread of misery, and drinks the cup of baleful grief: but when God gives the burdened conscience ease, and communicates a knowledge of his favor, then the man tastes that the Lord is good. 2. *When the love of God is shed abroad in the heart.* When we feel that we love him because he first loved us. 3. *When the promises are applied to our hearts by the power of the Holy Ghost.* In seasons of inward conflict or outward opposition.

III. SOMETHING ENJOINED. "O taste and see," &c. This invitation, request, or admonition is.

1. *Divine in its origin.* David wrote it, who was a warrior, a politician, a monarch, and a divine; but he wrote it under the influence of the Holy Ghost, and therefore it is God that speaks to us in the affectionate language of the text.

2. *Reasonable in its nature.* We are endowed with powers and faculties capable of this exercise; we can taste and see that the Lord is good; and what God has rendered us capable of doing, it is reasonable that we should do. The inferior orders of beings see nature smiling around them, but the Lord of nature they cannot see: they taste their rich pastures, but the goodness of God they cannot taste.

**3.** *Pleasurable in its exercise.* Sometimes we contemplate the divine character with trembling awe; God comes out of his place to punish the inhabitants of the earth for their iniquity. He rides in the whirlwind, and directs the storm; and we hear the voice of God, and are afraid: but to taste and see that the Lord is good, produces feelings of another description; feelings of pleasure, which can never be exceeded on earth, and enjoyments which can only be paralleled in heaven.

**4.** *Profitable in its result.* This is the only method by which we can enjoy God. The more we taste and see of the goodness of God, the more contentment we shall possess in our stations, and the more resignation to the allotments of God's providence. By tasting and seeing the goodness of the Lord upon earth, we shall be prepared for these exercises in heaven, and we shall anticipate with exquisite delight the period, when we shall see as we are seen, and know as we are known.

INFER,

1. That there is something more in religion than the mere profession, or outward form: there is the exercise of mental powers: a tasting and seeing the Lord is good. This is personal, and known only to ourselves.

2. How wretched those are who forego these pleasures, and refuse to comply with the requisition in the text,—who know nothing but animal gratification and sensual pleasure.

3. Those who enjoy personal piety, are anxious for others to realize the same enjoyment, and are ready to say to their families, friends, and neighbors, " O taste and see that the Lord is good."

4. If the Lord is good, let us learn the design of that goodness. Rom. ii. 4.

---

### PURITY NECESSARY TO SALVATION.

**Jer. v. 14.**—Oh Jerusalem, wash thine heart from wickedness, that thou mayest be saved. How long shall thy vain thoughts lodge within thee? (Sk.)

WHEN Jeremiah was called to the prophetic office, the moral state of the Jews was awfully degenerate and deplorable. As a nation, they had forsaken "the fountain of living water," and abandoned themselves to idolatry and every species of wickedness. Their defection and disobedience greatly displeased the God of their fathers, and caused him to chastise them for their impiety, and permit them to be carried captives into Babylon, under the galling yoke of their enemies. But previous to that calamitous event, the Lord sent his servants the prophets, to give them timely warning, and exhort them to immediate repentance. Such was manifestly the import and design of Jeremiah's commission, which he faithfully executed, in the midst of opposition and extreme discouragement. In the text and context he earnestly entreats the inhabitants of Jerusalem and Judea to return unto the Lord their God as the only way to be preserved from the *tyranny* of their enemies, and cleansed from the *impurity* of their iniquities ;—" O Jerusalem, wash thine heart," &c. But these words will strictly apply to mankind universally, as fallen and polluted sinners; and explicitly suggest and declare the natural depravity of the human heart— the spiritual purity which the Lord requires— and the absolute necessity of personal holiness. Let us observe.

I. THE NATURAL DEPRAVITY OF THE HUMAN HEART ;—" Wash thine *heart* from wickedness." By the *heart*, we may here understand all the faculties of the soul, and passions of the mind ; and by the "*wickedness* of the heart," the total corruption and moral defilement of human nature. But this doctrine is frequently misrepresented, and often denied, and must therefore be explained and proved ; as a position founded in *truth*, and confirmed by *evidence*.

1. *This doctrine requires definition.* When we maintain that man by nature is *wholly* depraved, and destitute of all spiritual goodness, we do not mean to deny that he may not be endued with some *comparative* and *moral* excellencies of natural disposition and mental attainments. It is evident, from a very partial acquaintance with mankind, that many in their natural state possess highly intelligent minds, liberal sentiments, amiable tempers, and benevolent hearts ; but no man by nature is *spiritually good*, or pleasing to God. All are deeply fallen, polluted, and prone to every evil thought, word, and work, Eph. ii. 3. This depravity of the heart includes *the entire absence of the divine image.* God made man originally in his own likeness, in knowledge, righteousness, and true holiness ; but through sin we have become ignorant, corrupt, and ungodly, both in heart and life, Rom. iii. 12–18 ; Eph. iv. 18.—*A natural aversion to God and godliness.* Hence there is in the unregenerate heart a deep rooted dislike and hatred to the purity of religion, and the sacred exercises of spiritual devotion, which fully proves that " the carnal mind is enmity against God ; for it is not subject to the law of God, neither indeed can be," Col. i. 21.—*A universal propensity or disposition to evil.* The mind, the will, the conscience, and the affections, are altogether alienated from God, and *naturally* inclined to resist his truth, and indulge in all the polluted habits of vice, and unhallowed pleasures of sin. Such is the *original* degeneracy and internal wickedness of every human being by nature, Job xv. 16 ; John iii. 6 ; Rom. i. 29—32. But,

2. *This doctrine demands evidence.* It is sometimes much easier to state a position, than to prove it ; but in the case before us, the latter is no more difficult than the former. It is so obvious a truth, that man is a fallen and sinful creature, that it cannot be denied without a manifest contempt of reason, violation of conscience, and rejection of scripture.—*It is divinely revealed.* It is explicitly taught by Moses and the prophets, and by Jesus Christ and his apostles. They are perfectly unanimous in their sentiments and representations of this humiliating subject. They assure us that " every imagination of the thoughts of the heart is only evil continually ;—the heart is deceitful above all things, and desperately wicked ;—from within, out of the heart of man, proceedeth all evil ;—that which is born of the flesh is flesh ;—the body of sin shall be destroyed, even the old man, which is corrupt according to the deceitful lusts," &c., Mark vii. 20—23. *It is practically exemplified.* In every age and nation, " the wickedness of man has been great in the earth." The heathen moralists acknowledged the fact, but could not account for its origin and prevalence. Revelation, however, explains the subject ; and the various afflictions and miseries to which human nature is incident, fully demonstrate that we are " children of wrath, shapen in iniquity, and conceived in sin."—*It is deeply lamented.* The pious sincerely mourn over " the flesh which lusteth against the spirit." and earnestly desire and pray for its utter destruction ; that they may be " redeemed from all iniquity, and purified unto the Lord a peculiar people," Psa. li. 2, 3, 7. As closely connected with the doctrine of moral depravity, we may consider,

**II. THE SPIRITUAL PURITY WHICH THE LORD REQUIRES;**—" O Jerusalem! wash thine heart from wickedness,—how long shall thy vain thoughts lodge within thee?" This affectionate and impressive address is highly instructive, and evidently implies,

1. *The possibility of obtaining purity of heart.* If it were impossible, the exhortation would be superfluous and vain; but it certainly is attainable, and therefore ought to be earnestly desired, and diligently sought. This will appear *from the design of redemption;* which was to " open a fountain for sin and uncleanness, and to purge our consciences from dead works, to serve the living God," Heb. ix. 13, 14; 1 Pet. i. 18, 19.—*From the ability of the Saviour;* who, by the characters he sustains, and the offices which he executes, is infinitely qualified to " save unto the uttermost, and redeem his people from all their iniquities," John i. 16; 1 Cor. i. 30.—*From the promises of scripture,* in which the Lord engages freely and fully to save them that believe, " by the washing of regeneration, and the renewing of the Holy Ghost," Ezek. xxxvi. 26, 27; 1 Pet. i. 4.—And *from the experience of believers;* whose hearts are purified by faith, " as vessels unto honor," sanctified, and meet for the master's use, and " prepared unto every good work," Rom. vi. 22; 1 John i. 7.

2. *The important duty of seeking purity of heart.* " O Jerusalem! wash thine heart," &c. This exhortation or command does not imply that we can cleanse ourselves from the stains of iniquity, but simply inculcates an immediate and diligent use of the means of grace, as necessary to obtain salvation, Ezek. xviii. 31. That " our hearts may be washed from wickedness," *we must repent of our sins:* for without repentance there is no forgiveness, nor peace with God, Isa. lv. 7; Acts iii. 19.—*We must believe in Jesus Christ;* for it is only by faith that we can realize an interest in his redeeming benefits, and participate the cleansing efficacy of the blood of sprinkling, Acts xxvi. 18; Heb. xii. 24.—*We must give ourselves unto prayer;* for the Lord will be inquired of for every blessing; and hence we should humbly and fervently pray, that we may be " washed and sanctified in the name of the Lord Jesus, and by the Spirit of our God," Psa. li. 10; 1 Thess. v. 23.—*We must also seek the Lord without delay;* for " how long," saith the Almighty, " shall thy vain," wicked, unbelieving, and impenitent " thoughts lodge within thee?"—O Jerusalem! O sinners! cleanse your hands and purify your hearts in the blood of the Lamb, for now is the day of salvation, Isa. lv. 6; 2 Cor. vi. 2. This duty is strongly enforced by,

**III. THE ABSOLUTE NECESSITY OF PERSONAL HOLINESS;**—" That thou mayest *be saved.*' Purity and happiness are inseparable. We are saved by being *purified;* and hence said Christ to Peter, " If I wash thee not, thou hast no part with me."

1. *Personal holiness is a necessary property of religion.* It is very possible to assume the profession and form of godliness, whilst we are entire strangers to its vital energy and power. And it is to be feared that many rest in the *letter,* without the *spirit* of christianity; and have a name to live, while they are *spiritually* dead. But pure and undefiled religion does not consist in the barren speculations of the deluded enthusiast, nor in the external ceremonies of the formal professor, Gal. vi. 15; it principally resides in the *heart,* enlightening, enriching, and hallowing every power of the soul unto the Lord; and directing every desire, disposition, and pursuit, to the glory of his name, 1 Cor. vi. 19, 20; 1 Pet. i. 15, 16. Without this *inter-*

*al purity* and spirituality of mind, the profession of religion is **an empty**
parade, and can profit us nothing, Rom. xiv. 17.

2. *Personal holiness is a necessary meetness for heaven.* Reason teaches
**us** that there must be a similarity and agreement between the *faculty* of enjoyment and the *object* enjoyed. Now God is essentially just and holy, and
therefore can never be the *portion* of impenitent and unholy souls. The
scriptures also assure us, that " without holiness no man can see the Lord ;"
"for nothing that defileth, or maketh a lie, can in any wise enter into the
kingdom of God," Matt. v. 8 ; 1 Cor. vi. 9, 10. Deliverance from the guilt,
the power, and the pollution of sin, is a doctrine uniformly taught by divine
revelation,—is personally confirmed in the experience of the saints,—and is
absolutely necessary to obtain complete and eternal *salvation* in the world to
come.

These reflections should excite deep humility and self-abasement as fallen
sinners, and promote an earnest application to Jesus the Mediator of the new
covenant, whose " blood cleanseth from all unrighteousness."

---

## THE GOSPEL CALL.

Matthew xxi. 28—33.—But what think ye? A certain man had two sons; and he came to
the first, and said, Son, go work to-day in my vineyard," &c. (Sk.)

IN these verses our Saviour shows by the parable of two sons, that penitent publicans and harlots were in a far more eligible state or condition for receiving the gospel, than self-righteous persons. For understanding this parable, it is necessary to consider generally and briefly, that our Saviour, by
the first of these sons, represents publicans, harlots, tax-gatherers, and sinners
of all descriptions, who convinced of their awful state and danger, by the
preaching of the word, proved far better than at first they promised, turning
away from all their iniquities, and readily and heartily embracing the gospel ;
and by the second son, he represents the learned scribes and the self-righteous pharisees, who promised fair, and performed nothing. This parable was
designed for the reproof and correction of the scribes and pharisees ; and therefore our Saviour appeals to themselves, that out of their own mouth he might
judge and condemn them.

I. AN INJUNCTION ;—" Son, go work to-day in my vineyard." This
*certain man*, who had two sons, is intended to represent God. He came to
the first, and said, "Son, go work to-day in my vineyard." Here we have
the Father's command, *Go work*—thou must not be idle. Go work in *my
vineyard*, thou must be employed where I appoint thee. Go work *to-day*,
thou must do it immediately. This command of God concerns all of us: we
are enjoined to go and work to-day in his vineyard,—to make religion our
present business. Here we may observe,

1 *That true religion is a work ;* and though hard and difficult, yet pleasant
and profitable. " Strait is the gate, and narrow is the way which leadeth unto life," Matt. vii. 14. Yet the " ways of wisdom are ways of pleasantness,
and all her paths are peace," Prov. iii. 17. God's " commandments are not
grevious," 1 John v. 3 ; and "in keeping of them their is great reward," Ps.
xix. 11.

**2.** *That the gospel or ministerial call to this work requires and demands present obedience.* "Go work *to-day.*" To-morrow may be too late. "To-day if ye will hear his voice harden not your hearts," Heb. iii. 15. We are called to "work while it is day;" for "the night cometh when no man can work," John ix. 4. The brevity of human life, and the important work of our salvation to be accomplished while it lasts, are considerations which should occupy the attention, and deeply impress the heart of every one.

**3.** *That this call is full both of authority and affection;* because it is the command of a *Father,* and it is directed to us as *children.* "Go, son, work to-day in my vineyard." He calls him *son,* to remind him of his own authority, to oblige and dispose of him as he pleases, to excite him to reverence, confidence, affection, and obedience; and to assure him, on his compliance, subjection, and faithfulness, and of all paternal regards, and an ample remuneration. What encouragement is here given to sinners, to devote themselves to God and his service!

II. THE ANSWER OF THE SON;—"He said, I will not: but afterwards he repented and went."

**2.** *This answer of the son is a very unfeeling and impertinent one.* He might have been more respectful; and if he had not a mind to go, might have excused himself in more modest language, and not given a direct refusal, saying, *I will not.* This is the voice of corrupt nature, the language of folly and madness; and shows us the entertainment which the gospel injunctions meet with from the majority of those persons who are thus addressed. We see here a picture of the state of fallen man, the prevalence of the carnal mind, and how unwelcome the salvation of Christ is to practical sinners. They even treat him with most censurable neglect, and insolent contempt.

**2.** *But afterwards he repented, and went.* Some persons will not go from their word, lest they should be deemed inconsistent. Afterwards the son repented;—better late wise, than never wise. He changed his mind, from a conviction that he had done wrong: the immediate effect is obedience, he *went* into his father's vineyard. The gospel call meets with peremptory refusals from multitudes of those who hear it; they refuse "him that speaketh from heaven," Heb. xii. 25; which conduct exposes them to the greatest peril, —"How shall we escape if we neglect so great salvation?" Heb. ii. 3. Obedience is the sure way of escaping danger, and the only evidence of a change of heart. Well it is when profligate sinners amend their ways, and turn to God. *He repented;* and as a proof of it, *went* into the vineyard.

**3.** *Though this change of mind in him involves in it a contradiction, yet his conduct in this instance can be justified on the soundest principles both of reason and revelation.* On what grounds can a life of sin and disobedience be vindicated? Not on any correct view of man's responsibility while in this world; nor on the doctrine of a suitable retribution beyond the grave. Sin brings disgrace on the character of man, and renders him the subject of guilt and misery.

III. THE FATHER CAME TO THE SECOND SON, AND SAID, "Go, work to-day in my vineyard."

**1.** *This son had the same kind of call given him that the other had.* The same call, as to the sense of it, is given to all who are favored with the gospel; but it is very different in its effects, for to some it is "the savor of death unto death," while to others it is "the savor of life unto life," 2 Cor. ii. 15, 16. He answered, "*I go, sir; and went not.*" This answer is very different from that of his brother. He called his father "sir," expressive of respect and complaisance, and promised ready obedience. He did not say, I will go, but "I go," promptly, immediately, now. But he *went not;* he spake well, but did nothing : saying and doing are two things. His answer should be ours; we should say from the heart, *We go :* but then we should take care that we act according to our profession of obedience.

2. *The command of our heavenly Father should be received with great reverence ;* and men should express their gratitude for such a gracious call, by a ready compliance. But alas ! many who make a pompous profession of obedience are the most reluctant to fulfil their engagements. How many are there in the christian world, who profess that they know God according to the holy scriptures, but daily deny him in their spirit and temper, as well as t.eir words and works. What a deception ! Their foundation is sand, which will give way, and the whole imaginary structure fall down. And what will they do, when God calls them to judgment?

Hence we learn, that the religion of many persons consists only in good purposes and resolutions ; but this will not avail, for they only are blessed who " do his commandments," as an evidence of possessing saving grace. Let us therefore secure the inward principle of saving grace, that we may be assisted to glorify God in all our works.

<hr />

## ISRAEL EXHORTED TO RETURN TO THE LORD.

Hosea xiv. 1, 2.—O Israel, return unto the Lord thy God ; for thou hast fallen by thine iniquity. Take with you words, and turn unto the Lord : say unto him, Take away all iniquity, and receive us graciously : so will we render the calves of our lips. (Sk.)

THE conduct of God towards Israel, and Israel's conduct towards God, form the most interesting topics with which the Old Testament abounds. David declared that God had not dealt so with any nation; and as a confirmation of this, we need only review the series of wonders and miracles which adorn their whole history. And yet their conduct towards God excites almost equal astonishment, in the serious and contemplative mind. Their repeated murmurings and abominable idolatries often provoked the Divine Being to pour out his indignation upon them, but in wrath he remembered mercy. He raised up prophets, and sent them forth as the ambassadors of peace, to warn the people of their danger, and to call them to repentance. Hosea was a man of this description, who lived in the days of Uzziah, Jotham, Ahaz, and Hezekiah, kings of Judah. An epitome of his general message we have in the text. "O Israel, return," &c. We notice here,

I. AN AWFUL FACT STATED ; "Thou hast fallen by thine iniquity." The term *fall* is used literally, when we speak of a body descending from a higher to a lower situation : thus we say, the fall of a leaf, or the fall of a stone. But when the fall of angels or of man is mentioned, we understand the term figuratively : so we apply it in the text, "Thou hast fallen by thine iniquity.' To explain this, we observe, God is a being of infinite dignity, and is called the Most High ; not because he occupies the most exalted sphere in a local sense, but because he is above all in his natural and moral perfections. Holy angels and glorified spirits, being most like God in the purity of their natures, are considered as surrounding his throne, and standing in his presence ; while the devil and his angels, who are farthest removed from all moral rectitude,

**are most** degraded, cast down to hell, into a bottomless pit of fire and brimstone. A state of sin is a low estate; and when a man turns from good to bad, he is considered as fallen. Thus Israel had,

1. *Fallen from their allegiance to God.* There was a period in their history, when the Lord was their King, and they were under his immediate government; "but they rejected him that he should not reign over them," 1 Sam. viii. 7. "They have set up kings, but not by me," &c., Hos. viii. 4.

2. *Fallen from his worship.* "They had their molten images of silver, and idols," &c., Hos. xiii. 2. "They sacrificed upon the tops of mountains," &c., iv. 12, 13. And they were "joined to idols," iv. 17.

3. *Fallen from the enjoyment of his favor.* The Lord had a controversy with them, and was fixed to punish them, &c., Hos. xii. 2. "They have sown the wind, and they shall reap the whirlwind," viii. 7. "I will meet them as a bear bereaved of her whelps," xiii. 8. "Fallen by *thine* iniquity," The iniquity by which they fell was *personal.* "O Israel thou hast destroyed *thyself,*" xiii. 9. "Israel is an empty vine," &c., x. 1. It was *mental.* "Their heart was divided," x. 2. Whoredom and wine had taken away their heart, iv. 11. It was *practical.* They rejected knowledge, forgot the law of God, practised swearing, lying, killing, stealing, and committing adultery; they had troops of robbers among them; and there was no truth nor mercy, nor knowledge of God in the land, iv. 1, 2, 6.

II. AN AFFECTIONATE EXHORTATION URGED. "O Israel, return unto the Lord thy God." Here observe,

1. *The persons addressed;*—"*Israel.*" A people once highly favored, but now degraded. Had the prophet used language expressive of their moral character, he might have designated them by the most odious epithets; but he calls them "Israel," to remind them of what they once were, the import of their name, and the high honor which God had put upon them. What affectionate men were God's prophets! How faithful, and yet how kind!

2. *The nature of the address;*—"Return." This supposes previous wandering. The people of Israel had wandered like a treacherous wife, who had forsaken her husband, Hos. ii. 5; they had gone after other lovers, but disappointment had attended them, ver. 6. Now the prophet invites them to "return." Have we acted the part of Israel? Oh let us return—now—with all our hearts—in the spirit of faith and prayer.

3. *The object to whom they were to return;*—"Unto the Lord thy God.' The Lord, who has the sole right to rule and govern thee; "thy God," who called himself thy God, Psa. l. 7;—who acted towards thee as a God, in defending thee in danger,—comforting thee in distress,—directing thee in difficulty,—and providing for thee in necessity. Gratitude, affection, justice, honor, safety, and comfort, should induce those who have wandered from God to return to him.

III. INSTRUCTIVE DIRECTION ADMINISTERED;—"Take with you words," &c. Prayer may be offered unto God without words, 1 Sam. i. 13. But Israel was here directed to take *words,*—not bullocks nor sacrifices; these we may not all have in possession, but *words* we have at will. *Words of sincerity* should be taken, when we approach to God, not speaking what we never mean; hypocrisy is hateful in his sight. *Appropriate words,* such as best accord with our feelings and desires. *Words of humble confession.* David, Daniel, and the prodigal, will furnish us with words of confession. *Words of petition.* These the prophet records; say unto him, "Take away all iniquity." Iniquity was the cause of their fall, and in returning to God they were to pray for its removal.

1. *Take it away from our affections, that we may no longer love it.* Sinners love sin; there is a bent and tendency towards it in the carnal mind. God alone can take away that desire after sin from our hearts.

2. *From our consciences, that we may no longer labor under the burden of it.* Sin induces guilt, and renders us liable to punishment; God threatens sinners with hell. Awakened sinners groan under the burden of sin, and say, "Take away all iniquity."

3. *From our lives, that it may not have dominion over us.* God has promised to redeem Israel from all his iniquities, Psa. cxxx. 8. "How shall we that are dead to sin live any longer therein?" Rom. vi. 2.

4. *From our hearts, that we may be dead to it.* This is the subject of the prayer;—"Take away *all* iniquity." God can do this, for he is almighty; and because he directs us to pray for it, we may infer his willingness to answer our prayer.

"Receive us graciously." This is another part of the prayer which Israel was directed to offer unto God.

1, *Receive our prayers graciously.* One of the heaviest judgments which God can inflict upon sinners in this world, is to reject their prayers. This he may justly do, and laugh at our calamity, &c. It is all of grace that he deigns to receive our prayers.

2. *Receive our persons graciously.* Receive us into thy *family.* Sin has rendered us aliens and enemies, and we are by our iniquities children of wrath; but receive *us*, and put us among thy children. Receive us into thy *favor.* Our iniquities have rendered us liable to thy heavy displeasure; but oh forgive us, heal our backslidings. Receive us into union with thyself. Our iniquities have separated between us and thee; but cast us not off from thy presence. In the margin this is read, "Take away all iniquity, and give good." God is good—all good; and he gives good; and "no good thing will he withhold from them that walk uprightly."

IV. RETURNS OF GRATITUDE EXPRESSED ;—"So will we render the calves of our lips." By this expression we understand the fruit of our lips, "giving thanks to his name," Heb. xiii. 15. When the Jews received signal favors from God, they were accustomed to offer animal sacrifices, such as calves and bullocks, as returns of gratitude, 1 Kings iii. 4, 15 ; but "we will render the calves of our lips." "Thou desirest not sacrifice," &c., Ps. li. 16.

1. *Gratitude is a debt which all owe to God.* All the benefits with which our being is crowned, flow from God, and flow freely, liberally and constantly. Gratitude is the expression of obligation ; and as our obligations to God know no bounds, our gratitude should know no end.

2. *Gratitude is a debt which gracious souls are ready to pay.* Fully to discharge this debt is impossible; but, like the woman in the gospel, they do what they can. When God takes away our iniquity, and receives us graciously, our first feelings are those of praise, Isa. xxxviii. 18, 19. As a proof that we "render the calves of our lips," let us render the homage of our hearts, and the actions of our lives.

Learn, 1. *That neither our civil nor religious privileges will preclude the possibility of falling by iniquity.* Whoever rose higher by the former than Israel ? or whoever sunk deeper by the latter?

2. *That those who have fallen by iniquity should be induced to return to the Lord their God.* God invites them to return—promises to receive them—and gives direction by the prophet in the text how they should return.

3. *Those whose iniquity is taken away should individually say,* "Bless the Lord, O my soul." Psa. ciii. 2, 3.

## JESUS WEEPING OVER PERISHING SINNERS.

**Luke** xix. 41, 42. And when he was come near, he beheld the city, and wept over it, saying, If thou hadst known, even thou, at least in this thy day, the things which belong unto thy peace! but now they are hid from thine eyes. (Sk.)

1. WHEN we see a man weeping, of whom but little is known by us, it is natural for us to set our imagination in exercise, that we may be able to ascertain the probable cause or causes of his distress. We very readily suppose that he is a man *weak* in his *intellects*, and liable to be thus affected by every unpleasant occurrence, however trifling;—or he has committed some heinous *crime*, and his conscience is wrung by bitter remorse;—or he is now overwhelmed by the pressure of some recent *affliction* in his *circumstances ;*—or some great calamity has befallen his *friends*, and the tears we behold are tears of sympathy.

2. Our text exhibits to our view a man in tears. But be not hasty in your conclusions: these tears are not indicative of *mental imbecility*, for in him dwelt all the treasures of wisdom and knowledge.—These tears are not expressive of *remorse*, for in him was no sin, and in all his deportment he was holy, harmless, and undefiled.—These tears are not occasioned by *personal afflictions*, they have no reference to himself.—They are not occasioned by the calamities of his *friends*, for their case, even at the worst, is very hopeful.—Why then does he weep? The reason is, he sees his *enemies*, his open and avowed enemies, obstinately bent on their own destruction. It is this that fills his heart with sorrow, his eyes with tears, and his mouth with this affecting language. " When he came near," on his last visit to Jerusalem, " He beheld the city," that city, the inhabitants of which had despised, rejected, and reviled him, and were now forming designs against his life. Well knowing the dreadful judgments by which this city would soon be laid desolate, he most compassionately lamented " and wept over it, saying, If thou hadst known," or, " oh that thou hadst known, even thou, in this thy day, the things which belong unto thy peace! but now they are hid from thine eyes." This lamentation, it appears, was lost on the Jews in general, but it is recorded for our instruction; and under the divine blessing it may prove highly beneficial to us, by teaching us,

I. THAT GOSPEL BLESSINGS ARE CONDUCIVE TO THE PEACE OF MANKIND. They are the things which belong unto our peace. Here let us more particularly observe,

1. *What those things are to which our Lord refers.* That they are those blessings which he had called " the lost sheep of the house of Israel" to enjoy, but which they had obstinately rejected, is evident from similar complaints, see Matt. xiii. 14, 15; xxiii. 37; John v. 40. They include the blessings of grace in this world; and the blessings of glory in the eternal state.—*The blessings of grace in this world.* Deliverance—from bondage, condemnation, and guilty fears, Psa. cxvi. 16: Isa. xii. 1; Psa. xxxiv. 4; and *holiness*—both of heart and life, Obadiah 17; Rom. vi. 22.—*The blessings of glory in the eternal state.* An eternal life of rest, felicity, honor, and security, Rom. ii. 6, 7. Let us also observe,

2. *How these things are conducive to our peace.* They belong unto our peace as they produce sweet tranquility of mind, Eccl. ii. 26. This arises from *peace with God*, Rom. v. 1; *peace of conscience*, 2 Cor. i. 12; a *peaceable disposition*, James iii. 18; the *joy of victory*, Rom. viii. 37; 1 Cor. xv. 57; and the joy of *hope*, Rom. v. 2 and xiv. 17. Our text teaches us,

71

**II.** That these blessings must be known to be enjoyed:—"Oh that thou hadst known," &c. The knowledge thus necessary, must be,

1. *A speculative knowledge;* that is, we must have a correct view of them, as they are exhibited in God's word,—For we are naturally *without* them, Rom. iii. 16—18.—We must *seek* them to *obtain* them, Job xxii. 21; Isa. xxvii. 5.—And we must *understand* them in order that we may *seek* them aright: we must understand the nature of them; the necessity of them; and the way to obtain them, Prov. xix. 2. The knowledge here required must also be,

2. *An experimental knowledge.* This is evident—From the *testimony of inspired apostles,* 2 Cor. v. 1; xiii. 5; 1 John v. 19.—And from the *nature of gospel blessings;* spiritual sight, liberty, and health, must be experienced to be enjoyed. Our text teaches us,

**III.** That a season is afforded us for acquiring the knowledge of these blessings.

1. This season is here called *our day,* because it is the time in which we are called to labor for the blessings of peace, John vi. 27; Phil. ii. 12, 13; 2 Pet. iii. 14.

2. This season is *favorable for seeking the things here recommended;*—for they are set *before* us, Deut. xxx. 19, 29;—we have *strength* promised to seek them with, Isa. xl. 31;—and we have *light* to seek them in, John xii. 36. Hence, we should also recollect,

3. *This season is limited;* it is only a *day.* It began with the exercise of our reason; it may be terminated either by death, the general judgment, the loss of our mental powers, or the departure of God's Spirit, Jer. vi. 8; and while it remains, it should be promptly improved, John xii. 35; Matt. xxiv. 44. Our text also teaches us, with respect to gospel blessings,

**IV.** That it is God's will they should be enjoyed by us. This is certain,

1. *From the wish of Christ;*—"O that thou hadst known," &c. Such a wish we find often repeated by God in his word, and expressed in the kindest manner; see Deut. v. 29, xxxii. 29; Isa. xlviii. 18.

2. *From the tears of Christ.* These demonstrate the *sincerity* of his *wish,* Deut. xxxii. 4;—the great *importance* of *godliness,* 1 Tim. iv. 8;—and the *dreadful doom* of *impenitent sinners,* Rom. ii. 8, 9.

3. *And from the visitations of Christ;* see ver. 44. He visited us by his *incarnation,* Luke i. 78, 79;—and he still visits us by the strivings of his *Spirit*— the gifts of his *providence,* Acts xiv. 17—and the ministry of his *word,* 2 Cor. v. 20; Luke xix. 10. Hence we learn,

**V.** That all who seek these blessings aright, will obtain them.

1. *To seek them aright, is to seek them as God requires:*—with respect to *time,* now while our day of visitation lasts, Job xxii. 21:—with respect to *manner*—by faith in Christ, John v. 28, 29;—by receiving Christ, John i. 12;—coming to God by him, Heb. vii. 25;—and abiding in him, 1 John ii. 28.

2. *All who thus seek them will certainly obtain them;* for Christ *died* for the chief of sinners, Zech. xiii. 1. He *calls* them to seek salvation, Isa. i. 16—18; and *engages* not to *reject* them, John vi. 37. Only those shall perish who despise him, Acts xiii. 41; and all such must perish, because they obstinately reject the only remedy, Prov. xxix. 1; John iii. 17. Hence our text finally teaches us,

**VI.** That the rejection of these blessings is punished with destruction.

1. *This is evident from Scripture:*—for all mankind by nature are sinners, Rom. iii. 23. As sinners, they are exposed to destruction, Prov. x. 29; and by impenitence, the only means of salvation are neglected, Heb. x. 26, 27.

2. *And it is evident from facts.* These Jews, through impenitence, became the victims of divine vengeance; and so must all impenitent sinners, 2 Thess. i. 7—9.

### APPLICATION.

1. *Examine yourselves.* Do you enjoy the things which belong unto your peace? Gal. vi. 4,

2. *If not, seek them*—on *God's terms*, Acts xx. 21;— with your *whole heart*, Jer. xxix. 13;—and *without delay*, Job. xxxvi. 18.

3. *If thus seeking, expect salvation*—from Christ's *all-sufficiency*, Heb. vii. 25; and from his *goodness.* Recollect he visits you—weeps over you —wishes your salvation—has bled for you—and now waits on you, Rev. iii. 20.

---

### PROMPTITUDE OF CHOICE RECOMMENDED.

Joshua xxiv. 15.—Choose you this day whom you will serve. (Sk.)

THE text contains a most important piece of advice, addressed to a highly privileged people, by a most distinguished character, on a very memorable occasion. The speaker was Joshua, the successor of Moses, who was invested with his miraculous powers, and high prerogative. The period at which the text was spoken, was when he contemplated the near approach of death; and the individuals to whom it was addressed, were the elders of Israel, their heads, their judges, and their officers. There are seasons when the force of truth acquires additional energy; when the time, the place, and the circumstances, combine their influence to give permanency to the impression produced in the mind; and the period before us was one of those occasions. Imagine a venerable old man, grown grey-headed in the service of his God, and in active benevolence for the good of his nation; a man high in repute for his personal prowess, for his uniform and consistent character, for the splendor of his talents, for his disinterested integrity, rehearsing in the ears of the heads of Israel, the wonderful conduct of God towards them, reminding them of their degraded origin, "Your fathers dwelt on the other side of the flood," &c., ver. 2. Of the plagues inflicted on Egypt for their sakes, ver. 6, 7. How God defeated the design of Balaam, who came to curse the people, but was constrained to bless them altogether, ver. 9, 10. And he also reminded them of what God had done for them since they inhabited the land of Canaan. "Now therefore," said he, "fear the Lord," &c., "and if it seem evil unto you to serve the Lord. choose you," &c. Three things we will notice, the *act*, the *period*, and the *motives* for choice.

I. LET US NOTICE THE ACT OF CHOICE.

1. *Our choice should be divine in its object.* We should choose the Lord for our God. Choose God for our *sovereign*, that he may govern us, and that we may submit to his authority, and dispensations. For our *guide*, that

he may direct us amidst all the intricate snares of this world. For our *husband*, that we may be married to him. For our *portion*, that we may be satisfied with his favor, and for our *pattern*, that we may imitate him. O how many choose other objects!

2. *Our choice should be rational in its character.* It should be the result of rational conviction; the religion of some people lies solely in their passions, their hearts have been affected, their passions touched, and without counting the cost, or calling in the aid of their intellectual faculties, they commence their religious course, and join some body of professing christians; but alas! when persecution comes, they are offended, and their profession vanishes as the morning cloud, and as the early dew. Let us wisely consider what we are doing, so that we may be able to give an answer to every man who asketh us a reason of the hope that is in us.

3. *Our choice should be decisive in its nature.* In reference to many things in human life, we are called upon to hesitate in making our choice; and after we have made it, we are left in doubt as to its result. "For who knoweth what is good for man in this life?" But this cannot be the case, in reference to the subject before us. We all know that if we do not choose God for our portion, we must be inevitably ruined; and under the influence of this conviction, we should be so decided in our choice, as not even to have a longing wish for the world, or a single thought of returning again to its vain pursuits in quest of happiness.

4. *Our choice should be practical in its operations ;*—"Choose you this day whom ye will *serve.*" Having chosen God, you must serve him—*totally*, with soul and body ; *uniformly*, not merely on the Sabbath, or among the friends of piety, but always and every where ; *consistently* evince that you serve him. "Let others *see* your good works."

II. Let us notice the period of our choice ;—"Choose you *this day,*" &c.

1. *We should make our choice this day, because of the criminal neglect of which we have been guilty.* As soon as reason dawned upon our minds, and we were capable of making a choice, we ought to have chosen God for our portion, and have been uniform in our attachment to him, from that time to the present. But the days of our youth passed away in the total neglect of God; we purposed when arrived at maturity, to choose the good part; but alas! here also many of us failed, and now some of us are old, and probably have never yet been decidedly pious. Oh what culpable neglect attaches to us!

2. *We should make our choice this day, from a view of the shortness and uncertainty of our time.* "Time is short," our days are as a handbreadth, swifter than a post. We may die to-day, our departure may be sudden. Death often gives no signal of his approach; but should we have a lingering affliction, that is not a proper time to choose whom we shall *serve.*

3. *We should make our choice this day, because the present is the only time when God has promised the aids of his Spirit.* The power of choice is from God; that power is the effect of his gracious operations in us. But his Spirit will not always strive with us. God may be provoked to give us up to a reprobate mind. "Now is the accepted time."

4. *We should make our choice this day, because the difficulty of choosing will increase in proportion to our neglect of it.* Sin is a disease; the longer that disease prevails, the more inveterate it becomes. Sin is slavery; the longer we continue in it, the faster our chains are riveted, and the more difficult it is to burst them asunder.

**III.** LET US NOTICE THE MOTIVES FOR CHOICE. Joshua gave this charge to Israel; it is given to us now.

1. *The capacity which we have for choice, is a reason for its exercise.* God gives nothing in vain. Had we ranked no higher than brutes, and possessed nothing superior to blind instinct, the power of choice would have been precluded; but we are men, endowed with rational faculties, and capable under the influence of the divine Spirit of choosing God, and serving him.

2. *The perilous state in which we are without this choice, is another motive.* How miserable is a man without God! He who has never chosen God for his portion, has no interest in him, no union with him, no salvation from him. God is to him no refuge, Christ no Saviour, the Holy Ghost no comforter: heaven is no inheritance of his; ruin must inevitably seize his soul, if he continues in a course of sin.

3. *The happiness that results from our choosing God, should prompt us to comply with the requisition in the text.* He who has chosen God is in a state of safety and tranquility. His guilt is pardoned, his soul is renewed, his hope is like an anchor, sure and steadfast, cast within the veil, whither the forerunner is for him entered. The Lord's portion is his people, and Jacob is the lot of his inheritance.

Conclude by inquiring, What choice have we made? Where are our affections placed? Whom do we serve? What is our chief good? Some worship mammon. Some serve the devil. Expostulate with such. Why make such a choice? The world cannot make you happy. With the devil you will be tormented if you die in sin. Exhort those who have chosen God to cleave to him. Amen.

---

## OUR LORD'S CONDESCENSION TO SINNERS.

**Rev.** iii. 20. Behold, I stand at the door, and knock : if any man hear my voice, and open the door, I will come in to him, and sup with him, and he with me. (S. S.)

THE ways of man are often made a standard whereby to judge of God—
Hence many foolishly "think him to be such an one as themselves"
But "his thoughts and ways are infinitely above ours"
This is remarkably manifest in the passage before us—
It is usual for inferiors to wait on their superiors—
The greater their inferiority, the more patience is expected of them—
But here the God of heaven waits upon his sinful creatures—
The declaration is made even to the Lukewarm Laodiceans—
It unfolds to our view,
I. THE WONDERFUL CONDESCENSION OF CHRIST TO SINNERS.
He represents himself as coming to them to be their guest—
But we must understand his words in a spiritual sense—
The hearts of natural men are shut against Christ.
Mankind have their hearts full of vile lusts and passions—
They utterly exclude Christ from his rightful habitation—
They bar the door against him by prejudice and unbelief—
He however condescends to seek admittance into them.
He "knocks" in various ways "at the door" of their hearts—
He intreats, promises, threatens, and expostulates by his *word*—

He awakens attention by the secret energy of his *Spirit*—
He calls also by alarming dispensations of his *providence*—
But the generality disregard his voice.
They are asleep, and even " dead in trespasses and sins"—
If awakened, they endeavor to lull themselves asleep again—
If they cannot do this, they rest in frivolous excuses, Cant. v. 2, 3.
Thus do they studiously and determinately resist his will—
Nevertheless he " stands" patiently waiting their leisure.
He might well depart at their first refusal—
But he knows how dreadful their state would then be—
He therefore " waiteth to be gracious" unto them—
On many he has waited a long series of years, Acts xiii. 18.
Of most it may be said as of Israel of old, Rom. x. 21.
This is a fact worthy of our highest admiration.
Well might he call us to " behold" it with wonder—
How wonderful, that the Creator should so condescend to a creature !—
How wonderful, that the Judge should become suitor to the criminal !—
How wonderful, that the self-sufficient God should seek in such a way to bless those who are inexpressibly vile and helpless !—
This must excite our admiration to all eternity—
The adorable goodness expressed in it will appear further by considering,
II. THE MERCIES HE DESIRES TO IMPART TO THEM.
He requires nothing of sinners but what he will enable them to perform.
He looks for no worthiness or merit in them—
He only desires that they " hear his voice, and open to him"—
He will himself " unstop their ears," and " incline their hearts"—
If indeed they obstinately persist in rejecting him, they cut themselves off from any hope in his mercy—
Upon their yielding to his solicitations, he will bless them.
The metaphor of a guest is still kept up—
It is a common metaphor in scripture, John xiv. 23.
The " supping" implies the most familiar intercourse with the soul—
This our Lord will vouchsafe to those who open their hearts to him— -
He will delight himself in the exercise of their graces, Cant. iv. 16.
He will communicate to them his richest consolations—
He will cause them to exclaim with the prophet, Zech. ix. 17.
Nor will he withhold these mercies on account of their past conduct.
He will with equal readiness become the guest of all—
No unworthiness or past obduracy shall hinder him—
He has declared this in the most express terms, "If *any* man." See also Isa. lv. 1 ; Rev. xxii. 17.
He has proved it in the most remarkable instances, 2 Chron. xxxiii. 9, 12, 13; 1 Tim. i. 13, 16.
There is a cloud of living witnesses ready to attest it—
We shall conclude with an ADDRESS to
1. Those who are living in a careless state.
You are yet strangers to the heavenly guest—
But this arises only from your own negligence and supineness—
Christ has been long knocking at the door of your hearts—
Every vile lust has been admitted, whilst HE has stood without—
May you never have that threatening fulfilled to you ! Prov. i. 24—31
Let every one obey the prophet's exhortation, Isa. lv. 6.
2. Those who are awakened from it.

What a mercy is it that you have heard the Saviour's voice !—
Let it be your daily endeavor to open your hearts to him—
Guard against unbelief, which above all bars the door against him—
Let the sins which are offensive to him be put away—
Then shall the fact which so offended the Jews be realized in you, Luke xix. 7.
Thus shall you enjoy the most endearing fellowship with Jesus—
And you shall ere long "sup with him" in a better place, Rev. xix. 9.

---

## AN EXHORTATION TO HOLINESS.

1 Peter ii. 11, 12.—Dearly beloved, I beseech you, as strangers and pilgrims, abstain from fleshly lusts, which war against the soul; having your conversation honest among the Gentiles: that whereas they speak against you as evil doers, they may, by your good works which they shall behold, glorify God in the day of visitation. (S. S.)

THE privileges of a sincere christian are exceeding great—
And the possession of them is secured to him by God himself, 1 Pet. i. 5.
His security however does not supersede the need of watchfulness—
On the contrary he is called to a continual warfare—
He needs therefore to be frequently reminded of his duty—
Hence Peter, having set forth the honors and privileges of God's people, proceeds to press upon them the practice of holiness—
We propose to explain and enforce the apostle's exhortation.
I. EXPLAIN
The manner in which it is introduced is worthy of notice.
A concern for the souls of men is characteristic of a pious minister—
Paul and John were eminent patterns in this respect—1 Thess. iii. 8; 3 John 4.
Peter exemplifies it in the passage before us—
He unites the tenderness of a father with the fidelity of an apostle—
The first part of it respects their "abstinence from fleshly lusts."
Impurity, intemperance, sloth, &c., are fleshly lusts—
Nor can any abstain from them without much prayer and vigilance—
This is enforced by two very important considerations.
Christians are "strangers and pilgrims" in the world—Psa. xxxix. 12; Heb. xi. 13.
This consideration strongly enforces abstinence from sin—It shews the folly of the Epicurean system, 1 Cor. xv. 32.
Moreover fleshly lusts "war against the soul"—
They destroy its dignity, its peace, its liberty, its salvation—
This should make us extremely careful to abstain from them—
The latter part of the exhortation respects positive holiness.
The christians were scattered through the Gentile world—
Their conduct therefore would be watched with a jealous eye—
On this account the apostle cautions them with respect to the whole of their deportment—
He exhorts them to maintain an honorable conduct in all things—
A very powerful motive is suggested to confirm this also—
Christians were universally represented as the worst of men, 1 Cor. iv 13

An unbecoming conduct in them would have confirmed this prejudice—
But a blameless conversation might conciliate esteem—
It might even be the means of converting their persecutors—
It would do so if God at the same time should visit them with his mercy*—
In this case it would cause them to glorify God—
This consideration might well operate as a motive to holiness—
St. Peter elsewhere urges it in this very light, 1 Pet. iii. 1.

II. ENFORCE.

Christians, however advanced, have need of this exhortation—
We therefore would address it to you with all earnestness—
We would not however forget the affection and tenderness due to you—
First then we beseech you to abstain from fleshly lusts.
Who amongst you is free from their baneful influence?
Who does not see that abstinence from them is necessary?—
Guard then against their first risings in the heart—
Beg of God that you may have grace to mortify them all—
We intreat you to consider,
1. Your present state and condition in the world.
You are here only as "strangers and pilgrims"—
You profess to be seeking "a city that hath foundations"—
You do not take up your rest in an inn, when on a journey—
Do not then retard your progress heaven-wards by sensual gratifications—
2. The dreadful tendency of fleshly lusts.
Who has not experienced the misery they bring upon us?—
Who does not know the consequence of indulging them?—
Let this thought make you flee from them with abhorrence—
We further beseech you to maintain an honorable conversation.
A few holy actions or dispositions will not suffice—
Religion must operate uniformly and universally—
Let the whole of your conversation therefore be blameless, Phil. ii. 15.
Nor need you despair of walking thus if you depend on Christ Phil. iv. 13.
For consider,
The tendency of such a life to remove prejudice.
The world is as ready to speak evil of christians as ever—
Nor will they regard your conduct in the church or closet—
They will enquire how you fill up your relative duties—
The sight of your blameless conduct will silence them, 1 Pet. ii. 15, and
iii. 16.
The possibility that others may be converted by means of it.
Certainly many would be hardened by misconduct on your part—
On the contrary, some may be won by your good conversation—
At all events God will be glorified by means of your good works—
Let this stimulate you to unwearied watchfulness and care.

* This seems to be meant by "the day of visitation:" See Luke i. 68, 78.

## PAUL'S DISCOURSE BEFORE FELIX.

Acts xxiv. 25.—And as he reasoned of righteousness, temperance, and judgment to come Felix trembled, and answered, Go thy way for this time ; when I have a convenient season, I will call for thee. (S. S.)

MEN usually persist in sin without duly reflecting on its consequences—
Hence the peace which they enjoy, notwithstanding they are exposed to the displeasure of the Almighty—
Yet the voice of warning and reproof will sometimes alarm them—
Too often, however, the alarm is only of short duration—
This was the case of Felix, when awakened by the preaching of Paul,
I. THE SUBJECTS OF THE APOSTLES DISCOURSE.
He was sent for to explain the principles he professed—
But he was not satisfied with gratifying the curiosity of his hearers—
He endeavored to reach their consciences, and convince them of their sins—
On this occasion he spoke of " righteousness, temperance, and judgment to come."
These subjects were well adapted to his audience—
Felix and Drusilla were both of an abandoned character*—
They needed to be "persuaded by the terrors of the Lord"—
Nor was it probable they would regard the tidings of salvation, unless they were first made sensible that they were lost sinners, Matt. ix. 12, 13.
Hence the apostle endeavored to prepare their minds for the gospel—
On these subjects he " reasoned."
He shewed the nature and extent of the duties—
He shewed the evil and danger of transgressing them—
He shewed the certainty and strictness of the future judgment—
A suitable lesson for avarice, iniquity, and oppression !—
And suitable, too, to every child of man !—
What degree of success attended this effort will appear from,
II. THE EFFECTS IT PRODUCED.
We read not of Drusilla being at all affected with the word—
But we are told of Felix, that he " trembled."
What a wonderful sight ! the judge trembling before his prisoner !—
He had sinned in unnumbered instances, and was obnoxious to God' wrath—
He now heard of the day of retribution, and of the sentence of condemnation under which he lay—
And now, though he feared no earthly tribunal, he was shaken with terror and with guilt—
And was there not cause for trembling?
He was not, however, faithful to his convictions.
One might have hoped that he would have cried out like those of old, Acts ii. 37.—
But he sought to efface the impression made upon his mind—
He put off his attention to his soul to a more " convenient season."
What madness was here, to depend on the morrow in a concern of such importance !—

* Felix had induced Drusilla to forsake her own husband, and to marry him . he was moreover exceedingly avaricious and oppressive.

What season could be so convenient as *that* he then enjoyed?—

His conscience was then affected, and the Spirit was striving with him—

Moreover, he had then a faithful and inspired instructor before him—

Was he more likely to repent when he had seared his conscience, quenched the Spirit, yielded to Satan, and confirmed his evil habits?—

But his future interviews with the apostle was of no avail—

One of the last acts of his government was marked with oppression and
avarice—

Nor did he spare the innocence which he confessed, and admired, Ver.
26, 27.—

A melancholy instance of judicial blindness!—

APPLICATION.

Let this history serve as a CAUTION to us,

All of us have known, in some measure, the motions of God's Spirit—

All of us have felt, at times, some general apprehensions respecting the
account which we must give at the day of judgment—

But how many have silenced their convictions, in hopes of finding some
more convenient season for attending to them!—

And how many have died before the hoped-for opportunity arrived!—

Let us beware of this device of Satan, whereby he upholds his kingdom
in the world*—

Let us remember that the same temptations will recur, and the same motives influence us at future periods—

Let us attend to that salutary advice of the apostle, Heb. iii. 13–15.

And let us seek, without delay, that godly sorrow which worketh repentance unto salvation, 2 Cor. vii. 10.

---

## AN EXHORTATION TO CARELESS SINNERS.

**Eph. v. 14.** Awake, thou that sleepest, and arise from the dead, and Christ shall give
thee light.  (S. S.)

THERE is a harmony in the Scriptures which many overlook and destroy—

Detached passages are often wrested to establish a favorite system†—

But the various truths of God should be viewed as they stand connected
with each other—

There would then be diversity indeed, but no contrariety between them‡—

This observation will throw light, as on many other parts of Scripture, so
on that before us in particular; in which we have—

I. A COMMAND.

The Scripture abounds with useful and instructive metaphors—

Our state is here represented under the images of sleep and death—

* He does not tempt any to resolve that they will never repent; but takes the more plausible method of insinuating that they will have a more convenient season for repenting.

† Calls to duty are supposed to imply the sufficiency of man to do the will of God; while
the confessions or petitions of the saints, and the promises of divine aid given to them, are
brought to justify a negligence in the use of means.

‡ God gives a *command*, Ezek. xviii. 31. David, knowing his duty, and feeling his inability to perform it, had long before presented this to God in the form of a *petition*, Ps. li.
10. And God, to encourage such applications to him, *promises* to work in us that which he
requires of us, Ezek. xxxvi. 26

*Sleep* implies a state of *inactivity* and *security*.

**Men** are busily employed about their worldly concerns—
But a lamentable supineness prevails with respect to spiritual things—
The generality do not apprehend their souls to be in any danger—
Death, judgment, heaven, and hell, do not seem worthy their notice—
God's threatenings against them are denounced without effect—
They are like Jonah, sleeping in the midst of a storm—
Hence they are described as "at ease from their youth," Jer. xlviii. 11.
To the same effect is the testimony of him that searcheth the heart, Ps. x. 4, 5.

*Death* includes the ideas of *impotence* and *corruption*.

An inanimate body cannot perform any of the functions of life—
It has within itself the seeds and principles of corruption—
The soul also, till quickened from the dead, is in a state of impotence—
It is incapable of spiritual action or discernment, John xv. 5; 1 Cor. ii. 14.
Its powers and faculties are altogether vitiated, Rom. vii. 18.
Whatever is loathsome and offensive to God proceeds from it, Mark vii. 21, 22.
So true is that humiliating declaration! Job. xv. 14—16.

Yet, notwithstanding this state appears so desperate, we must address to every one that is under it, the command, "Awake," &c.

Your inactivity and security involve you in the deepest guilt—
Your corruption of heart and life provokes the majesty of God—
Nor is your impotence any excuse for your disobedience—
It is your love of sin that disables you for duty—
Nor is God deprived of his right to command, though you have lost your power to obey—
Let every one then strive to comply with this heavenly call—
They who exert their feeble powers may expect divine assistance*—
To convince us that none shall fail who use the appointed means, God enforces his command with

II. A PROMISE.

Sleep and death are states of intellectual *darkness*—
Hence *light* is promised to those who obey the divine mandate—
*Light* in Scripture imports knowledge, Isa. viii. 20; holiness, 1 John i. 7; comfort, Ps. xcvii. 11; and glory, Col. i. 12.
And all these blessings shall they receive from Christ, the fountain of light, Mal. iv. 2; John i. 9.

Knowledge.

Spiritual knowledge every natural man stands in need of—
Nor is it attainable by the teaching of men, or the efforts of genius, Matt. xi. 25.
We can receive it from none but Christ, Matt. xi. 27.
Hence Christ invites us to come to him for it, Matt. xi. 29.
Nor shall an application to him ever fail of success, Psa. xxv. 9; Prov. ii. 3—6.

Holiness.

A despair of attaining this deters many from seeking it—
They think their inveterate habits cannot be rooted out, Jer. ii. 25.
But Christ is our "sanctification" as well as our wisdom, 1 Cor. i. 30.

---

*See Matt. xii. 10, 13. The man with the withered hand was unable to stretch it forth; but in attempting to obey, he was endued with strength.

His very name encourages us to expect deliverance from him, Matt. i. **21.**
And he will fulfil the promises which he has made to this effect. Mic. **vii.**
19; Isa. i. 25.

Comfort.

A sense of guilt shall yield to holy joy, Isa. xxix. 19 ; and lxi. 3.
Deplored weakness shall be succeded by a divine energy, Isa. xxxv. 5, 6.
Our delight in him shall be spiritual and exalted, Isa. li. 11, and lviii. 11
I* shall far transcend all earthly pleasures, Psa. lxxxiv. 10, and iv. 6, 7.

Glory.

Our Lord will not confine his blessings to this world, Psa. lxxxiv. 11.
He will raise his people to thrones of glory, Rev. iii. 21.
He will cause them to participate his own inheritance, Rom. viii. 17.
He will be the ground and object of their joy for ever, Isa. lx. 19 20.

APPLICATION.

What greater encouragement can any one desire ?—
What richer promises can any one conceive ?—
How suited are they to our necessities !—
Let every one consider the command as addressed to himself; "Awake,
Thou"—
Let all our powers and faculties be called forth to action—
In exerting ourselves let us expect the promised aid—
Thus shall we be eternal monuments of Christ's power and grace—

---

## CHRIST'S OFFER OF THE SPIRIT.

John vii. 37, 38.—In the last day, that great day of the feast, Jesus stood and cried, saying.
If any man thirst, let him come unto me, and drink. He that believeth on me, as the
scripture hath said, out of his belly shall flow rivers of living water. (S. S.)

OUR blessed Lord incessantly labored for the salvation of men—
Nor could their ungrateful returns at all divert him from his purpose—
His life was sought, and he knew that persons were sent to apprehend him.
Yet, instead of rejecting them with abhorrence, he sought to win them by
love—
And importuned them to accept his richest blessings—
His address to them on this occasion contained,

I. AN INVITATION.

The time and manner of the invitation are worthy of notice.
This was a day of peculiar sanctity, and of uncommon festivity*—
And it seems that some customs, not required in the original institutions
of the law, obtained among the Jews at that time†—

* It was the eighth and last day of the feast of tabernacles, Lev. xxiii. 34. 36.

† It is said that on this day they went annually to the pool of Siloam, and drawing water
from thence returned with it in procession to the temple, where they poured it out with all
possible demonstrations of joy. At what time this custom arose, it is not easy to determine ; but probably it commenced after the Babylonish captivity ; and was adopted in reference to that prediction, Isaiah xii. 3. Nor is the design of it precisely known : but it seems
most likely that they then commemorated the giving of water out of the rock in the wilder
ness · and called upon God for rain, which was so necessary to them at that season. Perhaps the more spiritual among them, might pray also for those spiritual blessings, which
their promised Messiah was appointed to bestow. These circumstances served as the foundation of our Lord's address, and reflect much light upon it.

**Happy** to improve the opportunity, Jesus stood in the most conspicuous place, and, with an exalted voice, claimed their attention—

And, despising equally the censures of the uncharitable, and the persecutions of the proud, he made them fresh overtures of mercy—

The invitation itself was beyond measure gracious and kind.

While they only panted for his blood, he longed for their salvation—

He pointed himself out to them as the only fountain of living waters—

And assured them of his readiness to impart whatsoever they stood in need of—

He excepted none from his offers, provided they did but "thirst" for his blessings—

What could have a more conciliatory effect on his blood-thirsty murderers?

Lest, however, his invitations should be slighted, he enforced it with,

II. A PROMISE.

He first explained what he meant by "coming to him."

It was not a mere outward, but an inward and spiritual application, that he wished them to make to him—

They were to "believe in *him*," as possessing all fulness in himself—Col. i. 19.

And as the person appointed of the Father to convey blessings to them—Psa. lxxii. 17.

In a full persuasion of this truth they were to come to him by faith—

And to "draw water with joy from this well of salvation"—

For their encouragement he promised them a rich effusion of his Spirit.

By "living water" our Lord meant the gift of his Spirit—Ver. 39.

That "rivers of this living water should flow out of his belly," imported, that the believer should have a constant spring of consolation within him which should refresh all who came within the sphere of his influence—

Of this blessed truth the scriptures had abundantly testified*—

And our Lord now confirmed it to them by a most solemn promise—

He assured them, as he had before done the Samaritan woman, that his communications to them should prove a source of unutterable and endless joy—John iv. 10, 13, 14.

We shall further IMPROVE this subject by addressing,

1. Those who have no desire after spiritual blessings.

Alas! how many are there who are insatiable in their thirst after earthly things; but never once desire the blessings which Christ is exalted to bestow!

Perhaps too they think that they contract no guilt by their neglect of him—

But it is with no small indignation that God speaks of their conduct, Jer. ii. 13.

Nor would their folly be hidden from themselves, if they only considered what "broken cisterns" the sources of their comfort have invariably proved—

O that they would drink of the living fountain before they experience the want of one "drop of water to cool their tongues!"—

2. Those who desire spiritual blessings, but know not where to go for them.

Many, like those whom our Lord addressed, look no further than to the outward duty—

But he directed their eyes to himself as the true Siloam, John ix. 7, the only fountain of good—

---

* Some, because our Lord's words are not found in scripture, καθὼς εἶπεν ἡ γραφη with ὁ πιστεύων εἰς ἐμὲ; (translating εἶπεν, hath *required*) but there are many passages that speak to the same effect, though not in his express terms. See Isaiah xliv. 3.

Thus must we also direct you to faith in Christ, as the one means of obtaining blessings from him—

Whatever delight you may take in duties, you must remember that ordinances are but the medium of communication between Christ and you—

And that the benefits you receive will be proportioned to the faith you exercise on him—

3. Those who desire spiritual blessings, but fear that Christ is unwilling to impart them.

Too many are discouraged because their prayers are not answered instantly—

They conclude themselves so unworthy as to have excited nothing but aversion in the heart of Christ towards them—

But are you unworthy? and were not they also to whom the text was addressed—

Have you waited long in vain? and is there not a special promise given for your encouragement?—Isa. xli. 17, 18.

Have you nothing to present to Christ in return? Then he bids you come without money and without price, Isa. lv. 1; Rev. xxii. 17.

Will it be an unparalleled act of mercy? Then is it that new thing which he has undertaken to perform, Isa. xliii. 19, 20.

Fear not then, but renew your application to him with increased fervor—

And your soul shall ere long " be as a watered garden, and like a spring of water, whose waters fail not"—Isa. lviii. 11.

---

## THE WORK OF REDEMPTION A MOTIVE TO CONVERSION.

Isaiah xliv. 22.—Return unto me; for I have redeemed thee.  (S. S.)

It is almost incredible that rational beings should ever be so stupid as to cut down a tree, and carve out of it the image of a man, and, after having roasted their food with a part of it, bow down to the residue as to a God—But it is yet more astonishing that Jehovah, having been thus insulted, should invite the offenders to mercy, and urge them to accept it—Yet it is in this connexion that the text stands; and it may well be addressed to *us*; since, however free we be from gross idolatry, we all have worshipped and served the creature more than the Creator—Let us then fix our attention upon,

I. The invitation.

Our defection from God is too manifest to need much proof—Shades of difference there may doubtless be between different individuals; but all have turned aside from God, and gone astray like sheep that are lost—But we are here invited to return to him,

1. With penitence.

The example of the Prodigal is that which we ought to follow—The consideration of our departure from God should fill us with shame and sorrow, and our idolatrous attachment to the creature humble us in the dust—This is the direction which God himself has given us, Hos. xiv. 1, 2; and it is to such humiliation alone that his promises of acceptance are made, Job xxxiii. 27.

2. With faith.

We are not to come to God with a mind full of doubts and suspicions, but with a full persuasion of his readiness to receive us—To what purpose is it to put away our contempt of his authority, if we deny or question the riches of his grace? Our conviction of his love and mercy should be as strong as possible; Mark ix. 22, 23; and we should with the most confident assurance rely on the death of Christ as a full, perfect, and sufficient sacrifice for all our sins—

3. With love.

God delights in a willing people; he would not have us regard him as a severe Master, but as a loving Father: instead of accounting his commandments grievous, we should consider his services as perfect freedom—Our disposition should be like that of Jesus when first he undertook our cause, Ps. xl. 7, 8;—Nor indeed can any thing but an unreserved surrender of ourselves to his service prove the truth of our repentance and the sincerity of our faith—

The full import of this invitation will be seen by considering,

II. THE MOTIVE WITH WHICH IT IS ENFORCED.

It is the Lord Jesus Christ who addresses to us the word of the text, See verse 21;—Now if he had enforced his invitation with a threatening of everlasting punishment, it would have called for our most attentive regard: but the motive here urged has tenfold energy—It may be considered,

1. As a tie upon our gratitude.

The redemption of Israel from Egypt, though great, was not to be compared with that which is wrought for us by the blood of Christ—The obligations which we lie under exceed all computation—Well therefore may this stupendous mercy be urged as an inducement to return to God—Indeed, this motive duly considered, could not fail of producing the desired effect—Suppose a prodigal, having left his father's house, and squandered away his substance, had been seized by his creditors and sold for a slave: suppose his father full of compassion, had gone, at the risk of his own life, and given all that he possessed as the price of his son's redemption: suppose the son returning to his evil ways, and actually going to sell himself again to his former master; if his father should follow him, with the invitation in the text, could he fail of success? Must not his son have an heart of adamant, if he could withstand such a solicitation?—The application of this to our own case is easy; O that we may realize the idea for our good!—

2. As an encouragement under our fears.

Notwithstanding the numberless proofs which God has given us of his readiness to forgive sin, we are apt to think him hard and inexorable—But the argument here used may well dissipate our unbelieving fears—Let us conceive the Saviour, at the very instant of his resurrection, meeting one of his murderers, and importuning him, by the very wounds which he had made, to accept of mercy, and assuring him that, if he would believe, the blood that he had shed, should cleanse him from the guilt of shedding it: could that man entertain a doubt of the Saviour's willingness to shew mercy?—This very thing is done to us, whose sins were the real occasion of Jesus' death: he meets us in the word, and, with his wounds yet exhibited before our eyes, addresses us in the words of the text—Let all unworthy conceptions of him then be put away, and every soul return to him as able and willing to save us to the uttermost—

APPLICATION.

*Careless sinners* overlook, alas! all these considerations—But if they would consider the Saviour as addressing *them*, and as following them with these

**words** into all their retirements, yea, into all their resorts of gaiety and dissipation, what a damp would such a reflection cast on all their vicious appetites and unhallowed enjoyments!—Methinks it would not be possible for them long to withstand the influence of such a thought—— —To *backsliding professors* these words must be applied with tenfold emphasis—How pungent must such an invitation be to those, who, having once experienced the efficacy of the blood of Christ, have relapsed into a lukewarm Laodicean state!—How shocking must their ingratitude appear, and how great their folly!—Let all such, if such there be amongst us, attend to this gracious call, and return without delay, to their duties, their priviliges, their enjoyments

---

## THE NEARNESS OF SALVATION A MOTIVE TO DILIGENCE.

**Rom. xiii. 11.**—Now it is high time to awake out of sleep : for now is our salvation nearer than when we believed.   (S. S.)

THE nearness of eternity may well excite us to improve the present hour—
This is a consideration as proper for believers as for unbelievers—
By it the apostle stimulated to activity the christians at Rome—
We shall consider,
I. HIS EXHORTATION.
Persons, at their accustomed hour, arise from their beds, come forth to the light, and engage in the duties of their respective callings—
Now "it is high time" for us, (as the apostle tells us, and "we know,")
1. To shake off our stupor.
The wise virgins, no less than the foolish, slumbered and slept—Matt. xxv. 5.
And the most zealous christians at times are apt to grow remiss—Rev. ii. 2—4.
But it becomes us all to resist this propensity to the utmost—
And to redeem every moment of our time for God—
2. To take a view of our prospects.
What glorious prospects has God set before us in his word!—
Should we not then be surveying them with admiration and joy?—
Should we be sleeping, when Christ and heaven are open to our view?—Luke ix. 29, 32.
Surely we should be ever standing as on Pisgah's top—Deut. iii. 25, 27.
3. To prosecute our duties.
The christian's work demands the utmost energy of his soul—
Unless we engage with our whole hearts, we can never discharge the offices of love—*
And are not multitudes around us "perishing for lack of knowledge?"—
Are not many of the saints also in need of consolation and support?—
What time then is there for loitering when so much is to be done?—
That the exhortation may have due influence upon us, let us consider,
II. THE ARGUMENT WITH WHICH IT IS ENFORCED.
Every day, and every hour, the believer draws "nearer to"
1. The termination of his conflicts.

* *These* are particularly referred to.  Compare ver. 8, 10, with the text.

The nearer a racer comes to the goal, the more he stretches forth for the prize—

And shall not the christian be animated by the thought, that all his temntations, trials, difficulties are nearly ended?—

Well may he endure with patience, or exert himself with vigor, when the moment of his eternal rest is nigh at hand—

2. The period of his probation.

God has fixed the precise time for our continuance in his service—

And when that is arrived, we must "give account of our stewardship"—

Should we not then improve our talents with all diligence?—

It is in this way alone that we can hope to "give up our account with joy"—

3. The consummation of his hopes.

What does the christian look for, but a perfect conformity to God's image, and a complete possession of his glory?—

And perhaps a few days, or hours, may bring him to the enjoyment of it all—

Blessed thought! who that entertains it, must not glow with ardent desire for the moment of his dissolution?—Phil. i. 23.

And redouble his exertions to finish the work assigned him?—2 Pet. iii. 11, 12.

APPLICATION.

It is high time also for *unbelievers* to awake; for "their damnation slumbereth not"—2 Pet. ii. 3.

If they sleep a little longer, where, oh! where will they awake?—Luke xvi. 23, 24.

With what propriety may we address you, as Joshua did the Jews!—Josh. xviii. 3.

~~~~~~~~~~~~

# CHAPTER III.

## THE WORK OF GRACE.

### OF THE PARDON OF SIN.

Psalm cxxx. 4.—There is forgiveness with thee.  (H.)

THE doctrine of pardon is of pure revelation; it is not to be known by the light of nature; "As many as have sinned without law." Rom. ii. 12. Nor is this a doctrine of the law, which gives not the least hint of pardon, nor any encouragement to expect it. As many as have sinned in the law shall be judged by the law, condemned without any hope of pardon. Rom. ii. 12. Every transgression and disobedience of the law, or word spoken by angels, received a just recompense of reward; that is, proper and righteous punishment. Heb. ii. 2. Nor does the law regard a man's repentance, nor admit of any. He that despised Moses's law, died without mercy! Heb. x. 28. But the doctrine of pardon is a pure doctrine of the gospel, which Christ gave commission to his disciples to preach. Luke xxiv. 47; Acts xxvi. 18. Concerning which may be observed,

**I.** The proof that may be given of it, that there is such a THING AS PAR-DON OF SIN.

This is asserted in the text, "There is forgiveness with thee;" and by Daniel, "To the Lord our God belong mercies and forgiveness, full and free pardon of sin." Dan. ix. 9. It is a blessing provided and promised in the covenant of grace; "I will be merciful to their unrighteousness, and their sins and their iniquities I will remember no more;" Heb. viii. 12; it is the gracious proclamation the Lord has made of his name; "The Lord, the Lord God, merciful and gracious." Ex. xxxiv. 7. Christ was set forth a propitiation, through faith in his blood, for the remission of sins. Rom. iii. 25; Matt. xxvi. 28; Eph. i. 7. And Christ is "exalted to be a prince and a Saviour, to give repentance;" Acts v. 31, and it is, by his orders, published in the gospel; to which may be added, the numerous instances of it; the Israelites, who, as they often sinned, God had compassion on them, and forgave their iniquities, Psa. lxxviii. 38; and xcix. 8, and of David, Manasseh, and others, and of Saul the blasphemer, the persecutor, and injurious person; and of other notorious sinners. Ps. xxxii. 5; 1 Tim. i. 13; Luke vii. 37, 47. It is in this way God would have his people comforted, when burdened and distressed with their guilt and sin, Isa. xl. 1, 2; Matt. ix. 2; and they are favored with a comfortable experience of it, and peace of soul from it; Psa. lxxxv. 1—3; Rom. v. 11; they are directed to pray for it, Psa. xxxii. 5; and li. 2, 7—9; Dan. ix. 19; Matt. vi. 12. Pardon of sin is a branch of redemption by the blood of Christ. Eph. i. 7.

**II.** The phrases by which the PARDON OF SIN is expressed, and which will serve to lead into the nature of it.

1. By lifting it up, and taking it away; "Blessed is he whose transgression is forgiven, is lifted up, taken off from him. and carried away." Psa. xxxii. 1. Sin lies upon the awakened sinner, as a burden too heavy for him to bear: which is taken away by the application of the blood of Christ.

2. By the covering of it: "Blessed is he whose sin is covered." Psa. xxxii. 1. "Thou hast forgiven the iniquity of thy people, thou hast covered all their sin." Psa. lxxxv. 2. Sin is something impure, nauseous, and abominable, in the sight of God, and provoking in the eyes of his glory, and must be covered out of sight; and this cannot be done by any thing of man's; not by his righteousness, which is but rags, a covering too narrow to be wrapped in, and can no more hide his nakedness, than Adam's fig-leaves could hide his; nay, it is no better than a spider's web; and of which it may be said, "Their webs shall not become garments." Isa. lix. 6. Sin is only covered by Christ, who is the antitype of the mercy-seat which was a lid or cover to the ark.

3. By a non-imputation of it; "Blessed is the man to whom the Lord imputeth not iniquity!" Psa. xxxii. 2, does not reckon it, nor place it to his account, nor bring any charge against him for it, nor punishes for it; but acquits him from it.

4. By a blotting of it out: in such language David prays for the forgiveness of sin; "Blot out my transgressions—and blot out all mine iniquities!" Psa. li. 1, 9, and in the same way God declares his will to forgive the sins of the people; "I, even I, am he, that blotteth out thy transgressions!" Isa. xliii. 25, which language is used either in allusion to the crossing of debt books, drawing a line over them; or to blotting out a man's hand-writing to a bond or note, obliging to payment of money; hence the phrase of "blotting out the hand-writing of ordinances that was against us." Col. ii. 14. Sins are debts, and these are numerous, and sinners poor, and unable to pay;

God for Christ's sake freely forgives; "I have blotted out, as a thick cloud." Isa. xliv. 22. Sins may be compared to clouds, for their quantity, their number being many; for their quality being exhaled out of the earth and sea, mount up to heaven, cause darkness, and intercept light; sin rises out of the earthly minds of men, who mind earthly things, and who are like the troubled sea, which cannot rest: and the sins of some, like those of Babylon, reach up to heaven, and call for wrath and vengeance to come down from thence; sin causes the darkness of unregeneracy, and is often the reason of darkness to such who have been made light in the Lord; it intercepts the light of his countenance and of Christ, the Sun of Righteousness: now, as a cloud is dispersed and dissipated by the breaking forth of the sun, which, overcoming the cloud, scatters it, so as it is seen no more: in like manner, through the rising of the Sun of Righteousness, with healing in his wings.

5. By a non-remembrance of it: "And their iniquities will I remember no more!" Heb. viii. 12; Isa. xliii. 25. God forgives and forgets; having once forgiven them, he thinks of them no more.

6. By making sin, or rather sinners, white as snow; so David prays, "Wash me, and I shall be whiter than snow." Psa. li. 7. So the Lord promises, "Thy sins shall be as white as snow." Isa. i. 18. "Her Nazarites are purer than snow." Lam. iv. 7.

III. What sins are pardoned? Sins both with respect to quality and quantity.

1. For quality; they are called trespasses. Sin is a walking on forbidden ground, for which a man must suffer, unless forgiven; and transgressions of the law of God; a passing over and going beyond the bounds and limits prescribed it: and iniquities, which are contrary to the rules of justice and equity; and sins, errors, aberrations, strayings from the rule of God's word: when God is said to forgive iniquity, transgression, and sin, it takes in every kind and sort of sin; sins are called abominations; not that they are so to sinners, for they delight in them; but to God, to whom they are so very disagreeable. Sin is defined, a transgression of the law, 1 John iii. 4, a breach, a violation of it; which accuses of it, pronounces guilty for it, and curses and condemns; and is only forgiven by the Lawgiver, who is able to save and destroy. Sins are sometimes represented as debts: because being committed, they oblige to the debt of punishment, which God remits; "Who forgiveth all thine iniquities." Psa. ciii. 3; Isa. xxxiii. 24; Mal. iv. 2.

2. For quantity; all trespasses, sins, and transgressions are forgiven. Col. ii. 13; Psa ciii. 3. Some are more secret, some more open, some less, others greater, more daring and presumptuous; some sins of commission, other sins of omission; but all are forgiven. See Isa. xliii. 22—25.

IV. The efficient cause is God, and not any creature, angels nor men.

It is not in the power of men to forgive sin; one man may forgive another an offense, as committed against himself; but not as committed against God: saints ought to forgive one another's offenses that arise among them; as God, for Christ's sake, has forgiven them. Eph. iv. 32: Col. ii. 13.

2. There is nothing a man has, nor can do, by which he can procure the pardon of sin, either for himself, or for others:

1. No man, by his riches, and the multitude of his wealth. can give to God a ransom for himself, or his brother make atonement and satisfaction for sin, and obtain the pardon of it. Riches profit not in the day of wrath: bags of gold and silver will be of no avail.

**2.** Nor is pardon of sin to be obtained by works of righteousness: could it, it would not be of grace; for grace and works are opposed to each other; men would be saved by works, contrary to the scriptures, since pardon is included in salvation, and that is by grace, and not works.

**3.** Nor is pardon procured by repentance; they are both gifts of grace; and though given to the same persons, the one is not the cause of the other, at least, repentance is not the cause of remission; for true, evangelical repentance flows from, and in the exercise of it, is influenced by the discovery and application of pardoning grace. See Ezek. xvi. 63; Luke vii. 37, 47. Nor is pardon procured by faith, as the cause of it; faith does not obtain it by any virtue of its own, but receives it as obtained by the blood of Christ. Acts x. 43; xxvi. 18.

**4.** Nor is it procured by a submission to the ordinance of water baptism; baptism neither takes away original sin, nor actual sin, not as to the guilt thereof, as the case of Simon Magus shows; for though the three thousand are directed to be baptized in the name of Christ, for the remission of sins; and Saul was advised by Ananias to arise, and be baptized, and wash away his sins, Acts ii. 38; xxii. 16, yet the meaning is not, as if remission of sins were to be obtained by baptism; but that by means of this ordinance, they might be led to the sufferings, death, and bloodshed of Christ, represented in it.

**3.** God only can forgive sin; it is his sole prerogative; it belongs to him, and no other. Mark ii. 7; Isa. xliii. 25; Dan. ix. 9. And this appears from the nature of sin itself; it is committed against God; and none but he against whom it is committed can forgive it. Who is a God like unto him that pardoneth iniquity? Mic. vii. 18. Saints in all ages never made their application to any other. Psa. li. 1; Dan. ix. 19; Matt. vi. 9, 12; Acts viii. 22.

**V.** THE EFFECTS OF PARDON, THAT IS, WHEN APPLIED; FOR THE EFFECTS OF IT ARE NOT SENSIBLY PERCEIVED, UNLESS APPLIED; which are,

**1.** Peace of conscience; when sin is charged upon the conscience, and there is no sight and sense of pardon, there is no peace; but no sooner is there a view of interest in justification, by the righteousness of Christ, and pardon by his blood, but there is peace. Rom. v. 1.

**2.** Cheerfulness of spirit: when sin lies as a heavy burden, without a view of pardon, the mind is depressed; it is filled with gloominess, as in the case of Cain: a wounded spirit who can bear? But when the Lord says, "Son or daughter be of good cheer, thy sins are forgiven thee!" cheerfulness takes place; the spirits are raised; the head is lifted up. Psa. li. 8.

**3.** Comfort of soul: whilst a gracious soul, under a sense of sin, apprehends that God is angry with him, he has no comfort; but when he manifests his pardoning grace, then he concludes his anger is turned away, and he is comforted: "Speak ye comfortably to Jerusalem." Isa. xl. 1, 2.

**4.** Access to God with boldness and confidence; a soul, under the weight and pressure of the guilt of sin, moves heavily to the throne of grace; and when he comes there, cannot lift up his eyes; but, looking downward, and smiting on his breast, says, God be merciful to me a sinner; but when it has a view of the blood, righteousness, and sacrifice of Christ, it comes with liberty, boldness, and confidence. Rom. v. 1, 2.

**5.** Attendance on divine worship with pleasure and delight: this flows from a sense of forgiveness of sin, and is one end of it; "There is forgiveness with thee, that thou mayest be feared." Psa. cxxx. 5; Heb. xii. 28.

**6.** Love to God and Christ is raised, promoted, and increased, by an application of pardon. Luke vii. 47.

**7.** Evangelical repentance, and the exercise of it, are much influenced by pardon of sin being applied. Ezek. xvi. 63.

**8.** Thankfulness of soul for such a mercy; than which there cannot be a greater: if a man be truly impressed with the sense of it, he will call upon his soul, and all within him, to bless and praise the Lord for all his benefits; and particularly for this, who forgiveth all thy iniquities! Psa. ciii. 2, 3.

---

## ON CONVERSION.

### Acts iii. 19.—And be converted. (H.)

CONVERSION, though it may seem, in some respects, to fall in with regeneration, yet may be distinguished from it. Regeneration is the sole act of God; conversion consists both of God's act upon men, in turning them, and of acts done by men, under the influence of converting grace; they turn, being turned. Regeneration is the motion of God towards and upon the heart of a sinner; conversion is the motion of a sinner towards God, as one expresses it. In regeneration men are wholly passive, as they are also in the first moment of conversion; but by it become active; it is therefore sometimes expressed passively: Ye are returned or converted, 1 Pet. ii. 25; and sometimes actively; A great number believed, and turned to the Lord, Acts xi. 21, and when it, the body of the people of the Jews, shall turn to the Lord, which has respect to their conversion in the latter day. 2 Cor. iii. 16.

I. WHAT CONVERSION IS AND WHEREIN IT LIES: The conversion to be treated of is not,

1. An external one, or what lies only in an outward reformation of life and manners, such as that of the Ninevites, for this may be where internal conversion is not, as in the Scribes and Pharisees.

2. Nor is it a mere doctrinal one, nor a conversion from false notions before imbibed to a set of doctines and truths which are according to the scriptures; so men of old were converted from Judaism and heathenism to christianity: but all that were so converted to a doctrinal sense were not true and real converts; some had "the form of godliness without the power, a name to live," &c.

3. Nor the restoration of the people of God from backsliding, when they are in a very affecting and importunate manner called upon to return to the Lord; Jer. iii. 12, 14, 22; Hos. xiv. 1—4; so Peter when he fell through temptation, and denied his Lord, and was recovered from it by a look from Christ, it is called his conversion, Luke xxii. 32. But,

4. The conversion under consideration, is a true, real, internal work of God upon the souls of men.

1. In the turn of the heart to God, of the thoughts of the heart; which are only evil, and that continually, and about evil things, not about God, and the things of God: God is not in all their thoughts, nor in any of the thoughts of wicked men; but when converted, their thoughts are about their state and condition by nature, about their souls, and their eternal welfare; it is a turn of the desires of the heart which before were after vain, sinful lusts and pleasures; but now after God and communion with him, after Christ

and salvation : of the affections of the heart, which before were inordinate, and ran in a wrong channel, towards God, their hearts being circumcised to love him ; and whom they love with their whole hearts and souls, because he first loved them. Conversion is a turn of the mind from carnal things to spiritual ones, and from earthly things to heavenly ones ; yea, it is a turn of the will, which before conversion is in a very bad state, is stubborn and inflexible, biassed to and bent upon that which is evil, and averse to all that is good ; but in conversion God works in men both to will and to do of his good pleasure.

2. Conversion lies in a man's being turned from darkness to light ; the apostle was sent to turn them from darkness to light, Acts xxvi. 18, that is, to be the instrument or means of their conversion, by preaching the gospel.

3. From the power of Satan unto God, as in the above place. Acts xxvi. 18. Satan has great power over men in an unconverted state, his seat is in their hearts, which are the palaces in which he rules ; he works effectually with great power and energy in the children of disobedience ; but now in conversion they are turned from his power, he is dispossessed of them, and his armour taken from him in which he trusted ; the prey is taken out of the hands of the mighty.

4. Conversion lies in turning men from idols, to serve the living God ; not merely from idols of silver and gold, of wood and stone, as formerly, but from the idols of a man's own heart, his lusts and corruptions ; with respect to which the language of a converted sinner is, what have I to do any more with idols ? this is a blessing bestowed in conversion. Unto you first, God having raised up his Son Jesus, sent him to bless you, in turning away every one of you from his iniquities.

5. Conversion lies in turning men from their own righteousness to the righteousness of Christ ; not from doing works of righteousness, for such converted persons are most fit for, and most capable of, and are under the greatest obligations to perform : but from depending upon them for justification before God, and acceptance with him.

6. Conversion lies in a man's turning to the Lord actively under the influence of divine grace : and by this phrase it is often expressed in scripture, as in Isa. x. 21 ; Acts xi. 21 ; 2 Cor. iii. 16 ; men being thoroughly convinced that there is salvation in no other but in Christ, that it is in vain to expect it elsewhere ; they turn to Christ as their Lord and lawgiver, and submit to his commands, renouncing all other lords, and their dominion over them ; and though in their natural state they are like sheep going astray, in conversion they are returned to Christ, as the great shepherd and bishop of souls.

II. THE CAUSES OF CONVERSION.

1. The efficient cause, which is not man, but God.

1. Not by the power of man ; what is said of the conversion, or turning of the Jews from their captivity, is true of the conversion of a sinner, that it is not by might, nor by power, that is, not of man, but by my Spirit, saith the Lord of Hosts. Zech. iv. 6. Men are dead in a moral sense whilst unconverted ; they are dead in trespasses and sins, which are the cause of their death ; and their very living in them is no other than a moral death : nor can they quicken themselves, and unless they are quickened, they cannot be converted. Conversion is such an alteration in a man as is not in his power to effect ; it is like that of an Ethiopian changing his skin, and a leopard his spots. Such things are never heard of, as a blackmoor becoming white, and a leopard becoming clear of his spots ; and as unlikely is it, that a man should

convert himself. Jer. xiii. 23. A tree must first be made good, so as to bring forth good fruit.

2. Nor is conversion owing to the will of men; the will of man, before conversion is in a bad state; it chooses its own ways, and delights in its abominations, it is in high pursuit after the desires of the flesh and of the mind. Conversion is denied to be of the will of men; as the whole of salvation is not of him that willeth, so this part of it in particular; regeneration, with which conversion, in the first moment of it, agrees, is not the will of the flesh, nor of the will of man, but of God. Rom. ix. 16; John i. 13.

3. God only is the author and efficient cause of conversion. He that made man's heart, and formed the spirit of man within him, he only can turn their hearts, and frame and mould their spirits, as he pleases; the heart of a king, and so of every other man, is in the hand of the Lord; he makes his people willing in the day of his power, to do what they had before no will nor inclination to do, and yet they act most freely; the man-slayer did not more willingly flee to a city of refuge to shelter him from the avenger of blood, than a sinner, sensible of his danger, flees to Christ for refuge, and lays hold on the hope set before him.

2. The moving or impulsive cause of conversion, is the love, grace, mercy, favor, and good will of God; and not the merits of men; for what is there in men before conversion, to move God to take such a step in their favor; see 1 Cor. vi. 9—11; Eph. ii. 2—4.

3. The instrumental cause, or means of conversion, is usually the ministry of the word; sometimes, indeed, it is wrought without the word, by some remarkable, awakening providence or another, and sometimes by reading the scriptures; but, for the most part, it is through the preaching of the word; hence, ministers are said to turn many to righteousness: and the apostle Paul says, he was sent by Christ unto the Gentile world, to turn men from darkness to light; and this is done both by the preaching of the law and the gospel. The law of the Lord is perfect, converting the soul, Ps. xix. 7, the preaching of the law is made use of by the Spirit of God, to convince of sin, for by the law is the knowledge of sin; though some take this to be rather preparatory to conversion, than conversion itself, which may be ascribed to the gospel. Received ye the Spirit by the works of the law? that is, by preaching the doctrine of obedience to it; or, by the hearing of faith? that is, by the doctrine of the gospel, preaching faith in Christ; which is therefore called the word of faith, and by which it comes; for faith comes by hearing, and hearing by the word of God; Gal. iii. 2; Rom. x. 8—17; but then, the preaching of the word of the gospel is not sufficient of itself to produce the work of conversion in the heart: men may hear it, and not be converted by it; for who is Paul, or who is Apollos, but ministers, or instruments, by whom ye believed? 1 Cor. iii. 5.

III. THE SUBJECTS OF CONVERSION.

Lost sinners redeemed by Christ are the subjects—I will hiss for them, by the ministry of the word, and gather them, which is another phrase for conversion, because I have redeemed them. Zech. x. 8. Sinners shall be converted unto thee; Ps. li. 13; sinners by nature and by practice, and some of them the worst and chief of sinners; and therefore the wonderful grace of God is the more displayed in their conversion. 1 Cor. vi. 11; 1 Tim. i. 3, 14, 15.

## REGENERATION CONSIDERED IN ITS CAUSES AND BENEFITS.

**1 Pet. i. 3—5.**—Blessed be the God, and Father of our Lord Jesus Christ, which according to his abundant mercy, hath begotten us again unto a lively hope, by the resurrection of Jesus Christ from the dead. To an inheritance incorruptible, and undefiled, and that fadeth not away, reserved in heaven for you, who are kept by the power of God, through faith, unto salvation, ready to be revealed in the last time. (S. S.)

THE ungodly may be patient, but are seldom joyful, in affliction—

Their happiness almost entirely depends on outward circumstances—

But the regenerate have sources of joy peculiar to themselves—

Nor can they be in any state wherein they have not abundant cause to bless God—

The persons to whom St. Peter wrote, were scattered abroad, and in a state of persecution—

Yet he begins his epistle to them, not in terms of pity and condolence, but of praise and thanksgiving.

I. THE CAUSES OF REGENERATION.

Regeneration is a spiritual and supernatural change of heart—

But the text requires us to consider it not so much in its nature, as in its causes—

The *efficient* cause of it is God.

God under the Old Testament dispensation, was the God of Abraham—

Under the gospel, he appears under the more endearing title, "the God and Father of our Lord Jesus Christ"—

He is our God and Father also in and through Christ Jesus—

In this relation he is considered as begetting us again—

And he certainly is the Father of our spirits, both in their first formation, and in their subsequent renovation, Compare Heb. xii. 9, with Eph. ii. 10.

The *final* cause or end is our present and eternal happiness.

God begets his people to "a lively hope" *here*—

Their hope is widely different from the cold and carnal hope of the unregenerate—

He has prepared for them also an "inheritance" *hereafter*—

And this inheritance is unspeakably glorious—

Not corruptible, as earthly "treasures, which moth and rust will corrupt"—

Not defiled, like the earthly Canaan, by wicked inhabitants—

Not fading, by use, age, or enjoyment, like the pleasures of sense—

The *instrumental* cause is the Lord Jesus Christ,

Christ is the medium of every blessing, whether of grace or glory—

Our blessings are generally represented as imparted through his death—

But here, as in many other places, they are ascribed to his resurrection—

His resurrection assured to us the acceptance of his sacrifice—

It is also a pledge and earnest of the resurrection of all his members—

Besides, it enables him both to intercede for us, and to send the Spirit to us—

His Word and Spirit are, indeed, the more immediate instruments which God uses—

Yet more remotely may the Resurrection of Christ be considered as the instrumental cause of our regeneration—

The *moving* cause of it is his mercy.

God has not respect to any goodness or merit in the creature—

He is actuated only by his own grace and "mercy"—

Of this the conversion of a soul is a marvelous display—

If the state of a converted person be compared with that of one unconverted, or of one that has perished, he will appear to have experienced " abundant mercy"—

They who have experienced this change are sure to possess at last the benefits connected with it.

II. The security of the regenerate.

Some even of the regenerate are ready to doubt whether God will bestow on them the inheritance they hope for—

Others fear they shall fall short of it through their own frailty—

But God has secured to them the full and everlasting enjoyment of it—

The inheritance is " reserved for them."

Earthly inheritances may be taken away by fraud and violence—

Not even crowns or kingdoms can boast of any stability—

But the saints inheritance is in heaven—

There it is out of the reach of all enemies—

God himself keeps it for his people, as their unalienable right—

They also are kept for it.

They are weak and helpless in themselves—

They are surrounded also with hosts of enemies—

But they commit themselves to God " by faith"—

In so doing they interest the power of God on their behalf—

God keeps them according to his promise, Isa. xxvi. 3 ; Jer. xxxii. 40.

God keeps them as in an impregnable garrison*—

God keeps them unto their full and final salvation—

Infer,

1. How happy are God's people here !

The change they have experienced in regeneration is truly blessed—

The prospects they enjoy are bright and glorious—

Their security enhances these blessings—

What then need they regard in this world ?—

Surely they should rejoice, though in the midst of tribulations—

Let every one then, when encompassed with troubles of whatever kind say, " Blessed be God, who hath begotten me again"—

2. How happy will God's people soon be !

Their inheritance, though at a distance, is a consolation to them—

The very hope of it fills them with joy unspeakable—

It will do this, even under the heaviest afflictions—

What sensations then will the full enjoyment of this inheritance excite !—

What joy will that be when it is without any alloy of sin or sorrow !—

But let us remember, that " we must be born again" in order to have any title to this inheritance, John iii. 3.

If we continue unregenerate, we shall inherit a far different portion—

But if we have really experienced the new birth, we are heirs of glory—

And the salvation reserved for us is " ready to be revealed"—

Let us then labor to secure this glorious inheritance—

And look for it with holy ardour and eager expectation—

This seems to be the import of the word οҫҗҗμένҗ

## CONVERSION A GROUND OF THANKFULNESS.

Rom. vi. 17.   God be thanked, that ye were the servants of sin ; but ye have obeyed from the heart that form of doctrine which was delivered you.   (S. S.)

EXEMPTION from the punishment of sin is doubtless an inestimable blessing—

But deliverance from its power is equally precious—

The most advanced christians greatly delight in this part of salvation—

Hence St. Paul thanks God for bestowing this mercy on the church at Rome—

We shall consider from the text,

I. THE CHARACTER OF ALL WHILE IN AN UNCONVERTED STATE.

All are " servants of sin" till they receive converting grace.

All indeed are not slaves to the same sin—

Some are led captive by their lusts and passions—

Others are drawn away by the pleasures and vanities of the world—

Others are under the dominion of pride and self-righteousness—

But all without exception are alienated from the life of God, Eph. iv. 18.

All are full of unbelief and self-sufficiency—

This, however humiliating, is an indisputable truth.

The scriptures every where assert this respecting fallen man, John viii. 34 ; Rom vi. 16, with the text.

The most eminent saints confess it to have been their own case, Tit. iii. 3

Experience proves it with respect to ourselves—

The very excuse which men offer in extenuation of their sins, viz. " tha they *cannot* live as God requires," establishes this truth—

But it does not remain so in regenerate persons ; as appears from

II. THE CHANGE THEY EXPERIENCE IN CONVERSION.

God instructs them in " the form of sound doctrine."

They hear the declarations of God in his word—

They are enlightened by the Spirit to understand them—

They have the word applied with divine efficacy to their souls—

This form of doctrine they " obey from the heart."

They yet indeed feel a law of sin in their members—

But " they no more serve sin" willingly as before—

On the contrary, " they now delight in the law of God"—

They obey it, not in appearance only or by constraint, but willingly and without reserve—

They are now cast, as it were, into the mould of the gospel.

This is the force of the original; and is the marginal version—

This is also the case, wherever the gospel takes effect, Col. i. 6.

The wax has every lineament of the seal, and the coin of the die—

So do they resemble God, who are renewed by the gospel, 2 Cor. iii 18.

The blessedness of this change will appear if we consider,

III. HOW GREAT A CAUSE OF THANKFULNESS SUCH A CONVERSION IS.

The apostle thanks God that they were no longer slaves of sin.

Sin is at all times a ground of shame and sorrow, Rom. vi. 21.

Paul esteemed it so in his own particular case, 1 Tim. i. 13.

Every saint of God views it in the same light—

St. Paul therefore did not mean that their subjection to it was a ground of thankfulness—

But the subject of his thanksgiving is, that the Romans, who once were slaves of sin, were now entirely devoted to God—

This is a ground of unspeakable thankfulness on many accounts.

1. On account of *the moral change* in the persons themselves.

What can be more deplorable than to be a slave of sin !—

What can be more amiable than to have all our actions and affections corresponding with the the word of God ?—

Surely this is a ground of thankfulness—

2. On account of *the effects* of this change *on society.*

How much better member of society must a child of God be than a slave of sin !—

How much happier would the world be, if such a change were general !—

On this account therefore it became the apostle to be thankful—

3. On account of *the eternal consequences* that must follow this change.

They who die slaves of sin must suffer its punishment—

They are now the children of the devil, and must soon be his companions in misery, John viii. 44.

But the regenerate are children and heirs of God—

Surely eternity will scarcely suffice to thank God for this—

We shall conclude with a suitable ADDRESS,

1. To the unregenerate.

All who have not been freed from sin are of this number—

Alas ! the friends of such have little cause to thank God for them—

They have rather reason to weep and mourn, Jer. xiii. 17.

They may indeed bless God that the stroke of vengeance has been delayed—

O that all such persons might know the day of their visitation !—

Let all cry to God for his converting grace—

Nor let any rest in an external or partial change—

Nothing but a cordial compliance with the gospel, and a real conformity to it, will avail us in the day of judgment—

2. To the regenerate.

The foregoing marks have sufficiently characterized these persons—

Such persons will do well to reflect on the mercy they have received—

The recollection of their past guilt will serve to keep them *humble*—

A consciousness of their remaining infirmities will make them *watchful*—

A view of the change wrought in them will make them *thankful*—

Let the regenerate then adopt the words of the Psalmist, Ps. ciii. 1—3.

Let them beware of ever returning to their former ways, 2 Pet. ii. 20, 21.

Let them press forward for higher degrees of holiness and glory, Phil. iii 13, 14.

3. To those who doubt to which class they belong.

Many, from what has been wrought in them, have reason to hope—

Yet, from what still remains to be done, they find reason to fear—

Hence they are long in painful suspense—

But let such remember, that sin, if truly lamented and resisted, does not prove them unregenerate, Jam. iii. 2.

On the contrary, their hatred of it, and opposition to it, are hopeful signs that they are in part renewed—

Nevertheless, let them endeavor to put this matter beyond a doubt, 2 Pet. i. 10.

Let them look to Christ as their almighty deliverer, John viii. 36.

Let them pray for, and depend upon, his promised aid, 2 Cor. xii. 9,

## THE IMPORTANCE OF SANCTIFICATION.

Col iii. 11.—Christ is all, and in all.* (H. H.)

In order to ascertain the true sense of any passage of scripture, two things are to be attended to : we should mark the scope of the context, and compare the terms or phrases with similar passages of Holy Writ.  By separating these canons of interpretation, we shall often overlook the true meaning of God's word, and put upon it a forced construction; whereas, if we unite them, we shall almost always find its just import.

It is undeniable that the verses which precede and follow our text refer to sanctification; see ver. 1—14 ; nor is there any thing which properly relates to our justification : and therefore we have a strong presumptive ground for interpreting the words of our text in reference to the new nature, which is spoken of in the verse immediately before it: nor could any thing but the peculiarity of the expression lead one for a moment to look for any other sense.  But it seems that to interpret the word " Christ," as meaning the image of Christ, or the New Man, is to take a great, and almost an unwarrantable, liberty with scripture.  Nevertheless, if we compare some other passages with the text,† we shall find that we are fully authorized to put this construction upon it, and that there is no necessity to understand it in any other way than that which the context so evidently requires.

The meaning then of the words before us is simply this.  We should be daily putting off our old and corrupt nature, and be putting on a new and holy nature; because nothing else will be at all regarded by God : whatever advantages we possess, we have nothing, if we be not holy : on the other hand, whatever disadvantages we labor under, we shall suffer no loss, if we be holy : for the image of " Christ" on the soul " is all, in all" persons, and under all circumstances : where that is, God will be pleased ; and where that is not, he will be eternally displeased.

In order to confirm this momentous truth, we shall shew, that, in the eyes of God, *our restoration to the divine image " is all in all."*  It is,

I. THE ONE SCOPE OF ALL HIS PLANS—

What did he design in the redemption of the world at large?

When first he determined to rescue man from perdition, he decreed that he would " create us anew in Christ Jesus *unto good works*, in which he ordained that we should walk."  Eph. ii. 10.

The means which he used for the accomplishment of our salvation had especial respect to this end, not to save us *in* our sins, but *from* them.  Matt. i. 21 ; Acts iii. 26.

---

* The author has formerly treated this text as Commentators in general have done, in reference to our justification before God.  But he apprehends on further consideration, that it refers rather to our sanctification.  In either sense, the position is true, that " Christ is all ;" but the latter interpretation seems more exactly to convey the mind of the Spirit in this passage.  The reader, by comparing the two statements, will be enabled to judge for himself.

† See 2 Cor. xiii. 5, where " Christ in us" must be understood of his image, because it is that whereby we are to ascertain whether we be in the faith.  See also Gal. iv. 19, where " Christ formed in us" cannot be understood of Christ *personally*, but of Christ *spiritually*, i. e. of his image.  Above all, see Rom. xiii 14, where the very metaphor which occurs in our context, is used.  " Put on the new man," says our context, " for Christ," i. e. the putting on of Christ, or of the new man, " is all."  And, in the passage referred to, 's the very expression, " Put ye on the Lord Jesus Christ."

He sent his only dear Son to take our nature, and in that nature to live, to die, to rise again. But in all this he aimed, not at our happiness merely, but our restoration to the image which we had lost. Gal. i. 4; 1 Pet. i. 18, 19, and ii. 24; Tit. ii. 14. This is specified in terms peculiarly strong and energetic, in order that we may not overlook this truth as if it were only of secondary importance. Eph. v. 25—27.

He gave his Holy Spirit also for the same end: he gave him to humble us, John xvi. 8—11, to renew us, Tit. iii. 5, 6, to mortify all our vile lusts and passions, Rom. viii. 13, to fashion us after the divine image,* and to perfect that image in our souls. 2 Cor. iii. 18.

What does he design in imparting that redemption to individuals?

Wherefore did he choose any of us from before the foundation of the world? It was "that we might be holy, and without blame before him in love." Eph. i. 4. Why has he revealed his grace in our hearts? It was to "teach us, that, denying ungodliness and worldly lusts, we should live righteously, soberly, and godly in this present world." Tit. ii. 11, 12. If he apply his promises to our souls, or hide his face from us, it is alike for our profit, that we may be partakers of his holiness." 2 Cor. vii. 1, with Heb. xii. 10. Whatever be his dispensations towards us, "this is his will, even our sanctification;" 1 Thess. iv. 3; and this is his ultimate design in all, even to "carry on the good work he has begun," Phil. i. 6, to "sanctify us wholly," 1 Thess. v. 23, and to "perfect that which concerneth us." Psa. cxxxviii. 8.

But holiness is also,

II. The one object of his regard—

Nothing but that is regarded by him in this world—

The external ordinances of religion are not only worthless, but even hateful, in his sight, if destitute of solid piety. Isa. i. 11—16. On the other hand, the smallest particle of genuine goodness is not overlooked by him. 1 Kings xiv. 13. Even the semblance of it has sometimes been rewarded by him, in order that he might shew to mankind how great a value he has for it, where it really exists. 1 Kings xxi. 29. One single disposition is declared by him to be of great price in his sight. 1 Pet. iii. 4. The purposes which have never been realized in act, are highly commended by him. 1 Kings viii. 18. And wherever he sees a person laboring to do his will, he invariably reveals to him his love in a more abundant measure, John xiv. 23, and communicates to him his richest blessings. Isa. lviii. 10, 11.

Nothing but that will be regarded by him in the world to come—

When we shall stand at the judgment-seat of Christ, the inquiry will be, not, what we have professed, but what we have done: Matt. vii. 21—23, and xxv. 31—46; and a Gentile who has served God according to the light that he enjoyed, will be preferred before the christian, who has not made a suitable improvement of his superior advantages. Rom. ii. 25—27. Apparently trivial occurrences will be noticed in that day; and rewards will be dispensed, not according to the greatness and splendor of our actions, but according to their intrinsic qualities, and to the principle evinced by them. Matt. x. 42. We must not indeed imagine that there is any *merit* in our poor services, for there is imperfection in them all; and, "if we had done all that is commanded us, we should be only unprofitable servants:" but God delights in holiness; and wherever he beholds it, he will, of his own

---

*Eph. iv. 23, 24, with 2 Cor. i. 22. A "seal" is an impress of the divine image; and an "earnest" is the commencement of heavenly purity and joy.

grace and mercy, bestow upon it a proportionate reward, exalting those to the highest thrones in glory, who have made the greatest improvement of the talents committed to them. Matt. xxv. 19—23.

There will be no distinction made, except what is grounded on the different degrees of conformity to the divine image which the different individuals have attained. God will not respect the circumcised more than the uncircumcised, or the rich and learned more than the poor and illiterate. In all persons equally the image of Christ will be sought for; and the possession, or want of it. will determine their eternal state : " Christ will then be, as he now is, all, and in all.

We conclude with INQUIRING, *Who amongst you is like-minded with God?*

1. Ye children of this world—

How far are ye from according with God! With him, *Christ* is all; with you, *the world.* If ye may but enjoy the pleasures, the honors, the riches of the world, ye care not about the image of Christ: to be rich in faith and good works is no' the object of your ambition: *that* you leave to the old, the sick, the enthusiasts. But ah! if Christ be *all*, as indeed he is, think what a vanity ye are pursuing: think how poor ye will be in the day of judgment; and how you will then execrate your present ways. Be persuaded to be wise in time: and beg without delay that " Christ may be made unto you wisdom, and righteousness, and sanctification, and redemption." 1 Cor. i. 30.

2. Ye self-deceiving professors—

How many are there in the church, who will talk about Christ, and speak of him as the ground of all their hopes, while yet they are shamefully destitute of his image! Yes, grievous it is to say, that there are " many vaintalkers and deceivers" now, as well as in the apostolic age; many that are proud and passionate; many that are earthly-minded and covetous; many that are unchaste and lewd ; many that are deceitful in their words, and dishonest in their dealings; many in short, whose tempers, and dispositions, and conduct, are a disgrace to their profession. Know ye, if such there be here present, that ye are as unlike to God as Satan himself is; and that all your knowledge, all your experiences, and all your professions, will only aggravate your condemnation, if you die in your present state. Job xxxvi. 13. You do well to rely on Christ, and to make him your *all* in point of dependence ; but know for a certainty, that, however you may pretend to trust in him, you never can be saved by him, unless you become new creatures : 2 Cor. 5, 17; for "without holiness no man shall see the Lord." Heb. xii. 14.

3. Ye true believers—

You can appeal to God that you are like-minded with him in this grand point; and that you desire as much to be saved from sin, as to be delivered from hell itself. This is a blessed evidence that ye are born of God. 1 John iii. 10. While ye are thus panting after holiness, ye have nothing to fear; your faith is sound, James ii. 22, your hope is scriptural, 1 John iii. 3, and saving. Rom. v. 5, and viii. 24. Go on then from grace to grace, from strength to strength. 2 Pet. iii. 18. Be daily putting off the old man with its lusts, ver. 8, 9, and putting on the new man with all its characteristic graces. Ver. 12, 13. Be "growing up thus into Christ in all things as your living Head," Eph. iv. 15, till you have arrived at " the full measure of the stature of Christ :" ib. ver. 13 ; and when you have attained a perfect meetness for the enjoyment of your God, you shall be like him, and with him for ever. 1 John iii. 2.

## THE EXCELLENCY AND EFFICACY OF THE GOSPEL.

2 Cor. iii. 18. But we all with open face beholding, as in a glass, the glory of the Lord, are changed into the same image, from glory to glory, even as by the Spirit of the Lord. (S. S.)

The Jews, when compared with the heathen world, were highly privileged—

But the dispensation under which they lived was in every respect inferior to that of the gospel—

The apostle, in vindicating his own character, incidentally mentions the blessings which the Corinthians had experienced by means of his ministry—

Hence he takes occasion to set forth the superior excellency of the gospel above the law—

In confirmation of this point we will consider,

I. THE EXCELLENCY OF THE GOSPEL.

In the context the law is spoken of as a ministration of condemnation—

Whereas the gospel is a ministration of the Spirit and of righteousness—

It is a revelation of the " glory of the Lord."

The law was in some degree a manifestation of the divine glory—

It displayed, however, chiefly the majesty and holiness of the Deity—

But the gospel displays the love and mercy of God—

It exhibits all the perfections of God harmonizing and glorified in the work of redemption—

Thus it is a revelation of the glory of God in the face of Jesus Christ, 2 Cor. iv. 6.

It manifests this glory to the soul.

Moses veiled the divine lustre which shined in his face—

This was an intimation to the Jews that they could not comprehend the full scope of the law which he published, ver. 13.

But this veil is taken away by Christ, ver. 14.

The gospel reflects Christ's glory as a mirror reflects the sun—

We behold that glory " with open, i. e. *unveiled* face"—

This is the common privilege of "all" who believe—

Nor is it more excellent in its discoveries than in its effects.

II. THE EFFICACY OF IT.

The apostle ascribes a wonderful efficacy to the gospel—

Experience attests the truth of his declarations—

It transforms the soul into the divine image.

A view of Jehovah's glory caused the face of Moses to shine—

So a view of Christ's glory in the gospel changes our hearts—

It renews us after the very image of our Lord and Savior—

It does this, notwithstanding we may have been hitherto most abandoned—

Every fresh discovery which it makes to us of Christ's glory increases that effect.

The first exercise of faith in Christ makes a great change—

But subsequent views of his glory advance the work of sanctification—

In this way is our progress in holiness carried on to perfection—

This power, however, it derives wholly from " the Spirit of the Lord."

The gospel has not that power in itself—

Were its power inherent, it would operate uniformly on all—

But its operation is dependent on the will of God, 1 Cor. xii. 11.

The word is called " the sword of the Spirit"—

It is the Spirit's instrument whereby he subdues souls to the obedience of faith—

Every fresh effect produced by it arises from the concurring operation of the Spirit—

Yet, as it is the great instrument whereby the Spirit works, the effects are properly ascribed to—

INFER,

1. How great a blessing it is to have the gospel preached to us

Nothing else will produce the effects here ascribed to the gospel—

The terrors of the law may alarm, but will not sanctify the heart—

But the mild accents of the gospel win the soul—

A manifestation of Christ's glory constrains us to obedience—

Let all rejoice therefore in hearing the glad tidings—

Let all endeavor to experience these glorious effects—

2. Whence it is that many make so small a proficiency in holiness.

Many truly desire to advance in holiness—

But they seek it in dependence on their own strength—

Hence they make a small proficiency in the divine life—

They should rather use the means prescribed in the text—

They should be often occupied in surveying the glory of Christ—

The discoveries of his glory would do more than all their legal exertions—

Let every eye therefore be fixed on him, till the effects appear both in our hearts and lives—

Our views of him ere long shall be incomparably brighter, 1 Cor. xiii. 12

Then the effects also shall be proportionably increased, 1 John iii. 2.

---

## THE GOSPEL FREES MEN FROM SIN AND DEATH.

Rom. viii. 2.—The law of the Spirit of life in Christ Jesus hath made me free from the law of sin and death. (S. S.)

THE world in general account it liberty to live loose to their passions—

But such freedom is indeed the sorest bondage to sin and Satan, Rom. vi. 16.

None possess true liberty but those who are freed by Christ, John viii. 36.

The state of the demoniacs when healed by Christ resembled theirs, Luke viii. 35.

Paul was made a glorious example of it to all ages—

He was once under condemnation, both because he adhered to the covenant of works, and was governed by his own impetuous will—

He now rejoiced in a freedom from the sin that he had indulged, and from the curse to which he had subjected himself—" The law of," &c.

We shall first *explain*, and then *improve* the text.

I. EXPLAIN IT.

It is not needful to state the various interpretations given of the text—

We shall adopt that which seems most easy, and agreeable to the context—

We will begin with *explaining the terms*.

" The law of the Spirit of life in Christ Jesus" is the gospel covenant as confirmed to us in Christ, and revealed to us by the Spirit.

The "Spirit of life" is the Holy Ghost, who is the author and preserver of spiritual life, John iii. 5. Eph. iii. 16.

The "law" of the Spirit is the gospel as revealed and applied by him—
It is called a law because it has all the essential properties of a law*—
It is often spoken of as a law both by prophets and apostles, Isaiah ii. 3 Rom. iii. 27.

It is said to be the law of the Spirit " in Christ Jesus," because the blessings of the gospel are treasured up in Christ, confirmed to us through Christ, and received by us from Christ, Col. i. 19 ; 2 Cor. i. 20 ; John i. 16.

" The law of sin and death" may be understood either of the covenant of works or of our indwelling corruption.

The covenant of works is a " law" to which all are by nature subject—
It is called the " law of sin and death," because both sin and death come by that law†

Our indwelling corruption also operates as "a law" within us, Rom. vii 23.

It invariably hurries us on to " sin and death," Rom. vii. 5.

We shall next *explain the proposition contained in the terms.*

The proposition is, that " the gospel frees us from the curse of the law, and from the dominion of sin."

When we embrace the gospel we cease to be under the covenant of works, Rom. vi. 14, latter part.

We then partake of all the blessings which Christ has purchased for us—
We are liberated from the condemnation due to sin, Rom. viii. 1.

We are freed, through the aid of the Spirit, from the power of sin, Rom. viii. 13 ; and vi. 14, former part.

This proposition is to be understood as extending to all believers.

It is not true with respect to the apostles only—
It was exemplified in all the first converts‡—
And is experienced still by every sincere christian—
The text thus explained is capable of most useful improvement.

II. IMPROVE IT.

It is replete with very important *instruction.*

It shews us the wretched state of every unregenerate man.

We are all in bondage to "the law of sin and death"—
We are justly subjected to the curses of the broken law, Gal. iii. 10.

We are also led captive by our own corrupt appetites—
Even St. Paul himself was in this very state, Rom. vii. 9.

Let us then humble ourselves under a conviction of this truth—
It declares to us the only method of deliverance from that state.

It was the gospel which freed the apostle—
The same will avail for every other person—
We must however " obey the gospel," and receive it as our " law of faith"—

* A law is a precept enforced with sanctions ; and such is the gospel : it is a precept, 1 John iii. 23 ; and it is enforced with the most encouraging and awful sanctions, Mark xvi. 16.

† Without that law there had been no transgression, and consequently, no sin (which is the transgression of a law ;) nor death (which is the penalty inflicted for transgression)— Compare 1 John iii. 4. Rom. v. 13. 1 Cor. xv. 56. Hence it is called " the ministration of death and condemnation." 2 Cor. iii. 7, 9.

‡ One hour they were full of guilt and wickedness ; the next they were rejoicing in the pardon of their sins, and in the practice of all holy duties. Acts ii. 46, 47

We must look for its blessings from Christ through the Spirit—

In this way we may all adopt the language of the text in reference to our own happy existence—

It affords also abundant matter of *reproof.*

It reproves those who despond as though there were no hope for them.

Many think their guilt too great to be pardoned, and their lusts too strong to be subdued—

But Paul's case was intended to prevent such desponding fears, 1 Tim. i. 16.

Let none therefore any more complain like those of old, Ezek. xxxvii. 11.

Every one may find encouragement in the power and mercy of God, Isa. lxi. 1.

It reproves also those who speak against an assurance of faith.

It would indeed be presumptuous in some to profess an assurance of faith—

But God is desirous that all his people should enjoy it, 1 John v. 13.

Let not any one therefore reprobate it as presumption—

Let every one rather seek the assurance expressed in the text—

It may administer *comfort* also to many sincere christians.

Many are yet fighting against their manifold corruptions—

And because they obtain not a perfect deliverance, they tremble under apprehensions of the divine wrath—

But Paul himself bewailed bitterly his indwelling corruption, Rom. vii. 24.

Yet that did not prevent him from rejoicing in the partial freedom he experienced—

Let upright souls take comfort from this reflection.

## TRUE BELIEVERS THE CHILDREN OF GOD.

Gal. iii. 26.—For ye are all the children of God, &c. (H.)

In the context the apostle shows the superior excellency of the gospel dispensation to that of the law. Those who were under it, were "shut up," &c. Ver. 23. It was only as a schoolmaster, &c. Ver. 24. The blessings of heaven are no longer confined to one nation, but extend to all ; ver. 28; and especially to all true believers—"For ye are all the children of God," &c. I shall,

I. Consider the sonship of believers under the gospel.

I need scarcely observe, that believers are not the sons of God in the same sense as our blessed Lord, whose generation is ineffable ; being one in nature, perfections, and glory with the Father.—But,

1. In common with the other intelligent creatures of God. In this respect, they have all one Father. In a peculiar manner, he is the Father of Spirits. In the intellectual powers, moral endowments, and immortality of the soul, they resemble him, for these are his image. Hence angels are called his sons, and Adam, the son of God; nay, the whole human race is said to be his off-spring. Acts xvii. 29.

2. They are children of God by their external profession, and a peculiar relation to him. In this sense, Israel is called his first-born, and his son, Hos. xi. 1 ; Matt. ii. 15.

3 This sonship consists chiefly in their regeneration and adoption. By the last, there is a change in their state. Formerly they were the slaves of Satan, and rebels; but now the friends of God, as was Abraham. By regeneration there is a change in their principles, disposition, and practice. They are born again, 1 Peter i. 23, and are partakers of the divine nature. The resemblance is real, though greatly inferior to the original. Hence, God is not ashamed to be called their God, nor is Christ ashamed to call them brethren. Which leads me to observe,

4. That this sonship is not a mere title or mark of distinction, but has privileges the most excellent annexed to it: there is no condemnation to them: they are his temples; led by his Spirit; abide in their Father's house; yea, in his heart and love; but particularly,

They have a title to incorruption and immortality, or a blessed resurrection. The body must die, but it is redeemed as well as the soul; was his habitation, while here, through the Spirit, and an instrument in his service; and he will raise it again. Rom. viii. 23.

They are born to a great inheritance. Though children of wrath by nature, yet, in virtue of adoption, they are heirs of salvation with eternal glory. They are heirs of God himself, Rom. viii. 17, and have indeed a goodly heritage. Psa. xvi. 5.

5. This sonship is equally the privilege of every believer in Christ. "Ye are all the children of God," says the apostle. They may be distinguished from each other, as to external circumstances in life, spiritual gifts and graces, but their filial relation is the same.

6. It is a privilege of which they are conscious, and hence they enjoy the comfort of it: with holy confidence, they cry, Abba, Father; Gal. iv. 6; and delight in approaching to him, with a childlike holy boldness in prayer.

II. How IT IS THAT THEY ATTAIN TO THIS PRIVILEGE AND DIGNITY.— The text says, by faith in Christ Jesus. To illustrate this, it may be proper to recollect,

1. That in the state of primitive innocence, Adam was truly the son of God: he resembled God. Gen. i. 27. This resemblance was effaced by sin, his former relation to God as his son then ceased, and he was turned out of God's family and garden as a rebel, while he and his numerous progeny became children of disobedience and wrath.

2. It is by faith, or a supernatural revelation only, that we are informed how this high prerogative of sonship may be regained. This surpassed the capacity of the wisest philosopher, and even of angels themselves. It is brought to light by the gospel. Gal. iv. 4, 5.

What a marvellous climax, and cluster of divine prodigies are here! Recount them with admiration! The mission and incarnation of God's own Son—his abject condition as a servant, under the grievous yoke of the law—himself a ransom for the slaves of sin—these slaves taken into fellowship with himself—to whom he grants this divine filiation!

3. We become the children of God, when we cordially believe in Christ: we are thereby brought into union with Christ, and into a dear relation to God, as his Father and ours. We are then born of God, and have the principle or seed of the life of God in the soul; and, consequently, are his children, and in an adopted state; suitable to that relation. John i. 12. To conclude.

1. From what has been said, let me address the children of God in the words of the beloved apostle. 1 John iii. 1. Be astonished ye heavenly principalities and powers, to see such base-born slaves, and rebellious crea-

tures taken into the family of God; rank in dignity with you, and made heirs of the same inheritance. Unmeasurable love!

The immunities and glory of the adopted state are beyond description. It is an adoption procured at an infinite price, and elevates to high honor. "Is it a light thing," said David, "to be the king's son-in-law?" But what is this when compared to that of being the sons and daughters of the Almighty.

2. Forget not the love and duty, submission and service, that results from this relation. If I be a father, says God, where is mine honor?

Should not this filial relation reconcile you to the cross, though heavy? It is the lot assigned by Infinite Wisdom, and sent in great kindness. Heb. xii. 6.

Are you indeed of the same family and Father? What a mighty motive is this to love as brethren, to be pitiful, and courteous, and kindly affected one to another, forbearing and forgiving one another, &c.

While mingled here with the children of this world, be watchful least you imbibe their spirit, learn their ways and vices, stain your character, and be a scandal to your profession. Remember that you have in you the blood-royal of heaven, and being washed in the blood of Jesus from your sins, return not to wallow in the mire—That ye may be blameless. Phil. ii. 15.

3. How insipid, alas! are subjects of this kind to the generality even of gospel hearers! Show them how to acquire a fortune, &c., and they will be all attention; but publish the riches of God's gracious adoption, they relish it not. Blinded sinner, what a fatal choice dost thou make! What though thou hadst the wisdom of a Solomon, the wealth of a Crœsus, the beauty of an Absalom, and were as high in dignity and power as ever Haman was, if thou art not a child of God, thou shalt at last lie down in sorrow, and be brought out of the grave to the day, the dreadful day of the perdition of ungodly men.

---

## THE INCREASE OF CHRIST'S KINGDOM.

John iii. 30.—He must increase. (H.)

THESE are the words of John the Baptist, in answer to a complaint which his disciples made concerning Christ, who, it appears, was baptising great multitudes; v. 26; afraid, perhaps, that he would eclips the glory of their Master. John tells them, that he had told them before that he was not the Messiah, but his forerunner; and that now he was come, his joy was fulfilled, v. 29. He, says he, must increase. I shall consider,

I. WHAT THE INCREASE OF CHRIST'S KINGDOM AND GLORY IS WHICH WE ARE TO EXPECT.

It is the increase of his mediatorial kingdom. and the manifestation of his glory in the world. This implies,

1. The spread of gospel light through the world. It is in this way the man of sin is to be destroyed, 2 Thess. ii. 8, and the earth filled with heavenly knowledge. Hab. ii. 14.

2. That many burning and shining lights will be employed for this purpose—men full of holy fire an zeal for God, willing to run all hazards, by sea and land, to spread the glo r of Christ, Dan. xii. 4.

**3.** That the number of Christ's subjects shall be greatly increased; this will be to his honor, Prov. xiv. 28. His arrows will be sharp in the hearts of his enemies, and his converts numerous as the drops of dew. Ps. cx 2, 3.

4. That truth shall triumph over error: that infidelity, Deism, Arianism, Socinianism, and popery, with all its superstition, shall then give way before the blaze of the Sun of Righteousness.

5. The increase of true piety, when the followers of Christ shall be wholly devoted to him—manifesting holy tempers, holy conversation, and a holy life.

6. An increase of zeal and public spirit among Christians. They shall boldly confess Christ before men ; use every resource, and exert all their powers, to promote the good of mankind.

II. THE TIMES AND SEASONS OF THIS GLORIOUS INCREASE.

1. The apostolic age was the most remarkable time that was ever known ; when every sermon made new conquests and additions to the church, till every city and corner of the vast Roman empire was filled with christians. But,

2. We have promises of a more full and glorious increase of Christ's kingdom in the latter day, or towards the end of the world, Dan. ii. 28—44 ; vii. 27.

The image represents the four grand monarchies. The Babylonian, is the golden head ; the Medo-Persian, the breast and arms of silver ; the Macedonian, or Grecian, the belly and thighs of brass ; and the Roman, the legs of iron, &c. which was to break and bruise all the rest; Dan. ii. 40 ; but, in its last stage, was itself to be divided into ten lesser kingdoms, represented by the ten toes ; and in another vision, by ten horns. Chap. vii. and Rev. xvii.

Then follows the establishment of the Messiah's kingdom. This is the stone mentioned Dan. ii. 34, which is to become a great mountain, and fill the world, v. 35. A kingdom which will swallow up all others and be established forever. Ver. 44.

These ten toes, horns, or kings, shall oppose the Lamb in his grand designs ; but he shall overcome them by the word of his power, and shall range themselves under his banner ; shall hate the whore of Babylon, the church of Rome, and make her desolate. Rev. xvii. 12—16.

Then shall the kingdoms of the world become the kingdoms of Christ. Rev. xi. 15.

The great river Euphrates will be dried up, to prepare the way for the kings of the east. Rev. xvi. 12.

The blindness of the Jews will be removed, and the fulness of the Gentiles shall come in. Rom. xi. 1, 25, 26.

Jerusalem shall be rebuilt, and be holy. Isa. lx. 10, 12, 13, 21.

The Jews shall be gathered out of all countries where they are dispersed Ezek. xxxvi. 24, 28.

All nations shall be gathered together to see his glory. Isa. ii. 2.

There shall be no more war between nations. Isa. ii. 4.

When these prophecies are fulfilled, what a glorious increase will it be to the Mediator's kingdom and glory ! Then shall be accomplished the overthrow of Babylon and Antichrist, the destruction of the Turkish empire, the bringing in of the Jews, with the fulness of the Gentiles !

Glorious period ! and we have ground to expect that we are arrived at the eve of that eventful period. Hence the establishment of Bible and Missionary So ieties, and the lively interest which rich and poor, and even **crowned** heads, are taking in the spread of the gospel to the ends of the earth. indeed, such a public spirit for doing good was never before, to the same extent, witnessed in the Christian world. This appears to be the dawn of a glorious day.

But previous to this glorious event, there will be

1. A very general defection in the churches of Christ; 2 Pet. ii. 1; which, in many instances, is awfully the case already.

2. There will be great numbers of infidels, and profane scoffers, deriding serious godliness, and contemning the promises. 2 Pet. iii. 3, 4.

3. Great troubles in the world, and great fear and distress in the church. Dan. xii. 1; also Matt. xxiv., and Luke xxi.

4. Great security among the enemies of Christ, and the Romish harlot is lifted up with pride. Rev. xvii. 7, 8.

5. A marvellous revolution in one of the ten horns, Rev. xi. 13: or one of the ten kingdoms: this is understood by many of the kingdom of France. Then shall Christ arise, and his enemies be scattered.

III. The reasons why Christ must increase.

1. Because it is the purpose and promise of God. Promised to the church. Jer. xxiii. 5. To Christ himself. Ps. ii. 8; and cx. 1, 2 And he will not alter. Ps. lxxxix. 34, 34.

2. Because for this very purpose God made the world, and he hath committed to Christ the administration of Providence. Isa. ix. 6. To secure the accomplishment of the glorious promises. Matt. xxviii. 18; Eph. i. 22.

2. Because Christ is the beloved of the Father. Matt. iii. 17. He fulfilled his will in the redemption of the world. Phil. ii. 8. And has obtained a name above every name, &c. Phil. ii. 8—10. To conclude, I would observe.

1. Under these circumstances it is in vain for any one to attempt to stop this glorious work. He must increase. Ps. ii. 1—4.

2. What encouragement we have to pray, as our Lord directs, "Thy Kingdom come."

3. How encouraging is the prospect to the friends of Christ? The church will outlive all its enemies. Christ must overcome, he must triumph.

4. And let every one, in their different spheres of action, do all they can to increase the Redeemer's glory. Dreadful shall be the state of those who are unconcerned in this great work. Amos vi. 1, 6; Esther iv. 14

---

## THE SINNER'S FAITH.

Luke vii. 50.—And he said to the woman, Thy faith hath saved thee; go in peace. (S. S )

To associate with the ungodly world is by no means expedient for those who have been redeemed out of the world. Yet there is a certain degree of intercourse with them which is both proper and desirable. There is a medium between an affecting of their society for our own gratification, and a contemptuous separation from them. Our blessed Lord has exhibited, as in every thing else, so in this also, a perfect pattern. When invited by a Pharisee to dinner, he accepted the invitation with a view to instruct him and Jo him good : and when a woman who had been a notorious sinner came to him at the Pharisee's house, he did not refuse her admission to his presence, but received with kindness the expressions of her regard, and imparted to her both the blessings and the comforts of his salvation.

The particular notice which our Lord took of the woman's *"faith,"* and the reward he gave her on account of it, leads us naturally to consider,

I. The marks and evidences of her faith

The first thing that calls for our attention is,

1. Her zeal.

She had doubtless seen many of our Lord's miracles, and heard many of his discourses; and though she was not yet one of his avowed followers, yet, having received good to her soul, she was desirous of honoring him to the utmost of her power. For this purpose she sought him out in the Pharisee's house, and went to him with a full determination to shew him some signal mark of her regard.

Now this argued no little zeal. She was of the weaker sex, and therefore the more liable to be condemned as officious, impertinent, and obtrusive. She was of a notoriously vile character, and therefore still more obnoxious to insult and contempt. But unmindful of these things, she went uninvited, to the house of a proud Pharisee (where she was least of all likely to meet with any favor) and (indifferent to the construction that might be put upon her conduct by any censorious spectators, or even to the treatment she might receive from them) in the presence of the whole company expressed to him all that was in her heart.

And what was it that enabled her thus to "despise all shame," and to triumph over the fear of man? Doubtless it was her faith: for the apostle says, "This is the victory that overcometh the world, even our faith."

2. Her humility.

Though she was bent on executing her pious purpose, she was solicitous to do it in as private and modest a manner as she could. She therefore went behind him as he lay upon the couch,* and, having easy access to his feet, placed herself there, without attracting the notice of the company, or interfering with the conversation that might be passing at table.

This also was a strong mark and evidence of her faith. She knew his august character, and felt herself unworthy to enter into his presence; yea, she accounted it the very summit of her ambition to be permitted to kiss his feet. It was in this way that the faith of the centurion and others shewed itself: Luke vii. 6, 7 ; Mark v. 25—28 ; and though, through the remaining pride and ignorance of their hearts, young converts often, like Jehu, seek the notice and applause of men, humility will always be found to exist in the soul in exact proportion to our faith.

3. Her contrition.

No sooner had she placed herself near the Saviour, than all her sins presented themselves to her mind, and filled her with deep compunction. Instantly she burst into a flood of tears, with which she bathed, as it were, the feet of her Lord, while she embraced them, in hopes of finding mercy from the friend of sinners.

Now it is the property of faith to "look on him whom we have pierced, and mourn." Zech. xii. 10. Yea, the more lively faith any have possessed, the more abundant has been their self-loathing and se'f-abhorrence. Jes

They did not sit at table as we do, but lay on couches.

xlii. 6; Isa. vi. 5; 1 Tim. i. 15. We cannot doubt therefore but that **faith** was the principle from whence her humiliation flowed.

4. Her love.

While she wept over the Saviour's feet, she wiped them with the hairs of her head, and kissed them, and anointed them with odoriferous ointment. It was not possible for her to manifest stronger tokens of her affection.

And was not this also an evidence of her faith? Had she been an unbeliever, she would have seen " no beauty or comeliness in Jesus" that deserved her admiration : Isa. liii. 2; but believing in him, she accounted him " fairer than ten thousand, and altogether lovely," Cant. v. 10, 16, according to that declaration of the apostle, To them that believe, he is precious. 1 Peter ii. 7.

5. Her confidence.

She would not have ventured to approach the Pharisee in this manner, because she knew that he would despise her in his heart, and dismiss her with scorn. But she felt no apprehension of such treatment from the Saviour. She well knew his condescension and compassion ; and therefore without reserve, and without fear, she cast herself upon his mercy.

In this too she shewed the strength of her faith. Unbelief would have suggested many doubts ; Will he receive me? Will he deign to look upon such an abandoned wretch? But faith enabled her to approach him under a full persuasion, that " whosoever came to him should in no wise be cast out."

It was not in vain that she thus approached the Saviour ; as we shall see, while we consider,

II. The fruits and consequences of her faith.

Though despised and condemned by the Pharisee, she was well rewarded by her Lord. She obtained from him.

1. The pardon of her sins.

Numerous as her iniquities had been, they were all in one moment blotted from the book of God's remembrance. Jesus, who "had all power on earth to forgive sins," pardoned all her offences, and " cast them, as it were, behind him into the very depths of the sea." What a blessed fruit and consequence of her faith was this ! Had she been subjected to all the evil treatment that could have been shewn her, she would have had no reason to regret that conduct by which she had obtained so inestimable a blessing.

And was this peculiar to her? Shall not we also have our iniquities forgiven, if we apply to him in humility and faith? Shall the greatness of our sins be any bar to our acceptance with him, if we repent and believe? Let the word of God be deemed worthy of any credit, and all such apprehensions will vanish in an instant— — —Acts xiii. 39 ; Isa. i. 18.

2. An assurance of her acceptance.

Twice did our Lord repeat to her the joyful tidings, that her sins were pardoned, and that her soul was saved ; and to confirm it, he bade her depart in peace. What a cordial must this have been to her drooping spirit ! How transported must she have been with the joyful sound ! And what comfort must she enjoy through life in a sense of the divine favor, and in a prospect of the divine glory !

But neither was this peculiar to her. It is true, that many real christians never attain to this high privilege : but it is owing to the weakness of their faith : if their faith operated as hers did, if it shewed itself in such humility, such contrition, such love, such confidence, such zeal, they also should hear him say to them, " Be of good cheer ; thy sins are forgiven thee." What though he should not utter it by an audible voice from heaven, can he not reveal it to the soul by his Spirit, and enable us to say, "My beloved is mine, and I am his?" Cant. ii. 16. Yes: let us only glorify him to the utmost of our power, and he will give us a peace that passeth all understanding, Phil. iv. 7, and a full assurance of hope unto the end." Heb. vi. 11. See also 2 Tim. i. 12, and iv. 8.

3. Everlasting happiness and glory.

In the declaration of Jesus she received both an earnest and a pledge of her eternal inheritance. Nor can we doubt but that after waiting her " appointed time upon earth," she was admitted to the enjoyment of her Lord in heaven, not any longer to weep at his feet, but to sit with him on his throne, and to participate his glory.

Thus also shall it be with all who truly believe: "they shall never perish, but shall have eternal life"———John iii. 16.

From this history we may LEARN,

1. The nature of faith.

We cannot too carefully enquire into the nature of faith; for there is nothing respecting which so many, and such fatal, mistakes are made. Faith is not a mere assent to any doctrines whatsoever; but it is a living principle in the soul, which evidences itself by precisely such a regard to Christ as this woman manifested on this occasion. Would we then ascertain whether our faith be genuine and saving? let us enquire whether it lead us to Christ, in spite of all obstacles from without or from within, with humility and contrition, with love and confidence? For in proportion as we abound in these graces, or are destitute of them, we either possess, or are destitute of, a living faith.

2. The excellence of faith.

Admirable were the graces which this woman exercised; yet not one of them was noticed by our Lord: he overlooked them all; and noticed that only *which was least apparent, and which every one else would have overlooked*, namely, her faith. He knew that this was the root or principle from whence all her other graces sprang. It was this that led her so to honor him; and therefore he determined to honor it. And must not that be excellent which he so highly regarded, so studiously searched out, and so eminently distinguished?

But what is it that he here assigns to her faith? it is nothing less than the saving of her soul: he passes by all her other graces as having no weight or influence whatever in her justification before God, and specifies her "*faith*" as that which "saved" her. Is it possible to bestow a higher commendation on it than this?

If it be asked, why faith is thus distinguished above all other graces? we answer, it is because faith unites us unto the Saviour, and interests us thereby in all that he has done and suffered for us: but this cannot be said of any other grace whatever; and therefore, though every other grace *adorns* the soul, no grace but faith will *save* it.

Let us all seek to attain right sentiments on this most important point, and pray with the apostles, "Lord, increase our faith."

3. The condescension of Christ to believing penitents.

If a person of an abandoned character, however changed in his conduct, should come to us when in the midst of company, and that company of a higher order and a pharisaic cast, and should express such affection for us, our pride would be apt to rise; and, while we blushed for the degradation we seemed to suffer, we should be ready to condemn him for his impertinent intrusion, or perhaps to suspect that he was deranged in his mind.  But Jesus accounted himself honored by the testimonies of the woman's regard: and, though he could not but know what reflections would be cast upon his character on account of his kindness to her, he vindicated her conduct, and richly recompensed her kind attentions.

Thus will he do to every believing penitent.  He will compensate the scoffs of an unbelieving world by manifest tokens of his approbation.  He will not regard the quantity or quality of a man's past offenses; but will speak peace to his soul, and in due time " wipe away all tears from his eyes" for ever.  O that we might all consider this, and experience it to our eternal joy !

## THE NATURE, SOURCE, AND MEANS OF SPIRITUAL PEACE.

Haggai ii. 9.—In this place will I give peace, saith the Lord of Hosts.  (B.)

IF this might be said of the temple at Jerusalem, where the sacrifices of bulls and goats were offered which could not take away sin, the prayers of Old Testament saints were put up, and the Law of Moses was read and expounded; the words may with, at least, equal, if not greater propriety be used of every place under the New Testament dispensation,—a dispensation much more perfect,—where the sacrifice of Christ, which does put away sin, and procure peace with God, is offered, the gospel of peace is proclaimed, the prayers of the New Testament saints are put up and presented through our great Hight Priest, and the Spirit of peace and love is bestowed.— —

Inquire we,

I. INTO THE NATURE OF THE PEACE HERE SPOKEN OF.

To understand this promise, we must observe, that man is by nature a' enmity with God.—All are sinners.  Rom. iii. 23.—All are under wrath. Rom. i. 18: Eph. ii. 1—3.—There is an enmity on the part of man towards God.  Rom. viii. 5—7; Col. i. 21.—Hence, guilt is charged, and condemnation and wrath denounced upon him by God.

The peace here intended includes,

*Peace with God; i. e.* forgiveness, acceptance, reconciliation with him Rom. v. 1.—When this is witnessed to the soul, by the Spirit of God, the enmity is removed, or the will is subdued, and the affections are brought into captivity to the obedience of Christ; whence spring " love, joy, peace, long-suffering, gentleness, goodness, faith, meekness, temperance."— —

*Peace of conscience;* arising from the pardon of past sin, and power over sin.  Rom. viii. 1—3; 6, 12—15.— —

A *peaceful, serene,* and *tranquil* state of mind; the will and affections being subdued, and all the tempers changed, and sanctified.  Col. iii. 12—15; Phil. iv. 7.— —

*Peace with all men;* injustice, oppression, guile, fraud, covetousness, pride, anger, and other causes of discord and strife, being removed.— —

How great the excellency of this peace, and the blessedness of those that possess it !— —

II. WHO IS THE AUTHOR OF THIS PEACE, AND THE WAY IN WHICH HE WILL GIVE IT.

*It is* not *ourselves.*—Our own works cannot purchase it, nor reconcile God to us. They are all of them imperfect, stained with sin, and instead of procuring favor, deserve divine wrath.—Our own strength and endeavors, and our abstinence and religious duties, of whatever kind, cannot remove the enmity on our part, and reconcile us to God.—Nothing that we have done or can do, can pacify or give peace to an awakened conscience ; can produce a really peaceful state of mind; or destroy those evil dispositions, which are the grand hinderences of peace among men.

It is not *others ;* not their absolutions, prayers, or advices.— —

It is the *gift of God.* He is its author.—It comes from him as a free gift.— — —His mercy passes by our past sins, and pardons them ; thus wrath on his part is removed. His spirit removes our enmity to him‘ witnesses the pardon of sin, and gives us power over it. Hence we have peace with God, peace of conscience, tranquility of mind, and peace with all men. —But it comes through Christ, the blood of his cross, and the pacification made thereby. Tit. iii. 4—6; Col. i. 20; Eph. ii. 13, 14.— —How inestimable the ransom by which we obtain this blessing !— —

III. Who are the subjects of it ; or, the persons to whom he will give it.

It is purchased by Christ for all, and offered to all. 2 Cor. v. 18, 19; Isa. lvii. 19.

But it cannot be possessed by the wicked. Isai. lvii. 20. "God is angry with the wicked every day." Psa. vii. 11. Hence, the necessity of repentance.*

It cannot be the portion of the unbeliever. John iii. 18—36. Hence the necessity of faith.†

Repentance and faith are both the gifts of God, and must be sought in the use of prescribed means, as hearing the word and prayer. We hence obtain the light concerning the method of justification and peace ; the sufficiency and grace of Christ are revealed by the Spirit, and our hearts are drawn to him.

IV. The place where he will give it, and the time when.

At all times and places may be considered as holy under the gospel. John iv. 21.

Nevertheless when and where the gospel is preached, and prayer offered to God, repentance and faith are usually given, and Christ in his word and Spirit is peculiarly present. Matt. xviii. 20 ; xxviii. 20.

---

## THE LIFE AND WALK OF A CHRISTIAN.

Galatians v. 25.—If we live in the Spirit, let us also walk in the Spirit. (B.)

As true christianity is divided into two grand branches, and is partly experimental and partly practical ; so, there are two particulars which are chiefly deserving of notice in the character of a real christian ; his inward life and his outward conversation. With regard to both of them, he differs essentially, I do not say, merely from profane and immoral persons, but from all

---

* Describe the nature and fruits of repentance.

† Describe the nature of faith, and the change consequent upon it.

that are carnal and worldly, from all that are not true christians, possessed of the genuine religion of Christ. And no wonder, for the spring and rule of his life and conduct are essentially different in him from what they are in them. They are influenced and directed by the powers of nature, he by the principles of grace; they by the spirit of the world and the customs and habits of men, he by the Spirit of God and the example and laws of Christ. Hence the exhortation of the Apostle in Eph. iv. 17—23, and in the text.—Consider we,

I. THE INWARD LIFE OF A CHRISTIAN.

"If we live in," or rather by, "the Spirit." It is evident the Apostle does not here speak of the life common to all men; for if he had, he needed not not have made a supposition, "if." He does not speak, therefore, of natural life, whether animal or rational, consisting in the union of soul and body, and supported by breathing, the circulation of the blood and other fluids, by the reception of food and use of exercise. Nevertheless this is, in a sense, in and by the Spirit of that God who at first "breathed into our nostrils the breath of life," and "in whom we live move and have our being;" Acts xvii. 28. But he speaks of spiritual and eternal life,—the life which man lost by the fall, Gen. ii. 17, and of which by nature we are all destitute. Eph. ii. 1—3; Col. ii. 13.—This life consists in the knowledge of God, John xvii. 3; his love; 1 John iv. 16; his favor; Psa. xxx. 5; his image; Eph. iv. 24; his heavenly, spiritual, and divine nature.— —By this spiritual life we have a title to eternal life, a meetness for it, and a foretaste of it —As to the vast importance of this life, it is the end of Christ's incarnation, 1 John iv. 9; John x. 10, of his miracles, his doctrine, and of divine revelation, especially of the gospel, John xx. 31; of the gift of the Holy Spirit, John xiv. 16—19. Indeed—we live by the Spirit, termed a quickening Spirit, John vi. 63; "a Spirit of life." Rom. viii. 2; the living water, John iv. 10—14; vii. 37, 38; the water of life, Rev. xxi. 6; xxii. 17. Hereby we are awakened, convinced, humbled, converted, and made to experience repentance unto life; living faith. Col. ii. 12, 13; in the living and true God, the gospel, the Lord Jesus, and the promises whereby "the just live;" Heb. x. 38; Gal. ii. 20; an interest in Christ and union with him, John xvii. 20, 21; John xiv. 20; 1 Cor. xii. 13; when we are brought into this union, and only then, we have life, 1 John v. 11, 12; justification unto life, Rom. v. 18; regeneration on our entrance into this spiritual life; sanctification by the same Spirit, 1 Pet. i. 2, whereby this life is continued and perfected.—Those who attain this experience are said to pass from death unto life.—This life is maintained, as well as communicated by the Spirit. If he be grieved, quenched, and done despite unto, it is lost. It is maintained also by the use of means, as the animal life is supported by breathing, food, exercise.— —

Thus we "live in the Spirit," in union and intercourse with the Spirit, which lives and dwells in us, as our bodies live in the air or light of this world.

II. THE WALK OF A CHRISTIAN.

The walk of a christian includes his tempers, words, and works, or his whole deportment. And this walk is by the Spirit. See ver. 16—26.—By the guidance of the Spirit, including that of God's word and providence, Rom. viii. 14.—The support of the Spirit affords courage, fortitude, resolution, power. Eph. iii. 16. The influence and drawings of the Spirit are necessary to it. Christians walk "after the Spirit." Rom. viii. 1—4. "In

the Spirit;" in the graces and fruits of the Spirit, in love, joy, peace, long-suffering, gentleness, goodness, faith, meekness, temperance, ver. 22.—
APPLICATION TO THE HEARERS.

Let me inquire,—Do you live by and in the Spirit? Do you walk by and in the Spirit? If you do not *live* you do not *walk* in the Spirit: we cannot walk without life. If you do not *walk* you do not *live* in the Spirit, or your spiritual life is in a very feeble, dying state. How great the misery of those who do not both *live* and *walk* in the Spirit, and the happiness of those that do! in regard of their own comfort, the glory of God, and the edification of others!— —

It should here be shown how the blessing is attained and retained.

## THE GOOD WORK OF GOD IN THE SOUL.

Philippians i. 6.—He which hath begun a good work in you will perform it until the day of Jesus Christ. (B.)

THE steadfast and consistent profession, which was made by the Philippian christians, "from the first day" of their conversion, until the time he now wrote to them, a period of about twelve years, without ever being turned aside, or dishonoring their holy calling, afforded St. Paul the most heartfelt satisfaction, and a confident expectation that God would carry on the work he had so favorably begun in them, till it should attain perfection, and issue, at the second coming of Christ, in their everlasting glory.— —
Inquire we,

I. WHAT IS THIS WORK?

It is wrought in us; not only in the church of Christ in general, but in each individual member of it in particular; in the mind and heart, Heb. xiii. 21; 2 Thess. i. 11. Thus it is distinguished from the works of God wrought for us, as those of creation, providence, redemption, justification.— This work wrought in us is performed in every faculty or power of our inward man. It is a work of illumination in the understanding, gradual and increasing; of conviction and awakening in the conscience; of quickening and animating the affections; producing humiliation, shame, sorrow for, and hatred to, sin; esteem, desire, hope, joy, in regard to holiness and the divine author of it;—of conversion, implying the subjection of the will; the mortification, restraint, and due regulation, of the appetites and passions; change in all the dispositions. It is a work, producing divine graces in us, as repentance, spoken of 2 Cor. vii. 10, 11: faith, John vi. 29; 1 Thess. i. 3; 2 Thess. i. 11; Col. ii. 12: hope, 1 Pet. i. 3: love, to God and man, Rom. v. 5; 1 Thess. iii. 12: humility, resignation, patience, contentment, meekness, gentleness, long-suffering, and purity of intention and affection, and universal holiness, or a renewal after the divine image, 2 Cor. iv. 16; Tit. iii. 5.—In general, this work is wounding and healing; killing and making alive; pulling down and building up; breaking up the ground and sowing; stripping and clothing. Acts xiii. 41.

II. HOW DOES IT APPEAR THAT THIS IS A GOOD WORK?

It is painful in its commencement; for a discovery of our sinfulness and guilt, conviction of sin, humiliation, shame, grief for it, are not pleasing to nature; but though not joyous, like affliction at first, it afterwards yields most pleasant fruit; producing, even on earth, peace hope, joy, love, **and** other happy affections, Ps. cxxvi. 5.—It is good, as to its author, God, from whom nothing but good can proceed.—It is good as it respects his motive for working it, love to us.—It is good as to the means and agents, by whom it is effected in us, Christ, the Spirit, the word. 1 Thess. ii. 13. The end is good, even eternal salvation.— —

III. WHAT ARE THE PROOFS THAT THIS WORK IS BEGUN?

Many of these are mentioned by the apostle in the context.—"Fellowship in, (or through) the gospel, till now:" ver. 5; a participation with others in the blessings of it, manifested in their hearing, reading, meditating, understanding, and receiving the word, and not departing from it, like the way-side and stony-ground hearers; also, uniting in fellowship with the people of God.—Believing in Christ, ver. 29. The work of faith being in a measure wrought in them, and of consequence the new birth, John i. 12; 1 John v. 1, love, 1 John iv. 7, victory over the world, 1 John v. 4, 5; ii. 15, purity. Acts xv. 9.—Suffering willingly for the gospel, like the apostle, and thus being " partakers of his grace," ver. 7, 29, not forsaking him in his bonds, and when he stood up in defence of the gospel, but sharing in the reproach and persecution he endured; the faith and patience they thus exercised, proving the reality of their grace.—Rejoicing in Christ, ver. 26.—"Shining as lights in the world" by their unblamable and useful life, chap. ii. 15.— —

IV. ST. PAUL'S CONFIDENCE THAT GOD WOULD CARRY ON HIS WORK IN THEM.

If God had not been willing to carry it on, he would not have begun it.— It is true, God works by means; but they were willing to use, and did actually use, and resolved to continue to use, the means.—Their perseverance, however, was not infallible. See ch. ii. 12, 13; Gal. v. 4.— —

APPLICATION.

*To sinners.* Is this good work begun?—You answer, "I do so and so." But what hath God done? hath he wrought in you to will and to do? Is it a good work, to rail, to lie, to cheat, &c.; to be proud, self-willed, discontented, envious, &c.?—*To mourners.* "He will not break the bruised reed." Matt. xii. 20. He hath wrought in you repentance, he will work faith: he hath convinced, he will convert; he hath wounded, he will heal; Hos. vi. 1; he hath brought down, and given sorrow, he will exalt and cause joy.—*To believers.* The work is but begun: the foundation is laid, that the superstructure may be raised: the tree is planted, that it may bear fruit; the child of God is born of his Spirit, that he may grow up from a babe to a young man and a father; the laborer is hired into the vineyard, that he may work.

---

THE SUCCESS OF THE GOSPEL IN THE DAYS OF THE APOSTLES.

Acts xii. 24.—But the word grew and was multiplied. (Sk.)

WHEN Christ appeared on earth, he was opposed to the wicked Jews; and, after his ascension into heaven, his holy apostles were opposed both by Jews and Gentiles. The heathen nations raged, and the professing people of God imagined a vain thing; but the Lord laughed them to scorn, and had

**them** in derision, Ps. ii. 1—4. Herod the king persecuted the church, be cause it pleased the Jews; but when he robbed God of his glory, by allowing the people to pay him divine honors, he was eaten up of worms, ver. 23. Let us consider the opposition which was made to the word in those days: its rapid success; and the principal means of its extensive promulgation.

I. THE WORD WAS OPPOSED.

1. *By the word we may understand the gospel of God our Saviour.* This was sent in the first instance to the Jews. Hence the apostle Paul said to the Jews at Antioch, "Men and brethren, children of the stock of Abraham, and whosoever among you feareth God, to you is the word of this salvation sent," chap. xiii. 26. It is fitly called a word of salvation, as it explains the cause of salvation; points out the terms of salvation; explains its nature and extent; and offers salvation to all who believe, Mark xv. 16.

2. *Jewish prejudices opposed the gospel.* The Jews were fond of pomp and parade; they admired the letter of the law; but they were proud, formal, and carnal. No wonder that they opposed that word which required humility, Luke xiv. 11. They could not endure the spirituality of the gospel, Rom. ii. 28, 29. And their prejudices were strong against regeneration; because they were ignorant of its nature, and were under the dominion of sin and death, John iii. 3; Rom. vii. 24.

3. *Heathenish superstitions were opposed to the word.* They had imaginary gods without number; they had priests whom they revered, and who kept them in darkness; and they had an impure worship to which they were superstitiously attached. Christianity took away their gods, exposed their priests, and threw down their idolatrous temples and altars. Can we wonder that they rose up in arms against the word? Their craft was in danger; for the preaching of the gospel turned the world upside down, Acts xvii. 6.

4. *Human learning was opposed to the word of God.* The Greeks and Romans excelled in learning; but that learning produced bad effects. They were self-confident, proud, and apt to boast. The gospel was plain, clear, and simple; and it rendered all their fine reasonings, and all their displays of oratory, completely useless. Hence they could not endure it. It appeared to them foolishness, and unworthy to be received by philosophers, who imagined they knew more than either the Jewish prophets or Christ and his apostles.

5. *The devil opposed the gospel, by his influence and agency on the hearts of men.* Thousands, who were ignorant of his devices, were led by him into error and sin. He stirred up all his servants, whether Jews or Gentiles, to oppose the word. We have an instance of this kind in *Elymas*, whom Paul called a child of the devil, because he perverted the right ways of the Lord, under the influence and agency of that wicked spirit, Acts xiii. 8—10.

6. *In spreading the word, the apostles had to endure many grievous afflictions, both from wicked men and evil spirits.* They were treated with scorn and contempt; they suffered bonds and imprisonment, hunger and nakedness, hardships and deaths, 1 Cor. iv. 11—13; 2 Cor. iv. 8—11. But they were strengthened and supported by the Lord; and their labors were crowned with success.

II. OPPOSITION DID NOT PREVENT THE RAPID SUCCESS OF THE GOSPEL; FOR THE WORD GREW AND WAS MULTIPLIED.

1. *The word is fitly compared to good seed.* Our Lord used this figure

in his parable of the sower, where he says, "The seed is the word of God, Luke viii. 11. And the apostle Paul says, in reference to a preached gospel, " We have sown unto you spiritual things," 1 Cor. ix. 11.

2. *This seed was sown by the apostles in prepared hearts;* and it cannot bring forth good fruit unless the heart be prepared. When men repent, and seek the Lord, the *fallow ground* of their hearts is broken up, Hos. x. 12. The sinner is then convinced of sin; mourns under a sense of sin; and inquires, " What must I do to be saved?" Acts xvi. 30.

3. *When the word sinks into the heart, and takes deep root, it produces holy tempers and holy actions;* and when we abound in these, the word grows in us, and our prayers go up to God with acceptance. " If ye abide in me, and my words abide in you, ye shall ask what ye will, and it shall be done unto you," John xv. 7. Then we see the grace of God in its wondrous effects. How it grows we know not; but we have sufficient proof of its growth, when we see the blade, the ear, and then the full corn in the ear, Mark x. 28.

4. *The word is multiplied when many are converted to God by the instrumentality of converts.* One grain may produce *fifty*, and another a *hundred*. In those days one convert was frequently the honored instrument of bringing many to Christ, so that the word spread in all directions. Every member of the church felt it his duty to do what he could for his Lord and Master; and when this is the case, the word multiplies, by the blessing of God, Acts viii. 4.

II. But what were the principal causes of the extensive promulgation of the gospel in the age of the apostles?

1. *The extraordinary gifts of the Spirit, conferred on the apostles, and on many in the church, promoted the success of the gospel.* They spake with tongues, and wrought miracles; a plain proof that God was with them, and that he was the Author of that religion which they taught and enforced, Acts vi. 7, 8.

2. Another cause of the rapid spread of the gospel in those days, was *the burning zeal of the apostles and primitive Christians.* They were always zealously affected in a good cause, Gal. iv. 18. Under the influence of this principle, they were diligent in the use of means; they were courageous; and did all things heartily as to the Lord, Col. iii. 23.

3. *Divine power attended the word.* This was absolutely necessary; for without that power nothing could have been accomplished, 1 Cor. ii. 4. Paul planted, and Apollos watered; but God gave the increase, 1 Cor. iii. 6; 1 Thess. i. 5. And when the word was clothed with divine power, it was " sharper than any two-edged sword," Heb. iv. 12.

4. *The holy tempers, and the holy conduct of the apostles, and of the first believers, produced powerful effects on the hearts of the people.* They were patient in sufferings; meek under provocations: and ever ready to forgive injuries. They were diligent in business; just in their dealings; and faithful to their promises. And when men saw their " good works, they glorified God," Matt. v. 16.

5. *The unity of the church gave success to the word.* They were closely united in affection, and all aimed at the same things, namely, the glory of God and the salvation of men. Their love to one another was proverbial. When the world saw this, and considered it as the fruit of christianity, many believed, and turned from dumb idols to the *living God*, Heb. x. 24.

6. *Persecution promoted the cause of Christ, and gave success to the word.* It discovered the *vileness* of the persecutors, and the real *worth* of

118

the persecuted. The one was *abhorred*, and the other *admired*. Hence the word of those holy and injured persons took effect; and it was frequently said, "The blood of the martyrs is the seed of the church."

7. *Judgments poured out on wicked men, and on persecutors, gave success to the gospel.* When Ananias and Sapphira were struck dead, "Great fear came upon all the church, and as many as heard these things," Acts v. 11. When Herod died by the visitation of God, the word grew and was multiplied; and when Elymas was struck blind, Sergius Paulus believed the word, Acts xiii. 12.

8. *The united prayers of the church gave success to the word.* All were crying out day and night, "Thy kingdom come." All prayed for the prosperity of the word, 2 Thess. iii. 1. And much prayer must be offered up in one day, if we would see a revival of religion, and a rapid spread of christianity, Heb. iii. 2.

### INFERENCES.

1. How widely different was the propagation of Christianity from that of Mohammedism! The one was by the force of truth, and holy example; but the other was by the sword, and acts of violence!

2. The effects of primitive times have reached us in these last days. We have the truth which was then taught; we have christian ordinances and christian ministers. Miracles have ceased; but grace still abounds, 1 Tim. i. 15.

3. We lay no claim to apostolical gifts; but God has opened a wide door, in our day, for the spread of his gospel. Let us imitate the piety and zeal of the first christians; and may we live to see the blessed days of the Son of man! Amen.

---

### THE CENTURION'S SERVANT HEALED.

Luke vii. 6, 7.—Then Jesus went with them: and when he was not far from the house, the Centurion sent friends to him, saying unto him, Lord, trouble not thyself: for I am not worthy that thou shouldest enter under my roof; wherefore neither thought I myself worthy to come unto thee: but say in a word, and my servant shall be healed. (S. S.)

NOTHING makes a wider breach among men than a difference in political and religious opinion—

But mutual good offices would greatly counteract this evil—

Though we can never hope to soften the rancour of all, we may by persevering kindness conciliate the esteem of many—

We have before us a remarkable instance of the efficacy of such conduct—

The Centurion was an heathen, an officer of an hostile nation, stationed in Judea to keep the Jews in subjection—

But instead of oppressing the Jews he had shewed them much favour-

He, in his turn, needed their good offices on behalf of his servant—

And they gladly became his advocates and intercessors—

They even prevailed on Jesus to work a miracle on his behalf—

To elucidate this miracle we shall consider,

I. THE CENTURION'S CHARACTER.

Soldiers, for the most part, are unfavorably circumstanced with respect to religion—

But here was one, though an heathen, whose character may well put to shame the greater part of the christian world—we may observe,

1. His love to his fellow-creatures.

His servant was grievously afflicted with the palsy nigh unto death—Compare Matt. viii. 6, with Luke vii. 2.

In this disorder, persons can do nothing for others, or even for themselves—

And in such a state, even dear friends and relatives are ready to think the care of one an heavy burthen—

Yet this Centurion administered to his servant with the tenderest affection—

And interested all he could in the promotion of his welfare—*

What could the servant himself have done more for the kindest master?

2. His piety towards God.

He had not embraced either the doctrines or discipline of the Jewish church—

But he had learned to acknowledge the only true God—

And he was glad to promote the worship of God, even though he himself did not acquiesce in the peculiar mode in which he was worshipped—

He even built a synagogue for the Jews at his own expense, ver. 5.

What an admirable pattern of liberality and candor!—

How different from those who will not do any thing without the pale of their own church!—

Surely he never afterwards regretted that he had so applied his wealth—

3. His low thoughts of himself.

He did not arrogate any thing to himself on account of his rank and authority—

Nor did he value himself on his benevolence to man and zeal for God—

While others judged him worthy that a miracle should be wrought for him, he accounted himself unworthy of the smallest favor—

This was the reason of his forbearing to wait on our Lord in person—†

How lovely does such an one appear in the eyes of God and man!—

4. His exalted thoughts of Christ.

He judged our Lord to be too holy to admit of converse with an heathen

He believed also that Jesus could effect whatsoever he pleased, by a word, and at a distance, without the intervention of any means, ver. 7.

Nor did he doubt but that universal nature was subject to his will far more than the most obedient soldier could be to the commands of his officer, ver. 8.

Thus did he ascribe to Jesus a power proper to God alone, Deut. xxxii. 39.

Well might our Lord's address to the discreet Scribe have been applied to him, Mark xii. 34.

Such a character as this could never meet with a repulse from Jesus.

II. THE KINDNESS VOUCHSAFED TO HIM BY OUR LORD.

Instantly at the request of the elders Jesus set off to the Centurion's house—

He who, though repeatedly importuned, declined to visit a *Nobleman's son*, John iv. 46—50, went, at the very first summons, to attend upon a *Centurion's servant*—

* He applied to some of the Jewish elders to use their interest with Jesus on his behalf.

† On our Lord's near approach to the house, the same humility that had kept the Centurion from going to him, compelled him, as it were, to go, lest he should seem guilty of disrespect. Compare Matt. viii. 13, with the text

And no sooner met the Centurion, than he richly recompensed his assiduity.

1. He expressed his admiration of the Centurion's faith.

We never hear of Jesus admiring the things of this world—

He rather checked in his disciples such ill-judged veneration, Mark xiii. 1, 2.

But when he beheld the Centurion's faith, " he marvelled at it"—

Not that such exercise of grace was *really* unexpected by him—

Jesus both knew what was in the Centurion's heart, John ii. 25, and had planted there the very grace which he exercised, John i. 16.

But Jesus, as our exemplar, would teach *us* what to admire—

And shew us that the smallest portion of true faith cannot be estimated too highly, 2 Peter i. 1.

Our Lord declared in his very presence, that this faith had not been equalled by any even of the Israelites themselves, ver. 9.

Such approbation from *his* mouth could not fail of comforting the afflicted Centurion—

2. He wrought the desired miracle in confirmation of his faith.

By a simple act of his will he restored the servant to perfect health—

And told the Centurion that it should " be to him according to his faith"—

Thus he removed the distress of the family in an instant—

Thus too he confirmed the faith which had shone forth so nobly—

And shewed that we could never expect too much at his hands—

What advantage for *eternal* life did the Centurion derive from hence !—

With what lively hope might he apply to Jesus for the healing of his soul !—

We can never suppose that such love and piety, such humility and faith were left to perish—

No, verily—That declaration shall be found true to all eternity, 1 Sam. ii. 30.

3. He declared that many such persons should be saved, while many, with clearer light and higher privileges, should be cast out.

They who profess the true religion may be called " the children of the kingdom"—

But how many of them are destitute of the attainments this heathen had made !—

How many would have imitated that vile Amalekite rather than him !— 1 Sam. xxx. 13.

How many grudge the necessary *contributions* for *keeping up* the houses of God !—*

What doubting of Christ's power and grace, yea, what a proud conceit too of their own worthiness, is to be found among professing christians !—

Surely what our Lord said respecting the unbelieving Jews shall be realized in christians of this character, Matt. viii. 12.

And the humbler heathens, who walked agreeably to the light that they enjoyed, shall be preferred before them—

Nor can we doubt but that the Centurion, in reference to whom these things were spoken, shall be among that blessed number—

APPLICATION.

Let us then learn to plead earnestly for ourselves— — —

---

* What a contrast to him who, *entirely at his own expense, erected* a synagogue *for people of another communion !*

Nor let a sense of unworthiness keep us from carrying our wants to Jesus— — —

Let us also sympathize with, and intercede for others—

Job, like the Centurion, found benefit from his own intercessions—Job xlii. 10.

Nor shall *our* supplications be in vain either for ourselves or others.

~~~~~~~~~~~~~~~~~~~~

## JAIRUS' DAUGHTER HEALED.

Luke viii. 50.—When Jesus heard it, he answered him, saying, Fear not : believe only, and she shall be made whole. (S. S.)

AFFLICTIONS may well be deprecated by us as painful to flesh and blood—
But they are often the means of humbling us before God—
Multitudes came as suppliants to our Lord who would never have regarded him if they had not felt the pressure of disease or trouble—
The rich in general were the most backward to acknowledge him—
But they found that in the hour of affliction none other could do them good—
Hence occasionally we see the opulent presenting their supplications before him—
Nor did he reject the suit of any, whether they were rich or poor—
The answer he gave to a ruler of the synagogue is recorded in the text—
And it will naturally lead us to notice the rulers's faith.
I. How IT WAS TRIED.
Jairus (such was his name) had much to try his faith.
He had an only child (twelve years of age) in dying circumstances—
Having heard much of our Lord's miracles, he applied to him on behalt of his daughter—
And earnestly requested him to come and restore her health—
But while he was returning with Jesus to his house, his servants brought tidings that the child was dead—
This was a dreadful shock to the parent's feelings—
And might have utterly destroyed all his hopes—
Thus it is that the faith of God's people is often tried.
They are enabled to make application to their God and Saviour—
But the storm in the meantime gathers thick around them—
Their difficulties so increase, that their hopes seem almost blasted—
They have cried for pardon, and find only an increasing sense of guilt—
They have prayed for deliverance from corruption or temptation, and experienced the assaults of Satan more violent than ever—
Thus they are almost ready to think that God has cast out their prayer, and shut up his tender mercies from them—
It was in this manner that holy Job was tried—
Yea, the experience of most, however diversified, is generally found to agree in this. Ps. cvii. 5, 6, 12, 13, 18, 19, 26, 27, 28.
But this accumulated trouble, was permitted for the further exercise of the uler's faith.
II. How IT OPERATED.
He was enabled humbly and confidently to depend on Jesus.

It was his faith that first led him to Jesus for help—

Nor, when his case seemed desperate, did he give up his hope—

It is probable that our Lord might perceive some rising apprehensions in his mind—

But he sustained him instantly with that encouraging word, " Fear not"—

Jairus expected now that his child should be raised as from a sleep—

The idea of sleep, however, only called forth the derision of the mourners—

Such was the fruit of their ignorance and unbelief—

But the ruler himself resembled the father of the faithful, Rom iv. 18, 20, 21.—

It is in this way that true faith will ever shew itself.

It will surely lead us to Jesus for relief—

It will make us humble and importunate in our supplications to him—

We shall not presently turn from him because our difficulties increase—

We shall rather adopt the expressions of holy Job, Job xiii. 15.

Unbelief may prompt us to deride what we do not understand—

But faith will make us acquiesce in God's declarations, though we carnot fully comprehend them—

And expect the accomplishment of his promises, however his providence may appear to contradict them—

Jesus did not fail to respect the faith that honored him.

III. How it was rewarded.

Jesus answered the ruler to the full extent of all his wishes.

Our Lord reproved the excessive lamentations of the people—

And encouraged them to expect the restoration of the child—

But he would not suffer those who had derided him to be spectators of the miracle—

He took with him, however, persons sufficient to attest it—

He favored the believing parents with admission to behold it—.

And restored their daughter, as it had been from sleep, in their very presence—

The child arose instantly, and walked as in perfect health—

For their further conviction he ordered food to be given to the child—

By this also he intimated, that though she was restored by a miracle, she was to be kept alive by natural means—

What a rich reward was this to the believing suppliant—

Nor shall any one who asks in faith, be disappointed.

Our Lord has commanded us to ask in faith, Mark xi. 24.—

And has assured us that petitions, so offered, shall be answered by him Matt. xxi. 22.—

Things the most impossible to man, shall, if they will conduce to our good and to God's honor, be effected by the prayer of faith, Mark ix. 23.—

Crimes the most atrocious that ever were committed, shall be pardoned, Acts xiii. 39.

Lusts the most inveterate that ever enslaved a soul, shall be subdued. isai. lxi. 19. 1 Cor. vi. 11.

The dead in trespasses and sins shall be raised, like Christ himself. to a new and heavenly life, Eph. i. 19, 20, with ii. 5, 6.

Nor shall they fail of attaining eternal happiness in heaven, John. iii. 15 Isaiah xlv. 17.

Application.

Every man must expect trouble in this vale of tears—

The dearest friends must look forward to a day of separation—
But let every trouble drive us to the compassionate Jesus—
And every want be spread before him in prayer, Phil. iv. 6.
We are not now indeed to expect *miraculous* interpositions—
Nor ought we to ask for *temporal* blessings in an unqualified manner—
We should commit the concerns of this life to his all-wise disposal—
But for *spiritual* blessings we cannot be too importunate—
Nor can our faith in his word be too strong—
What he said to Martha he still says to us, John xi. 40.—
The advice of Jehosaphat is the best direction we can follow, 2 Chron
xx. 20.—
Let us not then limit his tender mercies—
If we resemble the Samaritan lord, we shall fare like him, 2 Kings vii.
2—17.
Let us not in renewed troubles be like the unbelieving Jews, Ps. lxxviii
20.—
But let us bear in mind that encouraging declaration, Eph. iii. 20.—
And determine henceforth to live like the apostle, Gal. ii. 20.

---

### GROWING IN GRACE.

2 Peter iii. 18.—But grow in grace, and in the knowledge of our Lord and Saviour Jesus
    Christ. To him be glory, both now and for ever, Amen. (Sk.)

ONE of the most pleasing traits in the character of a genuine christian pastor, is his generous, disinterested concern for the present and everlasting welfare of those whom the chief Shepherd has committed to his care. And it
is peculiarly delightful to find the same disposition operating with unabated
vigor, amidst an almost endless variety of cares and troubles, and after many
years of separation have elapsed. This heavenly temper is more or less observable in all the epistles of the New Testament. Hear Paul's declaration
to the Thessalonians, "For now we live, if ye stand fast in the Lord."
Hear also how he felt, and how he prayed for the Ephesians; see chap. iii.
13—19. In the same spirit, Peter, also, endeavors to guard his christian
converts against the principles and practices of infidels and scoffers, by pressing on their attention the importance of activity and perseverance in the
great business of the soul's salvation, "Wherefore the rather, brethren, give
diligence," &c., chap. i. 10—13. And in conclusion he says, "But grow
in grace," &c. This is a subject to be *explained, recommended,* and *practised.* We therefore inquire,

I. WHAT IS MEANT BY GROWING IN GRACE? The word grace means
favor, kindness, friendly affection. Hence the phrase, so common in scripture, of finding grace in the eyes or sight of a person, Gen. xxxiv. 11; 2
Sam. xvi. 4; Esther ii. 17. And hence, as it respects God, we are said to
be "*justified freely* by his *grace,*" Rom. iii. 24. But the word is also variously applied to the *operations* and *effects* of this free favor. We at present
consider it in two senses. First, As it expresses that *state* or *condition* of
adoption and reconciliation into which believers are brought, Rom. v. 1, 2.—
And, secondly, As it denotes *divine assistance,* afforded "in time of need,"
2 Cor. xii. 9, through which the believer is "*strengthened* with might by

the Spirit in *the inner man*," Eph. iii. 16. Here we must be indulged in a few remarks.

1. This state of reconciliation, &c., is not that of mankind in general; but is contra-distinguished from a state of *nature*, in which evil principles produce works of wickedness, which, as well as the workers of them, "God's soul hateth," Psa. xi. 5. " By nature we are children of wrath," Eph ii. 3, "and God is *angry* with the wicked," &c., Psa. vii. 11; Isa. xii. 1—3.

2. Wherever there is that *relative* change, by which a penitent is adopted into the family of God, there is also a *real* change in the man's principles and practice ;—a change of *nature*, as well as of condition. Indeed, the real change, which begins in repentance, whereby we sorrow for, hate, and forsake sin, precedes that faith whereby we believe with the heart unto righteousness ;—and which farther purifies the heart, Matt. iv. 17; Acts xx. 21. Yet,

3. The change is not so complete as not to admit of improvement; therefore the text says, " *Grow* in grace." As grace means free favor, this may refer to an advancement in the favor of God. God loves, and must love holiness. It is his own nature; and the more of it any person has, with the greater complacency does God regard him. He calls Abraham his friend; and John was " the disciple whom Jesus (peculiarly) loved." But the principal idea intended to be conveyed, seems to be that of improvement. Illustrate by the example of "little children," &c., John i; Eph. i. 12—14. The growth here enjoined, may well include, and must consist with, 1. An improvement in knowledge ;—" the knowledge of our Lord and Saviour Jesus Christ," that ye may be freed from the mistakes, confusion, and imbecility of infancy; and that your views of his *person* and *work*, and of your christian privileges, may be more *correct*, Eph. iv. 13, 14,—more clear, chap. i. 17—19,—and more comprehensive, chap. iii. 14—19. This will be attended with, 2. A corresponding improvement in *strength ;* from childhood—to *youth*—to *maturity.* "The righteous shall be stronger and stronger," Job xvii. 9. And 3. An improvement in *usefulness*,—that, in uniting in yourselves the experience, firmness, prudence, &c., of mature age, with parental solicitude, ye may be *nursing fathers* to the church, and " mothers in Israel." With a view to recommend the subject, we inquire,

II. What are the advantages of growing in grace ? The improvement is,

1. *A personal advantage.* The christian's life is, in a great measure, made up of *doing* and *suffering.* An increase of grace will enable him to *do* the will of God more *easily*, and more *effectually*, Col. i. 9, 10; and to *suffer* it more *patiently* and *cheerfully*, v. 11. It is,

2. A *social* advantage. Society will be so far preserved from the baleful effects of *error, inconsistency,* &c. And many *good* things will be *done*, and *well done*, in the world, the church, the family, &c., which would otherwise be left undone, Phil. i. 9—11. Hence it is,

3. An advantage to *the cause of religion.* There is a pathos in the address, and an energy in the pious actions of an *eminently holy and thriving* soul, that can hardly fail to take effect.

4. It will advance *the glory of God.* It is he, who, through Jesus Christ, bestows grace, whereby we serve him acceptably ;—and " serve our generation" according to his will ;—and *endure* as seeing the Invisible, Matt. v. 13—16. Wherefore to him, as the *Origin* of good, and according to the

apostle's wish, to "our Lord and Saviour Jesus Christ, *as Mediator*, be glory, both now and for ever." Amen.

But this is a subject to be reduced to practice. It remains, therefore, that we inqure,

III. WHAT ARE THE MEANS OF GROWING IN GRACE? On this subject we may avail ourselves of what experience teaches us concerning the means which conduce to bodily health and improvement; among which are, proper care—proper nutriment—and proper exercise.

1. Proper *care*. This is so necessary, that before your children are capable of taking care of themselves, you anxiously keep them out of the way of harm. Observe, here, Paul's solicitude; "As a nurse cherisheth her children," &c., "*warning* every man;"—"we *charged* every one of you," &c., 1 Thess. ii. 7—11; Col. i. 28. And when we reach the years of discretion, we still find it necessary to guard against pestilential effluvia, accidential injuries, destructive practices, &c. So should we, in spirituals, avoid the pestilential atmosphere of the wicked;—"take heed, lest we fall;"— "flee youthful lusts, which war against the soul," &c., 1 Cor. xv. 33; Prov. iv. 14, 15.

2. Proper *nutriment ;*—rejecting, of course, what is *useless ;* and, more especially, whatever is *deleterious*. Much of what is useless, and much of what is poisonous, is to be met with, both in *conversation* and in *print*. Reject it; and seek that which will afford nourishment:—in, 1. Hearing and reading *the word*, 1 Pet. ii. 2. 2. Biography of persons whose pious *life*, and happy *death*, have exemplified the truth of scripture. 3. *Christian conversation*. 4. *Prayer;* and, in fine, every appointed or prudential means of grace.

3. Proper *exercise*. Without this, the most robust *body* will sink rapidly into the hands of the physician; and through them, into the grave. So, "health of mind is exercise; not rest." By reason of *use*, our senses are exercised to discern both good and evil, Heb. v. 13, 14; see also Matt. xiii. 12; Luke xix. 20—26. Have you a measure of faith, love, humility, patience? &c. *Use* grace, and *have* grace.

Remind *the sinner* of the awfulness of his case. "The *wrath* of God is revealed," &c., and it *abideth* on *him*, Rom. i. 18; John iii. 36; 2 Thess. i. 8, 9.

Let *the feeble-minded* remember, that grace admits of growth. "Who hath despised the day of small things?" Isa. xl. 11; Heb. iv. 15, 16.

On *adult believers*, the necessity of a farther growth should be urged—to prevent *apostasy*, ch. i. 1—9, and iii. 17,—to prevent *perdition*, ch. ii. 20; John xv. 6. And they may be *encouraged*, by the hope of "an entrance, ministered unto them abundantly, into the everlasting kingdom of our Lord and Saviour Jesus Christ," ch. i. 10, 11.

---

SPIRITUAL HEALTH.

Isa. liii. 5.—With his stripes we are healed. (Sk.)

FOR the transcendant importance of its matter, and the minuteness and accuracy of its prophetical descriptions, this chapter occupies an unrivalled eminence amongst the writings of the Jewish seers Here we have the humility of the Redeemer specified, ver. 2 ;—the contemptuous ideas of men respecting him described, ver. 3 ;—the acuteness of his sufferings asserted, ver 8, 9:—the patience with which he endured his peerless sorrows antici pated, ver. 7 ;—and the grand design of the whole announced, ver. 4, 5, 6. Yea, such is the luminous and evangelical glory which pours upon our astonished vision in this portion of Scripture, that we almost forget that its inspired author lived near seven hundred years before the important events which he predicted took place ; we are inadvertently rather inclined to associate him with the eye witnesses of the sorrows of the Son of God. Under the influence of these considerations, we do not wonder that even the licentious Rochester, when immured in the chamber of affliction, should, by a calm investigation of this chapter, have been fully convinced of the authenticity of those Scriptures which had before constituted the butt of his profane ridicule; and, through divine mercy, rendered capable of subscribing to the words of our text, "With his stripes we are healed." With fervent aspirations to God for his blessing, let us proceed to discuss this truly interesting passage, in which we have,

I. A LAMENTABLE DISEASE ASSUMED.

II. AN INFALLIBLE PHYSICIAN SPECIFIED.

III. HIS MODE OF OPERATION DESCRIBED.

IV. AN EXTRAORDINARY CURE ASSERTED.

1. As there can be no cure effected where no disease exists, the assumption of disease is inseparably connected with this passage. The sacred Scriptures abound with figurative modes of expression ; hence the diseases of the body have been used as a medium of representing the moral pravity of human nature, Isa. i. 5, 6; Jer. viii. 21, 22. In attending to the prophet's figure, we shall consider the spiritual disease of man, as,

1. *The baneful result of transgression.* When God had formed man of the dust, and breathed into him the breath of life, he pronounced him "very good," and doubtless this approving testimony had both a moral and a physical application ; but, alas! how are the mighty fallen !—how unlike the production of a holy and omniscient Being !—Man unhappily violated the paradisiacal commandment—mingled his pristine glory in the abyss of ruin—and introduced a hideous train of ills, of every shape and size :—and among these, a fixed inveterate aptitude to evil, holds a very prominent place, Gen. iii. 1—8 ; Rom. v. 12.

2. *Universal in its prevalence.* Some diseases of the body affect particular parts ; others diffuse their influence through the whole system. This moral disease pervades the whole man ; every member of the body, and every faculty of the soul, is thoroughly infected and deranged, Gen. vi. 5, Job xviii. 4; Mark viii. 21, 22 ;—and these baneful effects of the fall are diffused through the whole human kind. As totally as the man is fallen and depraved, so is the whole of his species involved in ruin ; infancy—childhood—youth—and tottering age—present indisputable evidence in proof of this humbling fact, Isa. liii. 6 ; Rom. iii. 10, 11, 23.

3. *Hereditary in its descent.* Some diseases of the body are unhappily entailed on posterity, and are transmitted in regular succession from father to son :—of this nature is the moral malady assumed in our text :—it has descended in one unbroken line, from the first guilty pair in Eden's garden, down to your preacher and his present audience ;—hence no happy intervening age of paradisiacal innocence has adorned the page of history ;—hence the biographical details of ages have not broken the painful monotony of human guilt, by the exhibition of one happy individual in a state of unmixed,

underived, pristine purity. The lineaments of moral pravity in the father, have been strikingly manifest in the son, Gen. iv. 1—8, viii. 21.

4. *Incurable by human energy.* The diseases of the human body frequently baffle the utmost skill of the medical science. All the wisdom and power of man have been exercised to impede the progress of this spiritual malady, but to little or no purpose; the senators of Greece and Rome have enacted laws, and the philosophers of both countries have disseminated their ethics abroad; but the radical principle of evil in the human breast has defied all their efforts—nothing less than a Divine Physician can effect a cure, Job. xiv. 4; Jer. xiii. 23.

II. An infallible physician specified. Man has not been abandoned to his spiritual self-induced malady, without hope or help;—mercy has interposed—a physician has been provided—and one possessing the most ample qualifications, John iii. 14—17. He is,

1. *Infinite in wisdom.* Wisdom is necessary in order both to understand the disease, and properly to apply the remedy. Jesus, our Divine Physician, is "the wisdom of God."—He comprehends our spiritual affliction in all its ramifications—he cannot be deceived by false appearances, for "he knoweth what is in man, and needeth not that any should tell him," Jer. xvii. 9, 10; John i. 1—5, 14.

2. *Impartial in his attendance.* Man, in every station in life, is susceptive of partial feeling; the medical profession cannot be expected to be free from its influences. The splendor of the palace, and the grandeur of nobility, are more attractive than the humble cottage of the peasant; but the physician before us, is equally attentive to high and low—rich and poor—learned and illiterate;—yea, and is able to attend to the necessities of all at the same moment, Ezek. xxxiii. 17—19; Mark x. 46—52; Luke vii. 1—10.

3. *Ever easy of access.* Medical practitioners of great celebrity, in order to secure leisure for the purposes of health and domestic duties, are obliged to render themselves inaccessible at certain periods; but Jesus, the infallible Physician of souls, is ever easy of approach. This appears evident from his kind invitations, Isa. i. 18; Matt. xi. 28, 29;—his solemn declarations, Ezek. xxxiii. 11, 12; Matt. xxii. 37;—and his gracious promises, John vi. 37; 1 John i. 9;—as also from the uniform testimony of experience, in all ages, Psa. xxxiv. 18; cxviii. 21; Rom. x. 12, 13.

4. *Gratuitous in his practice.* It is just and proper that the exercise of skill and attention should be reasonably remunerated. But such is the peculiar excellence of this spiritual Physician, that a cure can only be obtained on gratuitous terms. The salvation of the gospel is "without money and without price;" and this method of deliverance is exactly adapted to our ruined condition, Isa. lv. 1, 2; Rom. iii. 24; Eph. ii. 8—10.

III. His mode of operation described;—"With his stripes." The stripes which were inflicted on the blessed Redeemer, were connected with that death to which he gave himself for the life of the world, when "he bore our sins in his own body on the tree." This atonement, and faith in this atonement, are the only means of a sinner's acceptance with God; the only method by which a cure can be obtained, John iii. 36. This method is,

1. *Divine in its appointment.* It is not the fruit of the human imagination; the production of councils, or synods, however learned, or important: but the offspring of Jehovah; it comes to us under the sanction of the Deity, Isa. xxviii. 16; John iii. 16, 17.

2. *Easy in its application.* Not animal oblations—tedious pilgrimages—a course of painful penance—nor any of the other inventions of human

error;—but "repent and believe." The power is given, and its exercise is required, Acts iii. 19; xvi. 31.

3. *Universal in its adaptation.* The gospel way of salvation is admirably suited to all the possible constitutions, situations, and conditions of men, of every "nation, kindred, people, and tongue," Rom. x. 4—13 : Acts ii. 9—11; 37—42.

4. *Infallible in its efficacy.* No case is too intricate, none too desperate, to admit of a cure: no individual in any age of time, ever made a scriptural application and was disappointed. The antediluvian saints realized its efficacy by an anticipating faith; the evangelists and apostles by immediate application; and believers since, by a retrospective reference to the sacrifice of Christ, have proved that he is " able to save to the uttermost them that come to God by him."

IV. An extraordinary cure asserted;—" We are healed." Were mortal ears susceptible of celestial testimony, the loud hosannas of the blood-washed throng on high would amply support this assertion; and multitudes of terrestrial saints would echo back the sound! Can we from experience adopt the sentiment?—This cure may be considered, as,

1. *Radical in its nature.* The cure effected by this Physician is not the removal of external symptoms, while the principle is unrenovated; not breaking off a few gross evils, while the seat of depravity is untouched; but, the understanding is enlightened; the will divinely influenced; the affections properly directed; the imagination spiritualized; and the memory sanctified; in short, the heart entirely changed, Ezek. xxxvi. 26; 2 Cor. v. 17.

2. *Convincing in its evidence.* Whenever a cure is effected there are visible proofs of such restoration; so in the case before us, when a sin-sick soul has made application to Jesus Christ in a scriptural manner, and has realized his saving efficacy, the effect is manifest; the faculties have received a new tone, and this renovation appears in holy tempers, spiritual conversation, and an upright, conscientious, line of conduct, Gal. v. 22—24; 2 Pet. i. 5—7.

3. *Happy in its influence.* Of this there cannot be a doubt entertained for a moment. Personally, the peace of God is enjoyed; divine support under affliction experienced: succor in the hour of temptation realized; and the joys of heaven anticipated. In the family the sacred scriptures are read; prayer regularly offered; diligence and economy promoted; and the salvation of dependants sought. In reference to the world, intercession is offered up, exhortation and reproof are administered; and religion recommended by pious example, Rom. v. 1; Josh. xxiv. 15; 1 Thess. ii. 10.

This subject tends, 1. To promote humility. 2. To produce self-examination. 3. To excite to fervent gratitude. 4. To encourage the desponding penitent.

## GROWING IN GRACE.

2 Thessalonians i. 3.—We are bound to thank God always for you, brethren, as it is meet. because that your faith groweth exceedingly, and the charity of every one of you all towards each other aboundeth. (Pr.)

PERHAPS there is no christian society now on earth to whom this language is fully applicable; and it may be, if Paul had been writing to us, or to other christians of the present day, he would have adopted a different mode of address. It is nevertheless true, that among the primitive churches, they were not all alike prosperous, spiritual, and happy; but that at Thessalonica was one of the most amiable, and deserving of commendation. ——— It is a mercy however if these blessed fruits are found amongst us in any degree, and it is profitable for us to take the best examples presented in the scriptures, that we may learn our own defects, and be led to imitate what is more excellent.

1. Observe, in giving "thanks to God" for their growth in faith and love, the apostle plainly intimates that it was by *the grace of God* they were what they were. Though all that is evil in us belongs to ourselves, yet all that is good in us is of God alone, even that which is commanded and required at our hands.

2. The growth of faith and love plainly supposes that sanctification *is progressive*. It is like the kingdom of heaven in the world, which is compared to a grain of mustard seed, and a little leaven that leaveneth the whole lump. But if we had no inherent sanctification, and none but what is in Christ, this could not be true. Some indeed have endeavored to comfort themselves, and to comfort others, while in a low declining state, by certain examples in scripture; but it is our safest and best way to take examples of the most exalted kind.

3. The growth of faith is here connected with that of *brotherly love*, as a cause is connected with its effect. Certainly, if we grow in faith, we shall also grow in love; because the same principle which attaches us to the truth, will attach us to one another for the truth's sake. Christ is the centre of union; all who love him are taught of God to love one another.

I. ATTEND TO SOME OF THE EVIDENCES OF THIS GROWTH IN GRACE, MENTIONED IN THE TEXT.

Growth in grace is here supposed to be *visible*, or the apostle could not have seen it. It becomes visible by the fruits of righteousness which it produces; and if this be true of us, others will perceive it. Acts iv. 13.

1. Growing in faith will be seen in our taking increasing pleasure *in the means of faith*, the word of God. ——— We shall find delight in reading and hearing it, and it will be to us the joy and rejoicing of our hearts. Psa. i. 2, 3; Prov. vi. 20—23. The word of Christ will dwell in us richly in all wisdom, and be received as the ingrafted word. Col. iii. 16. Seasons of public instruction will be attended with delight, and we shall not hear the word from custom, but from far higher motives. Isa. ii. 2.

2. It will appear in a growing attachment to *the doctrines of Christ*, who is himself the great object of faith. ——— If a man could speak with great eloquence, he might please a certain description of hearers; but if Christ be not his theme, he would fail to please those who believe in him, for to them he is precious. 1 Peter ii. 7. When therefore it is chiefly the manner, and not the subject of address that is regarded, it bespeaks a religion too much

like that of the Corinthians, and not that of the Thessalonians.   1 Cor. ii. 4, 5.

3. Growing in faith consists in an *increasing acquaintance* with the mind of God in his word, as the ground of faith. —— We may be brought to believe the gospel in one day, but it is the work of a whole life to become rooted and grounded in the truth; to know not merely what we believe, but why; and to be able to say with Paul, "I know whom I have believed." We may believe what is true, from being told that it is so; but it will do us very little good, unless we perceive the authority on which it rests, and the principle by which it is supported in the scriptures of truth.   Our faith must not stand in the wisdom of men, but in the power of God.

4. It will be evident by increasing *patience* and *submission*, under all the ills of life. —— This was noticed in the Thessalonians, amidst the persecutions and tribulations which they endured, ver. 4.   If we faint in the day of adversity our strength is small, and our faith is weak.   Matt. xiv. 31.

5. By an increasing *weanedness from the present world.* —— This is the victory that overcometh the world, even our faith, both in prosperity and adversity.   John also speaks of those as being strong, who have overcome the wicked one, and have the word of God abiding in them.   1 John ii. 14, v. 4.

5. Growing in faith appeared in the *love they had one to another* for the truth's sake. —— Christians may live together without discredit, and esteem each other as friends; but to love as brethren, and as christians, is quite another thing.   They may also love one another from being of the same mind, and yet not love on account of their being of the mind of Christ. —— Or if there be true christian love existing, it may not "abound," as it did among the Thessalonians; yet this is necessary to prove that our faith "groweth exceedingly."

II. CONSIDER THE IMPORTANCE OF THE SUBJECT.

1. Growing in faith and love brings *glory to God*, verse 12.   Bearing much fruit honors him, and recommends the gospel to others.   John xv. 8.

2. It has an influence upon the *ministry of the word*, which is highly desirable. —— It is next to impossible to preach to some people, who instead of growing in faith have no faith at all, and Paul himself found it so. Heb. v. 11. —— But oh how different, where the souls of the people may be seen as it were in their countenances, and glisten in their eyes.   Rom. i. 11, 12; Acts xi. 23.

3. If we do not make some progress in religion, we shall be *declining* and going backward. —— There is no standing still in this race, no intermission in this warfare.   If we grow not in faith and love, the seeds of indifference and unbelief will spring up and grow in their stead; will choke the word, and render it unfruitful.

4. If we do not grow in grace, our religion will at best become *doubtful*, and we shall have cause to tremble for the issue.   Heb. x. 38. —— It is the character of all true believers that they are making advancement in the divine life, and growing up in the image and likeness of God.   Prov. iv. 18; 1 Pet. ii. 2; 2 Pet. i. 10, 11.

If there be some who have neither faith nor love, and are utterly unconcerned about it; what must be said to such?   We must go on preaching the gospel, warning them to flee from the wrath to come, and leave the consequences.

## CHRISTIAN PERFECTION AN OBJECT OF PRAYER AND OF HOPE.

Heb. xiii. 20, 21.—Now the God of peace, that brought again from the dead our Lord Jesus, that great Shepherd of the sheep, through the blood of the everlasting covenant,
make you perfect in every good work, to do his will; working in you that which is well-
pleasing in his sight, through Jesus Christ. (Pr.)

The believing Hebrews were in a very unsettled state : many of them had
gone back, and others were hesitating.    Hence there were many practical
disorders among them, and a general tendency to apostacy.    Hence also the
numerous warnings given them in various parts of this epistle : ch. ii. 3. iv.
1, 11.    But after all this, the apostle closes his address with the prayer in
the text, which is presented to God under the most endearing character.

This prayer is applicable to us as well as to them ; for we also are the subjects of many defects, and need to offer up the same request.

I. CONSIDER THE BLESSINGS PRAYED FOR.

The apostle here gives us a picture of what christians should be, and
should aspire after.    Let us therefore pray—

1. That we may be " made perfect."———— The word means to set right,
to restore and put in order, as in Gal. vi. 1: it therefore applies to the disorders among the Hebrews and other christians. ———— It does not so much express what we shall be hereafter, as what we may be in this world ; and points
out that lovely uniformity of character which accompanies great grace.    If
we examine ourselves, we shall find many things wanting, or so imperfect as
to need much to be done for us, to make us what we should be. ———— Some
appear to be pious and devout, but are deficient in benevolence ; they abound
in the duties of the first table of the law, but are deficient in the second.
———— Some have knowledge, but little zeal, and are cold hearted ; while
others abound in zeal, which is not according to knowledge. ———— Some
are tender and affectionate, but wanting courage and fidelity. ———— To
abound in all the fruits of the Spirit, so as to exhibit a lovely uniformity of
character, is to be " made perfect ;" and this is unspeakably desirable.

2. Perfect " in every good work." ———— If we be christians, we are engaged in many good works : such as preaching, praying, hearing, reading,
acts of kindness towards men, and of charity to the poor. ———— But there
is a manner of doing these things which gives a sort of perfection to the
christian character : if our minds are set in order, they will all be done in the
spirit of the gospel, and in a manner very different from what they would
otherwise be. ———— There is such a thing as speaking the word " as we
ought to speak ;" and of praying " as we ought." Ephes. vi. 20. Rom. viii.
26 ; xii. 8.

3. Perfect in every good work " to do his will." ———— We may be much
occupied in religious concerns, and yet not do the will of God in them.
———— Sometimes for want of taking his word as our rule : we may go
a round of religious duties, because others do the same, without any reference
to the will of God. ————.Sometimes the motive may be deficient : we may
do many things from nothing but mere vanity, self-righteousness, or a desire
to be seen of men. ———— But if we are " made perfect," we shall do the
will of God from the heart.

4. We are taught to pray that the Holy Spirit may " work in us that which
is well-pleasing in his sight." ———— It is not in our corrupt nature to attain
these things, without the influence of the Holy Spirit : it is he that excites
desire in prayer, resolution in labor, and that makes us perfect in every good

**word** and work. —— It is he that works faith in us by the promises, patience by sanctified affliction, and hope by the prospect of eternal life.

5. That all may be accepted " through Jesus Christ." —— None are accepted but as believing in him; and no works of ours, but for his sake.

III. THE ENCOURAGEMENT WE HAVE TO PRAY FOR THESE BLESSINGS.

In offering up this prayer for the believing Hebrews, the apostle directed them and us to pray in the same manner, and from the same motives.

1. Great encouragement is derived from *the pacific character of God*, as " the God of peace." This view of the divine character is essential to our drawing near to him; and through a Mediator, there is now peace on earth, and good will towards men. —— It is now with the world as it was with mankind after the deluge, when God accepted the sacrifice of Noah. Gen. viii. 20, 21.

2. From *the proofs* of his being the God of peace; " having brought again from the dead our Lord Jesus." —— This is a doctrine of unspeakable importance, and supported by the clearest evidence. —— 1. The resurrection of Christ is represented in the Scriptures as an act of almighty power, or as one of the greatest efforts of omnipotence. Ephes. i. 20. —— 2. It is represented as a judicial release or discharge. Rom. iv. 25. —— Simeon was kept as a hostage, having been surety for his brethren; but when they returned to Egypt, he was brought forth from prison, which was a sign of peace. God's having raised up Jesus from the dead, was declaring himself satisfied; it was smelling a sweet savor, as in Noah's offering. —— Hence he was "raised for our justification," after being " delivered for our offences."

3. *The character* in which *Christ was raised up*; as "the great Shepherd of the sheep." He that raised the Shepherd from the grave, can raise us also from death, and gather together the scattered sheep. Ephes. i. 18. —— It implies also that Christ has a people given him of the Father, and that for their salvation he went through all his sufferings: as such he died and rose again. —— Paul was a shepherd, and did all he could, and there were other shepherds also; but Christ is the " great Shepherd" of the sheep; and God having brought them forth, it was in love to the flock.

4. *The ground* of his resurrection is *the sacrifice* he offered on the cross. —— God's having raised him from the dead, was a proof of his having accepted the sacrifice in our stead; and this affords a powerful plea in prayer. —— It is this which the ascended Saviour presents as the ground of his own intercession; and all our supplications must be founded on the same plea.

5. The blood which he shed, being " the blood of the everlasting covenant," affords additional encouragement in prayer. —— This language may apply to the covenant made with Christ, as it is expressed in another passage, Zech. ix. 11: or to the covenant made with us through him, and which stands opposed to the covenant of works made at Sinai. —— Covenants with sinful creatures have been made through the medium of sacrifices, and the covenant of grace is founded in the blood of the Mediator; and through it, it is that we have the cup of blessing.

## THE OBJECTS, DESIGN, AND REQUISITION OF GOSPEL GRACE.

Acts xxvi. 17, 18.—I send thee, to open their eyes, and to turn them from darkness to light; and from the power of Satan unto God, that they may receive forgiveness of sins, and inheritance among them which are sanctified by faith that is in me. (Sk.)

1. THESE words occur in the relation given by the apostle Paul of his conversion to christianity; an event which was often referred to by himself, and has since been often appealed to by others, as a check to infidelity. It appears that the apostle's conversion was effected by means of our Lord's *personal* appearance to him. This personal appearance of Jesus, some considerable time after his death, proves the certainty of his *resurrection;* and his resurrection proves that he is the *Son of God*, the promised Saviour of the world, Rom. i. 4. Thus we have the fullest proof that christianity is of God, and that Paul was divinely commissioned to teach it.

2. The narrative of this remarkable conversion being so important, we cannot but feel well pleased with that repetition of it which we find in this book: especially as each account of it contains some interesting particular, not mentioned in the others. When St. Luke records this event in the 9th chapter, he informs us what the Lord said to Ananias, ver. 10--16; when St. Paul relates it himself in the 22d chapter, he informs us what Ananias said to him, ver. 12—14, and when he repeats it in this chapter, he informs us what our Lord said to him, ver. 15—18, "I am Jesus," &c. "I send thee to open their eyes," &c. These words teach us,

1. THE OBJECTS OF GOSPEL BENEVOLENCE,—or the persons to whom the gospel is sent. This we learn from the words which immediately precede our text, and from the text itself: here we are informed both who they are, and what they are.

1. *Who they are;*—They are the people, and the Gentiles. "Delivering thee," &c., ver. 17. By *the people* is meant the *Jewish nation*, who were God's chosen people, Deut. vii. 6;—a peculiarly favored people, Deut. xxxiii. 29;—and a sinful people, who became rebellious, ungrateful, and degenerated, Isa. i. 2—4. To this people the gospel was first preached by Christ's command, Luke xxiv. 47;—and to this people will the gospel yet be preached with the happiest success, Rom. xi. 25, 26. By the *Gentiles* are meant *those nations of the earth which are not of Jewish extraction.* To them also the Messiah was promised, Isa. xlix. 6; for their benefit he was manifested in the flesh, Luke ii. 10, 11, 32; to them also the gospel is sent by repeated injunctions, Luke xxiv. 47; Mark xvi. 15; Matt. xxviii. 19; on their receiving the gospel, Christ redeems them from sin, Acts x. 34, Rev. vii. 9, 10; and they are promised to Christ for his inheritance, Psa. ii. 8. The people and the Gentiles must therefore include *all mankind;* and hereby we are assured that God wills the salvation of all the human race, Ezek. xxxiii. 11; 1 Tim. ii. 4. Having seen who they are to whom the gospel is sent, let us now observe,

2. *What they are,*—or in what state the gospel finds them. *They are in darkness;* for the gospel is sent to open their eyes, &c. They are in the darkness of *ignorance*, respecting the nature, necessity, and way of salvation, Psa. cvii. 10, 11. They are in *darkness;* for they have closed their eyes by a deliberate rejection of divine light, John iii. 19, 20; Matt xiii. 15; and they are blinded by Satan, 1 Cor. iv. 4. *They are subject to the power of Satan.* This they evidently are, being *inhabited* by him, Eph ii. 2;—*devoted* to his service, John viii. 44;—and *governed* by his will, &,

**Tim.** ii. 26. *They are condemned criminals;* under a sentence of eternal death, John. iii. 18; Ezek. xviii. 20. *They are a disinherited family;* for they have justly forfeited their title to heaven, Rom. iii. 23; and they have no well-grounded hope of it, Eph. ii. 12. Thus our state, through sin, is alarming; but God has remembered us in mercy, Psa. cxxxvi. 23. Of this our text also assures us, by teaching us,

II. THE DESIGN OF THE GOSPEL MISSION,—or the purposes for which it was sent.

1. *It is sent to open our eyes, and to turn us from darkness to light.*— *To open our eyes;* by calling our attention to the care of our souls, as the most important business of our lives, Matt. vi. 33; 1 Tim. iv. 8; Matt. xvi. 26. *To turn us from darkness to light;* by engaging us to come to Christ for illumination of mind, Eph. v. 14; Matt. xi. 29; John viii. 12.

2. *It is sent to turn us from the power of Satan unto God.* To *turn us from the power of Satan;* from his *dominion,* by subduing our evil habits, 2 Cor. x. 4, 5; and from his *service,* by effecting an entire reformation in our conduct, Tit. ii. 12. To *turn us unto God;* with humble *contrition,* Luke xv. 18; with earnest *cries* for mercy, Luke xviii. 13; with *affiance* in his compassion, Psa. xiii. 5, and lii. 8; and with due *subjection* to his authority, Rom. vi. 13.

3. *It is sent that we may receive forgiveness of sins.* Gospel forgiveness implies, *full* forgiveness of all our past sins, both secret and open, Acts xiii. 38, 39. *Affectionate* forgiveness; such as exempts us from the punishment due to sin, and interests us in God's paternal favor, Psa. xxxii. 1, 2; Luke xv. 22—24. *Assured* forgiveness, which is attested by the Holy Spirit, Isa. xii. 1; Rom. viii. 16.

4. *It is sent that we may receive inheritance among them which are sanctified.* To be *sanctified,* is to be *separated from sin;* and *devoted to God's service,* Rom. vi. 22. This sanctification the gospel *requires,* 1 Thess. v. 23, 24, and iv. 7; and what the gospel requires, it instrumentally *produces,* Obad. 17; John xvii. 17. The *inheritance* of those which are *sanctified,* is *two-fold;* a gracious inheritance in this life, 1 Cor. iii. 21–23; and a glorious inheritance in heaven, 1 Peter i. 3—5. And *all who obey the gospel enjoy this inheritance,* Psa. lxxxiv. 11; Acts xx. 32. That we may ensure the enjoyment of this inheritance, our text teaches us,

III. THE DUTY OF GOSPEL SUBJECTS ;—or the means by which its blessings are appropriated. All its benefits are obtained by faith in Christ; "By faith that is in me." Here observe,

1. *What faith in Christ implies.* It appears from God's word that it implies—*Coming* to Christ, for rest from sin and its consequences, Matt. xi. 28; John v. 35. *Receiving* Christ, as our Teacher, Sovereign, and Redeemer, John i. 12; Matt. xi. 29. *Trusting* in Christ, for full salvation, pardon, acceptance, holiness, and heaven, Isa. xxviii. 16; Eph. i. 13. *Abiding* in Christ, till he comes to glorify us, 1 John ii. 28; Heb. xii. 2. And *walking* in Christ, by seeking all he calls us to enjoy, Col. ii. 6; Phil. iii. 12.

2. *The propriety of requiring faith in Christ as the means of salvation.* This is evident, because faith in Christ tends to inspire its subjects with the most profound *reverence for God,* who will not be approached by us without a Mediator, Psa. lxxxix 7; Heb. xii. 28, 29; with *dread of sin,* which rendered Christ's sufferings necessary, that we might be saved consistently with God's rectitude, Heb. ii. 10; Rom. iii. 25, 26; with *confidence in God;* who has graciously given us the earnest of salvation, in the gift of

his Son, Rom. viii. 32 ; with *gratitude* to God, for his redeeming goodness, 2 Cor. v. 14, 15 ; 1 Cor. vi. 19, 20; Rom. xii. 1 ; and with deep *humiliation*, through a consciousness that our salvation is ascribable only to divine grace, Eph. ii. 8, 9; Tit. iii. 5—7.

### APPLICATION.

1. *From the duty of gospel subjects, learn the importance of faith in our Lord Jesus Christ.—It is important,* as none can be saved without it, John. iii. 36; Mark xvi. 15, 16. Hence, *seek salvation in no other way* but that of faith in Christ; not on the ground of mere mercy without a Mediator; for God will not admit sinners into his presence on these terms, John xiv. 6; not on account of your sufferings, for these being the effects of sin, can never remove their cause ; not on account of your good morals, for you cannot atone for past offences by the imperfect fulfilment of present duties, Psalm cxliii. 2. *Rest in nothing short of faith in Christ.* Not in partial reformation, nor in correct opinions, nor in the mere outward form of godliness. Now actually come to Christ, receive him, and trust in him, Acts xxii. 16. *Persevere in the exercise of faith;* its continuance is necessary, Heb. x. 37.

2. *From the design of the gospel mission, learn your privileges as believers in Christ. Consider the blessings* you are called to enjoy ; these are illumination, conversion, pardon, sanctification. *Examine yourselves;* are you thus turned from darkness to light; from the power of Satan unto God? have you received forgiveness of sins? are you sanctified,—redeemed from sin, and devoted to God? have you heaven in prospect? can you say with the apostle, 2 Cor. v. 1 ; 1 Peter i. 3. *Expect* those blessings, if exercising faith in Christ; they are purchased for you, promised to you, and are now ready to be imparted, John xi. 40; Luke xiv. 17.

3. *From the objects of gospel benevolence, learn your duty as the followers of Christ.* As his professing followers you are called to *imitate him,* Phil. ii. 5; 1 John ii. 6. Like him, have *compassion* on perishing sinners ; whether relatives, the rising generation, adult neighbors, or the heathen world. However distinguished, their case is truly pitiable; for they are blind, enslaved, perishing, helpless, and hopeless, Job vi. 14. *Impart gospel truth to them,* that they may be healed of their diseases, and saved from their destructions, Psa. cvii. 20. *Your consistent christian zeal will be attended with the happiest results.* Hereby you will concur with God in fulfilling the Messiah's request, Psa. ii. 8; you will promote the glory of God, Isa. lxi. 1—3; and you ensure eternal honor to yourselves, Daniel xii. 3; 1 Peter v. 3.

---

## THE NATURE AND EFFECTS OF TRUE RELIGION.

James iii. 17.—The wisdom that is from above, is first pure, then peaceable, gentle, and easy to be entreated, full of mercy and good fruits, without partiality, and without hypocrisy. (H. H.)

RELIGION, like a tree, must be judged of by its fruits—
That which savors of pride, earthliness, or sensuality, is not of God—
Its character is justly drawn in the words before us—It is,

**I. Holy in its nature—**

Religion, above all other things, is entitled to the name of "wisdom"—

It enlightens the mind, informs the judgment, regulates the life—

And he who lives under its influence, is wise in the estimation of God himself—

Being from above, it resembles its divine author—

Religion is a beam issuing from God the fountain of light—

And, as "in him is no darkness at all," so neither is there any thing impure in that which flows from him—

It may be mixed with sin, but in its own nature it is "pure"—

And, in proportion as it prevails, it will dissipate the clouds of ignorance and sin—

All "spiritual or fleshly filthiness" will surely vanish before it, Matt. v. 8 Acts xv. 9; 2 Cor vii. 1.

In consequence of this it is,

**II. Useful in its tendency—**It renders us,

1. Amiable in our spirit—

Though men differ widely in their natural tempers, yet the unregenerate are, on many occasions, quarrelsome, fierce, implacable—

But as soon as ever religion exerts its influence on our minds, we mortify these unhallowed tempers, and become "peaceable, gentle, and easy to be entreated"—

From thenceforth it is the delight of our souls to cultivate and promote peace, to maintain in ourselves a meek and quiet spirit, and to exercise, as occasion may require, forbearance and forgiveness to all around us—

2. Benevolent in our conduct—

Compassion and diligence are inseparable attributes of true religion—

The real christian is not, like the barren fig-tree, covered with the leaves of an outward profession, but destitute of fruit—

He labors to abound in every good word and work, and to benefit to the utmost the bodies and souls of his fellow creatures—

His heart is "full" of love, and out of the abundance of his heart he both speaks and acts—

It is within us a living principle, that is,

**III. Uniform in its operations—**It extends,

1. To duties without limitation—

The grace of God will not admit of "partiality" in our obedience—

It will stimulate us to difficult and self-denying duties, as well as to those which are more easy and pleasant, 1 Tim. v. 21.

And will make us as solicitous to do what is right towards strangers or enemies, as towards our own friends or partizans, 1 Tim. v. 21.

2. To desires without reserve—

Religion penetrates to the inmost soul, and regulates all our motives and principles of action—

The person whose *outward* conduct *only* is good, is in God's sight no other than a "whited sepulchre"—

The man whose heart is right with God, will watch against all selfish ends, and endeavor to act with a single eye to the glory of his God—

**Infer,**

1. How unjustly is religion condemned in the world!

Many consider religion as destructive of all personal and social happiness—

But what is there in this representation of religion that deserves such a character?—

137

Let the world call it *folly* if they will; but God accounts it " *wisdom*"—

2. What reason have the most godly to blush and be ashamed!

We must not estimate our religion by our opinions so much as by our practice—

Doubtless we must build on Christ as our only foundation; but we have no evidence of an union with him any further than we raise upon him this holy superstructure—

Alas! what poor builders have the very best of us been; and how little progress have we made when we judge by this test!—

3. What need have we to wait continually upon our God in prayer!

This wisdom is "from above," and can be derived from God alone—

And how can we obtain it of him, but in the exercise of prayer?—

Let us then ask it of him, who has promised to impart it "liberally, and without upbraiding," James i. 5.

~~~~~~~~~~~

## STABILITY THE GIFT OF GOD.

**Psa.** lxvi. 8, 9.—O bless our God, ye people, and make the voice of his praise to be heard; which holdeth our soul in life, and suffereth not our feet to be moved. (H. H.)

THE blessings of Providence, when uninterruptedly continued, are scarcely noticed: it is only when the loss of them has been painfully apprehended, or actually sustained, that we consider how much we were indebted to God for them. What were the particular trials that had been endured by David or the Jewish nation, we cannot precisely determine: but it is evident, that the deliverance vouchsafed to them had made a lively impression on the Psalmist's mind. Compare ver. 1, 2, with ver. 10—12. The words of our text would furnish exceedingly profitable meditations, if we confined them to their primary import; since the preservation of our life and health, amidst the many seen and unseen dangers with which we are surrounded, demands our most grateful acknowledgments. But a subsequent part of the psalm shews clearly that the writer had respect also to spiritual blessings; ver. 16; and therefore we shall draw your attention more especially to them; and shew,

I. WHAT A MERCY IT IS TO BE UPHELD IN THE WAYS OF GOD.

We feel somewhat of the obligation conferred upon us in our first awakening and conversion; but are by no means duly sensible how much we owe to our God for our daily preservation. But we shall learn better to appreciate this mercy if we consider,

1. To how many snares and dangers we are exposed!

We have frequent occasion to advert to the temptations with which we are encompassed in the world; and to notice the still greater dangers we experience from the corruptions of our own hearts; and the additional conflicts which we have to sustain with all the powers of darkness. We dwell not therefore so particularly on those things at this time; but rather mention the danger to which we are exposed even from lawful things. It is not only allowable, but highly proper, to prosecute our worldly callings with diligence; and to cultivate the tenderest regard for our wife or children: yet both the one and the other may engross too much of our hearts, and become hinderences to us in our journey towards heaven. Our food, our sleep, our studies.

our recreations, may become snares, if we be not continually on our guard. It is therefore an unspeakable mercy to be upheld in the midst of such manifold temptations.

2. How many in like circumstances with ourselves, have fallen—

We are living in the full enjoyment of divine ordinances, and of whatever can conduce to the welfare of our souls. But are we therefore secure? Look back to the apostolic age: see how many then were seduced by error, Tit. i. 11; 2 Tim. ii. 18; or disheartened by the fear of man, 2 Tim. i. 15, and iv. 16; Matt. xxvi. 73, 74; or turned aside by the love of this world, Matt. xiii. 22; 2 Tim. iv. 10; or overthrown by unbridled passions. 1 Tim. v. 11, 12; 2 Sam. xi. 4. What reason then have we to adore the grace that has preserved *us!*

3. What would be the probable consequence of our falling—

Some who have fallen have been restored speedily; John xxi. 15—17; and some after a lapse of time; 2 Sam. xii. 13; but thousands have fallen to rise no more. The progress of declension is for the most part rapid. The heart becomes averse to holy duties: from secret neglects proceeds a backwardness to social conference and public ordinances. The conscience is gradually weakened, till it ceases to perform its office, or speaks in so faint a voice, that it is scarcely heard. The besetting sin then gains an entire ascendant, and leads him captive; till at last, God, filled with indignation against the base apostate, "gives him up to a reprobate mind," Ps. lxxxi. 11, 12; and either cuts him off by a sudden stroke, Prov. xxix. i; Acts v. 5, 10, or leaves him to protract a miserable existence, merely that he may bear testimony against his own impieties, and proclaim to those around him the foretastes which he already feels of his eternal destiny. Eccl. v. 17; with Prov. xiv. 32.

Such examples we have seen*: what a mercy it is that we ourselves, instead of being warned by others, are not made a warning to others!

4. What occasion we have given to God to let us fail—

Let us call to mind our own backslidings; our secret neglects; our tampering with temptations; our indulgence of evil passions; our vain-confident presumption: is it not wonderful that God has not long since said respecting us, "Let him alone;" Hos. iv. 17; "My Spirit shall strive with him no longer." Gen. vi. 3: "He likes not to retain God in his knowledge; so I will give him up!" Rom. i. 28.

If we be convinced of these things, let us proceed to consider,

II. THE DUTY OF THOSE WHO EXPERIENCE THIS MERCY—

There can be no doubt on this subject. If our souls have been upheld in life, we should,

1. Acknowledge God in our steadfastness—

"Who is it that has made us to differ" from others? 1 Cor. iv. 7. Have we by nature any more strength than they? or have we of ourselves a more abundant measure of goodness? No: it is "by the grace of God we are what we are; 1 Cor. xv.10; we have been as much indebted to his protecting hand, as a new-born infant is to its mother's care. We should then acknowledge, that "of him our fruit is found; Hos. xiv. 8; Isai. xxvi. 12; that "it is he that hath wrought us to the self-same thing;" 2 Cor. v. 5; and that to him belongs all the glory of our stability. Ps. lxii. 8; and xxvi. 12.

---

* This was preached on occasion of a person that had made a profession of religion, going back to drunkenness, and dying in a drunken fit. See other examples, 1 Cor. x 6—11.

2. **Bless and adore** him for his great goodness—

It is not by cold acknowledgments merely that we are to requite the Lord, but by fervent and devout thanksgivings. It is not possible for language adequately to express the obligations we owe to him: and therefore we should call upon " all that is within us to bless his holy name."

Nor should we be content with doing this ourselves: we should invite the whole creation, as it were, to join us. We should labor to stimulate all to love and serve him; and to make his name known to the very ends of the earth. Isai. xii. 4—6, or xlii. 10—12. See also *the text.*

It is in this way that we should endeavor at least, as much as in us lies, to " render unto the Lord according to the benefits" he has conferred upon us.

3. **Walk humbly and carefully** before him—

We must not presume upon the kindness of our God, or imagine that, because we have been upheld hitherto, we are in no danger of falling: if we had attained the stability of St. Paul himself, " we must keep our body under, and bring it into subjection, lest we become cast-aways ourselves." 1 Cor. ix. 27. To neglect this were to tempt God. God has warned us plainly, that " he will be with us no longer than we continue with him; that if we forsake him, he will forsake us." 2 Chron. xv. 2. We therefore must not be high-minded, but fear; 1 Cor. x. 12; and take heed lest we fall; Rom. xi. 20; and " watch and pray lest we enter into temptation." Matt. xxvi. 41. If we would have our God to keep us, we must be careful to " keep ourselves." Ver. 18, with Jude 20, 21. We must look at the fearful examples that are before our eyes; Luke xvii. 32; Heb. iv. 11; and tremble lest we ourselves become similar monuments of instability, and of God's deserved wrath.

4. **Commit ourselves continually** to him—

God has engaged to " keep the feet of his saints;" 1 Sam. ii. 9; and directed us to commit ourselves to him for that purpose; 1 Pet. iv. 19; and assured us, that, if we do so, " he will establish our goings." 2 Chron. xx. 20. We should commend ourselves therefore to his gracious care and protection. We should say with David, " Hold thou up my goings in thy paths, that my footsteps slip not: Ps. xvii. 5: " Hold thou me up, and I shall be safe." Ps. cxix. 117. To this we are encouraged by our past experience of his mercy: we may from the kindness already shewn us, safely infer the continuance of it to our souls. Ps. lvi. 13. If we can say, " He hath delivered," we may properly add, " In whom we trust that he will yet deliver us." 2 Cor. i. 10.

But here arise two important QUESTIONS, which it is of the utmost importance to resolve:

1. Are our souls really alive to God?

In vain shall we speak of having " our souls upheld in life," if they have never yet been quickened from the dead. Let us then seriously, and as in the presence of God, inquire, Whether we have been made partakers of a new and living principle, whereby we have been enabled to die unto sin, and to live unto God? Let us not mistake a mere approbation of religion for real regeneration: we must have become new creatures, having new views, new pursuits, new desires, and new prospects, if we have been truly born again: 2 Cor. v. 17; and if this change have not been wrought within us, we are yet in our natural and unconverted state; we may have " a name to live, but are really dead" before God: notwithstanding we may have been preserved from any flagrant violation of our duty, we are yet " dead in trespasses and sins.'

**2.** Supposing that we are on the whole alive to God, have "our feet really been kept from falling?"

We must ascertain this fact, before we can cordially thank God for it. And is it indeed true of all who profess religion amongst us, that they have been kept? Have none of us acted unworthy of our high calling? Has there been nothing in our tempers, nothing in our worldly transactions, inconsistent with our profession? Or, supposing our outward conduct to have been unimpeachable, have there been no secret sins, which we have reason to mourn over; nothing for which we ought to blush and be confounded before God? Perhaps, if we look inward, we shall find more occasion to bewail our falls, than to bless our God for having kept us from falling.

But, if conscience testify that we have indeed walked uprightly before God, then let us imitate the example in the text, and not only bless and magnify him ourselves, but endeavor also to "make the voice of his praise to be heard" throughout the world.

---

## STEADFASTNESS IN GOD.

Phil. iv. 1.—My brethren, dearly beloved and longed for, my joy and crown, so stand fast in the Lord, my dearly beloved. (H. H.)

St. Paul was a man of feeling, a man of love. He felt for all: for those whom he saw perishing in sin, he would willingly have endured all that men or devils could inflict, if only it might be instrumental to their salvation. Rom. ix. 3. For those who belonged to Christ, even though they had never seen his face in the flesh, he had great conflicts, striving if by any means he might promote their eternal welfare. But towards those who had been converted by his ministry, he felt as a father towards his children: he could say, "God is my record how greatly I long after you all in the bowels of Jesus Christ." Phil. i. 8. To such is this epistle addressed; as indeed the words of our text clearly evince. Such an accumulation of tender expressions can scarcely be found in the same space in all the Book of God. But what is the drift of them all? Why does he so labor to convince the Philippians of his love, and to conciliate their regards to him? it was, that they might be stirred up to give the more earnest heed to his exhortations, and to "stand fast in the Lord."

To be "in the Lord" is the character of every believer: he is united unto Christ by faith, and is engrafted into him as a branch of the living vine. But our blessed Lord cautions us again and again to "abide in him," and warns us against the danger of separation from him. John xv. 1—6. In like manner we are frequently exhorted to "stand fast in the Lord;" and so to continue in the faith grounded and settled, that we may not be moved away from the hope of the gospel."

To you then we would now address the exhortation, and say, Stand fast in,

I. Your allegiance to him—

Many things will conspire to draw you away from Christ—

The world, with its vanities on the one hand, and its terrors on the other, will assault you continually— — —the flesh also will operate to bring you into subjection to all its basest lusts— — —Nor will Satan be idle : he, with all his confederate hosts, will strive, by innumerable wiles and temptations, either to subvert your principles, or to vitiate your practice— — —It is a warfare into which you are brought, when once you enlist under the banners of Christ; and you must expect all manner of conflicts to your dying hour.

But you must be steadfast in your adherence to him—

You must be "good soldiers of Jesus Christ," and never cease to fight till you have obtained the victory. Neither hopes nor fears, neither joys nor sorrows, must be suffered to alienate you from him, or to damp your zeal in his service. True it is that the Lord gives you many great and precious promises, that he will keep you, and that nothing shall ever separate you from his love. Rom. viii. 35—39. But this is not to encourage supineness : but rather to make you more earnest in your application to him for protection and support. With the example of Demas before you, you should never cease to fear, lest you also should "fall from your own stedfastness," 2 Pet. iii. 17, and "be corrupted from the simplicity that is in Christ." 2 Cor. xi. 3. Aware of your danger, you must "fight the good fight of faith," and "cleave unto the Lord with full purpose of heart." "You must be faithful unto death, if ever you would obtain the crown of life."

Stand fast also in,

II. YOUR DEPENDENCE ON HIM—

From this also you are in danger of being drawn—

There is in us a continual proneness to self-confidence and self-dependence We are ever ready to lean to our own understanding to guide us— — —our own righteousness to justify us— — —our own strength to preserve us — — —It is a great matter to have the soul brought to a simple reliance upon the Lord Jesus Christ for every thing.

But we must live altogether by faith on Christ—

He is "Head over all things to his church," and has all fulness of blessings treasured up in him for our use. Eph. i. 22, 23; Col. i. 19. "He is made of God unto us wisdom, and righteousness, and sanctification, and redemption;" and from him must we receive them all, John i. 16, that in, and by, and for all, His name may be glorified— — —Isa. xlv. 24, 25.

Nor must any thing be suffered to weaken,

III. YOUR EXPECTATION OF HIS FUTURE ADVENT—

To that day there is a particular reference in the preceding context—Ch iii. 20, 21.

We are apt to lose sight of that awful day—

This is evident, from the remissness and negligence with which the things of eternity are pursued. Could we be dull and slothful with that day before our eyes ?— — —Could the allurements or terrors of the world have any influence upon our hearts, if we knew and saw that the Judge was at the door ?— — —

But we must stand continually in a state of preparation for it—

To wait for Christ's second coming is the habit of mind to which every believer is brought: 1 Thess. i. 9, 10; and in proportion as it is formed in the mind, is the progress which we have made in the divine life. 1 Cor. i. 7. We should not give way to sloth, like the foolish Virgins; but have "our loins girt, and our lamps trimmed, and ourselves as those who wait for the coming of their Lord." We should look forward with a holy longing for that day, as the termination of all our conflicts, and the consummation of all our joys, Tit. ii. 13; 2 Pet. iii. 12,— — —and comfort ourselves with the assured expectation that then we shall be ever with the Lord. 1 Thess. iv. 17, 18. With that period before our eyes, we shall " be diligent to be found of him in peace, without spot and blameless." 2 Pet. iii. 14.

Permit me, in CONCLUSION, to urge this matter, after the example of the apostle in my text.

~~~~~~~

## JOYFUL IMPORT OF THE GOSPEL.

Acts viii. 8.—And there was great joy in that city. (Pr.)

THE christian church has from its infancy been subject to great vicissitudes, and like the moon it has continually waxed and waned. When the disciples first found the Messiah they were full of joy; when he was crucified they were covered with a cloud of darkness; but when he arose from the dead their hopes and joys revived again. The work of grace at Jerusalem, in the conversion of so many thousands, makes them a little heaven upon earth; but soon a storm of persecution followed. See the blessed Stephen stoned to death, and Saul making havoc of the church, verse 2. Yet out of all this evil much good arises, and now there is another triumph to the cause of truth and righteousness. " Philip went down to Samaria and preached Christ unto them—and there was great joy in that city."

I. IT IS DESERVING OF REMARK, THAT THE SEAT OF THIS HOLY TRIUMPH WAS " THE CITY OF SAMARIA."

Well may it be said, " the wilderness and the solitary place shall be glad for them, and the desert shall rejoice, and blossom like the rose;" for such indeed was the city of Samaria.

1. Its inhabitants consisted partly of *heathens* and partly of *apostate Jews,* who had a sort of half heathenised religion among them. They had been a superstitious and degenerate people from the time of Salmanezer, and such they still continued. 2 Kings xvii. 33, 34. ———— They set up a temple on mount Gerizzim in opposition to that on mount Moriah, and carried on a kind of worship which Christ condemned. John iv. 22. ———— They had also manifested the greatest aversion to the Jews, and to Christ and his followers as being of that nation. Luke ix. 51—53. A hopeless and inveterate people!

2. Yet this very city is celebrated for its *reception of the gospel*, and was one of the first to surrender to the arms of truth. ———— On the report of the woman, after the interview at Jacob's well, the Samaritans showed a disposition to listen to the gospel, and they received the Saviour very courteously. John iv. 39—42. And now when Philip went down and preached Christ to them, " the people with one accord gave heed unto those things which Philip spake, hearing and seeing the miracles which he did," ver. 6. ———— Thus was fulfilled the prediction of our Lord to the woman of Samaria, and also to his disciples. John iv. 23, 35. Thus also the Lord builds up Jerusalem, and gathers together the outcasts of Israel. Psa. cxlvii. 2. Isa. lvi. 6—8.

II. THE JOY WHICH NOW PREVAILED IN THE CITY OF SAMARIA IS FULLY ACCOUNTED FOR BY THE CAUSE WHICH PRODUCED IT

Joy is never excited but on some great occasion, and the seasons of religious joy are distinguished by some interesting or extraordinary occurrence Such was the joy and gladness at the preparation for building the temple of Jerusalem, 1 Chron. xxix. 9: at Hezekiah's passover, 2 Chron. xxx. 25, 26: at the rebuilding and dedication of the city wall, Neh. xii. 43; at the birth of Christ, Luke ii. 10—14; at the appearance of the star to the eastern magi, Matt. ii. 13; and at the ascension of our blessed Saviour, Luke xxiv. 52. All these were great events, and furnished an abundant source of joy and rejoicing.

We may therefore expect something great and interesting in the present instance, to fill a whole city with joy ——— and what was it? Answer, the glad tidings of the gospel: that Christ was come, that he died for sinners, that he had risen again, that he had ascended above all heavens, and lived to make intercession for transgressors; that through faith in him there was now forgiveness and acceptance with God, and this news was proclaimed to all nations.

Some may say that these are common things, and they have been proclaimed in other cities as well as in Samaria, and we have all heard of them before. ——— Be it so: if you have cordially received them, there is enough to occasion great joy; and if they have not produced such an effect, it is because they have not been fully realized by faith.

Let us then recapitulate the leading facts of the gospel, and observe the glad tidings contained in them—

1. Is it not ground for joy that *the Lord is come into the world to save sinners?* ——— This is what the church was looking for, nearly four thousand years. This was the great theme of prophetic inspiration, from age to age; and what Israel was commanded to rejoice in, even from the days of old. Zech. ix. 9. The prospect of our Saviour's advent inspired not only the ancient church, but even the whole creation with joy and gladness. Psa. xcvi. 11—13. ——— If therefore Samaria had not exulted in this great event, there would have been no sympathy, no correspondence with the ancient believers, and of course no evidence of their belief in its existence or reality. ——— If we also profess to believe in the coming of Christ, and the great objects of his appearance, and are still indifferent and unaffected, it proves our faith to be utterly vain. Shall glory to God in the highest, peace on earth, and good will to men be nothing to us; and yet shall we be allowed to call ourselves christians!

2. Is it not ground for joy that *Christ has laid down his life for us,* and redeemed us unto God by his blood? ——— It is true his death caused sorrow to the disciples for a time; but when they understood the design of that great event, their sorrow was turned into joy. ——— Consider in what light this interesting truth is held up to us in the scriptures. "But now in the end of the world hath he appeared, to put away sin by the sacrifice of himself—When he had by himself purged our sins, he sat down on the right hand of the Majesty on high." Heb. ix. 26, i. 3. On this inestimable sacrifice is founded a new and everlasting covenant, promising forgiveness, and securing eternal life to all that believe. Heb. viii. 10—12; 2 Cor. v. 18, 19; John iii. 16. ——— This is the source of the first hope and joy to an awakened sinner, and it has turned the sorrow of many into gladness. We may afterwards derive comfort from a consciousness of believing in Christ, and being interested in him; but the first is from looking to him, looking out of ourselves, and beholding the Lamb of God that taketh away the sin of the world

144

**3.** Is it not a matter of great joy that *Christ is risen from the dead?*— This proves that he was the true Messiah, that his sacrifice is accepted, and that justice is fully satisfied. "The God of peace brought again from the dead that great Shepherd of the sheep, through the blood of the everlasting covenant—and raised him up and gave him glory, that your faith and hope might be in God." Heb. xiii. 20; 1 Pet. i. 21. —— The resurrection of Christ is also the pattern and the pledge of our own resurrection, and is therefore on this account a matter of joyful exultation. 1 Cor. xv. 20; Phil. iii. 21.

**4.** Is it not matter of joy too, that *Christ has ascended into glory:* and that he ever liveth to make intercession for us? —— On this ground it is that he is able to save to the uttermost all that come unto God by him. Heb. vii. 25. If any man sin, we have an advocate with the Father. 1 John ii. 1. —— Having entered into his glory, he is become heir of all things, and possesses the power of enriching his church, and of ruling in the midst of his enemies. Psa. lxviii. 18; cx. 1, 2; Ephes. i. 20—22.

**5.** That through faith in his name there is *forgiveness of sin, and acceptance with God?* —— The import of the gospel is, Believe in Jesus, and ye shall be saved; submit to his righteousness, and ye shall be accepted, whatever be your past sins, or present unworthiness. Look off from all duties of your own, and plead that obedience with which God is well pleased. Come unto me, says Jesus, and ye shall find rest to your souls—and him that cometh I will in no wise cast out. John vi. 37. —— If such tidings do not gladden the heart, it is only because we have neither part nor lot in the matter.

**6.** Is it not a source of joy that this gospel *is now sent to all nations?* —— Salvation originated with the Jews; theirs were the covenants, and the giving of the law; and of whom, as concerning the flesh, Christ came. But the Gentiles were to be grafted in, and to partake of the root and fatness of the olive tree; and now there is a community of privileges and of blessedness.

**7.** Was it not a special matter of joy to the Samaritans, that *they themselves had believed the gospel?* —— If Israel of old rejoiced that they were willing to build the house of the Lord, much more may we rejoice to see the spiritual temple edified and built up, especially if our hands also are in the work. —— Philip the evangelist rejoiced in the success of his labor, the Samaritans rejoiced in the doctrines of the cross, and that the kingdom of God was come nigh unto them.

### REFLECTIONS.

1. If then the gospel bring tidings of great joy, why is it reproached as tending to gloom and melancholy? Can any thing be more unreasonable or unjust.

2. Why do individuals despond, while there is such an exhibition of mercy? Because they do not hearken to the gospel, nor receive the record which God hath given of his Son.

3. Why do not christians possess more joy and peace in believing? Because we have not more religion, do not live more under the influence of the gospel. Lord increase our faith.

145

## THE SUBJECTS OF DIVINE GRACE EXHORTED TO CLEAVE UNTO THE LORD.

Acts xi. 23. Who, when he came, and had seen the grace of God, was glad, and exhorted them all, that with purpose of heart they would cleave unto the Lord." (Sk.)

THESE words are evidently connected with the preceding verses, and the whole paragraph from, ver. 19, claims our serious attention;—"Now they which were scattered abroad," &c. In this relation we observe,

1. *A display of God's perfections in the extension of his kingdom*, ver. 19—21. Of his *truth ;* in protecting his church amidst cruel persecution, Matt. xvi. 18 :—his *goodness ;* in sending the gospel to both Jews and Gentiles, Psa. cvii. 20, 21 :—his *wisdom ;* in promoting his own glory by the malice of his enemies, Psa. lxxv. 10 :—his *power*, in giving abundant success to the labors of his servants.

2. This account teaches us *the true nature of a christian church*, ver. 22.-—The church is capable of *hearing* and *acting ;* for the church heard that some of the Gentiles were converted to the faith of Christ, and sent Barnabas to visit them, and confirm them in the faith. Therefore the church cannot mean a building set apart for divine worship, as some suppose ; but a company of professing Christians united to assist each other in seeking the power of godliness, Acts ix. 31, and xii. 5. As a missionary of the church, Barnabas came to Antioch ; "Who when he came, and had seen the grace of God," &c. By what Barnabas thus saw, and felt, and did, we are instructed to observe,

I. THAT THE CONVERSION OF SINNERS TO GOD, IS JUSTLY ASCRIBABLE TO HIS GRACE. This is evident from the subjects, the benefits, and the causes of conversion.

1. *The subjects of conversion are sinners*—who have *rebelled* against God, Isa. i. 2, 3,—who have cherished and manifested *enmity* of heart against God, Rom. viii. 7; Col. i. 21; and who have justly *forfeited* every favor at God's hand, Lam. iii. 22.

2. *The benefits of conversion are various.* Conversion is a *turning* to God, and implies both a *deliverance* and a *translation*, Col. i. 13.—*A deliverance from Satan ;* from his service and dominion, Rom. vi. 14, 22.— And *a translation into the kingdom of Christ ;* by the enjoyment of pardon, which entitles them to the kingdom of heaven, Col. i. 14 ; Tit. iii. 6 ;— and of purity, which fits them for the kingdom of heaven, Col. i. 12.

3. *The causes of conversion are meritorious, efficient, and instrumental.*—The *meritorious* cause is *Christ's mediation*, through which we are pardoned, Eph. iv. 32.—The *efficient* cause is the *Holy Spirit*, 1 Cor. vi. 11, which is God's free gift, Luke xi. 13.—The *instrumental* cause is *faith*, Acts xxvi. 18, which ascribes all it receives to the grace or favor of God, Eph. ii. 8 : Tit. iii. 4, 5 ; 1 Cor. xv. 10. Our text teaches us,

II. THAT WHERE THE GRACE OF GOD IS ENJOYED, IT WILL BE SEEN IN ITS EFFECTS ;—"When he came, he *saw* the grace of God." The grace of God may be, and is seen,

1. *In the tempers of its subjects, or the dispositions of their minds.* Where grace reigns, pride, and unkindness, and unmercifulmess, will be subdued, Col. iii. 12—14.

2. *In the conversation of its subjects ;* this is pure, and profitable, Eph. iv. 22 : Col. iii. 16, 17.

3. *In the actions of its subjects ;* these are godly, righteous, and temperate, Tit. ii. 12.

**4.** *All who profess to enjoy the grace of God, should be careful thus to show it.*—On principles of *prudence;* that their own eternal salvation may be secured, 2 Pet. i. 5—10.—On principles of *piety;* that God may hereby be glorified, Matt. v. 16; 1 Pet. xi. 11. 12.—On principles of *benevolence;* that their weak brethren may be strengthened, Heb. xiii. 13, and that their pastors may hereby be comforted, 1 Thess. iii. 8; 3 John, ver. 4.—As an excitement to holy diligence, on this generous principle, our text teaches us,

III. THAT WHEN THE GRACE OF GOD IS SEEN, IT AFFORDS PLEASURE TO WELL-DISPOSED MINDS;—" When he saw the grace of God, he was *glad;*" and his joy was both pious and pure.

1. *His joy on this occasion was pious.* It was the joy of a saint excited by seeing the grace of God manifested, and sinners saved. He was glad— As *" a good man,"* or a *lover of mankind;* because hereby many were benefitted; being raised to a state of safety, happiness, and honor, Rom. v. 1; Eph. ii. 1—6; and the welfare of the civil state was also promoted, Prov. xiv. 32. He was glad—As *a holy man;* for he was *"full of the Holy Ghost."* Hence he was glad. because the felicity of angels was hereby augmented, Luke xv. 10. Christ was hereby most pleasingly satisfied, Isa. liii. 10, 11; and God was hereby glorified, Isa. lxi. 1—3. He was glad—As a *faithful man;* for he " was *full of faith."* Hence, he confidently expected the fulfilment of God's word, Ps. ii. 8. He beheld in these converted Gentiles, the earnest of Christ's universal dominion; and could exclaim with David, Psa. lxxii. 19, 20.

2. *His joy on this occasion was pure.* He was glad—though the subjects of this grace were Gentile *strangers;* it was not the joy of *bigotry:* and though *he* was not the *instrument* of their conversion; it was not the joy of *self-complacency.*

3. *His joy on this occasion was exemplary;* worthy of our *imitation.* Wherever the grace of God is seen we should rejoice: without *bigotry,* this is *unchristian,* Eph. v. 24; and without *envy,* for this is *devilish,* James iii. 14—16. Our text teaches us,

IV. THAT CLEAVING UNTO THE LORD IS THE INDISPENSABLE DUTY OF ALL CHRISTIAN CONVERTS.

1. *By the Lord is meant our Lord Jesus Christ;* who is our *Guide,* Ps. xlviii. 14,—our *Sovereign,* Matt. xxiii. 8;—our *Strength,* Psa. xlvi. 1;—and our *Foundation,* Isa. xxviii. 16.

2. *It is the duty of Christian converts to cleave unto the Lord.* Cleave unto him—By habitual *attention,* Acts iii. 22, 23;—by persevering *obedience,* Heb. v. 9; Psa. cvi. 3; by importunate *prayer,* Heb. iv. 16;—and by entire *dependance,* 1 Pet. ii. 5, 6; Jude, ver. 21, 22.

3. *All christian converts should thus cleave unto him.—All,* of every *age;*—of every religious *attainment;*—and of every *station* in the church John. xv. 5; Heb. iii. 12.

4. We should thus cleave unto the Lord *" With purpose of heart."* This should and must be the object of our deliberate *choice,* Deut. xxx. 19, 20;—of our steadfast *resolution,* Josh. xxiv. 15;—and of our incessant care, 1 John ii. 28; Phil. iii. 16. Our text teaches us,

V. THAT AFFECTIONATE EXHORTATION IS CONDUCIVE TO THE STEADFAST PERSEVERANCE OF BELIEVERS IN CHRIST;—" He *exhorted* them," &c Here we may observe,

1. *To whom this exhortation should be addressed.* As cleaving unto the Lord is a duty required of all christians, so we find *all* of every description, exhorted in the oracles of God. *Private* christians are urged to this,

John xv. 4 ; Col. ii. 6 ; and *public* characters are also thus stimulated to exertion, 1 Tim. iv. 16.

2. *By whom this exhortation should be employed.* It should be given—By all those to whom the *care* of souls is *committed*, 1 Cor. xiv. 3 ; Col. i. 28 ;—and by all *private* Christians, in their mutual communications, Heb. iii. 13, and x. 24, 25.

3. *How this exhortation should be enforced.* It should be urged, by the consideration—of *our* own total *insufficiency*, Jer. x. 23 ; 2 Cor. iii. 5 ;—of *Christ's all-sufficiency*, Heb. vii. 25 ;—of *Satan's malice*, who purposes and seeks to destroy us, 1 Pet. v. 8, 9 ;—of the dreadful *evils* to which *apostacy* would expose us, Heb. x. 38 ; Rev. iii. 11 ; 1 Chron. xxviii. 9 ;—and of the *blessings* with which God is engaged to crown *unfainting perseverance*, Gal. vi. 9 ; 2 Pet. i. 10, 11.

---

## THE GREATNESS AND PRECIOUSNESS OF THE PROMISES.

Pet. i. 4.—Whereby are given unto us exceeding great and precious promises; that by these ye might be partakers of the divine nature, having escaped the corruption that is in the world through lust. (S. S.)

COMMENTATORS are not agreed with respect to the connexion of these words—*

Nor is it of any great importance for us to enter into the difficulties of it—

The words themselves, whatever the precise connexion of them may be, are replete with instruction and comfort—

We shall take occasion from them to consider,

I. THE EXCEEDING GREATNESS AND PRECIOUSNESS OF THE PROMISES.

God, in infinite mercy, has given us many "promises"

Fallen man could not claim any thing at God's hands, Psa. cxliii. 2.

We were deserving of nothing but his wrath and indignation, Psa. cxxx. 3

But he was pleased to send his own Son to die for us—

And for the sake of Christ has promised us many blessings—

These promises are "exceeding great"

They offer the pardon of all our sins, Isa. i. 18.

They warrant us to expect strength for the performance of all our duties, 2 Cor. xii. 9.

They call us to enjoy the most intimate fellowship with God, 2 Cor. vi. 16

They assure us of everlasting happiness and glory, John x. 28.

Neither are the wants of the body, or the conveniencies of life overlooked, Matt. vi. 33; 2 Pet. i. 3; 1 Tim. iv. 8.

No wonder then that they should be "precious"

We cannot ascertain their full value—

But every true christian can adopt the language of David, Psa. cxix. 111

But the preciousness of them will further appear, if we consider,

II. THE END FOR WHICH THEY ARE GIVEN.

God would have us to be partakers of the divine nature.

---

* Some connect δι' ὧν with "glory and virtue" in the preceding verse, and understands it thus ; " by which glorious energy of the gospel are given to us," &c. Others, understanding the third verse parenthetically, connect δι' ὧν with "God and Christ" in verse 2, and translate the words "by whom," &c.

The divine nature does not import the divine essence—
Nor does it mean a personal union with God—
To partake of the divine nature in these respects was the peculiar honor of Jesus Christ—
But the divine nature has respect to the moral perfections of the Deity—Col. iii. 10.
Of these God would have us to partake abundantly—
It is for this end that he has given the promises.
He does not intend merely to save us from destruction—
He has laid a plan for our everlasting happiness—
But holiness is essential to happiness—
We could not enjoy his presence, if we did not bear his image—
He has therefore given us promises, in order to make us holy—
And the promises, if duly applied, always operate in this manner—
Their suitableness to this end will be manifest, while we contemplate.
III. The effects they invariably produce.
There is a dreadful "corruption in the world through lust"
The desires of men are altogether vitiated—
The indulgence of them produces much corruption in the world—
But God's people "escape" this corruption.
They are not free from all sin—
But they do not live under the allowed dominion of any—
They flee from temptation with fear and trembling—
This is the description given of the saints at Sardis, Rev. iii. 4.
And this is the universal operation of true religion, James i. 27.
They escape it through the operation of the promises.
They have not in themselves a power to keep themselves pure—
But God promises "grace sufficient"—
They therefore trust in his promises, and plead them in prayer—
In so doing, they experience their cleansing efficacy—
Hence St. Paul urges the promises not merely as a motive to holiness, but as the means of attaining it, 2 Cor. vii. 1.
Infer,
1. How foolish are they who neglect Christ!
Christ is the person in whom all the promises are ratified and confirmed. 2 Cor. i. 20.
Nor can we be interested in one promise, unless we be united to Christ—
What madness then is it to neglect that blessed Saviour!—
What unspeakable blessings do the thoughtless world despise!—
Let us "awake from our sleep, and arise from the dead"—
Let us seek Christ with our whole hearts—
All things are ours, if we be his, 1 Cor. iii. 22, 23.
2. How mistaken are they who seek for holiness merely in a way of mortification, or in the exercise of their own powers!
Many seek long after holiness without attaining it—
The reason of this is, that they do not seek it in God's appointed way—
God has given them promises by which they may be made holy—
But they are afraid to embrace them till they can see themselves holy—
Thus do they, in fact, reverse the appointment of God himself—
Let such, however, submit to God's method of imparting a divine nature—
Let them embrace the promises as sinners, that they may become saints—
3. How highly privileged are the people of God!
Whatever is needful for them, in time or eternity, is secured—

For their consolation God has confirmed his promises with an oath, Heb. vi. 17, 18.

And all of them can, like Solomon, attest his fidelity, 1 Kings viii. 56.

Let them therefore treasure up his promises in their hearts—

Let them do this for advancement in holiness as well as comfort—Psa. cxix. 11.

Thus shall they be enabled to say with David, Psa. xvii. 4.

And in due season shall that most precious of all the promises be fulfilled, John xii. 26.

~~~~~~~~~

# CHAPTER IV.

## CHRISTIAN GRACES.

### THE INESTIMABLE PRIVILEGES OF BELIEVERS.

1 John iii. 2.—Beloved, now are we the sons of God, and it doth not yet appear what we shall be: but we know that, when he shall appear, we shall be like him; for we shall see him as he is. (S. S.)

Our Lord was hated, reviled, and persecuted unto death—

But we see how glorious was his person, and how exalted his character—

In the same manner his followers are treated with contempt—

But God declares their state to be the most honorable upon earth—

To this effect St. John represents them as slighted by man and honored by God—

I. The present state of believers.

The scripture speaks of believers in the most exalted terms—

They are not merely servants, but "sons of God"—2 Cor. vi. 18

This they are,

1. By adoption.

Every believer was once a child of wrath, Eph. ii. 3.

But God takes whom he will into his own family, Eph. ii. 19.

He adopts them as his sons, and makes them heirs of his glory, Rom. viii. 15, 17.

2. By regeneration.

Once they had only a carnal mind that is enmity against God, Rom. viii. 7.

But they have been born again of the Holy Spirit, John i. 13.

They are renewed after the image of their heavenly Father, Col. iii. 10.

They enjoy this state "*now*"

Rich and poor, learned and unlearned, partake alike of this honor—

Nor does God withhold it from any on account of their remaining infirmities—

Even now, while the world despises them, does God own his relation to them—

What an unspeakably blessed state is this!

How different is it from the state they were once in!—

How great the privileges which they enjoy by means of this relation!—

How sweet the sense of this relation often is to their souls!—

To what a glorious state does it lead them in a better world—
Well might the apostle break forth in wonder and admiration, 1 John iii. 1.
Yet, blessed as it is, it falls infinitely short of what it will be,

II. THEIR FUTURE STATE.

Very little is known respecting this.
We can form no idea of spiritual and glorified bodies—
We cannot imagine how extensive will be the capacities of the soul—
We have very faint conceptions of perfect holiness and perfect happiness—
Even one who had seen Christ transfigured, says, "It doth not appear,"
&c.—
Yet there are some things revealed to us.
We shall see Christ, not merely by faith, but with our bodily eyes, Job
xix. 25—27.
Not veiled as formerly, but in all his glory—
We shall resemble him in all his imitable perfections—
This resemblance will result from our sight of him—
Even " our bodies shall be fashioned like unto his glorious body"—
This shall be fully accomplished at the great day of his appearing—
These things we may be said to " know"
We have already experienced the earnest of them in our hearts—
When we believe in him we have views of him, which we had not before—
These transform the soul into his image, 2 Cor. iii. 18.
Our Lord has given us the fullest assurance of these things, John xvii. 24.
St. Paul also leaves us no room to doubt, 1 Cor. xv. 49; Col. iii. 4.

INFER,

1. How wonderfully different the lot of believers and unbelievers!
Believers are the children of God—
Unbelievers are the children of the wicked one, John viii. 38, 44.
Believers can form no adequate conception of the happiness that awaits
them—
Unbelievers have no idea of the misery to which they are hastening—
How different will be the appearance of each in that day !—
How different their sentiments on seeing Christ upon his judgment-seat !—
For what different ends will their capacities of soul and body be enlarged!
What a different state will they experience to all eternity !—
Let none defer calling upon God for mercy—
Let all seek his regenerating grace, and an admission into his family—
If we believe in Christ these blessings shall be ours, John i. 12.
2. How bright the prospects of the true christian !
The christian's warfare will soon be over—
Then will come a blessedness which he cannot now conceive—
Another day may bring him to the full possession of it—
Let these prospects animate every pious soul—
Let none suffer their minds to be drawn away by the things of time—
Let every one stand ready to take his flight, 2 Pet. iii. 12.
Let the beloved apostle be our example, Rev. xxii. 20.

## THE LIGHT IN WHICH CHRIST REGARDS HIS FOLLOWERS.

John xv. 15.—Henceforth I call you not servants; for the servant knoweth not what his lord doeth; but I have called you friends; for all things that I have heard of my Father, I have made known unto you. (S. S.)

KNOWLEDGE of every kind is excellent and useful—

But that of religion far transcends all other—

Hence we are commanded to pay a peculiar respect to those who labor in the word and doctrine. 1 Thess. v. 12.

Hence also our Lord himself, having revealed to his disciples the whole will of God, adduces his fidelity in this respect as one of the strongest tokens of his affection for them.

I. IN WHAT LIGHT CHRIST REGARDS HIS FOLLOWERS.

The state of believers under the gospel differs widely from that of those under the Mosaic dispensation—

*They* were in the condition of servants, but *we* of friends—

Christ assures us that from "henceforth" his people should be regarded by him in that light—

He has taken away from us the yoke of the ceremonial law.

This was an exceedingly heavy burden, Acts xv. 10.

But Christ has delivered his people from it, Gal. v. 1.

He has imposed only two rites, and those easy and instructive—*

His service is perfect freedom, 1 John v. 3; Matt. xi. 30.

He has delivered us from a sense of guilt.

The offerings of a Jew afforded no assurance that God had accepted him, Heb. ix. 9.

They were rather so many remembrances of his sin, Heb. x. 1—3.

But Christ has freed *us* from the pains of a guilty conscience, Heb. x. 14.

He has set us at liberty also from a servile spirit.

The Jews could not enter into the most holy place—

None could go there but the high priest; and he only on' one day in the year; and then not without blood, Heb. ix. 7.

But now all believers are priests, Rev. i. 6.

The vail which separated the most holy place was rent at the death of Christ—†

All therefore may enter thither without fear, Heb. x. 19—22.

He has put us into the state of adult sons.

Believers under the law were like minors, or children under age, Gal. iv. 1—3.

But *we* are brought to the full possession of our privileges, Gal. iv. 6, 7

Our Lord proceeds to prove his assertion.

II. WHAT EVIDENCE WE HAVE THAT HE DOES SO REGARD US.

He still carries on the comparison between servant and friends—

He points out one particular wherein he has eminently distinguished us, and exalted us above all the Jewish saints—

He has revealed to us the perfections of God.

These were but little known to the Jews—

But Christ has more clearly revealed them—

He has declared them to us in his discourses, John i. 18.

* Baptism and the Lord's Supper.

† It was rent in twain from the top to the bottom at the very time of the evening sacrifice, by means of which it was opened to the view of all the worshippers in the temple.

**He** has exhibited them in his life, Heb. i. 3.

He has shewn us the way of acceptance with him.

This was but obscurely shadowed under the law—

Many even rested in the ceremonies themselves—

But Christ has plainly declared himself to be the way to the Father, John xiv. 6.

He has expressly told us that we have acceptance through his blood, Mat* xx. 28, and xxvi. 28.

He has unfolded to us the privileges of God's people.

The Jews were encouraged by temporal promises—

But "life and immortality are brought to light by the gospel"—

Christ has fully opened to us our present privileges, John xiv. 23, and our future prospects, John xvii. 24.

He has "made known all which he himself had heard of the Father"

At that time he had not absolutely revealed *all*, John xvi. 12.

But he had declared all which he had been commissioned to reveal, or was necessary for them to know—

And he completed his revelation soon afterwards—

This was a most undeniable evidence of his friendship.

Servants are not admitted to the secret views and designs of their masters—

But Christ has made known to us all the mysteries of his Father's counsels, Col. i. 26, 27.

What abundant evidence of his friendship does this afford!

INFER,

1. How should we esteem the holy scriptures!

It is by the scriptures that Christ declares to us the Father's will—

In them therefore we see the strongest testimony of his love—

The written memorials even of a creature's love are dear to us—

Of what inestimable value then should we account the word of Christ!—

Let us regard it with the same affection as David did, Psa. xix. 10.

Let it "dwell richly in us in all wisdom," Col. iii. 16.

2. What love and honor should we shew to Christ!

We should not consider him *merely* as a lord and master—

We should rather view him as our dearest friend—

Let us then delight ourselves in communion with him—

Let us open to him all our cares, wants, fears, &c.

Let us give him that best proof of our regard, a willing and **unreserved** obedience, John xv. 14.

---

## CHRIST PRECIOUS TO BELIEVERS.

1 Pet. ii. 7.—Unto you therefore who believe, he is precious. (S. S.)

THERE is a great difference between the views of natural and spiritual men—

This exists even with respect to things temporal; much more in those which are spiritual and eternal—

It appears particularly with respect to Christ—

Hence St. Peter represents him as disallowed of some, but chosen by others—

This was designed of God, and agreeable to the prophecies—
And it justifies the inference drawn from it in the text—
We shall shew,

I. THAT CHRIST IS PRECIOUS TO BELIEVERS.

We might suppose he would be so to all men ; but he is not—
Nevertheless he is so to all that truly believe—
The history of the Old Testament affords abundant proof of this—
Abraham rejoiced to see his day, though at a distance, John viii. 56.

Job delighted in death as the means of introducing him to his presence, Job. xix. 25—27.

Moses esteemed reproach for his sake, Heb. xi. 26.

David regarded nothing in earth or heaven in comparison of him, Ps. lxxiii. 25.

Isaiah exulted in the prospect of his incarnation, Isa. ix. 6.

The New Testament scriptures confirm it.

The virgin, while he was yet in her womb, sang his ·praises, Luke i. 47.

The angels congratulated the shepherds on his incarnation, Luke ii. 10.

The just and devout Simeon after seeing him, could depart in peace, Ib. ver. 29, 30.

John baptist, as the bridegroom's friend, rejoiced in his voice, John iii. 29.

How precious was he to that Mary who was a sinner! Luke vii. 38.

St. Paul counted all as dung for the knowledge of him, was willing to be bound, or to die for him, and knew no comfort like the expectation of being with him, Phil. iii. 8 ; Acts xxi. 13: 1 Thess. iv. 18.

The glorified saints and angels incessantly adore him, Rev. v. 12, 13.

The experience of living saints accords with that of those who have gone before—*

The world even wonders at them on account of their attachment to him—

II. WHY HE IS SO PRECIOUS TO THEM.

They have reason enough for their attachment—
They love him *for his own excellence.*
He is infinitely above all created beauty or goodness—
Shall they then regard these qualities in the creature, and not in him?—
Whosoever views him by faith cannot but admire and adore him—
They love him *for his suitableness to their necessities.*
There is in Christ all which believers can want—
Nor can they find any other capable of supplying their need—
Hence they delight in him as their " all in all"—
They love him *for the benefits they receive from him.*
They have received from him pardon, peace, strength, &c.
Can they do otherwise than account him precious?—
We may rather wonder why all do not feel the same attachment.

III. WHY HE IS NOT PRECIOUS TO OTHERS.

There certainly exists no reason on his part; he is good to all—
But unbelievers cannot love him.

1. Because they have no views of his excellency.

The god of this world has blinded them that they cannot see him, 2 Cor. iv 4.

How then should they esteem him, whose excellency they know not?—

---

* There are many to whom he is preciousness itself; who account him as the pearl of great price, desire to know more of him, grieve that they cannot love him more, think af flictions good when they lead to him, and despise all in comparison of him.

They must of necessity be indifferent to him, as men are to things of little value—

2. Because they feel no need of him.

Christ is valuable only as a remedy, Isa. xxxii. 2.

Nor can any man desire him as a physician, a fountain, a refuge, unless he feel some disease, some thirst, some danger—

APPLICATION.

All, who have any spiritual discernment, feel a love to Christ—

He is beloved of the Father, of angels, and of saints—

None but devils and unbelievers despise him—

And shall any, who do not account him precious, be objects of his regard ?—

Surely his final decision will correspond with that declaration, 1 Sam. ii. 30.

Let all then believe in him, that he may become precious to them—

Nor let any be dejected because they cannot delight in him as they wish—

The more we love him, the more shall we lament the coldness of our love—

In a little time all the powers of our souls shall act without control—

Then shall we glory in him with unrestrained and unabated ardor.

---

## THE FRUITS OF GOD'S FAVOUR.

Hos. xiv. 5—7.—I will be as the dew to Israel: he shall grow as the lily, and cast forth his roots as Lebanon. His branches shall spread, and his beauty shall be as the olive-tree, and his smell as Lebanon. They that dwell under his shadow shall return; they shall revive as the corn, and grow as the vine: the scent thereof shall be as the wine of Lebanon. (S. S.)

THERE are instances of beautiful imagery in the scriptures equal to any that can be found in the works of the most renowned authors—

They are enhanced too by the importance of the subjects they contain—

In both respects the passage before us deserves peculiar attention—

Imagination cannot conceive a richer display of divine blessings than God here vouchsafes to his church and people—

I. THE FAVOUR WHICH GOD WILL SHEW HIS PEOPLE.

The metaphor of "dew" is at once simple and sublime—

The benefits of the dew are but little known in this climate—

But in Judea the metaphor would appear very significant—*

For some time after the creation, dew supplied the place of rain, Gen. ii. 6.

And, after rain was given, it still remained of great use—

The scriptures speak of it as an important blessing—See Gen. xxvii. 28, 39, and Deut. xxxiii. 13.

They represent the withholding of it as a calamity and curse, 2 Sam. i. 21

The communications of God to his people are fitly compared to it.

It distils silently and almost imperceptibly on the ground—

Yet it insinuates itself into the plants on which it falls—

And thus maintains their vegetative powers—

* Where the rains are periodical, and the climate hot, the dews are more abundant.

In the same manner God's visits to his people are secret—*
But he gains access to their inmost souls, 2 Cor. vi. 16.
He cheers and revives their fainting spirits—
And thus he fulfils to them his own most gracious promises, Isa. lviii. 11.
Were his communications refreshing only, and not influential on the con-
duct, we might be afraid of enthusiasm—
But his favor invariably discovers itself by,
II. Its FRUITS AND EFFECTS.
The effects of the dew are seen by the progress of vegetation—
The descent of God's Spirit on the soul produces
Growth.
The "lily" springs up speedily, but is of short duration—
The cedars of "Lebanon cast forth their roots" to a great extent—
Thus the soul that is refreshed with divine communications—
The quickness of its growth often excites admiration—
Its stability defies the assaults of earth and hell—
While it "spreads its branches," and displays its vigor in every good
word and work—
Beauty.
There is peculiar grace and "beauty in the olive-tree"—
And such is there in the soul that communes much with God—
What a lustre was there on the face of Moses, when he came from the
mount!—Exod. xxxiv. 30.
And how is the lively christian "beautified with salvation?"—
His outward conduct is rendered amiable in every part—
His inward dispositions of humility and love are ornaments which even
God himself admires, 1 Pet. iii. 4.
He is transformed into the very image of his God, Eph. iv. 23, 24.
Nor shall his beauty be ever suffered to decay—†
Fragrancy.‡
Lebanon was no less famous for its odoriferous vines than for its lofty ce-
dars—
And does not the christian diffuse a savor all around him?—2 Cor. ii. 14.
How animated his discourse when God is with him!—
How refreshing and delightful to those who enjoy his conversation!—‖
How pleasing is it also to his God and Saviour! Mal. iii. 16; Cant. iv. 16
In proportion as he lives near to God, he fulfils that duty, Col. iv. 6.
Fruitfulness.
The "corn and the vine" are just emblems of a christian's fruitfulness—
They often wear the most unpromising appearance—
Yet are thay "revived" by the genial influences of the sun and rain—
Thus the christian may be reduced to a drooping or desponding state—
But the renewed influences of God's Spirit will revive him—
They make him "fruitful in all the fruits of righteousness"

* He comes not in the wind, the earthquake, or the fire, but in the small still voice, 1
Kings xix. 11, 12.

† Psa. i. 3. The olive, as an evergreen, retains its beauty; and in this respect also is a
fit emblem of the true christian.

‡ This is twice mentioned in the text, and therefore deserves peculiar notice.

‖ See him before the sun has exhaled the dew, or the world abated the fervor of his affections; and how does he verify that saying! Prov. xvi. 24.

They too, who "dwell under *his* shadow," and are most nearly connected with him, will participate his blessings—*

INFER,

1. How honorable and blessed is the christian's state!
Often is he favored with visits from above, John xiv. 23.
And glorious are the effects produced by God upon him—
The whole creation scarcely affords images whereby his blessedness may be adequately represented—
Who then is so honorable? who so happy?—
Let all endeavor to maintain a sense of their high privileges—
And to "walk worthy of the calling wherewith they are called"—
2. How hopeful is the state of those who wait on God!
The promises in the text were given as an answer to prayer—
And they are made to all, who, "like Israel," plead with God—
If the dew be withheld from others, it shall descend on them, Judges vi 37, 38.
Its descent shall accomplish the utmost wishes of their souls—
They shall soon experience the fulfilment of that word, Isa. xl. 31.

---

## EVERY CHRISTIAN POSSESSES THE SPIRIT OF CHRIST.

Rom. viii. 9.—Now if any man have not the Spirit of Christ he is none of his. (B.)

AN important and alarming declaration, which the professors of christianity would do well to consider maturely, and lay to heart; and particularly those who content themselves with a form of godliness, while they are destitute of the power of it. The apostle had just observed, "ye are not in the flesh," in a natural and unregenerate state, under the government of your animal appetites and passions, or of your corrupt nature, "if so be that the Spirit of God dwell in you;" for wherever he dwells, he governs, having regenerated our corrupt nature, and imparted a principle of genuine and true holiness. Then he adds, "Now," or, *but* "if any man have not the Spirit of Christ," residing in him, and forming him to such a temper and behavior, as characterizes a disciple of Christ, whatever that man's profession may be, "he is none of his."—But let us inquire,

I. WHAT IS IMPLIED IN BEING CHRIST'S.

There is a sense in which all men are *his;* viz. by right of creation; John i. 3; Col. i. 16; of preservation; Col. i. 17; of redemption. 1 Cor. vi. 20. But the apostle is to be understood in another and further sense. His true followers belong to him, as subjects to a prince; Psa. ii. 8; Matt. xxii. 11; Phil. ii. 11; as servants to a master; ch. xiv. 7—9; 2 Cor. v. 14, 15; as friends; John xv. 13—15; as brethren and sisters; Heb. ii. 11, 12; as children to a father; Heb. ii. 13; as a spouse to a husband; ch. vii. 4; 2 Cor. xi. 2; Eph. v. 25—32; Rev. xix. 7; as branches to a tree; John xv. 1; or as members to the head of the body. 1 Cor. xii. 12, 27; Rom. xii. 5; Eph. i. 22, 23.

* If he be a master, a parent, and especially a minister, the benefit of *his* revivals will extend to many.

## II. What is meant by the Spirit of Christ.

Not, as some think, merely the mind of Christ, but the Holy Ghost, the Spirit of God, is here intended. See context. This is called the Spirit of Christ, because he had it, and has it without measure; John iii. 34; Rev. iii. 1; he has purchased it for his followers by his death, the price of our redemption; he has received it for them; Psa. lxviii. 18; Acts ii. 33; he has promised it to them. As the Holy Spirit is the promise of the Father, emphatically, Acts i. 4, so also of the Son. Luke xxiv. 49; John xiv. xv. xvi. How great the consolation of this to those who are desiring and looking for these sacred influences, that they were purchased and received for us by our friend, kinsman, brother, husband, and are promised by the Amen, the faithful and true witness! He actually confers it. John iv. 10; vii. 38; Acts ii. 38, 39.— —

## III. How it appears that we must have this Spirit in order to be Christ's.

We cannot be Christ's unless we know him; John .x. 14, 27; but we cannot know him without the Spirit of Christ. Matt. xi. 27; Gal. i. 16; John xvi. 14.—We cannot be Christ's unless we love Christ; 1 Cor. xvi. 22; but we cannot love him without that Spirit, the fruit of which is love. Gal. v. 22; Rom. v. 5.—We cannot be Christ's unless we obey him; 2 Cor. v. 15; Rom. xiv. 7; John xv. 14, xiv. 21; Heb. v. 9; but we cannot obey him without the inspiration and aid of his Spirit. John xv. 5; 2 Cor. iii. 5.—We cannot be Christ's without we have an interest in him, and be able to say, "My Beloved is mine, and I am his;" but this interest in him we cannot have without his Spirit. 1 Cor. xii. 13:—We cannot be Christ's without union with him, such as branches have with a tree, or members with their head; but this we cannot have without his Spirit.—We cannot be Christ's unless we have his mind in us; but this we cannot have without his Spirit; meekness, long-suffering, goodness, &c., being fruits of the Spirit.— We cannot be Christ's without we be new creatures; 2 Cor. v. 17; Eph. iv. 21—24; and it is impossible we should be so without his Spirit. Tit. iii. 5.

In conclusion observe,

How important a matter for inquiry to each, whether he has received the Spirit of Christ, and is the subject of his enlightening, gracious, and sanctifying operations, in consequence of which he is brought to know, love, and serve the Lord Jesus, to have an interest in him, and union with him, and to be "created in him to good works."— —How needful and indispensable a duty to apply to Christ, to whom is entrusted the dispensation of the Spirit, that we may obtain, and having obtained, may receive more and more of his influence and grace. Perceiving the necessity and excellence of this gift we must ask for it, we must thirst, John vii. 37, we must believe. Gal iii. 13, 14.

---

## WALKING WITH GOD.

### Gen. v. 24.—And Enoch walked with God. (Sk.)

Of this excellent man, but little is recorded in the word of God; four verses in this chapter, one in the epistle to the Hebrews, and two in the epis-

**tle of Jude**, contain all that we learn respecting him. These records inform us,

1. *That he was the seventh from Adam;* or his descendant of the seventh generation. So the apostle pronounces him, Jude 14.

Hence he must have been contemporary with Adam, and probably enjoyed familiar converse with him during more than two hundred years ; for Enoch was born in the six hundred and twenty-second year of the world, and Adam did not die till the year nine hundred and thirty. And converse with one who could, and no doubt did, so fully inform him respecting the creation, fall, and redemption of man, must have been a great privilege.—He was also favored with the good examples of the Patriarchs; of Seth, Enos, Cainan, Mahalaleel, and Jared, his pious father, whose piety may be fairly presumed from the name he gave his son; for the name Enoch signifies to instruct, initiate, or dedicate; and intimates that Jared had dedicated him to God from his birth, and was concerned to train him up in the way he should go. Thus in Enoch God's word was exemplified, Prov. xxii. 6. But amidst these advantages, he also witnessed the prevalence of ungodliness in the earth; for he lived when men both acted and spoke wickedly against God: these he faithfully warned, "saying, Behold," &c., Jude 14 15. Hence we learn.

2. *That he was a prophet:* He "prophesied.' This he did

By predicting future events; particularly the general judgment.—And by teaching sacred truth—reproving sin—warning the rebellious—and encouraging God's "saints" to hope for glory with him.

3. We also learn *that he was the pious head of a family;* "And Enoch lived," &c., v. 21, 22. He walked with God both in his single and in his marriage state.—He did not shun society to become pious, nor forsake society to practise godliness; but amidst the business and cares of a numerous growing family, he still carefully and resolutely walked with God. This leads us to notice,

I. His GENERAL CHARACTER: He walked with God. Here let us consider,

1. *What walking with God supposes.* To discover this, we must observe,—All mankind are naturally fallen; In Adam, Rom. v. 18; and by their own personal transgressions, Psa. xiv. 2, 3.—Our degeneracy implies enmity of heart, and actual rebellion against God, Rom. viii. 7; Isa. i. 2.—Consequently, agreement with God must precede our walking with him, Amos iii. 3. This agreement must include the removal of our guilt by God's forgiving mercy, Mic. vii. 18; and the removal of our enmity by a gracious circumcision of heart, Deut. xxx. 6; Rom. viii. 16, and v. 1, 5; 1 John iv. 19.

2. *What walking with God implies.* It must imply,

*Faith in God*, Heb. xi. 5, 6. Faith in him as our proprietor, who has a just claim on our services, Psa. xcv. 3, 6, 7, 8; and faith in him as our Redeemer, all-sufficient to bless and keep us, Gen. xvii. 1, and xv. 1.

*A conformity to God's way;* That *way prescribed in his word*, Psalm cxix. 30. The way of communion with him through Christ, John xiv. 6; Heb. x. 19—22. And that way *suggested by his relations and perfections.* The way of grateful self-dedication, Rom. xii. 1, and of humble affiance, 1 Pet. v. 7.

The *habitual recollection of God's presence*, Psa. xvi. 8; Prov. iii. 6.

The *enjoyment of his manifested favor*, Heb. xi. 5; Psa. lxxxix. 15, 16. Hence observe,

3. *Some advantages which result from walking with God.* As

Guidance in difficulties, Prov. iii. 6. ' He shall direct," &c., Psa. **xxxii.** 8—Preservation from falling, Psa. xvi. 8.—Assistance in weakness, Isa. xli. 10.—Comfort in afflictions, Psa. xlvi. 1, and xciv. 19.—And improvement in piety, Prov. iv. 18. Having observed what is implied in this good man's general character, let us, for our farther instruction, consider.

II. SOME PECULIAR CIRCUMSTANCES CONNECTED WITH IT; Particularly,

1. *The period of its commencement, and the time of its continuance.*

It *commenced* in what may be c sidered his *early youth;* when he had not lived the twelfth part of the then usual age of man. This shows us, that early piety is acceptable to God, Prov. viii. 17. Seek it, Eccl. xii. 1; for early habits are most easily formed, and most lasting, Lam. iii. 27.—It *continued at least three hundred years.* This teaches us—That the pleasures of religion never cloy, Psa lxiii. 3, 4; and that God's grace is sufficient for the longest pilgrimage, Job xvii. 11.

2. *The relations under which it was sustained.* The relation of—a *family governor.* Hence, we see the falsehood of three common suppositions. First, "That solitude is necessary to piety." This is an error of superstition; as christians we are called to sociability, Matt. v. 14—16. Secondly, "That religion is injurious to social duties and comforts." This is an error of prejudice, which is confuted by many living characters, Prov. xii. 26. Thirdly, "That we serve God only when we engage in acts of devotion." This is an error of ignorance; for we also serve God acceptably, when we serve mankind in obedience to him, Acts xiii. 36; Gal. v. 13, and vi. 2, 10. This character was also sustained by Enoch, under the relation of—a *public teacher.* From this example, we learn, that teachers of others should be careful to walk with God themselves;—in domestic life, that they may engage their families in God's service, Josh. xxiv. 15:—in public life, that their labors may be blessed by God, Psa. li. 12, 13; Mal. ii. 6.

3. *The scenes amidst which it was preserved.* These were examples of prevailing ungodliness; when piety was generally reproached. Thus, when iniquity is general, it is our duty to be singular, Exod. xxiii. 2, for we are called by God to be a peculiar people, Tit. ii. 14; Rom. xii. 2.—A resolute confession of God in the face of an opposing world, is highly pleasing to him, Heb. xi. 5. "He pleased God," Numb. xiv. 24; Matt. x. 23. Those who honor God are honored by him, 1 Sam. ii. 30. This appears from,

4. *The glorious event which succeeded this holy walk.* "God took him." He was translated body and soul to heaven, without seeing death.—This removal was *gainful to him;* it perfected his felicity. So the death of all true believers is followed by the eternal consummation of all their happiness, Phil. i. 21, 23; Luke xxiii. 43.

It was *honorable to God.* To his wisdom, in discriminating characters; to his goodness, in rewarding the faithful; and to his truth, in fulfilling his promises. So is the death of all his saints, Psa. cxvi. 15, and lviii. 11.

It was *beneficial to mankind.* It teaches mankind in all ages, that *there is another and a better world reserved for the righteous:*—as the ascension of Elijah and our Lord did afterwards, Heb. xi. 16; 1 Pet. i. 3, 4, 5.

That *piety is extensively profitable;* being evidently conducive to our eternal, as well as to our present welfare, 1 Tim. iv. 8.

That *the redemption of our bodies as well as our souls is certain.* For we see God able and faithful to fulfil his engagements, Hos. xiii. 14; Phil. iii. 2.

That *an early removal, is no loss to the righteous.* For what is taken from time. is added to a blissful eternity. Rev. vii. 14—17.

And that *a sudden removal, when God appoints it, is no cause of terror to those who die in him;* for to all such characters sudden death becomes sudden glory, Rev. xiv. 13; 2 Cor. v. 8; Isa. lvii. 1, 2.

This interesting example teaches us,

1. *That to walk with God, is the common privilege of mankind.*—For what Enoch did, God calls us to do in his word, Jer. vi. 16; Mic. vi. 8; and the grace enjoyed by him is also free for us, Rom. x. 12.

We have free access to God through Christ, Eph. ii. 18; 1 Pet. iii. 18. And strength to walk with God is promised by him, Zech. x. 12.

2. To *walk with God is the indespensable duty of mankind.* For none can dwell with God hereafter, but such as walk with him here, Psa. v. 4, 5.

3. To *walk with God is the highest interest of mankind.* It is the sure and only way to heaven, Psa. lxxxiv. 11. Like Enoch, set yourselves to walk with God:—desire it, Psa. cxix. 5;—and in God's strength resolve on it, Psa. cxvi. 9, 18.

---

## PRACTICAL RELIGION ENFORCED.

John xiii. 17. If ye know these things, happy are ye if ye do them. (H. H.)

So little was the virtue of humility understood among the Heathen, that neither the Greeks nor Romans had a word whereby to express the idea. The lowliness of mind and poverty of spirit which we admire as the summit of christian excellence, they would have accounted meanness and pusillanimity. But our blessed Lord has instructed us in a far clearer manner than the philosophers of old could do, and has illustrated every one of his instructions by his own example. The act of condescension that is recorded in the chapter before us, very strongly exemplifies the virtue of which we are speaking: though Jesus was the Lord both of heaven and earth, and his disciples were no higher than poor fishermen, he made himself their servant, and performed for them the meanest office, even that of washing their feet: and then told them that such was the spirit which he would have them cultivate, and such the conduct he would have them pursue towards all their fellow-disciples. He declared, moreover, that such views of christian excellence, attended with a corresponding practice, would prove to them a source of the richest happiness.

We shall not however confine our views to this particular virtue; but shall take occasion from the words of our text to point out, in a more general manner, the connexion between "knowing and doing" the will of God. We shall shew,

I. THEIR WORTHLESSNESS WHEN SEPARATE—

As for doing, without knowing, the will of God, that is impossible; since knowledge is, and must be, the foundation of all practice. No act can be a religious act, unless it be done with a direct reference to the will of God ordering and directing it to be done. But knowledge may exist without practice: but when it does so, it is altogether worthless.

1. It has no intrinsic excellence—

The devils have knowledge in common with us, and probably to a far greater extent: but do they possess any thing that is truly good? *Virtue is* good, even though it reside only in the mind, and have no scope for exercise; but *knowledge*, when considered without reference to practice, is as empty and worthless as ignorance itself.

2. It is productive of no good—

The science of astronomy, and the knowledge of the magnet, are among the most useful of human attainments: but of what use would they be, if not applied to practical purposes? In the same manner, the knowledge of medicine would never benefit any one, if it were not improved for the healing or preventing of disorders. Thus it is also with respect to divine knowledge. We may be able to delineate all the perfections of God, to trace all the ways of his providence, and to open all the wonders of redemption; we may be able to descant upon virtue, in all its bearings and relations: yea, as the apostle says, we may " understand all mysteries and all knowledge;" and what are we the better for it all, or what good do we effect by it, if it float only upon the mind, and never operate upon our life and conversation? We are only " as sounding brass or as tinkling cymbals." If it be said, that, by communicating our knowledge, we may influence others; *this* only amounts to what we are insisting on, that knowledge is of use only in reference to practice; and, that it then only does good. when it stirs men up to a suitable improvement of it.

3. It only aggravates our condemnation—

We are assured, that, " to him that knoweth to do good, and doeth it not, to him it is sin." Jam. iv. 17. Exactly as much good therefore as " *sin*" does us, so much does unimproved knowledge. Knowledge is a talent, of which we are to give an account: and " to whom much is given, of him will the more be required." The man who knew his Lord's will, and did it not, was beaten with many stripes: while the ignorant offender was beaten with comparatively few. Luke xii. 47, 48. Thus shall we find it in the day of judgment. If on the one hand, unavoidable ignorance will be considered as an extenuation of our guilt, so, on the other hand, will unsanctified knowledge prove a fearful aggravation of it.

We would not, however, depreciate either knowledge or practice; but rather point out,

II. THEIR EXCELLENCE WHEN COMBINED—

When connected with each other as the root and the fruit, they have an efficacy,

1. To please God—

The fruits of righteousness that spring from an enlightened mind, are truly acceptable to God. Heb. xiii. 16; 1 Pet ii. 5. They answer the end for which he originally gave us to his Son, Eph. i. 4, and ii. 10, and for which his Son laid down his life. Tit. ii. 14. There is not any one act that can flow from just views of ourselves and of Christ, which God will not behold with complacency, and accept with joy. Matt. x. 42; Jer. ix. 24.

2. To bring comfort into the soul—

Works of piety are like the incense which, when offered by the priest, not only honored God, but also regaled the offerer. It is truly said, (though many who admire the expression have very inadequate notions of its import,) that religion's " ways are ways of pleasantness and peace," and that " in keeping God's commandments there is great reward." Who ever set himself to serve and honor God, without finding that " the work of righteousness was peace, and the effect of righteousness was quietness and assurance for ever?" It cannot fail but that those who abound in the exercise of virtue, must have the testimony of their own consciences respecting it; and wher-

**over** that is, there must be a never-failing source of joy and peace. 2 Cor. i. 12.

3. To embolden us in reference to the day of judgment—

That there is no *merit* in our works is certain: and if we were to found our hopes of acceptance with God upon them as meritorius, we should delude ourselves to our eternal ruin. Nevertheless we are authorized to expect that God will deal with us *according to* our works: and, if we have the testimony of our own consciences that it is our endeavor to " walk worthy of God unto all pleasing," we may "assure our hearts before him," and "have confidence towards him" in reference to his future judgment. 1 John iii. 18—21, and iv. 17. Knowing in our own souls that we have fought a good fight and kept the faith, we may say without doubt or fear, " Henceforth there is laid up for me a crown of righteousness, which the Lord, the righteous Judge, shall give me." 2 Tim. iv. 7, 8.

4. To augment our everlasting happiness—

Who need be told, that men will be rewarded in proportion to their improvement of their talents? Luke xiv. 14, and xix. 16, 17; 1 Cor. iii. 8. This is so plain a truth, that it cannot be denied; and so encouraging a truth, that it ought not to be concealed. A life of holiness is even now recompensed by the richest consolations; but its full value will be known only in heaven.

From this subject we shall take occasion to,

1. Condole with the ignorant—

We have before observed, that knowledge is the parent of all acceptable obedience. What then must be your state while you are ignorant of those great things which belong unto your peace? God himself has told you, that you will find " no favor" at his hands, Isa. xxvii. 11, but will inevitably and eternally perish. Hos. iv. 6. Do but reflect on the condition of a soul that finds " no favor" at the hands of an angry God: surely " better were it for that person that he had never been born."

2. Counsel the enlightened—

Value not yourselves upon your knowledge, if you have not a practice suitable to it: for, it is " not the hearer of the law that is just before God, but the doers of the law shall be justified." Rom. ii. 13. You may say, " Lord, Lord," and profess to have known and served him in many things; but you can never enter into the kingdom of heaven, if you have not cheerfully and unreservedly performed his will. Matt. vii. 21, 23. Take care therefore that you " be not hearers only of his word. deceiving your own selves; but be doers of it also; for then only shall ye be blessed in your deed." Jam. i. 22—25.

3. Congratulate the practical Christian—

" Happy are ye," God himself being witness. Every prominent feature of your character has been mentioned by our Lord as a distinct and certain ground of blessedness. Matt. v. 3—12. You are fitly "compared to a wise man who built his house upon a rock." Matt. vii. 24—27. Compare the difference between such a man, and a foolish man that builds his house upon the sand: and you will then see your own happiness in a just point of view. Hold on then in this good way; and " as you have learned how to walk and to please God, see that ye abound more and more." 1 Thess. iv. 1.

## FRUITS OF RIGHTEOUSNESS.

**Phil. i. 11.**—Being filled with the fruits of righteousness, which are by Jesus Christ unto the glory and praise of God. (Sk.)

SUCH was the apostle's desire and prayer for the Philippian christians. He had previously preached among them the gospel of Christ; and witnessed the demonstration of its power in their personal salvation. But when he wrote this epistle, he was a "prisoner of Jesus Christ for the Gentiles." Through the malice of his enemies, he was not permitted either to engage in the public work of the ministry, or to visit the churches of the saints. But his devout and zealous spirit could not be confined in the contracted precincts of his degraded dungeon. While he was detained from his regular ministerial labors, he wrote some of his most excellent epistles, to establish and encourage the primitive believers, in the faith and hope of the gospel. And to his pastoral instructions, he added fervent prayers and intercession for the welfare of his christian brethren. The text constitutes a part of a comprehensive prayer, which he offered to "the God of all grace," for the Philippian church: the whole of which is appropriate and sublime, and well adapted for general utility. The words selected for our present consideration, regard the nature—the fruits—the author—and the results of righteousness.

I. THE NATURE OF RIGHTEOUSNESS. We may observe, First, *The term righteousness is diversified in its meaning.* To ascertain its precise signification, we should consider the different objects of its application. Sometimes it refers to the Divine Being, and signifies the purity of his nature, and the perfection of his works, Psa. cxlv. 17. It also applied to the Redeemer, both in his personal and mediatorial character, 2 Cor. v. 21. We also read of the righteousness of the law, which implies uniform obedience to all its precepts and ordinances, as a perfect rule of moral rectitude, Eph. i. 6. Righteousness is also possessed by a man as a believer, and it is *relative* in its character—*internal* in its principle—and *practical* in its influence. This is the evangelical righteousness of faith in Christ. Phil. iii. 9.

Secondly, *Righteousness in the text signifies personal holiness.* Sin has corrupted all our moral powers, and rendered our souls unholy. But when we believe in Christ, we are freely justified and "saved by the washing of regeneration, and the renewing of the Holy Ghost." The divine nature is imparted, which consists in "righteousness and true holiness," as a meetness for "the inheritance of the saints in light." Thus, the work of God in the souls of his people, is called, "the *work of righteousness*, and the *kingdom of righteousness*, and grace reigning *through righteousness* unto eternal life."

II. THE FRUITS OF RIGHTEOUSNESS. This part of our subject, suggests the following truths. First, *Christian righteousness is productive of gracious fruits.* These fruits are both *internal* in the heart, and *external* in the life. The apostle speaks of the former, the latter will follow as a natural consequence. The fruits of righteousness include the exercise of unfeigned faith—peace which passeth all understanding—the love of God shed abroad in the heart—the testimony of a good conscience—the humble, heavenly mind of Christ—the implantation of every spiritual grace—joy unspeakable, and fully of glory—the indwelling, and operations of the Spirit, producing holy principles and dispositions, which practically appear "in all holy conversation and godliness.

**Secondly.** *The fruits of righteousness are abundant and progressive.* Hence the apostle prays that the Philippians might be *filled* with those fruits, which implies an *increasing plenitude* of grace and holiness. Perhaps he had reference to a very fruitful tree, that has all its branches laden with rich fruit, in a high state of perfection. It is certain, all the righteous are *really*, though not *equally* fruitful. Some bring forth "thirty, some sixty, and some an hundred fold." To be *filled* with the fruits of righteousness, is to realize *exalted degrees* of piety—to grow in every christian attainment—to "comprehend the breadth, and length, and depth, and height, of the love of Christ; and be *filled* with all the fulness of God." There is a *fulness* of grace here, and of glory hereafter, which we should desire and pray to enjoy.

III. The author of righteousness. It is "by Jesus Christ." We are naturally unrighteous, and therefore all our righteousness, as christians, is of the Lord, through the mediation of the Saviour. First, *Righteousness is purchased by Jesus Christ as our Redeemer.* For this purpose, he was manifested in the flesh—fulfilled the righteousness of the law—died a sacrifice for the sins of the world—"made reconciliation for iniquity—and brought in everlasting righteousness, which is unto, and upon all them that believe." Jesus Christ having thus opened a new and living way of pardon and salvation, is justly styled, "The Lord our righteousness;" because by his atonement, he has *merited* righteousness and eternal glory for perishing sinners, Rom. iii. 22—26.

Secondly, *Righteousness is derived from Jesus Christ as our Saviour.* It is only through *believing* we can be saved; and faith is counted for righteousness, by virtue of the precious blood of Christ, that ratified the everlasting covenant. In him there is a plenitude of grace for the salvation of sinners; and when we believe in his name, he is "made unto us wisdom, righteousness, sanctification, and redemption." We receive of his fulness every grace and blessing to constitute us *relatively*, *personally*, and *practically* righteous. And through union with him, and participation of the influences of his Spirit, we become fruitful in righteousness, "that we may be sincere, and without offence, till the day of Christ," John xv. 1—8.

IV. The results of righteousness. "Unto the glory and praise o God." The *essential glory* of the divine essence is infinite, and therefore unchangeable; but the *manifestation* of his *glorious perfections* is the original design of all his works. Consider, First, Righteousness is "to the glory and praise of God," *in the scheme of redemption.* In this, we behold the *glory* of the wisdom, power, love, mercy, justice, and holiness of God displayed; in creating, preserving, redeeming, and saving rebellious sinners. God is evidently *glorified* in the origin, author, work, design, and effects of our redemption. His glory is thus made manifest, both to angels and men. Psa. lxxxv. 10; Luke ii. 14; 2 Cor. iii. 18.

Secondly, Righteousness is "to the glory and praise of God," *in the subjects of salvation.* They are conscious that all their good comes from him: and therefore, they gratefully ascribe praise and adoration unto him for all his benefits, Psa. ciii. 1—5. And in all their designs and deportment they "show forth his praise, do all to his glory, and glorify him in their bodies and spirits, which are his." And in the kingdom of heaven they will ascribe salvation, glory, honor, and power, unto God and the Lamb, for ever and ever, Rev. i. 5, 6. Let these observations stimulate our desires—promote our devotion—and inspire us with praise.

## JACOB'S DYING CONFIDENCE.

Genesis xlix. 18.—I have waited for thy salvation, O Lord. (Sk.)

THE history of the patriarch Jacob is well known, and forms a very important and interesting portion of sacred biography. It is replete with admonitory caution and consolatory encouragements, which are highly profitable for the instruction and comfort of the saints. In the early part of his life, he was favored with the religious tuition and example of his eminently pious father, whose distinguished character is stamped with immortal renown in the imperishable annals of revelation. But notwithstanding the many advantages which he enjoyed in his youth, he did not on some occasions maintain that strict integrity of conduct, which is according to godliness. Yet it is evident, from the general aspect of his deportment, that he was deeply imbued with the spirit of holiness, and piously devoted to the God of his fathers. He firmly believed in the promised Messiah, and was repeatedly privileged with special tokens of the divine mercy and approbation. This chapter records the closing scene of his protracted life and labors, and contains his dying requests and solemn charges to his children, intermixed with various predictions of the future events connected with the twelve tribes of his family. And in the midst of his departing advices and devotions, he exclaimed in the text, with holy confidence and joy, "I have waited for thy salvation, O Lord." Thus this venerable patriarch commended his soul into the hand of his covenant God, in sure and certain hope of a blissful immortality beyond the grave. In attempting an improvement of his dying appeal, we shall notice,

I. THE IMPORTANT OBJECT FOR WHICH THE PATRIARCH WAITED—"Thy salvation." Some suppose that Jacob refers merely to temporal deliverances, but it is much more probable that he desired the complete salvation of his soul, through the divine Shiloh: which includes all the blessings of grace here, and of glory hereafter. In this general and extended sense of the term, salvation may be considered as only commenced in a state of probation, and perfected in the world of retribution.

1. Salvation is present in its commencement. It is the work of grace already begun in them that believe. It is not only a future portion joyfully anticipated, but also a present privilege actually enjoyed. The Lord now personally saves his people from the guilt, the power, and the pollution of sin, Eph. i. 7; Rom. vi. 14; Titus iii. 5;—from the curse and condemnation of the law, Rom. viii. 16; Gal. iii. 13;—from the tyranny and kingdom of Satan, Acts xxvi. 18; Col. i. 13;—from all their malicious and powerful enemies, and under every affliction and calamity of human life. Isa. liv. 17; 2 Cor. xii. 9. This salvation is progressive in its character, and admits of continual increase in christian knowledge, purity, and happiness. But this glorious state of grace is only the beginning and pledge of its final perfection.

2. Salvation is future in its consummation. Though the righteous are now initially saved from moral evil, and participate "holiness, without which no man shall see the Lord," yet they are not actually delivered from natural evil while in a probationary state. In the present world they are always surrounded with enemies, exposed to dangers, and subject to complicated trials. Here we have no continuing city, but seek one to come. "There remaineth a rest to the people of God." He saved them through every

period of their mortal existence; in the dark valley of the shadow of death; and in the great day of his wrath, when he shall come "to make up his jewels," Heb. ix. 28; Col. iii. 3, 4. Their bodies also shall be changed and fashioned like unto Christ's glorious body, and with their immortal spirits shall be *fully* and *eternally* saved from sin and all its direful consequences, to the perfect and endless fruition of the Deity, in whose "presence there is fulness of joy, and pleasures for evermore," Rom ii. 7. Such was the comprehensive and dignified object of Jacob's pious anticipation; and the source from whence he expected to derive it will appear by considering,

II. THE GLORIOUS BEING IN WHOM THE PATRIARCH CONFIDED—" *Thy* salvation, O *Lord*." He did not trust in the virtues of his ancestors nor expect salvation on the ground of his descent from Abraham, "the father of the faithful." He exercised implicit confidence in the Lord Jehovah, as the origin and donor of every blessing. He knew that salvation was solely a divine achievement, and therefore emphatically called it, " *Thy* salvation, O *Lord*."

1. *Salvation is divinely devised and provided.* When we had destroyed ourselves, in God was found our help. He piteously beheld our perishing condition, as depraved and guilty sinners, and in infinite wisdom and mercy devised a glorious scheme of reconciliation through the intervention of a Divine Mediator, 1 Tim. ii. 5, 6. By the actual accomplishment of his scheme of redemption, the perfections of the Creator are glorified—the moral law is practically magnified—a perfect atonement is made for sin—and eternal salvation is amply provided in Jesus Christ, for "the world that lieth in wickedness," John iii. 16; Acts v. 31; 1 Tim. i. 15. "Glory to God in the highest, and on earth peace, good will towards men!"

2. *Salvation is divinely revealed and promised.* It was primarily announced to our original progenitors in paradise, and was subsequently made known to the patriarchs and prophets, but is now more fully brought to light by the superior dispensation of "grace and truth," Col. i. 26—28. And it is not only explicitly revealed for our instruction, but is also graciously promised for our encouragement. The Lord faithfully engages to bestow every blessing of the covenant of grace on them who "unfeignedly repent, and believe his holy gospel," Isa. lv. 6, 7; Matt. xi. 28, 29; Acts xvi. 31. And all the divine promises are exceeding great and precious in their nature and effects, and infallibly certain in their authority and fulfilment. God is not slack concerning his promise, for his word is true from the beginning, 2 Cor. i. 20.

3. *Salvation is divinely imparted and realized.* Omnipotence alone is adequate to save the soul from sin and ruin. All human efforts, however wise and salutary, are totally inefficient and hopeless, 2 Cor. iii. 5.—But the infinite Jehovah is both able and willing to redeem us from all our iniquities. He can enlighten the darkest mind—pardon the most aggravated guilt,—renovate the hardest heart—and save to the uttermost all them that believe in his name. He is the only *Author* and *Finisher* of the salvation of his people, and from him every good and perfect gift freely descends, Eph. ii. 8, 9. He begins and completes the work of righteousness; and it will ever remain an important and consoling truth, that "salvation belongeth unto the Lord." In him therefore, like Jacob, we should put our trust, and patiently expect his saving grace. And for our direction and encouragement, the text specifies,

III. **The sacred exercise in which the patriarch was occupied.**— " *I have waited* for thy salvation," &c. This language expresses the gracious state of mind in which this excellent saint both lived and died. He long waited for salvation according to the will of God, and was not disappointed. Let us therefore follow his pious example.

1. *We must wait for salvation patiently.* We have all gone astray from God "like lost sheep;" and have incurred his righteous displeasure. We are condemned by his law, and obnoxious to his wrath: but if we return unto him with penitent and obedient hearts, he will have mercy upon us, and abundantly pardon our sins, Luke xv. 20—24. Thus Jacob humbled himself before his God, and devoutly acknowledged that he was "less than the least of all his mercies," chap. xxxii. 10.—Genuine repentance is invariably necessary to obtain salvation, and it is only by thus *seeking* and *waiting* for it, that we participate its personal benefits, Hosea xiv. 1, 2, 4.—"The Lord is nigh unto them that are of a broken heart, and saveth such as be of a contrite spirit."

2. *We must wait for salvation believingly.* This is the only way of obtaining an interest in the Redeemer.—Abraham "believed God, and it was counted to him for righteousness." Jacob's faith was strong and vigorous, by which he fully credited the divine declarations, and gladly embraced the promised Saviour. Genuine faith is unchangeably the same, and is essentially connected with the salvation of our souls, John iii. 18, 36. It is a principle of *credence, affiance,* and *appropriation.* It is not a mere *opinion* of uncertain speculation, but an *habitual* and *vital* exercise of the mind, by which we are enabled confidently to exclaim, "Lo, this is our God; we have waited for him, and he will save us; this is the Lord; we have waited for him, we will rejoice and be glad in his salvation."

3. *We must wait for salvation importunately.* This primitive patriarch was an eminently devout character. A remarkable instance of this appears when he wrestled with the Lord, and nobly declared, "I will not let thee go, except thou bless me;" and as a mighty prince "he had power with God and prevailed."—Prayer is still indispensably necessary, and uniformly attended with certain success, Psa. xci. 15, 16. It must be sincere, humble, spiritual, fervent, and faithful. By thus *waiting upon* and *for* the Lord, he will assuredly hear our cries, and save us from all our troubles, Psa. xl. 1—3, l. 15.

4. *We must wait for salvation perseveringly.* It must be a patient, continual, and confident expectation of divine mercy, in all the appointed means of grace, and under every vicissitude of human life.—Thus good old Israel, after waiting for the Lord through a long series of years, and having found him a never-failing refuge and portion, he was at last enabled to die triumphantly in the faith, by which he had previously lived, joyfully declaring, "I have waited for thy salvation, O Lord."—"Mark the perfect man, and behold the upright; for the end of that man is peace."

We may learn from this subject the necessity of seeking salvation—the excellency of genuine religion—and the blessedness of "dying in the Lord."

## AN INTEREST IN GOD THE MOST EFFECTUAL ANTIDOTE TO FEAR.

Gen. xv. 1. Fear not, Abram, I *am* thy shield, *and* thy exceeding great reward. (Sk.)

"THE Lord loveth the righteous." How demonstrable is this consolatory truth! He designates them by the most endearing titles. He confers upon them the most invaluable privileges. He permits them to hold with himself the closest communion. He manifests the most affectionate solicitude, to convince them of the deep interest he takes in their most minute affairs. God's conduct towards Abram abundantly illustrates the verity of these remarks.—The preceding chapter presents the first record of martial contest that has been transmitted to posterity; in which Lot, the nephew of Abram, and all his goods, had fallen into the hands of an unprincipled and ferocious soldiery. The tidings were conveyed to Abram, who most promptly armed his servants, amounting to three hundred and eighteen, and pursued after the conquerors; and, by a most judicious attack, succeeded in defeating them; and what to him was more desirable, in rescuing Lot, and his family, from their hands, and recovering all the spoils. "After these things, the word of the Lord came unto Abram, &c., saying, Fear not, Abram," &c. It would be natural for Abram, thus circumstanced, to fear lest the enemies whom he had routed should rally their forces, and by superior numbers overpower him; the text was therefore to him peculiarly appropriate. We will, in reflecting on it, consider,

1. THE PERSON ADDRESSED. Abram—a character rendered memorable for Faith—Prayer—Hospitality—and Obedience.

1. *Abram was a man of genuine faith.* The faith of Abram was *divine* in its object, "he believed God," Rom. iv. 3. *Unshaken* in its exercise, his faith was tried, Heb. xi. 17; but he staggered not, Rom. iv. 20. *Operative* in its principle, Heb. xi. 18. *Realizing* in its prospect, "he looked for a city," Heb. xi. 16. He is termed "faithful Abram."

2. *Of importunate prayer.* Witness the intercessions which he urged on behalf of Sodom. In these we perceive *feelings of profound self-abasement of soul,* "I am but dust and ashes." Gen. xviii. 27. *Sympathies of deep commiseration.* He saw the terrible storm of indignation ready to burst on Sodom. *Appeals repeatedly urged on the Divine Being.* "I will speak yet but this once," Gen. xviii. 32. But *principles of perfect submission.* Not a murmer of discontent is heard.

3. *Of cordial hospitality.* See Gen. xviii. 2—7. Kindness to strangers is highly commendable. The accommodations now provided for travellers were in the days of Abram unknown: but even in the apostolic age hospitality was deemed a praiseworthy virtue, Rom. xii. 13; Heb. xiii. 2; 1 Pet. iv. 9.

4. *Of uniform obedience.* His personal piety secured to him the high encomium of a "Friend of God." In reference to his domestic arrangements, the Lord declared, "I know him that he will command his children," &c., Gen. xviii. 19. And as to his general character, by works was his faith made perfect, Jam. ii. 22.

II. THE ADMONITORY PROHIBITION URGED. "Fear not, Abram." This prohibition cannot be designed to suppress the passion of fear; a passion common to human nature, and in our present state as necessary as it is common. Nor was it intended to divest Abram of that cautionary mode of conduct, which provides for safety in the time of danger. Much less are we to imagine that the prohibition includes that holy, reverential awe of the Divine

Being, which should be deeply fixed in our minds, Prov. xxiii. 17, xxviii. 14. But the fear prohibited is the apprehension of evil, attended with that uneasiness, anxiety, and torment, which are its usual concomitants.

1. *There is a fear of persecution.* The revilings of men, and the fines, penalties, and punishments which have been inflicted upon the righteous in various ages, have produced in their minds feelings of deep anxiety. Our Lord sought to arm his disciples against this kind of fear, Luke xii. 4. God said to Abram, "Fear not."

2. *There is a fear of poverty.* The disciples of Christ are chiefly "the poor of this world," Jam. ii. 5. Want often stares them in the face, and their fears are frequently excited, lest they should be deprived of the bread that perisheth, see Luke xii. 22—30. How far Abram was subject to this fear it is impossible to determine. In the early periods of the world commerce was unknown—the luxuries of life were few—famines were frequent and want prevailed to an alarming degree. Abram sojourned in a strange land, and might have been deprived of the common necessaries of life.

3. *There is the fear of pain.* Suffering is man's inevitable lot. The human body in its tendency to dissolution necessarily suffers, and where is the individual that has not indulged a painful presentiment in reference to the pain of dying? God said to Abram, "Fear not," Rev. ii. 10.

III. THE ENCOURAGING ASSURANCE ANNEXED. "I am thy shield," &c. This was designed as an antidote to fear. The shield anciently was a piece of defensive armor, usually composed of wood covered with leather, sometimes overlaid with plates of gold or brass.—The use of the shield was to defend the body against the darts of the enemy. God was Abram's defence, and he has been the defence of his people in all ages.

1. *He defends their persons.* Their *bodies.*—See Daniel in the den of lions; the Hebrew children in the fiery furnace; Paul when suffering shipwreck. Their *souls* in temptation.—"There hath no temptation taken you," &c., 1 Cor. x. 13; 2 Pet. ii. 9. From the power of evil. "The Lord shall preserve thee from evil," Psa. cxxi. 7; John xvii. 15.

2. *He protects their substance.* "Hast thou not made a hedge about him?" &c., Job. i. 10; "There shall no evil befall thee," &c., Psa. xci. 10. If God be our shield, our defence is *certain;* "The Almighty shall be thy defence," &c., Job xxii. 25; "My defence is of God," Psa vii. 19, lix. 9. Our defence is *universal.*—The shields of the people defended one part of the body only. God defends his people as the hen doth her brood, Luke xiii. 34. "He shall cover thee with his feathers," Psa xci. 4. *Constant.*—The earthly warrior may be divested of his shield; God will never leave his people. "He that keepeth Israel," &c., Psa. cxxi. 4.

3. *God is the reward of his people.* The king of Sodom had offered Abram rewards for interposing in his behalf; these he had rejected, saying that he would not even take a thread, Gen. xiv. 23. But God promises Abram that *he* will be his reward; *He is the author of his people's reward.* Their reward is not wages for service performed; but recompense freely and graciously given; infinitely surpassing all their claims, on the ground of any supposed worthiness; *He is the giver of their reward:* "the rewarder of them," &c., Heb. xi. 6. He appoints their kingdom, gives them their crown, places them on their throne, &c., Luke xxii. 29; Rev. ii. 10, iii. 21. *He is the object of their reward.* It is not their wonderful escape from perdition, nor the splendor of heaven, nor the society of angels, that will constitute their reward; but it is the possession of God, the light of his countenance, the consciousness of his love, and the enjoyment of his nature:

hence God is their portion and their heritage, and they are heirs of God. He is their *exceeding* great reward; exceeding all earthly rewards in the dignity of its origin—the vastness of its nature—the certainty of its communication—the felicity of its possession—and the perpetuity of its existence.

From the subject we learn,

1. *The security and safety of God's people.* God is their shield; they live in a world of enemies, and are surrounded by dangers, seen and unseen; but "the name of the Lord is a strong tower, the righteous runneth into it, and is safe."

2. *Their tranquility and happiness.* God is their reward; perhaps they have little to expect in this world but painful exercises; but their all is treasured up in God; and from his bounty and benevolence they cannot expect too much.

3. *The fearless confidence with which they should be inspired.* What can they fear, while God is their *shield* and their *exceeding great reward?* shall they fear tribulation, or distress, or famine, or nakedness, or peril, or sword? "Nay, in all these things, *they* are more than conquerors through him that hath loved *them*."

ON PATIENCE.

Tim. vi. 11.—Follow after patience. (H.)

AMONG all the graces that adorn the soul of a christian, like so many jewels of various colors and lustres, there is not one more brilliant than this of patience: not one that brings more glory to God, or contributes so much towards making and keeping peace on earth; not one which renders a christian more happy within himself, or more agreeable to all about him. Even they who themselves possess it not, are sure to commend it in others. They set their seal to the truth, though by so doing they condemn their own practice. Consider,

I. THE NATURE OF PATIENCE.

Patience is a holy behaviour in affliction: it is not an insensibleness of present evils, nor an indifference to future good—"no affliction for the present is joyous." Our Lord himself was sensible of his sufferings, nor should we be coldly affected to the blessings for which God has caused us to hope; that would be a reflection on the excellency of the blessings—would make us negligent in our endeavors to obtain them.

Christian patience is a disposition that keeps us calm and composed in our minds, and steady in the practice of our duty, under the sense of our afflictions, or the delay of our hopes. It is sometimes called long-suffering, or, a length of mind. It is directly opposite to hastiness of spirit.

1. Patience secures the possession of our souls in every circumstance that tends to discompose our minds. Patience is a soul enjoying itself in every condition, an even sea in all winds; a serene soul in all weathers; a thread even spun with every wheel of Providence. Our Lord exhorts his disciples, when he had foretold the sufferings and dangers to which they would be exposed, "In patience possess ye your souls." Smart trials, or the deferring of our hopes, are apt to make our hearts sick; patience guards the soul, and keeps it sedate and sober under every affliction.

**2.** Patience prevents hasty and rash conclusions, ei.ner from **present** trouble, or the suspension of desired good. We are prone to make **hasty** conclusions from present appearances, and to charge the Lord foolishly : to question the truth of his promises, if they are not accomplished in our way and time ; or to suspect his mercy and goodness, because afflictions are our present lot. Psa. lxxvii. 7—9. Patience disposeth us to rest in God ; I reckon the sufferings—"He who hath delivered, and doth deliver, will yet deliver." The patient soul is neither without tears, nor without hope ; neither over sensible, nor under sensible ; affected with all, cast down with nothing : quiet when tossed, very quiet when extremely tossed ; expecting his salvation from God, when none can be had from man. "Though he slay me." Patience is a soul at rest in God ; substance gone, Ziglag burnt, all mourning, many murmuring—stoning—David makes up all in God. 1 Sam. xxx. 1—6.

**3.** Patience will fortify against any unlawful methods for accomplishing our deliverance or desires : the impatient endeavor by any means to obtain their wishes.—When the Philistines were coming against Saul with a formidable army, and his own people were much discouraged, he would not wait for deliverance in God's time and way. 1 Sam. xiii. 5, 14. Patience restrains from unlawful expedients ; "He that believeth shall not make haste"—"The Lord will provide," is the language of patience under the greatest sufferings.

**4.** Patience disposes the soul to perseverance in the way of duty, whatever discouragements may arise from the pressure of afflictions, or the deferring of hopes. This is the most essential part of patience, to persevere in our christian course, whether afflictions attend us, or whatever it may cost us. The impatient are apt to "faint and weary in their minds," and grow remiss : "but the righteous shall hold on his way ;" hence we are exhorted to "run with patience the race that is set before us."

III. Endeavor to recommend this grace to your esteem, and excite you to the attainment of it.

**1.** Patience is a virtue common to us with God. Long-suffering is his darling attribute ; and what is dear in his sight, ought to be no less precious in ours. And how marvellous is his patience, who daily pours his blessings on those who as daily offend, affront, and dishonor him! "he makes his sun to rise on the evil and on the good ;" he does not exclude the worst of us from those blessings, to which the best of us have no title. For the benefit of the impious as well as the pious, the ungrateful as well as the grateful, the seasons take their rounds, the elements work together, the light and heat exert their friendly influence, the fountains send forth their salutary streams, and the pastures flourish. The gospel is still preached to those who slight it ; the cup of salvation is still held forth to those who have so often dashed it from them ; and although God be provoked every day, he holds his hand, and waiteth to be gracious—although he have the power in his own hands, and the weapons of his indignation are all ready, he defers to strike ; and while judgments sleep, mercy calls night and day to sinners, "Why will you die?" His truth is denied ; his Son crucified : and his long-suffering is made an argument against his existence ; and he is still patient, "What is man, then, that he should complain?"

**2.** The patience which we so much admire in God, shone forth yet more amazingly in the person of his Son. Was ever patience like that patience, which descended from a throne of glory, bore a long imprisonment in the womb, to sanctify sinners ; and lay in a stable to bring them to a kingdom !

Behold the Master baptized by his servant; and, with his disciples, he lived not as their Lord, but as the servant of all. How tenderly did he bear with their ignorance and infirmities, leading them gently as they were able to follow him; how patiently did he bear the contradiction of sinners, how was he wounded, who heals every disease, how was he fed with gall and wormwood, who reaches out to his people the fruits of paradise and the cup of salvation; and, at his crucifixion, when the heavens were confounded, and the earth trembled, "He opened not his mouth;" he endured without murmuring all that earth and hell could inflict, till he had put the last stroke to the most finished picture of perfect patience, and prayed for his murderers.

3. The patience thus practised by Christ is enjoined by his gospel, being indeed the badge of that gospel and its professors; "Ye have heard," says our Lord. Matt. v. 43. "Follow after patience"—"In patience." 1 Pet. ii. 21—23.

4. We find all the saints of God, who have been eminent for their faith in Christ, to have been as eminent for their patience, without which their faith must have failed in the day of trial: it being not through faith alone, but "through faith and patience," that they "inherited the promises." Faith begat patience, which, like a dutiful child, proved the support of its parent. Patience preserved Noah's faith all the time the ark was building and while it floated on the waters; through patience Abraham endured the severest trial that ever faith was put to; through patience, Jacob, persecuted by his brother, left his father's house; through patience, Joseph endured and forgave the ill treatment of his brethren; through patience, Moses, so often abused and insulted by a stiff-necked people, still entreated the Lord for them; through patience, David would not slay his implacable enemy, Saul; through patience, Job endured the loss of all things. We are compassed about with a cloud of witnesses, who, through the patience of Jesus Christ, "wandered about in sheep-skins." Heb. xi. 37, 38.

5. The present state of man renders the practice of this virtue absolutely necessary, if we would enjoy any happiness here or hereafter. Could we live in the world without sufferings, then were there no need of patience. But thus runs the sentence, Gen. iii. 17, "Cursed is the ground." Every man, from him that sitteth on a throne, to the man that lieth in a dungeon, must have labor and sorrow; and tribulation admits of no remedy but patience. The christian has need of patience—for "he that endureth to the end shall be saved." Wo unto you that have lost patience; and what shall ye do when the Lord shall visit you! Patience is the only armor that is proof against all assaults, and he who has it well buckled on, needeth not to fear any adversary.

6. And lastly, let me set before you, in one view, the incomparable excellences and advantages of this lovely grace. Patience commends us to God, and keep us his; patience is the guardian of faith, the preserver of peace, the cherisher of love, the teacher of humility; patience governs the flesh, strengthens the spirit, sweetens the temper, stifles anger, extinguishes envy, subdues pride; she bridles the tongue, restrains the hand, tramples on temptation, endures persecutions; patience produces unity in churches, and harmony in families; she comforts the poor, and moderates the rich; she makes us humble in prosperity, and cheerful in adversity; she teaches us to forgive those who have injured us, and to be the first in asking forgiveness of those we may have injured.

If, therefore, to be like unto God; if to be conformed to the image of Christ; if to follow the precepts of the gospel; if to write after the copy of the saints; if to render our present state comfortable, and ensure our **final** salvation; if to enjoy the incomparable excellences and advantages of patience: if these things are desirable, let us from henceforth give ourselves to the pursuit of this virtue, let us "follow after patience." And for this purpose let us adore and emulate the long-suffering of our God; let us contemplate and transcribe into our practice the patience of Jesus Christ; let us study and fulfil the precepts of the gospel; let us look at and emulate the examples of the saints; let us consider and alleviate the sorrows of our pilgrimage; let us seek until we obtain the heavenly grace of patience, with all her benefits and blessings conferred on her by Jesus Christ; into whose patience the Lord direct our hearts, until she have her perfect work in the salvation of our souls through the same. Amen.

## CHRISTIAN FORTITUDE.

2 Pet. i. 5.—Add to your faith virtue. (H.)

THE apostle supposes those to whom he wrote to have obtained like precious faith with him and the other apostles, ver. 1, *i. e.* to believe the gospel as well as they. He proceeds to exhort them to give all diligence in building a proper superstructure upon their belief of the gospel. That which he recommends consists of seven important articles. The first mentioned, and which he immediately connects with faith, is virtue. "Giving all diligence, add to your faith virtue."

Some would understand virtue in a general sense for a universal regularity of mind and manners, or a disposition to all virtuous actions.—I take the word virtue in a more limited sense here, to mean the particular disposition of christian fortitude. What could more naturally be pressed upon us after faith, or a belief of the gospel, than courage in the profession of it, and in a practice correspondent to it? And what could more aptly follow upon this, than that we should add to our virtue, or courage, knowledge? or a growing acquaintance with the doctrines and duties contained in the rule of our faith, that our courage and resolution may not be ill-placed?

I. EXPLAIN THE NATURE OF CHRISTIAN COURAGE, OR FORTITUDE.

Courage, in general, is a temper which disposes man to do brave and commendable actions, without being daunted at the appearance of dangers and difficulties in the way. The christian life being a warfare, gives the principal occasion and opportunity to show christian courage. It is nothing else but to behave as "good soldiers of Jesus Christ." 2 Tim. ii. 3.

To explain it more particularly, it will be proper to shew,

1. For what it is to be exercised. For the cause makes it a christian grace. It is courage in Christ's cause; that is in maintaining the profession of the christian faith, and adhereing to the practice of our duty, as far as we are convinced of the mind of God. 1 Tim. i. 18, 19.

But it must necessarily be presupposed, that we are careful to inform ourselves well about the mind and will of God, relating both to faith and practice, that our courage may not be blind and rash, without a good foundation to support it.

**And,** indeed, without such diligent inquiries, we are hardly like to be courageous in an hour of trial, whatsoever resolutions we may seem to have, while difficulties are at a distance.

2. Against what christian courage is to be exercised. It supposes oppositions, trials, and dangers in our way: else there would be no occasion for it. It is a temper, for which there will be no room in heaven; and the need of it now ariseth from our present condition, as in a state of conflict.

1st. The power, the subtilty, and activity of the powers of darkness, call for courage in a christian. Upon this the apostle founds an exhortation to be strong, or courageous. Eph. vi. 10, 12.

2dly. The oppositions from within ourselves require courage. Our own irregular inclinations and affections and passions are difficult to be overcome.

3dly. The several discouragements or dangers we may meet with from other men, in the way of our duty, and even for our duty, make courage necessary. Solomon tells us, "that the fear of man bringeth a snare." Prov. xxix. 25. Courage is to overcome this snare. Acts xx. 24.

3. Wherein, or in what acts and instances it should express itself.

Insensibleness of difficulties or dangers is not a proper expression of it. It is not expected of a christian that his apprehension of these things should be less quick than other people's, or that he should have no natural reluctancy to them. Without that, there would be no trial of his courage. Nor are we to expose ourselves unnecessarily to dangers. We should exercise courage in conjunction with christian prudence, though it ought not to be under the restraints of carnal policy. It would rather be imprudence than duty, to act, in time of persecution, as some primitive christians did, who ran uncalled to the heathen tribunals, and cried, "I am a christian," on purpose that they might obtain the honor and reward of martyrdom. It is delivered as an ordinary rule by Christ himself to his disciples, when he foretells the persecutions that would await them. Matt. x. 23. Though circumstances may sometimes vary the case, and make even this inconsistent with duty. Nehemiah was so situated. Neh. vi. 11. Christian courage is to exert itself in such ways as these:

1st. In deliberate and vigorous resolutions for God and our duty, upon counting the cost. This is all that can be done, when difficulties and dangers are not actually present; seriously to consider them, and, upon balancing matters, to determine for a firm adherence to our Master, whatever it may cost us. Luke xiv. 26—30. The same thing Barnabas inculcated upon the church of Antioch. Acts xi. 23. Such a noble ardour in Paul was a bright part of his character. Acts xxi. 13.

2dly. In the suppression of distracting fear of evils at a distance. The coward often fears where no fear is; and, as well as the slothful man, creates to himself many imaginary dangers. Prov. xxii. 13. The brave soldier of Christ does not anxiously take thought about the morrow, but leaves future events to God's ordering. Psa. cxii. 7, 8.

3dly. In a vigorous application to our christian work, notwithstanding the stated and constant difficulties and oppositions attending it. Though Satan would hinder, and the world ensnare, and a corrupt heart resist, a courageous christian goes on as one resolved to conquer or die; striving to enter in at the strait gate. Luke xiii. 24; Matt. xi. 12.

4thly. In readiness to undertake hard and difficult services, when God calls to them. Such as may be eminently for the honor of God or the advantage of our generation, though we may foresee few to help us. Psa. xciv.

**16.** Or when duty obliges us to go upon an ungrateful errand. **Isa. vi. 8.** And especially when visible dangers await us, not to decline a service of which we are capable. Heb. xi. 27.

5thly. In a uniform steadiness of conduct under all the trials we actually meet with. It is no great expression of courage in common life, to talk big when dangers are remote, though he should meet suffering with a trembling heart; yet, if he stands his ground in the hour of temptation, he has the truest courage. As it has been observed of some of the bravest soldiers, they have come with a trembling hand into the battle, but when once engaged have done wonders.

II. WHAT MAY BE INTENDED IN THE EXHORTATION TO ADD VIRTUE, OR COURAGE, TO OUR FAITH.

This may intimate the imperfection of our faith, without this superstructure upon it. It is necessary to be added to our faith, in order to our acceptance with God. Rom. x. 9. Faith is dead, if it produce not a correspondent profession and course of action.

But that which I principally apprehend to be designed is, to intimate the just reason which our faith gives for christian courage. Christian faith is most fit to inspire with christian fortitude. For instance,

1. Faith discovers divine Providence as engaged for us, and with us, in all our difficulties. God frequently animated his servants under the Old Testament in hard services, by an assurance of his presence: Gen. xxvi. 24; Isa. xli. 10; Dan. iii. 17; like the Jewish nurses in Egypt, these were not afraid of the king's commandment. Faith will support us in the greatest dangers by this reasoning, "If God be for us, who can be against us?" Heb. xiii. 5, 6; 1 John iv. 4.

2. Faith proposes the divine Spirit, as directly provided to help our infirmities. Particularly for this very purpose, to inspire us with needful courage Eph. iii. 16. Agreeable to that ancient promise. Psa. xxvii. 14.

3. Faith represents our main enemies as already vanquished, and as having their chief power broken. The Captain of our salvation hath personally overcome them, and as the head of his church too. Col. ii. 15; John xvi. 33. Hence the intention of God in sending his Son, is represented to be, 'that we should be saved from our enemies." Luke i. 71, and ver. 74, 75.

4. Faith gives us particular assurance, that our trials shall not exceed our strength; either the strength we have, or that which shall be imparted. 1 Cor. x. 13.

5. Faith sets in view greater evils to be feared from our cowardice, than can be feared from our adherence to God. Christ elegantly sets these the one over against the other. Luke xii. 4, 5; Heb. x. 38, 39. And the fearful, who choose always to be in the rear in danger, stand in the front of those who " shall have their part in the second death." Rev. xxi. 8. One would think this necessity, and the impossibility of escaping without it, should make even a coward to fight.

6. Faith assures us of the certain and glorious success of our courage. That our endeavors against our powerful enemies shall issue in a full conquest. Rom. xvi. 20. And though now a saint, after all his struggles, may have frequent occasion to mourn over the body of death, he may be assured that God " will deliver him from it, through Jesus Christ our Lord." Rom. vii. 24, 25. "And death itself, the last enemy, shall be destroyed." 1 Cor. xv. 26. And unspeakable rewards shall be the prize of the conquerors. We strive for mastery, not as uncertain what we are to obtain by it, but for an incorruptible crown. 1 Cor. ix. 25, 26; xv. 58.

**7.** Faith represents to us the noblest examples of such holy fortitude upon the same principle: all the excellent of the earth, particularly that noble collection of worthies, whose brave exploits are recorded in Heb. xi. The glorious apostle Paul himself; and, above all, the Captain of our salvation, who was an illustrious pattern of invincible courage in his work: he feared the face of no man in the course of his ministry, but boldly reproved sin and sinners. His enemies could not help owning it. Matt. xxii. 16; John vii. 25, 26. Consider him, that endured such contradiction of sinners against himself, lest ye be wearied and faint in your minds. Heb. xii. 2, 3.

Upon the whole,

1. Consider this grace of fortitude as a matter of the utmost importance in the christian life. The variety of oppositions and difficulties in our way make it necessary. We shall never make any considerable progress in the divine life without it, nor ever do much for God or our generation. 2 Tim. i. 7.

2. Cultivate therefore your faith, in order to the forming of your minds to holy fortitude. Frequently contemplate the establishing motives of the gospel, which are so full and apposite; and by prayer and frequent reviews of the grounds of your faith, endeavor to confirm your hope in the gospel.

3. Use all farther additional means to fortify your minds. Be prepared for the worst, by counting frequently the cost. Make clear the goodness of your case, for which you may be called to exert your courage. Make sure of the goodness of your state, and carefully exercise a good conscience

---

## THE PRESENCE OF CHRIST THE HAPPINESS OF THE SAINTS.

Psalm xvi. 11.—Thou wilt show me the path of life. In thy presence is fulness of joy, &c. (H.)

THESE words originally belong to Christ, being applied by David to him, in the spirit of prophecy, as will evidently appear from the connexion in which they stand. They are also applicable to the real Christian, and are expressive of the happiness and joy he expects in a future state. Joy is the soul's rest and satisfaction in the enjoyment of a suitable good. Such as the good and enjoyment are, such will be the joy. The most perfect enjoyment of the most perfect good, must, therefore, cause the most perfect joy. Such is the joy of the blessed in heaven. It consists in being in Christ's immediate presence, and partaking of that fulness of joy, and those pleasures which are at his right hand for evermore.

Consider,

I. THE CHARACTER OF THOSE WHO SHALL BE THUS BLESSED: they are such as,

1. Repent of their sins, and are converted: who cease to do evil and learn to do well. Upon these the times of refreshing shall come from the presence of the Lord. Acts iii. 19.

2. Believe in Christ, with a divine, practical, purifying faith. Rev. vii. 14, 15.

3. Upright in their profession and performance of commanded duties, both to God and man. Ps. cxx. 13.

**4.** His servants, who follow him as their Lord and Master, and his imitable life as their copy and pattern. John xii. 26.

**5.** To conclude this head, if any require, as the Psalmist did, who shall ascend into the hill of the Lord? I answer as he did; he that hath clean hands, &c. Ps. xxiv. 3, 4.

II. WHEREIN THEIR BLESSEDNESS CONSISTS; and according to the text, it is occasioned, by being in the presence of God; and by that fulness of joy and pleasure, which are at his right hand.

The presence of God here spoken of, is

**1.** The presence of his glory, the most conspicuous lustre of his excellencies, or his perfections shining in the highest excellency of their brightness. Jude 24.

**2.** The presence of his face, as it is in the original text; "In thy face, or being before thy face, is fulness of joy." The presence of his glory, which is hidden here, will be unveiled in heaven, and presented openly to view, without veil or shadow. 1 Pet. iv. 13. For we shall see him face to face, &c. 1 Cor. xiii. 12.

**3.** His immediate presence; no longer manifested through obscuring mediums; here we have his presence in creatures, in providences, and in ordinances; but in heaven we shall enjoy him immediately, and without the intervention of means. Rev. xxi. 22, 23; xxii. 5.

**4.** His countenancing presence, so the apostle explains the text. Acts ii. 28. It is his presence as a pleased friend, father, and husband. To these he gives the presence of his pleased face, without a frown, and the light of his countenance without an intervening cloud. As his anger kindleth hell, so his favor, the light and smiles of his countenance, make heaven, see Rev. xxi. 3, compared with Zeph. iii. 17.

**5.** His fixed and abiding presence: we shall be forever with him, and he shall dwell among us. Rev. vii. 17.

**6.** His influxive and efficacious presence: a glimpse of it made the face of Moses shine. As it is reflected in the glass of the gospel; it changeth them that behold it into the same image from glory to glory; much more will it change you, who shall stand before his face in heaven, into the most perfect likeness of him in holiness and happiness your natures are capable of. 1 John iii. 2.

Their happiness is also occasioned by those joys and pleasures which are at God's right hand. Heaven is a situation of joy and pleasure, very different from our present situation, which is a state of tribulation and distress. John xvi. 33. The joy and pleasures of the heavenly world are,

**1.** Spiritual and heavenly. Not carnal or earthly. Our bodies shall be spiritual, so far, as not to need any of these supports and refreshments they do now. There will be no need of sleep, of meat and drink, of marrying and giving in marriage; but we shall be as the angels of God in heaven. Matt. xii. 25; 1 Cor. vi. 13. The more noble senses of seeing and hearing, the pleasure of which is mixed with reason, shall subsist, be spiritualized, and eternally satisfied with glorified objects, the chief of which shall be the glorified body of the Son of God. It is the joy of the Lord the saints enter into, the same for kind, though not for degree.

**2.** Pure, without mixture. Here there is a mixture of good and evil. Heaven and hell are the extremes. Hell is a place of animated torment, heaven of unmixed joy: no sin there: no temptation or occasion of sinning: no serpent hissing in that paradise; all sorrow and cause of sorrow shall be done away. Rev. vii. 16; xxi. 4.

**3.** A multitude without number. There is not only a removal of every evil, but the presence and enjoyment of every good. The blessedness of heaven is resembled by every real good known to us here, all the glory and honor of the kings of the earth shall be there. Rev. xxi. 24—26. God who is an infinite and universal good, will feast his saints with fresh discoveries and communications of delight and wonder. Isa. lx. 19.

**4.** Full without any want. There every one shall enjoy a whole heaven, with all the felicities of it, and are blessed in every part in soul and body! all our wants shall be supplied, and our desires satisfied. Ps. xvii. 15.

**5.** Constant without diminution or interruption. Here our best enjoyments are often changeable and interrupted: but the joys of heaven shall never fade away. 1 Pet. i. 3, 4. God who is the source of their happiness remains unchangeably the same. The saints are fixed in his presence, and their happiness shall not be diminished on account of their number; as in nature, every man hath a sun to himself, the same as if there were but one man in the world. Nor will it be diminished on account of the length of the enjoyment; for the divine presence is an eternal spring of pleasure. Psalms xxxvi. 9.

**6.** Perpetual. They are pleasures for evermore; all the felicities of hea ven are everlasting; everlasting consolation, everlasting joy, everlasting habitations, everlasting life. It is this that maketh heaven to be heaven indeed; all its pleasures would be imperfect without it. It is an exceeding and eternal weight of glory. 2 Cor. iv. 17.

Improvement.

**1.** Hence see the folly and madness of those who seek their portion in this life; in carnal and sensual gratifications; dreadful will be their state at last. Ps. xcvii. 3; Matt. xxv. 41.

**2.** Let such glorious views and expectations comfort the heirs of glory in the midst of all their tribulations. 2 Cor. iv. 17·

**3.** Let it excite all such to diligence and activity in the ways of God. This is the very use the apostle makes of this doctrine. 1 Cor. xv. 58; Heb. xii. 1, 2.

---

## THE CHRISTIAN'S DESIRE TO SEE GOD'S GLORY.

Exod. xxxiii. 18.—And he said, I beseech thee show me thy glory. (H.)

THESE are the words of Moses, a man singularly favored of God, by the manifestation of himself he made to him; and still desiring to be more so, here expresses that desire in prayer to him. Perhaps he might desire too much; more than he in his present state could bear; and so far his request was denied, ver. 22. The request that Moses here makes, as duly regulated, is graciously answered, ver. ⸴ By his goodness, is there meant his glory; as the LXX render it, ' will pass before thee with my glory;" thou shalt have a transient view of it, but the full discovery is reserved for a future state: and how this matter was to be conducted, see in verses 21, &c. Doubtless, a great deal of God, and his goodness, is to be seen and known upon earth; but far, very far short of what will be enjoyed in heaven; and the more of his goodness we experience here, the more insatiable is our desire after more.

By divine assistance, I shall consider,

I. WHAT IS MEANT BY GOD'S GLORY, WHICH THE CHRISTIAN DESIRES TO SEE.

1. It is glory, in his gracious conduct to sinners, in and through his Son. Any other discovery of God would be dreadful and terrifying, and instead of desiring it he would deprecate it. "God is a consuming fire," and, as such, inaccessible without Christ. 1 Tim. vi. 16. But Jesus has revealed him in the most amiable and endearing manner; John i. 18. in this way his glorious goodness is abundant. Ex. xxxiv. 6. It is in his wounds that we are secured from flaming wrath. Through him it is, that the glory of God shines, not with a destroying. but reviving light; and only as standing within this rock, we are able with comfort to behold it.

2. It is his glory, as manifested to his soul in pardoning mercy and love. It is pleasing to the Christian, to see the glory of God's goodness, in reconciling the world to himself by the death of his Son; 2 Cor. v. 19. but much more satisfactory for him to see the glory of God, as revealed to his own soul, so as to be able to say with Paul, "In whom we have redemption," &c. Eph. i. 7. This is his abundant goodness, as expressed chap. xxiv. 7. It is called the secret of the Lord. Job xxix. 4; Prov. iii. 32.

3. It is his glory, as manifested to the soul, making him a partaker of the divine nature. 2 Pet. i. 4. Improving and increasing; 2 Cor. iii. 18. this is called the mind of Christ; Phil. ii. 5. and the Spirit of Christ. Rom. vii. 9. It is called the beauty of the saints; Ps. xlv. 11. and it is that salvation with which God beautifies the meek; Ps. cxlix. 4. and by which they are prepared to see his glory in heaven. Matt. v. 9.

II. WHERE DOES THE REAL CHRISTIAN WISH TO SEE THE GLORY OF GOD.

1. In all his ordinances in this world, especially in the assembly of his saints. There God has promised to be. Ex. xx. 24. There he gives the most glorious communications of himself; and after these the Psalmist expresses the most vehement desire. Ps. xlii. 1, 2. He there alludes to the assemblies of his people. as he explains it. Ps. xxvii. 4.; and again Ps. lxiii. 1, 2. How much of the glory of his perfections are seen in his sanctuary? particularly in prayer and praise, when the hearts of his saints are warmed, enlarged, and raised to himself, while he supplies them with fresh strength, life, and comfort. And when his word is read, opened, and applied, what impressions are made? what effects are produced? How much of his glory has been displayed in this way?

But the glory of God, in his perfections, eminently shines in the ordinance of the Lord's supper; where Jesus Christ is eminently set forth as crucified before our eyes, suffering, bleeding, and dying, in our room and stead.

2. Much of God's glory is here to be seen. The glory of his wisdom, in devising the wonderful scheme of man's redemption, so as the seeming contrary pleas of his attributes might be adjusted, sin punished, the law magnified and made honourable, and yet the rebel pardoned. And when none else could, God himself found a ransom, appointing his own Son, in our nature, by dying, to become our Saviour; "Wherein," &c. Eph. i, 8. And seeing this, in the commemoration of his death, believers have been made to cry out, "O! the depth," &c. Rom. ii. 33.

3. How glorious is the discovery here made of his justice and holiness, in the satisfaction made for sin by the voluntary death even of God's own beloved Son to make way for sinners being pardoned and saved. And, considering who he was, and what he bare, and how he was treated, that we might be spared the ruin of the offending angels, the drowning of the old

world, the burning of Sodom, and the punishment of sinners in hell for ever, do not altogether show forth the justice and holiness of God, like the sufferings and death of Christ, on the account of lost sinners.

4. Here divine grace is to be seen in its brightest lustre. In its freeness, without our merit, and against the highest provocation. In its condescension, in resolving to save us, however unworthy. In its sovereignty, passing by angels, and providing a Saviour for man. In its riches, as extendng to all mankind. John iii. 16.

5. Here is displayed the glory of God's faithfulness to his promises; in his being present in his ordinances, giving his people fresh light, strength, and comfort; and thus, in a sensible way, renewing his covenant with them, and assuring them, that all the blessing of it are theirs.

6. The Christian desires to see the glory of God above. Phil. i. 23. 2 Cor. v. 1, 2. The glory of the Lord sometimes fills his house, and his ordinances here below, which believers are admitted to see to their comfort and joy; but this is only preparatory to the inconceivably greater displays that will be made in heaven, which they expect, and earnestly desire. 1 John iii. 2; 1 Cor. xiii. 12.

III. WHY DOES THE CHRISTIAN DESIRE TO SEE HIS GLORY?

He desires to see it in his ordinances here,

1. Because the glory of God is transforming. The more he sees God in the manner described, the more he shall be like him. Some rays, as it were, were left upon him; and the disciples were so much raised above themselves, that it was remarked, " they have been with Jesus." Acts iv. 13.

2. The glory of God, thus shown to the Christian, is most reviving. Not any thing in this world can give that comfort to the soul, which the manifestation of God can do. Ps. iv. 7.

And the Christian wishes to see this glory in heaven,

1. Because it will be most clear and full. The manifestations which God will make of himself above, if communicated here, would dissolve our present frame; we could not see his face and live. Here, "his loving kindness is better than life." What then will it be when manifested in heaven?

2. The glory to be revealed above will be most satisfying. It is called a fulness of joy, and pleasures for ever; Ps. xvi. 11. and this David speaks of, as what he desired above every other thing. Ps. xvii. 15.

3. The manifestations of this glory in heaven, will be permanent and everlasting. The glory of God will be eternally open, and the saints shall eternally behold it, and that with the highest delight, without interruption, and without end.

Lastly, let us pray for it. And thus express our desires after it, for desire is the very life and soul of prayer: and those desires should be expressed to God who alone can show us his glory. And those desires should be expressed, especially in the assemblies of the saints, and with uncommon vehemence of desire, saying, " O Lord, I beseech thee, show me thy glory." And thus we shall express the high value we put upon it, and may reasonably expect a favorable answer. And to our prayers for clear manifestations of his glory, let us add our praises for those which we have already received; and thus begin the work of heaven while we are upon earth, in the hope of dwelling with God in heaven, to behold his glory for ever.

## HONOUR AND PRIVILEGE OF THE SAINTS.

**Psalm. iv. 3.**—But know that the Lord hath set apart him that is godly for himself. (Pr.)

David's greatest troubles were on account of his religion, though he was not without trouble in other respects.— — —He was persecuted for his piety ; and his elevation to the throne of Israel raised him up many enemies who were inclined to dispute his right.— — —But he intimates that he did not usurp the government: it was God that anointed him king over Israel, and who set him apart for that purpose.— — —In vindicating his own claims, he asserts the honour and the privilege of all the saints—that God hath set them apart for himself.

Let us notice the character here givin of the saints—and the privilege with which it is connected.

I. ILLUSTRATE THE CHARACTER IN THE TEXT, OR INQUIRE WHAT IT IS TO BE TRULY "GODLY."

Godliness is that which immediately relates to God : it has him for its object, and in it we are made partakers of a divine nature.

True religion is by the apostle distributed into three parts, corresponding with the precepts of the moral law, which requires us to love God, our neighbors, and ourselves. Tit. ii. 12. To live "soberly," concerns ourselves, and consists in the government of the passions.— — —To live "righteously," respects our conduct towards others, and consists in our doing to them as we should wish they would do unto us. To live "godly," refers to our conduct towards God, and consists in making him the object of our veneration.— — —The two former may exist without the latter, but the latter cannot be without the former.

More particularly,

1. To be godly is to be like God— — —to imitate his moral character, and to bear a resemblance to it— — —to think, and act, and feel, in some measure, as he does— — —to be of one mind with him, in the great principles of moral government.— — —God is necessarily the friend of holiness, and the enemy of sin; to be godly is to be the same, according to our measure, hating the evil and choosing the good.— — —God is infinitely kind and merciful ; he is good to all, and his tender mercies are over all his works : and it is essential to true godliness that we be pitiful, kind and courteous, full of compassion, and gracious. Psa. cxii. 4. Matt. v. 44, 45. James i. 27. — — —God also is ready to forgive, slow to anger, and abundant in goodness and in truth: to be godly is to be like him, and to possess the same spirit.

2. To be truly godly is to live in the fear of God— — —to walk as in his sight— — —to have a special regard to his presence— — —seeking his approbation in all things.— — —Not only to conduct ourselves wisely before men, but to walk before the Lord with a perfect heart. Hence that command to Abraham, Gen. xvii. 1, and this only is true religion.

2. Godliness consists in making the will of God the rule of our life, the reason and motive of our obedience.— — —It is not merely what we do in religion, but why we do it, that makes it acceptable in the sight of God. If we read, or hear, or pray, and do all this from custom, or the force of example only, it is not godliness.— — —We may abound in religious observances ; but if we have no regard to the will of God, it is no better than will-worship.— — —Hence that serious interrogation : "Did ye do it unto me, saith the Lord of Hosts." Zech. vii. 5.

**4.** It is to make the glory of God the end of all we do— — —there is no godliness without this.— — —If we repent of sin merely on account of its consequences, as affecting ourselves, it is not sorrowing after a godly sort. — — —Love to God is not genuine, unless it has the excellence of his character for its object.— — —True godliness feels for the glory of God, and is deeply interested in its advancement.

**5.** If we be godly, we shall seek communion with God— — —shall delight in secret duties, in drawing near to him, and displaying all our heart before him.— — —Much intercourse with heaven is essential to the life and power of true religion.

**6.** To be godly is to make the enjoyment of God our chief portion, our ultimate bliss— — —relinquishing every other object in comparison of this — — —making his friendship our all in all and desiring his loving-kindness as better than life. This only is true godliness.

II. CONSIDER THE PRIVILEGES OF THE GODLY: "THE LORD HATH SET HIM APART FOR HIMSELF."

**1.** They are "set apart," as the first-born of Israel, and their firstfruits, by being devoted to the Lord— — —as the whole nation of Israel, who were chosen to be a peculiar people; or as the tribe of Levi, who were to be the Lord's inheritance.

**1st.** This consecration is accomplished by effectual calling, "being chosen from the beginning, through sanctification of the Spirit, and belief of the truth."— — —All that are truly godly are chosen out of the world, separated from the world, and ordained that they should bring forth fruit. John xv. 16.

**2dly.** They are also set apart in a way of providence, and God has a special regard to them in all his dispensations.— — —Though he will make an end of his enemies, he will not make a full end of them.— — —When he destroyed the old world, he set apart Noah for himself; and when Sodom was consumed, he did the same by Lot.

**2.** It is not without design that the godly are thus disting*ished.— — — The Lord hath set them apart "for himself."

**1st.** That he may be glorified— — —"This people have I formed for myself, that they may show forth my praise."— — —They are God's witness before the world, to testify of the goodness of his government. and the exceeding riches of his grace— — —to give evidence of his truth and faithfulness, and of the efficacy of the blood of Christ.

**2dly.** That they may be finally saved, and become his everlasting portion. They are his, and he will set them apart in the last day, from the rest of the ungodly world— — —then he will gather up his treasure, and burn up the wicked as stubble. Mal. iii. 17.

Let sinners "know" this, that however they may treat the godly in this life, God is their friend, and he will delight in them to do them good.

Let the godly themselves "know" it for their comfort, and be assured that they are placed under divine protection.

## ASSURANCE OF FAITH.

**Psalm xxxv. 3.**—Say unto my soul, I am thy salvation. (Pr.)

David was now suffering persecution, both from the tongue and from the hand of his enemies : ver. 1, 11. The beginning of the psalm is a continued prayer for divine interposition, where, under the form of an imprecation on his enemies, he pleads for his own protection and safety. The words of the text, which form a part of his supplication, appear to be interjected, as referring to his spiritual salvation; and could he but be assured of this, it would inspire him with courage against his enemies, and with confidence in the divine interposition on his behalf. But whether so understood or not, the passage may afford us some profitable reflections—

I. ALL OUR SALVATION, FROM FIRST TO LAST, IS FROM THE LORD.

He alone is the salvation of his people, and it ought to be expected only from him. Jonah ii. 9. He is pre-eminently the God of salvation, and this is his memorial in all generations.— — —Temporal deliverances are from him. Ask Daniel, who restrained the fury of the lions? Ask the Hebrew children, who quenched the violence of fire? Ask Jonah, who brought him out of the whale's belly? They would all answer, it was the Lord's doings, and marvellous in our eyes. 2 Cor. i. 9.

That salvation especially which is spiritual and eternal, can belong only to the Lord : all others are excluded from having any hand in it. Isa. v. 16; Eph. ii. 8.— — —The way of salvation is of his contrivance; he alone hath found a ransom, and devised means, that his banished ones be not expelled from him : all is the effect of his infinite wisdom and mercy. Eph. ii. 4. 5.— — —All the blessings of salvation, from its commencement in our justification, to its consummation in glory, are of his providing. The foundation of this building, and the headstone, are brought forth by him, who is wonderful in counsel, and mighty in working.

II. A KNOWLEDGE OF INTEREST IN GOD'S SALVATION IS ATTAINABLE, OR DAVID WOULD NOT HAVE PRAYED FOR IT.

It is true, all good people do not attain this assurance ; some of them live and even die without it ; yet it is attainable.— — —Comparative ignorance and unbelief are the chief preventives. ——— Some have actually attained · I know, says Job, that my Redeemer liveth. I know, says Paul, in whom I have believed. Primitive believers knew that when their earthly house should be dissolved, they had a building of God, eternal in the heavens. 2 Cor. v. 1.— — —A knowledge of interest in this salvation, is one of the principal objects of Holy Scripture. Rom. xv. 4; 1 John v. 13. It brings us to a conviction of our need of Christ, to our knowledge of him as. the only Saviour, to an acceptance of him in that character, and to a happy persuasion of our interest in his great salvation.— — —Those who do not actually enjoy this assurance, possess, notwithstanding, the principle from which it proceeds—faith, hope, a conscience purified by the blood of Christ, and. unfeigned love to the brethren. 1 John iii. 14; iv. 12.— — —If the certainty of our salvation were not attainable, we should not be commanded or encouraged as we are to seek after it. Heb. vi 11 ; 2 Pet. i. 10.

III. AS AN ASSURANCE OF SALVATION IS POSSIBLE, SO IT IS ALSO HIGHLY DESIRABLE.

This appears from David's seeking so earnestly after it : "Say unto my soul, I am thy salvation." The thing speaks for itself, what a satisfaction it would afford to be assured that we are going to heaven. What an antidote against the corroding cares and perplexities of life; what a source of contentment in the midst of poverty and want, and of joy in every tribulation. Hab. iii. 17; 2 Cor. iv. 17, 18.— — —What confidence would it inspire, in all our approaches to the mercy seat. Psa. lxiii. 1; Heb. x. 22. Those who are assured of their interest in Christ, come to God as to their best and only friend, as children to their father. Eph. iii. 12.— — —This assurance is friendly to persevering holiness: nothing tends more to promote obedience, and a universal conformity to the will of God. 2 Peter i. 10; Psalm xxvi. 3.

IV. THE WAY TO OBTAIN THIS ASSURANCE IS, PARTLY BY SPEAKING TO GOD, AND PARTLY BY HIS SPEAKING TO US.

1. By speaking to God, as David does in the language of text, Prayer, fervent and constant prayer, is the principal means of clearing up our evidence. It is this that makes our face to shine, like the countenance of Moses, when descending from the mount. If we would meet the King of kings, we must do as when we wish to meet a friend; we must wait upon him in his walks. Thus David says, My soul follows hard after thee; and it was not long before he obtained what he so ardently desired. Ps. lxiii. 8. For every spiritual blessing, God will be inquired of and he must be sadly mistaken who thinks he has obtained assurance in any other way. When Peter was praying upon the house top, the sheet was let down; and while Daniel was on his knees, the angel brought him good tidings. Dan. ix. 23. And as assurance can only be obtained in this way, so in this way only can it be preserved. God would not leave Jacob, so long as Jacob said, I will not let thee go.

2. By God's speaking to us: "Say unto my soul, I am thy salvation." So that in order to this assurance, God and the soul must meet and converse together.— — —The testimony that David wanted, was personal and particular: Say unto "my soul," I am thy salvation. Jer. xxxi. 3. How is it that thou wilt manifest thyself to us, and not unto the world: yet so it is. When the Lord Jesus spake to Saul, in the way to Damascus, the voice was so immediately directed to him, that though his companions heard the sound, they understood not the speech.— — —The testimony is internal and spiritual, the Spirit bearing witness with our spirit, that we are the children of God. Men speak to the outward ear, but God has access to the "soul," and in the hidden parts can make us to understand wisdom. Rom. viii. 16-— — —When God speaks, it is not only encouraging, but effectual. There is no vocation, no consolation, like that which reaches to the heart. When God speaks, we not only hear but feel. Luke xix. 5, 6; xxiv. 32.

1. See what it is that alone can satisfy the soul of a good man. God gives to Esau a lordship, to Saul a kingdom, to Judas an apostleship, and they are satisfied. David also had a kingdom, but was not content: "Say unto my soul, I am thy salvation."

2. This prayer includes all other blessings. If God be our salvation, we have enough; all our desires are fulfilled, all our wants supplied.

3. Let those who have this assurance be thankful, but let them remember that it can be maintained only by habitual intercourse with God, and that it will need to be frequently renewed.

## ORIGIN, PROGRESS, AND END OF TRUE RELIGION.

Phillippians iii. 12.—Not as though I had already attained, either were already perfect; but I follow after, if that I may apprehend that for which also I am apprehended of Christ Jesus. (Pr.)

THERE is an intimate connection between justification by the righteousness of Christ, and sanctification by the Holy Spirit; for in the same breath in which the apostle prays for the one, he also prays for the other.— — —Some who are advocates for free justification, deny both the doctrine of sanctification and progressive holiness: but here they are united.

Three things are taught us in the text; namely—the origin—the progress—and the end of true religion.

I. THE ORIGIN OF TRUE RELIGION IN THE SOUL: this consists in our being "apprehended of Christ Jesus."

The word signifies *seizing*, or laying hold of one, or taking him as it were into custody. Thus it is used in Acts xii. 4. 2 Cor. xi. 32.

Here the term is used figuratively, and alludes to Paul's being met with in his way to Damascus. Acts ix. 4, 5.— — —Thus it is that the Lord meets with poor sinners: sometimes by trying events in providence, as in the case of Manasseh and Ephraim. Jer. xxxi. Sometimes by the word preached, as in the case of Peter's hearers. Acts ii. Some who have attended the word from motives of curiosity, have thus been taken, like Zaccheus, and unable to relinquish their convictions.— —Sometimes they have been overtaken at the mouth of the grave, and are apprehended, like the Phillipian jailor. Acts xvi. 29, 30. Sometimes by bringing them into difficulties which call their sin to remembrance, as in the case of Joseph's brethren. Sometimes by what is seen in godly people, the heart is taken captive, and " won by their conversation." Sometimes by solitary reflection, and so gradually as scarcely to know when or how.

But by whatever means it is, if Christ "apprehends" us, we are taken captive and held fast, not against our will indeed, but are sweetly constrained to surrender up ourselves to him. Christ will not lose his prisoner when he has taken him.

In whatever way our conversion is effected, or by whatever means, God is the first moving cause: true religion does not begin with any act or exercise of ours. Like lost sheep, we do not seek him till he first seeks us.— We should never find the way to God of our own accord; his word indeed exhorts us to seek him, and it is both our interest and our duty to do so: yet every real christian must say with Paul, "By the grace of God I am what I am." He that first loves us, first moves us to himself. Phil. ii. 13. 1 John iv. 10—19.

II. THE PROGRESS OF TRUE RELIGION: "that I may apprehend that for which also I am apprehended of Christ Jesus."

Though we are passive in being "apprehended," yet we then become active, and are drawn forth to "apprehend." Hence Paul, when taken captive, cried out, Lord what wouldst thou have me to do?

1. Observe, every thing we feel or do in religion here *is imperfect*.—Repentance, faith, love, obedience, all is imperfect: we know not but in part, and we prophecy but in part. Every kind of holiness is the same, and it is a mercy to be assured that such are not rejected. Matt. xii. 20

2. True religion teaches us *to feel and own it*, instead of pretending to the contrary.— — —If Paul had " not attained," it is presumption in any of

us to think we have: all pretences to entire freedom from sin are contrary to the Scriptures, to truth, and to universal experience. They indicate great ignorance of God's holy law, and of our own hearts. We shall always have occasion for that prayer: "Forgive us our debts, as we forgive our debtors."

3. Though perfection is not attained, it is of the nature of true religion to oe *pursuing after it.*— — —Here are several phrases by which this idea is expressed—"I follow after"—"forgetting the things that are behind"— "reaching forth to those which are before"—"pressing towards the mark." All these allure to a race, and are expressive of the utmost desire to win the prize.

1. These terms imply that true religion is something positive; that it not merely consists in our being kept from evil, or remaining barren and unfruitful, but in something absolutely good.

2. That it is essential to true religion to be progressive, and to follow after perfection, though at a humble distance from the mark.— — —Wo to him that is at ease in Zion, and pleads for imputed sanctification, as well as for imputed righteousness.

3. That it interests the soul, like one who is running in a race: "reaching forth."—These terms describe the earnest breathings of the soul, and its longing after more holiness, like what is expressed in ver. 10.

III. THE END OF TRUE RELIGION: to "apprehend that for which we are apprehended."

We are apprehended "for" this purpose, that we might win the prize, and lay hold of it. This prize is a holy state; it is heaven, and eternal life, which believers finally attain.

1. Observe the encouragement for perseverence. Eternal life is before us: think of this in times of temptation, of persecution, and of arduous duty: let that fortify and animate us.

2. The connexion there is between our being effectually called and finally saved, or between grace here and glory hereafter. We are apprehended for this very purpose; and whom he justifies, them he also glorifies. Psa. lxxxiv. 11. Rom. viii. 30. 2 Cor. v. 5.

~~~~~~~~~~~~~~~~~

## CHRISTIAN EDIFICATION.

2 Peter i. 5—8.—Giving all diligence, add to your faith virtue, and to virtue knowledge, and to knowledge temperance, and to temperance patience, and to patience godliness, and to godliness brotherly kindness, and to brotherly kindness charity. For if these things be in you, and abound, they make you that ye shall neither be barren nor unfruitful in the knowledge of our Lord Jesus Christ. (Pr.)

GREAT things are here ascribed to the knowledge of God, and of Jesus our Lord, ver. 2: "grace and peace are hereby multiplied." All things pertaining to life and godliness are derived from hence, ver. 3. By it we are interested in exceeding great and precious promises, ver. 4. Yet we must not rest in knowledge, but add to it what is recommended in our text.

I. OBSERVE WHAT IS HERE SUPPOSED TO BE THE FOUNDATION OF THE CHRISTIAN CHARACTER, EVEN "FAITH."

Peter had before spoken of faith, and ascribed to it two qualities; namely, "its preciousness," verse 1, as having relation to a precious Saviour; and its being the same in all good men, under whatever dispensation they have lived, and whether they be weak or strong in faith: it still is "like" precious faith "with us."

The term "add" to your faith, denotes that faith must be first, as the foundation of all the rest; and indeed it is this which forms the basis of the Christian character. Jude 20.

More particularly, observe—

1. Nothing but faith will support the building. What is the virtue of heathens, and unconverted men?— — —What is the virtue of Jews and deists in modern times; or of nominal Christians?— — —It is destitute of all the graces mentioned in our text: it has nothing of temperance, patience, godliness, kindness, or charity belonging to it.— — —All attempts to build up men in holiness without faith, are utterly vain: we may build, but it must come down again. Faith in the Son of God is the foundation of all.

2. Faith is sufficient for this purpose: it is the root from whence all the graces grow, and the spring which waters and makes them fruitful. ———— No sooner did the murderous Jews believe in him whom they had crucified, than all these graces began to appear. Acts ii.— — —The profligate heathens the same; and thus it is to this day. When a sinner ready to perish embraces the gospel, he is from thence a new creature, cast in a new mould. Let him cease to oppose the gospel, and begin to obey it from the heart, and he becomes the servant of God, and his fruit unto holiness. Rom. vi 17—22.

II. NOTICE WHAT IS TO BE BUILT ON THIS FOUNDATION, OR ADDED TO IT.

"Giving all diligence." We must not stop at faith, for faith without works is dead: it is inoperative, and has no influence on the life. Such however is the faith of multitudes of nominal Christians, and of many also who make an open profession of religion.

"Giving all diligence." This implies that we shall not grow in grace, without care and close attention. Sloth and carnal ease will reduce our souls to a state like that of the vineyard of the sluggard, which is overgrown with weeds.— — —It is in grace as in nature; though the utmost diligence will fail without the blessing of God, yet neither will he give his blessing without diligence: the diligent soul shall be made fat, and he that watereth shall also himself be watered. Prov. xi. 25. xiii. 4.— — —Grace will not grow spontaneously; but must be watched and watered, by prayer and holy carefulness. Isai. xxvii. 3.

More particularly—

1. The first stone to be laid on your holy faith is "virtue."— — —We use this word for moral excellence in general, as distinguished from vice, or what is unlovely; but seems here to have a more specific meaning.— — — It is a military term, and denotes courage, fortitude or resolution: if it were what is generally meant by virtue, it would include all that follow in the text, and so could not be distinguished from them.

Give all diligence, that he may not be feeble, but strong in the grace that is in Christ Jesus: not like the fearful and unbelieving, but like those who took joyfully the spoiling of their goods. Like Peter and John, who waxed bold to speak the word of the Lord, or like him who witnessed a good confession.

2. The next is "knowledge."— — —This is to regulate virtue or courage; energy and zeal without knowledge, would be dangerous. Even

love itself requires to be under its direction. Phil. i. 9. Courage in a soldier, without knowledge to guide it, would be misapplied: let all your zeal and energy therefore be under the regulation of God's word. As soldiers, know your dangers in order to avoid them; your enemies and their devices, to be able to meet and overcome them; your obligations, in order to fulfil them.— — —In times of trial, heaven "expects every man to do his duty."

3. "Temperance." This denotes the right government of the appetites and passions. Also in giving to others admonition and reproof, so as to be angry and sin not. Psal. cxli. 5. Our Lord himself affords a kind and gentle reproof, in his conduct towards his disciples; and Paul in dealing with the Corinthians. Gal. vi. 1. 1 Cor. iv. 21. Ephes. iv. 31, 32.

4. To these must also be added "patience," which denotes the enduring of evil; as afflictions, persecutions, and reproches; and in this we have the example of Christ. 1 Pet. ii. 20—23. Also in waiting for the coming of the Lord. James v. 7. 1 Thes. i. 10.

5. "Godliness," or piety. This is to be like God, to bear his image, to be of his mind, to love him, fear him, and keep his glory in view. This runs through the whole of the Christian character.

6. "Brotherly kindnes." This is that sweet disposition which feels towards the poorest Christian as a brother, in sympathising, and in rejoicing with him. Col. iii. 12. James i. 9, 10.

7. "Charity," or that candid disposition which thinketh no evil; which puts the best possible construction on the conduct and actions of others, and which envieth not— — —a spirit of meekness and love. 1 Cor. xiii.

III. THE NECESSITY OF THESE ADDITIONS, THAT WE MAY "NEITHER BE BARREN NOR UNFRUITFUL.

It is here supposed that we may possess some knowledge of our Lord and Saviour Jesus Christ, and yet be very barren withal: and if the building be not raised in the manner that is here expressed, we shall be so.

1. That we be "not barren." A person may be said to be barren when he bears no fruit, or when there is nothing positive in his religion; a sort of negative character.— — —But nothing merely negative will do: he has apparently put off the old man, but not put on the new: he was once like a wilderness, full of briers and thorns; and now is like a barren heath. Jer. xvii. 5, 6. Matt. xii. 44.

2. That we be "not unfruitful." A person is unfruitful when he bears little fruit, and barren when he bears none at all; a field may have some fruit, and yet not be fruitful.— —— God requires not merely the existence of true religion in the heart, but that it should grow exceedingly: and that "these things should be in us, and abound." 2 Thess. i. 11. 2 Pet. iii. 18.

---

## GLORYING IN THE CROSS.

Galatians vi. 14.—God forbid that I should glory, save in the cross of our Lord Jesus Christ, by whom the world is crucified unto me, and I unto the world. (Pr.)

IT is a mark of false religion, that it leads men to glory in something else, and not in the Lord. The Jews valued themselves on circumcision, and their being the children of Abraham. The false teachers in the churches of Galatia displayed a great deal of vain-glorying, desirous of making a fair show in the flesh: ver. 12. They wished to ingratiate themselves with the Galatians, and to supplant the apostles. But Paul wholly disclaimed every thing of this kind, and declares his great object to be to glory in nothing but the cross of Christ. The language he employs is very strong, and expressive of the holy ardour of his mind, as will appear in the following particulars.

1. He considers the cross of Christ *as an object of glorying.* Had he consulted the opinion of the world, he would have found that it was the great shame of christianity. "Christ crucified was to the Jews a stumbling block, and to the Greeks foolishness."— — —It was Satan's design, in effecting the crucifixion of our Lord, to overwhelm his cause with contempt. It might therefore have seemed enough for Paul to say, God forbid that I should ever be ashamed of my Lord, though he was crucified: but instead of this, he accounts it an object of exultation.

2. It is with him *the only object* of glorying. Many would have thought that Paul might have gloried in some other things: his descent from the tribe of Benjamin, his zeal, his literary acquirements, his office, labors, success and reputation as an apostle.— — —He was formed to take a leading part in whatever he undertook. When an enemy to the gospel, he breathed out his whole soul in threatenings and slaughter against the church of God. When he became a friend, he was equally ardent in his defence.— — —Yet in none of these things would he glory, but in the cross of Christ.

3. He bears the most emphatic protest *against glorying in any thing else:* "God forbid!" Far be it from me to think of any other object. This mode of speaking is not used lightly. It is of the nature of a solemn oath, and applied to things which he held in the greatest abhorrence: so that those things with which others were elated, and in which they gloried, he most solemnly abjured. It would have shocked him to have valued himself on such grounds, or to have had his heart divided between Christ and the world. His language is, "Be HE my ambition, my joy, my hope, my life, my all !"

Oh what christians should we be, if our eye were thus single : if the things which make a fair show in the flesh, were regarded by us as they were by Paul.— — —"The world is crucified unto me, and I unto the world." I am as a dead man, and the world is dead to me : it has lost all its charms in my view, and it ceases to have any influence over me.

I. ENQUIRE WHEREIN THIS CRUCIFIXION TO THE WORLD CONSISTS, AND WHAT ARE THE CHARACTERS IN WHICH THIS SPIRIT IS EXEMPLIFIED.

1. Certainly not in those who are *eaten up of the love of the world,* and whose sole concern it is to increase their wealth.— — —Yet there are men of this description, and that under a profession of the gospel. Some make haste to be rich, regardless of the means : others who are poor, may be of the same disposition, fretting and murmuring against God, and thinking hard of their lot.

The man who is dead to the world is one who is content with his portion : more concerned to devote what he has to the glory of God, than to increase it.— — —It is not him who can find no time for God and religion : but he who in all his ways acknowledges him, and sets the Lord always before him.— — —It is not him who retires from the world, like a monk or a hermit; but he who while in the world, devotes his all to God, and walks as in his sight.

Let but all our concerns and undertakings in life be subordinate to the interests of religion, and they will rather aid than hinder our christian course

Such a one may say with Paul, "The world is crucified unto me, and I unto the world."

2. This spirit is certainly not found in men whose grand object it is to *secure the approbation of the world*, and to gain popular applause. The opinion of the world is to some men the oracle in which they trust: under its smiles they live, and under its frowns they die. Hence their principal concern is to secure the approbation of men by temporising principles, and by every means of servile conformity.

But not so Paul: with him it was a light matter to be judged of man's judgment, or to enjoy the smiles of the rich and the great.— — —The man who is crucified to the world, is he whose chief concern it is to be approved of God: he who can bear adversity without being unduly depressed, and prosperity without being elated by it.

3. It is not found in those who *mix something worldly with their religion*, in order to make it palatable, that the offence of the cross may cease. This has been a principal source of corruption, in doctrine and in worship: great pains have been taken by false teachers and false professors, to render the doctrine of the cross more grateful to the carnal heart. The judaising teachers did this, and may have done it since.

To be as Paul, is to lay aside all carnal reasoning and worldly policy, and as new-born babes desire the sincere milk of the word: to keep the ordinances as they were at first delivered, and to maintain the purity of gospel worship and discipline.

II. THE MEDIUM THROUGH WHICH THIS DEADNESS TO THE WORLD IS ACCOMPLISHED: "by the cross of Christ."

We may indeed be dead to the world, through the failure of mere natural powers, the infirmities of age, or the progress of disease; or from chagrin and disappointment, we may take delight in nothing.— — —But this is not the spirit inculcated by the example of Paul. The crucifixion of which he speaks is like that of a lesser light obscured by a greater: a little joy swallowed up by that which is unspeakable and full of glory.

1. Our *first believing in Christ crucified* produces this effect.— — —The love of former sins is relinquished: the things that have charmed us, charm us now no more: the company we once sought is no more desired: the riches, the honors, the pleasures of the world are no longer what they used to be: we say of all these things, get ye hence!— — —A new set of objects is now set before us, a new set of feelings is now excited: we have better riches, more abiding honors, more enduring substance, more refined pleasures, and delights.

2. The more deeply we enter into *the doctrine of the cross*, the more dead shall we be to every thing but Christ.— — —Paul at the latest period of life "counted all things but loss, for the excellency of the knowledge of Christ," and that he might still go on to "know him."— — —The wonders of the cross have fixed the admiration of angels, and, and produced in them a comparative indifference to every other object. Eph. iii. 10. 1 Pet. i. 12.— — —Be this my study on earth: my theme in heaven!

## CHARACTERISTICS OF TRUE RELIGION

**Isa. xliv. 5** —One shall say, I am the Lord's : and another shall call himself by the name of Jacob : and another shall subscribe with his hand unto the Lord, and sirname himself by the name of Israel.

It is remarkable how God, in his dealings with his people, mixes judgment with mercy. It was but a little before, that the prophet had foretold the captivity of Israel ; and the godly amongst them must have been greatly dejected by the tidings ; for what would become of the cause of God ? For their encouragement however, their return is afterwards predicted, ch. xl. 1 : and here, though the last chapter speaks of giving "Jacob to the curse, and Israel to reproach," yet many great and precious promises are intermixed : ver. 1.

1. The Lord calls them by endearing names : " Jacob my servant, and Israel whom I have chosen," ver. 1. He loved them notwithstanding all their provocations

2. He reminds them of his having " made and formed them ;" not merely as creatures and as men, but as a nation and people peculiar to the Lord. He formed them for himself, to show forth his praise.

3. He teaches them to draw inferences that he would " help them and bless them," and their posterity after them ; and still he would remember his holy covenant, ver. 3.

4. Instead of their being swallowed up by the heathen, the time would come when the Gentiles should be accounted the seed of the church, and should " spring up as among the grass," ver. 4 : and though not born of Abraham, they should say, " I am the Lord's." What promises are these ! That which stumbled the carnal Jews, and even some of the primitive disciples, had been the support and comfort of the fathers of the church. Jer. xvi. 19.

Our text contains not only a promise of the conversion of the Gentiles to the God of Israel ; but this promise affords a lively description of the nature of conversion itself, and furnishes *several interesting characteristics of true religion*—

I. It is PERSONAL.

All that is here said is spoken of *individuals*. " One" and " another' shall say, " I" am the Lord's. Many things are mentioned in the context, and elsewhere, of God's having chosen Israel as a *people ;* but that did not avail to their salvation. There was even then a distinction between Israel after the flesh, and after the Spirit ; between Israelites " indeed," and such as were so in appearance only ; and the children of the promise were counted for the seed. Psa. lxxiii. 1 ; Johh i. 47 ; Gal. iv. 28 ; Phil. iii. 3.

God has also favored our *nation* with the gospel, and we are called christians ; but those only are such who have believed with the heart unto righteousness.— — —The Lord favors some *towns* more than others ; but religion is still a personal thing, and not national or parochial. Some *families* are also highly favored in succession, one generation after another ; yet religion is still personal, and there is no trusting to mere external privileges. Matt. iii. 9.

II. It is CORDIAL, or with the whole heart.

It includes the entire renunciation of every idol, and a full surrender of ourselves to the Lord.— — —It begins in the heart : there is such a thing as being called " by the name of Israel," and swearing by the God of Israel;

**yet not in truth,** nor in righteousness. Isa. xlviii. 1. The Lord always had a right to our hearts, though he possessed them not; true conversion will lead us to say, " I am the Lord's."

1. Some for example have been given up to *open abominations.* They have been the slaves of brutal passions, wallowing in sin, and devoted to every species of iniquity; like the Corinthians who were madly set upon their idols.— — —But grace reaches many of these; and now they are washed and sanctified, in the name of the Lord Jesus, and by the Spirit of our God. 1 Cor. vi. 11.— — —The consequence of this is, a voluntary surrender of themselves to be the Lord's.

2. Others have been wholly *devoted to the world.* The love of money was the ruling passion; all their hearts and all their time was swallowed up in the cares of the world, and they were worshippers of the unrighteous mammon.— — —Yet we have seen in some of these, the love of the world giving way to the love of God, and a willingness to count all things but loss for Christ. Luke xix. 8; Phil. iii. 8.

3. Some have been in the highest degree *self-willed* and perverse. If reproved, they could not bear it; and he that reproved the scorner only got to himself a blot. Their tongues were their own, and they loved all devouring words.— — —But when religion reached the heart, these have become as little children, and all their pride has been abased. Now they are willing to sit at the feet of Jesus, and be numbered with his humble followers.

4. Some have felt a sensible and *strong aversion to God,* and every thing that is serious. They hated to think of him, or to be where he is worshipped; family prayer was a burden to them, and they wished to be free from the yoke of domestic authority.— — —Yet such as these have been reconciled by the blood of the cross, and have given themselves up to God.

5. Others have been peculiarly prejudiced against those *doctrines and ordinances* that are the nearest to the truth, and have proclaimed war against their author— — —Yet we have seen some of these brought to submit, and embrace those very truths they once opposed. Thus the scribes and pharisees who believed, joined the sect that was every where spoken against.

6. Not a few have been remarkable for their *carelessness and negligence* about their souls and eternal things. They have been light-minded, poor thoughtless creatures. Nothing had any effect upon them: they were not grieved for the affliction of Joseph, but drank their wine in bowls, and chaunted to the sound of the viol. Amos vi. 6.— — —But we have seen their careless ones made to think, and lay their folly to heart, and eventually to say, We are the Lord's.

III. TRUE RELIGION IS DECIDED.

Here is no hesitation; the surrender is full and unreserved. The language is not, I will or may be, but " I am" the Lord's. ——— There are many cases of an opposite description, which we have frequent occasion to observe.

1. Some persons remain in *suspense,* between God and the world. They have had many convictions: the kingdom of heaven is near them, and they are not far off: and yet they have gone back to the world, to see whether they cannot make better of it.

2. Some still cleave to *their own righteousness,* and cannot wholly give it up. But true religion will constrain us to part with every thing, to be the Lord's.

3. Others take *no decided part* in religion. If God's cause prosper, they have no joy, no part in it. If it decline they do not mourn. These per-

sons do not consider God's cause as their own, nor do they feel when it is dishonored.

True religion is the opposite of all this; it is decidedly for Christ, and makes his cause our own. Its language is, Thine are we, David, and on thy side, thou son of Jesse. 1 Chron. xii. 18.

IV. IT IS SOCIAL.

They shall "call themselves by the name of Jacob, and sirname themselves by the name of Israel." Those who are joined to the Lord will naturally feel a union with them that love him. Jacob and Israel were then the people of God; and the language of these converts would be, "We will go with you, for we have heard that God is with you." Zech. viii. 21 —23. There is a cleaving to the people of God, like that of Ruth to Naomi. Ruth i. 16.

There have been times and places in which, for a person to "subscribe" himself an Israelite or a Christian, would require a considerable sacrifice, and would cost him his liberty or his life. Yet true religion will cause us to cleave to the people of God, even in the worst of time. Mal. iii. 16; Acts iv. 23, ix. 26; Heb. xi. 25.

V. IT IS INFLUENCED BY EXAMPLE.

"One" shall say, I am the Lord's, "and another" shall call himself by the name of Jacob: "and another shall subscribe with his hand unto the Lord."——— It is here implied, that one person resigning himself unto the Lord and his people, would be the means of exciting others to do the same. The conversion of one sinner is oftentimes the occasion of converting another, and the obedience of one is followed by that of others. Hence the importance of social and family religion. ——— We are greatly influenced by example; and it is frequently seen, that if those who sustain a religious character live in the neglect of gospel ordinances, others will plead their conduct in justification of themselves, and consider them as of no importance. So on the contrary, if faithful and diligent in following Christ, others will be induced to follow the example.

Let us remember—1. That we must either be the Lord's or Satan's. *Servants* we must be: choose ye therefore this day whom ye will serve.—2. If we become the Lord's, it must become voluntarily : it must be the surrender of the heart, and of all we have to him.

---

## CHRISTIAN CONTENTMENT.

Philippians iv. 11.—I have learned, in whatever state I am, therewith to be content.

THIS was the declaration of a great man of God : and it will be happy for us to aspire after his example. The Philippians had been very kind to him, in ministering often to his necessities, and he took it well at their hands: yet he wished them to know that he made no great account of the good things of this life, but could do without them.

It is not the language of boasting, however, of his own strength ; no, he was indebted to Christ for all: ver. 13.—— — —This is a lesson which but few have learned, but which is of great importance for us to study daily.

EXPLAIN THE NATURE OF CHRISTIAN CONTENTMENT, AND WHEREIN IT CONSISTS. ·

It does not consist in insensibility or indifference, as to our situation in the present life. Paul himself felt the hardships to which he was subject, and prayed to be delivered from them. He was keenly sensible of "the thorn in the flesh," and besought the Lord that it might depart from him. He also felt the injuries of men towards him, and prayed to be delivered out of the hands of the wicked and unreasonable. But he considered his lot in life as the will of God; and deeming that alone to be sufficient, he was quite content.

More particularly—

1. To be content is to be *satisfied with our station in life*, without envying those who are above us, or in superior circumstances.— — —Men in general are seeking great things for themselves, and make it their leading object to ascend up into the higher stations of society: but christian contentment is satisfied with its lot.— — —The former description of persons are always looking at those above them, and feel envy; while the latter look at those below them, and feel thankful.— — —The former is a sort of ambition which no means can gratify.

2. It is to be satisfied *in all the vicissitudes which may attend us in our station.*— — —If prosperous, we shall be thankful: if adverse, we shall consider that the hand of the Lord is in it. There is much self-deception in supposing that we should be content in another situation, if wholly discontent in that which we already occupy; though nothing is more common than for persons to imagine, that if they were only in such and such circumstances, then they should be happy, but it is all delusion.

Paul says, "In whatsoever state I *am*;" and the exhortation is, Be content with such as "ye have;" not with what ye might be, or might have.——— It may be that we are poor, afflicted, oppressed: and can these things be agreeable? No, not in themselves: but viewed as the cup which our Father has given us to drink, and considering the whole of our lot as of divine appointment, we may feel content, let it be whatever it may. ——— This spirit too will humble us under the calamities which may befal the nation or the world; knowing that there is no evil in a city, and the Lord hath not done it. Amos iii. 6. 1 Thess. iii. 3.

3. It is made up of *resignation, humility, and thankfulness.* ——— The language of true contentment is, "Thou Lord shalt choose our inheritance—I will bear the indignation of the Lord—If he say, I have no delight in thee, here I am—The Lord is my portion, saith my soul, therefore will I hope in him."

II. NOTICE THE EMINENT EXAMPLE OF CONTENTMENT AFFORDED US IN THE LIFE OF PAUL.

Much of the meaning and force of language depends on the character and situation of the speaker. ——— If Paul had been in high life, in a state of affluence and ease, his words would have no force. But he was not: and what is more, his poverty and affliction were the effect of his religion, and his love to Christ. ——— He might have been otherwise, but he counted all things but loss for him. ——— Many persons circumstanced, as Paul was would have felt more keenly than he did.

The situations through which he had to pass were of no ordinary description, as may be seen by the enumeration given us in 2 Cor. vi. 4—10, and xi. 23—27. ——— Are we poor? so was he. Are we destitute and hungry? so was he. Are we afflicted and oppressed? so was he. And yet his language is, "I have learned, in whatsoever state I am, therewith to be content"

195

III. The way in which he attained this desirable state of mind: "I have learned"

It was not natural to him; but he received it, he "learned" it. And where did he learn it? Not at the feet of Gamaliel, nor while a pharisee; but in the school of Christ, and at the foot of the cross.

1. He learned it from *the precepts of God's word.*———He understood that it was God's right to govern, and ours to obey: that every thought is to be brought into subjection to him. This lesson also David learned, and taught to others. Psalm xxxvii. 1—7.

2. He learned it from *the principles of the gospel,* and so learned it as to make it his own. He learned it especially from the doctrine of the cross, by which he was crucified to the world, and the world to him. Gal. vi. 14.

3. From *the example of Christ himself.* ——— He who was rich, for our sakes became poor—The cup which my Father giveth me, shall I not drink it—He was meek and lowly in heart: a man of sorrows and acquainted with grief. ——— This was Paul's pattern, and he copied after it.

1st. It glorifies God and the gospel, to trust all in his hands, and to rely on its faithfulness and truth. The contrary disposition tends to dishonour both.

2dly. How much does this spirit of contentment promote our own happiness, and the happiness of others. What a blessed world would this be, if such a spirit universally prevailed.

3dly. It has the promise of God's presence: "Be content with such things as ye have, for he hath said, I will never leave thee nor forsake thee." Heb xiii. 5,

~~~~~~~~~~

## ADVICE TO THE AFFLICTED.

Psalm lxi. 2·—From the end of the earth will I cry unto thee, when my heart is overwhelmed: lead me to the Rock that is higher than I. H. H·

In whatever situation we be, we shall find both consolation in the promises, and direction in the examples that are recorded for our use in the Sacred Writings. But in seasons of affliction principally will the holy Oracles be found precious, because they exhibit to us God's dearest children in similar circumstances, and point out to us the means, which they, in their troubles, found effectual for their relief.

In recommending the example of David, we shall,

I. Mention some seasons wherein our hearts are apt to be overwhelmed—

This is a vale of tears to all: but to some more especially,

1. From temporal calamities—

Bodily pains, loss of friends, 2 Sam. xviii. 33.; embarrassed circumstances, will weigh down the spirits even of the best. And though, at times, religion will enable them to triumph in the midst of all their tribulations, yet its more common operation is, to moderate their grief, to produce resignation in their souls, and to sanctify the affliction to their spiritual advancement.

2. From spiritual troubles—

The *first convictions* of penitents are often accompanied with the deepest anguish; insomuch that, if God did not support them by a hope of his mercy, they might, like Judas, destroy themselves in utter despair. Their *subsequent views* a'so *of their in-dwelling corruptions* are frequently attended with such dejection, as quite to enervate the body and overwhelm the soul. Isai. xxxv. 3. 4. Rom. vii. 24. If to these be added *the hidings of God's face*, the soul may have a foretaste even of hell itself in the miseries that it endures. Ps. lxxvii. 2—9.

3. From the near prospect of death—

To a person enjoying the Divine presence, death has no terrors, Phil. › 21, 23: it is a welcome messenger, that cannot come too soon. But to one in spiritual darkness and desertion, it is inexpressibly dreadful; and the whole world would appear but a small price to pay for the respite of a few days. The ungodly, it is true, too often die as insensible as the beast: but the godly, who know the terrors of the Lord, cannot pass through that dreary valley without extreme horror, unless they have an inward witness of their acceptance with God. Ps. lv. 4, 5, and perhaps Isai. xxxiii. 10—14.

The example in the text may serve as a model, while we endeavour to,

II. SHEW HOW WE SHOULD CONDUCT OURSELVES IN THOSE SEASONS—

1. To speake *generally*, we should betake ourselves to prayer—

God is the only source of strength and consolation. If we apply to the creature in our distress, we shall invariably find him but a broken reed. Hos. v. 14; Isai. xxxi. 3. On the contrary, the pressure that is on our minds will, for the most part, increase: or, if the trouble be removed, the removal will prove a heavier judgment than its continuance. But if we apply with humility to a throne of Grace, the desired effect will almost instantly appear. Isai. lxv. 24. There is no trouble from which prayer has not extricated the sons of men: it prolonged the life of Hezekiah, 2 Kin. xx. 1—6.; brought Jonah from the bottom of the sea, Jonah ii. 1—7; and restored to peace the tempest-tossed soul of David. Ps. cxvi. 3—8. For us also, if it be fervent, it shall effectually prevail, Jam. v. 16: there is no disquietude which it shall not pacify, "no sorrow which it shall not turn into songs of joy. Ps. l. 15. Wherever we are therefore, even "at the very ends of the earth," and however circumstanced, we should make our requests known unto God, in order to the attainment of solid peace. Phil. iv. 6, 7.

2. More *particularly*, we should beg of God to lead us to the Saviour—

David, though a king, had no sufficiency in himself: he was forced to look to one higher than himself, even to Jesus, the Rock of his salvation. Ps. lxxxix. 19. But how should he come to Jesus, unless the Father should draw him? John vi. 44. Hence he prayed so fervently, that God would "lead" him to that Rock. Thither then must we also go; for there alone can we find stability. Does guilt appal us? nothing but the blood of Jesus can compose our mind. Acts xvi. 29—31. Do temptations harass us? nothing but his grace can enable us to withstand them. 2 Cor. xii. 9. Do accumulated troubles threaten to overwhelm us? we can both do and suffer all things, if HE strengthen us, Rom. viii. 37; yea, we shall be more than conquerors through him that loved us, ib. Like a shipwrecked mariner standing on a rock, we may defy the waves that roar beneath our feet. Such was the experience of David himself, Ps. xl. 1—3; and such shall be ours also, if thestorms that threaten us drive us for security to that place of safety. Let us then, in every affliction, look to Jesus as our help; and, with a deep impression of our inability to go to him aright, let us cry unto God, "Lead me to the Rock that is higher than I!"

ADDRESS,

1. Those who experience no overwhelming troubles—

However serene the sky at present be, no man knows how soon a storm may arise. But supposing our voyage through life be ever so favourable, it must come to an end: and what shall we do in the hour of death without an interest in Christ? Above all, what must become of us, if we be not fixed upon that Rock at the day of judgment? Let us then improve our tranquil hours in securing an establishment on Christ Jesus; that, however suddenly calamities may come, or death may summon us into the presence of our God, we may be found standing immoveably on the Rock of ages. Then, like Noah, shall we rejoice in God's favour, when thoughtless myriads shall be overwhelmed in the deluge of his wrath.

2. Those who are bowed down under trouble—

You are but too apt to carry your complaints to men, instead of spreading them before God. What wonder then you find no deliverance? Has not David told you, that this was his very experience; and that nothing but the use of this remedy afforded him relief? Ps. xxxii. 3—5. Chide then, and resist, your backwardness to prayer. Lay the blame, not on God, who is willing to impart help, but on yourselves, who are unwilling to implore it. Your troubles are sent on purpose to drive you to the Saviour, whom, in a time of prosperity, you are too prone to neglect: and if you suffer them to produce that effect, you shall soon number them among your richest blessings.

---

## GODLINESS WITH CONTENTMENT.

1 Tim. vi. 6.—Godliness with contentment is great gain. (H. H.)

To the great dishonor of christianity, there are many professors, and even preachers of it, who are more intent on promoting their own temporal interests, or the interests of their party, than on advancing practical religion in the world. Of such persons St. Paul is speaking in the context: and he enjoins Timothy to withdraw himself from them, as from persons who disgraced the christian name, by giving reason to people to conclude, that "they supposed gain to be godliness." In opposition to such characters, the apostle reverses that which he had stated as their opinion; and declares, that though gain was not godliness, godliness was gain, yea, "great gain," if it were joined "with contentment."

In vindication of this sentiment, we shall shew,

I. WHAT WE ARE TO UNDERSTAND BY "GODLINESS."

The frame of mind which we may conceive the angels to enjoy, would be by no means suited to our state: we are sinners, redeemed sinners; and therefore "godliness" must include such a frame of mind as becomes persons in our condition. In this view, it implies,

1. An affiance in God through Christ—

This is the fountain of all true religion. Whatever a man may possess without this, he has not one particle of real godliness. If we could suppose him to be as just and honest, as kind and amiable, yea, as devout and fervent as ever man was, still, if he had not the heart of a sinner, of a sinner justly condemned, and delivered from condemnation solely ɔy the blood of **Christ,** he would be utterly destitute of true religion.— — --

2. A devotedness to God in Christ—

This must spring from the former: for though faith and practice differ from each other, as much as the root of a tree does from the fruit it bears, yet we must by no means separate them, since they are equally essential to real godliness. A reformation of the external conduct, or a partial surrender of the heart to God, will not suffice : if we would be approved by God, we mus have our whole selves, body, soul, and spirit, sanctified" to his service.— — —And as Christ is the only Mediator through whom we approach to God so must Christ, that is, God in Christ, be our only Lord and Governor.

When we have just views of the nature of godliness, we shall see,

II. ITS CONNEXION WITH CONTENTMENT—

Such godliness as has been described must bring contentment with it, since all who possess it must feel,

1. A consciousness that they deserve the miseries of hell—

No person can have an entire affiance in God through Christ, till he have felt his desert of God's wrath and indignation. And can such a person be discontented with any lot that may be assigned him ? Must he not, even in the most afflicted situation, say, " Shall a living man complain, a man for the punishment of his sins ?" Will he not call every affliction light, yea, lightness itself, in comparison of the misery he deserves ? Will he not, under the presure of the heaviest calamities, thank God that he is not in hell ?

2. A sense of infinite obligation to God for mercies received—

One who has within him the constituents of real godliness, must see himself to be infinitely indebted to God for the gift of his dear Son, for the knowledge of salvation by him, and for the prospect of everlasting glory. His sense of these mercies cannot but be heightened also by the consideration, that they were never once offered to the fallen angels, nor accepted by the great majority of those to whom they have been offered. Can such an one repine that he has a less measure of health, or riches, or temporal conveniences than others, when he is so far exalted above them in things of infinitely greater moment ?

3. A willingness to be conformed to the image of Christ—

No true disciple of Christ expects or wishes to be in a state different from that which his Lord and Master experienced when on earth. But what was the condition of Jesus in the world ? Did he live in ease and affluence and honor ? No ; " he was despised and rejected of men, a man of sorrows and acquainted with grief." He subsisted oftentimes on the benevolence of his friends and followers ; and often had not as much as " a place where to lay his head." Who that reflects on this, will murmur at his lot, even though nothing but poverty and persecution should await him ? Will he not check the first risings of discontent with this obvious reflection, " The disciple cannot be above his Lord : it is sufficient for the disciple that he be as his Lord ?"

The connexion of godliness with contentment being thus plain, let us, consider,

III. THE ADVANTAGE OF IT AS SO CONNECTED—

St. Paul tells us, that " godliness is profitable unto all things, having the promise of the life that now is, and of that which is to come." Let us view it then,

1. In reference to this life--

Money has obtained the excusive title of "gain:" but godliness has an incomparably greater right to that appellation. There are three principal ends for which money is considered as valuable ; namely, to provide present gratifications, to secure against future troubles, and to benefit our children or dependents. But in these respects it cannot for one moment stand in com petition with godliness,—that godliness I mean which is connected with contentment. Suppose money to afford ever such high gratifications, (though it is very much over-rated by the generality,) will not pardon of sin, peace of conscience, and the enjoyment of the divine presence, far outweigh them all ? Suppose money to afford effectual relief in trouble, (though it cannot assuage our pain either of mind or body,) what consolations can it afford equal to those which result from godliness and contentment ? The utmost that money can do, is to procure some outward relief ; whereas the piety above described will convert every cross into a comfort, and every trouble into a fountain of joy. We are ready to acknowledge that money has its uses, and very important uses too, in reference to our children or dependents, (though it not unfrequently is a curse to them rather than a benefit,) yet even in this view it is far'inferior to religion: for the godly and contented man will instruct his children and dependents in those principles which he has found so beneficial to himself: and who can duly estimate the benefit of such instructions, confirmed and enforced by such an example ? Who can value sufficiently the intercessions of such a friend ? Suppose a dying man to address his surviving relatives, " I have not wealth laid up for you in my coffers, but I have thousands of prayers treasured up for you in heaven, which, I trust, will come down in blessings on your heads, when I lie mouldering in the dust: I have engaged my God to be the husband of the widow, and the Father of the fatherless ; yes, my dear wife and children, I have intreated *him* to take care of you; and I believe that my prayers have not gone forth in vain :" I say, such a legacy would be far better than thousands of silver and gold.

Thus in every view for which money is coveted, godliness with contentment is a richer portion.

2. In reference to the world to come—

The blindest worldling in the universe is not foolish enough to think that "riches will profit him in the day of wrath." In the words following the text this point is established beyond all contradiction ; " For we brought nothing into this world, and it is certain that we can carry nothing out." Here therefore all competition ceases ; and " gain" must be confessed to belong exclusively to the godly and contented mind.

Address,

1. Those who boast of contentment, while they are destitute of godliness—

That persons may feel contentment while enjoying all that they can wish, we readily acknowledge. But we have not real contentment, unless we could be contented with any change of circumstances which God might see fit to appoint. Nor indeed can this fruit spring from any thing but real godliness. Therefore the complacency which many take in their own fancied contentment, while they are uninfluenced by vital godliness, is a delusion, which, if not rectified in time, will issue in the most fearful disappointment and misery.

2. Those who profess godliness, but manifest a worldly or discontented spirit—

The tree must be judged by its fruits. In vain are the highest pretensions to christian experience, if we be not dead to the world, and resigned to the will of God. O brethren, how many professors of godliness have, " through

9 *desire* to be rich, Βυλόμενοι πλυτεῖν, ver. 9—11, fallen into snares and temptations, and into foolish and hurtful lusts, which have drowned them in destruction and perdition!" Remember, that "the love of money is the root of all evil, which while some have coveted after, they have pierced themselves through with many sorrows." But thou man of God, flee these things, and seek rather to be "rich towards God."

3. Those who profess both godliness and contentment—

Know, that you have a richer portion than crowns or kingdoms. You never can have occasion to envy any man. Only seek to grow in these divine graces. Give yourselves up wholly to God; and "having food and raiment, be therewith content." Verse 8. Godliness is "durable riches;" and one grain of contentment is worth a talent of gold. Let it appear, Beloved, that you live under a full persuasion of these things; and that your ardor in pursuit of heaven is accompanied with a proportionable indifference about the things of time and sense.

---

### THE FRUITS AND EFFECTS OF HOPE.

1 John iii. 3.—Every one that hath this hope in him, purifieth himself, even as he is pure. (H. H.)

THE people of God are but little known to an ungodly world: instead of being considered according to their true character, they are regarded as hypocrites, enthusiasts, and disturbers of their brethren's peace. But this is easily accounted for: the world know not God; and therefore it is no wonder that they know not his people. But the saints themselves have a very inadequate conception of the honor that is put on them, or of the glory that is reserved for them. They know indeed that they are sons of God; but they have very little idea of what is comprehended in that relation: and as to their eternal state, they can form no precise judgment respecting it; they only know, in the general, that they shall be like God, and be with him for ever. Yet, though so little known to the world and to themselves they have marks whereby they may be clearly distinguished; they may be known by their uniform endeavors after holiness. To this effect the apostle speaks in the words before us; from which we shall take occasion to consider,

I. THE CHRISTIAN'S HOPE—

Christ is the fountain and foundation of a sinner's hope: without Christ, all must have perished: nor has the most eminent saint any more hope than a fallen angel, except as he is interested in the merits of Christ. But through *him** the believer has a glorious hope;

1. That he is a child of God—

Christ, having purchased us with his own blood, has reconciled us to God, and made us his children. He teaches his followers to consider themselves as standing in this relation to God, not merely like the angels who are his sons by creation, but in a more exalted manner by regeneration and adoption: and he teaches them to expect from him throughout their whole lives the blessings suited to that high dignity.— — —Verse 1; John i. 12, 13; **Matt. vi. 6, 8, 9, 31, 32, 33.**

*The text does not say, ἐν ἑαυτῷ in himself, but ἐπ᾽ αὐτῷ in him, that is, in Christ.

**Now** the true Christian hopes that he is brought into this happy state, **and** that he shall receive from God all those endearing tokens of affection which the relation of sonship emboldens him to expect. This hope of his is founded partly on the merits of his Saviour, and partly on the internal evidence which he has, that he is interested in the Saviour. The mere circumstance of Christ having laid down his life for him, would not be a sufficient ground for him to number himself among the family of God: but when he has the testimony of his own conscience that he has sought acceptance with God through the death of Christ, then he is enabled to indulge a hope that the privileges annexed to such a state belong to him.

2. That he shall be with God, and like him, for ever—

The blessings which the saints enjoy are not confined to this life: "Being sons of God, they are also heirs; heirs of God, and joint-heirs with Christ." Rom. viii. 15—17. "Though they know not yet what they shall be, they know that, when they shall see him, they shall be like him: for they shall see him as he is." Verse 2. The time is coming, when they shall all be introduced into his immediate presence, and be with him, and like him for ever. This also is an object of the Christian's hope.— — —He believes that this is the heritage of the saints; and that "what God hath promised, he is able, and willing, to fulfil."

That this is no barren hope, will appear from,

II. THE EFFECT IT PRODUCES IN HIM—

Every Christian will endeavor to purify himself to the uttermost—

The Christian cannot wilfully live in any known sin: he will search out his corruptions, in order to subdue them; and his duties, in order to fulfil them.— — —He will propose to himself the Lord Jesus Christ as his pattern; and though he can never hope to attain absolute perfection in this life, he will not rest satisfied with any thing short of that. He would gladly be "holy as God is holy, and perfect, even as his Father in heaven is perfect." He considers how the Lord Jesus acted in reference to his God: how in reference to man; and what tempers he manifested in the whole of his deportment;— — —then he labors to follow *his* example, and to "walk in all things as he walked."

To these endeavors he will be stimulated by his hope in Christ:

He cannot endure to think himself a child of God, and yet act like a child of the devil: he cannot please himself with a prospect of enjoying and resembling God in a future life, without seeking communion with him and a resemblance to him in the present world. He will feel himself impelled to holiness by *a sense of duty;* he knows he cannot be saved in any other way. Ps. xxiv. 3, 4; Matt. v. 8; Heb. xii. 14; Rev. xxi. 27; by *a sense of gratitude;* 1 Thess. ii. 12; 2 Cor. v. 14, 15; yea, moreover, by *a love of holiness itself.*— — —Ps. cxix. 128.

We must not however imagine that it is by any power of his own that he thus "purifies himself;" the duty and the exertion are his: James iv. 8: but the power, both to will and to do, proceeds from God alone. Phil. ii. 13.

We shall improve this subject,

1. For conviction—

All profess to have a hope in Christ: but before we conclude that to be well-founded, we must examine what fruits it produces: Are we seeking after universal holiness? Are we contented with no measure of holiness short of perfection itself? Are we setting the Lord Jesus before us, and taking him for our pattern in all our tempers, and in our conduct towards God and man? This is the criterion by which St. John himself teaches us to judge of our hope: ver 6—10: and St. James confirms it—by declaring, that, if in any one point (the not bridling of our tongue, for instance,) we allowedly deviate from this path, our religion is vain. Jam. i. 26. O consider this, lest your hope be only as the spider's web, that will be swept away with the besom of destruction!

2. For encouragement—

Though we must not think our hope well-founded, unless it produce in us the fruits of righteousness, yet we must not imagine that our righteousness is to be *the ground* of our hope, or even *our warrant* to hope in Christ. The only ground of our hope must be found in Christ, and in the promises which God has made to those who believe in him We must go to Christ *as sinners;* and then he will enable us to live *as saints.* This distinction is clearly marked in the text: our hope in Christ is to precede, not to follow, the purification of our hearts: and our holiness is to be the fruit, not the root, of our hope. The same distinction is made by St. Paul also, who, having spoken of our sonship with God, says, "Having therefore these promises, let us cleanse ourselves from all filthiness both of flesh and spirit, perfecting holiness in the fear of God." 2 Cor. vii. 1. See the same also by St. Peter, 2 Pet. i. 4. We must not wait till we are cleansed, and then embrace the promises: but first embrace the promises; and then make use of them for the cleansing of our souls.

What encouragement does this afford to those who feel the corruption of their hearts, and who, if their own purity were to be *the foundation* of their hope, would be in utter despair! Go then, how polluted soever ye are, and seek pardon and sanctification at the hands of Jesus; and you shall find him "faithful and just, to forgive you your sins. and to cleanse you from all unrighteousness." 1 John i. 9.

---

## HAPPY ISSUE OF SANCTIFIED AFFLICTION.

Psa. xcvii. 11.—Light is sown for the righteous, and gladness for the upright in heart. (Pr.)

THE mode of expression used in this passage is common in Hebrew poetry, which consists of a double sentence, the latter part of which is illustrative of the former. "Light" is here put for gladness, and "righteous" for the "upright in heart."— — —The whole is designed to teach us, that the most upright of men must expect a portion of darkness and sorrow for the present; but that it shall sooner or later come to a happy issue. All our enjoyments arise from contrast: if there were no darkness and sorrow here, light and gladness would not be what it will be hereafter.

I. NOTICE A FEW OF THOSE SORROWS WHICH ATTEND THE GODLY IN THE PRESENT STATE, AND OBSERVE THEIR HAPPY ISSUE.

There is abundant reason to expect a portion of darkness and sorrow in this life, because—

1. If we now sustain the character of "the righteous and the upright in heart," yet this was *not always the case with us;* and much of our present darkness and sorrow may be the bitter fruit of former sins.— — —Though God may have forgiven us, yet he may also continue to take vengeance on our inventions: personal and relative troubles may be the consequence. Ps. xcix. 8.— — —Manasseh must walk in darkness and sorrow, and seeing the fruits of his sin all his days

Yet if found "righteous" before God, we shall be forgiven, and all this darkness shall be turned into light. God may chasten us here, but it will only be for a time: he will hide his face, but it will only be for a little moment, and the indignation shall be overpast. He will wipe away all tears from the faces of his people, and sorrow and sighing shall be heard no more. Psa. xxx. 5. Isa. xii. 1; liv. 7, 8; lvii. 16—19. Rev. vii. 17; xxi. 4.

2. Though "upright" on the whole, yet there have been *deviations in our conduct* since we were made "righteous," and many backslidings from God: and our present darkness and sorrow may be the fruit of these.— — —David had much of this in his latter days: the sword departed not from his house · and it may be so with us. Many eminent characters have at different times been driven aside into temptation, or some unexpected evil, which has darkened their sky, and eclipsed both their evidences and their comforts— — —Some easily besetting sin indulged, or some created good idolized, will eat up all our religion, and bring sorrow and darkness with it.

But if we be truly "righteous," things will come to a happy issue at last

3. Irrespective of particular sins, it pleases God in the present state *to humble and try us* by various dark dispensations of providence. Israel were to have the good land, but they must go through the wilderness to possess it. This was a dark passage, but the Lord led them about, that he might try them, and know what was in their hearts. Deut. viii. 3.

God sometimes brings his people into *dark and trying circumstances*, into situations from whence they can see no way of escape.— — —This was the case with Job: yet the Lord lighted his lamp at last, even in this world. Job xlii. 12; James v. 11.— — —Thus also with Judah in her captivity, Lam. iii. 5—9: yet the cloud was dissipated at last: and there are many such seasons in our life, if we did but keep a register of God's mercies.

Sometimes the Lord brings upon us a load of *relative grief and trouble*, such as we cannot unbind or get rid of.— — —Unhappy connections, disobedient children, become a source of overwhelming distress. Thus Jacob's grey hairs were brought with sorrow to the grave: at least the latter part of his life was greatly embittered by this means.— — —Unhappy connections in religion, union without fellowship in the Spirit, attended with discord and evil surmisings, are likewise productive of similar effects.

But if we are truly "upright," all these things will end well at last.

4. A large portion of sorrow and darkness that a good man endures in this life, *arises from what he has within him*, and continually carries about with him; even a body of sin and death, which makes him truly wretched.— — —Hence we are often in the dark in secret duties, in reading, and hearing the word.

But if upright all this shall be removed. God shall bruise Satan under your feet shortly: faith shall be finally victorious: we must therefore hope to the end, for the grace that shall be brought to us at the revelation of Jesus Christ. 1 Pet. i. 13.

Much darkness and sorrow also attend *the church of God*, collectively, as well as individual believers.— — —Israel was long in Egypt, but the Lord brought them out at last with a high hand: in Babylon also, but the day of their redemption came.— — —The church has often been in persecution, but God has confounded all them that rose up against it. So now, Christ will one day gather out of his kingdom all things that offend. Matt. xiii. 41—43.

II. CONSIDER THE GROUND OF OUR HOPE FOR SUCH AN ISSUE.

"Light is *sown* for the righteous, and gladness for the upright in heart;" and therefore, sooner or later, it shall spring up.

1. It is sown in the *gracious purposes* of heaven.— — ~ -God has "prepared" things which ye have not seen, for them that love him: goodness is "laid up" for them that fear him, and trust in him before the sons of men. Ps. xxxi. 19. Cor. ii. 9. Col. i. 5.

2. It is sown for us in *the mediation of Christ*. All his sorrows are the seeds of joy to us: this is the procuring cause of all our comforts, both here and hereafter. All that he has done and suffered on earth, and all that he is now doing in heaven, will issue in the joy of his people: and what a harvest of light and gladness will arise! Ps. lxxii. 16.

3. In *the promises of God*.— — —The seed is sown, the word is gone out of his lips, and shall not return— — —pardon, preservation, and eternal life. Isa. lv. 11, 12.

3. In *the tears of godly sorrow*.— — —Christ's sorrows were the seeds of merit, these of meetness; but each will have their fruit.— — —Godly sorrow generally issues in hope and joy, even in this world, and shall end in everlasting life. Ps. cxxvi. 5, 6. Gal. vi. 8.

5. The very *troubles and trials themselves*, under which the righteous groan, being burdened, are the seeds of future joy, and shall work for them a far more exceeding and eternal weight of glory. 2 Cor. iv. 17.

1. Let us then be reconciled to affliction, and patiently wait for the light and gladness that will soon arise. Ps. xxx. 5.

2. Under all our trials, let us be chiefly concerned to be "upright in heart," and all will issue well. Ps. xlix. 14.

3. Wo to the unbeliever: darkness and sorrow are sown for him, and he himself is continually sowing the seeds of eternal misery! Prov. i. 30, 31

---

### THE PLEASURES OF TRUE PIETY.

Prov. iii. 17.—Her ways are ways of pleasantness, and all her paths are peace. (Pr )

WHATEVER be our age or circumstances in life, pleasure is the object after which the heart of man inspires: but the greater part of earthly enjoyments are unaccompanied with peace. They are surrounded with innumerable snares, and there is death in the cup. The great concern therefore is to enquire after a species of enjoyment, in which these bitter ingredients are not found, and where pleasure and peace are both united. This is found in true religion, and in that only.

I. ILLUSTRATE AND CONFIRM THE TRUTH TAUGHT US IN THE TEXT.

Here we shall notice what are the ways of true religion, and how they are accompanied with pleasure and peace—

1. The first of these ways is *the fear of the Lord*.— — —This is the beginning of wisdom, and of all true religion in the heart.— — —This in now-testament language is the same thing as repentance towards God, and faith in our Lord Jesus Christ.— — —Whatever there may be of religion without this, is not walking in wisdom's ways. You may read, and hear the word, and attend on means of grace; but you are not in her ways, without repentance and faith; and whatever pleasure you may find in all this, it is altogether spurious.— — —Walking in wisdom's ways is the beginning of a new life, a setting out for heaven in the path that truth has set before us.

The sorrow of repentance may be bitter for a time, but it is a bitter **sweet.** The pleasure of weeping at the foot of the cross exceeds every other pleas ure.— — —The Philippian jailor, amidst all his distress, rejoiced, believing in God. The Eunuch no sooner found the truth, than he went on his way rejoicing. Acts viii. 39, xvi. 34. This pleasure is also mingled with solid peace. Rom. v. 1, xv. 13.

2. Another part of wisdom's ways consist in *searching into the mind of God*, or the glorious truths of the everlasting gospel.— — —There is a source of intellectual enjoyment in studying the works of creation: but what a difference in contemplating this subject with and without a God, and the world with and without a providence. But in the gospel we find a greater work than all these. The work of redemption is the richest of all subjects, and engages the attention of angels. Eph. iii. 17.

Here also peace is connected with pleasure: here is a christian feast, and no danger of excess.

3. Another part consists in *walking in Christian fellowship.*— — —And oh how good and how pleasant a thing it is for brethren to dwell together in unity. Ps. cxxxiii.— — —Friendship and affection are the source of true enjoyment amongst rational creatures; and happiness can be found only in proportion as they exist. But religion opens a new source, and presents us with new and additional motives for affection and esteem, and so of pleasure; and by this means it heightens and endears all our attachments. David and Jonathan would not have been so united in soul, but for the influence of religious principle.

Here also is peace. No fear of the union being dissolved by death, but peace and joy may reign for ever.

4. Devoting ourselves *to the interest of Christ*, and laboring by every means in our power to promote it, is another of the ways of true wisdom. — — —If thy heart be with his heart, his interest will be yours; and then you will find pleasure in it, like that of the returning captives. Ps. cii. 14. Or like the builders of Jerusalem, who had a mind to work. Neh. iv. 6.

In this path we shall find peace as well as pleasure: the satisfaction arising from the service of Christ exceeds every other satisfaction.

5. Wisdom leads us in the way of *doing good to mankind in general.* — — —It fills us with compassion for the poor, with sympathy towards the afflicted, and induces us to seek the good of all: and this is the way of true blessedness.— — —A man of an envious or malignant spirit, may find some pleasure in gratifying it, by tormenting others; but he can have no peace. The heart and conscience are at variance.

But to love mankind, and do good, is sweet.

6. *Taking God's will as our rule* in all the affairs of life, and leaving consequences, is another part of wisdom's ways.— — —To do right, and leave it: to say, Thou shalt guide me with thy counsel: in all our ways to acknowledge him. Herein true pleasure and peace are found. Beasts of prey may shift for themselves; but the sheep of his pasture must know the shepherd's voice, and follow him. Ps. xxiii. John x.

7. Submitting with *meekness and contentment* to all the appointments of providence.— — —Such was the example of our Saviour; and if we learn of him, we shall find rest to our souls. Half the misery that is in the world arises from discontent.— — —How true then are the words of our text.

II. INFERENCES FROM THE SUBJECT.

1. We may learn from hence, how to estimate the *carnal pleasures* of a wicked world.— — —In all their mirth and levity, in all their dissipation,

do they find pleasure?— — —They may : but have they inward peace? No : how little therefore does it deserve the name of happiness.

2. How unreasonable are the *objections made to true religion*, as if it were unfriendly to our interests or our happiness.— — —This is one of the deceptions which Satan passes on a deluded world.

3. What reason to *congratulate* those who are walking in wisdom's ways, and who are decided in their hearts for God.— — —The lines have fallen to them in pleasant places, and they have indeed a goodly heritage.— — —. Yours also is true enjoyment: be your portion mine.— — —Yours also is only the beginning of pleasure, but the foretaste of what is still to come. Ps. xiv. 11.

4. Hear what the testimony of Wisdom is to all. "This is the way, walk ye in it." Nothing but destruction and misery will be found in any other. Rom. iii. 16—17.

## LOVE TO THE NAME OF THE LORD.

Malachi iii. 16.—Then they that feared the Lord, spake often one to another, and the Lord hearkened and heard ; and a book of remembrance was written before him, for them that feared the Lord, and that thought upon his name. (Pr.)

WHEN religion is in a low state at any particular period, it is considered as an excuse for the want of holy activity.— — —Many seem to think there is but little hope of doing any thing to purpose ; and that if we can but just keep alive in such a Laodicean state of the church, it is all that can be ex- pected.— — —How different the lesson taught us in this passage? In a time of general corruption, when the priests themselves had depraved the law— — —were enemies to true religion— — —and the common people like them— — —there were a few of another spirit.

1. Observe their *character :* they were such as " feared the Lord."— — —While all around them were practical atheists, they felt the importance of true religion.

2. What they *did :* they " spake often one to another."— — —Not con- tent with public opportunities, they sought each other out, stirred one another up, and delighted in each other's good.

3. How their *minds* were employed: " they thought upon his name."— — —Thinking is not opposed to speaking, but to forgetting.— — —The Lord's name was dear to them : they were concerned for its glory, and grieved for its dishonor.

4. What the Lord did *for them :* " he hearkened and heard."— — — They met together privately, as the sorrowful disciples did for fear of the Jews: but there was one that hearkened— — —heard— — —and approved.— — — What is more, it was " written before him"— — — according to the custom of eastern kings, who kept records of all that was done for their honor. Esther vi. 1.

Enquire what is included in our thinking on the name of the Lord—— and what advantages will arise from it.

I. EXPLAIN WHAT IS MEANT BY THINKING ON THE NAME OF THE LORD IN A WAY THAT HE APPROVES.

This expression is descriptive of the nature of true religion.— — —What is *repentance* towards God, but thinking on his name with grief for having dishonored it.— — —What is *faith* in Christ, but thinking on his name with delight, as revealed in the gospel.— — —What is *love* to God, but thinking on his name affectionately, and with the highest satisfaction.

More especially, it includes an earnest and habitual concern for God's *cause and interest in the world*, and for the spread of the gospel. ——— The name of the Lord is more deeply interested in this, than in all other things besides, and therefore it requires more of our thoughts. ——— When David thought of his name, his heart was set on the prosperity of the Messiah's kingdom. Ps. lxxii. ——— Here God is glorified in the highest ——— the gospel is the overflowing of his blessedness.

More particularly—

1. If we think on the name of the Lord in a way that he approves, *all we do in religion will be directed to his glory.* ——— We may be zealous in holy duties—praying, reading, hearing the word—with a view to our own name. ——— This is not religion, but mere vanity. ——— In the conduct of Mary, Zachariah, and Elizabeth, we see how dead they were to their own honor, and how alive to the glory of God. Their souls did magnify the Lord, and rejoice in God their Saviour. ——— John also was willing to decrease, that the Saviour might increase. This only is true religion.

2. If we think on the name of the Lord, *we shall reckon no sacrifice too great for it.* ——— He who has but little affection for his holy name, will think much of what he gives ——— much of what he does to promote its glory ——— and much of what he may suffer on account of it. ——— The opposite of all t'is is true religion. Acts xxi. 13.

3. It implies that *we seek our own spiritual advantage in subordination to it.* ——— Many are coming and going to the house of God, merely to get comfort and cannot find it. ——— Primitive christians sought first the kingdom of God, and his righteousness ——— cultivated a public spirit ——— laid themselves out for usefulness ——— and were filled with joy and peace in believing. ——— They thought of nothing but Christ, and his name. This was the substance of their doctrine ——— the life of their religion ——— the source of all their enjoyments. ——— Hence they had no distressing doubts and fears. If we take care of God's honor, he will take care of our peace.

II. OBSERVE IN WHAT MANNER GOD REMEMBERS THOSE WHO REMEMBER HIM, OR THINK UPON HIS NAME.

God is not unmindful of any of his creatures, nor does he need a book of remembrance; but he will think of those to do them good, who think of him.

1. The Lord generally employs those who *love his name* as instruments in *promoting its glory.* ——— All the great things that have been done in the church, have been done by characters of this description. ——— Those that honor me, I will honor: but wo to the idol shepherd. Zech. xi. 17.

2. In seeing his holy name glorified, they find *their own reward.* ——— The pleasure of the Lord shall prosper in their hand: what else is their hope or joy. 1 Thess. ii. 19, 20.

3. Their labors shall be *remembered for good* in this life, and even when they are gone to their grave. ——— They are of one heart with God: their zeal is united with his zeal, and their labors shall not be in vain in the Lord. ——— The seed sown shall spring up, and future generations shall bless their memory.

**4.** At *the last day* the Judge will bring forth the book t at was written before him, and read it in the presence of an assembled world. Matt. xxv. 21 —23. Heb. vi. 10.

1. There is no true religion but where the name of the Lord is loved and adored.

2. No hope of being useful in the cause of God without a portion of this spirit.

------

### BLESSEDNESS OF SPIRITUALITY.

Romans viii. 6.—But to be spiritually minded is life and peace.  (Pr.)

EXPERIENCE teaches us, that our greatest happiness consists in drawing near to God; that the love of God is its own reward; yet how prone are we to live at a distance from him.

There are some, however, in whom this spirituality wholly prevails : as among the blessed above, where all is life and peace.— — —In this world it prevails only in part, even in the best of men.  We have much carnality within us : all our powers, principles, and actions are infected by it.— — — Yet if we have any true religion, we are in some degree spiritually minded. We mind the things of the Spirit, and walk after the Spirit.— — —This is essential to denominate us christian.

Consider wherein this spirituality consists—and the blessedness connected with it.

I. EXPLAIN WHAT IT IS TO BE "SPIRITUALLY MINDED."

- This subject, like some others in religion, is better felt than described . experience here is the best teacher.

1. To be spiritually minded is to have a *discernment of the holy beauty and excellence of heavenly objects.*— — —Spiritual things are spiritually discerned.  1 Cor. ii. 14.  2 Cor. iv. 6.— — —While in a carnal state, the mind is blinded by pride, by prejudice, by the vanities of the world It can see no beauty in spiritual objects : the holy character of God possesses no interest.  There is no form or comeliness in the Saviour, that we should desire him— — —nothing desirable in the blessings of salvation— — —nothing lovely in the holy law or glorious gospel— — —in the worship, or in the people of God— — —no congeniality between the state of the mind, and the moral excellence of these objects.— — —But a spiritual mind can discern and feel their beauty and their worth : and in proportion to our spirituality, such will be our relish,— — —Nothing contributes more to our understanding and enjoying the Scriptures, than this state of mind.  Then it is that we can exclaim with David, as in Psalm cxix. 103. cxxxix. 17.

2. It is such a state of mind as to *live as it were on spiritual enjoyments.* These are its food, and its treasure.— — —The desires of a carnal mind are nourished by carnal and sensual objects : but a spiritual mind is taken up with heavenly delights.  The truths of the gospel are the food on which it lives, and the mind is hereby weaned from earthly objects.— — —The affections are now set on things above.  Self-denial becomes more easy, and the ills of life are borne with greater patience and fortitude.

**3.** Spirituality is a state of mind which *delights in spiritual exercises* — — —reading, hearing, meditation, and prayer.— — —The more spiritually minded we are, the more we shall delight in holy duties, especially in those which are most spiritual; in close dealing with God and our own souls.

**4.** A spiritual mind will be apt to *turn every thing to spiritual purposes.* — — —It is the property of a carnal mind to convert every thing into carnal purposes; it finds food in every thing to gratify a sensual taste.— — —A worldly minded man does the same; he possesses the unhappy ingenuity of rendering every thing subservient to his worldly interest, and never loses sight of that.— — —A spiritual mind will be similarly disposed towards spiritual things: it derives instruction from every event, finds a sweetness in a thousand objects overlooked by others, like the bee that sips the honey from every flower. ———— It turns all the mercies of God into matter of praise, all his judgments into matter of humiliation, and even the depravity of mankind into pity, lamentation, and self-reflection. It takes food out of the eater, and sweetness out of the strong.

II. THE ADVANTAGES ARISING FROM THIS STATE OF MIND.

It is "life and peace;" in its own nature—in its immediate effects—producing the most heavenly feelings and enjoyments.

**1.** Spiritual mindedness is accompanied with much *peace with God.*— — —It gives a holy and heartfelt satisfaction, a disposition to rejoice in God, in all his perfections, and in his universal dominion.

**2.** It is accompained with much *peace of conscience.*— — — It reconciles us to ourselves, and diffuses a sweet and holy calm. Oh that peace which passeth all understanding: how does it keep the heart and mind through Christ Jesus.

**3.** It diffuses life and peace under the most *trying circumstances.*— — —It is this which makes our heaviest burdens light, and gives a sweetness to every bitter cup.— — —Patience, humility, and love will all perform their part.

**4.** It will give life and peace even in a *dying hour.* Then will its advantages more especially be felt.— — —With what sacred peace and calmness did this state of mind enable Jacob to take his leave of the world, Gen. xlix. 18, Zachariah, Luke ii. **29.** Paul, 2 Tim. iv. 6.

How important to cultivate this state of mind; by reading, by prayer, by watchfulness, by hearing the word, by delighting in the return of sacred opportunities.

---

## HAPPY STATE OF THE PRIMITIVE CHURCH.

Acts iv. 33.—Great grace was upon them all. (Pr.)

THE power and the glory of the gospel may be seen in looking back on the times of the apostles: and such and more abundantly will be its glory in the latter day. ———— It is peculiarly interesting to behold such a number brought to repentance, by such weak instruments too, and after the cause of Christ had been loaded with reproach by the crucifixion. Oh what a change and what a scene.

It is difficult to give the precise meaning of the text, or to know by what

**words** to express it. We may form some idea of it by what we have **now** and then seen in some very eminent christians, and perhaps it is better judged of by comparison than in any other way. If great grace be seen in **a** minister, it makes his face to shine like that of Moses; or if in a private christian it makes him appear lovely, like one adorned in all the beauties of holiness.

We shall now seek an illustration of the text, by enquiring wherein such eminent grace appeared in these primitive believers.

Oh that by looking back on their conduct, we may be led to mourn over our great deficiency, and see from whence we are fallen, and repent.

1. Great grace appeared in their *earnest and united supplications*. ——— They had much communion with God in prayer, and this holy exercise was with them habitual. Acts i. 14. ——— On any extraordinary occasion, if they were in trouble or suffered persecution, prayer was their first and last resort: ch. iv. 31. ——— When Peter was in prison, prayer was made for him by the whole church, ch. xii. 5: and when Paul and Silas were imprisoned at Philippi, they spent the night in prayer: ch. 25. ——— When these primitive christians parted from each other they prayed together, though it was on the sea shore: ch. xxi. 5. ——— They were also much devoted to private prayer, ch. x. 9: and great grace will lead to much intercourse with heaven.

2. It appeared in their *stedfast adherence to the apostle's doctrine.*——— Great grace will prepare our hearts to understand the word, for it is that unction which teacheth all things; that which forms and adapts the mind to every part of the gospel. ——— Indifference to divine truth is always a sign of little grace, or of the total want of it; and it becomes us seriously to enquire whether our hearts are prepared for all we meet with in the apostles' doctrine. ——— A stedfast continuance in the truth is also a trial of grace. Not a continuance, indeed, in our own belief, because it is our own; for that may be where there is no grace; but to enter into the spirit of the apostles' doctrine, and to abide in it from love.

3. In a constant adherence *to the worship and service of God.* Acts ii. 42, 46. ——— Real religion was the object of supreme regard, and serving the Lord was their proper element: ch. iv. 46. All hands found some employment. ——— Peter and Paul viewed the whole world as lying before them, and they longed to go forth in the warfare: and wherever they went they made the service of Christ their proper business, whether on shipboard or in prison. ——— The History or Acts of the Apostles is full of their labours and travels for Christ; and churches were planted by them in almost every place. Ch. xiii. xiv.

4. In their great *love one to another.* ——— They were all of one heart and one soul: ch. iv. 32. They had all things common, neither said any of them that ought of the things which he possessed was his own. ——— This practice, however, continued only for a short time, during a special season of necessity. There were afterwards both rich and poor among them, but still they were of one heart. ——— Previous to their receiving the gospel they were at enmity with each other, and divided into sects and parties; but now all this was forgotten. Oh how interesting to see what religion can do!

5. These primitive christians were *full of holy joy* and peace in believing, and they triumphed in every place: ch. ii. 46. ——— Now was that prophecy fulfilled: " Behold, I create Jerusalem a rejoicing, and her people a joy " Samaria also was made glad with the tidings of salvation: ch. viii 8.

—— They had found the Messiah, had obtained mercy, and now they rejoice in serving him.

6. Their *spirit and deportment* were such as recommended their religion to the word: ch. ii. 47. —— They abounded in those christian graces which are lovely even in the eyes of men in general. They were neither surly nor morose, but pitiful, kind and courteous; easy to be entreated, full of mercy and good fruits, without partiality, and without hypocricy. Their conversation was such as becometh the gospel, and they adorned the doctrine of God our Saviour in all things.

What reason have we to mourn, that we so little resemble these holy men —— Oh how far do we come short of their ardent zeal, their love to Christ and the souls of men —— Yet let us be thankful for a little of that spirit which appeared so eminently in them. —— Bless God for the gospel, for the way of salvation, for the ordinances of Christ, for brotherly love and christian fellowship. Lord, increase our faith.

## CHRISTIAN COMPASSION.

Hebrews xi. 12, 13.—Wherefore lift up the hands which hang down, and the feeble knees; and make straight paths for your feet, lest that which is lame be turned out of the way; but let it rather be healed. (Pr.)

THE defection among the believing Hebrews seems to have arisen in part from the persecutions they met with on account of the gospel. They had been greatly oppressed by their unbelieving countrymen, and though they had not been called to resist unto blood, yet they had suffered " the spoiling of their goods," in the beginning of their profession. This at first they nobly endured, but afterwards fainted. Like their forefathers in the wilderness, when trouble overtook them, some of them were for going back, and others were disheartened.

The words of the text are taken from Isa. xxxv. 3, 4, and are addressed to the believing Hebrews as an admonition to comfort and encourage one another. The disheartened among them are compared to such as had been running in a race, or sustaining a protracted conflict till their knees began to tremble, and their hands to hang down; and in this condition, those who are strong ought to bear the infirmities of the weak.

I. NOTICE THE RELIGIOUS STATE OF THOSE WHO ANSWER TO THE DESCRIPTION GIVEN IN THE TEXT.

Were we to compare christians in general of the present day with those of the first ages, it would appear that they are grown weak and faint. We have but little of the zeal and activity which characterised the primitive church. The duties of religion are but faintly regarded, our resistance of evil is irresolute and undecided, and our fortitude in trials and adversities bears but little comparison with theirs.

The description, however, is more particularly applicable to certain individual cases and characters amongst us, who need the compassion of their brethren, under their various difficulties and discouragements.

1. Some are ready to faint under difficulties and *troubles of a worldly nature.* —— With all their toil, and care, and industry, though they rise up early, and sit up late, and eat the bread of carefulness, they are scarcely

able to ge along: and not casting all their care upon him who careth for them, the oad becomes too heavy, and they sink beneath the burden. —— Y if we keep near to the Lord, such things may be endured. Some pool people are very happy amidst all their privations, while others are faint an I weary in their course.

2. Some are discouraged through distrust, and *groundless fears of future ills.* —— In addition to the troubles they already feel, they anticipate future ones which may never come. Thus David, in the former part of life, was rendered perpetua.'y uneasy by the apprehension that he should one day perish by the hand of Saul. —— But if we could leave the future, with God we should be happy, and by encountering our difficulties only one at a time we should get through them all at last. Matt. vi. 34.

3. Others are distressed not only with the difficulties of life, but from being under *the chastening hand of God.* —— They could bear injustice and oppression from the hands of men; but when providence seems to be against them, they are utterly dismayed, and their strength is dried up. Flesh and heart fail them; and not finding sufficient relief in the promises, they faint in the day of adversity. —— These things may be borne, however if God be with us; but if left to ourselves, our hands will soon hang down, and our knees be feeble.

4. Some are disheartened by repeated opposition from *the enemies of religion* —— Though the laws of our country do not now admit of open persecution, there is nevertheless a great deal of enmity, reproach and unkindness to be endured oftentimes from friends and near relations for the sake of truth and of a good conscience. —— This also may be borne, if we live near to God, and duly estimate the importance of christian principles; otherwise we shall soon grow weary and faint in our minds. It was well with these Hebrews while they were warmly attached to the gospel: but when they began to give that up, their strength failed them.

5. Some are greatly discouraged by *inward conflicts*, arising from the evil propensities of their own hearts. —— It is more difficult to sustain this warfare than all the troubles that assail us from without. David could meet his numerous enemies in the field, and was not afraid of ten thousands of his people who set themselves against him: but when compassed about with his own iniquities, his heart utterly failed him, and he was not able to look up. Psal. xl. 12. —— Some easily besetting sin, arising from constitution or peculiar circumstances in life, is sufficient to destroy the comfort of a believer, and almost to annihilate his hope. Whether it consists in an inordinate love of the world, or the indulgence of some sordid appetite, it interrupts communion with God, cuts off supplies of grace from above, and so weakens and relaxes all the energies of vital religion. The hands hang down, and the knees are feeble.

6. A *departure from evangelical truth* has weakened the strength of some by the way, and left them shorn of their dignity and glory.— — — The relinquishment of any of the leading doctrines of the gospel, or mixing them up with a portion of error, tends as certainly to enfeeble the christian graces, and to destroy the stimulus to holy activity, as the indulgence of sin itself. Gal. v. 7—9.— — —If we begin to think less of the evil of sin, if we feel less our need of a divine Redeemer, and cease to go to God by him as lost and perishing sinners; if in this case we are christians at all, we shall soon grow faint and feeble, and exhibit little more than the mere form of godliness.

7. The despondency of some good people arises no doubt from a natural

*gloominess in their constitution,* which disposes them to dwell **on the dark side** of every subject, rather than on the other.— —They think of their own unworthiness, and forget the worthiness of the Saviour. They are overtaken by some temptation, fall into sin, and forget that there is an Advocate with the Father. John ii. 1.— — —Partial or contracted views of the gospel, which hide from us the allsufficiency of Christ, and fix our attention chiefly on ourselves, have a most discouraging tendency. Heb. vii. 25.

II. THE DUTY OF CHRISTIANS TOWARDS ONE ANOTHER UNDER THESE DISCOURAGEMENTS. "LIFT UP THE HANDS WHICH HANG DOWN, AND THE FEEBLE KNEES."

Though this exhortation is chiefly applicable to ministers, whose office it is to strengthen the weak, and to comfort the feeble-minded, it also points out the duty of all christians towards one another.— — —How much soever it may be neglected, it is unquestionably one of the great ends of christian society and fellowship, that we should be helpers of each other's faith and joy in the Lord.

1. In order to perform this duty aright, it is necessary to exercise much *tenderness and forbearance* towards those who are labouring under great discouragements.— — —Let the strong bear the infirmities of the weak, remembering that they are a part of the mystical body of Christ. 1 Cor. xii. 21, 25. The compassionate tenderness of the great Shepherd of the flock, is left as a pattern for our imitation. Isai. xl. 11. Matt. xii. 20.

2 Another way in which our compassion may be exercised is to point out to one another *the directions and consolations of the gospel,* according as the case may require; and here the tongue of the learned is necessary, to speak a word in season to him that is weary.— — —Are any discouraged by outward difficulties? Let them cast all their care on him who careth for them; let them commit their way unto the Lord, and be careful for nothing; but in every thing by prayer and supplication make their request known unto God. He that taketh care for the greater, will take care of the less.— — —Is the hand of the Lord gone out against any of our brethren? Let us relieve their own despondency by pointing out the end to be answered by afflictions; let us remind them of the sufferings of Christ, and of the weight of glory that shall follow.— — —Are any grieved and oppressed by irreligious connections? Remind them of him who endured the contradiction of sinners against himself, lest they be weary and faint in their minds— — —Are any disheartened and cast down on account of inbred corruption? Tell them to be looking still to Jesus, and to maintain the conflict till death: the God of peace shall bruise Satan under their feet shortly.— — —Does the weakness and faintness of any arise from a partial relinquishment or misconception of the gospel truth? Endeavour to instruct and teach them in all wisdom, restoring them in a spirit of meekness and love.— — —Does discouragement arise from a proneness to view the dark side of things? Turn to them the other side also. God's thoughts are not as our thoughts, nor his ways as our ways.

3. Let us be concerned to *remove the stumbling-block out of the way,* and so to " make straight paths for their feet." It is here intimated that the defection and irregularities of some of these Hebrews, became a stumbling-block to the rest. They had departed in some measure from the simplicity, of the gospel, and so were the occasion of "turning the lame out of the way."— — —If those who have been of longer standing in the church, begin to turn aside, or grow weary in their course, it will discourage the weak, and become a snare to the unwary.— — —In order therefore to heal

and strengthen others, it is needful above all things that we ourselves are found walking humbly with God; a zealous and holy example cannot fail to revive and quicken those who come within its influence. Hos. xiv. 7.

1. Let us learn from hence, that all our difficulties and discouragements in the ways of God arise from ourselves, and from the evil that is in the world. They originate in a departure from God, or from the simplicity of the gospel: and if we keep near to him, nothing can hurt us. His ways are ways of pleasantness, and all his paths are peace.

2. How lovely and how interesting is christian society, whose object it is to strengthen and encourage each other in the way to heaven: and how wretchedly defective must it be, if it has not this tendency.

3. How essential to the christian character are brotherly kindness, charity, and a disinterested but affectionate concern for the spiritual and everlasting welfare of our fellow christians. If their comfort and success be not an object of the tenderest solicitude, we are strangers to the benevolent spirit of the gospel.

---

### TRUE RELIGION THE SOURCE OF JUSTICE AND BENEVOLENCE.

Gen. xlii. 18.—This do and live: for I fear God.

The history of Joseph never fails to be interesting, as often as we read it. Here we have an account of his brethren, coming the first time into Egypt to buy corn. On this occasion he spoke roughly to them, and put them in prison, but afterwards released them. His conduct towards them may be seen in verse 14 to 17.

1. Observe, his design in saying to them, " I fear God," when he com mitted them to prison, was to convince them that he did not do it wantonly or in cruelty; but that his conduct in this instance was regulated by the purest motives, and that they had no reason to expect any injustice at his hands.

2. What an effect it must have had on them, to find that there was a man in Egypt who feared the God of their fathers; a man too in a high and honorable station, and who was lord over all the land.— — —They themselves had lived in a religious family, and did not fear him.

3. Notice the connexion there is between fearing God, and dealing justly and mercifully with men. This has been verified in all ages; true religion is the parent of humanity, and of genuine benevolence.

I. INQUIRE WHAT IS INCLUDED IN THE FEAR OF GOD.

This term is descriptive of the whole of true religion, which is thus frequently expressed in various parts of the Old Testament.— — —If Joseph had lived in gospel times, he would probably have said, " I believe in Christ;" and the meaning is much the same.

Religion however does not consist in slavish fear or dread of the Almighty. in trying to please him as a hard master, or in praying to avert his vengeance. These are the feelings of an idle unprofitable servant, and not of a true believer.

But true religion is called the fear of God, because

1. It chiefly consists in a sacred and solemn dread of the Supreme Being; deep and reverential regard for his holy name, his worship, and authority

— — —Its tendency is to fill the mind with mingled sentiments of love and awe : where this is wanting, there is no genuine religion.

2. True piety produces tenderness of conscience, as one of its principal fruits and evidences— — —a fear to neglect what God requires, or to trifle with his commands, as well as the dread of doing what he has forbidden. — — —It is therefore with infinite propriety that all true religion is called the fear of the Lord.

3. Though under the gospel, fear is not the predominant spirit of believ ers, but love and joy ; yet even there it is necessary, and neither love nor joy, nor any other part of true religion can exist without it.— — —We are exhorted to perfect holiness " in the fear of God," and this must accompany our highest joys.— — —This is the great preservative, both against presumption and despair. Heb. xii. 28.

II. CONSIDER ITS INFLUENCE ON OUR CONDUCT TOWARDS MEN : " This do, and live ; for I fear God."

It is a fact well known in former times, that where the fear of God was not, there was no security for justice and mercy towards men. Hence the conduct of Abraham, when he came to Abimelech at Gerar. Gen. xx. 11. This also is true of magistrates, and public rulers in general.— — — Hence the conduct of the unjust judge, mentioned by our Lord, Luke xviii. 4.— — —Even David, when he had lost his tenderness of conscience towards God, became cruel to Uriah, and also to the Amorites. 2 Sam. xii. 31.

On the contrary, where the fear of God prevails, there we shall find justice and humanity towards men : the kings of Israel were on this account esteemed to be merciful men. 1 Kings xx. 31.

As masters, it will make us kind ; as parents, tender : as friends, faithful ; as members of society, peaceable and well-disposed.

And how is this to be accounted for ?

1. True religion, or the fear of God, impresses the mind with a sense of its accountableness. Without this, a man considers only himself ; with it, a king will feel that he has a King above him ; and a master, that he also has a Master in heaven.— — —Under this conviction, those who have little to fear from others, will fear God ; and their conduct in the highest stations will be regulated by it. Neh. v. 15.— — —The principle that makes us feel that we are stewards, and must shortly give an account, is above all others adapted to inspire us with the love of justice and benevolence.

2. The fear of God will render us sensible of our own faults and failings, and of our need of mercy.— — —Such will be quickly aware that they owe ten thousand talents, and cannot therefore think of taking a fellow servant by the throat, and saying, Pay me what thou owest. Genuine religion will impart to us a spirit of meekness and kindness, and make us ready to forgive. Thus also it wrought in Joseph.

3. The fear of God is mixed with holy love : such therefore who possess this principle, will feel benevolently towards all that bear the divine image — — —whether as creatures, who are formed after his natural likeness, or as those who bear a resemblance to his moral nature.

1. We may from hence learn in what way we may hope to see the general state and condition of the world ameliorated · ·each men truly to fear God, and all the rest will follow of course.

2. We are here furnished with a rule for self-examination : the criterion of all genuine piety is the fear of God, disposing us to the exercise of justice and mercy towards men.

3. Whether we fear God or not, we are in his hands : by him we must be judged. and he will reward every man according to his works

## APOSTLES' PRAYER.

**Luke xvii. 5-–The apostles said unto the Lord, Increase our faith. (Pr.)**

The occasion of this prayer seems in this place to be the exhortation previously delivered, and which required the performance of a difficult duty, ver. 4. In this view it is highly proper, as faith is the grand moving principle by which every holy duty is performed. But whatever were the immediate occasion, the prayer itself is adapted to every part of the christian life.

I. CONSIDER THE GENERAL IMPORT OF THE PRAYER: "LORD, INCREASE OUR FAITH."

1. Faith has respect to *revealed truth,* as its immediate object; and in the New Testament it more especially relates to Christ, as the substance of all the promises.— — —He was the great object in whom they believed. Thus Peter's confession, " We believe and are sure that thou art that Christ, the Son of the living God."— — —Faith in the all-sufficiency of Christ is that to which the promise of miraculous healing was addressed : " Believest thou that I am able to do this? If thou canst believe, all things are possible."— — —It was this which failed the disciples in the hour of danger : " Oh ye of little faith." Matt. viii. 26.

2. In praying for an increase of this principle, the apostles acknowledged that *their faith was weak.*— — —So indeed it appeared in a time of trial ; and so does ours too frequently, if the strength of faith, as well as its genuineness, is to be judged of by its fruits.

3. In praying for more faith, they also acknowledged *their own insufficiency* to produce it.— — —Faith is indeed our duty, and unbelief a sin ; but like every thing else that is truly good, it is all of grace: and it is God that worketh all our works in us. Ephes. ii. 8. Phil. ii. 13.

4. In directing their prayer to Christ, they virtually *acknowledge his divinity.*— — —To give or to increase faith is more than any mere creature can accomplish. A minister may offer evidence for the truth to be believed: but he can neither impart faith, nor increase it.— — —Christ alone is the author and the finisher of faith. Heb. xii. 5.

5. This prayer might in some measure be answered at the time, but was more especially so after our Lord's ascension.— — —When he came to the crown, he blessed his followers: he gave gifts unto men, and an abundance of his Holy Spirit. Acts ii. 33.

II. THE REASONS WHICH RENDER THIS PRAYER SUITABLE TO ALL CHRISTIANS.

If we are truly the followers of Christ, yet our faith is weak at best, and needs to be increased, and that for various reasons—

1. On account of its influence in obtaining *other spiritual blessings ;* for they are bestowed according to the measure of faith.— — —In performing *miraculous cures,* our Lord always looked at this. Many looked at worldly distinctions, but he did not: his eye was on the faith of the party. Matt. ix. 2. Acts xiv. 9, 10.— — —When he hesitated, it was for unbelief. Mark ix. 23, 24.— — —It is so in the bestowment of *spiritual blessings :* they are given in answer to the prayer of faith. Psal. xxxi. 19. Mark xi. 24.— — —The answer to successful prayer will also be found to be of this description. Gen. xxxii. 26.

2. Its influences under *dark and trying providences.*— — —Nothing but faith can sustain us under them. Ps. xcvii. 2. What could Jacob have done

but for the influence of faith? "I will surely do thee good," the promise said; yet nothing but evil appeared. —— What could he have done afterwards, when his children seemed to be taken away, in whom the promises were to be fulfilled? —— What could the pious captives have done in Babylon, had they not been sustained by faith in the divine word. Hab. ii. 3. —— What could we do amidst dark and threatening providences, and when Zion is covered with a cloud, were it not for the support which faith derives from the promises?

3. Its influence on the *deep mysteries of divine truth*, which faith only can receive and apply. Truth is like a deep fountain, and faith is the only means of drawing from it: it lies far beyond the reach of the carnal mind, and even of the greater part of modern christians. —— The doctrine of Christ crucified, of God manifest in the flesh, and the wondrous extremes which meet in the person and work of Christ, are like an immense ocean. The powers of reason could do nothing here; and reason, if she attempted to fathom it, would soon be drowned.— — —But faith is like a little bark, borne along the mighty waves, and conducts us safely into harbour.— — — The only enquiry of a true believer is, hath God said it? Then I receive it: Lord, increase our faith!

4. Our *spiritual enjoyments*, as they are derived wholly from the promises, are proportioned to the degree of faith.— — —The consolations themselves are no less now than in primitive times. Christ is the same yesterday, to day and forever: the gospel is the same, our prospects are the same. If our enjoyments are not the same, it is owing to the want of faith— — — What christians might we be, had we but more of this! Instead of God's house being a house of mourning, it would be a house of joy: instead of dragging on heavily, we should run in the way of his commandments with enlargedness of heart: instead of fretting under the frowns of the world, we should rejoice in every tribulation. Rom. v. 2, 3.— — —The promises are full for this life, as well as for that which is to come. We only want faith to realize and enjoy what God has given us in his word.

4. The influence of faith *on our life and conduct*, renders this prayer peculiarly suitable and important.— — —Without faith it is impossible to please God: nothing is done right, nothing is acceptable. Where it is weak, and mixed with much unbelief, it will leave us lifeless and inactive.— — — This also is the case where any of the leading doctrines of the gospel are doubted or denied. The Galatians ceased to run well, when their minds had been corrupted from the simplicity that is in Christ. Gal. v. 7, 15, 16 — — —On the contrary, where faith is lively, all will be alive. Heb. xi. — — —The disciples in our Lord's life time believed a little, and did a little: but afterwards how great the difference!— — —As preachers and as hearers, in prosperity and in adversity, faith in God is the life of all activity, and of submission to his will.

6. Its importance *in the hour of death*, renders it unspeakably desirable. — — —We know nothing of hereafter but by faith: with much of this we shall be prepared to meet the last enemy, and shall even desire to be offered up. Lord increase our faith! 2 Tim. i. 2.

## COMMUNION OF SAINTS.

Romans 12.—That I may be comforted together with you, by the mutual faith both of you and me. (Pr.)

THE communion of saints was esteemed of such importance amongst early christians, as to make it an article of faith ; and where the spirit of it is preserved it still forms a charming part of the christian religion.

Our text gives us a brief description of it. Paul longed to see the christians at Rome, having as yet only heard of them by report. When going up to Jerusalem, he observed, he went not knowing the things that should befal him there, save that in every place bonds and afflictions awaited him. He wished to go to Rome, but little thought of being sent thither as a prisoner. In this epistle written from Corinth, he proposed taking them in his way to Spain, and promised himself much satisfaction in the interview. His hope was, that their mutual faith would be a comfort to each other.

I. ENQUIRE WHAT THERE IS IN THE FAITH OF MINISTERS TO COMFORT PRIVATE CHRISTIANS.

When christians see their minister, they expect to hear something concerning " the faith ;" and Paul takes it for granted it would be so with these christians at Rome.

Now there are three things in the faith of the ministers of the gospel, which tend to comfort the minds of the godly—

1. Its being *scriptural and decided.* ——— If the faith which we preach were antiscriptural, it might comfort the sinner and the hypocrite, but not the real christian ; to him it would be matter of grief. ——— If we dwelt in speculations, it might amuse and interest an ingenious mind ; but there would be no solid food for the godly. ——— Now the apostles were decided : they spoke what they believed and were assured of, and had not followed cunningly-devised fables; and it is this in the ministry of the word now, which affords comfort. ——— To see a minister decided on scriptural grounds, speaking the things of which he himself has been fully assured, is to see a guide who is well acquainted with his way, or a pilot who is conversant with his chart. ——— The opposite of this is distressing. ——— To see a guide stumbling in the dark, not knowing truth from error, but who now tells you this is the way and then that, and is at a loss to know what he should believe, must excite fear and distrust, and not comfort. ——— But Paul's gospel was not yea and nay ; but yea and amen in Christ Jesus. 2 Cor. i. 17—20.

2. Its being given them not for themselves only, but *as a public trust to be imparted*, renders it a source of comfort to believers. ——— In this respect Paul considered himself as "a debtor," both to the wise and the unwise : ver. 14. ——— He was entrusted with the " unsearchable riches of Christ," not for his own use merely, but that he might proclaim them among the Gentiles as an almoner. Eph. iii. 8. ——— He himself was poor, yet making many rich : he was afflicted and persecuted, in order that he might comfort others 2 Cor. i. 6 ; vi. 10.

3. Its being a *living principle in their own souls ;* the truth on which they live, and have ventured their own eternal all. 1 Tim. iv. 6. ——— Without an experimental acquaintance with the truth, there would be very little to edify and comfort others, whatever might be our attainments and gifts in other respects. ——— Its coming from the heart makes it interesting to the hearts of others : hence it is that an experimental ministry yields comfort to real christians, and no other ministry can do it. 1 Thess. i. 5, 6.

**II.** Notice what there is in the faith of private christians to comfort the ministers of Christ.

It is necessary that they should receive comfort, as well as impart it: and
the faith of christians tends to do this, and that for the following reasons—

1. It furnishes them with *sentiments and feelings* in their preaching,
which nothing else could do. ——— A believing, spiritual, attentive, and affectionate auditory, whose souls are engaged, tend to inspire thought and feeling in the preacher, which no previous preparation could excite. ——— So
on the contrary, when unbelief, carelessness, or conceit appears, it tends to
chill the soul, which is like a vessel confined in port for want of a gale. Heb.
v. 11.

2. In the faith of private christians also we see the *travail of our Redeemer's soul,* and this gives us comfort. ——— If we love him, we cannot
but rejoice in the success of his gospel. Every other consideration is of
very inferior importance compared with this, however agreeable our circumstances may be.

3. In it we see also the *fruit of our own labors;* an answer to many
prayers, and to many endeavors for the good of others. ——— This is highly
encouraging to a faithful minister; and without it he spends his strength in
vain. Isa. xlix. 4. Gal. iv. 19. 1 Thess. ii. 19.

4. In it we see the *pledge of your salvation;* and in proportion as we love
your souls, this must comfort us. ——— As fellow creatures, as friends, as
the relatives of dear friends, we cannot but love you: to see therefore the
evidence of your conversion and salvation, is our highest enjoyment and reward. 1 Thess. ii. 8. 3 John 4.

**III.** What there is in the common faith of both to comfort one
another.

Common blessings are the best of blessings; and those blessings which
ministers possess, not as ministers, but as christians in common with the rest,
are the best of all. ——— What Paul desired for his own soul, is common
to the meanest christian. Phil. iii. 8.

Now there are three things in the common faith of both ministers and
christians, which tend to their mutual comfort—

1. *Its unity.* ——— Those who have never seen each other's faces in the
flesh, yet when they come to converse together, will soon find their hearts to
be one. ——— Paul had often felt thus, even when at a distance from christian friends. Col. ii. 5. ——— But he would feel much more from a personal interview; and hence he longed to see these believing Romans. that he
might be comforted by " the mutual faith" of one another.

2. The *interesting nature of the truth believed,* has this tendency. ———
" This is a faithful saying, that Christ Jesus came into the world to save sinners—God was manifest in the flesh—God so loved the world." – ——— It
is from the belief of this gospel, that there is now no condemnation. Hence
we become the sons of God, and hence the hope of eternal life. ———
These are things of the utmost importance; and being such, like a company
of strangers who find themselves all embarked in the same ship, and going
together, the mutual belief of them affords mutual comfort.

2. The promised *presence of Christ,* which attends such meetings of the
godly for communion with each other, furnishes another source of mutual
enjoyment. ——— It is only where Christ meets with his people, that real
happiness can be found.

REFLECTIONS.

1. Learn the necessity of *faith in Christ,* in order to christian communion
Unbelievers, or mere nominal christians, possess no fitness for it:

there is neither any bond of union, nor any medium of receiving or imparting christian comfort.

2. The necessity of *communicating* faith, in order to enjoy the benefit of christian fellowship. —— That kind of discourse which tends to explain and render truth interesting, is of importance in promoting both the union and comfort of the godly.

3. If the fellowship of saints on earth be so desirable, what will it be *in heaven ;* where no darkness will be felt, no discords, no calamities, no painful separations shall take place any more !

## THE BLESSEDNESS OF FOLLOWING CHRIST.

John viii. 12.—I am the light of the world : he that followeth me, shall not walk in darkness, but shall have the light of life. (Pr.)

THERE were many pretended lights in the world, as there are now, and many who followed those wandering stars : but Christ is the origin of all true intelligence, the fountain of light and life to all his people. Like the lesser planets, they borrow all their light from him ; while he alone is as the mid-day sun.

I. CONTEMPLATE THE CHARACTER WHICH OUR LORD ASSUMES : "I am the light of the world."

The Jews objected to it, and do still object, ver. 13 ; and if he were a mere prophet, as some have said, and only a man, though inspired, the assumption in the text would indeed be inadmissible.

Our Lord not only distinguished himself from all false lights, and false prophets, but from all the servants of God that ever came before him, as in John i. 7—9.— — —They only shone with borrowed rays: his light is original and underived.— — —Their light was confined to time and place: his is universal, "the light of the world." Jews and Gentiles, rich and poor, learned and ignorant, all derive their light from him : those under the Old Testament, and those under the New.

More particularly—

1. Christ's being the light of the world means *what he is to others, as revealed in the gospel.*— — —The divine nature is sometimes expressed by this term, as when it is said, "God is light, and in him is no darkness at all :" but here it denotes what Christ is to the world.— — —If the light had been confined to his personal appearance, the sun would have been set when he left the earth. Instead of this, the light shone still brighter after his ascension than before : and it shall continue to shine, still more and more, unto the perfect day.

2. Christ as revealed in the gospel, sheds a light on *the character and designs of God.*— — —But for him, we should have known but little of his moral attributes; it is the Son that has "declared him," and it is in his face that we behold the glory of the Lord. John i. 18, xvii. 26 ; 2 Cor. iv. 6.

By the law written on our hearts we might have known something of the justice of God, and seen the terror of his majesty, sufficient to inspire us with dread, at the thought of appearing before him : but this would have been all. Whereas now, we see him gracious and glorious, a just God and yet a Saviour: glorified in the highest, and sending peace on earth.

**3.** The revelation of Christ casts a light on *the former dispensations.* — — —How dark and inexplicable would have been the types and shadows of the law, the prophecies and providences attending the Jewish church, had they not been followed by the doctrine of the cross.— — —The disciples themselves were all in the dark, till Jesus opened their understandings, and expounded to them all things written in the law and the prophets concerning himself. Luke xxiv. 25—27.

**4.** The doctrine of Christ affords the clearest discovery of *the way of a sinner's salvation,* so that it is now traced as with a sunbeam.— — —That faithful saying of Paul's, "that Christ came into the world to save sinners," casts more light on this subject than all the labors of man could possibly have effected.— — —Philosophy did nothing towards it. Even old testament believers saw only as through a glass darkly: but in the gospel we behold it all with open face.— — —Now, how clearly is the way of life revealed. The word is nigh thee, in thy mouth: and in thy heart: believe on the Lord Jesus Christ, and thou shalt be saved.

II. CONSIDER THE BLESSEDNESS OF THOSE WHO FOLLOW HIM: "they shall not walk in darkness, but have the light of life."

1. "Walking" implies that *life is a journey.* We are not at home, but travelling to another world.— — —There are many ways that lead to death, and but one that leads to endless life: hence the great importance of having the true light to guide us.

2. The promise implies that *many walk in darkness,* even all that follow not this light.— — —They go on stumbling, not knowing the way, nor whither they are going: all is doubtfulness, and dreadful uncertainty.

3. Those who follow Christ shall have *the light of life,* even that which not only illuminates, but cheers and quickens them along the road.

"Following" Christ supposes our believing on him. It is to follow him as the Shepherd of the flock, as disciples follow their Master; or rather, as a traveller who sees the light and follows after it, like the children of Israel who were guided by the pillar of fire through the wilderness.

1. Compare their state with that of *the heathen world.* They know nothing of the way, nor whither they are going; but vainly imagine that when they leave the world, they shall transmigrate into other bodies. But Christians know the way. John xiv. 3, 4.

2. Compare their state with that of merely *nominal Christians,* who know not the way, nor whither they are going, notwithstanding the objective light with which they are surrounded.

3. In comparisen of such as *follow Christ partially,* and not wholly, they may be said not to walk in darkness.— — —Some are blown about with every wind of doctrine, and are always at sea, without a compass or a guide.

In order to follow this light, we must be convinced of our own ignorance aud need of a guide. Pride and unbelief have darkened the understanding, and those who think they see are made blind. John ix. 39—41.

## PRIVILEGES OF CHRIST'S FLOCK.

**John x. 9.**—I am the door: by me if any man enter in, he shall be saved; and shall go in and out, and find pasture. (Pr.)

Were we to enquire which is the true church; who are the ministers of Christ, and which is the way of salvation; we may learn it from this chapter. —— The Jews indeed pretended that they only were the people of God; that their priests were the only ministers, and that salvation was confined to them. —— But our Lord shows that those only are the true church which are his sheep, and who enter in by him; that those only are true shepherds who believe in him, and lead sinners to him; and that this is the way of salvation.

I. THE CHARACTER OF THOSE WHO TRULY BELONG TO THE FLOCK OF CHRIST.

They are such as enter in by Christ, "the door" of the sheepfold; that is, by *faith* in him. Many have entered in by *birth:* they were born in a christian land, and so are called christians. Thus it was with the Jews, who rested on their being the children of Abraham. —— Others have entered into the fold by a mere *profession* of christianity: but coming in by "the door" is essential to our being Christ's sheep. All professions of religion come to nothing where this is wanting. John xiv. 6.

What is it then to enter in by "the door?" In general, it is to embrace Christ; to receive the truth in love, and that in three respects—

1. It is to embrace Christ *exclusively*, to the rejection of every other way of salvation. The way of salvation by the cross of Christ, is the great offence to the world; but he is "the door," and there is no other way of entering into eternal life. —— Other things may be dispensed with, but this is indispensable: we may differ in minor matters and may agree to differ: but "what think ye of Christ;" is a question of vital inportance.

This has been the way of salvation from the *beginning*. All the promises made to the fathers included Christ: the promise of the woman's Seed —— of the Seed to Abraham, and all nations being blessed in him —— the blessings promised to David in the everlasting covenant, had an immediate reference to Christ, and he was the substance of them all.

—— There is no other way of admission but by *faith in him*, as an atoning Saviour. This was clearly taught by the distinction made in the offerings of Cain and Abel, and this difference was observed throughout the whole of the Mosaic economy. —— There is no other way *now:* the concurren language of the new testament is, "He that hath the Son, hath life; and he that hath not the Son of God, hath not life." John iii. 36. 1 John v. 12

2. It is to embrace Christ *practically*, so as really to "enter in" by the door into the sheepfold. This is to be doers of the word, and not hearers only. —— Many stand and lie about the door, who never enter in: they think of it, but do not like such a narrow way, or they put it off to some other time. —— To such however he is still a door of hope, and a refuge to the lost.

3. It implies that we do it *socially*. In entering in by the door, we enter into the fold among the sheep, and become one with God's people.

II. THE PROMISE MADE TO SUCH: "THEY SHALL BE SAVED."

The great question with a fallen creature is, What shall I do to be saved? And this is the answer: Christ is the way, and you must embrace him as such: there is no other way.

223

Consider its importance—

1. *We are lost*, whether we be saved or not. ——— As a sheep upon the mountains is lost from the shepherd and the flock, so are we lost; and should never find the way to God, but should wander and perish for ever. Isai. liii. 6. Ezek. xxxiv. 11, 12.

2. If we be not saved, *our loss will be incalculable.* Our sins are upon our head, and we must die in the pit. ——— Other losses may be estimated, but this cannot: what shall a man give in exchange for his soul.

3. *If we be saved*, the good will be inestimable. It is salvation with eternal glory. ——— It includes not only deliverance from all evil, but the enjoyment of all good. 1 Cor. ii. 9.

III. THE PRIVILEGES WHICH SUCH ENJOY IN THIS WORLD: "they go in AND OUT, AND FIND PASTURE."

1. Observe, those who have once entered in by the door into the sheepfold, *will go in again and again.*— — —The same gospel that first quickened us, will quicken us afterwards: the same food that first fed us, will still be our meat and drink. John vi. 64, 68.

2. Those who are in Christ, have *rich pastures* provided for them: the word and ordinances of God's house, and the green pastures in which he leads them for his name's sake. Psal. xxiii 2. Cant. i. 7. Isai. xlix. 10.

3. They have *free and secure access* to them, under the care of the great Shepherd; who guards their souls from beasts of prey, and will cause them to lie down in safety. Ezek. xxxiv. 13—15.

1. Let us learn the great importance of coming to Christ, and taking his yoke upon us: let us beware we do not stop short of this.

2. See to it that our religion has a right beginning; that we enter in by " the door," and in no other way.

---

## CHRISTIAN HOPE AND CONSOLATION.

2 Timothy i. 12.—I know whom I have believed, and I am persuaded that he is able to keep that which I have committed unto him against that day. (Pr.)

PAUL was at this time a prisoner at Rome, and in the immediate prospect of martyrdom. But he was not ashamed of the cause in which he suffered, nor afraid of death in its most terrific forms: ch. i. 8. iv. 6. Oh how enviable was his situation! Some men desire to die great, that their names may live; or rich, that their families may be distinguished. But after all, who would not join with Balaam here; " Let me die the death of the righteous, and let my last end be like his!"

The general import of the words before us is, that Paul well knew the ground on which he stood, and felt satisfied in it.—He does not speak of himself as an apostle, but as a christian; and therefore what he says is applicable to all who believe in Jesus.

1. VIEW THE GROUND OF THE CHRISTIAN'S HOPE AND CONSOLATION; "I know whom I have believed"—

Paul stood firm and happy here, and many others have done the same: let us see wherein this confidence consists—

1. It arises from *a consciousness* that we believe in Christ, and have committed our souls into his hands, as a sacred trust until that day.— — —Much

is made of faith in the Scriptures; and what is it? It is to give credit to, or to receive the testimony of another; and as the testimony of Jesus respects himself as the only way of salvation, we cannot credit him without confiding or trusting in him. The words of Paul therefore are the same as if he had said, "I know whom I have *trusted*."— — —We may believe the testimony of Peter or Paul, but Christ alone is the object of our confidence: hence it is explained by "committing" a trust into his hands.

Can you remember *the time* when first convinced of your guilty and un-done condition, and of salvation being in no other; and when you first began to trust in him and commit all to him?— — —Or if not the time, you are conscious that you have *no other hope:* it is not once only, but often, that you have committed your soul into the hands of the Saviour.

2. This comfort arises from the persuasion that *Christ is all-sufficient* for the purposes for which you have reposed your trust in him.— — —The text does not so much relate to the act, as to the object of faith. Paul was not thinking so immediately of his believing, though of that he was conscious, as of him in whom he believed: and this is the principal source of conso-lation.

It greatly concerns us to know in whom we have put our trust: none but real christians enjoy this satisfaction.— — —Others do not know where their trust is: they trust in they know not what, and know not whom.— — — Some in their idols, some in departed saints, others in their own supposed goodness: but all this is trusting in they know not what, and know not whom.

Let us then consider Jesus, and his all-sufficiency, as the exclusive ground of the christian's hope:—

1. It is that Saviour to whom *all the prophets* have borne witness: the seed of the woman, the seed of Abraham—the Son of David.— — —He of whom Isaiah wrote, whose glory he foresaw, and whose sufferings he fore told. John xii. 41. Acts x. 43. Rom. ix. 5. 1 Pet. i. 10, 11.

2. Jesus is that Saviour in whom *all the godly* in all ages have put their trust, and have looked to him alone for salvation. Acts iv. 12; Heb. xi. 13. All the martyrs, all the good men we have ever known, put their trust in this almighty Saviour; and it affords the highest satisfaction to feel ourselves on the same ground.

3. It is him who in the fulness of time came into the world, and lived and *died for us*. This is the foundation that God hath laid in Zion, and our hopes are founded on a rock. 1 Cor. iii. 11; 1 Pet. ii. 6.

4. A Saviour who may be depended on for *his all-sufficiency* to save. His proper divinity renders him the object of our highest confidence: "He is able to keep that which we commit to him."— — —He also has an acquired ability, and an official authority, to save unto the uttermost, all that come unto God by him. Heb. vii. 25.

5. He is one that may be depended on for *his veracity* and truth. You may safely trust him, for he is the Amen, the faithful and true witness.— — —We know whom we have trusted: trust him, oh ye perishing sinners.

6. He is one *whose love* is equal to his power. What he can do he will do.— — —He speaks with great affection to those who have committed themselves to him. They are given to him of God, as well as by their own voluntary surrender: and of this sacred charge he says, "I will lose noth ing, but will raise it up at the last day."— — —He will also present them faultless before the presence of his glory with exceeding joy. John vi. 39. Jude 24.

**II.** The importance of enjoying this consolation under all the trials of life, and more especially in the near approach of death.

Paul felt it in his imprisonment, and therefore he was "not ashamed;" and as one who was now ready to be offered up, he knew whom he had trusted.

1. If the gound we stand on be *not firm*, at death we must sink forever. It is dreadful to be at a loss then, not knowing in whom we have believed, or where we have placed our trust.

3. Death often comes *unawares*, or if not, that is not a time for thought. Our house requires to be set in order, but much more our souls to be committed into safe hands.

3. Where this is the case, death is disarmed of its terrors, and we may join in the song of victory. 1 Cor. xv. 55—57.

---

## HUNGERING AND THIRSTING AFTER RIGHTEOUSNESS.

Matt. v. 6.—Blessed are they which do hunger and thirst after righteousuess; for they shall be filled. (H. H.)

Men naturally desire happiness: but they know not in what it is to be found. The philosophers of old wearied themselves in vain to find out what was man's chief good. But our blessed Lord has informed us wherein it consists: it is found in holiness alone; which, when embodied, as it were, and exercised in all its branches, renders us completely blessed. In this sense we understand the words of our text; wherein are set forth,

I. The distinctive character of a christian—

It is a gross perversion of Scripture to interpret this passage as relating to the righteousness of Christ: for though it is true that every Christian desires to be clothed in that righteousness, and shall, in consequence of that desire, obtain his wishes, yet it is not the truth contained in the words before us: they certainly relate to that inward righteousness which every Christian must possess, and to that "holiness, without which, no man shall see the Lord."

Now the character of every Christian is, that he desires holiness,

1. Supremely—

Other desires are not eradicated from the human breast: the natural appetites remain after our conversion the same as before, except as they are restrained and governed by a higher principle. In proportion, indeed, as religion gains an ascendant in the soul, those words will be verified, "He that eateth and drinketh of the water that Christ will give him, shall never thirst." John iv. 14. But from the very commencement of the Divine life, all earthly things sink in the Christian's estimation, and are accounted as dung and dross in comparison of the Divine image. In this sense "Christ is all" to him, Col. iii. 11.\*: and he can say, "Whom have I in heaven but thee? And there is none upon earth that I desire in comparison of thee "

2. Constantly—

While other desires remain in the heart, they will of course occasionally rise in opposition to the better principle: but the prevailing desire of the soul is after holiness. "The flesh may lust against the spirit and seem for

\* Christ here means the image of Christ.—

a moment to triumph over it: but "the spirit will lust and strive against the flesh," Gal. v. 17. till it has vanquished its rebellious motions. The needle may be driven by violence from its accustomed position: but its attractions are ever towards the pole; and it will never rest till it has resumed its wonted place. Its momentary diversion serves but to prove its fixed habitual inclination. In like manner, temptation itself, in rousing up the soul to action, calls forth its heavenly tendencies, and displays the holy energies with which it is endued.

3. Insatiably—

Every other desire may be satiated; but the more of spiritual nourishment we receive, the more will our hunger and thirst after it be increased. St. Paul himself could not sit down contented; but forgetting what he had attained, he reached forth for higher degrees of holiness. Phil. iii. 13. It is only "when we awake up after the perfect likeness of our God, that we shall be satisfied with it." Ps. xvii. 15.

Truly enviable will this state appear, if we consider,

II. The blessedness annexed to it—

To be filled with good and nutritious food is the utmost that the bodily appetite can desire. It is in this sense that we are to understand the promise in the text. The person who hungers and thirsts after righteousness, shall be made,

1. Truly righteous—

There is a negative kind of holiness, which is neither pleasing to God nor profitable to man: it consists merely in an abstinence from open sin, and a discharge of external duties. But real holiness pervades the whole man: it comprehends the whole circle of divine graces: it reaches to the thoughts and desires of the heart; and assimilates us to God in all his communicable perfections. Now this is that with which the true Christian shall be filled: in all his dispositions towards God and man, he shall be changed: he shall not only be delivered from all that would injure his character among men, but shall be "transformed into the very image of his God in righteousness and true holiness."

2. Progressively righteous—

That degree of perfection to which Christians may attain, is not gained at once. All the members of the new man, as well as of the material body, do indeed exist at the moment of our birth: but they are then in a state of infantine weakness: and their arrival at a state of maturity is a gradual work. Now this work shall be advanced in the souls of those who earnestly desire it: "they shall hold on their way, growing stronger and stronger. Job xvii. 9; and like the risen sun, "shining brighter and brighter unto the perfect day." Prov. iv. 18. "The Lord will perfect that which concerneth them," Ps. cxxxviii. 8. and "carry on his work until the day of Christ." Phil. i. 6.

3. Perfectly righteous—

Though absolute perfection is not to be attained in this life, yet every righteous person may expect it, as the completion of his wishes, and the consummation of his bliss. The moment that his soul is released from this frail tabernacle, it shall bid an everlasting farewell to sin and sorrow. The hunger and thirst which characterize him in this world, will then cease for ever: there will remain to him no heights unattained, no wishes unaccomplished: his soul will be "*filled*" with the desired good, yea, filled to the utmost extent of its capacity.

APPLICATION—
Are there *those who, instead of hungering and thirsting after righteousness, despise it?* Tell me, will ye despise it in the day of judgement? will ye despise it, when ye shall see the difference that is put between the godly and the ungodly? And what is that which ye prefer to it? Can ye say of your pleasures, your riches, or your honours, what our Lord says of righteousness? shall ye certainly be filled with those things? or if ye were, would they ever render you truly blessed? Go, ask of Solomon, or ask of any who have made the experiment; and see whether, in their sober moments, they will not confess those things to be " vanity and vexation of spirit?" O " spend not your money any more for that which is not bread, nor labour for that which satisfieth not; but eat ye that which is good, and let your soul be satisfied with fatness." Isai. lv. 2, 3.

Are there *those who rest in a form of religion?* Know that it is not the form, but the power, of godliness that God requires. The Pharisees of old abounded in outward duties; but " except your righteousness exceed theirs, ye shall in no case enter into the kingdom of heaven." That which you must desire, that which you must attain, is an universal change both of heart and life : " you must become new creatures: old things must pass away, and all things become new."

Are there *any discouraged because of the small proficiency they have made in holiness?* Doubtless this is a matter of lamentation to the best of men. If indeed we are excusing ourselves, and pacifying our consciences from the idea that in this frail state we cannot but commit sin, we are deceiving our own souls; for " he that is born of God, sinneth not;" John iii. 9. that is, he *allows not* himself in any sin, whether of excess or defect; whether of commission or of omission. But if "our souls are really athirst for God, and we are panting after him, as the hart after the waterbrooks," we need not fear. God will ere long " fill the hungry with good things:" " he will satisfy the longing soul, and replenish every sorrowful soul." The very idea of hunger is a painful sensation of want; and if holiness be the object of that appetite, all *shall be* well, yea, and all *is* well: " that soul is blessed, and *shall be* filled."

---

## CONSOLATION TO THE DISTRESSED.

Ps. xl. 17.—I am poor and needy; yet the Lord thinketh upon me. (H. H.)

THAT part of the Holy Scriptures which most fully opens the exercises of the heart is the book of Psalms. There we see a man of God unbosoming himself before his Maker, and declaring all his hopes and fears, his griefs and consolations. Sometimes he speaks in the person of the Messiah, and sometimes in his own person: sometimes his words are applicable both to the one and the other. These varieties often appear in the very same psalm : some parts of which exclusively relate to the type, or to the antitype; and other parts are common to both. It is thus in the psalm before us. That it refers to the Messiah, there can be no doubt; because it is applied to him by God himself.* Yet there are in it some expressions, which

* Compare ver. 6—8, with Heb. x. 5—7.

should rather be explained in reference to David only. The twelfth verse in particular must be understood in this way: and the circumstance of all the following verses being repeated in another place, and formed into a distinct psalm by themselves, Ps. lxx., is a strong reason for referring them also to him principally, or perhaps to him alone. In the words of our text we notice,

I. HIS COMPLAINT—

David on some occasions was reduced to great straits and difficulties with respect to his temporal concerns; but he was also much tried in his spirit: and the complaint before us seems to have arisen from,

1. A sense of his guilt—

In verse 12, he speaks of "his iniquities having taken such hold upon him, that he was not able to look up; that they were more than the hairs of his head, so that his heart failed him." It is very probable that he alluded in some measure to those dreadful enormities which he had committed in the matter of Uriah. But he would not consider those actions merely as insulated and detached, but rather as indications of the extreme depravity of his heart:* and in reference to *that* he might well say of himself, "I am poor and needy." Indeed, who that knows any thing of the spirituality of God's law, or of his own innumerable departures from it, can use any other language than that in the text? Was Adam poor when despoiled of the Divine image through the commission of one sin; and are not we, whose iniquities are more than the hairs of our head? Was he needy when banished from Paradise, and doomed to eternal death; and are not we, who from our very birth have been "treasuring up wrath against the day of wrath?" Though God has forgiven us, it does not become us to forget what we are in ourselves, but to go softly before him all our days, repenting in dust and ashes.

2. A sense of his weakness—

David had other enemies than those who opposed his regal authority. He complains in another psalm, "Iniquities prevail against me:" Ps. lxv. 3: and he found it exceeding difficult to subdue them. On this account also he used the expressions in the text. He felt himself poor and needy in reference to every thing that he accounted good. He lamented especially his want of wisdom, and strength, and righteousness. Hence he cried, "Open thou mine eyes;" "O give me understanding in the way of godliness!" "Hold thou me up!" "hold up my goings in thy ways, that my footsteps slip not!" "Enter not into judgment with thy servant, O Lord! for in thy sight shall no man living be justified." Similar to this is the experience of all the saints. All are insufficient of themselves for any thing that is good; and the man who was stripped, and wounded, and left half dead, Luke x. 30, was but a faint emblem of the man who, feeling in himself innumerable corruptions, is unable to mortify so much as one of them, except as he is aided from above, and strengthened by communications of the Spirit of Grace. St. Paul himself lamented his state in reference to this; yea, he even surpassed the Psalmist in his humiliating confessions and mournful complaints. Rom. vii. 24.

But in the midst of all this, we view with pleasure,

II. HIS CONSOLATION—

He considered that God's thoughts were exercised upon him—

God is not an inattentive observer of any of his creatures: but "his eyes are more especially upon the righteous." Ps. xxxiii. 18, 19, and xxxiv. 15. As "his eyes were upon the promised land from one end of the year even

*In this light he speaks of them in Ps. li. 5.

to the other," Job. xxxvi. 7; Deut. xi. 12, so are they upon his own people in every place and in every age. He says, "I know the thoughts that I think towards you, thoughts of good and not of evil, to give you an expected end." Jer. xxix. 11. He thinks of his people with *tender compassion*—with *anxious care*—with *joyful complacency*. How tenderly did he listen to the effusions of Ephraim's sorrow! Jer. xxxi. 18—20, and Hos. xiv. 8. With what anxiety does he sit, as a refiner, to watch the vessel which he is purifying in the furnace, lest it should by any means suffer injury by the process that was intended only for its good! Mal. iii. 3.— With what exultation too does he say, "To this man will I look, even unto him that is poor, and of a contrite spirit;" as though not all the angels in heaven could engage his attention in comparison of such a sight! David was sensible, that in the midst of all his spiritual distress he was not forgotten of his God; but that he was, notwithstanding all his unworthiness, an object of his paternal care.*

What comfort must such a consideration afford him!

Surely greater consolation could scarcely be conceived than that which would arise from this source. What must it be to have *unsearchable wisdom* contriving for his good!— — —*almighty power* ready to execute whatever Divine wisdom should judge expedient!— — —*unbounded mercy* pleading, that his sins and frailties may not provoke God to withdraw his loving-kindness from him!— — —and, lastly, *unchanging faithfulness* demanding on his behalf the accomplishment of all the promises!— — —The consideration of these things must of necessity check every desponding fear, and constrain him to exclaim, "Why art thou cast down, O my soul, and why art thou disquieted within me? Hope thou in God; for I shall yet praise him, who is the health of my countenance, and my God." Ps. xlii. 11. And every one who can realize this one consideration, has within himself an antidote for every fear, and a balm for every wound.

ADDRESS,

1. Those who know little of David's experience—

The generality of those who are called Christians would be ready to despise any one who should express himself like the inspired Psalmist. They would suppose that he was under the influence of a weak deluded mind But let them not congratulate themselves on their fancied superiority; for they only betray their own ignorance. Rev. iii. 17, with Mic. iv. 12. Let them rather seek to know themselves, that, being made sensible of their destitute condition, they may be made rich in Christ Jesus. 1 Cor. i. 30.

2. Those whose feelings are like his—

While you are complaining of your poverty, God is saying, "But thou art rich." Rev. ii. 9. The truth is, that the more we are sensible of our guilt and helplessness, the more ready God is to help and deliver us: "The hungry he filleth with good things; but the rich he sends empty away.' Indeed he paints the most destitute condition that can be imagined, on purpose that he may administer consolation to us under it. Isa. xli. 17, 18. If any then be cast down as though there were no hope, let them plead with him as David did: Ps. cxlii. 1—7; and they shall soon find by happy experience, that "God's thoughts and ways as far exceed ours, as the heavens are above the earth."† ‡

* He knew it from both his past and present experience, Ps. xxxi. 7, with verse 5.
† See Ps. lxxii. 12, 13, which may be illustrated by Jonah i. 6, 15, & ii. 1—10.
‡ If this were a subject for a *Charity Sermon*, the *Application* should be altered, and another substituted, recommending the audience to imitate God by thinking of the distresses of their fellow creatures

## l ANIEL'S CONFESSION.

Dan. ix. 3—7.—And I set my face unto the Lord God, to seek by prayer, and supplications, with fasting and sackcloth and ashes: and I prayed unto the Lord my God, and made my confession, and said, O Lord, the great and dreadful God, keeping the covenant and mercy unto them that love him, and to them that keep his commandments; we have sinned and committed iniquity, and have done wickedly, and have rebelled, even by departing from thy precepts and from thy judgments; neither have we hearkened unto thy servants the prophets, which spake in thy name to our kings, our princes, and our fathers, and to all the people of the land. O Lord righteousness belongeth unto thee, but unto us confusio of faces, as at this day. (H. H.)

FROM the earliest period, even from the time that God first had a visible church in the world, there have been particular seasons set apart for humiliation, and fasting, and prayer. In the christian church, the appointment of of forty days at this part of the year (Lent) for that purpose is of great antiquity.* The two days with which this season commenced were observed with peculiar solemnity: the one (Shrove Tuesday) was spent in recollecting and confessing† their sins; the other (Ash Wednesday) in fasting and supplication. That these institutions were carried to a very foolish excess, and that they degenerated into very absurd superstitions, under the reign of Popery, is readily acknowledged: but they were good in their origin; and our church has wisely retained such a portion of them as might tend to the real edification of her members: and if we were more observant of them than we are, we should find substantial benefit to our souls. But alas! we have run into an opposite extreme, insomuch that not only the observances are laid aside, but the very intention of them is almost forgotten: and instead of complying with the design which is intimated in the names given to the days, we render them perfectly ridiculous, by substituting a trifling change in our food for the most solemn acts of devotion before God.‡

Hoping however that on *this* day we are disposed to humble ourselves before God, we shall,

I. ILLUSTRATE THIS CONFESSION OF DANIEL—

*The manner in which he made his supplications* is deserving of particular attention—

He " set his face unto the Lord God:" he did not rush into the divine presence without any previous meditation, but endeavored to have his mind impressed with reverence and godly fear, that he might " not offer to his God the sacrifice of fools."

He " sought God by prayer and supplications, with fasting, and sackcloth, and ashes." By mortifying the body, he endeavored to aid the labors of his soul. Both the one and the other had been defiled by sin; and therefore he strove to make them partners in humiliation before God. Nor can we doubt but that the fervor of his prayers was greatly assisted by the bodily privations which God himself has so often prescribed for this very end.

Nor must we overlook *the remarkable representation which he gave of the divine character* on this occasion—

* The number of days for fasting was not always precisely the same as now: but the appointment itself may be traced almost to the times of the apostles.

† The word " *shrove*" is from the old English word " *shrive*," which signifies *to confess.*

‡ This is evident from the customs of having salt fish on Ash Wednesday, and pancakes on Shrove Tuesday. The latter in all probability arose from the people being reminded, or perhaps summoned, by a bell, to confess all their sins, παν κακόν. From hence it was called the παν κακόν, or *pan-cake* bell. Alas! how widely have we deviated from the intention of those who first enjoined the observance of that day!

He mentions in very expressive terms both *the Majesty* and *the goodness* of God; the one for the abasing, the other for the encouraging, of his soul. What words can more strongly paint *the Majesty* of God? In various other passages, God is called " the great and terrible God :" Neh. i. 5, and ix. 32, and Deut. vii. 21 ; and well may he be addressed in such terms ; for " who knoweth the power of his anger?" Let us only call to mind the judgments he has executed on sinners ; on the rebel angels : on the antediluvian world ; on Sodom and Gomorrah ; on the Egyptian first-born ; on Pharaoh and his hosts ; yea, on the Jews in Babylon, which was the point referred to in the text ; and we shall confess that " God is very greatly to be feared."

Yet he was not unmindful of the divine *goodness*. Notwithstanding God is angry with the wicked, he has " made a covenant" with his Son, wherein he engages to " shew mercy unto all that love him and keep his commandments." Now this covenant he has never violated ; this mercy he has never refused to one who by faith laid hold on that covenant, and showed forth his faith by his works. And Daniel mentions this, in his address to God, as the ground on which he presumed to approach him, and ventured to hope for acceptance with him.

*His confession before him* is also worthy of notice, as being expressive of the deepest humility and contrition—

'So deeply did he bewail his own sins and the iniquities of his people, that he strove by the most diversified expressions to make known his hatred of them : " We have sinned, and have committed iniquity, and have done wickedly, and have rebelled, even by departing from thy precepts, and from thy judgments ; neither have we hearkened to thy servants the prophets, which spake in thy name."

Here he distinctly acknowledges to God *their transgression of his commandments*, and *their contempt of his reproofs*. These were indeed a just ground for his humiliation ; since to no other nation had such a revelation of God's will been given, or such messages of mercy sent. Happy was it for him, and happy for the nation, that the reason of their chastisements was thus discovered ; and that, by knowing wherein they had erred, they had learned wherein they were to amend their conduct!

There is yet one thing more on which we must make our remarks, namely, *his justification of God in all his dealings with them*—

Nothing but equity is ascribed to God ; nothing but shame is taken to themselves : " O Lord ! righteousness belongeth unto thee ; but unto us confusion of face." He does not utter one word in extenuation of their guilt, or one complaint against the divine judgments : he declares rather, that to whatever extremities God might proceed, he could not but be righteous ; and that, whatever mercies they might experience at his hands, nothing but the deepest self-abasement could ever become them. Thus he gives the most decisive evidence of true repentance, and exhibits an admirable pattern for penitents in all ages.

Having briefly illustrated this confession on Daniel, we shall,

II. FOUND UPON IT SOME SUITABLE AND APPROPRIATE OBSERVATIONS—

1. We have the same sins to confess—

Without entering into any distinctions founded on the different terms which are here accumulated, let us only take the general division before mentioned, and call to mind *our transgression of God's commandments*, and *our contempt of his reproofs*.

Which of the commandments have we not broken? We may perhaps imagine, that, though we may have violated some, we are guiltless respecting others. But alas! if we take our Saviour's exposition of them, and remember, that an angry word is murder, and an impure look adultery, we shall find reason to bemoan our transgression of them all.

Nor is it any small aggravation of our guilt that we have despised those warnings and invitations which he has sent us in the gospel. The ministers of Christ have testified against our ways from Sabbath to Sabbath, and from year to year: yet how few have "hearkened to their voice!" how few have turned from their evil ways! how few have heartily embraced his salvation, or devoted themselves unfeignedly to his service! Let us in particular enter into our own bosoms, and consider what improvement we have made of the truths delivered to us.— — —If we do this in sincerity, we shall be at no loss for matter of humiliation before God.

2. We have the same God to go unto—

We do not like to think of God's *majesty*; but he is, as much as ever, "a great a terrible God:" the apostle justly observes, "Our God is a consuming fire." Let us not dream of a God *all* mercy: the Deity is just, as well as merciful; and it will be found "a fearful thing to fall into the hands of the living God."— — —

On the other hand, the *goodness* of God is unalterable. He is still merciful to all who lay hold on his covenant; and will assuredly fulfil to them all the promises of that covenant. Heaven and earth may fail; but not a jot or tittle of his word shall ever fail.— — —

Let us entertain just conceptions of the divine character; and we shall have a frame of mind suited to our condition; we shall be under the joint influence of hope and fear; of hope without presumption, and of fear without despondency.

3. We ought to approach him in the same manner—

We should carefully prepare our minds for communion with God. The neglect of this is the reason that we so seldom obtain real fellowship with him. We should not lay aside, as it is to be feared we do, the duty of fasting; we should set apart seasons for more than ordinary humiliation; and more especially improve those seasons which are set apart by public authority.

We should search out our iniquities with diligence: and, instead of leaning to the side of self-vindication, should learn to justify God and to condemn ourselves. Nor shall we ever have our hearts right with him, till we can say, "God will be righteous, though he should cast me into hell; and nothing but confusion of face will become me, even though I were as holy as Daniel himself."

Let us then begin the employment this day, under a full assurance, that "he who thus humbleth himself under the mighty hand of God, shall in due time be lifted up."

---

## HUMAN WEAKNESS SUBSERVIENT TO THE POWER OF CHRIST.

2 Cor xii. 9.—Most gladly therefore will I rather glory in my infirmities, that the power of Christ may rest upon me. (Pr.)

The false teachers, who had perverted the minds of the Corinthians, did all in their power to traduce the character and talents of the apostle Paul, alleging that his bodily presence was weak, and his speech contemptible. The apostle modestly admits, that he did not use "enticing vords of man's wisdom," nor "come to them with excellency of speech;" and as to his talents and general appearance, he would say nothing. But if he must imitate their boasting, he would glory in the very things for which he was despised.

1. Then observe *the object* of his glorying, even "his infirmities." Rv these he does not mean his moial weaknesses, or sinful infirmities, but those natural defects and outward disadvantages which attended him; his affliction, reproaches, and persecutions, as it is explained in ver. 10.

2. *The reason* why he would glory in his infirmities, "that the power of Christ might rest upon him." Not that they were in themselves desirable, but they furnished an occasion for God to impart his grace, and Christ his power. Hence the apostle could say, when I am weak then am I strong; even as the consolations of the gospel are more powerfully felt in a season of adversity. When in necessities, Christ makes it up with his presence, and causes every thing to turn to our spiritual advantage.

I. NOTICE A FEW INSTANCES in which our being humbled, and made to feel our own weakness, prepares us to receive in a larger degree, the power and the grace of Christ.

It is God's usual way to empty us of ourselves, before he fills us with his own fulness; to render us weak, before we are made strong; to kill, before he makes alive.

1. A sense of our own weakness and insufficiency precedes *our first participation of divine strength and consolation.* — — —While Paul was alive without the law he felt no need of Christ, but when he died to his former hopes he began to live. The reason why many find no rest to their souls is, they are not weaned from self-righteousness, and have not been emptied from vessel to vessel. They are not helpless in themselves, and God till then withholds his help. Till then there is no coming to Christ, for those only come who are ready to perish.

2. A sense of our own weakness and insufficiency, during our progress in the divine life, *constantly precedes the communication of grace and strength.* — — —If in seeking heavenly wisdom we are wise in our own eyes, we shall not find it. If in times of temptation we are self-confident, we shall be left to fall as Peter did: but if with Jehoshaphat we feel that we have no might against this great host, and our eyes are upon the Lord, we shall be strengthened from above. If in serving our generation by the will of God we are self-sufficient, and depend upon our own zealous exertions, we shall soon be exhausted: but if we have no might of our own, we shall wait upon the Lord, and renew our strength. Isa. xl. 29—31; 2 Chron. xx. 12.

3. When ministers are most deeply sensible of their own insufficiency, *that is the most likely time for God to bless their labors.* — — —If they imagine themselves well prepared for their engagements, it is most probable they will fail in their attempts; and when they have the greatest expectation of doing good by their exertions, that is seldom the time for God to work. If ever they are strong in the Lord, and in the power of his might, it is when self is utterly renounced and annihilated; and hence the Lord often blesses his servants when their hands are weak, and their hearts are faint.

4. When the servants of God collectively are reduced to a small number, and their strength seems to be dried up, *then it is often God's time to work.* — — —When Gideon's army was strong, that was not the time to defeat the Midianites; but when reduced to three hundred, the Lord gave them the victory. When great expectations have been raised from the number and

strength of those eng.ged in any religious undertaking, it has often been the same; to show that it is not by might, nor by power, but by my Spirit, saith the Lord of hosts. Zech. iv. 6.— — —When God would raise up the Jewish nation, he did not call a number of them at once; but he called Abraham alone, and blessed him. Isa. li. 2. When he would set up Christ's kingdom, he did not convert a great multitude, and send them forth to preach: he called twelve poor fishermen, and endowed them with power from on high. 2 Cor. iv. 7.

II. OBSERVE HOW THE INFIRMITIES AND ILLS of life are hereby converted into good to us, and become an object of glorying.

Infirmities, reproaches, and distresses, if they do but humble us and wean us from the world, will turn to our advantage.

1. In this view primitive Christians had must reason to glory in *the sufferings* they endured for Christ's sake, for at no period was there such a display of the power and grace of Christ, or so rich an enjoyment of the divine presence and blessing.

2. In this view we also may glory in some of our *heaviest afflictions*, as they have been the means of laying us low, and bringing us near to God. Many have been purified in that furnace, and can look back to it as the best season in their whole lives.

3. We may also for the same reason rejoice in some of our most painful *losses and disappointments*. It was never better with the Jewish church, as to spiritual prosperity, than when in captivity in Babylon. In the loss of all created good, she could rejoice in the Lord as her portion, and quietly wait for his salvation.

4. In this view we may have to glory *in the prospect of death itself*. Here every human hope vanishes, and flesh and heart must fail. Man then appears in the lowest state of humiliation and nothingness, possessing no hope but in the Lord: and that is often the time when the power and grace of Christ rest most eminently upon his people. That is a time when many a weak and drooping christian has been made to triumph, and the feeblest of all have taken the prey. The last and most formidable enemy is made the messenger of greater good than all that have gone before. Most gladly therefore may we glory in our infirmities, that the power of Christ may rest upon us.

---

## ENCOURAGEMENT TO PURSUE THE CHRISTIAN RACE.

Hebrews xii. 3.—For consider him that endured such contradiction of sinners against himself, lest ye be wearied and faint in your minds. (Pr.)

KNOWING the difficulties which these Hebrew converts had to encounter, and the weakness of their faith, the apostle watches over them with the utmost solicitude, endeavoring to comfort and encourage them by the example of our blessed Lord, as he had done in a former instance: ch. iii. 1.

We may here observe—1. That such things may befal us in our christian course, as to render us weary and faint in our minds. The cause itself is good, but there are many adversaries.—2. To grow weary and faint in our minds, is a very dangerous symptom. It often leads to apostasy: many a

**one** has first begun to tire, and then to turn back.—3. It becomes us to **watch** carefully against it, and to arm our minds by the example of Christ.

I. NOTICE A FEW INSTANCES IN WHICH WE ARE IN DANGER OF GROWING WEARY AND FAINT IN OUR CHRISTIAN COURSE.

1. In reference to *a close and humble walk with God*, we are prone to draw back and grow weary.— — —The happiest seasons in religion have not sufficient influence to keep us always near to God, and desirous of communion with him. After a diligent attention to the word, a more constant engagedness in holy duties, after some special instances of self-denial, a more affecting sense of our own depravity, and of the pardoning mercy of God, how prone we are to grow cold, to draw back, and to sink again into worldly-mindedness and carnality.

2. It is the same also with respect to *public duties.*— — —Those who preach the word are in great danger of sinking into discouragement, if they labor without any visible success. Isaiah complained that so few believed his report, and both Jeremiah and Elijah were on the point of giving up their work.— — —In hearing the word, if not edified and comforted, we are prone to grow weary and dull, and to think that our hearing is all in vain.— — —In prayer, if the blessings we desire appear to be withheld, we are soon discouraged, though we ought always to pray and not to faint.— — — So difficult is it to walk by faith, and live by faith: to believe the promises, and to stay ourselves upon the Lord.

3. When *persecution or reproach* overtake us in our race, we are much in danger of turning back.— — —It is easy to follow Christ when things go well, and the world is at peace with us: but if called to forego our temporal interest, to lose some of our friends, and those of our own house become our enemies, we shall be in danger of growing faint and weary in our course. When thus beset, some have been utterly discouraged, and have gone back again into the world.

4. When burdened and oppressed with *a weight of worldly cares*, and brought into unexpected difficulties, the same danger attends us.— — —In the early part of life, when free from burdens of this sort, we can go on our way rejoicing, and find the path without a thorn; but when filled with perplexing cares at a subsequent period, it is not so easy. Injuries and disappointments corrode the heart, unkindness and unfaithfulness exhaust our energies, and we move on slowly and heavily in the ways of God, faint and weary in our minds.

5. When struggling with *various temptations*, it is the same.— — —If there were no enemy to annoy, if no lion in the way, no Canaanite in the land, and no snares laid for our feet, we could proceed with alacrity and delight. But when burdened with temptations from day to day, with a load of indwelling sin, and our opposition becomes feeble and inefficient, we are in great danger of growing weary, if not of turning back.

6. *Long continued affliction*, is likewise attended with great discouragement.— — —Those who enjoy uninterrupted health do not know what others feel, who are under God's afflicting hand, and scarcely know what it is to be free from trouble. These things are apt to produce great discouragement, and even Job felt that they destroyed the hope of man: ch. xiv. 19.

7. When laboring under *a painful sense of guilt*, the mind is covered with gloom and darkness, and the heart is faint.— — —While all is peace within and without, while the conscience is kept tender, and the heart is right with God, it is easy to go forward: but when burdened with a sense of our many backslidings, and great unprofitableness, we are in danger of growing faint and weary, and of slackening in our course.

II. Consider the example of Christ as exhibited for our encouragement.

1. *What he had to endure* in his race, even "the contradiction of sinners against himself."— — —He was not only contradicted in words, but in actions. The whole of his doctrine, work, and conduct met with continual opposition; he was tempted in all points, and tried every way. He was laughed at by Herod, tempted by the devil, reviled by the Jews, smitten by the rabble, scourged by Pilate, and put to death.— — —Whatever opposition or difficulty we may meet with, it is nothing when compared with his; he met with "such contradictions," as no one besides ever did.

2. Consider *who it was* that endured all this, and *from whom* he endured it.— — —He was not only good and kind, as men may be; he was "holy harmless, undefiled, separate from sinners, made higher than the heaven;" the Son of God, the brightness of the Father's glory, and the express image of his person.— — —It is no wonder if we who are sinful, and were sometime foolish, and disobedient, should meet with such treatment; but that he should be subject to obloquy and contempt, is wonderful indeed. Affecting is the thought, that one of such infinite dignity, wisdom, and purity should be contradicted, blasphemed, and persecuted; and all this by "sinners," by sinners whom he come to save!

3. *The manner* in which he bore all this: he "endured" it.— — —He was a man of sorrows, and acquainted with grief, he hid not his face from shame and spitting. He endeavoured to bring sinners to the knowledge of the truth, and amidst all their hard sayings he expostulated with the utmost forbearance. He never gave up his course of holy obedience and meek submission, till he had finished it with joy.

4. Consider *for whom he endured it.*— — —For our sakes, and for ours only; it was in love to our souls that he suffered himself to be reviled, and evilly entreated. What a motive to endure for his sake, whatever opposition we may meet with, and why we should not be weary nor faint in our minds.

Let us learn from hence the necessity of keeping Christ's example in view, and of studying his character, in order to our perseverance in the ways of God.

Let those who contradict and blaspheme beware of the consequences, for they will soon have to give an account of all the hard speeches, which they have spoken against him. Jude. 15.

---

## THE BELIEVER'S INWARD WITNESS.

1 John v. 10.—He that believeth in the Son of God, hath the witness in himself. (S. S.)

The testimonies which God has given to his Son are numerous and convincing. There are three in heaven, and a similar number on earth, who bear record, that Christ is the Saviour of the world, ver, 7, 8, 11. But the believer has a distinct witness within himself; a witness, which gives a clearer insight into divine truth than any other, and fixes it with deeper conviction upon the mind. What this witness is will best appear, by considering what that is, of which it testifies.

It testifies of Christ, not only that he is a Saviour in general, but, more particulary, that he is

### I. A NEEDFUL SAVIOUR

The believer feels within himself such a load of guilt, such inability to remove it by any sufferings or obedience of his own, and such utter unsufficiency for any good thing, that he is sensible he must perish, if "help be not laid for him upon one that is mighty." Ps. lxxxix. 19. As for his attempting to satisfy divine justice, or to discharge the debt he has incurred, he sees that the very thought of it is folly and madness. Nor has he any hope of ever renewing his own corrupt nature: as well might he think to change the leopard's spots, or the Ethiopian's complexion. Jer. xiii. 23. Hence, when he hears of Jesus as a Saviour, he acknowledges from his inmost soul, that such an one was needed by him, and that, without such an one, he never could have entertained a hope of mercy.

### II. A SUITABLE SAVIOUR

When the believer compares his own necessities with the scripture representations of Jesus Christ, he perceives a wonderful correspondence between them, insomuch that there is nothing in Christ either superfluous or defective. Is the believer blind and ignorant? Christ is his wisdom. Is he guilty? Christ is his righteousness. Is he polluted? Christ is sanctification unto him. Is he enslaved to sin and Satan? Christ is his complete redemption. 1 Cor. i. 30, Rev. iii. 17, 18. Is Christ represented as bread to the hungry, and drink to the thirsty; as a Physician to heal, a Fountain to cleanse, a Sun to enlighten, a Shepherd to keep, &c. &c.? the believer feels within his own bosom that, which renders Christ precious to him in each particular view. He can find nothing in Christ, which his own necessities do no call for; nor any want in himself which Christ is not exactly qualified to supply.

### III. A WILLING SAVIOUR

In the whole circle of the Christian's experience there is not any thing which does not throw light upon this subject. If he ask himself, What did I, to induce Jesus to take upon him my nature, and to die in my stead? What was there in me either of merit or of strength, that I should be stopped in my career of sin; that I should be pardoned, sanctified, and saved through his meritorious death, and his almighty grace? Did I choose him before he chose me? John xv. 16. Do I not daily give him abundant reason to cast me off; and is it not of his own mere mercy that he still maintains my peace with God? Surely then mercy is his delight, and the exercise of it, his chief glory.

### IV. AN ALL-SUFFICIENT SAVIOUR

The believer is a wonder to himself; a bush burning, and unconsumed; a spark kept alive in the midst of the ocean: nor do the works of creation appear to him a stronger evidence of the almighty power of God, than his own preservation in the ways of godliness does, of the all-sufficiency of Christ. He cannot reflect on his errors and corruptions, his temptations and enemies, his falls and recoveries, but he is constrained to admire the efficacy of that grace, which alone has kept him, or alone restored him. As the woman who touched his garment, felt instantly within herself a proof of his ability to heal, Mark v. 28, 29. so the believer daily and hourly feels within himself a most indubitable testimony of Christ's "ability to save him to the uttermost."

### OBSERVE FROM HENCE

1. How wonderfully has God, in the constitution of his gospel, consulted the benefit of the poor!

Suppose erudition or strength of intellect ha. been necessary to the obtaining of divine knowledge, how melancholy had been the condition of the weak and illiterate! But the gospel is like the hidden manna, which is to be known only by its taste, or the name upon the white stone, which can be read only by those who have actually received it. Rev. ii. 17. The broken and contrite heart, with an humble faith in Christ, will give an insight into the gospel, infinitely beyond all that books can impart, or the learned of this world obtain. Matt. xi. 25, 26. Let the poor then know, and duly improve, this their high privilege, their inestimable benefit.

2. How easily may we determine whether we be believers or not!

We need only consult our own consciences, and enquire whether we have an inward witness of the gospel salvation? Let not any one, however, suppose, that we are speaking of an inward persuasion of our interest in Christ. In that, we may easily deceive ourselves: but, in the former, we cannot. The inward witness gathers strength in proportion to our proficiency, and will exist, yea, will be perfected, in heaven itself.

3. What comfort we may derive even from our own corruptions!

Doubtless there is no ground of comfort in our corruptions, simply considered. Nevertheless, as reflecting light upon the gospel salvation, and especially as illustrating the power and grace of Christ, they may afford us some consolation. When they rage, then we may rejoice that there is one able to pardon our transgressions, and to heal our backslidings: and when, through grace, they are mortified, then we may rejoice that we are living witnesses of Christ's faithfulness and all-sufficiency.

---

### THE LIBERTY WHICH CHRIST GIVES HIS PEOPLE.

John viii. 36.—If the Son therefore shall make you free, ye shall be free indeed. (S. S.)

We are exceedingly backward to acknowledge our true state and condition—
In consequence of this we disregard the remedy provided for us—
And deprive ourselves of all the blessings of salvation—
Nevertheless our gracious Saviour endures us with much long-suffering—
And repeats to us the overtures of love and mercy—
Thus he acted towards those who denied their need of freedom—
Thus also he addresses himself to us at this time—
It will be profitable for us to consider,
I. IN WHAT RESPECTS WE ARE IN BONDAGE.
We of this nation may justly boast of our civil freedom—
But we are, like all the rest of our species, under spiritual bondage
1. Under the curse of the law.
The law of God requires perfect and perpetual obedience—
It denounces also a curse against us for every transgression—Gal. iii. 10
Its precepts have been violated by us in ten thousand instances—Rom iii. 19, 23.
We all therefore, without exception, are obnoxious to its curse—
This may well be considered as a state of wretched bondage—Gal. iii. 23

2. Under the power of sin.

Sin has infected all the members of our body, and the faculties of our soul—Ps. liii. 3.

What can be conceived to argue a state of slavery so much as this—John viii. 34.

This construction is so obvious, that no Christian can doubt respecting it—Rom. vi. 16.

The church of old confessed her iniquities to have been a sore bondage—Isai. xxvi. 13.

And St. Paul himself could find no better image wherby to express the evil and bitterness of his indwelling corruptions—Rom. vii. 14, 23.

3. Under the tyranny of Satan

The influence of Satan over us is often denied and ridiculed—

But the wickedness of men is ascribed in scripture to his agency—Eph. ii. 2.

And every impenitent sinner is expressly said to be in bonadge to him—2 Tim. ii. 26.

4. Under the fear of death.

Many will shew a contempt for death on a field of battle—

But all fear it in its more gradual approaches—

Hence even the bravest are averse to meditate on death and judgment—

This is declared to be a state of wretched bondage—Heb. ii. 15.

Surely the Egyptian or Chaldean yoke was light in comparison of this—

Yet all may obtain a release from this yoke

II. How WE MAY BE DELIVERED FROM IT.

Vain are all attempts to liberate ourselves by our own strength

*We cannot make satisfiction for one single breath of the law—*

To do this, were beyond the power of the highest archangel—

Nothing but the blood of Christ can ever atone for sin—Heb. x. 4, 11, 12, 14.

*We cannot by any means renew and sanctify our own hearts—*

There is not in us a sufficiency even to think a good thought—2 Cor. iii. 5.

Our inclination and ability to do good can come from God alone—Phil. ii. 13.

*It is not in the power of fallen man to resist the assaults of Satan—*

There is provided for us armour of an heavenly temper—

And in that alone can any man hope to obtain the victory—Eph. vi. 11, 13.

*We are no less unable of ourselves to disarm death of its sting—*

In spite of all our efforts its terrors will appal the stoutest heart—

But " the Son" of God is able and willing to deliver us

Christ, as " the Son," is heir and Lord of all things—Heb. i. 2.

The very intent for which he came into the world was to give us liberty—Isai. lxi. 1.

He has paid down his own life as *the price* of redemption—1 Peter i. 13, 19.

And therefore may claim us as his " purchased possession"—

He is also commissioned to liberate us *by* his *power*—Luke x'. 20—22

All fulness resides in him for this very purpose—Ps. lxviii. 18.

Nor will he withhold this blessing from any believing soul—John. 13.

Unspeakably blessed are they to whom this blessing is vouchsafed

**III.** WHAT GLORIOUS LIBERTY WE MAY OBTAIN.

The liberty which sinners enjoy is merely ideal—

But that which Christ will give, is real and substantial—᾿Οντως.

1. He will free us from all our bondage.

*The law shall never be suffered to execute its curse upon us*—Rom. viii. 1.

Christ gave himself up as our surety, on purpose to redeem us from it—Gal. iii. 13.

It shall have no more power over us than a dead man over the wife that survives him—Rom. vii. 1—4.

*Sin also shall be cast down from the throne which it has erected within us*—

Nor, though it may renew its assaults, shall it ever regain its dominion— Rom. vi. 6, 14.

Christ will never suffer this great end of his death to be frustrated— Tit. ii. 14.

*Satan himself too shall yield to the all-conquering arm of Jesus*— Rom. xvi. 20.

And flee from the face of the very meanest of his saints—Contrast 2 Tim. ii. 26. with James iv. 7.

*Nor shall death appear any longer formidable as an enemy*—1 Cor. xv. 55.

It shall be accounted our gain, and numbered among our treasures— Phil. i. 23. 1 Cor. iii. 22.

2. He will introduce us to a state of perfect freedom

There is "a glorious liberty into which God's children shall be brought"—

Christ will pour into their hearts a spirit of adoption—Rom. iii. 15.

And admit them to the most intimate fellowship with himself—Rev. iii. 20.

The most difficult duties also he will render pleasant to their souls— Ps. cxix. 32.

Nor will he confine his blessings to this present life—

To all eternity shall his redeemed delight themselves in him—

Their capacity of enjoyment shall be inconceivably enlarged—

And every power be freely exercised in its proper functions—

INFERENCES.

1. How glorious a Saviour is Jesus Christ!

There is no bond-slave whom he will not liberate—

He offers too this liberty "without money, and without price

He even esteems himself glorified in conferring it upon us—

Let us all admire and adore his goodness—

And by faith apply to him for this perfect freedom—

2. How just will be the condemnation of those that perish!

None ever perish but through their own fault—

Their condemnation is the consequence of their obstinate attachment to the bonds in which they are held—John iii. 19.

O that men would reflect how they will one day condemn themselves!—

Let it be remembered that such offers of mercy will never be made to us in the eternal world—

This is a day of grace; but there will come a day of vengeance—Isai. xxi. 2.

Let every one then lay the blame where it is justly due—

And follow without delay the salutary advice of David—Ps. ii. 12.

~~~~~~~~~~~~

## BELIEVERS ARE CHRIST'S PROPERTY.

### 1 Cor. iii. 23.—Ye are Christ's. (S. S.)

TRUE Christians, however poor in this world, are inded the richest people in the universe—There is not any thing of which they have not the best use and enjoyment—All things temporal, spiritual, and eternal, belong to them—Yet they are not so rich in the property they possess, as they are in being themselves the property of another—The Apostle is enumerating in a climax the privileges of Christians—And having said that all things are theirs, he adds, as a more exalted privilege, that they are Christ's—To eiucidate this truth, we shall consider.

I. WHOSE WE WERE.

The whole creation properly belongs to God—But mankind have alienated themselves from him—Nor, what ever difference may have been made between us and others by the grace of God, is there any difference between us by nature—As long as we continue unregenerate we belong

1. To ourselves

The natural man disclaims God's authority over him—And thinks himself at liberty to live to himself—This was once the state even of the apostles themselves—Tit. iii. 3. Nor is there one amongst us who was not once a rebel like unto them—Our understanding, will, and affections, we used as altogether our own—The members of our bodies too we employed wholly in our own service—Even in our religious actions we regarded self rather than God—Zech. vii. 6. With respect to all our talents of time, money, influence, &c. we said, " They are our own, who is Lord over us?"—Ps. xii. 4.

2. To the world

The world has an entire ascendancy over us by nature—

We adopt its maxims, follow its fashions, and obey its dictates—The pleasures, riches, and honours of it are the idols which we worship—What more can be wanting to constitute us its vassals?—Rom. vi. 16. Our Lord himself declares, that all such persons are, not merely the friends, but the property, of the world. John. xv. 19.

3. To Satan

Satan rules in all the children of disobedience—Eph. ii. 2. He leads them captive at his will—2 Tim. ii. 26. Hence he is called the god of this world—2 Cor. iv 4. And who amongst us has not fulfilled *his* will?— This then manifests us to have been his children—1 John iii. 8, 10. And, if we be not converted by divine grace, it may still be said to us, as it was to the Jews of old, Ye are of your father, the devil. John viii. 44.

By conversion, however, we are brought back to our rightful owner.

## II. Whose we are.

Christ is the heir and sovereign Lord of all things—Both men and devils are subject to his controul—But believers are his in a more peculiar manner—They are his people, Tit. ii. 14. his bride, Rev. xxi. 9. his very member—Eph. v. 30.

1. By donation from the Father

The Father, from eternity, chose a people for himself—Eph. i. 4. These he gave to Christ to be redeemed by him—John xvii. 6. And secured them to him by an everlasting covenant—Ps. lxxxix. 34—36. To his eternal purpose we must trace the distinction made between them and others—2 Tim. i. 9. And ascribe all our salvation to him alone—1 Cor. xv. 10.

2. By his own purchase

Though salvation is freely given to us, it was purchased for us at a most invaluable price—Christ gave his own life a ransom for us—The price he paid was no less than his own blood—1 Pet. i. 19. This is the great subject of praise in heaven—Rev. v. 9. Nor should it ever be forgotten by us on earth—

3. By the drawings of the Holy Spirit

No man, of himself, would go to Christ for salvation—All who are his, are drawn to him by the Spirit—John vi. 44. It is the Spirit who quickens and renews our souls—To him alone must we ascribe the power and the glory—Zech. iv. 6.

4. By their own voluntary surrender

All Christ's people are made willing to be his—Ps. cx. 3. They willingly renew their baptismal covenant—And give themselves up to him at his holy table—This they consider as their reasonable service—Rom. xii. 1. Yea, they rejoice in it as their highest privilege—This is the peculiar character of all true Christians —Jer. i. 5.

### Learn hence

1. The Christian's character

How different from what he himself once was, and the generality still are !— — —

2. The Christian's privilege

The most eminent Christians were once in as miserable a state as any—But now, how altered their condition!—How *happy* are they in comparison of what they were!—How infinitely preferable is Christ's service to Satan's!—And how rich the recompense they will receive from Christ in comparison of any the world could have given!—How *secure* too are they in the hands of Christ!—None shall be able to pluck them from him—John x. 28, 29. They shall assuredly be kept by the Father's power—John xvii. 11. 1 Pet. i. 5. And shall finally participate the Saviour's glory—John xvii. 24. Let them all therefore rejoice, and adore their God—Nor let them regard the frowns of an ungodly world—If Christ owns them, it signifies little who disowns them—

3. The Christian's duty

If we belong to Christ, we ought to live as his people—We should devote to ourselves, and all that we have, without reserve—This was the manifest end for which he bought us—Tit. ii. 14. Let every one then remember whose he is, and whom he is bound to serve—Nor let any one presume to alienate the Saviour's property—All that we have and are, should be employed for him—Our duty is summed up in the apostle's exhortations—1 Cor. vi. 20.

## THE PRIVILEGES OF CHRIST'S FLOCK.

Luke xii. 32. Fear not, little flock; for it is your Father's good pleasure to give you the king-dom. (S. S)

Among the many faculties which exalt man above the brute creation, that of being able to look into futurity is by no means the least.—But while this in many instances elevates him with hope, in many other instances it depresses him with fear.—Hence he is often filled with anxiety to secure the good he hopes for, and to avert the evil which he dreads.—To discountenance this solicitude, and to teach men to live dependent upon God, is the scope of our Lord's discourse before us.—And, in the text, he fortifies his own peculiar people against fear and anxiety, by reminding them of the distinguishing favor of God towards them, and the glorious provision he has made for them. To elucidate his words we shall enquire,

I. Why the Lord's people are called "a little flock."
The metaphor of sheep is often used to characterize the followers of Christ.—Ingenuity might easily suggest a variety of particulars wherein the parallel between them may be drawn.—But, to limit our views within the strictest bounds of propriety, we observe that

They are called "a flock" principally from the peculiar regard shewn them by the Lord.
All who love and fear God, once "went astray like sheep that are lost." But they have been brought home by Christ, the great and good shepherd. And have been united together by him in one fold.—They are kept inclosed, as it were, and distinct from the world.—They "hear their shepherd's voice and follow him."—He "leads them into pastures" which he himself has provided for them. He administers to all their wants, "strengthening the diseased, healing the sick, and binding up the broken hearted." Ezek. xxxiv. 16. The lambs he carries in his bosom, and gently leads them that are with young." Isa. xl. 11. And, however they may feed in different pastures, he considers them all as under his peculiar care—

They are called "a little flock" because they are but few in number.
In every age and every place their numbers have been small.—They are "the few that find the narrow way."—When indeed they shall be all assembled at the last day they will be more than the stars of heaven or the sands upon the sea shore for multitude. Rev. vii. 9. But before that period they will receive an astonishing increase.—The whole earth shall be overspread with them; and that too in successive generation for a thousand years. Rev xx. 4. Till that day of God's power they will be a little flock when compared with the herds of the ungodly.—At present they are only "like the gleanings of the olive-tree, two or three upon the topmost branch." Isa. xvii. 6.

Interested as we must be in what relates to them, let us enquire,
II What they have to fear.
They are not exempt from the common calamities of life.—In some respects they are more exposed to them than other people.—They have reason therefore to fear

1. Wants
Though man may provide for to-morrow, he cannot secure what he has provided.—Hence all are so desirous of placing themselves as far as possible out of the reach of any disastrous contingencies.—In making such provision the true Christian labors under many disadvantages.—He cannot use

those means of acquiring wealth which the generality of the world employ without any scruple.—He cannot devote *all* his time, and *all* his attention to secular engagements.—He dares not neglect his soul, even if he could gain the whole world by it.—Moreover, he has many in the world who would be glad enough to ruin him; but few, very few, that will exert themselves much to help him forward.—On these accounts he may at times be tempted to indulge excessive care, and to harbor fears of want and embarrassment.

2. Sufferings.

The flock of Christ are not only subject to the trials incident to our present state, but are liable to many sufferings peculiar to themselves.—They are " as sheep in the midst of wolves."—Often among themselves are found some that are " wolves in sheep's clothing."—Above all there is " a roaring lion ever seeking to devour them."—Now Christians are not only weak when opposed to Satan, but also when opposed to the world.—They cannot contend with carnal weapons. 2 Cor. x. 4. " The servant of the Lord must not strive."—The rebuke given to Peter when fighting for his Master sufficiently ties their hands from standing in their own defence. Matt. xxvi. 52. Their only weapons are faith and patience.—They are to conquer indeed, but it is by suffering even unto death. Rev. xii. 11. Well therefore may they entertain fears respecting these things.—For if they be not well armed with the mind that was in Christ, 1 Pet. iv. 1, they will faint in the day of adversity—

But the exhortation in the text leads us to enquire further.

III. WHY, NOTWITHSTANDING THEIR DANGERS, THEY SHOULD NOT FEAR.

God has " provided for them a " kingdom."

God condescends to call himself their " Father."—And deals with them as his children.—He has " prepared for them a kingdom" that is infinitely superior to all the kingdoms of this world.—The glory of it cannot be expressed or conceived; nor will the duration of it ever end. Heb. xii 28. This he has given to them for their inheritance.—It is *his determination* to invest them with it, and *his delight* to preserve them for it.—His almighty power is ever exercised for this purpose. 1 Pet. i. 4, 5. Yea, his whole heart and soul are engaged in accomplishing his gracious intentions. Jer. xxxii. 41.

This is a very sufficient antidote to all their fears.

Why should they be afraid of *want*, who have God for their Father, and a kingdom for their inheritance?—Can it be supposed that he who provides for the evil and unthankful, and sustains the ravens that call upon him, will neglect his own children?—Will he, who *of his good pleasure* bestowed upon them all the glory of heaven, refuse them what is necessary for their present sustenance?—Why too should they be afraid of *sufferings*, since " not a hair of their head can perish," " nor can even a sparrow fall to the ground, without the permission of their Father?"—If he see fit to let loose the enemy for the trial of their faith, will he not support their courage, and make them " more than conquerors?"—Besides, will not their " light and momentary afflictions work out for them a far more exceeding and eternal weight of glory?" " And will not a kingdom abundantly compensate all their trials?"—Surely then they should dispel all fears; and commit themselves into the hands of a faithful God. Pet. iv. 19.

ADDRESS,

1. The flock of Christ.

God would have you without carefulness. 1 Cor. viii. 32. He bids you cast all your care on him who careth for you. 1 Pet. v. 7. And shall God be so concerned about relieving your fears, and you not be concerned to honor him?—O chide your unbelieving thoughts, and say, Why art thou disquieted, O my soul?—Jehovah is my shepherd, I shall not want; Jehovah is my Father, I will not fear. Ps. xxiii. 1, 4. Surely if you reflect on the promises he has made to you, it will be impossible for you ever to be cast down again.—"Ye, my flock," says he, "the flock of my pasture, are men; but I am your God, saith the Lord God." Ezek. xxxiv. 31. "When you pass through the waters, I will be with you, and through the fire, you shall not be burnt." Isa. xliii. 2. See also John x. 27, 28. Consider, "If God be for you, who can be against you?"—O be careful for nothing; but in every thing by prayer and supplication with thanksgiving, let your requests be made known unto God; and the peace of God which passeth all understanding shall keep your hearts and minds through Christ Jesus, Phil. iv. 6, 7.

2. The herds of this world.

Shall we address you in the language of the text, Fear not? Alas! not only the scriptures, but also your own consciences would condemn us.— You may possibly have no particular cause to dread either wants or sufferings in this world, (though you cannot tell what may befal you before you die) but may you not have to "dwell with everlasting burnings," and want even "a drop of water to cool your tongue" in that world to which you are hastening?—Know assuredly, that your numbers will not screen you from the vengeance of an angry God.—If you be not of those who have put themselves under the care of the good shepherd, you will be considered as goats, and be forever separated from the flock of Christ—"He will set the sheep on his right hand, and the goats on his left."—You will then find to your cost, that not God, but Satan was your Father; and that with Satan must be your portion. John viii. 42, 44. It is not without much regret that God *now* gives you up to that misery. Hos. xi. 8. But in the last day he will find as much satisfaction, and be as much glorified, in your destruction, as in the salvation of his elect.—He now complains, "Thou hast wearied me with thine iniquities;" but then he will say, "Ah! I will ease me of mine adversaries." Isa. i. 24. Seek then to become the sheep of Christ—Beg him to bring you home to his fold, and to feed you in his pleasant pastures.—Then shall we all become one fold under one shepherd, and feed beside the living fountains of water to all eternity.

---

## A SENSE OF WEAKNESS CONDUCIVE TO STRENGTH.

2 Cor. xii. 10. When I am weak, then am I strong.—(S. S.)

THERE are many things in scripture which appear inconsistent and contrary to truth. Christ is represented as God, and yet a man; as the Lord of David, and yet his son; as a lion, and yet a lamb. And, as his persons is thus variously described, so is his work. He is said to heal us by his own stripes, and to give us life by his death. But, however strange such expressions may seem, they contain many important truths. In the same manner the apostle's words, which we have now read, may be thought to imply a contradiction: but they accord with the experience of all God's people, and justly deserve the most attentive consideration.

In discoursing on this paradoxical assertion, we shall *illustrate, confirm,* and *improve* it.

**I. ILUSTRATE IT.**

A part of David's history will help to elucidate the words before us

When the champion of the Philistines defied, and terified, the whole army of Israel, David, "a stripling," without armor, defensive or offensive, (except a sling and a stone,) went forth against him; and, though unused to war himself, entered into combat with that experienced and mighty warrior. But the weaker he was in himself, the more confident was he in his God: and instead of being intimidated by the threatening aspect, and, boasting determinations of his adversary, he was as assured of victory, as if he had seen his enemy already under his feet. 1 Sam. xvii. 45—47.

But the context will give the best clue to the apostle's meaning.

St. Paul laboured under a heavy trial, which he calls a thorn in his flesh, ver. 7, 8. Apprehensive that this would counteract his usefulness in the world, he cried most earnestly to the Lord Jesus Christ to remove it from him. But his Lord, not judging it expedient to grant him his request, promised him (what was incomparably b tter) more abundant communications of grace, whereby he should obtain in a more advantageous manner the desire of his soul. Observe the effect—Paul remained as weak as ever; but being persuaded that Christ's power should be the more magnified through his weakness, he was satisfied; yea, rather, he made *that* a matter of joy and triumph, which had just before been a source of the greatest trouble. He was well assured that, however unable he was in himself either to bear his trials, or to fulfil his duties, he could not but succeed, when his almighty friend was pledged to succour and support him.

The apostle's assertion being equally applicable to all believers, we shall

**II. CONFIRM IT.**

A sense of weakness necessarily tends to make us strong, inasmuch as it makes us

1. Watchful against temptations,

If we conceive ourselves to be strong, we shall be fearless of temptation; and by exposing ourselves to it, shall be in greater danger of falling: whereas, if we feel our utter weakness, we shall not only pray, "Lead us not into temptation," but shall carefully shun the places, the books, the company, that may ensnare us. Like Joseph, we shall not parly with the tempter, but flee in haste: or, if we cannot flee, we shall oppose our enemy at first; and thus vanquish that, which, if it had time to gather strength, would soon vanquish us.

2. Importunate in prayer,

It is the sick alone who calls for a physician; they who are strong in their own conceit, will never pray in earnest; but he who feels his need of divine assistance will seek it at a throne of grace. Now if we do not pray for God's aid, we cannot receive it; and therefore in the hour of trial shall surely fail. But, if we pray with importunity and faith, we shall obtain the things we ask for; and consequently shall be upheld, while others fall. It was by this means that Paul obtained strength; "he prayed to the Lord *thrice:*" the answer vouchsafed to his petition dissipated all his fears, and strengthened him with might in his inner man: and similar means will always be attended with similar success.

3. Dependent on Christ,

In proportion as we fancy ourselves strong, we must of necessity confide in our own strength; the consequence of which may be sufficiently seen in the

247

repeated falls of Peter. But, if we are conscious that we are wholly without strength, and can do nothing of ourselves, we shall be more simple and uniform in our dependence on Christ. Now Christ will never suffer those, who trust in him to be confounded. He would consider it as an impeachment of his own veracity, if he did not give them "grace sufficient for them:" consequently, we never are so truly strong, as when we are deeply convinced of our own utter impotence.

This truth enters deeply into the experience of all the Lord's people: we shall therefore endeavour to,

III. IMPROVE IT.

Among the various lessons which it teaches us, let us especially learn two,

1. Not to be too much elated on account of any manifestations of the divine favour.

Paul was caught up into the third heavens; but soon afterwards we behold him crying, with much anguish of mind, under a severe affliction. Thus it may soon be with us. Indeed the seasons most distinguished by God's favour to us, are often most distinguished also by Satan's malice. It was immediately after they had received peculiar tokens of God's love, that he assaulted Paul, ver. 4. and Peter, Matt. xvi. 17, 23. and Christ himself. Matt. iii. 17. and iv. 1. Let us then, when most highly favoured, "rejoice with trembling,"Ps. ii. 11. and not while harnessed, boast as if we had put off our armour. 1 Kings xx. 11.

2. Not to be too much dejected on account of our manifold infirmities.

Jacob was lamed by God himself, that he might know he had not prevailed by his own strength. Gen. xxxii. 25. And Paul had a thorn in the flesh given him, "lest he should be exalted above measure." Now our infirmities are very painful: but they are necessary, in order to keep alive in our minds a remembrance of our own weakness and vileness; and if we do but carry them to God in fervent prayer, he will glorify himself by means of them, and "perfect his strength in our weakness." "Let the weak then say, I am strong; Joel iii. 10. let them "be strong in the Lord, and in the power of his might; Eph. vi. 10. and, doubtless, they shall receive that effectual succour, which believers, in all ages, have experienced, Heb. xi. 34. and shall invariably find their "strength according to their day" of trial. Deut. xxxiii. 25.

---

## BENEFITS ARISING FROM GOD'S RETURN TO THE SOUL.

Isai. xxx. 26.—Moreover the light of the moon shall be as the light of the sun, and the light of the sun shall be sevenfold, as the light of seven days, in the day that the Lord bindeth up the breach of his people, and healeth the stroke of their wound. (S. S.)

THE dispensations of providence, if rightly improved, are calculated to promote our spiritual welfare.—The Jews derived many instructive lessons from the dealings of God with them in Egypt and the wilderness.—But God here promises that more abundant knowledge and joy by means of their deliverance from the Assyrian host.* The grandeur, however, of the words

* That this is the literal import of the passage appears from ver. 31. compared with ver. 25, 26.

before us evidently shews, that the prophet had respect to blessings, which no temporal deliverance was able to convey.—We shall therefore endeavour to point out some other seasons when this promise receives its fuller accomplishment.

1. AT THE FIRST RECONCILIATION OF THE SOUL TO GOD.

The convictions of an awakened conscience are as deep wounds to the soul.

Sin, though it be honey in the mouth, becomes gall in the stomach—Peter, Judas, and David in particular, shew what "*wounds*" it will make in the soul—Ps. xxxii. 1—6. Nor can any one view it aright, without, having his heart broken with a sense of its malignity—

But reconciliation with God heals these wounds.

The blood of Christ is that "balm of Gilead," which never was applied in vain—Jer. viii. 22. It operates as the sight of the brazen serpent on the dying Israelites, to restore to life and vigour those, whose state seems altogether desperate—John iii. 14, 15. David, after the foulest transgressions declared his persuasion of its efficacy to cleanse even him—Ps. li. 7, 8. And all who are reconciled to God through Christ, experience its ful. effects—Luke iv. 18. 1 Pet. i. 8.

And this is a season, wherein the knowledge and joy of the soul are much enlarged.

Till this great event is accomplished, the views of the soul are very contracted; nor is it acquainted with any joy but what is carnal.—But no sooner has this taken place, than the light of the knowledge of the glory of God shines into the heart, and all his perfections are admired and adored.—Now also the excellency of the gospel salvation is discovered; and the reasonableness of a life devoted to God is deeply felt.—Now is a new and inexhaustible source of happiness opened to the soul; and its peace and joy flow down like a river.—And all the pleasures that it ever enjoyed in the ways of sin, are no more in comparison of its present consolations, than the faint "light of the moon" to the invigorating rays of the meridian "sun"—

But this promise has a further accomplishment.

II. AT ANY RETURN OF GOD TO THE SOUL AFTER A SEASON OF DARKNESS AND DESERTION.

God finds it necessary sometimes to hide his face from his people, and thus to wound their souls afresh.

How the loss of God's presence afflicts a pious soul, may be seen in the lamentations and complaints, which the most eminent saints have uttered on such occasions. Job tells us, that God's arrows stuck fast in him, and that the poison of them drank up his spirit. Job vi. 4. And David even "roared for the disquietness of his heart." Nor are there wanting at this day many, whose experience accords with the description which that eminent saint has given of his—Ps. xlii. 3, 4, 6, 7, 9.

But the return of God binds up this breach.

The deliverence from such a state is compared by our Lord to the joy that succeeds the pangs of childbirth—1 John xvi. 21. Nor can its effects upon the soul be more fitly represented than in the language of the Jews on their return from Babylon—Ps. cxxvi. 1—3.

And this also is another season of peculiar instruction and comfort.

By this the soul obtains much deeper discoveries of its own corruptions; Job xlii. 5, 6. and more encouraging views of God's power and faithfulness—Isai. xxv. 1, 4. The depths of Satan's device also are more clearly discerned.—And, if its joys are less ecstatic than before, they are more pure and refined—

The full accomplishment of the text will take place,

III. AT THE HOUR OF DISSOLUTION.

God never entirely withholds his chastening rod in this world.

The whole of this life is a state of discipline — — —

But at death there is an end of every thing that is penal, or painful.

Whatever wounds may have pained us here, death will heal them all Rev. xxi. 4.— — —

Then will this promise be fulfilled in its utmost extent.

What amazing discoveries will be made to the soul on its first dismission from the body! And with what inconceivable raptures will it be transported, as soon as ever it shall enter the gates of heaven! Whatever it may have heard of the blessedness of the saints, it will surely say, that not a thousandth part had been declared to it. Then shall those descriptions given by the prophets, all be realized—Isai. lx. 19. 20. Rev. xxi 23. and xxii. 5. As for the joys it experienced below, they shall appear as nothing in comparison of those it will then possess.—What they tasted here, was through the medium of ordinances, and mixed with frequent sorrows, and, at best, of short duration.—But what they possess in heaven, will be immediate, unmixed, and everlasting—

INFER,

1. They, who have never yet been wounded in their souls on account of sin, are yet strangers to all spiritual light and happiness.

They may be conversant with all the depths of philosophy, and all the pleasures of sense.—But the unhumbled and unbelieving soul is yet blinded by Satan, nor has even the glimmering light of the moon with respect to spiritual concerns—2 Cor. iv. 4. and 1 Cor. ii. 14. Let such then beg of God to open the eyes of their understanding; and let them seek those convictions of sin, whereby they shall be disposed to admit, and to love, the truth—

2. They who feel a wounded spirit, should labour to improve their convictions to the uttermost.

Too many endeavour to silence the accusations of conscience, and to drown its voice in business or pleasure.—But if we knew how ready God is to heal the broken spirit, and what unspeakable benefits would ultimately flow from our convictions, surely we should cherish them with care, and improve them with diligence.—Let us then not "heal our wounds slightly," but go to the blood of Jesus?—Then, "though weeping may endure for a night, joy shall come to us in the morning," even that "joy which is unspeakable and full of glory."

--------

## ALL THINGS WORK FOR GOOD TO GOD'S PEOPLE.

Rom. viii. 28.—We know that all things work together for good to them that love God, to them who are the called according to his purpose. (S. S.)

TRUE believers have the greatest encouragement to draw nigh to God—

They have supernatural assistance when pouring out their hearts before him—

**And** are assured by God himself that their prayers shall be heard—

Yea, sometimes, like the Israelites in Egypt, the more they renew their requests, the more they find their burdens increased—Exod. v. 6—8.

Hence, like them, they are also sometimes ready to murmur and despond—Ib. ver. 20, 21.

But, by grace they are enabled to wait patiently the Lord's leisure—

And invariably, in the issue, the clouds which they so much dreaded, burst in blessings on their heads—

This St. Paul declares to be the experience of all true believers—

His words lead us to shew.

I. THE CHARACTER OF TRUE CHRISTIANS.

Christians are sometimes described in the scriptures by their regard for God, and sometimes by God's regard for them—

The text leads us to speak of them in both points of view,

1. Their regard to God.

The "loving of God" is a character peculiar to true Christians—

Others are represented rather as "haters of God" and enemies to him in their minds—Rom. i. 30. Col. i. 21.

But they, who are partakers of his grace, have their natural enmity removed—

They behold his excellency, and are sensible of their obligations to him—

Hence they love him, and strive to love him with their whole hearts—

2. God's regard for them.

Their regard for him sprang not from any good dispositions in themselves—

It resulted purely from the manifestations of God's love to them—

He formed "purposes" of love to them from all eternity—Jer. xxxi. 3.

In due time he "called" them by his grace, and made him his people—

And this distinguishing favour is the true source of their love to him—

To this effect both our Lord and his beloved apostle testify—John xv. 16. 1 John iv. 19.

To the eternal purposes of God therefore, and not to the inclinations of our carnal minds, all the good that is in us, be traced—

To persons of this description the apostle announces,

II. THEIR PRIVILEGE.

It is under sufferings that the superiority of the Christian's state is to be seen to the greatest advantage—

Of them the apostle speaks; and declares that, of whatever kind they be, they shall work for the good of them that love God.

The Christian may be called to bear the heaviest *afflictions*—

But they shall bring him to consideration, stir him up to prayer, wean him from the world, and lead him to seek his rest above— — —

He may be assaulted also with the most distressing *temptations*—

But these will shew him the evil of his heart, and the faithfulness of his God—

They will also teach him to sympathize with his tempted brethren—

Even *death* itself will be among the number of the things that shall prove beneficial to him—

This is the most formidable enemy to fallen man—

It cuts him off from all means and opportunities of salvation, and seals him up under endless and irremediable misery,—

But to a true Christian it is a most invaluable treasure—1 Cor. iii. 22.

It puts a period to all his sorrows and temptations, and introduces him to the immediate, everlasting enjoyment of his God—

Nor need we doubt of this blessed truth.

The apostle speaks of it not as a matter of conjecture, but of certainty—

As he knew it, so may "we know" it, from the declarations and promises of God—Ps. xxv. 10.

Both David and Paul have attested it also from their own experience—Ps. cxix. 71. Phil. i. 19.

Nor is there any Christian in whom it has not been realized—

It is not however *singly* or *separately* that all things work for good, but as taken "*together*" in a collective view—

Separately considered, many things may have wrought for evil, by producing sinful tempers or actions—

But when viewed as connected with *all* their effects and consequences, the most untoward circumstances will be found to have wrought for good—

This subject naturally suggests,

1. A rule whereby to judge of our election of God—

Our election of God can be known only by its effects, 1 Thes. i. 4, 5.

To ascertain it, we must enquire whether we have been *called* by his grace.

And whether, in consequence of that call, we *love God* supremely?—

If we experience these effects, we may safely conclude, that God has entertained eternal purposes of love towards us.—

But if we trace not these effects, our pretensions to an interest in his electing love is a fatal delusion.—

Let them, in whom these evidences are found, rejoice; but rejoice with trembling.—

2. A ground of consolation for the afflicted.

Afflictions are not at the present joyous, but grievous—

And under them we are ready to say, "All these things are against me"—

But the scripture tells us, "the trial of our faith is precious"—1 Pet. 1. 7

Let the afflicted then consider what "good" may be accruing to them—

Their troubles may be working so as to discover, prevent, punish, or destroy *sin*— — —

Or they may be working to impart, exercise, strengthen, or perfect *grace*— — —

What reason, in either case, have the afflicted to take comfort!—

We think little of inconveniencies if they do but promote our *temporal* interest—

Should we then be averse to any trials that may tend to our *spiritual* advantage?—

Let us wait to see "the end of the Lord," and be solicitous rather about our future benefit, than our present ease—

3. A strong incentive to love and serve God.

Things are never represented as working for the good of the wicked—

On the contrary, their temporal blessings are often cursed to them—

Yea, even spiritual blessings only aggravate their guilt and condemnation—2 Cor. ii. 16.

Christ himself proves, not a Saviour, but a stumbling-block to them—1 Pet. ii. 7, 8.

But for God's people, all things, sin excepted, work for good—

Should they not then love him for such distinguished mercy?—

Can they ever do enough for him, who so marvellously overrules all events for them?

## A CONSCIENCE VOID OF OFFENCE.

Acts x .iv. 16.—And herein do I exercise myself, to have always a conscience void of offence, towards God and towards men. (Sk.)

THE Jews charged the apostle Paul with high crimes, and employed Ter-tullus, an orator, to bring accusations against him before Felix, the governor. Tertullus flattered Felix, and abused Paul; but produced no proof of guilt in the holy apostle. The answer of Paul was manly, correct, and convinc-ing. He had nothing to fear. His conduct had been pious and circumspect; for he had exercised himself "to have always a conscience void of offence both towards God and men."—But what is implied in a conscience void of offence?—And how should we exercise ourselves to have such a conscience;

I. WHAT IS IMPLIED IN A CONSCIENCE VOID OF OFFENCE?

1. *Conscience is the secret testimony of the soul, whereby it approves things that are good, and condemns those that are evil.* A good conscience is purified by the blood of Christ, 1 Tim. i. 5; Heb. ix. 14. An evil con-science is loaded with guilt, Heb. x. 22. And a hardened conscience does not feel the evil of sin, 1 Tim. iv. 2. Conscience has a rule of action; it compares action with that rule, and draws inferences from the comparison.

2. *To have a conscience void of offence, three things are necessary:—* First, a good rule of conduct; secondly, an impartial comparison of our conduct with that rule; and thirdly, a conviction that there has been a con-formity of conduct to our rule. In that case, conscience does not charge us with wilful crimes; but assures us of innocence and rectitude. Advocates for sin, whether professors or profane, will not allow that any man has a conscience void of offence, but surely the grace of God is sufficient to keep us from all sin, 1 Cor. xv. 34.

3. *That man who has a conscience void of offence towards God, is in-wardly pious, and practises all the duties of piety.* He believes in God, Heb. xi. 6; he fears God, Ps. cxxviii. 1; he loves God, Matt. xxii. 37, 38; he prays to God, Phil. iv. 6; he trusts in God, Isa. xxvi. 4; he praises God, Isa. xii. 1; and he worships God in spirit and in truth, John iv. 24. These are the principal duties of piety; and when we engage in them with true sincerity, we have a conscience void of offence towards God.

4. *He who has a conscience void of offence towards men, carefully fol-lows two rules:*—First, he injures no man, either in his person, in his prop-erty, or in his character; and, secondly, he does all the good which is in his power to every man with whom he is connected, both in word and deed. He loves all men, he prays for all, and he is ready to forgive injuries and in-sults. While he walks humbly with his God, he is careful to do justly to men, and is ever ready to exercise mercy, Mic. vi. 8.

II. HOW SHOULD WE EXERCISE OURSELVES TO HAVE A CONSCIENCE VOID OF OFFENCE?

1. Let us use those means by which we may *obtain an enlightened con-science*, that we may understand our duty both to God and men. To this end carefully examine the word of God, which is the only safe guide of hu-man conduct. Without this blessed book, we fall into error and sin; we dishonor God and injure men: and vainly imagine that we are doing what is fit and right. Thus Saul thought it right to do many things against the church: but he did those things in ignorance and unbelief, Acts xxvi. 9; 1 Tim. i. 13.

2. It should be an invariable rule with us, *to do nothing at any time, or*

253

*under any circumstances, contrary to the dictates of conscience.* **When** we act contrary to our views of things, we are self-condemned. If the conscience be not sufficiently enlightened, we should not venture to act against its warnings. Every one should be persuaded in his own mind that what he does is right; for if this be not the case, he cannot be guiltless before the Judge of all the earth. Whatsoever men do, without a conviction of its lawfulness, is sin to them; for whatsoever is not of faith is of sin, Romans xiv. 22, 23.

3. In this holy exercise we should *abstain from the appearance of evil;* for if we yield to any thing which our own mind condemns, or to any thing which appears evil in the eyes of wise and good men, we shall soon fall into great and gross sins, 1 Thess. v. 22. For this reason we should steadily follow what we deem to be right, even in *little things;* and scrupulously avoid evil of every kind and degree. If this rule be constantly followed, we shall seldom deviate from the path of duty.

4. That we may keep a conscience void of offence, let us *be careful not to enter into temptation.* We may be tempted to evil without our own consent, and without sin; but if we enter into it, we become guilty before God. We should resist the first attack of an enemy. Temptation when first presented to the mind is generally weak, and we are strong; but its strength increases and ours diminishes, when we enter into it. For this reason we should not enter into it at all, lest we be overcome in an evil hour, Matt. xxvi. 41.

5. As a farther help in this important work, *let us be vigilant.* We are surrounded by enemies, who are ready to seize every favorable moment to draw us from our duty. Let us look out for them, that we may not be taken by surprise. Watch against all evil, whether inward or outward; watch for opportunities of doing good: and watch for the coming of Jesus to judge the world. The admonition of our Lord will never be out of season, " What I say unto you, I say unto all, Watch," Mark xiv. 37.

6. To watchfulness let us add *prayer.* Let us pray for wisdom to conduct us safely through difficult circumstances, James i. 5. Let us pray for courage and strength, that we may be able to overcome all evil; and for that comfort and consolation which may be necessary for us in our trials and temptations. He who is always in the spirit of prayer, cannot live in any known sin; and for this reason, let us " pray without ceasing," 1 Thess v. 17.

7. It is essentially necessary, in this blessed exercise, to *avoid secret sins.* These are fully known to God, Ps. xc. 8. He will bring them into judgment, Eccles. xii. 14. Secret sins lead to open wickedness; and he who sins in the dark will soon transgress in open day. No man who lives in secret sin, whatever his pretensions are, has a conscience void of offence And his sin, though artfully concealed from men, will be sure to find him out, Num. xxxii. 23.

8. While we *set God before us,* in his justice and purity, and in his awful majesty and glory, we shall be careful to keep a conscience void of offence. This is our duty, and our privilege, Gen. xvii. 1; Ps. xvi. 8. His eyes are constantly upon us, and he hates all evil. Our love to him produces a hatred of evil; and if our love be without dissimulation, we shall abhor and detest it, Ps. cxvii. 10; Rom. xii. 9.

9. Let us *be conversant with death and judgment.* These are solemn subjects; they should occupy our thoughts in the morning when we awake; throughout the day, when we are engaged in business; and in the evening,

**when** we retire to rest. While this is the case we shall be careful **neither** to offend God nor to injure man.

10. And lastly, *we should exercise ourselves daily in meditations on the happiness of heaven, and the torments of hell.* There is a heaven of light and glory for good men; and there is a hell of darkness and shame for the wicked, Rev. xxi 23; Ps. ix. 17. He who has a good conscience, is an heir of immortal blessedness; but he whose conscience is loaded with guilt, is an heir of death and hell, Rom. vi. 23. Serious reflections on these subjects will keep us from sin.

### INFERENCES.

1. While we keep a conscience void of offence, *we enjoy the approbation of God,* and are happy in his love, Ps. xi. 7.

2. When this is the case, *our minds are at rest,* and we enjoy that peace which passeth all understanding, Phil. iv. 7.

3. This takes away the *fear of man.* which brings a snare to the soul, and enables us to look every one in the face without a blush of guilt.

4. And while the conscience is void of offence *we are holy, happy and useful,* and all things go well with us both for time and eternity, Isa. iii. 10. May we all enjoy this invaluable blessing, through Jesus Christ our Lord, Amen.

---

## THE EXCELLENCY OF UNION.

Psalm cxxxiii. 1.—Behold, how good and how pleasant it is for brethren to dwell together in unity.   (Sk.)

AMONGST the numerous excellencies which are connected with true religion, the delightful union of which it is productive holds a very distinguished place. Through the influence of religion, men whose condition in life, disposition of mind, mode of education, and regular habitudes, have been not only widely different, but also directly opposed to each other; have become so closely united, that even Heathenism, with all its inveterate opposition to revealed truth, has been constrained to attest, "See how these christians love !" And this interesting union has not been confined to the christian dispensation, but was manifestly a striking feature in the piety of rural and patriarchal times; and it also constituted a distinguished excellency in the Jewish church. David bears testimony to its existence in his day, exclaiming in the spirit of admiration, "Behold how good and how pleasant it is," &c. It is very probable that this psalm was composed on the termination of that civil war, which had so long prevailed between the two houses of Saul and David: yet this language may very properly be applied, in reference to the harmony of religious societies or christian churches. In thus using this portion of Scripture we shall,

I. DEFINE THE NATURE OF SCRIPTURAL UNION.
II. ASSERT ITS TRANSCENDENT EXCELLENCE. And,
III. SPECIFY THE MEANS OF ITS PROMOTION.

I. DEFINE THE NATURE OF SCRIPTURAL UNION. This union may be considered as including—*Sentiment—Affection—Design—and Operation.*

1. *A oneness of sentiment.* Whilst the different denominations of christians, in consequence of their early associations and impressions having been widely different, entertain notions contrary to each other on various subjects of minor importance, yet on the grand essential truths of christianity they are one. The fall, and consequent depravity of man ; the divinity and atonement of Christ, the necessity and reality of the operations of the Holy Ghost, and justification by faith alone, are doctrines which form a kind of central point, at which the christian tribes meet, and sing,

> " Let names, and sects, and parties fall
> And Jesus Christ be all in all."

This is manifest by their writings, their public ministrations, and their union of defence when these truths are assailed.

2. *A union in point of affection.* All those who are the "children of God by faith," maintaining the same common principles, influenced by the same powerful motives, participating the same spiritual enjoyments, and bearing the same divine image, are the subjects of a mutual and tender affection, which expresses itself by various acts of kindness ; such as administering to each other's necessities, steadily watching over each other's interests, studiously labouring to promote each other's happiness, and patiently bearing with each other's infirmities, Rom. xii. 5—10 ; Heb. vi. 10 ; 1 Pet. i. 22 ; Gal. vi. 2 ; Heb. x. 32—34 ; 1 John iii. 16, 17.

3. *A sameness of principle, and a union of heart, are very naturally productive of a similarity of design.* And Christians generally, and with steady uniformity, purpose to secure their own final salvation—to endeavour instrumentally, to effect the salvation of their friends and neighbours—to extend the kingdom of the Redeemer in the earth, having for their ultimate object the glory of God, Acts xxiv, 16 ; Rom. x. 1, xiv. 7, 8 ; 1 Cor. x. 31.

4. *Operation.* In this distinguished age of light and glory, the followers of Christ generally agree to merge their little differences on minor points of faith, in a unity of effort, to accomplish the grand object of their mutual purpose. If we turn our attention to school institutions, to Bible societies, and to Missionary establishments, we shall delightfully behold christians of all denominations rallying round the common standard, and marching on to certain conquest.

II. ASSERT ITS TRANSCENDENT EXCELLENCE. There are many things which are very good, but not pleasant ; while other things, which, to the vitiated inclinations of a depraved heart, appear delightful, are in reality injurious and destructive ; but scriptural union is both "good and pleasant." This will appear, if we consider,

1. *Its moral fitness.* The union of the christian church is in exact agreement with the nature and perfections of God, John iii. 16 ; 1 John iv 8—10. Correspondent with the great designs of mercy in the gospel of Christ, Eph. ii. 13 ; Col. i. 20—22. And strictly congruent with the harmony of the heavenly world, Rev. vii. 9—17.

2. *Its pleasing appearance.* Whilst discord and hostility offend the eye, and pain the heart of the thoughtful observer, union, of whatever description, tends to excite the most pleasurable sensations in the breast : but this is more especially the case when tranquillity pervades a religious society. When materials originally so discordant are brought into a state of delightful harmony, the scene is highly pleasing, and produces admiration, excites lively joy, and elicits sentiments of gratitude. The Psalmist felt the influ-

ence of such a scene, and made use of the most odoriferous compound, as a figure by which to describe the effect which was produced upon his mind.

3. *Its beneficial influence.* Union ever tends to augment the happiness of its possessor,—to recommend divine truth to mankind,—to extend the kingdom of Christ in the earth,—and to give strength and stability to the christian course, Rom. xvi. 16, 19 ; 2 Cor. xiii. 11.

III. SPECIFY THE MEANS OF ITS PROMOTION. In promoting christian union there are,

1. *Some things to be avoided.* If we would have peace in our own bosoms, and live in peace with our christian brethren, we must steadily avoid a spirit of evil surmising: and guard against hard and uncharitable thoughts, in reference to our fellow professors, resolutely resisting every inclination to evil speaking and detraction. If we indulge thoughts which are inconsistent with that "charity" which "thinketh no evil," we shall involve ourselves in condemnation, and be in the way of speaking those words, and performing those actions, which will prove destructive to the union and happiness of the church, Eph. iv. 1, 2, iv, 26, 27, 31 ; James iii. 13—18, iv, 11. In order to preserve christian harmony.

2. *There are some things to be performed.* As we are regularly dependant upon God for strength and support, it is of the utmost importance that we maintain constant communion with him by fervent prayer ; also that we uniformly regulate our conduct and conversation by that infallible directory which infinite wisdom has furnished, making the sacred Scripture our constant guide at all times ; steadily and conscientiously using every means which has a tendency to unite us more closely to our christian brethren. Finally, above all, let us labour to " grow in grace, and in the knowledge and love of God," so shall we be preserved from every evil, and regularly demonstrate " how good and how pleasant it is for brethren to dwell together in unity." This subject,

1. Excites to close and serious self-examination.

2. Teaches us that discord in religious societies impedes the progress of the gospel.

3. Describes a line of conduct for us in the future part of life.

---

### EARLY PIETY EXEMPLIFIED IN JOSIAH.

2 Chronicles xxxiv. 3.—While he was yet young, he began to seek after the God of David his father. (Sk.)

IT was the observation of an inspired apostle, that " not many wise men after the flesh, not many mighty, not many noble, are called." God's people have generally been an afflicted and a poor people " the poor have the gospel preached to them," and " God hath chosen the poor in this world, to be rich in faith and heirs of the kingdom which he hath promised unto them that love him." But the individual exhibited to our view in the text, was differently circumstanced. He was a king, and sat upon a throne, and reigned over a great people ; and though many acts of his life are inimitable by us, yet in the view in which the text represents him, he is eminently worthy the attention of the junior part of my congregation. We will therefore notice three things,

**I.** THE OBJECT AFTER WHOM JOSIAH SOUGHT;—" The God of David his father."

**II.** THE MANNER HOW HE SOUGHT AFTER THAT OBJECT; which will be seen by referring to this chapter.

**III.** THE PERIOD OF LIFE WHEN HE DID IT:—"While he was yet young," &c.

**I.** THE OBJECT AFTER WHOM JOSIAH SOUGHT. Josiah sought after the God of David his father. Josiah lived four hundred years subsequently to David, but being David's remote descendant he is considered as his son. Also, when one person imitates another, by a familiar mode of speech, he is represented as his son. Abraham was the father of the faithful. " Ye are of your father the devil, because his works ye do." Josiah imitated David, see ver. 2. God was David's God

1. *God was David's teacher.* David was a man of extensive information, his knowledge was various; he knew much of God and his works; much of men and things; but he was indebted to God for his instruction. " The Lord is my delight," &c. Ps. xxvii. 1. " Thou through thy commandments hast made me wiser than mine enemies." " I will thank thee, O Lord, who hast given me counsel." David's soul was dark and ignorant by nature, but God instructed and taught him great things out of his law.

2. *God was David's comfort.* He was involved at times in great trouble; he had tasted the wormwood and the gall; the waves and billows had gone over him; he had experienced personal, family, and national trouble. But he had applied unto God, and was enabled to say, "In the multitude of my thoughts within me, thy comforts delight my soul." " Bless the Lord, O my soul," &c. Psa. ciii. 1, 2.

3. *God was David's delight.* David seemed totally at a loss to express the ardency of his attachment unto God. " O God thou art my God," &c. Psa. lxiii. 1. " As the hart panteth after the water brooks," &c. Psa. xlii. 1, 2. When deprived of the public ordinances of religion, he appeared even to envy the sparrows who made their nests near unto the house of the Lord, Ps. lxxxiv. 3.

4. *God was David's defence.* David had many enemies; they who hated him, he said, " were more than the hairs of his head." " But the Lord," said he, " is my rock, and my fortress, and my deliverer," &c. " When I cry unto thee then shall mine enemies turn back,"&c. Thus, Jehovah was the God of David, and after him Josiah sought; but let us describe,

**II.** THE MANNER HOW HE SOUGHT AFTER GOD. Information on this subject we collect by perusing his history.

1. *He sought God from a deep conviction that his conduct, and the conduct of Israel generally, was highly offensive to God, and that they were exposed to imminent peril.* For in his reign, while they were repairing the temple, they found a copy of the book of the law, and by reading that, and comparing their conduct with it, they saw the criminality of their lives; and that wrath was ready to come upon them. Let us read our Bibles, and compare ourselves with the records of revelation.

2. *He sought God in deep self-abasement of soul.* When he heard the book of the law read, he rent his clothes, and wept, see ver. 19, 27. Humility best becomes those who seek the Lord; a view of our sins, a consciousness of danger, a consideration of the majesty and glory of God, all should tend to humble us.

*He sought God by destroying the idols out of the land.* Manasseh the grandfather of Josiah had reared up altars for Balaam, made groves, and worshipped the hosts of heaven. And Amon his father, had worshipped the carved image which Manasseh had made; but Josiah purged the land from idols, ver. 3, 4. Here we cannot exactly imitate him, but we should purge our hearts from idols: every human being is addicted to idolatry, to love the creature rather than the Creator; but God will have no rival, he will not give his glory to another.

3. *He sought God by restoring his true worship, and frequenting it.* The house of God had been neglected and forsaken, but Josiah got workmen, and builders, and artificers in great numbers, and they repaired the temple; and Josiah restored the passover, and the people celebrated it, "so that there had been nothing like it since the days of Samuel, neither did any of the kings of Israel keep such a passover as Josiah kept." Here too our conduct must necessarily vary a little from that of Josiah's; but those who would seek God, should frequent his public ordinances. These we have in abundance.

4. *He sought God with all his heart :*—"For like him, there was no king before him that turned to the Lord with all his heart, and with all his soul," &c. 2 Kings xxiii. 25 Here we must fully imitate Josiah; God demands our hearts, our whole hearts, and we must turn to him heartily, and in the most unreserved and decided manner.

III. The period of life when he did it:—"While he was yet young," &c. "He was eight years old when he began to reign; and he reigned eight years, and then he began to "seek," &c. We should seek God while we are yet young, because,

1. *God is the best object whom we can seek.* "All nations before him are as nothing; and they are counted to him less than nothing and vanity." To whom then will you liken God? Examine all the objects which men are accustomed to seek after, and say which of those objects can be compared with the Lord?

2. *Youth is the best time for seeking God.* It is the *most acceptable* time with God, "I love them that love me, and those that seek me early shall find me." It is the *most pleasant* time with us. The yoke of Christ is then peculiarly easy, and his burden more than ordinarily light. How hard and difficult it is for old sinners to seek God! It is the only certain time we can command. How few live to see old age. "Man that is born of woman is of few days and full of trouble:" thousands die daily—life is but "vapour that appeareth for a little time and then vanisheth away." Let me then persuade you, young people, to imitate Josiah. Reflect on the advantages attendant on such a mode of conduct. *There are personal advantages ;* seek God, and you will find him,—seek God, and you will live. *There are relative advantages ;* Josia's conduct stimulated others to seek God, and perhaps thousands and tens of thousands were benefited by his example. We cannot promise ourselves such extensive usefulness, but we may all be useful in a greater or less degree. How many of you, young people would gladden your parents by seeking the Lord! How useful might you be to your juvenile companion! But many young persons perceive no necessity for seeking the Lord; but this necessity exists, whether you see it or not. Oh! how awfully are you deceived! Others attach a degree of meanness to this exercise. To such we say, look at Joseph, Samuel, Solomon, Abijah, Daniel, Timothy, &c. But some have suffered the morning of their lives to pass away without seeking God: to such we address a word of exhortation, reproof, and encouragement.

## YOUTHFUL PIETY.

**Jer.** ii. 2, 3.—Go, and cry in the ears of Jerusalem, saying, Thus saith the Lord, I remember thee, the kindness of thy youth, the love of thine espousals, when thou wentest after me in the wilderness, in a land that was not sown. Israel was holiness to the Lord, and the first fruits of his increase. (P.)

Now, in order that we may have our minds duly affected with the subject, it will be necessary,

I. To CONSIDER THE RICH AND GLOWING DESCRIPTION OF YOUTHFUL PIETY WHICH IS HERE GIVEN.

It is figurative language; but the figure is formed from reality, and Israel devoted to the God of Abraham is what the prophet intended to describe. And what is it in reference to youthful piety which God remembers?

1. *Its ardent affection;* "I remember the kindness of thy youth ;" the glow of strong feeling which characterized thee. Young people feel greatly that which occupies their attention: the religion of the young is seldom the cold philosophic speculation or experience of age.

2. That the deep interest which you felt in religion was apparent in *a union of the soul to Christ.* "I remember the love of thine espousals." The Redeemer won you by his love; you felt the bond, and devoted yourselves to the Saviour.

3. Character of youthful piety; *it is a going after God.* "When thou wentest after me," &c. Your religion was not an invention of your own; it was not some worldly plan. It was the religion of the Scripture; it was clothed with an authoritative, "Thus saith the Lord."

4. Acceptable youthful religion is *not discouraged by difficulties and troubles.* When was it that Israel went after the Lord? "In the wilderness, in a land that was not sown." When there were no corn fields to gladden the eyes, and no water to quench the thirst; when they had nothing to live upon but the word, and presence, and Spirit of God. True religion is not that of fashion and custom, but that which God requires.

5. *The religion of an accepted youth is a religion of holiness.* Holiness is the character which he adopts, the atmosphere in which he breathes. "Israel was holiness unto the Lord."

Such is a brief description of the early piety which God delights to view in young people who are called by his name. I hasten

II. To NOTICE THE ASPECT WHICH THE DIVINE REMEMBRANCE OF YOUTHFUL PIETY MAY HAVE ON DIFFERENT CIRCUMSTANCES OF LIFE.

*You* may forget it, but HE never does. Your book of remembrance may be reduced to ashes, but his book remains, and every character in it is indelible. Two views may be taken of this remembrance.

1. *A view of approbation.* What a delightful view of early religion is this, that it is remembered with approbation! "I remember thee!"—And when is it that almighty God remembers with approbation and pleasure these traces of early piety?

*When you are successfully struggling with the temptations of the world.* I know that youth are exposed to strong temptations; but when you are struggling hard to maintain that integrity of character of which the world aims to deprive you; when you cultivate tempers which make you a derision to those around you; when you renounce pleasure rather than displease God; when you hold fast the beginning of your confidence steadfast unto the end, however it may be assailed and shaken : then God is well pleased.

and he says, "I remember thee, the kindness of thy youth," &c. Your early religion was not in vain; the impressions made in youth accompany you in your course of duty, and you still walk humbly with your God.

*When you act under their influence in promoting the cause of truth and holiness.* A pious youth is seldom slothful. Let a plan of usefulness be proposed, and who shall engage in it?—the young. They may not have all the means and all the prudence of the more aged, but theirs is the activity.

*When its possessors are sunk into deep affliction.* When laid on beds of sickness, and the world seems to be receding, O what delightful support do they then derive from the kindness of their youth, and the love of their espousals! And when they meet with disappointments in life; when difficulties rise in their path, and they know not which way to turn, what a satisfaction to think on the way in which they have walked before God!

*When young people come to be old people.* This will be the case if God permit; and I earnestly wish it may be so with those whom I address. Then, the remembrance of youthful piety taken by the blessed God, sheds a richer and a calmer satisfaction over the mind of the aged disciple, than anything else in the world can possibly yield.—And, finally,

*In a dying hour.* I need not carry the thought beyond this point. And tell me, which will afford greatest pleasure to the mind; that the Father of spirits has been loved and honored, or that he has been forsaken? Then, oh then it is he says with tenderest compassion, "I remember thee, the kindness of thy youth, &c.; and I will put under thee the everlasting arms, and will become thy portion for ever."

But this is the favorable side of the subject; and I should be unjust to my subject, and to the consciences of my hearers, if I were to leave it here. For the remembrance of youthful piety taken by God, may be

2. *A remembrance of regret and displeasure.* We are allowed to speak of the great God after the manner of men. He may act as though this were the language of his heart. I am afraid it is not necessary to go into the land of imagination, or to go beyond mournful facts, to demonstrate that many young persons, who appeared to be decidedly religious, have awfully sunk away. Some have gone into immoralities of the most flagrant character: others have become the disciples of a flimsy infidelity; and others who have not gone such lengths, have yet sunk down from the heights of piety into worldly conformity. Surely, I need not stay to *prove* this! Many of you can think of circumstances which prove all these particulars: you can remember one and another of your friends, dear to you as brothers and sisters, who have gone astray from the right path. Now, the truth is, God remembers these as much as he remembers the others; and it was to those in such a state that the words of the text were intended to be addressed. God is displeased, whether we think of it or not. That young man may have hardened himself in forgetfulness and sin, but let him know that God has it written in his book, that that young man is gone astray from his first principles. God is displeased; and very few who admit the being of a God, could bear in a solitary moment, or on the bed of sickness, or on the borders of the grave, to think of God's being displeased with them, without the deepest awe!

Let it be observed that the *day of divine desertion is not come.* You may have left God, but he has not left you. He has devised many means to bring you back. Sometimes he chastens your bodies with pain on the bed of sickness; at another time he plants difficulties around you which you cannot get through; sometimes he drives you to read your bibles; sometimes he brings you to hear a plain address like the present, when you are led to imagine that the preacher knows you intimately, and is describing your individual case. But if warnings be slighted, if providences be overlooked, if all means employed are in vain, if the youth determinately goes on to perdition;—the end will be dreadful indeed!—Such an end as will lead him to "mourn at the last, and to say, How have I hated instruction, and my heart despised reproof!" And to say it when "the harvest is past, when the summer is ended, and you are not saved!"

Such is the subject;—it is part pleasing and part painful—You may set the one against the other.

And now, there are various characters present whom I must address. Some here may say "The preacher has told my story, he has described me." O cannot some of you say "Wisdom's ways are ways of pleasantness, and her paths are paths of peace?" If so, go on your way rejoicing.

And cannot others say, and does not conscience oblige you to say, "We began with as good prospects as any around us, but the world beguiled us, and led us to our ruin!"—No, not to your ruin, if now you are wise enough to perceive your mistake, and apply to the only remedy.

And are there not some *thoughtless* ones here who will not properly apply to themselves what has been said? But, why not? What! my young friends, are you living among the professors of religion, and have *you* not devoted yourselves to God? Is there no kindness of youth, no going out after him, no following him, through the wilderness, no consecrated holiness, no first fruits? O, let me urge you to seek the Lord; and to seek him *now*, or it may be too late. Death is at the door;—the Judge is at the door, and you may be removed to judgment! O, why will you not accept the blessings of the gospel, and apply to that Saviour who would not reject you!

And now, *religious* young persons, I *congratulate* you; but I must also *warn* you. If you think yourselves secure, you are in more danger than others. Study your way; study your own hearts; study the religion of scripture. Be warned,—be animated,—be encouraged,—be faithful unto death.

There are some here who are in the *very bloom of life*, who can scarcely have had such feelings as have been described. O be persuaded now to come to Christ. He loves little children; he says, " Suffer little children to come unto me, and forbid them not.', He "gathers the lambs in his arms, and carries them in his bosom;" and the sooner you devote yourselves to him, the more likely are you to escape temptations. None are too young to die :—none are too young to live to Him in whose hands are " the keys of death and hell."

*Look forward to the judgment of the final day.* The book of remembrance will then be opened, and each will be judged according to what is written in that book. He that is ready for death, is ready for judgement, which will follow death.

Finally, let me entreat young and old ;—and let the impression sink deep into my own heart ;—to " give all dilligence that we may be found of Him in peace, without spot and blameless." And to Him be praise and glory for ever and ever, *amen and amen!*

## GENUINE RELIGION ILLUSTRATED.

**2 Thessalonians i. 11, I2.**—Wherefore also we pray always for you, that our God would count you worthy of this calling, and fulfil all the good pleasure of his goodness, and the work of faith with power: that the name of our Lord Jesus Christ may be glorified in you, and ye in him, according to the grace of our God and the Lord Jesus Christ. (Sk.)

THE passions are the chief springs of that activity which every where appears. Of these, hope and fear, as they awaken desire, or produce concern, and in either case create uneasiness, are among the principal causes which determine our various pursuits. But no subjects appear so calculated to excite those passions, as the joyful or awful prospects the gospel opens to our view. Do worldly enjoyments charm us? How much more inviting, "an inheritance incorruptible," &c; angelic company, "fulness of joy, and pleasures for evermore." Do earthly things alarm us? The day approaches when we shall see "A God in grandeur, and a world on fire." "For the Lord Jesus shall be revealed," &c, ver. 7—10. In reference to this revelation, and its important issues, the apostle says, "Wherefore also we pray," &c, in which he seems to direct our attention to pure religion, in its nature,—source,—producing and sustaining principle,—end,—and measure.

I. RELIGION IN ITS NATURE ;—a *worthiness.* "That our God would count you *worthy of this calling,*"—of the glorification mentioned, ver. 10. While we should carefully guard against self righteousness, we should be equally watchful against an opposite error, which, under the guise of humility, would lead us to abolish some of the most essential distinctions between the sinner and the saint; and should testify with the apostles, 2 Cor. v. 14—17; Eph. ii. 1. 10; 1 Thess. ii. 11, 12; 1 John iii. 9. Agreeably to these declarations is the character in ver. 10. *"His saints"* in whom he shall be glorified. This expresses,

1. *Their previous worthiness of condition.* They are in this life *sanctified ones :* that is, set apart from *common* uses, from worldliness as well as wickedness, to *sacred* service, 1 Peter ii. 9 ; Heb. xiii. 15; Rom. xii. 1 ; 1 Cor. x. 31. Nay they are children, heirs of God, &c, Gal. iv. 4—7. And having been thus honorably related, and so consistently employed, they are counted worthy to be approved and exalted, Matthew xxv. 23, 34—36, 40. And it expresses,

2. *Their previous worthiness of disposition;* their aptitude or meetness for glory. The word saint, (from *sanctus,*) means chaste, divine, heavenly, as well as sacred. Such the qualities of genuine christianity. 'Tis the circumcision *of the heart,* Rom. ii. 29; a transformation by the *renewing of the mind,* Rom. xii. 2 ; Eph. iv. 23 ; a participation of *the divine nature,* 2 Pet. i. 4. In *itself* pure and peaceable, James iii, 17 ; in *its operations* godly and benevolent, Phil. iii. 3 ; James i. 27. Contrast this with the *vileness* of sin, and with the inherent *worthlessness* of forms, creeds, &c.

II. RELIGION IN ITS SOURCE ; *the goodness of God ;* his free, spontaneous favour. "That he would fulfil *all the good pleasure of his goodness."*

1. Here is an intimation that all their present religious views and feelings were the effects of divine grace. Hence the apostle prays, that God would count, or make, them worthy (Whitby, Doddridge, and A. Clarke,) of his kingdom, ver. 5, by *fulfilling* what he had begun.

2. That all is of grace will appear, if we contemplate man, as existing only in *the intention of his Maker,* or as really existing in his *state of in-*

*nocence.* Neither innocent man, nor innocent angel can have any *rightful claim*, on even a continuance of being. But,

3. Still less, if possible, has *fallen, sinful* man any good thing as matter of right. 'Tis of mercy that we are not in hell: Yet,

4. 'Tis " our Father's good pleasure" that we should *get religion*, Prov. iv. 7; Isa. lv. 1—3; Matt. vii. 7—11 ;—that we should *keep religion*, 1 Thess. v. 21; 1 Tim. i. 19; Rev. ii. 25, iii. 11 ;—that we should *improve in religion*, 2 Pet. i. 5—8, iii. 18;—and that we should *continue to improve*, 2 Cor. iv. 18; Eph. iii. 18, 19. Thus is fulfilled, or completed his 'pleasure,"which is " good,"—in its *author, operation, end,* 2 Cor. iv. 17. This doctrine hides pride from man. " Salvation is of the Lord."

III. RELIGION IN ITS PRINCIPLE ;—*faith.* " The work *of faith* with power." By faith here, we may understand the grace of faith, Heb. xi. 1; exercised on the word of faith, Gal. i. 23. This is,

1. *The producing principle* of religious affections and practice, Heb. xi. 6. It is such credence given to God's declarations, as determines the judgment and heart; and leads the subject of it to fear what is threatened, Heb. xi. 7 ;—to do what is commanded, Heb. xi. 8. 17 ;—and to expect, seek, embrace, what is promised, Heb. xi. 13, 19 ; Eph. ii. 8.

2. *The sustaining principle* of religious affections, &c. It sustains under threats and sufferings, Heb. xi. 35—39. It sustains against the smiles and allurements of the world, Gen. xxxix. 9; Heb. xi. 24—26. It "worketh by *love*," Gal. v. 6; 1 John iv. 19;—by *peace* and *joy*, Rom. v: 1, 2 ;—by *patience, hope,* &c, Rom. v. 3—5. In short, it attaches the heart to Him who is the" author and finisher of faith ;" and at times wafts the soul to the upper regions, were jt breathes a purer air, dwells amidst brighter prospects, and hears the hallelujahs of the blessed: so that its return to earth is felt as a return to pilgrimage and banishment, which the same faith, nevertheless, enables it patiently to bear, Heb. x. 35—39.

IV. RELIGION IN ITS END ;—"That the name of our Lord Jesus Christ may be glorified in you and ye in (or by) him." The end is twofold:

1. *The glory of the Redeemer :*—" glorified *in you."* *At present:* his *love* appears glorious in his interesting himself about you ;—his *wisdom* in in instructing you ;—his *holiness* in making you saints :—his *power* in preserving and protecting you ;—his *faithfulness* in fulfilling all his engagements, &c. This also refers to *hereafter.* " when he shall come to be glorified in his saints," &c. verse 10. " He shall change our vile body, like unto his glorious body," &c. Phil. iii. 19, 20. The saints shall shine, *by reflecting* his radiance, and thus bring glory to his name.

2. *The glory of the redeemed :*—"and ye in him." This may apply to, 1. The glorified bodies they shall receive. 2. The glorious perfection of their minds ; freed from all ignorance, error, and moral taint. 3. The glorious distinction with which they shall be favoured, Col. iii. 4. And, 4. The glorious company and mansions to which they shall be raised, Heb. xii. 22, 23 ; Rev. iii. 21. And it should be remarked, that the glory which they have through him, and that whereby he is glorified in them is glory derived from him, or resulting to him *in his character of Redeemer,* as the representative of the triune Deity. This the redeemed feel and acknowledge ; hence their praises of both him that sitteth upon the throne and the Lamb, Rev. iv. 8—11, v. 11—14. This is certainly very much for us poor, sinful, wretched, dying worms to expect. But consider,

V. RELIGION IN ITS MEASURE OR RULE OF DISPENSATION ;—"according to the grace of our God, and the Lord Jesus Christ." This exactly and fully meets your case. For,

1. Are you *poor, insolvent, destitute of good?* It is "according to" the *freeness* of "the grace of God," &c. Luke vii, 42; Titus iii. 3—7.

2. Are you *guilty* and *vile?* It is "according to the" *riches* of "the grace," &c. Eph. i. 6, ii. 4—7. See "*the grace of our God,*" John iii. 16; "*the grace of the Lord Jesus Christ,*" 2 Cor. viii. 9; Eph. v. 2. Nothing farther could be given. God's thoughts are not as ours, &c. Rom. v. 6—12.

3. Are you *weak* and *ignorant?* It is "according to" the *tenderness,* the *sufficiency,* and *constancy* of "the grace," &c. Isa. xl. 11; 2 Cor. xii. 9; Heb iv. 15, 16.

4. Are you *still doubtful and distressed?* It is "according to" *the former operations* of the same rich "grace;" in the cases of David, Manasseh, Paul, and others, who "had *much* forgiven," and were greatly blessed.

*Careless sinner,*—how will you meet that awful revelation? verse 7—9.

*Formalists,*—remember that you have to do with him "who trieth the reins and the heart." Unless the heart be renewed, he will not "account you worthy" of his unsuffering spiritual kingdom.

*Penitents,*—press into the enjoyment of happy piety. Grace is given you, and "he giveth more grace."

*Believers,*—be thankful, and expect a farther and more powerful "work of faith;" till "*all the good pleasure*" of divine goodness be fulfilled in you. Jude 24, 25.

---

## THE FAITH AND HOPE OF JOB IN HIS REDEEMER.

Job xix. 25—27.—For I know that my Redeemer liveth, and that he shall stand at the latter day upon the earth: and though after my skin worms destroy this body, yet in my flesh shall I see God: whom I shall see for myself, and mine eyes shall behold, and not another; though my reins be consumed within me. (Sk.)

THIS celebrated text has been variously interpreted. While some, without any solid proof, have considered it as an interpolation, others have limited its meaning to the return of temporal felicity to Job; but if we carefully examine the preceding chapters, it will appear that he had no hope of deliverance from his calamitous circumstances, in the present world. Yet, while he was weighed down by a heavy load of afflictions, and misrepresented by his mistaken friends, he looked forward to the coming of his Redeemer; and had a comfortable assurance that he would avenge his wrongs, raise him from the dead, and bless him with the beatific vision. First, Job had a living Redeemer; secondly, he thought his afflictions would terminate in death; but, thirdly, he had a joyful hope of a happy resurrection from the dead.

1. JOB HAD A LIVING REDEEMER.

1. *The work of a redeemer is great and highly important.* First, *he pays a price* for the lost possession of his brother: "If thy brother be waxen poor, and hath sold away some of his possessions, and if any of his kin come to redeem it, then shall he redeem that which his brother sold," Lev. xxv. 25. Secondly, he saves and delivers him: "He saved them from the hand of him that hated them, and redeemed them from the hand of the ene-

my," Psa. c¡i. 10. Thirdly he vindicates and avenges his brother: "**The** revenger of blood himself shall slay the murderer," Num. xxxv. 19.

2. *Christ is the Redeemer of men.* He bought us with his blood. We " were not redeemed with corruptible things as silver and gold, but with the precious blood of Christ, as a Lamb without blemish and without spot," 1 Pet. i. 19. He saves and delivers his people from the guilt and power, and from the pollution and punishment of sin. He " gave himself for us, that he might redeem us from all iniquity, and purify unto himself a peculiar people, zealous of good works," Tit. ii. 14. And he will vindicate and avenge his church: in allusion to this he says, " The day of vengeance is in mine heart, and the year of my redeemed is come," Isa. lxiii. 4.

3. *The Son of God, our great Redeemer, was living in the days of Job;* and he had a saving interest in him, in the afflictions which he suffered, from the devil and from men. He says, " My Redeemer liveth." If our Lord had no existence prior to his incarnation, Job should have spoken in the future tense, saying, " I know that my Redeemer shall live ;" but he spake correctly, for his Redeemer was then living. He had glory with the Father " before the world was," John xvii. 5. He was rich in a prior state of existence, yet for our sakes " he became poor," 2 Cor. viii. 9. He was the only be gotten Son of the Father, John iii. 16.

4. *But how does it appear that the Redeemer of Job was the Son of God?* From these words, " he shall stand at the latter day upon the earth." This could not be affirmed of any *goel*, or kinsman of Job, who was then living; but the prediction, if applied to Jesus, is exceedingly appropriate. It was in *part* fulfilled when he appeared in our nature; for " when the fulness of time was come, God sent forth his Son, made of a woman, made under the law,," Gal. iv. 4. But it will be *completely* fulfilled when he arises in judgment; for the words may be rendered, " *he shall arise*" from his seat, and stand upon his feet, as a judge, to give sentence or to execute judgment. This was the posture in which judges always delivered their sentence; and hence we frequently read, in the Scriptures, of God arising to judgment, Job xxxi. 14; Psa. lxxiv. 22, lxxxii. 8.

5. *Job knew his divine Redeemer.* But how did he attain that knowledge? It might be by tradition. God had promised a Saviour and deliverer, and that promise was handed down from one generation to another. Besides, the promise which was given to Abraham, " In thy seed shall all the nations of the earth be blessed," was probably well known to Job; but it is most probable he knew his Redeemer by immediate revelation. God might make a discovery of this great truth to him,—first, to support him in his unparal leled affliction ; and, secondly, to comfort and encourage the church in after ages

II. Pious Job thought his affliction would terminate in death.

1. *When he spake the words of the text, his skin was destroyed.* He fell into the hands of Satan by the permission of the Lord: and he smote him with sore boils, from the sole of his foot unto his crown, chap. ii. 6, 7. These were fiery eruptions, or ulcerous eating sores, which destroyed the skin. "And he took him a potsherd to scrape himself withal." For *scrape*, says a learned author, the Chaldee and Arabic use a word commonly applied to pulling leaves and bark off from the tree. How deplorable was the state of Job, when scraping himself with potsherds! Well might he say, " Have pity upon me, have pity upon me, oh ye my friends !" verse 21.

2. *After his skin, he expected his whole body to be destroyed.* The word *worms* is not in the original, but is supplied by the translators; they

266

**seem** to have conjectured that his skin was destroyed by worms, and that they would proceed to destroy the body. How far this opinion is correct, we know not; but Job certainly had an idea, that the destruction of the whole body would speedily follow the destruction of the skin. The word *body* is also supplied, and properly, because that was certainly intended.

3. *Death and the grave, with their solemn attendants, closes every earthly prospect of that deeply afflicted, but eminently holy man.* He afterwards said, " I know thou wilt bring me to death, and to the house appointed for all living," Job xxx. 23. And we also must die; but when we know not. These bodies, however beautiful and strong, will perish in the grave. " The righteous perisheth, and no man layeth it to heart," Isa. lvii. 1. But, like Job, he hopes to rise again.

III. JOB HAD A JOYFUL HOPE OF A RESURRECTION FROM THE DEAD.

1. He positively affirms, that, after the destruction of his body, he *should see God in his flesh.* But how can that be the case, either with him or others, if the dead rise not. Man was created with a body, and will live in an embodied state, to all eternity ; but that cannot be without a resurrection; because his earthly and material frame returns to dust, as a sad punishment of his apostacy from God, Gen. iii. 19. How God will raise the dead is unknown; but the fact is certain. It was revealed to Job, and has been indubitably proved by the resurrection of Jesus. With these eyes of flesh we shall see God our Saviour. What a happy sight! Then the sorrows of life will be past, death will be destroyed, and a blessed eternity will follow !

2. I shall see for *myself,* he says, " and mine eyes shall behold, and not another." Good men wish well to all ; but they claim the blessings of grace and glory as their own. Others, no doubt, will see and enjoy the Redeemer ; but I shall see and enjoy him for myself. He will appear in my cause ; he will deliver me from death and the grave ; he will vindicate my character ; and he will avenge me of my foes. And all this will take place, though my reins, or vitals, are consumed within me ; for all things are possible with God ; and he who made the world can raise the dead.

### INFERENCES.

1. Jesus has been the hope of pious men in all ages. Abraham rejoiced to see his day, "and he saw it and was glad," John viii. 56. Moses and all the prophets foretold his coming ; and gave witness, " that through his name whosoever believeth in him shall receive remission of sins," Acts x. 43.

2. He is our only Redeemer and Saviour. We are lost, but he came to seek and to save us; we have enemies, but he has conquered them ; we are dead, but we may live by him for ever.

3. It is both our duty and our privilege to renounce our own righteousness; to trust in him only ; to love and honor him ; and to follow him in the regeneration, through evil report and good report. Amen.

## THE POOR MAN'S ACCOUNT OF HIMSELF.

**Ps. xxxiv. 6.**—This poor man cried, and the Lord heard him and saved him out of all his troubles. (Sk.)

THERE is an important reality in religion, which is enjoyed by all true believers. They do not follow cunningly devised fables, but receive the truth as it is in Jesus. They are enlightened, quickened, pardoned, adopted, and "renewed in righteousness and true holiness." And having obtained mercy of the Lord, they highly extol the riches of his grace. They become zealous in his cause, and greatly rejoice in the prosperity of Zion. They recommend religion to all around them, and earnestly desire the universal extension of its influence. And hence David, as a subject of saving grace, breathes in this psalm a spirit of " burning charity" and fervent zeal. In the preceding context he invites all men to unite with him to magnify and praise the Lord for all his benefits ; and in the text he encourages them, by the consideration of his own successful application to the throne of grace :—" This poor man cried," &c. These words describe—a humble character—a gracious privilege—and a happy deliverance.

I. A HUMBLE CHARACTER;—" This *poor man.*" It is highly probable that David here speaks of himself. Notwithstanding the dignity of his station as *a king*, he was deeply humble before God as a *saint*. Though he was not *temporally poor* as a man, he was *spiritually poor* and destitute as a sinner; and *consciously poor* and dependant as a believer. This language was therefore, a faithful description of his humble state and experience, as the man after God's own heart. It is also uniformly applicable to two distinct characters of mankind, and may be justly adopted,

1. *By the contrite penitent.* Such are thoroughly convinced of their depravity and sinfulness; and that naturally in them "dwelleth no good thing." They are entirely destitute of all the spiritual riches of knowledge, purity, and happiness; and are ignorant, guilty, polluted, and miserable, Rev. iii. 17. They are " without Christ, having no hope, and without God in the world." What an awful state of poverty and wretchedness is this! And yet such is the deplorable condition of all mankind by nature!—And those who truly feel their sinful and perishing state, readily acknowledge their total destitution of spiritual good; and their utter insufficiency to please God, or save themselves. And hence the true penitent frequently exclaims, " Wo is me! for I am undone—God be merciful to me a sinner—Lord, save. or I perish," Ps. li. 17 ; Isa. lxvi. 2.

2. *By the humble believer.* Though such characters are partakers of the ' unsearchable riches of Christ," they are still needy and dependant. They have many wants to be supplied,—many evils to be removed,—many enemies to overcome,—many difficulties to encounter,—many blessings to secure,—many dangers to escape,—many duties to perform ;—and without Christ they can do nothing. Hence they deeply feel their helplessness and dependance on God, and have no confidence in the flesh. They are grateful for what they already enjoy ; but their present attainments are very deficient. They have not already attained, neither are already perfect. Though they are " poor and needy, yet the Lord thinketh upon them for good." They are poor in spirit, but rich in faith, and heirs of heaven. The text also specifies.

II. A GRACIOUS PRIVILEGE ;—" This poor man *cried,* and the Lord *heard him.*" David was a man of eminent devotion. In all his afflictions and

**trials,** he had recourse to God, and gave himself unto prayer. Nor did he pray in vain. In the case before us he mentions,

1. *The object of his worship;*—"The *Lord*." He was no profane idolater, but a devout worshipper of the God of Israel. He had *correct views of his character*, as the only object of religious adoration, and the Giver of every good and perfect gift, Ps. xviii. 1—3. He was *acquainted with his will;* and hence he knew that it was both his duty and interest to wait upon him, and worship him in the beauty of holiness, Ps. xcv. 6, 7. He also *trusted in his name*, and expected salvation from him, Ps. lxii. 1, 2. He therefore carefully cultivated a spirit of prayer, and lived in holy fellowship with the covenant God of his fathers.

2. *The nature of his devotion;*—He "*cried* to the Lord." This intimates *earnestness*. He did not merely ask, nor seek; but he *cried* and *agonized*, like a person deeply distressed, or earnestly engaged in an important pursuit, Gen. xxxii, 24—26.—It includes *confidence*. He believed that God both *could* and *would* help and deliver him. He had frequently found it good to draw near unto him, and was therefore encouraged to trust in him for every blessing, Ps. cxxxiii. 1, 2.—It also implies *perseverance*. His crying to the Lord was not a *single* or *occasional* act of devotion; but his *regular* and *daily* practice, Ps. cxix. 164. He felt the constant necessity of divine succor and protection, which induced him fervently, faithfully, and diligently, to cry unto the Lord for mercy, and grace to help in time of need.

3. *The success of his prayer;*—"And the Lord *heard* him.' He is never inattentive to the cries and tears of his people, Isa. lix. 1.—"His eyes are over the righteous, and his ears are open unto their prayers."—He sees all their desires,—understands their "groanings which cannot be uttered,"—and hears all their supplications and thanksgivings both in public and in private, Ps. xl. 1.—He *accepts* their prayers. They approach him in the way of his own appointment, and worship him in spirit and in truth, Prov. xv. 8.—He *answers* their prayers. This was the case with the Psalmist; he "cried to the Lord," and he saved him in the day of trouble. The answers of faithful prayer are always *certain, seasonable,* and *compassionate;* for "like as a father pitieth his children, so the Lord pitieth them that fear him," Psa. xci. 15, 16; Matt. vii. 11; 1 John v. 14, 15.—The text records,

III. A HAPPY DELIVERANCE;—"The Lord *saved him* out of all his troubles."—Whether David here refers to some particular season of calamity or not, is uncertain; but his declaration is highly consolatory, and suggests the following instructions for the encouragement of the saints.

1. *They are frequently subjects of troubles.* This requires no argument to prove it: the Scriptures assure us, that this has always been the case; and experience sufficiently corroborates the fact. Yea, "many are the afflictions of the righteous," in this vale of tears.—They are subject to the common trials of human life, and are often chastised by the Lord for their profit in holiness, Heb. xii. 6—11.—They are frequently exercised with personal, domestic, spiritual, and temporal troubles; all of which are designed to "work together for their good."

2. *They are supported under their troubles.* They are not left to bear them alone; the Lord is with them, and into his hands they commit the keeping of their souls. They approach him with confidence, and find him to be their "refuge and strength, a very present help in trouble," Isa. xliii. 2; and lxiii. 9.—In their most trying seasons, his grace is sufficient for them, and will encourage them to possess their souls in patience. Hence

they feel fully resigned to the will of God, trusting in his wisdom and goodness, and "cast all their care upon him, for he careth for them."

3. *They shall be delivered from their troubles.* Thus the Psalmist and all the primitive saints, were saved from their sins and enemies, and out of all their troubles and afflictions. And God still delivers his people from many of their troubles while here, which they gratefully acknowledge with David in the text, Ps. ciii. 1—4. But whilst they are in a world of tribulation, their deliverance is not complete. "There remaineth therefore a rest to the people of God;" where they shall be perfectly safe from all their troubles, both of body and mind, and "God shall wipe away all tears from their eyes," Isa. xxxv. 10.

This subject suggests,

1. The awful state of the prayerless, Job xxi. 15.—Arise and call upon God, that you perish not.

2. The manner in which we should come unto God.—It must be humble, fervent, and incessant. And,

3. The consolation and encouragement of the righteous. "Lift up your heads, for your redemption draweth nigh."

---

## THE FATHER HONORS THE SERVANTS OF HIS SON.

John xii. 26.—If any man serve me, him will my Father honor. (Sk.)

EARTHLY monarchs are the fountains of temporal honors; but God is the fountain of eternal honors. The God and Father of our Lord Jesus Christ honors all who serve his beloved Son; and the honor which he confers, is as much above what the world can give, as the heavens are above the earth. Nor is this all; for while the honors which men receive of one another, are lost in death, those which God bestows, run on for ever. The servants of Jesus are now despised, as insignificant and worthless persons; but ere long they will shine as the brightness of the firmament Dan. xii. 3.

I. MAKE A FEW OBSERVATIONS ON THE SERVICE OF CHRIST.

1. *Jesus has high claims on our services.* He created us : for "all things were made by him; and without him was not any thing made that was made," John i. 3. And is it not right that our Creator should govern us? Surely the creature is bound to obey the Author of his being! But he has claims on our services as our Redeemer; "For ye are bought with a price : therefore glorify God in your body, and in your spirit, which are God's;" 1 Cor. v. 20. It will not be denied, by any man of reflection, that we should serve him, who has bought us with his precious blood. 1 Pet. i. 18, 19.

2. *He is our only Master;* "One is your Master, even Christ," Matt. xxiii. 8. Now, as a master has a right to command, and as servants are bound to obey, those who refuse obedience to Jesus, cannot, consistently, call him Master. The church is a house or family, and Christ is the governor of the house. The family is placed under his guidance and government, and every one should do what he commands. If his authority be denied, and if his commands be disobeyed, the whole family will fall into disorder; and when a house is divided against itself, it cannot tand, Matt. xii. 25.

**3.** *Our Lord is a good Master.* His work is pleasant in itself, and easy to his servants. He says, "My yoke is easy, and my burden is light," Matt. x. 30. He affords plentiful support to his servants, so that they never hunger, nor do they ever thirst, John vi. 35. And he will give great rewards, Rev. xxii. 14. These are things which are most agreeable to servants. Hence, when we voluntarily enter into service, we inquire after the character of the master; the nature of his employments; the support which he affords; and the rewards which he offers. We are aware that every blessing bestowed by our Master is the effect of grace; but it is as much our own as if we had merited it, and yet we humbly own that we are but unprofitable servants, Luke xvii. 10.

**4.** *The servants of Christ should obey him in all things.* His work is various: but whatever he commands is absolutely necessary. One serves him in the ministry of the word, and is ready, at his command, to go into all the world to preach the everlasting gospel, Mark xvi. 15. Another is employed in defending his cause by sound argument, being set for the defence of the gospel, Phil. i. 17. And all are required to practice those evangelical duties which relate to themselves, to men in general, and to God in particular; or, as the apostle Paul says, to "live soberly, righteously, and godly, in this present world," Titus ii. 12. Thus all are *employed;* all are *well* employed; and all are *constantly* employed.

**5.** *We should serve Christ in a right way.* Faithfulness is expected in a servant: and we should be faithful in all things, 1 Cor. iv. 2. Cheerfulness is necessary; a gloomy temper shows dissatisfaction, and is a reflection on our Master. Constancy and perseverance are necessary; for "he that endureth to the end shall be saved," Matt. x. 22. What we do, should be done with a single eye; "The light of the body is the eye: if therefore thine eye be single, thy whole body shall be full of light," Matt. vi. 22.

**6.** *We should be ever ready to obey the Son of God.* Paul, the apostle, required Timothy to be "*instant in season, and out of season.*" 2 Tim. iv. 2. The ear should be constantly open to hear the commands of Christ; and the heart should be constantly disposed to obey him. whether it be convenient or inconvenient to ourselves. When eastern despots command their slaves, it is a common reply, "To hear is to obey." And shall not we be always ready to obey our Lord, the moment we hear his voice.

II. CONSIDER THE HONORS WHICH THE FATHER CONFERS ON THE SERVANTS OF HIS SON.

**1.** *The service of Christ will not procure the honors of the world;—* "If ye were of the world, the world would love his own; but because ye are not of the world, but I have chosen you out of the world, therefore the world hateth you," John xv. 19. Learning, conquest, and wealth, are honored by men of the world; but holy obedience to Jesus Christ, is despised and contemned by men in general. But the servants of Jesus sit loose to human honors; they desire the good opinion of the wise and holy, but the good opinion of others is no credit to any man.

**2.** *If any man serve Christ he is honored with the friendship of God.* He has fellowship with the Father and with the Son, 1 John i. 3. Abraham was called the friend of God; and "they which be of faith are blessed with faithful Abraham," James ii. 23: Gal. iii. 9. "The Lord spake to Moses face to face, as a man speaketh to his friend;" and he is a friend to the truly pious, who sticketh closer than a brother, Exodus xxxiii. 11; Prov. xviii. 24. The friendship of great men is deemed an honor; but what is that when compared with the friendship of God?

3. *Every servant of Christ is honored with the special presence of God.* "If a man love me, he will keep my words: and my Father will love him, and we will come unto him, and make our abode with him," John xiv. 23. God dwells with the servants of Jesus, to direct their path in life; to defend them in the hour of danger; and to comfort them in the hour of affliction. His presence is a high honor, of which no man is worthy; but true believers enjoy it as their privilege, through the merit of Christ. God is at their right hand, and therefore they cannot be moved, Ps. xvi. 8. And he is with them in the waters and fires of affliction, Isa. xliii. 2.

4. *The servant of Christ is honored with a new nature.* All the tempers and dispositions of the soul, which are accounted great and good, are planted in his heart. He is generous to all who are in want; brave in the Christian warfare; pure in all his motives and ends; faithful to God and man; and upright in all his dealings. He is a dear child of God, and as far as grace enables him, he is a follower of God, Eph. v. 1. And is there any honor equal to this?

5. *Lofty titles are conferred on the servants of Christ.* They are called *elect*, or chosen; and are *precious*, or valuable, 1 Pet. ii. 6. They are called *sons* of God, 1 John iii. 2. They are the *bride* of Christ, Rev. xxi. 9. All their titles are expressions of real worth; and not like the flattering titles which are given to men, Job xxxii. 21. They are men of God; "a chosen generation, a royal priesthood, a holy nation, and a peculiar people," 1 Pet. ii. 9.

6. *The servant of Christ will be honored by the Father in the hour of death.* In death, the honors of the world come to an end; but in that awful hour the good man is highly honored. God is with him; holy angels minister unto him; he is about to be advanced to high preferment; and he is holy and happy. He can say, "My flesh and my heart faileth, but God is the strength of my heart and my portion for ever," Psa. lxxiii. 26.

7. *Honor will be put upon the servants of Christ in the end of the world.* They will rise to glory, 1 Cor. xv. 43. They will stand approved in the day of judgment, 1 John iv. 17. They will be openly invited to inherit the kingdom of God, Matt. xxv. 34. They will be assessors with Christ in the judgment, 1 Cor. vi. 2. Yea, they will judge angels, ver. 3.

8. *And eternal honors will be conferred on them in the kingdom of God.* When time is swallowed up in the ocean of eternity, they will wear the crown of life, James i. 12. They will be honored with the presence of God and the Lamb; with the society of angels and saints; with great personal glory; with high employments; with exalted seats; and with immortality, Rev. xxi. 3. 4.

### INFERENCES.

1. Christian honors infinitely surpass the honors of the world. They are real, substantial, great, and durable; but those of the world are imaginary, empty, trifling, and momentary.

2. Human honors are frequently obtained by war, bribes, flattery, wealth and power; but divine honors are obtained by repentance, faith, holiness, and the grace of God in Christ Jesus.

3. Proud men will be humbled; their greatness will perish with the world. Therefore, "Let not thine heart envy sinners: but be thou in the fear of the Lord all the day long," Prov. xxiii. 17.

4. We should set a great value on divine honors; and if human honors fall to our lot, we should be humble. And while we are honored, either by providence or grace, let us give the glory to God, 1 Tim. i. 17

## THE PIOUS SUFFERER EXHORTED TO GLORIFY GOD.

**1 Pet.** iv. 16.—Yet if any man suffer as a Christian, let him not be ashamed; but let him glorify God on this behalf. (Sk.)

IN the latter part of the first age, the rage of Jews and Gentiles was exceedingly stimulated by the prevalence of the gospel; the apostles, therefore, considered themselves as especially called to comfort and encourage their suffering brethren. With this view, Peter reminded the disciples of Christ of the obligations they were under to suffer for their religion, and suggested a variety of motives to persuade them to do it cheerfully. See context; also chap. iii. 14—18. We are not in similar circumstances with the first christians; hence, the danger of our religion being superficial; yet, if any man's piety and decision of character subject him to suffering, "let him not be ashamed." We may therefore state,

I. WHAT IS IMPLIED IN SUFFERING AS A CHRISTIAN.

II. WHY CHARACTERS WHO THUS SUFFER SHOULD NOT BE ASHAMED.

III. THEIR DUTY UNDER SUFFERING CIRCUMSTANCES.

1. WHAT IS IMPLIED, &c. The term christian, was given to the disciples of Christ first at Antioch, and is used in three places only in the New Testament, viz. here; in Acts xi. 26; and xxvi. 28. It imports nothing less than an experimental and practical believer in the Lord Jesus Christ. To suffer as a christian, is,

1. *To suffer in the character of a christian.* Where piety has its seat n the heart, it will appear in the life; hence believers are the salt of the earth, to spread a salutary influence; and save the world from moral putrefaction:—the light of the world; as such they are to shine brighter and brighter to the perfect day;—a city set on a hill, to be seen and identified by all, Matt. v. 13—16. It was never the design of the Head of the church that any of its members should seclude themselves from society, John xvii. 15. It is the duty of all who believe in Christ to confess him before men, Matt. x. 32, 33; and to conceal our religion is a tacit denial of Christ, and opposed to the doctrine of our text.

2. *To suffer for discharging the duties of a christian.* Christianity frees its possessors from the slavery of custom; they are governed by the high principles of religion. In the service of God, like Joshua, xxiv. 15, and Daniel vi. 10, they are undaunted. Whatever is the opinion of the world, the work of God is to them of paramount importance. In domestic life, they are faithful, conscientious, and obliging; as religious characters, they are fixed in their views, and bold in their profession; in the civil world, they are true and just in all their doings, embodying principle and conscience in each action; while, as subjects of the realm, they are peaceable and quiet. If, therefore, such a conduct subject them to suffering, "let them not be ashamed."

3. *To suffer in the spirit of a christian.* If human enemies rise against you, think it not strange, but "in patience possess ye your souls," Luke xxi. 19. Should their unkindness and sin lead to an unjust impeachment of your character, the injury of your person or circumstances, suffer not the spirit of revenge to betray you into sin "Recompense no man evil for evil," Rom. xii. 17; but, if it be possible, "live peaceably with all men," ver. 18; and "if thine enemy hunger, feed him," ver. 20, 21. Like your Lord, be ready to forgive, and show that you have added to your courage, patience, &c. 2 Pet. i. 5—7. Let not persecu

273

tion either in its mild or terrific forms, intimidate you; remember him, "who, when he was reviled, reviled not again." &c. 1 Pet. ii. 23; take also for your example the apostles of our Lord, who would say, "Being reviled, we bless," &c. 1 Cor. xii. 13. Let that mind be in you which was also in Christ Jesus, Phil. ii. 5. Let us therefore consider,

II. WHY CHARACTERS WHO THUS SUFFER SHOULD NOT BE ASHAMED.

1. *Because they suffer innocently.* "If any man suffer as a murderer, or as a thief, or as an evil doer, or as a busy body in other men's matters," he has cause to be ashamed; but if innocent, his record is with God, and he partakes of that satisfaction which is the good man's inheritance, Prov. xiv. 14. Let the craft and subtlety of the devil and man be directed against you, the shield of innocence will repel every dart. "Blessed are ye when men shall revile you, and persecute you, and shall say all manner of evil against you falsely for my sake," &c. Matthew v. 10—12.

2. *They suffer in a good cause.* Not like the man whom justice has arrested for dishonesty—the law condemned for perjury, or sentenced to death for murder; theirs is the cause of truth, justice, mercy, benevolence, and piety. Their business is to get good, and do good—to injure no one by word or deed; and while their motto is "Holiness to the Lord," and in all things seek to glorify him who has bought them with his blood, they should not be ashamed.

3. *They suffer from the purest motive.* Their conscientious exactness is not the result of fostered peculiarity, or with a view to be singular. God is their witness, that with sincerity and simplicity they wish to walk before him. His will is their law—his glory their end; and they esteem the approbation of God more than any thing this world can afford.

4. *They suffer for a blessed Master.* He is a high Priest who is touched with a feeling of their infirmities, Heb. iv. 15; and what they suffer for him, though painful, will conduce to their good, Rom. viii. 28; 2 Cor. iv. 16—18. "Think it not strange concerning the fiery trial which is to try you," &c. ver. 12, 13; "for unto you it is given, in the behalf of Christ, not only to believe on him, but also to suffer for his sake," Phil. i. 29; "and if we suffer, we shall also reign with him," 2 Tim. ii. 12.

4. *They suffer in imitation of the brightest examples.* Look at the catalogue of patriarchs, kings, priests, and prophets, Heb. xi. whose intrepidity, faith, patience, and purity, they follow. They have a noble army of martyrs before their eyes; and as their great example, a suffering Saviour, Heb. xii. 1—3. Let us therefore consider,

III. THEIR DUTY UNDER SUFFERING CIRCUMSTANCES; viz. to "glorify God on this behalf." We are not, however, to suppose that man can add any thing to the essential glory of God; but they are to glorify God by,

1. *Devoutly acknowledging Him and his gifts,* 1 Chronicles xxix. 11, 12; confessing him "worthy to receive honor, glory, might, and majesty,' Rev. iv. 11. The very circumstance of their suffering should prompt them to this.

2. *By firmness in the day of trial.* Let them consider Him who endured the contradiction of sinners against himself, and not be discouraged; let nothing shake their firmness, 1 Cor. xv. 58; but imitate the example of the disciples, who continued with their Lord in his temptations, Luke xxii. 28, 29. When the service of God demands their attention, let not secondary considerations discourage them. He who, for fear of persecution, or for the sake of his temporal interest, abandons religion, shall lose his soul; and he who, in the time of persecution, abjures the religion of

**Christ,** is not only in danger of losing his soul, but his life, Matt. **x. 39;** " He that findeth his life, shall lose it." That was literally fulfilled **in** Archbishop Cranmer, who, for confessing Christ against the devil and **the** pope, was ordered to be burnt: to save his life, he recanted, and was, notwithstanding, burnt. In the service of God we must persevere, fearless of consequences. Honor God, and God will honor you, 1 Sam. ii. 30.

3. *By a faithful and patient endurance of suffering.* Should conflicts increase, friends forsake, and enemies combine against you, "rejoice inasmuch as ye are partakers of Christ's sufferings,"&c. ver. 13. Think it not strange if an ungodly world should hate you, John xv. 18. " All that will live godly in Christ Jesus, shall suffer persecution," 2 Tim. iii. 12; therefore, "in your patience, possess your souls," Luke xxi. 19. "Let patience have her perfect work," James i. 4: and glorify God in the exercise of that grace which his own hand has planted, and which his providence has suffered to be exercised.

To this act of glorifying God, they are encouraged from

1. *The declarations and promises he has made.* These are many, great, and various, Isaiah xli. 10, xliii. 1, 2, liv. 17; Matt. x. 32; James i. 12; Rev. ii. 10, xxii. 7.

2. *The honor it will confer upon them.* Let the warrior wave his bloodstained laurel, boast of the immensity of his possessions, purchased by the gore of his fellow men, and spread his fame from pole to pole ;—a nobler award awaits *them ;* their names shall continue when the annals of history are destroyed—their inheritance will not fade away—their memorial will endure for ever, 1 Pet. i. 3—5 ; Ps. cxii. 6.

### IMPROVEMENT.

1. *Let us examine our experience by this test.* Do I believe in, **and** love the Lord Jesus Christ? Am I modestly, yet boldly, confessing him before the world? Can I patiently and cheerfully suffer for his sake?

2. *Let us encourage ourselves in the Lord.* In such a cause, for such a Master, with such promises, and in the strength of grace, let us pursue our course. Victory, rest, and glory, are before us.

3. *Let us pray for our persecutors.* Their state is awful—it is danger-ous. May the Lord our God grant them repentance unto life.

---

### WALKING IN TRUTH.

3 John 4.—I have no greater joy than to hear that my children walk in truth. (Sk.)

MINISTERS of our Lord Jesus Christ are appointed to watch over the souls of men ; and the great day is fast approaching, when they must give an account of the charge committed to their care, Heb. xiii. 7. The apostles of our Lord excelled in the discharge of this duty; and those who are called to the same work, should copy after their example; then, being influenced by the apostolic spirit, they will rejoice *greatly*, like the beloved John, when their children enjoy spiritual health, and walk in truth. The joys of the apostle, both as a Christian and a minister, were many and great; but he asserts, in our text, that he had no greater joy than to hear that his children walked in truth.

I. THE CHILDREN OF THE APOSTLE JOHN WALKED IN TRUTH. **His children** were real Christians, both in heart and life; and all such walk in truth. But, as Pilate said to Jesus, "What is truth?"

1. *Truth refers to our thoughts, words, and actions.* Our thoughts are true, when we think of things as they are; our words are true, when we speak as we think; and our actions are true, when they are conformable to the Holy Scriptures; for then we "obey the truth," Rom. ii. 8. That we may *think* correctly, let us examine things carefully, 1 Thess. v. 21; that we may *speak* exactly, let us keep the door of our lips, Ps. cxli. 3: and that we may *act* the truth, let us live as in the immediate presence of the Lord, Ps. xvi. 8.

2. *The word of God, including both the Old Testament and the New, is a revelation of the truth.* That blessed book is the only infallible rule of faith and practice: but the word *truth*, in our text, may particularly refer to the gospel of God our Saviour, which, as a system of truth, is the perfection of all previous revelations, Gal. iii. 1. "The New Testament," says Locke, "has God for its author; salvation for its end; and truth, without any mixture of error, for its matter."

3. *Jesus Christ, our Divine Teacher, is called the Truth.* In his humble birth, holy life, painful death, blessed resurrection, and glorious ascension, all the promises, prophecies, and types of the Old Testament, relating to the Messiah, were *fully verified;* and while he dwelt on earth, he taught the truth of God in all its beauty and fulness. We read Socrates, Plato, Seneca, Cicero, and other eminently learned men, with caution, because there is a mixture of truth and error in all their works; but when we read the discourses of our adorable Saviour, we feel confidence and assurance, because he knew all things, and taught the way of God in truth, Matt. xxii. 16.

4. *To walk in truth, implies a strict conformity to its sacred dictates, in our experience, and in all our works and ways.* Here it may be observed, that God has not revealed truth merely to amuse us, or to satisfy our curiosity, but with a view to practical purposes; that it is one thing to believe and profess truth, and another to walk in it, Rom. i. 18; that faith and practice, so often *separated*, should be constantly *united;* and, finally, that he walks in truth, in every point of view, who has an enlightened understanding, a renewed heart, an edifying conversation, and a holy conduct, Isa. ii. 5; Ps. ci. 2; Eph. iv. 29; Rom. vi. 4.

5. *Those who walk in truth should be careful to hold it fast.* Solomon says, "Buy the truth, and sell it not," Prov. xxiii. 23. Rather part with wealth, fame, and even life, than truth. Be valiant for it, Jer. ix. 3; let your loins be girt with truth, Eph. vi. 14; be established in the truth, 2 Pet. i. 12; do nothing against the truth, 2 Cor. xiii. 8. That you may hold it fast, carefully recollect that it makes you *free*, John viii. 32; and that you are sanctified and purified through the truth, John xvii. 17; 1 Pet. i. 22.

6. *We should examine ourselves daily, whether we be in the truth, and how it affects our life and conversation..* Our knowledge is limited, and ever will be so: but are our views, as far as they extend, agreeable to truth; Is our experience in unison with the revealed truth of the written word? Are we advancing in sound and true experience? Is our conduct, in all things, consistent with truth? These inquiries, by the blessing of God, will promote our *love* of truth, and lead us to *honor* and obey it in all its requirements.

II. JOHN HAD NO GREATER JOY THAN TO HEAR OF HIS CHILDREN WALKING IN TRUTH.

1 *Joy implies gladness and exultation either in the possession or prospect of something which we deem good and excellent.* It is a lovely passion in a pious person; it exhilarates the spirits, even in afflictive and trying circumstances, 1 Cor. vi. 10; and produces a flowing tide of the most pleasurable feelings. No matter what our external circumstances may be; for, if we have religious joy in our hearts, we are substantially happy, and like Paul and Silas, can praise God at midnight, in a prison, though loaded with chains, Acts xvi. 25.

2. *Men of the world, who mind only earthly things, feel joy and gladness in the things of time and sense.* They are joyful and glad when their corn and their wine are increased, Ps. iv. 7; they joy in their own labor, and in their carnal pleasures, Eccl. ii. 10; they joy even in their vile hypocrisy and artful deceptions, Job xx. 5; yea, "folly is joy to him that is destitute of wisdom," Prov. xv. 21. But this joy, like the crackling of thorns under a pot, is but a sudden blaze, which is soon extinguished, Eccles. vii. 6. The *unsanctified* joy of Hamon was of short duration; and that which made his heart glad, led him to a gallows, Esther v. 9; vii. 10.

3. *But pious men joy in spiritual and eternal blessings,* more than in *the good things of this life, which are passing away.* The blessed operations of the Holy Ghost in their hearts are abundant sources of pure joy, Rom. xiv. 17; they joy in the God of their salvation, Heb. iii. 18; they receive the word with joy, 1 Thess. i. 6; they count it all joy when they fall into divers temptations or trials, James i. 2, and their joy is unspeakable and full of glory, 1 Pet. i. 8. It is similar to the joys of the blessed in heaven, and a sweet anticipation of eternal bliss; it is intended to comfort and cheer the hearts of the pious in this world of sin and sorrow; and, being furnished with matter of joy in every state, they are commanded to rejoice evermore, and in every thing to give thanks, 1 Thess. v. 16.

4. *Ministers of the gospel joy in the followers of Jesus, and especially in those whom they have been instrumental in turning to the Lord.* The apostle Paul expresses his *feelings* on this subject in the following words; "Ye are our joy and glory," 1 Thess. ii. 20. Under the influence of human weakness, a minister may feel joy when the people praise his sermons and extol his gifts; but, in his best moments, nothing affords him so much joy as the success of his labors, in the conversion of sinners, and the edification of saints. He rejoices in the prosperity of believers, as a parent rejoices in the prosperity of his children; for they are his hope, his joy, his crown of rejoicing, 1 Thess. ii. 19.

5. *It is certain that the beloved John, whose piety far exceeded that of most men, had many pure and exalted joys.* Among these we may notice —his union with Christ—his high and holy calling, as an apostle of our Lord—his fellowship with the church—his spirituality and heavenly-mindedness—reflections on his personal acquaintance with Jesus, and the distinguishing marks of his Master's love to him—and his prospects of a happy and glorious immortality. Inspired with these joys, and allowing that he had no other, he was happier far than the most elevated of those mortals whose only portion was in the present world; and in such a frame of mind as those joys produced, might look down on all the mighty sons of earth with pity and compassion.

6. *But he had no greater joy than to hear that his children walked in truth.* He does not say he had no *equal* to that, but he had none which was *greater.* But why did he rejoice so greatly in the consistent character and conduct of his children? The following reasons may be assigned:—

277

*God* was *glorified* in their fruit, John xv. 8;—the *truth* was *exalted* and *acknowledged* before men, Tit. i. 1;—the *ministry* was *honored*, 2 Thess. iii. 1;—they were *happy* in a consistent conduct, Rev. xxii. 14;—they were *useful* in the world, Rom. ii. 10; and John had the pleasing prospect of their being his *confidence* at the coming of the Lord, 1 John ii. 28. Baxter observes that " true ministers rejoice more for the welfare of men's souls, than in their procuring wealth and worldly honors."

7. *The joyous feelings of the holy apostle would carry him forward in his great work with increasing ardour.* The world, the devil, and sin, oppose every faithful minister; but he fights the good fight, and gains the victory, 2 Tim. iv. 7. 8. Bonds and afflictions abide by him; but he is not moved; he rejoices in his work, and counts not his life dear unto him. that he may finish his course with joy, and the ministry which he has received of the Lord Jesus, Acts xx. 23, 24. Such was the experience of the apostle Paul, such was the experience of John the Divine, and may this be the happy experience of every christian minister.

8. *Happy are the people who are favoured with a minister, whose greatest joy is their prosperity in pure religion.* Their best interests lie near his heart; he carefully teaches them the truth; he constantly remembers them in his prayers; he visits them in their afflictions; he sets them a good example; and watches over them in the Lord with constant care. Such ministers are worthy of double honor, 1 Tim. v. 17; and whatever treatment they meet with among men, they will be highly honored in the day of judgment.

---

## CHRISTIANS REQUIRED TO CONTEND FOR THE FAITH.

Jude 3.—Beloved, when I gave all diligence to write unto you of the common salvation, it was needful for me to write unto you, and exhort you, that ye should earnestly contend for the faith which was once delivered unto the saints. (Sk.)

This epistle was written by Jude, " a servant of Jesus Christ," in the gospel ministry, to them who were "sanctified," or separated from an idolatrous world, " by God the Father, and preserved in Jesus Christ," from dangerous errors and wicked practices; and who were "called" to embrace the doctrines, engage in the duties, and share the privileges of genuine Christianity; and he devoutly prays that mercy, peace, and love, might be multiplied unto them. They were beloved by him, as all true believers should be by Christian ministers; and under the influence of Divine inspiration, he gave all diligence to write unto them on that salvation which is common to all who believe, whether they be Jews or Gentiles; but found it particularly needful to exhort them to contend earnestly for the faith which was once delivered unto the saints; because many seducing teachers had crept in among them unawares.

I. WHAT IS THAT FAITH WHICH WAS ONCE DELIVERED UNTO THE SAINTS?

1. *It is not a set of mere notions and opinions, founded on human reason, and supported by powers of oratory.* The heathen philosophers were famous for speculative notions, but were strangers to the truth as it is in Jesus. They had vast stores of human learning, but were ignorant of the God who

gave them being: and all men, nowever learned, who are in a state of nature, are ignorant of their Maker: for "the natural man receiveth not the things of the Spirit of God: for they are foolishness unto him; neither can he know them," 1 Cor. ii. 14.

2. *The faith of a Christian implies, either that act of his mind, by which he gives credence to revealed truth; or, by a usual metonymy, the objects of his faith, including all the doctrines of Christianity.* The credence which he gives is founded on satisfactory evidence. He has examined the *character* of Christ and his apostles, and finds they were worthy of credit; he has examined the *doctrines* which they taught, and finds them worthy of God; he has examined the miracles which they wrought in open day, and before multitudes of witnesses, as proofs of their mission from God, and finds them to be *real* and highly important facts; and he has examined the prophecies which they delivered, and finds them exact predictions of future events. On these and other important grounds, he gives full credit to all the truths which they taught. The principal doctrines which he believes may be summed up in a few articles: such as, the being and perfections of God, Matt. v. 48; the government of the world by divine providence, Matt. x. 29, 30; the original purity and happiness of man, Gen. i. 27; his awful apostacy from God, 1 John v. 19; the atonement of Jesus Christ, 1 John ii. 2; the influences of the Holy Spirit on the hearts of men, Gal. v. 22, 23; justification by faith, Rom. v. 1; the necessity of inward and outward holiness, 1 Thess. v. 23; a resurrection from the dead, John v. 28, 29; a day of judgment, Acts xvii. 31; and eternal rewards and punishments, Matt. xxv. 46.

3. *This faith was once delivered to the saints.* It was delivered in *part* by the Jewish prophets; but *fully* by Christ and his apostles, Heb. i. 1, ii. 3, 4. It was delivered to holy persons, no only to illuminate their own understandings, but that they might communicate it to others, and thereby enlighten the nations which were in darkness and in death, Matt v. 15.

4. *Besides this faith or belief of truth, there is a living and working faith, which has been delivered by Christ and his apostles, as a term or condition of salvation.* This faith implies a *knowledge* of Jesus in his mediatorial undertakings; an humble *dependence* on him as our atoning sacrifice; and a receiving of him in all his sacred offices and characters, Mark xvi. 15; John i. 12; Rom. x. 10. Faith in the *doctrines* of Christianity precedes *saving* faith; but he who believes the truth, without being influenced by it both in heart and life, has only a dead faith, James ii. 26; while he whose faith is active and operative, is brought into spiritual life and divine love, Gal. ii. 20, v. 6; and thus faith purifies the heart, Acts xv. 9.

II. How should the saints contend for faith?—

1. *The faith of a Christian is worth contending for, being of great value, and of vast importance to man.* It brings him out of darkness into light: teaches him the knowledge of himself and of God his Saviour: and opens to his view a blessed and glorious immortality, 2 Tim. i. 10. Without this faith we should be buried in gross ignorance, frightful superstitions, and destructive delusions.

2. *The Christian faith has many opposers, and we must prepare to meet them in the field of battle.* This faith is opposed by Jews, Infidels, Mohammedans, and Heathens. Let us defend it by sound arguments, drawn from the written word. This is our weapon, and when skilfully used, will either convince our enemies, or put them to flight. They will not easily yield to logic, metaphysics, or oratory; but the sword of the Spirit, which is the word of God, will carry all before it, Eph. vi 17

**3.** *Contend earnestly for the faith of the Lord Jesus Christ, which is placed in your hands as a sacred deposite, to be preserved in its purity.* Some who contend for the faith *ex officio*, neither seem to believe it themselves, nor to wish others to believe. To them the doctrines of the cross have no charms; they are lovers of filthy lucre, and would surrender the faith for wealth and honor. But when we consider that the present happiness of men, and their future prospects, depend on their receiving and holding fast the truth, we are awakened to a holy *zeal*, and contend for the faith with a sacred *ardor*.

**4.** *But though we contend with earnestness, let us carefully avoid carnal weapons and angry passions.* Mohammed contended for *his* faith with the sword; the Roman Catholics have contended for *their* faith by racks and tortures; but the real Christian, in a spirit of meekness, contends 'not with carnal weapons, but those which are mighty, 2 Cor. x. 4. He uses sound words and potent arguments, and is able " both to exhort and convince gainsayers," Tit. i. 9.

**5.** *Never contend merely for the sake of victory, but with a view to do good.* He who aims at nothing but victory, is proud and vain; and would undertake to defend either truth or error, for the sake of a triumph. The man of God has better motives and ends in all his contentions; he constantly aims at the good of men and the glory of God; and when these objects are not likely to be promoted, he retires and mourns in secret. The apostle Paul was set for the defence of the gospel, Phil. i. 17; and it is very observable, that when he was brought before kings and great men, his only object was to prove the truth, and win them over to the cause of Christ, Acts xxvi. 28, 29.

**6.** *Beware of little petty controversies about either nonessential things, or things beyond the reach of human intellect.* Many questions which have agitated the church in all ages, have been foolish and trifling; and others have been profoundly deep and unfathomable. When we contend for that which is important and within our reach, we keep in the line of duty; but when we engage in disputes on fanciful and deeply mysterious things, we miss our way, and injure the cause which we profess to support. Such were the vain janglings which the apostle Paul condemned, 1 Tim. i. 3—7.

To conclude:—

Let us be thankful to God for his holy word, which is an infallible rule both of *faith* and *practice ;* let us believe what he has revealed, though we cannot in every instance understand the mysteries of our faith; let us seek no new doctrine, but carefully study that which has been delivered to the saints; let us arm our minds with *plain* and *solid* arguments, to defend this faith against the subtle and malicious attacks of infidels and heretics; let us bend all our force in support of *vital* truths; let us transmit our faith, in its purity and simplicity, to the rising generation; and, above all, let us contend for that faith which unites the soul to Christ, and which is, " the *substance* of things hoped for, and the evidence of things not seen," Heb. xi. 1.

## FAMILY RELIGION.

Gen xviii. 19.—I know him, that he will command his children and his household after him, and they shall keep the way of the Lord, to do justice and judgment; that the Lord may bring upon Abraham, that which he hath spoken of him. (B.)

IN the context we have a lively picture of the hospitality, simplicity, benevolence, and liberality of the ancient patriarchs, ver. 1. This appearance of God to Abraham seems to have had in it more of freedom and familiarity, and less of grandeur and majesty, than those of which we have hitherto read, and, therefore, more resembled that great visit, which, in the fulness of time, the Son of God was to make to the world. God knew and approved his piety and integrity, and was assured he would employ his authority, as a father and a master, for the promotion of religion and justice, and would communicate the knowledge he acquired, for the benefit of those under his charge.

Let us consider,

I. THE LIGHT IN WHICH ABRAHAM APPEARS IN THIS PASSAGE ; and how he was qualified for the duty here ascribed to him.

He appears,—A man of *knowledge;* not, perhaps, in the jargon of language, the refinements of sciences, the niceties of history, or the subtilties of speculation ; but in matters of the greatest moment to his own present and everlasting salvation, and that of others, namely, in religion and morality, here termed the "way of the Lord," "justice and judgment."— — —

A man of *piety.* He not only understood the way of the Lord ; but he loved, experienced, and practised it. Hence his concern and endeavor to impress it upon others. Without personal religion in the heads of families, we cannot expect they will sincerely and perseveringly endeavor to promote it in their children or servants. — — —

A man of *virtue.* Justice and judgment were as dear to him, and as much practised by him, as the "way of the Lord." He did not make doing his duty to God, a reason for neglecting his duty to his neighbor ; nor, what God had joined together did he put asunder.— — —

A man of *authority.* "He will command his children and his household after him." Observe the respect and obedience he enforced, and his great influence over his family.

This was owing to his *station.* God had made him their head, and they had been taught to acknowledge and revere the appointment of God.

His *knowledge* and *wisdom.*— — —

His known and approved *piety.* They knew God was on his side, and that if they opposed him, God would resent it.

His consistent *virtue.*— — —

A man of *fidelity.* Whatever knowledge, piety, virtue, or authority he had, he faithfully employed for *his* glory, who entrusted him with them, and to the end intended,—the good of others, and especially of his own family.

A man of *diligence.* He appears evidently to have been laborious in this duty.

II. THE NATURE OF THIS DUTY ; or his endeavors for the good of his family.

He not only prayed *with* and *before* his family, but interceded for them as a *priest.* This the ancient patriarchs and holy men of old did. They were priests in their own houses. Job i. 5. So should every master of a christian family be. Indeed every private christian is a priest unto God. (Enlarge respecting praying with and for every member of our family.)

He was a *prophet* in his family. He instructed them: not in matters of mere speculation, nor doubtful disputation,—this were foolish and unprofitable,—but in matters of experimental and practical religion and virtue.

He taught them the "way of the Lord," *i. e.* God's way towards them, as a Creator, Preserver, Benefactor, and their way towards God, or piety, and godliness; the true knowledge, fear, love of God, obedience to his commands, patience under his dispensations, contentment in all estates, the time being short, deadness to the world and sin, and devotedness to God; and, in order to all this, repentance towards God, and faith in Christ. (Here show how the being and attributes of God may be demonstrated even to children from the works of creation, &c. the truth of the scriptures also, and of christianity, &c.)

He taught them *virtue*, "to do justice and judgment,—truth, justice, mercy, charity, flowing from the love of our neighbour, and the love of God. Children should be taught to consider all men as allied to each other, being creatures of one Creator, made of one blood, partaking of one nature, mortal, immortal, bought by the Redeemer, &c. Also, children should be early accustomed to sincerity, veracity, strict honesty, plain dealing, pity to those in distress, a forgiving spirit, a readiness to relieve those in want. In order to this, as well as to the health of their own bodies, and the peace of their own minds, they should be taught temperance, chastity, self-denial, &c.—

Abraham taught his family, lastly, not barely to know these things, but to do them.

Now upon whom must this be inculcated?—Upon *children*. Deut. iv. 9. If our children be the Lord's they must be educated for him. If they wear his livery, and be called by his name, they must do his work. Wha' hypocrisy is it to dedicate our children to God in baptism, and promise they shall "renounce the devil and all his works, the vain pomp and glory of the world, with all covetous desires of the same, and the carnal desires of the flesh, so that they shall not follow, nor be led by them," and afterwards to take no care that they may fulfil it!—Upon *servants*. Abraham had born in his house, three hundred and eighteen servants, Gen. xiv. 14, *trained*, or, as the Hebrew word means, *catechized*. Our servants are entrusted to our care, and should be taught and directed by us, while in our family.

But how must our children and servants be instructed? Deut. vi. 6. &c. By conversation, advice, exhortation, reading, hearing, catechizing, &c. and especially teaching them to "know the scriptures." 2 Tim. iii. 15. Further,

He was a *king* in his house, and used authority.—He not only recommended these things, and advised, and set before them the advantages on the one hand, and the miseries on the other, of the conduct which they might pursue, but he solemnly enjoined and insisted on these things, on pain of incurring his displeasure, as well as that of God. He not only used *doctrine*, but *discipline*, Eph. vi. 4. He not only informed the understanding of his children and domestics, as it might gradually open, by doctrine, and reminded and admonished them, but he persuaded, turned, and subdued the will to God and man, as far as possible, by discipline, rewards, punishments, or corrections, especially with regard to his children.

III. How PLEASING IT WAS TO GOD, and the blessed consequences there-of to Abraham and his family.

Observe—The reason why God would hide nothing from Abraham. "For I know him," &c. Abraham was communicative of his knowledge, and improved it to the good of those under his care, and therefore God resolved to make communications to him.

The way to the accomplishment of God's promises; "That the Lord may bring upon Abraham that which he hath spoken of him."

Family blessings arise from family religion;—Temperance, frugality, industry, discretion.

Peace, quietness, love, harmony.

The favour, protection, care of God, his direction and aid.

All necessaries. Psalm xxxvii. 25. Matt. vi. 33.

Prosperity, as far as will be for good for us and our families.

Our prayers are heard.

Afflictions are sanctified to us, and we are supported under them.

We make a comfortable progress together in the ways of God, and receive many spiritual blessings.

We shall meet in his presence and kingdom hereafter, and spend an eter nity together.

The sad reverse when this course is not taken.

Hence arise family curses—Intemperance, prodigality, idleness, impru-dence.

Strife, contention, hatred, disturbance.

The displeasure of God, &c. and his curse on all we do.

Not even necessaries, perhaps, but beggary and want

Nothing prospers.

Our prayers are rejected.

We are abandoned of God in our afflictions, and hardened by them.

We go forward miserably in the ways of the Devil.

We shall meet at the left hand of the Judge in the great day, and in hell, amidst everlasting strife and misery.

---

## CONFESSING CHRIST BEFORE MEN.

**Matt. x. 32.**—Whosoever, therefore, shall confess me before men, him will I confess also before my Father which is in heaven. (Sk.)

"ALL that will live godly in Christ Jesus shall suffer persecution." This apostolic maxim has been illustrated and established by the records of the Christian history in all ages. The carnal mind being "enmity against God" is decidedly hostile to the holy constitution and renovating designs of the gospel. Hence the annals of the church have been stained with the blood of martyrs, who with pious magnanimity have preferred immolation on the altar of bigotry, rather than violate the sacred rights of conscience. Of this course of suffering and death, Jesus Christ most fully apprized his follow-ers, when he planted Christianity in the earth, Matt. x. 16—22. At the same time furnishing them with the most ample encouragement, steadily to persevere in the path of duty which lay before them; by referring to his own reproach and suffering, ver. 24, 25:—to the circumscribed extent of their enemies' malevolent influence, ver. 28;—to the minute care of Divine

providence, ver. 29—31;—to the awful consequence of timidity and cowardice, ver. 33, 39;—and to the honorable and highly advantageous result
of Christian magnanimity. The last description of encouragement is contained in the passage before us, in discussing which, we shall have to consider,

I. THE NATURE OF THAT CONFESSION WHICH CHRISTIANITY REQUIRES.

II. THE HONORABLE DISTINCTION WITH WHICH A STEADY COURSE OF
CHRISTIAN FORTITUDE WILL BE CROWNED.

I. THE NATURE OF THAT CONFESSION WHICH CHRISTIANITY REQUIRES.
This interesting confession includes various considerations, viz.

1. *An open avowal of the person and Messiahship of Christ.* The sacred Scriptures represent Jesus Christ as that "Word" which "was in the
beginning with God," and which "was God;" the "Alpha and Omega, the
beginning and the end, the first and the last;" and yet was "made flesh,"
and dwelling among the inhabitants of the earth, for the purpose of human
redemption. Therefore, those who scripturally "confess Christ before men,"
unequivocally acknowledge his "eternal power and Godhead," and yet gratefully consider the mysterious union of the Divine nature with the human, as
a luminous display of the love of God to fallen man; and as the divinely
appointed means of rescuing him from everlasting perdition. And this they
are not ashamed publicly to avow and support; in opposition to the presuming pride of human reason, which absurdly affects to reject and deny that
which it cannot comprehend, John i. 1—3, 14, x. 30, xiv. 11; Col. i. 16,
17; John iii. 16; Phil. ii. 5—8. But as devils have thus confessed Christ,
saying, "We know thee who thou art, the Holy One of God," it is necessary to proceed farther, and notice.

2. *A conscientious adherence to the fundamental doctrines of Christianity.* In every theory which the human mind is capable of embracing, there
are certain grand principles which are individually essential to the existence
and consistency of the whole. So the Christian character, while it has for
its ground-work, a conscientious avowal of the person and messiahship of
Christ, includes in its superstructure, a sincere confession of the deep-rooted
depravity of the human heart, and its consequent moral imbecility, Gen. iii.
8—19; Jer. xvii. 9, xiii. 23; 2 Cor. iii. 5;—of the atonement and mediation of Christ, as the only legitimate medium of access to God, Isa. liii. 4,
5; 1 Pet. ii. 24; Rom. v. 11; Heb. vii. 24, 25; Rom. v. 1, 2;—of the
reality of the Holy Spirit's influence, as a principle of spiritual light, renovation, life, and holiness, Eph. i. 17, 18, ii. 1; Rom. xv. 13; Ezek. xxxvi.
25;—of the justification of the penitent sinner through faith in our Lord
Jesus Christ, John iii. 16—18; Rom. iii. 24—27, iv. 2—8; Gal. ii. 16,
iii. 6—12;—and of holiness of heart and life, as the evidence of faith, and
a meetness for the felicities of the heavenly world, 1 Cor. vi. 11; 1 Pet. i.
13—16; 1 Thess. iii. 13; Heb. xii. 10, 14; Col. i. 12.

3. *A declaration of the benefits received.* The true believer in the Lord
Jesus Christ, having been made the partaker of innumerable blessings at the
hands of his Divine Master, gratefully acknowledges his obligations, and
with pious solicitude inquires, "What shall I render unto the Lord for all
his benefits?" And he evinces his gratitude to God, by *aspirations of
praise;—by carefully guarding the good which he has received;—by em-
ulating more exalted enjoyments;—*and *by publishing, for the good of
others, what God has done for him.* Ps. xxxiv. 1, 2; 1 Cor. xv. 57; Phil.
iii. 8—16; Ps. lxvi. 16; Rom. x. 10; Acts xxiv. xxvi.

4. *Zealously supporting the cause of Christian truth.* No man can
properly "confess Christ before men," without feeling a lively concern for

**the** promotion of the gospel in the earth. This pious zeal manifests itself, by *owning, adhering to, and kindly aiding the followers of Christ*, John xiii. 35;—*by administering affectionate reproof to the ungodly*, Lev. xix. 17; Eph. v. 11;—*by exhibiting an example of Christian excellence to the world*, Matt. v. 13—16;—*by contributing pecuniary support*, Prov. iii. 9; Luke viii. 3;—*and by submitting to reproach and suffering*, when circumstances require it, Acts vii. 54—60, xx. 24, xxi. 13; 2 Cor. xii. 23—33.

II. THE HONORABLE DISTINCTION WITH WHICH A STEADY COURSE OF CHRISTIAN FORTITUDE WILL BE CROWNED. "Him will I confess also before my Father which is in heaven." Although man is by nature a rebel against the Majesty of heaven; yet the subject of vital godliness is owned, and highly distinguished by his God, even whilst journeying down the vale of life; by the ample supplies which are furnished; the invulnerable defence with which he is favored; the divine enjoyments of which he is the partaker; and the animating hope with which he is inspired. But the blessed Redeemer doubtless refers to that solemn period, when,

> " The Judge, descending, thunders from afar,
> And all mankind are summon'd to his bar ;"

that tremendous "day when God shall judge the secrets of men by Jesus Christ," " who will render unto every man according to his deeds." At that awful period of final decision, the Redeemer " will confess" his followers before assembled worlds, by

1. *An act of separation.* In the present condition of man, the Christian has to maintain a frequent intercourse with that class of his fellow creatures, who are under the influence of sinful habits and immoral dispositions; and this necessary intermixture is sometimes productive of painful sensations, and moral danger. Even in the silent grave the dust of the righteous and the wicked, in an intermixed state, rests till the morning of the general judgment, "when the dead shall be raised," and an eternal separation take place between " those who serve God, and those who serve him not," Matt. xxv 31—33; Luke xvi. 26.

2. *By an approving plaudit.* The Lord Jesus Christ, in the character of Judge, will publicly *own the persons*, and *approve the conduct* of those, who have boldly asserted his right, and suffered in his cause. Before angels, devils, and men, he will bear testimony to their faithfulness, and introduce them to those regions of unalloyed delight, where the " wicked cease from troubling, and the weary be at rest," Matt. xxv. 23, 34—40.

3. *By making them partakers of his glory.* Such is the amazing condescension of the "Captain of our salvation," that although it is through strength divine, that the Christian overcomes his enemies; perseveres in the path of righteousness; and achieves a final conquest; yet he addresses him, and acts towards him, as though the whole were effected solely by unaided human energy. He does not remind him of his dependence, and his obligations; but makes him the partaker of his honors, his throne, and his felicity. And this glory is *inviolable, eternal,* and yet *progressive,* John xiv. 1 2, 3; Matt. xxv. 46; Rev. iii. 5, 21, v. 10.

From this subject we learn,

1. That the human heart is, by nature, decidedly nostile to the spirit of the gospel.

2. That an entire change is essential to a scriptural confession of Christ.

3. That the Christian cannot ultimately be a loser by suffering for righteousness' sake

## CHRISTIAN HOPE.

**Romans v. 5.**—And hope maketh not ashamed ; because the love of God is shed abroad in your hearts by the Holy Ghost which is given unto us. (Sk.)

THE uniformity of christian experience, and its harmony with the sacred scriptures, furnish the most powerful arguments in opposition to the subtle sophisms of infidelity. Though the conditions of men widely differ, yet all those who are under the influence of that "faith which worketh by love," bear the same divine "image and superscription;" and though the several denominations of christians cannot harmonize on some minor points of theory, modes of worship, and forms of church government; yet they all find a central point at which they can meet, in the union of that christian experience described by the apostle in the verses preceding the text. In the passage before us, and its interesting context, the true believer recognises the foundation of his experience, in the atonement and resurrection of Christ, chap. iv. 25 ; the means of its existence and progress in that faith which is " of the operation of God," chap. v. 1, 2 ; its interesting gradation, ver. 3, 4 ; and its pleasing influence. Let us proceed to consider,

I. THE NATURE OF CHRISTIAN HOPE.
II. THE EFFECT WHICH IT PRODUCES.
III. THE REASON WHICH IT ASSIGNS.

In giving a general idea of hope, we may consider it as implying the *approbation* of its object; either on account of its real or imaginary excellence;—the *possibility* of possessing that object;—the *desire* of attainment; and a *pleasurable sensation of mind*, commensurate with our estimate of the object, and our prospect of possessing it. In confining our attention to christian hope, it will be necessary to consider,

I. *The magnificence of its object.* The hope of the christian is an object infinitely superior to every thing of an earthly kind; it quits terrestrial scenes; it mounts on high ; approaches the throne of the Eternal ; and fixes on the " glory of God" as its object. The term "glory" is sometimes associated with *conquest*, and in this sense it is the distinguished object of the believer's hope. That adorable Being, whose perfections he emulates is the universal conqueror ; and through him the christian hopes to overcome all opposition, triumph over every enemy, and seize the victor's palm in the regions of immortality, Rom. viii. 73 ; 1 Cor. xv. 57. " Glory" is sometimes descriptive of *grandeur*, and such are the exalted expectations of the christian, that he hopes to participate in the grandeur of his triumphant Redeemer, and vie with the sun when beaming forth in all his noontide refulgence, Dan. xii. 2, 3 ; Matt. xiii. 43 ; Rev. iii. 21. But by " the glory of God," the believer more generally understands the participation of *celestial felicity;* the eternal enjoyment of the unveiled glories of the Deity ; comprehending the entire exclusion of every species of evil, the perfections of society, and the consummation of happiness, Matt. xxv. 34 ; 46 ; 1 Pet. i. 3, 4. But as ungodly men sometimes profess to have hopes of heaven, it is of considerable importance that we attend to,

2. *The purity of its motive.* The hope of the righteous is influenced by a motive widely different from, and superior to, that which excites the feeble and groundless expectation of the sinner. Whilst the wicked hope to go to heaven merely that they may escape that punishment which is the just award of their rebellious conduct ; the righteous have the same object in view, and hope to attain it from principles of *love to God, attachment to his*

*people,* delight in holiness, and an ardent desire to enjoy the presence of Jehovah, 2 Cor. v. 1—4; Phil. i. 23.

3. *The solidity of its basis.* The hope of the christian is not founded on a supposed goodness of heart, nor on a comparative superiority of character, nor yet on the mercy of God simply considered, for he remembers the righteous claims of divine justice : and therefore the basis of his hope is, the atonement of Christ, and a lively interest in, and union with the " true vine," John xv. 4, 5; Rom. v. 1, 2, viii. 1—9; Gal. ii. 20.

II. THE EFFECT WHICH IT PRODUCES:—"maketh not ashamed." Although every true believer in the Lord Jesus Christ is ashamed of his former sinful practices, of his late ungodly associates, and of every thing inconsistent with the holy constitution of the gospel; yet he is "not ashamed,"

1. *Of Jesus Christ and his truth.* He humbly acknowledges his need of him as an all-sufficient and a present Saviour; with holy gratitude and pious exultation he confesses his interest in his dependence upon, and his obligation unto him. He is zealous for the extension of christian truth in earth, and in various ways labours to advance his Master's interests among men, Matt. x. 32 ; Rom. i. 16 : Gal. vi. 14 ; 1 Tim. i. 15, 16.

2. *Of the reproach which is connected with christianity.* Suffering and reproach have been connected with the progress of christian truth in all ages, and the records of the christian church have been stained with the tears and blood of the magnanimous soldiers of the cross, who, fearless of all consequences, have steadily avowed their attachment to their divine Master. Yea, they have rejoiced in having been permitted to participate in the sufferings of their Lord, Acts vii. 54—60, xx. 24, xxi. 13 ; Heb. xi. 35—40.

3. *Of his christian brethren.* The genuine follower of the Lord Jesus Christ, considers all who bear the image of his Master, however poor and afflicted they may be, as members of his heavenly Father's family, fellow heirs of the same eternal inheritance, and partakers of like precious faith with himself. He acknowledges them by acts of social intercourse, by participating in their sorrows, and by administering to their necessities, John xiii. 34, 35 ; Rom. xv. 1, 2 ; 1 John iv. 11, 12, 20, 21.

4. *Of pious exertion in the cause of Christ.* This the christian considers to be a duty incumbent upon him, and for the purpose of aiding this cause, he prudently declares what God has done for him ; administers affection, admonition, and reproof to his fellow creatures ; and engages in the regular ordinances of christianity according to his ability ; crowning the whole with incessant prayer to God for the prosperity of Zion, Psa. lxvi. 16, cxxii. 6; 1 Cor. ix. 19—22.

III. THE REASON WHICH IT ASSIGNS;—"Because the love of God is shed abroad in our hearts," &c. The religion of the gospel is a reasonable thing, and all its effects are strictly consistent with that divine source from which they proceed, and its highly honored subjects are "able to give a reason of the hope that is in them."

1. *The strength of its evidence.* The residence of the Holy Spirit in the breast of the christian, furnishes him with an indubitable evidence of the heavenly origin and divine reality of his religion. The skeptic may cavil, and the sneering infidel may object, but the

> " Christian dwells, like Uriel, in the sun
> Meridian evidence puts doubt to flight,
> And ardent hope anticipates the skies."

The Spirit of love dwelling in his heart, bears ample testimony to his presence there, Rom. viii. 14—17; 2 Cor. vi. 16; Gal iv. 6. And this internal conviction is accompanied by external operations of corresponding character, as *spirituality of temper and disposition; obedience to the divine commandments; resignation to the divine will;* and *zeal for the divine glory,* Gal. v. 22—24; 1 John iv. 13—21.

2. *The fulness of that enjoyment with which it is connected.* " The love of God" is pleasingly adapted to the intense cravings of an immortal spirit; and when this love " is shed abroad in the heart," it produces happiness the most pure, the most satisfactory, and the most permanent. The burden of native guilt is removed, peace is experienced, joy fills the heart, and the expanding soul has large anticipations of celestial felicity, "rejoicing in hope of the glory of God," Romans v 11, xiv, 17; 2 Tim. iv, 6—8.

This subject tends,

1. To promote inquiry respecting out interest in this hope.
2. To elicit sentiments of gratitude from those who possess it.
3. To stimulate to diligence those who are " without hope.'

---

## WATCHFULNESS, A PREPARATION FOR THE COMING OF CHRIST.

**Mark** xiii. 35, 36.—Watch ye therefore : for ye know not when the master of the house cometh, at even, or at midnight, or at the cock crowing, or in the morning ; lest coming suddenly he find you sleeping. (B.)

I name these words as the subject of a discourse, at this time, because I think nothing happens by chance ; that the superintending providence of God is over all things, especially over the death of mankind, and that in a signal manner, when any individuals are suddenly and unexpectedly removed from this world. I think, likewise, that such dispensations are peculiar calls and warnings to the living to " prepare to meet their God ;" and that it is the duty of those who " watch for souls," to endeavor to improve such events, and thus, in a certain sense, to be " workers together with God."

The Author, (having here mentioned several instances of sudden death, which had recently occurred,) then proceeds to consider,

I. WHAT WE ARE TO UNDERSTAND BY THE COMING OF THE MASTER OF THE HOUSE.

By " the master of the house," here, is meant Christ, as it is also in Luke xiii. 25. The world in general, and the visible Church in particular, and especially the spiritual part of it, are his house. Eph. i. 20—25; Heb. iii. 3—6.

His coming is represented in Scripture in different lights, and for different purposes.

In this chapter of Mark, and in the 24th chapter of Matthew, and the 21st of St. Luke, he is represented as coming to judge and punish the Jewish nation, his visible church of old, or his house, for rejecting him. Deut. xviii. 19, comp. with Acts iii. 23; Heb. xii. 15.

In other places he is represented as coming to judge all mankind at the last day. Ver. 24, 26 ; 2 Pet. iii. 3—12.

He is said to come. when he visits in a peculiar way, whether in judgment or mercy, any nation, or church, or any particular member of it. Rev. ii. 5, 16 ; iii. 3.

He comes to each of us at death. Rev. i. 18 ; ii. 25 ; iii. 11.

It is this last coming of Christ to which I would especially call your attention. For it is of the greatest importance to us, since—It will separate us from all below, from our occupations, enjoyments, possessions, families, relations, and friends, and even from our own bodies.—It will finish our state of trial, and determine our condition for ever ; for, you know, we are here on our trial for eternity.—It will bring us into the unseen and eternal world, a new, untried, unknown state.—It will place us in the presence of God, that we may receive his smile or frown, may enjoy the effects of his favor and friendship, and communications of bliss from him, or feel the effects of his wrath, and find him to be a consuming fire.—It will make a most astonishing change in our circumstances.—It often comes suddenly, and gives no warning.— —

II. What is that watchfulness which is recommended as a preparation for his coming.

It implies life, spiritual life, in opposition to that sleep of death which is mentioned, Eph. v. 14 ; which text compare with Eph. ii. 1.— —

It implies a lively sense of the reality and importance of spiritual and eternal things, such as persons awake have of temporal things, the seeing, feeling, tasting them, so to speak, in opposition to that insensibility about them, which is implied in spiritual sleep.

It implies a thoughtfulness, care, and concern about them, in opposition to that thoughtlessness and unconcern about them, which is natural to us.— —

It implies a sense of our danger from our enemies, visible and invisible ; from the Devil, the world, persons and things, the flesh, our own hearts, and the standing on our guard, in opposition to security of mind, and foolish peace.— —

It implies activity, and the vigorous exercise of every grace and virtue, as repentance, faith, hope, love, patience, &c., in opposition to indolence and sloth.— —

III. The vast importance of this watchfulness, as a preparation for every dispensation of divine Providence, and especially for death.

The spiritual life, and lively sense of the things of God, which are comprehended in this watchfulness, form a preparation for every event of Providence, as for temporal losses or gains, honor or dishonor, sickness, or health, &c,—We are thus armed against every enemy and assault.—We are fitted for every duty to God, our neighbor, and ourselves.—We are also in this way prepared for death.—

Does death separate us from all below ? We are prepared to be thus separated, being dead to the world, and our wills being resigned to the will of God. Does it terminate our state of trial? We are prepared to have it terminated. Does it bring us into the invisible world? We are ready for that world ; our thoughts and affections have gone before us, and we have made provision, and laid up treasure there. Does it bring us into the presence of God? The watchful are prepared for his presence, having by grace, through faith, ensured his favor, his friendship, his image, an acquaintance and fellowship with him. Does it make an astonishing change in our circumstances? The watchful are prepared for that change, having acquired a meetness for, and an earnest of heaven in their hearts. Does it often come suddenly, and give no warning? The watchful are habitually expecting it, and therefore are not surprised by its arrival. —— ——

But very different is the case with the unwatchful.—Suppose them, first, *unconverted* persons. If awakened on the borders of the grave, they are thrown into the greatest confusion and dismay ; they are carried away from all those sensual possessions and enjoyments on which they once doted ; their state of trial is ended, and they can never afterwards be quickened to spiritual life and renewed in holiness ; they awake into a life worse than dying.—— ——Suppose them *righteous*. By their improvident slumbering they darken their evidences, and render their state uncomfortable ; they cannot expect any peculiar support or consolation at a dying hour, or in the time of affliction ; they are often left to wrestle with sore temptation ; they make dismal work for bitter repentance on a sick and death bed ; they have the misery of reflecting that they have omitted many duties to God and man which now can never be performed, have not attained those degrees of holiness they might have attained, and although they do not finally perish, they have deprived themselves of the reward they might have enjoyed. As they bring little glory to God in life, so they do him no honor in their death, and leave little comfort to their friends concerning them. Perhaps they leave them in doubt whether they are saved or lost.

IV. How we may be enabled to take this advice, and to "watch ;" and what are the means leading to that end.

We must not presume on a long life, which is a most dangerous temptation, and an abundant source of unwatchfulness ; but we must set before us, and have always in view, the shortness and uncertainty of the present life, and the certainty and nearness of death.—We must remember, that unless we were lords of our own lives, and could appoint the time of our death, we can never be exempt from the duty of a wakeful and active attention to our spiritual and eternal interests.—Those whose constitutions are peculiarly feeble, or whose circumstances or employments expose them to peculiar danger, or who are arrived at old age, should consider themselves as being under especial obligations to be watchful.—We must be particularly on our guard against our own nature, and every person and thing around us, which tends to lull us asleep, and against sensuality and worldly cares. Luke xxi. 34.— We must remember that thousands are found sleeping, even thousands of professors, at the coming of their Lord.—We must pray much ; a duty frequently inculcated in connection with watchfulness. Ver. 33 ; Luke xxi. 36 ; Eph. vi. 18.— ——

## HOLY ARDOR.

Psalm lxiii. 8.—My soul followeth hard after thee. (Sk.)

To mankind in general this passage must be quite unintelligible. "God is not in all their thoughts, consequently they neither desire nor seek him. They might use the text with great propriety to express their attachment to the world, and its various objects—" Riches, honors, power, pleasures, our souls follow hard after *you*." It is only the christian that can truly adopt this language as his own. But even among professing christians too many are strangers to such sacred fervours—many feel them but too seldom—and few, if any, appreciate them aright. It will therefore be proper.

I. To DESCRIBE THIS STATE OF EXPERIENCE. It implies,

1. *A renunciation of the world.* This results from a conviction of its vanity. No man can follow God and the world at once, Matt. vi. 24; Luke xvi. 13; 1 John ii. 15. But we never renounce the world till we feel its vanity, and sensibly apprehend the fallacy of its *pretensions*—the unsatisfying nature of its *enjoyments*—the uncertainty and shortness of its *tenure.* In renouncing the world, however, we do not neglect its lawful concerns— shun human society—or despise the blessings of Providence. But we withdraw all *dependence* upon it—all *improper detachment* to it—and all *anxious cares* concerning it.

2. *A deliberate choice of God,* as the only adequate good of the soul. The soul must have some supreme object—The creature renounced, it can only cleave to the Creator, whom it now views as the sovereign Good, *suitable* to its nature—*adequate* to its wants—*perm·nent and secure* in possession.

3. *A vehement and intense desire after him.* This is the sense of the text. Perhaps the Psalmist alludes to a thirsty hart seeking the cooling brook, ver. 1; Psa. xliii. 1. The soul longs ardently to *know* God in Christ more explicitly—to be more perfectly *conformed to his image*—to have more *intimate communion* with him, and finally to *enjoy him* in all his plenitude for ever.

4. *The exercise of faith and hope.* God can only be known by faith— and unless we believe he is to be found, we shall never seek after him, Heb. xi. 2. The soul *apprehends* him as its God in Christ, and fully *anticipates* all the enjoyments which it desires. And in this exercise of faith and hope there is *present delight.*—The soul divinely sustained (" thy right hand upholdeth me") cheerfully and eagerly follows after God in the path of duty— in prayer, hearing, and all his ordinances. We are now led,

II. To INVESTIGATE THE REASONS WHY IT IS SO RARE.

It is obvious few christians enjoy this experience; at least it is only *occasionally,* and not *generally,* that their hearts are in this state. The principal causes of their languor are,

1. *Inattention to the state of their own hearts.* They are not recollected;—they do not examine themselves closely. Hence they are ignorant of their real condition, and do not keenly feel their wants.—But unless we are deeply sensible of our need of God, we shall never follow hard after him.

2. *Permitting the objects of sense to make too deep impressions.* These naturally tend to blunt the edge of holy desire, and to divide and weaken the soul. Whatever convictions may have been received of the vanity of the world, it will again obtain the ascendency without much watchfulness and firm resistance.

3. *Neglect of the instituted means.* This indeed is often the *effect* of losing spiritual ardor. But it is more frequently the *cause.* When we imagine that the holy flame will burn without the aid of additional fuel, and without fanning it by frequent approaches to God, we fall into a dangerous, and too often fatal snare.

4. *The indulgence of wrong dispositions, &c.* Unbelief, pride, vain curiosity, levity, censoriousness, uncharitable or useless conversation, &c. all these, like water, tend to damp and weaken, if not wholly to extinguish the desire for God

These are the principal reasons why David's experience is now so rarely enjoyed. But surely if christians knew how to value this state aright, they would never permit these causes so frequently to deprive them of it. In order to induce them to resist these hinderances, and to cultivate this state of soul, let us proceed,

III. To REPRESENT IT AS THE MOST DESIRABLE EXPERIENCE. Innumerable are the advantages which result from it. We can only name a few

1. *It is the best security against the allurements and troubles of the world.* A heart earnestly pursuing God has no leisure to gaze on the seductive charms of temporal good, and no disposition to pierce itself with the thorns of worldly solicitude. Comparative indifference to all but God, disarms both pleasure and pain of their power to injure, while the soul, free and disentangled, rapidly moves on in her heavenly course.

2. *It renders every duty delightful.* In this state nothing is done through custom, formality, or any other inferior motive—but every duty is performed with the highest views. God in Christ is aimed at in all—and oh ! how sweet is prayer or praise, reading or hearing, meditation or christian conversation, or even the commonest affairs of life, when we thus do all " in the name of our Lord Jesus," &c. Col. iii. 17.

3. *It prepares us for the largest communication.* We always receive from God what we earnestly and faithfully seek from him, Luke ii. 9, 10. In proportion, therefore, as our souls are enlarged by holy desire, humble faith, and earnest expectations, will be the divine communications unto them By this holy fervor the soul throws itself open to receive all the fulness of God, the shoreless, fathomless ocean of good.

4. *It advances our sanctification, and consequently qualifies us for heaven.* Detaching us from the creature, fixing us upon the Creator, leading us to communion and fellowship with him, we naturally imbibe more and more of *his Spirit,* become more and more transformed into *his likeness*—All sin vanishes from his powerful presence—pure universal love occupies our whole hearts, and thus we become meet for our inheritance among the saints in light.

Let us conclude by addressing,

1. Those whose hearts are wholly set upon the world. You cleave to visible objects, and entirely neglect your Maker, Benefactor, and Redeemer —your Sovereign, Lawgiver, and Judge. Oh consider—*the excess of your folly*—you prefer shadows to realities, vexation of spirit to peace of mind —misery to bliss. *The baseness of your ingratitude*—you reject your only friend, and side with his enemies. *The enormity of your guilt*—you idolize the creature, and pour contempt upon the Creator.—*The imminence of your danger*—you are exposed to the fierceness of the divine displeasure, to all the torments of hell, Jer. xvii. 5; John iii. 31.

2. Lukewarm and unstable professors—you are if possible more culpable than the former—Consider how inconsistent your character is with your *obligations*—your *engagements*—your *profession*—and your *interest.*

3. Ardent spiritually-minded christians—go forward—fear not the imputation of enthusiasm—fear no disappointment. Believe the promise—cherish the most sanguine hopes—Delight yourselves in the Lord, and he shall give you the desires of your hearts, Matt. v. 6; Rev. xxi. 6.

## THE POOR AND CONTRITE THE OBJECTS OF GOD'S FAVOR.

Isai. lxvi. 2.—To this man will I look, even to him that is poor and of a contrite spirit and trembleth at my word. (S. S.)

It often happens that accidental distinctions serve men as grounds of confidence towards God—

Many found their hopes on no better basis than Micah did—Judg. xvii. 13.

The Jews in particular thought themselves assured of the divine favor because of God's residence in their temple*—

But God shews them the folly of their notions†—

And declares the character of those, who alone shall be considered by him with any favorable regard.

I. Who are the ojects oe the divine favor?

Men choose for their companions the rich and gay—

But those, whom God regards, are of a very different character—

1. They *feel themselves destitute of all good.*

It is not temporal, but spiritual poverty, that distinguishes God's people—

They have discovered their total want of spiritual *wisdom*—Prov. xxx. 2, 3.

They are constrained to acknowledge that they have no *righteousness* of their own—Isai. lxiv. 6.

And that they are "without *strength*" for obedience—Rom. v. 6. 2 Cor. iii. 5.

They unfeignedly adopt the language of St. Paul—Rom. vii. 18.

Nor do they hope for mercy but as the *free gift* of God‡—

2. They *bewail the many evils they have committed.*

They have been made to see that sin is hateful to God—

And they have felt the bitterness of it in their own consciences—

They know experimentally the sensations of David—Ps. xxxviii. 4, 6, 8.

They loathe themselves for all their abominations—Ezek. xxxvi. 31.

Nor are their convictions merely occasional or transient—

They are *habitually* of a tender and "contrite spirit"—

3. They *pay a reverential regard to every word of God.*

They dare not say like the idolatrous Jews—Jer. xliv. 16.

They rather resemble the man after God's own heart—Ps. cxix. 161.

If the word be preached, they "receive it as the word, not of man, but of God"—

They hear the *threatenings* like the meek Josiah—2 Chron. xxxiv. 19, 27.

They attend to the *promises* with an eager desire to embrace them—

To every *precept* they listen with an obedient ear.‖—

---

* Hence that common boast among them, Jer. vii. 4.

† Ver. 1, 2. The import of which is, How can you think that I, an infinite Being, who myself created those things of which you boast, can be allured by an earthly structure to continue my presence among you, if you persist in your evil ways?

‡ They say not, like the servant, Matt. xviij. 26. but desire to experience the clemency shown to insolvent debtors, Luke vii. 42.

‖ Luke Cornelius, Acts x. 33. and Paul, Acts xxii. 10. yea, the angels in heaven, Ps. ciii. 20.

These, though generally considered by the world as weak and super-stitious, are not overlooked by the Supreme Being.

II. THE PECULIAR REGARD WHICH GOD SHEWS THEM.

The "eyes of God are in every place beholding the evil and the good"—
But he "looks to" *these*, in a far different manner from *others*—
This distinguishing favor implies,

1. Approbation of them.

From the proud and self-sufficient, God turns his face—James iv. 6.
But he "despises not the broken and contrite in heart"—Ps. li. 17.
Though so exalted in himself, he will not disdain to notice them—
His approbation of such characters stands recorded for ever—Luke xviii. 13, 14.
His reception of the prodigal is an eternal monument of the regard he will shew to *every* repenting sinner—

2. Care over them.

Wherever they go, his eye is upon them for good—2 Chron. xvi. 9.
He watches them in order to deliver them from danger—Ps. xii. 5.
He watches them in order to comfort them in trouble—Ps. cxlvii. 3.
He watches them in order to relieve them in want—Isai. xli. 17, 18.
He watches them in order to exalt them to happiness and honor—1 Sam ii. 8.

3. Delight in them.

There are none on earth so pleasing to God as brokenhearted sinners—
Their sighs and groans are as music in his ears—Ps. cii. 19, 20.
Their tears he treasures up in his vial—Ps. lvi. 8.
He dwells with them as his dearest friends—Isai. lvii. 15.
He rejoices over them as a people in whom he greatly delights—Zeph. iii. 12, 17.
He saves them *here* by the unceasing exercise of his power—Ps. xxxiv. 15. 18.
And reserves for them *hereafter* an inheritance in heaven—Matt. v. 3.
Nor shall the fewness of such characters render them at all less the objects of God's regard.
It must be acknowledged that they are but few—
But if there were only *one* in the whole world, God would find him out*—
Not all the splendor of heaven, nor all the acclamations of angels, should for a moment divert God's attention from him—
Though he were despised by all the human race, yet should he be amiable in the eyes of his Maker—
Nor should he want any thing in time or eternity—
Never shall that declaration in any instance be falsified—Ps cxxxviii. 6.

INFER,

1. How should we admire the condescension of God!

If we view only the material world we may well stand astonished that God should regard such an insignificant creature as man—Ps. viii. 3, 4.
But, if we contemplate the majesty of God, we cannot but exclaim with Solomon—1 Kings viii. 27.
Let then the declaration in the text lead our thoughts up to God—
Let us adore him for so clearly describing the objects of his favor.
And let us express our admiration in the words of David—Ps. cx. 5—8.

---

*"To this *man*, &c. even to *him*, &c."

2. How shou'd we desire to attain the character that is pleasing to God!
The poor and contrite are *exclusively* beloved of God—
If he look on others, it is only as he did on the Egyptians, Exod. **xiv.**
**24, 25.**
And how dreadful must it be to have *such* an enemy!—
But how delightful to have an *almighty, omnipresent* guardian!—
Above all, how awful must it be to have *him turn his face from us* in the
day of Judgment!—
Let us then endeavor to humble ourselves before God—Isai. ii. 11.
And rest assured that the promised mercy shall in due time be fulfilled to
us—James iv. 10.

---

## THE REWARD OF CHRIST'S FOLLOWERS.

Matt. xix. 27.—Then answered Peter and said unto him, Behold, we have forsaken **all**,
and followed thee; what shall we have therefore? (Sk.)

WHATEVER enterprize we engage in, it is equally rational and just duly to
consider the general merits of its character and the probable results of its
issue. This is more especially the case when we embark in any cause
which is likely to involve the most interesting and important consequences.
Now this is unquestionably the character of religion, which is the one thing
needful to every human being. In making choice therefore of this momentous subject, we should "first count the cost," and then willingly renounce
every thing which is incompatible with its possession, or it is impossible to
realize its personal benefits. This is evidently the doctrine that is taught in
the preceding context, and which gave rise to the language of the text. The
Saviour having described the snares of affluence, and asserted the impossibility of those who trust in riches to enter into the kingdom of heaven, (as
strikingly exemplified in the case of the young ruler, with whom he had
been conversing,) Peter, with his usual zeal and boldness, "answered and
said, Behold, we have forsaken all," &c. These words clearly unfold the
true character of Christ's disciples, and distinctly suggest the evils they renounced—the example they follow—and the reward they anticipate.

I. THE EVILS THEY RENOUNCE;—"Behold, we have *forsaken all*," said
Peter. And though Christ does not require all his followers to forsake their
secular occupations and become ministers of the gospel as the apostles did,
yet there are many things which we must renounce for his sake, or we cannot be his disciples, Matt. xvi. 24.

1. *We must forsake all our sinful practices.* As impenitent sinners, we
"live after the flesh according to the course of this world, fulfilling the desires of the flesh and of the mind," Eph. ii. 2, 3. But as the followers of
Christ, we must mortify the deeds of the body, "cease to do evil, and learn
to do well." Every vicious habit must be fully abandoned, however painful
to human nature, Matt. v. 29, 30.—Whatever is offensive to God and injurious to the soul, must be freely sacrificed to our best interests on the altar
of conscience and truth.—"Let the wicked forsake his way, and the unrighteous man his thoughts." All sin of every description must be faithfully renounced, as utterly inconsistent with Christian discipleship, Tit. ii. 11, 12.

2. *We must forsake all our ungodly associates.* While we are of the

world we are companions of the wicked, are actuated by the same carnal principles, and governed by the same worldly maxims. But when Divine grace apprehends and subdues sinners, and convinces them of the vanity and corruption of the world, they immediately "come out from among them, and are separate, and touch not the unclean thing," 2 Cor. vi. 17, 18. And though religion does not forbid every kind of intercourse with the wicked, yet it teaches its subjects the evil and danger of making them their constant associates and intimate friends, 2 Cor. vi. 14—16; James iv. 4. And hence, like David, they become companions of them that fear the Lord, and their delight is with the excellent of the earth.

3. *We must forsake all our unholy attachments.* Religion regards the heart as well as the life. We must not only be outwardly separated from sin and sinners, but also inwardly renewed in the spirit of our minds, Eph. iv. 22—24. An undue attachment to the world was evidently the ruin of the hopeful young man whose character and conduct are recorded in this chapter. He loved his possessions, and was unwilling to give up every thing for Christ, ver. 21, 22; Matt. x. 37, 38. But his faithful disciples "crucify the flesh with its affections and lusts," and gladly forsake sin in all its diversified forms and fascinating snares. The text also asserts,

II. The example they follow ;—" We have forsaken all and *followed thee*." The apostles followed Christ, both *literally* and *morally*, as his personal attendants and approved disciples. They gladly received his word, acknowledged his Messiahship, and obeyed his injunctions. In these respects we also ought to be "followers of God as dear children."

1. *We should follow Christ as our teacher, by embracing his gospel.* He is an infallible prophet, and teaches the way of God perfectly. "He spake as never man spake," Matt. vii. 28, 29.—His word is spirit and life, and able to save the soul. It must be received believingly, gratefully, experimentally, and practically "as the power of God unto salvation," John viii. 31, 32.—As willing and obedient disciples, we must affectionately imbibe, and duly improve, all the instructions of his word and Spirit, "Hear ye him."

2. *We should follow Christ as our Sovereign. by obeying his precepts.* He is the King of Zion, and sways his sceptre in his church.—As our Redeemer, Saviour, and Judge, he justly demands the obedience of mankind, 1 Cor. vi. 19, 20.—We must obey him decidedly, cheerfully, faithfully, and constantly.—In vain do we profess to be *taught* by him, and trust in him, if we do not *obey* him. Obedience is the genuine test of discipleship, Matt. vii. 20. "Ye are my friends if ye do whatsoever I command you."

3. *We should follow Christ as our pattern, by imitating his example.*— "He did no sin, neither was guile found in his mouth; for he fulfilled all righteousness."—His example is perfect, extensive, intelligible, and distinctly recorded by the evangelists for our instruction and encouragement.—As far as possible we should imbibe the spirit that he manifested, uniformly follow the example which he left for our imitation, John xiii. 15; 1 Pet. ii. 21. We shall thus "walk as he also walked," and rejoice with all his disciples in,

III. The reward they anticipate ;—" What shall we have therefore?" Whatever motive might prompt this important inquiry, the Saviour kindly gave a full and explicit answer in the following context, by which we are taught,

1. *Following Christ will secure our personal salvation.* They "shall inherit everlasting life," ver. 29.—Now it is impossible to obtain the inheritance of glory without a previous possession of saving grace, Heb. xii. 14.

**Those** who reject Christ, are condemned already; but such as embrace and follow him "are saved by grace through faith." They take his yoke upon them, and find rest unto their souls, Matt. xi. 28—40. Conformity to his image and will, constitutes both the purity and felicity of his followers.

2. *Following Christ will secure our temporal interests.*—He assured his disciples that whatever worldly advantages they might sacrifice for his sake, they would certainly "receive manifold more in the present life," ver. 29. Though he did not promise them riches, he engaged to supply all their necessities.—Religion always casts a friendly influence over all our temporal concerns, and makes "all things work together for our good." It insures every blessing, both for life and godliness, for this world and the next, Ps. lxxxiv. 11; Matt. vi. 33; 1 Tim. iv. 8.

3. *Following Christ will secure our eternal happiness.* He therefore distinctly promised this to the apostles, in his answer to Peter, ver. 28. This promise is certainly glorious in its import, and infallible in its accomplishment. It is the end that crowns the work. Christians have respect to the recompense of reward, and follow Christ from earth to heaven. He is now precious to their souls, and soon they will appear with him in glory everlasting, John xiv. 2. 3; 1 John iii. 2.

Are we the followers of Christ? Do we follow him fully, or at a distance? Let his enemies repent and believe, and escape the wrath to come. But let the saints rejoice, and "follow on to know the Lord."

---

## THE BLESSEDNESS OF FEARING GOD.

Eccl. viii. 12 —Surely I know that it shall be well with them that fear God. (S. S.)

NOTHING certain can be determined respecting God's favor from the outward dispensations of his providence, Eccl. ix. 1.

The wicked seem on the whole to prosper more than others, Psa. lxxiii. 5, 12.

Nevertheless the godly are by far the happier persons, Ps. lxxiii. 15.

It is of them only that the assertion in the text can be made—

We propose to shew,

I. WHO THEY ARE THAT FEAR GOD.

This, we may suppose, would be a point easy to be determined—

But, through self-love and Satan's devices, many mistake respecting it—

The characters described in the text may be distinguished by the following marks :—

1. They stand in awe of God's judgments.

Once they disregarded the displeasure of the Almighty—Ps. x. 5.

They would not believe that his threatenings would be executed—

But now they have learned to tremble at his word—Isai. lxvi. 2.

Awakened by his Spirit, they exclaim with the prophet—Isai. xxxiii. 14

The scriptures uniformly represent them in this light—Acts xvi. 29. and Ps. cxix. 120.

2. They embrace the salvation offered them.

In their natural state they felt no need of a physician—Rev. iii. 17.

They saw no suitableness in the remedy which the gospel offered them—1 Cor. i. 23.

Their pride would not suffer them to submit to its humiliating terms, **Rom x. 3.**

But now they gladly embrace Christ as their only Saviour—

They flee to him, as the murderers did to a city of refuge—

This is the description given of them in the inspired volume, Heb. vi. 18.

3. They endeavor to keep all the commandments.

If ever they obeyed God at all, they served him only to the extent the world would approve—

Where the lax habits of mankind forbade their compliance with the divine command, they were afraid to be singular—

But they dare not any longer halt between God and Baal—

They have determined, through grace, to follow the Lord fully—

The language of their hearts is like that of David, Ps. cxix. 5, 6.

This was the very ground on which God concluded that Abraham feared him, Gen. xxii. 12.

These marks clearly distinguish those who fear God from all others.

The *formal Pharisee* has never felt his desert of condemnation, Luke xviii. 11.

The *merely awakened sinner* has never truly embraced the gospel, Acts xxiv. 25, and xxvi. 23.

The *hypocritical professor* has never mortified his besetting sin, Acts viii. 23.

It is *the person* alone, *who fears God*, that unites in his experience a dread of God's wrath, an affiance in Christ, and a love to the command ments·—

Such persons, notwithstanding appearances, are truly blessed.

II. IN WHAT RESPECTS IT SHALL BE WELL WITH THEM.

They are not exempt from the common afflictions of life—

They have in addition to them many trials peculiar to themselves—

Yet it goes well with them.

1. In respect of temporal good.

They have a peculiar enjoyment of *prosperity*—

The ungodly find an emptiness in all their possessions, Job. xx. 22.

But the godly have not such gall mixed with their comforts, Prov. x. 22. 1 Tim. vi. 17.

They have also peculiar supports in a season of *adversity*—

The wicked are for the most part miserable in their affliction, Eccl. v. 17

If kept from murmuring, it is the summit of their attainments—

But the righteous are enabled to glory in tribulation, Rom. v. 3.

And cordially to approve of God's dispensations towards them, 2 Kings xx. 19.

2. In respect of spiritual good.

They possess a peace that passeth all understanding—

They are filled with a joy utterly unknown to others, Prov. xiv. 10.

The work of sanctification is gradually carried on within them, 2 Cor. iv. 16.

As they approach towards death they grow in a meetness for heaven—

And are serene and happy in the near prospect of eternity, Psa. xxxvii. 37.

3. In respect to eternal good.

Who can set forth their felicity in the eternal world?—

Who can even conceive the weight of glory preparing for them .—

How will their faith be lost in sight, and their hope in enjoyment!—

Then indeed will that truth be seen and felt by them, Ps. cxliv. 15.

These things are far from being " cunningly devised fables."

**III. WHAT ASSURANCE WE HAVE THAT IT SHALL BE THUS WELL WITH THEM.**

No truth whatever is capable of clearer demonstration—

The topics from whence it might be proved are innumerable—

We shall however confine ourselves to three.

**1. The fitness of things requires it.**

No man can seriously think that there is one portion to the righteous and the wicked—

There is no well ordered government on earth where this is the case—

Much less can we suppose it possible in the divine government—

To imagine such a thing, is to strip the Deity of all regard to his own honor—

We may be sure that there shall be a distinction made in favor of his servants, Mal. iii. 18.

**2. The promises of God insure it.**

All *temporal* good is expressly promised to those " who fear God," Psa. xxxiv. 9.

All *spiritual* good also is given them as their portion, Ps. xxv. 12, 13.

Yea, all *eternal* good is laid up for them as their unalienable inheritance, Ps. ciii. 17.

All the promises are made over to them in one word, 1 Tim. iv. 8.

Can any one doubt a truth so fully established?—

**3. The experience of all that ever feared God attests it.**

Who ever found it unprofitable to serve the Lord? Jer. ii. 31.

What truly devoted soul was ever forsaken by him? Isa. xlix. 15.

Who ever complained that the means, by which he was brought to fear God, were too severe?—

Or that any affliction, that increased and confirmed that fear, was too heavy?

David indeed did at one time question the position in the text—

But on recollection he condemned himself for his rashness and ignorance—

And acknowledged that his vile suspicions contradicted the experience of God's children in all ages, Ps. lxxiii. 12—15, 22.

On these grounds we " assuredly know" the truth declared in the text.

We do not *surmise it as a* thing *possible*—

We do not *hope it as* a thing *probable*—

We *absolutely know it as infallibly certain*—

We are not surer of our existence than we are of this truth—

Without hesitation therefore we deliver our message, Isa. iii. 10, 11

O that the word may sink deep into all our hearts!—

And that we might from experience unite our testimony to Solomon's, Prov. xxviii. 14.

We beg leave to ask, whether they who fear *not* God, have any such assurance in their favor?

We are aware that they will entertain presumptuous hopes—

And that, in opposition to God's word, they will expect happiness—

But does the boldest sinner dare affirm that he *knows* it shall be well with him?—

His conscience would instantly revolt at such falsehood and blasphemy—

Let those then, that fear not God, stand self-condemned—

Let them flee unto their God and Saviour with penitence and faith—

Let them so live as to preserve the testimony of a good conscience—

And then, however enlarged their expectations of good may be, they shall never be disappointed, Isa. xlv. 17.

## THE JOY OF THE LORD IS OUR STRENGTH.

Neh. viii. 10.—The joy of the Lord is your strength.   (S. S.)

The preaching of God's word is a very ancient ordinance—
In the context we have a description of the manner in which Nehemiah conducted it—
These means of instruction were useful in that day—
Nor are they less necessary in every place and age—
People need, not only reproof for what is wrong, but direction in what is right—
The Jews wept bitterly at the hearing of the law—
But Nehemiah corrected their sorrow as ill-timed—
And exhorted them to rejoice in God, who had done so great things for them—

I. What reason we have to rejoice in the Lord.
God is often said to rejoice over his people—Zeph. iii. 17.
But the joy here spoken of must be understood rather of that which we feel in the recollection of God's goodness towards us.
The Jews at that season had special cause for joy in God.
They had been miraculously delivered from Babylon—
This temple had been rebuilt in twenty years, and the worship of God restored—
And now, after seventy years more, the wall of the city was finished—
They had been enabled to surmount innumerable difficulties—ch. iv. 27.
They had prospered, even to a miracle, in their endeavors—ch. vi. 16.
These were tokens of the divine favor, and pledges of its continuance—
They were therefore called upon to rejoice with gratitude and confidence—
Nor was their sorrow, however just, to exclude this joy—
Such reason also have all the Lord's people to rejoice in the Lord,
They have experienced a redemption from sorer captivity—
And been delivered by more stupendous means—
Every day's preservation too is, as it were, a miracle—
Yet the work of their souls is carried on in spite of enemies—
Yea, *is expedited through the means used to defeat it*—
Surely then they should say, like the church of old—Ps. cxxvi. 3.
Moreover, these mercies are pledges and earnests of yet richer blessings—
They may well confide in so good and gracious a God—
They have indeed still great cause for sorrow—
Yet is it their duty to " rejoice *always* in the Lord"—Phil. iv. 4.
To promote and encourage this, we proceed to show,

II. In what respects this joy is our strength.
We are as dependent on the frame of our minds as on the state of our bodies—
Joy in God produces very important effects.
1. It disposes for action.
Fear and sorrow depress and overwhelm the soul—Isai. lvii. 16.
They enervate and benumb all our faculties—
They keep us from attending to any encouraging considerations—Exod. vi. 9.
They disable us from extending relief to others—Job ii. 13.
They indispose us for the most necessary duties—Luke xxii. 45.

300

We cannot pray, or speak, or do any thing with pleasure—
On the contrary, a joyous frame exhilarates the soul—Prov. xvii. 22.
David well knew the effect it would produce—Ps. li. 12, 13.
And every one may safely adopt his resolution—Ps. cxix. 32
2. It qualifies for suffering.
When the spirit is oppressed, the smallest trial is a burthen—
In those seasons we are apt to fret and murmur both against God and man—
We consider our trials as the effects of divine *wrath*—
Or, overlooking God, we vent our indignation against the instruments he uses—
But when the soul is joyous, afflictions appear light—Heb. x. 34. & xii. 2.
How little did Paul and Silas regard their imprisonment!—Acts xvi. 25.
How willing was Paul to lay down his very life for Christ!—Acts xx. 24.
This accords with the experience of every true christian—Rom. v. 2, 3, and 2 Cor. vi. 10.

APPLICATION.

1. Let us not be always brooding over our corruptions.
Seasonable sorrows ought not to be discouraged—
But we should never lose sight of all that God has done for us—
It is our privilege to walk joyfully before the Lord—Ps. cxxxviii. 5. & cxlix. 5. & lxxxix. 15, 16.
If we abounded more in praise, we should more frequently be crowned with victory—2 Chron. xx. 21, 22.
2. Let us carefully guard against the incursions of sin.
It is sin that hides the Lord from our eyes—Isai. lix. 2.
Joy will not consist with indulged sin—Ps. lxvi. 18.
Let us then " mortify our earthly members" and our besetting sins—
Let us be girt with our armor while we work with our hands—Neh. iv. 17, 18.
Nor ever grieve the Spirit, lest we provoke him to depart from us—
3. Let us be daily going to God *through Christ.*
If ever we rejoice in God at all, it must be through the Lord Jesus Christ —Rom. v. 11.
It is through Christ alone that our past violations of the law can be forgiven—Col. i. 20.
It is through Christ alone that the good work can be perfected in our hearts—Heb. xii. 2.
And, since " all things are *through* him, and *from* him, let them be *to* him also"—Rom. xi. 36.

---

## THE CHRISTIAN SOLDIER'S WARFARE.

Ephesians vi. 12.—For we wrestle not against flesh and blood, but against principalities, against powers, against the rulers of the darkness of this world, against spiritual wickedness in high places. (Sk.)

In this epistle, St. Paul reminds the Ephesians of their great obligations to God, on account of the gracious favors in which they were interested:

and having strongly urged them to a holy deportment answerable to their principles, their profession, and their privileges, he in conclusion exhorts them to "be strong in the Lord, and in the power of his might," ver. 12.

The *reason* why we should be "strong in the Lord," he assigns in our text. In improving and applying which let us consider,

I. THE ENEMIES WITH WHOM, AS CHRISTIAN SOLDIERS, WE ARE CALLED TO CONTEND. The term "christian soldiers," is thus employed, because in this paragraph, our apostle represents our present state as a warfare. Here we are instructed to observe,

I. *Our enemies are spirits;* not composed of flesh and blood. We wrestle not with flesh and blood, but with spirits. This implies, that *they are not material and compound beings*, but simple and immaterial; and as such, are capable of unwearied exertion. *They are not objects of sight and sense*, but invisible and impalpable; able to assault us when unperceived by us. *They are not inert in their natures*, but active and restless in the execution of their mischievous devices, Job i. 7; Matt. xii. 43. *They are not, and cannot be, subject to dissolution;* but, as spirits, they must be immortal. Here we are taught to observe,

2 *Our enemies are wicked spirits. They are maliciously wicked;* bent on injuring us. This is evinced *by their names:* a fallen spirit is called the *devil*, or calumniator; because he slanders men to God; he slanders God to men; and slanders men to each other. This he does for the purpose of sowing discord between God and his creatures, 1 Pet. v. 8. He is called *satan*, an adversary; because he sets himself up to oppose us. He is called an *enemy;* because he is filled with enmity against us, Rev. xii. 12. He is called the *old serpent;* because in this form he tempted Eve, Rev. xii. 9. He is called *Abaddon*, and *Apollyon*, the destroyer; because he desires and seeks our destruction, Rev. ix. 11. Their malice is also evinced *by their employment*. They go about seeking to destroy us: they seek to destroy our comfort, by depriving us of peace and joy in believing, 1 Pet. i. 6. They seek to destroy our piety, by divesting us of faith, hope, love, and purity, Luke xxii. 31. They seek to destroy our *usefulness*, by drawing us into sin, and rendering us stumbling blocks to those around us, Heb. xii. 15. They seek to destroy our *souls*, by engaging us in their service here, and bringing us to their own hell, hereafter, Matt. xxv. 41. *They are daringly wicked;* they are wicked spirits in high places: they first rebelled against God even in heaven itself; there was war in heaven, Rev. xii. 7. And they still approach the most sacred places that they may injure us; they assault us amid the avocations of civil and domestic life; in our religious retirement; in God's house; and even at his table, John xiii. 27.

3. *Our enemies are formidable spirits,*—being possessed of such qualities as are calculated to inspire terror. They are formidable on account of their *number;* it is not one enemy only that we have to contend with; we wrestle, or struggle against principalities. That our enemies are numerous is evident from the cause of the demoniac, Luke viii. 30, who was possessed by a whole legion of them.

> "From thrones of glory driven, by flaming vengeance hurl'd,
> They throng the air, and darken heaven, and rule this lower world."

And it appears that numerous as they are, all of them are united, employed, and instructed to seek the ruin of mankind. They are formidable on account of their *strength:*—they are justly called "powers." Their power or ability to effect mischief, is evident from the case of Job, i. 12, ii. 6.

They are formidable on account of their *weapons*, being armed with fiery darts; their injections are tipt with poison, and hurled with fury. They are formidable on account of their *extensive influence*,—being rulers of the darkness of this world. The ignorance and sinfulness of mankind are subject to them, and employed against us. They are formidable on account of their *wiles*, see ver. 11; for they are naturally sagacious; and must have acquired much skill by long experience. Having considered our enemies, let us observe,

II. IN WHAT MANNER WE ARE INSTRUCTED TO CONTEND WITH THEM. From what our apostle adds on this subject, our duty is evident.

1. *We must contend with them in the armor of God.* This armor must be *all put on*, ver. 11, 14, 17. The whole of it is absolutely necessary; if any part be wanting, whether it be the girdle,—the breast-plate,—the greaves,—the helmet,—the shield,—or the sword,—the consequence must be fatal to us. This armor we must *retain* till our warfare is past, 1 Tim. i. 18, 19. This armor we must *take* and use whenever assaulted, ver. 13.

2. *We must contend with them in the spirit of prayer and watchfulness*, ver. 18. Pray with *all prayer*, that you may be strong in the Lord; that you may be girded by his wisdom and assisted by his power in all temptations. And *watch* thereunto, with all perseverance; that you may not at any time fall into the snares of your enemies, Mark xiii. 37; 1 Thess. v. 6; Eph. v. 16.

3. *We must contend with them in the exercise of firm resistance.* You must wrestle with them; in doing this, *get* all the strength you can by prayer, and *use* it, by striving against sin. Let your resistance be *early;* never enter into any league, truce, or parley with the enemy: resist him at his first approach, 1 Thess. v. 22; let your resistance be *courageous;* expect certain victory, Psa. lxviii. 1, 2; 1 Cor. xvi. 13; and let your resistance be *unwearied*, till you conquer, Psa. xviii. 37, 38. That you may be animated to persevere in this warfare, consider,

III. THE REASONS BY WHICH WE SHOULD BE INDUCED THUS TO CONTEND. Thus contend,

1. *Because the most important objects depend on this contention.* Your *steadfastness* depends on it, for your enemies seek to cast you down, Psa. cxviii. 13: your *liberty* depends on it, for they contend with you for the mastery, 2 Tim. ii. 5; your *glory* depends on it, for they contend with you about heavenly places, Rev. iii. 11; your *eternal life* depends on it, for they aim at murdering your souls, John viii. 44; the best *interests* of your *connections* depend on it, for it is likely to be well or ill with them, as it proves with you, Deut. v. 29; Prov. iii. 33; and without *contention*, these objects cannot be secured, Matt. xi. 12.

2. *Because victory is certain to the faithful soldiers of Christ.* Victory over the *world*, 1 John v. 4; victory over *sin*, 1 John i. 7; victory over *satan*, Rom. xvi. 20; victory over *tribulation*, Rom. viii. 35—37; and victory over *death*, 1 Cor. xv. 55—57. Thus contend,

3. *Because victory will be attended with certain glory.* A *glorious rest* from all painful toil and contention, Rev. xiv. 13; *glorious exemptions* from all penal evil, Rev. ii. 11, and from all natural evil, Rev. xxi. 4: and *glorious honors*, comprising the public approval of Christ our judge, Rev. iii. 5; a glorious *throne*, Rev. iii. 21; a glorious *crown*, Rev. ii. 10; and a glorious *kingdom*, Luke xii. 32; Dan. vii. 18.

## THE CHRISTIAN'S TRIUMPH.

1 Corinthians xv. 57.—-But thanks be to God, which giveth us the victory through our Lord Jesus Christ.—-(Sk.)

IN the preceding verses of this truly interesting chapter, our apostle has been meeting the sophisms and cavils which the infidels and skeptics of his day opposed to divine truth; and, with the ability of "a master in Israel," has illustrated and defended that important doctrine of revelation, the resurrection of the dead. And in the close of a luminous and cogent train of argumentation, he directs our attention to the powerful influence of the religion of Jesus Christ at those most solemn of all periods, the hour of death, and the morning of the final judgment: the passage immediately before us forming a kind of ejaculatory conclusion to the whole, expressive of the most lively sentiments of gratitude, for that transcendent victory which the believer, through the " Captain of (his) salvation," is enabled to achieve

These words present to our serious consideration,

I. THE CHRISTIAN'S GLORIOUS TRIUMPH.

II. THE MEANS BY WHICH IT IS ACHIEVED.

III. THE MOTIVES TO GRATITUDE WHICH IT FURNISHES.

I. THE CHRISTIAN'S TRIUMPH naturally leads us to consider,—*the enemies encountered,—the conflict sustained,—*and *the success experienced.*

1. *The enemies encountered.* Victory supposes a state of warfare, and consequently assumes the existence of enemies. The christian proposes the attainment of the image of God, and the promotion of his glory: together with the enjoyment of a celestial inheritance beyond the grave; and whatever is opposed to the nature of his object, and impedes its accomplishment, may very properly be denominated his adversary. The world with its terrific frown, or its alluring and deceitful smile; the corruption and treachery of the human heart, and the mighty powers of hell, are united in close and potent combination against the christian, and the heavenly object of his pursuit. This enmity is inveterate in its nature, and perpetual in its operation, Jer. xvii. 9; John xv. 19; Rom. viii. 7; 1 Pet. v. 8.

2. *The conflict sustained.* The warfare in which the christian is engaged requires the most prompt and vigilant exertion. In order to maintain his ground, and ensure success, his resistance must be *firm ;* no compromise can be allowed; no pacific overtures can exist with safety; to hesitate and parley, is to give way to the enemy, and relinquish the palm of victory. It must be with *steady perseverence :* the conquering christian maintains a firm opposition; not for a few months or a few years only, but he goes on from conquest to conquest, till his captain calls him from the field, to his eternal reward. In the spirit of *humble dependence ;* though he puts forth all his energies,—gives all diligence,—firmly and perseveringly maintains his post,— yet his hope of success is founded in the wisdom, power, and faithfulness of his divine leader, 1 Pet. v. 9; 2 Pet. i. 5—10; and iii. 17; Rev. ii. 10; and xii. 11.

3. *The success experienced.* Sustaining this conflict with this constant steady reliance on his God, the christian's conquest is *certain ;*—the nature of the gospel economy, the omnipotence and truth of Jehovah : and the luminous testimony of every age of time, all unite to ensure this victory. It is *complete* and *perfect* in its nature ;—the believer triumphs over the world, and self, and sin ;—the sting of death is extracted, and the fear of it destroyed ;—he exults over the falling powers of darkness ;—quits terrestrial scenes ;

—ascends to the throne of the Deity ;—and receives the victor's crown at the hand of the captain of his salvation, 1 John iv. 4—18; 1 Cor. xv. 55, 56; 2 Tim. iv. 6—8; Rev. iii. 21.

II. THE MEANS BY WHICH THIS TRIUMPH IS ACHIEVED. It is through the operation of divine beneficence in the gospel of Jesus Christ. Hence this conquest may justly be considered.

1. *Divine in its origin.* Man in his natural state. has no disposition for this conflict; nor does he inherently possess that strength which is necessary for conquest;—yea, so far is this from being the case, that all his inclinations and energies are in unison with those of the enemies of God, and decidedly hostile to the cause of truth, Gal. v. 19—21; therefore, both the disposition for conflict, and the strength for conquest, are derived,— they flow from the exhaustless fountain of goodness, through the channel of gospel provision, Jer. xiii. 23; 1 Cor. iv. 7; Ephes. ii. 1—8.

2. *Free in its communication.* "The *gift* of God." Every blessing bestowed upon man by the author of good, is communicated freely; because man is the subject of guilt and condemnation, and has nothing of a meritorious nature to recommend or entitle him to the notice of Jehovah;—nor can he, in any way, ever remunerate or benefit a Being who is self-existent, self-dependent, and eternal;—one who is in his own nature perfectly and independently happy, Isa. lv. 1; 2 Tim. i. 9.

3. *It proceeds through the medium of sacrifice.* " Through our Lord Jesus Christ." God is a being who is just as well as merciful: man, by transgression, has violated the rights of divine justice, and offered insult to this perfection of the Deity:—justice required satisfaction; but poor insolvent, self-ruined man could render none. Jesus Christ became our "surety;" "he bore our sins in his own body on the tree." Justice is honored: yea—

> " Here the whole Deity is known ;
> Nor dares a creature guess,
> Which of the glories brightest shone,
> The *Justice* or the *Grace.*"

See Isa. liii. 4—6; John i. 29; Rom. v. 8; Tit. ii. 14; 1 Pet. ii. 24.

III. THE MOTIVES TO GRATITUDE WHICH IT FURNISHES. The most lively gratitude is ever due from man to God, for the manifold favors which he continually receives at his hands; but the anticipation of this victory ought, above every other consideration, to excite the christian to sing, " Bless the Lord O my soul, and all that is within me praise his holy name;" because of

1. *Our entire unworthiness.* Man being in his natural state a rebel against God,—opposed to his government,—his holiness,—and his truth,—in short, decidedly hostile to all the perfections of his nature,—has nothing to expect, on the principles of justice, but the satisfaction of its claims, by an interminable perpetuity of suffering; for a being thus circumstanced to be delivered from this just extremity of wo, and to be enabled to triumph over " the last enemy," and participate the felicities of heaven, ought to call forth bursts of grateful adoration, Ps. xxxiii. 1.

2. *The amazing love which is displayed in this triumph.* The value of a gift is materially augmented, and the obligations to gratitude increased, by the difficulties and sacrifices which may be connected with its communication. Though nothing is difficult to the " Lord God Omnipotent," yet there is a sacrifice connected with the process of human redemption, of the most unparalleled description;—the Father delivered up his Son to poverty,

ignominy, and death, in order to extricate rebellious man from the gulf of ruin, John iii. 16; Rom. v. 8—11; 1 John iii. 1.

**3.** *The glorious result of this victory.* The believer not only experiences a victory over the world and sin, and triumphs over the fears of death, but also enters the regions of immortality ; mingles with seraphic bands ;—participates the glory of the Redeemer ;—beholds, with ceaseless rapturous gaze, the transporting perfections of Jehovah;—swells the song of salvation;—and drinks full draughts at that exhaustless stream of joy which issued from the throne of God, Matt. xxii. 30 ; 1 Pet. i. 4; Rev. iii. 21, and vii. 15, 16, 17. Surely a victory replete with such blissful consequences demands the highest strains of praise from those who have a lively anticipation of it.

This subject, 1. Suggests the institution of a minute inquiry respecting the part we are taking in this warfare. And,

**2.** Furnishes ample consolation to the conflicting, suffering soldier of Christ.

----

## HOPE IN DEATH.

Proverbs xiv. 32.—The righteous hath hope in his death. (Sk.)

The most part of this book of Proverbs consists of short independent sentences, spoken by Solomon, the wisest of men, and as the Jews tell us, in the middle age of his life, when his understanding was in its greatest vigor, and under the inspiration too of the Holy Spirit of truth. Coherency of the parts, and dependence of one thing upon another, is not to be expected in a book of aphorisms ; for every sentence is to be taken by itself, and includes an entire sense. We come therefore immediately to the words of the text,—" The righteous hath hope in his death." We shall,

I. Attend to the character of the persons that have hope in their death.

II. Speak as to the object of their hope, or show what things they hope for.

I. Attend to the character of the persons that have hope in their death :—" the righteous."

1. On the mention of this character, that passage of the apostle is apt to offer itself to our minds, " *There is none righteous, no not one,*" Rom. iii. 10. Where then are the righteous persons to be found, that have hope in their death ? We must consider, that the apostle, in the place quoted, means the legally righteous ; none such indeed are to be found on earth ; but Solomon here speaks of those that are righteous in a gospel sense, and many such are to be found.

2. *All men are now in a fallen state.* God made the first man perfect, Eccl. vii. 29 ; after his own image, Gen. i. 27; in integrity or righteousness, which was his honor ; but he did not abide in the state in which he was made. The law that was given him to observe, he soon transgressed, though furnished with full ability to keep it; and so lost his innocence, or legal righteousness, made himself sinful, and brought guilt and moral pollution upon all his natural offspring. So that there is none righteous so as to be innocent and sinless: not one ; all are conceived and born in sin, Psa. il 5, and so are sinners by nature. And as to practice, " there is not a

just,' or righteous, " man on earth that doeth good, and sinneth not," in a legal sense, Eccl. vii. 20.

3. *Yet every true believer in Christ is righteous, according to the covenant of grace.* Every believer in Christ is in him, and has rigteousness imputed to him, 1 Cor. i. 30. It pleased God on the fall of the first Adam, to set up his Son as a second Adam, that " as by the offense of one judgment came upon all men to condemnation, even so by the righteousness of one the free gift came upon all men to justification of life :" that " by one man's disobedience many were made sinners, so by the obedience of one shall many be made righteous," Rom. v. 18, 19. God hath made Christ, who knew no sin, a sin offering for us, that we might be made the righteousness of God through him, 2 Cor. v. 21. This system was the contrivance of infinite wisdom, originated in the free grace of God, is a doctrine that could be only known by divine revelation, in which it is exhibited in the clearest light: "the righteousness of God, by the faith of Jesus Christ, to all and upon all that believe," Rom. iii. 22. Believers in Christ are justified before God; their guilt is taken away; they are constituted righteous, restored to the divine favor, enjoy inward peace, and possess a title to heaven.

4. *Believers in Christ have also an inherent righteousness wrought in them by the Holy Spirit.* They are renewed by the Holy Ghost, Tit. iii. 5 ; and made partakers of divine nature, 2 Pet. i. 4. Though free justification and entire sanctification are different degrees of a work of grace on the heart, yet the former is preparatory to the latter; and even the former blessing is inseparably connected with the reign of grace within. " Sin shall not have dominion over you, for ye are not under the law, but under grace," Rom. vi. 14. All that live in the favor of God are graciously fitted for a life of holiness. They are created in Christ to good works, Eph. ii. 10 ; and with their new nature they have the Spirit of God put within them, to cause them to walk in his statutes, Ezek. xxxvi. 27.

5. *Believers in Christ are not only habitually righteous by their regeneration, but they endeavor to be actually righteous in imitation of Christ.* Being united to him, and led by his Spirit, they endeavor to walk as he walked. And the apostle says, " He that doeth righteousness is righteous, even as he is righteous," 1 John iii. 7. Being born again, born from heaven, they are in the way of faith and holiness tending thither. They delight in the law of God after the inward man, and endeavor a conformity to it in the whole course of their actions. What God requires they sincerely try to render to him, the superlative love of their heart, and the impartial and constant obedience of their lives. These now are the righteous persons who have hope in their death.

II. Show the object of their hope, or what things they hope for in their dying moments. Hope is an expectation of something future and good, which God has promised; and the expectation of it is attended with pleasure and delight, in proportion to their thoughts of its excellency, and to the assurance with which they expect to enjoy it. Accordingly, the christian's hope is called " the rejoicing of hope," Heb. iii. 6. We shall mention a few things the righteous hope for in their dying moments.

1. *They hope for the gracious presence of God with them in that solemn crisis.* And indeed they never more need his reviving, supporting, and protecting presence, than when called to walk through the valley of the shadow of death. Their hope of this necessary and important blessing

is founded on such promises as these: "I will never leave thee, nor forsake thee," Heb. xiii. 5; "This God is our God for ever and ever: he will be our guide even unto death," Psa. xlviii. 14. "My flesh and my heart faileth : but God is the strength of my heart, and my portion for ever," Psa. lxxiii. 26. It is the consciousness of this gracious presence of God with them in their latter end that fortifies them against desponding fears, and refreshes their souls with light and comfort, when all other things appear dark and gloomy about them. Hence, David says, "Yea, though I walk through the valley of the shadow of death, I will fear no evil; for thou art with me; thy rod and thy staff they comfort me," Psa. xxiii. 4. From this promised grace and powerful presence of God, they hope for safety in their passage from this to the future world.

2. *They hope for the immediate admission of their souls into heaven:* that having guided them with his counsel during life, He will at death receive their spirits into glory, Ps. lxxiii. 24, to dwell in his presence, where there is fulness of joy, and pleasures for evermore, Ps. xvi. 11; where all evil is excluded, and all good is present, to fill the largest extent of their desires and wishes. The hope of this is founded on several promises: "If I go and prepare a place for you, I will come again, and receive you unto myself; that where I am, there you may be also," John xiv. 3. Christ in his testament, which is of force and unalterable by his death, appoints to his saints a kingdom, into which being risen, he as forerunner, is for them entered, with a declared purpose to prepare for their coming, and to keep open the way by his intercession. Hereupon their death comes under his direction and ordering, as having the keys of death and the invisible world. And when he sends death for the souls of believers, they have the like privilege that Stephen had, of committing them into his hand, as ready to receive them, and present them with acceptance to the Father. And thus being "absent from the body they are present with the Lord," which is far better, 2 Cor. v. 8; Phil. 1. 23; added to the "spirits of just men made perfect," Heb. xii. 23; and so they enter into the joy of their Lord, Matt. xxv. 21.

3. *The righteous, in death, hope for the resurrection of their bodies in the appointed season, to a glorious immortality.* The hope of this they found on that declaration, "This is the Father's will who hath sent me, that of all which he hath given me I should lose nothing, but should raise it up at the last day," John vi. 39. The apostle says, "I have hope towards God, that there shall be a resurrection of the dead, both of the just and unjust," Acts xxiv. 15. Though the believers go down to the grave, they do not lose their relation to Christ, but remain united to him. They sleep in Jesus, and under his eye as guardian of the dust, which, however scattered, is precious and sacred; and them that sleep in Jesus will God bring with him, 1 Thess. iv. 14. Christ's resurrection is the pattern and pledge of the resurrection of the bodies of the saints, and will infer it as desirable and blessed. Christ being risen from the dead is become the first fruits of them that sleep, 1 Cor. xv. 20; and as he rose in glory, they shall in this respect be conformed to him, Phil. iii. 21. All this the righteous die in the hope of, and therefore can freely deposit their flesh in the dark and silent grave, where it shall rest in hope; foreseeing that eventful time, when it shall be raised from thence with unspeakable advantage, every way suited to the noblest operations of the perfected soul, and to all the important uses of the resurrection state.

4. *The righteous in their dying moments have a hope of eternal life,*

*and complete salvation of their entire nature, soul and body, reunited at the resurrection; of all the promised glories of the heavenly state.* Eternal life is the great promise of the gospel. "This is the promise that he hath promised us, even eternal life," 1 John ii. 25; and, "in hope of eternal life," Tit. i. 2. All the hopes of christian believers look towards this, and centre in it. These are some of the chief things the righteous hope for in death.

APPLICATION,—

The use that we are to make of this subject is obvious. Let us labor to be righteous persons, in order to our having hope in our death; to have our sins pardoned through faith in the sacrifice of Christ, our souls sanctified by the Holy Spirit, and then to be holy in all manner of conversation. To this end, let us beg of God, in the name of Christ, for the Holy Spirit to assist us in the exercise of faith, to renew our nature, and enable us to walk in newness of life. And being on impartial trial, that we are real christians, let us live and die "waiting for the hope of righteousness," as the apostle describes the believers in his day, Gal. v. 5.

~~~~~~~~~

## THE CHRISTIAN PILGRIMAGE.

1 Chron. xxix. 15.—For we are strangers and sojourners, as were all our fathers. (O.)

IN the preceding part of the chapter, we find king David, after having by his own example and entreaty requested the princes and the people to offer liberally in behalf of the house of God, who is not confined to temples made with hands, but fills heaven and earth, and the temple of the universe itself with his presence.—Hence the doxology begins at the 10th verse—

In the sequel we shall attend,

I. TO THE CONDITION OF THE PEOPLE OF GOD IN THIS WORLD—they are strangers and sojourners.

II. THEIR AVOWAL OF IT—"we are strangers and sojourners."

I. The saints are strangers and sojourners on the earth, because they are born from above—born not of corruptible seed but of incorruptible, which is the word of God, by the resurrection of our Lord Jesus from the dead: begotten again unto a lively hope of the heavenly inheritance—

They are born from above, having the blood-royal of heaven running in their moral veins: and therefore with a loftiness of sentiment becoming their high descent, naturally aspire after their native land. Having discovered something more noble than any thing which this world can afford; they leave to others the vain and the inordinate pursuits of its riches, its pleasures and its honors—

The saints are strangers and sojourners upon the earth, because they are absent from their best friends. An individual going to a foreign country, has generally few if any friends in that country. So in like manner christians have many foes, but comparatively few friends in the present world: their nearest and dearest and best friends in heaven. There dwells God their Father—Jesus Christ—the Holy Spirit—the sons of light, angels and archangels—Abraham, Isaac and Jacob—the prophets—the twelve apostles—the noble host of martyrs—all our pious friends.

They may be called strangers and sojourners, because their inheritance is in heaven. Strangers have generally no landed property or possessions in the foreign countries through which they travel—

So in like manner, the people of God have no portion in this world—their inheritance is in heaven—

Convinced, therefore, of the unsatisfactory notion of all earthly enjoyments, they look out for something more substantial—

The well-founded and lively hope of soon entering upon the enjoyment of this glorious inheritance, sustains them in every trial, wipes the tear from the eye that is dim with sorrow and sustains and animates and cheers them amidst all the ills of life—

The saints are strangers and pilgrims on the earth, because they are surrounded by many enemies and exposed to many dangers—

They find, in the natives of the country through which they pass, inveterate enemies. They are different in their moral pedigree; the men of the world are the children of the wicked one, love and serve him.—But they are the children of the Most High and as such serve and worship him, submit to his authority and obey his laws. This causes the children of the world to persecute the saints of God.—But besides the seductions of a wicked world, they have likewise to encounter the fierce assaults and the fiery attacks of the wicked one from without: while powerful corruptions lodge within their own breasts, throwing numerous barriers in the way of their progress towards heaven—

The people of God may be styled strangers and sojourners on earth, because they are making progress on their way towards heaven. A traveller is always desirous to reach the place of his destination and for this purpose is bending his course towards it.

So in like manner, the spiritual sojourners notwithstanding the great opposition and the numerous enemies which they have to encounter, will always be making progress in their journey—

The saints are strangers and sojourners on the earth, because their continuance here is short and uncertain. As the stranger only turns aside for the night, and in the morning pursues his journey, so the continuance of the spiritual traveller in this world is short and uncertain, Job xiv. 18, 19.

Human life even when protracted to its utmost verge is but a hand-breadth and a span. It has now decreased in a ten-fold proportion to what it once was; but even when prolonged to its former period, it was but a point—it was nothing when compared with eternity—

The saints, like strangers and pilgrims, will forget all their sorrows, and reflect with pleasure on the dangers of their earthly pilgrimage, when they reach their eternal home. As a traveller forgets all the hardships, which he endured on his travels, when he arrives at his native country, and recounts with pleasure his adventures, his difficulties and dangers to his admiring friends and beloved family—as the tempest-tost mariner—as the warrior—

So shall the saints forget their sorrows, and recall with pleasure the dangers of their earthly pilgrimage when they arrive at their Father's house—

II. THEIR AVOWAL OF IT.

They confess it by their words, as well as by their actions—Abraham confessed that he was a stranger and sojourner with the children of Heth. Jacob confessed it to Pharaoh—David—Moses—

They confess it likewise by their actions. It frequently happens that men say one thing and mean another, so that their actions belie their words. But christians by their garb and language, by their practice and profession, by their sorrows and joys, and the whole tenor of their conduct, plainly testify to the world that they are strangers and pilgrims on earth.

## IMPROVEMENT.

If we regard this world as a strange country, through which we are passing to our native home, we should endeavor to sustain as little injury by the way as possible—

Let us abstain from fleshly lusts that war against the soul—

If we we are really strangers and pilgrims, we will strive to be suitably prepared for our journey and make ample provision for that better country to which we are travelling—

It becomes strangers and pilgrims to endure, with patience and fortitude, all the ills they meet with in their journey heavenward—

If we view this world only as a scene of our pilgrimage, and heaven as the place of our eternal abode, we should above all things be solicitous about the way that leads to it—

If we are strangers and pilgrims here, we ought to maintain a deportment like those who belong to a better country·—

If we are strangers and pilgrims here, we should love one another as brethren and assist one another by the way—

---

## CHAPTER V.

## CHRISTIAN DUTIES.

### ON THE ACCEPTABLE SERVICE OF GOD.

Hebrews xii. 28.—We receive a kingdom which cannot be moved, let us have grace, whereby we may serve God acceptably, with reverence and godly fear. (B.)

THE Apostle having stated, in the foregoing verses, the pre-eminent privileges and prospects to which true believers in Christ are admitted, and having shown, by a reference to the prophecy of Haggai, ch. ii. 6, the stability and permanence of the New Testament dispensation, which is to remain to the end of time as the only form a Divine worship and religion acceptable to God, from which alone men can obtain a certain and bright prospect of everlasting glory, he adds the words of the text, as a practical inference from his argument. See ver. 18—27.— —Consider,

I. WHAT IS IMPLIED IN SERVING GOD, AND WHEN IT MAY BE SAID WE SERVE HIM ACCEPTABLY.

To serve God is to worship him. Matt. iv. 10; Luke iv. 8; 1 Sam. vii. 3. See particularly Heb. ix. 1. where ordinances of Divine worship are termed "ordinances of Divine service;" and ver. 9, where worshipping God is termed "doing service;" and Acts xxvi. 7, where the twelve tribes, worshipping God statedly, are said to "serve him night and day." But what is it to worship God? It is to do him homage *outwardly*, by attending his appointed ordinances, public and domestic; *inwardly*, acknowledging, and being sensible of our dependence on him for life, and breath, and all things, temporal and spiritual: of our obligations to him as our Creator, Preserver, &c.; for all we are, (our members, senses, faculties;) for all we have; (time, talents, blessings;) for all we hope for, in this world or the next; of his absolute power and authority over us, as our Lawgiver, Governor, and Judge.—It is to venerate his matchless glories; to adore and praise him with seriousness and solemnity, awe, and self-abasement, with joy and delight.—It is to feel in ourselves, and manifest to others, affections and dispositions suited to his Divine attributes, and the blessed relations in which he stands to us. (Explain this, and show that this alone is worshipping in spirit, and therefore in truth. John iv. 23, 24; Phil. iii. 3.)—In prayer, it is to ask only for what we really need, and what his word authorizes us to ask, and to do so with sincerity, fervency, and perseverance, and in faith.—It is to give thanks with gratitude of heart :—to hear, read, and meditate on his word with sincere desire, concern, and resolution, through God's help :—to understand, believe, and experience the efficacy of it, and to practice what we hear :—to receive the Lord's supper with faith and devotion, so as to "feed on Christ in our hearts with thanksgiving." This, and only this, is to worship acceptably,— —

It is to be subject and obedient to him, as a servant to a master, Rom. vi. 16; xii. 1.—We must yield ourselves to him. Rom. vi. 19, intelligently, willingly, entirely, and irrevocably, to be his subjects, servants, sons, and daughters, to which relations we are invited. This implies, that we no longer yield ourselves to the world, the flesh, sin, Satan, but to the Lord, with desire that he would, and in confidence that he does, accept us through his Son. Hereby we are joined to the Lord to serve him. Isa. lvi. 6. As his servants, we must give evidence of our subjection and obedience to his will in all things universally ; Ps. cxix. 6; constantly. 1 Cor. x. 30.—In holiness, Luke i. 74, towards God; dying to, and delivered from the power of sin, Rom. vi. 18, the world, Gal. vi. 14, our own wisdom, will, and carnal inclinations. Gal. ii. 20. This implies, to be dedicated to God, employed for him, conformed to him.—In righteousness towards our neighbor, including truth, justice, mercy, charity, and its fruits.— —

It is to serve his cause ; that which he is carrying on in the world : advancing his glory, and the present and everlasting good of mankind, by promoting the progress of his gospel, or of his truth and grace among men. John xii. 26.— —

As to the properties of this service.—It must be in sincerity and truth; Josh. xxiv. 14; termed by David, " a perfect heart." 1 Chron. xxviii. 9.— With reverence and godly fear, (text,) from a sense of his presence, Luke i. 75, before him, his glory, wisdom, power, eternity, immensity. supremacy. To which should be added, a watchful fear of our enemies, Prov. xxviii. 14. and a jealous fear of ourselves. Heb. iv. 1.—In confidence, or without a slavish fear; Luke i. 74; Rom. viii. 15; 2 Tim. i. 7; and a confidence arising from the mediation of Christ, Justification through him, Rom. v. 1, and the testimony of our conscience. 1 John iii. 21.—In humility of mind, Acts xx. 19; Mic. vi. 8, arising from a deep sense of the distance between him and us, and a consciousness that we are unworthy to be permitted to serve him, and that our best services are unworthy of his acceptance.—In resignation under all his dispensations, persuaded that his providence is over all ; that all his dispensations are wise, just, and gracious ; that his eye is upon each of his servants; that he puts each of them in his proper place, and will make all things work for their good.—In meekness, gentleness, &c. towards all men, even enemies.—All our services are to flow chiefly from love as their principle, to be guided by the Divine will as their rule, and directed to the glory of God as their end. 1 Cor. x. 31. Thus they will be performed with a " willing mind," 1 Chron. xxviii. 9; Matt. vi. 24, and the service of God will be perfect freedom.— —

## II. The reasonableness and importance of thus serving him.

Every part of this service is reasonable, Rom. xii. 1, being different from the unreasonable services of the heathen in the worship of their gods, their bloody, lewd, ridiculous, unmeaning rites; the expensive, burdensome, shadowy, and hardly intelligible sacrifices and ceremonies of the Jews.— The christian's service of faith, love, and obedience is highly reasonable. For faith has for its object, not lies, but truth; love has beauty, excellence, goodness; and obedience commands, which are wise, holy, good. Few ceremonies are enjoined, and those most significant, as the sabbath, baptism, and the Lord's supper. Thus it far exceeds the service of the tabernacle and temple, though of Divine institution.— —

It is reasonable we should perform this service.—In justice: for we are God's by right of creation, preservation, and redemption.—In gratitude; for his numberless and great benefits.—Its infinite importance appears in that it is *our great interest*, in time and eternity.— —

## III. How we may be enabled to serve the Lord as above described.

We must "have grace."—*Enlightening* grace. In order to our serving God, we must "know" him 1 Chron. xxviii. 9, must be acquainted with him; must know ourselves, or we shall not be humble, resigned, meek, as we ought to be; must know the Mediator, through whom alone we can come to God; must know God's will, or we cannot do it; and must know the truths of the gospel in general, which have a connexion with, and influence on our serving God.—*Quickening* grace; awakening the mind to a sense of the certainty and importance of spiritual and eternal things; convincing, humbling, begetting repentance unto life, a living faith, union with Christ, a spiritual mind.—*Pardoning* grace. See Heb. ix. 15. Without this we cannot serve God with confidence, hope, love, joy, peace, &c.— *Renewing* grace; for a currupt tree cannot bring forth good fruit, nor an impure fountain send forth clear streams. The heart must be changed, that the life may be changed: and we must be "created in Christ Jesus unto good works," if we would walk in them. Eph. ii. 10.—*Strengthening* grace; inspiring fortitude, resolution, constancy, and power to resist the devil, overcome the world, crucify the flesh, conquer the power of sin, and the fear of death; and enabling us to do, and persevere in doing, the whole wil of God.— —*Comforting* grace; supporting us in the midst of reproaches, injuries, losses, afflictions, the death of relatives and friends, and the various trials and troubles which we shall certainly meet with, chiefly by immortal hopes, and an earnest of heaven in our hearts.— —

## CHRISTIAN PROFESSORS SHOULD IMITATE CHRIST.

1 John ii. 6.—He that saith he abideth in him ought himself also so to walk, even as he walked. (B.)

MANKIND, even in these christian countries so called, seem to be but too generally comprehended in two classes,—one consisting of persons who make no serious profession of true religion at all; and the other of those who make an empty, or, at least, inconsistent profession of it. With persons of the former class I have nothing to do on the present occasion; indeed it is not easy for a preacher of the gospel to have to do with them at any time, for they will take care not to come within the sound of his voice. But to the latter, many of whom are commonly present from time to time in all places of Divine worship, and therefore are probably here, I will address myself, especially on one point, the vast importance of imitating and resembling him, in whom we profess to believe, and whose disciples we regard ourselves. I am the more inclined to speak on this subject, because I am apprehensive that it is one much overlooked among some professors; and that on this account true and vital religion is greatly on the decline with them. Indeed, if I know anything of the christian world, it is verging fast towards Antinomianism. Men are beginning, more and more, to content themselves with mere doctrinal christianity, and to rest satisfied with right notions of those things in their heads, which they ought to experience in their hearts, and practice in their lives. This anti-christianism was beginning to pervade the church even in the Apostle's days, and some of them, especially St. James and St. John, used their utmost efforts to check the encroaching evil. This is evident from the general tenor of their epistle. As to St. John, it appears from many passages of this his first epistle, and especially from the paragraph from whence I take my text.— —Inquire we,

I. WHAT IT IS TO "ABIDE IN HIM?" AND WHO MUST BE UNDERSTOOD AS SAYING THAT THEY ABIDE IN HIM?

To abide in Christ, is to continue—in those relations in which, as children of God, we stand to him, as his disciples, his subjects, his servants, his friends, his brethren, his spouse.—In an interest in him as a Teacher, a Mediator, and a Saviour, being enlightened, reconciled, and saved by him; as our wisdom, righteousness, sanctification, and redemption.—In union with him, as the foundation on which we are built, the true vine of which we are branches, the living head of which we are members.— —

The Apostle does not speak here merely of saying in word, but of professing, and even of saying in our heart, or thinking respecting ourselves that we "abide in him." Now those who profess to abide in faith, in Christ and the Gospel, or to continue to be believers, do in effect profess to abide in him, for all true believers are in him. Gal. ii. 20; Rom. xi. 20; Rom. i. 16; 1 John v. 13.—All who profess to abide in hope, viz., an hope of eternal life, profess to abide in him; for all hope of eternal life, that is well grounded and lively, flows from union with Christ. Col. i. 27, 28.— All who profess to abide in love, profess to abide in him. 1 John iv. 16. Love is the fruit of the Spirit of Christ dwelling in us, Gal. v. 22, and can only be where he is.—All who profess to be in a justified state, profess to abide in him; for those to whom "there is no condemnation," "walk not after the flesh, but after the spirit," and "the law of the Spirit of life in Christ Jesus hath made them free from the law of sin and death." Rom. viii. 1, 2; 1 John v. 11, 12.—All who profess to be regenerated, or converted, or created anew, profess to abide in him; for only those that are "**in Christ**" are new creatures; 2 Cor. v. 17; and those that are **created unto** good works, are "created in Christ Jesus." Eph. ii. 10.— —

II. IN WHAT SENSE, AND IN WHAT RESPECTS, SUCH OUGHT TO "**WALK EVEN AS HE WALKED.**"

To "walk," here is a figurative expression, intended as in numberless other passages, to signify our spirit and conduct, all our dispositions, words and actions—and that towards God, our neighbor, and ourselves. If we profess to abide in Christ, or think we abide in him, we ought to take care that we be conformed to his example, in our tempers, words, and works. John xii. 26; Phil. ii. 5; Col. ii. 6; 1 Pet. ii. 21; text.

In what respects ?—In seriousness of mind; not gloominess, or sullenness, or moroseness, but habitual seriousness, solemnity and awe, knowing that we are always in the presence of God, and on the verge of death, of judgment, and eternity, and that we have no light matters, but matters of everlasting moment, to attend to and insure. Thus Christ walked, and thus we ought to walk. In watchfulness, as conscious of the various dangers and the enemies which surround us. In self-denial.—In a spirit of abstraction and separation from the world. Jam. iv. 4; Matt. vi. 24; John xvii. 14, 16.—In spiritual-mindedness.—In love to God; John xiv. 31; 1 John iv. 16, 19; to his people; Eph. v. 1, 2; John xv. 12, 13; 1 John iv. 7; to all men, even our enemies. Luke xxiii. 34.—In zeal. John ii. 17.—In humility before God and man. Matt. xi. 29.—In resignation and patience before God. Matt. xxvi. 39, 42, 44.—In meekness and gentleness towards man. 2 Cor. x. 1; 1 Pet. ii. 23.—In a long-suffering and forgiving spirit. Eph. iv. 31, 32.—In a merciful, compassionate, and sympathizing disposition. Matt. xiv. 14; John xi. 35; Heb. ii. 17; iv. 15.—In blamelessness. Heb. vii. 26.—In usefulness, employing every grace and gift, and all our time and talents, for the glory of God, and the good of our fellow creatures. Acts x. 38; John iv. 34.—In temperance and chastity. In purity and universal holiness. John viii. 46; Heb. vii. 26.— —

[Conclude, by showing how we may be conformed to his example, and walk as he walked.]— —

---

## THE DUTY OF CASTING OUR CARE ON GOD.

1 Pet. v. 7.—Casting all your care upon him, for he careth for you.  (S. S.)

INEXPERIENCED christians are generally partial in their views of religion—

They often exalt one duty, to the neglect, if not the exclusion of another—

But a proficiency in the divine life will discover itself by the united exercise of the various, and apparently opposite, graces—

Faith will not exclude fear, nor meekness fortitude—

Every grace will be limited and tempered by some other—

The soul must be humbled before God in dust and ashes—

Yet should it rely on him with most implicit confidence—ver. 6, 7.

**I. THE DUTY OF CHRISTIANS.**

Christians have learned "not to seek great things for themselves"—
Hence they are free from the corroding cares of avarice and ambition—
But they still have many grounds of care.
They cannot but feel some concern respecting their bodily wants—
The casualties of life may also occasion some uneasiness—
But they have other cares far more weighty and important—
They see many dishonoring their holy profession—
They feel within themselves also "an evil heart of unbelief"—
Nor are they ignorant of satan's devices to overthrow them—
Moreover, they frequently anticipate future evils—
And tremble, lest in the day of adversity they should faint—
Thus do they torment themselves with anxious and desponding fears—
It is their duty, however, to "cast their care on God."
To cast their care upon any creature would be fruitless—
And it would involve them in the deepest guilt—Jer. xvii. 5.
God alone is able to sustain their burthen—
On him they are commanded to cast it—Ps. lv. 22.
They must do so in the exercise of faith and prayer—Phil. iv. 6, 7.
Nor are any cares whatever to be excepted, "Cast *all*,"&c.
None are so small but they shall be regarded, none so great but they shall
be alleviated—
There is a backwardness in many to comply with this duty.

**II. THEIR ENCOURAGEMENT TO PERFORM IT.**

God extends his care to the whole creation—
But in a more especial manner careth for his people—
He conducted the Jews through the wilderness—
He interposed for them in all their dangers—
He supplied their every want—Ps. cv. 39—41.
Thus, though less visibly, he still regards those who trust in him—
He watches over them for good—2 Chron. xvi. 9.
He limits and restrains all their adversaries—Ps. lxx. vi. 10.
He sympathizes with them in all their afflictions—Isa. lxiii. 9. Heb
v. 15.
He imparts to them all temporal and spiritual blessings—Ps. lxxxiv. 11.
He hears and answers all their supplications—John xv. 7.
He accounts them his most inestimable treasure—Mal. iii: 17.
He communes with them as his sons and daughters—2 Cor. vi. 18.
He takes upon him the management of all their concerns—Isa. xlvi. 4.
What encouragement does this afford us to trust in him!
Our guardian and protector is infinitely *wise*—Isa. xxviii. 29.
He knows what trials we stand in need of—
He can suit all the circumstances of them to our necessities—
He can overrule them for our eternal benefit—
He is possessed of *almighty* power, Job xl. 2.
There is no difficulty from which he cannot extricate—Isa. l. 2, and
xliii. 13.
Nor duty which he cannot enable us to discharge—
Should we, for whom such wisdom and power are exercised, be anxious?
—Isa. xl. 27, 28.
Moreover he is *good* and gracious.
What innumerable blessings has he already bestowed upon us!
He has even given his own Son to die for us—

What then can we have to fear, if we trust in him?—Rom. viii. 32.

Above all, he is a *faithful* God.

He has promised seasonable protection and strength—Isa. liv. 10. Deut. xxxiii 25. 1 Cor. x. 13.

And is not his word a sure ground of confidence?—2 Sam. xxii. 31. Heb. x 23.

Surely then we should be filled with consolation rather than with care—Heb. vi. 18.

INFER,—

1. How needful is it that all should acquaint themselves with God!

Gaiety and dissipation may bear up the spirit in prosperity—

But God alone can comfort us in adversity—Job xxxv. 10.

At the hour of death we shall all need divine support—

Let the careless then begin to reflect upon their state—

Let them provide a refuge against the day of trouble—

Let them follow that salutary advice—Job xxii. 21.

2. How happy would christians be if they rightly enjoyed their privileges!

It is their privilege to be " without carefulness"—1 Cor. vii. 32.

If they trusted in God as they ought, nothing could disturb them—Isa. xxvi. 3.

Hence that exhortation to joy in God—Ps. v. 11, 12.

Let the afflicted saints then commit themselves to him—Mic. v. 4.

Let them know that duty is theirs, but events are his—

Let them, in the face of all difficulties, adopt the words of Joshua—Numb. xiv. 9.

Let them, with Hezekiah, repose themselves on God—2 Chron. xxxii. 7, 8.

~~~~~~~~~~~~~

## THE NECESSITY OF PRAYER

Ezek. xxxvi. 37.—Thus saith the Lord God : I will yet for this be inquired of by the house of Israel, to do it for them ; I will increase them with men like a flock. (Sk.)

THERE is a very striking analogy between the natural and the spiritual world ; between the productions of nature, and the operations of divine grace. In the former, a variety of means are necessary for the attainment of providential mercies; and in the latter, the duties of religion are essentially connected with the enjoyment of its personal privileges. In both cases the ends are made to depend on the means, which by virtue of the divine appointment and influence, are rendered efficient and successful. This is particularly evident in the important duty of prayer. The Lord has graciously promised innumerable blessings to mankind in his word : but in order to obtain them, we must earnestly call upon his name, with penitent and believing hearts. This chapter contains various promises, both of temporal and spiritual blessings to the Jews, which are also generally applicable to the Gentiles; but we are assured in the text, that they can only be realized by faithful prayer;—"Thus saith the Lord God," &c. These words will lead us to consider,

I. THE BLESSINGS FOR WHICH WE SHOULD INQUIRE;—"I will yet *for this* be inquired of by the house of Israel." This language manifestly refers to the inestimable benefits promised in the preceding context. Whatever God promises we may humbly desire and pray for, both for our own salvation and the welfare of all mankind.

1. *We should pray for ourselves.* We are sinful, indigent, and dependent creatures. God only can supply our wants and satisfy our desires. To him we must come, and devoutly inquire for every blessing which our circumstances need, 2 Cor. ix. 8; Phil. iv. 19.—Such as pardoning mercy—adopting love—quickening power—sanctifying grace—the indwelling Spirit—the consolations of piety,—ver. 25—27;—Ps. li. 9—12.—for light in darkness—strength in weakness—succor in temptation—assistance in duty—guidance in difficulty—peace in trouble—victory over enemies—triumph in death—and a blissful immortality beyond the grave, Ps. lxxxi. 10; Phil. iv. 6; Heb. iv. 16. For these and all necessary and promised blessings, for body and soul, for time and eternity, we must incessantly seek, and inquire of "the God of all grace."

2. *We should pray for the church of God.* Good men regard all the subjects of piety as brethren, Eph. iv. 4—6.—They feel interested in each other's welfare, and desire the peace and prosperity of Zion, Psa. cxxii. 6—9.—They pray for the extension and stability of her borders—the increase of her converts—and the unity and progression of her members, Hab. iii. 2; Eph. iii. 14—21; Phil. i. 9—11. Many such prayers have been offered by the pious, for the church of Christ in all ages, Ps. cxviii. 25; Isa. lxii. 67; Rom. xiii. 15.

3. *We should pray for the world.* We are commanded to "love our neighbors as ourselves," and "pray for our enemies;" even for those who "despitefully use and persecute us," Matt. v. 44. The Lord assures us that he will "give his Son the heathen for his inheritance," &c.; and that "the earth shall be filled with the knowledge and glory of his name," Ps. ii. 8; Isa. xi. 9; Jer. xxxi. 34. Encouraged by such declarations, we should "pray for all men; for kings, and for all that are in authority;"—for the universal dissemination of divine truth—and the glorious triumphs of the Redeemer's kingdom, in every nation, kindred, tongue, and people, Ps. xliii. 3; Isa. lxii. 1; Matt. vi. 10; Rev. xi. 15. If such are the the blessings for which we should inquire, we may observe,

II. THE MANNER HOW WE SHOULD INQUIRE FOR THEM. This is highly necessary, both for our instruction and encouragement. And for the proper discharge of this important duty the Scriptures furnish every needful direction, by which we are explicitly taught to inquire of the Lord.

1. *In the method which he appoints.* We cannot approach unto him acceptably, but through Jesus Christ, who is the high priest over the house of God for ever, John xiv. 6; Heb. vii. 17. He has sprinkled the mercy seat with his own precious blood, and "now appears in the presence of God for us." Through his mediation, under the influence of the Holy Ghost, we have constant boldness of access to the throne of grace, Rom. viii. 26, 27; Eph. ii. 18. This is the new and living way, which is divinely consecrated for mankind, to the "Father of mercies," Heb. iv. 14—16, chap. x. 19—22.

2. *With devout dispositions of mind.* The Lord looks at the heart, and when we enter into holy converse with him, we should inquire for the blessings of salvation *sincerely*, without hypocrisy, Matt. xv. 8; *humbly*, with reverence and godly fear, Ps. lxxxix. 7; *fervently*, with holy ardor, Gen. xxvii. 26;—*affectionately*, with hearts filled with love to God, and good

will to all mankind, Matt. vi. 14, 15; and *believingly*, in the lively exercise of faith, Matt. xxi. 22; 1 John v. 14, 15.

3. *In every situation of human life.* Whatever stations we occupy, or however different the circumstances in which we are placed, prayer is indispensably necessary. In private retirement, Matt. vi. 6;—in our families, Joshua xxiv. 15;—in the public ordinances of the gospel, Ps xxvii. 4;— and in our daily occupations, we should " pray always, with all prayer, and every where, lifting up holy hands without wrath and doubting," Eph. vi. 18; 1 Tim ii. 8.

4. *With diligent perseverance unto death.* We are invariably dependent on God, and continually need his special direction and blessing, as sinful and helpless creatures. Without him we can do nothing; and though he has promised every needful benefit, yet for all these things he will be inquired of to do them for us. And hence, we ought to " pray without ceasing, and in every thing give thanks," Rom. xii. 12. And in this sacred exercise, we shall be greatly encouraged by considering,

III. The reasons why we should inquire of the Lord. These are various; but we select the following only:

1. *Prayer is an ordinance of divine authority.* If it should be said, Why inquire of the Lord who knows our wants, and is ever ready to do us good? the text affords an appropriate answer to all such vain objections;— " *Thus saith the Lord God,*" &c. Every duty which is distinctly revealed and divinely enjoined, is unquestionable in its authority, and imperious in its claims. Now this is certainly the case in reference to prayer. The Lord commands us to pray, Ps. v. 14, 15; Jer. xxix. 12; Luke xviii. 1;—he promises to hear and answer prayer, Ps. xci. 15, 16;—and he directs us how to pray, Matt. vi. 9—13.—If therefore we restrain prayer before him, we impeach his wisdom, despise his authority, and reject his ordinance, Job xxi. 14, 15.

2. *Prayer evinces the dependence of the creature on the Creator.* It powerfully reminds us of our own insufficiency, and the all-sufficiency of the Almighty, 2 Cor. iii. 5.—We feel innumerable wants which we cannot supply but we are taught to " ask and receive, that our joy may be full." We thus at once discover our utter indigence and dependence as finite beings, and the absolute necessity of praying *to*, and " trusting *in* the Lord Jehovah, in whom is everlasting strength."

3. *Prayer demonstrates the connection between duty and interest.* As intellectual beings, we are capable of moral actions and spiritual enjoyments. The Lord is therefore pleased to suspend the blessings he promises, on the performance of the duties he enjoins; and it is only by complying with the latter, that we can realize the former, Ps. xxxiv. 17; Jer. xxxiii. 3. This inseparable connection admirably displays the wisdom and goodness of God in the salvation of his people.

We may conclude by warning the prayerless of their danger,—and encouraging the devout to " continue instant in prayer."

## PERSEVERANCE AND WATCHFULNESS IN PRAYER.

Eph. vi. 18.—Praying always with all prayer, &c. (H.)

THE believing Ephesians are here taught by the apostle what they have to expect in this world ; nothing less than a constant warfare, and that too with no common enemy, as may be seen by the description given, verse 12. He would not have them, however, be discouraged by the view of either the multitude or the strength of their opposers, nor yet to trust in the least degree to their own wisdom and strength, verse 10, when christians can do this, in the exercise of a strong faith, they may despise all the efforts of their most potent and malignant foe, and exult in the beautiful language of the apostle, " If God be for us," &c.

To manage the arduous conflict with success, it is requisite we should put on "the whole armor," verse 13, which the apostle describes; and then he introduces the words of my text: " Praying always," &c. intimating, that it was not enough to be duly apprized of the nature and strength of the enemy, and to have on the armor of defence ready for the attack ; but even then there must be much and constant prayer to God for wisdom, courage, and ability, to persevere in the conflict; for having once entered the field under Jesus, the Captain of our salvation, we must never think of obtaining peace, or putting off our armor, till we have reached the blissful shores of our heavenly Canaan, and can join in that delightful triumph of the church, Rev. xii. 10, 11. In our text the apostle directs the Ephesians—

I. To PRAY WITH ALL PRAYER.—What is the import of this expression? It may be considered under two ideas.

There are divers kinds of prayer. They are all important; none of them can be slighted with propriety by the real christian. They occupy distinct and separate stations in the good man's general sphere of action, and it should be his care to keep them from clashing one with the other. As in a well-constructed piece of mechanism every wheel and every pin has its proper station, and performs its office in a regular manner, all operating to the production of one grand effect; so it is in religion. 1 Cor. xiv. 33. We are not to be at home engaging in private prayer, when duty calls us to public prayer, &c. It is natural to infer, from the view we have been taking of prayer, what a burden religion must be to a worldly man. With the real christian it is exactly the reverse: he can say with truth, that the service of his God " is perfect freedom."

Prayer is composed of a variety of parts. Some arrange these under a smaller, and some under a larger number of particulars. From the examples of prayer which we have in the old testament, and also from the manner in which Christ taught his disciples to pray, I am led to divide the parts of prayer into—Adoration, Confession, Petition, and Thanksgiving.

1. When we approach God in prayer, it should be with sentiments of profound veneration : he is the infinitely great and eternal God, and we are creatures but of yesterday : he is the holy and righteous God, and we sinners by nature and by practice. If then we know who and what God is, when we come near to his throne we shall adore and worship him in the most humble manner. A view of his majesty and greatness will penetrate our souls with godly fear, and a sense of the riches of his mercy will inspire us with trust and confidence. Our souls will feel much of that temper which is manifested in the language of Nebuchadnezzar, Dan. iv. 34, 35.

2. Another part of prayer is *confession*. The deep depravity of our nature, Jer. xvii. 9, and the numberless sins which proceed from that corrupt source, furnish abundant matter for this part of prayer. The fifty-first Psalm, the language of the returning prodigal, and of the publican who went into the temple to pray, are among the finest examples of genuine confession—of that kind of confession which the scriptures connect with salvation, inasmuch as it is said, "If we confess our sins," &c. 1 John i. 9.

3. The next branch of true prayer is *petition*. Man is an indigent creature in every respect, and can never be addressed in a more suitable language than Rev. iii. 17. He is, therefore, in himself the most forlorn and dependent creature; but it is only the christian who sees and feels, and, consequently, acts in conformity to this humbling truth; he comes as a beggar to the door of mercy.

4. The last branch of prayer is *thanksgiving* and *praise*. This is mentioned in a very distinct manner by the apostle. Phil. iv. 6. This branch of the subject may be divided into two parts. In the first there is a particular and direct acknowledgment made to God for the mercies received. We may illustrate this point by the language of David, Ps. ciii. 2, 3. The other branch of thanksgiving is more general. We have examples of this in Matt. vi. 13; Jude 24, 25.

II. IN THIS TEXT THE APOSTLE RECOMMENDS "PRAYING ALWAYS;" every work of the good man's hand should be prefaced, accompanied with, and followed by prayer. Acts vi. 4; 1 Thess. iii. 10.

In this part of the subject I shall particularly urge upon you constancy and perseverance in prayer.

1. To you who have in past times bowed your knee to the God and Father of our Lord Jesus Christ, and now live prayerless, we say, "Ye did run well, who did hinder you." Gal. v. 7. Such persons may be thus addressed, "Thou castest off fear." Job xv. 4. The Jews were an awful instance of this, as appears by Ps. lxxviii. 34—37.

The temporary and short-lived nature of the disposition of some men to pray, may be seen in the case of affrighted mariners, whose distress and conduct, when in danger of shipwreck, is beautifully described, Ps. cvii. 23—30. But no sooner is the storm ended, and they find themselves in safety, than they utterly forget the God on whom they called.

Such also is the prayer of the man who is affrighted by the grand and awful representations which the Almighty is pleased sometimes to make of himself in earthquakes, inundations, yea, even in ordinary storms of thunder and lightning.

Again, The subject is illustrated by the prayers of the sick man, who, while his recovery is yet doubtful, is constant and devout in his supplications: but all his devotions evaporate on the first symptom of returning health; to such persons may be applied the words of our Lord, Matt. xii. 45.

We address this part of our subject to backsliders in general. You, in times past, sought God by prayer, not only in the public assembly of his saints, but also in your closet; but now you have lost all the good impressions you once had, though, like Felix, whilst the preacher reasoned of righteousness, &c. Acts xxiv. 25. Though, like Herod, you heard the word gladly, and did many things, Mark vi. 20, yet now you set truth and conscience at defiance. If this is your character, what are you better than an apostate? How awful is your state! How justly may the words of scripture be applied to you! 2 Pet. ii. 21, 22.

**2.** I come now to urge constancy and perseverance in prayer on those christians who are often tempted to leave it off. The scriptures would not have abounded with such exhortations as 1 Thess. v. 16; Rom. xii. 12, where it not that the soul is liable to be discouraged by difficulties and temptations.

Sometimes they are tempted to this by their want of liberty and enlargement in prayer:—others are discouraged in prayer, because they feel so many short comings and imperfections in their prayers. You forget, christian, too much and too often, that your prayers do pass through the hands of Jesus Christ, and are perfumed with the incense of his merit: Rev. viii. 3, 4, others are tempted to give up seeking the Lord by prayer, because he delays to answer them. These are often crying out, Lam. iii. 44; Hab. i. 2. Yet remember, Hab. ii. 3. We have also many striking instances, in which the Lord has kept his people long praying and waiting, before he has vouchsafed to say, "Be it unto thee even as thou wilt." David relates his own experience, Ps. xl. 1—3. And it is also related of Abraham, Heb. vi. 15.—See Rom. viii. 24, 25; and James v. 7, 8. Be not, then, christian, discouraged by not receiving an immediate answer to your petitions: go on praying; the Lord is not slack concerning his promises:—and you have abundant proof, that "praying breath is never spent in vain."

III. Our text recommends watching unto prayer; the nearness and importance of the connexion between prayer and watching is plain, by the frequency of those passages in which they are jointly recommended to the christian, Luke xxi. 36; Col. iv. 2; 1 Pet. iv. 7. This apostle knew, by fatal experience, the vast importance of what he here recommended. It has been exemplified in the experience and practice of the saints. Neh. iv. 9.

1. The christian should watch for opportunities to pray, or he will bu seldom find them.

2. In prayer we should watch over our own hearts, which are so deceitful and unstable. Prov. iv. 23.

3. Watch against hinderances to stated seasons of prayer. We are in danger of this from many sources.

4. Watch against intruders which would disturb you while exercising in prayer. If it is your desire to "attend upon the Lord without distraction," you must be constant and diligent in this duty. Gen. xv. 11.

5. Watch against the great enemy of souls, who is ever going about either to destroy them, or to disturb them in their religious exercises, which instrumentally subserve their eternal salvation. Job i. 6; Zech. iii. 1.

6. Watch for an answer to prayer. Too many, when they have finished prayer, rise up and go their way, and think no more about the matter. Not so the good man; he, like David, will not only say, "Show us thy mercy, O Lord, and grant us thy salvation:" but he will add, "I will hear what God the Lord will speak." &c. (Compare 1 King xviii. 1. 41—46, with James v. 17, 18.) So let us be looking and watching for an answer to prayer.

IV. Christians should pray in or with the Spirit. Praying "in the Spirit," either means praying under the influence of the Holy Ghost, or with divine fervor.

In speaking of divine fervor in prayer, I notice,

1. That it is urged by a variety of scriptures in which prayer is spoken of, all of which imply an earnest and vigorous exercise of the mind. To pray is to "pour out" the heart, Ps. lxii. 8; to "wrestle with God," Gen. xxii. 24; to "cry," Ps. ix. 12; to "sigh and groan," Ps. xii. 5; to

"strive," Rom. xv. 30 ; to "give God no rest," Is. lxii. 7; and in the text, it is "supplication in the Spirit." In all these places we are taught that true prayer is very fervent and importunate.

2. Earnestness and fervor in prayer may be urged by the consideration of the value of the blessings for which we pray ; nothing less than "grace and glory."

3. We may take an argument to be fervent in prayer from the arduous nature of the conflict in which we are engaged.

4. Fervency in prayer is recommended by examples recorded in the word of God. Gen. xxxii. 26. 28. We have also a striking example of fervent prayer in the woman who came to our Lord, Matt. xv. 22 ; Luke xxii. 44.

V. WHEN A CHRISTIAN MAINTAINS A LIFE OF PRAYER ACCORDING TO THE DIRECTIONS GIVEN IN THIS TEXT, it will produce a very advantageous influence upon his spiritual warfare, and assist him in the use of the armor which God hath provided.

1. By thus exercising ourselves in prayer we shall *stand* firm in the day of battle. He that is much with God in prayer, stands not only on even, but on elevated ground, and must ultimately have the advantage.

2. Praying always with all prayer has a tendency to inspire the soul with *courage* in this arduous conflict. Living near to God in prayer makes the soul as bold as a lion ; hence Elisha, who was a man of much prayer, when his house was surrounded by a host, was enabled to say to his servant, "Fear not." 2 Kings vi. 6.

3. They who pray always, and with all prayer, will be *skilful* and *active* in the use of the christian armor.

4. Abounding in prayer has a tendency to keep our armor bright and fit for use ; yea, it gives the christian soldier a promptness for action. By the means of prayer, the girdle of truth and the breastplate of righteousness are girded on tight; the helmet of hope, and the shoes of peace, fit well, and become proof against the most furious assaults ; and the shield of faith, and the sword of the Spirit, are grasped with a firm hand, and are wielded with energy.

5. It is by fervent and persevering prayer that the believer finally obtains the victory in every conflict. Whilst we cleave to the Lord with purpose of heart, and watch in prayer, satan gains little or no advantage over us --. To conclude,

1. Are we engaged in this holy warfare, with the description of which our text is connected? we shall not "endure hardness, as good soldiers " 2 Tim. ii. 3, but as we pray always and with all prayer.

2. What an awful state is yours, who have been induced to commence a life of prayer, either through the pressure of adverse providences, or the temporary alarms of your consciences, and have fallen back into a state of total indifference and irreligion. Isa. xxvi. 16. Ah, thoughtless sinner ! thou wilt be in trouble again, and then with what face wilt thou return to a throne of grace.

Our last reflection is for the comfort and encouragement of God's praying people : keep on in the holy exercise : exemplify that sentence, "faint, yet pursuing." Let thy soul be animated with the pleasing thought, that Christ prays for thee, and the Holy Spirit makes intercession within thee. Through all the changes of the christian life, be this thy constant practice, "Praying always with all prayer,' &c.

## THE DUTY OF PERSEVERING IN PRAYER.

Luke xviii. 1.—Men ought always to pray, and not to faint.  (S. S.)

THE efficacy of prayer is continually exhibited in the sacred writings—
And every incitement to it is afforded us—
Nevertheless we are prone to faint in the performance of it—
To encourage our perseverance in it our Lord delivered a parable—
Waving all notice of the parable itself, we shall consider,
I. OUR DUTY.
To be always in the act of prayer would interfere with other duties—
That which is here inculcated, implies that we pray —
Statedly.
Regular seasons for prayer should be fixed—
Except in cases of absolute necessity, Matt. ix. 13, they should be adhered to—
We should constantly acknowledge God *in the public assembly*, Heb. x. 25.
We should maintain his worship also *in our families**
Nor should we on any account omit it *in our closets*†—
Occasionally.
There are many particular occasions which require us to pray—
*Prosperity*, that God may counteract its evil tendency, Prov. xxx. 9.
*Adversity*, that we may be supported under it, James v. 13.
Times of *public distress or danger*, to avert the calamity, 2 Chron. vii. 14.
Habitually.
We should maintain a spiritual frame of mind—
We may have a disposition for prayer in the midst of business—
Nor will secret ejaculations prevail less than solemn devotions‡—
To pray thus is our duty; " We ought," &c.
It is a duty we owe *to God*.
He, our Creator, Preserver, and Redeemer, has commanded it—
Nor can anything absolve us from our obligation to obey—
We owe it also *to our neighbor*.
The edification of Christ's mystical body depends, not only on the union of every part with the head, but on the whole being fitly framed together, and on every joint supplying its proper nourishment, Eph. iv. 16; Col. ii. 19.
But if we be remiss in prayer, we shall be incapable of administering that benefit, which other members have a right to expect from us‖—
We owe it *to ourselves*.
A "spirit of supplication" is as necessary to the soul, as food to the body—

* Abraham and Joshua were noted for their attention to family religion: Gen. xviii. 19: Josh. xxiv. 15, and our Lord's example is worthy of imitation; he not only expounded his parables to his disciples in private, but prayed with them.  See Luke ix. 18, which means, "he was at a distance from the multitude, and praying with his disciples."

† How frequent the stated seasons shall be, must be left to our own discretion, David's example is good, Ps. lv. 17.  But as the morning and evening sacrifices were called the *continual* burnt-offering, so they may be said to pray *always* who pray at those returning seasons.

‡ Compare 2 Sam. xv. 31, with 2 Sam. xvii. 14, 23.  See also Neh. ii. 4, 6.

‖ Samuel had a deep conviction of this truth; 1 Sam xii. 23.

Nor can we feel any regard for our souls, if we do not cultivate it—
It is, however, by no means easy to fulfil this duty.

## II. THE DIFFICULTIES THAT ATTEND IT.

When we set ourselves to the performance of it, we shall find difficulties—
Before we begin to pray.

*Worldly business* may indispose our minds for this employment—
*Family cares* may distract and dissipate our thoughts—
*Lassitude of body* may unfit us for the necessary exertions—
We may be disabled by an invincible *hardness of heart*—
A *want of utterance* may also operate as a heavy discouragement—
By these means many are tempted to defer their religious exercises—
But to yield to the temptation is to increase the difficulty—
While we are engaged in prayer.

The *world* is never more troublesome than at such seasons—
Something seen or heard, lost or gained, done or to be done, will generally obtrude itself upon us when we are at the throne of grace—
The *flesh* also, with its vilest imaginations, will solicit our attention—
Nor will *satan* be backward to interrupt our devotions*—
After we have concluded prayer.

When we have prayed, we should expect an answer—
But *worldliness* may again induce a forgetfulness of God—
*Impatience* to receive the desired blessings may deject us—
*Ignorance* of the method in which God answers prayer may cause us to disquiet ourselves with many ungrounded apprehensions—
*Unbelief* may rob us of the benefits we might have received, James i. 6, 7.

Whatever obstructs God's answers to prayer, disqualifies us for the future discharge of that duty—

## APPLICATION.

Let us not expect victory without many conflicts—
Let us remember the effect of perseverance in the case of Moses, Exodus xvii. 11—13.
Above all let us attend to the parable spoken for this end, Luke xvii. 2—8.
So shall we be kept from fainting under our discouragements—
And God will fulfil to us his own promise, Gal. vi. 9.

---

*He has various devices whereby he strives to accomplish his purpose. He will suggest "it is needless to pray:" or, "it is presumption for so great a sinner to ask any thing of God:" or, "it is hypocrisy to ask, when the heart is so little engaged." Sometimes he will inject into the christian's mind the most blasphemous and horrid thoughts; and at other times tempt him to admire his own fluency and enlargement in prayer. Such are the "fiery darts" with which he often assails the soul, Eph. vi. 16.

## LOOKING TO CHRIST INSEPARABLY CONNECTED WITH SALVATION.

Isa. xlv. 22.—Look unto me, and be ye saved, &c. (H.)

By grace ye are saved. Eph. ii. 8. Now that faith, which is the instrumental cause of our salvation, is spoken of, in the sacred scriptures, by various metaphorical expressions: sometimes it is borrowed from earthly things, and particularly from the actions of the body. Matt. xi. 28; Isa. lv 1; Rev. xxii. 17. Or, as the manslayer, being closely pursued, &c. Heb. vi. 18.—Sometimes from the conduct of a dutiful and loyal people towards their royal sovereign, upon his entering among them, in his own territories. John i. 11, 12.—Sometimes the metaphor is taken from the ear; and faith is expressed by hearing his voice, as an impoverished, dying wretch, would hear of plenty and life. Isa. lv. 3. And sometimes the metaphor is taken from the eye, as in the text, and faith is represented as looking to Christ.

I. EXPLAIN THE DUTY HERE EXPRESSED BY THE METAPHOR OF LOOKING.

We are to observe, in general, that a man's looks often indicate his condition and frame of mind. By virtue of that strange union between the soul and the body, the dispositions of the one are often discovered by the emotion and appearance of the other. The eye, in particular, is a mirror, in which we may see the various passions of the mind; and is a kind of silent, yet significant language, that conveys to others those inward exercises which the tongue does not, or perhaps cannot express: hence we can understand a look of sorrow and compassion, a look of joy, and the look of a perishing supplicant. If an agonizing patient casts an eager look upon his physician, he understands it to be a silent petition for relief. When a dying husband fixes a wishful, tender look, upon his surviving half, and those other selves, his children, they know the melting language, and feel its resistless energy. And when a drowning man casts a wild and eager look towards a boat coming to his relief, we understand it to be the language of earnest importunity for speedy help.

Hence it follows, that looking to Christ implies those suitable dispositions and exercises of heart towards him, which are expressed by the earnest and significant looks of persons in a distressed condition towards their deliverer.

And, in such a case, it is natural to conceive a person expressing, by his looks, a particular and distinct knowledge, of his deliverer—an importunate cry for his assistance—a wishful expectation of it—an humble dependence on him for it—a universal submission to him—a hearty love and approbation of him—a joy and gratitude for his deliverance.

And these dispositions and exercises of mind towards Christ, I presume, are intended in the text by looking to him.

1. Looking to Christ implies a particular notice and distinct knowledge of him. John xvii. 3; Isa. liii. 11; xxvii. 11; Hosea iv. 6; 2 Cor. iii. 18

2. Looking to Christ implies an importunate eagerness for relief from him. Ps. xxv. 15. As a child falling into the hands of a murderer, on the sight of a parent coming to its help, so are we desired to look to Christ: this implies a sense of our need of him. Ps. cxxi. 1; Jonah ii. 4; John ii. 14, 15.

3. Looking to Christ implies a wishful expectation of deliverance from him. Isa. xvii. 7; Ps. cxxx. 6; Acts iii. 4, 5; Matt. xv. 22. 28.

4. Looking to Christ implies an humble dependence upon him for salva-

tion. This supposes a deep sense of our own utter inability; then **we see** no ground for self-confidence, when we shall place our trust in Christ alone: 2 Chron. xx. 12: Micah vii. 7. John xiii. 15.

5. Looking to Christ means a universal, cheerful submission to his authority. Ps. cxxiii. 1, 2.

6. Looking to Christ implies our hearty approbation of him as a Saviour. Love is often expressed by a look. 2 Sam. xxiii. 5.

7. Looking to Christ implies joy and gratitude. Ps. ciii. 1, 2.

II. URGE THE DUTY BY SEVERAL WEIGHTY CONSIDERATIONS.

It is the duty of saints and sinners, in all ages and places, to the end of the world; and the arguments to enforce it can never be exhausted; those in this copious text are sufficient.

1. It is salvation that is offered. "Look and be saved."

2. This salvation may be obtained upon low terms; it may be obtained by a look. "Look and be saved."

3. It is Immanuel, our incarnate God, that invites and commands us to look to him and be saved. We may trifle with the commands of a usurper, and reject the treacherous invitations of an enemy; but dare we trifle with the injunctions, dare we refuse the gracious invitations of our supreme Lord and heavenly King? Rom. xiv. 9. 11; Phil. ii. 9. 11.

4. It is Immanuel we are to look unto. "Look unto me." He is the glorious, attractive object we are called to behold. Ps. lxix. 20; cxlii. 4. And looking will not be in vain; for,

5. He is able to save us, upon our looking to him. "Look unto me and be saved, for I am God." And who can give us greater security of salvation? "If God be for us, who can be against us?"

6. Look unto him, for he is God, and there is none else. This implies that there is salvation in no other. Job. v. 1.

And lastly, We must look unto him, or drop into hell. Look to him! For we are particularly invited, being especially meant by the "ends of the earth." Therefore, "Look unto him and be saved all ye ends of the earth;" more especially backsliders, sensible sinners, &c

---

## NOAH'S OBEDIENCE.

Genesis vi. 22.—Thus did Noah; according to all that God commanded him so did he. (Sk.)

BIOGRAPHICAL researches are peculiarly interesting.—They teach us to form a proper estimate of mankind, and the various features in the human character; they convey correct ideas of the strong and capacious powers of the soul, and are eminently calculated to inspire us with a noble ambition to follow the most worthy and renowned of our species. There are some men, however, whose characters excite a more than common interest in our minds, especially those who have lived in a remarkable era of the world—who have accomplished some mighty achievement—and whose designs have met with the peculiar sanction of heaven: such was the subject of our text, Noah:—a man who witnessed the most desolating scourge which ever visited the world—who brought to perfection one of the most stupendous pieces of mechanism that was ever reared by human hands—and whose life was preserved as a reward for his obedience.

The text contains a high commendation of his character.—"Thus did Noah," &c. We will consider,

I. THE RULE OF NOAH'S OBEDIENCE, "All that God commanded." Mankind need a rule for their conduct. This rule should possess the following characteristics :—

1. *It should come forth from God, and have the Divine sanction.* No man can be a rule to himself ; as he did not produce himself, is not dependent on himself, nor solely accountable to himself. No man can be an absolute rule for another ; for all men are defectible, and subject to mutation : but a rule for human manners and conduct, should be perfect and immutable. The commandments found in the Bible, are God's commandments. The men who wrote them received them from God: some orally, others by inspiration ; " God said to Noah," verse 13. The prophets prefaced their messages, by declaring, " Thus saith the Lord."

2. *It should be practical in its requirements.* A rule whose demands are impossible to be observed, is a contradiction. God's commandments are all practicable. He is not a hard Master: "His yoke is easy, and his burden is light." " His commandments are not grievous." But we must not judge of their practicability by the infirmities of our flesh ; or the weakness of our reason ; but by the power of God—the energies of grace—and the attainments of the saints. God charged Noah to build the ark ; had human reason been consulted he would never have made the attempt.

3. *It should be plain and circumstantial in its phraseology.*—No man can act according to a rule which he does not understand. God's commandments are easily comprehended. The Bible may present mysterious things, and things inexplicable; but there is no precept mysterious, no commandment abstruse. Read the charge to Noah in the preceding verses, examine the commandments of God generally, plainness and perspicuity are their uniform characteristics.

4. *It should be beneficial in its results.* Human nature revolts at the idea of living by a rule which does not bear upon our personal interest. God never has laid, nor ever will lay, an injunction upon a human being which militates against his own happiness. God's commandments are the emanations of his love, and the welfare of mankind is their ultimate object; the precepts given to Noah serve to illustrate this. See Psalm xix. 11; Rev. xxii. 14.

II. THE NATURE OF NOAH'S OBEDIENCE. "According to all that God commanded him, so did he."

1. *Noah's obedience was pious in its principle.* Actions are the result of principles. The tree must be made good, before the fruit can be good. To suppose that a man will obey God, whose heart is not right before him, is a palpable absurdity. " Noah found grace in the eyes of the Lord." " Noah was a just man, and perfect in his generations, and Noah walked with God." Oh, how vain are all attempts to obey God without loving him !

2. *Noah's obedience was prompt and decided in its acts.* No sooner does the inspired writer close the account of the Divine admonition to Noah, than he immediately adds, " Thus did Noah;" Heb. xi. 7. It is said, he was "moved by fear;" and fear is always prompt in its acts. There is too commonly a culpable reluctance in our obedience, especially when the cros

res in the way; but, like David, we should make haste, and delay not to keep God's commandments, Psalm cxix. 60.

3. *Noah's obedience was laborious in its exercise.* To build an ark, not less than five hundred and twelve feet long, eighty-seven wide, and fifty-two high, and the interial capacity of which, according to Calmet, was 357,600 cubical cubits, was a prodigious undertaking, and required immense labor; the labor of the head to contrive, and the hands to accomplish. And does not our obedience to God require labor? Read Matt. xi. 12; John vi. 27; Heb. iv. 11. Is there no labor required in making the sacrifices which God demands;—in exercising the graces which he approves;—and in performing the duties that he requires? Here must be the exercise of the understanding, to know the commandments of God; of the will to submit to their authority; and of the faculties of the mind, and members of the body, to practise them.

4. *Noah's obedience was universal in its extent.* He did "according to *all* that God commanded him." A failure of the most trivial kind would have defeated his whole design; and endangered his own life, and the lives of all who were with him in the ark. His obedience was therefore exact, and he was attentive to do *all* that God commanded him. Oh, what a pattern for us to follow! Our obedience should be as broad as the commandment, James ii. 10.

5. *Noah's obedience was persevering in its course.* Impediments were most certainly thrown in his way. Were there no doubts that assailed his mind as to the possibility of the scheme? Were there no insults heaped upon him? Were there no temptations to relinquish the undertaking, during the long period of a hundred and twenty years? But Noah, not only began and continued, but finished his undertaking. We also shall have obstacles to meet with, in the course of our obedience; but we must persevere, hold on, and finish our course with joy, Matt. xxiv. 13.

6. *Noah's obedience was successful in its object.* The end crowned the action. His life was preserved as the reward of his toils and labors, and persevering efforts. See him shut up in the ark, secure in Divine protection, a world of water around him, millions of dead floating on its surface, the dwellings of men for ever demolished, and nature all in ruins.

Learn from the subject,

1. What terrible desolations sin makes in the world, and how the severity of God was displayed in making the very elements conspire to the destruction of those who had slighted the Divine counsels.

2. How tenderly God cares for his servants, and how easily he can provide means for their safety.

3. How much human security depends upon human exertion. The way of duty is the way of safety. Had Noah dared to disobey God, he would have perished in the flood. "Blessed are they that do his commandments"

## SOBRIETY.

1 Thess. v. 6.—Let us be sober. (Sk.)

In the context the apostle exhorts the converts at Thessalonica to a variety of Christian duties, personal and relative, suitable to their state and privileges as Christians in general, and to their belief and expectation of Christ's second coming to judgment in particular. One of these personal duties we have in the text—*sobriety;* and as the apostle deemed it requisite to urge this on the attention and practice of one of the primitive churches, it is no less applicable to Christian ministers and people in the present day. In speaking of this duty, we shall describe,

I. THE VIRTUE OF SOBRIETY.

1. *This virtue has a principal regard to a man's self, and is equally adapted to persons of all ranks, characters, ages and sexes.* Speaking generally, it consists in observing those rules, and walking according to those methods, whereby they may secure and preserve their own health, ease, and reputation: it is to keep within those bounds which God has fixed for the right government of ourselves, our appetites, and passions, avoiding all inordinary excesses.

2. *Sobriety relates to the whole man, body and mind.* As to the mind, it bounds and moderates our thoughts of ourselves, and enjoins us to take the measure of our own worth from what we have received from God, and not from any opinion that others may entertain or express of us. It requires that we have a low and modest opinion of ourselves, and guards us against pride, self-conceit, haughtiness, vain glory, and ostentation. We are not to have an overweening conceit of our own abilities, not to contemn others, not to be insolent or imperious, not to stretch ourselves beyond our line. In this sense of the word *sobriety*, the apostle recommends to every man among the Christians at Rome, "not to think of himself more highly than he ought to think, but to think soberly, according as God hath dealt to every man the measure of faith," Rom xii. 3.

3. *As to the body, it consists in a regular and moderate desire, pursuit, and use of sensible enjoyments, such as are allowed for the promotion of its health and sustenance.* The correct notion of sobriety lies in neither denying the body what is useful and proper for it, as God is pleased to bless us with the necessaries and comforts of life; nor going beyond our necessities and stations, merely to gratify a sensual appetite, or, as the apostle expresses it, "using the world as not abusing it," 1 Cor. vii. 31.

4. *The apostle in the text considers the word in a more restrained sense, relating only to the use of meats and drinks, in opposition to gluttony and drunkenness.* I think it is evident from the context that this is his meaning; for immediately after the text, he adds, "They that sleep, sleep in the night; and they that be drunken, are drunken in the night: but let us, who are of the day, be sober." As if he should say, The heathen, with whom is the night or moral darkness, who want the cheering light of the gospel of Christ, indulge themselves in riot and excess: but let us Christians, who are of the day, enjoying the luminous rays of evangelical truth, be sober, for that is one of the rudiments it teaches, Tit. ii. 12.

5. *So that to be sober, in a limited point of view, is to use meats and drinks moderately, and for the purposes for which the almighty Donor bestows them.* The chief design of which is to render us capable of performing the duties of religion, as well as those of civil and domestic life, and do-

ing good to others according to our ability, means, and opportunity. **We** should, therefore, use the gifts of divine Providence, so as neither our reason nor health may be injured by them. To be sober, is to keep a strict and constant guard on our appetite, that we neither offend by a luxurious costliness in the quality, or excess in the quantity of those blessings granted for the nourishment and support of the earthly frame. To this purpose are the words of Solomon, when tempting dainties are set before us; "When thou sittest to eat with a ruler, consider diligently what is before thee: and put a knife to thy throat, if thou be a man given to appetite. Be not desirous of his dainties: for they are deceitful meat," Prov. xxiii. 1—3. Also he says, "Look thou not upon the wine when it is red, when it giveth his color in the cup, when it moveth itself aright. At the last it biteth like a serpent, and stingeth like an adder," ver. 31, 32.

II. PRODUCE SOME REASONS TO ENFORCE THE PRACTICE OF IT.

1. *It is amiable and commendable.* A man governing himself by the rules of temperance, checking his sensual appetite restraining his inclination, especially when in the midst of plenty and affluence, is a character of peculiar interest. Such a person fills his station in life with credit to himself, and answers the design of God, in giving him reason to be the guide and director of his actions. How gratifying it is to behold a man whom providence has favored with the means of procuring whatever his heart may desire, habitually to deny himself, subdue wrong propensities, limit and restrain himself to what is consistent with and conducive to his health and support, without any excess. He that thus gains a conquest over himself, deserves a higher encomium than he that conquers a city or country. "He that ruleth his spirit, is better than he that taketh a city," Prov. xvi. 32. The conquest of ourselves is more glorious; for one gained by reason, is more noble to an intellectual creature than one gained by force.

2. *The contrary vices are odious and full of deformity.* In their progress they dethrone reason, and reduce the man to a level even with the brute. Reason is the glory of human nature, by which we are distinguished from animals, in the right use of which we are enabled to conduct ourselves with reputation and benefit; but to hurl this noble power from her legitimate, seat, by giving heed to the demands of a low craving appetite, is the highest reproach.

Historians inform us, that the Lacedæmonians, in order to fortify their children against intemperate habits, exposed their slaves when in a state of intoxication, to their contempt and derision. And really, if a drunkard would but conceive the ridiculous figure he makes, either as staggering along the streets, or disgorging his nauseous load, or stunning the company with noise and impertinence, he would not be in charity with himself till he had cleared away this worse than brutal conduct by repentance and reformation.

These vices are a gross abuse of providential blessings, perverting them to purposes quite contrary to the intention of the Divine Author in bestowing such favors. They also occasion a serious abuse of precious time, which is dishonorable and disgraceful to a rational creature, who should know better how to value its worth. Life is vastly important, and the opportunities for performing its essential duties are fleeting and uncertain, and, when past, cannot be recalled. It becomes, therefore, a reasonable creature, rather to endeavor to recover lost time, by future attention and diligence, than squander away more, by associating with extravagant company, and indulging in riot and excess. See 1 Pet. iv. 3.

3. *Excess in meats and drinks, is an inlet to all manner of wickedness.*

331

He who loses the government of himself, and the proper exercise of his understanding, by gluttony and intoxication, what crimes is he not capable of committing, and under the influence of what restraints is he to prevent such conduct? Intemperance is the parent of impurity. "Be not drunk with wine, wherein is excess," Eph. v. 10, or, an unbridled dissolution of manners. It prompts men to injure others, excites to quarrels and contentions, and often leads to immediate destruction. "Who hath wo? who hath sorrow? who hath contentions? who hath babbling? who hath wounds without cause? who hath redness of eyes? They that tarry long at the wine; they that go to seek mixed wine," Prov. xxiii. 29, 30. It opens a way to the commission of the grossest crimes, and therefore Solomon adds, at the 33rd verse, "Thine eyes shall behold strange women, and thine heart shall utter perverse things." In a word, it is fraught with innumerable evils.

4. *A luxurious life produces fatal effects.* It causes the ruin of health and constitution,— human life is shortened by its pernicious influences. The consequences often are, violent inflammation of the blood, the bloated dropsy, the shaking palsy, consumption, fevers, &c., the forerunners of death. Whatever pleasure intemperate persons may pretend to enjoy in gratifying their passions, they will experience bitterness in the end, when the bones are full of the sin of their youth : "And thou mourn at the last, when thy flesh and thy body are consumed," Prov. v. 11. It also ruins the reputation of men, as well as their estate and family affairs. "The drunkard and glutton shall come to poverty," Prov. xxiii. 21. And then, last of all, it ruins the soul, without deep contrition and faith in Christ; for the apostle declares, such "shall not inherit the kingdom of God," 1 Cor. vi. 10. To avoid all this mischief, to which an intemperate indulgence of our sensual appetites exposes us, "let us not sleep, as do others; but let us watch and be sober."

III. SUBJOIN A FEW DIRECTIONS TO THAT ÉND.

1. *Let us consider ourselves as under the all-seeing eye of God.* As David did, set the Lord always before us, knowing that all things are naked and open to his eyes with whom we have to do, Heb. iv. 13; and that he sees through all the like artifices by which we would excuse or cover any irregularities. Did we daily consider this, it would be a happy expedient to prevent all excesses.

2. *Let us secure a saving interest in Christ and carefully keep in view his shining example.* He lived on plain provisions, and always maintained strict temperance both in eating and drinking: he never once exceeded in the least the bounds of regularity. He was sometimes at feasts, being invited, but even then he recommended by his example the doctrine he taught his disciples; "Take heed to yourselves, lest at any time your hearts be overcharged with surfeiting and drunkenness," Luke xxi. 24. Herein, as well as in many other things, he has left us an example, which we should aspire to follow.

3. *Let us avoid as much as possible the society of intemperate persons, and never in one instance choose them for our companions.* "Be not among winebibbers; among riotous eaters of flesh," Prov. xxiii. 20, lest you learn their ways, and insensibly fall into their sins. Bad company in this, as in all other cases, is most pernicious; for those who are contaminated with vice, will endeavor to corrupt others, and triumph in their success.

4. *We must use the greatest caution in those circumstances, where we are in the greatest danger.* One of which is, when we are entertained by our superiors. The honor we are then apt to think done us, and the temptation presented to gratify our appetite, is very likely to make us forget the

snare, and run into excess out of complaisance to the company.
in such a case, to be particularly on our guard, since no pretence
to men, however highly distinguished, will justify our breach of
mands of God.

5. *Let us think frequently on the future judgment, and the strict account we must then give of our behaviour to the righteous Judge.* Intemperate persons must give a sad account of their abuse of providential
blessings, which they should have received with thanksgiving, and used
with moderation. In this particular then, "Let our moderation be known
unto all men. The Lord is at hand," Phil. iv. 5.

## THE DUTY OF GIVING THE HEART TO GOD.

Prov. xxiii. 26.—My son, give me thy heart.   (H. H.)

THIS address, however it may be considered in some respect as delivered
by Solomon to his son, must certainly be understood as proceeding from
him who is wisdom in the abstract, wisdom personified, even from the Lord
Jesus Christ, Prov. viii. 1, 22—32; and as directed generally to all the
children of men, but especially to those who regard him as their sovereign
Lord. And though the more immediate object of the address may seem
scarcely suited to this view of it, (because those who are possessed even of
incipient piety may seem less likely to fall into the snare which is there
spoken of,) yet the caution is necessary for youth of all descriptions; and,
as a general lesson, it teaches us, that there is no snare whatever into which
we may not fall, if our hearts be not given up to God; and that the only
sure way of being kept from sin of every kind, is, to give the heart to
God.

Taking the words then as addressed by the Lord Jesus Christ to all who
acknowledge his paternal authority, we will proceed to mark *the extent and
reasonableness of this command.*

I. THE EXTENT OF IT—

To give our heart to God, implies that we give him,

1. The affections of the soul—

Those should all centre in him, and in him alone. Him we should desire
as our supreme good, and in him should we delight as our chief joy— — —
We should be able to say with David, "Whom have I in heaven but Thee?
and there is none upon earth that I desire besides thee." Ps. lxxiii. 25.

2. The confidence of the mind—

If there be any thing besides God in the whole universe, on which we
rely, we do not really give our heart to him. To trust, though in ever so
small a degree, in an arm of flesh, argues a departure of heart from God.
Jer. xvii. 5. We should confide altogether in his wisdom to guide, and
his power to uphold us, in his goodness to supply our wants, and his truth
to fulfil to us the promises of his word. We should "trust in him with all
our heart, and not lean either to our own understanding" or strength: we
should consider him as alone able to help us, and as all-sufficient for our
utmost necessities.

3. The service of the life—

Without this, all else is vain. Obedience is the certain fruit of love to

God, John xiv. 15, 21; yea, it is altogether identified with it: "This is the love of God, that ye keep his commandments." 1 John ii. 3—5, & v. 3. To the man that has given his heart to God, no commandment can be grievous. ib.

The extent of the command being ascertained, we proceed to shew,

II. THE REASONABLENESS OF IT—

To surrender up our whole selves to God, is called by St. Paul, "a reasonable service." Rom. xii. 1. And reasonable indeed it is;

1. Because of his right over us, as our Creator—

God "made all things for himself: all that we are, and all that we have, was given us by him, to be improved for his glory. How then can we with propriety alienate any thing from him? A potter feels himself entitled to the use of the vessel which his own hands have made: and has not God a right to all the services that we can render him? Of all that have truly given their hearts to God, it may be said, "No man liveth to himself; and no man dieth unto himself: but whether we live, we live unto the Lord; and whether we die, we die unto the Lord: whether we live therefore or die, we are the Lord's." Rom. xiv. 7, 8.

2. Because of his mercies towards us, as our Redeemer—

The Lord Jesus Christ has "redeemed us to God by his own blood:" and by this has acquired a new right over us. To this effect the Apostle says, "Ye are not your own; ye are bought with a price: therefore glorify God with your bodies and your spirits, which are his." 1 Cor. vi. 19, 20. And in another place he gives this as the duty of every man according to the dictates of his most deliberate judgment: "The love of Christ constraineth us, because we thus judge, that, if one died for all, then were all dead; and that he died for all, that they who live should not henceforth live unto themselves, but unto him who died for them, and rose again." 2 Cor. v. 14, 15. Was he mistaken in his judgement? and are we at liberty to alienate from him what he has purchased at so great a price?

3. Because of his relation to us, as our Father—

If we profess to have been born again, and begotten to God by his word and Spirit, then are we yet further bound to him by the relation he sustains towards us: "What manner of love is this, wherewith the Father hath loved us, that we should be called the sons of God?" Can we have learned to cry, Abba, Father, and doubt whether the giving of our hearts to him be a reasonable service? The utmost then we can do to serve and honor him is no more than our bounden duty.

4. Because of the utter worthlessness of all his competitors—

What is there worthy to be compared with him? The whole creation is but as "a broken cistern that can hold no water." Shall we then, "for any thing that is in it, forsake the Fountain of living waters?" Survey the choicest blessings that the world affords; and they are all "vanity and vexation of spirit." Are these then to stand in competition with him who is the unfailing and only source of all blessedness? The more we see the vanity of all created good, the more we shall see the reasonableness of giving our hearts to God alone. We must not only not love our father or mother more than him, but must "*hate* every earthly relative, yea, and our own lives also, *in comparison* of him." Luke xiv. 26.

ADDRESS,

1. In a way of affectionate invitation—

In this view we may take the words of our text, even as an invitation to us from the Lord Jesus Christ to set our affections on him alone. And how astonishing is it that he will accept such hearts as ours! If we of ourselves had presumed to offer them to him, how justly might he have rejected and despised the offering! Yet behold, he solicits it at our hands! And what can such an offering add to him? Does he need any thing from us? or can we add any thing to him? Oh then admire and adore this astonishing condescension; and let him not woo your souls in vain.

2. In a way of authoritative injunction—

This command of Almighty God is not to be trifled with. Let none presume to withstand it, or to delay his obedience to it: for if we obey it not, we never can behold his face in peace. 1 Cor. xvi. 22. Attend to it then; and see that ye obey it in truth. Give not to your God and Saviour a divided heart; for such an offering he will not accept: but give yourselves *wholly* to him; and so shall that promise be fulfilled to you; "I will be a Father unto you, and ye shall be my sons and daughters, saith the Lord Almighty."

~~~~~~~~~~

## THE DUTY OF WATCHFULNESS ENFORCED.

Mark xiii. 32—36.—But of that day and that hour knoweth no man, no, not the angels which are in heaven, neither the Son, but the Father. Take ye heed, watch and pray: for ye know not when the time is. For the Son of Man is as a man taking a far journey, who left his house, and gave authority to his servants, and to every man his work, and commanded the porter to watch. Watch ye therefore: for ye know not when the master of the house cometh, at even, or at midnight, or at the cock-crowing, or in the morning; lest coming suddenly he find you sleeping. (H. H.)

ON different occasions, but especially at the close of his life, our Lord taught his disciples to look forward to a future period, when he would assuredly come again. He specified two objects for which he would come; the one was, to destroy Jerusalem; and the other, to judge the world: and, inasmuch as the former of these advents was typical of the other, he blended them both together, and thereby raised in them an expectation that they should take place at the same time. The truth is, that though the one was accomplished within forty years, and the other, notwithstanding more than eighteen hundred years have already past, remains yet to be accomplished at some distant and unknown period, they are both equally present in the mind of God, "with whom a thousand years are as one day, and one day as a thousand years:" And it is also true, that the day of death is to every man, *in effect*, as the day of judgment: so that the union of the two periods in their minds, notwithstanding their distance from each other, was strictly just, as it respected God, and highly salutary as it respected them. Not but that our Lord did make a clear distinction between the two periods: for in v. 30, he says, "This generation shall not pass till all *these things* (relative to the destruction of Jerusalem) be done; and then, in a way of contrast, he adds, "But of *that day* and *that hour*, namely, the day of judgment, knoweth no man." It is in reference to this latter period that he speaks in the words of our text; in discoursing on which we shall consider,

I. THE DUTY INCULCATED—

Watchfulness and prayer are often united in the holy scriptures as duties of the first importance. In themselves they are different; but in their exercise they are inseparable : neither would be of any avail without the oth *r*: prayer without watchfulness would be hypocritical ; and watchfulness without prayer, presumptuous. We shall therefore combine the duties, as though it had been said. *Watch in the exercise of prayer.* And that we may yet further simplify the subject, we shall not enter into a detail of particulars, but rather follow the general ideas of our text ; and shew,

1. What we should watch and pray *against*—

Here we must include *every thing which has a tendency to lull us asleep.* We see how intent men are on all the things of time and sense : the lust of the eye, and the pride of life, so occupy them, that they find no time nor inclination for spiritual concerns— — —

Against these then we should "watch and pray:" we should watch, to prevent them from gaining an ascendant over our hearts ; and cry mightily to God to keep us from yielding to their influence. Seeing how the whole world is led captive by them, we should tremble for ourselves ; and day and night intreat God rather to leave us destitute of all earthly things, than to give us over to the love of them, or suffer them to deprive us of eternal happiness— — —

2. What we should watch and pray *for.*

*To be found ready,* at whatever moment our Lord shall call for us, should be the one object of our ambition. With this view, we should seek to be found in Christ, not having our own righteousness, but that which is of God through faith in Christ. Not. content with a general hope of acceptance through Christ, we should wash our every sin, yea our every duty also, in the fountain of his blood, which must cleanse us from the " iniquity even of our holiest actions. We should seek also to " be renewed in the spirit of our minds," and to be transformed into " the image of our God in righteousness and true holiness." No attainments should ever satisfy us: if we were as holy as Paul himself, we should, like him, "forget the things that are behind, and reach forward towards that which is before." With a view to progressive holiness, we should carefully " abide in Christ," " living by faith on him," and receiving daily out of his fulness grace for grace : assured, that without him we can do nothing, but through him shall be enabled to do all things. In a word, we should seek to be ever ready to meet our God ; yea to be "looking for, and hasting unto the coming of that day," when we shall be summoned to his tribunal, and receive our eternal doom— — —

For the attainment of this happy frame of mind, we should be watching our progress in the Divine life, and praying day and night *to God* to perfect in us the work that he has begun— — —

Let us next attend to,

II. THE CONSIDERATIONS WITH WHICH IT IS ENFORCED—

These may be comprehended in the two following :

1. The uncertainty of the time when our Lord shall call us—

The time of the general judgment is unknown to the holy angels : nor was it revealed even to the Messiah himself for the purpose of communicating it to us.* And there was good reason why it should be concealed ; because if it had been represented as at a great distance of time, men might have become secure ; whereas the idea of its speedy arrival tended to quicken all to holy exertion. In like manner the uncertainty of the time of our

* As God, one with the Father, he knew all things ; but as the Mediator, he received his instructions from the Father, and delivered nothing but what he had before received. John xiv. 49. Rev. i. 1.

**death** has a very salutary effect; since it necessitates us to be always ready. The idea of a man going a long journey, and leaving his servants their appointed work, and ordering them to expect him every moment till they see him, justly illustrates this point. There is not a moment of our lives when we may sit down secure. The night was divided into four watches, which terminated at evening, at midnight, at the cock-crowing, and in the morning. Now at no one of these periods are we sure that we shall not be summoned into the presence of our God.

What a consideration is this to enforce the duty in our text! Who that reflects one moment on the possibility of his being called this night to the judgment-seat of Christ, must not desire to be found in the exercise of watchfulness and prayer?— — —

2. The awfulness of being found in a sleeping state—

In the parable of the ten virgins we are informed what we must assuredly expect, if we indulge in careless security; we shall be shut out from the marriage-supper of our Lord, and be "cast into outer darkness, where is weeping and gnashing of teeth." It will be to no purpose to plead, that we were not engaged in any wicked projects. We were "slothful servants," and therefore are justly regarded as "wicked:" we were unprepared, and therefore are justly cut off from all further opportunity to prepare for our great account; we treated heaven with contempt, and therefore we are consigned to the miseries of hell— — —

Who that contemplates these tremendous consequences, must not determine with God's help to watch and pray through the whole remainder of his days?— — —

Our Lord's concluding admonition, "What I say unto you I say unto all, Watch," will lead us to *address* some different descriptions of persons:

1. The old—

Is so much of your time gone, and will you not improve the remainder?— — —

2. The young—

What security have you against death, that you should delay so necessary a work?— — —

3. The afflicted—

God sends your afflictions on purpose to awaken you from your slumbers, and to stir you up to heavenly pursuits: What an aggravation will it be of your guilt, if these dispensations pass away unimproved!

4. The backslidden—

What an awful thing is it, that, instead of having advanced in the Divine life, you have lost in a good measure the life which you once had! Attend to God's admonition to the church of Sardis, lest he execute upon you the judgment that he threatened to inflict on them, Rev. iii. 2, 3.— — —

5. The more stedfast christian—

Experience proves that the exhortation to "watch" is not less necessary for you than for others. How many who are on the whole pious, grieve, by their unwatchfulness, their Divine Master! Be on your guard against such a slothful way of seeking him as his Bride was found guilty of, Cant. iii. 1; nor think to justify your sloth by such frivolous excuses as were urged by her. Cant. v. 2, 3. If you act like her, like her you will reap the bitter fruits in the hidings of his face. Cant. iii. 1—4. & v. 2—6. To you then no less than to others I would say, "Sleep not as do others, but watch and be sober." 1 Thess. v. 6—8.

## WE SHOULD WATCH FOR OUR LORD'S SECOND COMING

Mark xiii. 37.—What I say unto you I say unto all, Watch.  (H. H.)

GOD is pleased to speak to us, not only in his word, but by the dispensations of his providence.  Calamities, whether foreign or domestic, whether public or personal, are sent by him to awaken our drowsy consciences, and to stir us up to a remembrance of our latter end.  By all of them, whether menaced only, or actually inflicted, he addresses us, as Jesus did his disciples (whom he had forewarned of the evils coming upon Jerusalem, and hereafter also upon the whole world), " Watch therefore, for ye know not when the Master of the house cometh."

On a subject like this we should in vain attempt to speak any thing new.  But though we may do no more than remind ycu of truths with which you are already well acquainted, it will not be unprofitable for me to suggest to your thoughts,

I. THE UNCERTAINTY OF THE TIME WHEN OUR LORD WILL COME TO JUDGMENT—

Our Lord, in illustrating what he had been speaking respecting the day of judgment, compares himself to a master leaving his house, and appointing his servants their work, and commanding his porter to watch, in order to admit him without delay at whatever moment he should return.  He represents the precise time of his return to judgment as unknown to men, or angels, or even to himself; (so far at least, that the Holy Spirit, by which he was anointed to his prophetic office, had not communicated it to him as any part of the revelation which he was to make known to men ;) and from thence inculcates the necessity of incessant watchfulness.  Now, as the time of death is to us the commencement of our eternal state, and as it is equally unknown to us as the judgment itself, we shall direct our attention more particularly to that.

But what shall we say on such a subject as this ?  It needs neither proof nor elucidation: nor can any words make the uncertainty of life more evident, than the observation and experience of every man have already made it.  We appeal to your observation of what takes place around you :  Does not our Lord call men to death and judgment at every age, and often when his summons is least expected?— — —We appeal to your experience : Can you not recal to your minds many accidents which might have proved fatal? and do you not see, that you are yet liable every day and hour to be taken away by disease or accident?— — —

Instead of dwelling on so obvious a truth, we will endeavor to point out,

II. OUR DUTY ARISING FROM THIS CONSIDERATION—

Thrice in the space of a few verses does our Lord repeat the same injunction, " Watch," see ver. 33.  To enforce this, we would say,

1. Expect the second coming of your Lord—

Put not from you, as you are too apt to do, the thoughts of death and judgment, but cherish them in your minds, and labor to get them impressed upon your hearts.  Reflect upon their *uncertainty*, as to the precise period of their arrival, their *nearness*, their *awfulness ;* and keep yourselves, as it were, in the daily and hourly expectation of them— — —

2. Prepare to meet him—

Two things are indispensable for all who would behold his face in peace, namely, " repentance towards God, and faith in our Lord Jesus Christ."  These must be experienced by you— — —neither the one nor the other can be dispensed with.— — —Get a deep repentance therefore, and a lively faith : and rest not in any state short of that which the scriptures require, and the primitive christians actually attained.

3. Guard against any measure of drowsiness which may interrupt or render doubtful your preparation for him—

It will be a fearful thing if the Master of the house "should find you sleeping." Yet who amongst us is not apt at times to be "weary in well-doing?" "The wise virgins, as well as the foolish, slumbered and slept:" yea, even the Apostles slept, when our Lord had bidden them watch. We should therefore "exhort one another daily, and so much the more as we see the day approaching:" and, instead of giving way to sloth, should use all possible means, to "strengthen the things which remain that are ready to die."

Address,
1. The careless—

How many continue such in spite of all the warnings which they have received from sickness in themselves, or the sudden deaths of others! But what will they think of their conduct, when once they are taken hence? If any one of us knew that a thief would certainly come this very night to break into his house, would he lay himself down to sleep as at other times? Should we not watch, and use our utmost efforts to frustrate his designs? Why then do we not act thus in reference to our souls? Are our souls of less value than our property, or the concerns of time than those of eternity? Are not the consequences of unwatchfulness sufficiently awful? Matt. xxiv. 48—51. And is not our real danger increased, rather than diminished, in proportion to our security? 1 Thess. v. 3. Prov. vi. 9—11. To every one then who is unconcerned about his eternal state, and unprepared to meet his God, we address the reproof which even heathen mariners gave to a prophet of the Lord: "What meanest thou, O sleeper? arise and call upon thy God, if so be that God will think upon thee, and thou perish not." Jonah i. 6.

2. The half-awakened—

Pardon the term : it is but too appropriate to the states of many, who, if good wishes would carry them to heaven, would not come short of it; but when God calls them to run, and strive, and wrestle, and fight, will not exert themselves in the way that requires. Nevertheless God's word is true; "The kingdom of heaven suffereth violence, and the violent take it by force:" "Many shall *seek* to enter in, and shall not be able;" none shall succeed but those who "*strive*." Guard then against the fate of the foolish virgins, who were not aware of their want of Divine grace, till it was too late to obtain it. Matt. xxv. 8—13. Let the Apostle's exhortation sink down into your ears, Rom. xiii. 11—14, and adopt instantly the resolution of the Prophet, "I will stand upon my watch-tower, and will watch to see what God will say to me, and what I shall answer when I am reproved" Hab. ii. 1.

3. The professing people of God—

Think not yourselves above the exhortation in our text: "What we say unto some, we must say unto *all*, Watch." See what a caution our blessed Lord addressed to his own Apostles, Luke xxi. 34—36: and then say, whether *any* caution can be too strong for *you*. Many who have appeared to run well, have turned back again; and not a few have died without ever returning to the good way from which they have departed. Be ye then on your guard, "lest, having known the way of righteousness, ye turn from the holy commandment delivered unto you." Beware of imitating the slothful conduct of the Spouse in Solomon's Song, lest, like her, you provoke your heavenly Friend to depart from you. Cant. iii. 1 & v. 2—6. Watch unto prayer with habitual persevering earnestness. Eph. vi. 18. You know the truths we have insisted on; act therefore agreeably to them, and to your holy profession. 1 Thess. v. 2, 4—8. "Have your loins continually girt, and your lamps trimmed, and yourselves as those who wait for the coming of their Lord."*

---

## THE DUTY OF HOPING IN GOD.

**Ps cxxx. 7, 8.**—Let Israel hope in the Lord; for with the Lord there is mercy, and with him is plenteous redemption. And he shall redeem Israel from all his iniquities. (S. S.)

THAT advice which flows from experience is at all times most worthy of our attention. In this view the words of our text claim peculiar regard. David, in the Psalm before us, records a very signal deliverance which he had recently experienced, probably from an overwhelming sense of his own guilt and corruption; and, having informed us what methods he had used to obtain deliverance, and how effectual they had proved for his restoration to happiness, he recommends the adoption of them to all the people of God under all difficulties whatsoever; and assures them, that they shall not in any instance fail of success: "Let Israel," &c.

He sets before us,

I. OUR DUTY.

Hope in God, as men generally use the term, is nothing more than an unfounded expectation that God will save us, whatever be our state, and whatever be our conduct. But a scriptural hope implies a suitable regard to the things we hope for, and to him in whom our hope is placed. It implies,

1. That we pray to him with fervour.

This was united with the Psalmist's hope; ver. 1, 2; and it must also be with ours. Matt. vii. 7, 8. To pretend to hope in God while we neglect to spread our wants before him, is the grossest hypocrisy, and the most fatal delusion. Ezek. xxxvi. 37.

2. That we wait for him with patience.

It was in this manner that David exercised his hope. Ver. 5, 6. Nor can we act otherwise, if we be sincere in our profession. Rom. viii. 25. To be impatient, is an unequivocal mark of unbelief, and despondency. Isa. xxviii. 16; 1 Sam. xiii. 11, 12. But to wait patiently the Lord's leisure is the office and evidence of faith and hope. Hab. ii. 3.

3. That we depend on him with steadfastness.

The promises of God to those who seek him, must be the ground of our hope. Ver. 5. We are not to regard difficulties of any kind, as though they could prove any obstacle to God. However circumstances, both within and without, may seem to justify despair, we must "hope beyond and against hope," παρ' ἐλπίδα Rom. iv. 18; Job xiii. 15; Isa. i. 10, assured that, as nothing is impossible with God, so not one jot or tittle of his word shall ever fail

---

* Supposing this were a *funeral* Sermon for a truly pious person, some little mention of his character might be made here.

This duty being of infinite importance, and of universal obligation, let us consider,

II. OUR ENCOURAGEMENT TO PERFORM IT.

If we look inward, we shall find nothing but discouragement. But if, with David, we look to God, we may find abundant encouragement.

1. In his attributes.

While justice bears a frowning aspect, mercy smiles on the repenting sinner. God has opened a way for the exercise of his mercy in perfect consistency with the demands of justice; and to exercise it is his delight. Mic. vii. 18. This attribute is as essential to his nature as wisdom, or power, or any other. Exod. xxxiv. 6, 8. Nor needs he to have it excited by a view of our misery; (much less by any meritorious services of ours) it is ever " with him;" and is ready to manifest itself towards all those who call upon him. Rom. x. 12.

2. In his works.

" Redemption" is the crown of all his works : and this also is with him, that he may impart it to those who groan under their sore bondage. Yea, with him is " plenteous" redemption: he himself as our near kinsman, (bone of our bone, and flesh of our flesh, Eph. v. 30.) has the right of redemption vested in him : Lev. xxv. 25, 47, 48, 49; and having ability to pay the price, he will discharge our debt, and restore us, not only to liberty, but also to the inheritance which we have so basely alienated.

3. In his word.

The declaration of his determined purpose by an inspired writer, is equivalent to an express promise. And, if the extent and certainty of this promise be considered, what an encouragement will it afford us to hope in God ! There is no limitation whatever to the promise, provided, like " Israel" of old, we wrestle with God for the performance of it. Gen. xxxii. 24—28. However numerous and inveterate our iniquities may be, they shall "all" be pardoned, and "all" subdued. Isaiah i. 18.

APPLICATION.

1. To prevent any abuse of this subject, we shall *guard* it.

The repetition of the name "Israel" distinctly marks the characters to whom the text is more immediately to be applied. It is the *praying, waiting*, and *depending* sinner that is exhorted to hope in God: and it is he alone who can expect redemption at the hands of God. Let such therefore see their duty and their privilege : but let those who live in the habitual neglect of God know, that their " hope is as a spider's web, that shall soon be swept away with the besom of destruction." Job viii. 13, 14.

2. To impress the subject more deeply on our minds, we shall *enforce* it.

The advice here given is the most *suitable* that can be given, and if followed, will be *productive* of the greatest *happiness*. Were any of us directed to indulge an hope from our own endeavors, we should soon perceive the folly of such advice. Every day and hour would bring us fresh occasion for despair. But in God there is nothing wanting : he has the *right*, the *power*, and the *will* to redeem us. Nor, if we trust in him, shall we ever be confounded. Isaiah xlv. 17.

Let us therefore not limit either the mercy or power of our God, but putting away all self-righteous hopes, Phil. iii. 3. or unbelieving fears, Ps. xlii. 11. let us repose an unlimited confidence in our merciful and faithful Redeemer,

341

## THE DUTY OF THE CHURCH AS MARRIED TO CHRIST.

Ps. xlv. 10, 11.—Hearken, O daughter, and consider, and incline thine ear; forget also thine own people, and thy father's house. So shall the King greatly desire thy beauty: for he is thy Lord; and worship thou him. (S. S.)

Every change of situation brings with it many correspondent duties—
That of marriage in particular requires a sacrifice of other attachments—
It binds each party to renounce whatever habits or practices may be found inconsistent with their mutual happiness—
Such sacrifices are more eminently necessary for those united to Christ*—
To this effect God addresses the church in the words of our text—
We may consider,

I. THE DIRECTION GIVEN TO THE CHURCH.

The church is, by adoption, by regeneration, and especially by her union with the Lord Jesus Christ, become the "daughter" of God—2 Cor. vi. 18.
She is here addressed by him under that affectionate appellation—
Nor is it possible for a father to give more salutary advice—
Or to deliver it in more persuasive terms; "Hearken, consider, incline," &c.
The direction itself is of a very peculiar nature.
The Jews were permitted to marry the heathen virgins whom they had taken in war—
But they were to allow them the space of a month to forget their own relations—Deut. xxi. 10—13.
Thus the captives, weaned from former habits, might become loving companions, and obedient wives—
In reference to this law, the church is exhorted to forget her friends—
She has been taken captive by Christ, who makes her the first overtures of marriage—
But his union with her is incompatible with carnal attachments—
She can never love and obey him as she ought, till her heart be weaned from all other lovers—
It is given to every individual in the church of God.
Every wife is to forsake her parents, and cleave to her husband—Gen ii. 24.
Much more is it needful for the soul to forsake all for Christ—
To him we are espoused by our own voluntary surrender—2 Cor. xi. 2.
Nor will he be satisfied with a divided heart—Hos. x. 2.
Ungodliness and worldly lusts must be entirely renounced—Tit. ii. 11. 12, and 1 Pet. iv. 2, 3.
The companions of our unregenerate state must be forsaken—2 Cor. vi. 14—17.
Our very parents, yea, even life itself, must be hated, when they stand in competition with him—Luke xiv. 26.
The change in our actions and effections must be entire—2 Cor. v. 17.
And we must subscribe from our hearts the terms proposed to us—Hos. iii. 3.
This injunction will not appear harsh, if we attend to,

* The psalm before us is a kind of nuptial hymn; the former part of which recites the excellencies and glories of the heavenly Bridegroom, and the latter celebrates the praises of the church, which is his bride.

## II. The arguments with which it is enforced.

God deals with us in all things as intelligent beings—
And labors to persuade us by rational considerations.

1. It is our highest interest.

Though the church is vile in herself, she is complete in Christ—Col. ii. 10.

He has given orders for her thorough purification—Esther ii. 3.

When she is presented to him, she is cleansed from all the filthiness of her former state—Eph. v. 25—27.

Hence she is exceeding beautiful in h's eyes—Song iv. 9—11.

And he feels a longing desire after communion with her—Song ii. 14.

No bridegroom ever so much rejoiced over his bride, as he over her—Isa. lxii. 5.

More especially is he delighted with her when he sees that her heart is whole with him. Prov. xi. 20.

How powerful an argument is this with an ingenuous soul!—

What can influence a wife more than to know that her conduct will conciliate the esteem of her husband?—

And what can delight a regenerate soul so much, as to please Christ?—

Let this hope then animate us to renounce all for him—

And to address him in the words of holy David—Ps. lxxiii. 25

2. It is our indispensable duty.

The husband is to be considered as a Lord over his wife—1 Pet. iii. 6.

To him she owes an humble obediential reverence—Eph. v. 33.

Christ also is the supreme head and Lord of his Church—

No limits whatever are to be set to his authority—

We must " worship" and serve him equally with God the Father—John —v. 23.·

Let us then at least shew him that regard, which we ourselves expect from a fellow-creature—

A husband will not endure a rival in his wife's affections—

Shall we then " provoke the Lord himself to jealousy" by carnal attachments ?—

Let us not dare in such a way to violate our nuptial engagements—

When any thing solicits a place in our hearts, let us utterly reject it—

And let us exercise that fidelity towards him, which we have ever experienced at his hands—

Address,

1. Those who are endeavoring to unite the love of the world with the ove of Christ.

The interests of the world, and of Christ, are altogether opposite—

Our Lord declares them to be absolutely irreconcilable—Matt. vi. 24.

St. James also represents even a wish to reconcile them, as an incontestible proof of enmity against God—Jam. iv. 4.

As Jesus deserves, so he demands our whole hearts—Prov. xxiii. 26.

Let us not then " mock him, and deceive ourselves"—

If the Lord be God, let us not serve Baal, but him—1 Kings xviii. 21.

And let us unite in imitating the repentant Jews—2 Chron. xv. 12.

2. Those who are desirous of uniting themselves to Christ.

It is a great honor indeed which ye aspire after—

Yet is it offered to the vilest of the human race—Ezek. xvi. 3, 4, 5, 8.

But you must get a change of raiment, that you may not dishonor your new station—Zech. iii. 3—5.

Labor then to " purge out all remains of the old leaven"—
Be on your guard, lest after having escaped the pollutions of the **world,**
you be again entangled with them and overcome—2 Pet. ii. 20.
" Remember Lot's wife" that you may shun her example—
So shall you enjoy the sweetest fellowship with Jesus—
And live in the fruition of him to all eternity*—

***

## THE DUTY OF WALKING IN THE LIGHT.

**John xii. 35, 36.** Yet a little while is the light with you. Walk while ye have the light, lest darkness come upon you: for he that walketh in darkness, knoweth not whither he goeth. While ye have light, believe in the light, that ye may be the children of light. (S. S.)

THE perverseness of men in resisting the means of conviction, is apt to beget an asperity in the minds of their instructors, and to make them cease from their labors of love. But we are required "in meekness to instruct them that oppose themselves." And our blessed Lord affords us in this respect an admirable example. He had plainly told the Jews, that he must be crucified: and their very answer shews that they understood his meaning. But, instead of receiving the information aright, they cavilled at it, and concluded from thence that he could not be the Messiah, ver. 32—34. Our Lord did not judge it proper at that time to afford them any farther means of conviction, when they had so abused those that were already afforded them: but he most affectionately warned them to improve their present advantages, before they should be finally withdrawn from them.

The words being equally applicable to us, we shall consider,

I. THE EXHORTATION.

Christ is here spoken of as "the light."

We might consider the term " light" *in general*, as referring to the gospel: but *here* it undoubtedly relates to Christ himself. John i. 9, and viii. 12, and xii. 46. He is justly characterized by this name, not only as being the eternal fountain of light, but as enlightening the world by his doctrines and life.

" In him," under this character, we are to " believe."

All that he has spoken respecting his person, work, and offices, together with all his promissory, or threatening declarations, should be received by us without gainsaying, and be relied upon without hesitation.

" In him" also we ought to " walk."

We view earthly things in the light of the material sun; and avail ourselves of its light, every step we take. Precisely thus should we act with respect to Christ, "the Sun of Righteousness." We should view sin and holiness, time and eternity, yea, every thing without exception, in the light that HE, by his word and conduct, reflects upon it. Nor should we take any one step in life, without a direct reference to his word as our rule, and his life as our example.—1 John ii. 6.

To render this exhortation more impressive, let us consider,

II. THE ARGUMENTS WITH WHICH IT IS ENFORCED.

* This subject, and all others of a similar nature, must be treated with extreme care and delicacy.

There are three topics mentioned in the text, from whence we may urge this important duty,

1. From the shortness of the time that we shall enjoy the light.

The Jews now had the light; but it was to be extinguished within the space of four days. Hence our Lord *repeatedly* urges this consideration. "Walk, *while ye have the light.*" And how strongly does this argument apply to us! You have the light at present, yea, even greater light than the Jews enjoyed under the ministry of Christ: (for there were many subjects, which he did not fully open; and the things he did utter, could not be perfectly understood, till the day of Pentecost; whereas you have Christ exhibited to you in all his glory; and the fulness, the freeness, the suitableness of his salvation constantly set before you.) But how soon may it be removed from you, or you from it! Rev. ii. 5. Amos viii. 11, 12. O then, "*while ye have the light*, believe, and walk, in the light."

2. From the danger we incur by disregarding the light.

If we will not attend to the voice of Christ, a "darkness will come upon us," even "darkness that may be felt." They who never have had Christ preached unto them, are indeed in an awful condition; but by no means so awful as that, of those who have despised the gospel, ver. 39, 40. The darkness of which the text speaks, is *judicial*, sent them by God as the punishment of their iniquity; and the very light that shines around them, serves only to increase their blindness, and to aggravate their guilt. 2 Cor. ii. 15, 16. 2 Thess. ii. 11, 12. In this state, "they stumble at the noonday," and wander, "not knowing whither they go;" till at last they fall into that pit of destruction, where is weeping, and wailing, and gnashing of teeth for evermore.

Should not then the dread of such a state lead us to a just improvement of our present privileges?

3. From the benefit arising to those who rightly improve the light.

By "children of light" we may understand either *children of God* (who is light) or, *truly enlightened persons.** In either sense the general import is the same, namely, that, by believing in Christ, we shall attain the knowledge and enjoyment of God. Compare this state with that of those who are in darkness; and how great will this benefit appear!

Shall not then this blessed prospect allure us to embrace the gospel? Or shall we still prefer sin and misery to holiness and glory?

APPLICATION.

Let us no longer withstand the solemn warnings, and affectionate exhortations of the Lord Jesus; but improve to the utmost this accepted time, this day of salvation.

---

*Thus υἱοὶ ἀπειθείας is used; Eph. ii. 2, and τίκνα κατάρας, 2 Pet. ii. 14, is so translated, as υἱοὶ φωτὸς may be here.

## DILIGENCE IN DUTY NECESSARY TO BE FOUND OF GOD IN PEACE.

2 Pet. iii. 14.—Wherefore, beloved, seeing ye look for such things, be diligent, that ye may be found of him in peace without spot and blameless. (H.)

THE Apostle is speaking, in the preceding verses, of the drowning of the world by water, the coming of the day of the Lord, the destruction of the world by fire, and of a better state of things, in answer to the scoffers of the last days, who said, "Where is the promise of his coming? Since the Fathers fell asleep all things continue as they were." Verse 4. The words are an inference, or conclusion, from these promises. "Wherefore, beloved, since ye looked for such things." I shall have occasion to consider the context, in speaking to the words; what I propose is, to draw forth the sense of them in the several parts of which they consist.

I. IT IS HERE SUPPOSED THAT WE MUST BE JUDGED, and that an inquiry will be made into the states of men. This is implied in the expression, "being found in him;" i. e. by him as judge, or before him, when he shall come. The apostle uses the same expression in the same sense. Phil. iii. 9. The term relates to the final judgment, when the great inquiry shall be made, and the states of men determined. The future judgment is particularly represented and described in Scripture; I shall give you a short view of it to engage and affect your minds.

1. The time of it is appointed. The apostle here speaks of the day of judgment, and the coming of the day of God; chap. ii. 9; iii. 12; the period is determinately fixed; Acts xvii. 31; but of that day and hour knoweth no man. When the period arrives, there will not be a moment's delay; and it will come too soon, come when it will, for those who scoff at the seeming delay.

2. The judge is ordained. This our Lord himself tells us. John v. 22, 27; and again, Rom. ii. 16; 2 Cor. v. 10. The Saviour of sinners is to be Judge of sinners. His appearance will be very glorious, and with great magnificence and grandeur. Luke ix. 26.

3. The rule of judgment is fixed, or the measure of proceeding at that day. We are to be tried by the gospel of Christ, and not by the law of innocence. If he were to enter into judgment with us, and to be strict to mark iniquity, no living creature could be justified, or stand before him. The whole world must be condemned at his bar, and upon the ground of rigorous justice. But we shall be judged by the gospel of Christ, and according to the gracious constitution of the new covenant; so the apostle says. Rom. ii. 16. The apostle James is more direct, chap. i. 25. where he calls the gospel the law of liberty; also, the perfect law of liberty. chap. ii. 12. And which the apostle calls the law of faith, Rom. iii. 27. in opposition to the law of works, which accepts of true believers in Christ, or sincerity of heart, without absolute perfection, and with many imperfections. This is included in the books which shall be opened; Rev. xx. 12. and according to which he will judge the world in righteousness.

4. The persons to be judged are the whole world or the whole race of sinful man. All who died in Adam, shall be judged by Christ, as well as made alive by him; for they are raised in order to be judged. All nations are to be gathered before him. Matt. xxv. 32. We are all to appear before him; 2 Cor. v. 10. the small and great, Rev. xx. 12.

5. The matter of judgment or the cause to be tried, is expressed in the most comprehensive terms; Eccl. xii. 14. and this is the constant language

of the gospel. 2 Cor. v. 10. So that every man shall be rewarded according to his deeds; Rom. ii. 6. being judged according to their works. Rev. xx. 13; xxii. 12. God will judge the secrets of men by Jesus Christ; the most retired transactions of their lives, and the workings of their thoughts and desires, which lie concealed in their own breast, and fall not under the notice of others; and every idle word which men shall speak, they shall give an account thereof, Matt. xii. 36; *i. e.* every evil word, which is either false or hurtful.

6. And then there is the final issue and event of judgment; *i. e.* rewards and punishments. To the righteous it will be, "well done good and faithful servant, enter thou into the joy of thy Lord; and come ye blessed." &c. Matt. xxv. 34. 41. To the wicked it will be, "thou wicked and slothful servant; cast the unprofitable servant into outer darkness, there shall be weeping and gnashing of teeth; and, go, ye cursed," &c. verse 46. The execution of the sentence will immediately follow, "for these shall go away into everlasting punishment, but the righteous into life eternal." They each shall go to their respective, final, and unchangeable state; and so, from the consequence of it, it is called the eternal judgment. Heb. vi. 2.

II. I OBSERVE, THAT A CHRISTIAN'S GREAT CONCERN is to be found of his judge in peace, and without spot and blamleess. Here is a double expression used, which evidently refers to two different things, of the greatest importance.

1. It refers to our justification and acceptance with God, which is the state of every true believer. There can be no peace in the day of judgment to a fallen sinner, but in the way of forgiveness. We must be pardoned and justified through the blood of Christ; for that is the measure of our present acceptance with God, which will be the rule of the final judgment; so the apostle says; Phil. iii. 9, which is parallel to that of the apostle. Acts xiii. 39; also Gal. ii. 16. Thus we are brought into a state of friendship with God for being justified by faith; Rom. v. 1, we have peace with God.

The consequence of this is, peace of mind; a composed frame of mind, without the uneasiness of doubt, or torment of fear, or dread of divine displeasure. A blessed serenity of mind, arising from the testimony of conscience to their own sincerity, and the witness of the Spirit to their relation to God. They have that peace of God which passes all understanding; which none of the troubles of life, or fear of death, nor the presence of the Judge, or the terror of judgment, can disturb.

And this will appear in a peaceable frame of mind towards others: in good-will towards all men, fervent love to all the children of God. Heb. xii. 14.

I shall only farther add, that although the believer is justified already, yet we are most properly justified at the final judgment, when it will be most solemn and most complete.

2. It refers to our sanctification and holiness. This is the import of the other expression, "without spot and blameless." This may refer to our present sanctification, which is called the sanctification of the Spirit, &c. Eph. i. 4. For this end God has chosen believers; Phil. ii. 15; and they are to keep themselves unspotted, &c. James i. 27. This was the character of Zachariah and Elizabeth. Luke i. 6. And as such Jesus Christ will present them to himself at last. Eph. v. 27; also 1 Thess. iii. 13. It is a great act of the mediation of Christ, towards his members, not only to "wash them in his own blood, but to present them pure and faultless at last." This certainly was the grand end of his whole undertaking; see Titus ii.

347

**4**; also 1 Peter iii. 18. Paul represents it as the highest ambition of the christian's heart; 2 Cor. v. 9, and the greatest blessing he could wish for others. Phil. i. 10.

III. THAT IN ORDER TO OUR BEING FOUND OF OUR JUDGE IN PEACE we must be diligent. It is a work of labor and care, and not to be done with idleness and sloth. Men may sit still and perish; but they must be diligent who would be saved. Consider this diligence according to the scripture account of it, in the following instances.

1. There must be the due exercise of our natural faculties and reasonable powers. Those, we readily admit, are weakened and disordered by sin; but divine assistance is promised by God, who is the God of nature as well as grace. We are reasonable creatures, when we are not holy creatures, and can act as men, when we cannot act as saints, and in order to being such, see Deut. xxxii. 29; Isa. xlvi. 8; Hos. v. 4; 1 Cor. xiv. 20; Phil. ii. 12.

2. The improvement of the talents and enjoyments of life. Every man has his proper talents, besides his natural powers, though in different degrees, for which he must account at last. Matt. xxv. 14; Luke xix. 13. Such are life and health, acquired knowledge and experience, liberty and opportunity, possessions and prosperity, interest and credit in the world. Those who improve therein shall be commended, Matt. xxv. 21, and those who do not improve them shall be punished, ver. 25. We are only stewards of our talents; Luke xvi. 2, and our Lord advises a proper use of them; ver. 9; also the apostle, 1 Tim. vi. 17.

3 We must perform the proper duties of our place and station. John ix. 4. In this sense our Lord pronounces his servants blessed; Matt. xxiv. 46, and this the apostle recommends. 2 Pet. i. 10. Faithfulness in the way of duty is a good preparation for the coming of the Lord 1 Cor. xv. 58.

4. There must be watchfulness against sin. So our Lord directs his disciples in this case: Luke xxi. 34, in this view he often requires watchfulness. Matt. xxvi. 41, 42; Mark xiii. 37. The apostle abounds with exhortations to sobriety and watchfulness. 1 Thess. v. 6, 8; Pet. iv. 7; Heb. xii. 15, 17. And the judge is represented saying, "Behold I come, blessed is he that watcheth and keepeth his garments." Rev. xvi. 15.

5. The use of appointed means, or institutions of worship. These are properly means of grace. Thus we must be found in the daily practice of prayer. Luke xviii. 1; also xxi. 36. We must converse with the word of God; Heb. ii. 1; 2 Pet. i. 19, and the apostle says, that " God is a rewarder of them who diligently seek him," or come to him in any way of worship or service. Particularly the Lord's Supper is a perpetual memorial, not only of the death, but of the coming of Christ. 1 Cor. xi. 26. Thus, by frequent converses with God in the ordinances of his worship, and receiving communications from him, we are formed to a more spiritual frame, and serious habit of mind, and in a nearer fitness for the coming of the Lord. Hereupon,

6. There must be the exercise and improvement of suitable graces, or proper dispositions of mind. 2 Pet. i. 5; iii. 18. Particularly faith; Heb. vi. 1; also hope; Heb. vi. 11; 1 Pet. i. 13; and looking; Tit. ii. 13; Heb. ix. 28; Jude 21, and in this chapter, ver. 12.

IV. I SHALL CONSIDER THE MOTIVES and reasons of this diligence here suggested and referred to. This is intimated in the words of connexion, " Wherefore, beloved, seeing ye look for such things; *i. e.* the things which he had been speaking of, or the arguments of his foregoing discourse. The great ideas in his mind at that time were,

1. The destruction of the present world, ver. 7, to be accomplished by a deluge of fire; also, ver. 10, the whole globe of the earth shall be set on fire, and whatever belongs to it, and has been infected with sin. All the works of nature and of art, the stately buildings and proud palaces, the monuments of vanity, ambition, and curiosity, which have endured for many ages, and stood the longest injuries of time; all the grandeur and glory of this world, the pageantry and show of it, will be then destroyed and consumed to ashes, and there will be no remainder or ruins of them left; "for the heavens shall pass away," &c., ver. 10.

There will be a universal conflagration; heaven and earth will be all on fire at once, and make one burning vault, one funeral pile: it will be the funeral of the world. What will be the terror of the affrighted inhabitants! no place of refuge! Yea, the fire which will consume the world, will destroy the wicked, ver. 7. Now, how forcible is the reason? Be diligent to be found of him in peace, when the great day of his wrath shall come.

2. The expectation of a better state, ver. 13. He represents it as the common expectation of christians, grounded on the promise of God; " we, according to his promise, look for it, a new heaven and a new earth." Isa. lxv. 17. Heaven and earth will be alike, at least for a limited time, and become a glorious state, in which only righteousness and righteous persons shall dwell. And the expectation of such a state of things should operate as a powerful motive, that we may not come short of the glory of God, but be fit to partake of it, and share in all the blessedness of it. Let us, therefore, according to our Lord's direction, " watch and pray, that we may be accounted worthy to escape all these things which shall come to pass, and to stand before the Son of man." And, in the words of the apostle, " Give diligence, so an entrance shall be ministered abundantly into the everlasting kingdom; and, let us labor to enter into that rest, lest any man fall after the same example of unbelief."

---

## CONSTANCY CROWNED BY CHRIST.

### Rev. ii. 10.—Be thou faithful, &c.   (H.)

THESE are the words of our Saviour to the angel or pastor of the church of Smyrna; and they divide themselves into two parts, a precept and a promise. The precept is in these words— " Be thou faithful unto death." The promise in these— "And I will give," &c. There is the work in the one, and the reward in the other. I shall,

I. CONSIDER THE DUTY HERE RECOMMENDED. Faithfulness here, relates to the Lord Jesus Christ; our being true to our profession of his religion—to our repeated engagements with him to be his—our attachment to him, and our obedience to his commands—to continue therein to the end of our life. The necessity of this will appear, when we consider that,

1. Not to persevere, is a curtailed sacrifice, a maimed service, and such as God will not accept. No maimed beast was to be presented in sacrifice. Lev. xxii. 21, 22.

2. Inconstancy and instability is an argument of unsoundness and insincerity. Prov. xvii. 17

**3.** Christ persevered for us, and therefore we ought to persevere for him John xiii. 1. He is not only the beginning, but finisher of faith. Heb xii. 2. He held out to the last gasp. John xix. 30.

**4.** It is a rule in civil law, that it is as nothing that holdeth not. A will unfinished is no will; a deed, unless it be signed, sealed, and delivered, is no deed.

**5.** The former part of our life yieldeth to the latter; and the latter part of our life carrieth away from the former. Ezek. xviii. 21, 22. And so on the other side also, ver. 24.

**6.** The end of every thing is all in all. Ps. xxxvii. 37; lxxiii 17. The grand end of living should be, to make a good end, to be found in peace. 2 Pet. iii. 14.

**7.** It is perseverance alone that carries away the crown: unless we are faithful unto death, there is no crown of life for us. Christianity is compared to a race. Heb. xii. 1. It is not he that cometh first, but every one that holdeth out to the last is crowned. Matt. xxiv. 13; Mark xiii. 13.

**8.** God himself is eternal, from whom we expect our reward; and the reward we look for is everlasting. "What hath levity and inconstancy," saith Augustine, "to do with eternity?"

And if we would be faithful to Christ, our master, and hold out in our christian course to the end, we must,

**1.** Enter upon it with resolution: we must count the cost. Luke xiv. 28—30. Lay our accounts with the worst, and prepare for it. Luke xiv. 33. It is for want of this that many, who at first ran well, have been hindered.

**2.** Labor after sincerity. That which is counterfeit will not last long. Ps. lxxviii. 37; 1 Tim. iv. 1.

**3.** Be careful to keep a good conscience; 1 Tim. 1. 19; iii. 9, which some have cast away. 1 Tim. i. 19.

**4.** Slight no sin. Every sin, however small, comparatively speaking, is of a deadly nature. The mote must be cast out as well as the beam. Matt. vii. 3, 4.

**5.** Be jealous of thine own weakness; trust not too much to thine own strength. This was Peter's fault, and we know how foully he fell. Matt. xxvi. 33—35; John xiii. 37. And his fault is left upon record, as a warning to us.

**6.** Shun evil occasions. By unwatchfulness in this, thousands relapse into sin. 2 Pet. ii. 20. See David's case. Ps. cxlii. 3. Satan has his snares in our meat, drink, apparel, recreation, lawful delights, our trading, traffic, buying, and selling: we walk among snares, Job xxii. 10, and had need tread warily, Prov. iv. 25, 26, and walk wisely. Eph. v. 15.

**7.** Be much in prayer to God for support. Matt. xxvi. 41. It is from him that we must receive strength to stand. Eph. vi. 10, 11, 13. Thus prayed David. Ps. lxxxvi. 11.

**8.** Keep the fear of God alive in thy soul. Pray with David, Ps. lxxxvi. 11, and God will fulfil his promise. Jer. xxxii. 40.

**9.** Take heed of standing still; for he that begins to stand still, will soon draw back. 2 Pet. iii. 17. And to prevent it, grow in grace, ver. 18. If we be not growing, we are decaying.

**10.** Walk in humility. Take heed of pride. Remember Uzziah; 2 Chron. xxvi. 16, remember Hezekiah. 2 Chron. xxxii. 25, 26. It is a deadly poison, exceedingly displeasing to God, 1 Pet. v. 5, and destructive to the work of grace in the soul.

11. Consider the short time that this laborious course is required of us; it is only till death; and, as our life is short, that employment cannot be long that is to end with it. Not that our fidelity to Christ shall ever end, but our trials in consequence of it shall; they are but light and momentary. 2 Cor. iv. 17.

12. Be often surveying the royal reward promised in the text, as well as in other parts of the word of God. This was the case with Moses; Heb. xi. 25, 26, and the apostle. 2 Cor. iv. 8, 10, 16, 18. The reward is sure. Gal. vi. 9. It was the case with our Saviour, whose example we may safely imitate. Heb. xii. 2, 3. How important the apostle's advice. Heb x. 35.

II. THE GRACIOUS PROMISE HERE GIVEN—"I will give," &c.

1. He that promises is Christ, ver. 8, and he is well able to make it good. Matt. xxviii. 18: Rev. ii 16, 18; iii. 21. He is the Amen, true and faithful. Rev. iii. 14. Those who are faithful to Christ shall find him faithful to them. Heb. x. 23.

2. What he gives is a free gift. We owe him all that we do, or can do Rom. viii. 12. We can claim nothing of him as our right. Rom. xi. 35, 36. He does not owe us so much as thanks. Luke xvii. 9, 10. Of his mere bounty he will not suffer us to go unrewarded.

3. The gift promised is a crown; 2 Tim. iv. 8, it is a kingdom. Luke xii. 32; Matt. xxv. 34. Who would not strain hard for a crown?—Who would not endure much for a kingdom?

4. This crown is a crown of life; not like the crowns that earthly kings wear, that cannot save them from disease and death. They may die, and do die. Ps. lxxxii. 7; cxlvi. 3, 4. But this is a crown that giveth life to him that hath it, and keepeth him in life that weareth it.

5. The life that this crown giveth (though not expressed here) is an eternal, everlasting life. Matt. xxv. 46. It is an incorruptible crown. 1 Peter i. 4.

I shall now conclude with some improvement of the subject. And,

1. How ample shall be the recompense of the persevering christian! This crown of life—of eternal life, will indeed be a glorious compensation for all his sacrifices, services, and sufferings which he has performed and endured for the sake of Christ. Matt. ix. 27, 28; Mark x. 28—30; Luke xvi. 26, 33.

2. How deplorable the state of those who have forsaken their first love; Rev. ii. 4, 5, who run well for awhile, and then give over; Gal. v. 7, who begin in the Spirit, and end in the flesh; Gal. iii. 3, who put their hand to the plough, and then look back. Luke ix. 62, as Lot's wife did towards Sodom; Gen. xix. 26, that, like Demas, follow Paul awhile, Col. iv. 14, and return again to the world, 2 Tim. iv. 10, and turn away from the holy commandment. 2 Pet. ii. 20—22. Returning like the dog to his vomit, and the sow that was washed to its wallowing in the mire, ver. 22. Their last state is worse than the first. 2 Pet. ii. 20; Matt. xii. 45.

3. Let us consider what we lose if we give over, as well as what we gain, if we persevere. Hold fast, that no man take thy crown. Rev. iii. 11. And what a painful reflection will it be, to think that we have deprived ourselves of a crown, of a kingdom, of eternal felicity, for perhaps a mere trifle, the pleasures of sin, which are but for a season.

4. Be admonished then to hold fast, &c.; ver. 25, to cleave to God; Acts xi. 23, to give all diligence, &c. Heb. vi. 17. And seeing that we know these things, &c. 2 Pet. iii. 17, then may we be faithful unto death, and receive, at last, the crown of life.

## PEP EVERANCE IN RELIGION THE CHRISTIAN'S DUTY.

Judges viii. 4.—Faint, yet pursuing. (H.)

FIT me to this for the arms of the Christian; descriptive of the fatigue he endureth, and of his resolution to persevere. Though the words relate to quite another matter, yet they may, without any impropriety, be accommodated to the great purpose of animating us to the duties of our christian profession.

I. Briefly describe the christian's warfare.

The life of a real disciple of Jesus is frequently thus represented in scripture. 1 Tim. i. 13; vi. 12; 2 Tim. ii. 3. He is engaged in the cause of God and Christ; of truth and liberty. His enemies are, the devil; 1 Pet. v. 8, the world, evil passions and corruptions; enemies numerous, subtle, powerful who give no quarter. If they cannot conquer, will do their utmost to afflict, distress, torment; the conflict is often fierce and violent. Christ is the Captain under whom he fighteth; his weapons are, " the shield of faith," &c.; the object is the overthrow of sin.

A noble warfare this! and shall in the issue, be crowned with joy, &c.

II. The various temper and conduct of the christian; the reason of his many discouragements on the one hand; and of his resolution to persevere on the other. " Faint, yet pursuing."

1. View him as he is, sometimes faint and spiritless. The most intrepid soldier may, on some occasions, tremble; and the man whose constitution is the most robust and healthful, cannot always boast an exemption from faintness. No wonder that such, at certain intervals, is the sad experience of the christian in regard to the concerns of religion. His hands are feeble and his soul melts like wax; his spirit languisheth, and his strength faileth; and this may, perhaps, be ascribed,

1. To the past toils and labors he has endured.

2. To the want of proper refreshment. 1 Sam. xiv. 31; Isa. i. 10. The apostle was just at the point of fainting. 2 Cor. xii. 9.

3. Through the dread of being overcome. 1 Sam. xxvii. 1.

2. Resuming his wonted courage, and, in the strength of divine grace, resolving to pursue. He will not ignominiously submit: no, he will keep the field, maintain the conflict, push the victory. A brave resolution. He considereth what will be the consequence of submitting, on the one hand, and of pursuing, on the other. In order to animate the timorous in the pursuit, reflect,

1. What will be the effect, should you throw down your arms, yield to the enemy, and apostatize from your profession.

1. You will lose the advantage you have already gained. 2 John 8; Gal. iii. 3, 4; iv. 15; v. 7.

2. Be overcome; and here shame and misery present themselves to your view. This ought to excite to action. Luke xiv. 29, 30; Matt. xii. 43—45; 2 Peter ii. 20, 21; Heb. x. 26—29.

2. In order to quicken and enliven, amidst the fatigues and dangers of this spiritual war, consider,

1. The goodness of the cause in which you are engaged; the cause of God. It is called, " A good fight of faith."

2. The seasonable and effectual support you may depend on receiving. 2 Kings vi. 15, 16; Isa. xli. 10; 2 Cor xii. 9; Isa. liv. 17; Heb xiii. 5, 6; Ps. lx. 12.

Christ is also your Captain; and in his character, conduct, and example, you have every possible encouragement. Matt. xii. 20.

You may also notice your weapons; you need not to meet the enemy naked. Eph. vi. 10—18.

3. The triumph that shall succeed; the prospect of this should animate you. Rev. xxi. 7.

Inferences.

1. That undisturbed rest and tranquility are not to be expected here.

2. That the Christian may be reduced very low, but not be overcome.

3. Let those who have as yet felt little faintness in their conflict; take heed how they presume. Isa. xl. 29, 30.

Lastly, Ever remember the encouragement you have to pursue. Clad in armor of proof, led by a Captain of unconquerable magnanimity, supported by a numerous body of saints, all shouting, " The sword of the Lord and his Christ;" angels waiting for the event, and a cloud of witnesses, on every side, marking your conduct; and you yourselves pouring out incessant cries to heaven to prosper the enterprize: thus advancing, relying on the power and faithfulness of God, what have you to fear? Victory, complete victory shall crown the day; be persuaded, therefore, " though faint, yet to pursue "

---

## GOD'S CLAIM ON OUR OBEDIENCE.

Exod. v. 2.—Who is the Lord, that I shall obey his voice? (Sk.)

In the verse immediately preceding our text, we find Aaron delivering this message to Pharoah,—" Thus saith the Lord God of Israel, Let my people go, that they may hold a feast unto me in the wilderness." To this message, Pharaoh answers in the words before us, " Who is the Lord, that I should obey his voice, to let Israel go? I know not the Lord, neither will I let Israel go." The words imply, that as Jehovah was not an Egyptian Deity, and consequently not the professed object of Pharaoh's worship, he therefore concluded that he was under no obligation to obey Jehovah's voice. This conclusion teaches us, that ignorance of God is a most alarming evil, as it leads to daring rebellion against God; and this, if persisted in, must be attended with certain destruction, Prov. xxix. 1.

But the inquiry in our text, though at first employed in an avowed contempt of God, will admit of improvement favorable to piety. In attempting to make this improvement, under the divine blessing, let us consider some particulars relative to God's voice; and his claims on our obedience to it.

I. Some particulars relative to God's voice.

By the voice of God is meant the declaration of his will concerning mankind. Here therefore it may be proper to consider,

1. *The persons to whom he speaks—mankind.* "Unto you, O men," &c Prov. viii. 4.—He speaks to men as his *favorite* creatures, whose welfare he desires. This appears from his wish, Deut. v. 29. "O that there were," &c;—from his commands, Isa. xlv. 22; Acts xvii. 30.—his declaration, Ezek. xxxiii. 11.—his complaints, John v. 40; Matt. xxiii. 37,—and his threatenings, Prov. i. 24—26.—He speaks to men as *ignorant* creatures; who need his instruction in order that it may be well with them, Isa

lx. 2, and xlviii. 16, 17 ; Jer. x. 23, and xxxviii. 20.—He speaks to men as *improvable* creatures ; who are intrusted with a gracious talent, Luke xix 12, 13, and thereby capable of choosing the path of piety, Deut. xxx. 19. 20 ; Jer. vi. 16.

2. *The means by which he speaks.* These are his *works*, and his *word.* —God speaks to us by his *works*, His works of *creation*, Ps. xix. 1 These prove his existence, Heb. iii. 4, and display his perfections ;—his infinite power, goodness, and wisdom, Rom. i. 20. " The invisible things," &c.

> " The meanest pin in nature's frame,
> Marks out some letter of his name ;—
> Across the earth, around the sky,
> There's not a spot, or deep or high,
> Where the Creator hath not trod,
> And left the footsteps of a God."

And by his works of *providence.* His indulgences lead us to repentance, Rom. ii. 4 ; his corrections and judgments teach us lessons of righteousness, Isa. xxvi. 9. Micah vi. 9. God's works should therefore be attentively considered by us, Isa. v. 12, 13.—God speaks to us also by his *word*, Heb i. 1, 2. By this it is his purpose to judge us at the last day, John xii. 48, and by this our whole deportment should now be governed, James ii. 12 Taht we may thus conform to the will of God, let us consider,

3. *What he says to us.* He speaks to us variously, according to our various states, as sinful—submissive—and reclaimed creatures.—As *sinful creatures*, who transgress his laws, he speaks to us in the language of reproof ; charging us with rebellion, Isa. i. 1, 2, and ingratitude, Deut. xxxii. 6, and in the language of warning ; showing us that we are rejected by him, Prov. xv. 8, 26; under his curse, Gal. iii. 10; and under the sentence of eternal death, Ezek. xviii. 20; Rom. vi. 21.—As *submissive* creatures, who desire to obey him, he speaks to us in the language of kind authority, Isa. lv. 6, 7; Matt. xi. 28, 29 ; of encouragement, i. 16—18 ; and of caution against delay, Ps. xcv. 7, 8.—As *reclaimed* creatures, restored to his favor and service, he speaks to us in the language of instruction, Micah vi. 8; Tit. ii. 12 ; and in the language of consolation, Isa. xl. 1 ; Ps. lxxxiv. 11. Let us consider,

4. *With what design he speaks.* This is to engage our obedience.— His works teach us to glorify him as God, Rom. i. 21.—His word requires practical piety, as man's indispensible duty, 1 Sam. xv. 22; Matt, vii. 21 ; James i. 22, 25. The obedience thus required, must be *prompt*, without delay, Job xxii. 21. *Universal*, without defect, Ps. cxix. 6. *Persevering*, without intermission, Rom. ii. 7, and *humble*, without arrogance. It must be humbly ascribed to divine grace, Isaiah xxvi. 12; humbly presented through Christ, for acceptance, 1 Pet. ii. 5 ; and humbly acknowledged as unprofitable at best, Luke xvii. 10. Such being the obedience which God requires, let us consider,

II. HIS CLAIM ON OUR OBEDIENCE TO HIS VOICE. These will appear by answering the inquiry here instituted ; " Who is the Lord, " &c.

1. *He is our indisputable Proprietor.* He becomes thus—By right of *creation ;* he is the Lord our Maker. Ps. xcv. 6, 7, and c. 3.—And by right of *preservation ;* sustaining us by his constant agency on us, and care for us, Job x. 12 ; Acts xvii. 28; Ps. cxlv. 15. 16. Hence we are obliged to obey God on principles of *equity*, Ps. cxix. 73.

**2.** *He is our acknowledged Sovereign.* This he is by our baptismal covenant, and by open, deliberate profession of subjection to him, Deut xxvi. 17. Obedience to God is therefore due on principles of *fidelity*, 2 Tim. ii. 19 ; Eccl. v. 4.

3. *He is our best Friend, and kindest Benefactor.* This is evident— From his various *providential indulgences*, Ps. lxviii. 19.—From his *redeeming mercy*, by which eternal salvation is provided for a perishing world, John iii. 16; 2 Cor. viii. 9.—And from his *gracious influence*, which is freely givin to all who ask it, Luke xi. 13. Hence obedience to God is due on principles of *gratitude*, Rom. xii. 1.

4. *He is the Disposer of our eternal destiny.* As such,—he is *omniscient*, to observe all our deportment—all our actions, words, and thoughts, Ps. cxxxix. 1—4; Job xxxiv. 21, 22.—He is *just*, to recompense all characters, 2 Cor. v..10 ; John v. 28, 29.—He is *powerful*, to execute all his purposes ; both of mercy and vengeance, James iv. 12. Hence we should obey God on principles of *prudence ;* that we may secure the approbation of our Judge, 1 John ii. 18. The *while* God remains our Proprietor, our Sovereign, our Friend, and our Judge, his claims must be admitted. And this admission, *justifies scriptural piety from reproach—demonstrates the evil of irreligion—and encourages the hope of penitents.*

1. *It justifies scriptural piety from reproach.* By scriptural piety is meant, that obedience which God requires in his word ; obedience, seasonable in its commencement ; universal in its extent ; constant in its exercise ; and humble in its pretensions. This is frequently reproached by the ungodly as irrational, disgraceful, injurious to our interests, and a source of melancholy.—But compliance with the demands of justice cannot be unreasonable ; the exercise of fidelity and gratitude cannot be disgraceful ; the acquisition of godliness cannot be injurious, 1 Tim. iv. 8 ; nor can melancholy arise from a smiling conscience, and cheerful hope, Matt. xi. 19 ; 1 Pet. ii. 15.

2. *It demonstrates the evil of irreligion*, or inattention and disobedience to God's voice. This is too common in all ages, Job xxi. 14, 15. It is an evil in itself, as all who are guilty of it are sacrilegious, treacherous, ungrateful, and mad self-destroyers, Eccles. ix. 3. It is an evil in its consequences ; being attended with remorse here, and torment hereafter, Rom. iii. 16, 17, 18. Though kings set the dreadful example, and whole nations follow it, neither their dignity nor number can exempt them from vengeance, Isa. xxx. 33 ; Ps. ix. 17.

3. *It inspires penitence with hope.* God's voice encourages them to hope—for gracious illumination, Prov. i. 23 ; for redeeming mercy, **Ps. cxxx,** 7, 8 ; and for eternal life, Ezek. xviii. 27, 28 ; Rev. xxii. 14. " **Blessed**," &c.

## THE FATHER'S CHARGE.

**Ephesians vi. 4.**—And ye fathers, provoke not your children to wrath: but bring them up in the nurture and admonition of the Lord. (Sk.)

IF we consider our state and circumstances in the world, we cannot fail to be reminded, that we all stand in a twofold relation. We are related to God in an absolute sense, as creatures are related to their Creator; and in a subordinate sense, we are related to each other, as husbands and wives, parents and children. And from every relation in life, there are duties and obligations which necessarily arise, the performance of which is of the utmost importance to the happiness of man, and the wellbeing of society. From the indissoluble relation in which we stand to God, spring the duties of love, reverence, and obedience: and from the connexion which we have with each other, arise obligations, which though of minor importance, are yet of essential utility. The text is addressed to fathers; a class of men who fill most responsible stations in the world; and on whose conduct the tone of morals through all the gradations of society most essentially depends. There can be, therefore, no impropriety in addressing such individuals from the pulpit.—Two things claim their attention,

I. THE DUTIES WHICH PARENTS OWE TO THEIR CHILDREN.

II. THE OBLIGATIONS THEY ARE UNDER TO PRACTICE THOSE DUTIES.

The duties which parents owe to their children, may be distinctly understood, by adverting to the circumstances in which children are placed, on their introduction into the world.

1. *Children are weak and helpless, and totally incapable of caring for themselves; and hence arises the first duty which parents owe them, that of feeding and clothing them.* The weakness of infancy is proverbial. See the helplessness of little children; oh, how mean and degraded is our origin! There is scarcely an animal in existence, that has not, in this sense, the advantage of man. Parents must feed their children.—How pitiable are the circumstances of those parents, whose extreme indigence precludes the possibility of their performing towards their offspring the first duty in nature. Children should be fed, not pampered. The plainest food is the most wholesome, and the most nutritious. The children of the poor, who are fed on the coarsest food, and clothed with the coarsest raiment, or scarcely clothed at all, are the very pictures of health; the rosy cheeks, the sprighty features, the vigorous constitution, all unite to proclaim the utility of plain food and fare.

2. *Children are ignorant, and without understanding; hence they should not only be fed, but taught.* The mind of an infant is a perfect blank, devoid of all intelligence, and even unconscious of its being; but in proportion as the capacities of children expand, and their minds are rendered capable of receiving knowledge, they should be instructed; and who so proper to teach children, as parents. This is the doctrine of the text; *nurture* and *admonition*, signify, discipline and instruction.—Children should be taught *early;* it is scarcely possible to begin too soon:—*familiarly;* according to their comprehension:—*affectionately;* show them by your conduct how deeply you are interested in their welfare;—*extensively;* whatever concerns their duty; such as propriety of conduct—consistency of character—add the rules of moral conduct.

3. *Children are unruly, and therefore must be governed.* This duty devolves upon parents. Children are fond of having their own will; and

nothing is more difficult than to conquer that headstrong obstinacy which is common to children. But they must be governed, and brought into subjection; and it is as much the duty of parents to govern their children, as it is to feed or clothe them. The dispositions of children vary exceedingly; some may be governed by love, others must be subdued by fear; this makes correction necessary, Prov. xix. 18; xxix. 15: Heb. xii. 9.

4. *Children are prone to evil, and therefore must be restrained.* Eli's sons made themselves vile, and he restrained them not; he mildly reproved them, when he ought to have effectually restrained them; and for this, God punished him with the extirpation of his whole race. Oh! if God were to deal thus with every parent, who treads in the steps of Eli, how many families would have their names cut off from the earth! There are many parents who encourage both by precept and example, the prectice of evil in their children; who let them go where they will, and do what they will, without control or restraint. Having briefly hinted at the duties which parents owe to their children, let us notice,

II. THE OBLIGATIONS THEY ARE UNDER TO PRACTICE THOSE DUTIES.

1. *They should do it for their own sake.* For the credit of their *own charactars*. What greater disgrace can attach to a parent, than the neglect of his children? To take no pains to cultivate their minds, to improve their manners, or to save their souls. For their *personal comfort:*—how loud and bitter are the complaints uttered by parents against their children, and how deep the anguish endured on their account. Children may become sources of unspeakable pleasure, or occasions of grievous torment to their parents; but a vast proportion of the misery which they endure, originates in the criminal neglect of their offspring.

2. *They should do it for their children's sake.* We take it for granted that parents love their children, but how do they manifest that love? Perhaps by letting them have their way: that is, in other words, permitting them to go quietly to the devil.—Perhaps by leaving them large property; that is providing food for their pride, and poison for their souls. To bring up our children in the nurture and admonition of the Lord, is to do what we can to make them *wise*, to make them *good*, and to make them *happy*.

3. *They should do it for society's sake.* The children of the present age, will be the men and women of the future age; and the morals of society, half a century hence, will depend, as far as human calculations can go, on the manner in which parents now bring up their children. The seed which is now sown, will then be ripened for the harvest. Those who neglect to practice the advice in the text, not only accelerate the ruin of their children, but do their utmost to make them nuisances and pests to society, wherever their lot may be cast.

4. *They should do it for God's sake.* Children are a heritage of the Lord; they are his property; he is the father of their spirits; but he puts them under the care of their earthly parents, and they are to train them up for him, that they may know, love, and serve him all their days.

CONCLUSION.

1. Learn how careful the apostles were to instruct their converts, not only in the matters of faith, but rules of conduct descending even to the most particular duties of domestic life.

2. The practicability of a religious education. What is here enjoined is possible to be done. Children may be "brought up in the nurture and admonition of the Lord." There may be a thousand petty shifts, to which

ignorant and idle parents may resort to palliate their sins; but the inference from the text is plain.

3. How awful is the responsibility of parents, fathers especially.—*Ye fathers*, the text is God's voice to you; Oh hear it, reverence it, put it into practice!

---

## THE HAPPY RESULT OF WAITING PATIENTLY FOR THE LORD.

Ps. xl. 1—3.—I waited patiently for the Lord; and he inclined unto me, and heard my cry. He brought me up, &c. (Sk.)

By the prophet Hosea, we hear God complaining, "My people are destroyed for lack of knowledge." From this complaint it appears that *ignorance is destructive;* and numerous facts concur in attesting the same melancholy truth. Some through ignorance of their *state*, remain unconcerned about salvation; some, through ignorance of their *duty*, omit to use the means which are appointed and required by God for obtaining salvation; and others, through ignorance of their *privileges*, conclude there is no hope, and sink into inactive despair of salvation.

Our text is therefore of peculiar importance, as it is exactly calculated to prevent or remove that ignorance which is so fatal to the best interests of mankind. Here we behold a description of our state as sinners, and learn the *necessity* of salvation; a description of our duty, as subjects of a divine Redeemer, and learn the *way* of salvation; a description of our privileges, as gospel penitents, and learn the *attainableness* of salvation. "I waited patiently for the Lord," &c. These verses teach us,

I. Our state as sinners. This we learn from David's state as a sinner, which he describes by the simile of a man fallen into a deep sounding pit; with his feet stuck fast in the miry clay at the bottom of it. This striking figure teaches us that our state, as sinners, is a state of deep declension—of total defilement—of imminent danger—and of utter helplessness.

1. *It is a state of deep declension;* we are deeply fallen. *We are fallen* from the most desirable enjoyments. Man, as the creature of God, while he retained his original rectitude, was the subject of holiness, peace, and hope; but having all sinned, and come short of the glory of God, we have lost our peace and hope, with our purity—we know not the way of peace, Rom. iii. 17, 18;—and we are without hope, while without Christ, Eph. ii. 12;—"the crown is fallen from our head: wo to us that we have sinned." *We are deeply fallen*, into a pit of noise or sounding, as the words may be rendered, a pit that sounds by reason of its great depth. We are deeply sunk in *depravity*, or evil propensities—for we are at enmity against God, our parent, benefactor, and redeemer, Rom. viii. 7. We are deeply sunk in *transgression*; for we have expressed the enmity of our hearts against God, by wilful rebellion against him in our lives, Dan. ix. 9, 10. We are deeply sunk in *condemnation;* for we are under the curse of God, Gal. iii. 10; and the sentence of eternal death, Ezek. xviii. 20. We are deeply sunk in *misery*; for the pit into which we have fallen is a horrible one. The darkness of ignorance—the pangs of remorse—and the agitations of guilty fear—all concur to produce the most dreadful horror, Ps. cxix. 120.

2. *It is a state of total defilement.* The miry clay of sin defiles *all the*

*faculties of the sinner's mind;*—unto them that are defiled and unbelieving nothing is pure; but even their mind and conscience is defiled, Tit. i. 15;—their understandings, wills, and affections are corrupted—and out of the evil treasure of their hearts, they bring forth evil things. Consequently sin defiles—*all the powers of the 'sinner's body.* These also are yielded as instruments of unrighteousness unto sin, Rom. vi. 13; so that we are all as an unclean thing, Isa. lxiv. 6.

3. *It is a state of imminent danger.* While we remain in this horrible pit certain destruction awaits us. Destruction *awaits* us—for we have justly merited it by our sin, Rom. vi. 23—and it is justly threatened by a holy God, Prov. x. 20. And destruction is *certain* if we remain here, for the earnest of it is already given us, John iii. 36.

4. *It is a state of utter helplessness.* As, with respect to the perishing object here described, the pit into which he is sunk is so deep, that the top of it is far above his reach—the clay so confines his feet that he cannot climb —if help come to him it must be from above—and he cannot expect deliverance, unless he obtains it by earnest cries;—so it is with perishing sinners. Salvation is *above* the reach of human *efforts*, Ps. cxxx. 4, and cxlii. 2;—our help can come only from *heaven*, Ps. cxxi. 1, 2; and we cannot obtain deliverance unless we cry for it, Ezek. xxxvi. 37. This we learn also from the words of our text, which teach us,

II. OUR DUTY AS THE SUBJECTS OF A DIVINE REDEEMER. This we learn from David's example, "I waited," &c. Like him,

1. *We must make " the Lord" the object of our pursuit*; for the salvation which we need consists in the enjoyment of God. Being exposed to destruction, we need his *delivering mercy*, Ps. xvi. 4.—Being defiled, we need his *purifying influence*, Ps. li. 10.—Being deeply fallen, we need his *restoring grace* to raise us, Ps. cxlii. 6, 7.—As it is from the Lord alone that salvation cometh, so like David,

2. *We must wait for the Lord.* This must be done,—By *penitent application* to him, like the prodigal, Luke xv. 18, 19.—By *earnest application;* we must cry to him, Jer. xxix. 13.—By *confident dependence*,—on the foundation laid by God, Isa. xxviii. 16,—and on the promises made by him, Heb. x. 19, 22. Like David,

3. *We must wait patiently for the Lord.* Patient waiting implies,-Humble *consciousness* and *acknowledgment* of our *demerit*, Gen. xxxii. 10. —*Entire resignation* to God's method of operation on our minds; that he may dispense his saving benefits and comforts as he pleases, Ps. lxxviii. 40, 41.—*Unfainting perseverance* in seeking him, Luke xi. 9, and xviii. 1—7. According to these promises, the words of our text teach us,

III. OUR PRIVILEGES AS GOSPEL PENITENTS. These we learn from David's success, "He inclined unto me," &c. As gospel penitents expect,

1. *An interest in God's gracious regards.* He will incline unto you.—He will incline his *ear* to your cry, Prov. xv. 8; Ps. cxlv. 18, 19.—He will incline his *heart* to compassionate your misery, Ps. ciii. 8, 13 —He will incline his *hand* to save and help you, Matt. xiv. 30, 31; Isa. xli. 10.

2. *Expect the enjoyment of most desirable favors.* Even—complete *deliverance* from danger and pollution; "He will bring you," &c., Ps. xci. 14—16:—firm *establishment* on the rock, Christ, Ps. xvi. 8; 1 Peter v. 10:—and sacred *consolation;* he will put the new song into your mouth; that which David sings, Ps. ciii. 2, 3;—and Isaiah predicts, Isa. xii. 1. 2.

3. *Expect a capacity for extensive usefulness.* "Many shall see it," &c.—When divine grace is enjoyed, it may and should be *seen*, Acts xi. 23;

**Isa. lx. 1.**—When the grace of God is seen in its effects and fruits, it leads those who behold it to glorify God, Matt. v. 16.

In applying this subject, recollect,

1. *The suitableness of gospel salvation to our natural state.* We are fallen, polluted, weak, and miserable; and by this salvation, we are raised, purified, strengthened, and comforted, 1 Cor. i. 30; Col. ii. 9, 10.

2. *The necessity of waiting for God,* in order that we may obtain his saving benefits. This he expressly requires of us, Ps. xxxvii. 34.

3. *The certain success of gospel penitents:* from God's declaration. Lam. iii. 26:—from his kindness to all such, Luke xi. 10; and from his perfections, Rom, x. 12; Ps. c. 5. "The Lord is good," &c.

---

## SUBMISSION TO GOD

James iv. 7.—Submit yourselves therefore to God. (Sk.)

JAMES was accustomed to deliver his instructions in laconic sentences, where little was said, but much meant; the words few, but the sense comprehensive and important: a very cursory perusal of this epistle will sufficiently confirm the truth of this observation. The text however may be considered as a practical illustration of it; "Submit yourselves therefore to God." In order to profit by this highly important admonition we will endeavor to,

I. EXPLAIN THE NATURE OF THE SUBMISSION HERE ENJOINED

II. URGE THE REASONS FOR REDUCING IT TO PRACTICE.

I. EXPLAIN THE NATURE OF THE SUBMISSION HERE ENJOINED.

1. *We should submit to God in his authoritative sway.* God is a great King, "and his kingdom ruleth over all:" as a sovereign, he hath revealed laws, sanctioned by the highest authority, founded in immutable justice, and conducive to human happiness; to these laws we should submit, by forsaking sin, believing in Christ, reverencing God, loving our neighbor, &c.

2. *We should submit to God in his gracious influences.* God is the God of Grace. His Spirit strives with man, illuminates his understanding, convinces him of sin, subdues his will, and sanctifies his affections. "Submit yourselves therefore to God." His Spirit may be quenched, the light that is in you may become darkness, "I have called, and ye refused," &c. Prov. i. 24. In submitting to God, prize the teachings of his Spirit, cherish his holy influences, covet earnestly the best gifts, and shun whatever will wound your consciences, or vex the Holy One of Israel.

3 *Submit yourselves to God in his providential dispensations.* Your circumstances are various: some are afflicted in body—some are oppressed with poverty—others sustain painful bereavements. Here you are too frequently accustomed to murmur, to look at the situations of others with envy, and to entertain unworthy thoughts of God. But submission becomes you; it is God who afflicts, and he doeth it in mercy; cease therefore to complain, and humbly acquiesce in all his dispensations. This submission should be *voluntary.* There is a willing, and a forced submission. God will humble every man, either by his grace or justice; but we should willingly submit our understandings to his instructions, &c. It should be *universal;* there is a submission due to parents by children to masters by

servants, to princes by subjects, to husbands by wives, but these submissions are partial and temporary; but the submission in the text is universal; it admits of no exceptions, and knows no limits. It should be *constant*, at all times, in all circumstances, and in all situations.

II. Urge the reasons for reducing it to practice.

1. *We urge it from a consideration of the greatness and goodness of the Being to whom you are called to submit.* It is God, whose greatness is unsearchable, and whose power is infinite; who is above all and through all, and in you all; whose goodness is equal to his power, and whose will is holy, just and good.

2. *We urge it on the ground of relationship and obligation.* God is your Creator, you are his creatures; God is your Father, you are his children; God is the Sovereign, you are his subjects: submission therefore becomes you. In addition to this, you owe your all to God; your life, and clothes, and food; your personal and relative comforts all come from Him: gratitude therefore should bind you to submit to God.

3. *We urge it for the sake of your personal happiness.* Happiness supposes the removal of guilt from the conscience: submit to God's method of saving sinners, and you will be justified by faith. It supposes the regeneration of the nature; submit to the influences of the Holy Ghost, and you will be "born again of the Spirit," &c. It supposes internal tranquility: submit to God, and you will experience "the eternal sunshine of the spotless mind."

4. *We urge it from a consideration of the punishment which inevitably follows the crime of non-submission to God.* There is not one truth within the whole compass of religion more incontestably proved than this, that God will punish his enemies; and a refusing to submit to God, is the surest proof of personal enmity to him. The original sin of Adam, "that brought death into the world and all our wo," was non-submission; and the crime of apostate spirits was of the same description; and those who refuse to submit to God, must be punished by him, Luke xxi. 27.

The text should *suggest an inquiry*, Do we submit to God? Alas! how little submission there is to God in the world! Some violate his laws—others reject his counsel—others murmur at his providence. What is our character?—The text should *produce conviction*. We have all been found among the number of those who have neglected to submit to God; this should teach us our *folly*, our *ingratitude*, and our *danger;* and it should also excite deep remorse, genuine humility, &c. The text should *direct our conduct*. What else need we *know*, than how to submit to God? What *else* need we *do*, than practice this submission? What else need we covet to *enjoy*, than a consciousness of having submitted to God?

---

## SUBMISSION TO BEREAVING PROVIDENCES.

Job i. 21.—The Lord gave, and the Lord hath taken away, blessed be the name of the Lord. (Pr.)

The affliction and the patience of Job are set before us as an example, and there is scarcely any case that can occur, but something in his complicated trials will be found to correspond with it. His afflictions were sent, not so much in consequence of any particular sin, as for the trial of his faith. God is represented as glorying in him, and satan answers by alleging that his religion was all founded in self-interest. The Lord therefore consents that trial should be made: the trial was made, and it turned to the honor of Job.

However painful any affliction may be, while we are exercised by it, yet when it is over we often perceive that all was wise and good; at least we see it so in others. In Job's trials in particular, God was glorified, satan confounded, and the sufferer comes forth as gold.

That which supported him under all, was the power of religion, the value of which is never more known than in the day of adversity. This is the armor of God, which enables us to stand in the evil day; and having done all, to stand. That which enabled Job to take every thing well at the hand of God, was the love he bore to his holy name; and that name he blessed and adored, under all his bereavements.

There are two things in the text particularly worthy of notice :—The spirit of submission exemplified in the conduct of Job, and the principles on which that submission was founded.

I. THE SPIRIT OF SUBMISSION, UNDER BEREAVING PROVIDENCES, EXEMPLIFIED IN THE CONDUCT OF JOB.

There are several particulars in this case which serve to show the greatness and severity of Job's affliction, and the aboundings of the grace of God towards him, which enabled him to endure it all with so much meekness and submission.

1. The *Degree of his afflictions.* The objects taken away were more than were left, and seemed to leave him nothing to comfort him; his whole substance, his whole family, excepting one who only served to increase his distress. After this he is grievously afflicted in his own person: still he is submissive and resigned: chap. ii. 10.— — —We may have had our losses, in property, in children, and in valuable friends; but we have not lost our all. We have also had personal affliction, but it has been mixed with mercy; not like Job's unattended with any alleviating circumstance.

2. His trouble came upon him *suddenly and unexpectedly,* and completely reversed his former circumstances.— — —It was all in one day, and that a day of feasting too, when every thing appeared promising around him. Prosperity and adversity are like two opposite climates: men can live in almost any temperature, if but inured to it; but sudden reverses are insupportable. Hence it is we feel most for those who have seen better days, when they fall into poverty and want.— — —Yet we see that Job calmly submitted to all his trials and bereavements, and even blessed the name of the Lord. And shall not we copy his example? We have never experienced his trials, nor does God usually deal thus with any of his people; his strokes are more gradual, and less severe than in the present instance. We often witness the dying pains and sorrows of our friends, till they and we are made willing to part; thus the load is gradually diminished, so that we are able to bear it. But it was not so with Job, and therefore his submission is the more remarkable.

3. Though Job was eminently pious, it is doubtful whether *his children were so* in any degree, and this would render the bereavement far more severe.— — —It is a great alleviation to our affliction, when those who are removed by death have given us reason to hope that they are now with God, and that they sleep in Jesus. But this consolation appears to have been denied to Job, who in the day of his calamity had manifested a godly jeal-

ousy over his children, which indicated his apprehension that all was not right, chap. i. 5 : and how much this must have added to his affliction cannot he described. Yet we hear him say, The Lord gave, and the Lord hath taken away: blessed be the name of the Lord.

4. His submission also appears in a *holy moderation* which attended his griefs.— — —A man of no religion would have been distracted, or have sunk in sullen despair. A heathen would have cursed his gods, and perhaps have committed suicide, being filled with rage and disappointment.— — — But Job, fully sensible of his affliction, and feeling it in every point, still in patience possesses his soul. He rises from the earth, rends his mantle, shaves his head, and prostrates himself before the Lord.

5. Amidst all his sorrow and distress, he preserves a holy resolution *to think well of God*, and even blesses his holy name.— — —Losses and trials are sent to prove us, and we have no more religion than we actually possess and manifest in the day of affliction. If half that religion so generally professed were submitted to this test, it would be found lamentably deficient; and this probably is the reason why some towering professors feel so little for their brethren in adversity.

II. THE PRINCIPLES ON WHICH JOB'S SUBMISSION WAS EVIDENTLY FOUNDED.

There is something in the meek and humble resignation of a good man in the day of trouble, very different from that of other persons. Some sort of patience and submission is found amongst men in general, but not like that which real piety produces. There is the patience of despair, and a submission to fate ; but Job's was of a very different description.

1. He considers *all that befel him as God's doing*, and this calms and quiets his spirit.— — —He overlooks instruments and second causes, which would have given to his losses the character of injuries, and have filled him with indignation ; and therefore he does not say the Chaldeans and Sabeans had done him this injustice, but " the Lord gave, and the Lord hath taken away." Seeing and confessing his hand, answered every objection : and however trying to the dispensation, it is the Lord, let him do what seemeth him good.— — —This is true submission, to have no will of our own, but to have it lost and swallowed up in the will of God, even in those things that are most contrary to our natural inclination. " I opened not my mouth," said David, " because thou didst it."

2. He recollects that *all he had was from the hand of God ;* that it was merely a gift, or rather lent for a time, to be employed for his glory.— — — " The Lord gave," says the patient sufferer. These cattle, these children were not mine, though I called them so : in taking them away the Lord has only resumed his own, and left me as I was before, naked as from the dust I came.

3. He feels thankful that thay were *once given him to enjoy*, though now they are taken from him.— — —Supposing we are not allowed to enjoy our mercies for ever, or without interruption; were they not mercies while we did enjoy them? We may see reason to bless God that ever we had property, or children, or friends to enjoy, and that we possessed any of them so long as we did ; though now, by the will of providence, we are deprived of them all.

4. Even when bereaved of every earthly comfort, he considers God as *worthy of his gratitude and adoration*.— — —Job could bless the hand that took away, as well as the hand that gave ; and this must have been a special act of faith. We may not be able at present to see the mercy con-

tained in any of our bereavements, yet in the end we may see it, as was the case with Jacob, when Joseph was sold into Egypt. But Job already sees enough to assure him, that all his afflictions should be overruled for good, and should promote his spiritual and eternal welfare.

### REFLECTIONS.

1. How wise then and how needful, to choose the better part which shall never be taken from us; to set our affections on things above, where all is durable and lasting; and not on things on the earth, which are all fading from our sight, and quickly passing away.

2. Afflictions, if not sanctified, will only tend to aggravate our guilt. They are the voice of God, calling us from earth and sense; the discipline which our heavenly Father employs, to make us partakers of his holiness; and if despised or disregarded, will leave us worse than we were before.

3. The example of Job teaches us that a spirit of despondency and discontent in a time of trial, is utterly inconsistent with true religion; yet how many there are that faint in the day of adversity, and who, instead of deriving consolation and support from the promises of the gospel, are utterly inconsolable, and sink into gloom and despondency.

4. While we admire the patience and submission of Job, we cannot but abhor the unfeeling conduct of his friends, who with only a small proportion of his piety could pass unwarrantable censures upon his character, and withhold from him those succors which humanity itself demanded. Job vi. 14.

---

## PAUL'S PRAYER FOR HIS COUNTRYMEN.

Rom. x. 1.—Brethren, my heart's desire and prayer to God for Israel is, that they might be saved. (Pr.)

PAUL's conversion subjected him to the suspicion that he was an enemy to his country, a disaffected man, and of a most uncharitable judgment concerning his brethren, the Jews. This is no uncommon thing, though it is somewhat strange that a man cannot embrace the gospel, and begin to love Christ supremely, but he must immediately be suspected of the want of love towards mankind. Paul however repels the charge with the most solemn attestation, appealing to the Searcher of hearts for the sincerity of his motives, and for the ardent love he bore to his countrymen. Rom. ix. 1—3. In return for all their unkindness towards him, he longs and prays for their salvation; and in this he imitates the example of his blessed Lord, who desired the forgiveness of his murderers. It is christianity alone that can inspire such sentiments, and give such an example to the world.

I. ENQUIRE WHAT IT WAS THAT MADE THE APOSTLE SO DESIROUS OF THE SALVATION OF HIS COUNTRYMEN.

1. He considered *the danger they were in of perishing*, and being lost for ever — — —Had there been no danger, and religion were only a matter of opinion, there would have been no need for such anxious solicitude. But a good man beholds multitudes all around him going on in darkness, he foresees the consequences that must follow, and is anxious if possible to avert them. — — —Paul also knew the terrors of the Lord, he considered the import of the threatenings, was assured of their certainty, and that God was in real earnest, however poor thoughtless sinners might be disposed to trifle.

When Aaron saw men dying of the plague in the Israelitish camp, he ran in with a censer before the Lord, and stood between the living and the dead. Paul in like manner interposed his labors and his prayers to save his impenitent countrymen from eternal ruin, and every real christian will do the same.

2. *The love of Christ* constrained him to seek the salvation of souls, and to labor for their welfare.— — —He considered what Christ had done in giving himself for us; what humiliation, what sufferings, and what an ignominious death he had endured for our sakes; and the heart of this holy apostle was touched with the example, and stimulated to every exertion for the salvation of souls. 2 Cor. v. 14, 15.

3. The *magnitude of salvation itself*, is sufficient to justify all the anxiety which the apostle manifested.— — —Who can tell how great this salvation is, or what the soul is capable of suffering or enjoying in the eternal world? A period may arrive when the suffering of one soul shall be greater than that of the whole creation, from the beginning to the end of time; and who then can conceive of the unutterable importance of an interest in the salvation of the gospel?— — —Something of it may be seen in the price paid for our redemption, and in the bitter agonies of Christ in the garden and on the cross; but there is a depth in his sorrows which we cannot fathom, a dignity and a glory in his person which transcends our highest conceptions.

4. The apostle was influenced by a concern for *the glory of God*, which is inseparably connected with the salvation of sinners.— — —There is joy in heaven over a sinner that repenteth, and joy on earth; and the father of the prodigal rejoices that his lost son is found. When a sinner is brought to submit to God's government, to bear his image and likeness, and is received into the bosom of his family, the riches of his grace are illustrated, and his glory revealed. The conversion and salvation of sinners are the reward of Christ's sufferings, the travail of his soul, which he was to see, to his joy and satisfaction. Paul therefore, and every other true believer, would long for the salvation of souls, that Christ might be glorified.

5. There were *some peculiar reasons* in the present case, that so powerfully awakened the apostle's sympathy, and which it will be proper briefly to notice—

1. It is natural for a christian to feel especially for the souls of *his own countrymen*, who have a more immediate claim upon his regard; and this was the case with Paul. Persons who inhabit the same part of the world, or live in the same neighborhood, contract that sort of partiality which the love of country creates; and it is not the office of religion to destroy, but to improve and elevate those sympathies, by imparting to them its own benevolent qualities. Hence our Lord felt for Jerusalem more than for any other city; and Paul for " Israel," because they were his own people. Luke xix. 41, 42.

2. Among his countrymen he had *numerous acquaintances*, whom he saw to be in danger of perishing through unbelief, and it was natural he should feel much on their account. When we look around and see many of those with whom we spent our early days, and formed our earliest intimacies, still strangers to the gospel; and walking according to the course of this world, we cannot but lament their unhappy condition, and long to see them brought home to God.

3. We are led to feel more still for our *near relations and friends*, if any of them are left in the gall of bitterness, and in the bonds of iniquity. This can never fail to be the case, where religion has its proper influence on the heart. Our brethren, our parents, our children, must necessarily lie near

our hearts, and the thoughts of an eternal separation is insupportable. Jeremiah was pained at his very heart, and his bowels were troubled within him, to think of the destruction of Jerusalem; but how much more, to think of the destruction of soul and body in hell. Moses could not endure to leave Hobab his father-in-law behind him in the wilderness; nor could David contemplate the destruction of his rebellious son, without being overwhelmed with grief. Neither could Paul view the state of many of "his kinsmen according to the flesh, without having great heaviness and continual sorrow of heart." Rom. ix. 1—3.

II. Briefly notice the means which the apostle employed for the conversion and salvation of his countrymen.

If we use no means, it is a proof, that our desire for the salvation of others is not sincere.

1. Paul labored incessantly *in word and doctrine*, to bring them to the knowledge of the truth; and he did this amidst reproaches, necessities, and persecutions; encountering every difficulty and discouragement, that he might win them to Christ. Acts xx. 19—21. And though we may not be called to public services, we are required to bear witness to the truth, and meekly to instruct those who oppose themselves, in the hope that repentance may be given to them. 2 Tim. ii. 25. An admonition seasonably and prudently administered, has in many instances been attended with good effect.

2. A holy and *exemplary life*, adorning the doctrine of God our Saviour in all things, is a blessed means of fixing the attention of others upon the reality and importance of religion; and Paul did not fail to exemplify the doctrine which he preached. 2 Cor. i. 12; 1 Thess. ii. 10. If we desire, therefore, the salvation of those around us, let them see our good works, and glorify our father who is in heaven. 1 Pet. iii. 1, 2.

3. Fervent and *importunate prayer*. Though we cannot command success, God can give it; and if we were more fervent in prayer, our labors would be more successful. Primitive christians abounded in this holy exercise, and Paul himself affords an illustrious example: "Brethren, my heart's desire and prayer for Israel is, that they might be saved."

---

## LOVE TO THE BRETHREN.

**John xv. 12.**—This is my commandment, That ye love one another, as I have loved you. (H. H.)

THE law and the gospel are in perfect unison with each other: the law, *as a covenant*, sends us to the gospel, that we may obtain mercy with God; and the gospel sends us back again to the law, *as a rule of life*, that, by obeying its commands, we may honor and glorify our God. The loving our neighbor as ourselves was enjoined by the law, and indeed was a summary of all the duties of the second table.* Our blessed Lord, enjoining the same duty from new considerations, calls it "a new commandment," and emphatically *his* commandment; that so we may be led to examine it with stricter attention, and to regard it with deeper reverence: he says, in effect, Labor constantly to fulfil that old commandment of the law; and,

*Compare Lev. xix. 18, with Rom xiii. 8—10, & Gal. v. 14.

that you may never want either a directory to guide, or a motive to animate, you in your exertions, take my love to you as the *reason* and *pattern* of your love to each other.

To elucidate his words, we shall shew,

I. How CHRIST HAS LOVED US—

We must, of course, content ourselves with a few hints only of a subject, which has a height and depth, and length and breadth that can never be comprehended, never explored. Consider then the love of Christ to us:

1. How free!

Who ever did any thing to it? It exerted itself towards us long before we had any existence in the world. Who can do any thing *now* to merit it? We deserve to forfeit it every day and hour; but to earn an interest in it is beyond the power of man. We have nothing of our own but sin; and that would be a poor price to pay for the love of Christ. Indeed, if we deny the freeness of his grace, we rob him of the brightest jewel in his crown.

2. How tender!

There is not one of his people, however weak and afflicted, whom he does not watch over with more than parental tenderness, "carrying the lambs in his bosom, and gently leading them that are with young." Yes: "we have not an High-priest who cannot be touched with the feeling of our infirmities:" "in all our afflictions He is afflicted:" if we are stricken by the hand of persecution, He feels the blow, Acts ix. 4: "he that toucheth us, toucheth the apple of His eye." In every possible state he sympathizes with us, as a head with the members, and never fails to succour us with "grace sufficient for us."

3. How abundant!

If we regarded only the temporal blessings we receive at his hands, we must confess his love to us to be very abundant. But who can contemplate his unwearied intercessions at the right hand of his Father, or the incessant communications of his Spirit to their souls, and not stand amazed at the exceeding riches of his grace and love? And besides all this, he is "preparing mansions for us in his Father's house," and training us up daily, that we may be counted worthy to inhabit them for ever and ever. Well is his love represented as "passing knowledge!" Eph. iii. 10.

4. How costly!

Free as his love was to us, it was not exercised by him but at an expense that exceeds all calculation. Before it could operate for our advantage, he must leave his heavenly glory, assume our fallen nature, endure the scoffs and insults of his own creatures, and "pour out his soul unto death" as a sacrifice for sin. And would he pay this amazing price, in order to redeem our souls from death and hell? Yes, he undertook and executed the mighty work; and never drew back till he could say, ' It is finished."

From contemplating this stupendous mystery, let us proceed to inquire,

II. IN WHAT RESPECTS HIS LOVE TO US IS A PATTERN FOR OUR LOVE TO EACH OTHER—

The love which the saints should bear to each other is of a sublime nature, very different from that which they owe to the world around them.* To resemble that of Christ to us, it should be,

1. Disinterested—

Our love to the saints should not be confined to those of the same church

* The two are carefully distinguished from each other. Gal. vi. 10; 1 Pet. ii. 17.

or party, nor should it have respect to any pleasure or advantage that we expect to derive from them; for this is only a refined species of self-love, Matt. v. 46, 47: it should respect them only as children of our heavenly Father, as members of Christ our living Head, and as joint-heirs of the same eternal glory. It should be proportioned to their piety, rather than to any other endowments; and be occupied in advancing their happiness, not only as much as our own, but oftentimes in preference to our own. It was thus that the love of Christ operated towards us; and it is proposed for our imitation more especially in this point of view; "Mind not every one his own things, but every one also the things of others. Let this be in you which was also in Christ Jesus." Phil. ii. 4, 5.

2. Sympathizing—

We are all passing through a vale of tears, "born to trouble as the sparks fly upward." Hence we need each other's care and assistance through the whole of our lives. The kindness of friendship is a remedy which God has put within our reach, to enhance our joys and to alleviate our sorrows: we should therefore enter into the concerns of others, and feel them as our own; "weeping with them that weep, and rejoicing with them that rejoice." By this, we are told, we shall more especially comply with the injunction in the text; "Bear ye one another's burthens," says the Apostle, "and so fulfil the law of Christ." Gal. vi. 2.

3. Beneficent—

Love must not interest merely the feelings of the mind: it must exert itself in acts correspondent to the occasions on which it is exercised. Is our neighbor distressed? we must relieve him: Is he ignorant? we must instruct him: Is he weak? we must strengthen him: Is he fallen? we must raise him up: Has he shewn some infirmities? we must bear with him. Has he offended us? we must forgive him. Are there any opportunities whatever of doing him good? we must gladly and speedily embrace them. It is in this way also that the Apostle urges us to imitate our Lord and Saviour: "Put on, as the elect of God, holy and beloved, bowels of mercies, humbleness of mind, meekness, long-suffering; forbearing one another, and forgiving one another, *even as Christ forgave you*, so also do ye." Col. iii. 12, 13.

4. Self-denying—

That love which will exert itself only in things that are easy and pleasing to oneself, is not worthy the name of love. A truly christian affection will lead one to "condescend to men of low estate;" to visit the chambers of the sick; to enter into the dungeon of the prisoner; to cut off some of one's superfluities in order to supply the necessities of others; to do good in return for evil; to expose oneself to the derision of a thoughtless world, in order to be instrumental in turning some of them from the evil of their ways; and "to lay down, if need be, even our own lives for the brethren." This was the way in which St. Paul manifested his love, 1 John iii. 16; and in which we also after the example of our Lord, are called to manifest ours. Phil. ii. 17, 18.

This being the way in which our love may resemble his, we shall shew you,

III. The obligation we are under to follow that pattern—

Our blessed Lord has enjoined a conformity to him in these respects,

1. As an act of obedience to him—

He does not *recommend* such love as decorous and beneficial, but *commands* it as a duty which he will on no account dispense with. He stamps his own authority upon it; intimating thereby that he will make it a subject of particular inquiry in the day of judgment. Indeed the decision at the last day is represented as turning principally upon this point; they who for his sake have abounded in offices of love being made *exclusively* the objects of his favor, while they who have neglected them are marked as objects of his indignation and abhorrence. If therefore we have any regard to his authority, or any dread of his everlasting displeasure, we must see the importance of following the example of his love.

2. As an evidence of our love to him—

Having in another place enforced this duty in terms similar to the text, he adds, that the exercise of brotherly love is the distinctive badge of our profession, the habit whereby all his followers must be known. 1 John xiii. 34. 35. To the same effect his loving and beloved disciple also speaks, declaring that our profession of love to God is mere hypocrisy without this, 1 John iv. 20; and that without this we can have no assurance, no evidence, that we have passed from death unto life. 1 John iii. 14, 17, 19. Shall we then at once write " *Hypocrite*" upon our foreheads? Shall we be contented to be ranked with " murderers, who certainly have not eternal life abiding in them?" 1 John iii. 15. If not, we must see the necessity of imitating Christ, who " has left us an example that we should follow his steps."

INFER,

1. How little true religion is there in the world!

So far is love to the saints from being the common disposition of mankind, that almost all are rather filled with hatred against them: and where candor prevails over the enmity of the human heart so as to subdue its workings, there yet is a total want of that disinterested, sympathizing, beneficent, and self-denying love, which characterizes a true christian.———

2. What reason have even the saints themselves to be ashamed before God!

Let the most zealous and active christian compare his love with that of Christ: how poor and defective will his best efforts appear! Alas! alas! how often are things found among professing christians that are not only defective, but directly contrary to love! Beloved brethren, let us study more carefully St. Paul's description of love, 1 Cor. xiii: and above all, let us contemplate more the love of Christ to us; so shall we feel its constraining influence, and be stimulated to the exercise of this delightful duty

SUPERIOR IMPORTANCE OF RELIGIOUS ENGAGEMENTS. (Pr.)

Neh. vi. 3.—I am doing a great work, so that I cannot come down.

Nehemiah was truly engaged in a great work, and was chiefly employed in effecting the reformation of Israel, after their return from Babylon. Such also was his magnanimity, that he could not be content to live in a court, while Jerusalem lay waste. He comes to the holy city with the returning captives, and begins to rebuild its walls with all his might. The greatness of the work however did not consist merely in rebuilding the walls, but in the important ends to be answered by it; it was the city of the living God, and the seat of public worship. Yet no sooner had he commenced the undertaking, than he meets with opposition. Some of the neighboring heathen tried to put him in fear; they also allured him, in the hope of diverting him from his purpose: but to all these he answered as in the text.

The conduct of Nehemiah on this occasion is worthy of example, and in this view we may apply it to ourselves.

I. CONSIDER THE CHRISTIAN AS ENGAGED IN A GREAT AND ARDUOUS WORK.

Though it is not in every respect like that of Nehemiah, it bears some relation to it. There are many great undertakings in the world, and many works of art which men call great; but they dwindle into insignificance, when compared with the work in which Christians are engaged. The cause of God in the world is of unspeakable importance, and the soul of man is of more consequence than the whole material creation.

More particularly—

1. Every christian is represented *as engaged in a race*, as running for an immortal prize, and this is an arduous undertaking.— — —It is no great thing indeed to enter upon the race; many do that who never win the prize. It is easy to set out in the ways of God, and to go on till we meet with some difficulty or some temptation: but it is a great matter " so to run as to obtain," and to "endure to the end." This requires no ordinary degree of zeal and fidelity. 1 Cor. ix. 24—27.

2. Christians are engaged in *an arduous contest with all the powers of darkness*, and wrestle not merely with flesh and blood.— — —It requires but little courage to begin the contest; many do that who are overcome at last Many put on the harness who do not put it off with honor, and endure for a time only, till overcome by some great temptation. But to fight the good fight of faith, and to lay hold on eternal life, is indeed an arduous enterprize. Here no success can be expected, unless we are made strong in the Lord, and in the power of his might. Oh to be faithful unto death, to finish our course with joy, and to be more than conquerors through him that loved us! Eph. vi. 10—13.

3. They are *engaged in the work of saving others*, as well as in seeking their own salvation.— — —Real christians do not wish to go to heaven alone; seeking the good of others is of the essence of true religion. No man is converted for his own sake, but that he may bring others to the knowledge of the truth; and when the Lord blesses his people, it is that they may become a blessing. Luke viii. 39. And what are all the works of men, compared with the salvation of an immortal soul, and seeking the everlasting welfare of those about us?

4. The proper employment of a christian is *the spread of the gospel*, and carrying on the cause of God in the world.— — —This is the work in which the prophets and apostles were engaged, in which Christ himself was engaged, and for the accomplishment of which the whole system of providence is directed. The work committed to Moses and Aaron was but a faint emblem of this, and the work in which Nehemiah and Ezra were engaged was all preparatory to it. The labors of the apostles and early christians were all employed in laying the foundation; it is for us to raise the superstructure, and to bring forth the topstone with shoutings, Grace, grace unto it.

II. THE WORK IN WHICH WE ARE ENGAGED IS SURE TO MEET WITH OPPOSITION, and it becomes us not to be diverted from it, but to say with Nehemiah, " I am doing a great work, and cannot come down."

God's work must be first and chiefly regarded, it must be our supreme end, and all others subordinated to it. Many are convinced that the concerns of the soul are of the greatest importance; they know that they must be converted, must be born again, must be brought to repentance, or perish everlastingly; and they fully intend to seek the Lord, but at present it is not convenient, for something hinders. Thus it is with many a thoughtless youth, who sees and feels his danger; and with many a busy tradesman, who would attend to the concerns of his soul, but urgent worldly calls prevent. Thus alas it is too frequently with the real christian, when tempted to the neglect of duty. But how much better is the answer of Nehemiah to all such impediments: I am doing a great work, and cannot come down.

1. In particular, *christians are engaged in seeking the Lord*, in waiting upon him in secret; and when they would draw near at the appointed season, something in the family, or in a way of business intervenes, and the work of God is suspended. But all these things should be regarded as an effort of the enemy to draw us aside from the path of duty, and cause the work of God to cease. Let us rather say with Abraham, "Tarry ye here, while I go up yonder to worship;" or answer like Nehemiah in the text.

3. Christians are employed *in relieving the distressed*, and in contributing to the support of the cause of God: but when they think of doing these things, some temptation is apt to present itself in order to prevent. We can do but little good without some self-denial, and if not prepared for this, the work of God must cease.

3. While engaged in doing good, *we are exposed to injuries from men*, as Ezra and Nehemiah were. There will always be some Tobiah or Sanballet, who will seek to hinder the work of God, but it behoves us to regard them not. When Whitfield was persecuted and abused for preaching in a seaport town, previous to his departure for Georgia, he was advised by his friends to stop and prosecute the offenders: but he replied that he had no time for such an undertaking, he must be about his Master's business.

4. The *enjoyments of life* too often call off our attention, or unfit us for religious duties. Of these we must beware; and if truly engaged for God, we shall have no time to lose in mere worldly amusements, but shall find enough in religion to engage all our time and all our thoughts. The work of God is great and large, and demands all our energies, and all our strength.

### IMPROVEMENT.

1. Let christians be careful to guard against a light and trifling spirit, as totally incompatible with the solemn duties of christianity, and the right improvement of time.

2. Let the thoughtless sinner well consider the consequence of continuing to neglect the great concerns of his soul. How ready will such be another day to curse the vanities which led them to ruin and perdition. Seek the Lord while he may be found, and call upon him while he is near.

## MOTIVES TO CHRISTIAN DILIGENCE.

Eccles. ix. 10.—Whatsoever thy hand findeth to do, do it with thy might; for there is no work, nor device, nor knowledge, nor wisdom, in the grave whither thou goest. (Pr.)

THIS counsel comes with the greater force, from a man who himself had not been idle in his day, and much of whose zeal had been expended in building a house for God. It is true, that on reviewing many of his own labors, he saw much vanity attached to them; yet he did not mean by this to encourage despondency or inactivity, or he would not have used the urgent and impressive language of the text.

I. ILLUSTRATE AND EXPLAIN THE EXHORTATION.

Many things are said in scripture, especially in the New Testament, which may seem to depreciate the works of men, yet true religion is far from being unfriendly to good works.

Properly to understand this language, three or four things require to be noticed—

1. Nothing must be done with a view of *superceding the work of Christ.* If we think to gain the favor of God, or the forgiveness of our sins, by any works or doings of our own, we deceive ourselves, and stumble at the stumbling-stone. Rom. ix. 32. x. 3.

2. Whatever is done *must be done in faith,* in order to its being acceptable to God. When it was asked, what shall we do that we may work the works of God; the answer was, This is the work of God, that ye believe on him whom he hath sent. John vi. 28, 29. Without faith it is impossible to please God. Heb. xi. 6.

3. Whatever is done *must accord with the revealed will of God,* or we cannot be his servants. Worldly men would take up the words of the text, and go into every kind of evil; power and not justice, being the only principle that gives law to their conduct. But we are not at liberty to do as we please, so long as there is one Lawgiver, who is able to save and to destroy.

4. In selecting the objects of our zeal and labor, we must have *a special regard to what providence places within our reach,* or "whatsoever our hands find to do." Many things may be within the reach of another, that come not within our sphere; and it is one of the vanities of human life to be always thinking of what we would do, if in other circumstances, while the good we might do is neglected or overlooked. Much depends on a proper selection of labor, according to the talents or opportunities we may enjoy. One may have wealth, and with that he may do much good. Another is poor, but he can pray, and give counsel. Another has wisdom or influence, and the liberal will devise liberal things. One can preach, and another can open a door for the gospel, in his town and neighborhood. One may contrive, and another execute. Moses and Aaron did well together, neither of them would have done so well apart. Paul was a preacher, and left others to baptize, while he carried the gospel round about unto Illyricum. Let us consider also how much is left undone in the world, in the church, in the family, in the neighborhood where we dwell, and what labors our hands might find to do.

5. Having found what to do, *we are required to do it with all our might.* This includes at least two things.— — —1. That we do it *without delay.* Many things which our hands find to do at one time, may not be practicable at another; and therefore will not be done at all, if not done immediately. Opportunities are a call from God; they pass by, and return no more.— —

—2. That we do it in *good earnest.* If we look into the history of the church, we shall find that all the great things which have been done, were done by men who were in real earnest, and who labored with all their might. When God would redeem Israel, it was by one who was prepared to sacrifice a kingdom and a crown in his service, and who esteemed the reproach of Christ greater riches than the treasures of Egypt. And when he would bring his people into Canaan, it was by a man " who followed the Lord fully," and who nobly said, " We are well able to go up and possess the land. Also when Jerusalem was to be rebuilt, it was by a man who put not off his clothes, and by a people who had a mind to work. And by whom was the gospel at first diffused throughout the earth? By men who counted not their lives dear unto them, that they might testify the gospel of the grace of God. By whom was the reformation undertaken in the sixteenth century? By such men as Luther, whose zeal and whose labors were indefatigable. By whom has the gospel been carried into foreign parts, and bibles distributed in all languages? By missionaries and by agents of a kindred spirit.

The motives by which the exhortation is enforced.

1. We are *hastening to the grave.* Every step we take, every hour we pass, we are going thither. Other things may be uncertain, as, whether we are going to heaven or hell; but this is certain nor do we know how soon we may reach the end of our journey.

2. When we come thither, *all our activity for God or man is at an end:* "for there is no work, nor device, nor knowledge, nor wisdom, in the grave whither thou goest." There is no more to be done for the souls of men, nor for their temporal interest, nor for the cause of Christ in the world.

What a loud call then is this to *sinners.* Life is the only time to escape the wrath to come; this time is now in your hand, if you have but a heart to improve it. A door is now open, but by and by it will be shut for ever The throne of grace is now accessible, but ere long it will be converted into a judgment seat. Christ is the way of life and salvation, but the way will be of no use when we have arrived at the end of our course, and the scene of life is closed for ever.

It is also a loud call to *chris'ians,* to redeem the time, and live wholly to the Lord. There is much to do, and the time is short; let us therefore labor with renewed diligence, and be as those who wait 'or their Lord

---

### THE CHRISTIAN WARFARE.

Ephesians vi. 11—13.—Put on the whole armor of God, that ye may be able to stand against the wiles of the devil: for we wrestle not against flesh and blood, but against principalities, against powers, against the rulers of the darkness of this world, against spiritual wickedness in high places. Wherefore take unto you the whole armor of God, that ye may be able to withstand in the evil day, and having done all, to stand. (Pr.)

In the time of danger, when a powerful and malignant enemy is seeking our destruction, it would be natural to arm ourselves against him, that we may withstand the meditated attack. As christians we are engaged in a more important conflict than any pertaining to this world. " Wrestle not with flesh and blood," not with mortal men like ourselves, but with evil spirits and evil things. Hence we are called to be on our guard, to put on the armor which is provided for us, and to take good heed to the direction given us.

I. CONSIDER THE DANGER TO WHICH WE ARE EXPOSED : ver. 12.

As it is in other cases, so it is in this ; our greatest danger lies in not feeling our danger, and so not being prepared to meet it.

1, View *the enemy* we have to contend with. He is one who bears an *inveterate hatred* against us, and seeks nothing less than our destruction or eternal overthrow.— — —He hates us as God's creatures, but especially as those who have been rescued from his power, and taken up arms against him : nothing now will satisfy him but our eternal ruin.— — —It is therefore a struggle of life for life : if we do not overcome him he will overcome us. It is in vain to think of being neuter, or making peace with him.

2. He is *mightier* than we are ; and unless we have help from above, we are no match for him.— — —We know but little of the power of wicked spirits, abstractly considered ; but viewed as the god of this world, satan has all its temptations in alliance with him.— — —We know what power there is in these : with these he has cast down many mighty, yea many strong men have been slain by him.— — —With these he overcame our first parents, and with these also he attacked the second Adam, though in vain.

3. He is an *artful enemy.*— — —We are told of the " wiles of the devil," hiding his designs, and falling upon us when we least expect it. We are in his net before we are aware, and when providence seems to smile upon us. Deut. viii. 12.— — —He studies our propensities, and suits his temptations to them. Ephes. iv. 14.

4. He is *invisible.*— — —If he were " flesh and blood," like ourselves, we might beware : but his influence is like the nightly pestilence, which walks in darkness.— — —When least suspected, danger is nigh.

5. He is *near us,* as it were within our gates. The safety of a nation menaced by an enemy, often depends on his being kept at a distance, by walls or seas, of fortresses of defence. But here it is supposed that the enemy has entered into our borders, and that we have no other resource left but to struggle as it were for life.— — —It is not a contest with a distant enemy, but a kind of closing conflict : " we wrestle."

6. What is still worse, he has *a strong party within us.*— — —He was victorious with our first parents, when this was not the case, and when he had no party within : much greater therefore is the danger now.— — —If we do not obtain the victory, we shall ourselves be overcome, and perish in the conflict.

7. On *the issue* of this warfare depend all our hopes.— — —If we "stand" not in this, our loss when defeated can never be retrieved.

II. THE ARMOR PROVIDED FOR US : ver. 13.

Three things may here be observed—

1. In general, this armor is *the grace of the gospel,* believed and trusted in : this is opposed to human might or strength : ver. 10.— — —In common warfare it is usual for the commanders to persuade their enemies to think highly of their strength : but in this it is quite the reverse. We must go as Israel was always taught to do, as having no might of our own, but deriving all our strength from the Lord. 2 Tim. ii. 2.

2. It is described as *a whole or perfect armor,* sufficient to defend us in every part.— — —" Truth" is the girdle to strengthen us : " righteousness" a breastplate : the " gospel" of peace as shoes, by which we shall be able to trample upon the lion and the adder, the young lion and the dragon ; " faith" is a shield ; " salvation," or the hope of eternal life a helmet.—

374

—— —All this armor is to be drawn from the truths of the everlasting gospel.

**3.** The *use to be made of it is*, that we may be able to "withstand," and to face the enemy. There is no armor for the back : he that fleeth is wholly defenceless, and must inevitably fall.

III. THE NECESSITY OF "PUTTING ON" THIS ARMOR, OR "TAKING" IT TO OURSELVES : ver 11.

Armor is of no avail, unless it be used. The application of the gospel is that which proves our security.—— — —Some persons make no use of it: and others a bad use : but it must be our concern to make a good use of it. —— — —Use it in prayer, in other duties, in afflictions, in temptations : its truths, its promises and directions, will avail us in the whole of our warfare.

IV. THE INDUCEMENT TO DO SO ; "THAT WE MAY WITHSTAND IN THE EVIL DAY, AND HAVING DONE ALL, TO STAND."

It is here supposed that there are times of *special danger*, called "the evil day."— — —Times in which we are attacked with peculiar force ; such as seasons of persecution and temptation. It was an evil day to Joseph, when solicited by his faithless mistress ; but he successfully withstood.— — —It was an evil day to Nehemiah, when Sanballat and others came to hinder the work of the Lord ; to our Saviour, when the prince of this world came against him ; and to the martyrs when they had to resist even unto blood, striving against sin — —But they withstood in the evil day ; and having done all, they were enabled to keep their ground.

Some of God's servants, through neglecting their armor, have been *foiled* in the day of battle : of this there are many affecting examples.

The phrase, "having done all to stand," is very impressive : this is to keep the field at last. It is this which gives decision to a battle : we may be overcome, but if we overcome at last, it will be well.— — —We may obtain a victory now and then, and yet be finally conquered ; and "having done all," to fall at last.— — —Oh of what importance is it to be finally victorious !

These weapons are not only necessary in the spiritual warfare, but also in temporal dangers ; and though we may never be exposed to scenes of military conflict, we must all in some form or other have to encounter the king of terrors ; and for this, nothing can prepare us but " taking to ourselves the whole armor of God."

---

## CHRISTIAN GENEROSITY.

**Galatians vi. 2.**—Bear ye one another's burdens ; and so fulfil the law of Christ. **(Sk.)**

"THE heart is deceitful above all things," as well as "desperately wicked," and is therefore to be watched over with the most scrupulous jealousy ; otherwise there is danger, lest under the semblance of piety and religious zeal, we should be led to indulge rancorous and unholy passions. Thus the apostle seems to have thought, or rather to have felt : whence the *caution*, chap. v. 13—16 : whence also the *exposure* of the fruits both of the flesh and the Spirit, ver. 19—23 ; and the *exhortation*, from chap. v. 25, to the text ; in which we have an important duty, enforced by a powerful motive.

I. THE DUTY ENJOINED ;—" Bear ye one another's **burdens.**" The word "burden" denotes something which, by uneasy pressure, exhausts the strength and spirits of the person who is oppressed by it; and it may apply,

1. To *a weight of labor or bodily toil*. This is the effect of the original transgression, Gen. iii. 19. Thus were the Israelites *burdened*, Exod. i. 11. The pressure of this kind of burdens we may bear for "one another" by manual assistance, which even the poorest may give, by procuring the requisite help, or pecuniary aid, which would render the *excess of* labor unnecessary.

2. To *a weight of personal affliction;* in which "the corruptible body presseth down the soul," and, as in Job's case, the patient is a burden to himself, Job vii. 20. The pressure of this may be relieved by medical aid, (which a little experience and attention would enable many, who have not been bred to the profession, to afford,)—by kind attendance,—the soothing, sympathizing language of friendship,—or the considerations which religion affords, Heb. x. iii. 2; James i. 27.

3. To *a weight of domestic afflictions and cares*. This was a part of Job's overwhelming case, chap. i. 13—19. Here our text particularly applies to members of families, who should "bear one another's burdens," by manifesting a fellow feeling, in promptly and cheerfully lending a helping hand to lighten the common load of pain and trouble; and in suggesting those encouragements which affection, reason or religion may furnish. Not so Job's wife, who by endeavoring to deprive him of his only remaining support, contributed to make his "stroke heavier than his groaning," chap. ii. 9, and xxiii. 2.

4. To *a weight of providential losses, poverty, embarrassment, oppression, &c.* In reference to this, the Lord directs, Isa. lviii. 6, to "undo the heavy burdens," &c. This may be effected by public subscription, Acts xxiv. 17; 1 Cor. xiv. 1—3; by private contributions, James ii. 15, 16;— by furnishing materials for industry to work upon;—by judicious advice, suitable encouragement, remonstrance with oppressors, &c. Isa. lviii. 6, 7; Job xxix. 11—13; 1 John iii. 16, 17.

5. To *a weight of guilt and corruption*. So the Psalmist, Psa. xxxviii. 4, "For mine iniquities are gone over my head; as a heavy burden they are too strong for me." In this case christian sympathy is particularly demanded. "A wounded spirit who can bear?" 'Tis true every convinced sinner must bear this load for himself; yet it is often in the power of others materially to assist such. You find one of this character on the brink of despair: long has he been thus; and he fears he shall never obtain mercy:— *a relation of your own past experience* may serve to show him that his case is not desperate. Another may be painful because his distress has not been more distressing, and is therefore afraid that his repentance is not genuine. Here the experience of such as have had their hearts gently "opened" may be of vast benefit, Acts xvi. 14, 29—34. In every such case, we should point to "the Lamb of God," John i. 29; 1 John ii. 2; and bear their burdens in prayer *for* and *with* the humble penitents; and expound unto them the way of God more perfectly; Acts xviii. 26; showing, at once, the tenderness of the Saviour, Isa. xlii. 3, and the freeness and suitableness of his salvation, Isa. liii. 4—6; Rom. iv. 5.

6. To *a weight of temptation*. This may come *immediately* from satan, Matt. iv. 1; or, *mediately*, from persecuting men, from the world generally, from family connections, from the church, Matt. x. 36; Phil. iii. 18. In this case also, when the soul is "in heaviness through manifold temptations," the exercise of christian prudence and sympathy are requisite and beneficial. A friend, formed for adversity, may detect and expose the

devices of satan; may direct in affairs of difficulty; and, by advice and exhortation, support the soul of him that is ready to faint, and thus prove that "two are better than one," Eccl. iv. 9; Rom. xv. 1; 1 Thess. v. 14.

7. To *a weight of infirmities:* which is thought to be the apostle's more particular meaning in this place. These may belong to the *body,* worn down by labor, want, disease, or age, Eccl. xii. 3—5; or to the *mind,* wanting a clear and quick apprehension, a retentive memory, steady resolu tion, &c. By one or other of these infirmities your weak brother is *burd ened;* therefore you should *pity* rather than upbraid him; and, as making his burden your own, *help* his *infirmities* rather than *punish* them as *crimes.* If, in addition to this, we *conceal the infirmities* of others, when, in conse- quence of such concealment, we expose ourselves to the blame which would otherwise fall on them, and thus take *the inconvenience on ourselves,* we then emphatically "bear one another's burdens," 2 Cor. xi. 29. In general we should have respect to circumstances, and administer our relief in the most proper *mode, measure, time.*

*Propriety* recommends this duty; we are children of the same family, members of the same body, &c.—*Personal advantage* recommends it; it improves the best and happiest feelings of the heart.—*Christianity* recom- mends it; "So fulfil the law of Christ." Thus we are brought to consider,

II. THE ENFORCING MOTIVE. It is usual as well as proper in the apostles to enforce their advice and injunctions by a reference to the pre- cepts and practice of Christ. Instance in liberality, 2 Cor. viii. 9; humility, Phil. ii. 4; generous sympathy, and mutual support; thus our text, "Bear," &c.. "and so *fulfil the law of Christ.*" We do not know of any law of Christ enjoining this duty in precisely these words, yet there is much in the teaching of our Redeemer to enforce both the principle and the practice. Hence we observe that the apostle's requirement is,

1. *Worthy of the character of Christ,* inasmuch as it is a *law of equity.* We who have so many burdens, of which a part must be borne by others, and of which we wish them to bear a part, ought to bear in return, Matt. vii. 12.—*A law of benevolence.* "Let every man seek another's wealth," Luke x. 37; 1 Cor. x. 24.—*A law of general utility,* by which society is benefited, the sum of evil being lessened, and that of happiness increased.

*It is congenial with the spirit of Christ.* "Let this *mind* be in you," &c. Phil. ii. 5. "He hath *loved* us." "Ye know the *grace* of our Lord Jesus Christ," &c. "Put on therefore, as the elect of God, *bowels of mercies, kindness, humbleness of mind,*" &c. Col. iii. 12, 13.

3. *It is agreeable to the example of Christ.* Mark the sacrifices he made for the welfare, the salvation, of the *poor* and the *unworthy;*—conde- scending to become man, to labor, to suffer, and to die, John xiii. 13; Phil. ii. 6—9; Heb ii. 14—16.

4. *It is deducible from the precepts of Christ.* "A new commandment give I unto you, that ye love one another: as I have loved you," &c. John xiii. 33, 34. Perhaps this is the very "law" to which the apostle refers. And Jesus calls it "*my* commandment," John xv. 12, 17. It comprehends and is the substance of every other, Gal. v. 14. Hence "love is the ful- filling of the law," Romans xiii. 10, and "the end of the commandment," 1 Tim. i. 5.

5. *It has and shall have the approbation of Christ.* As King and Law giver he has said, and in the day of judgment will say, "Blessed are the merciful, for they shall obtain mercy," Matt. v. 7, and xxv. 34—40.

INFER,

1. Seeing that our text expresses the peculiar genius of the religion by which we hope for salvation, the subject should awaken inquiry, 1 John iv. 19—21.

2. If examination should happen to lead us to humiliating views of past short-comings, &c. it should also lead to unreserved and constant obedience; which may be supported by a consideration of what we owe to *ourselves*—our *brethren*, Heb. xiii. 1, 2;—our *Saviour*, who regards what is done to his followers, as done unto himself, Matt. xxv. 40;—and to *our God*, who expects such return for his love, 1 John iv. 9—11.

~~~~~~~~~~

## THE BEST EXERCISE.

1 Tim. iv. 7.—Exercise thyself rather unto godliness. (Sk.)

WHATSOEVER things were written aforetime, were written for our learning. The text therefore, though primarily addressed by St. Paul to Timothy, may be beneficial to us. There are exercises which belong exclusively to the ministerial character, but as godliness is designed to be a general blessing, and is the same in every clime, and through every age, the exercise recommended in the text is binding on us all. We will therefore notice,

I. THE OBJECT OF THE TEXT;—"godliness."

II. THE ATTENTION IT CLAIMS;—"Exercise thyself," &c.

III. THE MOTIVES THAT SHOULD EXCITE US TO A COMPLIANCE WITH THIS ADVICE.

I. THE OBJECT OF THE TEXT IS "GODLINESS." This is sometimes understood in a restricted sense, as having reference to one part of our duty only; hence it is mentioned in connection with other things, "Follow after righteousness, godliness, faith," &c. "Add to your faith virtue," &c., "and to patience godliness," &c.. 1 Tim. vi. 11; 2 Pet. i. 6. "Godliness," in its true etymological sense, signifies *right worship;*—worship *right in its object.* Some worship the work of their hands—others "the host of heaven,"—some worship they know not what,—others worship devils. "But thou shalt worship the Lord thy God." "Worship the Lord in the beauty of holiness." *Right in its subject.*—Forms of worship are necessary: Moses bowed his head and worshipped; Joshua fell on his face, and worshipped; but "God is a Spirit, and they that worship him must worship him in spirit and in truth." The homage of the heart is the only acceptable worship to God. *Right in its rule.*—Every thing relative to divine worship, must be regulated by the Divine precepts; the institutions of Christ, and not the inventions of men, must be the rules of our worship. The bowing to a crucifix, crossing with holy water, repeating Ave Marias, and all that ridiculous mummery peculiar to popery, is not right worship, because it has no sanction from the Bible. But *godliness* has been generally defined as being conformity to God: moral likeness to our Maker. Absolute resemblance to God is impossible; God is an infinite being; and eternity, immensity, and infinity, are incommunicable attributes. Likeness to God may be considered in having the understanding illuminated with his light, the heart renovated by his spirit, and the life regulated by his word.

**II.** THE ATTENTION IT CLAIMS;—"Exercise thyself," &c. We should exercise ourselves to *gain, retain, and recommend* godliness.

1. *Exercise thyself to gain godliness.* No man is naturally possessed of godliness; we are totally unlike God. Godliness is not to be gained by a few cold wishes, or languid desires. "*Exercise* thyself;" this is a word of great importance, it is borrowed from the practice of those who contended for the Olympic garland; who cast away every impediment, and strained every nerve to win the prize. There is much in godliness that demands the exercise of the human understanding, for "great is the mystery of godliness." Exercise yourselves to know all you can of godliness; its doctrines, its principles, and its practices. In order to this, give attention to reading— to hearing—to meditation—to prayer. Not only to gain the knowledge, but the enjoyment of godliness. It is a blessing to have a right judgment in all things, but knowledge of itself will not do; we must enjoy God, and dwell in God, and have God dwelling in us.

2. *Exercise thyself to retain godliness.* Some, after having sought it with many tears and much earnestness, seem unconcerned about retaining it. To hold it fast, *set a high value upon it.* To prize it too highly is impossible; there is no overrating it. *Seek for an increase of it.* The most advanced christian may yet advance; godliness possesses infinite attractions, and prospects interminable; and he who is not advancing is declining. *Stand aloof from the society of those who would rob you of your treasure.* If you possessed a large sum of money, or a rich collection of gems, pearls, and diamonds, you would not like to travel a road infested with robbers; and if you were obliged to, you would take heed to secure a guard, and get yourself well armed. Apply this to our subject, and exercise yourself unto godliness, to keep it in possession.

3. *Exercise thyself to recommend godliness.* Many are totally destitute of this invaluable treasure. They are ignorant of its vast advantages; and they are in extreme danger without it. Remember it is an important part of godliness, to love your neighbors as yourselves, and as you have been prompted under the influence of self-love, to seek this godliness for your own benefit; you are bound to recommend it to others. Do it by your conversation. Talk of it to your children, to your families, and to your neighbors. Do it by your holy lives. Exemplify in your conduct the purity of its principles. Let others see your good works, &c.—This exercise should be *spiritual;* all the powers of the immortal spirit should be engaged in it.—*Pre-eminent;* it should be our first and most important business.—*Habitual;* we should be always at it.—And, *Persevering;* we must be "faithful unto death."

**III.** THE MOTIVES THAT SHOULD EXCITE US TO A COMPLIANCE WITH THIS ADVICE.

1. *Because this is the best exercise.* God is the best being; the participation of godliness, makes us resemble God; and every other exercise of which man is capable, is frivolous when held in competition with this. It is the best exercise; as it engages the best powers of man, and these powers are directed to the noblest object.

2. *It is the most honorable exercise.* Some think the exercise of godliness mean, and despicable; but who are they that draw this conclusion? Are they persons who have studied its character? No, they are men who hate godliness, because godliness condemns them. Is there no honor in treading in the footsteps of the most illustrious characters who have ever lived,—patriarchs, prophets, evangelists, apostles, and martyrs, "of whom the world was not worthy?" Is there no honor in that exercise which will

most effectually secure to us the possession of the divine nature? Which will "make us kings and priests unto God;" sons and daughters of the Lord Almighty?

3. *It is the most satisfactory exercise.* Bodily exercise is often irksome and laborious; and produces a weariness of the flesh; but the work of right-eousness is peace, and the exercise of godliness yields secret satisfaction. What a comfort to have a conscience void of offence towards God and man! To know that we are working out our salvation! That we are walking in the narrow way that leadeth unto life; and returning to Zion with singing, and everlasting joy upon our heads.

4. *It is the most rational exercise.* There are many irrational exercises in the world, exercises that injure the constitution, ruin the health, and destroy the soul; but as godliness is profitable unto all things, that exercise must be most rational, which tends to secure this invaluable treasure.

5. *It is the most successful exercise.* How often are our exercises in this world unsuccessful; our labors frustrated; and our expectations blasted! but the exercise used in reference to godliness will be successful. They that ask shall receive, and they that seek shall find. We have the promises of an immutable Being to ensure success.

In conclusion we observe, there are in our congregations,

1. Some who have never begun the exercise recommended in the text. To such we say, You are capable, under the influence of Divine grace, of exercising yourselves unto godliness; you have means afforded you: you are very guilty in neglecting your salvation so long; if you procrastinate much more, your ruin will be inevitable; the longer you delay, the more difficult the work will be, and the less time you will have to accomplish it. Oh seize the present moment, and now begin this long neglected, but deeply important exercise.

2. Some who have begun, but have relaxed in the exercise; who have put their hand to the plough, but have looked back. Oh stir up the gift of God that is within you! Pray for the quickening influences of the Holy Ghost; and "give all diligence to make your calling and election sure."

3. Some who have begun, and continued to exercise themselves unto god-liness. "Hold fast the beginning of your confidence steadfast unto the end, for in due season ye shall reap if ye faint not."

---

## THE FIGHT OF FAITH

1 Timothy vi. 12.—Fight the good fight of faith. (Sk.)

THE apostle, in the chapter before us, after enjoining certain duties, and giving a caution against anti-christian teachers, proceeds to show the value of godliness with contentment: and he does this by contrasting it with the love of money, which is the root of all evil; "which, while some have coveted after, they have erred from the faith," ver 8, 9, 10. Covetousness being criminal and disgraceful in all, but especially in the ministers of religion; the apostle advised Timothy, as a man of God, to flee from it, and from all the vices which it occasions; and to pursue righteousness, godliness, faith, love, patience, and meekness, ver. 11. He then adds "Fight the good fight of faith," or, as some read it, "agonize the good agony"—"Combat the good combat of faith;" which terms are quite agonistical, and refer to the eagerness with which those who entered in the Grecian games, struggled for, and laid hold on the prize. In impressing this subject, we may notice,

I. The christian's warfare.
II. Its peculiar character.

I. The christian's warfare.—It is *Defensive* and *Offensive.*

1. *Defensive.* He has to contend with, 1, *A depraved nature.* "The carnal mind is enmity against God," Rom. viii. 7. "The flesh lusteth against the spirit," Gal. v. 17. Pride, anger, envy, jealousy, hatred, malice, revenge, and all other dispositions contrary to the mind of Christ, must be opposed and overcome, Rom. xii. 21; Rev. iii. 12; xxi. 17. 2. *The temptations of satan.* These are various; hence he is styled "the accuser of the brethren," Rev. x. 12; "a roaring lion, seeking whom he may devour," 1 Peter v. 8; the "prince," and "the god of this world," "the prince of the power of the air," &c. John xii. 31; 2 Cor. iv. 4; Eph. ii. 2. These armies he commands, and varies his mode of operation, according to circumstances: hence he presented a Babylonish garment, &c. to Achan, Jos. vii. 21;—Bath-shebah to David, 2 Sam. xi. 2—4;—and thirty pieces of silver to Judas, Matt. xvi. 15. But whatever are his temptations, we are commanded to resist, steadfast in the faith, 1 Pet. v. 8; Jam. iv. 7.

3. *The allurements of the world.* Its spirit, maxims, and fashion, Rom. xii. 2; 1 Pet. iv. 2, 3. This warfare is also,

2. *Offensive.* Hence the christian has to attack satan's strong holds, 2 Cor. x. 4. These are, 1. *Ignorance.* Numbers are so deluded, as to imagine that ignorance will excuse them for neglecting religion; but this is their condemnation, they are ignorant, not of necessity but choice, John iii. 19. Others say, "Ignorance is the mother of devotion;" and use their utmost efforts to prevent the human family from being benefited by that book which was designed to be "a lamp unto our feet, and a light unto our path," Psa. cxix. 105. The duty of christians, is to combine their efforts to remove or prevent this evil. The means are—the circulation of the sacred scriptures—a living ministry—the instruction of youth—the distribution of tracts, &c.—2. *Prejudice.* Nothing more effectually fortifies the mind against truth than this; and to overcome it, you must exercise prudence, meekness, patience, and love. With these graces, connect scriptural and sound argumentation, associated with correctness of principle, and conduct. —3. *Pride.* To some religion is degrading—it will stain their honor—rob them of their reputation; and thus Christ is to some a stumbling block, and unto others foolishness, 1 Cor. i. 23; the pride of human reason will not suffer them to receive the doctrines of the cross. These you must combat with the hallowed weapons of truth, which will admit of no system of religion but that which God has revealed, 1 Cor. iii. 14.—4. *Love of the world,* ver. 10. To overcome this, you must show the importance of spiritual things compared with temporal things &c. Take care, however, to connect with your utmost exertions, unceasing and ardent prayer to God, for the convincing influence of the Holy Ghost, without whose aid nothing is wise, or strong, or good. Let us therefore notice,

II. Its peculiar character. It is designated,
First, "*A fight of faith.*" It is a fight of faith as opposed,

1. *To physical exertion.* You are not to rally your forces, and combine your energies, to oppose an earthly power, or destroy the bodies of the

children of men; bnt rather to promote your own salvation, and that of others. It imports a mind determinately opposed to sin and satan, pursuing holiness and heaven, Eph. vi. 12.

2. *Mental speculation.* It is possible for a man to be well acquainted with the theory of christianity—to be a giant in literature—an able abettor of the truth—a wise disputant on theological subjects—a successful antagonist in the controversial field, and, after all, a stranger to inward religion. This was not the case with our apostle: he was not a mere theorist, 1 Cor. ix. 26, 27; Phil. iii. 14. This fight of faith imports a mind reconciled to God, Col. i. 21, 22;—a union with Christ by faith, Gal. ii. 20;—and the exercise of every grace, Eph. vi. 13—18.

3. *Doubtful uncertainty.* In an earthly campaign, a successful issue is uncertain. Troops may be well disciplined, under a judicious commander, and every thing ominous of success; but circumstances over which neither the commander nor his troops have any control, may determine the conflict, and place the victorious expectant in the hands of his enemies. But in this fight nothing can endanger those who are *immutably faithful;* "he that shall endure unto the end, the same shall be saved," Matt. xxiv. 13; Rev. ii. 10.

Secondly, "*A good fight of faith.*" This will appear when we consider,

1. *The authority by which it is sanctioned.*—"All scripture is given by inspiration of God," 2 Tim. iii. 16. This text therefore, considered in connection with other texts of equal import, proves that it is sanctioned by the highest authority, 1 Tim. i. 18, 19; Rev. iii. 11, 12, ii. 7.

2. *The aid afforded during the period of exercise.* In military operations, a sanguinary engagement protracted in its duration, induces debility, and exhaustion; and will not admit of those supplies necessary for recruiting strength and invigorating the spirit; but in this warfare the supplies are seasonable, and sufficient, Prov. iii. 6; Isa. xli. 10; 2 Cor. xii. 9.

3. *The security given.* In prosecuting this warfare, according to the rules laid down in the holy scriptures, you may say with an apostle, "Who shall separate us from the love of Christ?" &c. Rom. viii. 35—39. "No weapon that is formed against you shall prosper," Isa. liv. 17. "When the enemy shall come in like a flood, the Spirit of the Lord shall lift up a standard against him," Isa. lix. 19.

4. *The final triumph.* Instance the case of the apostle, "I have fought a good fight," &c. 2 Tim. iv. 7, 8, "Death shall be swallowed up in victory," 1 Cor. xv. 54—57. The conqueror shall be enthroned, Rev. iii. 21.

INFERENCES.

1. *This warfare will neither admit of substitution, nor cessation of arms.* The command is *personal* in its application, and *perpetual* in its obligation.

2. *This is the greatest encouragement.* Christ is your commander—the Holy Spirit your helper—the scriptures your directory—angels your guardians—saints your companions; and heaven the inheritance reserved for you, 1 Pet. i. 3—5.

3. *A refusal to fight is open rebellion against God.* Consider this ye sinners, and while the treaty of reconciliation is open, 2 Co. v. 20, humble yourselves before God, and implore mercy.

## REMEMBRANCE OF THE POOR RECOMMENDED

Galatians ii. 10.—We should remember the poor. (Sk.)

THE leading topics of the christian ministry are frequently inculcated, and by judicious hearers, generally understood, and distinctly remembered. The fall of man, the redemption of the world, the necessity of regeneration, and the final rewards of virtue and vice, are subjects, which in a direct or indirect manner, breathe in every sermon you hear, in every prayer you offer, and in every hymn you sing. But there are other subjects of a subordinate character, clearly stated in the sacred volume, which though they may not form articles of your faith, yet stand as rules for your practice, and are too important to be discarded from the pulpit. Among those we may notice the reciprocal duties that arise from the various relations in which we stand to society ; and one of the least regarded. though not the least in importance, is the practice recommended in the text, " We should remember the poor." We will,

I. EXAMINE THE NATURE OF THE ASSERTION.
II. STATE THE OBLIGATIONS WE ARE UNDER TO COMPLY WITH IT.
III. ANSWER OBJECTIONS.

I. EXAMINE THE NATURE OF THE ASSERTION. We need not spend a moment in describing the poor: alas! they describe themselves. You daily witness the scantiness and poverty of their apparel, their pale and emaciated forms ; and you hear their piteous plaints, and the tale of their complicated woes. But we should,

1. *Remember the work of the poor.* On these the curse entailed by sin, daily rests ; in the sweat of their face they eat bread, till they return unto the ground. *Their work is irksome and laborious.* See their hands, worn hard with incessant toil; their faces bathed in profuse sweat ; and their bodies bent, not so much with the weight of years, as with the pressure of ponderous burdens. *Their work is often destructive to health.* Many are plunged in mines ; view the confined situation in which they labor, the unnatural posture in which they pursue their work, the noxious damps that infect the air in which they breathe, and the incessant streams that distil upon their wearisome bodies. Huge masses of rocks often burst around them, and bury them alive in their subterraneous vaults ; and even if they escape these awful accidents, what multitudes go prematurely ι the grave. *But their work is chiefly beneficial.* They labor for the public benefit. Consider the labors of the mechanic, the husbandman, and the artizan.

2. *Remember the deprivations of the poor.* Here note, the means of instruction which are placed beyond their reach. The children of the poor are sent to work, as soon as they can earn a scanty pittance, with little or no learning, except what they get from Sunday schools. They read but little, partly for want of books, and partly for want of inclination. They are deprived in many instances of the common necessaries of life ; view the miserable huts and hovels in which they reside ; in low damp situations where the wintry winds howl through the broken casement: view their tattered vestments amid the rigors of winter, and their coarse food scantily administered, and scarcely sufficient to satisfy the demands of exhausted nature.

3. *Our remembrance of the poor should be founded on a personal acquaintance with their circumstances.* We should visit their abodes, and find out the retreats of wretchedness. It should be attended with a compassionate feeling towards them. " Indeed Sir," said a person of large prop-

erty, "I am a very compassionate man ; but to tell you the truth, I do not know any person in want." The fact was he stood aloof from the poor, and kept out of their way.—And it should be accompanied by relief. Many say "Depart in peace, be ye warmed, and be ye filled ;" but never administer the blessings which the poor need. We cannot do all we would, but let us do what we can. Cannot we retrench a little from our food ? Or give them some garments ? Or employ them in our farms, or at our merchandise ?

II. State the obligations we are under to comply with it.

1. *The dictates of humanity require it.* There is a chord in human hearts, that vibrates to the touch of misery ; hence all human beings occasionally remember mercy. The sufferings even of brutes excite compassion. The Jews had a law which required them to help an ox or an ass in distress, Deut. xxii. 4. And shall we show mercy to a brute, and neglect a man ? The poor are our brethren, one God hath created us, one Saviour hath redeemed us, one heaven will receive us, if faithful unto death.

2. *The demands of duty require it.* The laws of God have made this imperative upon us. The texts that bear upon this point are numerous Deut. xv. 7—9; Dan. iv. 27 ; Luke vi. 36—38 ; Matt. vii. 12 ; 1 John iii. 17. Consider the connection of the text. The saints at Jerusalem were exceedingly oppressed by poverty. A contribution had been made for them in Macedonia, and in Achaia ; St. Paul had written to the Romans concerning them ; Peter, James, and John, wished to "remember the poor;" "the same, (said Paul) I also was forward to do."

3. *The rights of justice require it.* The common opinion is, that "the poor are solely dependent on the rich for a scanty pittance; and that men of affluence are independent; have independent fortunes," &c. But the reverse of this is the truth. Men who do nothing, are mere drones in the hive of society, who live upon the labors of others. To the poor we are most deeply indebted. Who erect our houses? Who form our clothes? Who procure our food? Do not the poor? therefore remember them. Justice requires this at your hands.

4. *The claims of interest require it.* Every man is obligated to pursue that course of conduct, which will most effectually subserve his present and final happiness. Is it not our interest to imitate God ? God remembers the poor : his Son was poor; his disciples were poor; to the poor the gospel was preached ; God hath chosen the poor. Angels are mindful of the poor; they visited poor shepherds—they conducted the soul of poor Lazarus to paradise. God will bless those who remember the poor, Psalm xli. 1, 2 ; Prov. iii. 9, xix 17 ; Isa. lviii. 10, 11.

III. Answer objections.

1. "*My circumstances are impoverished, and I have nothing to spare.*" What nothing ?—Think of the poor widow, and her mites. Read the account of her to whom Elijah applied for a morsel of bread, 1 Kings xvii. 11, 12.

2. "*Charity must begin at home.*" But remember it should not *end* at home. The proper sphere of charity is abroad; the ties of relationship bind us to look at home; but benevolence looks abroad on all the suffering sons of humanity, and stretches forth her hands to relieve them.

3. "*I have a right to do what I will with my own.*" But what is your own? Are you not a steward? Is not God the universal proprietor of all things? Will he not call you to an account how you have spent his goods? It is not optional with you to give or not to give ; God has made it imperative on you.

4 "*The poor do not deserve to be remembered.*" But their merit is not the ground or rule of our benevolence. We are to "be merciful, as our Father in heaven is merciful;" and what if God had dealt with us according to our merit? How do we know, that the poor do not deserve what we give them? We do not know their value or their real characters.

Conclude with a *word of advice* to the *poor;* to excite them to economy, to submission to their superiors, and gratitude to their benefactors.—And a *word of comfort* to induce them to bear their lot of poverty, during the period of their mortal pilgrimage, with patience and resignation to God.

---

## LIBERALITY TO THE POOR.

Luke iii. 10, 11.—And the people asked him, saying, What shall we do then? He answereth and saith unto them, He that hath two coats, let him impart to him that hath none; and he that hath meat, let him do likewise. (H. H.)

In order to understand the true meaning of any part of scripture, the strictest attention must be paid to the context. If this rule be not observed, there is scarcely any thing which may not be sanctioned by the inspired volume; and the most contradictory positions may appear to stand on equal authority. Suppose, for instance, the question in our text be taken, as other apparently similar questions must be taken, namely, as an inquiry into the way of salvation; we shall make John the Baptist return an answer directly contrary to the whole tenor of the Gospel. When the gaoler asked Paul and Silas, "What he must do to be saved?" they answered, "Believe in the Lord Jesus Christ, and thou shalt be saved." Acts xvi. 30, 31. *This is the only true answer that can be given to that question;* for "there is no other name under heaven given among men whereby we can be saved." but the name of Jesus Christ. Acts. iv. 12. But if we look into the context. we find that John the Baptist had been "preaching the baptism of repentance for the remission of sins," ver 3; or, in other words had been preaching salvation by Jesus Christ, exactly as the apostle Peter, and indeed all the Apostles, did on the day of Pentecost.* Then, seeing multitudes coming to him for baptism, and apprehending that the great majority of them were taking up a profession of religion upon very light and erroneous grounds, he cautioned them strongly against a presumptuous confidence on the one hand, or an unproductive and hypocritical profession on the other; and exhorted them, if they would not experience the fate of a barren tree, to "bring forth fruits worthy of repentance," ver. 7—9. In reply to this, the people ask, "What shall we *do?*" That is, *What fruits shall we bring forth*, in order to evince our sincerity?† And the direction which John gives them, is an answer exactly suited to the occasion: it is to this effect; "If you would approve yourselves sincere and upright in your profession of faith in the Promised Messiah, shew forth your faith by your works, and, above all, by an abounding exercise of love."

Having thus prepared our way by a view of the context, and having as-

* See the people's inquiry, and Peter's answer, Acts ii. 37, 38.

† See the Greek, ver. 8—10. This will remove all doubt: for they adobt the very same term as John had used.

certained what the Baptist's design was in giving the people the direction in our text, we shall proceed to the more distinct consideration of his answer, and shall open to you,

I. ITS IMPORT—

It is manifest that the direction given by him is figurative, and therefore not to be taken in its strict and literal sense. But we must not therefore imagine, that we are at liberty to disregard it, as though it had no force at all. There can be no doubt but that the Baptist intended to inculcate a very tender compassion towards our indigent fellow-creatures, and a very enlarged exercise of liberality for their relief. To obtain, with as much precision as the subject is capable of, the true import of his words, we shall adduce from other parts of scripture, but especially from the writings of the same Evangelist.

1. Some other passages of similar tendency—

First, we shall notice one or two that are also figurative, Luke xii. 33, 34. & xiv. 12—14.— — —There can be no doubt but that these require a very high degree of liberality to the poor, since they were actually practiced *in their strictest sense* by the first christians, Acts ii. 44, 45, & iv. 32—37.— — —From these we may turn to others that are more plain, Luke vi. 38. & xi. 41.— — —What an accumulation of words is there in the former of these passages to encourage our compliance with the precept; and what a gracious benediction in the latter!— — —To *the rich* there is an especial charge given to be bountiful, 1 Tim. vi. 18, 19; but it is not to them only that this duty belongs; but to those also who gain a daily subsistence by their manual labor, Eph. iv. 28. To all, according to their ability, it equally appertains; for, on the foresight of a dearth in Judea, all the disciples of Antioch, every one according to his ability, contributed instantly to their relief, Acts xi. 28—30.

2. Some examples which are set forth for our imitation—

That of Zaccheus is particularly to our purpose, because he was just converted to the faith of Christ, and because our blessed Lord himself acknowledged this heavenly disposition to be an evidence of his having actually obtained acceptance with his God, Luke xix. 8, 9.— — —But the example of the Mecedonian churches is yet more pertinent; because it is an example, not of an individual, but of whole churches; and those, not in a state of ease and opulence, but of great affliction and deep poverty; and because it is expressly set forth for the imitation of others, who are called up to imitate it, *in order to prove the sincerity of their love to Christ*, 2 Cor. viii. 1—4, 8, 9. By carefully comparing these several passages, we see clearly what our duty is: we are not required to burthen ourselves in order to ease others, but so to participate their burthens that they may partake of our ease, ib. ver. 13, 14: thus to "bear one another's burthen is eminently to fulfil the law of Christ, Gal. vi. 2.

Having thus marked the import of the injunction in our text, we proceed to shew,

II. ITS REASONABLENESS—

The whole of God's "law is good," and the service it requires is reasonable. But the duty enjoined in our text, though arduous to a selfish mind, is particularly reasonable. For consider,

1. What obligations we owe to God for the superior comforts which we enjoy—

It is God who assigns to all their lot, not only in respect to the situation in which they are born, Acts xvii. 26, 28, but in all the changes, whether prosperous or adverse, which they experience through life, 1 Sam. ii, 6, 7. Whatever therefore we have above others, " it is God alone who has made us to differ," 1 Cor. iv. 7. And how eminently is this the case with respect to the ravages of war which during these last twenty years have desolated almost the whole of Europe, but have never reached our happy land! Compare our state with that of a great part of Germany at this present moment,* and then say, whether a compassionate regard for our suffering fellow-creatures be not called for at our hands, and whether such an expression of it as our text requires, be at all unreasonable? Methinks, it is not possible to have even the most indistinct view of our obligations to God, without saying from our hearts, " What shall I render unto the Lord for all the benefits that he hath done unto me ?"

2. What we ourselves should desire, if we were reduced to the state in which myriads of our fellow-creatures now are—

It is not easy to place ourselves in the situation of persons of whom we hear only by report: but yet we may conceive what we ourselves should desire, and what we should think reasonable, if we were perishing with cold and nakedness and hunger, whilst others, embarked in the same cause with ourselves, were exempt from those sufferings, and were enjoying comparative ease and affluence: Should we not wish them to stand forth for our relief? Should we not think it reasonable, that their exertions should rise in proportion to our necessities, and that they should almost literally fulfil the precept in our text, the man who had two coats imparting to us who had none, and that he who had meat should do likewise? Let us adopt for our principle the golden rule, and " Do unto others, as we would they should do unto us."

What our blessed Lord and Saviour has done for us—

This is the consideration which St. Paul himself suggests in reference to this very point, 2 Cor. viii. 9. O consider, " how rich he was" in the possession of his Father's glory ; and how " poor he became," " not having so much as a place where to lay his head," but dying under the curse that was due to our sins. Consider too what his object was ; namely, that we, who deserved to be in hell without a drop of water to cool our tongues, might through his poverty be rich, and possess all the glory of heaven. Does such love as this require no return? When this very Saviour tells us, that what we do unto the least of his brethren, he accepts as done to himself, shall we think any requisition hard, or any sacrifice too great? Truly, not only our property, but even our life itself, may well be sacrificed for him, 1 John iii. 16; and we should account ourselves happy in proportion as we have an opportunity to advance his glory in the world.

But instead of dwelling any longer on the general reasonableness of this precept, we will proceed to notice,

III. ITS SUITABLENESS TO THE PRESENT OCCASION—

Rarely, if ever, has greater occasion for charitable exertions existed than at present.†— — —Now therefore we might justly call upon you to comply with our text almost in the literal sense. But, waving that, we must urge you to adopt the *principle* that is there inculcated— — —and to bear in mind, that " he who soweth sparingly, shall reap also sparingly, and he who soweth bountifully shall reap also bountifully. Let every man do ac-

---

* This Sermon was preached in 1814, on occasion of a collection for the relief of the most grievous distresses in Germany.

† Here the particular occasion should be opened at considerable length.

cording as he is disposed in his heart, not grudgingly or of necessity ; for God loveth a cheerful giver," 2 Cor. ix. 6, 7.　Do not however forget the important distinctions with which we began the subject.　It is to glorify Christ, and to shew the sincerity of your love to him, that we invite you ;— not to purchase heaven by your alms.　Bear that in mind ; and God will not forget it in the day of judgment.

---

## A CALL TO WATCHFULNESS AND SOBRIETY.

1 Thess. v. 6.—Therefore let us not sleep as do others, but let us watch and be sober. (Sk.)

EVERY thing in this world is liable to degenerate.　The richest soil would, if neglected, be soon overrun with weeds.　The most laudable institutions, if not watched over, would be desecrated from their original purpose.　The firmest and best constructed buildings, are subject to decay.　Metals of the finest polish are liable to be tarnished, and Christians of the most exalted piety, may fall from their own steadfastness, and degenerate into lukewarmness and apostacy.　On this principle, we justify all the cautions, warnings, and admonitory precepts found in the apostolic writings.　In the last of these, we include the text ; "Let us not sleep," &c.　We have here.

I. A STATE ADVERTED TO ;—" *Sleep, as do others.*"

II. A COURSE OF CONDUCT DESCRIBED ; " Watch, and be sober."

III. AN OBLIGATION TO PURSUE IT INTIMATED :—" Let us not sleep— but *let* us watch," &c.

I. A STATE ADVERTED TO ;—" *Sleep.*"　This is the state of sinners : their moral condition is variously described, as being a state of darkness— bondage—death, &c.　Here, they are considered as being asleep, &c.

1. *Those who are asleep, are insensible of their state, and unconscious of all the objects that surround them.*　They have eyes, but they perceive no objects ; ears, but they hear no sound ; hearts, but they feel no sensations. How descriptive is this of the state of sinners !　To their worldly concerns, they are broad awake ; all eye, all ear, all attention ; but in reference to the interests of their souls, a deep sleep has fallen upon them.　They are unconscious of the immediate presence of God with them—insensible of his amazing love—of their moral condition as sinners—of the duties that devolve upon them—of the dangers that await them—and the privileges they are called to realize.

2. *Those who are asleep, are motionless and inactive.*　Powers the most vigorous may be in their possession ; blessings the most inestimable may be within their grasp, and business the most important may devolve upon them ; yet no efforts are called forth, no energies are roused—such is the state of sinners.　For the accomplishment of worldly objects they are ever on the alert, but in reference to their spiritual interests, they are motionless and inactive ; a death-like torpor rests upon them : they hear of heaven, but make no efforts to enter in at the strait gate, and walk in the narrow way that leadeth to life ;—they hear of hell, but they give no diligence to escape its tremendous punishment ;—they are told of their duty, but to do it they manifest no concern.

**3.** *Those who are asleep, are often the subjects of illusion and deception* What senseless dreams delude them! How many airy nothings swim before their eyes! How many pleasing and painful thoughts occupy their minds as destitute of reason, as they are of reality! Nothing can be more characteristic of the condition of sinners. Their whole life is a dream. Delusions deep as hell bind them fast; and all their ideas of God, of themselves, of sin, and religion, misery, and happiness, are the phantoms of error, and the creatures of imagination.

**4.** *Those who are asleep, are frequently exposed to dangers which they have no power to escape.* Hence sleep is a defenceless state. Men may bolt their doors, yet thieves often enter and surprise them. But sinners are exposed to dangers infinitely more dreadful. They are taken already in the snare of the devil, and they are liable every moment to be arrested, and hurried down to perdition. Such is the state adverted to in the text. Let us notice,

II. THE COURSE OF CONDUCT EXPRESSED ;—" Let us watch and be sober."

1. *Watchfulness is opposed to sleep, therefore let us be wakeful.* Complying with the requisition of the apostle, "Awake thou that sleepest," &c. Rousing ourselves from that delusive slumber into which sin has thrown us. Let us awake, and keep awake.

2. *Watchfulness is opposed to thoughtlessness and stupidity, therefore let us be considerate and thoughtful.* Our worldly business claims our thoughts; but our souls, our God, our salvation, our duties, and privileges, possess higher claims. To these we should bend our thoughts, with deep concern and solicitude.

3. *Watchfulness is opposed to indolence and sloth, therefore we should be diligent.* "Slothfulness casteth into a deep sleep." We have much to do for our neighbors, ourselves, and our God, and we must work while it is day.

4. *Watchfulness has reference to danger, therefore we must be prepared to meet its attacks.* Our enemies are wakeful and vigilant, and always waiting to attack us to advantage. Let us always be on our guard, and watch as sentinels at the post of duty.

5. *To watchfulness we must add sobriety.* Be sober, that is temperate ; avoid gluttony and intoxication : eating and drinking are designed to nourish the body ; but we may make our table a snare, and convert our aliments into poisons. Be sober, that is calm and dispassionate : holding your tempers and passions in subjection, never suffering wrathful dispositions to surprise you.

III. AN OBLIGATION TO PURSUE IT INTIMATED ;—" *Let us* not sleep, but *let us* watch," &c We must regard this as an apostolic precept; an expression of this kind, in some cases, amounts to little more than advice or counsel ; but when a superior gives it to a dependent, and especially when God by the ministry of his servants, imparts it for our instruction, it is a law from which we dare not swerve.

1. *Our circumstances call us to comply with this requisition.* We need not sleep, but we may watch ; the power and the obligation go together, we are not circumstanced as heathens are, nor as Jews, or Papists, or Mohammedans are. Our privileges are superior, therefore we should not sleep as do others.

2. *Our profession demands obedience to it.* Hear the apostle : " Ye are all the children of light, and the children of the day, "&c., ver. 5. " For they that sleep, sleep in the night," &c., ver. 7. We profess the christian

religion; this prohibits sin, therefore we should not sleep as others; this prescribes duties, therefore we should watch and be sober.

3. *Our personal security should bind us to observe it.* Sinners are in a state of dreadful danger; their imaginary peace is no security against its attacks, ver. 3. Safety and duty are inseparable, "Watch and be sober," this will insure protection.

4. *Our eternal happiness is connected with the performance of this duty.* —"Blessed are those servants whom the Lord when he cometh shall find watching."

Here then we discern,

1. The essential difference between the righteous and the wicked; the latter are asleep in their sins, the former are watching, &c.

2. That the christian religion binds us to the practice of a holy singularity; we must not do as others, but do what God has enjoined.

---

### A CHARGE TO THE RICH.

1 Timothy vi. 17—19.—Charge them that are rich in this world, that they be not high-minded, nor trust in uncertain riches, but in the living God, who giveth us richly all things to enjoy; that they do good, that they be rich in good works, ready to distribute, willing to communicate: laying up in store for themselves a good foundation against the time to come, that they may lay hold on eternal life." (Sk.)

THE holy scriptures contain advices and instructions suited to every sort and condition of men. And God's ministers are charged with messages to all;—some of these messages are mild and agreeable,—and others are the very reverse: so that in some cases, great and excellent messengers have shrunk from their duty, see Jer. xx. 7—18;—Jonah i. 3;—but they dare not refuse, Ezek. ii. 5—8, iii. 17; Jer. i. 8, 17. Allow me then to deliver the message contained in the text; by attending to the *subjects*, the *nature*, and the *execution* of the charge.

I. THE SUBJECTS OF THIS CHARGE;—"the rich." Whatever difficulty may be found in the appropriation of the term *rich* to individuals; it is sufficiently obvious, that there are rich as well as poor. Riches are opposed to poverty;—and as poverty signifies scantiness, penury, want;—so riches imply abundance, a store, more than enough.

1 *There may be a thousand gradations of riches:* from the least superabundance, to the largest sum that a mortal ever possessed. But that man must be ranked among the rich, who can command the necessaries, conveniencies, and comforts of life, and still have something to spare.

2. *Riches are strongly desired by mankind.* And the rich are frequently envied by their inferiors. And if man might be viewed merely as an inhabitant of this world, such conduct would hardly be censurable But the word of God, which connects eternity with time, and man with eternity, shows that religion is a thing essential to the happiness of the present and of the future state. Speaking of riches and poverty, in a way suited to these momentous associations, declares advantages peculiar to the poor, and dangers peculiar to the rich. Some of the latter, with the way to avoid them, form,

II. THE NATURE OF THIS CHARGE. Which comprehends,

*The dangers specified.*

1. *Highmindedness.* It is exceedingly difficult for a person to be rich and not to think the more highly of himself on *that* account. Solomon asserts, that the rich man is "wise in his own conceit," Prov. xxviii. 11; and Ezekiel, "that the heart is lifted up because of riches," chap. xxviii. 5. The manner in which such are honored, and the advantages which their riches give them, lead to ideas of superiority, and thus tend to generate and to nourish this ostentatious evil.

2. *"Trust in uncertain riches."* Trust in riches, is mentioned in the scriptures as a very dangerous sin, see Mark x. 24; Prov. xi. 4, 28, xxiii. 5. And the rich are much exposed to *this* danger;—because riches may procure many worldly comforts;—they may banish many apparent evils. And to trust in any thing rather than in God, is the common fault of man. Let us now endeavor to understand from the apostle,

*The way to avoid these dangers.*

1. *Trust in the living God. Hold* your possessions as *uncertain*, but *depend* on God, who cannot fail. He gives even the riches: he gives all things;—the enjoyment, the zest. He alone can enable us really to enjoy what we have. How few enjoy even riches! "Trust in the living God;" because, if riches fail, he can in the absence of riches, give sweet enjoyment. *Trust in God!* This is of more value than any quantity of riches; implicit dependence on God is greater security against want. than any extent of worldly property.

2. *Employ your riches in doing good.—Liberally;—*"rich in good works." Be in good works what you are in worldly possessions, abounding.—*Promptly;—*"*ready* to distribute." Some people who are very *able*, are never *ready.—Extensively;—*"ready to *distribute*." We often hear of, what we may be allowed to call, home-charity; but the apostle here enforces distributive charity. So the Psalmist, "He hath dispersed, he hath given to the poor," &c. Psa. cxii. 9.—*Freely—*"willing to communicate." How hardly are some persuaded to give, even a little!

Observe the different words which the apostle uses:—*Distributing*, appears to signify *general charity*. Give extensively; not to one or two persons or things, but to every laudable institution to which your means will extend.—*Communicate;* be *socially* benevolent. Be willing to share your good things with your fellow creatures. Be *hospitably* benevolent, see 2 Cor. ix. 5: Rom. xii. 13; 1 Tim. iii. 2; Tit. i. 8; 1 Pet. iv. 9.

3. *Live for eternity;—*"Laying up in store for themselves a good foundation against the time to come." *Laying up*, is a phrase which surely the rich understand. Laying up *for themselves.—*For whom are you *laying up*? see Psa. xxxix. 6; Matt. xxv. 40; Heb. vi. 20; 2 Cor. ix. 6—"That thay may lay hold on eternal life." *Riches* will not secure life. They permit their owners to perish; but a proper use of riches will end in everlasting life, see Luke xvi. 9. The apostle adapts his language and his ideas remarkably to the rich. They may still be *rich*,—thay may *lay up*,—they may still *trust in*,—and still aim at *high* things. Oh that the rich were wise, that they understood these things! Oh that their *riches*, their *trust*, their *laying up*, their *high views*, were all consecrated to God, But whether they will hear, or forbear to hear; *we* must not shrink from,

III. The execution of this charge. It is easy to charge the *poor;* but when the rich are the subjects, who will dare to say plain things to them? Their property, their dignity, their very appearance forbid. But the command is. "Charge *the rich*." Allow us then, oh ye rich! not as "lords over God's heritage," but as messengers of the Most High, to charge you.

Recollect,—that though your riches give you great worldly advantages, they also expose you to very serious dangers; "How hardly shall they that have riches enter into the kingdom of God!" Unsanctified riches always prove a curse to their owners. Would you enjoy any of their real advantages? then, "Honor the Lord with your substance, and with the first-fruits of all your increase, Prov. iii. 9.

Beware of high-mindedness; and remember, that though some rich men are wise and good; yet riches *may* be associated with any thing, and almost every thing, that is mean, and low, and vile.

Recollect, too, that there is but one way of salvation, for the rich and the poor. Repentance towards God, and faith in the Lord Jesus Christ, are essential to your salvation.

Finally, remember that a great day of reckoning and of judgment will come, when God will judge every man according to his works.

---

### THE CHRISTIAN'S DUTY AND HOPE.

1 Peter i. 13.—Wherefore gird up the loins of your mind, be sober, and hope to the end, for the grace that is to be brought unto you at the revelation of Jesus Christ. (Sk.)

ONE of the evidences of the truth and divinity of the christian religion is, that it obtained establishment in the world, not only without any assistance from human governments, or from the corrupt principles of human nature, but in opposition to both the one and the other. Nature loves sensual indulgence; christianity requires self-denial. Nature shrinks from pain and persecution. But the early christians had, in consequence of their profession, to endure fiery trials, ch. iv. 12. Hence the encouragements and supports afforded them in the former part of the chapter; and hence the exhortation to "a patient continuance in well doing," contained in our text itself; which points attention to the christian's duty, and his expectation.

I. THE CHRISTIAN'S DUTY;—"Gird up the loins of your mind, be sober, and hope to the end."

1. "*Gird up,*" &c. Here is an allusion to the manner in which persons in eastern countries usually disposed of their long flowing garments, when circumstances would not admit of their wearing them at full length. This was the case; that is, they confined what was loose and inconvenient by means of the girdle about the loins.

(1.) *In their journeying.* So Exod. xii. 11; 1 Kings xviii. 46; 2 Kings iv. 29. The advice, therefore, reminds us of our present state of *pilgrimage*, as ch. ii. 11. We are but too much disposed to call our lands our own, and to take up our rest here. But the text tells us that we should hold ourselves in readiness to leave the world. *Convinced*, like the Psalmist,—"I am a stranger," &c., Psa. xxxix. 12,—we should, like him and other ancient worthies, "*declare plainly*" our conviction and desires, Heb. xi. 13—16, by *acting* accordingly. "Gird up the loins;" have all things, whether temporal or spiritual, in readiness, as Israel to leave Egypt, &c., 2 Kings xx. 1; 2 Tim. iv. 6—8.

(**2**.) *This "girding up," &c., was practised by servants, when they wait-ed on their masters.* "*Gird* thyself and *serve* me." See Luke xii. 35, 37, xvii. 8. In this view it may denote that *cheerful and ready devotion* with which the christian, renouncing self-will and self-pleasing, should ever ask, "Lord, what wilt thou have me to do?" He should gird himself for any service, however mean, laborious, painful, or protracted, ch. ii. 13—21.

(3.) *Soldiers girded themselves for battle.* "Having your loins girt about with truth," Eph. vi. 14. This shows us the christian in his *militant state,* engaged in warfare with his three-fold enemy; and reminds us,—that oppo-sition is to be expected, ch. iv. 12—14;—that we should be always prepared for resistance, ch. v. 8, 9;—and therefore should have all the accompani-ments of the girdle of truth; namely, "the breastplate of righteousness," &c., Eph. vi. 10—17; and thus prepared, and praying always, verse 18, should *follow our captain,* and be led to certain victory.

2. "*Be sober,*" (or vigilant, Parkhurst,) a state equally distant from stu-pidity and carelessness, on the one hand, and the rashness of intoxication on the other. The opposite of intoxication by *strong drink.* Drunkenness, a swinish, abominable, ruinous practice, Isa. xxviii. 1—8; Prov. xxiii. 31, 32; 1 Cor. vi. 10. The opposite of intoxication *by excessive passion,* whether fear, anger, love or any other, Prov. xvi. 32; James i. 19. And consequent-ly the opposite of intoxication by *worldly cares,* compounded of unholy love, desire, fear, anxiety, &c., in fearful and fatal mixture; or by *carnal pleasure,* which enervates and destroys, Luke xxi. 34; Isa. v. 11, 12; 1 Tim. v. 6.—This wakeful sobriety is *valuable,* inasmuch as it enables a per-son to see his danger, and to provide against it; and to perceive his advant-ages, and avail himself of them. And it is *necessary;* because without this the mind must be so distracted, as to be a prey to every enemy; and espe-cially to our vigilant and crafty spiritual foes.

3. "*Hope to the end.*" We speak here of the *duty* of hoping or trusting amidst difficulties and discouragements. God gives grace; it is our place to exercise it on proper grounds afforded. Here they had to repose on the *work of redemption performed,* ver. 3, 16; the *word of promise afforded,* ver. 10—12, 25; and the *blessed effects* already produced in their experience, ver. 7, 8. This leads us to

II. THE CHRISTIAN'S EXPECTATION;—"The grace that is to be brought," &c. The word "grace," means any favor or benefit; the *revelation* of Jesus Christ, his coming to judgment, called ver. 7, "his *appearing.*"

1. The word "*revelation,*" seems to refer to his *appointment* by him who makes the revelation,—the eternal Father who has appointed the day, and committed all judgment to the Son, Acts xvii. 31; 1 Tim. vi. 15, 16.

2. And it would lead us to consider the *manner,* the *purposes,* and the *results* of this revelation.—The manner *awfully glorious:* in the Judge's announcement, attendants, equipage, &c. Not now as formerly, Isa. liii. 2; John i. 10, but with the trump of God, angels, flaming fire, &c., Luke ix. 26; 1 Thess. iv. 16, 17; 2 Thess. i. 7, 8; Rev. xx. 11—13.—The purpo-ses *awfully righteous:* to manifest the holiness and equity of God's govern-ment;—to convince and confound the ungodly,—and to vindicate the right-eous against the accusations of Satan and his sons, Matt. xxv. 1—40. Jude 15; Rev. xii. 9, 10.—The results *awfully transporting or terrific:* Matt. xiii. 41—50, xxv. 41—46. In the one case, all the bliss of heaven; in the other, all the woes of hell.

3. But this will be throughout to the saints, a revelation *of grace* Their bodies shall be *graciously* changed, Phil. iii. 12. In the separation, they

50

*shall* be *graciously* placed on the right. In *gracious* accents shall their **Redeemer** express his approval. Angels shall *graciously* conduct them; and Jesus graciously "present them before the presence of his glory;" &c. And in every case the grace shall be heightened *by contrast.* We would therefore,

1. Propose the solemn questions, Rom. ii. 3—10.
2. Enforce the important advice, "Acquaint *now*," &c., Job xxii. 21. And then urge the apostle's exhortation in our text, and join in his prayer, chap. v. 10, 11.

~~~~~~~~~~~~~

## THE SABBATH

Exodus xx. 8.—Remember the Sabbath day, to keep it holy. (Sk.

EVERY command of God is reasonable as it is divine; and is enjoined no less from regard to human happiness, than to secure the glory of the great Lawgiver. Those generally termed the ten commandments, stand prominently conspicuous in the sacred volume; and from the manner in which they were announced, the frequency with which they are introduced, and their essential connection with all good conduct, they present the strongest claims on our attention. You are aware, that our text forms a part of this sacred code, that it stands among these commandments, and is found in a part of the divine records which gives an account of God's delivering his law to mortals; and that it has the sanction which accompanies the mandates of heaven.

*The institution of the Sabbath-day,* and *the manner in which we should regard it,* are the topics which our text embraces; and those which now demand our serious attention.

THE INSTITUTION OF THE SABBATH.

1. By the Sabbath, we understand, a day rendered sacred, on account of divine appointment, and comprising, successively, a seventh portion of our time.
2. The institution of such a day, is not only divine; but, in order of time, it is prior to all other institutions which have a moral bearing on human conduct. Indeed, we trace its origin to the highest possible date, for the first seventh day was a Sabbath; blessed, sanctified, and kept: see Gen. ii. 2, 3.
3. No farther mention is made of the Sabbath-day, until Exod. xvi. 23, where it is referred to in such a manner, as shows, that Moses, at least, was well acquainted with its sacred character. Renewed sanction was given to this ordinance, when, as in the account before us, it was announced among, and made one of the ten words, or commandments, delivered with such awful authority as the context records. It is observable, however, that this command, in its introduction, is referred to as a thing well known; so much the word "remember," naturally suggests.
4. Admitting that there were peculiarities connected with the observance of this day among the Jews, and that some other days were termed Sabbaths in the Jewish ritual; suppose that some superstitious pretences respecting this day, when our Saviour was upon earth, were exploded by him; see Matt. xii. 1; Luke vi. 1, and xiii. 10; and John v. 1; and that he who

is the Lord of the Sabbath, changed the day from the seventh to the first; the day on which he arose from the dead; see John xvi. 12; Acts i. 2, 3; Matt. xxviii. 1; Acts xx. 7; 1 Cor xiv. 1; Rev. i. 10; will any, or all of such circumstances, bear us out in the disregard of an institution, so sacredly enjoined by God, and so importantly useful to the man? As well might we reject the precepts of justice because the Author of our mild dispensation substituted "Resist not evil," in the place of, "An eye for an eye, and a tooth for a tooth;" or leave off divine worship, because an apostle said, "Let no man judge you, in respect of an holy day, or of the new moon, or of the Sabbath-days;" and abandon all christian ordinances, because the weak, or the wicked, blend superstition with observance, and are reproved by heaven for such conduct.

5. The manner in which a violation of this day was punished, Num. xv. 32—36; the reproofs given to those who treated it with inattention, Neh. xii. 17, 18; Ezek. xx. 21, xxii. 8, and xxiii. 38; and the promise made to such as should keep it holy, Isa. lvi. 2, 4, 6, 7, and lv. 13, 14; show, that the man who trifles with the sacredness of its appointment, exposes himself, in no small degree, to the divine displeasure. Let me, therefore, have your continued, and most serious attention, while I endeavor to show,

II. THE MANNER IN WHICH WE SHOULD REGARD IT. This is expressed in the text, by the words, "keep it holy;" which must signify—*that the day should be separated from all common uses; and that it should be dedicated to services of a religious nature.*

1. *The former of these ideas is minutely illustrated in the subsequent part of the commandment;* "In it thou shalt not do any work," &c. From which we learn, that the Sabbath is as much violated by us, if we employ our servants, or cattle, in ordinary purposes on that day, as if we were thus engaged ourselves. It is necessary, however, to observe, that works of real necessity were allowed: and that this is rendered evident—by the very nature of things;—by the conduct of those who were most strict in their attention to the Sabbath;—and by the sanction of the Lord Jesus himself; see Matt. xii. 11; Luke xiii. 15; John vii. 22.

2. *The dedication of the day to religious services,* is next to be considered. That such an idea is contained in the phrase, "keep it holy," appears evident from the following consideration:—As no common occupation was to engage the time or attention of individuals on this day, something religious must, or idleness would be the necessary consequence. *It appears demonstrable from Leviticus* xxiii. 2, 3, that on this day, the worship of God was to be publicly celebrated; and that such worship was to engage the attention of the people in their dwellings.—*The usages of the Jews,* as recorded by the evangelists, make it clear, that they did employ the Sabbath for such a purpose; see Luke iv. 16, and xiii. 10, and vi. 3.—And *the conduct of the apostles* shows, that under the christian dispensation, the seventh day, or the first, was regularly occupied in the worship of God: see Acts xiii. 14—42, and 44, and xvi. 13, xvii. 1, 2, xviii. 14, and xx. 7. *The custom of the church of Christ,* in all ages, might be adduced; but this appears unnecessary, as the most common reference to ecclesiastical history will satisfy any candid inquirer.

3. That works of mercy and of charity, whether they respect the bodies or the souls of men, are suitable exercises for some parts of the sacred day, none, I presume, will question. However, *to keep the Sabbath-day holy,* is not merely to abstain from common concerns, and to give regular attention to the externals of divine worship, but amidst all, to *worship God in*

*spirit and in truth;* and to consider the day and the services, as **peculiarly** belonging to God.

Let me exhort you, then "Remember the Sabbath-day, to keep it holy."

Do not *forget* the sacred day; or merely remember it, to treat it with profanity.

Remember it—because God commands you to do it;—because it is a most salutary institution;—because the Sabbath is a day highly honored of God;—because awful judgments have arrested many in the profanation of it;—because it is a type of heaven's eternal rest.

---

## OBSERVANCE OF THE SABBATH ENJOINED.

**Isaiah lviii. 13, 14.**—If thou turn away thy foot from the Sabbath, from doing thy pleasure on my holy day; and call the Sabbath a delight, The holy of the Lord, Honorable; and shalt honor him, not doing thine own ways, nor finding thine own pleasure, nor speaking thine own words: then shalt thou delight thyself in the Lord; and I will cause thee to ride upon the high places of the earth, and feed thee with the heritage of Jacob thy father: for the mouth of the Lord hath spoken it. (H. H.)

THAT the observance of the Sabbath was intended to be of universal and perpetual obligation, does not admit of any reasonable doubt. It was enjoined to man in Paradise: and the commandment relating to it, when renewed to man at Mo int Sinai, was, like all the other moral commandments, written by God himself on tables of stone. The Jewish prophets spake of it as to be continued under the gospel dispensation: see ch. lvi. 1, 4, 6; and the apostles evidently continued the observance of it, transferring it only from the last day of the week to the first, in commemoration of our Lord's resurrection from the dead, and of the work of redemption which was thereby completed. See John xx. 19, 26. Acts xx. 7. 1 Cor. xvi. 2. The ceremonial laws relating to it are abrogated; but the moral part of it is as much in force as ever.

In the passage before us we may see,

I. IN WHAT LIGHT WE SHOULD VIEW THE SABBATH—

The estimation in which it should be held is here variously expressed: we are taught to account that day,

1. Holy—

Whatever was consecrated to God under the law was accounted holy: it was separated from all profane or common use, and was employed solely for the ends and purposes for which it had been thus set apart. Thus the Sabbath, being consecrated to the especial service of God, is called in our text "God's holy day;" and, "The holy of the Lord." In the New Testament also it is called, "The Lord's day." Rev. i. 10. Hence it is obvious, that every part of it is to be regarded as the Lord's property, and to be improved for him alone. We should feel a veneration for it, precisely as we should for any thing else that had been dedicated to the Lord: and, as we shudder at the impiety of Belshazzar in using, at a feast, the sacred vessels which he had taken from Jerusalem, though he himself was not a worshipper of Jehovah; much more must we, who acknowledge the sanctity of the Sabbath, shudder at the thought of alienating any portion of it from Him, to whom it exclusively belongs.

**2. Honorable—**

If any man, under the law, had regarded the temple, the sacrifices, and the vessels of the sanctuary, in no other light than as a common house, or common utensils, or common food, he would have been considered as greatly dishonoring God. Thus the very sanctity of the Sabbath should render it "honorable" in our estimation; and we should labor to "honor it" by every possible expression of our regard.

3. Delightful—

The arrival of that day should be greeted by us with holy joy : we should say, "This is the day that the Lord has made·; we will rejoice and be glad in it." If we could suppose an angel sent down to this lower world to labor in some common occupation, and permitted every seventh day to return to his heavenly abodes, and spend that day in the employments suited to his taste, with what delight would he look forward to the stated returns of that day! So should it be with us ; and so it *will* be, in proportion as we have attained to the views and dispositions of those blessed spirits. Not that we should delight in it merely as a day of rest to the body, but as a day wherein God calls us, like Moses, to come up and commune with him on his Holy Mount: and, instead of abridging it. or complaining of it as long and wearisome, we should rather say, with Peter, "It is good for us to be here :" and should almost regret the arrival of the period when we must descend from the Mount, to the less-pleasing occupations of time and sense.

But we will proceed to state more particularly,

II. In what manner we should employ it—

In what manner we should *not* employ it, is here distinctly told us—

Worldly business, and carnal pleasure, and unprofitable conversation, are all expressly proscribed: "we must not do our own ways, nor find our own pleasure, nor speak our own words." On all the other days of the week we may find time for these things ; but on the Sabbath-day they are to be excluded altogether. It is a grievous mistake to imagine, that after the public services of the day we are at liberty to engage in vain pursuits, invented only to beguile the time, which otherwise would be a burthen upon our hands : there are pursuits proper to the day ; and in them exclusively should our time be occupied. We do not mean to say, that such things as can neither be anticipated nor postponed may not be done with innocence : for even under the law, a latitude was allowed in relation to "what every man must eat." Exod. xii. 16. In reference to such things as are really necessary, we are authorized to say, that "God will have mercy, and not sacrifice :" but it becomes all to be on their guard, that they do not deceive their own souls ; for God can easily distinguish the hidden motives of the heart ; and will surely judge our actions as good or evil, according as their quality shall be found in his eyes. If the infringement of the Sabbath be reluctant, as in the extinguishing of a fire, or in the exercise of compassion to man or beast, it is well; but if we be actuated by considerations of ease, or interest, or pleasure, to alienate from God any of that time which ought to be consecrated to his service, we may be assured that we must answer for it in the day of judgment.

Our one aim on that day must be, to "honor God"—

The services which we are to render to our God on that day are various, and all compatible with each other. The first undoubtedly are *private :* we should give ourselves in a more peculiar manner to reading, to meditation, to prayer. On every day we should search the scriptures, but more especially on that day; applying them to our own hearts, examining ourselves by them, and intreating God to make them effectual for the conversion and salvation of our souls. From our closets we should go to worship God in *public*, and to testify before all, our regard for his authority, and our delight in his service. Whilst engaged in the various offices of prayer, or hearing of the word, or of communicating at the table of the Lord, we should be particularly careful that the frame of our minds be suited to the employment in which we are engaged; lest, whilst we profess to be serving God, we be found only mocking and insulting him by hypocritical professions. In the intervals, when we are disengaged from private or public duties, we may relieve our minds, and improve our time, in such as are of a social nature. The visiting of the sick, the comforting of the afflicted, the instructing of the rising generation, and, above all, the endeavoring to teach our children and servants, and to "bring them up in the nurture and admonition of the Lord," are services well pleasing to God, and admirably suited to the sanctity of that holy day. It is much to be feared that this latter duty in particular is sadly neglected, even in religious families; and that the great predilection that has been manifested by the religious world for public services, has brought into disuse those more self-denying offices which formerly occupied a considerable portion of the Sabbath-day. But, in whichever of these duties we are occupied, our great aim must be, to "honor God;" demeaning ourselves as in his more immediate presence, and endeavoring to approve ourselves to him as faithful servants.

And shall the Sabbath, in this view of it, be accounted a day of gloom! No; we shall have far other sentiments of it, if we consider,

III. THE BENEFITS WE MAY EXPECT FROM A DUE OBSERVANCE OF IT—

Whatever reference there may be in our text to the return of the Jews from their captivity in Babylon, we cannot doubt but the promises here made have a higher and more spiritual import. In them we are assured, that, if we really keep the Sabbath as we ought, we shall be blessed with,

1. Delight in God—

There is not any thing which God more delights to honor than a due observance of the Sabbath. We may perform the outward duties of that day, and reap no material benefit: but if we truly and earnestly endeavor to honor God in the way before described, God will draw nigh to us, and reveal himself to us, and fill us with joy and peace in believing. And here we confidently make our appeal to all who have ever labored to spend a Sabbath to the Lord, whether they have not found such a measure of grace and peace flowing into their souls, as has abundantly recompensed their utmost exertions? Who must not acknowledge that one day thus spent in the courts and in the service of Jehovah, is better than a thousand passed amongst the vain delights of this world? Ps. lxxxiv. 4, 10. And where the Sabbath is thus habitually honored, we will venture to say, that such happiness will at times flow into the soul, as David experienced, when he said, "My soul shall be satisfied as with marrow and fatness, whilst my mouth praiseth thee with "joyful lips:" Ps. lxiii. 5; yes, "they shall be satisfied with the fatness of God's house; and he will make them drink of the river of his pleasures." Ps. xxxvi. 8.

2. Victory over our spiritual enemies—

This seems to be the import of that expression, "I will cause thee to ride upon the high places of the earth:" compare Deut. xxxii. 13, and xxxiii. 29; and it shall be fulfilled to all who conscientiously improve their Sabbaths to the glory of their God. Too many of those who profess religion, are, it must be confessed, scarcely, if at all, advancing in the divine life: their evil dispositions still retain such an ascendant over them, as to make them go on heavily all their days. But, if we were to inquire how they spent their Sabbaths, and what efforts they made to glorify God in their public, private, and social duties, we should soon find the reason of their slow progress. As our Lord said of some particular evil spirits, "These go not out, but by prayer and fasting," so we may say of the evils which are predominant in many professors of religion. They do not give way, because such slight efforts are made upon the Sabbath to subdue them. If that day were truly and entirely devoted to the Lord, Satan would no longer retain the ungodly as his vassals, nor be able to exert so much influence over those who have professedly cast off his yoke.

3. The full possession of the heavenly Canaan—

That land which was given to Jacob for his inheritance, was typical of the Canaan that is above, which truly "floweth with milk and honey." And it may be safely affirmed, that no person who conscientiously employed his Sabbaths here, ever did, or ever can, fall short of the heavenly rest. Thousands who have perished by the hand of the public executioner, have traced their shame and misery to a neglect of the Sabbath: but never was an instance known of one who duly improved his Sabbaths being left to die under the dominion of his sins. Indeed the services of the Sabbath cannot possibly consist with indulged and wilful sin: on the contrary, they are both a preparation for heaven, and a foretaste of it: on earth the saints behold their God by faith, but in heaven they will behold him face to face: on earth they, as it were, learn and rehearse their parts: and in heaven they will join the full chorus of saints and angels in everlasting hallelujahs to God and to the Lamb.

SEE hence,

1. How reasonable are the requirements of God in his gospel!

Had God required six days out of the seven to be spent in such exercises, it would have been highly reasonable that we should obey him: how much more when he gives us six for earthly business, and requires only one to be consecrated entirely unto him! If the services of that day were ever so painful, they might well be claimed by Him who has done such great things for us: and how much more when they are so delightful and so profitable! Grudge him not then that day, nor any portion of it: but let it be wholly and unreservedly devoted to his service.

2. How just will be the condemnation of those who disobey them!

A person who has attained to fifty years of age, has had *above seven years of Sabbaths.* O what blessings might not have been secured in that time, if all those Sabbaths had been sanctified to the Lord! and what judgments does not he merit, who has wasted all of them in a wilful neglect of God! Little as we think of Sabbaths now, we shall find ere long, that the profaning of them has greatly increased our guilt and misery. The Lord grant that this day may not pass away as so many others have done, unprofitably to our souls; but let it be to every one of us a preparation for our eternal rest!

## CHILDREN INSTRUCTED TO FEAR GOD.

Psalm xxxi v. 11.—Come, ye children, hearken unto me; I will teach you the fear of the Lord. (B.)

Such was once the language of a king, a "man after God's own heart," and a prophet. What a commendation is contained in these words of all schools and institutions, the object of which is the religious instruction of children and young persons!

Inquire we,

I. What we are to understand by " the fear of the Lord."

" Fear," like hope, desire, love, joy, or sorrow, is an affection of the human soul, and is good or bad, laudable, or the contrary, according as the object by which it is excited is good or bad, and according to the degree in which it is excited. The fear here spoken of has God for its object, and cannot be excessive, if it be of the right kind. For, we can no more *fear* than we can love, or desire, or rejoice in him too much, or expect too great things from him; supposing our fear of him be rational and scriptural.

It must not be a fear of terror or dread, unless we be going on in sin, and be under its guilt and power, in which case it is quite proper we should be afraid of his wrath.— — —

Nor is it a fear of timidity, dejection, and discouragement; unless that we must be discouraged from hoping for prosperity, protection, or happiness, while we continue in a state of enmity and disobedience to him.

Nor is it a fear of diffidence, distrust, or suspicion, as if he would not fulfil his promises, or make good his word.

But it is a fear of reverence; from a sense of his glory and majesty. Jer. x. 7; Heb. xii. 28.—Of awe and concern, from a sense of his power, wisdom, holiness, justice, and of our ignorance, sinfulness, and guilt. Jer. v. 21, 22. Matth. x. 28.—Of subjection; termed a "godly fear;" Heb. xii. 28; from a sense of his goodness, as well as power and wisdom, producing a disposition to obey him. Isa. l. 10.—Of watchfulness and circumspection; from a sense of his omnipresence and omniscience. Prov. xxviii. 14.

With respect to the properties of this fear, we may observe, it is awakening, alarming, humbling, restraining from evil, constraining to good.

The whole of religion is here meant by the fear of God. This is generally termed the " fear of God" in the Old Testament, Gen. xx. 11. xlii. 18. Ps. xix. 9, and the " love of God" in the New. Gal. v. 6. 1 Cor. xiii. 13.— — —

It is religion in the heart, and in experience; in opposition to that in the head, and in speculation merely.—In reality and in practice; in opposition to that in profession, and in pretence.—Internally, and in power; in opposition to that externally, and in form.—In its principle and source, therefore, steady and permanent; in opposition to that which is assumed, inconstant, and transitory.

II. How it appears that it is of importance to teach this to children and others.

It is infinitely reasonable that we should reverence a Being so glorious, stand in awe of one so powerful and holy, be subject to one so good, be watchful under the eye of one so omniscient. All the divine perfections and the relations in which he stands to us, show the reasonableness of the particulars above mentioned, as comprehended in the fear of God.

400

It is in its beginning, the "beginning of wisdom ;" in its progress, the progress of wisdom. Thus David, Ps. cxi. 10, Solomon, Prov. i. 7, ix. 10, and Job, ch. xxviii. 28.

This, and only this, raises man above the brute creatures. They reason, in a measure, as well as man, but are not capable of religion. It is this, above every thing, which ennobles, and perfects human nature.

It provides a remedy for the follies and actual misconduct, into which we naturally fall, in the government of our minds and actions, as also the irregularity and exorbitancy of the appetites and passions.— — —

It imparts a higher excellence and value to all human attainments, and directs us, in the employment of them, to regard the interest of our fellow creatures, and the glory of God.— —

It is the means of providing, most effectually, for our comfort in the present life, and for our everlasting felicity in the next.— — —

Hence it appears that it is our interest to possess this religion.—*Temporally ;* "Godliness having the promise of the life that now is, as well as of that which is to come ;" of the necessaries of life; Matt. vi. 33 ; of all things useful, Ps. lxxxiv. 11, xxxii. 9, 10 ; of deliverance from trouble, ver. 4—6, 19—*Spiritually ;* It makes us partakers of the unsearchable riches of Christ ; pardon, the divine favor, adoption, regeneration, progressive renovation, direction in our difficulties, protection in dangers, ver. 7, answers to prayer, deliverance from troubles, ver. 15—18.

Therefore, it is our happiness. We have thereby peace with God, peace of mind, hope of immortality, joy in the Holy Ghost, communion with God, the fellowship of saints, the moderate enjoyment of the creature.

Consider the honor of it. It may, indeed, be attended with reproach among the ignorant and wicked but it is truly to our honor, as it is so reasonable and excellent, and as we thus imitate the wisest and best men that ever lived, the angels of God, and even Christ himself ; nay, and thus we become godlike. It will be our eternal glory. Hereby, and hereby only, is our nature advanced to the dignity of which it is capable.—

Consider its amiableness in all, especially in young persons.—

Now, if religion be thus reasonable, wise, advantageous, happy, honorable, we cannot have it too soon —And it is peculiarly for the honor of God, the good of society in general, and the comfort and advantage of their parents and friends in particular, and their own individual comfort, that children and young persons should be religious.

Hence piety towards God, benevolence to man, especially to the rising generation, and even self-interest, should induce us to say, with the royal Psalmist and Prophet, "Come, ye children, hearken unto me: I will teach you the fear of the Lord." I will do it myself, or I will do it by my substitute.—I will contribute from my fortune to have it done, or I will attend myself and see it done. I will promote it every way in my power.

III. How IT MAY BE TAUGHT THEM BEST, MOST SURELY, AND MOST LASTINGLY.

By instruction.—We must instruct them to know themselves, their ignorance, weakness, guilt, depravity.—To know God, his nature and attributes and the relations in which he stands to his creatures.—To know Christ, in his person, and offices, his love, and sufferings.—

We must instruct them to know the way of salvation, the will of God, their duty, and their happiness—To know the scriptures in order thereto.— To read and meditate. 2 Tim. iii. 15, 16.

401

By reproof, exhortation, corrections, rewards.—

By showing them a good example in all respects.—

By praying with and for them, and putting them on praying for themselves, and habituating them to public, social, family, and private worship.—

---

## GLORIFYING GOD IN ALL THINGS.

1 Cor. x. 31.—Whether therefore ye eat, or drink, or whatsoever ye do, do all to the glory of God. (P.)

THE word of God is of inestimable value, as it furnishes us with a comete directory how we may glorify God, and enjoy him for ever. The general rule contained in the text will afford particular direction to every lively christian who is anxious to know how he may best glorify him whose name he bears. The particular occasion of the words may be learned from the context; but they are fully applicable to us, and we may found upon them this grand maxim, that *it is the duty of christians, in all their actions, whether civil or religious, to aim at the glory of God.* It is impossible, indeed, to add to, or diminish from the essential glory of God. No mortal can, by any exertion, add to the splendor of the meridian sun; and it would be equally foolish for any mortal to imagine that he can add any thing to the glory of God. Yet it is not enough for us to be passive instruments here. The heavens, the animal, vegetable, and mineral tribes, display the glory of God *silently;* man is to do it *actively.* Christians are formed anew for this express purpose, that they may be a holy and peculiar people, zealous of good works. Let us apply the maxim I have stated,

I. To RELIGIOUS DUTIES. We are to glorify God,

1. By *believing in the Lord Jesus Christ*—"This is the work of God, that we believe in his Son Jesus Christ." Not to believe God, is to dishonor him—to make him a liar. The gospel is an authoritative system; it is revealed for the *obedience* of faith. Thus Abraham, by being strong in faith, glorified God: in how many instances he did this, his history will inform you. Like him, we must believe that God's promises are true, and that they shall be performed.

2. By *our repentance.* Impenitence dishonors God, by supposing that he winks at sin, or that he does not observe it. By making confession of sin, we give glory to God. We glorify his holiness, by which he hates sin; his omniscience, by which he discovers it. Thus the prodigal honored his father by his confession and his hopes; thus the publican glorified God, while the pharisee glorified himself; thus the thief on the cross honored Christ, and thus all true penitents honor him.

3. By *our obedience* in general. And here true faith is manifested, for faith works by love. God is pleased to esteem himself glorified by the *worship* of his people—"Give unto God the glory due unto his name worship before him in the beauty of holiness." God is dishonored in the world by idolatry, and by the homage rendered to the creature, and it becomes christians to be seen in public engaged in acts of solemn worship. *Prayer* is an act of homage, for in it we own that all our supplies are from him. *Praise*— "Whoso offereth praise, glorifieth me." In the ancient dispensation, all that

could excite to gratitude was employed, and it should be still more so in the christian church—*by a devout observance of his holy day,* Isa. lviii. 13,—by an *attentive hearing of his word:* thus Mary honored Christ more than Martha—by *reading* his word with simplicity—by making a *public profession* of our attachment to him—by *uniting with his people*—by *celebrating his dying love.*

4. By *our calm submission* to his chastening rod. None can hope to be exempt from these visitations. But if we "have had fathers of our flesh which corrected us, and we gave them reverence, shall we not much rather be in subjection to the Father of spirits, and live?" He is the ruler of the world, wise and good; it is our duty to glorify him in the fire, when we receive evil from his hand as well as when we receive good. Thus Job glorified him, and said, "The Lord gave, and the Lord hath taken away, blessed be the name of the Lord." Apply the maxim,

II. To CIVIL OR COMMON ACTIONS. Generally speaking, we are to glorify God in these actions, by doing all *in love;* for love is the fulfilling of the law—by our meekness, our patience, our usefulness. Thus we are to "let our light so shine before men, that they, seeing our good works, may glorify our Father which is in heaven."

But more particularly we are to glorify God,

1. In our *actions.* In order to this, they must be *lawful;* they must be pursued at *lawful times*—not performed on the Sabbath, for instance; and in a *lawful degree:* we shall not glorify God by destroying our health, by neglecting the private or public duties of religion, by inattention to our families, &c. We glorify God in the common actions of life.

By *aiming in them all at obedience to his will, and submission to his appointments.* Servants and masters are thus exhorted to serve the Lord Christ, and to do all in his name.

By *seeking for his blessing on all our endeavors.* "Go to now, ye that say we will go into such a city, and continue there a year, and buy and sell, and get gain; for that ye ought to say if the Lord will, we shall live, and do this or that."

By *ascribing all our success entirely to him.* We must not burn incense to our own net. Herod dishonored God when he was so elated with the people's shouting. So did Nebuchadnezzar when he said, "Is not this great Babylon that I have built by the might of my power, and for the honor of my majesty?" So all dishonor God who ascribe to themselves the contrivance, the execution, the completion of their works. We should glorify God,

2. In our *enjoyments.* "Whether ye eat or drink," &c. Not by *excess,* for this would dishonor God and ourselves too, but

By *humbly acknowledging our unworthiness,* as did the poor old woman, who, while eating her crust by the side of a brook of which she was about to drink, exclaimed, "All this and Christ too!" When we sit down to our tables, it becomes us to say, with David, "Who am I, O Lord God, and what is my house, that thou shouldst thus deal with me?"

By *adoring the bounty of God* in bestowing these things upon us. We are to regard them not as the purchase of our money, but as the gifts of his bounty, who as a parent supplies the wants of his children.

By *considering the love of Christ,* who was poor and destitute and self-denying, that we might have all things richly to enjoy.

By *aiming to employ our health* and strength and life to the service of God, that so in all things we may adorn the gospel of God our Saviour.

By *rising from the enjoyment of vanishing pleasures to the contemplation of heavenly satisfactions.* Looking up to Christ as the food of the soul, and longing for the day when we shall eat bread and drink wine in the kingdom of God. INFERENCES —

1. *How is man fallen?* If it be the duty of all to glorify God in all things, what a wretched being is man become! There are some who never perform one action to the glory of God. How displeasing, how dishonorable to God!

2. *How do we all stand in need of pardoning mercy!* We have not only committed *sinful* actions, but what has been *good*, has been done without proper motives, and with too much of self. When we read, when we pray, when we hear, when we give alms, we have often sought our own honor and advantage more than the glory of God. Let us seek forgiveness then.

3. *How necessary is regeneration!* If man by nature is indisposed to seek the glory of God, how important is it that he should be made a new creature, that new powers and dispositions should be infused into his soul, that the love of God should be shed abroad in his heart!

4. *How important is it to bear the rule of the text in mind continually.* Amidst the many things which present themselves to our notice, some are altogether unlawful, and others are inexpedient; but this maxim would always determine us, and set us right. Should two duties present themselves to us at the same time, we need only ask this plain, simple question, " By which of these actions shall I most glorify God?"

---

## CHAPTER VI.

## WARNINGS.

### SINNERS ADMONISHED.

**Prov. i. 23.**—Turn you at my reproof: behold, I will pour out my Spirit unto you, I will make my words known unto you. (Sk.)

VARIOUS are the means which the Lord employs to convince the wicked of the error of their ways, and bring them to a knowledge of divine truth. He has not only sent his Son, to seek and to save that which was lost, but he also waits to be gracious; and is " long-suffering, not willing that any should perish, but that all should come to repentance." He, therefore, invites the most abandoned to participate the blessings of his salvation, and encourages them to believe, by the most powerful persuasions and captivating motives;—he mercifully pities the folly, and justly complains of the incorrigible obstinacy of the impenitent;—he frequently visits them with the tokens of his displeasure, and faithfully warns them of the danger to which they are exposed;—but as he is "good to all," he suspends the execution of his wrath, and gives them *space* to repent and believe the gospel; —and as he hath no pleasure in the destruction of sinners, he kindly admonishes them to escape the ruin of sin, and graciously promises the richest blessing to the truly penitent. Such is evidently the import of his affectionate address to mankind, in the language of the text, " Turn you at my reproof," &c. These words also describe the Lord's dealings with his sinful creatures in reference to—*the reproofs he administers—the submission he requires—and the encouragement he imparts.*

I. THE REPROOFS HE ADMINISTERS;—"Turn you at *my reproof*." We are surrounded with faithful admonishers, who are all *arranged* and *employed* by God, to win the hearts of the disobedient to the wisdom of the just. He reproves us,

1. *By the scriptures.* His word contains the most *pointed* and *salutary* admonitions; it records the appropriate cautions and solemn warnings of Moses and the prophets—of Jesus Christ and his apostles, Rom. xv. 4; 2 Tim. iii. 16, 17.—It also repeatedly sends us for instruction and reproof to the works of creation—to admonitory examples of impiety—and the awful solemnities of death and the grave, Isaiah i. 2, 3; Prov. vi. 6; Matt. xi. 20—24; Deut. xxxii. 29; Eccl. ix. 10;—we are faithfully reproved in every part of the sacred writings. Let us hear and live.

2. *By ministers.* They are sent to warn the wicked of their danger, and show them the way of salvation.—They zealously persuade men by the terrors of the Lord, and encourage them by the promise of the Gospel; —as "ambassadors for Christ," they pray you, in his stead, to be reconciled to God. You have often heard their reproofs—witness their labors—and beheld their tears. But have you taken warning? Have you believed their report? Have you realized the truth of their message? Acts xxvi. 18; Col. i. 28.

3. *By conscience.* This in an *internal* and *universal* monitor—it is always with us, and cannot be silenced—it is a *witness* to all our proceedings, and irresistibly *arraigns* and *condemns* the guilty culprit, Rom. ii. 15. It speaks with *sovereign authority*, and its awful criminations fill the trembling sinner with inexpressible *anguish* and *bitterness* of soul, Prov. xviii. 14. Has it not often accused you of crimes, alarmed your fears, and warned you of approaching danger? Does it not frequently testify of your sinful state, and assure you that except you repent you must perish?

4. *By providence.* There is a perfect *harmony* between the purposes of God, and the arrangement of his works. "Day unto day uttereth speech, and night unto night showeth knowledge." The Lord often reproves us by pious parents—family connections—and godly neighbors. He also admonishes us, by afflictions and difficulties, to teach us the frailty of nature—the folly of sin—and the vanity of the world. The continual dissolution of our fellow-mortals, speaks loudly to survivors, and says to all, "prepare to meet your God—be ye also ready," &c. The *gracious design* of the Divine reprover will appear by considering,

II. THE SUBMISSION HE REQUIRES. "*Turn you* at my reproof." Through sin we have all forsaken the Lord, and "gone astray like lost sheep;" but he kindly *reproves* our folly, and *invites* us to return unto him,

1. *With penitent hearts.* We cannot come to him on the ground of *innocence* or personal worthiness; and as *guilty sinners* we ought to approach him "with broken and contrite hearts;" which are sacrifices highly becoming the creature, and always acceptable to the Creator, Ps. li. 17.—Genuine repentance includes—conviction of sin—humiliation of soul—compunction of spirit—holy indignation and shame—and humble confession to God, Luke xv. 17—19; 1 John i. 8, 9. "Repent ye, therefore, and be converted."

2. *With believing minds.* Jesus Christ is the *only way* to the Father, and the *medium* of all spiritual blessings;—through him, therefore, we

must return to God, *believing* in his name, and *trusting* in his merits;—it is by faith we credit the gospel—embrace the Saviour—and realize salvation, John iii. 18: Acts xvi. 31. " He that believeth shall be saved ;" for Christ is "able to save them to the uttermost that come unto God by him."

3. *With fervent devotion.* The Lord must be sought by earnest prayer, as the object of adoration and the source of blessedness ; though he knows our necessities, yet he will be inquired of for the communication of his blessings. We should call upon him sincerely—humbly—confidently—fervently—and diligently.—Prayer eminently distinguishes the character of every returning penitent, and God will assuredly hear and answer their requests, Luke xviii. 13 ; Acts ix. 11 ; Matt. vii. 7, 8.

4. *With prompt obedience.* The service of God, and the paths of sin, are *incompatible*, and can never be reconciled, Matt. vi. 24;—we must, therefore, cease to do evil, and learn to do well.—Religion requires a *universal* renunciation of the *principles* and *habits* of vice, and an entire devotedness to God, both of heart and life, Isa. lv. 6, 7 ; Titus ii. 12 ; Luke i. 74, 75. We should be induced thus to turn to God by,

III. The encouragement he imparts. " Behold I will pour out my Spirit," &c. This promise is highly important and comprehensive. The participation of the Holy Ghost is an inestimable privilege which includes every *holy principle* that he implants, and every *gracious disposition* which he inspires. The Spirit of God is,

1. *A convincing Spirit.* Under *this* character he is poured out upon all mankind, John xvi. 8—11. It is his special province to open the eyes of our understanding, that we may understand the scriptures ;—by him the Lord makes "known his *words* unto us ;"—he imparts a spiritual *discernment*, that we may discover our real state and character, and comprehend " the truth as it is in Jesus," 1 Cor. ii. 10—12.

2. *A quickening Spirit.* He removes the death of sin, and infuses the life of grace ;—he graciously dwells in his people, and by his *vital influence* they are born again, and become new creatures ;—he witnesses their adoption, and fills them with " the fruits of righteousness," Rom. viii. 15, 16; Gal. v. 22, 23. It is the Spirit *quickeneth* and *giveth life* and peace to the soul, Eph. ii. 1.

3. *A comforting Spirit.* All real consolation is *divine* in its author, and *spiritual* in its nature ;—it is the immediate *production* and fruit of the Holy Ghost, Rom. xiv. 17 ;—he communicates ample support and comfort in every time of need ;—he is. therefore, repeatedly styled "the Comforter." Through his sacred energy, we receive joy and peace in believing; and " rejoice evermore—pray without ceasing—and in every thing give thanks."

4. *A sanctifying Spirit.* He is justly denominated the " Spirit of holiness ;"—all his operations are *hallowing*, and productive of christian *purity ;*—he transforms the soul into the image and glory of God, Titus iii. 5 ; 2 Cor. iii. 18.—His baptismal fire *consumes* sin, and *purifies* the sinner, Matt. iii. 11, 12 ;—he sanctifies his people *wholly*, and preserves them *blameless*, unto the coming of our Lord Jesus Christ, 1 Thess. v. 23. Let us therefore now consider our ways, and turn unto the Lord, that we may receive the gift of the Holy Ghost, which he has promised to them that repent and call upon his name, Luke xi. 13.

## A CAUTION AGAINST DECEPTION.

Deut. xi. 16.—Take heed to yourselves, that your heart be not deceived.  (Sk )

It is one essential characteristic in christian charity, that it "suffereth long and is kind." It not only suffers all the insults, provocations, and maliciousness of a persecuting world; but all the frailties, imperfections, and errors of the children of God. And never was there a more illustrious example of this long-suffering charity than Moses, who dictated the sentiment in the text. He had for a series of years borne with the insults of Israel. He had instructed them in their ignorance, he had reclaimed them in their wanderings, he had interceded for them in their dangers, and now, though about to be taken from them, and go up unto mount Nebo, over against Jericho, to die there; yet he is most tenderly concerned for their future welfare. In this chapter, after having reminded Israel of what God had done for them, ver. 4, 5, 6, 7, he directs them to consider what he was about to do, verse 10. And knowing the propensity which they had to neglect their immortal interests, and turn aside after other gods, he urges upon their attention the sentiment in the text, "Take heed to yourselves," &c. We notice here,

I. An evil anticipated. That of having the heart deceived.

II. A caution urged against it. "Take heed to yourselves," &c.

To be deceived is to be imposed upon, deluded, brought into error, so as to be led to entertain ideas and sentiments inconsistent with the truth. Men generally are liable to be deceived. We may be deceived *concerning ourselves;* we may think of ourselves more highly than we ought to think, and give ourselves credit for the possession of virtues to which we are total strangers: we may be vain in our imaginations, suppose that we are wise, when in God's sight we are fools; and think ourselves safe, when danger is at the very door. We may be deceived, *concerning God.* Concerning *his nature;* we may say in our hearts that there is no God, or imagine that God is altogether such a one as ourselves. Concerning *his laws;* we may think that they are not as pure, as spiritual, and as extensive as they really are. We may be deceived *concerning religion.* We may substitute mere morality, a sound creed, or a pompous profession, instead of a saving conversion to God, and a sanctification of the soul to his service. These, with a thousand other deceptive suggestions, and erroneous thoughts, may occupy our minds, and lead us astray. In proof of the possibility of deception in reference to the concerns of our souls, we observe,

1. *The scantiness and imperfection of human knowledge.* Absolute knowledge precludes the possibility of deception; if we knew every thing, and every thing perfectly, we could not be deceived. But what little we do know, we know very imperfectly. With the objects of sense we are most intimately acquainted, but our eyes, and ears, and palate, and feelings, have deceived us. Religion requires the exercise of the intellectual faculties, and as our knowledge is so limited and defective, we may be deceived. We infer it.

2. *From the deceitfulness of the heart.* "The heart is deceitful above all things." A deceived heart turns us aside. Hence we are in love with deception, and will not come to the light that our deeds might be manifest. When Elisha told Hazael of the horrible acts of cruelty that he would commit in after life, he so far thought it impossible that he should ever arrive at such a climax in crime, as to rip up women with child, that he said, "What!

Is thy servant a dog that he should do this great thing?" 2 Kings viii. 12 13. The possibility of being deceived, appears,

3. *From the deceitfulness of sin.* Sin is deceitful. It promises rewards, but pays punishment; and it would lose its power, could we strip it of its deceit. Hence it seldom appears in its own native character, or is designated by its own legitimate title. Revenge is called honor; covetousness, frugality; luxury and extravagance, good living; lust and obscenity, innocent liberties; and there is scarcely a crime committed, but what has some of its malignity softened down, to render it more fascinating and deceptive; and as proofs of the deceitfulness of sin, we might advert to the pleas and subterfuges to which men resort in order to conceal it from the public eye, or lessen its evil when detected. Because sin is so deceitful, we are liable to be deceived. We infer it also,

4. *From the deceitfulness of the world.* The great mass of mankind are involved in deception. Every sinner is a deceiver, he deceives himself, and labors to deceive others. He sports himself with his own deceivings. Would men deliberately prefer darkness to light, bondage to liberty, peril to safety, and misery to happiness, if they were not most awfully deceived? Would acts of sin, and crimes of the most heinous character be extolled, and idolized; and acts of piety be defamed and scandalized, if delusions deep as hell had not seized their unhappy subjects? How few men *appear* to be what they are in reality! How many would shudder at the thought of appearing in their true character! How much moral deformity is often concealed beneath a decent, and perhaps a religious exterior! How many whited walls and painted sepulchres present themselves to our view! We are also liable to be deceived,

5. *From the deceitfulness of the devil.* The devil is the most deceitful being in existence. All the deception upon earth owes its origin to his influence. He is the deceiver of the nations. He deceived Eve, the mother of us all, and he has been practicing the same infernal policy, in all climes and ages. And his success has been without a parallel. Such are the reasons we have for believing that our hearts may be deceived. But the text assumes that this deception is an evil pregnant with very pernicious consequences. And this appears from the consideration, that *those whose hearts are deceived are involved in a state of the most palpable error.* Error of any kind is to be deplored. What tradesman would wish to make errors in his accounts? What scholar that would not guard against error in his sums? But these errors are trivial, when compared to the grievous error in which those are involved whose hearts are deceived; who are deceived concerning their souls, their salvation, and their God. Nor is this all; those whose hearts are deceived, are exposed to extreme danger. "He that converteth a sinner from the error of his ways, shall save a soul from death." The death of the soul is a tremendous death; a double death, a second death; and to this death every sinner whose heart is deceived is constantly exposed: "Wo unto them that call evil good," &c.: "therefore as the fire devoureth the stubble," &c., Isa. v. 20—24. See the verse subsequent to the text. Let us examine,

II. THE CAUTION URGED AGAINST THIS DECEPTION. "Take heed to yourselves," &c.

1. *Be alive to a sense of your extreme danger.* No man will use caution where he suspects no danger. Our senses furnish us with intimations of the dangers to which the body is exposed; but alas! to the dangers of the soul, though infinitely more alarming, we are too frequently insensible

Who that surveys the mirth, and jollity, and merriment of the multitude would at all suspect that they were in any danger, or exposed to any peril? But who that reads the Bible with attention can fail to be convinced, that we are threatened with the most tremendous punishment? Now in order that we may take heed to ourselves, let us be broad awake to our danger. Let us consider what we are,—how deeply fallen! Let us weigh well our circumstances, dangers, and enemies; this will lay the foundation for caution and circumspection.

2. *Seek for the illuminating and sanctifying influences of the Holy Spirit.* The mind of man is so completely darkened by the deceitfulness of sin, that he has naturally no perceptions of his danger; but the Holy Ghost opens the eyes of our understanding, and we see the truth, and begin to know ourselves. But illumination alone is not sufficient; our powers must be renewed, we must become new creatures in Christ Jesus. Your danger may be perceived, but without the renewal of your hearts in righteousness, you will possess no mental energy to avoid it. The Holy Ghost will illuminate and sanctify you. O seek his influence by fervent, importunate prayer. "Take heed to yourselves."

3. *By the constant practice of self-examination.* Examine yourselves whether ye be in the faith. Whether you have the fruits of faith. Whether you are the followers of them who through faith and patience have inherited the promises Examine yourselves *faithfully:* self-love leads us to look partially on ourselves;—*frequently:* never suffer a day to pass over your heads without an investigation of your conduct. It was the advice of an old heathen,

> " Let not the stealing god of sleep surprise,
> Nor creep in slumber o'er thy weary eyes,
> Ere every action of the former day,
> Strictly thou dost and righteously survey."

" Take heed to yourselves,"

4. *By watching over yourselves.* "Watch and pray." " Be ye there fore sober, and watch unto prayer." " Watch thou in all things." These are scriptural directions, and were addressed to the primitive saints. Watchfulness will lead you to keep a strict guard over your thoughts. Your thoughts will wander on forbidden objects, but by watchfulness you will detect them: vain, foolish, and lascivious thoughts will seek to obtrude on your attention. Take heed to yourselves in reference to your words and actions.

Conclude, by urging the text on the attention of hearers of all descriptions.

People of all ages, young and old.—Of all circumstances, rich and poor.—Of all relations, husbands and wives, parents and children, masters and servants.—Of all callings, preachers and people.—" Take heed to yourselves.'

409

## THE FOLLY OF A FRUITLESS PROFESSION

Luke vi. 46.—Why call ye me Lord, Lord, and do not the things which I say? (S. S.)

The honor of Christ and the salvation of our souls depend on our having right views of the gospel!—

We cannot therefore too earnestly insist on the doctrine of justification by faith in Christ—

Nevertheless we should constantly urge the practice of good works as the fruits and evidences of our faith in Christ—

The folly of expecting salvation while we neglect them is strongly represented by our Lord in the text—

I. Shew who they are that deserve the censure in the text—

The heathens have less to aggravate their sins than christians—

The greater part of those who live in countries that are evangelized are obnoxious to this censure—

1. Mere nominal christians deserve it.

Many are Christ's as having been devoted to him in baptism—

By the appellation of christians they profess to be his followers—

But they are in no respect subject to his will and word—

Christ commands them to "seek first the kingdom of God," &c. and they seek it last—

2. Formal, self-righteous persons deserve it.

Many will go far in the outward duties of religion—

They will profess too a veneration for the name of Christ—

But he calls them to regeneration, John iii. 3, and they deny their need of it—

He bids them live by faith on him, and it proves an hard saying—John vi. 53, 60.

They are satisfied with the form of godliness, without the power—

3. False professors deserve it.

None are so worthy of reproof as they—

They will talk much of their 'ependence on Christ—

They will profess perhaps to have experienced much of his power and grace—

They may even glory in the recollection of his truth and faithfulness—

But in the midst of all, they can be proud, covetous, passionate, censorious, unforgiving, deceitful and dishonest—

To such the text may be applied with peculiar energy—

Such persons ought to be addressed with all plainness of speech.

II. Expostulate with them on the folly of their conduct.

The service of God is justly called a "reasonable service"—

But a fruitless profession is most unreasonable—

No reason can be assigned "why" persons should rest in such a state.

1. Is not a conformity to Christ's precepts practicable?

Many allege that such strictness as he requires is unattainable—

We allow that absolute perfection is not to be expected in this world—

But an unreserved devotedness of ourselves to God is attainable—

Thousands of the saints of old have walked thus with God—

There is a cloud of living witnesses who exemplify this conduct—

God has promised grace to all who seek it diligently—

2. Is not obedience to him necessary?

We may be good citizens if we possess only the virtues of heathens.—

But an unfeigned regard to Christ is necessary to constitute us christians—
St. Paul has fully declared the inefficacy of outward religion—Rom. ii. 28, 29.

Judas and the foolish virgins awfully exemplified it—Matt. xxv. 3, 11, 12.

Our Lord has warned us all respecting it—Matt. vii. 21—23.

3. Will not a feigned allegiance be discovered by him?

We may easily deceive our fellow-creatures—

But every motion of our hearts is visible to Christ—Heb. iv. 13.

Nor can the most specious appearances deceive him—John ii. 24, 25.

In his final judgment he will shew that he was privy to our most secret thoughts and desires—1 Cor. iv. 5.

4. Shall we not wish at last that we had been sincere and upright?

The reproach which attends the exercise of real religion, may make us satisfied with the form of it at present—

But in the day of judgment we shall see our folly—Wisd. v. 1—9.

We shall not know what to reply to this question then—

The vain excuse we now make we shall not even dare to offer—

APPLICATION.

Let all then seek to become christians indeed—

Let us not be afraid to confess our Lord before men—

But let our lives be consistent with our professions—

Let us trust in the Lord as simply as if obedience were *not* required—

Let us obey the Lord as zealously as if obedience *only* were required—

---

## THE EVIL AND DANGER OF BACKSLIDING.

Hos. iv. 16.   Israel slideth back, as a backsliding heifer.   (H. H.)

SUCH is the influence of bad example, that it is extremely difficult to withstand its attractions, even at the time that we behold its fatal effects. Israel, or the ten tribes, from their first apostacy under Jeroboam, were irreclaimably addicted to idolatry.   The prophet finding his efforts vain with respect to them, turns to Judah, and intreats that they would not tread in the steps of Israel,* who, like an untamed and refractory bullock, had entirely cast off the yoke, and refused all subjection to Jehovah.

Humiliating as this account of Israel is, it is but too just a representation of the christian world, whose conduct is utterly unworthy of the name they bear, and from whose ways we cannot stand at too great a distance.

To impress this awful truth upon your minds, we propose to shew,

I. WHEN WE MAY BE SAID TO RESEMBLE A BACKSLIDING HEIFER—

We owe submission to our heavenly Master; but give too much reason for the comparison in the text.   This resemblance may be seen in us

1. When we will not draw in God's yoke at all—

Unconverted men in every age and place are rebels against God, Exod. v. 2.   Ps. xii. 4.   Jer. ii. 31, & vii. 24; and, though all are not equally

* Ver 15.   At Gilgal and at Bethel, where God had formerly been worshipped, idols were now set up.   The prophet, exhorting Judah not to go to those places, calls Beth-el, (the house of God,) Beth-aven, (the house of vanity.)

profligate in their manners, all are equally averse to spiritual employments: the law of God is considered as imposing on them an intolerable yoke, to which they will not, they cannot submit. Rom. viii. 7. They are indeed subjected to it against their will; but neither chastisements nor encouragements can prevail upon them to draw in it: on the contrary, like a ferocious bullock, they are insensible of favors, and they fret at rebukes. Jer. xxxi. 18.

2. When we draw in it only by fits and starts—

Many appear willing to obey God in a time of sickness, Isa. xxvi. 16, or after some signal deliverance, Psa. cvi. 12, 13, or under an impressive sermon, Exod. xxiv. 3, 7, Jam. i. 24, or during a season of peace and tranquility: Matt. xiii. 21: but, as soon as ever the particular occasion that called forth their pious resolutions has ceased, or they find that they must suffer for Christ's sake, they forget the vows that are upon them, and return to their former state of carelessness and indifference. Psa. lxxviii. 34—37. They renew their resolutions perhaps at certain seasons; but "their goodness is as the morning dew, or as the early cloud that passeth away." Thus, like a heifer that will draw for one moment and will not the next, they are, in the strongest sense of the words, unprofitable servants.

3. When we grow weary of the yoke—

It is not uncommon for persons to go on well for a season, and yet draw back at last. They grow weary of *performing their duties*, of *exercising their graces*, of *mortifying their lusts*. If they maintain an observance of public duties, they become remiss in those of the family and the closet: their delight in the scriptures languishes; their meditations are cold; their devotions formal. Their faith, their hope, their love operate with less vital energy: and their besetting sins, whatever they were, regain their strength, and resume their ascendancy. These are like a horse or bullock, which, after having yielded to the yoke for a season, becomes restive and ungovernable, and disappoints thereby the expectations of its owner.

Lest the frequency of these characters should tempt us to think favorably of them, we proceed to shew,

II. THE EVIL AND DANGER OF SUCH A STATE—

We shall notice,

1. The evil of it—

A backslidden state, in whomsoever it is found, is exceeding sinful; but in those who have made some profession of religion, it is attended with peculiar aggravations.

*It is a contemning of God;* of his Majesty, which demands our subjection, and of his mercy, which would accept and reward our poor services. And it is in this light that God himself frequently complains of it. Numb. xi. 20; 1 Sam. ii. 30, and 2 Sam. xii. 10; Ps. x. 13.

*It is a justifying of the wicked;* for it says to them, in fact, "I was once as you are, and thought I should become happier by serving God: but I find by experience that there is no profit in serving him; and therefore I am returning to your state, which is, on the whole, the happier and more desirable."

*It is a discouraging of the weak.* Little do false professors think how much evil they do in this way. Mal. ii. 8. Many are induced to follow their example in some things, under the idea that they are innocent; and are thus drawn from one sin to another, till they make shipwreck of a good conscience, and utterly turn away from the faith.

And need we multiply words any further to shew the evil of backsliding from God? Well does God himself call it "a wonderful and a horrible thing." Jer. v. 30.

2. The danger of it—

*This is an iniquity which God marks* with peculiar indignation; Jer. ii 19, 21, 22; and never fails to visit it, sooner or later, with some awful token of his displeasure.

*The first symptoms of declension lead,* if not speedily mourned over and resisted, *to utter apostacy.* Prov. xiv. 14. The disposition to backslide will soon increase, till it become inveterate, and, unless by a marvellous interposition of God himself, incurable.

*The misery that will be incurred by means of it will far exceed all that have been endured, if no profession of religion had been ever made.* "If any man draw back," says God, "my soul shall have no pleasure in him: he " draws back to certain and everlasting perdition:" Heb. x. 38, 39; and "it would have been better for him never to have known the way of righteousness, than, after having known it, to turn back from it." Matt. xii. 45. 2 Pet. ii. 21.

Let these consequences be duly weighed, and nothing need be added to shew us the importance of "holding fast our profession without wavering.'

To IMPROVE this subject, we shall,

1. Assist you in ascertaining your state before God—

Since all are "bent to backslide" more or less, it is of great importance to inquire of what kind our backslidings are, and to see whether they are merely the infirmities of an upright soul, or the revolt of an apostate. It is indeed difficult to determine this with precision; yet something may be said to aid you in this inquiry.

Examine diligently the *cause,* the *duration,* and the *effects* of your backslidings. Those of the sincere arise from the weakness of their flesh, while yet their spirit is as willing as ever: but those of the hypocrite proceed from a radical disaffection to the ways of God. Those of the sincere continue but a little time, and are an occasion of greater diligence: those of the hypocrite remain, and become the habit of his soul. Those of the sincere humble him in the dust: those of the hypocrite produce a blindness of mind, a searedness of conscience, and a hardness of heart.

But though we thus discriminate for the information of your judgment, we recommend all to stand fast in the Lord, and to guard against the first risings of spiritual decay. Gal. vi. 9.

2. Give a word of counsel to those in different states—

*Are you altogether backslidden from God?* O return to him, and take upon you his "light and easy yoke!" He invites you with all the tenderness of a father; Jer. iii. 12, 14, 22; he declares himself exceedingly averse to punish you according to your desert; Hos. xi. 7, 8; and he promises to "heal your backslidings, and love you freely." Hos. xiv. 4.

*Are you drawing in his yoke?* Bless and adore your God, who has inclined and enabled you to do so. It is his power, and his power alone, that has kept you hitherto: 1 Pet. i. 5; and therefore he must have all the praise. And in order to your continued stedfastness, reflect often on the evil and danger of backsliding; I may add too, on the comfort and benefit of serving God. Surely He is a good Master. Let but your hearts be right with him, and "none of his commandments will appear grievous to you:" 1 John v. 3; on the contrary, you will find that "*in* keeping his commandments there is great reward," Psa. xix. 11, and that your labor shall not be in vain with respect to the eternal world. "Be ye faithful unto death, and he will give you a crown of life." Rev. ii. 10

## ADVICE TO BACKSLIDERS.

**Rev.** iii. 2.—Be watchful, and strengthen the things which remain, that are ready to die.
(S. S.)

THE epistles to the churches of Asia seem descriptive of the state of the several churches at the time they were written—
But they are for the most part applicable also to other churches—
There are too many societies of christians that resemble that at Sardis—
There was much profession and but little life among them—
This our Lord signified to them in the letter he dictated to St. John—
ver. 1.
On account of it he gave them the salutary admonition in the text.
I. WHEN IT MAY BE SAID THAT THE THINGS WHICH REMAIN IN US ARE READY TO DIE.
It is here supposed that there were some good things in the Sardian church, though they were much on the decline—
What is said therefore of their being "dead" must be understood rather in reference to their *frame* than their *state*—
The things which remain in us are ready to die, *when our graces languish*—
The exercise of our graces is a sure test both of the reality and degree of our spiritual life—
We may form a judgment by examining,
Our faith.
The office of faith is to realize invisible things—
When it is vigorous it discovers the comparative value of heaven and earth—
It regards the promises and threatenings of God as certain—
Hence it stimulates the soul to an active pursuit of its chief good—
But many decline in their apprehension of divine things—
They neither see so clearly, nor feel so powerfully the truths of God as they once did—
They consequently relax their diligence in the ways of God—
Such persons are evidently in the state of those at Sardis—
Our hope.
Faith sees the reality, and hope anticipates the enjoyment of heavenly things—
When hope is lively it serves as an anchor of the soul—
It keeps us from fainting under the trials we meet with—
But oftentimes it is suffered to grow dead—
Then the future prospects are less valued—
Earthly things also rise in importance—
We are more discouraged with any difficulties—
We lose our enjoyment of heavenly things—
In this state the things that remain are ready to die—
Our love.
Love is as wings to the believing soul—
It carries us on with ardor and delight—
It makes us entertain low thoughts of all we do—
It excites us to still greater exertions—
But when it decays, we lose our fervor—
Duties become a burden and a task—

They are performed with less frequency and spirituality—
We endure with less concern the hidings of God's face—
We are more indifferent respecting his return to our souls—
What can more strongly indicate the dying state of a soul ?—
Moreover, the things which remain are ready to die, *when our corrup-tions increase.*

Graces and corruptions are as the scales of a balance—
The growth of corruption argues the decay of the divine life—
And such decay is manifest,
1. When our besetting sin resumes its ascendency.
It is the effect of grace to mortify and subdue our besetting sin—
But that sin is rarely if ever extinguished in this world—
It is generally the first that discovers our declensions—
When that regains its power, we are sure that it is ill with the soul—
2. When our natural hardness and obduracy of heart return
Divine grace brings a tenderness of spirit—
It shews itself by humiliation and contrition—
But sin will blind the eyes, and harden the heart—
In this state we shall feel less compunction *in* or *after* the commission of sin—
When conscience thus fails in its office we are in a dying state indeed—
3. When we are unwilling to be reclaimed
A heart duly impressed desires the light—
But persons in a backslidden state often feel averse to it—
They are backward to be told of their faults—
They are ready to palliate and excuse them—
They willingly expose themselves to the temptations of sin—
This is the worst symptom that a *living* soul can experience—
May God now accompany with his blessing,
II. OUR LORD'S ADVICE TO PERSONS IN SUCH A STATE.
None can more need advice for their bodies, than these for their souls.
1. Be watchful,
Against self-deception
There are many things which may hide our condition from us—
We may easily mistake gifts for graces—
We may attribute to God's Spirit what results from the operation of natural principles—
We may be less sensible of decay because it happens to be gradual—
The heart will suggest many plausible excuses—
It may satisfy itself also with hopes of a speedy revival—
But "be not deceived ; God is not mocked"—
Against the occasions of sin.
Many fall by means of their excessive care about worldly business—
Others decline through mixing too much with worldly company—
Too free an use even of lawful things injures many—
But all decay through a neglect of sacred duties—
Be watchful then against occasions of sin—
See the effect which they have produced upon you—
Resist them in future on their first appearance—Prov. iv. 14, 15.
2. Strengthen the things that remain.
Go to Christ for his Spirit.

Christ is the only source of spiritual strength*
In vain will be all human endeavors without his aid—
Go then, and plead with him that promise—Jer. iii. 22.
" 'They that dwell under his shadow shall return," &c.—Hos. **xiv. 7.**
Exercise your graces more diligently.
Every thing improves by exercise—
Put forth therefore your faith, your hope, your love—
'Stir up the gift of God that is in you"—
You will then experience the truth of that promise—2 Pet. i. 10. 11.
Lay home upon your heart the most powerful considerations.
Think how uncomfortable a declining state is ι how dishonorable **to**
God, and dangerous to your own souls!
Consider that if God ever restore you, he may do it in such a **way as**
shall be extremely terrible and distressing—
But what if he should "come at an unexpected hour ?"—
Let instant attention then be paid to the direction following **the text—**
Rev. iii. 3.
Address,
1. To those who have no marks of life in them.
They who are in a declining state are in great danger—
If they be not restored "their last state will be worse than their begin-
ning"—
What danger then must they be in who exercise no graces, and indulge
numberless corruptions !—
Oh! repent, ere it be too late—
2. To those who are enjoying the divine life.
" Be not high-minded, but fear," and be watchful—
"Work out your own salvation with fear and trembling"—
If it be difficult to proceed, it is still more so to recover lost ground—
Remember your strength consists in depending upon Christ—
When you are weak in yourselves then only are you truly strong—
Comfort yourselves with that description of your almighty Guardian—
Jude 24.

---

## ON EATING AND DRINKING OUR OWN DAMNATION.

1 Cor. xi. 27, 29.—Whosoever shall eat this bread, and drink this cup of the Lord unworthily, shall be guilty of the body and blood of the Lord. . . . . . For he that eateth
and drinketh unworthily, eateth and drinketh damnation to himself, not discerning the
Lord's body.  (S. S.)

THE more excellent any thing is, the greater is the guilt contracted by tne
abuse of it—
A contempt of the law is not so bad as a contempt of the gospel—Heb.
x. 28, 29
An irreverent attendance on divine ordinances is exceedingly sinful—
But to profane the Lord's supper is worse, inasmuch as that institution is
more solemn and brings us nearer to God—

*Rev. iii. 1. "He hath the seven spirits of God," i. e. a fulness of all the gifts and
graces of the Spirit, with a power to dispense them in all their perfection and variety.

Hence when St. Paul repr 'ved the former, he spake mildly—1 Cor. xiv 33, 40.

But when he reproved the l: tter, he spake with great severity—

I. WHAT IT IS TO EAT THE BREAD, AND DRINK THE CUP OF THE LORD UNWORTHILY.

To understand this, we should enquire how the Corinthians behaved—*

The abuses of which they were guilty are impracticable now—

Nevertheless we may imitate them in our spirit and temper—

Like them we shall eat and drink unworthily if we do it,

1. Ignorantly.

The Corinthians did not discriminate between the common and religious use of the consecrated elements—

Many at this time also partake without discerning the Lord's body—

They, not remembering his death, defeat the end for which the sacrament was instituted—

2. Irreverently.

The customs of our country do not admit of our meeting in the tumult uous way that was practiced at Corinth—1 Cor. xi. 21.

But many are altogether as destitute of reverence and sacred awe—

A light, worldly, impenitent heart is unbecoming that solemnity—

Such a frame, if habitual, makes us partake unworthily—

3. Uncharitably.

The rich did not impart of their provisions to the poor—1 Cor. xi. 22.

We also may be equally destitute of christian love—

We may be haughty, injurious, unforgiving, &c.—

Such a frame wholly unfits us for the Lord's table—Matt. v. 23, 24

4. Sensually.

The Corinthians made it an occasion for intemperance and excess—

Though we cannot imitate them in this, we may be as carnal as they—

A want of spirituality and affiance in Christ makes our service carnal—

Nor can such a service be acceptable to Him who will be worshipped in spirit and in truth—

To attend at the Lord's table in such a manner is no slight or venial offense.

II. THE CONSEQUENCE OF SO DOING.

The consequences mentioned in the text respect,

1. The guilt we contract.

They were "guilty of the body and blood of our Lord" who crucified him, as are they also who apostatize from his truth, Heb. vi. 6.

They too are involved in the same guilt who partake unworthily of the Lord's supper—

They manifest a contempt of this sacrifice, Heb. x. 29.

What dreadful iniquity is this!—

How carefully should we abstain from the commission of it!—

2. The punishment we incur.

The word "damnation" imports temporal judgment†—

Eternal damnation is by no means a necessary consequence of this sin, Matt. xii. 31.

---

*Ver. 20—22.—Their conduct seems at first sight to be absolutely inconsistent with a profession of christianity. But, having been accustomed to such behaviour in their feasts during their Gentile state, they were as yet too much addicted to their former habits.

†The apostle explains his meaning in the following verse; "for, for this cause," &c. and he tells us that it was a chastisement inflicted to keep them from eternal condemnation, ver. 32.

Yet if it be unrepented of, no doubt this punishment will follow—

And we may expect some spiritual or temporal judgments for it *here*—

We should therefore examine ourselves well before we attend the table of the Lord, ver. 28.

ADDRESS,

1. Those who urge this as an excuse for neglecting the Lord's supper.

There are many who under this pretext cover their own unwillingness to yield themselves up to God—

But God will not admit their vain excuses—

The habitual neglect of their duty insures the punishment which they desire to avoid—

Let all then devote themselves to the Lord in the use of all his instituted ordinances—

2. Those who are really kept away by a fear of incurring this punishment.

Many are kept from the table by a sense of their own unworthiness—

But to be unworthy, and to partake unworthily, are very different things*—

Yet if we have partaken unworthily in past times, let us humble ourselves for it; and then may we come again with joy—

This has been the experience of many, 2 Chron. xxx. 15—23, and may be ours also.

---

## THE CONSEQUENCES OF NEGLECTING PRAYER.

Isai. lxiv. 7. There is none that called upon thy name, that stirreth up himself to take hold of thee : for thou hast hid thy face from us. (S. S.)

MAN is encompassed with dangers from which no human foresight can deliver him—

He is oppressed with wants which no creature can supply—

It is to God that he must look for the blessings which he needs—

But he is naturally so averse to prayer, that he will bear all his own burthens rather than apply to God for relief—

On this account it is that so many faint under their afflictions—

And this was the ground of God's controversy with his people,

I. THE NATURE OF PRAYER.

Prayer is represented in the scriptures by a variety of expressions—

It is here set forth under the idea of "calling upon God."

Petitions, either with or without a form, are not worthy the name of prayer, if they be unattended with a devout spirit—

Prayer is a work of the heart rather than of the lips—

It supposes that we feel our wants, desire to have them supplied, and believe that God is able and willing to relieve them—

It is also described as a "taking hold of God."

---

* A rebel against a mild and merciful prince is unworthy of pardon: but if ne receive with gratitude the pardon offered him, and return to his allegiance, he receives it worthily. Thus we are *unworthy* of the smallest mercies, and much more of the children's bread : but if we receive this bread with humility, gratitude, and an increasing devotedness of heart to God, we receive it as we ought, that is, *worthily.*

God has set himself, as it were, before us in tne promises—
There we may lay hold on him by faith—
We may address him as the patriarch of old—Gen. xxxii. 26.
And this is the mean prescribed by God for the obtaining of his blessings
—Isai xxvii. 5.
It is further called a "stirring up of oneself" to lay hold on God.
It is no easy thing to gain access to God in prayer—
We engage in it for the most part with much reluctance—
Our thoughts wander, ere we are aware, and in spite of our endeavors to
fix them—
We seem to lose the accustomed energy of our minds—
We need again and again to stir up our sluggish hearts—
When we consider the duty in this light, we shall see reason to lament,
II. THE GENERAL NEGLECT OF IT.
Many live entirely without prayer.
They are wholly occupied with worldly concerns—
They are not sensible of any *spiritual* wants—
They rely on their own industry for *temporal* advancement—
They acknowledge not before God either their sins or their necessities—
Others only occasionally lift up their hearts to heaven.
They will cry under the pressure of some heavy affliction—Isai xxvi. 16.
But they resemble those spoken of by the prophet—Hos. vii. 14.
Like metal from the fire they soon return to their former hardness—Ps·
lxxviii. 34—37.
After some signal deliverance too they will praise God—
But, like the Israelites, they will soon forget his mercies—Ps. cvi. 11—13.
Some will maintain with constancy an external regard to this duty—
They will repeat their accustomed form at stated seasons—
Or they will offer a few general and cold petitions—
And with this outward act they will rest satisfied—
They feel no pleasure in the duty, but perform it as a task—
But there are few indeed who pray to God aright.
There is a remnant now, as there was in the prophet's days *—
There are some who "stir up their souls to lay hold on God"—
But these are few when compared with the bulk of mankind—
They may be said comparatively to be "none" at all—
To counteract this evil we proceed to set forth,
III. THE CONSEQUENCES OF THIS NEGLECT.
The tokens of God's displeasure, which those in the text experienced,
will be experienced by all who neglect prayer—
God will surely "hide his face from them."
He will not reveal to them his glory.
He reveals himself to his people as he does not unto the world—John
xiv. 22.
He shines into their hearts to discover to them his glory—
But he will vouchsafe no such mercy to those who call not upon him—
His perfections are to them rather an object of terror than of admiration—
He will not manifest to them his love.
He often "sheds abroad his love in the hearts" of those who seek him—
But the neglecters of prayer "intermeddle not with their joy"—Prov
xiv. 10.

---

* Isai. viii. 18. The prophet certainly did not mean to include them in his censure.

They are strangers to the Spirit of adoption—
They rather banish God from their thoughts, and wish like the fool*—
He will not communicate to them his blessings.
His faithful worshippers have all the blessings of grace and glory—
But others have no part or lot with them—
The blessings they do enjoy are turned into a curse unto them—
And to eternity must they ascribe their misery to their own neglect

APPLICATION.
They, who live without prayer, should consider these things,
This offense has been awfully marked by the indignation of God‡—
How bitter must be the reflections of those who perish through this neglect!—
Surely all should seek the Lord while he *may* be found—
They also, who are formal in prayer, should lay them to heart.
These, as being more liable to deceive themselves, are in greater danger—
Our prayers must be fervent in order to be effectual—James v. 16.
If we would enter into heaven, we must press into it with violence—Matt. xi. 12.
Nor should this subject ever be forgotten by those who profess godliness.
Unless we stir up ourselves continually, we shall soon lose the divine presence—
We cannot guard too much against formality in prayer—
Let us be encouraged by God's gracious declaration ‖—

———————

## MEN'S PROUD CONTEMPT OF GOD.

Psalm, x. 4, 5.—The wicked, through the pride of his countenance, will not seek after God. God is not in all his thoughts: his ways are always grievous: thy judgments are far above out of his sight: as for all his enemies, he puffeth at them. (S. S.

PRIDE, when manifested in a flagrant manner, universally excites disgust; so hateful is it, when divested of the specious garb in which it is generally clothed. But though all hate pride, when it appears in others, few are sensible how much it reigns within their own bosoms. In our converse with man, this evil disposition is ready to shew itself on every occasion: but in our conduct towards God, it is the fruitful parent of habitual neglect, and atheistical contempt. This is affirmed in the passage before us, in which we may notice,

I. THE STATE OF THE WICKED.

It is not easy to conceive a more humiliating description of their character than that given us by the Psalmist:
They " will not seek after God."

* Ps. xiv. 1. The words in Italics are not in the original.

† If all the souls that are banished from the divine presence were asked, " Wherefore has God hid his face from you?" they must assign the reason that is given in the text.

‡ Ps. lxxxi. 10—12. " God gave them up:" to what? to their enemies? to death? or to immediate and eternal condemnation? No; to what was worse than even that, " their own hearts lust," that they might " treasure up wrath against the day of wrath."

‖ Prov. xv. 8. God is not more pleased with the songs of angels than with the sighs and groans of a contrite soul.

420

God invites them to seek his face, and promises that he will be found of them; but they cannot be prevailed upon either by promises or threats: they will seek with eagerness an earthly object, that may make them happy; but they account God unworthy of any notice or regard, Job xxxv. 10.

" He is not even admitted into their thoughts."

It is astonishing to what a degree men often banish God from their minds. They will pass days, months, and even years, without one reverential thought of him, unless when they are alarmed by some awful providence, or awakened by some faithful discourse: and *then*, unless the grace of God prevent them, they will cast him out of their minds again as soon as possible, and drown their thoughts in business or dissipation, Job xxi. 14, 15.

They account " his ways," as far as they know them, "grievous."

When urged to devote themselves to God in sincerity and truth, they conceive that such a state is unattainable, or, at least, incompatible with the common duties and offices of life. They call the indulgence of their lusts, liberty; and the exercise of vital godliness, an intolerable bondage. Every part of the divine life is irksome to them, and *that* too, not occasionally, but " always," without any change or intermission.

The "judgments of God are far above out of their sight."

By the "judgments" of God we understand his word and works. Now these are not only out of their sight in some particulars (for they are incomprehensible in some respects even to the most enlightened saints) but they are altogether foolishness unto them, 1 Cor. ii. 14. When the mysteries of redemption are opened, they are esteemed by them as " cunningly devised fables:" and when the marvellous interpositions of Providence are insisted on, they are ready to exclaim, with Ezekiel's hearers, " Ah! Lord God, doth he not speak parables?" Ezek. xx. 49.

" As for all their enemies, they puff at them."

If God himself threaten them as an enemy, they disregard his menaces. The denunciations of his wrath are deemed by them unworthy of any serious attention. They even puff at them with contempt and disdain. They quiet all their fears, saying, like them of old, " Tush, God shall not see; neither will the Almighty regard it:" Ps. xciv. 7. " I shall have peace, though I walk in the imagination of my heart," Deut. xxix. 19.

In order to account for this state of things, let us trace it to,

II. THE REAL SOURCE OF THEIR WICKEDNESS.

We might trace this practical atheism to men's ignorance and unbelief: but the Psalmist suggests to us the original ground and occasion of it: it all arises from the pride of their hearts.

Men are *too good*, in their own apprehension, *to need* God s *mercy*.

They will confess that they are not altogether so good as they might be; but they do not think they deserve God's wrath and indignation. Why then should they trouble themselves to ask for mercy at his hands, when they are in no danger of suffering his judgments?

They are also *too strong to need his aid*.

They imagine, that they can repent when they please, and that, whensoever they resolve, they can easily carry their resolutions into effect. If they thought that "without God they could do nothing," and that " he must give them both to will and to do," then there were reason for imploring his assistance: but, when they acknowledge no such dependence upon God, wherefore should they seek his aid?

Moreover, they are *too wise to need the teachings of his Spirit*.

They see perhaps their need of a revelation to discover to them the mind and will of God; but, when that is once given, they are not conscious that they need a spiritual illumination to discover the truths contained in it. They suppose their reason to be as sufficient for the investigation of spiritual, as of carnal things: and under that persuasion, they consider all application to God for the teachings of his Spirit, as enthusiastic and absurd.

Finally, they are *too happy to need the divine presence.*

They are occupied with carnal pleasure, and wish for nothing beyond it. If only they can have the undisturbed indulgence of their appetites, it is, to them, all the paradise they desire. As for the light of God's countenance, and the manifestations of his love, they know not what is meant by such things; they suppose that they exist only in the pretensions of hypocrites, and the conceits of fanatics.

In short, like those of Laodicea, they possess such an imaginary sufficiency within themselves, that they have no need of God at all, Rev. iii. 17. And hence it is that they care not to have God in all their thoughts.

INFER,

1. How astonishing is the depravity of human nature!

If all be not equally addicted to gross sins, all are equally " without God in the world," Eph. ii. 12: all have a " carnal mind that is enmity against God," Rom. viii. 7. Alas! What a picture of human nature! Let "every mouth then be stopped, and all the world become guilty before God," Rom. iii. 10, 11, 12, 19.

2. How great is the change that takes place in conversion!

The state of a converted soul forms a perfect contrast with that of the wicked. " Old things pass away, and all things become new." Let all then ask themselves, Am I now devoting myself to God, as once I did to the world; and despising the world, as once I despised God? This were indeed "a new creation," 2 Cor. v. 17.

3. How necessary is conversion in order to an enjoyment of heaven!

There must be within ourselves a meetness for heaven before we can enjoy it, Col. i. 12. Let not those then, who banish God from their thoughts, and cast off his yoke, suppose that they could be happy in heaven, even if they were admitted there. If they would delight themselves in God for ever, they must obtain in this world a conformity to his image, and a delight in his commandments.

---

## THE CERTAINTY THAT SIN WILL FIND US OUT.

Numb. xxxii. 23.—Behold ye have sinned against the Lord: and be sure your sin will find you out. (S. S.)

THE fear of punishment, if not the best, is certainly the most common preservative from sin—

Under the Mosaic dispensation it was the principal motive with which the divine commands were enforced—

Nor did St. Paul, though so well acquainted with the liberal spirit of the gospel, think it wrong to " persuade men by the terrors of the Lord"—

The words before us, therefore may, not improperly, be addressed to us*—
We may take occasion from them to consider,

I. IN WHAT MANNER WE HAVE SINNED AGAINST THE LORD

It would be endless to attempt an enumeration of all the sins we have committed—

We shall confine ourselves to that view of them which the context suggests.

The sin against which Moses cautioned the two tribes was, unfaithfulness to their engagements—

And, a preferring of their present ease to the executing of the work which God had assigned them—

Now we promised at our baptism to renounce the world, the flesh, and the devil—†

These promises *then* made for us, we have renewed at our confirmation and at the Lord's table—

But how have we kept the covenant which we have thus solemnly entered into?—

Have we not maintained that friendship with the world which is enmity with God? James iv. 4.

Have we not rather sought to please than to mortify our carnal appetites? Tit. iii. 3.

Has not the god of this world led us captive at his will? Eph. ii. 2. 2 Tim. ii. 26.

And is not such a life one continued violation of our baptismal engagements?—

But the sin referred to in the text, will scarcely bear any comparison with ours.

The Israelites were to maintain a warfare with men; we with the devil, Eph. vi. 12.

They were to fight for an earthly portion; we, an heavenly, 1 Cor. ix. 25.

They might have urged that *their* aid was unnecessary, when *God* was engaged—

And that, after all, the prize was an inadequate reward for such fatigue and danger—

But, can we hope to conquer without exerting our own powers?—

Do we suppose that God will subdue our enemies without our concurrence?—

Or can we say that the prize held forth to us is not worth the contest?—

If our engagements be more solemn, our work more noble, and our reward more glorious than theirs, our sin in disregarding all must be proportionably greater—

Yet who amongst us must not confess that he has forgotten all his vows?—

Behold then, we may say to all, "Ye have sinned against the Lord"—
Nor are we to suppose that our sin will always pass unnoticed.

---

* The tribes of Reuben and Gad had solicited permission to have the land of Jazer and of Gilead for their portion instead of any inheritance in the land of Canaan. Upon their promising to fight in conjunction with the other tribes until the whole of Canaan should be subdued, Moses acceded to the proposal; but warned them withal, that if they receded from their engagement, they should assuredly meet with a due recompense from God.

† See the Church Catechism.

II. WHAT ASSURANCE WE HAVE THAT OUR SIN SHALL FIND US OUT.

Sin may be said to find us out when it brings down the divine judgments upon us.

Conscience, stupified or seared, often forgets to execute its office—

Nor speaks, till God, by his Providence or Grace, awaken it—

Sometimes years elapse before it reproves our iniquities—Gen. xlii. 21, 22

Sometimes it testifies to our face as soon as our sin is committed—Matt. xxvi. 74, 75, and xxvii. 3, 4.

Whenever it thus condemns us, our sins may be said to find us out—

But the expression in the text imports rather the visitation of God for sin—

There is a punishment annexed to every violation of God's law—Ezek xviii. 4.

And sin then finds us out effectually when it brings that punishment upon us—

That it will find us out, we have the fullest possible assurance.

*The perfections of God's nature* absolutely preclude all hope of impunity.

If he be omnipresent, he must see; if omniscient, remember; if holy, hate; and if just, punish the violations of his law—

If he be possessed of veracity and power, he must execute the judgments he has denounced—

*The declarations of his Word* abundantly confirm this awful truth—Isa iii. 11. Rom. ii. 9 ; Ps. xxi. 8 ; Prov. xi. 21.

Sin leaves a track which can never be effaced; and evil, however slow-paced, will surely overtake it—Prov. xiii. 21 ; Ps. cxl. 11.

However scoffers may exult in their security, their ruin is fast approaching—2 Pet. ii. 3, and iii. 4, 9, and Deut. xxix. 19, 20.

*The remarkable instances* of sin being detected and punished in this world afford a strong additional testimony—

David and Gehazi, though so studious to conceal their guilt, had their iniquity marked in the punishment inflicted for it—2 Sam. xii. 9—12 ; 2 Kings v. 26, 27.

When according to human calculations, it was above two millions to one that Achan would escape, the lot fell on him by an infallible direction—Josh. vii. 14—18.

How much more then shall the most hidden things be brought to light hereafter !—

*The appointment of a day of final retribution* puts the matter beyond a possibility of doubt—

For what end can there be such a period fixed but that the actions of men may be judged—

And for what end can they be judged, but that every man may receive according to his deeds—Eccl. xii. 14.

We may then emphatically say to every sinner, "*Be sure, &c.*"—

INFER,

1. How earnest should we be in searching out our own sins !

We think little of evils which have been committed by us long ago—

And imagine that they are effaced from God's memory as well as from our own—

But every action, word and thought is noted in the book of his remembrance—

He sees the transaction of former years as if they had this moment passed—

All our iniquities are viewed by him in one accumulated mass—

Nor does he abhor them less than in the very instant they were committed—

Let us not then pass them over, or palliate them, as youthful follies—

Let us remember how exactly the Lord's threatenings were executed on the Israelites in the wilderness—Numb. xxxii. 10—13.

And endeavor to avert his judgments while space for repentance is allowed us—

Let us mourn over our innumerable violations of our baptismal covenant—

Let us lament our solicitude about a present portion, our aversion to fight the Lord's battles, and our indifference about the heavenly Canaan—

We must repent of these things, or lie under the guilt of them for ever—Ps. l. 21 ; Luke xiii. 3.

2. How thankful should we be that a way of escape is provided for us !

It is not sin lamented, but sin unrepented of, which will find us out—

There is a city of refuge provided for those who will flee to it—Heb. vi. 18.

The man, Christ Jesus, is an hiding-place from the impending storm—Isa. xxxii. 2.

If we flee to him, we may be sure that sin shall NOT find us out—

*Every perfection of the Deity* is pledged to save a believing penitent—1 John i. 9.

We are confirmed in this hope by the most *positive declarations of scripture*—Isa. vliv. 22 ; Mic. vii. 19 ; Heb. viii. 12.

We have most *authentic and astonishing instances* of sin forgiven—2 Sam. xii. 13 ; Luke vii. 47, and xxiii. 43.

And *the day of judgment* is appointed no less for the complete justification of believers than for the condemnation of unbelievers—2 Thess. i. 9, 10.

Let this blessed assurance then dwell richly on our minds—

Let it encourage us to take refuge under the Saviour's wings—Matt. xxiii. 37.

Let an holy confidence inspire those who have committed their souls to him—2 Tim. i. 12.

And let all rejoice and glory in him as able to save them to the uttermost—Heb. vii. 25.

## THE SIN OF MAKING LIGHT OF CHRIST.

### Matt. xxii. 5.—But they made light of it.  (S. S.)

WE are apt to condemn the Jews as blind and obstinate, because they rejected Christ in spite of the clearest evidence in his favor—but we ourselves are more guilty than they, because we enjoy much greater advantages for understanding the gospel than they did, and yet are as regardless of it as they were.

Our blessed Lord illustrated their conduct by a marriage-feast, to which they who were invited, refused to come.  The same invitation is sent to us ; and we, no less than they, " make light of it "

To bring home a conviction of this upon our minds, we shall shew,

I. WHAT ARE THE BLESSINGS WHICH WE ARE INVITED TO PARTAKE OF God is here represented as having made a marriage for his Son.

The figure of a marriage union is often used to represent the connection that subsists between Christ and his church—Jer. iii. 14; Hos. ii. 19, 20. He is the bridegroom, and the church is his bride—Isa. liv. 5; Rev. xxi. 9. And the connexion is then formed, when the church gives up herself to Christ as her head and Lord, and by faith becomes so united to him as to be one flesh, Eph. v. 30—32, or to speak more properly, "one spirit with him"—1 Cor. vi. 17.

The feast prepared on the occasion contains all the blessings of grace and glory.

There is nothing that can nourish or delight the soul which God has not prepared for the bride on her union with Christ—Isa. xxv. 6. She instantly becomes related to him, and is considered in all things as his daughter, an object of his affections, and a partaker of his inheritance.—Let any one enquire, What is there that my soul can desire in time or eternity? and he shall find it all set before him, that he may freely and richly enjoy it.—

To a participation of this feast we are sent to invite you.

In one view, they to whom we are sent, are the bride; but in another view, they are the guests.—The commission God has given to his servants is to "go out into the highways and hedges, and to bring in as many as they can find."—To you therefore we come, declaring that no unworthiness on your parts shall exclude you, provided you put on the wedding garment, which the Master of the feast has prepared for you.—Accept the invitation; and all the blessings of salvation shall be yours.—Pardon, peace, strength, and whatever else can comfort the weary, and support the weak, shall become the daily, the everlasting food of your souls.—

To evince how much our message is disregarded, we proceed to shew,

II. WHO ARE THEY THAT MAKE LIGHT OF THE INVITATION.

Among the numberless classes that might be mentioned, two only shall be selected;

1. They who satisfy themselves with excuses for declining it.

The persons, mentioned in the context, excused themselves on account of "their farms or merchandize."—But their pleas, however satisfactory in their own eyes, were not admitted by God.—On the contrary, he declared them to be "unworthy ever to taste of his supper."—Now what excuses has any man more urgent than these?—And if these were of no avail in their case, what right have we to think, that the plea of worldly business will be admitted in our favor?—If the prosecuting of our worldly business were really incompatible with the enjoyment of God, there can be no doubt which we ought to prefer.—He was "a *wise* merchant, who having found a pearl of great price, sold all that he had and bought it."—But our duties to God and to the world are by no means irreconcilable with each other.— And therefore the resting in such vain excuses shews, that we make light of the salvation offered us—

2. They who do not accept it with all thankfulness.

Blessings, like those set before us in the gospel, ought to be regarded as of the first importance.—Indifference towards them is a positive contempt of them.—If a slave, whom we had ransomed at a great price, and to whom we offered liberty, and affluence, and honor, should express no gratitude, no joy on the occasion, should we not think that he "made light of" our proffered kindness?—But what bondage is so dreadful as that in which we are held by sin and satan? or what liberty is like that of God's children? or what comparison is there between the riches and honors of this world, and those which are imparted to us on our union with Christ?—If then our joy and gratitude excited by the gospel salvation, be not in some measure proportioned to its value and importance, we cannot but be considered as making light of it—

Nor will this be thought a venial matter, if we duly consider,

III. THE FOLLY AND SINFULNESS OF THEIR CONDUCT.

But what words can sufficiently express this? for they make light of,

1. That which is of the greatest possible value.

Estimate the blessings of salvation either *positively* by the price paid for them, or *comparatively* by weighing them, as it were, in a balance against all other things, and then see what it is that they despise.—Only consider, that every one of those blessings was bought with blood, with the blood of God's co-equal, co-eternal Son, a price infinitely exceeding ten thousand worlds.—Is there no guilt, no folly in disregarding things of such inestimable value?—Bring into competition with them all that the world can give; and it will be found lighter than the dust upon the balance, yea, " altogether lighter than vanity itself."—Well therefore does the apostle put that unanswerable question, " How shall ye escape, if ye neglect so *great* salvation?—Heb. ii. 3.

2. That without which they can never be happy.

The creature, at best, is but as a " broken cistern : in vain shall any one go to it for solid happiness, Jer. ii. 13.—" There is not, there cannot be, any true peace to the wicked," Isa. xlviii. 22.—Let any man try to make himself happy, while the guilt of all his sins continues to lie upon him, and he is in awful suspense about his eternal state : he may be thoughtless as a child, or stupid as a beast; but he cannot be happy.—And if this be the case in the midst of all his gaiety, what will be his situation in a dying hour?—At all events, supposing him ever so happy in life and in death, how will he feel himself on his first entrance into the invisible world?—Will he who made light of the marriage-feast on earth, sit down with boldness at " the marriage supper of the Lamb in heaven?"—Will all those employments to which he was averse in this world, be at once his joy and delight, as soon as he passes into the world above?—If he disregarded earthly things, he would have reason on his side; because he might be happy in God, even though he were destitute of every thing else : but to hope for happiness without God is a desperate delusion; and consequently, to make light of the invitations of the gospel is nothing less than madness itself—

3. That which they are sure to value, when it will be gone beyond recovery.

*Here* men are of very different sentiments ; some accounting godliness the one thing needful, and others despising it as enthusiasm and needless singularity.—But in the eternal world there is no such diversity of opinion : the saints in glory are fully confirmed in the judgment they had formed on earth ; and the wicked in hell are fully convinced of their error ; the one know by their enjoyments how good it was to obey the heavenly call ; and the other know by their sufferings, what " a fearful thing it is to fall into the hands of the living God."—What then is it but madness to make light of that, which we are so sure to value when there remains to us no longer any possibility of attaining it?—Wisd. v. 4.

Let due weight be given to these considerations, and we shall need nothing more to convince us either of the folly or sinfulness of slighting the invitations of the gospel—

APPLICATION.

It is to be feared that, after all, many will persist in their infatuated conduct —But we would at least make one more effort to reclaim them ; and beg of God to render his word effectual to their conversion.—

Know then that the marriage supper is now prepared ; and we, as God's servants, come in his name to invite you to it.—We invite you *all* : the rich, the poor ; the old, the young ; the moral, the immoral.—We announce to you, that all things are ready. Are *ye* then not ready ?—If ye say, " We have not a suitable garment ; we declare to you, that the Master of the feast has provided garments for all his guests ; and that ye need only to be clothed with the unspotted robe of Christ's righteousness, and ye shall instantly be acceptable in the sight of God.—Put away then your excuses : receive thankfully the invitation sent you : and begin to feast upon those spiritual provisions that shall nourish your souls unto life eternal.—

---

## THE MANIFESTATION WHICH CHRIST HAS GIVEN OF THE FATHER.

John i. 18.—No man hath seen God at any time; the only begotten Son, which is in the bosom of the Father, he hath declared him. (S. S.)

THE knowledge of God is the great source of blessings to mankind
But the heathen world were altogether ignorant of him—
Nor were the Jews themselves fully instructed concerning him—
To make a full revelation of him to the world was a part of that work which was reserved for Christ himself—
And this office he performed, to the unspeakable comfort of this church and people—
The evangelist unites his testimony with that of John the Baptist in confirmation of this truth—
We shall enquire,

I. WHAT CHRIST HAS DECLARED OF THE FATHER.

God himself is invisible to the eye of sense—1 Tim. vi. 16.
Even Moses was permitted to see only his backparts—Exod. xxxiii. 23.
But Christ had a peculiar relation to the Father as " his only begotten son ;" and a most intimate acquaintance with him, as being from all eternity, and at that very hour, " in his bosom"—
He has made known the Father to us, and declared,

1. His nature.
Mankind had gross conceptions of the Deity as a material being—
But Christ has assured us of his perfect *spirituality*—John iv. 24.
Nor was the *Unity* of God clearly ascertained among the Gentiles—
But Christ has left no room for doubt upon this subject—Mark xii. 29.
He has moreover revealed to us a *Trinity* of persons in the Godhead—
He has affirmed in the plainest terms his own Oneness with the Father—John x. 30.
He has spoken of the Holy Ghost as co-existing with himself and with the Father—John xv. 26.
And has joined the Three together as equal in authority and honor—Matt. xxviii. 19.
Thus has he enabled us by faith to " see him who is invisible"—

2. His perfections.

God had long since proclaimed his own name to Moses—Exod. xxxiv. 6, 7.

But Christ has afforded us more abundant discoveries of all his attributes—

He has clearly shewn us that his goodness is unbounded, Matt. v. 45 his sovereignty uncontrolled, Matt. xi. 25, 26, his power irresistible, Matt. xxvi. 53, his justice inflexible, ib. 42, his mercy infinite, John iii. 16, 17, and his truth inviolable—Luke xvi. 17.

There is not any thing relating to his Father, the knowledge of which could be at all serviceable to us, that he has not revealed—John xv. 15

He did not however merely utter these things like the prophets of old.

II. How HE DECLARED HIM.

Christ had formerly spoken of God in and by the prophets—1 Pet. i. 11 But now he declared the Father in a different manner.

1. By exhibiting a perfect pattern of him.

He was himself an exact resemblance of the Father—Heb. i. 3.

And in his conduct exhibited every perfection of the Deity—John viii. 29

Hence a sight of him was, in fact, a sight of the Father himself—John xiv. 7—9.

2. By making known his counsels.

Much of the Father's counsels had lain hid from the foundation of the world, or had been very imperfectly revealed—

Christ opened them to his hearers as they were able to bear them—John xvi. 12.

He made known God's intention to admit the Gentiles into his church—Matt. viii. 11, 12.

And assured us that the most abandoned of mankind should be cordially received the very instant he returned to God—Luke xv. 20.

But that none of whatever character could be saved, unless they sought acceptance with God through his mediation—John xiv. 6.

Thus by these declarations he has enabled us to attain a more perfect knowledge of the Father's mind and will—

3. By exerting a secret energy on the minds of men.

No man could know the Father unless Christ revealed him inwardly by his Spirit, as well as outwardly by the world—Matt. xi. 27.

His very disciples understood not until he opened their eyes—Luke xxiv. 45.

Nor can we attain to a true knowledge of God in any other way—

The " word must come to us in power and in the Holy Ghost," or it will come in vain—1 Thess. i. 5.

But when applied by his Spirit, it shall teach us plainly of the Father—John xvi. 25.

INFER,

1. How glorious a person must Christ be.

The description given of him shews his superiority above every created being—

He is not the Son of God by creation, as the angels are, nor by regeneration and adoption, as men; but by an inexplicable generation, his "only-begotten"—

And, as well in his incarnate as in his pre-existent state, was continually " in the bosom of the Father"—John iii. 13.

Nor was any other worthy to reveal the Father to us—

Let us then entertain just conceptions of his worth and dignity—

And manifest our delight in him as the saints in heaven did—Rev v. 5—9.

2. How precious ought the scriptures to be to us!

Job and David had but a small portion of the scriptures in their hands—

Yet did they value them above every thing in the world—Job xxviii. 12· Ps. cxix. 72.

How much more should we, who possess the sacred oracles entire!—

In these is recorded every thing that Christ has declared—

And by these we may be made wise unto salvation—2 Tim. iii. 15.

Let us then search them with diligence, and treasure them up in our hearts—

Nor let a day pass without digging into those invaluable mines—Prov ii. 4.

3 How inexcusable are they who are ignorant of God!

It is to our shame that many of us are still ignorant of God—1 Cor. xv. 34.

We have not that knowledge of him that produces correspondent affections towards him—

But what excuse can we offer in extenuation of our guilt?—

Has not Christ declared the Father in order that we might know him?—

And is he not willing also to reveal him in us by a powerful energy on our souls?—

Some, doubtless, are more guilty than others in proportion as they have possessed means of instruction—

But all will find the consequences of their ignorance most tremendous— 2 Thess. 1. 8.

Let all begin then to enquire after God with their whole hearts—

Nor rest till they have attained that knowledge of him which is life eternal—John xvii. 3.

---

## CHRIST THE ONLY FOUNDATION.

1 Cor. iii. 11.—Other foundation can no man lay, than that is laid, which is Jesus Christ. (S. S.)

THERE is not any thing more injurious to the church of God than a party-spirit: yet even in the apostolic age did it begin to distract the Christian community. At Corinth it prevailed, and rose to an alarming height: and St. Paul was obliged to exert all his influence in order to counteract it. He reminded the partisans, that, as "God's building," they should be cemented together with brotherly love: that they should study to shew themselves worthy of the place they held in the church, in expectation of that day when all their works should be tried by fire; and that, instead of fomenting strifes and divisions, they should unite with each other in cleaving stedfastly to the one foundation, whereon they stood.

The declaration in the text is plain, and of infinite importance.

To enter more fully into it we shall consider,

1. WHAT FOUNDATIONS MEN LAY FOR THEMSELVES.

Every man has some foundation for his hope. Though there are many shades of difference in the sentiments of different men, yet their grounds of hope may be reduced to two;

1. Their own goodness.

Some think that nothing but gross sin can expose them to the wrath of God. They therefore congratulate themselves as having never done any thing to merit his displeasure. Others imagine that they may trust in the good works that they have done. They have, in their own apprehension, been regular in their duties to God and man : nor can they conceive that *they* should have reason to fear. Thus, like the Pharisee of old, they thank God that they are not as other men ; and are filled with self-complacency, because they are punctual in the observance of certain duties, Luke xviii. 11, 12.

2. Their own works and Christ's merits united.

Many, who see, that their own works cannot justify them according to the strict tenor of the law, yet hope that they will, according to the milder demands of the gospel. If they see that these will not suffice, they will look to Christ to supply their deficiencies. If they see, that such an union is impracticable, and, that Jesus must be their only foundation, they hope, however, that he will save them for their works sake. Thus they either avowedly profess to participate with Christ the honor of their salvation ; or, while they pretend to give the honor of it to him, they look for the original and moving cause of it within themselves. Like the Judaising christians, Acts. xv. 5, or the Gentiles whom Peter misled, Gal. ii. 12, 14, they unite the law to Christ ; as though Christ needed to have something superadded to him, to render his death effectual. At all events, if they find their error in this respect, they will regard their works as *their warrant* to believe in Christ ; and will expect mercy at his hands, not so much because his grace is free and all sufficient, as because they have something in themselves, which may deserve his notice and regard.

These plans of salvation however will be found very erroneous, if we enquire,

II. What is that foundation which god has laid?

Nothing can be more clear, than that he has not laid either of those, which have been before mentioned.

He often describes his people as performing good works : and often prom ises them, under that character, eternal life. But he always represents us as sinners, and as standing in need of his mercy. And he has sent his Son into the world for that very reason, because none could obtain mercy by any works of their own. Nor has he clearly shewn, that works are *wholly* to be excluded from the office of justifying. He has told us that salvation must be wholly of grace or wholly of works, Rom. xi. 6. That every degree of boasting is excluded from that salvation which he has revealed, Rom. iii. 27; Eph. ii. 8, 9. And that the persons, whom he justifies, are ungodly, and without any works whatever to recommend them, Rom. iv. 5.

Christ is the one foundation which he has laid in Zion.

He "has set forth his Son to be a propitiation for sin :" and every sinner is to build his hope on Christ alone. Christ is the foundation laid in the covenant of grace, Gen. xvii. 19 ; Heb. viii. 6. The same is laid in all the promises, Gen. iii. 15, and xxii. 18 ; 2 Cor. i. 20. The same was exhibited in all the types.* The same is laid also in the gospel, 1 Pet. ii. 4—6. We are expressly told that there is no other, Acts iv. 12. Nor indeed can there be any other to all eternity.

The necessity of building upon this will appear, while we consider,

* The Paschal Lamb, the Scape Goat, &c.

431

### III. Why no other can be laid.

Many reasons might easily be assigned: but one or two may suffice.

1. Any other would be unworthy of the divine architect.

God himself is the architect, ver. 9; and must have all the glory of beginning and perfecting this building. But, if men were to found their hopes on any thing but the Lord Jesus Christ, they would have whereof to glory, Rom. iv. 2. So far as respect was had to any merit in them, so far might they ascribe the honor to themselves. Even in heaven their song must differ from that of the redeemed. Instead of giving *all* the glory to God and to the Lamb, Rev. v. 13, they must take a portion of it to themselves. But this would be utterly unworthy of God to suffer. Indeed he has told us that he never can nor will suffer it, 1 Cor. i. 29, 31; Eph. ii. 8, 9. We may be sure therefore that no such way of salvation shall ever be established, as leaves man at liberty to boast. We shall be rewarded *according to* our works, and in some respect *for* our works; but the only ground of acceptance, either for our persons or our services, is in Christ alone, Eph. i. 6.

2. No other would support the weight that is to be laid upon it.

Whatever our souls need in time or eternity must be derived from that, which is the foundation of our hope. Our pardon must be obtained by it; our peace flow from it; our strength and righteousness be given us on account of it; and eternal glory be bestowed on us, as the reward of it. And can we build our hope of such things in any degree on our own works? Can we, who, if we had done all that is commanded us, should be only unprofitable servants, imagine, that we can in any respect merit such things, when we have done nothing that is commanded us, at least, nothing perfectly, or as we ought to have done it? Surely such an hope would soon appear to be a foundation of sand; and would infallibly disappoint us to our eternal ruin. Yea, the very persons who build on such a foundation, almost invariably deny, that any man can be assured of his acceptance with God; they account such an assurance to be an enthusiastic delusion; which is a clear acknowledgment of the insufficiency of *their* foundation to bear this weight.'

Infer,

1. How needful is it to enquire what foundation we are upon!

If we build but a common habitation, we are careful on what foundation we raise it. How much more care should we exercise, when we are building for eternity! Let us enquire, whether we have been deeply convinced of the insufficiency of our own goodness, and of the impossibility of uniting any works of ours with Christ's atoning sacrifice? And let us examine whether Christ's obedience unto death be our only hope, our only confidence? We never can be saved unless, with Paul, we utterly renounce the filthy rags of our own righteousness, and desire to be found clad in Christ's unspotted robe, Isa. lxiv. 6; Phil. iii. 9.

2. How secure are they who are built upon the Lord Jesus Christ!

Christ, on whom they stand, is justly called "a *tried* stone, and a *sure* foundation," Isa. xxviii. 16. He never yet failed those who trusted in him.

The vilest of mankind have found him able to save them to the uttermost. He is a Rock to those who trust in him; nor shall the gates of hell prevail against them, Matt. xvi. 18. Let all believers then rejoice in their security; and hold fast the profession of their faith without wavering, Heb. x. 23.

3. How careful should we be, what superstructure we raise upon him!

While Christ is the foundation of our hope, we are also to build upon him all our works. But our works will all be tried by fire. If they be not such as tend to his glory, they will be burnt up as hay, and wood, and stubble. If they be truly good, they will stand the trial, like gold, or silver, or precious stones, ver. 11—14. Let us then give diligent heed to our works. We may suffer loss *in* heaven, though we should not suffer the loss *of* heaven, ver. 15. Let us then seek "a full reward," 2 John 8. While we renounce good works *in point of dependence*, let us practice them *from love to our Redeemer.* Thus shall we put to silence our adversaries ; and dorn the doctrine of God our Saviour

---

## HATRED OF CHRIST IS HATRED OF THE FATHER.

John xv. 23.—He that hateth me, hateth my Father also. (S. S.)

MEN are ever disposed to palliate their sins, and, by representing them under some specious name, to conceal their real enormity—But God calls every sin by its proper name, and speaks of it with just abhorrence—Covetousness in his eyes is not prudence, but idolatry : Eph. v. 5; a disregard of his presence is not mere inadvertence, but a denial of his most essential attributes : Ps. x. 11, 13; and a contempt of his gospel is not a venial ignorance or inattention, but an absolute hatred both of Christ and of the Father—To confirm this truth we will endeavor to shew,

I. WHO THEY ARE THAT HATE CHRIST.

It may be thought that none but Jews can be guilty of hating Christ, and that the bearing of his name is a sufficient testimony of our regard for him.—But there are too many who, notwithstanding they have been baptized into his name, are yet "enemies to him in their minds."—Certainly we must number among his enemies,

1. Those who disregard his gospel.

The gospel of Christ ought to be universally received as "glad tidings of great joy."—But the greater part of mankind feel an aversion to it.—Some dislike its fundamental doctrine of salvation by faith, and represent it as injurious to the interests of morality.—Others hate the duties it enjoins, and traduce it as requiring a state of mind totally incompatible with the discharge of our offices in social and civil life.—Many even of those who approve of the gospel in their judgment, are yet very far from experiencing its power in their souls.—They enjoy not its promises, they fulfil not its precepts, they know not its renovating, sanctifying effects.—It may be asked, Are all these persons haters of Christ ? Let Christ himself answer that question.—He states, that a practical renunciation of his authority is a proof, that they are enemies to him in their hearts, and will cause them to be treated as his enemies in the day that he shall judge the world—Luke xix. 14, 27.

2. Those who neglect his ordinances.

Our Lord has promised his peculiar presence to us while we seek him in the ordinances of his own appointment.—Should not then the hope of enjoying his presence endear the ordinances to us, and make us regard them as our most inestimable privilege ?—But how are they regarded by the generality amongst us ?—Does not worldly business or pleasure often detain us needlessly from the house of God ! And when we are assembled for worship, do not our thoughts rove to the very ends of the earth, so that, though we "draw nigh to God with our lips, our hearts are far from him?"—Are not almost all persons cold and remiss in secret prayer?—And is not family religion either banished altogether, or conducted with such formality as to render it irksome and unprofitable?—Our Lord left it as his dying command that we should often partake of bread and wine in remembrance of his body broken and his blood shed for us—Yet is not his table either shamefully deserted, or else profaned by impenitent, unsanctified communicants?—And what construction must we put on such conduct? Our Lord plainly tells us, that he considers them as his enemies, and that none of those who thus despise his invitations, shall ever taste of his supper—Luke xiv. 18, 24.

3. Those who persecute his people.

Persecution is not carried now to the same extent that it has been in former ages—But has it ceased?—Experience proves that there is the same enmity in the hearts of men against the faithful servants of God as ever there was—There are many at this day who are true descendants of Cain and Ishmael—And, as long as there shall be an unconverted man upon earth, it will be found, that they, who are born after the flesh, will persecute those who are born after the Spirit—Gal. iv. 29. If they do not kill the saints, they will "revile them, and separate them from their company, and say all manner of evil against them falsely for Christ's sake"—And are not such persons enemies to Christ? Yes; he considers himself as the real butt of their malice—Saul thought that he was justly punishing some wild fanatics when he dragged the christians to prison and to death; but Jesus said to him, Saul, Saul, why persecutest thou *me?*—Acts ix. 4. And the prophet tells us that whosoever toucheth the Lord's people, toucheth the apple of his eye—Zech. ii. 8.

The extreme enormity of their conduct appears in this,

II. That the hatred of Christ is, in fact, a hatred of the Father also.

Christ is essentially "one with the Father;" and as "whosoever had seen Christ, had seen the Father," so, "whosoever hateth Christ must of necessity hate the Father also"—But it is evident in other points of view that they hate the Father; for they hate

1. His authority.

God commands all men to believe in his Son, to "kiss him" with holy reverence, and to honor him even as they honor the Father—Ps. ii. 12. John v. 23. But the unequivocal language of those who comply not with his command is, "We will not have this man to reign over us;" "Who is the Lord that we should obey him? we know not the Lord, neither will we obey his voice"—Whatever they may pretend, they are not deceived through unavoidable ignorance, or impelled by irresistible force to reject Christ: they do it from a rooted aversion to the Father himself, and evince by their conduct the truth of that declaration, "The carnal mind is enmity against God; for it is not subject to the law of God, neither indeed can be"—Rom. viii. 8, 7.

2. His image.

The word, the ordinances, and the people of God, all bear upon them the impression of God's holiness—And this is the very ground of that aversion which rises against them in the hearts of the ungodly—The gospel is disliked as requiring so much purity and self-denial—The worship of God could be easily tolerated, if an outward form would suffice; but the spirituality and devotion necessary to an acceptable performance of this duty, cause the carnal heart to revolt from it as irksome—If the saints too would countenance the world in its sinful practices, the offense of the cross would cease; but they "make their light to shine before men;" and on this accour t they, whose deeds are evil, hate, revile, and persecute them.—Now this clearly proves, that holiness itself is their aversion, and consequently that the image of God, which principally consists in holiness, is hateful to them—Will any say, it is hypocrisy that they hate, and not holiness? Wherefore then were Christ and his apostles so universally the objects of cruel persecution? Was there any guile in him? Was he not "the brightness of his Father's glory, and the express image of his person?" and walked not his disciples in his steps? It is certain, not only that the image of God is hated by the enemies of Christ, but that every thing that bears his image is hated by them *on that very account,* and *in proportion* as it exhibits a resemblance of him—

3. His very existence.

It is vain indeed to entertain the thought that God could be annihilated—But, if we could suppose for a moment that it were declared from heaven, "There is no God;" would not the tidings excite a general satisfaction?—Would not all the haters of Christ congratulate themselves that there was no God to call them to an account, none to punish them for their iniquities?—Would they not look forward to an unrestrained indulgence of their lusts with pleasure, instead of weeping for the loss of their best and dearest friend?—Yes; as the enemies of Christ exulting in his crucifixion, so would all who hate him rejoice, if the Father also were utterly extinct—That this is no fanciful idea will appear from the declaration of God himself, "The fool hath said in his heart, No God!"—Ps. xiv. 1.

INFER,

1. How desperate is the wickedness of the human heart!

Wherefore is it that men are so full of enmity against Christ and his Father? Is it for having given us his dear Son that they hate the Father; or do they hate Christ for laying down his life for us?—Many good things has he done; for which of them do we reject him?—O let the haters of God blush and be confounded; let them abhor themselves for all their iniquities, and abominations—

2. What a dreadful place must hell be!

Here the wickedness of men is restrained by the preventing grace of God—But in hell it will rage without control—How will all the miserable spirits then vent their malice! How will they gnaw their tongues and blaspheme their God?—Rev. xvi. 9. May *we* never know this by bitter experience—

3. How astonishing is the tender mercy of our God

One would suppose that God should feel nothing but indignation against such an ungrateful world—But behold! he "waiteth to be gracious unto them;" he sends them offers of pardon; he even entreats and "beseeches them to be reconciled to him"—2 Cor. v. 20. O let his goodness lead us to repentance—Let us cast away the weapons of our rebellion, and bow to the sceptre of his grace—So shall we yet be numbered among the friends of God, and be living monuments of his mercy to all eternity.

## THE EVILS OF THE TONGUE.

James iii. 6.—The tongue is a fire, a world of iniquity. So is the tongue amongst our members, that it defileth the whole body, and setteth on fire the course of nature; and it is set on fire of hell. (S. S.)

AMONGST the most important of subjects must be reckoned the government of the tongue. The consideration of it is well calculated to convince the profane, to pluck off the mask from hypocrites, to humble the sincere, and to edify every description of persons. St. James, who intended his Epistle as a corrective to the abuse that prevailed in the christian church, insisted strongly upon this subject: and, in the words before us, has given us such a description of the tongue, as, if it had proceeded from any other than an inspired writer, would have been deemed a libel upon human nature. In order that the text may be fully understood, we shall shew,

I. THE TRUE CHARACTER OF THE HUMAN TONGUE.

The Apostle tells us "it is a fire."

Fire, in its original formation, was intended for the good of man; and, when subordinated to his wishes, is highly beneficial: but its tendency is to consume and to destroy. Thus the tongue was at first made for the Creator's praise; but through the introduction of sin, that member, which was, and, if well used, yet is, the glory of man, Ps. lvii. 8, is become "an instrument of unrighteousness" and all iniquity.

Fire also, even the smallest spark, is capable of producing incalculable mischief; such mischief as it may not be in the power of man to repair. Thus also will one single motion of the tongue, ver. 3, 4. It may so irritate and inflame a man, as to change him instantly into a savage beast, or an incarnate devil: and, if the whole world should labor to remedy the evil, it would mock their endeavors.

He further adds, that it is "a world of iniquity."

There is not any sin whatever, which does not stand in the nearest connexion with the tongue, and employ it in its service. Search the long catalogue of sins against God; then inspect those against our neighbor; and, lastly, those against ourselves; and there will not be found one, no, not one, that has not the tongue as its principal ally. See Rom. iii. 13, 14.— — — All iniquities whatever centre in it, and are fulfilled by it: so justly is it called, "A world of iniquity."

Its character will yet further appear by considering,

II. ITS EFFECTS.

1. These are defiling.

Sin, as soon as ever it is conceived in the heart, defiles the soul: but when it is uttered by the lips, "it defileth the whole body." Utterance gives solidity and permanency to that, which before existed in idea, and might have passed away: and, inasmuch as the tongue has every other member at its command to execute, according to their several powers, the things it has divulged, the whole man is become a partaker of its guilt and defilement, Eccl. v. 6; Mark vii. 20—23. And, though all its communications are not equally polluting, yet is there a stain left by means of them, a stain, which nothing but the Redeemer's blood can ever wash away.

2. Destructive.

To such an astonishing degree has this fire gained the ascendant, that it has "inflamed the whole course of nature." Look at *individuals*; what malignant passions has it kindled in them! Visit *families*; what animosities, and inextinguishable feuds has it produced! Survey *churches:* and you will find the unhallowed fire burning even in the sanctuary of God;[*] and sometimes too, even in the very censers of his ministers, alluding to Lev. x. 1. Cast your eyes round upon whole *nations;* and you will perceive that, times without number it has kindled the flames of war, and spread desolation through the globe.[†]

To prove that this account is not exaggerated, we shall point out,

III. THE REASON OF ITS PRODUCING THESE EFFECTS

The tongue "itself is set on fire of hell."

Satan is the source and author of all the evils that proceed from the tongue. Does it falsify? behold, it does so at the instigation of that wicked fiend, "the father of lies," Acts v. 3; John viii. 44. Does it discourage men from the prosecution of their duty? It does so, as the devil's agent, Matt. xvi. 23. Does it accuse and scandalize the people of God? Who but satan is the author of such calumnies? Rev. xii. 10. Does it disseminate error? the propagator of that error is satan's minister, however he be transformed into an angel of light, 2 Cor. xi. 3, 13, 14, 15. Does it encourage any bad design? It is the devil himself who speaks by it, 1 Kings xxii. 21, 22. In every sin that it commits, it is actuated by "the prince of the power of the air, the spirit that now worketh in all the children of disobedience, Eph. ii. 2. Its whole "wisdom is earthly, sensual, *devilish*, ver. 15. It comes from hell, and leads to hell: and, if God were to withdraw his restraints here, as he does in hell, it would speedily produce a very hell upon earth.

This alone can account for the effects that proceed from it.

Doubtless the wickedness of the heart may account for much: but, if the flames were not fanned by satannic agency, we can scarcely conceive that they should rage with such an irresistible force, and to such a boundless extent.

INFER,

How great must be the evil of the human heart!

The heart is the fountain, in which "the evil treasure is;" Matt. xii. 35. the tongue is only the channel in which it flows. If the channel then be so vile, what must the fountain be? Yet every one of us has this tongue in his mouth, and this heart in his bosom: and, if God should leave us without restraint, there is not one of us but would proclaim all the evil of his heart, as the most loathsome sensualist, or most daring blasphemer.

2. How much do we need the influences of the Holy Spirit!

It is absolutely impossible for man to tame this unruly member, ver. 7, 8, Yet restrained it must be, if ever we would be saved, James i. 26. What then shall we do? shall we sit down in despair? God forbid. The Holy Spirit will help our infirmities, Rom. viii. 26, and Christ will give us his Spirit if we call upon him. Let us then look to Christ; and we shall prove by sweet experience, that his "grace is sufficient for us," 2 Cor. xii. 9, and that "through him strengthening us we can do all things." Phil. iv. 13.

3. How careful should we be of every word we utter!

Immense injury may we do by one unguarded word. We may take away a character which we can never restore, or inflict a wound which we can never heal. On this account we should "set a watch before the door of our

---

[*] By means of heretics, cavillers, and proud disputers, and others who cause divisions and dissensions.

[†] What has not been perpetrated under the influence of those two words, liberty and equalit—

lips," Ps. cxli. 3. Nor is this a matter of expediency merely, but of necessity; for God has warned us that we shall account of every idle word, and, that by our words we shall be justified, and by our words we shall be condemned, Matt. xii. 36, 37. and v. 22, last clause. Let us then be utterly purposed that our mouth shall not offend, Ps. xvii. 3. Let our tongue be as choice silver, or a tree of life, to enrich and comfort the Lord's people, Prov. x. 20, and xv. 4. Let our "speech be alway with grace seasoned with salt" for the honor of God, and the good of our fellow creatures, Col. iv. 6; Eph. iv. 29.

## THE FOLLY OF VAIN EXCUSES.

**Prov. xxiv. 11, 12.**—If thou forbear to deliver them that are drawn unto death, and those that are ready to be slain; if thou sayest, Behold, we knew it not; doth not he that pondereth the heart consider it? and he that keepeth thy soul, doth not he know it? And shall not he render to every man according to his works? (H. H.)

OFFICIAL influence is a valuable talent: but to use it aright is often very difficult, and painful to the feelings. Hence those who are possessed of it, are apt to shrink back, when the exercise of it is likely to involve them in much trouble; and they will connive at abuses, which they cannot easily prevent. For such connivance they have excuses ever ready at hand; "They were not aware of the circumstances;" or, "They thought their interposition would be to no purpose." But power and responsibility are inseparable: and the magistrate who neglects his duty, must give an account of such neglect to God, and have his excuses weighed in the balance of the sanctuary. To succor the needy, and to relieve the oppressed, is a sacred duty, which no man can neglect, but at the peril of his soul: and to deceive ourselves with vain excuses is folly in the extreme.

We shall not however limit our views of this subject to magistrates, but shall extend them generally to all those excuses which men make for their neglect of acknowledged duties; and shall consider,

I. THE EXCUSES BY WHICH MEN DECEIVE THEIR OWN SOULS.

None are so hardy as to deny their obligation to serve God: yet the great mass of mankind will plead excuses for their neglect,

1. Of religious duties.

"They have not time to attend to their spiritual concerns." Not time? For what then is their time given them? and what other business have they in comparison of this? But, if they would speak the truth, is not their disregard of religion to be traced rather to their want of inclination to spiritual things———their want of faith in the divine records———their want of all fear of God, and all concern about their souls?———How vain then their plea of want of time, when their neglect arises from a total alienation of their hearts from God!

2. Of moral duties.

The duties of sympathy, of compassion, of activity in succoring the distressed, are mentioned in our text. Now for the neglect of these duties, such as the visiting of the sick, the instructing of the ignorant, the relieving of the needy, and the comforting of the afflicted, men will plead ignorance, inadvertence forgetfulness, inability. But is there not a great degree of criminality attaching to us, if we do not search out the poor and afflicted, on purpose to alleviate their distresses?— — —And is not the true cause of our supineness, that we have no love to our fellow-creatures, no zeal for God, no gratitude for redeeming love?— — —It is in vain to think that our neglects are venial under any circumstances, and more especially when they originate in cowardice, and sloth, and selfishness.

Seeing then that such excuses are vain, let us mark,

II. THE FOLLY OF RESTING IN THEM.

Were there no God to call us into judgment, our delusions would be of less consequence: but there is a God by whom all our excuses will be weighed; and he,

1. Will judge with truth.

He looketh not at the outward appearance; "He searcheth the heart and tries the reins," and is privy to the most secret workings of our minds. We may easily deceive ourselves; but him we cannot deceive. See how forcible is the appeal made to us in our text. Can we have any doubt whether he sees our conduct, or forms a correct estimate of it? Let us remember, that "he will bring to light the hidden things of darkness, and make manifest the counsels of the heart;" and that, whatever our judgment be, his will be according to truth.

2. Will award with equity.

Here again the appeal is strong, and carries conviction with it. We are sure that "God will judge the world in righteousness," and "give to every man according to his works." "Whatsoever we have sowed, that shall we also reap: if we have sowed to the flesh, we shall of the flesh reap corruption; but if we have sowed to the Spirit, we shall of the Spirit reap life everlasting."

Let this subject TEACH us,

1. To be jealous over ourselves with a godly jealousy.

We are apt to think that conscience is a safe guide, and that we may rest satisfied with its testimony; but conscience is corrupted by the fall, as well as all the other faculties of the soul. It is blinded, bribed, partial, and in many instances "seared as with an hot iron." Hence it is that "every man's way is right in his own eyes." Paul thought he ought to do many things contrary to the name of Jesus; and was applauded by his own conscience, whilst he was sinning against God with all his might. Be not therefore satisfied merely because you feel no condemnation in your own minds; but beg of God to enlighten your conscience, that it may guide you aright, and keep you from those delusions which would involve you in everlasting ruin.

2. To live in daily expectation of the future judgment.

Ask yourselves, not merely, What do I think of this or that conduct; but, What would God say to it, if I were instantly summoned to his tribunal? Such a question as this would often lead you to a very different estimate of yourselves from that which you have formed; and the consideration of his recording every thing in order to a future judgment would tend to keep you vigilant in all your conduct. Walk then as in his sight, and be satisfied with nothing which you are not well assured will satisfy him.

## CAUTION AGAINST DECLENSION IN RELIGION.

**Matt. xxiv. 12, 13.**—Because iniquity shall abound, the love of many shall wax cold: but he that shall endure unto the end, the same shall be saved. (H. H.)

THESE words are a part of the discourse which our Lord held with four of his disciples in private, after he had retired from the temple to the Mount of Olives. Compare Mark xiii. 1—4 with Matt. xxiv. 1, 2. Being in full view of the temple, his disciples were struck with the magnificence of its appearance, and expressed to him their admiration of it: from whence he took occasion to foretell the speedy destruction of it, and to give them signs whereby they should ascertain the approach of the judgments which awaited their whole nation. At the same time he gave them instructions for their own support and comfort under all the trials which they themselves should endure previous to that time. He told them what evil treatment they should meet with from the enemies of his gospel; and what difficulties they should encounter from his pretended friends. Their trials *from without* we considered in another discourse: * those *from within* we propose for our present consideration.

In the words before us our Lord suggests to his disciples,

I. THE DANGER OF SPIRITUAL DECLENSION.

Independent of the proneness of man at all times to backslide from God, there is a danger arising to us from the conduct of those with whom we stand connected. The bitterness of persecution, or abounding of corruption, may operate to abate our zeal in the service of our God; but the falls and offenses of those who profess religion have a peculiar tendency to discourage the people of God; and it is to this, we apprehend, our Lord more espe cially refers.

Such events must be expected in every age.

If we consult the holy scriptures, we shall find that, even in the apostolic age, multitudes who were once hopeful, declined from the ways of God, and made shipwreck both of faith and of a good conscience, 2 Tim. i. 15, and ii. 17, and iv. 10 — — —And what is there to prevent a recurrence of the same evils? As long as the heart of man is so evil and so treacherous, it will ever be prone to start aside from God, even as a broken bow— — —

Whenever they do happen, they tend to quench the love even of the most established.

Great disappointment is felt by all the members of the christian church: and every one feels a portion of that disgrace which the instability of any member brings upon the whole body. From the frailty of some, the fidelity of others begins to be questioned: evil surmisings arise: a coolness and distance are occasioned among the brethren: the communion of the saints is interrupted; and their associations for holy exercises are less frequented, or less enjoyed, Heb. x. 24, 25. Divisions then ensue: each leader endeavors to increase the number of his partisans: and thus all that union and harmony which should characterize the family of Christ is destroyed.

Hence arises also a coldness of heart towards God himself and a loss of fellowship with him— — —In a word, the almost inseparable effect of an irruption of iniquity into the church of God is, that "the love of many at least, if not of all, will wax cold." One single "root of bitterness springing up will trouble and defile many." Heb. xii. 15

* On Luke xxi. 17—19, which in Doddridge's Harmony of the Gospels, immediately precedes the text.

Such danger always existing, we proceed to suggest,

II. A PRESERVATIVE AGAINST IT.

Two things are certain, namely, that *on our continuance in well-doing our salvation depends;* and, that *by our continuance in well-doing our salvation is secured:* and the consideration of these two points will, under God, prove an excellent antidote against all the dangers to which we can be exposed.

Consider then, that,

1. *On* our continuance in well-doing our salvation *depends.*

To this truth the whole voice of scripture bears witness. We know full well that there are many promises made to the people of God; and that of those who have been given to Christ he will lose none. But it were a dreadful perversion of those promises, to think that we can be saved in any other way than that of "a patient continuance in well-doing." Rom. ii. 7. We must not attempt to make void the most positive declarations of holy writ, Ezek. xviii. 24, and xxxiii. 12, 13; Heb. x. 26, 27, 38, 39 — — — but must learn, like the apostle Paul himself, to make them an incentive to unwearied watchfulness and diligence, 1 Cor. ix. 27.— — —

2. *By* our continuance in well-doing our salvation *is secured.*

The promise in our text is absolute and universal: and throughout every part of scripture God says to us, "Be thou faithful unto death; and I will give thee a crown of life"— — —We need not disquiet ourselves about God's fulfillment of his promises: let us only attend to our own duties, and leave him to accomplish his own word in his own time and way. We shall find at last that "not a jot or tittle of his word has ever failed"— — —The words of our text were fulfilled literally to *every true disciple* at the destruction of Jerusalem, when *every apostate* perished. A refuge was provided for the whole body of christians, at Pella, and a way was opened for their escape thither: and so it shall be in the day of judgment, when Christ's faithful servants *universally*, and they *only*, shall be saved.

3. The consideration of these truths would be an effectual preservative against spiritual declension.

Suppose iniquity to abound ever so much, what is that to *us*, except as a matter of grief and lamentation for the persons who commit it? Let the iniquity shew itself in any *persons*, or in any *degree*, it is no reason that our love to God and man should wax cold: it should rather operate as a reason for us to stir up our love to a flame, in order to impede the progress of the corruption, or at least to prevent its assaults upon our own souls; as travellers in a wilderness kindle fires around them, in order to protect themselves from the assaults of ravenous and ferocious beasts. At all events, however much any persons may injure their own souls, and endanger their own salvation, it becomes us to take care that they do not destroy or injure us— — —

ADDRESS,

1. Let us above all things cultivate a spirit of love.

This is the characteristic feature of all God's children; and the want of it, whatever else we may possess, proves us to be only as sounding brass or as tinkling cymbals, 1 Cor. xiii. 1—3. A growth in this is the surest evidence of our growth in grace, 2 Thess. i. 3, 4.— — —and by this, more than by any thing else, is our establishment in the divine life secured, 1 Thess. iii. 12, 13.— — —Let us then "take care lest any root of bitterness spring up in our hearts;" and let us daily "put on charity, which is *the bond of perfectness.*" Col. iii. 14.

2. Let us beg of God the assistance of his Holy Spirit.

441

The consideration of our final happiness depending so entirely on our own continuance in well-doing, would be discouraging, if we did not know, that God has promised to us the aids of his Spirit; and that "the grace of Christ shall be sufficient for us." See how graciously the Lord supported Paul, when all his christian friends had forsaken him in his greatest extremity : "At my first answer no man stood with me, but all men forsook me : I pray God that it may not be laid to their charge : notwithstanding, the Lord stood with me, and strengthened me." 2 Tim. iv. 16. Thus shall you find him present with you in every hour of trial, and be made "more than conquerors through him that loved you."

---

## THE SINFULNESS OF MURMURING AGAINST GOD.

**Prov. xix. 3.**—The foolishness of man perverteth his way, and his heart fretteth against the Lord. (S. S.)

THE wickedness of the heart is deep and unsearchable—
They who do not watch its motions, have no idea of its depravity—
But they who diligently examine it may discover many evils—
And by the light of God's word attain considerable knowledge—
The disposition mentioned in the text deserves special attention.
I. ILLUSTRATE THE DISPOSITION HERE SPOKEN OF.
The careless and ungodly world are ever ready to cast blame on God.
1. On account of their sins.
They give the rein to every evil thought and desire—
————expose themselves to every kind of temptation—
. ————lay innumerable stumbling-blocks in their own way—
And thus become enslaved by vicious lusts and appetites—
Against these iniquities God denounces his judgment—
But the slaves of sin continue hardened in their evil ways—
They condemn even God himself as the author of their sins—
This was the conduct of Adam immediately after the fall*—
And it is too often imitated by his guilty descendants—
2. On account of their sorrows.
Sorrow is entailed on all as the punishment of the first transgression—
But most of the afflictions which men suffer are brought on them by their own folly—
Some involve themselves in distress through sloth or intemperance—
Others ruin themselves by imprudence and extravagance—
But all under their calamities "fret against the Lord"—
They are full of invectives against those that have been the more immediate occasions of their trouble—Numb. xvi, 11, 41.
They consider their lot as hard and severe—
And thus do they reflect on Providence rather than on themselves—
Cain, the first-born of Adam, indulged this malignant spirit—Gen. iv 13, 14.
Nor are there any sons of sorrow who do not follow his example—
Nor are believers themselves wholly free from this disposition.

*Gen. iii. 12.  He obliquely condemns God for giving the woman to him

They watch and pray against their besetting sin—

Yet are sometimes brought under the power of it—

On these occasions they are tempted to fret against the Lord—

They are ready to expostulate with him like those of old—Isa. lviii. **3.**

They forget how justly they might have been eternally forsaken—

And that the remaining power of their sins is the consequence both of former habits, and of present neglects—

Under afflictions also they feel too much proneness to murmur—

What sinful impatience did the holy Elijah manifest!—1 Kings xix. **4.**

Even Job himself preserved not wholly a becoming temper—Job vii. **15, 16.**

This disposition however is most hateful in the sight of God.

II. THE EVIL OF IT.

It betrays the most *deplorable ignorance.*

God is not, nor can be, the author of sin—

He maintains in all things the character given of him—Deut. xxxii. **4.**

Hence St. James shews the folly of casting blame on God—James i. **13, 14.**

Nor can God punish any of us more than our iniquities deserve—

Hence the expostulation of the prophet is unanswerable—Lam. iii. **39.**

Besides, to fret against God is not the way to interest him in our behalf—

Nor will it tend to the peace and composure of our own spirits—

It is as unprofitable to us as it is unjust towards him—

True wisdom would teach us to humble ourselves in his presence—

And to renew our supplications with greater earnestness—

This conduct is as sure to succeed, as the other is to fail of success—Prov. xxviii. **13.**

It manifests the most *obstinate impenitence.*

Both sins and sorrows ought to produce humility—

When they increase our rebellion, our state is almost desperate—Isa. i. **5.**

How awfully does such a temper characterize God's enemies!—Rev. xvi. **9.**

And make us resemble those that are consigned over to perdition!—Matt viii. **12.**

Surely nothing more heinous can be laid to our charge—

Nor any thing more speedily fit us for destruction—

It evinces the most *consummate arrogance.*

To fret and murmur is, in fact, to reprove God—

God himself considers it as a direct attack upon him—Mal. iii. **13, 14.**

And can any thing be more presumptuous in such worms as we?

St. Paul reprobates this impiety with holy indignation—Rom. ix. **20.**

And every one who allows himself in it, must answer it at his peril—

We conclude with suitable ADVICE.

1. Let us search into the occasions of our sins and sorrows

We may be surprised into sin by a sudden temptation—

But may trace our fall to preceding unwatchfulness—

Nor can we expect God to keep us, if we neglect to keep ourselves—

We are rarely earnest enough in using the means of safety—

We are too backward to meditation, prayer, and fasting—

Our afflictions also may have come without any misconduct on our part—

But who has not merited them by his sins?—

Men should only be considered as instruments in God's hands—Ps. xvii **13, 14**

And the consideration of his will should silence every murmur—2 Sam. xvi. 10.

2. Let us always be careful to justify God.

We may not always be able to account for his dispensations—
But we should not on that account doubt the equity of them—
Whatever we suffer, we should not " charge God foolishly"—
Under the darkest dispensations we should say as the Psalmist—Ps. xxii. 2, 3.

If we wait we shall see the wisdom of many things which now seem utterly inexplicable—

We may rest assured that David's assertion shall be verified—Ps. li. 4.

3. Let us see what improvement may be made of our troubles.

There is no rod which has not a voice to us—
Our very sins may be permitted, in order to humble us—
And to make us more thankfully cleave to the Saviour—
Our trials, of whatever kind, are to purge away our dross—
And to fit us for eternal rest—
To view them in this light will greatly compose our minds—
Instead of fretting against the Lord, we shall be thankful to him—
And instead of increasing our misery, we shall make it a mean of joy.

---

## THE FOLLY OF CREATURE-CONFIDENCE.

Hos. v. 13.—When Ephraim saw his sickness, and Judah saw his wound, then went Ephraim to the Assyrian, and sent to king Jareb: yet could he not heal you, nor cure you of your wound. (S. S.)

MEN continually provoke God to chastise them, but rarely make a due improvement of his chastisements. Instead of turning to God, they dishonor him more by applying to the creature under their distress rather than to him. The ten tribes, when punished for their willing compliance with Jeroboam's edicts,* sought repeatedly to the Assyrians for help instead of humbling themselves before God: but they found, as " Judah" also did on similar occasions, that their confidence in the creature served only to involve them in shame and disappointment.

Taking the text simply as an historical fact, we deduce from it two observations, which deserve our consideration.

I. MEN, IN TIMES OF TROUBLE, ARE PRONE TO LOOK TO THE CREATURE FOR HELP, RATHER THAN TO GOD.

This was one of the most common and heinous sins of the Jewish nation :† and it is universal also amongst ourselves.

1. In troubles of a temporal nature.

* Ver. 11, 12. God consumed them as moth does a garment, or as a rottenness the bones, secretly, slowly, gradually, effectually.

† Sometimes they relied on Egypt; Isaiah xxx. 1—3, and xxxi. 1. Sometimes on Assyria (as Manahem did on Paul, 2 Kings xv. 19, and Ahaz did on Tiglath-pileser, 2 Kings xvi. 7,) and sometimes on themselves, Isaiah xxii. 8—11. "Jareb" here certainly means the king of Assyria : but whether it was his proper name, or a name given him by the prophet, is uncertain. It means *Defender*, and might be applied to him in a taunting manner. In this view it would be a very severe sarcasm. See 2 Chron. xxviii. 20.

In *sickness of body*, we lean, like Asa, 2 Chron. xvi. 12, on the physician. In *distress of mind*, we complain and murmur; but forget to pray, Gen. iv. 13, 14. In *straitened circumstances*, we expect relief from friends. or our own exertions. God is invariably our *last* refuge.

2. In spiritual troubles.

Under *conviction of sin*, we betake ourselves to the observance of duties. and make resolutions to amend our lives, instead of fleeing to Christ as the refuge of lost sinners, Isaiah lv. 2. In *seasons* also *of temptation*, or *desertion*, we adopt a thousand expedients to remove our burthens, but will not cast them on the Lord, 1 Sam. xvi. 14—16. Though foiled ten thousand times, we cannot bring ourselves to lie as clay in the potter's hands; but will rest in the means, instead of looking simply to God in the use of means.

But the longer we persist in it the more we shall find, that,

II. THE CREATURE CANNOT AFFORD US ANY EFFECTUAL SUCCOR.

There are circumstances indeed wherein friends may be instrumental to our relief: but they can do,

1. Nothing *effectual*.

The consolations which are administered by man, or by the vanities of this world, are poor, empty, transient, Jer. ii. 13. Not the whole universe combined can ever bring a man to "glory in tribulations," Rom. v. 3, and to say with Paul. "I take pleasure in them for the sake of Christ:" 2 Cor. xii. 10, as soon might they enable him to stop the sun in its course, as to reduce to experience the paradoxes of that holy apostle, 2 Cor. vi. 10.

2. Nothing *of themselves*.

It is not a little humiliating to see how weak are man's endeavors to heal either the disorders of the body, or the troubles of the soul, when God is pleased to withhold his blessing. The best prescriptions, or the wisest counsels, are even lighter than vanity itself. Reasonings, however just and scriptural, have no weight: advice, however sweetened with love and sympathy, is rejected: the very grounds of consolation are turned into occasions of despair, Ps. lxxvii. 2, 3. When God says, "Let there be light,' there is light: but till then, the soul is shut up in impenetrable darkness Job xxxiv. 29.

ADDRESS,

1. Let us guard against this sinful propensity, both in our national and personal concerns.

We cannot but see how prone we are, as a nation, to rest on human alliances, and human efforts. Would to God we could correct this fatal error, and trust more entirely in the great disposer of all events!

As individuals at least we may, and must, correct it. If we would have the blessing of God, and not his curse, we must renounce all creature-confidence, and trust in him alone. Jer xvii. 5—8. See David's example, Ps. lx. 11, and cxxi. 1, 2.

2. Let us especially rely on Christ as the healer of our souls.

He is "the healer of the nations," Rev. xxii. 2, "Jehovah, who healeth us," Exod. x. 29; there is no physician besides him; nor any balm, but his blood. We may use whatever means we will, either to pacify our conscience, or to purify the heart; but we shall find that they can "not heal us, nor cure us of our wound." But Christ is all-sufficient: he can in one moment purge us by his blood, and renovate us by his Spirit. To him then let us look with humble, uniform, unshaken affiance.

## AGAINST SELF-CONFIDENCE.

1 Cor. x. 12.—Let him that thinketh he standeth, take heed lest he fall.  (S. S.)

The things which are recorded in the holy scriptures are written, not for the entertainment, but for the real improvement, of our minds.  Doubtless, as gratifying our curiosity, there is no book under heaven so interesting as the Bible: but as exhibiting what must be realized in our own experience, as shewing us our duties and our difficulties, our helps and our remedies, our punishments and our rewards, it claims, infinitely beyond all other books, our unremitting attention.  In this view the apostle, having mentioned the misconduct of the Israelites in the wilderness, and the destruction which they brought upon themselves by means of it, founds upon their history this solemn admonition; " *therefore* let him that thinketh he standeth, take heed lest he fall."

From these words we may learn,

I. That all, even the most eminent, are liable to fall.

The most distinguished characters of antiquity have fallen*———They have betrayed their weakness in those very points, wherein their eminence chiefly consisted†———Who then amongst us will presume to say, " I am in no danger of falling?" ‡———

II. That the more self-confident we are, the more likely we are to fall.

Self-confidence naturally emboldens us to rush into temptation———And necessarily provokes God to leave us to ourselves———By means of the former, our occasions of falling are greatly multiplied: by means of the latter, our ability to stand is utterly withdrawn‖———God, for his own honor's sake, is concerned to let us fall, in order that we may know and confess, that our sufficiency for any good thing is derived from him alone§———

III. That, if we would be kept from falling, we must look well to our steps.

As in a slippery path peculiar caution is required, and an inattention to our steps will probably issue in some painful accident, so more especially is it necessary to use circumspection in the path of duty.  Who can tell the snares and temptations that beset us?  Who can tell what may be the consequences of any step we take?  Who can reflect on all the circumstances that arose from one single glance of David's eye, and not feel himself exposed to continual danger?  The most important events of our lives may be traced to some trivial cause, some matter of pure indifference: and events,

* *Noah*, Gen. vi. 9, with ix. 21.  *Lot*, 2 Pet. ii. 7, 8, with Gen. xix. 33—36.  *David*, Acts xiii. 22, with 2 Sam. xi. 4, 5, 15.  *Solomon*, (who was called Jedediah, the beloved of the Lord, 2 Sam. xii. 24, 25.) 1 Kings xi. 1—9.

† *Abraham*, Rom. iv. 20, with Gen. xii. 12, 13, and xx. 2. 11.  *Job*, Jam. v. 11, with Job iii. 3.  *Moses*, Numb. xii. 3, with xx. 10, 11.  *Jeremiah*, Jer. ix. 1, with xx. 8, 9.  *Paul*, Acts xx. 24, with xviii. 9. 10 ; when he seems to have been struck with a panic.

‡ John iv. 14, and 1 Pet. i. 23, shew the proper qualities and tendency of *grace* ; but do not at all affect what the scriptures elsewhere affirm to be the tendency of our inherent *corruption*.

‖ We have a striking example of this in Peter, who to gratify his curiosity went into the midst of his enemies, and was then left to experience his own weakness, Matt xxvi. 58, 74

§ Thus he acted towards the Israelites  Deut. i. 42—44.

equally or more important, perhaps no less than the everlasting salvation of our souls, may depend on the very next step we take. Surely then we should in "all things be circumspect:" Exod. xxiii. 13; we should "take heed to our ways;" we should walk in an humble dependence on God for direction and support; we should cry to him continually " hold thou up my goings in thy paths, that my footsteps slip not." Ps. xvii. 5.

We shall conclude this subject with a few words of ADVICE.

1. To those who are offended at the falls of others.

Many, when they see a professor of religion act amiss, are ready to impute his misconduct to the gospel itself, as though christianity were only a cloak for hypocrites. But, considering the temptations that surround us, and the corruptions that are within us, it is rather a wonder that any stand, than that some should fall. We mean not to justify, or to extenuate, the sins of any: but we desire that religion should not be represented as promoting that, which it utterly condemns. Let the blame fall on those who merit it, and not be cast indiscriminately on all who profess godliness. Let Judas be branded as a traitor; but let not the odium of *his* offense attach to all the other apostles, and to their divine master.

2. To those who are endeavoring to walk uprightly before God.

It is of considerable use to persons when walking on slippery ground, to have hold of each other, that if one slip, the other may afford him immediate assistance. Many falls and bruises have been escaped by these means. Thus it is of great importance to christians to walk together in love, each helping to support his neighbor, and receiving help from others in the time of need. Eccl. iv. 9, 10. Let all then watch over one another with a godly jealousy. If one fall, let others endeavor instantly, in meekness, to raise him up. Gal. vi. 1. Above all, let every one know in whom his strength is; and pray continually, "hold thou me up and I shall be safe." Ps. cxix. 117.

" Now to him, who is able to keep us from falling, &c. be glory and majesty, dominion and power, both now and ever. Amen." Jude xxiv. 25

~~~~~~~~~~

## AGAINST HYPOCRISY.

Job xx. 4—7.—Knowest thou not this of old, since man was placed upon earth, that the triumphing of the wicked is short, and the joy of the hypocrite but for a moment; Though his excellency mount up to the heavens, and his head reach unto the clouds? yet he shall perish for ever, like his own dung: they which have seen him shall say, Where is he? (S. S.)

PREJUDICE or passion will miserably warp the judgment—

It will hide from us what we might know, and cause us to pervert what we do know—

Never was this more strongly exemplified than in the friends of Job—

Had they calmly considered, they might have comforted him in his affliction—

But, by a hasty misapplication of acknowledged truths, they most unjustly and cruelly condemned him—

Job had hinted to them the evil and danger of their conduct—Job xix 28, 29.

447

And Zophar, irritated at the caution, replies with great severity—

His words however, though misapplied, suggest to us two very important truths respecting sinners.

I. THEIR PROSPERITY IS TRANSIENT.

Of sinners, some *make no profession* of religion, and others *a false profession.*

Each of these characters may enjoy, for a while, great prosperity.

The *profane* are often exalted to places of dignity and power—

They prosper in all their labors for wealth and preferment—

They not only despise, but perhaps persecute the godly—

They "triumph," as though no evil should ever happen unto them—

This the Psalmist saw with deep regret—Ps. lxxiii. 3—12.

*Hypocrites* also frequently are held in estimation—Rev. iii. 1.

They are objects of envy to many an humble and contrite soul—

They will boast of experiences which might well be coveted—

And even attain considerable heights of joy—Matt. xiii. 20.

Their "excellency may mount up to the heavens, and their heads reach unto the clouds"—

But their prosperity will be of short duration.

Death will speedily seize upon the most stout-hearted sinner—

Then all, which he gloried in, shall come to an end—

None of his "pomp shall follow him," or his "wealth be carried with him"—

The hypocrite also shall have a period put to his dissimulation—

He shall soon appear in his proper character—

The all-seeing God will discover the secrets of his heart—

Nor is this time at any great distance—Deut. xxxii. 35.

In comparison of eternity, the duration of his joy will be "but a moment."

Then will they experience a sad reverse.

II. THEIR RUIN WILL BE TREMENDOUS.

The ungodly will in due time be visited for their offenses—

They will then "perish,"

1. To their own eternal shame.

Many portions of scripture appear to us indelicate—

But God's representations of sin are surely just—

And well calculated to make us nauseate and loathe it—

Such is his description of the *ways* of sinners—2 Pet. ii. 22.

And such his declaration respecting their *end*—Compare Rev. iii. 16, with the text.

They will perish under circumstances of disgrace and ignominy—

Christ will not deign to own them before his Father—Matt. x. 33.

The angels will come forth to execute the vengeance of God upon them—

The saints would even "thrust them out of heaven" if they should seek admittance there—Luke xiii. 28.

The damned themselves will insult them with bitter taunts—Isa. xiv. 9—16.

Nor shall they ever cease to be objects of contempt and abhorrence—

This is told us in the plainest terms—Prov. xiii. 5; Dan. xii. 2.

Nor while they retain, as they must, their character, is it possible that their situation ever should be changed—Rev. xxii. 11.

2. To the astonishment of all that knew them.

The question "Where is he?" refers primarily to the utter extinction of the ungodly—

But it may well be considered also as an expression of surprise—
The *wicked* little think where their course will terminate—
If the rich man's request had been granted, Luke xvi. 23, 27. 28, what reply would his surviving brethren have made so soon as that in the text*—
The *hypocrites* also often escape detection in this world—
Perhaps they were celebrated, after their departure, as eminent saints—
We may conceive that their dearest friends, or their associates in holy exercise, may enquire after them in heaven—
What surprise and horror must seize them, when they hear of the doom which the heart-searching God has passed upon them !†—
ADDRESS—"KNOW YOU NOT THIS ?"
*Know* you not that this has been so from the beginning of the world ?
Does not the word of God assert, that " it shall be ill with the wicked ?" Isa. iii. 11 ; Ps. ix. 17.
Does not the most authentic history in the world prove it to have been so ?‡
Does not conscience itself testify that it shall be so still ?—
If you know, do you not *consider* this ?
Can any thing be more worthy of our consideration ?—
If we have " but a moment," should we not improve that moment ?—
Are we willing to perish in this ignominious and awful manner ?—
Let us live no longer in the neglect of religion.
The gratifications of sense can last but for a little time—
But the consequences of neglecting God will endure for ever—
Surely the care of the soul is the " one thing needful"—
Nor let us rest in a " form of godliness" without experiencing " its power."
It will avail us little to deceive our fellow-creatures—
The higher we have been in their estimation, the deeper will be our disgrace—
Let us then go to Christ for the remission of past sins—
Let us approve ourselves to him in future, as " servants that need not be ashamed."—
And labor to be " sincere and without offense until his coming again."

* They would most probably have exclaimed, " *Where is he !* in hell! lifting up his eyes in torments! Is it really so? We never could have thought it: we had no doubt but that he was happy : he seemed to us as worthy and blameless a character as any: nor had he himself any doubts but that he was going to heaven."

† If a minister is to have those as his " joy and crown of rejoicing," who were truly converted by his ministry, we may, not improperly, suppose a degree of disappointment, if he miss those, concerning whom he had entertained the most sanguine hopes. We may suppose him, upon the first discovery, to say, " *Where is he !* What, HE in hell! I often feared that I myself should go thither ; but who would have thought that HE should ?" The Lord grant that this may never be realized by any of us!

‡ Where are now the antediluvian scoffers, the haughty Pharaoh, the treacherous Judas, the worldly-minded Demas, the heretical Hymenous ? &c.

## A CAUTION AGAINST DEPARTING FROM GOD.

Heb. iii. 12—14.—Take heed, brethren, lest there be in any of you an evil heart of unbelief, in departing from the living God. But exhort one another daily, while it is called to-day lest any of you be hardened through the deceitfulness of sin. For we are made partakers of Christ, if we hold the beginning of our confidence stedfast unto the end. (S. S.)

THE consideration of the fullness and sufficiency of Christ, is that which animates the believer in all his conflicts: yet it is on no account to supersede our own care and watchfulness: on the contrary, it affords us the greatest encouragement to watch, because it ensures success to us in our endeavors, which without his almighty aid, would be of no avail—In this view it is that the inspired writer calls us to "consider the Apostle and High-Priest of our profession, Christ Jesus, who was not merely a servant, like Moses, but a son, the heir and Lord of all, yea, the very builder of that spiritual house, of which we profess ourselves to be a part"—On this truth he grounds the exhortation in the text,* in which he suggests,

I. A SOLEMN CAUTION.

Difficult as it is to come to God, we find it easy enough to depart from him—We should therefore be on our guard.

1. Against any departure from him.

While men are yielding to temptation, and turning aside from the ways of God, they cherish an hope that they may still preserve their interest in his favor, though they be not studious to do his will ·But a departure of any kind, whether from the faith or practice of christianity, is nothing less than a departure from him who is the only source of life and happiness— We cannot therefore be too much on our guard against any secret declensions, which are so dishonorable to him whom we profess to love, and so destructive of our present and eternal welfare—

2. Against that unbelief from whence all declensions arise.

As faith is that which brings us to God, and keeps us stedfast in our adherence to him, so unbelief separates us from him, and, in proportion as it is harbored, invariably alienates us from the life of God—Whatever be the more immediate object of that unbelief, whether we attempt to lower the strictness of God's precepts, or question the veracity of his promises or threatenings, it proceeds equally from "an evil heart," and brings with it the same pernicious consequences; it is a root of bitterness, which, if it be permitted to spring up, will cause every devout affection to wither and decay —We must therefore labor to eradicate it, if we would not eat for ever its bitter fruits—

That his caution may have its due effect, the apostle prescribes,

II. THE MEANS OF IMPROVING IT.

Sin is of a deceitful and hardening nature.

When "a backslider in heart" commits a sin, many thoughts will arise in his mind to palliate the evil, and to make him think that it will not be attended with any important consequences—Soon he begins to doubt whether the thing be evil at all; and, ere long, to justify it from the peculiarity of his circumstances—At first he felt some remorse; but presently his conscience becomes less tender, till at last it is altogether seared and callous; so that, notwithstanding he be miserably departed from God, he is regardless

---

* All the words between "Wherefore," in ver. 7, and the text, are a parenthesis: we must therefore connect the text thus; "Wherefore" "take heed," &c.

of his loss, and insensible of his danger—Who that has ever noticed the workings of his own heart, has not found, what a bewitching and besotting thing sin is? yea, who has not often seen reason to bewail its deceitful, hardening effects?—

To guard effectually against it we should watch over each other.

Sin, from the foregoing qualities, naturally hides itself from our view, and renders us inattentive to the means of prevention—But ignorant as we often are of our own spirit, we see clearly enough the defects of others; yea, perhaps we condemn with severity in others the very things which we allow in ourselves—To watch over each other therefore, and to warn each other of those declensions which we either see or apprehend, is a most valuable service; and, if performed with discretion and love, it can scarcely fail of producing the happiest effects—This is a duty to which God has solemnly called us in his word; Lev. xix. 17, and it is to be a part of our "daily" work—Our time for it will be very short: either we or our brother may be speedily removed; and our opportunity of benefiting his soul may be lost for ever—We should exhort one another therefore "daily, while it is called to-day;" and, though it is often an unpleasant office, we should use all fidelity in the execution of it—By this means we may restore a brother before he has relapsed too far, and preserve him from that departure from God, which would otherwise terminate in his destruction—

Still further to enforce the caution given us, the apostle adds

III. A MOTIVE TO REGARD IT.

Our final participation of Christ's benefits depends on our stedfastness in the pursuit of them.

Without entering into the question, whether God has decreed the final perseverance of the saints, we may be fully assured, that none can obtain salvation but by persevering in the way of holiness to the end of life: the scriptures continually speak this language, "He that endureth unto the end, the same shall be saved:" "but if any man draw back, my soul shall have no pleasure in him"—Matt. xxiv. 13; Heb. x. 38. It is true that believers are already *in a measure* "partakers of Christ:" but the complete enjoyment of his benefits is reserved for the future life: and we must not only have a scriptural and well-founded confidence at first, but must keep it stedfast even to the end, in order to attain that full possession of our inheritance—

If any thing can stimulate us to caution, surely this must.

Eternity is at stake, and depends on our present condition: according as we approve ourselves to the heart-searching God, will our state be fixed for ever—Is it not madness to be remiss and careless under such circumstances? Would any one, who should have reason to think his house were on fire, sit still without endeavoring to find out the latent grounds of his alarm? And shall we know our proneness to unbelief, and not guard against its operation, lest it lead us to apostacy? Shall we acknowledge the deceitful, hardening nature of sin, and not exhort each other to mortify and subdue it?—Surely if we have the smallest concern for our souls, we shall not only regard the caution given us in the text, but labor to improve it in the way prescribed—

ADDRESS,

1. Those who have never come to God at all.

The foregoing subject is *in itself* applicable to those only who profess religion; but it may be accommodated to those also who make no such profession; for if they who have come to God are in danger of departing from him, and they who have enjoyed a scriptural confidence, may lose it; if they, who have believed, may "make shipwreck of their faith," and they, who have "begun in the Spirit, may end in the flesh:" if they, who have "begun to run well, may be hindered," and they, who have "escaped the pollutions of the world, may again be entangled therein and overcome;" and, lastly, if they who "have been enlightened, and have tasted the good word of God and the powers of the world to come, may so fall away as never to be renewed unto repentance;" What must become of those who have never experienced any of these things? Can they be safe? Can they have any scriptural hope of heaven? If the strongest have so much need of caution, and the most circumspect such reason to fear the deceitful, hardening effects of sin, surely the careless have need to tremble, lest they "die in their sins," and "be driven away in their wickedness"—If all, except two, of those who came out of Egypt, perished in the wilderness, can they hope to enter into the land of Canaan, who have never once come forth from their spiritual bondage?—The point is clear; may God enable us to lay it to heart, and to consider it with the attention it deserves!—

2. Those who are conflicting with their spiritual enemies.

Much has already been spoken to you both in a way of caution and direction: we beg leave to add a word of encouragement—The thing, against which you are chiefly guarded, is unbelief; because *that* is the true source of all apostasy—We now would say, Be strong in faith giving glory to God —"Faith is the shield wherewith you are to quench the fiery darts" of your enemies—Only believe; and Omnipotence will come to your support—Only believe; and you shall experience "the mighty working of *his* power, who raised Christ from the dead"—Commit yourself to him "who is able to keep you from falling; and he will present you faultless before the presence of his glory with exceeding joy."

---

## DANGER OF RELIGIOUS INDECISION.

Luke ix. 61.—Lord, I will follow thee; but let me first go bid them farewell which are at home at my house. (Pr.)

WHEN the marriage supper was provided, and the guests were invited, they all with one consent began to make excuse. And here, out of three that were invited to follow the Saviour, two are for pleading some delay; one wanted to go and bury his father, and the other to take leave of his friends. There is always something or another to hinder us in the path of duty, and to weaken our resolutions in following the Lord fully: it is therefore our wisdom to see the danger, and to guard against it. For this purpose let us

Consider the resolution mentioned in the text, and what are its principal defects.

1. He wished to follow Christ, but there was something of more urgent necessity that must first be attended to.—Thus the sick oftentimes resolve to reform their lives when they recover, but remain as before. The youth wishes to be religious but thinks that so grave a subject had better be deferred to old age. He must have a little more pleasure in his early days, and then he will attend to the concerns of his soul, will repent and obey the gospel. The servant must be free from his master, and then he thinks of becoming the servant of God. Some are for putting matters off for a few years, others only for a few days, when they shall be more at liberty from present diffi-

452

culties and engagements.———The folly of all this is very apparent: the concerns of the soul are of as much importance at this moment as they can be at any future time; life is uncertain, and every delay is a step towards final impenitence. Heb. iii. 8.

2. The person who formed the resolution in the text, evidently made it in his own strength.—Here is no reference whatever to divine assistance, no dependance upon the Lord, no seeking for grace to help in time of need, but an unqualified and self-confident resolution. "Lord, I will follow thee." How easy and how vain are such promises, yet how frequently do they meet our observation. The children of Israel said, " we will serve the Lord;" but considered not that his service requireth the renunciation of all their idols, and of all their sins. Josh. xxiv. 19. And in order to follow Christ we must deny ourselves and take up the cross, which grace only can enable us to do. John xv. 5.

3. The resolution when formed, seemed to depend on the consent of his friends, for though he speaks only of taking his leave, he probably wished to know whether they approved of the step he was about to take. Had he been influenced by proper motives, instead of leaving them behind, he would rather have endeavored to bring them with him, to follow Jesus in the way. Thus did Andrew and Philip, John i. 40—45; the woman of Samaria, John iv. 28—30; and others. Luke viii. 39.———But here was no seeking first the kingdom of God and his righteousness, no forsaking all for Christ, but a cleaving to worldly connexions rather than to him. Matt. x. 37.

4. Instead of following Christ cheerfully and with all his heart, he appeared somewhat dejected at the thought, and must go and take leave of his friends, as if he were about to die, and should see them no more. Such are the melancholy apprehensions which some persons entertain of true religion; they imagine it would be injurious to their worldly interest, and unfit them for the common duties and enjoyments of life, and that therefore they must take a final leave of the concerns of the present world.———Whereas, by cleaving to the Lord we should be better prepared to serve our generation, and to enjoy the blessings of providence. Religion improves all the relations, and heightens and endears to us all the comforts of life. Eccles. ix. 7.

5. By going home to his friends, he would expose himself to great temptation, and be in danger of breaking the resolution already formed. They would upbraid him with folly for attaching himself to a sect every where spoken against, and to a person so generally despised.———Paul consulted not with flesh and blood, neither must we, if we would follow the Lamb withersoever he goeth. Gal. i. 16. Those who are on the Lord's side must be as Levi, they must not know their own kindred. Deut. xxxiii. 9.

1 This subject may serve as a warning to those who trifle with the calls of the gospel. Here was a looking back, a lingering after the world, and Christ pronounces such to be unfit for the kingdom of God : verse 62.

2. Nothing but a decided attachment to Christ, and a determination to sacrifice all for his sake, can constitute us his disciples.

3. Let us beware of the ensnaring influence of worldly connexions, and of every inordinate affection; for these, rather than grosser evils, are the ordinary impediments to our salvation. Matt. xvi. 26.

## UNGODLY PROFESSORS ADMONISHED.

James iv. 8.—Draw nigh to God, and he will draw nigh to you: cleanse your hands, ye sinners, and purify your hearts, ye doubled-minded. (Pr.)

In the early period of the christian church it was said, that "great grace was upon them all:" but as things proceeded, many were found amongst them who were mere professors, having nothing of religion but the form.

Such was the case in James' time.—His epistle is addressed to the believing Jews; but in writing to them, he at the same time addresses himself to unbelievers among them, as in the language of our text.— — —He supposes indeed that they did not live without prayer; but that when they prayed, they received not, because they asked amiss; ver. 3.— — —He also describes them as being of a worldly spirit, and double-minded in all their ways. Hence the pointed language now before us.

I. Consider the characters addressed.

1. Though they were professors of religion, they are considered as far from God.—In all their prayers and religious duties, they never "draw nigh to God," have no communion with him; and though belonging to the church, they are living without God in the world.— — —Characters of this description are still to be found in every christian society.

2. Their "hands" and their "hearts" are supposed to be defiled.—They had not laid aside all malice, and all guile, and hypocrisy, and envies, and all evil speakings, that as new-born babes they might desire the sincere milk of the word. 1 Pet. ii. 1, 2. They are still under the power of darkness, and the dominion of sin: their hands are full of oppression and fraud, and their hearts full of impurity.— — —They live after the flesh, and war after it; fulfilling the desires of the flesh and of the mind.

The apostle calls them "sinners," though they may profess to be saints, and be numbered with the people of God.

3. Under a profession of religion, they were nevertheless "double-minded;" halting between God and Baal, and were sometimes this, and sometimes that.— — —When conscience is awakened by the application of some powerful truth, or by the occurrence of some alarming providence, then they are on the Lord's side.— — —When in the company of pious people, they can be pious too: but when they are in the world, and mix with worldly company, they are on the side of the world. 1 Kings xxii. 4.

II. The counsel given them: "Draw nigh to God—cleanse your hands—purify your hearts."

And what does all this denote? Some may think it sufficient to answer,—pray to God, and reform what is amiss in your conduct.— — —This indeed is included, but this is not all; it includes repentance towards God, and faith in our Lord Jesus Christ.

1. The exhortation supposes that God is accessible through a mediator, for without this there would be no invitation to "draw nigh."— — —If no mediator were provided, we should be like the fallen angels, without hope: the name of the Lord could not have been invoked, with any assurance of success.— — —But the blood of Jesus Christ his Son cleanseth from all sin: we may therefore draw nigh to him, though we are "sinners," great sinners and have offended against light and knowledge.— — —The fountain is opened for sin and uncleanness, and we may wash and be clean.

2. Though exhorted to "cleanse our hands and purify our hearts," these acts are not preparatory to repentance and faith, but the very things them-

selves.———No other way of drawing nigh to God has the promise of acceptance: no other cleansing will purify the heart.———The in luence of some inferior principle may be sufficient to cleanse the hands, but no the heart; but the cleansing will only be partial, and not lasting.

Genuine repentance will both cleanse the hands and the heart.——— Weeping at the Saviour's feet, a Magdalene was made clean; and of the impure Corinthians it is said, but ye are sanctified, ye are justified. in the name of the Lord Jesus, and by the Spirit of our God. 1 Cor. vi. 11. Isai. xxx. 21, 22.

A sinner under the first conviction generally reforms his conduct, and casts away his open sins; but his heart can only be purified by faith; and without this, there can be no entering into the kingdom of God. Matt. v. 8.

III. The encouragement to comply with this advice: "God will draw nigh to you."

This language does not imply that man is the first mover in the great affair of salvation: far from it. We are apprehended of Christ, before we apprehend him: he draws us, and we run after him. John vi. 44, xii. 32. Phil. iii. 12.

But it does suppose that repentance precedes forgiveness, and believing in Jesus.———The Lord may draw near to us in his secret influence on the heart, and does so before we draw near to him; but not in a way of fellowship and communion———not as a God pardoning iniquity, and giving rest to the soul. We must come to Christ by faith, before that can be obtained. 2 Cor. vi. 17. 18.

How important are these words: "I will draw near to you"———what condescension, for the great God to draw near to a worm of the dust; yes, near to you; as a father, a friend, and a guide———near to you in death, when every other friend must take their leave. Ps. xlviii. 14.

Oh what a state, for a sinner to be called to die, when no one can help him but God, and for God to be afar off!

---

### THE SCORNER REPROVED.

Proverbs xiv. 9.—Fools make a mock of sin.  (Pr.)

In the esteem of this pious philosopher, religion is the highest wisdom, and sin the greatest folly. Such is the general purport of his characteristics; but in the text especially, he has marked with the most degrading epithet a species of levity deserving of the severest rebuke. It is not enough for some men that they are sinners: they must add folly to their depravity, and treat the greatest of all evils as a light and trifling concern.

I. Enquire who they are that may be said to "make a mock at sin."

1. They are those who excuse or palliate the evil of their own conduct, treating sin as a light matter, and saying of it as Lot did of Zoar, is it not a little one.———Some plead nature, some custom, some necessity, and others example: but as the prophet said, will ye plead for Baal? Is it possible to excuse or justify so great an abomination? Every attempt to conceal its enormity, to throw the blame on others, or on the circumstances in which

we are placed, is a fearful sign of impenitence, and of that inconsiderate levity which the wise man so severely reprehends. Proverbs xxviii. 13.

2. Those make a mock at sin who can commit it without regret, and glory in their shame, instead of being humbled for it. Phil. iii. 19.———There are scorners who turn sin into a jest, and even boast of their wickedness. Prov. x. 23.— ——Injuries done to fellow men, such as are adapted to fill the mind with horror and detestation, are too often made the subject of unfeeling ridicule. 2 Sam. ii. 14—16; Prov. xxvi. 18, 19.———Some will dare to sin for the diversion of others, and to commit acts of public injustice for the sake of a little popularity. Hos. vii. 3. Acts xii. 2, 3; xxiv. 27.

3. Those who rush into sin upon the slightest temptation, show how lightly they regard it, and with what contempt they treat the divine authority. The profane Esau could sell his birthright for a mess of pottage, and the covetous Judas betray his master for thirty pieces of silver Zech. xi. 13. From such mean and mercenary motives do men sacrifice their conscience and their souls; and not only sell themselves to work wickedness, but sell themselves for nought.

4. Some make a mock at sin by scoffing at their reprovers, and treating them with utter disdain. Such was the conduct of Ahab towards Micaiah, and of Herod towards John the Baptist. 1 Kings xxii 8; Mark vi. 18, 19. On the same principle, parental authority is frequently despised, and ministerial fidelity treated with levity and scorn. Prov. xiii. 1.

5. How lightly some men regard sin may be seen in their rejection of the atonement, and substituting in its stead their own endeavors to appease the divine anger, and to commend themselves to God. All self-righteousness is founded in light thoughts of sin, and leads to a rejection of the only way of salvation. Prov. vii. 36.

6. Some even go so far as to take pleasure in the sins of others, and turn into a scene of mirth what will issue in lamentation and woe. Hab. ii. 15. It is sufficiently evil to mock at human suffering, but inconceivably more so to mock at that which leads to endless perdition; first to tempt men to the commission of sin, and then to be diverted with their impiety.

II. THE FOLLY AND DANGER OF SUCH CONDUCT.

It is sufficiently to our shame that we are sinners; but it is the height of folly to make a mock of sin.

1. Because of its intrinsically evil nature. Sin had its origin in the bottomless pit, 1 John iii. 8; whence it issued, and infected the nature of man, and is opprobiously termed "the filthiness" of the flesh and of the spirit. 2 Cor. vii. 1. It is the disgrace of our nature, and by it we have debased ourselves even unto hell. Isai. lvii. 9. It is the sum of all evil: from hence proceed evil thoughts, evil speaking, an evil conscience, and evil deeds. It is worse than death, for death would have no sting without it; and worse than hell, for it is sin that creates the never-dying worm, and the fire that cannot be quenched.

2. The present consequences of sin show the extreme folly of making light of it It is pregnant with all the evils that exist in the world, of whatever kind or degree; and who can calculate this mighty sum? Whatever calamity befals a sinner in the present life, it may truly be said to him in the language of the prophet, "thy way and thy doings have procured these things unto thee." Jer. iv. 18. The ruin and distress brought upon the conscience has induced others, besides Judas, to cast themselves directly into hell, to get rid of their horror and despair. And even where sin is re-

pented of and pardoned, it brings unutterable distress upon the soul. **Ps. xxxviii. 3.**

3. The sufferings of Christ for sin, and the price paid for our redemption, awfully demonstrate the folly and madness of making light of sin. Behold the Son of God prostrate in Gethsemane, witness his agony and bloody sweat; see him on the cross, and hear his dying cries; and then say whether the cause of these sufferings can be regarded with indifference, or be made a matter of idle jest. No where does the evil of sin appear so great as in the sacrifice of the Son of God. Isai. liii. 4, 5.

4. The final ruin and destruction which sin will bring upon the soul in a future world. Could we descend into the dark and silent chambers of the grave, and behold the bodies of the wicked crumbling into dust, and becoming a prey to rottenness and worms; could we draw aside the veil that conceals from us the world of spirits, and plunge into all the thickest horrors of the bottomless pit, and see the justice of God pouring out a tempest of fire upon lost souls to all eternity; surely we could not be disposed to make a mock at sin, or live any longer in a state of impenitence and unbelief. A fire is kindled in his wrath, that shall burn to the lowest hell.

Let mockers beware then, lest their bands be made strong, and they be left to wonder and perish.—Be not deceived: God is not mocked: whatsoever a man soweth, that shall he also reap. Those who now deride religion, and make a mock at sin, will find that God also will laugh at their calamity, and mock when their fear cometh. Prov. i. 25—27.

---

## FATAL ISSUE OF FINAL IMPENITENCE.

Job ix. 4.—Who hath hardened himself against him, and hath prospered. (Pr.)

Bildad, one of Job's friends, considered his complaints as amounting to a rebellion against God: ch. viii. 3. Job is greatly moved at this, and disowns the charge with abhorrence. " He is wise in heart, and mighty in strength; who hath hardened himself against him, and hath prospered?"

The words however imply, that there is such a thing as for a man so to harden himself as to contend with God: and that where this is the case it is certain to come to a dreadful issue.

I. ENQUIRE WHEREIN THIS HARDNESS OF HEART CONSISTS.

1. The word signifies a spirit that is *obstinate and incorrigible;* full of perverseness, keeping up a contention with God.— — —In scripture language it is being stiff-necked, and uncircumcised in heart and ears. Neh. x. 16, 17; Acts vii. 51.

2. It is descriptive of that *rebellious spirit*, which discovers itself under the various dispensations of God, both in a way of mercy and of judgment. — — —Thus Pharaoh acted: sometimes he seemed humble and willing to submit: but when the judgment was withdrawn, he resumed his former resolution, and continued to harden himself against God.

3. There is also a *judicial hardness* to which sinners are liable, in a way of righteous judgment for their iniquities.— — —God is said to have hardened Pharaoh's heart; not that he produces evil in the mind of man, which is utterly impossible, James i. 13: but through man's perverseness, the divine dispensations make him worse instead of better.— — —If the

457

providences of God do not soften the human mind, it generally becomes thereby more hardened. Thus also the gospel produces a similar effect, where its influence is rejected : and instead of being a savor of life unto life, it becomes a savor of death unto death. 2 Cor. ii. 16

This is not owing to any defect in the gospel, or in the dispensations of God towards us ; but to the depravity of the human heart, wh ch perverts the means of salvation into those of destruction.— — —Hence this impenitent hardness is ascribed to man, as well as to God ; to show that God has no influence in the matter, so as to affect man's free agency and accountability,

II NOTICE SOME OF THE INSTANCES IN WHICH THIS SIN IS STILL COMMITTED.

Ineffectual and dangerous as it is for any one to harden himself against God, it is a sin no less prevalent than formerly ; and it will become us to notice the different ways in which it operates, that we may be warned against it.

1. It appears in indulging *hard thoughts of God*, of his government and of his holy law : in esteeming him as a hard master, and is considering sinful propensities as an excuse for sinful actions, though no one thinks of excusing the offense of others against himself on the ground of such a plea.— — —The indulgence of such thoughts lead on to final impenitence.

2. It manifests itself in a rejection or *dislike of God's way of salvation*. This impenitent aversion is directed against its freeness, as placing all men alike on a level.— — —Against its sovereignty, in that God should have mercy on whom he will have mercy : and its language is, " why doth he yet find fault?"— — —This was the stumbling block to the hardened and unbelieving Jews. Isa. vi. 9, 10 ; Rom. ix. 29—33.

3. Persisting in an evil course, *amidst many convictions and fears*, is another instance of this sort of depravity.— — —Pharaoh knew that he was wrong, and yet he dared to persist. Many have great light and strong convictions, yet they have loved idols, and after them they will go.— — —Some under threatening afflictions will do the same.

4. This hardness of heart appears in the *resistance that is offered to the hand of God in providence* instead of being humbled under it.— — — The great end of adverse providences is to make us willing to accept the punishment of our iniquity. Lev. xxvi. 41.— — —Instead of this, many are like Ephraim, a bullock unaccustomed to the yoke : and when their plans are frustrated, they still persevere in rebellion against God. Isa. ix. 10.— — —This is desperate wickedness, and braving the divine judgments. It is an evil thing to be haughty in the day of prosperity, but more so in a day of adversity : this is incorrigible wickedness.

5. *Presumptuously tempting God*, amidst the most affecting means of salvation, is another instance of this hardness of heart. It was thus with Israel in the wilderness. God spared them time after time, yet they rebelled against him. They were warned of this impenitence and unbelief, five hundred years afterwards, Ps. xcv. 8—11 : and after a thousand years more, the same warning was repeated, but without effect, for they perished in their unbelief. Heb. iii. 12.

III. THE FATAL ISSUE OF FINAL IMPENITENCE : " Who hath hardened himself against him, and prospered ?

1. The longer you continue in this state, the *more hardened* you will become, till at last you will be past feeling. Ephes. iv. 19. This is the natural effect of unbelief, and sinning against God.

2. This also is the way in which God *punishes men* for their impeni-tence. Isa. vi. 8. And if God should give you up to this state, where would you be at last!

3. *The end* of this impenitence and hardness of heart is fearfully described by an apostle. and should warn us of our danger. Rom. ii. 5—9.

Let it be remarked however, that these awful consequences proceed on the supposition that this impenitence is finally persisted in, and that mercy is promised to the returning sinner, Isa. lv. 7.— — —Many have been brought to drop the controversy with God, as Ephraim did, and have found mercy, Jer. xxxi. 19, 20. And all other impenitent sinners are invited and en-couraged to follow his example, Isa. xlvi. 12, 13.

---

### DANGER OF SELF-DECEPTION.

Proverbs xiv. 12.—There is a way which seemeth right unto a man, but the end thereof are the ways of death. (Pr.)

However diversified the pursuits of men, all are in search of happiness. Some seek it in the things of this life, and leave the concerns of futurity unheeded. This their way seems wise to them, in making sure of what is, though it can scarcely appear to themselves to be "right." Others are seek-ing the gratification of their depraved appetites in a way that is opposite to their own consciences, and this therefore cannot seem to be right. The text then must be understood of those who think well of their own way, but who are under a gross deception. It is a painful thought, that there not only are multitudes who know that they are in a wrong path, but many more who think they are right even while "the end thereof are the ways of death."

The following considerations may account for this kind of self-deception, or show how it is that men walking in a wrong way, may, nevertheless think it to be right.

1. Much of this is to be attributed to the *influence of education.*— — — We are not aware of the innumerable instances in which we are influenced by the principles imbibed in early life, yet this first bias of the mind may make things appear to be right, which in themselves are utterly wrong, and lead to fatal consequences. How else could it be accounted for, that Saul of Tarsus should not only be induced to persecute the church of God and waste it, but to think that he ought verily to do it? Thus it is that many are attached to certain forms and systems of religion, because they have been brought up to them, and for no other reason. In different places, but from a similar cause, paganism, mahomedanism, corrupted judaism, popery, and other superstitions, are all thought to be right, though the end thereof are the ways of death. Being the religion of their forefathers, it has altogether the appearance of being right. It is the same where the truth is only par-tially received, and some of its leading doctrines rejected; and where they teach for doctrines the commandments of men.

2. This kind of deception arises in part from *the power of example,* and the countenance of the generality.— — —The example of those around us has an inconceivable influence on our principles and conduct. A variety of things positively evil, and which might easily be known to be so, appear nevertheless to be right, because they are practiced and pursued by a large

portion of mankind. Setting our affections on things on the earth is a great evil, condemned in the scriptures : and yet this is the way of the world. The wicked boasteth of his heart's desire, and blesseth the covetous whom the Lord abhorreth. To a great majority of the Jewish nation it seemed right to be of the same religion as their rulers, though it included a rejection of Christ and his gospel; and it is much the same with the great bulk of other nations.

3. The *favorable opinion which good people may form of us*, may make our way seem to be right.— — —Our chief acquaintance may be with serious people, we may go with them to the house of God, and enjoy a portion of their esteem. They may hope that we are the followers of Jesus, and treat us as such; and so we may conclude that we are right, and that all is well. This seems to be the case with the foolish virgins, who in the parable are associated with the wise. But if we wish not to be deceived, we must not trust to the judgment or good opinion of any one, but desire that God would search us and set us right.

4. Many a way seems to be right, merely *because it is our own way.* — — —It is the way which we have chosen, and to which we have been accustomed. It is often seen in temporal things, that a man thinks his way to be right, because it is his way ; and it is much more so in the concerns of religion. Hence many evils may cleave to us, and we see nothing of their sinfulness. We may even be altogether selfish and covetous, and not be aware of it; full of pride, and not perceive it; worldly-minded, vain and conceited, and yet think that all is right.

5. The *resemblance between real religion and what has only the appearance of it*, may be another cause of this deception.— — —In many instances this will make a way appear to be right, though it is leading us on to destruction. Self-righteousness has a seemly appearance, and promises fair for the kingdom of heaven ; for it will be pleaded that we must be religious and devout, and do something towards our salvation. Yet it is certain, that by the works of the law shall no flesh living be justified.— — —Those who rest in a few delusive impressions and feelings, by which the heart is moved, but not changed, may flatter themselves with being the subjects of true religion ; and those also who possess a mere speculative acquaintance with the gospel, are often very confident of being right, and of having truth on their side.— — —Those who rest in a partial reformation, and who comply with some of the duties of religion, may think that all is safe and right, while they are strangers to the love of God, and not renewed in the spirit of their mind.— — —Now the end of all these things is death ; yet they seem to be right, and bear some resemblance to true religion. Thus, in innumerable ways are we in danger of being deceived, and falling into perdition.

Let us then look well to our way, and see that it be such as God has marked out for us in his holy word. Let us examine well our motives, and see that we are influenced by better principles than those of mere education, or example, or the good opinion of others. See that our hearts be truly right with God, and that we are walking in the way that is everlasting.

## A CAUTION TO HEARERS.

Luke viii. 18.—Take heed, therefore, how ye hear. (B.)

THIS caution is an inference from the preceding parable of the Sower.—
In the parallel passage of St. Mark, iv. 24, it is, "Take heed *what ye*
hear." We shall explain and enforce the caution in both these senses.—
I. TAKE HEED WHAT YE HEAR.
This both concerns all ministers of the word, and all hearers.—
It is the indispensable duty of ministers to take heed what they preach.—
That their doctrine be *true*, that they may not deceive their hearers —That
it be *important*, that they may not trifle with them.—That it be *suitable* to
their state and character, that they may "rightly divide the word of truth,
and give to every description of hearers their portion of meat in due season.
Hearers should take heed what they hear. They must not take it for
granted that what they hear is *true, important, and suited to their state and
character;* but must bring it to the test of the holy scriptures, and examine
it thereby. For this purpose they should read the scriptures, and endeavor
to make themselves well acquainted with them, and understand them. And
if they find that, according to the divine oracles, the doctrines which they
hear answer the above description, they must so "take heed what they hear"
as to attend to it, and consider it maturely, that they may thoroughly understand and lay it to heart, and that it may have its designed effect upon their
spirit and conduct.—
Our Lord's caution, however, according to this Evangelist, implied another
thing, equally important :
II. TAKE HEED HOW YE HEAR.
Take heed, that you do not hear so inattentively, and in such a prayerless
state of mind, as not to understand, nor afterwards meditate on the word, and
so receive the seed as by the "way-side." Matt. xiii. 19. That having
heard and understood in a measure what you heard, and being affected
thereby, you do not rest in any ineffectual and transient impressions made on
your mind, and, therefore, be offended and fall away in time of trial and
temptation; but that the truth be deeply fixed in your mind, and that you
may have "root in yourself." Matt. xiii. 20, 21. That you guard against
the cares of the world, the love of deceitful riches, the vain pleasures of
life, and "desires after other things;" those pernicious weeds, which in so
many choke the springing blade, or forming ear, so that no fruit is brought
forth to perfection. Matt. xiii. 22.
But hear—in *simplicity of intention*, having a single eye to the glory of
God and your own salvation, present and eternal.—In *sincerity of heart*,
truly and earnestly desiring to discover and put away every error, and every
sin, and to know and do the whole will of God.—In *humility*, conscious
that you are unworthy to know the great and important things revealed in
the gospel, respecting the will of God, and the way of salvation from such
great misery to such great happiness; unworthy that God should speak to you
by his Son, and his inspired Prophets, Apostles, and Evangelists. We should
think ourselves undeserving that a nobleman, still more a king, or an angel,
should speak to us; how much more that Christ, or God, should make known
to us his will.—Hence you should hear with *reverence*, remembering it is
God's word, and that you are in God's presence, and under God's eye.—
With *seriousness*, persuaded the truth you hear is no light matter; but for your
life, your better and everlasting life. Would you not hear with seriousness

461

the advice of a skillful physician respecting your health, or of a lawyer concerning your property? And will you not hear with equal, nay with greater seriousness, what concerns you infinitely more?—With deep *attention;* let no sentence, or even word, that is uttered, escape you, and fail not afterwards seriously to consider what you have heard, and to examine yourself thereby. With *prayer*, while hearing, and before, and after you hear, " for the spirit of wisdom and revelation;" Eph. i. 17; persuaded " the things of God knoweth no man but by the Spirit of God." 1 Cor. ii. 11, 14. Hear with *faith*, firmly believing the certainty and importance of what is taught you from the oracles of God, always remembering the " word preached" does not profit those who hear it, in whom it is not " mixed with faith." Heb. iv. 2. With *love* to the truth, though searching and cutting, though disagreeable to your mind, like a bitter medicine to your taste, or giving pain like a lance which opens an imposthume.—With *meekness* with a calm, unruffled, peaceful mind, that what you hear, may prove an " ingrafted word, able to save your soul." Jam. i. 21. Above all, hear with a fixed *resolution*, formed in the strength of grace to be a " doer of the word and not a hearer only," to practice all you hear, as far as you see it to be agreeable to the word and will of God.

## NONCONFORMITY TO THE WORLD.

Romans xii. 2.—And be not conformed to this world. (Sk.)

THE christians at Rome, to whom St. Paul dedicated this epistle, had made considerable improvement in religion, and obtained great celebrity in their profession; they were the *beloved of God*, and their faith was *spoken of throughout the whole world.* To seek renown for personal beauty, or some exterior embellishment, is the genuine offspring of worldly vanity; but to be emulous to approve ourselves unto God, and obtain the *honor of all his saints*, is a principle which religion only inspires, and christians only enjoy. St. Paul had never seen the Roman in the flesh, but as he had the care of all the churches, he mentioned them always in his prayers—had often purposed to visit them; and to evince how deeply he was interested in their welfare, he sent them this epistle, which contains not only a statement of the sublime doctrines of christianity, but a clear view of experimental and practical godliness, together with the most affectionate exhortations to excite them to duty. St. Paul had *no dominion over their faith*, and therefore he begins his chapter thus, " I beseech you," &c, verse 1. The text is a part of this request, and therefore we will endeavor to show,

I. THE NATURE OF THAT CONFORMITY TO THE WORLD WHICH THE TEXT PROHIBITS. By the phrase *this world*, we understand the ungodly part of mankind, all unregenerate persons, whether openly profane, or pharisaically moral. They are thus denominated either to show that worldly objects engross all their attention, or else to distinguish them from those who are not of this world, John xvii. 14. The prohibition against conformity to *this world*, is not be understood absolutely, or practiced rigorously; it is not *ceremonial*, consisting in " meats or drinks," or external forms and habits; nor is it *civil*, leading us to abandon all intercourse with the world; to retire from the haunts of men, and shut ourselves up in cloisters or nunneries. No: christians are to be the lights of the world; and they must go where their light will shine to the best advantage; they are the salt of the earth, and the salt must be diffused to preserve the mass from putrefaction. But the conformity here prohibited is *moral*, and may be reduced to the following points.

1. Be not conformed to the spirit and temper of the world; live not under the influence of carnal dispositions or ungodly tempers: what these are, the scriptures clearly state, Mark vii. 21—23; Gal. v. 19—21. Such are the genuine fruits produced by that "root that beareth gall and wormwood," and such the corrupt streams that flow from the impure fountain of the human heart.

2. Be not conformed to this world in the maxims by which you are governed, or the rules by which you are directed. The miser has his maxims of worldly prudence and carnal policy; the hero has his maxims of worldly honor; the pleasure-taker has his maxims of carnal gratification. Remember your actions are not to be directed by such rules, nor your characters formed by such models; if you study worldly maxims, it should be with a design to perceive their inconsistency with those rules you profess to follow.

3. Be not conformed to this world in your company. As men of business, you may and must resort to marts of trade and places of public merchandise, and as mechanics or husbandmen, you may be obliged to labor for the bread that perisheth, in company with the men of this world. But form no unnecessary alliance with them, make no choice of them for your companions, 2 Cor. vi. 17, 18; Eph. v. 11; James iv. 4, and,

4. Most of all, be not conformed to this world in your practices; all such as are inconsistent with your allegiance to God, your duty to your neighbor, and love to yourselves.

II. Assign some reasons for its prohibition.

1. *Duty prohibits it.* The text is the voice of God, it is the expression of his will. The same sovereign power that said "thou shalt do no murder," said "be not conformed to this world." You owe your all to God, his you are, and his will you are bound to obey; but by conformity to this world, you run counter to his will, and as much as lieth in you thwart his designs.

2. *Profession prohibits it.* The vows of God are upon you; your baptismal engagements bind you to renounce the pomps and vanities of this wicked world, &c. By the profession of christianity, you tacitly acknowledge that you are aiming to be like Christ; and how far he was from conforming to this world, the writings of the four evangelists sufficiently attest, John viii. 23, xviii. 36. By profession you engage to imitate the saints, and the stripes and tortures they endured from the world are indisputable evidences that conformity *to this world* was not their crime.

3. *Self-love prohibits it.* This is not such a world as we may safely imitate; it is a theatre of folly, a stage of vice, one great aceldama of blood and cruelty. The world lieth in wickedness; it is not merely sunk in the gulfs of wickedness, but lies there contentedly buried in sin, like the earth in the universal deluge; and by conforming to this world you take the most direct steps to plunge yourself into that condemnation which will be the portion of the ungodly.

4. *The love of your neighbor prohibits it.* By conforming to this world, you countenance crime, and strengthen the cause of wickedness; you give it settlement, succession, and perpetuity; you embolden others to sin, and

as sin and misery go together, you swell the aggregate of human wo, and people the regions of the damned.

5. *The interests of religion prohibit it.* By conforming to this world you stab your own peace, and wound your own conscience; you grieve the Spirit of God; you cause the friends of Zion to mourn; you turn the lame out of the way, and make the enemies of christianity triumph.

III. How MAY THIS CONFORMITY BE PREVENTED?

1. *By the regeneration of our natures;* read the close of the verse. This is a divine work, but prayer will secure the agency of that Being who effects it, John iii. 6; Matt. vi. 11.

2. *By the exercise of devout meditation* and daily prayer.

3. *By guarding against temptation,* keeping out of its way, being "all eye, all ear, all watchfulness."

4. *Above all, by a constant dependance on God.*

Conclusion.—1. The spirit of christianity is a totally distinct thing from the spirit of the world. 2. Our living in the world is no argument why we should be like the world; see Lot, Noah, Daniel, &c. 3. The charge of singularity should never frighten us from our duty. Let us not be fools for the sake of avoiding being called such, nor be damned for the sake of company.

---

### AN ADDRESS TO THE FALLEN.

**Rev.** ii. 5.—Remember from whence thou art fallen, and repent, and do the first works; or else I will come unto thee quickly, and will remove thy candle-stick out of his place, except thou repent. (Sk.)

THESE words are a part of an epistle which was dictated by the Lord Jesus Christ, and addressed by the apostle John to the church of Ephesus; a church that had been formed by the apostles themselves, and that had advanced to a state of eminence under their particular inspection. See Acts xviii. 19—21, and xix. and xx. 16—38, and epistle to the Ephesians. Favored as this church had been, it became necessary, about forty years after its establishment, to address its minister and its members in the language which you have heard.

Falling from God has ever been man's prevalent fault;—in almost every part of the sacred volume we find cautions, admonitions, or threatenings respecting it;—our text refers to this evil,—it is an address to the *fallen;*—and from it we are led—*to consider their fall,* and *the means by which they may rise again.*

I. THEIR FALL. The word *fall* is striking; it is that which is so frequently used to express man's first departure from God. In the text it is synonymous with the various expressions used by the sacred writers, to signify declension from God and his ways. Our departure from God may, in its nature and in its degree, be different. Let us therefore rather take a general view of the subject, than confine our ideas to the particular fault charged on this church, (in verse 4;) and rather connect our ideas with individuals, than refer them to whole communities; not forgetting that what describes the state of a fallen individual, may illustrate the condition of a fallen church.

It is a fall—*from the favor and the approbation of God;*—where the soul lived under the smiles of the divine countenance; into a state of guilt and condemnation. Compare Psalms xxvii. and li.

*From the image of God;*—where knowledge, righteousness, and holiness adorned the mind, and rendered it peaceful and happy, into a state of inward depravity; where evil principles—unholy passions—sinful dispositions—and bad tempers again darken, disturb and torment the soul.

*From the love of God;*—where the best the strongest affections of the soul, were turned towards, and fixed on the greatest and best of beings; into a state, where all these are drawn towards, and fixed on, the degraded creature, and the perishing world.

*From a state of vigor, and holy zeal in the cause of God;*—where faith was active, love was warm, prayer and praise were fervent, and where efforts to do good were strong and constant: into a state of religious supineness; where the soul is no longer vigorous towards God; and where forms, sounds, and cold wishes, are substituted for prayer, praise and holy zeal.

It is *frequently* a fall *from rectitude of heart and life,* into the practice of immorality.

From having enjoyed the approbation, the respect, the love of the church, such persons become, to the people of God, mere objects of commiseration.

Oh, what a fall! They *were ascending* toward heaven: but see! they *now descend* towards hell.

Such a sight may gratify fiends. Bad men may say—"so would we have it." But over such the pious mourn; and the gracious, the merciful God speaks to such in the language of paternal compassion, Hos. xi. 8; and in our text, Jesus, who would raise them again, addresses them thus, "Remember," &c.

Fallen as they are, they need not perish. Oh, that they may take heed to the things which they hear! and from the following part of the subject, may they understand, and by the grace of God, use,

II. The means by which they may rise again!

"*Remember—from whence thou art fallen.*" Strange as it may be, the fallen do *forget,* or seem to forget, their former situation. Sin dreadfully deceives and hardens. See 2 Sam. xii. 1—7; Heb. iii. 7—14; Rev. iii. 17. But it is essential to the rise of any fallen professor, that he remember *from whence* he hath fallen; without this he can have no proper view of the nature and the extent of his fault.

*Remember,*—poor, fallen soul!—thou *once* wast a child of God, and couldst call God *thy* father. Thou *didst* live in a state of favor, of union, and of intimacy with thy God and Saviour.—Thou *wast* humble patient, meek, happy, loving, and beloved. Thy soul *did* aspire heavenward; and standing as on an eminence, thou couldst *look down* on created good, as perishable, trifling, diminutive, and mean; and turning thine eyes upward, by faith thou couldst almost behold the glory of heaven; while holy meditation, and spiritual desire really carried thee beyond the present life. Or, suppose that thou didst not rise quite so high:—hast thou not left *so much* of what was great and good, that thy soul is filled with sorrow and regret for that which thou hast lost? Dost thou not say, "Oh that it were with me as in days that are past!" We rejoice that thou art made thus sensible of thy present circumstances.—*Now,* take the following advice.

*Repent*—of thy fall. Falling is in itself a great sin, Jer. ii. 19. *Repent,* on account of the injury that thy fall hath done to thyself, to the people of God, to the cause of God. Repent *sincerely* and *deeply.* Read the fifty-first Psalm, and understand what deep and sincere repentance is. Many returning backsliders seem not to be affected, as they should be, on account of their fall. When fallen, there is no rising again without repentance.

"*Do thy first works.*" Leave off thy sins ; break from thy sinful associates. Have recourse to prayer, especially to private prayer. Use diligently the means of grace. Above all, go to Christ, the only Saviour, as thou didst first go. Cry mightily for salvation. Believe, *again* believe on the son of God. *Renew thy former zeal.*

Oh ! how difficult it is to acknowledge the depth of one's fall ;—to begin anew. How many never effectually rise again, because they *will* be viewed as though they had never fallen.

The above advice is urged by the following awful threat ;—

"*Or else I will come.*" Such an intimation is always very weighty. See Luke xx. 19 ; Rev. xxii. 12.

"*I will come—quickly.*" Though the Lord Jesus is long suffering, having given time for repentance, and that time being nearly expired, he will *quickly* come. See ver. 21, 22 ; Isa. i. 5 ; Prov. xxix. 1.

"*I will remove thy candlestick out of his place, except thou repent;*" see chap. i. 12, 20, and ver. 1. I will withdraw divine light, divine influence, and leave the fallen church in its degraded state ; so that a lifeless ministry, and lifeless forms, shall be followed by darkness, and by death. See Isa. v. 5, 6. A threat long since executed on the Ephesian church :—a threat that will ere long be put in force against thee, poor fallen professor, "except thou repent." *O that thou mayest awake, and call upon God, that thou perish not!*

What a lesson is our text, for fallen professors, and for fallen churches !

But who are so backward to learn, as those that are thus fallen ? The reason is obvious. See chap. iii. 17.

Yet *the fallen* are the most pitiable objects of commisseration in the world.

---

### FOLLOWING THE MULTITUDE PROHIBITED.

Exodus xxiii. 2.—Thou shalt not follow a multitude to do evil. (Sk.)

WHATEVER was written aforetime was written for our instruction. But the most important parts of divine revelation, and those with which we ought to be most intimately acquainted, are the precepts ; which comprise the whole of a man's duty, and delineate with a critical exactness, a moral map of the road which he has to travel. The precepts of the Bible are of two kinds; those which positively illustrate what we are obligated to do, and those which negatively describe what we are to leave undone : the text is of the latter description. which, though found in the Old Testament, and among the code of laws which God gave to the Jews, is not of less importance to us than it was to them ; we will therefore, in endeavoring to profit by it,

I. OFFER A FEW THOUGHTS FOR THE PURPOSE OF EXPLAINING ITS NATURE

II. URGE REASONS TO INDUCE US TO OBSERVE IT.

III. IMPART ADVICE FOR THE DIRECTION OF THOSE WHO WISH TO ESCAPE THE ENSNARING WILES OF THE MULTITUDE.

In explaining the text, there are two general observations which we have to make. First, something assumed. Secondly, something implied. It is assumed that the multitude do evil: it is implied that we are in danger of copying their example. First, *The multitude do evil.* Evil, is either moral or natural;—sin, or its consequences. The former is to be understood here; this is the most common import of the term, Gen. vi. 5; Isa. i. 16; Rom. xii. 9. That the multitude do evil, may be inferred, 1. *From the review of past ages.* Look at the example of the old world, when all flesh had corrupted its way; at Sodom and Gomorrah, when ten righteous persons could not be found amidst that vast population. God, indeed, in after ages, chose a people for himself, but even in reference to these, Isaiah said, "Except the Lord of Hosts had left unto us a very small remnant, we should have been as Sodom," Isa. i. 9. And if iniquity abounded among a people so highly distinguished, what could be expected from heathen nations, who were involved in the deepest darkness, and corrupted by the vilest idolatries? 2. *From the cruel persecutions which have been raised against the righteous in various ages of the world.* What these were in ancient times we learn from Heb. xi. 35—38. But why have the people of God been thus persecuted? because the multitude do evil. The reason why Cain slew his brother was, his works were evil, and his brother's righteous: and the prevalence of persecution has been a standing evidence of the truth we attempt to establish. 3. *From the common conduct of mankind.* Is not vice more general than virtue? Does not evil abound more than good? Is not the world followed with more avidity than religion? See how plays, and amusements, are sought after; what oaths are sworn, what lies are told, what thefts are committed, and what abominations are practiced?

Secondly, The precept in the text suppose, that *we are in danger of copying the example of the multitude.* We may infer this, 1. *From the innate tendencies which we have to evil.* The "imagination of man's heart is evil:" evil has its seat there; and if the fountain be evil will not the stream be evil? Look at little children, who have not been corrupted by the manners of th emultitude, yet what tendencies to evil are evinced, and dispositions to evil displayed in their conduct! 2. *From the prevalence of bad example.* Man is an imitative creature, and easily prevailed upon to imbibe the spirit, and copy the example of those with whom he may associate, and especially, when that example is in unision with his inclinations: hence we are not only disposed to evil, but have facilities to the practice of evil; we are like disordered people in a hospital, surrounded by the dying and the dead, breathing the very atmosphere of disease, putrescence, and death. The practice of the multitude renders vice familiar to our thoughts, and gradually wears off the abhorrence with which we once beheld it. 3. *From a variety of melancholy facts.* The multitude who now do evil, were not always such adepts in depravity; when they first entered into the broad way, their feet were not swift to do evil; they proceeded with hesitating steps, for none become completely wicked on a sudden, but by practice they became hardened in their crimes, and like the wicked whom they followed

II. URGE REASONS TO INDUCE US TO OBSERVE IT.

The multitude doing evil are represented as guides, which men are accustomed to follow; but the reasons why we should not imitate them, are, 1. *They are unlawful and unconstituted guides.* The text itself sufficiently proves this. "Thou shalt not follow," &c. This is God's positive injunction to *thee;* it is personal, and absolute; and wilt thou not revere His authority? God's will is law, and should be regarded as an invariable rule of action; and to "follow a multitude," &c., is to act in direct opposition to God.

2. *They are bad guides.* The principles by which they are actuated are vile, vicious, and ungodly principles: pride, anger, malice, revenge, and all the bad passions that infest the mind: the practices they pursue are bad practices; the way they travel is a bad way. By following "a multitude to do evil," you will become like them, and by yielding to the current of vice, you render that current stronger, for carrying forward others to ruin.

3. *They are dishonorable guides.* For the credit of your characters, you ought not to follow "a multitude," &c. In all ages, the most honorable men have been those who have dared to be singular, and stood aloof from the degenerate crowd, unterrified by their frowns, and untempted by their smiles. Follow a multitude to do evil, and you will dishonor your character, stain your reputation, and involve yourselves in eternal disgrace.

4. *They are unprofitable guides,* "What fruit had you in those things whereof ye are now ashamed?" Evil is a most unprofitable concern, Isa. xlviii. 22. We seldom embark in any enterprise without an eye to profit, but here you may calculate with moral certainty upon the loss of all that is valuable and profitable, for time and eternity.

5. *They are dangerous guides.* We all believe that there is a dreadful hell, a place and state of insufferable pain and punishment; and every evil doer is preparing himself for that punishment; treasuring up wrath against the day of wrath; his steps are taking hold on hell, and he is going down to the chambers of death. By following a multitude to do evil, you endanger your souls, and accelerate your ruin.

III. Impart advice for the direction of those who wish to escape the ensnaring wiles of the multitude.

1. *Get your minds deeply and thoroughly impressed with the awfulness of your situation.* Dangers unseen will be unavoided. Consider your ways; reflect on your past conduct; converse with your own hearts; thoughtlessness is one of the greatest evils in existence, and nothing is more common. Without consideration, you will be irresistibly captivated to do evil.

2. *Seek the regenerating grace of God.* Our carnal natures are wholly inclined to evil; "that which is born of the flesh, is flesh."—Oh! pray for the renewing influence of the Holy Ghost. The Ethiopian may as well attempt to change his skin, or the leopard his spots, as you can cease from doing evil without a change of heart.

3 *Be on your guard against the seductive wiles, and insinuating influence of the multitude.* Sinners will entice you; but come out from among them; have no communion with the unfruitful works of darkness, Ps. i. 1.

4. *Follow the happy few who strive to do good.* The church and the world form two societies, acting in direct opposition to each other; in one of these societies you *must* be; there is no standing neuter. On one side, be your allegiance, your honor, and your interest; on the other, your guilt, your shame, and your punishment. Can you hesitate for a moment where to take your stand? He that is not with Christ, is against him. Show that you are with Christ by being with his people. Oh, say, "This people shall be my people, and their God my God."—

Infer,

1. That the measures of right and wrong are not to be determined by the majority. Good and evil are fixed immutable principles; and their natures are unchangeable, whether many or few follow them.

468

2. What gratitude is due to God, for the revelation of his will, which marks the boundaries of right and wrong; and for the gift of his Son to redeem us from this present evil world: to whom be glory for ever and ever. Amen.

~~~~~~~~~~~~~~~~~

### THE REDEEMER'S COMPLAINT.

John v. 40.—And ye will not come unto me that ye may have life. (Sk.)

WHEN we seriously contemplate a future state of existence, we are over-powered by the magnitude and awful grandeur of the important objects it presents. When in imagination we launch forth from the shore of time, into a boundless of eternity, we feel our need of some one, who shall be constantly present with us, to afford us support, and to make us happy. But to whom shall we turn? Our fellow men are as destitute and feeble as ourselves. Nor is there any being who can meet our necessities, but that God whose potent arm sustains the keys of death, and the invisible world. Against him we have sinned; and can we hope for so much favor at his hands? His word reveals him gracious and merciful. He has given his Son to be our Redeemer. Our Redeemer has procured for us all we need. He offers us what he has procured, "without money and without price;" and even complains "ye will not come unto me, that ye might have life." This complaint suggests several important considerations. Herein,

I. WE HAVE OUR NATURAL STATE EVIDENTLY IMPLIED;—the opposite of 'life;"—a state of DEATH. This representation is frequently made by the scripture writers, who uniformly speak of the unregenerate, as being "*dead in trespasses and sins.*" The representation applies,

1. To the sinner's *judicial state.* We are under the law to God, our rightful sovereign;—have broken his law by open rebellion, as well as by omissions of duty; of course, we are subject to the penalty which the law denounces; and that penalty is *death.* "The soul that sinneth shall die." Thus a condemned criminal, who has forfeited his life to justice, and now waits the time of execution, is *dead in law.* Hence ministers are said to be "the savor of death unto death;"—and the law is denominated the "ministration of *death* and of *condemnation,*" 2 Cor. ii. 16, and iii. 7—9. The term death, applies,

2. To the sinner's *spiritual state.* Accordingly the apostle says, "you hath he *quickened,* who were dead," &c, Eph. ii. 1—5. Here we find several points of agreement between a state of death, and that which it is employed to represent. We select two;—death is a state of *insensibility,* and *inaction.* A corpse is *insensible* to any *insult* or *indignity* that may be offered to it;—would be insensible if in the midst of a *conflagration,* nor does it feel any honors done it, or intended to be done. So a person spiritually dead, feels not the *vile insult* which satan, the "father of lies," and the *most deeply fallen,* offers to both his *understanding* and his heart, when he employs him in his *dirty* and *degrading* drudgery. He is insen-sible of his *danger* of that hell on the breaking brink of which he totters:— and of his *privileges* as a ransomed son of Adam, and the happiness and honor to which he is invited, both *here* and *hereafter.* He neither feels

*shame* and *regret* for his base rebellion, nor *love* and *gratitude* for what Jesus has done and suffered on his account. A corpse is totally *inactive;*—so the dead sinner makes no effort to escape misery, or to secure eternal bliss.

3. The word "death" applies remotely to the *eternal state* of the finally impenitent;—"the second death,—everlasting destruction from the presence of the Lord," Rev. xx. 6, and xxi. 8; 2 Thess. i. 7—9. But,

II. WE ARE POINTED TO THE SOURCE OF LIFE. "Ye will not come to me."

1. Jesus is the source of *legal life;*—of that pardon or justification, by which the sinner's sentence is reversed. "By him, all that believe are *justified from all things,*" Acts xiii. 38, 39. "There is now *no condemnation;*" for "he was wounded *for our* transgressions;"—"died *for us;*"—"suffered, the just *for the unjust;*" therefore, "by his obedience many shall be *made righteous.*" See also Acts xxvi. 18; Eph. i. 7; Col. i. 14.

2. He is the source of *spiritual* life. . "I am *the vine,* ye are *the branches.*" From him believers derive their *vitality,* their *feeling,* their *vigor,* their *fruitfulness* in good works. Hence the apostle, in one place says, "I live: yet not I; but *Christ liveth in me;*" and in another, reminds the pious christian, that when Christ, who *is our life,* shall appear, he also shall appear with him in glory," Gal. ii. 20; Col. iii. 3, 4. From this, it follows, that,

3. He is the source of *eternal life.* "Though he were as a Son, yet learned he obedience by the things which he suffered; and being made perfect, he became the *author of eternal salvation* unto all them that obey him, Heb. v. 8, 9. He *purchased* life eternal, John iii. 14, 15; Rom. v. 1, 2. He *teaches the way* to it, John vi. 68. He, by his Spirit, *qualifies for* it, Rom. viii. 9: John xvii. 3; 2 Cor. v. 17. He will *dispense* it, John x. 27, 28: Matt. xxv. 31—46. In our text,

III. WE ARE INSTRUCTED HOW TO OBTAIN THE LIFE WE NEED. "Ye will not *come* unto *me.*" The "coming," thus recommended, implies,

1. *A change of situation.* The sinner, who was "*alienated,*" and "*far off;*" now *forsakes* his way of wickedness—*approaches* the Saviour; "*draws nigh*" unto God through him; and takes his station within the pale of the church, Prov. xv. 29; Col. i. 21; Eph. ii. 13.

2. It implies, also, *a change of object.* Formerly, he looked for *happiness,* to wealth, honor, worldly connections, &c; and for *salvation,* to a poor Pharisaic righteousness of his own; but now, for both happiness here, and salvation hereafter, he is found "looking *unto* Jesus," Phil. iii. 7—9. Coming to Jesus may perhaps, require,

3. *A change of company.* If your companions will accompany you, well. If not, you must come out from among them, and be separate, 2 Cor. vi. 17. On the other hand, if we wanted to obtain an interview with an earthly prince, from whom we hoped for such favors as none but himself could bestow, we should most gladly avail ourselves of the company and advice of persons who had, in *circumstances similar* to ours, *sought,* and *found admittance* to his presence, and had *presented* their *petition,* and been *graciously accepted.* Apply this thought; and avail yourselves of the *experience* and *assistance* of those who have already come to Jesus, and found him able and willing to save, and who now say, "Come thou with us; and we will do thee good," &c. This coming also supposes,

4. *Confidence* in the Redeemer's power and goodness.

5. *Earnest desire* of obtaining his salvation; and, consequently, a *readiness* to make *every sacrifice*, and to use *every* necessary *means* in order to o'tain it. From our text,

IV. WE LEARN WHAT IS THE IMMEDIATE CAUSE OF MAN'S ETERNAL DESTRUCTION;—" Ye WILL not come unto me." Concerning the freedom of the human will, there have been endless disputes. This is not a time and place to enter at length into the controversy; yet we may offer a few remarks.

1. It is a settled point, that no man can come to Jesus, except the Father draw him, John vi. 44.

2. The question, therefore, is not whether a person may become converted without God's grace; but whether he may not so *reject* the counsel of God against himself, Luke vii. 30, and *resist* the Holy Ghost Acts vii. 51, as to *frustrate* the grace of God? Gal. ii. 21.

3. In answer to this, it may be said, that the language of our text is that of *reproof*. Now, reproof supposes, that the reproved could have acted otherwise, and better than they have done: if they could not, then the blame rests, and the reproof should also rest, somewhere else. But,

4. This point is more fully determined, by Matt. xxiii. 37. " O Jerusalem, Jerusalem, how often *would* I have gathered thy children together, and *ye would not.*"

5. On this principle, God " is justified in his sayings;" and exonerated from the charge and suspicion of being the author of sin; while man appears to be wholly chargeable with both that, and his own perdition.

Lastly. On this principle, and, indeed, even on the opposite one, every sincerely seeking soul may derive from the text the greatest encouragement If you *will* come, you have free liberty and pressing invitation to do so; " Ho, *every one* that *thirsteth*, come ye to the waters." Isa. lv. 1. " The spirit and the bride say, come. And let him that heareth say, come. And let him that is athirst, come. And *whosoever will*, let him take the water of life freely," Rev. xxii. 17.

---

## THE JUDGMENT.

Romans xiv. 10.—We shall all stand before the judgment seat of Christ. (P.)

Our church, during the present season of advent, commemorates our Lord Jesus Christ's first coming " in great humility," to " give his life a ransom" for sinners; and I know not how to improve the present occasion better, that by directing your attention to his second advent, when He will come to be " glorified in his saints"—to be admired by all—and to pass the final and irrevocable sentence upon the whole family of man. To that awful time, the words of the text apply.—" For we must all stand before the judgment seat of Christ Lend me then your prayerful attention, whilst I consider,

I. THE CHARACTER OF THE JUDGE.

II. THE PERSONS TO BE JUDGED

III. THE EVIDENCE AND PROCESS BY WHICH THE JUDGMENT WILL BE CONDUCTED. And,

IV. THE SENTENCE ITSELF.

## I. The character of the judge.

And here I would have every one bear in mind, that what we here say are not matters of trifling import, nor are they idle chimeras as some would have them ; neither are they the mere inventions of man ; but the verities of God's word : they are of eternal importance. The scene here portrayed, is one in which we must all bear a part ; in which the preacher before you must answer for a large share of responsibility committed to his charge, and you, his hearers, for what you hear.

Who will preside on the occasion ?—The Lord Jesus Christ—the Son of God—the Son of God in our nature—our " elder Brother," who came into the world to accomplish our redemption,—who took our nature upon him, and " gave his life a ransom for our sins."

We are informed by himself, that all judgment is committed to him,— " The Father judgeth no man, but hath committed all judgment to the Son." The same is the doctrine of the text,—" For we must all appear before the judgment seat of Christ." Our Saviour says, " When the Son of man shall come in his glory, and all his holy angels with him, then shall He sit on the throne of his glory—Matt. xxv. 31. And an inspired Apostle bears his testimony to this point, Acts xvii. 31. St. John says, in the close of the Apocalyptic vision, referring to the glorious appearance of the Son of God from heaven, Rev. xi. and xx.

Here we behold the Redeemer on his throne of glory, a throne which never had been sullied by impurity or wrong, but of which it may truly be said, ' Righteousness and judgment are the habitation of his throne."—There will be no place for sin after this solemn day, " For the heavens shall pass away with a great noise, and the elements shall melt with fervent heat ;" the glittering stars rush from their orbits, and all created matter be consumed.—

> " And like the baseless fabric of a vision,
> Leave not a wreck behind."

" Behold he cometh with clouds, and every eye shall see him, and they also which pierced him, and all the kindreds of the earth shall wail because of him."

What a wonderful change will then take place ! No longer we behold him the " man of sorrows, and acquainted with grief ;" his sufferings are over—the days of his humiliation past—the atoning blood has ceased to flow —he no longer stands a captive at Pilate's bar ; but now comes to pass sentence on Pilate himself. Then shall we see him " robed in dreadful majesty," making the " clouds his chariots," and riding upon the " wings of the wind."

Then let the Jews repeat their cry, " Crucify him, crucify him,"—let them bow the deriding knee before him and say, " If thou be the Son of God, come down from the cross."—Let the sensualist, and the scoffer at religion, come and meet their Judge—let the hypocritical professor of an holy and spiritual religion tell his idle creed, and show his piety ;—his heart fails him—he now first discovers religion to be a reality, and essential to the welfare of man, and comes from God—he will now be convinced that the Son of God was what he professed to be, " God blessed for ever."

We notice,

## II. The persons to be judged.

The text says all. That Almighty Being, who first created all things by his power, now collects the scattered atoms of his creatures, that body and spirit may re-unite. The Apostle says, " For we must all appear before the judgment seat of Christ." What an assembly will that be !

Europeans and Asiatics, the swarthy sons of Africa, and the scattered tribes of America; the Jew, Turk, Pagan, Infidel, and Christian, will then stand on one common basis, and be judged according to the light which each has possessed, or the dispensation under which he has been privileged to live.—And each for himself, give "account of the deeds done in the body, whether they are good or bad."

In this assembly, we must all bear a part, and take our place; here all distinction but one solitary one, must for ever cease.

Let me, my brethren, call upon you here, to enquire what would be *your* feelings were you at this moment called upon to approach your God?

There is but one way for sinners, by which this dreadful disclosure may be avoided—by which those sins can be washed away; and that is by *now* fleeing to your Saviour, by covering them with his blood; otherwise you must eternally perish

Throw down then, I beseech you, the "arms of your rebellion"—turn to the Redeemer, who came "to seek and to save that which was lost." "Through Him, all your iniquities shall be blotted out," of the book of God's remembrance, and "be cast into the depths of the sea."

III. The evidence and process by which the judgment will be conducted.

"I saw the dead, small and great, stand before God; and the books were opened." The language is figurative, but plain. We are not to suppose that God, to whom the past, present, and future are alike, will require records or remembrances;—all things are open to him. But here he stoops to the capacities of our nature, and speaks "after the manner of men," according to the proceedings in earthly courts, where books are kept and evidences heard. At that awful day, many books will be opened. Time will not allow me to enlarge much on the subject, I will name but a few,

1. The book of *providence* will be clearly opened, and its mysteries explained.

2. The book of the *Moral Law*, and God's dealings towards all his intelligent creatures.

Such an one is not to be found. All have not received the gospel of Christ, and full salvation is alone revealed through that gospel. According to the privileges you have enjoyed, will your comparative guilt be weighed; and the wicked be eternally condemned.

The law demands perfect love to God and man;—consider what the law requires.

3. The book of *the scriptures*. God has given to the world these "treasures of wisdom and of knowledge," their object is to direct the sinner to the Saviour, to reveal a full and free salvation to all; none are excluded from its offers, all are invited to "throw down the arms of their rebellion," to believe and be saved.

4. The book of *conscience*. Conscience is a principle implanted in the mind, and is emphatically called "the Vicegerent of God."

IV. The sentence to be pronounced. The sentence will be short but decisive, and tremendous in its consequences. See Matt. xxv. and realize in your minds the scene before you.

The sentence is as decisive as it is awful.

Having now considered the subject before us, let me offer one or two remarkes by way of application; and,

1. The supreme importance of an interest in Christ.

2. The vast importance of good works, Matt. xxv. 41—45.

## CHAPTER VII.

## THE CONSEQUENCES OF SIN.

### THE EVIL OF SIN.

Jeremiah ii. 19.—Know therefore and see, that it is an evil thing and bitter, that thou hast forsaken the Lord thy God, and that my fear is not in thee, saith the Lord God of hosts. (Pr.)

SIN has not only entered into the world, but is become universal. Every individual is the subject of it, every heart is tainted with it. Had it been otherwise, we should have been more sensible of its evil nature, and more shocked at its deformity. But seeing all are alike diseased, it is but little thought of, and we are not sufficiently aware of its evil tendency. And though it is universal, yet if we obtain not a cure, its malignity will prove no less fatal on that account.

I. ENQUIRE WHEREIN SIN CONSISTS, ACCORDING TO THE DESCRIPTION OF THE PROPHET.

It is here summed up in two things: "forsaking the Lord our God"—and "his fear not being in us."— — —We may see the difference between man's view of sin, and God's view of it. Man regards the evil of sin chiefly as it consists in outward conduct, and as it affects himself or his own interest. But God traces it to its source, as originating in the disposition of our hearts towards him.

1. Every sinner has *forsaken* God.— — —He does not desire him as his portion, but other things in preference.— — —He is not mindful of his favor, nor thinks it worth seeking after; but esteems the friendship of a fellow creature more than his. Like a prodigal son, he has no love to his father, nor concern about his honor. Every sinner says in his heart, "No God." He is nothing but enmity against him: the throne of heaven would not stand secure, if it depended on the sinner, whether God should reign or not. Such is the evil of having forsaken him.

2. As God is not loved, so *neither is he feared*, at least not in such a way as to depart from evil. "My fear is not in thee, saith the Lord God of hosts."— — — Because he forbears, and sentence is not executed speedily, the hearts of the sons of men are set in them to do evil. No evil is avoided, merely out of regard to his authority, but from selfish motives only.

3. From these two sources proceed *all the evils that are in the world.* — — —Forsaking God has been the cause of every abomination: hence all the wars, oppression, and injustice, between nations and individuals.— — — From the same source also arises a rejection of Christ and the gospel; a contempt of religion, and of religious people.— — —Hence also that hardness, and indifference to the gospel, in many who attend upon it.— — —Hence the most solemn warnings and tender expostulations are without effect, and all the mercy of the Saviour is neglected and despised.

II. CONSIDER THE EVIL AND BITTER NATURE OF SIN.

On some accounts, it is very difficult for us properly to understand and feel this part of the subject. The subject itself is incomprehensible, and we are too much blinded by our own depravity to see the evil there is in it.

However, there are a few mediums by which we may form some idea of its magnitude.

1. We may "know and see how evil and bitter a thing sin is," *by th*

*precepts of God's holy law,* which forbid it; and we must measure it by this rule to see what evil there is in it.— — —Men generally estimate the evil of sin by what is commonly esteemed in the world, or commonly practiced amongst men, and by what is allowed to be harmless and excusable. — — —But we must appeal to the law and to the testimony. The world is a poor judge of what is right, as well as of what is true: the word of God is the only criterion by which to judge. Rom. vii. 7.— — —What a pure and happy world would this be, if cemented by love. How much would it then resemble heaven.— — —how evil and how bitter is the reverse.

2. We may "know and see" *by the awful threatenings of God's word,* by which it stands condemned. Deut. xxviii. 15.— — —The Lawgiver of the world has connected punishment with every offense: and could a Being of infinite goodness curse the creatures he has made, if sin were not an evil of inconceivable magnitude!— — —Could a small evil raise such wrath, and kindle such a burning flame? God is displeased with nothing else but sin; and here his anger burns to the lowest hell.

3. We may know and see *by the bitter sorrows of true penitents.*— — —Oh what anguish of soul has it occasioned in those who have been brought to "know and see" its evil nature.— — —Hear the groans of David, see the tears of Peter, and the deep distress of many others. Psa. xxxviii. 1—6; li. 1—4; Zech. xii. 10.

4. Know by *the bitter fruits it has already produced.*— — —Great is the misery of man upon him; but sin is the cause of all.— — —What a catalogue of diseases, oppressions, hardships, and disappointments; the whole creation groaning under the load of human misery.— — —Yet all this is only some of the first effects of this evil and bitter thing.

5. By the still more bitter fruits *it would have produced,* if God had not restrained it.— — —Every city and town would then have been a Sodom. God's authority would be driven out of the world: all mankind would be hateful and hating one another.— — —But, with all that we see and know, we see not a thousandth part of the evil that would result, if God had not said to the waves of this mighty ocean, Hitherto shalt thou go, and no farther.

6. By the *bitter pains of eternal death.* There shall be weeping and wailing, and gnashing of teeth— — —the worm dieth not, and the fire is not quenched— — —the smoke of their torment ascendeth up for ever and ever.— — —This is the hell of fire which sin has kindled.

7. Know it also by the *bitter sufferings of the Son of God*— — —What means that bloody sweat in the garden.— — —What is the meaning of those awful words upon the cross, "My God! My God! why hast thou forsaken me!"— — —But who can estimate the full evil of sin by this comparison: the Saviour in sorrow drowned, but not in sorrow lost!

III. ENFORCE THE EXHORTATION : "Know therefore and see that it is an evil and bitter thing."

1. Unless we know and see this, we can *neither know nor see the salvation of God.*— — —This indeed is the reason why it is so little regarded: the whole need not a physician, but they that are sick.

2. Without a knowledge of the evil of sin, we shall *neither repent of it nor depart from it* to any good purpose.— — —It is only as we are impressed with this conviction that we can be kept from sinning against God, or be made to loathe ourselves in his sight.

3. If we know and see it not truly in this world, we shall be made to

*know and see it to our cost* in the world to come.— — —Sooner or later we must realise the nature and extent of this awful subject.

4. If we are brought to know and see it aright, *we shall come to Christ;* and herein will be the proof of our knowledge being in some measure what it ought to be. John vi. 45.

~~~~~~~~~~~~~~~~~~~~~~

## DREADFUL EFFECTS OF CARNALITY.

Romans viii. 6.—To be carnally minded is death. (Pr.)

WHILE the apostle exhibits in this chapter a brief view of the leading doctrines of the gospel, and the privileges of the godly, he is careful at the same time to show their holy nature, and practical effect.— — —If there be no condemnation, it is to those who " walk not after the flesh."— — —If all things work together for good, it is to them that " love God."— — — If the righteousness of the law is fulfilled in our justification, our sanctification is no less implied : and all carnality is inconsistent with the spirit and design of the gospel, yea, it is death itself.

That carnality has this tendency, may be seen in its effects. It destroys all activity for God, and so produces spiritual death. It fills the world with misery, and destroys all our hopes and happiness. It exposes us to the wrath to come, and so to death eternal.

Where carnality wholly prevails, it produces these effects totally : where it partially prevails, they exist in a partial degree.

I. CARNALITY, IN PROPORTION AS IT OPERATES, PRODUCES STUPIDITY, OR INACTIVITY FOR GOD.

1. The very *essence* of that spiritual death which pervades the heart of the unregenerate, consists in the prevalence of this carnality. To what else can we attribute insensibility under judgments— — —amidst so many mercies— — —unconcern about eternal things———unwillingness to come to Christ———living without God in the world.

2. Where carnality *partially* prevails it produces similar effects, only in a less degree. Its tendency is to render us inactive in holy duties, by weakening and destroying the principles of action : nothing can be done without it.

3. One of these principles is holy *love:* but carnality damps the sacred fire, cools and weakens our resolutions.

4. Another is *hope:* the hope of success in the Lord's service, and of heaven hereafter, is essential to holy activity.———But carnality beclouds our prospects, and hides the objects of hope from our view.

5. *Faith* is also a powerful spring of action : nothing makes us more alive to God than a realising view of invisible objects. Heb. xi.———But carnality weakens our hands, and destroys the energy of faith.

6. Conscious *integrity*, or walking before God, enlivens the christian in his course. Righteousness is the girdle of his reins, it strengthens him for action.———But carnality enervates the mind, produces pusilanimity, inaction and sloth.

7. Spiritual *joy* inspires the soul with courage, with holy ardor and delight in the ways of God.———But carnality is death : it weakens all the springs of action, and paralyzes the whole soul.

476

II CARNALITY, IN PROPORTION AS IT OPERATES, PRODUCES MISERY.

1. We need only consider the state of those who are *wholly* under the dominion of a carnal mind, and we shall see what are its effects.———— There we shall see men ever seeking after happiness, but never able to obtain it.————Men at war with themselves; conscience and inclination at perpetual variance; continual fear and suspense about futurity.————Every affliction gives alarm: they are afraid to know themselves, or their true state, or to think closely about the concerns of their souls. They are loaded with guilt, and are self-condemned.————Oh, to be carnally minded is death ————worse than death.

2. Where this principle only *partially* prevails, it operates in the same, and produces similar effects.————Guilt and darkness, misery and death, are its natural consequences. It causes distance from God, unfits us for communion with him, and casts us out of his sight; and this is the essence of all other misery.

What peace could Jonah have, when he had disobeyed the commandment of the Lord. What happiness could David find, after he had killed Uriah with the sword.————Whither can we go for comfort, apostate from our God!

III. CARNALITY TENDS TO RUIN IN THE WORLD TO COME, AND TO DEATH ETERNAL.

Left to pursue its course, this would be its final issue. Rom. vi. 23; James i. 15.————Eternal death is the just desert of sin, its proper wages, its natural effect, and penal reward.————It is enmity with God: it says to him, Depart from us: and he will say, Depart ye cursed.

Eternal death is the privation of all good, the endurance of all evil.———— Carnality leads to this: it rejects the only remedy, the only refuge, and plunges the soul into the gulf of perdition.

It has the same tendency wherever it exists, and in whatever degree ————If the issue be not the same, it is because that tendency is counter acted. Like poison in the blood, its fatal effects may be prevented; but if it take its course, it will end in death.

How dangerous to seek relief from misery in carnal pleasures. They are bought at the hazard of the soul: the end of these things is death.

---

THE DIFFICULTY OF SALVATION A JUST GROUND OF APPREHENSION
TO THE UNGODLY.

1 Pet. iv. 18.—If the righteous scarcely be saved, where shall the ungodly and the sinner
appear? (S. S.)

EARNESTNESS in the concerns of religion is often thought unnecessary— But the attainment of salvation is by no means easy— This appears from the representations which the scriptures give of religion;—a race, a warfare, &c. The difficulties implied in these metaphors may well alarm the careless— With this view St. Peter suggests the awful query in the text— I. HIS ASSUMPTION. The apostle did not mean to express a doubt, but rather to assume a position which he deemed incontrovertible—

The point he assumes is, that the righteous are saved with difficulty.

The truth of this position will appear, if it be considered that the righteous are not saved without,

Deep afflictions.

God's people in all ages have been afflicted—Zeph. iii. 12.

They have much to endure on account of their religion—2 Tim. iii. 12.

But their trials are beneficial to them—1 Pet. i. 7.

They scarcely ever make any great proficiency without them—Ps cxix. 67.

They always in the issue acknowledge them as blessings—Ps. cxix. 71.

Severe conflicts.

The christian finds much opposition from without and from within—Eph vi. 12.

No attainments whatever put him without the reach of trials—

St. Paul, long after he had been caught up into the third heavens, felt the severest conflicts in his soul—Rom. vii. 15, 23.

They are more or less, the lot of every christian—Gal. v. 17.

And, though painful, they are necessary for us all—1 Pet. i. 6.

None can attain salvation without them, Heb. xii. 8; yet all find it extremely difficult to bear them without fainting—

Powerful assistances.

Nothing less than almighty power can uphold the christian—

This the most righteous men have freely acknowledged—Ps. cxix. 117.

Hence the preservation of the saints is ascribed to God alone—1 Pet. i. 5.

How mistaken then are they who think the attainment of salvation easy !—

Surely if the righteous find the way to heaven so difficult, the ungodly have reason to tremble for their state.

II. THE INFERENCE HE DRAWS FROM IT.

The different characters in the text are the same as those mentioned in the preceding verse—

The question respecting the latter implies that their destruction must be.

1. Certain.

This is constantly affirmed throughout the holy scriptures.

The ungodly shall appear at the judgment-seat of Christ—2 Cor. v. 10.

But they shall not be united with the righteous—Ps. i. 5.

They shall be separated from them for ever—Matt. xxv. 46.

It is deducible also from the foregoing assumption.

The righteous are justified by the blood of Christ, renewed by the Spirit of God, and are striving with all their might, &c.—

The ungodly are unpardoned, unsanctified, unimpressed—

It is impossible that these should have the same end—Isai. iii. 10, 11.

We will appeal to the ungodly themselves, and leave them to say, " where they shall appear ?"—

The want also of many advantages for salvation is a further ground for it.

The righteous have sanctified afflictions, victorious conflicts, and all-sufficient assistances—

The ungodly remain unaltered by afflictions, unacquainted with spiritual conflicts, nor do they even seek God's assistance—

Surely if *those* be *scarcely* saved, *these* cannot be saved *at all*—

2. Dreadful.

St. Peter refers to the fiery trial of persecution in particular as rendering the christian's way to heaven so difficult—

He mentions it as permitted of God for the purging of his church—

He infers from it the dreadfulness of their destruction who oppose or re-ject the gospel—

This inference naturally follows—

If such be the *salutary purgations* of God's *friends*, what must be the *vindictive chastisements* of his *enemies?*

If such things come on his friends in this state of *probation*, what shall come on his enemies.at the time appointed for final *retribution?*

If such be the visitations experienced by his friends *in the day of mercy*, what must his enemies expect *in the day of his wrath?*—

We may *improve* this subject,

1. For conviction.

Every one should inquire into his own character, state, and end *—

Let none rest till they can satisfy their consciences on scriptural grounds—

2. For consolation.

The difficulty of the salvation of the righteous implies however, that, though scarcely saved, they are saved at last—

This is a blessed and consolatory truth †—

Let all then under their difficulties commit themselves to God—1 Pet. iv. 19.

---

### THE GREAT SIN OF REJECTING CHRIST.

**John xv. 22.**—If I had not come, and spoken unto them, they had not had sin: but now they have no cloak for their sin. (S. S )

EVERY sin is committed against an infinitely good and gracious God—

Yet the stoical doctrine of the equality of sins is not therefore true—

Guilt may be aggravated or diminished by a variety of circumstances—

Hence our Lord denounced peculiar woe against Chorazin and Bethsaida—

To the same effect he speaks concerning the Jews in the text—

I. How GREATLY AGGRAVATED THE SIN OF THE JEWS WAS IN REJECTING CHRIST.

Sin admits of so many degrees of malignity, that one may be considered as no sin in comparison of another—

Not that any man can be absolutely without sin—1 John i. 8.

Nor is any man really excusable in the sight of God—Rom. i. 19—21.

But *comparatively* some may be said to "have no sin"—John ix. 41.

Thus it was with those whom our Lord spake—

If he had not come to them, they might have pleaded a want of the necessary means of salvation—

But our Lord's preaching rendered them wholly inexcusable—

---

* Am I righteous, that is, justified, sanctified, and striving for the heavenly prize? Am I improving afflictions, maintaining conflicts, and receiving assistances from God? Have I reason to hope that I shall appear at the right hand of the judge; or am I still unprepared to meet my God?

† John x. 28. This may be well illustrated by the narration of Paul's shipwreck, when all the crew, having been given to him, were, though with great difficulty, saved. Acts xxvii. 44.

They could not plead any want of
Instruction
Our Lord often spake in parables—
This was the means of inflicting judicial blindness on the proud—Luke vii. 10.
But it was well calculated for the instruction of the humble—
Besides, he delivered many things in the simplest terms—
Evidence.
Our Lord wrought many and stupendous miracles—
He performed them by a touch, a word, and even at a distance—
His miracles were as benevolent as they were open and undeniable—
Those who wished to descredit them, imputed them to the agency of satan—
Our Lord mentions them as aggravating the guilt of those who rejected him—ver. 24.
Warning.
There was no want of fidelity on our Lord's part—
He warned the people in the plainest and most awful manner—John viii. 21, 24.
Encouragement.
Every one that thirsted for his benefits was invited by him—John vii. 37, 38.
He offered to give *spiritual* life to all who would come to him—ibid.
He promised also to crown them with eternal happiness and glory—John xii. 26.
If *they* were thus without excuse, it becomes us to consider,
II. HOW MUCH MORE INEXCUSABLE WE ARE IF WE REJECT CHRIST.
Christ has come and preached to us by his word and ministers—
And many reject him after the example of the unbelieving Jews—
Though we be not avowed infidels, we *practically* reject Christ, when we do not receive him for all the ends and purposes for which he was sent—
And if we do so, our guilt is peculiarly aggravated—
We have not any Jewish prejudices to encounter.
The Jews had received their law from God—
They had been accustomed to expect a temporal Messiah—
Yet they saw a man altogether destitute and despised—
And beheld the law of Moses superseded by a new religion—
His works indeed should have obviated all these difficulties—
But we have not these difficulties to contend with—
We profess that the gospel is from God—
We profess that Christ's kingdom is of a spiritual nature—
We profess that his cross is his own glory, and his church's hope—
We see the whole design of God unfolded.
The Jews had only partial and contracted views—
They could not reconcile many seeming contrarieties—
The disciples, even after Christ's resurrection, were at a loss to account for the occurrences they had seen—Luke xxiv. 21.
But we behold the counsels of God completed—
The various prophecies are all accomplished—
The characters and offices of Christ are opened—
The great ends of his incarnation and death are effected—
The glory of God, as shining in his face, is fully displayed—
We have witnessed the success of the gospel.

Those to whom our Lord spake, saw his ministry despised—
The great and learned of their nation rejected him—
His followers were only a few, and those of the lowest class—
But we have seen the "grain of mustard become a large tree"—
The gospel has spread to the remotest corners of the earth—
It has triumphed over the prejudices and passions, the interests and pow-
ers, of the world—
Its influence is yet daily exhibited before our eyes—
How heinous then must be our guilt if we reject him !
Surely our " sin must be of a crimson or a scarlet die"—
Address,
1. Those who make excuses for their neglect of Christ.
With what foolish and weak excuses do men deceive themselves*—
Surely God will not be deceived by these—
What cloak for your sin will you find when he shall call you to account ?—
Will you plead a want of instruction, evidence, warning, or encourage-
ment ?—
Know that in that day you will be speechless—Matt. xxii. 12.
Your love of sin and hatred of the light are the true causes of your reject-
ing Christ—John v. 40.
And this will be the ground of a more aggravated condemnation—John
iii. 19.
2. Those who desire to attain the saving knowledge of him.
It is a great mercy to have such a desire formed in the heart—
But beware of cloaking or extenuating your sin—
Remember that awful yet encouraging declaration—Prov. xxviii. 13.
Confess your sin with all its aggravations—
There is a virtue in the blood of Jesus to cleanse you from it all—1 John
i. 7.

---

## THE SIN AND FOLLY OF GRIEVING THE HOLY SPIRIT.

Eph. iv. 30.—Grieve not the Holy Spirit of God, whereby ye are sealed unto the day of
redemption.  (B.)

THIS is one of the most necessary cautions, and most comprehensive and
useful directions to be found in the oracles of God.  None are of more
general utility, or more needful to be inculcated and regarded.  For all our
saving knowledge in divine things, our holiness and happiness, depend on
the Spirit of God, and a proper conduct towards him.  The subject therefore
is of the deepest importance, and deserves our most serious consideration.
To set it in a just point of view, consider we,

* We may notice a few : " I have not time."  For what is time given ?—" I am not
able."  Do you do what you can ?—" It is time enough yet."  Shall you certainly live,
and have the grace you now slight offered you again ?—" I have the majority on my side."
Are you not then in the *broad* road? and will associates mitigate your pain ?—" Professors
are hypocrites."  Is that a reason *you* should not be sincere ?--" God is merciful."  To
whom ? the *impenitent* !

THE CONSEQUENCES OF SIN.

I. WHAT IS HERE MEANT BY THE "HOLY SPIRIT OF G D," AND HOW HE SEALS US TO THE DAY OF REDEMPTION

By "the Holy Spirit of God," here, is meant that divine person or principle, to which every thing excellent is ascribed in scripture, or to his influence or inspiration.—All the life and motion in the universe, Gen. i. 2; particularly vegetable, animal, rational, and spiritual life.—Skill in arts. Exod. xxxi. 3.—Especially every gift, truly and durably good, and perfective of our nature, as illumination, the scriptures themselves, and the true knowledge of them, and of divine things, 1 Cor. ii. 11—14; Eph. i. 17; regeneration, John iii. 5, 6; including awakening, conviction, mourning, repentance, faith, an inward, universal, continued, and progressive change: direction, help, and succor, Rom. viii. 14, 26.—All our comfort and consolation, Rom. xv. 13.—Progressive and perfect sanctification, Tit. iii. 5; 2 Thess. ii. 13; 1 Pet. i. 2.—A knowledge of our title to, a preparation for, and an earnest of heaven.—For he "seals us to the day of redemption;" he marks us out for the Lord, stamps his image upon us, and preserves us to, and ensures to us, eternal and full redemption.—And yet men are wont to grieve this author of all good!

II. WHAT IS IMPLIED IN GRIEVING HIM, AND HOW THIS IS GENERALLY DONE.

Three expressions are used in scripture on this subject, which, though nearly related to each other, do not mean the same thing.—Doing "despite to the Spirit," Heb. x. 29; treating the Holy Spirit with contumely and affront: viz. blaspheming him, as by imputing the miracles wrought by his agency to the devil, calling his ordinary operations and grace a delusion of the devil, enthusiasm, &c.; persisting to sin wilfully in spite of all his remonstrances, Heb. x. 26.—"Quenching the Spirit." In allusion to fire, which is quenched or damped, by pouring water upon it, by heaping earth or ashes upon it, and whatever is not combustible; by withholding fuel from it, or by neglecting to stir it up. So may the Holy Spirit be quenched.—"Grieving the Spirit." By behaving unkindly towards him; as we grieve a friend, when he comes to warn us of danger, and urge us to flee to a place of safety, and we will not take warning and flee, Gen. xix. 12—14; when he comes to give us instruction and direction, and we refuse to receive it, as the Jews treated the prophets of old; to offer us help, and we reject the help offered, Matt. xxiii. 37; to invite us to partake of privileges and blessings, and we doat on trifling vanities, and disregard the invitation, John v. 40; Luke xiv. 16. To apply this. Our friend will be grieved and pained, not on his own account, but on ours; not merely or chiefly because we are enemies to him, but because we are enemies to ourselves; and the more he loves us, the more will he be grieved, and in the end will withdraw from us, and give us up.— —

But to proceed to the persons by whom, and the manner wherein, that is generally done.—We observe, it is done by the impenitent, when called to repentance by the word; the Spirit accompanies the word, and they feel relentings, but relapse into their besetting sins, fly into company, or plunge into business:—when visited by affliction; the Spirit of God works with his providence, and they are humbled, and form resolutions; they recover, and forget them, and "their goodness is like the morning cloud." Isai. vii. 13, lxiii. 9, 10.—By the penitent, when invited to come to Christ and believe in him: the Spirit draws them by the word and the advice and exhortations of the saints, but, through indolence, they rest in outward reforma tion. or through unbelief sink into despondency, and "reject the counsel of

God against themselves;" how slow are we to believe unless we see signs and wonders!— —By believers. They have properly received the Spirit, and are sealed by him, as the text signifies; but often grieve him, by yielding to unbelief, and slavish fears; by pride and self-confidence, by the love of the world, by care and business, by evil tempers as discontentment or anger, by indulging in vain thoughts and trifling conversation, misemploying time and other talents, as health, and money, neglecting to do good, and so doing evil.— —

III. THE SIN, FOLLY, AND MISERABLE CONSEQUENCES OF GRIEVING THE HOLY SPIRIT.

*The sin of it.*—It is an act of undutifulness and injustice. It may be compared with the sin of grieving a kind and faithful friend, a loving and tender father, an affectionate husband.—An act of ingratitude. The Spirit is the author of all spiritual and eternal blessings to us, as we have seen: he is God's greatest and best gift, next to the gift of his Son. The gifts of God's providence, the scriptures, and the means of grace, and even our redemption by Christ, are all lost upon us without the Spirit, who alone can enlighten, quicken, regenerate, direct, comfort, and seal us to the day of redemption. What is the greatness of the sin of grieving this author of all good to us; the Spirit; the Holy Spirit: the Holy Spirit of God!— —

*The folly of it.*—It may be compared with the folly of grieving a friend, whose direction and help we continually want, a father, on whom we are dependant; a husband, without whom we cannot live happy. If we grieve the Spirit, we grieve our only guide to heaven, forsaken of whom, we shall miss our way and never arrive there;—the only physician of our fallen souls, by whom being given up, we shall remain sick for ever; our only help against our enemies, being deserted of whom, we shall be overcome and destroyed;—our only comforter in our troubles, without whom we shall certainly sink under them;—the only one that can "seal us to the day of redemption;" and not being sealed, we shall want the knowledge of our title, and our chief qualification for heaven. Ezek. ix. 4.— —

*The miserable consequences of it.*—So far as we grieve him, we remain ignorant, sinful, guilty, depraved, weak, and wretched.—Persisting to grieve him, we are doubly lost, as we should have been lost if the Spirit had not visited us at all; we are in a superadded condemnation, because when "light is come into the world, we loved darkness rather than light," and rendered all God had done for our recovery vain: viz., the word of God, the means of grace, the death of Christ.— —

INFER,

The great goodness of God, whose Spirit is grieved, because man will resolve to sin and perish!—The amazing perverseness of man, to whom it is as natural to grieve the Spirit as to breathe!— —

Apply the whole to the impenitent, to mourners, to believers; and exhort from motives of gratitude and self-interest.

## THE CONSEQUENCES OF SIN.

Hos. viii. 7.—They have sown the wind, and they shall reap the whirlwind. (S. S.)

MISERY is attached to sin as its inevitable consequence—

This connection does not always appear to a superficial observer—

On the contrary transgression often seems productive of happiness—

And obedience, to be a source of much affliction and trouble—

But, whatever conclusions we may be led to draw from present appearances, we are sure that the wicked are not happy—

Nor have they any reasonable expectation of happiness in the eternal world—

The Israelites had forsaken the true God for idols—

And God warned them of the judgments which would ere long come upon them—

But the declaration in the text may be understood as a general position—

We shall take occasion from it to shew,

I. WHO MAY BE SAID TO SOW THE WIND.

To " sow the wind" is a proverbial expression for laboring in vain—

It is applied to idolaters, because the silver and gold lavished on idols was unprofitably spent—

And it may well be applied to all who seek happiness in a way of sin.

1. To sensualists.

They expect to find much comfort in the indulgence of their lusts—

Hence they yield themselves up to all the gratifications of sense—

But they find that such pursuits can afford them no real happiness—

While they forsake the fountain of living waters they hew out to themselves only broken cisterns that can hold no water—Jer. ii. 13.

Solomon, with the amplest means of enjoyment, confessed this—Eccl. ii. 1. 10, 11.

And we may address that appeal to all the votaries of pleasure—Rom. vi. 21.

2. To worldlings.

The lovers of this present world seem to follow something substantial—

They hope to obtain, not a momentary gratification, but solid and lasting benefits—

They promise to themselves the acquisition of ease, and affluence and respect—

But riches are justly, and on many accounts, termed "uncertain"— 1 Tim. vi. 17.

No dependence can be placed on their continuance with us—Proverbs xxxiii. 5.

Our cares are also generally multiplied by means of them—

But if they were more conducive to happiness now, what shall they profit in the day of wrath ?—Prov. xi. 4.

What advantage has he now, who once took such delight in his stores—Luke xii. 19.

Or he, who placed his happiness in sumptuous fare, and magnificent apparel ?—Luke xvi. 19, 23, 24.

Surely all such persons will find ere long, that they "sowed the wind"—

3. To formalists.

The performance of religious duties seems more calculated to make us happy—

It is certain that no one can be happy who disregards them—
But a mere round of services can never satisfy the conscience—
" The form of godliness without the power" will avail little—
It will leave the soul in a poor, empty, destitute condition—
Some indeed delude themselves with an idea that it will secure the divine favor—
And, under that delusion, they may be filled with self-complacency—Luke xviii. 11, 12.
But if God send a ray of light into the mind, these comforts vanish—
A sight of sin will speedily dissipate these self-righteous hopes—Rom. vii. 9.
Nor will any thing satisfy an enlightened conscience but that which satisfies God—
There was but one remedy for the wounded Israelites in the wilderness—John iii. 14, 15.
Nor can a wounded spirit ever be healed but by a sight of Christ—
4. To false professors.
Many wish to be thought religious, when they are destitute of spiritual life—
They perhaps are zealous for the doctrines of the gospel, and for their own particular form of church government—
But they are not solicitous to live nigh to God in holy duties—
Nor do they manifest the efficacy of religion in their spirit and conduct—
Yet, because of their professing godliness, they think themselves possessed of it—
And buoy up themselves with expectations of happiness in the world to come—
Alas! what disappointment will they one day experience!—Matt. xxv. 11, 22.
What will it avail them to " have had a name to live while they were really dead ?"—
Or to have " cried, Lord, Lord, while they departed not from iniquity ?—
The pains they have taken to keep up a profession, will all be lost—
Nothing will remain to them but shame and confusion of face—
From the seed which they sow we may easily perceive,
II. WHAT THEY MAY EXPECT TO REAP.
" A whirlwind" is a figure used to represent extraordinary calamities—Prov. i. 27.
And such is the harvest which they will reap in due season—
Their calamities will be,
1. Sudden.
The corn ripens gradually for the sickle; and its fate is foreseen—
But the destruction of the ungodly cometh suddenly and at an instant.
They indeed have many warnings from all which they see around them—
But they put the evil day far from them, and think it will never come—2 Pet. iii. 4.
Thus it was with the whole world before the deluge—
Though Noah preached to them for many years, they would not regard him—
And were taken by surprise at last, as much as if no notice had been given them—Matt. xxiv. 38, 39.
Thus also it will be with all who reject the gospel salvation—

Solomon has expressly declared it in reference to those who sow discord—Prov. vi. 14.

And St. Paul has asserted it respecting all that live in a neglect of God. 1 Thess. v. 2, 3.

2. Irresistible.

Sinners of every description can withstand the word spoken by their fellow-creatures—Ezek. xx. 49.

But they will not be able to resist God when he shall call them into judgment—

Then, if the whole universe should enter into a confederacy to protect one sinner, they would fail in their attempt—Prov. xi. 21.

There is not any thing more irresistible to man, in some climates, than a whirlwind—

Yet far less power shall the ungodly have to avert the wrath of God—

They will be carried to destruction as the chaff before the wind—Ps. i. 4, 5.

And call in vain to the rocks to fall upon them, or the hills to cover them—Rev. vi. 15—17.

3. Tremendous.

Nothing can be conceived more dreadful than the desolation made by whirlwinds—

Yet this suggests a very inadequate idea of the ruin that will come on the ungodly—

The raining of fire and brimstone on Sodom and Gomorrah must have been exceeding terrible—

But even that was light, when compared with the vials of God's wrath which will be poured out upon the ungodly world—

Who can comprehend the full import of that threatening in the Psalms?—Ps. xi. 6.

Who can form a just idea of the judgment denounced by Isaiah—Isa. v. 24.

May we never experience such dreadful calamities !—

May we tremble at the apprehension of them, and seek shelter in Christ! —Isa. xxxii. 2.

INFER,

1. How earnest should we be in redeeming time.

The present hours are given us that we may sow for eternity—

Every action, word and thought is as seed that will spring up hereafter—

According to what we sow now, we shall reap at the last day—Gal. vi. 7, 8.

Every moment increases our " treasure of wrath," or our " weight" of glory"—

How should we be affected with this consideration !

Let us lay it to heart, and " walk not as fools, but as wise men"—Eph v. 15, 16.

And let that just expostulation shame us to a sense of duty—Isa. lv. 2

2. How blessed are they who are living to God !

There is not a work which they perform for him that will not be rewarded—

God would esteem himself unjust if he made them no recompense—Heb. vi. 10.

However small and insignificant the service be, it shall not be forgotten—Matt. x. 42.

Some perhaps may complain, that they cannot do any thing for God

And. that they can only weep for their unprofitableness—

486

But the sighs and tears of the contrite are " precious seed"—
They will spring up to a glorious and abundant harvest—Ps. εxxvi. 6.
Let the humble then go on "sowing in tears till they reap in joy"—
Let them persist in their labor, assured that it shall not be in vain—1 Cor. xv. 58.

---

## THE END OF UNBELIEVERS.

1 Pet. iv. 17.—What shall the end be of them that obey not the gospel of God. (S. S.)

MANY are the troubles of the righteous : and though their afflictions are not always penal, yet they are for the most part to be considered as paternal chastisements, and as the judgments which God inflicts on his own household with a view to their advancement in faith and holiness—But though they are to be regarded in this favorable light by the sufferers themselves, they have a very awful aspect upon the world at large ; for, as the Apostle intimates, if God's paternal chastisements be often so severe, what must his vindictive judgments be ? If judgment first begin at the house of God, what must the end be of them that obey not the gospel of God?—To impress this solemn consideration upon our minds, we shall shew,

I. WHO THEY ARE THAT OBEY NOT THE GOSPEL.

To ascertain this, it will be proper to state briefly what the gospel requires.

The gospel supposes men to be in a state of guilt and misery, obnoxious to the wrath of God, and incapable of delivering themselves from it—It proposes to them a remedy of God's appointment : it sets forth Jesus as an all-sufficient Saviour ; and declares that sinners of every description may be washed in his blood, and renewed by his Spirit—But, if we will not apply to him by faith, and thankfully accept his proffered benefits, it dooms us to destruction under the aggravated guilt of despising, and trampling under foot the Son of God—The commission which our Lord gave to his disciples, Mar. xvi. 15, 26, and the answer given by Paul to the awakened jailor, Acts xvi. 30, 31, abundantly confirm this view of the gospel, and shew that a cordial acceptance of Christ as our only Lord and Saviour is the sum and substance of a christian's duty—

According to this statement, very many will be found disobedient to the gospel.

1. They who neglect Christ altogether.

This is so obvious a truth that the mention of it seems needless and absurd : but experience proves that the most abandoned sinners, and most avowed infidels, are often insensible of the guilt which they contract—Be it known however, that their excuses or objections will avail them nothing in the day of judgment : their whole lives were one continued act of disobedience to the gospel ; and they will most assuredly be numbered amongst the enemies of their incarnate God—Their rejection of him, whether in principle or practice, will be a decisive evidence of their guilt—

2. They who unite something else with him as a foundation for their hope.

The gospel requires us to renounce all dependence on our own works—However good our works be, they must never for one moment be considered as justifying us before God, either in whole or in part—In Christ alone must be all our hope; and if we attempt to unite any thing of ours with his perfect righteousness, we shall not only not add to our security, but shall altogether invalidate all which Christ himself has done for us—St. Paul asserts this in the plainest terms, Gal. v. 2, 4; and from the fullest conviction of its truth desired to be found in Christ, clad with his righteousness and his only—Phil. iii. 9.

3. They who, while they profess to follow Christ, dishonor him by their conduct.

Many there are who with apparent zeal cry, Lord, Lord, who yet are far from doing the things which he commands—Many alas! "profess to know him, but in their works deny him:" they are observant of outward duties, but inattentive to their spirit and temper: instead of being meek and lowly, patient and forgiving, and solicitous only to honor God, they are proud and passionate, covetous and worldly, and studious rather to be thought christians than really to deserve the name—Let such know that they "amidst all their appearances of religion deceive themselves, and their religion is vain"—James i. 26. By neglecting to walk as Christ walked they disobey the gospel, as much as if they rejected him altogether—

To awaken such from their slumbers, we proceed to shew,

II. WHAT THEIR END SHALL BE.

The peculiar manner, in which the apostle speaks of their "end," intimates that it will be dreadful,

1. Beyond expression.

In the text St. Peter infers from the trials, which God suffers to come upon believers *here*, the far greater miseries that shall be endured by unbelievers *hereafter*—But his very mode of suggesting this inference shews, that the two states could scarcely admit of any comparison: for what are any transient pains of body inflicted by the most ingenious cruelty of man, when compared with the eternal torments both of soul and body, which will be inflicted on the wicked by the hand of an incensed God?—St. Paul institutes a similar comparison, and, like St. Peter, leaves our imagination to supply what no language could possibly express—Heb. x. 29. There are indeed terms used in scripture to represent to us the misery of the damned—They are represented as "cast into a lake of fire and brimstone," "where the worm of an accusing conscience dieth not, and the fire of God's wrath is not quenched:" they "weep and wail and gnash their teeth;" and the "smoke of their torment ascendeth up for ever and ever:" But, awful as these expressions are, they convey no adequate idea of the misery sustained by those who have perished in unbelief: we must say of that, as St. Paul says of the things he heard and saw in the third heavens, that it is unutterable—2 Cor. xii. 4.

2. Beyond a doubt.

The apostle appeals to our own consciences for the truth of the inference which he suggests—He says, in effect, What must the state of unbelievers be? Can it be the same with that of obedient believers? Will God put no difference between those who serve him, and those who serve him not? Has not the scripture plainly declared the end of those who disobey the gospel? And are we not constrained to acknowledge the equity of that sentence, which the contemners of Christ are taught to expect?—Shall not an angel from heaven be accursed if he presume to preach any other gospel, Gal. i. 8, and can we hope to reject the gospel with impunity? Our wishes are doubtless in opposition to the declarations of God; but in our judgment we must approve of them; and we shall surely be silent in the day, that they shall be enforced, even though we ourselves be the unhappy monuments of God's displeasure—

We may *learn* from hence,

1. How to improve the dispensations of God's providence.

In God's providential dealings the most eminent christians are often involved in public calamities, or bowed down under a load of personal afflictions—On the other hand the enemies of God often triumph, and revel in a fullness of all earthly enjoyments—But the intelligent christian will see in these dispensations the certainty of a future day of retribution, when the wicked shall receive the just reward of their wickedness, and he himself be exalted to an inconceivable state of bliss—He will argue thus: If God so afflict his children in the day of his mercy, how will he punish his enemies in the day of his wrath? And if he so prosper his enemies and load them with benefits in this vale of tears, what prosperity and happiness must he have reserved for his friends in the regions of glory? If crowns and kingdoms be the portion of many who disregard and despise him, what shall be the inheritance of those who honor and obey him?—Such are the reflections suggested in the text; and such are the considerations which every dispensation, whether joyous or grievous, should excite in our minds.

2. How to judge of our state before God.

Mere morality is by no means a sufficient criterion whereby to judge of our state: we may be free from gross violations of God's law, and yet be far from yielding obedience to the gospel—Let us then enquire whether we be obeying the gospel by a simple dependence upon Christ, and by a spirit and temper suited to our profession? This is the test to which we must bring ourselves, since we shall be tried by it at the last day—In vain will be our morality, if Christ be not our only foundation; and in vain will be our professed adherence to Christ, if we do not adorn the gospel by an holy conversation—Let us then examine ourselves, that we may know beforehand what our end shall be—And let all earthly comforts or troubles be improved as means of exciting us to flee from the wrath to come, and to lay hold on eternal life.

---

## THE CHARACTER AND END OF A SENSUALIST

Luke xii. 20, 21.—But God said unto him, thou fool! this night thy soul shall be required of thee: then whose shall those things be which thou hast provided? so is he that layeth up treasure for himself, and is not rich toward God. (Sk.)

How must these words have struck the ears, and have sunk into the soul of the person to whom they were addressed! Fancy to yourselves a man wholly engaged by the affairs of this life;—quite unconcerned about his situation as a dying mortal, and as a creature accountable to God;—his salvation—his immortal concerns—entirely neglected;—at night, and alone, ruminating and contriving thus,—"what shall I do," &c., ver. 17—19, when—sudden and unexpected—he hears that voice, from whose sentence there is no appeal, saying, "fool! this night thy soul shall be required of thee," &c. But why did I say, *fancy* all this? When all that was worldly and thoughtless in this man, it probably realized in the disposition and conduct of many present, who differ from him, not in character, but in situation.

489

against him the sentence of death had just been pronounced; against you it is not yet uttered. Thanks be to God that it is not! You are still in a land of hope. Oh! suffer me to expose the impropriety and danger of your conduct, by describing—*the folly of this person; and the manner in-which God treated him.*

I. THE FOLLY OF THE PERSON MENTIONED IN THE TEXT: The meaning of the word " fool," as it is here applied, may be discovered by consulting the following passages; Deut. xxxii. 6; Psa. xciv. 8; Prov. xiv. 9; Rom. i. 21—25; Tit. iii. 3; Jer. xvii. 11. Thus understood, *folly* is wickedness; and the folly of this man consisted in,

1. *His making the things of this life his chief good.* That he did this, is manifest, from the whole of what is said respecting him.—The world was his god:—it had his heart;—all his wishes centred in it;—his thoughts were absorbed by its concerns:—he appears to have known no higher gratification than that which arose from eating, drinking, and making merry. How wicked was all this! It implies a total want of regard for God, Psa. lii. 7. If he were not a covetous man—one who is never satisfied—he was evidently a sensualist, who lived only for himself: see Rom. viii. 6, 13, and xiii. 14; Gal. vi. 7, 8. Besides, how foolish to depend on uncertain riches! Prov. xxiii. 5, and xi. 28; Jer. ix. 23. Can any measure of them keep off sickness, infirmities, or the ' thousand other ills that flesh is heir to?' Can they prolong life, or set death at defiance? Job xxxvi. 18, 19. Such conduct tends to sensualize the very spirit. Hence, another proof of this man's folly, is manifest in,

2. *His supposing that worldly goods would satisfy his soul.* Though he appears to have believed that he had a soul, his ideas of its nature must have been very gross; or could he have said " *soul,* thou hast much goods; eat, drink, be merry?" The folly of such conduct will appear, if we consider—*the nature of the soul.* It is a spiritual, and a rational principle, Gen. i. 27, and ii. 7; Job xxxii. 8. Can the gross materials that feed the body satisfy the soul?—*The capacities of the soul.* They, on account if its very nature, are so vast, that no measure of created good can possibly satisfy them.—*The duration of the soul.* It is immortal, everlasting, Eccl. xii. 7; Matt. x. 28. Can perishable things—such as earth affords—earth that will itself be destroyed, satisfy the immortal soul of man? Such foolish conduct, as that already described, naturally leads to another species of folly, that of,

3. *Presuming on continued, on long life.* He said, " soul, thou hast much goods laid up *for many years.*" How infatuated must that man have been, who could thus calculate! see Psa. xlix. 11—13. Do we not *see* mortals arrested, and borne to their graves, at every stage of life! How frequently do we *hear* the sighs and groans of the dying :—we *feel* pains, infirmities, and decays of nature, which are sure harbingers of death ;—and in the death of relatives and friends, we almost *taste* the deadly draught; and yet men will, with confidence, calculate on long life!

4. *Thus one species of folly or of wickedness leads to another.* Men make created things their chief good; then persuade themselves that such things will satisfy even their souls: this is naturally followed by a wish to enjoy them for many years; and then they persuade themselves, that for many years they shall enjoy them. Persons of the above description do not always pass for wicked men, Psa. xlix. 18, but in the sight of God, their conduct is highly offensive, Jer. xvii. 5, as will appear from,

II. THE MANNER IN WHICH GOD TREATED THE SUBJECT OF THIS FOLLY. We have in the Bible such numerous intimations of the goodness, the mercy, and the longsuffering of God, as should correct the ideas of those, who, being penitent, would despair of his mercy; and of those whose severe dispositions would lead them to describe the blessed God only as a terrible sovereign. But we have, on the other hand, such intimations of God's justice, and of the exercise of the divine displeasure towards the impenitent, as should alarm the boldest offender; and correct the errors of those, who, by a species of humanity, would question the divine prerogative to punish, let the guilty escape, and even annihilate hell itself. The circumstance under consideration speaks awful things.

1. *This man was called away* SUDDENLY. "God said unto him, *this night* thy soul shall be required of thee." Sudden death had been considered an evil; hence that petition in the liturgy, "from sudden death, good Lord, deliver us." In whatever light it may be viewed, as it respects the righteous, to the wicked it must be terrible. It finds them unprepared; it snatches them from all they love; it hurries them, in their sins, before the bar of God. See Prov. xiv. 32.

2. *He was called away* UNEXPECTEDLY. He had been calculating only on life and worldly enjoyments; on living long and enjoying much. What a terrible, and unexpected arrest! Even a good man cannot fail to be seriously affected by such a circumstance. See 2 Kings xx. 1—8; Isa xxxviii. 9.

3. *He was called away* AMIDST A PROFUSION OF WORLDLY GOODS. "Much goods laid up," was his language. Some in a state of wretchedness, misery, and want, without calculating on future consequences, have sought and have welcomed death, as a kind of deliverer from present wo. However dreadfully mistaken, such, though unprepared, have left the world without regret. But this man loved life: he had, to use a common phrase, "made his fortune," and was going to enjoy life. Ah! in what period, and in what circumstance could death be more unwelcome? See Job xx. 22, 23; Eccles. vi. 1, 2.

4. *He was called away* BY LANGUAGE THAT STRONGLY EXPRESSED THE DIVINE DISPLEASURE. The language is truly *cutting*. *He* had said, "*soul* thou hast," &c.; *God* said, "thy *soul* is required." *He* had calculated on "*many years;*" *God* said, "*this night* thy soul shall be required." *He* had said, "soul, *thou hast* much goods;" God said, "*whose* shall these things be?" *He had acted a part the most foolish;* and God addressed him by the cutting appellation, "*fool.*" He had passed through his day of grace, *totally neglecting salvation;* and *God summoned him away, unrenewed and unforgiven.* What a dreadful circumstance! and yet from the remainder of our text, we are led to fear that circumstances of this kind are not uncommon; for "*so is he that layeth up treasure for himself, and is not rich toward God.*"

The following reflections urge themselves on our attention:

1. Worldly prosperity is so far from being a proof of personal goodness, or of the divine favor, that the subjects of it may be so wicked as to incur sudden and severe destruction. See Psa. lxxiii. 2—12, 18, 19.

2. The proper enjoyment of life does not depend on large possessions, verse 15.

3. Rich men are, on account of their riches, in peculiar danger—of living without God—of indulging in sensual gratifications—of presuming on long life—and of neglecting their souls.

4. Life is uncertain.—It is therefore our highest wisdom to be living for eternity. Oh that men, instead of inquiring, as they too often do, in the

language of worldly concern, and of worldly anxiety, "what shall we do?" would thus inquire after salvation. Then would we gladly point them to Jesus the mighty Saviour, to religion the true riches, and to heaven the only sure depository, for what is truly valuable in time or in eternity.

---

## A DESCRIPTION OF THE WICKED, AND THE HELL INTO WHICH THEY SHALL BE TURNED.

Psa. ix. 17.— The wicked shall be turned into hell, and all the nations that forget God. (Sk.)

THE authorized topics afforded to God's ministers, for instruction and reproof, are various and dissimilar. Revelation presents innumerable subjects to our view; all of which, though not of equal importance, are worthy of the deepest attention and the most implicit confidence; some of these are the themes of every gospel minister, and the delight of every christian congregation—the love of God to the world—the atonement of Christ for sinners—the invitations of the gospel to the most unworthy—and the heaven prepared for the saints, are truths of the most pleasing aspect, and the most encouraging character. Happy should we be in beholding all who sit under our ministry, charmed, converted, and drawn to God by the publication of these truths; but, alas! many are yet hardened through the deceitfulness of sin. These we must persuade by the terrors of the Lord, or "save with fear, pulling them out of the fire." Many are yet wicked; these must be told of the punishment which they are preparing for themselves—this is their " portion of meat" which must be administered " in due season,"—and this is the only apology we make for laying before you the awful affirmation chosen for the text; " The wicked shall be turned into hell," &c. Here observe,

I. THE CHARACTERS SPECIFIED ;—" The wicked, and all the nations that forget God." Scripture is its own interpreter; and in describing the characters spoken of in the text, we will be guided by this rule, and compare spiritual things with spiritual. By the wicked, then, we understand,

1. *All those who willfully violate the plain and positive precepts of God.* Such as intemperate persons, who eat or drink to excess, Nah. i. 10; Joel i. 5; Luke xii. 34; Rom. xiii. 13; Eph. v. 18. Profane persons, whose mouths are full of cursing and bitterness, Exod. xx. 7; Matt. v. 34; James v. 12. Liars, Zech. viii. 16; Colos. iii. 9; Rev. xxii. 15. Profaners of the Sabbath, who prostitute that holy day in purposes of pleasure or business, Exod. xx. 8; Isaiah lvi. 2, and lviii. 13. Dishonest persons, who deprive their neighbors of their property, by acts of theft or extortion; taking advantage of their ignorance or necessity, to enhance the price of their goods, Exod. xx. 17; Matt. x. 19; 1 Thess. iv. 6.

2. *Among the wicked we must include all the persecutors of the people of God.* Such was Pharaoh, who said, " The Lord is righteous, and I and my people are wicked;"—such was Manasseh, who shed innocent blood very much, and " who wrought much wickedness," 2 Kings xxi. 6;—such was Haman, who meditated a plan for the destruction of all the Jews from India even unto Ethiopia, and who is designated as " this wicked Haman:"—and such were the Jews in the days of our Saviour, whom he denominated a " wicked generation," and concerning whom Peter said, " Ye have taken, and by wicked hands " &c., Acts ii. 23.

3. *In the list of wicked persons we also rank all hypocrites, and impostors in religion;* who profess to know God, but by works deny him. Such were the Pharisees, who came to our Lord, Matt. xxii. 15; but Jesus "perceived their wickedness," &c.; for though they made clean "the outside of the cup and platter, their inward part was full of ravening and wickedness," Luke xi. 39.

4. *All must be denominated wicked who are unregenerate.* Wickedness is not a superficial defect, but a profound radical principle, deeply rooted in the heart of man, which is said to be "desperately wicked:"—the crimes we have enumerated are a few only, of the fatal fruits produced by this root of bitterness. Man, considered as a fallen creature, is not merely inclined to wickedness, but his inward part is very wickedness: and this applies not only to a few individuals, but to all; for "the world lieth in wickedness:" and unless your hearts have been washed from wickedness, in the fountain opened for sin and uncleanness, you must be included in the characters specified in the text. But, in addition to the wicked, we have "all nations that forget God."—Perhaps this expression refers to heathen nations, whose gods were idols, Psa. xcvi. 5; but how far the whole inhabitants of any nation forget God we cannot determine. Nations are composed of individuals, and every man who forgets God (whatever be his country, clime, or language) must be included here. The latter part of the text may be considered as explanatory of the former—the wicked are they who forget God. David's description of a wicked man is, "God is not in all his thoughts," Psa. x. 4;—he forgets God in the character of a *Sovereign,* and refuses to walk in his law, Psa. xii. 4;—as a *Benefactor,* he renders not again according to the benefit done unto him, 2 Chron. xxxii. 25;—he forgets *the all-prevailing presence of God,* so as to have no consciousness that God seeth;—he forgets *the word of God*—to its precepts he never conforms—with its invitations he never complies—its promises he never embraces—and its threatenings he never fears. Having described the characters specified in the text, let us consider,

II. THE AFFIRMATION MADE CONCERNING THEM;—"They shall be turned into hell." Here we may remark three things—the *place* into which they shall be turned—the *manner* how it will be done—and the *certainty* of the affirmation. The place is *hell,* שאול a word used sometimes to describe the grave, or a separate state of departed spirits, Gen. xxxvii. 35; Psa. xvi. 10; but more commonly descriptive of that place of punishment into which the souls of the wicked shall be thrust, when discharged from the body, Luke xvi. 23. The holy scripture, which must be our sole guide in all things that relate to the eternal world, gives us various ideas concerning this awful state of being.

1. *It describes the place of punishment.* It is called "outer darkness," Matt. viii. 12;—a lake of fire, burning with brimstone, Rev. xix. 20, xx. 10;—a bottomless pit, Rev. ix. 1, 2, xx. 1, 2;—blackness, Jude 13;—the mist of darkness, 2 Pet. ii, 17, xx. 1, 2;—a furnace of fire, Matt. xiii. 42.

2. *The nature of the punishment.* It will be inflicted by fire—fire unquenchable, Matt. iii. 12; Luke iii. 17. The pain produced by fire, is the most intolerable that the body can sustain; even when it only touches a part of our flesh, how exquisite is the torment we feel; what then must the punishment of the damned be, who will be cast into a lake of fire? But there will be in hell, deep mental anguish; "there the worm dieth not," Mark ix. 43. This metaphor is used to describe the inward agonies, which the soul must sustain from the stings of conscience. Something of this kind is

intimated by Homer, who, in describing the sufferings of **Tityus in hell,** says,

> "Two rav'nous vultures, furious for their food
> Scream o'er the fiend, and riot in his blood,
> Incessant gore the liver in his breast,
> Th' immortal liver grows, and gives the immortal feast."

*Odyss.* b. xi. 709.

The Roman poets, like the Grecian, describe furies as avengers of wickedness in hell. They represent these furies, as old, squalid, meagre, and pale they clothe their bodies with black garments; affix to their heads vipers in stead of hair, and arm their hands with scorpions, whips, and torches, &c. In hell, the wicked will also be punished by the just judgment of God. Who can read such texts as the following, without being struck with horror at the view of their punishment? Deut. xxxii. 23—41; Psa. xi. 6; Jer. xxiii. 19; 2 Thess. i. 7—9; Rev. xiv. 9—11.

3. *The exquisite sense of punishment which the wicked will feel.*— "There shall be weeping and gnashing of teeth, when ye shall see Abraham, and Isaac, and Jacob, and all the prophets in the kingdom of God; and you yourselves thrust out," Luke xiii. 28; Matt. xiii. 42, xxii. 13, and xxiv. 51. Weeping and wailing, in the view of that eternal loss which they had sustained, for they shall see Abraham, &c., in the kingdom of God;—and from a consciousness that they might have shared in the same blessedness;—and "gnashing of teeth," with undescribed agony, and inward vexation, for having plunged themselves into that place of torment; with envy at the saints, and every expression of rage and malice against God and goodness.

4. *The companions of their punishment.* Besides the fearful and unbelieving, the abominable, murderers, whoremongers, sorcerers, idolaters, liars, thieves, drunkards, and revilers, 1 Cor. vi. 10; Rev. xxi. 8, of which the wicked will be composed: they will be associated with "the devil and his angels," Matt. xxv. 41. The devil, who is described as an old serpent—an adversary—a dragon—and a roaring lion;—"his angels," his messengers:— these will be the tormentors of the wicked, Matt. xviii. 34. Their tempters here, will be their tormentors in hell; they will probably remind them of their folly—of their crimes—and of the heaven they have lost, and "toss their infamy from tongue to tongue."

5. *The perpetuity of their punishment.* The fire of hell is unquenchable, and the worm is deathless. The punishment is everlasting; the great gulf that intervenes between paradise and perdition, is impassable; and the crimes of the wicked, after death are unpardonable, Matt. xii. 32, xxv. 42, 2 Thess. i. 9; Rev. xiv. 11.

"The wicked shall be turned into hell;"—this shall be done,

1. *Unexpectedly.* A few indeed have presentiments of their approaching punishment, and forebodings of their impending doom; but the great mass of the wicked are lulled to sleep by the fascinating charms of sin, and the dreadful delusions of the devil;—are led on blindly towards destruction; and, contrary to all their expectations, are turned into hell.

2. *Suddenly.* How many are cut off in a moment! Death suddenly seizes upon them, and they go down *quick* into hell, Psa. lv. 23. And though many of the wicked may linger on to old age, yet the stroke of death is sudden, Psa. lxxiii. 19; Prov, xxix. 1; 1 Thess. v. 3.

3. *Irresistibly.* The expression in the text conveys an idea of violence and impetuosity; *turned*, or hurried headlong into hell; driven by death into

494

the territories of perdition. The destruction of the wicked will come upon them as a whirlwind, Prov. i. 27. They will be bound hand and foot, and taken away and *cast* into outer darkness, Matt. xxii. 13.

The certainty of the affirmation in the text, may be inferred,

1. *From the general consent of mankind.* The idea of future punishment has been almost universal, from the remotest periods of antiquity; and it cannot be supposed that men of different ages, and distant countries, would agree on this point, if the idea had not rested on grounds of wide extent, discernible to the understandings of men in general.

2. *From the justice of the moral Governor of the universe.* In the present state of things, evil goes unpunished in a thousand instances, either by human or divine justice; but the Judge of all the earth will do right, and will not suffer the eternal laws of right and wrong to be violated with impunity; and as the wicked are not punished here, the righteousness of God will induce him to turn them into hell.

3. *From the moral unfitness of the wicked for any other situation.* They must die, and heaven or hell must receive them; but they are totally unfit for the former, and completely prepared for the latter. Heaven is the region of holiness, and the habitation of the great King; but into his presence they cannot come, for evil shall not dwell with him; they cannot even *see* God; to hell they *must* go, this is the reward of their hands, the meed of their toil, and the wages of their iniquity.

4. *The certainty of the affirmation is incontestibly proved from the Bible.* Psa. lxxv. 8; Matt. xxv. 41. We conclude by observing—How awful is the state of the wicked! Language fails to describe the horror and punishment that await them; and what is most to be deplored, they have no knowledge of their danger. Oh how amazing is the infatuation that has seized them!—But what deep commiseration should christians feel in contemplating the circumstances of their wicked neighbors, and especially the awful state of heathen nations! Oh what efforts should they make to save souls from death!—and what praise should they offer to God, who has plucked them as brands from the burning, and saved them from those things of which they are now ashamed.

---

# CHAPTER VIII.

## THE BLESSEDNESS OF RELIGION.

### THE CITY OF GOD

Psalm lxxxvii. 3.—Glorious things are spoken of thee, O city of God. (Sk.)

ALTHOUGH the whole of this Psalm literally refers to the ancient city of David, it is undoubtedly an encomium on the glory and privileges of the gospel church, of which Jerusalem was a type. Jerusalem was exalted and fortified by its situation, but much more so by the favor and protection of Jehovah, ver. 1, 2. "He loved the gates of Zion more than all the dwellings of Jacob." What Jerusalem *was*, that the christian churcl. now *is*—Built by God "upon the foundation," &c., Eph. ii. 20. He loves her beyond the kingdoms and empires of the earth, which rise and fall only to subserve his purposes concerning her. But although Jerusalem was eminently typical of the church on earth, it was no less so of the triumphant church above.—We shall therefore contemplate the words of our text,

I. IN THEIR LITERAL REFERENCE TO THE JEWISH METROPOLIS. Jerusalem was truly the "city of God;"—the city which he particularly chose— to which he paid especial regard. Hence "glorious things" were spoken of her. She was beautiful for situation, magnificent in her buildings, the delight of the nations, and the joy of the whole earth. She was the emporium of Jewish commerce, and the seat of oriental learning. Above all others, the following glorious things were spoken of this city:

1. *There was the seat of the civil government.* There were the splendid courts of the kings of Judah. "There," says the Psalmist, "are set the thrones of judgment," &c.—There the princes and nobles resided— thence issued the mandates by which the people were governed, &c.

2. *There the divine ordinances were celebrated.* There was the ark, the altar, the sacrifices, the stupendous temple of Solomon, and the testimony of Jehovah—There were the singers, the musicians, and the priests—Yea, there were the visible symbols of the divine glory, and the king of heaven dwelling in the midst of his people, 2 Chron. vii. 16; Ps. xlviii.

3. *There was the general rendezvous of all the Israelitish tribes.* Three times a year all the males came up to worship at Jerusalem. How interesting to see such multitudes all assembled to praise the Lord in the beauty of holiness, playing on sacred instruments, singing, making solemn processions, &c.

4. This city received a *glorious name,* "vision of peace;" and was at length honored with *the presence of our Lord,* "the Prince of Peace."

II. IN THEIR SPIRITUAL APPLICATION TO THE CHURCH OF CHRIST. St. Paul styles this, "Jerusalem which is from above, which is the mother of us all"—of all believers, Gal. iv. 26. Hence Christians are represented as "fellow citizens," Eph. ii. 19. Now of this spiritual city, the antetype of Zion, glorious things are spoken:—

1. *That she is gloriously founded by the living God.* The church exists by his good pleasure and purpose. The plan was formed in the divine counsels, and fulfilled by the divine hand. 1. She is built upon Jesus the sure foundation and precious corner stone. 2. He purchased the church with his own blood. 3. Instituted all her ordinances. 4. Quickens every member by his own spirit. 5. Protects and supports her by his power, and, 6. Designs by all the wonders of his providence and grace to establish her for ever.

2. *That she possesses glorious privileges.* All ancient enfranchised cities had various immunities and privileges—but none ever had such as are enjoyed in the church. Some of these are, 1. Spiritual illumination. The church is to the world as *Goshen to Egypt.* 2. Justification by faith. 3. The peace of God. 4. Divine love. 5. Joy in the Holy Ghost. 6. Protection from danger. 7. Triumph over enemies. 8. Inestimable riches, and glorious dignities. 9. The constant presence and favor of Christ.

3. *That she contains glorious inhabitants.* Suitable to the dignity of the founder, and the value of the privileges, is the character of the denizens. 1. They are all *free,* Gal. iv. 31. 2. They are a *heavenly race,* born of God, 1 John iii. 1. 3. *A holy people.* 4. *Priests and kings,* 1 Peter ii. 9; Rev. i. 6. 5. *Heirs of God, and joint heirs with Christ,* Rom. viii. 17; Ps. xv.

4. *That glorious promises shall be accomplished in her.* See a summary of these, in that magnificent prophecy, Isa. lx.

III. IN THEIR GRANDEST TYPICAL REFERENCE TO HEAVEN ITSELF. Heaven is emphatically "the city of the Great King"—the "city which hath foundations"—"which is to come."—The city which the ancient patriarchs sought, and which St. John saw in vision, and afterwards described.

The future state of the saints is represented by various figures, calculated to convey the sublimest ideas of its perfection—a mansion—inheritance— crown, throne, &c.—But it is a *place* as well as a *state*. Though the essence of Deity pervades immensity, yet every other nature being finite, it is ne- cessary there should be a *local* display of his glory, in some central point, where all the happy intelligences of the universe may be collected. That place is heaven; and glorious things are spoken thereof in the oracles of God. It is,

1. *Surpassingly grand in magnificence.* There the throne of the Su- preme Glory is erected—and there the manifestations of Deity are witnessed— The sun is a splendid object here—the radiance of the stars, and the beauty of the firmament, impress our senses strongly—but these, and all other resplendent objects which glitter in mortal eyes, have no glory by reason of that which excelleth. See Rev. iv. and xxi. 9, to xxii. 5, where this glory is minutely described.

2. *Absolutely complete in its enjoyments.* This will clearly appear when we consider that it comprises,

1. The perfect exclusion of all evil—
2. The utmost perfection of body and soul!—
3. The visions and fruition of God and Christ—
4. The most glorious and amicable society—
5. The most pleasing engagements.—

3. *Eternal in its duration.* Being built by Jehovah, it rests upon his own goodness, power, and truth—an immovable basis. "The saints shall reign for ever and ever."—Believers "shall not perish, but have everlasting life;" God "who had given us the hope of eternal life by Christ Jesus be- fore the world began," cannot lie, or deny himself, Titus i. 2, 3.—This is the brightest gem in the crown of righteousness—the most radiant star in the constellation of future glory.

IMPROVEMENT. How important to be citizens of the spiritual Jerusalem, the gospel church! It was an honor and a privilege to be a denizen of ancient Jerusalem—how much greater to belong to this holy community; especially as this also qualifies us for the Jerusalem above.—

2 How cheerfully should christians welcome death! It will release them from earth and send them home to their Father's house! Purified by the blood of Jesus, they should hail the day of dissolution.

> "O happy day—that breaks our iron chain!
> That manumits,—that calls from exile home!
> That leads to nature's great metropolis,
> And re-admits us, through the guardian hand
> Of elder brother, to our Father's throne!
> Who hears our advocate, and through his wounds
> Beholding man, allows that tender name."—"'Tis this," &c.

3. How foolish those who remain strangers to, and foreigners from the church, and thereby exclude themselves from heaven.

## THE CHRISTIAN CONDUCTED TO GLORY

Psalm lxxiii. 24.—Thou shalt guide me with thy counsel, and afterward receive me to glory. (Sk.)

WHEN at the Divine command the Israelitish host forsook the land of Egypt, and entered upon the wilderness of the Red Sea, Jehovah was pleased to guide them as a flock by the hands of Moses and Aaron, but more especially by the mysterious pillar, which was as a cloud by day, and as a fire by night. By this instrument he safely led them through the sea—through the difficulties and perils of the wilderness—and conducted them to the frontiers of Canaan ; then dividing Jordan before them, he received them into the land of rest, "the land flowing with milk and honey, which is the glory of all lands." These circumstances afford our text a striking illustration, as they form a beautiful emblem of the christian's journey through life, under the guiding and protecting hand of Jehovah, who at length divides the stream of death for his ransomed to pass over, and receives him into the Canaan of everlasting repose. The Psalmist had been tempted to envy the wicked, ver. 2, 15 ; but having vanquished the temptation, he labored to turn it to an advantage by increasing in humility, in love to God, and confidence in his care. In the text he beautifully opposes his own character and end to that of the wicked. 'Instead of following the devices of my own heart like the wicked, "thou shalt guide me with thy *counsel.*" Instead of being like them cast down into destruction when life is ended, "thou shalt receive me to *glory.*"' The text therefore expresses,

I. A GOOD MAN'S CONFIDENCE FOR THIS LIFE. "Thou shalt guide me with thy counsel." Counsel frequently means advice or instruction, frequently design or purpose. Either of these would apply here; but there is another signification, which embraces both the former, and extends much farther. Counsel is properly that which adapts means to the end. When we have an important design to accomplish, we have recourse to counsel, which provides suitable means to secure our object. Now the great end which God proposes concerning us is our salvation. To accomplish this, his counsel has provided means, viz. his providence, word, and Spirit. Hence, to be guided by his counsel, is to follow,

1. *The leadings of his providence.* God holds the reins of government in his own hands, and regulates human affairs. His various dispensations plainly mark out to attentive minds the path in which they should walk as to their earthly concerns, viz., their *employments, situations,* and *objects of pursuit.* No man can be guided by the Divine counsel who does not move in this providential road. When we get out of the way of God's appointment, we resemble a dislocated limb, for every motion gives us pain, Prov. iv. 26.

2. *The directions of his word.* The Bible explicitly reveals "the whole counsel of God." It affords ample information on every point relative to our duty, or interest; our present, or future felicity. It exhibits the way of life so luminously, that "the wayfaring man, though a fool, need not err therein." "Thy word is a lamp unto my feet, and a light unto my path." It is our only rule of faith, and of practice. It points *guilty* man to the atoning blood for *pardon.* It directs *polluted* man to seek the regenerating, purifying *influences of the Holy Spirit.* It opens to *miserable* man the richest source of *consolation ;* and unfolds to *mortal* man an interminable prospect of "glory, honor, and immortality."

3. *The teaching of his Spirit*, John xvi. 13. This is always in perfect conformity with the written word, nor can it possibly be contradictory thereto. But the Spirit is sent to open our understandings, that we may comprehend the scriptures; to apply their doctrines and general rules to particular characters and cases; and to render the truth vital, penetrating, and efficacious. He emphatically speaks to the heart through the dispensations of providence, and the ministry of man, as well as by secret illuminations, impressions, and attractions. "Thou shalt guide me with thy counsel." The Psalmist's language pleasingly marks,

1. His *humility*. "*Thou* shalt guide me," for I cannot guide myself.' See his humiliating confession, ver. 22. Equally convinced is the christian now, "that it is not in man who walketh to direct his steps;" he dares not trust his own understanding or heart; 'Whither,' he exclaims, 'my erring judgment, and my impetuous passions, whither, would you conduct me, if I were left to your guidance? Alas! experience returns a melancholy answer to this question. Oh my God! *thou*, thou only shalt guide me with thy counsel. I will trust in thee with all my heart, and not lean unto my own understanding. I will acknowledge thee in all my ways, that thou mayest direct my paths.'

2. His *submission and acquiescence*. 'However unpleasing to flesh and blood, I cheerfully follow thy guidance.' When a man is led or guided, he is not driven, dragged, or constrained: he voluntarily follows his conductor. The christian is not compelled to follow the divine counsel; he willingly consents and submits to it. This is a diposition essentially necessary, for God often conducts us through paths which cause every natural feeling to recoil.

3. His *strong assurance*. "Thou *shalt* guide me," &c. He had no doubt of being safely conducted, notwithstanding all his ignorance and weakness. Thus the christian, distrusting himself, is nevertheless fully assured that God will guide him securely through all vicissitudes of time, Isa. lxiii. 9; Deut. xxxii. 10, 11, 12.

II. A GOOD MAN'S CONFIDENCE FOR ETERNITY. Thou shalt "afterward receive me to glory." All the vast machinery of providence, and the still more wonderful economy of grace, tend to this grand purpose, to prepare the soul for glory. This is God's ultimate end in all. And when the christian arrives at the brink of that dark flood, which all must pass; his God is there, to bring him in safety through, and to receive him on the shore of everlasting deliverance, where he is crowned with unwithering honors, and filled with ineffable delight. He is received,

1. To a *glory of condition*. Contrast the meanness of his condition on earth, with the unsearchable riches, the immortal beauty, and the radiant majesty, to which he is the legitimate heir in the eternal state. Contrast also the imperfection of his intellectual powers, and the scantiness of his knowledge here, with the vigor of the former, and the immensity of the latter, in glory.

2. To a *glory of charity*. While here, the christian was regarded as base and mean. He was degraded, vilified, and slandered. Reproach and ignominy marked his career. But God renders his character glorious. In heaven all acknowledge him as a saint—a son of God—an heir of God—a priest—a king of glory.

3. To a *solid, substantial glory*. Earthly glory is an empty bubble, calculated only to glitter and deceive. But this is "a *weight* of glory," a

satisfying reality; the honor which comes from God, and which is suited to the dignity of man.

4. *To a permanent, unfading glory.* "An *eternal* weight of glory." When the sun shall lose his radiance, when the stars shall be extinguished, and all nature dissolved, then shall the christian shine with undecaying lustre, and be adorned with immortal splendors. His life and happiness, and glory, shall last forever, Matt. xiii. 43; Rom. ii. 7—10.

Such is the design of God. A design directly opposite to that of satan, who wishes to guide men by the counsels of the ungodly, the corruptions of their hearts, and his own suggestions, to everlasting perdition. Into which of these designs have we entered? Our tempers, conversation, and life, have already decided this question. Whose counsel shall guide us for the future? May we all reply,—' we will follow the counsel of the Lord!' Amen.

---

## THE CHRISTIAN'S HAPPINESS.

1 Peter i. 8, 9.—Whom having not seen, ye love; in whom, though now ye see him not, yet believing, ye rejoice with joy unspeakable, and full of glory; receiving the end of your faith, even the salvation of your souls. (H. H.)

THE world often wonder that christians do not conform to the vices of the age—1 Pet. iv. 4.

And are yet more surprised that any should be willing to suffer for the sake of their religion—

But every christian is actuated by a principle of love to Christ—

This principle even gathers strength from the opposition it meets with—

The apostle is writing to those who were in heaviness through manifold temptations—

He declares, however, that their trials were promoting their eternal good—

He then shews that they were supported under them by their attachment to Christ—

In his words we may see,

I. THE STATE OF TRUE CHRISTIANS—

Christians cannot be distinguished better by any thing, than by their regard to their divine Master:

1. They love Christ—

Once, like the ungodly around them, they were enemies to Christ and his cross—Phil. iii. 19.

They "saw no beauty in him, for which he is to be desired"—Isa. liii. 2.

But now he is truly precious to their souls—1 Pet. ii. 7.

They claim him as their best friend and portion—Cant. v. 10.

This is the character of every true christian—Eph. vi. 24.

If any answer not to this character, they are, and must be, accursed—1 Cor. xvi. 22.

2. They rejoice in Christ—

They have a good hope, if not a full assurance, of an interest in him—

They have access to him in their secret duties—

They receive strengthening and refreshing communications from him—

They rejoice in him, as their faithful and almighty Friend—Phil. iv. 4.

Their joy in him is " incapable of being fully declared"*—

It is a "glorified" joy, such as the saints in heaven possess†—

Every christian indeed does not experience the same measure of joy; nor is any one at all times alike joyful—

But no one is a christian, who does not esteem the light of the Redeemer's countenance above every other good—Ps. iv. 6, and lxxiii. 25.

That their felicity may be more generally experienced, we proceed to state,

II. THE MEANS BY WHICH THEY ATTAIN IT.

Paul was favored with a sight of Christ at the time of his conversion—

But this is not the way in which the christian's state is attained—

Many suppose, that if they could have a personal interview with Christ, they should love him, and rejoice in him—

But a sight of him with the bodily eyes only never produced this effect—

Many who even heard his discourses, and beheld his miracles, were amongst his bitterest enemies—

The christians to whom St. Peter wrote had never seen Christ—

The apostle *twice* mentions this circumstance, to shew that their regard for him did not arise from any personal acquaintance with him—

Faith is the only mean whereby we are brought to this love and joy—

It is only by faith that we can behold the excellency of Christ—

It is only by faith that we can apply his merits to ourselves—

It is only by faith that we can receive his gracious communications— Eph. iii. 17.

Repentance will lead to this state; and obedience spring from it—

But it is faith only that will prevail to bring us into it—Rom. xv. 13.

To increase our ardor in pressing forward to this state, let us consider.

III. THE BLESSEDNESS OF THOSE WHO HAVE ATTAINED IT—

The salvation of the soul is the great " end of our faith"—

Present comforts are desirable; but eternal happiness is that which the christian has principally in view—

It is to this that he looks forward, under his first convictions—

This is the end for which he cheerfully endures all his privations and conflicts—

In every possible state he has an eye to this, as the consummation of all his hopes and desires—

This blessed object is already attained by all true christians—

They do not wait for it till they arrive in heaven—

Their full reward indeed is reserved for another world—

But believers have the foretastes of heaven already communicated to them—

Yea, their love to Christ, and their joy in him, are an earnest, as well as pledge, of their eternal inheritance—

INFER,

1. What a rational character is the christian!

He is thought an enthusiast, for loving and rejoicing in Christ—

And they who have no such love or joy appropriate to themselves the name of *rational* christians—

But we are willing to meet our adversaries on this ground, and to submit our sentiments to this test—

If to admire supreme excellence, to love infinite amiableness, and to

---

* ἀνεκλαλήτω.　　　　† δεδοξασμένη.

rejoice in unbounded goodness, be a *rational* employment; yea, if **the glori-**fied saints and angels be rational; then the christian is a *rational* character; and the more so, in proportion as he loves and rejoices in Christ: and their adversaries are most *irrational*, in that they can love and rejoice in the things of time and sense, and yet feel no love to, nor any joy in, our adorable Lord and Saviour—

Let those who are now despised as enthusiasts, think who will be accounted *rational* in the day of judgment?

2. How clearly may we know, whether we be real christians, or not !

There are certainly different degrees of faith, love, and joy—

But every true christian experiences them in some measure—

This is decided by an authority that cannot be doubted—Phil. iii. 3.

Let us then examine what is the supreme object of our affections, and chief source of our joys—

Nor let us ever conclude well of our state, unless we can adopt from our hearts the language of St. Paul—Phil. iii. 8.

3. How highly should we value the ordinances of the gospel !

Faith, as has been shewn, is the mean of filling us with ardent love, and joy unspeakable—

And how is faith to be produced in our hearts, but by the preaching of the gospel?—Rom. x. 14.

Let us then love the ordinances of religion, and diligently attend them—

Let us come to them *with the express view* to have our faith, our love and our joy increased—

And let us judge of our improvement of them by the degree in which we experience these effects from them

---

### EXTENT AND SOURCE OF THE CHRISTIAN'S POWER.

Phil. iv. 13.—I can do all things through Christ which strengtheneth me.  (H. H.)

THERE are in the sacred writings many various, and apparently opposite, representations of the christian's state: he is mournful, yet happy; sinful, yet holy; weak, yet possessed of a derived omnipotence.  These paradoxes are incomprehensible to the world at large: but the solution of them is easy to those who know what man is *by nature*, and what he is *by grace*, and what are the effects which flow from the contrary and contending principles of flesh and Spirit.  Nothing can be more incredible, at first sight, than the assertion in the former part of our text: but, when qualified and explained by the latter part, it is both credible and certain: yea, it presents to our minds a most encouraging and consoling truth.

In elucidating this passage, we shall shew,

I. THE EXTENT OF A CHRISTIAN'S POWER.

Using only such a latitude of expression as is common in the holy scriptures, we may say concerning every true christian, that he can,

1. Endure all trials.

In following his divine Master, he may be called to suffer reproaches, privations, torments, and death itself.  But "none of these can move him." When his heart is right with God, he can "rejoice that he is counted worthy to suffer shame for his Redeemer's sake :" Acts v. 41; he can "suffer the loss of all things, and yet count them but dung :" Phil. iii. 8; under extreme torture, he can refuse to accept deliverance, in the prospect of " a better resurrection :" Heb. xi. 35 ; he can say, "I am ready to die for the Lord's sake ;" Acts xxi. 13 ; and when presented at the stake as a sacrifice to be slain, he can look upon his sufferings as a matter of self-congratulation and exceeding joy, Phil. ii. 17, 18; 1 Pet. iv. 12, 13.

2. Mortify all lusts.

Great are his inward corruptions ; and many are the temptations to call them forth : but he is enabled to mortify and subdue them. Gal. v. 24. " The lust of the flesh, the lust of the eye, and the pride of life," are very fascinating : but " the grace of God, which has brought salvation to his soul, has taught him to deny them all, and to live righteously, soberly, and godly in this present world." 1 John ii. 15, 16, with Tit. ii. 13, 14. " By the great and precious promises of the gospel, he is made a partaker of the divine nature," 2 Pet. i. 4, and is stirred up to " cleanse himself from all filthiness, both of flesh and spirit, and to perfect holiness in the fear of God." 2 Cor. vii. 1.

3. Fulfill all duties.

Every different situation brings with it some correspondent duties : prosperity demands humility and vigilance ; adversity calls for patience and contentment. Now the christian is " like a tree that is planted by the rivers of water, and bringeth forth its fruits *in its season*." Psa. i 3. It is to this change of circumstances that the apostle more immediately refers in the text: "I have learned," says he, " in whatsoever state I am, therewith to be content. I know both how to be abased, and I know how to abound : everywhere, and in all things, I am instructed both to be full, and to be hungry , both to abound, and to suffer need. *I can do all things*." Ver. 11—13. The christian knows that all his duties are summed up in love to God, and love to man: he is assured, that no changes in his condition can for one moment relax his obligation to approve himself to God in the execution of these duties : and he endeavors to avail himself of every wind that blows, to get forward in his christian course.

But in reference to all the foregoing points, we must acknowledge, that all christians are not equally advanced; nor does any christian so walk as not to shew, at some time or other, that " he has not yet attained, nor is altogether perfect." Phil. iii. 12. We must be understood therefore as having declared, rather what the christian " *can* do," than what he actually does in all instances. " In many things he still offends ;" Jam. iii. 2 ; but he aspires after the full attainment of this proper character : in the performance of his duties, he aims at *universality in the matter, uniformity,in the manner*, and *perfection in the measure* of them.

The christian's power being so extraordinary, we may well inquire after,

II. THE SOURCE FROM WHENCE HE DERIVES IT.

The christian *in himself* is altogether destitute of strength—

If we consult *the scripture representations* of him, we find that he is " without strength," Rom. v. 6, and even " dead in trespasses and sins." Eph ii. 1. Nor, after he is regenerate, has he any more power that he can call his own ; for " in him, that is, in his flesh, dwelleth no good thing." Rom. vii. 15, 18, 19.

If *our Lord's assertion* may be credited, " without him we can do nothing ;" we are like branches severed from the vine. John xv. 5.

If *the experience of the most eminent apostle* will serve as a criterion, he confessed, that he "had not *of himself* a sufficiency even to think a good thought; his sufficiency was entirely of God." 2 Cor. iii. 5.

His power even to do the smallest good is derived from Christ—

"It has pleased the Father, that in Christ should all fullness dwell," Col. i. 19, and that "out of his fullness all his people should receive." John i. 16. It is he who "strengthens us with all might by his Spirit in the inner man:" Eph. iii. 16; it is he who "gives us both to will and to do." Phil. ii. 13; Heb. xiii. 21. If we are "strong in any degree, it is in the Lord, and in the power of *his* might." Eph. vi. 10. Whatever we do, we must give him the glory of it, saying. "I live; yet not I, but Christ liveth in me:" Gal. ii. 20; "I have labored; yet not I, but the grace of God which was with me:" "by the grace of God I am, what I am." 1 Cor. xv. 10.

Nor is it by strength *once* communicated, that we are strong; but by continual communications of grace from the same overflowing fountain. It is not through Christ who *hath strengthened*, but who *doth strengthen* us, that we can do all things.* We need fresh life from him, in order to the production of good fruit; exactly as we need fresh light from the sun, in order to a prosecution of the common offices of life. One moment's intermission of either, would instantly produce a suspension of all effective industry.

From that source he receives all that he can stand in need of—

Christ is not so prodigal of his favors, as to confer them in needless profusion: he rather apportions our strength to the occasions that arise to call it forth. Deut. xxxiii. 25. He bids us to renew our applications to him; and, in answer to them, imparts "grace sufficient for us." 2 Cor. xii. 9. There are no limits to his communications: however "wide we open our mouth, he will fill it." Psa. lxxxi. 10. He is "able to make *all* grace abound towards us, that we, having *all-ways all*-sufficiency in *all* things, may abound unto *every* good work:" 2 Cor. ix 8; he is ready to "do for us exceeding abundantly above all that we can ask or think." Eph. iii. 20. "If only we believe, *all* things shall be possible unto us:" Mark ix. 23; we shall be "able to quench *all* the fiery darts of the devil," Eph. vi. 16, and "be more than conquerors over *all* the enemies of our souls." Rom. viii. 37

The uses to which we may apply this subject, are,

1. The conviction of the ignorant.

Many, when urged to devote themselves to God, reply, that we require more of them than they can do; and that it is impossible for them to live according to the scriptures. But what ground can there be for such an objection? Is not Christ ever ready to assist us? Is not omnipotence pledged for our support? Away with your excuses then, which have their foundation in ignorance, and their strength in sloth. Call upon your Saviour; and he will enable you to "stretch forth your withered hand:" at his command, the dead shall arise out of their graves; and the bond-slaves of sin and satan shall be "brought into the liberty of the children of God."

2. The encouragement of the weak.

A life of godliness cannot be maintained without constant watchfulness and strenuous exertion. And there are times when "even the youths faint and are weary, and the young men utterly fall." But "if we wait upon our God we shall certainly renew our strength, and mount up with wings as eagles." Isa. xl. 30, 31. If we look "to Him on whom our help is laid," Psa. lxxxix. 19, the experience of David shall be ours: "In the day when

* ἐνδυναμοῦντι.

504

I cried, thou answeredst me, and strengthenedst me with strength in my soul." Psa. cxxxviii. 3. Let not any difficulties then discourage us. "Let the weak say, I am strong;" Joel iii. 10; and the stripling go forth with confidence against Goliath. Let us "be strong in the grace that is in Christ Jesus," 2 Tim. ii. 1, and "his strength shall assuredly be perfected in our weakness." 2 Cor. xii. 9.

---

## OUR TIMES IN GOD'S HAND.

Psalm xxxi. 15.—My times are in thy hand. (H. H.)

*mt 99 Jan.*

To the ungodly it is a satisfaction to deny the providence of God, and to cut him off, as it were, from any connection with his creatures. But the saints find a rich consolation in the thought that God reigneth. This it is which reconciles them to the evils they endure, and fortifies them against those which they have reason to apprehend. David, in the psalm before us, complains that there were many who "took counsel together against him, and devised to take away his life." But he comforted himself in the reflection, that, however *man* might be his enemy, *God* was "his God;" and that however bitterly his enemies might be enraged against him, "his times were not in *their* hands, but in *God's;*" and, consequently, that they could do nothing against him but by his permission.

From this view of the text we are led to notice,

I. OUR DEPENDENCE ON GOD.

*Job + satan*

God is the Governor of the universe: he appoints the stars their courses; he makes the raging elements to fulfill his will, Ps. cxlviii. 8; he imposes a restraint upon the most savage beasts, causing them to suppress, 1 Kin. xiii. 28, or forget, Dan. vi. 22, their instinctive ferocity, or over-ruling the exercise of it, for the preservation, John i. 17, or destruction of men, 2 Kin. ii. 24, as he sees occasion. The affairs of men he more especially controls. In his hands are,

1. The occurrences of life

There is nothing really casual or contingent in the world. It is God that disposes of us from our earliest infancy to the latest hour of our lives. "He determines the bounds of our habitation, Acts xvii. 26. If we are called to the possession of wealth, or deprived of it by any untoward circumstances, it is "the Lord who gives, and the Lord who taketh it away, Job i. 21. If we enjoy health, or pine away in sickness, it is "the Lord who both wounds and heals, who kills and makes alive," 1 Sam. ii. 6, 7. "There is neither good nor evil in the city, but the Lord is the doer of it," Am. iii. 6. Even the falling of a hair of our head, trifling as it is, takes not place but by his appointment, Matt. x. 30.

2. The seasons of death.

To every man "there is an appointed time upon earth, Job vii. 1: there are "bounds which he cannot pass, Job xiv. 5. "God holdeth our souls in life, Ps. lxvi. 9: and "when he taketh away our breath, we die, and return to the dust," Ps. civ. 29. Youth and health are no security against the stroke of death: the most vigorous constitutions are soon broken, when God is pleased to afflict us, Job xxi. 23—25: the skill of physicians, however useful when attended with his blessing, is of no avail, Mark v. 26. So

*Roman 8:28*
*all things work together*

numerous are the occasions of death, that no caution can possibly avoid them: "a man may flee from a lion, and a bear meet him; or he may go into a house for safety, and a serpent bite him," Amos v. 19. When God "requires our souls," we must surrender them at his call," Luke xii. 20. Our days are protracted to an advanced age, if he be pleased to uphold us; if not, our course is finished as soon as ever it is commenced. It is "in God, and in God alone, that we live, and move, and have our being," Acts xvii. 28.

But though these ideas are certainly comprehended in the text, its more immediate scope is to declare,

II. OUR SECURITY IN GOD.

We have already observed, that the words of the text were introduced by David as a consolatory reflection, under the cruel treatment which he had received from friends and enemies. We are therefore taught by them to assure ourselves,

1. That none can destroy us before our time.

We appear to be, yea, we really are, in the midst of many and great dangers. But however we may be encompassed with enemies, they cannot prevail against us till the Lord's time for our removal is come. David was continually exposed to the rage and jealousy of Saul, who repeatedly cast a javelin at him, and hunted him incessantly with armed hosts "like a partridge upon the mountains." Yet though he was often in the most imminent danger, 1 Sam. xxiii. 26, and certainly would have been betrayed by the men of Keilah, ib. ver. 11, 12, yet God watched over him, and kept him in perfect safety. Many sought to apprehend our Lord; but "they could not lay hands on him till his hour was come," John vii. 30. & viii. 20; Luke xiii. 33: and even then Pilate "could have had no power against him, unless it had been given him from above," John xix. 11. Paul was in perils innumerable, "and in deaths oft," 2 Cor. xi. 23—27: once he was stoned, and even left for dead, Acts xiv. 19, 20; but none could take away his life, till he had finished the course marked out for him. Thus we also are immortal, till our work is done. We are surrounded with "chariots of fire and horses of fire," 2 Kin. vi. 17: yea, "God himself is a wall of fire round about us," Zech. ii. 5. And sooner shall successive bands of enemies be struck dead upon the spot by fire from heaven, 2 Kin. i. 10—12, than one of the Lord's little ones shall perish, Matt. xviii. 14.

2. That none shall hurt us without his permission.

As we depend on God for our happiness as well as for our existence, so are both our being and our well-being secured by him. Satan could not touch the person or the property of Job, till he had obtained leave of God to do so, Job i. 12, & ii. 6. "Nor can any weapon that is formed against us, prosper," Isa. liv. 17, any further than our God shall see good to permit it. "His angels encamp round about us," Ps. xxxiv. 7, and have an especial charge to "keep us in all our ways, that we dash not our foot against a stone," Ps. xci. 11, 12. "Neither the arrow that flieth by day, nor the pestilence that walketh in darkness, can hurt us. Thousands may fall at our side, and ten thousands at our right hand; but it shall not come nigh us," ib. ver. 5—7.

We are not indeed at liberty to rush needlessly into danger, from an expectation that God will deliver us; (this were to "tempt the Lord our God,") Matt. iv. 6, 7; but in the path of duty we have nothing to fear: we may "tread upon the lion, the adder, or the dragon;" Ps. xci. 13; Acts xxviii. 3—6: we may drink poison itself, Mark xvi. 18, or suffer ourselves to be committed to the flames, without experiencing the smallest injury, Dan. iii. 25—27: nothing in the whole universe can "harm us, if we be followers of that which is good," 1 Pet. iii. 13: if God see fit to keep us, we are as safe "in a den of lions" as in a house of friends.

From this subject we may *learn*,

1. To seek God without delay.

There is no period of life when we can call one day, or one hour, our own. We are altogether "in God's hands;" and, if he withdraw his support for one moment, we perish, as certainly as a stone gravitates to the earth. Shall we then, when so entirely dependent on our God, provoke him to cast us out of his hands? Shall we continue to despise his patience and forbearance, till he swear in his wrath that our "time shall be no longer?" Rev. x 6. Think, how many have lost the time afforded them, and how bitterly they now bewail their folly: and beg of God, that he would "so teach you to number your days, that you may apply your hearts unto wisdom." Ps. xc. 12.

2. To serve him without fear—

We are too apt to keep back from serving God through fear of the persecutions we may endure from man. But, if our times be in God's hands, all our concerns must be there too; and nothing can befall us but by his appointment. "Who art thou then, that thou shouldest be afraid of a man that shall die, and forgettest the Lord thy Maker?" Isa. li. 12, 13. Are we not told, that "the wrath of man shall praise him; and that the remainder of it he shall restrain?" Ps. lxxvi. 10. Be bold then for God; "set your face as a flint against the whole world," Isa. xlix. 7—9, and trust in him for protection. He will not indeed screen you from all trials; because it is on many accounts necessary that you should feel them, 1 Pet. i. 6: but he will suffer none to come upon you which he will not enable you to bear, none which he will not sanctify to your eternal good, 1 Cor. x. 13

3. To trust him without carefulness.

It is foolish as well as impious to distrust God, or to murmur at any of his dispensations. In whose hands could the disposal of all events be placed so much to our advantage, as in his, who possesses infinite wisdom to devise what is best, and infinite power to effect it? Would we be made the sport of chance or fortune? or would we have our present and everlasting concerns left wholly to our own management? If we are not fit to regulate our temporal affairs till we attain the age of manhood, how much less can we ever be competent to take the reins of God's government into our own hands, and to order the affairs of his kingdom. But our times will be in God's hands, whether we acquiese in it or not. Let us therefore contentedly leave ourselves to his all-wise disposal, assured, that "he doeth all things well," and will make "all things to work together for good to them that love him."

---

## THE SECURITY OF THOSE WHO DWELL IN GOD.

Psalm xci. 9, 10.—Because thou hast made the Lord, which is my refuge, even the Most High, thy habitation, there shall no evil befall thee. (H. H.)

It is scarcely possible to conceive any terms more strong, or any images more lively, than those in which the scripture represents the privileges of believers. We need look no further than to the psalm before us for a confirmation of this truth. Indeed, according to the view given of this psalm by a learned Prelate, there is, in the first verses of it, an emphasis which cannot be surpassed. * And the whole may be considered as the believer's charter, in which all his privileges are contained, from his first acceptance with God to the consummation of his happiness in glory.

We have in the words of our text a just description of the believer:

I. His EXPERIENCE.

The true christian is one who has been "turned from darkness unto light, and from the power of satan unto God." Being once brought to God, he "makes the Most High his habitation." He regards God, not merely as reconciled to him, but as affording him what a dwelling-house affords to its possessor,

1. Free access.

A person goes familiarly to his house at all times, not doubting but that he shall gain a ready admission into it. He considers it as his own, and feels that it exists only for his accommodation. It is thus that the believer goes to God as his God: he has "access to him with boldness and confidence:" he is certain that, when he calls, he shall receive an answer; and " when he knocks, the door will be opened to him." In this precise view the Psalmist speaks of God; "be thou my strong habitation, whereunto I may continually resort." Ps. lxxi. 3.

2. Necessary provision.

Every man, whatever be his situation in life, expects to find in his own house the things suited to his necessities. He does not seek his meals at the houses of his neighbors, but in his own; and he returns home at stated seasons to partake of them. And whither does the believer go for daily supplies of bread for his soul? It is in Christ Jesus that his fulness is treasured up, and in him the believer expects to find the "grace that is sufficient for him." God invites him to come to him for the express purpose, that he may be filled and satisfied with good things: "Wherefore do ye spend your money for that which is not bread? Hearken diligently unto me, and eat ye that which is good, and let your soul delight itself in fatness." Isai. lv. 2.

3. Sure protection.

If storms descend, or dangers menace, we take refuge in our house, and find it a place of safety. Thus "the name of God also is a strong tower, to which the righteous runneth and is safe." Prov. xviii. 10. It is to himself that God invites us, when he says, "Come my people, enter thou into thy chambers, shut the door about thee, and hide thyself for a little moment, until the indignation be overpast." Isai. xxvi. 20. And that this was a primary idea in the mind of the Psalmist, appears from the very words of the text, wherein he calls God "his refuge," and from the whole scope of the psalm, from the beginning to the end. With this also agrees the beautiful description given of Jesus by the prophet, as "an hiding-place from the wind, and a covert from the tempest." Isai. xxxii. 2.

4. Sweet repose.

To this house a man retires from the noise and bustle of the world; and there he lays himself down to rest after the fatigues of the day. Home, though inferior in many respects to places of temporary residence, is to al-

* Bishop Horne reads the two first verses thus: "He that dwelleth &c. who abideth under &c who saith of the Lord," &c. Then at the end of ver. 2, he supposes the Psalmist to break off abruptly, and, instead of continuing his description, to address himself to the person before described; "Surely he shall deliver thee."

most all persons the most agreeable, because there they are most at ease. And such is God to the believer. "In every place, God is to him as a little sanctuary," Ezek. xi. 16; where he finds himself at rest. He carries his wants to God, and "casts all his care on him," and enjoys peace which passeth all understanding. In this sense he says *for his own encouragement,* "Return unto thy *rest,* O my soul:" and attests *for the glory of his God,* "Lord thou hast been our *dwelling-place* in all generations." Ps. xc. i.

In connexion with this experience of the believer, let us consider,

II. His privilege.

The expression in the text seems to exceed the bounds of truth: but the more it is examined, the more will it be found to be strictly true. The man who makes God his habitation shall have no evil befall him:

1. None here.

No *casual* evil shall befall him. There is no such thing as chance: every thing, even to the falling of a sparrow, is ordered of the Lord. As for the children of God, "their heavenly Father hath given his angels charge over them, to keep them in all their ways;" see ver. 11, 12; and if any thing were to happen to them, *they* (the angels) would contract a fearful responsibility for their neglect. We must not however imagine that believers are at liberty to rush into needless dangers; for our Lord, when tempted by satan to cast himself from a pinnacle of the temple in expectation that the angels would preserve him from injury, replied, "Thou shalt not tempt the Lord thy God:" but nothing can happen to them except by the divine appointment: they are hid in the shadow of their Father's hand, and "their very hairs are all numbered."

But it may be thought that *penal* evil may come to them. This however we utterly deny. That they may be "visited with the rod," we readily acknowledge: but there is great difference between the vindictive arm of an incensed judge, and the gentle chastisements of an indulgent parent. The cup that may at any time be put into their hands may be bitter; but it has not in it one drop of wrath: it is altogether mixed by love; and not an ingredient can be found in it, which they themselves shall not one day confess to have been salutary and beneficial.

In short, no *real* evil shall befall them. That they may have troubles, is certain: that their troubles may be heavy and accumulated, is also certain. But who accounts even the amputation of a limb *evil,* if it be the only and infallible method of preserving life? Much less then are any sufferings to be accounted evil, which the believer can ever be called to sustain: for he shall never endure any, which shall not work for good to him in this life, and be the means of increasing his weight of glory in the next. Rom. viii. 28, and 2 Cor. iv. 17.

2. None hereafter.

It is in this life only that the believer can meet with even the semblance of evil: when he goes hence, he is instantly placed beyond the reach of harm. No sin, no sorrow, no pain, no temptation, no weariness, no want, can ever be felt by him in the mansions of bliss. He will there enjoy for ever one unclouded day; and his happiness will be without alloy, without intermission, without end. Rev. xxi. 4.

To render this subject more instructive, we shall add a word,

1. Of direction.

Christ, in reference to the sheepfold of his church, says, "I am the door; if any man enter in by me, he shall be saved, and shall go in and out, and find pasture." John x. 9. The same figure we may apply to the subject before us: "Christ is the door;" he is "the way to the Father;" and "no man cometh unto the Father, but by him." To those who come to God in any other way, he is not "a refuge," or "habitation," but "a consuming fire." Heb. xii. 29. But if we believe in Christ, then "will he dwell in us, and we shall dwell in him:" John vi. 56; yea, "he will be our house of defence, to save us for ever." Ps. xxxi. 2.

2. Of warning.

Who, except the believer, can apply to himself the promise in the text? As for the unbelieving and disobedient, they are in danger every hour: they know not but that God's wrath may break forth against them the very next moment to their destruction. Of this they are certain, (whether they will believe it or not,) that in a little time his judgments shall overtake them, and the greatest of all evils shall befall them, unless they repent. O that they would be prevailed upon to flee for refuge to the hope that it set before them! O that they would now seek to be "found in Christ!" Then should the destroying angel pass over them, and "they should dwell safely, and be quiet from the fear of evil." Prov. i. 33.

3. Of encouragement.

The weakness of men's faith often robs them of the comfort which it is their privilege to enjoy. Why should a believer be afraid of thunder and lightning? Were he but sensible what a protector he has, he would feel assured that no evil could come unto him. How varied are God's promises to him in the psalm before us! How diversified also are the assurances given him by Eliphaz in the book of Job! Job v. 19—24. Let him only commit himself to God, and he has nothing to fear. Let us then, beloved, have faith in God; and let those words of David be our song in this land of our pilgrimage; "God is our refuge, &c.; therefore will we not fear, though the earth be removed, and though the waters be carried into the midst of the sea: &c." Ps. xlvi. 1—4.

~~~~~~~~~~

## THE TRIUMPHANT SONG OF THE REDEEMED.

**Rev.** i. 5, 6.—And from Jesus Christ, who is the faithful witness, and the first begotten of the death, and the prince of the kings of the earth. Unto him that loved us, and washed us from our sins in his own blood, and hath made us kings and priests unto God and his Father; to him be glory and dominion for ever and ever. Amen.

THE Saviour having appeared in a vision to St. John, in "the isle of Patmos," he commanded him to write appropriate epistles to "the seven churches in Asia," to reprove their evils, correct their errors, and encourage their hopes. He therefore introduced the subjects of his addresses by an affectionate salutation in the name of the triune Jehovah; and having distinctly specified the Father and the Holy Spirit, he solemnly adds in the text, "and from Jesus Christ, who is the faithful witness," &c. These words strikingly illustrate the *mediatorial character* of Jesus Christ—the *exalted privilege* of his believing people—and the *personal influence* of redeeming grace. Let us observe,

I. THE MEDIATORIAL CHARACTER OF JESUS CHRIST. This is admirably described by the apostle, in the words before us; in which he faithfully re presents the various offices that he executes, as the mediator of the new covenant.

1. *He is the prophet of his church.* Hence he is denominated, "the faithful *witness.*" A *witness* is one who either *reveals* what was previously unknown, or *attests* what has been already announced. In both these respects Jesus Christ is "given to be a witness to the people." He has distinctly revealed the true character and will of God—the astonishing scheme and work of redemption—and the only way of salvation and eternal life, John iii. 16—18. The writings of Moses and the prophets were fully accomplished in him, for they "testified beforehand the sufferings of Christ, and the glory that should follow." The comparative darkness of the law is passed away, and the meridian light of the gospel now shineth. The sun of righteousness hath arisen on the moral world, to give light to them that sit in darkness and the shadow of death. As a teacher come from God, he "spake as never man spake;" and as an immutable witness, he still externally reveals and personally attests divine truth, both by the medium of his word, and the influence of his spirit, Rom. viii. 14—16; 2 Tim. iii. 16, 17. The testimony of Christ is invariably true, for he is the *faithful witness*, whose veracity is infinite, and fidelity infallible. He has brought life and immortality to light by the gospel; he guides his people into all truth, and makes them wise unto salvation, Isa. liv. 14.

2. *He is the high priest of our profession.* This is evidently intended, when he is called, "the first begotten of *the dead.*" His death and resurrection were important parts of his priesthood, and essentially connected with the salvation of sinners. An atonement was absolutely necessary, and therefore Jesus Christ in matchless love, "took upon him the seed of Abraham, to make reconciliation for the sins of the people." By his *sacrificial death*, he fully atoned for our iniquities, and opened a new and living way to the Father, Heb. x. 18—22. He also rose again for our justification, and is now "the resurrection and the life, having obtained eternal redemption for us." He is therefore emphatically, "the first begotten of the dead," because he is the first, who ever rose to die no more; and his resurrection clearly demonstrates the efficacy of his sacrifice, and is the strongest pledge of the blissful immortality which awaits his people in the world to come, Luke xxiv. 46, 47; 1 Cor. xv. 20. As the high priest over the house of God, Christ is our "advocate with the Father," and the altar which sanctifieth both the giver and the gift. Through him alone we have access to the throne of grace; and our persons and services are accepted by virtue of the life and death of him, who once suffered for our sins, and now "ever liveth to make intercession for us," John xiv. 6; Heb. iv. 14—16.

3. *He is the sovereign of the universe.* His dominion is supreme and unlimited, reaching through all space, and extending to all duration. He is therefore justly acknowledged "the prince of the kings of the earth;" for by him "kings reign, and princes decree justice." An *essential* God, his kingdom ruleth over all things, and he *only* sways the sceptre of universal empire, and sustains supremacy of character, as "the king of kings, and Lord of lords." And as "the mediator between God and man," he has founded a kingdom of grace, in which he triumphantly reigns for the salvation of mankind, Dan. ii. 44; Matt. iii. 2. This kingdom is spiritual in its character, and perpetual in its duration. All other empires are worldly and perishing; but the kingdom of Christ "is not of this world, and shall never be destroyed." The Almighty King of Zion reigns *universally* in the world—*mediatorially* in his church—*spiritually* in the hearts of his

people—and *eternally* in the glory of heaven, Heb. i. 8; Rom. xiv. 17; Matt. xxv. 34. His reign is infinitely wise, holy, just, merciful, and gracious. What a transcendently glorious and amiable Sovereign! Let us therefore consider.

II. THE EXALTED PRIVILEGE OF HIS BELIEVING PEOPLE;—"Unto him that loved us," &c. This inspired description of the nature and properties of Christian salvation, is highly appropriate and comprehensive; and distinctly specifies,

1. *The divinity of its origin;*—"Unto *him* that *loved us*." God is unquestionably the source of all possible good, and from him every blessing descends. When he beheld the miserable and perishing state of mankind, he remembered us in infinite mercy, and graciously sent his Son to be the Saviour of the world, John iv. 9, 10. Jesus also loved us, and "gave himself a ransom for all, to be testified in due time." What unspeakable love has he manifested to fallen sinners! Consider his amazing incarnation, sufferings, crucifixion, resurrection, ascension, and intercession at the "right hand of the majesty on high," 2 Cor. v. 14, 15, viii. 9. His love contains unfathomable breadths, and lengths, and depths, and heights, which neither angels nor men can perfectly comprehend! This spontaneous and unparalleled love is the originating cause of all the ineffable blessings of present and eternal salvation, Eph. ii. 4—6.

2. *The excellency of its character;*—"And *washed* us from *our sins*." All sin is moral contamination. It not only contracts guilt, but also defiles every power both of body and soul. Hence it is called, "uncleanness, corruption, defilement, the pollution of the world, and filthiness of flesh and spirit," Mark vii. 21—23. From these stains of guilt and depravity Christ saves all his faithful followers. The work of grace is *already begun* in their hearts. Their iniquities are freely and fully forgiven, and they believingly participate the cleansing efficacy of the blood of sprinkling, 1 John i. 7. Present salvation therefore includes both the justification of our *persons*, through the righteousness of Christ, and the sanctification of our *nature* by the spirit of holiness, Jer. xxiii. 6; Titus iii. 5. Pardon and purity are *equally* necessary, and are *actually* enjoyed by those who have "tasted that the Lord is gracious," and are saved "by the washing of regeneration, and the renewing of the Holy Ghost," 1 Cor. vi. 11; Tit. ii. 14.

3. *The efficacy of its medium;*—"And washed us in *his own blood*." This is the only possible way in which sinners can be saved; "for without shedding of blood, there can be no remission." Every spiritual blessing is attributed to the blood of Christ. We are *redeemed, justified, adopted, washed*, and ultimately *glorified*, through "the *blood* of the everlasting covenant," Rom. iii. 24, 25; 1 Pet. i. 19; Rev. vii. 14. This medium of salvation was *typified* by the whole sacrificial dispensation of the Jews, which was a shadow of good things to come. But Jesus Christ has now *personally* "opened a fountain for sin and uncleanness," and saves his people not *ceremonially* by the blood of legal sacrifices, but *meritoriously* by his own "most precious blood," which was shed for them, Heb. xii. 14. This blood possesses not only an *atoning virtue*, for the expiation of sin, but also, a *cleansing efficacy*, which purifies the soul; for "the blood of Jesus Christ cleanseth from all unrighteousness."

4. *The dignity of its subjects;*—"And hath made us *kings* and *priests* unto God and his Father." Divine grace both saves and dignifies its possessors; it raises them from the ruin and misery of sin, to a state of glory and virtue. They are anointed spiritual *kings*, having already received a

kingdom of grace; and are the legitimate heirs of the kingdom of heaven, Col. i. 13; Heb. xii. 28. They are also consecrated *priests*, "to offer up spiritual sacrifices, acceptable to God through Jesus Christ." They receive this honor that cometh from God only, and participate all the inestimable dignities and privileges of the glorious gospel of peace, 1 Pet. ii. 9, 10. The believing recipients of salvation, are thus divinely honored and blessed; and are made by the blood and Spirit of Christ, "a royal and holy priesthood unto God and his Father." Surely, "happy art thou, O Israel; who is like unto thee, O people saved by the Lord!" This will lead us to notice,

III. THE PERSONAL INFLUENCE OF REDEEMING GRACE;—"To him be glory and dominion for ever and ever. Amen." This lively description of supreme majesty and power to the redeemer, may be regarded as,

1. *The language of admiration and love.* The believer discovers inexpressible perfection and glory, in the person and character of the Saviour; and therefore regards him, as the object of his intense desire and devout attachment. A *personal* apprehension of his infinite grandeur and goodness deeply affects the minds of Christians, and fills them with unutterable raptures of wonder, love and joy. The believing contemplation of his divine glories, redeeming works, and saving offices, powerfully attracts and captivates their hearts, and triumphantly subdues them to the sceptre of his kingdom. They gladly embrace him as an object altogether lovely and glorious; readily acknowledge the supremacy of his glory and dominion; and joyfully "count all things but loss, for the excellency of the knowledge of Christ Jesus the Lord," Gal. vi. 14; 1 John iv. 19.

2. *The language of gratitude and praise.* A participation of the unsearchable riches of Christ is invariably accompanied with grateful and affectionate dispositions of the heart. The doctrine of salvation by grace necessarily excludes boasting, and inspires the profoundest gratitude and thanksgiving. Though the obligations of believers to the redeemer are infinite and indescribable, they sensibly feel their overwhelming influence, and often gratefully exclaim, "bless the Lord, O my soul, and forget not all his benefits;" "unto him that loved us," &c. Their unfeigned gratitude is *practically* displayed, by their love to the Saviour's person,—obedience to his word,—zeal in his cause,—praise for his goodness,—and joyful anticipation of his kingdom, Ps. cxvi. 12—14; 1 Pet. i. 8, 9.

3. *The language of adoration and delight.* Jesus Christ is inexpressibly glorious and precious to them that believe. He is their "wisdom, righteousness and sanctification, and redemption." He is the object of their confidence,—the author of their salvation,—and the source of their happiness; they exultingly glory in his cross,—devoutly honor him as they honor the Father,—supremely adore the perfections of his character,—and greatly delight in the exercises of his worship, Prov. iii. 17; Phil. iii. 3. The text is their triumphant felicity and song in the house of their pilgrimage; and will ultimately constitute the blissful theme of their ceaseless hallelujahs, in the "house not made with hands, eternal in the heavens." Let all the redeemed therefore, believingly and piously add, *Amen.*

This subject displays the exalted dignity of the redeemer,—unfolds the nature and method of salvation,—and affords ample consolation to them, that "follow the Lamb whithersoever he goeth."

65

CHRIST THE BELIEVER'S LIFE, AND DEATH THE BELIEVER'S GAIN.

Philippians i. 21.—For me to live is Christ, and to die is gain.  (Sk.)

WHEN St. Paul uttered this sentiment, he was a prisoner for Jesus Christ, deprived of his liberty, and under the control of his persecuting foes; but his soul was not bound : the Philippians were inexpressibly dear to him ; he, had them in his heart; they were his joy and his crown; and he longed after them all in the bowels of Jesus Christ: and their love to him, if less ardent, was not less sincere.  Hearing of his deprivations, they voluntarily raised a contribution among themselves, and sent it to him by the hand of Epaphroditus their minister; in return, St. Paul sent them this admirable epistle.  In the preceding verses to the text, he assures them that the things which had happened to him, were so far from impeding the progress of truth, that they had "fallen out," &c., ver. 12 ; and that his fellow helpers in the ministry were more confident by his bonds, ver. 14.  He then, after expressing his confidence that all his sufferings would have a favorable issue, verse 19, 20, utters the devout and elevated sentiment in the text; "For me to live," &c.  We have here two things :—

I. CHRIST THE BELIEVER'S LIFE.

II. DEATH THE BELIEVER'S GAIN.

"For me to live is Christ."  This is in effect saying,

1. *Christ is the Author of my life.*  'Two kinds of life has double-natured man.'  We all live as animal and rational beings, and have capacities for the performance of animal and rational actions.  But believers live in a more exalted sense, and possess a higher life, a life of which Jesus Christ is the immediate Author.  Once they were devoid of this, and even dead while they lived ; they saw objects, heard sounds, tasted food, performed actions, and did all that was necessary as members of civil society and citizens of the world; but they had no spiritual senses, they saw not God, they heard not his voice, they tasted not his love, and they had no feeling of the powers of the world to come.  But when they were dead in sin, Christ quickened them.  "The hour is coming," &c., John v. 25.  "I am the resurrection and the life," &c., xi. 25.

2. *Christ is the principle of my life.*  Every kind of life, whether vegetable, animal, or spiritual, depends upon some principle from which it springs ; for life is but the effects of some latent and operative cause.  Christ not only lights up the lamp of spiritual life, but he feeds the flame, and supplies the oil by which it burns.  Christ, dwelling in our hearts by faith, becomes the principle of our life.  "I am the living bread," &c., John vi. 51.  "Except ye eat the flesh," &c., ver. 53.  "I live, yet not I, but Christ liveth in me," Gal. ii. 20.  "When Christ, who is our life," &c., Col. iii. 4.  "He that hath the Son," &c , 1 John v. 12.  We are as much dependant on Christ for spiritual life, as plants are dependant on the earth for vegetable life, or the body is dependant on the soul for animal life.

3. *Christ is the model of my life.*  Christians are not lawless beings who walk at random, or live according to the course of the world.  No, they regard Christ as their pattern, and they study to be like him.  They do this, because they know that the life of Christ was the most dignified and glorious life that was ever led upon earth, and that there is every thing great and good in the imitation of so illustrious a character.—Because the Spirit of Christ within them, excites them to follow the example of Christ without.—Because they love Christ, and love leads them to imitate the beloved object,—and they

know that the profession of christianity lays them under strong obligations to follow the Lord Jesus. "He that saith he abideth in him, ought himself also," &c., 1 John ii. 6.

4. *Christ is the end of my life.* Carnal men are most commonly selfish men; they seek their own, and not another's wealth; their own ease, or their own glory, or their own pleasure, engages all their attention, and occupies all their time; and they live as fully to themselves, as if they were the authors of their own being, or the arbiters of their own fate. But believers consider Christ as the end of their life; from a consciousness that they owe their being to Christ, and that he formed them for his glory, and redeemed them by his blood: they surrender themselves to his service; whether they eat or drink, or whatever they do, the glory of Christ is their great object: they renounce their own ease, to sustain the cross of Christ: they sacrifice their own reputation for the reproach of Christ: and count not their lives dear unto themselves, so that they may advance the honor of Christ: with the apostle they can say, "None of us liveth unto himself," &c., Rom. xiv. 7, 8.

II. DEATH IS THE BELIEVER'S GAIN. "To die is gain." We must distinguish here, between the act of dying and the consequences of death. There is every thing in death, considered in itself, that is appalling and dreadful. *Look at death in its deprivations.* Here the tenderest bonds of affection are dissolved; the most endearing relations ended; and the deepest pangs of parting endured. *Death in its agonies.* How inadequate is human language to describe the pains of the dying; what deep waters go over them! how hard the struggle they endure! *Death in its degradations.* What can be more exquisitely beautiful than a human body adorned with youth, flushed with health, and fired with vigor, the eyes sparkling with joy, the heart dancing with gladness, the pulse beating high with expectation, and the cheeks glowing lovelier than the virgin rose. But in death all is changed! all degraded! a putrid mass of inanimate matter is all that is left; a receptacle for worms, a prey for corruption, a heap of dust! So that if there were nothing beyond death, it would be no gain to die; for death in itself is a sore evil, and a most terrible curse inflicted upon mankind. But as it is gain to die, pronounced so by an inspired apostle, we must infer that there is another state of being to which death introduces us. In illustrating this subject, we consider the evils from which we are delivered,—and the blessings with which we shall be crowned.

First, The evils from which we are delivered.

1. *Death delivers us from the pains and miseries of the present life.* Man is born to trouble, and suffering is his lot upon earth. He suffers in his body; what numerous ills life is heir to! He suffers in his mind; how many things would his spirit and put him to grief! He suffers by commiseration; his friends and fellow creatures suffer, and he weeps with those that weep. What a suffering man was St. Paul! Hear his tale of wo: "Of the Jews, five times received I forty stripes save one," &c., 2 Cor. xi. 24. Nor was this all, he was a man of feeling; "Who is weak, and I am not weak? who is offended, and I burn not?" "What mean ye, to weep, and break my heart?" Acts xxi. 13. But in heaven there is no pain; "sorrow and sighing shall flee away, and God shall wipe away all tears from our eyes."

2. *Death frees us from all the imperfections of our mortal state.* Our knowledge here is very imperfect and defective; we know but in part: and the little knowledge of which we are possessed is frequently obtained by hard study and intense thought; and this defective knowledge renders us liable to

mistake, to entertain wrong opinions of men and things; and a mistake in judgment frequently induces errors in practice. Paul withstood Peter to the face, because he was to be blamed. But to die is gain. "In heaven we shall know even also as we are known." 'There knowledge grows without decay.' That is the region of perfection, and there error can find no entrance.

3. *Death terminates the conflicts of our christian warfare.* Believers are now engaged in a most perilous contest. Their enemies are principalities and powers, &c., Eph. vi. 12. The issue of this conflict sometimes appears doubtful; "without are fightings and within are fears:" but when death comes, the fight is finished, the victory won, and the believer goes to his vast reward that awaits him in the skies.

Secondly, The gain to which the text refers, comprehends the acquisition of all possible good.

1. *It will be universal. In the situation;* we exchange houses of clay for everlasting habitations. *The society;* we leave behind our weeping companions, to greet he blood besprinkled bands on the eternal shore. *The enjoyments*; here the purest pleasures are often interrupted, and may be finally forfeited. There our enjoyments will flow on like a river, pure as the source from whence they spring. *In our capacities;* here we have blessings, but sometimes cannot enjoy them; there the body will be immortal, and the soul capacitated for enjoyments the most elevated and enlarged. *In employments;* the occupations of this world are sordid and laborious; there we shall sing the praises of God, contemplate the mysteries of his nature, the variety of his works, and the glory of his government.

2. *It will be incalculable.* There is no gain upon earth that may not be estimated. We have figures and numbers, and arithmeticians who can form estimates and make calculations to any amount. But who can calculate the value of heavenly joys! the worth of immortal pleasures!

3. *It will be eternal.* It is not the gain of a moment, or even an age, but the gain of eternity, and of all eternity can give. Gain that can never be forfeited, nor diminished in value. Earthly goods cease to give their possessors pleasure, in proportion to the duration of the period they possess them. Worldly joys cloy the appetite, and pleasures cease to please; but the happiness of heaven will increase in value to eternity.

In conclusion we observe,

First, *If Christ is the believer's life, how happy and desirable is his state!* 'What hath the world to equal this?' What life is so honorable, so profitable, and so glorious! How strange it is that we have so few candidates for such a life! Is this your life? Why should not the apostle's experience be yours? There is no state of christianity that belonged exclusively to any order of men. You may be as holy as apostles. If Christ is not your life, you are not christians; you may have been baptized into the christian name, and accustomed to attend christian ordinances; but in the benefits of christianity you have no share, and to the rewards of christianity you have no title. O what a miserable, worldly, sensual life is yours!

Secondly, *If death is the believer's gain, should not this more than reconcile us to the thoughts of dying?* Many look at death in the pains and agonies it inflicts, and tremble with fearful apprehensions. These we may never realize; many die as tranquilly as they sink into the arms of sleep: but should death be even as dreadful as we anticipate, 'tis useless 'to die a thousand deaths in fearing one.' Let us look at the promises of God, read the experience of dying saints, and especially "endure as seeing him who is invisible."

Thirdly, *If to die is gain, how selfish to indulge inconsolable grief for our departed friends, who have passed into the skies.* 'O the pain, the bliss of dying!' the bitterness of death is with them for ever passed, and the bliss of now dying is their unalienable portion.

---

## THE HAPPINESS OF DYING IN THE LORD.

Revelation xiv. 13 —And I heard a voice from heaven, saying unto me, Write, Blessed are the dead, &c. (H )

THESE words are a voice from heaven, concerning the future state of those that die in Christ; and surely none are better qualified to comfort those who are left behind, than one of the heavenly company.

Our blessed Lord tells his disciples, when sinking into despondency at the idea of his leaving them, "If ye loved me, ye would rejoice, because I said, I go unto my Father," John xiv. 28; so when the believer dies, he goes to be with him: and, that we may not sorrow as those who have no hope, the text tells us, that they are not lost by ceasing to live in this world, but, are advanced to an infinitely better life than this: "Blessed are the dead," &c.

Consider,

I. WHAT IT IS TO DIE IN THE LORD, AND WHO MAY BE SAID TO DO SO. This may be said of the martyrs who die for the Lord, and seal the truth of their profession with their blood. It is applicable also to all real christians, who are united to Christ, and die the members of his mystical body: these die in the Lord. And, in order to this,

Something is previously necessary.

1. That they be quickened and made alive by the Lord    John v. 20, 21; Eph. ii. 1.

2. That they be pardoned, justified, and sanctified.  1 Cor. vi. 11.

3. That they walk after him.  Heb. xii. 2; 1 Pet. ii. 21.

4. That they live to him, as they receive all from him.  2 Cor. v. 14, 15; Phil. i. 21.

Something is implied.

1. That we die in submission to his will, when, where, and how he pleases.  Rom. xiv. 7, 8.

2. In dependence upon him for life and immortality.

3. A sincere desire to be with him.  Phil. i. 23.

II. WHEREIN THEIR BLESSEDNESS CONSISTS; and the text tells us, that, "They rest from their labors."

1. Arising from the evils to which they were subject in this world: disease, pain, want, &c.  "Many are the afflictions," &c.  Ps. xxxiv. 19. All shall be left behind at death.  Rev. xxi. 4.

2. From satan's temptations.  After death they shall be placed beyond the reach of his fiery darts.  2 Cor. iv. 4.  These they shall have left in the field of battle, and be "where the weary are at rest."  1 Pet. v. 8 Job iii. 17.

3. From the persecution of the ungodly.  John xv. 20.

**4.** From the remains of the carnal mind, wanderings in duty, and the im perfections of the best of our religious services.

" Their works follow tl em."

All the works they have done for God and his Christ, to advance his glory, prepare themselves for his kingdom, and serve his interest, and to help on others to it. These works shall follow after, so as to enter with them, and that in the most endearing manner.

**1.** In God's faithful remembrance of them all. Heb. vi. 10 ; Mal. iii. 16.

**2.** In the recompense of reward, which God will bestow. 1 Cor. xv. 58.

III. WHY THIS MESSAGE IS SO SOLEMNLY PROCLAIMED BY ".A VOICE FROM HEAVEN."

**1.** To let an unthinking world know what becomes of the friends of Christ when they die.

**2.** To assure believers that death is no hinderance to their happiness ; but the certain, though awful, way to it.

**3.** To leave it on record, to the end of time, for the assurance of every christian, that their rest is not here, and to excite them to look after one remaining.

APPLICATION.

**1.** Are the dead, who die in the Lord, blessed? how miserable are they who die out of him : and if the former are blessed immediately, henceforth from the time they die, so the latter must be wretched immediately upon their dying.

**2.** How much better to a believer is the day of his death, than the day of his birth; seeing he is born to labor, but dies to rest!

# INDEX OF SCRIPTURE